ENCYCLOPAEDIA JUDAICA

ENCYCLOPAEDIA JUDAICA

SECOND EDITION

VOLUME 16
Pes–Qu

Fred Skolnik, *Editor in Chief*
Michael Berenbaum, *Executive Editor*

MACMILLAN REFERENCE USA
An imprint of Thomson Gale, a part of The Thomson Corporation

IN ASSOCIATION WITH
KETER PUBLISHING HOUSE LTD., JERUSALEM

THOMSON
GALE

Detroit • New York • San Francisco • New Haven, Conn. • Waterville, Maine • London

THOMSON
GALE

ENCYCLOPAEDIA JUDAICA, Second Edition

Fred Skolnik, *Editor in Chief*
Michael Berenbaum, *Executive Editor*
Shlomo S. (Yosh) Gafni, *Editorial Project Manager*
Rachel Gilon, *Editorial Project Planning and Control*

Thomson Gale
Gordon Macomber, *President*
Frank Menchaca, *Senior Vice President and Publisher*
Jay Flynn, *Publisher*
Hélène Potter, *Publishing Director*

Keter Publishing House
Yiphtach Dekel, *Chief Executive Officer*
Peter Tomkins, *Executive Project Director*

Complete staff listings appear in Volume 1

For more information, contact
Macmillan Reference USA
An imprint of Thomson Gale
27500 Drake Rd.
Farmington Hills, MI 48331-3535
Or you can visit our internet site at
http://www.gale.com

LIBRARY OF CONGRESS CATALOGING-IN-PUBLICATION DATA

Encyclopaedia Judaica / Fred Skolnik, editor-in-chief ; Michael Berenbaum, executive editor. -- 2nd ed.
v. cm.
Includes bibliographical references and index.
Contents: v.1. Aa-Alp.
ISBN 0-02-865928-7 (set hardcover : alk. paper) -- ISBN 0-02-865929-5 (vol. 1 hardcover : alk. paper) -- ISBN 0-02-865930-9 (vol. 2 hardcover : alk. paper) -- ISBN 0-02-865931-7 (vol. 3 hardcover : alk. paper) -- ISBN 0-02-865932-5 (vol. 4 hardcover : alk. paper) -- ISBN 0-02-865933-3 (vol. 5 hardcover : alk. paper) -- ISBN 0-02-865934-1 (vol. 6 hardcover : alk. paper) -- ISBN 0-02-865935-X (vol. 7 hardcover : alk. paper) -- ISBN 0-02-865936-8 (vol. 8 hardcover : alk. paper) -- ISBN 0-02-865937-6 (vol. 9 hardcover : alk. paper) -- ISBN 0-02-865938-4 (vol. 10 hardcover : alk. paper) -- ISBN 0-02-865939-2 (vol. 11 hardcover : alk. paper) -- ISBN 0-02-865940-6 (vol. 12 hardcover : alk. paper) -- ISBN 0-02-865941-4 (vol. 13 hardcover : alk. paper) -- ISBN 0-02-865942-2 (vol. 14 hardcover : alk. paper) -- ISBN 0-02-865943-0 (vol. 15: alk. paper) -- ISBN 0-02-865944-9 (vol. 16: alk. paper) -- ISBN 0-02-865945-7 (vol. 17: alk. paper) -- ISBN 0-02-865946-5 (vol. 18: alk. paper) -- ISBN 0-02-865947-3 (vol. 19: alk. paper) -- ISBN 0-02-865948-1 (vol. 20: alk. paper) -- ISBN 0-02-865949-X (vol. 21: alk. paper) -- ISBN 0-02-865950-3 (vol. 22: alk. paper)
1. Jews -- Encyclopedias. I. Skolnik, Fred. II. Berenbaum, Michael, 1945-
DS102.8.E496 2007
909'.04924 -- dc22

2006020426

ISBN-13:

978-0-02-865928-2 (set)	978-0-02-865933-6 (vol. 5)	978-0-02-865938-1 (vol. 10)	978-0-02-865943-5 (vol. 15)	978-0-02-865948-0 (vol. 20)
978-0-02-865929-9 (vol. 1)	978-0-02-865934-3 (vol. 6)	978-0-02-865939-8 (vol. 11)	978-0-02-865944-2 (vol. 16)	978-0-02-865949-7 (vol. 21)
978-0-02-865930-5 (vol. 2)	978-0-02-865935-0 (vol. 7)	978-0-02-865940-4 (vol. 12)	978-0-02-865945-9 (vol. 17)	978-0-02-865950-3 (vol. 22)
978-0-02-865931-2 (vol. 3)	978-0-02-865936-7 (vol. 8)	978-0-02-865941-1 (vol. 13)	978-0-02-865946-6 (vol. 18)	
978-0-02-865932-9 (vol. 4)	978-0-02-865937-4 (vol. 9)	978-0-02-865942-8 (vol. 14)	978-0-02-865947-3 (vol. 19)	

This title is also available as an e-book
ISBN-10: 0-02-866097-8
ISBN-13: 978-0-02-866097-4
Contact your Thomson Gale representative for ordering information.
Printed in the United States of America

10 9 8 7 6 5 4 3 2

TABLE OF CONTENTS

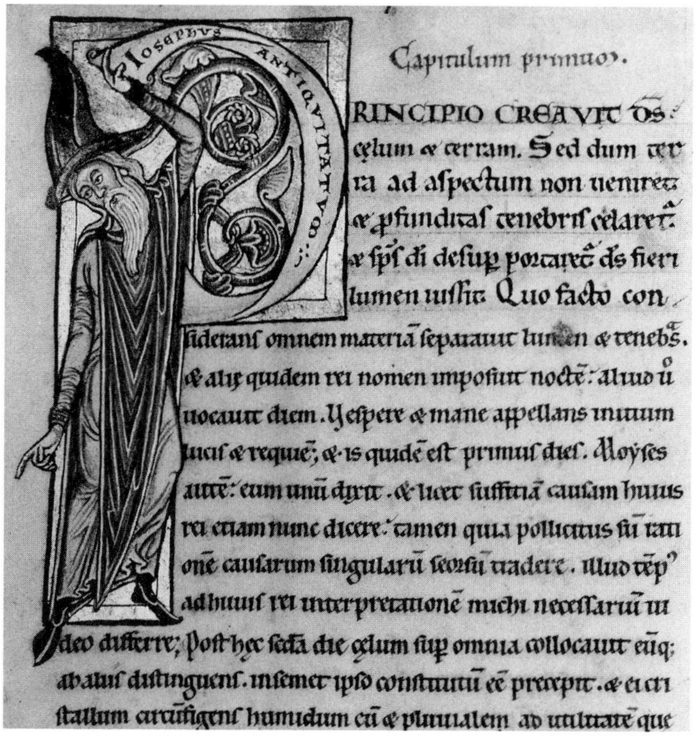

Initial letter "P" of the word Principio *in a Latin manuscript of* The Antiquities of the Jews *by Josephus Flavius, France, 12th century. The figure in the illuminated letter is wearing the medieval Jewish pointed hat. Paris, Bibliothèque Nationale, Cod. Lat. 5047, fol. 2, column 2. Photo Bildarchiv Foto Marburg, Marburg-Lahn.*

PES-PY

PESAḤIM (Heb. פְּסָחִים; "paschal lambs"), third tractate in the Mishnah, Tosefta, and two Talmuds, of the order *Mo'ed*. *Pesaḥim* deals, in ten chapters, with the laws concerning the *Passover festival.

Pesaḥ refers primarily to the paschal sacrifice, but was applied also to the festival itself. This tractate deals with both subjects, the sacrificial service (chaps. 5–9), leavened and unleavened bread (chaps. 1–4), and the *seder* (chap. 10). In geonic times the tractate was still divided correspondingly into two parts called *Pesaḥ Rishon* and *Pesaḥ Sheni*. The two parts were afterwards combined and given the name *Pesaḥim* (in the plural). In the Munich manuscript, the tenth chapter appears as the fourth, so that the "practical" chapters follow one another consecutively. There is clear evidence that the two parts of this tractate were not redacted in the same school, and there are definite differences between them. They contain conflicting topics and even those which are similar differ in details and even halakhically. The redaction of the tractate *Pesaḥim* took place relatively later than that of the other tractates and its Talmud already utilized the edited Talmud of many other tractates. The *mishnayot* of the second part are very old and refer to events from the time of the Second Temple and the early authorities. The Mishnah of the first part, though it is of later redaction, contains *halakhot* which were a subject of dispute between the latest of the **zugot* and the first of the *tannaim*, as can be proved from the parallel passages.

The following are the contents of the chapters. Chapter 1 deals with the "search" for leaven (*bedikat ḥameẓ*) and its removal. Chapter 2 continues the subject and then goes on to discuss certain aspects of the making of the *matzah* and questions relating to **maror and *ḥaroset*. Chapter 3 opens with a list of various foods containing *ḥameẓ* (e.g., beer made from barley), then reverts again to problems of the search for leaven and its removal, especially in the event of the eve of Passover falling on a Sabbath. Chapter 4 opens with the ruling that abstention from work on the eve of Passover depends on local customs. It then lists various *halakhot* which depend on local customs. Chapter 5 is mainly concerned with determining the time for slaughtering the paschal lamb and other aspects of the sacrificial service. Chapter 6 deals with the sacrificial arrangement when the festival falls on a Sabbath, and with related problems. Chapter 7 deals with the roasting of the paschal lamb, and discusses problems touching on ritual impurity affecting the persons participating in the sacrifices. Chapter 8 considers the question of a person slaughtering the paschal lamb on behalf of another person, and the qualifications of the persons involved. Chapter 9 touches first on the question of Second Passover (cf. Num. 9:10–11), but then discusses a variety of other problems, such as the interchange of a paschal lamb. Chapter 10 considers the arrangement of the *seder* night.

In the Tosefta, this tractate is also divided into ten chapters. An aggadic point of particular interest is how King Agrippa took the census of the people assembled in Jerusalem on the occasion of a Passover pilgrimage (4:3; also 63b). There is *Gemara* in the Palestinian and Babylonian Talmuds. The *Gemara* of the Babylonian Talmud contains a considerable amount of *aggadah*. The following are worthy of note: the insistence on refined language (3b); expressions of extreme antagonism between scholars and ignoramuses (49a–b); arrogance and anger make a scholar lose wisdom and a prophet his prophecy (66b); there is an advantage in the existence of a Diaspora, insofar as it makes a concentrated attack on Israel's existence impossible (87b, also 118b on the causes of Diaspora); and finally mention should be made of the story of the appointment of Hillel as *nasi* (66a). The English translation in the Soncino Talmud is by H. Friedman (1938).

BIBLIOGRAPHY: Epstein; Tanna'im, 323–36; Ḥ. Albeck, *Shishah Sidrei Mishnah*, 2 (1958), 137–42.

[Arnost Zvi Ehrman]

PESAḤSON, ISAAC MORDECAI (1876–1943), a pioneer of the *Bund in Russia and Poland. Pesaḥson was born in Shklov but his family settled in Warsaw, where his father, a descendant of the founder of the *Ḥabad ḥasidic movement, officiated as rabbi. As a youth Pesaḥson belonged to a group of Jewish Populist and Marxist intelligentsia. In 1893 he assisted in the publication of the first Yiddish May Day manifesto. During the 1890s, in contact with I.L. *Peretz, he instructed circles of workers in socialist studies. In 1897 he was active in bringing about the merger of Polish-born Jewish members of the Polish Socialist Party (*PPS) and the Union of Jewish Workers in Warsaw led by J. *Mill, whose members came from Lithuania. After the establishment of the Bund, he worked for it in Lodz, utilizing his familiarity with Polish ḥasidic life. Subsequently, he was alternately imprisoned on various occasions or active for brief periods in Warsaw and Lodz. He escaped from Siberia and worked with the Bund "committee abroad." During the 1905 Revolution, he worked again in Lodz, and was a Bund delegate at the Fifth Convention of the Russian Social Democratic Labor Party (London, 1907). From 1909 until his death he lived in Bedzin, western Poland. From 1917 he was a member of the central committee of the Bund in Poland. He was employed as secretary of the Jewish community in his town and pursued his activities for the Bund until he was murdered during the Nazi occupation. Under the pen name, *An Alter Bakante*, he published reminiscences on the beginnings of the Jewish workers' movement in Warsaw and Lodz in *Der Yidisher Arbeter*, 10 (1900), 27–36; 25 *Yor* (1922), 35–36; and *Royter Pinkos*, 2 (1924), 159–64.

BIBLIOGRAPHY: A. Brandes, *Keẓ ha-Yehudim be-Ma'arav Polin* (1945); I.S. Hertz (ed.), *Doyres Bundistn*, 1 (1956), 262–9; I.S. Hertz et al. (eds.), *Geshikhte fun Bund*, 3 vols. (1960–66), index.

[Moshe Mishkinsky]

PESANTE, MOSES BEN ḤAYYIM BEN SHEM TOV (d. 1573), author and self-appointed emissary of Safed who traveled in Turkey and the Balkans between 1565 and 1573. He was murdered in Greece.

Pesante was the author of *Ner Mitzvah*, a commentary on the *azharot* of Solomon ibn *Gabirol (Constantinople, 1567; second edition with additions, Salonika, 1569); *Yesha Elohim* (Constantinople, 1567), including an exposition of the *Hoshanot* and their relevant customs together with the laws of *lulav*, and the *piyyutim* for the Rejoicing of the Law; and *Ḥukkat ha-Pesaḥ*, a commentary on the Passover *Haggadah* (Salonika, 1569). Among his unpublished works are a commentary on the order of *Zera'im* of the Jerusalem Talmud and novellae to the tractate of *Kiddushin*.

BIBLIOGRAPHY: Yaari, Sheluḥei, 236.

[Samuel Abba Horodezky]

PESARO, city in north-central Italy on the Adriatic Sea. A rabbinical responsum attests to the existence of a Jewish community there in 1214. We can assume that Jews had settled in the city even earlier, attracted by its commercial importance. Pesaro's Jewish residents were engaged in crafts, moneylending, and local and regional trade.

The establishment of a public loan bank (*Monte di Pietà) in 1468 caused only minimal harm to local Jewish enterprises. Moneylending to the poor was the most conspicuous but by no means the most important, of the manifold activities of Jewish bankers. In fact, Jews supplied floating capital to local artisans and merchants and provided financial support to farmers in anticipation of the crops. Jews also lent large amounts of money at low rates of interest to local municipalities, eminent personalities, and noblemen. These loans were generally granted solely on the basis of written receipts, and without a *pegno* (guarantee). In the second quarter of the 16th century, a few Levantine and Portuguese merchants settled in Pesaro and engaged in international and regional commerce in wool textiles and leather.

When the Jews were expelled from the Kingdom of Naples in 1541, a branch of the Sarfati family, related to the *Abrabanels, settled in Pesaro and engaged in local commerce and financial activities. They described themselves as Neapolitan Jews and joined the local "Italian" congregation.

In or around 1549, Leone (Yehudah), son of Samuel Abrabanel, moved to Pesaro from Ferrara, after a bitter quarrel with his mother, Benvenida, who opposed his relations with Luna, a Portuguese Jewess of exceptional beauty whom he later married. Amatus Lusitanus called her the "divina."

In 1548, Manoel Lopes Bichacho, formerly a leader of the Portuguese Nation in Antwerp, settled in Pesaro, where he obtained a *condotta* (banking license) from Guidobaldo, duke of Urbino.

According to Samuel Usque, in 1549, when the duke of Ferrara expelled from his city all the recent arrivals, Manoel Bichacho persuaded Duke Guidobaldo to allow some of them to settle in his lands.

In 1550, Manoel was allowed to include up to 35 merchants in his *condotta*. This was the rather unusual beginning of the Portuguese Nation in Pesaro.

In 1556, in the wake of the persecutions against the former *Marranos of *Ancona, several of them fled to Pesaro. This group included the famous physician Amatus Lusitanus; the poet Diogo *Pires (*alias* Isaiah Cohen); Yom Tov Atias (*alias* Alvaro de Vargas) and his son Jeronimo, editors of the famous *Biblia Española de Ferrara*, and Rabbi Yuda Ibn Faraj who later acted as ambassador of the Portuguese Nation of Pesaro to the Jewish communities in the Levant.

After the death of the 26 martyrs of Ancona, Gracia and Joseph *Nasi conceived a famous plan to engage in an open commercial war against the Church, boycott the Ancona entrepôt, and develop the city of Pesaro as a new center for maritime trade between Italy and the Levant. Unfortunately, the port of Pesaro did not have adequate facilities and was not deep enough for big merchant ships to berth in it. Furthermore, there were bitter differences among the Jewish merchants in the Levant, some of whom did not participate in the boycott of Ancona. Consequently, the daring program failed.

The duke of Urbino was embittered and disappointed by the unfulfilled attempts at developing the port of his city. In March 1558, Guidobaldo, overwhelmed by diplomatic pressure from the Church, decreed the expulsion of all the former Marranos, including those who had already been living in Pesaro before the Ancona affair. The duke took revenge against Manoel Bichacho and seized all the properties and goods belonging to him and his family. The punitive provisions were carefully enforced. Italian Jews, however, were not persecuted and enjoyed a period of prosperity. Angelo, son of Zaccaria di Volterra, obtained the license of the bank which had formerly belonged to his family and later to Emanuel Bichacho. He also received the job of ducal cashier. Duke Guidobaldo was so pleased with Angelo's performance that he praised him publicly and granted him a "perpetual" exemption from local taxes.

Sephardi Jews were later readmitted and continued to engage, as before, in trade with the Levant. They built a richly decorated synagogue officially designated as "Spanish and Levantine," but commonly called "Portuguese."

After the expulsion of Jews from the Papal States in 1569, several refugees found shelter in Pesaro. In 1631, when the Duchy of Urbino fell under papal rule, the oppressive legislation that applied in the States of the Church was extended to Pesaro. In 1634, Jews were segregated in a ghetto and compelled to wear a yellow badge. The new regulations forbade the Jews to own real estate, and drastically reduced their permitted commercial activities to the *arte strazzaria* (i.e., trade in secondhand clothes). Jews were not allowed to employ Christians. Jewish physicians were no longer licensed to practice medicine among Christians. As a consequence, many Jews left the city. Their number shrank from 630 in 1628 to barely 500 in 1656. The Jewish population continued to decrease in the following century and totaled only 406 persons in 1747. However, in the 18th century, the enforcement of the oppressive legislation was somewhat relaxed. Several bankers obtained, for a price, special licenses enabling them to establish commercial offices and their residences in the center of the city, outside the ghetto. Prominent among the new entrepreneurial class was Salvatore della Ripa, merchant, banker, and communal leader.

In 1797 when French forces occupied Pesaro, the gates of the ghetto were opened. The Jews were declared full citizens and replaced the yellow badge with the tricolor cockade. When the French army withdrew from the city, a mob attacked the Jewish quarter and ransacked the synagogues.

When the rule of Church was fully reinstated, the old restrictions were renewed, at least nominally. Nonetheless, several Jews where permitted to engage in various commercial and industrial activities. According to the 1824 National Industrial Statistics, Bonaiuto d'Ancona employed 60 women in his spinning factory with a yearly production of 1,400 pounds of extra-fine silk, most of which was exported to England. Alessandro Bolaffi and Iacob Foligno were engaged in the silk industry and grain trade. Other merchants dealt in wool garments, leather, and skins, and a variety of other goods. However, alongside a few rich families, many others were impoverished and received financial help from the Jewish community.

After his ascent to power, Pope Leone XII (1823–29) reinforced the oppressive rules with great obstinacy. All previous concessions were revoked. Jews were compelled to sell any real estate they had acquired. Many rich families left the States of the Church and moved to more hospitable places. The sons of Zaccaria della Ripa settled in Florence, where they had already established the headquarters of their banking activities. However, they kept their house and their offices in Pesaro and continued to support the local Jewish community, which faced serious economic problems as it had been deprived of most of its wealthiest members.

In 1860 Pesaro was annexed to the kingdom of Italy and the Jews were emancipated. Many families moved to the center of the city. In 1869 there were only 160 Jews in the area of the former ghetto. At the beginning of the 20th century the Jewish population of Pesaro numbered only 60. By 1940 there were only a few individuals. The building of the Italian Synagogue was severely damaged by an earthquake in 1930 and was later demolished.

During World War II no Jews were deported from the city of Pesaro. A few Jews joined the Italian partisans and fought in the war of liberation against the occupying German army. Small groups of foreign Jews lived scattered throughout the large province of Pesaro. Some of them had succeeded in reaching Italy from far-away localities in Germany and Poland. Others had handed themselves over to the Italian army in Croatia in order to find shelter from the Ustasha militias and German troops. They were arrested by the Italian military police, who did not hand them over to the SS but confined them to "internment camps" in Italy. However, such camps did not exist in the district of Pesaro. Jewish refugees lived in private homes or hotels. They were nominally obliged to appear every day before the local police but, in truth, they enjoyed almost complete liberty with the tacit consent of the Italian police headquarters in Pesaro. When the German army retreated from the region, the SS arrested a group of Jews hidden in the hospital of Urbino. These prisoners were executed at the airport of Forli.

In 1944 Pesaro was liberated by the Allied forces. The 7th British Army included an all-Jewish unit: the *Jewish ("Palestinian") Brigade, which fought the Germans under the blue and white Zionist flag. There were indescribable scenes of emotion in Pesaro, as everywhere else, when the surviving Jews met the soldiers displaying the Magen David and the word "Palestine" on their shoulder straps. The Jewish soldiers reopened the Sephardi Synagogue and celebrated religious services – the last ones to be held in a city with almost no Jewish population left. This synagogue is owned by the Jewish community of Ancona, which donated the magnificent wooden *Aron ha-Kodesh* to the Jewish community of Leghorn. Part of the *bimah* was moved to the Levantine Synagogue of Ancona. The remains of the prayer hall are considered a national monument. Complex restoration works have been executed by the local municipality, and the stucco ornaments of the vaulted ceiling were restored to their original splendor. Two ancient wall paintings depicting the city of Jerusalem and the encampment of the Jews at the foot of Mount Sinai were also restored.

The abandoned cemetery on the steep slopes of Mount S. Bartolo was cleared from rampant vegetation, its terraces rebuilt and reinforced, the sepulchral stones dug up.

[Aron Leoni (2nd ed.)]

Hebrew Printing

Pesaro occupies an important position in the history of Hebrew publishing. *Abraham b. Ḥayyim "the Dyer" worked in Pesaro before moving to Ferrara in 1477. In 1507 Gershom Soncino opened a printing house in Pesaro and worked there with some interruptions until 1520. He produced, besides books in Italian and Latin, an impressive range of classical Hebrew texts: some 20 Talmud treatises, a complete Bible (1511–17), Pentateuch or Bible commentaries by Baḥya (reprinted three times), by Moses b. Naḥman (Naḥmanides), Levi b. Gershom, David Kimḥi, Isaac Abrabanel as well as an edition of Nathan b. Jehiel's *Sefer Arukh* (1517). Some of these works appear as issued by the "Sons of Soncino."

[Ariel Toaff]

BIBLIOGRAPHY: Roth, *Italy*, index; Idem. *The House of Naci, Doña Gracia*, index; Kaufman, in REJ, 16 (1888), 231–39; idem, in: JQR, 4 (1892), 509–12; Adler, in: REJ, 89 (1930), 98–103; D.W. Amram, *Makers of Hebrew Books in Italy* (1909), 104 ff.; H.D. Friedberg, *Ha-Defus ha-Ivri be-Italyah* (1956²); A.M. Haberman, *Ha-Madpisim Benei Soncino* (1933), 37–39, 50–60. **ADD. BIBLIOGRAPHY:** A. Leoni, in: *Sefarad*, 59 (1999), 77–100; M.L. Moscati Benigni, in: *Itinerary ebraici* (1999), 118–31; A. Leoni, "La Nazione Portoghese ad Ancona e Pesaro," in: I. Zorattini (ed.), *Identità dissimulata* (2000), 27–98; R.P. Uguccioni, (ed.), *Studi sulla Comunità Ebraica di Pesaro* (2003).

PESARO, ABRAMO (1818–1882), Italian revolutionary and communal leader. Pesaro was born in Ferrara where as a young man he established a cultural and vocational training center. In 1846 he belonged to the local committee which organized a rising against the papal government and was a member of the National Assembly of Mazzini's short-lived Roman republic of 1849. After the failure of the 1848 Revolution he lived in Venice until the establishment of the kingdom of Italy in 1861. Afterward he returned to Ferrara where he was active in both Jewish and general public life. He published various monographs on Italian Jewish history, in particular a work which is still the only history of the Jews of Ferrara (2 pts., 1878, 1880).

BIBLIOGRAPHY: Milano, Italia, index; Milano, Bibliotheca, nos. 1255–60.

[Menachem E. Artom]

PESHAT (Heb. פְּשָׁט), word which came to mean the plain, literal meaning of a text, as opposed mainly to *derash, the homiletical interpretation, but also to any other method than the literal. According to W. Bacher (*Die exegetische Terminologie der juedischen Traditionsliteratur*, 2 (1905), 112ff.) it was *Abbaye, in the first half of the fourth century, who first made a distinction between *peshat* and *derash* as separate methods of exegesis, while Dobschuetz regards the word as the innovation of the academy of Pumbedita as a whole, including Abbaye, Joseph, and Rava. An examination of the one clear instance in which Abbaye advances two interpretations, one of *peshat* and one of *derash* (Sanh. 100b), however, does not bear out the assumption that the word indicates the literal meaning (cf. Loewe in bibliography, p. 163–4). Similarly, the frequently quoted statement, *ein mikra yoẓe middei peshuto*, "a text cannot be taken from the meaning of its *peshat*" – Shab. 63a; Yev. 11b, 24a – does not necessarily imply that *peshat* means the literal exegesis. In point of fact in parallel passages where one uses the verbal form *peshat*, the others use *darash*, or *shanah*, or *matne* (Heb. and Aramaic respectively for "studied," or "repeated"; Num. R. 18:22; Gen. R. 10:7 ed. Theodor Albeck p. 81, and notes), while in two interpretations given by R. Dimi to a biblical passage (Gen. 49:11–12) that which is called "the *peshat* of the verse" *(peshta de-kera)* is much further removed from the literal meaning than the other interpretation given (Ket. 111b; cf. also Kid. 80b; Er. 23b; Ar. 8b). Actually the rabbis had only two major methods of biblical exegesis, that of *halakhah* and that of *aggadah*, neither of which depended upon literal exegesis and in most instances deviated from it.

The basic meaning of the root of the word *peshat* in biblical Hebrew is "to flatten out," with the secondary meaning "to extend" or "to stretch out" (hence the meaning "to make a raid" – Job. 1:17), and from this was derived the talmudic meaning of "to expatiate upon," or "to propound." In context, *peshat* in talmudic literature seems to mean not the plain meaning but "the teaching recognized by the public as obviously authoritative, since familiar and traditional" (Loewe) or "the usual accepted traditional meaning as it was generally taught" (Rabinowitz). The present meaning of *peshat* is probably due to Rashi's biblical commentary, in which he was the first sharply to differentiate between the homiletical interpretation which he called *derash* and the literal meaning to which he gave the name *peshat*.

BIBLIOGRAPHY: W. Bacher, *Die exegetische Terminologie der juedischen Traditionsliteratur*, 2 (1905), 173; L. Dobschuetz, *Die einfache Bibelexegese der Tannaim* (1893), 11–15; L. Rabinowitz, in: *Tradition*, 6 no. 1 (1963), 67–72; R. Loewe, in: *Annual of Jewish Studies* (1965), 140–85.

[Louis Isaac Rabinowitz]

PESHER (Heb. פֵּשֶׁר), word meaning "interpretation." It occurs only once in the Hebrew Bible: "Who is as the wise man? and who knoweth the interpretation of a thing?" (Eccl. 8:1). However, the Aramaic word *peshar* occurs 31 times in the Aramaic portion of Daniel, where it mainly refers to dream interpretation.

In Qumran texts, it usually occurs after a biblical quotation, introducing its interpretation. As such it refers to a particular technique of interpretation which may be paralleled to midrashic exegesis.

What is distinctive of Qumran is both the systematic application of such a technique to a given prophetic work and its specific purpose. On the one hand, it had the result of creating a fixed literary structure, mostly known from the "continuous" *pesharim*. Those works quote one "prophetic" book verse by verse, each verse being followed by its interpretation, aiming at giving the plain meaning of the Prophet's words as a whole. On the other hand, their aim is to read historical and eschatological events into the biblical prophecies, understanding them as describing their own sect's situation on the verge of the *eschaton*.

Such an attitude to the biblical text (i.e., God's words) is already exemplified by the book of Daniel, where the term *peshar* is linked to the noun of Iranian origin *raz*, which appears nine times in the Aramaic portion of Daniel. Nebuchadnezzar's dream of the great image of four metals is a *raz* which cannot be understood until the *pesher* is supplied. Both the *raz* and the *peshar* are given by divine revelation; the *raz* is the first stage of the revelation, but it remains a mystery until the second stage, the *peshar*, is forthcoming.

Raz and Pesher

Both *raz* and *pesher* are common terms in the Qumran texts. Repeatedly in the *Thanksgiving Psalms God is praised because He enabled the psalmist to understand His wonderful mysteries (*razim*), by which His eschatological purposes seem especially to be meant. In the Qumran commentaries on various biblical books or parts of books this *pesher* pattern is particularly manifest. The first stage of divine revelation was imparted to the biblical writer, but it remained a mystery (*raz*) until the second stage, the interpretation (*pesher*), was imparted to the Teacher of Righteousness (and by him to his disciples). Thus, in the *Habakkuk Commentary*, it says that "God commanded Habakkuk to write the things that were coming on the last generation, but the fulfillment of the epoch He did not make known to him. And as for the words, that a man may read it swiftly; their interpretation (*pesher*) concerns the Teacher of Righteousness, to whom God made known all the mysteries (*razei*) of the words of His servant the prophets" (1Qp Hab. 7:1–5, on Hab. 2:1ff.). This is completely in accordance with the statement at the beginning of the Damascus document, that God raised up for the righteous remnant "a Teacher of Righteousness to lead them in the way of his heart, that he might make known to the last generations what he was going to do to the last generation" (CD 1:10–12). Not until the two parts of the revelation, the *raz* and *pesher*, are brought together is its meaning made plain. The revelation, moreover, is predominantly concerned with the time of the end, the last generation of the current epoch. Three basic principles of Qumran interpretation have already shown themselves:

(1) God revealed His purpose to the prophets, but did not reveal to them the time when His purpose would be fulfilled; this further revelation was first communicated to the Teacher of Righteousness.

(2) All the words of the prophets had reference to the time of the end.

(3) The time of the end is at hand.

Contemporary Interpretation

Much then of what the prophets had to say was believed to be in a kind of code; it could only be decoded when the Teacher of Righteousness was provided with the key. Knowledge of the context of the prophet's own day, which a modern exegete would regard as indispensable for understanding his message, was irrelevant; the historical context which made his words intelligible was the interpreter's own situation and that of the period immediately following. Isaiah might prophesy the downfall of the Assyrian, Ezekiel might foretell the rise and fall of "Gog, of the land of Magog," Habakkuk might describe the invasion of his land by the Chaldeans; but in these and other instances the reference is not to enemies of Israel in the respective prophets' days but to the great gentile power which would oppress the people of God at the end-time, regularly designated the *Kittim in the Qumran texts. For example, in a commentary on Isaiah (4QpIs[a]), the advance and overthrow of the Assyrians in Isaiah 10:24ff., are interpreted as the eschatological "war of the Kittim." The leader of the Kittim (or so it appears, for the manuscript is badly mutilated) goes up from the plain of Acre to the approaches of Jerusalem. This is followed by the quotation of Isaiah 11:1–4 which is properly interpreted as the "shoot of David" who is to arise in the latter days to rule all the gentiles, including "Magog," but takes his directions from the priests. (This is in line with the Qumran picture of the age to come, in which the priesthood, and especially the "Messiah of Aaron," will take precedence over the Davidic Messiah, whose main function is to lead his followers to victory in battle.) In line with the interpretation of the Assyrians as the Kittim in this commentary is the quotation of Isaiah 31:8 in the *War Scroll (1QM 11:11ff.) with references to the destruction of the Kittim ("Then shall Asshur fall with the sword, not of man, and the sword, not of man, shall devour him").

The Habbakuk Commentary

The best-preserved of the Qumran commentaries is that on Habakkuk from Cave 1, and it provides the largest number of examples of this *pesher*-interpretation. The description of the Chaldeans in Habakkuk 1:6–17 is applied almost clause by clause to the Kittim. The Kittim, in their swift advance, overthrow all who stand in their way, and subdue them to their own dominion. They take possession of many lands and plunder their cities, "to possess dwelling places that are not theirs." Nor do they rely on military power alone to accomplish their ends: "With deliberate counsel all their device is to do evil, and with cunning and deceit they proceed with all the nations." "They trample the earth with their horses and their beasts; they come from afar, from the islands of the sea, to devour all the nations like vultures, and they are never satisfied… With wrath and anger, with hot passion and fury, they speak to all the nations." They impose heavy tribute on the nations, to be paid year by year, and thus they denude the lands of their wealth. In war they are completely ruthless; their sword regards neither age nor sex. Yet, as the prophet says, they are the agents of divine judgment against the ungodly; in particular, they are sent to punish the wicked priesthood of Jerusalem, who oppressed the godly and plundered the poor; they will deprive these priests of their ill-gotten gain and afflict them as they had afflicted others. Other parts of the Qumran commentary on Habakkuk apply the prophet's words to internal conflicts in Judea – especially to the conflict between the *Teacher of Righteousness and the *Wicked Priest, with some reference to other groups and leaders active at the same time as these. It rarely happens that the prophet's words lend themselves so literally to the commentator's purpose as do Habakkuk's words about the Chaldeans. Elsewhere the text is atomized to serve that purpose; one variant will be preferred to another on the same principle. Where other procedures fail, the text is allegorized: if in Habakkuk 2:17 mention is made of the Chaldeans' cutting down the cedars of Lebanon for military equipment and depriving the beasts there of their natural shelter, "Lebanon" is the council of the community and the "beasts" are "the simple ones of Judah, the doers of the law," while their devastator is the Wicked Priest.

Other Examples

Another example of allegorization appears in the commentary on Micah from Cave 1, where the words of Micah 1:5b ("What are the high places of Judah? Are they not Jerusalem?") are interpreted as "the Teacher of Righteousness, who teaches the law to his council and to all who offer themselves for enrollment among the elect of God." Several instances of *pesher*-interpretation are found in the Damascus document: once the actual term is used, where the *pesher* of Isaiah 24:17, "Terror (*paḥad*) and the pit (*paḥat*) and the trap (*paḥ*) are upon thee," is said to be "the three nets of Belial… in which he catches Israel by making them look like three kinds of righteousness – namely fornication, wealth, and pollution of the sanctuary" (CD 4:12–19). The document called 4Q *Testimonia* quotes three passages from the Torah (Ex. 20:21, Samaritan text; Num. 24:15–17 and Deut. 33:8–11) with apparent reference to the eschatological prophet, prince, and priest respectively, and then quotes Joshua's curse on the rebuilder of Jericho with reference to a son of Belial and his two sons; the text, unfortunately, is so fragmentary and allusive that the identity of the "son of Belial" remains in doubt: almost every member of the Hasmonean dynasty from Mattathias to Aristobulus II has been suggested, as have also Antipater, Herod, and even Vespasian. Alongside 4Q *Testimonia* the documents called 4Q *Florilegium* and 4Q *Patriarchal Blessings* provide examples of messianic interpretation. To those who had grasped the basic principles of the *pesher* received and taught by the Teacher of Righteousness, the sacred text was luminous; those who tried to understand it otherwise still groped in darkness.

The Historical Implication of the Pesharim

As already suggested above, the authors of the *pesharim* believed that the Prophets (including Moses and David) actually described the sect's own times as being the end of days (or at the least, the last days before the end). As a result, they aimed at ascribing every feature derived from the biblical text to figures and groups that were their contemporaries.

Thus it is of the utmost importance to succeed in identifying these groups and figures. Unfortunately, they are recalled not by names but by sobriquets. And the most secure identifications are the vaguest from the chronological point of view. Hence, the "Yaḥad" is called Judah, while Ephraim points to the Pharisees and Manassseh to the Sadducees. The Chaldeans recalled in the book of Habakkuk are said to be the "Kittim." The only exception is the "Lion of Wrath" mentioned by Nahum: from the historical event alluded to, it may be securely inferred that this figure is Alexander *Yannai having his opponents crucified, in 88 B.C.E. However, the *pesher* provides no further indication about the involvement of the "Lion of Wrath" in the history of the sect.

As a whole, the Teacher of Righteousness lived in the time of the Wicked Priest who persecuted him, and the sectaries saw the domination of the world by the Kittim as a sign of the coming of the end (cf. Nb 24:24). If we only knew who were the Kittim and who was the Wicked Priest, we would be able to reconstruct the history of the sect. Most scholars think the noun *Kittim* is a sobriquet for Romans (especially in Nahum), but they nevertheless usually assume that the sect was founded before Roman times. The Wicked Priest is variously identified with one Hasmonean ruler or another, if not with Herod, Jesus, or Paul. As a result, the Teacher of Righteousness' time variously is ascribed to the 2nd century B.C.E.–1st century C.E.

BIBLIOGRAPHY: F.F. Bruce, *Biblical Exegesis in the Qumran Texts* (1960); Fitzmyer, in: *New Testament Studies* (1960–61), 297ff.; J. de Waard, *A Comparative Study of the* OT *Text in the Dead Sea Scrolls and in the* NT (1965); K. Elliger, *Studien zum Habakkuk-Kommentar vom Toten Meer* (1953); Osswald, in: ZAW, 68 (1956), 243ff.; F. Noetscher, *Zur theologischen Terminologie der Qumran-Texte* (1956); O. Betz, *Offenbarung und Schriftforschung in der Qumransekte* (1960). **ADD. BIBLIOGRAPHY:** W.H. Brownley, "The Jerusalem Habakkuk Scroll," in: BASOR, 112 (1948), 8–18; M.H. Segal, "The Habakkuk 'Commentary' and the Damascus Fragments (A Historical Study)," in: JBL, 70 (1951), 131–47; M. Burrows (ed.), *The Dead Sea Scrolls of St Mark's Monastery* (1951); L.E. Toombs, "The Early History of the Qumran Sect," in: JSS, 1 (1956), 367–81; J.M. Allegro, "*Thrakidan*, the 'Lion of Wrath' and Alexander Janneus," in: PEQ, 91 (1959), 47–51; M. Stern, "*Thrakidas* – about Alexander Jannaeus' Nickname in Josephus Flavius' Writings and Syncellus' Ones," in: *Tarbiz*, 29 (1960), 207–9 (Heb.); J.D. Amusin, "Ephraïm et Manassé dans le Pesher Nahum," in: RQ, 4 (1963), 386–96; A. Dupont-Sommer, "Le commentaire de Nahum découvert près de la mer Morte (4Qp Nah): Traduction et Notes," in: *Semitica*, 13 (1963), 55–88; S.B. Hoenig, "Dorshé Halaqot in the Pesher Nahum Scrolls," in: JBL, 83 (1964), 119–38; A. Dupont-Sommer, "Lumières nouvelles sur l'arrière-plan historique des écrits de Qumran," in: *Eretz Israel*, 8 (1967), *E.L. Sukenik Memorial Volume*, 25*–36*; D. Flusser, "The *Pesher* of Isaiah and the Twelves Apostles," in: *Eretz Israel*, 8 (E.L. Sukenik Volume; 1967), 52–62 (Heb.); J.M. Allegro, *Qumran Cave 4: I (4Q158–4Q186), Discoveries in the Judaean Desert*, 5 (1968); D. Flusser, "Pharisees, Sadducees and Essenes in *Pesher Nahum*," in: *G. Alon Memorial Volume* (Tel Aviv, 1970), 133–68; J. Strugnell, "Notes en marge du volume V des 'Discoveries in the Judaean Desert of Jordan,'" in: RQ, 7 (1969/1971), 211–18; J. Baumgarten, "Does *TLH* in the Temple Scroll refer to Crucifixion?" in: JBL, 91 (1972), 472–81; D. Pardee, "A Restudy of the Commentary on Psalm 37 from Qumran Cave 4," in: RQ, 8 (1973), 163–94; Y. Yadin, "Pesher Nahum (4Q pNahum) Reconsidered," in: IEJ, 21 (1971), 1–12; J. Murphy-O'Connor, "The Essenes and Their History," in: RB, 81 (1974), 215–44; idem, "Demetrius I and the Teacher of Righteousness," in: RB, 83 (1976), 400–20; J.D. Amusin, "The Reflection of Historical Events of the First Century B.C. in Qumran Commentaries (4Q61; 4Q169; 4Q166)," in: HUCA, 48 (1977), 123–52; W.H. Brownlee, *The Midrash Pesher of Habakkuk*, in: SBLMS 24 (1979); M.P. Horgan, *Pesharim: Qumran Interpretations of Biblical Books* (CBQ Monograph Series, 8, 1979); D. Flusser, "Pharisäer, Sadduzäer und Essener im Pescher Nahum," in: K.E. Grözinger et al. (eds.), *Qumran: Wege der Forschung* (1981), 121–66; J.M. Baumgarten, "Hanging and Treason in Qumran and Roman Law," in: *Eretz-Israel*, 16 (1982), 7–16; W.H. Brownley, "The Wicked Priest, the Man of Lies and the Righteous Teacher – The Problem of Identity," in: JQR, 73 (1982), 1–37; D. Dimant, "Qumran Sectarian Literature," in: *Jewish Writings of the Second Temple Period* (CRINT II. 2, 1984), 505–8; I. Fröhlich, "Le genre littéraire des *Pesharim* de Qumrân," in: RQ, 47:12 (1986), 383–98; M. Kister, "Concerning the History of the Essenes. A Study of the Animal Apocalypse, the Book of Jubilees and the Damascus Covenant," in: *Tarbiz*, 56 (1986), 1–18 (Heb.); B. Nitzan, *Megillat Pesher Habakkuk* (1986); M. Fishbane, *Biblical Interpretation in Ancient Israel* (1988); idem, "Use, Authority and Interpretation of Mikra at Qumran," in: M.J. Mulder and H. Sysling (eds.), *Mikra, Text, Translation, Reading and Interpretation of the Hebrew Bible in Ancient Judaism and Early Christianity* (1988), 339–78; S. Talmon, *The World of Qumran from Within* (1989), 11–52, 142–46, 186–99; F. Garcia-Martinez and A.S. van der Woudde, "A 'Groningen' Hypothesis of Qumran Origin and Early History," in: *Revue de Qumran*, 14 (1990), 521–42; D. Dimant, "Pesharim, Qumran," in: *Anchor Bible Dictionary* (1992), 5:244–51; L.H. Schiffman, "Pharisees and Sadducees in *Pesher Nahum*," in: *Minḥah le-Naḥum. Biblical and Other Studies Presented to Nahum M. Sarna in Honour of his 70th Birthday* (1993), 272–90; G.J. Brooke, "The Pesharim and the Origins of the Dead Sea Scrolls," in: *Methods of Investigation…*, (1994), 339–54; J.C. VanderKam, *The Dead Sea Scrolls Today* (1994); I. Fröhlich, *Time and Times and Half a Time: Historical Consciousness in the Jewish Literature of the Persian and Hellenistic Eras*. JSP Supplement 19 (1996); A.S. van der Woude, "Once Again: The Wicked Priests in the *Habakkuk Pesher* from Cave 1 of Qumran," in: RQ, 65–68 (*Milik vol.*; 1996), 375–84; G.J. Brooke, "Isaiah in the Pesharim and Other Qumran Texts," in: C.C. Boyles and C.A. Evans (eds.), *Writings and Reading the Scroll of Isaiah. Studies of an Interpretive Tradition*, vol. 2, part 3, *The Interpretation of Isaiah in Late Antiquity* (1997), 609–31; H. Eshel, "The History of the Qumran Community and Historical Details in the Dead Sea Scrolls," in: *Qadmoniot*, 114 (1997), 86–93 (Heb.); G. Vermes, *The Complete Dead Sea Scrolls in English* (1997); M. Kister, "A Common Heritage: Biblical Interpretation at Qumran and its Implications," in: M.E. Stone and E.G. Chazon (eds.), *Biblical Perspectives: Early Use and Interpretation of the Bible in Light of the Dead Sea Scrolls. Proceedings of the First International Symposium of the Orion Center for the Study of the Dead Sea Scrolls and Associated Literature, 12–14 May 1996*, 101–11. Studies on the Texts of the Desert of Judah 28 (1998); J.C. Vanderkam, "Identity and History of the Community," in: P.W. Flint and J.C. Vanderkam (eds.), *The Dead Sea Scrolls after Fifty Years: A Comprehensive Assessment*, (1999), 2:487–533; S.L. Berrin, "Lemma/Pesher Correspondence in Pesher Nahum," in: L.H. Schiffman, E. Tov, and J.C. VanderKam (eds.), *The Dead Sea Scrolls: Fifty Years after Their Discovery 1947–1997. Proceedings of the Jerusalem Congress, July 20–25, 1997* (2000), 341–50; H. Bengtsson, *What's in a Name? A Study of Sobriquets in the Pesharim* (2000); L.H. Schiffman and J.C. Vanderkam (eds.), *Encyclopedia of the Dead Sea Scrolls*, 2 vols. (2000): M. Bernstein, "Interpretation of Scriptures," in: EDSS (2000), 1:376–83; idem, "Pesher Habakkuk," in: EDSS (2000), 2:647–50; idem, "Scriptures," in: EDSS (2000), 2:832–42; S.L. Berrin, "Pesharim," in: EDSS (2000), 2:644–47; G.J. Brooke, "Prophecy," in: EDSS (2000), 2:694–700; T.H. Lim, "Kittim," in: EDSS (2000), 1:469–71; idem, "Liar," in: EDSS (2000), 1:493–94; idem, "Wicked Priest," in: EDSS (2000), 2:973–76; G. Doudna, *4Q Pesher Nahum. A Critical Edition*, JSP Sup. Series 35, Copenhagen International Series 8 (2001); H. Eshel, "The Kittim in the *War Scroll* and in the Pesharim," in: D. Goodblatt, A. Pinnick, and D.R. Schwartz (eds.), *Historical Perspectives / From the Hasmoneans to Bar Kokhba in the Light of the Dead Sea Scrolls* (2001), 29–44; D. Dimant, "Not Exile in the Desert but Exile in Spirit: The Pesher of Isa. 40:3 in the *Rule of the Community*," in: *Meghillot*, 2 (2002), 21–36; J.H. Charlesworth, *The Pesharim and Qumran history: Chaos or Consensus?* (2002); J.H. Charlesworth et al. (eds.), *The Dead Sea Scrolls: The Pesharim, Other Commentaries and Related Documents*, *PTSDSSP 6B* (2002); T.H. Lim, *Pesharim* (2002).

[Frederick Fyvie Bruce / Emanuelle Main (2nd ed.)]

PESIKTA DE-RAV KAHANA (Aram. פְּסִיקְתָּא דְּרַב כָּהֲנָא), one of the oldest of the homiletic Midrashim. The word *pesikta* means "the section" or "the portion." The *Pesikta de-Rav Kahana* contains homilies on portions of the Torah and *haftarah* readings for the festivals and special *Sabbaths. There are two editions of this text which are similar in the following order of contents: Chapter 1, on Torah readings for Ḥanukkah; Chapters 2–6, on Torah readings for the special *Sabbaths and *Parashat ha-Ḥodesh*; Chapters 7–12, on Torah readings for *Passover and *Shavuot; Chapters 13–22, 24, 25, on readings for the 12 *haftarot* of the three Sabbaths of "reproof" (before the Ninth of *Av) and the seven Sabbaths of "consolation" (after the Ninth of Av); and an additional two (this section is often referred to in rabbinical literature as "The Midrash דש״ח נו״ע אר״ק שד״א," an acronym consisting of the first letters of each of the *haftarot* (see Tos. Meg. 31b)). Chapters 23 to the end consist of Torah readings for *Rosh Ha-Shanah and the *Day of Atonement; *haftarah* readings for the Sabbath of Repentance, *seliḥot*; Torah readings for *Sukkot, Shemini Aẓeret.

In 1832 L. *Zunz, in an ingenious work of scholarship, demonstrated the existence of *Pesikta de-Rav Kahana*, as distinct from the *Pesikta Rabbati and the *Pesikta Zutarta*, although there was no text or manuscript available to him. On the basis of references and readings in the medieval *Yalkut Shimoni* and especially in the *Arukh*, Zunz even went so far as to propose an order of contents of 29 chapters. Chapter 1, on Rosh Ha-Shanah, was followed by the festivals and special Sabbaths in the normal cycle of the year. It has since been demonstrated, on the basis of its language and of rabbis and place names mentioned, that the *Pesikta* is a Palestinian text, probably of the fifth century. In 1868 Solomon Buber published an edition of the *Pesikta* based on four manuscripts. The discovery of these manuscripts represented a remarkable confirmation of Zunz's basic proposition – the existence of the *Pesikta*. However, the arrangement of chapters in Buber's edition, as indicated above, begins the cycle of the year with the chapter on Ḥanukkah.

The confirmation of the original structure of the *Pesikta* was made possible by the discovery of a new Oxford manuscript of the 16th century. It is the only one of the manuscripts which has a table of contents beginning the cycle of the year with the chapter on Rosh Ha-Shanah, almost exactly as Zunz surmised in his arrangement of the order of chapters.

The name of the work is somewhat obscure. Zunz and Buber believe that the authorship was attributed to Rav Kahana because of a reading in the 12 chapters beginning with the Sabbath after the 17th of Tammuz. The first chapter in this unit opens as follows: "'The words of Jeremiah' (Jer. 1:1) R. Abba b. Kahana opened…." An alternative theory that is suggested now is based on the opening lines in the chapter of Rosh Ha-Shanah in two manuscripts which open with a reference to Rav Kahana. If the *Pesikta* begins with Rosh Ha-Shanah, it is correct to assume that the name *Pesikta de-Rav Kahana* was based on a version which made its first reference to this *amora* in its opening lines.

There are six known manuscripts of the *Pesikta* (three from Oxford, and one each in Carmoly, Casanatense, and Safed). An analysis of their contents in terms of the Palestinian tradition of the portion of Torah which is read on a particular festival, or the reading for a second day (non-Palestinian; see *Festivals), yields the conclusion that the new Oxford manuscript, which begins with Rosh Ha-Shanah, is a consistently closer reflection of the tradition of Palestine where the *Pesikta* originated.

This manuscript, reflecting an old, original source, has many excellent readings on individual words and phrases. However, its special importance derives from the order of chapters which renders it possible to establish the original structure of the *Pesikta*. It is almost exactly the same as the remarkable prediction made by Zunz, at a time when a copy of the *Pesikta* was not available. However, in the new Oxford manuscript, an excerpt of the chapter on Shavuot and the chapter on *Simḥat Torah come at the very end of the manuscript, after the chapter for the last Sabbath of the year. This would indicate that these two chapters for the second day of a holiday, observed outside of Palestine, were not part of the original *Pesikta*, which is of Palestinian origin. In all probability, a later scribe came upon these two chapters, which are similar in style (although definitely of later origin) to the *Pesikta*, and attached them as an addendum to the manuscript. Each of the six manuscripts has such addenda within a chapter or complete chapters attached which are not to be found in the other manuscripts. This practice by scribes of adding material similar to the books which they were copying was not uncommon in ancient times.

It may therefore be concluded that the original order of the *Pesikta* chapters followed the cycle of the Jewish calendar, beginning with Rosh Ha-Shanah and concluding with the Sabbath before Rosh Ha-Shanah, as found in the new Oxford manuscript and anticipated some 130 years ago by Zunz.

BIBLIOGRAPHY: *Pesikta de-Rav Kahana*, ed. by B. Mandelbaum (1962), introd.; Zunz, Vortraege; *Pesikta de-Rav Kahana*, ed. by S. Buber (1868), introd.; *Midrash Va-Yikra Rabbah*, ed. by M. Margulies, 5 (1960), xiii; Goldberg, in: KS, 43 (1967/68), 68–79.

[Bernard Mandelbaum]

PESIKTA RABBATI (Aram. פְּסִיקְתָּא רַבָּתִי), a medieval Midrash on the festivals of the year. It has been printed several times, and a critical edition, with introduction, commentary, and indices was published by M. Friedman (Ish-Shalom) in 1880. Further fragments were published by S.A. Wertheimer (in *Battei Midrashot*, 1 (1950), 260–4), and L. Ginzberg (in *Ginzei Schechter*, 1 (1928), 172–81; all future references are to Friedman's edition). The word *pesikta* means "section," and this Midrash consists of a series of separate sections, on the pentateuchal and prophetic lessons of festivals, unlike most other *Midreshei Aggadah* (e.g., some of the *Rabbot*) which are continuous commentaries to the Bible. It is called *Rabbati* ("the greater") probably in contrast to the earlier *Pesikta (de-Rav Kahana).

In Friedman's edition, the *Pesikta Rabbati* consists of some 47 sections, but considerably more homilies, as some sections consist of (parts of) several homilies (e.g., section 10). Seven or eight sections deal with *Ḥanukkah (2–8 or 9); sections 10–15 (or 16) with the Sabbaths preceding *Passover; 17–18 with Passover itself; 20–24 are a Midrash on the Ten Commandments (*Shavuot); 26–37 deal with the Sabbaths of mourning and comforting and the Ninth of *Av; while 38–48, bearing the superscription "*Midrash Harninu*," deal with *Rosh Ha-Shanah and the *Day of Atonement. Thus this Midrash spans the year from the Day of Atonement, omitting only *Sukkot. Probably, in its original form, the Midrash covered the full year, but now the end has been lost.

It has five entire sections in common with the earlier *Pesikta* (15–18 and 33, and also part of 14), but otherwise is totally different both in style and structure. Thus, while the *Pesikta de-Rav Kahana* has no halakhic passages, no fewer than 28 homilies of the *Pesikta Rabbati* have halakhic exordia, many (1–14, 39–45, 47) beginning with the formula *"*Yelammedenu Rabbenu*," followed by proems beginning "*Kakh pataḥ R. Tanḥuma*." This demonstrates clearly the *Pesikta Rabbati's* relationship to the *Tanḥuma-Yelammedenu* literature. Furthermore, it has been shown that the formula "*Kakh pataḥ R. Tanḥuma*" does not mean that what follows is a statement by R. Tanḥuma, but merely that this passage is taken from the *Tanḥuma* (*Yelammedenu*).

So far it has been discovered that two major sources are represented in the *Pesikta Rabbati*: (1) the *Pesikta de-Rav Kahana*, and (2) the *Tanḥuma-Yelammedenu*. Sections 20–24, which Ha-*Meiri calls *Midrash Mattan Torah* ("the Midrash on the giving of the Torah"), differ in style and structure from the rest of this work, and seem to form one unit. The proem in section 20 is strikingly individual in both its style and content. This work emerges, then, as a composite one, a compilation whose main body of source material is from the *Tanḥuma-Yelammedenu*.

In the first homily, one of the *Yelammedenu* sections, 845 is indicated as the date of the composition of the work. (The other date there – 1219 – is clearly the gloss of a later reader or copyist, perhaps *Eleazar of Worms, who made much use of this Midrash.) However, since this work is considered a composite one, possibly reflecting several periods of editing, this date is evidence only for the composition of the *Tanḥuma-Yelammedenu* stratum. The source material is all Palestinian, and though the precise date and place of compilation have not yet been fixed with certainty, modern scholarly opinion tends to view the *Pesikta Rabbati* as a Palestinian work of the sixth or seventh century.

The complete English translation of the *Pesikta Rabbati* by Braude (1968) takes into account, inter alia, the readings of Ms. Parma 1240 (completed in the year 1270) and Ms. Casanata 3324 (of the 17th century).

BIBLIOGRAPHY: W.S. Braude, *Pesikta Rabbati* (1968), translation and introduction; L. Prys, *Die Jeremias Homilie Pesikta Rabbati* (1966); idem, in: JQR, 52 (1961/62), 264–72; idem, in: PAAJR, 30 (1962), 1–35; B.J. Bamberger, in: HUCA, 15 (1940), 427–8; V. Aptowitzer, *ibid.*, 8–9 (1931–32), 383–410; Mann, Egypt, 1 (1920), 48; Zunz-Albeck, Derashot, 117–21, 376–89.

[Daniel Sperber]

PESOTTA, ROSE (1896–1965), third woman vice president of the International Ladies Garment Workers Union (ILGWU), anarchist, and labor activist. The second of eight children (originally named Rachelle), she was born in Derazhnya in the Ukraine to observant parents, Masya and Isaack Peisoty. Immigrating to the United States in 1913 to avoid an impending arranged marriage, she lived with an elder sister and became a seamstress. As an activist in Local 25 of the ILGWU she quickly became a leader, attending the Bryn Mawr Summer School for Women Labor Activists, Brookwood Labor College, and the Wisconsin Summer School. In 1933 Pesotta was sent to Los Angeles to organize union shops and in 1934 she was elected the only woman vice president of the Board of the ILGWU. Her charisma, rhetorical skills, and innate love and sympathy for the workers won her many ardent followers. Her leadership style was colorful; she encouraged seamstresses to model the clothes they sewed as they marched in picket lines and had children of striking workers carry protest signs in support of their parents. She provided food, music, and parties for striking workers. In Cleveland in 1937 Pesotta was slashed and beaten by anti-union thugs; she later became deaf in one ear from an altercation in Flint, Michigan. Her activism took her to Seattle, San Francisco, Milwaukee, Buffalo, Boston, and Montreal and she also assisted other unions in organizing efforts.

Pesotta became an anarchist activist early in life, writing for the journal *Road to Freedom* and working to overturn the convictions of Sacco and Vanzetti. She believed in decentralization and self-government for workers and found it hard to reconcile these beliefs with work in a union bureaucracy, where she felt marginalized as a woman and an anarchist. Her friend Emma *Goldman provided her with support and intellectual guidance for her labor and anarchist activism. Finally in 1942, after being undermined by a fellow vice president in her work in Los Angeles, Pesotta left the General Executive Board of the ILGWU. Eventually she returned to the sewing machine, working briefly for the Anti-Defamation League and the American Trade Union Council of the Histadrut. Pesotta was romantically involved for a time with Powers Hapgood, a labor organizer for the United Mine Workers Union and other unions, and she was married briefly to Albert Martin, also known as Frank Lopez, whom she met during the Sacco and Vanzetti case. Pesotta, whose books include *Bread upon the Waters* (1944; rep. 1987) and *Days of Our Lives* (1958), died in Miami, Florida. In her eulogy Gus Tyler wrote: "She was born to lead. She was fated to rise from the machine and to guide her fellow workers in the age old struggle for human dignity."

BIBLIOGRAPHY: A. Kessler Harris, "Organizing the Unorganizable: Three Jewish Women and Their Union," in: *Labor History* (Winter 1976), 5–23; E. Leeder, *The Gentle General: Rose Pesotta, Anarchist and Labor Organizer*. Albany (1993).

[Elaine Leeder (2nd ed.)]

PESTSZENTERZSEBET (Hung. **Pestszenterzsébet**), town, formerly a suburb of Budapest, Hungary. A Neologist congregation was founded there toward the end of the 19th century. In 1901 a synagogue was erected and in 1903 a *talmud torah* was founded. A school was opened in 1922 and existed until the Holocaust. B. Krishaber was rabbi of Pestszenterzsebet from 1900 to 1950. The Jewish population numbered 21,953 in 1910; 3,293 in 1920; 7,000 in 1929; 4,522 in 1936; and 3,978 in 1941. Most of the Jews in Pestszenterzsebet were laborers but some were occupied in commerce or were members of the liberal professions.

During World War II, after the German occupation (March 19, 1944), the 3,000 Jews in Pestszenterzsebet were among the last to be deported to Auschwitz, on July 8. Very few returned, and in 1969 only six Jews were living there.

BIBLIOGRAPHY: B. Krishaber, in: *Zsidó Évkönyv*, 1 (1927), 131–3.

[Baruch Yaron]

PESUKEI DE-ZIMRA (Aram. פְּסוּקֵי דְזִמְרָא; lit. "verses of song/praise"; cf. Shab. 118b; Soferim 18:1, ed. Higger), in the Ashkenazi rite, the Psalms and cognate biblical passages recited in *Shaḥarit* immediately following the morning *benedictions; the Sephardi, Yemenite, and Italian designation is *Zemirot*. The liturgical pattern requires meditation prior to formal prayer (Ber. 32a, cf. Bet. 5:1) in order to achieve the required state of mind; the recitation of the *Pesukei de-Zimra* is in place of such meditation (Tosafot ad loc.). The Ashkenazi practice is to enclose the *Pesukei de-Zimra* between the two blessings, *Barukh she-Amar* and *Yishtabbaḥ*. On weekdays, they comprise I Chronicles 16:8–36, plus a lectionary of 23 verses from Psalms; Psalm 100; another lectionary, mostly from Psalms, beginning *Yehi khevod*; Psalms 145–50; a doxology formed by the final verse of Psalms 89, 135, and 72:18–19; I Chronicles 29:10–13; Nehemiah 9:6–11; and Exodus 14:30–15:18, 19, plus three divine kingship verses. On Sabbaths and festivals, Psalm 100 is omitted while Psalms 19, 34, 90, 91, 135, 136, 33, 92, and 93 are added before *Yehi khevod*. Also the prayer *Nishmat kol ḥai is recited before *Yishtabbaḥ*.

There is considerable variation in the other rites, especially for Sabbaths and festivals, reflecting the relatively late development of a custom not mandated by the Talmud. The expression *pesukei* ("verses") rather than *pirkei* ("chapters") suggests that "originally not whole Psalms but selections from them were prescribed" (J. Mann in HUCA, 2 (1925), 276). Liebreich distinguished two stages of evolution: before the inclusion of Psalms 145–50, and thereafter. The sages lauded "those who complete the *Hallel* [Psalms] daily" (Shab. 118b). Special merit was attached to reciting Psalm 145 (*Ashrei*). Psalms were publicly recited in both Temples, but *Pesukei de-Zimra* did not become integral to synagogue worship until geonic times. Only a reader and two respondents are required for their public recitation (Mid. Ps. 113:3).

BIBLIOGRAPHY: Abrahams, Companion, xxix–xxxix; Elbogen, Gottesdienst, 81–87; K. Kohler, *Studies, Addresses and Personal Papers* (1931), 141–6; Idelsohn, Liturgy, 80–84; Liebreich, in: PAAJR, 18 (1948/49), 255–67; idem, in: JQR, 41 (1951), 195–206; E. Levy, *Yesodot ha-Tefillah* (1952^2), 132–8.

[Herman Kieval]

PETAḤ TIKVAH (Heb. פֶּתַח תִּקְוָה), city in Israel's Coastal Plain, 7 mi. (12 km.) E. of Tel Aviv. In the 1870s a number of observant Jews from Jerusalem decided to become farmers and establish a village called Petaḥ Tikvah ("Gateway of Hope"), after Hosea 2:17. They initially set out to purchase a tract of land near Jericho, but did not obtain the consent of the Turkish Crown to the transfer of ownership. Not abandoning their plan, in 1878 they chose an area of 3,400 dunams near the Yarkon River course, adjoining an Arab village called Mulabbis and owned by a Greek. The area looked attractive with its greenery, uncommon for the country in those days. Disregarding warnings of the danger of malaria there, the settlers acquired the land and thus laid the ground for the first Jewish village in the country, which later became known as "the mother of the moshavot." The founders, Joel Moses *Salomon, David *Gutmann, and Yehoshua *Stampfer, succeeded in mobilizing additional settlers, but soon malaria wrought havoc, the first harvests were disappointing, and quarrels broke out within the group. In 1882 Petaḥ Tikvah numbered 10 houses and 66 inhabitants. As health conditions became unbearable, the settlers had to transfer to the neighborhood of the Arab village Yehud further south.

In 1883 *Bilu immigrants renewed settlement on the site of Petaḥ Tikvah itself. They again had to withstand immense difficulties caused by their own lack of farming experience and financial means, frequent raids of Arab neighbors, and the hostility of the Turkish authorities. Baron Edmond de *Rothschild soon came to their aid and enabled them to embark on the drainage of the swamps. The direction of the moshavah passed from the local committee into the hands of the Rothschild administration. This step soon became a source of tension between the officials and the settlers, until Rothschild decided (in 1900) to transfer the moshavah to the *Jewish Colonization Association (ICA). The danger of Arab attacks, causing bodily harm to settlers, damage to homes and other property, and the malicious practice of pasturing Arab flocks on Jewish fields prompted the settlers to organize a first guardsmen's group, headed by Abraham *Shapira, which succeeded in securing the village and driving off the marauders. The drainage of the swamps and planting of citrus groves led to an improvement in the economic situation and attracted more settlers and Jewish laborers.

In 1891 Petaḥ Tikvah numbered 464 inhabitants, and in 1900 there were 818. The moshavah was regarded as a center by the nascent Jewish labor movement, and in 1905 the ground was laid there for the Ha-Po'el ha-Ẓa'ir and Aḥdut ha-Avodah parties. In World War I, Petaḥ Tikvah came in between armies of the Central Powers (Turkey and Germany) and Allied lines before it was taken by the British in 1917. After the war, the moshavah absorbed many immigrants and in 1920 received municipal council status. In May 1921 an Arab attack on Petaḥ Tikvah was repulsed by a defense force consisting mainly of local youth, assisted by British troops, and four young men, among them Avshalom *Gissin, were killed. In 1930, it attained a population of 8,768. Its growth was accelerated further in the

1930s, thanks to its central location within the Jewish settlement zone, resulting in a population of 20,000 in 1938 and in the attainment of city status in 1939. Petaḥ Tikvah became the marketing center of its region's farming produce and established industries, which, initially, were based mainly on agricultural raw materials. Also in the 1930s underground Jewish defense organizations had headquarters in Petaḥ Tikvah.

With the expansion of its built-up area Petaḥ Tikvah gradually absorbed adjoining workers' quarters and villages (e.g., Maḥaneh Yehudah, Ein Gannim, Kefar Gannim, Kefar Avraham, Sha'ariyyah). After 1948, the city's expansion proceeded at an even quicker pace, bringing the population to 45,000 in 1953, 54,000 in 1961, and 83,200 in 1970. In the mid-1990s the population was approximately 151,100, and by the end of 2002 it had increased to 172,600, making it the seventh largest city in Israel, ranging over an area of 15 sq. mi. (39 sq. km.). Its location on the outer ring of the Tel Aviv conurbation deeply influenced Petaḥ Tikvah's character. Although industry, with large enterprises in metals, rubber tires, textiles, food, and other branches, constituted the city's main economic foundation, farming still played a role, as the environs belonged to Israel's central citrus-growing area. Today, there is little farming in the PetaḥTikvah area. However, efforts to limit Petaḥ Tikvah's expansion over additional farmland in the vicinity, which was among Israel's most productive soil, resulted, from the 1960s, in denser and higher building in the city. Petaḥ Tikvah's industrial area has been expanded to include branches of some of the largest firms in Israel, such as Osem, ESI, Intel, IBM, etc.

Two large hospitals, Beilinson and Ha-Sharon, are within Petaḥ Tikvah's city limits. An important cultural institution has been Yad la-Banim, which is dedicated to the fallen in all stages of Israel's defense. In 1980 the institution was awarded the Israel Prize for special contribution to the state and society, with its founder, Baruch Oren, receiving special mention. According to the Israeli statistics bureau, Petah Tikvah is rated medium-high socio-economic status. The average salary in 2000 was slightly below the national average.

[Shlomo Hasson / Shaked Gilboa (2nd ed.)]

PETEGORSKY, DAVID W. (1915–1956), political scientist, administrator. Born in Ottawa, Canada, to Leon and Beckie (Wolinsky) Petegorsky, he was valedictorian at his graduation from Yeshivah College, 1935, and was ordained rabbi in 1936 at the age of 21, receiving the highest level of ordination (*yore yore*; *yadin yadin*) from Dr. Bernard Revel. He earned a Ph.D. in Political Science at the London School of Economics in 1940 and was in London during the first year of the war. Petegorsky taught government at Antioch College in Ohio, 1940–1941. From 1942 to 1945, he returned to his native Canada for wartime service, first on the National Film Board and then as director of the industrial division of the Canadian Wartime Information Board. In 1945, he went to New York as executive director of the American Jewish Congress at the age of 30, supervising an experienced staff, many of whom were much more his senior in both age and experience and tested by the war years. In this capacity he refined the Jewish position on civil rights, created imaginative ways to apply modern social research to intergroup relations, and charted new directions for the fight against antisemitism at a time in the immediate postwar period when, seemingly inexplicably, antisemitism was on a sharp decline and young American Jews, who had fought as Americans for their country expected full participation in American society. He wrote books and articles on history and political science, including *Left Wing Democracy in the English Civil War* (1940), *Strategy for Democracy* (with J. Donald Kingsley, 1942), *Combatting Racism* (1947), and *The Jewish Community* (1948). Petegorsky died July 15, 1956, just months after his 40th birthday. He was considered one of the most brilliant products of the first generation of Yeshiva College alumni (which was only established seven years before he received his degree) and among the most constructive minds in American Jewish public service. An endowed chair in the Political Science department at Yeshiva University was established in his name by many of the men with whom he went to college.

[Matthew Schwartz (2nd ed.)]

°**PETER OF BLOIS** (c. 1135–after 1204), Christian theologian. Born in France, Peter lived in England from 1169, writing there his treatise *Contra perfidiam Judaeorum* (c. 1200). The work was composed at the request of a friend who complained that he was surrounded by heretics and Jews with whom he was often compelled to engage in argument without always being able to refute them. The treatise is divided into 34 chapters and quotes as authorities not only the Bible but also the Church Fathers, and the *Sibyl. The final passages quote both Jewish and pagan authors, and include the apocryphal text on Jesus attributed to *Josephus. The prestige enjoyed by Peter, whom several of his contemporaries designated as a "new Church Father," while his works came to be regarded as models of style, helped to gain his treatise a wide circulation.

BIBLIOGRAPHY: PL, 207 (1855), 825–70; J. de Ghellinck, *L'essor de la littérature latine*, 1 (1946), 132–5.

[Bernhard Blumenkranz]

°**PETER OF CLUNY** (also named **Peter the Venerable**; **Petrus Venerabilis**; c. 1090–1156), abbot of Cluny, France. Peter was a contemporary of *Bernard of Clairvaux, a prolific author, and counselor of kings and princes. On the eve of the Second Crusade, because of his advice to King *Louis VII to adopt harsh measures against the Jews, the authority of the abbot of Clairvaux had to be exerted for their protection. Peter was associated with the translation of the Koran into Latin carried out in Spain. His travels to Spain resulted in two polemical treatises against Islam, and in an anti-Jewish polemic, *Adversus Judaeorum inveteratum duritiam* (completed c. 1140). This work is set in the form of a dialogue and refers three times to oral *disputations with Jews. It is based mainly on the views of *Petrus Alfonsi, from whom Peter was the first in France to borrow criticisms alleging the "foolishness" and "insanities" of the Talmud and the midrashic texts. Peter, however, also refers to other texts not mentioned by Petrus Alfonsi. As he had no knowledge of Hebrew Peter could not have read the texts himself, but the source from which he drew them is unknown. The most important passage mentioning Jewish contemporaries is a reference to a "Jewish king" in Rouen. Thirty-four manuscripts of this work (some of them translations) have been preserved, testifying to its popularity.

BIBLIOGRAPHY: PL, 179 (1899), 507–650; G. Constable and J. Kritzeck, *Petrus Venerabilis* (1956); S. Lieberman, *Sheki'in* (Heb., 1939).

[Bernhard Blumenkranz]

PETERS, ROBERTA (1930–), U.S. opera singer, recitalist, and master teacher. Peters was born in New York City, the daughter of Ruth (Hirsch), a milliner, and Sol Peterman, a shoe salesman. She began performing at 20 at the Metropolitan Opera, where she achieved the longest tenure of any soprano in the opera house's history, giving more than 500 performances in over 20 roles. Peters, who performed to great acclaim throughout the world, was known for a broad and varied repertoire which ranged from opera to lieder, and included both art and folk songs. Her famous roles included the Queen of the Night in Mozart's *The Magic Flute*, Rosina in his *The Barber of Seville*, and Gilda in Verdi's *Rigoletto*. She was heard frequently on the *Voice of Firestone* radio broadcasts and appeared for a record 65 times on television's *The Ed Sullivan Show*. Caught in Israel during the Six-Day War, she and her colleague Richard *Tucker performed for soldiers.

Peters, who was involved in many philanthropic efforts for general and Jewish causes, established a scholarship fund at Hebrew University. After a brief marriage to fellow opera star Richard Merrill in 1952, Peters married real estate investor Bertram Fields in 1955. Peters, who published a memoir, *Debut at the Met* (1967), with Louis Biancolli, received numerous awards and honorary degrees. In 1991, she received a presidential appointment to a five-year term on the National Council of the Arts.

BIBLIOGRAPHY: M.B. Edelman, "Roberta Peters," in: P.E. Hyman and D.D. Moore (eds.), *Jewish Women in America*, vol. 2 (1997), 1046–48.

[Judith R. Baskin (2nd ed.)]

PETHAHIAH OF REGENSBURG (12th century), traveler; son of Jacob ha-Lavan and brother of *Isaac b. Jacob ha-Lavan of Prague, both tosafists. His permanent home appears to have been in Regensburg (Ratisbon), although he was also connected with Prague. About 1175 he set out on his travels, making his way through Poland and Russia to Crimea, from there to Tartary, Khazaria, Armenia, Kurdistan, Babylonia, Syria, and Ereẓ Israel. During his journey he made notes of his experiences. However, the contents of his book of travels were not written by Pethahiah but by others according to the stories they heard directly from him. The writer does not speak in the first person but relates the events in the name of the traveler. Apparently the book was written by several people, one of whom was *Judah b. Samuel he-Hasid of Regensburg. The writers did not record the whole of Pethahiah's narrative, but a summary of what he related or those parts which they considered the most important.

The book says nothing on Pethahiah's journey to Crimea and little on Crimea and Tartary. The major part of the narrative is devoted to his travels in Babylonia, Syria, and Ereẓ Israel. Some scholars consider that his destination was Babylonia, and that he was seeking a refuge there for his persecuted brethren in Europe. There is however no basis for this. The narrative indicates that Pethahiah was a wealthy man whose principal objective was to make a pilgrimage to Palestine and to pray at the tombs of the righteous. In a letter of recommendation which he requested of the *gaon* of Babylonia, the latter wrote that "in every place where he comes, they should guide him and point out the site of the tombs of the scholars and the righteous." However, besides the holy tombs in Babylonia, he found a large and alert Jewish settlement with a flourishing spiritual life, a firmly established *exilarch, and a respected *gaon* who could implement his instructions by force. This autonomous power, and the methods of study at the great yeshivah there, left a tremendous impression on the German traveler, and he related all of this in detail. When he told of the Babylonian *gaon*, he emphasized, in addition to his erudition, his political power and princely deportment.

In contrast to Babylonia, he found only a poor and oppressed community in Ereẓ Israel. The crusaders who had conquered the country in 1099 had annihilated the Jewish settlements in Jerusalem, Hebron, and other places, and the remnants had fled to Syria and Egypt. The traveler did not therefore dwell on at length or the writer did not note down the details of the Jewish population in Palestine. Of the country's settlements, principally mentioned are Tiberias, Acre, Jerusalem, and Hebron. In Jerusalem he found only one Jew, Abraham the Dyer, whose services were needed by the crusaders. Pethahiah's main descriptions of Palestine concern the holy places and the reports and traditions about them. He does not tell anything of his return journey, and it appears that he traveled by sea, passing through Greece.

The story of Pethahiah's travels was published for the first time in Prague in 1595 under the title *Sibbuv* ("Circuit") and has been published in its original form 24 times. It has also been translated into Judeo-German, Latin, French, German, English, and Russian. The best editions are the first, and that of L. Gruenhut (1905, with German translation), which is based on manuscripts and on the first edition.

BIBLIOGRAPHY: E.N. Adler, *Jewish Travellers* (1930), 64–91 (includes excerpts from the *Sibbuv*); A. Yaari, *Mas'ot Ereẓ Yisrael* (1946), 48–55, 762–3.

[Avraham Yaari]

PETIḤAH (Heb. פְּתִיחָה; "opening"), the ritual of opening the Ark in the synagogue during services to take out the Torah scroll(s) for the reading of the Law, and (particularly in Ashkenazi synagogues) to recite prayers of special importance or solemnity, especially on the High Holidays (e.g., the prayer *Avinu Malkenu and the entire *Ne'ilah service on the Day of Atonement). In the Reform ritual other special prayers (e.g., for the welfare of the government) are also recited before the open Ark. The custom of the *petiḥah* may be a remnant of the ritual in the talmudic period when in times of danger and need (pestilence, drought), the Ark was carried to the town square where special penitential prayers were recited (see Ta'an 2:1, 2, etc.). Mordecai Jaffe (in his *Levush Tekhelet* to Sh. Ar., OḤ 133) explains the custom of the *petiḥah*: "The high priest entered the Holy of Holies in the Temple once a year, on the Day of Atonement, in order to stress the special sanctity of that day; therefore the most significant prayers are recited before the open Ark to stress their special importance." The congregants rise for all prayers which are recited when the Ark is open.

°**PETLYURA, SIMON** (1879–1926), Ukrainian nationalist leader held responsible for not having stopped the wave of pogroms which engulfed the Jews in the Ukraine in 1919 and 1920. Petlyura, who was born in Poltava, was active in the Ukrainian Social Democratic Workers' Party. During the Russian Revolution in 1917, he was one of the leaders who organized Ukrainian soldiers into nationalist battalions. When the Ukrainian puppet state, set up by the Germans, fell in November 1918, Petlyura was among those who established the "directorium" (provisional government) to protect the independent Ukraine against its many enemies. From February 1919 he was chairman of the government and also chief *atamàn* (commander) of its army. With the retreat of his forces before the Red Army in the winter of 1919, his units turned into murderous bands and perpetrated mass killings of Jews in the Ukrainian towns and townlets (*Zhitomir, *Proskurov, and elsewhere). Petlyura did little to stop the wave of mob violence which became endemic within the Ukrainian army and the gangs of rebellious peasants, connected with his government. In October 1919 the remnants of Petlyura's forces fled to Poland. The following year he made a treaty with the Poles, set up his headquarters in *Kamenets-Podolski, and joined in the Polish war against the Soviet Union. After peace was made between the U.S.S.R. and Poland, Petlyura continued to maintain his government and the remnants of his army in exile. In the summer of 1921, Vladimir *Jabotinsky conducted negotiations with Petlyura's representative for the establishment of a Jewish militia to defend the Jewish population, should Petlyura's forces return to the Soviet Ukraine (the "Jabotinsky-Slavinsky Agreement"). From 1924 Petlyura was a political émigré in Paris, where he headed Ukrainian anti-Soviet organizations. On May 26, 1926, he was assassinated in the street by a Jew, Shalom *Schwartzbard. In 1927, after a dramatic trial, in which the Jewish tragedy in the Ukraine was amply documented, Schwartzbard was acquitted by a court in Paris. Ukrainian nationalists consider Petlyura an outstanding leader and claim that he personally could not be held responsible for the pogroms, because of the anarchical conditions of the revolutionary period.

BIBLIOGRAPHY: Committee of Jewish Delegations, *The Pogroms in the Ukraine* (1927); E. Tcherikower, *Di Ukrainer Pogromen in Yor 1919* (1965), index; J.B. Schechtman, *Rebel and Statesman*, 1 (1956), 399–415; A. Revutsky, *In di Shvere Teg oyf Ukraine* (1924); A. Shul'gin, *L'Ukraine et le cauchemar rouge* (1927); J. Reshetar, *The Ukrainian Revolution* (1952), index; Hunczak and Szajkowski, in: JSOS, 31 (1969), 163–213.

[Yehuda Slutsky]

PETRA (Gr. "rock," a translation of the Heb. *sela*), a ruined site in Edom, 140 mi. (224 km.) S. of Amman, 60 mi. (96 km.) N. of Elath. It is assumed that the biblical Sela was situated farther north (II Kings 14:7). In later sources (Jos., Ant., 4:161; Tosef., Shev. 4:11) it is called Rekem, a derivation of the Nabataean name *Raqmu*. Petra is situated in a broad valley, which is approached from the east by a long, narrow, and winding canyon, the Sīq, also called the Wadi Mūsā, which has several confluents in the plain of the city. The valley is surrounded by steep rocks of reddish Nubian sandstone. The place is safe from attack once the Sīq and its continuation to the west, the still narrower and more difficult Sayl al-Ṣiyāgh, are barred. The earliest settlement is indicated by Edomite pottery found at the top of a rock called Umm al-Biyāra in the southwestern part of the site. This rock served mainly as a place of refuge, the last time during the attack on the Nabateans by Antigonus. Owing to its secure position, Petra was adopted by the Nabatean kings as their capital; the caravan routes from the Syrian desert, Elath, Gaza, and the Mediterranean converged there. In 106 C.E. the city was incorporated into the Roman Empire, remaining the capital of the region – Provincia Arabia – until the time of Hadrian, who endowed it with the title of *metropolis*. Papyri discovered in the caves of the Judean Desert reveal that Petra had a senate and archives, and that it was visited by the Jewish inhabitants of the province; possibly, a number of Jews lived there. When the capital of Arabia was transferred to Bosrah, the city began to decline. In the time of Diocletian (late third century), it was included in Palestine and in the fifth century became the *metropolis* of the province of Palaestina Tertia. It disappeared from history in Arab times, apart from a brief Crusader interlude when it was known as *Li Vaux Moyse* ("the valley of Moses"). Its ruins were discovered by Burckhardt in 1812. It has since been explored by numerous scholars, in particular by R.E. Brünnow and A. von Domaszewski, G. Dalman, Th. Wiegand, S. and A. Hersfield, D. Kirkbride, and P.J. Parr. The first plan of Petra was made by W. von Bachmann in 1921, and a new accurate and measured map has been prepared in recent years by the architect C. Kanellopoulos. In the early 1980s Z. Muheissen made a study of the water-management systems of Petra and its vicinity. A major study of the architecture of Petra and its decorations was made by J. McKenzie and published in 1990. Excavations between 1988 and 1997 by B. Kolb have uncovered residential buildings close to ez-Zantur. Since 1993 major excavations have been undertaken at the Great Nabataean Temple and elsewhere by M.S.

Joukowsky. A number of Byzantine churches have been investigated in an ACOR project led by P. Bikai, with the discovery in 1993 of an amazing cache of Greek papyri from the sixth century in one of the churches (St. Mary).

In the center of the plain of Petra are the remains of the town, which is partly surrounded by a wall extending from the southern suburb of al-Katūte to the tower sanctuary on ʿArqūb al-Hīsha in the east. The remains are mainly Hellenistic (Nabatean) and Roman, with additional Byzantine remains extending towards the north ridge. After 106 C.E., al-Katūte was abandoned and the town life was concentrated in the main colonnaded street (with shops) in the bed of the Wadi Mūsā. On the northern side of this street are, from east to west, two nymphaea and pool near the issue of Wadi al-Matāha, a "royal palace," and the Temple of the Winged Lions or Temple of Al-Uzza ("gymnasium"). On the southern side the "Trajanic Arch" leads to the "upper market" (agora) surrounded by a porticoe, with another market further west (the "middle market"), the Great Temple, with a lower temenos in front of it, and with an adjacent pool and garden complex (the so-called "lower" market) and a public bath. A triumphal arch (the "Temenos Gate") crosses the street not far from the bath, with towers to the north and south. Beyond it is the "Small Temple" and further to the west the Temple of Dushares, also known as Qaṣr al-Bint Farʿun ("the castle of Pharaoh's daughter"), one of the best-preserved buildings at Petra; it is a temple *in antis* on a podium with pronaos, cella, and an adytum in three parts. Another remarkable structure is the rock-cut theater close to the Siq, which was excavated in 1963. It consists of three tiers of seats with a *scenae frons* resembling that of the theater at Beth-Shean. Of principal interest at Petra are the rock-cut facades. Some of these may belong to temples (as e.g., the famous al-Khazna in the Sīq – recently additional chambers have been found at a lower level below the steps) and dwelling houses, but above all, they belong to monumental tombs of the kings and princely merchants of the city, including that of the Roman governor, Sextus Florentinus. At least 800 tombs are known. These facades are imitations of the *scenae frons* of the Hellenistic theater with several tiers of columns usually crowned with the type of capital known as Nabatean. The lowest tier has a doorway and mock windows and often, an inscription. The second tier is divided into round or square pavilions with broken gables and a tholos crowned by an urn in the center. There are also several "high places" and numerous rock carvings of a religious nature at and near Petra.

BIBLIOGRAPHY: R.E. Bruennow and A. v. Domaszewski, *Die Provincia Arabia*, 1 (1904), 125–428; G. Dalman, *Petra und seine Felsheiligtuemer* (1908); idem, *Neue Petra-Forschungen* (1912); A. Kammerer, *Petra et la Nabat-ène* (1930); S. and A. Horsfield, in: QDAP, 7 (1938), 1ff.; 8 (1939), 87ff.; 9 (1942), 105ff.; G.L. Harding, *The Antiquities of Jordan* (1959), 114–35; D. Kirkbride, in: ADAJ, 415 (1960), 117–22; Parr, in: PEFQS, 89 (1957), 5ff.; 91 (1959), 106ff.; 92 (1960), 124–35; Wright, *ibid.*, 93 (1965), 124ff. **ADD. BIBLIOGRAPHY:** W. Bachmann, T. Watzinger, and T. Wiegand. *Petra, Wissenschaftliche Veröffentlichungen des Deutsch-Türkischen Denkmalschutz-Kommandos* (1921); C.M. Bennett, "The Nabataeans in Petra," in: *Archaeology*, 15 (1962): 233–43; I. Browning, *Petra* (1982); R.E. Brünnow and A. von Domaszewski, *Die Provincia Arabia* (3 vols) (1904–1909); G. Crawford, *Petra and the Nabataeans: A Bibliography*, ATLA Bibliography Series (2003); P.C. Hammond, *The Nabataeans: Their History Culture and Archaeology* (1973), 11; J.S. McKenzie, *The Architecture of Petra*. British Academy Monographs in Archaeology (1990); P.J. Parr, "Sixty Years of Excavation in Petra: A Critical Assessment," in; First International Conference, The Nabataeans. Oxford, 26–29 September 1989, in: ARAM, 2 (1990), 1 and 2:7–23; J. Starcky, "Pétra et la nabatène," in: *Dictionnaire de la Bible*, Supp. 7 (1966), 886–1017; J. Taylor, *Petra and the Lost Kingdom of the Nabataeans* (2001); F. Villeneuve, "Pétra et le royaume nabatèen," in; *L'historie*, 11 (1979), 50–58; F. Zayadine, (ed.), *Petra and the Caravan Cities*. Proceedings of the Symposium organized at Petra in September 1985 (1990); Z. Al-Muheisen and D. Tarrier, "Water in the Nabatean Period," in: ARAM, 13–14 (2001–2002): 515–24; T.S. Akasheh, "Ancient and Modern Watershed Management in Petra," in: ANE, 65:4 (2002), 220–24; L.A. Bedal, "Desert Oasis: Water Consumption and Display in the Nabatean Capital," in: ANE, 65:4 (2002), 225–34; M.S. Joukowsky, "The Petra Great Temple: A Nabatean Architectural Miracle," in: ANE, 65:4 (2002), 235–48; J. Bodel and S.K. Reid, "A Dedicatory Inscription to the Emperor Trajan from the Small Temple at Petra, Jordan," in: ANE, 65:4 (2002), 249–50; C. Kanellopoulos, "A New Plan of Petra's City Centre," in: ANE. 65:4 (2002), 251–54; B. Kolb, "Excavating a Nabatean Mansion," in: ANE, 65:4 (2002), 260–64; M.A. Perry, "Life and Death in Nabatea: The North Ridge Tombs and Nabatean Burial Practices," in: ANE, 65:4 (2002), 265–70; P.M. Bikai, "The Churches of Byzantine Petra," in: ANE, 65:4 (2002), 271–76; M. Lehtinen, "The Petra Papyri," in: ANE, 65:4 (2002), 277–78.

[Michael Avi-Yonah / Shimon Gibson (2nd ed.)]

°**PETRIE, SIR WILLIAM MATTHEW FLINDERS** (1853–1942). British archaeologist well-known for his work in Egypt, as well as in Palestine. In 1880 he visited Egypt for the first time and in 1882 he was engaged in establishing the exact measurements of the Giza pyramids. In Palestine he conducted excavations at Tell el-Ḥesī in 1890 on behalf of the Palestine Exploration Fund, pointing out for the first time that a mound was not a rubbish heap, as some scholars believed at that time (notably C.R. Conder), but represented the superimposed strata of ancient settlements with a sequence of identifiable cultural materials and pottery dating from different ages. Petrie did many of the drawings and plans himself, even going as far as making his own "pinhole" cameras. One of his invented cameras is shown at the Museum of Photography in Bath. Beginning in 1897, Petrie undertook excavations in Egypt on behalf of the Egypt Excavation Fund. He excavated and identified, among many others, a number of Pre-Dynastic sites (where he applied his method of sequence dating), the early royal tombs at Abydos, discovering the Sinaitic inscriptions and the Greek city of Naucratis. In the process Petrie also studied many aspects of ancient Egyptian life, such as the use of papyri in mummification. From 1893 to 1935, Petrie served as professor of Egyptology at University College in London. He excavated during the winter and published the results in the summer, eventually producing over 100 reports. In 1926 he founded the British School of Archaeology in Egypt, which supported several excavations in Palestine. Among the sites excavated by Petrie in southern Palestine are Tell el-Jemmeh (1926), Tell el-Farah (south) (1927–29) and Tell el-ʿAjjūl (1929–31), from which he achieved valuable results, despite his mistaken identifications of the sites. His works include, in addition to numerous excavation reports, *Hyksos and Israelite Cities* (1906); *Egypt and Israel* (1906); *Methods and Aims in Archaeology* (1904); *A History of Egypt* (6 vols., 1894–1905); *The Arts and Crafts of Ancient Egypt* (1909); *Social Life in Ancient Egypt* (1923); *Religious Life in Ancient Egypt* (1924); *Seventy Years in Archaeology* (1931), an autobiography. He was knighted in 1923 and spent the last years of his life in Jerusalem and at the American School of Oriental Research (now the Albright Institute). Petrie was a constant follower of the popular 19th-century eugenics movement that correlated human intelligence with measurement of skull size. He died in Jerusalem and was buried in the Protestant cemetery on Mount Zion (within the property of the present-day Jerusalem University College); his head, however, was removed, following his dying wishes, and taken to London, where it is now located in liquid preservative in a large glass jar within the collections of the Royal College of Surgeons.

ADD. BIBLIOGRAPHY: E.P. Uphill, "A Bibliography of Sir William Flinders Petrie (1853–1942)," in: JNES, 31 (1972), 356–379; J.A. Callaway, "Sir Flinders Petrie: Father of Palestinian Archaeology," in: *Biblical Archaeology Review*, 6:6 (1980), 44–55; M.S. Drower, *Flinders Petrie: A Life in Archaeology* (1985); V.M. Fargo, "Sir Flinders Petrie," in: *Biblical Archaeologist*, 47 (1984), 220–23; L.C. Martin, "The Flinders-Petrie Archaeological Camera," in: *The British Journal of Photography*, 98 (1950); S. Gibson and T. Rajak, "Tell el-Hesi and the Camera: The Photographs of Petrie and Bliss," in: PEQ, 122 (1990), 114–32; N.A. Silberman, "Petrie, William Matthew Flinders," in: *The Oxford Encyclopedia of Archaeology in the Near East*, 4 (1997), 308–9; S. Gibson, "Sir Flinders Petrie," in: *Eretz Magazine*, 52 (1997), 51.

[Michael Avi-Yonah / Shimon Gibson (2nd ed.)]

PETROGRAD CONFERENCE, seventh national conference of the Russian Zionists and the first after the February 1917 Revolution. It opened on June 6, 1917. Five hundred and fifty-two delegates, representing 140,000 shekel holders from 680 cities and towns, took part in the conference. In the new Russia, the conference demonstrated the growing power of Zionism among Jewry and defined the Russian Zionists' attitude toward the problems of the World Zionist movement and the upbuilding of Ereẓ Israel. It discussed the specific problems of the Russian Jews under the democratic regime with the hope of expanding the movement, which up to that time had acted mainly illegally. Jehiel *Tschlenow and Menahem *Ussishkin were elected as presidents of the conference. In his programmatic address, Tschlenow said that the main task of the conference was to lay the foundations for Jewish national autonomy in Russia, as well as to emphasize the Jewish people's aspiration to return to Ereẓ Israel. Ussishkin spoke of the need to immediately mobilize Jewish capital for settlement work, especially for the purchase of land, and to train pioneer workers. Alexander *Goldstein proposed the holding of a referendum in order to prove to the world that Ereẓ Israel was the desired country of every Jew. The proposal was enthusiastically accepted. Isaac *Gruenbaum and Julius Brutzkus delivered speeches based on the *Helsingfors Program for Zionist Diaspora activities in light of the new situation in Russia. There was a trenchant debate about the authority and character of the Jewish community as the nucleus of self-government. When the conference rejected Gruenbaum's proposal to exclude religious matters from the control of the communal boards, a 40-delegate group of his followers declared that none of them would enter the movement's executive bodies. According to one resolution a Zionist was allowed to be a member of another political party, as long as it was not Jewish and provided that it was approved by the local branch of the Zionist movement. Another resolution read that the Zionist Organization would participate in the elections as an independent party. The conference agreed that educational and cultural actions should be recognized as one of the main tasks of Zionist work, and the Tarbut society should be recognized as the only institution to do this work. This seven-day conference was the last free countrywide expression of the Russian Zionist movement before the October Revolution of the same year became the starting point of its persecution and liquidation.

BIBLIOGRAPHY: Y. Gruenbaum, *Ha-Tenu'ah ha-Ẓiyyonit*, 4 (1954), 98–108; B. Dinaburg (Dinur), in: *Sefer Tschlenow* (1937), 46–48; J. Tschlenow, *ibid.*, 363–74; A. Raphaeli (Ẓenẓiper), *Ba-Ma'avak li-Ge'ullah* (1956), 19–24.

[Arie Rafaeli-Zenziper]

PETROLEUM AND OIL PRODUCTS. In modern times Jews took part in the development of the oil industry, some in pioneering the extraction of oil and trade in its products in their respective countries, and some in financing the industry abroad.

Eastern Galicia

Oil prospecting and the development of the oilfields of eastern Galicia from the middle of the 19th century was due to a large measure to the initiative of Jews. In *Borislav the first attempts to find petroleum were made by a Jew, Schreiner, before the middle of the 19th century. Ozocerite, which became a substitute for the expensive beeswax in the manufacture of candles, was then discovered there. Ozocerite candles were soon extensively marketed in the region. The great demand for ozocerite led many Jews in *Drogobych to acquire plots of land in Borislav to extract it. Thousands of Jews streamed from surrounding townlets and villages to work there, in primitive conditions. The work was performed in two shifts of 12 hours each; women and children also were employed on the easier tasks. Abraham Schreiner, son of the discoverer of petroleum in Galicia, attempted to separate the petroleum from the earth admixture. After many failures, he succeeded in establishing the first petroleum refinery in Borislav in 1854. Many railway companies then ordered petroleum from him for lighting their carriages and stations. Thus he became the world's first "petroleum king" until the destruction of his refinery in a fire in 1886.

In the 1880s the enterprise, capital, and modern methods of corporations drove out the Jewish entrepreneurs with their inadequate means and primitive methods. As a result, 5,000 Jewish workers in Borislav addressed themselves to the second Zionist Congress in Basle in 1898, described their plight, and requested assistance for *aliyah* to Ereẓ Israel. Some Jews were still active in the oilfields of Galicia between the two world wars.

Czarist Russia

As the oil wells in czarist Russia were situated outside the *Pale of Settlement Jews were at first unable to participate in the industry. Later on Jewish chemists succeeded in entering the petroleum trade and subsequently also the industry. By 1910, 15% of oil extraction was carried out by Jews, as well as 44% of the manufacture of kerosene, 32% of the manufacture of lubrication oils, and 49.6% of the trade in oil products on the Baku exchange.

During the second half of the 19th century Jews were engaged in the transportation of petroleum. The Jewish petroleum company Dembo & Kagan, whose owners were A. Dembo of Kovno and Kh. Kagan of Brest-Litovsk, laid the first oil pipeline in Russia in 1870. They set up a petroleum refinery in a suburb of Baku and established relations with shipping companies of the Caspian region which transported the oil by sea, whence it was expedited by rail throughout Russia. Because of the monopolistic position of the Nobel Company in the Caucasus, Dembo & Kagan could only operate for five years, after which it was compelled to confine itself to the marketing of oil.

The brothers Saveli and Mikhail Polyak and the engineer Arkadi Beylin, in partnership with the Rothschild Bank, founded the Mazut Company of Baku, later amalgamated with the Shell Company. The Rothschild house also financed the Batum Oil Association, founded after the construction of the Trans-Caucasian railroad and owned mainly by Jews. The *Pereire family of Paris invested considerable sums in the oil fields of the Caucasus. A.M. Feigel, one of the initiators of the petroleum trade in Baku, organized, with A. Beylin, a syndicate of oil companies to compete with the American Standard Oil. The Dembat brothers succeeded in publicizing mazut as a cheap fuel oil for ships and locomotives. They were the first Jews to be permitted by the Russian government, in appreciation of their activities, to acquire oil wells. With Baron Horace Guenzburg, they established the Volga-Caspian Petroleum Company.

Czechoslovakia

In Czechoslovakia Jews were active in oil refining, and in general branches of the trade and industry. The Kralupy refinery on the river Vltava was established by Jindřich Eisenschimel and Ludvik Heller. The refinery owned by David Fanto was prominent in the industry by 1924. The Vacuum Oil Company was headed by Charles Wachtel and Bedřich Stránsky, who transferred their affairs to New York in 1939.

England

Marcus *Samuel, Viscount Bearstead, played a central role, sometimes in cooperation with the house of Rothschild, in developing the trade and transportation of petroleum and oil on a large international scale from 1897. In 1907 he founded the Shell Royal Dutch Company together with Royal Dutch, which launched England as an oil power. He was one of the first to initiate the haulage of petroleum through the Suez Canal. During World War I, he played a role of prime importance in the supply of oil to the British Navy. Sir Robert Waley *Cohen was active in the Shell Company from 1901, and in 1905 was appointed director of the Asiatic Petroleum Company. From 1907 he served as director of the Anglo-Saxon Petroleum Company. During World War I he served as adviser on oil affairs to the Army Council.

France

In addition to the investments of the house of Rothschild of Paris and the Pereire family, Alexandre Deutsch founded the Société de Pétrole, and his sons Emile (1847–1924) and Henri (1846–1918) *Deutsch de la Meurthe succeeded him. Henri published a work on petroleum and its use and headed the petroleum industry exhibit at the Paris International Exhibition in 1889.

United States

The role of Jews in the petroleum industry in the U.S. was negligible. The petroleum industry in the U.S. was in the hands of a small number of Protestant families which did not as a rule hire Jews. The Arab boycott after 1948 strengthened this tendency not to employ Jews so as to avoid friction with the Arab oil states. Exceptions were the *Blaustein family, founder of the American Oil Company and Armand *Hammer with his Occidental Petroleum Corporation.

For petroleum and oil products in Israel, see *Israel, State of: Economic Affairs.

BIBLIOGRAPHY: N. Shapira, in: *Gesher*, 5 (1959), 122–9; H. Landau, in: *YIVO Bleter*, 14 (1939), 269–85; I.M. Dijur, in: J.G. Frumkin et al. (eds.), *Russian Jewry; 1860–1917* (1966), 140ff.; J.C. Pick, in: *Jews of Czechoslovakia*, 1 (1968), 375; R. Mahler, *Yehudei Polin Bein Shetei Milḥamot ha-Olam* (1968), 107.

°**PETRONIUS, PUBLIUS**, governor of *Syria, 39–42 C.E. Petronius was ordered by Emperor Caligula to place his statue in the Temple at Jerusalem and to use force if necessary to overcome the resistance of the Jews. When they learned of the order, the Jews flocked to Petronius' headquarters at Acre to plead for annulment of this decree. Realizing that the Jews were prepared to sacrifice their lives, Petronius wrote to Caligula advancing reasons for a delay in installing the statue. The response was an impatient command to carry out the imperial order immediately. Meanwhile, as a result of Agrippa I's intercession, Caligula was prevailed upon to rescind his instructions. Unaware of this, Petronius again wrote to Caligula, who, in a rage, ordered him to commit suicide: this order reached him, however, after the news of Caligula's murder in 41 C.E. Petronius's friendship toward the Jews was demonstrated again when some Greek youths of the city of Dora set up a statue of the emperor in the local synagogue. In response to Agrippa I's remonstration Petronius ordered the magistrates of the city to send him the offenders; he enjoined them to allow everyone freely to practice his ancestral faith. Petronius' conduct is indicative not only of a desire to preserve order in the Roman provinces but also of his favorable attitude toward Judaism, which is ascribed by *Philo to his search for knowledge and to his close contact with Jews in the provinces of Syria and Asia, where he had previously been as proconsul.

BIBLIOGRAPHY: Philo, *De Legatione ad Caium*, 31, 33; Jos., Ant., 18:261–309; 19:301f.; Pauly-Wissowa, 37 (1937), 1199–201, no. 24; Schuerer, Hist, 207–10, 219; Stern, in: *Zion*, 29 (1964), 155–67.

[Lea Roth]

°PETRONIUS ARBITER, GAIUS, Roman author and a companion of Nero in some of his pleasure ventures. Petronius links Jewish circumcision with the pierced ears of the Arabs and with the chalked faces of the Gauls (*Satiricon*, 102). In a poetic fragment he says that the Jews revered a porcine deity (*Fragmentum*, 97, in *Poetae Latini Minores*, ed. by Baehrens, 4 (1882), 98; = no. 24 in Loeb edition (1913), p. 354). This may be an allusion to Jewish abstinence from pork, or Petronius could be really ascribing a pig-god to Jews either out of ignorance or malice. He writes also of circumcision whereby Jews distinguish themselves from non-Jews and of the oppressive laws of the Jewish Sabbath. Some take this to refer to Sabbath observance, though most commentators regard it as an allusion to the mistaken notion, common to many Roman writers, that the Jews fasted on the Sabbath (cf. Strabo, Augustus, Trogus Pompeius, and Martial).

BIBLIOGRAPHY: Reinach, Textes, 266.

[Jacob Petroff]

PETROV, VALERI (Mevorakh; 1920–), Bulgarian poet, playwright, screenwriter, author of plays for children. Petrov was born in Sofia into a family of intellectuals. His father was Prof. Nissim Mevorakh, the outstanding Bulgarian jurist and diplomat. Petrov graduated from Faculty of Medicines at Sofia University and, after four years of work in Rome as a cultural attaché, finally abandoned the medical profession in favor of poetry, writing with great virtuosity in an accessible though highly poetic language.

Among his best-known poems are "Palechko," "Krai sinioto more" ("Around the Blue Sea"), "Juvenes dum sumus," "Na pat" ("On the Way"), "Tavanski spomen" ("Attic Memory"), "Na smiah" ("For Fun"), "Dajd vali – slanze gree" ("It Is Raining – The Sun Is Shining"), "V mekata esen" ("In the Soft Autumn"), "Sbogom, tate" ("Good-bye, Dad"). These were collected in *Jivot v stihove* ("Life in Poems") and *Raztvoren prozoretz* ("Opened Window").

In the theater Petrov also sought new forms, combining prose and poetry, drama and music, the sad and the joyful. His plays include *Kogato rozite tanzuvat* ("When the Roses Dance"), *Teatar, liubov moia* ("Theater, My Love"), and *Chestna musketarska* ("Honest Musketeer's"). For children he wrote *Biala prikazka* ("White Story"), *Kopche za san* ("Button for a Dream"), *Meko kazano* ("To Put It Mildly"), *V lunnata staia* ("In the Moonlit Room"), and *Puk!*, which was an international success.

Petrov's cinema scripts helped create some of Bulgaria's best films, such as *Na malkia ostrov* ("On the Little Island"), *Slanzeto I siankata* ("The Sun and the Shadow"), *Rizar bez bronia* ("A Knight without Armor"), and *Lo-Ho-Ho*. Petrov also devoted his energies to poetic translation, including the complete works of Shakespeare in eight volumes and Goethe's *Faust*. He was the recipient of numerous awards, including Bulgaria's highest state honor, *Stara planina I class*, and the French *Ordre des Arts et des Lettres*.

[Emil Kalo (2nd ed.)]

PETRUS ALFONSI (Aldefonsi; b. 1062), Spanish Converso, physician, polemicist, and author, possibly born in Huesca. Known as Mosé or Moisés Sefardi before his conversion at the age of 44, he assumed the new name of Petrus Alfonsi (Aldefonsi) because his conversion took place on St. Peter's Day and his baptismal patron was King Alfonso I of Aragon. He spent the second half of his life in England, where he was physician to King Henry I. Petrus introduced the Oriental apologue to Western Europe through his *Disciplina Clericalis*, a collection of some 34 stories belonging to the traditional literature of the Orient (translated into English under the title *The Scholar's Guide*). He was also the author of a polemical treatise, *Dialogi… in quibus judaeorum opiniones… confutanur* (Bibliotheca Patrum, 22 (1677), 172ff.), which he wrote to defend his conversion.

These dialogues, cast in the mold of classic apologetics, take place between a Jew and a Christian, named respectively Moses and Peter, the two figurations of the author before and after his baptism. The work, divided into 12 chapters, begins with an attempt to prove that the Jews were only partially observing the Law of Moses. The author also touches upon Islam, to demonstrate its falsehoods. From chapter 6 on, he explores the concepts of the Trinity, the Immaculate Conception, the Incarnation, and the supposed fulfillment of prophecies with the birth of Jesus. Chapters 10 to 12 treat of the crucifixion, resurrection, and ascension of Jesus of Nazareth. The final arguments are that Christianity is not contrary to Mosaic Law. Additionally, Petrus was a noted astronomer and translated scientific works from the Arabic.

BIBLIOGRAPHY: Baer, Spain, 1 (1961), 59; Ashtor, Korot, 2 (1966), 172–3; G. Díaz-Plaja, *Historia general de las literaturas hispámcas…*, 1 (1949), 194, 285–6; J.M. Millás Vallicrosa, *La Obra astronómica de Mosé Sefardi* (1937); idem, in: *Sefarad*, 3 (1943), 65–105; F. Ainaud de Lasarte, *ibid.*, 359–76; H. Schwarzbaum, *ibid.*, 22 (1962), 17–59, 321–44; 23 (1963), 54–73; J.J. Jones and J.E. Keller, *The Scholar's Guide* (1969).

[Kenneth R. Scholberg]

PETSCHEK, Bohemian family of financiers and industrialists, for half a century owners of one of the leading coal mining companies in central Europe. MOSES BEN ISRAEL (1822–1888), its founder, moved from his native village, Pečky (hence the family's name), to nearby Kolin, where ISIDOR (1854–1919), JULIUS (1856–1932), and IGNAZ (1857–1934) were born. Moses made his fortune mainly in real estate. In 1871 he acquired stock in a lignite mining company in Most (Bruex) and in 1876 moved to Prague. The real pioneer of the Petschek family's entry into the coal industry was Ignaz, who began his career as a bank clerk. After an apprenticeship with J.E. *Weinmann in Ústí nad Labem (Aussig an der Elbe), he founded his own coal marketing agency there. In 1890 Ignaz was selling up to 7 million tons of lignite a year. In 1906 he bought his first mines. The business of Isidor and Julius, conducted from Prague, became known as "Grosser Petschek" while Ignaz's firm was known as "Kleiner Petschek"; they were competitors and acquired interests in many other branches of industry and finance throughout Europe. Both groups, but mainly Ignaz's, acquired coal mines during the post-World War I inflation years, and subsequently, with 50 other German mining firms, formed a syndicate, in which they themselves controlled 50% of all the output. After World War I the Prague group (Julius and Isidor) founded their own bank.

After Julius' death, the Prague group was owned by seven families, and in 1938 by 40, who transferred their property to a specially created British corporation, and as such in 1937 opened negotiations with their Nazi competitors. In May they succeeded in selling the property at a huge loss for $4.75 million in hard currency. Subsequently they also sold the majority of their possessions in the Sudeten area, including 24 coal mines, their sales organization, and 30% of the north Bohemian coal output. All the Prague Petschek families moved to England in July 1938, and later to the U.S. The property of the Ústí branch, managed by Ignaz's son Karl, was too large to be acquired by the Germans and the family tried to withstand them. When the Nazis occupied Ústí (1938) they immediately appointed a German executor (trustee) and in spring 1939 the property was sold by the German Reich as restitution for 3 billion Reichsmark allegedly defrauded from taxes due in Germany. The Hermann *Goering Werke organized a special firm, known as Subag, to include both groups. During the German occupation of Prague the Petschek residence was taken over by the Gestapo. The Petschek possessions became state-owned after World War II.

BIBLIOGRAPHY: F. Pinner, *Deutsche Wirtschaftsfuehrer* (1925), 305–6; J. Stoessler, in: H. Gold (ed.), *Die Juden und Judengemeinden Boehmens in Vergangenheit und Gegenwart* (1934), 22; *Jews of Czechoslovakia*, 1 (1968), index; R. Hilberg, *Destruction of the European Jews* (1967²), 61, 81; K. Kratochvíl, *Bankéři* (1962).

[Meir Lamed]

PETTER BEN JOSEPH (12th century), tosafist. Petter came from Carinthia in Austria and was a pupil of *Samuel b. Meir and of his brother, Jacob *Tam. He participated in the editing of R. Tam's *Sefer ha-Yashar*, to which he made additions. Petter maintained a halakhic correspondence with R. Tam and with *Isaac b. Melchizedek of Siponto and it is probable that the quotations from the latter in the *Sefer ha-Yashar* were included by Petter. He was also an associate of *Isaac ha-Lavan, who quotes him in his *tosafot*. Most of the statements of Petter in the printed *tosafot* also appear in the *Sefer ha-Yashar*. He met a martyr's death at an early age during the Second Crusade, and Jacob of Bonn eulogized him in the highest terms.

With regard to the unusual name of Petter borne by a pupil of R. Tam, it is interesting to note that R. Tam accepts the medieval legend that Peter (Simon Caiaphas) was a devout Jew who sacrificed himself in order to effect the separation between Judaism and Christianity, and is the author of the prayer *Nishmat, a legend whose authenticity had been rejected by R. Tam's grandfather, Rashi (see *Maḥzor Vitry*, ed. by S. Hurwitz (1923²), 282 n. 5, 362 n. 5).

BIBLIOGRAPHY: Urbach, Tosafot, 191–3.

[Israel Moses Ta-Shma]

PETUCHOWSKI, JAKOB JOSEF (1925–1991), U.S. rabbinic scholar and theologian. Petuchowski was born in Berlin and brought to England from Germany in a "children's transport" before the outbreak of World War II. Living in London from 1939 to 1947, he studied with Isaac *Markon and Leo *Baeck and earned a B.A. from the University of London while holding a variety of jobs in the Jewish community, including education director of the Youth Association of Synagogues in Great Britain, social worker in the Windermere DP camp, chaplain to the DP Tuberculosis Sanatorium, and Hebrew and religion teacher at the West London Synagogue. In 1948, Petuchowski immigrated to the United States, where he received his B.H.L. (1949), M.H.L. and ordination (1952), and Ph.D. (1958) from *Hebrew Union College. He served as rabbi of Temple Emanuel in Welch, West Virginia, and Beth Israel Synagogue in Washington, Pennsylvania, before returning in 1956 to HUC to join the faculty as a lecturer in Jewish theology. In 1974, he was appointed professor of theology and liturgy, and in 1981 he became the Sol and Arlene Bronstein Professor of Judeo-Christian studies. He was the first director of Jewish studies at HUC-JIR in Jerusalem (1963–64) and a visiting professor of Jewish philosophy at Harvard University Divinity School, Oxford University, Antioch College, Theologische Fakultat Luzern (Switzerland), and *Tel Aviv University.

Petuchowski's writings reflected a rather traditional theological perspective and thus served as a bridge between the Reform movement and the rest of the Jewish world. In his *Ever Since Sinai*, he articulated a belief in the authority of revelation and *halakhah*, while interpreting both concepts in terms of the evolutionary process of Jewish tradition throughout the ages, of which Reform is simply another stage. Though initially severely critical of secular Zionism, particularly in his *Zion Reconsidered* (1966), Petuchowski's attitude toward Israel as a legitimate continuation of Jewish history became far more positive after the *Six-Day War. A fellow of the American Academy of Jewish Research, Petuchowski wrote more than 35 books and monographs and contributed to several encyclopedias and numerous periodicals. His thought exerted great influence within the U.S. Reform movement and in Germany, where he worked with Christian theologians to improve German-Jewish relations after the Holocaust. He encouraged the program of Judaic studies at the University of Cologne, which awarded him an honorary Ph.D. in 1979, the same year he received an honorary D.L. degree from Brown University. In 1985, 22 Catholic and Protestant theologians published a German volume in his honor, titled (in translation) *Judaism Is Alive – I Have Encountered: Experiences by Christians.*

Petuchowski's major works include *Ever Since Sinai: A Modern View of Torah* (1961, 1979); *Prayer Book Reform in Europe: The Liturgy of European Liberal and Reform Judaism* (1969); *Heirs of the Pharisees* (1970); *Understanding Jewish Prayer* (1972); *Theology and Poetry* (1978); *Studies in Memory of Joseph Heinemann* (1981); *When Jews and Christians Meet* (co-editor, 1989); *Studies in Modern Theology and Prayer* (published posthumously, edited by Elizabeth and Aaron Petuchowski, 1998).

[Bezalel Gordon (2nd ed.)]

PEVSNER, ANTON (**Antoine**; 1886–1962) and **NAUM NEHEMIA** (**Gabo**; 1890–1977), Russian sculptors. The two brothers were born in a village near Orel, south of Moscow. Anton Pevsner studied at the academies of art in Kiev and St. Petersburg, while Gabo went to Munich to work for a civil engineering degree. From 1911 to the outbreak of World War I Anton Pevsner was in Paris, where the painter *Modigliani was among his friends. In 1917, the brothers returned to Russia and were appointed professors at the Academy of Art in Moscow. They now emerged as the leaders of Constructivism, a movement related technically and aesthetically to architecture and engineering. In 1920, they published their Realist Manifesto, which set out the theoretical foundations of Constructivism. When the Soviet state began to demand that artists apply their talent to political propaganda, the Pevsner brothers refused. In 1923 they immigrated to Paris. Here they collaborated on settings and costumes for a Diaghilev ballet and repeatedly showed their work together. In 1931 Anton Pevsner was a cofounder of the Abstraction-Creation group in Paris, and from 1946 to 1952 was an active member of the Salon des Réalités Nouvelles. In 1948 Gabo, who had settled in the United States, lectured at the Graduate School of Design, Harvard University.

The work of these two sculptors is closely related. While in their early works figurative elements still appear, their mature work is entirely nonfigurative. Anton preferred to work in metal, usually bronze, to get the solidity and permanence that are lacking in the materials – plastic and nylon – often used by his brother. The creations of both are characterized by strong rhythm, and by the movement of free forms into dynamic new shapes.

BIBLIOGRAPHY: C. Giedion-Welcker, *Contemporary Sculpture* (1961), index; idem, *Antoine Pevsner* (Eng., 1961); A. Pevsner, *Biographical Sketch of my Brothers, Naum Gabo and Antoine Pevsner* (1964); Museum of Modern Art, New York, *Naum Gabo-Antoine Pevsner…* (Eng., 1948).

[Alfred Werner]

PEVSNER, SIR NIKOLAUS (1902–1983), British architectural historian. Born in Leipzig, he studied at various German universities. After working as assistant keeper at the Dresden Art Gallery (1924–28) and as lecturer in art history and architecture at the University of Goettingen (1929–33), he emigrated to England when Hitler came to power. He was a lecturer and later (1959–69) professor of fine art at Birkbeck College, London, as well as Slade professor of fine art at Cambridge (1949–55) and professor of fine art at Oxford (1968–69), and was also an honorary fellow of St. John's College, Cambridge. Books such as his classic *An Outline of European Architecture* (1942) helped spread a knowledge of architectural history, and his *Buildings of England* series, published in many county volumes between 1958 and 1973, which called attention to the English architectural heritage, became one of the best-known series of works on Britain's heritage ever written. These made Pevsner a household name among educated people in Britain. Pevsner gave many talks on BBC radio, including the 1955 Reith Lecture. He was knighted in 1969. Pevsner was one among a surprising number of German Jewish refugees who not merely adapted to England but, in a sense, became British icons.

BIBLIOGRAPHY: Hughes-Santon, in: *Design*, 222 (June, 1967), 56–57. **ADD. BIBLIOGRAPHY:** ODNB online.

PEVZNER, SAMUEL JOSEPH (1879–1930), Russian Zionist and pioneer in Palestine. Born in Propoisk, Belorussia, Pevzner was a delegate to the First Zionist Congress (1897) and a member of the *Democratic Fraction. He contributed to *Ha-Shilo'aḥ and other Hebrew papers under the pen name Shemu'el Ben-Natan. Pevzner graduated as an engineer from the Berlin Technical College and in 1905 emigrated to Ereẓ Israel. He settled in Haifa and was one of the builders and developers of the town. Together with N. *Wilbuschewitz and S. Itzkovitz, he established the Atid factory, the first modern enterprise for the manufacture of oil and soap. He was one of the founders of Hadar ha-Carmel, the central Jewish quarter in Haifa, and head of its development committee from 1922 to 1927. Pevzner was also active in the development of the *Technion and the Reali High School in the town; a member of the community council; and a delegate to the *Asefat ha-Nivḥarim.*

BIBLIOGRAPHY: H. Aharonovich, *Hadar ha-Karmel* (1958), 7–21; Tidhar, 1 (1947), 354; I. Klausner, *Oppoziẓyah le-Herzl* (1960), index; S. Levin, *Iggerot* (1966), index.

[Yehuda Slutsky]

PEWTER PLATES. Pewter vessels began to spread through Europe in the 16th century when the tin mines became more fully exploited. In the 17th century they were most commonly found in the homes of peasants, laborers, craftsmen, and middle class merchants. At that time also, pewter vessels spread to Jewish homes in Western and Eastern Europe, both among the working classes and the middle classes. Only a few of the wealthy could afford to use silver, glass, or crystal plates, and Jews in distant villages in Eastern Europe and the impoverished Jewish town dwellers continued to use pottery and wooden dishes. The smooth surface of pewter and its malleability appealed to the artist. The non-Jewish artist decorated pewter plates with subjects taken from Greek mythology, Christianity, and the Old and New Testaments; and the Jewish artist drew his inspiration from his own world, from Jewish tradition, Jewish life, and biblical stories. On the Passover *seder* plate, he depicted scenes such as members of a Jewish family reclining at the *seder* table, the Paschal sacrifice, the sages reclining at Bene Berak, and the four sons of the *Haggadah*. A tradition of Jewish wooden plates apparently preceded the pewter, as a 15th-century plate from Germany has been discovered. The origin of the Passover *seder* plate can be traced through the dress and appearance of the reclining figures. The edge of the plate was generally decorated with Passover symbols, such as the order of the *seder* ceremony – the washing of the hands, etc. – or there were designs of the zodiac and various plants and animals of symbolic significance. Most Jewish pewter plates are full of self-expression, charm, and individuality. Pewter plates were also used for the Purim gift offerings (*mishlo'aḥ manot*). These were decorated with illustrations and quotations from the Book of Esther. Mordecai was depicted riding on the king's horse which was inscribed with the Hebrew passage, "and of sending portions one to the other" (Esth. 9:22), and the plate often bore the Pisces sign of the zodiac, the sign of the month of Adar. There were pewter plates for *Havdalah*, bearing the *Havdalah* benedictions. They often showed a Jew performing the *Havdalah* ceremony with his family. These illustrations are based on those in *minhagim* books and illuminated manuscripts. There are certainly pewter plates for *Kiddush*, showing the father of the house making the blessing over the wine, with the whole family sitting around the Sabbath table, but many of these have been lost. Though these pewter plates served their various purposes, throughout the year they decorated the Jewish home, adding to the Jewish sentiment and atmosphere. There were also plates which were mainly intended to adorn the Jewish home. The most popular subjects for these were biblical stories such as, for example, the selling of Joseph, and this too was common in Persia. The Hebrew letter was also improved upon through the decorating of pewter plates as it had been neglected to a great extent after the invention of printing. In the late 18th century, pewter vessels were replaced by earthenware and glass, which began to spread through Europe. These were easier to clean, shinier, and more suited to the tastes of the Rococo and later periods.

BIBLIOGRAPHY: L.A. Mayer, *Bibliography of Jewish Art* (1967), index, s.v.

[Yizhak Einhorn]

PEYREHORADE (Heb. פיניי׳א אורראדה), town in Landes department, S.W. France. A number of Marranos established themselves in Peyrehorade, at the latest by 1597. Under the name "Portuguese merchants," they formed a community around 1628, when they acquired a plot of land for a cemetery. In 1648, when a partial expulsion was decreed, there were 42 Jewish families (about 200 persons) in the town. In about 1700 only about 15 families remained there. Subsequently the number of Jews evidently increased because in 1747 the community, which from then on is openly referred to as Jewish, acquired a second site for a cemetery. The existence of a synagogue is confirmed about 1728 (at the latest, 1747). The community, by then well organized, had its own butchery and a ritual bath (*mikveh*), and supported three societies, the Sedaca, concerned with charitable activities, the Hebera, responsible for burial of the dead, and the Yesiba, dedicated to study. The Jews of Peyrehorade played an active role in the French Revolution. When the consistories were created, the community was at first attached to Bordeaux and later to Bayonne. In 1826 a third cemetery was acquired, which was also used by the Jews of the surrounding areas. (In 1970 all three cemeteries were still in existence.) From 1826 Jews began to leave the town, and the synagogue was sold in 1898, its furnishings being later removed to the synagogues of Biarritz and Bayonne. A few Jews were still living in Peyrehorade at the outbreak of World War II.

BIBLIOGRAPHY: Gross, Gal Jud, 453; E. Ginsburger, in: REJ, 104 (1938), 35–69; G. Nahon, *Communautés judéo-portugaises du sud-ouest de la France* (mimeographed, 1969), passim.

[Bernhard Blumenkranz]

PEZINOK (Slovak **Pezinok**; Hung. **Bazín**; Ger. **Poesing, Boesing**), town in Slovakia (part of Czechoslovakia 1918–1991; since then the Slovak Republic). In 1450 Jews were permitted to live in Pezinok, which was inhabited by Germans and Slovaks. In 1529 Counts Wolfang and George von Pezinok and St. George, who were heavily in debt to Jews, began to imprison local Jews. When the mutilated body of a young boy was found, it was deemed an act of Jewish ritual murder. The imprisoned Jews were tortured in the main square until they confessed to the murder and other crimes. On May 21, 1529, some 30 men, women, and children were burned at the stake. Only children under 10 were pardoned and were converted to Christianity. The pardon granted to the victims by Emperor Ferdinand I reached them late. Jews were prohibited to live in Pezinok or even spend a night. In 1540 the Protestant reformer Andreas *Osiander published a booklet repudiating the Pezinok blood libels and incriminating the count who started it. The booklet was attacked by Johann Eck and repudiated by Martin *Luther.

In 1609 the counts of the Palffy family allowed Jews to settle on their land and in Cajla (Zeile). They allowed them to build a synagogue and to lead a communal life. The prohibition to live in Pezinok, except for the Palffy estates, continued until 1840; the community prospered but was forced to pay a "toleration tax." In 1843 a German-language private school was opened; in 1856 it was taken over by the Jewish community. In 1874 a new synagogue was built; it was destroyed in 1958.

In 1781 there were 88 Jews on the Palffy estate. The census of 1785/87 lists 304 Jews. In 1830, there were 220; in 1840 there were 271; in 1850 there were 280. In 1857 there were 540. In 1880 there were 321 Jews in Pezinok; in 1919, 359; in 1930, 418; and in 1940, on the eve of the deportations, the Jewish community numbered 235.

In spite of the economic prosperity and flourishing communal life (after the 1868 Hungarian Jewish Congress, the community chose the Orthodox path), the Jews were on shaky ground. In 1848–49, during the Spring of Nations, anti-Jewish disturbances swept the city. In 1918, at the end of the World War I, antisemitic demonstrations, abuse, and looting hit parts of Slovakia. Czechoslovak troops (the Legions) rescued the Jews of Pezinok and helped recover some of their property.

Between the wars, Jewish communal life flourished, although the congregation was sometimes unable to pay its employees. The congregation had a variety of social, philanthropic, and religious installations. The Zionist movement and the Jewish party were active in Pezinok.

Everything changed after March 14, 1939, with the proclamation of Slovak independence. German SS units entered Pezinok. On May 18 the Hlinka Guard (the Slovak Storm Troopers) assembled Jewish men in the synagogue, forcing them to demolish it and destroy the holy books. Jews were attacked in the streets and in their apartments. They were subjected to discriminatory legislation – their property was appropriated by gentiles and their belongings were legally looted.

In 1941 there were 175 Jews. In the summer of 1942, the Jews were deported to Auschwitz. German troops blew up the ancient cemetery, and the pulverized tombs were used as gravel in highway construction. The Germans used the empty space to train their dogs. Only a lapidarium was left to symbolize the former cemetery.

Few Pezinok Jews returned. In 1947 there were 45 Jews. Sixteen local Jews participated in the anti-Nazi struggle. After 1948–49 most of the Jews emigrated, largely to Israel.

Maurice *Loewy, the French astronomer, member of the French Academy and for a time its president, was born in Pezinok.

BIBLIOGRAPHY: M. Stern (ed.), (1893); H.L. Strack, *The Jews and Human Sacrifice* (1909), 204–5; J.C. (May 12, 1939), 30; MHJ, 1 (1903), nos. 329, 333, 335, 336, 338; 5 (1959); 8 (1965); 9 (1966); 10 (1967), index s.v. *Bazin*; V. Turcan, "Zidia v dejinach Pezinka," in: *Vestn* 1:45 (January 1984); D. Dvoraova, "Zhlbin archivov, Pezinsky pogrom" in: *Historická Revue*, 1:4, 34. E. Bárkány-L. Dojc, *Zidovské nábozenské obce na Slovensku*, (1991), 67–73.

[Yeshayahu Jelinek (2nd ed.)]

PFEFFER, LEO (1910–1993), U.S. professor of constitutional law and constitutional lawyer. Pfeffer, who was born in Hungary, the son of an Orthodox rabbi, was taken to the U.S. in 1912. He studied law at New York University and practiced privately from 1933 to 1945, when he accepted a position on the legal staff of the Commission of Law and Social Action, the legal and political arm of the *American Jewish Congress. In 1947 he became assistant-director of the Commission and in 1957 its director, as well as general counsel of the American Jewish Congress. In 1964 Pfeffer became special counsel of the Congress. From 1965 to 1980, he became professor of constitutional law and chairman of the political science department at Long Island University. He co-founded the Lawyers Constitutional Defense Committee (which later became part of the American Civil Liberties Union), an organization formed to provide legal services in defense of civil rights.

A noted lecturer on constitutional issues, Pfeffer was recognized as a specialist in the area of church-state relations and religious liberty. He participated as counsel in numerous cases decided by the U.S. Supreme Court and other of the nation's appellate courts involving these issues. Pfeffer's writings include: *Church, State and Freedom* (1967^2); *The Liberties of an American* (1963^2); *Creeds in Competition* (1958; with Anson Phelps Stokes); *Church and State in the U.S.* (1964); and *This Honourable Court* (1965).

[Julius J. Marcke]

PFEFFERKORN, JOHANNES (**Joseph**; 1469–after 1521), apostate and anti-Jewish agitator. Originally from Moravia, Pfefferkorn claimed to have been educated by a relative, Meir Pfefferkorn, a *dayyan* in Prague. A butcher by profession, he was convicted of burglary and theft, but released on payment of a fine. After his release, at the age of 36, he and his wife and children were converted to Christianity in Cologne (c. 1504), where he found employment. He put himself under the protection of the *Dominicans, who were quick to make use of him in their campaign against the Jews and their literature. Between 1507 and 1509 Pfefferkorn wrote a number of anti-Jewish tracts: *Judenspiegel* ("Jews' Mirror"), in which, incidentally, he spoke out against the *blood libel; *Judenbeichte* ("Jewish Confession"); *Osterbuch* ("Passover Book"); and *Judenfeind* ("Enemy of the Jews"). All were also published almost simultaneously in Latin translation. The treatises certainly betrayed a thoroughgoing ignorance of rabbinic literature. Pfefferkorn demanded the suppression of the Talmud; prohibition of usury; forced attendance at *Sermons to Jews (longstanding Dominican objectives); expulsion of the Jews from the last German cities which had sizable Jewish communities – *Frankfurt, *Worms, and *Regensburg – unless such attendance took place (they were in fact expelled from Regensburg in 1519); and their employment in the most menial tasks only.

Through the influence of Emperor Maximilian's pious sister Kunigunde, and the support of the Cologne Dominicans, Pfefferkorn gained access to the emperor and in 1509 was empowered by him to confiscate any offending Jewish books, including prayer books, with the exception of the Bible. The confiscations took place on Friday, Sept. 8, 1509, in Frankfurt and subsequently in Mainz, Bingen, and other German cities. When the archbishop of Mainz, the Frankfurt city council, and various German princes intervened on behalf of the Jews, Pfefferkorn addressed a petition to the emperor (*Zu Lob und Ere* – "In Praise and Honor," 1510, also in Latin) in defense of his cause. Though the vacillating emperor ordered the return of the confiscated books, six weeks later, on May 23, 1510, he was apparently influenced by an alleged *Host desecration and blood libel at *Brandenburg, and under pressure from his sister, he ordered the appointment of an investigating commission.

The Pfefferkorn-Reuchlin Controversy

The commission was headed by the archbishop of Mainz, who appealed to theological faculties of Cologne, Erfurt, Heidelberg, and the famous scholar and humanist Johannes *Reuchlin, whose aid Pfefferkorn had tried in vain to enlist earlier. Pfefferkorn was to communicate the results to the emperor. When Pfefferkorn learned that Reuchlin's opinion would be favorable to the Talmud he assailed him in his *Handspiegel wider und gegen die Juden* ("Hand Mirror," 1511). Reuchlin replied in his *Augenspiegel* ("Eye-glass," 1511), strongly attacking Pfefferkorn and his backers, and thereby starting one of the great literary controversies of history, in reality a battle between the reactionary and the liberal parties within the Church. It occurred at a time when the tide of humanism was rising, and most German humanists rallied to Reuchlin's side. Erasmus, the Rotterdam humanist, though not exerting himself on Reuchlin's behalf, termed Pfefferkorn "a criminal Jew who had become a most criminal Christian." In September 1511 Pfefferkorn preached against the *Augenspiegel* outside a Frankfurt church, but the main battle was now fought between Reuchlin and the Cologne theologians. When the emperor visited Cologne in 1512, Reuchlin's enemies obtained from him an interdiction against the *Augenspiegel*, and in the same year Pfefferkorn issued his *Brandspiegel* ("Burning Glass"), an even more vituperative attack on Reuchlin and the Jews. Reuchlin submitted a further defense; the emperor imposed silence on both sides in June 1513.

The conflict echoed in the papal court and Pope Leo X set up a special ecclesiastical tribunal at Speyer to deal with the matter (November 1513). The judgment of March 1514, favorable to Reuchlin, was torn down by Pfefferkorn in Cologne, and in the same year he published a further tract, *Die Sturmglocke* ("Alarm Bell"); however, he was taken to task for breaking the silence imposed by the emperor. A scandal connected with another apostate named Rapp was used by Ulrich van Hutten, Crotus Rubianus, and other supporters of Reuchlin to discredit Pfefferkorn and in 1516 they issued the *Epistolae Obscurorum Virorum* ("Letters of Obscure Men"), a virulent but effective satire on Pfefferkorn, the Dominicans, and all they stood for. In retaliation Pfefferkorn published his defense (*Beschirmung…*, 1516, also in Latin) and a further attack on Reuchlin (*Streibuechlein* – "Polemic") in the same year. In 1520 the pope finally decided against Reuchlin, though by this time the proceedings were so far removed from the original controversy against Jewish literature that the decision did not interfere with David *Bomberg's first printing of the Talmud, then in process in Venice. Pfefferkorn fired his last triumphant shot in 1521 with *Eine Mitleidige Clag* ("A Pitiful Complaint"), which Graetz describes as the most impudent and obscene of all his lampoons, and for which the printer, but not the author, was imprisoned. The outpourings from the other side were equally intemperate. Though his opponents were exaggerating somewhat when they described Pfefferkorn as a complete ignoramus, his knowledge of Jewish sources was minimal and his acquaintance with Latin nonexistent. Leading historians have come to the conclusion that Pfefferkorn received substantial help in the preparation of his treatises from his Dominican mentors. The effect of the episode was to bring about a considerable decline in the prestige of the Church. As S. Baron has pointed out, it was not merely by coincidence that Martin *Luther promulgated his thesis in 1517, at the height of the Pfefferkorn-Reuchlin controversy. The name Pfefferkorn became proverbial for unprincipled denigrators of their own origin and faith.

BIBLIOGRAPHY: Baron, Social^2, 13 (1969), 184ff., Graetz, Gesch, 9 (1891^4), index; Graetz, Hist, 4 (1894), 422ff,; K.H. Gerschmann, in: *Zeitschrift fuer Religions-und Geistesgeschichte*, 21 (1969), 166–71; S.A. Hirsch, *Book of Essays* (1905), 73–115; idem, *Cabbalists and Other Essays* (1922), 197–215; I. Kracauer, *Geschichte der Juden in Frankfurt*, 1 (1925), 247ff.; A. Freimann and F. Kracauer, *Frankfort* (1929), 48–59; H.L. Strack, *Das Blut* (1911^8), 171–2; M. Spanier, in: ZGDJ, 6 (1936), 209–29; A. Kober, *Cologne* (1940), 168ff.; M. Brod, *Johannes Reuchlin und sein Kampf* (1965), index.

°PFEIFFER, ROBERT HENRY (1892–1958), U.S. Protestant Bible scholar and Assyriologist. Pfeiffer taught at Harvard University from 1922, after serving in the ministry of the Methodist Church from 1916 to 1919. He directed the Harvard-Baghdad School excavations at Nuzi, Iraq (from 1928), and from 1931 served as curator of the Harvard Semitic Museum.

Pfeiffer is mainly known for his *Introduction to the Old Testament* (1941, 1952^2) and its sequel *History of New Testament Times, With an Introduction to the Apocrypha* (1949). These works and his *The Books of the Old Testament* (1957) show a marked influence of his major professors at Harvard, George Foot Moore and William R. Arnold. It was the influence of the latter and the writings of A. Klostermann that led him to isolate the earliest Hebrew historical source that includes II Samuel 9–20 and I Kings 1–2, published as *The Hebrew Iliad* with general and chapter introductions by William G. Pollard, and to claim that the priest Ahimaaz, the biographer of David, was "the father of history," history being defined as a narrative of past events dominated by great ideas. Pfeiffer's works in the field of Assyriology included *The Archives of Shilwateshub* (1932); *Excavations at Nuzi*, volumes 2 (1933) and 4 (with E.R. Lacheman, 1942); *One Hundred New Selected Nuzi Texts* (with E.A. *Speiser, 1936); and *State Letters of Assyria* (1935).

Pfeiffer wrote a number of papers on literary, philological, and historical critical problems of the Bible. His comments on New Testament subjects followed the methodology of his teaching, which was distinguished by a traditional Christian approach. He was editor of the *Journal of Biblical Literature*, 1943–47.

[Zev Garber]

PFORZHEIM, city in Baden, Germany. The first reference to the presence of Jews dates from the 13th century. In 1267 the discovery of the corpse of a drowned girl gave rise to a *blood libel against the Jewish community, and their communal leaders were killed. Their martyrdom was extolled in religious verse and the day of their death (20th Tammuz) set aside as a fast day. The community was almost annihilated during the *Black Death persecutions of 1349. In the 15th century a few **Schutzjuden* lived in Pforzheim. In the early 16th century J. *Reuchlin, the renowned humanist, intervened on behalf of the Jews of Pforzheim with Margrave Philip I (1479–1533). Expelled with all the Jews of *Baden in 1614, they returned in 1670. The handful of Jewish families in Pforzheim in the 18th century dealt mainly in cattle, leather, and cloth. Prior to 1812, worship was conducted in a private home, but in that year a synagogue was built. It remained in use until 1893, when a new synagogue was built, later renovated in 1930. A cemetery was consecrated in 1846 and a school founded in 1832. The community increased from 101 in 1801 to 287 in 1875 and continued to grow, in part due to the flourishing jewelry industry; by 1900 it had reached 535, and by 1927 around 1,000. By June 1933 the Jewish population had fallen to 770 (1.1% of the total population). In the 20th century Jews were important in the financial and industrial life of the city. With the rise of Nazism, Jewish enterprises were boycotted and the community was further depleted through emigration, largely to the U.S. and Ereẓ Israel. On Nov. 10, 1938, the synagogue was desecrated and partly demolished. One hundred and eighty-three Jews were deported to the *Gurs concentration camp on Oct. 22, 1940; 21 returned after the war. They were affiliated with the *Karlsruhe community and possessed a new cemetery. A memorial was erected in 1967 on the site of the synagogue. In 1976 there were 120 Jews in the city. In 1994 a Jewish community was founded in Pforzheim, which numbered 434 in 2004. The majority of the members are immigrants from the former Soviet Union. A new community center functioned from 2006.

BIBLIOGRAPHY: *Germania Judaica*, 2 (1968), 654–5; F. Hundsnurscher and G. Taddey, *Die juedischen Gemeinden in Baden* (1968); Salfeld, Martyrol, index; PK, Germanyah; G. Braendle (ed.), *Gurs – Vorhoelle von Auschwitz. Antisemitismus in Pforzheim 1920–1980* (1980); idem, *Die juedischen Mitbuerger der Stadt Pforzheim* (1985); G. Braendle and W. Zink, *Juedische Gotteshaeuser in Pforzheim* (1990); M. Preuss, *Der juedische Friedhof auf der Schanz in Pforzheim* (1994); G. Braendle, *Juedisches Pforzheim. Einladung zur Spurensuche* (Orte juedischer Kultur) (2001). **WEBSITES:** www.alemannia-judaica.de; www.jgm-net.de/Baden/pforzhm.html; www.israelitische-kultusgemeinde-pforzheim.de.

[Larissa Daemmig (2nd ed.)]

PFORZHEIMER, CARL HOWARD (1879–1957), U.S. businessman, public servant, and bibliophile. Pforzheimer, who was born in New York City, established in 1901 a brokerage business that became well known for its underwriting of oil securities at a time when the U.S. financial community generally regarded such issues as a poor risk. Active in Westchester County public affairs, he served as chairman of the Westchester County Emergency Work Bureau (1931–35); the Westchester County Commission on Government, whose work subsequently led to the promulgation of Westchester's Home Rule Charter; and the Westchester County Planning Commission. Pforzheimer was a trustee of the Jewish Publication Society of America and of Montefiore Hospital, and a supporter of the Jewish Division of the New York Public Library. He was a rare-book and manuscript collector who assembled one of the finest private collections in the U.S. (including a Gutenberg Bible). Pforzheimer compiled a three-volume catalog of his collection for scholarly use.

PHALSBOURG, little town in Moselle department, N.E. France. Between 1680 and 1691, Louis XIV's minister, Louvois, authorized two Jewish families to settle there; these increased to four in 1702, eight in 1747, and 12 in 1770; on several occasions they were threatened with expulsion. Two Jews acquired merchants' licenses in 1768 and this right was ratified by the Conseil d'Etat. The synagogue was erected in 1772 and rebuilt in 1857; the cemetery dates from 1796. From 1807 until around 1920 Phalsbourg was the seat of a rabbinate (which also served the neighboring communities of Sarrebourg, Mittelbronn, Lixheim, etc.) whose incumbents included Mayer Heyman (1827–37), the model for the Reb-Sichel of Erckmann-Chatrian, and Lazare *Isidor (1837–47), future chief rabbi of France. From the close of the 19th century the Jewish population decreased from 159 in 1880, to 89 in 1931, and 48 in 1970. During World War II, nine Jews of Phalsbourg died when they were being deported and two were shot.

BIBLIOGRAPHY: D. Kahn, in: *Revue juive de Lorraine*, 8 (1932), 253–6.

[Gilbert Cahen]

PHARAOH. The Egyptian expression *per ꜥo* ("the Great House"), transcribed and vocalized *pirꜥu* in Akkadian and *parꜥo* in Hebrew, did not originally designate the king of Egypt, but rather his palace, and was used in this sense in Egyptian texts until the middle of the 18th dynasty (c. 1575–1308 B.C.E.). Circumlocutions were frequently used to specify the king in the texts of the 18th dynasty, and during the reign of the great conqueror and empire-builder, Thutmosis II (c. 1490–1436 B.C.E.), *per ꜥo*, i.e., the palace, began to appear as another such designation, just as in more modern times "The Sublime Porte" meant the Turkish sultan. The Egyptian texts never used this designation, however, as part of the official titulary of the king, although from the 22nd dynasty on (c. 945–730 B.C.E.), it was regularly added, in popular speech, to the king's personal name. In the non-Egyptian sources, particularly in the Bible where it occurs not infrequently, Pharaoh always means the king of Egypt, although frequently the earlier usage, without the addition of the king's personal name, is followed. Attempts have been made by modern scholarship to identify the Pharaoh of the oppression and of the Exodus with various rulers of the 19th dynasty, but unanimous consensus on the identity has not yet been reached.

[Alan Richard Schulman]

PHARAOH AND THE EGYPTIANS IN THE AGGADAH

Influence of Jews' Experience in Roman Egypt

Rabbinic references to the biblical Egyptians are almost invariably hostile and they are probably strongly colored by the unfortunate experiences of the Jews in Roman Egypt. Ancient Alexandria was the birthplace of racial antisemitism and the scene of major pogroms in 38, 66, and 116–117 C.E. Egyptian Jewry outside of Alexandria was massacred toward the end of Trajan's reign. The Egyptians, even more than the Greeks, were, according to Josephus, the Jews' bitterest enemies and the originators of the worst libels against them.

The rabbis, accordingly, depicted the ancient Egyptians as uniformly evil and depraved – ugly both in appearance and character. Thus, when Abraham approached Egypt, he is said to have warned Sarah that Egypt was a center of sexual immorality (Sifra 7:11, end; Jos., Ant., 1:162). Moreover, Abraham pointed out, they were entering "a country whose inhabitants are ugly and black" (Gen. R. 40:4), evidently a reflection of the racial contempt harbored by the relatively fair-skinned Semites for the darkskinned Hamites.

When Pharaoh, "this wicked man" (Tanḥ. B., Gen. 33), took Sarah for himself, he was, according to the Midrash, duly informed by her that she was a married woman; but this did not deter him from trying to seduce her (Gen. R. 41:2). He was, however, whipped by an angel and stricken with leprosy.

Leper Motif

Leprosy figures repeatedly in the punishments inflicted or threatened on the Egyptians. The Pharaoh of the oppression became a leper and sought to cure himself by bathing in the blood of Hebrew children specially slain for this purpose (Ex. R. 1:34). Also, the Egyptian people were smitten with leprosy along with the inflammation of boils (*ibid.* 11:6). The leper motif was probably a literary vengeance for the Egyptian calumny that the Israelites of the Exodus were lepers (Jos., Apion, 1:229, 233ff., 305ff.), while the slaughter of the Hebrew children in Egypt evidently alludes to the atrocities committed in the course of the Jewish uprising and its suppression in 116–117 C.E.

Potiphar's Wife

Not surprisingly, Potiphar's wife becomes, in rabbinic literature, the seductress par excellence, a shameless, wicked woman (Ruth R. 6:1), who behaved "like an animal," was willing to murder her husband (Gen. R. 87:4–5), and went to fantastic lengths to win Joseph's love (Yoma 35b; Sot 36b).

Potiphar and Pharaoh

Even Potiphar, who according to the biblical account, bestowed many favors upon Joseph, as well as the Pharaoh who raised the Hebrew prisoner to the position of vizier and welcomed his family to Egypt, are treated by the rabbis with disdain and even outright hostility. Potiphar, "an Egyptian – a cunning man" (Gen. R. 86:3), had purchased Joseph for the purpose of sodomy, and was appropriately punished by castration (Sot. 13b). He was not even justified in having Joseph imprisoned, despite his wife's accusations, for he knew Joseph to be innocent, and, indeed, told him so (Gen. R. 87:9). When Joseph became ruler of Egypt, he sentenced his former master to lifelong imprisonment (Mid. Ps. to 105:7).

Pharaoh and Judah

Pharaoh, repeatedly consigned by the Midrash among "the wicked" (Gen. R. 89:4), was said to have been charged by Judah with making false promises and indulging in pederasty, and in his anger Judah threatened to kill both Joseph and Pharaoh and, indeed, to destroy all Egypt (*ibid.* 93:6). Judah's furious threats no doubt personify and reflect the savage fighting in Egypt and Cyrene during the Jewish rising in 116/117 C.E.

Pharaoh and Joseph

Even Joseph had scant respect for his royal benefactor. Whenever he wanted to make a false oath, he would swear in Pharaoh's name (Gen R. 91:7). When presenting some of his brothers to Pharaoh (Gen. 47:2), Joseph chose the weakest among them in order to avoid having them drafted into Egyptian military service. This Midrash seems to reflect rabbinic opposition to Jewish mercenaries who for centuries had been serving Egypt's rulers.

Oppression and Enslavement of the Hebrews

In line with the anti-Egyptian attitude of the rabbis, the Pharaoh of the oppression was depicted by some as identical with the Pharaoh of Joseph's time. He was not "new" (Ex. 1:8), only his anti-Israelite decrees were new. It was not that "he knew not Joseph" but in his ingratitude he deliberately ignored the fact that Joseph had ever existed, and he gratuitously initiated the persecution of the Hebrews (Sot. 11a). Thus, even the best of the Pharaohs who had promoted Joseph and invited the Israelites to settle in Egypt, turned out to be a wicked rogue.

According to one rabbinic view, however, the initiative to oppress and enslave the Hebrews was taken not by Pharaoh himself but by his Egyptian subjects. At first he opposed this plan on the grounds that "were it not for Joseph we would not be alive"; but the Egyptians deposed him, restoring him after three months on the express condition that he would do as they wished (Ex. R. 1:8). This interesting interpretation was probably designed to justify the severe punishment of the Egyptian people.

Having cunningly enslaved the Israelites, Pharaoh imposed on them increasingly onerous tasks, often endangering their lives, and brutally burning or immuring infants and even adults in unfinished buildings whenever the Israelites failed to complete their work quota (Sot. 11a–b; Ex. R. 1:10–11, 18:9).

Casting of Hebrew Infants into River

The decree to cast the infants into the river (Ex. 1:22) applied to the Egyptians, too, because Pharaoh was misled by his astrologers who were not sure whether the savior of Israel would be a Hebrew or an Egyptian (Sot. 12a), a legend which must have been influenced by the Egyptian stories that Moses was an Egyptian. The Hebrew girls who were to be spared were meant to be reserved to satisfy the sexual appetites of the Egyptians (Ex. R. 1:18).

Egyptian Immorality

Pharaoh is also charged with having claimed divine honors for himself (*ibid.* 8:12; Tanh. B., Ex. 16) – a normal practice among Egyptian rulers down to Roman times – and with an attempt to seduce the Hebrew midwives (Ex. R. 1:15).

Egyptian immorality is a constantly recurring theme in rabbinic literature, due presumably to actual observation of the contemporary Egyptian scene. The killing of the Egyptian taskmaster by Moses (Ex. 2:12) was justified by the rabbis on the grounds that the Egyptian had violated the wife of the Hebrew slave and, having been detected by her husband, was on the point of beating him to death (Ex. R. 1:28; Lev. R. 32:4; cf. Targ. Ps-Jon., Lev. 24:10). Even when the Egyptians were pursuing the Israelites into the Red Sea, they were like "inflamed stallions" driven on by expectations of sexual orgies.

Only Pharaoh's daughter who rescued Moses from the river is given favorable treatment, and her bathing in the river is interpreted as ritual immersion for the purpose of proselytization (Sot. 12b; Ex. R. 1:23). Although a firstborn, she was saved because of Moses' prayer (Ex. R. 18:3).

Legend of Moses' Taking Pharaoh's Crown

The legend of the infant Moses taking Pharaoh's crown and placing it on his own head (Ex. R. 1:26, et al.) apparently alludes, not as is commonly believed, to the plagues that Moses was to bring on Egypt, but to the messianic redemption when the kingdoms of the gentiles – including that of the Egyptians – would disappear. Significantly, an early Midrash predicts that all the plagues of Egypt would be repeated in Rome (Tanḥ. B., Ex. 15b, 22a–b).

Moses' Treatment of Pharaoh

Despite Pharaoh's overweening arrogance, Moses was commanded by God to treat him with the deference and respect due to a king (Ex. R. 7:3), a widely current political concept promoted by those rabbis who favored cooperation with the Roman authorities as being ultimately in the best interests of the Jews. Nevertheless, Pharaoh cut a sorry figure during the Exodus when he was thoroughly humbled, being compelled to look for Moses and Aaron at night, mocked and derided by the Hebrew children, and begging Moses to take the Israelites out of Egypt (Mekh., Bo, 13; Tanh. B., Ex. 26). This humiliation as well as the ten plagues and the drowning of the Egyptian host in the Red Sea were, however, well-deserved.

Depiction of Plague of Firstborn

The plague of the firstborn, in particular, is depicted in lurid colors. None could escape, for even the lowest classes hated the Hebrews and desired their humiliation and persecution (Mekh., Bo, 13: Tanh. B., Ex. 22). Only those Egyptians who joined the "mixed multitude" (Ex. 12:38), celebrated the Passover with the Israelites, and left Egypt with them, were saved from the plague (Ex. R. 18:10).

Jewish animosity toward the Egyptians found eloquent expression in the Passover *Haggadah*, where the plagues which befell the Egyptians – both in Egypt and at the Red Sea – were homiletically multiplied many times over (cf. Mekh., Amalek, 2; Ex. R. 23:9).

Conciliatory Spirit of Later Rabbis

In the light of such bitter Egyptian-Jewish enmity, it is all the more remarkable that within little more than a century after the bloodbath of Egyptian Jewry, R. Jonathan, a fervently patriotic rabbi, is reported to have said that when the ministering angels wished to chant a song of praise before God at the time when the Israelites were saved at the Red Sea, He rebuked them, saying, "The work of my hands [the Egyptians] is drowning in the sea, and you want to chant a song before me!" (Sanh. 39b; Meg. 10b). Although the parallel versions in the Palestinian Midrashim (Ex. R. 23:7; Tanh. B. II, 60; Mid. Ps. to 106:2) transfer God's concern from the Egyptians to Israel, it appears that R. Jonathan's statement, as preserved in the Babylonian Talmud, is the original version. Indeed one of the reasons for which, on Passover, the entire *Hallel* is recited only on the first day is that on the seventh day the Egyptians were drowned (PdRK 189). In the same conciliatory spirit, some rabbis believed that Pharaoh was not drowned in the Red Sea, but lived to become king of Nineveh and lead the people in repentance in response to Jonah's warning (PdRE 43; Mekh., Be-shallaḥ, 6; cf. Jonah 3:4ff.).

[Moses Aberbach]

IN ISLAM

Pharaoh of the *Koran is the king who oppressed the people of Israel in *Egypt; Musā (*Moses) and Hārūn (*Aaron) negotiated with him. In accordance with the counsel of his advisors, among them Hāmān, Pharaoh ordered that all male children be killed (Sura 2:46; 7:137). Āsiya, the wife of Pharaoh, adopted Moses, who had been found in an ark (28:9). Pharaoh believed that he was god and therefore ordered Hāmān to erect a tower which would reach the heavens, thereby enabling him to wage war against the god of Moses (28:38; 40:38). He severely penalized those who returned to God, including his righteous wife (7:111; 26:45). A description of the mission of Moses and Aaron is found in Humayya's. Several conversations which Moses and Aaron had with Pharaoh are given in the *Koran. There is a great degree of similarity in content between Humayya's description and the dialogue of Sura 20:49–56. Pharaoh conspired to kill Moses (Sura 26:33). One of the believers, who is not mentioned by name, attempted to save Moses (40:29). The unbelieving wives of the believers Noah and Lot are contrasted with Pharaoh's wife, who unlike her husband, was a believer (66:10–11). When Pharaoh saw his people drowning in the sea, he repented and believed in Allah (10:90–92).

Indeed, it is not explicitly stated in the Book of Exodus that Pharaoh drowned; this can be deduced from Psalms 136:15. Therefore, there is a suggestion in the *aggadah* that Pharaoh was saved. Humayya, however, knew that Allah did not take notice of Pharaoh's prayer and that he drowned (34:19). This view also appears in Muslim legend. After Pharaoh asked to repent, Gabriel closed Pharaoh's mouth with the mud of the sea, thus making him unable to repeat the verse: "I believe that there is no god but He in whom the people of Israel believe" (10:90). Muslim legends greatly influenced later Jewish *aggadah*. *Muhammad obviously was confused concerning Āsiya, since she plays the same role in the Koran as Pharaoh's daughter does in the Bible. Pharaoh was very cruel to her because she was an Israelite. Various stories are related about her death: she was cast down upon a rock; Pharaoh whipped her to death, but she did not feel the pain.

[Haïm Z'ew Hirschberg]

BIBLIOGRAPHY: A.H. Gardiner, *Egyptian Grammar* (1957³), 71–76. IN THE AGGADAH: Ginzberg, Legends, 7 (1938), 368–70 (index). IN ISLAM: Ṭabarī, Tafsīr, 20 (1328 A.H.), 19–22; Thaʿlabī, *Qiṣaṣ* (1356 A.H.), 140–68; Kisāʾī, *Qiṣas* (1356 A.H.), 195–224; G. Weil (ed.), *The Bible, the Koran, and the Talmud* (1846); J. Horovitz, *Koranische Untersuchungen* (1926), 56; J.W. Hirschberg, *Juedische und christliche Lehren im vor-und fruehislamischen Arabien* (1939), 61–62, 129–34.

PHARISEES (Heb. פְּרוּשִׁים, *Perushim*), a Jewish religious and political party or sect during the Second Temple period which emerged as a distinct group shortly after the Hasmonean revolt, about 165–160 B.C.E. They were probably successors of the Hasideans (or *Ḥasidim), an earlier Jewish sect which promoted the observance of Jewish ritual and the study of the Torah. The Pharisees considered themselves the traditional followers of Ezra, whom they cherished, after Moses, as the founder of Judaism, maintaining the validity of the Oral Law as well as of the Torah as the source of their religion. They tried to adapt old codes to new conditions, believed in a combination of free will and predestination, in the resurrection of the dead, and in recompense for this life in the next. At first relatively small in number, the Pharisees came to represent, by the first century C.E., the religious beliefs, practices, and social attitudes of the vast majority of the Jewish people. They attempted to imbue the masses with a spirit of holiness, based on a scrupulous observance of the Torah, by spreading traditional religious teaching. So greatly did the religious values prevail over the political in the Pharisaic framework that, in contrast to the *Zealots, they were willing to submit to foreign domination – so long as it did not interfere with their inner way of life – rather than support an impious government of their own.

Origin of the Name

The meaning of the word "Pharisee" is uncertain. It is generally believed that the name derives from a Hebrew stem, *parash* ("to be separated"), hence "Pharisee" would mean "the separated ones" or the "separatists" (cf. Kid. 66a, where this meaning is clearly implied). According to some scholars, "Pharisee" would mean "those who are set apart", i.e., avoiding contact with others for reasons of ritual purity, or those who "separated themselves" from the heathens (Gal. 2:12ff.) and from the heathenizing tendencies and forces in their own nations, such as the *Sadducees.

History of the Pharisees

The Pharisees' first bid for power was made in a period two centuries after the Babylonian exile during the struggle to remove the Temple and religious control from the sole leadership of the aristocratic Sadducees. The inception of the synagogue worship traced to this time is seen as an attempt by the Pharisees to undermine the privileged authority exercised by the Sadducees. Ceremonies originally part of the Temple cult were carried over to the home, and learned men of non-priestly descent began to play an important role in national religious affairs. While the priesthood exhausted itself in the round of Temple ritual, the Pharisees found their main function in teaching and preaching the law of God.

The conflict between the lay and priestly factions of the supreme council and tribunal, the Sanhedrin, regarding the interpretation of the Torah when decisions were required on questions arising in daily life, gave the Pharisees the opportunity to incorporate popular customs and traditions into the Temple cult and the religious life of the people. In general, the Pharisees admitted the validity of an evolutionary and non-literal approach toward the legal decisions and regarded the legal framework of the Oral Law as equally valid as the Written Law. A serious conflict eventually developed between the Pharisees and the Sadducees over the approach to these problems, and two distinct parties emerged, with theological differences entangled with politics. The antagonism between Pharisees and Sadducees extended to many spheres outside the religious domain and eventually became a fundamental and distinctive one. Under John Hyrcanus, the Pharisees were expelled from membership in the Sanhedrin and branded with the name *Perushim*, "the separated ones." They took the name as their own, but used its alternate Hebrew meaning, "the exponents" of the law. Pharisaic strongholds of learning were later founded by such "exponents" as Shammai and Hillel, and Ishmael and Akiva.

By the time of the Hasmonean revolt, it had become evident that the Pharasaic theological doctrines were giving utterance to the hopes of the oppressed masses and affecting the entire life of the Jews. This hope was especially seen in doctrines which included belief in the resurrection of the dead, the Day of Judgment, reward and retribution in the life after death, the coming of the Messiah, and the existence of angels, and also divine foreknowledge along with man's free choice of, and therefore responsibility for, his deeds. These beliefs touched on the theological foundations of life.

Concept of God

Based on the sayings of the prophets, the Pharisees conceived of God as an omnipotent spiritual Being, all-wise, all-knowing, all-just, and all-merciful. They taught that God loved all His creatures and asked man to walk in His ways, to act justly, and to love kindness. Though all-knowing and omnipotent, God endowed man with the power to choose between good and evil. He created in him two impulses, a good one and a bad, advised him to do good, and gave him the Torah as a guide. Since God was transcendent, He could not be comprehended in anthropomorphic terms, nor could His totality of being be designated with a name. Several terms were used merely to describe some attributes of God. The Pharisees spoke of God as "The Creator of the World" (*Bore Olam*), "the Place" (*Ha-Makom*), "the Divine Presence" (*Shekhinah*), and so forth.

Free Will and Divine Retribution

In opposition to the Sadducean belief that God took little cognizance of and little interest in human affairs, the Pharisees held that everything in the world was ordained by God, but that man had it in his power to choose between good and evil. Although "fate does not cooperate in every action," and although God could determine man's choice of conduct, He left the choice open to man himself. In talmudic reports the followers of the Pharisees declare, "Everything is in the hands of God but the fear of God" (Ber. 33b), and although "everything is foreseen, yet freedom of choice is given" (Avot 3:16). As the Talmud puts it, "If man chooses to do good, the heavenly powers help him. If he chooses to do evil, they leave the way open to him" (Shab. 104a). This belief in man's responsibility for his actions led to the Pharisaic doctrine of divine retribution. For the Pharisees, man would be rewarded or punished in the next life according to his conduct. This belief in divine retribution also rests on the more basic idea that man's existence is not limited to this life alone.

Resurrection

According to the Talmud and the New Testament, the Pharisees believed in the resurrection of the dead. This belief in another world makes possible the belief in divine justice in the face of apparent injustices on earth. Ideas of immortality and resurrection are generally attributed to Greek or Persian origins, yet to the Pharisees it was a genuine Jewish belief based on passages in the Torah.

Place of the Torah

For the Pharisees, the Torah God gave to Moses consisted of the Written and the Oral Law, and both were truth. The divine revelations in the first five books of Moses were supplemented and explained by the prophets and the unwritten tradition, and were intended to guide men in the right way of life. The Torah, they felt, was the center of their teachings and sufficient for all men and all times. Their view of the law was that its commandments were to be interpreted in conformity with the standard and interpretation of the rabbis of each generation, and to be made to harmonize with advanced ideas. Therefore, when a precept was outgrown, it was to be given a more acceptable meaning, so that it would harmonize with the truth resulting from God-given reason. The law must be understood according to the interpretation of the teachers who are endowed with God-given reason to do so. When the letter of the law seemed to oppose conscience, it was to be taken, accordingly, in its spirit. The Mosaic law of "an eye for an eye", for instance, was interpreted to refer to monetary compensation and not retaliation. The Pharisees generated a ramified system of hermeneutics and found no great difficulty in harmonizing Torah teachings with their advanced ideas, or in finding their ideas implied or hinted at in the words of the Torah. It was due to this progressive tendency, therefore, that the Pharisaic interpretation of Judaism continued to develop and remain a vital force in Jewry.

For discussion of the evolution of the Oral Law and its relation to the Torah, see *Oral Law and *Talmud.

Synagogue Worship

The Pharisees believed that, since God was everywhere, he could be worshiped both in and outside the Temple, and was not to be invoked by sacrifices alone. They thus fostered the synagogue as a place of worship, study, and prayer, and raised it to a central and important place in the life of the people, rivalling the Temple.

Relation to the New Testament

While the Pharisees, as a whole, set a high ethical standard for themselves, not all lived up to it. It is mistakenly held that New Testament references to them as "hypocrites" or "offspring of vipers" (Matt. 3:7; Luke 18:9ff., etc.) are applicable to the entire group. However, the leaders were well aware of the presence of the insincere among their numbers, described by the Pharisees themselves in the Talmud as "sore spots" or "plagues of the Pharisaic party" (Sot. 3:4 and 22b). The apostle Paul himself had been a Pharisee, was a son of a Pharisee, and was taught by one of the sect's most eminent scholars, Gamaliel of Jerusalem. Pharisaic doctrines have more in common with those of Christianity than is supposed, having prepared the ground for Christianity with such concepts as Messianism, the popularization of monotheism and apocalypticism, and with such beliefs as life after death, resurrection of the dead, immortality, and angels.

The active period of Pharisaism extended well into the second century C.E. and was most influential in the development of Orthodox Judaism. The Pharisees were deeply earnest in the religion of their forefathers, represented the most stable elements in their religion, and were most instrumental in preserving and transmitting Judaism. Unlike the Zealots, they rejected the appeal to force and violence, believing that God was in control of history and that every true Jew should live in accordance with the Torah. It is not surprising, therefore, that the Pharisees devoted much of their efforts to education. After the destruction of Jerusalem in 70 C.E., it was the synagogues and the schools of the Pharisees that continued to function and to promote Judaism.

BIBLIOGRAPHY: GENERAL: J.W. Lightly, *Jewish Sects and Parties in the Time of Jesus* (1925); R.T. Herford, *Judaism in the New Testament Period* (1928); G.F. Moore, *Judaism in the First Centuries of the Christian Era*, 3 vols. (1927–30); S. Zeitlin, *History of the Second*

Jewish Commonwealth: Prolegomena (1933); idem, *Rise and Fall of the Judean State*, 2 vols. (1962–67); H. Wheeler Robinson, *History of Israel* (1938); Alon, Toledot; Baron, Social², 1–2 (1952); N.H. Snaith, *The Jews from Cyrus to Herod* (1956); D. Daube, *New Testament and Rabbinic Judaism* (1956); Schuerer, Hist; A. Posy, *Mystic Trends in Judaism* (1966); J.L. Blau, *Modern Varieties of Judaism* (1966): R. Kaufman, *Great Sects and Schisms in Judaism* (1967). PHARISEES: Schuerer, Gesch, 2 (1907⁴), 447ff., incl. bibl.; I. Abrahams, *Studies in Pharisees and the Gospels*, 2 vols. (1917–24; repr. 1967); R.T. Herford, *Pharisaism: Its Aim and Method* (1912); idem, *Pharisees* (1924); idem, in: *Judaism and the Beginnings of Christianity* (1924); idem, *Truth about the Pharisees* (1925); H. Loewe, in: W.O.E. Oesterley (ed.), *Judaism and Christianity*, 2 (1937, repr. 1969); L. Baeck, *Pharisees* (1947); J.Z. Lauterbach, *Rabbinic Essays* (1951), 23–162; Klausner, Bayit Sheni, index, s.v. *Perushim*; R. Marcus, in: JBL, 73 (1954), 157–61; L. Finkelstein, *Pharisees*, 2 vols. (1962³), incl. bibl.; A. Finkel, *The Pharisees and the Teacher of Nazareth* (1964); L. Bronner, *Sects and Separatism during the Second Jewish Commonwealth* (1967); W.D. Davies, *Introduction to Pharisaism* (1967).

[Menahem Mansoor]

PHAROS (near Alexandria), an island just over half a mile from *Alexandria, on which stood the lighthouse of Pharos, regarded as one of the wonders of the ancient world. According to the "Letter of Aristeas" (par. 301), the Septuagint was translated there, and there the Jewish community of Alexandria also assembled to hear the translation and accept it (*ibid.* par. 308–11). Philo stresses the excellent qualities of Pharos which were ideal for the needs of the translators – cleanliness, peace and tranquility, solitude, and closeness to nature. Philo also relates that a festive ceremony was held annually on the island in commemoration of the translation. Both Jews and non-Jews participated in the festivity where they gave thanks and prayed to God and then spent the whole day on the shore (Philo, II Mos. 35–44).

BIBLIOGRAPHY: *Aristeae, ad Philocratem epistula*, ed. by P. Wendland (1900), 301, 308–11; Schuerer, Gesch, 3 (1909⁴), 144, 428, 610.

[Uriel Rappaport]

PHASAEL (d. 40 B.C.E.), older brother of *Herod the Great. He appears to have been more moderate than Herod. Having received from his father, *Antipater, the governorship of Jerusalem when Herod was appointed governor of Galilee, Phasael exercised firm rule coupled with discretion. Notwithstanding Josephus' generous appraisal of his character, Phasael, together with Herod, was twice accused before Mark Antony by Jewish deputations. The latter were singularly unsuccessful and on the second of these attempts Herod and Phasael were, in fact, appointed tetrarchs. Both he and Herod strove from the outset to remove the vestiges of Hasmonean domination in Judea. *Antigonus, who succeeded in gaining Parthian assistance in his efforts to reestablish his family's rule over Judea, laid siege to Phasael and Herod in Jerusalem. Phasael, accompanied by the high priest Hyrcanus II, allowed himself to be inveigled into the Parthian camp in 40 B.C.E., and both were imprisoned by the Parthians. Hyrcanus was physically disfigured to prevent his serving in the priesthood, and Phasael took his own life by dashing out his brains – this is the official Herodian account but it is more probable that he was killed in battle while trying to escape. The present-day Tower of David in Jerusalem's Old City is probably the site of the Phasael tower of Herod's palace.

BIBLIOGRAPHY: Jos., Ant., index; Schuerer, Hist, 109, 113–5; A.H.M. Jones, *Herods of Judaea* (1938), 28, 35–36, 38–42; A. Schalit, *Hordes ha-Melekh* (1964), index.

[David Solomon]

PHASAELIS, settlement and estate founded by King Herod in the Jordan Valley N. of Jericho and named after his elder brother Phasael, who died in 40 B.C.E. (Jos., Wars, 1:418). The place was renowned for its palm groves and dates (Pliny, *Natural History*, 13:4, 44). Herod bequeathed Phasaelis to his sister Salome; she in turn willed it to the empress Livia, the wife of Augustus; from Livia, the estate of Phasaelis passed to her son Tiberius and remained imperial property throughout the period of the Roman and Byzantine empires. It is shown on the Madaba Map with an accompanying date palm. In Byzantine times, hermits lived there; a church of St. Cyriacus in Phasaelis is mentioned by Moschus (*Pratum spirituale*, 92) and Cyriacus of Scythopolis (*Vita Sabae*, 29). The site is identified with Khirbat Faṣṣa'il, which has remains of water channels, an aqueduct 1¼ mi. long, water mills, building foundations, and Roman roads.

BIBLIOGRAPHY: Schuerer, Gesch, 2 (1907), 204; Abel, in: RB, 10 (1913), 235; Alt, in: PJB, 23 (1927), 31; Avi-Yonah, Geog, 120. **ADD. BIBLIOGRAPHY:** Y. Tsafrir, L. Di Segni, and J. Green, *Tabula Imperii Romani. Iudaea – Palaestina. Maps and Gazetteer.* (1994), 202–3.

[Michael Avi-Yonah]

PHEASANT, the game bird *Phasianus colchicus*. The pheasant was known in Greek as Φασιανός and hence in mishnaic Hebrew as פַּסְיוֹנִי (*pasyoni*). It is not mentioned in the Bible, although pseudo-Jonathan identified it with the biblical שְׂלָו (*selav*; Ex. 16:13), which is, however, the *quail. The pheasant was originally found in Asia, from the shores of the Caspian Sea to Manchuria and Japan. It was brought to Europe and America where, acclimatized in forests, it became a notable game bird. The Romans set great store upon its flesh, and it is told that when the emperor Hadrian doubted whether there were also pheasants in Ereẓ Israel, R. Joshua b. Hananiah produced some to prove to him "that Ereẓ Israel lacks nothing" (Eccles. R. 2:8, no. 2). Whether these particular pheasants existed in a wild state in the country or were bred cannot be determined, although from other sources it is evident that they were bred together with peacocks (Tosef., Kil 1:8), this having been a sign of wealth (Eccles. R. 7:8). The pheasant is listed in the Midrash among those rare delicacies, the taste of which the manna could acquire should a person yearn for it (Num. R. 7:4). In connection with the command to honor one's father, it was said: "One may give his father pheasants as food, yet this drives him from the world, while another may make him grind in the mill, and this brings him to the world to come" (Kid. 31a). In several communities in

Europe the Jews ate the pheasant, which has the characteristics of a *kasher* bird. An attempt was made in recent years to breed it in Israel, but the rabbinate cast doubt on its *kashrut* for lack of local tradition to that effect (see *Dietary Laws).

BIBLIOGRAPHY: Lewysohn, Zool, 213f.; Feliks, in: *Teva va-Arez,* 8 (1965/66), 326–32.

[Jehuda Feliks]

PHERORAS (d. c. 5 B.C.E.), son of Antipater and Cypros, younger brother of Herod the Great. During the war of Herod against Antigonus, Pheroras was put in command of the Roman soldiers and charged with fortifying Alexandrion, and was later appointed by Herod tetrarch of Transjordan. Pheroras was actively involved in the intrigues in the court of Herod. Together with his sister Salome, he did everything in his power to accentuate the differences between Herod and the sons of *Mariamne the Hasmonean. Herod hated Pheroras' wife and demanded that he divorce her. Unwilling to accede, Pheroras was compelled to return to his tetrarchy where he died by poisoning. After his death his wife testified that he had plotted to poison Herod.

BIBLIOGRAPHY: Jos., Wars, 1:181, 308, 475ff.; Jos., Ant., 14:121; 15:362; Schuerer, Hist, 150, 153, 156; Klausner, Bayit Sheni, 4 (1950[2]), 58, 153, 155–7, 162f.; A. Schalit, *Koenig Herodes* (1969), index.

[Edna Elazary]

PHILADELPHIA, fifth largest city in the United States, in the State of *Pennsylvania. The area's Jewish population (2001), sixth largest in the nation, was estimated at 206,000.

Origins of the Jewish Community

Jews came from New Amsterdam to trade in the Delaware Valley area as early as the 1650s, long before William Penn founded the colony of Pennsylvania in 1682. Several individual Jews were transient in Philadelphia by 1706. Permanent Jewish settlement began in 1737 with the arrival of Nathan *Levy (1704–53) and his brother Isaac (1706–77), who were joined in 1740 by their young cousins David *Franks (1720–93) and Moses (1718–89). Nathan Levy and David Franks established a successful mercantile firm known for its shipping and import-export activity. Barnard *Gratz (1738–1801) arrived in 1754 and went to work for David Franks. Gratz, with his brother Michael *Gratz (1740–1811), the two best known Philadelphia colonial Jews, created a prosperous business enterprise which specialized in western trade. Jewish communal life may be dated from 1740, when Nathan Levy secured a grant of ground on Spruce Street between Eighth and Ninth Streets for Jewish burial. Informal services were undoubtedly conducted early in the 1740s, but it is probable that no organizational structure existed until about 1761, when a Torah scroll was borrowed for the High Holy Days from Shearith Israel Congregation of New York City. At first, services were conducted in a rented house on Sterling Alley; after 1771, in a building on Cherry Alley. The oldest extant document utilizing the name Mikveh Israel Congregation is dated 1773, although the name was probably adopted prior to that.

Revolutionary Period

Nine or 10 Jewish merchants, led by the Gratz brothers, signed the Non-Importation Resolutions of Oct. 25, 1765. While a majority of Philadelphia's Jews supported the Revolutionary cause, a few were Tories, among them David Franks, who served as deputy commissary of prisoners and was expelled by the Continental authorities in 1780 for his pro-British sympathies. During the war Jews were active as suppliers to the troops, as brokers for the government (e.g., Haym *Salomon), and as military figures. The highest commissioned rank achieved by Jews was that of lieutenant colonel, held by both Solomon *Bush and David S. Franks, the latter having had the misfortune of serving as aide-de-camp to Benedict Arnold at the time of his treachery, but innocent of complicity. After the evacuation of the city by the British in 1778, Philadelphia became a center for Jewish refugees from Charleston, Savannah, and New York City. Gershom Mendes *Seixas became the community's hazzan in 1780. The city's first real synagogue building, 30 × 36 feet, was erected on the north side of Cherry Street between Third and Sterling and dedicated in 1782. After the end of the war, many of the out-of-towners returned home, including Seixas, who went back to his New York City congregation, and the Philadelphians were left holding a large mortgage, resulting in public appeals for funds in 1788 and 1790. Among the contributors were Benjamin Franklin, scientist David Rittenhouse, and political leader Thomas McKean, a signatory of the Declaration of Independence.

In 1783 the leaders of Mikveh Israel Congregation unsuccessfully attempted to change the requirement in the Pennsylvania constitution of 1776 that officeholders take an oath swearing belief in both the Old and New Testaments. Another effort led by Jonas *Phillips in 1789 was successful, and the 1790 state constitution prohibited only atheists from holding state office. Phillips was also the author of a communication to the Constitutional Convention of 1787 urging the recognition of full legal equality for members of "all Religious societies," later guaranteed by the First Amendment of the U.S. Constitution. The fact that both the Declaration of Independence and the Constitution were adopted in Philadelphia gave the Jews of the community a sense of close relationship to the founding of the nation which was the first in the modern world to grant the full range of rights and prerogatives of citizenship to Jews. President George Washington, answering a letter of congratulations sent to him in 1790 by Philadelphia's Manuel *Josephson on behalf of Mikveh Israel and its sister congregations of New York City, Charleston, and Richmond, also recognized that "the liberal sentiment toward each other which marks every political and religious denomination of men in this country stands unparalleled in the history of Nations."

Early 19th Century

The growth of the Jewish community of Philadelphia, like that of other major cities, was comparatively slow until about 1830. There may have been as many as 1,000 Jewish men, women, and children in the town at the time of Cornwallis' surrender, but this swollen population swiftly scattered, and so large a number was not again reached until about 1830. It is estimated that at the time of the 1820 census there were about 500 Jews in Philadelphia, of whom a little less than half were immigrants. Some of these foreign born felt uncomfortable at the Sephardi services of Mikveh Israel and in about 1795 instituted their own Ashkenazi form of worship, under the name German Hebrew Society. In 1802 they formally organized themselves as Rodeph Shalom Congregation. Philadelphia thus became the first city in the Western Hemisphere to break the unitary pattern of one congregation in each community. In 1819 Rebecca *Gratz and women from Mikveh Israel established the Female Hebrew Benevolent Society, the first non-synagogue charity in the country, which is active today. By 1825 these two congregations had spawned a handful of independent benevolent societies. Rebecca Gratz, Simha Peixotto, Rachael Peixotto Pyke, and other women in response to Protestant missionaries founded The Hebrew Sunday School Society in 1838. In 1848 there were about 4,000 Jews in the city, a figure which probably doubled by 1860, when Mikveh Israel and Rodeph Shalom had been joined by five more congregations: Beth Israel (1840, merged into Beth Zion in 1964); Keneseth Israel (1847); Bene Israel (1852, disbanded 1879); Beth El Emeth (1857, dissolved about 1890); and Adath Jeshurun (1858).

National Influence of the Community During the 19th Century

Beginning with the election of Isaac *Leeser to the pulpit of Mikveh Israel in 1829, and continuing until about 1906 when the *American Jewish Committee was formed in New York City in partnership with Philadelphia Jews, the Philadelphia Jewish community was innovating, pioneering, and, in many ways, the most influential Jewry in the U.S. Religiously, the dominant pattern was a moderate traditionalism. In spite of New York City's numerical superiority – and perhaps because New York's Jewry was so immense and diverse as to be unmanageable, uncontrollable, and diffuse – it was in Philadelphia that new ideas for the shaping of U.S. Jewish communal life were tested. Such creative religious and lay leaders of Philadelphia as Leeser, Sabato *Morais, Abraham *Hart, Moses Aaron *Dropsie, Mayer *Sulzberger, and Joseph *Krauskopf were as concerned with the future and fate of Jewish life throughout the country as they were with developments on the local scene. Other factors which contributed to the achievements of Philadelphia's Jews were the city's tradition of intellectual and cultural excellence, which spurred its Jews to match the activity of their non-Jewish neighbors; the geographical location of the city and its commercial and financial links with the South and Midwest, which brought it into frequent and instructive contact with Jews in other parts of the country; and a less frenzied pace of life than New York City's, which perhaps granted the leisure and perspective necessary for intelligent assessment of current and future needs. At any rate, it was in this community that Leeser's *Occident*, prayer book, and Bible translations were published – sources of incalculable Jewish cultural and religious enrichment throughout the country. It was in Philadelphia that Leeser issued a call for an organized U.S. Jewish community in 1841. In 1845 he organized the American Jewish Publication Society in Philadelphia, and, upon its failure, and that of a New York-based successor organization, the present Jewish Publication Society was formed in 1888. Leeser's Hebrew Education Society high school, the first in the land, was founded in 1849. He also opened the first Jewish theological seminary in the country, Maimonides College, in Philadelphia in 1867. The first U.S. Jewish teachers' college, Gratz College, established under the provisions of the will of Hyman *Gratz (1776–1857), began in 1897. In Philadelphia, too, *Dropsie College (later University), the first postgraduate institution for Jewish learning in the world, was opened in 1907, bringing to Philadelphia as its president the learned Cyrus *Adler, who for several decades was the representative of U.S. Jewry. In New York the Jewish Theological Seminary was founded by a Philadelphia rabbi, Sabato Morais, who was its first president.

[Bertram Wallace Korn]

Mass Immigration and Communal Chaos

Philadelphia's concern for national Jewish undertakings was virtually overwhelmed by the East European immigration, which began to pour into the city toward the end of the 19th century. A fairly homogenous community of approximately 12,000 in 1880 was inundated by 15 times its number within 35 years: There were upward of 200,000 Jews in the city by 1915. A majority of Philadelphia's Jewish immigrants came from the Ukraine. East European Jews were the largest immigrant group in Philadelphia by 1920. The process of Americanization, adjustment, and integration began all over again, accompanied by a vast proliferation of lodges, landsmannschaften, synagogues, and societies, numbering more than 150 in 1904 and twice that in 1920. Most of the community energy was channeled into social welfare and personal aid. The Jewish Foster Home (1855) and the Jewish Hospital (1866), formerly fairly modest institutions, struggled to keep pace with incessant need. Jewish women formed the Jewish Maternity Hospital in 1871. Another Jewish medical institution, Mt. Sinai Hospital, was created in 1900 to serve the immense Jewish population in south Philadelphia. The Jewish Sheltering Home (1882) developed into the Home for the Jewish Aged (1899). Single middle-class women led by Fanny Binsingwanger established the Young Women's Union to assist the new immigrants, opening what eventually became the Neighborhood Centre, a settlement house at 4th and Bainbridge in 1900. In 1901, with Jacob *Gimbel of the department store family as its first president, the new Federation of Jewish Charities was formed through the merger of a number of societies, including the United Hebrew Charities (founded in 1869) which had been supported by the proceeds of an annual Hebrew Charity Ball since 1855.

Federation of philanthropic endeavor did not, however, connote communal unity. As wide a gulf as anywhere in the nation existed between German and East European Jews, between Reform and Orthodox, and between Zionists and anti-Zionists. Within the field of philanthropy itself, family and business associations of the German Jews, and anti-, or at least non-Zionist views continued to dominate the Federation of Jewish Charities (FJC) until the end of World War II. The German Jews kept aloof from the newer immigrants in the Mercantile Club (1853) and Philmont Country Club (1906), where their social gatherings were held; only in the Locust Club (1920), beginning in the 1940s, were social distinctions overlooked and, ultimately, ignored. In religious life, leaders such as Orthodox Rabbi Bernard L. *Levinthal and Reform Rabbi Joseph Krauskopf were personally friendly. However they rarely joined together except for specific causes as when they sold war bonds together during World War I, stood for election in the American Jewish Congress campaign of 1917, or supported expansion of Jewish education. Philadelphia, essentially a conservative city, preserved traditional characteristics dating back to colonial times; it also maintained social barriers that excluded Jews longer than in most other cities.

Toward a United Community: Post-World War I

After the war, Jews from the immigrant neighborhoods of Port Richmond, Northern Liberties, and South Street, relocated to heavily Jewish areas including South Philadelphia, Strawberry Mansion, and West Philadelphia. Organized Jewish education, largely community-sponsored, expanded after the war. The Associated Talmud Torahs, founded by the short-lived Kehillah (1911–early 1920s) in 1919 educated mostly boys and the Hebrew Sunday School Society enrolled mostly girls. In addition, numerous Yiddish supplementary schools, including Zionist, socialist, and communist branches opened by the 1920s.

The Reform and Orthodox movements were relatively weak. By the mid-1930s there were about more than 100 Orthodox congregations (many quite small); over 30 Conservative, and two Reform synagogues. English-speaking traditional synagogues, as well as some fairly liberal ones, identified as Conservative. With the exception of Mikveh Israel, few English-speaking Orthodox congregations existed until the late 1930s.

Overseas events provided the catalyst for cooperation. In June 1919, tens of thousands of Jews demonstrated against pogroms in the new state of Poland. In the 1930s under the impact of the depression, of overseas needs provoked by Hitlerism, and of the simultaneous rise of U.S. antisemitism, the Philadelphia Jewish community began to coalesce. In 1937, the first Allied Jewish Appeal campaign was conducted for funds to assist the *yishuv* and the victims of German oppression, supported by 9,000 donors raising $258,000. In 1938 the second AJA drive, just after *Kristallnacht, reached 37,000 donors, including many working class and lower-income Jews able to give small amounts, raising $741,000. In 1939, there were 48,000 donors to the AJA, 74% of whom contributed less than $10. A total of $902,000 was raised that year.

Overseas needs drove the expansion of Jewish fundraising during and after World War II. For the first time, a community structure with mass participation was established on an ongoing basis. A council of local defense agencies was organized, resulting in the establishment of the Jewish Community Relations Council in 1938. Zionism, long only a small part of the Jewish scene, was growing in influence. Judge Louis Levinthal became head of the national Zionist Organization of America in 1943. Rose Bender (1895–1964) became the first woman executive director of a ZOA office in 1945. In the same period, the anti-Zionist American Council for Judaism (ACJ; 1943) was founded by Philadelphia rabbis and laymen, among them leaders of the Federation.

Post-World War II: Community Change

Throughout the post-war period, Philadelphia Jewish life centered on Jewish neighborhoods and the dominant pattern of moderate traditionalism. Unlike some American cities, even at the close of the century close to half the Jews lived in the city of Philadelphia itself, with others living in contiguous inner-ring suburbs. In these neighborhoods, informal interactions reinforced synagogues and Jewish organizations.

Following World War II, many Jews relocated to newer Jewish neighborhoods in the city (West Oak Lane, Mt. Airy, Overbrook Park, and especially the Northeast) or to inner ring suburbs such as Elkins Park–Old York Road and Lower Merion. Established synagogues moved, and new Jewish institutions were founded. Older Jewish neighborhoods, including Strawberry Mansion and South Philadelphia, declined due to the attractions of newer housing and in the former case racial conflict.

The merger in 1944 of several children's agencies into the Association for Jewish Children, was the first of a number of steps in the gradual restructuring of the community. The three Jewish hospitals merged into the Albert Einstein Medical Center in 1951. At the same time, many leaders were ambivalent about religious expression. The hospital's Frank Memorial Synagogue, opened in 1901, was closed in 1957. (An increased interest in Jewish identity led to its restoration in 1984.) Old hostilities and loyalties were overcome through the final merger of the Federation of Jewish Charities and the Allied Jewish Appeal into the Federation of Jewish Agencies (FJA) in 1956.

Jewish education began to shift from communal auspices to congregational ones, still largely neighborhood-based. Akiba Hebrew Academy, a community secondary school, opened amid controversy in 1946. An Orthodox day school opened the same year and a Solomon Schechter day school (Conservative) opened in 1956. Gratz College reorganized and moved from North Philadelphia into a new building in Logan in 1962.

The Young Men's Hebrew Association and the Neighborhood Center were united in 1965, with a projected network of leisure time agencies throughout the metropolitan area. By 1970 most of the old institutional rivalries had been forgotten.

The younger leaders did not know whose grandmother had been Ukrainian, or whose great-grandfather had been German. Money for Israel was raised and bonds for Israel were sold in the very synagogues whose former rabbis had created the anti-Zionist ACJ. Although a local Synagogue Council had failed in the 1950s, a flourishing Board of Rabbis testified to increased cooperation among Conservative, Orthodox, Reform and from the 1970s, Reconstructionist rabbis. The FJA itself had moved far beyond its conceptual origins as a fund-raising agency and was functioning vigorously in broad areas of social planning.

1970s and 1980s: Transitions and New Voices

Philadelphia Jewish life continued to be neighborhood-based, even with increasing dispersion. By 1970, the Jewish population was concentrated in the Center City, Greater Northeast, Old York Road Suburban, West Oak Lane–Mt. Airy, Wynnefield, and Main Line sections, with growing centers in Levittown and Norristown.

There were over 100 congregations in the Philadelphia area of which approximately 50 were Conservative, 45 Orthodox, and 15 Reform. Some of the Orthodox congregations were quite small, and some were served by Conservative rabbis. While two of the largest Reform congregations in the country were located in Greater Philadelphia, the dominant religious thrust of the community was Conservative. Since most Reform congregations were formed after the war, they had fewer internal struggles regarding modifying the more radical reforms instituted by some older Reform congregations. Several Conservative congregations (including Adath Jeshurun, Beth Hillel-Beth El, and Germantown Jewish Centre) include participatory ḥavurah *minyanim* led by members, established in the 1970s and early 1980s. A resurgent interest in Orthodoxy was stimulated through work of branches of the Lubavitch movement and by a nationally known talmudic yeshivah established in Philadelphia by students of Rabbi Aaron *Kotler in 1952.

By the late 1960s, barriers to Jewish participation in civic and professional life were declining. Representative Jews were appointed to the boards of practically every bank in the city, as they had long served on the boards of the community's cultural and educational institutions. Many major corporations were actively soliciting applications for employment as executive trainees from young Jews, and almost every major law firm included a few Jews. In law, medicine, and other prestigious Philadelphia professions, Jewish leaders and pioneers were numerous. For example, in 1971, Martin Meyerson was named president of the University of Pennsylvania, the first Jewish head of an Ivy League college. Marvin Wachman served as president of Temple University from 1973 to 1982. Arlen *Specter served as district attorney (1966–74) and later as U.S. senator from 1981. His wife, Joan Specter, was a city council member (1980–1996.) David Cohen (1914–2005) was a formidable liberal member of city council from 1968 to 1971 and 1980–2005.

Although Jews occupied a significant place in the political and economic life of the area, Jews themselves were still rigorously and consciously excluded from most of the town and country clubs which represented the last strongholds of old Philadelphia "society."

By the 1980s, declining social boundaries meant that Jews no longer needed to affiliate with Jewish social clubs or charities. Increasingly, a challenge was to bring younger participants and potential donors into Jewish life.

[Bertram Wallace Korn / Robert P. Taback (2nd ed.)]

Philadelphia continued national leadership in several areas. Local Holocaust survivors established one of the first outdoor public monuments in the U.S. in Center City in 1964. Local Jews played leading roles in the Soviet Jewry movement, and an annual rally each year was a prominent event in the 1970s and 80s.

The Jewish Renewal movement created one of its centers from the 1970s, stimulated by Rabbi Zalman *Schachter-Shalomi as well as by Rabbi Arthur *Green and Arthur *Waskow, all of whom lived in West Mount Airy. Other new organizations, including the National Havurah Committee, the Shomrei Adamah Jewish ecology movement, and the Shalom Center were based there. The Federation of Reconstructionist Congregations and Havurot joined the rabbinical college in Philadelphia in 1987.

By the 1980s, Jewish population had shifted again. In 1986, the Federation opened Mandell Education Campus in Melrose Park, including Gratz College (about 2 miles (3 km) north of its former home), the new Auerbach Central Agency for Jewish Education, day care, a Conservative day school, and other agencies.

A 1984 study estimated that about 53 percent of area Jews lived within the Philadelphia city limits. Sixty percent of the area's Jews were concentrated in four areas: Northeast Philadelphia, Center City, the City Line area, and the northern suburbs. The dominant religious group remained Conservative. Amy *Eilberg, the first woman Conservative rabbi, was from the city and served in Philadelphia congregational and chaplaincy positions in the 1980s.

The 1990s and Beyond: Dispersion and New Initiatives

Geographic dispersion increased by the 1990s. In 1996–97, 48 percent of Jewish households were within the city, a number in decline. A few urban neighborhoods such as Mt. Airy and Center City, and some inner suburbs such as Lower Merion and Elkins Park-Old York Road, maintained significant Jewish populations, as did the Orthodox enclaves in the city's Northeast and Overbook Park. These were a declining percentage of the region's Jewish population. Outside these neighborhoods, most Jewish movement was to suburban areas marked by commuting synagogues rather than neighborhood synagogues – only a few members lived within a mile or two (1.6–3 km) of the congregation.

Philadelphia Jewish life has been neighborhood-based. Increasing population dispersal meant that fewer Jews had neighbors or classmates who were Jewish. The Jewish community struggled to define itself with less geographic concentration. The Federation structure was changed to include four quasi-autonomous suburban regions, serving Bucks, Montgomery, Chester, and Delaware counties. The Jewish Community Centers determined that building new physical structures was no longer efficient after the 1980s and established four JCCs without walls in suburban counties. The Philadelphia Geriatric Center, renamed the Abramson Center for Jewish Living, relocated from urban Logan adjacent to Albert Einstein hospital, to suburban North Wales in 2002.

In 1990 the Federation of Jewish Charities adopted the name Jewish Federation of Greater Philadelphia. The Federation and some of its agencies began to place greater emphasis on Jewish values, education, and observance. The *Jewish Exponent*, founded 1887, is the official organ of the Federation, which also publishes *Inside*, a quarterly magazine.

The community showed continued vitality. Since 1990, several new Reconstructionist and Orthodox congregations opened in the city itself and in the suburbs. Existing congregations in the suburbs from all movements expanded, although there were closures and mergers, particularly in Northeast Philadelphia. Six neighborhoods had *eruvim* (Sabbath boundaries) in 2005. Both one Reform and one Conservative congregation opened *mikva'ot* after 2000. The Conservative movement continued a major role, with 38% identifying as Conservative, 28% as Reform, 12% as no denomination, 5% traditional, and 4% each as Orthodox, Reconstructionist, and secular humanist in 1997. Philadelphia was the only major U.S. city where the Conservative Rabbinical Assembly played a major role in *kashrut* supervision. Almost all Conservative congregations were formally egalitarian by the 1990s, but only a handful of women rabbis served that movement locally, unlike the Reconstructionist and Reform movements. There was a low level of formal affiliation. In 1997 only 37% of the population was affiliated with a synagogue.

A 2002 survey found 97 synagogues (excluding 8 in Chester county): 33 Orthodox, 28 Conservative, 21 Reform, 8 Reconstructionist, and 7 "other." Many of the synagogues and Jewish community centers have day care or nursery school programs. There are six elementary Jewish day schools, a middle school, and three high schools. Most children received their education in supplemental congregational schools. The Community Hebrew Schools, descendant of the 1838 Hebrew Sunday School Society, announced plans to close in 2006.

[Lillian Youman and Robert P. Taback (2nd ed.)]

Jews were prominent in the wider community and government, particularly from the 1990s onward. Judith Rodin, president of the University of Pennsylvania from 1994 to 2004, was the first woman to head an Ivy League university. Stefan Presser (1953–2005), a forceful advocate for the poor and disabled and for church-state separation, served from 1983 to 2004 as legal director of the Pennsylvania American Civil Liberties Union. Christie Balka served from 1997 as executive director of the Bread and Roses Community Fund, an umbrella group raising funds for local social change organizations. Shelly Yanoff, an advocate for health care for children, was executive director of Philadelphia Citizens for Children and Youth from 1986.

In the 1990s, Jews held the city's three highest elected offices, as well as serving in Congress, the state legislature, and as leaders in suburban communities. Edward *Rendell served as the first Jewish mayor of Philadelphia (1992–99), and later as governor. Lynne Abraham, a former judge, was district attorney of the city from 1991 and Jonathan Saidel was elected city controller four times from 1990. Allyson Y. Schwartz was a state senator representing the city and suburbs from 1991 to 2005, when she took office as a U.S. congresswoman for a city-suburban district. Businessman Sam Katz was the unsuccessful Republican candidate for Philadelphia mayor in 1999 and 2003.

Jewish population declined from an estimated 240,400 (256,100 people living in Jewish households, including non-Jews) in 1983–84 to 206,100 in 1996–97 (241,600 in Jewish households.) The decline (including some movement to Southern New Jersey) would have been greater had not some 30,000 immigrants arrived from the former Soviet Union, especially Ukraine. In 1996–97 12% of Jewish residents (15,200 people) lived in "poor" households with incomes under $15,000. Including these, almost 23% of the population (57,000 people) lived in low-income households. There were many elderly Jews, new immigrants, and single parents among the poor and near poor.

Philadelphia remained a center for Jewish studies. In addition to Gratz College and the Reconstructionist Rabbinical College, opened in 1968, several other centers were established. Dropsie University, affected by the rise of Judaic studies in secular universities, closed in 1986, eventually becoming the University of Pennsylvania Center for Advanced Judaic Studies. Temple University established the Feinberg Center for American Jewish history in 1990. The Philadelphia Jewish Archives Center opened in 1972. The National Museum of American Jewish History, opened on Independence Mall in 1976, planned a major expansion in 2005.

[Robert P. Taback (2nd ed.)]

BIBLIOGRAPHY: E. Wolf and M. Whiteman, *History of the Jews of Philadelphia* (1957). **ADD. BIBLIOGRAPHY:** D. Ashton, *Rebecca Gratz: Women and Judaism in Antebellum America* (1997); L. Sussman, *Isaac Leeser and the Making of American Judaism* (1995); M. Friedman (ed.), *Jewish Life in Philadelphia, 1830–1940* (1983); idem (ed.), *When Philadelphia Was the Capital of Jewish America* (1993); idem (ed.), *Philadelphia Jewish Life, 1940–2000* (20032); G. Stern (ed.) *Traditions in Transition: Jewish Culture in Philadelphia, 1840–1940* (1989); *Summary Report: Jewish Population Study of Greater Philadelphia, 1996–1997*; J. Schwartz, "Census of U.S. Synagogues," in: AJYB 2002; A. Harrison, *Passover Revisited: Philadelphia's Efforts to Aid Soviet Jews, 1963–1998* (2001): R. Tabak, "The Transformation of Jewish Identity: The Philadelphia Jewish Experience, 1919–1945" (Ph.D. diss., Temple Univ. 1990); R. Peltz, *From Immigrant to Ethnic Culture: American Yiddish in South Philadelphia* (1998); D. Ashton, *The Phila-*

delphia Group and Philadelphia Jewish History: A Guide to Archival and Bibliographic Collections (1993); H. Boonin, *The Jewish Quarter of Philadelphia: A History and Guide, 1881–1930* (1999).

PHILADELPHIA, JACOB (b. 1720 or 1735–after 1783), Colonial American physicist, mechanic, and kabbalist. Philadelphia's family name and the year when he assumed the name of his native city is unknown. He may have been educated by a Dr. Christopher Witt, a Rosicrucian mystic and anchorite survivor of the German Pietist mystic sect known as the "Women of the Wilderness." Witt was known to be a correspondent of the Duke of Cumberland, who later became Philadelphia's patron in England. After his patron's death in 1758, Philadelphia toured England, lecturing and conducting experiments to great acclaim, and later lectured throughout Europe. Considered a powerful magician by the ignorant, Philadelphia nevertheless refused to lecture at the University of Goettingen (1777) after a satirical poster campaign derided him as a miracle worker and magician. He supposedly last lectured in Switzerland in 1781. In 1783 he applied to the Prussian court for a license to form a Prussian-American trading company.

BIBLIOGRAPHY: J.F. Sachse, in: AJHSP, 16 (1907), 73–83; J.R. Marcus, *Early American Jewry*, 2 (1953), 83–89.

PHILANTHROPY.

Introduction

At the close of the 18th century the communal system of fund raising for charity with authority vested in the charity overseers (*Gabba'ei Ẓedakah*) – to tax members of the community in order to ensure appropriate giving – was on the verge of collapse in many European communities. The situation in Rome was typical. "The enormous indebtedness of the Roman community was, in part, due to these expenses for public welfare, which in the early decades of the 18th century equaled or exceeded the total income from communal taxation" (S. Baron, Community, 2, 346–50). The financial condition deteriorated with the rise of absolute states which imposed ever harsher taxes on their subjects. The spread of secularism and individualism, and the appearance of Haskalah (Enlightenment) and Reform also tended to weaken the cohesiveness of the community and reduce its authority to exact adequate sums for their communal functions. Moreover, there were duplication and waste in fund raising and in social services due to absence of coordination between the community, the benevolent societies, and the individual donors who espoused their own favorite projects – a situation which had grown apace (see Finances, *Autonomous).

State Taxation for Jewish Communal Services

In the 19th century states altered the procedures for tax collections for communal purposes. In Russia, which then included Poland, with the dissolution in 1844 of the **kahal* (the autonomous Jewish community) a Russian government ukase forced the Jewish communities to turn over to the municipalities control of their tax collections and administration of their financial affairs and charitable institutions. A remnant of the authority left to them was the recommendation of tax collectors who frequently bade for these potentially profitable posts. The burden of caring for the needy, the poor, and the sick, and for the education of the children, became increasingly more difficult to bear as the number of expelled Jews and the mass emigration of breadwinners reached vast proportions in the 1880s. Revenue for charity and education became dependent primarily on the share given to the community from government taxes, of which they could never be sure, and on limited income from private donations and payment for synagogue honors. Among the taxes imposed by the government one of the most oppressive was the *kasher* meat tax (**Korobka*) and the *candle tax (see *Taxation). Revenues from these taxes were divided between the state and the community to cover expenditure for social welfare, maintenance of educational institutions, and other communal activities. Frequently the share of taxes due the community was diverted by the authorities to build a road or erect a church, and often an inordinate portion of the funds collected went into the pockets of the Jewish tax collectors.

Voluntary Associations or Benevolent Societies in Modern Times

Voluntary associations or benevolent societies continued in modern times to play the important part which they had had in the Middle Ages for raising funds for specific religious, social, and educational services. Where communal charity systems were weakened or broke down completely, voluntary associations filled their place as well as they could and frequently adapted themselves to changing conditions. In England, where plans to introduce state taxation in 1795 and 1802 were withdrawn, many of the voluntary associations in the 19th century were organized on the pattern of voting societies found in the general community. An annual subscription to the association of four or five shillings entitled a subscriber to one vote which could be used to vote for himself or for someone else when benefits were to be distributed. An alternative procedure to voting was drawing the winning ticket from a box or by using a special "wheel," made for that purpose. The Bread, Meat, and Coal Society (Mashvah Nephesh, founded in 1779 and still in existence in 1970) introduced an element of self-help for the poor by arranging that subscriptions could be paid weekly at the rate of one farthing. A total annual subscription of 4s. 4d. gave the subscriber the chance to draw 12 tickets, each of which entitled him to 1s. 9d. worth of bread, meat, and coal.

The *fraternal organizations or Friendly Societies, all mutual benefit associations, were an important form of voluntary association. Many older voluntary associations ceased to exist, as central welfare and fund-raising agencies took over their functions, and as governments assumed responsibility for direct aid to individuals. Nevertheless, many new voluntary associations rose to provide help to those afflicted by disease, supply funds for research in medicine and other vital fields, provide care for the children of a growing number of working mothers, support programs for prevention of juvenile delinquency, ensure better facilities and more scientific treatment for the care of the aged, the chronic sick, or the convalescent, and help meet every humanitarian need which a changing world made urgent.

Fund Collectors on the Local Communal Level

In the early modern period communal collectors still made their rounds, as they had done in mishnaic and medieval times, to gather the obligatory contribution for the communal charity fund, and congregational collectors visited homes to ensure payment for synagogue honors. As in the Middle Ages, voluntary benevolent societies had collectors to collect dues or donations or the coins deposited in their boxes placed in the homes of members. Collectors for authorized societies were also permitted to use their collection boxes in front of the synagogue on Purim or the Ninth of Av. Burial societies assigned collectors at cemeteries at funeral or memorial services, and this practice is continued in traditional cemeteries. Until the middle of the 19th century the majority of communal collectors appear to have served without compensation, thus fulfilling their obligation to do charity.

In the second half of the 19th century many charitable organizations employed collectors, and the practice continued to grow until community leaders in the 1920s recognized its wastefulness. Though in 1970 fund collectors were still working for some local charity organizations, the number had been reduced sharply.

France

Coordination in the administration of charity and fund raising was first achieved in 1809 in the emancipated community of Paris, when seven benevolent societies in that city were amalgamated. At the direction of the Consistoire, they created the Société d'Encouragement et de Secours (from 1855 officially named the Comité de Bienfaisance Israélite de Paris). From the beginning the Comité recognized that it could not rely solely on the resources provided by the Consistoire, for although the Napoleonic regime had permitted the Consistoire to tax members of constituent congregations, it had not obligated every Jew to join a congregation and pay taxes to support the charitable and other services of the community. The offerings for the privilege of sharing in the Torah reading, the fees for other synagogue honors, and the collections from the charity boxes in the congregation, proved no adequate supplement to the limited tax revenues. Shortly after its establishment, the Comité undertook to secure annual subscriptions over a three-year period, with a minimum requirement of 18 francs payable monthly from regular members and 30 francs from those known as honorary members. After a good effort the first year, the campaign lagged, and it was only when the community began to see the benefits of coordination, substitution of preventive social techniques for palliative measures, training of the young for productive work, and building of essential institutions such as an almshouse, a hospital, and an orphanage, that an increasingly larger number of members of the community began to subscribe more generously to the appeals of the Comité. Among the many new subscribers were those in the new voluntary associations founded after the Comité had been organized. When finally given representation in the Comité, they proved to be among the most enthusiastic contributors and workers. A lottery for raising funds from the general community was instituted in 1843, but this device became less significant as fund raising began to depend on annual subscriptions, large-scale donations, trusts, endowments, and legacies. Two significant endowments were made by the Rothschilds, one for the acquisition and maintenance of a hospital in 1841 and another for an orphanage founded by the family in 1855. Other Jewish philanthropists followed their example and made large-scale donations and endowments in succeeding years. After the liberation of France in 1944, the *American Jewish Joint Distribution Committee (JDC), with the cooperation of French Jewish leaders, established the Comité Juif d'Action Sociale et de Reconstruction (COJASOR); most of the resources were supplied by JDC. In 1946 the Comité de Bienfaisance resumed its full activities, including fundraising, but was still dependent in largest measure on the JDC and other foreign Jewish agencies. In 1949 the Fonds Social Juif Unifié de France was created as the national fund-raising and distributing body. Until 1964 the Fonds received additional large financial support from the Material Claims Conference and steadily diminishing aid from the JDC. In 1966, 1,600 heads of families in France contributed $1,600,000. After the Six-Day War in 1967 the Fonds Social combined with Aide à Israël (*Keren Hayesod) to form the Appel Juif Unifié, a single national fund-raising agency to help meet the budgets of both the Fonds Social and the Jewish Agency.

England

The Sephardi community was the first to coordinate its charity work in England and established its Board of Guardians in 1837. In 1966 the name was changed to the Spanish and Portuguese Synagogue Jewish Welfare Board. This board acted independently of the Ashkenazi community and relied for its funds on a portion of the Finta (a tax levied on the class of membership known as Yehidim) and on donations, trust funds, and legacies.

In 1859 the Board of Guardians for the Relief of the Jewish Poor (renamed the Jewish Welfare Board in 1963) was established in London to coordinate charity work for the immigrant poor of the three oldest Ashkenazi congregations: the *Great Synagogue (1690), the Hambro (1706), and the New Synagogue (1761). To prevent poverty the Board immediately introduced new measures by granting loans to help poor Jews become self-supporting and by providing training for young Jews to work in handicrafts and industry. Conduct of the Board was gradually placed in the hands of professionally trained workers. The Board was subsequently called upon to supervise the work of a number of institutions, which in turn made subventions to it. Aid societies, the first of which was the East End Aid Society (1902), budgeted either all or part of their income to finance the Board's operations. In 1968 there were 15 such societies. Despite its efforts to achieve coordination on a total community level, the Board had not succeeded by the end of 1969 in securing the assent of the voluntary associations and the many institutions which conducted independent campaigns, to the establishment of a fully centralized metropolitan fund-raising and distributing agency, or a fund-raising and distributing agency on a national basis, as in France.

Germany

Founded in 1869, the *Deutsch-Israelitischer Gemeindebund (Union of German-Jewish Congregations) was Germany's first federated but not all-inclusive body devoted to advancing Jewish education and performing charitable work, combined with guidance and material support to its member congregations. While its revenues were basically derived from the taxes which the government required every Jew to pay for support of his congregation's religious, educational, and social programs, it also benefited from private donations, etc. Simultaneously, Unterstuetzungsvereine (aid societies) and institutions raised funds and individual contributions for their special projects. World War I reduced the capability of the German Jewish community to give adequate aid to its members and to refugees from eastern European lands. Inflation wiped out the fortunes of many wealthy contributors, income from congregational taxes was reduced by 50%, and the coffers of the benevolent societies and institutions were emptied. Aid by the American Jewish Joint Distribution Committee (JDC) was forthcoming, but limited by its commitments elsewhere. To meet the crisis, the Zentralwohlfahrtstelle (Central Welfare Office) was established in 1917 as a roof organization covering many but not all social welfare agencies, voluntary associations, and institutions. Substantial savings resulted nevertheless from elimination of duplication in services and competition in fund raising. Following coordination, there were larger grants from synagogue tax funds (e.g., in 1926, 52% of the total congregational budgets in Berlin was allocated to charity and education) and greater contributions from individuals, institutions, and associations.

Hitler's rise to power in 1933 altered the situation drastically. The Reichsvertretung der deutschen Juden ("National Committee of German Jews"), formed in 1933, founded the Zentralausschuss fuer Hilfe und Aufbau ("Central Committee for Relief and Reconstruction"), as an all-embracing welfare organization, but the sharply reduced capacity of German Jewry to support its work is indicated by its revenue for 1936, namely $1,287,500 of which $737,500 came from JDC and other welfare agencies.

In 1938 the congregations which had been a primary source of funds were deprived of their privileges as public, legal corporations with authority to tax their members for upkeep of religious requirements, education, and social welfare, and were denied the tax exemption previously enjoyed by all religious institutions. Voluntary membership dues and donations were their only source of income. Moreover, with emigration of the affluent, and increasingly vast requirements for relief and emigration, the congregations rapidly lost their capability to share significantly in bearing the communal burden. In 1938, both in Germany and occupied Austria, $12,000,000 was spent on relief and emigration; a large share came from foreign Jewish sources and the remainder from the sale of communal and institutional property. In 1939 the Reichsvertretung der deutschen Juden was compelled to change its name to Reichsvertretung der Juden in Deutschland, and the government decree of July 4, 1939, forced upon it the responsibility, among others, for expediting emigration and providing social welfare assistance, a responsibility it bore until 1941, with the greatest difficulty, despite help from JDC which was permitted to carry on its relief and emigration work during this tragic period. The relief, rehabilitation, and emigration of the remnants of German Jews in the concentration camps after World War II, and of other displaced persons, were made possible by foreign agencies.

In the late 1960s there were approximately 38,000 Jews in the Federal German Republic and West Berlin. A central welfare office in Frankfurt handled the requests for help of the very few needy ones.

Russia

In August 1914, a coordinated fund-raising body, Yekopo (Yevreiski Komitet Pomoshchi Zhertvam Voiny; "Jewish Committee for the Relief of War Sufferers") was formed in St. Petersburg (Leningrad) to bring relief to Russian Jews, mainly those forcibly evacuated from the front areas to the Russian interior. In its first three years of operation it raised 32,000,000 rubles through contributions from 300 communities which taxed their members, individual donations, government subsidies, and in later years through assistance from JDC. With these funds it aided 250,000 Jews and, before ceasing its operations in 1921, had raised and spent over 50 million rubles to provide for the needs of most of Russia's charity-supported 1.5 million Jews, such as health services, social and economic assistance, educational programs for children, homes for refugees, and support of institutions. Yekopo cooperated with *ORT and *OSE in many of their endeavors. Yekopo ceased to exist in Soviet Russia in 1921, but a branch office functioned in Vilna until 1924.

[Morton Mayer Berman]

United States

The promise made to Peter Stuyvesant by the first boatload of 23 Jews who arrived at New Amsterdam in 1654, that they would care for their own poor, meant simply that they would act as did the other religious denominations in the village. The charitable activities of the few American Jews during the 17th, 18th, and early 19th centuries were centered in the synagogues. They consisted of the maintenance of cemeteries, aid to transients and a few needy local cases, and the freeing of Jewish redemptioners and indentured servants. The few known instances of Palestinian emissaries (*meshullaḥim*) visiting the colonies and the early republic exemplify aid to Jews overseas. The first charitable institution was the Hebrew Orphan Asylum of Charleston, South Carolina, established in 1802.

During the German Jewish immigration of the mid-19th century, the scope of Jewish charity expanded and became structurally separate from the synagogue. Almost every local community had a Hebrew Relief Society, or Hebrew Benevolent Society, and a feminine counterpart. Fraternal orders such as B'nai B'rith, Brith Abraham, and Kesher shel Barzel provided scheduled assistance to ill or bereaved members and their families. Several institutions, such as B'nai B'rith's Jewish Orphan Asylum in Cleveland, reached beyond local boundaries, and there were occasional appeals for emergency aid in the U.S., and for overseas Jewry, especially from Sir Moses *Montefiore; but before 1900 Jewish philanthropy was local.

The great historic coincidence was the encounter of the European Jewish tradition with the American idea of voluntarism. Early observers of the American scene commented on a distinctive characteristic of Americans, that voluntary groups take into their hands the creation of voluntary organizations to meet their own needs. Jewish communal traditions of autonomy and mutual assistance found fertile soil for growth in American voluntarism.

The great underlying force which created the distinctive American Jewish philanthropy was large-scale immigration from eastern Europe. Beginning in the 1880s, the immigrants coming in the tens of thousands yearly, with their special needs and their problems of adjustment to American life, molded American Jewish philanthropy. Its institutional structure derives from the expansion of earlier charitable organizations and the establishment of new ones. Thus, the numerous local Hebrew Relief Societies raised and spent far more money than earlier, and one by one changed their name to Jewish Social Service Association (or Bureau), reflecting the greater refinement and professionalization of their operations.

The American impulse toward efficiency and the Jewish conviction of communal responsibility coalesced disparate and often rival institutions into combined effort. This began with the establishment of the first Jewish philanthropic federation in Boston in 1895. It was a strikingly simple concept: funds would be raised and disbursed jointly to the agencies to meet the needs. The agencies, invariably supported by federations, included services to families and children, hospitals, free loans, settlement houses, and sundry aid groups. Jewish philanthropic federations were established in most American Jewish communities; New York City's was the largest and one of the last to be established, in 1917.

The few local agencies in the first federations joined on the common platform of efficiency in fund raising and coordination of local services. But the federation idea contained seeds of future development. The early federations began rudimentary social planning for the Jewish community, designed to explore the need for new services and old ones which could be dispensed with. The founding and expansion of federations occurred during a period of professionalization of the art of helping and the emergence of social work as a new profession. Jewish social workers provided the professional skills for the expansion of services. During its existence from 1927 to 1936, the Graduate School for Jewish Social Work in New York City trained professional social workers for service in the Jewish community.

The National Conference of Jewish Social Service (later Welfare), founded in 1899, became the professional organization. Professional journals were published, beginning with *Jewish Charities* (1910) and progressing to the *Journal of Jewish Communal Service* (1956). The National Conference of Jewish Charities, established in 1900, became the Council of Jewish Federations and Welfare Funds in 1932, providing planning and statistical data and recommendations.

The "Great Depression" of the 1930s marked a watershed in American philanthropic history. The magnitude of impoverishment forced the government into granting material relief, and the voluntary agencies gave up this function. The 1920s and 1930s witnessed severe disputes between pro-Zionist advocates of higher allocations to Palestine, and non-or anti-Zionists dominating the Joint Distribution Committee and providing most of the funds, whose views prevailed that most of the money go to European relief and to projects in Soviet Russia. Yet it was during the 1930s that the scope of organized Jewish philanthropy expanded both geographically and functionally. As the world emergency grew with the rise of Nazism, disparate agencies aiding Jews were brought together in the *United Jewish Appeal and subsequently made the desperate condition of eastern European Jewry the dominant cause in local campaigns of Jewish federations. After 1941, the European Holocaust and the struggle of Israel brought about ever closer agreement on the allocation of funds overseas. At the same time most federations broadened to include within organized Jewish philanthropy the support of Jewish education, community relations activities, Jewish vocational services, and national agencies that served the entire American Jewish community. New York City remained the exception and maintained a separate Federation and United Jewish Appeal. This period's expansion of the budgeting and planning activities of local federations necessitated constant assessment of priorities, and required decisions on new programs.

At the close of World War II in 1945, when the full dimensions of the European Holocaust were revealed, American Jewish philanthropy faced its greatest challenge – to provide the vast sums required to rescue the survivors and to build up the Jewish state for the redemption of the Jewish people. It responded with funds unequaled in the history of philanthropy anywhere.

In 1946 the United Jewish Appeal raised approximately $100 million, in 1948, $150 million, in addition to approximately $31,265,000 and $43.6 million in the respective years for the needs of the larger federations. Between 1939 and 1968 the United Jewish Appeal raised $2,035 billion for Israel and overseas Jewry, largely through allocations from combined campaigns in local Jewish communities throughout the United States.

The Federation's role broadened to the point where it was widely recognized as "the organized Jewish community." Philanthropy began to serve as the organizing principle for the voluntary Jewish community, especially in cities where the federations and Jewish community councils merged during the 1950s and conducted a single campaign for local, national, and overseas needs. Debate mounted during the 1960s over the proper proportion of local funds to be divided among hospitals, social services, and recreational institutions on one hand, and Jewish educational and cultural services on the other. In 1968 the range of concerns stretched across the spectrum of local, national, and international Jewish needs, ranging from services to the individual and family to programs designed to insure the survival of Judaism. The dollar figures reflect the vastness of scope. In 1969 the annual campaigns of Jewish federations totaled $266 million (including $104 million in the Israel Emergency Fund). In addition approximately $40 million were raised in endowment and capital funds campaigns.

Not all of American Jewish philanthropic endeavor in 1969 was within the federation orbit. Substantial groups remained outside either from choice or tradition; in 1969 these groups raised approximately $100 million. They included institutions of higher learning, many national agencies, pro-Israel organizations and others, but not synagogues which collected and disbursed millions of dollars annually themselves.

The funds allocated by federations represented only a fraction of the money disbursed by the agencies which receive them. In addition, these agencies' expenditures derived from other sources of income: dues; tuition; fees; and various governmental bodies and third-party payments. Therefore, the Jewish gross national philanthropic product, inclusive of all of these funds, was substantially in excess of a billion dollars in 1969.

Contemporary philanthropic services under Jewish auspices utilized the highest professional skills of American society in medicine, social work, public relations, and other areas. The collection and disbursement of funds to support these services was elevated to a high art by the Jewish group in the U.S. Concepts of fund-raising became sophisticated, and efforts were skillfully elaborated to raise maximum sums. The result, however, was ultimately based on fundamental Jewish commitments to philanthropy and the growing affluence and homogenity of the Jewish population which made possible a broad consensus on the needs.

One of the distinctive Jewish contributions to philanthropy in America was the recognition that federated fund-raising produced greater results for all participants. The general community also recognized this and the Community Chest movement used the Jewish Federation as its model.

Fund-raising goals were raised by the continuous education of the Jewish community to the dimensions of the needs and their responsibility to meet them. The capstone of the structure resides in the development of the responsibility of leaders. Achievements in the philanthropic campaigns have been based on the willingness of leadership to elevate the levels of giving by setting the pace through their own contributions. When this "leadership by example" takes place, matching contributions follow. In this way the Jewish group has demonstrated that it can implement its high ethical imperatives with pragmatic programs.

For Federation and other activities in the last third of the 20th century, see *Foundations.

[Charles Zibbell]

Canada

The first central fund-raising campaigns in Canada were conducted in 1917–18 by *Montreal's Federation of Jewish Philanthropies (renamed the Federation of Jewish Community Services and the Allied Jewish Community Services) and by *Toronto's Federation of Jewish Philanthropies (now known as the United Jewish Welfare Fund of Toronto). Funds at that time were raised exclusively for local social welfare, health, and recreational services (Jewish centers and children's camps). In 1937–38 the United Jewish Welfare Fund of Toronto began to campaign also for local Jewish education, the national work of the Canadian Jewish Congress, and the Hebrew Immigrant Aid Society ("HIAS"), as well as for the operations of a number of overseas agencies, including those in Ereẓ Israel.

In 1951 the United Israel Appeal and UJRA of the Canadian Jewish Congress combined their fund-raising activities in the United Jewish Appeal which then joined with the welfare funds in Toronto, Montreal, and other communities for raising funds in which they were to share. For this purpose Toronto and several other communities adopted the name of the United Jewish Appeal, and Montreal called its campaign the Combined Jewish Appeal.

Argentina

The Ashkenazi Ḥebra Kadisha ("The Holy Society"), founded strictly as a burial society in 1892, had evolved by 1949 into the Buenos Aires Kehillah, the central communal body. In 1956, it was renamed the Asociación Mutual Israelita Argentina-Communidad de Buenos Aires (briefly AMIA) which became the community's central fund-raising and distributing agency, financing nearly all its religious, social, and cultural activities. Half of its 1967 budget of $2,350,000 was devoted to support the Buenos Aires' Jewish educational system, in which 60% of the pupils were children of parents who paid low dues and were not enrolled in AMIA's membership of 42,000. Its main income, however, came from the sale of burial plots in its cemetery, over which it had exclusive control. While always generous in serving the needy, AMIA demanded of the wealthy what they could afford to pay and, in the case of individuals who had failed in their obligation to support the community, its demands were extremely high.

Israel

In the State of Israel with its state financing of religious needs (of all denominations), as well as its social services as an evolving welfare state, fund-raising of the usual Jewish Diaspora type became marginal. In 1970 there was no central local or national fund-raising body in Israel, with the result that much costly overlapping and duplication occurred in fund-raising campaigns. The Tel Aviv Council of Social Agencies, a consultative body, and the Israel Fund Raisers' Association in 1969 undertook, but without success, to coordinate the separate fund-raising efforts along the lines followed in western communities.

Fund-Raising by International Organizations
The traditional concern and sense of responsibility of Jews for the well-being of their people wherever they dwell prompted them in modern times to establish organizations which devoted themselves on an international level to one or more of the following activities:

(1) seeking emancipation of Jews or protecting their rights;

(2) helping them to overcome their economic and social plight by building schools for educating their children and training them vocationally, and giving immediate relief in grave situations;

(3) facilitating their emigration when they suffered persecution from pogroms and insurmountable poverty.

The outstanding international organizations founded in the mid-19th century were the *Alliance Israélite Universelle, the *Anglo-Jewish Association, the *Israelitische Allianz zu Wien, and the *Hilfsverein der deutschen Juden.

The Alliance Israélite Universelle organized committees in western Europe and the United States, and later in the local communities where it carried out its programs, as well as in Jewish communities in other parts of the world. With the help of these committees it raised funds through dues or annual subscriptions, special appeals for donations, trusts, legacies, and endowments. For nearly four decades the principal sources of support were Baron Maurice de *Hirsch and his wife, Baroness Clara. The Alliance received from the baron 4,595 shares (at £100 per share) of the capital stock of the *Jewish Colonization Association (ICA) which entitled it to a voice in the direction of ICA's program, but these funds were used only for the work of ICA.

The *Anglo-Jewish Association (London, 1871) adopted aims similar to those of the Alliance Israélite Universelle. Its income came from dues, donations, trust funds, legacies, endowments, and earnings from an annual ball.

Four dominant organizations established in Europe set themselves one specific goal in their service to deprived, sick, or oppressed Jews. *ORT (St. Petersburg, 1880, with headquarters subsequently in Berlin, 1921, where it became the World Ort Union; Paris, 1933; and Geneva, 1943), directed its efforts initially to rehabilitating and retraining Russia's impoverished Jewish masses.

The Russo-Jewish Committee for Relief of Jewish Refugees (London, 1882) was organized to deal with the large-scale influx of immigrants after the outbreak of pogroms in 1881 and the May Day Laws of 1882. The Committee required funds for settling a number of refugees in England and making it possible for a larger number to migrate to the United States and Canada. Other funds were raised by the Russo-Jewish Committee in cooperation with the Board of Jewish Guardians to deal with immigrants who settled in London. In 1891, with the outbreak of pogroms in Russia, funds especially raised for immigrant work were virtually exhausted. Another meeting was convened at the Guildhall and $486,000 were donated to be used primarily but not exclusively for sending Jews westward. ICA provided additional resources to assist the Russo-Jewish Relief Committee, principally for the resettlement of immigrants in countries on both the North and South American continents. From 1890 to 1905 funds were raised for immigrants fleeing from famine in Galicia in 1890, economic and social restrictions in Romania in the early 1890s, and from pogroms in Russia in 1903 and 1905; but a year later when the Alien Act of 1905 went into effect, England ceased to be a transient center for mass Jewish immigration, and activity on behalf of immigrants was limited almost exclusively to help those who had reached English shores to be absorbed into the economic and cultural life of the United Kingdom.

The Jewish Health Society *OSE (St. Petersburg, 1912) moved its central committee to Berlin in 1922, where it was connected with ORT, embracing committees established in Berlin and London (1920) and in other communities in 1921 and 1922, Paris, 1934, and Geneva, 1943, and returned to Paris after World War II. It was founded to promote the health of Russian Jews by using preventive medical measures and giving instructions in hygiene, but was forced by the Soviet government in 1919 to liquidate its work in Russia. After World War I, it extended its work to Poland (where the organization was called TOZ), Lithuania, Latvia, and Romania, and secured additional support from its branches in those countries and from supporting committees which it established in a number of countries, but the largest measure of aid came from JDC.

The *Central British Fund for German Jewry (since 1944, the Central British Fund for Jewish Rehabilitation and Relief) was organized in London in 1933 to raise funds to help German Jews meet the crisis in Nazi Germany. It engaged in operations to help them emigrate and reestablish themselves in England, Palestine, and other countries open to immigration. From 1933 to 1935 the fund campaigned under its own name; from 1936 to 1939 as the Council for German Jewry; from 1940 to 1943 as the Central Council for Jewish Refugees; and from 1939 to 1943 again under the original name of the Central British Fund for German Jewry.

In 1944, the Central British Fund became the Central British Fund for Jewish Relief and Rehabilitation, extending its help to destitute Jewish communities in Italy and Greece, and made use of radio and television as well as other publicity media to bring its appeal to the community.

Organizations which devoted themselves to one specific area of service but did not conduct independent campaigns for their work included:

(1) Emig-direkt (Berlin, 1921, the United Committee for Jewish Emigration) which was organized by the World Relief Conference (Carlsbad, 1920; this organization raised limited funds for relief and reconstruction work in central, eastern, and southeastern Europe), and HIAS. Emig-direkt drew its major financial support from JDC, ICA, and other organizations. It was succeeded by

(2) *HICEM (Paris, 1927, a name formed from the initials of the three agencies which established it, HIAS, ICA, and Emig-direkt, the last of which associated itself in 1934). HICEM gave assistance to Jews emigrating from Europe and found places for them in various countries.

(3) American Joint Reconstruction Foundation (1924), a joint operation of JDC and ICA for economic rehabilitation of Jews in central and eastern Europe through provision of loans and other constructive measures. Also treated as an American organization is AgroJoint (American Jewish Joint Agricultural Corporation, created by JDC in 1924 and liquidated in 1951) for resettlement of Jewish tradesmen and businessmen declassed by the Soviet government in agricultural colonies in Crimea and Ukraine.

Old Type Fund Collection for Ereẓ Israel

On the international level, old-type emissaries and fund collectors for Ereẓ Israel were known as *meshullaḥim* (see *Sheliḥei Ereẓ Israel).

The excessive costs in the employment of *meshullaḥim* and their uneconomic use in Palestine of the funds collected by them have been reported on exhaustively (Proceedings of the U.S. National Conference of Jewish Charities, Cleveland, 1912). The costs were not less than those which had prevailed in earlier centuries. Some communities accepted responsibility for collecting the funds themselves. After the establishment of the State of Israel in 1948 the number of old-type fund-raising emissaries fell to a vanishing point. The state's program for social welfare, health, education, and social security, and the supplementary services of such agencies as the Jewish Agency, Hadassah, WIZO, Histadrut, Moeẓet Ha-Poalot, Malben-JDC, and others drastically reduced the need for old-type fund-raising for Ereẓ Israel's philanthropic needs. The few *meshullaḥim* now turned their efforts chiefly to capital fund-raising for new buildings and expansion of their programs. Many local committees abroad continued to collect funds for maintenance of yeshivot, *talmud torahs*, orphanages, homes for the aged, hospitals, and other institutions and sent their collections directly to the institutions in Israel. Other committees abandoned their fund-raising in return for an allocation to their institutions by a community welfare fund agency. JDC, which is a partner in the *United Jewish Appeal, for some years made a sizable allocation through its Cultural Committee for Israel Institutions in Jerusalem for the support of yeshivot in Israel, refugee rabbis, scholars, and their dependents. It has also subsidized various research and publication projects on biblical and talmudic subjects. In 1969 JDC spent close to one million dollars to aid 132 yeshivot in Israel, with an enrollment of over 18,000 students. The charity box (*kuppah* of mishnaic origin) and the charity plate (*ke'arah*) were still in use in modern times. It was reported that in 1900 there were more than 250,000 *ḥalukkah* boxes bearing the name of Rabbi *Meir Baal ha-Nes in homes, synagogues, and communal gathering places. From it evolved in the Zionist era the most widely used box in the Jewish world: the Jewish National Fund blue box for land purchase in Palestine (later, in Israel) which was introduced after the founding of the JNF in 1901.

Zionist and Modern Israel Fund Raising

The *Bilu, organized in the 1880s by a group of young Russian Jewish students committed to pioneer and settle on the land in Palestine, made the first modern effort to raise funds for Zionist purposes. They succeeded in establishing 25 branches with a total of 525 members, but achieved very little success in fund raising which depended on membership dues, earnings from literary and musical evenings, and meager donations.

The Ḥovevei Zion ("Lovers of Zion"; Russia, 1882), members of the *Ḥibbat Zion movement, met relatively greater, but not startling, success in fund-raising. The Ḥovevei Zion organized societies – first in Russia and Poland and later in Germany, England, and the United States – to help existing settlements and establish new ones in Palestine. Their membership consisted of middle-class and poor Jews and was not able to provide large sums; some sold their belongings to add to the funds which would make possible their own settlement in Palestine. The Ḥovevei Zion collected dues, canvassed for donations in homes and shops, and, when permitted by the few not antagonistic rabbis, made appeals in the synagogues. Wherever possible they collected funds in the synagogue, on the eve of the Day of Atonement and the Ninth of Av. They established congregations of their own where they were free to propagate their ideas and raise funds, but fared no better than the Bilu in their efforts to persuade wealthy Jews to support their cause. The situation improved through the intercession of Rabbi Samuel *Mohilever, founder of the first Ḥibbat Zion movement in Warsaw, and after Baron Edmund de *Rothschild began to provide funds on a munificent scale to save struggling older settlements. Some of these had been founded by Ḥovevei Zion and new ones were organized. In 1890 came another favorable turn for the Ḥibbat Zion movement, when the Russian government gave its approval for the formation of a society for the support of Jewish tillers of the soil and artisans in Syria and Palestine (see *Odessa Committee), a step that made it easier to get some help from those who had been concerned about supporting the illegal movement.

It was not until the 1890s that Ḥovevei Zion was able to win the support and leadership of men of status in England like Elim *d'Avigdor, who in 1891 joined the Ḥibbat Zion movement and became its head; his kinsman, Colonel A.E.W. *Goldsmid, who succeeded him in the leadership; and others, among them Reverend Simeon *Singer, Sir Joseph *Sebag-Montefiore, and Lord Swaythling. These men, who contributed themselves, were able to persuade other well-placed people to do so.

The Jewish National Fund (Keren Kayemet le-Israel), the *World Zionist Organization's first instrumentality for fund-raising, was founded in Basle in 1901 by the Fifth World *Zionist Congress. It was created to raise funds for the purchase of land in Palestine and its development for settlement and agriculture. In its first decade the JNF introduced the blue box for coin collections in homes, synagogues, and wherever Jews met publicly; the Golden Book in Jerusalem for inscription of the names of men and women in return for specific contributions, or of individuals in whose honor contributions were given; stamps, of which there have been over 4,000 varieties, sold for use on letters, synagogue tickets, contract documents, and even used for postage in Israel immediately before the State of Israel postal system was established in 1948; and flags, tags, and flowers which contributors received as gifts on special occasions. The "sale" of trees for planting in Israel has proved to be one of the JNF's most productive fundraising methods. The *Keren Hayesod-*United Appeal was created in London in July 1920 at a Zionist conference convened by Chaim Weizmann to raise funds for the World Zionist Organization. The Zionist Executive and later the Jewish Agency Executive were responsible for the conduct of the activities generally performed by states, including security, until the founding of the State of Israel in 1948, when the operations of the Jewish Agency were limited chiefly to immigration, absorption, and settlement. The Keren Hayesod, which had first functioned directly under the aegis of the World Zionist Organization, became the financial arm of the Jewish Agency in 1929, with the formation of the enlarged Jewish Agency which included non-Zionists as members. At one time there were branches in 70 countries, and in 1970, owing to political changes in certain countries, there were 54, but this number did not include the U.S. where UJA campaigned independently of the Keren Hayesod.

In the years between 1920 and 1948 total Keren Hayesod UJA income in the United States amounted to $143,000,000, of which UJA raised 70% and Keren Hayesod 30%. From 1948 to 1970, both organizations raised $1,990,000,000 of which 65% came through UJA and 35% from other countries through Keren Hayesod.

Other fund-raising for Israel was conducted by various organizations such as WIZO and the *Histadrut (General Federation of Labor, Israel).

Fund-raising was also done in Diaspora countries by Israeli schools of higher learning, yeshivot, hospitals, general health and social welfare agencies, orchestras, museums, and many other groups. The principal schools of higher learning in Israel, namely, The Hebrew University, Technion (the Israel Institute of Technology), Tel Aviv University and Bar Ilan University, and the Weizmann Institute of Science do their fund raising through societies of friends or committees set up for this purpose.

*Magen David Adom ("Red Shield of David," Tel Aviv, 1930) is Israel's equivalent of the Red Cross. It meets its own maintenance and operating costs with income from an annual lottery and from subsidies from the government of Israel and local authorities, which together provided from 15 to 16% of its budget.

Support from societies of friends, committees, and individuals in many countries took the form of contributions in kind (ambulances, medical supplies, and equipment) and contributions in cash for Magen David Adom's building program, which envisaged completion of 17 new structures early in the 1970s.

The Modern Campaigns and Their Goals

There are various kinds of major fund-raising campaigns, all of which are conducted annually, except for the biennial campaigns of the Israel United Appeal and the United Communal Fund in South Africa, which occur in alternate years. These include:

(1) The independent campaign conducted by a communal federation or welfare fund for local social welfare agencies, other local institutions, and at times also certain national organizations. The goals for these campaigns are set by the local federation or welfare fund.

(2) The independent campaign conducted by authorized representative local committees on behalf of national or international organizations (Keren Hayesod, Jewish National Fund, WIZO, ORT, Histadrut, and others). The goals set for an independent campaign in a community are determined by agreement between the authorized committees located in a country and the national or international organizations. The time of year to be devoted to the independent campaign is decided upon after consultation between the local federation or welfare fund and the local committee representing the national or international body. In Australian communities the Board of Jewish Deputies allots appropriate periods to various national or international campaigns.

(3) The combined campaigns for local, national, Israel, and overseas needs conducted by local federations and welfare funds or through their fund-raising agencies (e.g., United Jewish Appeal in Toronto, Combined Jewish Appeal in Montreal). The principal parties to these campaigns are the local federations or welfare funds and the Keren Hayesod. Allocations to national organizations and overseas agencies are made upon application. The goal is set by the local fund-raising body in consultation with the national committee representing the Keren Hayesod acting for the Jewish Agency (in Canada the national committee is the United Israel Appeal of Canada, Inc.), after taking into account the allocations to be granted to other beneficiaries whose applications have been approved.

(4) The Joint Campaign, which is limited strictly to Israel's needs, conducted in Great Britain and Ireland (Joint Palestine Appeal-JPA) and in Israel (United Appeal in Israel-HaMagbit ha-Me'uḥedet be-Yisrael). Partners in these campaigns are the Keren Hayesod and the Jewish National Fund. In the JPA campaign, a limited number of allocations to other Zionist fund-raising agencies is made by the Keren Hayesod from its share. The campaign goal is set after consultation

between the administrative committee of JPA in London and the Keren Hayesod, the Jewish Agency, and the Jewish National Fund head offices in Jerusalem. For the Israel Joint campaign the goal is set by the two partners (the Keren Hayesod and the JNF) and neither makes any allocation to any other agency.

[Morton Mayer Berman]

Women and Philanthropy

The Hebrew Bible establishes the precedent for women's charitable work, both in its commandments to help the needy and in narratives highlighting female acts of *gemilut ḥasadim* (loving kindness). Rebekah's kindness toward Eleazar, for example, results in her marriage to Isaac (Gen. 24: 12–27). Proverbs 31:21 praises the ideal wife who "gives generously to the poor;/Her hands are stretched to the needy." According to the rabbis, women are naturally compassionate (Meg. 14b); they are also said to be more responsive to the needy than men (Ta'an. 23b).

Dedications and inscriptions in ancient synagogues provide early evidence of Jewish women's communal donations. Although these inscriptions give little insight into whether leadership and positions of power accompanied female philanthropy, they demonstrate that women, often independently, helped determine the financial life of their communities (Brooten).

The Cairo *Genizah* preserves the bequests of *Wuhsha, a 12th-century businesswoman. Her donations (10% of her estate) were designated for Cairo synagogues, Jewish charitable institutions, and needy individuals. Both in the Middle East and in Europe, medieval and early modern Jewish women of means contributed Torah scrolls and other sacred books to the synagogue, as well as funds for oil and upkeep. Although major donations may have come from prosperous women, often widows, women of more modest means regularly donated ceremonial objects and needlework in the form of Torah binders and Torah curtains.

*Dulcea of Worms (d. 1196) is described as preparing thread and gut to sew together books, Torah scrolls, and other religious objects. She is also said to have bathed the dead and to have sewn their shrouds, a quintessential act of loving kindness in Jewish tradition. At the end of the 17th century, organized groups of women assumed responsibility for preparing deceased members of the community for burial, mirroring already established male associations (see **Ḥevra Kaddisha*).

In the 19th century, middle class Jewish women in Europe formed charitable organizations, a shift from the largely individual nature of earlier women's philanthropy. These groups, which ranged from patrons of orphan asylums to free loan societies, to dowry clubs for poor brides, mirrored the social and philanthropic patterns of non-Jewish bourgeois women. The early 20th century saw the establishment of national women's organizations for philanthropic purposes, including the *Juedischer Frauenbund in Germany (1904) and the Union of Jewish Women in England (1902). Its predecessor, the Jewish Association for the Protection of Girls and Women, was established in 1885.

Jewish women in the United States followed American models in defining their charitable organizations. The first formal American Jewish women's association, the Female Hebrew Benevolent Society of Philadelphia, was founded by Rebecca *Gratz, with her mother and sister, in 1819. Later, synagogue-based "Sisterhoods of Personal Service" were founded in response to the needs of the massive influx of Jewish immigrants from eastern Europe.

In 1893, the *National Council of Jewish Women became the first body to link local chapters into a national organization. Taking on women-centered issues like immigration, settlement, education, and the battle against white slavery, the NCJW connected middle class Jewish American women, primarily of central European descent, to their eastern European coreligionists. In 1995, more than a century after its founding, NCJW absorbed a feminist organization (U.S. Israel Women to Women) in an effort to expand its work in Israel.

By the end of the 19th century, when professional social workers increasingly assumed responsibility for serving the needy, earlier, local organizations gave way to more inwardly-focused synagogue sisterhoods or auxiliaries, where tasks were domestically linked and less public. Women raised funds for synagogue furnishings and education and were charged with expanding the reach of synagogue life. Reform leaders established the *National Federation of Temple Sisterhoods in 1913. The Conservative (*Women's League) and Orthodox movements followed suit in 1918 and 1926, respectively.

*Hadassah, the Women's Zionist Organization of America, was founded in 1912. Focusing on health initiatives in Palestine, Hadassah raised more funds and engaged more members (heavily eastern European) than any other American women's organization. In 1925, the predecessors of *Amit and *Pioneer Women (now Naamat) also formed Zionist groups. *ORT (Organization for Rehabilitation through Training), established in 1927, focused women's funds and voluntarism towards international education initiatives.

During World War I, American Jewish women formally became part of local Federation work. Women's Divisions were created in Boston (1917, reestablished in 1930), Philadelphia (1918), and New York (1920), paralleling the Businessmen's Divisions. Throughout the 20th century, Women's Divisions thrived nationwide, raising a large percentage of Federation, and eventually United Jewish Appeal, budgets. Despite their successes, these divisions were commonly considered a source of "plus giving," providing funds over and above the male partner's gift. The 1970s witnessed a rejection of the parallel power structure represented by Women's Divisions; approximately ten Federations closed these fundraising vehicles, but all were reinstated in the 1980s.

Federation funds raised by Women's Divisions are ordinarily included in general allocations. During the late 1990s, concluding that issues important to women and girls were not being appropriately funded by community allocations, female philanthropists established Jewish Women's Foundations. In their first ten years, more than 20 such funds have raised over $35 million to fund services that are specifically directed to the needs of girls and women.

U.S. women's philanthropic impact also reaches beyond single gender organizations, although women remain poorly represented in the upper echelons of Jewish philanthropic leadership in the first decade of the 21st century. While a number of individual women were substantial contributors to the Jewish community, women accounted for only 25% of board memberships and 12% of presidents in North American Jewish communal organizations.

See also *Charity.

[Deborah Skolnick Einhorn (2nd ed.)]

BIBLIOGRAPHY: GENERAL: B.D. Bogen, *Jewish Philanthropy* (1917), 38–58; E. Frisch, *A Historical Survey of Jewish Philanthropy* (1924); I. Abrahams, *Jewish Life in the Middle Ages* (1932²), ch. xvii–xviii; Baron, Social, 3 vols. (1937), index s.v. *Charity*; Baron, Community, 2 (1942), 290–350; C. Roth, *Jewish Contribution to Civilization* (1938), ch. on "Charity," 287–315; Elbogen, Century, index s.v. *Philanthropy*; I. Chipkin, in: L. Finkelstein (ed.), *The Jews, their History, Cult and Religion*, 2 (1949), 713–44. COUNTRIES: ARGENTINA: J.X. Cohen, *Jewish Life in South America* (1941); J. Shatzky, *Comunidades Judias en Latinoamerica* (1952); AJYB, 69 (1968), 394–404. CANADA: L. Rosenberg, *Two Centuries of Jewish Life in Canada 1760–1960* (= AJYB vol. 62, 1961); F. Hutner, *Fund Raising in Canada* (1969). ENGLAND: L. Wolf, *Essays on Jewish History*, ed. by C. Roth (1934); C. Roth, *The Great Synagogue London 1690–1940* (1950); V.D. Lipman, *Social History of the Jews in England 1850–1950* (1954), index; idem, *A Century of Social Service 1859–1959* (1959), index; S.D. Temkin, in: AJYB, 58 (1957), 3–63. FRANCE: L. Berman, *Histoire des Juifs de France* (1937); L. Kahn, *Histoire des écoles communales et consistoriales israélites de Paris (1809–1884)* (1884); J. Kaplan, in: AJYB, 47 (1945/46), 71–118; 49 (1947/48), 319–22; Z. Szajkowski, *Analytical Franco-Jewish Gazetteer* (1966). GERMANY: J.R. Marcus, *Rise and Destiny of the German Jew* (1934), index; A. Ruppin, *Jewish Fate and Future* (1940), index; H. Schwab, *A World in Ruins* (1946). ITALY: Vogelstein-Rieger, passim; Roth, Italy, index s.v. *Charity*. PALESTINE AND ISRAEL: H. Szold, in: *National Conference of Jewish Charities, Proceedings* (1910–12); R. Gottheil et al., *ibid.*; A. Greenbaum, *The American Joint Distribution Committee and the Yeshivot in Israel* (1964). RUSSIA: L. Greenberg, *The Jews in Russia*, ed. by M. Wischnitzer, 1 (1944); 2 (1951), index; H.L. Sahsovich et al., in: *National Conference of Jewish Charities, Proceedings* (1908). U.S.: H.L. Lurie, *A Heritage Affirmed; the Jewish Federation Movement in America* (1961); R. Morris and M. Freund (eds.), *Trends and Issues in Jewish Social Welfare in the United States* (1966); S.P. Goldberg, *Jewish Communal Services* (1969); AJYB, passim. ORGANIZATIONS: See also articles on individual organizations. ALLIANCE ISRAÉLITE UNIVERSELLE: *Les Cahiers de l'Alliance Israélite Universelle*, esp. no. 168 (Jan. 1969). ANGLO-JEWISH ASSOCIATION: *Annual Report*, 13 no. 1 (March 1969). BILU: N. Sokolow, *Hibbath Zion* (Eng., 1935), ch. 42. BOARD OF GUARDIANS (Spanish and Portuguese Synagogue Jewish Welfare Board, London): *Report* (1969). BOARD OF GUARDIANS AND TRUSTEES FOR RELIEF OF THE JEWISH POOR, LONDON (Jewish Welfare Board, London): *Annual Report* (1968) and Letter, Public Relations Officer (Oct. 8, 1969). DEUTSCH-ISRAELITISCHER GEMEINDEBUND: Wilhelm, in: YLBI, 2 (1957), 61–63; Sandler, *ibid.*, 76–84. HEBREW UNIVERSITY: B. Cherrick, *Report on Fund Raising* (1969). HICEM: M. Wischnitzer, *Visas to Freedom. The History of Hias* (1956). HILFSVEREIN DER DEUTSCHEN JUDEN: Z. Szajkowski, in: JSOS, 13 (1951), 47–70; 19 (1957), 29–50; 22 (1960), 131–58. ḤOVEVEI ZION: A.M. Hyamson, *Palestine. The Rebirth of an Ancient Nation* (1917), 5–123. **ADD. BIBLIOGRAPHY:** B. Brooten, *Women Leaders in the Ancient Synagogue* (1982); S. Chambré, "Parallel Power Structures, Invisible Careers and the Changing Nature of American Jewish Philanthropy," in: *Journal of Jewish Communal Service* 76:3 (2000); idem, "Philanthropy," in: P.E. Hyman and D.D. Moore (ed.), *Jewish Women in America* (1998), K. Goldman. *Beyond the Synagogue Gallery* (2000); M. Kaplan, *The Jewish Feminist Movement in Germany* (1979); idem, *The Making of the Jewish Middle Class* (1991); L.G. Kuzmack. *Woman's Cause* (1990); F.M. Loewenberg. *From Charity to Social Justice* (2001).

°**PHILIP**, name of six kings of France.

PHILIP II or PHILIP AUGUSTUS, king of France from 1180 to 1223. All Philip's biographers agree that he detested the Jews, an attitude formed by stories he had heard in his childhood about Jews murdering Christian children. Soon after his accession, he ordered the imprisonment of all the Jews in the kingdom, and it was only in exchange for a large ransom that they were set free. Early in April 1182, in order to bolster the treasury before going to war, Philip ordered the expulsion of the Jews from his kingdom; Jewish real estate was confiscated and most of it sold on behalf of the royal treasury; synagogues were converted into churches (as was the case in *Paris and *Orleans); and debtors were absolved of their obligations to Jews on condition that they paid the treasury one-fifth of the monies owed. The king persecuted the Jews even beyond the borders of his kingdom: in 1190 he attacked in *Champagne the Jewish community of *Bray-sur-Seine (or Brie-Comte-Robert), putting to death almost 100 persons. When he authorized the return of the Jews to his kingdom in 1198, it was for purely financial reasons. At the same time as he guaranteed the Jews freedom to trade with Christians by forbidding priests to excommunicate those Christians who dealt with them, he also initiated the practice of assigning an official seal to every locality which contained an important Jewish community, for the purpose of regulating loans. An ordinance of February 1219 prohibited any loan to persons whose only source of income was their own labor. This was an attempt to put a stop to loans taken for personal consumption only; previously loans of this type were granted if paid back in three annual sums. Loans offered against pledges were not subject to compulsory registration, but the list of articles which could not be accepted in pledge was extended to cover not only church appurtenances but also agricultural tools and beasts of burden.

PHILIP III THE BOLD, king from 1270 to 1285. Shortly after his accession, Philip followed the example of his father and predecessor, *Louis IX, and in 1271 ordered his officers to enforce the wearing of the Jewish *badge. His father's policy is again reflected in an ordinance, probably issued in 1272, which prohibited the Jews from engaging in all kinds of moneylending and directed them either to pursue permitted commercial activities or to work with their hands. If there were any attempts by Jews to engage in agricultural work or handicrafts, these were in any event doomed in practice from 1280 when

Christians were forbidden to enter into their service. The most disastrous of Philip's decrees from the socioeconomic point of view was that issued in 1283, forbidding the Jews to reside in smaller places.

PHILIP IV THE FAIR, king from 1285 to 1314. The various changes in Philip's policy toward the Jews were all motivated by the sole purpose of furthering the interests of the monarchy and the kingdom. Thus, asserting royal power and challenging the Church, in 1288 he reminded his officers that the number of charges for which the Jews could be tried by the ecclesiastical courts was very limited, and he called upon them not to collaborate in any unjustified prosecutions. However, in February 1291 he ordered the expulsion of all the Jewish exiles who had arrived from England and *Gascony: Since they had been stripped of all their belongings before they arrived, the kingdom could not derive any profit from them. On April 1 of the same year, seeking to strengthen the economic status of the large towns, he renewed the order prohibiting the Jews to live in the small localities. As a step toward legal standardization, on September 23 he dismissed all the special judges of the Jews. He took action against Jewish moneylenders on Jan. 31, 1292, but only in order to expropriate the debts owed to them. When Philip decided to protect the Jews from extortion and hindrances in their trade, his measure applied to the Jews owned by the king, for he wished to be the only one to profit from them. The practical reasons for the compulsory concentration of the Jews in special quarters put into force in 1294 were revealed in 1306. Philip's only decree that arose from religious scruples and carried no material advantage was that of 1299 directed against missionary efforts on the part of the Jews and "their blasphemies and evil spells."

The king's essentially mercenary interest in the Jews was finally manifested on June 21, 1306. An oral command called on John of Nogaret, John of Saint Just, and the seneschal of Toulouse to organize the arrest of all the Jews of the kingdom, the seizure of their belongings, and then their expulsion. A written order of the same day required all the prelates, barons, and officers of every degree to lend their assistance to these three persons in the execution of their mandate. The date had been fixed for July 22 and the secret was so well guarded that not one Jew escaped. The Jews had not even left the kingdom when Philip issued his regulations for public auction of their real estate. In the eventuality that treasures hidden by the Jews in these buildings might be discovered, such finds were reserved for the treasury. Claiming that there was a judicial distinction between the Jews of the king and those of the lords, some of the latter resisted the order to expel "their" Jews. The king easily overcame their objections by promising them the lion's share of the spoils. Immediately after the expulsion of 1306, a number of Jews were given safe-conducts to return to the kingdom in order to cooperate in the recovery of their debts. Subsequently they too were driven out in 1311. It has been said that by expelling the Jews, Philip committed not only an evil act but also made a bad bargain. The second part of this statement can hardly be substantiated: nine years later the Jews were once more to be found in France; they were again expelled in 1323, while the royal treasury continued, until 1325, to collect the debts due to the Jews which had been confiscated in 1306.

PHILIP V THE TALL, king from 1316 to 1322. Of this king's few ordinances concerning the Jews, the first (April 1317) was the most favorable: it protected them against abusive imprisonment, guaranteed their right to dispose of their own estates, and exempted them from wearing the Jewish badge outside their homes. In the course of Philip's brief reign, three major events affected the situation of the Jews. During the uprising of the *Pastoureaux in 1320, the king, together with the ecclesiastical authorities, exerted his power to the utmost to protect the Jews. In 1321 the Jews of several localities were accused of having poisoned the wells and fountains in collusion with the lepers. Philip appointed a commission of inquiry on July 21 and numerous trials ensued – as well as massacres without even the travesty of a trial. An enormous fine – at first established at 150,000 livres and consequently reduced to 120,000 – was imposed on French Jewry. Finally, Philip decided on a new expulsion of the Jews from France, although this measure was not enforced until 1323, during the reign of his successor.

BIBLIOGRAPHY: Philip Augustus: A. Cartellier, *Philipp II August*, 4 vols. (Ger., 1899–1922); Baron, Social², index; E.J. de Laurière et al. (eds.), *Ordonnances des Rois de France*, 1 (Paris, 1723); vol. 11, indexes; H.F. Delaborde (ed.), *Recueil des actes de Philippe Auguste*, 3 vols. (1916–66). Philip III the Bold: L. Berman, *Histoire des Juifs de France* (1937), 114ff.; *Ordonnances des Rois de France*, 1 (Paris, 1723), 312–3; vol. 12, 323. Philip IV the Fair: L. Lazard, in: REJ, 15 (1887), 233–61; I. Loeb, in: *Jubelschrift... H. Graetz*, 1 (1887), 39–56 (Fr.), incl. bibl. notes; L. Berman, *Histoire des Juifs de France* (1937), 116–24; G. Saige, *Juifs en Languedoc* (1881), index s.v. *Philippe le Bel; Ordonnances des Rois de France*, 1 (Paris, 1723), index. Philip V the Tall: P. Lehugeur, *Histoire de Phillippe le Long*, 1 (1897), 428–35; B. Blumenkranz, in: *Archives Juives*, 6 (1969/70), 36–38; *Ordonnances des Rois de France*, 1 (Paris, 1723), index, s.v. *Philippe le Long*.

[Bernhard Blumenkranz]

PHILIP OF BATHYRA (first century C.E.), son of Jacimus and grandson of Zamaris, rulers of Bathyra in the district of Trachonitis. He was a friend of Agrippa II, who appointed him commander of the army in Bathyra. Josephus describes him as "excelling in combat and... possessing other virtues which could bear comparison with any other man" (Ant., 17:30). When war broke out in Jerusalem and the peace party requested help from Agrippa, Philip was dispatched at the head of 3,000 cavalry. They occupied the upper city, but with the arrival of the *Sicarii under *Menahem b. Judah, Philip's forces were driven out of the fortress of Antonia and compelled to take refuge in the palace of Herod. After a short time, they surrendered on receiving a promise that they would be permitted to leave the city in peace. Philip, fearing that he would be put to death, hid for four days in Jerusalem and by a subterfuge succeeded in escaping from the city and reaching Gamala. This saved him from the intrigues of Varus who was plotting against him. After the dismissal of Varus, he returned with his troops to Bathyra where he was charged with the task of preventing the inhabitants from joining the revolt against the Romans. When Vespasian and Agrippa II visited Tyre, its inhabitants accused him of surrendering the palace of Herod and the Roman garrison to the Jews, and Vespasian ordered him to be sent for trial before Nero. Nothing more is known of him. Two of his brother's daughters were the only inhabitants of Gamala who escaped death by hiding from the Romans.

BIBLIOGRAPHY: Jos., Wars, 2:421, 556; 4:81; Jos., Ant., 17:30; Jos., Life, 46ff., 59–60, 177, 179–84, 407.; Drexler, in: *Klio*, 19 (1925), 277–312; Schalit, *ibid.*, 26 (1933), 67–95.

[Edna Elazary]

PHILIPPINES, island republic off the coast of S.E. Asia. Marranos are known to have lived in Manila among the early Spanish settlers, and they soon came under the surveillance of the Spanish Inquisition. The first public auto-da-fé was held in Manila in 1580, but it is not known whether there were Jews among the seven persons accused. In 1593 two Marrano brothers, Jorge and Domingo Rodriguez, old-established residents of Manila, appeared at an auto-da-fé held in Mexico City because the Inquisition did not have an independent tribunal in the Philippines. They were sentenced to imprisonment. At least eight Marranos from the Philippines are known to have been tried by the Inquisition by the end of the 17th century.

Significant Jewish immigration to the Philippines did not begin until the last quarter of the 19th century. The first Jews known to arrive on the islands were the three brothers Levy, natives of Alsace, who went to Manila in the early 1870s to establish a jewelry business and brought additional people for their store. They were joined by groups of Turkish, Syrian, Lebanese, and Egyptian Jews, by families from Russia and Central Europe (either directly or via Harbin and Shanghai), and by U.S. Jews in the first few decades of the 20th century. By the early 1930s the Jewish community numbered approximately 500. The Manila congregation, organized formally in 1922, purchased land for a synagogue and a burial plot, and in 1924 erected Temple Emil, named after a benefactor, Emil Bachrach. As a result of strenuous activity by the community, the friendliness of the then governor of the Philippine Commonwealth, Manuel Quezon y Molina (who donated some land for the purpose of refugee settlement), encouragement by the U.S. authorities, and the lack of better alternatives, the Philippines became a center for refugees from Nazi persecution. By the end of World War II the Jewish community had grown to more than 2,500. Among the refugees were a rabbi, Joseph Schwartz, and a cantor for the community. Late 1944 and the first two months of 1945 were calamitous for the Jewish community. The Japanese had used the synagogue and adjacent hall as an ammunition store, and both buildings were completely destroyed in the fighting. Ten percent of the Jews fell victim to atrocities perpetrated by the retreating Japanese or to the shelling of the advancing Americans. After the war the community reorganized, and its temple was rebuilt. In 1968 the community numbered approximately 250, about a quarter of whom were Sephardim. In 2005 there were still around 250 Jews there, mostly Americans and Israelis. The community had a rabbi, *mikveh*, and Sunday school.

[Walter Zanger / Ernest E. Simke]

Relations with Israel

The Republic of the Philippines was the only Asian country to vote for the partition of Palestine in 1947, and it recognized the State of Israel in 1949. Relations between the two countries have been cordial. Formal diplomatic ties developed from the exchange of honorary consuls and honorary consuls-general in the early 1950s, to nonresident ministers in the later 1950s, the establishment of an Israel legation in Manila in 1958, and finally to the appointment of resident ambassadors in Manila and Tel Aviv in 1962. An aviation agreement was signed between the two countries in 1951, a friendship treaty was contracted in 1958, several consular agreements and a technical-aid agreement were signed in 1964. Technical cooperation includes the participation of Israeli experts in the establishment of a model village.

Israel has sent experts to the Philippines in the service of various UN agencies, and Philippine trainees in community development, agriculture, and cooperation studied in Israel. Tens of thousands of Philippine nationals work in Israel, most visibly as caretakers.

[Shaul Tuval]

BIBLIOGRAPHY: G.A. Kohut, in: AJHSP, 12 (1904), 145–56; N. Robinson, *Jewish Communities of the World* (1963), 46; H.C. Lea, *The Inquisition in the Spanish Dependencies* (1908).

PHILIPPSON, German-Jewish family of prominent rabbis, scholars, educators, journalists, doctors, bankers, and scientists. Their family tree goes back to 16th-century Poland, where *Joshua Hoeschel ben Joseph (c. 1578–1648) had been chief rabbi of Cracow. His great-grandson was the Talmud scholar Jacob Joshua *Falk (1680/81–1756), chief rabbi of Berlin, Metz, and Frankfurt/Main, who strongly opposed the Shabbatean movement. After 1750, the family settled in Arnswalde (Neumark, Prussia). Falk's grandson, the Talmud scholar Reb Phoebus (Philipp) Moses Arnswald (d. 1794), moved to Sandersleben (Anhalt-Dessau) upon his marriage, earning his living as a peddler. His children were the first to change "Phoebus" into the German "Philipp" and called themselves Philippson.

Arnswald's son MOSES (ben Uri Phoebus) Philippson (1775–1814) received an Orthodox upbringing in Halberstadt, Brunswick, and Frankfurt/Main and, from 1790, became a tutor in Bayreuth and later Burgkunstadt. He was attracted to the works of Moses *Mendelssohn and German literature. In 1799, he was appointed teacher at the newly founded *Freischule* at Dessau. In order to supplement his meager income he began printing books and selling them at fairs; among them were various sermons and translations from the Bible, a Hebrew reader "*Kinderfreund*" (1808), the renewed **Me'assef* (1808–12), then edited by Shalom *Cohen, and other ventures. He died of typhus, aged 39, before completion of his Hebrew-German and German-Hebrew dictionary, leaving behind four small children: Phoebus (1), Johanna, Ludwig (2), and Julius (3).

[Johannes Valentin Schwarz (2nd ed.)]

(1) Moses Philippson's eldest son, PHOEBUS MORITZ (1807–1870), was educated at the Franzschule and Gymnasium in Dessau, took his doctor's degree at Halle University, and practiced medicine at Magdeburg, from 1835 as a country doctor at Kloetze (Altmark). He published the first medical study on cholera (1831) and literary works, which he partly contributed to the periodicals of his brother Ludwig from 1834. His novel *Die Marannen* (1855) and his *Biographische Skizzen* (1864/66) are particularly worth mentioning. MORITZ Philippson (1833–1877) continued the medical career of his father Phoebus as an army-doctor, settling down in Berlin. Phoebus' granddaughter PAULA (1874–1949) became one of the first woman doctors in Germany but, from 1921, applied herself to classical studies where, from 1936, she made her mark in Greek mythology. In 1933, she moved to Basel where she died at the age of 75.

[Max Gottschalk / Johannes Valentin Schwarz (2nd ed.)]

(2) LUDWIG PHILIPPSON (1811–1889), the second son of Moses, achieved renown as the founder of the *Allgemeine Zeitung des Judenthums* (AZJ, 1837–1922), which he edited until his death. Ludwig was an avid student of both Hebrew and classical literature in Dessau and Halle. After graduation from Berlin University (1829–33), aged 22, he took up the position of a preacher and teacher in the *Magdeburg Jewish community. Though following the practice of *Reform Judaism – he preached in German and introduced the organ and the rite of confirmation – he tried to steer a middle course between Reform and *Orthodoxy. He was among the initiators of the *Rabbinical Conferences of Brunswick (1844), Frankfurt/Main (1845), and Breslau (1846), but was critical of their decisions. One of his projects was the establishment of a modern institution for training scholars, rabbis, and teachers. From 1834 Philippson started editing several periodicals, first the monthly *Israelitisches Predigt- und Schulmagazin* (1834–36), followed by his famous AZJ, the most important Jewish weekly of the 19th century, which was also dedicated to the struggle for emancipation in all parts of Germany and Europe and fought discrimination and antisemitism. From 1839–53, he published a popular translation and commentary of the Bible, which went through three editions (1858^2, 1878^3), together with a revised edition illustrated by Gustav Doré (1875). Along with I.M. *Jost, A. *Jellinek, and others he founded the *Institut zur Foerderung der Israelitischen Literatur* (1854–73), whose main achievement was the publication of H. *Graetz's *Geschichte der Juden* (1853–76). In 1862, he had to resign as rabbi of Magdeburg because he had become almost blind. He moved to Bonn, where he continued his journalistic and literary work until his death. He was among the founders of the Israelitische Bibelanstalt (1862), the *Deutsch-Israelitischer Gemeindebund (1869), and the *Hochschule fuer die Wissenschaft des Judentums (1872). Ludwig Philippson had nine children. Three of his sons attained fame in their respective fields:

[Johannes Valentin Schwarz (2nd ed.)]

(2a) MARTIN EMANUEL PHILIPPSON (1846–1916) was a historian and a communal leader in Berlin. Born at Magdeburg, he studied in Bonn and Berlin, where he later worked as a teacher, volunteered in the Franco-Prussian War (1870/71), and was finally appointed assistant professor at Bonn in 1875. However, when Emperor William I would not sanction the appointment of a Jew, he took a professorship at the Free University of Brussels (1878), and eventually became rector there. In 1890, he was forced to resign this post in the face of agitation by anti-German and radical students, and returned to Berlin as a private scholar. From 1891, he devoted his energies to Jewish communal affairs and to his writing. He was chairman of the *Deutsch-Israelitischer Gemeindebund (1896–1912) which, in 1906, initiated the Gesamtarchiv der deutschen Juden; chairman of the *Gesellschaft zur Foerderung der Wissenschaft des Judentums (1902), which commissioned his three-volume *Neueste Geschichte des juedischen Volkes* (1907–11, 1930^2); and chairman of the *Verband der deutschen Juden (1904). He also headed the *Hochschule (Lehranstalt) fuer die Wissenschaft des Judentums. In all, he published some 12 studies in modern history, especially on Prussia, but their scholarship has been sharply questioned by fellow historians.

[Herbert A. Strauss / Johannes Valentin Schwarz (2nd ed.)]

(2b) FRANZ MOSES PHILIPPSON (1851–1929), the seventh child of Ludwig, was a Belgian banker, financier, and communal leader. Born in Magdeburg, he was sent to Brussels in 1865 to work as a clerk in the *Errera banking house. In 1871, he established his own bank in Belgium and directed it for over 50 years until his death. Involved from the beginning in the Belgian colonization of Africa, he was an administrator of the Belgian Congo railways in 1889, becoming its president in 1924, and was founder of the Banque du Congo Belge (1909) and its vice president from 1911 to 1919. Philippson was president of the Brussels Jewish community and a leader of Belgian Jewry, from 1918 as president of the *Consistoire Central Israélite de Belgique. He represented the Brussels community on the administrative council of the *Jewish Colonization Association (ICA) from 1896, becoming vice president in 1901 and president in 1919. He made an important contribution to Jewish colonization efforts in Argentina and Brazil. He died in 1929 in Paris. Franz's first son, MAURICE (1877–1938), was professor of zoology and physiology at Brussels University; his second son, JULES (1881–1961), became head of the firm F.M. Philippson & Co. after the death of his father. PAUL PHILIPPSON (1910–1978), son of Maurice, was also a banker and Jewish leader in Belgium. Born in Brussels, he was an officer in the Belgian Forces (1940–45); president and founding member of the Service Social Juif (from 1945); president of the Jewish community of Brussels (1945–63); chairman of the Consistoire Central Israélite de Belgique (from 1963); and chairman of the Social Service Commission of the European Council of Jewish Communities.

[Max Gottschalk / Johannes Valentin Schwarz (2nd ed.)]

(2c) ALFRED PHILIPPSON (1864–1953), the youngest son of Ludwig, born at Bonn, became a geographer and geologist. As a student of Ferdinand von Richthofen (1833–1905), the founder of modern geography, he followed his teacher from Bonn to Leipzig University, where he took his doctor's degree (*Studien ueber Wasserscheiden*) in 1886, aged 22. In the course of a distinguished career he specialized in the east Mediterranean region, particularly Greece and Asia Minor. In 1891, he was appointed university lecturer at Bonn, 1899 assistant professor. Since a full professorship was denied to him as a Jew, he accepted a chair at Basel University in 1904, finally becoming head of the department of geography. In 1906, he was called back to Halle, and in 1911 to Bonn. In 1929, upon his retirement, his pupils and admirers published a volume of geographical essays in his honor. Several of his many books have become classics of regional geography, among them: *Der Peloponnes* (1892), *Zur Morphologie des rheinischen Schiefergebirges* (1903), *Das Mittelmeergebiet* (1904, 1922⁴), *Europa* (1905, 1928³), *Grundzüge der allgemeinen Geographie* (1921/24, 1930/33), *Das fernste Italien* (1925), and *Das byzantinische Reich als geographische Erscheinung* (1939). In 1933, he was awarded the Great Gold Richthofen Medal by the German Geographical Society. He continued to play a leading role in German geographical research until he was banned from the university and all other scientific bodies by the Nazi regime. In 1942, at the age of 78, he was deported to *Theresienstadt but managed to survive. In 1945, despite terrible suffering, he returned to his scientific activities, which he continued to his death in Bonn, aged 89. In this last period he produced two of his best works: *Die Stadt Bonn. Ihre Lage und raeumliche Entwicklung* (1947, 1951¹²), an outstanding work on urban geography, and *Die griechischen Landschaften* (1950–59).

[Mordechai Breuer / Johannes Valentin Schwarz (2nd ed.)]

(3) JULIUS PHILIPPSON (1814–1871), the younger brother of Ludwig, who was only three months old when their father Moses died, became a businessman at Magdeburg. Of his six children, HEINRICH (1849–1908) became a businessman at Magdeburg, too. EMIL (1851–1906) studied modern languages and comparative philology in Bonn, Berlin, and Leipzig, where he took his doctor's degree. Since he was barred from an academic career, he accepted an offer from the Philanthropin in Frankfurt/Main in 1874, till he became headmaster of the Jacobsonschule at Seesen in 1886. ROBERT (1858–1942) studied philosophy and classics in Bonn, Leipzig, and Berlin, where he took his degree in 1881. He followed his brother Emil to the Frankfurt Philanthropin, till he was admitted to the Wilhelmsgymnasium at Magdeburg as the first Jewish teacher in the Prussian province of Saxony. He retired in 1923. In 1942, aged 84, he was deported to Theresienstadt, where he died a week after his arrival. Robert's oldest son JULIUS (1894–1944), who was dismissed as a teacher in 1933, joined the Socialist underground movement Internationaler Sozialistischer Kampfbund (ISK), until he was caught by the Gestapo in 1937. He was later deported to Auschwitz, where he died from exhaustion. JOHANNA PHILIPPSON (1887–1977), a daughter of Heinrich, chose a career as a teacher, from 1930 holding a senior position at the Elisabethschule in Berlin until she was dismissed in 1933. Thereafter, she taught at the schools of the Jewish community. In 1939, she immigrated to London, where she engaged in adult education and contributed to various periodicals. In 1962, she published a detailed study in the *Leo Baeck Institute Year Book* on "The Philippsons, a German-Jewish Family 1775–1933." Their history, as she wrote, "seems typical of many German Jewish families: the very rapid inhaling of German civilization, the high degree of assimilation, and the abrupt ending."

[Johannes Valentin Schwarz (2nd ed.)]

BIBLIOGRAPHY: G. Salomon, *Lebensgeschichte des Herrn Moses Philippsohn* (1814); Ph. Philippson, *Biographische Skizzen*, 1 (1864); M. Kayserling, *Ludwig Philippson* (1898); M. Philippson, in: JJGL, 14 (1911), 84–108; J.C. Dornfeld, in: CCARY, 21 (1911); J. Feiner, *Ludwig Philippson* (1912); Wininger, 5 (1930), 17–25; *Festschrift... A. Philippson* (1930); *Biographie Coloniale Belge*, 3 (1952); J. Rosenthal, in: S. Federbush (ed.), *Hokhmat Yisrael be-Ma'arav Eiropah*, 1 (1958), 399–408; J. Philippson, in: LBIYB, 7 (1962), 95–118; E.G. Lowenthal, in: LBI Bulletin, 8 (1965), 89–106. **ADD. BIBLIOGRAPHY:** J. Philippson, in: H. Liebeschütz and A. Paucker (eds.), *Das Judentum in der Deutschen Umwelt, 1800–1850* (1977), 243–91; E. Friesel, in: LBIYB, 31 (1986), 121–46; H.O. Horch, in: LBI Bulletin, No. 86 (1990), 5–21; G. von Glasenapp, in: A.B. Kilcher (ed.), *Metzler Lexikon der deutsch-jüdischen Literatur* (2000), 459–61; A. Mehmel, A. Brämer, I. Fischer, in: NDB, 20 (2001), 395–401.

PHILIPSON, DAVID (1862–1949), U.S. Reform rabbi. Philipson was born in Wabash, Indiana, and received his early education in Columbus, Ohio. Entering Hebrew Union College, Cincinnati, in 1875, he was one of the first group of rabbis who received their ordination in 1883. After serving as rabbi of Har Sinai Congregation, Baltimore, from 1884 to 1888, Philipson returned to Cincinnati to become rabbi of the B'nai Israel Congregation in 1888, remaining there for the rest of his life. He became the leader and the embodiment of Classical Reform Judaism, believing in the Jewish mission and universalism. Philipson participated in the conference which drew up the Pittsburgh Platform (1885); he was a founder of the Central Conference of American Rabbis, serving as president in 1907–09; and he was an influential figure in – but never president of – Hebrew Union College, where he taught for many years, and in the Union of American Hebrew Congregations. He chaired the joint CCAR-HUC Commission on Jewish Education for 39 years (1903–43), which published widely used resource material and textbooks for the Reform movement. Not a profound thinker, Philipson was productive in the literary field. His most important work was *The Reform Movement in Judaism* (2nd ed. 1931; repr. 1967). He also wrote *The Jew in English Fiction* (5th ed. 1927) and edited *The Letters of Rebecca Gratz* (1929). He was a member of the board of translators of the Jewish Publication Society for the translation of the Holy

Scriptures (1916), an editor of *Selected Writings of Isaac M. Wise* (1900), and translator of *Reminiscences of Isaac M. Wise* (1901, 1945). An autobiography, *My Life as an American Jew*, appeared in 1942, and a volume of occasional writings, *Centenary Papers*, in 1919. *My Life as an American Jew* gave voice to the double-edged nature of American Judaism, Philipson was not just a Jew, but an *American* Jew. There was something uniquely American about his Judaism. Philipson verbalized and gave a universal dimension to the optimism of the prospering Midwest Jews among whom he lived and, surviving most of its exponents, came to be regarded as a representative spokesman of "classic" Reform Judaism.

BIBLIOGRAPHY: D. Philipson, *Reform Movement in Judaism* (1967), introd. by S. Freehof.

[Sefton D. Temkin]

PHILISTINES (Heb. פְּלִשְׁתִּים), a people of Aegean origin occupying the south coast of Palestine, called Philistia (פְּלֶשֶׁת, *peleshet*) in the Bible, and often at war with the Israelites. The name Philistine is first found in the Egyptian form *prst* as one of the "Sea Peoples" who invaded Egypt in the eighth year of Ramses III (c. 1190 B.C.E.). In Assyrian sources the name occurs as both *Pilišti* and *Palaštu/Palastu* (also *Palaštaya*). The Septuagint, when not translating it as "strangers" (*allopsyloi*), usually renders it as *phylistiim* (i.e., in Genesis–Joshua).

In biblical tradition, the Philistines came originally from *Caphtor (Crete: Jer. 47:4; Amos 9:7; cf. Deut. 2:23). This tradition is buttressed by the fact that part of the Philistine coast was called הַנֶּגֶב הַכְּרֵתִי, "the Negeb of the Cherethites" (I Sam. 30:14), and by the occurrence of Cretans in parallelism with Philistines (Ezek. 25:16; Zeph. 2:5), but there is no direct archaeological proof for it. The Philistines participated in the second wave of the "Sea Peoples" who, according to Egyptian reports, ravaged the Hittite lands, Arzawa, the Syrian coast, Carchemish, and Cyprus, and threatened Egypt during the reigns of Merneptah and Ramses III. The excavations at Hattusas (Boghazköy) and Ugarit have shown that these cities were destroyed at the end of the Late Bronze Age (c. 1200) and tablets discovered at Ugarit and archaeological finds on Cyprus give evidence of this troubled period. Of the "Sea Peoples" only the Philistines, who settled along the Palestinian coast, and the Tjeker, who occupied Dor according to the Wen-Amon story (c. 1050), can be positively identified. The others – Shekelesh, Denyen, Sherden, and Weshesh – have only been conjecturally identified. These peoples, displaced from their original homelands, assimilated the Minoan–Mycenean culture patterns of the Aegean world.

"Philistia" or the "Land of the Philistines" is that part of the coastal plain of Palestine which lies between Tel Qasīle and the Wadi Ghazza, about 6 mi. (c. 10 km.) south of Gaza. (See Map: Philistine Pentapolis). The Philistine pentapolis consisted of Gaza, Ashkelon, Ashdod, Gath (Tell al-Ṣāfī = Tel Ṣafit; Rainey, Schniedewind, Dothan), and Ekron (Khirbat al-Muqanna'/Tel Miqne). The references to Philistia and the Philistines in Genesis 21:32, 34 and Exodus 13:17; 15:14;

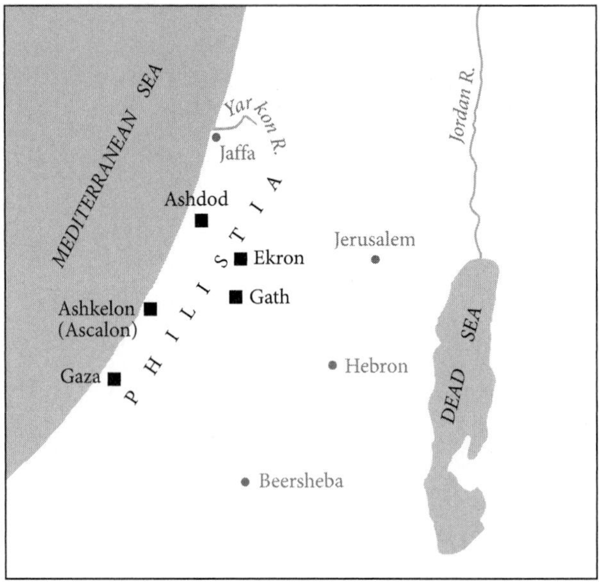

The Philistine Pentapolis.

23:31 are anachronistic. The Greeks, familiar at first with the coastal area, gradually applied the name Palestine to the whole of the country. The Philistines depicted on the walls of the temple of Ramses III at Medinat Habu in Egypt are dressed in a kind of Aegean kilt and wear a plumed headdress with chinstraps. Similar depictions from Late Bronze Age Cyprus have been found. The Philistine ship is unusual while the wagon and chariot fit well-known forms. The clearest sign of Philistine presence is "Philistine pottery," whose chief types are buff-colored craters, beer jugs with spouted strainers, cups, and stirrup vases with a white wash or slip on which are painted reddish-purple or black geometrical designs, or metope-like panels with stylized swans preening themselves. These are found from the beginning of the 12th century to the late 11th century B.C.E. in Philistia itself, in adjacent sites of the Negev (e.g., Tell el-Fāriʿa) and the Shephelah (ʿAyn Shams), and in cities occupied by them (e.g., *Gezer, Tell Belt Mirsim, Meggido, Afulah, and Tell al-Naṣba). Similar pottery was also found at Tell Deir ʿAllā in the Jordan valley. Analysis has shown that from the beginning Philistine pottery was a local product using local techniques with strong points of contact with the Mycenean IIIC1 wares discovered at Enkomi and Sinda on Cyprus and the other sub-Mycenean wares of Cyprus and Rhodes. Anthropoid clay coffins also signal Philistine presence (e.g., Tell al-Fāriʿa and Beth-Shean). According to the Bible, the Philistines had a monopoly on metal working (I Sam. 13:19–21) in the days of Saul, and smelting furnaces have been found at Ashdod, Tell Qasīle, Tel Ḥamma, and Tell Mor. Archaeologically, however, it appears that during Iron Age I, iron was a precious metal that did not come into mass production until the tenth century, with bronze surviving as the main utilitarian metal (Rainey, 130).

The excavations at Ashdod have uncovered as yet undeciphered seals in the Cypro-Minoan script from the 12th–11th centuries. Tablets in a related script were also found at Deir ʿAllā. From the ninth century on, a variant of the Phoenician-Hebrew script was used in Philistia. A seventh-century temple inscription of Achish (Ikayaus; Gitin, Dothan, and Naveh; Rainey, 255) the ruler of Ekron (*šr ʿqrn*) is written in a Canaanite dialect, and dedicated to a goddess Potgaya (Demsky reads Potnia, "Mistress" in Greek). A few words that may be native Philistine have been identified. These are *seranim*, used of the five princes of the Philistine confederacy which has been equated with the Greek *turannos*, of pre-Hellenic or Asiatic origin; *kobaʿ* / *qobaʿ*, "helmet," connected with Hittite *kupakhi*; and *ʾargaz*, "chest," "ark." Two Philistine names in biblical accounts set in the period of the early monarchy have possible Asiatic connections – *Goliath with Alyattas and *Achish, king of Gath, a contemporary of David, with either the Homeric proper name Anchises (Esarhaddon and Assurbanipal refer to Ikaus[u] of Ekron), or with the sense "Achaean," i.e., "Greek." The spelling of "Achish" in the Ekron inscription is identical to the biblical spelling. The other names, from the later period, are usually Canaanite (e.g., Ahimilki, Sidqa (צדקא on a seal), Mitinti (מתת on a seal), and Hanun). Soon after coming to Palestine, the Philistines adopted a Canaanite dialect, and this in turn gave way to Aramaic. Ashdodite (Neh. 13:24) refers to such a local (Canaanite?) dialect and an ostracon from the late fifth century reading *krm zbdyh* was found at Ashdod. The recurrence of the non-Semitic name Ikayaus in the Assyrian sources and in the Ekron inscription may point to a cultural revival perhaps inspired by the presence of Greeks in Canaan, by nostalgia (cf. Hezekiah and Josiah's reforms), or both.

The Philistines were uncircumcised and were, therefore, despised by the Israelites (Judg. 14:3; 15:18; I Sam. 17:26; 18:25). Among other recognizable cultural traits are certain peculiar burial practices, with Mycenean connections; the replacement of goat meat and mutton in their diets by pork and beef; the division of their cities into zones; and the development of a central city plan (Ashdod had a drainage system and a municipal garbage dump outside the city walls).

Various ritual objects found at Ashdod and Gezer are closely related to similar objects from the Aegean, but all the Philistines' gods known from the Bible have Semitic names. According to the Bible the Philistines had temples to Dagon in Gaza and Ashdod (Judg. 16:23; I Sam. 5:1–7), to Astarte (Ashtoreth) in Ashkelon (Herodotus 1:105), and to Baal-Zebub in Ekron (II Kings 1:1–16). A Philistine temple discovered at Tell Qasile built about 1150 and rebuilt several times shows Aegean as well as Canaanite influence. Excavations at Ashdod revealed a stylized image of a female deity with small breasts, merged into a high-backed chair. Though the deity's name is unknown she is now commonly referred to as "Ashdoda." An elegant and monumental temple with a large hearth, reflective of Aegean practice, was found at Ekron. Literary sources refer to Philistine temples as late as the Hellenistic period (I Macc. 10:83; Diodorus Siculus 2:4).

The Philistines also achieved a reputation as soothsayers (Isa. 2:6). The Philistine pentapolis, until its defeat by David, was ruled by *seranim*, "leaders," who acted in council and were able to overrule the decision of any individual *seren* (I Sam. 29:1–7). The Philistines were able to muster large, well-armed troops of foot soldiers, archers, and charioteers (I Sam. 13:5; 29:2; 31:3) and also elements of the autochthonous population and mercenaries (David – I Sam. 27–29; the Rephaim – II Sam. 21:18–22). Individual combat (Goliath – I Sam. 17:4–10) and shock troops were used by the Philistines (I Sam. 13:17–18; 14:15). In the later period they were ruled by "kings" (Jer. 25:20; Zech. 9:5).

After being repulsed by Ramses II, the Philistines first settled the coast of Palestine. Ashkelon, Ashdod, Gath, and Gaza, known from older sources, were captured by the Philistines from their Canaanite inhabitants, perhaps with the tacit permission of the Egyptians. They may also have served as part of the Egyptian garrison at Beth-Shean. The tradition concerning *Shamgar son of Anath's killing 600 Philistines may stem from this time (Judg. 3:31). Ekron may have been a newly founded Philistine city, and the excavations at the Philistine-founded Tell Qasīle and at Ashdod attest their building activity during this period. There are no reports of any opposition to the Philistines on the part of the inhabitants of the coastal cities. The Philistine expansion into adjacent areas in the Shefelah and the Negev from about 1150 on is demonstrated by the abundance of their pottery found there. The ensuing pressure upon the Danites and Judahites is reflected in the *Samson saga (Judg. 13–16), and toward the middle of the 11th century, they were able to encroach upon the hill country, destroy Shiloh, and capture the ark. They devastated part of western Palestine, and occupied Gibeath-Benjamin, Megiddo, and Beth-Shean. Under Samuel (I Sam. 7:7–14) and Saul, at the beginning of the latter's reign (c. 1020), some respite from the Philistines was obtained. The Philistine return to power is highlighted by the Goliath pericope (I Sam. 17), but the freedom of David and his band as auxiliaries of Achish of Gath points up Philistine weakness (I Sam. 27). After the defeat of Saul at Gilboa, the Philistines were able to reestablish control over part of the land as far north as Beth-Shean, but David, after being anointed as king over all Israel, was able to use his knowledge of Philistine strategy to defeat them and to drive them back to Gezer (II Sam. 5:17–25). David subdued the city of Gath (I Chron. 18:1) and imposed vassalage upon it; Gath supplied him with faithful warriors like *Ittai the Gittite (II Sam. 15:18–22; 18:2). Mercenary troops from the other independent Philistine cities, such as the Cherethites and Pelethites (see below) under the command of Benaiah son of Jehoiada, joined the ranks of David's personal army.

Philistine history was now the history of individual cities, rather than that of a people acting in concert. It is quite possible that in the course of their battles with Saul and David, the ruling Philistine military class had been wiped out and that strong assimilation with the native Canaanite population had already taken place. Except for Achish of Gath, mentioned in I Kings 2:39–40, who is most probably the same person as the ruler of Gath under whom David served, and Ikausu of Ekron, a contemporary of Ashurbanipal of Assyria, all the known subsequent Philistine rulers have Semitic names. The typically Philistine pottery of the Early Iron Age disappears, and the pottery and other artifacts found in the following Early Iron Age III levels is the same as that found elsewhere in Palestine. The Philistines were, on the whole, limited now to their pentapolis and the immediate coastal area. Reduced to a secondary role, their hold over the sea coast was broken, and Phoenician maritime expansion became possible. The vassal status of Gath remained unchanged at the beginning of the reign of Solomon (c. 960), as can be seen by the ease with which Shimei son of Gera moved into and out of that city (I Kings 2:39–40). Toward the end of the United Monarchy and the early part of the divided Monarchy, Egyptian influence in Philistia may be surmised from the campaign of an unnamed Pharaoh of the 21st Dynasty at Gezer (I Kings 9:16–17) and the use made by Sheshonk I (biblical *Shishak) of Gaza as the starting point of his campaign in Palestine (c. 917), as reported in his itinerary. During the next 50 years *Gibbethon (Tell Malāt, near Gezer), which was held by the Israelites, was the site of border battles, involving troops of relatively large numbers, between them and the Philistines (I Kings 15:27; 16:15–17). During the reign of Jehoshaphat the Philistines paid tribute to Judah (II Chron. 17:11), but were able to make incursions into Judahite territory and raid the king's household, carrying off his son Jehoram (II Chron. 21:16–17). It is also clear, from these scant references, that Arabian tribes now occupied the territory to the south of Philistia.

During his raid into Judah in about 815, Hazael of Aram was able to capture the city of Gath (II Kings 12:18). The first definite reference to Philistia in Assyrian sources dates from the reign of Adad-nirâri III (810–783), who boasts of having collected tribute from Philistia (Palastu) in his fifth year. Uzziah successfully raided Philistine territory and, according to the biblical report, tore down the walls of some cities (as shown archaeologically at Ashdod) and set up garrisons of his own (II Chron. 26:6–7). Although no destruction of the city is reported, except in the enigmatic reference in Amos 5:2, Gath lost its former importance. Gath is not listed in the various prophetic condemnations of the Philistines (Jer. 25:20; Amos 1:6–8; Zeph. 2:4; Zech. 9:5–8), and had, in all likelihood, come under the rule of Ashdod. During the reign of Ahaz, the Philistines once again raided Judah and occupied cities in the Shefelah and the Negev (II Chron. 28:18; cf. Isa. 9:11; 14:28–32). However, Tiglath-Pileser III invaded Philistia in 734, sacked Gaza, and forced vassalage on Hanun, its king, and upon Mitinti of Ashkelon (text in Rainey, 229; Ehrlich, 176–89). *Sargon II stormed Gaza in 720, after Hanun had participated in the anti-Assyrian coalition, exiled Hanun, and made Gaza once again a vassal city. Tribute from various Philistine cities is recorded in Assyrian records of this period. In 713, Azuri of Ashdod was deported for treachery and was replaced by his brother, Ahimiti, but the Ashdodites placed a local usurper, Iamani, on the throne. Iamani fortified Ashdod and, by forming an alliance including Philistia, Judah, Edom, and Moab, he precipitated an attack in 712 by Sargon. This campaign is referred to in Isaiah 20:1. The capture of Ekron and Gibbethon is portrayed on wall reliefs from Dur-Sharrukin; Ashdod, Ashdod-Yam, and Gath were also captured. Excavations at Ashdod have uncovered fragments of a basalt victory stele erected by Sargon and also show that the walls of the city were destroyed at this time. Ashdod was temporarily converted into an Assyrian province. According to II Kings 18:8, Hezekiah invaded Philistia and attacked Gaza. In Ashkelon, Sidqa replaced the loyal ruler while Hezekiah was in alliance with the people of Ekron who handed over their king, Padi, to him. The Ethiopian rulers of Egypt in all likelihood planned to move into the south of Philistia. In 701, Sennacherib invaded southern Palestine and captured the cities of Beth-Dagon, Jaffa, Bene-Berak, and Azor and their capital Ashkelon; deported Sidqa and his family and imposed a new king; and punished the patricians of Ekron, restored Padi to his throne, and rewarded the faithful kings of Ashdod, Ekron, and Gaza with a strip of Judahite territory in the Shefelah. The traditional dislike of the Philistines, reflected in both the Prophets and the Psalms, was intensified by their participating in the Phoenician slave trade during this period (Joel 4:1–8). During the rest of Sennacherib's reign Philistia served as a buffer zone between Assyria and Egypt. During the reigns of Esarhaddon and Ashurbanipal, the kings of Gaza, Ashkelon, Ekron, and Ashdod are listed among the loyal vassals of Assyria who supplied corvée workers and troops to the Assyrian army. The constant passage of Assyrian troops through Philistia in the campaigns against Egypt guaranteed the tranquility of the area.

After the breakdown of Assyrian might, the Philistine cities, particularly Ashdod, were under strong Egyptian pressure (Herodotus 1:157). Archaeological discoveries have made it probable that Josiah annexed part of northern Philistia near Yavneh-Yam. There is also a tradition of an invasion of Scythians who destroyed the temple of Astarte in Ashkelon (Herodotus 1:105). Philistia was overrun by the Egyptians under Neco, who conquered Gaza in about 609–608 (Herodotus 1:159; cf. Jer. 47:1). The Philistines were allied with Egypt against Nebuchadnezzar of Babylon, as is now clear from the Aramaic letter found at Saqqarah from Adon (of Ashkelon?) to Pharaoh, but Ashkelon was laid waste and her king exiled in 604 by Nebuchadnezzar. Nebuchadnezzar put out any remaining sparks of Philistine independence. He deported both rulers and people, as has been shown by the mention of the kings of Gaza and Ashdod and the princes of Ashkelon in various lists from Babylon (cf. Jer. 25:20; 47:2–7; Zeph. 2:4–7; Zech. 9:5–6). The later history of the cities Ashdod (Azotus), Ashkelon (Ascalon), and Gaza is of Persian and then Hellenistic cities with a highly mixed population. Only the territorial name *Palestine connected them with their Philistine past.

The Cherethites and Pelethites (הַכְּרֵתִי וְהַפְּלֵתִי) were a section of David's personal army who joined him after he had defeated the Philistines. They were part of his retinue after he was established in Jerusalem. Their commander, *Benaiah son of Jehoiada, is listed as a member of David's administrative corps (II Sam. 8:18; 20:23). Their absolute loyalty to David was proved by their accompanying him on his flight from Jerusalem (II Sam. 20:7). Their faithfulness was again proved in their supporting the selection of Solomon as king (I Kings 1:38–44). The name Cherethite most probably meant Cretan and alluded either to the Aegean origin of part of the "Sea Peoples" who settled along the south coast of Palestine with the Philistines or to a group of Cretans settled there by the Egyptians. They probably dwelt in the area to the southeast of Philistia proper, which is once alluded to as the Cretan Negev or the Negev of the Cherethites (I Sam. 30:14). The Pelethites were, in all likelihood, recruited from the ranks of the Philistines with whom David had served during his stay in Ziklag. The form "Pelethite" (*peleti*) for "Philistine" (*pelishti*) is explicable as a formation modeled on "Cherethite" (*kereti*). In the two passages in which the Cherethites are in parallelism with the Philistines, it is not clear from the context whether the terms are synonymous or if separate peoples are meant (Ezek. 25:16; Zeph. 2:5). The Carians were a people originating in southwest Anatolia whose services as mercenaries in Egypt and elsewhere, from the early seventh century on, is well known. Their script has not yet been deciphered, nor is their history before this period known. There may very well be a connection between them and the enigmatic Carites (הַכָּרִי) of II Kings 11:4, 19 who were considered loyal to the royal house in the story of Joash. The variant reading "Carites" (כָּרִי) for Cherethites (כְּרֵתִי) in the *ketiv* of II Samuel 20:23 is in all likelihood an error.

Archaeological excavation has revealed the Philistines to have been a highly sophisticated ancient people, both materially and commercially. They developed trading networks between Canaan and the rest of the Mediterranean world. Ekron produced both utilitarian and high-quality tableware as well as wine. By the seventh century B.C.E. Ekron was the largest producer of olive oil in the ancient Near East. Nonetheless, despite their impressive historical accomplishments, the Philistines, "because of their confrontation with the hill people known as the Israelites… acquired a negative historical image that still retains its symbolic power" (Dothan, CANE II, 1279).

[Jonas C. Greenfield / S. David Sperling (2nd ed.)]

In the *Aggadah*

Most Midrashim are concerned with the alliance made of Abraham and Isaac with Abimelech, king of the Philistines (Gen. 21 and 26). Abraham is criticized for concluding an alliance with him. The Midrash tells that as a punishment for the seven sheep he sacrificed in making this covenant, the Philistines would one day slay seven righteous men – Samson, Hophni, Phinehas, and Saul with his three sons; they would destroy seven holy places; they would retain the holy Ark in their country as spoils of war for a period of seven months; and, furthermore, only the seventh generation of Abraham's descendants would be able to rejoice in the possession of the land (Gen. R. 54:4). Jacob did not stay in Philistia lest he too be compelled to make an alliance with the Philistines, thus delaying the conquest of the Holy Land (*ibid.* 68:7). David was not bound by his forefathers' covenant with Abimelech, since the Philistines' stopping of the wells which Abraham had dug constituted a breach of this agreement (Mid. Hag. to Gen. 26:28). However, they came to him with the bridle of a mule, which Isaac had given to Abimelech as a pledge of this covenant (PdRE 36). David commanded the Sanhedrin to investigate the claim carefully, but it was declared unfounded. Moreover, the Philistines of his day were not the descendants of the Philistines who had concluded the treaty; they had immigrated from Caphtor at a much later date (Mid. Ps. 60, 1).

After the capture of Samson the Philistines brought their wives to him in the Gaza prison in the hope that he might sire children who would be as strong as he (Sot. 10a). When they took the Ark, they said contemptuously: "The God of the Israelites had only ten plagues which he expended upon the Egyptians, and he no longer has it in his power to do us harm." As a result they were afflicted with a new plague consisting of mice crawling forth out of the earth and gnawing their entrails (Sif. Num. 88).

BIBLIOGRAPHY: R.A.S. Macalister, *The Philistines, Their History and Civilization* (1913); B. Mazar, *The Philistines and the Rise of Israel and Tyre* (1964); B. Mazar (ed.), *World History of the Jewish People*, 3 (1971), 164–79; G.E. Wright, in: BA, 29 (1966), 70–86; H. Tadmor, in: BA, 29 (1966), 86–102; W.F. Albright, *The Amarna Letters from Palestine-Syria, The Philistines and Phoenicia* (1966); T. Dothan, *Ha-Pelishtim ve-Tarbutam* (1967); H.J. Franken, in: CAH², vol. 2 (1968), ch. 26; R.D. Barnett, in: CAH, vol. 2 (1969), ch. 28; M. Dothan, in: D.N. Freedman and J.C. Greenfield (eds.), *New Directions in Biblical Archaeology* (1969); R. Hestrin, *The Philistines and the Other Sea Peoples* (1970). IN THE AGGADAH: Ginzberg, Legends, index. **ADD. BIBLIOGRAPHY:** T. Dothan, *The Philistines and their Material Culture* (1982); N. Sandars, *The Sea Peoples: Warriors of the Ancient Mediterranean* (1985); T. Dothan and M. Dothan, *People of the Sea: The Search for the Philistines* (1992); R. Drews, *The End of the Bronze Age: Changes in Warfare and the Catastrophe ca. 1200 B.C.* (1993); H. Katzenstein, in: ABD, 5:326–28; T. Dothan, *ibid.*, 329–33 (illustrated); idem, in: CANE II, 1267–78; A. Kuhrt, *The Ancient Near East c. 3000–330 BC* (1995), 386–93; C. Ehrlich, *The Philistines in Transition* (1996); T. Dothan, S. Gitin, and J. Naveh, in: IEJ, 47 (1997), 1–16; W. Schniedewind, in: BASOR, 309 (1998), 69–77; J. Naveh, in: BASOR, 310 (1998), 35–37; A. Demsky, in: JANES, 25 (1998), 1–5; E. Oren (ed.), *The Sea Peoples and their World* (2000); A. Rainey and R.S. Notley, *The Sacred Bridge Carta's Atlas of the Biblical World* (2005). For extensive bibliography on Ekron with illustrations see: http://www.aiar.org/docs/EkronSummary.pdf.

PHILLIPS (originally **Pheibush**), early American family. The Phillips family was founded in America by JONAS PHILLIPS (1736–1803), born in Buseck in the Rhineland, who arrived in Charleston, South Carolina, in 1756 as an indentured servant of Moses *Lindo, a merchant. He became a freeman in 1759, lived in Albany, where he failed in business, and moved to New York where he was a *shoḥet*. Phillips subsequently engaged in business and was admitted as a freeman in New York City in 1769. A patriot who subscribed to the Non-Importation Resolution, Phillips left New York when it was threatened by the British and enlisted as a private in the Philadelphia militia in 1778. After the war Phillips continued as a merchant in Philadelphia and was elected president of Mikveh Israel Congregation. He took part in signing petitions addressed both to the governments of Pennsylvania and the United States asking civil rights for Jews. Phillips had 21 children, a number of whom died in infancy; a grandson was Mordecai Manuel *Noah.

MANUEL PHILLIPS (d. 1826), son of Jonas, studied medicine at the University of Pennsylvania and served as assistant surgeon in the War of 1812. He died in Vera Cruz.

NAPHTALI PHILLIPS (1773–1870), another son, was born in Philadelphia and became president of Mikveh Israel Congregation at the age of 25. He moved to New York in 1801 where he served Shearith Israel Congregation in a similar capacity for 14 terms. Naphtali Phillips was the first of a group of Jewish newspaper publishers in the United States, owner of New York City's *National Advocate*. He worked in the Customs House for 30 years. Phillips was the father of 15 children.

ZALEGMAN PHILLIPS (1779–1839), another son of Jonas, was a graduate of the University of Pennsylvania. Admitted to the bar in 1799, he was the first Jewish lawyer in Pennsylvania.

BIBLIOGRAPHY: Rosenbloom, Biogr Dict, s.v.; E. Wolf and M. Whiteman, *History of the Jews of Philadelphia* (1957), index; H. Simonhoff, *Jewish Notables in America* (1956) index, especially 49–52 on Jonas and 145–48 on Naphtali Phillips.

[Abram Vossen Goodman]

PHILLIPS, LAZARUS (1895–1986), lawyer, businessman and member of the Senate of Canada. Phillips was born into an establishment Montreal Jewish family. A member of Montreal's uptown Jewish elite, he graduated from McGill University in 1918, after service in the Canadian Officers Training Corps. He served on the Headquarters Staff of the Canadian Siberian Expeditionary Force in 1918–19 before returning to Montreal to practice corporate law, first in the offices of Sam *Jacobs, Liberal member of Parliament for Montreal's Cartier riding. In 1923 Phillips became a partner in the firm and was named King's Counsel in 1930. Phillips was also active in the Liberal Party, an able fundraiser and well connected in Ottawa. His one foray into electoral politics was ill-starred. He was the Liberal candidate in the hotly contested 1943 by-election in Montreal's Cartier riding, where he and CCF candidate David *Lewis were both defeated by Fred *Rose, the Communist (Labor-Progressive) candidate.

Phillips was active in various local Jewish philanthropies and served on the boards of numerous corporations. For the better part of 30 years Phillips was also chief legal counsel to Sam *Bronfman and was often the public face of the Seagram empire. In 1968 he was appointed a Liberal Party member of the Senate of Canada, the first Jew from Quebec appointed to the upper house. This was an appointment long coveted by Sam Bronfman and the Phillips appointment was something of a personal disappointment to Bronfman.

[Gerald Tulchinsky (2nd ed.)]

PHILLIPS, SIR LIONEL (1855–1936), South African financier and mining magnate. Born in London, he emigrated to South Africa (from England). He settled in Kimberley in 1875 and started work as a diamond sorter. In 1881 he became a director of the Griqualand West Diamond Company. He joined the leading mining house of Hermann Eckstein and Company in 1889 and succeeded Eckstein as head of the firm. In 1891 he was president of the Chamber of Mines and he played an important part in the financial organization and technical development of the gold mines. Phillips was one of the four members of the Reform Committee who, after the fiasco of the Jameson Raid (1896), were sentenced to death. The sentences were commuted to a fine of £25,000 and banishment. He returned to South Africa after the Boer War, was a member of the first Union Parliament (1910–15), and was created a baronet in 1912. During the disturbances accompanying the Rand strike of 1913 he was severely wounded. Phillips' views on contemporary affairs are given in *Transvaal Problems* (1905) and *Some Reminiscences* (1924). On his retirement he settled at the Cape. Phillips and his wife Dorothea Sarah Florence Alexandra Ortlepp laid the foundations of the Johannesburg Art Gallery collection and of the Michaelis Gallery in Cape Town.

BIBLIOGRAPHY: G. Saron and L. Hotz (eds.), *Jews in South Africa* (1955), index. **ADD. BIBLIOGRAPHY:** G. Wheatcroft, *The Randlords* (1985), index; P. Struik, *Art and Aspirations: The Randlords of South Africa and Their Collections* (2002).

PHILLIPS, MARION (1881–1932), British politician. Born and educated in Melbourne, Australia, the daughter of a solicitor, Marion Phillips moved to Britain in 1904, where she received a doctorate at the London School of Economics. She was employed by Sidney and Beatrice Webb as a researcher on the London poor and joined the Fabian Society as well as suffragette and pro-labor organizations. From 1912 she was actively involved in politics, serving as a Labour councillor in London. Phillips was especially concerned with Labour's policies towards women and was the author of a pioneering work, *Women and the Labour Party* (1918). In 1929 she was elected Labour Member of Parliament for Sunderland, one of the first woman Labour MPs and the first Australian woman to win a seat in any national parliament. She was also the first Jewish woman to serve in the British Parliament. Marion Phillips lost her seat at the 1931 general election and died of stomach cancer at the age of only 50.

BIBLIOGRAPHY: ODNB online; ADB.

[William D. Rubinstein (2nd ed.)]

PHILLIPS, NATHAN (1892–1976), Canadian politician. Phillips was born in Brockville, Ontario, the descendent of a pioneer Canadian Jewish family. He graduated from high school at 16 and in 1913 at age 21 graduated from Osgoode Hall Law School in Toronto. A member of the Toronto law firm of Phillips and Phillips, Phillips acted as crown counsel at various Ontario Assizes and in 1929 was appointed king's council, the youngest in Ontario. Phillips was also a member of the Conservative Party and unsuccessfully ran for federal and provincial office. He was more successful in municipal politics. He was a member of Toronto City Council for 36 years, and won two back-to-back terms as mayor of Toronto, serving from 1955 until his retirement in 1962. Phillips' election as mayor was notable in that he was not only the first Jewish mayor of Toronto or any other major Canadian city, but he was also the first politician to break the Orange Order's iron hold on the political power of Toronto. His term as mayor marked a turning point in the city, a transforming moment when Toronto shifted from being a staunchly Protestant, Anglocentric, and conservative city to become a modern cosmopolitan and thriving metropolis. Fittingly, Phillips was popularly dubbed "mayor of all the people." Determined that his city should have a new showcase City Hall, he won approval for an international design competition that was ultimately won by Finnish architect Viljo Revell with a strikingly avante-garde design. The large public square in front of the building is named for Phillips. Phillips was a member of several service groups including the Masonic Order, the Order of Eagles, and the Lions and Kiwanis Clubs. He was president of Toronto Lodge B'nai B'rith and honorary president of the Holy Blossom Temple Brotherhood and was the recipient of the Human Relations Award from the Canadian Council of Christians and Jews in 1959.

[Frank Bialystok (2nd edition)]

PHILLIPS, PHILIP (1807–1884), U.S. congressman and jurist. The son of an immigrant from Germany, Phillips, who was born in Charleston, South Carolina, began studying law there in 1825, and was admitted to the South Carolina bar in 1828. As a delegate to the South Carolina "nullification convention" of 1832, Phillips, a unionist, strongly opposed Southern secession over the slavery issue. Phillips was elected to the South Carolina state legislature in 1834 but moved the following year to Alabama, where he served in the legislature from 1844 to 1853. In 1853 he was elected as a Democrat to a two-year term in the House of Representatives in Washington, thus becoming the second U.S. Jew to sit in Congress. Phillips was admitted to the bar of the Supreme Court in 1850 and during his stay in Washington argued many cases before the Court. With the outbreak of the Civil War in 1861, he and his non-Jewish wife were placed under house arrest in Washington because of the latter's openly pro-Southern sympathies. However, later that year they were permitted to move to New Orleans. After Lee's surrender Phillips returned to Washington, where he continued to practice law. Among his published legal works was his *Statutory Jurisdiction and Practise of the Supreme Court of the United States* (1872).

Although Phillips was secretary of the Charleston Reform Society of Israelites during his residence in that city, his association with Jewish life appears to have been tenuous. He did, however, head a Jewish delegation to President Buchanan in 1857 to petition for the repeal of the anti-Jewish clauses contained in the American-Swiss treaty of 1855.

BIBLIOGRAPHY: B.A. Elzas, *Jews of South Carolina* (1905), passim; J.R. Marcus, *Memoirs of American Jews 1775–1865*, 3 (1955), 133–96.

PHILLIPS, REBECCA MACHADO (1746–1831), pioneering American communal leader. Phillips was born in Reading, Pennsylvania, the eldest of two daughters of María Caetena (Zipporah), and Rev. David Mendes Machado, refugees of the Portuguese Inquisition who had returned to open Judaism in London. Her maternal grandfather, Samuel Nunes Ribeiro, had been a prominent court physician in Lisbon and later a founding member of Governor Oglethorpe's Savannah colony established in 1733, while her father served as cantor of New York's Congregation Shearith Israel and taught in its school. The family's Crypto-Jewish legacy was largely preserved by Rebecca's mother and female relatives, who transmitted accounts of escape from the Inquisition and maintained syncretic Catholic/Jewish rituals long after their return to open Judaism.

Rebecca's father died in 1747 and her mother subsequently remarried, producing a half-sister. In 1762, at age 16, Rebecca wed Jonas Phillips (1735–1803), an Ashkenazi merchant 11 years her senior, and moved with him to New York, where the first of their 21 children was born. Along with Zipporah Levy (1760–1832), daughter of Hayman Levy and wife of Benjamin Mendes Seixas, who also bore 21 children, Rebecca holds the fertility record among early American Jewish women. Most of her children survived to adulthood.

After some years of financial hardship, the Phillips family emerged prosperous from the Revolutionary War; by the early 1780s Jonas was the second wealthiest Jew in Philadelphia, where the family had relocated after the British occupation of New York. A staff of indentured servants, slaves, and a wet nurse permitted Rebecca to devote some of her energies to the synagogue and larger communal affairs. In 1782, she raised funds to purchase ritual objects for the newly founded synagogue, Mikveh Israel. Rebecca made several personal donations over the years, including a scroll of Esther. In 1801 she became a founding member of the Female Association for the Relief of Women and Children in Reduced Circumstances, a Philadelphia organization whose Jewish and gentile members provided food and clothing to indigent women and children. In 1820 she served as first directress and one of 13 managers on the board of the Female Hebrew Benevolent Society of Philadelphia, founded in 1819 to assist the Jewish poor. Rebecca assumed a more central role in household affairs after the death of her husband in 1803. Contemporary reports allude to the high status and respect she enjoyed during her latter years.

BIBLIOGRAPHY: A. Ben-Ur, "The Exceptional and the Mundane: A Biographical Portrait of Rebecca Machado Phillips, 1746–1831," in J.D. Sarna and P. Nadell (eds.), *Women and American Judaism: Historical Perspectives* (2001), 46–80; N.T Phillips, "Family History of the Reverend David Mendez Machado," in: *Proceedings of* *the American Jewish Historical Society* 2 (1894), 45–61; M.H. Stern. *First American Jewish Families: 600 Genealogies, 1654–1988* (1991).

[Aviva Ben-Ur (2nd ed.)]

PHILLIPS, WILLIAM (1907–2002), U.S. editor and writer. Born in New York, Phillips attended City College and earned a master's degree at New York University (1930). He completed some graduate work at Columbia while an instructor in English at NYU. Phillips is best known as a co-editor of arguably the most influential of the "little" magazines, the *Partisan Review*. Phillips and co-editor Philip *Rahv founded the *Partisan Review* in 1933 as the literary modernist organ of the John Reed Club. The criticism, poetry, and fiction that appeared in the magazine was intended at first to complement the more overtly political magazine *New Masses*. After nine published issues associated with the John Reed Club, *PR* broke with the organization because of ideological differences related to the Moscow Purge Trials. Phillips and Rahv, who had refused to subordinate their literary standards to Communist Party ideology, reestablished *Partisan Review* as an independent journal in December 1937. After breaking from the John Reed Club, *PR* remained committed for a period to independent Marxist, anti-Stalinist principles. Circulation of the magazine never topped 15,000, but its profound influence on American intellectual life is undeniable. Historians have described *PR* as intensely urban, anti-Stalinist with a Trotskyist bent, New York-dominated, and overwhelmingly Jewish. The magazine brought together, in Phillips's words, "writers committed to modernism and literary innovation, and radical social and political thinkers, most of whom were either non-Communist or anti-Communist." Phillips himself wrote for *PR* and other magazines (sometimes under the penname "Wallace Phelps"), and his memoir, *A Partisan View*, appeared in 1983, but he is better known as an editor who brought to the public the works of influential writers including Hannah *Arendt, Saul *Bellow, Clement Greenberg, Irving *Howe, Delmore *Schwartz, Lionel *Trilling, and many, many others. Although *PR* had lost its central place of influence by the 1960s (Rahv left the magazine in the late 1960s and died in 1973), Phillips and his second wife, Edith Kurzweil, continued to edit the magazine until his death in 2002. The final issue of *Partisan Review*, a tribute to Phillips, was published in 2003.

BIBLIOGRAPHY: T.A. Cooney, *The Rise of the New York Intellectuals: Partisan Review and Its Circle* (1986); J.B. Gilbert, *Writers and Partisans: A History of Literary Radicalism in America* (1968); W. Phillips, *A Partisan View: Five Decades of the Literary Life* (1983); A.M. Wald, *The New York Intellectuals: The Rise and Decline of the anti-Stalinist Left from the 1930s to the 1980s* (1987).

[Daniel Greene (2nd ed.)]

PHILLIPSON, IRVING JOSEPH (1882–1955), U.S. Army officer. Graduated from West Point in 1904, Phillipson saw action in the Philippines in 1906–07 and in the Meuse-Argonne battles of World War I. In World War II he was chief of staff of the Second Corps Area and in 1941 was promoted to major general. In 1942 he was sent to Washington to plan and administer the aid to be given to the wives and dependents of soldiers. Phillipson introduced many needed reforms in this field.

PHILO (The Elder), author of a Greek epic entitled *On Jerusalem*. He is sometimes identified with the Philo the Elder mentioned by Josephus (*Contra Apionem* 1:218) and Clemens of Alexandria (*Stromata*, 1:141, 3). If so, his presumed date can be conjectured from the fact that these list him after *Demetrius (fl. 221–204 B.C.E.) and before *Eupolemus (fl. 161–157). It is, however, by no means certain that the two are identical, since Philo was a common name. Of Philo's lengthy epic of 14 (or four) books, only three fragments consisting of a total of only 24 lines survive. About half of the lines are unintelligible, either because of faulty transmission of the text or because of the author's own obscurity. The view that the obscurity was intentional must be rejected.

Mras explains the first fragment as dealing with Abraham's circumcision and the binding of Isaac. Because the patriarch was the first to perform circumcision according to statute, God made a covenant with him. Gutmann rejects this interpretation, as based on a too heavily emended text. But Gutmann's own interpretation of the first four lines as a statement of the Torah's antedating the creation of the world has been questioned. The remaining six lines of Fragment I, however, appear clearly to deal with the binding of Isaac, the appearance of the angel, and the slaughtering of the ram, though the details are not quite clear. Fragment II depicts the remarkable fountains that watered Jerusalem. Similar accounts, contrasting the dry parched surroundings of the city with the wealth of water in the city itself are found in the Letter of *Aristeas (88–91) and in a fragment from Timochares, the author of a *Life of Antiochus* (IV?). Philo's poem can also be compared with that of Theodotus, a Samaritan epicist, describing the marvelous streams that watered the valleys of the holy city of Shechem. Philo's poem, however, does not restrict itself to Jerusalem, but ranges widely through biblical lore. Fragment III records Joseph's rule in Egypt. If the author of the poem *On Jerusalem* is identical with the historian mentioned by Clemens, it is reasonable to assume that Philo dealt with chronology in a manner similar to Eupolemus, and that perhaps again, like Eupolemus, wrote in Jerusalem.

BIBLIOGRAPHY: K. Mras (ed.), *Eusebius, Praeparatio Evangelica* (1954), 9:20; 24; 37; J. Gutmann, *Ha-Safrut ha-Yehudit ha-Hellenistit*, 1 (1958), 221–44.

[Ben Zion Wacholder]

PHILO (Pseudo-) or **LIBER ANTIQUITATUM BIBLICARUM**, conventional ascription and title of a Latin translation of an early Jewish chronicle. With extensive omissions, modifications, and additions, the chronicle retells biblical history from Adam to Saul's death (the archetype has lost its ending and how much followed remains uncertain). The length of the work makes it impracticable to list its chief innovations; for an outline see L. Cohn and G. Kisch (see bibl.). The period until the Exodus is briefly treated; additions and omissions are so distinct from those of *Jubilees that it has been suggested that Pseudo-Philo was correcting and supplementing that book. Especially notable are the strangely sympathetic account of Balaam, Moses' apocalyptic testament, the revisions of Joshua 22:7ff. and Judges 17–21, the novel careers of the first judge (called Kenez, as in Josephus' *Antiquities*) and his successor Zebul, Phinehas' installation of Eli, his ascension (to return as Elijah), and additional prayers, speeches, and visions, etc. throughout.

The title *Liber Antiquitatum Biblicarum* is probably a late assimilation of "Philo's" historical work to Josephus' *Antiquities*. The author (Jewish, not Christian) does not adopt any pseudepigraphical mask. He is probably from Palestine, not the Diaspora, and is totally devoid of classical allusions. The manuscript's ascription to Philo of Alexandria is impossible.

Liber Antiquitatum Biblicarum is usually dated shortly after 70 C.E., the strongest argument being Moses' prediction (19:7) that the First Temple would be destroyed on the 17th of the 4th month; it is plausible, though not inevitable, that this presupposes the cessation of the *Tamid* ("the daily offering") on that date in 70. Such a date would suit the linguistic parallels with II *Baruch and IV *Esdras, but the *Liber Antiquitatum Biblicarum* is demonstrably the source from which the other two have borrowed. Pseudo-Philo's Hebrew biblical text, furthermore, suggests an earlier date for at least much of the material. A few Septuagintal, Proto-Lucianic, and Palestinian readings have been noted by earlier scholars, but their number is far greater. That the translator, influenced by some form of Greek Bible, substituted its text for that of Pseudo-Philo is impossible, as such readings occur in passing allusions as well as in long quotations. More probably, the author himself used a notably pre-Masoretic form of Hebrew text – how late could he have done this? Further indications of date are unusable until the chronological system is explained.

Pseudo-Philo appears to be supplementing Chronicles with a history principally about Israel's cultic and national leadership from the Exodus until David. His real purpose is unclear, especially since the end is missing. The work is usually taken as a haphazard aggadic collection, with some unspecified educational or pious purpose, and the fact that many additions have parallels elsewhere suggest that not all the *aggadah* was created *de novo*. Its importance lies in the fact that it is one of the oldest substantive midrashic works extant. A. Spiro expounds it as a systematic attempt to replace the canonical history of pre-Davidic times by a version apter for anti-Tobiad and anti-Samaritan polemic. The anti-Tobiadism may be imaginary; some anti-Samaritanism is certain (there are even intriguing parallels with later Samaritan chronicles), but whether this controls the whole composition is disputable and the reason for the omissions is not yet apparent.

The affinities in Pseudo-Philo's theology and vocabulary need study; "mystical Jewish Hellenism" and "Essene Gnosis" are not too helpful characterizations. A coincidence (23:2) with Jubilees-Qumran on the date of the Feast of Weeks could be important for identifying its background and praxis; but other analogous indicators have not yet been noted.

The work survives in whole or in part only in some 20 late Latin manuscripts, but is older, having been translated (second to fourth century C.E.) via Greek from Hebrew. No clear traces of either Greek or Hebrew survive; the Hebrew form in *Chronicles of Jerahmeel* was retroverted from an important lost Latin manuscript. Strangely enough the work appears to have been unknown to the *Church Fathers. After early printings, *Liber Antiquitatum Biblicarum* was almost completely neglected until 1898. Among Jewish writers until this period it was known only to Azariah de *Rossi. The work of emendation, begun by M.R. James and L. Ginzberg (*The Biblical Antiquities of Philo*, 1970), can be systematically perfected and a critical text established. Much of the work (including chronological data and proper names presumably important for Pseudo-Philo's purposes) is as yet obscure, though it is not irremediably corrupt.

BIBLIOGRAPHY: M.R. James (ed. and tr.), *Biblical Antiquities of Philo* (1917; reprinted 1971, with a lengthy prolegomena by L.H. Feldman correcting and supplementing James on many points); L. Cohn, in: JQR, 10 (1898), 277–332; G. Kisch (ed.), *Pseudo-Philo's Liber Antiquitatum Biblicarum* (1949); Ginzberg, Legends, 7 (1938), 537–9; A. Spiro, in: PAAJR, 20 (1951), 279–355; L.H. Feldman, *Scholarship on Philo and Josephus (1937–1962)* (1963); M. Delcor, in: DBI, supplément 7 (1966), 1354–75.

[John Strugnell]

°PHILODEMUS (c. 110–c. 40/35 B.C.E.), Epicurean philosopher from Gadara in Palestine. He founded a school at Herculaneum, Italy, and may have been a teacher of *Horace. He wrote Cynic diatribes. According to Hadas (see bibl.) his erotic poetry shows some parallels with the Song of Songs.

PHILO JUDAEUS (**Philo of Alexandria**; c. 20 B.C.E.–50 C.E.), Jewish exegete and philosopher of outstanding importance for Jewish Hellenism and early Christianity. Little is known about the details of his personal life. It is clear, however, that he belonged to an extremely wealthy and distinguished Alexandrian family with connections to the Herodian dynasty and the Roman court. His brother was the high official and banker Alexander, known through Josephus, and his nephew, Alexander's son, was *Tiberius Julius Alexander. In 40 C.E. Philo headed a delegation of the Jewish community of Alexandria to the Roman emperor Gaius Caligula, in order to alleviate the situation of the Jews after the outburst of violence in the city. Moreover, Philo once visited Jerusalem, offering a sacrifice in the Temple. Philo's works, which he wrote in Greek, show intimate familiarity with Hellenistic culture and education. His Jewish training seems to have derived from growing up in a traditional Jewish home, but apparently did not include knowledge of the Hebrew language.

Living at a crossroad of cultures in Alexandria, just before rabbinic Judaism emerged and Christianity became a visible phenomenon, Philo is highly significant for a variety of reasons. Initially, he made a clear statement on Jewish identity in the midst of a multicultural metropolis, indicating patterns of negotiating Judaism with general culture. Moreover, Philo's Bible exegesis was extremely rich and methodologically diverse, offering invaluable insights into the state of Jewish Bible interpretation before rabbinic exegesis became normative. His philosophy is intrinsically connected to his exegesis, having developed mostly in the context of interpreting Scripture. Philo engaged in the contemporary discussion, offering an original approach that became especially relevant for subsequent Christian thinkers. His eyewitness reports of the events under Tiberius and Caligula, as well as his descriptions of the *Essenes and the *Therapeutae, are precious and in many respects exclusive sources of information. The former two provide a particular Jewish perspective from the province of the Roman Empire, which complements Josephus Flavius' reports from the capital. Finally, Philo's statements on women are crucial for a proper understanding of the history of gender issues.

Writings

Most, but not all, of Philo's vast output has been preserved by the Christian Church in the original Greek. Some treatises have survived only in Armenian and Latin translations. Philo's works are usually divided into the following categories:

I. Philo's exegetical works, probably written for a Jewish audience.

These are again subdivided into three categories, which, however, should not be seen as absolute divisions, since each contains pieces of exegesis belonging to the other categories.

1) The Exposition of the Pentateuch, beginning with the creation story and leading through a treatment of the Patriarchs to a systematic discussion of the legal material. Philo explains that the Pentateuch, although a law code, opens with the story of creation, because this story shows that Mosaic Law is in harmony with the Law of Nature. Everyone living in accordance with the Torah thus becomes a "loyal citizen of the world."

2) The Allegorical Commentary on select biblical passages from the book of Genesis, consisting of 18 extant treatises. Disregarding the plot and context of the biblical stories, Philo progresses in a highly associative manner, transposing biblical verses into philosophical-mystical concepts.

3) *Questions and Answers on Genesis and Exodus* (preserved fragmentarily in an Armenian and Latin translation). Following the Hellenistic genre of Question and Answer Literature, which flourished in Alexandria, especially in connection with the interpretation of Homer, Philo closely follows the biblical text, raising difficulties on certain details and providing answers that confirm Scripture. These treatises are valuable also for their numerous references to other Jewish exegetes whose work has not survived in any other source.

II. General philosophical writings, probably addressed to a non-Jewish as well as a Jewish audience. In these treatises Philo hardly ever refers to Scripture, instead discussing themes of topical concern, such as *The Eternity of the World* or *Providence*. In another work he focuses on the notion of *Every Good Man Being Free*. These treatises show intimate familiarity with Hellenistic genres of philosophical discourse, such as the dialectical style, which demands that divergent views be discussed before the writer presents his own ideas. These works moreover indicate Philo's desire to participate in the general discussion, reaching out to contemporary intellectuals in Alexandria.

III. Eye-witness reports of contemporary events. Two extant treatises describe the turbulent years of unrest and violence in Alexandria (*Flaccus, On the Embassy to Gaius*). These are not historical treatises in the strict sense, because they did not aim at describing contemporary reality or discussing the reliability of the sources at hand, but rather at encouraging fellow Jews by a theologically appealing narrative. Philo also described a group of Jewish philosophers, both women and men, who had settled near Alexandria (*On the Contemplative Life*). Highly sympathetic to their life-style, he provides the only extant information about this group (*Therapeutae).

Jewish Identity

It has often been assumed that Hellenistic Jews were confronted with an existential dilemma of having to choose between two diametrically opposite cultures: Jewish monotheism, commitment to a specific people, legal code, and revealed Scriptures, on the one hand, and Greek rationalism, sense of beauty, and universal individualism, on the other. This image has increasingly been challenged. It has become clear that ancient Jews living in Alexandria may not have felt such a dichotomy. Instead, they seem to have been proud of both their heritage and their participation in the general culture. They creatively modernized their Scripture and tradition, choosing from the diversity of the Hellenistic environment whatever seemed suitable.

Philo expressed his pride in the Mosaic tradition by claiming that it is the best constitution. The particular laws of Judaism, such as Sabbath observance and kosher food regulations, reflect in his view Natural Law (Opif. 1–5). Anyone seeking to live a rational life in accordance with Nature will come to accept the Torah. The Jews are thus placed at the top of a hierarchy of cultures. Next rank the Greeks whose culture and philosophy Philo deeply appreciated. His numerous references to the sports and theater suggest that he regularly participated in these activities. He was moreover familiar with Homeric, Platonic, Aristotelian, Stoic, and Pythagorean writings. These, however, were not seen as alternatives, challenging his own tradition, but rather as expressions of ideas akin to the highest truth which Moses had recognized. Of the Stoics Philo explicitly said that they copied certain ideas from the Torah (Lib. 57). Plato's *Timaeus* was quoted in his interpretation of *Genesis* as if it naturally belonged to the Jewish hermeneutic endeavor (Opif. 21).

At the bottom of humanity, in Philo's view, are the Egyptians. Reflecting contemporary Roman prejudice, he never tired of stressing their unreliability, the beastly nature of their religious life, their materialism, and their inherent tendency to political unrest (Dec. 79–80, Fuga 19, Mos. 2:194–95). The Egyptians became Philo's ultimate Other against whom he outlined the contours of Jewish identity. The Romans also played a special role. Unlike the Egyptians, however, they appear as benefactors, who brought civilization and proper government to the world. Philo praised especially Augustus, even to the extent of describing and celebrating the temple in his honor in the harbor of Alexandria (Legat. 143–51). Philo felt that the Jews are akin to the rulers of the world, sharing their values as well as their wide physical distribution throughout all civilized countries.

Philo defined Jewish existence in the Diaspora by reference to the model of the *metropolis*. For Jews, he writes, "the holy city where stands the sacred Temple of the most High God" is the mother-city whence they have gone to settle in numerous other places, which have become their "fatherland" (Flac. 46). Jews living outside the homeland thus have a twofold commitment, namely to their place of living as well as to Jerusalem. This, however, does not imply a "Zionist" orientation, because Philo considered Diaspora Jews to be intellectually more at leisure and, therefore, better equipped to engage in the elevation of the mind commanded by Moses. He neither recommended living in Ereẓ Israel nor did he look to Jerusalem for spiritual guidance. Other exegetes mentioned by him, as far as can be established, are fellow Alexandrians rather than teachers from Ereẓ Israel. The Temple played a central symbolical role, uniting the Jews all over the world, but was also of concrete theological importance, as Philo did his best to prevent its desecration by Caligula's statue.

Philo was observant and encouraged his fellow Jews to be so as well. His treatises on the Decalogue and the Special Laws discuss the *mitzvot* under 10 headings, providing spiritual justifications for each one of them. Unlike medieval Jewish philosophers, such as *Saadiah Gaon and *Maimonides, Philo did not yet distinguish between rational and revealed commandments, but stressed self-restraint (*enkrateia*) as the value underlying all of Mosaic legislation. Philo also confronted a group of radical allegorizers among the Jews of Alexandria, who argued that the law no longer needs to be implemented once its spiritual meaning is recognized (Migr. 89–93). Philo responded to this approach by stressing the need of community life based on the *halakhah*. The latter, however, was locally colored and not necessarily identical to the *halakhah* in Ereẓ Israel. In Leg. 2:232, for example, Philo, in accordance with Roman law in Hellenistic Egypt, assumes that the death penalty for the stubborn and wicked son is to be decided by both parents rather than a law court.

Philo's construction of Jewish identity was only one of the many voices of Alexandrian Judaism. While the works of most other Jews have not survived and can only fragmentarily be reconstructed, Philo's writings are largely extant thanks to his popularity among the Christians. His statement on Jewish identity, however, was unheard for many centuries. It was during the Enlightenment and the period of *Wissenschaft des Judentums that his position became relevant again. Isaac M. *Jost, Heinrich *Graetz, and others identified him as a paradigmatic "modern" Jew who successfully combined Jewish tradition and general culture, thus foreshadowing the Golden Age of Spanish Judaism in the Middle Ages. In the eyes of some he also appeared as a welcome alternative to rabbinic Judaism, providing an early example of the dichotomy that many German Jews felt between their own "enlightened" religion and the "primitive" traditionalism of Polish Jews. The philosopher Moses *Mendelssohn could thus appear as a "German Philo."

Exegesis

Philo's exegesis must be appreciated against the background of the ongoing hermeneutic efforts among Egyptian Jews. In the third and early second century B.C.E., the main types of Philonic exegesis are already visible in the sources: *Aristobulus is the first known interpreter who suggested an allegorical approach to Scripture which, he hoped, would solve the problem of the biblical anthropomorphisms; *Demetrius for the first time recorded difficulties in the biblical text for which he provided learned answers; *Artapanus wrote free paraphrases of biblical stories, adapting them to the ideals of his own time and environment. Philo also mentions numerous other interpreters without, however, identifying them more specifically. They seem to be contemporaries living in Alexandria and can be divided into two main groups: allegorical readers whose work Philo generally appreciates, and literal readers some of whom provoked Philo's anger, apparently because they adopted text-critical methods from Homeric scholarship. Philo thus assumes a relatively conservative position, insisting on the integrity of the biblical text and the absolute value of its contents. He is in fact the first Jew known to have formulated ideas of canonicity, suggesting that the Torah in its Greek translation (*Septuagint) was a perfect emanation of the Divine Logos.

Most famous and influential are Philo's interpretations of the story of creation and the Patriarchs. In both areas he enriched Scripture with motifs from Greek literature. Philo rewrote the story of creation by inserting a distinctly Platonic perspective. Relying on Plato's *Timaeus*, he argued that such a beautiful world could only have been created as a copy of an ideal model. Distinguishing between an active cause and the passive material, which is shaped into ever new forms, Philo describes the activity of God as initially creating the ideal cosmos in His own mind and then modeling the material cosmos in its image (Opif. 1–25). The question of *creatio ex nihilo* is not yet on the horizon, and Philo naturally seems to assume preexisting matter on the basis of Gen. 1:2. Furthermore, raising the same question as the rabbis in Genesis Rabbah (chap. 8), Philo contemplates the expression "let us make man" (Gen. 1:26). He solves the problem of the plural expression "us" by suggesting that God left the creation of man with his obvious imperfections to assistants, so as not to be responsible for the origin of evil (Opif. 72–76).

The stories of the patriarchs and Moses are retold with a view to producing biographies of ideal heroes. While the biographies of Jacob and Isaac are lost, the extant examples show a definite pattern. Philo distinguishes a main feature in each character and arranges the biblical material accordingly. Joseph, for example, is treated as the perfect statesman, whereas Moses is identified as the paradigmatic legislator and prophet of the Jews. This style of biography according to types of careers anticipates Plutarch's famous series of Greek and Roman biographies a generation later. In this framework particular attention is paid to the childhood of each hero, taken to indicate the talents that will later become publicly visible. Moses is thus said to have avoided any childish play or Egyptian dainties while growing up at Pharaoh's court. Fitting his future role, he was from the beginning drawn to serious learning, recollecting in his soul rather than acquiring outside knowledge from his teachers (Mos. 1:18–24). Abraham became the prototype of the person elevating himself above the material realm, recognizing God and even experiencing His gracious presence in what must be identified as a mystical experience (Abr. 68–80).

Worthy of particular attention are also Philo's allegorical interpretations. Sarah and Hagar, for example, are interpreted respectively as sovereign philosophy and servile school studies (Congr. 1–126). Anticipating some of Moses *Mendelssohn's thoughts in the *Biur*, Philo moreover interpreted the tree of knowledge as the virtues planted by God in man's soul (All. 1:56–62). The snake in the Garden allegorically represents lust (All. 2:59). Joseph's colorful coat is allegorized as a symbol of the politician's diversity and ultimate lack of principles (Somn. 1:210–20, 2:10–14). Sarah's pregnancy prompted by God symbolizes for Philo the soul's impregnation by the Divine spirit (Abr. 99–102). These examples show that Philo's allegorical exegesis usually translates biblical motifs into narratives about the human soul, which are meant to complement their literal sense. In this area Philo often refers to other interpreters, sometimes calling them "natural philosophers" (Abr. 99). He is thus in good company, providing his own particular perspective in a well-established field of Jewish Bible exegesis in Alexandria.

Philosophy

Living in the capital of Hellenistic scholarship, Philo was familiar with the philosophical discussion of the day. He was immensely well read, reaching even such minor treatises as Ocellus' still extant *On the Nature of the Universe* (Aet. 12). While he has often been described as an eclectic writer, who gathered more or less randomly ideas floating around, he actually has a special philosophical profile. His most outstanding characteristic is his enthusiastic appreciation of Plato as distinct from Aristotle. This position must be recognized as an unusual and novel preference in an environment overwhelmingly dominated by a deep syncretism with a strong Aristotelian orientation. It was this preference for Plato that rendered Philo particularly popular among Christians. The Church historian *Eusebius relied on Philo when interpreting Christianity as a religion akin to Platonism, but diametrically opposed to Aristotle. These Platonic tendencies later also suggested to Azariah de *Rossi that Philo may be a proto-type of Medieval Jewish mysticism (Kabbalah).

Philo was familiar with the ongoing discussion of the classical philosophical works and hoped to make a lasting contribution to it. He took a particularly pronounced position on the hotly debated issue of the nature of the cosmos. Rejecting the Aristotelian notion of an eternal world and the Stoic assumption of ever recurring destructions and re-creations of the cosmos as well as Epicurean atomism, Philo emphatically called for a return to Plato's *Timaeus* (Aet. 7–16). He complained, however, that even among Plato's students this treatise was commonly read metaphorically, and thus taken as supporting Aristotle's notion of an eternal cosmos (Aet. 7–16). Philo dismissed such readings as "falsifying" Plato's original intention, which he hoped to recover. He stressed that, according to Plato, the world had really been created as an image of an ideal model, and under the "providence" of the creator god, who was therefore called "Father and Maker." This view of things, Philo insisted, closely corresponded to the Mosaic version, which, however, had been written down much earlier. Fending off Aristotelian influence was also a major concern when Philo interpreted the biblical creation account for a Jewish audience. Obviously fearing that Aristotle had already left a deep impression on the Jewish community of Alexandria, he urged his readers not to abandon the idea of a real creation. He urged that the assumption of an eternal cosmos eliminates the notion of Divine providence and thus renders true piety impossible (Opif. 9–11).

Philo's Platonic tendency is moreover visible in his distinction of a spiritual realm which is opposed to the world of the senses and material entities. Truth can only be attained on the upper, intelligible level, while the concrete world of common experience is governed by "opinion" or "probability." Given the imperfection of the material realm, Philo maintains an extreme transcendentalism regarding God whom he describes as "...transcending virtue, transcending knowledge, transcending the good itself and the beautiful itself" (Opif. 8) and as "...better than the good, more venerable than the monad, purer than the unit..." (Praem. 40). Whereas Philo sometimes speaks of God's goodness and other attributes (All. 1:5), he generally insists that God is "without quality," has no name, and is unknowable (ibid 36). This last tenet is not meant in an agnostic way. On the contrary, man has to strive to know God and God is the only object worth knowing. But whereas it is easy to know that God is, we cannot know what He is (Spec. 1:32).

Man can hope to make progress in this area when looking at God's intermediary powers and involvement in the world. God's foremost intermediary is the *Logos, His rational part as well as His speech. Philo adopted this term from Stoic philosophy, where it referred to the Divine power immanent in the world and was sometimes identified with Zeus. Philo used this term in a new way, referring to that aspect of God which is active in the creation of the world and remains involved in earthly matters. At times the Logos is identified with the place in the mind of God where the ideal cosmos is created (Opif. 24), while on another occasion it is identified with the high priest (Somn. 2:185ff.). Similarly, the doctrine of God's two "powers," mercy and justice, is built up into a system of intermediaries. Abraham's three guests, mentioned in Gen. 18:2, are thus identified as God and His two powers (Q *Gen.* 4:2). Only at a close look does Abraham discover that they are one.

Man being created in the image of God, and thus with a divine spark, he can hope to encounter Him and, on occasion, even enter into a Corybantic trance which allows for a temporary union of the human mind with God. Following the example of Abraham, man has to leave for this purpose "his land, his kinfolk and his father's home," i.e., the body, the senses, and the whole material realm, as far as humanly possible (Migr. 1ff.). Unlike the moral struggle of the Stoic sage, which leads to "apathy" and freedom from the passions, Philo's student becomes jubilant and even surging into frenzy (Plant. 38). His soul becomes ecstatic, being filled with Divine spirit (Somn. 2:254) This experience is described in intensely erotic terms, which recall the terminology of contemporary mystery cults, namely as a union between God and the soul issuing forth Divine ideas in man's mind (Cher. 43–50).

Some Pythagorean features can be identified in Philo's philosophy. Foremost among these is his interest in numbers and their metaphysical significance. Philo, for example, makes a long excursion in his interpretation of the biblical creation account, devoting approximately 40 paragraphs to the meaning of the number 7 (Opif. 89–128). Adducing evidence from diverse realms, Philo thus hopes to show that the Mosaic account discloses the deeper structure of the cosmos, which can be expressed in numerical terms. Furthermore, Philo mentions some precious pieces of Pythagorean exegesis. Their original writings all having been lost, he is the earliest extant writer to mention Philolaus and the Pythagorean interpretations of Athena and Zeus as numbers (Opif. 99–100, Leg. 1:15). It has sometimes been suggested that Philo's ascetic tendencies may be Pythagorean in origin. Yet his position significantly differs from theirs: while they recommended asceticism as an end in itself, prescribing for their students long periods of abstention from sex, food, and other instinctual needs, Philo never doubted the legitimacy of bodily needs. On the contrary, he recognized sexuality as a necessary requirement of marriage as well as reproduction, and therefore did not worry about an excess of lust within that framework (Spec. 3:32–63).

Eye-Witness Accounts of Contemporary Events

Philo witnessed important events of the Second Temple Period and, like virtually all upper-class intellectuals during the Hellenistic period, he took an active part in politics. Philosophy and involvement in real life were by no means mutually exclusive, even though Philo once complained in an often quoted sentence that politics took him away from contemplation (Spec. 3:1). The titles of Philo's extant accounts, *The Embassy to Gaius* and *Flaccus*, suggest that they contain the proceedings of the embassy, which Philo himself headed, as well as a profile of the Roman governor. The truth, however, is that both treatises are focused elsewhere. In the *Embassy* Philo is overwhelmingly concerned to explain the benefits of Roman rule, while in *Flaccus* he shows Divine retribution effecting initially the punishment of Flaccus and then his religious conversion. Both reports are often seen as apologetic texts addressing a Roman audience, perhaps even the emperor himself. But it is rather obvious that they were not intended for foreign readers, but for Jews back home. Philo was confronted with increasing criticism from Alexandrian Jews, who even sent a second embassy in order to present a more militant view in Rome. Others altogether despaired of Roman rule and took to armed street fights. Philo made efforts to counter these trends, explaining how benevolent Rome was for the whole civilized realm. God, moreover, providentially protected the Jews and liberated them from such aberrations as Gaius and Flaccus.

Philo's reports are often compared to those of the historian Flavius *Josephus. Scholars argue which one is the more authentic and original, some opting for Josephus' copying from Philo, while others suggest that Josephus' account, even though written later, is closer to the truth. One example may suffice to illustrate the difficulty. Philo tells us that Gaius was so adamant about his plan to set up his statue in the Jerusalem Temple that Agrippa's intervention only produced a feigned reversal, while in reality Gaius continued to make preparations until God caused his assassination (Legat. 333–37). Josephus, on the contrary, reports that Agrippa's intervention was truly successful (AJ 18:289–304). Philo's version may well have originated from his overall desire to stress Divine providence, reassuring his readers that patience was called for. In any case, Philo's account perfectly fits his overall story of a beneficial Roman government that was temporarily deranged by an emperor who had given in to Egyptian lures.

Gender Issues

Philo has sometimes been identified as the "father of Western misogyny," because he embedded Classical Greek prejudices in authoritative Scripture and thus transmitted them to the Church Fathers as well as the rest of European culture. Such judgment can rely on Philo's acceptance of Aristotelian biology. He assumed that the role of the female in procreation is merely passive, providing a material and nourishing environment for the active sperm donated by the male (Ebr. 73, 211). Philo applied this concept to the spiritual realm, suggesting that virtue and *enkrateia* belong to the masculine and thus active realm (Abr. 100–1). God is conceived of as masculine, while the soul of the male student is "impregnated by His sperm" (Cher. 43–45). Philo's view of Eve was anything but egalitarian: he considered her to be the addition of sense-perception and lust to a mind that had hitherto enjoyed the bliss of pure spirituality and masculinity (Opif. 151). Philo moreover had little sympathy for contemporary Jewish women, whom he was happy to confine to the culturally and inferior *gynaikon* (Flac. 89). His position in this respect is especially remarkable, since the Classical ideal of a wife never leaving her quarters had in Hellenistic Egypt been replaced by a far more open atmosphere, where women could assume public roles, such as queen, priestess, and even head of a philosophical school.

On the other hand, however, one must appreciate that, within an obviously patriarchal framework, Philo showed a relatively great interest in biblical women. Sarah, for example, was treated by him with remarkable empathy and respect. He praised her for her stoic endurance of hardships (Abr. 245–46) and suggested that she immediately grasped the Divine nature of the visiting "messengers" whom Abraham still took as regular guests (Abr. 111). Josephus, by contrast, consistently minimized all references to Sarah (as well as other biblical women), taking her, for example, altogether out of the scene with the messengers by stressing the presence of other servants who prepared the cakes for the guests (JA1:197). Moreover, we owe to Philo the earliest extant testimony to Jewish women philosophers, who were part of the Therapeutae. These women were not only versed in reading and writing, but also participated in the regular spiritual and exegetical activities of the group. Philo, on the whole, was highly sympathetic to this group. Nothing in his description suggests ambivalence concerning the women's activities.

Influence

Apart from Josephus, no ancient Jewish source mentions Philo, although there may be traces of Philonic influence in rabbinic Midrash, such as R. Oshaiah Rabbah's saying in *Genesis Rabbah* 1:1 echoing Philo, Opif. 16. The medieval Midrash Tadshe (in: A. Jellinek, *Beit ha-Midrash*, 3 (1967), 164–93) draws largely on Philonic material, while the first Jewish writer who mentions him is Azariah dei *Rossi. Philo had a much greater influence on Christianity, not on the New Testament itself but on the Church Fathers, such Clement of Alexandria, Origen, Ambrose, and many others. They eagerly drew on his exegesis and adopted many of his concepts. However, owing to their different approach, many of his distinctly Jewish notions were translated into Christian terms. H. Wolfson estimated Philo's influence to be very significant, arguing that his reconciliation of philosophy and revelation resurfaced in all monotheistic religions, whether it was with or without direct knowledge of his texts. This thesis, however, can hardly be proven, since Philo is not directly mentioned and the "Philonic" structure of thought which Wolfson identifies may well have developed out of a parallel synthesis of the Bible and Greek philosophy.

BIBLIOGRAPHY: F.H. Colson and G.H. Whitaker (tr. and eds.), *Philo* (Complete Works), 12 vols. (1953–63). **ADD. BIBLIOGRAPHY:** J. Morris, The Jewish Philosopher Philo, in: G. Vermes, F. Millar, M. Goodman. *Emil Schürer. The History of the Jewish People in the Age of Jesus Christ* (1987) vol. 3, 2 809–90; M.R. Niehoff, *Philo on Jewish Identity and Culture* (2001); E. Birnbaum, *The Place of Judaism in Philo's Thought. Israel, Jews, and Proselytes* (1996); D.T. Runia, *Philo of Alexandria. On the Creation of the Cosmos according to Moses. Introduction, Translation and Commentary* (2001); P. Borgen, *Philo of Alexandria: An Exegete for His Time* (1997); Carlos Lévy (ed.), *Philon d'Alexandrie et la Langage de la Philosophie* (1998); J. Dillon, *The Middle Platonists* (1977); P.W.V.D. Horst, *Philo of Alexandria. Philo's Flaccus. The First Pogrom. Introduction, Translation and Commentary* (2003); J.E. Taylor, *Jewish Women Philosophers of First-Century Alexandria* (2003); D. Sly, *Philo's Perception of Women* (1990); G. Sterling, *The Jewish Plato. Philo of Alexandria, Greek-speaking Judaism and Christian Origins* (forthcoming). CLASSICAL WORKS OF CONTINUOUS IMPORTANCE: H.A. Wolfson, *Philo: Foundations of Religious Philosophy in Judaism, Christianity, and Islam*, 2 vols. (1940); S. Belkin, *Philo and the Oral Law* (1940). **ADD. BIBLIOGRAPHY:** I. Heinemann, *Philons griechische und juedische Bildung* (1932); E. Bréhier, *Les Idées philosophiques et religieuses de Philon d'Alexandrie* (1925); D.T. Runia, *Philo of Alexandria and the Timaeus of Plato* (1986); Y. Amir, *Die hellenistische Gestalt des Judentums bei Philon von Alexandria* (1983).

[Yehoyada Amir and Maren Niehoff (2nd ed.)]

°PHILO OF BYBLOS (also called **Herennius Philo**, 64–161 C.E.), Greek author of a Phoenician history. Philo claimed that his history was a translation from the Phoenician of Sanchuniathon, whose sources go back to before the Trojan War. Many quotations from his history concerning religion are found in Eusebius' *Praeparatio Evangelica* (1:9, 22–10; 8). He is also said to have written, among other works, a history of the Jews in which he criticized Hecataeus of Abdera. Only fragments of his work survive.

PHILOSOPHY. In his article on the Jewish involvement in philosophy in the *Dictionnaire des sciences philosophiques*, written over a century ago, Solomon *Munk pointed out that the Jewish mission to know God and to make Him known to the world was not basically involved with philosophy. After surveying the part played by Jews in philosophy, he concluded that "the Jews, as a nation, or as a religious society, play only a secondary role in the history of philosophy." As a nation or as a religious society this may be true, but even when Munk wrote it was not the case that Jewish participation in philosophy had been insignificant. Since his day the participation of Jews in philosophical activities has become extremely important.

It used to be said that the peculiarly Jewish role in philosophy had been that of middleman, transmitting the ideas of one culture to another, as some Jewish scholars had done in Spain, translating Arabic thought into forms available to Christian Europe. This, of course, was only part of the Jewish involvement in philosophy in the Middle Ages. Since the Renaissance many thinkers of Jewish origin have made central contributions to philosophy, and have played seminal roles in the development of modern Western thought. Some have played roles as Jews; others, who are of Jewish descent, have functioned as individual intellectuals, or sometimes as Christian thinkers.

14th to 17th Centuries

It may have been because they could not function within the Jewish nation or the Jewish religious society that many intellectuals of Jewish origin from Spain and Portugal, functioning in Iberia, Italy, France, and Holland, developed crucial philosophical views. Being spiritually dispossessed, and forced into an alien Christian intellectual world, the Marrano intellectuals may have been led into a more profound philosophical examination of their situation, and through it to a new evaluation of man's place in the cosmos. The drama of the forced conversions, the expulsion of the Jews from Spain, and the terror of the Inquisition created a class of Marrano thinkers trying to find their place in the world, trying to find meaningful values, and trying to use the intellectual tools of the Christian world they found themselves in to justify their appreciation of the nature and destiny of man. In Spain and Portugal, the efforts of many Jewish Conversos now went into explorations of theology and philosophy to find a viable and significant theory. From the time of *Pablo de Santa Maria (converted in 1390), until well into the 17th century at least, Iberian intellectuals of Jewish origin were in the forefront in developing creative interpretations of the human scene, trying to define a Christian view that they could participate in. Most of the novel theories developed during Christian Spain's Golden Age were the product of this group. Spanish scholasticism, with its emphasis on universal law and natural rights, started from the views of Francisco de *Vitoria, and was developed by the humanists, Las Casas and Alonzo de la Vera Cruz. Spanish Erasmianism, with its emphasis on liberal Christianity, Christianity without theology, and a Christianity based on moral teachings rather than doctrines, was mainly a convert view. The Jesuit obedience theory was set forth by Diego Lainez, a theologian of Jewish ancestry. Christian kabbalism as a justification of the position of the New Christians was developed by Luis de *Leon, showing the role of Jewish Christians in an apocalyptic age.

Outside of Spain, exile thinkers of Jewish origin played an important role in philosophical thought. Judah *Abrabanel in Italy provided a major statement of Renaissance Platonism that was influential all over Europe. Juan Luis *Vives in the Lowlands was one of the chief exponents of humanism. It has been suggested that Montaigne's closest friend, the French humanist Etienne de la Boétie (1530–1563), was of Marrano origin. His *Discours de la servitude voluntaire* (1576; Eng., *Anti-Dictator*, 1942) is a plea for human freedom and dignity against the tyranny of rulers and is the first modern statement of nonviolence as a means of protest.

The Marranos who settled in Amsterdam in the 17th century had been trained in Christian philosophy, and debated their problems in terms of European philosophical thought. *Manasseh Ben Israel, known as the Hebrew philosopher, provided the main perspective through which philosophers like Mersenne, Grotius, and Cudworth saw Jewish ideas in philosophical terms. Within the Jewish community of Amsterdam, Marrano intellectuals like Uriel da *Costa and Juan de *Prado raised basic philosophical challenges not only to Judaism, but to the whole framework of revealed religion. Coupled with the radical biblical criticism of Isaac *La Peyrère, their criticisms led to the formulation of a new basic metaphysical ideology for a naturalistic nonreligious world in the theory of Baruch *Spinoza. Spinoza, starting from issues raised by heretical thinkers within the Jewish world in Holland, quickly developed a rationalistic, scientific metaphysics to explain the cosmos in terms of logic, psychology, and the 'new science.' Spinoza's naturalism soon became one of the fundamental presentations of the ideology of modern man, greatly affecting the materialists of the Enlightenment, the German idealists, and other movements. Spinoza has become the symbol of the pure modern philosopher, persecuted by religious orthodoxy, but preserving his philosophical ideals and mission. One of his opponents, *Orobio de Castro, tried to provide a philosophical defense of Judaism against Prado, Spinoza, Catholicism, and the liberal Christianity of Limborch and John Locke. Orobio de Castro, originally a professor of metaphysics in Spain, played a significant role in late 17th-century thought, influencing Locke, Bayle, and Fénelon.

18th to 19th Centuries

Philosophical activity in Amsterdam died out in the 18th century. The last thinker of note was Isaac de *Pinto who challenged *Voltaire's antisemitism, and Enlightenment atheism. His most influential work was in proposing the theory of modern capitalism against Hume and Mirabeau. He was one of the very first to understand the role of credit and circulation in the modern economic world.

The Enlightenment world, starting in Germany, led to another level of Jewish participation in philosophy. As Jewish intellectuals were emancipated and could participate in the full range of gentile society, they began to apply themselves to philosophical problems, especially of an ethical and general religious nature. The first to make his entry into the general philosophical scene in Germany was Moses *Mendelssohn. His writing on aesthetics, psychology, metaphysics, and philosophy of religion made him a central figure in Enlightenment thought, influencing his close friends, Theodor *Lessing and Immanuel *Kant. Mendelssohn sought to show that 18th-century Deism, the universal religion of reason, was the same as essential Judaism. In the spirit of the Enlightenment, he advocated religious toleration and equality for the Jews. Mendelssohn became a symbol in the general philosophical world of the enlightened and liberated Jew, who could contribute greatly to the mainstream of culture.

A Jewish doctor, Marcus *Herz, a friend of both Kant and Mendelssohn, played an important role in the development of Kant's philosophy. He was Kant's official "advocate," and discussed the latter's theories with him as they were being formed. Lazarus *Bendavid, at the end of the 18th century, became one of the major expositors of Kant's philosophy. One of the first, and most important, critics of Kant's views was the Lithuanian émigré, Solomon *Maimon, who came to Germany, learned philosophy, and offered a skeptical critique of Kant. Kant considered Maimon's views to be the most astute of any of his opponents, and some of his theories regarding the creative function of the mind became important in the development of German idealism.

People of Jewish origin only begin to play a role in the course of the development of 19th-century German thought around the middle of the century. Moses *Hess and Karl *Marx redirected German idealism into a materialistic socialist ideology. Julius *Frauenstadt became Schopenhauer's main follower, exponent, and editor of his writings. Adolf *Lasson was one of the very few advocates of Hegelianism. One of the founders of neo-Kantianism, Otto *Liebmann, attacked the various metaphysical theories after Kant, and urged a return to the master. As a result of his efforts the neo-Kantian movement developed, and one of its most important leaders was Hermann *Cohen, head of the Marburg school. Cohen emphasized a panlogistic transcendental version of Kant's thought, as opposed to some of the speculative metaphysical interpretations. Cohen stressed the objective side of Kant, and sought to justify a priori knowledge of nature and values. He also tried to identify Kantian ethics with liberal socialism. Cohen played a very significant role in the development of German philosophy. One of his students, Arthur *Liebert, edited the journal *Kantstudien*, in which many of the discussions of neo-Kantianism took place.

In the course of the 19th century, Jews were gradually able to attend the universities and hold positions in them (often only if they were converts). They began to participate in the full range of intellectual activities. Jacob *Freudenthal of Breslau became one of the foremost scholars of ancient thought, both Greek and Hebrew, as well as one of the most important Spinoza scholars. Adolphe *Franck in France, the first Jewish professor at the Collège de France, a follower of Victor Cousin, made important contributions in the history of thought, philosophy of religion, and philosophy of law. Xavier *Léon founded the *Revue de métaphysique et de morale* to combat positivism and encourage speculative philosophy. The reform rabbi, Felix *Adler, started the *Ethical Culture movement, and played an important role in formulating and advocating a humanistic nonreligious ethical view.

20th Century

By the end of the 19th century secularization and assimilation had proceeded to the point where large-scale participation by Jews in philosophy was possible since antisemitic barriers were gradually being removed. Jewish intellectuals could devote their energies to trying to give philosophical interpretations of man's situation and his achievements. Many of the most original theories in 20th-century philosophy are the products of thinkers of Jewish origin, who have come to play a larger and larger role in European thought.

Starting with Henri *Bergson at the end of the 19th century, some of the major speculative philosophers have been Jews. Bergson's *Creative Evolution* and Samuel *Alexander's *Space, Time and Deity* have been two of the most prominent efforts to develop metaphysical systems in terms of modern knowledge. Vladimir *Jankélévitch in Paris, starting from Bergsonism, continued to try to find metaphysical meaning in human existence. Léon *Brunschvicg devoted himself both to historical scholarship and to maintaining the idealistic tradition in France. Karl *Joel developed a system called "the new idealism" in Germany. In America Paul *Weiss has been developing an original metaphysics influenced by Whitehead, and Mortimer *Adler has been advocating neo-Thomism. Nathan *Rotenstreich, in Jerusalem, has been setting forth a theory about human nature and the bases of values. The neo-Kantian movement in its many forms was led by Jewish thinkers, the most prominent of whom were Ernst *Cassirer and Leonhard *Nelson. Cassirer set forth a developmental Kantianism. Nelson, founder of the New Fries School, emphasized the psychological side of Kantianism. Other major figures who came out of the neo-Kantian movement were Emil *Lask, Franz *Rosenzweig, Samuel Hugo *Bergman, and Fritz *Heinemann. The phenomenological movement, which has been so important in 20th-century thought, was started by Edmund *Husserl. Seeking an unshakable foundation for human knowledge, he developed his phenomenological method and transcendental phenomenology. Max *Scheler applied the phenomenological approach to Catholic doctrines and to social psychology. Edith *Stein (who became a nun), influenced by Scheler, combined Thomism with phenomenology and existentialism. Aron *Gurwitsch has emphasized the application of phenomenology to psychology, Adolf *Reinach to the philosophy of law, and Moritz *Geiger to aesthetics. Herbert *Spiegelberg wrote the history of the phenomenological movement, and was a leading exponent of it in America along with Fritz *Kaufmann. Emanuel *Levinas, one of those who introduced phenomenology into France, played an important creative philosophical role in the contemporary European scene. Jewish thinkers, and some of Jewish origin, have played important parts in the existentialist movement. Jean *Wahl in France was a leading spokesman and theoretician. Martin *Buber was one of the most important figures in religious existentialism. The writings of Simone *Weil have played a significant role in postwar Christian existentialism. Jacques *Derrida was the founder of postmodern deconstructionism. George *Simmel was one of the most important figures in the naturalistic movement, both for his biological and Darwinian interpretation of Kant, and for his theory of sociology. Wilhelm *Jerusalem followed out some of the implications of pragmatism, Darwinism, and positivism. In America, Morris Raphael *Cohen, Horace *Kallen, and Sidney *Hook have developed some of the naturalistic ideas of James and Dewey.

In radical philosophy some of the major figures have been Jewish thinkers who have developed new interpretations of Hegel and Marx. Gyorgy *Lukacs, Ernst *Bloch, and Walter

*Benjamin set forth creative versions of Marxism, extending its insights into many cultural fields. Alexandre *Kojève has played a most important role in reinterpreting Hegel's thought. Herbert *Marcuse combined *Freud's and Marx's views, including those of the early Marx, into a powerful critique of modern society that was very influential on New Left thinkers. On the other side, two thinkers of Jewish origin were leaders of Russian Orthodox thought in Russia. Semyon *Frank, originally a Marxist, developed a metaphysical defense of Christianity. Lev *Shestov was a leading anti-rationalist fideist. Among non-Marxist social philosophers and social critics, Jewish thinkers have also made significant contributions. Julien *Benda criticized the role of the intellectuals. Elie *Halévy wrote against the tyrannies of fascism and communism. Hannah *Arendt analyzed the bases and nature of totalitarianism, and the nature of political freedom. Chaim *Perelman has done important work on the nature of justice.

In the analytic philosophical movement, which has been important in the English-speaking world, philosophers of Jewish origin have been in the forefront. One of the first proponents of linguistic analysis was Fritz *Mauthner. Leaders of the logical positivist movement included Herbert *Feigl, Philipp *Frank, and Friedrich *Waismann. Ludwig *Witgenstein established himself as one of the towering figures of 20th-century philosophy. The work of the logician Alfred *Tarski was also most important in this movement. Among the important American analytic philosophers are Max *Black, Nelson *Goodman, Arthur *Pap, and Morton *White. Thinkers of Jewish origin have played basic roles in 20th-century work in the philosophy of science and logic. Emile *Meyerson developed a philosophical view of the world based on modern science. Sir Karl *Popper has been one of the most important in evaluating the nature of science and the problems involved in gaining scientific knowledge.

In the area of historical studies and interpretations of philosophy, Jewish scholars have been in the forefront throughout this century. They have developed the best of European scholarship and have provided some of the most important ways of understanding various philosophical traditions, as well as editing some of the basic texts. Raoul *Richter wrote an important history of skepticism from antiquity onward. George *Boas wrote on Greek philosophy and on French thought. Hans *Jones, through his demythologizing method, helped in the understanding of Gnosticism. Richard *Waltzer examined the transition of Greek thought into Arabic philosophy. Shlomo *Pines wrote on Arabic and Jewish medieval philosophy. Harry Austryn *Wolfson examined the religious philosophical tradition from Philo, through the Church Fathers and medieval Islamic, Jewish, and Christian thought up to Spinoza. Raymond *Klibansky was influential in medieval and Renaissance studies. Paul O. *Kristeller was a leading figure in the many areas of Renaissance studies. One of Ernst Cassirer's contributions was a monumental study of the development of the modern problem of knowledge from the Renaissance onward. He also wrote on English Platonism and the philosophy of the Enlightenment. Alexandre *Koyré was a leading figure in the study of the history of science from the Renaissance onward, as well as an important Descartes scholar. Leon *Roth wrote important interpretations of Descartes and Spinoza and showed their relationship to Maimonides' thought. R.H. Popkin wrote on the history of skepticism from the Renaissance to the Enlightenment. David *Baumgardt did important work on the philosophy of Jeremy Bentham, and Elie Halévy wrote the basic study of British philosophical radicalism.

The historical scholarship done on German thought from Kant onward is too copious to mention in detail. Neo-Kantians, especially, have studied the development of German philosophy extensively, and much of the basic work on Kant, Fichte, Hegel, and Schelling, has been done by scholars of Jewish origin.

Participation in philosophy by Jews has grown rapidly, especially in this century. Jewish concern with fundamental issues about man and the world has, no doubt, contributed to this, as has the growing toleration in academic-intellectual circles, especially in the West. The decline of Christianity as a central factor in European philosophy has also made it more possible for Jews to play a role in this area. At the present time in America, and to a lesser extent in England and France, among younger philosophers there are many important figures of Jewish origin who will probably play a most significant role in the decades to come. In Central Europe there are few Jewish intellectuals left, and in Eastern Europe they are being driven from their positions.

BIBLIOGRAPHY: L. Magnus, *The Jews in the Christian Era* (1929), 241–8, 330–65, and passim; C. Lehrmann, *L'élement juif dans la pensée européenne* (1947), 43–66; A.A. Roback, *Jewish Influence in Modern Thought* (1929), 333–53, 401–40, incl. bibl.; H.G. Gadamer, in: L. Reinisch (ed.), *Die Juden und die Kultur* (1961), 78–90; H. Landry, in: S. Kaznelson (ed.), *Juden im deutschen Kulturbereich* (1959), 242–77; A. Altmann, in: L. Finkelstein (ed.), *Jews, Their History, Culture, and Religion*, 2 (1960[3]), 954–1009.

[Richard H. Popkin]

PHILOSOPHY, JEWISH.

This article is arranged according to the following outline:

WHAT IS JEWISH PHILOSOPHY?

Jewish philosophy is described or defined in various ways, depending on the philosopher's or historian's understanding of both Judaism and philosophy. In general, the question of "what is Jewish philosophy?" would have been alien to the medieval Jewish philosophers, who saw themselves as engaging not in something particularly "Jewish" in a cultural sense, but in philosophy as a science, indeed as the "mother of sciences." As "lovers of wisdom," they understood the truth to transcend cultural or religious boundaries, and had no problem agreeing with and borrowing from the classical Greek and medieval Arab philosophers. Moses *Maimonides thus states explicitly that he borrows from "the words of the philosophers, ancient and recent, and also from the works of various authors, as one should accept the truth from whoever says it" (Introduction to the *Eight Chapters on Ethics* (Commentary to Mishnah Avot)), an attitude reiterated by Shem Tov ibn *Falaquera (13th century): "A person should learn whatever he is capable [of learning] from those who speak the truth, even if they are non-believers, just as one takes honey from a bee" (*Epistle of the Debate*, p. 13); "It is appropriate to accept the truth from any person, even if he is on a lower level than oneself or from another nation … It is not proper to look at the speaker, but rather at what is said" (*Book of Degrees*, pp. 11–12). These positions reflect similar views expressed by Islamic thinkers, such as the early Arab philosopher al-*Kindi ("We ought not to be ashamed of appreciating the truth and of acquiring it, wherever it comes from, even if it comes from races distant and nations different from us. For the seeker of truth, nothing takes precedence over the truth" (*Al-Kindi's Metaphysics*, ed. A. Ivry, pp. 57–58)) and Maimonides' contemporary *Averroes, who regarded the study of philosophy, including that of the non-Muslim ancients, "regardless of whether this other one shares our religion or not," as a religious obligation, and that to forbid the study of philosophy because of its foreign source is like denying a thirsty person water, so he dies of thirst, just because some people have choked on water (cf. *Averroes on the Harmony of Religion and Philosophy*, ed. G. Hourani, pp. 46–49).

The customary modern assignment in universities of philosophy to the humanities, rather than to the natural sciences, would also have violated the classical and medieval self-perception of the philosophers. It is, however, precisely that categorization of philosophy as one of the humanities, and not as an empirical, natural science, which renders philosophy subject to particular cultural influences and forms of expression, such as literature, history and the arts, and makes possible the historical and cultural question, "What is Jewish philosophy?"

There is no clear consensus among Jewish philosophers and scholars of Jewish philosophy regarding the proper definition of the field. The approaches to our question are not necessarily mutually exclusive, and, therefore, we find thinkers and scholars who may support more than one approach. The responses to "what is Jewish philosophy" include a denial of "Jewish philosophy" as an oxymoron; purely biographical or linguistic criteria; religious "philosophy of Judaism"; harmonizing Judaism and philosophy; essentialist message vs. method; and contextual criteria, including Jewish sources, motives, audience, and impact. All of these approaches, in turn, raise further questions.

For some philosophers, including Leo *Strauss and Emmanuel *Levinas, and for some scholars, like Joseph *Sermoneta and Zev Levy, philosophy (at least when it deals with purely philosophical questions of logic, ethics, esthetics, epistemology and the like) is essentially a universal discipline, like physics, and therefore "Jewish philosophy" is an oxymoron. Levinas, for example, accordingly regarded his philosophical and his Jewish writings to be different and basically unrelated genres (although many of his interpreters and readers, Levy included, question that dichotomy in Levinas' self-evaluation).

When moving to biographical or linguistic criteria, presumably a non-Jew cannot produce Jewish philosophy – but is any philosophy produced by a Jew *ipso facto* Jewish philosophy? A Jew who plays football is not usually considered to be playing Jewish football, so does the accident of Jewish birth automatically mean that a Jew who philosophizes is engaging in Jewish philosophy in any meaningful sense? Or should the thinker's Jewish identity be regarded as a necessary but not sufficient criterion for determining the Jewishness of his or her philosophy? Similarly, is the fact that philosophy is written in Hebrew or another Jewish language a sufficient criterion for determining the Jewishness of the philosophy, as suggested by no less of a scholar than Jacob *Klatzkin (whose *Oẓar ha-Munaḥim ha-Filosofiyim* (*Thesaurus Philosophicus Linguae Hebraicae*, 1928–33) remains a classic reference book for students of medieval Jewish philosophy)? Does translating works of non-Jewish philosophers into Hebrew "convert" their philosophy and make it Jewish? Are the Greek works of *Philo, the Arabic works of all the medieval philosophers from *Saadiah Gaon to Maimonides, and the books written by modern Jewish philosophers in European languages, not to be considered Jewish? Returning to the biographical criteria, how are we to regard such philosophers as *Abner of Burgos, who wrote some of his works in Hebrew, but converted to Christianity; Abu al-Barakat al-Baghdadi, who converted to Islam; or freethinkers like *Hiwi al-Balkhi, who attacked all religion, including Jewish; or Baruch *Spinoza, who was excommunicated? Is their philosophy Jewish in some sense, and if so, only prior to their apostasy, critique or excommunication?

Jewish sources, audience, motivation and impact have also been suggested as criteria for defining Jewish philosophy, but raise similar difficulties. Jewish philosophers frequently and explicitly cite non-Jewish sources (as mentioned above); they may intend to be read by one group but in fact be read by another; and in some cases (among 20th-century thinkers, notably Martin *Buber and Abraham Joshua *Heschel), although their thought is overtly Jewish in content, it frequently has a significant impact upon certain trends in Christian thought.

Emil *Fackenheim is among those who have suggested that Jewish philosophy refers to the combination of an essential Jewish message with the general philosophical method; the message is the ethical teaching of the classical prophets of ancient Israel, and the method is that of Socrates, Plato, and Aristotle. While undoubtedly accurate when applied to such philosophers as Fackenheim himself, such a definition has less obvious application when the subject of the philosophizing is something other than ethics, and deals with questions such as cosmology or creation vs. eternity, which may be hinted at in various books of the Bible, but are by no means central to the concerns of the prophets.

The idea that Judaism has some identifiable and definable essence, presumed by Fackenheim, becomes much more pronounced in the essentialist approach of such scholars as Julius *Guttmann and Alexander *Altmann, for whom Jewish philosophy is the religious philosophy of Judaism, in other words, where Judaism has a religious essence and is the subject of the philosophical inquiry. Guttmann's classic book, still unrivaled in its scope as the work of a single author surveying Jewish philosophy in all its periods, is, therefore, deliberately called *Philosophies of Judaism* (although in the German original, and in the expanded Hebrew translation from which the English was prepared, the title appears in the singular, *Die Philosophie des Judentums*), and not a "history of Jewish philosophy." For Guttmann, "Since the days of antiquity, Jewish philosophy was essentially a philosophy of Judaism… This religious orientation constitutes the distinctive character of Jewish philosophy" (*Philosophies*, p. 4). "The great majority of Jewish thinkers made the philosophic justification of Judaism their main subject" (*ibid*, p. 55). As R.J.Z. Werblowsky points out in his introduction to the English translation of Guttmann's *Philosophies*, "The very title of the book contains a programme and betrays its basic orientation – that of the philosopher of religion. The philosopher of religion philosophizes about religion, just as the philosopher of law philosophizes about law … Judaism is something given, a datum, something that is there before the philosophers begin to philosophize about it" (*Philosophies*, pp. viii–ix). In Guttmann's view, the unique character of Jewish life in the Diaspora prevented the development of a "Jewish philosophy" in the way that French or German philosophy evolved. This view was explicitly shared by Alexander Altmann: "It would be futile to attempt a presentation of Judaism as a philosophic system, or to speak of Jewish philosophy in the same sense as one speaks of American, English, French or German philosophy. Judaism is a religion, and the truths it teaches are religious truths. They spring from the source of religious experience, not from pure reason" ("Judaism and World Philosophy," in: L. Finkelstein (ed.), *The Jews: Their History, Culture and Religion*, 2 (1949), 954). Guttmann's and Altmann's essentialist definition is shared by such scholars as Leon *Roth, S.B. *Urbach, and Eliezer *Berkovits. It also underlies the approach of Arthur Hyman, who served as editor of the Jewish philosophy division of the first edition of the *Encyclopaedia Judaica* (1971) and who wrote the original Jewish Philosophy entry: "Jewish philosophy may be described as the explication of Jewish beliefs and practices by means of general philosophic concepts and norms. Hence it must be seen as an outgrowth of the biblical and rabbinic traditions on which Judaism rests as well as part of the history of philosophy at large."

Hyman then recognized the need to modify this essentialist position to make it more flexible: "This description must, however, be expanded to include the general philosophic literature in Hebrew produced by Jews in the latter part of the Middle Ages and the various secular philosophies of Jewish existence formulated by modern Jewish thinkers. General philosophers who happened to be Jews or of Jewish extraction are not considered part of the tradition of Jewish philosophy. Whereas the biblical and rabbinic traditions were indigenous products of the Jewish community, Jewish philosophy arose and flourished as Jews participated in the philosophic speculations of the external culture. Significant religious and philosophical differences distinguish ancient and medieval from much of modern Jewish thought; nevertheless, the subject matter of Jewish philosophy may be divided into three parts. First, as interpretation of unique aspects of Jewish tradition, Jewish philosophy deals with such topics as the election of Israel; the revelation, content, and eternity of the Torah; the special character of the prophecy of *Moses; and Jewish conceptions of the Messiah and the afterlife. Second, as philosophy of religion, it investigates issues common to Judaism, Christianity, and Islam (as well as to certain kinds of metaphysics), such as the existence of God, divine attributes, the creation of the world, the phenomenon of prophecy, the human soul, and general principles of human conduct. Third, as philosophy proper, it studies topics of general philosophic interest, such as the logical categories, the structure of logical arguments, the division of being, and the nature and composition of the universe. Historically, Jewish philosophy may be divided into three periods: (1) its early development in the Diaspora community of the Hellenistic world, from the second century B.C.E. until the middle of the first century C.E.; (2) its flourishing in Islamic and Christian countries during the Middle Ages from the tenth until the early 16th century; and (3) its modern phase beginning in the 18th century and continuing to the present. Its prehistory, however, begins with the Bible."

The essentialist approach to defining Jewish philosophy clearly and unequivocally answers our question of what is Jewish philosophy: it is a philosophy of Judaism (i.e., a philosophy whose subject of inquiry is Judaism), and it is a philosophy which verifies, or in the very least, accords with, Judaism, which is understood to be an invariable given, prior to and transcending changing philosophies, whether its essence is presumed (as in Guttmann) or defined explicitly (as in Berkovits).

A modification of the essentialist approach is offered by Colette *Sirat, who maintains both of these essentialist conditions, and according to whom "only the combination of philosophy and Jewish tradition forms Jewish philosophy … The essence of Jewish philosophy is the harmonizing of a particular system of thought with the Jewish sources" (*Jewish Philosophical Thought in the Middle Ages* (Heb.), 1975, p. 8). Sirat further modified her definition a decade later, in the revised and expanded English edition of her book, to provide greater recognition of the manifold spectrum of Jewish opinions: "One can say that the history of Jewish philosophy in the Middle Ages is the history of the efforts of Jews to reconcile philosophy (or a system of rationalist thought) and Scripture… The harmonizing of these two systems of thought in one unique verity was the theme of almost all Jewish medieval philosophy" (*A History of Jewish Philosophy in the Middle Ages*, p. 5).

Despite its clarity, the essentialist approach, even in its modified harmonizing form, presupposes a Jewish essence, or a definitive Jewish tradition, although it generally avoids defining that essence and tradition. As with the *via negativa* to the divine attributes, it seems far easier to determine what Judaism is not (eg., it is not Christianity or Islam) than what it is, and attempts at a positive definition, like that proposed by Berkovits (the irreducible facts of the events of revelation) are far from universally accepted and tend to be more prescriptive than descriptive. Moreover, limiting philosophy to an explication or verification of given truths undermines the openness which is basic to the philosophical method and weakens, if not eliminates, the distinction between philosophy and theology – a distinction Maimonides insisted upon in his critique of the *Kalām (Islamic theology), which attempts to make reality conform to its hypotheses, rather than adapting its hypothesis to reality (*Guide of the Perplexed* 1:71). The essentialist approach also makes it difficult to account for a richness of varied and even opposing points of view in Jewish philosophy on many questions, for example on such questions as creation, free will and proofs of God, and for Jewish philosophers disagreeing with each other (Maimonides vs. Saadiah Gaon) while agreeing with much of non-Jewish thought (respectively Aristotelianism or Mu'tazilite Kalām). Furthermore, the assumption of the essentialists that there is a continuous and uniform tradition that we may call "Judaism" or "the Jewish tradition," which must then be harmonized with foreign philosophy, does not provide an adequate paradigm for dealing with the prior encounters in each generation or period of that "Judaism" or "Jewish tradition" with foreign cultures, and the ways in which foreign elements were always adopted by Judaism and adapted to its needs. The ideas or values perceived as novel, foreign, or heterodox in one period came, in later periods, to be an integral and organic part of what was perceived to be orthodox Jewish tradition, as the case of Maimonides himself demonstrates.

A third approach to defining Jewish philosophy – between the formalism of purely biographical or linguistic criteria on the one hand, and essentialism on the other hand – suggests that Jewish philosophy is to be understood as philosophy in a Jewish context. The contextual approach shares with essentialism a rejection of external formalist criteria which indicate nothing of the content of the philosophy, and shares with formalism a rejection of the essentialist reduction of Jewish philosophy to philosophy of Judaism and agreement with Jewish tradition. Zev Levy, who regards "Jewish philosophy" as an oxymoron when the philosopher is dealing with universal and purely philosophical questions, acknowledges that a philosophy can be Jewish contextually, when it relates to the destiny of the Jewish people and expresses Jewish cultural creativity. The contextual criteria for making such an assessment include sources and influences (the dimension of the past, whether the philosopher's ideas grew out of the collective experience of the Jewish people), the intended audience or the philosopher's motivation (the dimension of the present, whether the philosopher is attempting to address Jewish concerns, or whether Jewish concerns motivate the philosophizing), and impact (the dimension of the future, whether the philosopher's ideas had an impact on subsequent Jewish thought) – questions for which there may not always be a clear and unequivocal answer, especially for recent philosophers whose impact cannot yet be gauged. Such philosophy may be Jewish in a narrow sense, if it deals with overtly Jewish issues, or in a broader sense, if it deals with any questions, but does so within a Jewish context. As Aviezer *Ravitzky suggests, what is common is the question, not the answer. Jewish philosophy, he suggests, "is a philosophy which deals with a certain *problem* (or more precisely, a certain type of problem), namely the confrontation or encounter of the nonphilosophic Jewish sources and the non-Jewish philosophic sources … That is, it deals with the problem of the existence of the Jew as a Jew confronted by his universal philosophic knowledge and consciousness… The problem which motivates the rise of Jewish philosophy is the encounter of two *traditions*, the Jewish tradition and the philosophic tradition" ("On the Study of Medieval Jewish Philosophy," in *History and Faith: Studies in Jewish Philosophy* (1996), 4, 7).

RECENT HISTORIES OF JEWISH PHILOSOPHY

An essentialist approach to defining Jewish philosophy was possible so long as histories were written by one author with a consistent overview of what is Jewish philosophy. Julius Guttmann's *Philosophies of Judaism* retains its unique status as the only attempt by a single author to provide such a total and consistent survey of Jewish philosophy in all its periods. Subsequent scholars (such as Harry Wolfson, Shlomo Pines, and Alexander Altmann) focused their scholarly attention on particular thinkers and specific issues, and did not write general histories. Others (such as Jacob Agus, Raphael Jospe, Nathan Rotenstreich, Norbert Samuelson, Eliezer Schweid, Kenneth Seeskin, Colette Sirat, S.B. Urbach) generally wrote only histories or text books relating to a given period (medieval, modern, or contemporary), although Joseph Blau wrote a popular overall survey, *The Story of Jewish Philosophy* (1962) and Norbert Samuelson also wrote a general text book, *Jewish Philosophy: An Historical Introduction* (2003), presenting at least a few representatives of different periods.

With the rapid growth in recent decades of interest in, access to, and availability of Jewish philosophy, including previously unknown or unpublished manuscript material, and with increasing emphasis on specialization, the kind of total overview achieved by Guttmann is unlikely to be replicated, and recent overall histories and anthologies, not limited to one period or one topic, have been collective efforts of teams of scholars, and have appeared with accelerated frequency, as have recent encyclopedias.

Earlier 20th-century histories of Jewish philosophy, written by single authors, appeared once every generation – roughly once every 35 years. Isaac *Husik's *History of Medieval Jewish Philosophy* was published in 1916. Guttmann's *Philosophies of Judaism*, which first appeared in German in 1933, was revised and expanded in Hebrew and published posthumously in 1951 (and the Hebrew was the basis for the 1964 English translation). The expanded and revised English version of Colette Sirat's *History of Jewish Philosophy in the Middle Ages* appeared in 1985. These later works do not share Guttmann's essentialist approach, and, as collective works, have tended to a more inclusive, contextual presentation. Colette Sirat's 1975 Hebrew and 1985 English histories already broke new ground by devoting a chapter to astrology. The 1997 *History of Jewish Philosophy* (Routledge *History of Word Philosophies*, Vol. 2), edited by Daniel H. Frank and Oliver Leaman, which includes a team of 35 authors, takes this inclusivistic trend further by incorporating under Jewish philosophy discussions of its historical, social and cultural contexts (chapters 6, 13, 22, 23, 25); political philosophy (ch. 18); mysticism (ch. 19); Jewish nationalism (ch. 31), and Zionism (ch. 32); the Shoah (ch. 36); and Jewish feminist thought (ch. 38).

The loss of a consistent theoretical overview provided by a single author may, therefore, prove to be a gain for our understanding the history of Jewish philosophy. Research in recent decades has tended to blur the already unclear demarcations between strictly philosophical and other types of thought. Moreover, the historical fact is that, in some cases, the more purely philosophical and theoretical works exerted less influence on the Jewish community of their day and on subsequent Jewish history and thought than did works which, while including philosophic terminology and doctrines, are not themselves strictly philosophical.

In the paradoxical tradition of 19th-century German-Jewish *Wissenschaft des Judentums, which (in the words of Leopold *Zunz) sought to provide a scientific "account of what has already been sealed away," while rapidly disappearing Jewish books could still be found, and thereby contributed to a renaissance of Jewish literature and learning, Isaac Husik concluded his early 20th-century history with the pessimistic comment, "There are Jews now and there are philosophers, but there are no Jewish philosophers and there is no Jewish philosophy." Husik had little idea how his own book, and those which came after it, would play a role in the revitalization in the 20th century of the study and practice of Jewish philosophy.

[Raphael Jospe (2nd ed.)]

BIBLICAL AND RABBINIC ANTECEDENTS

Although the Bible and the rabbinic literature contain definite views about God, man, and the world, these views are presented unsystematically, without a technical vocabulary, and without formal arguments in their support. Hence, it is more appropriate to speak of biblical and rabbinic theology rather than philosophy. Nevertheless, Jewish philosophers of all periods held that their opinions were rooted in the Bible and the rabbinic writings, and they quote these literatures extensively in support of their views. Interestingly, quotations from the Bible far outnumber those from the rabbinic writings, so that one may speak of a certain "Bible-centeredness" of Jewish philosophy. In quoting the Bible, Jewish philosophers often imposed a philosophic rigor on its vocabulary and thought that is not immediately apparent from the literal reading of the text. However, besides quoting the Bible, certain philosophers also had a theory concerning the nature of this document. Aware that the world view of the Bible is rather simple and unphilosophical, they found it difficult to accept that the Bible lacked philosophical sophistication. If God created man with reason, the discoveries of the human mind must be related in some fashion to the content of divine revelation. Hence, they viewed the Bible as twofold: on its literal level it was addressed to philosophers and non-philosophers alike, and thus it had to speak in a manner intelligible to all; but behind its rather simple exterior it contained a more profound meaning, which philosophers could discover by proper interpretation. This esoteric content is identical, fully or in part, with the teachings of philosophy. In assuming this methodological principle, Jewish philosophers resembled Jewish mystics, who discovered secret mystical teachings behind the literal biblical text. We may now examine some representative biblical passages which Jewish philosophers cited to support their views. (For a fuller picture the reader may refer to the indexes of biblical passages appearing in Saadiah Gaon, *The Book of Beliefs and Opinions*, tr. by S. Rosenblatt (1949); Judah Halevi, *The Kuzari*, tr. by H. Hirschfeld (1964); Moses Maimonides, *The Guide for the Perplexed*, tr. by M. Friedlaender (1904²; repr. 1956); Joseph Albo, *Sefer ha-Ikkarim*, ed. and tr. by I. Husik, 4, pt. 2, 1930).

Bible

Of verses concerning God that were cited by Jewish philosophers, perhaps the central one was "Hear, O Israel: the Lord our God, the Lord is one" (Deut. 6:4), which was held to refer to God's uniqueness as well as to His simplicity. The opening of the Decalogue – "I am the Lord thy God" (Ex. 20:2, Deut. 5:6) – was understood as a declaration of God's existence, and, by some, even as a positive commandment requiring the affirmation of the existence of God. God's omnipotence was indicated by the verse: "I know that Thou canst do all things, and that no purpose of Thine can be thwarted" (Job 42:2), and His omniscience, by the verse: "His discernment is past searching out" (Isa. 40:28). That God is incorporeal was derived from the verses: "… for ye saw no manner of form" (Deut. 4:15) and "To whom then will ye liken Me, that I should be equal?" (Isa. 40:25), and that His essence is identical with His existence, from the verse: "I am that I am" (Ex. 3:14). How God can be known was derived from a story concerning Moses. Moses had asked God to show him His ways and then he had requested that He show him His glory. God granted Moses the first of these requests, but denied him the second (Ex. 33:12ff.). This story was interpreted to mean that God's glory, that is, His essence, cannot be known by man, but His ways, that is, His actions, can be known.

Of passages and verses concerning the universe, the creation chapters (Gen. 1–2) were interpreted as stating that the world was created out of nothing and in time. The creation of the universe was also derived from the verses: "I have made the earth, and created man upon it; I, even My hands, have stretched out the heavens, and all their hosts have I commanded" (Isa. 45:12) and "It is He that hath made us, and we are His" (Ps. 100:3). That the celestial spheres are animate and rational was deduced from the verse: "The heavens declare the glory of God" (Ps. 19:2), and the verse: "The sun also arises, and the sun goes down, and hastens to his place where he arises" (Eccles. 1:5) was seen as a description of the daily motion of the uppermost celestial sphere, which produces day and night. That the heavens and the earth are finite was derived from the verses: "... from the one end of the earth even unto the other end of the earth" (Deut. 13:8) and "... from the one end of heaven unto the other ..." (Deut. 4:32). From four terms appearing in Genesis 1:2 it was deduced that the sublunar world consists of the four elements: earth (*ereẓ*), air (*ru'aḥ*), water (*mayim*), and fire (*ḥoshekh* – ordinarily darkness, but here interpreted as fire). Reference to the composition of these four elements of matter and form and to the succession of forms in matter was seen in the verses: "Then I went down to the potter's house, and, behold, he was at his work on the wheels. And whensoever the vessel that he made of clay was marred in the hand of the potter, he made it again another vessel, as seemed good to the potter to make it" (Jer. 18:3–4). Somewhat more fancifully, Abraham and Sarah, respectively, were identified with form and matter.

Other verses provided a description of human nature. The verses: "See, I have set before thee this day life and good, and death and evil ... therefore choose life, that thou mayest live ..." (Deut. 30:15–19) were frequently quoted in support of the notion that man possesses freedom of choice. That man's essential nature is his reason was derived from the verse: "Let us make man in our image..." (Gen. 1:26), and that wisdom distinguishes him from other creatures, from the verse: "He that teaches man knowledge" (Ps. 94:10). That man has five senses is indicated by the verses "They have mouths, but they speak not; Eyes have they, but they see not; They have ears, but they hear not; Noses have they, but they smell not; They have hands, but they handle not ..." (Ps. 115:5–7). "For the life of the flesh is in the blood ..." (Lev. 17:11) refers to the nutritive faculty of the human soul, and "Notwithstanding thou mayest kill and eat flesh within all thy gates, after all the desire of thy soul ..." (Deut. 12:15), to the appetitive. Some interpreted that man's ultimate goal in life is to understand God from the verses: "Know this day, and lay it to thy heart, that the Lord, He is God in heaven above and upon the earth beneath ..." (Deut. 4:39) and "Know ye that the Lord He is God" (Ps. 100:3); but others invoked the verse "And thou shalt love the Lord thy God ..." (Deut. 6:5) to show that man's final goal is the love of God. That man should be modest in his conduct is indicated by the verse: "The righteous eateth to the satisfying of his desire ..." (Prov. 13:25), and that the middle way is the best is shown by the verse: "... and thou shalt walk in His ways" (Deut. 28:9). While many other verses and passages were cited in support of these and other teachings, Jewish philosophers were also interested in whole chapters and complete biblical books. The theophany in Isaiah 6 and the account of the divine chariot in Ezekiel 1 and 10 were used as descriptions of God and the angelic realm. Of special interest were the more philosophical books of the Bible, including Proverbs, Job, Song of Songs, and Ecclesiastes, on which numerous philosophical commentaries were written, especially in the late Middle Ages.

Rabbinic Literature

Since the Greek philosophers had appeared by the time the rabbis of the Talmud formulated their teachings, it may be asked whether the rabbinic literature reveals any Greek philosophical influence. While the rabbis had some acquaintance with Greek philosophical ideas, particularly with those of the Stoics (in popular versions), it has now been shown that the rabbis were not familiar with formal philosophy (see S. Lieberman, in: *Biblical and Other Studies*, ed. by A. Altmann (1963), 123–41). The names of the major philosophers are absent from the rabbinic writings, and the only philosophers mentioned by name are Epicurus and the obscure, second century cynic Oenomaus of Gadara. In the tannaitic literature the term "Epicurean" (*apikoros*) is used, but it seems to refer to a heretic in general rather than someone who embraces Epicurus' doctrines. H.A. Wolfson, the modern historian of philosophy, stated that he was unable to discover a single Greek philosophic term in rabbinic literature (Wolfson, *Philo*, 1 (1947), 92). Talmudic scholar Saul *Lieberman replied to Wolfson: "I want to state more positively: Greek philosophic terms are absent from the entire ancient Rabbinic literature" ("How Much Greek in Jewish Palestine?," in: A. Altmann (ed.), *Biblical and Other Studies* (1963), 130). In his *Greek in Jewish Palestine* (1942) Lieberman wrote that "Certain elements on most of the Greek sciences of that time were known to the rabbis in Palestine, and the formulations and the definitions in natural sciences are very similar to those of the Greek scholars. But here again there is no evidence for rabbinic quotations from first-hand sources; all their information may have been derived from secondary sources" (pp. 1–2). In the case of the rabbis and the Gnostics, according to Lieberman, the situation is similar: "Certain basic teachings of the rabbis were not entirely foreign to the rabbis ... However, even in this domain the early rabbinic literature never mentions a single Greek 'philosophic' term used by the Gnostics" (*ibid*, pp. 132, 141).

This conventional view has been challenged by Jacob *Neusner in a series of studies. While acknowledging that there are no overtly philosophical terms in rabbinic literature, that the rabbis never cite any Greek philosophical text, and that it is unlikely that they had direct personal or literary contact with philosophy, Neusner argues that "a sizeable portion of the Mishnah is philosophical in method, manner of formulating results, and ... in specific philosophical program," and that when read philosophically, the Mishnah's arguments coincide with Aristotle's rules of classification, and its issues and positions are congruent with those of Greek philosophy. Neusner concludes, therefore, that the Mishnah is philosophical in method (which he sees as similar or parallel to Aristotelian classification), medium and message (which he compares to the Neoplatonic unity of being) (*Judaism as Philosophy*, 1990; reissued as *The Method and Message of the Mishnah*, 1997). In Neusner's analysis, Wolfson and Lieberman, by looking only at the trees, thus missed the forest. The Mishnah, in his view, is philosophy and not theology because it doesn't merely cite Scripture, but analyzes its truths rationally. In the Mishnah, as in Aristotle, God serves as a principle but is not involved in the system of classification of natural reality. But what follows the Mishnah is theology, not philosophy, because the later rabbinic literature appeals to citations of Scripture and of the Mishnah for authority, not to reason (*The Transformation of Judaism*, 1992). Neusner later extends the argument to the *Gemara* as well. He sees the Mishnah as philosophy (especially natural history) in form of a law code, and the *Gemara* also as philosophy, specifically dialectical analysis, in the form of a commentary on the Mishnah, but reiterates that his claim is "congruity," i.e., similarity, and not direct continuity or contact between the rabbis and Greek philosophy (*Jerusalem and Athens: The Congruity of Talmudic and Classical Philosophy*, 1997). In Neusner's view, the concrete cases of law, at least in some cases, thus reflect a "philosophical template," in which diverse subjects yield an orderly system of abstract thought (*Intellectual Templates of the Halakhah*, 2006).

Jewish philosophers cited rabbinic sayings, as they did biblical quotations, for support of their views, once again imposing a philosophic rigor that the sources, on literal reading, lacked. To indicate that attributes describing God in human terms must be interpreted allegorically, philosophers invoked the saying: "The Torah speaks in the language of the sons of man" (Yev. 71a; BM 31b). How circumspect one must be in describing God is shown in the following story:

Someone reading prayers in the presence of Rabbi Ḥanina said "God, the great, the valiant and the tremendous, the powerful, the strong, and the mighty." Rabbi Ḥanina said to him, "Have you finished all the praises of your Master? The three epithets 'the great, the valiant, and the tremendous,' we should not have applied to God, had Moses not mentioned them in the Law, and had not the men of the Great Synagogue followed and established their use in prayer; and you say all this. Let this be illustrated by a parable. There once was an earthly king who possessed millions of gold coins; but he was praised for owning millions of silver coins. Was this not really an insult to him?" (Ber. 33b).

To show that the substance of the heavens differs from that of sublunar beings the philosophers cited R. Eliezer's saying: "The things in the heavens have been created of the heavens, the things on earth of the earth" (Gen. R. 12:11). Similarly, that the heavens are animate beings was derived from a passage in *Genesis Rabbah* (2:2) which states in part "... the earth mourned and cried on account of her evil lot saying, 'I and the heavens were created together, and yet the beings above live forever, and we are mortal.'" The saying "The world follows its customary order" (Av. Zar. 54b) was taken as confirmation that a natural order exists in the world.

Other rabbinic sayings deal with human nature. The saying: "All is in the hands of heaven except the fear of heaven" (Ber. 33b; Nid. 16b) is interpreted to mean that, while certain natural dispositions are fixed in man, his actions are free. That there is a correlation between what man does and the fate he suffers is supported by the sayings: "There is no death without sin, and no sufferings without transgression" (Shab. 55a) and "A man is measured with the measure he uses himself" (Sot. 1:7). The spiritual nature of the afterlife is taught in the saying of Rav: "In the World to Come, there is no eating, no drinking, no washing, no anointing, no sexual relations, but the righteous sit, their crowns on their heads, and enjoy the radiance of the *Shekhinah*" (Ber. 17a). Many other citations could be added to this list.

Of special interest are two esoteric rabbinic doctrines known respectively as "the account of creation" (*ma'aseh bereshit*) and "the account of the divine chariot" (*ma'aseh merkavah*). While it is clear that, historically speaking, these two doctrines were forms of Jewish gnosticism (see Scholem, *Mysticism*, 40ff.; idem, *Jewish Gnosticism, Merkabah Mysticism, and Talmudic Tradition*, 1960), philosophers saw in them philosophical truths. Maimonides goes so far as to identify *ma'aseh bereshit* with physics and *ma'aseh merkavah* with metaphysics, holding that the rabbis were conversant with philosophic doctrines but presented them enigmatically.

For editions and translations of philosophic works described below, the reader is referred to the entries appearing under individual philosophers' names. The modern scholarly literature concerning individual philosophers is also listed there.

HELLENISTIC JEWISH PHILOSOPHY

Jewish philosophy began, as has been noted, in the Diaspora community of the Hellenistic world during the second century B.C.E. and continued there until the middle of the first century C.E. It arose out of the confrontation between the Jewish religion and Greek philosophy (particularly the Stoic-Platonic tradition) and had as its aim the philosophic interpretation of Judaism. It also had an apologetic purpose: to show that Judaism is a kind of philosophy, whose conception of God is spiritual and whose ethics are rational. Jewish philosophers polemicized against the polytheism of other religions and against pagan practices. In spite of their philosophic interests they maintained that Judaism is superior to philosophy (see H.A. Wolfson, *Philo*, 1 (1947), 3–27). Philo of Alexandria is the only Jewish Hellenistic philosopher from whom a body of works has survived; all the other materials are either fragmentary or only allude to philosophic or theological topics. The dating of these other materials also presents considerable difficulties. The language of Hellenistic Jewish philosophy was Greek. Jewish Hellenistic culture may be said to have begun with the Septuagint, the Greek translation of the Bible. The translation of the Pentateuch dates from the third century B.C.E. Some scholars have held that this translation already manifests philosophic influences (*ibid.*, 94, n. 39).

The first Jewish philosopher appears to have been *Aristobulus of Paneas (middle of second century B.C.E.), who wrote a commentary on the Pentateuch, fragments of which have been preserved by Christian Church Fathers. He argues that Greek philosophers and poets derived their teachings from the wisdom of Moses, and he interpreted the Bible allegorically. He held, for example, that the expression "hand of God" refers to God's power. He maintained that wisdom (the Torah) existed prior to heaven and earth and that God's power extends through all things. He gives a symbolic interpretation of the Sabbath and comments on the symbolic character of the number "seven." The letter of *Aristeas, a pseudepigraphic account of the history of the Greek translation of the Bible, which incidentally polemicizes against paganism, states that God's power is manifested throughout the world, praises the mean as the best course of action, holds that the help of God is necessary for the performance of good deeds, and advocates the control of passions. The author also presents moral interpretations of the ritual laws, holding that such laws are designed to teach man righteousness, holiness, and perfection of character. II Maccabees mentions cryptically resurrection and creation out of nothing. IV Maccabees, evidently written by someone familiar with Greek philosophy, particularly with the teachings of the first-century B.C.E. Stoic Posidonius, maintains that reason can control the passions, illustrating this theme through examples from Jewish history. The author cites the Stoic definition of wisdom and identifies wisdom with the Law. The Sibylline Oracles (in their extant form a combination of Jewish and Christian teachings) denounce paganism and mention the resurrection and the messianic age. The Wisdom of Solomon, which is patterned after Hebrew Wisdom Literature, contains occasional philosophic terms and arguments. The work polemicizes against idolatry, holding that it is a source of immoral practices. H.A. Wolfson (*Philo*, 1 (1947), 287–9) maintains that the author's conception of wisdom is the same as Philo's conception of the logos (see below), although others have argued that the two conceptions are different. According to Wolfson, wisdom first existed as an attribute of God, then as an independent being created by God prior to the creation of the world, and, finally, as immanent in the world. God created the world out of formless matter. Man can love righteousness, God, and wisdom, and the love of wisdom is manifested in the observance of the Law. The attainment of wisdom also requires the help of God. The righteous are rewarded with immortality, while the wicked shall perish.

Philo of Alexandria

*Philo (c. 20 B.C.E.–c. 50 C.E.), who was well versed in Greek philosophy and poetry, presented his views in a series of commentaries on passages of the Pentateuch, works on biblical topics, and independent philosophic treatises. He was influenced largely by Platonic and Stoic ideas, and his philosophy also has a mystical streak. Because of its unsystematic presentation, his philosophy has been interpreted in several ways. Some consider Philo merely a philosophic preacher, others a philosophic eclectic, still others a mystic. H.A. Wolfson, in his *Philo* (on which what follows is based), presents him as a systematic philosopher who is the founder of religious philosophy in Judaism, Christianity, and Islam. Wolfson describes philosophy from Philo to Spinoza as essentially Philonic (*Philo*, 1 (1947), 87–115). (For a discussion of Philo's knowledge of Hebrew and of Palestinian Jewish traditions, see *Philo*, 1 (1947), 88–93.)

BIBLICAL EXEGESIS. The Bible for Philo was the revealed word of God which had an apparent and a hidden meaning: the apparent meaning was addressed to the masses, while the hidden meaning was reserved for students of philosophy. To discover these two meanings Philo used the literal and allegorical methods of interpretation. Most biblical passages lend themselves to both kinds of interpretation, but Philo insists that anthropomorphic descriptions of God must be interpreted allegorically. While he interprets certain parts of the creation story only allegorically, and while he allegorizes biblical names, persons, and events, he also appears to accept biblical narrations in their literal sense. Philo's attitude toward the laws of the Pentateuch is complex and depends on one's evaluation of the nature of Alexandrian *halakhah*. In some passages he maintains that one must observe the totality of Mosaic law, but in others he states that such laws as that requiring the return of a pledge before sunset (Ex. 22:25–26) are trivial in their literal sense and must be understood allegorically.

GOD, LOGOS, AND THE WORLD. Philo's conception of the world is based on Platonic notions, particularly as interpreted and systematized by Posidonius. Characteristic of this approach is the opinion that there exist intermediary beings between God and the world. God, according to Philo, transcends the world. He is one (both in the sense of unique and simple), self-sufficient, eternal, incorporeal, and unlike His creatures. He is good, but He is not identical with the idea of the good of which Plato spoke. In His essence He is unknowable, indescribable, and unnamable; the terms used by Scripture to describe Him are properties referring to His actions. To explain creation and the structure of the world, Philo uses the Platonic notion of "ideas." These ideas, according to him, exist first as patterns in the mind of God, then as incorporeal beings between God and the world, and finally as immanent in the world. Since ideas must inhere in a mind, Philo posits a logos (also called wisdom) in which the ideas inhere. Like the ideas, the logos exists in three forms: as an attribute of God, as an incorporeal being existing between God and the world, and as immanent in the world. The ideas are patterns of things, but they are also causes producing these things; in the latter sense they are called powers. God created the world because He is good, and He created it freely and by design. He first created the incorporeal logos, also called intelligible world, and then the perceptible world. The perceptible world was created out of matter, but it is not clear whether Philo held that this matter was created or uncreated. Creation is not a temporal process, and when it is said that God is prior to His creation it is meant that He is its cause. To create the world God used the self-existent logos, but everything is said to have been created by God Himself except man's body and his irrational soul. The immanent logos, while inhering in the material world, is still immaterial. It produces the laws of nature; but since God created these laws, he can change them if he so desires, and this makes miracles possible.

SOULS. When God created the world, He created with it incorporeal rational souls of varying degrees of impurity. The souls which had greater purity remained incorporeal and became the angels which are God's messengers; the less pure souls were joined to bodies and became the souls of men. The human soul is active in sensation and cognition and it possesses free will. Upon death, the human soul may ascend to the upper realm, where it may come to rest among angels, in the intelligible world, or even beyond this, close to God, Immortality is the gift of God.

KNOWLEDGE AND PROPHECY. Basing himself on Plato, Philo speaks of three kinds of knowledge: sensation or opinion, rational knowledge derived from sensation, and the knowledge of ideas. However, whereas Plato describes knowledge of ideas as recollection, Philo identifies it with prophecy. Prophecy, which is said to come from God, can come in three possible ways: through the Divine Spirit, through a specially created divine voice, or through angels. Prophecy can be accompanied by frenzy and ecstasy, and it is here that Philo's mystical inclination comes to the fore. There are also three kinds of prophetic dreams which correspond to the three kinds of prophecy. Prophecy through an angel can come to a non-Jew, prophecy through the Divine Spirit can also come to a non-Jew provided he has attained moral and intellectual perfection, but prophecy through the voice of God is reserved for Jews. Prophecy has a fourfold function: prediction of the future, expiation of the sins of the people, promulgation of law, and vision of incorporeal beings.

ETHICS AND POLITICS. Philo accepts the philosophic notion that happiness comes through the acquisition of the moral and the intellectual virtues; but he holds that human laws achieve this purpose only imperfectly, whereas the Law of Moses, divine in its origin, achieves it perfectly. The good life is not so much life in accordance with virtue but life in accordance with the Law. The Law contains the philosophic virtues, but adds to them additional ones of its own, such as faith, humanity, piety, and holiness, as well as prayer, study, and repentance. Obedience or disobedience to the Law leads to reward or punishment, respectively, which are, for Philo, individual. Philo presents Jewish law in the light of Greek political theories. The Law of Moses is the constitution of a state initiated by Moses. In this state there live citizens and noncitizens of various kinds. The state is ruled by a king, a high priest, and a council of elders. However, since this state is based on God's Law, God is the real ruler, and earthly rulers only administrate and interpret the divine Law. This state was originally only a state for the Jewish people, but it also provides the pattern for an ideal society (still composed of states) which will come to be in messianic times. Philo influenced the teachings of Church Fathers such as Clement of Alexandria, Origen, and Gregory of Nysea, but his works remained unknown to Jewish philosophers of the Middle Ages. Whatever influence he may have had on them came through the indirect transmission of his ideas. It was only in the 16th century that, through Azariah dei Rossi, his works became known once again among Jews.

MEDIEVAL PERIOD

Medieval Jewish philosophy began in the early tenth century as part of a general cultural revival in the Islamic East, and continued in Muslim countries – North Africa, Spain, and Egypt – for some 300 years. The Jews of the period spoke, read, and wrote Arabic and thus were able to participate in the general culture of their day. Although Jews produced a rich literature on biblical and rabbinic subjects and much poetry, they did not produce an extensive scientific and philosophical literature of their own. The extant literature was adequate for their needs, and their major speculative efforts were devoted to investigating how Judaism and philosophy were related. Most of their philosophic works were written in Arabic. Toward the end of the 12th century the setting of Jewish philosophy began to change. The Jewish communities in the Islamic world declined, and communities hospitable to philosophic and scientific learning developed in Christian lands, particularly Christian Spain, southern France, and Italy. As a result, Arabic was gradually forgotten, and since, with some notable exceptions, Jews had little occasion to learn Latin, Hebrew became the language of Jewish works in philosophy and the sciences. Thus, whereas in Muslim countries Jews were part of the mainstream of general culture, in Christian lands they had to foster a general culture of their own. In this period, while Jews continued to write works investigating the relationship of Judaism and philosophy, they now also produced an extensive literature devoted to purely philosophic topics. As a first step they translated into Hebrew the extensive Arabic philosophical literature of the previous period. Then they commented on the newly translated works, summarized them in compendia and encyclopedias, and composed their own treatises and books. Jewish philosophy during this period was largely based on sources from the Islamic philosophic tradition, but some Jewish philosophers were also influenced by the views of Christian scholastics. The second period in medieval Jewish philosophy lasted until the early 16th century.

Sources and Translations

The philosophic literature available during the Islamic period was based on works studied in the late Hellenistic schools. As the Islamic empire expanded, these schools came under Muslim rule, and the works studied in them were soon translated into Arabic. At times these translations were made from Greek originals, but more often from intermediary Syriac translations. A number of works were translated more than once. The translators, most of whom were Nestorian and Jacobite Christians, were active from about 800 until about 1000. (For an account of these translations see R. Walzer, *Greek into Ara-*

bic, 1962.) Of Platonic works translated, the most important were the *Timeaus*, *Republic*, and *Laws*, but Arabic translations of some other dialogues are extant. Perhaps the most important influence was exercised by the works of Aristotle, all of which were known, except for the *Dialogues* and *Politics*. Together with the works of Aristotle there were translated works by his commentators *Alexander of Aphrodisias, *Themistius, Theophrastus, Simplicius, and John Philoponus. There were also translations of works by Galen, some of which are no longer extant in the original Greek. The neoplatonic tradition was represented by the *Theology of Aristotle*, a collection of excerpts from Plotinus' *Enneads*, and the *Liber de Causis*, a collection from Proclus' *Elements of Theology*, as well as by other neoplatonic writings, some of which have been discovered only recently. There were also translations of the Hermetic writings. In addition, philosophers of the period were familiar with Epicurean, Stoic, and skeptic teachings (see *Epicurus, *Stoicism, and *Skeptics), which, however, reached them through the reports of other authors rather than through translations of original works. Jewish philosophers were similarly influenced by the works of Islamic philosophers of the period, including Al-Kindī Al-Rāzī, *Al-Fārābi, *Avicenna (Ibn Sīnā), Al-*Ghazālī, *Avempace (Ibn Bājja), and *Averroes (Ibn Rushd). However, Averroes influenced medieval Jewish philosophy during its second period rather than its first. Jews were familiar, also, with the collection known as the "Epistles of the *Brethren of Sincerity," and they knew the writings of Sufi mystics.

Main Schools

Paralleling Islamic philosophers, Jewish philosophers of the Islamic period may be divided into four groups: followers of the Muʿtazilite branch of the *Kalām, Neoplatonists, Aristotelians, and philosophical critics of Aristotelian rationalism. In the work of one philosopher, at times doctrines from several schools were mixed. Before expositions of the opinions of individual philosophers are given, the characteristics of each of the four groups will be briefly described.

MUʿTAZILITE KALĀM. Muʿtazilite Kalām arose in Islamic circles toward the end of the eighth century. Its views developed out of reflections on problems posed by Scripture. The two major problems were the unity of God and God's justice, and because of their concern with these problems, Muʿtazilites were also called "Men of Unity and Justice." The first problem arose from the observation that the Koran affirms that God is one, yet describes Him by many attributes; the second, from the observation that God is omnipotent and omniscient (which seems to imply that God causes everything in the world including man's actions), yet punishes man for his wrongdoing. To solve the first problem, the Muʿtazilites set out to show that God can be described by many attributes without violating His unity; to solve the second, that, although God is omnipotent and omniscient, man's freedom and, hence, responsibility for his actions are not precluded. These two interests were broadened to include discussions of other aspects of God and human nature. Muʿtazilites also addressed themselves to more theological problems, such as the nature of different kinds of sinners and the afterlife. Since the Muʿtazilites' speculations derived from a concern with scriptural problems, they did not formulate a systematic philosophy as the neoplatonists and later the Aristotelians did. Philosophy was for them a way of solving scriptural difficulties, and they made use of any philosophical argument that might be of help. Hence, their philosophic speculations were eclectic, and a philosopher would make use of Platonic, Aristotelian, or Epicurean arguments as the need arose. Characteristic of Muʿtazilite works is their division into sections devoted to the unity of God and His justice. Also characteristic are proofs of the existence of God based on proofs of the creation of the world and the division of scriptural commandments into rational and traditional. In reaction to the Muʿtazilites, a more orthodox kind of Kalām, known as Ashʿarite (founded by Al-Ashʿarī, d. 935), arose. While Ashʿarite Kalām was known to Jewish philosophers and is cited by them, it appears that there were no Jewish Ashʿarites. The Ashʿarites were known for their insistence on the absolute omnipotence and omniscience of God, which led them to deny the existence of laws of nature and human free will. However, to safeguard God's justice and man's responsibility, they formulated the doctrine of "acquisition," according to which man, while not causing his acts, can do them willingly or unwillingly.

NEOPLATONISM. Neoplatonism was characterized by the doctrine of emanation, which states that the world and its parts emanated from a first principle, God, in a manner analogous to the emanation of rays from the sun or streams of water from a living fountain. To safeguard the absolute unity of God, Neoplatonists posited a first emanation, identified by some with wisdom (logos) and by others with will, which was between God and the world. Drawing on an analogy between man, the microcosm, and the world, the macrocosm, Neoplatonists posited a number of spiritual substances, such as intellect, soul, and nature, between the first emanation and the world. Some Neoplatonists also held that the spiritual world, no less than the visible, is composed of matter and form. Neoplatonism is marked by the insistence that God is completely above the created order and thus can be described only by negative attributes. Some Neoplatonists held that the world proceeds by necessity from God and is contemporaneous with Him, while others, making concessions to Scripture, affirmed that the world is the product of God's will and is posterior to Him. In their conception of man, Neoplatonists subscribed to the duality of body and soul. The soul originates in the upper region and in some way is forced to join the body. It is man's purpose in life to free the soul from the body, thus making it possible for it to rejoin the upper region from which it came. This "purification" is accomplished through practice of the moral virtues and through philosophic speculation. Neoplatonic ethics generally are ascetic.

ARISTOTELIANISM. *Aristotelianism was based on the premises that the world must be known through observation and that this knowledge is gained through study of the various speculative and practical sciences. The speculative sciences, which deal with the nature of reality, are divided into physics, mathematics, and metaphysics; the practical sciences, which deal with human conduct, are divided into ethics, economics, and politics. Logic is the prerequisite instrument of all the sciences. The physics of the Aristotelians is based on an analysis of the many changes taking place in the world. These changes are explained through the four causes – the material, efficient, formal, and final causes. The world is divided into the celestial and the sublunar regions. The sublunar world is one of generation and corruption, and everything in it is ultimately reducible to the four elements – earth, water, air, and fire. Sublunar beings are divided into minerals, plants, animals, and rational beings, and all of them are composed of matter and form. By contrast, the celestial region, not subject to generation and corruption, is immaterial, and the only motion occurring within it is the locomotions of the celestial spheres. The celestial region is made up of its own element – the so-called fifth element. It consists of the various celestial spheres in which are set the sun, moon, planets, and fixed stars. Each sphere consists of a body governed by an incorporeal soul and intelligence. The earth is fixed at the center of the universe and the celestial spheres revolve around it. All organic beings – plants, animals, and human beings – are governed by an internal principle of motion called a soul. In man, the most complex organic being, the soul possesses nutritive, sensory, appetitive, imaginative, and rational faculties, or powers. The highest faculty is the rational, and to develop it is the purpose of human life. The rational faculty starts as the potential intellect and through exercise becomes the actual intellect and, finally, the acquired intellect. The agent in the production of human knowledge is the active intellect, which in the Islamic and Jewish traditions is identified with the lowest of the celestial intelligences. The active intellect also produces prophecy in men who have the required preparation. While there are some variations in particulars, Islamic and Jewish philosophers subscribe to this general scheme. Metaphysics is viewed as the study of being qua being, that is, of the highest categories, and also as a study of the incorporeal beings, that is, of God and the incorporeal intelligences, which are identified with the angels of Scripture. Morality is viewed as the acquisition of the moral and intellectual virtues. The moral virtues, which, generally speaking, consist of following the mean, are acquired by habituation and thereby become second nature. They are a prerequisite for the attainment of the intellectual virtues, the final goal. While in their ethics Aristotelians followed the traditions of Aristotle, in their political philosophy they followed Plato. They accepted the notion Plato set forth in the *Republic*, that mankind may be divided into three classes – men of gold, men of silver, and men of bronze – and identified the first class with the philosophers, who can understand by means of demonstration, and the other two classes with those who can only follow arguments of persuasion. For Plato, the state is founded by a philosopher-king, who in the Islamic and Jewish traditions is identified with the legislative prophet.

Critics of Aristotelianism

The critical reaction to philosophy was marked by the attempt to show, on philosophic grounds, that philosophers had not made good their claim to have discovered physical and metaphysical truths. The fact that philosophers could not agree on these truths was taken as evidence that they had failed. However, while the critics rejected physics and metaphysics, they accepted the principles of Aristotelian logic.

Saadiah Gaon

The first Jewish philosopher of the Middle Ages was *Saadiah Gaon (882–942), head of the rabbinical academy of Sura (near Baghdad). Influenced by the Muʿtazilites and relying on Platonic, Aristotelian, and Stoic notions, he undertook to formulate a Jewish Kalām. His major philosophic work, which, in Muʿtazilite fashion, is divided into a section on divine unity and a section on divine justice, is his *Book of Opinions and Beliefs* (*Emunot Ve-De'ot; Kitāb al-Amānāt wa al-Iʿtiqādāt*), but his philosophical opinions are also found in his commentary on *Sefer Yeẓirah*, his commentary on the Bible, and in his polemics against Hiwī al-Balkhī. Saadiah wrote his *Book of Opinions and Beliefs* to rescue his contemporaries from the doubts that had befallen them and to lead them from being men whose beliefs were based on religious authority alone to becoming men whose beliefs were also confirmed by arguments of reason. Since these were his goals, he began with a methodological preface devoted to an analysis of doubt and how it may be remedied, a definition of belief (the opposite of doubt), and a description of sources of knowledge – sense perception, self-evident first principles, inference, and reliable tradition – which enable one to distinguish true from false beliefs. In typical Muʿtazilite fashion, Saadiah began the book proper (treatise 1) with four proofs for the creation of the world; from the finiteness of the world, from its composition, from accidents, and from the nature of time. Typical of these proofs is the one from finiteness. According to this argument, the finite nature of the universe requires a finite force preserving it, and everything possessing a finite force must have a beginning in time. Saadiah goes on to show that from the creation of the world it follows that it was brought into being by a creator who is distinct from it, and that this creator made it out of nothing. It was part of Saadiah's method to refute current opinions which differed from his own, and thus he adds the refutation of 12 other cosmogonic theories which he considered wrong. Saadiah next demonstrates that God is one (treatise 2). However, despite His unity, God is described by a multiplicity of attributes, such as life, power, and knowledge. According to Saadiah, these attributes only serve to explicate the divine nature and do not suggest that any multiplicity exists in God. God must be described by many attributes because human language cannot find one word describing them all. In his discussion Saadiah takes issue with dualistic and trinitarian conceptions of God. God's kindness toward His creatures requires that He provide them with a law, adherence to which will guide them to earthly happiness and to eternal bliss (treatise 3). This law, the Torah, contains commandments of two kinds: rational, such as the prohibitions against murder and theft, which reason can also discover on its own, and traditional, such as the Sabbath and dietary laws, which must be revealed through the will of God. Rational commandments are general and require particular traditional commandments for their implementation; and traditional commandments upon examination are also found to have certain reasons. The promulgation of the divine precepts requires the existence of prophets, whose mission is confirmed by the miracles they perform. However, the prophecy of Moses is confirmed not only by miracles but also by the reasonableness of the law he brought. This law is unchanging and cannot be abrogated.

Man, Saadiah held, is the goal of creation, and divine justice requires that he be free. He offers two kinds of arguments for the existence of human choice: first, man experiences himself to be free, and there is no evidence that his acts are compelled; second, holding man responsible for his acts requires that he be free. Since man is free, God justly rewards and punishes him. God's foreknowledge is compatible with human freedom, for to foreknow something is different from causing it. Invoking Muʿtazilite models again, Saadiah (treatise 5) discusses different categories of righteous and wicked men. Among them is the penitent, who accomplishes repentance in four steps: renunciation of sin, remorse, the quest for forgiveness, and the assumption of an obligation not to sin again. The sufferings of the righteous are explained as "sufferings of love" (*yissurin shel ahavah*), that is, their sufferings in this world will be compensated by the reward they will receive in the next. (Maimonides later attacked this doctrine.) Man's soul originates at the time of the formation of the body, and its place of origin is the human heart (treatise 6). The substance of the human soul is akin to that of the celestial sphere. The latter section of the *Book of Opinions and Beliefs* is devoted to eschatological issues, and Saadiah's discussion follows traditional Jewish lines. He accepts the doctrine of the resurrection of the body and offers numerous arguments in its support (treatise 7). The resurrection will occur after Israel has been redeemed. The redemption (treatise 8) may take place in two ways. If the time appointed for the Exile passes before Israel repents, God will first send the Messiah from the house of Joseph. Great calamities will befall the Jews, but in the end they will be redeemed by the Messiah from the house of David. Should Israel repent before the completion of the appointed time, the Messiah from the house of David may come right away. In the messianic era, Israel will return to its land and the Temple will be rebuilt. The Christian claims that the Messiah has already come are false. The final stage is the world to come (treatise 9), in which the righteous will be rewarded and the wicked punished. Man's body and soul will remain together in the world to come, and life in that world is eternal. Saadiah concludes his book with an appendix (treatise 10) describing how man should conduct himself in this world.

Other Rabbanite Followers of Kalām

Although Saadiah remained the major Jewish exponent of Muʿtazilite Kalām, other Jewish philosophers made use of kalamic teachings. In Rabbanite circles, kalamic influences were evident until the rise of Aristotelianism in the 13th century, while among Karaites, Kalām provided the dominant philosophy throughout the Middle Ages. David ibn Marwān *al-Mukammiṣ, probably an older contemporary of Saadiah, combined kalamic, Platonic, Aristotelian, and Neoplatonic teachings in his *ʿIshrūn Maqālāt* ("Twenty Treatises"), a work only partially preserved. His views are also cited in *Judah b. Barzillai al-Bargeloni's commentary on *Sefer Yeẓirah*. Al-Mukammiṣ cites the kalamic formula: "God is knowing, but not with knowledge; living, but not with life," interpreting it to mean that God's attributes are identical with each other and with His essence. Following the Neoplatonists, he adds that God's attributes must be understood as negations. Kalamic and Greek philosophic influences are also found in the Bible commentary (extant in fragments) of *Samuel b. Hophni (d. 1013), head of the academy of Sura. He also held that God's attributes are identical with His essence, and, again following the Muʿtazilites, he teaches that only prophets can work miracles. *Nissim b. Jacob b. Nissim ibn Shahin of Kairouan, a younger contemporary of Samuel b. Hophni, uses Muʿtazilite doctrines at the beginning of his introduction to his commentary on the Talmud. *Hai Gaon (d. 1038), last head of the academy of Pumbedita, was also acquainted with Muʿtazilite doctrines, but took issue with some of them. For example, he criticized Samuel b. Hophni for limiting miracles to prophets, holding that pious persons can also perform them.

[Arthur Hyman]

Karaites

Karaite speculative thought has generally mirrored Rabbanite speculative thought, and discussions of philosophical interest can be found both in treatises fully devoted to the subject, of which there are not many, as well as in works belonging to other genres, such as exegesis, law, and poetry. The first Karaites generally did not formulate clearly their theological views, and there is some indication that some objected to rationalism. By the 10th century, Karaites came under the influence of Muʿtazilite Kalām, and both the legalist, Yaʿqub al-Qirqisani, and the exegete, Japheth ben Eli, incorporated Kalamic ideas into their works. Only in the late 10th and early 11th century did Karaites write separate speculative treatises incorporating fully the ideas and terminology of the Basran Muʿtazilites, most notably Abd al-Jabbar. In the 11th century, the outstanding Karaite philosophers were Joseph b. Abraham al-*Baṣīr (author of *Kitab al-Muhtawi* and *Kitab al-Mansuri*) and his disciple *Jeshua b. Judah, whose views were similar. They believed that rational knowledge of God precedes belief in revelation; only after it has been established that God exists, that He is wise, and that He is omnipotent, is the truth of revelation guaranteed. A similar rationalism is manifest in their conception of ethics: they maintained that various specific moral principles are self-evident upon reflection, e.g., that good should be done and evil avoided, that one should be grateful, and that one should tell the truth. This awareness is independent of revelation, since even those who deny God and revelation adhere to these principles. The moral law is binding not only for man but also for God, a point which is central to their theodicy. They also adopted the Kalamic view that the world is composed of atoms, and the atomic theory can be used to prove the creation of the world, and, thereby, the existence of God.

Al- Baṣīr's influence among Karaites remained strong for almost 300 years, kept alive by Byzantine Hebrew translations of his works and a number of independently written Hebrew treatises, which propounded his ideas. In the late 13th century, Maimonidean Aristotelianism began making inroads into Karaite thought. The main figure to attempt an accommodation between the Karaite tradition of Kalām and Maimonides' *Guide of the Perplexed* was *Aaron ben Elijah of Nicomedia, author of *Eẓ Ḥayyim* ("Tree of Life," written in 1346). Although he ostensibly objected to Greek philosophy as undermining Judaism, he incorporated many Aristotelian ideas (form and matter, separate intellects, causality) into his work. Aaron defended the intellectual honesty of his Karaite predecessors, against Maimonides' assertion that those Jews who adopted Kalām did so for theological, not scientific, reasons, but on many issues, such as prophecy and theodicy, he followed Maimonides' lead. Like some Rabbanite post-Maimonideans, Aaron also criticized Maimonides for positions which he felt were too radical, such as negative theology and the assertion that creation of the world cannot be demonstrated. By the late 15th century, Karaite Kalām had all but disappeared from Byzantine Karaite thought, but traces of it remained in more popular Karaite presentations of theology.

Karaite thinkers also engaged in dogmatics, generally listing ten articles of faith. The first such list was written by Judah *Hadassi (fl. 1149); a similar, but eventually more authoritative, list was presented by Elijah *Bashyazi (Bashyatchi; d. 1490). Dogmatics was especially important since ritual slaughterers were obligated to hold clear conceptions of Karaite theology in order for their meat to be ritually acceptable.

[Daniel J. Lasker (2nd ed.)]

Isaac Israeli

Neoplatonism in Jewish philosophy appeared at the same time that Kalām did. The first Neoplatonist was the renowned physician Isaac b. Solomon *Israeli (c. 855–c. 955), who flourished in Kairouan. Influenced by the Islamic philosopher al-Kindī and various Neoplatonic writings, he composed *Kitāb al-Ḥudūd (Sefer ha-Gevulim*; "Book of Definitions"), *Kitāb al-Jawāhir* ("Book of Substances"), *Sefer ha-Ru'aḥ ve-ha-Nefesh* ("Book on Spirit and Soul"), *Sha'ar ha-Yesodot* ("Chapter on the Elements"), and *Kitāb al-Ustuquṣṣāt* ("Book on the Elements"). In Latin translations some of these works influenced Christian scholastic thought. According to Israeli, God, the Creator, in His goodness and love created the world in time and out of nothing. The means of creation were His power and His will, which for Israeli are attributes of God, not separate hypostases. Two simple substances, first matter and first form, or wisdom, come directly from God. It appears that these two principles combine to form the next hypostasis, intellect; but Israeli also affirms that first matter and form have no separate existence but exist only in the intellect. Intellect is followed by three distinct hypostases of soul – rational, animal, and vegetative. The next hypostasis is nature, which Israeli identifies with the sphere or heaven. This hypostasis is the last of the simple substances and holds a position intermediate between these substances and the perceptible world. The four elements of the lower world are produced from the motion of the sphere or heavens. Israeli distinguished three stages in the creation of the world: creation proper, which produces only first matter, first form, and intellect; emanation, which produces the four spiritual substances; and causality of nature, which produces the world below the heavens. Israeli's philosophy of man is based on the Neoplatonic notion of the human soul's return to the upper world from which it came. The soul's ascent proceeds in three stages: purification, which consists of turning away from appetites and passions; illumination by the intellect, which produces wisdom defined as knowledge of eternal things; and union with, or adherence to, supernal wisdom (not God), at which stage the soul becomes spiritual. Union with supernal wisdom can be accomplished even in this life. Israeli identifies union with the religious notion of paradise, and he holds that the punishment of sinners is that their souls cannot ascend to the upper region but are caught in the fire extending below the heavens. Israeli distinguishes between philosophy, which is the quest for wisdom, and wisdom, which is the final goal. Discussing the prophet, Israeli sees no sharp distinction between him and the philosopher: both are concerned with the ascent of the soul and with guiding mankind toward truth and justice. Israeli distinguishes three kinds of prophecy, which are in ascending order: voice (*kol*), spirit (*ru'aḥ*), and speech (*dibbur*). Many of Israeli's ideas are cited and developed in the commentary on *Sefer Yeẓirah* by his disciple, *Dunash ibn Tamim.

Solomon Ibn Gabirol

The most important Jewish Neoplatonist was Solomon ibn *Gabirol (c. 1020–1057, possibly 1070); beginning with him the setting of Jewish philosophy shifted to Spain. Also an important Hebrew poet, Ibn Gabirol presented his philosophy in *Mekor Ḥayyim* ("The Source of Life"; *Fons Vitae*), *Tikkun Middot ha-Nefesh* ("The Improvement of the Moral Qualities"), and his Hebrew philosophical poem, *Keter Malkhut* ("The Kingly Crown"). The Arabic original of *Mekor Ḥayyim* is no longer extant, but the work was preserved in a full Latin translation and in a Hebrew paraphrase of the 13th century by Shem Tov b. Joseph *Falaquera. The Latin translation was circulated widely in Christian scholastic circles, and, possibly because the work was a pure philosophic treatise lacking biblical and rabbinic citations, its author, known as Avicebron or Avemcebrol, was considered a Muslim or an Arab Christian. Divided into five treatises, *Mekor Ḥayyim* deals mainly with different aspects of the principles of matter and form, though it also contains incidental accounts of other aspects of Ibn Gabirol's thought. It reveals influences of Neoplatonic writings as well as of the pseudo-Empedoclean writings. Ibn Gabirol's conception of God is Neoplatonic in that it emphasizes that God is beyond the world and can be known only through negations. According to *Mekor Ḥayyim*, from God, called First Substance, emanates the divine will or wisdom (logos); but, according to *Keter Malkhut*, wisdom and will as successive emanations are distinct. Next come universal matter and form. According to some passages, universal matter emanates from God, and universal form, from the will; according to others, both principles emanate from the divine will. Three spiritual substances, intellect, soul, and nature, and then the perceptible world follow. According to some interpreters, Ibn Gabirol introduced the notion of the will to give a voluntaristic complexion to the doctrine of emanation, while according to others, he subscribed to the view that emanation proceeds by necessity from God. Another characteristic doctrine of Ibn Gabirol is the notion that all beings other than God, including the spiritual substances, are composed of matter and form. Ibn Gabirol's account of matter and form is ambiguous. There are passages in which he accepts the Aristotelian notion that matter is the substratum for change, while form determines the essence; but there are other passages in which he maintains that the essence of something is determined by its matter, while the forms produce differences between substances having the same material principle. In typical Neoplatonic fashion, Ibn Gabirol presents the goal of human life as the soul's return to the upper sphere, which is accomplished through proper conduct and philosophic speculation. In his *Tikkun Middot ha-Nefesh*, he discusses 20 moral qualities (four for each of the five senses) and tries to relate them to the four humors of the human body. Ibn Gabirol's philosophic views influenced later kabbalistic thought.

Baḥya Ibn Paquda

Toward the end of the 11th century, *Baḥya b. Joseph Ibn Paquda wrote his *Sefer Torat Ḥovot ha-Levavot* ("Guide to the Duties of the Hearts"; *Kitāb al-Hidāya ilā Farāiʾḍ al-Qulūb*), a devotional manual which achieved great popularity among Jews. The work was influenced by Neoplatonism, Kalām, the *hermetic writings, and Sufi literature, and Baḥya readily quoted stories and sayings from Islamic, as well as Jewish, sources. Baḥya's work rests on a distinction between "duties of the limbs" (*ḥovot ha-evarim*), religious commandments that require overt actions, and "duties of the hearts" (*ḥovot ha-levavot*), those commandments which require specific beliefs and inner states (intentions). He holds that the latter are commanded by the Torah no less than the former. In the ten chapters of his work he discusses the following duties of the hearts: belief in God's unity; examination of created beings, which leads to an understanding of the divine goodness and wisdom manifest in nature; service of God; trust in God; sincerity in serving God; humility; repentance; self-examination; abstinence; and, finally, love of God. Baḥya defines and describes these traits and provides practical guidance for their attainment. Using a Kalām distinction, Baḥya divides the duties of the limbs into rational and traditional commandments, while the duties of the hearts are all rational. Although Baḥya's work is largely practical, he also insists on theoretical knowledge, holding that knowledge of God is a necessary prerequisite for practicing the other duties of the hearts. Hence, he devotes the first chapter of his work to kalamic proofs (based on Saadiah) demonstrating the creation of the world and the existence and unity of God. Of the proofs for the creation of the world, Baḥya prefers the one from composition. God's unity, he holds, is different from all other unities, and His essential attributes (existence, unity, and eternity) are to be considered as descriptions of God's actions. Similar views were later expressed by Maimonides. Of special interest is Baḥya's discussion of abstinence, one of the most extensive in Jewish philosophic literature. Baḥya acknowledges that there is a general abstinence for all mankind that is practiced to improve man's physical, moral, and political conditions, but maintains that there is also a special abstinence required of the adherents of the Torah. This special abstinence requires the rejection of everything that is not necessary for the satisfaction of man's natural desires and has as its goal the control of man's desires and the subsequent development of his intellect. However, Baḥya's asceticism is moderate. Disapproving of those who separate themselves from the world or confine themselves to their homes, Baḥya recommends that one participate in the social endeavors of his fellow men and restrict asceticism to his personal life. The final goal is the love of God, which Baḥya defines as the soul's turning to God so that it may cleave to His upper light. The soul is a simple spiritual substance, which was implanted by God in the body, but which wants to free itself from bodily desires and pain in order to attain a spiritual state.

PSEUDO-BAḤYA. A work written between the middle of the 11th and 12th centuries entitled *Kitāb Maʿānī al-Nafs* ("On the Nature of the Soul") was attributed to (Pseudo-)*Baḥya, but it is not by him. Influenced by Neoplatonic and hermetic (Gnostic) teachings, the work describes the origin of the world by emanation and the nature of the soul. The soul is a spiritual substance, independent of the body, which comes from the upper world to which it wants to return. In its descent, the soul acquires influences from the various regions through which it passes, and they account for differences between the souls. It is also polluted by the body in which it inheres. Return to the upper world is accomplished by practicing moral virtues and acquiring knowledge. The book contains a description of the afterlife, including the punishments of various kinds of sinners.

Abraham bar Ḥiyya

*Abraham b. Ḥiyya (first half of the 12th century), who lived in Spain and was the author of works on mathematics and astronomy, was the first to write philosophical works in Hebrew. His philosophic ideas, influenced by Neoplatonism and Aristotelianism, are found in his *Hegyon ha-Nefesh ha-Aẓuvah* ("Meditation of the Sad Soul") and in his messianic treatise *Megillat ha-Megalleh* ("Scroll of the Revealer"). Central to the former work is a discussion of repentance; in general, his interests are more ethical and theological than philosophic. Abraham b. Ḥiyya subscribes to the doctrine of emanation, but, differing from earlier Neoplatonists, he interposes a world of light and a world of dominion between God and the three spiritual substances. His conception of matter and form is Aristotelian: he holds that these principles exist only in the corporeal world, not in that of the simple substances. In *Hegyon ha-Nefesh*, Abraham b. Ḥiyya divides the fates of souls after death into four categories: souls that have acquired intellectual and moral perfection will ascend to the upper world; souls that have acquired intellectual, but not moral, perfection will ascend only to the sphere below the sun, where they will be afflicted by the sun's fire; souls that have acquired moral, but not intellectual, perfection transmigrate to other bodies until they have acquired knowledge; and souls that have neither perfection will perish with their bodies. However, in *Megillat ha-Megalleh*, he denies the transmigration of the soul and makes the afterlife more dependent on moral perfection. In *Megillat ha-Megalleh*, Abraham b. Ḥiyya formulates a theory of history reminiscent of Judah Halevi's theory and of Christian speculation. The history of the world can be divided into six periods corresponding to the six days of creation. There is also an analogue to the Christian notion of original sin: God created Adam with three souls, rational, appetitive, and vegetative. Before Adam sinned the rational soul existed independently of the other two souls, but afterwards it became dependent on them. After the flood, God freed the rational soul from its dependence on the vegetative soul, but not from its dependence on the appetitive soul. However, in each generation the rational soul of one man achieved independence, and this was the state of affairs until the time of Jacob. In Jacob the rational soul was so pure that all of his descendants, first his 12 sons and later all of Israel, received a rational soul independent of the lower two souls. This is Abraham bar Ḥiyya's explanation of the election of Israel, though he does not deny that there may also be righteous persons among the gentiles.

Joseph Ibn Ẓaddik

*Joseph Ibn Ẓaddik of Cordova (d. 1149) was the author of *Sefer ha-Olam ha-Katan* ("Book of the Microcosm"), an eclectic Neoplatonic work with Aristotelian and kalamic influences, apparently written as a handbook for beginners. In the four parts of the work he discusses the principles of the corporeal world and its constitution, the nature of man and the human soul, the existence of God (derived from the creation of the world) and His attributes, and human conduct and reward and punishment. His thought shows similarities to that of Saadiah, Israeli, Baḥya, Pseudo-Baḥya, and Ibn Gabirol, though he does not mention them, and he attempts to refute opinions of the Karaite Al-Baṣīr. With Ibn Gabirol, he affirms that spiritual beings are composed of matter and form, but he defines the matter of spiritual beings as the genus of a species rather than as a distinct principle. However, he does not mention Ibn Gabirol's universal matter and universal form. Like Ibn Gabirol, Ibn Ẓaddik mentions the divine will, but for him, it appears to be identical with the essence of God rather than a separate hypostasis. He criticizes Al-Baṣīr's notion that the divine will is a substance that God creates from time to time. For his proof of the creation of the world he selects the Kalām proof from accidents, but he describes God in Neoplatonic fashion as an absolute unity beyond the world and as incomprehensible. Yet, he also holds that God can be described by attributes that are identical with His essence. These attributes in one respect describe God's actions, and in another, His essence; as describing His essence, they must be understood as negations. The attributes of action are important for providing models for human conduct. For example, as God is good and merciful, so man should be good and merciful. A similar orientation is found in his account of human happiness. He begins by saying that the knowledge of the supernal world and God is the goal of human life; but then he seems to consider this knowledge only as preliminary to proper conduct. Ibn Ẓaddik's account of the soul's fate after death is derived from Israeli (see above).

Moses and Abraham Ibn Ezra

Moses *Ibn Ezra (c. 1055–after 1135) was important mainly as a poet and critic, but he presented some philosophic opinions in his *al-Maqāla bi al-Ḥadīqa fī Maʿnā al-Majāz wa al-Ḥaqīqa* (partially translated into Hebrew as *Arugat ha-Bosem*). Ibn Ezra was fond of quoting sayings (often incorrectly attributed) of such authorities as Pythagoras, Empedocles, Socrates, and Aristotle, and he preserved some Arabic quotations from Ibn Gabirol's *Mekor Ḥayyim* (see S. Pines, in *Tarbiz*, 27 (1957–58), 218–35). His orientation was Neoplatonic, and he employs the notions that man is a microcosm and everything in the upper world has its counterpart in man; the soul's knowledge of itself leads to the knowledge of the Creator; God is a unity above all unities, and, unknowable as He is in Himself, He can only be known by metaphors; the rational soul is a substance which must take care of the body; and others.

Abraham *Ibn Ezra (c. 1089–1164) was important as a grammarian, as an author of works on arithmetic and astronomy (including astrology), and as a biblical commentator. He was the author of *Sefer ha-Shem* and *Yesod Mora*, on the names of God and on the commandments, but his philosophic views are scattered throughout his biblical commentaries. He often presented his opinions in enigmatic language. Ibn Ezra was profoundly influenced by Neoplatonic doctrines, which in his formulation have at times a pantheistic ring; for example "God is the One; He made all and He is all." Like Ibn Gabirol, he held that everything other than God is composed of matter and form, and he alludes as well to the divine will. Speaking of creation, Ibn Ezra affirmed that the world of the intelligences and angels, as well as that of the celestial spheres, is coeternal with God, and only the lower world was created (through emanation). The human soul comes into being from the spiritual substance known as the universal soul, and, if worthy, it can become immortal by being reunited with that soul and being absorbed by it. Destruction is the punishment of unworthy souls. Like the Islamic Aristotelians, Ibn Ezra held that God's knowledge extends only to species, not to individuals. God's providence, also general, is transmitted through the influences of the heavenly bodies, but individuals who have developed their souls and intellects can foresee evil influences caused by the celestial spheres and avoid them.

Judah Halevi

*Judah Halevi (before 1075–1141), ranking with Ibn Gabirol as one of the two most important Hebrew poets of the Middle Ages, wrote a philosophic work whose full title is *Kitāb al-Ḥujja wa al-Dalīl fī Naṣr al-Dīn al-Dhalīl* ("The Book of Argument and Proofs in Defense of the Despised Faith"); but it is popularly known as *Sefer ha-Kuzari*. Like the Islamic philosopher al-Ghazālī, with whom he seems to have shared a common source, he is critical of Aristotelian rationalism. (By Judah Halevi's time, Aristotelianism was important in Islamic philosophy, but not yet in Jewish philosophy.) For Judah Halevi, historical experience, rather than physical and metaphysical speculations, is the source of truth, and religious practices are more important than beliefs and dogmas. Composed as a narrative, Judah Halevi's book has as its subject the conversion of the king of the Khazars to Judaism in the first half of the eighth century. Judah Halevi's views emerge in a dialogue between the king and the *ḥaver*, a Jewish scholar who acts as the author's spokesman. Judah Halevi relates that the king had a dream in which an angel appeared to him telling him that his intentions were pleasing to the Creator, but not his deeds. At first the king interpreted the dream to mean that he should be more zealous in his observance of the Khazar religion; but when the angel appeared with the same message a second time, he understood that he was to look for a new way of life. He invited an Aristotelian philosopher, a Christian, and a Muslim; only after he had found their presentations unsatisfactory did he feel compelled to invite the Jew, a member of the "despised faith" (*Kuzari*, 1:10). His conversation with the *ḥaver* convinces the king to convert to Judaism (2:1). Most of the five treatises of Judah Halevi's book are devoted to the *ḥaver*'s explanation of the Jewish religion.

GOD. Judah Halevi's point of view emerges from the *ḥaver*'s opening statement that Jews believe in the God of Abraham, Isaac, and Jacob, who publicly performed many miracles for them and who gave them the Torah. When the king asks the *ḥaver* whether he should not have begun with such speculative principles as "God is the creator and governor of the world," the *ḥaver* replies that to begin with such principles bring one to a rational religion, which is subject to many doubts. Only a religion based on the experience of God's manifestation in historical events is certain and free from doubt (1:11–29).

PROPHECY. Closely related to his conception of God is Judah Halevi's account of prophecy and the nature of the Jewish people. Unlike Neoplatonists and Aristotelians, who tended to describe prophecy as a natural activity of the rational faculty or of the rational and imaginative faculties combined, Judah Halevi views prophecy as the activity of a separate faculty beyond the natural faculties of man (1:31–43). God created Adam with this faculty, and it was transmitted by heredity first to individuals such as Noah, Abraham, Isaac, and Jacob; then to the 12 sons of Jacob and their descendants; and, finally, to the Jewish people as a whole (1:95). Possession of the prophetic faculty is the distinguishing feature of Israel's election, and even a convert, though equal to the born Jew in all other respects, cannot attain the prophetic gift (1:27). A sign of the inadequacy of philosophy is that no prophets were found among the philosophers (1:99). While for Judah Ḥalevi prophecy is primarily a gift of God and not the result of natural processes, he attaches two conditions to its attainment: prophecy can be attained only in Ereẓ Israel or (to account for prophets who prophesied outside Ereẓ Israel) the content of the prophecy, at least, must be about Ereẓ Israel; and only those who observe the divine commandments can be prophets (2:8–14).

PIETY. Piety is the main theme of Judah Halevi's philosophy of man. Man does not attain closeness to God, his goal in life, by pursuing philosophic speculations, but by faithfully adhering to the commandments of God. Accepting the Kalām's distinction between rational and traditional (divine) commandments, Judah Halevi holds that all men must observe the former; however, in his view they have only a preliminary function, and true guidance to human happiness is provided only by the latter (2:45–48). The servant of God is like a ruler: he apportions to each part of his body and soul its due (3:1ff.). While Judah Halevi advocates moderation in eating and drinking and control of appetites, his outlook is not ascetic. Man's joy on the Sabbath and the festivals is no less pleasing to God than his affliction on fast days (2:50). Prayer is the nourishment which sustains the soul from one prayer time to the next (3:5).

ATTITUDE TOWARD PHILOSOPHY. Judah Halevi is against philosophy as a way of life, but he is not against philosophic speculations altogether. It has already been noted that he accepts the philosophic notion of rational commandments. Philosophic distinctions appear also in his discussion of God. As YHWH, God can be known only through revelation, but as *Elohim*, the ruler and guide of the universe, He can be discovered also through philosophic speculation (4:1–3). Like the philosophers, Judah Halevi holds that anthropomorphic and anthropopathic terms applied to God must be interpreted, and he states that divine attributes must be understood as negations, relations, or attributes of action (2:2). Judah Halevi holds that philosophy was known among Jews in ancient times, as can be seen from *Sefer Yeẓirah*, which tradition attributed to Abraham; but Abraham wrote this book before he received his revelation (2:66; 4:24–25). At the request of the king, the *ḥaver* explains the principles of Aristotelian philosophy and of the Kalām (treatise 5), but he points out once again the superiority of revelation. The *ḥaver* also discusses human free will (5:20), and at the end of the book (5:22ff.) he declares his intention to go to Ereẓ Israel.

Ḥibat Allah

*Ḥibat Allah Abu al-Barakāt al-Baghdādī (second half of 11th century–first half of 12th century; flourished in Baghdad), whose philosophy has only recently been studied by S. Pines, was the author of a commentary on Ecclesiastes and of a philosophic work *Kitāb al-Muʿtabar* ("The Book of What Has Been Established By Personal Reflection"). He converted to Islam at the age of 60, but the two works mentioned seem to have been written while he was still a Jew. Subjecting the doctrines of the Aristotelian philosophers to a critical review, he presents novel notions of his own on physical, psychological, and metaphysical questions.

Nethanel al-Fayyūmī

*Nethanel al-Fayyūmī (d. about 1165; flourished in Egypt or Yemen) composed a work entitled *Bustān al-ʿUqūl* ("Garden of Intellects"), which attempts to introduce doctrines of the Islamic Ismāʿīliyya sect into Jewish thought. It is notable in particular for its unusual pluralistic views of religion (Ch. 6).

Abraham Ibn Daud

By the middle of the 12th century Jewish philosophy entered its next phase and, under the influence of the Islamic philosophers, Al-Fārābī, Avicenna, and Avempace, turned toward Aristotelianism. Abraham b. David ha-Levi *Ibn Daud (c. 1110–1180), was the first Jewish Aristotelian. He wrote his major philosophical work, *al-ʿAqīda al-Rafīʿa* ("Sublime Faith," translated into Hebrew as *Ha-Emunah ha-Ramah*, and a second time as *Ha-Emunah ha-Nissa'ah*, 1161) to explain the doctrine of free will to a friend; but, in fact, he discusses a variety of philosophical and theological topics. The work was strongly influenced by Avicenna and highly critical of Ibn Gabirol. Asserting that Judaism and philosophy are identical in their essence, Ibn Daud begins with an explanation of Aristotelian metaphysical, physical, and psychological notions (treatise 1). Having explained these notions philosophically, he cites scriptural verses that in his view allude to these notions. He proceeds to use them for an exposition of six topics: the existence of God, His unity, divine attributes, God's actions (including creation), prophecy, and the allegorical interpretation of terms comparing God to creatures (treatise 2). The work concludes with a brief discussion of ethical matters (treatise 3). To prove the existence of God, Ibn Daud uses the Aristotelian proof from motion and the Avicennian proof from necessity and contingency. According to the first proof, the analysis of motion in the world leads to a prime mover; according to the second, the contingent character of the world leads to a being necessary through itself. God, as necessary existent, is one both in the sense of being unique and of being simple. The attributes applied to God cannot have any positive meaning, but must be understood as negations or relations. Following Aristotle he holds that every change or process requires an underlying matter, but differing from Aristotle (for whom the world is eternal), he holds that God created a first matter, out of which he subsequently created the world. In a different vein, he cites aspects of the doctrine of emanation to explain the creation of the world, insisting, however, that emanation occurs not by necessity but by the free will of God. In psychology, Ibn Daud, like Avicenna, taught that the human intellect is an individual substance, not just a corporeal predisposition, as other Aristotelians believed. It is this substance as a whole that becomes immortal, not only that part known as the acquired intellect. The active intellect, the lowest of the celestial intelligences, is a cause for the actualization of the human mind, and it is also the effect of the active intellect on the mind of man that enables him to prophesy. Unlike Maimonides, who assigns to the imagination the important role in the prophetic inspiration, Ibn Daud, like Judah Halevi, restricts prophecy to the Jewish people and limits it to the land of Israel. Most difficult from the theological point of view is Ibn Daud's account of the knowledge of God: in order to safeguard man's freedom of choice, he willingly admits that God's knowledge is limited.

Maimonides

Ibn Daud was soon overshadowed by Moses *Maimonides (1135–1204), the greatest Jewish Aristotelian and the most prominent figure of medieval Jewish thought. Maimonides discusses his philosophy in popular fashion in parts of his halakhic works, his commentary on the Mishnah and *Mishneh Torah*, and in some treatises; but he reserves its technical exposition for his *Guide of the Perplexed* (*Dalālat al-Ḥāʾirīn; Moreh Nevukhim*). In formulating his views he drew on Aristotle and his Hellenistic commentators, and on the Muslims Al-Fārābi, Avicenna, and Avempace. Maimonides wrote his *Guide* for a faithful Jew, who, having studied philosophy, was perplexed by the literal meaning of biblical anthropomorphic and anthropopathic terms applied to God and by parables appearing in the Bible. Maimonides shows this person that his perplexities can be resolved by correct interpretation. Hence, the *Guide* is devoted in part to the philosophic interpretation of the Bible, but beyond that, to revealing the inner, i.e., philosophic, meaning of the Torah – as Maimonides puts it, to "the science of the Law in its true sense," or to the "secrets of the Law." Maimonides believed that the philosophic content of the Bible should be revealed only to an intellectual elite, not to the masses, and thus he wrote his work in an enigmatic style (*Guide*, 1: Introd.).

DIVINE ATTRIBUTES. In accord with his exegetical program, Maimonides begins his *Guide* (1:1–49) with an interpretation of difficult biblical terms, showing that even such terms as "to sit," "to stand," and "to eat" (applied in the Bible to God) have a spiritual sense. From exegesis he proceeds to exposition, selecting as his first topic the attributes of God (1:50–60). Medieval philosophers held that attributes applied to substances are of two kinds: essential, such as existence and life, which are closely related to the essence; and accidental, such as anger and mercifulness, which are incidental to the essence. The Avicennian tradition, which Maimonides followed, maintained, in addition, that both kinds of attributes are distinct from the substances to which they are applied, and, hence, introduce multiplicity into that which they describe. How, then, can attributes be applied to God, Who is one in the sense of being simple? After considering a number of possibilities of how attributes may be applied, Maimonides comes to the conclusion that essential attributes in the case of God must be understood as negations and accidental attributes as descriptions of His actions.

GOD. Before presenting his own views concerning the existence, unity, and incorporeality of God and the creation of the world, Maimonides offers a summary and critique of the Kalām's discussion of these four topics (1:71–76). His exposition rests on Aristotelian physical and metaphysical principles (2: Introd.), and he sets down four proofs, current in his day, for the existence of God: the proofs from motion, from the composition of elements, from necessity and contingency, and from potentiality and actuality (casuality). All of them start with some observable property of the world and conclude that a prime mover, a necessary existent, or a first cause (all of which are identified with God) must exist. These proofs for the existence of God lead in turn to proofs for His unity and incorporeality (2:1).

CREATION. Maimonides next discusses the incorporeal intelligences, which he identifies with the biblical angels, the celestial spheres (2:2–12), and then the creation of the world (2:13–26). A good part of his exposition is devoted to showing that the Aristotelian arguments for the eternity of the world are not conclusive demonstrations; they only attempt to show that eternity is more plausible than creation. Maimonides' own position is that the human mind is incapable of conclusively demonstrating the eternity of the world or its creation and can only present plausible arguments for either view. An examination of these arguments reveals that those for creation are more plausible, and on this basis Maimonides accepts the doctrine of creation *ex nihilo* as his own. He finds additional support for his opinion in the teachings of Scripture. Although the world has a beginning in time, it will not have an end (2:27–29).

PROPHECY. In the introduction to the *Guide* Maimonides incidentally discussed the nature of the prophetic experience, likening it to intellectual illumination; in the present section (2:32–48) he is interested in the psychology of prophecy and in its political function. Prophecy, for Maimonides, appears to be a natural phenomenon occurring when man's psychological faculties, particularly his intellect and imagination, have reached a certain perfection. God's role is limited to keeping someone who has met all the prerequisites from becoming a prophet. The prophet requires a well-developed imagination, because besides being a philosopher, he is also a statesman who brings a law, as in the case of Moses, or admonishes the people (who must be persuaded by arguments of the imagination) to adhere to a law, as in the case of the other prophets. Moses as a prophet is singular and so is his law, since through it one can attain intellectual as well as moral perfection. Maimonides concludes the portion of the *Guide* devoted to physical and metaphysical topics with an interpretation of the divine chariot (*merkavah*) described in Ezekiel chapters 1 and 10 (3:1–7).

EVIL AND DIVINE PROVIDENCE. The first topic of practical philosophy is the existence of evil (3:8–12), which Maimonides defines as the absence or privation of good. There is more good than evil in the world; of the three kinds of evil – natural evil, such as earthquakes, political, such as wars, and moral, such as the various vices – the majority, i.e., political and moral evils, can be remedied by man. Closely related to the question of evil is that of divine providence (3:16–21). Maimonides rejects the opinions of the Epicureans that everything is due to chance; the Aristotelians that there is no individual providence; the Ashʿarites that there is only individual providence, extending even to animals and minerals; and the Muʿtazilites that individual providence includes animals but not minerals; and he presents instead the views of the Torah. All Jews are agreed that God is just, that man is free, and that individual providence extends only to man. According to Maimonides' understanding of the Jewish view, individual providence depends on the development of the human mind, that is, the more a man develops his mind the more he is subject to the providence of God. Maimonides also holds that any suffering in this world is punishment for some prior sin, rejecting the doctrine of *yissurin shel ahavah*, according to which God may afflict man in this world in order to reward him in the next. Maimonides interprets the Book of Job in the light of his discussion of providence, showing how the characters of the book symbolize the various viewpoints about providence that he had discussed (3:22–24).

ANALYSIS OF THE TORAH. Rejecting the Muʿtazilite distinction between commandments produced by reason (*mitzvot sikhliyyot*) and those coming from the will of God (*mitzvot shimiyyot*), Maimonides maintains that all the commandments of the Torah are the result of the wisdom of God. Hence, all are intelligible, some (*mishpatim*) easily, others (*ḥukkim*) with difficulty. However, Maimonides adds that particular commandments, which by their very nature are not subject to reason, were stipulated by the will of God. The Torah has two purposes: the well-being of the soul (intellect) and the well-being of the body, by which he means man's political and moral well-being. The well-being of the soul is achieved through assent to true beliefs, such as the existence and incorporeality of God, which are true in themselves. However, there are also necessary beliefs, such as that God gets angry at those who disobey Him, whose main function is to motivate men to obey the Law. Reasons for moral laws can easily be found, but it is more difficult to explain the numerous ritual laws found in the Bible. Maimonides explains many of them, for example, the biblical prohibition against wearing garments made of wool and linen combined, as reactions to ancient pagan practices (3:25–50). He concludes his *Guide* with a supplementary section on the perfect worship of God and man's perfection (3:51–54).

THE MESSIAH. Maimonides barely refers to eschatology in the *Guide*, but he develops his views on the subject in other works. The Messiah is an earthly king descended from the House of David, who will bring the Jews back to their country, but whose main task will be to bring peace and tranquility to the world, thereby facilitating the full observance of the Law. The Messiah will die of old age; he will be succeeded by his son, and the latter, by his son, and so on. No cataclysmic events will take place in messianic times; the world will continue in its established order. In that time the dead will be resurrected with body and soul united, but later they will die again. The central notion of Maimonides' eschatology is *olam ha-ba* ("the world to come"), where the intellect will exist without the body and contemplate God.

Hebrew Translators of the 13th Century

When, after the period of Maimonides, the setting of Jewish philosophy shifted to Christian countries and its language became Hebrew (see above), the philosophic literature produced by Jews during the preceding period was translated from Arabic into Hebrew, as were many scientific and philosophic works written by Muslims (see Steinschneider, Uebersetzungen). Among the translators of this vast literature were Judah, Samuel, and Moses ibn Tibbon, Jacob Anatoli, Jacob ben Makhir, and *Kalonymus ben Kalonymus. Maimonides' *Guide* was the most influential work translated; next in importance were Averroes' commentaries on the works of Aristotle. Of the 38 commentaries that Averroes composed, 36 were translated into Hebrew (see H.A. Wolfson, in: *Speculum*, 38 (1963), 88–104). Under Averroes' influence, Jewish philosophy turned toward a more extreme rationalism (for details see below), and some Jewish philosophers attempted to harmonize the opinions of Maimonides and Averroes on topics on which these two philosophers differed.

Maimonidean Controversies

Maimonides' attempt to formulate a rationalistic account of Judaism produced controversies between his followers and their opponents that lasted throughout the 13th and into the early 14th century. The controversy reached such intensity that the two sides excommunicated each other, and they even went so far as to call in the Church authorities, who burned the *Guide* and *Sefer ha-Madda* in 1232. Another highlight was the ban of Solomon b. Abraham *Adret, issued in 1305, which prohibited the study of physics and metaphysics before the age of 25 (for an account of these controversies, see *Maimonidean Controversy). During the early 13th century, some philosophers were still active in the Islamic world. Joseph b. Judah ibn *Aknin (flourished in Morocco), Maimonides' younger contemporary, composed a number of talmudic and philosophic works, among them a commentary on the Song of Songs, a commentary on *Avot*, and a work on moral philosophy, *Ṭibb al-Nufūs al-Salīma wa Muʿālajat al-Nufūs al-Alīma* ("The Hygiene of the Healthy Souls and the Therapy of Ailing Souls"), which contains an interesting account of the content and order of religious and secular studies among Jews. Joseph b. Judah ibn Sham'un (d. 1226), the disciple for whom Maimonides wrote his *Guide*, composed a small metaphysical work on the necessary existent, how all things proceed from it, and on creation. The early portion of the work follows Avicennian Aristotelianism, and the latter portion, the teachings of Kalām. It is likely that the kalamic section predated Ibn Sham'un's acquaintance with Maimonides. *Abraham b. Moses b. Maimon (1186–1237), Maimonides' only son, followed the teachings of his father and defended them against opponents. However, in his *Kitāb Kifāyat al-ʿAbidīn* ("Comprehensive Guide for the Servants of God"), he advocates a Sufi-like Jewish pietism.

SAMUEL IBN TIBBON. In southern France, Samuel ibn *Tibbon, the translator of the *Guide* and other works, composed *Perush me-ha-Millot ha-Zarot*, a philosophical glossary for the *Guide*, philosophical commentaries on Ecclesiastes and Song of Songs, and *Ma'amar Yikkavu ha-Mayim* (on Gen. 1:9), devoted to physical and metaphysical topics. He favored the allegorical interpretation of the Bible, and is said to have held that the Bible was primarily for the masses.

JACOB ANATOLI. Jacob *Anatoli (13th century), active as a translator at the court of the emperor Frederick II, wrote *Malmad ha-Talmidim*, a philosophical commentary on the Pentateuch. In this work he quotes the Christian scholar Michael Scot (he even cites the emperor), and he shows acquaintance with Christian literature and institutions. He followed the allegorical interpretation of Scripture and preached philosophical sermons publicly. This earned him the anger of the anti-Maimonists.

SHEM TOV BEN JOSEPH IBN FALAQUERA. Shem Tov b. Joseph ibn *Falaquera (c. 1225–c. 1295), translator and author of many works devoted largely to ethics and psychology, also wrote *Moreh ha-Moreh*, a commentary on Maimonides' *Guide*. In this commentary he corrects Ibn Tibbon's translation of the *Guide* on the basis of the Arabic original, and he cites parallel passages from the works of Islamic philosophers, particularly from Averroes. In his *Iggeret ha-Vikku'aḥ*, a dialogue between a philosopher and an opponent of philosophy, he justifies the study of philosophy. In his *Sefer ha-Nefesh* he follows Avicenna, but in his encyclopedic work *De'ot ha-Pilosofim* he follows Averroes. He translated and condensed Ibn Gabirol's *Mekor Ḥayyim* from Arabic into Hebrew.

JOSEPH IBN KASPI. Joseph ibn *Kaspi (c. 1279–c. 1340), prolific author of biblical commentaries, lexicographic works, and books on philosophy, wrote a commentary on the *Guide*, consisting of an exoteric and esoteric part entitled, respectively, *Ammudei Kesef* and *Maskiyyot Kesef*. This commentary was influenced by that of Shem Tov b. Joseph ibn Falaquera and in turn influenced later commentaries on the *Guide*. He accepts doctrines associated with the teachings of Averroes, such as the identity of religion and philosophy, the eternity of the world, and the natural interpretation of miracles, but he tries to modify these doctrines in a way that distinguishes him from such extreme rationalists as Moses of Narbonne and Levi b. Gershom.

Hillel ben Samuel

*Hillel b. Samuel (c. 1220–1295), one of the first Jewish philosophers in Italy, translated from Latin to Hebrew the Neoplatonic work *Liber de causis* and composed *Tagmulei ha-Nefesh* ("The Rewards of the Soul"). Since he knew Latin, he was able to draw on the opinions of Christian scholastics, particularly those of Thomas Aquinas. In Aristotelian fashion, Hillel defined the soul as the entelechy of a natural organic body, but, following Avicenna and the Neoplatonists, he held that the soul is a substance that emanates from God through the intermediacy of the supernal soul. He also cites Averroes' opinion that there is only one universal soul for all men, from which individual souls emanate like rays from the sun. However, on the question of the material or potential intellect he criticizes Averroes, using arguments offered by Aquinas. Averroes had argued that there exists only one such intellect for all men, but Hillel argued that each person has his own material intellect. On the question of the active intellect, Hillel accepts the opinion of the Islamic and Jewish Aristotelians, for whom the active intellect was the lowest of the celestial intelligences; in this he differed from Aquinas, who held that each person has his own active intellect. According to Hillel, only the rational part of the soul is immortal, and its ultimate happiness consists in union with the active intellect. In its immortal state the soul retains its individuality. Hillel also composed a commentary on the 26 propositions appearing at the beginning of the second part of Maimonides' *Guide*.

Isaac Albalag

Isaac *Albalag (second half of 13th century, probably lived in Spain) translated Al-Ghazālī's *Maqāṣid al-Falāsifa* (a compendium of the teachings of Avicenna) into Hebrew and presented his own views in a commentary on the work entitled *Tikkun ha-De'ot*. A follower of Averroes, who accepted such doctrines as the eternity of the world, he has also been described as a proponent of the theory of the "double truth," advocated by Latin Averroists. Like the Latin Averroists he distinguished between two coexistent independent truths, philosophic truth and prophetic truth, and he held that the two can contradict one another. However, he does not cite in his work any instance of such contradiction (see G. Vajda, *Isaac Albalag* (1960), 251ff.). His outlook is not completely clear, but it seems that his own view on a given topic is always that of philosophy. He maintained that speculative truths are the province of philosophy, not of Scripture. The Torah has as its sole purpose the moral and political guidance of the masses and contains no speculative truths, even by implication. Nevertheless, Albalag offers philosophic interpretations of the Bible; for example, he explained the story of creation in accordance with the doctrine of the eternity of the world. In a somewhat different vein, he states that if philosophic and prophetic truths contradict each other, both should stand, and one should say that the prophetic truth is unintelligible.

Abner of Burgos and Isaac Pollegar

The first half of the 14th century saw a debate concerning the freedom of the will initiated by *Abner of Burgos. Abner, who converted to Christianity, presented his views in *Minḥat Kena'ot*; although the work was written after his conversion, it seems clear that he held the same views when he was still a Jew. Following Avicenna, whose opinions he knew through their summary in al-Ghazālī's *Maqāṣid al-Falāsifa*, he held that human acts no less than natural occurrences are causally determined. Although the will has the ability to choose between alternatives, any given choice is determined, in fact, by causes influencing the will. Causal determination of the will is also required by God's omniscience and omnipotence: were human actions undetermined until the moment of decision, God could not foreknow them, and, also, His power would be limited. Abner tried to justify the existence of divine commandments and reward and punishment: divine commandments can be among the causes affecting the will, and reward and punishment are necessary consequences of human actions. Abner viewed biblical and rabbinic statements affirming freedom of the will as concessions to the understanding of the masses. Isaac *Pollegar, who knew Abner personally, attacked his determinism in his *Ezer ha-Dat*. According to Pollegar's solution, which contains difficulties of its own, there is a correlation between the divine and human wills, such that at the moment man wills to do a certain act, God also wills that it be accomplished. In willing that the act be accomplished, God also knows it. Yet, although this knowledge begins in time, there is no change in God. Whatever the difficulties of this position, it is clear that Pollegar tried to defend the freedom of the will by limiting God's foreknowledge. Levi b. Gershom (see below) solved the problem in a more radical fashion. Holding that God's knowledge extends only to species and not to individuals, he excluded man's action from God's knowledge, thereby safeguarding human freedom.

Moses of Narbonne

Moses b. Joshua of Narbonne (d. after 1362) was another participant in the debate. He wrote commentaries on works by Averroes and other Muslim philosophers (including al-

Ghazālī's *Maqāṣid*) and also an important commentary on Maimonides' *Guide*. Although he held Maimonides in high esteem, he criticized a number of his doctrines, which under the influence of Al-Fārābi and Avicenna had a Neoplatonic complexion; he opposes these doctrines with the more strictly Aristotelian teachings of Averroes. His critique of Abner is found in *Ha-Ma'amar bi-Veḥirah*, and he also discusses human freedom in other works. However, his position is not completely clear. In some passages he holds in agreement with Maimonides that God's knowledge extends to particular human acts without determining these acts; in others he holds that God knows only species, not individuals. The latter opinion was probably Moses' real view.

Levi ben Gershom

*Levi b. Gershom (1288–1344), also known as Gersonides, mathematician, astronomer, and biblical commentator, wrote supercommentaries on many of Averroes' commentaries on Aristotle (still unpublished) and was the author of a philosophic work, *Sefer Milḥamot Adonai* ("The Book of the Wars of the Lord"). The most important Jewish Aristotelian after Maimonides, he was influenced by Averroes, though he is also critical of some of his views (see below). In *Milḥamot* Levi discusses in great detail and with scholastic subtlety topics that in his view Maimonides had not discussed sufficiently or had solved incorrectly. In the six parts of his work he deals with immortality of the soul; foretelling the future; God's knowledge of individual contingent beings; the celestial bodies, their movers, and God; and the creation of the world. *Milḥamot* is formally devoted to these six topics, but, together with his other works, it indicates Levi's general philosophy.

IMMORTALITY. Levi begins his discussion of immortality (treatise 1) with an extensive review and critique of various theories concerning the intellect. The Aristotelian philosophers had distinguished between the material or passive intellect, the active intellect, and the acquired intellect. Rejecting Themistius' and Averroes' opinions concerning the passive intellect, Levi accepts an opinion close to that of Alexander of Aphrodisias, namely, that the passive intellect is a predisposition inhering in the sensitive soul and comes into being with each individual man. Under the influence of the active intellect, the lowest of the incorporeal intelligences, the passive intellect is actualized and becomes the acquired intellect. While the passive intellect dies with the body, the acquired intellect is immortal. Differing from Averroes, for whom immortality was collective, Levi holds that each acquired intellect retains its individuality in its immortal state.

PROPHECY. The ability to foretell the future was accepted as an established fact by the adherents of religion and philosophers alike, and Levi set out to explain this fact (treatise 2). Maintaining that there is a continuity between the celestial and terrestrial world, Levi holds that terrestrial events, particularly those related to man, are caused by the celestial spheres. Since the events of human life are thus ordered, it is possible that there are certain individuals who can foretell them. However, Levi is not a complete determinist. Discussing the problem of celestial (astrological) influences from another perspective, he holds that man is free in choosing his actions and that those who understand the laws of the celestial spheres can avoid the evil influences they may have. Since the active intellect both actualizes the human intellect and is a cause in the production of sublunar substances and events, it also causes knowledge of the future. In men who have strongly developed intellects the active intellect produces prophecy; in men who have strongly developed imaginations it causes (indirectly) divination and true dreams.

PREDESTINATION AND DIVINE PROVIDENCE. Discussing God's knowledge of individuals in the sublunar world (treatise 3), Levi is critical of Maimonides. Maimonides held that God knows particulars and met the objection that this seems to introduce a change in God by holding that God's knowledge is completely different from ours. Levi took this objection seriously and denied that God knows particular individuals. God only knows the order of nature. Closely related to God's knowledge of individuals is the question of providence (treatise 4). Levi rejected the theories that God's providence extends only to the species or that it extends equally to all men; he maintained that it extends only to those individuals who have developed their intellect. Like Maimonides, he held that the more an individual develops his intellect, the more he is subject to providence.

DIVINE ATTRIBUTES. Levi's account of the celestial spheres, their movers, and God (treatise 5) need not detain us, except for one aspect of his account of God, namely divine attributes (5:2, 12; see also 3:5). Maimonides, following Avicenna, had denied that attributes applied to God can have any positive meaning. Levi, following Averroes, accepted the alternative that Maimonides had rejected. Holding that essential attributes are identical with the essence to which they belong, Levi maintained that to understand such attributes positively does not introduce a multiplicity into God. He also held that such attributes (life, knowledge, and so on) whether applied to God or man have the same meaning, though they are applied to God primarily and to creatures derivatively.

CREATION. In his account of creation (treatise 6), Levi agrees with Maimonides that Aristotle's proofs for the eternity of the world are not conclusive arguments, though Aristotle's arguments are the best offered so far. However, against Aristotle, Levi presents a number of arguments designed to show that the world is created, among them one from the finiteness of time and motion. (Levi also rejects the Neoplatonic theory of emanation.) However, Levi differs from Maimonides and most Jewish philosophers in denying creation *ex nihilo*, holding that the world was created out of a formless matter coexistent with God, though this matter is not a principle paralleling God. He concludes his *Milḥamot* with a discussion of miracles and prophets, which reflects his general rationalistic temper.

Ḥasdai Crescas

Judah Halevi and Ḥibat Allah Abu al-Barakāt al-Baghdādī had criticized the doctrines of the Aristotelians, but the most significant critique within the mainstream of Jewish philosophy was that of Ḥasdai Crescas (d. 1412?). Although Crescas was critical of certain Aristotelian notions, he did not oppose philosophic speculations altogether; in fact, he proposed philosophic notions of his own to replace the Aristotelian notions he rejected. Nevertheless, in his conception of Judaism he emphasized observance of commandments and love of God rather than intellectual accomplishments. His critique of Aristotle as well as his own philosophy are found in *Or Adonai* ("The Light of the Lord"); he also wrote a work in Spanish criticizing Christianity, which has been preserved in Hebrew as *Bittul Ikkarei ha-Noẓerim* ("Refutation of the Dogmas of the Christians").

BASIC PRINCIPLES OF JUDAISM. Maimonides' formulation of 13 principles of Judaism sparked a lively debate in the late Middle Ages. Taking issue with Maimonides, Crescas uses his own account of such principles as the framework of his book. According to Crescas, the basic principles of all religions are the existence, unity, and incorporeality of God (treatise 1). These are followed by six principles required for a belief in the validity of the Torah: God's knowledge of existing things, providence, divine omnipotence, prophecy, human freedom, and purpose in the Torah and the world (treatise 2). Next come eight true beliefs, which every adherent of the Torah must accept, and a denial of which constitutes heresy: creation of the world, immortality of the soul, reward and punishment, resurrection of the dead, eternity of the Torah, superiority of the prophecy of Moses, efficacy of the Urim and Thummim (worn by the high priest) in predicting the future, and the coming of the Messiah (treatise 3). The book concludes with 13 questions on topics ranging from whether there exists more than one world to the existence of demons.

SPACE AND INFINITY. Crescas' critique of Aristotle is found largely in an exposition and critical evaluation of the 26 physical and metaphysical propositions with which Maimonides had begun the second part of his *Guide* (see H.A. Wolfson, *Crescas' Critique of Aristotle*, 1929). Of special interest are Crescas' conception of space and infinity. The Aristotelians had defined place (rather than space) as the inner surface of a surrounding body; they had argued that there are no empty spaces (vacuum) in the world, and that the universe is finite and unitary. They also had held that an actual infinite cannot exist. Taking issue with them, Crescas set out to show that empty space without bodies can exist (it is identical with extension), that a vacuum can and does exist, that space beyond our world exists, and that there can be more than one world. He also differed from the Aristotelians in maintaining that an actual infinite (space, quantity, magnitude, time) can exist.

EXISTENCE OF GOD. Crescas' acceptance of the existence of an actual infinite raised questions concerning the Maimonidean (Aristotelian) proofs of the existence of God. Since the proofs rested on the proposition that an actual infinite is impossible, Crescas rejected them. However, he retains the proof from necessity and contingency, which to his mind is independent of the disputed principle. In view of difficulties, he also substitutes proofs of his own for the unity and incorporeality of God. Against Maimonides, Crescas affirms the possibility of positive attributes applied to God.

PROVIDENCE AND FREEDOM. God's knowledge, according to Crescas, extends to particulars; He knows the nonexistent and He knows future contingents without removing their contingent character. Crescas also upholds individual providence and states that man's true reward or punishment, dependent on obedience or disobedience of God's will, is given in the hereafter. A similar attitude also determines Crescas' conception of prophecy. God can inspire whomever he wishes, but the one chosen for prophecy is someone who follows the Torah and loves God. Of special interest is Crescas' conception of human freedom. While Maimonides and Levi ben Gershom in different ways safeguarded the freedom of human actions, Crescas' solution is more deterministic. He holds that everything in the world is the result of prior causes and affirms that God's omniscience requires that the object of His foreknowledge come to pass. Human actions are caused by a will determined by other causes, not by an undetermined will. Crescas tried to mitigate this position by stating that commandments, training, and other factors are among the causes influencing the will and that, despite being determined, the will in its own nature is contingent. Crescas' anti-Aristotelian stance is also apparent in his doctrine of man. In place of development of the intellect as the main purpose of human life is the observance of God's commandments; not philosophic speculation but the love and fear of God bring immortality to man. It is the soul that is immortal, not the acquired intellect.

Simeon ben Ẓemaḥ Duran

After the period of Crescas, medieval Jewish philosophy declined. It became more eclectic and most philosophers accepted a more orthodox religious position. Simeon b. Ẓemaḥ *Duran, talmudist and author of a philosophic theological work, *Magen Avot*, generally followed the moderate rationalism of Maimonides, though, like Crescas, he maintained that divine attributes can have a positive meaning, that immortality comes through observance of the commandments, and that divine providence extends to all men. In the introduction to his commentary on Job, entitled *Ohev Mishpat*, Duran also contributes to the discussion of dogmas. Emphasizing the centrality of a belief in revelation, Duran listed three dogmas, the existence of God, revelation, and reward and punishment, which became the foundations of Joseph Albo's philosophy.

Joseph Albo

Joseph *Albo (15th century), a student of Crescas, presented his views in *Sefer ha-Ikkarim* ("Book of Principles"), an eclectic, popular work, whose central task is the exposition of the principles of Judaism. Albo, following Duran, held that there are three basic principles (*ikkarim*) necessary for the existence of a divine law: the existence of God, revelation, and reward and punishment. From these principles follow eight derivative principles (*shorashim*): from the existence of God there follow God's unity, incorporeality, timelessness, and perfection; from revelation, God's omniscience and prophecy and authentication of the prophet; from reward and punishment, individual providence. The denial of these principles, no less than the denial of the first three, makes one a heretic (*kofer*). There are, furthermore, six branches (*anafim*): creation *ex nihilo*, the superiority of Moses as a prophet, immutability of the Torah, guarantee of immortality through the observance of any one commandment, resurrection of the dead, and the coming of the Messiah. Although it is proper that every Jew accept these branches, and although their denial makes him a sinner, it does not make him a heretic. Albo also criticizes the opinions of his predecessors concerning principles of Judaism. *Sefer ha-Ikkarim* is divided into four treatises. The first deals with the general principles of laws, the three *ikkarim*, and how a genuine divine law can be distinguished from a spurious one; each of the other three treatises is devoted to an exposition of a basic principle and of the principles derived from it. In his preliminary discussion (*Ikkarim*, 1:7ff.) Albo distinguishes three kinds of law: natural, conventional, and divine. Natural law is the same for all persons, times, and places; conventional law is ordered by a wise man in accord with reason; divine law is given by God through a prophet. It is only divine law that can lead man to true happiness and immortality. Albo's work contains explicit and implicit polemics against Christianity (for example 3:25), which are very likely the result of his participation in the debates at Tortosa and San Mateo (1413–14).

Shem Tov Family, Abraham Shalom, and Isaac Arama

The tension of the age is well illustrated by the Shem Tov family. Shem Tov b. Joseph *Ibn Shem Tov (c. 1380–1441), a kabbalist and opponent of Greek philosophy, attacked in his *Sefer ha-Emunot*, not only such extreme rationalists as Albalag and Levi ben Gershom, but even more fiercely Maimonides himself. His son Joseph b. Shem Tov *Ibn Shem Tov (d. c. 1480), who greatly admired Aristotle and Maimonides, tried to rehabilitate philosophy by improving its rapport with religious Orthodoxy. He attempted to show that Aristotle really believed in individual providence, and that when Aristotle stated that man's happiness comes through contemplation, he had in mind only happiness in this world, leaving room for happiness in the next dependent on the observance of the Torah. Shem Tov b. Joseph *Ibn Shem Tov, who bore the same name as his grandfather, continued his father's philosophical interest in a commentary on Maimonides' *Guide* (composed 1488), in which he defends Maimonides against the attacks of Crescas. His contemporary, Abraham *Shalom, in his work *Neveh Shalom*, also defended Maimonides against Crescas. Isaac b. Moses *Arama (1420–1494) wrote a philosophic-homiletical commentary on the Pentateuch, entitled *Akedat Yiẓḥak*.

Isaac and Judah Abrabanel

The last Jewish philosopher in Spain was the statesman Isaac *Abrabanel (1437–1508), who went into exile with his fellow Jews in 1492. He admired Maimonides greatly (he wrote a commentary on the *Guide*); nevertheless he opposed the rationalistic interpretation of Judaism. Thus he held, for example, that prophecy was caused by God Himself, not by the active intellect. His attitude also emerges in his work *Rosh Amanah*, in which he defends Maimonides' 13 principles with great subtlety against all those who had taken issue with them; but in the end he states that only the commandments of the Torah count. Abrabanel's account of history and political life was novel. In his commentary on the beginning of Genesis he held that God willed that man be satisfied with what nature provides and concentrate on cultivation of his spirit. However, men were dissatisfied and produced civilizations to gain further possessions. These civilizations distracted them from their true goal. Abrabanel had a similar attitude toward the state. Man's condition, as ordained by God, was to live in loose associations, but as man's desires increased, he organized states. States are evil in themselves, since they detract man from his true goal. After the expulsion of the Jews from Spain, Jewish philosophy continued in Italy, where it had begun in the 13th century. Abrabanel, in fact, wrote his most important works in Italy. His son Judah *Abrabanel, known as Leone Ebreo (c. 1460–after 1523), under the influence of Renaissance Platonism, wrote a general philosophic work entitled *Dialoghi di Amore* ("Dialogues of Love"). Earlier, an Italian Jew, *Judah b. Jehiel (Messer Leon; 15th century), had written a work on rhetoric in Hebrew, which drew on Aristotle, Cicero, and Quintillian. He also wrote on logic.

Elijah Delmedigo

Elijah *Delmedigo (c. 1460–1497), born in Crete, lived for a time in Italy, where he exchanged views with Christian Platonists. He had lectured at the University of Padua, and at the request of *Pico della Mirandola he translated works by Averroes from Hebrew into Latin. He also wrote independent works on philosophic topics, including *Beḥinat ha-Dat* ("The Examination of Religion"), a work based on a treatise by Averroes, in which he investigated the relation of philosophy and religion. Like Averroes, he held that the masses must accept Scripture literally, while philosophers may interpret it. However, he denied philosophers the right to interpret the basic principles of Judaism. Like the Latin Averroists, he envisaged religion and philosophy as independent disciplines that may be mutually contradictory. If this should happen, the philosopher must accept the teachings of religion. He modified this position by maintaining that it is permissible to interpret philosophically doctrines which do not affect a basic principle and by affirming that, in fact, basic principles do not conflict with reason.

Joseph Delmedigo

Joseph Solomon *Delmedigo (1591–1655), a descendant of Elijah, was influenced by the theories of Galileo; but he did not free himself completely from certain medieval notions. He accepted the heliocentric theory of the universe and also denied that there is any distinction between the celestial and terrestrial realm. He criticized the Aristotelian notion of form, holding that material substance and its qualities are adequate to explain the world. He also rejected the Aristotelian notion that incorporeal movers of the spheres exist. His conception of the soul follows the Platonic notion that the soul is a substance joined to the body, and his view of the active intellect follows Aquinas' view that it is located within the individual human soul. In addition to defending these philosophic views, Delmedigo also defended the Kabbalah, though he mocked its superstitions.

Influences on Christian Thought

Two Jewish philosophers, Gabirol and Maimonides, influenced Christian thought extensively through Latin translations of their major works. Gabirol's *Mekor Ḥayyim* was translated into Latin as *Fons Vitae* in the middle of the 12th century; Maimonides' *Guide* was translated as *Dux* (*Director*) *Neutrorum* (*Dubitantium, Perplexorum*) about a century later. Gabirol's *Fons Vitae*, together with the writings of Augustine and of Islamic philosophers, molded the Neoplatonic component of Christian scholastic thought. *William of Auvergne, while disagreeing with some of his views, described Gabirol as "one of the noblest of all philosophers," and he identified Gabirol's (divine) will with the Christian logos. Gabirol is also considered a proponent of the doctrine of the multiplicity of forms, according to which several substantial forms exist within a given substance. However, by far the best known of Gabirol's teachings was his notion that spiritual substances (the angels and the human soul), no less than corporeal substances, are composed of matter and form. This doctrine became the subject of a lively debate among scholastics. Among those who accepted Gabirol's view were *Alexander of Hales, Bonaventure, and *Duns Scotus; among those who rejected it were *Albertus Magnus and Thomas *Aquinas. In general the Franciscans accepted this doctrine, the Dominicans rejected it. Among Christian scholastics who were influenced by Maimonides were Alexander of Hales, William of Auvergne, Albertus Magnus, Thomas Aquinas, Meister *Eckhart, and Duns Scotus. Aquinas, for example, was influenced by Maimonides in his account of the relation of faith and reason, in his proofs for the existence of God, and in his opinion that the creation of the world in time cannot be demonstrated by philosophic arguments. However, he polemicized against Maimonides' opinion that all essential attributes applied to God must be understood as negations, against his description of the celestial movers, and against his identifying angels with the incorporeal intelligences.

Christian Scholastic Influences on Jewish Thought

Islamic philosophy and its Greek antecedents provided the foundations for medieval Jewish philosophy during its two phases. There were also Christian scholastic influences on Jewish philosophers who knew Latin: for example, Hillel b. Samuel was influenced by Aquinas and Albalag, by the Latin Averroists. But even those Jewish philosophers who did not know Latin had, in time, access to scholastic thought through Hebrew translations. As was to be expected, the works translated dealt with philosophical rather than theological topics. Among the scholastics from whose works translations were made were Albertus Magnus, Thomas Aquinas, Aegidius Romanus, Peter of Spain, and William of Ockham. Among the translators were Judah *Romano, Elijah *Habillo, and Abraham Shalom. S. Pines has advanced the view that, while Jewish philosophers do not cite works by late medieval scholastics, they were familiar with the problems they discussed. He has argued that physical and metaphysical notions of Duns Scotus, Buridan, Oresme, Albert of Saxony, and William of Ockham influenced Jedaiah ha-Penini Bedersi, Levi b. Gershom, Joseph ibn Kaspi and Hasdai Crescas (S. Pines, *Scholasticism after Thomas Aquinas and the Teachings of Ḥasdai Crescas and his Predecessors*, 1967).

MODERN PERIOD

Introduction

Modern Jewish philosophy shared with Hellenistic and medieval Jewish philosophy a concern for relating general philosophy to Judaism, and it discussed some of the same problems that had been discussed in earlier Jewish philosophy; but, at the same time, it differed from Hellenistic and medieval Jewish philosophy in several respects. For one thing it differed in its conception of Jewish tradition. For Hellenistic and medieval Jewish philosophers, Judaism, with its Oral and Written Law, was the revealed word of God which was binding in its totality for all times. While there were modern Jewish thinkers who accepted the traditional position, most of them considered Judaism a creation of human thought, intuition, or feeling, which had developed in history and, which, while containing a perennial core, also contained parts which could be discarded in modern times. Then again, it differed in its conception of science and philosophy. Hellenistic and medieval Jewish philosophers accepted the notion of a geocentric universe with a sharp distinction between its terrestrial and celestial parts – a universe that manifests design and purpose. Modern Jewish philosophers accepted the notion of a heliocentric universe with no distinction between its terrestrial and celestial parts, a universe governed by the necessary laws of nature. Moreover, pre-modern Jewish thinkers saw no sharp distinction between science and philosophy, had strong metaphysical interests, and emphasized that the development of the human mind was the purpose of human life and morality was only a prerequisite for the fulfillment of this goal. Modern Jewish philosophers saw science as distinct from philosophy, and while those following the idealist tradition retained metaphysical interests and emphasized the primacy of intellectual cognition, there were many who denied the possibility (or at least the importance) of metaphysics, emphasizing instead the study of ethics and the centrality of proper conduct for attaining the goal of human life. It can readily be seen that it was easier to reconcile pre-modern philosophy with Jewish teachings than modern philosophy. The Enlightenment and the Emancipation also had a significant impact on modern Jewish thought. For example, the Enlightenment notion of a religion of reason which, consisting of rational beliefs and practices, was addressed to all men, was adopted by a number of Jewish philosophers of the modern period. Some, Mendelssohn for example, accepted this notion and investigated to what extent historical Judaism was identical with the religion of reason and to what extent different. Others, such as Hermann Cohen, went so far as to maintain that Judaism was the ideal embodiment of the religion of reason. The process of secularization initiated by the Enlightenment also had its impact on Jewish thought. While modern Jewish philosophy was still largely a religious philosophy, there arose Jewish thinkers who attempted to formulate secular philosophies of Judaism, and for whom Judaism was a culture or a social philosophy rather than a religious tradition (see also *Haskalah).

The impact of the Emancipation was felt in Western rather than in Eastern Europe, for in the East the Jewish community retained its social (even its political) identity into the 20th century. The progressive political and social emancipation of the Jews posed special problems for Jewish thinkers, one of these being the nature of the Jewish group. While pre-modern Jewish thinkers had no difficulty in accepting the notion that the Jews were a people, many modern Jewish thinkers considered Judaism a religion and the Jews a religious society (*Religionsgemeinschaft*), thereby emphasizing that only their religion distinguished Jews from other citizens. The Emancipation also influenced the concept of the Messiah. Whereas in classical Jewish thought the Messiah was a king from the House of David who would bring the Jews back to their own land, most modern Jewish thinkers gave up the belief in a personal Messiah, speaking instead of messianic times when all mankind would be united in justice and righteousness.

Another factor that influenced modern Jewish philosophy was the emergence of distinct religious groups within Judaism. While in former times, too, there were different groups within Judaism, e.g., Sadducees and Pharisees, and Rabbanites and Karaites, Jewish philosophy for the most part moved within the mainstream of classical rabbinic tradition. However, in the 19th century there developed three distinct groups within Judaism, each of which had its philosophers. *Neo-Orthodoxy upheld the classical formulation of Judaism but attempted to make modern culture relevant to Jewish concerns. The positive-historical school (which was to become in the United States in the 20th century the *Conservative movement) was committed to classical Jewish tradition but at the same time studied Judaism from a historical-critical perspective, maintaining that Judaism was subject to evolutionary development. Liberal (*Reform) Judaism was committed to a program of change, holding that the core of Judaism was ethics (ethical monotheism) and that ritual was subject to abrogation and change.

One further factor was the rise of modern antisemitism. In the case of some Jewish thinkers (Hermann Cohen is a notable example) it was antisemitism that aroused their interest in Jewish thought. Antisemitism also produced in certain thinkers a despair of the promise of emancipation, which, together with the emergence of modern nationalism and classical Jewish messianic expectations, produced Zionism which advocated the reestablishment of a Jewish state, preferably in Ereẓ Israel. In its philosophic component modern Jewish thought followed the main currents of modern and contemporary Western philosophy, rationalism, Kantianism, idealism, existentialism, and pragmatism. There were also influences derived from British empiricism and positivism. Whereas medieval Jewish philosophy consisted of movements which had a certain continuity and structure, modern Jewish thought represents mainly the efforts of individual thinkers. In Western Europe the language of Jewish philosophy was the language of the country in which the philosopher lived, while in Eastern Europe its language was largely Hebrew.

Spinoza

Baruch (Benedict) *Spinoza (1632–1677) has sometimes been described as the first modern Jewish philosopher, but he cannot be considered part of the mainstream of the Jewish philosophic tradition. When in his *Theologico-Political Treatise* he set out to separate philosophy from religion (Introd., ch. 7, 14), he denied the possibility of a religious philosophy of any kind. Moreover, the pantheistic system of his *Ethics*, with its identity of God and nature, cannot be said to be in harmony with Jewish beliefs. Nevertheless, there are good reasons for including him in an account of Jewish philosophy: his ideas were influenced by medieval Jewish philosophers, particularly Maimonides and Crescas; he polemicized against the medieval understanding of such ideas as prophecy and miracles; modern Jewish philosophers discussed his ideas (pro and con); and his biblical criticism became one of the foundations of the liberal interpretation of Judaism to which many modern Jewish philosophers subscribed. From his medieval predecessors Spinoza accepted the distinction between a philosophic elite which can understand through reason and the masses which can understand only through imagination. Spinoza wrote his *Ethics* for philosophers, its object being to show that the good life and human happiness can be attained through reason without recourse to historical religion. (In the five parts of the *Ethics* he discusses God (1), mind (2), passions (3, 4), and human freedom (5).) Spinoza rejects the notion of a personal God who acts by will and design. Instead, God is an impersonal being who acts out of the necessity of His (Spinoza often retains theistic language) own nature and determines everything through His infinite power. God possesses an infinity of attributes, of which thought and extension are known to man; He also possesses modes. Everything that exists appears to be an aspect of God. The world and man lack any purpose other than to function in accordance with their necessary causes. Man also lacks free will. The greatest obstacle to the good life is enslavement to the passions, but man can free himself from this enslavement by understanding and controlling the passions. Philosophic understanding is the goal of human life, and Spinoza describes its highest form as "the intellectual love of the mind toward God." In his *Theologico-Political Treatise* Spinoza manifests a twofold interest in religion. He attempts, on the one hand, to show that philosophy is independent of religion, and, on the other, to show the ruler that he may enforce religious practices while granting the philosopher the freedom to philosophize. To show philosophy's freedom from religion, Spinoza develops a new method for interpreting the Bible. Holding that the Bible is a human document composed by different authors, at different times, and under different circumstances (a critical view he attributes to Abraham ibn Ezra), he maintains that it must be interpreted in accordance with ordinary canons of historical and literary exegesis. The new method brings him to the conclusion that the Bible is intellectually rather naïve (a product of the imagination rather than of reason), so that one should not expect to find any philosophical profundities in it. In spite of this evaluation, Spinoza does not reject the Bible altogether. While he held that the biblical religions had sunk to the level of superstition, and while he maintained that most of the biblical precepts could be discarded, he also stated that the Bible contains a viable core useful for the instruction of the masses. The Bible in its noblest core teaches "obedience to God in the singleness of heart and the practice of justice and charity." The Bible also contains seven dogmas of universal faith – God's existence, unity, omnipresence, power and will, man's obligation to worship God, salvation, and repentance – belief in which leads the masses to proper actions. While some of the dogmas reflect philosophic notions discussed in the *Ethics*, Spinoza presents them in the *Treatise* as products of the imagination. Spinoza applies his critical method primarily to the Hebrew Bible, but it can be applied to Christian Scripture as well. It appears that he considered Christianity a better embodiment than Judaism of the purified biblical religions which he favored. Jewish ceremonial law, political in its function, lost its validity with the destruction of the Jewish kingdom and hence was no longer obligatory. In passing he envisages the possibility that under the right conditions the Jews may once again establish their state.

Moses Mendelssohn

Moses *Mendelssohn (1729–1786), champion of Jewish emancipation, translator of the Pentateuch into German, and biblical commentator, is generally considered the first Jewish philosopher of the modern period. Born in Dessau, where he was trained in traditional Jewish learning, he came to Berlin in 1743 and there acquired, through private study, knowledge of classical and modern languages, mathematics, and modern philosophy. His traditional training provided him with extensive familiarity with the medieval Jewish philosophers (whom he cites in his writings), and his modern training acquainted him with the thought of Locke, Leibniz, and Christian Wolff. As philosopher, Mendelssohn followed the pre-Kantian German Enlightenment, sharing with it the conviction that metaphysical knowledge is possible. He wrote on metaphysics, psychology, aesthetics, and also literary criticism. His main philosophical works were *Phaedon* (patterned after Plato's dialogue of the same name; 1767) and *Morgenstunden* (1785). In the former work he offered arguments for the immortality of the soul, and in the latter he discussed proofs for the existence of God.

Mendelssohn might never have presented his views on Judaism had it not been for the challenge of the Swiss theologian Johann Kaspar Lavater. In 1769 Lavater published his German translation of Charles Bonnet's *La Palingénésie philosophique* under the title *Untersuchung der Beweise fuer das Christenthum*, and in his introduction he challenged Mendelssohn to refute Bonnet's arguments or accept Christianity. Mendelssohn, who was not given to polemics, reluctantly accepted the challenge and in his reply professed his unshakable belief in Judaism and pointed out that Judaism tolerantly held that salvation is possible for all men, while Christianity limited salvation to its adherents. Mendelssohn presented his views on religion and Judaism more fully in his *Jerusalem* (1783), a work influenced by Spinoza's *Theologico-Political Treatise*. Like Spinoza, Mendelssohn (in the first part of the work) advocated the separation of state and church, holding that, while both contribute to human happiness, the state governs man's relation to his fellow man and the church man's relation to God. Ideally, the state should govern by educating its citizens, but practically it must compel them to obey the laws. The church should not possess secular power or own property and should promote its teachings only through instruction and admonition. Religion is a personal matter, and both state and church must guarantee freedom of conscience. In the second part of *Jerusalem*, Mendelssohn discusses the nature of religion and Judaism. Religion, for him, is the Enlightenment religion of reason which consists of rational and moral truths discoverable by all men. It is inconceivable to Mendelssohn that a benevolent God should restrict salvation to the adherents of a particular historical religion; salvation must be available to all men. Judaism, then, is not a revealed religion but revealed legislation. Insofar as it is a religion it is the religion of reason. However, whereas Spinoza had held that Jewish law had lost its validity with the cessation of the Jewish kingdom, Mendelssohn maintained that it was still binding for Jews; what has changed since the destruction of the Temple and the ancient Jewish state is only Jewish law's political enforceability, not its inherent divine authority. If there were to be changes, only a new revelation from God could make them. It is the purpose of Jewish law to preserve pure religious concepts free from idolatry, and it still fulfills this purpose in the modern world. It also serves to keep the Jewish community together. The Law compels man to action but also stimulates him to contemplation. Judaism consists of three parts: religious truths about God, His rule, and His providence, addressed to man's reason (but these are not presented as compelled beliefs); historical truths disclosing the purposes of the Jew's existence; and laws, precepts, commandments, and rules of conduct, the observance of which will bring happiness to individual Jews as well as to the Jewish community as a whole.

Kant, Schelling, Hegel

The two most important general philosophic influences on 19th- and (to some extent) 20th-century Jewish thought were the critical philosophy of *Kant and the idealistic philosophies of *Schelling and *Hegel. Kant was important for his denial of speculative metaphysics; for his sharp distinction between theoretical and practical (moral) philosophy; for making God, freedom, and immortality postulates of practical reason; for his account of duty, the categorical imperative, and the autonomy of the will; and for closely connecting ethics and religion. The idealist philosophers were important for affirming the spiritual nature of all reality and for their notion that history presents the progressive self-realization of spirit. Jewish philosophers used these philosophies in varying ways and combinations, holding that Judaism is the best embodiment of the religion of reason (Kant) or the religion of spirit (idealists).

Solomon Formstecher

Solomon *Formstecher (1808–1889), rabbi and leader of the Reform movement, developed his philosophy in *Die Religion des Geistes* (1841), a work combining idealist philosophy with a special concern for ethics. From Schelling he accepted the notion of a world soul which is manifest in the phenomena of nature; but, whereas for Schelling the world soul was bound to nature, Formstecher emphasized its transcendence and identified it with God. However, there is another manifestation of the world soul, and that is spirit, whose main characteristics are self-consciousness and freedom. When spirit becomes conscious of nature it produces physics; when it becomes conscious of itself it produces logic. There exists an ideal for spirit in each realm: aesthetic contemplation in nature; moral action in the realm of spirit. Corresponding to the two realms there are two forms of religion: the religion of nature, which considers the world as containing divine forces or which identifies nature with God; the religion of the spirit, which considers God as transcendent. There are also two corresponding goals for human life: for religion of nature it is to become one with God; for religion of the spirit it is to become like Him through moral actions. Historically, paganism embodied the religion of nature, Judaism, the religion of spirit. There exist two kinds of revelation: prehistoric revelation which consists of the ideal that spirit can attain, and historical revelation which is the gradual attainment of this ideal. Historical revelation occurs in natural religion as well as in the religion of the spirit; but in natural religion it comes to an end with the cognition of a God bound to nature, while in spiritual religion it tends toward the cognition of the transcendent God. The religion of the spirit is identical with absolute truth. (Formstecher does not succeed very well in harmonizing the idealist notion that man's final goal is understanding, with his emphasis on ethics.) The religion of the spirit is the religion of the Jews, but it had a historical development. Since Judaism developed in a pagan world, the religion of the spirit had to be the religion of a specific people. However, as Judaism progressed from objectivity to subjectivity (which consisted in the spirit's becoming more and more conscious of itself), it gained greater universalism. This occurred at first through the destruction of Jewish national life. However, since the world was still hostile, Judaism had to maintain its identity, but now as a theocracy of law. Formstecher maintained that the process of becoming more and more universal was about to come to an end in the modern world which was marked by the emancipation of the Jews, and the absolute truth of spiritual religion was about to emerge.

But spiritual religion also had to penetrate natural religion, and this occurred through Christianity and Islam. Since Christianity addressed itself to the pagan world, it combined the religion of the spirit with the thought of paganism. The history of Christianity is the struggle between Jewish and pagan elements. As Christianity developed historically, it freed itself more and more from its pagan elements. Since Christianity, even in the modern world, has not completely freed itself from these accretions, there is still room for Judaism as a separate religion. However, both religions strive toward the realization of the religion of the spirit. Judaism can prepare itself by stripping itself of its particularistic elements and its ceremonial law.

Samuel Hirsch

Samuel *Hirsch (1815–1889), rabbi and Reform leader, presented his views in *Die Religionsphilosophie der Juden* (1842), a work influenced by Hegel. Hirsch considered it the task of philosophy to transform the content of religious consciousness into the content of spirit (mind), and for him religious and philosophic truth are identical. Central to Hirsch's thought is the notion of freedom. Man, by understanding himself as an "I" standing over against nature, becomes aware of his freedom. However, this freedom is abstract and must be given content. One such content is natural freedom, his ability to do whatever he desires. Hegel held that abstract and natural freedom were in conflict and that this conflict was ingrained in man. Not so Hirsch. He tried to preserve abstract freedom for man by holding that alternate courses of action are open to him. Man may sacrifice his freedom to nature, or he may control nature by means of his freedom. These courses of action have as their concomitants two kinds of awareness of God. According to both, God is the giver of freedom, but according to the first view nature becomes the divine principle; according to the second view God transcends nature. Understanding nature as divine produces paganism; understanding God as transcendental produces Judaism. Hirsch now analyzes the history of religion in a manner reminiscent of Formstecher. But whereas for Formstecher, paganism, being the partial recognition of spirit, has some redeeming features, for Hirsch, it does not. Whatever development paganism has, it is only to show its nothingness. Judaism also had a development, but only because it originated in a pagan world (Abraham lived in that world); but once it had become free by recognizing that the true nature of religion is moral freedom, no further development was necessary. In early times Judaism required prophecy and miracles to show that God is master of nature; but once the threat of paganism had passed these were no longer necessary. The only miracle still apparent is the continuous existence of the Jewish people. There is, however, a kind of development in Judaism, for once one has discovered the truth of ethical freedom for oneself one wants to spread it to others. This Judaism attains, not by missionizing but by bearing witness to its faith. There existed, however, a tendency to bring Jewish beliefs to the pagan world in an active fashion, and Jesus made this his task. Jesus still moved within the world of Judaism, but a break came with Paul. When Paul formulated a doctrine of original sin and redemption through Jesus, Christianity severed its ties with Judaism. Only when the work of Paul is undone will Christianity be able to fulfill its true mission. When Christianity reaches that stage it will be essentially identical with Judaism. However, even in messianic times, when Israel will become one with all mankind, it will retain a structure of its own.

Nachman Krochmal

Nachman *Krochmal (1785–1840), a representative of the East European Haskalah, presented his philosophy in his posthumously published (1851) Hebrew work *Moreh Nevukhei ha-Zeman* ("Guide of the Perplexed of the Time"). In this work Krochmal does not present his views in any great detail, and a good portion of the work is devoted to an analysis of Jewish history and literature, but his thought may be gathered from the introductory chapters (1–8) and from his discussion of the philosophy of Abraham ibn Ezra (ch. 17). Krochmal was influenced by German idealism, but scholars have debated whether the primary influence was Hegel or Schelling. He differed from Formstecher and Hirsch by emphasizing the speculative rather than the ethical content of religion, and he also differed from them in not accepting the distinction between nature and spirit, and between the religion of nature and the religion of spirit. For Krochmal all religions are concerned with the self-realization of human consciousness and all religions accept a belief in spiritual powers. Even the idolator does not worship the physical likeness but the spiritual power it represents. All religions are religions of the spirit and they differ only in degree. Yet there is a distinction between Judaism and other religions: Judaism is concerned with infinite "absolute spirit" (Krochmal's term is "the absolute spiritual"), while other religions are only concerned with finite spiritual powers. Krochmal affirms the identity of religious and philosophical truth, the only difference between them being that religion presents this truth in the form of representation, while philosophy presents it in conceptual form. There is, however, a distinction between Judaism and the other religions: Judaism had an awareness of absolute spirit from its beginnings, while the other religions were only aware of partial spiritual powers. Judaism underwent development; but this development was only a progression from a representational understanding of the absolute spirit to a conceptual understanding of it. The world for Krochmal is a world of spirit, and even inanimate nature is only a concretization of spirit. Since all existence is spirit, and since true existence can only belong to absolute spirit, i.e., God, the world is said to exist in God. This gives a decidedly pantheistic complexion to Krochmal's thought. He mitigates it somewhat by affirming that the world is descended (emanated) from God. This descent is the true meaning of the biblical account of creation. God creates the world by limiting Himself, thereby separating Himself from the world; nevertheless, His being, as has been noted, still permeates the world. The act of divine self-limitation appears to be a spontaneous act. Krochmal also interprets prophecy within the framework of his thought. Prophecy is the connecting of the human spirit with the divine and it can exist in all men; those in whom the connection exists strongly become prophets in actuality. The prophets also have the ability to predict the future, but they can only predict the future close to their own time. Thus Krochmal denies that the second part of Isaiah was written by the same prophet as the first; the author of the first was too far removed in time from the events described in the second part. He also professes a belief in miracles in the sense of direct divine intervention, but how this can be reconciled with the rest of his philosophy is not too clear.

Corresponding to his general philosophy, Krochmal also develops a philosophy of history. Each of the historical nations is subject to a spiritual power which determines its history and its culture. The gods in which each nation believes are an embodiment of this spiritual principle. Each nation undergoes a three-stage development: growth, maturity, and decline. Decline sets in when desire for luxury and power increases. Once a nation has declined, it ceases to exist and another nation comes to the fore. The accomplishments of the nation which has ceased to exist are often absorbed by the nation which takes its place (for example, the accomplishments of Greece by Rome); however, the Jewish nation manifests the triad – growth, maturity, and decline – it is the eternal people, exempt from extinction. Once a triadic period has come to an end a new one begins. Israel is exempt from the fate of other nations, because it had a belief in absolute spirit from the beginning. This belief makes Israel the teacher of all mankind and this is Israel's mission in the world. The spirit of the Jewish people flows from absolute spirit, and it is said that God dwells in Israel and that God's spirit rests on Israel. Krochmal divides Jewish history into four periods: the first extended from the period of the Patriarchs to the Babylonian Exile; the second from the Babylonian Exile to the revolt of Bar Kokhba; the third, which is not too clearly described, ended in the 17th century; and the fourth cycle was still going on in Krochmal's time.

S.D. Luzzatto

While Formstecher, Hirsch, and Krochmal attempted to harmonize idealism and Judaism, Samuel David *Luzzatto (1800–1865), translator of the Bible into Italian and biblical commentator, was an outright opponent of philosophic speculation. He agreed with Mendelssohn that Judaism possesses no dogmas, but, unlike Mendelssohn, he affirmed that moral action leading to righteousness is the purpose of all (even the ritual) commandments. While he does not hold that Judaism lacks beliefs altogether, he considers it the function of religious beliefs to induce moral actions. It is conceivable to him that some religious beliefs may be false. Ethical activity, according to Luzzatto, springs from the feelings of honor and pity. In his *Yesodei ha-Torah* ("Foundations of the Torah," published posthumously in 1880) he enumerates three principles of Judaism: the feeling of pity, reward and punishment, and the election of Israel. The first of these is the basic principle; the other two have only an auxiliary function. A belief in reward and punishment is necessary because without it man would be governed by the evil part of his nature; the election of Israel is important for motivating Jews to ever higher ethical practices. Luzzatto distinguishes between Judaism, which aspires to moral action, and "Atticism," which has understanding as its goal. He maintains that cognition of God lies beyond the capacities of man, but he also holds that the existence of God can be demonstrated philosophically.

S.L. Steinheim

Solomon Ludwig *Steinheim (1789–1866), physician, poet, and philosopher, was also an outright opponent of philosophic rationalism. In his *Offenbarung nach dem Lehrbegriff der Synagogue* (4 vols., 1835–65) he defended the thesis that religious truth is only given through revelation. This meant to him not only that reason is inferior to revelation, but that when reason examines the contradictions contained within its content, it must recognize its own insufficiency. Revelation is not the product of human consciousness but comes from without, from God. (Steinheim does not deny that religion possesses cognitive content; but this content can only come through revelation, not through rational processes.) The truth of revelation is not confirmed by external signs but by reason, which clearly recognizes the superiority of revelation, and also that revelation meets human needs better than philosophy. Philosophy differs from religion in that philosophy conceives of all reality in terms of necessity, while religion understands it in terms of freedom. Corresponding to these approaches are two kinds of religion: natural religion which conceives of God as subject to the necessity of His own nature and as dependent on the matter on which he acts; revealed religion which understands God as the Creator Who, unbounded by necessity, creates the world freely and out of nothing. Creation, according to Steinheim, is the first principle of revelation; other principles are freedom, immortality of the soul, and (very likely) the unity of God. Steinheim applies the two conceptions of religion to the historical religions: paganism is the embodiment of natural (philosophical) religion; Judaism is the embodiment of revealed religion; and Christianity is a mixture of the two. As revealed religion, Judaism emphasizes, besides the cognitive principles mentioned before, human freedom and moral activity. Hence in his conclusions concerning the content of the Jewish religion, Steinheim differs little from Formstecher and Hirsch; but whereas the latter two philosophers saw Judaism grounded in reason, Steinheim sees it grounded in revelation.

Moritz Lazarus

Moritz *Lazarus (1824–1903), writer on psychology and philosophy, devoted *Die Ethik des Judentums* (*The Ethics of Judaism*; vol. I, 1898; vol. II, published posthumously, 1911) to the philosophic interpretation of Jewish ethics. The avowed purpose of the work is to use philosophy to give a structured account of Jewish ethics; but he also uses philosophic concepts to analyze its content. He derives his main notions from Kant, but he gives these notions a psychological interpretation. From Kant, Lazarus accepts the notion of the autonomy of ethics, but to Lazarus this only meant that the sphere of ethics is independent. Whereas for Kant the autonomy of ethics further implied that ethics is independent of the emotions, Lazarus maintained that ethics is grounded in the emotions of duty and obligation. Religious ethics differs from philosophical ethics in that it recognizes God as the author of ethical imperatives. However, if ethical imperatives are given by God, ethics is no longer autonomous but heteronomous. Lazarus tries to solve this difficulty by stating that God is also subject to ethical imperatives. What God commands is right, but not because He commands it: rather He commands it because it is right. Judaism is essentially religious ethics, and even the ritual commandments have an ethical purpose. Jewish ethics are ethics for the individual, but even more for society. Lazarus also interprets the idea of holiness. God is holy, not because He is mysterious or remote but because he represents moral perfection. Man becomes holy through ever increasing moral activity.

Hermann Cohen

Hermann *Cohen (1842–1918), founder of the Marburg school of neo-Kantianism, presented his views on religion in *Der Begriff der Religion im System der Philosophie* (1915) and his views on Judaism in *Die Religion der Vernunft aus den Quellen des Judentums* (published posthumously in 1919). While, in accordance with the development of his thought, Cohen's works on religion and Judaism were written only after he had retired from the University of Marburg (where from 1873–1912 he had a distinguished career) and had moved to Berlin (1912), he had strong Jewish loyalties throughout his life. As the title of Cohen's last work shows, he considered Judaism as the religion of reason, that is, in the Kantian sense, of practical reason; but, as will be seen, he tried to introduce into this conception the more personal aspects of the religious life. During the Marburg years Cohen wrote works commenting on the philosophy of Kant and also systematic works of his own. In his views on ethics, he followed Kant in holding that ethics is only concerned with the general category of man as a moral being, not with individual man in his singularity. In Cohen's Marburg system there is no room for religion as an independent sphere; it is merely a primitive form of ethics which will disappear once ethics has developed sufficiently. While Cohen always maintained that Judaism should preserve its religious identity, during the early years at Marburg he found little difference between it and liberal Protestantism. While Cohen left no special place for religion in his early thought, he did speak of God. God, for him, is not a metaphysical substance but an idea bridging the gap between morality and nature. Man's moral reason tells him that his ethical task is unending, but he has no guarantee that nature is eternal, so that he can fulfill this task. The idea of God provides this guarantee. Cohen is well aware that this conception of God has little to do with the scriptural notion of a personal God, but he praises the Hebrew prophets for contributing to the progress of mankind through their non-mythological conception of God, through their concern for ethics, and through their belief in the coming of the Messiah, which for Cohen is the symbol for mankind's advance toward ever greater moral perfection. Cohen conceived of ethics more as social ethics than personal ethics.

Cohen's conception of religion underwent a marked change. Whereas in his previous writings he had denied the independence of religion, in his *Begriff der Religion* he assigns to religion a separate domain. Ethics only knows humanity (moral man), but it does not know individual man. Yet the individual's feeling of sin and guilt possesses a reality of its own, and this feeling must be removed, so that man may recapture his moral freedom. Religion accomplishes this task by teaching that man can free himself from sin through remorse and repentance and by fostering a belief in a merciful God who is ready to forgive. Cohen emphasizes that atonement is gained through human efforts and not, as in Christianity, through an act of grace on the part of God. He praises the latter prophets, primarily Ezekiel, for having formulated these religious truths. Cohen's conception of God underwent a change as well. Whereas in his early thought he had described God as an idea, he now identifies God as being. In fact only God is being; the finite changing world standing over against Him, is becoming. Though being and becoming, God and the world, always remain distinct, there exists between them a relation, described by Cohen as "correlation." The world cannot exist without God; but God also has no meaning without the world. Cohen considers God as the origin of the world and man, and he uses this thought to explain creation and revelation. Creation refers to the dependence of the world on God (Cohen does not conceive of creation in temporal terms); and revelation refers to the dependence of the human mind on God. (Redemption refers, as has already been seen, to mankind's progress toward the ethical ideal.) Cohen's notion of "correlation" is well illustrated by his understanding of the "holy spirit." He rejects the Christian belief that the holy spirit is a separate substance, describing it instead as a relation between man and God. God's holiness is the model for human action, and man becomes holy by imitating God. "Correlation" is also illustrated by the saying that man is God's partner in the work of creation. In his final work Cohen applies all these distinctions to an interpretation of Jewish beliefs and practices which combines a concern for ethics and the unity of God (ethical monotheism) with the more personal elements of religion which have been described.

Franz Rosenzweig

The first half of the 20th century saw the emergence of Jewish *existentialism, whose major proponents were Buber and Rosenzweig. Franz *Rosenzweig (1886–1929) studied the philosophy of Hegel as part of his university education, and his doctoral dissertation was a substantial scholarly work entitled *Hegel und der Staat* ("Hegel and the State"). However, even during his student days Rosenzweig became dissatisfied with the rationalism of Hegel and looked for the meaning of life in the existence of the concrete individual and in religious faith. He contemplated converting to Christianity, but resolved to remain a Jew (1913) and embarked upon the intensive study of Jewish sources which he continued throughout his life. (During the year that followed he came under the influence of Hermann Cohen.) During the first World War he fought in the German army, and during those years he sent his philosophic reflections home on postcards to his mother. These became the basis for his major work *Der Stern der Erloesung* (1921; *The Star of Redemption*, 1971). In 1921 he was struck by a disabling disease, but he continued a creative life until his death. Rosenzweig formulated his philosophy in opposition to Hegelian rationalism. According to Hegel thought preceded being, and humanity was more important than the individual man. By contrast Rosenzweig maintained that being (existence) was primary, and that the concrete individual was of supreme importance. He advocated a "new thinking" which, standing between theology and philosophy, began, not with abstract concepts, but with the suffering, anxiety, and the longing of the individual man. Philosophy, Rosenzweig states, had claimed to still man's fear of death; but death is still real and man is still afraid. Philosophy up to Hegel, according to Rosenzweig, had attempted to describe the world as a unitary whole, trying to show that the three elements given in human experience – God, the world, and man – share one essence. The various periods of philosophy differed in that ancient philosophy derived God and man from the world, medieval philosophy, the world and man from God, and modern philosophy, God and the world from man. All these attempts to unify the world, according to Rosenzweig, have failed, and the three elements of experience remain distinct. But while none of these elements is reducible to one of the others, reflection discloses that they stand in relation. God's relation to the world is creation, God's relation to man is revelation, and man's relation to the world is redemption. In creation, which for Rosenzweig is not a unique but an ongoing event, God shows that He is not a hidden God; in revelation He shows His love for man, which, in turn, leads man to a love of his fellowman; and man's love for his fellow leads to the redemption of the world. While Rosenzweig thought of redemption as occurring at the end of time, he also held that redemption may be experienced in the here and now. The three elements of experience, which so far have been discussed without reference to the historical religions, also provide the substance of these religions. In paganism God, man, and the world remain distinct, but in the scriptural religions they stand in relation. When speaking of the scriptural religions, Rosenzweig has in mind Judaism and Christianity, both of which are in his view valid. They differ, however, in that Judaism is conceived as the "eternal life," Christianity as the "eternal way." The Christian is born a pagan, who, through baptism, becomes a Christian. He is joined to other Christians through a common faith and he must go out to convert the world to his belief. The Jew is born a Jew, and it is his task to lead the "eternal life" of his people. Whereas the Christian is immersed in history, the Jew is beyond it. At present, Judaism and Christianity possess only partial truth, but God's full truth will be revealed at the end of time. While the relation between God and man is marked by love, for the Jew this relation is also governed by law. Rosenzweig advocates that the Jew must study the traditional body of law with seriousness and respect, but he does not demand blind obedience to it. He upholds the right of the individual to decide which laws to obey, maintaining that each Jew must appropriate of the Law whatever he can; however, his criterion should not be ease of life. (It is interesting to note that throughout his life Rosenzweig observed more and more of traditional Jewish law.)

Martin Buber

Martin *Buber (1878–1965) is perhaps best known for his philosophy of dialogue, a form of existentialism. In formulating his philosophic views he drew on his extensive knowledge of the Bible, Ḥasidism, and comparative religion, and he applies his philosophic findings to contemporary social and political issues. His dialogical philosophy is described in his *Ich und Du* (1923; *I and Thou*, 1937). Buber begins by holding that man has two attitudes toward the world, and these two attitudes are determined by two "primary words" – I-Thou and I-It, which refer to relations, not to their component parts. An I-Thou relation is one between two subjects (persons) and is marked by reciprocity and mutuality. An I-It relation is one between a subject (person) and an object (thing) and is one in which the subject dominates and uses the object. Buber also envisages that there can be I-Thou relations between men and animals and even inanimate beings; while I-Thou relations between men often deteriorate into relations of I-It. In fact, Buber considers human life dynamic: I-Thou relations deteriorate into I-It relations, and a new effort is required to make them I-Thou relations once more. Buber also evaluates critically much of modern social and economic life; for in the modern world human relations have often sunk to the level of I-It. While human I-Thou relations cannot be sustained continually, there is one I-Thou relation that suffers no deterioration: it is the relation between man and the Eternal Thou, God. Buber does not attempt to demonstrate by philosophic proof that there is an Eternal Thou, for the Eternal Thou can only be recognized by one who is sensitive to it. God, the Eternal Thou, is not hidden but is present in every dialogic situation and speaks through it; He is not encountered in supernatural occurrences but in the events of everyday life. Buber finds this view of the Eternal Thou in Ḥasidism. The dialogue between man and God is not accomplished in isolation from life, but is best attained in the life of a community. To establish a community is a central Jewish task. Judaism is to be the community within which God dwells and it is to be the bearer of the kingdom of God. Buber's dialogic stance can also be seen in his account of revelation. He rejects the traditionalist view according to which the biblical account of revelation is literally true; but he also rejects the critical view according to which it is only symbolic. Revelation contains both history and symbol; it is the record of the meaning that the historical event had to the one experiencing and reporting it. Perhaps one of the most problematic parts of Buber's thought is his attitude toward Jewish law, on which he exchanged letters with Rosenzweig. As has been seen, Rosenzweig requires the serious study of Jewish law and the appropriation of as much of it as possible. Buber sees no such necessity. Since man's existential response to any given situation is primary, he can refer to a particular commandment if it speaks to that situation; but in itself the commandment has no special claim. Buber also differs from Rosenzweig in his conception of Christianity. Whereas Rosenzweig considered Judaism and Christianity parallel, Buber cannot accept the Christian claim. That the Messiah should have come, as Christianity claims, is inconceivable to the Jew; just as the Jew's stubborn refusal to believe that the Messiah has already come is unintelligible to the Christians.

[Arthur Hyman]

Developments in the Late 20th Century

THE JEWISH PEOPLE. The focus of Jewish philosophy in the late 20th century was neither God nor the individual, but the Jewish people. A generation after the Holocaust and the proclamation of the State of Israel, Jewish thinkers – in the Diaspora and in Israel – are urgently inquiring into the meaning and purpose of Jewish peoplehood.

TWO DIASPORA THINKERS. In North America Emil *Fackenheim published a bold programmatic work, *Encounters Between Judaism and Modern Philosophy: a Preface to Future Jewish Thought* (1973). In it he charges that modern Western philosophy – in its British empiricist, Kantian, Hegelian, and existentialist traditions – has, despite its aim of universality and impartiality, been prejudiced in favor of Christianity and against Judaism. To liberate Judaism from such Christian prejudices, Fackenheim stages a series of merciless encounters between Judaism and modern philosophy. The result of these encounters is not only a critique of modern Western philosophy, but an indictment of modern Western civilization. Fackenheim vigorously turns the tables on modern Western civilization, which had assumed that it could fairly judge Judaism. "Ever since the Nazi Holocaust," he declares, "it is Western civilization that is on trial" (p. 5).

Fackenheim argues, among other things, that modern Western philosophy has generally failed to recognize that Judaism, unlike Christianity, is a religion not of individuals but of a people, and that unlike Christianity its driving eschatological hope is not the salvation of souls in the hereafter but the Messianic redemption in history. The faith of the Jewish people, he emphasizes, has its stake in history.

It is precisely on the grounds of history that Fackenheim launches his frontal attack on modern Western philosophy. He contends that modern Western philosophy, with its notions of "enlightenment" and "progress," has been unable to come to terms with modern history: it has been wholly unable to comprehend the radical evil of Nazism. Even Hegel, "the greatest modern Christian philosopher" (p. 81), left no room in his description of the modern world for the appearance of radical anti-Spirit (p. 157).

Judaism, however, with its biblical and rabbinic categories, can recognize Nazism for what it is: idolatry, the idolatry of *Volk* and *Führer*, "the most horrendous idolatry of modern time and, perhaps, of all times" (p. 175). Citing the rabbinic dictum, "one who repudiates idolatry is as though he were faithful to the whole Torah," Fackenheim describes Judaism as the "uncompromising opposition to idolatry" (pp. 173, 189). It follows for him that the radical manifestation of idolatry in Nazi Europe demands one clear Jewish response: a radical commitment to remain a Jew, which constitutes a witness against modern idolatry. According to Fackenheim, such a post-Holocaust commitment to remain a Jew, whether "secular" or "religious" demands a *secular* self-reliance in the face of God's inaction and silence, but it also demands a *religious* hope, if not in the traditionally awaited Messianic redemption, then at least in a future in which no second Holocaust will occur. The faith of the Jewish people thus continues to have its stake in history. Fackenheim further argues that the "commingling of religiosity and secularity" today characterizes not only the individual Jew, but also the State of Israel, which is "collectively what the survivor is individually" (p. 167).

In a number of passionate lectures and essays, Fackenheim elaborated on his conviction that the Jewish response commanded by the Holocaust is the *commitment of the Jewish people to life*, a commitment whose chief expression is the existence of the State of Israel, and whose theme is "I shall not die but live, and declare the works of God" (Ps. 118:17). (See "Israel and the Diaspora *or* The Shofar of Rabbi Yitzchak Finkler of Piotrkov," *The Yaacov Herzog Memorial Lecture*, McGill University, Montreal, 1974.)

In France, Emmanuel *Lévinas published a revised edition of his *Difficile Liberté* (1976). This second edition contains several new essays and omits some dated material. Lévinas' discussion of the place of Judaism in contemporary society is similarly connected with a severe judgment on modern western civilization. He speaks of "a crisis of humanism" in the West brought on by the inhuman events of our century. Post-Hitlerian man, in his desire for autonomy, has indiscriminately sought liberty everywhere, until he has finally liberated himself from responsibility to others and has fallen into a lawless, egoistic anti-humanism. Judaism, by contrast, is the "extreme humanism of a God who demands much of man." This humanism of Judaism is founded on the biblical doctrine of "the irreducibility and the supremacy" of man, and on the difficult liberty "engraved on the Tablets of the Law" (see Avot 6:2). Judaism, Lévinas insists, is intransigently ethical and social. "Jewish man [unlike Heidegger!] discovers man before he discovers landscapes…": he first encounters Being when he encounters the naked human *face* of the other (pp. 40, 45, 364–65). Understood so, Judaism represents a defiant challenge to contemporary anti-humanism.

Lévinas's focus on ethics and society leads him to emphasize the significance of Jewish peoplehood. Judaism, he explains, does not mean a spiritualized or interiorized "humanism without nation" or "idealism without danger" (p. 288); rather, it is the destiny, the responsibility, the obligation of the Jewish people. The State of Israel, built out of the passion to recommence after all had been consumed, bears witness to the will of Jews to expose themselves to danger, and to sacrifice themselves, in order to confront their responsibility and obligation. "The Zionist dream – which issued from the most faithful, the most durable, and the most improbable of nostalgias – went back to the very sources of Revelation, and was an echo to the highest expectations" (p. 286).

Judaism, concedes Lévinas (p. 42), may today refer to a "culture" or even to a faint "sensibility," but he insists that in its foundation Judaism remains a religion, whose divine – and therefore humanistic! – Law, the Torah, is making supreme ethical and social demands, here and now on the individual Jew, on the Jewish people, and on the State of Israel.

FIVE ISRAELI THINKERS. In Israel, several thinkers emerged, addressing themselves mainly to questions concerning Jewish peoplehood in general, and Zionism in particular.

The book which caused the most controversy was Yeshayahu *Leibowitz' *Yahadut, Am Yehudi, u-Medinat Yisrael* ("Judaism, Jewish People, and The State of Israel," 1975), a collection of essays and topical lectures from 1943 to 1974. Leibowitz, whose approach to Judaism is heavily influenced by Maimonides, has argued consistently throughout the years that Judaism knows only one value: the service of God out of love, as expressed in the Torah and the commandments. It therefore follows, for him, that the Jewish state is not a value in itself. He even goes so far as to contend that "seeing the state as a value is the essence of the fascist conception" (pp. 181, 243, 270). To his mind, no state should ever be considered as more than an instrument. Similarly, he argues, the Jewish people should not be considered a value in itself. He thus freely criticizes "the sacred cow of national unity" (pp. 188,

273), noting that the Jewish religion – that is, the Torah and the commandments – has always divided the Jewish people (prophets vs. kings, pietists vs. Hellenists, Rabbinites vs. Karaites, religionists vs. secularists).

Zionism, as understood by Leibowitz, is a political, not a religious phenomenon. Its aim was to liberate the Jewish nation from the rule of the Gentiles and to achieve for it independence in its Land. This political aim having been spectacularly achieved, the only meaning today of Zionism lies in the strengthening of the bonds between the independent nucleus of the Jewish people and the majority of the people who still live dispersed among the nations (pp. 245–48). Zionism, according to Leibowitz, cannot be considered a religious phenomenon, since its adherents – many of whom were heretics or atheists – were not as a whole motivated by the intention of serving God. Religious significance, he stresses, presupposes intention, and thus cannot be assigned retroactively (p. 404). Denying religious significance to Zionism, he also denies Messianic meaning to the State of Israel. Time and again he quotes Maimonides' admonition (*Hilkhot Melakhim* 12:2) that one ought not to preoccupy himself with the rabbinic homilies concerning the Messiah since "they lead neither to fear [of God] nor to love [of Him]." He ferociously polemicizes against the "modern Sabbateanism" of those who turn religion into a means to justify nationalistic interests (e.g., the claim to all of Judea and Samaria), and for whom the "nation has become God, and the homeland Torah" (p. 271).

Yet, notwithstanding his denial of religious significance to Zionism and of Messianic significance to the State of Israel, Leibowitz declares that the renewal of Jewish independence in the Land of Israel has brought about a religious revolution. The religious significance of the Jewish state lies not in the political fact of its existence, but in the task with which it confronts and challenges the Jewish nation. He explains that in the Diaspora the Jews were not responsible for the political, social, and economic factors of the world in which they lived, and so the Torah did not have the opportunity to deal with the fundamentals of actual human existence. "Now – and only now, with the attainment of the independence of the Jewish nation – will Judaism be tested, as to whether indeed it has a 'Torah of life' in its hand" (p. 96).

For Leibowitz, therefore, the religious significance of the State of Israel lies in the fact that it provides a framework for the struggle on behalf of the Torah. It is the struggle, not the state, which has intrinsic value. "Certainly there is no guarantee ... that the struggle on behalf of the Torah within the framework of the state will be crowned with success, but even so we are not free to desist from it, for this struggle is itself a supreme religious value, independent of its results" (p. 208).

Detesting Messianic euphoria, Leibowitz teaches a hard-nosed political Zionism, and a heroic, infinitely demanding Judaism.

Another book which has roused wide discussion in Israel on the question of Jewish peoplehood and Zionism is *Devarim Bego* ("Explications and Implications," 1975), a potpourri of essays written over a span of more than half a century by Gershom G. *Scholem, the world-renowned expert in the history of Kabbalah and Jewish mysticism. Among these essays are not only erudite studies on various aspects of Jewish thought, but also recent original enquiries into the meaning of Judaism and Zionism. Some of the essays appeared also in an important English collection, *On Jews and Judaism in Crisis* (1976).

In "Israel and the Diaspora" (which appears in both volumes), Scholem asks whether Zionism ought to be seen as a rebellion against the previous life of the Jewish people, or as the historical continuation of that life. His answer is that though Zionism is both, its most important aspect is that of continuation. "We [Israelis] are first and foremost Jews, and we are Israelis as a manifestation of our Judaism." He calls for "a synthesis between tradition and the new values growing out of the reality of the Jewish people in Israel." As a corollary to his giving precedence to Jewish peoplehood over Israeli nationhood, he sees Israel and the Diaspora as "two partners," and he pleads for the building of bridges between them. The strongest bond today between them, he believes, is not tradition or religion, but the unfathomable trauma of the Holocaust. It follows that the "common denominator" of Israel and the Diaspora is education, which must create a living Judaism, the synthesis of tradition and reality.

In "Reflections on Jewish Theology" (also included in both books), Scholem explores what such a "synthesis" would mean. Traditional Judaism, as he sees it, unfolded in three stages: The Bible, the rabbinic tradition, and the Kabbalah. He pointedly does not include the philosophic tradition (e.g., Saadiah, Maimonides, Crescas, Mendelssohn) which he considers to be merely "apologetic." According to him, Judaism is characterized by "religious concepts" like Creation, Revelation, and Redemption, and by "moral concepts" like the love and fear of God, humility, and sanctity. These "moral concepts" underlie the commandments of the Torah and constitute religious ethics. Secularization conflicts not only with the "religious concepts" but also with the "moral concepts," the latter being based on – or at least related to – the former. For example, sanctity has no secular meaning, for it points to "a teleology of Creation."

The implication of Scholem's analysis is that the decision for or against secularism determines whether it is possible to retain the traditional "religious ethics" of Judaism. Moreover, according to him, it also determines whether the goal of Zionism should be for Jews to be "a nation like all the nations" or "a holy nation." Scholem's position is unequivocal; he decides for religion against secularism; he argues in favor of retaining the religious ethics; and he champions a Zionism whose goal is "a holy nation" (cf. *On Jews*, pp. 36, 55).

Scholem, to be sure, does not advocate any current Orthodoxy, nor does he believe that the "religious concepts" of Creation, Revelation, and Redemption – which must be given meaning if Jewish religious ethics is to be founded – can be sustained today on the basis of the Bible, the rabbinic tradition, or even the Kabbalah. However, he seems to suggest that a fourth stage of Judaism is possible. This stage would come about in Zion out of the dialectic between Judaism and the secularized world. Judging from hints in Sholem's' writings, this stage will be a new – previously unimaginable – kind of mysticism, which will be able to re-interpret audaciously the "religious concepts" for tomorrow even as the Kabbalah had audaciously reinterpreted them for yesterday.

Scholem's Zionism is revolutionary in its vision of a new kind of holy community in Zion, while it is conservative in that the religious ethics of that community will at root be those of traditional Judaism. His Zionism is, indeed, fundamentally the historical continuation of the previous life of the Jewish people, but it is still in a meaningful sense a rebellion against that life. In his works on the Kabbalah, Scholem has shown how the great Kabbalists conservatively maintained the traditional religious concepts while reinterpreting them with a radical novelty which bordered on heresy. What he has found to have happened in the Kabbalah, he hopes will happen once again in Zion.

If Leibowitz's discussion of the fateful national questions confronting Jews today is propelled and guided by a mighty religious vision derived from Maimonides, and if Scholem's is propelled and guided by one derived from the Kabbalah, Nathan *Rotenstreich's – in sharp contrast – is controlled by sobriety, cautiousness, and a determination to avoid one-sidedness or tendentiousness. An eminent Kantian scholar and for many years recognized as one of the most serious Zionist theorists, Rotenstreich – always a prolific writer – published in the 1970s three books on contemporary Jewish issues: *Al ha-Kiyyum ha-Yehudi ba-Zeman ha-Zeh* (*On Contemporary Jewish Existence*, 1972); *Iyyunim ba-Ẓiyyonut ba-Zeman ha-Zeh* (*Studies in Contemporary Zionism*, 1977); and *Iyyunim ba-Maḥashavah ha-Yehudit ba-Zeman ha-Zeh* (*Studies in Contemporary Jewish Thought*, 1978).

At the center of Rotenstreich's discussions is the desire to understand the relationship between Jewish tradition and present Jewish existence. In order to do this, he seeks in *On Contemporary Jewish Existence* to clarify just what is Jewish tradition. Defining "tradition" as the network of beliefs, ideas, and lifestyles which precede the man living in the present, Rotenstreich notes the danger that, the more man identifies with tradition, the more he denies independent meaning to his present. Modern secular Judaism, including Zionism, is according to Rotenstreich a reaction against the dominance of the religious tradition in the Jewish community: it is an attempt to free the present from the domineering religious past, and to assert the present as an active independent historical factor. However, he argues, this reaction was an overreaction, for the religious elements in the Jewish tradition cannot be wholly denied if one wishes fully to participate in Jewish culture. Indeed, according to Rotenstreich, merely speaking Hebrew and living in the Land of the Bible force the modern Israeli to confront the Jewish religious tradition. But what elements in this tradition are indispensable? What meaning can this tradition have today for would-be "secular" Jews in the Diaspora and, more especially, in Israel?

In his *Studies in Contemporary Jewish Thought*, Rotenstreich tries to throw light on these questions by examining the approaches of several modern Jewish thinkers, including such major Orthodox figures as Abraham Isaac Kook, Joseph Dov Soloveitchik, and Yeshayahu Leibowitz. Ultimately, Rotenstreich – like Scholem – speaks about a dialectic between the religious past and the secular present. However, the weight he gives to the religious past is not nearly as great as that given it by Scholem. Rotenstreich speaks about "a modest, not a total, Renaissance of Judaism" (p. 37). He calls for an examination of the traditional Jewish sources in order to determine what elements in them are "relevant" to present Jewish existence. Since the determination of relevance to present Jewish existence presupposes an understanding of that existence, Rotenstreich maintains that the task of modern Jewish philosophy cannot be only, as in the past, the interpretation of the Jewish sources, but also the interpretation of present Jewish existence.

This interpretation of present Jewish existence is the purpose of *Studies in Contemporary Zionism*. Directing his attention to the relationship between Israel and the Diaspora, Rotenstreich argues that the brute facts of contemporary Jewish existence in the 1970s render problematic the time-worn metaphor of Israel's "centrality." From the cultural point of view, he explains, it is not clear that Israel is the center of the Jewish world, and in any case it has not become the ideal "spiritual center" envisioned by Aḥad Ha-Am. More significantly, he argues, Diaspora Jews in liberal democratic societies like the United States, who enjoy freedom and material comfort, and who on the whole have no desire to leave their homes and to immigrate to Israel, have – especially since the Yom Kippur War – come more and more to see their relationship to Israel as being based on their support for their brethren in distress. These Jews, notes Rotenstreich, are identifying not with the State of Israel, but with the plight of the Jews in Israel. They are, in other words, increasingly coming to think that Israel needs the Diaspora as a support more than the Diaspora needs Israel as a cultural center. Instead of the unrealistic metaphor of centrality, Rotenstreich advocates that of the birthright; Israel's right to priority over the Diaspora is not dependent on whether or not it happens to be seen as the cultural center but on the unequivocal fact that it alone represents the great effort of Jews to reenter history as a collective. Rotenstreich contends that the metaphor of the birthright is closer to classical Herzlian Zionism than that of centrality, because it stresses the significance of national sovereignty. Immigration to Israel, he concludes, is to the advantage even of the free and prosperous Western Jews, "if they want to serve the historical existence, and to prefer the struggle for the place of the Jewish people in the world over their own everyday existence" (pp. 50–51).

No holds are barred in Rotenstreich's thought, and classical Zionism is forced to grapple both with the traditional Jewish past and the difficult Jewish present.

Leibowitz, Scholem, and Rotenstreich, born in Europe, had formed their basic ideas on Judaism and Zionism before they arrived in the Land of Israel. Eliezer Schweid, on the other hand, is a sabra, and he has given eloquent and thoughtful expression to the crisis in Jewish identity which is acutely experienced by many native-born Israelis.

Schweid, who taught Jewish philosophy for years at The Hebrew University of Jerusalem, published numerous essays and books, among them: *Le'umiut Yehudit* ("Jewish Nationalism," 1972); *Ha-Yehudi ha-Boded ve-ha-Yahadut* ("Judaism and the Solitary Jew," 1974); *Beyn Ortodoksiah le-Humanizm Dati* ("Orthodoxy and Religious Humanism," 1977); *Toledot ha-Maḥashavah ha-Yehudit ba-Et ha-Ḥadashah* ("A History of Jewish Thought in Modern Times: Nineteenth Century," 1977); and *Demokratiah ve-Halakhah* ("Democracy and Halakhah," 1978).

In *Judaism and the Solitary Jew*, Schweid describes the predicament of the modern Jew who – like most Israelis – has been given a secular education and is largely ignorant of traditional Judaism. A typical modern man, the modern Jew is at first happy to be an individual, an atom in and of himself. He seeks freedom from external limitations, from commitments to his family, to his nation, to his past, to his Jewishness. His atomism, however, is soon undermined by such existential questions such as, "How shall I educate my children?" He then realizes that his break with his Jewishness has caused him to be limited by a lack of cultural plenitude, which in turn limits his freedom, his creativity, and his self-respect. He realizes, in short, that in his striving to free himself from limitations, he has paradoxically been limiting himself!

It is, thus, the awareness of cultural deprivation which, according to Schweid, leads the modern Jew to reject individualism, and to seek out the Jewish community. He discovers, however, that there is today no one Jewish community, but many fragmented communities, none offering the cultural wealth he needs. Frustrated in his vital search for community, the modern Jew – no longer happy to be an individual – experiences dire alienation, and becomes "the solitary Jew."

In trying to recover his national identity, the modern solitary Jew, according to Schweid's analysis, finds himself in at least one respect in a better position than his modern solitary European counterpart. For his Jewish nationalism, like other ancient nationalisms, is rooted in religion, that is, it is essentially cultural and spiritual; while European nationalisms (having been deprived of their distinctive religious content by the supra-national medieval Church) are rooted in nothing but the state. However, just because it is essentially religious, Jewish nationalism poses a problem for the modern solitary Jew which European nationalism does not pose for the modern solitary European. The modern Jew seeks to embrace his Jewish national tradition, but finds it beyond reach, because it is a religious tradition, and he – as modern man – has no faith. The existential predicament of the modern solitary Jew thus turns into a problem of faith in God. Here, however, Schweid argues dramatically that the very decision of the solitary Jew to break out of his individualism and to affirm his familial, communal, and national commitments is already an expression of faith in God because it is an expression of faith in life in its totality, and the beginning and the end of all true faith is itself faith in God!

Having argued that religion is possible for the modern solitary Jew, Schweid now finds himself faced with the same question posed by Scholem and Rotenstreich: What is Judaism? His answer is: "Judaism is Scripture, Mishnah, Talmud, Midrash, medieval scriptural and rabbinic exegesis, the responsa literature, the philosophic and kabbalistic speculative literature, and even modern literature in all its genre, including the belletristic, to the extent that it is based on the previous sources and related to them"(p. 91). All these sources are, for Schweid, "Torah," and Judaism is, in one word, Torah.

It is a fact, however, contends Schweid, that the Torah and the national life have in modern times been tragically ripped asunder. To reunite them requires audacious innovation, no less audacious than the innovation of the Mishnah over against the Bible, or of the Gemara over against the Mishnah, or of the medieval speculative literature over against biblical and rabbinic literature. His call for an audacious revival of Judaism is thus similar to Scholem's (but without the kabbalistic bias), and in obvious contrast to Rotenstreich's measured call for "a modest renaissance."

But whence is this audacity to come? Orthodoxy, Schweid laments, has not been sufficiently open to the new life of the Jewish nation, and thus has been incapable of the audacity requisite for renewing the Torah. In an attempt to understand whether such audacity might be possible, Schweid has investigated the history of modern Orthodox thought. He believes that he has found an example of openness to modernity and *halakhic* audacity in Ḥayyim *Hirschensohn, whose views he analyzes in *Democracy and Halakhah*.

Schweid's thought, which begins with modern secular individualism and moves through secular nationalism toward a yet unrealized religious nationalism, poses a powerful challenge both to the Jewish secularist and to the Jewish religionist.

If Schweid raises questions of Judaism and Zionism from the point of view of a sabra, André Neher's *U-ve-khol Zot: Nevertheless* (1977) raises them from that of a recent immigrant. *Nevertheless* is the first Hebrew collection of essays published by the noted French-Jewish existentialist, who immigrated to Israel after the Six-Day War. It contains analyses of biblical and contemporary themes and reflections on his *aliyah*.

In France, he remarks, he had loved Jerusalem from afar, as one dreams of a distant fiancée, but now he has joyously consummated the marriage (p. 216). Having left the rich universal culture of France, Neher asks whether the move to Jerusalem might not cut him off from humanity as a whole and harness him to "the particularism of the solitary Jew" (p. 218). His reply, citing Judah Halevi, is that the Jewish people is the heart of universal human history, and Jerusalem the heart of the Jewish people. In Jerusalem, where God is worshipped by

Jews, Christians, and Muslims, the utopian, Messianic, universalistic vision of Isaiah is being realized every day: "My house shall be called a house of prayer for all peoples" (Isa. 56:7). The culture of France is a universal one, but that of Jerusalem is much more so!

Neher's discussions of contemporary Israel are permeated with a powerful consciousness of Jewish history and vocation. In immigrating to Israel, he chose to go up on the King's highway, "the highway of the God who acts in world history and in the history of the Jewish people" (p. 57). According to him, the Six-Day War – preceded by days of anxiety and concluded with victory – wrought a revolution in modern Jewish existence by uniting Jews and strengthening their ties to Judaism. Again, according to him, the Yom Kippur War – which began when Israel's enemies, after the old antisemitic pattern, struck on the holiest of Jewish days, and throughout which Israel stood in dreadful isolation, and which in all this recalled the horror of the Holocaust – painfully emphasized that the State of Israel must be seen in the perspective of "the metaphysics of Jewish history." However, the awareness that in Jewish history holiness has often been bound up with tragedy does not, for Neher, mean that hope should give way to fatalism. We, the builders of the Third Commonwealth, must, like our forefathers who built the Second Commonwealth, affirm "Nevertheless" (Neh. 10:1), and apply ourselves to our task in faith (p. 19).

Neher does not think that any good will come of the current attempts to find a definition of Jewishness. Judaism cannot be defined, because it points to the infinite. "I am a Jew not only in accordance with how I see myself. Nor only in accordance with how I am seen by others. I am a Jew in accordance with how I am seen by God!" (pp. 29, 45).

Common to the thought of Leibowitz, Scholem, Rotenstreich, Schweid, and Neher is the conviction that Israeli nationhood has meaning only within the framework of Jewish peoplehood. This conviction, moreover, seems to reflect popular feeling in Israel today. Israelis seem more and more to be defining themselves as "Jews first, Israelis second." The once fashionable slogan "I am an Israeli not a Jew" is rarely heard today. Israelis now generally see their future as tied not to that of their Arab neighbors but to that of Diaspora Jewry. The Aḥad Ha-Amian vision of Zionism as the evolutionary continuation of previous Jewish history and traditional Jewish values seems to have almost completely obscured the Berdyczewskian vision of Zionism as the revolutionary break with previous Jewish history, the transvaluation of Jewish values, and the creation of something radically new. Over the past half-dozen years, there hardly has been any serious effort to argue the primacy of Israeli nationhood over Jewish peoplehood. One notable exception is A.B. Yehoshua's essay, "A Return to Ideology" (*BiTefuẓot ha-Golah*, Winter 1975). Needless to add, the Canaanite movement of Yonatan Ratosh has today no appreciable following. It is not yet clear whether the growing assimilation of Israeli nationhood to Jewish peoplehood is to be understood as a negative or a positive phenomenon. It may, of course, be understood as a sign of Israeli insecurity and weakness, that is, as failure of nerve, whose etiology is in the trauma of the Holocaust, but which was aggravated by the awful days of isolation before the Six-Day War, and which was brought to a critical state by the shock of the Yom Kippur War. However, it may also be understood as a sign that the Jews in the Land of Israel, having achieved political independence, are now ready to recapture and to renew their ancient, sacred heritage.

JEWISH LAW – *HALAKHAH*. A second question which, after that of Jewish peoplehood, has occupied Jewish philosophers over the past half dozen years, is that of Jewish law, the *halakhah*. To some extent, the current interest of Jewish philosophers in the *halakhah* has itself grown out of their interest in Jewish peoplehood. Rotenstreich, for example, was led by his analysis of Jewish peoplehood to examine some problems concerning the *halakhah* in his *Studies in Contemporary Jewish Thought*, and Schweid was led by his analysis of Jewish peoplehood to write his *Democracy and Halakhah*. However, it would surely be an exaggeration to say that the current philosophic interest in the nature of the *halakhah* is entirely the product of a prior philosophic interest in the nature of Jewish peoplehood. In recent years, particularly in North America, there has been a growing interest among many Jews in the spiritual significance of the *halakhah*. This interest has manifested itself even in the Reform camp, where various attempts are now being made to create a "Reform *halakhah.*"

Recent philosophic discussion concerning the nature of the *halakhah* has been largely inspired by the work of Joseph B. Soloveitchik and Yeshayahu Leibowitz. Soloveitchik has sought to describe the *halakhah* as a conceptual system which, analogous to mathematical physics, is both related to the world and yet self-contained, and he has sought to describe the halakhist as autonomous, creative, and free (see e.g., Lawrence Kaplan, "The Religious Philosophy of Rabbi Joseph Soloveitchik," *Tradition*, vol. XIV, Fall 1973). Leibowitz has sought to distinguish the *halakhah* from other phenomena, particularly from ethics and secular civil law.

One stimulating contribution to the philosophic discussion of the *halakhah* is *Maimonides: Torah and Philosophic Quest* (1976), by David Hartman, a student of Soloveitchik, who served for 15 years as a rabbi in Montreal and then taught Jewish philosophy at The Hebrew University of Jerusalem, during which time he also founded and headed the Shalom Hartman Institute. His book, ostensibly about Maimonides, is better seen as a new Maimonidean attempt to recapture the spiritual sensitivity of the *halakhah*. According to Hartman's Maimonidean analysis, the *halakhah* is based on the universal human aspirations of the love and knowledge of God, and seeks to create a moral, historically conscious *community* in which these aspirations may be realized. The *halakhah* is thus seen as operating simultaneously on spiritual and political levels. Hartman believes that the philosophic analysis of the *halakhah* has particular significance in the light of the political renaissance of the Jewish people in the land of Israel and expresses the hope that his book "will encourage renewed discussion on the political implications of halakhic thought" (p. x). He has pursued the themes of *halakhah* and community in several essays (see, e.g., his "*Halakhah* as a Ground for Creating a Shared Spiritual Language," *Tradition*, vol. 16, Summer 1976).

However, philosophizing about *halakhah* has not been confined to its advocates. In his highly polemical *Teokratiah Yehudit* ("Jewish Theocracy," 1976), Gershon Weiler, professor of philosophy at Tel Aviv University, and a zealous secularist, argued that the *halakhah* is in irreconcilable opposition to the modern state, and that consequently the Jewish religion is subversive to the State of Israel. Not surprisingly, Weiler's book roused violent antagonism among religionists, who charged that Weiler, who has no formal training in rabbinics, should never have written a book about a subject of which he is flagrantly ignorant. Criticism of the book, unfortunately, became in the main a hunt for errors of fact, misunderstandings of texts, and other mistakes, and thus avoided confrontation with Weiler's main thesis. Yet it cannot be denied that *Jewish Theocracy* is – despite its author's intent – an invitation to renew discussion on the political implications of halakhic thought.

Recent philosophic interest in the *halakhah* has also been connected with new developments in the discipline of the philosophy of law, which in the past two decades has been given increasing attention, especially in Britain and America, but also on the continent. Several young Jewish philosophers, involved in the fruitful work going on in this discipline, have begun to apply its methodology to the study of the *halakhah*. They are raising questions concerning obligation, responsibility, rights, intention, freedom, justice, fairness, equity, and so on (see, e.g., Yehuda Melzer's essay and Yeshayahu Leibowitz's reply to it in *Iyyun*, 23 (Oct. 1975)). Mention should be made here of the excellent work being carried out in the clarification of legal concepts of the *halakhah* by Aharon Lichtenstein, an eminent disciple (and son-in-law) of Soloveitchik and head of the Har-Eẓion Yeshivah in Israel (see, e.g., his essay in Marvin Fox, ed., *Modern Jewish Ethics*, 1975). Yet the analysis of the *halakhah* in terms of the philosophy of law remains an almost virgin field. Perhaps it will have to be plowed before any progress can be made toward the audacious renaissance of Judaism called for by Scholem and Schweid, or maybe even before any progress can be made toward the "modest renaissance" called for by Rotenstreich.

MAN'S RELATIONSHIP WITH GOD. With Jewish philosophic activity focused primarily on the question of Jewish peoplehood and secondarily on that of Jewish law, the existential questions concerning man's relationship with God have during the past half-dozen years receded into the background. Yet it has been precisely these questions which until recently have most occupied 20th century Jewish philosophers, and which indeed have most enriched 20th-century Jewish philosophy. Ever since Martin Buber's early publications more than 70 years ago, modern Jewish philosophy has been in large measure under the dual influence of Ḥasidism and existentialism. One of the most popular and compelling of those Jewish philosophers to write under the influence of Ḥasidism and existentialism was Abraham Joshua *Heschel (1907–72). Himself a descendant of distinguished ḥasidic rabbis, Heschel developed an exciting philosophy of Judaism rooted in ḥasidic mysticism and Kierkegaardian existentialism. His writings ranged over Bible, rabbinics, medieval Jewish philosophy, Kabbalah, Ḥasidism, Yiddish culture, religious existentialism, and Zionism. Yet it may be that there is no more suitable introduction to his lifework than his two posthumous publications: *Kotzk: In Gerangl far Emesdikeit* ("Kotzk: The Struggle for Integrity," 1973), a two-volume study in Yiddish of the mysterious ḥasidic master, Rabbi Menahem Mendl of Kotzk, known as "the Kotzker"; and *A Passion for Truth* (1973), an English condensation of the Yiddish study. In these works, Heschel recalls the ḥasidic teachings which he had learned as a youth, and which underlie his mature thought. It seems proper to conclude this summary of the past half-dozen years of Jewish philosophy with a discussion of Heschel's portrait of the Kotzker.

Heschel speaks of a struggle which has raged within him since his youth between the Ba'al Shem Tov (c. 1690–1760), the founder of Ḥasidism, and the Kotzker (1787–1859). The Kotzker, he writes, was both the climax and the revolutionary antithesis of the ḥasidic movement (*A Passion*, p. 10). To Heschel, the Ba'al Shem Tov meant love, while the Kotzker meant truth. The Ba'al Shem Tov meant "emphasized love, joy, and compassion for this world," while the Kotzker "demanded constant tension and unmitigated militancy" and "insisted … that to get to the truth a man must go against himself and society" (pp. 10–11). The Ba'al Shem Tov "dwelled in my life like a lamp, while the Kotzker struck like lightning" (p. xv). The Kotzker reminded Heschel of the Prophets of Israel (pp. 10, 15, 307–10), or perhaps it would be more accurate to say that the example of the Kotzker taught Heschel how to appreciate the Prophets. The image of the Kotzker which arises from Heschel's study is similar to the image of the prophet which arises from his celebrated work, *The Prophets*. The Kotzker was "anti-social, shocking, an enemy to all established convention and propriety"; he sought "to jolt minds out of their complacency … to unsettle, to question accepted habits of thought"; he "held moral cowards in contempt"; he was ruthless in his demand for honesty and justice; he was disgusted by egoism and had no patience for those who sought in religion their own personal salvation; and he insisted that "man was created to exalt Heavens!" (pp. 263–67, 310–11), In *The Prophets*, Heschel had written of the phenomenon of "moral madness," and he reverts to this theme. He explains that the man of moral and religious sensitivity, who refuses to ignore the mendacity and cruelty of society, and who seeks to bring about radical social change, lives under unbearable tensions, and finds it impossible to be comfortable and happy while others are suffering and oppressed. Moral and religious sensitivity, argues Heschel, may thus cause madness, a madness which might be the only normal reaction to "the madness that has overtaken so-called normal society" (pp. 205–08, 313).

Heschel also compares the Kotzker with his contemporary, the Danish Christian existentialist Søren Kierkegaard. He observes that both took the concrete existence of individual man as the basis of their approach to reality; both gave the will predominance over the intellect; both "knew that faith constituted a demand rather than a consolation or comfort; both held that the goal and requirements of faith must not be adapted to the weakness of human nature, but that human nature must be raised to a level of greatness; and both contended that "the essence of religion is warfare … against spiritual inertia, indolence, callousness" (pp. 108, 120, 124–25, 183). Heschel also calls attention to differences between the Kotzker and Kierkegaard, and argues that these are mostly due to differences between Judaism and Christianity. For example, while both suffered intense agony, the Christian Kierkegaard's agony was rooted in a sense of guilt due to Original Sin, while the Jewish Kotzker – who, of course, did not accept the dogma of the Original Sin – was "plagued by a more radical agony, the awareness that God was ultimately responsible for the hideousness of human mendacity" (p. 256). Heschel seems here to be suggesting that the doctrine of Original Sin prevents the Christian from radically confronting existence, and thus true religious existentialism is impossible in Christianity, but possible in Judaism. Throughout all his writings, Heschel has presented a Judaism which teaches man to love life and to rejoice in the world, but which at the same time exposes him to existence in all its agony and sublimity. Judaism, for Heschel, is at one and the same time the Ba'al Shem Tov and the Kotzker.

A Passion for Truth, like Heschel's other English works, is written in an aphoristic, poetic style, whose easy readability contrasts with the difficult, sometimes frightful, thoughts it expresses. The two-volume Yiddish work is written in a beautiful Yiddish, rich in rabbinic Hebrew elements, and is an expression of Heschel's love for the language and his desire to contribute to its philosophic literature.

[Warren Zev Harvey (2nd ed.)]

WOMEN AND GENDER IN JEWISH PHILOSOPHY

Gender has not been considered relevant to Jewish philosophy, even though Jewish philosophers held strong beliefs about women and some philosophers employed "the feminine" as a central trope of their philosophy of Judaism. Under the impact of feminism, however, new attention has been paid to gendered language in Jewish philosophy, its hidden philosophical assumptions, and socio-cultural implications. The new research has documented the extent to which philosophy contributed to the negative perception of women, thereby adding to the marginalization of women in traditional Jewish society. In addition to exposing the gender inflection of Jewish philosophy, a few feminist Jewish philosophers have also proposed new approaches to *halakhah* that call for inclusion of women in the interpretative process and prescribe egalitarianism. Despite these innovative efforts, a systematic engagement of Jewish philosophy with feminist philosophy is still in its early stages, and only time will tell if feminist philosophy will enrich Jewish philosophy as an academic discipline and as a constructive endeavor.

Jewish Philosophy in Antiquity

Interestingly, gender stood at the foundation of the Jewish philosophical tradition, because in the Bible wisdom (*ḥokhmah*) was personified as a female. Feminine wisdom is the ideal which the male lover of wisdom seeks to obtain through the devotion to learning. Given the gender difference between the pursuer of wisdom and his goal, the pursuit of wisdom was couched in erotic terms and obtaining wisdom was expressed in metaphors of conjugal union. The feminization of wisdom reflected a certain social reality of patriarchy in ancient Israel as much as it prescribed certain social norms and attitudes. Because the pursuit of wisdom was perceived as masculine activity, in ancient Israel the learned elites of priests, scribes, and sages comprised men only.

The origins of the feminine portrayal of Wisdom cannot be determined with certainty. It is very possible that the Egyptian belief in Maat, the cosmic order of the universe which was identified with the goddess Isis, was the immediate source of Proverbs 8 and Ben Sira 24, because the cult of Maat/Isis was very popular in the Ptolemaic period during which the biblical canon received its final form. However, Ben Sira gave it a Jewish coloration when he equated Wisdom, who was with God at the creation of the world, with the Torah of the sacred tradition. In the Wisdom of Solomon, Lady Wisdom was depicted as a principle of order that "reaches mightily from one end of the earth to the other, and She orders all things well" (8:1). In a language that suggests familiarity with Neo-Pythagoreanism and Middle Platonism, the author turns wisdom into a hypostasis, an emanation of God's glory that acts as His agent in creation, pervading the entire cosmos while remaining intimately close to God (7:24; 8:1, 3). Wisdom is identical with the divine mind through which God acts (9:9) and contains the paradigmatic patterns of all things (9:8). In this sense, Wisdom is identical with divine providence over the created cosmos. Because Wisdom is personified as a female, the male lover of wisdom makes her his "bride" and "spouse," enjoying intimate kingship with her (8:9; 7:28; 8:16). Since Wisdom is an attribute of God, intimacy with her entails a mystical union with God. Earthly women, however, could either hamper the attainment of this lofty goal or assist it. Thus Proverbs 7:6–21 depicts the "strange woman" as a seductive female who steers the young student of wisdom away from the "straight path," while her antagonist, the "woman of virtue" (Pr. 31:10–31), represents the diligent woman with good managerial skills who frees her husband to study Torah and devote life to the pursuit of wisdom. These negative and positive stereotypes of women were perpetuated throughout the Jewish philosophical tradition in commentaries written on Proverbs during the Middle Ages.

*Philo of Alexandria (15 B.C.E.–ca. 50 C.E.) drew on Jewish Wisdom tradition while being immersed in Greek and Hellenistic philosophy. Philo was the first to offer a systematic allegorical interpretation of the Bible in light of Greek philosophy. With Philo began the allegorical reading of the creation narrative in Genesis whose inner meaning was understood in psychological categories: biblical "Adam" and "Eve" represent the powers of the human soul (*Allegorical Interpretation of Genesis*, II, 18.37; Sarah Pessin "Loss, Presence, and Gabirol's Desire: Medieval Jewish Philosophy and the Possibility of a Feminist Ground," in *Women and Gender in Jewish Philosophy* (2004), pp. 34–38). For Philo, "Adam" is a figurative expression of the rational part of the soul, whereas "Eve" represents sense perception that gives rise to the passion, hence she is referred to as "the mother of passion." The main passion, pleasure, is symbolized by the serpent (*naḥash*), who is the main obstacle for the pursuit of wisdom. For Philo both sense and passion are irrational aspects of the soul that must be subordinated to reason, whose activities are portrayed in masculine terms. As ruler, the reasoning aspect of the soul emerges as authoritarian and controlling, the "husband" and "father" who as lord of the household must keep the wife and children in line, namely Eve and her daughters, the passions.

According to Philo not only is the pursuit of wisdom the exclusive domain of men, reason itself is masculine in contrast to the feminine aspects of humanity, sensation and desire. These gender paradigms pertain not only to the powers of the human soul but also to society: reason belongs to the intellectual few, whereas the passions are associated with the vulgar masses. As much as the philosophical life necessitates the control of the (feminine) passions by (masculine) reason, so do the masses need to be controlled by the philosopher-ruler, because they are prone to fall under the sway of the passions. All hierarchical relations (in the individual, the society, and the cosmos) are expressed in gender categories where the ruler is always male and masculine traits constituted the ideal, and, conversely, the ruled is always female and feminine traits are viewed necessarily as short of the ideal. Despite these hierarchies, and almost against his will, Philo discusses an actual egalitarian community of Jewish contemplatives, the Therapeutae of Lake Mareotis in which women devoted themselves to the life of wisdom alongside men (*The Contemplative Life*, VIII: 68–69).

Medieval Jewish Philosophy

While Jewish philosophers in the Middle Ages did not have direct access to Philo's works, they perpetuated many of the themes and assumptions of his gendered metaphysics and anthropology. When Jewish philosophers reflected about the human species they referred to it by the universal 'Man,' taking for granted that the male of the species is the standard of the human species as a whole. The female of the human species was deemed to be less than the male on account of her defective rationality. Whether the perception of women as intellectual inferior was caused by the exclusion of women from Torah study in rabbinic Judaism, or rather by the influence of Greek and Hellenistic philosophy (for example, Aristotle in *Generation of Animals* I, 20:727a 15; II, 4:737a 25; *Politics* I, 13:1260a 12–14) cannot be easily determined. Nevertheless, even though medieval Jewish philosophers assumed that the philosophical life is for men only, their use of gender categories, "femininity" and "masculinity," was rather flexible. A given entity could be regarded as "feminine" in one context and as "masculine" in another, determined by its function: whatever was active was considered to be "masculine," while that which was passive, or being acted upon, was considered "feminine." This gendered metaphysics was presupposed by all medieval Jewish philosophers, whether they endorsed a Neoplatonic schema or an Aristotelian one.

In the Neoplatonic strand of Jewish philosophy gender configured in psychological theories. Since the seeker of wisdom was always male, it is no coincidence that the human soul of the male philosopher was always referred to as female. This gendered language was further exacerbated by the fact that in Hebrew all nouns referring to the soul (i.e., *nefesh*, *ruaḥ*, and *neshamah*) are feminine terms. Nonetheless, even though the human soul was always taken to be female, it could function in "masculine" or "feminine" ways: toward the body, the soul acts as a masculine power, ruling it and governing it so as to ensure proper behavior. By contrast, vis-à-vis the (masculine) God of Israel, the human soul in a "feminine" way when she receives the divine efflux by virtue of which one acquires knowledge and wisdom. Not surprisingly, Neoplatonic Jewish philosophers such as Moses *Ibn Ezra, *Solomon ibn *Gabirol, and *Judah Halevi, who developed systematic philosophical anthropology, also produced powerful religious poetry that expresses the yearning of the feminine soul to unite with God. However, in regard to corporeal women, Neoplatonic Jewish philosophers saw them *as a class* to be intellectually deficient. For example, *Bahya ibn Pakuda explains the revelation of the Law as follows: the revealed Law is necessary for the "education and management [of Man] to help him overcome his desires until he grows up and his mind strengthens. The same is true of women and the weak-minded among men, both of whom cannot be easily managed by the mind because its rule is impotent over them. They need a moderate rule, one they can bear without being impossible for them to grasp." (*Duties of the Heart*, ed. Menachem (1973), p. 187) For Baḥya, and Saadiah Gaon before him, all women are intellectually deficient and require divine revelation to make known truths that are beyond their limited intellectual competence.

In medieval Jewish Aristotelian philosophy the binary relationship between the active vs. passive principles was given a general abstract formulation in the metaphysics of matter and form. All existents are comprised of matter and form, where matter signifies that a thing is, namely its corporeality, and form signifies what a thing is, namely, its essence. By identifying form with male and matter with female, the Jewish

Aristotelians made gender categories more rigid, shaping an entire range of gender stereotypes. Matter was believed to be inherently unstable and unable to exist by itself without form, and in turn, form was said to give matter its identity. When this gendered metaphysics was applied to men and women, it lent support to the claim that men must rule over women and that marriage is the ideal institution for the social relations between the sexes.

*Maimonides was the first Jewish philosopher to apply this gendered metaphysics to Scriptural interpretation, beginning with the creation narrative of Genesis. Reading Scripture allegorically, Maimonides identifies "Adam" as the form of the human species, whereas "Eve" stands for matter. Prior to the sin of disobedience Adam was engaged in contemplation of truth, but the separation between matter and form in the sin entailed an epistemic shift to moral distinction between good and bad (Guide I, 2; I, 6; I, 17). "Eve," the material dimension of the first being represents the cause of the sin and, more broadly, the life governed by passions which is characteristic of ordinary human beings. In Guide II, 30 Maimonides elaborated on his philosophical anthropology identifying the imagination with femaleness. Reading the Genesis narrative in light of Genesis Rabbah 8:1 and Midrash Pirqey Eliezer 13, Maimonides suggests that the "serpent" is the appetitive power that was controlled by the imagination (represented in the Midrash as Samael), that tempted Eve (i.e., matter) to irrationally desire and even lust after the fruit of the forbidden Tree of Knowledge Good and Evil (Sarah Klein-Braslavy, *Maimonides' Interpretation of the Adam Stories* (1986), pp. 209–26). In Maimonides' interpretation of Genesis, when Eve was separated from Adam, the power of imagination was no longer controlled by reason. As a result, Adam shifted away from contemplation of truth to moral knowledge of good and bad, which is of lower epistemic level. The goal of human life, therefore, is to regain the form of the human species, which had been lost in the sin of disobedience, by perfecting the human intellect through the study of philosophy. The resulting intellectual perfection ensures entry into the "world-to-come," a cognitive state of contemplation.

While all human beings are born with the capacity to reason, which Maimonides identified with the "image of God" (Gen. 1:26), not all humans actualize that capacity. Those who do not cannot be considered fully human. On the intellectual capacity of women, however, Maimonides' left for posterity an ambiguous legacy. On the one hand, he states categorically that women possess a "feeble mind" (*Guide* III, 37) that makes them more prone to be governed by the emotions and desires, but, on the other hand, he included the prophetess Miriam among the very few who reached intellectual perfection (*Guide* III, 51). Maimonides was equally ambiguous on the question of women's education: on the one hand, he treats women as a group whose rationality, like that of children, is defective and excludes them from the performance of certain *mitzvot* (*Mishneh Torah*, Talmud Torah 1:1; Keriat Shema 4:1; Berakhot 5:6; Sukkah 6:1; Edut 9:1). But, on the other hand, he envisions a situation in which women study Torah and even teach Torah (Talmud Torah 1:13), even though they should not be compensated for it. Mainly Maimonides was concerned with women in the context of the institution of marriage whose primary purpose was reproduction. Within the marital institution, sex should be carefully regulated according to the strictures of *halakhah*, because sexuality and sensual pleasures in general are obstacles for the attainment of the ultimate end of human life, the contemplation of God (*Guide* III, 33). While sexual intercourse between husband and wife must be free of coercion, between husband and wife there is no equality: he must rule over her and the children, and she must strive to function as the ideal "woman of virtue."

In post-Maimonidean philosophy the association of women with matter, the belief that they are rationally inferior, and their exclusion from the study of philosophy were further accentuated, resulting in full blown misogyny. A typical example was Shem Tov ibn *Falaquera whose *Sefer ha Mevakesh* (The Book of the Seeker) used the trope of the young seeker of wisdom to introduce the reader to the various sciences, as well as to promote the values of the philosophical life. The characters in the novels stand for specific professions (e.g., merchant, soldier, artisan, physician, rabbi, or poet), and all of them are men. Similarly, the persons who represent various intellectual disciplines (e.g., ethics, grammar, poetry, arithmetic, geometry, optics, astronomy, music, logic, physics and metaphysics) are all men. Falaquera's allegorical tale accurately represents the social reality of his time: these professions were not practiced by women, who were largely excluded from the public spheres and from cultural pursuits. But Falaquera further contributes to the denigration of women by portraying them as the cause of men's sins and transgressions. Under the influence of ibn Bajja, Falaquera depicted the perfect man as a solitary philosopher who is estranged from society and who attains intellectual perfection because he subdues his appetites, controls his emotions, and lowers his human interaction to the necessary minimum. In his philosophical reflections on human perfection, *Sefer ha-Ma`alot*, and *Sefer Shelemut ha-Ma`asim*, Falaquera made clear that attainment of moral perfection does not constitute the ultimate end of human life (Raphael Jospe, "Rejecting Moral Virtue as the Ultimate Human End," in: *Studies in Islamic Judaism Traditions* (1986), pp. 185–204). Even if women attain such perfection, they are categorically excluded from the final perfection of the intellect.

The negative perception of women was further developed in the semi-philosophical literature written in rhymed prose for the amusement of men. Written in rhymed prose, the literary debate on the merits and demerits of women portrayed the woman as either totally beautiful or utterly ugly; perfectly virtuous, or vicious and hateful; loyal and nurturing wife or a licentious seductress, a facilitator of the pursuit of wisdom or an obstacle to it (Talyah Fishman, "A Medieval Parody of Misogyny: Judah ibn Shabetai's Minhat Yehuda Sone ha-Nashim," in: *Prooftexts* 8 (1988), 89–111). The grotesque depiction of women highlights negative traits such as greed, possessiveness, vanity, foolishness, fickleness, and untrustworthiness. Designed to produce comic relief, for which purpose it employed exaggerations and distortions, Hebrew rhymed prose treated the woman as the rejected Other, thereby expressing the fears, anxieties and aspiration of Jewish men in a Christian-dominated society. In Christian polemical literature of the Middle Ages, circumcised Jewish men were viewed as feminized aberrations of nature and were even said to menstruate (Joshua Trachetenberg, *The Devil and the Jews* (Philadelphia, 1941), pp. 50, 149). The feminization of a group was just one way of denigrating and invalidating it.

A similar dynamic operated during the *Maimonidean Controversy of the 13th century about the legitimacy of philosophy within traditional Jewish society. Especially during the last phase of the controversy (1303–06), when the question was no longer whether or not to study philosophy but rather how to define the appropriate relationship between traditional Jewish topics and the various branches of philosophy in the context of the Jewish curriculum (Gad Freudenthal, "Holiness and Defilement: The Ambivalent Perception of Philosophy by Its Opponents in the Early Fourteenth Century," in: *Micrologus*, 9 (2001) (= *The Jews and the Sciences*) (Florence, 2001), pp. 169–93). In a male-dominated society, where women were the ever-present "Other within," both sides of the controversy imaged philosophy as a "foreign woman," and both framed the relationship between Torah and philosophy in terms of power relations between a mistress and her female servant. Philosophy is commonly referred to as an "alien women" and the students of philosophy as the "children of alien women" (Abba Mari of Lunel, *Minhat Qenaot* (Pressburg, 1838)). It follows that a Jew who studies philosophy is like one who enters an illicit sexual union with a foreign woman. The offspring of this form of idolatry offspring must not be allowed to enter the community. The idolatrous nature of the study of philosophy is conveyed most forcefully by images taken from the prophecy of Hosea, in which Israel is likened to a disloyal licentious wife, who whores after other men and whose shame is exposed by the prophet "in front of her lovers" (Hos. 2:12). Studying philosophy is portrayed as a sexual sin as well as a sin of disobedience and betrayal of God. Less severe are the pronouncements that portray philosophy as Hagar, the boastful concubine of Sarah, who improperly challenged the lawful wife, Sarah, and was forced to flee from Sarah's justified wrath. In this imagery, there is nothing wrong with philosophy per se, but with the brazen character of the philosophers who challenge the proper hierarchy between philosophy and Torah.

The Maimonidean Controversy ended with a ban on the study of philosophy under the age of 25, but the study of philosophy continued unabated as philosophy became more technical. In the 14th century, gender categories continued to inform Jewish philosophy especially in biblical philosophical commentaries that followed the guidelines of Maimonides' hermeneutics. Commentaries on the Song of Songs (e.g., by Moses ibn *Tibbon, *Immanuel ben Solomon of Rome, and *Levi Ben Gershom) identified the female beloved not with the community of Israel but with the human soul. For Gersonides, for example, the Song of Songs was a philosophical parable about the pursuit of ultimate felicity that culminates in the knowledge of God (Menachem Kellner (ed. and trans.), *Commentary on Song of Songs: Levi ben Gershom (Gersonides)* (1998), pp. xv–xxxi). The biblical text is understood as two simultaneous dialogues: one between the human material intellect and the Active Intellect, and the other between the faculties of the soul and the material intellect. The two dialogues are connected: as the material intellect desires to conjoin with the Active Intellect it must enlist the aid of the other faculties of the soul in this quest. In these hierarchical relations, that which is superior ontologically or epistemologically is always masculine, and that which is inferior always feminine.

From the 13th to the 16th centuries Jewish philosophers (e.g., Zerahiah She'altiel *Gracian Hen, Judah *Romano, *Immanuel of Rome, Levi ben Gershom, *Shemariah ben Elijah of Crete, Benjamin ben Judah ben Joab of Rome, Isaac ben Moses *Arama, David *Ibn Yahya and others) perpetuated the dichotomy between the "strange woman" and the "woman of virtue" in their commentaries on Proverbs. Lady Wisdom was identified with theoretical wisdom, whose knowledge (by the male philosophers) led to the immortality of the soul; the perfect wife illustrated practical reasoning and the cultivation of moral virtues, necessary for the attainment of theoretical knowledge, and the "strange woman" symbolized the desires of the body and other material pursuits that hinder the lover of wisdom (Julia Schwartzmann, "Gender Concepts of Medieval Jewish Thinkers and the Book of Proverbs," in: *Jewish Studies Quarterly*, 7 (2000), 183–200). The philosophical commentaries on Proverbs perpetuated the view of women as intellectually imperfect and inferior to men and made normative the subordination of women to their husbands. A marked departure from this negative perception was Judah *Abrabanel's Italian best-seller, *Dialogi di amore*, in which the female protagonist, Sophia, engages in a philosophical dialogue with the male protagonist, Philo, acting as a teacher of wisdom. Abrabanel's positive portrayal of a female seeker of wisdom reflects both the conventions of Renaissance courtier literature as well as a new social reality in which patrician women had greater access to education in the liberal arts (Merry E. Wiesner, *Women and Gender in Early Modern Europe* (2000^2), 143–74).

Toward Modernity

Ironically, it was the very otherness of philosophy in traditional Jewish society that enabled a few Jewish women to study the liberal arts (in preparation for the study of philosophy) long before they were allowed to study halakhic texts. In Renaissance Italy, women of merchant-bankers families received such learning, and some of them functioned as patronesses of learning. To one such woman, Laura, the wife of Jehiel of Pisa, David ben Judah Messer *Leon composed his commentary on Proverbs, *Shevaḥ Nashim* (Praise of Women). After his forced departure from Naples in 1494 he asked her to provide for his livelihood in Constantinople. To make his plea effective, he praised her along with other illustrious women of Greek and Roman mythologies and Dante's beloved, Beatrice, and identified her with the industrious and generous Proverbial "woman of virtue" (Hava Tirosh-Rothschild, *Between Worlds: The Life and Thought of Rabbi David ben Judah Messer Leon* (1991), pp. 73–77). A more famous patroness of learning was ex-converso Doña Garcia *Nasi, who supported many educational institutions in the Ottoman Empire. In eulogizing her and other illustrious women, Moses Almosnino praised female learning and had no qualm asserting that the departed soul of these women will enter the "world-to-come" (*Me'amez Ko'aḥ*, Venice 1588). Contrary to Maimonides, for whom inclusion in the "world-to-come" was predicated solely on attainment of intellectual perfection, Almosnino posited the perfection of the will as a condition of religious perfection. Although women lacked formal philosophical training, they could experience religious perfection, because it was predicated not on the intellect but on the will and on acts of faith.

With the dawn of modernity and the Emancipation of the Jews in the 19th century, Jewish society and culture underwent profound transformation through processes of acculturation and assimilation. As Jews acquired the basic markers of the larger society such as language, dress, and values, they gradually dissolved their minority status through intermarriage or conversion (Paula E. Hyman, *Gender and Assimilation in Modern Jewish History: The Roles and Representations of Women* (1995). Modernity offered the Jewish female greater access to secular education, entry into the liberal professions and the sciences, and participation in political movements such as socialism and communism (Harriet Freidenreich, *Female, Jewish, Educated: The Lives of Central European University Women* (2002). While women in traditional Jewish society of Eastern Europe remained relatively uneducated, in western and central Europe daughters of assimilated Jewish families enrolled in the philosophy faculty of secular universities, and very few of them (e.g., Edith *Stein, Simone *Weil, and Hannah *Arendt) became professional philosophers. However, it is debatable whether these philosophically-trained Jewish women composed Jewish philosophy: Edith Stein and Simone Weil converted to Catholicism, and Hannah Arendt, who was committed to Zionism, was also deeply critical of traditional Judaism.

Arendt's case in particular illustrates the complexity of defining Jewish philosophy. On the one hand, she grew up in an assimilated Jewish home and had little knowledge of Judaism, but when she began her philosophical career she was concerned about "how to do [philosophy] if one is a Jewish woman." Defining herself as a political theorist rather than a philosopher, she regarded her Jewishness as a matter of ethnicity rather than religion. On the other hand, Arendt developed her distinctive method of doing philosophy through storytelling as a critique of western philosophy. Her biography of Rahel Levin *Varnhagen (1771–1809), a Jewish woman who converted to Christianity and held an intellectual salon in Berlin, was a deliberate attempt to philosophize in a new way (*Rahel Varnhagen: The Life of Jewess* (1957)). While Arendt did not produce a philosophy of Judaism, she was a Jewish philosopher. Yet, for most Jewish women in the first half of the 20th century, to be Jewish and educated in Jewish philosophy was a contradiction in terms. This was the case at least until Jewish Studies began to flourish as an academic discipline first in the State of Israel and later in North America. Several women (e.g., Sara Heller-Willensky, Rivkah Schatz-Uffenheimer, Rivkah Horwitz, Collette Sirat, and Edith Wyschogrod) helped establish Jewish philosophy as academic field, but, with the exception of Wyschogrod, they wrote history of Jewish philosophy rather than constructive philosophy.

Modern Jewish Philosophy

While Jewish philosophy remained the exclusive domain of men until the end of the 20th century, at least two of them – Franz Rosenzweig and Emmanuel Lévinas – made the category of "the feminine" central to their philosophical project. These philosophers were either closely associated with Martin Buber (i.e., Rosenzweig) or deeply influenced by Buber (i.e., Lévinas), and all three philosophers took for granted the bourgeois model of female domesticity which dominated Europe in the late 19th and early 20th centuries. Against this cult of domesticity it is not surprising to find that early 20th century Jewish philosophers use the category of "the feminine" in their analysis of Judaism and in their reflections on the human condition. More intriguingly, the three Jewish philosophers employed the category of "the feminine" as a Jewish critique of Western philosophy, which is both Christian and masculine. Buber, Rosenzweig, and Lévinas proposed a new approach to philosophy (*Das Neue Denken*), which challenged the universalizing and totalizing tendencies of western philosophy and offered an alternative, dialogical philosophy. In this regard, their philosophy parallels that of Hannah Arendt.

Buber's alternative was philosophy as an art of living a life of dialogue through an I-Thou relationship. The philosophy of dialogue rejects all forms of objectification, abstraction, or logical constructs, characteristic of traditional philosophy. By contrast, scientific knowledge, including metaphysical knowledge, is typified as an I-It relation, but it falls short of grasping reality because the Thou escapes rational inquiry. Since Buber's philosophy rejected objectification, his dialogical philosophy could not recognize gender differences. I-Thou relationship is not limited to men, and in fact it often occurs in heterosexual love relationship, although this relationship too reverts to I-It mode. In a philosophy of dialogue there is room for women as equal partners of dialogue, as persons who must never be objectified and treated as the means to an end. Socially speaking, the ideal arrangement is the egalitarian communities of the early kibbutzim in which men and women were (in theory at least) equal. Notwithstanding his egalitarian vision, Buber's language to describe relational self was carried out in androcentric terms: the "interhuman" was "between man and man" and the "I" in the I-Thou relations was always "a *man* who needs the other in order to be *himself*." Gender differences were subsumed under the category of "the human" expressed in masculine language.

Buber's colleague and co-translator of the Bible, Franz Rosenzweig, creatively built on medieval poetry of Judah Halevi, medieval commentaries of Song of Songs, and Western philosophy to articulate a novel philosophy of Judaism. In *Star of Redemption*, Part II, Book Two, Rosenzweig applied the category of "the feminine" to the Jewish people as a whole (Leora Batniztky, "Dependency and Vulnerability: Jewish and Feminist Existentialist Constructions of the Human," in: *Women and Gender in Jewish Philosophy*, pp. 127–52, esp. 138–42). The Jewish collectivity, like real women, has a special ontological share in revelation: as an eternal people the Jews have one task only, to worship God in prayer. Unlike other nations that are still moving toward the accomplishment of this goal, the Jewish People has already achieved it, because, like the "most feminine woman," they are naturally disposed to revelation. As much as a woman is a-priori ready for eternity (a view for which Rosenzweig can offer no empirical proof), so are the Jewish people a-priori eternal. In the case of both actual women and the actual Jewish People, the "natural" provides a kind of transcendental condition for the supernatural. As a woman embodies a natural openness to the supernatural realm of love, so the Jews embody in their blood God's revelation to them. Rosenzweig constructs Judaism as the feminized rootless Other that has contributed to the creation of Christian masculine culture. Batnitzky shows that for Rosenzweig, "Judaism is not just 'feminine,' but in remaining 'homeless,' she, namely, Judaism, makes Christianity and the nations of the world more 'feminine.' By not allowing Christianity to become totalitarian, Judaism forces Christianity to remain somewhat rootless and thereby more 'feminine', Jewish and ethical" (ibid, p. 142).

The category of "the feminine" is even more central in the philosophy of Lévinas, who was deeply indebted to Buber and Rosenzweig but attempted to go beyond them. For Lévinas the relation to the Other is irreducible to comprehension; it takes place in acts of speech, in a face-to-face relation with the Other. To learn to acknowledge what one cannot know and to respect the separateness of the other person is to acknowledge the transcendent of the other person. The task of ethics is the fundamental obligation to the Other. Lévinas's ethics is genderized because he identified the feminine with radical alterity. The feminine is presented as an exemplar or ideal figure of alterity; she is the Other *par excellence*. This claim means first that the feminine is not defined in terms of its opposition to the masculine; it has its own positive essence, and second that this positive essence is alterity. Lévinas did not sufficiently distinguish between these two meanings of alterity, but he definitely presented the alterity of the feminine as irreducible and absolute; it cannot be bridged or diminished; it cannot be negated or reduced. Lévinas defines the very mode of being of the feminine as "withdrawal into mystery" as "hiding" and "modesty" (*Time and the Other*, trans. Richard Cohen (1987), p. 87) The relation to the feminine is a relation with what "slips away from the light" with what escapes comprehension and understanding. The Other escapes knowledge or understanding because the recognition that the relation to the Other (a form of transcendence) is irreducible to comprehension.

Lévinas's celebration of the feminine has generated a lot of attention among feminist (mostly non-Jewish) philosophers, while also posing a challenge to feminists. Should feminists endorse it because Lévinas privileges the feminine and gives her a certain priority, or should feminists note that his portrayal of the feminine functions in a way that ultimately re-inscribes feminine in a traditional trope that benefits men more than it does women? Or perhaps feminists should reject Lévinas's appeal to feminine alterity as too much mystification? The feminist engagements with Lévinas are not conclusive on this point. Simone de Beauvoir (*The Second Sex*, trans. H.M. Parshley (1952) and later Luce Irigaray ("Questions to Emmanuel Lévinas, in: *The Levinas Reader*, ed. Margaret Whitford (1991), pp. 178–89; "The Fecundity of the Caress: A Reading of Lévinas, *Totality and Infinity*, 'Phenomenology of Eros,'" in *Feminist Interpretations of Emmanuel Lévinas*, ed. Tina Chanter (2001), pp. 119–44) took Lévinas to task precisely because he posited the woman as the paradigm of the Other. These feminist critics argued that his analysis of the Woman and his use of the feminine as a trope in his philosophy of the Other perpetuated the negative perception of women in traditional patriarchal society, considering them always as an object rather than a subject and viewing them as that which the (male) Self is not. To construe the woman as the "absolute Other" was no bonus to women but a continuation of patriarchy; the Self is always defined by men who speak from their located perspective but universalize it as the norm of humanity.

Recently some philosophers, such as Tina Chanter, Catherine Chalier, and Clair E. Katz, have offered more positive readings of Lévinas showing how Lévinas' philosophy of the Other could be useful to feminist thinking. Contrary to many feminist readers of Lévinas who ignore his Jewishness, Claire E. Katz argues that knowledge of Lévinas' Jewish sources (biblical, rabbinic, and philosophical) is necessary if one is to correctly understand how the feminine functions in his philosophy. According to Katz, Lévinas "uses the feminine as a transcendental structure. The feminine creates the dwelling, the welcoming, and habitation, thus providing the means of enjoyment and sensuality that are interrupted by the ethical" ("Reinhabiting the House of Ruth: Exceeding the Limits of the Feminine in Levinas," in: *Feminist Interpretations of Levinas*, p. 147). Elsewhere Katz explains why Lévinas chose the trope of maternity as the epitome of ethical relations which goes beyond the eros of philosophy, uniting enjoyment and responsibility ("From Eros to Maternity: Love, Death, and 'the Feminine' in the Philosophy of Emmanuel Levinas," in: *Women and Gender in Jewish Philosophy*, pp. 153–75). Lévinas's ethics, with its focus on maternity, was a Jewish alternative to Western philosophy's conception of life as being-toward-death, exemplified by the philosophy of Heidegger. Katz concludes that Lévinas did not exclude woman (or women) from ethical relationship. In fact it was "his Hebrew roots [that] give him profound insight into the obligation and responsibility of the Other, for those who are most vulnerable. And yet it is his Judaism that precisely allows his inadequate view of women to merge and take hold." Lévinas's project, therefore, is of use to feminists but not in a straightforward and simplistic manner. He offers feminists "an opportunity to see feminist concerns in a different light and to see a wider range of what those concerns might be" (*ibid.*, p. 171).

Lévinas's philosophy of the Other has generated as well non-feminist philosophical engagements by two female Jewish philosophers, Catherine Chalier and Edith Wyschogrod. By juxtaposing Lévinas and Kant, Chalier implicitly endorses Lévinas's critique of Kant's understanding of the moral subject and moral autonomy on the basis of the Jewish sacred tradition (*What Ought I To Do?: Morality in Kant and Levinas*, trans. Jane Marie Todd (2002)). Lévinas' ethics as first philosophy arose from his personal experience of the barbarism and savagery of the 20th century manifested "through nuclear, chemical and biological warfare, through death camps, through concentration and labor camps and by means of conventional weapons," which Edith Wyschogrod appropriately labeled as the "death event" (*Saints and Postmodernism: Revisioning Moral Philosophy* (1990), p. xiv). She responded to the "new historical horizon" not only by subjecting the modern "kingdom of death" to close philosophical analysis in her *Spirit in Ashes: Hegel, Heidegger, and Man-Made Mass Death* (1985), but also by articulating a postmodern ethics that is grounded in the lives of saints. Deliberately moving away from moral theory into the specific "pathways" or "journeys" of saints' lives, Wyschogrod's narrative philosophy, which is informed by literary theory and comparative literature, offers "a three pronged critique of theory: a pragmatic criticism of moral theory; an ontological criticism of its infrastructure; and a criticism of normative reason as belonging to the philosophy of reflection" (*Saints and Postmodernism*, p. xxv). While Wyschogrod's philosophy engages mostly non-Jewish philosophical and literary texts and includes no hermeneutics of Jewish sacred texts, her philosophical project emerges from the problematics of the Shoah, making her the most important post-Holocaust female Jewish philosopher.

Feminist Jewish Philosophy

During the last two decades of the 20th century, Judaism and Jewish philosophy were transformed by the rise of feminism, including Jewish feminism. Jewish women demanded and largely received an end to centuries of discrimination and exclusion and gained access to formal religious education, communal leadership roles, and participation in public ritual. At the forefront of feminist Jewish thought stood the theologian Judith Plaskow who insisted, contrary to other Jewish feminists, that the problem of women in Judaism is primarily theological rather than sociological. She charged that Judaism is a male-centered tradition because women were deliberately excluded from the process of interpretation. The sacred texts of Judaism do not express the will of God, but rather the interpretation of the will of God by men who deliberately excluded women from the process of interpretation. In order to address the injustice done to women by the Jewish tradition itself, Plaskow re-envisioned Judaism when women take their rightful place in the community of interpreters and offer new readings of Scriptures and the rabbinic tradition (*Standing Again at Sinai* (1981)). Plaskow's feminist critique of traditional Judaism was indebted to non-Jewish feminist theologians, to Liberal Christian theologians such as Paul Tillich, and to Buber's dialogical philosophy. However, precisely because Plaskow construed the Jewish feminist critique as a theological and midrashic discourse, Jewish philosophers did not take her critique to be sufficiently philosophical and did not engage her philosophically.

In the 1980s and 1990s Jewish feminist theologians (e.g., Ellen Umansky and Laura Levitt) followed Plaskow's lead, engaging the Jewish tradition both critically and constructively. Early feminist writings reexamined biblical and rabbinic sources, highlighted the presence of women that the tradition ignored, explored the historical development of the tradition in regard to perceptions of women, and constructed their own feminist Midrashim in which women were the main actors. Although this work articulates a distinctive Jewish feminist discourse that changed the practice of Judaism (especially in North America), scholars of Jewish philosophy regarded feminism as a political ideology that has little to do with Jewish philosophy. The reluctance to engage feminist philosophy reflects a deeper debate about the meaning of philosophy as an intellectual inquiry in the postmodern age and about the discipline of Jewish philosophy within Jewish Studies (Hava Tirosh-Rothschild, "'Dare to Know': Feminism and the Discipline of Jewish Philosophy," in: Lynn Davidman and Shelly Tenenbaum (eds.), *Feminist Perspectives on Jewish Studies* (1994), 94–117). Only a handful of (male) Jewish philosophers (e.g., Kenneth Seeskin, Steven Katz, Michael Oppenheim) recognized the merits of feminist philosophy and its implication to the future of Jewish philosophy.

Two feminist thinkers, Rachel Adler and Tamar Ross, articulated a systematic theology of Judaism informed by philosophical models. Rachel Adler's *Engendering Judaism: An Inclusive Theology and Ethics* (Boston, 1998) engages Judaism from the perspective of philosophy of law. Inspired by the work of the legal theorist, Robert Culver, Adler seeks to articulate a theory of *halakhah* that includes women and honestly deals with the historical development of Judaism over time. For Adler, the task of "engendering Judaism," namely, of honoring gender differences as equal in value, will have to engage men and women cooperatively, and its primary mode is the narrative. She endorses the values of "equal respect, inclusivity, diversity and pluralism," and not only re-reads rabbinic sources in light of them but also proposes new rituals that reflect them. As a Liberal Jew who is committed to halakhic life, Adler defines the task for feminist praxis and theory as an articulation of "a world of legal meaning in which the stories, dreams, and revelations of Jewish women and men are fully and complexly integrated" (p. 35). This task includes not only new readings of revelatory stories but also new rituals to inculcate equality between men and women.

Tamar Ross shares Adler's goal but offers philosophical arguments for it within the boundaries of Orthodox Judaism. Inspired by Wittgenstein's philosophy of language, *Expanding the Palace of Torah: Orthodoxy and Feminism* (2004) presents a theory of revelation as "cumulative." For Ross, revelation is a product of an interpretative community that selectively treats the received tradition. It is the community that determines which meaning is normative and/or authoritative, and it is the entire community that determines what the will of God is. *Halakhah* is not the mechanical application of eternal pre-existing legal principles to changing conditions, but the ever-changing interplay between texts, social reality, and shifting hermeneutic and moral assumptions. Community practice and social reality are thus part of the process by which the collective negotiates its normative consensus (Yoel Finkelman, "A Critique of *Expanding the Palace of Torah: Orthodoxy and Feminism* by Tamar Ross," in: *The Edah Journal*, 4:2 (2004): 1–10). Ross calls on contemporary Orthodox feminists to gradually alter not only the place of women in Orthodoxy but the very texture of interpretation and religious life. Feminists can help forge a new religious language that is less biased, but to do so they must become learned in every area of sacred tradition. As women make their voices and concerns more central as the interpretive community, they will gradually rewrite the ground rules by which Orthodox Jewry plays the language game of Torah and *mitzvot*.

While feminist Jewish philosophy is still in its infancy, the number of women who study, teach, and construe Jewish philosophy is quite impressive, including Francesca Alberitini, Leora Batnitzky, Ruth Birenbaum, Almut Bruckstein, Jean Cahan, Catherine Chalier, Idit Dobbs-Weinstein, Amirah Eran, Barbara E. Gali, Resianne Fontaine, Yudit K. Greenberg, Ruth Glassner, Hannah Kasher, Claire Katz, Sarah Klein-Braslavy, Gitit Holtzman, Nancy K. Levene, Diana Lobel, Sandra M. Lubarsky, Sarah Pessin, Heidi Ravven, Randi Rashkover, Tamar Ross, T.M. Rudavsky, Susan Shapiro, Julia Schwartzmann, Suzanne Last Stone, Hava Tirosh-Samuelson, Edith Wyschogrod, and Laurie Zoloth. Some of these scholars (especially in Israel) define themselves strictly as historians of Jewish philosophy and attest little interest in or even hostility to feminist philosophy, while others (especially those who focus on modern Jewish philosophy in the U.S.) engage feminist philosophy in their own work as constructive Jewish philosophers. A recent anthology, *Women and Gender in Jewish Philosophy*, edited by Hava Tirosh-Samuelson (2004), includes many of the women listed above. Retaining a critical posture toward Jewish philosophy as well as toward feminist philosophy, the participants of the volume demonstrate the possibility of a fruitful dialogue between Jewish philosophy and feminist philosophy. The volume engages past Jewish philosophers (e.g., Philo, Ibn Gabirol, Maimonides, Gersonides, Baruch Spinoza, Hermann Cohen, Buber, Rosenzweig, and Lévinas) and the sub-disciplines of philosophy (e.g., epistemology, metaphysics, ethics, political theory, philosophy of law, and theology) in light of feminist philosophy. Without reaching consensus about Judaism, Jewish philosophy, and feminism, the volume demonstrates that when women are allowed to philosophize they can and do enrich Jewish philosophy.

[Hava Tirosh-Samuelson (2nd ed.)]

BIBLIOGRAPHY: For information concerning editions of texts, translations, and books, monographs, and articles dealing with topics in the thought of a particular philosopher, see entry on that philosopher. BIBLIOGRAPHY: J. Kaplan, *2000 Books and More: an Annotated and Selected Bibliography of Jewish History and Thought* (1983). HISTORIES OF JEWISH AND GENERAL PHILOSOPHY: A. Altmann, "Jewish Philosophy," in: S. Radhakrishnan (ed.), *History of Philosophy, Eastern and Western*, 2 (1953), 76–92; S.H. Bergman, *Faith and Reason* (1961); J.L. Blau, *The Story of Jewish Philosophy* (1962); F. Copelston, *A History of Philosophy*, 8 vols. (1950–66); T. De Boer, *The History of Islam* (1903); M. Fakhry, *A History of Islamic Philosophy* (1970, 1983); D.H. Frank and O. Leaman (eds.), *History of Jewish Philosophy – Routledge History of World Philosophies*, vol. 2 (1997); D.H. Frank, O. Leaman, and C.H. Manekin, *The Jewish Philosophy Reader* (2000); E. Gilson, *History of Christian Philosophy in the Middle Ages* (1955) incl. bibl.; R. Goldwater (ed.), *Jewish Philosophy and Philosophers* (1962); Guttmann, Philosophies; Husik, Philosophy; M. Horten, *Die Philosophie des Islam* (1924); A. Jospe (ed.), *Studies in Jewish Thought: An Anthology of German Jewish Scholarship* (1981); R. Jospe, *Filosofyah Yehudit bi-Ymei ha-Beinayim*, 1: *Yesodot* (2005); idem, *Filosofyah Yehudit bi-Ymei ha-Beinayim*, 2: *Ma'avarim* (2006); idem, *Filosofyah Yehudit bi-Ymei ha-Beinayim*, 3: *Rambam* (2006); idem, *What Is Jewish Philosophy?* (1988; 1990); idem (ed.), *Paradigms in Jewish Philosophy* (1997); E. Fackenheim and R. Jospe (eds.), *Jewish Philosophy and the Academy* (1996); R. Jospe and S. Wagner (eds.), *Great Schisms in Jewish History* (1981); I. Kajon (ed.), *La Storia della Filosofia Ebraica* (1993); A. Kilcher and Otfried Fraisse, *Metzler Lexikon Juedischer Philosophen* (2003); Munk, Mélanges; S.H. Nasr and O. Leaman (eds.), *History of Islamic Philosophy*, vols. 1 and 2 (*Routledge History of World Philosophies*, vol. 1 (1996); S. Pines, "Jewish Philosophy," in: *Enyclopedia of Philosophy*, 4 (1967), 261–77; N. Rotenstreich, *Jewish Philosophy in Modern Times* (1968); M.M. Sharif (ed.), *A History of Muslim Philosophy*, 2 vols. (1963–66), incl. bibl.; B. Geyer (ed.), *Die patristische und scholastische Philosophie* (1928, repr. 1951); R. Walzer, "Islamic Philosophy," in: S. Radhakrishnan (ed.), *History of Philosophy, Eastern and Western*, 2 1953), 120–48; repr. in: R. Walzer, *Greek into Arabic* (1962); idem, in: A.H. Armstrong (ed.), *Cambridge History of Later Greek and Early Medieval Philosophy* (1967), 643–69; W. Watt, *Islamic Philosophy and Theology* (1962); J. Weinberg, *A Short History of Medieval Philosophy* (1964); G. Vajda, *Introduction à la penseé juive du moyen âge* (1947), incl. bibl.; idem, *Juedische Philosophie* (1950); N. Samuelson, *Introduction to Modern Jewish Philosophy* (1989); idem, *Jewish Philosophy: An Historical Introduction* (2003); E. Schweid, *Toledot ha-Hagut ha-Yehudit ba-Et ha-Ḥadashah: Ha-Meah ha-19* (1977); idem, *Jewish Thought in the Twentieth Century: An Introduction* (1992); K. Seeskin, *Jewish Phi-*

losophy in a Secular Age (1990); C. Sirat, *A History of Jewish Philosophy in the Middle Ages* (1985); idem, *La Philosophie Juive Médiévale en Pays de Chrétienté* (1988); idem, *La Philosophie Juive Médiévale en Terre d'Islam* (1988); idem, in: P. Wilpert (ed.), *Die Metaphysik im Mittelalter* (1963), 126–1135 (bibliographic information on medieval Jewish philosophy between 1950 and 1960). For the current literature the reader is referred to *Kirjath Sepher*, bibliographic journal. STUDIES: A. Altmann, *Studies in Religious Philosophy and Mysticism* (1969); I. Efros, *The Problem of Space in Medieval Jewish Philosophy* (1917); idem, *Ha-Pilosofyah ha-Yehudit bi-Ymei ha-Beinayim: Munaḥim u-Musagim* (1969); idem, *Ha-Pilosofyah ha-Yehudit bi-Ymei ha-Beinayim: Shitot ve-Sugyot* (1965); J. Guttmann, *Das Verhaeltnis des Thomas von Aquino zum Judentum und der juedischen Litteratur* (1891); idem, *Die Scholastik des dreizehnten Jahrhunderts in ihren Beziehungen zum Judenthum und zur juedischen Literatur* (1902); J. Guttmann, *Dat u-Madda* (1955); idem, in: MGWJ, 78 (1934), 456–64; I. Heinemann, *Die Lehre von der Zweckbestimmung des Menschen im griechisch-roemischen Altertum und im juedischen Mittelalter* (1926); idem, *Ta'amei ha-Mitzvot be-Sifrut Yisrael*, 2 vols. (1954–56); S. Horovitz, *Die Psychologie bei den juedischen Religionsphilosophen des Mittelalters von Saadia bis Maimuni*, 4 vols. (1898–1912); A. Hyman and J. Walsh, *Philosophy in the Middle Ages: The Christian, Islamic, and Jewish Traditions* (1967) incl. bibl.; A. Hyman, in: *Arts libéraux et philosophie du moyen âge* (1969), 99–110; D. Kaufmann, *Geschichte der Attributenlehre in der juedischen Religionsphilosophie des Mittelalters von Saadia bis Maimuni* (1877); idem, *Die Sinne: Beitraege zur Geschichte der Physiologie und Psychologie im Mittelalter* (1884); M. Kellner, *Dogma in Medieval Jewish Thought* (1986); idem, *Must a Jew Believe Anything?* (1999); D. Lasker, *Jewish Philosophical Polemics Against Christianity in the Middle Ages* (1977); R. Lerner and M. Mahdi, *Medieval Political Philosophy* (1963); A. Melamed, *Philosopher-King in Medieval and Renaissance Jewish Political Thought* (2003); S. Pines, *Beitraege zur islamischen Atomenlehre* (1936, 1946[2]); idem, *Nouvelles études sur Awhad al-Zamān Abu'l Barakāt al-Baghdādī* (1955); idem, "Translator's Introduction," in: *Guide of the Perplexed* (1963); A. Ravitzky, *Al Da'at Ha-Makom: Meḥkarim ba-Hagut ha-Yehudit u-ve-Toledoteha* (1991); idem, *Dat u-Medinah be-Maḥshevet Yisrael* (1998); idem, *Derashat ha-Pesaḥ le-Hasdai Crescas* (1988); idem, *History and Faith: Studies in Jewish Philosophy* (1996); idem, *Iyyunim Maimoniyim* (1996); idem, *Ḥerut al ha-Luḥot* (1999); E. Rosenthal, *Griechisches Erbe in der juedischen Religionsphilosophie des Mittelalters* (1960); Scholem, Mysticism: *On the Kabbalah and its Symbolism* (1965); idem, *Jewish Gnosticism, Merkabah Mysticism and Talmudic Tradition* (1960, 19652); M. Schreiner, *Der Kalām in der juedischen Literatur* (1895); D. Schwartz, *Ha-Ra'ayon ha-Meshiḥi ba-Hagut ha-Yehudit bi-Ymei ha-Beinayim* (1997); idem, *Setirah ve-Hastarah ba-Hagut ha-Yehudit Bi-Ymei ha-Beinayim* (2002); idem, *Astrologya u-Magya ba-Hagut ha-Yehudit bi-Ymei ha-Beinayim* (1999); idem, *Yashan be-Kankan Ḥadash: Mishnato ha-Iyyunit shel ha-Ḥug 'a-Neoaplatoni be-Filosofya ha-Yehudit ba-Meah ha-14* (1996); idem, *Kame'ot, Segulot u-Sikhaltanut ba-Hagut ha-Yehudit Bi-Ymei ha-Beinayim* (2004); idem, *Emunah u-Tevunah* (2001); idem, *Studies on Astral Magic in Medieval Jewish Thought* (2005); M.B. Shapiro, *The Limits of Orthodox Theology: Maimonides' Thirteen Principles Reappraised* (2004); C. Sirat, *Les théories des visions surnaturelles dans la penseé juive du Moyen-Âge* (1969); L. Strauss, *Philosophie und Gesetz* (1935); idem, *Persecution and the Art of Writing* (1952); idem, *Spinoza's Critique of Religion* (1965); G. Vajda, *L'amour de Dieu dans la théologie juive du Moyen Age* (1957); idem, *Recherches sur la philosophie et la Kabbale dans la pensée juive du Moyen Age* (1962); E.E. Urbach, *Ḥazal–Pirkei Emunot ve-De'ot* (1969; Eng., *The Sages, their Concepts and Beliefs*, 1975).), incl. bibl.; H.A. Wolfson, *Philo Foundations of Religious Philosophy in Judaism, Christianity and Islam* (1947); idem, *The Philosophy of the Church Fathers*, vol. 1 (1956; 1964[2]); idem, *Religious Philosophy* (1961); idem, *The Philosophy of Spinoza* (1934); idem, *The Philosophy of the Kalam* (1976); idem, *Repercussions of the Kalam in Jewish Philosophy* (1979); *Harry Austryn Wolfson Jubilee Volume* (1965), Eng. section, 39–46. For publications in the field of Jewish philosophy by S. Pines, E. Schweid, J. Sermoneta see *Reshimat ha-Pirsumim ha-Maddaiyyim shel Ḥavrei ha-Makhon le-Madda'ei ha-Yahadut* (1957–68). **ADD. BIBLIOGRAPHY:** J.B. Agus, *Jewish Identity in an Age of Ideologies* (1978); E. Alexander, *The Jewish Idea and its Enemies: Personalities, Issues, Events* (1988); A. Altmann, *Essays in Jewish Intellectual History* (1981); E. Berkovits, *Major Themes in Modern Philosophies of Judaism* (1974); idem, *Crisis and Faith* (1977); E.B. Borowitz, *Renewing the Covenant: a Theology for the Postmodern Jew* (1991); A. Cohen and P. Mendes-Flohr (eds.), *Contemporary Jewish Religious Thought: Original Essays on Critical Concepts, Movements, and Beliefs* (1986); E.L. Fackenheim, *Encounters between Judaism and Modern Philosophy: a Preface to Future Jewish Thought* (1973); idem, *To Mend the World: Foundations of Future Jewish Thought* (1982); M.A. Fishbane, *Judaism: Revelation and Traditions* (1987); S. Freedman, *Life as Creation: a Jewish Way of Thinking about the World* (1993); J. Neusner, E.S. Frerichs, N. Sarna (eds.), *From Ancient Israel to Modern Judaism: Intellect in Quest of Understanding; Essays in Honor of Marvin Fox*, 4 vols. (1989); N. Gillman, *Sacred Fragments: Recovering Theology for the Modern Jew* (1990); R. Gordis, *The Dynamics of Judaism: a Study in Jewish Law* (1990); B. Greenberg, *On Women and Judaism: a View from Tradition* (1981); B. Herring, *Jewish Ethics and Halakhah for Our Times: Sources and Commentary*, 2 vols. (1984–1989); A. Green (ed.), *Jewish Spirituality: From the Sixteenth Century Revival to the Present* (1988); I. Twersky and B. Septimus (eds.), *Jewish Thought in the Seventeenth Century* (1987); S.T. Katz, *Historicism, the Holocaust, and Zionism: Critical Studies in Modern Jewish Thought and History* (1992); W.E. Kaufman, *Contemporary Jewish Philosophies*,(1975); H. Kushner, *To Life!: a Celebration of Jewish Being and Thinking* (1993); L. Kushner, *The Book of Words: Talking Spiritual Life, Living Spiritual Talk* (1993); D. Marmur, *The Star of Return: Judaism after the Holocaust* (1991); N.N. Glatzer (ed.), *Modern Jewish Thought: A Source Reader* (1978); R. Link-Salinger (ed.), *Of Scholars, Savants, and their Texts: Studies in Philosophy and Religious Thought: Essays in Honor of Arthur Hyman* (1989); R. Patai, *The Jewish Mind* (1977); G. Rose, *Judaism and Modernity: Philosophical Essays* (1993); D.B. Ruderman, *Jewish Thought and Scientific Discovery in Early Modern Europe* (1990); J. Sacks, *Tradition in an Untraditional Age: Essays on Modern Jewish Thought* (1990); N.M. Samuelson, *Judaism and the Doctrine of Creation* (1994); Z. Schachter-Shalomi, *Paradigm Shift: From the Jewish Renewal Teachings of Reb Zalman Schachter-ShalomiI* (ed. by Ellen Singer; 1993); K. Seeskin, *Jewish Philosophy in a Secular Age* (1990); R.M. Seltzer, *Jewish People, Jewish Thought: The Jewish Experience in History* (1980); D.S. Shapiro, *Studies in Jewish Thought* (1975); E. Starobinski-Safran, *Le Buisson et la Voix: Exegese et Pensée Juives* (1987). WOMAN AND GENDER: A. Brenner (ed.), *Feminist Companion to Wisdom Literature* (1993); C.V. Camp, *Wisdom and the Feminine in the Book of Proverbs* (1985); C. Chalier, *Figures du feminine: lecture d'Emmanuel Lévinas* (1982); idem, *La perseverance du mal* (1987); I. Dobbs-Weinstein, "Matter as Creature and as the Source of Evil: Maimonides and Aquinas," in: L.E. Goodman (ed.), *Neoplatonism and Jewish Thought* (1992), 217–35; E.C. Katz, *Levinas, Judaism and the Feminine: The Silent Footsteps of Rebecca* (2004); M. Kellner, "Philosophical Misogyny in Medieval Jewish Philosophy – Gersonides vs. Maimonides," in: *Jerusalem Studies in Jewish Thought* (= Sermoneta Jubilee Volume, 1998), 113–28; A. Melamed, "Maimonides on Women: Formless Matter or Potential Prophet?" in: A. Ivry, E.R. Wolfson, and

A. Arkush (eds.), *Perspectives on Jewish Thought and Mysticism … dedicated to the memory … of Alexander Altmann* (1998), 99–134; A. Nye, *Philosophia: The Thought of Rosa Luxemburg, Simone Weil, and Hannah Arendt* (1994); M. Peskowitz and L. Levitt (eds.), *Judaism since Gender* (1997); M. Oppenheim, "To Notice the Color of Her Eyes: Facing the Feminist Jewish Critique," in: idem, *Speaking/Writing of God: Jewish Philosophical Reflections on the Life with Others* (1999), 53–82; J. Plaskow, "Jewish Feminist Thought," in: D.H. Frank and O. Leaman (eds.), *History of Jewish Philosophy* (1997), 885–94; H. Ravven, "Creating a Jewish Feminist Philosophy," in: *Anima*, 12:2 (1986):, 99–112; G. Rose, *The Broken Middle: Out of Our Ancient Society* (1992); T.M. Rudavsky, *Gender and Judaism: The Transformation of Tradition* (1995); S.E. Shapiro, "A Matter of Discipline: Reading for Gender in Jewish Philosophy," in: M. Peskowitz and L. Levitt (eds.), *Judaism since Gender* (1997), 158–78; J. Schwartzman, "Was She Created in the Image of God Too? The Medieval Philosophical Interpretation of the Creation of Woman," in: *Da'at* 39 (1997), 79–82 (Heb.); J.E. Taylor, "The Women 'Priests' of Philo's *De Vita Contemplativa*," in: J. Schaberg, A. Bach, and E. Fuchs (eds.), *On the Cutting Edge: The Study of Women in Biblical Worlds: Essays in Honor of Elisabeth Schüssler Fiorenza* (2004), 102–22; E. Umansky, J. Plaskow, and C.P. Christ (eds.), "Creating Jewish Feminist Theology," in: *Weaving the Visions: New Patterns of Feminist Spirituality* (1989); E. Wyschogrod, *An Ethics of Remembering: History, Heterology, and the Nameless Others* (1998); idem, *Emmanuel Levinas: The Problem of Ethical Metaphysics* (2000); N. Yavneh, "The Spiritual Eroticism of Leone's Hermaphrodite," in: J.R. Brink, M.C. Horowitz, and A.P. Coudert (eds.), *Playing with Gender: A Renaissance Pursuit*, 85–98.

°PHILOSTRATUS (b. c. 172 C.E.), a native of the island of Lemnos, he studied rhetoric in Athens and later joined the literary and philosophic circle in Rome of Empress Julia Domna, wife of Septimius Severus. She commissioned him to write a literary life of Apollonius of Tyana, whom he presented as a divinely inspired sage, prophet, and reformer along Pythagorean lines. The work has several comments on the separateness of the Jews and on their bloody revolt against the Romans under Vespasian.

PHILO VERLAG (named after *Philo of Alexandria), German-Jewish publishing house (1919–38), founded in Berlin as the publishing arm of the *Central-Verein deutscher Staatsbürger jüdischen Glaubens (C.V.). The originally intended name, "Gabriel-Riesser-Verlag," was rejected by the *Riesser family. According to the C.V.'s ideology, the Philo Verlag was to publish apologetic literature, both in a scientifically reliable and outwardly attractive form, in order to fight antisemitism and broaden the knowledge of Judaism among Jews and non-Jews, focusing on the description of Jewish history and the contribution of Jews to German life and culture. The Philo Verlag was first managed by Ludwig *Holländer (1877–1936), then syndic of the C.V. and editor of its monthly organ, *Im Deutschen Reich* (1895–1922), which was continued by the Philo Verlag as a weekly under the title *C.V. Zeitung* (1922–38). From 1923–38, Holländer and his successor Alfred Hirschberg (1901–1971) were assisted by Lucia Jacoby (1889–1944). Within 20 years, more than 100 pamphlets and books of both Jewish and non-Jewish authors appeared and, besides a press information service, several periodicals were published, including *Der Morgen* (1925–38), first edited by Julius *Goldstein (1873–1929), and the revived *Zeitschrift für die Geschichte der Juden in Deutschland* (1929–37), edited by Ismar *Elbogen (1874–1943) and others. In 1933 however, when fighting antisemitism became both hopeless and dangerous, the Philo Verlag changed its strategy, concentrating on publications which could deepen Jewish knowledge and consciousness and give both intellectual and practical orientation. The Philo "Library" (*Kleine Philo-Bücherei*) and handbooks like the *Philo-Lexikon* (1935–37, 1–4, reprinted 1982), the *Philo-Zitaten-Lexikon* (1936), and the *Philo-Atlas* (1938, reprinted 1998), a guide to Jewish emigration, served these various purposes. The Philo Verlag was closed by the Gestapo on November 10, 1938.

ADD. BIBLIOGRAPHY: A. Hirschberg, in: LBIYB, 7 (1962), 39–74; *Lexikon des Judentums* (1971²), 625–26; S. Urban-Fahr, *Der Philo-Verlag 1919–1938…* (2001).

[Ernst Gottfried Lowenthal / Johannes Valentin Schwarz (2nd ed.)]

PHINEHAS (Heb. פִּנְחָס), name of three biblical figures:

(1) Son of *Eleazar, son of *Aaron the priest (Ex. 6:25; cf. genealogies in Ezra 7:1–5; I Chron. 5:28–41; 6:35–38). When the Israelites suffered a plague in punishment for indulging in the orgiastic Baal-Peor cult, Phinehas slew Zimri son of Salu and Cozbi daughter of Zur, a prince of Midian, and thereby stopped the plague. By virtue of this act, Phinehas and his descendants were granted "a pact of priesthood for all time" (Num. 25:1–18). The memory of this event is reflected even in later sources (e.g., Ps. 106:30–31; Ecclus. 45:23–24; I Macc. 2:26, 53). Phinehas is encountered next in the war against the Midianites when, equipped with sacred utensils, he was sent by Moses to act as priest in the campaign (Num. 31:1–6). At the period of the Conquest, Phinehas, together with ten of the princes of the tribes that had settled west of the Jordan, formed a delegation to Reuben, Gad, and the half-tribe of Manasseh who had erected an altar on the east bank of the Jordan. There had been some suspicion that these tribes had defected from the Lord (Josh. 22:9–34). Phinehas appears to have been selected for this task because of his battle against the cult of Baal-Peor. At any rate, the issue was settled amicably. In the story of the Israelite war against the tribe of Benjamin over the incident of the concubine in Gibeah, it is stated that Phinehas served before the ark in Beth-El, and that through him the Israelites received an affirmative answer from God to their question as to whether to continue the war (Judg. 20:27–28). Many scholars believe these verses not to be part of the body of the narrative but additions by a later editor. It is related of Phinehas that he had been superintendent of the gatekeepers (I Chron 9:20). This is probably to be understood as indicating that Phinehas was considered to have been their patron. Phinehas' death and burial place are not recorded, though Joshua 24:33 does state that "Eleazar the son of Aaron died, and they buried him in the hill of his son Phinehas… in

Mount Ephraim." This passage may have been reworked by a later editor. The formula is surprising since the usual statement about the dead is that he was buried "with his fathers." E. Auerbach believes that originally the site was known as the grave of Phinehas, and that Eleazar's name was attached to it as a result of a later tradition. Indeed, according to both Jewish and Samaritan tradition, Phinehas is also buried at this hill. Eusebius (Onom. 2:14) identified the location as being 5 mi. (8 km.) from Gophna on the way to Shechem (see *Aaron for genealogy of the house of Aaron). A family of priests named Gershom, directly related to Phinehas, existed as late as the time of Ezra, returning with him from the Exile (Ezra 8:2; cf. *Gershom). According to I Esdras (5:5), the priests Jeshua son of Jehozedek and Joiakim son of Jeshua were associated with the house of Phinehas.

(2) A priest, one of the sons of Eli, at Shiloh, brother of Hophni (e.g., I Sam. 2:34). See *Hophni and Phinehas.

(3) The father of Eleazar, who was one of the assistants of Meremoth son of Uriah the priest. This priest weighed the sacred vessels brought by those who returned with Ezra from the Exile (Ezra 8:33; cf. I Esd. 8:62).

The name Phinehas derives from the Egyptian *panḥśj*, meaning "the Nubian," which was also employed as a proper name in Egypt, especially for residents of Nubia.

[Ephraim Stern]

Phinehas (1) in the *Aggadah*

Because of the major problems arising out of occasional cases of apostasy (TJ, Ḥag. 2:1) or fornication with pagan women (Sanh. 9:6; Sanh. 82a), Phinehas is, for the most part, highly praised in rabbinical literature for the "zeal" which he displayed in slaying Zimri and the Midianite woman whom he had caught in the act (cf. Num. 25:6ff.). While Moses, who had himself married a Midianite woman (albeit before the Sinai covenant), was humiliated and unable to cope with the situation (Sanh. 82a; Gen. R. 96:3; Num. R. 20:24, et al.), Phinehas remembered the *halakhah* that "he who cohabits with a gentile woman is struck down by zealots" (Sanh. 9:6). Seeing that even the most warlike tribes refused to punish the transgressor, Phinehas resolved to take the law into his own hands (Sif. Num. 131; TJ, Sanh. 10:2, 28d). The rabbis could not agree whether Phinehas had acted with or without Moses' permission – the issue at stake being whether a disciple could, in an emergency, decide a case without reference to his master (Sanh. 82a). In view of the unequivocal biblical approval of Phinehas' deed (Num. 25:10ff.), the legitimacy of the act could not be seriously questioned. Indeed, no less than 12 miracles were said to have been wrought in aid of Phinehas – otherwise he could not have successfully accomplished his mission (Sif. Num. 131). The rabbis, moreover, interpreted Psalms 106:30 in the sense that Phinehas had argued with God concerning the injustice of inflicting a plague on Israel which carried off 24,000 people (cf. Num. 25:9). When the angels wanted to push Phinehas away, God defended him: "Let him be; he is a zealot and the descendant of a zealot" (viz. Levi; cf. Gen. 34:25ff.). The Almighty also bestowed high praise on Phinehas when the tribes of Israel, especially Simeon, tried to cast aspersions on him, taunting him with his descent from Jethro (through Putiel; cf. Ex. 6:25) who had "fattened calves for idolatry" (Sanh. 82b; Sif. *ibid.*).

There were, nevertheless, rabbis who had some legal reservations concerning the summary execution carried out by Phinehas. According to one view, Phinehas had acted "against the will of the Sages," who had therefore intended to put him under the ban but were restrained by "the holy spirit" which proclaimed "the covenant of a perpetual priesthood" (cf. Num. 25:13) for Phinehas and his descendants (TJ, Sanh. 9:9, 27b). Both Palestinian and Babylonian rabbis stated explicitly that anyone consulting them about how to act in a similar situation would not be instructed to emulate Phinehas' example (Sanh. 82a). The implied disapproval is evident in the rabbinic speculations on hypothetical events which might have had an adverse effect on Phinehas' legal position: "If Zimri had separated (from his Midianite mistress) and Phinehas slain him, Phinehas would have incurred the death penalty, and if Zimri had turned upon Phinehas and slain him, he would not have been liable to the death penalty, since Phinehas was a pursuer [seeking to take his life]" (*ibid.*).

Notwithstanding the legal irregularities of Phinehas' unauthorized zeal, the rabbis accorded Phinehas a prominent place in Jewish history. He was chosen to accompany the Israelites in their campaign against Midian to complete the good deed he had begun by slaying the Midianite woman (Num. R. 22:4), and also to avenge his maternal grandfather Joseph, who had been sold into slavery by the Midianites (Sif. Num. 157; Sot. 43a; cf. Gen. 37:28, 36). It was Phinehas who miraculously slew Balaam (Sanh. 106b; cf. Num. 31:8 and Targ. Ps.-Jon. ad loc.). He was also one of the two spies sent by Joshua to Jericho (cf. Josh. 21:1ff.), where he managed to make himself invisible like an angel; and he was in fact identical with the angel sent to the Israelites at Bochim (Num. R. 161:1; cf. Judg. 2:1ff.). This must probably be connected with the identification of Phinehas with Elijah (both having been distinguished for their "zeal and their peacemaking missions"; cf. Num. 25:11ff.; I Kings 19:10, 14; Mal. 3:23ff.), whose transformation into an angelic being is predicated in Malachi 3:1, 23 (PdRE 47; Targ. Ps.-Jon. to Ex. 6:18; Num. 25:12; Num. R. 21:3, et al.). He is, accordingly, the forerunner of the Messiah (Targ. Ps.-Jon. to Num. 25:12, et al.). The criticism leveled against Phinehas for failing to annul Jephthah's fatal vow, thereby causing the death of Jephthah's daughter (Gen. R. 60:3; Lev. R. 37:4, et al.), in all probability reflects the rabbinic attitude to certain priests in the talmudic age and has no bearing on Phinehas' personality even as viewed through rabbinic eyes.

[Moses Aberbach]

BIBLIOGRAPHY: North, Personennamen, 63; T. Melek, in: AJSLL, 45 (1929), 165; K. Moehlenbrink, in: ZAW, 52 (1934), 189, 217–9; C. Simpson, *The Early Traditions of Israel* (1948), 322. IN THE AGGADAH: Ginzberg, Legends, 3 (1911), 383–9; 6 (1928), 137f.; 7 (1938), 37f. (index).

PHINEHAS, guardian of the Second Temple treasury in the last days of the Temple. Josephus (Wars, 6:387–91) relates that with the seizure of Jerusalem and the Temple (70 C.E.) Phinehas, taken prisoner, "disclosed the tunics and girdles worn by the priests, an abundance of purple and scarlet kept for necessary repairs to the veil of the Temple, a mass of cinammon and cassia, and a multitude of other spices mixed and burnt daily as incense to God. Many other treasures were also delivered up by him, with numerous sacred ornaments." Phinehas was not the sole Temple custodian to disclose the sacred treasures of the Sanctuary. He was joined by one of the priests, Joshua (Jesus) son of Thebuthi. Both officials were granted pardons by the Romans in reward for their services. The mishnaic list of officials in the Temple (Shek. 5:1) includes a Pinḥas al ha-Malbush ("Phinehas, the guardian of the wardrobe"), who is probably the same person.

BIBLIOGRAPHY: Graetz, in: MGWJ, 34 (1885), 193–205; Schuerer, Gesch, 2 (1907), 332f.; Klausner, Bayit Sheni, 5 (1951^2), 272.

[Isaiah Gafni]

PHINEHAS BEN ḤAMA HA-KOHEN (mid-fourth century), Palestinian *amora*. In the Jerusalem Talmud and *Genesis Rabbah* he is known as R. Phinehas, while in the later Midrashim he appears with his full name: Phinehas (ha-Kohen) b. Ḥama. Though born and brought up in Palestine, he was familiar with the genealogy of both Babylonian and Palestinian families (Kid. 71a), and showed his preference for the former (*ibid.*). He appears to have resided in the town of Sikhnin where his brother Samuel is recorded to have died (Mid. Sam. 9:3), and he probably lived to an old age (Kid. 71a and Rashi *ibid.*).

In the *halakhah*, Phinehas was primarily a pupil of R. Jeremiah, details of whose ritual practice he records (e.g., TJ, Kil. 4:4, 29b; TJ, MK 1:2, 80b; TJ, Ket. 6:7, 31a). He was a colleague of R. Yose, with whom he often debated halakhic points (TJ, Yev. 1:2, 2d, et al.), and his main pupil in *halakhah* was Hananiah (of Sepphoris) who handed down most of his halakhic statements (see TJ, Dem. 3:1, 23b). Phinehas transmitted many aggadic aphorisms in the name of earlier *amoraim*, especially those of the previous generation – Hilkiah, Ḥanin, Reuben, and others. His own *aggadot*, both aphorisms and homiletic exegesis, are also extensive, and he often added a light anecdote to his homily to bring home the moral. In what appears to be a polemical reference to Christianity he declared, "While other laws decree that one must renounce one's parents to pledge allegiance to the king (cf. Matt. 10:35–37), the Torah says, 'Honor thy father and thy mother'" (Num. R. 8:4). His deduction from Job that "Poverty in a man's house is worse than 50 plagues" (BB 116a) may well be a bitter reflection on current economic conditions, and he laments the moral decline of the nation in its contemporary promiscuity (Lam. R. 1:11, no. 39) and gambling (Mid. Ps. to 26:7). His maxim that only one who does not leave after him a son of his own caliber is truly dead (BB 116a) is indicative of his keen concern for right education; and his best-known maxim is that "the name a person gains for himself is worth more than the one endowed him from birth" (Eccles. R. 7: 1, no. 4).

BIBLIOGRAPHY: Bacher, Pal Amor, 3; Hyman, Toledot, s.v.; Ḥ. Albeck, *Mavo la-Talmudim* (1969), 347–8.

[Benjamin Cohen]

PHINEHAS BEN JACOB HA-KOHEN (Kafra), eighth century Palestinian *paytan*. He is apparently the last in the list of the "early poets" given in *Saadiah Gaon's *Sefer ha-Agron*. As the acrostic to one of his *piyyutim* implies, he came from Kafra, near Tiberias, and his connection with Ereẓ Israel is further indicated in his *piyyutim* by the representation of a number of customs in force only in that country. His assumed identification with R. Phinehas, head of the academy, who is mentioned among the early masoretes, is possible, but not sure. A prolific poet, Phinehas wrote his works approximately in the second half of the eighth century, at least after 748. Most of his compositions were found in the Cairo *Genizah*. The critical edition of Sh. Elitsur (2004) includes more than 140 *piyyutim* of many diverse genres. Outstanding among them are *Kiddush Yeraḥim, piyyutim* for all the months of the year, a series of *piyyutim* concerning the 24 divisions of kohanim, and two monumental *kedushta* for Shemini Aẓeret. The *Kedushta* contains an important and colorful amount of midrashic matter; the sources of some of these Midrashim are unknown. Phinehas' style places him in the school of Eleazar *Kallir, but his expression is usually simpler and his poetry original. In only a few compositions does he use many neologisms and an obscure style, with typical strange paytanic forms.

BIBLIOGRAPHY: A. Harkavy, *Zikkaron la-Rishonim ve-gam la-Aḥaronim*, 5 (1892), 112–5; A. Marmorstein, in: HḤY, 5 (1921), 225–8; 6 (1922), 46–47; M. Zulay, in: YMḤSI, 1 (1933), 150–62; idem, in: *Yerushalayim*, 4 (1953), 51–81; H. Yalon, in: *Ginzei Kedem*, 5 (1934), 191–2; M. Margalioth, in: BJPES, 8 (1940/41), 97–104; idem, in: *Tarbiz*, 29 (1960), 339ff.; A. Scheiber, in: JQR, 42 (1951/52), 213–4; idem, in: *Goldziher Memorial Volume*, 2 (1958), 55; E. Fleischer, in: *Sinai*, 59 (1966), 215–26; 61 (1967), 30–56; 66 (1970), 224–60. **ADD. BIBLIOGRAPHY:** E. Fleischer, *Hebrew Liturgical Poetry in the Middle Ages* (Hebrew; 1975), passim; idem, in: *Ha-Yoẓerot* (1984), 113ff., 129; T. Beeri, *The "Great Cantor" of Bagdad* (Hebrew; 2002), 83ff.; Sh. Elitsur, *Piyyuṭe Rabbi Pinḥas ha-Kohen* (2004).

[Ezra Fleischer / Angel Saenz-Badillos (2nd ed.)]

PHINEHAS BEN JAIR (second half of second century), *tanna* renowned both for his saintliness and his ability to work miracles. He was a son-in-law of *Simeon b. Yoḥai, with whom he studied, and achieved a reputation as a keen halakhist (Shab. 33b). Nonetheless, few of his halakhic statements are recorded, and he is better known as an aggadist. Indeed his legendary saintliness made him, like his father-in-law, a prominent aggadic personality. His place of residence was "a city in the south," probably Lydda, from where he testified that he used to go down with his friends to Ashkelon (TJ, Yev. 7:3). In several passages, Phinehas is reported as traveling to redeem captives and being deflected from his mission neither by a river in flood (which he is said to have parted miraculously), nor by a pressing invitation to dine with Judah ha-Nasi (Ḥul. 7a; 7b). Phinehas was famed for his great independence, and it was said of him that from the day he grew up he would not eat from his father's table, let alone that of another. "Not that I have taken a vow to that effect," he protested wryly to Judah ha-Nasi, "Israel is a holy nation, and worthy for one to break bread with it. But one wants [to give] and has not, and another has but does not want to give. You both have and want, so with you I shall eat!" However, even here, when he saw that Judah had white mules on his estate, which were regarded as dangerous, he turned away and would not eat (Ḥul. 7b). The grandeur of the court was not for him.

Phinehas took a gloomy view of the moral and material state of Israel in his time. "Since the Temple was destroyed," he lamented, "learned and free men are put to shame, the mighty and the informers have vanquished, and none seeks Israel's welfare, and we have no one to rely upon but our Heavenly Father" (Sot. 49a). He was strict not only in his personal discipline but also in halakhic decisions for others, and would not join with Judah ha-Nasi in allowing work on the land in the Sabbatical Year (TJ, Ta'an 3:1). Even Phinehas' donkey was celebrated for its piety and the tale that it refused to eat untithed corn is developed by the Talmud into a general proposition, "If God does not bring a stumbling block through even a beast of the righteous, how much more will He not bring a stumbling block through the righteous themselves!" (Ḥul. 5b). A number of tales told about him, including the one about his donkey, are also told of his contemporary, *Ḥanina b. Dosa. *Midrash Tadshe*, a late Midrash dealing with symbolic interpretations of the vessels of the Tabernacle, was also attributed to Phinehas as it opens with one of his sayings. In the Zohar, Phinehas appears as a particularly revered member of Simeon b. Yoḥai's mystic circle, though here he is represented as Simeon's father-in-law and not his son-in-law (Zohar 3:240, 2 and 288).

Fittingly, Phinehas is the author of the famous ladder of saintliness: "Caution [against evil] leads to Eagerness [for good], Eagerness to Cleanliness, Cleanliness to Purity, Purity to Asceticism, Asceticism to Holiness, Holiness to Humility, Humility to Fear of God, Fear of God to Attainment of the Holy Spirit [divine inspiration], and Attainment of the Holy Spirit to Resurrection of the Dead" (Sot. 9:15). A millennium and a half later, this dictum was amplified as the path to holiness by Moses Ḥayyim *Luzzatto in his classic ethical work *Mesillat Yesharim*, and in this way it became the guiding principle of the *Musar movement.

BIBLIOGRAPHY: Bacher, Tann; Hyman, Toledot; Heilprin, Dorot, 2 (1905), 313–4; A. Epstein, *Mi-Kadmoniyyot ha-Yehudim (Kol Kitvei, 2)* (1957), 130ff.; I. Konovitz, *Ma'arekhot Tanna'im*, pt. 4 (1969), 101–6.

[Benjamin Cohen]

PHINEHAS BEN JOSEPH HA-LEVI (13th century), Hebrew poet and *paytan* in Toledo. According to some scholars Phinehas was the brother of *Aaron ha-Levi of Barcelona to whom the *Sefer ha-Ḥinnukh* is attributed. He was one of the rivals of Todros b. Judah *Abulafia in the court of Don Caq de la Maleha. To entertain Don Caq, Todros from time to time conducted a poetic controversy with Phinehas in the course of which they exchanged with one another 35 short poems, generally filled with contempt and faultfinding. While the poems themselves have little literary value, they are of great importance for knowledge of the contemporary mode of life and society. In one of his poems, published in Abulafia's *Gan ha-Meshalim ve-ha-Ḥidot*, Phinehas addresses Don Caq and attempts to persuade him to renew his benefactions toward him; he had been driven away, in his opinion, through the effort of Todros, and had fallen victim to a base charge. His **azharot* for the Sabbath preceding Rosh Ha-Shanah, *Elohim Niẓẓav ba-Adat El* ("God stands in the divine congregation"), together with their *reshut, Asir Tikvah le-Keẓ Yamim* ("Prisoner of hope for the end of days"), was published in the *maḥzor* according to the custom of Catalonia (Salonika, 1526). It is not known whether he is identical with the poet Phinehas ha-Levi, also called Don Vidal Profiat, who lived in Spain in the 13th century and who forsook poetry, devoting himself to agriculture. His friend, the poet Abraham *Bedersi, who regarded agriculture as degrading labor, derided him with great contempt in one of his poems, and even rejoiced at his misfortune when all his produce went up in flames.

BIBLIOGRAPHY: Davidson, Oẓar, 4 (1933), 461; idem, in: *Tarbiz*, 2 (1931), 90–100; A. Neubauer, in: MGWJ, 20 (1871), 455–9; Schirmann, Sefarad, 2 (1960²), 449–53; idem, in: *Sefer Yovel Y. Baer* (1960), 161f.

[Abraham David]

PHINEHAS BEN SAMUEL (known also as "**the man of Kefar Habta**"; first century C.E.), high priest before the destruction of the Temple, 67–70 C.E. Phinehas was appointed to his office by the casting of lots. Until then the appointment was made only from among the families of distinguished birth. However, within the framework of the democratic reforms introduced by the Zealots, the selection of the high priest was made by casting lots in order to abolish the rule of these families (in this they relied on the ancient tradition in I Chron. 24:5). The lot fell on Phinehas who belonged to the watch of Jachin. Josephus censures him and says that "he scarcely knew what the high priesthood meant," for he was a farmer who tilled the earth (Wars, 4:155). This statement is to be treated with caution, however. In talmudic sources Phinehas is mentioned as a son-in-law of the house of the *nasi* (Tosef. Yoma 1:6), and the view that he was not learned in the affairs of the priesthood cannot be accepted (Klausner). This act of the Zealots gave rise to great bitterness and was the cause of civil war between them and the other parties among the people.

BIBLIOGRAPHY: Klausner, Bayit Sheni, 5 (1951²), 208f; Jos. Ant., 4, ch. 3.

[Edna Elazary]

PHLORINA (formerly **Florina**), city in Greek Macedonia, near the former Yugoslav border. In the 17th and 18th centuries there was a Jewish community in Phlorina, of which little is known.

In the 17th century Phlorina had a Sephardi community whose members maintained economic relations with Salonika, Kastoria, and Karditza. At the end of the 18th century, Rabbi Joseph Baruch stood at the head of the community and consulted with Rabbi Yitzhak Samuel of Salonika on halakhic matters. It is not known when the Jewish community ceased to exist. The community was reestablished in 1912. In that year many Jews from Monastir migrated to Phlorina. Additional Jews arrived in World War I, especially when Monastir was under siege in 1916/17. In sum, some 60 families from Monastir established themselves in Phlorina, and Baruch Kamhi, a butcher from Monastir, became community president.. In 1914, the Phlorina Jewish community numbered 100 families. In 1917 a Jewish school was established. At the beginning of the 1920s, the Jewish community turned to Salonikan Chief Rabbi Ben Zion Meir Ḥai *Ouziel, who, together with other influential Jews in Salonika, influenced the Ministry of National Economy to change the market day from Saturday to Wednesday, but in Phlorina the local Greek-Orthodox population ignored the ruling. In 1921–22, local Muslims and Greek-Orthodox attacked the Jews over this issue. The events were covered in the world and Jewish press. In 1923, while many Jewish merchants began working on the Sabbath; others were prompted to emigrate. In 1924–25, the Greek government banned work on Sunday and the Jews of Phlorina were further pressed to earn a living. Only some 50 families remained, with most leaving for Monastir. The Jews were merchants, dealers in old clothes, greengrocers, cobblers, etc. In the mid-1920s, the local Zionist organization, Achdut B'nai Zion, was formed and in the 1930s the Theodor Herzl Club was active. Blood libels erupted annually at Easter time from 1925 to 1927. Three local Jews fell in the Greek army in the Albanian campaign against the invading Italians in late 1940–early 1941. In 1940 there were 400 Jews in Phlorina; 372 of them were deported by the Nazis. On April 30, 1943, the Jews were arrested, sent to Salonika, and from there by train to their deaths in Birkenau, where they arrived in mid-May 1943. Some 60–70 Jews had fled previously, in early 1943, to the nearby mountains, and several Jews fought in the resistance. In 1948 the number of Jews was 64, and in 1958 it was seven. Small enclaves of Phlorina Jews concentrated in Tel Aviv and Jerusalem; Brooklyn, New York; and Sao Paulo, Brazil. An annual ceremony for the community's Holocaust victims is conducted at the Cave of the Martyrs on Mount Zion, Jerusalem.

BIBLIOGRAPHY: J. Angel, in: *Almanakh Izraelit* (Ladino, 1923), 79–80; Rosanes, Togarmah, 4 (1935), 267–8; M. Molho and J. Nehama (eds.), *In Memoriam*, 1 (1948), 106–7, and passim; idem, *Sho'at Yehudei Yavan 1941–1944* (1965), index. **ADD. BIBLIOGRAPHY:** Y. Kerem, "Florina," in: *Pinkas ha-Kehillot Yavan* (1999), 319–22.

[Simon Marcus / Yitzchak Kerem (2nd ed.)]

PHOENICIA, PHOENICIANS.

Names

(a) The Greek name *Phoinike* (*Phoinix*) is first mentioned by Homer, and is subsequently well attested in the writings of Greek historians who consistently refer it to the eastern Mediterranean coast; in Homer, Phoenician is synonymous with Sidonian. Though the exact extent of the region called Phoenicia cannot be determined, the name is clearly the Greek equivalent of Canaan. One should also compare the Septuagint's at times mechanical translation of Canaan(ite) by Phoenicia(n) in Exodus 6:15; 16:35; Joshua 5:1, 12; and Job 40:30; as well as the parallel passages Mark 7:26 (Syro-Phoenician) and Matthew 15:22 (Canaanite); and the replacement of Canaan by Phoenicia in coins of the second century (see below). Some scholars derive the Greek name from *phoinix*, "crimson, purple," so that *Phoinike* is "the land of purple" (see *Canaan). Another possibility is to derive the Greek from Egyptian *fenkhu*, "loggers," "woodcutters," in keeping with the Phoenician foresting of the cedars of Lebanon. The Bible (I Kings 5:20) informs us how skilled the Sidonians were at lumberjacking (Scandon and Xella apud Krings, 632).

(b) The name Canaan(ite) is first attested in sources from *Mari in Syria in the 18th century B.C.E. (J. Sasson, BA, 47 (1984), 90) down to the early 12th century B.C.E.; after that, except in the Bible or writers under its influence, it virtually vanishes. Exceptions are a Babylonian lexical text (c. 1100 B.C.E.), a final Egyptian reference (c. 900 B.C.E.), and two coins of the second century B.C.E. (in what is probably the corresponding Greek version of these coins, Phoenicia replaces Canaan; see above). These last witnesses prove that the name was not forgotten among the natives; besides, Greek writers are familiar with *xna* both as the eponymous hero of the Phoenicians and as the latter's name for their native land, and Augustine testifies that even in his day Punic peasants still called themselves *Chanani*.

Though the interpretation of the evidence is disputed, in its earliest occurrences Canaan is a region along the Levantine coast, and its borders were probably around the Nahr el-Kebir (Eleutheros River) in the north, and the area above Carmel in the south; only in northern Galilee around Hazor does it seem to have reached inland to any extent. Biblical usage, though it occasionally reflects the original restriction to the coast (Num. 13:29; Deut. 1:7; Josh. 5:1), commonly refers the name Canaan(ite) to all of Palestine and part of Syria (e.g., Gen. 10:15ff.; Num. 13:17ff.); however, this represents a later development, which was probably connected with colonization of the interior. The beginnings of this broader reference can be observed in Egyptian sources of the late 14th and 13th centuries; it is doubtful, however, whether Canaan was ever the name of an Egyptian province either embracing all of the Egyptian territory in Syria and Palestine, or, in the el-Amarna period, located in the south with its center at Gaza, though both views have their proponents (see *Canaan).

The origin of the name, a problem intimately associated with its etymology, remains a non liquet ("unclear"). Certainly Canaan was associated very early with one of the land's principal industries, the manufacture of purple dye from the Murex shellfish so plentiful along the coast; already in the Nuzi documents "Canaanite" is the designation of a variety of purple-dyed wool. This association is also reflected in the Greek name Phoenicia (see above). The problem is whether this connection with purple dye is primary (so W.F. Albright, hypothetical *kn*ʿ, "Murex"; otherwise B. Mazar, "merchant" (*kn*ʿ + Hurrian suffix), whence "merchant of purple [his staple]," etc.; S. Moscati, geographical term (origin unknown), whence derived meanings). No solution is without its difficulties; the last is best supported by parallels (cf. morocco, cordovan, etc.).

The Land

Geography played a very important role in the political and cultural history of Canaan. Lying between Egypt, Asia Minor, and Mesopotamia, and opening Asia to the Mediterranean world, Canaan was a confluence of cultures and of necessity deeply involved in the political ambitions and struggles of its neighbors. Its topography, however, led to political fragmentation; Canaan was never a state, and it was destined to centuries of vassalage under one or other of the surrounding colossuses.

To the east, most of Canaan was locked in by Lebanon, and the long, thin strip of coastal lowlands (c. 125 mi. = 200 km.) was often broken by gorges or promontories. Only at the mouth of the Eleutheros was there a plain of any size. There was one river, the Litani, besides a number of perennial streams; none of them was of use agriculturally. The climate, however, was warm (present monthly lowest median 50° F), with ample rainfall from October to April (annually in modern times, c. 40–24 in. from north to south). The climate and soil were favorable for the cultivation of wheat, barley, olives, figs, grapes, and other fruits. The densely forested hills and mountains provided excellent timber – the famous cedars, junipers (*Juniperus excelsa*, Heb. *berosh*; cf. I Kings 5:22, 24), firs, cypresses, and oaks. Sand from the shore would be the basis of a glassmaking industry, while from the sea itself came the source of the precious dye.

People and Language

Though there is much evidence for human habitation of Canaan as far back as the Paleolithic period, fixed settlements were apparently founded only in the pottery-Neolithic period, and, therefore, relatively late in the Syro-Palestinian picture. The lag was probably due, in part at least, to the necessity of clearing this section of the coast of forests before cultivation of the land was possible. Relics of the earliest settlers are the non-Semitic place-names in early written sources, like Uzu/Ushu (Palaityros on the mainland), Ammia, and Ullaza. However, most Canaanite cities bear names which certainly, or very probably, are Semitic: Tyre (the island city), Sidon, Beirut, Byblos, Batron, Irqata, Yarimuta, Sumur. In view of the tenacity of place-names, which tend to survive despite ethnic shifts in population, Canaan must have first been settled on a large scale by Semites. They were probably an offshoot of the Semitic inhabitants of Palestine and southern Syria, whose occupation of these areas goes back to the fourth millennium, and the penetration into Canaan proper was probably not much later – roughly, around 3000 B.C.E. Racially, as far as can be judged from the meager evidence, these Semites were mixed and, in this respect, indistinguishable from their predecessors; later, around 1500 B.C.E., a shift from the prevalence of a dolichocephalic to a brachycephalic type is observable, thus reflecting the more complex cultural relations of the period.

Of the language of the first settlers, except that it was Semitic, nothing is known. There is a stratum in the *Ugaritic lexicon which for a West Semitic language has an unusually close affinity with Akkadian; perhaps it is a survival of the earliest speech in the Syro-Palestinian area. The first real evidence for the language spoken in Canaan comes from the Execration Texts, shards (c. 1900 B.C.E.), or figurines (c. 1825 B.C.E.) inscribed with the names of rebellious rulers and their localities in Palestine and Canaan. These newcomers, another wave from the Syro-Arabian desert, usually called *Amorites, were also Semites and constituted another level of Semitic settlement. Their language, with dialectal differences, was identical with that of the Semites, who, in a long process of infiltration and finally invasion, seized power and set up a string of local dynasties from Babylonia to the borders of Egypt. Classification of this language in terms of the later developments which produced Canaanite and Aramaic is impossible; it is best simply called West Semitic. The question as to what happened to this language, i.e., whether it became the language of the earlier inhabitants (cf. *Aramaic), or disappeared, as in Babylonia, in favor of the established local language, unfortunately remains unanswered. The answer is crucial for the history of the Canaanite language which first emerges around 1400 B.C.E. At this time, "the language of Canaan" (Isa. 19:18) began to develop those specific features which would distinguish it from Aramaic. Their center of diffusion seems to have been Canaan itself; many of them appear only later, and then sporadically, in the north (Ugarit). The process of evolution continued – somewhat in contrast to Hebrew, a related dialect, which tended to be more conservative – and produced Phoenician. This was the language which was brought by the colonists to the western Mediterranean and became Punic.

History to 1200 B.C.E.

Canaanite history falls into two periods: approximately 3000–1200 B.C.E., and approximately 1200–332 B.C.E. In the first, Canaan, by and large, was in language, religion, art, and social and political institutions indistinguishable from Palestine and a large part of Syria. With the coming of the Philistines, and Arameans, and the emergence of the Israelites, the situation was profoundly changed, and the coastal Canaanites, who carried on the Late Bronze Age city system which had mostly been swept away by the 13th century catastrophe, had an identity thrust upon them such as they had never known. They became, as this new situation may be conveniently designated, Phoenicians. They maintained this identity until they were submerged by Hellenism, an event that may be dated to Alexander the Great's conquest. The date of course is too exact; such a change is never effected in a single blow, and there are always survivals, especially in religion; besides, the erosion of the old order had begun before the appearance of the conqueror. However, Hellenism, best symbolized by Alexander, was new, pervasive, and a turning point.

Early in the third millennium, Canaan was already in close contact with Egypt, which was to dominate so much of its history; Byblos became the center of an intense trade in timber, and by the Sixth Dynasty (c. 2305–2140 B.C.E.) was virtually an Egyptian colony. Such it remained with little or no interruption, despite periods of Egyptian weakness, until approximately 1740 B.C.E. Though the point is controversial, the political control evident at Byblos probably extended, though somewhat loosely and with some oscillations, to the rest of Canaan and Palestine. It probably continued during the *Hyksos rule of Egypt (c. 1670–1570 B.C.E.), and then after a brief period of independence following the expulsion of the Hyksos, it was resumed again with Egyptian expansion under Thutmosis I (1525–c. 1512 B.C.E.) and its consolidation under Thutmosis III (c. 1504–1450 B.C.E.). Within little more than a century, most of Canaan fell to the state of Amurru, which eventually became a Hittite vassal, and thus part of the Hittite empire (see *El-Amarna). However, under Seti I (c. 1318–1301 B.C.E.) and Rameses II (c. 1301–1234 B.C.E.) it was reconquered once more, probably in its entirety. Finally, with the invasion of the Sea Peoples, in approximately 1200 B.C.E., the Egyptian yoke was broken forever.

Internal Development to 1200 B.C.E.

In this long period there were other influences on Canaan besides the Egyptian. Contacts with the Aegean world are demonstrable by 2000 B.C.E., and they became particularly close in the 14th–13th century when, after the fall of Cnossus, the Myceneans conducted a vigorous trade with the entire eastern Mediterranean littoral. Relations with Mesopotamia go back even further, probably to the early third millennium, but almost certainly to around 2400 B.C.E.; and three centuries later one hears of a messenger of the "governor" of Byblos at Drehem in Babylonia (though the title should not be taken as implying the suzerainty of the Sumerian Third Dynasty of Ur). The arrival of the Amorites, already noted, added the deep cultural tie of language and religion, which commerce only strengthened; in the *Mari texts of the 18th century, Byblos is involved (along with Aleppo, Carchemish, Qatna, and Ugarit) in the movement of timber, resinous substances, wine, olive oil, and grain from Syria and Canaan to the kingdom on the Middle Euphrates.

The Amorite invasion also marks an important stage in the formation of the system of small city-states which became so characteristic of Syro-Palestine in the second millennium, and then, after the rise of the nearby national states in the Iron Age, continued in Phoenicia. The Execration Texts show the transition from a semi-nomadic stage – which is reflected in the earlier group – when the cities were probably not yet taken, and two or three sheikhs divided the authority over the environs, to a completely settled stage – attested in the later groups – when the cities had fallen and, with a couple of exceptions, there was a single ruler. Since the shift to monarchy is so widespread and so quick, it suggests the adoption and diffusion of an already prevailing institution. Acceptance of the institution, however, was hardly effected without important concessions, mainly in the form of land grants to the sheikhs who had helped in the conquest; at first, therefore, the king may have been only *primus inter pares*, as in early Assyria. The roots, therefore, of the city-state system probably go back to the third millennium; its feudal character began with, or was strongly reinforced by, its adoption by the Amorites.

This development may have received in Canaan, as in other parts of Syria and Palestine, further impetus in the period between approximately 1700 and 1500 B.C.E., when the Indo-Iranian chariot warriors, called *maryannu*, were introduced to the area and their services secured for the crown by grants of fiefs. At least in the following period all Canaanite kings still bear Semitic names, and never is a *maryannu* associated with the coastal cities of Canaan. However, for whatever the causes, by the 14th century B.C.E. one finds strong social unrest in Canaan as attested by the el-Amarna Letters; the half-free class who worked the land are escaping, and popular revolutions with assassination of the king are not unknown.

[William L. Moran / S. David Sperling (2nd ed.)]

The Transition

With the rise of a new dynasty in Egypt (the 19th), the southern part of Phoenicia fell again under Egyptian dominion. Seti I (c. 1318–1301 B.C.E.) speaks of conquering Asia, and mentions, among others, Tyre and Uzu (Ushu = Palaityros). Although Seti advanced as far as Kadesh on the Orontes, there is no evidence that Egypt could retain its hold on that vast Asian territory, for in the time of Seti's son, Rameses II (c. 1301–1234 B.C.E.), Kadesh was firmly in Hittite hands. Yet Egypt continued to rule the southern part of Phoenicia. In a famous treaty, the Egyptian and Hittite kings divided Syria and Phoenicia into two spheres of influence. The borderline may have passed north of Byblos (cf. Papyrus Anastasi I; Pritchard, Texts, 475 ff.). The following peace was of great importance for the cultural and material development of Phoenicia, and its overseas trade reached a peak.

1200–1000 B.C.E.

In the last years of Merneptah (1234–1224 B.C.E.), there is reference to the first waves of the invasions of the Sea Peoples into the countries of the Fertile Crescent. In the days of Rameses III (1182–1151 B.C.E.), these invasions brought with them the destruction of all the coastal towns of the eastern shore of the Mediterranean Sea. The archaeological evidence shows the total destruction of Ugarit, and the Egyptian sources speak about the conflagration of Arvad. According to a Tyrian source preserved by Josephus, there were 240 years from the founding (of Tyre) until the reign of Hiram (Ant., 8:62). This date is confirmed by Justin, who says that the king of Ashkelon (= Philistines) defeated the Sidonians, who fled and founded the town of Tyre, one year before the fall of Troy (Justin, *Trogi Pompei Historiarum Philippicarum Epitoma*, 18:3, 5). These independent sources agree that Tyre was refounded at the very end of the 13th century or the very beginning of the 12th century B.C.E. Certainly there was no new foundation, but the tradition teaches us that a juncture occurred in Phoenician history. It may be suggested further that from now on the name Sidonian was applied to the Phoenicians generally.

Emergence – First Contacts with Israel

At the beginning of the 11th century, Tiglath-Pileser I (1114–1076 B.C.E.) of Assyria arrived at the Phoenician coast. He mentions Lebanon and the towns of Arvad, Byblos, and Sidon. The story of Wen-Amon (in the first quarter of the 11th century B.C.E.; Pritchard, Texts, 25ff.; COS I, 89–93) shows the low political prestige of Egypt in the coastal towns at that time, a fact which is clearly expressed by the king of Byblos. Also the comparison of Byblos with Sidon shows Sidon's political and mercantile position. The first suggestion of contact between the tribes of Israel and the Phoenicians comes from about half a century earlier. In the Song of Deborah, the tribe of Dan already lives in the north (cf. the sequence of the tribes which did not participate in the struggle, Judg. 5:16–17), and the close relationship between the tribe of Dan and the Phoenicians can be seen from the verse: "And why did Dan remain in ships?" (Judg. 5:17), which Taeubler (*Biblische Studien*...(1958), 89ff.) interprets to mean that the Danites were seasonal workers in the harbors of Phoenicia. In the days of David there were already intermarriages with the Phoenicians (II Chron. 2:13). Similarly, there must have been intermingling between the tribe of Asher and the Phoenicians, for it says, "The Asherites dwelt among the Canaanites...for they did not drive them out" (Judg. 1:32), while the whole of the Valley of Acre and the southern Phoenician coast remained in Phoenician hands. It appears that at the end of the period of the Judges, Tyre rose to the position of the leading city on the Phoenician coast, and in the following 300 years it exercised a certain supremacy over the southern Phoenician coastal towns; W.F. Albright suggests that from this time Tyre became the capital of Phoenicia. Furthermore, Albright has propounded that it was Abibaal, the father of Hiram, who in a kind of alliance with David, destroyed the sea power of the Philistines, while David defeated them on the mainland. An alliance was formed between Hiram and Solomon (I Kings 5:15ff. = II Chron. 2:2[3]ff.), though given the superiority of Phoenician seamanship it is likely that the Phoenicians were the dominant partner (Cogan). Archaeological support is provided by finds of Phoenician wares in Israel in tenth–ninth-century contexts (Kuhrt, 408). This included the supply of Phoenician lumber and technology in exchange for Israelite agricultural products, and led to a joint venture by sea to Ophir (see *Trade and Commerce).

Height and Decline – 1000–750 B.C.E.

From the days of *Hiram the Great (c. 969–936 B.C.E.) Phoenician history, as known, becomes the history of Tyre. The external proof is the change of title: while Hiram is still called "king of Tyre" in the Bible, Ethbaal (c. 887–856 B.C.E.), the father-in-law of Ahab, is called "king of the Sidonians" (I Kings 16:31). The reign of Hiram also saw the beginning of the Phoenician colonial mercantile empire, which culminated in the foundation of Carthage in North Africa (c. 814–813 B.C.E.). By the marriage of Ahab with Jezebel, daughter of Ethbaal, the culture and religion of Phoenicia penetrated Samaria (I Kings 16:32ff.), and later by the marriage of Athaliah with Joram of Judah they also penetrated Jerusalem (II Kings 8:18; 11:18). Yet Phoenicia proved to be a haven to Elijah (I Kings 17:10). Among the allies who banded together with Hadadezer of Damascus, Irḥuleni of Hamath, and Ahab of Israel, against Shalmaneser III of Assyria at the battle of Karkar (853 B.C.E.), were the northern Phoenician towns, Arvad, Arka, Usanata, Shian, but not Byblos, Sidon, or Tyre. It may be assumed that the king of the Sidonians, ruling over the whole coast from Byblos to Acre, was behaving exactly like his predecessors and successors and avoiding a fight on the continent; his strength was in his fleet. The poem on the "Ship Tyre" in Ezekiel 27, though from a later period, may preserve some memories of Tyre at the zenith of her power. From the first years of Adad-nirari III (810–783 B.C.E.), Tyre and Sidon were among the tributary countries. The question is whether Tyre and Sidon formed a single unit, or were two different states. Tyre's leading position on the Phoenician coast is shown by the fact that it is always mentioned first in all the Assyrian lists from the days of Ashurnaṣirpal II (883–859 B.C.E.), even after the Assyrians definitely set up an independent kingdom of Sidon in the third year of Sennacherib, and it is also always mentioned first in all the pre-Exilic biblical sources (cf. Isa. 23; Jer. 47:4; Zech. 9:2).

750–538 B.C.E.

From the days of Tiglath-Pileser III (744–727 B.C.E.), a change in the Assyrian policy toward its neighboring states can be observed. One after another, the states were turned into Assyrian provinces (on the Phoenician coast, Sumuz became the main seat of the Assyrian governor). Only the main Phoenician city-states, such as Arvad, Byblos (the name of whose king is mentioned for the first time after a gap of 140 years), and Tyre, still remained "independent," certainly because of their commercial importance. In those days, another formidable enemy appeared – the growing colonial power of the Greek city-states in Cyprus, southern Italy, Sicily, and Sardinia. However, in the eyes of the prophets, Tyre was the "crowning city, whose merchants are princes, whose traders are the honorable of the earth" (Isa. 23:8; cf. Zech. 9:3).

While Shalmaneser V (726–722 B.C.E.) tried to break the power of Tyre by "liberating the subjugated towns (like Sidon, Acre, etc.)," Sargon II (721–705 B.C.E.) came to an understanding with "the king of the Sidonians," i.e., the king of Tyre. Sennacherib separated Sidon from Tyre and set it up as an independent kingdom (in 701 B.C.E.), but after an unsuccessful revolt in the days of Esarhaddon, Sidon became an Assyrian province (in 677/76 B.C.E. for about 45 years). Again the whole struggle against the imperialistic Assyrian forces was borne by Tyre alone. After a short interlude, when the Egyptian pharaoh Neco tried to reestablish Egyptian suzerainty in Greater Syria, including Phoenicia, he was defeated by Nebuchadnezzar at Carchemish (605 B.C.E.), and thus Babylon became the overlord of the Phoenician coast. At the beginning of the sixth century B.C.E. the west again revolted, with Egypt's support. After the fall of Jerusalem (586 B.C.E.), Nebuchadnezzar turned to the Phoenician cities and laid siege to Tyre as the main city of the coast (cf. Ezek. 26ff.). This siege lasted 13 years (Jos., Apion, 1:156), and ended in a conditional surrender (cf. Ezek. 29:18). At this time, the Phoenician colonies in Spain and Sicily, looking in vain for help from the mother-city against the growing Greek colonization, turned to Carthage, and with this move the real independent history of Carthage began. The contact with Tyre still continued, but now it took only a religious form. An annual tribute was sent from the daughter colony to the mother Tyre for Melkart (Melqart), literally, "the king of the city," i.e., the lord of Tyre (for the possibility that "city" in the god's name means "netherworld" see S. Ribichini, DDD, 563–65).

538–64 B.C.E.

According to Herodotus, the Phoenician towns opened their gates to Cyrus the Great of their own free will (*Persian Wars*, 3:91). From this time, Sidon, where the Persian king had one of his palaces, became the leading city of the Phoenician coast (cf. Ezra 3:7; I Chron. 22:4). The hegemony of Sidon is shown by the hierarchy of the command of the Persian fleet, since the king of Sidon is mentioned before the kings of Tyre and Arvad (Herod., *ibid.*, 7:96, 98). Territorial rights to parts of the coast (mostly to the south, in Palestine) were granted to the main Phoenician towns, and Sidon, Tyre, and Arvad together, founded the city of Tripolis. Here the Phoenician cities now held assemblies, and together dealt with the Persian government. The cruel suppression of the great revolt of Sidon (about 350 B.C.E.) by Artaxerxes III was not forgotten by the Sidonians, who opened their gates to Alexander the Great. Tyre, in contrast, sustained a siege of nine months before it was conquered (332 B.C.E.) by Alexander, who built a dike from the coast to the island. Since that time, Tyre has been situated on a peninsula. During the wars of the successors of Alexander, the Diadochoi, the Phoenician coast not only changed hands from the Seleucids to the Ptolemies but the main cities also exploited these quarrels to become independent and counted the years accordingly (Tyre from 274 B.C.E., and a new era from 126 B.C.E., Sidon from 111 B.C.E., Beirut from 81 B.C.E.). In 64 B.C.E. the Phoenician coast was incorporated into the Roman Empire, with certain special rights for both Sidon and Tyre. In the last years of the Second Temple in Jerusalem, the Phoenicians are called anti-Jewish by Josephus (Apion, 7:70). Still, from the time of the Maccabees until the destruction of the Temple, the Tyrian coinage (*kesep ṣōri*) because of its purity and reliability was the official standard for specific payments whose amounts were defined in the Bible (Tosef., Ket. 13:3).

Phoenician Colonization

The Phoenician colonization – which was, in fact, Tyrian colonization, for none of the other Phoenician cities established colonies – was quite different from that of the Greeks. Its main purpose was the securing of trading posts. It may be assumed that it started with the establishment of such centers in Cyprus. One of the oldest, if not the oldest, Phoenician settlement there was the town of Citium/ Kition (modern Larnaka), the *Kittim of the Bible (cf. Gen. 10:4), which may have been called Utica (cf. Jos., Ant., 8:146). It is said that its inhabitants revolted against the mother-city, Tyre, and were subdued by Hiram, the contemporary of King Solomon. From Cyprus, the Phoenicians penetrated, via Rhodes, to the Aegean Sea (according to Greek mythology Cadmus of Tyre came to Boeotia and introduced a number of arts, of which the most important was writing – Herod., *Persian Wars*, 5:57–58; cf. also the Phoenician merchantmen in the poems of Homer). According to Thucydides (*Peloponnesian War*, 6:2), the Phoenicians at one time had settlements all around the island of Sicily, although later they withdrew to the southwest. From Sicily they spread out to Sardinia in the north, and by way of the islands Malta and Gozo, southward to North Africa (Utica and Carthage), and from North Africa westward to Spain. It is possible that the Phoenician merchants reached Spain as early as the tenth century during the reign of Hiram (W.F. Albright, 1961, in bibl. against B. Mazar who thinks they date from the time of Ethbaal, about the middle of the ninth century). Josephus has preserved a notice that Ethbaal founded two colonies, one on the Phoenician coast itself and one in Lybia (Ant., 8:324). This Phoenician colonization of North Africa is not only reported in the classical literature, but also reflected in the Talmud and Midrash, and much later in the early Christian historiography as "an expulsion of the Canaanites by Joshua" (cf. H. Lewy, in: MGWJ, 77 (1933), 84ff.). The climax of Phoenician colonization was the foundation of Carthage according to tradition in 814/813 B.C.E. Thus far archaeological evidence is found no earlier than the second half of the eighth century. About the middle of the seventh century, the Carthaginians, the descendants of the Phoenicians, and the native populations took under their protection the Tyrian colonies, which were now endangered by the Greek colonization. Unlike the Greek colonial movement, Tyre's greatness rested on her mercantile colonies, which remained subjects of the mother-city. They paid their annual tithes to Melkart in Tyre, for Melkart, or the Tyrian Baal, now became also the chief deity in each colony.

EXPLORATION AND COMMERCE. The geographical conditions of Phoenicia dictated the pursuits and undertakings of its inhabitants; sea trade, fishing, and small industry. The Phoenicians claimed that they invented the building of ships and the art of fishing. The magnificent forest of Lebanon provided the wood for the ships, and the introduction of iron made it possible to build larger and more seaworthy ships, called "ships of Tarshish," which gave an impetus to more distant voyages. From the beginning of the tenth century, we can trace Phoenician colonization via Cyprus, to the western part of the Mediterranean – Sicily, Malta, North Africa, Sardinia, Corsica, and Spain – but it appears that the dates of the classical historians, who ascribe Phoenician colonization to the beginning of the 11th century, must be lowered by more than 100 years. Many Semitic names, however, have preserved the memory of Phoenician colonization, e.g., Cition (= Kittim) in Cyprus, Utica (= Watiga) and Carthage (qart-Ḥadasht) in North Africa, Cadez (= Gadar) and Tartessos (= Tarshish) in Spain. The Phoenicians actually founded only trading posts (this is the original meaning of Tarshish according to Albright) which engaged not only in trade, but also in a search for raw materials. The Phoenicians brought their own manufactures to the West, but to a far greater extent they acted as middlemen, transporting incense and spices from Arabia. These overseas expeditions were undertaken by guilds of merchantmen, with the king acting as representative both of the state and of the merchants (cf. *The Journey of Wen-Amon*; Pritchard, Texts, 25ff.; COS I, 89–93). The trips to *Ophir undertaken by Hiram and Solomon in partnership are the most famous examples of these expeditions. Ophir was apparently on the African coast, in the general region of Somaliland (Albright, Arch Rel, 133; cf. I Kings 9:28; 10:11, and for Jehoshaphat's aborted attempt, I Kings 22:49). The daring of the Phoenicians as sailors is shown by the expedition they made at the command of Pharaoh Neco, circumnavigating Africa by sailing south from the Red Sea and home through the Pillars of Hercules. Herodotus, who writes about this (*Persian Wars*, 4:42), discounts as incredible what in fact is the proof of its truth, namely, the fact that the Phoenician sailors claimed to have seen the sun on the right, i.e., to the north. Another famous voyage was made by Hanno from Carthage to Central Africa (approximately, Ivory Coast), at the beginning of the fifth century B.C.E.

INDUSTRY AND ART. The most famous industry of the Phoenicians was the manufacture of purple dye (it is possible that the name "Phoenicia" was derived from the industry; see above). Second in importance was weaving; the multicolored garments of the Phoenicians are mentioned in nearly all tribute lists of the Assyrian kings. Furthermore, the Phoenicians excelled in handicrafts: ivory objects, metalwork, metal statuettes and small stone sculptures, jewelry, and seals. Although the Phoenicians are credited with the invention of glass, it appears that they only developed the technique of its manufacture, for which they became famous in classical times. The purpose of all these handicrafts was not aesthetic but commercial. This is one of the reasons for the mixed styles, mostly borrowed from the neighboring countries and adapted to the taste of the customers. The Phoenicians were also famous as builders and architects (cf., e.g., the Temple of Solomon).

Religion

Little is known about the Phoenician religion (C. Bonnet and P. Xella apud Krings, 316–33; P. Scmitz, ABD, 5:357–63). Although over 6,000 inscriptions in Phoenician and Punic (overseas Phoenician) are known, there are no hymns, prayers, or god lists. Mostly, the inscriptions mention some specific deities, clients, and rituals. The excavations at *Ugarit in northern Syria of the late second millennium B.C.E. have brought to light many religious texts, myths, and rituals, which have enriched modern knowledge. The head of the pantheon was El, and his wife was Asherat of the Sea. In the poems about Baal and his sister Anath, their war against the gods of the underworld is recorded. These Ugaritic texts confirm to some extent the short notes of Philo of Byblos, which are quoted by Eusebius (*Praeparatio Evangelica*, 1:10, 7), about the Phoenician religion, and show a certain amount of continuity. At the same time much changed over a millennium thanks to Phoenician colonization resulting in increased contact with other cultures and the penetration of Hellenistic culture. In general each city-state had its own chief deity: El in Ugarit, Dagon in Arvad, the Lady of Byblos in Byblos, Eshmun in Sidon, Melkart in Tyre, Baal (Melkert)-Hammon in Carthage. The most important goddesses were Astarte, in the east, and Tanit/Tinnit, in the west. B. Mazar has noted that from the first half of the tenth century, a new deity appears in the pantheon, Baalshamem. Baalshamem may be identified with the Greek Zeus, whose temple is mentioned by Menander and Dius (Jos., Apion, 7:113, 118). Mazar suggests that this new deity should be connected with the colonial movement (cf. also the group of gods connected with navigation in the seventh-century treaty between Esarhaddon and Baal, king of Tyre: Baalshamem (Roellig, DDD, 149–51), Baalmadge ("Lord of Fishery"), and Baal-saphon (Niehr, DDD, 152–54)). The gods Eshmun (Ribichini, DDD, 307–9) and Melqart (Ribichinini, DDD, 563–65) are also newcomers unknown in the second millennium. There is no doubt that the Phoenician temples bore similarities to the Temple of Solomon, with two main pillars in front (cf. Jos., Apion, 1:118; Herod., *Persian Wars*, 2:44; and graphically, Harden, in bibl., *The Phoenicians*, pl. 50). The Phoenicians buried their dead in coffins as a rule, but there is also some archaeological evidence that they burned them. It is known that in Carthage the custom of infant sacrifices prevailed, which may have some connection with the cult of *Moloch (cf. II Kings 23:10). An inscription found at Incirli in Turkey may contain a reference to Moloch and human sacrifice (Kaufman and Zuckerman apud Holm).

Language and Literature – Later Period

The Phoenician language, which was spoken for more than 2,000 years, belongs to the northwest Semitic group. It is strongly related to Hebrew. As late as the fifth century C.E. there was to be found in North Africa a rustic dialect based on the Punic language, which is a descendant of Carthaginian, itself a descendant of the Phoenician language. The earliest Phoenician alphabetic text comes from the 11th century

B.C.E.; we already find here the *alphabet of 22 consonants. Greek tradition tells us that the Phoenicians invented the alphabet, since it was from the Phoenician merchants that the Greeks learned alphabetic writing. At the courts of the Phoenician kings, archives were kept, dealing with historical events (cf. Jos., Ant., 8:144ff., 324; 9:283ff.; Apion, 1:159ff.) and mercantile accounts (cf. *The Journey of Wen-Amon* (Pritchard, Texts, 25ff.); the correspondence between Hiram and Solomon (I Kings 5:15ff.). The Phoenician merchants were opposed to any descriptions of their voyages, with one exception: "The Periplus of Hanno," which has come down in its Greek translation (*Hannōnis Periplūs*). The epigraphic material from Phoenicia and from its colonies is very scarce. The most famous inscriptions are the sarcophagus of Aḥiram, king of Byblos (beginning of the tenth century B.C.E.); the Yeḥawmilk stele (about the middle of the fifth century); the sarcophagi of Tabnit and of Eshmunezer of Sidon (generally dated to the middle of the fifth century, but probably from the times of the Ptolemaic kings). Yet the longest Phoenician inscription on stone was discovered not in Phoenicia itself but in Cilica at Karatepe. It is a bilingual (Hittite and Phoenician) building inscription, of 62 lines (probably mid-eighth century B.C.E.). Another Phoenician inscription comes from Zinjirli, in northwest Syria (the building inscription of Kilamuwa, king of Y'dy), and dates from the second half of the ninth century. Other Phoenician inscriptions (some of which are bilingual) have been discovered in Cyprus, Rhodes, Sicily, Sardinia (e.g., the so-called Nora stone), Malta, Egypt, and even Attica. Examples of Phoenician writings occur on the coins of the main Phoenician towns, such as Arvad, Beirut, Byblos, Marathus, Ptolemais-Acre, Sidon, and Tyre. For a survey of Phoenician inscriptions see D. Vance, in: BA, 57 (1994), 110–20.

[H. Jacob Katzenstein / S. David Sperling (2nd ed.)]

BIBLIOGRAPHY: GENERAL: G. Contenau, *La civilisation phénicienne* (1949²); O. Eissfeldt, in: Pauly-Wissowa, Supplement, 20 (1950), 350–80; W.F. Albright, in: G.E. Wright (ed.), *The Bible and the Ancient Near East* (1961), 328–62; D. Harden, *The Phoenicians* (1962); S. Moscati, in: *Accademia Nazionale dei Lincei, Rendiconti della classe di scienze morali*, ser. 8, vol. 18 (1963), 483–506; idem, *The World of the Phoenicians* (1968); J. Gray, *The Canaanites* (1964). NAMES: E.A. Speiser, in: *Language*, 12 (1936), 124ff.; S. Moscati, in: AB, 12 (1959), 266–9. LAND: E. de Vaumas, *Le Liban*..., 1–2 (1954). PEOPLE AND LANGUAGE: G. Garbini, *Il semitico di nord-ovest* (1961); M. Noth, in: *Welt des Orients*, 1 (1947–52), 21–28; M.J. van Liere and H. Contenson, in: AASOR, 14 (1964), 125–8. HISTORY: Alt, Kl Schr; I.J. Gelb, in: JCS, 15 (1961), 27–47. RELIGION AND HIGHER CULTURE: Albright, Arch Rel, 68–94; T.H. Gaster, *Thespis* (1950); A.S. Kapelrud, *Baal in the Ras Shamra Texts* (1952); H. Frankfort, *The Art and Architecture of the Ancient Orient* (1954); M.H. Pope, *El in the Ugaritic Texts* (1955); P. Matthiae, *Ars Syra* (1962); H. Donner and W. Roellig, *Kanaanaeische und aramaeische Inschriften* (KAI), 1–3 (1962–64); J.B. Peckham, *The Development of the Late Phoenician Scripts* (1968). **ADD. BIBLIOGRAPHY:** GENERAL: V. Krings (ed.), *La civilization phénicienne et punique* (HdO; 1995). BIBLICAL CONNECTIONS: M. Cogan, *I Kings* (AB; 2000); M. Greenberg, *Ezekiel 21–37* (2000), 528–99. HISTORY: B. Peckham, in: ABD, 5:349–57; R. Drews, *The End of the Bronze Age: Changes in Warfare and the Catastrophe ca. 1200 B.C.* (1993); A. Kuhrt, *The Ancient Near East c. 3000–330 B.C.* (1995), 401–10. RELIGION: C. Bonnet and P. Xella apud Krings, 317–33; R. Clifford, in: BASOR, 279 (1990), 55–64; P. Schmitz, in: ABD, 5:357–63; T. Mettinger, in: BASOR, 293 (1994), 84–87; A. Cooper, EncRel, 10 (2005), 7128–33 (incl. bibl.); T. Holm, in: *ibid.*, 7134–35 (incl. bibl.). LANGUAGE: Z. Harris, *A Grammar of the Phoenician Language* (1936); J. Friedrich and W. Röllig, *Phoenizisch-Punische Grammatik* (1999); C. Krahmalkov, *Phoenician-Punic Dictionary* (2000); idem, *A Phoenician-Punic Grammar* (HdO; 2001).

PHOENIX, capital and largest city of Arizona. Its Jewish population in 2002 was 83,000, the 13th largest in the United States and growing. The first known Jew in Phoenix was Dr. Herman Bendell, who arrived in 1871, a year after the town was laid out, as Superintendent of Indian Affairs for the Arizona Territory. The first Jewish settlers came in 1872: Emil Ganz, a Civil War veteran, who was elected Mayor of Phoenix in 1887; Michael and Joseph *Goldwater (Goldwasser,) who founded a family mercantile dynasty that grew from a wilderness outpost into a statewide chain; Other early arrivals were Hyman Goldberg, his sons Aaron and David, and his brother Isaac (1875); Adolph, Leo, and Charles Goldberg (1879); Wolf Sachs; Joe Melczer; Selig Michelson, postmaster from 1908 to 1912; Gus Hirschfield; Harry Friedman; Pincus Kalsman; I.J. Lipson; and Isaac Rosenzweig. Aaron Goldberg, sat in the ninth and tenth territorial legislatures (1899–1901,) authored the bill that made Phoenix the capital, and his brother, Hyman was elected to the 19th and 20th legislatures. Barnett E. Marks, a young lawyer, who also organized the first Sunday school, later became assistant U.S. attorney for Arizona (1927–28.) Both Barnett and his wife, Freeda, were elected to the state legislature (1922.) Jews have been active in the political and civic life of the city. Rabbi Abraham Krohn of Beth Israel was memorialized in the city in 1958 when it named a public housing development for him. The mayor of Phoenix in 2006, Phil Gordon, was an active member of the Jewish community.

Informal Jewish worship services began in 1906 in a room over Melczer's saloon under the leadership of Barnett Marks. Temple Beth Israel was begun in 1921 as the first synagogue in Phoenix with funds raised by local sections of B'nai B'rith and the National Council of Jewish Women, which had been organized in 1917. Temple Beth Israel relocated to a new building in 1949. The original sanctuary was used as a Baptist church until 2002 when it was acquired by the AZ Jewish Historical Society with plans for restoration. Jews began coming to Phoenix for their health around 1920. The Jewish population increased dramatically after World War II as soldiers who had been stationed in Arizona returned to the state with their families. The city became one of the fastest-growing cities in the country, a major southwest trading center, and a haven for winter residents from all parts of the U.S. It is estimated that 2,000 Jewish families move to the Phoenix area yearly. There are over 40 congregations – Orthodox, Conservative, Reform, Humanistic, and Jewish Renewal. The Jewish Federation of Greater Phoenix supports 11 constituent agencies including the Bureau of Jewish Education, Council for Jews with Special Needs, Greater Phoenix Va'ad HaKashrut, Hillel at Arizona State University, Jewish Community Foundation, Jewish Family and Children's Service, King David School, Kivel Campus of Care, Pardes Jewish Day School, and two Community Centers. The community also has two other day schools: Phoenix Hebrew Academy and Jess Schwartz Community High School. The Federation has a very strong Israel office stressing programming, travel opportunities, and economic partnerships. The Phoenix Sister City Commission accepted a partnership with Ramat Gan in Israel (2005.) Cities of Scottsdale, Tempe, Chandler, Gilbert (all east of Phoenix) and Surprise (west of Phoenix) have growing Jewish communities. Surrounding retirement communities are Sun City, Sun City West, Sun City Grand, and Sun Lakes. (Other organized congregations in Arizona are in Flagstaff, Kingman, Lake Havasu, Prescott, Sedona, and Yuma.) According to a demographic study conducted in 2002 the Jewish population in Greater Phoenix included approximately 83,000 in 44,000 Jewish households, a 138% increase since 1984.

BIBLIOGRAPHY: J. Stocker, *Jewish Roots in Arizona* (1954); F.S. Fierman, in: AJA, 16 (1964), 135–60; 18 (1966), 3–19; *Phoenix Jewish News* (1947–2005); *Arizona Post* (1946–2005); Risa Mallin, Arizona Jewish Historical Society.

[Bernard Postal / Risa Mallin (2nd ed.)]

PHOENIX. The Greek legend of the phoenix, the fabulous bird that lives forever, is mentioned in apocalyptic literature with various addenda, as for example that "its food is the manna of heaven and the dew of the earth, and from its excrement the cinnamon tree grows" (III Bar. 6: 13). Some contend that the *ḥol* mentioned in Job 29:18 is the phoenix. It is so translated in the Septuagint, while the Midrash explains it as referring to that bird "which lives for a thousand years. At the end of a thousand years fire comes out of its nest and consumes it, and leaving behind of itself about the size of an egg, it reproduces limbs and lives again." Another view holds that after a thousand years "its body is consumed, its wings moult," and it renews itself (Gen. R. 19:5). This idea of a bird's renewing itself after a great age is applied elsewhere to the griffon *vulture (Ps. 103:5). However, it is not definite that in Job *ḥol* refers to the phoenix, since it may mean sea sand which is "eternal."

BIBLIOGRAPHY: Lewysohn, Zool, 352f., no. 501; N.H. Tur-Sinai, *Sefer Iyyov* (1954), 250.

[Jehuda Feliks]

PHOTIS, village marked on the Madaba Map between Orda and Elusa on the Gaza-Elusa road. It has been identified both with the Aphtha of Josephus (Jos., Wars 4: 155) and with the Aphta of Johannes Rufus (*Plerophoria*, 48; in *Patrologia orientalis*, vol. 8, p. 100), the more likely identification. The ancient site of Photis has been established at Khirbat Fuṭays, east of Gaza, with the remains of a settlement and a church; close by is the Monastery of Silvanus. In the Wadi Fuṭays are the remains of Byzantine silos. The moshav Pattish was founded on the site in 1950.

BIBLIOGRAPHY: M. Avi-Yonah, *Madaba Mosaic Map* (1954), 73; Avi-Yonah, Geog, 169. **ADD. BIBLIOGRAPHY:** Y. Tsafrir, L. Di Segni, and J. Green, *Tabula Imperii Romani. Iudaea – Palaestina. Maps and Gazetteer.* (1994), 203.

[Michael Avi-Yonah / Shimon Gibson]

PHOTOGRAPHY. The first photographer known to be of Jewish birth was Solomon Nunes *Carvalho, an American who in 1853–54 served as artist-photographer with John C. Frémont's expedition to the Far West. However, the 19th century did not produce many photographers with Jewish backgrounds. Jews took their place as photographers on the world scene in the 20th century. Among the inventors, the names of Leopold *Mannes and Leopold *Godowsky, the musician-scientists who in 1933 produced Kodachrome, and five years later Ektachrome, rank high. Polaroid, one of the most ingenious of all photographic devices, was invented by Edwin H. *Land. The list of distinguished Jewish photojournalists, beginning with Erich *Salomon, who originated candid photography with the first of the miniature cameras invented in the early 1920s, through John Heartfield (1892–1968), who, in montage photographs of vitriolic satire, blasted the Nazi hierarchy in various German publications until he was forced to flee for his life in the early 1930s, to the ubiquitous magazine photographers, is an extensive and impressive one.

The biggest pool of talented recorders of big world stories is to be found among the staff of *Life* magazine. Alfred *Eisenstaedt, who joined *Life* in 1936 when it was founded, had, by 1969, covered more than 2,000 assignments, and more than 90 of his photographs had been used as *Life* covers. Other famous Jewish staff members included Eliot Elisofon (1911–1973), Fritz Goro (1901–1986), Dmitri Kessel, Ralph Crane, Yale Joel, Ralph Morse, David E. Scherman, and Bernard Hoffman. The equally gifted free-lance photographers whose pictures regularly appear in the pages of *Life* as well as its sister magazine, *Time*, have also included extraordinarily gifted photographers such as Cornell Capa, Bruce Davidson (1933–), Elliot Erwitt (1928–), Burt Glinn (1926–), Philippe *Halsman, Archie Lieberman, Arnold *Newman, and Arthur Siegel (1913–1978). *Look Magazine* had on its staff such brilliant photographers as Arthur Rothstein (1915–1985), while Alex Liberman became the photographer-artist-art director for *Vogue*. Free-lance photojournalists work through photo agencies. Two of the leading ones in 1970 were Rapho-Guilumette, directed by one of the ablest administrators in the field, Charles Redo, and Magnum Photos by Inge Bondi. Among the great number of Jewish photo-journalists belonging to these two agencies have been Joe Rosenthal (1912–1981), of the Associated Press, who took the dramatic "Raising of the Flag on Mt. Suribachi in Iwo Jima, 1943"; Diane Arbus (1923–1971), whose photographs of transvestites were exhibited at the Museum of Modern Art, New York, in 1968; Morris Rosenfeld, photographer of yacht races; Robert Frank (1924–), known for his pictures of the seamy side of U.S. life; Ben *Shahn, whose photographs for the Farm Security Administration were later used as themes for his famous posters and paintings; and Arthur Rothstein, Edwin Rosskam (d. 2006), and Charles Rotkin (1916–2004), who all photographed the American dust bowl for FSA during the depression years of the 1930s.

Photography has dominated fashion and product photography since the 1940s. The remarkably versatile Irving Penn (1917–) had a flair for graceful, bold compositions, and like Richard Avedon (1923–2004) and Eliot Elisofon was an adventurous explorer and unique stylist in fashion photography. Through unconventional lighting, exaggerated poses, startling costumes, and exotic backgrounds, fashion photographers all over the world have created eye-catching images that have more than once changed female attire everywhere. Two emerging talents in fashion photography at the end of the 1960s were Melvin Sokolsky and William Klein (1926–). Architectural photography, which requires a highly developed sense of design, and the ability to plan a series of photographs from strategic vantage points at exact moments during the day or night, found an exceptional practitioner in Ezra Stoller. Abstract images, found in objects ordinarily ignored, became the "new reality" of Aaron *Siskind, who, as head of the photography department of the Illinois Institute of Technology and founder of the Society for Photographic Education, exercised considerable influence as teacher-photographer. A gifted student of Siskind's at IIT, Len Gittleman, became head of photography at Carpenter Center, Harvard University. Other members of the Society for Photographic Education have been Martin Dworkin of Columbia University, Bernard Freemesser of the University of Oregon; Jerome Liebling (1924–) of the University of Minnesota; Jerry Uelsmann (1934–) of the University of Florida; and Ralph Kopell of the State College of Iowa. It is not surprising that photographers of war and battle should rank as distinguished cameramen. David *Seymour (Chim; 1911–1956) was such a person – he died in the Sinai Campaign of 1956; Robert *Capa was another – he died in 1954 in the Indochina War; and among the first casualties in the Six-Day War of 1967 was Paul Schutzer (1930–1967), a staff photographer of *Life*. Combat photographers have inner discipline, and it was this same quality which caused the death in an air crash of Dan Weiner (1919–1959), who flew out in a storm to cover an assignment in the Kentucky mountains, and of Camilla Koffler (Ylla), the famous photographer of wild animals, who was killed in an accident in 1970 while photographing a wild bullock in India.

Photography, which unites art and science, was a child of the Industrial Revolution. It was the first art in history to owe its very existence to a scientific instrument. However, it would be wrong to think of science-minded Fritz Goro or Roman *Vishniac as cold and factual reporters of the modern world. They are poets who have drawn upon technology at its most advanced to reveal the poetry of an emerging world of thought and feeling. Photography was born largely as a result of the efforts of portrait painters to find some reliable means of getting an accurate likeness.

Portrait photography has been a big industry for over a century. The giants in portrait photography are few, but Arnold Newman and Philippe Halsman, two Jews, are certainly among them. So too are Eliot Elisofon, Alfred Eisenstaedt, *Izis in France, and Alfred Stieglitz. They all share the one essential quality that makes a portrait photographer, the ability to interpret a complex personality creatively, discovering something fresh and important to say. Newman is a master of symbolism that underlines and reinforces his central message. Halsman is a brilliantly inventive and witty graphic artist whose chosen medium is light.

There have been some distinguished Jewish curators, editors, journalists, and critics of photography, especially in the last three decades. Among these are Grace Mayer, curator of photography, the Edward Steichen Memorial Collection, at the Museum of Modern Art, New York, from 1962; Jacob Kainen (1909–2001), curator of prints and drawings, The National Collection of Fine Arts, Washington, DC; Eugene Ostroff, curator of photography, Smithsonian Institute, Washington, DC; Lewis Walton Sipley (1897–1968), director, American Museum of Photography, Philadelphia, Pennsylvania; Margaret Weiss, photography critic for the *Saturday Review*; Jacob Deschin (1900–1983), photography critic for the *New York Times*; David B. Eisendrath, science-oriented columnist of *Popular Photography*; Helmut Gernsheim (1913–1995), photography historian of London, England; and Albert Boni, who assembled and edited the comprehensive photographic bibliography published in 1962, *Photographic Literature*.

[Peter Pollack]

While no definitive "Jewish" photography style emerged, many of the practitioners of landmark photographic images were Jewish. Among them were Nan *Goldin, Annie *Leibovitz, Garry *Winogrand, and Helen *Levitt, who continued to be active into her nineties. At least two European-born photographers, Helmut *Newton and Andre *Kertesz, did significant work as Americans.

In Israel

The early photographers in Ereẓ Israel included Yaakov Ben Dov, Alfred Bernheim, and Shemuel Josef Schweig. Among the contemporary photographers working in Israel are many doing press work and producing picture books on the Holy Land. Among them are Werner Braun, David Rubinger, Micha Bar Am, Peter Merom, and David Harris.

CAMERA JUDAICA

Introduction

The great upsurge of interest in photographing Jewish subjects and in the understanding of photography as documenting the many facets of Jewish life in the past is a phenomenon of more recent years. More exactly, one could speak of a wave of renewed interest, a reinforced presence of photographs aimed at recording Jewishness and Jewish existence, and of a more outspoken use of old photographs as an instrument to safeguard Jewish memory. One feels today a more conscious and concerted involvement of photographers, photo-editors, and curators in an effort to interpret Jewish life through photography than ever before. The age of Jewish photography has arrived.

Moreover, and complementarily, in our age of the threefold domination of the cultural and social life by the camera – through photography (and photojournalism), through film (fiction and documentary), and through television and video – Jewishness itself seems to strive to express its presence in an image-oriented, visible dimension. The emancipated appearance on the one hand, and on the other the admired "sabra with an 'Aryan' look" (cf. the Paul Newman-alias-Ari ben Canaan ideal in the film "Exodus") evolves into a more expressive "Jewish is Beautiful" ideal. The latter is sometimes characterized by an ungroomed haircut-cum-beard often adorned with a big "*Chai*" sign (or a larger-than-life *Magen David*) and sometimes crowned with a *yarmulke*. Photogenic Judaism of the 1970s and 1980s is more visually aggressive than its 1950s–1960s predecessor. The once most powerful expression of the attitude to photography of Orthodox Jews, the refusal to be photographed, is today increasingly limited to the narrowest fringe. The "we have the right to be different" expression of Judaism has become more outward-projected and less abstract. The cameras were there, among other factors, and played their role.

The beginning of the New Wave in Jewish photography could be set in 1974. Three important photographic books, all relating to contemporary Jewish history, appeared in that year, independently of each other. In the German-speaking area, photographer and photo-editor Franz Hubmann published his *Jewish Family Album*. Germanic and bourgeois in its spirit and composition, the album mainly represented the West European Jewish Family. A photographic social history, it ended (significantly, as we will see) before 1939. In New York, journalist and writer Abraham Shulman compiled and created another family album, *The Old Country*. His book focused on the poor cousin, eastern European Jewry. Also in New York in 1974, Leyzer Ran compiled and composed a two-volume documentation about pre-war Vilna, *Jerusalem of Lithuania*. Here the photographs and other documents represented mostly the organized Jewish life, including its destruction and the resistance. Hubmann, Shulman, and Ran, the three compiler-authors, created, through photographs, different views of the Jewish experience. And yet, the books share certain traits that remain discernible in photographic books and exhibitions of later years.

In 1976, Abraham Shulman, perhaps encouraged by the reception of his *Old Country*, published *The New Country*, depicting Jewish immigration and early days in America. Also in 1976, the Jewish Museum in New York exhibited *Image Before my Eyes*, a photographic history of Jewish life in Poland between 1864 and 1939 (again), prepared by the YIVO Institute of Jewish Research in New York. Lucjan Dobroszycki and Barbara Kirshenblatt-Gimblett turned it into a book in 1977; a year later, the book was itself turned into a film. By the same time, a collective of young American Jews sponsored an amateur-photography contest that led to the publication of a book entitled *Behold a Great Image*, published by the Jewish Publication Society of America in 1978. In the same year, the Diaspora Museum in Tel Aviv opened its doors to the biggest Jewish photography exhibit/slide show/gallery ever created. This was the year in which the introduction of the image into the realm of representing Jewishness reached its culmination. To the more traditional and religious reader, this statement might sound like a heresy; in reality, there is a transformation. The process goes on, both in compilation and new photography. In 1980 and 1984, the sociologist Gerard Silvain published in Paris, in French, two large volumes based on his collection of (mostly photographic) postcards. The first, *Jewish Images and Traditions*, includes a thousand postcards illustrating Jewish life. The other, *Two Destinies in the Diaspora*, juxtaposes two fictional life stories, one Ashkenazi, the other Sephardi, also based on postcards. Also in the 1980s, the Diaspora Museum initiated three worldwide contests in photographing Jewish life. At the same time, the Museum assigned several photographers to take pictures relevant to contemporary Jewish history and sociology. In 1985 Yeshayahu Nir's book *The Bible and the Image, the History of Photography in the Holy Land 1839–1899* appeared; its popularized Hebrew version *Jerusalem and Ereẓ Israel: In the Footsteps of Early Photographers* appeared in Israel in 1986. In both editions, Jewish attitudes toward photography are discussed; the latter focuses on Jewish life in pre-Zionist and pre-Mandatory Palestine.

There is little doubt that these books and exhibitions represent less than a carefully orchestrated effort, more than a fad or a fashion. They embody a spontaneously growing cultural movement that arises from certain needs, that focuses certain energies, responds to certain realities. They demonstrate that Jewish photography is a fact, definable as the body of photographic images of Jews and of their culture taken, "encoded," by Jews integrated in it and meaningful to a Jewish audience able to "decode" it. There exists, undeniably, a photographic discourse on Jewish life. It has its themes, motifs, tendencies, and ideologies.

Motifs, Past and Present

TYPES AND FACES. *Behold a Great Image*, the photography book that has contemporary Jewishness as its theme, offers perhaps the best starting-point for an introduction to a taxonomy of Jewish motifs in photography. The book is a clearly shaped statement that presents its theme in clearly delimited, ideologically charged terms; it was edited by a team of Jewish activists and militants who used pictures taken by many photographers, most likely all Jewish. Finally, it was published by a representative and prestigious Jewish publishing house.

One opens the book and sees, first and foremost, faces: a first reaction is, "These faces are me, these are my people, they received the Law together with me on Mount Sinai, we were together through the Inquisition and the ghetto, it is for them that we have taken to guns and have built a country."

The fact that one might be as far from religion as the authors are from atheism and still identify with these images may serve as evidence as to the validity of the opening sequence. Of the 28 faces depicted, the opening double spread and 11 more pictures do not carry any unequivocal graphic sign of Judaism. Faces in this context serve as signs of identity, and identification is axiomatic to photography. The act of recognition of the Self (or its part) in photographs of the other is the most general and basic function of photography in society and in culture.

The first section, "Faces," is followed by sections on "Children" and "Elderly"; this reads of course that Judaism is a family, a tribe, first and foremost. True, the book represents the editors' specific ideas influenced by "*Ẓedakah* collectives," engaged in voluntary social work. It draws both on feelings of compassion and on sentimentality, also axiomatic to much of photography. But the book's message goes beyond its narrow and immediate aims. In "Children" and "Elderly" and the following sections – "Hasidim," "Trade," "Food," "Demonstrations," "Cemeteries," and "Holocaust" – Family and Tribe become an ethnicity with its own garment, gastronomy, alphabet, political interest, and history. Many of these are perennial motifs in Jewish photography that can be found in retrospective photography books and in modern photographic monographs, and they invite a more detailed discussion.

Whoever enters the permanent exhibition at the Diaspora Museum is first touched by the show-window "Faces" that seems to welcome the visitor. It is a never-ending audiovisual display of Jewish "types," similar in its conception and impact to the opening sequence of *Behold a Great Image*. Gerard Silvain's *Jewish Images and Traditions* also opens with "types." And, as Silvain implies, the "Jewish type" is a problematic image. At the beginning of his compilation, there are three postcard-photographs entitled "The Eternal Jew," showing poor, bearded, French ambulant merchants and vagabonds. The photographed "types" that is to say, the models, are not Jewish; yet, they may "seem Jewish," especially in antisemitic eyes. According to Silvain, it was the oral tradition that assimilated such French "types" to Jews, the eternal wanderers. But ambiguities of perception are present even in responses to authentic images. A typical postcard brought later by Silvain shows a "Jewish type." Such postcards, having Jews and other "types" as subjects, were very popular in their time and had nothing denigrating in them. And yet one of the postcards carried an inscription and signature handwritten by the sender: "The town of Leopol (?) is half populated by these dirty Jews. Germaine." Silvain brings another postcard, from Algiers, that also shows in a characteristically typical and neutral manner a young Jewish woman. The handwritten note is quite different in spirit: "Pas mal. Hein! Levy."("Not bad, isn't it! Levy.") As the signatures indicate, the images – in both cases – were created in the beholders' eyes, and so were the connotations. However, although antisemitic propaganda richly used photographs of Jewish faces, none of the portraits used in *Behold a Great Image* or the Diaspora Museum slide show would attract antisemitic editors today. Jewish photography is actively and consciously involved in the de-caricaturization of the Jewish stereotype. True, very often this tendency leads to an excessive beautification and romanticization of the distinctive traits of the Jewish face. Nevertheless, many photographers of the past and the present portrayed "Jewish types" with sensitive eyes and minds. Some did it with a touch of greatness.

CELEBRATIONS, CUSTOMS AND STUDY: RITES. Few subjects seem as obviously belonging to the field of Jewish photography as weddings (the universally most preferred subject of the trade) and bar mitzvahs. Theirs is a powerful link: they are both memorable family events and graphically expressive rites. Weddings and bar mitzvahs are perceived as prestige-conferring social events in the time they occur, and the value of their depiction rises with time, as they find their way onto walls and into family-albums. The canopy above the bride and groom, the *tallit* on the youngster's shoulder, provide the Jewish color. It was no miracle that this subject developed into a full-fledged photographic genre.

New Year greeting cards are one of the oldest "holidays" and "Jewish Year" subjects in Jewish trade photography. For the amateur's camera Ḥanukkah candles are among the most favorite subjects of the Jewish year, with their light preferably reflected on children's faces. The environment of study, the yeshivah, the *ḥeder* and the Jewish scribe belong to this order of subjects. Jewish study and scripture is a religious practice, a celebration, one rite among others. Other powerful links are at work here: *ḥeder* means children, yeshivah and scribes – most often – elderly, all "graphic" types. Unfortunately, photography of rites became the very realm of schmaltz, with children, brides, and scribes, and without them.

An interesting innovation in this field was, a few decades ago, the clash between objects of rite with objects of modern life. Photography is profane, and so are most of its subjects. Images such as truck drivers in ḥasidic garments, a *yarmulke* on the head of a laboratory specialist, a *lulav* in the hands of a man in overalls, *tefillin* on the forehead of a tank commander have at once secularized Judaism and by the same token have spiritualized its secular dimension. Today, even this relatively new genre seems overworked and outworn, one kitschy cliché among others.

Greatness, authentic belief, and real cultural values are best served with straight, "documentary" or "anthropological" photographs, or with subdued, somewhat enigmatic images. Roman Vishniac's pictures from 1938 eastern Europe mostly belong to the first category. Nahum T. Gidal's photograph entitled, "The Night in Meron" (taken in 1935), which shows in semi-darkness a traditionally dressed man half leaning, half lying on a building's arched roof, is perhaps the best example of the second. Vorobeichic's 1931 constructivist photo-montage of bookshelves in the Vilna rabbinical library also touches the realm of mystery.

TRADES AND STREETS. The shtetl – wooden houses, twisted lanes, Jewish artisans and poor storekeepers – preserves the ever present images of our past. To be sure, in a few streets and in some trades the shtetl is well and alive even in our days. Jewish photographers detect and depict it as a curious mixture of relics from the past and of present-day decay, which it, most often, is. But then, photography has this curious power to pictorialize rubbish and romanticize poverty. If rites are the realm of schmaltz, the shtetl is the realm of nostalgia. The fact that old photographs survived the vagaries of time provides them with an additional aura – as if time itself survived with them. Nothing feeds nostalgia as exquisitely as old photographs. Given the extreme hardships, misery, and martyrdom of the old days, one must admit that old pictures feed warm feelings toward a world that never existed in reality.

The beauty of nostalgia, in spite of the appearances, is not a celebration of the past, a real longing to live again, in the future within the conditions of the past. It is a self-assuring celebration of memory itself. To turn old photographs, vital evidence of bygone times, into historical documents, therefore, necessitates a demystifying reading. This means to analyze and deconstruct the idealizing photographic techniques on the one hand, and the falsifying connotations of a selective memory on the other.

It is easy to enjoy the heartwarming old images, knowing that the "golden" olden days when Jewish poverty – often, utmost poverty – was a fact of life, are over. This is not the case when poor socio-economic status and low prestige persist. In 1975 Jerusalem's Israel Museum organized a large scale representation of Jewish life in Morocco. Some of the photographs that were to be included displayed poverty and connoted, moreover, "underdevelopment" and "primitiveness." A prominent Israeli investigator of folklore born in Morocco and involved in the preparation of the exhibition threatened to demonstrate violently his opposition to the enterprise should these photographs, whose authenticity he did not deny, be exposed. One senses behind this opposition an anxiety that they may have confirmed negative stereotypes concerning the Moroccan immigration still current in the more established strata of Israeli society. That such an opposition was never recorded among descendants of eastern-European poor Jews does not imply that the shtetl was less poor than the mellah, the Moroccan Jewish quarter. It indicates that it belonged, already, to a more distant past. It also indicates that the mellah did not find its Vorobeichic, Vishniac, and Gidal.

CEMETERIES. Cemeteries exercise a powerful attraction for Jewish photographers. There is hardly an illustrated book or an exhibition about Jewish communities where a photograph of tombstones – mostly taken from middle distance – is absent. Paradoxically they signify survival and continuity of the ethnic group. Old tombstones are signs of life, albeit of life gone, but they represent people and a people. With their Hebrew inscriptions, old Jewish tombstones signify survival of a culture, both in the eyes of Jews and of their opponents. Antisemites do not analyze signs. Their instincts tell them that by destroying and desecrating Jewish cemeteries they pose a potent threat to Jewish culture and life.

Nature, always present in photographs of cemeteries, plays a double role, of both adversary and catalyst. The photogeny of tombstones, even half-broken and half-lying, consists of their victory over grass and thistle that threaten to overgrow them and to condemn them to disappearance and oblivion. They signify victory of a cultural artifact over the surrounding nature. On the other hand, adorning the stones and their Hebrew letters with wild greenery, nature embraces them, "naturalizes" them, and turns them in to part of nature. The photogeny of old cemeteries consists of the dialectics of struggle and fusion of culture with nature, of memory with eternity. It adds to the Hebrew inscriptions – a symbol in itself – an immensely powerful second symbolic dimension.

SYNAGOGUES. *Behold a Great Image*, the starting point of our analysis, has almost exclusively in its synagogue section, photographs of wrecked synagogues and of synagogues converted into churches. None of the high-class houses of prayer or of other *shuls* in popular quarters is represented. This is an exceptional representation of the subject, a wrecked synagogue, in the Jewish repertory of symbols, means destruction, pogrom, *Kristallnacht*, Holocaust. An abandoned synagogue, in opposition, could mean disappearance of a Jewish community through emigration to another or more affluent country, perhaps *aliyah* to Israel; and in American inner cities, urban exodus toward better ecologies of a wealthy suburb. The particular treatment of synagogues in this book implies ideology. The message is that the latter exodus weakens the coherence of Jewish communities. This may be a plausible point, but the almost exclusive use of images of abandon and decay in living and prospering Jewish America seems to be a textbook case in photographic rhetoric and propaganda.

History, and its more recent chapters, turned the destroyed synagogue into a clearly determined and conventionally decipherable, decodable sign. It turned all old photographs of synagogues in eastern and central Europe from a view of a building of prayer into a view of a monument. The shift can be exemplified by one of Silvain's postcards, printed in his *Jewish Images and Traditions*. It is a photograph of the Great Synagogue in Frankfurt. Sent on October 22, 1899, it carries the following handwritten inscription and signature in French: "My dear Joseph, for an Israelite this card is a pleasure to have. Your brother, Isaac." Never again will this photography generate a similar feeling of joy over Jewish presence. The meanings that it carries today are of a more complex order. It is nostalgia, but also mourning, pride, anxiety, sorrow, elements of Jewish memory.

A synagogue also remains, of course, in all its aspects, a work of architecture and of decorative art. As such, it represents Jewish art, with all the ambiguities of this concept. It also represents the search for identity and status of a community, an ethnic community in a foreign and not always friendly world. Photographers can capture and differently emphasize any of these connotations. A symbol of Jewish religion, a subject charged with Jewish history and sociology, synagogues are and will remain a permanent motif in Jewish photography.

VANISHING COMMUNITIES. Since the 1940s, thousands of Jewish communities have ceased to exist. Many of these disappeared as the result of the Holocaust; some in mass emigration to Israel; others have been gradually abandoned as the Jews have slipped away to other homes, sometimes in the metropolitan areas of the same country. Often the descendants of these communities or other photographers have been motivated to photo-document the material remains. Some of this has been initiated by Beth Hatefutsoth.

The following extracts are taken from the descriptions of Temporary Exhibitions held in the Gallery of the Beth Hatefutsoth (the Diaspora Museum in Tel Aviv). They speak for themselves and the subject.

> Radauti, a town in northeast Romania, was once a busy trade center with a community of 6,000 Jews. By the late 20th century, only about 200 remained and their numbers continued to diminish as the older generation died and the younger generation left. This is one of the last places in Europe where many of the characteristics of the shtetl life still survive. The American photographer, Laurence Salzmann, spent two years in Romania, preparing his photographs on Jewish life in contemporary Radauti. His work portrays the Jewish life cycle, from circumcision to burial, religious life and cemeteries, economic life and community functions, and he follows two families as they leave Radauti and start a new life in Israel.
>
> Several centuries ago, Jewish life in the Caribbean thrived with activity. Descendants of Marranos, from Spain and Portugal, came to the region in the 17th century and established a chain of flourishing settlements. Today only a few remnants survive; Jewish community life is limited to a few centers. Elsewhere all that remains are ruins, tombstones, and memorial tablets. Beth Hatefutsoth sent out a small expedition to locate and document the remains. They visited Surinam, Curaçao, Coro (Venezuela), Barraquila (Colombia), Panama, Jamaica, Barbados, St. Thomas and St. Eustatius.

Ethnophotography of a people that had never stopped migrating and perhaps never will.

HOLOCAUST. There is a world of difference between the vanished Jewish communities of Radauti and the Caribbean on the one hand, and the vanished Jewish community of Poland on the other. Whatever remains of Polish synagogues or of the terrible sites on which death machinery had left its traces will most likely be photographed again and again by Jews who attempt vainly to apprehend the unacceptable. In contrast, such photographs will also be taken as an outcry to be turned into an ever-accusing evidence, an expression of protest of a people revolting against its historical conditions of existence.

Photographs taken during the Holocaust by Jewish photographers (only those are considered here) are of a different and unique kind. In one sense, they simply are historical documents, reports, and records of an event of unique dimensions. In another, they constitute a personal testimony of a photographer-eyewitness. In a third and utterly exceptional sense, they depict the photographers' own path toward death, a path shared with their portrayed subjects. "Doomed Photographers Reporting about Their Doomed Community" would be the appropriate title of their exhibition. Research, disclosure of official material, and state archives of all Allied powers, and accidental discoveries may lead to the uncovering of more such pictures than those presently known and published. And it is under the above mentioned title that such photographs will have to be studied and incorporated into the pantheon of Jewish Photography.

ISRAEL. The Jewish homeland is certainly the most diverse and most problematic subject of Jewish photography. Vested ideology is perhaps nowhere as powerful and influential as in this case.

The authors of *Behold a Great Image* again provide an interesting example of a clearcut and significant choice. Most of the photographs in their concluding chapter, entitled "Israel, the Land," show Orthodox Jews in their own secluded quarters. It is not difficult to fill in the verbal equivalent of their visual statement: Even in Israel, Jewishness is first of all a religion, and it is picturesque and ultraconservative.

Israel, the land, the state, the people, is in all its facets unique in Jewish history, culture, and experience. It is an important, perhaps central, though not yet fully crystallized, part of it. A Jewish photographer who depicts Israel, and this includes any theme and motif in Israeli life, is operating inside the culture. A controversial work may best exemplify this problem. Some of Joel Kantor's photographs of Israel exhibited at the Israel Museum in Jerusalem in the late 1980s (Kantor, born in Canada, had lived in Israel for some 15 years) show Israeli security forces brutalizing young Arabs. By their subject matter, esthetics and ethics, they belong to Jewish photography at its best.

Conclusion

First, a single photograph can only exceptionally express a culture's particular point of view by its formal organization. Only exceptionally can a single photograph disclose a photographer's approach to his subjects. Even more rarely will it reveal whether the photographer has operated within his own culture and was intimately acquainted with its values and points of view. But a photographic discourse of larger dimensions, such as an exhibition, a book, or a lifetime work, reflect these characteristics. Photography is vision of things, of people, of life, of the world, and as such, culturally determined. Even the most universalistic and universe-embracing photographic show ever created, "Family of Man," represented the Family in a perceptibly American, "WASP-ish" perspective. To bring another example of the influence of the photographers' cultural background on their work, British/Protestant 19th-century traveling photographers who visited the Holy Land depicted its biblical sites in the open countryside more often, and included in their pictures of famous landmarks more of the surrounding nature than their French/Catholic counterparts, who focused more closely on monuments and architecture. It is appropriate to observe this relation from another direction. Few audiences were as sensitive to Alter Kacyzne's photographs from the 1920s of Jewish Poland, or to Roman Vishniac's images from eastern European Jewish life in the 1930s, as the Jewish audience. And no gentile photographer has produced on this subject a collection as powerful and as penetrating as Kacyzne and Vishniac. True, Vishniac's collection owes part of its impact to its date – the eve of the Holocaust. But then, precisely, the close relationship to reality is typical of and inherent in the camera's work.

Second, preliminary definitions concerning Jewish photography may now be suggested. The first definition has to be restrictive and limited and formulated in the following manner: The basic body of Jewish photography is constituted by the pictures taken by Jewish photographers who explore and record Jewish life from an insider's point of view, and which appear to Jewish viewers as meaningfully expressing their shared concerns. The second definition has to provide Jewish photography with a broader perspective. It has to leave space for "unpopular" images, which like Kantor's, while relating to present-day Jewish concerns and values, might be rejected by a Jewish audience as too critical. it has also to leave space for more universal concerns of Jewish photographers, since such concerns are part of Jewish experience and culture. Last but not least, it has to leave space for gentile photographers who feel affinity toward Judaism and Jewish culture, perhaps the space English literature had for a Joseph Conrad, and American literature for a Vladimir Nabokov.

Golden is theory, and green the tree of life. The growth of Jewish photographic work during the coming decades and centuries, and the growth of a Jewish audience perceptive to it, will confirm – or reject – the ideas here suggested.

[Yeshayahu Nir]

BIBLIOGRAPHY: L. Dobroszycki and B. Kirshenblatt-Gimblett, *Image Before My Eyes, A Photographic History of Jewish Life in Poland, 1864–1939* (1977); N.T. Gidal, *Land of Promise* (1985); M. Grossman, *With a Camera in the Ghetto*, ed. by Z. Szner and A. Sened (1977); F. Hubmann, *The Jewish Family Album, The Life of a People in Photographs* (1974); L. Ran, *Jerusalem of Lithuania*, Illustrated and Documented (1974); Y. Nir, *The Bible and the Image, The History of Photography in the Holy Land 1839–1899* (1985); idem, *Bi-Yerushalayim u-ve-Ereẓ Israel, be-Ikvot Ẓalamim Rishonim* (1986); A. Shulman, *The Old Country* (1974); idem, *The New Country, Jewish Immigration in America* (1976); G. Silvain, *Image et Tradition Juives. Un millier de cartes postales, (1897–1917), pour servir a l'histoire de la Diaspora* (1980); idem, *Deux Destins en diaspora, Moi, Myriam Attias, Sepharade, Moi, Joseph Lewski, Ashkenaz* (1984); R. Vishniac, *Polish Jews, a Pictorial Record* (1947); M. Vorobeichic, *Ein Ghetto im Osten (Vilna)* (1931); G. Wigoder (ed.), *The First Years, Beth Hatefutsoth. The Nahum Goldmann Museum of the Jewish Diaspora* (1983).

PHRYGIA, district in central Asia Minor, part of the Roman province of Asia after the death of Attalus III (133 B.C.E.), the last king of *Pergamum. A Jewish community was established in Phrygia no later than the end of the third century B.C.E. According to Josephus, Antiochus III (the Great) transported 2,000 Jewish families from Mesopotamia and Babylonia to "the fortresses and most important places" of Phrygia and Lydia. These Jews were to serve as military settlers in support of the Seleucid monarchy, as the inhabitants of Phrygia had risen in revolt (cf. II Macc. 8:20: Babylonian Jews in the service of the Seleucid army against the Galatians). Favorable terms were granted the Jewish settlers. They were permitted to live in accordance with their own laws, and each was allotted land on which to build and cultivate. Generous exemptions from taxes were also granted, and Josephus thus considers the episode ample testimony to the friendship of Antiochus toward the Jews. The Jews of Phrygia undoubtedly had strong ties with Jerusalem and the Temple. On two occasions large sums of money which had been gathered in two cities of Phrygia, Apamea, and Laodicea, to be sent to the Temple were confiscated in 62–61 B.C.E. by the Roman governor Flaccus on the charge of illegal export of gold (Cicero, *Pro Flacco*, 28:68). A number of Jews from Phrygia resided in Jerusalem during the first century C.E. (Acts 2: 10). Several important Jewish inscriptions in Greek have been discovered in Phrygia, mostly from graves. One, dated 248–49 C.E. warns that if anyone should desecrate the tomb, "may the curses written in Deuteronomy [cf. ch. 27–29] be upon him." Nearly all the personal names are Greek, but the epithet "Joudaeos" is used several times and a *menorah* is carved on one stone. A tomb from Hierapolis, of the second or third century, states that the fee for any future additional internment is a donation to the Jewish community in Jerusalem.

BIBLIOGRAPHY: Schuerer, Gesch, 3 (1909^4), 6, 12, 17; V. Tcherikover, *Hellenistic Civilization and the Jews* (1959), 287f., 501; Schalit, in: JQR, 50 (1959/60), 289–318; Frey, Corpus, 2 (1952), 24–38.

[Isaiah Gafni]

PHYSICS. The material presented in this entry emphasizes those contributions which were important in arriving at verified present-day scientific results, rather than those that may have appeared important at the time. Unavoidably it will overlap in parts with material presented in the separate *Astronomy entry.

Introduction

Though rich, innovative, and highly creative, the Jewish intellectual contribution to civilization was initially an essentially humanistic and non-scientific "program," staying that way for more than 25 centuries, from the Patriarchs and Moses in the second millennium B.C.E. in the eastern Mediterranean to the great Jewish astronomers in the 10th–15th centuries C.E. at the other end of that sea. There was one exception, namely a marginal interest in astronomy, the "intercalation" sub-program motivated by repeated efforts aimed at the construction of an ever-improved calendar. Technically, this was a quest for better synchronization between the agriculturally important solar year and the timekeeping advantages of the lunar month, an aim which was indeed achieved in the present Jewish calendar, finalized by the end of the first century C.E.

It was only in the 10th century C.E. that a major change appears to have occurred involving the Jewish communities in Europe along the western Mediterranean, from the Iberian Peninsula and southern France to Italy, with science gradually approaching (but not achieving) the status of Torah studies. These regions constituted the interface between the crystallizing Christian national dynastic states of the western Roman Empire, as parceled out by its Germanic conquerors, and the Ummayad and Abbasid caliphates and other Muslim states established in Northern Africa.

The Jewish interest in science was part of a general regional reawakening some four centuries after the almost complete eradication of Greek science with its remarkable achievements over the one thousand years from Pythagoras to Diophantus – e.g., the realization that the earth is round and measurement of its radius by Erathostenes with a better than 0.5% precision, the understanding by Aristarchus of Samos of the heliocentric structure of our planetary system 1,800 years before Copernicus, or Archimedes' derivation of the laws of mechanics and hydrostatics – just to mention three examples from the third century B.C.E. All this would have been lost forever upon the closure of the Academy in Athens on the orders of Justinian in 550 C.E., if not for the transplantation of nine Academy scholars with some of their documentation to Mesopotamia at the invitation of Persian emperor Khushru Anushirvan and the founding of an academy outside of Christianity's reach. The institution survived the Muslim conquest, developed under the Ummayads, and flourished under the Abbasids, who established the central school in their palace. Their Spanish Ummayad rivals responded by creating a similar academy in Cordoba. The preservation and consolidation process had thus lasted almost half a millennium, when science made its re-entry into western Europe from the Muslim bridgeheads in Sicily and Spain. Being neither Christian nor Muslim, Jewish scholars for a while enjoyed the advantage of having access to the research centers on both sides of the divide, but the religious zeal in England and France throughout the Crusades and their aftermath brought about the total expulsion of Jews from these countries, which thereby remained "*judenrein*" for several centuries.

The second millennium C.E. did witness two periods of peak Jewish creativity in the sciences, separated by a figurative "black hole," the Dark Age of European Jewry, lasting from the 16th to the mid-18th centuries.

Jewish involvement in the physical sciences can thus be summarized as follows:

(1) Creative Humanism, no physical sciences: 15th century B.C.E.–10th century C.E.

(2) First creative era in science (astronomy and physics): 11th–15th century (Spain, S. France)

(3) Jewish Dark Age (Europe): 16th–mid-18th century.

(4) Second creative era in science (physics and astronomy): 19th century to present.

This can be further divided into two phases, according to the limitations on Jewish access to scientific research facilities, namely,

(a) a *restricted phase*, either

(a1) *formal* (through the Oath of Allegiance), or

(a2) *patronizing* ("they do not know how to behave …");

(b) *the fully emancipated phase.*

The transitions occurred at different periods in each of the western democracies (e.g., 1950 for full emancipation in the United States).

This chronology is followed in the present entry, with the Second Era section including three subsections dealing with special episodes: Nazi "Jewish Science" (1933–45), Nazi Germany and the Jewish initiative in the development of nuclear weapons (1938–46); and the "Scientists' Freedom of Movement" struggle in the U.S.S.R. (1971–91). It concludes with a survey of physics in modern Israel (from 1928).

From Antiquity to Sepharad (Humanism)

In its first 25 centuries (1500 B.C.E.–1000 C.E.), the creative Jewish cultural contribution effectively centered on humanism and its ethical, social or juridical realization, e.g. the idea of a weekly day of rest, moral codes (as in the Ten Commandments), the treatment of slaves, support for the weak, etc. Very little was achieved in the sciences, where both motivation and methodology remained purely pragmatic, whatever the activity. An example is the biblical value (I Kings 7:23) of 3 = ח for the ratio between circumference and diameter in a circle, a value indicating that it must have been determined experimentally, namely averaging between results of very rough measurements of the ratio in several round objects; the Masoretic editors (8th–10th century C.E.) noted the lack of precision and inserted an improved value in a footnote. Another example is R. Nehemiah's *Sefer ha-Middah*, a book which played an important role in the preservation of Greek geometry and its revival in the East under the Abbasid caliphate, yet without a single proof, only prescriptions. Compare this with Greek culture, where Archimedes provided a mathematical *proof* that the value of π, an important geometrical constant, lies between $^{22}/_{7}$ and $^{223}/_{71}$ (or between 3.1408 and 3.1428), while using a method that could be further extended to any degree of precision.

There is no real principle making it incompatible to be creatively involved both in humanistic culture and in science. There is even evidence that the conception of science as a worldview, i.e., the idea which emerged in sixth century B.C.E. Greece, that the physical world might be describable by laws of nature, was inspired by its humanistic analog, namely by the adoption of Solon's ethical code (human law), itself an imported offspring of the Middle Eastern ethical codes (Hammurapi, Moses, etc).

Returning to pragmatic scientific activity in early Jewish tradition, there is talmudic evidence in two cases for marked astronomical erudition, namely the *tanna* R. Joshua b. Hananiah in Judea (c. 40–100 C.E.) and the *amora* Mar Samuel of

Nehardea in Babylonia. Such erudition was essential to the establishment of the Jewish calendar. On the other hand, there is no evidence for any systematic observation and recording of astronomical data. Such recording was performed by the Sumerian, Egyptian, and other priesthoods and was directly related to their cults. This is still universally reflected in the seven-day week, established for the seven deities identified with the seven astronomical "wanderers" (Sun, Moon, and five planets seen with the naked eye – Mars, Mercury, Jupiter, Venus, Saturn; notice the strange order).

The strong biblical injunction against "worship of stars and zodiac signs" notwithstanding, there was no hesitation about applying the data to evaluate the various intercalations required to fit a lunar calendar to the solar year, a pragmatic task that was indeed performed efficiently.

The First Active Scientific Age: Sepharad and Provence

The first Jewish scientific era lasted from 1000 to 1500 C.E., with major contributions in astronomy and physics (as well as *medicine), all by scholars residing in Spain and southern France. It began with R. *Abraham bar Ḥiyya ha-Nasi ("the Prince") of Barcelona (d. 1136), author of three books on astronomy (in Hebrew) and continued with his pupil R. Abraham *Ibn Ezra (1089–1164).

A formal dimension was acquired by this "dynasty of learning" between 1152 and 1156, when a team headed by R. Isaac *Ibn Sa'id and R. Judah ben Moses Cohen, working in Toledo in the service of King Alphonso x of Castille, calculated and published the Alphonsine Tables. These tables were designed to track the movement of the planets, mainly for high-seas navigation.

The two most original and effective Jewish contributions were those of R. *Levi ben Gershom in Provence in the 14th century and R. Ḥasdai *Crescas in Aragon in the 15th. The last astronomer in this sequence was "Zacut," namely R. Abraham ben Samuel *Zacuto (1452–1515), a leading scholar at Salamanca in Castille, who, at the expulsion, was welcomed for a while in Portugal and was given the responsibility for the scientific work at Sagres. Four years later, however, he was expelled with all other Jews in Portugal.

The Portuguese Marrano Jewish philosopher Baruch *Spinoza (1632–1677), working in Holland, where his family returned to the Jewish faith, can be considered as an extension of the Iberian age. Although the Amsterdam Jewish community leadership eventually excommunicated Spinoza (1656) because of his position on religious dogma, his overall views in several contexts are now not far from those of non-fundamentalist modern Jewish religious thinkers, such as R. Abraham Isaac *Kook.

R. Levi ben Gershom of Bagnols (1288–1344) lived in Avignon in the south of France, a city which at that time was the seat of the papacy. Jewish scholars and historians generally designate Levi by the acronym RaLBag – while to the gentiles he is Maestre Leo de Bagnols, Leo Hebraeus, Gersonides – but the crater on the moon named after him by the International Astronomical Union reads "Rabbi Levi." (It is situated in a "Jewish quarter" which also has craters named after Ibn Ezra, Zacuto, and Einstein. In the Jewish world, Gersonides is generally cited for his teachings in religious philosophy – sometimes with a footnote stating "he also wrote 118 chapters in astronomy" (these works were translated from the original Hebrew into Latin by Mordecai Finzi, astronomer to the duke of Mantua). Levi earned his living as "mathematicus" (astrologer) in the service of the popes, the same function filled by Johannes Kepler at the emperor's court in Prague 200 years later, or by Galileo Galilei at the duke of Tuscany's court in Florence.

Rabbi Levi was one of the greatest astronomers (and one of the greatest scientists) in the Middle Ages after the lights of science were turned off in the Greek centers along the shores of the Mediterranean. The following are but a few of his accomplishments: He invented the sextant (naming it Jacob's staff, a term used in the British Merchant Marine until the early 18th century). He improved the camera obscura – the camera's ancestor. Predominantly, and contrary to social norms during the Middle Ages, R. Levi did not blindly accept dogma but tested every assumption with his instruments. He was criticized for this both in the Jewish world and by the secular astronomy establishment. In a brilliant experiment, in the spirit of 20th century philosopher Karl *Popper's (1902–1994) invalidation ("falsification") doctrine, R. Levi measured variations in the luminosity of Mars over a period of five years. He proved that there was no correlation between the observed variations in the luminosity and the variations which would be expected if the planet Mars were following the path according to the then current version of Ptolemy's (Claudius Ptolemaeus of the second century C.E.) geocentric model with its epicycles – a theory universally accepted in the Middle Ages. He therefore disproved that model, and thereby paved the way for the adoption of the Copernican system two centuries later.

The greatest Jewish medieval non-mathematical theorist in physics and cosmology was R. Ḥasdai Crescas (d. 1412) of Barcelona. Better known for his philosophy, which argued against mixing science with religion (in itself a view, close to modern approaches), his impact on the rebirth of physics was unique. Plato had discussed vacua, but Aristotle had then stated that "nature does not tolerate a vacuum," and throughout the Middle Ages physical thinking was non-reductive, always "effective," a priori assuming the presence of friction, air resistance, etc. Without a vacuum, however, one cannot define inertia and mass. In his book *Or Adonai* Crescas refuted Aristotle's arguments against the vacuum and presented an infinite empty space as the scene on which the physical world is enacted. Like Gersonides, he also assumed continuous creation and a multiplicity of worlds.

Pico della Mirandola (1463–1494), the one-man encyclopedic "team" who prepared the philosophical and scientific transition to the Renaissance, and who taught himself Hebrew and Arabic for that purpose, included an abstract of Crescas' book in his "900 theses." It was picked up by Giordano Bruno (1548–1600), who was burned at the stake specifically for spreading Crescas' notion of an infinite empty (presumably absolute) space. Galileo, however, could now "place" a moving body in this vacuum and invent inertia, while Newton could have a force act on the body and measure velocities and accelerations with respect to that space and define the concept of mass as a measure of inertia.

The Dark Age

CAUSES. The 15th and 16th centuries are among the darkest in Jewish history. It is not that the previous 400 years in western Europe had been an idyll. On the contrary, the Jews in France suffered several expulsions and three countrywide massacres (1214, 1251, and 1320), by the Pastoureaux, sweeping peasant rebellions that struck almost only the Jews because they were the only unprotected group in the population. And yet there were a few quieter spots, in particular in the papal possessions in and around Avignon, where a Jewish presence lasted until the area was annexed to France during the Revolution. But the 15th and 16th centuries represented a regression. Two physical catastrophes followed by spiritual letdowns in the four movements they inspired, as well as the mystically oriented transformation of Judaism which they brought about, all contributed to the regression in Jewish participation in the development of science. The two major disasters were (1) the expulsion from Spain and other territories ruled by the Spanish monarchs (1492) and from Portugal (1497), and (2) the massacres in southeastern Poland (with about 600,000 dead), by the rebel Ukrainian Cossacks (1648) under the leadership of hetman Bogdan *Chmielnicki.

To these we may add the four pseudo-Messiahs (David *Reuveni, 1490–1538; Solomon *Molcho, 1591–1532; *Shabbetai Ẓevi, 1636–1676; Jacob *Frank, 1726–1791) with the despair and conversions which followed the failure of each movement. Finally, there was the boost enjoyed by the mystic interpretation of Judaism with the rise of Ḥasidism, following the teachings of R. *Israel ben Eleazar Ba'al Shem Tov (1700–1760), a trend which lasted about a 100 years and which was not inducive to scientific thinking.

HASKALAH. One development running counter to these trends occurred in Berlin, namely the rise of the *Haskalah (Enlightenment) movement, following the lead of Moses *Mendelssohn (1729–1786). This was an attempt to develop a westernized interpretation of Judaism, emphasizing modern approaches to the study of Jewish classics (also as a shield against conversion), coupled with an assimilationist approach regarding dress, language, and other everyday aspects of life to produce "Germans of the Mosaic persuasion." It was made possible in Berlin by the relative liberalism in matters of culture and science of Voltaire's friend, the scholarly King Frederick II (the Great), whose academy included the key scientists of the era.

Moreover, while the norm throughout central Europe was for Jews to be confined to the ghettos and restricted to peddling as a "profession," 18th-century Germany with its heterogeneous multitiered political structure offered a number of channels – "protected" Jews who could go anywhere because they were paying their "protection taxes" to the emperor, other taxes to the various kings, etc. In 1763, Mendelssohn won a prize offered by the Prussian Royal Academy of Sciences in a competition consisting in an essay on a question in metaphysics, with Immanuel Kant coming in second. The event had an impact on Jewish youth, attracting them to the sciences. The intellectual transformation was shaped and polished in the salons of several Jewish ladies (Rahel Levin *Varnhagen, Henriette *Herz, and others). The movement started by Mendelssohn thus played an important role in the return of Jews to science, literature, etc., but it failed badly in the prevention of conversion. It is rather tragic to note that much of the creative cultural harvest would have lost any trace of its Jewish origins had it not been for its rejection by the Nazis, together with their reclassification of the authors as Jews even at a distance of two generations.

MITNAGGEDIM. The ḥasidic movement's rapid spread seemed to replace the "religion of learning" by one of hereditary dynasties of miracle-rabbis leading a following of ignoramuses. The spiritual leadership of classical Judaism in Lithuania, under the inspiration of *Elijah Gaon of Vilna (1726–1791), a leader revered for his spiritual creativity and his learning, organized a campaign aimed at stemming the growing mystical flood. After several decades of a bitter struggle, the conflict lost its "either/or" aspect and new trends appeared on the ḥasidic side, with a reemphasis on learning.

The Gaon was interested in science, considered himself fully knowledgeable in this matter, and promoted scientific studies as useful additions to Torah. However, the Jewish isolation and loss of contact were so great that what the Gaon meant in 1780 by "science" was Euclid's geometry and Aristotle's physics, having never heard of Descartes, Galileo, or Newton.

The Second Creative Period: Restricted Approach

To understand what happened to European Jewry around 1800, the reader should bear in mind the effective status of the Jewish population in central Europe, constrained to ghettos and to marginal professions. This state of affairs ended as a combined result of two roughly simultaneous "revolutions," namely the French Revolution (with its Napoleonic sequel) on the one hand, and the Industrial Revolution on the other. Napoleon's army reached every capital in Continental Europe at some time or other, and the reforms it either imposed or indirectly induced included the cancellation of employment and residence restrictions on the Jews. The Industrial Revolution created work and new white-collar jobs for bankers, financiers, accountants, clerks, lawyers, but also engineers of various specialties, etc. The autochthonous population generally preserved family traditions – nobility serving as professional army officers, peasants receiving farms from their parents and transferring them to their own children, etc. The white-collar jobs required literacy, but intellectual types in the nobility generally joined the Church.

The situation on the Jewish side was just the opposite: to the extent that anybody had risen above peddling and had some traditional family training, it was in moneylending, jewelry, or commerce, a preparation for banking and other financial professions. Males were all literate and with some preconditioning for logical structures, somewhat facilitating the study of law and mathematics. As a result, the 19th century established an emancipated Jewish middle class throughout central Europe, and yet this did not include a serious academic or scientific component, mainly because of the customary Oath of Allegiance required upon becoming an ordinarius (full professor), a throwback to medieval times. The Oath was taken with one's hand on a New Testament and was thus considered de facto religious conversion.

One way of participating in academic activities without swearing allegiance was to have a parallel occupation outside the academic world and occupy it after resigning from the university before the oath stage, and whenever possible to return after a few years and repeat the cycle. This was somewhat easier in mathematics and mathematical physics, which did not require special equipment for the professor to continue his research and preserve his knowledge in the non-academic phase.

Prominent examples are the mathematicians John Joseph *Sylvester (1814–1897) in England and Leopold *Kronecker (1823–1891) in Prussia. England was still in its "formally restricted" stage as far as Jewish emancipation went, and Sylvester, who studied at Cambridge, could not even get his B.A. until 1871, when he received it together with his M.A. He "meandered" between academic life and working in an insurance company, and later as a lawyer. By 1883, though, progress in emancipation had reached a level which enabled Sylvester to become a full professor at Oxford without converting. Kronecker's line was commerce and banking, with short appointments in academe, until progress in emancipation allowed him to receive a professorship in 1883. In a somewhat bizarre twist, Kronecker converted to Christianity shortly before his death.

The mathematician and theoretical physicist Karl Gustav Jacob *Jacobi (1804–1851) was the first Jewish scientist to be appointed to a special royal chair without having to take the Oath, which had just been abolished by Prussian Minister of Culture Wilhelm von Humboldt (brother of the geographer). Intellectually, the von Humboldt brothers had grown up in the intellectual salons of the ladies of the *Mendelssohn family and its periphery, a liberal milieu, and it was natural that they should regard the Oath as a medieval vestige. However, this was not the end of the story. In 1848 politically liberal Jacobi signed a petition calling on the king to put an end to his absolute rule. The king put an end to Jacobi's chair and Jacobi found himself in the street with his wife and seven children. One year later, Alexander von Humboldt intervened and the king reestablished the chair. However, Wilhelm had died and the new minister had reestablished the Oath, so that Jacobi took it and converted shortly before his demise.

By the end of the 19th century formal restrictions had been abolished almost everywhere, but they had been replaced by an unwritten numerical restriction policy. This was often represented as protection of the academic milieu against Jews in academe who "do not know how to behave," a phrase found in most appointment committee reports, such as the one dealing with Einstein's appointment in 1909 as professor at the University of Zurich, or that of the Princeton University Graduate School's admissions committee dealing with Richard Feynman's application (backed by his MIT professor): "We do not like to have many Jews in the graduate school because it is difficult afterwards to find jobs for them."

In the United States, the restrictive policy lasted till the mid-1960s when an incident involving MIT President Vannevar Bush and British mathematician G.H. Hardy (1877–1947) exposed the procedure and held it up to ridicule. Bush had fixed a ceiling of one Jew per department. In mathematics this position was occupied by Norbert *Wiener (1894–1964), but sometime in the 1950s the Department of Mathematics wanted to hire Norman Levinson, recommended by Hardy. This was vetoed by Bush in view of the restrictive policy of the institution. Some time later MIT awarded Hardy an honorary doctorate. In the ceremony, Hardy thanked "the Mass. Inst. of Theology" for the award and, when corrected, insisted, explaining, "Why else would a professor's religious appartenance matter at all?"

Further Advances

The restrictions notwithstanding, the children and grandchildren of the earliest white-collar Jewish generations gradually replaced *ḥeder* or yeshivah schooling with state education and found their way to the universities as students and then as temporary teachers, etc. The formalities constituting the obstacles in the admission threshold for Jews were sometimes more flexible in medicine and pharmacy, perhaps a vestige of the traditionally high reputation enjoyed by medieval Jewish medicine. In Austro-Hungary, this extended to chemical engineering, which is why famous theoretical physicists such as E. Wigner, E. *Teller, etc., were originally trained as chemical engineers. The combination of talent, intellectual curiosity, and the willingness to be satisfied with temporary and somewhat insecure positions resulted in the emergence of a sizable Jewish component in most European countries' research setup. Towards the end of the 19th century there were in the forefront of physics at least two future Jewish Nobel laureates, both experimentalists, Albert Abraham *Michelson (1852–1931) and Heinrich Hertz (1857–1894). Both of them, and more so, more recently, Dennis *Gabor (1900–1979) were investigating electromagnetic radiation in its overlap with optics, i.e., a field very remotely related to the traditional occupational expertise in lenses (itself probably an extension of diamond cutting and jewelry making) as exemplified by Spinoza. In France, the advance was more in the conceptual and abstract domain as represented by Henri *Bergson (1859–1941) in philosophy and Jacques *Hadamard (1865–1963) in mathematics.

The Einstein Era: Quantum Theory and Relativity

The more distinguished the Jews were, the greater their mark both within the system and outside it. Then a young German Jew, an employee of the Swiss Patent Office in Bern, published within the same year (1905) five articles in theoretical physics, each of which was a scientific high-water mark of the order of Newton's papers. This was Albert *Einstein (1879–1955), and his reputation grew accordingly after the experiments verifying his theory of gravity (1916), namely the general theory of relativity. His success attracted many a young Jew to physics.

Two conceptual revolutions occurred in physics in the first half of the 20th century, namely relativity and quantum mechanics. Einstein spearheaded both, almost single-handedly in relativity and with M. Planck and Niels *Bohr (1885–1962) in the quantum maze. Aside from Michelson's initial experimental exposure of the failure of classical mechanics for velocities close to light-velocity, Einstein was assisted at the mathematical end by the perception of his former teacher Hermann *Minkowski (1864–1909) and by his former classmate Marcel Grossmann; the first interesting application was achieved by astronomer Karl *Schwarzschild (1873–1916). All three were Jewish.

On the quantum front, aside from Niels Bohr, there was Max *Born (1882–1970), who led in the initial understanding of the mathematical results, John von *Neumann (1903–1957), who provided the mathematical consolidation of the new formalism, and Wolfgang *Pauli (1900–1958), whose "Pauli Principle," forbidding having at any one time more than one electron for any set of quantum numbers, provided a master-key to understanding atomic physics and the Periodic Table in Chemistry and applications in electronics.

The growing sophistication both in the conceptual toolkit of mathematical physics – and even more so in the rapidly evolving technological potentialities at the disposal of experimentation – forced 20th century physicists to split according to a two-dimensional repartition, namely theorists versus experimentalists in the abcissa and the ordinate going from high-energy nuclear physics (or the physics of particles and fields), to (low-energy) nuclear physics, atomic physics, molecular, nanotechnology, condensed matter, astrophysics, and cosmology (plus the environmental refocusing – geophysics, oceanography, etc.). A glance at the list of Nobel laureates in physics shows that they are evenly distributed on the above chessboard. In theory, Lev *Landau (1908–1968) and Richard *Feynman (1918–1988) have both covered several areas and produced the deepest insights. Eugene *Wigner (1902–1999) (and Giulio Racah) developed algebraic methods which played an important role in atomic, nuclear and particle physics. Feynman's impact was mostly in particle physics; other theorists who made important contributions in that area are Julian *Schwinger (1918–), Murray *Gell-Mann (1929–) (and Yuval *Ne'eman), Steven *Weinberg (1933–), Sheldon *Glashow (1932–), and David *Gross, also Maria Goeppert-Mayer in nuclear physics. The leading experimentalists in this field are Donald *Glaser (1926–), Leon *Lederman (1922–), Fred *Reines, Jack *Steinberger (1931–), Melvin *Schwartz (1932–), Martin *Perl (1927–), and Jerome *Friedman. In condensed matter physics, among the leading theorists are Vitaly *Ginsburg and Abrikosov. Isidor I. *Rabi (1898–1988) measured particle magnetic moments, while Felix *Bloch (1905–1983) turned them into a scientific and medical tool. Claude *Cohen-Tannoudji (1933–) developed methods of trapping single atoms, David *Lee (1931–) and Douglas *Osheroff advanced superfluidity.

One of the founders of modern cosmology was Alexander Friedman in the 1920s in the U.S.S.R., while Herbert Friedman was a pioneer in X-ray astronomy. Arno *Penzias discovered the cosmic background radiation. Ed Salpeter contributed to astrophysics and Jesse *Greenstein in astronomy.

Nazi Germany

The growth in size and in importance of the Jewish contribution to physics continued throughout the 20th century, yet it was also especially marked by several momentous events belonging to both Jewish and general history. As against the gradual opening of the world of science (and physics in particular) to Jewish students, teachers, and researchers, the coming to power of the Nazis in Germany in 1933 acted more like lightning. All Jewish professors in German state universities were fired immediately, with only Max Planck and David Hilbert protesting – admittedly Germany's two top gentile scientists, which may also partly explain their civic courage (Planck's son later participated in the officers' plot to kill Hitler and was executed). Two prominent experimental physicists, Philip E.A. von Lenard (1862–1947) and Johannes Stark (1874–1957), both of them Nobel laureates, and two leading mathematicians, Ludwig Bieberbach, best known for the "Bieberbach conjecture," and Oswald Teichmullern, an important topologist, identified with Nazi policy and actively joined the campaign for the eradication of "Jewish physics" and "Jewish mathematics." The exodus of Germany's Jewish scientists was complete, from Albert Einstein, who left in 1931, settling in at the Princeton, to Max Born, who went to Scotland instead of moving to Jerusalem, Einstein's entreaties notwithstanding.

Three remarkable female Jewish physicists provide a typical sample of Jewish destinies reminiscent of 1492: Emmy *Noether, mathematical physicist, worked with F. Klein at Erlangen and with Hilbert at Goettingen, and was famous for "Noether's theorem" linking conservation laws (e.g., energy, linear and angular momentum, electric charge, etc.) to invariance under symmetry transformations (for the above examples these are, respectively, time translations, spatial translations, rotations, phase modifications). Barred from getting a professorial appointment by the double barrier of her sex and religion, she immigrated to the United States in 1933.

Mariette Blau of Vienna, who developed the detection of cosmic radiation with emulsions, fled Austria with the *An-*

schluss (1938) for Sweden and later reached Mexico and the United States. Lise *Meitner (1878–1968), a physicist, collaborated with the chemist O. Hahn until 1933, then fled to Sweden. For many such cases, including that of her physicist nephew O. *Frisch, the Bohr Institute in Copenhagen served as a first stop when fleeing – until the start of World War II and the German invasion of Denmark. Between 1933 and 1938 Nazi de facto domination spread over central and southern Europe, causing the flight of most Jewish physicists, as well as non-Jews married to Jews (e.g., E. Fermi, H. Weyl) or children of one Jewish parent (e.g., H. Bethe, N. Bohr, W. Pauli). In Italy, formal racist legislation was decreed in October 1938.

Conceiving Nuclear Weapons – a Jewish Response to the Nazi Threat of Annihilation

Scattering neutrons off uranium, and having detected the presence of elements resembling barium and iodine, Enrico Fermi announced the production of new elements (93 & 94 in the Periodic Table) and was awarded the Nobel Prize in 1938. The Fermi family fled to the United States after the Nobel ceremony, except for wife Laura's father, a Jewish admiral, who returned to Italy and indeed died in a concentration camp. The other Jewish members of the Fermi group were Emilio *Segre (1905–1989), who left for the United States, and Giulio Racah, who immigrated to Israel.

Around that time (Christmas 1938), Lise Meitner was visited by her nephew O. Frisch. They discussed a letter from her former partner O. Hahn, who had redone Fermi's experiment and was certain that these new products were not new elements but indeed true barium and strontium! Meitner and Frisch then recognized nuclear fission.

The news arrived in Copenhagen upon Frisch's return and was brought to the United States by N. Bohr and Leon Rosenfeld. Here it caught the attention of Leo *Szilard (1898–1964), a Hungarian Jewish engineer turned physicist (eventually also one of the founders of molecular biology), who had earlier considered the possibility of fission in nuclei and now realized its military potential. Meanwhile, Frisch moved to England, so that early in 1939 two alarmed groups of Jewish physicists ("Central European refugee scientists" in the textbooks), now refugees in the United States and England, were going through a nightmare as they considered the possibility of German physics and an eventual nuclear weapon joined to Evil as personified by Adolf Hitler. In America, the Szilard group included Edward Teller (1908–2003), John von Neumann, and Enrico Fermi; in England, Otto Frisch, Rudolph *Peierls (1907–1995), and Joseph *Rotblat (1908–2005). Both groups tried to alert the respective governments. In the United States, Szilard used Jewish contacts, in particular financier A. Sachs, to get to President Roosevelt; at Sachs' request, they informed Einstein and got from him a signed letter explaining the danger and calling for preempting Germany in developing the new weapon, in order, at least, to achieve through deterrence some protection against its use. The entire effort resulted in the allocation of $6,000 for Fermi, for an experimental study of an eventual chain reaction. In England, however, the lobby reached and convinced Winston Churchill, who wrote to Roosevelt. Less than a week before the Japanese attack on Pearl Harbor, which drew America into World War II, the president, now convinced, authorized the Manhattan Project.

The Manhattan Project, an R&D and production ensemble, was directed by American Jewish physicist J. Robert *Oppenheimer (1904–1967), with Hans *Bethe (1906–2005) heading the Theoretical Division and E. Segre and R.P. Feynman, members of the original initiating group, and others participating.

A 1995 study of the project by A. Makhijani (*Bulletin of Atomic Scientists*) reports that the Pentagon decided a priori that the new weapons would not be used on the European front, for fear of Germany's capability for nuclear retaliation, but that they could be used on the Japanese front, as Japan was not considered as scientifically capable of developing nuclear weapons – but it was also decided not to inform the scientific leadership of the project "because they are Jewish and singly motivated by fear of Hitler's Germany"; eventually, Germany surrendered before the weapons were ready, and when President Truman weighed their use in Japan, several of the Jewish physicists signed a letter to the president suggesting they be used in a harmless demonstration rather than on a target, whether military or civilian. The Dutch Jewish physicist Samuel Goudsmit (1902–1978), co-discoverer of the electron spin, was put in charge of ALSOS, a military unit whose task was to find out what Germany might be doing in the nuclear weapons context.

Of course, other war needs continued in parallel, with important roles played by Isidore I. Rabi working on microwave radar, Theodore von *Karman (1881–1963) on aeronautics, etc. In all of these developments, including the Manhattan Project, Jewish physicists were doing their duty as American patriots. The frantic concern of the two refugee groups on both sides of the Atlantic and the resulting initiative should be counted as an intrinsic part of Jewish history, a response to Germany's extermination program, in the same category as the Warsaw ghetto revolt or the Jewish maquis in France.

The second nuclear confrontation was the Cold War (1950–90). Edward Teller initiated the development of the H-bomb, a nuclear fusion weapon based on an idea of Teller and S. *Ulam, a Polish Jewish mathematician.

Physics in Israel

BEGINNINGS. The first academic appointment in physics in modern Israel was that of Samuel *Sambursky in 1928 as assistant for physics in the Department of Mathematics at The Hebrew University of Jerusalem. Einstein had joined the founders' group in 1921 when he traveled with Weizmann to the U.S. to collect the basic funds, then in 1923 when he visited Palestine under the British Mandate.

The head of the Department of Mathematics was A.H. Fraenkel of Set Theory fame, and helped by Einstein and L.

Ornstein (Leyden, then Utrecht), he tried to attract quality personnel. The number of serious candidates rose considerably in 1933, when the Nazis came to power in Germany and all Jewish faculty members in all German universities were fired. For reasons of economy, however, HU President Magnes did not assign any priority to physics, and various candidates (F. London, F. Bloch, G. Placzek – who had planned to bring along his student – E. Teller) were effectively rejected. E. Wigner did stay one year, but left in order not to be in the way when a single position was made available for either him or L. *Farkas, a physical chemist (married with one child while Wigner was single). Farkas had arrived from Fritz *Haber's lab (Haber, of World War I chemical warfare repute, had been prevailed upon by Einstein to go to Jerusalem and was on his way, when he fell ill and died).

Finally, E. Alexander, an arrival from von Hevesy's Freibourg X-ray crystallography lab, with parallel theoretical experience in the study of symmetry in crystals, launched both the Physics Department at HU and a line of research which developed in all physics departments in the country, achieving important results, such as J. Zak's work, and culminating in D. *Shechtman's 1984 discovery of non-periodic ordering (pseudo crystals), both at the Technion. Alexander and Farkas created laboratories which fulfilled an important role in the defense of the eastern Mediterranean in World War II. Another physicist whose role was extremely useful in World War II and in Israel's War of Independence was E. *Goldberg, the former founder and director of Zeiss-IKON, the leading optics firm in Europe, and yet another refugee immigrant scientist fleeing Nazi rule. He founded Goldberg Instruments, the first high-tech firm in the country (renamed El Op after its merger with A. Jaffe's Rehovoth Instruments.

Condensed matter physics developed with the arrival of several key researchers: Cyril Domb, FRS, who joined Bar-Ilan University in the 1960s; Guy Deutscher from France; Alexander Voronel and Mark Azbel arrived from the U.S.S.R. after a difficult struggle, joining Tel Aviv University (TAU), which had been active in support of their struggle; M. Gitterman (Bar-Ilan) also arrived from the U.S.S.R., while Isaak Khalatnikov (TAU) and Pitaievski (Technion) arrived in the early 1990s, after Glasnost.

Racah, arriving in 1938, launched theoretical physics and, in particular, atomic physics and spectroscopy in the country. On the experimental side, research in nuclear chemistry (as the experimentation in the production of elements and isotopes came to be called) was initiated at the Weizmann (formerly Sieff) Institute by Israel Dostrowski, who had worked on these subjects in England in the early 1940s. He developed techniques for the separation of isotopes of hydrogen and oxygen. The Weizmann Institute soon became an important supplier of the latter, much in use in the study of organic processes.

Sometime after the founding of the state in 1948, the government established an Atomic Energy Board, with E.D. *Bergmann, a distinguished organic chemist and the director of the Weizmann Institute, as chairman. Bergman, Racah, and Dostrowski selected good students and placed them in high-quality research centers and under good tutors. Amos *de-Shalit and Igal *Talmi (nuclear structure), G. Yekutielli (cosmic rays), I. Pellah (reactors), and U. Habersheim (physics education) were selected and were joined by H.J. Lipkin, who had immigrated from the United States after receiving a Ph.D. in physics. They returned in 1954, but Ben-Gurion had meanwhile resigned and retired. His successors, Prime Minister Sharett and Defense Minister Lavon, did not share Ben-Gurion's enthusiasm for science and transferred the group to the Weizmann Institute against a payment of $100,000, the estimated investment in their studies (U. Habersheim returned to the United States).

De-Shalit and Talmi produced important results, and the Weizmann Institute had thus become a bridgehead for nuclear physics in Israel, soon to become the most active center for nuclear structure studies after the Bohr Institute in Copenhagen. By the end of 1957 it was "natural" to have a well-attended International Conference on Nuclear Structure in Rehovot, discussing the hottest topic of the decade, namely parity non-conservation, and with W. Pauli, T.D. Lee, Mme C.S. Wu, and Ben Mottleson of Copenhagen in attendance.

Theory needs to be close to experiment for good balance and this came next – a Tandem Van de Graaff electrostatic accelerator was started up, with Gvirol Goldring in the lead.

Ben-Gurion returned from his Sedeh Boker retreat in 1955 and the IAEC returned to its program, with two nuclear labs, and two reactors – a 1–5 MW "swimming pool" AMF enriched uranium reactor at Sorek, supplied by the United States and under its surveillance, and a 24 MW natural uranium "heavy-water" cooled one in Dimonah, purchased in France. In reactor physics, experiment (I. Pellah) preceded theory (S. Yiftah). Members of the former team now served as advisors, sometime after taking specific courses in France.

ROSEN, RELATIVITY, AND QUANTUM FOUNDATIONS. At the *Technion (Haifa, founded 1912) the Physics Faculty was established around 1955, after Nathan Rosen immigrated to the country. Rosen had worked for many years with Albert Einstein on a variety of subjects: gravitational radiation, "wormholes" (the "Einstein-Rosen bridge"), etc., in general relativity and "entanglement" in quantum mechanics (the Einstein-Podolski-Rosen ("EPR") paper). He had developed his own modification of GR (the "two fields" theory). The study in Haifa of the non-intuitive aspects of quantum mechanics, inspired by Rosen's continuing interest in EPR, strengthened with the arrival in Israel of David *Bohm, fleeing Senator McCarthy's House Un-American Activities Committee. Bohm left a year later for Bristol in the UK, but the seeds were planted. Two leading researchers in the foundations of quantum mechanics grew out of this, Yakir *Aharonov (TAU after 1967) and Asher Peres (Technion), the latter also a leading researcher in GR. Among the next generation in this "school," Lev Veidman (TAU) and Avshalom Elitzur (Bar-Ilan) have made important contributions. Michael Marainov (Technion) arrived from the USSR.

In general relativity and cosmology, the impact of Rosen's presence was felt in most physics departments, either through his students, as in Beersheva with Moshe Carmeli, or by the attraction of immigrant scientists, such as Gerald Tauber in Tel Aviv and his student Tsvi Piran or Jacob Bekenstein first in Beersheba and later in Jerusalem, a leader in the intersection of GR with thermodynamics, where his identification of a contribution to entropy generated by the gravitational field of a "black hole" opened up an entirely new chapter with profound conceptual aspects, as discussed in recent years by S. Hawking, L. Susskind (the "holographic" universe), S. Coleman ("Black Holes as Red Herrings"), and others.

Sometime in the 1970s new lines of research appeared: neural networks at HU, with David Horn at TAU. Chaos was treated by Ittamar Procaccia at Weizmann, Shmuel Sambourski (HU), and Max Jammer (Bar-Ilan).

COSMIC RAYS, PARTICLES, AND FIELDS. Cosmic ray physics developed with Y. Eisenberg, who had observed in 1958, in an emulsion that had been exposed to cosmic radiation, an "event" which was to be identified in 1962 with the omega-minus hyperon. He joined the Weizmann Institute in 1959; at the same time and in the same subdiscipline, Dan Kessler joined Sorek. At the Technion, Kurt Sitte, an experienced experimentalist, started an experimental cosmic ray group, short-lived because Sitte was arrested and tried for crimes against the nation's security. Paul Singer, joining in 1959–60, studied the theoretical issues involved, thus entering particle physics. While research in cosmic rays in Israel thus focused in the early years on the particle physics aspect, a new group was led by L. Dorman, who had immigrated from the USSR in the 1990s; their interest lay in the Earth's environment, the radiation belts, and the solar wind. The Emilio Segre Observatory collaborates with the Italian CR community.

Yuval Ne'eman (1925–2006), scion of several of the founding families of the modern Jewish resettlement (c. 1800, prior to organized Zionism, founded in 1897) and of the city of Tel Aviv (1909), after a career in the Israel Defense Forces, turned to physics at the age of 33, combining graduate studies at Imperial College with the duties of defense attaché in Israel's London embassy. Resigning from this position in May 1960 he "embarked on a highly speculative program" (in the words of A. Salam, his advisor, who advised against it), namely a search for a symmetry of the hadrons providing both a classification and dynamical couplings. The result, arrived at in October 1960, was submitted for publication early in February 1961. This was SU(3) symmetry (now renamed flavor-SU(3)) in a version based on the identification of the spin ½ baryons as an octet. It provided a hadron classification and an exact global-symmetry, also an effective local gauge-symmetry (mediated by a spin-1 massive vector-meson octet). The most elegant visualization of these octets sets them as 3 × 3 matrices. The octet's main competitor was the Sakata model, using the same SU(3) group, but with a different and a priori more popular algebraic normalization, namely assigning the best-known multiplet {p,n,/\} to the group's defining representation.

The octet global symmetry was tested in hundreds of predictions relating to the couplings and based on the Clebsch-Gordan coefficients of the group, but the final verdict was supplied by the discovery of the omega-minus hyperon, fitting the predictions exactly. The classification and symmetry were discovered simultaneously and independently by M. Gell-Mann, who called them "the Eightfold Way."

Back in Israel, as scientific director of the Sorek Laboratory, Ne'eman also organized a group combining technical service in the establishment with research in particle physics. With H. Goldberg of that group, Ne'eman constructed a mathematical model yielding precisely the observed set of representations; this model consisted in fixing as the basic "brick" the 3-dimensional defining SU(3) representation with a baryon-number B = ⅓ assignment (and fractional electric charges). We would also have to prepare the 3* anti-brick with B = –⅓. The B = 1 baryons are then in [3 (×) 3 (×) 3] = 1 + 8 + 8 + 10. The model was again discussed two years later as to the physical nature of these "bricks" by M. Gell-Mann (who named the "bricks" quarks) and by G. Zweig (who named them "*aces*").

Soon after this consolidation of the quark model it was tested and scored nicely through algebraic treatments based either on a nonrelativistic approximation, initiated by F. Gursey and L. Radicati, or applying an asymptotic limit, a method used by E. Levin and L. Frankfurt in Leningrad (1965; both were professors at TAU by 1990).

In the first two years after his return to Israel, Ne'eman lectured on particle physics at the Technion. Hebrew University, Weizmann Institute. C. Levinson and S. Meshkov, who were guests from the United States, worked with H.J. Lipkin on the SU(3) Elliott Model in nuclei, "transferred" to particle physics, and produced many of the predictions for both the Sakata and the Ne'eman/Gell-Mann models.

The first group of graduate students who worked with Ne'eman in particle physics then spent 1–2 years in leading centers – D. Horn and Y. Dothan at Caltech, H. Harari at SLAC, J. Rosen at BU, etc. – while a flux of guests and post-docs in particle physics arrived in Israel, L. Susskind, J. Rosner, J. Yellin at the new TAU, H. Rubinstein, M. Virasoro, at Weizmann, D. Lurie at the Technion, etc.

Generally speaking, an internal symmetry, and even more so a global one, is an extension of the kinematics and has to be grafted onto a dynamical theory. In London in 1958–60 this was Relativistic Quantum Field Theory (RQFT), which had been successfully applied to quantum electrodynamics in 1946–48, producing the most precise theory in physics.

Ne'eman was a guest at Caltech in 1963–65 and was impressed by the apparent rejection of Quantum Field Theory. R.P. Feynman, one of the heroes of that theory's success in the 1940s, had tried to extend it to quantum gravity and, encountering difficulties, had decided to do it first on the Yang-Mills gauge theory as a simplified model. He had then come across violations of unitarity off mass shell. The news spread to Berkeley, and G.F. Chew, the charismatic leader of particle physics in the 1950s and 1960s on the West Coast and sometimes everywhere in the United States, proclaimed Quantum Field Theory to have been a lucky accident of the 1940s, worthless beyond some special conditions. That verdict was accepted by the rank and file.

Luckily, QFT could still be used for leptons, and the first important step in unification, the Weinberg-Salam theory, was presented in its leptonic dress (1967–68). For the hadrons Gell-Mann had then invented current algebra, a way of preserving those features onto which one could apply the symmetry. Ne'eman himself developed similar structures in the mid-1960s (e.g., "the algebra of Regge residues" in the work with N. Cabibbo and L.P. Horwitz). Hadron dynamics now moved on to "S-Matrix theory" and the Bootstrap hypothesis. Between 1966 and 1970, Israel – the local group and its guests – was in the lead internationally: D. Horn (with C. Schmid and R. Dolan) provided the bootstrap with a mathematical embodiment, the "Finite Energy Sum Rules." Gabriele Veneziano, an Italian-Jewish graduate student at Weizmann, solved these equations, L. Susskind (at that stage a prospective immigrant from the U.S.) at TAU and Y. Nambu in Chicago showed that the Veneziano representation describes a quantum string. Harari at Weizmann with P.G.O. Freund in Chicago and G. Zweig at Caltech further developed the methodology, and M. Virasoro and H. Rubinstein at Weizmann enriched the string formalism. An international conference on "Dual Models" held in 1970 in Tel Aviv embodied the centrality achieved by particle physics in Israel in one decade. It was also a milestone in this first role of String Theory, here as a candidate theory for the Strong Interactions (1968–73).

The year 1970, however, was another "refocusing" year, when G. 't Hooft in Holland completed the renormalization of the Weinberg-Salam electroweak theory. That "infamous" breakdown of the unitarity of mass shell had been cured by its discoverer around 1962, when Feynman introduced ghost fields. Further work by B. deWitt, Slavnov, Taylor, Faddeev, and Popov had completed the cure, and now not only had 't Hooft finished the Yang-Mills case, he had also cleaned up the case of a spontaneous breakdown of that local gauge theory. Quantum Field Theory was now back with a vengeance.

In Israel, research in experimental particle physics is mostly done at CERN (Israel was granted Associated Membership in 1991, together with Russia, after a weaker association starting from 1971) and at DESY (Israeli formal association since 1983), with active groups at the Technion (J. Goldberg), TAU (G. Alexander, A. Levy, Y. Oren, G. Bela, E. Etzion, S. Dagan, O. Benary), Weizmann (G. Mickenberg, U. Karshon) plus medium energy groups at HU (A. Gal) and TAU (A. Yavin, P. Alster), etc. Theory groups are active in all these institutions.

GEOMETRICAL DEVELOPMENTS. In 1971, Yu. Golfand (who later immigrated to Israel) and E. Likhtman in Russia introduced supersymmetry, which was then "sharpened" by J. Wess and B. Zumino and by A. Salam and J. Strathdee. This was a new opening both in mathematics and physics. The Harvard mathematician S. Sternberg, visiting Tel Aviv University yearly and bringing in other visitors such as B. Kostant of MIT, etc., had already collaborated with Ne'eman on topics in current algebras, etc. In 1974, L. Corwin, Ne'eman, and Sternberg published a major exploratory study of "Graded Lie Algebras" which cleared the field and was soon followed by V. Kac's classification of the Simple Lie Superalgebras (the new name for the "Graded Lie Algebras"). Superalgebras avoided some of the "no-go" theorems forbidding mergers between spacetime and "internal" symmetries. One such application was supergravity, discovered in 1976 by D.Z. Freedman, S. Ferrara, and P. von Nieuwenhuizen and by S. Deser and B. Zumino. Gell-Mann and Ne'eman showed in 1976 that the gauge supersymmetry models with $N = 4h$ (max) (N the number of internal degrees of freedom, h(max) the highest helicity) are so severely constrained algebraically as to be possibly renormalizable or even finite. The $N = 4$ supersymmetric Yang-Mills ($h = 1$) is indeed finite and the $N = 8$ (built by E. Cremmer and B. Julia in 1978) is still the great hope in the "M-theory" of 1997 as the field theory limit of a string theory embedded in a Membrane.

Moreover, Ne'eman's work with T. Regge in 1977 introduced a new geometrical approach, the group manifold method. Ne'eman's French student J. Thierry-Mieg then showed (1979–81) that the "ghost fields" have a very useful geometrical interpretation (in a Yang-Mills theory) as the vertical component of the connection 1-form, while the unitarity-guaranteeing equations (BRS, etc.) just reproduce the Cartan-Maurer equations guaranteeing the horizontality of the curvature 2-forms. It also led Ne'eman (1979) to the concept of a "superconnection" – a concept independently introduced in mathematics by D. Quillen in 1985.

As a matter of fact, the geometric features present in much of algebraic physics – perhaps the most interesting aspect of Felix Klein's and Sophus Lie's (1872) Erlangen Program – first emphasized in GR, pervade gauge theories and spectrum generating algebras and have led both the string theorists and Ne'eman from the strong Interactions to gravity and back, though along different paths.

Ne'eman's collaboration with the Cologne group of F.W. Hehl, with D. Sijacki (Belgrade), R. Kerner (Paris), E. Mielke and A. Macias (Mexico), and others is the outcome of his discovery (1977) of world spinors, the infinite unitary spinorial reps of the double-covering of the SL(n, R) and of the covariance group, for long wrongly thought of as nonexistent. These have been used to describe Regge excitation sequences in strong interactions ("chromogravity"), where they are the only clear link, to date, between QCD and the features that characterized the S.I. in the S-matrix analytical continuation formalism. All of this may find applications in gravity too and has also somewhat overlapped with mathematical work by Shmuel Kaniel's group in Jerusalem and the cosmological studies of Eduardo Guendelman's group in Beersheba.

Ne'eman's 1979 superconnection introduced an internal supersymmetry SU(2/1) constraining the electroweak SU(2) × U (1); the same theory (though derived differently) was suggested independently and simultaneously by D. Fairlie. It predicts the Higgs mass to be M(H) = 2M(W), prior to radiative corrections. We note that with his various collaborators at Harvard, Cologne, Turino, Belgrade, etc., Ne'eman's TAU chair has been a source of innovative mathematical physics throughout the 1965–2005 period.

ASTRONOMY, ASTROPHYSICS, AND COSMOLOGY. There was no astronomy in Israel until 1965, although there were two young men who studied astronomy – Elia Leibowitz at Harvard and Raphael Steinitz in Holland – assuming that some day there would be such activity Israel. At TAU, Ne'eman started to develop several programs in parallel. Solar astronomy was undertaken, using a telescope on a roof at the TAU campus working in full conjunction with a Caltech telescope at Great Bear Lake in California under the guidance of H. Zirin. This was one of the first combined instruments providing 24-hour full coverage and thereby making it possible to follow eruptions, etc., throughout the entire season.

This small success (1967) was followed by a series of failed attempts in 1968–71. Still in solar astronomy, a special telescope – static and with a rotating mirror following the sun – was installed in a specially designed observatory (following advice from Kippenheuier) on another TAU campus roof, and another Israeli who had studied and now worked in France under Michard undertook to operate it, but "defected" for family reasons, and this initiative collapsed. A second attempt failed some years later, when an excellent instrument in an observatory in California became available due to the closure of that base. One of the main supporters of TAU, Raymond Sackler, undertook payment, and it was purchased at full price, but then the State of California authorities passed a law restricting the sale of scientific instrumentation belonging to the state, a restriction which included this case. In radio-astronomy, Arno Penzias, co-discoverer of the 30K "background radiation," spending a semester at TAU, developed a collaboration with a millimeter radioastronomical observatory at Bonn for N-S interferometry, but this scheme also collapsed due to the operators defecting, this time as a result of industry offering very much higher salaries.

Finally, after these three failures, a triumph was achieved late in 1971 with the inauguration of the George and Florence Wise (Optical) Observatory at Mitzpeh Ramon in the Negev at an altitude of 1000 m., with a 40″ wide angle Ritchie-Chretien reflector telescope with a Cassegrain mirror. The site was selected after a survey which covered the peaks from Mt. Sinai (where Abbott measured the solar constant around 1900) to Mt. Hermon. The Smithsonian Institute, under the leadership of F. Whipple, and with the active participation of M. Lecar, collaborated by supplying much of the auxiliary instrumentation for the project; the Israeli government paid for the building and TAU President Dr. George Wise and Mrs. Wise contributed the telescope. The outcome was beyond expectations: within the first three years there were three fairly spectacular results: John and Neta Bahcall produced the first optical identification of an X-ray pulsar (Hercules HR); Peter Wehinger and Susan Wykopf produced a spectroscopic validation of F. Whipple's conjecture that comet tails are made of water and hydroxil by direct analysis of the comet Kohoutek and an on the spot collaboration with Herzog in Canada and Herbig in California; the discovery of clouds of sulfur and phosphorus around Jupiter, announced by Wise Observatory (TAU) astronomers A. Eviathar, I. Kupo, and Y. Mekler was met with skepticism until NASA's Voyager radioed pictures of the fuming volcanoes on Jupiter's moon Io.

In the 1980s, H. Netzer and D. Maoz achieved the first precise measurements of the mass of black holes in active galactic nuclei. The Wise Observatory was then involved in several international collaborations that pursued these measurements extensively. Netzer, Maoz, and S. Caspi have since studied some of the largest black holes known to date. N. Brosh was involved in the discovery of extra-solar planetary systems by international collaborations in the 1990s. TAUVEX, a major instrumental setup for the exploration of the UV sky (quasars, etc.) built by EL-OP for TAU in 1991–95, was due to be orbited in 1996 on Soviet satellite together with 13 other experiments, but changes in the USSR first caused a postponement and finally a cancellation in 2000. The instrument is now due to be raised on an Indian satellite in 2008.

Israel Dostrovsky at Weizmann designed and built the gallium-germanium neutrino-detector for the International experiment at the Gran Sasso tunnel in Italy. This experiment brought the first solid verification of John Bahcall's claim about missing solar neutrinos.

In radio-astronomy, work on the sun is done by D. Eichler at Ben-Gurion University in the Negev and by L. Pustilnik at the Jordan Valley College.

Research in theoretical astrophysics was done by A. Finzi at the Technion, by G. Rakavy, Z. Barkat, Z. Cinnamon at HU, G. Shaviv, M. Livio (TAU, later at the Technion), M. Contini, J. Refaeli, B. Kozlovski, A. Yahil, U. Feldman, I. Goldman A. Kowacz at TAU, Y. Avny and M. Milgrom at Weizmann. M. Gelman (Technion) leads in space physics. Work in cosmology started with the discovery of the first quasars, when I. Novikov in the U.S.S.R. (1964) and Y. Ne'eman (1965) independently suggested that quasars are lagging-cores in the cosmological expansion. Ne'eman and G. Tauber further developed this model, while it became clear that it does not fit the quasars. This model was in fact a very simple precursor of the presently used Eternal and Infinite Multi-core Inflationary Cosmology suggested by A. Linde after A. Guth's inflation hypothesis. In recent years, work in cosmology is mainly conducted at HU under the leadership of Avishay Dekel.

[Yuval Ne'eman (2nd ed.)]

PIACENZA, city in northern Italy, formerly in the duchy of *Parma. Jewish moneylenders lived there in the 15th century and were attacked by the friars who condemned usury in their sermons. When **monti di pietà* were established here and in Parma in 1488–90, the Jews from both towns scattered throughout the country districts in order to carry on their business there. Thus, around Piacenza, the small communities (now extinct) of Monticelli d'Ongina, Fiorenzuola d'Arda, and Cortemaggiore came into being and were able to carry on even after 1570, at which date Jews were forbidden to live in Piacenza.

BIBLIOGRAPHY: Ravà, in: *Educatore Israelita*, 18 (1870), 169–80, 212–3; Loevinson, in: RMI, 7 (1932/33), 351–8; Milano, Italia, index; Roth, Italy, index; Zoller, in: RI, 7 (1910), 87–92.

[Attilio Milano]

PIAMENTA, MOSHE (1921–), linguist and Orientalist, professor emeritus of the Hebrew University of Jerusalem in Arabic language and literature. Piamenta distinguished himself in the research of colloquial Arabic and its dialects (chiefly of the syntax of Jerusalem Arabic) as well as of socio-anthropological aspects of Arab linguistics. Noteworthy, also, are his investigations of the Judeo-Arabic of Yemen and Baghdad, of expressions of the Islamic religion in Arabic words, terms, and ways of expression.

He received the Jerusalem Award (1994) and Israel Prize for scholarship in Oriental Studies in 1996.

Among his main works are *Shimmush ha-Zemannim, ha-Aspektim ve-ha-Derakhim ba-Lahag ha-Aravi ha-Yerushalmi* 2 (1964); *Studies in the Syntax of Palestinian Arabic* (1966); *Islam in Everyday Arabic Speech* (1979); *The Muslim Conception of God and Human Welfare as Reflected in Everyday Arabic Speech* (1983); *Dictionary of Post-Classical Yemeni Arabic* (1990–91); *Jewish Life in Arabic Language and Jerusalem Arabic in Communal Perspective: Lexico-Semantic Study* (2000).

BIBLIOGRAPHY: J. Rosenhouse and A. Elad-Bouskila (eds.), *Linguistic and Cultural Studies on Arabic and Hebrew. Essays Presented to Moshe Piamenta* (2001); *Jerusalem Studies in Arabic and Islam*, 29 (2005), ii–iv.

PIASECZNO, town in Warszawa province, Poland. During the 18th century there was a Jewish settlement in the town, but in 1740 King Augustus III prohibited the residence of Jews. In 1789 they were also forbidden to trade or be innkeepers in the town. After the abolition of this decree by the Russian government, the population of the town increased from 1,328 in 1865 to 5,604 in 1921. The latter figure included 2,256 Jews. An active Jewish life began after World War I and in 1932 a Zionist delegate was elected to head the community. Among the *ẓaddikim* of Piaseczno, R. Israel Jehiel Kalish (whose father R. Simḥah Bunem Kalish of Otwock died in Tiberias in 1907) was renowned at the beginning of the 20th century.

[Shimshon Leib Kirshenboim]

Holocaust Period

Before the outbreak of World War II, there were about 3,000 Jews in Piaseczno. The Jewish community was liquidated on Jan. 22–27, 1941, when all the Jews were deported to *Warsaw and shared the fate of that community. After the war the Jewish community was not reconstituted.

BIBLIOGRAPHY: K.K. Shapiro, *Sefer Esh Kodesh* (1960); M. Piekarz, *Ha-Te'udah ha-Ḥasidit ha-Sifrutit ha-Akharona al Admath Polin, Divrei ha-Rabbi mi-Piaseczno be-Getto Varsha* (1979).

PIATIGORSKY, GREGOR (1903–1976), cellist. Born in Yekaterinoslav, Ukraine, Piatigorsky became first cellist at the Imperial Opera. He left Russia in 1921 and from 1924 he was leading cellist of the Berlin Philharmonic Orchestra. He resigned in 1928 to tour as soloist, often appearing in recitals with Serge Rachmaninoff, Arthur *Schnabel, and Vladimir *Horovitz. He also formed a trio with Nathan *Milstein and Horovitz. In 1929 he settled in the U.S. and taught at the Curtis Institute in Philadelphia and later at Boston University.

One of the leading cellists of his generation, Piatigorsky made many arrangements for the cello and commissioned cello concertos from several composers – Paul Hindemith, Mario *Castelnuovo-Tedesco, and Serge Prokofiev. He visited Israel in 1954 for concerts with the Israel Philharmonic Orchestra and returned in 1970 for concerts together with Jasha Heifetz. His autobiography, *Cellist*, was published in 1965.

[Uri (Erich) Toeplitz]

PIATRA-NEAMT (Rom. **Piatra-Neamţ**, or **Piatra**), town in Moldavia, N.E. Romania. According to a local Jewish tradition, a synagogue existed there by the middle of the 16th century, and during the war against Turkey (1541–46), the Jews of Piatra-Neamt hid the ruler of Moldavia. The oldest tombstone dates from 1627 and the first entries in the *pinkas* (minute book) of the *ḥevra kaddisha* date from 1771. The *ḥevra* maintained a *talmud torah* and directed various communal activities. The Jews' Guild (see *Romania) was in charge of communal affairs. In 1819 the head of the guild was the assistant of the chief commissioner of the local police. There were 120 Jewish taxpayers in 1802. The number of Jews had risen to 3,900 (33% of the total population) in 1859 and 8,489 (c. 50% of the total) in 1907. In 1930 there were 7,595 Jews (24% of the total).

Antisemitism was prevalent from the 19th century on, and in 1821 the community suffered from Greek rebels who appeared in the area and robbed and murdered Jews there. The arrival of the Turkish army prevented a complete massacre of the community. In 1841, 48 Jews from the surrounding villages were arrested following a *blood libel. They were released by special order of the sultan on the intervention of Sir Moses *Montefiore.

The abolition of the **ḥakham bashi* system in 1834 and of the Jews' Guild was followed by a long period of chaos in Jewish public life; attempts to form a community failed because of quarrels among different Jewish groups and institutions which attempted to assume communal responsibility and leadership. In 1868 the police closed the *talmud torah* and the private *ḥadarim*, obliging the community to establish a modern school. A primary school was founded by the local *B'nai

B'rith in 1882 and functioned until 1885 when the *talmud torah* was reopened. In 1899–1900 the *Jewish Colonization Association contributed to the building of two schools, one for boys and another for girls, which in 1910 had 810 pupils.

In addition to the "Great Synagogue" there were 16 prayer houses, some of them belonging to specific craftsmen. A *hekdesh* (hostel for travelers) was turned into an old-age home in 1898 and a Jewish hospital was established in 1905.

Most of the commerce in Piatra-Neamt was conducted by Jews: in 1891 there were 417 Jewish commercial firms. Many Jews dealt in the agricultural products of the area, such as timber, cereals, and cattle. The majority of craftsmen were also Jews and some industries were also owned by Jews.

In 1894 a branch of Ḥovevei Zion was founded in the town. After 1897 groups of supporters of Herzl's political Zionism were formed there. The Hebrew weekly *Yizre'el* was published in Piatra-Neamt from 1882, as well as a Yiddish journal *Di Hofnung* (published three times weekly). Another Hebrew magazine, *Ha-Mekiẓ*, edited by the Hebrew author and teacher M. *Braunstein-Mibashan, and A.L. *Zissu, who was born in Piatra-Neamt, was published there from 1909. Jean *Juster and the historian of Romanian Jewry, M.A. Halevy (1900–1972), were also born in Piatra-Neamt.

Antisemitism was especially virulent in Piatra-Neamt between the two world wars. In 1925 synagogues, Jewish schools, and other institutions were looted, and in 1926 and 1928 the cemetery was desecrated. Corneliu *Codreaunu, head of the *Iron Guard, was elected to Parliament as deputy for Piatra-Neamt in 1931. In 1937, 26 out of 28 Jews practicing at the bar were dismissed. Despite these problems the community itself was more firmly organized between the two world wars. The two primary schools, serving 400 boys and girls in 1936–37, were amalgamated, and the community also supported a boarders' annex for 250 children. There were Zionist organizations of all shades.

The community of Piatra-Neamt survived World War II. In 1947 Jews numbered 8,000, declining to 5,000 in 1950. In 1969 about 300 Jewish families remained. There were two synagogues. About 100 Jews remained in the early 21st century.

BIBLIOGRAPHY: PK Romanyah, 208–16; J. Kaufman, *Cronica comunităţilor israelite din Judeţul Neamţu* (1929); *Almanahul ziarului Tribuna evreească*, 1 (1937/38), 273–4; E. Schwarzfeld, in: *Anuar pentru Israeliţi*, 7 (1884/85), 19; *Buletinul Bibliotecii Muzeului şi archivei istorice a Templului Coral, Bucureşti*, 2:1 (1936), 13–15.

[Theodor Lavi]

°PIATTOLI, SCIPIONE (1749–1809), Italian clergyman who later became a Polish statesman. He was born in Florence and lived in Poland from 1783. In 1789, on a tour of France, he supported the political demands of the third estate and was deeply impressed by the suggestion of *Malesherbes for an improvement in the situation of the Jews in Alsace. On his return to Poland in 1790, he made contact with the reformists in the Sejm, and took an active part in the formation of the constitution of May 3, 1791. His diplomatic qualifications led to his appointment as adviser to Stanislaus Augustus, the last king of Poland. Piattoli strove to rectify the unstable legal situation of Polish Jews, combining practical suggestions on behalf of the Jews with an effort to solve the king's personal financial debts. In September 1791 he proposed that Jews be given the right to buy land and houses, and juridical autonomy and the status of a separate urban class. For these rights the Jews were to pay the king's debts (about 20 million zlotys) in 10 annual installments. Piattoli first addressed his proposal to the leaders of the Jewish communities, then in Warsaw, asking them for their support. He also convinced certain statesmen, H. Kollątaj, A. Linowski, J. Jeziezski, and others, to discuss his plan in the Sejm. In 1792, however, Piattoli's proposal was opposed by urban representatives and those aristocrats who inclined toward Russia. The Sejm was dissolved on May 26, 1792 with the outbreak of war between Russia and Poland, and Piattoli's proposal lapsed.

BIBLIOGRAPHY: N.M. Gelber, in: *Nowe Życie*, no. 6 (1924), 321–3; A. D'Ancona, *S. Piattoli e la Polonia* (1915); *Encyklopedia Powszechna*, 20 (1865), 640–1. **ADD. BIBLIOGRAPHY:** M. Balaban, *Historja i literatura zydowska*,vol. 3 (1925) 424–28; A.Eisenbach et al., *Materialy do Sejmu czteroletniego*, vol. 6 (1969), 544–45.

[Arthur Cygielman]

PICA (The Palestine Jewish Colonization Association), society for Jewish settlement in Palestine, active between 1924 and 1957. In 1923, as a result of the rapid development of his settlement projects in Palestine, Baron Edmond de *Rothschild decided to establish a separate body to achieve his ideal. The new association, headed by his son James, took over from the *Jewish Colonization Association (ICA), which had managed the villages assisted by the Baron since 1900. PICA was officially recognized by the Mandatory authorities in 1924.

PICA founded and assisted Jewish settlement in the moshavot Pardes Ḥannah and Binyaminah, in moshavim such as Naḥalat Jabotinsky, Bet Ḥananyah, Shadmot Devorah, and Sedeh Eli'ezer, and in kibbutzim such as Ashdot Ya'akov, Ma'yan Ẓevi, and Kefar Glickson. It also engaged in swamp drainage (e.g., at Kabarah in 1925), afforestation (at Ḥaderah), stabilization of sand dunes, and agricultural research and modernization. It gave financial support to cultural institutions, including the Hebrew University and the Technion, and developed the industrial enterprises started by Baron de Rothschild, though it always tried in some way to link its efforts in industry with agriculture or land. After 1948 it modernized and expanded the Grands Moulins flour mill, Haifa, and the salt works at Athlit, as well as acquiring shares in Fertilizers and Chemicals, Haifa, and other enterprises. On the death of James de Rothschild in 1957, PICA wound up its operations and transferred its considerable property to the State of Israel.

BIBLIOGRAPHY: PICA, *Memorandum and Articles of Association* (1924); idem, *Memorandum Submitted to the United Nations Special Committee on Palestine* (1947); idem, *Exchange of Letters between Mrs James A. de Rothschild... and Mr. David Ben Gurion...* (1958); PICA: *Ha-Ḥevrah le-Hityashevut ha-Yehudim be-Ereẓ-Yisrael* (1957).

[Avital Levy]

°**PICARD, EDMOND** (1836–1924), Belgian lawyer and antisemite. Picard became an active advocate of socialism, then of antisemitic racialism, and attempted to forge an alliance between the two ideologies. He fought for the socialist cause between 1866 and 1907, when he left the Socialist Party, although he continued to call himself a socialist. In 1888 Picard visited Morocco on a diplomatic mission and from then on turned his talents as a writer to outright racialist propaganda. Observing Arabs and Jews there, he concluded that Semites and Aryans were irreconcilable races. In the following years he wrote *La Bible et le Coran* (1888), *Synthèse de l'antisémitisme* (1892), which was reprinted during the German occupation of Belgium in World War II, and *L'Aryano-Sémitisme* (1899), a collection of 19 articles previously published in the socialist daily *Le Peuple* under the bizarre title *L'Antisémitisme scientifique et humanitaire*. Picard abhorred any intermingling of races and urged Aryans to protect themselves from the "Semitic invasion." He presented Jesus as an Aryan and the Jews as Asians. Seeing no contradiction between antisemitism and socialism, he believed that brotherhood of the oppressed did not necessarily imply equality between all races. He was influenced by *Proudhon's anti-Jewish *ouvriérisme* and by *Gobineau, as well as by his Catholic education which provided a receptive ground for animosity toward the Jews. He succeeded in infecting the minds of leading socialists like Hennebicq (1871–1940) and Destrée (1863–1936); but thanks to the efforts of E. Vandervelde, L. De Brouckère, and C. Huysmans, the Socialist movement in Belgium officially proscribed antisemitism. Yet the Socialist Party newspaper, *Le Peuple*, never refused to print Picard's articles.

BIBLIOGRAPHY: R.F. Byrnes, *Anti-semitism in Modern France*, 1 (1950), index; Silberner, in: HJ, 14 (1952), 106–18.

PICARD, JACOB (1883–1967), German author and poet. Picard was born in Wangen, Wuerttemberg, and practiced law in Konstanz. He published two collections of verse, *Das Ufer* (1913), and *Erschuetterung* (1920), but turned seriously to literature when his legal career ended with the advent of the Nazi regime in 1933. He fled to New York via Soviet Russia and Asia in 1940. His lyrics expressed a traditionally religious outlook.

In 1936 he published his most important work, a collection of short stories entitled *Der Gezeichnete* (1936, reissued as *Die alte Lehre*, 1963; *The Marked One and Twelve Other Stories*, 1956), which described the folklore, piety, and traditions of Jews settled for centuries in the towns and villages of southern Germany. Some of his later poems were collected in *Der Uhrenschlag* (1960). A short autobiography, entitled "Childhood in a Village," appeared in the *Yearbook of the Leo Baeck Institute* (vol. 4 (1959), 273–93) and under the title "Erinnerung eigenen Lebens," in *Allmend*, 25/25 (1989) 5–38). In 1991 there appeared his *Werke* (in 2 vols., ed. by M Bosch).

ADD. BIBLIOGRAPHY: W. Braun, "Jacob Picard," in: J.M. Spalek et al. (eds), *Deutschsprachige Exilliteratur seit 1933*, 2 (1989), 772–82; M. Bosch and J. Grosspietsch (eds), *Jacob Picard: 1883–1967. Dichter des deutschen Landjudentums; Katalog zur gleichnamigen Ausstellung in der ehemaligen Synagoge Sulzburg* (1992); M. Brandt, "Gertrud Kolmar an Jacob Picard. Briefe aus den Jahren 1937–1939," in: *Juedischer Almanach des Leo-Baeck-Instituts* (1995), 136–149.

PICARD, LEO YEHUDA (1900–1996), Israeli geologist. Born in Konstanz, Germany, he earned his Ph.D. in geology from the University of Freiburg (1923). After a period of study at the University of Florence, he immigrated to Palestine in 1924. After initial employment by the Keren Kayemet, in 1925 he joined the staff of the Natural History Department of the newly founded Hebrew University of Jerusalem as the sole geologist among the three young staff members supervised by Otto *Warburg. During the period of this appointment he carried out research in Paris (1926) and, supported by the Royal Society, at Imperial College, University of London where he obtained his D.Sc. He returned to the Hebrew University where he was appointed lecturer (1934), head of the department of geology (1936), and professor in 1939. When Picard arrived in Palestine, Jerusalem was the only area in the country that had been fully surveyed. He carried out the first geological surveys of the Jezreel valley (the "Emek") and Haifa region and contributed to the first study of the mineral deposits of the Judean Desert. He later directed the comprehensive geological survey of Israel (1950–54). In addition to his general geological skills, he had special expertise in surveys for petrochemical and water resources. He also carried out research and teaching in paleontology. He played a major part in organizing the study and teaching of geology and geography after the establishment of the state and in insisting on high academic standards. There was great national and international demand for his services, and he made geological surveys for governments and organizations throughout the world including Europe, Africa, Asia, and South America. He also served as chairman or adviser on many national and international committees including UNESCO, the UN, and geological conferences, especially those concerned with the problems of arid regions. His publications on basic and applied geology were universally recognized for their research and educational distinction. His many awards included the Israel Prize for natural sciences (1958), election to the Israel Academy of Sciences and Humanities (1961), and membership in many national geological societies.

[Michael Denman (2nd ed.)]

°**PICART, BERNARD** (1673–1733), French artist and engraver. Picart settled in Amsterdam in 1710, partly to escape the restrictions to which, as a Protestant, he was subjected in Catholic France. He earned a place in the history of Jewish art by his realistic portrayal of Jewish religious rites. These constitute an invaluable record of Dutch Jewry in the early 18th century. Unlike Rembrandt and his circle, who were chiefly interested in the facial expressions of individuals, Picart sought out Jews in the synagogue and in their homes in order to acquaint himself with their ceremonies. In his picture of a Passover celebration the artist himself can be seen, hatless, participating in the meal. Picart used his sketches, the originals of which are in the Stedelijk Museum, Amsterdam, to make etchings with which he illustrated the section devoted to Jews in the first volume of an 11-volume work, *Cérémonies et Coûtumes Réligieuses de tous les Peuples du Monde* (Amsterdam, 1723). The engravings were often reproduced in various editions, and served as the basis for a series of imitations published by F. Novelli in Venice in 1789. Picart also engraved the title pages for some Hebrew works, such as the Amsterdam Pentateuch of 1725.

BIBLIOGRAPHY: A. Rubens, *A Jewish Iconography* (1954), 6, 14–22.

[Alfred Werner]

PICCIOTTO, family of merchants and community leaders from Leghorn, Italy. Of its members HILLEL ḤAYYIM (d. 1773) traveled to *Aleppo for the first time in 1732 and settled there in 1771. His son, ḤAI MOSES (d. 1816), author of *Va-Yeḥal Moshe* (Vienna, 1814), a collection of sermons and ethics, also died in Aleppo. He was the father of RAPHAEL (d. 1827), the Austrian consul in Aleppo for about 50 years; in 1818 he emigrated to Tiberias, where he died. In 1806 he was honored by Austria with the title of "Ritter von Picciotto." He was also the Russian consul in Aleppo. His son, Ezra (d. 1822), was the Austrian consul from 1818 until his death in the earthquake of Aleppo. He was then replaced by his brother ELIJAH, who held his position until 1840. A third brother, HILLEL, was Prussian consul in Aleppo from 1824. When Wolf Shorr visited the town in 1875, he found that this family provided "most of the envoys of Europe's kingdoms, such as Germany, Austria, Belgium, Sweden, Holland, and others." MOSES BEN EZRA (1818–1894) acted as Austrian, German, and Danish envoy in Aleppo and defended his brethren in 1875 at the time of the blood libel brought about by the Armenians.

MOSES HAIM (1806–1879) emigrated from Aleppo to London in 1843 and died there. He played an active role in the affairs of the Sephardi Bevis Marks community and was also its president. He was also a member of the Board of Deputies over a long period. During the Spanish-Moroccan War of 1859, when a great number of Jewish refugees fled to Gibraltar and the situation of the Jews in *Morocco worsened, a committee of support was formed in England and Moses Ḥaim was its emissary to report on the exact conditions of the Jews. His report was published under the title *Jews of Morocco Report* (London, 1861). His son, James (1830–1897), was a historian of English Jewry and also a hymnologist. He was for many years secretary to the Morocco Relief Fund. From 1872 onward he published in the *Jewish Chronicle* a series of discursive historical essays based to some extent on original sources. These were republished in volume form in 1875 under the title *Sketches of Anglo-Jewish History* – the earliest popular work on Anglo-Jewish history. He was among the founders of the Jewish Historical Society of England. Another member of the family, Joseph (1872–1938), was the first Jewish senator to be appointed by King Fuad of *Egypt (1924). He was also a member of the Chamber of Commerce in *Alexandria and a member of the Economic Council of the Egyptian government. As a Zionist, he was vice president of the "Pro-Palestine" Society founded in Egypt in 1918. For many years he was also the vice president of the Alexandrian Communal Board and president of the local B'nai B'rith.

BIBLIOGRAPHY: M. Franco, *Essai sur l'histoire des israélites de l'empire ottoman* (1897), 209, 232; A.M. Hyamson, *Sephardim of England* (1951), 294, 353, 399; J. Picciotto, *Sketches of Anglo-Jewish History* (1956^2), 15–22 (introd.); Hirschberg, Afrikah, 2 (1965), 306. **ADD. BIBLIOGRAPHY:** ODNB online.

[Haim J. Cohen]

PICHO (or **Pichon**), **JOSEPH** (d. 1379), *contador mayor* ("auditor general") of Henry II of Castile, Spain. He gradually rose in rank from being an adviser to Henry, before the latter seized power, to one of the foremost officials at court. In 1366 his signature appears on official documents, and a year later he was entrusted with an important mission, probably financial, to the king of Aragon. In 1369 Picho was appointed chief tax collector and made responsible for the crown revenues, while in 1371 he appears as chief tax farmer of Castile. In consequence of his governmental position he was vested with much authority which he abused at times. In 1379 certain Jews who were jealous of Picho's position obtained a writ issued in blank authorizing them to punish *informers. On the authority of this document Picho was convicted and executed. According to the evidence of the contemporary Spanish historian, Lopez de Ayala, the only available source for this episode, these events took place in Burgos, at the time of the coronation of Pedro III, the son of Henry. This angered the young king, and as a result the Cortes, at its session in Soria in 1380, abrogated the rights of criminal jurisdiction previously held by the Jews of Castile.

BIBLIOGRAPHY: Baer, Spain, 1 (1961), 366f., 376, 450; Baer, Urkunden, index, s.v. *Joseph Picho*; Neuman, Spain, index; H. Beinart, *Kevuẓot Illit u-Shekhavot Manhigot* (1966), 66.

PICK, ALOIS (1859–1945), Austrian army medical corps general, university professor, and president of the Vienna Jewish community. He was born in Karlin near Prague, studied medicine in Prague and Vienna, and graduated in 1883. After 1887 he served as army surgeon and military hospital director; in 1891 he became head of the ward for stomach and intestinal diseases in the Vienna General Hospital. He was appointed to the position of lecturer and professor at Vienna University after 1890. During World War I he was attached to the general staff, and attained the highest rank in the army medical corps. From 1920 to 1932 he headed the Vienna Jewish community, assisted by two vice presidents of the non-nationalist and Zionist groups. His respected and kind personality helped to reconcile party differences. He wrote books and numerous articles on internal medicine, among them *Vorlesungen ueber Magen und Darmkrankheiten* (1895–97) and, with Adolf Hecht, *Klinische Semiotik* (1908), both translated into English.

During his service in Herzegovina he was the first to describe a form of pappataci fever. He also wrote plays and poetry.

BIBLIOGRAPHY: Wininger, Biog, s.v.; I. Fischer, in: *Biographisches Lexikon der hervorragenden Aerzte* (1932).

[Hugo Knoepfmacher]

PICK, ERNST PETER (1872–1960), Austrian pharmacological chemist. Born in Jaromer, Bohemia, Pick worked until 1899 at the University of Strasbourg. He was head of the biochemistry department of the Serum Institute of Vienna from 1899 to 1911, and professor of pharmacology at the University of Vienna from 1911 to 1924. He was chief of the drug control department of the Austrian government from 1914 until the advent of the Nazis. In 1938 he went to the United States and was appointed professor of pharmacology at Columbia University (1939–46), as well as being attached to Mount Sinai Hospital, New York.

Pick's papers were largely concerned with serology, the breakdown of proteins, poisons, and various other fields of experimental pathology and pharmacology. He wrote *Biochemie der Antigene* (1912), *Biochemie der Antigene und Antikoerper* (1928), and co-edited *Die experimentelle Pharmakologie als Grundlage der Arzneibehandlung* (1933).

BIBLIOGRAPHY: *Arzneimittel-Forschung*, 7 (1957), 332; *Archives internationales de pharmacodynamie et de thérapie*, 132 (1961), 205.

[Samuel Aaron Miller]

PICK, ḤAYYIM HERMANN (1879–1952), Assyriologist and Mizrachi leader. Born in Schildberg, Poland, Pick was a pupil of F. Delitzsch at the University of Berlin. His doctoral dissertation was entitled *Talmudische Glossen zu Delitzschs assyrischen Handwoerterbuch* (1903). He was also ordained as rabbi by David Z. Hoffmann at the Rabbinerseminar fuer das Orthodoxe Judentum. Pick joined the Zionist movement in 1898 and the Mizrachi upon its foundation, serving as a delegate to several Zionist congresses. In 1904 he joined the department of Middle Eastern studies at the Prussian State Library, and in 1918 was appointed professor and *Bibliotheksrat* (library counsellor). He was the first Jew in the Prussian civil service to be permitted not to work on the Sabbath. Concurrently he acted as headmaster of the Lippmann Taus Hebrew College in Berlin.

Pick was very active in Mizrachi affairs in Germany until 1914. In World War I, he acted as chief military censor of the Jewish press in Poland. After the war he was temporarily attached to the German Foreign Office. In 1920 he was elected a member of the Mizrachi World Executive, serving for a time as its chairman. From 1921 to 1927 he was a member of the Jerusalem Zionist Executive and was appointed to its Immigration Department. At the height of the "*Grabski *aliyah*" he kept up an impassioned fight with the British high commissioner, Sir Herbert Samuel, over the politically motivated cutbacks in the allotment of immigration certificates. Pick was among the initiators of the Mizrachi Bank. Though unable to pursue his scientific work, he was able to found, together with S.H. Bergman, **Kirjath Sepher*, the bibliographical publication of the Jewish National Library.

From 1928 to 1934, upon returning to the Prussian State Library, he was again extremely active on behalf of the Mizrachi in the Berlin Jewish Community Council. The Nazis pensioned but did not dismiss him, on account of his wartime service. After returning to Jerusalem he was again elected to the Mizrachi World Executive (1935), heading its Ereẓ Israel Fund. Later he initiated and headed the Council for Refugee Rabbis that looked after hundreds of people. Pick's last years were darkened by a crippling illness, and by the confiscation by the Germans of his unique Assyriological library, including all the cuneiform texts that were to be the basis of his life's work – an Assyrian-Aramaic-Hebrew dictionary.

BIBLIOGRAPHY: *Ha-Ẓofeh* (Jan. 18, 1939), 3; *Deyokena'ot* (1962), 230–4.

[Pinhas Artzi]

PICK, JIŘÍ ROBERT (1925–1983), Czech author of satirical poetry and prose, publicist, playwright. Born in Prague, Pick spent 1943–1945 in the Theresienstadt concentration camp. He contributed to dozens of literary magazines and published many aphorisms, satirical sketches, fables, parodies, and avant-garde poetry for children. Some of his short stories, such as "Association of Animal Protection" (1969), and his plays *A Dream of Distant Lakes* (1981) and *An Unlucky Man in the Yellow Cap* (1982) are based on his time in Theresienstadt.

BIBLIOGRAPHY: A. Mikulášek, *Literatura s hvězdou Davidovou*, vol.1 (1998); *Slovník českých spisovatelů* (2000).

[Milos Pojar (2nd ed.)]

°**PICO DELLA MIRANDOLA, GIOVANNI** (1463–1494), one of the most remarkable figures of the Italian Renaissance. Pico was an influential thinker, a humanist scholar of note, a pioneer of Oriental studies, and the father of Christian *Kabbalah. Contemporaries with whom Pico associated include, among others, Elijah *Delmedigo, Flavius *Mithridates, Johanan Alemanno, Marsilio Ficino, Angelo Poliziano, and Girolamo Savonarola. Delmedigo translated several Averroist treatises for Pico. Mithridates instructed him in Arabic and Aramaic ("Chaldean"), and translated for him a considerable number of kabbalistic writings; his translations survive and are the likeliest literary sources of Pico's Christian Kabbalah. The most striking and, in the long run, most influential outcome of Pico's encounter with Jewish esoterism are his kabbalistic theses "according to his own opinion" (*Conclusiones cabalisticae secundum opinionem propriam*), which set out to confirm the truth of the Christian religion from the foundations of Jewish Kabbalah. They are included among the 900 theses derived from all branches of knowledge which he offered, in 1486, for public debate in Rome. The debate never took place, but the kabbalistic theses made a lasting impression, and may truly be considered to mark the beginning of Christian Kabbalah. What they amount to is as much a kabbalistic interpretation of Christianity as a Christian interpretation of the Kabbalah.

The Kabbalah, touched upon in Pico's *Oration on the Dignity of Man*, is discussed at great length in his *Apologia* (in *Commentationes*, 1496), where he defended 13 of his theses specifically condemned by the Church, one of which was the thesis that "no science can make us more certain of Christ's divinity than magic and Kabbalah." The *Heptaplus* (1489), a sevenfold interpretation of the biblical account of Creation, also shows kabbalistic traits. Pico owned many Hebrew books, and in his writings, particularly in his refutation of astrology (*Disputationes adversus Astrologiam Divinatricem*, 1495), he mentions various Jewish authors besides the kabbalists, notably Maimonides, Ibn Ezra, and Levi b. Gershom. The precise extent of Pico's knowledge of Hebrew and of his acquaintance with the Kabbalah are still open questions.

Editions of his works are *Opera Omnia* (Basle, 1572); *Opere*, ed. by E. Garin, vol. 1, *De hominis dignitate, Heptaplus, De ente et uno*, and *Scritti vari* (1942); vol. 2–3, *Disputationes adversus Astrologiam Divinatricem* (1946–52).

BIBLIOGRAPHY: E. Anagnine, *Giovanni Pico della Mirandola* (It., 1937); J.L. Blau, *Christian Interpretation of the Cabala in the Renaissance* (1944); U. Cassuto, *Gli Ebrei a Firenze nell'età del Rinascimento* (1918); E. Garin, *Giovanni Pico della Mirandola* (It., 1937); idem, *La cultura filosofica del Rinascimento italiano* (1961); idem, *Giovanni Pico della Mirandola* (It., 1963); P.O. Kristeller, in: *L'Opera e il pensiero di Giovanni Pico della Mirandola nella storia dell'Umanesimo*, Convegno Internazionale, vol. 1, "Relazioni" (Florence, 1965), 35–133 (the most complete up-to-date bibliography of Pico will be found on pp. 107–33); Scholem, in: *Essays Presented to Leo Baeck* (1954), 158–93; F. Secret, *Kabbalistes chrétiens de la Renaissance* (1964), index; idem, in: *Convivium*, 25 (1957), 31–47 (It.); Wirszubski, in: *Studies in Mysticism and Religion Presented to G. Scholem* (1967), 353–62.

[Chaim Wirszubski]

PICON, MOLLY (née **Maragret Pyckoon**; 1898–1992), U.S. actress in Yiddish and English. Born in New York, she made her name playing Yiddish roles on 2nd Avenue. She was at Kessler's Theater for several years and in 1935 went touring in vaudeville with her husband, Jacob Kalich. From 1942 she managed the Molly Picon Theater in New York. After World War II she visited the DP camps, went touring in Australia, South Africa, and Europe. In 1960 she was back on the English stage playing the lead in *A Majority of One* in London and appeared on TV and in films. In 1961 she scored a success on Broadway in the musical *Milk and Honey*, and in 1967 appeared in *How to be a Jewish Mother*. She appeared in the film *Fiddler on the Roof* in 1970, while in 1982 she won an Emmy Award nomination for her performance in the television drama *Grandma Didn't Wave Back*. Picon also appeared in the films *Cannonball Run* (1981) and its sequel *Cannonball II* (1984). As well as being an actress, Picon was also a songwriter and lyricist with nearly 100 songs to her name. Her book *So Laugh a Little* (1962) was written as a family biography.

[Rohan Saxena (2nd ed.)]

PIEDMONT, region in N. Italy which comprised the duchy of *Savoy (a kingdom since 1713), the duchy of Montferrat (under Savoy rule since 1709), the marquisate of *Saluzzo (under Savoy rule since 1598), and the municipalities of *Asti, *Chieri, Cuneo, and *Alessandria. The Jewish communities of Piedmont were formed or expanded following the expulsion of Jews from France in 1306, 1332, and 1394. Loan bankers were among the prominent people who settled in Piedmont. In 1430 Amadeus VIII determined the judicial status of the Jews in the duchy of Savoy, stipulating that in each city they were to live in closed quarters. The Jews were frequently subjected to special taxation: in 1551 the annual toleration tax was 500 gold crowns, increased to 14,000 in 1626, but subsequently reduced. In 1708 the Jews were ordered to file a complete inventory of their property every three years. About the middle of the 16th century there were 3,000–4,000 Jews in Savoy, somewhat less in Montferrat, and about 100 in Saluzzo. For a considerable payment, Emmanuel Philibert granted them the monopoly on *moneylending, which continued under his son Charles Emmanuel I. In 1624 there were about 100 Jewish loan-banks in Piedmont. The communities and the loan-bankers were often subjected to demands for exorbitant "gifts." Against a payment of 60,000 ducats a decree was issued in 1603 granting Jews permission to bear defensive weapons when outside the city of *Turin, in addition to the freedom to practice every profession including banking, commerce, and medicine (subject to the bishop's approval). In 1723–29 new enactments were issued, renewing the statutes of 1430 in a milder form, but extending the area to which they applied as a result of the extension of the state of Savoy. The Jews then formed a General Council of Jews (università generale degli ebrei) of Piedmont with branches in Turin, Casale *Monferrato, and Alessandria. In 1723 the Jews were forbidden to own real estate (the prohibition was slightly relaxed in 1729), and were compelled to live in the ghetto, which had been in existence in Turin since 1679. In Casale, *Vercelli, Chieri, Carmagnola, and Saluzzo, the outer walls of the ghettos were completed in 1724, while in Cherasco, *Acqui, and *Moncalvo, the walls were completed in 1730, 1731, and 1732 respectively. The dwellings in the Piedmont ghettos were generally arranged around a central courtyard (*ḥaẓer*), and every ghetto had a synagogue.

The constitution issued under Charles Emmanuel III in 1770 reenacted the statutes of 1430, 1723, and 1729, and during this period the voices of non-Jews, such as the publicist Giuseppe Compagnoni, were first raised in defense of Jews. In 1798 emancipation was introduced into Piedmont by French revolutionary forces, and in 1807, 13 rabbis from Italy attended the French *Sanhedrin in Paris. But after a short interval of well-being, Victor Emmanuel I restored almost *in toto* the 1770 constitution; in 1816 the re-creation of the ghetto was decreed. By then, however, attitudes had changed and men like Vincenzo Gioberti, Roberto and Massimo *d'Azeglio, Carlo *Cattaneo, and others pressed for Jewish emancipation. With the promulgation of the Piedmontese Constitution (Statuto) of 1848 by Prince Charles Albert, the Jews obtained full emancipation and began to participate more actively in political and cultural life. The rabbi of Turin, Lelio *Cantoni, started to reorganize the Jewish communities, and the Jewish publications *L'Educatore Israelita* (Vercelli, 1853–74), followed by *Il Vessillo Israelitico* (Cuneo, 1874–1922), made their appearance. In the middle of the 19th century a famous controversy arose over Rabbi Samuel Olper's project to introduce changes in Jewish religious practice. In 1840 and 1881 there were about 6,500 Jews in Piedmont; in 1911, 6,000; in 1931, 4,900; and in 1961, 6,618; and by 1970 this number dwindled to 1,820.

BIBLIOGRAPHY: G. Volino, *Condizione giuridica degli ebrei in Piemonte prima dell'emancipazione* (1904); M.D. Anfossi, *Gli Ebrei in Piemonte Loro condizioni giuridico-sociali dal 1430 all'emancipazione* (1914); G. Levi, in: RMI, 9 (1934), 511–34; 18 (1952), 412–37, 463–89; B. Terracini, *ibid.*, 15 (1949), 62–77; S. Foa, *ibid.*, 19 (1953), 542–51; 26 (1955), 38 ff.; 27 (1961), passim; 28 (1962), 92 ff.

[Alfredo Mordechai Rabello]

PIERLEONI, ex-Jewish family who first appeared in Rome shortly after the year 1000. The founder of the family, BARUCH, lent large sums of money to church dignitaries, thereby assuring himself of their protection. He and his son, LEO, became converts to Christianity. Leo's son, PIETRO DI LEONE (hence the name Pierleoni), continued to give financial backing to successive popes. Among his numerous sons was one, also called Pietro Pierleoni, who entered the Church. Thanks to his family influence, he became a cardinal in 1120 and pope in 1130, taking the name *Anacletus II. A turreted mansion in the vicinity of what was to become the Rome ghetto still bears the name of the Pierleoni family.

BIBLIOGRAPHY: J. Prinz, *Popes from the Ghetto* (1966), incl. bibl.; Milano, *Ghetto di Roma* (1964), index; Picotti, in: *Archivio storico italiano*, 100 (1942), 3–41 (on the supposed relationship of Gregory VII with the Pierleoni family).

[Attilio Milano]

PIERRE-BLOCH, JEAN (1905–1999), French Socialist politician, writer, and Resistance leader. Pierre-Bloch, who was born in Paris, contributed to the left-wing journal *Populaire* and in 1936 was elected Socialist deputy for the Aisne department. In 1937 he was vice president of a commission of enquiry into the problem of Algeria, which unsuccessfully advocated the consideration of the special demands of the Algerians, then under French tutelage. Pierre-Bloch volunteered for military service on the outbreak of World War II and was taken prisoner by the Germans in 1940. He escaped and joined the Resistance, becoming one of the leaders of the clandestine French Socialist Party. In 1941 he was condemned to death by the Vichy regime for helping to parachute arms into occupied France. Again he succeeded in escaping and in 1942 reached London, where he became chief of French counterespionage. Later in the war he went to Algiers, where he was appointed assistant commissioner for the interior. After the liberation he was a leading figure in the French Socialist Party (SFIO) and became director of the Société Nationale des Entreprises de Presse. From 1968 to 1992, he was president of the International League Against Racism and Anti-Semitism (LICA).

A prolific writer, Pierre-Bloch was the author of *L'Affaire Frankfurter* (1937), *Charles de Gaulle, premier ouvrier de France* (1945), *Liberté et servitude de la presse en France* (1952), *Carnet d'un voyageur en Israël* (1958), and *De Gaulle, ou le temps des méprises* (1969).

[Shulamith Catane]

PIESTANY (Slovak. **Piešťany**; Hung. **Pöstyén**; Ger. **Pistyan**), town in Slovakia (part of Czechoslovakia, 1918–1991; since then the Slovak Republic). Piestany's hot springs were already known to the Romans. In 1736, there were 12 Jewish families from Moldavia living on the estate of Count Forgacs. In 1774 there were 22 families, and in 1795 about 50. Religiously and administratively, they were part of the Vrbov congregation. In 1840 there were 105 Jews in Piestany; 375 in 1880; and 850 in 1910. In 1930 they numbered 1,344. In 1940, on the eve of the deportations, there were 1,559.

The mineral springs attracted many visitors. Jews were not permitted in the common bath but were relegated to the "Jewish bath house." The first congregation was founded in 1795. There were many visitors and they needed services, hence Jews discovered a source of income. They also rented estates, where they grew fruits and vegetables. Grateful to the Hungarian government, they displayed strong Magyar patriotism. During the Spring of Nations (1848–49), some volunteered for the Magyar army. After the Hungarian Jewish Congress of 1868, the congregation joined the Orthodox. Including the neighboring villages, the congregation numbered 1,800. By 1870 they had their own school, synagogue, *mikveh*, cemetery, and a *shoḥet*. In 1895 they built a new synagogue. They also established a *talmud torah* and a *ḥevra kaddisha*. After World War I the congregation expanded, adding a yeshivah; a kosher restaurant – mainly for guests of the spa; a home for the aged and a Beth Jacob school for religious girls.

During World War I, Jews were recruited into the army. At the end of the war, Piestany was hit by the wave of disturbances that beset Slovakia. A militia was able to handle the situation. When more violent disturbances erupted in 1910, the congregation appealed to President *Masaryk. In 1889 the Winter family took over management of the springs, turning it into a world-renowned spa. Alexander Winter developed the sleepy town into a first-rate health resort.

But there was no peace in the Jewish community. Rabbi Koloman Weber (1871–1931), who served as the president of the Orthodox Chancellery for Slovakia in Bratislava, encouraged extremist policies. Internal disturbances led to a split in the congregation in 1926. In addition to the Orthodox body, a Yeshurun congregation was established. They built their own synagogue, a *ḥevra kaddisha*, and other Jewish institutions. Quarrels between the two congregations continued until the deportations of 1942.

Delegates of Slovakian Jewry met in Piestany on March 13, 1919, to discuss their conditions in the new republic. The convention led to political and social reorganization of Jews in Slovakia. The Zionist movement flourished in Piestany in spite of Rabbi Weber's efforts to hinder it. The Zionist organization Ahavat Zion was founded in 1919 and, subsequently, the local branch of the Jewish party. Jews were regularly elected to the municipal board. The Jewish adult and youth movements included all major organizations active in the country. The writer Gieze *Vamos, who wrote in Slovak, gained national fame. His book, *The Broken Branch* (1934), bitterly criticized Jewish life in Slovakia.

Piestany was one of the centers of the Hlinka Guard, a Slovak form of Fascist storm troopers. When Slovakia's autonomy was proclaimed in September 1938, Jews without valid citizenship were expelled to the harsh wasteland of the Hungarian-Slovak border. Slovakia's proclamation of independence under the aegis of the Third Reich on March 14, 1939, was accompanied by violence in the streets. Anti-Jewish legislation and activities culminated in 1942 with the deportation of Jews to Poland. Some 1,500 Jews from Piestany and its environs were sent to extermination camps.

After the war, 250 returned. In June 1945, they established a single congregation. They elected a committee to conduct community life and reconstruct community buildings, such as the synagogue, *mikveh*, and kosher restaurant. During the wave of emigration from Slovakia in 1948–49, most of the Jews left Piestany. In 1959 there were 90 Jews in the city. In the late 1970s the synagogue was torn down. One of the three cemeteries was turned into a public park. In 1958 a kosher restaurant was opened for guests of the spa.

BIBLIOGRAPHY: R. Iltis (ed.), *Die aussaeen unter Traenen …* (1959), 180–4; S. Gruenwald, *Gedenkbuch der Gemeinden Piestany und Umgebung* (1969); E. Bárkány-L. Dojc, *Zidovské nábozenské obce na Slovensku*, (1991), 202–206.

[Yeshayahu Jelinek (2nd ed.)]

PIETY AND THE PIOUS. Because of its theocentric orientation, Judaism regards piety as the supreme virtue leading to man's highest good. Moreover, according to the Mishnah, the *ẓaddik* ("righteous person") is credited with contributing to the preservation of the world (Avot 5: 1). Although the term *ẓaddik gamur,* "the perfectly pious man" is found in talmudic literature (cf. RH 16b) and is contrasted with the *ẓaddik she-eino gamur,* "the imperfectly pious man," it is largely a theoretical designation, and on the principle that "there is none righteous upon earth who doeth only good and sinneth not" (Eccles. 7:20): no human being is regarded as the perfect paragon of piety.

In rabbinic literature a variety of terms is employed to distinguish between different types or degrees of piety. There is, however, no uniform system of ranking such terms as *yere het* ("sin-fearing"), *yere shamayim* ("God-fearing"), *ẓaddik* ("righteous"), and *ḥasid* ("pious"). For example, *Maimonides, explicating the term *ḥasid*, asserts that it carries overtones of excess or extremism not found in other terms describing piety (commentary to Avot 5:7; *Guide of the Perplexed*, 3:53), but in fact this is not always so. There are many instances when the term *ḥasid* describes what elsewhere would be called *ẓaddik* or *yere ḥet*.

Notwithstanding the wide range of definitions of piety one encounters in rabbinic literature, the emphasis on the service of God and the imitation of His ethical attributes appear to be a constant component of all the different types.

Although obedience to halakhic norms represents a necessary condition of piety, it is far from representing its perfection. It was expected that obedience to the law would inculcate such virtues as the *love and fear of God. R. Johanan, a Palestinian *amora*, attributed the destruction of Jerusalem to the failure of the Jews to observe the moral demands that extend beyond the strict requirements of the law. His contemporary, the Babylonian *amora*, Rav, indicated that even in civil litigation one must take into consideration the ethical-religious imperative of Proverbs 2:26, "to walk in the ways of the good and to keep the path of the righteous" (BM 83a). Moreover, abundant references to the special standards of piety, or the "Mishnah of the pious," are found in talmudic literature (BM 52b; Ḥul. 130b; Ter. 8:10). *Naḥmanides cites the talmudic statement "Sanctify yourself within the domain of the permissible" as evidence for his contention that even an individual who has not violated any of the specific and detailed rules set forth in the Torah may still be branded a scoundrel (commentary on Lev. 19:1).

Man's total commitment to the service of God, according to Judaism, extends over all areas of life. For example, R. Yose stated that all our actions should be performed for the sake of God (Avot 2:12). Rabbinic Judaism believed that performance of a religious act could be disciplinary, leading to higher religious sensitivity. This idea was manifested in the relatively positive attitude taken toward deeds inspired by impure motives. In contrast to Christianity's despair over the worthwhileness of human effort, resulting from the Pauline emphasis on original sin, Judaism holds an optimistic view of human nature. The individual is encouraged to perform an act even though it may originate in unworthy motives, because, ultimately, these motives may be transformed and the act performed for the sake of God (Pes. 50b).

The aim of all piety is the sanctification of life, not the withdrawal from it. There is relatively little endorsement of asceticism in rabbinic Judaism. A widely prevalent attitude is represented by the statement of the medieval philosopher, *Judah Halevi, that "contrition on a fast day does nothing to bring man nearer to God than joy on the Sabbath" (*Kuzari* 2:50). Similarly, Judaism generally recoils from tendencies designed to remove the pious from involvement with the community. Man's confrontation with God is not meant to lead to self-centeredness or a sense of isolation, but to participation in a holy community. This attitude is reflected in Hillel's maxim "Do not separate thyself from the community" (Avot 2:5). Moreover, according to a talmudic comment, the overall objective of the entire Torah was to promote peace and thus contribute to the improvement of society (Git. 59b).

Although rabbinic Judaism produced a number of extraordinary individuals endowed with special capacities for mystical union, apocalyptic visions, and saintliness, these aspects of piety were never recognized as displacing the normative component, which stressed faithful adherence to the Covenant as interpreted by the Oral Law. It was felt that the practice and, especially, the study of the Torah are not merely intrinsically valuable activities, but are also instrumental in refining man's character and lifting him to higher levels of piety. According to *Phinehas b. Jair, spiritual development reaches its climax when the individual becomes so attached to God that *Ru'ah ha-Kodesh* is conferred upon him (Av. Zar. 20b).

Maimonides held that faithful observance of the commandments is needed to inculcate the fear of God in man, while the contemplative virtues, climaxing in the intellectual apprehension of God, lead to the love of God (*Guide*, 3:52). Maimonides redefined the rabbinic notion of the *talmid ḥakham*, the scholar of the law, who, as early as the talmudic period, was regarded as the supreme religious model (see I. Twersky, in: *Jewish Medieval and Renaissance Studies* (1967), 106–18). For Maimonides, the true Torah scholar is not merely knowledgeable in *halakhah*, but is also proficient in science and philosophy. Accordingly, only he who combines obedience to the commandments with contemplative perfection can aspire to the state of true union with God.

For the medieval German ḥasid, *Judah he-Ḥasid, the love of God manifests itself in an entirely different fashion. It impels him to go beyond the legal requirements of the Torah, which makes concessions to human frailties and weaknesses. Instead, the truly pious will govern themselves by the "law of heaven," which makes far stricter demands than the "law of the Torah," addressed to the average individual.

The kabbalists' notion of piety stresses the craving for the mystical ideal of *devekut* (adherence to God), which to them represents the pinnacle of religious achievement. Unlike the complete mystical union which seeks the absorption of the self in the divine, the state of *devekut* preserves the separateness and self-identity of the individual. It is an act of communion, not a mergence, for the self is not divested of its responsibilities toward God. It is the function of the righteous individual to help bring about the *tikkun* (redemption of the world; see *Kabbalah).

In the ḥasidic movement special emphasis was placed on such personal components of piety as *kavvanah* ("intention" or "purposefulness" in prayer) and *hitlahavut* ("enthusiasm") in the attainment of the ideal of *devekut*. The charisma of the *ẓaddik*, renowned for his *devekut* rather than his knowledge of Torah, played a decisive role. It is for this reason that Gershom *Scholem observed that in the *ḥasidic* movement "personality takes the place of doctrine" (Mysticism, 344). The *ẓaddik*, by virtue of his special spiritual status, serves as the channel for the transmission of divine grace and plays a unique role in the redemption of the world. In the ḥasidic scheme, through attachment to the *ẓaddik*, the ordinary individual can participate in this task and achieve union with the "upper worlds."

BIBLIOGRAPHY: J.B. Agus, *The Evolution of Jewish Thought* (1959), passim; S. Belkin, *In His Image* (1960), passim; A. Buechler, *The Ancient Pious Men: Types of Jewish Palestinian Piety* (1968); L. Jacobs, *Jewish Values* (1960), passim; S. Schechter, *Studies in Judaism*, 2 (1908), 148–81; J.B. Soloveitchik, in: *Talpioth*, 1 (1944), 651–735.

[Walter S. Wurzburger]

PIG (Heb. חֲזִיר, *ḥazir*). Included in the Pentateuch among the unclean animals prohibited as food is the pig which, although cloven-footed, is a nonruminant (Lev. 11:7; Deut. 16:8). It is the sole unclean animal mentioned as possessing these characteristics. There are archaeological evidences (figurines and relics of bones) that the pig was eaten by the inhabitants of Canaan before the Israelite conquest. It was also offered as a sacrifice in idolatrous worship, provoking a protest from Isaiah (66:3), while those "eating swine's flesh, and the detestable thing, and the mouse" (66:17) apparently did so in a cultic ceremony. The pig symbolized something repulsive, and hence "as a ring of gold in a swine's snout, so is a fair woman that turneth aside from discretion" (Prov. 11:22). Other peoples, too, such as the Egyptians and the Sidonians, refrained from eating pig, which was also later prohibited to the Muslims. Abhorrence of the pig entered so deeply into the consciousness of the Jews that the expression *davar aḥer* ("another thing," i.e., something not to be mentioned by name) was used for it, at least as early as talmudic times (Ber. 43b; Shab. 129a) and in Aramaic as "that species." As early as *Antiochus Epiphanes it was decreed that the eating of swine's flesh was to be a test of the Jews' loyalty to Judaism (II Macc. 6:18). Following the incident in the days of Hyrcanus II when, instead of an animal fit for sacrifice, a pig was sent up the walls of Jerusalem during a siege, it was decreed: "Cursed be he who breeds pigs" (Sot. 49b; TJ, Ta'an. 4:8, 68c), and this prohibition was incorporated into the Mishnah (BK 7:7). Since the pig eats everything and finds its food everywhere, there arose the saying: "None is richer than a pig" (Shab. 155b). The pig suffers from various maladies: "Ten measures of diseases descended to the world, of which the swine took nine" (Kid. 49b). During a plague that afflicted pigs, R. Judah decreed a fast in Babylonia since "their intestines are like those of human beings," the fear being entertained that the plague would spread to people (Ta'an. 21b).

The domesticated pig, *Sus scropha domestica*, is descended from the wild boar, *Sus scropha*. Its domestication was a lengthy process, going back to ancient times. The pig formerly found in Ereẓ Israel differed from the present-day one whose various breeds were developed from strains brought from China about the middle of the 18th century. The wild boar (*ḥazir ha-bar*), which is found in Israel especially in Upper and western Galilee, damages plants and vegetables, and uproots the bulbs and tubers of wild flora. It is the "boar out of the wood" in Psalms (80:9–14), where reference is made to the ravages it causes to vines. The Tosefta (Kil. 1:8) states that "although the pig and the wild boar resemble each other, they are heterogeneous."

[Jehuda Feliks]

In Halakhah and Aggadah

In a *baraita* mentioned three times in the Babylonian Talmud (Sot. 49b; BK 82b; Men. 64b), the prohibition against rearing pig is joined with the prohibition against studying "Greek wisdom," and some scholars have queried the trustworthiness of this tradition and tend to the opinion that the incident referred to there – when the besiegers of Jerusalem sent up a pig to the besieged in place of the two lambs for the daily sacrifices – occurred during the siege of Jerusalem by Titus, when the subsequent prohibition against rearing pigs was decreed (cf. TJ, Ber. 4:1, 7b, where a similar story occurs about sending up a pig at "the time of the wicked kingdom"). It seems, however, that the prohibition against rearing pigs was already known in the days of the early Hasmoneans; it is possible that its source is to be found in a reaction to the decrees of Antiochus Epiphanes, who ordered a pig to be offered as a sacrifice (I Macc. 1:47) and pig's flesh to be eaten (II Macc. 6:18–7:42) and that the incident in the time of the Hasmonean brothers caused the prohibition to be stressed with greater emphasis.

The phrase "Cursed be the man who rears" is worthy of attention. It would appear that, with the increase of the non-Jewish population, Jews in Ereẓ Israel apparently engaged in the business of pig rearing. Of interest is the combination "pig-breeders and usurers" (Ber. 55a, and Rashi, ad loc.) both of which were regarded as providing an easy means of livelihood. Although there are many references in the *aggadah* to a feeling of revulsion and disgust toward swine flesh, the rabbis refrained from connecting the prohibition with this feeling. Eleazar b. Azariah expounded, "Whence do we know that a man should not say, 'I have no desire to eat swine's flesh,' but rather should he say 'I would like to eat it, but what can I do seeing that my Father in Heaven has decreed against it'" (Sifra, *Kedoshim*, Perek 11:22). A substitute was even given in a fish called *shibuta* "which resembles the pig" in taste (Ḥul. 109b; Tanh. *Shemini*, 12).

In the Midrash the Roman kingdom is called *ḥazir* ("pig"). It is possible that the name originated in the fact that the symbol of the Roman legion in Ereẓ Israel was the boar (see ARN[1], 34:100: "'The… boar out of the wood doth ravage it' [Ps. 80:14], refers to the Roman kingdom"; and cf. Mid. Ps. to 80:6). The Midrashim explain the name with reference to the characteristics common to Rome and to the pig: "and the swine because he parteth the hoof' – why is [Rome] compared to a swine? – To teach that just as a swine when it lies down puts out its hooves as if to say, 'see, I am clean,' so too the kingdom of Edom [Rome] acts arrogantly, and plunders and robs under the guise of establishing a judicial tribunal" (Lev. R. 13:5). Another "etymological" explanation states: "Why is [Rome] called *ḥazir* ['pig']… because it will eventually restore *haḤazir* ['the kingdom'] to its rightful owner" (Eccles. R. 1:9; Lev. R. 13:5). This statement was quoted in the Middle Ages by the people with the reading, "Why is it called a pig? – Because the Holy One will restore it to Israel" (i.e., declare it clean), and in this form it became a topic in Jewish-Christian polemics.

In Israel

The raising of pigs in the Holy Land was always regarded with abhorrence not only by Jewish religious circles but also by many outside the strictly religious camp. The Jewish National Fund's leases forbade pig raising on its land. The religious parties pressed for the prohibition of pig breeding by law, but in the early years of statehood it was left to local authorities to pass their own bylaws in this matter. When the Supreme Court, in a test case, ruled that such regulations were *ultra vires*, the religious parties pressed for, and secured, the passage of a special authorization law (5717/1956) to give the local authorities the necessary authority. There was still pressure for the prohibition of pig breeding on a national basis and in 1962 a law was passed forbidding the breeding, keeping, or slaughtering of pigs, except in Nazareth and in certain other named places with a sizable Christian population. In the early 2000s Kibbutz Lahav and Kibbutz Mizra were among the few Jewish pig breeders in the country.

BIBLIOGRAPHY: IN THE BIBLE: Lewysohn, Zool, 146–8 (nos. 170–2); F. Blome, *Die Opfermaterie in Babylonien und Israel*, 1 (1934), 120–5, nos. 117–21; F.S. Bodenheimer, *Animal and Man in Bible Lands* (1960), 51, 103. IN HALAKHAH AND AGGADAH: S. Kraus, in: REJ, 53 (1907), 15–19; Ginzberg, Legends, 5 (1925), Y. Baer, in: *Sefer Zikkaron le-Asher Gulak ve-li-Shemu'el Klein* 294; idem, *Perushim ve-Ḥiddushim ba-Yerushalmi*, 3 (1941), 35–40; (1942), 40, note by J.N. Epstein: Ḥ. Albeck, *ibid.*, 49; E. Wiesenberg, in: HUCA, 27 (1956), 233–93. IN ISRAEL: M. Elon, *Ḥakikah Datit* (1968), 20–23. **ADD. BIBLIOGRAPHY:** Feliks, Ha-Ẓome'aḥ, 228.

PIGIT, SAMUEL BEN SHEMARIA (1849–1911), Karaite scholar from Chufut-Qaleh, who was a descendant of Simhah Isaak *Luzki. He studied in Chufut-Qaleh and afterwards in Yevpatoria. He was a *ḥazzan* and a teacher of Torah in the communities of Karasubazar (1868–78), Simferopol (1878–82), and in Yekaterinoslav from 1882 until his death. Pigit was one of the last Crimean Karaite scholars who wrote Hebrew. He had a wide knowledge of Rabbanite literature and used in his pure Hebrew a great number of words, expressions, and quotations from the Talmud and from rabbinic literature. He was also interested in the research of Jewish studies. Some of his works were published: *Iggeret Nidḥei Yisrael* (St. Petersburg, 1894), which contains sermons and liturgical poems in Hebrew and the Karaite language, his own memories, and some information on the history of Crimean Karaites; *Davar Davur* (Warsaw, 1904; reprint Ramleh, 1977) includes Oriental fables and Karaite proverbs in his Hebrew translation from the Karaite language. He also published two poems in the Karaite language (K. Zh., 5–6 (1911), 15–16). Other works by Pigit that remained in manuscript and never published were lost. He had a large collection of manuscripts.

BIBLIOGRAPHY: B. Elyasevich, *Materialy k serii narody i kul'tury*, 14, kn. 2 (1993), 166–67.

[Golda Akhiezer (2[ed] ed.)]

PI-HAHIROTH (Heb. פִּי הַחִירֹת, Hahiroth), town E. of Baal-Zephon, near Migdol, in the East Delta of Egypt (Num. 33:7). At the beginning of the Exodus the Israelites encamped near Pi-Hahiroth, whose site is yet to be identified. A.H. Gardiner (see bibl.) suggests that the town's name is an alteration of Pr-

Ḥtḥr ("the house of Hathor"), mentioned in various Egyptian documents. The Septuagint translates Pi-Hahiroth either as "the mouth of Hiroth" – i.e., considering פִּי as the Hebrew word for "mouth" and not as part of the name – (cf. Num. 33:8, where the Hebrew text also omits פִּי), or as "the encampment" (cf. lxx, Ex. 14:2, 9), as though the Hebrew text did not use the name (Heb. פִּי הַחִירֹת), but rather a word meaning encampment.

BIBLIOGRAPHY: A.H. Gardiner, in: *Recueil d'études égyptologiques dédiées à la mémoire de Jean-François Champollion* (1922), 213; H. Gauthier, *Dictionnaire des noms géographiques contenus dans les textes hiéroglyphiques*, 2 (1925), 117; P. Montet, *La stèle du Roi Kamose* (1956), 115.

PIJADE, MOŠA (1890–1957), Yugoslav revolutionary and politician. Born in Belgrade, Pijade studied painting in Munich and Paris and returned to Belgrade as an art teacher. He joined the illegal Communist Party in 1920 and was imprisoned by the authorities the following year. On his release he continued his revolutionary activities and in 1925 was imprisoned for a further 14 years during which time he translated Marx's *Das Kapital.*

In 1940 Pijade was arrested for a third time but released shortly before the German invasion of Yugoslavia. Following the German conquest of Yugoslavia he organized the Communist partisans and set out the tasks of the People's Liberation Committee in a document known as the *Regulations of Foča*. Pijade was one of the closest associates of the Yugoslav leader Josip Broz Tito, and when the latter came to power after the liberation of Yugoslavia, Pijade was made president of the Serbian Republic, chairman of the Yugoslav National Assembly, and a member of the political bureau of the party central committee. He was helpful in allowing the departure of Jews to Israel with all their personal property and gave occasional advice to the leaders of the Federation of Jewish Communities.

BIBLIOGRAPHY: S. Bosiljčić and D. Marković, *Moša Pijade* (Serbian, 1960). **ADD. BIBLIOGRAPHY:** S. Marković, *Moša Pijade i njegovo vreme* (1968).

[Zvi Loker]

PIKE, LIPMAN EMANUEL (Lip; "The Iron Batter"; 1845–1893), U.S. baseball player, considered the first professional baseball player for openly receiving money to play. Pike was born in Manhattan, the second of five children to Emanuel, a haberdasher of Dutch origin, and Jane. The family moved to Brooklyn, where Pike and his siblings became engrossed in the newly invented American game of baseball. One week after his bar mitzvah in 1858, Pike appeared in a box score playing first base, while his older brother Boaz played shortstop. The Pike brothers played for various teams, including the renowned Brooklyn Atlantics. In 1866, the Philadelphia Athletics offered the 21-year-old Pike $20 per week to play third base. It exposed for the first time the widespread though hushed up system of paying supposedly amateur players to play baseball, thereby legitimizing the practice of play for pay. Pike played from 1866 to 1881, switching teams often throughout his career: he also played for Irvington, New Jersey (1867), New York Mutuals (1867–68), Brooklyn Atlantics (1869–70), Troy Haymakers (1871), Lord Baltimores (1872–73), Hartford Dark Blues (1874), St. Louis Brown Stockings (1875–76), Cincinnati Reds (1877–78), Providence Grays (1878), Worchester Ruby Legs (1881) for five games, and one last appearance with the New York Metropolitans of the American Association for one game on July 28, 1887, at the age of 42. While no statistical records exist of his career through 1870, Pike appeared in 425 National Association and National League games beginning in 1871, hitting .321 with a .465 slugging average. Standing only 5′ 8″ and weighing 158 pounds, Pike was known as both a powerful batter and the fastest base runner of his time. He led the league in home runs four times, including 1872, when his six home runs accounted for a sixth of the National Association's 35 home runs. So fast was Pike that on August 16, 1873, at Baltimore's Newington Park, he raced in a 100-yard dash against a horse named Clarence, and won. After his career was over, Pike followed his father and became a haberdasher in Brooklyn, but he remained involved in the game as a part-time umpire. One of his younger brothers, Jay (Jacob), played one game in the major leagues on August 27, 1877, and became the first Jewish umpire when he officiated in 1875 in the National Association.

[Elli Wohlgelernter (2nd ed.)]

PIKKU'AḤ NEFESH (Heb. פִּקּוּחַ נֶפֶשׁ; "regard for human life"), the rabbinical term applied to the duty to save human life in a situation in which it is imperiled. The danger to life may be due to a grave state of illness or other direct peril (*sakkanat nefashot*), or indirectly, to a condition of health which, though not serious, might deteriorate and consequently imperil life (*safek sakkanat nefashot*). *Pikku'aḥ nefesh* is a biblical injunction derived from the verse "Neither shalt thou stand idly by the blood of thy neighbor" (Lev. 19:16), and according to the Talmud it supersedes even the Sabbath laws (*pikku'aḥ nefesh doḥeh et ha-Shabbat*; Yoma 85a). One should be more particular about matters concerning danger to health and life than about ritual observances (Ḥul 10a). The strict rules of hygiene codified in the Shulḥan Arukh center around the principle of *pikku'aḥ nefesh* (YD 116). The rabbis interpreted the verse "Ye shall therefore keep my statutes and my ordinances which if a man do he shall live by them" (Lev. 18:5), that man shall "live" by these commandments, and not die as a result of observing them (Yoma 85b; Sanh. 74a).

The Talmud (BM 62a) discusses the problem of an individual faced with the choice of saving his own life or that of his companion, and mentions the example of two men in a desert with a supply of water sufficient for one only. Although *Ben Peturah advocated that neither should attempt to save his own life at the expense of the other but that both share the water, R. *Akiva, whose opinion prevailed, ruled that one should save one's own life and not share the water. Only when faced with a choice between death and committing idolatry, unlawful sexual intercourse, or murder is martyrdom to be preferred (Sanh. 74a–b). One must also sacrifice one's life rather than submit to what may be taken for a renunciation of faith through the violation of any religious law in public (Sanh. 74a–b; Sh. Ar., YD 157). In all other cases, the rule of *pikku'aḥ nefesh* takes precedence (Sanh. 74a–b; Maim., *Iggeret ha-Shemad* 3).

The rule that one may profane one Sabbath in order to save the life of a person and enable him subsequently to observe many others (Yoma 85b) is inferred by the rabbis from the verse "The children of Israel shall keep the Sabbath to observe the Sabbath" (Ex. 31:16). Thus, on the Sabbath (or a festival), every type of medical treatment must be accorded to a dangerously ill person, to the extent of even putting out the light to help him sleep (Shab. 2:5; Sh. Ar., OḤ 278). Equal efforts must be made even where there is only a possibility of danger to life (*safek sakkanat nefashot*, Yoma 8:6; ibid. 84b). Only in cases of minor illnesses or physical discomforts should violations of the Sabbath be kept to the minimum; if possible a non-Jew should perform these duties (Sh. Ar., OḤ 328:17). In all other instances, the medical treatment should be administered by a Jew, and those who are assiduous in their help, comfort, and work for the sick on the Sabbath, are deemed worthy of the highest praise (*ibid.*, 328:12–13). If a dangerously ill person is in need of food on the Sabbath, one should slaughter animals and prepare them according to the dietary laws, rather than feed him ritually forbidden food (*ibid.*, 328:14). If, however, it is deemed necessary for the recovery of the patient that he eat forbidden food, he is allowed to do so (*ibid.*, 328). A woman in confinement is considered dangerously ill for a period of three days after delivery. Should one of these days be a Sabbath, everything possible must be done to ease her pain and lessen her discomfort, including the kindling of a fire to warm her (Maim. Yad, Shabbat 2:13–14; Sh. Ar., OḤ 330:1, 4–6). A sick person is forbidden to fast on the *Day of Atonement if it is thought that this would seriously endanger his recovery. Moreover, even a healthy person seized by a fit of "ravenous hunger" which causes faintness (*bulmos*), must be fed on the Day of Atonement with whatever food is available (including ritually forbidden food (Sh. Ar., OḤ 618:9)) until he recovers (Yoma 8:6; Sh. Ar., OḤ 618).

BIBLIOGRAPHY: Eisenstein, Dinim, 291, 342–3.

PILCH, JUDAH (1902–1986), U.S. Jewish educator. Born in the Ukraine, he received a traditional Jewish education in Europe and his ordination as a rabbi in Turkey. He went to the United States in 1928. He received his M.A. degree from Columbia University and his Ph.D. at Dropsie College. He was on the faculty of the College of Jewish Studies at Chicago from 1929 to 1939; for the following five years he was director of the Jewish Education Association in Rochester, N.Y. After serving with the Jewish Education Committee of New York City and the Jewish Education Association of Essex County, N.J., in 1949 Pilch became associated with the American Association for Jewish Education (now the Jewish Educational Services of North America), and from 1952 to 1960 was the executive director. In 1960 he became the founding head of the Association's National Curriculum Research Institute. After his retirement, Pilch moved to Los Angeles, where he was on the faculty of the Institute of Religion at HUC/JIR.

In the early 1950s Pilch organized and led the first Jewish teachers' seminar to Israel. He was president of the National Council for Jewish Education (1945–1950), vice president of the Religious Education Association of the U.S. and Canada in 1953, and president of the National Conference for Jewish Social Service (1954–55). He was vice president of the Histadrut Ivrit (1934–38). Without compromising his devotion to Hebrew, he was also interested in Yiddish literature and served as dean of the Graduate Division of Herzlia–Jewish Teachers' Seminary in New York.

Pilch was a prolific writer in Hebrew, English, and Yiddish. Among his works are *Jewish Life in Our Times* (1943), *Teaching Modern Jewish History* (1948), *Between Two Generations: Selected Essays* (1977), and *The Weak Against The Strong* (1973). He edited the Jewish education department of the *Encyclopaedia Judaica.*

Pilch was widely recognized as one of the great leaders of Jewish education in the United States, belonging in the same echelon as Alexander *Dushkin, Israel *Chipkin, and Samson *Benderly. Like them, he combined a European, traditional Jewish education with Western culture, and expertise as a teacher and administrator. He brought to his positions and work an extraordinary single-minded devotion to the furtherance of Jewish education; he sought to pioneer in methodology and stimulated the preparation of newly designed textbooks and the exploration of teaching through technological advances.

[Milton Ridvas Konvitz (2nd ed.)]

PILCHIK, ELY EMANUEL (1913–2003), U.S. Reform rabbi. Pilchik was born in Baranowicz, Poland, and immigrated to the United States in 1920. He earned a B.A. from the University of Cincinnati in 1935 and was ordained and received his M.H.L. from *Hebrew Union College in 1939. HUC-JIR awarded him an honorary D.D. degree in 1964. In 1939, Pilchik joined the faculty of the University of Maryland, where he established a *Hillel Foundation, serving as its first director. He became assistant rabbi of Har Sinai Temple in Baltimore, Maryland (1940–42), before being appointed rabbi of Temple Israel in Tulsa, Oklahoma (1942–47), where his tenure was interrupted by service overseas as a chaplain in the United States Navy during World War II (1944–46). In 1947, Pilchik assumed the pulpit of Temple B'nai Jeshurun in Newark, New Jersey, becoming emeritus in 1981. He quickly became a regional Jewish leader, serving as president of the Essex County, N.J., Synagogue Council (1949–51) and Board of Rabbis (1951–52), as well as of the New Jersey Board of Rabbis (1955–57) and of the Association of Reform Rabbis of New York (1958–59). In the general community, he was appointed by the governor to serve on the New Jersey State Council on Economic Opportunity and served as chairman of the Newark Citizen's Housing Committee. On a national level, Pilchik was president of the Jewish Book Council of America (1954–58), and in the Reform movement, a member of the Executive Board of the *Central Conference of American Rabbis (1951–53) and of the Board of Governors of HUC-JIR. In 1977, he was elected president of the CCAR (1977–79). Pilchik is the author of *Hillel* (1951), *Maimonides' Creed* (1952), and *Duties of the Heart* (1953).

[Bezalel Gordon (2nd ed.)]

PILGRIMAGE. In Hebrew the term *aliyah* (lit. "going up") has been used since ancient times for pilgrimages to Jerusalem on the three festivals known as **shalosh regalim*). The Torah prescribes that all males must go up to Jerusalem "three times a year" on the three festivals – Passover, Shavuot, and Sukkot (Ex. 23:17; 34:23; Deut. 16:16; II Chron. 8:13).

For pilgrimages in the biblical period see *Passover; *Shavuot; and *Sukkot.

Second Temple Period

Hundreds of thousands of pilgrims from within Ereẓ Israel, as well as from the Diaspora, streamed to the Temple at each of the three festivals. The pilgrimage affected the life of every Jew, who might have to prepare for the occasion, and the journey and the accompanying sacrifices involved a not inconsiderable financial outlay. The inspiration derived from "the sojourn in the Temple courts," and from attendance at the rabbinical academies in Jerusalem, remained a powerful stimulus to the pilgrim after his return: "His heart prompts him to study Torah" (TJ, Suk. 5:1, 55a). Many of the new trends in Jewish spiritual life were ventilated in Jerusalem, and the pilgrim served as the vehicle for disseminating the ideas that were in constant ferment during the period. The pilgrimage had a considerable influence upon the life of the capital in a number of spheres; in the social sphere, from the presence there of Jews from every part of the Diaspora, and in the economic, from the vast sums spent by the thousands of pilgrims both for their own needs and on charity. It also had a national-political influence. The *aliyah* from all parts of Ereẓ Israel and the Diaspora strengthened the consciousness of national and social solidarity (Jos., Ant. 4:203–4). This national consciousness reached a new peak with the presence of the throngs of pilgrims in Jerusalem and made them even more sensitive to the humiliation entailed in their subjection to a foreign yoke. As a result of this sensitivity disorders and revolts were of frequent occurrence in Jerusalem during the festivals (Jos., Wars 5:243–4; Ant. 13:337–9).

The biblical injunction on the subject states: "Three times in the year shall all thy males appear before the Lord God" (Ex. 23:17; 34:23, Deut. 16:16). These passages were apparently not construed as mandatory, requiring *aliyah* thrice yearly, but as meaning that on these occasions it was a meritorious act to make the pilgrimage and in so doing offer up sacrifices, "and none shall appear before me empty" (*ibid.*). The tannaitic sources speak of the obligation of *aliyah le-regel* but not of a commandment to go up on every festival (Ḥag. 1:1, 6a). In any event it is clear that not all the male population of Ereẓ Israel, and certainly not of the Diaspora, made the pilgrimage three times yearly. Although both from the Talmud (Pes. 8b) and from Josephus (Wars 2:515) one might infer that the whole population of a city would participate in the pilgrimage, it was not general that the cities, even those near to Jerusalem, would be entirely emptied as a consequence of their Jewish population going on pilgrimage. On the other hand, there can be no doubt that a considerable number went up, especially from Judea (Wars 2:43). There is ample evidence of *aliyah le-regel* from Galilee, and it may be assumed that the number who came from the Diaspora was not as great as those from Ereẓ Israel. Philo mentions that "countless multitudes from countless cities come to the Temple at every festival, some by land, and others by sea, from east and west and north and south" (Spec. 1:69). Sources in the Talmud, Josephus, and the New Testament yield a long list of places, including Babylonia, Persia, Media, Alexandria, Cyrenaica, Ethiopia, Syria, Pontus, Asia, Tarsus, Phrygia, Pamphylia, and Rome, whose residents were to be found in Jerusalem during the festivals (ARN^2, 27, 55; Meg. 26a; Jos., Ant. 17:26; Acts 2:9–10). Both the inscription of Theodotus found in Jerusalem and the literary sources indicate that sometimes the inhabitants of a particular city would establish synagogues in Jerusalem and hospices for the pilgrims who required such facilities (Tosef., Meg. 3:6; Acts 6:9; M. Schwabe, in *Sefer Yerushalayim*, ed. by M. Avi-Yonah, 1 (1956), 362).

The Pilgrimage

The pilgrims often traveled in caravans which mustered in the cities of Ereẓ Israel and the Diaspora. The ascent of the joyful throng of celebrants to Jerusalem is already mentioned in a number of Psalms, such as Psalms 42, 84, and 122, which are songs of the pilgrim companies, and it is reflected in many rabbinic passages (cf. Lam. R. 1:17, no. 52). The procession on the occasion of the first fruits of Shavuot was particularly impressive: "Those who lived near brought fresh figs and grapes, but those from a distance brought dried figs and raisins. An ox with horns bedecked with gold and with an olive crown on its head led the way. The flute was played before them until they were near Jerusalem" (Bik. 3:3). Josephus relates that the pilgrims from Babylonia used to assemble in *Nehardea and *Nisibis and accompany the convoys transporting the annual half-*shekel* Temple dues on the journey to Jerusalem (Ant. 18:311–2). Women also took part, the biblical passage "all thy males shall appear" being understood merely as referring only to the duty of the men who alone were obliged to bring the obligatory sacrifices (Ant. 11:109; Luke 2:41–43).

The Rituals

The pilgrims arrived in Jerusalem several days before the festival; this was especially true of those from the Diaspora who had to undergo purification for over a week from the defilement incurred in alien lands (Jos., Wars 1:229; 6:290). The essence of the pilgrimage was the entry of the individual, or the group, into the Temple to worship there on the festivals, and the offering of the obligatory sacrifices enjoined in the precept that, "None shall appear before me empty." The tannaitic tradition expounded that the celebrant was obliged to offer the pilgrim's burnt offering, the festal offering which is counted as a peace offering, and the offering of rejoicing (Ḥag. 6b). The sacrifices were offered both on the first day or during subsequent days of the festival.

The Stay in Jerusalem

According to the *halakhah*, not only did the scriptural verse, "and in the morning you shall turn and go to your tent," enjoined with regard to the Passover pilgrim, oblige him to remain overnight in Jerusalem, but "in the morning" was interpreted as the morning after the last day of the festival. The pilgrim was thus obliged to stop over for the entire Passover week, and for the eight days of Sukkot (Zev. 11:7 and 97a; Tosef. Ḥag. 1:5). The celebrants used to stay in the capital itself, or in the adjoining villages, or encamp in tents erected in the surrounding fields (Jos., Ant. 17:217; Wars 2:12). During their sojourn in Jerusalem the pilgrims engaged in study of the Torah and participated in the common festive meals at which they ate the permitted sacrificial food – the peace offering, as well as the second tithe which had to be consumed in Jerusalem (Jos., Ant. 4:205). Greater leniency was applied to the law appertaining to ritual defilement during the festival, in order that the laws of ritual purity would not prevent social intercourse. Jerusalem was regarded as the common possession of the entire Jewish people, and householders in the capital were forbidden to take rent from the pilgrims, who however left them the hides of the sacrificial animals as a token of gratitude (Tosef., Ma'as Sh. 1:12 and 13; ARN[1] 35, 1 and 3). The sources indicate that a convivial atmosphere prevailed in the capital during the days of pilgrimages: "Nobody ever had occasion to say to his neighbor 'I have been unable to find a stove for cooking the paschal meals in Jerusalem,' or 'I have been unable to find a bed to sleep in Jerusalem'" (ARN *ibid.*).

[Shmuel Safrai]

Post-Temple Period

Pilgrimages to Jerusalem continued after the destruction of the Temple (cf. Ned. 23a). However, the joy that previously characterized these events was now combined with sorrow. When the pilgrims encountered the site of the ruined Sanctuary they rended their garments as a sign of mourning and recited the verse, "Our holy and our beautiful house, where our fathers praised Thee, is burned with fire and all our pleasant things are laid waste" (Isa. 64:10; MK 26a). Some even abstained from meat and wine on the day they saw Jerusalem in its destruction (Shevu. 20a). The rabbis, commenting on the verse, "These things I remember, and pour out my soul within me" (Ps. 52:5), compared the pilgrimages before and after the destruction. Previously, the Jews went up to Jerusalem along well-kept roads, the trees forming a covering over their heads, and under the protection of a government committed to God. Now they went through thorny hedges, exposed to the sun, and under the sovereignty of oppressive governments (Lam. R. 1:52). Nevertheless, the Jews continued their pilgrimages to the Temple site, and in 333 "the traveler of Bordeaux" described Jews pouring oil on a stone. In 392 Jerome related that Jews came to lament the destruction of the Temple, after paying for a permit to enter the Temple grounds (commentary on Zeph. 1:16). A fifth-century testimony reported a pilgrimage of over 100,000 Jews, made possible as a result of the sympathetic attitude of Anthenais Eudocia, wife of the emperor Theodosius II.

These pilgrimages continued throughout the Middle Ages, although on many occasions the Jewish pilgrims were subject to taxes and discriminatory regulations which were enacted against them by the Christian or Muslim overlords of the holy places. The ninth-century pilgrimages of Rabbi *Ahimaaz the Elder, of Venosa, Italy, are well known. The Persian traveler Nāṣir Khosraw (1047) stated that he saw Jews from Roman lands (Byzantium) coming to visit their houses of worship. The testimony of a pilgrim from Babylonia, Phinehas ha-Kohen (c. 1030), has also survived.

After Ereẓ Israel was conquered by the Muslims under Saladin (1187), the Jews were once again permitted to visit their holy places freely. Numerous pilgrims came from Damascus, Babylonia, and Egypt, and they remained in Jerusalem over Passover and Shavuot. Naḥmanides, in a letter to his son, wrote: "Many men and women from Damascus, Babylon, and their vicinities come to Jerusalem to see the site of the Holy Temple and to lament its destruction." The commandment of pilgrimage was also a factor in motivating the journeys of *Benjamin of Tudela and *Pethahiah of Regensburg in the 12th century, and *Jacob b. Nethanel and Judah *Al-Ḥarizi in the 13th. In his writing, Benjamin referred to the Dome of the Rock, standing "opposite the place of the holy Temple which is occupied at present by [a church called] Templum Domini… In front of it you see the Western Wall, one of the walls which formed the ancient Temple… and all Jews go there to say their prayers near the wall of the courtyard."

The number of pilgrims was greatly increased by the many exiles who settled in Turkish territory following the 1492 expulsion of the Jews from Spain. The tomb of Samuel the Prophet at Nabi Samwil (thought to be the biblical Ramah) was also a goal of their pilgrimages. Here they held annual celebrations similar to those which were instituted in Meron on *Lag Ba-Omer, a century later. In 1634, Gershom ben Eliezer Ha-Levi of Prague visited the Holy Land, and later recorded his experience in *Gelilot Ereẓ Yisrael* (Prague, 1824[4]). The most famous pilgrimage made to the Holy Land by early ḥasidic leaders was that of *Naḥman of Bratslav. His visit (1798–99) left such a profound impression upon him that, when he later returned to Poland, he remarked, "Wherever I go, I am still in Ereẓ Israel."

In modern times, the pilgrimages most beneficial to the Holy Land were those of Sir Moses *Montefiore. He made his first visit in 1827, and returned in 1838, 1849, 1855, 1866, and 1875. He made his last pilgrimage when he was 91 years old, and after each visit he intensified his financial support for the new *yishuv*. With the continuing development of the Jewish resettlement in Ereẓ Israel and the improvement in the means of long-distance transportation, Jews continued in ever-increasing numbers to visit the Holy Land.

With the conclusion of the armistice agreement following the Israel War of Independence (1949), it was agreed between Jordan and Israel that talks would follow immediately to enable "free access to the holy places" in Jerusalem, and the "use of the Jewish cemetery on the Mount of Olives." However, nothing ever came of this and Jerusalem remained a divided city. This caused difficulties for pilgrims who desired to visit the shrines in both countries. While Jordan finally did make some arrangements for Christian pilgrims to enter or leave through one of the crossing points (the main one being the Mandelbaum Gate in Jerusalem), Jewish pilgrims were not allowed into Jordan at all. Most distressing to Jews was the denial of access to the Western Wall. The main goal of the pilgrims then became the traditional Tomb of David on Mount Zion, from where they viewed the Old City of Jerusalem. Following the Six-Day War and the reunification of Jerusalem, the Western Wall was again reopened to Jews and became a magnet of pilgrimage.

Christian Pilgrimages

Christian pilgrimages to Ereẓ Israel became an established institution from the fourth century on and have continued almost uninterruptedly to the present day. The reports of the pilgrims had a wide influence, stimulating religious piety and curiosity about the Holy Land. They also provide an important source of information for the history of Ereẓ Israel, the political situation in various periods, its communities, sects, settlements, and social life. Despite its occasional anti-Jewish bias, the pilgrim literature also gives a general picture of Jewish settlement in Ereẓ Israel, supplementing and augmenting the Jewish sources in many details.

HISTORY. Ereẓ Israel became the Holy Land to Christians as the cradle of Christianity and because of its associations with the life of Jesus and the apostles. Nevertheless the Church never aspired to make Jerusalem the center of Christianity, and its symbolic significance was in its mystic-heavenly sense (see Gal. 4:24–26 and Rev. 21). The primacy of the mystical, heavenly Jerusalem in Christian thought on the one hand, and the concrete association of the Holy Land with the life and death of Jesus on the other, resulted in an ambivalent attitude to pilgrimages (see *Jerusalem, In Christianity). While popular piety and devotion naturally tended toward a veneration of the *holy places, many writers warned against the danger of a "carnal" and material misunderstanding of essentially spiritual realities. In fact, many early Church Fathers at first discouraged pilgrimage. Jerome declared that the gates of heaven were open to believers equally in Britain as Jerusalem (Ep. 58 *Ad Paulinum*). He mentions that St. Hilarion, who lived in the Holy Land for 50 years, prided himself on the fact that he had visited the holy places only once. However the ardent wish of Christians to visit the Holy Land was eventually accepted by Jerome, who settled in a cave near Bethlehem. In practice pilgrimage was first stimulated under Constantine (306–337), with the announcement by his mother *Helena of the discovery of the cross in Jerusalem, and the erection by Constantine of the magnificent rotunda at the traditional sepulcher of Jesus with an adjacent basilica (the *martyrium*). Christians thereupon readily identified other places mentioned in the New Testament associated with Jesus and the apostles. The sites were immediately sanctified, and shrines or churches built near them (cf. E. Robinson, *Biblical Researches in Palestine* [1841], 371). Some of these sites contained holy relics which also attracted an increasing stream of pilgrims, interrupted only by political insecurity or pestilence, and reaching huge proportions in the Middle Ages. The *Crusades were preeminently a pilgrimage of armies, aimed at liberating the holy places from the Muslims, whatever their accompanying political motives. The duty of caring for the protection and needs of pilgrims gave rise to the influential hospitaller orders, such as the Knights Templar and the Knights of Malta. In the later Middle Ages the religious factor diminished, to be replaced increasingly by commercial motives. Even in the ninth and tenth centuries the Muslim rulers had encouraged trade there, and Jerusalem became a large entrepôt between East and West. One result of the trading contacts between Europe and the East was the extension of the maritime power of the Italian republics, especially Venice and Genoa, during the Fourth Crusade (1202–04).

CHARACTER OF THE PILGRIMAGES. Jerusalem and Bethlehem remained the main centers of Christian pilgrimage, but there were others, especially in Galilee. However places in Galilee such as Nazareth, Capernaum, Magdala, or Kefar Kanna are not mentioned by early pilgrims, such as the Bordeaux pilgrim whose *Itinerarium Burdigalense* (written before 333) is the first pilgrim guide extant. This was probably because Galilee then still had a mainly Jewish population.

The chief incentive to pilgrimage remained religious. Pilgrimages were organized to gain remission of sins, as set penances, in fulfillment of vows, for atonements for crimes, for cures, and for the acquisition of relics. However they also fulfilled other purposes: the desire to see foreign lands, people and customs, love of adventure, and commercial profit. Thus, besides the thousands of the pious, the pilgrim movement attracted a bevy of adventurers, sick persons, and paupers. The journey of the pilgrim was fraught with danger. He faced local wars, attack by pirates or brigands, epidemics, bad sanitation, or arbitrary imprisonment by the local authority. In Venice in the 15th century he was given facilities to make his will before embarking. The departure of a pilgrim also posed a problem for the Church. It meant disruption of family life and the absence of a breadwinner or worker, while the conditions of the journey frequently brought a lowering of moral standards. The Church therefore insisted that pilgrims should obtain written authorizations from the bishop or abbot for their journey. If he met the Church's requirements, the pilgrim received its blessing and assistance.

THE LITERATURE. Once home, the pilgrim reported the glories of the holy places and the wonders he had seen and heard. These accounts circulated both by word of mouth and in written records or itineraries for the guidance of future pilgrims. Although until the end of the Middle Ages the oral accounts were predominant, as the vast majority of pilgrims were uneducated, a growing number of travelers recorded their journey and impressions. Roehricht's bibliography of Palestiniana in the main European languages lists 38 authors between the years 333 and 1000, 517 up to the year 1500, and nearly 2,000 between the years 1800 and 1878. Subsequently there has been an inordinate increase of such records.

The record usually followed a set scheme, providing a description of the Holy Land and the spiritual experiences of the pilgrims for those who had never been there. From the end of the 17th century, much was written for the purposes of religious propaganda. The authors frequently catered to their audience and supplemented their descriptions with embellishments and imaginary adventures, where reality and legend intermingle. However, many present an accurate if limited record, often closely resembling one another. The records fall into several different categories. Some are on-the-spot accounts of events as they occurred. Many were written down after the pilgrim's return, often on the basis of notes taken on the journey, which contained details omitted from his book. A large number were written on the basis of previous works, including many passages merely copied from them or with deliberate variations. The German cleric Ludolf von Suchem (1336–41) states that he did not see all that he wrote with his own eyes, but drew on ancient history books. *The Travels of Sir John Mandeville* (in the Holy Land, 1336) is a collection of earlier sources. Some writers quote their sources, and some copy them without acknowledgment. A number, especially in the early period, related their accounts to a third person who recorded them in turn. The account of the French bishop Arculfus (670) was recorded by an abbot in Iona, off Scotland.

Educated pilgrims and scholars later made independent investigations, instead of accepting everything they were told. Many, who reveal wide learning, relate the old traditions, but with reservations. Fynes Moryson (16th century), although criticizing the credibility of the tales told by the monks of the Latin monastery, was still deeply impressed and moved by what he saw. The pioneer of modern researches was the U.S. theologian, philologist, and geographer Edward Robinson (1838), who voiced a much stronger and well-founded criticism of the credulity accorded by the pilgrims down the ages, who had always seen the holy places through the eyes of their monastic cicerones. He considered that many sites had no historical basis and even contradicted the evidence of the New Testament. He also cast doubt on the traditions associated with Eusebius and Jerome, from which others had originated. Robinson therefore carried out his pioneer researches independently of the Christian orders in Ereẓ Israel.

[Yvonne Glikson]

Information on the Jews

Much of the information available on Jewish life in the Holy Land in earlier periods comes from the Christian pilgrim accounts. Thus, Jacobus de Verona (1335), an Augustinian friar, speaks of Jewish guides. Ludolf von Suchem states that Jews, but not Christians, were allowed on payment to enter the cave of Machpelah in Hebron, where the Patriarchs are buried. An anonymous Englishman (1345) tells of Jews living in caves near Jerusalem. Arnold von Harff, a German nobleman from Erft, though as prejudiced against the Jews as most of the early pilgrims, showed a more intelligent interest in them. Among "the very many" Jews in Jerusalem, with some of whom he entered into learned discussion, he found several natives of Lombardy knowledgeable about Christianity, three from Germany, and also two monks who had converted to Judaism. He learned some Hebrew, and his book reproduces the *alef-bet* and also a number of words and phrases in common use, from his transliterations of which it is clear that he learned them from people of central European origin. Pierre Belon (1547), a French physician of Mans, saw in Galilee Jews engaged in fishing; and he reports on newly established villages, where, he notes, they were converting wasteland into fertile areas.

Much is reported about Safed as a flourishing Jewish center. A Franciscan from Spain (1553–55), whose name is not known, found a Jewish population of 8,000–10,000 there. William Biddulph (1600), an English priest, mentions the Hebrew that was taught there (as well as in Salonika).

John Sanderson (1601), an English merchant, traveled with a Jewish merchant who hid his money in his clothes, some 12,000 ducats, of which 3,000 was for charity and for books in the Holy Land. The Franciscan Eugenius Roger (1629–34), who estimates 15,000 Jews in the country, including 4,000 in Jerusalem, divides them into two groups: the old-established Oriental Jews and the newcomers from Europe, particularly Spain, Germany, and Italy. There was little intermarriage between the two groups, the first being particularly doubtful of the authenticity of the Jewishness of those from Spain, "for they had been baptized, had for long lived as Christians and ate foods and drank drinks forbidden by the Law of Moses." Other communal troubles are reported by the Jesuit Michael Nau, who visited the land in 1665 and again in 1674. He found the Jews divided into the Rabbanites, who accepted the Talmud, and the Karaites and the Samaritans, who accepted only the Bible. Each complained to him about the other: "They hate one another with an unparalleled hatred. But there is one thing about which they must agree in Jerusalem, that is, that they must pay heavily to the Turks for the right to remain there."

A vivid description of the unhappy condition of the Jews in Jerusalem is given by Chateaubriand (1806–07): "isolated from the other inhabitants, abandoned to every kind of shame…, he suffers every humiliation without crying out against it, without a sound turns his cheek to him who strikes him," and Chateaubriand adds sympathetically that there is nothing more remarkable in the history of the nations than the survival of the Jews – a miracle "even in the eyes of a *philosophe*."

Another sympathetic observer is Alfonse de Lamartine (1832–33) who writes: "This land, if settled by a new Jewish people… is destined once again to become the Promised Land… if He who watches from above will return the people to it and give them the political privileges of peace and security." Robert Curzon (1834) states: "It is noteworthy that the Jews who are born in Jerusalem are completely different from those we see in Europe. Here they are of a blond race, light in movement, and, especially, refined in their conduct." At the same time John Lloyd Stephens (1835) tells of the fear under which the Jews lived in Hebron and Safed.

Edward Robinson remarks about Christian missionary activity among the Jews: "So far the efforts of the English mission have had only the most meager success." He also describes the devastation wrought by the great earthquake of 1837. Another visitor was William Bartlett (1842 and 1853) who gave exact descriptions of Jerusalem.

William Holt Yates (1843), London physician and Orientalist, exemplifies an attitude toward the country radically different from the pilgrims of the earlier centuries. He thinks that Palestine (and Asia Minor and Syria) would benefit by the mingling of the "natives" with Britishers, especially Scotsmen, and with Jews: "Although the Jews as a people have never particularly distinguished themselves in literature and science, they nevertheless have excellent qualities, if only these were properly recognized…" William Francis Lynch (1848), the U.S. naval officer celebrated for his account of his voyage of discovery to the River Jordan and Dead Sea, saw the only hope for Palestine in the dissolution of the degenerate Ottoman Empire and the settlement of the Jews.

Active in assisting Jews to settle was James *Finn (1853–56), who as British consul in Jerusalem made himself their protector. His own book and his consular reports are prime sources for knowledge of conditions. Among other events he describes the blood libel raised against the Jews.

Henry Baker Tristram (1863–64), English theologian, fellow of the Royal Society, and among the founders of the Palestine Exploration Fund, finds place in his important works on the flora and fauna of Palestine for descriptions of the Jews. But the most interesting of all for that period is the diplomat and statesman Laurence *Oliphant (1883–87), who gives a first hand account of the earliest pioneers of the modern resettlement, whom he greatly assisted.

Subsequently there are accounts of historians, theologians, journalists, surveyors, and archaeologists, from all over Europe and the United States, reference to which may be found among the records of the various scientific institutions. Visitors of literary fame who wrote of their impressions include W.M. Thackeray, Mark Twain, George Moore, G.K. Chesterton, Pierre Loti, and Herman Melville.

The flood of books by pilgrims of all kinds and all intentions and pretensions in recent times is overwhelming. As with the earlier pilgrims, the accounts of many of them are colored by their preconceived opinions. Other contemporary writers convey their experiences in the form of novels, detective stories, and thrillers, experiences which are often observed more authentically than in more solemn works.

[Semah Cecil Hyman]

BIBLIOGRAPHY: SECOND TEMPLE PERIOD: I. Elbogen, in: *Bericht der Hochschule fuer die Wissenschaft des Judentums*, 46 (1929), 27–46; S. Safrai, in: *Sefer Yerushalayim*, ed. by M. Avi-Yonah, 1 (1956), 369–91; idem, in: *Zion*, 25 (1959/60), 67–84. POST-TEMPLE PERIOD: K. Wilhelm. *Roads to Zion* (1948); S. Assaf and A.L. Mayer, *Sefer ha-Yishuv*, 2 (1944), 25–29; A. Yaari, in: KS, 18 (1941/42), 293–7, 378–80; idem, *Iggerot Erez Yisrael* (1943); idem, *Masot Erez Yisrael* (1946); Ya'ari Sheluḥei, index; M.A. Shulvass, *Roma vi-Yrushalayim* (1944), passim; idem, in: *Zion*, 3 (1938), 86–7; S.A. Horodezky, *Olei Ẓiyyon* (1947); S. Assaf, *Tekufat ha-Ge'onim ve-Sifrutah* (1955), 91–7; R. Mahler, *Divrei Yemei Yisrael* (1956), 117–31; Ben-Zvi, Erez Yisrael (1967³); S. Safrai, *Ha-Aliyyah le-Regel bi-Ymei ha-Bayit ha-Sheni* (1966); Ta-Shema, in: *Tarbiz*, 38 (1968/69), 398–9. CHRISTIAN PILGRIMAGES: R. Roericht, *Bibliotheca Geographica Palaestina* (new ed., 1963); P. Thomsen, *Palaestina-Literatur* (1908, 1956, 1960); T. Wright (ed.), *Early Travels in Palestine* (1948); M. Ish-Shalom, *Masei ha-Nozerim le-Erez Yisrael* (1966). **ADD. BIBLIOGRAPHY:** E.D. Hunt, *Holy Land Pilgrimage in the Later Roman Empire AD 312–460* (1982); J.E. Taylor, *Christians and the Holy Places* (1993); G. Stemberger, *Jews and Christians in the Holy Land. Palestine in the Fourth Century* (2000).

PILGRIM FESTIVALS (Heb. שָׁלוֹשׁ רְגָלִים, "three pilgrim festivals"), collective term for the three festivals of *Passover, *Shavuot, and *Sukkot. The duty of pilgrimage on these three occasions stems from the biblical injunction, "Three times a year shall all thy males appear before the Lord thy God in the place which He shall choose, in the feast of unleavened bread, and in the feast of weeks, and in the feast of tabernacles" (Deut. 16:16; and Ex. 23:17 where the festivals are not specified). According to the Mishnah, "All are under obligation to appear, excepting a deaf-mute, an imbecile, a child, one of doubtful sex, one of double sex, women, slaves that have not been freed, a man that is lame or blind or sick or aged, and one that cannot go up [to Jerusalem] on his feet" (Ḥag 1:1). The importance of the duty is stressed by Joshua b. Levi who stated, "all who perform the duty of pilgrimage are considered as if they had received the *Shekhinah" (TJ, Hag, 1:1, 76a). Besides the festive offerings made on these occasions (Lev. 23), it was also enjoined that "they shall not appear before the Lord empty. Every man shall give as he is able" (Deut. 16:16–17). The Mishnah ruled that the minimum value of each individual offering was to be three pieces of silver (Ḥag. 1:2).

In the times of the judges, the pilgrimages were made to Shiloh (I Sam. 1:3) and, after the construction of the Temple, to Jerusalem (I Kings 8:65; II Chron. 7:8–9). *Jeroboam, king of the northern kingdom of Israel, considered them such a threat to his authority that he established rival shrines at Dan and Beth-El (I Kings 12:26–33). After the return from Babylonia, Nehemiah reinstituted the practice of pilgrimage to Jerusalem on the festival of Sukkot (Neh. 8:15). Both Josephus (Wars 6:422–7) and the Tosefta (Pes. 4:3; also Pes. 64b) comment upon the large number of pilgrims to the Second Temple during Passover. According to the Mishnah, the fact that there was room for them all was a miracle (Avot 5:5). It seems that even Diaspora Jewry made the pilgrimage (Ta'an. 28a), and it was ruled that the prayer for rain should not be recited until 15 days after the conclusion of Sukkot in order to allow the last of the pilgrims to return to the Euphrates (Ta'an. 1:3).

In modern times, the tradition has been continued by individuals and groups from all over the country going up to Jerusalem, especially during the intermediate days of Sukkot. The center of pilgrimage is the *Western ("Wailing") Wall, but when access to it was barred pilgrims went to Mount Zion.

BIBLIOGRAPHY: S. Safrai, *Ha-Aliyyah le-Regel bi-Ymei ha-Bayit ha-Sheni* (1965).

PILICHOWSKI, LEOPOLD (1869–1933), Polish painter. Pilichowski left his native village of Zadzin for nearby Lodz, where he was helped by David *Frischmann, the Hebrew writer, who made it possible for Pilichowski to study in Munich. Later, he lived in Paris for a number of years, and in 1914 he moved to London. Pilichowski became a successful portraitist. He was filled with socialist and Zionist sentiments, and struggled to give pictorial expression to both. He painted the exploited wool dyers of Lodz, and the weary shopkeepers and artisans he met in London's Whitechapel. Many of his large pictures were crowded with pious Jews in a variety of moods and postures. His huge painting of *The Opening of the Hebrew University in Jerusalem* in 1925 has been frequently reproduced. Among the Jewish personalities he portrayed were *Bialik, *Einstein, Aḥad *Ha-Am, *Nordau, and *Weizmann.

[Alfred Werner]

PILLAR (Heb. עַמּוּד; from the root *ʿmd*, "to stand"), a column that stands perpendicular to the ground and generally serves to support the beams of a roof. In this article no distinction will be made between "pillar," "column," and "post." The pillar is used in construction in three ways (see *Architecture): (1) as a functional element in construction to support a large ceiling; (2) to emphasize an ornate door at the front of a building, or to emphasize the outline of a building; and sometimes (3) to take the place of a doorpost and support a massive lintel. Another type of support performing the same functions is the pilaster which does not stand free but is attached to and stands out from the wall. There is another type of pillar that stands alone and is not connected with any other structure; this type of pillar was designed to attract attention and to serve as a place around which a crowd could gather (II Kings 11: 14).

Pillars (posts) occupied an important place in the structure of the Tabernacle (Ex. 26–27). The pillars (posts) used in the Tabernacle were constructed of wood. During the period of the monarchy, pillars were used in palaces and the Temple. Halls are mentioned which contained rows of pillars (I Kings 7:6): pillars which served to support the roof; the symbolic pillars of Jachin and Boaz (I Kings 7:21; II Chron. 3:17); and copper pillars which stood at the entrance to the Temple (II Kings 7:15, 20, 22). Pillars that were functional elements in construction are mentioned in the story of Samson, who brought down the middle pillars of the palace of Dagon and in this way destroyed the entire building (Judg. 16:29).

Pillars were introduced into the Near East with the first experiments in enlarging covered structures. In Egypt they were first used as supports for roofing in the middle of the third millennium B.C.E. As early as this, pillars served not only as supports but also as ornaments of buildings, or as ornaments in themselves. In Mesopotamia pillars began to be used in the middle of the second millennium B.C.E.

Remains of pillars uncovered in various archaeological excavations in Ereẓ Israel and the discovery of plans of various buildings have revealed much about the function of pillars in ancient architecture. In a large structure at Ai dating to the early Canaanite period a row of pillar bases was discovered in one hall, which passed through the center of a long building. The function of these pillars was to help support the beams of the roof. In general, builders saw to it that the pillars inside buildings, whether of wood or stone, should be separated from one another in order to permit free passage among them. The pillars were set up in a place where they would not hide the inside of the structure from the entrance. In most cases, only the bases of the pillars, which could have served as foundations for both stone and wooden pillars, have been found in archaeological excavations. The pillars were sometimes made from one block, but generally from several stones placed one on top of the other. The use of pillars as supports for beamed ceilings is common also in the late Canaanite period. In one of the buildings discovered at Taanach a pillar was set up in the middle of a large area that could not be beamed from wall to wall, thereby shortening the distance between walls and making it possible to place short, strong beams between the pillar and the wall in order to build a roof over this area.

The use of pillars in the construction of houses and other types of buildings was widespread in the Israelite period. Buildings from this period have been found that are divided internally into four sections: three long sections that lie side by side forming an almost perfect square, and a fourth section, of approximately the same size, running across their ends. The long rooms were sometimes divided from one another by solid walls, but generally by rows of pillars. It appears that of the long rooms, the middle one was uncovered, being a type of court lined on either side by rows of wooden or stone pillars. The roofs of the two outer rooms were supported by the outside walls and the two rows of pillars that surrounded the court. These structures are common in Tell en-Naṣbeh, Tell Qasila, and other places. Larger structures of this type were found in Hazor. Another use of pillars inside a building was discovered in the structures of the stables of Megiddo in one of the Israelite strata. In the large network of stables, stone pillars arranged in rows at equal distances from one another were discovered. In each space between the pillars a water trough was discovered, and on the pillar itself a hole for tying a horse. These pillars had a threefold function; to support the roof, to serve as a place for harnessing a horse, and to divide the building into compartments for individual horses.

Square stone columns and pillars bearing "proto-Ionian" capitals are characteristic of the elaborate structures of the Israelite period. These capitals are decorated with a bas-relief of a double coil emanating from a central triangle. Discovered in strata from the beginning of the Israelite period in Jerusalem, Megiddo, Samaria, Ramat Raḥel, and Hazor, these pillars served as posts of gates. In addition to actual physical pillars, the Bible speaks of the *pillar of cloud and the pillar of fire that accompanied the Israelites during their journey through the desert (Ex. 13:22). The pillar of cloud is also described as standing at the door of the Tabernacle (Deut. 31:15). Metaphorically, in the poetic sections of the Bible, the heavens are described as standing on pillars (Job 26:11). In a poetic manner, the pillar is used metaphorically in the descriptions of the parts of the human body: "His legs are as pillars of marble set upon sockets of fine gold" (Song 5:15).

In the fifth and fourth centuries B.C.E., under the Persian rule, with the penetration of Greek influences into the Middle East generally and Ereẓ Israel in particular, many elements of classical architecture found their way into the local styles. Among these elements, the pillar holds an important place as a functional element in the structure of building or as ornamentation. Pillars appear both in private and public buildings, and also in tombs. In Ereẓ Israel pillars and capitals of different styles were in use simultaneously; for example an ancient specimen of a Doric pillar remained on a mural inside a Hellenistic tomb in Marissa. In Ereẓ Israel remains of pillars from the beginning of the Hellenistic era are rare. From the Roman period on, Hellenistic architecture spread greatly. During this period, particularly in the reign of Herod (37–4 B.C.E.), much building on the part of the king took place in Ereẓ Israel, almost all of which included elements of Roman architecture. In order to raise the level of the Temple Mount, Herod erected rows of large square pillars, remains of which exist underground southeast of the Temple Mount at the site known today as "Solomon's Stables." Examples of smooth monolithic pillars stand in the "colonnaded street" in Samaria. These pillars stand on square bases and their capitals seem to have been Corinthian. Corinthian pillars and capitals were set up by Herod in Herodium and in Masada in the northern palace. In this palace the pillars are not monolithic but are built in sections (drums) and covered with stucco intended to give the effect of marble. With the exception of the Temple and other stately buildings in Jerusalem, large pillars were not widespread in the country, as they were in other lands of the Roman Empire, large monumental structures being uncommon in Ereẓ Israel.

The use of pillars was more common in tombs of the Second Temple period. They are found in the tombs of the Sanhedrin and the tombs of the sons of Hezir in the Valley of Kidron in Jerusalem. In these places the pillars, like the whole tomb, are hewn out of rock. This style was also widespread in many other places both in the Judean Hills and Galilee, for example, in the cemetery in Bet She'arim. A different use was made of columns and pillars in "Absalom's Tomb" and in the "Tomb of Zechariah" in the Valley of Kidron, both monumental tombs from the time of the Second Temple. These monuments are partly or wholly hewn from the living rock and are cube-shaped, and their facades are beautified by half pillars and columns cut out of the rock. The capitals of the pillars in these two monuments are Ionic.

With the erection of synagogues in Galilee and Judea in the third and fourth centuries C.E., a mixture of styles in architecture came into use. The pillars, like the carvings and other decorations of the synagogue, were ornamented in a mixture of styles – an Oriental style that was the result of Persian influence, and a late Hellenistic style. This is the case with the capitals and other decorations of the synagogues of Capernaum, Kefar Baram, Chorazin, and others. In these places there are capitals in a number of styles, chiefly Ionic and Corinthian, used together in various parts of the structure. Worthy of mention are the widespread corner pillars in these early synagogues. In cross-section the pillars are heart-shaped and their function is to emphasize the corners of the rows of pillars. The synagogue pillars had two functions – to beautify the appearance of the portico and to support the slanted roof inside. In the synagogues in Galilee there were usually two rows of pillars: those of the halls are large and stand on square bases, while those of the upper (women's) galleries on the second floors are small and narrower. These are found in Kefar Baram, Chorazin, Capernaum, and other sites. While the interiors of the synagogues were decorated with columns, the facades of the early synagogues were decorated with pillars protruding from the walls, such as those found in Capernaum, Chorazin, Kefar Baram, and other places.

This mode of decoration was a continuation of the system of building of the Herodian era and is found on the monument erected over the cave of Machpelah in Hebron. It appears that the decorations with which the cave of Machpelah was adorned are a return to the motif that decorated the Temple Mount, though that was on a much larger scale. Circular pillars, mostly with Corinthian capitals, also decorated the insides of later synagogues from the fifth and sixth centuries C.E., such as those found at Bet Alfa, Beth-Shean, on the wall of Tiberias, etc. The pillar, being a conspicous element in the architecture of magnificent buildings, also served as decoration. Thus in many places pillars are portrayed in mosaics or paintings flanking the ark of the Law in the synagogues. They were found on the murals in Dura Europos, in the mosaics of Bet Alfa, Nirim, Beth-Shean, and elsewhere. Small marble pillars with delicate ornaments usually served to support the chancel screen before the ark. Such pillars were found out of their original places in a number of synagogues in Galilee and Judea. A series of pillars symbolizing the Temple appears on the coins of Bar Kokhba. These are usually portrayed as four pillars apparently carrying the exedra in front of the facade of the Temple.

In the Jewish world it was not customary to erect a pillar as a monument in memory of a person or enterprise. Pillars were used primarily for decorating splendid houses and as functional elements in construction, chiefly in synagogue buildings. Technically, the pillars used for this purpose were either monoliths, as in Samaria or Capernaum, or were built of sections, as in the synagogues in Chorazin and Kefar Baram and in the late synagogues. Apparently the pillars built of sections were to some extent an expression of the economic situation of the Jewish population in the first centuries C.E., when materials were poorer than in previous eras. When Herod built his monuments in Caesarea, Tiberias, Jerusalem, and other places, he erected huge monolithic columns whose production and also transportation were much more costly than the production and transportation of column drums.

BIBLIOGRAPHY: E. Sellin, *Tell Ta'annek* (1904), 3; A.G. Barrois, *Manuel d'archéologie biblique, Tomb*, 1 (1939), fig. 97; See excavation reports at: *Megiddo I* (R.S. Lamon and G.M. Shipton, 1939); *Samaria I* (G.A. Reisner et al.); *Hazor I* (Aharoni); *Ramath Rahel* (Aharoni, 1964).

[Ze'ev Yeivin]

PILLAR OF CLOUD AND PILLAR OF FIRE. The earliest traditions of the Exodus from Egypt refer to the pillar of cloud by day and of fire by night, which accompanied the Children of Israel on their way through the desert (Ex. 13:21–22). The visible symbol of the presence of God caused a panic among the Egyptians as it cut them off from the Israelites (Ex. 14:19b, 24a), and continued to guide and protect the latter uninterruptedly throughout their wanderings. Later generations remembered it as a special sign of divine favor (cf. Ps. 78:14), no less important than the parting of the Sea of Reeds itself. Another early tradition connected the cloud with the *Tent of Meeting. According to the view attributed by critics to the author of the Elohist account (E), the pillar of cloud served not as a regular escort marching at the head of the people, but as an intermittent presence, descending from time to time to the entrance of the Tent of Meeting when God conversed with Moses (Ex. 33:9–10; Num. 11:25; 12:5). The priestly authors, on the other hand, taught that "a cloud of the Lord" (not a pillar) with a fiery appearance by night, permanently covered the Tabernacle from the day of its completion, lifting only to signal the breaking of camp for a new journey (Ex. 40:34–38; Num. 9:15–23; 10:11–12, 34; 14:14). The Divine Presence in Solomon's Temple was similarly accompanied by the descent of the cloud (I Kings 8:10–11; cf. Ex. 16:10; Lev. 16:2) though the pillar of cloud and of fire did not accompany the Israelites into the Promised Land.

Various explanations have been sought for the origin of these traditions. Among them is the attested use of braziers filled with burning wood at the head of caravans or armies, sometimes placed before the tent of the chief or carried before him. Others derive the imagery from the *pillars before Solomon's Temple, which, they contend, were fiery cressets emitting clouds of smoke and flame by day and by night at the time of a festival. Still others point to the smoke that rose from the altar of the burnt offering as the origin of the representation. The most commonly accepted theory connects the pillar of cloud and fire with the theophany at Sinai, when the descent of the Lord was marked by a thick cloud (Ex. 19:9), by thunder, lightening, smoke, and fire. Attempts to provide a natural basis for this narrative have pointed to the possible existence of volcanic action in the vicinity of Sinai – which is highly unlikely – or to the sudden outbreak of a raging desert storm. In any event, there can be little doubt that the imagery is as old as the time of Moses, and that the cloud, and, in a lesser degree, the fire symbolism proved effective in communicating the presence of God to the people.

Post-biblical legend embellished the biblical account. Thus, not one but seven clouds descended at Sukkot to envelop and protect the Israelites, one on each of the four sides of the camp, one above and one below, and one which went before them to raise the valleys and lower the mountains. The Israelites were protected against the elements and wild beasts; even their garments did not wear out or become dirty. Eliezer maintained that the Festival of Sukkot commemorated the "clouds of glory" (Suk. 11b) which were considered among God's special creations in the "twilight" of the first six days (ARN^2 37, 95).

BIBLIOGRAPHY: G.B. Gray, *Numbers* (ICC, 1912), 85–86, 113, 212; Ginzberg, Legends, 2 (1910); 5 (1925); 6 (1928); S.R. Driver, *Exodus* (1953), 112–3, 147; L. Koehler, *Theologie des Alten Testaments* (1953), 8–9; R. Reymond, *L'Eau, sa Vie, et sa Signification dans l'Ancient Testament* (1958), 37ff.; M. Noth, *Exodus* (1959), 91ff.; A. Weiser, *Die Psalmen* (1959), 463; de Vaux, Anc Isr (1965^2), 295; H.J. Kraus, *Psalmen*, 2 (1966^3), 722; U. Cassuto, *A Commentary on the Book of Exodus* (1967), 158, 169, 336ff.; E.A. Speiser, in: J. Finkelstein and M. Greenberg (ed.), *Oriental and Biblical Studies* (1967), 106–12; T.H. Gaster, *Myth, Legend, and Custom in the Old Testament* (1969), 236–7.

[David L. Lieber]

PILPUL (Heb. פִּלְפּוּל), a collective term denoting various methods of talmudic study and exposition, especially by the use of subtle legal, conceptual, and casuistic differentiation. The word is derived from *pilpel* ("pepper"), indicating that these methods were employed in talmudic disputations by the more sharp-witted among the scholars (cf. *palpelan* – TJ, Hor. 3:7, 48c; *ba'al-pilpul* – BB 145b). In the talmudic period the term *pilpul* was applied to the logical distinctions through which apparent contradictions and textual difficulties were straightened out by means of reasoning (*sevarah*), leading to a more penetrating understanding and conceptual analysis. This method was distinguished from a mere cursory knowledge of the texts (*girsah*) and the oral traditions and teachings of the scholars of the past. The masters of *pilpul* would advance arguments and opinions of their own, though always based on the authority of tradition, while those strictly adhering to the texts and their traditional exegesis would reject the ways of the pilpulists, whose daring originality would sometimes lead them astray from plain reason and truth (cf. Er. 90a). Scholars hotly debated the question as to whose merits for the dissemination and advancement of Torah study were greater: *sinai*, i.e., he who faithfully preserved the established texts and traditions, or *oker harim*, i.e., he who "uproots mountains" in his intellectual struggle for clarity and logical harmony (cf. Ber. 64a). Nevertheless, it was generally agreed that *pilpul* was of vital necessity for establishing hermeneutical links between the Oral and the Written Torah, thus keeping tradition from error and oblivion (cf. Kid. 66b; BM 85b; Zev. 13a; Tem. 16a). It was also valued as a didactic method to sharpen the intellect of students (Avot 6:6; Ber. 33b; Er. 13a). Members of the high court (Sanhedrin) were required to be masters of *pilpul* (cf. Sanh. 17a). Babylonian scholars were especially noted for their subtle ways of *pilpul* and their acrimonious disputations, contrasting with the moderation of the Palestinian schools (cf. Pes. 34b; BM 85a).

The talmudic *pilpul* was thus suited to meet three principal needs. The first was to safeguard the unity of the Oral and Written Torah and to harmonize between the apparently differing opinions of the sages. This was based on the religious principle that both parts of the Torah tradition flowed from one single divine revelation and that consequently what appeared to be contradictory, repetitive, or redundant appeared so only because of the intellectual limitations of the students. The second was to keep up the vitality and relevance of the Oral and Written Torah in its traditionally fixed form in the face of changing times and circumstances. Finally, it made Torah study a permanent challenge to the intellectual powers of masters and students and kept it safe from routine and perfunctoriness. *Pilpul* enabled the gifted student to bring new elements into Torah study, and these were themselves considered part of the divine revelation (cf. Ned. 38a; Meg. 19b; TJ, Pe'ah 2:6; 17a; for examples of talmudic *pilpul* see JE, vol. 10, p.40.).

The Babylonian scholars of the geonic period continued to employ the methods of *pilpul*, though they were chiefly occupied with arranging, editing, and explaining the text of the Talmud, as did the early school of Ashkenazi commentators up to Rashi's generation. A new wave of *pilpul* rose in the tosafist schools of France and Germany, as well as in the Spanish schools of the 13th and 14th centuries. The same methods as had previously been applied in the Talmud, now served to harmonize apparently differing talmudic passages and opinions. This new vogue gave rise to adverse criticism among the Ashkenazi Ḥasidim who deplored the over-cleverness of sharp-witted scholars who substituted originality for truth and preferred the study of *tosafot* to that of the Talmud itself (cf. *Sefer Ḥasidim* ed. by J. Wistinetzki (1924^2), nos. 648, 1049, 1375, 1707, 1816, 1838).

The close of the tosafist era in the 14th century was followed by a short period during which scholars occupied themselves chiefly with the study and recording of the traditional laws and customs (*minhagim*) that had accumulated until then. However, the intrinsic dynamics of Torah study called for new intellectual challenges to be put to the restlessly searching minds of scholars and students. The traditional modes of study and disputation had become exhausted, and scholars strove to devise new modes in which they could distinguish themselves. In addition, yeshivah teachers became increasingly conscious of didactics and method in the education of rabbinical scholars. The prevailing spirit of humanism influenced scholars to seek intellectual independence while remaining faithful to the traditional sources. Thus the 15th and 16th centuries witnessed an unprecedented intensification of casuistic disputation. A clear distinction began to be made between lessons devoted to cursory study of the talmudic text and those given to intensive disputation. This was led by the head of the yeshivah and was of an essentially oral character, which accounts for the fact that very little of its content was recorded and preserved in manuscripts.

Some idea of the new modes of *pilpul*, which consisted mainly in the application of logical models and of increasingly sharper divisions and differentiations (*ḥillukim*), may be gained from treatises on talmudic methodology such as the *Darkhei ha-Talmud* by Isaac *Canpanton. Several new modes became known by the names of communities whose yeshivot specialized in them, e.g., Nuremberg and Regensburg. These methods are characterized by a penetrating inquiry into the minutest details of halakhic discussion as recorded in the Talmud. Each and every sentence is shown to convey some novel meaning of its own and no redundancy whatsoever is allowed. A problem set by one of the sages is not an indication of any doubt or ignorance but an attempt to test the knowledge and intelligence of his colleagues and students. Since all the sages are supposed to possess knowledge and intelligence of identical width and depth, the talmudic dialogue is shown to be an interplay of diverging attitudes and opinions rather than a series of questions and answers. Furthermore, the divergences are attributed to casuistic differentiations rather than to fundamental contradictions, and thus the basic unity and conformity of the spiritual world of the Talmud is preserved and safeguarded.

In the sphere of didactics diverse pilpulistic methods were innovated by which to heighten the students' powers of perception and imagination. Masters devised imaginary halakhic cases and problems and required their students to pass reasoned judgments. They also composed halakhic riddles, sometimes involving the most abstruse casuistry, which the students were required to solve. In the 16th and 17th centuries the ability to excel in pilpulistic disputation was the chief aim and mark of distinction of the yeshivah student. At a time when rabbinical learning had become widespread and rabbis as well as lay leaders were rivals for communal leadership, accomplished masters in the art of *pilpul* outshone less brilliant, if more conscientious, scholars and secured for themselves a paramount social status. In the spiritual sphere *pilpul* was reinforced by certain kabbalistic trends that glorified the contemplative, as against the pragmatic, attitude to study. The intuition of the scholars was seen as a form of divine inspiration. At the same time *pilpul* served a vital purpose in enabling rabbis to pass decisions on many new halakhic problems arising from the changing economic and political situation. Nevertheless, outstanding rabbis, such as *Judah Loew b. Bezalel (the Maharal), Isaiah *Horowitz, Ephraim *Luntschitz, and Jair Ḥayyim *Bacharach, severely criticized the universal "craze" for *pilpul* and *ḥillukim*. They had been preceded as early as the 15th century by the anonymous treatise on ethics known as *Orḥot Ẓaddikim*, which contained the first vigorous attack on the new ways of *pilpul* launched from within the circles of the Ashkenazi yeshivah. Though not opposed to *pilpul* as such, these rabbis resented the twisting of plain truth resulting out of the hairsplitting efforts of the most sharp-witted and argued that *pilpul* should serve the comprehension of the texts and not itself become an art. They also criticized the students' passion for personal honor and aggrandizement and questioned their authority to decide on halakhic matters, since their preoccupation with *pilpul* made them wholly dependent, in matters of religious practice, on the new codes such as R. Joseph Caro's Shulḥan Arukh. Thus it is not surprising that the critics of *pilpul* often expressed concern about the publication of these codes. Criticism was much more lenient regarding the application of *pilpul* to the exposition of the Bible and homiletic literature, since this was considered irrelevant to a true understanding of *halakhah*. Consequently, popular preachers used to strain their imagination by adducing the most complicated talmudic passages and controversies in order to throw new light on a story from the Bible or the Midrash. When toward the end of the 18th century the methods of *pilpul* seemed to have been exhausted, new ways of Torah study were opened by the school of the *Gaon* of Vilna, Elijah b. Solomon Zalman.

BIBLIOGRAPHY: *Orḥot Ẓaddikim* (Prague, 1581), ch. 27 (Sha'ar ha-Torah); J. Landau, *Sefer ha-Ḥazon* (appended to his *Agur*); Z. Margaliot, *Ḥibburei Likkutim* (Venice, 1715), preface; *Alilot Devarim*, in: *Oẓar Neḥmad*, 4 (1863), 177–214; A. Jellinek, in: *Bikkurim*, 1 (1864), 1–26; 2 (1865), 1–19; M. Reines, in: *Keneset Yisrael*, 3 (1888), 137–72; J.L. Fishman, *Ha-Noten be-Yam Derekh* (1903); H. Ehrentreu, in: JJLG, 3 (1905), 206–19; M. Tosfai, in: *Ha-Shiloaḥ*, 19 (1908), 138–46, 248–58, 329–35; Assaf, Mekorot; N.S. Grinspan, *Pilpula shel Torah* (1935); idem, *Melekhet Maḥashevet* (1955); Urbach, Tosafot; H.H. Ben-Sasson, *Hagut ve-Hanhagah* (1959), index s.v., L. Jacobs, *Studies in Talmudic Logic and Methodology* (1961); A.F. Kleinberger, *Ha-Maḥashavah ha-Pedagogit shel ha-Maharal mi-Prag* (1962); M. Breuer, in: *Sefer ha-Zikkaron le... ha-Rav Y.Y. Weinberg* (1969).

[Mordechai Breuer]

PILSEN (Czech **Plzeň**), city in W. Bohemia, Czech Republic; its Jewish community was one of the earliest in Bohemia. The first documentary record is a decree of 1338, signed by *Charles IV, in which the city's administrators were ordered, under penalty, to protect the Jews from molestation. In 1432 the community bought a plot from the city to be used as a cemetery. It also had a synagogue. Many transactions between Jews and Christians appear on the city records of the 15th century. In 1504 Jews were expelled from Pilsen as a result of a *Host desecration charge, and the city was granted the privilege *de non tolerandis Judaeis*. From then until 1848 Jews lived in surrounding villages and did their business in the town. Jews from all of western Bohemia and Prague attended the Pilsen markets, which became very important in Jewish life. In 1821–32 Jews were living without authorization in Pilsen, and in 1854 there were 249 Jews in the town. A Jewish cemetery was consecrated in 1856 and a synagogue in 1859. Anti-Jewish riots broke out in 1866. In 1870 the community numbered 1,207. Jews were instrumental in the development of the city into an industrial center of worldwide repute.

At the beginning of the 20th century the community was among the five largest and most affluent in Bohemia; a Moorish-style synagogue was erected in 1893. The community suffered from the conflicts between German liberal assimilationists, Czech Jews (see *Čechů-Židů, Svaz) and Zionists. In 1892 the first *B'nai B'rith Lodge of Bohemia was founded there. From 1918 the community supported two rabbis, one preaching in Czech and the other in German. **Sheḥitah* was forbidden in 1920 for "humanitarian" reasons. When the supreme court declared this prohibition illegal in 1934, the attempt to reintroduce *sheḥitah* failed because of the higher price for *kasher* meat. In 1921 there were 3,117 Jews in Pilsen and in 1930 the community numbered 2,773 (2.4% of the total population). In the fall of 1938 Pilsen became a refuge for many Jews from communities in the Sudeten area, occupied then by Germany, who were supported by funds previously designated for the building of an old-age home.

After the German occupation (March 1939) there were persecutions and arrests of Jews, and the Jewish cemetery was desecrated. A plan to destroy the synagogue was given up only because it would have caused the destruction of an entire city block. In 1940 the rabbi Max Hoch and one of the community functionaries were murdered. In 1942 more than 2,000 persons from all western Bohemia were concentrated in Pilsen and deported to the Nazi extermination camps. The synagogue's ritual objects were transferred to the Central Jewish Museum in Prague.

After World War II a community was reorganized in Pilsen, numbering 293 in 1948. A memorial for the 3,200 victims of the Holocaust from Pilsen and western Bohemia was dedicated at the new cemetery in 1951. The newly established community, considerably reduced in numbers, was still active in 1970 using the old synagogue and maintaining both cemeteries, and survived into the 21st century. It also administered the *Ceske Budejovice congregation.

BIBLIOGRAPHY: M. Hoch, in: H. Gold (ed.), *Die Juden und Judengemeinden Boehmens* (1934), 479–88; Bondy-Dworský, 1 (1906), nos. 213, 222, 255, 256, 258, 287, 307, 321, 322, 336, 423; R. Iltis (ed.), *Die aussaeen unter Traenen...* (1959), 243–5.

[Jan Herman]

°**PILSUDSKI, JÓZEF** (1867–1935), Polish statesman, first marshal of Poland. In the early years of his political life, Pilsudski came into contact with Jews, especially Jewish workers, and the PPS (Polish Socialist Party) founded by him even published a periodical in Yiddish, *Der Arbeter,* between 1898 and 1905. However, he was sharply critical of the *Bund, accusing it of "commercial and religious Jewish separation," of favoring Russification, and of opposing the Polish independence movement. Since he was fiercely anti-Russian, he dissociated himself from the pro-Russian antisemite Roman *Dmowski. When Pilsudski, supported by the left, seized power in 1926, the Jews hoped for improved conditions, and indeed the prime minister, K. Bartel, proposed the abolition of several cultural, religious, and economic restrictions on the life of the Jews. However, these proposals came to nothing; on the contrary, by a law of Oct. 4, 1927 the government interfered in internal Jewish affairs and curtailed the autonomy of the Jewish communities. As a result of the pressure of the ND (*Endecja), in 1931 further restrictions were placed on Jewish economic and social life. Now opposed to the left, Pilsudski formed a front with the land owners and did nothing to curb the antisemitic right wing. In 1934 the Pilsudski government signed a pact with Hitler's Germany, with tragic results for the Jewish community in subsequent years.

BIBLIOGRAPHY: P. Szwarc, *Józef Pilsudski* (Yid., 1936); S. Segal, *The New Poland and the Jews* (1938), index; R.L. Bruell, *Poland: Key to Europe* (1939), 297–99, 301; Y. Gruenbaum, in: EG, 1 (1953), 100–13; *Wielka Encyklopedia Powszechna*, 8 (1966), 669–71; J. Rothschild, *Pilsudski's Coup d'Etat* (1966). **ADD. BIBLIOGRAPHY:** C. Kozlowski, *Zarys Dziejow Polskiego Ruchu Robotniczego do 1948 roku* (1980), index; A. Ajnenkiel, *Od "Rzadow Ludowych" do przewrotu majowego 1918–1926* (1964), index; idem, *Polska po prrzewrocie majowym* (1980), index; A. Micewski, *W cieniu Marszalka Pilsudskiego* (1969), index.

PINA, JACOB (Manuel) DE (1616–c. 1675), Marrano poet. Born in Lisbon, Pina arrived around 1660 in Amsterdam, where he openly proclaimed himself a Jew and took the name Jacob.

The poems of his early Lisbon years were humorous in the main, for example the collection *La mayor hazaña de Carlos VI* and *Juguetes de la ninez y traversuras del ingenio* (1656). His later verse included several elegies, one dedicated to the scholar Saul (Levi) *Morteira (d. 1660), another to the martyr Isaac de Almeyda *Bernal (d. 1655), and a third to the martyred Spanish nobleman Lope de Vera y *Alarcon (d. 1644). Pina wrote in both Spanish and Portuguese.

BIBLIOGRAPHY: M. Kayserling, *Sephardim* (Ger., 1859), 204; Kayserling, Bibl., 89.

PINANSKI, ABRAHAM (1887–1949), U.S. lawyer and jurist. Pinanski, who was born in Boston, Mass., worked in the legal department of the Boston Elevated Street Railway Company (1910–12), and then practiced law privately from 1912 to 1930, becoming active in the Democratic Party. Appointed to the Massachusetts Superior Court in 1930, he instituted pretrial hearings to reduce case backlog and hasten court proceedings.

Pinanski, who was active in both Jewish and public affairs, was a member of the Sinking Fund Commission of Boston for five years; a trustee of the Boston Public Library; president of both the Hebrew Free Loan Society of Boston and the Jewish Child Welfare Association; and executive committee member of both the Association of Jewish Philanthropies and Beth Israel Hospital.

PINCAS, ISRAEL (Anton; 1935–), Hebrew poet. Born in Sofia, Bulgaria, Pincas moved to his grandparents following the death of his father. After his arrival in Palestine in 1944, he joined the Ben Shemen youth village and later served as an army reporter. He worked for a while as an editor for United Press and translator from various languages into Hebrew, and for many years ran two art galleries in Tel Aviv, acting also as adviser on contemporary art. His first collection of poems, *Arba'a-asar Shirim,* was published in 1961, followed by further collections, including *El kav ha-Masheveh* (1975), *Betokh ha-Bayit* (1978), *Geneologiyyah* (1997), and *Ba-Yam ha-Atik Shelanu* (1999). A member of the so-called "*Dor ha-Medinah*" ("The Generation of the State"), Pincas followed an individualistic path, keeping away from the literary mainstream. While his early poetry focuses on Mediterranean culture, his later works pursue a dialogue with his European heritage. Indeed, at times it seems that Pincas, whose poetry is suffused with longings for other cultures, quoting from European literature and often deploying the patterns of classical music, is more of a European poet writing in Hebrew than an Israeli one. And yet, in his seminal article "*Harẓa'ah al ha-Zeman*" ("A Lecture on Time," 1991), he recalls early experiences, underscoring his local, Israeli identity. Pincas was awarded the Prime Minister's Prize and, in 2005, the Israel Prize. Some of his poems have been translated into various languages, for instance *Discours sur le temps: Choix de poèmes* (1997).

BIBLIOGRAPHY: H. Yeshurun, in: *Ḥadarim*, 6 (1987), 141–150; A. Or, in: *Haaretz* (Oct. 30, 1992); M. Gluzman, in: *Haaretz Sefarim* (Aug. 16, 2000); N. Zach, in: *Hed ha-Ḥinukh*, 76:6–7 (2002), 45; A. Melamed, in: *Yedioth Aharonoth* (Apr. 14, 2005); R. Yagil, in: *Maariv* (Apr. 29, 2005); R. Weichert, in: *Haaretz* (July 1, 2005).

[Anat Feinberg (2nd ed.)]

PINCHERLE, MARC (1888–1974), musicologist. Born in Constantine, Algeria, Pincherle edited the periodicals *Le Monde Musical* (1924–27) and *Musique* (1927–30) and was secretary of the Société Française de Musicologie (1932–35) and its president (1948–56). He made outstanding contributions to the study of baroque violin music on which he also lectured at the Ecole Normale de Musique. His writings include *Les Violinistes Compositeurs et Virtuoses* (1922); *Corelli* (1933); *Antonio Vivaldi et la musique instrumentale* (2 vols., 1948); *Corelli et son temps* (1954; *Corelli, His Life, His Work*, 1956); *Vivaldi* (1955; Eng. transl. 1957), with an important thematic index; and *Histoire illustrée de la musique* (1959). He also published editions of baroque music.

PINCHIK, PIERRE (**Pinchas Segal**; c. 1900–1971), **ḥazzan*. Born in Zhivitov, Ukraine, the young Pinchik was sent to live with his grandfather in Podolia. His singing in the local yeshivah attracted the attention of one of his teachers who arranged for Pinchik to be taught music and piano and to study voice at Rostov. He became *ḥazzan* in Leningrad and subsequently made his way to the U.S., where his ḥazzanic talent was quickly recognized. His style was best expressed in his widely acclaimed performances and recordings of *Raza de-Shabbat*, which represent his successful attempt to evoke the mystical dimension of prayer.

PINCUS, GREGORY GOODWIN (1903–1967), U.S. biologist. Born in Woodbine, New Jersey, he pursued his interest in the genetics of physiological characteristics. In post-doctoral studies at Cambridge and the Kaiser Wilhelm Institute he began investigations of steroid control of reproductive cycles. After teaching appointments at Harvard, Cambridge, and Clark University, he rounded the Worcester Foundation for Experimental Biology in 1944 with H. Hoagland. As research director he pioneered development of the widely used oral contraceptive. Having discovered earlier that the hormone progesterone, present in increased amounts during pregnancy, prevented ovulation, Pincus tested some 200 progesterone-like compounds for their effectiveness as ovulation suppressors. In 1954 he and Dr. John Rock began clinical testing of the most promising of these. Their method proved to be virtually 100% effective in preventing conception. Its widespread adoption in the ensuing decade had great medical and sociological consequences.

Pincus was a member of the American Academy of Arts and Sciences (1939) and the National Academy of Sciences (1965). He wrote *The Control of Fertility* (1965), co-authored *Steroid Dynamics* (1966), and was editor of *Recent Progress in Hormone Research*, proceedings of the 1966 Laurentian Hormone Conference (vol. 23, 1967).

BIBLIOGRAPHY: *Current Biography Yearbook 1966* (1967), 314–6; *New York Times* (Aug. 23, 1967), 45.

[George H. Fried]

PINCUS, LOUIS ARIEH (**Louis Abraham**; 1912–1973), Zionist leader. Born in South Africa, Pincus practiced law from 1934 to 1948. He was chairman of the South African Zionist Socialist Party and co-founder of Habonim in the country. He was also vice chairman of the Zionist Federation (1940–48). Pincus settled in Israel in 1948 and served as legal adviser and general secretary of the Ministry of Transportation until 1949. From then until 1956 he was the first managing director of *El Al. He practiced law in Israel from 1957 and was a member of the central bodies of *Mapai, the *Histadrut, and Iḥud Olami from 1956. In 1961 he was elected a member of the *Jewish Agency Executive, and its treasurer. On the death of Moshe *Sharett in 1965, Pincus became acting chairman and at the 27th Zionist Congress (1966) was elected chairman of the executive. He was chairman of the Board of Governors of Tel Aviv University.

[Benjamin Jaffe]

PINCZOW (Pol. **Pínczów**; Rus. **Pinchov**; Yid. **Pinchev**), town in Kielce province, S.E. Poland. During the 16th–18th centuries Pinczow was a busy market town in Sandomierz province. The date of the foundation of the Jewish community is unknown, but the fact that it sent representatives to the *Councils of the Lands testifies to its significance in the 17th century. During the attacks led by the Polish hetman S. *Czarniecki (1656), the Jews of Pinczow suffered comparatively little since they took refuge with the local margrave, and were defended by his troops. The Pinczow district (*galil*) was included in the province of *Lesser Poland. One of the most interesting relics possessed by the community is the hand-written prayer book which was completed (according to an inscription) by a scribe named Elijah b. Samuel Gronenn in January 1614 (published by S. Dubnow in *Voskhod*, 14, no. 4 (1894), 149–50). Other records of later years mention martyrs who died as a result of blood libel accusations and during the massacres in the 1640s and 1650s. In 1765 there were 2,862 Jews registered in the district, most of whom lived in the town itself; there were 2,877 Jews (70% of the total population) in the town in 1856 and 5,194 in 1897; in the latter years there were 13,716 Jews in the whole district.

Holocaust Period

At the outbreak of World War II there were about 3,500 Jews in Pinczow. In October 1942, 3,000 Jews were deported to *Treblinka death camp. During the deportation, hundreds of Jews fled into the surrounding forests. About 100 joined the two Jewish partisan units headed by Michal Majtek and Zalman Fajnsztat. These units merged and operated in the vicinity until February 1944, when they incurred heavy losses near Pawlowice. After the war the Jewish community of Pinczow was not reconstituted.

BIBLIOGRAPHY: *Sefer Zikkaron li-Kehillat Pinchev* (1970); M. Baliński and T. Lipiński, *Starożytna Polska*, 1 (1845); M. Bersohn, *Dyplomataryusz dotyceący żydow w dawnej Polsce* (1910), S.V.; L. Lewin, *Judenverfolgungen im zweiten schwedisch-polnischen Kriege 1655–59* (1901).

PINE. One species of pine, the Aleppo pine *Pinus halepensis*, is indigenous to Israel. Other species of the same genus have been planted in the afforestation of modern Israel and as ornamental trees, among them the stone pine, *Pinus pinea*. The modern Hebrew name for the pine is *oren*, but this biblical name relates to a different species, the *bay tree. The Aleppo pine is one of the most beautiful forest trees of Israel. Only a few groves of it remain at the present day because it was felled for use as building material. Among the natural groves of this species is the Masrek ("comb") at Bet Meir in the Judean hills, so called because its high trunks, conspicuous on the horizon, look like a comb. The Aleppo pine was adopted as the most important forest tree of Israel, tens of thousands of acres being planted with it, because of its rapid growth, beauty, and abundant shade, as well as for its ability to grow on rocky ground. It is the *eẓ shemen* ("oil tree") of the Bible, as it is still called (in Aramaic) by the Jews of Kurdistan, and is so called because of its high turpentine content. Isaiah (41:19) mentions this tree among those that will fructify the wilderness on the path of the redeemed. In the time of Nehemiah its branches were used for covering the *sukkah (Neh. 8:15). Ben Sira (50:10) compares the high priest to its tall evergreen flourishing top. In the Temple the cherubim and the doors were made from its wood (1 Kings 6:23, 32). The pseudo-Jonathan Targum here renders *eẓ shemen* as olive tree, but it is impossible to make doors from the hollow trunk of the latter (see *Olive). Furthermore, the olive is mentioned in Nehemiah (8:15) together with the *eẓ shemen*; they cannot therefore be identical. Nor can the *eẓ shemen* be identified with the *Eleagnus angustifolia* (which in modern Hebrew is called *eẓ shemen*) since it does not fit the descriptions of *eẓ shemen* in the Bible and Mishnah. *Eẓ shemen* is enumerated among the four species of "cedar" (*erez*), i.e., conifers (RH 23a). In mishnaic times its boughs were used for kindling the beacons that announced the appearance of the new moon (RH 2:3). They were also used as firewood for the altar (Tam. 2:3). The needle-like leaves of the pine contain fibers from which is produced "forest wool." In the Mishnah this is called *lekhesh*, and it is mentioned among the fibers whose wick may not be used for the Sabbath lamp (Shab. 2:1, 20b; TJ, *ibid.* 4d).

The stone pine, though not indigenous to Israel, is grown as an ornamental tree and for its edible and tasty nuts. These nuts are called *iẓtrubalin* in the Mishnah, which states that they may not be sold to idolators on their festivals (Av. Zar. 1:5). They are liable to tithes (TJ, Ma'as. 1:2, 48d). In the view of *Saadiah Gaon the stone pine is the *tirzah* (JPS ilex; A.V. cypress) of Isaiah 44:14, mentioned as being used both for making idols and for firewood.

BIBLIOGRAPHY: Loew, Flora, 3 (1924), 40–47; J. Feliks, *Olam ha-Ẓome'aḥ ha-Mikra'i* (1968^2), 88–92. **ADD. BIBLIOGRAPHY:** Feliks, Ha-Ẓome'aḥ, 31, 113.

[Jehuda Feliks]

PINEDA, JUAN DE (d. 1486), Converso martyr, commander in the Order of Santiago, and the emissary of the head of the order, Juan Pacheco, to the papal court. Born into a poor Converso family in Córdoba, in his youth, Pineda worked as a tailor and was known as Juan de Baena. Nothing is known of how he rose in Spanish society. In 1486 he was tried by the Inquisition on charges of having practiced Judaism. Among the accusations brought against him was that he had declared in 1464, when the Turks and Pope Pius II were at war, that the redemption of Israel would come through the Turks. He was burned at the stake on Aug. 16, 1486 in Toledo.

BIBLIOGRAPHY: Baer, Spain, 2 (1966), 347ff.; Baer, Urkunden, 2 (1936), 468ff.

PINELES, HIRSCH MENDEL BEN SOLOMON (known as "**Shalosh**" from the last (Hebrew) letters of his name, Hir**sch** Mendel Pineles; 1806–1870), Galician scholar and writer. Pineles settled in Brody and joined the circle of young *maskilim* who gathered round Nachman *Krochmal. He perfected his German, and began to educate himself in philosophy, Greek, Latin, Arabic, and astronomy, specializing in mathematics and the calculation of the Jewish calendar. In 1853 he moved to Odessa, and in 1855 to Galati in Romania, where he lived until his death. He was an active member of the *Alliance Israélite Universelle and involved in its program in Romania.

Pineles began his literary career with a letter to Krochmal in 1836 published in *Kerem Ḥemed* (2 (1936), 108–113). He wrote the first critical article on Krochmal's *Moreh Nevukhei ha-Zeman* (in: *He-Ḥalutz*, 1 (1852), 123–4); and he published critical book reviews as well as numerous articles on a variety of subjects in *Kerem Ḥemed* (2 (1936), 125–9, 168–71), in *Ha-Maggid* (8–11 (1864–67)), *Yeshurun*, and elsewhere. For about 30 years he engaged in a fierce controversy with Ḥ.S. *Slonimsky on the method of calculating the Jewish calendar (see *Kerem Ḥemed*, 8 (1854), 27–37, 85–109).

Pineles is best known for his *Darkah shel Torah* (Vienna, 1861), a critical examination in 178 sections of the Mishnah and its interpretation, followed by a treatise on the Hebrew calendar including tables. The stated aim of the work was to justify the Oral Law and substantiate the words of the scribes where they deviate from the literal text. Pineles defended the Mishnah both against the authors of the Talmud, who honored it but distorted its plain meaning, and against the detractors of the Talmud, who attempted to find defects in it and to devalue it. He also sought to explain a number of difficult passages in the Babylonian and Jerusalem Talmuds. His work is characterized by critical acumen and boldness. Believing that some explanations given by the later *amoraim* distorted the original Mishnah, he attempted to interpret a number of *mishnayot* in a new way. His deviations from the traditional explanations of the *amoraim* were attacked by traditionalists, one of them being his brother-in-law, Moses b. Joel Waldberg, a leading banker in Bucharest (*Kakh hi Darkah shel Torah*, pt. 1, Lemberg, 1864; pt. 2, Jassy, 1868). Pineles, however, maintained that he had no heretical intent and himself attacked certain scholars for their extreme views – chiefly Abraham *Geiger for his *Urschrift und Uebersetzung der Bibel in ihrer Abhaengigkeit von der innern Entwicklung des Judenthums* (1857; a review of which is published at the end of *Darkah shel Torah*) and J.H. *Schorr – stressing his own attachment to tradition (*Darkah shel Torah*, no. 14, p. 19).

BIBLIOGRAPHY: Fuenn, Keneset, 286–8; Lachower, Sifrut, 2 (1929), 191, 311; B. Wachstein, *Die hebraeische Publizistik in Wien*, 1 (1930), 160–1; N.M. Gelber (ed.), *Arim ve-Immahot be-Yisrael*. 6 (1955), 211; Kressel, Leksikon, 613–4.

[Yehoshua Horowitz]

PINELES, SAMUEL (1843–1928), early member of Ḥovevei Zion and the Zionist Movement in Romania. Born in Brody, Galicia, the son of Hirsch Mendel *Pineles, he moved with his family to Galati, Romania, in 1863. Early in his youth he began his activity in the Ḥibbat Zion movement, and submitted to the central board of the Alliance Israélite Universelle in Paris periodical information and documents concerning Romanian Jewry. In 1881 he was elected to the board of the Romanian Association for the settlement of Ereẓ Israel. He took part in the conference of the settlement societies held in Focsani in January 1882 and was elected chairman of the central board, situated in Galati. Pineles did much for the Romanian immigrants and their two settlements in Palestine, Rosh Pinnah and Zamarin (later known as Zikhron Ya'akov). As chairman of the central board, he mobilized resources from Baron Edmond de *Rothschild for the purpose of purchasing lands in the Golan to be settled by Romanian Jews. He participated in all of the first ten congresses and was a member of the Zionist General Council. He was one of the founders of the *Jewish Colonial Trust. In 1909 he gave the *Jewish National Fund 30,000 francs, which he had received from Rothschild for the lands in the Golan acquired by Romanian members of Ḥibbat Zion. In 1920 he took part in the Committee for Jewish refugees who went to Galati after the pogroms in Ukraine. In 1965 his remains were reinterred in Jerusalem.

BIBLIOGRAPHY: I. Klausner, *Ḥibbat Ẓiyyon be-Rumanyah* (1958), index; L. Jaffe (ed.), *Sefer ha-Congress* (1950^2), 348–9.

[Israel Klausner]

PINES, MEYER ISSER (1881 or 1882–1942?), leader of the Territorialist movement in his youth, Yiddish writer, and journalist. Born in Mogilev, Russia, Pines grew up in Rozinay, Grodno district. He received his doctorate for his dissertation, *Histoire de la littérature judéo-allemande* (Paris, 1911), which was translated into Yiddish (Warsaw, 1911), Russian, and German. Israel *Zinberg and Ber *Borochov stamped the work as dilettantish, a judgment held also by later scholars. Pines is presumed to have died in a Russian deportation camp sometime after 1942.

BIBLIOGRAPHY: LNYL, 7 (1968), 149–51.

[Leonard Prager]

PINES, NOAH (1871–1939), Hebrew educator and writer. Born in Shklov, Russia, he studied at the yeshivah of Volozhin. At an early age, he became a teacher and established a modern *ḥeder* in Lublin at the beginning of the century. After completing his pedagogic studies in German and Swiss universities, he immigrated to Palestine (1919), taught in the Levinsky Teachers' Seminary of Tel Aviv, and served as its principal from 1923 until his death.

He published study manuals, articles, and essays on educational problems. His book *Ha-Zamir* (1903), children's poems for reading and singing, was an important innovation. A volume of his poems *Ẓilẓelei Erev* (1940) and a pedagogic work, *Ketavim Pedagogiyyim* (1941), were published posthumously.

BIBLIOGRAPHY: Kressel, Leksikon, 2 (1967), 619–20.

[Getzel Kressel]

PINES, SHLOMO (Solomon; 1908–1990), historian of philosophy and science. Born in Paris, Pines taught at the Institut d'Histoire des Sciences et des Techniques de l'Université de Paris from 1937 to 1939. He settled in Ereẓ Israel in 1940. From 1948 to 1952 he served in the Middle East division of the Israel Ministry for Foreign Affairs. In 1952 he began teaching at the Hebrew University and in 1961 Pines became professor of general and Jewish philosophy. He was a fellow of the Israel Academy of Sciences and Humanities, and in 1968 received the Israel Prize. He served as coeditor of the *Corpus Commentariorum Averrois in Aristotelem* of the Medieval Academy of America. The 20th volume of the philosophic journal *Iyyun* (1969) was dedicated to him on the occasion of his 60th birthday.

Pines wrote in the fields of Islamic philosophy and science, the Greek antecedents of Islamic philosophy and science, and Jewish philosophy. In his first book, *Beitraege zur islamischen Atomenlehre* (1936), he analyzed the atomic theories of the Muslim theologians. He wrote several detailed analyses of the thought of Abu al Barakāt ben Ali al-Baghdādī *Hibat Allah, a hitherto barely known critic of Islamic Aristotelianism. In the field of Jewish philosophy he published a new English translation of Maimonides' *Guide of the Perplexed* (1963) with an introduction tracing Maimonides' philosophic sources. In his *Scholasticism after Thomas Aquinas and the Teachings of Hasdai Crescas and his Predecessors* (1967) he proposed the thesis that late medieval Jewish philosophers, such as *Levi b. Gershom, *Jedaiah b. Abraham Bedersi (ha-Penini), and Ḥasdai *Crescas, were familiar with the philosophic and scientific doctrines of the late medieval Christian scholastics. In "Spinoza's Tractatus Theologico-Politicus, Maimonides, and Kant" (in: *Scripta Hierosolymitana*, 20 (1968), 3–54) he discusses the interrelation of Maimonides and Spinoza. He also published *A New Fragment of Xenocrates* (1961).

BIBLIOGRAPHY: For further information on his writings between 1957 and 1968 see *Reshimat ha-Pirsumim ha-Madda'iyyim shel Ḥavrei ha-Makhon le-Madda'ei ha-Yahadut* (1969), 82–84.

[Yehuda Landau / Arthur Hyman]

PINES, YEHIEL MICHAEL ("Michal"; 1843–1913), writer, early exponent of religious Zionism, and *yishuv* leader. Born in Ruzhany, Belorussia, into a family of prosperous merchants and Torah scholars, Pines was influenced in his youth by Mordecai Gimpel *Jaffe, an early leader of *Ḥovevei Zion, who headed a yeshivah maintained by Pines' family. He studied both traditional subjects and foreign languages and science, and the fusion of the two spheres of knowledge led to a romantic-religious outlook. Pines believed that Jewish life should be reformed, but he was opposed to deliberate, religious reforms that would undermine the foundations of tradition and increase assimilation. He thought that a reformed way of life would inevitably bring about certain changes of *halakhah* without affecting the sanctity of the Jewish religion. During the 1860s Pines developed these ideas in his controversy with M.L. *Lilienblum, *J.L. Gordon, and others, mainly through his articles in *Ha-Karmel, *Ha-Meliẓ, and *Ha-Levanon. The articles were collected in his book, *Yaldei Ruḥi* ("Children of

My Spirit," 2 vols., 1872), and his ideas were later expanded by *Aḥad Ha-Am, who restyled them in his own clear, polished language.

In 1877, while he was living at his father-in-law's home in Mogilev, Pines was asked by the Moses Montefiore Testimonial Fund in London to serve as its representative in Ereẓ Israel. He accepted eagerly, reached Jaffa a year later, and settled in Jerusalem (1878) at the home of his relative, Yosef *Rivlin, the secretary of the Va'ad Kelali (General Committee of the *ḥalukkah), thus arousing the enmity of Rivlin's many opponents in Jerusalem (Ḥasidim and *maskilim*, Sephardim, and religious extremists; the latter, supporters of Rabbi Y.L. *Diskin persecuted Pines and proclaimed him "excommunicated").

On behalf of his London sponsors, Pines conducted investigations into the spiritual, cultural, and particularly the economic problems of the *yishuv*, proposing the founding of an agricultural settlement, the building of houses and new quarters, and the establishment of artisan and industrial projects. The Montefiore Fund concentrated on granting aid for the construction of houses and Jerusalem was thus expanded through the building of several new quarters. Pines' letters to the Fund trustees appear in volumes 2 and 3 of *Mivḥar Kitvei Y.M. Pines* ("Selected Writings of Y.M. Pines") and in his *Binyan ha-Areẓ* ("Building of the Land"), volumes 1 and 2 (1934).

Pines tried to set up artisan and industrial projects with the help of Montefiore Fund loans, and with his own money as well, but they proved a failure and brought about his dismissal in 1885. (His son-in-law, David Yellin, was appointed to the same post in 1901.) In 1882 Pines became friendly with Eliezer *Ben-Yehuda who had just arrived in Ereẓ Israel, and together they established the Teḥiyyat Israel ("Israel Renaissance") Society, whose aim was, inter alia, to introduce Hebrew as a spoken language. When the first members of *Bilu arrived at the end of the same year, Pines became their patron and established the Shivat he-Ḥarash ve-ha-Masger ("Return of the Craftsmen and the Smiths") Society for them in Jerusalem. With Ḥovevei Zion funds he bought for them the lands for the settlement of *Gederah in 1884 and was the settlement's patron for several years. In 1885 K.Z. *Wissotzky appointed him a member of the executive committee of Ḥovevei Zion in Palestine. For several months in 1886 he edited *Ha-Ẓevi*, Ben-Yehuda's newspaper, while the latter was abroad, but the friendship between the two was affected by the outbreak of the violent controversy regarding the Sabbatical Year (*shemittah*), which fell in 1888/89. Although Pines' conservative attitude to this question aroused opposition in Ḥovevei Zion circles, he was elected in 1890 to the organization's executive committee in Jaffa, headed by Vladimir *Tiomkin. At about the same time Pines joined the *Benei Moshe Society, but its leader Aḥad Ha-Am, who wanted to prevent discussions of religious problems in the Society, advocated his departure from that group. In 1892, after a crisis in the activities of the executive committee of Ḥovevei Zion, Pines was dismissed and thereafter affiliated himself with the old *yishuv*, even becoming one of its main spokesmen. His views on nation and religion, which he then developed in his articles in *Ha-Ḥavaẓẓelet* and in special pamphlets, were shortly afterward adopted by the *Mizrachi Party. In 1893 he became a trustee of the Ashkenazi community's charitable institutions in Jerusalem, and the librarian and a teacher of Talmud in the Hebrew Teachers' college.

Pines was foremost a thinker, writer, and craftsman of Hebrew language and style. He displayed outstanding knowledge of biblical style and language (into which he translated various scientific books) and greatly influenced his brother-in-law and pupil, Ze'ev *Jawitz, who in turn influenced Ḥ.N. *Bialik. Pines was conversant with mishnaic style (see his *Mishnat Ereẓ Yisrael*), the medieval style rhyming prose, and the conglomerate style that he employed in his articles and his many letters to employers and to people who approached him with queries regarding settlement in Ereẓ Israel. *Yaldei Ruḥi* and some of his letters and articles appeared in the three volumes of *Kitvei Y.M. Pines* ("Writings of Y.M. Pines," 1934–39), edited by his sons-in-law, David Yellin and Yosef *Meyuḥas. His selected writings, *Mivḥar Kitvei Pines*, appeared in 1946, edited and with a preface by G. Kressel. Kefar Pines, a moshav in the Sharon Plain, is named for him.

BIBLIOGRAPHY: N. Sokolow, *Ḥibbath Zion* (Eng., 1935), index; A. Boehm, *Die zionistische Bewegung* (1935), index; G. Raphael, *Rabbi Yeḥi'el Mikha'el Pines* (1954); M. Michaeli, *Rabbi Yeḥi'el Mikhal Pines* (1928); A. Druyanow (ed.), *Ketavim le-Toledot Ḥibbat Ẓiyyon ve-Yishuv Ereẓ Yisrael*, 1 (1919), index; 3 (1932), index; Ḥ.N. Bialik, in: *Ha-Olam*, 7 no. 13/14 (1913), 23–25; I. Yellin, *Le-Ẓe'eẓa'ai*, 2, vols. (1938–41), passim; Y. Nissenbaum, *Ha-Dat ve-ha-Teḥiyyah ha-Le'ummit* (1920), 145–51.

[Galia Yardeni-Agmon]

PINHEIRO, MOSES (17th century), Shabbatean, born in *Izmir. A contemporary of *Shabbetai Ẓevi, Pinheiro studied talmudic and kabbalistic literature with him in their youth (1640–50). There is no indication that he supported Shabbetai Ẓevi's messianic claims in 1648. About 1650 he left Izmir and settled in *Leghorn, where he became a highly respected scholar. When the news of the Shabbatean awakening reached Italy, he became at once one of its most ardent spokesmen, continuing to believe that Shabbetai Ẓevi was Messiah long after his *apostasy. As delegate of the Leghorn community, he went to see Shabbetai Ẓevi in the summer of 1666, at the height of the excitement, but arrived in Izmir after the apostasy. There he received communications from both Shabbetai Ẓevi and *Nathan of Gaza which strengthened his faith. In March 1667 he returned to Italy with a delegation from three other communities. Nathan stayed at his house on his visit to Italy in 1668. Pinheiro, who was the center of the Shabbatean group in Leghorn, maintained a correspondence with Shabbetai Ẓevi over the years and also took an interest in Abraham *Cardozo. As shown by Abraham *Rovigo's notebook on Shabbatean matters (Ben-Zvi Institute, Ms. 2265), he was still considered a "believer" about 1690. When and whether he finally gave up his belief is unknown.

His daughter was the mother of the well-known kabbalist and Rabbi Joseph *Ergas, who kept silent about his grandfather's Shabbatean connections. Rabbi *Malachi ha-Kohen of Leghorn, Ergas' pupil, though an outspoken foe of the Shabbatean movement, praised Pinheiro highly for his piety and ascetic life in his foreword to Ergas' responsa, *Divrei Yosef* (1742). Several of Pinheiro's recollections on Shabbetai Ẓevi have been preserved.

BIBLIOGRAPHY: Scholem, Shabbetai Ẓevi, index; J. Sasportas, *Ẓiẓat Novel Ẓevi* (1954), index; I. Tishby, in: *Zion*, 22 (1957), 31–33; idem, in: *Sefunot*, 3–4 (1960), 93, 107; Freimann, *Inyenei Shabbetai Ẓevi* (1912), 45, 95.

[Gershom Scholem]

PINKAS (פִּנְקָס), record book of Jewish autonomous units, used mainly in the Middle Ages. The *pinkas* contained minutes of meetings, bylaws, lists of officers elected at the annual meetings, records of disciplinary actions against recalcitrant members, of tax assessments and fines, of trials, of unusual historical events, and an endless variety of other entries reflecting the life of the local community. Each community and each *ḥevrah, including artisan guilds, had its own *pinkas*, as did the *Councils of the Lands in Poland, Lithuania, and Moravia. *Pinkasim* of local communities and those of the Councils have been published.

BIBLIOGRAPHY: Baron, Community, 2 (1942), 113, index s.v. *Minute books*; I. Levitats, *Jewish Community in Russia, 1772–1844* (1943), index s.v. *Minute book*; A. Rechtman, *Yidishe Etnografye un Folklor* (1958), 193–240.

[Isaac Levitats]

PINKAS, DAVID ẒVI (1895–1952), Mizrachi leader and Israel politician. Pinkas was born in Sopron, Hungary, into a religious Zionist family, which settled in Vienna when he was a child. He became active in the Mizrachi movement and represented it as a delegate at the 13th Zionist Congress. In 1925 Pinkas settled in Palestine, became the manager of the Mizrachi bank, and, in 1932, was elected to the Tel Aviv municipal council, heading its Education Department from 1935. He was also a Mizrachi representative to the Asefat ha-Nivḥarim and the Va'ad Le'ummi, becoming treasurer and director of its department of Religious Communities and the Rabbinate. After the establishment of the State of Israel, he was elected to the First Knesset on behalf of the United Religious Front, and after the elections to the Second Knesset, in October 1951, he was appointed minister of transportation. In this capacity he regulated the austerity measures for fuel consumption and stipulated that all vehicles should not be driven two days a week, and that one of these days should be Saturday (the Sabbath). This regulation aroused sharp protest from extreme circles opposing "religious coercion."

BIBLIOGRAPHY: Tidhar, 2 (1947), 855–6.

PINKEL, BENJAMIN (1909–1992), U.S. aeronautical engineer. Pinkel was born in Gloversville, N.Y., and graduated in electrical engineering from the University of Pennsylvania (1930). He joined the National Advisory Council for Aeronautics where he was head of the engine analysis section (1938–42), the fuel and thermodynamic division (1945–50), and the materials and thermodynamic research division (1950–56). He was associate head of the aero-astronautics department of Rand Corporation from 1956. Pinkel was an early supporter of the superiority of jet propulsion and the gas turbine engine in aircraft design and a pioneer in rocket propulsion technology. Later in life he was interested in the philosophy of the mind in the light of scientific advances.

[Michael Denman (2nd ed.)]

PINNER, ADOLF (1842–1909), German organic chemist. Born in Wronke, then Germany, he studied for the rabbinate, but changed to chemistry. He was a professor at Berlin University from 1878 and also taught at Tieraertzliche Hochschule. He was director of the Patent Office of Ministry of Commerce (1885–1907). Pinner published extensively on organic chemistry topics, particularly alkaloids. His *Repetitorium der organischen, beziehungsweise anorganischen Chemie* (2 vols., 1872–73) was a standard textbook for many years. He also wrote *Die Imidoaether* (1892).

PINNER, EPHRAIM MOSES BEN ALEXANDER SUSSKIND (c. 1800–1880), talmudist. Born in Pinne (district of Poznan), Pinner studied Talmud under Rabbi *Jacob of Lissa. In 1831 he compiled an abbreviated form of the Talmud, *Kiẓẓur Talmud Yerushalmi ve-Talmud Bavli*. Pinner is best known for his ambitious scheme to translate into German the whole of the Talmud; he enlisted the moral support of some prominent rabbis, including Rabbi Moses *Sofer (Schreiber) of Pressburg, who eventually withdrew his name. It appears that Pinner maintained that Rabbi Nathan Marcus *Adler of Hanover (later of London) had undertaken to translate the difficult tractates *Eruvin* and *Yevamot* under this scheme, but Adler denied the existence of such an arrangement. In 1842 *Berakhot* was published in Hebrew with German translation. Czar Nicholas I lent his name to the project, together with other notables. The volume was dedicated to the czar, who had shown an unusual interest in the translation of the Talmud before Pinner's venture – and not with the best of intentions. No further volume appeared. Samuel David Luzzatto criticized the work somewhat adversely in *Kerem Ḥemed* (2 (1836), 174–82).

BIBLIOGRAPHY: S. Sofer (ed.), *Iggerot Soferim* (1928), pt. 2, 73–78; R.N.N. Rabinowitz, *Ma'amar al Hadpasat ha-Talmud*, ed. by A.M. Habermann (1952), 246–8.

[Alexander Tobias]

PINNER, FELIX (1880–1942), German economist and journalist. Born in Birnbaum (Posen), he engaged initially in economic and journalistic activities which also included a strong interest in the colonization of Palestine by German Zionists. In 1924 he became editor of the financial section of the *Berliner Tageblatt*, one of Germany's leading liberal dailies. He left Germany for the U.S. soon after Hitler's rise to power, but failed to integrate in his new surroundings. He took his own life, and that of his wife, in New York during a period of mental depression due to financial difficulties.

His principal publications are *Emil Rathenau und das elektrische Zeitalter* (1918); *Deutsche Wirtschaftsfuehrer* (1925, published under the pseudonym Frank Fassland); *Das Neue Palaestina* (1926); *Tannerhuette; der Roman einer Sozialisierung* (1928); and *Die grossen Weltkrisen…* (1937).

[Joachim O. Ronall]

PINNER, MORITZ (1828–c. 1909), U.S. antislavery activist in the Civil War period. Pinner was born in Prussia. He was one of a handful of immigrant Jews who played a significant local role in the founding of the Republican Party and in the propaganda efforts against slavery which helped to bring on the Civil War. He participated in abolitionist activities in Missouri as early as 1856, served as editor of Republican antislavery papers in St. Louis and Kansas City, and was a member of state and national Republican conventions in 1860. Said to have been offered a diplomatic post by Lincoln, Pinner preferred military service, although the reports of his commissioned service are confused.

BIBLIOGRAPHY: Kohler, in: AJHSP, 5 (1897), 152–3; Markens, *ibid.*, 17, (1909), 139–41.

[Bertram Wallace Korn]

PINS, JACOB (1917–2005), Israeli printmaker, born at Hoxter, Germany. Pins immigrated to Palestine in 1936 and spent five years working on the land before he took up art and studied under the great woodcut artist Jakob Steinhardt. His stark, dramatic woodcuts often convey an atmosphere of war. In style they show the influence of the Japanese color print. Bold and simple in black and white with few or no halftones, they nevertheless express a sense of volume and a third dimension. One of his favorite subjects was the city of Jerusalem. He was also a major collector of Japanese artwork.

PINSK, capital of Pinsk district, Belarus. The Jewish community there was established before 1506 by some 12 to 15 families (about 60–75 persons) from *Brest-Litovsk who settled in Pinsk instead of returning to Lithuania after the Jews were granted permission to return. Pinsk was then a Russian-Orthodox town and capital of a semi-independent principality. In 1506 Prince Feodor Yaroslavski granted the settlers the same rights enjoyed by the Jews of Lithuania, and the status of a community. The separate existence of the principality came to an end in 1521 and Pinsk was incorporated into Lithuania.

By 1566 the community consisted of about 55 families (approximately 275 persons; c. 7% of the total population). It numbered over 1,000 (c. 20% of the total) in 1648, and about 2,000 at the beginning of the 18th century, when they constituted the large majority of the town and controlled most of its life, there having been a severe decline in the Christian population during the second half of the 17th century. Subsequently the Jewish population numbered 13,681 in 1871 (77.7%); 21,819 in 1896 (77.3%); 28,063 in 1914 (72.5%); 17,513 in 1921 (74.6%); and 20,200 in 1939. Pinsk thus remained a "Jewish town" until the Holocaust.

Until 1648 the Jews of Pinsk were guaranteed the legal status of citizens, complete protection of their persons and property, freedom to engage in commerce, moneylending, and crafts, and the right to organize their internal life according to the precepts of their religion. The favorable geographical position of the region of Pinsk on the junctions of roads and waterways, and colonizing activity there during the 16th century, encouraged its development. Jews engaged in varied activities including the ownership (later lease) of estates, the lease of taxes and customs duties, commerce, moneylending, and crafts. The community leaders, descendants of the founding nucleus, mainly dealt in business connected with estates and engaged in moneylending. Later they entered the wholesale trade also, as well as the leasing of tax collection and customs duties. In the middle of the 16th century, Pinsk Jews took up the then thriving export of grain and forest products. In the 1560s Nahum Pesahovich was outstanding for the scope and variety of his business activities. As in the rest of the region, the Pinsk Jews benefited from the support of the Catholic nobles against the Russian-Orthodox Belorussian townsmen. In these circumstances the status granted to the Pinsk municipality under the *Magdeburg Law in 1581 did not greatly hamper the Jews though it contained several restrictions on their trade.

The leasing and subleasing of estates by Jews resulted in an increasing periphery of Jewish inhabitants who settled in villages and new townlets established around Pinsk which came under its jurisdiction within the structure of the *Councils of the Lands. The community consolidated and developed. As one of the three original leading communities of the Lithuanian Council, Pinsk played a prominent role in the shaping of the council's policy and activity.

The period between 1648 and 1667 was one of wars and misfortunes. At the time of the *Chmielnicki massacres, Pinsk was taken on Oct. 26, 1648. Scores of Jews there were murdered in the town and on the roads, though most of them managed to escape in good time and were thus saved. A number of those who had remained in the town became converted to Christianity, but later returned to Judaism. Before the capture of Pinsk by the Russians during the Polish-Russian War (1654–67), all the Jews fled, in general managing to save much of their property. In 1660 the community suffered again from the depredations of the Muscovite armies and the Cossacks: some Jews were murdered, and property was lost. In this period of troubles, the Pinsk community showed the resilience and vital forces inherent in Jewish society and community leadership. When the numbers of the Christian townsmen were reduced they retreated to the suburbs and villages, where many of them turned to agriculture, whereas the Jews of Pinsk timed and organized their escape (in 1648 and 1655) with relative success and took measures to preserve at least part of their property. With peace they rapidly resumed their activities in the town, taking up new livelihoods if their former ones were no longer viable. The community leadership energetically restored community life, helped the refugees, aided in the ransoming of prisoners, and renewed the educational network and Torah study.

From 1667 until the beginning of the 18th century, the economic situation took a turn for the worse. Large-scale leasing disappeared, numerous Jews became impoverished and were compelled to seek new occupations, and many Jews of Pinsk turned to dealing in alcoholic beverages, most of them as retailers in the town and villages. Jewish trade diminished in scale and in part converted to retail trade; credit became difficult and many had to borrow from noblemen. Even the community administration itself had to borrow from them and from church officials, and gradually sank under a load of debt. However, the number of Jews in Pinsk increased, and the proliferation of small Jewish settlements around Pinsk proceeded. The same social circles which had led the community before 1648 continued to do so until the close of the century. In these difficult times there were many scholars in Pinsk, and renowned rabbis held office. These include Naphtali Gunzburg (officiated from 1664), Israel b. Samuel of Tarnopol (from 1667), Joel b. Isaac Eisik Heilperin (1691), and Isaac b. Jonah Teomim Fraenkel (1693–1703). The rabbi and *Maggid* Judah Leib *Pukhovitser, who lived in Pinsk during the last third of the 17th century, exerted considerable influence.

The tense situation in Poland-Lithuania during the first quarter of the 18th century, the continuing economic crisis, and the burden of taxation and debts, gave rise to internal tensions within the community and to a conflict of interests between the community of Pinsk and its subordinate communities, whose numbers continued to increase during the 18th century. In 1719, controversies broke out between the council of the communities of the province of *Volhynia and the community of Pinsk over the jurisdiction of several village communities of northern Volhynia. With the official abolition of the Council of the Lands in 1764, almost all the subordinate communities rejected Pinsk's authority, and after a prolonged struggle the weakened central community lost control.

*Ḥasidism spread to Pinsk and *Karlin during the 1760s. Aaron b. Jacob of Karlin made Karlin a center of Ḥasidism equal in importance to *Mezhirech. Until the early 1780s, Ḥasidism was the predominating influence in Pinsk and Karlin. The community leadership adopted a neutral position toward Ḥasidism. However, under severe pressure by the community leadership of Vilna and *Elijah b. Solomon Zalman, the Gaon of Vilna, the leadership of Pinsk associated itself with the ban against the Ḥasidim at the fair of *Zelva in 1781. *Levi Isaac b. Meir of Berdichev was dismissed from his position as rabbi of Pinsk in 1785, but he had apparently already completed his official ten-year term of office. At the same time Solomon of Karlin also left Karlin for *Vladimir-Volynski (Ludmir). In 1785 *Avigdor b. Joseph Ḥayyim, an avowed opponent of Ḥasidism, was elected rabbi of Pinsk and district. However, he did not succeed in imposing his authority on the community, and the ḥasidic villages in the vicinity, so that the Ḥasidim regained their strength.

Under Russian Rule

In 1793 Pinsk was incorporated into Russia and became a district capital in the province of Minsk. The Ḥasidim then gained control of the community administration and dismissed R. Avigdor from his position. Under Russian rule the Jews of Pinsk and Karlin were granted equal rights with the townsmen, and a small number of Jews belonged to the merchant sector. At the beginning of Russian rule the economic activity of the Jews was reduced and their situation apparently became precarious. A change for the better began in the 1820s. From then on Pinsk played an important role as a center for the *salt trade of Lithuania and in the exploitation of forest resources for timber export. Prominent in the economic life and community leadership of Pinsk-Karlin at that time was Saul b. Moses Levin of Karlin (1775–1834), an avowed opponent of the Ḥasidim. During the 19th century the wealthiest merchants settled in Karlin, which gradually became a stronghold of the *Mitnaggedim*.

The economic improvement in Pinsk continued during the 1830s, helped along by the government's economic policy which, among other measures, paved the way for the development of industry and the agricultural output of the Ukraine, and created opportunities for export of its agricultural surpluses. Pinsk became a transit center for trade between southwestern Russia and the Baltic ports. Members of the Levin and *Luria families held a prominent place in this commerce. The Jewish merchant class was broadened, its capital increased, and a stratum of white-collar workers and agents from Pinsk in the service of its wealthy merchants became active throughout the Ukraine. This prosperity in Pinsk lasted until the 1870s. Much of the capital accumulated by the merchants of Pinsk was invested in the markets of the Ukraine. During the 1850s a number of Pinsk merchants put into service steamships for the transportation of goods and passengers. In the 1860s Moses Luria established a steam-powered oil press and mill. However, after the construction in the 1860s of the Kiev-Brest-Litovsk railroad, a severe crisis struck the city.

During the 1860s there were between 750 and 950 Jewish craftsmen in Pinsk. The philanthropist Gad Asher provided training for orphans and children of the poor in crafts, and the large number of Jewish artisans at this time was a feature of the city. In 1855 a Jewish agricultural settlement was established in the village of Ivanichi near Pinsk.

At the close of the 19th century members of the Luria family established nail and plywood factories. A match factory was established in 1892. Jewish workers were employed in the factories and a Jewish proletariat formed. Of the 54 industrial enterprises in Pinsk in 1914, 49 were owned by Jews. Industrialization was accompanied by an economic recovery in both commerce and crafts, in which Jews also predominated. Stirrings of the *Haskalah movement appeared in Pinsk with the beginning of the economic prosperity of the 1830s, and its influence gradually increased. A Russian government school for the children of Jews in the first category of merchants was founded in Pinsk in 1853, and during the 1850s to 1860s, 26 to 38 pupils studied there. During the same year a Jewish school for girls was established. In 1878 a private school, in which emphasis was placed on Hebrew studies, was founded by the *Kazyonny Ravvin* Abraham Ḥayyim *Rosenberg. During the early 1860s *talmud torah* schools were founded in Pinsk and Karlin whose curricula included the study of the Hebrew and Russian languages and arithmetic in addition to religious studies. Many were still educated in the *ḥadarim*. In 1888 a vocational school was founded in Pinsk. During the 1890s modern *ḥadarim* were founded under the tutelage of the Ḥovevei Zion, whose members included the young Chaim *Weizmann. Zionist and *Bund organizations were also formed in Pinsk in this period.

In Independent Poland

During the initial period of Polish rule after World War I, on April 5, 1919, the Poles executed 35 prominent Jews following a trumped up charge against them. Between the two world wars the majority of the Jewish population in Pinsk was Zionist in orientation while a minority adhered to the Bund and other parties. Many Jews emigrated to Ereẓ Israel, among them members of *Bilu including Aharon Eliyahu *Eisenberg, the founder of Reḥovot, and Ya'akov Shertok. The kibbutz *Gevat was founded in 1926 by pioneers from Pinsk. The Jewish educational network was widely extended. New schools were founded: the Tel Ḥai School of the *Po'alei Zion (with Hebrew and Yiddish as the languages of instruction); two *Tarbut schools, one in Pinsk and one in Karlin; and the Chechick gymnasium (Polish). The Hebrew high school Tarbut, founded in 1923, existed until the beginning of Soviet rule.

[Mordekhai Nadav]

Holocaust and Postwar Periods

When Pinsk was under Soviet rule from September 1939 to June 1941, the Jewish institutions, including political parties and schools, were closed down. Some of the Zionist and Bund leaders were arrested and many Jewish businessmen and members of the free professions were expelled from the city. A large number of Jewish refugees from western Poland found shelter in Pinsk, but were deported to the Soviet interior in 1940. Pinsk served as a stopover for many refugees trying illegally to reach Vilna. Pinsk fell to the Germans on July 4, 1941. A month later 8,000 Jewish men were rounded up and marched a few miles beyond the outskirts where they were murdered and buried in mass graves. A few individuals escaped from the mass graves. A similar *Aktion* was carried out a few days later against 3,000 Jewish men, including the elderly and children. They were executed in the nearby village of Kozlakowicze. After these executions a series of repressive economic measures were enforced. On one occasion the Jews of Pinsk were asked to hand over 20 kilograms of gold.

The first head of the *Judenrat was David Alper; he resigned after a short time and was executed in August 1941. He was succeeded by Benjamin Bokczański. A crowded ghetto was established toward the end of April 1942, where 13 square feet were allotted per person. Some 30 to 40 Jews a day died there from starvation and epidemics, and some risked their lives to bring in food to the ghetto. The Judenrat established a hospital, a public kitchen, and some places of work. In July 1942 all the patients in the Jewish hospital were murdered. Soon afterward, groups of Jews secretly organized resistance. On Oct. 28, 1942, the final *Aktion* took place and all the Pinsk Jews, with the exception of 150 artisans, were killed. During this *Aktion* a desperate attempt was made by the resistance group to break through the cordon of German soldiers. Some managed to reach the forests but were caught by the local population, and a very few succeeded in joining the partisans. On Dec. 23, 1942, the remaining 150 artisans were executed at the local cemetery and the ghetto was liquidated. The swamps and forests around Pinsk sheltered many Jews. Polesie served as a base for partisan activities in which many Jews who escaped from the ghettos and from execution participated either as individuals or as Jewish units. After the war, under the Soviet regime, community life was not renewed in Pinsk, although Jewish families settled there. In 1970 the Jewish population was estimated at 1,500. There was no synagogue. The last prayerhouse had been closed down by the police in 1966. The old Karlin cemetery, desecrated by the Nazis, was converted by the Soviet authorities into a park in 1959. The Jews did not comply with the request of the authorities to remove the bones for reinternment in the Pinsk cemetery.

[Aharon Weiss]

BIBLIOGRAPHY: S. Dubnow, *Pinkas ha-Medinah* (1925); I. Halpern, in: *Horeb*, 2 (1935), additions to the above work; idem, in: *Zion*, 3 (1938), 51–57 (*Yehudim ve-Yahadut be-Mizrah Eiropah* (1969), 48–54); M. Nadaw, in: *Zion*, 31 (1966), 153–96; 34 (1969), 98–108; idem, *Toledot Kehillat-Pinsk, 1506–1706* (dissertation, Heb. Univ. of Jerusalem, 1964); idem, in: Israel Historical Society, *Koveẓ Harẓa'ot* (1968), 159–77; A. Shochat, *ibid.*, 12 (1965), 121–33; Meir b. Samuel of Szczebreszyn, *Ẓok ha-Ittim* (Cracow, 1650); N.N. Hannover, *Yeven Meẓullah* (Venice, 1653); N. Tamir (ed.), *Sefer Edut ve-Zikkaron li-Kehillat Pinsk-Karlin*, 2 vols. (vol. 2, 1966; vol. 1 in print); S.M. Rabinowitz, in: *Talpiyyot* (1895); M. Wilenský, *Ḥasidim u-Mitnaggedim* (1970); H. Tchemerinsky, *Ayarati Motele* (1951); Ḥ. Weizmann-Lichtenstein, *Be-Ẓel Koratenu* (1948); A.A. Feinstein, *Megillat ha-Puraniyyot* (1929); J. Eliasberg, *Be-Olam ha-Hafikhot* (1965); C. Weizmann, *Massah u-Ma'as* (1949); idem, *Letters and Papers*, 1 (1968); M. Shomer Zunser, *Yesterday* (1939); B. Hoffman (ed.), *Toyznt Yor Pinsk: Geshikhte fun der Shtot* (1941); A. Luria, in: *YIVO Bleter*, 13 (1938), 390–428; M. Karman, *Mayne Zikhroynes; Hundert Yor Pinsk* (stencil, Haifa, 1953); Z. Rabinowitsch, in: *He-Avar*, 17 (1970), 252–80: *Pinsker Shtodt Luekh*, 2 vols. (1903–04); K. Kontrym, *Podroż Kontryma... odbyta wroki 1829 po Polesiu* (Poznan, 1839); S.A. Bershadski, *Russko-yevreyski arkhiv*, 1–2 (1882); idem, *Litovskiye yevrei* (1883); idem, in: *Yevreyskaya Biblioteka*, 8 (1880), 1–32 (suppl.); *Regesty i nadpisi*, 2 vols. (1899–1912); Yu. Janson, *Pinsk i yego rayon* (1869); I. Zelenski, *Materilay dlya geografii i statistiki Rossii: Minskaya guberniya*, 2 pts. (1864). HOLOCAUST AND POSTWAR PERIODS: *Sefer ha-Partizanim ha-Yehudim*, 1 (1958), index; M. Kahanovich, *Milḥemet ha-Partizanim ha-Yehudiyyim be-Mizraḥ Eiropah* (1954), index. **ADD. BIBLIOGRAPHY:** Shmuel Spektor (ed.), *Pinkas ha-Kehillot Poland*, vol. 5 – *Volhynia ve-Polesie* (1999).

PINSKER, LEON (Judah Leib; 1821–1891), leader of the *Ḥibbat Zion movement. Born in Tomaszow, Poland, Pinsker studied at the school of his father Simḥah *Pinsker, a Hebrew writer and scholar, in Odessa. He was one of the first Jews to attend Odessa University, where he studied law. However, he discovered that being a Jew, he had no chance of becoming a lawyer and studied medicine at the University of Moscow, returning to practice in Odessa in 1849. Pinsker was one of the founders of the first Russian Jewish weekly, *Razsvet* ("Dawn"), to which he was a regular contributor. The editors attempted to acquaint the Jewish population with Russian culture and encourage them to speak Russian. These aims were more strongly expressed in the weekly Russian-language publication *Sion*, which replaced *Razsvet* and of which Pinsker was one of the editors for about half a year. He was also one of the founders of the Odessa branch of the Society for the Dissemination of Enlightenment among Jews, whose aim was similar to that of the periodical. Pinsker contributed to the Russian-language weekly *Den* ("Day"), founded by the society, which called on Jews to assimilate into Russian society. The pogroms that began in 1871 in Odessa severely shook the enlightened Jews; the weekly stopped publication, and the Odessa branch of the society closed down. Thereafter, Pinsker concentrated on medicine and published a book in German on the medicinal value of the sea and the Liman spa at Odessa (Vienna, 1881). He also became prominent in local public life. When, after an interval of six years, the Odessa Branch of the Society for the Dissemination of Enlightenment was reopened, Pinsker was elected to its committee and helped to collect documentation on the history of the Jews in Russia.

The pogroms that broke out in southern Russia in 1881 and the undisguised antisemitism of the government had a profound effect on Pinsker and caused him to undergo a complete change of heart. He ceased to regard the spreading of Enlightenment and the Haskalah movement as the solution to the future of Russian Jewry, doubted the value of the emancipation of European Jewry, and did not believe that hatred of the Jews would be overcome by humanist ideals. He followed the debates in Jewish newspapers as to which countries were suitable for Jewish emigration. They discussed the need for an emigration organization, some demanding that Jewish emigration be channeled into one country in which a national center be created, in essence a Jewish state. Moses *Lilienblum was an advocate of the Ḥibbat Zion movement's demands that Jews immigrate to the Land of Israel. He saw antisemitism rooted in the fact that Jews were foreigners, a minority of strangers; Pinsker studied the problem of the fate of the Jewish people and reached similar conclusions. In his trip to Italy, to seek a cure for his heart disease (1882), he included visits to the capitals of Western Europe – Vienna, Berlin, Paris, and London – to discuss with leading personalities the need to channel Russian Jewish emigration into one country and to establish a national Jewish center. The chief rabbi of Vienna, Adolph *Jellinek, was unimpressed with the idea. In Paris, the leaders of the *Alliance Israélite Universelle rejected his suggestions; they supported immigration to the U.S., without territorial aims. The person most impressed with Pinsker's ideas was Arthur Cohen, a member of parliament and chairman of the Board of Deputies of British Jews in London. Together they emphasized the need to regard the Jewish question as an international problem and to win governments over to the idea.

It was at Cohen's suggestion that Pinsker published his famous work *"Autoemancipation." Mahnruf an seine Stammesgenossen von einem russischen Juden* (1882), in which he analyzed the psychological and social roots of antisemitism and called for the establishment of a Jewish national center. The book was intended to serve as a warning to his fellow Jews (*Stammesgenossen*) and was published anonymously, the author defining himself as "a Russian Jew." The book was written in a passionate style which forcefully expressed the author's deep anxiety for the fate of his people.

Pinsker first states that the reason for the old-new Jewish problem is the existence of the Jews as a separate ethnic entity among the nations, an entity which cannot be assimilated. The radical solution is the acquisition of a Jewish homeland, a country where they can live and which will be theirs, just like other nations. At best, Jews reach technical equality, but this legal change of status is not a real, social, emancipation. There are also economic reasons for antisemitism, because in competition, preference is given to one's own ethnic group and the foreigner is discriminated against. There is a saturation point to the number of Jews in each country, and when they exceed this point, persecution begins.

Pinsker directs his attacks against Western Jewry, the "diploma chasers" who view the dispersion of Jews throughout the world as a "mission." Moreover, the religious approach that the exile must be suffered in silence until the coming of the Messiah also weakened the desire for a Jewish homeland. He indicates that national consciousness has awakened in Russian and Romanian Jewry, in the form of a movement to settle in Ereẓ Israel. Pinsker did not wish to decide whether Ereẓ Israel or a territory in America should be chosen as a Jewish homeland, since he felt that a national Jewish congress should decide the matter. He hoped that the worldwide process of national awakening would be of benefit to the Jewish people and that other nations would help them achieve national independence. He called on Western Jewry and on its "existing alliances" (meaning the Alliance Israélite Universelle, the *Anglo-Jewish Association, etc.) to lighten the suffering of their brethren by founding a homeland and advocated the convocation of a National Jewish Congress to organize the new exodus. In order to settle destitute emigrants, a national fund should also be established.

The book had strong repercussions, both in Russia and abroad. The Ḥovevei Zion received it enthusiastically, though it had many opponents. Lilienblum attempted to convince Pinsker not to wait for a decision by Western Jewry, but to work immediately toward the realization of the plan in Ereẓ Israel. Pinsker, however, refused to make a decision as to the location of the homeland. Nevertheless, Hermann *Schapira, who accompanied Lilienblum, managed to win him over in the summer of 1883. Discussions, also attended by Max *Mandelstamm from Kiev and several others, led to the decision to work for the establishment of a center for Jewish settlement, in Ereẓ Israel if possible, and to convene a congress, with the participation of the Ḥibbat Zion movement, to choose a central executive committee. Afterward Pinsker held a meeting of community leaders at his house, and they chose a committee to organize the movement; he was elected chairman, with Lilienblum as secretary. The committee made contact with existing groups of the Ḥibbat Zion movement, and encouraged the establishment of new groups. The Warsaw branch of the movement was also active in organizing a convention, which met at *Kattowitz on Nov. 6, 1884, and was attended by members of the Ḥibbat Zion from Russia and abroad. Pinsker was chosen chairman of the convention, and in his opening speech he indicated the need for Jews to return to working the land. He did not mention national revival or independence, since this new movement wished to attract Western Jews. At his suggestion, the convention decided to found the Montefiore Association for the dissemination of the idea of agriculture among Jews and to engage their support for Jewish settlers in Ereẓ Israel. Pinsker was elected chairman of the temporary executive committee, whose seat was in Odessa.

Attempts to establish a central bureau of the Ḥovevei Zion outside Russia failed, and Odessa thus remained the center of the movement. Pinsker invited Lilienblum to become secretary of the Odessa office. The limited activities of the committee and its small income, which did not permit any large-scale settlement activity but served to support only a very small number of settlers; the lack of legalization of the committee's activities and internal feuds; and Pinsker's ailing health caused him to resign. He called a convention in Druskieniki (summer, 1887), at which he intended to hand in his resignation and then travel abroad to seek a cure. At the convention, relations worsened between the Orthodox and the *maskilim*. Pinsker handed in his resignation, but a majority of delegates asked him to continue at his post, and he agreed to do so. Six advisory wardens, including three rabbis, were elected to the leadership.

While abroad, Pinsker attempted to work for the movement. In Paris he met Baron Edmond de *Rothschild, who promised to help the *Petaḥ Tikvah settlement and to acquire land. Rothschild's associates told Pinsker that they would collaborate with the Ḥovevei Zion only if he headed it. As a result, Pinsker ceased to consider resigning immediately. The rabbis who were advisory wardens caused Pinsker considerable difficulty in their demands in religious matters. The declining situation in the movement and his failing health again caused Pinsker to consider resigning. He did not attend the convention held in Vilna in the summer of 1889 for he feared he would be persuaded to continue at his post. At this convention, Samuel *Mohilewer attempted to become head of the movement, but at Pinsker's suggestion in a letter to the convention, Abraham Gruenberg, a resident of Odessa, was chosen as active warden, together with Mohilewer and Samuel Joseph Fuenn. The center of the movement thus remained in Odessa.

In 1890, the Ḥovevei Zion was legalized in Odessa under the name Society for the Support of Jewish Farmers and Artisans in Syria and Palestine (see *Odessa Committee) and Pinsker was again asked to be its head. He agreed, despite his grave doubts about whether the new committee would succeed any better than the old one. While the committee was carrying on its first activities, the Ḥovevei Zion movement revived in Russia, and Jews began to settle in Ereẓ Israel as a result of worsening conditions of Russian Jewry and the expulsion of Jews from Moscow (1891). Pinsker began to hope that his dream would come true in Ereẓ Israel. However, the Turkish authorities issued a prohibition on immigration, and the movement underwent a crisis. The Jaffa committee, which represented the Odessa center, ran into debt, many acquisitions of land in Ereẓ Israel were cancelled, and the contributions of associations for settling the land were lost. Pinsker, who was pessimistic by nature, began to doubt whether Ereẓ Israel would serve as the solution for saving masses of Jews from persecution. He began to believe that the activities of Baron Maurice de *Hirsch, who founded the Jewish Colonization *Association (ICA) for the settlement of Jews in Argentina, might solve the problem.

Toward his death, he reached the conclusion that Ereẓ Israel would remain only the spiritual center of the Jewish people. He expressed these opinions in an article that he read to Lilienblum 20 days before his death and which was intended to serve as a supplement to the English edition of *Autoemancipation*, shortly to be published. Despite Pinsker's wish to publicize his new attitude, the article was never published. His funeral was the occasion for a large Jewish demonstration. In his will he left the sum of 16,000 rubles to various institutions, but only 2,000 rubles to the Odessa committee. In 1934 his remains were transferred and buried in the Cave of Nicanor on Mount Scopus in Jerusalem.

BIBLIOGRAPHY: B. Netanyahu, in: *Road to Freedom*… (1944), 7–73; N. Sokolow, *Ḥibbath Zion* (Eng., 1935), index; idem, *History of Zionism*, 2 (1919), index; A. Druyanow, *Pinsker u-Zemmano* (1953); idem, *Ketavim le-Toledot Ḥibbat Ẓiyyon ve-Yishuv Ereẓ-Yisrael*, 3 vols. (1919–32), index; Y. Klausner (ed.), *Sefer Pinsker* (1921); idem, *Ha-Tenu'ah le-Ẓiyyon be-Rusyah*, 3 vols. (1962–65); M. Yoeli, *J.L. Pinsker* (Heb., 1960); A. Hertzberg (ed.), *Zionist Idea* (1960), 178–98 and introd., passim; B. Dinur, *Mefallesei Derekh* (1946), 21–61; S. Breiman, in: *Shivat Ẓiyyon*, 3–4 (1953), 205–27.

[Israel Klausner]

PINSKER, SIMḤAH (1801–1864), scholar. Pinsker was born in Tarnow, Galicia. Educated at home by his father, an eminent preacher (*Maggid*), he at first engaged in commerce, but lack of success induced him to move to Odessa, where he became secretary to the local rabbi. He also founded in 1826 the first successful modern Jewish school in Russia, in which he taught Hebrew language and literature. At the same time he published a series of learned papers in the periodical *Orient*, and when the famous Karaite savant Abraham *Firkovich visited Odessa, Pinsker examined and described several of the ancient Hebrew manuscripts collected by him. His work eventually earned him gold medals from the Russian government and a pension from the Jewish community of Odessa. Relieved from the daily need to earn a living, Pinsker moved to Vienna in order to devote all of his time to research, and there in 1860 he published his major work, *Likkutei Kadmoniyyot*, a history of Karaism and Karaite literature, with copious extracts from hitherto unpublished Karaite works in Hebrew and Arabic. It is these original extracts which lend his work its permanent value. His own contribution is now largely antiquated, particularly his exaggerated idea of the role of the early Karaite scholars, whom he erroneously regarded not only as the sole founders of the study of Hebrew grammar and lexicography, but also as the pioneers in medieval Hebrew poetry and the precursors of the great Rabbanite poets in Spain, such as Ibn Gabirol and Judah Halevi. Some of Pinsker's misconceptions were the result of Firkovich's tendentious advice or were based on data forged by Firkovich in his zeal to magnify the otherwise very substantial contribution of Karaism to medieval Jewish learning. Pinsker subsequently returned to Odessa.

Pinsker's philological works are *Mavo el ha-Nikkud ha-Ashuri o ha-Bavli*, on the Babylonian Hebrew punctuation, with an appendix containing an annotated edition of Abraham *Ibn Ezra's *Yesod Mispar* (Vienna, 1863); and *Mishlei ha-Gizrah ve-ha-Beniyyah*, on mood and inflection of the Hebrew verb, edited posthumously by S. Rubin (Vienna, 1887). The edition of Abraham Ibn Ezra's *Sefer ha-Eḥad*, begun by Pinsker, was completed by M. Goldhardt and published in Odessa, 1867. His emendations to David *Kimḥi's *Mikhlol* are included in I. Rittenberg's edition of this work (Lyck, 1862). A catalog of Hebrew and Arabic manuscripts in Pinsker's library was published by J. Bardach as *Mazkir li-Venei Re-SHe-F* (Vienna, 1869). Pinsker was the father of Leo *Pinsker, author of *Autoemancipation*.

BIBLIOGRAPHY: A. Druyanow, in: *Ha-Tekufah*, 12 (1922), 215ff.; Zeitlin, Bibliotheca, 269.

[Leon Nemoy]

PINSKI, DAVID (1872–1959). Yiddish author. Born in Mogilev, Russia, Pinski moved to Moscow with his family at 14. He received not only a traditional but also an excellent secular education. He early became interested in literature and in socialism. After living briefly in Vitebsk, he pursued university studies in Vienna and later Berlin, also living in Warsaw, where writer I.L. *Peretz became his mentor. Pinski published his first stories in Mordecai *Spector's *Der Hoyzfraynd* and Peretz's *Yontif Bletlekh* in 1894. Pinski's early writing introduced the Jewish proletariat as a subject in Yiddish literature. He wrote his first full-length play, *Ayzik Sheftl* (1907), which Martin Buber later translated into German, shortly before moving to New York to edit the Socialist Labor Party's Yiddish newspaper *Abend Blat* with labor leader Joseph*Schlossberg. He also pursued a Ph.D. in German at Columbia University.

Pinski married Hudl (Adele) Koyfman in 1897, with whom he had three children, including a son who died at age seven. Hudl helped support the family as a masseuse while Pinski pursued his careers as a Yiddish author, editor, and activist. As activist, Pinski initially sympathized with the Jewish Labor *Bund. In 1912, he joined the Labor Zionist movement, helping to found that movement's North American branch, the Farband, in 1913 and served as its president (1918–21 and 1933–49). He played a role in organizing the Czernowitz Language Conference of 1908 and long proclaimed the slogan "Yiddish but also Hebrew for the Diaspora; Hebrew but also Yiddish in Ereẓ Israel." Pinski served as an editor of *Der Arbeter* (1904–1911), *Yidishe Vokhnshrift* (1912), and later the Farband newspaper *Der Yidisher Arbeter Shtime*, Po'alei Zion's *Der Yidisher Kemfer*, *Di Tsayt*; and the literary journal *Di Tsukunft*. One of his most famous protégés was the humorist Jacob Adler. Pinski also edited the 13-volume collected works of Peretz. He cofounded CYSHO (the Central Yiddish Cultural Organization) in 1941 and the All-World Jewish Culture Congress in 1948. In 1948, he served as president of International PEN's Yiddish section.

Pinski wrote over 25 full-length plays, three novels, scores of short stories and one-act plays, two volumes of travel essays, a screenplay, and one of the first histories of the Yiddish theater. Until the 1940s, he was perhaps the world's most frequently and widely translated Yiddish author. Key plays include *Di Familye Tsvi* ("The Tsvi Family" or "The Last Jew," 1904), written following the Kishinev pogrom, published and smuggled into Russia by the Bund; *Yankl der Shmid* ("Yankl the Blacksmith," 1907), his most frequently performed work, which he adapted into a film for director Edgar G. Ulmer in 1938; and *Der Oytser* ("The Treasure," 1908; Eng. 1915), perhaps his greatest work, a dark comedy about greed in a Jewish town that critic George Pearce Baker compared in achievement to Ben Jonson's *Volpone*. *Yankl der Shmid*, depicting a married blacksmith's relationship with his neighbor's wife, is considered the Yiddish theater's first exploration of illicit sexual passion. Pinski's plays were produced by some of the world's leading theatrical companies. *Der Oytser* was first produced by Max Reinhardt at Berlin's Deutsches Theater in 1911. The Theater Guild produced it in English translation by Ludwig Lewisohn in 1920, as well as *Dos Letste Sakhakl* ("The Last Reckoning," 1926). Konstantin Stanislavski selected Pinski's one-act *Der Eybiker Yid* ("The Eternal Jew") for the Habimah Theatre's inaugural performance in 1918. Other companies to produce Pinski's plays included the Provincetown Players, the Yiddish Art Theater, the Folksbine, and the Vilna Troupe.

Pinski revisited three major themes throughout his dramatic career, often in combination: Jewish history (including dramas about such figures as Noah, King David, Mary Magdalene, and the Baal Shem Tov), the lives of humble or working-class folk (e.g., *Der Oytser*), and the psychology of sexual desire (e.g. *Yankl der Shmid*; *Profesor Brenner*, 1918). Pinski's early drama employed naturalism: the play *Ayzik Sheftl*, about a frustrated inventor trapped in a factory job drew stylistic comparison with *Die Weber* by Gerhart Hauptmann, whom Pinski knew in Berlin. Later Pinski employed techniques of symbolism as well. Though he never abandoned an ethical viewpoint in his work, his characterization and action relied on psychological exploration rather than mere moral or political preaching. His first two novels, *Arnold Levenberg* (serialized in *Der Tog* in 1926; book 1938; Eng. 1928) and *Dos Hoyz fun Noyakh Edon* (1938; *The Generations of Noah Edon*, 1931), were well received in English translation and deal with assimilation in American Jewish life prior to the Depression. The second novel depicts the erosion of Jewish knowledge and practice in three generations of immigrant Noyakh Edon's family, the tragic emptiness in his children's lives, though they become well-educated and affluent Americans, and his grandson's belated suspicion that Judaism could have filled a void in his own life.

In 1949, Pinski settled in Haifa, Israel, where a street is named for him. His 80th birthday was a major state event. He continued to write until paralyzed by a stroke in 1956 and died a few months after his wife in 1959. While some critics find the quality of much of Pinski's prolific body of work to be uneven, he remains a major figure in the history of Yiddish literature, and Chaim Zhitlovski, among others, has classified Pinski as the fourth classic writer of Yiddish literature after Sh.Y. *Abramovitsh, *Sholem Aleichem, and I.L. *Peretz.

BIBLIOGRAPHY: Rejzen, Leksikon 2 (1927), 885–98; S. Niger, *Dertseyler un Romanistn* (1946), 282–319; Z. Zylbercweig, *Leksikon fun Yidishn Teater*, 3 (1959), 1762–806; M. Singer (ed.), *David Pinski Zikhrono li-Verakhah* (1960); S. Liptzin, *Flowering of Yiddish Literature* (1963), 118–30; C. Madison, *Yiddish Literature* (1968), 182–96, list of English translations, 525. **ADD. BIBLIOGRAPHY.** M. Shtarkman and L. Rubenshtayn (eds.), *Dovid Pinski: Tsum Tsentn Yortsayt* (1969); Sh. Rozhanski, in: *Di Goldene Keyt*, 135 (1993), 5–13; N. Sandrow (ed. and tr.), *God, Man and Devil: Yiddish Plays in Translation* (1999), 20–4, 184–9.

[Moshe Starkman / Ben Furnish (2nd ed.)]

PINSKY, ROBERT (1940–), U.S. poet and critic. Author of six collections of his own poetry and five important books of literary criticism, as well as translations of Milosz and Dante, Pinsky is the only American poet to have held the post of Poet Laureate Consultant to the Library of Congress for three consecutive years (1997–2000). The appointments to the position allowed him to bring to fruition what he called the Favorite Poem Project. Contrary to conventional notions of the philistinism of American culture, Pinsky believed that lyric poetry continued to be a vital presence in the lives of ordinary American citizens. Thus the Favorite Poem Project invited readers to send in short prose statements explaining why their favorite poem was important to them. From an abundant initial response various readers were selected for a series of video recordings that presented them reading the poems that they treasured. There followed two anthologies of those poems and a digital archive, the sum total of which bore witness to what Pinsky claimed was the hidden but vital presence of poetry far beyond the walls of the universities and research libraries.

Revealing an underground life of the spirit in the postmodern era is the central act of Pinsky's own poetry as well. His work assays and charts the life of the soul amid the swirling and always perplexing currents of the contemporary. Pinsky sometimes seems to wonder whether there is such a thing as a soul to worry about, but more often he measures the labors, passions, and effortful creations of human beings – however flawed – as visible and invaluable signs of the soul's existence. His restless intelligence, his abiding curiosity about how the soul fares – be it for good or ill – has been with him from his first book of poetry, *Sadness and Happiness* (1973), where he notes in the first poem the "terrible gaze of a unique/Soul, its need unlovable." The concern is still there in his most recent book, *Jersey Rain* (2000), in "The Haunted Ruin," where Pinsky writes that everything we touch leaves something of ourselves in it. Even in our machines, our computers and handsaws, there thus remains a residue of ourselves, a "machine soul."

Pinsky's skeptical, troubled but surprisingly firm faith that there is a soul has its analogue in his attitude toward God. All sorts of gods thickly populate his collections of poetry. They range from Yahweh to Shiva to Jesus to Hermes and beyond to various lesser spirits, prophets, heroes, and all those who traffic with the gods. Pinsky's religious themes are heterodox, ironic, and inclusive, but they are also nonetheless grounded in the intellectual inheritance of Judaism. Raised in what he has called "a nominally Orthodox" Jewish family, in a working-class neighborhood of Long Branch, N.J., Pinsky attended Rutgers for his B.A. and Stanford for his Ph.D. He taught at Wellesley College, the University of California, Berkeley, and then in the graduate creative writing program at Boston University. Thus there is also a streak of the scholarly in his work, for he seems to study Judaism (as well as any other religion or manifestation of culture) as part of the abiding human impulse toward meaning. The stance he takes in some of his poems reminds one of Job facing the whirlwind, a whirlwind that one might call God, or History, or Fate, or Civilization. The best example of this is in "The Figured Wheel," a poem that gives its name to the title of his *New and Collected Poems* (1996), where Pinsky stands stunned by an impersonal power, rolling through our lives and throughout history. It is also perhaps his sense that there are impersonal spirits moving in the world that led Pinsky also to his translation of Dante's *Inferno* (1994).

At other times, however, Pinsky seems a contemporary psalmist, praising the surprising ways in which the gods reveal themselves. In "To Television," from *Jersey Rain*, Pinsky likens the "boob-tube" to Hermes, and sings its praises for the strange comfort it sometimes brings, however bad the rest of its news may be. In this context, it is significant that Pinsky's book of prose *The Life of David* (2005) speaks of an "obdurate calculus of pain." That too is an essential part of his psalmlike poems. One hears the stern facts of human suffering woven through the very fabric of a poem like "Shirt," from *The Want Bone* (1990). Here the speaker fingers a shirt, admiring each part of its construction, and as he does he thinks of the fire at the Triangle Shirtwaist Factory in 1911, and recalls the photos of workers leaping from the windows, which then links him to thoughts of heaven and the afterlife, and the poetry of George Herbert, the English metaphysical, author of a poem called "The Collar." That thought brings him back to the shirt and a woman named Irma who has left a tag in it saying it was she who inspected this shirt. Up, down, and across the spans of human history, culture, and suffering, the poem not only praises the shirt, but all that is human and woven into that which we wear on our backs.

Yet for all the centrality of matters of soul and faith to Pinsky's work, there remains an equally firm and open-ended commitment to experience, to this world, to history, and to the turbulent vitality of lives lived. In meditations such as his book-length *An Explanation of America* (1980) or in the more recent "An Alphabet of My Dead" in *Jersey Rain,* one senses above all in this poetry an earned freedom of thought and feeling. As with William Carlos Williams, another great poet of New Jersey and urban America, one has the feeling that there is nothing in this world or the next that Pinsky conceives of as alien to poetry. Though fonder of traditional and more formal poetry than Williams was, Pinsky is nonetheless in the direct line of descent from Williams in regard to his sense of the vitality of the art. In his most important collection of essays, *The Poet and the World* (1988), Pinsky argues that "only the challenge of what may seem unpoetic, that which has not already been made poetic by the tradition, can keep the art truly pure and alive." The ongoing transformation of the apparently "anti-poetic" into poetry of the first order is one of the great revelations that the work of Robert Pinsky continues to offer.

BIBLIOGRAPHY: J. Longenbach, *Modern Poetry After Modernism* (1997); W. Spiegelman, *The Didactic Muse* (1989).

[Frederick J. Marchant (2nd ed.)]

PINSON, KOPPEL S. (1904–1961), U.S. historian. Born in Lithuania, Pinson was taken to the U.S. in 1907. He lectured at the New School for Social Research from 1934 to 1937, when he went to Queens College, N.Y., becoming professor of history in 1950. He was also history editor of the *Encyclopedia of the Social Sciences* (1929–35), and an editor of *Jewish Social Studies* (1938–61). In 1945–46, he was director of education and culture, Jewish Displaced Persons in Germany and Austria, United Nations Relief and Rehabilitation Association.

Pinson's principal scholarly interests embraced modern European history, with special emphasis on nationalism and modern Germany, and recent Jewish history. His contributions to general history were *Pietism as a Factor in the Rise of German Nationalism* (1934); *A Bibliographical Introduction to Nationalism* (1935); and *Modern Germany, Its History and Civilization* (1954). In Jewish studies, he edited a number of important books: *Essays on Anti-Semitism* (1946^2); *Yivo Annual of Jewish Social Science*, vols. 59 (1950–54); and notably *Nationalism and History* (1958), which made available in English Simon Dubnow's classic, *Essays on Old and New Judaism*. Pinson analyzed Dubnow's national theories and appraised his role as historian. Pinson was actively involved in the work of the *Yivo Institute for Jewish Research. He was also chairman of the modern Jewish history committee of the Jewish Publication Society of America.

[Oscar Isaiah Janowsky]

PINTER, HAROLD (1930–2005), English playwright, Nobel laureate. Born in Hackney, London, the son of a tailor, Pinter was on the stage from 1949 to 1957 under the name of David Baron, acting chiefly in repertory and with touring companies in Ireland. His first plays to become known were written for radio, a medium admirably suited to the rather sinister ambiguity of his early work. To this period belong *The Room, The Dumb Waiter,* and *The Birthday Party* (1958). The last play is symbolic of the universal guilt of man, with the central figure as a scapegoat. Pinter's subsequent plays include *The Caretaker,* produced in 1960, which is generally classed as a tragicomedy belonging to the genre of the "theater of the absurd." It shows a homeless tramp billeting himself upon two brothers, under the pretense of taking care of their home. He emerges, however, as a type of suffering humanity, making what may be felt to be excessive claims upon men's charity. *The Caretaker* was an outstanding success on stage, screen, and television. The plays Pinter wrote in the 1960s were dominated by the husband-wife relationship and several were acted by his wife, Vivien Merchant. *The Lover* (1963) depicts a marriage which can only function if both partners pretend that it is an illicit love affair. *The Homecoming* (1964), which won the New York Drama Critics Circle Award for best new play in 1967, is about an English intellectual who brings a new wife back from the U.S. to meet his crude, working-class family. In this phase of his writing, Pinter was concerned with the frailty of marital relationships, with the potential violence of family life, and with the impossibility of ever knowing or possessing a woman. His other plays include *A Night Out* (1960), *The Collection* (1961), *Tea Party* (1964), and *Old Times* (1971).

Pinter first became involved in writing screenplays when he adapted *The Caretaker* for the screen as *The Guest* in 1963. After that he earned two Academy Award nominations for best screenplay, for his adaptation of John Fowles' novel *The French Lieutenant's Woman* in 1981 and for his adaptation of his own play, *Betrayal*, in 1983. His adaptation of L.P. Hartley's novel *The Go-Between* won him a BAFTA award in 1971. Other screenplays include his 1968 version of *The Birthday Party* for the screen, *Reunion* (1989), *The Handmaid's Tale* (1990, based on a novel by Margaret Atwood), and *The Trial* (1993, based on Kafka's novel).

Pinter's later plays saw him shifting his focus away from the sinister underbelly of urban society and onto an upper-middle-class setting that more closely reflected his own milieu. In addition to *Betrayal* (1978), they include *No Man's Land* (1975). Pinter is also an occasional contributor of poetry to certain London journals, where he uses the pen name Harold Pinta.

In 2002 Pinter was made a Companion of Honour (CH). In later years he became well-known as a left-wing political activist over a range of international issues including Chile, Yugoslavia, and the 2003 Iraq War. After his divorce from Vivien Merchant in 1980, Pinter married the best-selling historian Lady Antonia Fraser. One of the most famous of all modern British playwrights, Pinter has attracted many biographical and critical studies, among them biographies by R. Hayman (1975), Michael Billington (1997), Martin S. Rega (1995), and Volker Strunk (1998). In 2005 he was awarded the Nobel Prize for literature.

BIBLIOGRAPHY: M. Esslin, *Theater of the Absurd* (1961); idem, *The People Wound: The Work of Harold Pinter* (1970); J.R. Taylor, *Anger and After* (1960).

[Philip D. Hobsbaum / Rohan Saxena]

PINTO, name of several families who originated in the small town of Pinto, whose Jewish community was subordinate to that of Madrid. Some Pintos arrived in *Morocco from the Iberian Peninsula, particularly from Seville, in 1492 and 1496 and from the Canary Islands during the 16th century. The latter were former Marranos who settled in Agadir and Marrakesh, where they ranked among the spiritual and lay leaders of the Jewish communities of those towns. R. JACOB (d. c. 1750), a disciple of R. Abraham Azulai and a well-known kabbalist, wrote a lengthy commentary on the Zohar. His son, R. ABRAHAM (d. after 1800), was a *dayyan* in Marrakesh. The latter's commentary on the tractate *Ketubbot* is often mentioned in the work *Sefer Ḥesed ve-Emet* (Salonika, 1803). There are many manuscripts of his responsa and *haskamot*. R. ḤAYYIM (d. before 1840) was chief rabbi of Mogador, where he was revered as a saint. Pilgrimages are still made to his grave. ABRAHAM BEN REUBEN (c. 1750) was one of the leaders of the Jewish community of Agadir. A financier, he wielded considerable influence; the sultan of Morocco entrusted him with economic missions to Europe. During the 19th century the Pintos were prominent in the communities of northern Morocco, especially in Tangier and later in Casablanca, where their commercial importance was considerable down to the present day.

BIBLIOGRAPHY: E. de Avila, *Be'er Mayim Ḥayyim* (1806), 70–71; Azulai, 67; J.M. Toledano, *Ner ha-Ma'arav* (1911), 161, 190.

[David Corcos]

PINTO, DE, family of Dutch jurists of Sephardi origin. ABRAHAM DE PINTO (1811–1878), Dutch jurist and public worker, was the elder brother of Aaron Adolf de Pinto. He graduated in law from the University of Leiden. He became editor of the law journal *Weekblad voor het recht* in 1835 and in 1840 founded the juridical review *Themis* which he edited for 36 years. De Pinto also published digests of several Dutch legal codes which served to make known the principles of Dutch law after the Codification of 1838. He was dean of the Order of Advocates in The Hague and a Hague municipal councilor from 1851 until 1878. As chairman of The Hague Sephardi congregation, De Pinto unsuccessfully favored cooperation between the Sephardi and Ashkenazi communities in contrast to many of his contemporaries. In 1850 he established the Maatschappij tot nut der Israëlieten in Nederland (Association for the Benefit of the Jews in Holland) for the promotion of educational and vocational training for poor Jews. AARON ADOLF DE PINTO (1828–1908) was a Dutch criminal lawyer. Born in The Hague, De Pinto graduated in law from the University of Leiden. As a high official at the Netherlands Ministry of Justice from 1862 to 1876, he was largely responsible for the adoption of a New Netherlands penal code which came into force in 1886, and for the Dutch East Indies Penal Code. In 1865 De Pinto initiated and drafted the law on the abolition of the death penalty. This was adopted in 1871, against the opposition of successive ministers of justice. Subsequently he drafted the law for the complete revision of the Netherlands code of civil procedure. Rejecting the offer of a professorship and the cabinet portfolio of justice, De Pinto became a member of the Supreme Court. In 1903 he was appointed vice president. From 1878 to 1901 he was an editor of the *Weekblad voor het recht*, and a founder of the Netherlands Association of Jurists. Among De Pinto's numerous publications are several on the Dreyfus trial, showing that it was being conducted in violation of French legal procedure. In 1885, at a lawyers' conference in Rotterdam, he championed the rights of the Romanian Jews. For many years he was chairman of the Maatschappij tot nut der Israëlieten in Nederland (founded by his brother), and in 1908 officially opened the Eighth Zionist Congress in The Hague.

BIBLIOGRAPHY: A.A. De Pinto, *Mr. Abraham de Pinto…* (1879).

[Henriette Boas]

PINTO, ISAAC (1720–1791), U.S. merchant and translator of prayer books. Emigrating to the U.S. from the West Indies, where one branch of the Pinto family was established, Pinto settled in Connecticut; an Isaac Pinto is listed in *Colonial Records of Connecticut* as living in Stratford during 1748. By 1751 Pinto was a resident of New York City and a member of Congregation Shearith Israel. Ezra Stiles, president of Yale College, identified him as a "learned Jew at New York." Pinto, who signed the Non-Importation Act, was a devoted patriot. The anonymous English translation in *Evening Services for Rosh-Hashanah and Yom Kippur* (New York, 1761) is attributed to Pinto; this rendering and his acknowledged translation in *Prayers for Sabbath, Rosh-Hashanah and Yom Kippur, with the Amidah and Musaph of the Moadim* of the Sephardi rite (New York, 1766) are the earliest English translations of Hebrew prayer books published in the New World. That a translation was needed indicates, in the view of Grinstein, a low level of Hebrew learning in the colonies at that time.

BIBLIOGRAPHY: D. de S. Pool, *Portraits Etched in Stone* (1952); I. Abrahams, *By-Paths in Hebraic Bookland* (1920), 171–7; L. Huehner, in: JE, s.v.; H. Grinstein, *Rise of the Jewish Community of New York* (1945).

[Leo Hershkowitz]

PINTO, ISAAC DE (1717–1787), philosopher and economist of Portuguese-Jewish origin. Born perhaps in Bordeaux, Pinto lived mostly in Holland. A widely cultured man with a combative pen, he defended the Jewish people against *Voltaire's *Dictionnaire Philosophique* article *"Juifs"* in his well-known *Apologie pour la Nation Juive* (Amsterdam, 1762). He sent a copy of this work to Voltaire, who thanked him but held to his opinions. Pinto's major work on economics is the *Traité de la circulation et du crédit* (Amsterdam, 1771), one of the great documents in the history of political economy, written in refutation of the physiocrats, who advocated an economy based mainly on agriculture. Other works by Pinto are his *Essai sur le luxe* (Amsterdam, 1762), *Précis des arguments contre les matérialistes* (The Hague, 1774), and *Du jeu de cartes* (1768), a short essay on card playing which he addressed to *Diderot. For his services in arranging favorable terms for English trade in India at the Treaty of Paris, which ended the Seven Years' War (1756–63), Pinto was lavishly rewarded by the East India Company a few years later (1767).

De Pinto was, as Voltaire said, a *philosophe* and a Jew. He had a broad general 18th-century education, as evidenced by two unpublished philosophical discourses from 1742. His attack on Voltaire, whom he admired, was more a defense of the Sephardim than of Judaism. He suggested that Voltaire's antisemitic criticisms were justified against the Ashkenazim, but that the Sephardim were cultured and enlightened. In economics, De Pinto opposed the physiocrats, and advocated (against Hume) the economically productive role of the national debt, and modern credit and commerce. Opposed by Adam Smith, he was seen by Dugald Stewart and Sir Francis D'Ivernois as an important new economist. Marx called him "the Pindar of the Amsterdam stock exchange" for his advocacy of speculation. Werner *Sombart regarded him as the beginner of the modern age of economics, and the first to understand the growth of credit. Sée claimed he was the first to say that speculation was useful. Hertzberg saw De Pinto's economics as a covert defense of the role of Jews in 18th-century economic affairs. De Pinto was a conservative in philosophy and politics. A Deist, he opposed D'Holbach's materialistic atheism as a menace to the social order. He offered proofs of the existence of God and the immortality of the soul (borrowing from Mendelssohn among others), but not appealing to any biblical evidence. His criticisms of the American Revolution opposed popular democracy and defended the economic rights of the colonial powers, and the need for them to join together to maintain peace and social harmony.

De Pinto was a Jew of the Enlightenment (he knew Voltaire, Hume, Diderot, Marat, among others). He was a genuine innovator in economic theory, and a moderate, tolerant, pacifistic conservative in its politics and philosophy. Manuscript 48A19 of Ets Haim library (Amsterdam) contains many unpublished works of De Pinto, including two philosophical discourses.

BIBLIOGRAPHY: M.B. Amzalak, *O economista Isaac Pinto* (1922); J.S. Wijler, *Isaac de Pinto, sa vie et ses oeuvres* (1923), incl. bibl.; A. Guenée, *Lettres de quelques juifs… M. de Voltaire* (Paris, 1769), letters 2, 3, and 4; *Biographie universelle*, 34 (1823), 484–6; Sutherland, in: *English Historical Review*, 62 (1947), 189; A. Hertzberg, *French Enlightenment and the Jews* (1968), index.

[Richard H. Popkin]

PINTO, JOSIAH BEN JOSEPH (1565–1648), talmudist and kabbalist. Born in *Damascus, Pinto was for the major part of his life rabbi in Damascus, but went to Jerusalem about 1617. In 1625 he decided to settle in Safed, but when his son died in the following year, he returned to Damascus. His teacher in subjects other than Kabbalah was Jacob *Abulafia, who ordained him. In Kabbalah he adhered closely to the system of Ḥayyim *Vital whose son, Samuel, was his pupil and subsequently married his daughter.

Pinto is best known for his *Me'or Einayim* (part 1, Amsterdam, 1643; part 2, Mantua, 1743), a commentary on *Ein Ya'akov* of Jacob *ibn Ḥabib. He also wrote *Kesef Nivḥar* (Damascus, 1605), sermons on the weekly scriptural readings; part 2, entitled *Kesef Mezukkak* (Venice, 1628), sermons and explanations of unusual rabbinic comments on scriptural passages; *Kesef Ẓaruf (ibid.*, 1629) on the Book of Proverbs; *Nivḥar mi-Kesef* (Aleppo, 1869), responsa. Some of his responsa were in a manuscript of the responsa of his son-in-law, Samuel *Vital, which was in the possession of Ḥ.J. Michael, while others were published in the responsa of Yom Tov *Ẓahalon (Venice, 1694). Some, which he wrote in 1646, were published in the *Yad Aharon*, part 1 (Smyrna, 1735), of Aaron *Alfandari. His *Kesef Nimas*, on Lamentations, and *Kevuẓot Kesef*, on the laws of marriage and the civil laws in the Shulḥan Arukh, are in manuscript. Joseph *Delmedigo mentions a biblical commentary by Pinto entitled *Kesef To'afot*.

BIBLIOGRAPHY: M.D. Gaon, *Yehudei ha-Mizraḥ be-Ereẓ Yisrael*, 2 (1938), 552–3, 743; Conforte, Kore, 49b; Fuenn, Keneset, 382–3; Rosanes, Togarmah, 3 (1938), 231–2; Frumkin-Rivlin, 1 (1928), 51 n. 1, 130; Benayahu, in: *Tarbiz*, 29 (1959/60), 74.

[Samuel Abba Horodezky]

PINTO, VIVIAN DE SOLA (1895–1969), English literary scholar and poet. The son of a tobacconnist on fashionable St. James's Street, London, Pinto became professor of English at the University of Nottingham (1938–1961) and specialized first in 17th-century studies and later in modern literature. His works include two volumes of poetry, *The Invisible Sun* (1934) and *This Is My England* (1941); *Crisis in English Poetry, 1880–1940* (1951, 1967[5]); and an edition of the poems of D.H. Lawrence (1964). He appeared for the defense in the famous 1960 obscenity trial in London of *Lady Chatterley's Lover*, and was a friend of many famous writers including Siegfried *Sassoon, to whom he was second-in-command on the Western Front in World War I.

PINTO DELGADO, JOÃO (**Mosseh**; d. 1653), Portuguese *Marrano poet, born at Vila Nova de Portimão. His grandfather, of the same name, was in government administration in the Algarve, as was João's father, Gonçalo Delgado. On two separate occasions, João lived in Lisbon. His parents, after going to Antwerp, settled in Rouen, c. 1609, where he later joined them. In 1633 some of the Portuguese New Christians in Rouen denounced others as Judaizers, and João and his father took refuge in Antwerp (a brother, Gonçalo, remained in Rouen). João moved to Amsterdam in 1634, followed soon after by his father. In the Dutch city he openly joined the Jewish community and was known as Mosseh Pinto (Delgado). Around 1636, 1637, and 1640, he was one of the seven *parnasim* of the *talmud torah*. João Pinto Delgado began his literary career in Lisbon, where he contributed poetry to works of a purely Catholic nature by João Baptista de Este and Luis de Tovar. In Rouen, in 1627, he published a collection of verse paraphrases of Old Testament books, *Poema de la Reyna Ester, Lamentaciones del Propheta Jeremias y Historia de Rut y varias poesías*, which he dedicated to Cardinal Richelieu. I.S. Révah has published parts of a manuscript autobiography, in prose and verse and written in Holland, in which Pinto Delgado attacked the Inquisition and Christian beliefs, and satirized those New Christians of Rouen who denounced others in 1633.

BIBLIOGRAPHY: João Pinto Delgado, *Poema de la Reina Ester...*, ed. by I.S. Révah (Lisbon, 1954); E.W. Wilson, in: JJS, 1 (1949), 131–42; C. Roth, in: *Modern Language Review*, 30 (1935), 19–25; idem, in: REJ, 121 (1962), 355–66; I.S. Révah, in: REJ, 119 (1961), 41–130.

[Kenneth R. Scholberg]

PIONEER WOMEN, international labor Zionist women's organization, known since 1981 as **Na'amat**. Founded in New York City in 1925, Pioneer Women appealed to idealistic and politically committed women who were part of the eastern European immigrant generation. The organization provided social welfare services for women, young people, and children in Palestine, helped new immigrants become productive citizens there, and encouraged U.S. Jewish women to take a more active part in Jewish community life and U.S. civic affairs. Although its business was originally largely conducted in Yiddish, the organization gradually shifted to English as it became increasingly acculturated to the U.S. scene. By 1936 it had chapters in 60 U.S. cities, with 10,000 members.

After World War II Pioneer Women broadened its field of endeavors, while at the same time moderating its original socialist and feminist ideology; nevertheless, it continued to cooperate with progressive and labor groups on behalf of liberal causes. In cooperation with its sister Israel organization, Mo'ezet ha-Po'alot, Pioneer Women maintained a large network of welfare and cultural projects in Israel. Pioneer Women also stimulated the formation of sister organizations in other countries. The World Union of Pioneer Women's Organizations, which was formed in Tel Aviv in 1964, had member sisterhoods in the United States, Canada, Mexico, Argentina, Brazil, Chile, Peru, Uruguay, Great Britain, Belgium, and Australia. The total world membership of Pioneer Women in 1970 was 150,000.

In later decades, Na'amat/Pioneer Women gradually lost many of its distinctive features, as most of its functions and goals were adopted by mainstream American Jewish groups and institutions. By 2005, U.S. membership in Na'amat had declined to approximately 25,000 from a peak of 50,000 in 1970. In the United States, Na'amat continues to conduct Jewish educational and cultural activities, publishes a quarterly journal, *Na'amat Woman*, and supports youth work through the *Habonim labor Zionist youth movement, founded in 1935. Habonim sustains a network of coeducational year-round activities and summer camps and serves as a training ground for many future leaders of American labor Zionism.

ADD. BIBLIOGRAPHY: M. Raider, "Pioneer Women," in: P.E. Hyman and D.D. Moore, *Jewish Women in America*, vol. 2 (1997), 1071–77.

[Gertrude Hirschler and Shoshana Hareli / Judith R. Baskin (2nd ed.)]

PIOTRKOW (Pol. **Piotrków Trybunalski**; Rus. **Petrokov**; Ger. **Petrikau**), town in Lodz province, central Poland; known from 1578 as Piotrkow-Trybunalski. Several anti-Jewish resolutions were passed at state conventions held in Piotrkow during the 14th to 16th centuries, including a series of limitations by the Sejm (Diet) of 1562. Jews settled in Piotrkow from the first half of the 16th century. In 1569 Jews were permitted by the king to settle in the suburbs of Piotrkow and trade at the fairs there on payment of 30 ducats to the Christian guild. The Jews were expelled following a *blood libel in 1590. During the greater part of the 17th century the municipality prevented Jews from entering Piotrkow, until 1679 when King John II Sobieski permitted Jews to return, to trade there, and to build a synagogue (completed in 1689). During the 1720s, under the first rabbi of Piotrkow, Eliakim Getz, a *ḥevra kaddisha* and Bikkur Ḥolim were organized. In 1744 Jewish self-defense against an attack by the mob was successfully led by Ephraim Fishel. The Jews of the community (about 800) were then compelled to leave the city and settle in the suburbs (Nowa Wiés). A *bet midrash* was founded there in 1765, and a large synagogue was built by the merchant Moses Kazin in 1781.

After the second partition of Poland in 1793, Piotrkow passed to Prussia. In 1808 there were in Piotrkow 1,817 Jews (46% of the total population), and in 1827, 2,133 Jews (45% of the total). After the opening of the Warsaw-Vienna railway line and the development of industries in the region, Jews founded weaving mills in Piotrkow. A growing Jewish proletariat was employed in the timber and textile industries, and in services. In 1857 there were 4,166 Jews (42% of the total population). In 1861 Jews obtained electoral and elective rights on the municipal council. In 1864 a Hebrew printing press was set up in Piotrkow, which in 1900 published the Jerusalem Talmud. Moses David *Szereszewski, the Lithuanian *maskil*, introduced the Ḥibbat Zion movement into Piotrkow in 1880. There were 30 *ḥadarim*, a *talmud torah*, two *battei midrash*, and a private secular school in this period. The Jewish hospital, founded in 1836, was also extended. In 1912 a Zionist workers' party was founded in Piotrkow. The community numbered approximately 5,400 in 1865, 9,370 (33.14%) in 1897, and by 1917 had increased to 14,890.

Some of the Jews who found shelter in Piotrkow during World War I left the town during the establishment of independent Poland (1918). In 1921 there were in Piotrkow 11,630 Jews (28% of the total population). Of the 33 members of the municipal council elected in 1919, seven were Jews. In the 1928 elections their number rose to eight. Between the two world wars new educational institutions were established in Piotrkow by the *Tarbut, CYSHO, and *ORT; and sports organizations (Maccabi, Shtern, etc.) and a musical society, Zamir, were formed. From 1924 the Zionist periodical *Unzer Tsaytung* was published in Piotrkow and Zionist and other youth movements gained in strength. In the elections to the community council in 1935 six representatives of the *Bund were elected. From 1924 to 1931, Meir Shapiro, leader of the Agudat Israel, served as rabbi of Piotrkow.

Holocaust Period

After the outbreak of World War II about 2,000 Jews, the majority of them young people, escaped from Piotrkow and attempted to find refuge in the larger towns and the Soviet-occupied zone. On Oct. 28, 1939, the Germans set up at Piotrkow the first ghetto to be established in Poland. Despite famine, disease, and terrorization, the population in the ghetto continued to increase as thousands of Jewish refugees arrived there, mostly from the regions annexed by the Germans. In April 1942 there were 16,469 Jews in the Piotrkow ghetto, of whom 8,141 had come from other localities, and by Oct. 15, 1942, there were about 25,000 Jews, including a large number of refugees from the surrounding townlets of Kamiensk, Wolborz, Serock, and others. Subsequently, in the course of one week, until Oct. 22, 1942, some 22,000 Jews of the Piotrkow ghetto were deported to the death camp of *Treblinka. About 4,000 Jews remained, half being workers in labor camps assigned to factories which worked for the German army. Some 2,000 others hid in the ghetto to escape the death transports. At the beginning of 1943 the Nazis carried out searches for those in hiding and found about 2,000 Jews, whom they murdered in the surrounding forests. In May 1943 about 500 Jews were taken from Piotrkow to the camps of Starachowice, *Radom, and others. Among those some 40 women and children were murdered on the spot. The remainder, numbering about 1,100, were concentrated into camps near the Karo and Hortensia glassworks and the Fischer & Co. timber enterprises. In November 1944 the last few hundred Jews in the ghetto were deported to the camps of *Buchenwald, *Bergen-Belsen, and *Mauthausen.

Several attempts had been made in the ghetto to organize resistance. Between 1942 and 1944, about 500 Jews escaped from the ghetto. They found refuge in the forests and within the organizations which fought the Germans. From the middle of 1943 a group of Jewish partisans was active in the vicinity of Piotrkow. The group succeeded in escaping from the labor camp attached to the Karo glassworks and held out until the retreat of the Germans from the region in January 1945. Jewish settlement in Piotrkow was not renewed after the war.

BIBLIOGRAPHY: A. Feldman, in: *Bleter far Geshikhte*, 1 (1938); Sz. Ashkenazy, *Ze spraw żydowskich w dobie kongresowej* (1913); M. Bersohn, *Dyplomataryusz Żydow w dawnej Polsce (1388–1752)* (1910), 179–80; *Dzieje ydów w Piotrkowie i okoliey* (1930); A. Eisenbach, in: BŻIH, no. 29 (1959), 72–111; A. Rutkowski, *ibid.*, no. 15–16 (1955), 75–182.

[Arthur Cygielman]

PIOVE DI SACCO, small town in Padua province, N. Italy. Piove di Sacco was the first town to admit Jews in this region. Before 1373 a moneylending bank was founded there by a Jewish consortium. In 1455, when the Jews of Padua were forbidden to lend money, they transferred their business to nearby centers, among them Piove di Sacco – where there had never been a ghetto. Piove di Sacco is of particular interest for its Hebrew press. In 1475 Meshullam Cusi Rafa ben Moses Jacob of nearby Padua and his sons set up a Hebrew printing press and were the first to issue a *Seliḥot* prayer book in nonvocalized square type (1475). In July 1475 they printed in folio form, the first volume of the first printed edition of *Jacob b. Asher's *Arba'ah Turim* – the second dated Hebrew book in Italy (now found at Padua's Biblioteca Civica Bp 6747). Meshullam died soon after, and his widow and sons Solomon and Moses continued printing the remaining volumes. After the second and third volumes were issued, the sons were imprisoned, apparently in connection with the *Trent blood libel, and their mother completed publication of the fourth volume alone (see *Incunabula). In 1905 Leone Romanin Jacur sat in the Italian parliament as the town's deputy.

BIBLIOGRAPHY: A. Ciscato, *Gli Ebrei in Padova* (1901), 21, 53, 158; G.B. De Rossi, in: *Annales Hebraeo-Typographici*, sect. 15, no. 2 (Parma, 1795); A. Vercesi and L. Dalla Rira, *Capitoli concessi da Francesco da Carrara… all'ebreo Abramo… in Piove di Sacco* (1900); S. Bassi, in: *Festschrift Bellini* (1959), 288–96. HEBREW PRINTING: D.W. Amram, *Makers of Hebrew Books in Italy* (1909), 22, 24, 26; Ḥ. D. Friedberg, *Toledot ha-Defus ha-Ivri bi-Medinot Italyah* (1956^2), 22–25; Milano, Bibliotheca, no. 1541.

[Alfredo Mordechai Rabello]

PIPERNO BEER, SERGIO (1906–1976), Italian judge and communal leader. Born in Rome, Piperno Beer took up a juridical career, reaching the rank of a councilor at the Court of Cassation, the highest court of Italy. During the period of racial persecutions (1938ff.), though dismissed from public service, he was active in DELASEM (Delegation for Assistance to Emigrants) and in the Italian liberal-secular movement Giustizia e Libertà (1943–44). After the liberation he was elected councilor of the Rome Jewish community and chaired the Communal Commission charged to investigate the case of the chief rabbi of Rome, Israel Zoller, who had converted to Christianity.

In June 1956 he was elected president of the Board of Italian Jewish Communities and in this office he worked for the Italian state's recognition of the rights of families who had lost members during Nazi persecutions, for the strengthening of institutions of Italian Jewry and their standing vis-à-vis the State, and for the revival of Jewish culture in Italy. He was active in the contacts with the Vatican before Ecumenical Council Vatican II and the declaration *Nostra aetate.* In the aftermath of the Six-Day War (1967) he helped with the emigration of the entire Jewish community of Libya, with the consent of the Italian government. Piperno Beer was reelected as president of the Board of Italian Jewish Communities in 1961, 1966, and 1974.

[Sergio DellaPergola / Robert Bonfil (2nd ed.)]

PIPES, RICHARD EDGAR (1923–), U.S. historian. Born in Cieszyn, Poland, Pipes migrated in his youth to the United States. He taught Russian history at Harvard, and was appointed professor. He also served as director of Harvard's Russian Research Center (1968–73). From 1974 until 1996 he held the position of Frank B. Baird Jr. Professor of History at Harvard. From 1997 he was the Frank B. Baird, Jr. Professor of History Emeritus at Harvard. Politically conservative, Pipes was included in President Ronald Reagan's U.S. Department of State transition team in 1980. He was the director of the National Security Council's East European and Soviet Affairs team (1981–82) and served as an expert witness in the Russian Constitutional Court's trial against the Communist Party in 1992.

Pipes' principal historical studies concern both Imperial Russia and the Bolshevik period, with special attention to intellectual and national questions. He was a member of the editorial boards of *Strategic Review, Orbis,* the *International Journal of Intelligence and CounterIntelligence, Continuity, Journal of Strategic Studies, East European Jewish Affairs,* and *Nuova Storia Contemporanea.*

His published works include *Formation of the Soviet Union* (1954), an important contribution to the study of the national question of Soviet Russia. He edited and translated *Karamzin's Memoir on Ancient and Modern Russia* (1959) and *Social-Democracy and the St. Petersburg Labor Movement 1885–97* (1963). He edited *Russian Intelligentsia* (1961) and *Revolutionary Russia* (1968). Among his other publications are *Europe Since 1815* (1970), *Soviet Strategy in Europe* (1976), *U.S.-Soviet Relations in the Era of Detente* (1981), *Russia Observed* (1989), *The Russian Revolution* (1990), *Communism: The Vanished Specter* (1993), *Russia under the Bolshevik Regime* (1994), *Three "Whys" of the Russian Revolution* (1996), *Prosperity and Freedom* (1999), and *Communism: A Brief History* (2001).

His son Daniel Pipes is a writer and commentator on Middle Eastern affairs.

[William Korey / Rohan Saxena and Ruth Beloff (2nd ed.)]

PIRKEI DE-RABBI ELIEZER, eighth-century aggadic work (see *Midrash), also called *Baraita de-Rabbi Eliezer* or *Haggadah de-Rabbi Eliezer* in medieval rabbinic literature because of its opening words: "It is related of *Eliezer b. Hyrcanus."

Character and Composition

The book is not a Midrash constructed on the verses of Scripture, but an aggadic narrative; the extant version is divided into 54 chapters, but this is probably not the whole book. It commences with an *aggadah* about the early days of Eliezer b. Hyrcanus, and then chronologically narrates events from the Creation until the middle of the journeys of the Children of Israel in the wilderness, concluding with *Miriam's leprosy and the *copper serpent. In the second half of the book, from Abraham onward, the narrative is related to the blessings of the **Amidah* prayer, but the last chapter terminates at the eighth blessing (for health). The book also refers to the 10 occasions when God descended to earth, but in their enumeration only reaches the eighth descent. It is therefore clear that the book as it survived is incomplete; but even in manuscript the only additional portion preserved is the second half of the last chapter.

Language and Date

The book is written in Hebrew – partially artificial – reminiscent of the geonic era, and contains a few Greek words. The author made use of the tannaitic literature, the Jerusalem Talmud, the *Midreshei Aggadah of the **amoraim*, and even of the Babylonian Talmud, as well as those Aramaic *Targums to the Scripture that originated in Ereẓ Israel. The author does not quote his sources, but tends to revise them completely – shortening, lengthening, and combining them freely. It is therefore not a collection or compilation of different sources, but a book with a unified and continuous narrative in which the personality of the author is clearly recognizable. The author was greatly influenced in both content and form by the *Apocrypha and Pseudepigrapha of the Second Temple period, particularly the books of the *Enoch cycle. His entire manner of narration and unique method of connecting *halakhah* and *aggadah* were influenced by the Book of Jubilees. *Pirkei de-Rabbi Eliezer* has thus preserved many ancient sources. It contains almost no names of *amoraim*, but falsely attributes sayings to many *tannaim. Pirkei de-Rabbi Eliezer* is therefore a pseudepigraphic work par excellence; the influence of apocalyptic works of the Second Temple period is well marked in that respect, as well as in its mystical air and in the descriptions of angels. The *halakhot* of the *calendar laid down in the Byzantine period and at the beginning of the Muslim era were already known to the author. The book is filled with the halakhic customs current in Ereẓ Israel at the beginning of the geonic period. It contains Arabic legends, and remarkable descriptions of the Muslim Omayyad dynasty, and looks forward to the downfall of this (Omayyad) caliphate as an omen of the end of the exile. All these indications prove that it was composed in Ereẓ Israel during the first half of the eighth century, just prior to the fall of the Omayyad dynasty, but before the rise of the Abbasid dynasty. Quotations from it are already found in the tractate **Soferim*, and in the work of *Pirkoi ben Baboi. The work also follows the model of the Arabic collections of biblical legends, in which narrative receives more emphasis than exegesis. *Pirkei de-Rabbi Eliezer* was first published in Constantinople (1514), and reprinted many times on the basis of the first edition. In the Warsaw edition of 1852, a valuable commentary by David *Luria was added. Many manuscripts have been preserved, and extracts from three of them were published by Higger in *Horeb*, 8–10 (1944–48), and one of them was translated into English by G. Friedlander (1916, 1965[2]).

BIBLIOGRAPHY: Zunz-Albeck, Derashot, 134–40.

[Moshe David Herr]

PIRKOI BEN BABOI (eighth–ninth century), talmudic scholar of the geonic era and author of a polemical halakhic work. A pupil of Abba, who was a pupil of *Yehudai, a *Gaon* of Sura, Pirkoi notes that it was only because of their teaching and tradition that he presumed to write to the scholars of Kairouan. His teacher Abba wrote the *Halakhot de-Rav Abba*, small fragments of which were published from the Cairo *Genizah by S. Schechter and J.N. Epstein. Some conjecture that Abba was one of the scholars of the Pumbedita Academy and that Pirkoi also apparently studied there. It was earlier assumed that Pirkoi b. Baboi meant "the chapters of [*Pirkei*] Ben Baboi," but Epstein showed that Pirkoi was a Persian personal name. According to Epstein, Pirkoi was born in Babylon, where he studied and wrote his *Iggeret*. According to Ginzberg, however, he was a native of Ereẓ Israel who studied in Babylon, where he settled and wrote his work. Fragments of the work were scattered in various libraries – St. Petersburg, Oxford, Cambridge – and were published from the *Genizah*, beginning in 1903, by various scholars such as Harkavy (*Ha-Goren*, 4 (1903), 71–74) and L. Ginzberg (Geonica, 2 (1909), 50–53), neither of whom identified the author. J. Mann, who added a third fragment, succeeded in indicating Pirkoi as the author; additional fragments were published by various scholars of the period including Solomon Schechter, J.N. Epstein, B.M. Lewin, Shraga Abramson, and S. Spiegel.

Pirkoi became renowned through his work *Iggeret*, which reflects his aspiration to make the Babylonian Talmud the authoritative code for world Jewry. Echoes of the long drawn-out struggle between the two Torah centers – Ereẓ Israel and Babylon – are heard in the polemical chapters of Pirkoi which constitute, in Ginzberg's view, the earliest halakhic work extant from the geonic era. Some were of the opinion that the *Iggeret* was sent to Ereẓ Israel, but more accepted the view of Lewin and Spiegel that it was sent to the countries of North Africa (around 812), where the customs of Ereẓ Israel were followed. Pirkoi's intention was to encourage them to accept the *halakhah* of Babylon and the customs of the two academies in Babylon. It is probable that Pirkoi's words in his *Iggeret*, "God established places of learning in all localities of Africa and of Spain and granted you the privilege of engaging in Torah study by day and by night," were directed especially to the people of Kairouan, which in the time of Pirkoi enjoyed tranquility and economic stability. The communal leaders and scholars of Kairouan endeavored to maintain places of learning in the town as well as in various localities in Spain. Emigrants who left Kairouan for Spain founded Torah centers there. Pirkoi complains about the pupils of the Babylonian academies who "learnt the customs of Ereẓ Israel," arrived in North Africa, and were then drawn after the ignorant customs and habits of Ereẓ Israel. In his view any custom or ruling which is not in accordance with the law and *halakhah* of the Babylonian Talmud is a consequence of the apostasy decreed by the wicked kingdom of Edom upon Ereẓ Israel. As a result Torah was forgotten by the inhabitants of Ereẓ Israel, and the Ereẓ Israel customs came to be "customs of apostasy." Pirkoi, as a "pro-Babylonian," stresses the superiority of the Babylonian academies as the only source in the world for the details of the Oral Law, and says that it is fitting that from them the Torah should go forth to Jews in all countries. In the opinion of many scholars (Lewin, Mann, Aptowitzer), this polemic of Pirkoi also had an anti-Karaite purpose: to ensure that the denial of the Oral Law by Karaites should not detach the Jews from the tradition customary in the Babylonian academies.

BIBLIOGRAPHY: S. Schechter, in: *Festschrift… D. Hoffmann* (1914), Heb. pt. 261–6; V. Aptowitzer, in: REJ, 57 (1909), 246ff.; idem, in: HUCA, 8–9 (1931–32), 382, 415–7; idem, *Meḥkarim be-Sifrut ha-Ge'onim* (1941), 13–17; J. Mann, in: REJ, 70 (1920), 113–48; idem, in: *Tarbiz*, 6 (1935), 78f.; J.N. Epstein, in: REJ, 75 (1922), 179–86; idem, in: *Madda'ei ha-Yahadut*, 2 (1927), 149–61; idem, in: *Tarbiz*, 2 (1931), 411f.; L. Ginzberg, *Ginzei Schechter*, 2 (1929), 504–73; B.M. Lewin, in: *Tarbiz*, 2 (1931), 383–405; Ḥ. Tchernowitz, *Toledot ha-Posekim*, 1 (1946), 109–12; Baron, Social[2], index s.v.; S. Abramson, in: *Sinai*, 50 (1962), 185f.; S. Spiegel, in: *H.A. Wolfson Jubilee Volume* (1965), Heb. pt. 243–74.

[Josef Horovitz]

°PIROGOV, NIKOLAI (1810–1881), Russian physician-surgeon and civic leader. From 1856 to 1858 he was a trustee for the Odessa education district and from 1858 to 1861 he served in the same capacity for Kiev. In south and southwest Russia he came into contact with the Jewish population and became their defender. In a letter to the Ministry of Education, dated Feb. 4, 1857, he argued for compulsory general education which would, at the same time, respect the religious sensitivities of the Jews. He proposed a cadre of Jewish teachers who would have the same rights as their non-Jewish colleagues, and opposed the idea that Christian trustees should be assigned to Jewish educational institutions. In his writings Pirogov pointed out the traditional respect of Jews for education and culture, and supported O. *Rabinovich and J. *Tarnopol in their efforts to publish a Jewish periodical in Russian. He also supported A. *Zederbaum for his publication of a Hebrew periodical.

BIBLIOGRAPHY: Morgulis, in: *Voskhod*, 5 (1881), i–iv, 1–13; Gessen, in: *Perezhitoye*, 3 (1911), 1–59; L. Greenberg, *The Jews in Russia*, 1 (1944), 102–3.

PIRYATIN, city in Poltava district, Ukraine. A Jewish settlement in Piryatin was first mentioned in 1630. The community was destroyed in the massacres of 1648 and not revived until the close of the 18th century, when it became a center for *Chabad Ḥasidism. The community numbered 464 in 1847 and grew to 3,166 (39% of the total population) in 1897. Apart from *ḥadarim* there was a Jewish school with separate classes for boys and girls. By 1926 the Jews numbered 3,885 (31.8%), dropping by 1939 to 1,747 (12.7% of the total population). About 100 families worked in a Jewish kolkhoz founded in 1929. The Germans entered Piryatin on September 18, 1941. On April 6, 1942 they murdered 1,600 Jews, and later another 1,400 from the environs, and refugees.

[Yehuda Slutsky]

PISA, city in Tuscany, central Italy. Benjamin of *Tudela found 20 Jewish families living there around 1165. It may be presumed that Jews had settled in the city even earlier, attracted by the possibilities offered by the close commercial ties between Pisa and countries of the Levant. Some of the Jewish tombstones embedded in the town wall, near the cathedral, date back to the middle of the 13th century. At the end of the 13th century an "Alley of the Jews" (Chiasso di Giudei) is recorded. In 1322 the Jews in Pisa were instructed to wear the distinguishing *badge but the regulation was apparently not strictly enforced. By the second half of the 14th century Pisa was in a state of political and economic decline, which culminated in its subjection to Florence in 1406. Around the same time, Vitale (Jehiel) b. Matassia of Pisa, a banker of Roman origin, began his activities in Pisa. The family he founded owned banks in Pisa and Florence, as well as branches in other towns, and for about 150 years dominated Jewish moneylending in Italy, as well as distinguishing itself in the cultural sphere (see Da *Pisa family). Some of its members had close connections with the Medici of Florence. In 1492 Jewish exiles from Spain who arrived in Pisa were assisted generously by the Da Pisa family. When a Christian loan bank (*Monte di Pietà) was opened in Pisa in 1496, Isaac b. Jehiel subscribed over half the founding capital, so that Jews were permitted to continue their moneylending activities, although only for a short period. As a result of the struggle between the Florentine Republic, which was hostile to the Jews, and the Medici, who were favorably disposed toward them, and the war of 1494–1509 between Pisa and Florence, the Jewish community of Pisa was considerably reduced in size. It began to recover in 1547 when Cosimo I de'Medici, duke of Tuscany, urged Jews and *New Christian fugitives from Portugal to settle in Pisa and *Leghorn, and some accepted the invitation. Larger numbers were attracted by the generous terms of the proclamation issued in June 1593 by the grand duke Ferdinand I de'Medici, addressed particularly to Sephardim and Marranos wherever they happened to live. Another proclamation, issued in October 1595 to the German and Italian Jews, who had then been driven from the territories of Milan, aroused little response. The Medici wished to promote Pisa as the market capital of Tuscany, with the port of Leghorn dependent on Pisa. However, Leghorn developed more successfully and also attained greater importance as a Jewish center, and in 1614 became independent of Pisa.

Samuel *Foa (or Fua), a member of the famous printing family of Sabbioneta, established a Hebrew press at Pisa toward the end of the 18th century, and was succeeded by Samuel and Joseph Moliho (1816ff.).

There were 600 Jews living in Pisa at the beginning of the 17th century, and half that number a century later. The number remained thereafter approximately the same, totaling 365 in 1840. Most of the Jews in Pisa were governed by the liberal patents of 1593 which granted, among other privileges, Tuscan citizenship ipso jure to any person admitted as a member of the community, and semiautonomous internal jurisdiction. The Jews in Pisa lived in relative tranquility, mainly engaging in commerce. In the 18th and especially the 19th century, they played an active part in developing industries, particularly the cotton industries which attracted a certain number of Jews there. The Jewish population numbered 700 in 1881.

[Attilio Milano]

Holocaust and Modern Periods

In 1931 the Jewish community of Pisa numbered 535. During the Holocaust, a dozen Jews, among them Rabbi Augusto Hasdà, were sent to extermination camps. Eight more Jews were deported elsewhere. On Aug. 1, 1944, the Nazis broke into the house of the president of the community, the well-known philanthropist Pardo-Roques, and massacred him together with six Jews who had taken refuge there. After the war, the community, including the towns of Viareggio and Lucca, had a membership of 312 Jews, which declined to 210 by 1969 and 100–200 at the beginning of the 21st century.

[Sergio Della Pergola]

BIBLIOGRAPHY: Cassuto, in: RI, 5 (1908), 227–38; 6 (1909), 21–30, 102–13, 160–70, 223–32; 7 (1910), 9–19, 72–86, 146–50; Toaff, in: *Scritti in memoria di Guido Bedarida* (1966), 227–62; Kaufmann, in: REJ, 26 (1893), 83–110, 220–39; 29 (1894), 142–7; 31 (1895), 62–73; 32 (1896), 130–4; C. Roth, *Jews in the Renaissance* (1959), index; Roth, Italy, index; Milano, Italia, index; Milano, Bibliotheca, index; D.W. Amram, *Makers of Hebrew Books in Italy* (1909), 396f.

PISA, DA, family of bankers, financers, and international merchants ranked among the best-known Italian Jewish families.

In 1393 MATASSIA DI SABATO, a member of the well-known Bet-El or Min-ha-Keneset Roman family, settled in San Miniato, a small town in Tuscany, under the Florentine government, where he opened a local bank. In 1406 his son VITALE JEHIEL of Matassia established his activities in Pisa, the city from which he derived his new family name. He opened other lending banks in San Gimignano, Prato, Colle di Val d'Elsa, and Arezzo. A scholar and lover of letters, he became known even outside Italy: Profiat *Duran recommended him to his disciple Judah Zark, who found hospitality at the da Pisa home.

After Vitale's death the banking activities were continued by his daughter GIUSTA (d. 1478) who married ISAAC DI

MANUELE DA RIMINI, who later assumed his wife's surname. Giusta managed the family company together with her husband and later with her son JEHIEL VITALE (d. 1490), who brought their activities to their greatest heights by obtaining, with other associates, an exclusive banking license for Florence. He opened loan banks in several other towns.

Jehiel Vitale was also known as one of the most noteworthy Hebrew personalities of his time and gained the favor of Lorenzo de' Medici. When the Franciscan friar *Bernardino da Feltre preached in Florence against the Jewish loan bankers, Vitale led a deputation of the Jews of the city before Lorenzo de' Medici and succeeded in averting an edict of expulsion (1488). Vitale had family connections with other important families (such as da S. Miniato, da Tivoli, da Fano and da Volterra) and was friendly with notables abroad, including Abraham Ḥayyun of Lisbon, Don Isaac *Abrabanel, and Joseph Yaḥia (d. 1497), whom the da Pisa house helped transfer goods from Lisbon to Ferrara. Vitale's house became known as a meeting place of scholars: among those who stayed there was Johanan *Alemanno, who tutored Vitale's sons.

The distinctive characteristics of the family were maintained also by Jehiel Vitale's sons ISAAC (d. 1511) and SIMONE SAMUEL (d. 1510). The da Pisa fortunes suffered only limited damage when the family was compelled to leave Tuscany after the downfall of the Medici (1494). When they returned to Florence, with Pope Leo x, the da Pisa were able to recover their properties and resume their banking activities in Tuscany.

Another outstanding member of the family was DANIEL (d. 1532), son of Isaac. He was active in Pisa, Florence, and Rome, where he was appointed gentleman and *familiare* of Pope Clemete VII, who entrusted him with the task of drawing up the new *takkanot of* the composite Roman Jewish Community. This code was approved in 1524.

Daniel welcomed David *Reuveni on his visit to Rome. Daniel had two brothers, SALOMON and ABRAM. The first developed wide-ranging banking activities from Tuscany to the Republic of Venice. Abram established his activities in Bologna.

VITALE JEHIEL NISSIM (d. 1574), son of Simone Samuel, was an eminent scholar, with profound knowledge of Scriptures, philosophy, Kabbalah, and astronomy. He wrote *Minḥat Kena'ot* (publ. by D. Kaufmann, 1898) aimed at demonstrating the superiority of religion over philosophy, and *Ma'amar Ḥayyei Olam*, a halakhic treatise on matters of finance (publ. in 1962 by G. Rosenthal under the title *Banking and Finance among Jews in Renaissance Italy*, with notes and biographical sketch). He lived in Pisa and on the vast farming estate that had belonged to the family for more than a century, in the hills surrounding the city. His house was open to the needy.

In 1554 SIMONE SAMUEL, son of Vitale Jehiel Nissim, graduated in medicine from the University of Pisa. Seven years later EMANUELE, son of Salomon di Isaac, obtained a university degree in Ferrara, by special privilege. Furthermore he was a member of the rabbinical academy in that city.

In the 17th century a branch of the family became established in Ferrara, under the rule of the Church. In the course of several generations their surname was simplified to Pisa.

In 1831 ZACCARIA OF ELIA PISA (1788–1833) founded a banking house in Ferrara under his name. In 1852 his sons LUIGI ISRAEL (1813–1895), LEONE LEOPOLDO (1812–1872), and GIUSEPPE (1827–1904) moved the family enterprise to Milan and developed it into one of the most important private banks in Italy. Between 1863 and 1914 the Bank Pisa was engaged in raising public-capital subscriptions and placed bonds issued by the state as well as by the railway companies. It was on the board of directors of such companies as the Strade Ferrate Meridionali (Southern Railways), the Navigazione Generale, and Edison.

UGO PISA, son of Luigi Israel (1845–1910), volunteered in the 1866 war. He entered a diplomatic career, led an economic mission to China and Japan, and was eventually appointed ambassador. He later became president of the Chamber of Commerce of Milan and senator of the Kingdom of Italy. The banking house of the family continued its operations well into the 1930s under the guidance of LUIGI DELLA TORRE (a grandson of Luigi Pisa), who was senator of the Kingdom (1913) and president of the ABI (Italian Banking Association).

From MOSES-ARON PISA, a brother of Zaccaria, descended the Roman line of the family, headed in the early 21st century by FRANCO PISA, an economist and international merchant. He engaged in the study of Jewish economic history and published several studies on the structure of local banks and their influence on regional economies. He also sponsored several cultural activities.

BIBLIOGRAPHY: U. Cassuto, in: RI, 5 (1908), 277–38; 10 (1913–14), 48–59: D. Kaufmann, in: REJ, 31 (1895), 62–73; Milano, *Italy*, index: idem, in: RMI, 10 (1935/36), 324–38, 409–26; Roth, Italy index. **ADD. BIBLIOGRAPHY:** F. Bonelli, *La crisi del 1907* (1971); A. Confalonieri, *Banca e Industria in Italia* (1979); M. Luzzati, *La casa dell'ebreo* (1985); S. Simonsohn, *The Apostolic See and the Jews* (1991), index.

[Menachem E. Artom / Aron Leoni (2nd ed.)]

PISCO, SERAPHINE EPPSTEIN (1861–1942), secretary and chief administrator of the National Jewish Hospital for Consumptives in Denver from 1911 through 1938. She should also be understood as a product of the late 19th century Jewish club women's movement, which transmuted traditional ideas about women's nurturing role into professional social work. Pisco was born in St Joseph, Missouri, to Max and Bertha Eppstein, who moved her and five siblings to Denver in 1875. In 1878, like so many women of her generation, she married a businessman many years older than herself, Edward Pisko, who was prominent in local politics, and had been president of the local B'nai B'rith lodge. Also like so many women of her generation she became active in Jewish women's charitable work, serving as president of the Jewish Relief Society and in 1896 helping Carrie Shevelson Benjamin found a section of the National Council of Jewish Women. She served on many Council committees, and when president she helped found a settlement house in the Colfax district, where she developed close relations with East European Jews and Italian immigrants. An excellent public speaker, in 1899 she represented the Women's Club of Denver at the National Conference of Charities and Corrections in Cincinnati, and also accepted a paid position as fundraiser for the newly opened National Jewish Hospital. Since most hospital officers did not live in Denver, when the secretary died suddenly in 1911, she was appointed his successor. She could assume this position with no medical training because sanitariums, treating a disease with no known surgical cure, lagged behind general hospitals as research-oriented teaching facilities whose medical staffs demanded control of budgets. When an audit revealed that her predecessor had embezzled funds, Mrs. Pisco used her reputation as leader of Jewish women's clubs to restore public confidence in the institution. She brought professional efficiency to the business office by removing it from her predecessor's law office to the hospital grounds, hiring women to replace men on her small staff, and using her network of female social work professionals at other Denver institutions to sustain her autonomy against the male medical staff. When nationally sponsored investigations of the hospital in 1912 and 1916 recommended that its administrative autonomy be subordinated to a citywide Jewish federation of charities, she persuaded Judge Julian Mack of Chicago that the hospital could best treat its patients by retaining its fundraising network and administration. Her correspondence with the president and treasurer of the hospital reveal extraordinary command of fiscal details, rhetorical irony when rebuffing the criticisms of male officers, and charm when persuading city officials to meet the hospital's needs. The hospital remained her life's work, and in 1925 the Women's Pavilion was renamed in her honor. When infirmities slowed her down she retired in 1938.

BIBLIOGRAPHY: J. Abrams, "Seraphine Eppstein Pisco (1861–1942)," in: P. Hyman and D.D. Moore, *Jewish Women in America, An Historical Encyclopedia* (1997), 1077–78; M.A. FitzHarris, *A Place to Heal, The History of National Jewish Center for Immunology and Respiratory Medicine* (1989); W. Toll, "Gender and the Origins of Philanthropic Professionalism: Seraphine Pisco at the National Jewish Hospital," in: *Rocky Mountain Jewish Historical Notes* (Winter/Spring 1991).

[William Toll (2nd ed.)]

PISGAH (Heb. פִּסְגָּה), mountain in Transjordan in the territory of the tribe of Reuben (Josh. 13:20). It lay on the border between the land of Sihon the Amorite and the territory of Reuben, northeast of the Dead Sea (Deut. 3:17; 4:49; Josh. 12:3). In the above passages, the reference is apparently to the slopes of Mt. Pisgah near the Dead Sea (Num. 21:20; 23:14; Deut. 3:27; 34:1). More precisely, they probably refer to the western slope of the mountain. The slopes of Mt. Pisgah served as an important junction for the roads in the area of the mountain ridge of Nebo. It is probably due to the area's geographic location that biblical sources emphasized its location within the borders of Israelite settlement. The "top of Pisgah" (Deut. 34:1) is identified with Ra's al-Siyāgha, west of Mt. Nebo (supposedly the Siyaran mentioned in one version of Targum Onkelos, Num. 32: 3: cf. "*Netinah la-Ger*," *ibid.*). This is the place from which Moses viewed the Promised Land before his death.

BIBLIOGRAPHY: Birch, in: PEFQS, 40 (1898), 110–1; A. Musil, *Arabia Petraea*, 1 (Ger., 1907) passim; I.S. Horowitz, *Ereẓ Yisrael u-Shekhenoteha* (1923) s.v. *Ashdot ha-Pisgah*; Abel, Geog, 1 (1933), 281, 379ff.

[Michael Avi-Yonah]

PISK, PAUL AMADEUS (1893–1990), musicologist, composer, and pedagogue. Born in Vienna, Pisk studied under Arnold *Schoenberg, Schreker, and Guido *Adler and received a doctorate in musicology from the University of Vienna (1916). He attained prominence as a musical journalist and as a spokesman for progressive German and Austrian composers. Pisk served as secretary of Schoenberg's Society (1918–21) and worked as editor for the *Musikblätter des Anbruch* (1920–28) and the *Wiener Arbeiter-Zeitung* (1921–34). He was a co-founder of the International Society for Contemporary Music (ISCM), and served as director of the music department of the Volkshochschule, Vienna (1922–34). In 1936 he had to immigrate to the United States, becoming a citizen in 1941. He held senior academic posts at various universities, and renewed contact with Schoenberg, *Milhaud, and Hindemith. Pisk composed about 100 works for orchestra, chamber groups and keyboard, dramatic pieces, and choral works. Pisk's compositions tend toward atonality, but do not employ 12-note techniques. Many of them employ folk melodies. Among his publications are a study of the masses of the 16th-century composer Jacobus Gallus (1918) and articles on Schoenberg, Berg, Webern, and modern music. He wrote (with H. Ulrich) *History of Music and Musical Style* (1963). Through a bequest of his the American Musicological Society established the Paul A. Pisk Prize.

ADD. BIBLIOGRAPHY: Grove online; *Baker's Biographical Dictionary* (1997). J. Glowacki (ed.), *Paul A. Pisk: Essays in his Honor* (1966).

[Naama Ramot (2nd ed.)]

PISSARRO, CAMILLE (1830–1903), French painter. Born into a Sephardi family which had migrated from Bordeaux to the Virgin Islands, he was sent to a boarding school in Paris at the age of 12. At 17 he returned to St. Thomas to become a clerk in his father's general store, but he wanted to be an artist, and ran away to Caracas, Venezuela. After a while he obtained his father's permission to study in France, and from 1855 until his death, he remained in, or near, Paris.

With his socialist-anarchist convictions, he regarded himself a citizen of the world, with no particular religious, racial, or national ties. His wife was of Catholic peasant stock. He was shocked and hurt by the *Dreyfus case, but more as a man of progressive political ideals than as a Jew. Pissarro became a staunch member of a loosely organized group that came into being in 1874 under the name of "Société anonyme des artistes, peintres, sculpteurs, et graveurs" which soon became better known as the "Impressionists." He participated in all of the Impressionists' eight group shows, received his share of abuse from public and press, and held the group together until 1886, after Cézanne, Renoir, and even the prime mover, Monet, had lost interest.

He took his guidance from Corot and Courbet, blending Corot's subtlety of atmospheric effect with the strength and solidity of Courbet. In 1865 he came under the spell of Manet. By that time he had already eliminated black and the siennas and ochers from his palette. In his mid-fifties, he was greatly influenced by Georges Seurat's pointillist technique, and for several years he experimented with the "divisionist" method of painting with little dots of primary color. Yet, he is chiefly known for his Impressionist landscapes and cityscapes. Pissarro thought he saw nature objectively but actually he rendered it just as much from feeling and knowledge as from dispassionate sight – rendered it in solidly constructed, architectural forms. Most of his canvases show a definite desire for order and organization, and a feeling for design. His work is uneven – perhaps more uneven than that of other artists, since he was forced to overproduce in his efforts to keep his family of eight from starvation.

All of Pissarro's sons – Lucien (1863–1944), Georges (1871–1961), Félix (1874–1897), Ludovic-Rudolpe (1878–1952), and Paul-Emile (1884–1972) – were gifted artists, but only one, LUCIEN PISSARRO, achieved a modicum of fame for his Impressionist landscapes and his woodcuts. Lucien played a major part in the introduction of Impressionist painting to England. Educated in France, he was trained by his father and in 1890 went to England, where he met William Morris, Charles Ricketts, and Charles Shannon who interested him in the art of book design. He later set up his own publishing firm, the Eragny Press, and collaborated with his wife in the production of beautifully illustrated books. Among his book productions was *The Book of Ruth and Esther.* Lucien's daughter Orovida (1893–1968) inherited his talent. She signed her work with her first name, and became known for her studies of animals.

BIBLIOGRAPHY: J. Rewald, *Pissarro* (Eng., 1963); idem (ed.), *Camille Pissarro: Letters to his Son Lucien* (1943); A. Werner, *Pissarro* (Eng., 1963); W.S. Meadmore, *Lucien Pissarro* (Eng., 1962). **ADD. BIBLIOGRAPHY:** T. Maloon, *Camille Piscarro* (2006).

[Alfred Werner]

PISTACHIO (Heb. בָּטְנָה; *botnah*), the tree and fruit of the *Pistacia vera*, a dioecious tree. The female tree produces reddish clusters of nuts with a white shell and a greenish kernel of delicate flavor. The word occurs only once in the Bible, in the plural, (Heb. בָּטְנִים (*botnim*)), among the "choice fruits of the land" sent by Jacob to the ruler of Egypt (Gen. 43:11). The Samaritan translation of the word is *biẓtekin*, i.e., pistachio. The Mishnah calls the tree *botnah* (Shev. 7:5) and its fruit *pistakin*. They were grown in Israel, and subject to tithes (TJ, Ma'as, 1:2, 48d). Two members of its genus, *Pistacia palaestina* and *Pistacia atlantica*, are indigenous to Ereẓ Israel but the fruit is hardly edible. It was customary, however, to graft the pistachio onto the branches of these species whose trees and fruit are called *botmin* (Ar. *but'm*) in the Talmud. The pistachio tree is similar to the latter, but its nuts taste like the almond, and in consequence the ancients thought it to be a hybrid of these two species (TJ, Kil. 1:4, 27a). In modern Hebrew *botnim* is used to designate peanuts. The identification is erroneous, for not only was the peanut brought from the Americas, but it is not a tree, as *botnim* definitely are, according to the Mishnah.

BIBLIOGRAPHY: Loew, Flora, 1 (1926), 190–200; J. Feliks, *Kilei Zera'im ve-Harkavah* (1967), 106–7; idem, in: *Olam ha-Ẓome'aḥ ha-Mikra'i* (1968^2), 64–65; H.N. and A.L. Moldenke, *Plants of the Bible* (1952), 319 (index), s.v. Pistachio and Pistacia. **ADD. BIBLIOGRAPHY:** J. Feliks, Ha-Ẓome'aḥ, 125, 179.

[Jehuda Feliks]

°**PISTORIUS (DE NIDA), JOHANNES** (1546–1608), German scholar. Pistorius was physician and adviser to the margrave of Baden-Durlach, whom he induced to support the Protestants; he himself later reverted to Catholicism, however, and entered the priesthood in 1591. He is mainly remembered for his *Artis Cabbalisticae, hoc est reconditae theologiae et philosophiae Scriptorum Tomus I* (Basle, 1587), a compendium of Christian mystical literature (including Johannes *Reuchlin's *De Arte Cabalistica* and Archangelus de Burgonuovo's commentaries on the "Conclusions" of Giovanni *Pico della Mirandola) which also contained a translation of Judah *Abrabanel's *Dialoghi di Amore.* A second volume, planned to contain major Jewish kabbalistic works, never appeared, probably as a result of Catholic objections to some of the material in the published compendium. The *Artis Cabbalisticae* was consulted by many later authors and is the most likely source of *Milton's knowledge of the Kabbalah.

BIBLIOGRAPHY: F. Secret, *Les Kabbalistes chrétiens de la Renaissance* (1964), 79–80; D. Hirst, *Hidden Riches...* (1964), index. **ADD. BIBLIOGRAPHY:** H.-J. Guenther, *Die Reformation und ihre Kinder* (1994).

[Godfrey Edmond Silverman]

PITHOM (Egyptian **Per Atum**, "House of the god Atum"), a city mentioned once in the Bible (Ex. 1:11) as one of the two treasury cities (see also *Ramses) which the Israelites were forced to build for Pharaoh. The identification of Pithom with the site of Tell el-Maskhutah near the eastern end of the Wadi Tumilat has been accepted for many years by a large number of scholars despite the lack of any definite evidence that the town located there, Tjeku (= biblical Succoth?), was called Pithom (Per Atum) earlier than the Egyptian 22nd Dynasty (c. 945–730 B.C.E.) or that Ramses II, the supposed pharaoh of the bondage, had built a completely new city there (as implied in Ex. 1:11). The 19th-Dynasty Egyptian text mentioning the "pools of Per-Atum of Merneptah which are in Tjeku" (Papyrus Anastasi IV, 4:56) may or may not refer to this city. An alternative identification of the site as Tell er-Ratabeh, about 22 miles west of Ismailia, has also been proposed and has been accepted by some. The most recent and most convincing identification depends on the Egyptians' use of *Per* (literally "house") in a wider, administrative context as the large region, under the control of the temple of a particular god. *Per* could then refer to a city sacred to that god, as did Per Amun to Thebes and Per Bastet to Bubastis. Since Atum was a manifestation of the sun god, Per Atum could very well have meant *Heliopolis (called On in the Bible). It is quite probable that the Beth-Shemesh of Jeremiah 43:13 is a Hebrew translation of Per Atum. Such an identification is well supported by the size, importance, and fame of Heliopolis.

BIBLIOGRAPHY: E.P. Uphill, in: JNES, 27 (1968), 291–316; 28 (1969), 15–39.

[Alan Richard Schulman]

PITIGRILLI (pen name of **Dino Segre**; 1893–1954), Italian author and journalist. After working on the staff of *L'Epoca* in Rome, Segre was a foreign correspondent in Istanbul and later founded two popular reviews, *Le Grandi Firme* and *Il Dramma*, in his native Turin. As Pitigrilli, he wrote novels and short stories which gained considerable notoriety in France as well as Italy for their erotic, often pornographic, themes and qualities, and their analysis, superficial though it was, of moral behavior. They include *La cintura di castita* (1921), *La vergine a 18 carati* (1924), *I vegetariani dell'amore* (1932), and *Dolicocefala bionda* (1936). During the Fascist era Pitigrilli became a police informer and, between 1934 and 1938, collaborated with the OVRA, Mussolini's secret police. As a result of these activities, he later had to seek refuge in Argentina. On his return to Italy after World War II, he ostentatiously embraced Catholicism and wrote anti-Jewish books such as *Mosé e il cavalier Levi* (1948).

BIBLIOGRAPHY: D. Zucáro (ed.), *Lettere all' OVRA di Pitigrilli* (1961).

PITTSBURGH, a leading industrial city in western Pennsylvania; in a metropolitan region of 2,500,000, the estimated Jewish population of Greater Pittsburgh (in 2002) was 54,000.

Early History

When the Quaker William Penn received the colonial charter for the area from Charles II in 1680 he incorporated a guarantee of religious freedom. Accordingly, many varied sects settled in Pennsylvania, including Jews. Among the early settlers were Joseph *Simon and Levy Andrew Levy.

After the Revolutionary War, the prosperous Philadelphia merchant David *Franks sent agents, among them Michael Gratz, with pack trains to Pittsburgh so often that their route was labeled Frankstown Road. They and several other Jews bought plots of land, apparently for speculation, and the map indicates a cluster of lots to the east marked "Jewstown," with another area near Sewickley marked "Gratztown." Most of the Jews, like other traders, came and went as itinerant peddlers, but a few remained, striking roots. The first known permanent resident of Pittsburgh to have Jewish ancestry was Samuel Pettigrew, son of Judith Hart, who settled in the town in 1814 and later served as mayor.

On the whole, however, economic difficulties caused by the diversion of river traffic by the Erie Canal kept Jewish immigration down. It was not until 1842 that Jews first met in a *minyan* for worship in a home near the Point. There is a dearth of records of this period, most having been destroyed in the great fire that swept the wooden town in 1845. In that year the Beth Almon Society was formed; land for a cemetery on Troy Hill was bought in 1846. With the building of a railroad in 1849, Jewish settlement began to increase. In 1852 there were 30 Jewish families in Pittsburgh, and six years later the number doubled. By 1854 a group meeting in a room over Vigilant Fire Department organized itself as Rodef Shalom, and in 1861 a building was dedicated on Hancock Street (later Eighth Street), where a Mr. Armhold served as reader, *mohel*, and *shoḥet*. German was the language of sermons and records, but the congregants showed willingness to modify practice regarding covered heads and mixed seating, among others. This caused dissension, and a new group was created in 1864, calling itself Etz Hayim, more conservative in practice. In 1861 Rodef Shalom brought a young English Jew, Josiah Cohen, to head its religious school an preach in English. He later became a distinguished judge.

With the outbreak of the Civil War, Pittsburgh grew in importance and population. From a handful, the number of Jews in 1864 became 750, nearly all of German origin. Ten of their men were in uniform. Women served on the Sanitary Commission, forerunner of the Red Cross. The United Hebrew Relief Society assisted returning soldiers and their families. Expanding heavy industry that was to make Pittsburgh the "Workshop of the World" drew great streams of immigration from Europe. The population had outgrown the Triangle and pushed upward, with stores on Fifth Avenue and small red-brick houses on adjacent streets on the "Hill." Some moved across the river to the town of Allegheny. More affluent Jews followed them there. By 1877 there were 2,000 Jews in Pittsburgh, many of them recent immigrants from Lithuania, sharing in the ferment of the industrial growth of the city and its environs. Many peddlers moved out to the surrounding towns, but all returned to the city for the Sabbath and holidays and for *kasher* food.

In 1885 a national group of leading Reform rabbis, led by Rabbi Isaac Mayer *Wise, met in Pittsburgh and articulated a series of points that were to be known as the *Pittsburgh Platform.

Eastern European Immigration

The Russian pogroms of 1881 set in motion the mass exodus which brought Russian Jews to America. Many thousands came to Pittsburgh, raising its Jewish population to 15,000 by 1905. The earlier residents received the penniless immigrants as their own, despite barriers of language and provincial manners. They doled out silver dollars for Sabbath meals, and helped to find lodgings and jobs. The Council of Jewish Women provided English teachers, gave guidance to homeless girls, and conducted classes in religion for children. The Gusky Orphanage was established, and various family and health services were founded. The Hebrew Free Loan Association assisted the newcomers with small sums to start them in business.

The rush of immigration brought an influx of well-educated Hebraic scholars from the yeshivot of Lithuania and Poland. In 1877 Rabbi Markowitz led the first of many Orthodox congregations. Rabbi Simon Sivitz founded the Shaare Torah Congregation and *talmud torah* in 1888. In 1901 Rabbi Aaron *Ashinsky led Beth Jacob and Beth Hamedrash Hagodol, and was a driving force in creating new agencies conducted in the Orthodox tradition, including the House of Shelter, Home for Aged, and Hebrew Institute. A variety of synagogues served Russian, Polish, Galician, and Hungarian groups. The demand for *kasher* food in a hospital and the need for professional openings for Jewish doctors inspired a group of women, led by Mrs. Barnett David, to inaugurate fund raising that led to the creation of Montefiore Hospital. The Irene Kaufmann Settlement was the recreation center for large numbers of immigrants. By 1912 a full complement of social agencies united in the Federation of Jewish Philanthropies, with headquarters on Fernando Street, easily accessible to the Yiddish-speaking community from the Hill. In that year there were 35,000 Jews in Pittsburgh. By the close of free immigration in 1925, there were 60,000 Jews in the area, many of whom had begun spilling over the margins of the Hill to Oakland, East End, and Squirrel Hill.

A complex community was growing. The Workmen's Circle fostered socialist ideas in an agnostic framework. Largely inspired by Rabbi Ashinsky, a vibrant Zionist movement flourished. A branch of the American Jewish Committee came into being; the B'nai B'rith lodges multiplied, and the American Jewish Congress added a note of militancy. Jewish War Veterans organized a Post.

Post-World War I

A new generation of young people, native American Jews, moved with enthusiasm and talent through the public schools, heading on to colleges and eastern universities. English was spoken everywhere, and prevailing American social amenities were the norm. Attendance at worship services dropped off and religious education reached a low ebb. But the Jews were playing an appreciable role in the growth of Pittsburgh. Parallel with the vast development of the steel industry, Jewish storekeeping had blossomed into great department stores – Kaufmann's, Kaufmann and Baer's, Rosenbaum's, Frank and Seder's. These and other Jewish names appeared among those who sponsored symphony concerts, art exhibitions, and other cultural events. Although the leading social clubs still practiced exclusion, Jews had created pleasant facilities for themselves and began to emerge on the political and social scene, a number serving with distinction in the judiciary, city-council, board of education, and state legislature.

With the Depression of the 1930s, the Jews were able to "take care of their own" through numerous agencies which were united in the Federation of Jewish Philanthropies. As the decade advanced and the urgency to provide help for German Jewry became evident, new service and fund-raising agencies were called into being. In 1936 the United Jewish Fund was established. Reacting to the Nazi tragedy, Pittsburgh received its share of refugees from Germany, responded with fervor to the effort to create a Jewish homeland, and raised unprecedented sums for overseas relief.

A total transfer of Jewish population had taken place from the Hill to Squirrel Hill and the suburbs. New structures housed the synagogues, old and new. Awakened by the Holocaust, a renewed zeal for Jewish education resulted in highly developed programs of the Hebrew Institute, Hillel, and the Advanced Jewish Study Program of the United Jewish Federation. Synagogues responded with emphasis on education and youth, as well as keen interest in the State of Israel.

In 1970 Pittsburgh Jewry numbered 45,000, a decrease attributable to a growing tendency to relocate in the suburbs. Leadership passed into the hands of a new generation, largely of eastern European origin. Rodef Shalom remained the largest and most prestigious congregation, although no longer dominated solely by the "German" families. Montefiore Hospital, with 500 beds, was a teaching arm of the University of Pittsburgh. The Symphony Orchestra included many Jews, players as well as the conductor, and many generous patrons. There were several hundred Jewish teachers and principals in the public schools, and many distinguished members of university faculties. Jewish names were outstanding in the city's history – Otto *Stern, Nobel prize winner; Alexander Silverman, glass chemist; Joseph Slepian, electrical engineer; George S. *Kaufman, dramatist; Jonas *Salk, discoverer of polio vaccine; Solomon B. *Freehof, rabbi; Samuel Rosenberg, artist; William Steinberg, conductor; and Immanuel Estermann, physicist.

[Lillian A. Friedberg]

A study by the United Jewish Federation of Pittsburgh in 2002 revealed the following information:

In 2002, there were 54,000 people living in 20,900 Greater Pittsburgh Jewish households. In 1984, there were 47,700 people living in 19,000 Jewish households. This represents an increase of 14% in the number of people living in Jewish households and 10% in the number of households. The number of Jewish people in Greater Pittsburgh has declined by approximately 6% since 1984, but, in context, the Allegheny County population decreased by 11.6% during a similar time period (1980–2000).

Contrary to the graying of American Jews, 48% of the Jewish community of Pittsburgh is under the age of 40, and of those age 22 to 39, 40% have moved to the city in the past 10 years. Thus Pittsburgh is attracting young Jews.

The study reveals that Squirrel Hill remains a very vibrant, stable, and desirable neighborhood for the community. The Squirrel Hill section of Pittsburgh accounts for 47% of the entire Jewish population in greater Pittsburgh. Unique in North America, this is a tightly knit and closely connected third generation community. Often grandchildren live in their grandparents' homes as the generational transition keeps homes in the family. The infrastructure built up before World War II – and enhanced since then – continues to serve the community. Notable is the stability of Squirrel Hill, a geographic hub of the Jewish community located within the city limits. Other Jews are dispersed throughout the community and less linked to it. The Jewish population of the South Hills comprises 14% of the total; the Eastern Suburbs, 13%; the Fox Chapel/O'Hara Township and sections of the North Hills, 9%; East End, defined as East Liberty, Highland Park, and Stanton Heights, 5%; and the Western Suburbs, 5%.

The Pittsburgh Jewish community still has a significant elderly population, with 18% over the age of 65; unlike most North American Jewish communities, this percentage is comparable to the population in the country as a whole and not disproportionate to it. Perhaps this can be accounted for by the large percentage of elderly Jews who have moved to warmer climates. One in four Jews over 65 lives alone and almost one half have no adult children in the area.

The study showed significant needs in the Greater Pittsburgh Jewish community among the Jewish poor and near poor; 59% of households with incomes under $25,000 report "fair" or "poor" health.

Regarding Jewish denomination, 41% of all Jewish respondents self-identified as Reform, 32% as Conservative, 7% as Orthodox, 2% as Reconstructionist, and 14% as "no denomination, just Jewish."

The quantitative study was based on telephone interviews with 1,313 Jewish households conducted between November 8, 2001, and February 1, 2002. A Jewish household was defined as a residence where at least one adult considered himself/herself to be Jewish.

Pittsburgh has 28 congregations, among them Orthodox, Conservative, Reform, and Reconstructionist, as well as Gay. There is a Jewish women's center as well. There are Hillel Foundations at the University of Pittsburgh, Duquesne, and Carnegie Mellon as well as smaller schools in the area. The community has two Jewish Community Centers, one in Squirrel Hill and one in South Hill. Its local newspaper is the *Jewish Chronicle*, which serves western Pennsylvania and West Virginia as well. There is a community day school as well as the Hillel Academy. Yeshiva Schools and Mesivta of Allegheny County serve the Orthodox community. The United Jewish Federation of Pittsburgh was one of the first to sponsor a Holocaust Resource Center, and Jewish Studies programs are found at Pittsburgh and Carnegie Mellon University.

[Michael Berenbaum (2nd ed.)]

BIBLIOGRAPHY: M. Taylor, *Jewish Community of Pittsburgh, December, 1938* (1941); A.J. Karp (ed.), *Jewish Experience in America*, 1 and 4 (1968), indexes.

PITTSBURGH PLATFORM. The Pittsburgh Platform was a formulation of principles agreed upon by the Reform movement in 1885 at the Pittsburgh Conference. The conference was called together by Kaufmann *Kohler of New York and was chaired by Isaac M. *Wise of Cincinnati, the foremost figure in *Reform Judaism. The Pittsburgh Platform symbolized the merger of the Eastern U.S. and Germanic-oriented wings of Reform Judaism. The Eastern wing had previously been led by David *Einhorn, Kohler's father-in-law; Wise led the Germanic-oriented wing, which was stronger in the western U.S.

The following points were agreed upon and became known as the Pittsburgh Platform:

> First – We recognize in every religion an attempt to grasp the Infinite, and in every mode, source, or book or revelation held sacred in any religious system, the consciousness of the indwelling of God in man. We hold that Judaism presents the highest conception of the God idea as taught in our holy Scriptures and developed and spiritualized by the Jewish teachers, in accordance with the moral and philosophical progress of their respective ages. We maintain that Judaism preserved and defended, midst continual struggles and trials and under enforced isolation, this God idea as the central religious truth for the human race.
>
> Second – We recognize in the Bible the record of the consecration of the Jewish people to its mission as priest of the one God, and value it as the most potent instrument of religious and moral instruction. We hold that the modern discoveries of scientific researches in the domains of nature and history are not antagonistic to the doctrines of Judaism, the Bible reflecting the primitive ideas of its own age, and at times clothing its conception of Divine Providence and justice, dealing with man in miraculous narratives.
>
> Third – We recognize in the Mosaic legislation a system of training the Jewish people for its mission during its national life in Palestine, and today we accept as binding only the moral laws, and maintain only such ceremonies as elevate and sanctify our lives, but reject all such as are not adapted to the views and habits of modern civilization.
>
> Fourth – We hold that all such Mosaic and rabbinical laws as regulate diet, priestly purity, and dress, originated in ages and under the influence of ideas altogether foreign to our present mental and spiritual state. They fail to impress the modern Jew with a spirit of priestly holiness; their observance in our days is apt rather to obstruct than to further modern spiritual elevation.
>
> Fifth – We recognize, in the modern era of universal culture of heart and intellect, the approaching of the realization of Israel's great messianic hope for the establishment of the kingdom of truth, justice, and peace among all men. We consider ourselves no longer a nation, but a religious community, and therefore expect neither a return to Palestine, nor a sacrificial worship under the sons of Aaron, nor the restoration of any of the laws concerning the Jewish state.
>
> Sixth – We recognize in Judaism a progressive religion, ever striving to be in accord with the postulates of reason. We are convinced of the utmost necessity of preserving the historical identity with our great past. Christianity and Islam being daughter religions of Judaism, we appreciate their providential mission to aid in the spreading of monotheistic and moral truth. We acknowledge that the spirit of broad humanity of

our age is our ally in the fulfillment of our mission, and therefore, we extend the hand of fellowship to all who operate with us in the establishment of the reign of truth and righteousness among men.

Seventh – We reassert the doctrine of Judaism, that the soul of man is immortal, grounding this belief on the divine nature of the human spirit, which forever finds bliss in righteousness and misery in wickedness. We reject as ideas not rooted in Judaism the beliefs both in bodily resurrection and in Gehenna and Eden (Hell and Paradise) as abodes for everlasting punishment or reward.

Eighth – In full accordance with the spirit of Mosaic legislation, which strives to regulate the relation between rich and poor, we deem it our duty to participate in the great task of modern times, to solve on the basis of justice and righteousness, the problems presented by the contrasts and evils of the present organization of society.

At its founding in 1889, the *Central Conference of American Rabbis (CCAR), the Reform rabbinical organization, adopted the platform in toto, and it remained the major statement of the basic tenets of Reform Judaism until its extensive revision by the CCAR in Columbus, Ohio, in 1937.

An examination of the platform indicates its religious optimism. It is prepared to accept the legitimacy of other religious perspectives; all religions have some truth, but Judaism has the highest truth. It places its emphasis on the Bible – in contrast to the Talmud – but the Bible is described not as divine revelation but as the consecration of the Jewish people to its mission. The third element of the platform affirms the moral codes of Jewish tradition but discards the obligations of non-moral, ritual dimensions of the tradition. It treats laws as utilitarian; modernity becomes the key to the acceptance of laws. The fourth principle rejects halakhic restrictions on diet, priestly purity, and dress. Again, modern sensibility becomes the standard. The fifth principle embraces modernity as the realization of Israel's dream of a messianic age, rejecting the return to Zion and the restoration of sacrifice. "We consider ourselves no longer a nation, but a religious community." These words reject Jewish peoplehood, the essence of the Zionist vision. Principle six regards Judaism as being in accord with reason and rejects the non-rational in religious life. The seventh principle rejects bodily resurrection and a belief in heaven and hell as alien imports into Judaism. And the final element of the platform asserts the agenda of religious liberalism, working for justice and righteousness.

These principles defined Reform Judaism for almost half a century and distinguished it from Orthodox Judaism and Conservative Judaism as well as from Zionism. The Pittsburgh Platform is often referred to as Classical Reform Judaism. Reform rabbis, even leaders of the movement, did not necessarily adhere to these principles. Many were more Zionist in their orientation. Some were more observant, but it gave an ethos to the movement, one that was significantly rejected in 1937 with the Columbus Platform and by generations thereafter.

[Michael Berenbaum (2nd ed.)]

PITTUM HA-KETORET (Heb. פִּטּוּם הַקְּטֹרֶת; "ingredients of the incense"), the initial words of a *baraita* (Ker. 6a and TJ, Yoma 4:5, 41d) which enumerates the various species of incense offerings in the Temple service every evening and morning (see: Ex. 30: 34–38). In the Ashkenazi liturgy, this talmudic passage is recited on Sabbaths and festivals at the end of the Musaf prayer immediately after the *Ein ke-Elohenu hymn; in the Sephardi ritual it is recited every morning and afternoon. The custom of reciting *Pittum ha-Ketoret* is based on a quotation in the Zohar (to Num. 224a), where it is stated that a person who recites the section of incenses will be spared death (see also: Num. 17:12 and Yoma 44a). In Provence (southern France), it was customary to recite *Pittum ha-Ketoret* at the departure of the Sabbath, after the *Havdalah* service, as a good omen for wealth and prosperity (Abraham ha-Yarḥi, *Sefer ha-Manhig*, ed. Berlin (1855), Hilkhot Shabbat, 75, 35a).

BIBLIOGRAPHY: G. Munk, *The World of Prayer* 1 (1961), 193; 2 (1963), 58–59; Eisenstein, Dinim, s.v.

°**PIUS X** (1835–1914), pope from 1903. Friendly to individual Jews and ready to acknowledge their philanthropic activities, he was, however, disdainful of Judaism and the Jewish people. On one occasion, while serving as bishop of Mantua, he prohibited the celebration of a solemn mass in honor of the king's birthday because the mayor had attended a prayer service in the synagogue on that day. The pope reacted bitterly to a festive address by Ernesto *Nathan, mayor of Rome, on Sept. 20, 1910, delivered on the occasion of the 40th anniversary of the occupation of Rome by Italian troops, and asked Catholics to pray for the Church "which was being attacked with impunity by its enemies." On Jan. 25, 1904, he received Theodor *Herzl in private audience, only to inform him that he could not support the aspirations of Zionism despite Herzl's expressed statement that Jerusalem, because of its holy places, would be extraterritorial. The pope declared: "The Jews have not recognized our Lord, therefore we cannot recognize the Jewish people," and settlement of Ereẓ Israel by the Jews, he felt, would only make it incumbent upon him to intensify missionary activities among them: "If you come to Palestine and settle your people there, we shall have churches and priests ready to baptize all of you."

BIBLIOGRAPHY: K. Burton, *The Great Mantle. The Life of Giuseppe Melchiore Sarto, Pope Pius X* (1950); T. Herzl, *Complete Diaries*, ed. by R. Patai, 5 (1960), index.

[Willehad Paul Eckert]

°**PIUS XI** (1857–1939), pope from 1922. Concerned about the safety of the holy places, Pius XI had misgivings regarding the Palestine mandate. A decree of the Holy Office (March 21, 1928) proscribed the Amici Israel Association (founded two years earlier) which, though missionary in its ideology, tried to promote better understanding of Judaism. The Holy Office declared the organization contrary to the spirit of the Church, finding fault specifically with its publication *Pax* *super Israel*, which called upon its members to promote rapprochement with the Jews, while avoiding all offensive references and stressing the fact that the Jews continue to be the Chosen People. At the same time, however, the decree also proscribed antisemitism on the basis that it is contradictory to Christian doctrine.

Although Pius XI did not respond to a plea submitted to him in 1933 by a Catholic convert from Judaism, Edith *Stein, to issue an encyclical on the so-called Jewish problem, he condemned racism repeatedly. To a group of Belgian pilgrims, whom he received on Sept. 8, 1938, Pius XI declared: "It is not possible for Christians to take part in antisemitism. Spiritually we are Semites." His efforts to protect the Jews in Fascist Italy against antisemitic actions met with some success. He also helped immigrants and on Jan. 14, 1939, called upon the envoys accredited to the Holy See to provide as many immigration visas as possible "for the victims of racial persecution in Germany and Italy." It was during his pontificate that La *Civilta Cattolica, a Jesuit organ which had previously been anti-Jewish, protested that the periodical had been misused by the Fascists.

BIBLIOGRAPHY: G. Lewy, *The Catholic Church and Nazi Germany* (1964); G. Schwaiger, *Geschichte der Paepste im 20. Jahrhundert* (1968); S. Friedlaender, *Pius XII and the Third Reich* (1966), index.

[Willehad Paul Eckert]

°**PIUS XII** (1876–1958), pope from 1939. Born Eugenio Maria Giuseppe Giovanni Pacelli, in Rome, he entered the Secretariat of State in 1901, was professor of ecclesiastical diplomacy at the Pontifical Ecclesiastical Academy from 1909 to 1914, undersecretary of state in 1911, archbishop of Sardes and apostolic nuncio to the Bavarian court in Munich in 1917, and nuncio to Germany in 1920 but moving to Berlin only in 1925. In 1929 Pacelli concluded a concordat with the State of Prussia. He became cardinal in 1929 and secretary of state in 1930. Cardinal Pacelli was instrumental in negotiating the concordat between the Holy See and the Third Reich, which was signed on July 20, 1933, by him and Vice Chancellor von Papen. His ambivalent stance during the Nazi period subsequently gave rise to considerable controversy (much of it engendered by Rolf *Hochhuth's play *The Deputy*; for a full analysis see *Holocaust and the Christian Churches). On April 10, 1945, he received Moshe *Sharett, director of the Political Department of the Jewish Agency, to discuss with him the "situation of the Jews in Europe and the future of the Jews in Palestine." His views on the situation in Ereẓ Israel found expression in the encyclicals *Auspicia quaedam* (May 1, 1948), *In multiplicibus curis* (Oct. 24, 1948), and *In redemptoris nostri* (April 15, 1949), in which he recommended that Jerusalem should be internationalized. His attitude toward the State of Israel was reserved. On June 10, 1948, the Congregation of Rites ruled that the term *perfidi Judaei* in the Good Friday liturgy be translated into the vernacular as "unbelieving" and not as "faithless" as it had been hitherto.

BIBLIOGRAPHY: D. Fisher, *Pope Pius XII and the Jews* (1963); E.R. Bentley (ed.), *The Storm over the Deputy* (1964); G. Lewy, *The Catholic Church and Nazi Germany* (1964); S. Friedlaender, *Pius XII and the Third Reich* (1966); L. Rothkirchen, in: *Yad Vashem Studies*, 6 (1967), 27–53; P.E. Lapide, *Three Popes and the Jews* (1967), 117–305; C. Falconi, *The Silence of Pius XII* (1970).

[Willehad Paul Eckert]

PIYYUT (Heb. פִּיּוּט; plural: *piyyutim*; from the Greek ποιητής), a lyrical composition intended to embellish an obligatory prayer or any other religious ceremony, communal or private. In a wider sense, *piyyut* is the totality of compositions composed in various genres of Hebrew liturgical poetry from the first centuries of the Common Era until the beginning of the Haskalah. In ancient times, the *piyyutim* were intended to replace most of the set versions of prayer and to serve as substitutes. They ensured variety of the obligatory prayers, mainly on Sabbaths and festivals. In a later period, when the prayers became fixed, sections of *piyyut* were interspersed in certain places within the set pattern of the prayers. Naturally, most of the very extensive *piyyut* literature is devoted to the adornment of the major holy days. However, during the early Oriental (eastern) period of the history of the *piyyut*, liturgical compositions were also produced in great abundance for regular Sabbaths, for simple fast days, and even for weekdays. Obligatory prayers were also embellished with special sets of *piyyutim* for private occasions, such as weddings, circumcisions, and mourning. (See Table: *Piyyut*.)

The History of the *Piyyut*

Piyyut literature began in Ereẓ Israel while the various versions of the obligatory prayers were crystallizing. Though the evidence from this period is limited, texts of ancient *piyyutim* are to be found scattered in talmudic sources, and *piyyutim* which apparently were composed during this period were absorbed into the established versions of the various rites of prayer. These ancient segments are recognizable by their lofty style and characteristic rhythm; they do not as yet use rhyme. The ancient compositions, known in part from the Cairo *Genizah* and in part from other sources, and similarly characterized by their style and rhythm, were also apparently composed during this period, which may be called "the period of the anonymous *piyyut*."

The earliest *paytan* known to us by name is *Yose b. Yose, who lived and worked in Ereẓ Israel in approximately the sixth century or even earlier. His works still retain the above-mentioned characteristics of the form; they do not employ rhyme, even though something similar to rhyme can be seen in his *teki'ot*, where similar words are employed as line endings. With Yose b. Yose begins the period of the *paytanim* whose names are known; the period is represented by a group of important poets from Ereẓ Israel, who all seem to have been functioning before Ereẓ Israel was conquered by the Arabs (636 C.E.). The most important of these *paytanim* are *Yannai, *Simeon b. Megas, Eleazar b. *Kallir, *Ḥaduta b. Abraham, Joshua ha-

Kohen, and Joseph b. Nisan from Shaveh Kiryatayim. During their period, the structural framework of most of the classical *piyyut* types was finally crystallized. Even after Ereẓ Israel was conquered by the Arabs, all the great *paytanim* worked in the East; from then until the beginning of the 11th century this literature flourished; a great quantity of *piyyutim* was produced. For the first time *paytanim* from abroad, such as Solomon Suleiman b. ʾAmr al-Sanjari, Nissi al-Nahrawani, *Saadiah Gaon, Joseph al-Bardani, and others, begin to appear. Outstanding among the *paytanim* of Ereẓ Israel are *Phinehas b. Jacob ha-Kohen from Kafra at the beginning of the period, and *Samuel ha-Shelishi b. Hoshana at its close. Toward the end of the period, creative activity spread to North Africa, which in the tenth and eleventh centuries became a fruitful extension of Oriental *piyyut*.

On European soil, the first blossoms of *piyyut* literature appeared in Byzantine southern Italy in the second half of the ninth century. Only a few *piyyutim* from among the creations of the early Italian *paytanim*, *Silano, *Shephatiah, and his son *Amittai, are now extant, but even these testify to an extensive and consolidated literary activity, which, despite a number of interesting points of originality, reveals blatant signs of the influence of Ereẓ Israel. The creative work of the *paytanim* of southern Italy became, in the tenth century, a basis for the development of *piyyut* in central and northern Italy. The *paytanim* working there, headed by *Solomon b. Judah ha-Bavli, created a precedent for Central European *piyyut*, whose major representatives henceforth worked in Italy, Ashkenaz (Germany), France, and Byzantine Greece. The most important region of Central European sacred poetry was Germany, where the *piyyut* developed impressively because of the activity of a number of great *paytanim* in the 10th–11th centuries, such as *Moses b. Kalonymus, *Meshullam b. Kalonymus (both of Italian extraction), *Simeon b. Isaac, and Meir b. Isaac. In the succeeding centuries, Ashkenazi *piyyut* continued to develop, and a number of important composers made major contributions to the literature.

The direct continuation of Oriental *piyyut* was in Spain, where, beginning in the middle of the tenth century, several generations of great composers functioned. Outstanding among these are Joseph *Ibn Abitur, Solomon ibn *Gabirol, Isaac *Ibn Ghayyat, Moses *Ibn Ezra, *Judah Halevi, and Abraham *Ibn Ezra. These Spanish *paytanim* attained impressive peaks of perfection. Even though creativity in the realm of *piyyut* did not cease in Central Europe, Northern Africa, or the East until the beginning of the Haskalah, the 13th century marks the beginning of the decline; later *paytanim*, despite their often impressive productivity, failed to create major works. Although some of their poetry was included in local prayer rites, most of it has been excluded from accepted prayer books.

Types of *Piyyut*

Piyyutim can be divided according to their liturgical purpose into a number of categories, differing in their histories and development, their structures, and their distribution. In different periods, certain types of *piyyutim* were more prevalent than others. The earliest and most important types of *piyyut* are the *kerovah* and the *yoẓer*. The *kerovah* is designed for inclusion in the *Amidah* prayer, while the *yoẓer* belongs to the benedictions before and after the **Shema* in the **Shaḥarit* service. The *kerovot* divide into a number of secondary categories, according to the types of *Amidah* to which they are attached: the *kerovah* of the daily *Amidah* is called *kerovat Shemoneh Esreh* because of the 18 blessings in that *Amidah*; that of *Musaf* or *Maʿariv Amidah* for Sabbaths and the holy days is called *shivata* because of the seven blessings in these *Amidot*; while that of the *Shaḥarit Amidah* of the Sabbath and holy days, which include a *kedushah*, is called *kedushata* (in ancient Ereẓ Israel, *kedushah* was said on Sabbaths and festivals only in the *Shaḥarit* service). Each of the types of *kerovah* has its own structural characteristics. The *kerovah*, mainly the *kedushata*, is thought of as the dominant type of ancient *piyyut*. The *yoẓer* is combined from several types of *piyyut*, according to the structure of the permanent prayers replaced or embellished by *piyyut*. The *yoẓer* enjoyed great circulation mainly in the second period of Oriental *piyyut*, between the seventh and eleventh centuries. Parallel to the *yoẓerot*, which were intended for *Shaḥarit*, there are also, during this period, *piyyutim* of *Maʿariv*, intended to adorn the blessings before and after the *Shema* in the evening service. This type of *piyyut*, however, was never widely employed.

Among the *kerovot* of the major holidays, a number of special types of *piyyut* for different occasions are found. These include *tekiʿata*, which adorns the **malkhuyyot*, **zikhronot*, and **shofarot* blessings in the *Musaf Amidot* for New Year; *Seder ha-*Avodah* (which describes the sacrificial service on the Day of Atonement during the time the Temple was in existence), in the *Musaf kerovah* of the Day of Atonement; or the **azharot*, which discuss the list of 613 *mitzvot* in the Torah, in the *shivatot* of *Musaf* for Shavuot. The *kerovot* for fast days include **seliḥot* (penitential), while the *kerovot* for the Ninth of Av include *kinot* (dirges). In some communities these *seliḥot* and *kinot* were removed in later periods from the *kerovot* and placed after them. *Seliḥot* were also composed for the Days of Penitence during the month of Elul and between New Year and the Day of Atonement. The special processions for the days of Tabernacles (Sukkot) were embellished with *hoshana piyyutim* (see **Hoshanot*). In the early period of *piyyut*, works were not composed to adorn religious ceremonies outside of the obligatory prayers, except for the Grace after Meals, and even in that case, they were probably intended, from the start, for use at communal festive meals or at meals for religious ceremonies. Similarly, *ashkavah piyyutim* were composed in this period (*aftarot*, or *ẓidduk ha-din*, "funeral services").

All the classical types of *piyyut* were cultivated to some

extent by the later European *paytanim*. However, the scope of the *piyyut* literature was greatly enlarged, mainly in Spain, by the creation of a number of new types of *piyyut*. The Spanish *paytanim* preceded the accepted patterns of the *yoẓer* with a number of *piyyut* passages which they interlaced in the prayer said on Sabbaths and festivals before the *yoẓer* prayers. These types are known as the *nishmat*, the *muḥarakh*, the *illufinu*, and the *kol aẓmotai*. The Spanish *paytanim* also cultivated the type known as *reshut* (pl. *reshuyyot*, "introductory *piyyutim*"), and they joined these works to the *Barukh she-Amar* prayer, to *nishmat*, to **Kaddish* after *nishmat*, to **Barekhu*, and so on. In addition to their extensive work with these types, the Spanish *paytanim* developed new types of special *piyyutim* for private religious ceremonies, such as Sabbath songs and **Havdalot*, as well as types of religious poetry intended to satisfy the spiritual needs of the individual. To a certain extent, the Ashkenazi *paytanim* followed them in these areas.

A considerable part of the creative efforts of the European *paytanim* was dedicated to the type known as *seliḥot* for fast days and days of penitence. Because of the great creative activity in this area, a number of secondary types within the category have been distinguished, some partly because of thematic distinctions and some because of formal distinctions. The early Oriental *seliḥah* recognized only the category *ḥatanu* (*seliḥot* of confession), and the *tokhaḥah* ("rebuke") as a secondary type. In a later period, the **Akedah* type was added to them, in which God's mercy is requested for Israel because of the merit of the binding of Isaac. According to structural distinctions, a number of secondary types of *seliḥot* are distinguishable, of which the important ones are the *pizmon* (a *seliḥah* with an opening refrain and a strophe), and the *mustagib* (a *seliḥah* in which a biblical passage appears as a refrain at the end of every verse). In specific sources, especially Ashkenazi, the *seliḥot* are distinguished by special names according to their place in the calendar, their composers, the way they are said, or the number of lines in their poetic phrases.

Language and Style

The style and the vocabulary of the *paytanim* vary in the different periods and different poetic schools. In the anonymous period of *piyyut*, the style followed the stylistic and lexical paths of the permanent prayers; the vocabulary is mostly biblical, even though some later linguistic bases – midrashic and talmudic – may be found in it. The style of the *piyyutim* is lucid and clear and contains little wordplay or rhetorical embellishment. With the work of Yannai, Hebrew sacral poetry becomes more and more expansive in its vocabulary and increasingly vague and flowery in its style. During the whole Oriental period of the *piyyut*, the composers used not only the whole Hebrew lexicon, with all its various layers and strata (to a certain extent, in the early *piyyut* creations, ancient Hebrew words with no mention in the sources are preserved) but they also adorned the *piyyut* with idioms and words of their own creation. The poetic novelties of language and form, which do not always fit the classical rules of Hebrew grammar, gave a singular stylistic character to the poetic creations, and frequently aroused harsh criticism. These *paytanim* (who are included among those of the Kallir school, so called after its major representative, the *paytan* Eleazar b. Kallir), often used a complicated set of terms, flavoring their works with an abundance of talmudic and midrashic material, or with (sometimes vague) allusions to this material. Thus, some of their works became enigmatic, constituting difficult exegetical problems. From a linguistic point of view, *piyyut* reached its peak in the works of Saadiah Gaon and his pupils, during the tenth and eleventh centuries. The *paytanim* of the "Saadiah school" were the most radical in establishing novel uses of language in their *piyyutim*.

As a reaction to the Saadianic style of exaggerated innovations, and probably under the influence of the new ways and principles of Andalusian arabized secular poetry and of philological studies, Hebrew sacred poetry in Spain crystallized within clearly biblical frameworks of language and style. The first of the Spanish *paytanim* composed their works according to the example of the later Oriental *paytanim*. In addition to the works written in this style, there exists a parallel group of works, written in the Spanish model in a language which strives to recognize only a biblical vocabulary and in a style which strives to free itself of talmudic and midrashic material and allusions to the teachings of the rabbis. The style of the Spanish *piyyutim* is impressively lucid and flexible, approaching the style of secular poetry; in this period, sacred poetry was notably influenced by secular poetry both in form and in lyrical means of expression. Solomon ibn Gabirol was instrumental in the process by which the *piyyut* was increasingly purified of the linguistic-stylistic exaggerations of eastern *piyyut*; the earliest of the Spanish *paytanim* whose work appears to be entirely within the new stylistic framework is Isaac Ibn Ghayyat. During this period, the style of writing of the Spanish *paytanim* greatly influenced the *paytanim* of other lands, such as North Africa, Yemen, Ereẓ Israel, Babylonia, and Provence. Certain traces of Spanish influence are found also in later Ashkenazi *piyyut*. In general, Central European *piyyut* remained faithful to the Kallir model in language and style. Even so, Italian and Ashkenazi poets were more restrained and moderate in their use of language and style. In the creations of the greatest of them, the poetic language reaches impressive heights of beauty and flexibility.

Rhyme and Meter

The ancient anonymous *piyyut* did not employ rhyme. The *piyyutim* composed during this period with the characteristic method of dividing each poetic line into four feet, each one having two or three stresses, are limited. With the beginning of the use of rhyme, or more specifically, with the period of the literary activity of Yannai, the *paytanim* concentrate much more on rhyme than on rhythm. Those of the Kallir school attained great virtuosity in their methods of rhyming and playing with rhyme, and this lowered the level and content of the creations, especially in the works of mediocre *paytanim*. A number of eastern *paytanim* wrote their works in a peculiar rhythmic system (known as *mishkal ha-tevot*), by establishing an identical number of words or stresses in every poetic line, but this method is found in only a few works, and was used more widely in the works of the first Central European *paytanim*, who also continued and developed the traditions of rhyme of the early Kallir school. It was the Spanish *paytanim* who introduced a precise method of rhythm in their *piyyutim*. Many of their works, mainly in the specific types of *piyyut* which originated in Spain, are subject to the quantitative method of meter – Arabic in its source – of secular poetry, but the major part of their work is in a unique meter created in Spain for sacred poetry. This is mainly syllabic, meting out to each line of poetry a specific fixed number of grammatical syllables. In Spain, however, the *paytanim* also continued to compose *piyyutim* without meter, particularly in the classical types of *piyyut*. Rhyme also developed impressively in Spain, particularly in the short types of *piyyut*, under the influence of the *ezor* (Muwassaha) type of secular poems. Many *piyyutim*, some metered precisely according to the example of the *ezor* type, some metered according to the special method of Spanish *piyyut*, have a variegated and rich rhyme, which competes successfully with the best achievements of Hebrew secular poetry in Spain.

Signatures

The first *paytanim* signed their *piyyutim* only with their own names. Later, they added patronymics and the places where they wrote; and, after a while, they added blessings and the like. At times, the *paytanim* also added the names of relatives.

Collections of *Piyyutim*

The extent to which *piyyutim* were incorporated into the prayer service differs in time and locality. In ancient times, there was fierce opposition to the *piyyut* literature, mainly from the great academy in Babylonia. Nevertheless, it appears that there was a wide use of *piyyutim* in most of the early eastern communities. During this period there were still no fixed collections of *piyyutim* for the use of various communities. Rather, each cantor recited *piyyutim* according to his taste and choice. Only in later periods, when the congregations took greater part in prayer services, was the set recitation of certain *piyyutim* for various liturgical occasions practiced. These fixed prayers, which multiplied, led to the collections of *piyyutim* (*maḥzorim*, books of *seliḥot*, and *kinot*) which established for every occasion passages of *piyyut*, whose recitation was repeated year after year. At first, each community established its own collection, usually by choosing *piyyut* passages and adding the works of local composers. In a later period, the distinctions between the collections of *piyyutim* of the various communities became increasingly blurred and, with the invention of printing, unified collections of *piyyutim* crystallized for different rites of prayer. (See table on following page.)

BIBLIOGRAPHY: Waxman, Literature, 1 (1960), ch. 9; 2 (1960^2), ch. 3; Zunz, Poesie; Zunz, Ritus; Zunz, Lit Poesie; Elbogen, Gottesdienst, 206–31, 280–353; Zulay, in: YMḤSI, 5 (1939), 107–80; Mirsky, *ibid.*, 7 (1958), 1–129; A. Mirsky, *Reshit ha-Piyyut* (1965); S. Abramson, *Bi-Leshon Kodemim* (1965); Davidson, Oẓar, index, s.v. names of *paytanim*; J. Yahalom, *The Syntax of Ancient Piyyut* (including Yannai) *as a Basis for its Style* (1974). **ADD. BIBLIOGRAPHY:** E. Fleischer, *Shirat ha-Kodesh ha-Ivrit bi-Ymei ha-Benayim* (1975); idem, *Ha-Yoẓerot be-Hithavvutam ve-Hitpatteḥutam* (1984); Sh. Elizur, *Piyyutei Eleazar be-Rabi Ḳilar ve-Yaḥasam li-Yeẓirato shel Eleazar Berabi Ḳilir* (1981); idem: *Paitan be-'Idan shel Mifneh: R. Yehoshu'a Bar Khalfa u-Fiyyutav* (1994); idem, *Shirah shel Parashah: Parashot ha-Torah bi-Re'i ha-Piyyut* (1999); N. Weissenstern (ed.), *Piyyutei Yoḥanan ha-Kohen be-Rabi Yehoshu'a* (diss., 1983); L. Weinberger, *Early Synagogue Poets in the Balkans* (1988); A. Mirsky, *Ha-Piyyut: Hitpatḥuto be-Ereẓ-Yisra'el u-va-Golah* (1990); idem, *Me-Ḥovot ha-Levavot le-Shirat ha-Levavot* (1992); R.P. Scheindlin, *The Gazelle: Medieval Hebrew Poems on God, Israel, and the Soul* (1991); I. Levin and A. Sáenz-Badillos, *Si me olvido de ti, Jerusalén… Cantos de las Sinagogas de al-Andalus* (1992); Z.Z. Breuer, *Shirat ha-Kodesh shel Rabi Shelomoh Ibn Gabirol: Tokhen ve-Ẓurah* (1993); Eleazar ben Judah, *Shirat ha-Roke'ah. Piyyutei Eleazar mi-Vermaiza*, ed. I. Meiseles (1993); A.V. Tanenbaum, *Poetry and Philosophy: The Idea of the Soul in Andalusian Piyyut* (1993); S. Kats, *R. Yiẓḥak Ibn Gi'at: Monografyah* (1994); E. Hollender, *Synagogale Hymnen: Qedushtaót des Simon b. Isaak im Amsterdam Mahsor* (1994); idem, *Clavis Commentariorum of Hebrew Liturgical Poetry in Manuscript* (2005); M. Zulay, *Ereẓ-Yisra'el u-Fiyyuteha: Meḥkarim be-Fiyyutei ha-Genizah*, ed. E. Ḥazan (1995); idem, *Mi-pi Paytanim ve-Shofkhei Siaḥ*, ed. Sh. Elitsur (2004); Sh. Spiegel, *Avot ha-Piyyut: Mekorot u-Meḥkarim le-Toledot ha-Piyyut be-Ereẓ Yisra'el*, ed. M. Schmelzer (1996); M. Zulay and E. Hazan, *Ereẓ-Yisra'el u-Fiyyuteha: Meḥkarim be-Fiyyutei ha-Genizah* (1995); E.D. Goldschmidt, *Meḥkerei Tefillah u-Fiyyut* (1996); David Ben-Hasin, *Tehilah le-David: Koveẓ Shirato shel David Ben-Hasin*; ed. A.E. Elbaz et al. (1996); idem, David Ben-Hasin, *Tefillah le-David: Azharot*, ed. A.E. Elbaz et al. (2000); idem, *Leket Shirei David Ben Hasin: …mi-Tokh Sifro Tehilah le-David* (2005); M. Ben-Yashar, *Siftei Renanot: Mivḥar Piyyutim le-Shabatot u-le-Mo'adim* (1996); Isaac ha-Seniri, *Piyyutei R. Yiẓḥak ha-Seniri*, ed. B. Bar-Tikva (1996); Y. David, J. Schirmann, et al., *Osef Shirei Kodesh: Ketav Yad mi-Sefarad u-mi-Arẓot ha-Magreb me-ha-Me'ah ha-14* (1997); W. van Bekkum, *Hebrew Poetry from Late Antiquity: Liturgical Poems of Yehudah* (1998); R. Halevi, *Shirat Yisra'el be-Teiman: mi-Mivḥar ha-Shirah ha-Shabazit-Teimanit* (1998); N. Katsumatah, *Sidrei Avodah le-Yom ha-Kippurim min ha-Dorot ha-Semukhim le-R. Se'adyah Ga'on* (1998); J. Yahalom, *Shirat Benei Yisra'el ba-Tekufah ha-Bizantinit ve-ad Kibushei ha-Ẓalbanim* (1996); idem, *Piyyut u-Meẓi'ut be-Shilheu ha-Zeman ha-Atik* (1999); I. Meiseles, *Shirat ha-Miẓvot: Azharot Rabi Eliyahu ha-Zaken* (2001); T. Beeri, *Ha-Ḥazzan ha-Gadol asher be-Bagdad: Piyyutei Yosef ben Ḥayyim Albaradani* (2002); N. Katsumata, *The Liturgical Poetry of Nehemiah ben Shelomoh ben Heiman ha-Nasi* (2002); idem, *Hebrew Style in the Liturgical Poetry of Shmuel Hashlishi* (2003); Y. Ratzaby, *Shirei R. Shalem Shabazi: Bibliografyah* (2003); M. Zulay, and S. Elizur, *Mi-pi Paytanim ve-Shofkhei Si'ah* (2004); M.D. Swartz and J. Yahalom, *Avodah: An Anthology of Ancient Poetry for Yom Kippur* (2005).

[Ezra Fleischer]

The following list contains:

1. Those *paytanim* and pre-modern poets who have individual entries in the Encyclopedia – included are those who are either primarily *paytanim* or famous as such;

2. Paytanim and pre-modern poets who do not have individual entries and who are not included in (1) Davidson's *Oẓar ha-Shirah ve-ha-Piyyut* (vol. 4, pp. 347) which was completed in 1933 (Davidson's additions were published in HUCA 12–13, 1937–38);

3. Paytanim and pre-modern poets who are in Davidson but on whom new material has been made available in the intervening years.

The list is alphabetical according to the first names.

The abbreviations used (other than standard) are the following:

Bernstein, Italyah – S. Bernstein, *Mi-Shirei Yisrael be-Italyah* (1939).

Bernstein, Piyyutim – S. Bernstein, *Piyyutim u-Faytanim meha-Tekufah ha-Bizantinit* (1941).

Habermann, Ateret – A.M. Habermann, *Ateret Renanim* (1967).

Schirmann, Italyah – J. Schirmann, *Mivḥar ha-Shirah ha-Ivrit be-Italyah* (1934).

Schirmann, Sefarad – J. Schirmann, *Ha-Shirah ha-Ivrit bi-Sefarad u-vi-Provence*, 2 vols. (1959–60[2]).

Schirmann, Shirim Hadashim – J. Schirmann, *Shirim Ḥadashim min ha-Genizah* (1965).

Simonsohn, Mantovah – S. Simonsohn, *Toledot ha-Yehudim be-Dukkasut Mantovah*, 2 vols. (1962–64).

YMḤSI – *Yedi'ot ha-Makhon le-Ḥeker ha-Shirah ha-Ivrit*, 7 vols. (1933–58).

Name	Place	Dates
Aaron b. Abraham of Offenbach Habermann, Ateret, 126–7, 225.	Germany	18th century
Aaron b. Isaac *Hamon		
Aaron b. Joshua ibn Alamani J. Schirmann, in: YMḤSI, 6 (1945), 265–85; S.D. Goitein, in: *Tarbiz*, 28 (1959), 343ff.; A. Scheiber in: *Sefarad*, 27 (1967), 269–81.	Alexandria	12th century
Aaron b. Mariyyon ha-Kohen M. Zulay, in: YMḤSI, 5 (1939), 178–80; idem, in: *Sinai*, 23 (1948), 214–28.	Acre	11/12th century
Aaron b. Moses Malti M. Benayahu, in: *Sefunot*, 3–4 (1969), 17.	Babylonia	16/17th century
Aaron b. Samuel ha-Levi A.M. Habermann, Amarai Kaḥ (1964).	Spain	14/15th century
*Aaron Hakiman		
Abner A.M. Habermann, in: *Sefer ha-Yovel… S. Federbush* (1961), 173–99.	Spain	14th century
*Abraham b. Daniel		
Abraham b. Daniel Buttrio M. Benayahu, in: *Rabbi Yosef Caro*, ed. by Y. Raphael (1969), 309–12, 323–5.	Italy	b. 1510
Abraham b. Gabriel Zafrana J.L. Weinberger, in: HUCA, 39 (1968), 19–22 (Heb. part).	Corfu	16th century
Abraham b. Isaac M. Zulay, in: *Sinai*, 25 (1949), 46–47.	Babylonia?	10/11th century
Abraham b. Isaac H. Schirmann, in: *Leshonenu*, 21 (1957), 212–9; S. Abramson, *ibid.*, 25 (1961), 31–34.	Italy	11th century
Abraham b. Isaac *Bedersi		
Abraham b. Isaac Da Pisa Bernstein, Italyah, passim.	Italy	16th century
Abraham b. Isaac he-Ḥasid Tawil S. Bernstein, in: *Tarbiz*, 15 (1944), 97, 101–7; idem, in: *Ha-Tekufah*, 32–33 (1948), 780; D. Yarden, in: *Sefunot*, 8 (1964), 259, 266–72.	Lybia	
Abraham b. Jacob H. Merhaviah, in: *Tarbiz*, 39 (1970), 277–84.	Germany	11/12th century
Abraham b. Jacob Habermann, Ateret, 18–19, 225.	Germany or France	12th century
Abraham b. Jacob Gavison R.S. Sirat, in: *Fourth World Congress of Jewish Studies Papers*, 2 (1968), 66–67.	Algiers	1520–1578
Abraham b. Joseph ha-Kohen M. Zulay in: *Sinai*, 28 (1951), 162.	Ereẓ Israel	11th century

Name	Place	Dates
Abraham b. Mattathias Schirmann, Italyah, 78–79.	Rome	12th century
Abraham b. Mereno ha-Kohen Bernstein, Piyyutim, 27–28.	Corfu	13th century
Abraham b. Moses Doresh A.M. Habermann, in: Maḥanayim, 30 (1956), 149, 151–2.		14th century
Abraham b. Samuel Schirmann, Sefarad, 2 (1960²), 457–58; S. Abramson, in: *Leshonenu la-Am*, 18 (1967), 67ff.	Spain	13th century
Abraham b. Samuel ha-Levi *Ibn Ḥasdai		
*Abraham b. Samuel he-Ḥasid (of Speyer)		
Abraham b. Shabbetai Kohen Schirmann, Italyah, 358.	Greece, Padua	1670–1729
Abraham b. Solomon ha-Levi Buqarat H.H. Ben-Sasson in: *Tarbiz*, 31 (1961), 59–71; A.M. Habermann, *ibid.*, 301.	Spain, Tunis	15/16th century
Abraham Di Medina M. Benayahu, in: KS, 35 (1960), 530.	Egypt	17th century
Abraham ha-Kohen A. Scheiber, in: *Zion*, 30 (1965), 123–7.	Babylonia	10th century
Abraham Ḥazzan Gerondi Schirmann, Sefarad, 2 (1960²), 291–4.	Spain	13th century
Abraham *Ibn Al-Rabib		
Abraham *Ibn Ezra		
Abraham Kohen N. Ben-Menahem, in: *Sinai*, 13 (1943), 363–5.	Crete	16th century
Abraham *Kurtabi (Kortabi)		
Abraham Maimin A.M. Habermann, *Toledot ha-Piyyut ve-ha-Shirah* (1970), 141; M. Benayahu, in: KS, 35 (1960), 528.	Safed	d. 1570?
Abu Ibrahim Isaac ibn Maskaran J. Schirmann, in: YMḤSI, 4 (1938), 277.	Spain	12th century
Abu Isaac Abraham *Harizi		
Abu Ishaq Ibrahim *Ibn Sahl		
Adonim b. Nissim ha-Levi N. Allony in: *Sinai*, 43 (1958), 393–4; Schirmann, Shirim Ḥadashim, 58–62.	Fez	10/11th century
*Ahimaaz b. Paltiel		
Ahitub b. Isaac J. Schirmann, in: YMḤSI, 1 (1933), 132–47.	Palermo	13th century
Akiva b. Jacob J.L. Bialer, *Min ha-Genazim* (1967), 69–77.	Frankfurt	1520?–1597
*Ali (b. David) M. Zulay, in: *Sinai*, 23 (1948), 214–28.	Orient	12/13th century
Ali b. Ezekiel ha-Kohen A.M. Habermann, in: *Sinai*, 53 (1963), 183–4, 191–2.	Egypt	11th century
*Alvan b. Abraham		
*Amittai		
*Amnon of Mainz		
Amram b. Moses Ḥazzan S. Assaf and L.A. Mayer (eds.), *Sefer ha-Yishuv*, 2 (1944), 54; Habermann, Ateret, 149, 212, 230.	Ereẓ Israel	10th century?
*Anan b. Marinus ha-Kohen		
Anatoli J. Schirmann, in: YMḤSI, 1 (1933), 106–7, 121–4.	Italy	12th century
Anatoli (Zerahiah) b. David Cazani J. Schirmann, in: YMḤSI, 1 (1933), 107; J.L. Weinberger, in: HUCA, 39 (1968), 27–29 (Heb. part).	Greece	12th century
*Aryeh Judah Harari		
Asher b. Isaac ha-Levi S.H. Kook, *Iyyunim u-Meḥkarim*, 2 (1963), 197–201; E.E. Urbach (ed.), *Arugat ha-Bosem*, of Azriel b. Abraham, 4 (1963), 15–16.	Worms	11/12th century
Avigdor *Kara		

Name	Place	Dates
Avtalyon b. Mordecai	Turkey	17th century
Azriel b. Joseph	Orient	13th century
Schirmann, Shirim Ḥadashim, 392–6.		
*Baḥya (Baḥye) b. Joseph ibn Paquda		
Barhun (Abraham; maybe *Abraham b. Sahalan)		
M. Zulay, *Ha-Askolah ha-Paytanit shel Rav Sa'adyah Ga'on* (1964), 35.		
*Baruch b. Samuel of Mainz		
Ben ha-Melekh ve-ha-Nazir		
Benjamin b. Abraham *Anav		
*Benjamin b. Azriel		
*Benjamin b. Ḥiyya		
*Benjamin b. Samuel ha-Levi		
*Benjamin b. Zerah	Germany	11th century
Habermann, Ateret, 176–7, 226.		
Benjamin Peraḥyah	Greece?	14th century?
Bernstein, Piyyutim, 36–39.		
Benveniste b. Ḥiyya al-Dayyan	Spain	12/13th century
J.L. Weinberger, in: HUCA, 39 (1968), 23–26 (Heb. part).		
Ben Zion Aryeh Gerondi	Padua	1763–1820?
Habermann, Ateret, 128–9, 226.		
*Berechiah b. Natronai ha-Nakdan		
Caleb b. Said	Babylonia	10th century
M. Zulay, in: *Sinai*, 25 (1949), 36–37.		
Daniel b. Samuel *Rossena		
*David b. Aaron ibn Ḥassin		
David b. Gedaliah	France or Italy	12th century
Habermann, Ateret, 173–4, 226.		
David b. Huna	Italy	10th century
S. Bernstein, in: *Sefer ha-Yovel, Meir Waxman* (1966), 45–58.		
David b. Nasi	Orient	11th century
J. Ratzaby, in: *Tarbiz*, 14 (1943), 204–13.		
David b. Saadiah ha-Kohen	Yemen	17th century
J. Tubi, in: *Ba-Ma'arakhah*, 11 (1971), no. 121, 18–19.		
David b. Samson	France	13th century?
H. Schirmann, in: *Kobez al-Jad*, 13 (1939), 43–44.		
David b. Yom Tov *Ibn Bilia		
David ha-Kohen	Spain or Provence	13th century
Schirmann, Sefarad, 2 (1956), 463–5; Habermann, Ateret, 175, 226.		
David *Ibn Paquda		
David Onkinerah	Salonika	16th century
J. Patai, in: *Kobez al-Jad*, 12 (1937), 75–119.		
Dosa b. Joshua ha-Ḥazzan		
S. Abrason, in: *Tarbiz*, 15 (1944), 55–59.		
Dunash b. Judah	Kairouan	11th century
N. Allony, in: *Sinai*, 43 (1958), 90, 387, 396–400; Habermann, Ateret, 94–95.		
*Eleazar		
Eleazar b. Abun	Ereẓ Israel	
S. Spiegel, in: YMḤSI, 5 (1939), 267–91.		
*Eleazar b. Ḥalfon ha-Kohen		
Eleazar b. Phinehas	Ereẓ Israel	
M. Zulay, in: YMḤSI, 5 (1939), 147–8.		
Eleazar ha-Ḥazzan	Ereẓ Israel	
M. Zulay, in: YMḤSI, 1 (1933), 155–6.		
Eleazar Hodaya	Ereẓ Israel	
E. Fleisher, in: *Tarbiz*, 36 (1967), 342 ff.		
Eleazar *Kallir		
Eleazar Kohen	Spain	
A. Scheiber, in: *Sinai*, 35 (1954), 183–6.		

Name	Place	Dates
Eliakim S. Bernstein, in: *Sefer Yovel li-Khevod S.K. Mirsky* (1958), 465–6, 478–9.	Crimea	14/15th century
Eliakim b. Abraham D. Pagis, in: *Sefer Ḥayyim Schirmann* (1970), 247–8.	Europe	14/15th century
Eliashib Joshua Provencale M. Benayahu, in: *Rabbi Yosef Caro*, ed by Y. Raphael (1969), 313, 340.	Italy	16th century
Eliezer b. Ephraim Urbach, Tosafot, 414–6.	Germany or France	13th century
*Eliezer b. Samson		
Eliezer de Mordo Bernstein, Piyyutim, 16–18; S. Simonsohn, in: PAAJR, 34 (1966), 106–8.	Corfu	17/18th century
Eliezer Gentili (Ḥefeẓ) Schirmann, Italyah, 398.	Italy	18th century
Eliezer Leizer b. Judah Loeb A.M. Habermann, in: *Maḥanayim*, 89 (1964), 20–23.	Germany	17th century
Elijah b. Abraham Bernstein, Piyyutim, 63–65.	Greece	15th century?
Elijah b. David Mazzal Tov Bernstein, Piyyutim, 65–67.	Corfu	1575–1625
Elijah b. Eliezer Delmedigo J.L. Weinberger, in: HUCA, 39 (1968), 34–37 (Heb. part).	Crete	16th century
*Elijah b. Eliezer Philosoph		
Elijah b. Menahem ha-Zaken A.M. Habermann (ed.), *Shirei ha-Yiḥud ve-ha-Kavod* (1948), 87–97.	Le Mans	11th century
Elijah b. Mordecai A. Mirsky, in: *Sinai*, (1969), 179–87.	Italy	10th century
Elijah b. Moses *Kapuzato		
Elijah b. Samuel A.M. Habermann, *Sefer ha-Yovel…* Ḥ. Albeck (1963), 160–76.	Macedonia	15th century
Elijah b. Shemaiah Schirmann, Italyah, 41–47; Habermann, Ateret, 22–24, 225.	Bari	11th century
Elijah b. Shalom, or, Samuel A.M. Habermann, in: *Haaretz* (Sept. 21, 1960).	Germany	13th century?
*Elijah Chelebi-ha-Kohen Anatolia		
Elijah of Buttrio M. Benayahu, in: *Rabbi Yosef Caro*, ed. by Y. Raphael (1969), 312–3, 326–39. ("En") Maimon *Galipapa	Italy	16th century
*Ephraim b. Isaac of Regensburg		
Ephraim b. Joab Schirmann, Italyah, 200–2.	Modena (Italy)	14th century
Ezekiel b. Ali ha-Kohen Albasir M. Zulay, in: YMḤSI, 3 (1936), 57–58; A. Mirsky, *Yalkut ha-Piyyutim* (1958), 60–63.	Persia, Iraq, or Egypt	11th century
Ezekiel (Hezekiah) David b. Mordecai *Abulafia (Bolaffi)		
Gamaliel b. Moses Schirmann, Shirim Ḥadashim, 126–9.	Egypt	12th century
Gershom b. Solomon b. Isaac J. Schirmann, in: *Kobez al-Jad*, 3 (1939), 41–43.	France or Germany	12th century
*Haduta b. Abraham ha-Efrati		
Hananel b. Amnon S.H. Kook, *Iyyunim u-Meḥkarim*, 2 (1963), 201–2.	Italy	10th century
Hananiah S. Bernstein, in: *Sinai*, 19 (1946), 213.	Orient	12th century
Hananiah Eliakim b. Asael Raphael Rieti Simonsohn, Mantovah, 2 (1964), 544.	Bologna and Mantua	1561–1623
Ḥarizi Habermann, Ateret 113, 226	Spain	
Ḥayyim b. Machir J. Schirmann, in: *Kobez al-Jad*, 13 (1939), 58–62; A.M. Habermann, *Gezerot Ashkenaz ve-Ẓarefat* (1946), 198–202.	Regensburg	13th century

Name	Place	Dates
Ḥiyya b. Al-Daudi	Spain	d. 1153/54
S. Bernstein, in: *Sinai*, 19 (1946), 99–104, 208–17, 313–37.		
Immanuel b. David *Frances		
Immanuel Benevento	Italy	16th century
I. Sonne, *Mi-Paulus ha-Revi'I ad Pius ha-Hamishi* (1954), 110–7.		
Immanuel b. Joseph	Spain	14th century
S. Bernstein, *Al Naharot Sefarad* (1956), 191–3, 269–70.		
*Immanuel b. Solomon of Rome		
Isaac, poet of *Ezrat Nashim*	Castile	13th century
Schirmann, Sefarad, 2 (1956), 87–96.		
*Isaac (Isḥak)		
Isaac *Al-Avani		
Isaac Amigo	Turkey	17th century
M. Benayahu in: KS, 35 (1960), 528–9.		
Isaac b. Abraham	Provence	13th century
G. Sed-Rajna, in: REJ, 126 (1967), 265–7.		
*Isaac b. Abraham ha-Gorni	Greece	15th century?
Isaac b. Abraham ha-Parnas		
Bernstein, Piyyutim, 67–71.		
Isaac b. Fayun	Egypt?	early poet
Habermann, Ateret, 120, 228.		
*Isaac b. Ḥayyim b. Abraham		
*Isaac b. Joseph ibn *Pollegar		
*Isaac b. Judah		
*Isaac b. Judah *Gerondi		
*Isaac b. Judah ha-Seniri		
Isaac b. Kalo [nymus?]	Romania?	14/15th century?
Habermann, Ateret, 148, 228		
Isaac b. Levi *ibn Mar Saul		
Isaac b. Moses Hezekiah ha-Levi	Italy	16th century
M. Benayahu, in: *Rabbi Yosef Caro*, ed. by Y. Raphael (1969), 317, 349–51.		
Isaac b. Solomon *Alḥadib	Spain, Syracuse,	14th century
I. Davidson in: *Tarbiz*, 11 (1940), 111; C. Roth, in: JQR, 47 (1956–57), 324.	Palermo	
Isaac b. Solomon he-Haver	Ereẓ Israel	10/11th century
M. Zulay, in: *Sefer Assaf* (1953), 303–6.		
*Isaac b. Yakar	Germany	12th century
A.M. Habermann, in: *Haaretz* (Sept. 25, 1955).		
Isaac b. Zerahiah ha-Levi Gerondi	Spain	13th century
Schirmann, Sefarad, 2 (1956), 285–90; A.M. Habermann, in: *Haaretz* (May 28, 1963).		
Isaac de Leon	Egypt	17th century
M. Wallenstein, in: *Sefer ha-Yovel, Tiferet Yisrael to I. Brody* (1966), 171–78 (Heb. part).		
Isaac ha-Ḥazzan b. Joseph	Ereẓ Israel?	10/11th century?
M. Zulay, in: *Sinai*, 16 (1945), 39–48.		
Isaac ha-Levi	Orient	13th century?
A.M. Habermann, in: *Eked*, 3 (1960), 91–98.		
Isaac Ḥandali	Crimea	15th century
S. Bernstein, in *Sefer Hadoar* (1957), 83–85; idem, in: *Sefer Yovel li-Khevod S.K. Mirsky* (1958), 466, 486–8.		
Isaac ibn Al-Shami	Spain	12th century
J. Schirmann, in: YMḤSI, 6 (1945), 259–60.		
Isaac *ibn Ezra		
Isaac *ibn Ghayyat		
Isaac ibn *Gikatilla	Spain	10/11th century
M. Zulay, in: *Tarbiz*, 20 (1950), 161–76.		
Isaac (Abu Ibrahim) *ibn Khalfun		
Isaac *ibn Kaprun		
Isaac *ibn Shuwayk		

Name	Place	Dates
Isaac Salmah	Turkey	16th century
J. Schirmann, in: KS, 12 (1935–36), 393.		
Isaac Samuel	Greece	18th century
J.M. Matza, *Aiannistika hebraika tragoudia* (1953), 55–56.		
Isaiah Hai b. Joseph *Carmi		
Ishmael Ḥanina b. Mordecai of Volmontono	Bologna, Ferrara	16th century
M. Benayahu, in: *Rabbi Yosef Caro* ed. by Y. Raphael (1969), 320–21, 357–58.		
*Israel b. Joel (Susslin)		
Israel b. Moses *Najara		
Israel Berechiah Fontanella	Rovigo, Reggio	d. 1763
R. Patai, *Shirei R. Yisrael Berekhyah Fontanella* (1933).		
Jacob	Ereẓ Israel	early poet
M. Zulay, in: YMḤSI, 1 (1933), 157; Habermann, Ateret, 119–20, 228.		
Jacob Al'ayin	Babylonia?	10/11th century
Habermann, Ateret, 182–228.		
Jacob Amron	Turkey	
M. Benayahu, in: KS, 35 (1960), 529.		
Jacob b. Abraham (Angelo d'Ascoli)	Italy	15th century
Schirmann, Italyah, 193–94.		
*Jacob b. Dunash b. Akiva		
*Jacob b. Eleazar		
Jacob b. Eliezer Guenzburg-Ulma	Ulm (Germany)	16th century
J.L. Bialer, *Min ha-Genazim* (1967), 63–69.		
Jacob b. Isaac Segre	Italy	16/17th century
M. Benayahu, in: *Rabbi Yosef Caro*, ed. by Y. Raphael (1969), 316, 348–9.		
Jacob b. Joab Elijah *Fano		
Jacob b. Judah	Germany	13th century
H. Peri, in: *Tarbiz*, 24 (1955), 426 ff.		
Jacob b. Judah ibn Ala'mani	Alexandria	12th century
S. Abramson, in: YMḤSI, 7 (1958), 163–81.		
*Jacob b. Naphtali		
Jacob Hai (Vita) Israel	Italy, Amsterdam	18th century
Schirmann, Italyah, 408–9.		
Jacob ibn Albene	Toledo	14th century
C. Roth, in JQR, 39 (1948–49), 123–50.		
Jacob Israel Bilgradi	Ferrara	18th century
Bernstein, Italyah, 86–90, 165–6.		
Jacob Kunat	Morocco	12/13th century
S. Bernstein, in: *Sinai*, 19 (1946), 214.		
(Jacob?) Manish b. Meir	Austria	17th century
J.L. Bialer, *Min ha-Genazim* (1967), 77–78.		
Jacob of Castilia	Spain, Fez	
S. Bernstein, in: *Aresheth*, 1 (1958), 15–16, 20.		
Jacob Tarfon	Salonika	16th century
H. Brody, in: *Minḥah le-David* dedicated to D. Yellin (1935), 205–220.		
Jeduthun ha-Levi		12th century
S. Assaf, in: *Minḥah li-Yhudah* to J.L. Zlotnik (1950), 162–9.		
Jehiel b. Abraham	Rome	d. before 1070
Schirmann, Italyah, 48–54; idem, in: *Scritti in memoria di E. Sereni* (1970), 92–107 (Heb. part).		
Jehiel b. Asher	Spain	14th century
Habermann, in: *Maḥanayim*, 82 (1963), 38–41; idem, Ateret, 191–3, 200–1, 228.		
Jehiel b. Israel Luria	Padua	16th century
M. Benayahu, in: *Babbi Yosef Caro*, ed. by Y. Raphael (1969), 315–6, 345–8.		
Jehiel b. Joab min ha-Anavim (Anav)	Rome	13th century
N. Pavoncello, in: *Miscellanea di Studi in memoria di D. Disegni* (1969), 190–2, 195–7.		
Jehiel b. Joseph	Germany	14th century
Urbach, Tosafot, 317.		

Name	Place	Dates
Jehoseph b. Hanan b. Nathan *Ezobi		
Jekuthiel J. Schirmann, YMḤSI, 6 (1945), 262.	Spain	12th century
Jekuthiel b. Isaac *ibn Hasan		
Jekuthiel of Vilna I. Tishbi, in: *Sefer Yovel le-Y. Baer* (1960), 385ff.	Italy	18th century
*Jerahmeel b. Solomon		
Joab S. Bernstein: *Sinai*, 19 (1946), 213–4; idem, in: *Ha-Tekufah*, 32–33 (1948), 774–5.	Syria	13th century
Joab Almagia C. Roth and C. Rabin, in: *Metsudah*, 5–6 (1948), 262–83.	Italy	18th century
Joab b. Benjamin Schirmann, Italyah, 135–6.	Rome	13/14th century
Joab b. Daniel Schirmann, Italyah, 133–4.	Rome	13th century
Joab b. Jehiel de Synagoga Bet-El Schirmann, Italyah, 170–1.	Rome	14th century
Joab b. Nathan b. Daniel de Sinagoga J.N. Pavoncello, in: *Scritti in memoria di E. Sereni* (1970), 119–32 (Heb. part).	Rome	13/14th century
*Joab the Greek		
*Johanan b. Joshua ha-Kohen		
Johanan-Judah (Angelo) Alatrino Schirmann, Italyah, 256–60.	Italy	16/17th century
Jonah ha-Kohan Rappa Schirmann, Italyah, 327–31.	Italy	17th century
Joseph (Abu `Amar) ibn Hasdai Schirmann, *Sefarad*, 1 (1959²), 171–5.	Saragossa	11th century
Joseph *Albaradani		
Joseph *Almanzi		
Joseph Baruch b. Jedidiah Zechariah of Urbino Schirmann, Italyah, 274–5.	Mantua, Modena and Busseto	17th century
Joseph b. Abraham Almosnino D. Yarden, in: *Sefunot*, 8 (1964), 258–60; 264–5.	Salonika?	15/16th century
*Joseph b. Asher (of Chartres)		
Joseph b. David ibn Suli S. Bernstein in: *Al Naharot Sefarad* (1956), 138–42, 144–5, 251–4; Schirmann, *Sefarad*, 2 (1960²), 485–8.	Toledo	d. after 1306
Joseph b. Isaac S. Bernstein, in: *Tarbiz*, 26 (1957), 465–8.	Orléans	12th century
Joseph b. Israel J. Ratzaby, in: *Yeda Am*, 12 (1967), 56–60.	Yemen	16th century
*Joseph b. Jacob		
Joseph b. Jacob (Abu Amr) *ibn Sahl		
Joseph b. Jacob ha-Levi N. Ben-Menahem, in: *Aresheth*, 2 (1960), 404–5.	Morocco	15/16th century
Joseph b. Jacob Kalai S. Bernstein, in: *Sinai*, 19 (1946), 214; J.L. Weinberger, in: HUCA, 39 (1968), 11–14 (Heb. part).	Crimea	13th century?
Joseph b. Joshua ibn Vives Lorki J.L. Weinberger, in: HUCA, 39 (1968), 15–18 (Heb. part).	Spain	14/15th century
*Joseph b. Kalonymus ha-Nakdan		
Joseph b. Mattathias S. Bernstein, in: *Tarbiz*, 7 (1936), 181–5.	Italy	13th century
Joseph b. Meir b. Ezra Bernstein, *Piyyutim*, 57–62.	Greece?	14th century?
Joseph b. Meir ibn Al-Muhadjir Schirmann, Shirim Ḥadashim, 215–6.	Andalusia	11/12th century
Joseph b. Moses *Alashkar		

Name	Place	Dates
Joseph b. Nathan Ḥazzan A.L. Katch, in: JQR, 58 (1967), 89–94, 60 (1968–9), 1–5; J. Schirmann, in: KS, 44 (1969), 427–8.	Germany	12th century
Joseph Ben-Ram M. Wallenstein, in: *Sefer Ḥayyim Schirmann* (1970) 116ff.	Egypt	17th century
Joseph b. Samuel Z!arefati (Giuseppe Gallo) M.D. Cassuto, in: *Meḥkarim le-Zikhron R.A. Kohut* (1935), 121–28 (Heb.part).	Florence	15/16th century
*Joseph b. Sheshet ibn Latimi		
*Joseph b. Solomon of Carcassonne		
*Joseph b. Solomon *Yahya		
*Joseph b. Tanhum ha-Yerushalmi		
Joseph Cibzio S. Olivetti, *Rassegna Mensile di Israel*, 25 (1959), 22–25.	Italy	17th century
Joseph Fiametta (Lehavah) J. Schirmann, in: *Zion*, 29 (1964), 101.	Italy	d. 1721
Joseph *Ganso		
Joseph ibn al-Shami H. Schirmann, YMḤSI, 6 (1945), 253–8.	Spain	12th century
Joseph *ibn Barzel		
Joseph *ibn Zabara		
Joseph *Kaspi		
Joseph *Kimh$i		
*Joseph Saul Abdallah		
Joseph Shalim Gallego		
Joseph Sofer S.M. Stern, in: *Zion*, 11 (1950), 141–3.	Spain	11th century
*Joshua Habermann, Ateret 158f., 227.	Ereẓ Israel	early poet
*Joshua b. Elijah ha-Levi		
Joshua b. Joseph ha-Kohen M. Zulay, in: *Haaretz* (Jan. 10, 1949); ibid. (Dec. 12, 1952)	Egypt	11th century
Joshua Ben-Zion Segre J. Schirmann, in: *Zion*, 29 (1964), 100.	Italy	1718–1798
Joshua ha-Kohen M. Zulay, in: *Alei Ayin* (1952), 89–90; E. Fleischer, in: *Tarbiz*, 36 (1967), 146ff., 342ff.	Ereẓ Israel	early poet
Joshua he-Haver b. Nathan E. Fleischer, in: *Tarbiz*, 38 (1969), 280–2.	Ereẓ Israel	11th century
*Josiphiah (Jehosiphiah) the Proselyte		
Judah M. Zulay, *Zur Liturgie der Babylonischen Juden* (1933); Habermann, Ateret, 121ff., 226	Egypt or Ereẓ Israel	9th or 10th century
Judah *Abrabanel (Leone Ebreo)		
Judah *al-Ḥarizi		
Judah b. Aaron *Kilti		
Judah b. Hillel ha-Levi M. Zulay, in: *Eretz Israel*, 4 (1956), 138–44; Habermann, Ateret, 123–4, 227.	Ereẓ Israel	10/11th century
Judah b. Isaac *ibn Ghayyat		
*Judah b. Isaac ibn Shabbetai		
Judah (Leone) b. Isaac *Sommo		
Judah b. Israel Berechiah Fontanella M. Zulay, *Zur Liturgie der Babylonischen Juden* (1933); 23–24, 67–68.	Italy	b. 1719
Judah b. Jo[seph] E. Fleischer, in: *Tarbiz*, 38 (1969), 280–1.		early poet
Judah b. Joseph Segelmesi S. Bernstein, in: *Horeb*, 12 (1956), 217–33.	North Africa	14/15th century
Judah b. Kalonymus b. Moses J. Schirmann, in: *Kobez al-Jad*, 13 (1939), 38–41.	Mainz	12th century
Judah b. Menahem Schirmann, Italyah, 76–77.	Rome	12th century

Name	Place	Dates
*Judah b. Menahem of Rome		
Judah b. Moses		16th century
Bernstein, Piyyutim, 62.		
Judah b. Moses Alfaqui	Turkey	16th century
J. Schirmann, in: KS, 12 (1935–36), 293, 521–3.		
Judah b. Moses *Leonte		
Judah b. Moses of Saltars	Italy	b. 1550?
M. Benayahu, in: *Rabbi Yosef Caro*, ed. by Y. Raphael (1969), 313–5, 341–5.		
Judah b. Samuel *Abbas		
*Judah Halevi		
Judah Levi Toabah	Salonika?	17th century
M. Attias, in: *Sefunot*, 1 (1958), 128–40.		
Judah Maẓli'aḥ Padova	Modena	d. 1728
J. Schirmann, in: *Zion*, 29 (1964), 102; G. Laras, in: *Scritti in memoria di A. Milano* (1970), 193–203.		
Judah *Zarco		
**Kalila and Dimna*		
Kalon ha-Romi	Byzantium	9th century
Schirmann, Shirim Ḥadashim, 424–6.		
*Kalonymus b. Judah the Younger		
Kalonymus b. Kalonymus (see *Kalonymus family)		
Kalonymus b. Shabbetai	Rome, Worms	1030–1096
Schirmann, Italyah, 62–67.		
Kalonymus ha-Nasi (see *Kalonymus family)	Italy	13th century
Kalonymus ha-Zaken	Italy	10th century
Leon b. Michael ha-Parnas	Greece	14th century
J.L. Weinberger, in: HUCA, 39 (1968), 30–33 (Heb. part).		
Leonte b. Abraham	Rome	12th century
Schirmann, Italyah, 70–73, 543.		
Leonte b. Moses	Rome	12th century
Schirmann, Italyah, 80–81.		
Levi b. Jacob *ibn Altabban		
Malkiel b. Meir	Greece or Italy	11th century
J.L. Weinberger, in: HUCA, 39 (1968), 45–51 (Heb. part).		
*Mattathias	Italy	13th century
Schirmann, Italyah, 179–81.		
Mazzal Tov b. David	Constantinople	15/16th century
I.D. Markon, in: *Sefer ha-Yovel ... A. Marx* (1950), 322.		
Meir *Abulafia		
Meir b. Abraham	Bulgaria, Safed	16th century
A. Marmorstein, in: *Alim*, 3 (1937), 15–16.		
*Meir b. Baruch of Rothenburg		
*Meir b. Isaac Sheli'aḥ Ẓibbur		
Meir b. Moses	Rome	13th century
J. Schirmann, in: KS, 37 (1962), 405, no. 1140.		
Menahem b. Aaron	Germany	12th century?
S.H. Kook, *Iyyunim u-Meḥkarim*, 2 (1963), 209–10.		
*Menahem b. Jacob		
*Menahem b. Jacob ibn Saruq		
Menahem b. Mordecai ha-Parnas Corizzi	Italy	
J. Schirmann, in: YMḤSI, 1 (1933), 101–5, 109–20.		
*Meshullam b. Moses	Mainz	d. 1094/5
A.N.Z. Roth, in: *Zion*, 28 (1963), 233–5; E.E. Urbach (ed.), *Arugat ha-Bosem* of Azriel b. Abraham, 4 (1963), 17, 52–54.		
Meshullam ha-Sofer	Italy	14th century
Schirmann, Italyah, 182–3.		
Mevorakh b. David	Ereẓ Israel	early poet
A. Scheiber, in: *Tarbiz*, 22 (1951), 167–73; 36 (1966), 92–93.		

Name	Place	Dates
Mevorakh b. Nathan	Ereẓ Israel	10th century
Schirmann, Shirim Ḥadashim, 29–30.		
Mevorakh ha-Bavli	Ereẓ Israel	11th century
A.M. Habermann, in: *Maḥanayim*, 44 (1960), 59ff.; idem, Ateret 143–4, 729.		
Meyuhas	Italy	16th century
J. Schirmann, YMḤSI, 1 (1933), 107, 125–27.		
Michael b. Caleb	Greece	11/12th century
J.L. Weinberger, in: HUCA, 39 (1968), 52–53 (Heb. part).		
Mordecai b. Berechiah Jare	Mantua	16/17th century
Simonsohn, Mantovah, 2 (1964), 522.		
*Mordecai b. Hillel ha-Kohen		
Mordecai b. Joseph	Worms	d. 1294
Schirmann, in: *Kobez al-Jad*, 13 (1939), 52–57.		
Moses	Ereẓ Israel	early poet
M. Zulay, in: YMḤSI, 5 (1939), 149–54; Habermann, Ateret, 140, 229.		
Moses *Abbas (ibn Abez)		
Moses b. Abraham *Dar'l		
Moses b. Abraham ha-Levi	Dara' (North Africa)	9th century
N. Allony, in: *Sinai*, 43 (1958), 394.		
Moses b. Benjamin Sofer	Rome	12th century
Schirmann, Italyah, 74–75.		
Moses b. Ḥiyya	Greece	12th century
J.L. Weinberger, in: HUCA, 39 (1968), 41–44 (Heb. part).		
Moses b. Isaac	Spain	11th century
H. Brody, in: *Keneset*, memorial volume to Ḥ.N. Bialik, 1 (1936), 410–5.		
Moses b. Isaac	Tyre	early poet
M. Zulay in: YMḤSI, 5 (1939), 171–4.		
Moses b. Isaac b. Jacob	Grenoble	13th century?
H. Schirmann, in: *Zion*, 19 (1954), 66.		
Moses b. Isaac Da *Rieti		
Schirmann, Italyah, 195–9.		
Moses b. Isaac *Remos		
Moses b. Israel Finzi	Italy	16th century
M. Benayahu, in: *Rabbi Yosef Caro*, ed. by Y. Raphael (1969), 317–8, 351–3.		
*Moses b. Jacob		
Moses b. Jacob (Abu Harūn) *ibn Ezra		
Moses b. Joseph	Rome	13th century
Schirmann, Italyah, 110–5.		
*Moses b. Kalonymus		
*Moses b. Levi		
Moses b. Maẓli'aḥ		
A. Mirsky, in: KS, 34 (1959), 363–7.		
*Moses b. Mevorakh		
Moses b. Naḥman (*Naḥmanides)		
*Moses (b. Nethanel) Nathan		
Moses b. Samuel b. Absalom	France?	12th century
S. Bernstein, in: *Tarbiz*, 10 (1939), 15–19.		
Moses b. Samuel ha-Kohen *Gikatilla		
Moses b. Shabbetai	Rome	11th century
Schirmann, Italyah, 60–61; Bernstein, Piyyutim, 41–44, 77–78.		
*Moses b. Shem Tov de Leon		
Moses b. Shem Tov *Gabbai		
Moses b. Shem Tov Ḥazzan	Spain, North Africa	14/15th century
A.M. Habermann, in *Tarbiz*, 14 (1943), 54, 67–69.		
Moses b. Shem Tov *ibn Habib		
Moses b. Solomon d'Escola *Gerondi		
Moses b. Zur	Morocco	17/18th century
N. Ben-Menahem, in: *Aresheth*, 2 (1960), 383–6.		

Name	Place	Dates
Moses ha-Kohen ibn Gikatilla	Spain	11th century
A. Scheiber, in: *Alexander Marx Jubilee Volume* (1950), 537–8 (Heb. part).		
Moses Ḥayyim b. Abraham Catalano	Padua, Montagnana	d. 1661
B. (C.) Roth in: *Kobez al-Jad*, 4 (1946), 99–101.		
Moses *ibn Al-Taqana		
Moses *Kilki		
Moses Mevorakh	Crimea	15/16th century
S. Bernstein, in: *Sefer Yovel li-Khevod S.K. Mirsky* (1958), 406, 479–86.		
Moses *Zacuto (Zacut)		
Mubbashshir b. Ephraim he-Haver	Orient	11th century
A.M. Habermann, Ateret, 160–1.		
Nahum	Spain?	13th century
Schirmann, Sefarad, 2 (1960^{2}), 459–62.		
Nahum b. Joseph al-Bardani	Babylonia	11th century
A. Scheiber, in: *Zion*, 30 (1965), 123.		
Nathan b. Isaac	Mainz	12/13th century
A.M. Habermann, in: *Haaretz* (Sept. 20. 1968).		
Nathan b. Samuel he-Ḥaver	Egypt	12th century
J. Schirmann, in: YMḤSI, 6 (1945), 291–7.		
Nehemiah	Orient	12/13th century
S. Bernstein, in: *Sinai*, 19 (1946), 215.		
Nehemiah b. Menahem Calomiti	Crete	15th century
M.D. Cassuto, in: *Sefer ha-Hovel... S. Krauss* (1936), 211–6.		
Nehemiah b. Solomon b. Heiman ha-Nasi	Babylonia?	10/11th century
M. Zulay, YMḤSI, 4 (1938), 197–246.		
Nethanel b. Naaman	Corfu	16th century
S. Bernstein, Piyyutim, 81–83.		
Nethanel b. Nehemiah Caspi	Provence	15th century
S. Bernstein, in: *Tarbiz*, 10 (1939), 26–29.		
*Nissi (Nissim) b. Berechiah al-Nahrawani		
*Ohev b. Meir ha-Nasi		
Perfet Zark	Spain	14th century
Schirmann, Sefarad, 2 (1960^{2}), 544–6.		
Pesaḥ b. Abraham ha-Kohen	Germany	13th century
E.E. Urbach (ed.), *Arugat ha-Bosem* of Abraham b. Azriel, 1 (1939), 281; 4 (1963), 122.		
*Phinehas b. Jacob ha-Kohen (Kafra)		
*Phinehas b. Joseph ha-Levi		
Raḥamim Kalai	Egypt	17th century
M. Wallenstein, in: *Sefer Ḥayyim Schirmann* (1970), 111–34.		
Raphael b. Isaac de-Faenza	Florence	15th century
Schirmann, Italyah, 203–5, 573.		
Raphael Joseph b. Johanan Treves	Italy	16th century
M. Benayahu, in: *Rabbi Yosef Caro*, ed. by Y. Raphael (1969), 318–9, 353–6.		
Rehabiah b. Judah	France	11/12th century
H. Brody, in: *Emet le-Ya'akov, Sefer Yovel...J. Freimann* (1937), 22–26.		
Rephaiah b. Judah Kohen	Orient	12th century?
S. Bernstein, in: HUCA, 16 (1941), 150–3.		
Reuben ha-Kohen Ḥazzan		
S. Abramson, in: *Tarbiz*, 15 (1944), 51–54.		
*Saadiah b. Joseph Gaon		
*Saadiah b. Joseph ha-Levi		
Saadiah b. Maimun *ibn Danan		
Saadiah *Longo		
Sahalul	Yemen	15th century
J. Ratzaby, in: *Afikim ba-Negev*, 2 (1966), nos. 15–16		
Sa'id b. Babshad ha-Kohen		10/11th century
Schirmann, Shirim Ḥadashim, 431–3, 482.		

Name	Place	Dates
Saj'id Darin (or Drin), Dinar J. Ratzaby, in: *Zion*, 20 (1955), 32–46.	Yemen	17th century
Salem (Salam) Abraham b. Isaac Simonsohn, Mantjovah, 2 (1964), 529–31.	Mantua, Venice	17th century
Samson b. Samuel Habermann, Ateret 202–3, 231.	Germany, Jerusalem	14th century
Samson Kohen Modon	Mantua	1679–1727
Samuel Schirmann, Shirim Ḥadashim, 134–5.	Egypt	13th century
Samuel Habermann, Ateret, 199, 230.	Germany or France	13th century?
Samuel Habermann, Ateret, 87–88. 109–12, 166, 194, 230.	Spain	13/14th century
Samuel *Archivolti		
Samuel b. Eliasaph	Rome	16th century?
Samuel b. Hananiah S. Abramson, in: *Sinai*, 36 (1955), 538–42.	Spain	11th century
Samuel b. Ḥayyim Bernstein, Piyyutim, 94–101.	Greece	13/14th century
Samuel b. Isaac Segan Leviyyah S.H. Kook, *Iyyunim u-Meḥkarim*, 2 (1963), 244–6.	Germany	11th century
Samuel b. Joseph *ibn Sasson		
Samuel b. Joshua Minz Biritaro M. Benayahu, in: *Rabbi Yosef Caro*, ed. by Y. Raphael (1969), 319–20, 356–57.	Mantua	16th century
Samuel b. Kalonymus ha-Ḥazzan E.E. Urbach (ed.), *Arugat ha-Bosem* of Abraham b. Azriel, 4 (1963), 60.	Germany	d. 1241
Samuel b. Moses Anav Bernstein, Italyah, passim.	Bologna	16th century
Samuel b. Moses ha-Dayyan A.M. Habermann, in: *Haaretz* (Sept. 27, 1964); J.L. Weinberger, in: *Tarbitz*, 38 (1969), 286–9.	Syria	15/16th century
Samuel b. Moses ha-Levi S. Bernstein, in: *Sinai*, 19 (1946), 216.	Orient	12/13th century
Samuel b. Moses min ha-Ne'arim (Dei Fanciulli) N. Pavoncello, in: *Miscellanea di Studi in Memoria di D. Disegni* (1969), 188–90, 192–5.	Italy	14th century
Samuel b. Shalom M. Zulay, in: YMḤSI, 3 (1936), 153–62; A.M. Habermann, *Toledot ha-Piyyut ve-ha-Shirah* (1970), 56.	Ereẓ Israel	8th century
Samuel b. Simeon A. Yaari, in KS, 16 (1939/40), 377–9.	Poland	17th century
Samuel b. Zadok ibn Alamani A. Scheiber, in: *Sefer Ḥayyim Schirmann* (1970), 394–6.	Egypt	12/13th century
Samuel David *Luzzatto		
*Samuel ha-Nagid		
*Samuel ha-Shelishi b. Hoshana		
Saul *Caspi		
Shabbetai S. Bernstein, in: *Horeb*, 5 (1939), 55.	Italy	16th century
Shabbetai b. Abishai Ḥabib Bernstein, Piyyutim, 88–89.	Corfu?	15th century
Shabbetai b. Moses Schirmann, Italyah, 39–40; Bernstein, Piyyutim, 74–77.	Rome	11th century
Shabbetai Ḥayyim (Vita) *Marini		
Shalem *Shabazi		
Shape b. Said (URU?) Y. Ratzaby, in: *Be-Ma'arakhah* (1969), no. 14–15.	Yemen	15th century?
Shealtiel b. Levi A.M. Habermann, in: *Haaretz* (April 18, 1968).	Germany?	13/14th century
*She'erit ha-Ḥazzan		

Name	Place	Dates
Shemariah b. Aaron ha-Kohen	Babylonia	12/13th century
N. Alloni in: *Sinai*, 58 (1966), 136–7; D. Yarden, *Sefunei Shirah* (1967), 144–8; J. Tubi, in: *Ba-Ma'arakhah*, 10 (1971), no. 119, 18–19.		
Shemariah of Rabyuano	Greece	12th century
J.L. Weinberger, in: HUCA, 39 (1968), 55–59 (Heb. part)		
Shem Tov *Falaquera		
*Shephatiah b. Amittai		
Sheshet	Provence	12th century
Habermann, Ateret, 96, 231.		
*Silano		
*Simeon b. Isaac		
*Simeon b. Megas ha-Kohen		
Simeon b. Ẓemaḥ *Duran		
Simeon Labi	Spain, North Africa	d. 1545
A.M. Habermann, in: *Maḥanayim*, 56 (1961), 42–45.		
Simḥah b. Samuel	Germany	12/13th century
A.M. Habermann, in: *Haaretz* (Aug. 19, 1963).		
Simḥah *Issachar		
Schirmann, Italyah, 350–3.		
*Sindabar		
Solomon Abu Ayyuv ibn Al Muallim	Seville, Morocco	11/12th century
Schirmann, Sefarad, 1 (1959²), 541–3.		
Solomon al-Kufi Ḥazzan		10/11th century
A.M. Habermann, *Be-Ron Yaḥad* (1945), 35.		
Solomon b. David ha-Rifi	Egypt	11/12th century?
N. Alloni, in: *Sinai*, 64 (1969), 22–23.		
Solomon b. Elijah Sharvit ha-Zahav ha-Levi	Salonika	15th century
A. Ovadiah, in: *Sinai*, 6 (1940), 78–79; S.H. Kook, *Iyyunim u-Meḥkarim*, 2 (1963), 216–9; I.M. Molho, in: *Oẓar Yehudei Sefarad*, 3 (1960), 80–82.		
Solomon b. Immanuel Da Piera or De Pierrelatte	S. France	14th century
M. Catane, in: KS, 42 (1966–67), 399–402; 43 (1967–68), 160.		
Solomon b. Isaac	Italy	14th century
Schirmann, Italyah, 186.		
Solomon b. Isaac (*Rashi)		
Solomon b. Isaac b. Meir Gaon	Syria	11th century
M. Zulay, in: YMḤSI, 5 (1939), 175–7.		
Solomon b. Isaac *Gerondi	Spain	13th century
S. Bernstein, *Al-Naharot Sefarad* (1956), 146–51, 254–6.		
Solomon b. Judah ha-Bavli		
Solomon b. Judah ibn *Gabirol		
Solomon (b. Judah?) ibn Ghiyyat	Spain	12th century
J. Schirmann, in: YMḤSI, 6 (1945), 261.		
Solomon b. Mazzal Tov	Constantinople	16th century
I.D. Markon, in: *Sefer ha-Yovel… A. Marx* (1950), 321–49; idem, in: *Melilah*, 3/4 (1950), 260–75.		
Solomon b. Menahem	Germany	13th century
D. Goldschmidt, in: *Maḥanayim*, 60 (1961), 62–63.		
Solomon b. Moses Dei Rossi	Rome	13th century
Schirmann, Italyah, 105–6.		
Solomon b. Reuben *Bonafed		
Solomon b. Said	Yemen	16th century
J. Ratzaby, in: *Oẓar Yehudei Sefarad*, 2 (1959), 85, 88.		
Solomon b. Samson	Germany	11th century
A.R. Malachi, *Bitzaron*, 50 (1964), 178–80.		
Solomon b. Sar Shalom	Yemen	16th century
J. Ratzaby, in: *Maḥanayim*, 40 (1959), 170–92.		
Solomon Ḥazzan	Italy	16th century
Bernstein, Italyah, 44–45, 146; A. Yaari, *Meḥkerei Sefer* (1958), 220, 225–6.		

Name	Place	Dates
Solomon ibn *Labi		
Solomon *ibn Zadbel		
Solomon Kohen	Orient	
Jabermann, Ateret, 216–7.		
Solomon Mevorakh	Turkey	16th century
S. Bernstein, in: *Horeb*, 5 (1939), 61–62; J.L. Weinberger, in: HUCA, 39 (1968), 60–62 (Heb. part)		
*Solomon Suleiman b. Amar		
*Tamar b. Menahem		
Todros b. Judah ha-Levi *Abulafia		
Yaḥya b. Abraham Harazi	Yemen	16/17th century
Y. Ratzaby, in: *Tagim*, 1 (1969), 54–59.		
Yakar b. Samuel ha-Levi	Cologne and Mainz	13th century
Urbach, Tosafot, 452–3; C. Sirat, in: REJ, 118 (1959–60), 131–3.		
*Yannai		
Yanon b. Ẓemaḥ	Syria	11th century
M. Zulay, in: *Sinai*, 28 (1951), 167–9; J.L. Weinberger, in: HUCA, 39 (1968), 3–10 (Heb. part).		
Yo'eẓ b. Malkiel	Germany	13th century
A.M. Habermann, *Gezerot Ashkenaz ve-Ẓarefat* (1946), 194, 264.		
Yom Tov (Bondi), Valvason	Venice	1616–1660
J. Schirmann, in: *Zion*, 29 (1964), 104.		
Yom Tov b. Isaac	France	12th century
J. Schirmann, in: *Kobez al-Jad*, 13 (1939), 35–37.		
Yom Tov Soriano	Spain	15th century
A.M. Habermann, in: YMḤSI, 3 (1936), 133–50.		
*Yose b. Yose		
Yudan b. Misatya ha-Kohen	Greece or Italy	10th century
Sefer ha-Mekorot (1970²), 128.		
Zadok b. Aaron ibn Alamani	Alexandria	12th century
S. Bernstein, in: *Sinai*, 19 (1946), 215; idem, in: *Ha-Tekufah*, 32–33 (1948), 77.		
*Zebidah family		
*Zechariah al-Dahiri		
Ẓedakah	Egypt	Medieval
N. Allony, in: *Oẓar Yehudei Sefarad*, 1 (1959), 54–61.		
Zedekiah b. Benjamin min ha-Anavim (Anav)	Rome	13th century
B. Dinur, in: *Sefer Zikkaron Aryeh Leon Carpi* (1967), 52–63.		
Ẓemaḥ b. Yanon he-Ḥazzan	Syria	11th century
M. Zulay, in: YMḤSI, 5 (1939), 132.		
Zevadiah	S. Italy	9th century
Schirmann, Shirim Ḥadashim, 422–4.		

[Abraham David]

PIZARNIK, ALEJANDRA (1936–1972), Argentinean poet. Born in Buenos Aires to a family of Jewish Russian immigrants, she published her first book of poetry in 1955. In 1960–64 she lived in Paris. Her fourth volume of poetry, *Arbol de Diana* ("Diane's Tree," 1962), established a distinctive style of short texts (verse and poetic prose) built in an intense language and surrounded by an expressive blank page. Among her books are *Los trabajos y las noches* ("Works and Nights," 1965); *Extracción de la piedra de locura* ("Extraction of the Stone of Folly," 1968); *El infierno musical* ("The Musical Hell," 1971); and the posthumous *Textos de Sombra y últimos poemas* ("Texts of Shadow and Last Poems," 1982), which includes unpublished texts. Also renowned is her prose book *La condesa sangrienta* (1971; *The Bloody Countess*, 1986), on the fascination/rejection of evil. Loneliness, existential anguish, intense but hopeless love, and the seduction and dangers of silence are her main themes, together with poetic creation as a longed-for means of salvation. Though she experienced her Jewish background as an important part of her complex identity, Jewish themes are not central in her texts and appear mostly in connection with the figure of her father. Pizarnik was a gifted translator of French poetry and wrote insightful articles on poetry and fiction. She suffered periods of mental instability; it is possible that her untimely death was voluntary. Pizarnik is one of the major Argentinean and Latin American poets of the century, and her wide influence has continued to grow. Her works have been translated into English, French, and Hebrew.

BIBLIOGRAPHY: I. Bordelois, *Correspondencia Pizarnik* (1998); C. Caulfield (ed.), *From the Forbidden Garden* (2003); F.F. Goldberg, *Alejandra Pizarnik: "Este espacio que somos"* (1994); F. Graziano (ed.), *Alejandra Pizarnik: A Profile* (1987); D.B. Lockhart, *Jewish Writers of Latin America. A Dictionary* (1997); F.J. Mackintosh, *Childhood in the Works of Silvina Ocampo and Alejandra Pizarnik* (2003); M.I. Moia, "Some Keys to Alejandra Pizarnik," in: *Sulfur*, 8 (1983); C. Piña, *Alejandra Pizarnik* (1991); T. Running, "The Poetry of Alejandra Pizarnik," in: *Chasqui*, 14 (1985).

[Florinda F. Goldberg (2nd ed.)]

PIZMON (Heb. פִּזְמוֹן, pl. פִּזְמוֹנִים, pl. *pizmonim*), a term transferred to Hebrew from Greek by way of Aramaic, meaning "adoration and praise," i.e., a poem praising God. It was first applied to the refrain in *piyyutim* in which either the first or the last line of the first stanza was repeated at the end of each stanza. Subsequently, the *piyyutim* themselves in which these refrains occur were called *pizmonim. Pizmonim* can be inserted almost anywhere in the liturgy; the Sephardi *paytanim* inserted them in the *kerovot* (the groups of *piyyutim* in the *Amidah*). In Spain the one who sang or read the *pizmon* before the congregation was called *pizmanana*. In a later period editors used the word *pizmonim* for poems and songs in general. The name often appears on the title page of collections of poems, particularly those printed in Oriental countries. In modern Israel the word is used to mean a popular song.

BIBLIOGRAPHY: Zunz, Poesie, 88–89, 367–8; Elbogen, Gottesdienst, 208; Schirmann, Sefarad, 2 (1956), 714.

[Abraham Meir Habermann]

PLACHY, SYLVIA (1943–), U.S. photographer. Born in Budapest, Hungary, Plachy immigrated to the United States with her parents in 1958 after waiting more than a year in Vienna for visas. Her father was a Catholic, the offspring of her aristocratic but impoverished grandmother's affair with a guard in the Hapsburg court. Her mother was Jewish and many relatives were murdered during the Holocaust. In the United States, the Plachy family settled in Queens, N.Y. Plachy started photographing in 1964 and over the next 40 years recorded the visual character of New York City along with its diverse occupants. She was a photographer for the New York weekly *The Village Voice* for 30 years, and for eight years she had a black and white photograph published there, near the contents page, usually without a caption. The longest-running series was called *Sylvia Plachy's Unguided Tour*, which later became a book (Aperture, 1990). Her words and images, along with pictures from her family album, combine for poignant effect in *Self Portrait with Cows Going Home* (Aperture, 2004), an autobiography of sorts, and an ode to both the exile's life and the land of her birth. Another book, *Red Light*, was a collaboration with the writer James Ridgeway about the sex industry. Her monthly column of writing and photographs in *Metropolis Magazine* was published as a book, *Signs & Relics* (1999). On successive trips back to Hungary and while traveling through other countries in the Eastern Bloc, sometimes on assignment, Plachy's camera captured traces of her real and imagined childhood with tenderness and yearning. She was also there in later decades to record the monuments as they fell; the empty frames in bureaucrats' offices that formerly held pictures of dictators and two Berlin teenagers pretending to be executed against a remnant of the Berlin wall. Plachy's mother had kept her own Jewishness a secret during the postwar years in Hungary. But Sylvia Plachy's Jewishness comes back to haunt her in images of her son, the actor Adrien Brody, who won an Oscar for his starring role in Roman *Polanski's Holocaust drama *The Pianist* (2002), based on the life of Wladyslaw Szpilman, a Polish Jewish musician who survived the war by hiding in Warsaw. Plachy's work is in most major museum collections and she has had one-woman shows around the world.

[Stewart Kampel (2nd ed.)]

PLACZEK, ABRAHAM (1799–1884), **Landesrabbiner* of Moravia. In 1827 he became rabbi in his birthplace, Přerov (Prerau, Moravia), and in 1832 in *Hranice (Maehrisch Weisskirchen). From 1840 until his death he was rabbi in *Boskovice. When Samson Raphael *Hirsch left the *Landesrabbinat* of Moravia in 1851, the provincial authorities appointed Placzek acting *Landesrabbiner*, declaring the election regulations of 1754 obsolete. He held the post until his death. By this act the *Landesrabbinat* was removed from *Mikulov after more than 200 years. Placzek was considered an outstanding talmudic scholar and was strictly Orthodox, supporting Solomon *Spitzer in his struggle against liturgical reform in Vienna (1872). Nevertheless he attempted to avoid open conflicts between the factions, both in Boskovice and in Moravia.

His son, BARUCH JACOB (1835–1922), succeeded him and became the last *Landesrabbiner* of Moravia. He taught at Jewish secondary schools in Germany for some years and was called as rabbi to *Brno (Bruenn) in 1860. He established a teachers' seminary offering a course in *ḥazzanut*, a project favored by his father, and was an adherent of moderate religious reform. Baruch published, partly under the pseudonym Benno Planek, various works on Jewish themes: *Im Eruw* (1867), poems, and *Der Takkif* (1895), a short novel documenting a Moravian Jewish quarter before 1848. He also published articles on natural science, mainly zoology.

BIBLIOGRAPHY: H. Gold (ed.), *Die Juden und Judengemeinden Maehrens…* (1929), 52 (a list of Baruch's works), and index; D. Feuchtwang, in: *Gedenkbuch… D. Kaufmann* (1900), 384; A. Frankl-Gruen, *Geschichte der Juden in Kremsier*, 2 (1898), 138–43, 174–6; *Dr. Blochs Oesterreichische Wochenschrift*, 28 (1911), 11–12.

[Meir Lamed]

PLAGUES OF EGYPT. The Bible has three accounts of the plagues (*maggefot*, Ex. 9:14; *negaʿim*, cf. Ex. 11:1; *makkot*, cf. I Sam. 4:8; cf. LXX, Targ.) that struck Egypt prior to the Exodus: a full, prose account is given in Exodus 7:14–11:10; 12:29–33, and brief, poetic ones in Psalms 78:43–51 and 105:27–36. The variations are set out in the Table: Plagues of Egypt listing the plagues and their effects. While the ten items of the Exodus narrative are distinctly separate, some of the items in Psalms

The Plagues Of Egypt

Exodus	Psalm 78:44–51	Psalm 105:28–36
1. Blood Nile; all water; fish died	1. Blood Nile; liquids	1. Darkness
2. Frogs nuisance to[3] men	2. Swarms[1] "consumed them"	2. Blood water; fish died
3. Lice nuisance to men and beasts	Frogs "ruined them"	3. Frogs nuisance
4. Swarms[1] nuisance to men; ruined land	3. *Ḥasil*[2] ate produce	4. Swarms[1], Lice } Nuisance
5. Pestilence killed livestock	Locusts ate "toil"	5. Hail, Fire } destroyed vines, figs, trees
6. Boils pained men and beasts	4. Hail destroyed vines	6. Locusts, *Yeleq*[2] } destroyed all vegetation
7. Hail and fire destroyed plants, men, and beasts	*Ḥanamel*[3] destroyed sycamores	7. Firstborn death
8. Locusts destroyed plants	5. Hail[4] destroyed beasts	
9. Darkness immobilized men	*Reshafim*[5] destroyed livestock	
10. Firstborn death	6. Death, Pestilence } Killed men[6]	
	7. Firstborn death[7]	

1 Heb. *'arov*; LXX: "dogflies"; R. Nehemiah (Ex. R.) "gnats and mosquitoes"; NJPS "swarms of insects." But Josephus (Ant., 2:303), R. Judah (Ex. R.), and Targ. "mixture of birds and beasts."
2 A kind (or stage of development) of locusts.
3 Meaning obscure; LXX: "frost"; medieval conjectures: "locust," "stones."
4 Symmachus: "pestilence" (*dever* for MT *barad*).
5 Traditionally "fiery bolts," but *Reshef* is a Canaanite plague-god, and *reshef* in Deuteronomy 32:24 (|| *qetev*) and Habakkuk 3:5 (|| dever) means "pestilence" (cf. note 4).
6 *Ḥayyatam* = nafsham, "their life" (Ibn Ezra; cf. Rashi); LXX, Targ. misconstrue as "their beasts".
7 Ibn Ezra joins to the preceding.

are but synonyms or components of plagues. Thus Psalm 105 lists ten items, but refers to seven plagues only. Psalm 78 lists 11 items, but only seven (or six) plagues. The climactic order in Psalm 78 is most satisfactory: nuisances, destruction of plant life, of animals, and of human beings. The order of Psalm 105 is similar, while in the Exodus account the ascending line is not consistently realized. The Psalms' divergence from Exodus has been ascribed to poetic license; the likelihood is, however, that it attests to independent, variant traditions (see further below).

Their Function

The leading motif of the plague series in the Exodus account is introduced in 7:5: "The Egyptians shall know that I am YHWH when I stretch my hand over Egypt…" Repeated variously (7:17; 8:6, 18; 9:14, 16, 29), it shows the plagues to be the answer to Pharaoh's challenge in 5:2: "Who is YHWH…? I do not know YHWH, nor will I release Israel." Intended, thus, as revelations of the nature and power of Israel's God, the plagues are distinguished from both magic and natural calamities. The magicians' failure to produce lice elicits from them the confession that "it is the finger of God" (8:15). The plagues' onset after an announcement or at a signal, and their removal by order, links them to YHWH, whose agents, Moses and Aaron, announced, signaled, and removed them in His name. The accumulation of disasters, their discriminating between Israel and the Egyptians (starting from 8:18), and the unprecedentedness of the last four plagues succeed in eliciting from Pharaoh's court increasingly frequent acknowledgments of God's authority (8:4, 21, 24; 9:20, 27–28; 10:7–8, 16–17, 24), ending with the release of Israel to worship Him (12:31–32). As 9:14–16 and 10:1–2 make clear, the reason for prolonging the series is not to secure Israel's release (which might have been achieved by one crushing blow), but to establish for all time the fame of YHWH and the folly of defying Him.

The Structure of the Narrative

The narrative evidences a deliberate, if imperfectly realized design:

(1) The plagues gradually intensify, beginning with nuisances, passing through destruction of livestock and crops, and ending with the death of human beings. The intensifica-

tion sometimes falters (e.g., boils after pestilence), and sometimes the effects of a plague transgress its proper limits (e.g., the death of men and beasts in the hail). These appear to result, on the one hand, from the combination of variant traditions, and, on the other, from a desire to aggrandize God (see further below). A comparison with the strategy of reducing a rebellious population is found in the Midrash: God used the tactics of kings against the Egyptians. First He cut off their water supply (blood), then He raised a clamor around them (frogs), then shot arrows at them (lice), then arrayed legions against them (swarms), then caused a pestilence, then threw burning naphtha at them (fever boils), then sent hosts against them (locusts), then incarcerated them in dungeons (darkness), then put to death their chiefs (firstborn; Tanḥ. *Bo* 4). Levi b. Gershom perceives cycles of increasing severity: God began with a harmless wonder (Ex. 7:8–13); when that failed, He spoiled their water – but not totally; next He sent the frogs, which caused discomfort; but that was less than the distress caused by the lice. A second round began with the swarms that attacked livestock and food; then pestilence that killed off the livestock; then boils that afflicted the body. A third round followed, starting with hail and locusts, wiping out the food supply, followed by darkness – a bodily affliction just short of death. The death of the firstborn climaxed the series.

(2) These rounds correspond to the formal division of the story into three sets of three plagues, capped by a tenth, in a pattern determined by an invariably recurring order of introductory clauses. Plagues one, four, and seven begin with God commanding Moses to stand before Pharaoh in the morning (at the Nile) to warn him; two, five, and eight begin with a command to enter Pharaoh's residence to warn him there; three, six, and nine begin with a command to bring on the plague without warning. Early perception of this pattern is reflected in R. Judah's mnemonic, cited in the *Haggadah*, דצ״ך עד״ש באח״ב (cf. also Rashbam to 7:26; Baḥya to 10:1).

(3) A certain design can also be discerned in the various agents who induce the plagues. In the first triplet Moses warns, but Aaron signals the coming of the plague; in each case the Egyptian magicians respond. The triplet continues, on an intensified level, the contest begun with the accreditation episode (7:10–12) between the very same characters. It is decided only in the third plague, when the magicians, unable to produce lice, confess it is the work of a higher power. In this contest, the principles – Moses and Pharaoh – are each represented by their seconds; when the magicians retire from the fray, Aaron does too (and when Aaron reappears in a subsidiary role in the sixth plague, the magicians momentarily reappear with him). In the last triplet Moses both announces and induces the plagues, thus enhancing his prestige as God's plenipotentiary in the negotiations that mark this climactic triplet (cf. 11:3). God directly brings on two plagues of the middle triplet – the third (boils), induced by Moses and Aaron, is asymmetrical – and the final firstborn plague. The reason emerges from an examination of the distinctive motif of each triplet.

(4) A purpose clause in the first member of each triplet adumbrates its distinctive motif. As the aim of the first triplet is to dispel the courtiers' notion that the power of the Hebrew envoys is magical, God fittingly admonishes Pharaoh before the blood plague: "By this you shall know that I am YHWH" (7:17). Two plagues of the second triplet explicitly (and the third implicitly) discriminate the Israelites from the Egyptians (8:18–19; 9:4, 6, 11). Such discrimination realizes the purpose stated in 8:18, "That you may know that I, YHWH, am in the midst of the land," for the presence of God – His overseeing providence (cf. Ex. 17:7; 33:5; Num. 14:42; Deut. 6:15; 31:17) – is typically manifest in the separation between the fates of the innocent and the guilty. The opening speech of the third triplet asserts that its aim is to let Pharaoh know "that there is none like Me in all the earth" (Ex. 9:14). The words are echoed four times in phrases expressing the unparalleled intensity of the first two plagues of the triplet (the last member (darkness) again is asymmetrical). There is a notable accumulation of motifs in the last plagues. Thus the last triplet twice refers to discrimination (in different words; 9:26; 10:23) besides its own motif, while the warning of the last plague mentions the last two motifs (11:6–7) and alludes to an intensified form of the first (11:8; the court will bow to Moses). That God directly brings on plagues of the second triplet suits its stated purpose of demonstrating God's presence in the land. The presence-discrimination motif is linked again to God's direct action in the last plague (11:4, 7; 12:12, 29). Where God's presence is to be felt, mediators are out of place.

(5) Design (without strict systematization) is also evident in the characterization of Pharaoh and Moses. Pharaoh's reactions oscillate erratically during the first two triplets between impassivity (7:23; 8:15; 9:7, 12) and insincere concessions (8:4, 21, 24). In the first plague of the third triplet he confesses guilt (9:27), and in the last two he negotiates seriously over Israel's release, as is indicated by his measured concessions at each stage (10:8, 11, 24). Moses' manner changes from a certain sportiveness (8:5) to pained rebuke (8:25), to disbelief (9:30), and finally, in negotiation, to provocative baiting that enrages Pharaoh (10:25–26).

Hardening Pharaoh's Heart

This drama is embedded in (and manages to overcome the stultifying potential of) a deterministic framework. God's policy of hardening Pharaoh's heart is announced in advance (7:3), and notice of its operation is repeatedly given (9:12; 10:1, 20, 27; 11:10). Some mitigation of it is probably to be seen in the fact that during the first five plagues Pharaoh's stubbornness is consistently represented as self-motivated (7:22; 8:11, 15, 28; 9:7; cf. Ex. R. 13:3: God hardened Pharaoh's heart from the sixth plague in order to punish him for his voluntary defiance during the first five; cf. further Maimonides, introduction to Avot, ch. 8; Yad, Teshuvah 6). But this still makes the last, worst plagues – an infliction of suffering on an involuntary sinner – paradoxical, since precisely in the last plagues Pharaoh's reactions are adequately motivated, perhaps even justifiable in view of Moses' provocations. There is here the parade example of the "two-level" view of history characteristic of biblical narrative. Human events are shaped by the will of God, yet they unfold in accord with the motives of actors who do God's will without realizing it (Gen. 45:5, 8; Judg. 14:4; I Kings 12:15). Thus God determined for His own purposes that Pharaoh should resist the plagues; indeed He saw to it. But Pharaoh conducted himself throughout conformably with his own motives and his own godless arrogance. God made it so, but Pharaoh had only to be himself to do God's will.

Interpretations of the Plagues

Attempts have been made to interpret the plagues in terms of ancient Egyptian beliefs or the natural conditions of Egypt. A Middle Kingdom description of anarchy speaks of the Nile's turning into blood (The Admonitions of Ipuwer; Pritchard, Texts, 441); a New Kingdom prophecy of the darkening of the sun (Nefer-rohu; Pritchard, Texts, 445). Philo and the Midrash understand the blood plague as an attack on the deified Nile (I Mos. 98; Ex. R. 9:9), and this clue has been followed by some moderns who look for the humiliation of Egyptian deities in the course of the plagues (e.g., Hapi, the Nile god; Ḥekt, a frog-headed goddess; Re, the sun god), though no hint of this is to be found in the biblical plague narrative. On the other hand, most of the plagues can be linked with local or seasonal phenomena. During its annual rise, in the summer, the Nile is reddened by organisms carried in it; swarms of frogs and insects follow the inundation (insects normally abound in Egypt); Egyptian boils were proverbial (Deut. 28:27); hail, though uncommon, has been known to fall in January – the time indicated by the agricultural data of Exodus 9:31–32; locusts may be blown across the country in winter or spring; three-day, palpable darkness conforms with the heavy sandstorms raised by the *ḥamsin* winds that blow in the early spring. Thus the plagues have been viewed as a miraculous intensification and concentration of local phenomena, crowded into a single year (Moses was 80 years old when they began (7:7), lived 40 years more, and died at the age of 120 (Deut. 34:7); cf. also Eduy. 2:10).

The Variant Versions

The narrative appears to combine two major versions of the plague series. Hence arose such inconsistencies as are found in the depiction of the agent, the signal, and the extent of the blood plague in Exodus 7:17–21 (cf. the dispute between R. Judah and R. Nehemiah in Ex. R. 9:11); such inconsequence as the skipping of the boils in the backward glance of 9:15, or the unmotivated reappearance of Aaron and the boils-afflicted magicians after the lapse of two plagues; and such asymmetry and stylistic differences as set lice, boils, and darkness apart from the rest of the plagues.

(1) One version began with the accreditation sign given by God to Aaron and Moses: Moses orders Aaron to turn his staff into a serpent; the magicians imitate the sign (7:8–13). The plagues proper follow;

(2) Moses orders Aaron to turn all the waters of Egypt to blood; this is imitated by the magicians (7:19–20*aa*, 21b–22);

(3) Moses orders Aaron to induce frogs; this is again imitated by the magicians (8:1–3, 11b (fragmentary));

(4) Moses orders Aaron to produce lice; the magicians fail and confess God's power (8:12–15);

(5) Moses, aided by Aaron, induces boils; the magicians are themselves afflicted and retire routed (9:8–12);

(6) Moses alone induces darkness, immobilizing everyone for three days (10:21–23, 27a (fragmentary));

(7) God strikes the firstborn (cf. 12:12, belonging to this version). In this conjecturally restored version (which, with the exception of item 6, agrees with conventional criticism's P) the agents of the plagues ascend climactically, the effects intensify steadily, and all before the last are designed to outdo and overwhelm rather than destroy. They are tokens of God's might rather than punishments.

The second version ran thus:

(1) After a morning warning, Moses turned the Nile into blood, which killed its fish; Pharaoh was unmoved (7:14–17, 20a*b*–21a, 23–25);

(2) After a warning in the palace... (there follows the other version of frogs); negotiation with Pharaoh (7:26–29 (gap), 8:4–11a (fragmentary));

(3) After a morning warning by Moses, God sends swarms of insects, separating the Israelites; negotiations (8:16–28);

(4) After a warning in the palace by Moses, God strikes Egypt's livestock with a pestilence, separating the Israelites (9:1–7);

(5) After a morning warning, heeded by some courtiers, Moses signals the onslaught of an unprecedented hail mixed with fire; negotiations (9:13–35);

(6) After a warning in the palace, followed by fruitless negotiation, Moses signals the coming of an unprecedentedly severe locust plague; Pharaoh asks relief just this once; further negotiations end in Moses' expulsion (10:1–19, 24–29);

(7) Moses announces the death of the firstborn (11:4–8), which comes that night (12:29–33).

This conjectured version (roughly consisting of the conventional JE) represents the plagues as increasingly severe injuries to Egyptian property and life, as blows designed to afflict the land. The story seems to have been expanded at times by reflective comment (9:15–16; 10:1b–2), or to broaden the scope of a plague (e.g., 9:19–21 includes men and beasts among the victims of the hail). The redactorial interweaving of the two accounts was relatively smooth once the first triplet was constituted on the basis of the overlapping of the two versions and the lice plague's deciding the issue posed in the accreditation sign. The formal pattern of that triplet determined the rest of the interweaving, the genial device of three triplets plus one (an expansion of the 3.3.1 pattern of Gen. 1:1–2:3) nicely accommodating the total of ten separate plagues. Since both versions were climactic, their fusion was on the whole reasonable, although it impaired thematic symmetry, stylistic unity, and strict progress of the narrative. The variant Psalms passages may attest to independent traditions of the plagues. The affinity of the listing in Psalm 78 to the reconstructed second version is particularly striking: both lack the three distinctive plagues of the first – lice, boils, darkness. The present Exodus narrative presumably represents an effort to create a standard account of the plagues, embodying maximally the data of the various traditions known to the author-redactor.

Midrashic Embellishment

The local color of a number of the plagues makes it plausible to assume that the traditions concerning them rose out of events that happened in Egypt. In time, the events were added to, embellished, and reflected upon, most likely in connection with the religious celebrations of the Exodus. The Passover laws of Exodus 12:26–27; 13:8 and the firstborn redemption rite in 13:11–16 suggest occasions for use of a liturgical formulation of the pre-Exodus events. Various statements of the plague series may have originated in and for such occasions, just as, in post-biblical times, the standard Exodus listing was taken up into the *Haggadah*. The tendency to enlarge the scope of the plagues – formally legitimized in the Midrash cited in the *Haggadah* ("How can you prove from Scripture that each plague was really four [or five] plagues…?") – shows itself already in the components of the Exodus narrative, e.g., while in one version the blood plague affects the Nile only, in the other it spreads to all the waters of Egypt. Similarly, just as the Exodus version of hail has already made it deadly to man and beast, so does Philo raise blood (1 Mos. 98) and Josephus raise lice, swarms (of beasts), ulcers, and darkness to the level of death-dealing scourges (Ant., 2:293ff.). The Midrash gives free rein to the imagination in this direction: the Egyptians' spittle and fruit juice turned to blood; their wood and stone household objects oozed blood (Ex. R. 9:11; Mid. Hag. to 7:19); the frogs castrated them (Ex. R. 10:4); deadly pestilence accompanied all the plagues (Ex. R. 10:2); the darkness lasted six days, and at its worst was so thick that no one could move a muscle (Ex. R. 14:3). The Midrash also enlarges upon the brief biblical reflections on the rationale of the plagues. The "measure for measure" interpretation is typical: blood – because they kept Israel's women from their post-menstrual immersion, to stop their childbearing (another view – because they cast the male infants into the Nile); frogs – because they made Israel clean and repair streets; lice – because they made them sweep homes and markets; mixture of beasts – because they made them catch wild beasts; pestilence – because they made them tend flocks; fever boils – because they made them tend baths; hail – because they made them tend fields; locusts – because they made them plant trees; darkness – so that they could not witness the burial of wicked Israelites; firstborn – because they enslaved Israel, whom God called "my firstborn son" (Ex. 4:22; Mid. Hag. to 10:2). Thus the plagues grew ever more marvelous "to spread the fame of God's great power… that Israel might realize that He is the Lord, and teach it to their descendants, so that this true belief might live on in Israel forever" (Ralbag, Comment., end of *Va-Era* and *Bo*).

BIBLIOGRAPHY: A. Macalister, in: DB, s.v.; J.C. Mihelic and G.E. Wright, in: IDB, 3 (1962), 822ff.; G. Hort, in: ZAW, 69 (1957), 84ff.; 70 (1958), 48ff.; H. Eising, in: *Lex tua veritas (Junker Festschrift*, 1961), 75ff.; G. Fohrer, *Ueberlieferung und Geschichte des Exodus* (1964), 60ff.; S.E. Loewenstamm, *Masoret Yeẓi'at Miẓrayim be-Hishtalshelutah* (1965), 25ff.; M. Greenberg, *Understanding Exodus* (1969), 151ff.; Ginzberg, Legends, 2 (1910), 341ff. **ADD. BIBLIOGRAPHY:** J. Hoffmaier, in: ABD II, 374–78; W. Propp, *Exodus 1–18* (AB; 1998).

[Moshe Greenberg]

PLAIN, BELVA (1919–), U.S. novelist. Born in New York and a graduate of Barnard College, Plain published her first book, *Evergreen*, in 1978 when she was almost 60. The book topped the *New York Times* bestseller list for 41 weeks and was adapted into a six-part television series. *Evergreen* spans three generations of an immigrant family. It was born, she said, when her children began asking questions about their forebears. Every one of Plain's books became national bestsellers. More than 25 million copies of her books were in print in the early part of the 21st century, and they appeared in 22 foreign translations. Before she became a novelist, Plain wrote short stories for major magazines. A history major in college, Plain used her background in her work. The Werner family saga, first unveiled in *Evergreen*, continued in *The Golden Cup* (1986), *Tapestry* (1988), and *Harvest* (1990). *The Sight of the Stars* was published in 2003.

[Stewart Kampel (2nd ed.)]

PLAMENAC, DRAGAN (1895–1983), U.S. musicologist of Yugoslav origin. He was born in Zagreb where he first studied law and took a degree. Thereafter, he turned to his early interest in music and studied composition in Vienna (1912) and Prague (1919), musicology with Pirro at the Sorbonne and with Hugo *Adler, one of the founders of modern musicology, in Vienna. He took his doctorate in 1925 with his dissertation on Ockegem's motets and chanson; in 1928 he began teaching musicology at the University of Zagreb. He went in 1939 to the U.S. as the Yugoslav representative to the International Musicological Society Congress in New York and decided to remain there during World War II. He became an American citizen in 1946. Plamenac was thereafter professor of music at different universities, mainly the University of Illinois (1954–63), where he received an honorary doctorate in 1976. Plamenac held several offices at the American Musicological Society and received a number of awards.

In his numerous writings Plamenac distinguished himself as a prominent researcher and editor of early music, namely that of the 14th and 16th centuries as well as the music of Adriatic coastal areas in the Renaissance and early Baroque period. His studies and editions of manuscripts provide important insights into the practice of those periods.

BIBLIOGRAPHY: Grove Music Online; MGG; G. Reese and R.J. Snow (eds.), *Essays in Musicology in Honor of Dragan Plamenac* (1969), including list of publications.

[Amnon Shiloah (2nd ed.)]

PLANE TREE (Heb. עַרְמוֹן; *armon*). The Oriental plane, *Platanus orientalis*, is indigenous to Israel and grows on the banks of rivers, especially in the north. It is one of the most beautiful of Israel's trees and is recognizable by its lofty trunk, spreading crest, and large leaves. Its Hebrew name is connected with the fact that its bark peels so that the trunk is left bare (*arom*). It grows also in Syria and Babylon; while sojourning with Laban in Mesopotamia, Jacob peeled "white streaks" off rods from the tree (Gen. 30:37). Ezekiel, who prophesied in Babylon, mentions it among the beautiful trees in "the garden of God" (Ezek. 31:8). The Targum (Gen. 31:37) rightly renders the word *doleva* ("the plane") and the Septuagint similarly has *platanos*. Rashi, however, identifies the *armon* with the chestnut, an identification which was accepted by European rabbis and by the biblical commentators, and it has been adopted in modern Hebrew. However, this identification is erroneous since the chestnut does not grow in Israel or in Mesopotamia. Beautiful plane trees are found especially on the banks of the River Dan and the River Senir, the sources of the Jordan. Particularly well known is the great plane tree at the Banias Falls which divides the falls in two.

BIBLIOGRAPHY: Loew, Flora, 3 (1924), 65–67; B. Cizik, *Oẓar ha-Ẓemaḥim* (1943), 224ff.; J. Feliks, *Olam ha-Ẓome'aḥ ha-Mikra'i* (1968^2), 120–1; H.N. and A.L. Moldenke, *Plants of the Bible* (1952), 391 (index), s.v.

[Jehuda Feliks]

PLANNING AND CONSTRUCTION. The laws of planning and construction occupy an important place in contemporary public law. This group of laws regulates the status of the various planning authorities, determines norms for the planning of communities, allocates areas for residence, industry and agriculture, establishes various norms regarding the construction of buildings and other facilities within the bounds of a community (such as for residential areas, agricultural regions, nature reserves, and waterside areas), and enumerates various conditions for the maintenance and preservation of buildings and other entities (such as trees, railways, roads, etc.) – especially in cases in which they are liable to cause harm to individuals or to the public.

Although the modern city is notably different from the city of ancient times, the sources of Jewish law over the generations set forth basic principles regarding the regulation of various aspects of planning and construction which are also appropriate – with certain appropriate changes – in contemporary times. In many cases, these principles of Jewish law have been incorporated within other laws, such as *Torts, *Acquisition, public and administrative law (see *Public Authority) and constitutional law (see *Rights, Human: Right to Title), *Unjust Enrichment, etc. Some of the laws of planning and construction were intended to prevent safety hazards, but many were intended to ensure the external appearance of the community, which should be attractive and pleasant for residential purposes. Initially, many of these obligations were specified in the framework of torts regarding private law and created rights and obligations of individuals, but they eventually became public obligations, binding all members of the community.

Thus, for example, it was ruled that commercial installations liable to cause damage to the public should be removed, or built at a safe distance from residential areas (see *Hazard). In many cases, such laws enable individuals to submit claims against others for damage caused to them, or to compel their removal (see *Nuisance).

In other cases, the *public* aspect of planning law is emphasized. Thus, for example, already in the Mishnah we find the requirement that a cemetery be located at a distance from urban centers (M. BB 2:8), the commentators differed however regarding the reason for that requirement: Some think that in this case, similar to other laws of nuisance, the reason is because of the offensive smell that is prevalent there, but others explain that it was meant to prevent distress to the city residents who might see the place (Rabbi Mordechai Yaffe, *Sefer ha-Levush*, YD 365). A similar directive was made in Israeli law, which specifies certain areas in which burials may be performed and prohibiting burial elsewhere (Public Health Ordinance; Planning and Construction Law, 5725 – 1965).

Owing to the wish to preserve "the city's beauty" – its external esthetics – a requirement was made to keep certain types of trees far from its borders (M. BB 2:7), for which the Talmud gives the following rationale: because these trees have many branches, and "it is the beauty of the city when there is open space around it" (BB 24b and Rashi, ad loc.). In the Jerusalem Talmud, there were those who explained that the reason for distancing such trees far from the city is that they have many branches, which create excessive shade for the city's residents (TJ, BK 2:7). Among the early Sages there were those who limit this rule to inhabited regions in the Land of Israel, where it is obligatory to preserve its beauty, while others extend it to include cities abroad as well (Ramban, Rashba and Ritba, on Bava Batra, ad loc.). Rashba, in his novellae (to BB 24b), set an important rule, according to which "Anything that has to do with aesthetics cannot be waived by the residents"; in other words, this is a mandatory rule having the character of *jus cogens*, being intended to maintain "the city's beauty," and therefore cannot be made a matter of their discretion.

The rules concerning the "city's beauty" were especially enforced in those cities given to the Levites, and this dictated their explanation of the biblical rule (Num 35:5), compelling one to leave an empty "plot" around the Levite cities. Rashi (Sotah 27b) interprets the rationale for this by saying that they wished to leave open space on the edges of the city, to leave "an expanse empty of sowing and houses and trees for the sake of the city's beauty, and to provide air for it." From other sources, it emerges that this empty space surrounded the town from all sides, and measured 1000 cubits (approximately 500 meters) in each direction. See Targum Onkelos to Num. 35:4–5; and Rashi to Eruvin 56b, s.v. *ẓe'i mehen*).

Another law stated with respect to the levitical cities prohibits changing the land's designation. Already in the Tosefta

(Arakhin 5:18) we read that "A plot should not be made into a field, and a field should not be turned into a plot." Rashi explains this (Arakhin 32b) with the rationale: "A plot should not be made into a field – because of [the imperative] of settling the Land of Israel, and this would be devastating, for it reduces sowing [the areas available for sowing]; and a field should not be turned into a plot – *because it ruins the town's aesthetic appearance*." In other words, the desire to maintain certain agricultural areas, as well as concern for the town's aesthetic appearance, requires the avoidance of changing the land's designation. Similar norms were set in Israel's Planning and Construction Laws.

Special rules were fixed for the *City of Refuge, which served as the place of residence for persons who had accidentally committed manslaughter. Although Jewish law does not generally establish criteria regarding urban density and the location of cities, this indeed was inter alia the rationale of the rule that the various cities of refuge should not be too close to one other but rather scattered at equal distances (Tosefta Makkot 3:3). The Tosefta (*ibid.*, 8) further states that: "These three towns [= Cities of Refuge] should not be built either as large cities or as small villages, but rather as medium-sized towns. They should not be built in places where there is no water. If there is no water there – water should be brought there. And they should not be built in places that are uninhabited. If the population has dwindled – other inhabitants should be brought and settled there instead of those who left. If their residents have dwindled – then priests (Kohanim), Levites and [ordinary] Israelites should be added to them." The Jerusalem Talmud (Mak. 2:6) adds that "If there is no market there, then one should be set up" – all in order that the person who accidentally committed manslaughter and finds refuge there should be able to live a normal life. Nevertheless, in order to prevent blood avengers from getting into the habit of coming to these towns, the practice of certain crafts – such as operating an oil press and producing oil, manufacturing glassware, rolling cords, and similar crafts – was forbidden in those towns (Tosef. and TJ, ad loc., and see *Human Rights: Freedom of Occupation).

Laws of this nature were also applied to the building of the Temple, such as the prohibition on building it during the night hours and the obligation to build it only from materials that were originally designated for this purpose (Yad., Beit ha-Beḥirah). Various limitations on construction works were imposed on special occasions. In addition to Shabbat and holidays, in the ancient sources construction was also prohibited on fast days, such as public fasts, and from the beginning of the month of Av until the 9th of the month, which is a period of mourning (Ta'anit 14b). In the later sources this prohibition was qualified and limited only to "building for the sake of joy." Rambam explained (*Commentary on the Mishnah*, Ta'anit 1:7: "planting for joy" (such as drawings and ornaments) refers to special buildings the wealthy make, or aromatic trees and so on planted by kings, but building for residence, and planting for the sake of fruits and for making a living, is not forbidden and is not prevented at all. The Jerusalem Talmud explains that if a building was about to collapse, it is permitted to rebuild it even in such times (TJ, Ta'anit 1:8). During the Intermediate Days of Festivals construction work was prohibited as well. The Tosefta cites an exception to this rule (Tosef. Mo'ed Katan 1:7) regarding a house that is liable to endanger its residents: "Should its wall be tottering on the brink of collapse into the public domain, then it should be toppled and rebuilt because of the risk to life." The same rule applies in those places where there are other dangers: "If the city walls have been breached – then it should be fenced off. If it has been fenced off and breached – then it should not be fenced off further. If it was close to the frontier [= border] – then it should be demolished and rebuilt in the usual way."

The sources of Jewish law indicate that certain institutions were originally built in certain locations. Thus, for instance, from many biblical sources we learn that the Court used to sit at the city gates, to enable convenient access. In the Midrash (*Pesikta Zutrata, Lekaḥ Tov, Ki Teẓe*) it was even taught that it is mandatory, and not merely a directive to be exercised voluntarily, that the Court sit at an the highest spot in the city.

A special norm was fixed regarding the construction of synagogues as well. As early as the Tosefta (Megillah 3:22–23) it was already stated that "The doorways of Synagogues are to be opened only towards the East, because in the Sanctuary the doors opened towards the East," and that "Synagogues are only to be built in the highest place in the city." However, as early a source as Rabbenu Tam (12th century) already qualified this law, stating that it had been applicable specifically in ancient times, "when people were accustomed to residing on and using the roofs, but in our times this prohibition should be qualified." At any rate, he too prohibited the construction of an apartment on a floor that was higher than the synagogue (Shabbat 11a, and Nov. Ritba *ibid.*). Testimony from medieval Jewish communities shows that, in certain cases, it was decreed that synagogues should be elevated or houses that were built at higher levels should be lowered (*Hagahot Maimoniyot*, to *Hilkhot Tefillah* 11:2; Sh. Ar., OḤ, 150, and Rema *ad loc.*, 3, and *Arukh ha-Shulḥan*, OḤ 150). During the period of the *aḥaronim* and certainly in modern times, when synagogues are frequently built in multi-storey buildings, various dispensations were made for this issue as well. For example Rabbi Joseph Caro cites Rabbi Jacob Ibn Habib – "In our times, when we are under Turkish rule, that we are not permitted to establish a permanent house for a synagogue; all the more we are not permitted to build one, and we are obliged to hide ourselves in low buildings, where the sounds [of prayer] are not to be heard because of the danger involved. Accordingly, even if there is a residential house above the house in which we customarily pray, this is not to be protested, on condition that they maintain cleanliness in the houses that are above the house of prayer." (*Beit Yosef*, OḤ 154; and see the Rambam's responsum in Resp. Pe'er ha-Dor 74; *Magen Avraham*, OḤ 150:2; and compare Rabbi Ben-Zion Ouziel, Resp. Mishpatei Ouziel, vol. 3, OḤ 19, and R. Ovadiah Yosef, Resp. Yabi'a Omer, vol. 6, OḤ, 26).

As a remembrance of the destruction of the Temple, it was enacted that when a person plasters his home, he should leave a certain area unpainted in remembrance of the destruction of the Temple (Tosef. Sotah 15:12; Tur, OḤ 560).

Other *halakhot* determine the need to distance one residential building from another for the sake of maintaining privacy (see * Rights, Human: the Right to Privacy). This *halakhah* is rooted in ancient sources. Commenting on the biblical verse (Num 24:2), "And Balaam lifted up his eyes, and he saw Israel dwelling tribe by tribe; and the spirit of God came upon him," the Sages remarked: "He saw that the openings [of their tents] were not facing each other, to prevent one person from looking into his neighbor's tent (Rashi, *ibid.*; BB 60a). Accordingly, the sages stated in the Mishnah (BB 3:7) that "In a courtyard which he shares with others, a man should not open a door facing another person's door, nor a window facing another person's window. If it is small, he should not enlarge it, and he should not turn one into two. On the side of the street, however, he may do so," because there, there is no risk that someone's privacy may be infringed

In all these rules, important status was granted to "the prevailing practice in that place" (see *Minhag), on condition that it isn't a "foolish practice" or a "mistaken practice." And thus, the Rashba (Rabbi Solomon Adret, Spain, 13th century), in his important responsum on the status of custom in Jewish law (Resp. Rashba, vol. 2, no. 268) wrote: "And we also learn from the custom of the land, even though it has not been [formally] agreed. As we have learned (M. BB 1:1): "In those districts where it is usual to build using unhewn stone, hewn stones, beams, or bricks, they must use such materials, all according to the custom of the district." And they explained: "Everything – including a light partition, made of thatch and straw," but he adds: "At any rate, if the custom was not to be particular at all with respect to the injury of visual trespass [into] homes and yards [= which damages the neighbor's privacy, see entry: *Damages], then this is a mistaken practice, and is not a [correct] custom. Because a person cannot waive his rights, except with respect to finances, of which a person is entitled to give of his own, or to sustain damage to his property. But he is not entitled to breach the fences [= prohibitions] of the Jewish people, and behave immodestly."

Special provisions of the Israeli planning and construction laws prevent a person from making changes in his house (such as closing a balcony or building an annex) without receiving a permit from the local committee for planning and construction. Similar principles exist in various provisions of Jewish law, as well as in local regulations for public welfare (see **Takkanot ha-Kahal*). The main principle was based upon the words of the prophet Jeremiah: "Woe unto him that builds his house by unrighteousness, and his chambers by injustice" (Jer 22:13). In other words: even a person building his own house must do so in accordance with principles of justice and law. In later generations, the Sages used this verse as a basis for various rulings with respect to planning and construction. Thus, for instance, the Italian sages stated that a person is not entitled to make changes to a house in his possession if his neighbors' rights to light and air would thereby be compromised (see, for instance, Resp. Haramaz of Rabbi Moses Zacuto, no. 37).

Other provisions of modern planning and construction laws require a person to demolish unstable buildings, which endanger their surroundings. A similar provision may be found in Jewish civil torts law. Already in the Mishnah it states that in such cases, "the Court determines a period of 30 days during which the owner of the property must demolish the unstable building, and if he does not do so, he will be charged with any damage that may be incurred as a result" (M. BM 10:4; Yad., *Nizkei Mamon* 13.19; and see Resp. Rashba, vol. 4., no. 114).

Various laws were legislated in the Mishnah and the Talmud, with respect to construction below the surface of the ground, intended to prevent hazards from the public. Thus, it is stated in the Mishnah (BB 3:8) that "It is not acceptable to make a hollow space under the public domain, such as pits, a trench or a cave," while Rabbi Eliezer allows making a cavity under the public domain, provided that it is provided with a sufficiently strong covering to bear the weight of a wagon laden with stones passing over it." And it is further stated in the Mishnah (*ibid.*) that "one must not make beams and balconies that protrude into the public domain unless one chooses to do so by withdrawing into his own area, and then the protrusions can be contained within his own area." The Talmud cites an opinion that qualifies this law, adding that if the protruding beams are higher than "a camel and its rider" – that is, in a sufficiently high place so as not to cause a disturbance to passers-by, then it is allowed. Indeed, Ritba, who was asked about this matter, rules that in places where "it was not customary" to have protruding beams, even if they are much higher than "a camel and its rider," they should not be extended (Resp. Ritba 125). However, in places where a custom existed to allow this, one cannot protest against a person who does so, and in certain cases he even acquires possessory rights (*Ḥazakah) and cannot be compelled to demolish what he has built (Resp. Rosh, 99:6).

Due to its unique character and status, special laws were made for *Jerusalem. Thus, for example, it was determined that in this city, even within private property, a person is barred from building with beams that protrude from the walls, or balconies or pipes that project into the public domain, because they are liable to contaminate or cause other harm to the pilgrims who come to the city (BK 82b; Tosef., Nega'im; *Avot de-Rabbi Nathan*, 35; Yad., *Beit ha-Beḥirah* 7:14; Resp. Rashba, 125). It was similarly prohibited to plant "gardens and orchards" within the city of Jerusalem, and trees should not be planted there, apart from "a rose garden that had been there since the days of the former prophets" (BK and Rambam, ibid.). This was decreed in order to prevent the fertilizing of the fields with manure, which creates an offensive odor, which would be liable to lead to the city's becoming "repulsive to the pilgrims and to all those who come to it from all over the land" (Responsa Radbaz, vol. 2, 633). Likewise, "kilns are not to be made in Jerusalem" – i.e., lime kilns for pottery – because the smoke blackens the city walls, which would be a disgrace, as it has been said of Jerusalem that it was the "paragon of beauty." Others interpret the reason for this rule so as to prevent the smoke from blackening the walls of the Temple (BK 82b; *Rashi* and *Shitah Mekubbeẓet*, ad loc.; Ḥaggigah 26a; Zevaḥim 96a; Yad., *Beit ha-Beḥirah* 7:14). It was further stated that "cemeteries should not be built within the boundaries of Jerusalem, apart from the tombs of the House of David and that of the prophetess Huldah, which have been there since the time of the earliest prophets" (Tosefta, *Avot de-Rabbi Nathan, ibid.* and Rambam, *ibid.*). Indeed, Radbaz (Rabbi David Ben Zimra – a rabbi in Egypt and the Land of Israel during the 16th century) wrote that during these times, when the Temple was not standing, and the laws of uncleanliness and purity no longer prevailed there, this prohibition was no longer in effect (Resp. Radbaz, vol. 2. 635).

A special chapter on the laws of planning and construction relates to compensation of a landowner who has suffered damage due to the change of designation or expropriation of his property (see, for example, Sections 188–197 of the Planning and Construction Law, 5725 – 1965, and the Lands Ordinance (Acquisition for Public Purposes), 1943). This principle complies with the values of a Jewish State, which require that landowners be given compensation even when the damage to his rights in the land is justified due to an opposing public interest, such as in cases of expropriation of the land for public purposes. The compensation can be monetary, in the manner ruled by Rambam (Melakhim 4:6) with respect to the king's right to expropriate land: "and he takes the fields and the olive trees and the vineyards for his slaves when they go to war … and gives their value [in money]" (see Hacohen; and *Rights, Human: Right of Acquisition), or by way of providing alternative land, in the manner that Ahab proposed to Naboth the Jezreelite (I Kings 21:2).

In the State of Israel

In Israeli law, the laws of planning and construction were regulated by a system of laws, the most important of which is the Planning and Construction Law, 5725 – 1965. Other laws establish various qualifications regarding the location of commercial and industrial facilities in residential areas, such as the Business Licensing Law, the Abatement of Nuisances (Noise and Pollution) Law, and municipal by-laws.

In several cases, the Israeli courts have found support and remedies from the sources of Jewish law for matters concerning planning and construction laws that they adjudicated. For example, one case dealt with the municipality's obligation to demolish an unstable structure (CA 2904/92 *Tel Aviv Municipality v. the Estate of the Deceased Leterhaus*, PD 50(1)754). Justice Tal cited the position of Jewish law, according to which one must distinguish between an unstable building that does not present an immediate danger, in which case the court is obliged to caution the owners and give them time to demolish it, and one that poses immediate danger. Thus, it is stated in the Shulḥan Arukh: "The wall and the tree … if they are unsound, the court gives him time to chop the tree and to demolish the wall. And how much time? Thirty days" (Sh. Ar., ḤM 416:1). The Rema, in his gloss on this passage, adds that "A time is set for him – only when the court has forewarned him. But without there having been a court [warning], even though his friends have cautioned him, it is considered as nothing … and if it is necessary and there are grounds to assume that it might harm others, then he should not be given time, and he is forced to remove the impending menace immediately."

In another case, the Supreme Court deliberated over the rights of demonstrators to demonstrate in a public area, while causing a nuisance to neighbors [CA 3829/04 *Israel Tuito, Chairman of Mikol Halev, Kikar Halehem, The Association for Reducing Social Disparities in Israel, et al. v. Municipality of Jerusalem*; (unpublished). Justice E. Rubinstein ruled that even the right to freedom of demonstration (see *Rights, Human: Freedom of Expression) is not unlimited, and should be prevented when its damage to the public is greater than its benefit. He found support for this ruling, inter alia, in the above-cited talmudic ruling, according to which the prohibition against of beams and balconies that protrude into the public domain does not apply when they are "higher than [the height of] a camel and its rider."

The Supreme Court likewise referred to the sources of Jewish law when it determined the obligation of the Local Planning and Construction Committee to avoid expropriating land areas from their owners unnecessarily and to compensate the owner in cases in which he incurs harm as a result of its actions (HC 2390/96 *Karasik et al. v. the State of Israel*, 55 (2) PD 625). In order to establish the landowner's proprietary rights, Justice Heshin referred, inter alia, to the biblical story of Ahab and Naboth the Jezreelite, which is discussed extensively in the sources of Jewish law. In another case (CA 8989/04, *Petach Tikva Local Planning and Construction Committee and others v. M. Zitman and Sons Ltd.*; unpublished), Justice. Rubinstein refers to the words of Chief Rabbi Ben Zion Meir Hai Ouziel, who wrote in connection with a similar matter on the eve of the establishment of the State of Israel:

> "Proposals for the Constitution of the State of Israel," in which it was stated, among other things, that "The State of Israel recognizes its obligation to protect all private and public property owners by their own acquisition or by inheritance, and denies the right to expropriate private or public lands in favor of the government if it is not located in a place where it is necessitated by public needs. And even in such cases, no land shall be expropriated save at its full price or in exchange for other similar land" (quoted in Rabbi Isaac Halevi Herzog, *Constitution and Law in the Jewish State*, vol. 1: *Administration of Rule and Justice in a Jewish State* [Hebrew], ed. I. Warhaftig, 251).

A special section of the Planning and Construction Law determines limits to injury and prohibits the destruction of buildings that have been designated for preservation due to their historic value (Section 76 and the Fourth Supplement to the Planning and Construction Law, 5725 – 1965). Similar provisions also exist in Jewish law with respect to the prohibition on damaging holy sites. Thus, for example, a prohibition was imposed on breaking one stone of the Temple, and it was prohibited to unnecessarily demolish a synagogue. This issue was deliberated in the Supreme Court, in the context of demolishing synagogues in *Gush Katif in wake of the disengagement plan of 2005, and Justice E. Rubinstein referred extensively to the sources of Jewish law when deliberating the matter.

The rabbinical courts, too, are occasionally required to address the laws of planning and construction, such as the question of whether a neighbor can force his neighbors to consent to additional construction in his apartment.

BIBLIOGRAPHY: M. Elon, *Ha-Mishpat ha-Ivri* (1988), 879–80; idem; *Jewish Law* (1994), 1073–74; *Enẓiklopedyah Talmudit*, 10:666–671; 25:304; Y. Ariel, "*Piẓẓuyim al Hafka'at Karka'ot*," in: *Emunat Etekha*, 25 (1999); Y.S. Blass, "*Piẓẓuyim Mifga'ei Mamon u-Sevivah*," in: *Teḥumin*, 19 (1999); A. Hacohen, "*Ve-Khi ha-Rabbim Gazlanim Hem? Al Hafka'at Mekarke'in u-Pegi'ah bi-Zekhut ha-Kinyan be-Mishpat ha-Ivri*," in: *She'arei Mishpat*, 1 (1997), 39–54; idem, "'*Ma-Nora ha-Makom ha-Zeh' – Mekomot Kedoshim: Bein Dat, Misphat u-Kedushah*," in: *Sha'arei Mishpat*, 3 (2003), 247–79; H.S. Shaanan, "*Ḥiyyuv Dayyar le-Haskim le-Tosefet Beniyyah shel Shekheno*," in: *Teḥumin*, 19 (1999), 60.

[Aviad Hacohen (2nd ed.)]

°**PLANTAVIT DE LA PAUSE, JEAN** (**Plantavitius**; 1576–1651), French Hebraist. Born into an aristocratic Protestant family, Plantavit was brought up in Nîmes and became pastor of Béziers. In 1604 he converted to Catholicism and later became bishop of Lodève. He left a detailed account of his Hebrew teachers, who included the erudite and prolific convert Philippe d'Aquin (born Mordecai Cresque de Carpentras, c. 1575–1650), Leone *Modena, Abraham Jedidiah Shalit of Ferrara, Elisha Mazzal-Tov of Modena, Jacob b. Moses Senior of Pisa, and Solomon b. Judah Ezobi of Carpentras. One of the outstanding Christian Hebraists of the age, Plantavit spent 30 years preparing his monumental *Thesaurus synonymicus Hebraico-Chaldaico-Rabbinicus* (Lodève, 1644–45), which gave the Latin equivalent of Hebrew and Aramaic terms, appropriate biblical references, and a wealth of synonyms. He also published *Florilegium Biblicum* and *Florilegium Rabbinicum* (both Lodève, 1645), in the latter of which he records his gift of a copy of the Zohar to his master, Philippe d'Aquin.

BIBLIOGRAPHY: F. Secret, *Les kabbalistes chrétiens de la Renaissance* (1964), 336–7.

[Godfrey Edmond Silverman]

°**PLANTIN, CHRISTOPHE** (c. 1520–1589), French humanist printer and publisher. Plantin, who was born near Tours, learned the book trade in Normandy and Paris. His Protestant sympathies led him in 1549 to the more congenial atmosphere of Antwerp in the Spanish Netherlands, where he devoted himself to fine printing from about 1555 onward. Plantin was, after Daniel *Bomberg, the outstanding 16th-century Christian printer of Hebrew books. By 1576 he operated 22 presses and was the leading printer-publisher of northern Europe. Following the "Spanish Fury" of 1576, he spent some years in France and Holland, eventually returning to Antwerp, where he died.

Plantin's greatest publishing achievement was the eight volume "Antwerp Polyglot," *Biblia Sacra hebraice, chaldaice, graece et latine…* (1568–72), an improved and expanded version of the first Complutensian Bible (Alcalà de Henares, 1514–17). The undertaking received the Vatican's approval in 1568 owing to fears of a rival project by Immanuel *Tremellius, a Jewish convert to Protestantism. The four volumes devoted to the Old Testament included revised texts of the Targums, and a Latin translation; the fifth covered the New Testament; and the last three volumes constituted the *Apparatus Sacer*, which included pioneering lexicons of Syriac and Aramaic. The introduction to the first volume, inspired by the prefaces to Daniel Bomberg's second Rabbinic Bible (1525), contains interesting Hebrew panegyrics by Benito *Arias Montano, Guy *Le Fèvre de la Boderie, and Gilbert Génébrard (one of the Polyglot's obliging censors). From every aspect, the work was a masterpiece of Bible scholarship, typography, and illustration. Hebrew punches were either especially cut by Guillaume *Le Bé or provided by the Bombergs. Of the 1,200 copies printed, 12 sets on vellum were prepared for Philip II of Spain, who made Plantin his Architypographer Royal, but never furnished the sum promised for naming the Bible in his honor. The "Antwerp Polyglot" was speedily denounced by Spanish obscurantists, who objected to its philological, rabbinic, and kabbalistic preoccupations, but it was cleared of suspicion in 1580. Plantin also printed Hebrew Bibles for export to Jewish communities in North Africa (1567) and may have issued the anonymous Hebrew prayer book which appeared in Antwerp c. 1577. His descendants maintained the press until 1875, when the Antwerp municipality transformed it into the present-day Plantin-Moretus Museum – a unique monument to Renaissance printing and publishing.

BIBLIOGRAPHY: C. Clair, *Christopher Plantin* (Eng., 1960); M. Rooses, *Christophe Plantin, imprimeur anversois* (1882); idem, *Correspondance de Christophe Plantin* (1883–84); S.H. Steinberg, *Five Hundred Years of Printing* (1955), index; *Gedenkboek der Plantin-Dagen 1555–1955* (1956); F. Secret, in: *Sefarad*, 18 (1958), 121–8; G.E. Silverman, in: JC (Jan. 8, 1960); B. Rekers, *Benito Arias Montano 1527–1598…* (1961); I.S. Revah, in: REJ, 2 (1963), 123–47.

[Godfrey Edmond Silverman]

PLANTS. Research into the flora mentioned in the ancient Hebrew literature is grounded on the basic assumption that within historical times no fundamental changes have taken place in the country's climate (see *Agriculture). This assumption, which allows conclusions to be drawn from present-day plants about the floral landscape of bygone days, is particularly important for identifying the flora of the Bible and of talmudic literature. The overwhelming majority of them can be identified with those of today, but, as with all the terms of biblical and talmudic realia, many and varied identifications and interpretations have been suggested for them. Modern botanical and philological studies have, however, helped greatly in arriving at a correct identification.

In the Bible

The Bible mentions about 100 names of plants, the bulk of them of Ereẓ Israel, the others being trees of Lebanon and tropical plants that yield an aromatic substance or were used in incense. (See Table: Plants in the Bible and Mishnah.) These names refer to specific plants, but some are generic names, such as *koẓ ve-dardar* ("thorns and thistles") and *shamir va-shayit* ("briars and thorns"). Although the biblical plants are chiefly those which were economically important, they are to a large extent mentioned fortuitously. The carob, for example, although undoubtedly grown at that time, is not mentioned in the Bible, while specific vegetables are mentioned in one verse only of the Bible; and these are the vegetables of Egypt for which the children of Israel longed during their wandering in the wilderness (Num. 11:5).

In Talmudic Literature

The Mishnah, the Talmuds, and the Midrashim add hundreds of names of plants to those mentioned in the Bible. They are particularly numerous in the Mishnah of *Zera'im* which treats of laws connected with agriculture. In the aggadic Midrashim, too, many plants are mentioned in simile and parable. In all, the ancient literature on Ereẓ Israel mentions close to 500 names of flora. The Babylonian Talmud refers to scores of plants of Babylonia and its neighborhood. In the Table: Plants in Bible and Mishnah, only one identification is given. Alternative suggestions of identification will be found in the individual articles.

BIBLIOGRAPHY: H.B. Tristram, *Natural History of the Bible* (1877[5]); J. Schwarz, *Tevu'ot ha-Areẓ* (1900); Loew, Flora; G. Dalman, *Arbeit und Sitte in Palaestina*, 7 vols. in 8 (1928–42); H.N. and A.L. Moldenke, *Plants of the Bible* (1952); J. Feliks, *Ha-Ḥakla'ut be-Ereẓ Yisrael bi-Tekufat ha-Mishnah ve-ha-Talmud* (1963); idem, *Kilei Zera'im ve-Harkavah* (1967); idem, *Olam ha-Ẓome'aḥ ha-Mikra'i* (1968[2]), contains additional bibliography. **ADD. BIBLIOGRAPHY:** Feliks, Ha-Ẓome'aḥ.

[Jehuda Feliks]

Plants and Products of Plants Mentioned in the Bible and Mishnah

English Name	Scientific Name	Hebrew name	Description of Plant	Reference
Acacia	Acacia albida	שִׁטָּה, שִׁטִּים	thorn tree	Ex. 26:15; Isa. 41:19, et al.
Alga	Chlorophyta	יְרוֹקָה	seaweed	Shab. 2:1
Almond	Prunus amygdalus (Amygdalus communis)	לוּז שָׁקֵד	fruit tree	Gen. 30:37 Num. 17:23; Jer. 1:11, et al.
Aloe	Aquilaria agallocha	אֲהָלִים אֲהָלוֹת אַלְמֻגִּים אַלְגֻּמִּים	fragrant tropical tree	Num. 24:6; Prov. 7:17 Ps. 45:9; Song 4:14; I Kings 10:11–12 II Chron. 2:7; 9:10–11
Amaranth	Amaranthus retroflexus	יַרְבּוּז	vegetable (herb)	Shev. 9:1
Amomum	Amomum cardamomum	חָמָם	tropical spice plant	Uk. 3:5
Apple	Pyrus malus	תַּפּוּחַ	fruit tree	Joel 1:12; Song 2:3, et al.
Artichoke	Cynara scolymus	קִנְרֵס	garden vegetable	Kil. 5:8; Uk. 1:6
Asafetida, Fennel	Ferula assafoetida	חִלְתִּית	herb whose gum fennel is used in spices and medicine	Shab. 20:3; Av. Zar. 2:7, et al.
Balm, Balsam	Commiphora opobalsamum	בֹּשֶׂם נָטָף צְרִי, צֳרִי קְטָף	the balsam shrub whose resin yields an aromatic substance	Song 5:1 Ex. 30:34 Gen. 37:25; 43:11, et al. Shev. 7:6
Barley	Hordeum sativum	שְׂעוֹרָה	cereal grass	Ex. 9:31; Deut. 8:8, et al.
Barley, two-rowed	Hordeum distichum	שִׁבּוֹלֶת שׁוּעָל שׂוֹרָה	cereal grass	Isa. 28:25 Kil. 1:1; Pes. 2:5, et al.
Bdellium	Commiphora africana	בְּדוֹלַח	tropical tree whose resin yields an aromatic substance	Gen. 2:12; Num. 11:7
Bean, broad	Vicia faba	פּוֹל	legume	II Sam. 17:28; Ezek. 4:9, et al.
Bean, hyacinth	Dolichos lablab	פּוֹל הַלָּבָן	legume	Kil. 1:1; Ma'as. 4:7, et al.
Bean, yard-long (asparagus bean)	Vigna sesquipedalis	פּוֹל הֶחָרוּב	legume	Kil. 1:2
Beet spinach	Beta vulgaris var. cicla	תֶּרֶד	garden vegetable	Kil. 1:3; Ter. 10:11, et al.
Bermuda grass	Cynodon dactylon	יַבְּלִית	weed	Kelim 3:6
Box	Buxus sempervirens	אֶשְׁכְּרוֹעַ	hardwood shrub	Yoma 3:9; Kelim 12:8; Neg. 2:1

Plants and Products of Plants Mentioned in the Bible and Mishnah (continued)

English Name	Scientific Name	Hebrew name	Description of Plant	Reference
Boxthorn	Lycium europaeum	אָטָד	thorny shrub	Gen. 50:10–11; Judg. 9:14–15, et al.
Broom plant	Retama roetam	רֹתֶם	desert shrub	I Kings 19:4–5; Job 30:4, et al.
Cabbage, garden	Brassica oleracea var. capitata	תְּרוּבְתוֹר	garden vegetable	Kil. 1:3
Cabbage, kale	Brassica oleracea var. acephala	כְּרוּב	hardy cabbage	Kil. 1:3; Ter. 10:11, et al.
Calamus, Indian sweet	Cymbopogon martini	קָנֶה הַטּוֹב קְנֵה־בֹשֶׂם קָנֶה	tropical aromatic plant	Jer. 6:20 Ex. 30:23 Isa. 43:24; Song. 4:14, et al.
Cane, biflorate	Saccharum biflorum	אַגְמוֹן	reed that grows near water	Isa. 9:13, 58:5, et al.
Caper	Capparis spinosa	צָלָף, קַפְרֵס אֲבִיּוֹנָה	thorny plant whose buds and fruit are used as spices Caperberry	Ma'as. 4:6 Eccles. 12:5, Ma'as 4:6
Caraway	Carum carvi	קַרְבוֹס (קַנְבוֹס)	vegetable used as a spice	Kil. 2:5
Carob	Ceratonia siliqua	חָרוּב	fruit tree	Pe'ah 1:5; Dem. 2:1, et al.
Castor-oil plant	Ricinus communis	קִיקָיוֹן	shrub whose seed yields oil	Jonah 4:6, 7, 9, 10
Cattail	Typha angustata	סוּף	marsh and water plant	Ex. 2:3; Isa. 19:6, et al.
Cedar	Cedrus libani	אֶרֶז	forest tree of Lebanon	Isa. 2:13; Amos 2:9, et al.
Celery	Apium graveolens	כַּרְפַּס	garden vegetable	Shev. 9:1
Chick-pea	Cicer arietinum	חָמִיץ אֲפוּנִים	legume	Isa. 30:24 Pe'ah 3:3; Kil. 3:2
Chicory	Cichorium intybus	עוֹלְשִׁין	garden vegetable	Shev. 7:1; Pes. 2:6
Chicory, wild	Cichorium pumilum	עוֹלְשֵׁי־שָׂדֶה	wild vegetable	Kil. 1:2
Cinnamon, Ceylonese	Cinnamonum zeylanicum	קִנָּמוֹן	aromatic tropical spice tree	Ex. 30:23; Prov. 7:17, et al.
Cinnamon, Chinese	Cinnamonum cassia	קִדָּה	aromatic tropical spice tree	Ex. 30:24; Ezek. 27:19
Cinnamon, Indo-Chinese	Cinnamonum laurei	קְצִיעָה	aromatic tropical spice tree	Ps. 45:9
Citron	Citrus medica	עֵץ הָדָר אֶתְרוֹג	fruit tree	Lev. 23:40 Ma'as. 1:4; Bik. 2:6, et al.
Colocasia	Colocasia antiquorum	קַרְקָס	vegetable with edible bulb	Ma'as. 5:8
Coriander	Coriandrum sativum	גַּד כֻּסְבָּר	herb whose seed is used as a spice	Ex. 16:31; Num. 11:7 Kil. 1:2; Ma'as. 3:9, et al.
Cotton	Gossypium herbraceum Gossypium arboreum	כַּרְפַּס צֶמֶר־גֶּפֶן	plant with fibrous fruit	Esth. 1:6 Kil. 7:2
Cowpea	Vigna sinensis	פּוֹל הַמִּצְרִי	legume	Kil. 1:2; Shev. 2:9, et al.
Cowpea, Nile	Vigna nilotica	שְׁעוּעִית	legume	Kil. 1:1
Cress	Lepidium latifolium	עֲדָל	garden vegetable	Uk. 3:4
Cress, garden	Lepidium sativum	שַׁחֲלַיִם	garden vegetable	Ma'as. 4:5
Crocus, saffron	Crocus sativus	כַּרְכּוֹם	plant used as a spice and for coloring	Song 4:14; Nid. 2:6
Cucumber, bitter	Citrullus colocynthis	פַּקּוּעוֹת	wild desert plant	II Kings 4:39; Shab. 2:2
Cucumber, squirting	Ecballium elaterium	יְרוֹקַת הַחֲמוֹר	wild herb	Oho. 8:1
Cumin	Cuminum cyminum	כַּמּוֹן	herb whose seeds are used as a spice	Isa. 2:25, 27; Dem. 2:1
Cypress	Cupressus sempervirens	גֹּפֶר תְּאַשּׁוּר	forest evergreen tree	Gen. 6:14 Isa. 41:19; 60:13, et al.
Daffodil, sea	Pancratium maritimum	חֲבַצֶּלֶת	fragrant wild flower	Isa. 35:1; Song 2:1
Darnel	Lolium temulentum	זוּן	weed grass	Kil. 1:1; Ter. 2:6
Dill	Anethum graveolens	שֶׁבֶת	plant used as a spice	Pe'ah 3:2; Ma'as. 4:5; Uk. 3:4
Durra	Sorghum cernuum	דֹּחַן	summer cereal	Ezek. 4:9; Shev. 2:7

Plants and Products of Plants Mentioned in the Bible and Mishnah (continued)

English Name	Scientific Name	Hebrew name	Description of Plant	Reference
Ebony	Diospyros ebenum	הָבְנִים	tropical hard wood	Ezek. 27:15
Emmer	Triticum dicoccum	כֻּסֶּמֶת	winter cereal	Ex. 9:32; Isa. 28:25, et al.
Eryngo	Eryngium creticum	חַרְחֲבִינָא	edible wild herb	Pes. 2:6
Fennel	Foeniculum vulgare	גְּפְנִין	herb used as a spice	Dem. 1:1
Fennel flower	Nigella sativa	קֶצַח	herb whose seeds are used as a spice	Isa. 28:25, 27; Eduy. 5:3
Fenugreek	Trigonella foenum- Graecum	תִּלְתָּן	cultivated legume used as forage or medicine	Kil. 2:5; Ter. 10:5
Fern, ceterach	Ceterach officinarum	דַּנְדַּנָּה	medicinal fern	Shev. 7:1–2
Fern, maiden hair	Adiantum capillus veneris	יוֹעֶזֶר	medicinal fern	Shab. 14:3
Fig	Ficus carica	תְּאֵנָה	fruit tree	Num. 20:5; Deut. 8:8, et al.
Fig, sycamore	Ficus sycomorus	שִׁקְמָה	fruit tree	I Kings 10:27; Isa. 9:9, et al.
Flax	Linum usitatissimum	פִּשְׁתָּן פִּשְׁתָּה	herb whose stem yields fiber and from whose seed oil is extracted	Josh. 2:6; Hos. 2:7; et al. Pe'ah 6:5
Frankincense	Boswellia carteri	לְבוֹנָה	tree yielding aromatic resin used in incense	Ex. 30:34; Isa. 60:6, et al.
Galbanum	Ferula galbaniflua	חֶלְבְּנָה	herb whose resin was used in incense	Ex. 30:34
Garlic	Allium sativum	שׁוּם	vegetable used as spice	Num. 11:5
Ginger, wild	Arum dioscoridis	לוּף שׁוֹטָה	wild vegetable	Shev. 7:1, 2, et al.
Gourd, Calabash	Lagenaria vulgaris	דְּלַעַת	vegetable with edible fruit	Kil. 1:2; Ma'as. 1:5, et al.
Grape vine	Vitis vinifera	גֶּפֶן עֲנָבִים	fruit shrub	Gen. 40:9; Num. 20:5, et al.
Graspea	Lathyrus sativus	טֹפַח	legume	Pe'ah 5:3; Kil. 1:1, et al.
Hawthorn	Crataegus azarolus	עֻזְרָר	wild fruit tree	Dem. 1:1; Kil. 1:4, et al.
Heliotrope	Heliotropium europaeum	עַקְרַבָּנִין	medicinal wild herb	Shev. 7:2; Er. 2:7
Hemlock, poison	Conium maculatum	רוֹשׁ,רֹאשׁ	poisonous herb	Deut. 29:17; Hos. 10:4, et al.
Hemp	Cannabis sativa	קַנְבּוֹס	herb whose stem yields fiber	Kil. 5:8; 9:1, 7
Henna	Lawsonia alba	כֹּפֶר	shrub which yields a dye	Song. 1:14; 4:13, et al.
Hyssop (v. marjoram)	Hyssopus officinalis	אֵזוֹב כּוֹחֵל	aromatic herb	Neg. 14:6; Par. 11:7
Iris	Iris germanica Iris pallida	אִירוּס	plant whose bulb yields an aromatic substance	Kil. 5:8; Oho. 8:1
Ivy	Hedera helix	קִיסוֹס	climbing evergreen vine	Kil. 5:8; Suk. 1:4, et al.
Jujube	Zizyphus vulgaris	שֵׁיזָפִין	fruit tree	Kil. 1:4
Jujube, wild	Zizyphus spina christi	צֶאֱלִים רִימִין	wild tree with edible fruit	Job 40:21–22 Dem. 1:1; Kil. 1:6
Juniper (savin high)	Juniperus exelsa	בְּרוֹשׁ בְּרוֹת	coniferous tree of Lebanon	Isa. 14:8; 37:24, et al. Song. 1:17
Knotweed	Polygonum aviculare	אֲבוּב־רוֹעֶה	medicinal wild herb	Shab. 14:3
Laudanum	Cistus ladanum	לֹט	shrub yielding aromatic resin	Gen. 37:25; 43:11
Laurel	Laurus nobilis	אֹרֶן	forest tree with aromatic leaves	Isa. 44:14
Lavender, Lavandula	Lavandula officinalis	אֱזוֹבְיוֹן	aromatic shrub	Shab. 14:3; Neg. 14:6, et al.
Leek	Allium porrum	חָצִיר כְּרֵישָׁה כַּרְתִּי	garden herb	Num. 11:5 Kil. 1:2; Shev. 7:1 Ber. 1:2; Suk. 3:6
Leek, wild	Allium ampeloprasum	כְּרֵישֵׁי שָׂדֶה	wild herb	Kil. 1:2; Uk. 3:2
Lentil	Lens esculenta	עֲדָשִׁים	legume	Gen. 25:34; II Sam. 17:28, et al.
Lettuce	Lactuca sativa	חֲזֶרֶת	garden vegetable	Kil. 1:2; Pes. 2:6, et al.
Lettuce, wild	Lactuca scariola	חֲזֶרֶת גַּלִּים	wild vegetable	Kil. 1:2

Plants and Products of Plants Mentioned in the Bible and Mishnah (continued)

English Name	Scientific Name	Hebrew name	Description of Plant	Reference
Lily, madonna	Lilium candidum	שׁוֹשָׁן, שׁוֹשַׁנָּה	aromatic flower	Hos. 14:6; Song. 6:2–3, et al.
Lily, Solomon's (black calla)	Arum palaestinum	לוּף	wild vegetable with edible bulb	Pe'ah, 6:10; Kil. 2:5
Love grass	Eragrostis bipinnata	חִילָף	weed used for making baskets	Kelim 17:17
Lupine	Lupinus termis	תֻּרְמוֹס	legume	Kil. 1:3; Shab. 18:1, et al.
Lupine, yellow	Lupinus luteus	פַּלְסְלוּס	legume	Kil. 1:3
Madder	Rubia tinctorim	פּוּאָה	climbing plant whose roots are used for dyeing	Shev. 5:4; 7:2, et al.
Mandrake	Mandragora officinarum	דּוּדָאִים	wild herb with aromatic fruit	Gen. 30:14–16; Song. 7:14
Marjoram, Syrian	Majorana syriaca	אֵזוֹב	aromatic wild plant	Ex. 12:22; Lev. 14:4, et al.
Mastic	Pistacia lentiscus	בָּכָא, בְּכָאִים	wild shrub	II Sam. 5:23–24; Ps. 84:7
Melon	Cucumis melo	מְלָפְפוֹן	garden vegetable	Kil. 1:2; Ter. 2:6, et al.
Melon, chate	Cucumis melo var. chate	קִשּׁוּת, קִשֻּׁאִים	garden vegetable	Num. 11:5; Kil. 1:2, et al.
Millet	Panicum miliaceum	פְּרָגִים	summer cereal	Ḥal. 1:4; Shev. 2:7
Mint	Mentha piperita	מִינְתָּא	herb used as spice	Uk. 1:2
Mudar	Calotropis procera	פְּתִילַת הַמִּדְבָּר	wild shrub with fibrous fruit	Shab. 2:1
Mulberry	Morus nigra	תּוּת	fruit tree	Ma'as. 1:2
Mushroom	Boletus, etc.	פִּטְרִיָּה	generic name for the mushroom species	Uk. 3:2
Mustard, black	Brassica nigra	חַרְדָּל	wild herb whose seeds are used as a condiment	Kil. 1:2
Mustard, field	Sinapis arvensis	לִפְסָן	wild herb	Kil. 1:5
Mustard, white	Sinapis alba	חַרְדָּל מִצְרִי	wild herb whose seeds are used as a condiment	Kil. 1:2
Myrrh	Commiphora schimperi Commiphora abyssinica	מוֹר	tropical aromatic tree	Ex. 30:23; Song 1:13, et al.
Myrtle	Myrtus communis	הֲדַס עֵץ עָבֹת	aromatic shrub	Isa. 41:19; 55:13, et al. Lev. 23:40; Neh. 8:15, et al.
Narcissus	Narcissus tazetta	שׁוֹשַׁנַּת הָעֲמָקִים(?)	wild flower	Song 2:1
Nard (Spikenard)	Nardostachys jatamansi	נֵרְדְּ, נְרָדִים	aromatic plant	Song 1:12; 4:13–14, et al.
Nettle	Urtica sp.	סִרְפָּד	stinging wild weed	Isa. 55:13
Oak	Quercus ithaburensis Quercus calliprinos	אַלּוֹן	forest tree	Gen. 35:8; Isa. 2:13, et al.
Oak, gall	Quercus infectoria (Boissieri)	מֵילָה	forest tree	Mid. 3:7
Oleander	Nerium oleander	הַרְדּוּפְנֵי	river bank evergreen shrub	Ḥul. 3:5
Olive	Olea europaea	זַיִת	fruit tree	Deut. 6:11; 8:8, et al.
Onion	Allium cepa	בָּצָל	garden vegetable	Num. 11:5
Orange, trifoliate	Poncirus trifoliata	קִדָּה לְבָנָה	tropical fruit tree	Kil. 1:8
Orchid	Orchis sp.	חַלְבְּצִין נֵץ־הֶחָלָב	flower with edible bulb	Shev. 7:2 Shev. 7:1
Palm, date	Phoenix dactylifera	תָּמָר דֶּקֶל	fruit tree	Ex. 15:27; Num. 33:9, et al. Pe'ah 4:1; Shab. 14:3, et al.
Papyrus	Cyperus papyrus	גֹּמֶא	aquatic plant	Ex. 2:3; Isa. 18:2, et al.
Peach	Persica vulgaris	אֲפַרְסֵק	fruit tree	Kil. 1:4; Ma'as. 1:2
Pear	Pyrus communis	אַגָּס קְרִיסְטוֹמֶלִין	fruit tree	Kil. 1:4; Uk. 1:6, et al.
Pear, Syrian	Pyrus syriaca	חִזְרָר	forest tree with edible fruit	Kil. 1:4
Pepper	Piper nigrum	פִּלְפֵּל	tropical aromatic plant used as a condiment	Shab. 6:5; Beẓah 2:8

Plants and Products of Plants Mentioned in the Bible and Mishnah (continued)

English Name	Scientific Name	Hebrew name	Description of Plant	Reference
Pine	Pinus sp.	תִּדְהָר(?)	coniferous tree	Isa. 41:19; 60:13
Pine, aleppo	Pinus halepensis	עֵץ שֶׁמֶן	coniferous forest tree	I Kings 6:23; Isa. 41:19, et al.
Pine, stone	Pinus pinea	תִּרְזָה	coniferous tree with edible kernels	Isa. 44:14
Pistachio	Pistacia vera	בָּטְנָה, בָּטְנִים	fruit tree	Gen. 43:11; Shev. 7:5
Plane	Platanus orientalis	עַרְמוֹן	river bank tree	Gen. 30:37; Ezek. 31:8
Pomegranate	Punica granatum	רִמּוֹן	fruit tree	Num. 20:5; Deut. 8:8, et al.
Poplar	Populus euphratica	צַפְצָפָה	river bank tree	Ezek. 17:5
Purslane	Portulaca oleracea	חֲלַגְלוֹגָה רְגֵלָה	wild herb used as a vegetable	Shev. 9:1 Shev. 7:1, 9:5, et al.
Quince	Cydonia oblonga	פְּרִישׁ	fruit tree	Kil. 1:4; Ma'as. 1:3, et al.
Radish	Raphanus sativus	צְנוֹן	garden vegetable	Kil. 1:5; Ma'as. 5:2, et al.
Rape	Brassica napus	נָפוּץ, נָפוּס	garden vegetable used as forage	Kil. 1:3; 1:5, et al.
Raspberry, wild	Rubus sanctus	סְנֶה	thorny climbing shrub	Ex. 3:2–4; Deut. 33:16
Reed, ditch	Phragmites communis	קָנֶה	river bank weed	Isa. 19:6, 35:7, et al.
Rice	Oryza sativa	אֹרֶז	annual summer cereal grass	Dem. 2:1; Shev. 2:7, et al.
Rocket, dyer's	Reseda luteola	רִכְפָּה	herb whose leaves and stem yield a dye	Ma'as. 5:8; Shev. 7:2
Rocket, garden	Eruca sativa	אוֹרֹת	medicinal herb	II Kings 4:39
Rose	Rosa, sp.	וֶרֶד	shrub with fragrant flowers	Shev. 7:6; Ma'as. 2:5, et al.
Rue	Ruta graveolens	פֵּיגָם	shrub used as a spice	Kil. 1:8; Shev. 9:1
Safflower	Carthamus tinctorius	חָרִיעַ קוֹצָה	herb used as a spice and for dyeing	Kil. 2:8; Uk. 3:5; Shev. 7:1
Saltbush	Atriplex halimus	מַלּוּחַ	desert shrub	Job 30:4
Savory	Satureja thymbra	סִיאָה	aromatic wild plant	Shev. 8:1; Ma'as. 3:9
Sesame	Sesamum orientalis	שֻׁמְשֹׁם	plant used as a spice and yielding oil	Shev. 2:7; Ḥal. 1:4, et al.
Shallot	Allium ascalonicum	בְּצַלְצוּל	garden vegetable used for seasoning	Kil. 1:3
Sorrel, garden	Rumex acetosa	לְעוּנִים	garden vegetable	Kil. 1:3
Spanish cherry	Mimusops balata	פַּרְסָאָה	tropical fruit tree	Shev. 5:1
Spelt	Triticum spelta	שִׁפּוֹן	cereal	Kil. 1:1; Ḥal. 1:1, et al.
Squill	Urginea maritima	חָצוּב	wild toxic onion	Kil. 1:8
Storax	Styrax officinalis	לִבְנֶה	forest tree	Gen. 30:37; Hos. 4:13
Sumac	Rhus coriaria	אוֹג	forest tree with edible fruit	Pe'ah 1:5; Dem. 1:1, et al.
Tamarisk	Tamarix, sp.	אֵשֶׁל עַרְעָר	desert and saline tree	Gen. 21:33; I Sam. 22:6, et al. Jer. 17:6; Ps. 102:18
Terebinth	Pistacia palaestina Pistacia atlantica	אֵלָה	forest tree	Gen. 35:4; Hos. 4:13, et al.
Thistle	Centaurea, sp.	דַּרְדַּר	prickly herb	Gen. 3:18; Hos. 10:8
Thistle, golden	Scolymus maculatus	חוֹחַ	prickly herb	Hos. 9:6; Prov. 26:9, et al.
Thistle, silybum	Silybum marianum	קִמּוֹשׂ	prickly herb	Isa. 34:13; Hos. 9:6, et al.
Thistle, sow	Sonchus oleraceus	מָרוֹר	bitter herb	Ex. 12:8; Lam. 3:15, et al.
Thorn	Calycotome villosa	חָרוּל	prickly shrub	Zeph. 2:9; Job 30:7, et al.
Thorn, camel	Alhagi maurorum	נַעֲצוּץ	prickly dwarf shrub	Isa. 7:19; 55:13
Thorn, gundelia	Gundelia tournefortii	גַּלְגַּל	prickly herb	Isa. 17:13; Ps. 83:14
Thorn, poterium	Poterium spinosum	סִירִים סִירָה	prickly dwarf shrub	Isa. 34:13; Hos. 2:8, et al. Ps. 58:10
Thorn, prosopis	Prosopis farcata	נַהֲלֹל	prickly dwarf shrub	Isa. 7:19

Plants and Products of Plants Mentioned in the Bible and Mishnah (continued)

English Name	Scientific Name	Hebrew name	Description of Plant	Reference
Thyme	Thymus capitatus	קוֹרָנִית	aromatic dwarf shrub	Shev. 8:1; Ma'as. 3:9
Tragacanth	Astragalus gummifer Astragalus tragacantha	נְכאֹת	dwarf shrub yielding a fragrant resin	Gen. 37:25; 43:11
Truffle	Ascomycetes- Tuberaceae	שְׁמַרְקָעִים	edible subterranean fungus	Uk. 3:2
Turnip	Brassica rapa	לֶפֶת	garden vegetable	Kil. 1:3, 9, et al.
Vetch, bitter	Vicia ervilia	כַּרְשִׁינָה	legume	Ter. 11:9; Shab. 1:5, et al.
Vetch, French	Vicia narbonensis	סַפִּיר	legume	Kil. 1:1
Walnut	Juglans regia	אֱגוֹז	fruit tree	Song 6:11
Watermelon	Citrullus vulgaris	אֲבַטִּיחַ	garden vegetable	Num. 11:5
Weed, ridolfia	Ridololfia segetum	בָּאְשָׁה	weed	Job 31:40
Wheat	Triticum durum Triticum vulgare Triticum turgidum	חִטָּה	cereal	Ex. 9:32; Deut. 8:8; et al.
Willow	Salix, sp.	עֲרָבָה	riverbank tree	Lev. 23:40; Ps. 137:2, et al.
Woad, isatis	Isatis tinctoria	אִסְטִיס	herb which yields a dye	Kil. 2:5; Shev. 7:1, et al.
Wormwood	Artemisia, sp.	לַעֲנָה	desert dwarf shrub	Deut. 29:17; Jer. 9:14, et al.

PLASENCIA, city in the Estremadura region of Spain, near the Portuguese border. The Jewish quarter was in the suburb of Jaraíz, and in the 13th century the Jewish community ranked with the flourishing communities in Castile. The Jews settled in Plasencia quite soon after its foundation at the end of the 12th century. From the beginning of the 14th century, restrictions issued against the Jews in Castile by the various *cortes*, or legislative assemblies, were also applied in Plasencia; for instance, those of the *cortes* of Medina del *Campo (1305), stipulating that no Jew was to farm taxes or acquire real estate from Christians. In 1313 Queen Dona María and the infante Pedro ratified the decisions of the *cortes* of Plasencia which prohibited the Jews from holding public office; furthermore, suits in which one of the parties was not Jewish were to be tried according to local and not Jewish law, and Hebrew documents would not be accepted as proof. Toward the end of the 14th century, there were 50 Jewish heads of families in Plasencia who paid the annual tax. The decline which overtook the Castile communities after the persecutions of 1391 was also felt in Plasencia.

In the mid-15th century several Jewish names appear among the tax farmers of Plasencia and the kingdom. Various documents give further details on the life of the community during the final period of Jewish residence in Spain. In 1490 a sum of 501,183 maravedis was levied on the community for the redemption of the Jewish captives of *Málaga. The monarchs were dissatisfied with the incomplete residential segregation of the Jews in Plasencia, and in 1491 they ordered that the decisions of the *cortes* of 1480 be stringently fulfilled. Even after the edict of expulsion of March 1492, the crown continued to collect money in payment of the debts which the Jews had left in the hands of various Christians. One of the collectors was Gernando Perez Coronel (formerly Meir *Melamed). The exiles from Plasencia, about 50 heads of families, left for Portugal; the synagogue was converted into the Santa Isabel church in honor of the queen; and the cemetery was sold to the local church. There was also a *Converso community in Plasencia, but little is known of it. An *auto-da-fé was held in the town in 1489 and Conversos from nearby *Trujillo were then burnt at the stake.

There were two synagogues in Plasencia. One was in the Mota, next to the alcázar, where San Vicente church stands now. This synagogue was confiscated in 1477 so that a Dominican monastery could be erected on the site in honor of Vicente Ferrer. After the confiscation of their synagogue the Jews built a new synagogue which was on Vargas Street.

BIBLIOGRAPHY: V. Paredes, in: *Revista de Extremadura*, 9 (1907), 499f., 556f.; Baer, Urkunden, 2 (1936), index; B. Netanyahu, *Don Isaac Abravanel* (Eng., 1953), 280, 285; F. Cantera y Burgos, *Sinagogas españolas* (1955), 266f.; Suárez Fernández, Documentos, index **ADD. BIBLIOGRAPHY:** E.C. de Santos Canalejo, *El siglo XV en Plasencia y su tierra. Proyección de un pasado y reflejo de una época*, (1981), 109–19, 194–204; idem, *La historia medieval de Plasencia y su entorno geo-histórico: la Sierra de Bejar y la Sierra de Gredos* (1986), 521–40.

[Haim Beinart / Yom Tov Assis (2nd ed.)]

PLASZOW, forced labor camp (*Zwangsarbeitslager Plaszow des SS – und Polizeifuehrers im Distrikt Krakau*) and, later, a *Konzentrationslager* (concentration camp). It was opened in late 1942 and built partially on the site of Cracow's two main Jewish cemeteries. Plaszow had only about 2,000 prisoners when it initially opened, though at its peak in the summer of 1944, it had about 25,000–30,000 prisoners, most of them Jews. But Plaszow was also an important transfer camp for Jews being sent to other camps, particularly nearby Auschwitz. Estimates are that 150,000 Jews passed through Plaszow, particularly during the summer of 1944 when Adolf *Eichmann was sending hundreds of thousands of Hungarian Jews to their death in Auschwitz. Estimates are that between 8,000 and 12,000 Jews died in Plaszow during the Holocaust.

Like most forced labor and concentration camps, Plaszow was laid out as a small city by the SS, meaning that it was a self-sustaining entity fully able to support its inmates and SS staff with the products it produced in its slave labor factories. During most of its history, Plaszow was commanded by Amon Goeth, a figure made famous by Steven Spielberg's film, *Schindler's List*. Goeth was a true monster who brutalized his Jewish work force. Goeth was also extremely corrupt and was removed as commandant in the fall of 1944 in the midst of an SS investigation into corruption in Plaszow and other concentration camps. Goeth was arrested at the end of the war and tried in Poland for war crimes. He was found guilty and hanged in Cracow in 1946.

Oskar *Schindler, a Sudeten-German businessman, operated a factory for Goeth, but not in the Plaszow camp. Schindler, who arrived in Cracow in the fall of 1939, ran, among other things, an enamelware factory, Emalia (*Deutsche Emailwarenfabrik Oskar Schindler*), about two miles from Plaszow. After Goeth brutally closed the Cracow ghetto in the spring of 1943, Schindler convinced Goeth to allow him to transform Emalia into a Plaszow subcamp, the *Schindler Nebenlager*. Schindler, who had begun using Jewish workers at Emalia in the fall of 1939, and relied heavily on a Jewish manager, Abraham Bankier, to run his enamelware factory, increased the number of Jewish workers substantially over the next four years. When Goeth ordered Schindler to shut down that portion of Emalia that employed Jewish workers in the summer of 1944, Schindler got permission to transfer a thousand Jews to a new factory in Bruennlitz in what is now the Czech Republic.

Unfortunately, most of the Jews who had worked for Schindler in Emaila never made it to Bruennlitz. After Schindler closed the Jewish portion of his Emalia factory, his Jewish workers were sent back to Plaszow and on to other camps. It was in Plaszow that the famed "Schindler's List" was written in the fall of 1944, though not by Schindler. Its architect was a Jewish orderly, Marcel Goldberg, who compiled two lists with the names of 700 men and 300 women. Those chosen from the remaining Jewish inmate population in Plaszow were then sent on separate transports to Bruennlitz via Auschwitz or Gross Rosen in October and early November 1944. Plaszow was finally shut down two months later after Soviet forces occupied Cracow.

Today, little remains of the former camp. Its grounds have been turned into a nature preserve, though a Soviet-style monument, the Polish Martyrs' Monument, rests at one corner of the former camp site. Nearby is a smaller monument to Plaszow's Jewish victims. The Jewish cemeteries are still part of the nature preserve, with open, desecrated graves. Poles live in the only buildings remaining from the camp, Amon Goeth's villa, and the "Grey House," the former camp prison. A McDonald's stands at the site of the camp's storehouse for property stolen from the camp's Jewish inmates.

BIBLIOGRAPHY: A. Bieberstein, Aleksander. *Zagada Ʃydów w Krakowie* (1985); D.M. Crowe, *Oskar Schindler: The Untold Account of His Life, Wartime Activities, and the True Story Behind the List* (2004); M. Kessler, *"Ich muß doch meinen Vater lieben, oder?: Die Lebensgeschichte von Monika Gö, Tochter des KZ-Kommandanten aus "Schindlers Liste"* (2002); M. Pemper, *Der rettende Weg. Schindlers Liste – Die wahre Geschichte* (2005); *Proces Ludobójcy Amona Leopolda Goetha przed Najwy szym Trybuna em Narodowym* (1947).

[David Crowe (2nd ed.)]

°PLATO AND PLATONISM. The influence exercised by the Greek philosopher Plato on posterity both directly and through his interpreters was enormous and has been detailed in a vast literature. The direct influence of Plato on Jewish circles is much less pervasive. It seems quite clear that Greek philosophical writings in general had little or no influence on biblical and rabbinic literature, though current popular philosophic notions evidently became known also in the Jewish world. In Alexandria, one of the great centers of *Hellenistic civilization, Philo in the first century C.E. was faced with the necessity of effecting a reconciliation between Greek philosophy and scripture. This he did by reading the principles of the Platonism of his day into the Pentateuch by interpreting the latter in an allegorical manner. Philo did not leave any direct impression on later Jewish literature until reintroduced by Azariah de' *Rossi in the 16th century. After the Hellenistic period Plato did not have a great influence on Jewish thought until the period of the Arabic translations from the Greek, at which time Jews shared in general humanistic culture.

Among the dialogues reported to have been translated into Arabic were the *Republic*, the *Timaeus*, and the *Crito*. Quotations in Arabic from the *Republic, Timaeus, Laws*, and *Symposium*, among others, have been identified. Another source was the synopses of certain of the Platonic dialogues by *Galen. *Maimonides quotes from Galen's "commentary" on the *Laws* (*Galeni Compendium Timaei Platonis*, ed. by P. Kraus and R. Walzer (1951), 101), and his contemporary and friend Joseph ibn *Aknin quotes from Galen's *Summary of the Republic (ibid.*, 100; and A. Halkin "Classical and Arabic Material in Aknin's 'Hygiene of the Soul'" in: PAAJR, 14 (1944), 135). However, it was mainly through the works of his later interpreters and followers that the doctrines of Plato had an effect on Jewish intellectuals in the Islamic cultural sphere, first of all through quotations and interpretation of Platonic doctrine occurring in the body of Aristotle's writings, and secondly through neoplatonic interpreters of Plato, mainly Plotinus and Proclus. The doctrines of Plotinus became known through the medium of the pseudepigraphical *Theology of Aristotle*, which consists of excerpts from the fourth, fifth, and sixth *Enneads* of Plotinus, as well as other works. The longer version of the *Theology of Aristotle* includes extracts from an as yet unknown neoplatonic work cited in the works of Isaac

*Israeli and translated partially into Hebrew by Abraham *Ibn Ḥasdai in *Ben ha-Melekh ve-ha-Nazir ("The Prince and the Ascetic"), which itself is a translation of an Arabic work which goes back to the legend of Buddha. Also interpolated in the longer version are texts relating to the doctrine of the Divine Will, which are not Plotinian and had an influence, along with the whole *Theology*, on Ibn *Gabirol in his *Fons Vitae*. The longer version is extant in Leningrad in three fragmentary manuscripts, all Arabic in Hebrew script, which testify to its influence on Jewish circles. In the early 16th century, Moses Arovas made a Hebrew as well as an Italian translation of the longer version. The Italian version was then translated into Latin and published in Rome in 1519.

*Avicenna utilized neoplatonic sources in the construction of his philosophic system and had a vast influence on philosophic circles, Jewish as well as non-Jewish. The influence of neoplatonism on Jewish mystical (kabbalistic) thought is also very great. A third major source of Platonic doctrine was through the works of al-*Fārābī, who seems to have been dependent on a tradition of Platonic interpretation which emphasized the political aspect of his thought. The influence of the *Republic* and the *Laws* as well as the *Statesman* are apparent in his political works. In his *Philosophy of Plato and Aristotle*, he summarizes briefly all of the dialogues and considers them from a political point of view. Extensive excerpts from this work were translated into Hebrew by the polymath 13th-century historian of philosophy, Shem Tov ibn *Falaquera. Maimonides in his *Guide* leans heavily on al-Fārābī in his attempt to explain the relationship which should obtain between philosophy and religion. Plato indirectly thus influenced the whole course of later Jewish medieval philosophy, which was mainly a reaction to the position taken by Maimonides in his *Guide*. Maimonides' esotericism in the *Guide* may also have been influenced by the tradition of Platonic esotericism common in Arabic philosophic literature.

The *Politics* of Aristotle was not known in the Arabic west, where Plato was the major classic of political philosophy. *Averroes composed an *Epitome of the Republic* in which he expresses interesting personal views more openly than he would in works addressed to a more religious audience, on the relationship between philosophy and politics. This work, along with Averroes' *Middle Commentary on the Nichomachean Ethics*, was translated by Samuel b. Judah of Marseilles into Hebrew in the 14th century, and marks the first time that a classical work of political philosophy was translated into Hebrew. The work was soon summarized by Joseph ibn *Kaspi, Samuel's contemporary, and exercised some influence on the course of later Jewish philosophy. In the 16th century the Jewish physician Jacob *Mantino translated it from Hebrew into Latin and it appears in the standard Latin editions of Averroes' works.

Another source of Platonic sentiments were the collections of the sayings of the philosophers, notably that of Ḥunayn ibn Ishāq, which was translated into Hebrew by Judah *Al-Ḥarizi in the 13th century. Joseph ibn Aknin includes a number of Platonic dicta in his "Hygiene of the Soul" (see Halkin, as above in: PAAJR, 14 (1944), 69ff.).

Finally, Judah *Abrabanel or Leone Ebreo, the son of Isaac Abrabanel, utilizes the basic ideas of Platonic philosophy in his *Dialoghi di amore*. Moses *Mendelssohn wrote on the immortality of the soul in his *Phaedon* (1767) and follows the Platonic dialogue of the same name.

BIBLIOGRAPHY: A.H. Armstrong (ed.), *Cambridge History of Later Greek and Early Medieval Philosophy* (1967); Walzer, in: EI², s.v. *Aflāṭūn*; Guttmann, Philosophies, index; H.A. Wolfson, *Philo, Foundations of Religious Philosophy…*, 2 vols. (1947), index; Plessner, in: *Tarbiz*, 24 (1954/55), 60–72; C. Roth, *Jews in the Renaissance* (1959), 128–36; Stern, in: *Oriens*, 13–14 (1961), 58–120; Maimonides, *Guide of the Perplexed*, tr. by S. Pines (1963), ixxvff. (introd.); E.I.J. Rosenthal (ed.), *Averroes' Commentary on Plato's Republic* (1966²).

[Lawrence V. Berman]

PLAUT (Flaut), HEZEKIAH FEIVEL (1818–1895), Hungarian rabbi. Born in Kolin, Plaut studied under Moses *Sofer of Pressburg, whom he venerated exceedingly, paying particular attention to every detail of his way of life so that he could emulate him. A profound talmudic scholar, Plaut was renowned for his piety. He engaged in halakhic correspondence with Hillel Lichtenstein, rabbi of Kolommya, Galicia, with whom he had studied. In 1849 he was appointed rabbi of Nagysurany and remained there until his death. Students from every part of Hungary came to study at the large yeshivah he established there. As rabbi of Nagysurany he was also rabbi for the whole region, which included the community of Nove Zamky (Ersekujvar). He spent a number of Sabbaths there every year and preached there despite the fact that the leaders of the synagogue had, against accepted custom, moved the reading desk from the center of the synagogue to the front of the ark. When a ban was eventually issued by the Orthodox Hungarian rabbis against even entering such a synagogue, he established a separate synagogue in the old style. Plaut had no children but brought up orphans as his own children.

He was the author of *Likkutei Ḥaver Ben Ḥayyim*, in 11 parts (1878–93), containing talmudic novellae, glosses on the four parts of the Shulḥan Arukh, a number of his responsa, eulogies, the glosses of the Ḥatam Sofer (Moses Sofer) on the Shulḥan Arukh, *Yoreh De'ah*, and the customs of Ḥatam Sofer and the latter's biography, as well as Plaut's correspondence with Hillel Lichtenstein.

BIBLIOGRAPHY: H.F. Plaut (Flaut), *Likkutei Ḥaver Ben Ḥayyim*, 1 (1878), introd.; P.Z. Schwartz, *Shem ha-Gedolim me-Ereẓ Hagar*, 2 (1914), 26b, no. 5; 3 (1915), 21bf., no. 13; A. Stern, *Meliẓei Esh*, 3 (1962), 27th Kislev, no. 219.

[Samuel Weingarten-Hakohen]

PLAUT, HUGO CARL (1858–1928), German bacteriologist. Born in Leipzig, Plaut settled in Hamburg in 1913 and became director of the Institute for Fungus Research. In 1918 he was appointed titular professor. He made his greatest contribution to medicine in 1896, when he described the etiology of trench mouth. Two years later H. Vincent of the Pasteur Institute described the same condition and it became known as the Plaut-Vincent disease or angina ulcero membranosa caused by fusiform spirochaeta. Of significance also were Plaut's works on streptococcus mocosus, streptothrix, and actinomyces. His publications include *Die Hyphenpilze oder Eumyceten* (1903, 1913^2), *Dermatomykosen* (1909), and *Mykosen* (1919). He also carried out fundamental work in veterinary medicine.

[Suessmann Muntner]

PLAUT, W. GUNTHER (1912–), U.S. Reform rabbi and author. Plaut was born in Munster, Germany, and earned his law degree at the University of Berlin in 1934. When Nazi decrees made a law career impossible, he switched to Jewish studies. He was tutored by Abraham Joshua *Heschel and attended the Hochschule (later, Lehranstalt) fur die Wissenschaft des Judentums. In 1935, Plaut and four other students accepted a lifeline – an invitation to study at *Hebrew Union College in Cincinnati, where he was ordained in 1939. HUC-JIR awarded him an honorary D.D. in 1964, followed by an honorary L.L.D. from the University of Toronto in 1977.

Plaut became rabbi of Congregation B'nai Abraham Zion (Washington Boulevard Temple) in Chicago (1937–48), taking a leave of absence in 1943 to enlist in the U.S. Army and serve as a chaplain in the infantry at the European front. He was present at the opening of the Dora-Nordhausen concentration camp in April 1945 and was awarded a Bronze Star.

Plaut's next pulpit (1948–61) was at Mt. Zion Temple in St. Paul, Minnesota, where he served as president of the Minnesota Rabbinical Association, was appointed to the Minnesota Human Relations Committee, and headed the Governor's Commission on Ethics in Government. In 1961, he was named senior rabbi of Holy Blossom Temple in Toronto, Canada, becoming senior scholar in 1977. He was also a founder and co-chairman of the Canada–Israel Committee (1975–76) and president of the Canadian Jewish Congress (1977–80). In the wider community, he served as president of the World Federalists of Canada (1966–68); as vice chairman of the Ontario Human Rights Commission (1979–85); and as a judicial officer in cases of human rights violations (1987). In the Reform movement, he chaired the Reform Jewish Practice Committee of the Central Conference of American Rabbis (1973–79), served as its vice president (1981–82), and as president (1983–85). He also served as vice president of the *World Union for Progressive Judaism and chaired the CCAR's Response Committee (1989–94).

Plaut was a prolific writer. A 1982 bibliography of his writings, compiled as a *Festschrift* titled *Through the Sound of Many Voices*, contained approximately 1,000 entries. In addition to chronicling the evolution of the Reform movement in *The Rise of Reform Judaism* (1963) and *The Growth of Reform Judaism* (1965), Plaut grappled with theological issues in *Judaism and the Scientific Spirit* (1962) and *The Case for the Chosen People* (1965). Other major books include *The Man Who Would Be Messiah* (1990); *The Magen David: How the Six-Pointed Star Became an Emblem for the Jewish People* (1991); *The Price and Privilege of Growing Old* (1999); and *The Reform Judaism Reader* (with Michael A. Meyer, 2001).

His masterpiece remains *The Torah – A Modern Commentary* (1981), which was praised by Robert *Alter as "the finest commentary [on the Torah] in English or, for that matter, in any language." He complemented it with *The Haftarah Commentary* (1996), which is used in Reform synagogues throughout the English-speaking world.

[Bezalel Gordon (2nd ed.)]

PLEAS.

Nature of Pleas

Talmudic law developed certain well-defined forms of pleading in civil cases (not unlike the *actio, formula*, and *exceptio* in Roman law). These forms of pleading constitute a catalog of causes of actions and defenses which could be applied in, and adapted to, all kinds of civil litigations. Unlike Roman law, pleas were not reduced to abstract terms, but expressed in direct language: for instance, the action of debt is rendered as the plea of "I have money in your hands"; the defense of payment is rendered as the plea of "I have paid." The law of pleas thus comprises the catalog of the various pleas and the provisions governing the applicability and effect of each particular one. However, in the sources there is no systematic differentiation between the two, and they will be considered together below. It often happens that not only the burden of proof (see *Evidence) or of taking the *oath will depend on the pleas chosen by the party but also the immediate outcome of the action, where in the circumstances a given plea is considered conclusive.

Pleas of the Plaintiff

Plaintiff's pleas, or causes of action, can be roughly divided into three classes: debt – "I have money in your hands"; or "I have a loan in your hands": or "I have wages with you"; chattels – "I have a deposit in your hands"; or "I have deposited this or that chattel with you"; or "you have stolen this chattel from me"; and oath – where the cause of action depends on accounts to be rendered and the defendant (e.g., an agent, executor, or guardian) is sued to verify his accounts on oath.

In order to be valid and to require a plea (or an oath) in reply, the plaintiff's plea must be such as to disclose a legally valid cause of action. Where a plaintiff would not be entitled to judgment, even though his plea be proved or admitted, no defense is called for. Thus, the plea "you promised to lend me money" – which is a promise unenforceable in law – or the plea "you insulted me" – which, if proved or admitted, could not bear weight in a case of damages – would be rejected as irrelevant from the outset.

Pleas of the Defendant

Whenever a cause of action has been pleaded by the plaintiff, "it is not a proper reply for the defendant to say, I owe you nothing, or you have nothing in my hands, or you are lying; but the court will tell the defendant to reply specifically to the plaintiff's plea and be as explicit in his defense as the plaintiff was in his claim: have you or have you not taken a loan from him?; has he or has he not made this deposit with you?; have you or have you not stolen his chattel?; have you or have you not hired him?; and in the same way with all other pleas. The reason is that a defendant may err [in law]… and believe that he is not liable to the plaintiff; therefore he is told: how can you say 'I owe him nothing'? maybe the law renders you liable to him and you do not know; you must submit to the judges explicit statements of fact, and they will advise you whether you are or are not liable. Even a great scholar is told: you do not lose anything by replying to his plea and explaining to us how it is that you are not liable to him; is it because 'the thing has never happened' or although 'it happened, it is because you already made restitution to him'" (Yad, To'en 6:1).

Defendant's pleas may roughly be divided into admissions and denials.

*Admissions are of three kinds:

(1) full and express admission of the whole claim – such an admission establishes the claim "like a hundred witnesses";

(2) partial admission and partial denial, with the result that the oath will be administered to the defendant;

(3) implied admission – plea of "I have not borrowed" is, on proof of the loan, taken as an admission that the defendant has not repaid the loan; or, a plea of "I have repaid" is, on proof of non-repayment, taken as an admission that a loan had been made (BB 6a; Shevu. 41b; Yad, To'en 6:3). For pleas of "feigning" or "satiation" to revoke out-of-court admissions, and for the effect of admissions in general, see *Admission.

Denials are also of three kinds: "no such thing has ever happened" – i.e., a total denial of the fact (the loan, the contract, the tort) underlying the cause of action; "I have paid" – i.e., an assertion that any liability which may have existed has already been fully satisfied; and "you have renounced the debt," or "the money you gave me was in repayment of a debt which you owed me, or was a gift" (Yad, To'en 6:2) – i.e., in the nature of a plea of confession and avoidance.

The general rules that the burden of proving his case rests upon the plaintiff (see *Evidence) and that, in the absence of such proof, the defendant has to take the oath to verify his denial, apply to all these pleas of denial. The presumption that a debtor will not lie in the face of his creditor was in the course of time superseded by the presumption that the plaintiff will not lodge a claim unless he has a cause of action. While by virtue of the former presumption the defendant would be believed on his oath, by virtue of the latter he was required to take the oath to disprove the plaintiff's claim (Shevu. 40b).

Plea of Repayment

In the case of the plea of repayment, the following special provisions should be noted:

Where the defendant pleaded repayment, it was not sufficient for the plaintiff to prove that he had given the defendant a loan, because a loan given before witnesses need not necessarily be repaid before witnesses (Shevu. 41b), and the claim would be dismissed on the defendant's oath verifying his plea. The same rule applied to claims on bills: where the signature of the defendant on the bill was proved or admitted, his defense of repayment would be accepted on his taking the oath (BB 176a; Yad, Malveh 11:3; Sh. Ar., ḤM 69:2); but some later jurists held that the plea of repayment was not available against a bill which was in the hands of the plaintiff, as it would normally have been returned or destroyed on payment (*Rema*, ḤM 69:2 and the references given there). The matter appears to be left to the discretion of the court in each particular case (Resp. Ribash, no. 454; *Siftei Kohen*, ḤM 69, n.14). Where the plea of repayment is inadmissible in law, e.g., where the loan or bill was made with formal *kinyan* (see *Acquisition, Modes of; ḤM 39, 3), the plaintiff will recover on the bill on taking the oath that it is still unpaid (Shevu. 41a; Yad, Malveh 14:2). Where a debt is repayable at a certain date, the defendant will not be heard to plead that he repaid it before that date because of the presumption that no debtor pays a debt before it matures (see *Evidence). The plaintiff will be entitled to recover without oath, on proof of the debt and of the time stipulated for repayment (BB 5a–b; ḤM 78:1).

In order to forestall pleas of repayment and their all too easy verification by oath, it became customary to stipulate beforehand either that repayment must be made in the presence of witnesses – in which case the plaintiff could recover without oath unless the defendant produced witnesses of repayment (Shevu. 6:2; Yad, Malveh 15:1; ḤM 70:3) – or that the plea of repayment should not be available to the defendant, and that the plaintiff should be entitled to recover on his assertion that he had not been paid (Yad, Malveh 15:3; ḤM 71:1).

Plea of Insolvency

Originally the law was that a debtor who pleaded that he was unable to pay was not required to take the oath, but the burden was on the creditor to discover property of the debtor on which execution could be levied (Yad, Malveh 2:1). However, when "defrauders increased and borrowers found lenders' doors closed," it was laid down that the debtor should take the oath that he possessed nothing and concealed nothing and that he would disclose any property coming into his hands (Yad, Malveh 2:2; ḤM 99:1). There are two noteworthy exceptions to this rule: a man reputed to be poor and honest will not be required to take the oath if the court suspects the creditor of desiring to annoy or embarrass him; and a man reputed to be a cheat and swindler will not be allowed to verify his plea on oath even though he volunteers to do so (Yad, Malveh 2:4; ḤM 99:4–5; see also *Execution, Civil).

Plea of Counterclaim

Where a plaintiff sues on a bill, it is no defense for the defendant to plead that the plaintiff is indebted to him on another bill: each sues and recovers on his own bill separately (Ket. 13:9; Yad, Malveh 24:10; Sh. Ar., ḤM 85:3). But where the defendant denies the bill sued upon by the plaintiff, his plea prevails that the plaintiff would not have made a later bill in favor of the defendant had he really been indebted to him (Sh. Ar. loc. cit.; but see Yad, loc. cit. and *Siftei Kohen* to Sh. Ar., ḤM 85, n. 7). Where the defendant pleads that the plaintiff already "has mine in his hands," the plaintiff is entitled to have his claim judged first, and the defendant's claim for restitution or to have one claim offset by the other will be adjudicated separately (BK 46b; Rashi and Tosef. thereto; Tur, ḤM 24:1; *Rema*, ḤM 24:1).

Identical Pleas

Where, in respect of a certain sum of money or of a chattel, both parties plead "this is mine," and both are in possession of it (i.e., each holds it with his hand), and none can prove previous or present title, both will have to take the oath that they are entitled to at least one-half of it, and then one-half will be judged to belong to each (BM 1:1; Yad, To'en 9:7; ḤM 138:1). Where the mutual "this is mine" is pleaded in respect of land, or in respect of a chattel not in the possession of either, the party who first succeeds in taking possession, even by force, cannot be ousted unless the other can prove that he has a better title to it (BB 34b–35a; Yad, To'en 15:4; ḤM 139:4). For this rule, which in effect legitimizes seizing by force, the Solomonic reason was given that it would only be the true owner who would go to the length of using force and facing the ensuing lawsuit (Resp. Rosh 77:1; *Beit Yosef*, ḤM 139, n.1; see also *Extraordinary Remedies).

Pleas of Law

As a general rule, pleas are assertions or denials of fact only; but there are some exceptions to the rule, two of which are noteworthy:

(1) the plea of "I do not want this legal privilege." Wherever the law confers a benefit on the class of persons to which the pleader belongs, he will be heard if he waives that benefit (Ket. 83a). Thus, the rule that a husband must maintain his wife in consideration of her handiwork for him was established in favor of his wife, and she may plead, "I will not claim *maintenance and I will not work" (Ket. 58b). Or, where a plaintiff is allowed by law to recover on taking the oath, he may plead, "I do not want the privilege of taking the oath," and have the oath shifted to the defendant (Yad, To'en 1:4; ḤM 87:12); and

(2) the plea of "I rely on the other view." Where the authorities are divided on a given question of law, the defendant is entitled to plead that the opinion most favorable to him should be adopted (*Keneset ha-Gedolah*, ḤM 25, *Beit Yosef*). This post-talmudic rule is based on the premise that the benefit of any possible doubt on what the law is must accrue to the defendant, the burden of establishing his case always being on the plaintiff (see also *Codification of the Law).

Weight of Pleas

Even where no evidence is available or forthcoming to substantiate a plea and even before such evidence is called for, the court will accept a plea as valid and conclusive in the following cases:

(1) Where the plea is fortified by a legal presumption (see *Evidence) or by generally recognized standards or patterns of conduct. For instance, the plea, "I have not been paid" is accepted as conclusive if fortified by the presumption that no debtor pays a debt before maturity (BB 5b).

(2) Where the plea is eminently reasonable (*sevarah*). The reasonableness cannot generally be determined from the particular circumstances of the case at issue, but rather from legal rules evolved for this purpose. Thus, a man's plea is not believed if by that plea he accuses himself of wrongdoing (Ket. 22a, 23b), unless he can adduce a good reason (*amtala*) for so doing. Where, by his own mouth, a man has taken upon himself a certain status or obligation which could not otherwise be proved against him, he is believed on his plea that that status has come to an end or that obligation has been performed, for "the mouth that obligated is the mouth that discharged" (Ket. 2:5). For instance, a woman who cannot otherwise be proved to have been married is believed on her plea that her marriage has been dissolved (Ket. 2:5; Yad, Gerushin 12:1; Sh. Ar., EH 152:6).

Witnesses whose attestation to a deed cannot be proved other than by their own testimony are believed on their plea that they were incompetent or coerced to attest (Ket. 2:3; Ket. 18b; Yad, Edut 3:6; ḤM 46:37), provided they did not plead that their incompetence was due to criminal conduct (Yad, Edut 3:7; ḤM 46:37). Opinions are divided on whether a defendant who admitted that a bill, which could not otherwise be proved, had been authorized by him, would be believed on his plea that he had paid the bill (BM 7a; Ket. 19a; BB 154b); the better opinion seems to be that, as long as the bill is in the hands of the plaintiff, it is presumed to be unpaid (Tur, ḤM 82:3), and the defendant's unsworn plea of repayment is not sufficient to discharge him (see above; and Rashi, Ket. 19a, s.v. *Ein ha-Malveh*). Similarly, a plea is believed if it was "in the hands" of the pleader to execute it by his own act (Sanh. 30a; ḤM 255:8).

(3) A particular brand of reasonableness is known as *miggo*, meaning something like "inasmuch": inasmuch as you could have succeeded by some other more far-reaching plea, the lesser plea, by which you likewise succeed, can be accepted as credible. "If A makes a certain statement which does not appear probable on the face of it, this fact will not tend to weaken his case, if he could have made another statement which would have appeared probable. If that other statement would have been acceptable to the court, the one that he actually makes must also be accepted, for had he wished to tell an untruth he would have rather made that other statement" (Herzog, Instit, 1 (1936), 250ff.). In the much shorter and clearer words of *Shabbetai b. Meir ha-Kohen (Shakh) in his "Rules of *Miggo*" (appended to his commentary *Siftei Kohen* to ḤM 82, hereinafter referred to as Rules), "he is known to speak the truth, for if he had wanted to lie, a better plea would have been open to him" (Rule 26). *Miggo* is the amoraic version and elaboration of the mishnaic "the mouth that obligated is the mouth that discharged" (cf. Ket. 2:2, 16a; the dif-

ferent problems of *miggo* are dealt with in the Shakh at the end of ḤM 82).

Miggo is, generally speaking, available in respect of pleas of defendants only (Rules 1, 14, 15); *miggo* is of no use against witnesses (Rules 5, 12); *miggo* is of use against a written deed (Rule 11); where the taking of an oath is prescribed (other than the post-mishnaic oath), *miggo* is not available in lieu of it, nor will it be allowed where the more far-reaching plea could have resulted in a Pentateuchal or mishnaic oath being imposed, for the actual plea may have been put forward only for the purpose of evading the oath (Rules 25, 28); *miggo* does not apply where it would contradict local custom in matters of commerce (Rule 2); both the more far-reaching and the actual plea must relate to the same subject matter (Rule 13); *miggo* does not operate retroactively (Rule 8); where the more far-reaching plea would obviously have been a lie, it cannot operate as *miggo* on the actual plea; nor will *miggo* be of any avail to strengthen a plea which is manifestly false (Rule 9); whether the *miggo* is of avail against presumptions of fact is discussed (Rules 10, 16); *miggo* is of no avail against any possessory title (*ibid.*); *miggo* is not allowed where the more far-reaching plea would have been "I do not know" (Rule 3); *miggo* is allowed only in respect of pleas which are outspoken and unambiguous (Rule 7); there are differences of opinion on whether *miggo* would be allowed where the pleader could have remained silent instead of pleading, and by remaining silent would have attained the same or a better result (Rules 19, 21); whether *miggo* is available where the more far-reaching plea would have been unreasonable or unusual, or would have been an affront or an impertinence to the creditor, is discussed (Rules 6, 22); *miggo* is not available where the more far-reaching plea would have incriminated the pleader (Rule 24); *miggo* is applied only to the plea of a single pleader: where the same plea is put forward by more than one, none can avail himself of *miggo* (Rule 4); *miggo* is allowed in respect of pleas of fact only, and not in respect of pleas of law (Rule 31); and where there recommends itself to the court a reasoning (*sevarah*) which appears (however slightly) better than *miggo* in the particular case before it, *miggo* may be discarded at the discretion of the court (Rule 32).

Rejection of Pleas

UNTRUSTWORTHINESS. Once a defendant has denied having taken a loan and the fact that he has is proved by witnesses, he will not be allowed to plead that he has repaid the loan (BM 17a; Yad, To'en 6:1; ḤM 79:5), provided the denial has been made in court (Yad, To'en 6:2; ḤM 79:9). The denial which proved untrue renders the pleader, insofar as the same subject matter is concerned, a "potential denier," *huḥzak*, whose pleas will no longer be accepted as trustworthy. The same rule applies where a debtor had admitted the debt and, when sued in court, denied it (ḤM 79, 10), provided the previous admission could not be explained away as unintentional (Sanh. 29b; Yad, To'en 6:6).

INCONSISTENCY. No alternative or inconsistent pleas are allowed (BB 31a; ḤM 80:1). While pleading in court, however, the pleader may rectify his plea and explain it or even substitute another plea for it, as long as his original plea has not been proved or disproved by evidence (Yad, To'en 7:7–8; Tur, ḤM 80:4). Statements made out of court are not regarded as "pleas" and may freely be contradicted by pleas in court (ḤM 79:9, 80:1).

PUBLIC POLICY. Pleas which may otherwise be perfectly legitimate may sometimes be rejected because their acceptance might lead to undesirable results from a moral, humanitarian, or economic point of view. Examples of purposes for which pleas might be rejected are: that a wrongdoer should not reap a reward (Ket. 11a, 39b; et al.); that the lenders' doors not be closed in the face of borrowers (Ket. 88a; Git. 49b–50a; BK 7b–8a; et al.); for the protection of open markets (BK 115a); that it be not too easy for a husband to divorce his wife (Ket. 39b); and that equity and generosity may prevail over strict law (BM 51b–52a; 83a; 108a; Ket. 97a; et al.).

Suggestion of Pleas

Where the defendant (or, in exceptional cases such as widows and orphans, the plaintiff) appears unable or unfit to formulate the plea which is open to him in the circumstances, the court will "open the mouth of the dumb for him" (Prov. 31:8) and enter the plea for the defendant of its own accord (Ket. 36a; Git. 37b; BB 41a; *Piskei ha-Rosh*; BK 1:3). The court will not, however, of its own accord enter for the defendant a plea to the effect that any admission made by him out of court was false or unintended (Yad, To'en 6:8; ḤM 81:21; but see *Rema*, ḤM 81:14).

BIBLIOGRAPHY: Gulak, Yesodei, 4 (1922), passim; Herzog, Instit, 1 (1936), 57f., 241, 250–5, 268; 2 (1939), 108, 117f.; ET, 1 (1951³), 140, 224–6, 253f., 255–7, 263–6, 267f.; 2 (1949), 52–55, 70f.; 3 (1951), 106–10; 4 (1952), 199–208; 5 (1953), 524–7; 6 (1954), 200; 7 (1956), 290–5, 321–8, 733–8; 8 (1957), 404–35, 722–43; 9(1959), 451–9, 722–46; B. de Vries, in: *Tarbiz*, 36 (1966/67), 229–38; Z. Frankel, *Der gerichtliche Beweis nach mosaisch-talmudischen Rechte* (1846); H.B. Fassel, *Das mosaisch-rabbinische Gerichtsverfahren in civilrechtlichen Sachen* (1859); Z. Freudenthal, in: MGWJ, 9 (1860), 161–75; M. Bloch, *Die Civilprocess-Ordnung nach mosaisch-rabbinischen Rechte* (1882); D. Fink, *Miggo als Rechtsbeweis im babylonischen Talmud* (1891); T.S. Zuri, *Mishpat ha-Talmud*, 7 (1921); Elon, Mafte'aḥ, 84–88; idem, in: ILR, 3 (1968), 437f. **ADD. BIBLIOGRAPHY:** M. Elon, *Ha-Mishpat ha-Ivri* (1988), 1:322–23, 502, 504ff., 533, 586, 811ff.; 2:1062–63, 1154, 1257–58, 3:1442–43, 1502; idem, *Jewish Law* (1994), 1:385–87; 2:612, 614ff., 649, 722, 993ff.; 3:1282, 1386, 1504–5; 4:1715–16, 1787, 1788; M. Elon and B. Lifshitz, *Mafte'aḥ ha-She'elot ve-ha-Teshuvot shel Ḥakhmei Sefarad u-Ẓefon Afrikah* (legal digest) (1986), 442–47; B. Lifshitz and E. Shochetman, *Mafte'aḥ ha-She'elot ve-ha-Teshuvot shel Ḥakhmei Ashkenaz, Ẓarefat ve-Italyah* (legal digest) (1977), 300–4.

[Haim Hermann Cohn]

PLEDGE.

The Concept

In Jewish law, in addition to the personal right of action against the debtor, the creditor also has a right of *lien on the latter's property. This lien automatically comes into being when the debt is created and is termed *aḥarayut* or *shi'bud nekhasim*. Sometimes the operation of the lien may be limited by the parties to a specified asset or part of the debtor's property, in one of two possible ways: either this distinct asset remains in the debtor's possession, in which case the lien is termed *apoteke*, or possession of the asset is surrendered to the creditor, which is termed *mashkon* ("pledge"). In both cases limitation of the lien to a distinct asset may be effected either so that it operates over and above the general lien on all the debtor's property, or so as to free all but the distinct asset from its operation; in the case of pledge, these two forms are referred to respectively as *mashkon stam* ("unconditional") and *mashkon meforash* ("express pledge"; Tur, ḤM 117:1).

Jewish law distinguishes between three types of pledge: a pledge taken when the debt is due for repayment, not in payment of it but as a security for its repayment; a pledge taken when the debt is established with the consent of both debtor and creditor, as security for repayment of the debt on the due date; and a pledge given by the debtor to the creditor for the latter's use and enjoyment of its fruits.

Taking a Pledge After Establishment of the Debt

There are various biblical enjoinders concerning taking a pledge from the debtor: "If thou lend money to any of My people, even to the poor with thee, thou shalt not be to him as a creditor; neither shall ye lay upon him interest. If thou at all take thy neighbor's garment to pledge, thou shalt restore it unto him by that the sun goeth down; for that is his only covering, it is his garment for his skin; wherein shall he sleep?" (Ex. 22:24–26); similarly, "When thou dost lend thy neighbor any manner of loan, thou shalt not go into his house to fetch his pledge. Thou shalt stand without, and the man to whom thou dost lend shall bring forth the pledge without unto thee. And if he be a poor man, thou shalt not sleep with his pledge; thou shalt surely restore to him the pledge when the sun goeth down, that he may sleep in his garment, and bless thee; and it shall be righteousness unto thee before the Lord thy God" (Deut. 24:10–13); and, "No man shall take the mill or the upper millstone to pledge, for he taketh a man's life to pledge" (Deut. 24:6). In their plain meaning, these passages refer to a debtor from whom a pledge is taken as such. These passages (which also lay down general principles concerning the creditor-debtor relationship; see *Execution, Civil) are the source of a threefold direction in matters of pledge and relate to articles which may never be taken in pledge; which may be taken in pledge but must be returned to a poor debtor when he needs them; and the prohibition against taking a pledge from a widow.

From the biblical prohibition on taking "the mill or upper millstone to pledge," the scholars deduced that it is forbidden to take in pledge "aught wherewith is prepared necessary food" (BM 9:13). They generally agree that the prohibition applies to utensils which are used in the actual preparation of "necessary food," such as a grain mill, certain cooking pots, an oven, and a sieve (Tur, ḤM 97:17), as well as water, wine, or oil jugs, "since this involves taking from a man a utensil which was fashioned for the actual preparation of necessary food for himself and his family, and this the Torah has forbidden, to save him hurt" (ḤM 97:11). In the case of things which do not meet this exact requirement but are used by a man to earn his livelihood, such as oxen for plowing and the like, some scholars hold that these may be taken in pledge, except for the essentials of his sustenance which must be left with the debtor, in terms of the rule of making an "arrangement" or assessment for the debtor (*Rema*, ḤM 98:8); other scholars hold that these things too fall into the category of "necessary food" and, therefore, may not be taken in pledge (Tur, ḤM 97:17; BM 113b; this opinion also conforms with the ordinary meaning of the statements in Tosef., BM 10:11 and those surrounding the discussion about a yoke of oxen and a pair of barber's shears, in BM 116a). With regard to articles which may be taken in pledge but must be returned to a needy debtor, Maimonides states "when a person takes a pledge from his neighbor [when the debt is due for payment] – whether through a court, or forcibly of his own accord, or with the debtor's consent – then if the debtor is poor it is a *mitzvah* to return the pledge to him if and when he be in need thereof; he must return to him the pillow at night to sleep thereon, and the plow by day to work therewith" (Yad, Malveh 3:15). Anyone who does not return a poor man's pledge when he needs it transgresses two prohibitions of the Torah and one positive precept.

It is in the interest of the creditor to take a pledge – notwithstanding his obligation to return it to the debtor when the latter is in need of it – in order that the debt shall not be wiped out in the Jubilee Year, just as a debt established against a pledge is not wiped out in order to recover payment of it on the death of the debtor, so that it should not be like movable property in the hands of orphans, which is not charged in the creditor's favor (Tosef., BM 10:9; BM 115a; Yad and Sh. Ar., loc. cit.). "Why then does he continue each day to take the pledge after he has returned it to the debtor whenever necessary? So that the debtor shall hurry to repay the debt because he is ashamed of having his pledge returned by the creditor day after day" (Tos. to BM 115a). In a dispute with R. Simeon b. Gamaliel, the scholars held that the creditor must return the debtor's pledge in this way as long as the debtor is alive; Gamaliel's opinion was that the creditor need only return the pledge during a period not exceeding 30 days; thereafter it must be sold through the court. All the scholars agree that if the creditor takes in pledge articles which are not essential to the debtor and therefore need not be returned to him from time to time, the creditor will be entitled to have the pledge sold through court, in similar manner to a pledge taken at the time of the establishment of the debt.

In the case of a widow, R. Judah held that the prohibition applies to all widows, rich or poor, giving to the word "widow" its ordinary meaning, since "he did not seek the reason for the scriptural law." R. Simeon, because "he sought the reason for the scriptural law," was of the opinion that the prohibition only applied to a poor widow, since the creditor would have to return her pledge if she needed it, and by entering and leaving her house from time to time would bring her into disrepute. The *halakhah* was decided according to R. Judah's opinion. Maimonides' opinion that the prohibition extends also to a pledge taken from a widow at the time the debt is established (Yad Malveh 3:1) is disputed in most of the codes on the grounds that the Torah deals solely with the question of a pledge taken when the debt is due for payment and that this is also to be deduced from the statements in the Talmud, even when the debtor is a widow (*Hassagot Rabad* and *Maggid Mishneh*, ad loc.).

The laws concerning a pledge of the debtor's property which the creditor takes after the debt is due as security for but not in payment of a debt are set out in detail in Scripture; although these laws were also dealt with in the Talmud and in the codes, by then they had become of less practical importance in daily life. The result was that the relevant laws came to be interpreted as applying also to the matter of actually satisfying a debt out of the debtor's property. (Maimonides, for instance, incorporates a number of matters pertaining to the *siddur le-va'al-ḥov* in his treatment of the above laws (Yad, Malveh 3:6) and this is done by other commentators also.) This process is particularly noticeable in the treatment of the prohibition against entering the debtor's home; the prohibition was interpreted in talmudic discussions and until the 12th century as applying also to the case of the creditor seeking to recover his debt, and only R. Tam interpreted the prohibition as applying solely to the case of entry for the purpose of taking a pledge.

In talmudic times, when the creditor came to take any of the debtor's assets after the debt was due, he generally did not do so in order to take a pledge, but rather as a means of recovering his debt. For this purpose too the scholars specified a number of articles which a debtor needed for the sustenance of himself and his family which might not be taken from him. From talmudic times onward it became most common for the pledge to be delivered by the debtor to the creditor at the time the debt was established.

Pledge Taken When the Debt is Established

The distinction drawn in Hebrew legal parlance in the State of Israel between the terms *mashkon* and *mashkanta*, pertaining to movables and to immovable property respectively, does not appear in the sources, where the term *mashkanta* is simply the Aramaic form of *mashkon* (although the distinction is already hinted at in earlier periods – see, e.g., Elon, Mafte'aḥ, note on p. 152).

Modes of Establishing a Pledge

The ancient form of pledge was apparently executed in the following manner: the debtor would sell one of his assets – land or movable property – to the creditor on the condition: "whenever I so desire I shall return the money and take it back." On receipt of the property the creditor would hand over the money; if, in the course of time, the money was returned by the debtor, the transaction constituted a loan and the property a pledge, otherwise the property would be forfeited to the creditor, presumably upon determination and expiry of a maximum period allowed the debtor for redemption of the property. This form of pledge also existed in other legal systems (Tosef., BM 4:4; Gulak, *Toledot ha-Mishpat be-Yisrael bi-Tekufot ha-Talmud*, 1 (*Ha-Ḥiyyuv ve-Shi'budav*), 62–65). A variation of this form of pledge was one in which the sale only came into effect upon the debtor's failure to make repayment on the date due (BM 63a). In the first case the creditor was entitled to sell the property after it had been delivered to him, although the debtor retained the right to redeem the property from a third party – i.e., within the period determined for this purpose; since the property had already been sold to the creditor, his usufruct thereof was not in conflict with the prohibition against *interest (see below). In the second case, however, it was forbidden for the creditor to sell the property before the agreed date of repayment and, therefore, according to some scholars, the fruits of the property were forbidden to the creditor, as amounting to interest, since the property had not yet been effectively sold to the latter. Common to both the above forms of sale was forfeiture of the property to the creditor upon the debtor's failure to return the money within the determined period (Gulak, 65–66). Forfeiture of this kind, although likely to have resulted in the creditor gaining property whose value exceeded the amount of the debt, was not regarded by the scholars as prejudicial to the debtor since the latter retained the option of selling the pledged property to a third party before the due date for repayment of the debt and then paying the creditor the exact amount only (Tos. to BM 65b).

In the later form of the pledge that was customary in talmudic times, the creditor was only entitled to recover out of the pledge – when the debt matured – the exact amount owing to him, and the remainder belonged to the debtor; conversely, if the value of the pledge was less than the amount of the debt, the creditor was entitled to recover the shortfall from the debtor. (Nevertheless, from a number of *halakhot* it is discernible that later, as early as amoraic times, forfeiture of the whole of the pledge continued to be practiced; see Gulak, 69–71.) It was customary for the parties to stipulate that the whole of the pledge be forfeited to the creditor upon the debtor's failure to repay the debt within a prescribed period, even if the value of the pledge exceeded the amount of the debt. Some scholars upheld the validity of such express conditions, but R. Judah held a contrary opinion: "In what manner shall this party become entitled to that which is not his!" (Tosef., BM 1:17). For part of the amoraic period some scholars maintained that the above condition was valid, but later the *halakhah* was decided to the effect that this condition was invalid because of the defect of **asmakhta* (BM 66a–b). A similar decision was made in the codes; namely, that this condition was invalid unless imposed in a special manner so as to obviate the defect of *asmakhta* (Yad, Malveh 6:4; Sh. Ar., ḤM 73:17).

Ownership and Responsibility for the Pledge

Property pledged by the debtor remains in his ownership, but cannot be alienated by him to another since it is not in his possession (Rashi, Pes. 30b). The debtor may, however, alienate the pledge to another in such manner that the *kinyan*, i.e., transfer of ownership, shall take effect after he has redeemed the pledge from the creditor, and then retroactively to the time of alienation; in addition, the debtor may immediately alienate that portion of the pledge which is in excess of the amount of the debt (Ket. 59a–b; Tos. to BM 73b, s.v. *hashata*; s.v. *hakhi ka-amar; Rema*, YD 258:7).

The creditor acquires a limited proprietary interest in the pledge (Pes. 31b; et al.), hence a marriage contracted by him through the means of a pledge he holds is valid (according to Maimonides, the creditor has *mikẓat kinyan*, "a measure of *kinyan*," in the pledge: Yad, Ishut 5:23). The creditor may assign to another the charge which he has on pledged property. According to the *posekim*, the creditor only has *mikẓat kinyan* in a pledge that is taken after the debt is established, and no *kinyan* whatever in a pledge taken at the time of establishment of the debt, so that a marriage contracted by the debtor through the means of pledged property of the latter kind will be invalid (Tos. to BM 82b, s.v. *emor*; *Rema; Siftei Kohen*, ḤM 72, n. 9; R. Isaac's above statement is also based on a passage dealing with a pledge taken after establishment of the debt).

Opinions were divided on the question of the creditor's responsibility for the pledge in his possession, some holding him liable as a bailee for reward and others regarding him as an unpaid bailee (BM 6:7). The majority of the *posekim* decided according to the first view: "hence if the pledge was lost or stolen, he will be liable for its value; if the value of the pledge equaled the amount of the debt, the one party will have no claim against the other; if the debt exceeded the value of the pledge, the debtor must pay the difference; but if the value of the pledge exceeded the debt, the creditor must refund the difference to the debtor; if the loss of the pledge was due to **ones*, the creditor must swear that this was the case, whereupon the pledger must repay the debt to the last penny" (Yad, Sekhirut 10:1; *Hassagot Rabad*, ad loc.; *Rema*, ḤM 72:2).

Use of the Pledge

The use of the pledge is forbidden to the creditor, since this is tantamount to taking interest on the loan. In the case of a poor debtor, if the nature of the pledge is such that it suffers only slight deterioration upon use and the return for its hire is great – for instance a plowshare or spade – the creditor will be entitled to hire the pledge to others and to apply the proceeds in reduction of the debt, since this is assumed to be convenient for the debtor. It is precisely to others and not to himself that the creditor may hire the pledge in this manner, lest he be suspected of using the pledge without reducing the debt accordingly. If originally, however, the parties stipulate with each other that the creditor might use the pledge and apply the hire in reduction of the debt, then he will be entitled to use the pledge himself, since anyone who knows that he holds a pledge will also know what he stipulated with the debtor. When the pledge consists of books, the use of the pledge is permitted by some scholars because it is a *mitzvah* to lend books for study, but other scholars include books in the general prohibition against the use of the pledged property (*Rema*, ḤM 72:1; and YD 172:1).

Recovering Payment out of the Pledge

When the debt matures the creditor must notify the debtor, before two witnesses, that the debt must be repaid and the pledge redeemed or else he will seek leave from the court to sell the pledge in satisfaction of the amount owing to him. The debtor, according to some of the *posekim*, has 30 days in which to make payment, failing which the value of the pledge is assessed by three knowledgeable assessors and "he [the creditor] shall sell it at the assessment price allowed by the above three and he is given the advice to sell it before witnesses, lest the debtor say that it was sold for more than the assessment price" (Yad, Malveh 13:3; Sh. Ar., ḤM 73:12–15). The creditor himself may not purchase the pledge, but some scholars aver that he may do so if the pledge is sold through a court of experts.

Pledge (Mortgage) with a Right of Usufruct in the Creditor's Favor

USUFRUCT AND THE PROHIBITION AGAINST INTEREST. In the case of a long-term debt in a large amount, land was generally given in pledge, to remain in possession of the creditor until the debt matured; this practice is illustrated in Nehemiah 5:3–5. According to the Jewish laws of interest, any benefit derived by the lender over and above repayment of the original amount of the loan is regarded as interest and prohibited (BM 5:9). Strict observance of the minutiae of the prohibition posed no particular economic hardship in the case of small short-term loans, but when large credits were involved it was difficult to deny the creditor the right to derive any benefit from the mortgaged land in his possession. In other legal systems it was customary for the creditor to enjoy the fruits of the mortgaged property by way of interest and the existence of this phenomenon in Greco-Roman laws was mentioned in the Talmud (TJ, BM 6:5). In order to ensure the availability of credit, the halakhic scholars sought to evolve special ways for the creation of a mortgage in a manner enabling the creditor to derive some usufructuary benefit from it without transgressing the prohibition against interest.

As already noted, the use and enjoyment of the pledge was permitted the creditor in case of a sale for return and – in the opinion of R. Judah – even in the case where the sale only came into effect upon the debtor's failure to make payment on the due date. This was because the property was regarded as sold to the creditor whereas the question of interest could only arise in the case of loan. The Babylonian *amoraim* regarded even the above cases as involving prohibited interest, since upon repayment of the debt the land would return to the debtor and the sale become voided retroactively (see BM 67a and Rif, *Halakhot*; Sh. Ar., ḤM 182:12; and *Ha-Gra*). A way

developments in the history of Hebrew liturgical poetry in Oriental Jewish communities in the 9th century, which helped bring to a close the period of classical liturgical poetry and led to the emergence of the post-classical period.

In 1977 A. Mirsky published *Piyyutei Yose ben Yose*, containing 11 *piyyutim*, which are certainly by him, and four which are also attributed to him. The volume includes a comprehensive introduction dealing with the period and works of Yose.

Developments in the 1980s

During the 1980s, a number of noted scholars in the field of Medieval Hebrew Poetry died, namely: A. *Scheiber, J. *Schirmann, N. Allony, A.M. *Habermann, G. *Vajda, H. Schwarzbaum, D. Jarden, D. Goldschmidt, D. Pagis, Y. *Heinemann, and A.L. Wilsker. Anthologies of articles from their estates, as well as memorial volumes, have begun to appear.

During the 1980s, the decade under review, editions of poetic texts from all the countries of the Diaspora as well as from Ereẓ Israel were published.

EDITIONS – POETRY. *Ereẓ Israel.* All the *piyyutim* of Yannai (Z.M. Rabinowitz); *piyyutim* of Eleazar Berabbi Kiler (S. Elizur). *Babylonia.* Rabbi Hai Gaon (Y. Hasida); Eleazar ben Jacob ha-Bavli (D. Jarden); Rabbi Judah Berabbi Benjamin (S. Elizur). *Byzantium.* Simeon bar Megas (Y. Yahalom). *Spain.* Joseph Bensuli (Y. David); A. Ibn Ezra (I. Levin); Y. Ibn Ezra (M. Schmelzer); Joseph Ibn Zaddik (Y. David); Samuel ha-Nagid (Ben Mishlei; D. Jarden); Isaac ibn Ghiyyat (Y. David); Judah Halevi (religious poems; D. Jarden); Jehiel ben-Harosh (Y. David); Isaac b. Solomon al-Ahdab (O. Raanan). *Provence.* Rabbi Zerahiah ha-Levi Gerondi (I. Meiseles). *North Africa.* Fradji Shawat (E. Hazan).

EDITIONS – TEXTS. *Prose and Rhymed Prose. "Isaac Polgarzer ha-Dat"* (J.S. Levinger); Shem Tov ben Isaac Ardutiel, *"Ma'aseh ha-Rav"* ("The debate between the pen and the scissors"; Y. Nini and M. Fruchtman); Berechiah ha-Nakdan, *Mishle Shu'alim* ("Fox Fables"; H. Schwarzbaum); *Sippurei ben Sira* (E. Yassif).

Monographs and Studies. Topics chosen focused on trends and aims in poetry and prose. (1) Poetry. The following poets and topics were studied and annotated: Judah Halevi (A. Doron; E. Hazan); Samuel ha-Nagid (T. Rosen-Moked; A. Zemach); M. Ibn Ezra (J. Dana); Erez Israel piyyut (Y. Yahalom); Saadiah Gaon (N. Allony); Eliezer Berabbi Kiler (S. Elizur). (2) Types of Hebrew secular poetry (I. Levin; T. Rosen-Moked; R. Tsur; R. Scheindlin; M. Itzhaki, Y. Feldman). (3) Types of Hebrew religious poetry and the *piyyut* of Erez Israel (E. Fleischer; D. Goldschmidt; J.J. Petuchowski). (4) Hebrew emblem-riddles in Italy (D. Pagis). (5) The history of Hebrew poetry in Spain, Provence, Italy (J. Schirmann) and Morocco (H. Zafrani).

Edited Texts. (1) V.E. Reichert, *The Tahkemoni of Judah al-Harizi*, an English translation, vol. I, Introduction and Gates 1–15 (Jer., 1965), 234 pp.; vol. II, Gates 16–50 (Jer., 1973), 443 pp.

(2) E. Hazan, *Shirei Fradji Shawat* (Jer., 1976), a critical edition of 91 poems by the most famous Hebrew poet in Tunisia, who apparently lived in the 17th century. He came to Tunisia from Fez, Morocco, and composed a total of 900 poems which were largely religious in nature. The real name of the poet was Raphael Malah, who adopted the equivalent Arabic name Fradji Shawat.

(3) Y. Hasida, *Rav Hai Gaon, Reshuyyot le-farshiyyot ha-Torah* (Jer., 1977), 63 pp.; the book contains 29 poems for sections of the Torah.

(4) R. Bonfils and A.M. Habermann (eds.), *Kalonymus ben Kalonymus, Megillat Setarim al Massekhet Purim* (Jer., 1977), a facsimile of the first edition published in Pesaro in 1513. Along with 24 pages of text there are 34 facsimile pages. The book contains an article by the translator M.D. Cassuto about Kalonymus in Rome and an introduction by Habermann on *Massekhet Purim*, its editions and printings.

(5) E. Romero (tr. and ed.), *Selomo ibn Gabirol, Poesia secular* (Madrid, 1978), 532 pp., with an introduction by Dan Pagis. This is a bilingual edition with selected texts, translations, and notes.

(6) S. Hopkins, *A Miscellany of literary pieces from the Cambridge Genizah Collection…Old Series, Box A 45* (Cambridge, 1978), 110 pp.; this work has facsimiles and copies, along with short introductions, and includes *piyyutim* by Kallir and a fragment from *Esa Meshali* by Saadiah Gaon.

(7) Y. David, *Piyyutei Yosef Bensuli* ("The Poems of Joseph Bensuli"), critical edition with introduction and commentary (Jer., 1979), 55 pp. Joseph Bensuli was an important Hebrew poet in Toledo, Spain, at the beginning of the 14th century. Fifteen liturgical collections found in Spain and elsewhere.

(8) H. Schwarzbaum, *The Mishle Shualim*, 658 p., bibliography, table of narrative types and table of narrative motifs plus a general index. In this comprehensive work the author presents not only competent translations of all the fables, but examines the various sources which influenced them and offers a comparative folkloristic analysis.

(9) Rabbi Shem Tov ben Isaac Ardutiel (or Don Santo de-Carrion), *Ma'ase -Harav* (*The Debate between the Pen and the Scissors*; Tel Aviv, 1980), 86 pp., edited with introduction, commentary, and notes by Y. Nini and M. Fruchtman.

(10) I. Levin, *Shirei ha-Kodesh shel Avraham Ibn Ezra* ("Religious Poems of Abraham Ibn Ezra," 1 (Jer., 1975), 522 pp.; 2 (Jer., 1980), 708 pp. Volume one contains 262 poems and volume two has 247 poems.

(11) M.H. Schmelzer, *Yizhak ben Avraham Ibn Ezra, Shirim* ("Isaac ben Abraham Ibn Ezra, Poems"; New York, 1980), 171 pp., edited on the basis of manuscripts, with an introduction and notes; the book contains a letter and 44 annotated poems.

(12) L.J. Weinberger, *Sefer ha-Selihot ke-Minhag Kehillot ha-Romaniyyotim* ("Romaniote Penitential Poetry"; New York, 1980), 248 pp.

(13) A. Saenz-Badillos, *Tešubot de Dunaš ben Labrat*, critical edition and Spanish translation (Granada, 1980), 124 + 164 pp.

(14) A. Scheiber, *Geniza Studies* (New York, 1981), 570 pp.

(15) *Amadis de Gaula* (*Alilot ha-Abir*), Hebrew translation by the physician Jacob di Algaba, first published Constantinople, c. 1541. Critical edition with introduction by Z. Malachi (Tel Aviv, 1981), 240 pp.

(16) Varela Moreno Ma Encarnacion, *Tešubot de Yehudi ben Šešet*, edited and translated with commentary (Granada, 1981), 117 pp.

(17) Y. David, *The Poems of Joseph Ibn Zaddik* (Jerusalem, 1982). Joseph Ibn Zaddik (1075–1149) was well known as a Hebrew poet in Cordoba, Spain, at the beginning of the 12th century. This critical edition of his extant poetry, in which 36 poems are collected for the first time, includes liturgical poems, eulogies, love songs, and four lamentation.

(18) D. Jarden, *Divan Shemuel Hanagid*; vol. 2, *Ben Mishlei* ("The Son of Proverbs"; Jerusalem, 1982), 478 pp.

(19) L.J. Weinberger (ed.), *Bulgaria's Synagogue Poets: The Kastoreans*, critical edition with introduction and commentary (Cincinnati, 1983), 175 pp.

(20) I. Levin, *Iggeret Hay Ben Mekitz by Abraham lbn Ezra*, a critical edition supplemented with a Hebrew translation of the Arabic original *Hay Ibn Yaqiẓan* by Abu Ali Alḥusain Ibn Abdalla Ibn Sina (Tel Aviv, 1983), 99 pp.

(21) J. Yahalom, *Piyyutei Shimon bar Megas* (Jerusalem, 1984). The poet Simeon bar Megas lived in Byzantine Palestine in the sixth or seventh century. He is the author of a cycle of over 150 *kedushot* based on the triennial cycle then current in Palestine. His writings constitute one of the few resources for information on Palestinian Jewry, its practices and customs, during the crucial period of transition from the Byzantine to the Arabic period. Simeon Bar Megas's 218 poems manifest a special ingenuity in vocabulary and inventiveness, in the use of neologisms, poetic form, and structures. They contribute also to knowledge of Palestinian Hebrew, which, according to the editor, was still spoken in Simeon Bar Megas's time, at least in the villages.

(22) J.S. Levinger, *Isaac Polgar, Ezer ha-Dat* ("A defense of Judaism"), a critical and annotated edition (Tel Aviv, 1984), 197 pp.

(23) D. Jarden, *Shirim Ḥadashim le-Rabbi Elazar ben Ya'akov ha-Bavli* ("New Poems of Rabbi Eleazar ha-Bavli"), based on manuscripts and printed editions (Jerusalem, 1984), 60 pp.

(24) I. Meiseles, *Shirat ha-Maor. The Poems of Rabbi Zerahia ha-Levy* (Jer., 1984), 186 pp. critical edition with commentary. The complete collection of the liturgical poems of Rabbi Zeraḥiah ha-Levi Gerondi is presented in this volume, which contains 51 poems collected from 145 manuscripts located in 32 libraries.

(25) L.J. Weinberger, *Jewish Poets in Crete* (Cincinnati, 1985), 211 pp., a critical edition with introduction and commentary.

(26) Y. Ratzaby, *A Dictionary of Judeo-Arabic in R. Saadya's Tafsir* (Ramat Gan, 1985), 151 pp.

(27) E. Yassif, *Sippurei Ben-Sira bi-Ymei ha-Beinayim* (Jer., 1985), 324 pp.

(28) *Ma'aseh Zofar*, an ancient story first printed in Salonika, c. 1600, republished by Z. Malachi (Lod, 1985), 72 pp., a limited edition of 100 copies.

(29) Y. David, *The Poems of Yehiel ben-Harosh* (1986), a critical edition with introduction and commentary (Jer., 1986), 65 pp. Rabbi Jehiel ben-Harosh was a theologian, a judge (*dayyan*), and also a poet of Toledo, Spain, during the 14th century. The poems of Ben-Harosh are offered here in a critical edition of extant works, 15 liturgical poems collected for the first time. The poet was, moreover, a witness of the 1391 massacre in Toledo, and his lamentations give a historical perspective of Jewry in the Middle Ages in Spain.

(30) D. Jarden, *Shirei ha-Kodesh le-Rabbi Yehuda Halevi* ("The Liturgical Poetry of Judah Halevi," vol. 1: The Winter Festivals (Jer., 1978); vol. 2, The Summer Festivals (Jer., 1980); vol. 3: Other Poems (Jer., 1982); vol. 4, Poems (Jer., 1986)). The four volumes of this edition include 550 poems. In addition to an introduction, a commentary, source references and parallels, and indices are provided.

(31) T. Alsina Trias, Olmo Lete, del. G., *El Diwan de Yosef ibn Saddiq*, according to the critical edition by Yonah David. Introduction, text, and notes (Barcelona, 1987), 116 pp.

(32) Z.M. Rabinovitz, *The Liturgical Poems of Rabbi Yannai according to the Triennial Cycle of the Pentateuch and the Holidays*, critical edition with introductions and commentary, vol. I: Introduction, Liturgical Poems to Genesis, Exodus, and Leviticus (Jer., 1985), 508 pp.; vol. II: Liturgical Poems to Numbers, Deuteronomy and Holidays and indexes (Jer., 1987); 444 pp.

(33) Y. David, *The Poems of Rabbi Isaac Ibn Ghiyyat (Lucena 1038–Cordoba 1089)* (Jer., 1987); the first anthology of 370 poems by this poet.

(34) Sh. Elizur, *Rabbi Jehuda Berabbi Binjaminis, Carmina Cuncta.* Ex codicibus edidit, prolegominis et notis instruxit (Jer., 1988), 319 pp.

(35) Sh. Elizur, *Kedushah ve-Sir Kedushta'ot le-Shabbatot ha-Neḥamah le-Rabbi Eleazar Berabi Kiler*, critical edition with commentary and epilogue (Jerusalem 1988), 109 pp.

(36) O. Raanan, *The Poems of Ishak ben Shlomo Al-Ahdab based on manuscripts and prints.* Critical edition with commentary (Lod, 1988), 152 pp. The 90 poems in this book represent a great variety of a didactic ethical nature and humorous and satiric elements. The poet was born towards the middle of the 14th century in Castile, Spain, and died after 1429, approximately at the age of 80.

(37) *The Piyyutim of Rabbi Musa Bujnah of Tripoli* (1989), 251 pp., were edited by Ephraim Ḥazan, who also wrote the introduction and notes. The book has two parts: the first describes North African Hebrew poetry and discusses the poet and his period, the genre of his poems and their language, while the second offers 109 *piyyutim* by this poet. Appendices provide a table of poetic meters, a list of sources, and an index to the *piyyutim*.

(38) *Pirkei Shirah*, from the treasure-houses of poetry and *piyyut* of Jewish communities, were produced by Yehudit Dishon and Ephraim Ḥazan (1990), 166 pp. The book includes, in addition to the introduction of the editors, chapters by Ya'akov Adler on the explication of a poem by Yosé ben Yosé; Yiẓḥak Meizlish on a heretofore unknown personal *bakkashah* by Zerahiah ha-Levi; Benjamin bar-Tikvah, on a *kerovah* by Rabbi Berachiah; Judah Razaby, on songs of praise by Joseph ha-Yerushalmi; Hadassah Shai, on a selection from a *maqāma* by Joseph ben Tanḥum ha-Yerushalmi: Aaron Mirsky, on poems of Israel Najara from his *She'erit Yisrael;* Ephraim Ḥazan on eight *piyyutim* by Mandil Avi-Zimra; Meir Wallenstein, on the character of Samuel Vitale according to a poetic letter by Moses Judah Abbas.

(39) Ezra Fleischer's *The Proverbs of Sa'id ben Babshad* appeared in 1990 (320 pp.). In this book the author publishes fragments of a major collection of proverbs, written by an unknown medieval Hebrew poet, Said ben Babshad, who flourished in Iraq or in Persia at the end of the 10th and beginning of the 11th century. The eleven chapters of the book, in addition to the texts themselves, summarize the progress of this research, the linguistic issues, ideology, and poetics as well as sources of influence upon which the poet drew. The proverbs were culled from 25 manuscripts located in 10 different collections, most prominently from the Cairo *Genizah*.

(40) *Ḥibbat ha-Piyyut* was edited by Eliyahu Gabbai. It is a selection of *piyyutim* representing different Jewish communities. The commentary was provided by Herzl and Balfour Hakkak. This is a second edition, and it appeared in 1990 (258 pp.). The book has 18 chapters.

(41) Federico Pe'rez Castro published *Poesia secular Hispano-Hebrea* (1989; 399 pp.), which contains translations of 92 Hebrew poems by nine of the most outstanding medieval Hebrew poets, from Menahem ibn Saruq to Judah Halevi. Included are notes and introductions to each poem, edited by H. Schirmann in his *Ha-Shirah ha-Ivrit bi-Sefarad u-ve-Provence.* There are also a general introduction and bibliography.

(42) Carlos del Valle Rodriguez wrote *El Divan Poetico de-Dunash ben Labrat. La introuducion de la metrica arabe* (1988), 543 pp. The book has, in addition to an introduction, six chapters: (1) Dunash ben Labrat the man; (2) the poetry of Dunash; (3) language of Dunash; (4) quantitative metrics; (5) a diachronic survey of Hebrew metrics; (6) the terminology of Hebrew poetry. Moreover, all of Dunash's poems (including those of doubted attribution) are printed according to N. Allony's edition. The author added two appendices which cite the most significant works treating Hebrew metrics [text opposite translation], and finally the volume ends with a bibliography, list of terms, and list of names.

Interpretive Works. (1) C.A. Colaḥan, "Santob's Debate between the Pen and the Scissors," Dissertation, University of New Mexico (1977), 360 pp.

(2) A. Doron, *"Kivvunim u-Megamot be-Ḥeker Shirato shel Yehudah ha-Levi,"* Dissertation, Tel Aviv University (1977), 240 pp.

(3) N. Ben-Menahem, *Inyanei Ibn-Ezra* (Jerusalem, 1978), 373 pp., an anthology of the author's articles on Abraham Ibn Ezra.

(4) E.D. Goldschmidt, *On Jewish Liturgy: Essays on Prayer and Religious Poetry* (Jerusalem, 1978), 494 pp.

(5) *Mishnato ha-Hagutit shel Rabbi Yehudah ha-Levi*, published by the Ministry of Education and Culture, the Department of Tarbut Toranit (Jerusalem, 1978), 242 pp. The book is divided into four sections: (a) the thought of Judah Halevi, a general discussion, (b) society and state, (c) historical thought, and (d) thought and experience. Eighteen contributors participated in the volume, which was dedicated to the 900th anniversary of the birth of Judah Halevi.

(6) J.J. Petuchowski, *Theology and Poetry: Studies in Medieval Piyyut* (London, 1978), 153 pp. The book contains ten *piyyutim* in the original language, as well as in English translation, accompanied by commentary.

(7) J. Schirmann, *Le-toledot ha-shirah ve-ha-dramah ha-ivrit* ("Studies in the History of Hebrew Poetry and Drama;" Jerusalem, vol. 1, 1979, 438 pp., vol. 2, 1980), 376 pp. A year before his death, Schirmann was able to collect the studies and essays which he had published from 1931 through 1978, and arrange them chronologically according to subject matter. Vol. 1 is devoted to early Palestinian *piyyut* and medieval Spanish and southern French poets. Vol. 2 deals with Hebrew poetry in Italy from its beginnings until approximately 1800, as well as with Hebrew drama during the 16th–18th centuries. The material has been revised and the biography of Judah Halevi rewritten on the basis of the *Genizah* finds of Shlomo Dov Goitein. This is a monumental work distinguished for its erudition, expertise, and meticulous care in dealing with the literary creativity of more than a thousand years.

(8) I. Levin, *Me'il Tashbeẓ, The Embroidered Coat: The Genres of Hebrew Secular Poetry in Spain* (Tel Aviv, 1980). The six chapters of the book are divided as follows: (a) the *qasida;* (b) the war poems of Samuel ha-Nagid; (c) songs of praise; (d) poems of glory; (e) poems of complaint; (f) poems of retribution, apology, and abuse.

(9) Z. Malachi, *Be-No'am Si'aḥ, Pleasant Words: Chapters from the History of Hebrew Literature* (Lod, 1983). This volume contains articles dealing with five types of subject matter: (a) studies in *piyyut;* (b) Hebrew poetry in Spain; (c) Medieval Hebrew fiction; (d) the Balbo family of Candia (Crete) in the 15th century; and (e) authors and books of Amsterdam.

(10) A. Ẓemach and T. Rosen-Moked, *Yeẓirah Meḥukhamah: Iyyun be-Shirei Shemuel ha-Nagid* ("Sophisticated Writing: a Study of Samuel ha-Nagid's Poems"; Jer., 1983), 158 pp. The authors analyze and explain 17 poems by Samuel ha-Nagid. The book includes three short introductions which treat various biographical, thematic, and methodological aspects of the poet's work.

(11) J. Dana, *Ha-Po'etika shel-ha-Shirah ha-Ivrit bi Sefarad bi-Ymei ha-Beinayim al-pi Rabbi Moshe ibn Ezra u-Mekoroteha* ("Of Medieval Hebrew Literature, According to Moshe Ibn Ezra"; Tel Aviv, 1983), 337 pp. The book contains, in addition to an introduction, chapters devoted to: (a) content and form, (b) the best poem is that which contains the greatest falsehood, (c) the ornaments in poetry, (d) the qualification and image of the poetic outline, (e) M. Ibn Ezra as poetical theorist and as poet, and (f) influence and originality in the poetics of M. Ibn Ezra. There are also a bibliography and indices.

(12) E. Fleischer, *Ha-Yoẓerot be-Hithavvutam u-ve-Hitpatteḥutam* ("The Yotzer, Its Emergence and Development"; Jerusalem, 1984), 795 pp. This is an illuminating and comprehensive scholarly treatment of a thousand years of the development of the *yoẓer* form, from its beginnings in Byzantine Palestine (c. the 6th century) to its decline in the European Jewish centers. Over two hundred unpublished selections from the Cairo *Genizah* are employed by the author, the first work of its kind in Hebrew.

(13) H. Zafrani, *Poesie juive au Maroc*, (ed. Yosef Tobi; Jer., 1984), 210 pp.

(14) A. Doron, *Yehuda Ha-Levi: Repercusion de su obra*, with a biographical sketch of Judah Halevi by Fernando Diaz Estaban (Barcelona, 1985).

(15) J. Dishon, *Sefer Sha'ashuim le-Yosef ben Meir ibn Zabara* ("The Book of Delight Composed by Joseph ben Meir Zabara"; Jerusalem, 1985), 292 pp.

(16) *Studies in the Work of Shlomo Ibn-Gabirol* (Zvi Malachi (ed.), Hanna David (co-ed.); Tel Aviv, 1985). The book contains two collections of articles. The first is dedicated to the philosophical elements in the poetry of Ibn Gabirol, while the second deals with the types of poems by him and the characteristics of his poetry. There were 12 contributors in addition to the editor.

(17) J. Yahalom, *Sefer ha-Shir shel ha-Piyyut ha-Ereẓ-Yisraeli ha-Kadum* ("Poetic Language in the Early Piyyut"; Jer., 1985), 218 pp. This study deals with the language of the early Ereẓ Israel *piyyutim* which struggled to maintain its independence between the natural needs of expression, rooted in the spoken language, and the archaic literary tradition characteristic of the *piyyutim*. During this confrontation there developed a new independent literary language which bridges the ancient times and the Middle Ages; its distinctive signs are developed and expanded in this work.

(18) Y. Silman, *Bein Filosof le-Navi: Hitpatteḥut Haguto shel R. Yehuda ha-Levi be-Sefer ha-Kuzari* ("Thinker and Seer: The Development of the Thought of R. Yehuda Halevi in the Kuzari"; Ramat Gan, 1985), 325 pp.

(19) T. Rosen-Moked, *Le-Ezor Shir* ("The Hebrew Girdle Poem (*Muwashshah*) in the Middle Ages"; Haifa, 1985), 245 pp.

(20) N. Allony, *Meḥkarei Lashon ve-Sifrut: Pirkei Sa'adiah Gaon* (Jer., 1986), 400 pp.

(21) E. Ḥazan, *Torat ha-Shir be-Fiyyut ha-Sefardi le-Or Shirat ha-Kodesh shel R. Yehuda ha-Levi* ("The Poetics of the Sephardi *Piyyut* According to the Liturgical Poetry of Yehuda Halevi"; Jer., 1986), 340 pp.; this work, with introduction, appendices and indices, discusses meter, rhyme, and euphonic word-texture: language, methods of formulation and imagery, and structural methods.

(22) Dan Pagis, *Al Sod Ḥatum* ("A Secret Sealed," Hebrew Baroque Emblem-Riddles from Italy and Holland; Jerusalem, 1986). This work deals with Hebrew riddles which developed in Italy and Holland in a 200-year period, 1650–1850. The ten chapters of the book cover: the field and its study; the origin of the emblem-riddle and foreign languages; the literary riddle as a social genre; the social role of the emblem-riddle; the "emblem-riddle" and related subjects; tricks of language; Aramaic, Hebrew, and the random interpolation of the key word; the body of the emblem-riddle; the unit of the false "solution," three emblem-riddles by Rabbi Moses Zacuto. There are also indices, bibliography, and an English summary.

(23) R.P. Scheindlin, *Wine, Women, and Death: Medieval Hebrew Poems on the Good-Life* (Philadelphia, New York, Jerusalem, 1986), 204 pp. The author presents the original Hebrew poem along with his own English translation, followed by commentary which explains its cultural context. Included are 31 poems, grouped into three categories: (a) Wine, description of or meditations on the wine party, a conventional Arabic social gathering; (b) Women, Golden Age poems of love and desire; (c) Death, mellow reflections on the brevity of life. Among the poets whose work is represented in this collection are: Samuel ha-Nagid, Solomon Ibn Gabirol, Moses Ibn Ezra, and Judah Halevi.

(24) M. Itzḥaki, *"Ani Hashar": Studies in Secular Poetry in Spain* (Tel Aviv, 1986), 133 pp. This work discusses a number of poems by Samuel ha-Nagid, Solomon Ibn Gabirol, Moses ibn Ezra, and Judah Halevi in the light of normative poetics of the period.

(25) I. Levin, *Ha-Sod ve-ha-Yesod* ("Mystical Trends in the Poetry of Solomon Ibn Gabirol"; Lod, 1986), 174 pp.

(26) Y. Feldman, *Bein ha-Kotavim le-Kav ha-Mashveh* ("Semantic Patterns in the Medieval Hebrew Qasida": Tel Aviv, 1987), 130 pages. The author analyzes through semantic deductions six *qasidot* by Moses Ibn Ezra and thereby demonstrates significant principles of structure which are based on two patterns of organization: opposition or polarization and comparison.

(27) M. Itzḥaki, *Ha-Ḥai Ge en ve-ha-Mawet Bozer* ("Man-the Vine; Death-the Reaper: The *Tocheha* Hebrew Admonishment Poetry of Spain"; Tel Aviv, 1987), 82 pp.

(28) R. Tsur, *Ha-Shirah ha-Ivrit bi-Ymei ha-Beinayim be-Perspektivah Kefulah: Ha-Kore ha-Versatili ve-Shirat Sefarad* ("Medieval Hebrew Poetry in a Double Perspective: The Versatile Reader and Hebrew Poetry in Spain." Papers in Cognitive Poetics; Tel Aviv, 1987), 221 pp. The book deals with medieval literature from three perspectives: (a) the analysis and evaluation of the poems as the result of interaction between the ideational generic figurative, and prosodic dimensions as objects of perceived meaning; (b) the skills necessary for a

versatile reader to be able to respond to a wide range of literary styles; (c) the contemporary reader's confrontations with the styles of a far-distant literary period.

(29) S. Elitzur. *Piyyutei Eleazer berabbi Kiler* (Jer., 1988), 430 pp.

Additional Bibliography on Individual Subjects. (1) *Todros ha-Levi Abulafia* (1989), 234 pp., was published by Aviva Doron. Todros ha-Levi Abulafia was born in Toledo some hundred years after the transfer of the Jewish cultural centers from Muslim Andalusia to Christian Spain. This book describes the poetry of the Hebrew-Castilian poet against the background of the cultural crossroads in which he lived and worked. The book comprises, in addition to an introduction, a selected bibliography, and three indices (poems treated in the book, subject, and name) eight chapters: (a) the author and his times; (b) Todros ha-Levi, a Hebrew author at the crossroads of literary streams; (c) national and religious expressions in the language of Todros's personal poetry; (d) time in his poetry; (e) the attitude of the poet towards his poetry; (f) love poems; (g) methods of structural and rhetorical design in his poems; (h) comments on a selection of poems from *Gan ha-Meshalim ve-ha-Ḥidot.*

(2) Rina Drory's *The Emergence of Jewish Arabic Literary Contacts at the Beginning of the Tenth Century* appeared in 1988. In addition to an introduction and summary, the book has six chapters: (a) the structure of the Jewish literary system at the beginning of the 10th century; (b) the consolidation of Hebrew and Arabic as the written languages for the Jewish literary system; (c) unequivocal literary patterns: Karaite patterns; (d) ambivalent literary patterns: wisdom proverbs; (e) biblical treatment; (f) the role of Saadiah Gaon in contacts with Arabic literature. Indices of names and of works conclude this important contribution to the field.

(3) *Yehuda Halevi*, a selection of critical essays on his poetry, selected with an introduction by Aviva Doron, was published in 1988, 285 pp. It has (a) studies into the biography of the poet by H. Schirmann, S.D. Goitein, and Yosef Yahalom; (b) articles on his poems – a total of 16 items by Ḥayyim Naḥman Bialik, Franz Rosenzweig, Ben-Zion Dinur, Michael Ish-Shalom, Yitzḥak Heinemann, Aryeh Ludwig Strauss, Yisrael Levin, Moshe Schwartz, Adi Zemaḥ, Aharon Mirsky, Reuven Zur, Dov Sadan, Ezra Fleischer, Ẓevi Malachi, Ephraim Ḥazan, and Aviva Doron; (c) five appendices – Samuel David Luzzatto's *Betulat Bat-Yehudah* (1840); a diwan by Judah Halevi; from Michael Sachs' *Religious Poetry of the Jews* (1845); Heinrich Ḥayyim Brody's *Rosh Davar'* to a *diwan* by the poet; and from Fritz Yitzḥak Baer's *The History of Jews in Christian Spain* (1945).

(4) *Abraham Ibn Ezra y su tiempo*, the acts of an international symposium held in Madrid, Tudela, and Toledo on February 1–8, 1989, 396 pp., appeared in 1990. This book contains the 45 lectures given by international scholars at the symposium held in honor of the 900th anniversary of the birth of Abraham Ibn Ezra.

Jubilee and Memorial Volumes. (1) *Shai le-Heiman* (*A.M. Habermann Jubilee Volume*), edited by Z. Malachi with the assistance of Y. David (Jer., 1977), 385 pp. This volume contains 21 articles, a bibliography of Habermann's works and an index to *piyyutim* he published, prepared by Y. David.

(2) J. Blau, S. Pines, M.J. Kister, S. Shaked (eds.), *Ḥakkirei Mizraḥ* (*Studia Orientalia, Memoriae D.H. Baneth Dedicata*) (Jer., 1979), 407 pp.

(3) G. Nahon and Ch. Touati, *Hommage a G. Vajda. Etudes d'histoire et de pensé juive édités par…* (Louvain, 1980), 604 pp. The 40 contributions dealt with Judaica studies.

(4) Z. Malachi (ed.), *Yad le-Heiman* (*The A.M. Habermann Memorial Volume*; Lod, 1983), 434 pp. The five sections of the book deal with Medieval Hebrew literature, the heritage of Eastern Jewry after the Expulsion from Spain, bibliography and study of the Hebrew book, the history of liturgy and customs, and the memory of Prof. Habermann.

(5) *Le-Zikhro shel Ḥayyim Schirmann,* published by the Israel National Academy of Science (Jer., 1984). The essays included are "The Position of Prof. Schirmann in the Study of Hebrew Poetry," by S. Abramson; "On Retribution and Redemption in the Religious Poems of Abraham Ibn Ezra," by I. Levin, and "Ups and Downs in Ancient Hebrew Poetry," by A. Mirsky.

(6) Z. Malachi (ed), *Be-Oraḥ Mada* (*Aharon Mirsky Jubilee Volume*, essays on Jewish Culture; Lod, 1986), 619 pp. In addition to a selected bibliography of the works of A. Mirsky, the book contains essays on Jewish studies, on Hebrew poetry in Spain and North Africa, on poetry and *piyyut* and culture.

(7) G.J. Blidstein, Y. Salmon, E. Yassif (eds.), *Eshel Beer-Sheva* ("Essays in Jewish Studies in Memory of Professor Nehemia Allony"; Beersheba, 1986), 371 pp. A bibliography of the works of Nehemiah Allony prepared by R. Attal is included.

Anthologies and Collections. (1) J. Rothenberg, H. Lenowitz, and Ch. Doria, *A Big Jewish Book; Poems and Other Visions of the Jews from Tribal Times to the Present* (New York, 1978), 633 pp.

(2) K. Bosley, *The Elek Book of Oriental Verse* (London, 1979).

(3) D. Pagis (ed.), *Ke-Ḥut ha-Shani* ("The Scarlet Thread; Hebrew love poems from Spain, Italy, Turkey and the Yemen"; Tel Aviv, 1979), 120 pp. an anthology of 99 poems by 23 poets, dating from the 10th to the 19th centuries. The poems are arranged in 12 sections by subject and motif rather than according to chronological order.

(4) *Abraham ibn Ezra Reader*, annotated texts with introduction and commentary, by I. Levin, edited by M. Arfa (Tel Aviv, 1985), 438 pp.

(5) Angel Saenz-Badillos and Judit Targarona Borras published an anthology, *Poetas Hebreos de-al-Andalus* (*Siglos x–xii*), in 1988, 232 pp. This is the first anthology of its type to appear in Spain: it offers selections from 12 of the greatest Hebrew poets of Spain, beginning with Menahem ibn Saruq

and ending with Abraham Ibn Ezra. The text, in an excellent translation, is accompanied by a selected bibliography.

(6) Aharon Mirsky's 731-page *Ha-Piyyut, The Development of Post-Biblical Poetry in Eretz-Israel and the Diaspora*, appeared in 1990. This large, excellent anthology contains 45 articles representing 40 years of research in the field. There are three sections to the book: (1) 16 articles on the sources of the prayers and the initial steps toward *piyyut* in the Bible; post-biblical poetry; poetry in the talmudic period; delineation of the characteristics of ancient poetry; the schools within ancient Hebrew poetry; the *piyyut* tradition in the Land of Israel; and other items.

(2) 15 articles on innovations introduced by early post-biblical poetry, including language and the poetic form; the significance of rhyme in Hebrew poetry; clarification and explication of the language of poetry, and so on;

(3) 14 articles on Hebrew poetry in Spain and Germany and the nature of the poetry which began anew in the eastern countries in the 17th and 18th centuries; evaluations of four important poets – Dunash ben Labrat, Rabbenu Gershom Meor ha-Golah, Judah al-Ḥarizi, and Israel Najara. The book ends with indices on subjects, *piyyutim* and *paytanim*.

Liturgy. (1) J. Heinemann and A. Shinan, *Tefillot ha-Keva ve-ha-Ḥovah shel Shabbat ve-Yom Ḥol* (Tel Aviv, 1977), 131 pp., deals with the weekday and Sabbath liturgy and includes explication, history, and discussion of their structure.

(2) J. Heinemann, *Prayer in the Talmud* (Berlin, 1977), a revised English edition of the 1964 Hebrew-language version.

(3) H.G. Cohen (ed.), *Ha-Tefillah ha-Yehudit* ("Prayer in Judaism: Continuity and Change"; Jerusalem, 1978), 292 pp.

(4) J. Heinemann, *Iyyunei Tefillah* ("Studies in Jewish Liturgy"; Jerusalem, 1981), edited by A. Shinan, 205 pp.

(5) A. Mirsky, *Yesodei Ẓurot ha-Piyyut* ("The Original Forms of Early Hebrew Poetry"; Jer., 1985), 134 pp., deals with ancient Ereẓ Israel poetry.

(6) A.M. Habermann, *Al ha-Tefillah* ("Essays on Prayers"), edited by Z. Malachi (Lod, 1987), 148 pp. This collection is made up of various essays on prayers published during the author's lifetime.

(7) The monumental (posthumous) work by D. Goldschmidt, *Meḥkare Tefillah u-Fiyyut.*

FACSIMILES AND BIBLIOGRAPHY. (1) D.S. Loewinger (ed.), *Osef Piyyutei Sepharad* ("Collection of Spanish Piyyutim"; Jerusalem, 1977), 264 pp. Facsimile edition based on Ms. 197 in the David Guenzberg Collection. Lenin Public Library, Moscow.

(2) J. Yahalom (ed.), *Kit'ei ha-genizah shel piyyutei Yannai* ("A Collection of Genizah Fragments of Yannai's Liturgical Poems"; Jerusalem, 1978), 214 pp.

(3) E. Koren, *The Alphabetical Index to Israel Najara's Poems* (Tel Aviv, 1978), 44 pp.

(4) D. Carpi (ed.), *Bibliotheca Italo-Ebraica: Bibliografia per la storia degli Ebrei in Italia 1964–1973*, collected by A. Luzzato and M. Moldavi (Rome, 1982).

(5) D. Pagis, E. Fleischer (eds.), Y. David (co-editor), *A Bibliography of the Writings of Prof Jefim (Haim) Schirmann (1904–1981)* (Jer., 1983), 48 pp.

(6) "Bibliography of the Writings of G. Vajda", in: *Da'at*, 10 (1983), 53–66,125–126.

(7) R. Attal, *Kitvei Professor Nehemya Allony* ("A bibliography of the writings of Prof. N. Allony"; Beersheba, 1984), 33 pp.

(8) Y. Ganuz, *Bibliografiyyah shel Kitvei Ḥayyim Schwarzbaum be-Ḥeker ha-Folklore ha-Yehudi ve-ha-Aravi*, in: *Yeda-Am*, 22 (1984; no. 51–52), 10–19.

(9) M. Beit-Arie, *The Only Dated Medieval Manuscript Written in England (1189 C.E.) and the Problem of Pre-Expulsion Anglo-Hebrew Manuscripts* (Appendix 1 by M. Banitt; appendix 2 by Z.E. Rokeaḥ), London 1985, 56 pp.

(10) Y. David, "A Decade of Research on Medieval Hebrew Literature," in: *Jewish Book Annual*, 43 (1985–1986), 107–117;

(11) J. Yahalom, *Maḥzor Ereẓ Yisrael, Kodex ha-Genizah* with a paleographic introduction by E. Engel, facsimile edition (1988), 148 pp.

(12) *Ḥeqer ha-Shirah ve-ha-Piyyut* ("Research in Poetry and Piyyut") 1948–1978, a cumulative index-bibliography was published by Ben-Gurion University in 1989. There are 451 pages in Hebrew and 31 in other languages. The editors were Gisella Davidson, Elhanan Adler, Pinḥas Ziv, and Amira Kehat.

(13) *The Catalogue of the Jack Mosseri Collection* appeared, edited by the Institute of Microfilmed Hebrew Manuscripts, with the collaborations of numerous specialists (1990), 407 pages, with a foreword by Claude Mosseri and a preface by Israel Adler. The catalogue contains, in addition to a concordance of call-numbers and indices of titles, subjects, authors, places, dates, languages, copyists and persons mentioned, and melody indications, a listing on *piyyut* and poetry-genres, subjects, and forms and incipits of the *piyyutim* and the poems.

[Yonah David]

Developments from 1990 to 2005

EDITIONS, HEBREW TEXTS. E. Fleischer, *Mishle Sa'id ben Babshad* (1990); A. Sáenz-Badillos & J. Targarona, *Šĕmu'el ha-Nagid. Poemas. I, Desde el campo de batalla (Granada 1038–1056)* (1990); A. Sáenz-Badillos, J. Targarona & A. Doron, *Judah ha-Levi, Poemas. Shirim* (1994); A. Sáenz-Badillos & J. Targarona, *Šemu'el ha-Nagid. Poemas. II, En la corte de Granada* (1998); N. Allony, *Shirim Genuzim: Shirim Ḥadashim mi-Genizat Kahir*, ed. J. Tobi (2001).

STUDIES, HISTORY, CRITICISM. R. Brann, *The Compunctious Poet* (1991); D. Pagis, *Hebrew Poetry of the Middle Ages and the Renaissance* (1991); F. Corriente & A. Sáenz-Badillos, *Poesía estrófica* (1991); A. Sáenz-Badillos, *El alma lastimada: Ibn Gabirol* (1992); D. Pagis & E. Fleischer, *Ha-Shir Davur 'al*

Ofanav: Meḥkarim u-Masot ba-Shirah ha-Ivrit shel Yeme ha-Beinayim (1993); A. Schippers, *Spanish Hebrew Poetry and the Arab Literary Tradition: Arabic Themes in Hebrew Andalusian Poetry* (1994); D. Bregman, *Shevil ha-Zahav: ha-Sonet ha-'Ivri bi-Tekufat ha-Renesans ve-ha-Barok* (1995); E. Hazan, *Ha-Shirah ha-'Ivrit bi-Ẓefon Afrikah* (1995); I. Levin, *Me'il Tashbeẓ: ha-Sugim ha-Shonim shel Shirat ha-Ḥol ha-'Ivrit bi-Sefarad* (1995); J. Schirmann, & E. Fleischer, *The History of Hebrew Poetry in Muslim Spain* (Heb., 1995).

T. Vardi, *"Adat ha-Nognim be-Saragosah, Shirat ha-Ḥol"* (diss. 1996); D. Bregman, *Ẓeror Zehuvim: Sonetim Ivriyyim mi-Tekufat ha-Renesans ve-ha-Barok* (1997); P. Fenton, *Philosophie et exégèse dans Le Jardin de la méthaphore de Moïse Ibn 'Ezra, philosophe et poète andalou du xiie siècle* (1997); S. Kats, *Benot-ha-Shir ha-Na'vot: Hebetim Po'etiyim, Ḥevratiyyim ve-Historiyyim bi-Yeẓiratam shel Meshorere-Sefarad* (1997); T. Rosen, *Shirat ha-Ḥol ha-Ivrit bi-Ymei-ha-Beinayim* (1997); J. Schirmann, & E. Fleischer, *The History of Hebrew Poetry in Christian Spain and Southern France* (Heb., 1997); I. Levin, *Tanim ve-Khinor: Ḥurban, Galut, Nakam u-Ge'ulah ba-Shirah ha-Ivrit ha-Le'ummit* (1998); J. Chetrit, *Piyiut ve-Shirah be-Yahadut Maroko: Asupat Meḥkarim al Shirim ve-al Meshorerim* (1999); R.P. Scheindlin, *Wine, Women, & Death: Medieval Hebrew Poems on the Good Life.* (1999); D. Bregman, *Sharsheret ha-Zahav: ha-Sonet ha-Ivri le-Dorotav* (2000); R. Drory, *Models and Contacts. Arabic Literature and Its Impact on Medieval Jewish Culture* (2000).

R. Brann, *Power in the Portrayal: Representations of Jews and Muslims in Eleventh- and Twelfth-Century Islamic Spain* (2002); S. Einbinder, *Beautiful Death: Jewish Poetry and Martyrdom in Medieval France* (2002); A. Tanenbaum, *The Contemplative Soul: Hebrew Poetry and Philosophical Theory in Medieval Spain* (2002); T. Rosen, *Unveiling Eve: Reading Gender in Medieval Hebrew Literature* (2003); A. Brenner, *Isaac ibn Khalfun: a Wandering Hebrew Poet of the Eleventh Century* (2003); J. Targarona & A. Sáenz-Badillos (eds.), *Poesía hebrea en al-Andalus* (2003); S. Elizur, *Shirat ha-Ḥol ha-Ivrit bi-Sefarad ha-Muslemit* (2004); M.M. Hamilton, S.J. Portnoy, et al. *Wine, Women and Song: Hebrew and Arabic Literature of Medieval Iberia* (2004); J. Tobi & M. Rosovsky, *Proximity and Distance: Medieval Hebrew and Arabic Poetry* (2004); Joseph ben Tanhum, *Arugot ha-Besamim*, ed. J. Dishon (2005).

TRANSLATIONS. M.J. Cano, Ibn Gabirol, Poesía religiosa (1992); C. del Valle, Isaac ben Jalfón de Córdoba: poemas (1992); M. Itzhaki, M. Garel, et al. Jardin d'Eden jardins d'Espagne: poésie hébraïque médiévale en Espagne et en Provence: anthologie bilingue (1993); P. Cole, Selected poems of Shmuel HaNagid (1996); L.J. Weinberger, Twilight of a Golden Age: Selected Poems of Abraham Ibn Ezra (1997); I. Goldberg, Solomon ibn Gabirol: a Bibliography of His Poems in Translation (1998); M. Itzhaki & M. Garel, Poésie hébraïque amoureuse: de l'Andalousie à la mer Rouge: anthologie bilingue (2000); P. Cole, Selected poems of Solomon Ibn Gabirol (2001).

[Angel Sáenz-Badillos (2nd ed.)]

BIBLIOGRAPHY: BIBLICAL: L. Alonso Schökel, *A Manual of Hebrew Poetics* (1988); R. Alter, *The Art of Biblical Poetry* (1985); idem, "The Characteristics of Ancient Hebrew Poetry," in: R. Alter and F. Kermode (eds.), *The Literary Guide to the Bible* (1987); A. Berlin, *Biblical Poetry through Medieval Jewish Eyes* (1991); idem, *The Dynamics of Biblical Parallelism* (1985); idem, "Introduction to Hebrew Poetry," in: *The New Interpreter's Bible*, 4:301–15 (1996); idem, "Motif and Creativity in Biblical Poetry," in: *Prooftexts*, 3 (1983), 231–41; idem, "Reading Biblical Poetry," in: M. Brettler and A. Berlin (eds.), *The Jewish Study Bible* (2004), 2097–104; *Biblia Hebraica Leningradensia*, ed. A. Dotan (2001); *Biblia Hebraica Stuttgartensia* (1977); M. Black, "Metaphor," in: M. Johnson (ed.), *Philosophical Perspectives on Metaphor* (1981), 63–82 (reprint of *Proceedings from the Aristotelian Society*, N.S. 55 (1954–55), 273–94; T.V.F. Brogan, "Poetry," in: A. Preminger and T.V.F. Brogan (eds.), *The New Princeton Encyclopedia of Poetry and Poetics* (1993), 938–42; G. Buccellati, "On Poetry – Theirs and Ours," in: T. Abush, J. Huenergard, P. Steinkeller (eds.), *Lingering Over Words* (1990), 105–34; W.T.W. Cloete, "The Colometry of Hebrew Verse," in: *Journal of Northwest Semitic Languages*, 15 (1989) 15–29; idem, "A Guide to the Techniques of Hebrew Verse," in: JNSL, 16 (1990), 223–28; idem, "Verse and Prose: Does the Distinction Apply to the Old Testament?" in: JNSL, 14 (1988), 9–15; T. Collins, *Line-Forms in Hebrew Poetry: A Grammatical Approach to the Stylistic Study of the Hebrew Prophets* (1978); H. Fisch, *Poetry with a Purpose: Biblical Poetics and Interpretation* (1988); J.P. Fokkelman, *Major Poems of the Hebrew Bible at the Interface of Hermeneutics and Structural Analysis* (1998); idem, *Reading Biblical Poetry: An Introductory Guide*, trans. I. Smit (2001); D.N. Freedman, "Pottery, Poetry, and Prophecy: An Essay on Biblical Poetry," in: JBL, 96 (1977), 5–26; N. Friedman, "Imagery," in: Alex Preminger and T.V.F. Brogan (eds.), *The New Princeton Encyclopedia of Poetry and Poetics* (1993), 559–66; P. Fussell, *Poetic Meter & Poetic Form* (1979); S. Geller, "The Language of Imagery in Psalm 114," in: T. Abush, J. Huehnergard, P. Steinkeller (eds.), *Lingering Over Words* (1990), 105–34; idem, *Parallelism in Early Biblical Poetry* (1979); S. Gevirtz, *Patterns in the Early Poetry of Israel* (1963); S.E. Gillingham, *The Poems and Psalms of the Hebrew Bible* (1994); G.B. Gray, *The Forms of Hebrew Poetry* (1972); J. Greenfield, "'The 'Cluster' in Biblical Poetry," in: *Maarav*, 5–6 (1990), 159–68; E. Greenstein, "Aspects of Biblical Poetry," in: *Jewish Book Annual*, 44 (1986–87), 33–42; idem, "Robert Alter on Biblical Poetry: A Review Essay," in: *Hebrew Studies*, 27 (1986), 82–94; *The Holy Scriptures* (Jerusalem, Koren Publishers Jerusalem Ltd., 1988); B. Hrushovski, "The Meaning of Sound Patterns in Poetry," in: *Poetics Today*, 2 (1980) 39–56; idem, "Prosody, Hebrew," in: *Encyclopaedia Judaica*, 13:1195–240 (1971); J. Kugel, *The Great Poems of the Bible* (1999); idem, *The Ideal of Biblical Poetry: Parallelism and Its History* (1981); idem, "Some Thoughts on Future Research into Biblical Style: Addenda to *The Idea of Biblical Poetry*," in: JSOT, 28 (1984), 107–17; K. Kenneth, "Recent Perspectives on Biblical Poetry," in: *Religious Studies Review*, 19 (1993), 321–27; F. Landy, "Poetics and Parallelism: Some Comments on James Kugel's *The Idea of Biblical Poetry*," in: JSOT, 28 (1984), 61–87; idem, "Recent Developments in Biblical Poetics," in: *Prooftexts*, 7 (1987), 163–205; M. Lichtenstein, "Biblical Poetry," in: B.W. Holtz (ed.), *Back to the Sources* (1984), 105–27; R. Lowth, *Lectures on the Sacred Poetry of the Hebrews* (1847); P.D. Miller, Jr., "Meter, Parallelism, and Tropes: The Search for Poetic Style," in: JSOT, 28 (1984), 99–106; J. Muilenburg, "Poetry: Biblical Poetry," in: *Encyclopaedia Judaica*, 13:671–93 (1971); A. Niccacci, "Analysing Biblical Hebrew Poetry," in: JSOT, 74 (1997), 77–93; M. O'Connor, *Hebrew Verse Structure* (1997); D. Orton (ed.), *Poetry in the Hebrew Bible: Selected Studies from Vetus Testamentum* (2000); S. Paul, *Amos* (1991); D.L. Petersen, David and K.H. Richards, *Interpreting Hebrew Poetry* (1992); E. Reiner, *Your Thwarts in Pieces, Your*

Mooring Rope Cut: Poetry from Babylonia and Assyria (1985); I.A. Richards, *The Philosophy of Rhetoric* (1936); E. Spicehandler, "Hebrew Poetry," in: A. Preminger and T.V.F. Brogan (eds.), *The New Princeton Encyclopedia of Poetry and Poetics* (1993), 501–9; *Tanakh: The Traditional Hebrew Text and the New JPS Translation* (1999²); W.G.E. Watson, *Classical Hebrew Poetry: A Guide to Its Techniques* (1995); idem, "Problems and Solutions in Hebrew Verse: A Survey of Recent Work," in: VT, 43 (1993), 372–84; idem, *Traditional Techniques in Classical Hebrew Verse* (1994); E.R. Wendland, "The Discourse Analysis of Hebrew Poetry: A Procedural Outline," in: E. Wendland (ed.), *Discourse Perspectives on Hebrew Poetry in the Scriptures* (1994); M. West, "Looking for the Poem: Reflections on the Current and Future Status of the Study of Biblical Hebrew Poetry," in: P. House (ed.), *Beyond Form Criticism: Essays in Old Testament Literary Criticism* (1992), 423–31; Z. Zevit, "Psalms at the Poetic Precipice," in: *Harvard Annual Review*, 10 (1986), 351–66; idem, "Roman Jakobson, Psycholinguistics, and Biblical Poetry," in: JBL, 109 (1990), 385–401. MEDIEVAL HEBREW SECULAR: SPAIN AND PROVENCE: For editions and studies of individual authors, see the individual articles. Davidson, Oẓar, 4 vols. (1924–33); second enlarged edition with general introduction by Ḥ. Schirmann (1970); Ḥ. Schirmann, in: KS, 26 onward (from 1950 onward), annual bibliography of research in secular and sacred poetry; Schirmann, *Sefarad* (1961²), an anthology of poetry in Spain and Provence, with an introduction on each poet, and a bibliography; idem, *La poésie hebraique du Moyen Age en Espagne*, in: *Mélanges de Philosophie et de Littérature juives* (1962), 171–210; idem, *Shirim Ḥadashim min ha-Genizah* (1965); idem, "Problems in the Study of Post-Biblical Hebrew Poetry," in: *Proceedings of the Israel Academy of Sciences and Humanities*, 2 (1967), 228–36; A.M. Habermann, *Toledot ha-Piyyut ve-ha-Shirah* (1970); B. Halper, *The Scansion of Mediaeval Hebrew Poetry*, in: JQR, 4 (1913/14), 153–224; J. Schirmann, "La métrique quantitative dans la poésie hébraïque du Moyen Age," in: *Sefarad*, 8 (1948), 323–32; D. Yellin, *Torat ha-Shirah ha-Sefaradit* (1939); S. Abramson, *Bi-Leshon Kodemim* (1965); D. Pagis, *Shirat ha-Ḥol ve-Torat ha-Shir le-Moshe ibn Ezra u-Venei Zemanno* (1970); J. Schirmann, "The Function of the Hebrew Poet in Medieval Spain," in: JSOS, 16 (1954), 235–52; J. Weiss, *Tarbut Ḥazranit ve-Shirah Ḥazranit* (1948); S.D. Goitein, "*Ha-Makamah ve-ha-Maḥberet – Perek be-Toledot ha-Sifrut ve-ha-Ḥevrah be-Mizraḥ*," in: *Maḥbarot le-Sifrut*, 5 (1951), 25–40; I. Goldziher, "Bemerkungen zur neuhebraeischen Trauerpoesie," in: JQR, 14 (1901/02), 719–36; J. Schirmann, "The Ephebe in Medieval Hebrew Poetry," in: *Sefarad*, 15 (1955), 58–68; I. Levin, "*Zeman ve-Tevel be-Shirat ha-Ḥol ha-Ivrit be-Sefarad bi-Ymei ha-Beinayim*," in: *Oẓar Yehudei Sefarad*, 5 (1962), 68–79; J. Schirmann, "Der Neger und die Negerin; Zur Bildersprache und Stottwahl der Spanisch-Hebraeischen Dichtung," in: MGWJ, 83 (1939), 481–92; S.M. Stern, *Hispano-Arabic Strophic Poetry*; studies selected and edited by L.P. Harvey (1974); D. Yellin, *Hebrew Poetry in Spain*, edited with an introduction by A.M. Habermann (vol. 3 of a proposed 7-volume edition of the writings of David Yellin); D. Pagis, *Change and Tradition in the Secular Poetry: Spain and Italy* (1976). **ADD. BIBLIOGRAPHY:** A. Sáenz-Badillos, in: *Miscelánea de Estudios Árabes y Hebraicos*, 50:2 (2001), 133–61; A. Tanenbaum, in: *Hebrew Scholarship and the Medieval World* (2001), 171–85; T. Rosen, in: *The Oxford Handbook of Jewish Studies* (2002), 241–94. ITALY: B. Klar (ed.), *Megillat Aḥima'aẓ* (1945); Schirmann, Italy; idem (ed.), *Ẓaḥut Bediḥuta de-Kiddushin* (1946); P. Naveh (ed.), *Kol Shirei Ya'akov Frances* (1969); S. Bernstein (ed.), *Divan le-Rabbi Immanu'el ben David Frances* (1932); C. Roth, *The Jews in the Renaissance* (1959); Y. David, *The Poems of Elya bar Shemaya*, Critical edition with introductions and commentary (1977). FRANCE AND GERMANY: I. Elbogen et al., *Germania Judaica* (1934); A.M. Habermann, *Piyyutei Rabbi Shimon bar Yiẓḥak* (1938); idem, *Gezerot Ashkenaz ve-Ẓarefat* (1966); idem, *Hebrew Poems of Meir of Norwich* (1966); idem, in YMḤSI, 2 (1936), 92–115; idem, in: *Sinai*, 15 (1945), 288–98; S. Spiegel, in: L. Finkelstein (ed.), *The Jews, their History, Culture, and Religion*, 1 (1960³), 854–92. MAQĀMA: Y. Ratzaby, *Yalkut ha-Maqama ha-Ivrit, Sippurim be-Ḥaruzim* (1974), selections from *maqamot* of 32 authors from Solomon ibn Zakbel to Bialik, with a detailed introduction and notes. PIYYUT: D. Goldschmidt, *Meḥkarei Tefilah* (1979); J. Yahalom, *The Syntax of Ancient Piyyut* (including Yannai) *as a Basis for its Style* (1974).

POGREBIN, LETTY COTTIN (1939–), U.S. feminist activist, prolific writer, and cofounder with Gloria *Steinem of the National Women's Political Caucus. Born in Queens, New York City, to Cyral (Halpern) and Jacob Cottin, Pogrebin was among the first girls to celebrate a bat mitzvah in Conservative Judaism (1952). A 1959 graduate of Brandeis University, she married Bertrand Pogrebin, a New York City lawyer, in 1963. Following her marriage, Pogrebin worked for Bernard Geis Associates, a publishing company, becoming director of publicity and vice president. Her experiences inspired her first book, *How to Make It in a Man's World* (1970). In 1971, Pogrebin helped found *Ms. Magazine* with Steinem. *Getting Yours: How to Make the System Work for the Working Woman* (1975), continued her concern for women's status in the workplace.

Pogrebin's writings reconciled feminist convictions with marriage and family life. A mother of twin daughters and a son (and later grandmother of six), Pogrebin discussed sex-role socialization and principles of nonsexist child-rearing in *Growing Up Free: Raising Your Child in the 80s* (1980) and *Stories for Free Children* (1982). She worked with Marlo Thomas to create *Free to Be You and Me*, a record, book, and television special of nonsexist songs and stories, for which she received an Emmy Award. In *Family Politics: Love and Power on an Intimate Frontier* (1983), Pogrebin argued against "family fetishists," who insisted on "the old-fashioned, confining, authoritarian family, or no family at all." Pogrebin elaborated on the meaning and politics of relationships in *Among Friends: Who We Like, Why We Like Them and What We Do with Them* (1987).

For the first two decades of her career, Pogrebin was not overt about her Jewish identity. Her disenchantment with Judaism began when she was barred from reciting **kaddish* following her mother's death when she was 15. In her memoir, *Deborah, Golda and Me: Being Female and Jewish in America* (1991), she chronicled her 1980s reconnection with Jewish life: "I decided it was worth the effort to incorporate the nice Jewish girl I was raised to be into the uppity woman I had become." Pogrebin's high-profile status in the secular feminist movement made the book a powerful example of a Jewish commitment that embraced feminist/liberal social activism. She also wrote a second memoir, *Getting Over Getting Older* (1997), as well as a critically acclaimed first novel, *Three Daughters* (2002).

Pogrebin's essays and articles have appeared in diverse publications, including the *New York Times*, *Tikkun*, the *Nation*, and *Good Housekeeping*. She was a leader in the National

Women's Political Caucus, the Ms. Foundation for Women, the International Center for Peace in the Middle East, Americans for Peace Now, Mazon: A Jewish Response to Hunger, and the New Israel Fund. She spoke out against antisemitism in the women's movement (*Ms. Magazine*, June 1982) and decried the United Nations declaration that equated Zionism and racism.

BIBLIOGRAPHY: S. Weidman Schneider. "Letty Cottin Pogrebin," in: P.E. Hyman and D.D. Moore (ed.), *Jewish Women in America* (1997), vol. 2, 1087–89; "Pogrebin, Letty Cottin," in: *Current Biography Yearbook* (1997).

[Wendy Zierler (2nd ed.)]

POGREBISHCHENSKI (known as **Pogrebishche** up to 1945, referred to by the Jews as **Pohorbishch** and in Polish documents as **Bohybryszcze**), town in Vinnitsa district, Ukraine. Jews settled in Pogrebishchenski at the beginning of the 17th century, and it is listed among the communities destroyed during the *Chmielnicki massacres of 1648. The community, restored at the end of the 17th century, suffered severely from the uprisings of the *Haidamacks in 1736 and 1768. There were 664 Jews in Pogrebishchenski in 1765 and 1,726 in 1847; the census of 1897 showed 2,494 Jews (39.5 percent of the total population). The 17th-century wooden synagogue, whose construction and appurtenances were renowned for their original artistic execution, attracted the attention of researchers of Jewish art. During the years of the civil war (1918–21), a Jewish *self-defense group was maintained, which prevented bands of peasants of the region from attacking Jews. In the summer of 1919 troops of *Petlyura conquered the locality and ordered the self-defense group to be disarmed. A few days later (on Aug. 22, 1919) an armed band of peasants commanded by Zeleny entered and gained control of the town, carrying out a massacre of the Jews which lasted several hours. About 400 people were murdered, many were wounded, and property was looted. There were 2,881 Jews (30 percent of the total) in the town in 1926, dropping by 1939 to 1,445 (15% of the total population). Between the world wars there was a Yiddish school and a Jewish council. Most of the artisans in the two cooperatives were Jews and did not work on Saturdays. The Germans occupied the town on July 21, 1941. At the end of July 40 Jewish refugees were killed, and a ghetto was established. On October 18, 1941 more than 1,750 were murdered. The remaining artisans were killed later.

BIBLIOGRAPHY: Committee of Jewish Delegations, *The Pogroms in the Ukraine* (1927), 231–3; E. Tcherikower, *Di Ukrainer Pogromen in Yor 1919* (1965), 261–3.

[Yehuda Slutsky]

POGROMS. Pogrom is a Russian word designating an attack, accompanied by destruction, looting of property, murder, and rape, perpetrated by one section of the population against another. In modern Russian history pogroms have been perpetrated against other nations (Armenians, Tatars) or groups of inhabitants (intelligentsia). However, as an international term, the word "pogrom" is employed in many languages to describe specifically the attacks accompanied by looting and bloodshed against the Jews in Russia. The word designates more particularly the attacks carried out by the Christian population against the Jews between 1881 and 1921 while the civil and military authorities remained neutral and occasionally provided their secret or open support. The pogroms occurred during periods of severe political crisis in the country and were linked to social upheavals and nationalist incitement in Eastern Europe. (Similar events also occurred during that period, though on a more limited scale, in the context of the antisemitic movements in Germany, Austria, Romania, and the Balkan countries, and of nationalist and religious fanaticism in *Morocco, *Algeria, and *Persia.)

The Jews of Russia were the victims of three large-scale waves of pogroms, each of which surpassed the preceding in scope and savagery. These occurred between the years 1881 and 1884, 1903 and 1906, and 1917 and 1921. There were outbreaks in Poland after it regained independence in 1918, and in Romania from 1921.

In the 1880s

The pogroms of the 1880s took place during the period of confusion which prevailed in Russia after the assassination of Czar Alexander II by members of the revolutionary organization Narodnaya Volya on March 13, 1881. Anti-Jewish circles spread a rumor that the czar had been assassinated by Jews and that the government had authorized attacks on them. The pogroms at first also received the support of some revolutionary circles, who regarded this action as a preliminary awakening of the masses which would lead to the elimination of the existing regime. The first pogrom occurred in the town of Yelizavetgrad (*Kirovograd), in Ukraine, at the end of April 1881. From there, the pogrom wave spread to the surrounding villages and townlets – about 30 in number. At the beginning of May, the pogroms spread to the provinces of *Kherson, Taurida, Yekaterinoslav (*Dnepropetrovsk), *Kiev, *Poltava, and *Chernigov. The most severe attack was perpetrated in Kiev over three days before the eyes of the governor general and his staff of officials and police force while no attempt was made to restrain the rioters. The pogroms in *Odessa were of more limited scope. During the months of July and August there was again a series of pogroms in the provinces of Chernigov and Poltava. During this period, the pogroms were mainly restricted to the destruction and looting of property and beatings. The number of dead was small. The attackers came from among the rabble of the towns, the peasants, and the workers in industrial enterprises and the railroads. At the end of this period, the government forces reacted against the rioters and in several places even opened fire on them, leaving a number of dead and injured. The pogroms occurred in a restricted geographical region – southern and eastern Ukraine. Here there was a combination of aggravating circumstances: the traditional rebelliousness among the masses; a tradition of anti-Jewish hatred and persecutions from the 17th and 18th centuries (the massacres perpetrated by *Chmielnicki and the

*Haidamacks), together with the presence there of homeless seasonal workers in the factories, railways, and ports; the rise of a rural bourgeoisie and local intelligentsia, who regarded the Jews as most dangerous rivals; and an extremist revolutionary movement which was unscrupulous in the methods it adopted.

After the pogroms in the spring and summer of 1881, there was a remission, although occasional pogroms broke out in various parts of the country. Among these was a severe pogrom in *Warsaw on the Catholic Christmas Day and an Easter pogrom in *Balta, in which two Jews were killed and 120 injured, and many cases of rape occurred. In *Belorussia and *Lithuania, where the local authorities adopted a firm attitude against the rioters, large fires broke out in many towns and townlets; a considerable number of these were started by the enemies of the Jews. The murder of individual Jews and even whole families also became a common occurrence during this period. On June 21, 1882, the new minister of the interior, Count D. Tolstoy, published an order which placed the blame for the pogroms on the governors of the provinces and declared that "every attitude of negligence on the part of the administration and the police would entail the dismissal from their position of those who were guilty." Isolated pogroms nevertheless occurred during the following two years or so. In the spring of 1883, a sudden wave of pogroms broke out in the towns of *Rostov and Yekaterinoslav and their surroundings. On this occasion, the authorities reacted with vigor against the rioters and there were several casualties among them. The last great outburst occurred in June 1884 in Nizhni Novgorod (see *Gorki), where the mob attacked the Jews of the Kanavino quarter, killing nine of them and looting much property. The authorities tried over 70 of the rioters and severe penalties of imprisonment were imposed on them. This marked the end of the first wave of pogroms in Russia.

The pogroms of the 1880s greatly influenced the history of Russian Jewry. In their wake, the Russian government adopted a systematic policy of discrimination with the object of removing the Jews from their economic and public positions. This was achieved either by restrictive laws (the *May Laws of 1882, the percentage norm of admission (*numerus clausus) to secondary schools, higher institutions of learning, etc.) or by administrative pressure, which reached its climax with the expulsion of the Jews from *Moscow in 1891–92. A mass Jewish emigration began from Russia to the United States and other countries. One reaction to the pogroms was the birth of a nationalist and Zionist movement among the Jews of Russia, while many of the Jewish youth joined the revolutionary movement. The year 1881, the first year of the pogroms, was a turning point not only for Russian Jewry but also for the whole of the Jewish people.

1903 to 1906

The second wave of pogroms was connected with the revolutionary agitation in Russia and the first Russian revolution of 1905. In its struggle against the revolutionary movement, the Russian government gave the reactionary press a free hand to engage in unbridled anti-Jewish incitement in an attempt to divert the anger of the masses against it toward the Jews and to represent the revolutionary movement as the result of "Jewish machinations." Monarchist societies, such as the *Union of Russian People, the Double-Headed Eagle Society, and others, which were referred to by the general name of the Black Hundreds, played a prominent role in the organization of the pogroms. The first results of this incitement were pogroms which occurred in Kishinev during Passover 1903, in the wake of the wild agitation propagated by the antisemitic local newspaper *Bessarabets*, edited by P. *Krushevan. This pogrom was accompanied by savage murders (45 dead and hundreds of wounded) and mutilations of the wounded and dead. About 1,500 Jewish houses and shops were looted. The pogrom angered public opinion throughout the world. Subsequently, a *self-defense movement was organized among the Jewish youth. Its organizers were mainly drawn from the Zionist socialist parties and the *Bund. In a pogrom which broke out in *Gomel in September 1903, the self-defense group played a prominent part in saving Jewish lives and property. In the fall of 1904, a series of pogroms was perpetrated in *Smela, *Rovno, *Aleksandriya and other places by army recruits about to be sent to the war against Japan and by the local rabble. In 1905, when the revolutionary movement gained strength, reactionary circles, with the support of the government, intensified the anti-Jewish propaganda, and an atmosphere of terror reigned in many towns of the *Pale of Settlement and beyond it. Occasionally pogroms occurred in reaction to revolutionary demonstrations, which the opponents of the revolution condemned as Jewish demonstrations. In February 1905 a pogrom took place in *Feodosiya, and in April of the same year in *Melitopol. A pogrom which took place in the provincial capital of *Zhitomir surpassed all these in scope (May 1905). However, the severest pogroms of this period took place during the first week of November 1905, immediately after the publication of the manifesto of the czar (October 1905), which promised the inhabitants of Russia civic liberties and the establishment of a state *Duma (parliament). On publication of the manifesto, spontaneous manifestations of joy broke out throughout Russia. The celebrants came from the liberal and radical elements of Russian society, while the Jews, who hoped to obtain rapid *emancipation, prominently participated in this rejoicing. In response to these manifestations, the reactionary circles organized popular processions of elements loyal to the regime; these were headed by the local civil and ecclesiastical leaders. In many places these processions developed into pogroms against the Jews (on some occasions, the non-Jewish intelligentsia was also attacked).

The most serious pogrom occurred in Odessa (with over 300 dead and thousands of wounded); another severe pogrom took place in Yekaterinoslav, where 120 Jews lost their lives. Altogether, pogroms were perpetrated in 64 towns (including, in addition to Odessa and Yekaterinoslav, Kiev, Kishinev, *Simferopol, *Romny, *Kremenchug, *Nikolayev, Chernigov,

*Kamenets-Podolski, and Yelizavetgrad), and 626 townlets and villages. About 660 of the pogroms took place in the Ukraine and Bessarabia, 24 outside the Pale of Settlement, and only seven in Belorussia. There were no pogroms in Poland and Lithuania. The total number of dead in these pogroms was estimated at over 800. The pogroms lasted only a few days. The most prominent participants were railway workers, small shopkeepers and craftsmen, and industrial workers. The peasants mainly joined in to loot property.

From the outset, these pogroms were inspired by government circles. The local authorities received instructions to give the pogromists a free hand and to protect them from the Jewish self-defense. Commissions of inquiry were appointed after the pogroms which explicitly pointed out the criminal inactivity of the police and military forces. After a while, it became known that pamphlets calling for the pogroms had been printed on the press of the government secret police.

Two further pogroms occurred in 1906. The first took place in *Bialystok in June. About 80 Jews lost their lives and the mob looted and murdered under the protection of the military and police forces, who systematically opened fire on the Jews. This pogrom occurred during the session of the first Duma, which sent a commission of inquiry to Bialystok. It also held a debate, in which direct responsibility for the pogrom was placed on the authorities. The second took place in *Siedlce in August and was directly perpetrated by the police and military forces. About 30 Jews were killed and 180 wounded. With the suppression of the first Russian revolution, the pogroms were brought to a halt until the downfall of the old regime in 1917.

The pogroms of 1903–06 stimulated a great nationalist awakening among the Jews of Europe, encouraged the development of organized self-defense movements among Jews, and accelerated Jewish emigration for the Second *Aliyah and the formation of the *Hashomer society in Ereẓ Israel.

1917 to 1921

The third wave of pogroms occurred during the years 1917–21, in scope and gravity far surpassing the two previous outbreaks. These attacks on the Jews were connected with the revolutions and the civil war which took place in Eastern Europe during this period. At the end of 1917, pogroms had already occurred in the townlets and towns within proximity of the war front. The riot was headed by groups of soldiers from the disintegrating czarist army, and consisted of unruly acts against Jews by drunkards and of looting. Many pogroms of this type occurred in the Ukraine after the declaration of its independence in 1918. The first pogroms to be accompanied by slaughter of Jews were, however, perpetrated by units of the Red Army which retreated from the Ukraine in the spring of 1918 before the German army. These pogroms took place under the slogan "Strike at the bourgeoisie and the Jews." The communities of *Novgorod-Severski and Glukhov in northern Ukraine were the most severely affected. After a short period of confusion, the Soviets adopted stringent measures against pogromists found in the ranks of the Red Army. In addition to a fundamental and comprehensive information campaign, severe penalities were imposed not only on guilty individuals, who were executed, but also on complete army units, which were disbanded after their men had attacked Jews. Even though pogroms were still perpetrated after this, mainly by Ukrainian units of the Red Army at the time of its retreat from Poland (1920), in general, the Jews regarded the units of the Red Army as the only force which was able and willing to defend them.

In the spring of 1919, at the time of the retreat of the Ukrainian Army before the Red Army which occupied Kiev, units of the Ukrainian Army carried out organized military pogroms in *Berdichev, Zhitomir, and other towns. These pogroms reached their climax in the massacre at *Proskurov on Feb. 15, 1919, when 1,700 Jews were done to death within a few hours. On the following day, a further 600 victims fell in the neighboring townlet of Felshtin (Gvardeiskoye). Those responsible for these pogroms went unpunished, and henceforward the Ukrainian soldiers considered themselves free to spill Jewish blood. The Jews regarded Simon *Petlyura, the prime minister of the Ukraine and commander of its forces, as responsible for these pogroms (in 1926 he was assassinated while in exile in Paris by Shalom *Schwarzbard). The general chaos which reigned in the Ukraine in 1919 resulted in the formation of large and small bands of peasants who fought against the Red Army. The commanders (atamans) of these bands occasionally gained control of whole regions. The Jews in the villages, townlets, and towns there were constantly terrorized by the peasants, who extorted money ("contributions") and supplies from them or robbed and murdered them. These atamans included Angell, Kazakov, Kozyr-Zyrko, Struk, Volynets, Zeleny, Tutunik, and Shepel. The ataman Grigoryev, who in May 1919 seceded from the Red Army with his men, was responsible for pogroms in 40 communities and the deaths of about 6,000 Jews in the summer of 1919. He was killed by Ataman Makhno, who led a peasant rebellion in eastern Ukraine and endeavored to restrain his men from attacking the Jews. One of the most notorious pogroms carried out by the peasant bands was that in Trostyanets in May 1919, when over 400 people lost their lives.

In the fall of 1919, there was a wave of pogroms committed by the counterrevolutionary White Army, under the command of General A.I. *Denikin, in its advance from northern Caucasus into the heart of Russia. This army, which sought to restore the old regime, proclaimed the slogan: "Strike at the Jews and save Russia." Its officers and soldiers made savage attacks on the Jews in every place which they occupied. The most sinister of these pogroms was in Fastov at the beginning of September 1919, in which about 1,500 Jewish men, women, and children were massacred. The soldiers of the White Army also perpetrated similar pogroms in other regions of Russia: in Siberia, where they were led by Admiral Kolchak and where the Cossack battalions of Baron R. Ungern-Sternberg gained notoriety for the systematic destruction of many communities in eastern Siberia and Mongolia; and in Belorussia, where Bulak-Balachowicz was in command in 1920. During 1920–21, when the Red Army gained control of Ukraine, the armed anti-Soviet bands still retained their full strength and the pogroms and brutalities against the Jews assumed a character of revenge, such as the massacre in Tetiev, in which about 4,000 Jews were put to death and the whole townlet was set on fire. The anti-Jewish movement set the total annihilation of the Jews as its objective and destroyed whole townlets. Only the military weakness of the attackers prevented a holocaust of Ukrainian Jewry.

During this period of pogroms, Jewish self-defense organizations were formed in many places throughout the Ukraine. The "Jewish Militia for War against Pogroms" of Odessa was renowned; it prevented pogroms in the largest community of Ukraine. Such groups were created in many towns and townlets but they were not always capable of withstanding military units or large armed bands. It was only after the consolidation of the Soviet regime that they received its support and played an important role in the suppression of the armed counter-revolutionary movement.

It is difficult to assess the scope of the pogroms during the civil war years and the number of victims they claimed. Partial data are available for 530 communities in which 887 major pogroms and 349 minor pogroms occurred; there were 60,000 dead and several times that number of wounded (according to S. Dubnow). The pogroms of 1917–21 shocked East European Jewry, as well as world Jewry. On the one hand, they rallied many Jews to the Red Army and the Soviet regime; on the other, they strengthened the desire for the creation of a homeland for the Jewish people and a powerful and independent Jewish force. This aspiration found its expression in the Zionist movement, the *He-Ḥalutz movement, and the *Haganah in Ereẓ Israel.

BIBLIOGRAPHY: Zionist Organization, *Die Judenpogrome in Russland*, 2 vols. (1909); Dubnow, Hist Russ, 3 (1920), index; Yevreyskoye istoriko-etnograficheskoye obshchestvo, *Materialy dlya istorii anti-yevreyskikh pogromov v Rossii*, 2 vols. (1919–23); I. Halpern, *Sefer ha-Gevurah*, 2 (1944), 104–58; 3 (1951), 1–229; E. Heifetz, *The Slaughter of the Jews in the Ukraine in 1919* (1921); Committee of Jewish Delegations, *The Pogroms in the Ukraine* (1927); L. Khazanovich, *Der Idisher Khurbn in Ukraine* (1920); E. Tcherikower, *Anti-semitizm un Pogromen in Ukraine 1917–1918* (1923); idem, *Di Ukrainer Pogromen in Yor 1919* (1965); J. Schechtman, *Pogromy dobrovolcheskoy armii na Ukraine* (1932); N. Gergel, *Di Pogromen in Ukraine* (1928); A.D. Rosenthal, *Megillat ha-Tevaḥ*, 3 vols. (1927–31); A. Druyanow (ed.), *Reshumot*, 3 (1923); R. Feigenberg, *A Pinkas fun a Toyter Shtot* (1926); *Yevreyskiye pogromy 1918–1921 – album* (1926); *He-Avar*, 9 (1962), 3–81; 10 (1963), 5–149; 17 (1970), 3–136.

[Yehuda Slutsky]

°POHL, OSWALD (1896–1951), *SS officer, formerly a naval paymaster head of the Wirtschafts-Verwaltungshauptamt (Economic-Administrative Main Office, WVHA). He joined the Nazi Party in 1926 and the SS in 1934. In 1934 he became head of the administrative office of the SS which dealt with all its financial and administrative matters. In 1939 he was appointed head of the construction office of the SS, including the concentration camps. His task was to develop the economic enterprises of the SS, which were essential to their operation. On Feb. 1, 1942, the officers under his charge were brought into the WVHA. In the spring of 1942 the Inspection Authority of the concentration camps was added to his responsibilities. Pohl aimed at financing all SS activities, including the Waffen SS, from the profits of SS-owned enterprises for which he utilized the slave labor of concentration camp prisoners and expropriated Jewish property. He had more than half a million slave laborers at his disposal which he could rent to industry as workers. Another source of income was gained from the belongings of murdered Jews, including their gold teeth. Pohl always urged longer working hours, less rest, and stricter supervision over the camp inmates. He enslaved prisoners of war contrary to international conventions. Since his concern was labor and since he was pressed for manpower, he even opposed the *RSHA policy for the total destruction of the Jews and advocated sparing able-bodied Jews from immediate death, so that they could be worked to death. This bought them a little time and enabled some to survive. Pohl was sentenced to death by the U.S. Military Tribunal in 1947 and hanged in Landsberg in 1951.

BIBLIOGRAPHY: IMT, Trial of the Major War Criminals (1949), index; *Trial of the War Criminals before the Nuremberg Military Tribunals*, 5. (1950), Case 4, against Pohl et al.; R. Hilberg, *Destruction of the European Jews* (1961), index; R.M.W. Kempner, *SS im Kreuzverhoer* (1964), 130–46; G. Reitlinger, *Final Solution* (1968^2), index.

[Yehuda Reshef / Michael Berenbaum (2nd ed.)]

POHORELICE (Czech **Pohořelice**; Ger. **Pohrlitz**), village in S. Moravia, Czech Republic. It had one of the most ancient Jewish communities in Moravia, and according to legend, the oldest. Although the earliest known documentary evidence for the existence of a Jewish settlement in Pohorelice dates from 1490, a Jewish community apparently already existed there at the beginning of the tenth century. At the close of the 18th century about 500 Jews lived in Pohorelice. From 1849 (officially from 1862) until the dissolution of the Austrian Empire in 1918, a local Jewish political authority also existed. From 1847 to 1918 the community supported a Jewish elementary school whose language of instruction was German. In 1930 the community numbered 277. The majority perished in the Holocaust. A transit camp for Jewish prisoners from Hungary existed in the town in 1944–45 from where they were sent to Theresienstadt and Bergen-Belsen. A synagogue built in 1854–55 was demolished by the Nazis. The cemetery was likewise destroyed; however, after the war it was restored. The Jewish community was not renewed. Berthold *Feiwel was born in Pohorelice.

BIBLIOGRAPHY: T. Haas, *Die Juden in Maehren* (1908); H. Gold (ed.), *Die Juden und Judengemeinden Maehrens* (1929), index. **ADD. BIBLIOGRAPHY:** J. Fiedler, *Jewish Sights of Bohemia and Moravia* (1991), 136–37.

[Chaim Yahil / Yeshayahu Jelinek (2nd ed.)]

POISON (Heb. חֵמָה, לַעֲבָה, מְרֵרָה, רֹאשׁ [רוֹשׁ], רַעַל, תַּרְעֵלָה; Akk. *imtu, martu*; Ug. *ḥmt*). The biblical terms for poison are derived mainly from two sources: types of poisonous plants and the poisonous venom of snakes and other reptiles. Many attempts have been made to identify the specific plants involved based on the translations of these terms in the Septuagint and the other ancient versions, but any conclusions based on this evidence must be considered extremely uncertain. The Bible itself offers no evidence whatsoever, since its usage of these terms is generally metaphorical, offering no identifying characteristics. Therefore, when discussing these various terms, this article will deal with the biblical usage and its ancient Near Eastern parallels rather than attempting to arrive at specific identifications.

La'anah, Rosh

The terms *rosh* ("gall") and *la'anah* ("wormwood") are often found in synonymous parallelism (Jer. 9: 14; 23:15; Amos 6:12) or in hendiadys (Deut. 29:17; Lam. 3:19). They are most often used metaphorically to represent the concepts of poison and bitterness. As her punishment for disobeying the Lord, Israel is forced to consume bitter food and drink (Jer. 8:14; 9:14; 23:15; Lam. 3:15), while a psalmist contends that his enemies are giving him such a hard time that he feels that he is being given bitter food (Ps. 69:22). Another common theme for which these terms are employed is the turning of justice into bitterness (Hos. 10:4; Amos 5:7; 6:12). The especially general nature of the term *rosh*, "gall," in the bible may be demonstrated by its usage in contexts referring to snake venom (Deut. 32:33; Job 20:16) and grapes (Deut. 32:32).

Ḥemah

The biblical term most commonly employed for the venom of snakes and other reptiles is *ḥemah*. In the Song of Moses, the calamity which befalls Israel as a result of God's judgment takes the metaphorical form of *ḥamat zoḥalei 'afar*, "the venom of snakes" (Deut. 32:24; for the meaning of *zoḥalei 'afar* cf. Micah 7:17), while later in the same chapter, *rosh* and *ḥemah*, which are parallels, are again used metaphorically: "the venom (*ḥamat*) of serpents is their wine, and the poison (*rosh*) of vipers ..." (Deut. 32:33). Elsewhere *ḥemah* is used for snake poison in Psalm 58:5 and for the venom of an unknown reptile (*'akhshuv*) in Psalm 140:4.

Both Akkadian (*imtu*) and Ugaritic (*ḥmt*) utilize an etymological and semantic equivalent of חמה as one of their regular words for "poison." The usage of Akkadian *imtu* is very close to the usage of biblical *ḥemah*. The following two passages illustrate the usage of *imtu* as "snake venom":

> 1. *azzūzâ izarri imta ana sursurru*
> *izarri imta*
> *imat ṣēri imassu*
> *imat zuqaqīpi imassu*
>
> She [Lamaštu] spits venom now and then,
> she spits venom suddenly,
> her venom is snake venom,
> her venom is scorpion venom (A. Falkenstein, *Literarische Keilschrifttexte aus Uruk* (1931), 33:21ff.).
>
> 2. *patûni šapti šinnašunu našâ imta*
> [Their] lips are open, their fangs carry venom (*Enūma eliš*, 4:53; Ps. 140:4).

Two Ugaritic texts (*Ugaritica*, 5 (1969), nos. 7, 8), which appear to be "serpent charms" contain, for the first time in Ugaritic, the substantive *ḥmt*, "poison, snake venom." This substantive is found more than 25 times in these two texts whose provenance has already been compared to such biblical passages as Jeremiah 8:17; Psalms 58:5; and Ecclesiastes 10:11. In the first of these two texts, an incantation formula consisting of six lines is repeated 11 times, each time invoking a different deity. While the translation of all the lines of this incantation is far from certain, the lines containing the noun *ḥmt*, while not without their difficulties, are relatively clear:

> *lnh mlhs/a'bd*
> *lnh ydy hmt*
>
> From him [the serpent], the conjurer shall destroy,
> from him, he shall remove the venom (*Ugaritica*, 5 (1969), 7: 5–6, 10–11, 16–17, 21–22, 27–28, 32–33, 37–38, 42–43, 47–48, 53–54, 59–60).

There are many biblical passages (e.g., Isa. 51:17, 22; Jer. 25:15; Job 21:20) where the substantive *ḥemah* is employed to evoke a double entendre based on its most regular meaning of "wrath" (e.g., Gen. 27:44–45; Deut. 29:22, 27; Isa. 63:3, 6; Jer. 21:5; *a'f*, "anger") and its less common denotation of "poison, venom" (see above). This usage is further demonstrated by the occurrence of such idioms as the "pouring out of God's wrath/poison" (e.g., Isa. 42:25; Jer. 10:25; Ezek. 7:8; Ps. 79:6) and "full of God's poison/wrath" (e.g., Isa. 51:20; Jer. 6:11). While there are no Akkadian passages where *imtu* could be translated "wrath," *The Assyrian Dictionary of the Oriental Institute of the University of Chicago* (7 (1960), 139) defines *imtu* in one of its meanings as "poisonous foam, slaver produced from the mouth of angry gods, demons, humans, and animals." (For a full discussion of the semantic range of words for "anger, wrath" in Semitic languages, see H. Cohen, in bibl.)

Mererah

The substantive *mererah* ("poison, venom, gall") is obviously connected with the root *mrr*, "to be bitter," and is generally used in the same way as *ḥemah* (see above). This is demonstrated by the Akkadian lexical equation *imtum* = *martum* (*malku* = *šarru*, 8:124; where *martum* is the Akkadian etymological and semantic equivalent of Hebrew *mererah*) as well as by the following biblical passages:

> Their grapes are grapes of poison (*rosh*); Their clusters are venomous (*merorot*) (Deut. 32:32; cf. Deut. 32:33 quoted above); The venom serpents (*merorat petanim*) is within him (Job 20:40; cf. all examples for *ḥemah*, "snake venom" quoted above); He pours out my gall (*mererati*) upon the ground (Job 16:13; cf. the idiom לשפך חמת יהוה quoted above); He has filled me with poison (*merorim*), sated me with wormwood (*la'anah*) (Lam.

3:15; cf. the idiom "the pouring out of God's wrath/poison" quoted above).

The Akkadian substantive *martu*, "gall," is used in the same way as *imtu*, *ḥemah*, and *mererah*, as may be seen from the following proverb which is somewhat parallel to Deuteronomy 32:32 (see above):

ina nāri tabbaššima mūka daddaru
appūnāma ina kirî tabšîma suluppaka martum

When you are in \a canal, the water around you is foul-smelling;
Furthermore, when you are in a palm grove, your dates are gall (W.G. Lambert, *Babylonian Wisdom Literature* (1959), p. 244, lines 19–24).

Thus, the biblical *ḥemah* (in its meaning of "poison, venom") and *mererah* must be considered poetic synonyms like the Akkadian *imtu* and *martu*.

Raʿal, Tarʿelah

The exact meaning of *raʿal* and *tarʿelah* is unknown. That it must refer to some kind of poison is clear from Isaiah 51:17, 22, where *tarʿelah* parallels *ḥemah*. The occurrence with *yayin* ("wine") in Psalm 60:5 *(yayin tarʿelah)* also fits in well with the usage of *ḥemah* and *mererah* as stated above. The other few passages (Isa. 3:19; Nah. 2:4; Hab. 2:16 [read והרעל, as in 1Qp-Hab]; Zech. 12:2) in which this substantive or its denominative verb occurs are far from clear, however, and offer nothing in the way of identification. What is clear from the little evidence is that the biblical *raʿal* cannot be derived from Aramaic *rʿl* ("to reel, tremble") because its usage is identical with that of two known biblical words for poison, *ḥemah* and *mererah*. While the etymology of the Modern Hebrew *raʿal* ("poison") is unclear (*raʿal* "poison" is almost nonexistent in the Talmud and Midrash), because its usage in modern Hebrew appears consistent with biblical usage, it is more likely that it is derived from the biblical term than from the Aramaic *rʿl*.

BIBLIOGRAPHY: Loew, Flora, passim; N.H. Tur-Sinai, *The Book of Job* (1957), 114–7; R.H. Harrison, *Healing Herbs of the Bible* (1966); A.L. Oppenheim, et al. (eds.), *The Assyrian Dictionary of the Oriental Institute of the University of Chicago*, 7 (1960), 139–41; W.G. Lambert, *Babylonian Wisdom Literature* (1960); M.C. Astour, in: JNES, 27 (1968), 13–36; C. Cohen, in: *Journal of the Ancient Near Eastern Society of Columbia University*, 2 (1969), 25–29.

[Chayim Cohen]

POITIERS, capital of Vienne department, W. France. The history of the Jewish community of Poitiers is almost entirely interwoven with that of *Poitou. During the 13th century, Nathan b. Joseph *Official was involved in a religious disputation with the bishop of Poitiers. An expulsion order against the Jews of Poitiers had already been issued in 1291 but it was canceled in exchange for a large sum of money. The community ceased to exist in 1306. The Rue de la Juiverie, the modern Rue Arsène-Orillard, was closed off by ogival gates which still existed during the 19th century. The cemetery was situated in the present suburb of Montbernage. According to local tradition, treasures buried by the Jews lay hidden there. On the eve of World War II, there were a few hundred Jews in Poitiers. Their numbers increased with the arrival of Jewish refugees from Alsace and Lorraine and later with the internees detained in several camps within the vicinity of the town. In 1970 the community consisted of about 100 persons.

BIBLIOGRAPHY: Gross, Gal Jud, 452f.; *Intermédiaire des chercheurs et curieux*, 39 (1899), 20; 40 (1899), 1104; J. Guerinière, *Essai sur l'ancien Poitou*, 1 (1836), 491; R. Brothier de Rolliere, *Poitiers – Histoire des rues* (1930), 293; Z. Szajkowski, *Analytical Franco-Jewish Gazetteer* (1966), 284.

[Bernhard Blumenkranz]

POITOU, region and former province of W. France, now included in the departments of Vendée, Deux-Sèvres, and Vienne. In the Middle Ages Jews lived in at least 20 localities in Poitou, the most important of which were *Poitiers, Niort, Vitré, Moncontour, Loudun, Bressuire, Lusignan, Montmorillon, and Thouars. Their presence is also recalled by a large number of sites named La Juderie, La Judrie, Les Judes, etc. The earliest evidence of Jewish settlement in Poitou dates from 1134 to 1143, with arrivals from Narbonne. After 1160 Jewish scholars from Poitou took part in the synod of Troyes convened by *Samuel b. Meir and Jacob b. Meir *Tam. One *takkanah* with which the scholars of Poitou were also associated referred to the custom of Narbonne Jewry connected with the dowry. When Poitou passed to English rule, the kings of England provided both individuals and groups of Jews (Niort, 1221) with letters of protection. Under French rule (1224) the Jews of Poitou (like those of Anjou, etc.) were attacked by the *Crusaders in 1236. Soon after he received Poitou in appanage, *Alphonse of Poitiers threatened the Jews with expulsion, but this was not carried out. In 1268, in order to finance his joining a Crusade, Alphonse had all the Jews of Poitou, as well as all those in his other territories, imprisoned and their belongings seized, extorting a ransom of 8,000 livres for their release. In 1269, following the example of *Louis IX, he imposed the wearing of the distinctive Jewish *badge. Although Poitou was incorporated into the kingdom of France in 1270, the Jews there were subjected to special decrees and were finally expelled in 1291, 15 years before their coreligionists in other parts of France. A few of them who returned in 1315 were among the first to be accused (1321) of collusion with the lepers (see *France). An even smaller number of Jews returned after 1359 (or more exactly after 1372 when Poitou was liberated by the English). Some Jews from Comtat Venaissin traded in Poitou during the 18th century.

BIBLIOGRAPHY: Gross, Gal Jud, 451; Finkelstein, Middle Ages, index; Dr. Vincent, in: *Revue d'histoire économique et sociale*, 18 (1930), 265–313; G. Nahon, in: REJ, 125 (1966), 167–211.

[Bernhard Blumenkranz]

POKI, JUDAH BEN ELIEZER CHELEBI (16th century), *Karaite scholar of Constantinople, a nephew of Elijah *Bashyazi. He traveled widely in order to study Karaite writings. In 1571 he was living at the house of the Karaite *nasi* in Cairo. In his *Sha'ar Yehudah*, on forbidden marriages (published by his son Isaac in Constantinople, 1581), he opposed the modifications introduced in this subject by Joseph ha-Ro'eh and Jeshua b. Judah. Poki is the only Karaite scholar of the period to uphold the *rikkuv* ("catenary") theory of forbidden marriages. He mentions also a second work, *Ve-Zot li-Yhudah*, on the determination of the new moon. Jedidiah Solomon of Troki refers in his *Appiryon* to a prayer book compiled by Poki, as well as works on poetry and grammar.

BIBLIOGRAPHY: A. Neubauer, *Aus der Petersburger Bibliothek* (1866), 65; I.D.B. Markon, *Texte und Untersuchungen* (1908), xvii.

[Isaak Dov Ber Markon]

POLACCO, VITTORIO (1859–1926), Italian jurist. Born in Padua, Polacco was professor of civil law at the University of Padua from 1885 to 1918 and at the University of Rome from 1918 until his death. He was renowned as a jurist and was invited to teach law and the history of religions to Prince Umberto of Savoy. Polacco was a member of the Italian Senate from 1910 and played an important part in the drafting of the Senate's legislation. He kept aloof from politics and aroused great interest when, in 1925, he delivered the only political speech he ever made in parliament, his subject being freedom of conscience and the protection of religious minorities. He wrote a number of legal works, including *Le Obbligazioni nel Diritto Civile Italiano* (1898); and *Delle Successioni* (2 vols., 1902), both of which ran into many editions, and *Contro il divorzio* (2 vols., 1892) in which he set out his opposition to divorce. Rome's Jewish elementary school was named after him.

[Giorgio Romano]

POLÁČEK, KAREL (1892–1945), Czech writer and journalist, a participant in the "Friday Visitors" literary gatherings of Karel Čapek and probably the outstanding Czech humorist after Hašek. Born in Rychnov nad Kněžnou, Bohemia, he began his career as a reporter in the law courts, where he gained insight into the ordinary people about whom he wrote in his short stories and novels. In these Poláček introduced many Jewish characters, mainly traders, salesmen, and commercial travelers, recording their way of life and mode of speech with accuracy and understanding. A number of these novels and stories became screen and TV successes. Poláček's first novel was *Dům na předměstí* ("The House on the Outskirts," 1928). One of his major works was the quintet *Okresní město* ("District Town," 1936), *Hrdinové táhnou do boje* ("Heroes Go into Battle," 1936), *Podzemní město* ("Underground Town," 1937), and *Vyprodáno* ("Sold Out," 1939); the fifth volume was completed but is known only in fragments. The work presents the panorama of a small Czech township. His volumes of short stories include *Povídky pana Kočkodana* ("Mr. Kočkodan's Tales," 1922), *Mariáš a jiné živnosti* ("Cardplaying and Other Professions," 1924), *Povídky izraelského vyznání* ("Stories of the Mosaic Persuasion," 1926), and *Život ve filmu* ("Life in the Movies," 1927). Two humorous novels are *Muži v offsidu* ("Men at Offside," 1931) and *Michelup a motocykl* ("Michelup and the Motorbike," 1935). His last novel had to be published under the name of a painter, Vlastimil Rada: *Hostinec u kamenného stolu* ("The Restaurant at the Stone Table," 1941). Other books were published after 1945, like the novel *Bylo nás pět* ("We Were Five," 1964). Poláček wrote two comedies, one of which, *Pásky na vousy* ("The Beard-binders," 1926), was produced by the Prague National Theater. During the Nazi occupation, Poláček was deported, first to Theresienstadt, later to Auschwitz. He probably died on his way to the Dora concentration camp in the winter of 1945. Poláček's *Sebrané spisy* ("Collected Works") were published in 1994–2002 in Prague in 22 volumes.

BIBLIOGRAPHY: O. Donath, *Židé a židovství v české literatuře* (1930); J. Kunc, *Slovník českých spisovatelů beletristů* (1957); Frýd, in: Terezín (1965), 206–18 (publ. by the Council of Jewish Communities in the Czech Lands). **ADD. BIBLIOGRAPHY:** *Českožidovští spisovatelé v literatuře 20. století* (2000); J. Firt, *Knihy a osudy* (1972); M. Jelimowicz, *Karel Poláček's Last Letter to Dora* (1984); J. Jelimowiczová, *Můj otec Karel Poláček* (2001); A. Mikulášek et al., *Literatura s hvězdou Davidovou*, vol. 1 (1998); T. Pěkný, "Karel Poláček (1872–1944?)," in: *Review of the Society for the History of Czechoslovak Jews*, vol. 5 (1992–93); T. Pěkný, "Karel Poláček," in: *Židovská ročenka* (1991–92); *Slovník českých spisovatelů* (2000); H. Svobodová, *Karel Poláček nezemřel* (2000); J. Škvorecký, *Karel Poláček* (1967).

[Avigdor Dagan / Milos Pojar (2nd ed.)]

POLACHEK, SENDER (also known as **Sender Minsker**; 1786–1869), Polish cantor. Born in Gombin, Polachek received instruction from Cantor Nahum Leib Weintraub, brother of Solomon *Weintraub. For over 30 years Polachek was cantor in Minsk (hence his additional name) and became famous for his melodic gifts. Having no knowledge of musical notation, he committed none of his works to writing, but he achieved an original style which deeply affected his hearers and which became known as the "Sender Steiger."

POLACHEK, SOLOMON (1877–1928), talmudic scholar and teacher. Polachek was early recognized as a precocious youngster and became widely known as the *illui* ("prodigy") of Meitshet where he studied. He entered the Volozhin yeshivah at the unusually early age of 12 and his bar-mitzvah was celebrated at the home of the head of the yeshivah, Naphtali Ẓevi Judah *Berlin. After the yeshivah was closed by the czarist government in 1892, Polachek studied with Ḥayyim *Soloveitchik in Brest-Litovsk and became "R. Ḥayyim's" most beloved pupil. Polachek also studied in the Slobodka yeshivah and at the "kibbutz" of Ḥayyim Ozer *Grodzenski in Vilna. Polachek mastered secular studies and modern Hebrew on his own and acquainted himself with the literature and problems of his time. In 1905, I.J. *Reines appointed him head of the Talmud department in the newly organized Lida yeshivah where the curriculum also included secular studies. After Reines' death in 1915 the entire burden of the yeshivah fell on Polachek. Shortly afterward, as a result of World War I, Polachek and the yeshivah were compelled to move to central Russia, where the school continued for five more years. During the war Polachek lost the notes he had amassed on over 1,500 different talmudic topics. After the war and the Bolshevik revolution, Polachek succeeded in escaping to Poland, where he became head of the Talmud department of the Taḥkemoni Rabbinical Seminary in Bialystok. In 1922 Polachek emigrated to America and accepted the position of senior *rosh yeshivah* in the Rabbi Isaac Elchanan Theological Seminary (the forerunner of *Yeshiva University). He was enthusiastically received by American Orthodoxy since he was the first renowned European talmudist who agreed to remain in the U.S. for the purpose of teaching Talmud in an advanced yeshivah. While in the U.S., he was a member of the *Union of Orthodox Rabbis and was active in the *Mizrachi movement. Polachek's *Ḥiddushei ha-Illui me-Meitshet* was published posthumouly in 1947.

BIBLIOGRAPHY: A. Rothkoff, in: *Jewish Life*, Nov.–Dec. 1967, 29–35; O. Feuchtwanger, *Righteous Lives* (1965), 119–21; O.Z. Rand (ed.), *Toledot Anshei Shem* (1950), 94; *Yahadut Lita*, 1 (1960), index s.v., 3 (1967), 75f.

[Aaron Rothkoff]

POLACHEK, VICTOR HENRY (1876–1940), U.S. editor and publisher. An executive with the Hearst newspaper chain for 40 years, Polachek began as a reporter in his native Chicago in 1893. He was appointed telegraph editor of the *Chicago Inter-Ocean* in 1897 and went to the *New York World* in 1898. He joined the Hearst organization in 1899, served on various papers of the chain in Chicago and New York, and in 1928 became manager of the Hearst Sunday newspapers. In 1931 he was given charge of circulation for all Hearst papers.

POLACK, JOEL SAMUEL (1807–1882), adventurer and author. Born in London, he was the son of the artist Solomon Polack (1757–1839). Before his arrival at Hokianga, New Zealand, in 1831, he had been an artist, Californian gold miner, South African ordinance officer, and Australian ship's chandler. His dominant personality enabled him to survive among the rough whalers and semi-cannibalistic Maoris of Hokianga and Kororareka, where he opened a store in 1833. He learned to speak Maori fluently, and won the confidence of the Maoris. In 1838 his Kororareka store containing military and naval explosives blew up and he returned temporarily to London. There he urged the colonization of New Zealand in evidence before a select committee of the House of Lords. *The Times* attacked Polack's New Zealand dealings, describing him as "a worthy and wandering offshoot of the seed of Abraham." Suing *The Times* for libel, he was awarded £100 damages. In 1838 Polack wrote *New Zealand*, being a narrative of travels and adventures in that country between 1831 and 1937, and *Manners and Customs of New Zealanders* in 1840. Both books, especially the second which is profusely illustrated by Polack himself, are valuable documentaries of New Zealand's precolonization history. Polack returned to New Zealand after the proclamation of British sovereignty in 1840, but soon left for the Californian goldfields. He died in San Francisco.

BIBLIOGRAPHY: *Journal and Proceedings of the Australian Jewish Historical Society*, 3 (1949–53), 142–51; Rubens, in: JHSET, 14 (1940), 108–12. **ADD. BIBLIOGRAPHY:** ODNB online; J. Chisholm, "Joel Samuel Polack," in: *Dictionary of New Zealand Biography.*

[Maurice S. Pitt]

POLAK, GABRIEL ISAAC (1803–1869), Dutch scholar, Hebrew author, and bibliographer. Born in Amsterdam, Polak served as head of a school there. He provided Dutch Jewry with accurate liturgical texts translated into Dutch.

Among these were a Pentateuch with *haftarot* and Rashi (1828; his *le'azim* translated into German), Sabbath prayers (1828), and *piyyutim* (*Torat Emet-Tikkun Soferim*, 1827, repr. 1937); *Amarot Tehorot* (biblical books with Dutch translation, 1862/63; also Job, with M.S. Polak, 1844); a *maḥzor* (1857^2), with commentary in Hebrew and Judeo-German and another edition with Dutch translation (with M.L. van Ameringen, 1850^2); *Areshet Sefatayim* (1960^{23}), a *siddur*; a Passover *Haggadah* (1930^9); *Ezrat ha-Sofer* (1866), a *tikkun*; and *Sefer Ḥayyim la-Nefesh* (1867). He also edited orders of service for Purim (1857), circumcision (1878), and the seventh of Adar (death of Moses; 1851), *Kinot* (1868), and *Seliḥot* (1869). Polak published a small Hebrew-Dutch dictionary, *Divrei Kodesh*, with S.E. Heigmans, in 1857^2. Among his other works were *Ḥukkei Ha-Elohim* (1841, 1883), on the 613 commandments; a translation with commentary of *Josippon (1868, with van Ameringen); an edition of a manuscript he discovered of Judah ibn Balam's *Sha'ar Ta'amei Sefarim Emet* on the accents of Psalms, Proverbs, and Job (1858); and an enlarged edition of Abraham Bedersi's (Bedarshi's) dictionary of Hebrew synonyms (1865). Polak completed H.A. Wagenaar's biography of Jacob Emden (1868), and annotated Menahem Mann b. Solomon's *She'erit Yisrael* (with L. Goudsmit, 1855), with notes on the history of Dutch Jewry. He also wrote Hebrew poetry and translated Dutch works into Hebrew (*Ha-Poret*, 1836; *Halikhot Kedem*, 1847; *Ben Gorni*, 1851). In addition, he wrote a biography of the Dutch Hebrew poet D. Franco-Mendes and published letters and essays by S. *Dubno, J.S. Reggio, S.L. Rapoport, and S.D. Luzzatto, maintaining contact with some of them. Among his bibliographical work is *Me'ir Einayim* (1864), a catalog of the M.L. Jacobson and M.B. Rubens collections in Amsterdam *Ḥok Shelomo* (1857), and catalogs of S.B. Rubens' collections in Amsterdam (1864).

BIBLIOGRAPHY: J.H. Gurland, in: *Ha-Maggid*, 12 (1869), no. 22, 175; no. 23, 181–2.

[Jacob H. Copenhagen]

POLAK, HENRI (1868–1943), Dutch trade unionist and socialist politician. Born in Amsterdam, he was the eldest of Mozes Polak and Marianna Smit's ten children. His father started out as a diamond polisher and became a rather prosperous jewelry manufacturer; his mother, daughter of a much respected antiquarian bookseller, developed a keen interest in Western literature. After a stay of three years in London, where he worked as a diamond cutter, Henri Polak settled in Amsterdam in 1890 with his London-born wife, Emily Nijkerk. As one of the first Jewish members of the small revolutionary socialist party, and as a diamond cutter, he tried for four years, with some success, to propagate socialism and trade unionism among the then 8,000 Amsterdam diamond workers (about 60% of whom were Jewish). In 1894, he was one of the 12 founders of the Dutch Social Democratic Party (SDAP) and after a general diamond workers strike became founder and president of the General Dutch Diamond workers Union (ANDB). Under his clever and enthusiastic guidance, the ANDB grew within a few years into the best-organized and most successful modern trade union of the Netherlands. Polak's prestige as a union leader resulted in the SDAP's electing him president during 1900–05. In 1905, Polak became founder and president of the World Alliance of Diamond workers. He retained both this presidency and that of the ANDB until the German occupation of Holland in 1940.

For a man like Henri Polak, socialist trade unionism meant not only striving for better tangible living conditions for the workers, but also improving the quality of life of the working classes by teaching them to take part in all kinds of social and cultural activities. In this respect he was a student of the English socialist artist William Morris, for whom he had great admiration. In the 1920s and 1930s Polak became, partly under Morris' influence, one of Holland's staunchest defenders of historical and natural monuments. Most Jewish workers viewed Polak as a cherished member of the family, as well as a leader of great ability and moral standing.

Although he never believed in the possibility of a Jewish state, after the World War I Polak became a member of the board of the Dutch chapter of the *Keren Hayesod. He considered the founding of a Jewish National Home (not a state) only a partial solution to the problem of the persecution of the Jews. From 1933 until the war Polak launched, both in his weekly column in the socialist daily *Het Volk* ("The People") and as a member of the Dutch Senate, unabatingly fierce attacks on the Nazis in Germany and Holland. As one of the few anti-fascist leaders, he took Julius *Streicher's threat to kill all the Jews seriously.

After half a year of imprisonment in 1940, Polak was put under house arrest until July 1942 in the home of a Dutch Nazi, who made his life as miserable as possible. At the start of the deportations of the Jews from Holland, Polak was unexpectedly set free. Although mentally unbroken, his physical health had deteriorated considerably. He died of pneumonia in the hospital at Laren in February 1943, just in time not to be deported. Emily died about two months later in Westerbork. Both were buried in the Jewish cemetery of Muiderberg.

BIBLIOGRAPHY: S. Bloemgarten, in: J. Michman and T. Levie (eds.), *Dutch Jewish History* (1984), 261–78; idem, in: A. Blok et al. (eds.), *Generations in Labour History* (1989); idem, *Henri Polak sociaal democraat 1868–1945* (1993), with English summary and extensive bibliography.

[Salvador Bloemgarten and Ruben Bloemgarten (2nd ed.)]

POLAK, JACOB EDUARD (1820–1891), physician and writer. Born in Bohemia, he studied medicine and science in Prague and Vienna and in 1851 was invited to Teheran by the Persian government to serve as professor of anatomy and surgery at the military college. In 1856 he was appointed court physician to Shah Nasr-el-Din. Polak returned to Vienna in 1860 and was associated with the general hospital there while acting as lecturer in Persian at the University of Vienna. When Nasr-el-Din toured Europe in 1872 he visited Polak, who is mentioned in the shah's "Diary" as his "good old friend." Polak wrote a number of important treatises in Persian on anatomy, surgery, ophthalmology, and military medicine, some of which became standard works. He also compiled a medical dictionary in Persian, Arabic, and Latin in order to provide the Persian language with a system of medical terminology, and composed a much-used dictionary, *Deutsch-persiches Konversationswoerterbuch* (1914).

A faithful and devoted Jew, Polak used his prestige and influence at the court of the shah in favor of his coreligionists. He drew the attention of European Jewry to the plight of the Jews in Persia at the time and proposed that the Alliance Israélite Universelle should send a Jewish representative to Teheran or establish a Jewish school there, as was ultimately done. Polak wrote extensively on various aspects of Jewish life in Persia; *Persien, das Land und seine Bewohner* (1865) and other publications contain important information about the Jews.

BIBLIOGRAPHY: P. Goldberg, *Dr. J.E. Polak: eine biographische Skizze* (1856); Fischel, in: JSOS, 12 (1950), 119–60.

[Walter Joseph Fischel]

POLAK, LEONARD (1880–1941), Dutch philosopher. Born in Steenwijk, Polak graduated in law, in 1925 became assistant professor at the University of Leiden, and in 1929 was appointed to the chair in philosophy at the University of Groningen. A rationalist and agnostic, Polak played an important part in the free-thought movement in the Netherlands. He followed the Marburg neo-Kantian school of philosophy holding that mechanical causality reigns in nature while freedom reigns in the realm of the spirit.

Polak wrote on important social questions such as the philosophy of war, the philosophy of punishment, sexual ethics, and religious divisions. His principal works include *Kennisleer contra materie-realisme* (1912); *De zin der vergelding* (1921); *Hegel's leer der straf* (1925); and *Noodlot en vrije wil* (1937). After World War II, Polak's works were collected in *Verzamelde werken* (4 vols, 1947).

BIBLIOGRAPHY: P. Spigt, *Leo Polak, een erflater van onze beschaving* (1946); L. van der Wal, *Herdenking van Leo Polak* (1946); F. Sassen, *Wijsgerig leven in Nederland in de twintigste eeuw* (1948^2).

[Richard H. Popkin]

POLAND, republic in E. Central Europe; the kingdom of Poland and the grand duchy of Lithuania united formally (Poland-Lithuania) in 1569. This article is arranged according to the following outline:

THE EARLY SETTLEMENTS

While Jews had visited the kingdom of Poland and been economically active there at an early stage of the country's consolidation, from the tenth century approximately, they had no contact with the grand duchy of Lithuania until King Gedimin conquered the regions of Volhynia and Galicia (as it was later called) in 1321.

Jews came to Poland mainly from the west and southwest and from the very beginning were of *Ashkenazi culture. Those in the regions conquered by Gedimin had come there from the south and the southeast, chiefly from *Kiev, and were thus influenced to a large degree by Byzantine Jewish culture patterns; some think that they could have had traces of *Khazar ethnic descent and culture patterns. Jews in the region of *Lvov and its environs were of the same provenance to a large extent. In the end the western Ashkenazi culture became dominant.

Polish-Jewish legendary tradition tells about a Jewish merchant, Abraham Prochownik (unlikely to mean "the gunpowder man," which would be completely anachronistic, but probably, "the dust-covered," an epithet found in the early Middle Ages in relation to merchants), who was offered the Polish crown around the middle of the ninth century, before Piast, the first, legendary, Polish king, ascended to the throne. According to another legend, at the end of the ninth century a Jewish delegation in Germany appealed to Prince Leszek to admit them to Poland. The request was granted after prolonged questioning, and later on privileges were granted to the immigrants. Although almost certainly formulated in their present version in the 16th–17th centuries – at a time of fierce struggle between Jewish and Christian townsmen (see below) – the legends do transmit meaningful historic elements. Jews did first come to Poland as transient, dust-covered merchants, and they did come there to escape the suffering and pressure brought to bear on them in the lands of the German Empire. The theories of some historians, that place-names like Żydowo, Żydatycze, Żydowska Wola, and Kozarzów indicate the presence of Jewish villages and peasants and even the presence of Khazar settlements in the regions where they are found, have been thoroughly disproved. The first Jews that the Poles encountered must certainly have been traders, probably slave traders, of the type called in 12th-century Jewish sources *Holekhei Rusyah* (travelers to Russia). Some of them may have stayed for years in Poland, giving rise to the legends and fixing their dates. The chronicler Cosmas of Prague relates that the persecutions of the First Crusade caused Jews to move from *Bohemia to Poland in 1098. From this point undisputed and datable information on Jews in Poland begins to appear. According to the chronicler Vincent Kadlubek, under Boleslav III heavy penalties were laid on those who harmed Jews bodily.

The first sizable groups and fixed communities of Jews settled and established themselves in the region of Silesia, then part of Polish society and culture but later Germanized. A large part of Jewish settlement in what was later consolidated as the kingdom of Poland came from Silesia, and a great proportion of the immigration from further west and from the southwest passed through it. As late as the 15th century Silesian Jewry kept its ties with Poland. Jewish settlement grew steadily, though at first slowly, in Polish principalities to the east of Silesia. Excavations in *Great Poland and near *Wloclawek have unearthed coins with Hebrew inscriptions issued under the princes Mieczyslaw III (1173–1209), Casimir II the Just (1177–94), Boleslav the Curly (1201), and Leszek the White (1205). Some inscriptions directly concern the ruler, like the

Hebrew legend "Mieszko King of Poland" (משקא קרל פולסקי) or "Mieszko Duke" (משקא דוכוס); others include the names and titles of the Jewish *mintmasters, one of them even with its honorific title of **nagid*; "of the [coining] house of Abraham the son of Isaac Nagid" (דבי אברהם בר יצחק נגיד); another showing that the Jewish mintmaster was settled in Poland: "Joseph [of] Kalisz" (יוסף קאליש). Minting money was an important social and economic function, and as some of the inscriptions indicate, these finds are evidence of a circle of rich and enterprising Jewish merchants in the principalities of great Poland and Mazovia in the 12th century, some of them in close contact with the princely courts, some priding themselves on their descent from old Jewish families or on their own role in Jewish leadership. Rulers were quick to realize what they could gain from such immigrants; in 1262 Prince Boleslav the Shy forbade a monastery in *Lesser Poland to take Jews under its sovereignty.

By that time, however, a new era had already begun in the history of the colonization of Poland in general and of the settlement of Jews in it in particular. From 1241 onward the Mongol invasions caused heavy losses in life and destruction to property in Poland. Subsequently, the princes of Poland eagerly sought immigrants from the west, mainly from Germany, and gave them energetic assistance to settle in the villages and towns. Various organized groups settled in the cities that were granted the privilege of living according to German Magdeburg *Law; thus Polish towns became prevailingly German in origin and way of life. Though the children of the immigrants became gradually Polonized, the traditions and social attitudes of the German town remained an active force and basic framework of town life in Poland of the 15th to 17th centuries. From the Jewish point of view the most important, and harmful, result of this basic attitude of the Polish towns was the tradition of the *guilds against competition and against new initiative in individual commercial enterprise and the activities of craftsmen. The townsmen also inherited a direct and bitter legacy of hatred of the Jews and the baleful and deeply rooted German image of the Jew.

Jews did not only come to Poland in the wake of the German *Drang nach Osten*, tracts of which are found in the 13th-century *Sefer Ḥasidim*, for instance, in the description of the creation of a new settlement in a primeval forest by Jews (*Sefer Ḥasidim*, ed. J. Wistinetzki (1924), 113, no. 371). For them the move was a continuation of and linking with earlier Jewish settlement in Poland. They also had compelling reasons stemming from the circumstances of their life in Western and Central Europe to leave their homes there and go to Poland-Lithuania. Their insecure position in this region was a compound of the atmosphere of fear and danger generated by the *Crusades, the insecurity of settlement caused by the *expulsions, the wave of massacres in Germany in particular between 1298 and 1348 (see *Rindfleisch; *Armleder; *Blood Libel; *Black Death; *Host, Desecration of), the insecurity and popular hatred in Germany and German-Bohemian-Moravian towns in the second half of the 14th century and the first half of the 15th, the tensions and dangers created by the *Hussite revolution and wars in Bohemia-Moravia and southern Germany in the early 15th century, and the worsening situation of Jews in the kingdoms of Christian Spain after the massacres of 1391. All these factors, combined with the success of the settlers in Poland-Lithuania, induced large and variegated groups of Jewish immigrants from various countries – Bohemia-Moravia, Germany, Italy, Spain, from colonies in the Crimea – to go to Poland-Lithuania long after the original German drive had died out. As Moses b. Israel *Isserles put it in the 16th century, "it is preferable to live on dry bread and in peace in Poland" than to remain in better conditions in lands more dangerous for Jews" (Responsa, no. 73). He even coined a pun on the Hebrew form of Poland (Polin), explaining it as deriving from two Hebrew words, *poh lin* ("here he shall rest").

The results of this immigration were evident almost immediately. In 1237 Jews are mentioned in Plock. The Jewish community of *Kalisz bought a cemetery in 1283, so it must have been organized some time before, as the fact that the first writ of privileges for Jews was issued in 1264 by the prince of Kalisz also tends to show (see below). A *Judengasse* (*Jewish Quarter) is mentioned in *Cracow in 1304, lying between the town market and the town walls, but there must have been a community in Cracow long before then for about 1234 "Rabbi Jacob Savra of Cracow that sits in Poland, a great scholar and fluent in the entire Talmud" put forward his own opinion against that of the greatest contemporary scholars of Germany and Bohemia. In 1356 there is a record of the Jewish community at *Lvov; in 1367 at *Sandomierz; in 1379 at *Poznan; in 1387 at Pyzdry; and about 1382 at *Lyuboml. In the grand duchy of Lithuania Jewish communities are found in the 14th century at *Brest-Litovsk (1388), *Grodno (1389), and *Troki (1398). The volume of immigration grew continuously. By the end of the 15th century more than 60 Jewish communities are known of in united Poland-Lithuania. They were dispersed from Wroclaw (*Breslau) and *Gdansk in the west to *Kiev and *Kamenets Podolski in the east. The number of Jews living in Poland by that date is greatly disputed: At the end of the 15th century there were between 20,000 and 30,000.

JEWISH LEGAL STATUS

The foundations of the legal position of the Jews in Poland were laid down in the 13th to 15th centuries. The basic "general charters" of Jews in Poland have their origin in the writ issued by Prince *Boleslav v the Pious of Kalisz in 1264. This "statute of Kalisz" (Pol. *Statut kaliski*) – as it is called in literature – was also an "immigrant" from the countries which Jews left to come to Poland, being based on the statute of Duke Frederick II of Austria and on derivative statutes issued in Bohemia and Hungary. The Jews are seen, accepted, and defended as a group whose main business is *moneylending against pledges. With the unification of Poland into a kingdom, King *Casimir III the Great strongly favored the Jewish element in the cities of Poland, the German element having proved untrustworthy under his father, the unifier of Poland, Ladislaus I Lokietek.

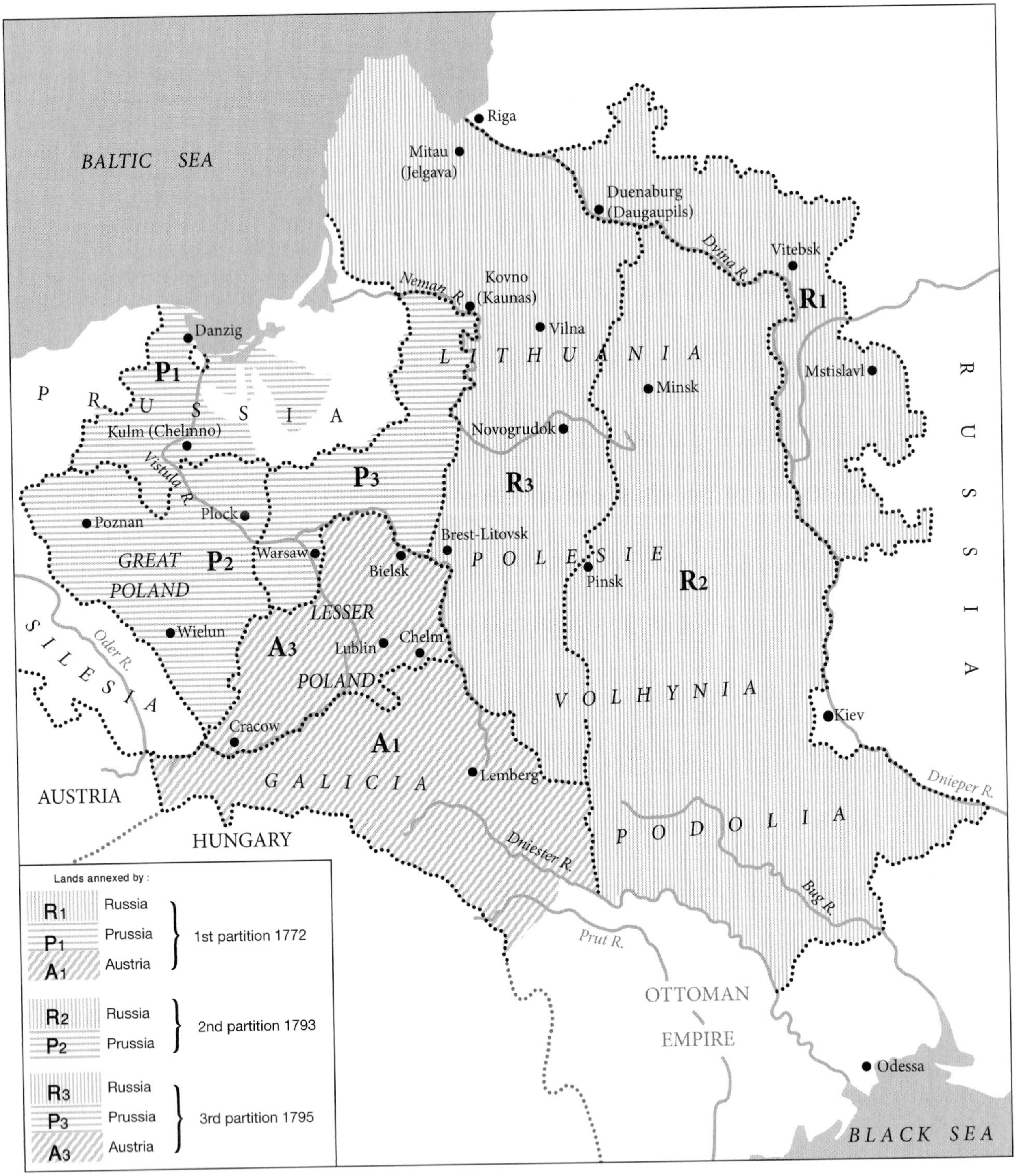

Map 1. The Partitions of Poland.

Casimir broadened the statute of Kalisz while ratifying it for the Jews of his kingdom (in 1334, 1364, and 1367). Yet basically the same conception of the Jews as **servi camerae regis* and as protected moneylenders remains throughout. The legal status of the Jews changed considerably in Poland, but not through any central reinterpretation of their rights and standing, which remained in theory based on and conceived of in terms of the Boleslavian-Casimirian statutes, codified and ratified by King Casimir IV Jagello in 1453. Throughout the 14th century, there was opposition to Jews accepting landed property as security for loans; while throughout the 15th century town and church tried to insist that Jews should wear the distinctive *badge.

On several occasions these undercurrents broke out in sharp and violent decisions and action. During the Black Death "All Jews ... almost throughout Poland were massacred" (*omnes judaei ... fere in tota Polonia deleti sunt*; Stanislas of Olivia in his *Chronica Olivska*, for the year 1349). The martyrs were defined by German Jews as "the communities and kingdom of Cracow, its scholars and population" (S. Salfeld, *Das Martyrologium des Nuernberger Memorbuches* (1898), 82). By that time hatred of the Jews was also widespread among the nobility. In the statute of Lesser Poland of 1347, paragraph 26 claims that "the aim of the perfidious Jews is not so much to take their faith away from the Christians as to take away their wealth and property." In 1407 the Cracow populace was diverted by the spectacle of a Jewish moneylender being led through the streets adorned with a crown set with forged coins – he was accused of forging currency – to be horribly tortured and burned in public. The citizens of Cracow claimed as early as 1369 that the Jews were "dominating" the town and complained of their cruelty and perfidy. In the main King Ladislaus II Jagello was hostile to Jews, though some of them were numbered among his financial and business agents, like Volchko, whom the king hoped in vain to bring over to Christianity.

Church circles were very active in their opposition to the Jews. Many priests and directors of monasteries, who had originally come from Germany, brought to Poland the hostile traditions concerning the city-dwelling accursed Jew. As early as 1267 the Polish Church Council of Wroclaw (Breslau) outlined its anti-Jewish policy; its main aim was to isolate the Jews as far as possible from the Christians, not only from the communion of friendship and table but also to separate them in quarters surrounded by a wall or a ditch: "for as up to now the land of Poland is newly grafted on to the Christian body, it is to be feared that the Christian people will more easily be misled by the superstitions and evil habits of the Jews that live among them" (*quum adhuc Terra Polonica sit in corpore christianitatis nova plantatio, ne forte eo facilius populus christianus a cohabitantium Iudeorum superstitionibus et pravis moribus inficiatur*; Aronius, Regesten, 302 no. 724). With various modifications, this was restated in subsequent Church councils. In the 15th century this ecclesiastical attitude found new and influential expression. Cardinal Zbigniew *Oleśnicki and the chronicler Jan *Długosz were the main leaders of the anti-Jewish faction. When Jewish representatives came to King Casimir IV Jagello to obtain the ratification of their charters, Oleśnicki opposed it vehemently. He invited to Poland "the scourge of the Jews," John of *Capistrano, fresh from his "success" in engineering a *Host desecration libel which resulted in the burning of many Jews and expulsion of the community of Wroclaw. In vain Capistrano tried to influence the king not to ratify the Jewish charters. Oleśnicki himself wrote to the king in support of his effort: "Do not imagine that in matters touching the Christian religion you are at liberty to pass any law you please. No one is great and strong enough to put down all opposition to himself when the interests of the faith are at stake. I therefore beseech and implore your royal majesty to revoke the aforementioned privileges and liberties. Prove that you are a Catholic sovereign, and remove all occasion for disgracing your name and for worse offenses that are likely to follow" (*Monumenta Mediaevi*, ed. Szugski, Codex Epistolaris s. XV, T. II past posterior p. 147). As a result of this pressure, the Nieszawa statute of 1454 decreed the repeal of all Jewish charters, but the repeal was short-lived. Perhaps central to the definition of the status of the Jews was the decision of King Sigismund I in 1534 that the Jews need not carry any distinguishing mark on their clothing. Despite the contrary resolution of the Sejm (Diet) of *Piotrkow in 1538, the king's decision remained.

Major changes in the status of the Jews occurred throughout the 16th and 17th centuries, but they came about either through the issuance of particular writs of rights by kings for towns and communities – both in favor of Jews as well as to their detriment (e.g., the *privilegia de non tolerandis judaeis* given to many towns in Poland) – or through the action of various magnates, whose power was continuously growing in Poland in these centuries. Some of the latter, nicknamed *Krolewięta* ("kinglets"), granted Jews many and costly rights in the new municipal settlements they were erecting on their expansive estates – the "private townships" of Poland, so-called in distinction to the old "royal townships." To a slight degree, change resulted from the new economic activity of the Jews, mainly in the east and southeast of Poland-Lithuania, and their move toward colonization there.

The foundations of the legal status of the Jews in the grand duchy of Lithuania were laid by Grand Duke Vitold in writs of law granted to the Jews of Brest-Litovsk in 1388 and to the Jews of Grodno in 1389. Though formally based on the rights of the Jews of Lvov in Poland, in letter and spirit these charters reveal an entirely different conception of the place of Jews in society. The writ for the Grodno community states that "from the above-mentioned cemetery – in its present location as well as on ground that might be bought later – and also from the ground of their Jewish synagogue, no taxes whatsoever will have to be given to our treasury." Not only are the Jewish place of worship and cemetery tax free – a concession that indicates interest in having Jewish settlers in the town – but also "what is more, we permit them to hold whatever views they please in their homes and to prepare at their homes any kind of drink and to serve drinks brought from elsewhere on the condition that they pay to our treasury a yearly tax. They may trade and buy at the market, in shops and on the streets in full equality with the citizens; they may engage in any kind of craft." Thus, in granting the Jews complete freedom to trade and engage in any craft, the grand duke gave them economic equality with the Christian citizens. He also envisaged their having agricultural or partially agricultural occupations: "As to the arable lands as well as grazing lands, those that they have now, as well as those that they will buy later, they may use in full equality with the townspeople, paying like them to our treasury." The Jews are here considered as merchants, craftsmen, and desirable settlers in the developing city. As the grand duchy merged with Poland to an ever-increasing degree, in particular in the formal, legal, and social spheres, the basic concepts of the *servi camerae* also influenced the status of Lithuanian Jews (as was already hinted at in the formal reference to the rights and status of the Jews of Lvov). In spite of this, the general trend in Lithuanian towns and townships remained the same as that expressed in the late 16th-century charters. In 1495 the Jews were expelled from Lithuania. They were brought back in 1503: all their property was returned and opportunities for economic activity were restored.

Thus, on the threshold of the 16th century, the gradually merging grand duchy of Lithuania and kingdom of Poland had both a fully worked out legal concept of the status of the Jews. In Poland, the whole conception was medieval to the core: Legally and formally the attitude to the Jews remained unchanged from their first arrival from the west and southwest. In Lithuania, on the other hand, from the start the formal expressions reveal a conception of a Jewish "third estate,"

Map 2. Major Jewish communities in Poland in 1931.

equal in economic opportunity to the Christian townspeople. Particular legal enactments in Poland took cognizance of the change in the economic role of the Jews in Polish society. In Lithuania the formal enactments were always suited to their economic role, and to a large extent the dynamics of 16th- and 17th-century development could be accommodated in the old legal framework.

ECONOMIC ACTIVITY

From the very first the Jews of Poland developed their economic activities through moneylending toward a greater variety of occupations and economic structures. Thus, by the very dynamics of its economic and social development, Polish Jewry constitutes a flat existential denial and factual contradiction of the antisemitic myth of "the Jewish spirit of usury." On the extreme west of their settlement in Poland, in Silesia, although they were mainly engaged in moneylending, Jews were also employed in agriculture. When the Kalisz community in 1287 bought a cemetery it undertook to pay for it in pepper and other Oriental wares, indicating an old connection with the trade in spices. As noted above, the Jewish mintmasters of the 12th century must undoubtedly have been large-scale traders. In 1327 Jews were an important element among the participants at the *Nowy Sacz fair. Throughout the 14th and 15th centuries Jews were occupied to a growing degree in almost every branch of trade pursued at that time. Jews from both the grand duchy of Lithuania and Poland traded in cloth, dyes, horses, and cattle (and on a fairly large scale). At the end of the 15th century they engaged in trade with Venice, Italy, with Kaffa (Feodosiya), and with other Genoese colonies in the Crimea, and with Constantinople. Lvov Jews played a central role in this trade, which in the late 15th and early 16th centuries developed into a large-scale land-transit trade between the Ottoman Empire and Christian Europe. Through their participation in this trade and their contacts with their brethren in the Ottoman Empire, many Jewish communities became vital links in a trade chain that was important to both the various Christian kingdoms and the Ottoman Empire. Lithuanian Jews participated to the full and on a considerable scale in all these activities, basing themselves both on their above-mentioned recognized role in Lithuanian civic society and on their particular opportunities for trade with the grand principality of *Moscow and their evident specialization in dyes and dyeing. Obviously, in all these activities, all links with Jewish communities in Central and Western Europe were beneficial.

During all this period Jews were engaged in moneylending, some of them (e.g., Jordanis *Lewko, his son Canaan, and Volchko) on a large scale. They made loans not only to private citizens but also to magnates, kings, and cities, on several occasions beyond the borders of Poland. The scope of their monetary operations at their peak may be judged by the fact that in 1428 King Ladislaus II Jagello accused one of the Cracow city counselors of appropriating the fabulous sum of 500,000 zlotys which the Jews had supplied to the royal treasury.

To an increasing extent many of the Jewish moneylenders became involved in trade. They were considered by their lords as specialists in economic administration. In 1425 King Ladislaus II Jagello charged Volchko – who by this time already held the Lvov customs lease – with the colonization of a large tract of land: "As we have great confidence in the wisdom, carefulness, and foresight of our Lvov customs-holder, the Jew Volchko … after the above-mentioned Jew Volchko has turned the above-mentioned wilderness into a human settlement in the village, it shall remain in his hands till his death." King Casimir Jagello entrusted to the Jew Natko both the salt mines of Drohobycz (*Drogobych) and the customs station of Grejdek, stating in 1452 that he granted it to him on account of his "industry and wisdom so that thanks to his ability and industry we shall bring in more income to our treasury." The same phenomenon is found in Lithuania. By the end of the 15th century, at both ends of the economic scale Jews in Poland were becoming increasingly what they had been from the beginning in Lithuania: a "third estate" in the cities. The German-Polish citizenry quickly became aware of this. By the end of the 15th century, accusations against the Jews centered on unfair competition in trade and crafts more than on harsh usury. Not only merchants but also Jewish craftsmen are mentioned in Polish cities from 1460 onward. In 1485 tension in Cracow was so high that the Jewish community was compelled to renounce formally its rights to most trades and crafts. Though this was done "voluntarily," Jews continued to pursue their living in every decent way possible. This was one of the reasons for their expulsion from Cracow to Kazimierz in 1495. However, the end of Jewish settlement in Cracow was far from the end of Jewish trade there; it continued to flourish and aggravate the Christian townspeople, as was the case with many cities (like *Lublin and *Warsaw) which had exercised their right *de non tolerandis Judaeis* and yet had to see Jewish economic activity flourishing at their fairs and in their streets.

CULTURAL AND SOCIAL LIFE

In Poland and Lithuania from the 13th century onward Jewish culture and society were much richer and more variegated than has been commonly accepted. Even before that, the inscriptions on the bracteate coins of the 12th century indicate talmudic culture and leadership traditions by the expressions used (*rabbi*, רַבִּי, *nagid*, נָגִיד). About 1234, as mentioned, Jacob Savra of Cracow was able to contradict the greatest talmudic authorities of his day in Germany and Bohemia. In defense of his case he "sent responsa to the far ends of the west and the south" (E.E. Urbach (ed.), in *Sefer Arugat ha-Bosem*, 4 (1963), 120–1). The author of *Sefer Arugat ha-Bosem* also quotes an interpretation and emendation that "I have heard in the name of Rabbi Jacob from Poland" (*ibid.*, 3 (1962), 126). Moses Zaltman, the son of *Judah b. Samuel he-Ḥasid, states: "Thus I have been told by R. Isaac from Poland in the name of my father.… thus I have been told by R. Isaac from Russia.… R. Mordecai from Poland told me that my father said" (Ms. Cambridge 669. 2, fol. 69 and 74). This manuscript evidence

Map 3. Provincial distribution of Polish Jewry in towns and villages (1931). Basd on data from R. Mahler, Yehudei Polin bein Shetei Milḥamot Olam, *1968.*

proves conclusively that men from Poland and from southern Russia (which in the 13th century was part of the grand duchy of Lithuania) were close disciples of the leader of the *Ḥasidei Ashkenaz. The names of Polish Jews in the 14th century show curious traces of cultural influence; besides ordinary Hebrew names and names taken from the German and French – brought by the immigrants from the countries of their origin – there are clearly Slavonic names like Lewko, Jeleń, and Pychacz and women's names like Czarnula, Krasa, and even Witoslawa. Even more remarkable are the names of Lewko's father, Jordan, and Lewko's son, Canaan or Chanaan, which indicate a special devotion to Ereẓ Israel.

By the 15th century, relatively numerous traces of social and cultural life in the Polish communities can be found. In a document from April 4, 1435, that perhaps, preserves the early *Yiddish of the Polish Jews, the writer, a Jew of Breslau, addresses "the Lord King of Poland my Lord." The closing phrases of the letter indicate his Jewish culture: "To certify this, have I, the above mentioned Jekuthiel, appended my Jewish seal to this letter with full knowledge. Given in Breslau, on the first Monday of the month Nisan, in Jewish reckoning five thousand years and a hundred years and to that hundred the ninety-fifth year after the beginning and creation of all creatures except God Himself" (M. Brann, *Geschichte der Juden in Schlesien*, 3 (1901), Anhang 4, p. lviii).

(דש צו בקינטניש האבע איך אֵי גננטר יקותיאל מיין יודיש זיגל אן דיזן בריבֿא מיט רעכטר ווישן גהאנגן. געגבן צו בריסלא אנדעמא אירשטן מאנטאג דש מאנדש ניֿסן איין יידישר צאל בֿונץ טאוזנט יאר אין הונדרט יאר אונ דר צו אין צעמא בֿינווא אונ׳ נויינציקשטן יאר נאך אנבגינן אונ׳ שיפֿפונגא אללר קריאטייר זונצו גוטא אליין)

Though Israel b. Ḥayyim *Bruna said of the Jews of Cracow, "they are not well versed in Torah" (Responsa, no. 55, fol. 23b), giving this as his reason for not adducing lengthy talmudic arguments in his correspondence with them, he was writing to one of his pupils who claimed sole rabbinical authority and income in the community of Poznan (*ibid.*, no. 254, fol. 103b). Israel b. Pethahiah *Isserlein of Austria writes, "my beloved, the holy community of Poznan." Two parties in this community – the leadership, whom Isserlein calls "you, the holy community," and an individual – were quarreling about taxation and Isserlein records that both sides submitted legal arguments in support of their cases (*Terumat ha-Deshen, Pesakim u-Khetavim*, no. 144). Great scholars like Yom Tov Lipmann *Muelhausen, who came to Cracow at the end of the 14th century, and Moses b. Isaac Segal *Mintz, who lived at Poznan in 1475, must certainly have left traces of their cultural influence there. Some of the responsa literature contains graphic descriptions of social life. "A rich man from Russia" – either the environs of Lvov in Poland or of Kiev in Lithuania – asked Israel Bruna, "If it is permissible to have a prayer shawl of silk in red or green color for Sabbath and the holidays" (Responsa, no. 73, fol. 32b), a desire fitting a personality of the type of Volchko. Something of the way of life of "the holy company of Lvov" can be seen from the fact that their problem was the murder of one Jew by another in the Ukrainian city of *Pereyaslav-Khmelnitski. As the victim lay wounded on the ground, a third Jew, Naḥman, called out to the murderer, Simḥah: "Hit Nisan till death" and so he was killed by being beaten on his head as he lay there wounded. The victim was a totally ignorant man, "he couldn't recognize a single [Hebrew] letter and has never in his life put on *tefillin*." The murderer was drunk at the time and the victim had started the quarrel; they were all in a large company of Jews (*ibid.*, no. 265, fol. 110a–b). The rough social and cultural climate of Jewish traders in the Ukraine in the middle of the 15th century is here in evidence. Moses Mintz describes from his own experience divorce customs in the region of Poznan (Responsa (Salonika, 1802), no. 113, fol. 129b). He also describes interesting wedding customs in Poland which differed in many details from those of Germany: "when they accompany the bride and bridegroom to the *ḥuppah* they sing on the way … they give the bridegroom the cup and he throws it down, puts his foot on it and breaks it, but they pour out the wine from the cup before they give it to the bridegroom. They have also the custom of throwing a cock and also a hen over the head of the bride and bridegroom above the canopy after the pronouncing of the wedding blessings" (*ibid.*, no. 109, fol. 127a). Thus, in the western and central parts of Poland there is evidence of an established and well developed culture and some learning, contrasting sharply with the rough and haphazard existence of Jews living southwards from Lvov to Pereyaslav-Khmelnitski.

Jewish culture in Poland and in Lithuania seems to have had a certain rationalist, "Sephardi" tinge, as evidenced both by outside reports and by certain tensions appearing in the second half of the 16th century. At the beginning of the 16th century the Polish chronicler Maciej Miechowicz relates that in Lithuania, "the Jews use Hebrew books and study sciences and arts, astronomy and medicine" (*Tractatus de duabus Sarmatiis* (1517), II: 1, 3). The cardinal legate Lemendone also notes that Lithuanian Jews of the 16th century devote time to the study of "literature and science, in particular astronomy and medicine." At the end of the 15th century, Lithuanian Jews took part in the movement of the *Judaizers in Muscovite Russia, whose literature shows a marked influence of rationalistic Jewish works and anti-Christian arguments. The Jewish community of Kiev – in the 15th and early 16th centuries within the grand duchy of Lithuania – was praised by a Crimean Karaite in 1481 for its culture and learning. In about 1484 another Karaite, Joseph b. Mordecai of Troki, wrote a letter to Elijah b. Moses *Bashyazi (Mann, Texts, 2 (1935), 1149–59) telling about a disputation on calendar problems between him and "the Rabbanites who live here in Troki, Jacob Suchy of Kaffa (Feodosiya) and Ozer the physician of Cracow" (*ibid.*, 1150). He closes his letter with ideas showing a decided rationalist tendency, "The quality of the sermon will be through the quality of the subject, therefore as we have none such more important than the Torah, for in it there is this teaching that brings man straight to his scientific and social success and the chief of its considerations is that man should achieve his utmost perfection, which is spiritual success; and this will happen when he attains such rational concepts as the soul, the active reason, can attain, for the relation between a phenomenon and its causes is a necessary relation, i.e., the relation of the separate reason to the material reason is like the relation of light to sight" (*ibid.*, 1159).

In Poland a dispute between two great scholars of the 16th century – Solomon *Luria and Moses *Isserles – brings to the surface elements of an earlier rationalist culture. Luria accuses yeshivah students of using "the prayer of Aristotle" and accuses Isserles of "mixing him with words of the living God … [considering] that the words of this unclean one are precious and perfume to Jewish sages" (Isserles, Responsa, no. 6). Isserles replies: "All this is still a poisonous root in existence, the legacy from their parents from those that tended to follow the philosophers and tread in their steps. But I myself have never seen nor heard up till now such a thing, and, but for your evidence, I could not have believed that there was still a trace of these conceptions among us" (*ibid.*, no. 7). Writing around the middle of the 16th century, Isserles tells unwittingly of a philosophizing trend prevalent in Poland many years before. A remarkable case of how extreme rationalist conceptions gave way to more mystic ones can be seen in Isserles' pupil, Abraham b. Shabbetai *Horowitz. Around 1539 he sharply rebuked the rabbi of Poznan, who believed in demons and opposed *Maimonides: "As to what this ass said, that it is permissible to study Torah only, this is truly against what the Torah says, 'Ye shall keep and do for it is your wisdom and understanding in the eyes of the gentiles.' For even if we shall be well versed in all the arcana of the Talmud, the gentiles will still not consider us scholars; on the contrary, all the ideas of the Talmud, its methods and sermons, are funny and derisible in the eyes of the gentiles. If we know no more than the Talmud we shall not be able to explain the ideas and exegetical methods of the Talmud in a way that the gentiles will like – this stands to reason" (see MGWJ, 47 (1903), 263). Yet this same man rewrote his rationalistic commentary on a work by Maimonides to make it more amenable to traditionalistic and mystic thought, declaring in the second version, "The first uproots, the last roots." Later trends and struggles in Jewish culture in Poland and Lithuania are partly traceable to this early and obliterated rationalistic layer (see below).

Polish victories over the Teutonic Order in the west and against Muscovite and Ottoman armies in the east and southeast led to a great expansion of Poland-Lithuania from the second half of the 16th century. In this way Poland-Lithuania gained a vast steppeland in the southeast, in the Ukraine, fertile but unpacified and unreclaimed, and great stretches of arable land and virgin forest in the east, in Belorussia. The agricultural resources in the east were linked to the center through the river and canal systems and to the sea outlet in the west through land routes. These successes forged a stronger link between the various strata of the nobility (Pol. *szlachta*) as well as between the Polish and Lithuanian nobility. In 1569 the Union of Lublin cemented and formalized the unity of Poland-Lithuania, although the crown of Poland and the grand duchy of Lithuania kept a certain distinctness of character and law, which was also apparent in the *Councils of the Lands and in the culture of the Jews (see below). With the union, Volhynia and the Ukraine passed from the grand duchy to the crown. The combined might of Poland-Lithuania brought about a growing pacification of these southeastern districts, offering a possibility of their colonization which was eagerly seized upon by both nobility and peasants.

1569–1648: COLONIZATION OF THE UKRAINE

The Polish nobility, which became the dominant element in the state, was at that time a civilized and civilizing factor. Fermenting with religious thought and unrest which embraced even the most extreme anti-trinitarians; warlike and at the same time giving rise to small groups of extreme anarchists and pacifists; more and more attracted by luxury, yet for most of the period developing rational – even if often harsh – methods of land and peasant exploitation; despising merchandise yet very knowledgeable about money and gain – this was the nobility that, taking over the helm of state and society, developed its own estates in the old lands of Poland-Lithuania and the vast new lands in the east and southeast. Jews soon became the active and valued partners of this nobility in many enterprises. In the old "royal cities" – even in central places like Cracow, which expelled the Jews in 1495, and *Warsaw, which had possessed a *privilegium de non tolerandis Judaeis* since 1527 – Jews were among the great merchants of clothing, dyes, and luxury products, in short, everything the nobility desired. Complaints from Christian merchants as early as the beginning of the 16th century, attacks by urban antisemites like Sebastian *Miczyński and Przecław *Mojecki in the 17th century, and above all internal Jewish evidence all point to the success of the Jewish merchant. The Jew prospered in trade even in places where he could not settle, thanks to his initiative, unfettered by guilds, conventions, and preconceived notions. The *kesherim*, the council of former office holders in the Poznan community, complain about the excessive activity of Jewish intermediaries, "who cannot stay quiet; they wait at every corner, in every place, at every shop where silk and cloth is sold, and they cause competition through influencing the buyers by their speech and leading them to other shops and other merchants." The same council complains about "those unemployed" people who sit all day long from morning till evening before the shops of gentiles – of spice merchants, clothes merchants, and various other shops – "and the Christian merchants complain and threaten." There was even a technical term for such men, *tsuvayzer*, those who point the way to a prospective seller (*Pinkas Hekhsherim shel Kehillat Pozna*, ed. D. Avron (1966), 187–8 no. 1105, 250 no. 1473, 51 no. 1476). Miczyński gives a bitter description of the same phenomenon in Cracow in 1618. Large-scale Jewish trade benefited greatly from the trader's connections with their brethren both in the Ottoman Empire and in Germany and Western Europe. It was also linked to a considerable extent with the *arenda system and its resulting great trade in the export of agricultural products.

Table 1. Growth of Jewish Settlement by Places and Numbers in the Colonization Period (Poland)

Województwo (district)	Before 1569 Places	Before 1569 Numbers	c. 1648 Places	c. 1648 Numbers
Volhynia	13	3,000	46	15,000
Podolia	9	750	18	4,000
Kiev	–	–	33	13,500
Bratslav	2	?–	18	18,825
Total	24	c. 4,000	115	51,325

Through the arenda system Jewish settlements spread over the country, especially in the southeast. Between 1503 and 1648 there were 114 Jewish communities in the Ukraine, some on the eastern side of the River Dnieper and list by S. Ettinger, in *Zion*, 21 (1956), 114–8); many of these were tiny. The table Growth of Jewish Settlement shows the main outlines of the dynamics of Jewish settlement in these regions of colonization (*ibid.*, p. 124).

The further the move east and southward, the greater the relative growth in numbers and population. The Jewish arenda holders, traders, and peddlers traveled and settled wherever space and opportunity offered.

Life in these districts was strenuous and often harsh. The manner of Jewish life in the Ukraine, which as we have already seen was uncouth, was both influenced and channeled through Jewish participation in the defense of newly pacified land. Meir b. Gedaliah of Lublin relates "what happened to a luckless man, ill, and tortured by pain and suffering from epilepsy.... When there was an alarm in Volhynia because of the Tatars – as is usual in the towns of that district – when each one is obliged to be prepared, with weapon in hand, to go to war and battle against them at the command of the duke and the lords; and it came to pass that when the present man shot with his weapon, called in German *Buechse*, from his house through the window to a point marked for him on a rope in his courtyard to try the weapon as sharpshooters are wont to do, then a man came from the market to the above mentioned courtyard ... and he was killed [by mistake]." The rabbi goes on to tell that a Christian, the instructor and commander of this Jew, was standing in front of the courtyard to warn people not to enter. The Jew was "living among the gentiles in a village" with many children (Meir b. Gedaliah of Lublin, Responsa, no. 43). There is reference to an enterprising group of Jews who went to Moscow with the armies of the Polish king during war, selling liquor (one of them had two cartloads) and other merchandise to the soldiers (*ibid.*, no. 128). Among the Cossack units there was a Jew about whom his Cossack colleagues "complained to God ... suddenly there jumped out from amongst our ranks a Jew who was called Berakhah, the son of the martyr Aaron of Cieszewiec." This Jew was not the only one in the ranks of the Cossacks, for – to allow his wife to marry – one of the witnesses says that "he knew well that in this unit there was not another Jewish fighter who was called Berakhah" (*ibid.*, no. 137). Life in general was apt to be much more violent than is usually supposed: Even at Brest-Litovsk, when the *rebbe* of the community saw a litigant nearing his door, he seized a heavy box and barricaded himself in for fear of harm (*ibid.*, no. 44).

Arenda did more than give a new basis to the existence of many Jewish families; it brought the Jews into contact with village life and often combined with aspects of their internal organizational structure. Thus, the Jew Nahum b. Moses, as well as renting the mills, the tavern, and the right of preparing beer and brandy, also rented for one year all milk produce of the livestock on the manors and villages. Elaborate and complicated arrangements were made for payment and collection of these milk products (S. Inglot, in: *Studja z historji społecznej i gospodarczej poświęcone prof. Franciszkowi Bujakowi* (1931), 179–82; cf. 205, 208–9). In contact with village life, the Jew sometimes formed a sentimental attachment to his neighbors and his surroundings. In 1602 a council of leaders of Jewish communities in Volhynia tried to convince Jewish arendars to let the peasants rest on Saturday though the Polish nobleman would certainly have given them the right to compel them to work: "If the villagers are obliged to work all the week through, he should let them rest on Sabbath and the Holy Days throughout. See, while living in exile and under the Egyptian yoke, our parents chose this Saturday for a day of rest while they were not yet commanded about it, and heaven helped them to make it a day of rest for ever. Therefore, where gentiles are under their authority they are obliged to fulfill the commandment of the Torah and the order of the sages not to come, God forbid, to be ungrateful [*livot* לִבְעֹט] to the One who has given them plenty of good by means of the very plenty he has given them. Let God's name be sanctified by them and not defiled" (H.H. Ben-Sasson, in *Zion*, 21 (1956), 205).

The interests of the Jews and Polish magnates coincided and complemented each other in one most important aspect of the economic and social activity of the Polish-Lithuanian nobility. On their huge estates the nobles began to establish and encourage the development of new townships, creating a network of "private towns." Because of the nature of their relationship with their own peasant population they were keen to attract settlers from afar, and Jews well suited their plans. The tempo and scale of expansion were great; in the grand duchy of Lithuania alone in the first half of the 17th century between 770 and 900 such townships (*miasteczki*) existed (S. Aleksandrowicz, in: *Roczniki dziejów społecznych i gospodarczych*, 27 (1965), 35–65). For their part, the Jews, who were hard pressed by the enmity of the populace in the old royal cities, gladly moved to places where they sometimes became the majority, in some cases even the whole, of the population. Since these were situated near the hinterland of agricultural produce and potential customers, Jewish initiative and innovation found a new outlet. Through charters granted by kings and magnates to communities and settlers in these new towns, the real legal status of the Jews gradually changed very much for the better. By the second half of the 17th century everywhere in Poland Jews had become part of "the third estate" and in some places and in some respects the only one.

Jews continued to hold customs stations openly in Lithuania, in defiance of the wishes of their leaders in Poland (see Councils of the Lands). Many custom station ledgers were written in Hebrew script and contained Hebrew terms (see R. Mahler, in YIVO *Historishe Shriftn*, 2 (1937), 180–205). Sometimes a Jew is found with a "sleeping partner," a Pole or Armenian in whose name the customs lease has been taken out. That some customs stations were in Jewish hands was also of assistance to Jewish trade.

This complex structure of large-scale export and import trade, the active and sometimes adventurous participation in the colonization of the Ukraine and in the shaping of the "private cities," in the fulfilling of what today we would call state economic functions, created for the first time in the history of Ashkenazi Jewry a broad base of population, settlement distribution, and means of livelihood, which provided changed conditions for the cultural and religious life of Jews. Even after the destruction wrought by the *Chmielnicki massacres enough remained to form the nucleus of later Ashkenazi Jewry. The later style of life in the Jewish *shtetl was based on achievements and progress made at this time.

INTERNAL JEWISH LIFE

The Councils of the Lands, the great superstructure of Jewish *autonomy, were an outgrowth of such dynamics of economy and settlement. Beginning with attempts at centralized leaderships imposed from above, appointed by the king, they ended with a central elected Jewish leadership. The aims, methods, and institutions of this leadership were intertwined with the new economic structure. Great fairs – notably those of Lublin and Jaroslaw – since they attracted the richest and most active element of the Jewish population, also served as the meeting place of the councils. Throughout its existence the Council of the Province of Lithuania cooperated with its three (later five) leading communities through a continuous correspondence with them and between each of them and the smaller communities under its authority. Here the council was adapting the organizational methods of large-scale trade to the leadership structure. The concern of the councils with the new economic phenomena, like arenda, is well known. They also concerned themselves with matters of security and morals which arose from the thin spread of Jewish families in Christian townships and villages. On the whole, up to 1648 a sense of achievement and creativity pervades their enterprises and thought. A preacher of that time, Jedidiah b. Israel *Gottlieb, inveighed against a man's gathering up riches for his children, using the argument of the self-made man: "The land is wide open, let them be mighty in it, settle and trade in it, then they will not be sluggards, lazy workers, children relying on their father's inheritance, but they themselves will try … to bring income to their homes, in particular because every kind of riches coming through inheritance does not stay in their hands … easy come, easy go.… through their laziness … they have to be admonished … to be mighty in the land through their trading: their strength and might shall bring them riches" (*Shir Yedidut* (Cracow, 1644), *Ẓeidah la-Derekh*, fol. 24a).

This buoyancy was based on a continuous growth of population throughout the 16th and the first half of the 17th centuries, due both to a steady natural increase thanks to improving conditions of life and to immigration from abroad resulting from persecution and expulsions (e.g., that from Bohemia-Moravia for a short period in 1542). As noted, the growth was most intensive in the eastern and southeastern areas of Poland-Lithuania, and it was distributed through the growing dispersion of Jews in the "private cities" and in the villages. At the end of the 16th century, Great Poland and Masovia (Mazowsze) contained 52 communities, Lesser Poland 41, and the Ukraine, Volhynia, and Podolia about 80; around 1648, the latter region had 115 communities. From about 100,000 persons in 1578 the Jewish population had grown to approximately 300,000 around 1648. It is estimated that the Jews formed about 2.5–3% of the entire population of Poland, but they constituted between 10% and 15% of the urban population in Poland and 20% of the same in Lithuania.

The dynamics of Jewish economic life are evident not only in the variety and success of their activities, but also in certain specific institutions and problems that reveal the tension behind their strain for economic goals which tended to entail risks. By the end of the 16th century, Jews were borrowers rather than lenders. Seventeenth-century antisemites – Miczyński and Mojecki – accused Jews of borrowing beyond their means and deceiving Christian lenders. From their accusations it is clear that much of this credit was not in ready cash but in goods given to Jewish merchants on credit. Borrowing was a real problem with which the Jewish leadership was much concerned. Many ordinances of the Councils of the Lands, of the provincial councils, and of single communities are preoccupied with preventing and punishing bankruptcy. Great efforts were devoted to prevent non-payment of debts to Christians in particular. Young men who were building up a family were especially suspected of reaching beyond their means. These ordinances tell in their own way the story of a burgeoning economy which is strained to dangerous limits, inciting in particular the young and the daring. A good name for credit was then a matter of life and death for the Jewish merchant. The great halakhist Solomon Luria was prepared to waive an ancient talmudic law in favor of the lender because "now most of the living of the Jews is based on credit; whereas most of those called merchants have little of their own and what they have in their hands is really taken from gentiles on credit for a fixed period – for they take merchandise [on credit] till a certain date – it is not seemly for a judge to sequester the property of a merchant, for news of this may spread and he will lose the source of his living and all his gentile creditors will come on him together and he will be lost, God forbid, and merchants will never trust him again. I myself have seen and heard about many merchants – circumcised and uncircumcised – to whom, because people said about them that they are a risk, much harm was caused and they never again could stand at their posts" (*Yam shel Shelomo, Bava Kamma*, ch. 1, para. 20). Because of the importance of credit the practice of a Jew lending on interest to another Jew became widespread in Poland-Lithuania despite the fact that it was contrary to Jewish law (see *usury). This necessitated the creation there of the legal fiction of *hetter iskah*, formulated by a synod of rabbis and leaders under the chairmanship of Joshua b. Alexander ha-Kohen *Falk in 1607. Widespread credit also led to the use of letters of credit specific to the Jews of Poland, the so-called **mamram* (Pol. *membrana, membran*; Heb. ממרמ"א, ממרים, ממרנ"י, in initials: ממ"א, מ"מ): the Jew would sign on one side of the paper and write on the other side "this letter of credit obliges the signed overleaf for amount x to be paid on date *y*."

Jewish cultural and social life flourished hand in hand with the economic and demographic growth. In the 16th and early 17th centuries Poland-Lithuania became the main center of Ashkenazi culture. Its *yeshivot were already famous at the beginning of the 16th century; scholars like *Ḥayyim b. Bezalel of Germany and David b. Solomon *Gans of Prague were the pupils of *Shalom Shakhna of Lublin and Moses Isserles of Cracow, respectively. Mordecai b. Abraham *Jaffe; Abraham, Isaiah, and Jacob b. Abraham *Horowitz; Eliezer b. Elijah *Ashkenazi; *Ephraim Solomon b. Aaron Luntshits; and Solomon Luria were only a few of the great luminaries of talmudic scholarship and moralistic preaching in Poland-Lithuania of that time. Councils of the Lands and community ordinances show in great detail if not the reality at least the ideal of widespread Torah study supported by the people in general. This culture was fraught with great social and moral tensions. Old Ashkenazi ascetic ideas did not sit too well on the affluent and economically activist Polish-Lithuanian Jewish society. Meetings with representatives of the Polish *Reformation movement, in particular with groups and representatives of the anti-trinitarian wing like Marcin Czechowic or Szymon *Budny, led to disputations and reciprocal influence. Outstanding in these contacts on the Jewish side was the Karaite Isaac b. Abraham *Troki, whose *Ḥizzuk Emunah* sums up the tensions in Jewish thought in the divided Christian religious world of Poland-Lithuania. It was Moses Isserles who formulated the Ashkenazi modifications and additions to the code of the Sephardi Joseph Caro. Isaiah b. Abraham ha-Levi *Horowitz summed up in his *Shenei Luhot ha-Berit* the moral and mystic teaching of the upper circles of Ashkenazi Jewry. Yet his writings, and even more so the writings of Isserles, give expression to the tensions and compromises between rationalism and mysticism, between rich and poor, between leadership and individual rights. To all these tensions, Ephraim Solomon Luntshits gave sharp voice in his eloquent sermons, standing always on the side of the poor against the rich and warning consistently against the danger of hypocrisy and self-righteousness. Fortified and wooden synagogues expressed the needs and the aesthetic sense of Jewish society of that time. In the old "royal cities" magnificent synagogue buildings were erected as early as the 16th century (e.g., the Rema synagogue at Cracow and the Great Synagogue of Lvov). Hebrew manuscripts were brought from abroad and some of them illuminated in Poland. Jewish printing developed early and many beautiful works were published. Various sources describe carnival-like Purim celebrations, and the fun, irony, and joy of life expressed in now lost folk songs and popular games and dramas.

FROM CHMIELNICKI TO THE FIRST PARTITION

The *Chmielnicki revolt and massacres of 1648–49, the Tatar incursions from Crimea, and the subsequent war with Moscow combined with the Swedish War to bring on the Jews of Poland-Lithuania approximately 30 years of bloodshed, destruction, and suffering. Thousands were killed, thousands forced to adopt Christianity. At the end of these convulsions, Poland-Lithuania had lost much territory in the east which of course was also lost for Jewish life and settlement. Thousands of refugees thronged westward, bringing heavy pressure to bear on charity and the very structure of Jewish society. The arrangements of the Councils of the Lands to prevent competition for arenda had to stand the severe test of diminished opportunities and increasing demand. Contemporary figures like Nathan Nata *Hannover saw in this catastrophe a fissure in Jewish life and institutions, as indicated by the tenor of his chronicle, *Yeven Metsulah*. In reality, Jewish cultural and social life in the second half of the 17th century and in the 18th continued to a considerable extent along the lines developed in the great era of the 16th and first half of the 17th centuries. Recent research has shown that *Pinsk, a community in the east of Lithuania, recovered from its troubles more completely and at greater speed than had been known before. But the dynamism had gone out of institutions and activities; inertia set in. Much that had been full of imminent promise of development and change before the disasters tended now to be petrified. Tensions that had been submerged in the buoyant pre-Chmielnicki times became more open, causing dissension and revolt. The councils and communities were burdened with the growing debts incurred mostly to meet unexpected demands for defense against multiplying libels and massacres, but at the same time the oligarchic structure within the community and the councils and the dominating attitude adopted by the larger communities toward the smaller ones – in Lithuania in particular – caused the lower strata of the population and the members of the smaller communities to suspect their in-

Table 2. Distribution of Jews in Poland According to Size of Communities in the 18th century

Region	Percentage of communities of less than 500	Percentage of communities of more than 500
Great Poland	91.7	8.3
Masovia	93.5	6.5
Lesser Poland	76.5	23.5
Lvov	61.7	38.3
Ukraine	85.0	15.0

Table 3. Economic Structure of Jewish Population in Poland-Lithuania in the 18th century

Region	Arenda and Alcoholic Beverages	Trade	Transportation	Crafts	Professions	Unspec.
Great Poland	1.8	6.1	–	41.7	12.4	38.0
Masovia	15.2	0.7	–	19.0	13.0	52.1
Lesser Poland	3.1	4.8	1.0	24.0	11.0	56.1
Lvov	2.8	3.0	3.2	20.5	12.5	58.0
Ukraine	28.9	3.6	2.0	27.0	14.5	24.0

tentions and greatly resent the increasingly heavy tax burden. Jewish economic activity continued to develop, though Jews in the "private towns" and on arenda in the villages came to feel more and more the heavy and capricious hand of the Polish nobles, who by that period had lost the vigor of earlier times and become tyrannical, petty lords.

Despite the loss of territory and the worsening of conditions, the Jewish population in Poland-Lithuania continued to grow both absolutely and, from many aspects, in its relative strength in the country. With the abolition of the Councils of the Lands in 1764, a census of the Jewish population was taken. Jews tried to evade being counted by any means available for they were certain that the purpose of the census was to impose heavier taxation on them, as they had every reason to suspect the intentions of the authorities. For this reason at least 20% should be added to the official figures. Accordingly in 1764 there were 749,968 Jews over a year old in Poland-Lithuania: 548,777 of them in Poland and 201,191 in Lithuania; 16.5% of the Jewish population of Poland lived in western Poland, 23.5% in Lesser Poland, and 60% in the Ukraine and neighboring districts; in Lithuania 77% lived in the western part and only 23% in the eastern, Belorussian districts. Taking into account the overall population of Poland, it can be seen that the concentration of Jewish population had shifted eastward in the 18th century to an even greater extent than in the early and successful 17th century. The census also shows that Jews lived mostly in small communities. (See Table 2: Distribution of Jews in Poland.)

As the entire Christian urban population of Poland-Lithuania was estimated at that time to be about half a million, and as the Jews were concentrated mainly in the townships and "private towns," there emerges a clear picture of a predominantly Jewish population in the smaller Polish-Lithuanian urban centers, at least 70% to 90% in many of these places.

The economic structure of the Jewish population at this time is shown in Table 3.

Although the predominance of unspecified professions does indicate the impoverishment of the Jews, it is largely an aspect of the evasive attitude toward the census. As this table does not include the village Jews, among whom the occupations of arenda and the production and sale of alcoholic beverages certainly predominated, only the following economic conclusions can be drawn with certainty: A considerable proportion of the Jews were engaged in crafts, and arenda and alcoholic beverages became more important as sources of livelihood as the Jews moved eastward and into villages (according to R. Mahler, *Yidn in Amolikn Poyln in Likht fun Tsifern*, 1958).

The Jewish population of Poland-Lithuania was still seething with creativity and movement in the 18th century. The messianic claims of *Shabbetai Ẓevi not only stirred the masses of Jews in 1665–66 but also left a deep impression on later generations. This is evident in the suspicion expressed about itinerant **maggidim* (it was also demanded that they be supervised), who were suspected of disseminating heretical and critical ideas. The personality and movement of Jacob *Frank made the greatest impact on the distressed population of Podolia, in the extreme southeast. From the same region too arose *Israel b. Eliezer Ba'al Shem Tov and the movement of *Ḥasidism he originated. Talmudic scholarship and traditional ways of life, which continued to flourish throughout the period, found a supreme exemplar in the vigorous personality and influence of *Elijah b. Solomon Zalman, the Gaon of Vilna, and in the way of life and culture originated by him and his circle in the Mitnaggedic Lithuanian yeshivot. At that time too the first influences of *Haskalah and *assimilation began to appear in Poland-Lithuania.

With the partitions of Poland (beginning in 1772), the history of ancient Jewish Poland-Lithuania comes to an end. During the agony of the Polish state, several of its more enlightened leaders – e.g., H. Kołłątaj and T. *Czacki – tried to "improve the Jews," i.e., improve their legal and social status in the spirit of western and European enlightened absolutism. With the dismemberment of Poland-Lithuania, their belated efforts remained suspended. Even when broken up and dispersed, Polish-Lithuanian Jewry was not only the majority and the cultural source of Jewish society in czarist Russia, but those elements of it which came under Prussia and Austria also served later as the reservoir of Jewish spirit and manpower which resisted the ravages of assimilation and apostasy in the German and Austrian communities in the late 18th and 19th centuries.

[Haim Hillel Ben-Sasson]

AFTER PARTITION

The geographic entity "Poland" in this part of the article refers to that area of the Polish commonwealth which, by 1795, had been divided between Austria and Prussia and which subsequently constituted the basis of the grand duchy of Warsaw, created in 1807. Following the Congress of *Vienna in 1815 much of this area was annexed to the Russian Empire as the semi-autonomous Kingdom of Poland, also known as Congress Poland. The kingdom constituted the core of ethnic Poland, the center of Polish politics and culture, and an economic area of great importance. It is to be distinguished from Austrian Poland (Galicia), Prussian Poland (Poznan, Silesia, and Pomerania), and the Russian northwestern region also known as Lithuania-Belorussia.

During and after the partitions the special legal status enjoyed by the Jews in Poland-Lithuania came under attack – while disabilities remained, efforts were made to break down the Jews' separateness and transform them into "useful" citizens. This new notion, brought to Poland from the west and championed by Polish progressives with the support of the tiny number of progressive Jews, advocates of the Haskalah, was clearly expressed during the debates on the Jewish question at the Four-Year Sejm (1788–92). The writings of H. Kołłątaj and M. *Butrymowicz demanded the reform of Jewish life, meaning an end to special institutions and customs (from the *kahal* to the Jewish beard), sentiments to be expressed later on

Table 4. Growth of Warsaw Jewry

Year	Number of Jews	Percentage
1781	3,532	4.5
1810	14,061	18.1
1856	44,149	24.3
1882	127,917	33.4
1897	219,141	33.9

Table 5. Lodz Jewry, Population

Year	Number of Jews	Percentage
1793	11	5.7
1856	2,775	12.2
1897	98,677	31.8
1910	166,628	40.7

by S. Staszic and A.J. *Czartoryski. The attack on "*l'état dans l'état*" as Czartoryski put it in 1815, was accompanied by an attack against Jewish economic practices in the village, which, it was claimed, oppressed and corrupted the peasantry. From Butrymowicz, writing in 1789, to the writings of Polish liberals and Jewish assimilationists in the inter-war period, there runs a common assumption: the Jews suffer because they persist in their separateness – let them become like Poles and both they and Poland will prosper. This assumption was also shared by many antisemites of the non-racist variety.

Some effort was made during the 19th century to implement this belief. For example, the *kahal*, symbol of Jewish self-government, was abolished in 1822, and a special tax on Jewish liquor dealers forced many to abandon their once lucrative profession. On the other hand Jews were encouraged to become agriculturalists and were granted, in 1826, a modern rabbinical seminary which was supposed to produce enlightened spiritual leaders. Moreover, in 1862 the Jews of Poland were "emancipated," meaning that special Jewish taxes were abolished and, above all, that restrictions on residence (Jewish ghettos and *privilegium de non tolerandis Judaeis*) were removed. Nonetheless, the legal antisemitism of Russia's last czars was also introduced into Poland: in 1891 aspects of N. *Ignatiev's *May Laws were extended to Congress Poland, resulting in the expulsion of many Jews from the villages, and in 1908 school quotas (**numerus clausus*) were officially implemented. In sum, during the 19th and early 20th centuries the policy of the carrot and the stick was employed. By the end of the pre-World War I era the stick had prevailed, making the legal status of Polish Jewry nearly identical to that of Russian Jewry. The efforts to assimilate Polish Jewry by legislation aimed at making it more productive and less separatist had virtually no impact on the Jewish masses.

The "Jewish question" in Poland and the legal efforts to deal with it were to a certain extent the result of the Jews' special demographic and economic structure. From the demographic point of view two striking tendencies may be observed. First, the natural increase of Polish Jews was greater than that of non-Jews, at least during most of the 19th century, leading to an increasing proportion of Jews within the population as a whole. In 1816 Jews constituted 8.7% of the population of the kingdom; in 1865, 13.5%. In 1897, despite the effects of large-scale Jewish emigration, 14 out of every 100 Polish citizens were Jews. This increase, attributable in part to the low Jewish death rate, was accompanied by the rapid urbanization of Polish Jewry. A few examples may suffice to illustrate this important process. Table 4 demonstrates the growth of Warsaw Jewry, where restrictions on residence were not entirely lifted until 1862.

A similar trend is found in Lodz, the kingdom's second city (see Table 5).

This remarkable urbanization – the result of government pressure, a crisis in the traditional Jewish village professions, and the economic attractions of the growing commercial and industrial centers – had the following impact on the Jewish population: In 1827, according to the research of A. Eisenbach, 80.4% of the Jews lived in cities and the rest in villages, while in 1865 fully 91.5% of Polish Jewry lived in cities. In the same year 83.6% of the non-Jewish population lived in the countryside. As early as 1855 Jews constituted approximately 43% of the entire urban population of the kingdom, and in those cities where there were no restrictions on Jewish settlement the figure reached 57.2%. The Jews, traditionally scattered, could claim with some justification that, by the end of the century, the cities were their "territory."

This demographic tendency meant that the traditional Jewish economic structure also underwent certain changes. Jews, of course, had always predominated in trade; in 1815, for example, 1,657 Polish Jews participated at the Leipzig fair compared with 143 Polish gentiles. During the course of the century, as the Jews became more and more dominant in the cities, their role in urban commercial ventures became more pronounced. Thus, in Warsaw, at the end of the century, 18 out of 26 major private banks were owned by Jews or Jewish converts to Christianity. A wealthy Jewish merchant and financial class emerged, led by such great capitalists as Ivan *Bliokh and Leopold *Kronenberg, who played a role in the urbanization and industrialization of Poland. On the other hand, the vast majority of Jews engaged in commerce very clearly belonged to the petty bourgeoisie of shopkeepers (of whom, in Warsaw in 1862, nearly 90% were Jews) and the like. In the same year, according to the calculations of the economic historian I. *Schiper, more than two-thirds of all Jewish merchants were without substantial capital.

Two tendencies must be emphasized with regard to the Jewish economic situation in the kingdom. First, it became apparent by the end of the century that the Jews were gradually losing ground to non-Jews in trade. Thus, for every 100 Jews in Warsaw in 1862, 72 lived from commerce, while in 1897 the figure had dropped to 62. For non-Jews, on the other hand, the percentage rose from 27.9 in 1862 to 37.9 in 1897. The rise of a non-Jewish middle class, with the resulting increase in competition between Jew and gentile, marks the beginning of a process which, as we shall see, gained impetus during the interwar years. Second, there was a marked tendency toward the "productivization" of Polish Jewry, that is, a rise of Jews engaged in crafts and industry. The following figures, which relate to the whole of Congress Poland, are most revealing: in 1857 44.7% of all Jews lived from commerce and 25.1% from crafts and industry, while in 1897 42.6% were engaged in commerce and 34.3% in crafts and industry. In this area, as in trade, the typical Jew was far from wealthy. For every wealthy Jew like Israel Poznański, the textile tycoon from Lodz, there were thousands of Jewish artisans (some 119,000, according to the survey of the *Jewish Colonization Association (ICA) in 1898) who worked in tiny shops with rarely more than one hired hand. It is noteworthy that for various reasons – the problems of Sabbath work, the antisemitism of non-Jewish factory owners, fear of the Jewish workers' revolutionary potential – a Jewish factory proletariat failed to develop. Even in Lodz and Bialystok the typical Jewish weaver worked in a small shop or at home, not in a large factory. One further development should be mentioned. By the end of the century a numerically small but highly influential Jewish professional class had made its appearance, particularly in Warsaw. This class was to provide the various political and cultural movements of the day, Jewish and non-Jewish, with many recruits, as well as to provide new leadership for the Jewish community.

The Jews, therefore, constituted an urban, middle class and proletarian element within the great mass of the Polish peasantry. There existed in Poland a long tradition of what might be called a "Polish orientation" among Jews, dating back to the Jewish legion which fought with T. *Kościuszko in 1794 and continuing up to the enthusiastic participation of a number of Jews in J. *Piłsudski's legions. The Polish-Jewish fraternization and cooperation during the Polish uprising of 1863 is perhaps the best example of this orientation, which held that Polish independence would also lead to the disappearance of antisemitism. The idea of Jewish-Polish cultural assimilation took root among the Jews of the kingdom far earlier than in Galicia, not to mention multi-national Lithuania-Belorussia. **Izraelita*, the Polish-Jewish periodical advocating assimilation, began publication in 1866, and a number of Jewish intellectuals like Alexander Kraushar hoped for the eventual merging of the Jews into the Polish nation. Such men took comfort from the views of a few Polish intellectuals, notably the poet Adam *Mickiewicz, who hoped and worked for the same event. The slogan "for our and your freedom" had considerable influence within the Polish-Jewish intelligentsia by the century's end.

The Jewish masses, however, had nothing to do with such views, knew nothing of Mickiewicz, knew little if any Polish, and remained (as the assimilationists put it) enclosed within their own special world. Here, too, as was the case regarding the economic stratification of Polish Jewry, a thin stratum separated itself from the mass. It was usually the offspring of the wealthy (Kraushar's father, for example, was a banker) who championed the Polish orientation, while the typical Jewish shopkeeper or artisan remained Yiddish-speaking and Orthodox. On the Polish side, too, Mickiewicz was a voice crying in the wilderness. It is true that the great wave of *pogroms in the Russian Empire was concentrated in the Ukraine and Bessarabia (although Russian Poland was not wholly spared); nor was there anything in Poland resembling the expulsion of the Jews from Moscow in 1891. Indeed, Russian antisemitism led to the influx of so-called Litvaks into the kingdom. But the rise of Polish national fervor, accompanied by the development of a Polish middle class, naturally exacerbated Polish-Jewish relations. The founding of the National Democratic Party (*Endecja) in 1897 was symptomatic of the growing antisemitism of the period. The economic and political roots of this antisemitism (not to mention the traditional religious factor) were clearly expressed in 1912, when the Jews' active support of a Socialist candidate in elections to the *Duma resulted in an announced boycott of Jewish businesses by the National Democrats. On the eve of World War I relations between Poles and Jews were strained to the utmost, a state of affairs which led to a decline in the influence of the assimilationists and a rise in that of Jewish national doctrines.

In comparison with Russia, specifically Jewish political movements had a late start in the kingdom. The Haskalah, progenitor of modern Jewish political movements, was far less influential in Poland than in Galicia or Russia. Warsaw, unlike *Vilna, Lvov, and other great Jewish cities, did not become a center of the Enlightenment; its Jewish elite, like the elite in Germany, tended toward assimilation. True, the city of *Zamosc was, for a time, a thriving Haskalah center, but Zamosc was part of Galicia from 1772 to 1815 and followed the Galician rather than the Polish pattern. Later on, the pioneers of Jewish nationalism and Jewish Socialism came from the northwest region (Belorussia-Lithuania) or the Ukraine. While in Lithuania the Jewish intelligentsia, though Russianized, remained close to the masses, in Poland the intelligentsia was thoroughly Polonized. Its members tended, therefore, to enter Polish movements, such as the Polish Socialist Party (*PPS). Thus the *Bund, although it succeeded in spreading into Poland in the early 20th century, remained very much a Lithuanian movement. It is striking that the so-called Litvaks played a major role in spreading the ideas of Jewish nationalism to Poland; it was they, for example, who led the Warsaw Ḥovevei Zion (*Ḥibbat Zion) movement, the precursor of modern Zionism. On the eve of World War I, however, Jewish political life in Poland was well developed. The Bund had developed roots in such worker centers as Warsaw and Lodz, while the Zionists felt strong enough to challenge, albeit unsuccessfully, the entrenched assimilationist leadership of the Warsaw Jewish community.

INDEPENDENT POLAND

As a result of World War I and the unexpected collapse of the three partitioning powers, Poland was reconstituted as a sovereign state. The final boundaries, not determined until 1921, represented something of a compromise between the feder-

Table 6. Decrease in the Percentage of the Jews in the Total Population in the Cities of Poland in the Interwar Period

City	Percentage of Jews in 1921	Percentage of Jews in 1931
Warsaw	33.1	30.1
Lvov	35.0	31.9
Vilna	36.1	28.2
Bialystok	51.6	43.0
Grodno	53.9	42.6
Brest-Litovsk	53.1	44.3
Pinsk	74.7	63.4

Table 7. The Natural Increase of Four Major Religious Groups in Poland in the Interwar Period

Religion	Natural Increase
Roman Catholic	13.1
Greek Catholic	12.5
Greek Orthodox	16.7
Jewish	9.5

alist dreams of Pilsudski and the more ethnic Polish conception of R. *Dmowski. To Congress Poland, purely Polish save for its large Jewish minority, were added Galicia, Poznania, Pomerania, parts of Silesia, areas formerly part of the Russian northwestern region, and the Ukrainian province of Volhynia. The new state was approximately one-third non-Polish, the important minorities being the Ukrainians, Jews, Belorussians, and Germans.

The heritage of the war years was a particularly tragic one for Polish Jewry. The rebirth of Poland, which many Jews had hoped for, was accompanied by a campaign of terror directed by the Poles (as by the invading Russian army in the early years of the war) against them. The Jews too often found themselves caught between opposing armies – between the Poles and the Lithuanians in Vilna, between the Poles and the Ukrainians in Lvov, and between the Poles and the Bolsheviks during the war of 1920. And it is probably no accident that the two major pogroms of this period, in Lvov in 1918 and in Vilna in 1919, occurred in multi-national areas where national feelings reached their greatest heights. The triumph of Polish nationalism, far from leading to a rapprochement between Jews and Poles, created a legacy of bitterness which cast its shadow over the entire interwar period. For the Poles the war years proved that the Jews were "anti-Polish," "pro-Ukrainian," "pro-Bolshevik," etc. For the Jews the independence of Poland was associated with pogroms. The legal situation of the Jews in independent Poland was, on the surface, excellent. The Treaty of Versailles, concluded between the victorious powers and the new states, included provisions protecting the national rights of minorities; in the Polish treaty Jews were specifically promised their own schools and the Polish state promised to respect the Jewish Sabbath. The Polish constitution, too, declared that non-Poles would be allowed to foster their national traditions, and formally abolished all discrimination due to religious, racial, or national differences. The Jews were recognized by the state as a nationality, something the Zionists and other Jewish nationalists had long fought for. There were great hopes that the Jews would be allowed to develop their own national institutions on the basis of national autonomy.

These hopes were not fulfilled. The two cornerstones of Jewish autonomy – the school and the **kehillah* – were not allowed to develop freely. The state steadfastly refused to support Jewish schools, save for a relatively small number of elementary schools closed on Saturday which possessed little Jewish content. The Hebrew-language *Tarbut schools, along with the Yiddish-language CYSHO (see *Education) network, were entirely dependent on Jewish support, and the diplomas issued by the Jewish high schools were not recognized by the Ministry of Education. The Jewish schools were successful as pedagogical institutions, but the absence of state support made it impossible for them to lay the foundation for a thriving Jewish national cultural life in Poland. As for the *kehillah*, projected by Jewish nationalists as the organ of Jewish national autonomy on the local level, it was kept in tight check by the government. While elections to the *kehillah* were made democratic, enabling all Jewish parties to participate on a basis of equality, the government constantly intervened to support its own candidates, usually those of the Orthodox *Agudat Israel. By the same token the government controlled the budgets of the *kehillot*. These institutions remained essentially what they had been in the preceding century, concerned above all with the religious life of the community.

Far from barring discrimination against non-Poles, the policy of the interwar Polish state was to promote the ethnic Polish element at the expense of the national minorities, and above all at the expense of the Jews, who were more vulnerable than the essentially peasant Slav groups. The tradition of *numerus clausus* was continued at the secondary school and university level, efforts were made to deprive the "Litvaks" of Polish citizenship, local authorities attempted to curb the use of Yiddish and Hebrew at public meetings, and the Polish electoral system clearly discriminated against all the minorities. All Jewish activities leading toward the advancement of Jewish national life in Poland were combatted; the government favored Zionism only insofar as it preached emigration to Ereẓ Israel, and in domestic politics tended to support the traditional Orthodoxy of Agudat Israel. Worst of all was the economic policy of the state.

According to official statistics, most likely too low, Jews made up 10.5% of the Polish population in 1921. The density of their urban settlement was related to the general development of the area. In less developed regions, such as East Galicia, Lithuania, and Volhynia, the Jewish percentage in the cities was very high, while in more developed areas, such as Central Poland (the old Congress Poland), the existence of a strong native bourgeoisie caused the Jewish percentage to be lower. As for the Jewish village population, it too was higher in backward areas, since the number of cities was naturally less. There were, therefore, substantial Jewish village populations in Galicia and Lithuania but not in the old Congress Poland (with the exception of Lublin province, economically backward in comparison with the other provinces of the region). The most striking development in the demography of Polish Jewry between the wars is the marked loss of ground in the cities. Table 6 illustrates this point. (See Map: Poland, 1931 and Map: Jews in Poland.)

Among the factors contributing to this decline was the Polish government's "colonization" policy in non-Polish areas, its changing of city lines to diminish the Jewish proportion, and Jewish emigration (though with America's gates shut this last factor was not very significant). Another major cause would appear to be the low Jewish natural increase, caused by a low birth rate. (Table 7 presents the natural increase of four major religious groups in interwar Poland.) Thus the process of Jewish population expansion in Poland ended, itself the victim of urbanization (which led, in turn, to a low birth rate). If the cities were Judaized during the 19th century, they were Polonized in the 1920s and 1930s.

The demographic decline of Polish Jewry was paralleled by a more serious economic decline. On the whole, Polish Jews between the wars continued to work at the same trades as their 19th-century predecessors and the tendency toward "productivization" also continued. The vast majority of those engaged in industry were artisans, among whom tailors predominated; those working in commerce were, above all, shopkeepers. What distinguished the interwar years from the prewar era was the antisemitic policy of the Polish state, which Jewish leaders accused of leading to the economic "extermination" of Polish Jewry. Jews were not employed in the civil service, there were very few Jewish teachers in the public schools, practically no Jewish railroad workers, no Jews employed in state-controlled banks, and no Jewish workers in state-run monopolies (such as the tobacco industry). In a period characterized by economic *étatisme*, when the state took a commanding role in economic life, such official discrimination became disastrous. There was no branch of the economy where the state did not reach; it licensed artisans, controlled the banking system, and controlled foreign trade, all to the detriment of the Jewish element. Its tax system discriminated against the urban population, and its support of peasant cooperatives struck at the Jewish middleman. Such specific legislation as the law compelling all citizens to rest on Sunday helped to ruin Jewish commerce by forcing the shopkeeper to rest for two days and to lose the traditionally lucrative Sunday trade.

More natural forces were also at work in the decline of the Jews' economic condition, e.g., the continued development of a native middle class, sponsored by the government but not created by it. According to research carried out by the *YIVO in 113 Polish cities between 1937 and 1938, the number of Jewish-owned stores declined by one, while the number of stores owned by Christians increased by 591. In the western Bialystok province, to cite another example, the number of the Jewish-owned stores declined between 1932 and 1937 from 663 to 563, while the number of Christian-owned stores rose from 58 to 310. These figures reflect both the impact of antisemitism (in the late 1930s the anti-Jewish boycott became effective) and the impact of the developing Polish (and Ukrainian) middle class.

The Jews' economic collapse in the interwar period bears witness to the disaster, from the Jewish point of view, inherent in the rise of exclusive nation-states on the ruins of the old multinational empires. Jews were employed in the old Austrian public schools of Galicia, but not in the Polish state-operated schools. They worked as clerks in the railroad offices of Austrian Galicia, but not in Poland. Thousands of Jewish cigarette factory workers in the old Russian Empire were dismissed when the Polish state took over the tobacco monopoly. It also demonstrates the extremely vulnerable position of the Jews vis-à-vis the other Polish minorities, largely peasant nations which did not compete with the Polish element. The urban Jewish population found itself in a situation in which the traditional small businessman was being squeezed out, while the policy of the state also ruined the wealthy Jewish merchant and industrialist. This was then the end of a process already discernible in the late 19th century, immeasurably speeded up by a state which wanted to see all key economic positions in the hands of "loyal" elements, i.e., Poles.

What was the Jews' political response to this situation? In the beginning of the interwar period the *General Zionists emerged as the strongest force within the Jewish community, thus reflecting the general trend in Eastern Europe toward nationalism and, in the Jewish context, reflecting the impact of the terrible war years. In the 1919 Sejm elections the list of the Temporary Jewish National Council, dominated by General Zionists, received more than 50% of those votes cast for Jewish parties. In 1922, when Jewish representation in the Sejm reached its peak, the percentage of General Zionists (together with the *Mizrachi) among the Jewish deputies was again over 50% (28 out of 46). The Jewish Club (Koło) in the Sejm, which claimed to speak for all Polish Jewry, was naturally dominated by General Zionists, who with considerable justice regarded themselves as the legitimate spokesmen of the community. General Zionism in Poland was divided into two schools, that of "Warsaw-St. Petersburg" and that of "Lvov-Cracow-Vienna." The former came of age in the revolutionary atmosphere of the czarist regime and consequently tended to be more extreme in its demands than the Galicians, who had learned their politics in the Austrian Reichsrat. The clash between Yiẓḥak *Gruenbaum, leader of the Warsaw faction, and Leon *Reich of Lvov was well expressed in the negotiations carried on between the Jewish Sejm Club and the Polish government in 1925. Gruenbaum, rejecting negotiations with antisemites and offering instead the idea of a national minorities bloc, found himself outnumbered in the club by adherents of Reich's position, namely that negotiations should be carried on in order to halt the deterioration of the Jewish position. In the end neither Gruenbaum's minorities bloc nor Reich's negotiations caused any improvements; the tragedy of

Jewish politics in Poland was that the government would not make concessions to the Jews so long as it was not forced to do so, and the Jews, representing only 10% of the population, could find no allies.

All General Zionists agreed on the importance of "work in the Diaspora," though Gruenbaum, the central figure in this work, was castigated by Palestinian pioneers as the apostle of "Sejm-Zionismus." They did not agree, however, on various aspects of Zionist policy; the efforts to broaden the *Jewish Agency and the nature of the Fourth *Aliyah caused a split within the Warsaw Zionists, Gruenbaum leading the attack on Chaim *Weizmann and upholding the young pioneering emigration while his opponents defended the "bourgeois" *aliyah* and Weizmann's conciliatory tactics toward non-Zionist Jewry. Gruenbaum's faction, Al ha-Mishmar ("On Guard"), remained in the minority throughout the 1920s, but the so-called radical Zionists returned to power in the 1930s following the failure of the Agency reform, the crisis in the Fourth Aliyah, and the stiffening of the British line in Palestine. The General Zionists, of course, did not monopolize Jewish political life in interwar Poland. On the right, non-Zionist Orthodoxy was represented by the Agudat Israel, which succeeded in dominating the Jewish *kehillot*, but its generally good relations with the government did not stem the antisemitic tide. On the left the dominant Jewish party was the Bund, which had disappeared in Russia but survived to play its last historic role as the most important representative of the Jewish proletariat in Poland. The Bund, like Gruenbaum's Zionist faction, also recognized the need for allies in the struggle for a just society in which, its leaders hoped, Jews would be able to promote their Yiddish-based culture. Such allies were sought on the Polish left rather than among the disaffected minorities, but the Polish Socialist Party (PPS), for reasons of its own, had no desire to be branded pro-Jewish. Unable to create a bloc with the Polish proletariat, the Bund devoted itself to promoting the interests of the Jewish working class and took a great interest in the development of Yiddish culture. Despite the fact that this party, too, was split into factions (the split turned chiefly on different attitudes toward the international Socialist movement), it was to grow in influence. Sharing the left with the Bund, though overshadowed by it in terms of worker allegiance, were the various Socialist Zionist parties, ranging from the non-Marxist *Hitaḥadut to the leftist *Po'alei Zion (the Po'alei Zion movement had split into right and left factions in 1920; in Poland the left was dominant, at least in the 1920s). The moderate Socialist Zionists were concerned mainly with the pioneering emigration to Ereẓ Israel, while the Left Po'alei Zion steered a perilous course of non-affiliation either with the Zionist organization or with the Socialist International. Its ideological difficulties with the competition of the anti-Zionist Bund (which went so far as to brand Zionism as an ally of Polish antisemitism) sentenced the Left Po'alei Zion to a relatively minor role among the Jewish proletariat, though its influence among the intelligentsia was by no means negligible.

Two other Jewish parties deserve mention. The Polish Mizrachi, representing the Zionist Orthodox population, enjoyed a very large following (eight of its representatives sat in the Sejm in 1922). The Mizrachi usually cooperated with the General Zionists, though its particular mission was to safeguard the religious interests of its followers in Ereẓ Israel and in the Diaspora. The *Folkspartei, on the other hand, never managed to make an impression on political life in Poland, though its intellectual leadership was extremely influential on the cultural scene. Both anti-Zionist and anti-Socialist, it could never attain a mass following.

The economic collapse of Polish Jewry, together with the rise of virulent antisemitism, led to the radicalization of Jewish politics in Poland. Extreme solutions to the Jewish question gained more adherents as the parliamentary approach clearly failed to lead anywhere; hence the growth of the pioneering Zionist movements – *He-Ḥaluẓ, HeḤaluẓ ha-Ẓa'ir, *Ha-Shomer ha-Ẓa'ir, and others – resulting in the large-scale emigration to Ereẓ Israel in the mid-1930s, and also the inroads of Communism among the Jewish youth. Another symptom of this radicalization was the great success of the Bund in the 1930s; by the late 1930s the Bund had "conquered" a number of major *kehillot* and was probably justified in considering itself the strongest of all Jewish parties. This spectacular success did not occur as a result of any apparent party success, since the efforts to improve the lot of the Jewish proletariat and to forge a bloc with the Polish left had failed. Rather, the Bund's success may be attributed to the rising protest vote against attempts to mollify the regime and in favor of an honorable defense, no matter how unavailing, of Jewish interests. Within the Zionist movement the process of radicalization was very clearly illustrated by the decline of the General Zionists and the rise of the Socialists and the Revisionists. In the elections to the 18th *Zionist Congress, held in 1933, the labor Zionists of Central Poland received 38 mandates and the General Zionists only 12. The same congress seated 20 Polish Revisionists, whose growing strength faithfully reflected the mood of Polish Jewry. In short, a transformation may be discerned of what might be called the politics of hope into the politics of despair. The slogans of *ḥaluẓiyyut* ("pioneering"), evacuation, and Communist ideology became more and more palatable as the old hopes for Jewish autonomy and the peaceful advancement of Jewish life in a democratic Poland disappeared.

By the late 1930s the handwriting was clearly on the wall for Polish Jewry, though no one could foresee the horrors to come. The rise of Hitler in Germany was paralleled by the appearance of Fascist and semi-Fascist regimes in Eastern Europe, not excepting Poland. A new wave of pogroms erupted along with a renewed anti-Jewish boycott, condoned by the authorities. The Jewish parties were helpless in the face of this onslaught, especially as the disturbances in Ereẓ Israel resulted in a drastic decline in *aliyah*. The political dilemma of Polish Jewry remained unresolved; finding no allies, Jewish parties could do little to influence the course of events. It should be recalled, however, that the role of these parties was greater than the narrow word "political" implies. Their work in raising the educational standards of Polish Jewry was remarkable, and the Jewish youth movements were able to supply to the new generation of Polish Jews a sense of purpose and a certain vision of a brighter future.

Polish Jewish history, from 1772 to 1939, reveals an obvious continuity. The Jews remained a basically urban element in a largely peasant country, a distinct economic group, a minority whose faith, language, and customs differed sharply from those of the majority. All attempts to break down this distinctiveness failed, and the Jews naturally suffered for their obvious strangeness. A thin layer of assimilated, or quasi-assimilated, Jews subsisted throughout the entire period, but the masses were relatively unaffected by the Polish orientation. In the end all suffered equally from Polish antisemitism. There were also several basic discontinuities. The rise of an exclusively national Polish state in 1918 was a turning point in the deterioration of the Jews' position, though the signs of this deterioration were already visible in the late 19th century. The rise of a native middle class, encouraged by state policy, put an end to the Jews' domination of trade and forced them into crafts and industry, resulting in the emergence of a large Jewish proletariat. Politically speaking perhaps the greatest change was the triumph within the community of Jewish nationalism, whether Zionist, Bundist, or Folkist, at the expense of the traditional assimilationist or Orthodox leadership. In this sense Polish Jewry followed the same course of development as the other peoples of Eastern Europe. It was a tragic paradox that these nationalist parties, which extolled the principle of activism and denounced the passivity of the Jewish past, also depended for their effectiveness on outside forces. Neither the Polish government nor the Polish left proved to be possible allies in the struggle for survival.

[Ezra Mendelsohn]

HOLOCAUST PERIOD

The outbreak of the war (Sept. 1, 1939) and the invasion of Poland by German troops were marked by immediate heavy loss of civilian (especially Jewish) life and material damage. Military operations caused the death of 20,000 Jews, while bombing destroyed some 50,000 Jewish-owned houses, factories, workshops, and stores in about 120 Jewish communities, in some of which 90–95% of the houses went up in flames. In Warsaw alone, in the first month of the war, 30% of the Jewish buildings were destroyed when entire Jewish neighborhoods burned down. A tremendous stream of refugees sought shelter in the large cities, particularly in Warsaw. Subsequently, tens of thousands of Jewish enterprises not destroyed in the bombing were now lost in liquidation measures, bringing the total amount of Jewish property and business concerns lost or destroyed to an estimated 100,000. Jewish losses on the battlefield totaled 32,216 dead (officers and enlisted men) and another 61,000 taken prisoner, the majority of whom died in captivity.

Military operations were still going on when the German army and SD Einsatzkommandos undertook a campaign of bloody repression (see *Holocaust, General Survey). They usually arrested a group of Jews or Poles, who were kept as hostages and eventually shot. Sometimes mock executions were staged, in which the victims stood for hours in suspense anticipating execution. Pious Jews had their beards removed by blunt instruments, which tore their skin, or had their beards burned off. Swastikas were branded on the scalps of some victims; others were subjected to "gymnastics," such as "riding" on other victims' backs, crawling on all fours, singing and dancing, or staging fights with one another. The Nazis took a special sadistic pleasure in violating religious feelings, deliberately choosing Jewish religious holidays on which to carry out their assaults.

They instituted a special campaign of burning down synagogues, or, after destroying their interiors, turned them into stables, warehouses, bathhouses, or even public latrines (see *Synagogues, Desecration and Destruction of). At *Bedzin the synagogue at the old market place was set on fire on Sept. 9, 1939. The flames spread to the neighboring Jewish houses, and as the area was cordoned off by soldiers and SS-men who did not permit anyone to escape or to fight the fire, 56 houses were burned down, and several hundred persons were burned to death. In some places, e.g., *Wloclawek and *Brzeziny, the president or rabbi of the community was forced to sign a "confession" that the Jews themselves started the fire and to pay heavy fines as punishment for the "arson." The tenants of the houses burned down were brought before a military court. Any Jew who tried to enter a burning synagogue in order to save the Torah scrolls was either shot or thrown into the flames. In many places the military staged *autos-da-fé* of Torah scrolls, Hebrew books, and other religious articles, and forced the Jews to sing and dance around the flames and shout that the Jews were to blame for the war. The Jewish communities were also compelled to bear the cost of tearing down the remaining walls of the houses and clearing the rubble. It is estimated that several hundred synagogues were destroyed in the first two months of the occupation.

At the same time, mass arrests of Jews were carried out in which thousands of men, women, and children were interned in "civilian prison camps" set up in synagogues, churches, movie houses, and the like, or put behind barbed-wire fences on open lots and exposed to the soldiers' cruelty and torture. Afterward the prisoners were sent on foot to larger centers (such as *Wegrow, *Lomza, *Sieradz, *Tomaszow Mazowiecki), where some were set free and others put on forced labor or deported to Germany. In the latter instance their transport to Germany was used for propaganda purposes, as in the case of groups of Jews from Kalisz and Wieruszow who were borne around German towns in trucks bearing the inscription: "These are the Jewish swine who shot at German soldiers."

Precise instructions issued by the High Command of the Wehrmacht on July 24, 1939, for the internment of civilian prisoners provided for the arrest of Jews and Poles of military age at the outset of the invasion. In practice, however, a wild huntdown of Jews was made, without regard to age. In the campaign of terror that followed, hundreds of civilians, Poles, and Jews (in *Czestochowa, *Przemysl, *Bydgoszcz, and Dynow) were slaughtered outright or imprisoned in buildings which were sealed and then set on fire or blown up, the imprisoned dying a horrible death (in Dynow, Lipsk-Kielecki, Mszczonow). No precise figures are available on the number of victims in this period of terror. In the rampage of persecution throughout Poland, people were taken off the streets or dragged from their homes and put on forced labor. They were tortured and beaten, and deprived of their human dignity when forced to perform such acts as cleaning latrines with their bare hands or, in the case of women, washing the floor with their own underwear. Normal life was paralyzed by the arbitrary arrests for forced labor even at a later stage, when forced labor was "regulated" and the still-existing communities or the Judenraete (see *Judenrat) had to provide labor contingents on the basis of an understanding reached with the various German offices or commands.

The systematic robbery of Jewish property involved the closing of all the Jewish shops in many towns, or enforced sale of the wares at nominal prices or against worthless receipts. To facilitate the identification of Jewish property, the chief of the civilian administration attached to the army, Hans *Frank, issued an order (Sept, 8, 1939) for all Jewish stores to display a Star of David or other appropriate inscriptions on their stores by the following day. Practically all Jewish communities were also forced to make large "contributions" of money, gold, silver, and jewelry. In many towns compulsory contributions were paid several times over. Large sums were extorted from wealthy individuals under threat of imprisonment. Whenever a Nazi "visit" to the offices of the communities took place, all the money in their safes was confiscated, e.g., in Warsaw on Oct. 5, 1939, when 100,000 zlotys ($20,000) were taken in this manner. "Legal" forms of robbery were also instituted. The civilian administrators attached to the occupation forces issued orders restricting the sums Jews could hold in their bank accounts, while the accounts themselves were blocked. Restrictions were also placed on the amount of cash a Jew could keep in his home. Jewish-owned property was frozen, Jews were prohibited from engaging in the textile and leather business, and their inventories were registered with the Nazi authorities. Any infringement entailed heavy punishment, including death.

Two decrees by Hitler (Oct. 8 and 12, 1939) provided for the division of the occupied areas of Poland into the following administrative units: (a) Reichsgau Wartheland, which included the entire Poznan province, most of the Lodz province, five Pomeranian districts, and one county of the Warsaw province; (b) the remaining area of Pomerania, which was incorporated into the Rechsgau Danzig-Westpreussen; (c) Regierungsbezirk Zichenau (Ciechanow) consisting of the five northern counties of Warsaw province (*Plock, *Plonsk, Sterpe, *Ciechanow, *Mlawa), which became a part of East Prussia; (d) Regierungsbezirk Kattowitz – or unofficially Ost-Oberschlesien (East Upper Silesia) – which included *Sosnowiec, Bedzin, *Chryzanow, and *Zawiercie counties and parts of *Olkusz and Zywiec counties; (e) the General Government of Poland, which included the central Polish provinces and was subdivided into four districts, Warsaw, Lublin, *Radom, and Cracow.

The areas listed under (a)–(d) were incorporated into the Reich. After the outbreak of the Soviet-German War, the Polish territories previously occupied by the Russians were organized as follows: (f) Bezirk Bialystok, which included the Bialystok, *Bielsk Podlaski, *Grajewo, Lomza, *Sokolka, *Volkovysk, and Grodno counties and was "attached" (not incorporated) to East Prussia; (g) Bezirke Litauen und Weissrussland – the Polish part of White Russia (today western Belorussia), including the Vilna province, which was incorporated into the Reichskommissariat Ostland; (h) Bezirk Wolhynien-Podolien – the Polish province of Volhynia, which was incorporated into the Reichskommissariat Ukraine; and (i) East Galicia, which was incorporated into the General-Government and became its fifth district.

The Jewish population of this entire area was 3,351,000, of whom 2,042,000 came under Nazi rule and 1,309,000 under Soviet occupation in September 1939. The ultimate fate of the Jewish population under Nazi rule was the same in all the areas, though the various administrative areas differed in the degree and pace of persecution, depending on local leadership (a Nazi principle of administration).

Reichsgau Wartheland

The area was subdivided into three *Regierungsbezirke* ("administrative districts") – Poznan, *Inowroclaw, and Lodz. On Sept. 1, 1939, it had 390,000 Jews (including 4,500 in Poznan, 54,090 in Inowroclaw, and 326,000 in the Lodz district – 233,000 in the city of Lodz). Like all Polish areas incorporated into the Reich, Wartheland was from the beginning designated to become "*judenrein*" (*Heydrich's "*Schnellbrief*" of Sept. 21, 1939). In a secret order to the *RSHA (Reichssicherheitshauptamt – Reich Security Main Office) and the high *SS and police officials, issued on Oct. 30, 1939, *Himmler fixed the period of November 1939–February 1940 for clearing the incorporated areas of their entire Jewish population and the majority of their Polish population as well. A similar decree was issued on Nov. 4, 1939, by Wartheland's Gauleiter Arthur Greiser.

Arrangements were made for the transfer of 100,000 Jews from its territory during this period. In fact, more than 50 Jewish communities were deported wholly or in part to the Lublin district between the fall of 1939 and May 1940; the larger communities among those deported were Poznan, Kalisz, Ciechocinek, *Gniezno, Inowroclaw, Nieszawa, and *Konin. In some towns the deportation was carried out in stages, with a small number of Jews remaining, engaged in work for the Nazi authorities. In some instances, the regime of terror drove the Jews to desperation, so that they chose "voluntary" exile. This happened in *Lipno and in Kalisz, where many Jews, unable to withstand the persecution, fled from the city in October and November 1939. In Lodz, over 10,000 Jews, including most of the Jewish intelligentsia, were deported in December 1939. For weeks the deportees were kept at assembly points, and had to supply their own means of subsistence, though they had been deprived of all their valuables. Large assembly points were located at Kalisz, Sieradz, and Lodz. There, the *Selektion* ("selection") took place in which able-bodied men, aged 14 and over, were sent to labor camps which had been established in the meantime, while women, children, and old men were deported in sealed freight cars to the Lublin and *Kielce areas. This occurred in the severe winter of 1939–1940, and upon arrival at their destination, some of the deportees were dead, others nearly frozen, or otherwise seriously ill. The survivors were bereft of clothing, food, and money. A few found refuge with relatives or friends, but most of them had to find places in the crowded synagogues and poorhouses. For the Jewish communities of the Lublin and Radom districts, the influx of deportees was a very heavy burden. Most of the deportees perished before mass deportation began.

GHETTOIZATION. At this time, a second campaign was launched to concentrate the Jewish population in ghettos. The first ghetto in Wartheland was established at Lodz, on orders given by *Polizeipraesident* (Chief of Police) Johannes Schaefer (Feb. 8, 1940). By the latter half of 1940, all the Jewish communities that had survived the mass deportations were sealed off in ghettos. Lodz ghetto had a population of 162,000 on the day of its establishment (May 1, 1940). The large ghettos in Wartheland included *Pabianice (with about 8,500 persons), *Kutno (7,000), *Belchatow (5,500), *Ozorkow (4,700), *Zelow (4,500), *Zdunska Wola (10,000), Wloclawek (where 4,000 were left after the deportations), and *Wielun (4,000). Lodz became a central ghetto (*Gaughetto*) for the entire province, absorbing Jews sent from ghettos that were liquidated or reduced in size, as well as from the Reich, *Vienna, and *Prague. Between Sept. 26 and Oct. 9, 1941, 3,082 Jews from Wloclawek and the vicinity arrived at Lodz Ghetto, and between Oct. 17 and Nov. 4, 1941, approximately 20,000 arrived from Vienna, Prague, Berlin, Frankfurt, Hamburg, Cologne, Emden, Duesseldorf, and Luxembourg. From May to August 1942, 14,440 "selected" Jews from liquidated ghettos arrived at Lodz.

From the end of 1942 until its liquidation in August 1944, Lodz was the only remaining ghetto in Wartheland. Its comparatively long existence was due to the fact that it became one of the largest industrial plants working for the Wehrmacht or private contractors. In August 1943, some 76,000 workers (about 85% of the entire ghetto population) were employed in 117 warehouses. According to the Nazi *Ghettoverwaltung* ("ghetto administration"), the total wages and production in 1942 reached a value of 27,862,200 RM ($5,572,440). Large tailor shops also existed at Pabianice, Belchatow, Ozorkow, and other ghettos in the Lodz district. Lodz Ghetto bore the imprint of its *Judenaeltester* ("Jewish elder") Mordecai *Rumkowski, who at an early stage imposed his rule over the ghetto. The ghetto was administered by division of the population into various socio-economic groups, each with a different status, in accordance with their status in the ghetto hierarchy or their usefulness for the war industry. In those areas of ghetto life in which the Nazis allowed the Jews autonomy, Rumkowski held absolute power.

PHYSICAL ANNIHILATION. Partial liquidation actions affecting certain categories of Jews, such as the sick and the old, began in Wartheland as early as the fall of 1940 (in Kalisz). In September or October 1941, experiments in the murder of Jews were carried out in Konin county, where Jews were forced into ditches and covered over with wet quicklime. On Dec. 8, 1941, the murder camp at *Chelmno began operation. On Jan. 2, 1942, Greiser's *Erlass, die Entjudung des Warthelands betreffend* ("Decree on Clearing all Jews from the Wartheland") was issued. In December 1941, the remaining Jews from *Kolo and Dabie were deported to Chelmno, followed in January 1942 by the inmates of the ghettos of Izbica Kujawska and other places. From Jan. 16 until mid-May 1942, numerous transports of Jews were dispatched from Lodz Ghetto to Chelmno. By May some 55,000 were murdered there. Between March and September 1942, all the remaining ghettos, with the exception of Lodz, were evacuated. Lodz ghetto was the scene of a bloody "action" against children under 10 years of age, the old, and the sick, resulting in the murder of 16,500 persons.

In mid-1943, Himmler and Albert Speer (Reich Minister for Armament and War Production) entered a long-drawn-out contest over the disposition of Lodz Ghetto. Himmler sought to incorporate the ghetto industries into the SS camp combine in the Lublin district, while Speer tried to retain a monopoly over this important industrial center. Their rivalry prolonged the existence of Lodz Ghetto until the summer of 1944, by which time Germany's strategic situation had deteriorated to such an extent that the evacuation of Poland was imminent. In August 1944, Lodz, the only ghetto still left in Europe, was liquidated and all its inmates, some 68,500 Jews, were deported to *Auschwitz.

Reichsgau Danzig-Westpreussen

This area, with a total Jewish population of 23,000, had few and small Jewish communities; e.g., *Danzig, *Torun, and *Bydgoszcz. The province became "*judenrein*" at a comparatively early stage. The Jews and Poles were exposed to a campaign of terror from the very beginning, which resulted in the massacre of part of the Jewish inhabitants. Others fled from the area, and the rest were deported to the General Government. The last transport of Jews (some 2,000 persons) from Danzig and Bydogszcz, including the surviving Jews of *Koenigsberg, arrived at the Warsaw Ghetto on March 10, 1941.

Regierungsbezirk Zichenau (Ciechanow)

According to the 1931 census, there was a Jewish population of 80,000 in the area of this newly created administrative district. In the first weeks of the occupation, a large number of

Jews from the towns near the German-Soviet demarcation line, e.g., *Ostrow Mazowiecka, Przasnysz, *Ostroleka, and *Pultusk, were forced to cross over to the Soviet zone. Their expulsion was accompanied by acts of terror, such as forcing the Jews to cross the Bug or the Narew rivers and opening fire on them, so that some people drowned or were shot to death. This group shared the fate of all the other Polish refugees in the Soviet Union. At the end of February 1941, about 10,000 Jews from Plock and Plock county were driven out, first passing through the Dzialdowo transit camp, where they were tortured and robbed, and from there to various towns in the Radom district, where within a year most of them died of starvation and disease. In Ciechanow, Mlawa, Plonsk, Strzegowo, and Sierpc, the Jews were segregated into ghettos, along with the few Jews left in towns whose Jewish populations had largely been expelled to the Soviet Union in the fall of 1939. These ghettos situated in the administrative area of East Prussia, ruled by the notorious Erich Koch, endured particularly harsh and bloodthirsty treatment, and the murder of members of the Judenrat and ghetto police was a frequent occurrence. In the fall of 1942 the ghettos were liquidated and the Jews dispatched to *Treblinka.

Regierungsbezirk Kattowitz (East Upper Silesia)
According to statistics published by the "Central Office of the Councils of Elders of the Jewish Communities in East Upper Silesia," comprising 32 communities, a Jewish population of 93,628 existed in these communities in March 1941. The largest among these were Bedzin (25,171), Sosnowiec (24,149), Chrzanow (8,229), Zawiercie (5,472), *Dabrowa Gornicza (5,564), and *Oswiecim (6,454). Jews played an important role in the life of this highly industrialized region (in mining, metallurgy, and textiles), and were heavily hit by the early-instituted "Aryanization" process.

A special office, the Dienststelle des Sonderbeauftragten der RRSS und Chefs der deutschen Polizei fuer fremdvoelkischen Einsatz in Oberschlesien, headed by Gen. Albrecht Schmelt (and commonly referred to as the Schmelt Organization), was in charge of sending the comparatively large number of skilled Jewish workers to German firms in Silesia and the Reich. No German firm was permitted to employ Jewish workers without the consent of the Schmelt Organization, and the latter maintained complete control over the Jewish "work effort." The German firms paid the Jewish workers at the normal rate (in this the Katowice (Kattowitz) area differed from the other occupied areas), but the workers received only a part of their wages and the firms had to submit the remainder to the Dienststelle. In 1942 the Schmelt Organization controlled 50,570 Jewish workers. When the evacuation of Jews from East Upper Silesia took place (starting May–June 1942), the Jewish workers were deported to Auschwitz, which was the major concentration camp as well as the largest industrial combine in Silesia.

The chairman of the Central Office of the Councils of Elders in Sosnowiec, Moshe Merin, exercised a decisive influence on the internal affairs of the Jewish communities and had considerable authority over the Judenraete (the Jewish councils). The formal ghettoization of East Upper Silesia did not take place until a comparatively late date. In Bedzin and Sosnowiec, for example, a closed ghetto was not established until May 1943, but it was liquidated by August 1943. These ghettos also absorbed the Jews left over from previous *Aussiedlungen* ("evacuation actions"). Merin was a consistent protagonist of the strategy of "rescuing" Jews by voluntarily providing the Nazi Moloch with contingents of victims to give others the chance of survival. He carried out this policy to its extreme, lending his own active cooperation, as well as that of the ghetto police, to the *Aussiedlungsaktionen*.

General Government
Originally, the General Government consisted of four districts, Warsaw, Lublin, Radom, and Cracow. When the district of Galicia was added, the Jewish population reached 2,110,000. The transfer of the administration from military to civilian authorities, which took place at the end of October 1939, did not alleviate the harsh conditions, for the uncontrolled terror of the first period was then replaced by "legally" imposed restrictions and persecution. The first proclamation, issued by General Governor Hans *Frank on Oct. 26, 1939, stated that "there will be no room in the General Government for Jewish exploiters," and from the very first day of his rule, Frank inundated the Jewish population with a flood of anti-Jewish measures. The personal rights of Jews were severely curtailed in all spheres of private and social life. Jews were deprived of freedom of movement, the right to dispose of their property, exercise their professions, and benefit from their labor. They were denied social and medical insurance benefits (which the antisemitic regime in Poland had granted them), religious observance (ritual slaughter and public worship), and a normal school education for their children. Finally, they lost the right to dispose of their own persons. Jews could no longer associate freely and Jewish societies, institutions, and organizations were disbanded and their property confiscated. The Judenrat, a quasi-representative body of the Jews, was established in their place by the Nazi authorities.

WARSAW DISTRICT. This district was divided into 10 counties, Warsaw, Garwolin, *Grojec, *Lowicz, *Skierniewice, *Sochaczew, Blonie, Ostrow Mazowiecki, *Minsk Mazowiecki, *Siedlce, and *Sokolow Podlaski. In the first half of 1940 the total Jewish population of this district was 600,000, of whom 400,000 lived in Warsaw. Its Jews were concentrated into ghettos in the western counties in 1940, and in the eastern counties in the fall of 1941. The Warsaw Ghetto was established on Nov. 15, 1940. The ghettos in the western part were of short duration. From the end of January to the beginning of April 1942, 72,000 Jews from this area were brought into the Warsaw Ghetto, where they lacked even the most rudimentary means for existence. With their arrival, the total number of refugees in the ghetto rose to 150,000, but the population was being constantly decimated by starvation and disease.

In the fall of 1941, the Jews in each of the eastern counties were concentrated into between five and seven ghettos. This step was in fact in preparation for *Aussiedlungsaktionen* which began with the Warsaw Ghetto on July 22, 1942, and continued until Oct. 4–6, 1942. In the General Government these actions, under the code name of "Einsatz Reinhard," were always carried out by special commando units (see Reinhard *Heydrich and *Holocaust, General Survey), headed by the SS and police chief of the Lublin district, Odilo *Globocnik. A decree issued by Frank on June 3, 1942, transferred the civilian authority's jurisdiction over the Jewish population in the General Government to Wilhelm Krueger, its chief of SS and police.

On the eve of its destruction, the Warsaw Ghetto contained 450,000 Jews, of whom approximately 300,000 were deported to Treblinka by Sept. 21, 1942. Officially, 35,639 Jews remained in Warsaw as workers in German factories, employees of the Judenrat, or policemen. In fact, some 60,000 were left, including those in hiding. It is to be noted that Himmler's order to Krueger of July 19, 1942, formally fixed the date of Dec. 31, 1942, as the final date for "cleansing" the General Government of the Jews. Between July 19 and 24, 1942, the Jews of *Otwock, Minsk Mazowiecki, and Siedlce were deported. Between September 22 and 27, most of the ghettos in the Sokolow Podlaski, Wegrow, and Minsk Mazowiecki counties were liquidated, followed, in the last days of October, by the remaining ghettos in the Warsaw district. Small groups of Jews tried to hide out on the "Aryan" side or in the countryside. In order to lull the intended victims into a false sense of security, Krueger issued a decree (Oct. 28, 1942) when the annihilation of the Jewish population in the district had been almost completed, providing for "residential quarters" in Warsaw and Siedlce. His aim was to influence the Jews in hiding to believe that these "newly established ghettos" which had already passed through a partial liquidation would now be a safe haven for the survivors. In this he was largely successful. The intolerable conditions in which the Jews found themselves, hiding out in the forests amid a hostile population, induced them to seek out and settle in the new "residential quarters." Only a short while later they were deported. The "new" Siedlce Ghetto, for example, did not last a month, and by November 25, Siedlce was *judenrein*. In November, too, the liquidation of most of the Jewish labor camps was begun and after "selections" the workers were deported to the Warsaw Ghetto. In the course of the *Aktion* on Jan. 18–19, 1943, the SS men met with armed resistance from the Jewish Fighting Organization and were forced to cease action for the time being. The Warsaw Ghetto, according to Himmler's decree (Feb. 16, 1943), was to be liquidated at the earliest possible date, and the workers and machinery were to be transferred to the Lublin SS camps.

LUBLIN DISTRICT. The 10 counties in the Lublin district – Lublin, *Biala Podlaska, *Bilgoraj, *Chelm, *Hrubieszow, *Janow Lubelski, *Krasnystaw, *Pulawy, *Radzyn, and *Zamosc – had a Jewish population of 250,000 in March–April 1941, including 55,000 refugees and deportees. In the beginning, the eastern part of the Lublin district was regarded as a "Jewish reservation" and Jews from parts of Poland that had been incorporated into the Reich, as well as from the Reich itself, from the Czech Protectorate of Bohemia-Moravia, and from *Austria were deported there on a systematic basis. Jozefow, Izbica Lubelska, Krasnystaw, and Zamosc were some of the towns which served as concentration points for these deportees. The local population was also displaced, generally in order to make room for the new arrivals. Even after this plan for the "Jewish reservation" had been given up, tens of thousands of Jews deported from Germany, Czechoslovakia, and Austria continued to stream into the district, to be "evacuated" to the *Belzec death camp, whose murder installations began functioning in March 1942.

The Nazi ideologists also regarded Lublin as a reservoir of "World Jewry," which presumably maintained secret links with Jewish communities everywhere (see *Hitler). As a result, the Lublin district was turned into an experimental station for various Nazi schemes for the annihilation of Polish Jewry. It was the headquarters of "Einsatz Reinhard" from where its "action groups" began their destructive march through the General Government. The first ghetto in the district was set up in the city of Lublin in April 1941. Since the area designated for the ghetto was too small to hold the approximately 45,000 Jews who were in Lublin at the time, the Nazi authorities forced over 10,000 to leave the city "voluntarily" and move to other towns in the district. The restricted area of the ghetto and its dense population caused epidemics and a high rate of mortality. In November and December 1941 there were 1,227 cases of typhus and the mortality rate that year was three times that of a year before the war (40.8 per 1,000).

In the second half of 1940, about 50 forced labor camps for Jews were established in the Lublin district for local Jews and Jews from other districts. In the winter of 1940–41, there were over 12,000 Jews in these camps. Many succumbed to the intolerable living and working conditions – starvation; wretched accommodations (usually in decrepit old barracks, stables, and barns); lack of hygiene; strenuous work (regulating rivers, draining swamps, and digging canals); and inhuman treatment by the camp commanders. In Osowa camp, 47 inmates were shot in July 1941 after two or three of them had contracted typhus. The Judenraete in ghettos from which the workers had come organized aid for them. The Warsaw Judenrat, for example, spent 520,000 zlotys ($104,000) in aid to the camps in 1940, and the Lublin Judenrat, 150,000 zlotys ($30,000). The "evacuation" campaign in this district preceded those in other parts of the General Government. In the period from March 17 to April 20, 1942, 30,000 Jews from Lublin Ghetto were deported to Belzec and murdered there, while 4,000 others were deported to the Majdan Tatarski Ghetto close to Lublin, which existed until Nov. 9, 1942. In the same period, 3,400 Jews from Piaski and 2,200 from

Izbica were dispatched to Belzec, preceded by about 17,000 Jews from Pulawy county (May 6–12). The ghettos which had thus been made *judenrein* became temporary collection points for Jews deported from the Reich, the Protectorate, and Vienna, and after a short stay there they were sent on to Belzec to be murdered.

Krueger's decree of Oct. 28, 1942, set up eight ghettos in the Lublin district, and like the ghettos in the Warsaw district, their existence was of short duration. By Dec. 1, 1942, five ghettos were left (Piaski, Wlodawa, Izbica, *Lukow Lubelski, and Miedzyrzec Podlaski) and the last of these was liquidated in July 1943. The Jewish workers remained in the concentration and labor camps until November 1943. On Nov. 3–7, 1943, 18,000 Jews were murdered in *Majdanek concentration camp, over 13,000 in the Poniatowa camp, and approximately 10,000 in the Trawniki camp, to which several thousands of Jews had been deported from Warsaw after the ghetto revolt in April 1943.

CRACOW DISTRICT. The Cracow district, consisting of 12 counties (Cracow, Debica, *Jaroslaw, *Jaslo, *Krosno, Miechow, *Nowy Sacz, Nowy Targ, *Przemysl, *Sanok, and *Tarnow), had a prewar Jewish population of over 250,000. By May 1941 this number dwindled to 200,000, in spite of the additional influx of 20,000 refugees and deportees from the incorporated areas, including Silesia, Lodz, and Kalisz, in the fall of 1939 and spring of 1940. The expulsion of Jews from the Cracow district, where the General Government capital was situated, was accelerated. In the first few months, Jews living in the border towns along the San River were expelled to the Soviet zone. From the spring of 1940 to November 1941, Jews living in the spas and summer resorts in Nowy Sacz and Nowy Targ counties were expelled, and from May 1940 to April 1941, 55,000 Jews left Cracow voluntarily or were driven out. The Jewish population thus became concentrated in an ever-decreasing number of places – in Cracow county, in seven townships and 10 villages, in Nowy Sacz in five places, and in the Nowy Targ county in seven.

The first ghetto was established in March 1941 in the Podgorze quarter of Cracow. A wall sealed it off from the rest of the city and the gates of the wall had the form of tombstones. The first "evacuations" took place in Cracow Ghetto, which underwent three such actions, on May 30–31, October 28, 1942, and March 13–14, 1943. In the final evacuation, 2,000 Jews were murdered on the spot, about 2,000 were deported to Auschwitz, and approximately 6,000 were sent to the nearby camp in *Plaszow, located on the site of two Jewish cemeteries. The first *Aktion* in Tarnow took place on June 11–13, 1942, involving 11,000 Jews. The Jews of Przemysl county were murdered on July 27–August 3 (after 10,000 Jews from the county had been concentrated in the city). At the beginning of August, the Jews from Jaroslaw were deported to Belzec, followed at the end of that month by deportation of the Jews from Cracow county, where at an earlier date the Jews from the ghettos in *Bochnia, *Wieliczka, and Skawina had been concentrated. In September 1942 approximately 11,000 Jews from Sanok county (earlier concentrated at a camp at *Izyaslav (Zaslav) were deported to Belzec or shot in the surrounding forests. That month the ghettos in Tarnow county were finally liquidated.

Krueger's decree of Oct. 28, 1942, setting up six ghettos in the Cracow district (Cracow, Bochnia, Tarnow, Rzeszow, Debica, and Przemysl), was immediately followed by murder "actions" there. From June to November 1942, a total of over 100,000 Jews were murdered, and by Jan. 1, 1943, according to official figures, 37,000 destitute Jews were left in "residual ghettos" and a number of camps. There were over 20 labor camps in the Cracow district, the largest at *Mielec (with 3,000 Jewish inmates on the day of its liquidation, Aug. 24, 1944) – and others in Pustkow (1,500), Rozwadow (1,200), Szebnie (2,000–2,500), and in Plaszow with two branches in Prokocim and Biezanow. Plaszow, a collection point for the Jews who survived the liquidation of ghettos and camps in the entire district, had 20,000 imprisoned there in the fall of 1943. In March 1944, large transports were sent from Plaszow to Auschwitz, Stutthof, Flossenburg, and *Mauthausen, while the 567 Jews left were liquidated in January 1945 together with the rest of the Jewish survivors from the Cracow district.

RADOM DISTRICT. The newly created Radom district, comprising the larger part of the Kielce province and parts of the Lodz and Warsaw provinces, had a Jewish population of about 360,000 on Sept. 1, 1939. In this district too the evacuation of the Jews proceeded at a rapid pace. First of all, the district had been heavily bombarded, and there were cities and towns in which up to 80% of the Jewish population had lost their homes and sought refuge elsewhere. Secondly, the deportations from the incorporated areas, the Protectorate (an undetermined number from Prague), and Vienna brought into the district large numbers of homeless Jews – 4,000 from Wartheland, about 10,000 from the Plock county, and 4,000 from Vienna. In 1941, the total number of refugees and deportees reached 70–75,000 (over 20% of the local Jewish population). In 1940–41, a kind of internal expulsion process went on in the district, e.g., in December 1940, when 2,000 Jews were expelled from Radom, and in October 1941, when several thousand were driven out from Tomaszow Mazowiecki.

The ghettos in this district were created at an earlier stage than in other parts of the General Government – in *Piotrkow at the end of October 1939, and in *Radomsko at the end of December that year. Ghettos were set up in March–April 1941 in the three large cities of the Radom district – in Radom (which in January 1941 had 28,000 Jews), Czestochowa (36,000), and Kielce (20,000). At the end of 1940 the ghetto of Tomaszow Mazowiecki was established (this town had 16,500 Jews in June 1940), divided into three different sections (the Radom Ghetto also consisted of two sections in two different quarters of the city). Many places were in ruins, causing severe overcrowding in the ghettos, and in some of the smaller ghettos there were as many as 12–30 persons to a room. In order to prepare for the *Aussiedlungen*, the Nazis concentrated the Jews in a few ghettos. In the first stage, the Jews who were still living in villages were expelled to the neighboring towns. In the second stage, the Jewish population from the smaller towns was concentrated in the large ghettos, and each of the 10 counties had several concentration points assigned to it. At the end of this stage, over 20,000 Jews were living in a few large, heavily guarded ghettos.

The first deportation, to Treblinka, took place on Aug. 5, 1942, in Radom. The Kielce Ghetto inhabitants were deported on August 20–24, and the Czestochowa Ghetto inhabitants, between Sept. 2 and Oct. 5, 1942. By Nov. 7, 1942, most of the Jews had been deported to Treblinka. On Jan. 1, 1943, according to a German source, there were only 29,400 Jews left in the four ghettos ("residential districts") in Radomsko, Sandomierz, *Szydlowiec, and Ujazd, provided for in Krueger's second decree (Nov. 10, 1942). These ghettos came to an end in January 1943. Only the Jewish slave laborers in the labor camps were left, mainly near the industrial concerns of Radom, Kielce, Czestochowa, Ostrowiec-Swietokrzyski, Skarzysko-Kamienna, Blizyn, Piotrkow, Tomaszow Mazowiecki, and other towns. These were in fact concentration camps run by the district SS and police chiefs, to whom the German factory owners directly paid the fees for exploitation of Jewish manpower (as was the case in the other districts also). Some of these camps went through a series of transfers and "selections" but continued to exist until the second half of 1944. The German *Hasag* factories in Czestochowa were still functioning as late as January 1945.

GALICIA DISTRICT. The district of Galicia, established in August 1941, comprised the *Stanislav and *Tarnopol provinces and the eastern part of the Lvov province, and consisted of 16 counties. The 1931 census report indicated a Jewish population in this area of 500,000. As a result of the great influx of refugees from Nazi-occupied Poland in the fall of 1939, the number of Jews had considerably increased, and it is estimated that at the outbreak of German-Soviet hostilities, there were 600,000–650,000 Jews in the area, taking into account the natural increase from 1931 to 1941. The German invasion was accompanied from the very beginning by the mass murder of Jews, initiated and perpetrated by local Ukrainians with the support and participation of the Einsatzkommandos and the German army. Pogroms took place in Lvov (on the "Petlyura Days," July 25 and 27), in Tarnopol, *Zolochev, and *Borislav. Many of the Jews living in the countryside, about 25% of the total Jewish population, were murdered in this period.

In the part of Galicia temporarily occupied by the Hungarian army (Kolomyya, Borshchev, and *Gorodenka), the situation was quite different, the Hungarian commanders taking the Jews under their protection and preventing murders from taking place. During the short period of German military occupation, until Aug. 1, 1941, when its civilian administration took over, several tens of thousands of Jews were killed. The civilian administration immediately introduced the anti-Jewish legislation applying to the General Government. In fact, some of the provisions of this legislation were applied even before a "legal" framework was created. The first ghettos were set up in the beginning of October at Stanislav (for about 30,000 Jews) and Tarnopol (18,000). These were followed in the spring of 1942 by ghettos in Kolomyya and Kolomyya county, and at *Chortkov. By the second half of 1942, ghettos existed in all the cities and towns, and a large part of their population had already been deported to Belzec. The last ghetto to be established was the one at Lvov, in August–September 1942, after several postponements. This came after the great *Aussiedlung* action, 36,000 surviving out of a population of about 150,000. Krueger's decree of Nov. 10, 1942, provided for 32 ghettos in the Galicia district, in Lvov, Stanislav, Tarnopol, Chortkov, *Stry, *Drogobych, *Sambor, Borshchev, *Zholkva, *Brody, Rava-Russkaya, *Rogatin, and *Skalat.

Large-scale physical extermination campaigns began in the second half of 1941 and were initially directed mainly against Jews in the professions and intellectuals. During the High Holiday period, on Oct. 12, 1941, about 10,000 Jews were shot to death at the Jewish cemetery of Stanislav. In November numerous executions took place in Lvov, when the first attempt was made to organize a ghetto there, and mass shootings occurred in Kolomyya county in December of that year. This is only a partial listing and it is estimated that some 100,000 Jews were murdered in July 1941–March 1942. In the latter month, the extermination camp at Belzec went into operation and from then until the end of 1942, about 300,000 Jews – 50% of the Jewish population of the district – were deported to Belzec or shot on the spot, or taken away for execution in the forests. The others remained for a short while in the ghettos and labor camps, and by June 1943 they were all liquidated. According to SS-*Gruppenfuehrer* Fritz *Katzmann's report on the "Final Solution" in Galicia, only 21,000 Jews were left in Galicia, distributed in over 21 camps, the largest of which was the Janowska Street camp in Lvov. Selected workers from liquidated ghettos were transferred to this camp in Lvov, while those who were no longer fit for work were executed in the vicinity. In the second half of 1943, nearly all the Jewish labor camps were liquidated and their inmates murdered. In this period, several thousand Jews who had been engaged in agricultural work were also murdered.

Bezirk Bialystok

This district, created in July 1941, was attached to but not incorporated in East Prussia. The chief of the East-Prussian provincial government was also appointed head of the civilian administration of the Bialystok district and the central provincial organs at Koenigsberg were responsible for all district affairs. The area of the district, practically identical with Bialystok province, was divided into seven counties: Bialystok, Grodno, Bielsk Podlaski, Grajewo, Lomza, Sokolka, and Volkovysk. The Bialystok district suffered two eruptions of war, on Sept. 1, 1939, and June 22, 1941. The first German occupation was restricted to the western part of the district and lasted only a fortnight, after which the area was turned over to the Soviets. The Soviet occupying forces imposed far-reaching changes in the economic, social, and political life of the Jews. The Jewish population of the district in September 1939 was estimated at 240,000–250,000. Later on, the district was flooded by a stream of refugees from the western and central part of Poland. Among the officials and specialists brought in from the Soviet Union, there were also a considerable number of Jews, and the total increase in population is estimated at 100,000. It may therefore be assumed that in June 1941 the district had a Jewish population of about 350,000.

The second German invasion was accompanied by mass murders, carried out by the *Einsatzkommandos* comprising Tilsit police battalions. These operated in the rear of the army and caused the destruction of entire communities (Jedwabne, *Kolo, Stawiski, *Tykocin, and others). In Bialystok, over 6,000 Jews were murdered between June 27 and July 13, 1941. The great synagogue was burnt down and at least 1,000 Jews who had been forced into it perished in the flames. Special murder campaigns were instituted against Jewish intellectuals. Antisemitic elements within the local Polish and Belorussian population, as well as among the Polish police which continued to serve under the occupying power, took an active part in the mass murder of Jews. (Even before the war, the influence of the Polish antisemitic parties had been especially strong in this area.) Most of the ghettos were established in August 1941. The larger among these were Bialystok (over 50,000), Grodno (25,000), *Pruzhany (12,000), Lomza (10,000), *Sokolka (8,000), and Bielsk Podlaski (7,000). Grodno Ghetto consisted of two parts, one inhabited by artisans and skilled workers and their families, and the other by the rest of the Jewish population. Each had its own Judenrat and ghetto police, but the chairman of the Judenrat of the artisans' ghetto had the title of *Generalobmann* ("chief chairman") and represented both parts vis-à-vis the authorities.

While the ghettos were in the process of formation, "selections" and mass slaughter of Jews often took place. In Szczuczyn, for example, the ghetto was inhabited almost entirely by women and children, most of the men having been killed. The overcrowding in the ghettos was phenomenal. In Czyzow, for example, 200 persons were squeezed into seven tiny houses. Systematic mass annihilation began on Nov. 2, 1942. In a single day, most of the ghettos were wiped out (except for Bialystok, Pruzhany, the first part of the Grodno Ghetto, *Krynki, and Sokolka). Before reaching their final destination at the extermination camp of Treblinka, the deportees were kept in assembly camps for a period of three to 10 weeks, during which many of them succumbed to the inhuman conditions. In November, 120,000–130,000 Jews were killed in the murder campaign. The *Aktionen* were renewed in February 1943, after the liquidation of the Pruzhany, Sokolka, and Krynki ghettos. In Bialystok Ghetto, the first "action" took place on Feb. 5–12, 1943, resulting in the deaths of 13,000 Jews, of whom 1,000 were killed on the spot. Over 40,000 persons were killed in the third phase of the extermination campaign. Bialystok Ghetto was the last in the district to be liquidated (Aug. 16, 1943). Armed resistance, organized by the Jewish Fighting Organization (see Mordekhai *Tenenbaum), was suppressed by German military forces, including tanks. Over 30,000 Jews were deported to Treblinka, Majdanek, and Auschwitz.

Generalbezirk Litauen und Weissrussland (Lithuania and Belorussia)

The Polish parts of these districts, which belonged to Reichkommissariat Ostland, consisted of almost the entire Vilna and Novogrudok provinces and of the northern portion of Polesie province. In 1931 this area was inhabited by over 230,000 Jews. From September to December 1939, a large number of refugees arrived in the area, especially in Vilna. For nearly 11 months (from Oct. 10, 1939, until the end of August 1940), Vilna and its environs formed a part of Lithuania. In August, the entire country was absorbed by the Soviet Union. Under Soviet occupation, thousands of Jews were arrested and deported to distant parts of the Soviet Union, but several thousand escaped to the United States, Palestine (see *Beriḥah), and *Shanghai. It is therefore impossible to determine the size of the Jewish population in June 1941. The larger communities in the Lithuania district were Vilna, Vileika, *Oshmyany, Sviencіany, and Trakai (*Troki); in the Belorussian district they were *Novogrudok, *Baranovichi, *Lida, *Slonim, *Molodechno, and *Stolbtsy. Like everywhere else in "Ostland," the military invasion brought in its wake large-scale murder by the *Einsatzkommandos*, in this case Einsatzgruppe A. In many places they had the assistance of locally recruited "Hiwis" (*Hilfswillige* – local volunteer units). On July 11–Dec. 24, 1941, 45,000 Jews were killed in Vilna (which in 1931 had a total Jewish population of 55,000). At approximately the same time, 9,000 Jews were slaughtered in Slonim; 5,000 in Vileika; 4,000 in Molodechno; 2,500 in Novogrudok; 1,800 in *Volozhin, and other places. During the murder campaign, or a short while later, ghettos were established where further mass executions took place (Vilna Ghetto was set up on Sept. 6, 1941). Many small communities were completely wiped out.

Ghettos continued to exist in Vilna, Vileika, Oshmyany, Novogrudok, Lida, *Glubokoye, Slonim, and Baranovichi, and in a few smaller communities from which Jews were dispatched to larger ghettos in the summer of 1942, in preparation for the second phase of the annihilation program. Vilna Ghetto was also used for this purpose. Jacob Gens, chief of the Vilna Ghetto and of the ghetto police, had some measure of jurisdiction over the smaller ghettos in "Wilnaland," and the Vilna ghetto police participated in the *Aktion* that took place in Oshmyany at the end of October 1942. In Belorussia the same procedure was initiated of concentrating the Jewish population of a certain area in one of the larger ghettos in preparation for murder "actions." Here there was an almost continuous murder campaign, with breathing spells only between one *Aktion* and the next. The longest such period of respite was granted to Vilna Ghetto, lasting from early 1942 until September 1943.

The final phase extended from August 1942, when the ghetto in Slonim was destroyed, until September 1943, when the Jews of Vilna, Novogrudok, and Lida were sent to their deaths. In the course of August and September 1943, about 10,000 Jews were deported from Vilna Ghetto to concentration camps in Estonia. Six thousand were murdered on September 23, and the ghetto was liquidated. Several thousand Jewish workers employed outside the ghetto were exterminated later (July 1944). Specialists and skilled workers were sometimes concentrated in certain houses in the liquidated ghetto or sent to labor camps. Such camps, containing the pitiful remnants of the liquidated ghettos of Belorussia, were located at *Koldychevo (near Baranovichi) and Kelbasin. They too ceased to exist at the end of 1943.

Generalbezirk Wolhynien-Podolien

Of the Polish territories, this district, which formed part of the "Reichskommissariat Ukraine," contained the larger part of the Polesie province and the entire Wolyn (Volhynia) province belonging to prewar Poland. The 1931 census of the population in this area indicated about 300,000 Jews. The larger communities were Pinsk, Brest, *Kobrin, *Kovel, *Dubno, *Rovno, *Lutsk, *Ostrog, *Kremenets, and *Vladimir-Volynski. Here too, a large influx of refugees came from Poland shortly after the outbreak of the war, while a certain number of Jews were moved by the Soviets to other parts of the U.S.S.R., so that it was impossible to determine the size of the population in June 1941. A mass slaughter in this district was carried out mainly by Einsatzgruppe C, commencing with the German invasion. The murder action at *Rovno was carried out on Nov. 5–6, 1941, when 15,000 Jews were shot. In general the local Ukrainian population cooperated in the annihilation campaign against the Jews.

Only a few communities escaped in the initial phase (one of these was Kovel). As was the case elsewhere, the surviving Jews were herded into temporary ghettos. Dubno Ghetto was among the first to be liquidated (May 27, 1942), and 5,000–7,000 Jews were killed. The first *Aktion* took place on May 10, 1942, and the handful of Jewish workers who survived it were shot on May 23, 1942. In Kovel the "city" ghetto was destroyed on June 2, 1942, with 8,000–9,000 victims, while the "workers'" ghetto in the city was liquidated on Sept. 18, 1942. Lutsk Ghetto came to an end on Aug. 20, 1942 (17,000 people murdered). In Kremenets, the ghetto's agony lasted for two weeks, starting on Aug. 10, 1942, in the course of which 19,000 Jews went to their deaths. In September, it was Vladimir-Volynski's turn (18,000 victims) and from October 28 to 31, the Jews of Pinsk Ghetto were murdered. As in "Ostland," the mass executions took place in the vicinity of the ghettos, in front of prepared mass graves, and were marked by extraordinary manifestations of sadism. The Ukrainian police displayed a murderous zeal in their cooperation with the Nazis. In the course of December 1942, the Jewish workers who had survived the mass executions were also liquidated. In a report on a trip in the Ukraine in June 1943, Hans Joachim Kausch of the Propaganda Ministry stated that the Jews of that area had been "completely" liquidated and throughout his entire stay there he had found only four Jews, working as tailors in an SD camp.

Demographic Total

Up to September 1939 Poland had a Jewish population of 3,351,000. Exact figures on the number killed between September 1939 and 1944 are not available, but the following account is a relatively well-founded estimate. Shortly after the end of the war, the Central Committee of Polish Jews began registering all surviving Polish Jews and by June 15, 1945, 55,509 had registered. Since some people registered several times with different local committees a round figure of 55,000 is assumed, which included a certain number of Jews who succeeded in returning to Poland from the Soviet Union. To this must be added 13,000 Jews in the Polish army formed in the U.S.S.R. in 1941, and approximately 1,000 Jews (out of 2,000) who had saved themselves by posing as "Aryans" and had not registered with the Jewish committees, bringing the total to 69,000. The number of Polish Jews who were saved by fleeing in September 1939 to the Soviet Union, to certain European countries, to Palestine, or to North and South America, or who survived the camps in Germany, is estimated at a maximum of 300,000 (250,000 of whom had fled to the U.S.S.R.). The sum total of surviving Polish Jews is therefore about 369,000, i.e., 11% of the prewar population, while 2,982,000 Jews were killed.

Jewish Resistance

Nazi plans called for a campaign of repression utilizing legal and economic restrictions and hard labor to bring about a rapid reduction of the Jewish population by pauperization, starvation, and epidemics. The Jews developed a system of self-defense to thwart the rapid achievement of the plans for their destruction, or at least succeeded in slowing down the realization of the Nazi program. Jewish resistance applied to all spheres of life – economic and spiritual; on an individual as well as on a collective basis; and in the final stage, when the Nazis resorted to the "Final Solution" (physical annihilation) of the Jews, it took the form of armed insurrections. In the economic sphere, the Jews succeeded in circumventing the regulations designed to isolate them from the gentile society, due to the fact that large numbers of Jews were put to work outside the ghetto. They established secret industries in the ghetto itself, by which they staved off rapid starvation and carried on business with the "Aryan" market. Foodstuffs were also smuggled into the ghetto by various means, often displaying astounding inventiveness. Jewish industrialists and artisans managed to obtain substitutes for all kinds of raw materials. In Warsaw Ghetto, for example, the export of wares produced in the ghetto workshops under orders of the German "Transferstelle" was in no proportion to that of articles produced in secret and exported without the knowledge of the official German office. The considerable gap between legal and illegal economic activities became characteristic of the economic situation in all the occupied areas. Officially the Jews were given the opportunity of working for the German economy only, military as well as civilian, for as long as this served the German war effort. In practice, many of the Jews, inured by a long tradition of existence under harsh conditions of persecution, and fortified by a powerful will to live, were able to break out of the economic straitjacket into which the Nazis had forced them and to surmount the dangers of the ghetto walls.

The Nazis were disappointed by the ability of the ghettoized Jews to adapt themselves to the abnormal conditions of their existence, and surprised that "so few" Jews were dying from "natural" causes and that there were no mass suicides. At a meeting of Nazi officials, held in Cracow on Aug. 24, 1942, General Governor Frank openly admitted: "By the way, I wish to state that we have sentenced 1,200,000 Jews to death by starvation; the fact that the Jews are not dying from hunger will only serve to speed up enactment of further anti-Jewish decrees." Thus, the Jews' vitality served to frustrate partially the biological war that the Nazis waged against them and was one of the causes for the Nazis' decision to resort to the "Final Solution."

Jewish aid organizations which existed before the war, such as the *American Jewish Joint Distribution Committee (JDC), *TOZ, and *CENTOS, the Yidishe Sotsiale Alaynhilf (YISA) founded in May 1940, and, after liquidation of the last in Oct. 1942, the Juedische Unterstuetzungsstelle (JUS), established formally in March 1943, were permitted by the General Government to carry on their activities in its area. The YISA set up a highly diversified system of social and medical assistance. Almost every ghetto provided some form of public assistance, such as soup kitchens and accommodation for deportees and refugees. As early as May 1940, according to an incomplete list, some 200 welfare committees were sponsored by the Judenraete, and their budgets were provided mainly by the JDC. These committees also collected funds, clothing, and other articles among local Jews. By the end of 1941 the YISA organization was active in over 400 localities in the General Government, maintaining 1,500 social and medical institutions and serving 300,000 adults and 30,000 children. This, of course, was not enough to cope with the demands posed by the constantly growing pauperization of the Jewish population and the continual influx of new arrivals (in some ghettos, 60% of the population was dependent on public assistance). The constant lack of nourishment and hygiene in the ghettos, which the Nazis set up in the most dilapidated parts of the towns, resulted in diseases and epidemics to which the entire Jewish population might have easily succumbed. However, health and sanitary departments were set up and maintained by the Judenraete and TOZ which in turn subsidized 117 hospitals and 123 out-patient clinics and sanitary posts. To prevent the spread of the epidemics to the "Aryan" city quarters, the Nazi authorities used police measures, the results of which were even worse than the epidemics. In fact the ghetto population was so weakened that a large loss of life could not be avoided. In Warsaw, Lodz, Lublin, and Kutno, 15–20% of the Jewish population died in the two or three years of the ghettos' existence.

The Jews also displayed moral resistance to the starvation and debilitating forced labor, whereby the Nazis hoped to divest the Jews of all interest in spiritual life and dehumanize them. Moral resistance took varied forms. Pious Jews convened in secret for prayers, disregarding the dangers thus incurred; yeshivah students continued their studies and held clandestine *minyanim* to which they took the orphans to recite *kaddish* for their deceased parents. They also abstained from using the public soup kitchens which under ghetto conditions were not kept *kasher*, despite the greater suffering this entailed for them. Nonobservant Jews had their own means of moral resistance. Teachers established clandestine student groups and conducted classes in private homes. Persons who had been active before the war in cultural societies established secret libraries, choirs, orchestras, and dramatic groups, and held lectures and celebrations of important historical anniversaries. The Judenraete also established schools, wherever the Nazi authorities did not put obstacles in their way. (According to a decree issued by Frank on Aug. 31, 1940, the Judenraete were to be permitted to run elementary and vocational schools, but with few exceptions were prevented from actually doing so by the local Nazi authorities.)

Intensive cultural and educational activities were carried on in the Warsaw ghetto by the Yidishe Kultur-Organizatsye and the CENTOS, and in Vilna Ghetto by the cultural department of the Judenrat. Lodz Ghetto also maintained a large network of schools until the summer of 1941 (45 schools with 500 teachers and an average monthly attendance of 10,300 children). In most ghetto schools the emphasis was placed on Jewish studies. The teaching of history and geography was prohibited. Cultural activities fulfilled the dual purpose of protecting the inhabitants of the ghetto, especially the youth, against the demoralizing atmosphere of the ghetto created by the Nazis, and of strengthening their resistance to Nazi attempts to deprive them of their human dignity.

Organized physical and armed resistance was closely linked to political activities in a number of ghettos, and took various forms. Illegal publications, including pamphlets, were issued periodically or singly, and were either handwritten or duplicated. (In Warsaw Ghetto, for example, incomplete reports indicate that from mid-1940 to April 1943, 40 illegal periodicals were issued by various illegal movements representing every shade of political opinion.) Organized secret listening-in to foreign broadcasts, to reduce the Jews' isolation from the outer world, provided information on the political and military situation, and served as a source of hope and encouragement. In some ghettos, political parties – particularly workers' parties, e.g., the Bund, Po'alei Zion, and the communists – actively opposed the Jewish ghetto administration, i.e., the Judenraete and the ghetto police. (In Lodz Ghetto, opposition to Rumkowski's regime took the form of street demonstrations and strikes in the ghetto workshops.) Opposition to the Judenraete was also voiced in the underground press. The parties' youth movements conducted a cultural education campaign among their secret membership.

At a later stage, when the mass deportations began, the movements made preparations for armed resistance to the deportation "action." It was on the basis of organizing armed resistance that the political parties began to cooperate. Thus, in Warsaw Ghetto, a Jewish Coordinating Committee was set up in October 1942, composed of representatives of all the Zionist parties (with the exception of the Revisionists) – who were united in the Jewish National Committee – and of representatives of the Bund. On Oct. 27, 1942, the Jewish Fighting Organization (ZOB) was established which united the above-mentioned Jewish parties and the communists under one command. The heroic revolt of Warsaw Ghetto (which lasted from April 19 until the end of May 1943) was the result of the collective, self-sacrificing efforts of the youth of almost all political parties. The Revisionist Jewish Military Organization took an active part in the fighting. Similarly, in Bialystok Ghetto, a united fighting organization was set up on the eve of the revolt that broke out on Aug. 16, 1943.

In Czestochowa, the planned revolt was frustrated when an unexpected deportation "action" (on Sept. 21, 1942) barred access to the bunkers where the arms were hidden. During the liquidation of Bedzin Ghetto, underground fighters of the Zionist youth movements fought against vastly superior Nazi armed forces from fortified bunkers until they all fell. In Cracow Ghetto, the fighting organization, consisting of Zionist and Communist youth, carried out acts of sabotage and direct attacks on the Germans (such as the armed attack against German officers in the Cyganeria Café on Dec. 23, 1942). In Vilna Ghetto, a United Partisans Organization was founded in January 1942, comprising in later stages members of all the political movements. Following the Gestapo demand for the surrender of the Vilna underground commander, Yiẓḥak *Wittenberg, in July 1943, the leadership of the organization was forced to give up the struggle inside the ghetto, and smuggled its members into the forests, where they set up a partisans' group under the name of *Nekamah* ("Revenge").

Revolts broke out in the extermination camps of Treblinka (on Aug. 2, 1943) and Sobibor (Oct. 14, 1943) in which large numbers of prisoners managed to escape (most of whom were later killed). These insurrections later brought the murder installations in those camps to a halt. An armed revolt of the Jews in the "Sonderkommando" in Auschwitz took place on Oct. 7, 1944.

[Isaiah Trunk]

PARTISANS. The guerilla warfare in Poland (i.e., within the area designated by post-World War II boundaries) was confined to the territories of the so-called General-Government and the province of Bialystok. The first Jewish attempts to organize partisan units were undertaken by the resistance movement of the *Warsaw Ghetto in spring 1942, but these, as well as some other early attempts, failed due to lack of experience and the lack of support from the local population. In July 1942, the Germans began to implement the so-called Operation Reinhard. At that time, mainly in the provinces of Lublin and Kielce, there began a spontaneous movement of thousands of Jews fleeing the townlets to the forests to escape deportation. Many of them formed groups that offered active resistance to the Nazis. Although numerically strong, they had very few arms and no supply bases at all. Those who managed to hold out through the winter of 1942/43 came in contact with the Polish underground, as in the course of spring and summer 1943 a number of Polish partisan units began to operate from the forests.

The attitude of the Polish partisans toward the Jews depended upon the political framework to which they belonged and the goodwill of local commanders. The closest relations were between the Jewish partisans and the Communist-dominated People's Guard (Gwardia Ludowa). About a dozen Jewish partisan units were subordinated to the command of that organization and later acted as its units. Among them were: partisan detachment "Chil" (known also as the Second Company of the "Holod" battalion), under the command of Yehiel Grynszpan, which operated in the eastern part of the Lublin province; detachment "Emilia Plater," under the command of Samuel Jegier, and detachment "Kozietulski," under the command of Mietek Gruber, in the northern parts of the Lublin province; detachment "Berek Joselewicz," under the command of Forst, in the southern part of the Lublin province; detachment "Lwy" ("Lions"), under the command of Julian Ajzenman (Kaniewski), in the northern part of the Kielce province; detachment "Zygmunt," under the command of Zalman Fajnsztat, in the southwestern part of the Kielce province; detachment "Iskra" ("Spark"), under the command of Lejb Birman, in Rzeszow province; and detachment "Mordecai Anielewicz" commanded by Adam Szwarcfus, Mordecai Growas, and Ingac Podolski, in the forests near Wyszkow (northeast of Warsaw) which was organized after the Warsaw Ghetto uprising by remnants of the Jewish Fighting Organization. Jews also constituted a significant percentage in a number of other units of the People's Guard.

Remnants of the fighters in the *Bialystok Ghetto uprising formed the partisan unit "Forwards" ("Foroys"), which was later part of a Soviet partisan brigade under the command of General Kapusta. The attitude of the Armia Krajowa (Home Army), sponsored by the Polish government-in-exile residing in London, and of the Peasants' Battalions ("Bataliony Chłopskie") were different. These organizations did not accept Jewish units, but some of them accepted individual Jewish fighters, while others often took part in the murder of Jews. The extreme right-wing National Armed Forces ("Narodowe Siły Zbrojne") were strongly hostile toward Jews, organized attacks against Jewish partisans, and murdered all Jews they found hiding in the forests. Some Jewish units managed to operate independently of any Polish underground organization. The greatest of them was the unit in the Doleza forests under the command of Abraham Amsterdam.

A number of Jews won great fame in various Polish partisan units, mainly in those belonging to the People's Guard. Among the best known are: Colonel Ignacy Robb-Rosenfarb (Narbutt), commander of the People's Guard in the Kielce region; Colonel Robert Satanowski, commander of a partisan brigade; Colonel Niebrzydowski, commander of the Peasants' Battalions in the Miechow region; Major Menashe Matywiecki, member of the general staff of the People's Guard; Alexander Skotnicki, commander of the "Holod" battalion; Yehiel Brewerman, commander of the detachment "Bartosz Glowacki," and Captain Lucyna Herz, the only Polish woman officer parachuted into the woods for partisan activity. Jews also played a significant role in the Special Attack Battalion, which organized parachute units for guerilla warfare in the rear of the German army. The commander of that unit was the Jewish officer Lieutenant Colonel Henryk Toruńczyk. Four of the 12 units parachuted into the forests during the summer and autumn of 1944 were commanded by Jewish officers: Robert Satanowski, Julian Komar, Joseph Krakowski, and Zygmunt Gutman (later known as one of the best partisan commanders in the Kielce province). The significant feature of the Jewish partisan movement in Poland was that almost all Jewish partisans started their guerilla activity at a very early period (second half of 1942), when the Polish partisan movement hardly existed; thus Jews constituted in the early period a high proportion of the partisans and guerilla fighters. Among the first nine partisan detachments organized at the beginning of 1943 in the Kielce province, four were Jewish units, with a number of Jews present in all other units. Later in spring 1944, when the partisan movement in Poland grew rapidly, thanks to the great flow of arms from England (for the Armia Krajowa) and from the Soviet Union (for the left-wing guerillas), the Jewish communities were already destroyed and there were no more Jewish youth who could fill the partisan ranks. (See also: *Partisans.)

[Stefan Krakowski]

Jewish-Polish Relations during the War

Relations between Jews and Poles in occupied Poland were complicated in nature, especially in the Polish underground movements. The entire Polish population was vehemently anti-German, but the vast majority of people were also violently antisemitic. In the first month of the war, antisemitism seemed to have completely disappeared out of hatred for the Nazis, but it reemerged soon afterwards.

The Polish political parties' attitude to the Jews before the war generally remained much the same during the entire period of occupation. The right-wing parties, led by the Narodowa Demokracja (Endecja) officially denounced Hitler's barbaric methods, but in fact remained antisemitic and regarded the Nazi "solution of the Jewish problem" in Poland with quiet satisfaction. The extreme right-wing radicals, the Obóz Narodowo-Radykalny (ONR) and the Falanga, rejoiced over Hitlerism and approved of the Nazi murders. They contended that the victims were no better than murderers, and deserved their fate. The Polish Socialist Party (PPS), on the other hand, and especially its left wing (RPPS) and the reorganized Communist Party (PPR) condemned the murder of the Jews in their illegal publications, took part in campaigns to aid Jews, and appealed to the Polish people to assist. A similar stand was taken by the Democratic Party and the People's Party, although the latter, formerly an important party, did not have a uniform approach. In general it identified itself with the stand taken by the Polish government-in-exile represented inside Poland by the Delegatura. The Delegatura also maintained contact with the Jewish National Committee and the Jewish Coordinating Commission. Through the Delegatura these Jewish bodies were able to keep in touch with Jewish political movements and organizations abroad.

Relations between the Jews and the Delegatura, initially quite friendly, deteriorated in the course of time. This was due to the Delegatura's negative attitude in regard to supplying the Jewish Fighting Organization with sufficient quantities of arms. It was not until the resistance of the Jewish Fighting Organization in Warsaw in January 1943 that the fighters at last received a small quantity of arms from the Delegatura. The strained relations with the Delegatura were partly the result of the reactionary and antisemitic groups' influence within the Polish underground, which grew in strength as the German front moved back toward Poland and a general anti-Soviet attitude came to the fore. (Anti-Soviet feelings among the Poles were also heightened by the story of the Katyn massacre, and the resulting break in Soviet-Polish diplomatic relations in the summer of 1943.) Anti-Jewish agitation among the Polish population was also fed by the reports of the situation of the Jews in Eastern Poland under the Soviet occupation, when Jews were appointed to official positions. The Delegatura also adopted a negative attitude to the Jewish partisan movement, refusing to support it or even to recognize its existence.

As the Soviet army drew near the Polish frontier, a rapprochement took place between the Sanacja (the ruling party of Pilsudski's successors) and the Endecja and between the Sanacja and such outright Fascist organizations as the ONR, whose military arm, the National Armed Forces (NSZ), was recognized in March 1944 as a component of the Delegatura's underground army, the Armia Krajowa. The NSZ went so far as to murder Jewish partisans and Jews who had succeeded in escaping from the slaughter taking place in the ghettos. More and more, an anti-Jewish tendency made itself felt in the official underground publications issued by the Delegatura.

The Nazi propaganda machine cleverly exploited the antisemitism existing among the Polish population. Reviving the old Polish slogan of "Żydo-Komuna," they identified Jews with Communism and succeeded in further poisoning the prevailing anti-Jewish feelings among the Poles. As a result, Jews who had been in hiding on the "Aryan" side were denounced to the Nazis. In many places Poles not only assisted in the search for Jews, but joined the Nazis in torturing and killing them as well. The Polish police, with hardly any exception, took part in the "actions" and on several occasions were themselves in charge of rounding up the Jews and dispatching them to the death camps.

There were, however, some social groups and individuals, from all segments of the population, who helped Jews at the risk of their own lives. The activities of the "Council for Aid to Jews," which provided "Aryan" documents and shelter in Polish houses, rescued children, and extended financial aid, helped some 50,000 Jews. There were more than a few individual Poles who had the moral strength to overcome the fear of death (the punishment for giving refuge to Jews) and the pressure exerted on them by the prevailing anti-Jewish climate of opinion, to stretch out a helping hand to the persecuted Jews. Some of these Poles, along with their families, had to pay with their lives for the courage they displayed in aiding Jews.

It may be concluded that the attitude of the Poles to the Jews was marked by both active participation in the murder of Jews and rescue efforts at great risk. The motives for these attitudes also varied from religious, humanitarian, or simply materialistic considerations, to a "biological" hatred of Jews. Of all the occupied countries, the percentage of Jews saved in Poland was the smallest, since the predominant attitude was hostile, while rescue was an exception to the rule.

[Isaiah Trunk]

AFTER WORLD WAR II

Rescue of Jewish Children

When Poland was liberated in 1945, thousands of orphaned and abandoned Jewish children were wandering through villages and in the streets of the towns. Many were found in Polish homes and in convents. Some had been baptized, and some had been exploited by the peasants as a source of cheap labor. The official Jewish committees (*komitety*) established institutions for homeless children. Jewish parents applied to the Jewish organizations for help in finding children, who had been entrusted to non-Jewish families in order to save their lives but later disappeared without trace. Some Poles refused to return Jewish children, either because they had become attached to them or because they demanded financial remuneration for maintaining the child and for the risk they had incurred in hiding Jews from the Germans. There were a few cases of Jewish children living under conditions of starvation and terror. With the mass repatriations from the Soviet Union, 31,700 children under 14 years of age returned to Poland, including many hundreds of orphans, who also needed immediate care. Three separate bodies worked to save Jewish children. The first of these, the official Jewish committees, acting under the auspices of the authorities, maintained 11 boarding schools with a total of 1,135 orphans, and day schools and nurseries which cared for about 20,000 children. The youth department of the committees cared for about 7,700 boys and girls. Material conditions were good, but education was oriented toward Polish assimilation. The second, the Jewish Religious Council (Kongregacja), sent people to redeem children from Polish homes, particularly at the request of religious relatives. These children were delivered to their relatives abroad, or sent to be adopted by Jewish families in the United States, Great Britain, and other countries. The third organization was established by the Zionist movement, and given the abbreviated name of the "Coordination" (Koordynacja). Its emissaries wandered through Poland to rescue children, very often risking their lives in doing so. The Koordynacja established four children's homes, which housed hundreds of children aged between two and 12. The older children were sent to "children's kibbutzim" of the youth movements. Funds were supplied mainly by the *American Jewish Joint Distribution Committee (JDC). The special psychological problems of the Holocaust period, such as fear and hatred of Jews, necessitated the establishment of a special seminary for educators at Lodz. The Koordynacja systematically sent children abroad, with the intention of finally enabling them to reach Palestine. By the end of 1947, more than 500 children had been taken out of Poland. Together with their teachers and educators they entered *Youth Aliyah institutions in Germany, Austria, and France, most of them settling later in the State of Israel. Scores of Jewish children are believed to have remained in Poland, mainly in Catholic institutions and convents.

[Sara Neshamith]

Renewal of Jewish Life

The first attempts to renew Jewish life took place in Lublin, the seat of the Polish Committee of National Liberation. In a manifesto issued on July 20, 1944, this committee published a solemn declaration assuring equal rights and full rehabilitation to the survivors of Polish Jewry. The Jewish Committee was formed to extend emergency aid to Jews converging on Lublin from the liberated parts of Poland. This group included adults who returned from the forests and other hiding places or who miraculously survived the concentration camps, and children who found refuge in convents or with individual Polish families. In October 1944 the Jewish Committee was renamed the Central Committee of the Jews in Poland and moved to Warsaw when the Polish capital was liberated. The committee was composed of representatives of the various Jewish parties and was presided over by the Zionist Emil *Sommerstein. At first it was primarily concerned with providing material assistance to the Jewish survivors and facilitating their return to a productive life. Before long, however, the committee extended the range of its activities to social and cultural spheres.

By 1945 it comprised 10 districts (*województwa*), two subdistricts, and about 200 local committees. Several dozen Jewish cooperatives, in a variety of trades, and 34 Jewish farms run by several hundreds of Jewish agricultural laborers were founded. A considerable number of Jewish weeklies and biweeklies, representing every shade of Jewish political opinion, made their appearance. Among them was the organ of the Central Committee, *Dos Naye Lebn*. An elementary school having Yiddish as the language of instruction with Hebrew as a compulsory subject was established in Lodz. There was also a society of Jewish writers, journalists, and actors in that city, while in Lower Silesia the Jewish Society for Art and Culture was formed. After the Zionist pioneering youth movements were reorganized, they established hundreds of training farms, children's homes, etc., and prepared their members for *aliyah*. In July 1945 the JDC entered the Jewish scene in Poland. Through the Central Committee, it subsidized a variety of social welfare agencies, emphasizing the care of children, the aged, and the sick. In addition the JDC provided food, clothing, and medicine to educational and cultural institutions, and supported a variety of plans to help able-bodied men and women become productive again. The following year, *ORT began its work in Poland, creating a network of vocational schools. In the medical field TOZ provided the assistance. At the beginning of 1946, this organization was running eight mobile clinics, seven hospitals, and medical aid stations in all major cities.

In addition to the 80,000 Jews already in Poland, over 154,000 Polish Jews were repatriated from the U.S.S.R. in the summer of 1946, bringing the total Jewish population of Poland close to 250,000. The Polish government and the Communist-dominated ruling party (the Polish Workers' Party – PPR) encouraged the Central Committee in its social and cultural activities and lent support to the Jewish efforts to establish new economic foundations and restore communal life. At the same time, the government placed no obstacles in the path of Jews who wished to emigrate. It permitted the Zionist movement to exist and displayed a friendly attitude to the aspirations of the *yishuv* in Palestine and later to the State of Israel. Polish government support (or at least tolerance), aid from world Jewry, and, especially, the growth of the community by mass repatriation from U.S.S.R., led many Polish Jews in the immediate postwar period to believe that the conditions being created in the "new" Poland would enable them to live a free and full Jewish life.

Cultural, Religious, and Economic Life

At first these hopes had some basis in fact. In 1946–47 two Yiddish theaters were founded – in Lodz and Wroclaw – and employed some 80 actors. In 1950 they joined forces as the Jewish State Theater with a government subsidy under the direction of Ida *Kaminska. The theater discontinued its activities after 1968, when most of the Jews emigrated from Poland. A publishing house and a literary monthly came into being. The Society for Art and Culture founded Jewish libraries, promoted amateur societies in various cultural fields, and arranged public lectures. The *Jewish Historical Institute embarked upon a program of collecting and publishing historical material on the Holocaust. According to figures published in the anniversary edition of *Dos Naye Lebn* (1945–47), the Central Committee's Board of Education served 34 Jewish schools staffed by 179 teachers and attended by 2,874 children. Jewish religious life was renewed in every town where Jews resettled. In prewar Poland there had been 2,000 rabbis, 8,000 ritual slaughterers and religious teachers, and 10,000 yeshivah students. Of these, only a few dozen rabbis, slaughterers, and about 100 yeshivah students survived the war, mainly in the U.S.S.R., but only a few of them refrained from emigrating and remained in postwar Poland. Nevertheless, the Union of Religious Communities was established, comprising some 30 communities. The Union attended to Jewish religious needs by refurbishing and using two synagogues which had not been destroyed – one in Warsaw and the other in Wroclaw – establishing prayer-houses in all the communities, providing *maẓẓot* for Passover, arranging for the supply of *kasher* meat, and founding *kasher* public kitchens. In cooperation with the Central Committee, the Union rededicated Jewish cemeteries and reburied according to Jewish rite the victims of Nazism buried in mass graves.

In mid-1948, the Union of Religious Communities formally joined the Central Committee of Jews in Poland. The cooperation between the two bodies, however, lasted only into the early 1950s, when the Stalinization taking place in the country also affected Jewish life and made the cooperation of secular and religious bodies impossible. By the end of 1960, there were 23 member communities in the Union, and by 1966 the number was reduced to 18. The number of individual members varied greatly from one community to another; thus, in Warsaw, there were only 20 registered members, while in Katowice there were 1,200 and in Wroclaw 2,000. The Union of Religious Communities was still in existence in 1969, but the mass emigration of 1968–69 reduced its membership severely. At the end of 1947, there were 200 Jewish cooperative societies, with a membership of 6,000. About 15,000 Jews were employed in communal institutions, coal mines, heavy industry, textile factories, and a variety of government and private factories; 124 Jewish families were employed on farms. By the end of 1946, ORT was conducting 49 different vocational courses staffed by 81 instructors and attended by over 1,100 pupils. Contact with Jewish communities outside of Poland was maintained by both the Central Committee and by the various Zionist groups which were active in the early postwar years. In the beginning of 1948, the Central Committee joined the *World Jewish Congress and participated in its meetings and conferences.

The Flight from Poland

The revival of a sound Jewish community life in Poland was the declared aim of those Jews who had been Communists before the war. They believed that the conditions were now ideal for the renewal of Jewish life and argued that a revived Jewish community would both demonstrate the vitality of the Jewish people and the failure of Nazism and other forms of antisemitism. The majority of Polish Jews, however, including those who were being repatriated from the Soviet Union, did not want to reestablish their lives in Poland, where the Nazis had found thousands of collaborators among the local population eager to cooperate in the extermination of the Jews. Moreover, pogroms continued even after the Nazi occupation ended. To most Polish Jews it was unthinkable to renew their life on the Polish soil soaked with the blood of millions of Jews. Thus tens of thousands of Polish Jews who fled from the U.S.S.R.

and Poland made their way to Romania and Germany in the hope of reaching Palestine. After the *Kielce pogrom this exodus took on an organized and semi-legal character. A coordinating committee for *aliyah* was formed from representatives of all Zionist groups to make arrangements for up to a thousand persons a day to cross the Polish border at three points in Lower Silesia near Kudowa. The operation lasted about six months, until the end of 1946 (see *Beriḥah). Thereafter, Jews encountered difficulties in leaving Poland, but emigration did not come to a stop. In 1949, when the Zionist parties were disbanded, all former Zionists were permitted to leave for Israel, and some 30,000 people took advantage of this opportunity. Thus, mass emigration continually depleted Polish Jewry from 1944 to 1950. The Central Committee, which did all in its power to combat this movement, was forced to accept the reality of a drastic decrease in the Jewish population.

Anti-Jewish Excesses

Jewish emigration from Poland was motivated not only by the recent tragic past and by prewar Zionist education, but also by the continuation of a clear and present danger to the Jews. There were murderous attacks upon Jews on Polish roads, railroads, buses, and in the towns and cities. The murders were committed by members of Polish reactionary organizations, such as the NSZ (Narodowe Sily Zbrojne). In cruelty and inhumanity, their crimes often equaled those committed by the Nazis. Beginning in 1945 the assaults upon Jews swiftly assumed mass proportions. In two pogroms – one in Cracow on Aug. 11, 1945, and the other in Kielce on July 4, 1946 – thousands of Polish men, women, and children ran amok in the Jewish quarters, killing in Kielce 42 Jews and wounding 50 others. The attacks spread throughout the country, and in 1945 alone 353 Jews were reported murdered. The wave of anti-Jewish excesses continued well into 1946 and reached its climax in the Kielce pogrom. The government and the ruling party issued declarations designed to placate the Jews and there were public protests against antisemitism by intellectuals and large parts of the working class. Above all, the Jewish Communists and the Central Committee of Jews in Poland tried to reassure the Jews that the government would stamp out the antisemitic underground. The Jews, however, did not heed the exhortations and raced for the borders. By the end of 1947, only 100,000 Jews remained in Poland.

The Soviet Example

A second factor discouraging any hope for a viable Jewish community in Poland was the rising tide of antisemitism in the U.S.S.R. Soviet antisemitism was at first disguised as a campaign against "rootless cosmopolitans." This was followed by the judicial murder of leading Jewish writers and artists and the total liquidation of Jewish cultural life in the Soviet Union. The campaign culminated in the so-called *Doctors' Plot (see *Antisemitism, in the Soviet Bloc). These Soviet developments had an immediate effect on the Polish scene. In 1948 the central committee of the ruling party, the PPR, on Moscow's initiative, accused its first secretary, Wladyslaw Gomulka, and his associates of rightist-nationalist deviation, and Poland became, more than ever, a Soviet satellite. The entire country was overrun by the Soviet secret police. Under these circumstances Poland's attitude toward its Jews could not be substantially different from the Soviet model.

Nevertheless, Stalinist antisemitism was effected in Poland without bloodshed and mass arrests. It was the cultural activities of Polish Jewry that were immediately affected, reduced in their scope, and adapted in their content to the new spirit. The Stalinization of Poland was carried out by a variety of measures. The existing workers' parties were merged into a single party, and all other parties were liquidated. The Soviet Union was glorified and its policies in internal and foreign affairs were slavishly copied. In all creative activities "socialist realism" became the rule. In the Jewish sphere, "unifications" and liquidations were carried out. The first to be liquidated were the Zionist parties and the Bund in November 1949. This was followed by a ban on the operation of the JDC and ORT, in spite of the assurance given by the Polish Committee of National Liberation in its manifesto of July 20, 1944, and the appeal in December 1945 by the Polish provisional government for foreign aid to be extended to Polish Jews. Similarly, the recognition of the JDC's work expressed in November 1946, when JDC director, Joseph *Schwartz, was awarded a high decoration by the government, no longer had any meaning.

An act of liquidation by "unification" affected the Union of Jewish Cooperative Societies, representing 200 societies, 15,000 workers, and substantial assets (originally financed by the JDC) which was forced to merge with the general Polish Union of Cooperatives. On May 16, 1949, a "recommendation" was made to the Central Committee of the Jews in Poland to secede from the World Jewish Congress. Finally, the Central Committee itself, whose continued existence as a seemingly independent representative body was not in harmony with the new trend, was ordered to merge with the Jewish Society for Art and Culture. The new organization bore the name Cultural-Social Association of the Jews in Poland (Kultur-Gezelshaftlekher Farband fun di Yidn in Poyln). All Jewish schools were nationalized in the 1948–49 school year, resulting in the further reduction of Jewish studies. Yiddish as the language of instruction and the teaching of Hebrew had already been eliminated. Such organizations as the Jewish Agency came to be regarded as "agents of imperialism," and any contact with them was highly suspect. The spiritual life of Polish Jews was now restricted to preoccupation with the "progressive" tradition. The mass emigration had resulted in a radical reduction in the number of district and local Jewish committees. Their total number dropped to 30. The largest concentrations of Jews were in Warsaw (about 8,000), Wroclaw (about 6,000), Lodz (about 5,000) and Szczeczin, Katowice, Cracow, Legnica, and Walbrzych.

In spite of these far-reaching quantitative and qualitative changes, the leaders of the Cultural-Social Association and the other Jewish establishments (such as the Historical Institute, the theater, the publishing house, the literary journal, and the newspaper *Folksshtime*), both in Warsaw and the provinces, did all in their power to maintain at least a modest level of Jewish activity. In fact, in the period 1950 to 1957, Jewish life in Poland was relatively stable. Even so, there were those in the association who, encouraged by the ruling party, sought to promote assimilation and achieve results.

1956–1967. Stalin's death in 1953 resulted in an easing of tension, but Gomulka's assumption of power, in 1956, completely transformed the Jewish scene in Poland. Revelation of the innumerable crimes committed in the U.S.S.R. during the period of Stalin's rule enabled the Jewish newspaper *Folksshtime* to publish a passionate protest against Soviet antisemitism and its destruction of Yiddish literature and culture. In Poland it was once more possible to foster Jewish literature and to reestablish contact with Jewish organizations abroad. The JDC and ORT returned to devote themselves primarily to the approximately 25,000 Polish Jews who were being repatriated from the U.S.S.R. under an agreement between Gomulka's government and the Soviet Union (along with hundreds of thousands of people who had been Polish citizens in 1939 but for some reason had not been repatriated after the war). Once again the JDC extended aid to the sick, the aged, and children. It also assisted various cultural institutions, including schools. ORT, for its part, reestablished its network of vocational training schools.

The great majority of Jews repatriated from the U.S.S.R. did not, however, have any intention of staying in Poland. Even before their departure from the Soviet Union, most of them resolved to move on from Poland, primarily to Israel. Similarly, thousands of long-established Jews now decided to leave Poland for good. Their decision was influenced by the antisemitic incidents that occurred soon after Gomulka's rise to power. Poland again allowed Jews to emigrate, and some 50,000 people left the country in 1958–59. In some cases, whole towns were emptied of their Jewish population, and the Jewish community in Poland was now reduced to about 30,000 people. Of those who remained some 3,000 were too old or too sick to earn their livelihood and were supported by the JDC, as were various children's homes, camps, and clubs. In addition, the JDC financed the Historical Institute, the Cracow Jewish Museum, cultural enterprises, the reestablishment of Jewish cooperatives, and the construction of a Jewish home for the aged.

The Jewish cooperative movement, revived after 1957 with help from the government and the JDC, was soon able to stand on its own feet and to transfer 20% of its yearly profits – ranging from one to two million zlotys – to the Jewish Cultural-Social Association. This situation prevailed until 1967.

Final Liquidation

In 1968–69, a fourth mass emigration of Jews from Poland took place, resulting in the virtual dissolution of the Jewish community as an identifiable and creative group. It also spelled the final disillusionment of those Jews who hoped the Gomulka regime would differ from the Soviet Union in its approach to the Jews. The Six-Day War (1967) and the March 1968 student riots in Polish university towns were seized by the Polish government as the opportunity to utilize popular antisemitism for its own political purposes. When the party faction called the Partisan Group, led by Minister of Interior Mieczyslaw Moczar, initiated antisemitic action in an attempt to oust Gomulka from power, the Polish Communist leader adopted a clearly defined anti-Jewish policy. In March 1968 Gomulka publicly declared those Jews whose loyalty wavered between Poland and Israel to be "rootless cosmopolitans" unworthy of holding public office. He reiterated, however, the principle that Israel-oriented Jews should be allowed to immigrate to the Jewish state. In the course of 1968, Jewish youth camps, schools, and clubs were disbanded. Jews were dismissed from whatever public positions they still held, and the Cultural-Social Association was reduced to a mere paper existence. Restrictions were placed even on the status of Yiddish, a language which had been used in Poland almost as long as Polish itself. Yiddish was declared a foreign language, with the result that any publication in Yiddish had first to be translated into Polish before it could be released for distribution. In practice this signified the end of the Yiddish publishing house "Yidish Bukh" and of *Yidishe Shriften*, the literary journal. The Yiddish newspaper *Folksshtime*, which formerly appeared four times a week, was now restricted to a weekly appearance. The JDC and ORT were again forbidden to operate in Poland, and the Jewish cooperatives were again handed over to the general Cooperative Union. The Jewish home for the aged, financed by the JDC, was turned into a general institution.

The liquidation of all organized forms of Jewish life was accompanied by a relentless antisemitic campaign carried through the press, radio, and television. The majority of Polish Jews, the tragic remnant of a community that had once numbered over 3,250,000 people, reacted to these events by choosing to emigrate. Since the Polish authorities allowed Jewish emigration only to Israel, and then only upon renunciation of Polish citizenship, many Jews who intended to immigrate to other countries (Canada, Australia, Scandinavia) ostensibly applied for papers and visas to Israel. Efforts to assure the continued existence of Jewish life in Poland were in vain. Young Jews, most of whom left the country, were especially shocked by the antisemitism displayed by leading Polish Communists. The few Jewish institutions still in existence in 1971 were devoid of all creative content and had been stripped of all authority. (See also *Cooperatives; *American Jewish Joint Distribution Committee; *ORT; *OZE; *Beriḥah.)

[David Sfard]

Later Developments

In the following two decades the Jewish population of Poland stabilized at around 6,000. There remained only a single synagogue in Warsaw and in the whole country there was no rabbi. The Jewish cemetery in Bialystok was transformed into a public garden and the famous Jewish cemetery in Warsaw was repeatedly desecrated by gangs who stole the marble from the graves.

The Social and Cultural Society of Jews in Poland came under the full control of the Ministry of Interior and almost all of its social functions were terminated. After the Jewish cooperatives were liquidated, the Polish government began to defray the rather modest budget of the society.

In 1976–77 the Jewish issue again became a motif in the official propaganda campaign which came on the heels of the Polish workers' protest movement against rises in food prices and the activities of the "Committee for the Defense of the Workers" and dissidents.

The prolonged instability of the situation resulted in intensified exploitation of the Jewish issue, and the press directly attacked and ridiculed Jewish religion, tradition, and customs with the result that Jewish life was compressed into a lifeless framework which, nevertheless, still continued to function. The Jewish Cultural-Social Committee remained in existence, as did the Jewish Historical Institute and the Jewish Theater. The newspaper *Folksshtime* also continued to appear. The institute received permission to resume publication of the academic journal *Yidishe Bletter*, whose publication had ceased several years earlier.

In the latter part of 1977 the Poles took several tactical steps to improve their image with regard to Jewish matters. In October and December 1977 the chairman of the Organization of Former Jewish Partisans and Fighters in Poland (Stefan-Shalom Greik, an Israeli), the chairman of Yad Vashem (Dr. Yitzḥak Arad), and a representative of Kibbutz Loḥamei ha-Getta'ot (Ẓevi Schneir) were invited to Poland in connection with the implementation of a plan to establish a Jewish exhibit hall in the former extermination camp at Auschwitz. It was the first time that the authorities in Poland displayed a readiness to permit Israeli institutions to participate in the implementation of the plan, and even to be assisted by the advice of Israeli experts. The Warsaw Institute of Jewish History was also invited to assist in drawing up the plan. The pavilion was opened at a ceremony held on April 17, 1978, in the presence of Polish authorities and Jewish delegations from Israel and the Diaspora. Its official name was "The Destruction and the Struggle of the Jews in Occupied Europe." In June, however, it was closed to the public, although it was claimed that the closure was only temporary to improve the amenities there, and that it would be opened to individuals on request.

A definite anti-Zionist, anti-Jewish tone was expressed in government propaganda used in its fight against the increased strength and demands of Solidarity in 1980 and 1981, although the current demographic distribution of Jews in Poland certainly did not warrant any such attacks. Individual Jews did participate in the Solidarity movement.

Poland's transition to a democratic system of government and a market economy which began in 1989 after nearly five decades of Communist rule took place against the background of economic crisis and industrial unrest. At the same time, the new freedom experienced by Polish society had an invigorating effect on the small, mostly elderly Jewish community that remained in the country. A significant renewal of Jewish cultural and religious life took place, and people previously estranged from Jewish tradition, especially among the young, began to acknowledge their Jewish identity. Communal and cultural activities were strengthened and encouraged by the renewal of ties with Israel and increasing contacts with world Jewry. Two important events exemplify this positive trend: The community acquired its first resident rabbi in over 20 years, and a Coordinating Commission of Jewish Organizations, which represented and acted on behalf of the whole community, was established. The new body brought together the Jewish Social and Cultural Association, the Mosaic Religious Association, the Jewish Historical Institute, the Jewish Theater, and the bi-weekly paper *Dos Yiddishe Wort* (formerly *Folkssztyme*).

A range of educational and cultural activities was provided by the Social and Cultural Association (TSKZ), which had branches in 15 cities. Courses in Jewish history and Yiddish as well as song and dance classes were held. The Jewish Historical Institute conducted research and published scholarly papers and books on the history of Jews in Poland. Welfare activities were carried out with the financial support of the JDC.

On the positive side of Polish-Jewish relations was the continuing interest in the history and culture of Polish Jews among the Polish intelligentsia. The awareness of the need to preserve the Jewish heritage and recognize the Jewish contribution to Polish culture originated in liberal Catholic, Protestant, and opposition circles in the 1980s.

Among the initiatives taken were annual weeks of Jewish culture, seminars on Jewish subjects, festivals of Jewish films, exhibitions as well as efforts to restore and maintain Jewish cemeteries and monuments. From the mid-1980s, in an attempt to improve their image abroad the Communist authorities encouraged Jewish studies. The Institute for the Study of the History and Culture of the Jews in Poland was created at Cracow's Jagellonian University in 1986. A number of conferences and symposia were held with the support of the state and the participation of Western, including Israeli, scholars. A large number of books on Jewish subjects were published to meet the growing demand. In post-Communist Poland, state authorities continued to support a range of cultural activities. A foundation called Eternal Memory was set up by the treasury for the restoration and preservation of Jewish cultural monuments.

The community, however, experienced a rising tide of antisemitism. The change to a pluralist democracy opened up opportunities for extremist nationalist groups using antisemitism as a tool in the political struggle. Their propaganda identified Jews with the Communist regime and blamed them for all the shortcomings of Polish life. The removal of restraints on freedom of expression meant that antisemitism was now openly voiced in public and everyday life with grass-roots antisemitism well attested in public polls.

Government and Solidarity personalities became targets of anti-Jewish campaigns, which drew attention to their real or alleged Jewish origins. At the time of the 1990 presidential and 1991 parliamentary elections these tactics were freely used even by the mainstream political groups. Antisemitic publications, including reprints of the notorious *Protocols of the Elders of Zion*, were distributed widely. Acts of vandalism at Jewish institutions, synagogues, and cemeteries multiplied as Polish skinheads sought to emulate their Western counterparts. The need to obtain economic assistance from the West, which acted as a brake on political antisemitism during 1980s, prompted President Walesa's initiative in 1991 to create a Council on Polish-Jewish Relations. An advisory body attached to the president, its function was to promote better understanding between Poles and Jews by drawing-up educational programs for Polish youth, organizing events and exhibitions, and providing a reaction to antisemitic incidents.

The continuing dispute over the Carmelite convent at Auschwitz had been at the center of the crisis in Catholic-Jewish relations from 1984 (see *Auschwitz Convent). The controversy was widely debated in the Polish press: a range of views from openly antisemitic to liberal was expressed revealing a disquieting level of prejudice and a lack of understanding between Poles and Jews. The crisis was finally resolved in 1993 with the relocation of the nuns at the convent.

While some elements within the Catholic Church supported right-wing Christian parties with known antisemitic tendencies, the Polish bishops, in an effort to improve relations, issued an unprecedented statement taking a clear stand against all manifestations of antisemitism. The episcopal letter, read in churches on January 21, 1991, presented Vatican II teachings on the relations between the two faiths and dealt with a number of controversial issues such as Polish responsibility for the Holocaust, alleged Jewish responsibility for Communism, and antisemitism past and present. At the same time the Catholic Seminary in Warsaw published a book on Judaism and the Jews for school teachers written in a similar spirit.

[Lena Stanley-Clamp]

By the mid-1990s most of the Jewish communities in Poland – Warsaw, Cracow (Krakow), Lodz, Stettin (Szcecin), Danzig (Gdansk), Kattowitz (Katowice), and Breslau (Wroclaw) – had synagogues. The eastern part of the country, once teeming with Jewish life and with great centers such as Lublin and Bialystok, probably had no more than 50 Jews. The Coordinating Committee of Jewish Organizations in the Polish Republic (KKOZRP) coordinated activities of the various Jewish bodies. Under the auspices of the Lauder Foundation, a club was established which organized many events for young people including Jewish summer camps and athletics. The Jewish groups included persons orphaned in the Holocaust and brought up by non-Jews and a veterans' organization. An important item on the agenda was the preservation of synagogues and cemeteries throughout the country. Many of these were in a state of disrepair or being used for secular purposes. Poland had a chief rabbi whose seat was in Warsaw and another rabbi for youth. A primary school and kindergarten were opened in Warsaw. Jewish courses were offered at the universities in Warsaw and Cracow. Warsaw's Jewish Historical Institute was an important archive and venue for cultural events while Cracow had a Center for Jewish Culture. The Warsaw Yiddish Theater was the only regularly functioning Yiddish theater in the world. Most of the actors were non-Jews. Poland was the scene of considerable Jewish tourism including pilgrimages to Holocaust sites, which bring many Jewish youth groups, such as the March of the Living.

In the early years of the 21st century, around 8,000 Jews were registered with the community, but it was estimated that as many as 30,000–40,000 had some Jewish ancestry.

RELATIONS WITH ISRAEL

Poland was among the first countries to recognize Israel (May 18, 1948). During the period preceding the establishment of Israel, Poland was unstinting in its support for the *yishuv*. At a convention of Soviet-bloc foreign ministers, the Polish foreign minister introduced a resolution congratulating Israel and condemning Arab aggression. Polish public opinion also strongly supported Israel and its struggle, as evidenced by resolutions passed by various public institutions, including the National Conference of Polish writers. Israel also received practical aid. In 1948, before the declaration of independence, a Haganah camp was set up in Poland, where 1,500 young Jews underwent preparatory military training before leaving for Israel. During the actual fighting, shipments of wheat were brought to Israel by a Polish boat. In August 1948 an Israel legation was established in Poland, one of Israel's first diplomatic missions.

The Change of 1950

The cooling of U.S.S.R.-Israel relations from 1950 affected relations between Poland and Israel. A certain ambivalence characterized Poland's attitude toward Israel, for, together with criticism of Israel on the international scene, particularly at the UN, there was also understanding and sympathy for Israel's problems and a courteous attitude in official relations, in contrast to the attitude of other member states of the Eastern bloc, even in 1950–55, which were particularly difficult years for Israel relations with East Europe. The change, which started to make itself felt at the beginning of 1950, was reflected in a decrease in the number of exit permits issued, although emigration from Poland never ceased altogether. Polish authorities began to display animosity toward the Israel legation, with a view to minimizing its contacts with Polish Jewry. During this period there were mass arrests and staged trials in a number of Eastern European countries, and, while the situation did not reach such proportions in Poland, police measures were intensified there and the Israel legation was put under police surveillance. A sharp turn of events occurred in 1953, when the Israel minister in Warsaw, A.L. Kubovy, who was stationed in Prague, was declared persona non grata as a result of a similar action taken against him by the Czechoslovak government after the *Slánský trial. Thereafter two other Israel diplomats were expelled.

Improved Relations in 1956

Wladyslaw Gomulka's ascension to power as secretary of the Communist Party in the fall of 1956 ushered in a liberalization in Poland's internal regime and a more independent foreign policy. Relations toward Israel improved primarily through an open emigration policy. Israel's problems were given more objective treatment in the press. In 1956 Israel again appointed a resident minister in Warsaw after a three-year period during which a chargé d'affaires headed the Israel legation. In 1963 the mission was elevated to the level of an embassy. After 1956 there was also a broadening of cultural and scientific relations in the form of reciprocal visits by individuals and delegations. Nevertheless, the Polish government maintained a constant reserve and did not respond to all of Israel's initiatives, sometimes even failing to implement plans they themselves had suggested. Thus, for example, cultural and scientific relations were not established on a formal basis, although such a step would have been justified by the extent of these activities. Nor was a Polish-Israel Friendship League set up in Poland, although an Israel-Polish Friendship League functioned in Israel.

Nevertheless, Poland was undoubtedly foremost among the East European countries in fostering relations with Israel, especially in the areas of culture, science, and information. Israel artists participated regularly in international music festivals in Poland, and many Polish performers appeared in Israel. Radio musical programs were exchanged. Exhibitions of Hebrew books were held in Poland, and Polish books were distributed in Israel. Regular exchanges of scientific publications took place, and individuals and figures in public life paid reciprocal visits. Exhibitions of graphic art were organized in Poland and in Israel. Of special note during the period between 1956 and 1967 were the tour of a Polish medical delegation in Israel; the visit to Israel of the chairman of the Polish Academy of Sciences; and the visit of the Israel ministers of health and welfare to Poland. After 1956 Israel participated regularly in the International Fair in Poznan. An information bulletin distributed by the Israel embassy influenced public opinion, and the Polish press often drew upon it.

In the political arena (e.g., in voting at the UN), Poland continued to identify with the U.S.S.R. but nevertheless was willing to support the election of Israelis for various functions in international agencies. Its spokesmen would point out that Poland's guiding principle was to foster relations both with Israel and with the Arab states, but neither at the expense of the other. An event in May 1966 seemed to herald a marked improvement in Polish-Israel relations and a development in Israel's relations with the entire Communist bloc: A convention of Israel diplomatic representatives in Eastern Europe was held in Warsaw with the participation of Foreign Minister Abba Eban. It was the first time that such a convention was held in a capital of the Eastern bloc, and Warsaw was willing to serve as its venue; it was also the first visit in an East European capital by an Israel foreign minister. Eban held discussions with the Polish foreign minister, Adam Rapacki, who displayed the attitude usually accorded an official foreign visitor.

The Six-Day War

Fairly normal relations were maintained between the two countries when the U.S.S.R. began escalating the Middle East crisis, which resulted in the Six-Day War. Significantly, a visit to Poland at the end of April by the Israel minister of welfare, heading a delegation for the establishment of the Auschwitz memorial, was handled in a way that reflected a change for the worse in Poland's attitude. The fact that the visit was not mentioned in the press was interpreted as one expression of the attempt to minimize the Jewish character of the Holocaust. In the first half of May, Polish newspapers and communications media were still presenting a balanced view of the Middle East crisis. A sharp change occurred, however, during the second half of the month. The press began to give unilateral coverage to the Arab-Soviet position. Grotesque accusations with antisemitic overtones were leveled against Israel and its leaders. On May 28 the president of Poland sent a message to Nasser expressing "full support for the struggle of the Arab nations." After that time, Poland's statements were characterized by an animosity toward Israel even more venomous than in other East European countries.

According to all indications, Polish public opinion generally supported Israel in its struggle for survival, but in the hands of groups competing for power in the party and in the Polish government, the Middle East crisis became a weapon for infighting, with the declared intent of displacing Jews from public positions. On June 12, 1967, following the Soviet Union's example, Poland notified Israel that diplomatic relations between the two countries were being severed, and inimical demonstrations against the Israel diplomats initiated by the authorities took place in sight of the diplomatic staff that came to take leave of the Israelis at the Warsaw airport. The Dutch embassy, which represented Israel's interests in Poland from that time, strongly protested against this behavior.

Immigration to Israel

In 1948 there were approximately 70,000–80,000 Jews in Poland. This number was swollen by thousands of Jews who returned from the U.S.S.R. in 1956–57 under the Polish-Soviet repatriation agreement. One of the major tasks of the Israel legation in Poland was the struggle on behalf of the majority of Jews who wished to migrate to Israel. Despite accusations leveled periodically by Polish authorities at the Israel legation and its staff for propagandizing and organizing the Jews for migration to Israel, there was continuous emigration. Between 1948 and 1949 the Polish authorities were issuing several hundred passports a month to Jews wishing to emigrate, especially to the aged, handicapped, and women left alone. Between 1949 and 1956 the number of passports issued decreased to a few dozen per month. The major years of Polish Jewish immigration to Israel were 1956–60 with their numbers reaching around 52,000. The peak year was 1957, during which some 31,000 Jews migrated to Israel. Despite the breakdown in diplomatic relations in June 1967, the Polish government continued to issue exit permits for emigration to Israel, but the motivation for this policy became more and more an antisemitic intent to "purge" Poland of its Jewish population.

Trade Relations

A trade agreement signed between Poland and Israel in 1954 was renewed annually until 1968. The numerous industrial and agricultural products traded were valued at approximately $4 million in both directions. Major Israel exports were citrus fruit and tires, with Poland exporting frozen meat, sugar, iron and steel products, and chemicals. Two Israel exports added in the later years were potash and cotton, which then exceeded the citrus export. During 14 years the scope of the agreement had doubled, in effect, and in certain years it had tripled. A shift in the trade balance in Israel's favor occurred in the first months of 1966 and continued thereafter due to a steep increase in the export of potash. Upon the severance of diplomatic relations, Poland was in debt to Israel for over $5 million, but despite its hostile attitude toward Israel it did not revoke the trade agreement of 1954, and it was automatically renewed in 1968. By then, however, the agreement was meaningless, with Israel having discontinued its exports to Poland to avoid increasing the Polish debt, which was, in effect, a credit extended to Poland without interest. In June 1968 the Israel government informed the Polish government of the revocation of the trade agreement. Poland's debt to Israel, then $2.7 million was repaid thereafter.

[Moshe Avidan]

Following the severing of commercial ties between Israel and Poland in 1968, the first exchange of goods between the two countries was renewed in 1976. Israel exported citrus to Poland ($834,000) and imported books ($5,000). In 1977 goods in the value of $1.5 million were exported to Poland and $600,000 worth of merchandise was exported from Poland to Israel.

In 1986 Poland was the first of the Communist bloc countries to re-open low-level diplomatic relations with Israel which had been severed since the Six-Day War. Interest sections dealing with visa regulations and cultural and economic ties were established in Warsaw and Tel Aviv. Full diplomatic relations were restored in 1990. A framework for the promotion of good relations was provided by the establishment of the Polish-Israeli Friendship Society. There was a steady growth in cultural exchanges and trade expansion. Poland has shown a strong interest in acquiring Israeli technology in the fields of agriculture, telecommunications, health, and hotel industry. There was an unparalleled growth in tourism, facilitated by direct air links, with Israelis visiting Poland in great numbers. President Walesa visited Israel in 1991 and President Herzog visited Poland in 1992. By 2003 Israel's exports to Poland had grown to around $95 million, with imports at $60 million.

[Lena Stanley-Clamp]

BIBLIOGRAPHY: G.D. Hundert and G.C. Bacon, *The Jews in Poland and Russia: Bibliographical Essays* (1984); POLAND (UNTIL PARTITION): Dubnow, Hist Russ, 1 (1916), 13–305; R. Mahler, *Toledot ha-Yehudim be-Polin* (1946); A. Polonsky (ed.), *The Jews in Old Poland, 1000–1795* (1993); I. Halpern (ed.), *Beit Yisrael be-Polin*, 2 vols. (1948–54); *Istoriya yevreyskogo naroda: Istoriya yevreyev v Rossii*, 11 (1914); I. Schiper, *Studya nad stosunkami gospodarczymi Żydów Polsce podczas śedniowiecza* (1911); idem, *Kultur-Geshikhte fun di Yidn in Poyln beysn Mitlalter* (1926); idem, *Dzieje handlu żydowskiego na ziemiach polskich* (1937); T.B. Heilikman, *Istoriya obshchestvennago dvizheniya yevreyev v Polshe i Rossii* (1930; rev. ed. of *Geshikhte fun der Gezelshaftlekher Bavegung fun di Yidn in Poyln un Rusland*, 1926); H.H. Ben-Sasson, *Hagut ve-Hanhagah* (1959). **ADD. BIBLIOGRAPHY:** A. Eisenbach, I. Pogonowski, *Jews in Poland: A Documentary History* (1993); A. Eisenbach, *The Emancipation of the Jews in Poland, 1780–1830: Tradition and Change in a Liberal Society*, (1979). AFTER PARTITION: Dubnow, Hist Russ; S. Segal, *The New Poland and the Jews* (1938); B. Johnpoll, *The Politics of Futility* (1967); W. Gliksman, *A Kehilah in Poland during the Inter-War Years* (1970); J. Shatzky, in: YIVOA, 7 (1962), 146–74; M. Mishkinsky, *ibid.*, 14 (1969), 27–52; Y. Gruenbaum, *Milḥamot Yehudei Polin* (1941); idem (ed.), EG, 1 (1953); idem, *Ne'umim ba-Sejm ha-Polani* (1963); J. Lestschinsky, *Oyfn Rand fun Opgrunt* (1947); idem, in: *Yidishe Ekonomik*, 1 (1937); 2 (1938); M. Linder, *ibid.*, 1 (1937); J. Shatzky, *Geshikhte fun Yidn in Varshe*, 3 vols. (1947–53); idem, in: *YIVO Bleter*, 36 (1952), 24–62; I. Halpern (ed.), *Beit Yisrael be-Polin*, 2 vols. (1948–54); N.M. Gelber (ed.), *Ha-Yehudim ve-ha-Mered ha-Polani* (1953); R. Mahler, *Ha-Ḥasidut ve-ha-Haskalah* (1961); idem, *Yehudei Polin bein Shetei Milḥamot ha-Olam* (1968); idem, *Divrei Yemei Yisrael, Dorot Aḥaronim*, vol. 2 bk. 1 (1970); A. Tartakower, in: Velt-Federatsye fun Poylishe Yidn, *Yorbukh*, 3 (1970); *Sbornik materialov ob ekonomicheskom polozhenii yevreyev v Rossii*, 2 vols. (1904); M. Wischnitzer, *Perezhitoye*, 1 (1908), 164–221; J. Kirszrot, *Prawa Żydów Królestwie polskiem* (1917); I. Schiper, *Żydzi Królestwa polskiego w dobie powstania listopadowego* (1932); idem, *Dzieje handlu żdowskiego na ziemiach polskich* (1937); idem, in: *Miesięcznik Żydowski*, 1 (1931), 513–29; 2 no. 4 (1932), 311–27; idem et al. (eds.), *Żydzi w Polsce odrodzonej*, 2 vols. (1932–33); L. Halpern, *Polityka żydowska w Sejmie i Senacie Rzeczypospolitej Polskiej* (1933); P. Friedman, *Dzieje Zydów w Łodzi od początków osadnictwa do roku 1863* (1935); E. Ringelblum, *Żydzi w powstaniu kościuszkowskiem* (1938); S. Bronsztejn, *Ludność żydowska w Polsce* (1963); A. Eisenbach et al. (eds.), *Żydzi a powstanie styczniowe* (1963); idem, in: *Społeczeństwo Królestwa polskiego*, 2 (1966), 177–316. **ADD. BIBLIOGRAPHY:** C.S. Heller, *On the Edge of Destruction: Jews in Poland Between the Two World Wars*, (1977); I. Lewin, *The Jewish Community in Poland: Historical Essays* (1985); L. Dobroszycki and B. Kirshenblatt-Gimblett, *Image Before My Eyes: a Photographic History of Jewish Life in Poland 1864–1939* (1977); HOLOCAUST PERIOD: Bernstein, in: *Algemeyne Entsiklopedye: Yidn*, 6 (1963), 165–242; Brustin-Bernstein, in: *Bleter far Geshikhte*, 1, nos. 3–4 (1948), 125–64; 3, no. 2 (1950), 51–78; 4, no. 2 (1951), 103–22; 6 no. 3 (1953), 45–153; Rutkowski, *ibid.*: 12 (1959), 75–118; Rutkowski and Brustin-Bernstein, in: BZIH, 38 (1961), 28–38; Winkler, in: *Bleter far Geshikhte*, 1 nos. 3–4 (1948), 3–40; Trunk, *ibid.*, 1 no. 1 (1948), 114–69; 1, no. 2 (1948), 14–45; 2 (1949), 64–166; idem, in: YIVO *Bleter*, 37 (1953), 58–100; idem, *Geshtalten un Geshenishn* (1962), 127–261; idem, *Lodzer Geto…* (1962), preface, conclusion, and list of documents in English; Żydowski Instytut Historyczny, *Dokumenty i Materiały*, 3 vols. (1946); P. Friedman, *Zagłada Zydów polskich w okresie okupacji hitlerowskiej 1939–1945* (1947); Podhorizer-Sandler, in: BZIH, no. 30 (1959), 37–108; Datner, *ibid.*, no. 60 (1966), 3–29; J. Kermisz, *Akcje i wysiedlenia* (1946); A. Eisenbach, *Hitlerowska polityka zagłady Żydów* (1961); idem, *Di Hitleristishe Politik fun Yidn-*

Farnikhtung, 2 vols. (1955); T. Berenstein et al. (eds.), *Eksterminacja Żydów na ziemiach polskich w okresie okupacji hitlerowskiej* (1957). FOR FURTHER READING IN ENGLISH: G. Reitlinger, *The Final Solution* (1962²), 143–53, 260–319 and passim, includes bibliography; R. Hilberg, *Destruction of European Jews* (1961), index; American Federation for Polish Jews, *Black Book of Polish Jewry* (1943); American Jewish Black Book Committee, *Black Book* (1945); Central Commission for War Crimes, Warsaw, *German Crimes in Poland*, 2 vols. (1946–47); M. Muszkat, *Polish Charges against War Criminals* (1948); A. Melezin, *Demographic Processes among the Jewish Population of Poland 1939–1945* (1948); J. Tenenbaum, *In Search of a Lost People* (1949); idem, *Underground, the Story of a People* (1952). PARTISANS: *Sefer Milḥamot ha-Geta'ot* (1954² = *The Fighting Ghettos*, partial trans. by M. Barkai, 1962); J. Tenenbaum, *Underground* (1952); Y. Suhl (ed.), *They Fought Back* (1968). RESCUE OF JEWISH CHILDREN IN POLAND: N. Orelovitch-Reznik, *Imma, ha-Muttar Kevar Livkot?* (1965); L. Kuchler-Silberman, *One Hundred Children* (1961); E. Mahler, *Yad Vashem Bulletin*, no. 12 (Dec. 1962), 49–56; J. Goldman, *Rabbi Herzog's First Rescue Journey* (1964), passim; S. Nishmit, *Dappim le-Ḥeker ha-Sho'ah ve-ha-Mered*, 2 (1952); *Tetikeyts-Baricht fun Tsentral-Komitet fun di Yiden in Poyln* (1947); *Farn Yidishn Kind* (1946); AFTER WORLD WAR II; P. Lendvai, *Communism without Jews* (1971), 89–239.

POLANSKI, ROMAN (Liebling; 1933–), film director, writer, and actor. Born in Paris, Polanski went to Poland with his parents at the age of three. During World War II, he managed to escape the ghetto, while his parents were sent to a concentration camp, where his mother died. As a young boy he survived in the Polish countryside, living with various Catholic families. In 1945 he was reunited with his father.

In the 1950s, still in Poland, he took up acting and also became a well-known filmmaker. He moved to Paris and made two films in England – *Repulsion* (1965) and *Cul-de-sac* (1966) – which won him international acclaim. Polanski also won several international awards for his film *Two Men and a Wardrobe* (1958). Among his other films are *Mammals* (1961); *Knife in the Water* (Oscar nomination for Best Foreign Language Film, 1962); and *Rosemary's Baby* (Oscar nomination for Best Adapted Screenplay, 1968), which showed his mastery of suspense and the macabre, as well as *The Fearless Vampire Killers* (1967), starring his wife, Sharon Tate.

In 1968 Polanski had gone to Hollywood – until 1969, when the circumstances of his life took on the nightmarish quality of his films. While Polanski was out of town his wife, who was eight months pregnant with their first child, as well as four of their friends, were brutally murdered at a party at their home by the Charles Manson gang. Polanski returned to Europe and continued to make films there, such as *Macbeth* (1971) and *What?* (1973). In 1974 he returned to the U.S. and made *Chinatown* (Oscar nomination for Best Picture and Best Director, 1974) and *The Tenant* (1976).

However, in 1977 he fled the country again, this time to avoid being incarcerated on a charge of statutory rape after having been involved in a sex scandal with a 13-year-old model. Living in Paris, Polanski continued to make films, such as *Tess* (Oscar nomination for Best Director, 1979), *Pirates* (1986), *Frantic* (1988), *Bitter Moon* (1992), *Death and the Maiden* (1994), *The Ninth Gate* (1999), and *The Pianist* (Oscar for Best Director, 2002).

He also acted, most notably in *The Fearless Vampire Killers*; *What?*; *Chinatown*; *The Tenant*; the French film *A Pure Formality* (1994); and the Polish film *The Revenge* (2002).

His autobiographical *Roman by Polanski* was published in 1984.

ADD. BIBLIOGRAPHY: J. Parker, *Polanski* (1993); V. Wexman, *Roman Polanski* (1985); B. Leaming, *Polanski, a Biography: The Filmmaker as Voyeur* (1981); T. Kiernan, *Repulsion: The Life and Times of Roman Polanski* (1980); I. Butler, *The Cinema of Roman Polanski* (1970).

[Jonathan Licht / Ruth Beloff (2nd ed.)]

POLANYI, JOHN C. (1929–), Canadian chemist and Nobel laureate. Born in Berlin, he moved to England in 1933 with his Hungarian parents, Michael and Magda. He graduated B.Sc. (1949) and obtained his Ph.D. (1952) in chemistry from Manchester University. After a post-doctoral research fellowship at the Canadian National Research Council Laboratories in Ottawa (1952–54) and Princeton University (1954–56) he joined the chemistry faculty at the University of Toronto where he was appointed professor in 1962 and continued to work there with his research group. Polanyi's research interests develop themes explored by his father, Michael *Polanyi, namely the atomic interactions that form the basis of chemical reactions. The theoretical basis for his earlier contributions was the computer integration of the classical equations of motion allied to the methodology of infrared chemiluminescence. In principle, this approach, termed "surface aligned photochemistry," analyzes the visible emission from a variety of molecules adsorbed to crystals in an ultra-high vacuum. He shared the 1986 Nobel Prize in chemistry with Dudley Herschbach and Yuan Lee. Subsequently Polanyi and his colleagues in their Toronto laboratory adapted laser techniques and reactive rather than inert adsorbing surfaces to analyze chemical reactions in even more detail occurring virtually instantaneously. Polanyi's many honors include the Centenary Medal of the British Chemical Society (1965), the Wolf Prize in Chemistry (1982), and the Royal Medal of the Royal Society of London (1989). He was appointed Officer of the Order of Canada (1974) and Companion of the Order of Canada (1979). He was elected to the Royal Society of Canada (1966), the Royal Society of London (1971), the American Academy of Arts and Sciences (1976), the U.S. National Academy of Sciences (1978), and the Pontifical Academy of Rome (1986). He received an honorary doctorate from the Weizmann Institute (1989). He has played a prominent part in many national and international organizations concerned with scientific research and education.

[Michael Denman (2nd ed.)]

POLÁNYI, KARL (1886–1964), economist and anthropologist. His scientific work was based on the place of economics in society, and the relation between production and distribution of goods. He also made a study of kinship and religion. Born in Vienna and educated in Budapest, Polányi was the foreign editor of the *Der Oesterreichische Volkswirt*, Austria's leading economic journal. Later he moved to England and in 1940 to America where he taught at Bennington College (Vermont) and New York. He was a socialist and in his later years the maintenance of peace became his major concern.

Polányi's writings include *The Great Transformation* (1945); jointly with A. Rothstein, *Dahomey and the Slave Trade* (1966); and *The Plough and the Pen-Writings from Hungary 1930–1956* (1963, jointly edited with Ilona Duczynszka).

BIBLIOGRAPHY: J. Helm (ed.), *Essays in Economic Anthropology Dedicated to the Memory of Karl Polanyi* (1965), includes biographies.

[Joachim O. Ronall]

POLANYI, MICHAEL (1891–1976) British physical chemist and philosopher. Born in Budapest, Polyani was educated at the extraordinarily successful Minta Gymnasium. He entered the University of Budapest to study medicine (1908) but his interest in physical chemistry largely dominated his student career and he spent the summer of 1912 at the Technische Hochschule in Karlsruhe, Germany, where he wrote his first papers on physical chemistry with Einstein's approval. He received his M.D. (1913) and returned to the Karlsruhe institute for the 1913–14 academic year, but joined the Austro-Hungarian Army as a medical officer on the outbreak of war in 1914. Diphtheria and other illness curtailed his military obligations, allowing him to complete his Ph.D. (awarded in 1919). Political upheaval linked to virulent antisemitism obliged Polanyi to leave Hungary to work in Karslruhe again (1919–20), and in Berlin at the Kaiser Wilhelm Institute for Fiber Chemistry (1920–23) and for Physical Chemistry and Electrochemistry (1923–33), eventually with a tenured position as "scientific member." After initial reservations, with the Nazi rise to power he moved to the University of Manchester, England (1933), as professor of physical chemistry with a brief to revitalize the chemistry department. A shift in his professional interests from the sciences to the humanities prompted a change in title to professor of social studies (1948) before his retirement in 1958. He was elected a senior research fellow at Merton College, Oxford (1959–61) and he continued to write, lecture, and travel as visiting professor in Europe and North America. He lived in Oxford until shortly before his death in Northampton. Polanyi's first scientific work concerned the interaction of molecules with a liquid surface, a process termed adsorption. His subsequent interests centered on the fundamental basis of molecular structure and the factors governing molecular association and dissociation. His theoretical insight was matched by technical innovations in crystallography and methods for studying gases at low concentration. His work had an important practical application in the British development of synthetic rubber during World War II. His work also explained the remarkable fibrous strength of cellulose. He was elected to the Royal Society of London (1944). Polanyi's interest in other fields dates from his student days. His philosophical studies explored the links between the physical universe and religious belief and were also largely concerned with the central role of personal morality in the face of eternal human imperfection. These beliefs were closely related to his conviction that scientists should have social concerns but intellectual freedom without constraints imposed by central planning. His early defense of what are now termed civil rights complemented his vigorous political opposition to communism and his support for Keynesian economics. Polanyi identified with Christianity mainly on moral grounds and he converted to the Roman Catholic Church (1919), although possibly for political reasons. He was not a practicing Catholic and was skeptical about biblical authority. Although he did not join any Jewish communal organizations and was opposed to Zionism, he gave talks to Jewish societies. He married Magda, a chemistry student, in a civil ceremony (1921) and they had two sons. Polanyi's extensive writings in all fields are listed in Scott and Moleski's enlightening biography *Michael Polanyi: Scientist and Philosopher* (2005).

[Michael Denman (2nd ed.)]

POLEMICS AND POLEMICAL LITERATURE. There were internal polemics with Jewish sectarians in the talmudic and post-talmudic periods, and a rich Jewish polemical literature in the Middle Ages. It does not include the continuous and sustained controversies which characterize rabbinical literature throughout the ages on the interpretation of the Oral Law. For this see *Conflict of Opinion. Polemics with non-Jews in the Bible, Talmud, and Middle Ages is discussed under *Disputation and Polemics and *Islam.

Talmudic Period

The talmudic literature is replete with details of polemics between the upholders of normative Judaism, the Pharisees and their successors, and the numerous sects which flourished at the time. Insofar as they are referred to by name, these are the *Samaritans, the *Sadducees, and those who are referred to under the generic name of **minim* (sectarians). Confusion exists as to the exact nomenclature and identification of the last two. As a result of *censorship, the original word in the Talmud had to be changed. Reference to the manuscripts as well as internal evidence provided by the context, show that the word *Ẓeduki*, Sadducee, which appears in the printed text refers to other sects. In addition, the word *min* applied to a wide range of sectarians, Judeo-Christians, Gnostics, Manicheans, Magi, etc. Thus whereas in the *Sifra* (Lev. 2) in the phrase "from here is provided an opening to the *minim*" the word refers to Gnostics who believed in dualism, the identical phrase in *Exodus Rabbah* 13:4 refers to those sectarians who denied the doctrine of free will. Jacob of Kefar Sakhnayya "of the disciples of Jesus of Nazareth" (these words, which are in the Mss., have been omitted from the printed text; Av. Zar. 17a) is referred to as a *min* in 27b. The Talmud states in the name of R. Naḥman "there are no *minim* among the gentiles" (Hul.

13b). The *minim* were all Jewish sectarians, and the Christian *minim*, Judeo-Christians.

There are a few polemics which can be definitely ascribed to Sadducees and Samaritans. With regard to the former, the Mishnah records a number of polemics between the Sadducees and the Pharisees in one of which Rabban Johanan b. Zakkai was the spokesman of the Pharisees. "The Sadducees said 'We cry out against you, O ye Pharisees' for they say 'the Scriptures render the hands unclean' [a typical rabbinic enactment]. Yet the writings of Hamiram [Homer?] do not render the hands unclean." In typical polemic vein Rabban Johanan carried the war into the enemy camp: "They say that the bones of the ass are clean, and the bones of Johanan the High Priest are clean" and the argument continues with the victory of the Pharisees (Yad. 4:6–8).

R. Eleazar b. Yose polemicized against the Samaritans by pointing out to them that the identification of Mt. Gerizim, the holy mountain, overlooking Shechem depends entirely upon the application of the *gezerah shavah*, an inference from analogy which was one of the 13 *hermeneutical rules evolved by the rabbis which the Samaritans rejected (Sot. 33b). Whereas this, like so many of the polemics in the Talmud, was a literary and academic controversy, the Midrash gives one with a Samaritan which belongs to a less refined sphere. R. Ishmael b. Yose, on a pilgrimage from Galilee to Jerusalem, came to Mt. Gerizim. There he met a Samaritan who asked him where he was bound. When he answered "Jerusalem," the Samaritan said "Is it not better for you to pray on this blessed mountain than that accursed one?" To which Ishmael retorted, "You are like a dog which digs up a buried carcass. It is because you know that there are idols buried here, which Jacob hid away [Gen. 35:4] that you are so full of fervor for this mountain" (Gen. R. 81:3; TJ, AZ 5:4, 44c). The polemics with the *minim* are legion in the rabbinical literature. They cover every biblical and theological topic including monotheism, dualism (Sanh. 38a), that "he who created the wind did not create the mountains" (Ḥul. 87a), freedom of will, and predetermination (see above); the validity of the principles of rabbinic exegesis (Ber. 10a); that the destruction of the Temple was a sign that God had rejected the Jewish people (obviously a Judeo-Christian, though the printed text has a Sadducee; Yoma 57a); and other topics.

One fact seems to emerge clearly from a consideration of the many polemics in the Talmud, namely that they were rarely if ever sought out by the rabbis. Almost invariably the challenge came from the sectarians. The sectarian who "used to annoy Joshua b. Levi greatly with his biblical texts" (Ber. 7a) represents the general attitude of challenge by them and only response by the rabbis.

In the Geonic Period

As was the case in the talmudic period, the rise of the various sects was the cause of various polemics. To a special category belongs *Saadiah Gaon's *Kitab al-Amanat* in which he answers the heretical opinions expressed by Hiwi al-Balkhi who lived in Persia in the last quarter of the ninth century. The fact that Saadiah found teachers in Babylonia teaching children from books based on Hiwi's biblical criticism makes it a contemporary polemic. The greatest polemic, however, in which Saadiah took a leading part, but which extended over at least three centuries, was against the *Karaite schism.

Polemical Literature of the Middle Ages

The literature of the period reflects this preoccupation with disputation, polemical works being composed in almost every literary form then used by Jews: e.g., poetry, homiletics, ethical literature, fiction, and halakhic writing. In addition, the polemic – a genre whose main purpose was to express the views of the conflicting parties – was developed.

Purely halakhic and rabbinic disputes were usually dealt with in the literature of *she'elot u-teshuvot* (rabbinic responsa) and other halakhic literary forms. Medieval halakhists followed the literary style and legal precedents found in the vast body of talmudic literature, in which almost every point of law was contested, clarified, and usually determined. Even in controversies touching basic beliefs and carried on with intense emotion, medieval Jewry accepted opposing views as at least worthy of consideration. For example in his *Hassagot*, *Abraham b. David, the leading rabbi of Provence, contested many of the legal decisions in Maimonides' *Mishneh Torah*. Yet when the celebrated code of laws was printed, the *Hassagot* were included, as if they were a commentary on Maimonides' text. Opposing views, therefore, were regarded as important and worthy of being studied by all rabbinical scholars. Sometimes halakhic controversies originated from political differences rather than legal ones; thus the contentions between the leading rabbis in Palestine and Babylonia in the time of Saadiah Gaon, carried on in the traditional halakhic literary forms, were in fact struggles for recognition as the supreme religious authority in the Jewish world.

Halakhic literary forms, however, were both inadequate and inappropriate for the resolution of basic ideological problems and new literary forms were used. One of the earliest literary documents recording a fierce ideological controversy is *Milḥamot ha-Shem* ("The Lord's Fight," 1830), a small tenth-century book by the Karaite writer, Solomon b. Jeroham. Part of the polemical literature of the Rabbanite-Karaite dispute, the work is a Hebrew reply to Saadiah Gaon's attack against the Karaites, though Arabic was usually the language in which this controversy was sustained. *Milḥamot ha-Shem*, like most medieval polemical works, is written in the literary form of a letter (see *Letters and Letter Writing). But whereas only the opening and concluding portions of such a letter were usually written in rhymed prose, this work is written entirely in that manner. The most striking characteristic of Solomon's book is its satirical nature; he quotes (and rhymes) passages from the Talmud and from the literature attributed to talmudic sages, including the **Shi'ur Komah*, to show how far these rabbinic sayings had strayed from the biblical text and from the accepted theological ideas of the times – even those accepted in

Saadiah's philosophical works. The three elements – the epistolary form, the rhymed prose, and the satirical statement of the main thesis – became the common feature in medieval Hebrew polemical literature.

Polemical literature in the form of a literary epistle served as the main vehicle of expression in one of the greatest controversies in medieval Jewry – the controversy over the writings of Maimonides, which began in the last year of Maimonides' life and continued throughout the 13th and the beginning of the 14th century, and especially during the years 1232–35 and 1304–05. The subjects of the controversy – the meaning of the anthropomorphic passages in the Bible and the talmudic literature, the reasons behind the commandments (*ta'amei ha-mitzvot*), the question of the resurrection and the nature of the afterlife, the existence of angels and demons, the problem of the creation *ex nihilo*, the allegorical interpretation of the biblical stories – were discussed in letters exchanged between the leading disputants. Most of the letters are written partly in rhymed prose, with some written completely so.

The use of the literary epistle resulted from the fact that the disputants usually did not intend to clarify the ideological, theological, or even exegetical problems over which the controversy arose. Their main aim was to disqualify the opponent as a competent judge in the issue, to prove that he does not have the requisite knowledge or awareness of the problems which would entitle him to be heard in the controversy. Thus, early in the 13th century, when *Aaron b. Meshullam of Lunel answered Meir b. Todros Abulafia ha-Levi's letters concerning Maimonides' alleged disbelief in the resurrection, he dedicated the bulk of his letter to a discussion of Abulafia's character, knowledge, and understanding, and a review of his own feelings about Maimonides and his critics. The small portion of the letter that actually deals with the problem of the resurrection says nothing more than that Maimonides' views do not differ from those of the Talmud and the *geonim*, especially Saadiah Gaon. The letter is entirely written in rhymed prose and makes extensive use of biblical and talmudic phrases, leaving no doubt that the writer intended to win the public over to his views mainly by the beauty with which he expressed his feelings. This form of polemic, therefore, encouraged not so much the clarification of the issues as the demonstration of the writer's personal qualities and literary ability, and the enumeration of his opponent's faults. Another example of the evasive character of the polemical epistle is *Naḥmanides' reply to the rabbis of northern France in the same controversy over Maimonides' *Guide of the Perplexed*. Naḥmanides did not address himself to the issues raised by the French rabbis, rather he concentrated on proving that the rabbis, being far removed from the culture of the Jews in Spain and the Provence, were not qualified to judge Maimonides. In addition, he said that the *Guide* was not written for them, but for the perplexed Jewish scholars in Spain who could not avoid contact with Greek and Arabic philosophy. In this letter, Naḥmanides did not reveal his own kabbalistic ideas nor make known his stand on the problems themselves. Neither his duties as a responsible rabbi, nor the conventions of the polemical letter required Naḥmanides to express his own opinions about the issues involved. Although other letters exchanged in this controversy deal more closely with the ideological problems, they never do so fully or exhaustively. Abraham Maimon, for example, in his letters collected as *Milḥamot ha-Shem* ("The Wars of the Lord," a very common name for a polemical work), treated some problems, especially the allegorical interpretation of biblical and talmudic passages, as did Abraham b. Samuel in his defense of Maimonides against the criticism of the French rabbis. But even in these cases the personal allusions and the flow of rhymed phraseology make up a great part of the letters. These conventions persist in the letters exchanged during the controversy in 1305, when Abba Mari *Astruc again raised the issue of the dangers stemming from allegorical interpretation and the study of philosophy. Astruc tried to organize a movement, to be headed by Solomon b. Abraham *Adret, to oppose these practices.

Ashkenazi Ḥasidism, which flourished during the Middle Ages among the Jews in Germany and northern France, also gave rise to controversy. An extant fragment of Moses b. Ḥisdai *Taku's detailed polemical work, *Ketav Tamim* ("Book of Righteousness," published by R. Kirchheim, in: *Oẓar Neḥmad*, 3 (1960), 54–99), indicates that the work pays almost no attention to literary form, the issues themselves being the writer's major concern, although inflamed accusatory language is sometimes used. Moses did not hesitate to declare that his opponents, who included *Judah he-Ḥasid, Saadiah Gaon, Maimonides, and Abraham *Ibn Ezra, were followers of the Karaites and the Christians who were destroying Judaism from within.

*Kabbalah, probably the most innovating Jewish ideology during the Middle Ages, aroused surprisingly little controversy when it began to flourish in Provence in the 12th century and in Christian Spain during the 13th century. From this period only one letter in clear opposition to the Kabbalah is extant. It is known that there was some disagreement among the kabbalists themselves over whether the Kabbalah should be discussed openly and brought to the attention of the Jewish community, or kept a secret known only to the selected few, the mystically inspired elect. Like most medieval disputes, these discussions were carried on in the form of letters.

During the 16th and 17th centuries both Jewish philosophy and Kabbalah again became objects of controversies, but with a larger part of the discussions now carried on in the form of special polemical books. Thus Joseph *Jabez, who wrote in Italy after the expulsion of Jews from Spain, termed the teachings of the Jewish philosophers as the cause of the conversion of thousands of Jews to Christianity during the 15th century in Spain. Isaac b. Judah *Abrabanel held somewhat similar views. Accusations and polemics against the philosophers are found in the works of many scholars up to and including Jacob *Emden and *Naḥman of Bratslav. Many polemical letters were written concerning the 16th-century controversy over whether the Zohar, the major work of the Kabbalah, should be printed. The opponents of publication comprised two groups:

the devout kabbalists, who thought that a work of kabbalistic mysticism should be kept secret in order to prevent the uninitiated from reading it; and the opponents of the Kabbalah in general, who opposed its printing in order to reduce the influence of the Kabbalah which they regarded as false. A few anti-kabbalistic works were written in Italy, the most notable being *Ari Nohem* by Leone *Modena who systematically sought to prove that kabbalistic beliefs were invalid and that the kabbalists' claim that their theory and literature are ancient, transmitted from the time of the *tannaim*, is historically untrue. Modena was one of the first to use methods of literary and historical criticism in polemics against the Kabbalah. Two other 16th-century controversies deserve mention. The first was initiated by Azariah de' *Rossi's *Me'or Einayim*, a critical study of Jewish history and tradition which claims that the accepted system of chronology, i.e., counting from the creation, has neither a historically nor a traditionally sound basis. For this view he was criticized both by Renaissance scholars and by traditional Jewish scholars like *Judah Loew b. Bezalel of Prague. Azariah answered his more learned critics in a special book, *Maẓref la-Kesef.*

During the 1530s dozens of polemical letters were written by supporters and opponents of the *semikhah*, the ordination of rabbis, after the rabbis of Safed tried to reinstate the tradition that had been broken early in the Middle Ages. The rabbis of Jerusalem, however, opposed this; participation in the controversy increased, engaging the attention of many rabbis from various countries. The participants tried to treat the controversy as a purely halakhic one and the language of the polemical letters exchanged on this problem is clearly halakhic. But there is no doubt that beyond the halakhic references lay the true question: Should the rabbis take upon themselves activities concerned with messianic times (the reestablishment of the *semikhah* was regarded as one of the events connected with the redemption) or should they wait patiently until the coming of the Messiah who will reinstitute the *semikhah* himself? A similar consideration probably lay behind the dispute over the printing of the Zohar, for it was believed that wide acceptance of the Zohar and its teachings was one of the signs indicating the approach of messianic times.

The fiercest controversies in Jewish history were those arising over Shabbateanism and *Ḥasidism. Although there was some 17th-century criticism of *Shabbetai Ẓevi and his prophet, Nathan of Gaza, even before the former was converted to Islam, it was neither intense nor widespread. After the conversion, however, the critics knew no bounds in their accusations against the Shabbateans, and for 150 years thereafter the persecution of believers in Shabbetai Ẓevi and those influenced by his teachings was carried out relentlessly by some of the greatest rabbis. Jacob b. Aaron *Sasportas, among the first to oppose Shabbateanism, published his collection of anti-Shabbatean epistles under the title *Ẓiẓat Novel Ẓevi* (though it was proven recently that he re-edited some of his early letters to make them more anti-Shabbatean than they originally were). Later, anti-Shabbateans concentrated their efforts on discovering scholars with Shabbatean sympathies and bringing about their excommunication (*ḥerem*). Thus, Moses *Ḥagiz accused Moses Ḥayyim *Luzzatto of Shabbateanism, the same charge Jacob Emden leveled against Jonathan *Eybeschuetz. Both Luzzatto and Eybeschuetz were defended against the accusation by a number of supporters, and the controversies raged for decades.

In the second half of the 18th century, the newly founded ḥasidic movement was also suspected of heretical and Shabbatean tendencies. This suspicion, one of the causes for the unflaggingly intense opposition to the movement, led to the *ḥerem* brought against the Ḥasidim in 1772, a ban which was renewed many times in the next 40 years. The Ḥasidim were mainly accused of disregarding the importance of traditional Talmud study and of abusing the traditional scholars. Rarely did Ḥasidism's opponents clearly express their real suspicion – that the ḥasidic movement was a new version of the Shabbatean and Frankist movements – a suspicion which was the underlying reason for the vehemence of the various *ḥerem* declarations, in the anti-ḥasidic epistles, and in the collections of letters and special polemical works written by the *Mitnaggedim*. It is to be noted that very little material in the vast anti-ḥasidic literature is concerned with the basic ideas of Ḥasidism. The *Mitnaggedim* attacked the Ḥasidim because of the way they behaved, or the way they believed they behaved, almost totally disregarding the ideology of the new movement. In this omission the *Mitnaggedim* followed the tradition of epistolary polemical literature since the early Middle Ages.

BIBLIOGRAPHY: I. Davidson (ed.), Solomon ben Jeroham, *Milḥamot ha-Shem* (1934); D.J. Silver, *Maimonidean Criticism and the Maimonidean Controversy* (1965), incl. bibl.; A. Halkin, in: *Tarbiz*, 25 (1955/56), 413–28; J. Sarachek, *Faith and Reason, the Conflict over Rationalism of Maimonides* (1935); Baron, Social², 5 (1969), 82ff.; J. Shatzmiller, in: *Zion*, 34 (1969), 126–44; Baer, Toledot, passim; S.Z.Ḥ. Halberstam, *Kevuẓat ha-Mikhtavim* (1875); G. Scholem, in: *Sefer Bialik* (1934), 141–62; I. Tishby, in: *Perakim*, 1 (1967), 131–82; J. Katz, in: *Zion*, 16 (1951), 28–45; S. Ginzburg, *Rabbi Moshe Ḥayyim Luzzatto u-Venei Doro* (1937); I. Tishby (ed.), Jacob Sasportas, *Sefer Ẓiẓat Novel Ẓevi* (1954); M.A. Perlmutter, *Rabbi Yonatan Eybeschuetz* (1947); M. Wilensky, *Ḥasidim u-Mitnaggedim* (1970).

[Joseph Dan]

POLEMON II (d. 74 C.E.), king of Cilicia. The Judean princess, *Berenice, widow of Herod of Chalcis, induced Polemon to undergo circumcision and marry her in an attempt to suppress rumors detrimental to her reputation. Polemon, with an eye to her wealth, accepted the proposal, but the marriage did not last long. Berenice deserted her husband, and the king, according to Josephus, "was relieved simultaneously of his marriage and of further adherence to the Jewish way of life" (Ant., 20:145–6). Polemon of Cilicia has been confused with Julius Polemon, king of Pontus from 37–63 C.E., who vistited *Agrippa I at Tiberias.

BIBLIOGRAPHY: IV. Magie, *Roman Rule in Asia Minor*, 2 (1950), 1407.

[Isaiah Gafni]

°**POLEMON OF ILIUM** (c. 202–181 B.C.E.), Greek author of a lost history in which the Exodus was used to date the mythological Greek king Apis, according to Eusebius, *Praeparatio Evangelica*, 10:10, 15.

POLGAR, ALFRED (1873–1955), Austrian essayist and critic. One of Austria's foremost prose stylists and drama critics, Polgar, who was born as Alfred Polak, was the son of a Viennese musician. He worked as a reporter and as drama critic for the *Wiener Allgemeinen Zeitung*. From 1918 he voiced his pacifistic views, which were influenced by his impressions of World War I, in the journal *Der Friede* and in monographs such as *Kleine Zeit* (1919) and *Schwarz auf Weiss* (1929). In 1925 he moved to Berlin, where he contributed to such eminent periodicals as *Die Weltbuehne* and the *Berliner Tageblatt*. He returned to Vienna upon the Nazis' accession to power in Germany, where he worked as a reporter for German-language foreign papers. In 1938 he fled to Paris and in 1940 he settled in the U.S. After 1949 he spent much of his time in Europe. In his years of exile and after the war Polgar was active as a translator, adapter, and cultural mediator. He died in a hotel while on a visit to Zurich.

A prolific and subtle writer, Polgar produced many brilliant *feuilletons*, impressionistic sketches, reviews, parodies, satires, and elegant short essays and vignettes in the style of Peter *Altenberg. Polgar collaborated with Egon *Friedell on the witty satirical plays *Goethe im Examen* (1908) and *Soldatenleben im Frieden* (1910). One of several collections of his short stories appeared in 1912 under the title *Hiob*. Polgar's collected critical writings appeared as *Ja und Nein* (4 vols., 1926–27, 1956), followed by *Handbuch des Kritikers* (1938, 1997). Collections of Polgar's work were compiled and published in six volumes under the title *Kleine Schriften* (1982–86), edited by M. Reich-Ranicki and U. Weinzierl, and *Das Grosse Lesebuch* (2003), edited by H. Rowohlt.

BIBLIOGRAPHY: K. Schuemann, *Im Bannkreis von Gesicht und Wirken* (1959), 133–70; F. Lennartz, *Deutsche Dichter und Schriftsteller unserer Zeit* (1959^8), 591–3; H. Kesten, *Meine Freunde die Poeten* (1959), 79–84; H. Zohn, *Wiener Juden in der deutschen Literatur* (1964), 57–60. **ADD. BIBLIOGRAPHY:** U. Weinzierl, in: *Taschenspiegel* (1979), 187–242; idem, *Alfred Polgar: Eine Biographie* (1985).

[Harry Zohn / Noam Zadoff (2nd ed.)]

POLIAKOV, LÉON (1910–1997), historian. Born in Saint Petersburg, Russia, Poliakov went to France in 1920. He was on the staff of the *Pariser Tageblatt* until 1939. During World War II he served with the French army. Participating in the establishment of the Centre de Documentation Juive Contemporaine, he became head of its research department after the war. In 1952 he was appointed research fellow at the Centre National de la Recherche Scientifique and in 1954 joined the Ecole Pratique des Hautes Etudes. Poliakov, one the first historians of the Holocaust, wrote extensively about it and paved the way for the scientific study of antisemitism from the 1950s. He was departmental editor of the first edition of the *Encyclopaedia Judaica* for the subject of antisemitism. Some of his books have been translated into English – *Harvest of Hate* (1954), *The Aryan Myth: A History of Racist and Nationalist Ideas in Europe* (1974), and his major four-volume *The History of Anti-Semitism* (2003). His other works include *Auschwitz* (1964), *Les banchieri Juifs et le Saint-Siège du xiii au xvii siècle* (1965) and *De l'antisionisme à l'Anti-semitisme* (1969). Poliakov also edited a number of works, including *La condition des Juifs en France sous l'occupation italienne* (1946) and, with Josef Wulf, *Das Dritte Reich und seine Diener; Dokumente* (1956) and *Das Dritte Reich und die Juden; Dokumente und Aufsaetze* (1955). He published his memoirs in 1981 (*L'auberge des musiciens*), and amongst his other books published later are *La Causalité diabolique: essai sur l'origine des persécutions* (1980) and *L'impossible choix: histoire des crises d'identité juive* (1995).

[Sylvie-Anne Goldberg (2nd ed.)]

POLICE OFFENSES, offenses arising in connection with the prevention of public mischief and for the maintenance of public security, as laid down in the Bible, that have formed the basis for elaborate regulations in later periods of Jewish law. Thus, the biblical injunction against false weights and measures (Deut. 25:13–15) led to the appointment of special inspectors who were authorized not only to enter shops and ascertain the accuracy of weights and measures in use, but also to impose penalties, e.g., *floggings or *fines. Similarly, the biblical injunction against *fraud (Lev. 25:14, 17) and *oppression (Lev. 19:13) led to the prohibition of profiteering and to the appointment of special officers charged with the supervision of prices (cf. Yoma 9a); and profiteers too were liable to be flogged. *Gambling and betting were prohibited as if they were species of larceny, and so were such potentially injurious acts as hunting in populated areas or taking animals already captured in the trap of another (Yad, Gezelah 6:8–12). The biblical injunctions for the protection of animals (Deut. 22:4, 6–7; Ex. 23:5) gave rise to the prohibition against hurting any living creature (BM 32a, b), and led to the elaboration of rules for the prevention of collisions between loaded animals in the street, and hence also between ships and vehicles (Yad, Roẓe'aḥ 13:11–12).

The injunction that "you shall not bring bloodguilt on your house" (Deut. 22:8) was interpreted as not limited to the traditional requirement of providing a *parapet for the roof lest anyone should fall from it, but as extending to any act or omission likely to endanger human life (Yad. loc. cit.). It is no excuse for a man to say that his conduct endangers himself too; even if he chooses to disregard his own safety, he cannot disregard that of others – and he is liable to be flogged if he does. Thus the supply or consumption of unclean or noxious food or water is prohibited (*ibid.*, 11:7–16), and so is the creation of any danger to the public (BK 27a–30a). There are also express provisions for the annual inspection of streets and thoroughfares by officers of the court to make sure they are not damaged by rain and are safe for traffic (Tosef. Shek 1:1). Where particular roads or journeys were dangerous, the court would appoint officers to accompany travelers and guard their safety; if they failed in watchfulness, the officers were regarded as if they had shed innocent blood (Yad. Evel 14:3). Where there were dangers of overcrowding or public licentiousness, court officers would mingle among the crowds to maintain law and order (Yad, Yom Tov 6:21).

The biblical prohibition against a woman putting on a man's clothing, and vice versa (Deut. 22:5), may have served as the authority and pattern for later regulations governing dress and appearance. As dressing in the clothing of the opposite sex was regarded as conduct conducive to sexual perversion, so was dressing in the gentile fashion regarded as a first step toward assimilation. Sumptuary laws against extravagance and luxury became increasingly frequent, not only to prevent the following of the practices of gentiles (cf. Lev. 20:23), but also to ensure humility in walking before God (cf. Micah 6:8). Penalties were imposed mostly as fines, but we find also public denunciations (see *Ḥerem). In some places, regulations were also laid down to make certain dresses or robes obligatory, e.g., for judges and notables (*Takkanot Mehrin*, 530). Generally, the biblical injunction to appoint executive officers in addition to judges (Deut. 16:18) was interpreted as imposing a duty to attach to each court "men with sticks and rods, standing at the service of the judges, to patrol markets and streets, inspect shops, rectify prices and measures, and redress all injury: they act only on the orders of the court, and when they detect a breach of law, they bring it before the court for adjudication" (Yad, Sanhedrin 1:1). It appears that until the destruction of the Temple, petty offenses were not, in Jerusalem, brought before the ordinary criminal courts, but before two or three police courts (*dayyanei gezerot*, Ket. 13:1), who were sitting full time and therefore (in contradistinction to judges) entitled to remuneration (Ket. 105a).

[Haim Hermann Cohn]

Offenses that Harm the Entire Public

Particular severity attaches to offenses that harm the entire public, or any undefined group of people. Their severity stems from the fact that when a person causes an injustice to the public at large or an unidentified person or persons, he cannot directly rectify the injustice, neither to a specific person, nor to the society at large. An example of such an offense is stealing from the public, regarding which the Sages said, "Theft from the public is more severe than theft from an individual, because one who steals from an individual can compensate him by returning what he has stolen, while a person who steals from the public cannot compensate them by returning what he has stolen" (Tos. to BK (ed. Zuckermandel) 10:14). Another example of theft which cannot be compensated is an act of fraud in weights and measures (see *Weights and Measures): Rabbi Levi said, "The punishments for offenses relating to weights and measures are more severe than for sexual offenses" (BB 88b). The reason is explained by the *posekim*: "The punishment for [offenses concerning] weights and measures is very severe, because it is impossible for one who weighs and measures to repent properly" (Sh. Ar., ḤM, 231: 19) – "Because it is impossible to restore [the amount improperly taken to its owners, since he cannot know to whom and how often he gave a [false] measure" (*Sema* to Sh. Ar., ḤM, 231:34). The offender's act can be redressed to a certain extent by his working in community service for the benefit of the public, but this is not considered full redress, which necessitates returning the full return of what he has stolen to the victim (*Rashbam*, BB 88b).

Based on these principles, the Israeli Supreme Court decided on a severe sentencing policy against public officials who embezzled public funds (Cr. A 291/81, *Ploni* v. *The State of Israel*, 35 (4) 438; per Justice Menachem Elon).

Different Aspects of Police Activities

MAINTAINING PUBLIC ORDER. The obligation to maintain public order has implications for the saving of life (*pikku'aḥ nefesh*), which, as is well known, overrides almost all biblical and rabbinical prohibitions. When a large public is concerned, the fear of jeopardizing lives is even greater. Thus, to prevent public damage and risk, even when the life threatening risk is not obvious, some authorities permit certain otherwise forbidden actions on Shabbat, precisely because the public is involved (Shab. 42b; *Ḥidushei Haran*, ad loc.; Yad, Shabbat 10: 25 and in *Maggid Mishneh,* ad loc.). Following the establishment of the State of Israel, these principles were relied upon to justify various aspects of police activity intended to maintain public order and peace, including various police activities on the Sabbath or operations entailing risk to the life of an individual in order to maintain the peace and security of the entire public.

THE PROHIBITION ON THE HUMILIATING OR INTERFERING IN THE WORK OF THE POLICE. The humiliation of policemen, who are officers of the court, is considered as contempt of court (see*Contempt of Court). A punishment of excommunication (see *Ḥerem) may be imposed on anyone found to have humiliated or interfered with the police in their work, even if based on the sole testimony of the policeman concerned. Policemen are exempt from liability if causing financial damage to a person who interfered in their work, and are even entitled to strike such individuals (Sh. Ar, ḤM 8.5., Rema, ad loc.).

[Menachem Elon (2nd ed.)]

BIBLIOGRAPHY: M. Block, *Das mosaisch-talmudische Polizeirecht* (1879); Frankel, Mishnah; C. Roth, in: JQR, 18 (1927/28), 357–83; ET, 3 (1951), 63f.; J.R. Marcus, *The Jew in the Medieval World* (1960), 193–7. ADD. BIBLIOGRAPHY: M. Elon, *Ha-Mishpat ha-Ivri* (1988), 1:636, 642, 649f, 654, 663, 995, 1102; idem, *Jewish Law,* (1994) 2:788, 795, 803f, 809, 815, 820; 3:1203, 1325; idem, *Jewish Law* (*Cases and Materials*) (1999), 213–17; S. Yisraeli, *Amud ha-Yemani* (1991) no. 17; D. Nativ and M. Slae, in: *Teḥumin*, 1 (1980), 372–96; U. Dasberg and Y. Rozen, "*Ha-Shabbat ba-Mishtarah*," in: *Teḥumin*, 2 (1981) 66; I. Warhaftig, "*Shimush be-Neshek Ḥam be-Pizzur Hafganot Allimot*," in: *Teḥumin*, 3 (1982) 371–76.

POLIER, SHAD (1906–1976), U.S. Jewish leader and civil rights advocate. Polier was born in Aiken, South Carolina. After graduating from the University of South Carolina with distinction, he continued his studies at the Harvard Law School, graduating in 1929, and got his master's degree in 1931. As a college student he was disturbed by cases of lynching which had taken place in his hometown, and devoted himself from then on to the cause of civil rights. He gained international fame in the famous Scottsboro case, in which eight black youths were sentenced to death on an allegation of rape of two white girls, preparing briefs on behalf of the defendants twice before the High Court. As a result he became active in the National Association for the Advancement of Colored People (NAACP), serving on the Executive Committee of its legal and educational defense fund. In 1948 he brought a personal suit against the Metropolitan Life Insurance Company, alleging that its Stuyvesant Town Development in New York was guilty of discriminatory practice in not admitting blacks. The case resulted in fair housing laws in New York. He led the fight that resulted in the first state Fair Education Law that was directed to ending discrimination in the admission of blacks on the basis of race or religion.

In 1945 Polier founded and became chairman of the commission on Law and Social Action of the American Jewish Congress, which conducted legal battles against antisemitism, segregation, racism and other discriminatory laws. In this capacity he fought and won a six-year battle against antisemitic job practices by Aramco, the Arabian-American Oil Company.

Polier occupied prominent positions in the World Jewish Congress, as a member of its Executive and Governing Council and Chairman of its Budget and Finance Commission, and finally as Honorary Chairman of its National Governing Council. He was also a member of the board of the Conference on Jewish Material Claims against Germany and of the Memorial Foundation for Jewish Culture. Polier's wife Justine, daughter of the late Rabbi Stephen *Wise, was for 35 years a judge of the New York Family Court, retiring in 1973.

POLIKER, YEHUDAH (1950–), Israeli rock-ethnic guitarist-singer. Poliker is one of the best-known artists in Israel, but it took him a long time, a lot of hard work, and a musical reincarnation to get to the top. He was born in the northern town of Kiryat Ḥayyim and began playing melodica and accordion as a young child. For a while he divided his leisure time between his musical explorations and goaltending for the local youth soccer team. When he received a guitar for his bar mitzvah the former won out and he soon began spending most of his time out of school honing his guitar skills.

When he was in high school he set up a band called FBI, which included a bass player called Banjo Kimḥi. This was followed by a band called The Phantoms, which broke up in 1968, when Kimḥi joined the army. Poliker enlisted a short while after but failed to win a place in the navy band, despite his advanced instrumental skills, because he could not read music. Poliker's stint in the army was short-lived, and he soon resumed his musical career, forming the Tigers in 1970. This group was a far more professional outfit. It lasted a full five years and, for a while, relocated to Tel Aviv before Poliker returned north to set up Bareket, with Kimḥi back on bass. Bareket mostly played covers but also began to perform some original material, and even released a couple of poorly received singles.

It was in 1980 that Poliker got his first big break when supergroup Brosh recruited him for a show with megastar pop singer Zvika Pik that ran for six months. That spot brought him to the notice of several leading figures of the Israeli music industry, including a producer by the name of Ya'akov Gilad. Gilad soon took a trip up north to see Poliker and his Bareket group for himself and was impressed. Shortly afterwards, Poliker and the band members moved to Tel Aviv, began working on a new album, and changed their name to Benzine. Benzine's debut recording, "24 Hours a Day," was a hit and the group was one of the leading rock bands on the Israeli scene until it disbanded in 1985.

With the passing of Benzine, Poliker took the biggest step in his career when he returned to the ethnic sounds his Greek-born parents had brought with them to Israel. In 1985 he released his first solo album, *Enayim Sheli* ("My Eyes"), which incorporated a mix of Greek songs and rock material. The record was an instant hit and Poliker had found his way to the hearts and ears of a much wider audience. In 1988, Poliker's career took another successful turn when he released *Efer ve-Avak* ("Ashes and Dust"). This was a very emotive album which included several songs with lyrics based on Poliker's parents' Holocaust experiences and Poliker's own feelings as the child of Holocaust survivors and on the hardships of growing up in Israel of the 1950s and 1960s.

Poliker was now a superstar and remained at the top, releasing more big sellers, like *Paḥot Aval Ko'ev* ("Less, But Painful") in 1990 and 1995's *Ha-Yeled Shebekha* ("The Child in You"), which included electronic and computer music.

[Barry Davis (2nd ed.)]

POLISH, DAVID (1910–1995), U.S. Reform rabbi, Zionist leader. Polish (pronounced like the household product, not the country) was born in Cleveland and received a B.A. from the University of Cincinnati in 1931. In 1934, he was ordained at Hebrew Union College, where he earned a D.H.L. in 1942 and was awarded an honorary D.D. in 1959. Already an outspoken Zionist at the time of his ordination, Polish was told by a Reform movement then indifferent (if not hostile) to Zionism that he would not be employed. Nevertheless, he became the rabbi of Congregation of Judah in Cedar Rapids, Iowa (1934–39), where he formed a statewide Zionist organization. After serving as director of the B'nai B'rith Hillel Foundation at Cornell University (1939–42) and rabbi of Temple Israel in Waterbury, Connecticut (1942–47), he assumed the pulpit of Temple Mizpah in Chicago, Illinois, where he introduced **seliḥot* services to the congregation, sparking interest in a traditional practice that was soon adopted by other Reform congregations. Polish became influential in the so-called neo-traditional movement, in which Reform Jews recovered many traditions and customs that the movement had earlier discarded; his 1957 book *Guide for Reform Jews* emphasized the importance of *mitzvot* in Reform Jewish observance.

In 1950, the still controversial Polish left Temple Mizpah to form Beth Emet – The Free Synagogue in the Chicago suburb of Evanston, named and modeled after the original Free Synagogue in New York City and conceived in the principle that the pulpit was free, i.e., the rabbi could sermonize about whatever he wanted to without fear of being dictated to by the lay leaders. Polish went on to reorganize the Chicago Rabbinical Association into the Chicago Board of Rabbis, serving as its first president (1958–60) and doing the same for the Chicago Board of Reform Rabbis. He was the first rabbi in Chicago – indeed, one of the first rabbis in the country – to invite Martin Luther King, Jr., to address his congregation: in early 1958, King, then 29, dined at the rabbi's home, spoke on the "Desirability of Being Maladjusted" and then slept at the temple, because he could not find a suitable hotel. In 1965, Polish joined King in his march for peace from Selma to Montgomery, Alabama.

Polish enjoyed the support of his congregants not only for his civil rights activism but also for his energetic advocacy of Zionism. At the urging of Stephen S. *Wise, he served as national chairman of the Committee on Unity for Palestine (1947), as well as president of the Chicago Zionist Federation (1975–76). He furthered the cause of Zionism in the *Central Conference of American Rabbis as a member of the executive board (1945–47; 1967–69; 1973–75), as well as chairman of the CCAR Committee on Projects for Palestine (1948). He also chaired the Committees on Liturgy (1959–61), Rabbinic Training (1967–69), the Future of the Rabbinate and the Synagogue (1969–72), Jewish Organizations (1973–75) and the Rabbi's Manual Committee (1986). He represented the CCAR at the Prime Minister's Conference in Jerusalem in 1968, where he delivered an address in Hebrew, and planned the first CCAR conference in Jerusalem in 1970. Symbolic of the triumph of his many years of lobbying the organization on behalf of Zionism and embracing tradition, he was elected vice president (1969) and then president of the CCAR (1971–73). During his tenure in office, the CCAR became a member of the World Jewish Congress (1972) and embarked on a series of dialogues with the *kibbutz movement in Israel, resulting in the establishment in the *Aravah of kibbutz Yahel (1977) and kibbutz Lotan (1983), both comprising young American *olim* and sabras and affiliated with Reform Judaism. As president, he testified before the U.S. Congress in favor of home rule for the District of Columbia (1972); he was later cited in the Salt II Treaty of 1979. In 1977, Polish was a founder of the Association of Reform Zionists of America and author of ARZA's Statement of Principles.

In 1980, Polish retired from Beth Emet, retaining the title founding rabbi, which he preferred to emeritus. He taught that year at the Los Angeles campus of HUC-JIR and subsequently at Northwestern University, where he was instrumental in establishing the Philip and Ethel *Klutznick Chair of Jewish Civilization in 1986. The senior editorial writer for the Chicago Jewish Sentinel, Polish was the author of nine books, including *Higher Freedom*, which won the Frank and Ethel S. Cohen Award from the Jewish Book Council of America in 1966 as an outstanding work in the field of Jewish thought. His major works are *A Guide for Reform Jews* (with Doppelt, 1957), *The Eternal Dissent* (1961), *The Higher Freedom: A New Turning Point in Jewish History* (1965), *Israel – Nation and People* (1975), *Renew Our Days: The Zionist Issue in Reform Judaism* (1976, based on his 1973 monograph *"Are Reform and Zionism Compatible?"*), (1989), and *Abraham's Gamble: Selected Sermons for Our Times* (1988). He also edited *The Reform Rabbi's Manual* (1988) for the CCAR.

BIBLIOGRAPHY: The Nearprint Files of the American Jewish Archives, Cincinnati.

[Bezalel Gordon (2nd ed.)]

POLISH LITERATURE.

Biblical and Hebraic Influences

Translations of the Bible played an important part in the development of Polish as a literary language. From the early 14th century onward, the Old Testament – particularly the Psalms – provided a major source of poetical inspiration in Polish literature and culture. Some of the best-known of these Polish versions of the Scriptures were the 15th-century Queen Sophia Bible; the 14th-century Floriański Psalter; the Calvinist Brześć (Radziwill) Bible (1562); Szymon Budny's Nieświez Bible (1572); and Fr. Jakub Wujek's classic Catholic Bible (1593–99), which injected the greatest concentration of biblical imagery and expression into the Polish language. Polish Bibles from the 16th century onward were mainly the work of Protestants, who also produced many paraphrases of biblical books such as the Psalms. New translations have been produced in the 20th century, and there have also been a few Polish Jewish versions of Old Testament texts, notably Song of Songs (1922) by Juliusz Feldhorn (1901–1943), who was murdered by the Nazis; and complete Old Testaments by F. Aszkenazy (1927–30) and S. Spitzer (1937). In Polish literature proper, the influence of the Bible may be detected during and after the Renaissance era in works such as *Żywot Józefa z pokolenia żydowskiego* ("The Life of Joseph," 1545), a biblical interlude by Mikolaj Rej, the Calvinist "father of Polish literature" who also published a verse translation of Psalms (1546); and the *Kazania sejmowe* ("Parliamentary Sermons," 1597) of the Jesuit Piotr Skarga. The impact of the Old Testament was most evident in the outstanding Polish poet of the Renaissance, Jan Kochanowski, whose works include *Pieśń o potopie* ("The Song of the Flood," 1558), *Zuzanna* (1562), and *Treny* ("Lamentations," 1580; English selections, 1920). Kochanowski's sensitive and beautiful version of Psalms, *Psałterz Dawidów* (1578), was the finest poetical work of its time and served as a literary model until the 19th-century romantic period. Some later Psalters by his followers and imitators were Maciej Rybiński's *Psalmy monarchy i pro-*

roka św. Dawida ("The Psalms of David, King and Prophet," 1598) and the paraphrase by Mikolaj Sęp-Szarzyński in *Rytmy* (1601). Some Polish writers were also interested in other books of the Bible, which they either translated or used as stylistic models. The staunchly Catholic poet and historian Wespazjan Kochowski celebrated the tenth anniversary of the battle of Vienna (in which King Jan III Sobieski defeated the Turks) with his *Psalmodia polska* ("Polish Psalmody," 1693), written in the form of biblical prose. There were also scores of dramatic works and interludes on biblical subjects belonging to the theatrical repertory of the Polish court from the 16th and 17th centuries onward.

LATER BIBLICAL WRITING. Scriptural phraseology, syntax, and imagery constantly recur in the works of Poland's greatest writers, particularly in the romantic era. Some notable examples are Adam *Mickiewicz's *Księgi narodu polskiego i pielgrzymstwa polskiego* ("The Books of the Polish Nation and Pilgrimage," 1832), Juliusz Slowacki's *Anhelli* (1838), and Zygmunt Krasinski's *Psalmy przyszłości* ("Psalms of the Future," 1845). Cyprian Kamil Norwid ranks next with his *Żydowie Polscy* ("Polish Jews"), which summarizes the history of the Jews from the time of Moses until the era of the struggle of the Poles and Jews ("Maccabees") against their common oppressors. Biblical books such as Isaiah, Jeremiah, and Job; figures such as Cain and Abel, Moses, Samson, Saul, David, Judith, and Daniel; historic sites such as Mount Ararat and Babylon; and even objects such as Samson's pillar or the prophet's staff were, for centuries, the poetical stock-in-trade of many Polish writers. These include Kazimierz Brodziński, Stefan Witwicki, Kornel Ujejski, Maria Konopnicka, Wladislaw Belza, Kazimierz Przerwa-Tetmajer, Stanislaw Wyspiański, Jan Kasprowicz, Leopold Staff, and Jan Dobraczyński. After Poland lost her independence, writers used biblical themes to discuss the present in the guise of an ancient historical setting, this being the only means of presenting the slavery into which the Poles had been forced, without exposing the authors to the wrath of foreign oppressors. Polish poets found in the Bible the moral values required by a people condemned to slavery, contempt, and humiliation. Biblical and other Jewish figures had the same function as those drawn from Greek and Roman mythology in the dramas of Stanislaw Wyspiański (*Daniel*, 1907) and Karol Hubert Rostworowski; *Opowiesci biblijne* ("Biblical Tales," 1963) of Kosidowski had a vast sale even in post-World War II Communist Poland.

The Image of the Jew

Evidence of an unfriendly attitude toward the Jews may be found in Polish literature of the 16th and 17th centuries, as well as in Catholic polemical literature of the Reformation period. This was also the case with epigrams and satires of the so-called bourgeois literature, in the satirical *Worek Judaszów* ("Judas' Sack," 1600) by Sebastian Fabjan Klonowicz, who was mayor of Lublin, and in *Wyprawa żydowska na wojne* ("The Jewish War Expedition," 1606), a comedy by an anonymous author. In writings of this type there are sometimes echoes of anti-Jewish riots, as in *Taniec Rzeczypospolitej Polskiej* ("The Dance of the Polish Republic," 1647), a rhymed chronicle by Gabriel Krasiński which describes part of the student riots at Kazimierz, the Jewish district of Cracow.

FAVORABLE PORTRAYALS. A markedly different attitude governs works about Jews during the period of the so-called Four-Year Sejm (1788–92) and at the beginning of the 19th century, which appealed for tolerance toward the Jews (see *Poland). This also characterized the first Polish social novel about Jews, *Lejbe i Sióra* ("Leib and Sarah," 1821), by Julian Ursyn Niemcewicz. Polish folk poetry also mentions Jewish participation in the Kościuszko revolt, one instance being the song about Berek *Joselewicz, the commander of a squadron of Polish lancers, who died a hero's death near Kock in 1809. The figure of the Jew and the Jewish problem both appear in the works of the great Polish romantic poets (Mickiewicz, Słowacki, and Z. Krasiński) and their imitators. Juliusz Słowacki portrayed the fate of the Jew as a human being – hated, alien, and condemned to shame, contempt, and death – in Judith, a character in his drama *Ksiądz Marek* ("Father Marek," 1843). Proud and conscious of her fate, she seeks revenge on her antisemitic persecutors. The third of the great romantics, Zygmunt Krasiński, symbolized the role of Jewish converts in the revolutionary movements of Europe in his historical drama *Nieboska Komedia* ("The Ungodly Comedy," 1835). The events preceding the outbreak of the November insurrection (1830) and its collapse inspired a rich political and polemical literature dealing with the problem of the Jews. Works of this type were *Au Peuple d'Israël* (1832), a French appeal by the historian Joachim Lelewel, who also wrote the booklet *Sprawa żydowska w roku 1859* ("The Jewish Question in 1859," 1860), defending the Jews against antisemitic attack; and papers by the Jew Ludwik Ozeas Lubliner, author of *Des Juifs en Pologne* (1839), *Obrona Żydów* ("The Defense of the Jews," 1858), and *Do Polaków Izraelitów, w Polsce* ("To Polish Israelites in Poland," 1862). Pro-Jewish works were also written by other romantics, such as Cyprian Norwid, Wladislaw Syrokomla, Mieczyslaw Romanowski, Aleksander Teofil Lenartowicz, and Wlodzimierz Wolski. Their sympathetic references to the Jews were often interwoven with others about Polish suffering under the foreign oppressor. In 1883 the poet Wladislaw Belza published poems of this kind about the Jews in his anthology *Żydzi w poezyi polskiej – głosy poetów o Żydach* ("Jews in Polish Poetry – Voices of the Poets on the Jews," 1906²), a work inspired by the Jewish assimilationist Agudas Achim society. The short-lived rapprochement between Poles and Jews before and after the outbreak of the January Revolution (1861–63) was reflected in poems by some Poles, such as Ludwik Mieroslawski, a nationalist politician and general, and in the verse of Jews like Henryk Merzbach and M. Epstein, who also participated in the uprising; but these were phenomena of minor literary importance.

THE JEWS AS A SOCIAL PHENOMENON. The deep changes in political outlook after the defeat of 1863 and the attitude adopted by literature of the so-called Positivist period toward everyday contemporary themes made Polish poets increasingly aware of the Jews and the Jewish problem, not only from the Polish point of view, but also as a specific, characteristic feature of contemporary society. The role of Jews in science, industry, commerce, and banking was reflected in Polish literature of the period. The radical development of Polish socialism on the one hand, and of Polish nationalism on the other, made the Jew a stock character – artisan, merchant, scholar, politician, journalist, or yeshivah student – and writers portrayed him according to their specific outlook. Polish poets, far from despising the Jews, pitied and defended them in their works. This was especially true of the Warsaw urban poet Wiktor Gomulicki, although such writers tended to overlook the Jewish world discovered by playwrights and prose writers. However, sympathetic insight was evident in the works of Poland's greatest poetess, Maria Konopnicka, who condemned antisemitic outrages in one of her novellas, and in *Żydzi* (1843), a play by Józef Korzeniowski. Much space was also devoted to the Jewish problem by prose writers such as Eliza *Orzeskowa, Klemens *Junosza, Józef Rogosz, and Ignacy Maciejowski (Sewer). Another leading writer, Boleslaw Prus, introduced two Jewish figures in *Lalka* (3 vols., 1887–89), the first important Polish realistic novel. Szlangbaum, a Jewish stereotype, is avaricious, ruthless, self-abasing before the rich, and self-confident with the poor, sacrificing everything for the sake of business; but the second Jew, Dr. Szuman, partly resembles the romantic hero of the novel. In his great historical novel *Faraon* ("The Pharaoh," 3 vols., 1895–96), set in ancient Egypt, Prus also alludes to the Jewish situation in contemporary Poland. In his weekly column in a Warsaw newspaper, Prus displayed a contradictory attitude, either attacking the Jews for their financial skill and resourcefulness or praising them for the same abilities, through which the Jews, unlike Polish Christians, served the interests of society in general. The Jew as a revolutionary social innovator was a figure created by the great radical prose writer Stefan Żeromski. In his novel *Ludzie bezdomni* ("The Homeless," 2 vols., 1900) he depicted the role of a Jewish physician in initiating the fight for reforms in stagnant Polish society. Żeromski's last novel, *Przedwiośnie* ("Early Spring," 1925), aimed against the right-wing Pilsudski regime, assigned a much more important task to the Jews as the co-authors of the Polish Communist movement. In Communism Żeromski saw a force capable of redeeming Poland's disinherited youth.

NEGATIVE PORTRAYALS. A different tendency also made its appearance from the late 19th century, some writers setting out to prove the destructive role of the Jews in the social, political, economic, and cultural life of Poland. Wladislaw Stanislaw Reymont (1867–1925) drew an unfavorable picture of the Jews in his novel *Ziemia obiecana* ("The Promised Land," 1899), where he showed the different cross sections of industrial life in Lodz during the period of czarist occupation. Both Jewish and German capitalists exploit the Polish working classes, which are thus denied the benefits of a native capitalism. Other hostile assessments were presented by Teodor Jeske-Choiński, a mediocre novelist and critic who expressed reactionary, clericalist opinions, and Roman Dmowski, the ideologist of Polish nationalism and a leader of the National Democratic movement, who played a major role in the propagation of antisemitism. Aleksander Świętochowski, once broadminded and progressive, joined the conservative, antisemitic groups of writers, as did the poet Andrzej Niemojewski, who edited *Myśl niepodległa*. In his youth Niemojewski had been a revolutionary democrat, but in his later years he joined the extreme reactionary, nationalist circles frequented by Adolf Nowaczyński (Neuwert), a playwright and pamphleteer of Jewish birth. Many antisemites were active as essayists and literary critics, although scarcely anyone of major importance campaigned against the Jews.

LATER TENDENCIES. After Poland attained independence and national sovereignty in 1918, new forms of social and artistic life came into being. At the same time the whole basis of political thought underwent a change under the impact of the new conflicts in a society liberated from foreign oppression. Polish poetry, which was revitalized during the years 1918–39, also echoed the voice of Polish Jewry. Some poets dedicated works to the Jews, whom they considered to be fellow citizens sharing common ideals determined by the same political program. In two pre-World War II poems, "*Księżyc ulicy Pawiej*" ("The Moon of Pawia Street") and "*Na śmierć rewolucjonisty*" ("On the Death of a Revolutionary"), Wladislaw Broniewski, a communist, sympathetically portrayed the life of the Jewish poor and the struggle of the Jewish revolutionaries who died in the cause of the Polish working classes. In his moving *Ballady i romanse*, written after a pogrom organized by the Nazis, Broniewski expressed his admiration for the Jews, while his "*Pamięci Szmula Zygielbojma*" commemorated Samuel *Zygelbojm who committed suicide in London in order to draw world attention to the destruction of the Jewish people by the Nazis. Artur Oppman (Or-Ot), a Warsaw poet, eulogized a certain Rabbi Jawor who chose to remain within the walls of the embattled Polish capital. Among its citizens he enjoyed "the credit of the ancient sons of Judah, the servants of Jehovah, and of the bards and knights." On the other hand, another outstanding poet, Konstanty Ildefons Galczynski, sometimes described the Jews in a satirical manner in poems such as his "*Sonata księżycowa rodziny Kon*" ("The Moonlight Sonata of the Kon Family"), "*Ballada o Aronku*" ("The Ballad of Little Aaron"), and "*Wilno, ulica Niemecka*" ("Vilna, the German Street"). Wanda Melcer's *Czarny ląd* ("The Black Land," 1896), a series of reportages written after a visit to the Jewish section of Warsaw, stressed the exoticism of Jewish customs, clothing, speech, behavior, and way of life. This account was not written for the sake of cheap sensation, but indicated the many aspects of a social problem.

PROTESTS AGAINST FASCISM. The upsurge of Polish antisemitism immediately before the outbreak of World War II found reflection in the satirical poetry of Antoni *Slonimski, whose *Dwa końce świata* ("Two Ends of the Earth," 1937) attacked racism and Fascism. Many leading Polish writers dealt with issues involving the Jews and fought antisemitic manifestations. They included members of the *Przedmieście* group founded in 1933: Jerzy Kornacki, Helena Boguszewska, Pola Gojawiczyńska, and Halina Górska. Allied with them were other writers and journalists who worked for weeklies such as *Oblicze Dnia, Epoka, Czarno na białym, Sygnały, Poprostu, Lewar,* and *Dziennik Popularny.* Weeklies ranging on the opposing side included *Prosto z mostu* and *Merkurjusz Ordynaryny.* In the battle against Fascism and antisemitism during the years preceding World War II many satirical poets took an active part. Among them were Jewish writers such as Antoni Slonimski, Juljan *Tuwim, Leon Pasternak (1910–1969), Stanislaw Jerzy *Lec, Jan *Brzechwa, Wlodzimierz Slobodnik (1900–1991), Lucian *Szenwald, Jerzy Jurandot, and Jerzy Kamil Weintraub (1916–1943); and non-Jewish writers such as Artur Marya Swinarski, and Eduard Szymański. After the defeat of the Nazi invaders, many Polish writers – Jews and non-Jews – devoted books to the "Final Solution" of the Jewish problem, as put into effect during the German occupation. Events in Poland two decades later, after the Israel-Arab Six-Day War of 1967, were reflected in "Israel" (1968), an outstanding poem by the émigré Polish writer Kazimierz Wierzyński, a member of the old *Skamander* literary group, and Czeslaw Milosz, émigré Polish writer.

The Jewish Contribution

Since Polish Jewry was almost entirely Yiddish-speaking until the early part of the 20th century, Jews who wrote in Polish were at first comparatively few. The pioneer of Jewish literary activity in Polish was the converted essayist Juljan *Klaczko. Two writers who followed his lead later in the 19th century were Wladislaw Ordon (Wladislaw Szancer, 1848–1914), a tragic figure of humble origin whose poems were once highly regarded, and the poet and historian Alkar (Aleksander Kraushar, 1843–1931), who translated works by *Heine. By the beginning of the 20th century, Jews had become more active in Polish literature, their participation being reflected in the symbolic figure of the Jewess Rachel in Stanislaw Wyspiański's drama *Wesele* ("The Wedding" 1901). The Jewish share in Poland's cultural life gained momentum during the first two decades of the 20th century, and particularly after the achievement of national independence following World War I. Those representing this trend include the poets Franciszka Arnsteinowa (1865–1942), Henryk Balk (1901–1941), Mieczysaw Braun, Julia Dickstein-Wielczynska (1880?–1943), Juliusz Feldheim (1901–1943), Zuzanna Ginczanka (1917–1944), Bruno *Jasieński, Cezary Jellenta (Napoleon Hirszband, 1861–1935), Boleslaw *Leśmian, Stefan Napierski (Stefan Marek Eiger, 1899–1949), Artur Prędski (Artur Pfeffer, 1900–1941), S.R. Stande, Jan Stur (Hersz Feingold, 1895–1923), L. Szenwald, and J.K. Weintraub. Among the novelists were Leo Belmont (Leopold Blumenfeld, 1865–1940), Henryk Drzewiecki, Halina Górska, Gustawa Jarecka (1908–1942), Alfred Aleksander Konar (Aleksander Kinderfreund, 1862–1940?), Bruno *Schulz, and Bruno Winawer. The last also wrote plays, as did Jasieński. Three early Jewish literary critics and historians were Samuel *Adalberg, Henryk *Biegeleisen, and Wilhelm *Feldman. Many of these writers died during the Nazi occupation of Poland, and among them also the famous children's writer and educator Janusz *Korczak. Both between the world wars and after 1945, Jews, or men and women of Jewish origin, continued to make an important contribution as poets, playwrights, novelists, short story writers, and literary historians and critics. Some who were active before World War II resumed their careers in Poland after the German defeat. Leading poets in this category were Jan Brzechwa, Mieczyslaw *Jastrun, Stanislaw Jerzy Lec, Tadeusz *Peiper, Tadeusz Różewicz, Antoni *Slonimski, Arnold Slucki, Juljan Tuwim, Aleksander *Wat, Adam Ważyk, Józef *Wittlin, Wiktor Woroszylski, and Stanislaw *Wygodzki. Of these, Slonimski maintained his independence of the Communist Party line on Zionism, while Wygodzki left Poland for Israel after the Six-Day War of 1967. Other poets included Stefania Grodzieńska (1914–), Leon Pasternak, Józef Prutkowski (Józef Nacht, 1915–1981), Wlodimierz Slobodnik, and Irena Tuwim (1900–1987), Juljan Tuwim's sister. Two major playwrights were the émigré satirist Marian *Hemar and the ex-Zionist convert Roman *Brandstaetter; others included Benedykt Hertz and Jerzy Lutowski (1923–1984). Kazimierz *Brandys, Adolf *Rudnicki, and Julian *Stryjkowski were leading novelists, the last specializing in stories of pre-World War I Jewish life; and others included Michal Maksymilian Borwicz (Maksymilian Boruchowicz, 1911–), whose anthology, *Pieśń ujdzie cało* ("The Song Will Prevail," 1947), contained Jewish songs of the occupation era, as well as Irena Krzywicka (1904–1994) and Stanislaw Lem (1921–). Hanna Mortkowicz-Olczakowa (1905–1967), who in 1936 published *W Palestynie: obrazy i zagadnienia* ("In Palestine: Pictures and Problems") on the situation of Palestinian Jewry, later wrote the biographical *Janusz Korczak* (1949; *Mister Doctor,* 1965). Some Jewish authors in other genres were the screenwriter Józef Hen (1923–), the émigré author and actor Henryk Grynberg, the satirist Karol Szpalski (1908–1963), and Krystyna Żywulska (1918–), author of *Przeżyłam Oświęcim* ("I Survived Auschwitz," 1946).

Polish Jews were also prominent as literary historians and critics, and as editors and publishers of important literary reviews which influenced cultural life, notably *Wiadomości Literackie* (edited by M. Grydzewski). Juljusz Kleiner (1866–1957), who wrote many literary monographs and standard textbooks on Polish literature, trained a whole generation of literary critics, including scholars such as Henryk Balk and Henryk Szyper (1900–1949). Some later writers of eminence in this field were Jan Kott (1914–2001), whose works on Shakespeare were translated into many languages; Henryk Markiewicz (1922–), a leading Marxist literary theorist; Maria Renata Mayenowa (1910–1988); Henryk Wolpe (1899–1967); and Wiktor Weintraub (1908–1988), who became professor of

Polish literature at Harvard University, U.S. Other authorities on Polish literary history and criticism included Rafal Marcel Blueth (1891–1939), Emil Breiter (1886–1943), Wilhelm Fallek (1888–1941), Ludwik Fryde (1912–1942), Dawid Jakub Hopensztand (1904–1943), Roman Karst (1911–), Jerzy Pomianowski (1921–), Artur Sandauer (1913–1989), and Henryk Vogler (1911–2005). A number of major writers and critics were also distinguished translators.

BIBLIOGRAPHY: *Udział żydów w kulturze*, 2 vols. (1938); J. Feldhorn, *Literatura polska wieku XVI a Żydzi* (1929); K. Bartosiewicz, *Antysemityzm w literaturze polskiej XVI i XVII wieków* (1940); T. Jeske-Choiński, *Żyd w powieści polskiej* (1914): W. Fallek, in: *Pamiętnik zjazda naukowego im. Jana Kochanowsskiego…* (1931), 383–471; K. Dresdner, in: *Miesięcznik Żydowski*, 2 pt. 1 (1932), 399–426.

POLITICS.

Introduction

Jewish involvement in national politics in the various countries in which they settled dates from the period of Jewish emancipation at the end of the 18th and the first half of the 19th century. In fact, personalities such as Joseph *Nasi, duke of Naxos, and Solomon *Ashkenazi held powerful positions in Ottoman politics in the late Middle Ages; Jewish ministers held office in medieval Spain; and Jews served as court advisers to various rulers in Holland, Germany, and Sweden. Nevertheless, professing Jews entered representative institutions of modern states only at a much later date. Until the Emancipation, Jews who were eager to hold political office were generally obliged to content themselves with participation in local government (as in Russia) or to convert to Christianity. The political emancipation of the Jews came in the U.S. from the late 18th century and in parts of Western Europe it was effected soon after the outbreak of the French Revolution. Thus, in Holland, Moses *Asser and Jonas Daniel *Meyer were appointed in 1797 to the legislative council and state council and, in Venice, following the overthrow of the oligarchy, the elected municipal council contained three Jewish members. In France and Germany, Jews were still generally excluded from political office but, even after the onset of reaction at the end of the Napoleonic Wars, it was clear that Jewish emancipation could not be long delayed. Soon after the 1848 revolutions in Europe, Jews were permitted to become members of representative institutions in nearly all major European states, outside the Russian Empire.

In English-speaking countries other than Britain and Canada, Jewish entry into political life developed more rapidly than elsewhere. The small Jewish community in the United States enthusiastically supported the revolutionary cause, and in 1775 Francis *Salvador was elected to the South Carolina Provincial Congress, probably the first Jew to be elected to a representative assembly in modern times. The Declaration of Independence, issued the following year, affirmed the principle of equality and Jews were freely admitted into all American legislative bodies from that time onward. No restrictions ever existed on Jewish political activities in Australia and South Africa, and Jewish pioneers in these territories were prominent in public affairs, as mayors of cities, legislators, and, in the case of Sir Julius *Vogel and Vabian *Solomon, as prime ministers. On the other hand, in Canada and Great Britain, where Jews received the right to serve as representatives in parliament in 1832 and 1851, respectively, they had previously been refused this right because they could not swear "on the true faith of a Christian," as the oath required.

Once admitted to parliament, Jews rapidly achieved top government posts in the democracies outside America and rose to ministerial rank in France in the 1850s (Achille *Fould), Holland in the 1860s (Michael *Godefroy), Australia in the 1870s (Sir Julius Vogel), Britain in the 1880s (Henry de *Worms), and Italy at the turn of the 20th century (Luigi *Luzzatti). On the other hand, professing Jews were generally deprived of ministerial status in Germany and Austria, but there was no discrimination against converts, and Franz Klein, Austrian minister of justice, was the only unconverted Jew to become a minister in a Central European national government before 1918. In America, on the other hand, Jews were not victims of discrimination, but neither were they as a rule sufficiently integrated into American society to participate in national politics.

One important reason why Jews did not hold ministerial posts in many states, especially before World War I, was that Jewish politicians were generally numbered among the opposition radical parties of the center and left. This was particularly true of Germany and Austria where, following the upheavals after World War I, a number of Jews who had been prominent in the Socialist parties assumed senior government positions. The same situation proved true of France and Britain, where Socialist administrations brought Jews into cabinets, but conservative governments rarely included any Jewish members. Thus, in France all three Jewish prime ministers professed varying shades of socialism, and in England, of ten professing Jews to become members of British cabinets (up to 1970), only Sir Keith *Joseph was a Conservative. A similar trend was noticeable elsewhere.

A number of reasons have been advanced for the Jewish tendency toward radical parties. One of the most obvious is that liberal and left-wing political groups have generally been far less hostile to underprivileged newcomers (as Jews generally were) than conservative parties. The Right associated itself with the Church, the establishment, and social tradition – three concepts with which Jews had no connection – and was frequently antisemitic, while the radical groups, committed to challenge the establishment and alter tradition, were obviously more attractive to Jewish voters and prospective politicians alike. This reason also explains why Jews found advancement in left-wing parties much easier than in rightist ones (e.g., Ferdinand *Lassalle, Eduard *Bernstein, Leon *Blum, and others). Even in 1970 it was as true as at the beginning of the 20th century, that Jews in Western Europe were found mainly in the Socialist and Liberal parties and in the United States in the Democratic Party.

In pre-revolutionary Russia Jews were officially discriminated against and deprived of the opportunity to air their grievances democratically. Many of them, particularly young intellectuals who did not choose to emigrate overseas or join the Zionist movement, were impelled toward revolution. The Socialist revolutionaries and both Menshevik and Bolshevik factions of the Social Democrats seemed to be the only real alternative to the autocracy of the czars, which openly professed antisemitism. Many middle-class Jews in Russia did vote for the liberal Constitutional Democratic (Kadet) Party, but many more supported political groups that sought not to reform, but to destroy the existing regime. As a result, a significant proportion of the Social Democratic party consisted of the Jewish *Bund, and among the leaders of the general revolutionary parties the number of Jews was also disproportionately high.

Undoubtedly, Socialist doctrine, with its emphasis on equality and the destruction of the ruling classes, had a considerable appeal to Jewish intellectuals fighting against discrimination. This proved true not only in Russia, but in other European countries amid the convulsions at the end of World War I. Jews practically dominated the short-lived Communist regimes in Hungary (Béla Kun) and Bavaria (Kurt *Eisner), and it is reasonable to assume that this fact contributed to their quick downfall, since they lacked support in the general population. They were murdered or forced into exile when the counterrevolutionaries took control. After World War II Jews were again prominent at the head of East European Communist regimes (*Rakosi became the party leader in Hungary, *Minc and *Berman leading members of the Polish Communist regime under Bierut, and a number of Jews held key ministries in Czechoslovakia). This was largely a result of the fact that during the Stalin period Moscow could rely more on Soviet-trained old Communists of the satellite countries, among whom Jews played a prominent part. These Jews, however, did not reflect the general political attitude of the Jewish population in those countries and ultimately, when the Stalinist regimes crumbled there, they mostly disappeared or were openly attacked, frequently with antisemitic allusions (particularly in Poland and Czechoslovakia). In the Soviet Union the number of Jews in the top leadership sharply declined from the great Stalinist purges of the 1930s onward. In contrast to the prominent position of individual Jews in the Communist movement, Jews were never active in other totalitarian regimes and hardly any right-wing dictatorships included Jewish ministers. Clearly, Jews could not be expected to support regimes whose policy was specifically antisemitic, and in other dictatorships not characterized by antisemitism, the authorities were nonetheless reluctant to number Jews in their party in order not to cause offense to antisemitic elements.

An important issue connected with the involvement of Jews in politics is the degree to which Jewish and national interests have clashed. In Germany most leading Jews generally accepted the principle that German national interests were of paramount importance (e.g., Levin *Goldschmidt), and were anxious to prove their loyalty to the state in the face of attacks by antisemites. Furthermore, Jewish politicians, with very few exceptions – mostly Zionists – were assimilationists and had no interest in Jewish affairs. Most Jewish Socialist politicians in Germany as well as Austria rejected Judaism and, either by converting to Christianity or professing atheism, demonstrated their detachment from any Jewish interests. On the other hand, in English-speaking countries, where Jews were less subject to antisemitic pressures and were not required to prove their social integration by assimilation, Jewish politicians were frequently prepared to oppose government policies even in face of accusations of "dual loyalty." In the United States and Great Britain Jewish political leaders repeatedly pressed their governments to take steps to stop antisemitic excesses in Central and Eastern Europe and help Jewish immigration and settlement in Palestine. Later, in the United States, Jews were also in the forefront of demands upon the government to increase its assistance to Israel in the face of Arab threats. In supporting Israel, Jewish politicians in English-speaking countries often clashed openly not only with the government of their country but also with their parties as, e.g., Labor MPs in Britain during the Sinai Campaign (1956) or Jewish supporters of De Gaulle in France after the Six-Day War of 1967. Jewish politicians in South Africa generally accepted Israel's clear stand at the UN against their government's apartheid policy. However, the degree to which Jewish politicians canvassed Jewish issues often tended to reflect the political advantage to be gained by it. Jewish politicians in New York City have an interest in the large Jewish vote; those in most parts of Europe are more conscious of the antisemites. Nevertheless, though Jewish interests have been pressed hard on occasion, Jews rarely organized themselves for solely political purposes and have in most instances denied the existence of a Jewish political interest. In some East European countries, before World War II, many Jews were elected to parliament as Jews, i.e., as representatives of the Jewish community or of Jewish parties, and in such cases there was no question of conflicting loyalties. In Hapsburg Austria-Hungary Jews had the choice of voting for the assimilationist Socialists, many of whose leaders were Jewish, or the Jewish, i.e., Zionist Party, while before and after World War I Jews from different political parties united to defend the Jews from state persecution. Although these groups never had substantial influence in general politics, they played an important part in maintaining the unity of the Jewish communities and providing a forum for airing Jewish grievances.

Australia

No discrimination existed against Jews in Australia and they played an important part in the early development of the Australian colonies. As a result, Jews were identified with Australian political life from the first years of self-government. The first Jew to be elected to an Australian legislative body was Sir Saul *Samuel, who became a member of the New South Wales legislative council in 1854. He was joined by Jacob Montefiore, who was elected in 1856 while the first Jewish members of the Victoria legislative assembly were Nathaniel Levi who was elected in 1860, Charles Dyte who represented Ballarat East from 1864 to 1871 and championed miners rights on the Ballarat goldfields, and J.F. Levien, who was a member of the Victoria parliament for over 30 years. Other prominent figures included Judah Moss *Solomon who represented Adelaide in the South Australian parliament from 1858 to 1874, Edward Cohen (1822–1877) who represented East Melbourne from 1864 until his death, and Ephraim Zox (1837–1897) who succeeded him as member for East Melbourne. Jewish representation in the 19th-century Australian parliament was out of proportion to their total number and in Adelaide where the Jewish population was only 500 there were four Jewish members of the legislative assembly (Judah Moss Solomon, Emanuel Solomon, Vabian Solomon, and Lewis Cohen). Four Jews also held ministerial posts in Australian colonial governments: Sir Saul Samuel was minister of finance and trade, Edward Cohen served as commissioner of customs, Sir Julian *Salomons became vice president of the New South Wales executive council, while Vabian Solomon was premier of South Australia for a short time in 1899.

When the first Australian federal parliament met in Melbourne in 1901 there were three Jewish members, Vabian and Elias Solomon, and Pharez Phillips. However, few Jews were subsequently elected to the Australian federal parliament, prominent exceptions being Senator Sam *Cohen, who was deputy leader of the Australian Labor Party, and Max Falstein. Many Jews played an important part in the various state parliaments, however, particularly in Victoria where several rose to the rank of minister, among them Theodore *Fink, minister without portfolio, Henry Isaac Cohen who held several ministerial appointments, Harold Edward Cohen who was minister of public instruction and solicitor general, and in New South Wales Abram *Landa who was successively minister of labor, housing, and cooperative societies. In addition, Matthew Moss was a minister in the government of Western Australia and Sir Asher Joel was a member of the New South Wales Legislative Council. Two Jews also acquired distinction as speakers of parliaments, Sir Daniel Levy being speaker of the New South Wales parliament and Sir Archie Michaelis (d. 1975) was speaker of the Victorian parliament. Most distinguished of all was Sir Isaac *Isaacs, chief justice of Australia, who was governor-general of Australia from 1931 to 1936, the first Australian-born governor-general and the first Jewish governor-general of any British Dominion territory. In subsequent years, fewer Jews have served in Australia's federal parliament, although four – Peter *Baume, Joe *Berinson, Barry *Cohen, and Sam *Cohen – have served in Australian cabinets since the 1970s. Sir Zelman *Cowen was governor-general of Australia in 1977–82.

[Isidor Solomon]

Austria

Although a few Jews were prominent in Austrian political society in the 17th and 18th centuries as court advisors to Hapsburg monarchs, Jews were not generally allowed to hold political posts until after the reforms which followed the outbreak of the 1848 Revolution. Five Jews were elected to the first revolutionary parliament of that year: Adolph *Fischhof, Joseph Goldmark, Abraham Halpern, Isaac Noah *Mannheimer, and Rabbi Dov Ber *Meisels. The suppression of the revolutionary movement, however, led to the renewal of restrictions on Jews and they were denied the right to hold government or municipal offices. These rights were restored in 1860 when liberal legislation allowed the Jews various civil liberties and two Jews, Ignaz *Kuranda and Simon Winterstein, were elected to the Reichsrat. In the same year Baron Anselm von *Rothschild was made a member of the Austrian upper house. The constitution of 1867 abolished all discrimination on the basis of religion, and for over half a century Jews suffered no legal restrictions on their entry into public life though anti-Jewish prejudice frequently acted as an equally effective bar. Except for Franz Klein who was twice minister of justice, no professing Jews held ministerial posts in the Hapsburg Empire until October 1918. In the half century between the promulgation of the constitution of 1867 and the collapse of the Hapsburg Empire, a number of Jews became prominent figures in Austrian politics. They included successful industrialists and bankers such as Simon Winterstein, Baron Anselm von Rothschild, Moritz von *Koenigswarter, and Rudolph *Auspitz. Most Jews were members of the German Liberal Party but toward the end of the century many turned to the new Social Democratic Party under Victor *Adler which acquired wide support among the Jews of Austria and rapidly became the target of antisemitic attacks. Among the leaders of the party were Wilhelm *Ellenbogen, Friedrich Austerlitz, and Otto *Bauer, all of whom pledged their sole allegiance to the Socialist cause, supported Jewish assimilation, and opposed all forms of Jewish nationalism, believing that this was an effective way of combating growing antisemitism. By contrast, Rabbi Joseph Samuel *Bloch formed the Union Oesterreichischer Juden to defend Austrian Jewry against the antisemites and on the two occasions he was elected to the Reichsrat fought strenuously against anti-Jewish discrimination. Following the granting of universal suffrage at the end of 1906 four Jews were elected to parliament as members of the newly formed Jewish National Party (*Volkspartei, Juedische) which advocated an independent Jewish policy and was pro-Zionist. Its members were Heinrich Gabel, Arthur Mahler, and Adolf Stand, all from Galicia, and Benno Straucher from Bukovina. During World War I many Jewish Socialists opposed the war and for most of the war were an ineffective minority, but the pro-Western liberal politician Joseph *Redlich became increasingly more important and was briefly minister of finance at the end of the war. With the creation of the Austrian Republic in November 1918, a Socialist government took office with the Socialist leader Otto Bauer as foreign minister. Bauer and Friedrich *Adler were among the party leaders to combat the threat of a Communist revolution which became a serious possibility as long as the short-lived Bolshevik regime of Béla Kun held power in Hungary. But though the Socialists retained their respectability as an anti-Communist party, the fact that a large number of their leaders were of Jewish origin, among whom were Julius *Braunthal, Robert Danneberg, and Hugo *Breitner, was a continual source of embarrassment to the party. Many Vienna Jews voted for the Socialist Party but many also supported the Zionist candidates of whom Robert *Stricker was elected to the Austrian National Assembly and three others were elected to the Vienna city council. The Zionist candidates were not subsequently successful, however, largely because the Jewish refugees from the eastern part of the old Hapsburg Empire, who were the least assimilated and the most pro-Zionist, were denied the right to vote at all. However, toward the end of the 1920s the Zionist parties gained strength in the Jewish communal elections while the Jewish Socialists declined in importance in both communal and national politics following the resurgence of the nationalist and later fascist parties. When Chancellor *Dollfuss assumed rule by executive decree, Jewish Socialist leaders like Braunthal and Breitner were among those temporarily imprisoned as part of the policy of destruction of the Social Democratic Party, but for a time Jews were allowed to become members of the Vaterlaendische Front. However, following the *Anschluss* with Germany in March 1938 Austrian Jews were deprived of all their political and civil rights and many fled the country to avoid arrest, among them Otto Bauer, Friedrich Adler, and Hugo Breitner. After World War II few Jews were active in politics in Austria, a notable exception being Bruno *Kreisky who became successively foreign minister, chairman of the Social Democratic Party, and in 1970, chancellor of the Austrian Republic, remaining in office until 1983.

Canada

Prior to the British conquest in 1759, Canada was a French colony. Only Roman Catholics were legally allowed to settle in the colony. Protestants and Jews were excluded. But when France ceded Canada to Great Britain at the Treaty of Paris in 1763, the common law of England became the law of the new British colony. Nevertheless, as a Jew Ezekiel Hart, first elected to the Legislative Assembly of Canada in 1808, was prevented from taking his seat and again in 1809. The Jews of Montreal petitioned the Legislature of Lower Canada for the recognition of a Jewish religious corporation. A "Jewish Magna Carta" of 1831–32 was passed in which it was declared that Jews were to be "entitled to the full rights and privileges of other subjects of His Majesty … and capable of taking, having, or enjoying any office or place of trust within this Province." Nevertheless, long before the passage of the 1832 Bill of Rights, a tradition of public service among the early Jews of Canada had already existed – as early as Aaron Hart, who was postmaster in Three Rivers in 1763, and in 1790 John Frank, chief of the fire brigade of Quebec.

The theoretical question of whether Jews possessed equal rights had long before been resolved by parliament in England where almost a full century earlier rights had been accorded Jews in 1740. In 1832 Jews in the British colonies of North America were granted naturalization although in Canada the problem was at first complicated by the absence of an oath-taking procedure appropriate to Jews. And even later, after the Law of 1832, it took Royal intervention to smooth the way. Thereafter, however, Jews could stand for and hold political office without any of the former impediments.

As early as 1871, Henry Nathan from Victoria, British Columbia, was elected a member of parliament in Ottawa. Almost a half-century would pass before another Jew, Samuel Jacobs from Montreal in 1917, was sent to Ottawa as an elected member of parliament. After World War I, Peter Bercovitch, Maurice Hartt and A.A. Heaps were elected in the House of Commons. During and after World War II, the numbers of Jewish members of parliament increased significantly, especially during the 1960s. Jews were elected for most parties, including Fred *Rose, the only Communist ever elected to the House. David *Lewis of the New Democratic Party was the only Jew chosen to lead a federal party. In 1969, Pierre Elliott Trudeau appointed the first Jew to a federal cabinet minister, Herbert *Gray, as minister without portfolio. Since that day, a government without a Jew in a cabinet post has become the exception rather than the rule. In 2005 two Jews were members of the federal cabinet, Justice Minister and Attorney General Irwin *Cotler, and Jacques Saada, who was the minister of the Economic Development Agency of Canada for the Regions of Quebec and minister responsible for the Francaphonie.

Jews have also been prominent in provincial politics. They have led major political parties in Ontario, Manitoba, and British Columbia. Dave *Barrett, leader of the New Democratic Party in British Columbia, went on to become the first Jewish provincial premier, serving between 1972 and 1975. There have also been many Jewish elected mayors of towns and cities across Canada, particularly in the smaller towns of Ontario, and in the West. The first Jewish mayor elected in the Province of Quebec was William Hyman of Gaspé in 1858. Vancouver elected a Jewish mayor, David Oppenheimer, in December 1887. He was a crucial figure in the creation of the services necessary for the city. In Toronto Nathan *Phillips, elected in 1952, was the first non-Protestant ever elected mayor of Toronto. His election was a major step in the transformation of Toronto from a solid and stolid outpost of British and conservative values to a modern pluralist metropolis. Philips served for eight years. Since then, Philip *Givens and Mel *Lastman have also served as mayors of Toronto. In 1955 Leonard Kitz was elected mayor of Halifax. In 2004, Stephen Mandel was elected mayor of Edmonton and Sam Katz mayor of Winnipeg.

The widening acceptance of Jews in civil society in the first decades after World War II encouraged politicians to appoint Jews to ranking public service positions. Prime among them was Louis *Rasminsky who, after some disappointments, was named the governor of the Bank of Canada in 1961; little more than a decade later, with Bora *Laskin pointed chief justice of the Supreme Court of Canada in 1973, the fact of Jews being appointed in the upper reaches of the public service was becoming so accepted that it hardly merited comment. This included the appointment of Jews to major diplomatic posts. Canadian Jews have, for example, served as ambassadors to the United States, Germany, Turkey, the United Nations, and to Israel and the Palestinian Authority.

As in other arenas of Canadian public life, such as the judiciary and the press, Jews have achieved a presence in Canadian politics and what was exceptional before World War II became increasingly commonplace by the late 1960s. In the early 21st century Jews were politically active in the Canadian public square from one ocean to the other and at all levels of government.

[Stuart E. Rosenberg / Richard Menkis and Harold Troper (2nd ed.)]

England

After the resettlement of the Jews in England in 1656, they enjoyed social freedom, but did not achieve full political emancipation until 1858. For a century and a half their exclusion from national and local government was shared by nonconformists and Roman Catholics, although these minorities were emancipated in 1818 and 1819, respectively. The insistence of the House of Lords on retaining the words "on the true faith of a Christian" in the parliamentary oath prevented Jews from sitting in parliament for almost 30 more years. Thus, before 1858 only converts or the descendants of converts were able to enter parliament or hold any state or municipal post. Nevertheless, the very fact that such men were permitted to sit in parliament testified to the fact that the bar was purely religious and not racial. Benjamin *Disraeli, for example, who was an active supporter of Jewish emancipation, was regarded as a Jew by many of his contemporaries and was the victim of social discrimination but not of any legal bars. In 1845 the Jewish Disabilities Removal Act allowed Jews to hold office in municipal government and two years later David *Salomons became an alderman of the City of London. In the same year Lionel de *Rothschild became the first Jew to be elected to parliament but was not allowed to take his seat. In 1851 Sir David Salomons was elected to parliament but was forcibly removed from the Commons Chamber after he had voted three times and even made a speech to explain his position. Eventually, a bill was passed in 1858 allowing each House to fix its own oath to be administered to a Jew; Lionel de Rothschild became the first Jewish member (but, incidentally, never made a speech). Lionel de Rothschild was one of eight Jewish MPs in the Liberal Party during the 19th century; the others were Sir David Salomons, Sir Francis Goldsmid, Sir Frederick Goldsmid, Sir Julian *Goldsmid (who sat for 30 years and became speaker of the House of Commons), Sir John *Simon, Sir George *Jessel, who, as solicitor general in 1871, became the first Jewish minister in a British government, and Arthur *Cohen. The first Jewish Conservative member was Saul Isaac, elected in 1874, who was followed by Lionel Louis *Cohen and Henry de *Worms, who as Lord Pirbright was made parliamentary secretary to the board of trade and undersecretary of state for the colonies. Jews at first found the road to political advancement easier in the more progressive Liberal Party, but after Disraeli became prime minister, the Conservatives became the party of reform. Nevertheless, most Jewish politicians were to be found in the ranks of the Liberal Party, among them Herbert *Samuel who became Chancellor of the Duchy of Lancaster, postmaster general, home secretary, and the first Jewish cabinet minister in Britain. Others included Rufus Isaacs, Lord *Reading, who was Lord Chief Justice of England and later viceroy of India, and Edwin *Montagu who was Chancellor of the Duchy of Lancaster, minister of munitions, and secretary of state for India. The decline of the Liberal Party in the 1920s led many Jews to switch their allegiance to the growing Labor Party and a number of Jews sat in parliament, first in the Liberal cause and later as Labor members. Among them were Harry *Nathan, who was minister of civil aviation in the Labor government after World War II, George Spero, and Barnett *Janner. Few Jews held important positions in the national governments of the 1930s, though a prominent exception was Leslie *Hore-Belisha, who was minister of war from 1937 to 1940. In the general election immediately after World War II the number of Jewish Labor members of parliament rose from 4 to 26. Considerable influence was also wielded by Harold *Laski who was chairman of the Labor Party. Jewish MPs from other parties were virtually eliminated, a notable exception being Phil Piratin (1907–1995), the only Jewish Communist in parliament in Britain. Jewish liberals were gradually eliminated by the failure of the party at elections while Jewish Conservative candidates tended to be passed over by the constituency associations, though Henry d'Avigdor *Goldsmid sat for many years in the Conservative interest and Sir Keith *Joseph became the first Jewish Conservative cabinet minister. Lord Reading had served in 1931 as foreign secretary in a national government and Leslie Hore-Belisha as a National Liberal in Conservative-dominated conditions. Several Jews became cabinet ministers in the Labor governments of 1945–51 and 1964–70. In the former Labor government under Clement *Attlee, Lewis *Silkin was minister of town and country planning; Emanuel *Shinwell was minister of fuel and power and secretary of state for war; Harry Nathan was minister of civil aviation; and George *Strauss was minister of supply. In the Labor government of 1964–70 there were more than 30 Jewish Labor MPs and Jewish ministers included John *Diamond and Harold *Lever, who held senior posts at the Treasury, and John *Silkin), who was minister of public building and works. In addition, several Jewish members who never held ministerial posts had considerable influence on Labor policy, in particular Sydney *Silverman and Ian Mikardo (1908–1993). Nevertheless, Jews played little part as Jews in the formation of government policy and there was never a "Jewish vote" even on the Palestine question during the last days of the British Mandate. A few Jewish women played a part in Jewish parliamentary life. Marion Phillips (1881–1932) was the first Jewish woman member, while Barbara Ayrton Gould (c. 1890–1950) was chairman of the Labor Party (1939–40). Two Jewish women were returned to parliament in 1970, Renée Short (1919–) for the Labor Party and Sally Oppenheim (1930–) for the Conservatives. Four women were among the first ten Jews to be made life peers: Dora Gaitskell (1909–1989), Beatrice Serota (1919–2002), Alma Birk (1917–1996), and Beatrice Plummer (1903–1972). The government of Margaret *Thatcher brought about a reversal of the traditional affiliation of most active Anglo-Jewish politicians with the Left. From her accession in 1979 there were now many more Jewish Conservative MPs than Laborites, with five Jews being members of her cabinet in the 1980s, among them the chancellor of the exchequer and the home secretary. Under her successor John Major, Sir Malcolm Rifkind served as foreign secretary. The Jewish presence in the Labor government of Tony Blair, which took office in 1997, has been much less marked. Michael *Howard became leader of the Conservative Party in 2003, stepping down at the end of 2005 after the Conservative election defeat.

Ireland

Robert *Briscoe, who represented the Fianna Fail Party, was the only Jewish member of the Irish parliament from 1927. On his retirement in 1965 he was succeeded by his son, Benjamin.

[Vivian David Lipman]

France

Before the French Revolution of 1789 Jews had neither civil nor political rights and very few took part in French public affairs. They were granted civil rights in 1791 and from then onward no formal bars remained before their advancement in politics, though for many years they were not active in public affairs largely because of the exclusiveness of French society. One of the first Jews in politics in France was Benjamin David (1796–1879), who was elected deputy for the department of Deux-Sèvres in 1834 and became mayor of his native city of Niort in 1846. The first Jewish minister was the banker Michel *Goudchaux who led the opposition to King Louis Phillipe's economic policy and himself became minister of finance in 1848, shortly before the revolution of that year. The famous advocate, Isaac *Crémieux, was another prominent opponent of the regime who participated in the revolution and was briefly minister of justice. After the revolution Achille *Fould served as minister of finance until 1852 when he became a senator and then minister of state, the first Jew in France to hold these positions. His three sons, Ernest Adolphe, Edouard Mathurin, and Gustave Eugène, and his grandson Achille Charles (see *Fould family) were subsequently elected to the chamber of deputies. During the Franco-Prussian War of 1870 two Jews came to the fore. Camille *Sée became secretary general of the Ministry of Interior in the government of National Defense and Leo *Frankel, a Hungarian émigré, was minister of labor in the Paris Commune. Subsequently, Jewish politicians tended to support socialist or radical parties largely because the royalist and clerical groups tended to be antisemitic. Thus Camille Sée was a member of the Republican Party as was David *Raynal, who was minister of public works in Gambetta's ministry in 1881 and later minister of the interior. Nevertheless, Jews were not particularly prominent in French politics at the end of the 19th century and the antisemitic attacks during the *Dreyfus case were directed more against Jews in the professions generally than against Jews in public affairs. Following the turn of the century, however, an increasing number of Jews served in Clemenceau's war cabinet from 1917 to 1919: Georges *Mandel, who was *chef de cabinet*, Edouard Ignace (1864–1924), and Louis *Klotz, the latter serving as minister of finance. After the war Klotz was raised to the senate, Abraham *Schrameck, formerly governor of Madagascar, became minister of the interior and minister of justice, and Maurice Bokanowsky was minister of commerce and industry from 1926 to 1927. Thereafter, however, most Jewish politicians tended to represent socialist parties, a notable exception being Mandel who served in several non-socialist cabinets before the outbreak of World War II and was minister of the interior until the fall of France. Salomon *Grumbach was a member of the Socialist Party central committee, Leon *Meyer was a Socialist minister of mercantile marine, and in 1936 Léon Blum became prime minister of France, the first Jew and the first Socialist to hold this post. Blum's cabinet included Jules *Moch as minister of public works and Jean Zay as minister of education. Blum was briefly prime minister of France after World War II as were the Radical Socialist René *Mayer and the Radical leader Pierre *Mendès France. France was thereby the only European state in which three Jews held the post of prime minister, each representing a different shade of socialist policy. In addition, Moch, René Mayer, and the Socialist Party leader Daniel Mayer all held posts in postwar French coalition cabinets until the end of the Fourth Republic in 1958 and the return to power of General de Gaulle. Few Jews held positions of influence during De Gaulle's term of presidency from 1958 to 1969 but following the election of Georges Pompidou as president in June 1969 two Jews were appointed to ministerial posts, Maurice *Schumann, as minister of foreign affairs, and Leo *Hamon as secretary of state to the prime minister. In subsequent years Simone *Veil became the most prominent Jew in French politics, serving in numerous cabinets and becoming president of the European Parliament in 1979.

The main Jewish organizations continued to follow the old tradition of not giving any directions on how to vote. Constituting about 1 percent of the French electorate, they could only play an important role in specific localities such as Paris and Marseilles. On the basis of analyses of voting behavior, it is known that the Jewish vote is spread among all parties, while Jews are active within the machinery of every party.

Germany

Although individual Jews acted as *Hoffaktoren* and *Hofjuden* (*Court Jews) to monarchs in a number of German states during the 17th and 18th centuries, acting both as advisers and financial agents, Jews played no part in German national politics until the middle of the 19th century, and almost no part in government until the 20th. Jews who converted to Christianity, however, enjoyed full political rights and rose to high office. Thus, Friedrich Julius *Stahl became leader of the reactionary Conservative Party and a firm opponent of political emancipation for his former coreligionists. Other converted Jews who rose to high office included Martin Eduard von *Simson, president of the Reichstag, Heinrich von Friedberg (1813–1895), Prussian minister of justice, and Karl Rudolf Friedenthal (1827–1890), Prussian minister of agriculture under the Empire. The first professing Jew to hold a public position in Germany was David *Friedlaender who was elected to the Berlin municipal council in 1809. Not until the 1840s, however, did the Jews gain electoral rights, including the right to vote for the German National Assembly and to be elected to the Assembly or to state parliaments. Jews participated in the liberal revolution in 1848, and among the Jewish representatives to the National Assembly held in Frankfurt after the revolution were Moritz *Veit and Gabriel *Riesser, who was vice president of the Assembly. Both were staunch champions of Jewish emancipation as were Fischel *Arnheim, the only Jewish member of the Bavarian Diet and Johann *Jacoby, an early leader of the liberal movement. The German states finally removed all political restrictions from the Jews during the 1860s and after the unification of Germany (1871) they were granted legal equality in most spheres. Nevertheless, they were still effectively excluded from holding government office and with the exception of Moritz *Ellstaetter, minister of finance in Baden from 1888 to 1893, no unbaptized Jew held ministerial office. On the other hand, Jews were very active in political life, being among the leaders of the progressive political parties. They were particularly well represented among the liberals, whom the Jews tended to favor. Thus Eduard *Lasker was one of the founders of the National Liberal Party and was influential in framing the social legislation of his regime while his colleague Ludwig *Bamberger helped organize the state finances. Other Jewish politicians included Max Hirsch, the trade unionist and advocate of popular education, Leopold *Sonnemann, a leader of the Democratic Party, Ludwig *Loewe, a founder of the Progressive Party in North Germany, and Wolf *Frankenburger, leader of the Liberal Party in Bavaria.

Toward the end of the 19th century Jewish politicians became increasingly prominent in left-wing parties. At the same time the political allegiance of German Jewry was itself undergoing a process of radicalization, moving from moderate to progressive liberalism, and eventually to Socialism, with the upper strata of Jewish society retaining a traditional allegiance to liberalism. Thus Jews were very prominent in the leadership of the Socialist Party though they formed but a fraction of the electorate. The party itself was founded by Ferdinand *Lassalle who adopted the ideology of Karl *Marx and formed the General German Workers Association (ADAV) which was the forerunner of the German Social Democratic Party. The Social Democratic Party was later much influenced by Eduard *Bernstein, who called for a fundamental revision of Marxist doctrine arguing that the party should work for social reform rather than revolution, and by Rosa *Luxemburg, who advocated workers' control by revolution and led the abortive Communist rising at the end of 1918. After the outbreak of World War I the German Social Democratic Party split into two factions, the majority supporting the war while the minority opposing the war included a number of Jews, among them, Hugo *Haase, president of the German Social Democratic Party in the Reichstag, Bernstein, and Luxemburg.

The prominence of Jewish left-wing intellectuals in German political life was successfully exploited by the antisemites and right-wing parties and revolutionary socialism became identified with Jewry especially since the Soviet and Hungarian revolutions after World War I were led by Jews. In Germany, too, Jews rose to high office in the revolutionary ferment that followed the collapse of the German Empire at the end of 1918. Paul Hirsch (1868–1938) was briefly prime minister of Prussia, Kurt *Eisner headed the revolutionary government of Bavaria and Hugo Haase and Otto *Landsberg were two of the six people's commissars in the first postwar government. In addition Paul *Levi succeeded Rosa Luxemburg as head of the Communist Party and the Communists included many Jewish members, among them Ruth *Fischer and Gerhart *Eisler. During this period of the Weimar Republic there were no restrictions on Jews holding political posts and four Jews held high ministerial office. Hugo *Preuss, one of the drafters of the Weimar Constitution, became minister of the interior, Otto Landsberg was minister of justice, Walther *Rathenau was foreign minister, and Rudolf *Hilferding minister of finance. The Nazis deliberately overstated the importance of Jews in German politics, however, and condemned the Weimar Republic as being the hated *Judenrepublik* dominated by Jews.

Soon after the Nazis came to power in 1933 all political parties were banned except the Nazi Party from which Jews were excluded. Jewish politicians were either arrested or forced to leave the country. After World War II a small number of Jews took part in German political life, among them Herbert *Weichmann who was president of the Bundesrat and Joseph Neuberger (1902–1977) who was minister of justice in North-Rhine-Westphalia. In East Germany the only figure of importance was Gerhart Eisler, who was for a time minister of information. Though for many years not a single professing Jew has been a member of the Bundestag, at the beginning of the 21st century there were a few well-known younger Jews active in political life, such as Michel Friedman for the Christian Democrats and Prof. Micha Brumlik for the Greens. Together with the late Ignatz *Bubis, a leading member of the Free Democrats, these most visible Jewish politicians all came from Frankfurt.

Holland

The first Jewish politicians in Holland represented William III of Orange in international diplomatic negotiations. Thus Samuel Palecke was made representative of the king of Morocco in Holland, Isaac *Belmonte was agent-general of the king of Spain to the Netherlands, and several Jews were involved in his negotiations to secure the British crown. Jews were not active in Dutch internal Politics, however, until after their emancipation in 1795, following the conquest by France and the formation of the Batavian republic. In 1798 Jews were given the right to vote and be elected to state offices and two Jews, H.L. Bromet and H. de H. Lemon, were elected to the national assembly, being the first Jewish parliamentarians ever. Subsequently, two Jewish lawyers held high government posts, Moses Salomon *Asser who became a member of the legislative council and Jonas Daniel *Meyer who was appointed to the state council during the reign of Louis Napoleon. In the first half of the 19th century Jews were represented in the city councils of Amsterdam, The Hague, and Rotterdam, but they did not enter provincial and national politics again. These local Jewish politicians were seen as the representatives of their communities. After 1848, when the Netherlands became a constitutional monarchy, Jews entered the provincial and national political scenes as well. One of them, Michael *Godefroi, became minister of justice and Samuel *Sarphati became a leading campaigner for social reform. In the 19th century Jewish politicians were foremost active within the liberal parties and from the end of the century on in the socialist parties as well. Jews elected to the second chamber of parliament included Abraham Hartogh (1844–1901), Samuel van den *Bergh, Abraham *Wertheim and Joseph *Limburg (1866–1940), all of whom were members of the Liberal Party. In the 20th century two Jewish women were prominent in Dutch politics: Aletta *Jacobs (1854–1929) and Betsy *Bakker-Nort (1874–1946), both of whom championed the rights of women. Several Jewish socialists sat in Parliament, among them A.B. *Kleerekoper, Henri *Polak, Ben Sajet, and the Communist Party chairman, David *Wijnkoop. However, only two Jews were appointed to ministerial posts before World War II besides Godefroi: Eduard van *Raalte, minister of justice at the beginning of the 20th century and Salomon Rodrigues de *Miranda who was socialist minister of housing in the 1930s. After World War II two more Jewish ministers of justice held office, Ivo *Samkalden being appointed in 1956 and 1965 and Carel *Polak taking office in 1967. Other prominent Jewish politicians included the ministers Sidney van den *Bergh (1959), Aaron Pais (1977–981), Ed van Thijn (1981–82, 1994), and Hedy d'Ancona (1989–94). Within the Second Chamber the leader of the Socialist Party, Jacques Wallage, was prominent as well as the liberal chairman of the Second Chamber, Frans Weisglas. In the post-World War II period Amsterdam had no fewer than four Jewish mayors: Ivo Samkalden (1967–77), Wim Polak (1977–83), Ed van Thijn (1983–94), and Job Cohen (from 2001).

[Bart Wallet (2nd ed.)]

Italy

In 1778 Jews were given the right to become members of municipal councils in Tuscany and this right was extended to other parts of Italy at the end of the century following the French invasion of Italy under Napoleon. Thus in 1796 the venerable oligarchic government of Venice was overthrown and a new municipality was elected that included three Jews: Moses *Luzzatto, Vita Vivante, and Isaac Grego. After the defeat of Napoleon at the hands of the Holy Alliance, Jews were deprived of their newly acquired civic equality and as a result actively supported the secret revolutionary forces, such as the *Carbonari* and Young Italy movements. In this respect Italy was the only 19th-century European state in which substantial elements of the Jewish population took up a political cause.

Following the outbreak of the 1848 Revolution, Jewish rights were restored in most parts of Italy and two Jews became ministers in the Venetian Republic, headed by the half-Jew Daniel Mantin: Leone Pincherle, minister of agriculture and commerce, and Isaac Maurogonato (1817–1892), minister of finance. In 1855 Isaac *Artom became private secretary to the Piedmontese prime minister Count Cavour and in the following year Sansone d'*Ancona became director of finance and public works in the government of Tuscany. When the reunification of Italy was completed in 1870, a number of Jews were members of the Italian parliament and by 1894 their numbers had increased to 15, representing a wide variety of political views. The number of Jewish deputies and senators never became large in proportion to the size of the Italian parliament but a number of Jews held important posts at the turn of the century. Luigi *Luzzatti served as minister of finance on several occasions and later became prime minister, the first Jew in modern times to achieve this distinction; Leone *Wollemborg was minister of finance for a short period in 1901, Guiseppe *Ottolenghi was minister of war from 1902 to 1903, and Ernesto *Nathan became mayor of Rome. The rise of Fascism after World War I virtually brought to an end Jewish involvement in Italian politics. Many Jews did support Mussolini at first but with the exceptions of Guido Jung, minister of finance (1932–35), and Aldo Finzi, who was assistant minister of the interior, none held important posts in his party or government and Jewish politicians of the left such as the socialist leaders Guiseppe Modigliani and Claudio *Treves (1869–1944) and the Communist Umberto *Terracini were systematically persecuted or forced into exile. When the Fascists became antisemitic in the late 1930s Jews were expelled from the Fascist Party, by then the only legal political party in Italy, and effectively excluded from all political activity. Political rights were restored to the Jews after World War II but only Terracini, who became a leading Communist figure in the Italian senate, played a significant part in Italian politics in the early postwar period. In later years, two Italian Jews were elected to parliament: Bruno Zevi on the Radical ticket in 1987 and Enrico Modigliani, a Republican, in 1992. In 1992, Oscar Luigi Scalfaro was elected president of the Italian Republic only two months after having been named the first president of the newly formed Italy-Israel Parliamentary Friendship Association.

Muslim States

TURKEY. Jews played an important part in Turkish politics in the 16th century, a few Jews acting as ministers and financial advisers, among them Joseph *Nasi, Duke of Naxos, Solomon *Ashkenazi, and Esther *Kiera. The decline in the status of Turkish Jewry from the beginning of the 17th century led to the exclusion of Jews from public affairs, and civil rights were not granted to Turkish Jews until the middle of the 19th century. Exceptional were the *Picciotto family of merchants, five of whom, Hillel, Raphael, Ezra, Elijah, and Moses ben Ezra, were consuls for European powers in Aleppo. In 1876, Daniel *Carmona became the first Jew to serve in the Turkish Parliament and in 1899 Behor *Ashkenazi became the representative of Turkish Jewry in the Ottoman Parliament, later becoming vice prefect of Istanbul and a member of the senate. A few Jews joined the Young Turk movement at the beginning of the century, among them Haim *Nahoum who was appointed chief rabbi of Egypt when the Young Turks came to power. After World War II Solomon Adato was the sole representative of Turkish Jewry in Parliament and after his death in 1953 he was succeeded by Henry Soviano.

EGYPT. Jews took little part in Egyptian affairs during the centuries that Egypt was under Turkish rule. One of the first Jews active in Egyptian politics in modern times was Joseph Aslan *Cattaui who worked with Sir Ernest *Cassel on engineering projects and was made pasha in 1912 and a member of the legislative assembly. He was appointed minister of finance and transport and later became a member of the senate. Other prominent Jews in Egyptian politics who were elected to the senate were Joseph *Picciotto, a leader of the Egyptian Zionist movement, and Cattaui's elder son, Cattaui Bey. Following full Egyptian independence after World War II, Jews were made to suffer for the government's anti-Zionist policy and no Jews held positions in the government or parliament.

IRAQ. Few Jews were prominent in politics in Iraq either during Turkish rule or after independence but a few were elected to the Iraqi parliament where at one time seats were specifically reserved for candidates elected by the Jewish community. The first Jewish representative from Iraq in the Turkish parliament was Menahem ben Salaḥ *Daniel who was appointed in 1876. Sir Ezekiel *Sassoon was the first Iraqi delegate to the Turkish Parliament after the Young Turk revolution and from 1920 to 1925 was Iraqi minister of finance during the British protectorate.

Following Iraqi independence in 1924, three Jews were elected to the Iraqi lower house and Menahem ben Salaḥ Daniel, at the age of nearly 80, was appointed to the senate. On his retirement in 1935 he was succeeded by his son Ezra. The number of Jews representing Iraqi Jewry was raised to six and many prominent Jewish businessmen were active in politics. The anti-Zionist campaign after World War II led to a change in government policy toward Iraqi Jewry. The right of separate Jewish representation in parliament was abolished and Jews were deprived of civil rights. Following the death of Ezra Daniel in 1952 no Jews sat in the Iraqi parliament.

MOROCCO. Jews were prominent in Moroccan state affairs during the reign of the Marinids (1269–1465). Two members of the Roggasa (or Waqqasa) family were influential ministers and toward the end of the dynasty *Aaron ben Batash was prime minister. In the 17th century Abraham Maimaran and Moses *Atar were ministers and advisors to King Mulay Ishmael. In the 18th century Samuel *Sumbal was advisor to the sultan on foreign affairs and his son Joseph Ḥayyim was Moroccan ambassador to London. Several members of the *Corcos family were advisors on financial and foreign affairs to five successive sultans during the 19th century, and Meir Macnin was ambassador to London. However, wealthy Jews no longer held a prominent place in state affairs during the period of the French Protectorate (1912–56). Following Moroccan independence in March 1956, Leon *Benzaquen was made minister of posts and David Benazeraf became a member of the advisory council. Growing Muslim nationalism acted as a brake on Jewish political activity from July 1957 to 1961 but after the accession of King Hassan II Jews once again held representative posts, David Amar as a senator and Meyer Obadia and Jacob Banon as members of the National Assembly.

TUNISIA. Although Jews held powerful economic and political positions in Tunisia in the Middle Ages, Jews were deprived of all their rights in the 16th century. Nevertheless, members of the Cohen-Tanudji family were advisors on foreign affairs to the bey and in the 19th century Abraham Belaish and Nessim *Samama were finance ministers. Several members of the *Valensi family were statesmen and one was Tunisian minister of war. In the 20th century Jews tended to support the French administration and many fought in the French army in World War I. Later many Jews joined the Zionist movement and some were active in the nationalist Destour Party, among them Albert *Bessis who was made minister of public works in the Tunisian cabinet upon independence and André Barrouch who was appointed to the cabinet on Bessis' resignation. The anti-Zionist campaign at the end of the 1950s led to Barrouch's resignation and a sudden decline in Jewish involvement in politics. Following the mass emigration from Tunisia in the 1960s, Jews ceased to take any part in Tunisian politics.

Poland

Until the end of the 18th century Jews played no part in public life in Poland. Their interests were bound up with those of the Polish Jewish community as a whole and in any case they were granted no civil rights in Polish society. The decline in the cohesion of the Jewish community, however, led to increasing involvement of the Jews in the large cities in Polish affairs and after the partition of Poland and the outbreak of the French Revolution a number of Jews joined the insurrection against the Russians in 1794, among them Berek *Joselewicz who commanded a force of 500 Jews in the defense of Warsaw. Nevertheless, though Jews fought in the army of Napoleon, they were not granted political rights in the Grand Duchy of Warsaw, nor, after 1815, when the Russians regained control over most of Poland. During the Polish insurrections of 1830 and 1831 Jews were again prominent as supporters of the revolutionary cause and following the suppression of the insurrection, Stanislaus Hernisz Ludwig Lubliner and Leon Hollandaerski were leaders of the group of émigré Polish leaders agitating abroad for Polish independence. In the 1860s Rabbi Dov Ber *Meisels, chief rabbi of Warsaw, organized the Jewish community's support for the Polish nationalist movement. He was arrested by the czarist authorities for closing the Warsaw synagogues as an act of solidarity with the Catholic leaders who closed the churches in defiance of the authorities. Meisel's funeral in 1870 was the occasion for a mass demonstration of Polish national feeling. Other Jewish revolutionary leaders were Henry K *Wohl who became head of a department in the insurgent government of 1863 and was later arrested and imprisoned and Bernhard *Goldman. Toward the end of the century a number of Jewish intellectuals joined the Social-Democratic Party of Poland and Lithuania, one of whose founders was Rosa *Luxemburg. The party's leaders included Herman *Diamand, Feliks *Kon, Herman *Lieberman, Adolf *Warski-Warszawski, and Boleslaw *Drobner, the last being among the many Jews to take part in the anti-czarist uprisings between 1905 and 1907. Following the granting of universal suffrage in the Austro-Hungarian Empire and the establishment of the Duma in Russia, Polish Jews were allowed to vote for and to be elected to the Austro-Hungarian Reichsrat and the Russian Duma. Herman Lieberman and Herman Diamond were elected to the Reichsrat in 1917 as representatives from Galicia and several Jews stood as candidates for the Duma. None was successful, however, largely because they attracted the Jewish vote only and also because they were officially opposed by the authorities. Furthermore in the elections to the fourth Duma, the Jews supported the Polish Socialist Party candidate en masse and this led to an organized boycott of Jewish traders in protest. After the outbreak of World War I, Jews ceased to play any part in politics in Russian Poland even after the Central Powers occupied the territory. Nevertheless Jewish representatives from Galicia sat in the Austro-Hungarian Reichsrat.

Following the declaration of Polish independence at the end of World War I the Polish government concluded a minorities treaty granting full equality to the Jews and other minorities and the provisions of the treaty were incorporated in the Polish constitution. In the first Sejm of 1922, 45 Jews were elected, six of them being elected to the senate. Jews represented Zionist parties, the non-Zionist Agudat Israel and the Polish Socialist Party, the last being the only non-Jewish political party which was not antisemitic. Most of the Jewish members of the chamber of deputies joined together to form a Jewish parliamentary club ("Kolo") headed initially by the Zionist leader Yitzḥak *Gruenbaum and were mainly concerned with attempting to improve the social and political condition of the Jews in the face of government-inspired antisemitism. Jewish Socialists, of whom Herman Lieberman and Boleslaw Drobner were among the leaders of the party, were more concerned with general Polish politics. In 1925 the Jewish club agreed to support the government on condition that the government acted to improve the condition of the Jews. However, when it became clear that the government had no intention of fulfilling its side of the bargain, most of the Jewish members rejoined the Socialists in opposition. Government policy became increasingly antisemitic and during the 1930s the number of Jews in the Sejm dwindled to seven and many of the Jewish Socialist leaders were imprisoned or exiled, among them Herman Lieberman who led the opposition to the government, Isaac *Schwarzbart and the Polish communist leaders Roman *Zambrowski and Adolf Warski-Warszawski.

The destruction of Poland on the outbreak of World War II and the Nazi Holocaust did not result in the end of political activity among Polish Jews. Adolf *Berman cooperated with left-wing political groups in Warsaw and fought in the Warsaw uprising of 1944. Herman Lieberman was briefly a member of the Polish government in exile in London and a number of Polish Jews who fled to the Soviet Union in 1939 held important position in the Soviet-sponsored Union of Polish Patriots and the Polish army in the U.S.S.R., among them Eugeniusz *Szyr, Stefan Wierblowski, Roman Zambrowski, Hilary *Minc, Jacob *Berman, and Drobner. On the formation of the Polish Committee of National Liberation in 1944, Drobner was made minister of labor and social care, the first Jew to hold a portfolio in a Polish government.

The liberation of Poland at the end of World War II led to the formation of a Provisional Government of National Unity in which the Communist Party with its prominent Jewish members played a key part. All discrimination against Jewish politicians ceased and when the pro-Communist Socialists merged with the Communists into the Polish United Workers Party, Boleslav Bierut became head of the party with two Jews, Jacob Berman and Hilary Minc, as close colleagues, the latter serving as minister of commerce and later as vice premier. Berman and Minc were, like Bierut, loyal supporters of Stalin and included several other Jewish Stalinists in the government and party, among them Szyr, Starewicz, and Wierblowski, and Julius *Katz-Suchy. Following the death of Bierut, however, and the rise to power of Wladyslaw Gomulka, Berman and later Minc were forced to resign. In the 1960s Zambrowski and Szyr held important party posts but the former was dismissed during the government-inspired antisemitic campaign of 1968 in which a number of Jews holding lesser positions were also forced to resign. By 1971, two Jews were left in the government – Szyr as deputy prime minister and Edward Sznajder, minister for home trade.

Russia

As early as 1783 Jews were given the right to hold municipal office in Belorussia. The right was extended to all parts of Russia in 1835 but was later limited to western Russia, where most Jews lived, so that Jews could not be elected as mayors or municipal chairmen, nor could they constitute more than a third of the number of municipal councilors even in areas where Jews constituted a majority of the inhabitants. Jews were thus prevented from playing an influential part in municipal affairs while they were completely excluded from national politics by the very nature of the autocratic and antisemitic czarist rule. As a result, many Jews, particularly among the secularly educated, joined or supported the illegal revolutionary organizations that sprung up in the 1870s. Their number included Pavel *Axelrod, Aaron Zundelevich, and O. Aptekman (see *Socialism). The abolition in 1882 of the right to vote for local councils or to be elected to them added impetus to the Jewish opposition to the regime. Several Jews were founders of the Narodniki (Populists) and of the Social Democratic Party (among them Axelrod and Lev Deutsch), both of which groups received wide support in Jewish assimilationist or semi-assimilationist circles. Most Jews, however, remained in purely Jewish frameworks; they were Orthodox, Zionists, or joined the *Bund. The failure of Nicholas II to make any substantial reforms brought about a resumption of revolutionary activity at the turn of the century. Jews held leading positions in the Social Democratic Workers Party but when the party split in 1903, most of the Jewish members, among them members of the Bund, joined the Menshevik group under Julius *Martov, among them Fyodor *Dan, Raphael *Abramowitz, and Grinevich, who from 1905 to 1917 was chairman of the All-Russian Council of Trade Unions. Jews were also prominent in two other political parties, the Socialist Revolutionary Party, which continued the heritage of the Populists, and the liberal Union of Liberation. The Socialist Revolutionary Party, formed in 1902, appealed mainly to the peasants as the Social Democrats appealed to the industrial workers. Its leaders included Chaim *Zhitlovsky, Grigori *Gershuni, and Mikhail Gots. The Union of Liberation was a radical liberal group who drew their support from the urban professional classes and attracted Jewish professionals such as the lawyers Maxim *Vinaver and Henry *Sliosberg. When the abortive 1905 revolution led to the setting up of the first *Duma, the Union of Liberation, called Kadet (short name for the Constitutional Democratic Party), formed the largest single political group, their 179 members including nine Jews. However, owing to changes in electoral law during the period of reaction, the party's strength in the later Dumas declined, and there was also a decline in representation of the small Jewish parties (Zionists, Folkspartei, Jewish People's Group, and Jewish Democratic Group), whereas Jewish socialists were not elected at all. The outbreak of revolution in February 1917 brought the immediate abolition of all restrictions against Jews, and four Jews from the Kadet and Menshevik groups were offered posts in Kerensky's provisional government, M. *Vinaver, L.M. Bramson, Fyodor Dan, and M.I. Liber. All refused on the grounds that the time was not yet ripe for Jews to enter a Russian government. On the other hand, A. Galperin was secretary of the provisional government and later Mark Vishniak became secretary of the Constituent Assembly, which was dispersed by force by the Bolshevik Soviet government

U.S.S.R.

In Lenin's first Soviet government Jews were prominently represented, not only among the Bolsheviks (e.g., *Trotsky, *Zinoviev, *Kamenev, *Sverdlov) but also among their left Socialist-Revolutionary partners in the short-lived coalition (e.g., the people's commissar for justice, Isaac *Steinberg). Jews were also strongly represented in republican and local soviets and in all echelons of the ruling party hierarchy. Some Jewish politicians in areas densely populated by Jews, and during the first stages of the *Birobidzhan experiment particularly those engaged in *Yevsektsiya work, could be regarded Jewish representatives, since they communicated mainly with the Jewish population or represented its interests. This situation changed quickly in the 1930s. The Yevsektsiya itself was closed down in 1930 and with the purges of the later 1930s most leading Jewish Bolsheviks were imprisoned and liquidated, together with other members of the Old Guard. Simultaneously, the last shreds of Jewish regional and cultural autonomy disappeared and the Birobidzhan experiment, as a "nascent Jewish republic," was practically abandoned. Prominent exceptions were Lazar *Kaganovich, a close associate of Stalin, and Maxim *Litvinoff, people's commissar for foreign affairs. During and after World War II, very few Jews remained in the Soviet top leadership. Under Stalin only Kaganovich was a member of the ruling circle and when Khrushchev assumed personal leadership in 1957 Kaganovich was declared a member of a subversive "anti-party group" and disappeared. No other Jew ever became a member of the policy-making bodies of the party, particularly the Politburo, which is the real government of the country. In 1962 the Jewish economist Venyamin *Dymshyts was appointed one of the six deputies of Soviet prime minister Khrushchev and put at the head of the central planning body *Gosplan*, but the post was without much political significance. Jews also practically disappeared from the middle and lower party hierarchy and the number of Jews in the representative organs of central and local government (both houses of the Supreme Soviet of the U.S.S.R. as well as the republican, regional, and local soviets) declined rapidly. By 1970 it was much below the percentage of the Jews in the total population, not only of the cities (where 95% of the Jews live) but even of the population at large. In the new Russia, after the fall of Communism, the so-called Jewish oligarchs achieved political influence in a cozy relationship with President Boris Yeltsin, but fell out of favor with his successor, Vladimir Putin.

[Binyamin Eliav]

South Africa

Although Jews first settled in South Africa in the beginning of the 19th century, for many years they played little part in South African politics. An exception was Benjamin *Norden, one of five brothers who emigrated from England in 1820 and became a municipal commissioner (city councilor) in Cape Town in 1840. Norden was narrowly defeated in the elections to the Cape parliament. Saul *Solomon was elected to the Cape parliament in 1854, 20 years after he and his brother Henry had converted to Christianity. He and Simeon *Jacobs, who was elected in 1866, campaigned for the separation of Church and State in Cape Colony. Four other Jews were elected to the parliament of Cape Colony, Julius and Joseph Mosenthal, Ludwig Henry Goldenschmidt, and Ludwig Wiener. Jews were also among the pioneers of some of the other South African colonies. One of the first settlers in Natal was Nathaniel *Isaacs who unsuccessfully canvassed a treaty between the Zulu monarch and the British crown as the basis for the European settlement of Natal. Another was Jonas Bergtheil, who emigrated to South Africa in 1834 and became the first Jewish member of the Natal legislative council. In the Orange Free State, Isaac Baumann, who arrived in South Africa from Germany in 1840, became chairman of the municipal board of Bloemfontein, and Adolphe Coqui, an immigrant from Belgium, negotiated the establishment of republican government for the Orange Free State after Britain announced that she was terminating her sovereignty over the territory. A third Jewish personality in the early days of the Orange Free State was Moritz Leviseur, who was elected to the provincial parliament in 1905 and became mayor of Bloemfontein in 1906. Leviseur was elected to the Union of South Africa parliament in 1921. The first Jewish parliamentarian in the Transvaal (Zuid-Afrikaansche Republiek) was M de Vries, a Dutch immigrant who was chairman of the Transvaal Volksraad (Parliament), 1872–73.

The discovery of diamonds and gold brought a number of Jews to prominence in South African politics. Barney *Barnato became a member of the Transvaal parliament and a personal friend of President Paul Kruger. Barnato did not commit himself in the Anglo-Boer dispute but his nephew Solly *Joel became a member of the reform committee which organized the Jameson raid. Barnato's cousin, Sir David *Harris, took Barnato's seat in the Cape parliament after the latter's death. He was one of six Jews elected to the first Union parliament in 1910, the others being Morris *Alexander, who was a member for over 30 years, Emile Nathan, Sir Lionel Phillips, C.P. Robinson, and Sammy *Marks, a member of the senate. Subsequent Jewish members of the Union parliament included Morris *Kentridge, the first Jewish Labor member of parliament, who sat continuously from 1924 to 1958, Leopold *Lovell, Hyman Davidoff, Sam Kahn – the first Jewish communist MP, who was unseated in 1952 following the Suppression of Communism Act, Bertha *Solomon, who advocated the cause of women's rights in parliament and initiated the Matrimonial Affairs Act of 1953, Abe Bloomberg and Charles Barnett. Jewish senators included: Franz Ginsberg, Fritz Baumann Adler, Alfred Friedlander, Hyman Basner, and Leslie Rubin. The 36-year parliamentary career of Helen *Suzman commenced in the Union Parliament in 1953 and continued after South Africa became a Republic in 1961. In 1959 she was a co-founder of the Progressive Party, which opposed the government's apartheid policy, and was the sole Progressive elected in the elections of 1961, 1966, and 1970. Other prominent Jewish parliamentarians after 1961 included Harry *Schwarz (1974–89), Ruth Rabinowitz (representing the opposition Inkatha Freedom Party from 1994), Ben Turok, and Tony *Leon (from 1989), who became Leader of the Opposition Democratic Party (later Democratic Alliance) after the 1999 elections. Four Jews have served as cabinet ministers. They are Henry *Gluckman, who served as minister of health in the *Smuts cabinet from 1945 to 1948, Louis *Shill (minister for national housing and of public works, 1993–94), Joe *Slovo (minister of housing, 1994–95), and Ronnie *Kasrils (minister of water affairs and forestry, 1999–2004, and from 2004 minister of intelligence). Two Jews have served as deputy cabinet ministers, Ronnie *Kasrils (deputy minister of defense, 1994–99) and Gill Marcus (deputy minister of finance, 1996–99).

South America

Before World War II Jews were not generally active in politics in South America, although in most South American states there were no legal bars to their entering parliament. They were handicapped by the fact that most were immigrants from Central and Eastern Europe and by deep-rooted antisemitism in many of the Catholic states. Nevertheless, a few Jews did achieve considerable prominence in political life. One of the first was Horacio *Lafer who was appointed Brazilian delegate to the League of Nations in 1928. He was a member of the Federal Chamber of Deputies from 1934 to 1964 and served as minister of finance and foreign minister in postwar Brazilian governments. Another important figure was Angel Faivovich *Hitzcovich who was elected to the Santiago municipal council in 1935. During a 30-year political career he was president of the Chilean Radical Party and vice president of the senate. The number of Jews in politics gradually increased after World War II, particularly in Argentina where the Jewish population was at one time over half a million. Several Jews represented the Argentine Radical Party (Union Civica Radical Intransigente) in the Chamber of Deputies, among them Santiago Nudelman, David *Blejer, who was undersecretary to the ministers of the interior and of labor, Isaac Breyter, David *Schapira, and Naum Jaroslavsky. Enrique Dickman and Adolfo Dickman were prominent socialist deputies. Few Jews were prominent in Argentine politics during the rule of the dictator Domingo Peron but an exception was Jose Alexenicer who was head of Peron's "Justice" Party in Cordoba and a member of the provincial parliament. In Chile, Miguel *Schweitzer, was minister of labor, and several other Jews were elected to the Chamber of Deputies. Among them were Jacobo Schaulson *Numhauser who was president of the Chamber of Deputies, and Daniel *Schweitzer, both of whom served as Chilean delegates to the United Nations. There were also two Jewish communist deputies in Chile, Adolfo Berman and Volodia Teitelbaum. Jews were also elected to parliament in Brazil where Marcos Melzer and Aarao Steinbruch sat in the Chamber of Deputies, while in Uruguay Jacobo *Guelman was a member of the senate as was Benazar *Serfaty in Venezuela. In Panama Max *Delvalle became first vice president of Panama and was president for two months in 1968 following a controversial decision of the National Assembly to remove the constitutional president. He thus became the only Jew ever to become president of a state (outside of Israel).

In South America in general, both the Foreign Office and the army remained almost closed to Jews, and the few Jewish ambassadors who served owed their appointment to personal friendships with the president in office.

In Argentina, after the establishment of a democratic regime in 1983, Raúl Alfonsín, a progressive and charismatic president, opened the doors to Jews: Bernardo Grinspun became minister of the economy and Mario Brodersohn district secretary; Adolfo Gass obtained a seat in the Senate, Marcelo Stubrin and César Jaroslavsky (the latter, head of the district bank) entered the Chamber of Deputies, and Jacobo Fiterman, ex-president of the Argentinean Zionist Organization, became secretary of public works in the Buenos Aires municipality. In the field of education and culture, traditionally a Catholic enclave, Marcos Aguinis became minister of national culture. Manuel Sadosky was minister of science. Under Menem additional Jews served in government: Moisés Ikonicoff (minister of planning), Enrique Kaplan (director of protocol), Néstor Perl (governor of Chubut), and Carlos Corach (presidential adviser).

In Brazil, before the Parliament was dissolved in 1968, six Jews representing various parties were elected to the federal legislature in the 1966 parliamentary elections. There were also Jewish politicians in the state legislatures and city councils. Horacio *Lafer was a leading Jewish political figure and served as finance minister and foreign minister of Brazil. A former federal deputy, Aarão *Steinbruch, was elected senator, the first Jew to be elected to that prestigious post. Under the government of Fernando Collor de Melo (1990–92, when the president was politically impeached), Celso Lafer was minister of foreign affairs. In the two terms of President Fernando Henrique Cardoso (1994 to 1998 and 1998 to 2002) numerous members of the Jewish community took an active part in the government.

[Paul Link / Efraim Zadoff and Roney Cytrynowicz (2nd ed.)]

United States

At the turn of the 21st century American Jews play an outsized role in American politics, representing a dramatic change from earlier eras. For example, when the first edition of the *Encyclopaedia Judaica* was published in the early 1970s, the section on United States politics cited three "facts in connection with Jews in American politics":

1) "Jews have not been prominent as political office holders, political appointees or party leaders";

2) "Jews have never expressly organized themselves for solely political purposes.... They were at pains to deny the existence of Jewish political interests";

3) "...[S]upport for liberal and left of center parties and candidates is proportionally higher among Jews...."

By 2006 two of the three "facts" were no longer facts. First, the American Jewish community in the last third of the 20th century became the most highly politicized ethnic/religious groups in America. As a result, during the first decade of the 21st century the Jewish community is highly over-represented among political opinion leaders – including such groups as major donors to the political parties, elected federal officials, political journalists, political consultants, and high-level political appointees. Second, Jewish organizations have become quite adept at trying to organize the community for political purposes, and most are not reluctant to speak about Jewish political interests.

The third fact of 1972 – the community's allegiance to liberal and left of center parties and candidates – remains true today. The Jewish community continues to strongly back the Democratic Party and its candidates. This remains true despite dramatic demographic changes in the community in 80 years; despite dramatic changes in Jewish public opinion between the early 1920s and the first decade of the 21st century; and despite the fact that the Democratic and Republican parties of the 1920s were entirely different from what they are today.

It is exceedingly difficult to reconstruct the political behavior of American Jews in the earliest days of the Republic – the Jewish community was tiny (2,000 people or .038% of the U.S. population in 1800), and historical Jewish voting data for this period is nonexistent. However, one can assume that most American Jews during the period were Jeffersonian or Jacksonian Democrats. In the first few decades after the adoption of the Constitution there were a handful of Jewish officeholders, all of whom were Democratic-Republicans (the earliest name for the Democratic Party). Jews were among the earliest leaders of the pro-Jeffersonian Tammany Hall, and an early 19th century speaker of the Pennsylvania House was a Jewish Jeffersonian. Probably the best-known Jewish politician of the age, Mordecai *Noah, started his career as a Democratic-Republican (he was appointed U.S. consul to Tunis by President Madison) and was an early supporter of President Jackson as well. Moreover, there is evidence that the Federalist Party used overtly antisemitic rhetoric in the hard-fought 1800 presidential elections as a means of attacking Thomas Jefferson's candidacy.

Between 1840 and 1860, the Jewish population grew from 15,000 (.09% of the population) to 150,000 (less than .5% of the population) largely because of immigration from German-speaking parts of Europe. In this era, Whigs (and by the late 1850s, Republicans) battled Democrats for political supremacy. There is anecdotal material that points to some Jewish support for the Whig party of Henry Clay – especially by the older Sephardi community. However, most of what is known about the period indicates that a majority Jews of this era were Democrats. Of the five Jews who served in the U.S. House of Representatives in the 1840s and 1850s, four were Democrats and one (the first Jewish Congressman, Lewis *Levin) was a member of the anti-Catholic American Party. Of the two Jewish U.S. senators who served in the same period, one – David *Yulee – was a Democrat. The other Jewish senator of the period, Judah *Benjamin (who went on to serve in the Confederate Cabinet), was elected in 1853 as a

Whig and re-elected in 1859 as a Democrat. The Rothschilds' agent in America, Augustus *Belmont, was appointed chairman of the Democratic National Committee in 1860 by Stephen Douglas and continued to serve as the chairman until 1872. As late as 1860, an Illinois state Jewish legislator who was helping Abraham Lincoln in his presidential campaign wrote about the Jews of New York as a constituency that had been voting 2–1 Democratic.

The roughly three-decade period from 1860 until 1896 was an intensely partisan era, which is usually characterized as the third American party system. In that era the country was evenly divided geographically – the south overwhelmingly Democratic and New England and the upper Midwest overwhelmingly Republican. At least one prominent political scientist has concluded that starting with Lincoln in 1860, American Jews swung their support over to the new Republican Party. Again, Jewish voting data is scarce for this period, and it appears as if the truth is a bit more complicated.

The Jewish population continued to grow, especially in New York City. By 1890 there were 475,000 Jews in America, representing 0.67% of the total population. There is evidence that in Midwestern cities like Chicago, the Jewish community began voting Republican by the 1860s. Many German Jews were attracted to the GOP but the newer Yiddish-speaking Jews probably did not have strong party loyalties. Meanwhile, the Jews of the South remained Democratic and the city with the largest Jewish population – New York – remained a largely Democratic stronghold in the latter half of the 19th century.

There were a few prominent Jewish political leaders in the period – men like Abe Reuf, the powerful Republican Party boss in San Francisco, and Oscar *Straus, who served as President Cleveland's minister to Turkey. Fourteen Jews served in Congress during this period. They included nine Democrats and five Republicans. A review of a larger database of 60 known Jewish officeholders during this period reveals a close partisan split between Democrats and Republicans.

In the first decade of the 21st century, Americans are used to an ideologically congruent party system – a reliably liberal Democratic Party and a reliably conservative Republican one. But this was not the case in the late 19th and early 20th centuries. In the first 60 years after the Constitution was ratified, it can be argued that the Jeffersonian and Jacksonian Democrats with their more egalitarian views on white manhood suffrage were more liberal than their Federalist and Whig opponents. By the time of the Civil War, however, the Democrats were largely the party of states rights and support for slavery. And in the years after the Civil War both parties supported economic policies that were pro-business. Thus Jewish support for one party or the other prior to the 1920s cannot be attributed to liberal or conservative proclivities of the community.

The election of 1896 ushered in a 35-year period of national dominance of the Republican Party. The minority Democratic Party in this era was made up of rural populists in the west and south and a few urban machines, like New York's Tammany Hall. This was also a period in which the Jewish community grew exponentially as poor Yiddish-speaking Jews from the Austro-Hungarian and Russian empires streamed into Ellis Island. By 1920 there were 3.15 million Jews in America – three percent of the total population – and in New York State the Jewish population became the key swing vote in city- and statewide elections. It is also during this period that one can start tracking the voting behavior of heavily Jewish voting districts.

Former Jewish Democratic businessmen like Oscar Straus (who was appointed the first Jewish cabinet official by Teddy Roosevelt) became Republicans in reaction to the populism of William Jennings Bryan. The newer and more numerous immigrant voters did not have strong partisan attachments. Sometimes they voted for Eugene Debs' new Socialist Party, and two Jewish Socialists were elected to Congress – Meyer London in New York and Victor *Berger in Wisconsin. Sometimes these immigrants voted for reform politicians (often these reformers were WASP-Republican politicians) in reaction to the graft of urban political machines. Sometimes these Jewish newcomers turned against WASP reformers who advocated Sunday blue laws and voted the machine politicians back into office. It is clear that in presidential elections, American Jews strongly backed Republicans Teddy Roosevelt in 1904 and Warren Harding in 1920, and more narrowly backed Democrat Woodrow Wilson in 1912 and 1916.

From 1896 through 1930, 15 Jewish Republicans, 15 Jewish Democrats, and two Jewish Socialists served in Congress. Two Jewish Democrats were elected governor in the west – Simon *Bamberger in Utah and Moses *Alexander in Idaho – and President Wilson appointed the "people's attorney," Louis D. *Brandeis, as the first Jewish Supreme Court justice in 1916.

Most people attribute the modern Jewish community's attachment to the liberal policies of the Democratic Party to the presidency of Franklin D. Roosevelt. However, the beginnings of this Democratic trend began a decade earlier in 1922. In 1920, Jews (as well as the rest of the country) voted overwhelmingly Republican in reaction to disillusionment with Wilson's Treaty of Versailles and a series of economic recessions. In the Congress that convened in 1921 there were 11 Jewish congressmen – 10 Republicans and one Socialist (in New York five Republican Jews and one Socialist were elected).

In 1922 former New York Governor Al Smith ran to avenge his defeat of 1920, and in winning he carried the Jewish vote overwhelmingly. Though Smith was a supporter of Tammany Hall, unlike many Tammany politicians he supported progressive labor legislation like the eight-hour day, and he opposed many of New York's blue laws. This was the perfect combination for New York State Jews, which at the time accounted for one-half of American Jewry. In the Congress, which convened in 1923 there were 10 Jewish congressman – four Republicans, five Democrats, and one Socialist. In New York State only one Jewish Republican survived, and four new Democrats were elected. From 1922 onward New York Democratic candidates were usually in the mold of Al Smith and Senator Robert Wagner – progressive reformers who ran with Tammany support – and the Jewish vote increasingly solidified as a Democratic bloc.

In 1928 the national Jewish vote split 72–28 in favor of Al Smith, the first non-Protestant (he was Roman Catholic) to run for president. In 1932 FDR carried the Jewish vote with 82%. In his first re-election he carried 85%, in his second re-election he carried 90%, and in 1944 he won 90% of the Jewish vote. Between 1948 and 1968 Democrats captured between 60% and 90% of the Jewish vote in each presidential election.

Jewish voting for Democrats at the state and national levels was perfectly understandable in the 1920s and 1930s. The New York Democrats and increasingly the national Democratic party was the party of liberalism, economic populism, and the "little guy." The Jewish population of the 1920s and 1930s was overwhelmingly poor and working class. However, after World War II the Jewish population was increasingly middle class and highly educated. Yet at the state and national levels, Republican candidates could not secure a respectable Jewish vote. Only at the municipal level could Republican candidates like Mayor Fiorello LaGuardia win a majority of Jewish voters.

Another development in this period was the rising importance of "reform" political clubs in cities like New York and Los Angeles. Though there were few Jewish professional politicians (Chicago's political boss Jake Avery was one of the exceptions) in this era, the amateur reformers became increasingly important in Democratic politics, and a disproportionate share of these reform leaders were Jewish. The other arena where Jews came to prominence was in the labor union movement. Sidney *Hillman was the most prominent of these labor leaders. In 1944, Hillman – as the head of the CIO's Political Action Committee – acted as one of FDR's most trusted political allies.

Between 1932 and 1970, a number of Jewish Americans became prominent at the highest levels of American politics. In the Senate five Jews served during this era – the most prominent being former Governor *Lehman of New York and Jacob *Javits of New York. Jews also became increasingly common as presidential cabinet officers – Henry *Morgenthau, Jr. in FDR's cabinet; Lewis *Strauss in Eisenhower's cabinet; Arthur *Goldberg and Abraham *Ribicoff, the sons of Jewish immigrants, not German-Jews, in the cabinet of Irish American John F. Kennedy, the first Catholic elected president; and Wilbur *Cohen, who served under President Johnson. Moreover, during this period presidents appointed Felix *Frankfurter, Benjamin *Cardozo, Arthur Goldberg, and Abe *Fortas to the highest court in the land. There was a tradition of a Jewish seat on the Court.

Though there were well-known Jewish personalities in the public arena in mid-20th century America, in 1950 politics was not considered a Jewish profession. Fifty years later American politics was a decidedly Jewish occupation.

In the last third of the 20th century, very significant changes took place in the role that Jewish Americans played in the political process. In 2005 Jews represented something less than 2% of the U.S. population. Yet in the same year they represented 11% of the U.S. Senate. In 1970 14 Jews were elected to the U.S. Congress; in 2004, 37 were elected. By the first decade of the 21st century Jewish Americans were significantly represented among the top political appointees and senior civil servants in the elite agencies of the U.S. government. At the same time a substantial proportion of top political journalists and nationally prominent political consultants (a new profession which largely replaced the political boss in American politics) were Jewish. Perhaps equally important, both major political parties (but particularly the Democrats) and their candidates for office were heavily reliant on contributions from Jewish Americans to help fund their election year expenditures.

This increase in the political roles played by Jewish Americans was complemented by a change in how Jewish Americans were "accepted" in American society. In the 1930s, Jewish Americans were subjected to some of the worst antisemitism in American history. In that decade Ivy League colleges and medical schools had strict quotas on Jewish enrollment, and at the same time many law firms and corporate management slots were strictly off-limits to American Jews. In 1937 the Gallup Poll found that only 46% of Americans were willing to vote for a Jewish candidate for president. By the 1970s most of these barriers to Jews in American life were gone, and by 1999 – according to Gallup – fully 92% of Americans were willing to vote for a Jewish candidate for president.

The list of Jewish Americans who rose to prominence on the American political scene in the last 40 years is so large that it is only possible to highlight the most famous in an article of this size. In the early 1970s Robert *Strauss was chair of the DNC, and between 1997 and 2005 three Jews (two Democrats and one Republican) were national party chairs. Richard Nixon appointed perhaps the most prominent secretary of state of the 20th century, Henry *Kissinger, in his second term. President Gerald Ford had two Jewish Americans in his cabinet. President Jimmy Carter, despite his periodic disputes with the organized Jewish community, appointed three Jews to his cabinet. President Clinton appointed five Jews to his cabinet, and there were at least as many Jewish appointees who held cabinet-rank positions. Moreover, both of Clinton's Supreme Court appointments – Ruth Bader *Ginsburg and Stephen *Breyer – were Jewish. As of 2005 President Bush had one Jewish American in his cabinet, but the director of his Office of Management and Budget and numerous senior White House and subcabinet appointees were Jews.

Some observers describe the chairman of the Federal Reserve Board as the second most powerful person in the world. From 1987 to 2006, that position was held by Alan *Greenspan. His successor, chosen by President Bush in 2005, was another Jewish American, Ben S. (Shalom) Bernanke. But perhaps the most widely-known Jewish political figure at the turn of the 21st century was Senator Joseph *Lieberman. In

August of 2000, Vice President Al Gore picked Lieberman as his vice presidential running mate. This was the first time in history that a Jewish American had been on the presidential ticket of a major American political party. Despite the concern of some that America was not ready for a Jewish president or vice president, Lieberman was widely credited with running a good campaign and was seen as an overall asset to the Democratic ticket that year. He began his acceptance speech as nominee with the proto-typical American Jewish phrase "only in America."

Not only did the doors of opportunity open for Jewish Americans in the last third of the 20th century, but Jews also became increasingly comfortable in publicly acknowledging their ethnic and religious background. The Six-Day War in 1967 engendered a great deal of ethnic pride and in the following decades the *American Israel Public Affairs Committee (AIPAC) became a major Washington lobbying institution that represented the Jewish community's very public commitment to fostering strong U.S.-Israel relations. In the late 1980s two partisan Jewish organizations – the *National Jewish Democratic Council (NJDC) and the *Republican Jewish Coalition (RJC) – emerged as an acknowledgement that Jewish Americans were now comfortable in asserting a particular Jewish agenda in the public arena. Moreover, a review of nearly any Jewish weekly at the turn of the 20th century would turn up a headline or two that asked the very public question, "What is good for the Jews?"

In the 1960s Milton Himmelfarb observed that "Jews live like Episcopalians and vote like Puerto Ricans." In the latter third of the 20th century, many commentators examined an American Jewish community that was one of the richest and most highly educated groups in America and predicted that such a minority was bound to become Republican. However, the GOP realignment among Jews never happened.

In 1968 Republican Richard Nixon captured about 17% of the Jewish vote in his run for president. Four years later against George McGovern the Nixon percentages doubled to 35%. Elsewhere Nixon was elected in a landslide. In the next four presidential elections the Jewish Republican vote bounced between 30% and 39% – the trend seemed to be away from the community's New Deal loyalties. Jimmy Carter received a plurality of Jewish votes and Jews voted in significant numbers of John Anderson, the third party candidate.

However, in 1992 George H.W. Bush only received approximately 12% of the Jewish vote, and in the next two elections, the Clinton-Dole-Perot election, the GOP garnered 16% and then 19% of the Jewish vote in the Gore-Lieberman-Bush-Cheney election. Between 2001 and 2004, the administration of President George W. Bush adopted a pro-Israel stance toward the ongoing violence in the Middle East. Republican political operatives openly targeted the Jewish vote as they prepared for the 2004 election. During the same time frame there were numerous predictions by Republican spokesmen and Jewish organizational leaders that the Jewish vote was about to shift to the Republican party. On election day 2004, John Kerry defeated George W. Bush in the Jewish community by a margin of 77% to 22%.

Why did the Jewish vote continue to be a reliable Democratic bloc at the presidential level in the 1990s and the first four years of the 21st century? The most important reason has to do with the nature of the two American political party coalitions. The modern Republican coalition's most dominant element has been evangelical Christians. Though this group is widely viewed as pro-Israel, the other issues it champions – opposition to abortion rights, gay rights, and the separation of church and state – clash with the issue agenda of the vast majority of American Jews. Republicans have tried to paint the Democratic Party as anti-Israel, but this has been unsuccessful as both parties in America are broadly seen as pro-Israel.

The progressive world-view that the vast majority of American Jews adhere to does not mean that Republican candidates can never win majorities in the Jewish community. Party-identification in 2004 was less strong than it had been in previous eras. Jews split along religious lines with Orthodox Jews voting far more often for George Bush than did their non-Orthodox counterparts. In municipal elections Republican candidates are often successful with Jewish voters. Moreover in the northeast states, where GOP candidates are often much less conservative than their brethren in the rest of the country, individual moderate Republicans have run fairly strongly in Jewish constituencies. But as long as the national GOP strongly identifies with conservative Christian constituencies, it will be hard for most state and national Republican candidates to compete effectively in the Jewish community.

By the first decade of the century, the American Jewish community played an unprecedented role in the politics of the United States. Jewish actors were placed in significant roles throughout the process. Unlike in Europe, antisemitism has not surged in recent years and American Jews are comfortable in running for office and even in asserting a Jewish agenda in the political process. Jewish public opinion remained much more liberal than most other segments of the American electorate and Jewish voting remained largely, if not universally, Democratic.

Antisemitic appeals by candidates have been fairly rare and largely ineffectual over the last few decades. When they are used they are usually the work of fringe candidates, or they are of the "whispering campaign" variety, or they have engendered an immediate backlash. Candidates, whose records on Jewish-related issues have been problematic, have tended to go out of their way to move toward a more pro-Israel, pro-Jewish point of view as they move into the mainstream. Of course, there have been exceptions such as Patrick Buchanan.

It is difficult to predict the future political landscape for the American Jewish community, but demographic trends provide a few hints. By 2001 Orthodox Jews comprised less than 10% of the Jewish electorate. However, given fertility rates it is expected that Orthodoxy will represent a larger percentage of the Jewish electorate in future decades. It is also the least progressive segment of the Jewish community. Moreover, if current overall rates of assimilation and lower birthrates persist, it will be very difficult for the Jewish community to be as influential in the political process by the latter half of the 21st century.

[Ira Forman (2nd ed.)]

ADD. BIBLIOGRAPHY: F.C. Brasz, in: *Studia Rosenthaliana*, 19 (1985), 299–311; J. Michman, *Dutch Jewry during the Emancipation Period 1787–1815, Gothic Turrets on a Corinthian Building* (1995); B. Wallet, in: *Zutot*, (2003), 173–77. L.H. Fuchs, *Political Behavior of American Jews* (1956); J.J. Goldberg, *Jewish Power; Inside the Jewish American Establishment* (1996); S.D. Isaacs, *Jews and American Politics* (1974); L.S. Maisel and I.N. Forman (eds.), *Jews in American Politics* (2001); K.F. Stone, *The Congressional Minyan: The Jews of Capitol Hill* (2000).

POLITISCHE GEMEINDE ("political community"), political group right conferred on Jewish communities in *Moravia. In Moravia Jews had for centuries been permitted to reside in a restricted number of locations only (52 according to the patent issued by Francis II on Feb. 15, 1798). These, and other restrictions, were abolished on March 4, 1849. On March 17, however, the *provisorisches Gemeindegesetz* ("provisional communities law") created 25 "political communities" (out of the 52 Jewish communities); the remainder were either placed under the jurisdiction of the local city or town authorities or merged with them (two additional political communities, Boskowitz (*Boskovice), and Holleschau (*Holešov), were created later, raising the total number to 27). The political communities were constituted as autonomous territorial units within the towns, having their own mayor and functionaries, municipal services, and right of taxation. Membership of the political community was hereditary. However as Jews tended to move out of the area of their former quarters while Czechs moved there instead, an anomalous situation was created, as for instance in Trebitsch (*Třebič), where of 1,342 persons living in 194 houses in 1921, only 178 were Jews. All the same, electoral rights for the political community were retained by Jews living elsewhere, either in the same town or in other localities.

The existence of the political communities was a factor in helping the Germans maintain an electoral majority in the country, since the political communities were represented in the municipal *curia* out of proportion to their numerical importance, and Jews, who tended to adopt German culture, generally supported Austro-German policies against the rising Czech national movement. The Czech parties tried to exclude the Jews from the assembly of municipal *curia* and to diminish their influence in the representation of the country (Landgemeindenkurie). It was indicated that in many cases there was no basis for the existence of a political community and that their existence was illegal because they were not territorial units. The political Jewish communities increasingly concentrated on political functions and ceased to be suitable for dealing with religious needs.

In 1880 the Austrian Ministry of the Interior ordered the amalgamation of the political communities with the local authorities, but this was not implemented because of the opposition of both Jews and Germans, which was given support by the courts. Ten years later a type of purely religious community, the *Kultusgemeinde*, was established by law. About 50 *Kultusgemeinden* were established in Moravia and they took over the religious functions of the political communities there. The political community, however, continued to exist until the dissolution of the Hapsburg Empire after World War I; 25 were liquidated by the Czechoslovak authorities in 1919–20, and the last two, Trebitsch and Misslitz (*Miroslav), in 1921. The institution of the political community was unique in retaining the features of the old Jewish communal autonomy within the modern political framework.

For map see *Moravia.

[Aron Moshe K. Rabinowicz]

POLITZER, ADAM (1835–1920), founder of modern otology. Politzer, who was born in Alberti, Hungary, studied at Vienna University where from 1870 to 1907 he was professor of otology. During his tenure Vienna became the center for study in otology for students from all over the world. His *Lehrbuch der Ohrenheilkunde*, published in 1878 was translated into many languages and his *Geschichte der Ohrenheilkunde* (2 vols., 1907–13) was the authoritative book in that field.

Politzer devised many new methods for diagnosing and treating ear diseases. He invented a method of opening a blocked eustachian tube (a method which bears his name all over the world), a method for illuminating the eardrum, an ear speculum, and a bag for inflating the middle ear. He also showed how to test for deafness in one ear. Politzer founded the Otologic Clinic at Vienna University and the Austrian Otologic Society as well as the journal *Archiv fuer Ohrenheilkunde*.

BIBLIOGRAPHY: S.R. Kagan, *Jewish Medicine* (1952), 493; *Biographisches Lexikon der hervorragenden Aerzte*, 4 (1932).

[Suessmann Muntner]

POLITZER, H. DAVID (1949–), U.S. physicist and Nobel laureate. He was born in New York City and educated at the Bronx High School of Science. He gained his B.S. from the University of Michigan, Ann Arbor (1969), and his Ph.D. in physics from Harvard University (1974) under the direction of Sidney Coleman. He joined the physics department of the California Institute of Technology, Pasadena, in 1975 where he became professor (1979) and head of department (1986–88). His research in theoretical particle physics was essential to the discovery of asymptotic freedom, the phenomenon in which the strong force binding quarks together increases when quarks move apart and decreases when they move closer together. This finding was influential in establishing the field of quantum chromodynamics that explains the interactions between quarks and gluons on the basis on their color charge, consisting of a color and an anti-color. These theories, largely validated experimentally, have the eventual aim of producing a standard model for the structure of matter throughout the universe. Politzer shared the 2004 Nobel Prize in physics with his collaborators David J. *Gross and Frank Wilczek.

Politzer played the role of the physicist Robert Serber in the 1989 movie *Fat Man and Little Boy* about the Manhattan Project. His Nobel lecture admirably describes the uncertainties in particle physics and the difficulties in attributing discoveries to individual scientists.

[Michael Denman (2nd ed.)]

POLLACK, EGON (1879–1933), conductor. Born in Prague, Pollack was chorus master at the German Theater there and later held posts at Bremen, Leipzig, and Frankfurt. From 1917 to 1932 he was principal conductor of the Hamburg Opera, which developed considerably under his direction. He conducted in Chicago (1931–32) and appeared as guest conductor in Cairo. He died in Prague of a heart attack while conducting *Fidelio*. Pollack was especially known as an interpreter of Richard Strauss. He also conducted Wagnerian opera and promoted the work of contemporaries.

POLLACK, ISRAEL (1910–1993), industrialist. Pollack was born in Transylvania and raised in Bukovina where he received a traditional education and studied in a textile school. He opened his first textile factory in 1935. In 1947 he moved to Chile, where in addition to his textile business, he was active in Jewish affairs and education. While in Chile he was the head of the Jewish Federation. In the early 1960s he established the Polgat textile works in Kiryat Gat, and in 1966 he arrived in Israel to serve as Polgat's CEO. Pollack was active in many public institutions. He was one of the founders of Klal Corporation, serving as its chairman. He was the chairman of the United Fund and a member of the university boards. In 1990 he received the Israel Prize for special contribution in national and social fields.

[Fern Lee Seckbach / Shaked Gilboa (2nd ed.)]

POLLACK, JACOB BEN JOSEPH (1460/70–after 1522), rabbi and first Polish halakhic authority. His name has given rise to the conjecture that he was born in Poland, but it appears that he was born in Bavaria. Pollack studied under Jacob Margolis in Regensburg, and was already known in his youth as a profound talmudist. He married Esther, the daughter of Moses and Rachel Fischel of Cracow, who acted as government tax farmers and were on intimate terms with the Polish royal court, upon whom they were able to exercise some influence. Pollack was appointed rabbi in Prague and was a member of the *bet din* together with Isaac Margolis, the son of his teacher. In 1492 an incident took place which roused a violent controversy. His wife's sister, Sara had been married while a minor to David Zehner of Buda, Hungary. Before she reached her majority she exercised her right of *me'un* (see *Child Marriage) to free herself from her husband and Pollack permitted her to remarry, in accordance with talmudic law, despite the fact that *Menahem of Merseburg had 50 years earlier enacted a *takkanah* abolishing *me'un*. This permission roused against him all the great contemporary scholars and he was laid under a ban. The only one to support him was Meir Pfefferkorn because Jacob Pollack's mother-in-law had used her influence to obtain the release from prison of his wife and children.

Pollack left Prague and went to Cracow where he opened the first yeshivah in Poland and transferred there the method of *ḥillukim* ("fine distinctions") that he had learnt from his teachers. At that time knowledge of the Talmud in Poland was generally at a low ebb, and the talmudists were not conversant with this method of study. He was given the sobriquet of *avi ha-ḥillukim*. In Cracow he was highly admired and immediately became one of the communal leaders. When in 1494 the king of Poland imprisoned the dignitaries of Cracow, Pollack and his father- and mother-in-law were among them. After his release he moved together with the whole of the Cracow community to Kazimierz, a suburb of the town. In 1503 he was appointed by King Alexander as rabbi of the whole of Poland, or Lesser Poland – the letter of appointment is not clear. But Pollack was to find no tranquility in this position either. The friction and quarrels between the two local communities of Polish and Bohemian Jews embittered his life. Under pressure from the king, separate rabbis were finally chosen for the two communities, R. Perez for the Bohemians and Asher Lemel, Pollack's brother-in-law, for the Polish. Pollack retained only the conduct of his yeshivah. In 1520 a dispute which broke out in Italy on a financial matter between Emanuel of Ferrara and Abraham Raphael of Bologna was brought before Abraham Mintz of Padua. One of the parties turned to Pollack and as a result Pollack excommunicated Mintz. Some two years later, Pollack became involved in a libel against Samuel, the court physician of Cracow, as a result of which he was compelled to flee. From this time all traces of him disappeared. However in the *Birkat Avraham* of Abraham b. Solomon Trebitsch-Ẓarefati of Constantinople, written in 1524, there is a commendation, without a date, which concludes with the words "I have signed here, says the 'quiet' and 'smooth' [the words are applied to Jacob in the Bible (Gen. 25:27) and are applied here to mean "innocent" and "free of sin"] Jacob b. Joseph Ashkenazi Pollack of Jerusalem." If the signature is indeed that of Jacob Pollack and was written in the same year as the commendation of Israel Dayana to the same work in 1532, then Pollack must have been in Constantinople that year on his way to Jerusalem. It is even possible that he settled in Ereẓ Israel before 1532, since he signs "of Jerusalem." The year of his death and his place of burial are not known. (Some think a tombstone found in Lublin with the inscription: "The *Gaon* Koppelman named Jacob ha-Levi…, the *gaon* Jacob b. Joseph died 23rd of Sivan 301" (1541) is his, however, it is doubtful whether Pollack was called Koppelman and nowhere is there mention of his being a levite.) No works by Pollack are known.

BIBLIOGRAPHY: Halberstamm, in: *Jeschurun* (ed. by Kobak), 5 (1865), Heb. pt. 153; Bruell, Jahrbuecher, 7 (1885), 31–37; M. Balaban, in: MGWJ, 57 (1913), 59–73, 196–210; idem, *Historja żydow w Krakowie*, 2 (1936), 105–18; J.L. Ritmann, *Ma'aneh* (1878), 20; Ḥ.N. Dembitzer, *Kelilat Yofi*, 1 (1888), introd. 2; Wetstein, in: *Ha-Maggid*, 5 (1896), nos. 17, 20–21; idem, in: *Sefer ha-Yovel… N. Sokolow* (1904), 278; idem, in: *Ha-Eshkol*, 6 (1909), 218–22; S.J. Fuenn, *Kiryah Ne'emanah* (1915²), 56; M. Straschun, *Mivḥar Ketavim* (1968), 168.

[Shlomo Tal]

POLLACK, MILTON (1906–2004), U.S. judge. Born in Brooklyn, Pollack earned undergraduate and law degrees at Columbia University. He joined the Wall Street firm of Gilman & Unger and was made a partner in 1938. In 1942 he brought a stockholder suit against General Motors, charging that senior executives had been given improper bonuses in cash and stock of more than $4.3 million. Eight named executives were forced to return the bonuses, plus $2 million in interest. Flushed with success, Pollack opened his own firm in 1945 and continued to practice, specializing in cases related to finance, until appointed a federal district court judge by President Lyndon B. Johnson in 1967. In a prominent case for New York City, Pollack issued a decision in 1977 that forced the Port Authority to allow the Concorde supersonic jet to land at Kennedy International Airport. Later, past the age of 80, he began hearing the massive civil litigation involving the bankruptcy of Drexel Burnham Lambert and the prosecutions on securities charges of Ivan *Boesky and Michael *Milken. In 1992, Pollack oversaw a settlement and then the distribution of $1.3 billion in settlement funds to creditors who purchased junk bonds through Drexel. Pollack continued hearing cases until two days before his death at the age of 97.

[Stewart Kampel (2nd ed.)]

POLLACK, SYDNEY (1934–), U.S. film director and producer. Born in Lafayette, Indiana, Pollack first learned his craft by directing many TV episodes of such programs as *Ben Casey*, *The Defenders*, *Dr. Kildare*, *The Fugitive*, and *The Naked City*. Pollack then initiated his career as a feature film director with *The Slender Thread* (1965), and over the past decades has directed varied cinematic fare, including *This Property Is Condemned* (1966), *The Scalp-hunters* (1968), *Castle Keep* (1969), *They Shoot Horses, Don't They?* (Oscar nomination for Best Director, 1969), *Jeremiah Johnson* (1972), *The Way We Were* (1973), *The Yakuza* (1975), *Three Days of the Condor* (1975), *Bobby Deerfield* (1977), *The Electric Horseman* (1979), *Absence of Malice* (1981), *Tootsie* (Oscar nomination for Best Picture and Best Director, 1982), *Out of Africa* (Academy Award for Best Picture and Best Director, 1985), *Havana* (1990), *The Firm* (1993), *Sabrina* (1995), *Random Hearts* (1999), *Sketches of Frank Gehry* (2005), and *The Interpreter* (2005).

Pollack produced more than 40 films, which include many of the above, as well as other successes such as *Songwriter* (1984), *The Fabulous Baker Boys* (1989), *Dead Again* (1991), *King Ralph* (1991), *Leaving Normal* (1992), *Sense and Sensibility* (1995), *Sliding Doors* (1998), *The Talented Mr. Ripley* (1999), *Iris* (2001), *Heaven* (2002), *The Quiet American* (2002), and *Cold Mountain* (2003).

He also acted in several films, such as *Tootsie*, Robert Altman's *The Player* (1992), Woody Allen's *Husbands and Wives* (1992), Stanley Kubrick's *Eyes Wide Shut* (1999), *Random Hearts*, and Roger Michell's *Changing Lanes* (2002).

BIBLIOGRAPHY: J. Meyer, *Sydney Pollack: A Critical Filmography* (1998); S. Dworkin, *Making Tootsie* (1983); W. Taylor *Sydney Pollack* (1981).

[Jonathan Licht and Ruth Beloff (2nd ed.)]

POLLAK, MIKSA (1868–1944), Hungarian rabbi and historian; born in Beled, Hungary. He was a rabbi in Sopron from 1894 until he was killed in Auschwitz.

His main works are *Die Juden in Wiener-Neustadt* (1927, earlier in Hung., 1892) and *Die Geschichte der Juden in Oedenburg* (1929, in Hung., 1896). Despite new sources, Pollak's works are still considered valid in their major conclusions. His other scholarly activities were centered on exploring biblical influences on great Hungarian poets – Arany János (1904), Tompa Mihály (1912), and Madách Imre (in IMIT, 1935–39). He also published a Hungarian translation of the prayer book. Pollak was an outstanding preacher; a volume of his collected sermons was published in 1938.

BIBLIOGRAPHY: A. Scheiber, in: MHJ, 11 (1968), 5–15.

[Alexander Scheiber]

POLLAK, MOSES HA-LEVI (1845–1888), Hungarian rabbi. Born in Szerdahely, Pollak studied under Judah Aszod and Abraham Samuel Sofer. In 1872 he was appointed rabbi of Bonyhad, where he established a yeshivah which attracted pupils from all parts of Hungary. He was one of the founders of the Orthodox community of Bonyhad, which he developed to a considerable extent.

Pollak was the author of *Va-Yedabber Moshe* (1894–95; photoprint New York, 1943), in five parts, on the Pentateuch and various talmudic themes; *Tikkun Moshe* (1894–99), in five parts, sermons and discussions on talmudic topics; and *Birkat Moshe* (1911) on tractate *Ḥullin*.

BIBLIOGRAPHY: P.Z. Schwartz, *Shem ha-Gedolim me-Ereẓ Hagar*, 2 (1914), 11b, no. 165; A. Stern, *Meliẓei Esh*, Marḥeshvan (1933), 122f., no. 287.

[Naphtali Ben-Menahem]

POLLAK, WALTER HEILPRIN (1887–1940), U.S. attorney. Born in New Jersey, Pollak was admitted to the New York bar in 1911 and entered private practice in New York City. During World War I he worked on the legal staff of the War Industries Board. He was a special assistant attorney general for the Arnstein bond theft case (1923–1924) and was counsel, consultant, and chairman of a number of important federal and state commissions. One of the most prominent lawyers at the U.S. bar, Pollak rendered services for the defense of those who were persecuted for unpopular views and causes, and inspired his younger associates to follow this same path. He helped in the drafting of the brief of Arthur Garfield Hays in the Scopes evolution case. He argued the Whitney and Gitlow free speech cases in the U.S. Supreme Court and in 1932 and 1935 was counsel before the Supreme Court in the Scottsboro case involving the issue of a fair trial for blacks in the South.

[Michael Hart Cardozo]

POLLAK, ZALMAN (1901–1985), cantor, composer, and instructor of cantorial music. Born into a rabbinic family in Patrovosla, then Hungary and later part of Yugoslavia, he studied in a *ḥeder*, and then in *yeshivot*, including the Pressburg yeshivah. He began singing with the choir of the Great Synagogue of Pressburg. Upon the conclusion of World War I he emigrated to Palestine and settled in Jerusalem. He led services in the Great Synagogue of the Ḥurvah of Rabbi Judah Ḥasid in Jerusalem and then served as cantor in Rishon le-Zion. From 1922 he was in Europe and was cantor in Yugoslavia (Sobotizia and Sarajevo) and in Vienna, Austria, where he was the chief cantor at the Kehillat Montefiore synagogue for almost five years. He advanced his cantorial education under Judah Leib Miller. After returning to Palestine in 1935 he was cantor at various synagogues in Jerusalem and Tel Aviv. His main efforts were directed at instructing the younger cantors. He wrote many works for passages from the services and his wife, Margalit, initiated the publication of his works, the first volume of which, *Nusaḥ le-Shabbat*, appeared in 1989, edited by Benjamin Glickman.

[Akiva Zimmerman]

POLLARD, SIDNEY (1925–1998), British economic historian. Born Siegfried Pollak in Vienna, the son of a salesman, Pollard came to England in 1938 on a *Kindertransport*; his parents perished in the Holocaust. Through the help of charities and British relatives, Pollard was able to study at the London School of Economics and then became one of Britain's most respected economic historians, holding the post of professor of economic history at Sheffield University from 1963 to 1981. Among his many works are *The Development of the British Economy, 1914–50* (1962), *The Genesis of Modern Management* (1962), *Peaceful Conquest* (1981), and *Britain's Prime and Britain's Decline* (1989). In 1971 Pollard was offered a chair at the University of California at Berkeley, but was barred from entering the United States because he had briefly been a member of the Communist Party in the 1940s, despite the fact that his books were emphatically pro-capitalist. From 1981 until 1990 he was professor of economic history at the University of Bielefeld in West Germany.

BIBLIOGRAPHY: ODNB online.

[William D. Rubinstein (2nd ed.)]

POLLARD AFFAIR. Jonathan Jay Pollard, an American Jew, born in 1954 in Galveston, Texas, the son of a distinguished scientist, was educated at Stanford and became an intelligence analyst with the U.S. Naval Intelligence Service in Suitland, Maryland, in late 1979. He rose in the ranks and had access to sensitive information. In May 1984 he was recruited by Israeli agents and for the next 18 months was "run" by a senior Israeli air force officer Colonel Aviem Sella, then on study leave in New York. Pollard provided Israel with a vast amount of information pertaining to Israel, the Middle East, and other countries, thus compromising the United States. This information was channeled through an independent intelligence unit called the Scientific Liaison Unit, which functioned in the Israeli Defense Ministry from the 1960s and was headed by a veteran Mossad operative, Rafael Eitan. During those 18 months Pollard was paid for his services, traveled to Israel and Europe, and was promised asylum in case of discovery. The Israelis argued that his recruitment and "running" were never authorized by any Israeli defense minister or the cabinet, though their denial was not widely regarded as credible in the United States.

When FBI agents began to follow Pollard and his wife, they fled to the Israeli embassy in Washington seeking asylum, but were ejected from the embassy's grounds and arrested on November 21, 1985. Their arrest and revelations were leaked to the U.S. media, and the extent of their operation and the Israeli involvement generated an extreme and furious reaction by the American leadership – including American Jewish leadership – and public opinion. There emerged a serious danger of an open confrontation between Israel and the Reagan administration and the U.S. Congress. The row that erupted required an immediate Israeli effort to stem the tide. By then the Israeli people were appalled over the details of this operation carried out by civil servants. The details of the affair could have created a major crisis with Israel's only major ally, and placed American Jews in a highly delicate situation.

The U.S. demanded cooperation from Israel in the investigation, and on December 1, 1985, Prime Minister Peres agreed to allow questioning of the Israelis involved by U.S. officials, to return all the documents taken by Pollard, to disband the Scientific Liaison Unit, and to punish the Israelis responsible. Pollard was never brought to trial. As part of a plea bargain, which provided for the limited – five-year – imprisonment of his then wife Anne, Pollard pleaded guilty to espionage charges in June 1986. But in spite of this he was sentenced in March 1987 to life imprisonment. The severity of his sentence remains a matter of considerable controversy even in the early 21st century.

The government charged Pollard with violating 18 USC 794 (c), the federal law that makes it a crime to deliver defense information to a foreign government "with intent or reason to believe" that the information is to be used "to the injury of the United States" or "to the advantage of a foreign nation." The indictment did not charge Pollard with injury of the United States but with the "intent and reason to believe that the [information] would be used to the advantage of Israel." Israel is clearly a foreign nation but an ally, not an enemy, of the United States, which is of moral significance though not necessarily of legal significance. Those involved in the Pollard case assumed that this distinction would result in a more lenient sentence than life imprisonment.

Between the time of the plea bargain and the actual sentencing the government submitted two Victim Impact Statements, one that was made public and one that was delivered in camera because of issues of national security.

The government argued in the Victim Impact Statement that the scope of what was revealed was great, that it threatened U.S. relations with its Arab allies, and that it diminished U.S. leverage with Israel. In short, the government argued that Pollard had done significant damage to the United States. In

January 1987 the government submitted a 46-page classified declaration from Secretary of Defense Caspar Weinberger that described in detail the harm Pollard's activities had allegedly caused national security. The contents of this submission have never been made public; a heavily redacted document was released, which alleges that Pollard "jeopardized … the sources of that information, by placing it outside a U.S.-controlled security environment." In addition, "U.S. combat forces, wherever they are deployed in this world, could be unacceptably endangered through successful exploitation of this data."

Then, on March 3, 1987 – the day before Pollard was to be sentenced – Secretary Weinberger submitted a supplementary declaration to the court, which included the following:

> It is difficult for me, even in the so-called "year of the spy," to conceive of a greater harm to national security than that caused by the defendant in view of the breadth, the critical importance to the U.S., and the high sensitivity of the information he sold to Israel… I respectfully submit that any U.S. citizen, and in particular a trusted government official, who sells U.S. secrets to any foreign nation should not be punished merely as a common criminal. Rather the punishment imposed should reflect the perfidy of the individual's actions, the magnitude of the treason committed, and the needs of national security.

The word treason – which was not part of the government's initial charge – was introduced by Weinberger for the first time, just prior to sentencing.

In a breathtaking display of poor timing, a few weeks before sentencing U.S. public opinion was again inflamed by the news that Rafael Eitan had been appointed chairman of the board of Israel Chemical Industries, a government corporation, while Aviem Sella was appointed to command a major air base, which meant promotion in rank, moves that seemed to belie Israel's formal claim that this was a rogue operation, unauthorized and wild. Following public outcry in the U.S., Sella resigned his post. Meanwhile public opinion in Israel demanded the appointment of an inquiry committee to investigate the evolution of the affair and to determine responsibility for this operation. The harshness of the Pollard sentence led the government to appoint a two-man committee (the Tsur-Rotenstreich Committee) on March 12, 1987, while a subcommittee of the Knesset Foreign Affairs and Defense Committee headed by Abba *Eban carried out its own separate and independent investigation. Both committees submitted their reports on May 26, 1987.

The Tsur-Rotenstreich committee felt that the entire cabinet should bear responsibility for the affair. In a secret annex it affixed blame on Prime Ministers Peres and Shamir and Defense Ministers Arens and Rabin for failure to exercise control and supervision over the Scientific Liaison Unit and recommended new procedures in intelligence operations. This body and the Knesset subcommittee felt that the involved civil servants, Eitan and Sella, acted injudiciously and far exceeded their authority, but also blamed the senior political echelon for lack of involvement in such operations and their failure to check the details pertaining to the source of the vast intelligence information flowing to Israel. Both committees severely criticized Israel's leadership for hasty actions and serious errors of judgment, although they justified their cooperation with the United States government.

American Jews were furious, most especially Israel's strongest supporters in Congress and in the Executive Branch and the bevy of Israel's supporters who worked in Washington to advance the U.S.-Israeli alliance. The avowed justification of Pollard that he was a Zionist and the exploitation of that commitment by Israeli agents – and perhaps even higher authorities – threatened the easy communications, the close friendships, and cooperative working relationships throughout Washington. The affair placed the American Jewish community in an embarrassing situation, their confidence in Israel's leadership seriously shaken, fearing that the affair could be used in the future by anti-Israel and anti-Jewish elements in America. Public opinion both in Israel and the U.S. felt however that the Israeli committees' reports basically amounted to a whitewash. Accusations by such eminent Israeli intellectuals as Shlomo Avineri that the Pollard case was the Dreyfus case redux only inflamed the tension. The differences were basic: Pollard was guilty, Dreyfus was framed, and American Jewry was not reticent about going public in defense of Jewish interests and confronting the administration, whether Democratic or Republican.

To some, Pollard was a hero. A fundraising effort on Israeli city streets brought more than $150,000 for the Pollard defense fund. Significant sums were raised to pay for ongoing litigation that reached not only the Court of Appeals but the Supreme Court. Those Israelis who sought to defend their country's actions argued that Israel was still under siege, fighting a battle against terror, and living in a fragile and turbulent Middle East. Israel's strategy rested on early warning with intelligence the key to that strategy. Denying Israel vital information was seen as hurting its vital security interests. In spite of the existing Israel-U.S. Strategic Understanding, some Israelis felt they were not being supplied with all relevant information.

These arguments did not convince many Israelis who felt that a monumental error had been committed and that Israeli leaders were not being required to pay the political price for their lack of judgment and involvement. It was feared that the affair would have long-term negative effects on Israel-American relations and the degree of trust and confidence once prevailing in these ties had been seriously compromised.

Over time, the anger generated by the Pollard Affair within American Jewry has faded; many who condemned him and the Israeli government now support clemency, and Pollard is a hero to some within the American Jewish community though not within the political establishment. Still, few relish the image of Pollard going to Israel and receiving a hero's welcome.

By the early 21st century all avenues of appeals had been denied at every level of the U.S. judicial system. The case had been litigated again and again. Pollard divorced his first wife and remarried. Pollard remained in prison, often in solitary confinement, angry at American Jewry for abandoning him, angry at Israel for leaving an agent in the field. His only hope was clemency, and it seemed that every time Israel made a major concession in the peace process such as in the Wye Agreement, the request for presidential clemency was made and then the American intelligence establishment used all of its considerable resources to pressure the president – as George Tenet and others did with President Clinton – not to acquiesce to the Israeli request. The case also has ongoing consequences, as in 2005 two AIPAC officials were indicted for passing on to the Israeli government secret information given to them by a Pentagon official. Painstaking efforts were made to distinguish their case from the Pollard Affair. No documents were passed, no funds were offered or received, and these men were not American officials but lobbyists who routinely trade in information.

In 2006 yet another appeal on behalf of Jonathan Pollard was presented to the U.S. Supreme Court.

[Meron Medzini / Michael Berenbaum (2nd ed.)]

POLLEGAR (Pulgar, Policar), ISAAC BEN JOSEPH IBN (first half of 14th century), Spanish scholar and philosopher. Pollegar's chief literary work was the *Ezer ha-Dat* ("Support of Faith"), consisting of five sections, which was published with an English summary by G. Belasco in 1906, while a variant text of the second section was published by E. Ashkenazi in *Ta'am Zekenim* (1854), 12–19. The purpose of the work was to answer the criticisms of certain schools of thought against Judaism. In the first and main section, the author sets forth the chief principles of Judaism, such as the superiority of Moses and the Torah, the world to come, and the Messiah, and rejects despair over the sufferings of Israel. Combating the apostate *Abner of Burgos, whom he had befriended in his youth, he refutes the latter's Christological interpretation of the *aggadah* by claiming that the *aggadot* are not binding and need not be taken literally. The second section consists in large part of a dialogue between an opponent of philosophical studies and someone who believes that philosophical studies should be pursued, and concludes with the author's reconciliation of Judaism and philosophy along Averroistic lines. In the third section, Pollegar opposes the view, usual in medieval Judaism, that human affairs are guided by the influence of the heavenly bodies, and attacks determinist views such as those expounded by Abner of Burgos. Pollegar attempts to solve the problem posed by Abner of the alleged contradiction between human freedom and divine foreknowledge by his theory of the mutual cooperation of the divine and human wills. The source of all action is the divine will. All of man's actions are founded upon the imitation of the divine will by the human. At the moment when human actions are realized, their completion is ordained by the divine will, and at the very same moment they become objects of the human will, which thus imitates the divine will. Since God's foreknowledge and the decision of His will exist within His essence at the same moment, neither precedes man's actions. God's knowledge, however, does not change, since knowledge of particulars originates in His all-embracing knowledge identical with his essence. The fourth section consists of an attack on various kinds of pseudosciences which conflict with true philosophy. This section includes a four-part critique of

(a) the philosophizers who do not really know philosophy yet mock religion,

(b) the kabbalists, criticized for their language, their belief in their tradition and its authority, and their alleged non-monotheism,

(c) those who see nature as an independent force, and

(d) believers in sorcery. In the fifth section Pollegar praises pure intellectual activity which, he states, can only be fully developed in the next world.

Pollegar also composed at least one treatise against astrology, a translation of the third book of Al-Ghazālī's *Maqāṣid al-Falāsifa*, and a reply to Abner of Burgos known as the *Iggeret ha-Ḥarifot* ("Epistle of Blasphemies"). He refers to commentaries on Genesis, Psalms, and Ecclesiastes, and also to a work called *Musar Banim* ("Discipline of Sons"); none of these is extant.

BIBLIOGRAPHY: Baer, Spain, index, s.v. *Isaac Policar*; idem, in: *Tarbiz*, 27 (1958), 278ff.; Guttman, Philosophies, 205–6; I. Loeb, in: REJ, 18 (1889), 63–70; G. Belasco, in: JQR, 17 (1905), 26–56; Zinberg, Sifrut, 2 (1956), 101ff.; Schirmann, Sefarad, 2 (1956), 520–3.

[Frank Talmage]

POLLIN, ABE (1923–), U.S. sports owner, philanthropist. Pollin's parents were immigrants from Russia who came to America as teenagers with no money and no knowledge of the English language. His father taught himself to read and write, and worked his way up as a plumbing and heating contractor, to the point where he became the largest contractor in Washington with 250 employees. He was the first chairman of Israel Bonds in Washington, and was present at the meeting on November 8, 1946, when money was collected to purchase the *Exodus* the next day. Pollin was born in Philadelphia, and moved to Washington, D.C., when he was eight, growing up seven blocks from Griffith Stadium. He graduated from George Washington University in 1945, and went to work for his family's construction company for 12 years. He then started his own construction company in 1957. In 1964 Pollin purchased the NBA's Baltimore Bullets for $1.1 million, the most anyone had ever paid for a team at that time, and then moved the team in 1973 to Landover, Maryland, near Washington, D.C. The Washington Bullets won the NBA championship in 1978. He later changed the name of the basketball team from Bullets to Wizards, three months after Yitzhak *Rabin was gunned down, saying "the name Bullets is no longer appropriate." In 1972, Pollin received an N.H.L. franchise that later became the Washington Capitals.

Pollin, chairman and CEO of Washington Sports & Entertainment, twice built a multi-million dollar sports and entertainment arena. On December 2, 1973, he opened the Capital Centre in Landover, Maryland, and 24 years later, on December 2, 1997, he opened the MCI Center in the middle of downtown Washington, D.C., which was a cornerstone in helping to revitalize the downtown area. Both arenas were considered state of the art facilities, the standard for new arenas throughout the world. By 2006, Pollin was in his 42nd season of ownership, making him the longest-tenured owner in the National Basketball Association.

Together with his wife, Irene, Pollin's philanthropic and humanitarian work was widespread: he served as chairman of the Advisory Council for UNICEF and was on the international board of the Red Cross; he was president of the Advisory Board of the American Foundation for Autistic Children, honorable chairman of the Salvation Army's Leadership Committee for Centers of Hope, a founding partner of the National Health Museum, and co-sponsor of the "I Have a Dream Foundation" through which he has personally guaranteed college education for some 60 students in Maryland. Pollin also works with business and government leaders in Washington to help the city's homeless population, and helps administer a host of D.C. programs including Abe's Tables, Food For Kids, Serving Seniors Thanksgiving Dinner, Pollin Award, Read To Achieve, Our House Rules, Annual Turkey Basket Giveaway, and The Wizards Kids 'n Kops program. Pollin and his wife established the Pollin Prize for Pediatric Research, administered by New York Presbyterian Hospital, and Irene Pollin, president and founder of the Linda and Kenneth Pollin Foundation, was founder and chairperson of the Sister to Sister – Everyone Has a Heart Foundation.

Pollin was awarded the Duke Ziebert Capital Achievement Award for helping to revitalize downtown Washington, and was the recipient of the Distinguished Civilian Service Award, presented by the U.S. Army; the 1996 Robert F. Kennedy-Martin Luther King, Jr. Award, presented by Coalition to Stop Gun Violence; the 1996 United Cerebral Palsy Achievement Award; and the 1997 Jewish Leadership Award.

[Elli Wohlgelernter (2nd ed.)]

POLLINI, BERNHARD (**Baruch Pohl**; 1838–1897), opera manager. Pollini began his career as a tenor (later baritone) in his native Cologne and while on tour with an Italian opera troupe, he became its manager. Subsequently he managed the Lemberg Theater and the Italian Opera in St. Petersburg and Moscow. Pollini directed the Hamburg City Theater from 1874 until his death. Under his leadership, it gained an international reputation both for its performances and for the many outstanding musicians, such as Gustav *Mahler, whom it first brought to public attention.

POLNA (Czech **Polná**), town in S.E. Bohemia, Czech Republic. Jews are mentioned in the vicinity in 1415 and two Jewish families in Polna itself in 1570. The town's law-manual of 1582 also contains a Jewish *oath formula. A cemetery was established in 1619. In 1681 Jewish and town representatives signed an agreement to build a Jewish quarter of 16 houses (one of its gates was still extant in 1970). The synagogue was built in 1684 and renovated for the first time in the 18th century. The register of synagogue seats was kept in the town archives. In a conflagration in 1863 the synagogue and 32 houses were destroyed. There were 27 Jewish families in Polna in 1724, and 541 Jews lived in the town in 1847. The synagogue was renovated for a second time in 1861. In 1869 there were 430 Jews in Polna, and 238 in 1890. Polna acquired a dubious notoriety through the *Hilsner blood libel case in 1899. In 1930 the community numbered 51 (1.2% of the total population). In 1942 the Jews remaining in Polna were deported to Nazi death camps. The synagogue equipment was sent to the Central Jewish Museum in Prague. Although no congregation was reorganized after the Holocaust, the synagogue and the Jewish cemetery remained extant. Restoration of the synagogue commenced in 1990s.

BIBLIOGRAPHY: H. Gold (ed.), *Juden und Judengemeinden Boehmens…* (1934), 508–11.

[Jan Herman and Meir Lamed]

POLONNOYE, town in the Khmelnitski (Proskurov) district, Ukraine. Jews are mentioned in 1601, and by the middle of the century it was an important community in *Volhynia. In 1648, the time of the *Chmielnicki massacres, when the Cossack armies approached the town about 12,000 Jews found refuge in its fortress, defending themselves, together with Poles, against the enemy. When the Cossacks overran the town about 300 Jews gathered in the *bet ha-midrash* and, led by the kabbalist R. Samson *Ostropoler, they wrapped themselves in their *tallitot* and met death with a prayer on their lips. The number of dead in the town was estimated at 10,000. In 1684 the owner of the town, Countess Lyubomirskaya, granted Jews letters-patent which authorized them to build houses in one of the town's quarters. They were also exempted from military service in exchange for a special payment in favor of the Christian inhabitants, "…with the exception of a general mobilization in the event of an attack by the enemy." In the 18th century the Jews suffered from attacks by the Haidamacks and from Polish and Swedish soldiers.

Polonnoye rapidly became an important commercial and spiritual center. During the second half of the 18th century, two of the pillars of Ḥasidism (and disciples of the Ba'al Shem Tov), Aryeh Judah *Leib ("The 'Mokhiaḥ' of Polonnoye," d. 1770) and after him, Jacob Joseph *ha-Kohen (d. 1782), held the rabbinical positions of the town.

Hebrew printers were active in Polonnoye between 1782 and 1820. Among them was Samuel b. Issachar Ber, who also printed in *Korets and *Shklov, and who transferred the press to *Ostrog in 1794. Another was Joseph b. Ẓevi ha-Kohen, active from 1800 to 1820, who founded another press in *Medzibezh, in 1815. Altogether some 90 works, mostly kabbalistic, ḥasidic, and ethical, were issued, some of the latter in Yiddish.

In 1847 there were 2,647 Jews in Polonnoye and, according to the census, there were 7,910 Jews (48.5% of the population) in 1897. In 1919 the town was at the center of the battle area between the Red and Ukrainian armies, and consequently, during Passover of that year, most of the inhabitants fled to nearby towns. In September calvary units of Budenny rioted, robbing and killing about 40 Jews. In 1926 there were 5,337 Jews (32.5% of the population) in Polonnoye, and their number dropped further by 1939 to 4,171 (30% of the total population. The Germans occupied the town on July 6, 1941, and after a month they executed 19 Jews as Communist agents. On August 23, 1941 they murdered 113, and in June 1942 they killed 1,200. In all the Germans murdered about 2,000 Jews. There was no information available on the presence of Jews in Polonnoye after World War II.

BIBLIOGRAPHY: N.N. Hannover, *Yeven Meẓulah; Sefer Zwihl [Novograd-Volynskiy]* (1962), 253–5 (Heb. part); Ḥ.D. Friedberg, *Toledot ha-Defus ha-Ivri be-Polanyah* (1950^2), 102–3.

[Yehuda Slutsky]

POLOTSK, city in Vitebsk district, Belarus, one of the oldest Jewish communities in Lithuania. There is evidence that Jews settled in Polotsk toward the end of the 15th century. In 1551 the Jews of the city were exempted from paying a special tax known as the *srebrzczyzna*. When Ivan the Terrible captured Polotsk in 1563, he ordered that all the Jews who refused to be baptized (around 300), should be drowned in the Dvina River. (Memorial prayers for these martyrs were recited in Polotsk each year on the 25th of Kislev.) The Jewish community was revived soon after, but in 1580, when the town adopted the *Magdeburg law, it forbade Jewish commerce and purchase of real estate within the city. Jews lived on six landholdings outside municipal jurisdiction. The Jewish community was destroyed in 1654 by Cossack rebels, but was rebuilt shortly after. When local residents complained in 1681 that the Jews were purchasing land within the city without paying municipal taxes, King John III Sobieski ordered them to pay. In 1765 there were 1,003 poll-tax paying Jews in Polotsk. The city was one of the earliest centers of Ḥasidism in Belorussia and *Israel ben Pereẓ of *Polotsk (a disciple of Dov Baer the Maggid of Mezhirich) was a leader of ḥasidic immigration to Ereẓ Israel in 1777. Polotsk had 2,600 Jews in 1815 (56.3% of the total population). The figure rose to 7,275 by 1847 and to 12,481 in 1897 (61% of the total). In the late 19th century the city became a center of anti-Jewish agitation, largely because several Russian Orthodox monasteries and an officers' training school were located there. When pogroms broke out in October 1905, the authorities prohibited Jewish self-defense activities in the city. There were 19,252 Jews living in Polotsk in 1910. The community maintained 23 synagogues, a *talmud torah*, and a Jewish high school. The *kehillah* (Jewish community organization) was abolished under Soviet rule in 1918, along with many other Jewish public institutions. In 1926 the number of Jews had fallen to 8,186 (32% of the total) and dropped further by 1939 to 6,464 (22% of the total population). The two Yiddish schools had 340 pupils, and a Jewish orphanage and kindergarten existed there. The Germans occupied the town on July 16, 1941. A ghetto was organized in August, but in September all Jews were moved to a closed camp near the village of Lozovka, where many died from hunger and disease. In December 1941 7,000 Jews of Polotsk and its environs were murdered. In 1970 the Jewish population of Polotsk was estimated at about 500. There was no synagogue.

BIBLIOGRAPHY: A. Arnin, in: B. Karu (ed.), *Sefer Vitebsk* (1957), 209–12; S. Ogurski (ed.), *1905 in Vaysrusland* (1925), 164–71; *Prestupleniya nemetsko-fashistskikh okkupantov v Belorussii* (1963), 285–6.

[Yehuda Slutsky]

POLOTSKY, HANS JACOB (1905–1991), Orientalist and linguist. Born in Zurich to Russian parents, Polotsky attended the universities of Berlin and Goettingen, studying Egyptology and Semitics. While at Goettingen he was employed at the "Septuaginta Unternehmen," in connection with Greek, Coptic, Syriac, and Arabic material. In Berlin he edited Manichaean texts in Coptic. These texts brought him into contact with Turkish (and Iranian) dialects. His interest in Ethiopic languages (Ge'ez, Amharic, Gouragé, Tigrina, etc.) widened when he began teaching at the Hebrew University in 1934, as professor from 1948. He received the Israel Prize in humanities (1965). In Jerusalem he discovered native speakers of Eastern Neo-Aramaic (modern Syriac) dialects, and thus became acquainted with this long-neglected subject. Being familiar with Russian besides many other European languages, he was able to use important Russian contributions in this field. The discovery of Greek Papyri in Israel (Naḥal Ḥever) provided him with the opportunity to return to Hellenistic Greek. Polotsky is the rare, if not the last, of a type of linguist whose achievements are outstanding in several language families. This enabled him to obtain remarkable results in such studies as his *Etudes de syntaxe Copte* where he solved problems that had been vexing generations of Coptologists, such as the use of the so-called "second tenses," which he approached through the comparison of Coptic texts with their Greek "Vorlage" and by adducing Arabic on French and English constructions of the type "it is who…" (cleft sentence). This type of work, using parallels from different language families, relied less upon dictionaries and grammars of the languages concerned than upon his own material which he collected himself. As an Egyptologist he made his mark with several important studies, e.g., *Egyptian Tenses* (the Israel Academy of Science and Humanities, Proceedings no. 5; 1965). Polotsky proceeds along the lines of synchronic description, following the Saussure school. Only after achieving his aim does he take recourse to comparative material, sometimes nailing down his results by employing diachrocical proofs. Since he never published an article on general linguistics, his approach to languages can be pieced together only by studying carefully all his articles, dealing with different languages. In his *Études de grammaire Gouragé*, he reconstructed a form that (he thought) had disappeared from Ethiopian dialects and had the satisfaction to learn that the "reconstructed" form does indeed exist in one of them. In his studies in modern Syriac he showed his first-hand knowledge of the different Neo-Aramaic dialects spoken near the sea of Urmia (in Iran and Iraq), and proved that synchronic problems of certain dialects can be solved by comparative dialectology plus the diachronic approach. In his article *Syntaxe Amharique et syntaxe Turque* (1960), a study of two languages which belong to two entirely different language families (Semitic and Uralo-Altaic), he showed how close they are in the field of syntax, without having had any contact with each other. While conversant with recent linguistic trends, including that of N. Chomsky, Polotsky tended toward the school of de Saussure. His *Collected Papers* were published by the Magnes Press of the Hebrew University (1971).

A bibliography of his writings appeared in H.B. Rosén (ed.), *Studies in Egyptology and Linguistics in Honour of H.J. Polotsky* (1964), ix–xi. Quite a few languages never dealt with by Polotsky in his articles are even more familiar to him than those mentioned, e.g., Latin (Classical and Middle) and, of course, Hebrew, biblical, mishnaic, that of the prayer book and of Israeli Hebrew. Polotsky is the linguists' linguist.

[Eduard Yecheskel Kutscher]

POLSHEK, JAMES (1930–), U.S. architect. Polshek received his bachelor's degree from Case Western Reserve University and masters in architecture from Yale University (1955). He established Polshek Partnership Architects in Greenwich, Conn., in 1963 and is now based in New York. Polshek also served for 15 years as dean of the School of Architecture, Planning and Preservation at Columbia University in New York.

Central to Polshek's view of architecture is the necessity of it being connected to community and tradition. Polshek has suggested that the "increasing homogenization" of architecture in the United States "brings despondence and is unhealthy. It indicates a loss of place." As a result, Polshek became an important critic of what he called the "bad quality of building today" that is due to a variety of problems, especially lack of vision by public leaders. Polshek's approach is to create architecture that "implements resolutions rather than creating oppositions," and must fulfill the aspirations of the institutions they house.

Polshek's most well-known projects are the William Jefferson Clinton Presidential Center in Little Rock, Ark., the Carnegie Hall renovation, and Zankel Hall expansion in New York, the Rose Center for Earth and Space at the American Museum of Natural History, the New York Times Printing Plant, the Santa Fe Opera Theater in New Mexico, the WGBH public television headquarters near Boston, the Newseum/Freedom Forum headquarters in Washington, D.C., the Omaha Performing Arts Center, and National Inventors Hall of Fame in Akron, Ohio.

The Clinton Library drew particular praise because of the choice of site in a downtown industrial zone, linked to downtown Little Rock by a 27-acre public park. On the other hand, a more modest, yet important renovation by Polshek Partnership was that of Symphony Space and the Thalia Theater on Manhattan's Upper West Side, which has a tradition of catering to avant-garde film and theater.

BIBLIOGRAPHY: S.S. Stephens, *James Stewart Polshek and Partners: Architecture, Planning, Interiors* (1992); Strauss and S. Sawyer (eds.), *Polshek Partnership Architects: 1988–2004* (2004).

[Stephen C. Feinstein (2nd ed.)]

POLTAVA, capital of Poltava district, Ukraine. Jews began to settle there at the close of the 18th century. In 1801 there were 18 Jewish merchants in Poltava and 292 Jews classed as townsmen (about one fifth of the total number of inhabitants). The community in Poltava and its environs numbered 2,073 in 1847. The number of Jews in the town doubled by the 1870s, and in 1897 reached 11,046 (20.5% of the total population), of whom a considerable number were from Lithuania and Belorussia. The Poltava community was one of the best organized and most progressive in Russia. It had 10 synagogues. Jews owned four large flour mills, most of the distilleries, some lumber warehouses, and two printing presses. At the close of the 19th century the *talmud torah* was converted into a modern elementary school, which was attended by 300 children who studied both religious and general subjects; its teaching staff included Alexander Siskind *Rabinovitz and M. Haezraḥi. There were also a girls' vocational school supported by the *Jewish Colonization Association, a yeshivah, and 20 *ḥadarim*. The community's hospital and clinic provided free services, and there were an old age home and a loan bank. The Jewish library contained 8,000 volumes. The influence of the Russian intelligentsia, led by the author V. Korolenko, prevented the outbreak of pogroms in Poltava during both periods of revolution in Russia in 1905 and 1917. There was a strong Zionist movement in Poltava, which was one of the foremost centers of the *Po'alei Zion movement in Russia; several founders of this party were born in Poltava and began their activities there: B. *Borochov, I. *Ben-Zvi, and Y. *Zerubavel (the last two were natives of Poltava). The ideological organ of the party, *Yevreyskaya Rabochaya Khronika* (founded in 1906), was published in Poltava, and the founding conference of Po'alei Zion was held there. Rabbi of Poltava from 1893 to 1917 was E.A. Rabinowich, a leader of the extreme Orthodox and a strong opponent of the Zionists. He published the religious monthly *Ha-Peles* (1903–06) and the weekly *Ha-Modi'a* (1910–15) in Poltava. The historian Elias *Tcherikower was born in Poltava.

Under the Soviet regime the fate of the community was the same as that of the rest of Russian Jewry. Until 1927 Poltava remained a center for printing of Jewish religious books (particularly *siddurim* and calendars). In 1926 among the 9,000 Jewish breadwinners, 2,415 were white collar workers, 1,862 craftsmen, and 1,676 simple laborers. Some 80% of the artisan union were Jews. Many were occupied in the large sock factory that supplied the entire Soviet Union. There were 2 Yiddish schools and a Yiddish section in the railroad school. The Jewish population numbered 18,476 (20.1% of the total) in 1926. It dropped by 1939 to 12,860 (10% of the total population).

The Germans entered the city September 18, 1941. Many Jews were successfully evacuated or escaped. A Judenrat was established, and the Jews were called to register. On September 25, 5,000 were murdered, and on November 23, after a new registration was ordered, 3,000 Jews were executed. In the following days Jews who evaded registration or hid were caught and executed. In the late 1960s the Jewish population was estimated at 5,000. There was no synagogue, the remaining one having been closed down in 1959 by the militia, which broke in, confiscated all religious articles, dispersed the congregation, and prohibited the holding of further gatherings. Subsequently Jews have prayed in private. There is a Jewish cemetery in Poltava. There are also two mass graves of Jewish martyrs murdered by the Nazis; one in which 13,000 bodies are buried, and in the other 7,000. The monuments there do not specify that all the victims were Jews.

Region of "Poltavshchina"

Jews began to settle in the region during the early 17th century in the process of Jewish participation in the colonization of Ukraine. By 1610 there was a Jewish community in Berezan (to the north of Pereyaslav), and within a few decades about a dozen Jewish communities were established in the districts of *Pereyaslav and Mirgorod, of which the largest were in Pereyaslav and *Lubny. Jews engaged in commerce and the leasing of estates, flour mills, liquor distilleries, breweries, and inns. There was strong competition from Christian townsmen, and during the *Chmielnicki massacres of 1648 these communities were among the first to be destroyed. After the region came under Russian rule Jews were not permitted to live there until the first partition of Poland in 1772. Individual Jewish families, however, settled in various estates under the protection of their owners despite frequent expulsions by the authorities.

After the first partition of Poland in 1772, Jewish settlement on the eastern bank of the river Dnieper was renewed, and by 1792 there were over 700 Jews in the region, most of whom lived on estates or in villages. In 1794 this region, which then formed part of the province of Yekaterinoslav, was incorporated within the *Pale of Settlement. In 1803 there were 82 Jewish merchants and 2,030 Jews classed as townsmen living in the province of Poltava, which was formed in 1802. The community of *Kremenchug was the largest in the district, and developed in particular owing to its position on the Dnieper, the main waterway from Lithuania to the south. It accounted in 1897 for 30% of the Jews in the province. In 1847, 15,572 Jews were counted in the 18 communities of the province (which also included the Jews in the small settlements and their environs). Their numbers increased as a result of a large emigration from Lithuania and Belorussia, and were estimated at 84,000 in 1881. The census of 1897 recorded 111,417 Jews (4% of the total population) in Poltava province (the lowest percentage of Jews in all the provinces of the Pale). The Russian-Ukrainian majority had a strong assimilationist influence on the Jews in the province, who were a minority in all the towns; it was only in Kremenchug that their numbers approached half the population. On the other hand, *Chabad Ḥasidism, which penetrated from the north, was an important spiritual influence (the tomb of *Shneur Zalman of Lyady, the founder of Chabad Ḥasidism, is in *Gadyach in Poltava province).

About one half of the Jews of the province of Poltava earned their livelihood from commerce (in contrast to 38.5% in the whole of Russia), and about 30 percent were engaged in crafts and industry. Commerce was principally conducted in grain and other agricultural produce. Although some Jews owned saw mills, brick-kilns, flour mills, alcohol distilleries, and other enterprises, the overwhelming majority of the workers in them were non-Jews. During the spring of 1881 pogroms occurred in the north of the province of Poltava. In 1905 a wave of pogroms swept across 52 settlements of the province. The most severely affected were Gadyach, Kremenchug, *Romny, and *Zolotonosha.

During World War I thousands of refugees and Jews expelled from the battle zone arrived in the province of Poltava and found refuge in the Jewish communities. During the Civil War, the communities of the western section of the province suffered especially from pogroms by bands of Ukrainians and the "volunteer army" of A.I. *Denikin. In 1926 there were approximately 93,000 Jews in the five districts (Kremenchug, Lubny, Poltava, *Priluki, Romny) of the former territory of the province of Poltava.

BIBLIOGRAPHY: S. Ettinger, in: *Zion*, 21 (1956), 107–42; Zionist Organization, *Die Judenpogrome in Russland* (1909); *Reshumot*, 3 (Berlin, 1923), 157–71; Y. Zerubavel, *Alei Ḥayyim* (1960), 14–124 passim, 233–5; B. Ḥaikin, in: J. Erez (ed.), *Sefer Z.-S.* (1963), 120–1.

[Yehuda Slutsky]

POLYAKOV, family of railroad builders and bankers in Russia, headed by the brothers Jacob, Samuel, and Eliezer. They originated in Dubrovno, Belorussia. JACOB (1832–1909) began his economic career as a liquor excise farmer and later went on to railroad construction. He participated in the founding of the Don-Azov and other Russian banks and also acted as the vice chairman of the *Jewish Colonization Association in Russia. He received a Russian title of nobility. SAMUEL (1837–1888) was one of the most important railroad builders in Russia. He was responsible for laying over 1,600 mi. (2,500 kms.) of railroads, including the Kozlov (Michurinsk)-Rostov and the Kursk-Kharkov-Azov lines, and strategic railroads in Romania during the Russo-Turkish War of 1877–78. He also founded the South Russian Coal Mining Society and several important banks (Moscow Estate Bank, Don Estate Bank, etc.). He contributed generously to Russian educational and cultural institutions and showed a special concern for technical education (he founded the first technical school for railroad construction in Yelets in 1867 and the first school for mining in Korsun). He was unpopular among Jews because of his refusal to employ Jewish workers in his enterprises, but toward the end of his life played a role in Jewish public life. He initiated the foundation of the *ORT organization, participated in negotiations with the minister of the interior P.N. *Ignatyev in 1881–82 and contributed to the construction of the synagogue of St. Petersburg. He received a Russian title of nobility. ELIEZER (1842–1914) constructed railroads in partnership with his brother Samuel and was one of the leading bankers in Moscow. He was president of the Moscow Estate Bank and in 1873 founded the Polyakov Bank. He invested large sums in the development of industries in Russia and Persia. Eliezer was president of the Jewish community of Moscow and received a Russian title of nobility. In 1908, after a crisis befell his enterprises, he was removed from the majority of them by the government.

BIBLIOGRAPHY: Y. Mazeh, *Zikhronot*, 2 (1936), 10–20.

[Yehuda Slutsky]

°POLYBIUS OF MEGALOPOLIS (c. 210–128 B.C.E.), the most notable of the Hellenistic historians. Polybius did not devote much space to the Jews or Judaism in his universal history. His detailed description of the fourth Syrian war (book 5) makes no mention of Jerusalem or Judea, although it gives a comparatively lengthy account of the conquest of Palestine. He does, however, discuss the Jews in the context of the fifth Syrian war, as attested in the fragment from book 16 of his history, preserved in Josephus (Ant., 12:3, 135–6). Here Polybius records among other achievements of Antiochus III that those Jews who lived near the Temple of Jerusalem allied themselves with him. From another passage (Jos., Apion, 2:53–54) it can be seen that a section of Polybius' work, now lost, also gave *Antiochus Epiphanes' impecunious state as his motive for plundering the Temple.

POLYKOFF, SHIRLEY (1908–1998), innovative advertising executive. Born the middle daughter of Russian Jewish immigrants, Polykoff began selling coats in a department store at the age of 11 and wrote her first advertising copy as a teenager while working at *Harper's Bazaar.* By 1929 she was earning money as a copywriter for a women's specialty shop and soon began writing catchy ads for other products, including "Chock Full O'Nuts, the heavenly coffee." Her most famous ad was written in 1955 for Clairol hair products. "Does she … or doesn't she? Hair color so natural only her hairdresser knows for sure," was tremendously successful and enriched both Clairol and Foote, Cone & Belding, the agency where Polykoff was employed. The Clairol ad budget grew from $400,000 to $33 million in one year. Polykoff, who colored her hair, credited her mother-in-law with the phrase. Polykoff continued with catchy ads such as "Is it true blondes have more fun?" and "If I've only one life, let me live it as a blonde!" During her marriage she had the agency hold her salary at $25,000, so as not to make more money than her lawyer husband, George Halperin. After his death in 1961, the agency increased her salary tremendously, in part as a result of her promotions within the agency. In 1968 she became the chairman of the creative board of Foote, Cone & Belding and a vice president. She went on to head her own advertising firm, Shirley Polykoff Advertising, Inc., one of the few women to do so. Polykoff was named Advertising Woman of the Year in 1967 by the American Advertising Federation, an award she considered her greatest honor; she received some 16 other awards, including a Matrix award for professional achievement in the media. Polykoff, who had two daughters and three grandchildren, wrote about her career in her book, *Does She … or Doesn't She? And How She Did It* (1975).

[Sara Alpern (2nd ed.)]

POMEGRANATE (Heb. רִמּוֹן, *rimmon*), the tree, *Punica granatum*, and its fruit. It is one of the seven choice fruits of Ereẓ Israel (Deut. 8:8), and among the fruits brought by the spies sent by Moses, as proof of the land's fertility (Num. 13:23). After the devastation of the land "the vine, the fig tree, and the pomegranate and olive tree" ceased producing their fruit (Ḥag. 2:19). The pomegranate, with its beautiful red flowers, decorative fruit, and its delicate flavor, was especially beloved by the poet of the Song of Songs, who mentions it six times. The loved one is compared to "a park of pomegranates" (4:13); her cheek (*rakkah*) to a "pomegranate split open" (4:3, 6:7), the reference being to a divided pomegranate, as the cheeks are called "the *rimmon* of the face" in the Talmud (Av. Zar. 30b). In the spring its large flowers are conspicuous in their beauty (Songs 6:11). The juice of pomegranates is a delicious drink (8:2). Adornments in the shape of the fruit embellished the hem of the robe of the high priest Aaron (Ex. 28:33–34) and the capitals of the pillars of the Temple (I Kings 7:18, 42). Three joined pomegranates also appear on the Hasmonean coins, and it also appeared upon the one *lirah* coin of modern Israel. A number of localities in Israel have its name: Ein Rimmon, Gat Rimmon, Sela ha-Rimmon, etc.

In the time of the Mishnah and Talmud, the pomegranate was one of the important plants, and details about it abound. It grew in nearly every region of the country, but the best were the pomegranates of the valleys (Tosef., Bik. 1:5). Those from Badan, apparently in the Wadi Badan near Shechem, won particular praise (Or. 3:7). Various species of it were grown (Tosef., Ter. 2:4) and there were both sweet and sour varieties (*ibid.* 5:10). Pomegranates were of different sizes (Kel. 17:5), but the average size was less than that of the average *etrog* (TJ, Naz. 1:4, 51c). It is noted that the pomegranate's "fruit is beautiful but not its tree" (TJ, Suk. 3:5, 53d). Unlike the seeds, the peel is very bitter, hence the pomegranate was used metaphorically for a pupil who selected only the good: "He found a pomegranate, ate the fruit and discarded the peel" (Ḥag. 15b). Schoolchildren sitting in their rows and learning Torah were compared to the compact kernels of the pomegranate (Song R. 6:11), and the Talmud interprets the Song of Songs 4:3 homiletically to the effect that "even the most empty of Jews is as full of good deeds as the pomegranate [is of kernels]" (Ber. 57a). The delicate beauty of pomegranate kernels found poetic expression in the description of the beauty of Johanan of whom it was said that anyone wishing to see it: "Let him bring a silver cup from the smelter, fill it with the kernels of a red pomegranate, surround it with a crown of red roses, and put it between the sun and the shade, he will then sense in its brilliance the beauty of Johanan" (BM 84a). The kernels were eaten fresh, or pressed into juice or they were dried and a sort of raisin made from them (Tosef. Shev. 6:29).

The peel of the pomegranate contains a dark brown dye that was used for dyeing (Shev. 7:3) and also as a test for invisible ink (Git. 19b; *narah* there being the Persian for pomegranate). Pomegranate trees are cultivated in Israel and are frequently to be seen near the houses of Arabs. In the valley of Beth-Shean extensive pomegranate orchards were planted but with doubtful success, since the pomegranate was attacked by pests.

BIBLIOGRAPHY: Loew, Flora, 3 (1924), 80–113; J. Feliks, *Olam ha-Ẓome'ah ha-Mikra'i* (1968^2), 48–51; H.N. and A.L. Moldenke, *Plants of the Bible* (1952), 319, index, s.v. **ADD. BIBLIOGRAPHY:** J. Feliks, Ha-Ẓome'aḥ, 151.

[Jehuda Feliks]

POMERANIA, former duchy, subsequently Prussian territory; divided between Poland and Germany since 1945. The earliest references to Jewish settlement in Pomerania date from the 13th century, when (in 1261) Duke Barnim I decreed that the clauses of the Magdeburg *Law concerning the Jews would apply to Stettin (*Szczecin) and the rest of Pomerania. It is recorded that in 1320 the Jews of Templin, Prenzlau, and Pasewalk enjoyed civic equality; indeed, until the *Black Death persecutions (1350) the position of Pomeranian Jewry was relatively favorable. Originally the Jews made their living as traders, later turning to moneylending. Nevertheless, in spite of the privileges of 1481 and a grant of residence to 22 Jewish families, Boguslaw X expelled them in 1492/3. On the other hand, Frederick William, the "Great Elector" (1640–88), extended an invitation to Jewish merchants who had been expelled from Vienna in 1670 to settle in his domains, and by 1682 at least four Jewish families were living in the part of Pomerania that was under Prussian rule. However, numerous complaints against Jewish business practices caused him to threaten Jewish expulsion in 1687/8. By then 15 families had been licensed to reside in Pomerania, the gentry frequently interceding on their behalf. Polish Jewry continued to immigrate to Pomerania in spite of obstructive regulations. In 1706 a rabbi was elected by an assembly of Pomeranian Jewry (46 licensed families), but the king appointed his own nominee to the position.

In the western half of Pomerania, intermittently under Swedish rule, harsher regulations against Jews were in force. From 1728, however, all laws of Prussia applied to the Jews of Pomerania, who at that time totaled about 325 persons. During that period the Jews were mainly engaged in the wool, wheat, and amber trades, and in peddling.

The communities grew after 1812 (c. 1,700 Jews) until 1880 (13,886), after which date they began to decline. In 1932 there were 7,760 Jews (0.4% of the total population) in 50 communities, 28% of whom lived in the modern industrial city of Stettin. During World War II the majority of Pomeranian Jews were deported and annihilated. After the war a community was renewed in Stettin.

BIBLIOGRAPHY: H. Loewe, in: *Zeitschrift fuer Demographie und Statistik der Juden*, 7 (1911), 146–9; L. Hiller et al., in: *Der Jugendbund* (Jan. 1931), 1–3; *Fuehrer durch die juedische Gemeindeverwaltung und Wohlfahrtspflege in Deutschland* (1932/33), 69–81; U. Grotefend, *Geschichte und rechtliche Stellung der Juden in Pommern von den Anfaengen bis zum Tode Friedrich des Grossen* (1931); B. Brilling, in: *Gemeindeblatt der Synagogen Gemeinde zu Stettin* (1932), no. 9; AJYB, 63 (1962), 376–7; *Germania Judaica*, 2 (1968), 658; S. Stern, *Der preussische Staat und die Juden* (1962), 1 Akten, 125–48, 385–414, 536; 2 Akten, 713–804. **ADD. BIBLIOGRAPHY:** *Der faschistische Pogrom vom 9./10. November 1938 – zur Geschichte der Juden in Pommern* (1989); L. Baecker, *Juden in Schwedisch-Vorpommern, Neuvorpommern von 1648–1871* (1993); W. Wilhelmus, *Juden in Vorpommern* (Reihe Geschichte Mecklenburg-Vorpommern, vol. 8) (1996); idem (ed.), *Flucht oder Tod. Erinnerungen und Briefe pommerischer Juden ueber die Zeit vor und nach 1945* (2001); J. Sziling (ed.), *Neighborhood Dilemmas. The Poles, the Germans, and the Jews in Pomerania along the Vistula River in the 19th and 20th Century* (2002); W. Wilhelmus, *Geschichte der Juden in Pommern* (2004).

[Henry Wasserman]

POMERANTZ, BERL (1900–1942), Hebrew poet. Pomerantz was born in the Polish village of Udrzyn. He studied in Vilna and later settled in Warsaw, where he unsuccessfully applied to the British authorities for an entrance visa to Ereẓ Israel. In December 1942, while hiding with a group of fellow Jewish escapees in the forest near the townlet of Janow, he was killed by German soldiers.

His work constitutes one of the most significant achievements in Hebrew poetry written in Poland between the two world wars. As distinct from the poetry of Bialik and his followers, Pomerantz's poems are in the modern manner. Composed in rhymeless *vers libre*, they are daringly figurative and evince a close affinity with the Yiddish poetry of the day which had been affected by German expressionism. His themes and preoccupations – nostalgic reminiscences of his native village with contrasting urban tableaux suggested by Warsaw (seen as the epitome of the city) – are in keeping with the spirit of his age. He is at his best when rendering visual impressions that are figuratively elaborated until they acquire the status of symbols of an uprooted, humiliated, poverty-ridden humanity. Although emotionally intense and figuratively hyperbolic, Pomerantz's language is also characterized by the concrete detail in its natural contours. His facility in perceiving metaphoric relationships never interfered with his ability to delineate what was actually observed and genuinely felt.

Pomerantz's poetry is closest to that of Ḥayyim *Lensky and Abraham *Shlonsky, but Pomerantz's work is more concrete than the latter's, as well as more intimate in tone. His longest poem, *Me-al ha-Hadom* ("From Above the Footstool"), is dedicated to the memory of his father, "whose grace lasted longer than his meal," as the poet puts it. This is an impressive work, moving in its simple sincerity, which has been compared with Bialik's *Yatmut* ("Orphanhood") cycle. *Bi-Sefatayim el ha-Sela* ("With Lips to the Rock"), his first book of poems, appeared in Warsaw in 1935. His second book, *Ḥallon ba-Ya'ar* ("A Window in the Forest"), the last to come out during his lifetime, was published in 1939 by the Stybel Publishing House in Warsaw. In Ereẓ Israel, his poems were regularly printed in the literary journal, *Gilyonot*. However, to make a living Pomerantz engaged in teaching, translation from Yiddish and Polish, and various forms of literary hackwork. Despite his trials, his poetry is never devoid of gentle and compassionate humanity nor does it ever become embittered or aggressive. His last poems, written in occupied Poland, were never recovered and were probably buried with him in the forest. Other works were published in 1966 under the title, *Shirim* ("Poems").

BIBLIOGRAPHY: S.Y. Penueli, in: *Gilyonot*, 26 (1951–52), 308–10; Y. Lamdan, *ibid.*, 28 (1953), 110f.; N. Peniel, in: B. Pomerantz, *Shirim* (1966), 7–26.

[Natan Zach]

POMERANTZ, FRED P. (1901–1986), U.S. garment manufacturer. Although his formal education never went beyond the sixth grade, Pomerantz was one of the apparel business's most prominent executives. His company, Leslie Fay Inc., was an industry giant, one of the first dress manufacturers to be listed on the New York Stock Exchange, and his products were sold in stores all over the U.S. Pomerantz, a native New Yorker, was a larger-than-life character who looked more like a boxer than a businessman. Rough-hewn in manner, he would arrive at his office in a chauffeur-driven, maroon Rolls-Royce with his initials on the license plates. The car was a gift to him from the workers at his factory in Wilkes-Barre, PA., where Leslie Fay was a major employer, at one time supporting almost 2,000 people. Pomerantz started working at the age of 11, doing odd jobs and learning how to cut fabrics. With his older brother, Michael, he operated a succession of coat, dress, and uniform companies and during World War II he produced uniforms for the U.S. military. In 1947 he launched his own business, using the government's sizing guidelines to make women's dresses, a category he felt was about to increase in importance as the country moved further away from a wartime environment. He called his company Leslie Fay, naming it after his daughter, and began turning out dresses, sportswear and coats in different price ranges with a variety of labels, including Leslie Fay, Kaspar for ASL, LF Petite, Leslie Pomer, and Breckenridge. The company prospered and in 1962, a public offering was issued. In the 1980s, Leslie Fay went through two leveraged buyouts and a second public offering. The first buyout was in 1982, when Pomerantz took Leslie Fay private for $54.5 million, selling it to his son, John, and other investors. It allowed Pomerantz to cash out his 30% stock interest in the company and he retired. His son succeeded him as chairman. Two years later a second buyout was completed, for $178.4 million. Following Pomerantz's death in 1986, Leslie Fay went public again. Its volume peaked at almost $900 million in 1991, but early in 1993, it was discovered that two company officials had fraudulently reported quarterly earnings. Corrected figures revealed huge losses. The stock price, around $12 a share when the scandal broke, eventually plummeted to less than 50 cents. Leslie Fay filed for bankruptcy in 1993 and remained there for five years before emerging with new owners. It changed its name to LF Brands in April 2003, then closed at the end of the year. Despite Pomerantz's limited education, his name became attached to two prominent schools. In the 1960s, a dormitory at Brandeis University in Waltham, Mass., was named for him and his wife, Gerta. In 1986, just a few months after Pomerantz died, his family contributed $1 million to the endowment fund of the Fashion Institute of Technology in New York and the school's Art and Design Center was named for him.

[Mort Sheinman (2nd ed.)]

POMERANTZ, SIDNEY IRVING (1909–1975), U.S. historian. Pomerantz was born in New York and taught at City College, rising to the rank of professor of history in 1960. He was a pioneer in the study of American urban history, with particular emphasis on the role of the press and business enterprise as determinants of metropolitan growth. His best-known work is *New York, an American City, 1783–1803* (1965^2).

The history department of the City University of New York has established the Sidney I. Pomerantz Prize for the best essay on the history of New York City written in an elective course.

ADD. BIBLIOGRAPHY: I. Yellowitz (ed.), *Essays in the History of New York City: A Memorial to Sidney Pomerantz* (1978).

POMI(S), DE' (Heb. מִן הַתַּפּוּחִים, *Min ha-Tappuḥim*), one of the four distinguished Roman families which, according to an ancient tradition, were brought by Titus from Ereẓ Israel to Italy (see title page of David de' Pomis, *Ẓemaḥ David*).

ELIJAH DE' POMI(S) (d. 1298), rabbi and possibly also head of the community in Rome, martyred on the 20th Tammuz 5058. The Inquisition sought to strike at the richer Jews since it considered them supporters of the Patrician Colonna family, who opposed Pope Boniface VIII (1294–1303). While denying that there was any basis for the allegation, Elijah allowed all suspicion to fall on him alone. He was burned at the stake and his family sought refuge in Spoleto. Two anonymous elegies on his death have been preserved.

DAVID DE' POMIS (1525–1593) was linguist, physician, and philosopher. Son of the learned R. Isaac, he was born in Spoleto. He received his early education from his father and later, at Todi, from his uncles Rabbi Jehiel (Vitale) and Moses *Alatino, both physicians who were well versed in philosophy. For six years David studied medicine and philosophy in Perugia, where he received his doctorate in medicine in 1551. He was rabbi and physician at Magliano near Rome, but on account of the edict of Pope *Paul IV forbidding Jewish physicians to attend Christians (1555), he moved from town to town in Italy before he settled in 1569 in Venice, where he published the greater part of his works. Pius IV (1559–65) gave him permission to attend Christians, a concession revoked by Pius V (1565–72) and later restored by Pope Sixtus V (1585–90). In his booklet *De Medico Hebraeo Enarratio Apologica* (Venice, 1588) David de' Pomis refutes the charges brought against Jews and Jewish physicians in particular by a bull of 1581 by Gregory XIII (1572–85). He stresses that according to the Bible and Talmud a Jewish physician must give help to every sufferer, and cites numerous instances of Jewish doctors who had distinguished themselves by their work and their loyalty. The volume ends with a selection of talmudic rules translated into Latin in order to prove that the Talmud should not be despised.

David de' Pomis is famous above all for the *Ẓemaḥ David*, a trilingual Hebrew, Latin, and Italian dictionary (Venice, 1587). The work, which is dedicated to Pope Sixtus V, contains numerous discourses of a scientific and historical nature; the preface embodies the author's genealogy and autobiography. Among his other works are a translation into Italian of Ecclesiastes with explanatory notes (Venice, 1571) dedicated to Cardinal G. Grimani; *Discorso intorno a l'humana miseria e sopra il modo di fuggirla* ("A Discourse on Human Suffering and How to Escape It"; Venice 1572), dedicated to Margaret of Savoy, was published as an appendix to this work. His medical works include a treatise on the plague (Venice, 1577) and another on maladies of old age (Venice, 1588) dedicated to the doge and senate of Venice; in the latter, he mentions a work on the divine origin of the Venetian Republic which has not been preserved; also lost were *Sukkat David* and *Migdal David* (mentioned in the preface to *Ẓemaḥ David*) and a treatise on the battering ram (mentioned under the name of תותק). His translations of Daniel and Job have never been published.

BIBLIOGRAPHY: Vogelstein-Rieger, 1 (1896), 255–7; 2 (1895), 259–60; H. Friedenwald, in: JQR, 32 (1941/42), 228–30; 407–8; idem, *Jews and Medicine* (1944), index s.v. *Pomis, David de*; C. Roth, *Venice* (1930), 95, 186–8; idem, *Jews in the Renaissance* (1959), 223–5; L. Muenster, in: *Revue d'Histoire de la Médicine Hebraique*, 7 (1954), 7–16, 125–36; Milano, Italia, 82, 633, 662; idem, *Il ghetto di Roma* (1964), 418, 422.

[Alfredo Mordechai Rabello]

POMMER, ERICH (1889–1966), German producer. After serving in the German army in World War I, by 1919 Pommer was directing the Deutsches Eclair (Decla) film company and had gathered a staff that included the director Fritz Lang and the set and costume designers who had been associated with the avant-garde Der Sturm group, Pommer's expressionist succés de scandale. *Cabinet of Dr. Caligari* (1919) was followed by *Dr. Mabuse* (1922); *Niebelungen* (1924), produced after Decla had merged with the German colossus of the industry, UFA; *Variety* (1925); *Metropolis* (1925/26); *Blue Angel* (1930); and *Last Laugh*. The day Hitler became chancellor of Germany, Pommer left the country for Paris, where he produced *Liliom* (1934) with Lang. In the 1930s he worked in England as an independent and in the United States for Fox, producing *Jamaica Inn* (1939) with Alfred Hitchcock and adapting the Sidney Howard play *They Knew What They Wanted* (1940). He worked again in Germany as an independent producer after the war.

POMPEII, city in Campania, Southern Italy. There is enough epigraphic evidence, mostly graffiti, to show that Jews lived in Pompeii as well as in the neighboring cities of Herculanum and Stabia, before its destruction in the eruption of Vesuvius in 79 C.E. It seems that most Jews arrived in Pompeii after 70 C.E. This assumption is corroborated by their humble status as freedmen, slaves, servants, or prostitutes. They bear traditional Jewish names such as Iesus, Ionas, Maria, and Martha. However there were also more affluent Jews like a certain Fabius Eupor, who bears the title *princes libertinorum*, or a certain Youdaikos, a wine merchant. It seems, according to epigraphic evidence, that the Jews took an active part in the municipal life of the city.

One of the houses excavated, called by the excavators "Casa degli ebrei" (N. 6, Reg. VIII, Ins. 6), exhibits wall paintings, which depicts the Judgment of Solomon. However it is possible that this painting in fact depicts a tale from Ancient Egypt, mediated by Hellenistic Alexandrine Art, and not a biblical episode. As the painting clearly caricatures the subjects, depicting them as pygmies, the owner was not Jew.

An interesting graffito (Reg. IX, Ins. I, n. 26) read "Sodom Gomor." It is possible that it was written during the eruption of Vesuvius. Another graffito bears the word Cherem in Latin, which may correspond either to *ḥerem* (ban) or *kerem* (vineyard).

BIBLIOGRAPHY: C. Giordano and I. Kahn, *Gli Ebrei in Pompeii, in Ercolano e nelle citta della campania Felix* (1965); Review by A.M. Rabello, in- *Labeo*, 13 (1967), 127); J. Daoust, in: BTS 126 (1970); Review by A.M. Rabello, in: RMI 37 (1971), 329. **ADD. BIBLIOGRAPHY:** A. Baldi, *L'anatema e la croce, Ebrei e Cristiani in Pompei antica* (1983); M. Della Corte, "Fabius Eupor, princes libertinorum e gli elementi giudaici in Pompei," in: *Atti dell'Accademia Pontiana*, n.s., 3 (1950), 347–53; J. Goodnick Westenholz, *Images of Inspiration, The Old Testament in Early Christian Art* (2000), 92–93; D. Noy, *Jewish Inscriptions of Western Europe*, 1 (1993).

[Alfredo Mordechai Rabello / Samuele Rocca (2nd ed.)]

°**POMPEIUS TROGUS** (c. first century B.C.E.), Roman historian of the Augustan age. His comprehensive *Historiae Philippicae* (perhaps completed in 9 C.E.), concentrating on the Macedonian-Hellenistic empires, is not extant. However, an abstract made by Justin in the third or fourth century C.E., and the prefaces to all 44 books, remain. The Jews are first discussed in Book 36 in the context of events in the reign of *Antiochus Sidetes. The account falls into three sections: antiquities (archaeology); a geographical description of Judea; and the history of the Jewish nation from the Persian period. The first section is a combination of the biblical account, a Damascene account, and the hostile Greek-Egyptian tradition. Pompeius Trogus emphasizes the close connection existing between the priesthood and the monarchy in Jewish affairs, and his work reflects the conditions prevailing under the Hasmonean monarchy. He undoubtedly had access to

Greek sources, evidently among them Timagenes. The preface to Book 39 shows that he also extended his history to later developments in Hasmonean Judea.

BIBLIOGRAPHY: Reinach, Textes, 250–8; I. Heinemann, *Poseidonios' metaphysische Schriften*, 2 (1928), 80–81; L. Ferrero, *Struttura e metodo dell' Epitome di Giustino* (1957), 120–3.

[Menahem Stern]

°POMPEY (Gnaeus Pompeius Magnus; 106–48 B.C.E.), Roman general and one-time triumvir with *Julius Caesar and *Crassus. In 64–63 B.C.E. Pompey effectively established Roman rule throughout Syria and Palestine. He ostensibly attempted to arbitrate between the Hasmonean factions, represented by the brothers *Hyrcanus II and *Aristobulus II, contending for supremacy in Judea. A third party, according to Diodorus (4:2; cf. Jos., Ant., 14:41), expressed preference for Roman domination which would allow for Jewish religious autonomy. Pompey, though receiving costly gifts from both the brothers, was only biding his time, and when the moment was opportune made his way to Jerusalem. The pro-Hyrcanus party opened the city gates to him. Aristobulus' faction (though he himself was now a prisoner of Pompey) resisted a siege of several months' duration. Both Jewish (Jos., *ibid.*, 64ff.) and pagan sources (Dio Cassius, 37:16) confirm that Pompey took advantage of the Sabbath day, on which Jews refrained from taking the offensive, to accelerate siege operations. The Temple appears to have been stormed in midsummer 63 B.C.E. According to Josephus Pompey entered the Holy of Holies on a "fast-day" but left it intact. There is evidence by Dio Cassius, however, that the Temple treasury was robbed by Pompey. Wholesale slaughter of the defenders took place and the country became tributary to Rome. With this, Jewish independence came to an end, save for the few fitful years of the Jewish War (66–70) and the Bar Kokhba War (132–135). A telling blow was the severance from Judean control of the vital coastal towns of Gaza, Jaffa, Straton's Tower (later Caesarea), among others, as well as Samaria (Ḥag. 25a) and large areas of Transjordan. This act was the prelude to *Gabinius' later subdivision of the country. Aristobulus was carried off to Rome in chains together with the members of his family, including his two sons, Alexander and Antigonus, the former escaping en route. Hyrcanus was rewarded by being granted the high priesthood and leadership of the nation.

The noncanonical Psalms of Solomon are generally attributed to the period of Pompey's capture of the city where this event is described. Pompey is regarded as the "alien to our race" and rod of God's wrath against Hasmonean usurpation of the Davidic throne (Ps. of Sol. 7–9). According to some scholars his era may also be the background of the first century C.E. *Pesher Habakkuk* of the Dead Sea Scrolls.

BIBLIOGRAPHY: Jos., Loeb (ed.), vol. 9, p. 762; Schuerer, Hist, index s.v.; T. Mommsen, *Roemische Geschichte*, 3 (1922^{13}), 143ff.; A. Schalit, *Ha-Mishtar ha-Roma'i be-Ereẓ Yisrael* (1937), index; Klausner, Bayit Sheni, 5 (1951^{2}), 315; A. Schalit, *Koenig Herodes* (1969), 7ff., 678f., 757f.

[David Solomon]

°POMPONIUS MELA (first century C.E.), Roman geographer. Referring to Near-Eastern countries (he calls the area Syria), he mentions Judea and singles out three ancient cities of its southern coastal plain (which he calls Palaestina): Gaza (Aza), Ascalon (Ashkelon), and Jope (Jaffa; *De Situ Orbi* 1:11).

[Jacob Petroff]

POMUS, DOC (Jerome Solon Felder; 1925–1991), U.S. blues singer and songwriter who helped define rock & roll and rhythm & blues music, lyricist and co-lyricist of some of the greatest songs in rock and roll history, including "This Magic Moment," "Suspicion," "Sweets for My Sweet," "Teenager in Love," and "Save the Last Dance for Me," one of the 25 most-performed songs in history; member of the Rock and Roll Hall of Fame. Born in the Williamsburg section of Brooklyn, New York, Pomus contracted polio at age nine and walked with crutches, but it did not hinder his career: he began performing as a teenager, and became one of the finest white blues singers of his time. At the age of 15, already playing saxophone and singing at jazz and blues clubs throughout the New York metropolitan area, he changed his name to hide his profession from his parents. Pomus recorded a number of blues-influenced singles for independent companies beginning in his late teens, none of which were hits. In 1956 he began to focus on writing songs, and soon formed a partnership with Mort Shuman, a pianist, to become one of the greatest songwriting teams in the history of American popular music. They wrote 12 songs a week, and a range of artists including B.B. King, the Drifters, the Mystics, Fabian, Bobby Darin, Dion and the Belmonts, Andy Williams, and Ray Charles cut Pomus' songs. Elvis Presley recorded at least 20 Pomus originals, including "Little Sister," "Viva Las Vegas," "Kiss Me Quick," and "A Mess of Blues."

The Pomus-Shuman partnership dissolved in 1965, and Pomus went into semi-retirement after a fall that left him confined to a wheelchair the rest of his life. He re-emerged in the mid-1970s, and worked with John Belushi to put together the band that supported the Blues Brothers. Pomus teamed with Dr. John (Mac Rebennack), and wrote the songs for his albums *City Lights* and *Tango Palace*. Pomus also co-wrote most of the material for B.B. King's album *There Must Be a Better World Somewhere*, which won a 1981 Grammy Award. Some of Pomus' songs were also used on the soundtracks of the films *Dick Tracy* and *Cry Baby*. Pomus estimated that during his career he wrote more than 1,000 songs, of which 100 were domestic and foreign Top Ten songs and more than 350 top-100 songs, that sold more than 250 million recordings. Pomus was given a Pioneer Award from the Rhythm & Blues Foundation, an organization he co-founded, the first white musician to be so honored. In 1995, a tribute album featuring recordings of 14 of his songs, *Till the Night Is Gone: A Tribute to Doc Pomus*, was recorded by artists including B.B. King, Bob *Dylan, Lou *Reed, Los Lobos, Roseanne Cash, and Dr. John. He was inducted into the Rock and Roll Hall of Fame in January 1992.

[Elli Wohlgelernter (2nd ed.)]

PONARY (Lithuanian: **Paneriai**), a resort area about 5 mi. (8 km.) from Vilna, where from July 1941 to July 1944, about 100,000 people were executed by the Nazis, with the aid of special Lithuanian units. The decisive majority of the victims were Jewish men, women, and children from Vilna and the surrounding area, as well as from other countries. In addition, a few thousand non-Jewish Soviet prisoners of war and civilians were killed there. In spite of the deceit that the Nazis staged to mislead the victims brought to Ponary, the nature of the place was known in the Vilna ghetto, as early as the fall of 1941, from reports of the few people who managed to escape during the executions. A frequently sung lullaby in the Vilna ghetto, "*Shtiler, Shtiler*" ("Quieter, Quieter"), by Shmerle *Kaczerginsky, included the line: "Many roads lead to Ponary, but no road leads back." On January 1, 1942, Abba *Kovner proclaimed in his call for resistance: "Of those taken through the gates of the [Vilna] ghetto not a single one has returned. All the Gestapo roads lead to Ponar [the forest seven miles outside the city], and Ponar means death.... Ponar is not a concentration camp. They have all been shot there. Hitler plans to destroy all the Jews of Europe, and the Jews of Lithuania have been chosen as the first line." His perception of the "Final Solution" came three full weeks before the *Wannsee Conference. It took 18 more months for the Vilna ghetto inhabitants to share his perceptions.

It is known from German documents and other sources that there were instances of resistance on the part of the Jewish victims at Ponary when they were taken out to be executed. In August 1943, the Germans returned to the site, in order to cover up the traces of their crime and began to dig up and burn the corpses. The work was carried out by a group of 70 Jews and ten Soviet prisoners of war, bound in chains. A secret group was organized among them and, during a period of about three months, its members dug a tunnel about 30 meters long with spoons and with their bare hands. On the night of April 15, 1944, this group carried out its escape. Only 13 managed to get away alive, and of these 11 reached the Rudniki forests, where they joined partisan units.

After the war a monument was erected to the memory of the victims and a museum was opened containing remains discovered at the place. An information bulletin entitled *Der Muzey in Ponar* was published for Jewish visitors (1966), who come in large numbers from throughout the world. In 1969 the singer Neḥamah *Lifshitz brought remains of Ponary victims to Israel, and they were placed in the Memorial Hall of Yad Vashem in Jerusalem.

[Dov Levin / Michael Berenbaum (2nd ed.)]

PONTECORVO, BRUNO (1913–1993), Italian nuclear physicist. Born in Italy, Pontecorvo studied at Pisa University and at Rome University, where he taught from 1933 to 1936. He then served with scientific institutions in France and in 1940 moved to the U.S., where he worked as an expert in radiographic prospecting for oil. In 1943 he became a member of the Anglo-Canadian atomic energy team in Montreal and worked under the Nobel prizewinner Enrico Fermi in the Chalk River atomic project, participating in research leading to the development of neutron physics. From 1948 he was in England as an associate in the Harwell Atomic Research Laboratory. In 1950 Pontecorvo defected to the Soviet Union, where he was put in charge of a team at the Joint Nuclear Research Institute. He became a member of the U.S.S.R. Academy of Sciences and won the Lenin Prize and Order of Lenin (both in 1963).

His main fields of research were neutron physics (1943–48), the production of pi-mesons from neutrons (1950–55), and the interaction of pi-mesons with nucleons. Among his publications are "Artificial Radioactivity Produced by Neutron Bombardment" (in *Proceeding of the Royal Society of London*, 1935); "Isomérie nucléaire produite par les rayons × du spectre continu" (with A. Lazard, in *Comptes rendus des séances de l'Académie des Sciences, Paris*, 1939); *O protsessakh obrazovaniya tyazholykh mezonov i chastits* ("Production Processes of Heavy Mesons and Particles," 1955); and *Slabye vzaimodeystviya elementarnykh chastits i neytrinov* ("Weak Interactions of Elementary Particles and Neutrinos," 1963).

BIBLIOGRAPHY: A.M. Moorehead, *The Traitors: The Double Life of Fuchs, Pontecorvo and Nunn May* (1952); *Prominent Personalities in the U.S.S.R.* (1968), s.v.

°PONTIUS PILATE, Roman governor of Judea from 26 to 36 C.E. Pilate held office at the time of Jesus' crucifixion. At the outset of his rule, he incurred the resentment of the Jews when his army, in Jerusalem for its winter encampment, brought into the city its standards bearing the imperial image (Philo, *De Legatione ad Gaium*, 38). This act utterly disregarded the religious sensibilities of the Jews, who staged a mass protest before Pilate in Caesarea. Pilate, who realized that his threats of force would not deter the Jews, yielded to their demands and had the standards removed from Jerusalem to Caesarea. He caused even greater bitterness by his appropriation of Temple funds in order to build an aqueduct. When angry crowds demanded the abandonment of the project, Pilate planted Roman soldiers among them. At a signal from him, the soldiers fell upon the demonstrators, killed and injured many of them, and crushed the resistance (Jos., Wars 2:177; Antiq. 18:60–62). The situation worsened when Pilate ordered his soldiers to attack the Samaritans who had gathered on Mount Gerizim for a religious ceremony. Many, including several of their leaders, were killed. The Samaritans sent a delegation to protest to L. Vitellius, governor of Syria. Vitellius ordered Pilate to Rome to account for his conduct to Emperor Tiberius and appointed Marcellus in Pilate's place, as well as alleviating taxation in Jerusalem. Before Pilate reached Rome, however, the emperor died and Pilate never returned to Judea.

Bloody riots in the time of Pilate are also hinted at in the New Testament, though there is no clear statement of the circumstances. Pilate is best known with regard to the crucifixion of *Jesus. According to Tacitus "Christus, the founder of the name, had undergone the death penalty in the reign of

Tiberius, by sentence of the procurator Pontius Pilate, and the pernicious superstition was checked for a moment…" (Annales XV, 44:2–5). According to the Evangelists, Pilate considered Jesus innocent of any crime. Jewish pressure alone is supposed to have caused Pilate to have him tried and executed. Christian sources, presumably motivated by a desire to place complete responsibility for the *crucifixion on the Jews, are generally sympathetic to Pilate. Josephus, however, is extremely matter of fact about Pilate's actions: "Pilate, upon hearing him [Jesus] accused by men of the highest standing amongst us, condemned him to be crucified." (Antiq. 18.64, though some scholars believe this passage to be a later interpolation into the text). This is in contrast to the account given in the epistle of Agrippa I (Philo, *ibid.*) which depicts Pilate as corrupt, cruel, and bloodthirsty. In Christian tradition, Pilate's death is attributed either to suicide or to execution by the emperor. A Latin inscription mentioning the emperor Tiberius and Pilate was discovered at Caesarea in 1961 ("…this Tiberium, Pontius Pilate, prefect of Judaea, did [or erected]…"); it clearly indicates that the title of the governors of Judea was also *praefectus* (see *Procurator). Coins minted by Pilate belong to the years 29–31 C.E.; it is unclear why he did not strike coins in the early years of his governorship (26–28 C.E.), or in his later years (32–36 C.E.). A lead weight from the time of Pilate and dated "Year 15 of Tiberius" is also known.

BIBLIOGRAPHY: G.A. Mueller, *Pontius Pilatus*… (Ger., 1888) contains earlier bibliography; Schuerer, Hist, index; M. Radin, *Jews among the Greeks and Romans* (1915), 280ff.; G. Lippert, *Pilatus als Richter* (1923); D.R. Fotheringham, *Suffered under Pontius Pilate*… (1930); Pauly-Wissowa, 40 (1950), 1322–23; J. Blinzler, *Der Prozess Jesu* (1951, 1955^2); P. Winter, *On the Trial of Jesus* (1961); R. Caillois, *Pontius Pilate* (Eng., 1963); Doyle, in: JTS, 42 (1941), 190–3; Vardaman, *ibid.*, 81 (1962). **ADD. BIBLIOGRAPHY:** A.H.M. Jones, *Studies in Roman Government and Law* (1960), 115; M. Stern, *Greek and Latin Authors on Jews and Judaism*, vol. 2 (1980), 89, 92 (for bibliography on the Caesarea inscription and on the *praefectus Iudaeae* title); Y. Meshorer, "Coins of the Roman Procurators of Judaea," in: *A Treasury of Jewish Coins From the Persian Period to Bar Kokhba* (2001), 167–76; M. Grant, *Jesus* (1977): 161ff; E.P. Sanders, *The Historical Figure of Jesus* (1993), 28ff.; J. Dominic Crossan and J.L. Reed, *Excavating Jesus* (2001), 268. For further literature see: *Jesus (bibliography).

[Lea Roth / Shimon Gibson (2nd ed.)]

PONTOISE, town in the department of Seine-et-Oise, France. Toward the close of the 12th century, the Jews of Pontoise were accused of having murdered a Christian child named Richard. In 1204 there was already an established Jewish community supervised by a Christian provost. Proof of the considerable financial activities transacted by the Jews of Pontoise was the introduction of a special royal seal which was to be affixed to all documents. Notable among the scholars of Pontoise was *Moses b. Abraham of Pontoise, the *paytan*, tosafist, and commentator on the Pentateuch and Talmud. Until World War II, there were about 30 Jewish families in Pontoise, but no community was established after the war.

BIBLIOGRAPHY: Gross, Gal Jud, 443ff.; J. Depoin, in: *Mémoires de la societé historique de Pontoise et du Vexin*, 36 (1921), 120f.; Z. Szajkowski, *Analytical Franco-Jewish Gazetteer* (1966), 274.

[Bernhard Blumenkranz]

PONTRÉMOLI, EMMANUEL (1865–1956), French architect. Born in Nice, Pontrémoli was appointed inspector of public buildings and state palaces in 1926 and from 1932 to 1937 was director of the École Nationale des Beaux-Arts, Paris. Among his works are the Museum of Natural History and the Institute of Human Paleontology, Paris, the synagogue at Boulogne-sur-Mer, and the Maison Grecque at Beaulieu-sur-Mer built for Theodore *Reinach.

POOL, DAVID DE SOLA (1885–1970), U.S. rabbi, civic and communal leader, and historian. Pool, who was born in London, pursued his rabbinic studies, first at Jews' College, London, and then at the Hildesheimer Rabbinical Seminary in Berlin. Pool went to the U.S. in 1907 to become minister of the Sephardi Congregation Shearith Israel in New York City, the oldest synagogue in the U.S. He served there until his retirement in 1956.

Pool's other posts and activities included: president of the New York Board of Rabbis (1916–17); member of Herbert Hoover's food conservation staff (1917); field organizer and director of army camp work of the Jewish Welfare Board during World War I (1917–18); U.S. representative of the Zionist Commission in Jerusalem to help implement the Balfour Declaration (1919–21); regional director for Palestine and Syria of the Joint Distribution Committee (1920–21); founder and director (1922) of the Jewish Education Committee of New York; president of the Union of Sephardic Congregations from 1928; president of the Synagogue Council of America (1938–40); chairman of the Committee of Army and Navy Religious Activities of the National Jewish Welfare Board (1940–47); vice president (1951–55) and president (1955–56) of the American Jewish Historical Society; and U.S. delegate to the NATO Atlantic Congress in London (1959).

Pool wrote several significant works and monographs in the fields of American Jewish history, religion, education, and Zionism, and edited and translated Sephardi and Ashkenazi Hebrew liturgical works. His works include: *The Kaddish* (1909; 1964^3); *Hebrew Learning Among the Puritans of New England Prior to 1700* (1911); *Capital Punishment Among the Jews* (1916); *Portraits Etched in Stone: Early Jewish Settlers, 1682–1831* (1952); *An Old Faith in the New World: Portrait of Shearith Israel, 1654–1954* (1955); *Why I Am a Jew* (1957); and *Is There an Answer?: An Inquiry in Some Human Dilemmas* (1966), the last three with his wife, TAMAR DE SOLA POOL (1893–1981). Mrs. Pool was national president of Hadassah from 1939 to 1943 and held executive positions with several other national and world Jewish organizations, among them the American Jewish Committee, the World Zionist Organization, and Youth Aliyah.

BIBLIOGRAPHY: D. de Sola Pool, in: AJHSP, 52 (1962), 3–7; idem, in: Jewish Theological Seminary of America, *Thirteen Americans: Their Spiritual Autobiographies* (1953), 201–17.

POONA, city 75 mi. S.E. of Bombay, India, formerly seasonal headquarters of the British government of Bombay. Poona's Jewish community, which was established in the middle of the 19th century, consisted of Arabic-speaking Jews who made Poona their summer residence and of *Bene Israel from Bombay. David *Sassoon built the synagogue Ohel David, and the Sassoon family endowed a hospital, infirmary, and leper asylum. The Bene Israel synagogue, known as Sukkath Shlomoh, was founded later. From 1870 Poona had a Hebrew printing press, publishing many works in Hebrew with Arabic translations for the Baghdadi Jews, and the Bene Israel published several liturgical works there. Once prosperous and numerous, the Jewish population has declined in recent years as a result of immigration to Israel.

BIBLIOGRAPHY: A. Yaari, *Ha-Defus ha-Ivri be-Arẓot ha-Mizraḥ* 2 (1940), 83–89. **ADD. BIBLIOGRAPHY:** J.G. Roland, *Jews in British India: Identity in a Colonial Era* (1989).

[Walter Joseph Fischel]

POOR, PROVISION FOR THE. The Bible makes frequent references to the obligation to help the poor, to render them material assistance, and to give them gifts. This obligation is mentioned in the Prophets (Isa. 58:7, 10; Ezek. 18:7, 16) and especially in the Wisdom Literature (Prov. 31:20; Job 22:5–9; 29:12–13; 31:16–20; cf. Ps. 112:9). The Wisdom Literature also urges consideration of the destitute, i.e., by making loans to them (Prov. 14:21, 31; 19:17; 28:8; cf. Ps. 37:21, 26; 112:5). Concern for the poor and hungry is one of the qualities of God Himself (Ps. 132:15; 146:7, etc.); Deuteronomy says that "He loves the sojourner, in giving him food and raiment" (10:18 – sojourners (Heb. *gerim*) were among the poor).

In post-Exilic times it was customary to give gifts to the poor on holidays (Esth. 9:22; Neh. 8:10). This obligation gained in importance in post-biblical times, and in the language of the rabbis, *ẓedakah* (originally "righteousness") came to mean giving to the poor. This meaning of *ẓedakah* appears already in Ben Sira (3:30; 7:10; 29:12; Tob. 4:7–11; 12:8–9), as well as in Syriac, *ẓedketa*, and in Arabic, *ṣadaqa*. In biblical usage, however, this meaning is not yet attached to *ẓedakah*.

Several gifts are mentioned in the Pentateuchal laws; some are to be given to the poor along with other people, while others are intended solely for the poor. Exodus 23:11 says of the produce of the seventh year: "… let the needy among your people eat of it, and what they leave let the wild beasts eat." According to Leviticus 25:6, these crops are eaten by masters and their slaves, and also by hired servants, sojourners, and strangers, i.e., the poor of the people. In Deuteronomy, the seventh year is a year for the release of debts (Deut. 15:1–2); a warning is given against withholding loans from the poor because of the proximity of the year of release (15:7–11; see *Sabbatical and Jubilee Year). Deuteronomy also commands that the poor be included in the celebration of the pilgrimage feasts (16:11, 14), which means that they must be allowed to partake of the eating of the sacrifices. Similarly, the poor are the recipients of the tithe of the third year, which, according to Deuteronomy, is not brought to the chosen city but is eaten in the local settlements hence the name of the year "the year of the tithe" (14:28–29; 26:12–15) and the rabbinic name of the *tithe "the tithe of the poor." The gifts which are specifically intended for the poor are mentioned in Leviticus (19:9–10; again briefly, 23:22 in conjunction with Shavuot, the festival of wheat harvesting) and in the laws of Deuteronomy (24:19–22). The rabbis derived from these passages four gifts from the vineyard – *pereṭ* ("individual grapes [fallen off during cutting]"), *shikhḥah* ("what is forgotten"), *pe'ah* ("[unharvested] edge"), and *'olelot* ("small single bunch [of grapes]"); three gifts from grain fields – *leqet* ("gleanings [of what is dropped by harvesters]"), *shikhḥah*, and *pe'ah*; and two from orchards – *shikhḥah*, and *pe'ah* (Tosef., Pe'ah 2:13).

According to the plain sense, Leviticus 19:9–10 designated two types of gift, both given from field and vineyard. The first gift consists of part of the produce which is to be left for the poor. The farmer is enjoined not to reap his entire crop, but to leave part of it unharvested for the poor: "And when you reap the harvest of your land, you shall not reap all the way to the edges of your field"; and the owner of a vineyard is commanded: "you shall not strip your vineyard bare" (Lev. 19:9–10). The *pe'ah* which is left in the field parallels the *'olelot* of the vineyard. The second gift consists of what falls to the ground during the harvesting: it is to be left there for the poor, as is written: "neither shall you gather the gleanings [*leqet*] of your harvest … neither shall you gather the fallen grapes [*pereṭ*] of your vineyard" (*pereṭ* in the vineyard is the same as *leqet* of the harvest, as the rabbis have explained).

Deuteronomy 24:19–22 refers to the second type of gift, exemplified, in the rhetorical manner peculiar to Deuteronomy, by produce of the field, olive grove, and vineyard. The prohibition against returning to gather the sheaf forgotten in the field is another version of the prohibition of total harvest in Leviticus. Similarly, the prohibition of beating the boughs of olive trees again and picking the vineyard again is the equivalent of Leviticus' ban on gathering up grapes fallen during the harvest.

Ruth's gleaning the *leqet* after the harvesters (Ruth 2), and the common reference to gleanings after the grape harvest (Judg. 8:2; Isa. 24:13; Micah 7:1, etc.) indicate that these laws were grounded in current practices. Various customs of other peoples have been compared: leaving the last sheaf in the field after the harvest in the superstitious fear that it contained the grain-demon and should therefore be left for strangers; or burial of a "corn baby," shaped out of a sheaf, in the field in order to assure the renewal of the crop the next year. Such conceptions, however, are alien to the Bible; its injunctions on behalf of the poor are given explicitly moral grounds. Permitting the widow to glean unhindered and giving gifts of oil to the poor are commended in Egyptian wisdom literature as approved by the gods ("The Instruction of Amen-em-opet," 28; in Pritchard, Texts, 424).

BIBLIOGRAPHY: W. Nowack, *Die sozialen Probleme in Israel* (1896), 12–16; F. Buhl, *Die sozialen Verhaeltnisse der Israeliten* (1899), 102–5; D. Hoffmann, *Das Buch Leviticus*, 2 (1906), 36–38, 240–1 (= *Sefer va-Yikra*, 2 (1954), 31–32, 168); P.J. Baldensperger, in: PEFQS (1907), 19; G. Beer, in: ZAW, 31 (1911), 152; J.G. Frazer, *The Golden Bough*, 2 (1911, 1932), 171ff., 232ff.; G.A. Smith, *Deuteronomy* (1918, 1950), 284; I. Schur, in: ZAW, 32 (1921), 154; M. Lurje, in: BZAW, 45 (1927), 61–62; P. Joueon, in: *Biblica*, 15 (1934), 406–10; N. Peters, *Die soziale Fuersorge im Alten Testament* (1936), 66–72; J. Hempel, in: BZAW, 67 (1938), index, s.v. *Armer*; H. Bolkestein, *Wohltaetigkeit und Armenpflege im vorchristlichen Altertum* (1936), 38–40, 53–54, 56ff.; C. van Leeuwen, *Le développement du sens social en Israel avant l'ère chrétienne* (1955), 173ff.; E. Kutsch, in: RGG, 1 (1957[3]), 617–8.

[Menahem Haran]

POPES. The earliest, semi-legendary popes, Peter and his immediate successors, were of Jewish birth, yet nothing specific is known of their relations with the Jews. The first pope reported historically to have entered into direct relations with Jews was SYLVESTER I (314–335), who is said to have discussed religious matters with a Jew named Noah and to have conducted a triumphant disputation with a number of Jews, headed by Zambri the magician, in the presence of Emperor Constantine. LEO I (the Great; 440–461) composed some polemical sermons nominally (though not really) directed against Jews. Nothing further is known of papal-Jewish relations until the time of *Gelasius I (492–496), who had in his service, perhaps as physician, a Jew named Telesinus, whom he called *vir clarissimus*, recommending one of his relatives, Antonius, in a letter to Bishop Quingesius. He also ordered an inquiry (496) into the complaint of a Christian slave who claimed he had been circumcised by his Jewish master.

By far the most important medieval pope as regards relations with Jews, as in other respects, was *Gregory I (the Great; 590–604), whose letters are replete with information on the subject. He may be regarded as the founder of the accepted papal Jewish policy in both its positive and its negative aspects. On the one hand Pope Gregory ordered that the Jews should not be molested, that they should be protected from violence and permitted the free exercise of their religion, and on the other hand he said the Jews should be restrained from exercising any semblance of authority over Christians, or from enjoying equal status with Christians, or any privileges beyond those guaranteed them by existing law (i.e., the laws of the Roman Empire after the triumph of Christianity). A letter he wrote to the bishop of Palermo opened, "In the same way as the Jews should not have license to practice in their synagogues anything more than is allowed them by the law, so they should not suffer any disability in that which is conceded to them." This position summed up papal policy and set the example for all later papal legislation on the matter. The statement was reproduced as a fixed rubric, *Sicut Judaeis*, in bulls of protection issued by popes of the later Middle Ages on at least 22 occasions. It is with Gregory I, moreover, that the papacy came to be recognized as the supreme authority of the Western Church and accordingly Jews outside *Rome, and even outside Italy, began to address appeals for protection to the various popes, primarily through the mediation of the Jews of Rome.

Succeeding popes carried out the policy laid down by Gregory I without, however, extending it. At times of danger to the Church and consequent internal reformation, the tendency was to emphasize the negative rather than the positive side of that policy. Thus STEPHEN III (768–772), protested against the privileged position of the Jews of *Narbonne, their possession of landed property, and their mingling with their Christian neighbors on equal terms. NICHOLAS I (858–867) prohibited the wearing of "Jewish vestments" (i.e., those based on Old Testament prescriptions) by Christian priests. *Leo VII (936–939), departing from the tolerant policy of his immediate predecessors, authorized the archbishop of *Mainz to offer the Jews of his diocese the alternatives of expulsion or apostasy. So far as is known, in the persecutions which took place throughout most of Europe early in the 11th century (in the wake of a report that the Jews had persuaded the Muslims to destroy the Church of the Holy Sepulcher in Jerusalem) the popes took no part. Although a spurious document connected with the event is ascribed to SERGIUS IV (1009–12) a very old Hebrew account tells how on the occasion of a persecution at Rouen the Jews appealed to the pope for protection. If the extant report is reliable, Pope *Benedict VIII (1012–24) must have condoned the persecution of the Jews of Rome (1020–21) on a charge of blasphemy which was supposed to have brought about an earthquake. On the other hand, *Alexander II (1061–73) admonished the Christian warriors setting out to fight the Muslims in Spain (1063) not to molest Jews, and in 1065 he reproved the ruler of *Benevento, in Italy, for forcibly converting the Jews of that city to Christianity. The reformist popes who succeeded Alexander, and who reverted to strict Church discipline, inevitably emphasized the repressive aspect of papal policy. In 1078 GREGORY VII (1073–85) renewed the canon laws against placing Jews in positions of trust, with a particular view to their employment as taxfarmers or mintmasters; he renewed the prohibition in a brief to *Alfonso VI of Castile in 1081. (The suggestion that this pope and his kinsman Gregory VI (1045–46) were of Jewish extraction is based on error: see G.B. Picotti, in *Archivio Storico Italiano*, 1942.)

The popes were not implicated in the persecutions in Europe at the time of the early Crusades, although URBAN II (1088–99) berated Emperor *Henry IV for permitting those Jews who had been baptized by force to return to their faith. Urban's position was based on the doctrine that although compulsion could not properly be used in the baptismal act, once performed the sacrament of baptism was irrevocable, however it had been carried out. In 1120 *Calixtus II (1119–24) issued the protective bull, or *Constitutio pro Judaeis*, beginning with Gregory the Great's words *Sicut Judaeis*, in which any sort of persecution of the Jews was condemned in unqualified terms.

Henceforth, for generations, this bull was often renewed by popes shortly after their accession, on the petition of the Jewish communities and presumably accompanied by gifts. In the next three centuries, the bull was reissued 21 times. Although his authority was not recognized elsewhere, ANACLETUS II, who was of immediate Jewish extraction and who for this reason was inveighed against by his opponents, maintained himself as pope in Rome between 1130 and 1138. It is possible that his career was the source of the medieval Jewish legend of the Jewish pope, Elhanan. Although his enemies lost no opportunity of calling attention to his Jewish origin, this had no lasting ill effects upon the Jews.

On his visit to Rome (c. 1165) Benjamin of Tudela found the Jews enjoying a favorable status. R. Jehiel, grandson of the author of the *Arukh* Nathan b. Jehiel, was then in the service of the reigning pope, *Alexander III (1159–81), who on his state entry into Rome (1165) had been greeted by the Jews, headed by their rabbis and bearing embroidered banners. However, this same pope presided over the Third *Lateran Council of 1179, which renewed the conventional canonical restrictions against Jews, forbidding them to exercise any authority over Christians or to live in close associations with them. The council marked the beginning of reform forced on the Church by the danger inherent in the development of the *Albigenses movement of southern France, in which Jewish influences were wrongly suspected

The reform reached its climax with the Fourth Lateran Council of 1215–16, convened under the auspices of Pope *Innocent III (1198–1216), who may be recognized as at least the systematizer, if not the founder, of medieval clerical antisemitism. He is also the most important figure in the history of relations between the papacy and the Jews after Gregory I. The anti-Jewish canons of the Fourth Lateran Council, while not necessarily enforced or obeyed forthwith, set a standard of policy which afterwards was kept constantly before the eyes of Christian rulers, especially by the *Dominicans, who established their order at about this time to combat heterodoxy and heresy. Even Innocent, however, did not overlook the other aspect of the traditional papal policy and confirmed the *Constitutio pro Judaeis* in 1199, which protected Jews against violence from the French crusaders. At the same time he contested the claims of the Holy Roman emperor, as the successor to their conqueror, Vespasian, to suzerainty over the Jews throughout Europe.

Although all, or almost all, Innocent's successors confirmed the *Constitutio pro Judaeis*, they usually attempted to secure the enforcement of the anti-Jewish canons of the Lateran Council. Honorius III (1216–27) was, however, forced by circumstances to permit the king of Castile to suspend the obligation of wearing the Jewish *badge as prescribed by this council, so as to prevent the Jews from migrating to Muslim realms. Under *Gregory IX (1227–41), who attempted to enforce the wearing of the badge in Navarre (1234), the papal offensive against the Jews was extended to Jewish literature, for it was with his authorization that the attack upon Jewish books and the Talmud was launched. Copies of the latter were sequestered pending an inquiry into its contents (1239; see Nicholas *Donin; *Jehiel b. Joseph of Paris). This was followed by its condemnation and sentence to burning, which apparently took place not only in France but also (under the pope's specific authority) in Rome (see *Talmud, Burning of). *Innocent IV (1243–54) repeated the condemnation of the Talmud in his bull *Impia judaeorum perfidia* of 1244. In 1253 he approved the archbishop's expulsion of the Jews from *Vienne in France for not obeying the Lateran decrees, and in 1250 he intervened to prevent the erection of a new synagogue in *Córdoba. On the other hand, in two bulls of 1246 he condemned in unqualified terms *blood libels which had begun to arise, and embodied his condemnation in the *Constitutio pro Judaeis*, which he issued for the second time that year. This condemnation remained an integral part of the text of the *Constitutio* whenever it was subsequently reissued by his successors. Although *Alexander IV (1254–61) attempted to enforce the Jewish badge and incited further attacks on the Talmud, he recognized also the value of the Jewish merchants for his treasury, and in 1255 relieved a number of them of all tolls throughout the papal possessions.

In the course of his brief papacy (1265–68) *Clement IV professed anxiety over the conversion of Christians to Judaism and authorized the *Inquisition to take measures against it, thus bringing Jews and the Inquisition into official contact for the first time (1267). A further extension of the Dominican offensive against Jews was approved by *Nicholas III (1277–80); in his bull *Vineam Soreth* (1279) he ordered that the Jews be compelled to listen to conversionist sermons. (There is, however, no evidence that this was enforced in Rome until much later.) This was the pope from whom the mystic Abraham b. Samuel *Abulafia sought to demand in person the release of the Jews from captivity, and was saved from the stake, according to his own account, only by the death of the pope at his summer residence at Soriano on the very night before Abraham entered the city to interview him. Boniface VIII (1294–1303) was the first pope recorded to have treated disdainfully the Jewish deputation who regularly came to congratulate the pope on his accession; he returned over his left shoulder the Torah Scroll presented to him with the scornful remark that they could not comprehend it. Under his pontificate, moreover, R. Elijah de *Pomis was put to death by the Holy Office in Rome, apparently for allegedly having helped the Colonna family in their rebellion. This instance opened up serious possibilities of blackmail, and in 1299 a bull was procured which excluded the Jews, regardless of their material means, from the category of "powerful persons" who could be denounced anonymously to the inquisitors. On the other hand, it was at this time, notwithstanding the canonical prohibition, that popes are first recorded as having Jews regularly in their employment as personal physicians. The first known case is that of the philosopher and translator, Isaac b. Mordecai ("Master Gaio"), who was in the service either of Boniface or his predecessor, Nicholas IV.

On the death of Boniface, there began the "Babylonian Exile" of the papacy at *Avignon (1309–77) which, along with the adjacent *Comtat Venaissin, had at that time finally become a papal possession by purchase. From this time onward, these papal territories in France were treated in much the same way as those in Italy, and Jews were consequently permitted to remain there when they were expelled from the rest of Provence. Not much is recorded about the policy toward the Jews of the first Avignonese pope, CLEMENT V (1305–14). His successor, *John XXII (1316–34), however, adopted a singularly antagonistic attitude toward Jews, although he did attempt to protect them at the time of the *Pastoureaux disturbances in 1320. John expelled Jews from certain places in the French papal dominions and temporarily (1321) from Rome itself. He converted former synagogues into churches, enforced the wearing of the Jewish badge (1317), encouraged conversion by permitting apostates to retain their property (1320), instituted special surveillance over converts to prevent backsliding (1317), and once more stirred up the French bishops against the Talmud (1320). John's successors proved themselves more favorably disposed toward the Jews. With them, there are records of Jews acting as tailors and parchment makers to the papal court in Avignon. *Benedict XII (1334–42) actively protected the Jews of Germany from a wave of massacres which broke out after a charge of the desecration of the *Host, by refusing to give credence to the charge without proper inquiry. *Clement VI (1342–52) was among the most benevolent of all medieval popes. Besides reconfirming the *Constitutio pro Judaeis* (as almost all other popes of the period had done), he condemned forcible baptism, and in 1348 he issued a benevolent edict protecting Jews in the widest terms from the fantastic accusations and brutal massacres which followed the *Black Death.

During the period of the great schism (1378–1417) the papacy was so absorbed in its own problems that it had little opportunity to occupy itself with the Jews. Hoping to score an impressive victory by having the Jews acknowledge the truth of Christianity, thereby to reinforce his personal status, the Spanish antipope *Benedict XIII established an almost frenetic anti-Jewish policy. It was he who was responsible for and presided over the disputation of *Tortosa (1413–14) and who instigated the persecutory movement, including condemning the Talmud and imposing wide-sweeping restrictions upon the Jews, which followed also in the Spanish Peninsula.

The Italian popes, however, influenced by the spirit of the Renaissance, reverted (with some exceptions) to a more tolerant policy. *Boniface IX (1389–1403), for example, had a succession of Jews in his employ as physicians and was responsible for a number of protective edicts, including one in 1402 which recognized the citizen rights of the Roman Jews. *Martin V (1417–31), with whose election the great schism ended, followed the example of Boniface, owing in part possibly to the influence of his Jewish physician, Elijah b. Shabbetai *Be'er. Martin greatly favored the Jews of Rome, prohibited forcible baptism, and even abolished the clerical prohibition on employing Jewish physicians. There is extant a drawing showing him greeting a deputation of Jews from Constance who came to welcome him to that city. This, however, was the period of intensified agitation against the Jews by the friars, led by John of *Capistrano, which could not fail to influence the papacy. In 1422 the alarmed Jews obtained a further edict of protection from the pope, and the friars were warned not to continue to incite the populace against them. (The edict was actually withdrawn a year later on the grounds that it had been obtained by fraud.) In 1427, as a result of reports that the Franciscan chapel on Mount Zion had been seized, the pope forbade Italian vessels to convey Jews to Palestine. A number of other unfavorable edicts led the Jews of Italy to organize countermeasures, backed by appropriately bestowed monetary gifts. This resulted in a very sweeping edict from the pope in 1429 protecting the Jews from the propaganda of the friars. The two conflicting currents, favorable and unfavorable, appear also in the policy of *Eugenius IV (1431–47) who, though at first renewing the privileges and safeguards of the Jews, was later forced to issue a bull putting into effect the severe decisions of the Council of Basle against Jews, forbidding them to practice handicrafts and moneylending, to engage in intercourse with Christians in any capacity, and even to study the Talmud. Once again there was a conference of Italian Jews and countermeasures (no doubt including bribery) were taken until the pope, persuaded that his policy was economically ruinous, withdrew the prohibitions. Restrictions were, however, renewed though apparently not enforced under the successors to Eugenius, *Nicholas V (1447–55) and & Calixtus III (1455–58), under whose rule the influence of Capistrano and the Observantine *Franciscans reached its climax. The humanist PIUS II (1458–64), who maintained the poet Moses da *Rieti in his service as his physician, was bent on a crusade against the Turks and therefore heavily increased taxation on the Jews.

With *Sixtus IV (1471–84) the Renaissance spirit triumphed in Rome, and for the next three quarters of a century relations between the popes and Jews were particularly close and cordial. Formally, of course, the popes had to conform to the external demands of unbending Christian orthodoxy. Thus Sixtus was nominally responsible for the introduction of the *Inquisition into Spain by his bull of 1478. On the other hand he had close personal relationships with Jews, as did his immediate successors down through the middle of the 16th century. Sixtus was interested to some extent in Hebrew literature and employed Hebrew copyists at the Vatican library. He also employed Jewish physicians, one of whom is said to have attempted a blood transfusion to save him in his last illness. In 1475 Sixtus initially refused to countenance a blood libel associated with the name of Simon of *Trent. The notorious *Alexander VI (1492–1503) permitted refugees from Spain to settle in Rome and had as his body physician Bonet de *Lattes, who dedicated his *Annuli… super Astrologiae utilitate* to him in 1493. JULIUS II (1503–13) extended his favor in the same manner to Samuel Sarfatti.

The climax in the favorable relations between the Jews and the Holy See was, however, reached with the popes of the house of Medici. *Leo x (1513–21) was so well disposed in fact that it was said that the Roman Jews considered his pontificate a presage of messianic times. Leo issued a notably benevolent edict in favor of the Jews in 1519, in which he repealed the obligation of wearing the Jewish badge in the papal dominions in France and allowed it to fall into disuse in Italy. He employed the converted Jewish musician, *Giovanni Maria, took a lively interest in Jewish literature, and permitted the printing of the Talmud. It is significant at this time that when Johann *Reuchlin made his appeal to the pope from the sentence of the Dominicans of Cologne, he requested the papal physician Bonet de Lattes, a Jew, to support him, such was the influence and esteem the latter enjoyed at the papal court. A kinsman and successor to Leo, *Clement vii (1523–34), showed even greater benevolence toward the Jews, so much so in fact that he was called "the favorer of Israel." He was especially noted for his close and friendly relations with David *Reuveni and Solomon *Molcho. His outstandingly favorable attitude was continued by his successor, PAUL III (1534–49), who invited refugee Marranos from Portugal to settle in Ancona and who employed Jacob *Mantino as his physician. The reluctance of the Medici popes to authorize the Inquisition in Portugal or to permit it to go into effect, although ultimately defeated, typifies the general tolerance of their approach to the Jews.

By now the spirit of the Counter-Reformation was beginning to make itself felt. *Julius III (1550–55) was personally friendly enough; he employed *Amatus Lusitanus as his physician, confirmed the rights of the Marranos of Ancona, condemned the blood libel, and prohibited the baptism of Jewish children without the consent of their parents. But the reactionary party led by Cardinal Caraffa, the embodiment of the Counter-Reformation, ultimately gained the upper hand. Before long this resulted in the establishment in 1553 of the House of *Catechumens (*Casa dei Neofiti*) in Rome at the expense of the local Jewish communities, the confiscation and burning of the Talmud (1553), the institution of the Congregation of the Holy Office with the surveillance of the Jews as one of its functions (1553), and the institution of a regular censorship of Hebrew books (1554). After the brief papacy (April 1555) of MARCELLUS II, Cardinal Caraffa himself became pope as Paul IV (1555–59), and the spirit of the Counter-Reformation triumphed with him and through his personal influence. The reaction against the Jews (especially in Rome and the Papal States, where he was able to carry his policy into effect) began immediately after his accession with the fanatical bull *Cum nimis absurdum* of 1555, which in effect drove the Jews out of civilized life and began the age of the *ghetto in Italy with all its horrors. Pope Paul IV was, moreover, personally responsible for the treacherous and faithless onslaught on the Marranos of Ancona, as a result of which some 25 were burned at the stake in the spring and summer of 1556. When he died on Aug. 18, 1559, there was a general reaction against his severity and a story is told that his overthrown statue was surmounted by a yellow hat such as he had imposed on the Jews of his dominions.

PIUS IV (1559–65), Paul's successor, brought a brief respite, and in 1562 he modified the severity of the enactments of his predecessor, even permitting the printing of the Talmud with certain omissions or, without them, under a different name (1564). He also induced the Holy Roman emperor to withdraw an edict of expulsion against the Jews of Bohemia, and eased living conditions in the newly established Roman ghetto by prohibiting the increase of rentals there. He was succeeded by Pius V (1566–72), who, as Cardinal Ghislieri, had formerly been at the head of the Roman Inquisition, in which capacity he led the assault on Jewish literature during the preceding decade. With him the policy of repression triumphed again; the regulations of 1555 were renewed and the concessions made by his predecessor revoked. In 1567/68 he forbade Jews of the Papal States to lend money at interest, and his bull *Hebraeorum gens* of 1569 expelled Jews from the smaller places in the papal dominions, with the exception of Rome and Ancona in Italy, and Avignon, Carpentras, and two other places in France. His personal zeal, moreover, was responsible for the introduction of the ghetto system into the duchies of Urbino and Tuscany (1570–71).

There were some slight ameliorations under *Gregory XIII (1572–85), but he was responsible for the renewal of the institution of the conversionist sermons which Jews were compelled to attend, and for the stringent prohibition of the practice of medicine by the Jews among Christians. The latter marked the end of the tradition of Jewish medical practitioners in the service of the Vatican, which had been commonplace since the 13th century.

There was again a brief favorable interlude under Sixtus V (1585–90), who made a determined attempt to restore the economic prosperity of the papal states and for that reason reversed the anti-Jewish policy of former popes, although before his election he had shown great severity against the Marranos when he was inquisitor in Venice. He had in his service as his majordomo Joao Lopes, a Marrano who had reverted to Judaism. He also granted Meir *Magino a monopoly for an improved method of silk manufacture, accepted the dedication to himself in David de' Pomis' dictionary, *Zemaḥ David*, and protected the Jews of the Papal States physically on more than one occasion. His bull *Christiana pietas* of 1586 revoked the persecutory edicts of his predecessors and permitted the Jews to return to the Papal States, to employ Christian servants as before, and to practice medicine. Moreover, he reversed the policy of former popes in regard to the practice of usury, permitting the opening of loan banks in the Papal States and issuing licenses or "absolutions" for Jewish moneylenders in various parts of Italy, which for the next 100 years provided a considerable income to the papal treasury. This favorable interlude was short-lived, ending soon after the death of Sixtus V. *Clement VIII (1592–1605) must at one time have been on friendly terms with Jews, for a Ḥannukkah lamp bearing his coat of arms as cardinal is preserved in the Victoria and

Albert Museum, London. Nevertheless, in the year after his accession he issued the bull *Caeca et obdurata* (1593), which reinforced once more the persecutory policy of Paul IV and Pius V, except for the prohibition on moneylending, which remained permissible for some time longer.

From this period on, for between 200 and 300 years, there was no intermission or change in the policy of the popes who, absorbed with fears for the position of Roman Catholicism in Europe, considered that the repression of the Jewish communities under their control was an essential part of Catholic orthodoxy. Still, they preserved something of traditional balance in protecting the Jews of their dominions from the physical violence and the more fantastic antisemitic allegations common elsewhere. Occasionally, they were successfully appealed to by the Jewish communities of other countries for protection against such violence and allegations. With the extension of the area of Italy politically subject to the pope, the Roman policy was extended to the Jewish communities of the duchy of Ferrara (in 1625) and to Urbino (in 1634) by Urban VIII (1623–44), who was responsible also for prohibiting tombstones in Jewish cemeteries. He also legalized forced baptisms in certain circumstances, declaring that the baptism of the head of a family could include, if he so desire, everyone in his household who were under age or dependent on him. Popes Innocent X (1644–55), Alexander VII (1655–67), and Clement IX (1667–69) enforced the policy somewhat less severely, the last named in his brief pontificate abolishing (in 1668) the humiliating race run by the Jews at carnival time. In 1674 *Clement X (1670–76) suspended the activities of the Portuguese Inquisition which were, however, renewed in 1681 by Innocent XI (1676–89). Innocent again (and this time finally) prohibited the practice of moneylending by the Jews of the papal possessions and suppressed their loan banks, a measure so harsh that its execution had to be twice postponed, eventually bringing the Jewish communities to the edge of ruin. At the same time this pope discouraged forced baptisms (which decreased somewhat under his rule) and in 1685 secured the release by the republic of Venice of the Jewish prisoners captured in the Morea.

With the 18th century conditions deteriorated still further. Renewed severity began under *Benedict XIII (1724–30) and *Clement XII (1730–40). The latter commissioned Cardinal Petra in 1733 to draw up a new anti-Jewish code, which introduced various new degradations, e.g., that the Jewish badge was to be worn even while traveling and that rabbis were not to be permitted to have any distinguishing costume. In 1766 this code was renewed and rigorously enforced by *Benedict XIV (1740–58) and the condition of the Jews of the papal dominions reached its nadir. The pope reinstituted rigorous measures against Hebrew literature, and in 1747 he ruled that a Jewish child once baptized, even against Church law, had to be brought up as a Christian. This ruling gave impetus to the scandal of forced baptisms, which from then on assumed tragic prominence in the history of Roman Jewry. Yet even this pontiff did not forget the nobler papal traditions. When in 1758 the Jewish communities of Poland appealed to him, through Jacob Selek, for protection against the wave of blood libels which were becoming a perpetual menace to their lives, he sympathetically referred the matter to the Holy Office of the Inquisition, an act which resulted in the famous report of Cardinal Ganganelli condemning the libel. In 1759 this report was presented to and approved by the next pope, *Clement XIII (1758–69), who communicated the findings to the papal nuncio in Warsaw and instructed him to protect the Jews from violence in this matter. Ten years later, Ganganelli himself became pope, as Clement XIV (1769–74). Profoundly moved by the misery into which the Jewish communities of the Papal States had fallen, he wanted to improve their economic condition. Among other reforms, he accorded Jews some freedom of occupation and released them from the immediate jurisdiction of the Inquisition. He showed marked favor to the Roman Jewish leader, Ezekiel Ambron. This proved to be only a brief interlude, however, for with his successor, Pius VI (1775–98), a complete reaction set in. The *Editto sopra gli ebrei* (1775) of Pius codified, reinforced, and intensified the whole of former, degrading anti-Jewish legislation, however barbarous it was, and went so far even as to forbid Jews from passing the night outside the ghetto, under pain of death. These were the conditions under which the Jews of the Papal States continued until the armies of the French Revolution overthrew the temporal power of the popes in 1797–98 and as a matter of course abolished all discriminatory legislation. After the overthrow of Napoleon, Pius VII (1800–23) led the way in the reaction which followed throughout Italy. (The papal possessions in the south of France, with control over the Jewish communities of that region, were by now lost.) To an antiquated religious obscurantism was now added the more cogent consideration that Jews were correctly suspected of sympathy with the liberal movement in Italian politics. From this time down to the overthrow of the temporal power of the papacy, the old policy of repression was renewed, from this point of view the Papal States now being the most reactionary area in Europe. Pope Pius VII returned from his long exile determined to reestablish the pre-revolutionary ecclesiastical regime down to the last detail, including the ghetto, conversionist sermons, and so on. Only the wearing of the Jewish badge, though nominally prescribed, was not actually enforced. Pius VII was, however, almost moderate as compared with his successor, Leo XII (1823–29), who revived the most fierce anti-Jewish prejudices, even to the point of having the gates of the ghettos restored and reenacting the *Editto sopra gli ebrei* of 1775. Pope Pius VIII (1829–30) found time in the course of his brief pontificate to forbid the Jews to enter into personal relations with Christians for any purpose except in the course of business. His successor, Gregory XVI (1831–46), even reimposed the carnival tax, which had replaced the old abuse of the Jewish carnival race, with all its degrading associations. In 1836 he expelled the few Jews who had settled "illegally" in Bologna. Pius IX (1846–78) began his pontificate as the hope of the liberal movement, introducing several measures for the amelioration of the position of the Jews of the Papal States. Later, however, he too turned to reaction, and though his personal attitude remained not unfriendly he kept to all of his predecessors' restrictions with an unabated vigor. Under him even the abusive forced baptism of children prevailed, the most notorious (but not the only or the last) instance being the infamous *Mortara case of 1858, in which the pope maintained an absolutely unyielding attitude.

After the fall of Rome and the end of the Church's temporal power in 1870, up to which time the policy of repression had continued in force almost unmodified, the relationship of the papacy with the Jews inevitably changed. It was no longer a question of political treatment in an area subject to direct papal rule, but of a general attitude toward them on the intellectual and theological plane, political influence being therefore indirect. The papal attitude was inevitably influenced to some extent by the natural sympathy of the Jews in Catholic countries with the secular and anti-clerical party and their natural antagonism to Church influence in education. Although Leo XIII (1878–1903) was guilty in 1895 of the blunder of sending his blessing to the clerical-antisemitic coalition in Austria, he did, on the other hand, try to some extent to moderate passions in France. In 1892 he called on all right-thinking persons in that country, including Protestants and Jews, to unite against the "enemies of religion and society," i.e., the Freemasons and secularists. *Pius X (1903–14), though no less opposed to modernism, was not as interested in political matters as his predecessor. Early in 1904 he received Theodor *Herzl in audience, his secretary of state subsequently expressing mild sympathy with the humanitarian, though not the political objectives of Zionism. Benedict XV (1914–22), on the other hand, though he vaguely endorsed the *Balfour Declaration in an interview with Nahum *Sokolow, afterward expressed grave concern over the control of the holy places in Palestine. *Pius XI (1922–39) was confronted with the problems which arose with the triumph of the Nazi movement in Germany and antisemitism in Italy, and expressed his disapproval of racism in the most outspoken fashion, declaring that "spiritually we are all Semites." In 1935, at the time of the revival of the blood libel in Germany, he formally accepted from Cecil Roth a copy of his new edition of Pope Clement XIV's report condemning the libel, thereby confirming in effect the declaration of his predecessor. His successor, *Pius XII (1939–58), though less outspoken at a period of greater danger and failing even to condemn publicly the deportations and annihilation of European Jewry, nevertheless, on the occupation of Rome by Germans in 1943, received many refugees in the Vatican, and thus set the example for, even if he did not inspire, the protection of the Jews of Italy by the Catholic population. His reaction to the establishment of a Jewish state was unfavorable, since this falsified the Catholic interpretation of prophecy. The personal relations of *John XXIII (1958–63) with individual Jews were cordial both before and after his elevation to the papacy, and as cardinal he showed active sympathy with the victims of Nazi persecution. Jews moreover shared in the atmosphere of tolerance toward non-Catholics which became manifest during his pontificate. Under his successor Paul VI (1963–1978), the Second Vatican Council adopted a schema deploring antisemitism and stating that the blame for Jesus' death must be attributed to some of his contemporaries and not to the Jewish people as a whole. The declaration was less forthright than had been advocated by John XXIII but its spirit led to important modifications in Catholic textbooks. In 1964 Paul visited Christian holy places in Israel for a day.

Paul VI was followed by John Paul I (1978) whose sudden death, a month after his election, cut short his papacy.

*John Paul II (1978–2005) succeeded John Paul I, his pontificate of 27 years becoming the third longest in Church history. The first Polish pope, the former Karol Wojtyla was a political activist who fought for justice and human rights and who vigorously opposed totalitarianism. Known as a defender of the Jewish people, his ideological focus, personal integrity, and lengthy tenure provided a stable platform for growth in Jewish-Catholic relations, as he sought to broaden the ecumenical and interreligious relations of the Church.

As a youth in Wadowice, he had extensive contacts with the Jewish community, a legacy which deeply informed his pontificate. As pope, he worked consistently to improve Jewish-Catholic relations, as well as Vatican-Israel relations. He was the first pope since Peter to visit a synagogue (the Great Synagogue of Rome in1986), a move seen as bridge-building by Jews and Catholics alike. During this visit, he acknowledged the filial ties of Christianity to Judaism, stating, "I am Joseph, your brother!" In June 1994, he established formal diplomatic relations between the Holy See and the State of Israel, a move that publicly acknowledged Israel's centrality for the Jewish people. In March 2000, he convened a Day of Pardon for the sins committed by Church members over the centuries, including all antisemitic actions, which he declared were "a sin against God and humanity."

John Paul II, the most widely traveled pope in history, made a historic visit to Israel in 2000. He visited Yad Vashem, where he paid homage to the victims of the Holocaust. At the Western Wall, he inserted a written apology to the Jewish people for antisemitic sins by Catholics into a crack in the wall.

John Paul II authored or commissioned several very important documents on the Churches' relations with the Jews including "We Remember: A Reflection on the Shoah" (1998; Commission for Religious Relations with the Jews). His focus was to affirm the special relationship between Christianity and the Jewish people and the permanent validity of God's on-going covenant with the Jews, as articulated in the groundbreaking work of the Second Vatican Council "Nostra Aetate." He challenged the Catholic Church throughout the world to repent of its past history of antisemitic actions and to strive for a fresh, deeper understanding of the Jews and Judaism within God's plan for salvation history, emphasizing the filial ties between Judaism and Christianity and denouncing supersecessionism. He was unafraid to ask if the Church's own attitudes allowed or encouraged the cataclysm of the Holocaust, and he diligently sought to battle against latent antisemitism in the Church. While affirming the right of the State of Israel to exist, the pope also established official contacts with the Palestine Liberation Organization, beginning in 1994, and culminating with the signing of a formal Basic Agreement in 2000. He opposed the invasion of Iraq in 2003, but welcomed its new government in 2004. Pope John Paul II also canonized more saints than any other pope in history. Two among them proved disconcerting in some Jewish circles: Edith Stein (d. 1942, canonized 1998), a Jewish convert to Catholicism who died in the Holocaust, and Pius XII (beatified though not yet canonized), who many felt should have done more to protect the Jewish people during the Holocaust.

BENEDICT XVI (2005–). The former Joseph Cardinal Ratzinger, an eminent theologian who served alongside John Paul II for many years as prefect for the Congregation of the Doctrine of the Faith, began his pontificate with a visit to the Roonstrasse Synagogue in Cologne, the oldest synagogue in northern Europe. During this visit, Benedict XVI, a German by birth, spoke out against "new signs of antisemitism" that are emerging in his home country, Europe, and throughout the world. This action is seen as an affirmation of the course of action and theological outlook begun during the Second Vatican Council, and continued in the ground-breaking work of Benedict's predecessor, John Paul II. In 2006 he visited Auschwitz, delivering a speech criticized by many for the failure to characterize the Holocaust explicitly as a crime of the German people against the Jews.

See entries on individual popes.

BIBLIOGRAPHY: E.A. Synan, *Popes and the Jews in the Middle Ages* (1965); S. Grayzel, *Church and the Jews in the XIIIth Century* (1933); idem, in: HJ, 2 (1940), 1–12; J. Parkes, *Conflict of the Church and the Synagogue* (1934); idem, *Jews in the Medieval Community* (1938); E. Rodocanachi, *Le Saint-Siège et les Juifs* (1891); I. Loeb, in: REJ, 1 (1880), 114–18, 293–8; M. Stern, *Urkundliche Beitraege ueber die Stellung der Paepste zu den Juden*, 2 vols. (1893–95); idem, *Die paepstlichen Bullen ueber die Blutbeschuldigung* (1893); P. Browe, *Judenmission in Mittelalter und die Paepste* (1942); K. Eubel, in: *Roemische Quartalschrift*, 7 (1903), 183–37.

[Cecil Roth / Claire Pfann (2nd ed.)]

POPLAR (Heb. צַפְצָפָה), tree. The *Populus euphratica* grows wild on the banks of the Jordan. Its leaves are usually broad though some are long and narrow, resembling those of the willow. In Israel the white poplar, *Populus alba*, is grown as an ornamental tree. It is a tall tree with a white bark, and the underside of its leaves are silvery white. This species, which flourishes on the banks of rivers, is one of the two that Ezekiel refers to as a tree growing by the side of water (Ezek. 17:5). It is possible that the white poplar was the *livneh* peeled by Jacob to place in front of the sheep (Gen. 30:37; but see *Storax). When stating that it was not permitted to use the poplar for the *willow branch, one of the *Four Species, the Talmud indicates its characteristics: "The poplar has a white stem, a round leaf, and an edge serrated like a sickle" (Suk. 34a), and notes that whereas the serrations of the leaf edges of the willow are small and dense, those of the poplar are like the teeth of a saw (Maim. Yad, Lulav 7:3–4). The warning against confusing the poplar with the willow was due to the fact that their names were interchanged.

BIBLIOGRAPHY: Loew, Flora, 3 (1924), 325–7, 338–9; J. Feliks, *Olam ha-Ẓome'aḥ ha-Mikra'i* (1968^2), 116–7. **ADD. BIBLIOGRAPHY:** J. Feliks, Ha-Tzome'aḥ, 135.

[Jehuda Feliks]

°**POPPAEA, SABINA**, second wife of Nero (62–65 C.E.). Josephus describes her as being sympathetic toward Judaism, even terming her a "god-fearing" woman (Ant., 20, 189–96). She twice interceded successfully on behalf of the Jews. When Josephus went to Rome in 64 C.E. to plead for the priests imprisoned by Felix, he was introduced to Poppaea by the Jewish actor *Aliturus. With her assistance the priests were freed and she bestowed many gifts on Josephus himself (Life, 16). On the second occasion she interceded on behalf of a delegation headed by the high priest *Ishmael b. Phabi, sent by the priests to Rome to appeal against a decision of the procurator *Festus, who had, at the request of *Agrippa II, ordered the demolition of a wall erected by the priests to prevent the king from viewing the proceedings in the Temple. Poppaea influenced Nero to uphold the appeal and the wall was allowed to stand. Tacitus, who makes no mention of her attitude toward the Jews, pictures Poppaea as a corrupt and cruel woman.

BIBLIOGRAPHY: Schuerer, Gesch, 1 (1901^3 and ^{4}), 579, 585, 591; 3 (1909^4), 64; Klausner, Bayit Sheni, 5 (1951^2), 26, 39, 167.

[Lea Roth]

POPPER, family of entrepreneurs and communal leaders in Bohemia. Members of the Popper family from Breznice, Bohemia, attended the Leipzig fairs from the late 17th century. WOLF POPPER, the "Primate of Bohemian Jewry," was in charge of the collection of taxes for 18 years (1749–67). His son ḤAYYIM (Joachim; 1720–1795) moved to Prague and was a successful merchant (woolens, potash, whalebone), banker, manufacturer, and co-lessee of the profitable tobacco monopoly. In 1775 he is mentioned as holding his father's position in perpetuity. Joachim Popper was a patron of literature and also donated large sums to philanthropy, maintaining a balance between Christian and Jewish causes. In 1790 he was ennobled as Edler von Popper in recognition of his contributions to the welfare of the state. On the day he received his patent of nobility he presented a petition to Leopold II requesting the introduction in Bohemia of the more liberal *Judenpatent* of Galicia, which included obligatory military service for Jews. However, a group of Prague Jews presented a counterproposal arguing against conscription. He suggested reform of the system of taxation in 1792, the same year he resigned from office. On his death he bequeathed large sums to charity, and provided for the creation of a synagogue in his home in which prayer and study were to be subsidized perpetually. He also stipulated that his firm continue to bear his name.

BIBLIOGRAPHY: S. Krauss, *Joachim Edler von Popper* (1926); idem, in: *Zeitschrift fuer die Geschichte der Juden in der Tschechoslo-*

vakei, 4 (1934), 40–44, 69–84; R. Kestenberg-Gladstein, *Neuere Geschichte der Juden in den boehmischen Laendern* (1969), index.

POPPER, DAVID (1843–1913), cellist and composer. Popper, son of a cantor, studied the violin at the Prague Conservatory but because of a shortage of cello students, he changed to cello and became a pupil of Julius Goltermann. At the age of 18 he was appointed assistant principal cellist of the Löwenberg Court Orchestra and at the age of 20 became famous as a concert artist after his first tour of Germany in 1863. From 1868 to 1873 he was first cellist at the Vienna Opera and the Vienna PO (the youngest player to hold such a post) and became a member of the Hubay Quartet. After 1896 he was professor at the Budapest Conservatory. He composed more than 75 works, including many solos for cello, which won favor among cellists. Among his compositions are four concertos for cello and orchestra (op. 8, 1871; op. 24, 1880; op. 59, 1880; op. 72, 1900); Requiem, op. 66 (1892); String Quartet, op. 74 (1905); and his manual *Hohe Schule des Violoncellspiels*, c. 1901 (a set of 40 studies that examine the positions of the left hand within a highly chromatic, Wagner-influenced setting) which remains in use until today.

BIBLIOGRAPHY: Grove Online; S. De'ak, *David Popper* (1980).

[Israela Stein (2nd ed.)]

POPPER, JOSEF (pseudonym, **Lynkeus**; 1838–1921), Austrian social philosopher, engineer, and inventor. Born in Kolin, Bohemia, Popper studied at Prague University. As a Jew, he was refused a teaching post at the university and worked for a while with the national railroads in Hungary. He then went to Vienna where, after a series of fairly humble jobs, he invented, at the age of 30, a device to prevent fur from accumulating on engine boilers. The meager profits from this and other inventions enabled him to devote his later years to writing on social reform. His pseudonym, Lynkeus, is the name of the keen-sighted, mythological, Argonaut helmsman.

As a scientist Popper was far ahead of his time. In 1862 he proposed a system for the electrical transmission of energy, but sent the monograph to the Vienna Academy of Sciences in a sealed letter to be opened 20 years later. He discussed the possible existence of quanta of energy before Max Planck enunciated the quantum theory; in 1884 he tried to relate matter and energy, 20 years before *Einstein's theory of relativity; and in 1888 discussed the possibility of lightweight steam engines for flying machines in a treatise, *Flugtechnik* (1889). In *Phantasien eines Realisten* (2 vols., 1899), suppressed by the Austrian government as "immoral," he anticipated, as Freud himself acknowledged, the fundamental basis from which the latter elaborated his theory of dreams.

Popper was best known, however, for his writings on social reform.

In his first work of this nature, *Das Recht zu Leben und die Pflicht zu Sterben…* (1878), he contrasted man's natural right to live with the alleged obligation to sacrifice himself when required to do so by the state. He denied that man has a duty to let himself be killed when ordered and, in *Die allgemeine Naehrpflicht als Loesung der sozialen Frage* (1912), advocated the right of the individual to live in freedom and dignity within the framework of a social system created for the benefit of its members. Popper's solution to social problems was the formation of a labor force (*Naehrarmee*) whose purpose was "producing or procuring all that physiology and hygiene show to be absolutely indispensable." This was to be regarded as a minimum contribution by every member of society. Popper's philosophy differed from Marxism, in that it was based on simple humanitarianism and common sense and endeavored to eliminate class hatred by a synthesis of socialism and realism. In trying to revive Voltaire's philosophy, he advocated a policy which in fact became crystallized in the modern welfare state.

Popper regarded metaphysics, theology, and traditional religion as harmful, and to be eliminated from an economically and socially reformed state. He saw religion, especially Christianity, as opposed to genuine individual human values, and believed that education, especially about the history of religions, could lead to a superstition-free culture.

Although he suffered considerable humiliation as a Jew, Popper refused to convert, and accused the German chancellor, Bismarck, of antisemitism in *Fuerst Bismarck und der Antisemitismus* (1886). He believed that only a Jewish state would eliminate antisemitism, and although he never took an active part in the Zionist movement he bequeathed his substantial collection of books to the National Library in Jerusalem.

Popper was a close friend of Albert Einstein, who described him as a "prophetic and saintly person" who had forecast that "the continued existence of mankind without organized planning is inconceivable." He was widely regarded as a genius, and a bust of him was erected in the Rathauspark in Vienna. It was destroyed by the Nazis in 1938. Popper's writings include *Die technischen Fortschritte nach ihrer aesthetischen und kulturellen Bedeutung* (1886), *Friedensvorschlaege, Schiedsgerichte, Voelkerbund* (1910), and *Krieg, Wehrpflicht und Staatsverfassung* (1921).

BIBLIOGRAPHY: J. Popper-Lynkeus, *Selbstbiographie* (1917); H.I. Wachtel, *Security for All and Free Enterprise: A Summary of the Social Philosophy of Josef Popper-Lynkeus* (1955), incl. bibl.; A. Gelber, *Joseph Popper-Lynkeus, sein Leben und sein Wirken* (1922); F. Wittels, *An End to Poverty* (1925); P. Edwards (ed.), *Encyclopedia of Philosophy*, 6 (1967), 401–7 (incl. bibl.); E. Relgis, *Der Humanitarismus und die "Allgemeine Naehrpflicht"* (1931).

[Josef J. Lador-Lederer.]

POPPER, JULIUS (1857–1893), Romanian explorer. Popper's father was the principal of the first Jewish school in Bucharest. After studying engineering in Paris, he went on a world trip during which he heard about gold deposits on Tierra del Fuego. His exploration of the island proved the stories to be true, and he accordingly designed a machine for extracting the gold. Establishing himself as ruler over the island, Popper gave it a code of laws and defended it against other adventurers.

POPPER, SIR KARL (**Raimund**; 1902–1994), philosopher. Popper was born in Vienna of Jewish parents who had converted to Christianity. In the early 1920s he worked with juvenile delinquents in Alfred *Adler's clinic in Vienna. In 1930 he became a secondary school teacher of mathematics and science. The rise of Fascism led to his leaving Austria in 1937, and until 1945 he taught philosophy at Canterbury University College, New Zealand, where he wrote *The Open Society and Its Enemies*. He then moved to the University of London, and in 1949 became professor of logic and scientific method at the London School of Economics. He was knighted in 1965, and in 1982 was made a Companion of Honour (CH). Popper's philosophical views were profoundly influenced by the Einsteinian revolution in physics.

As early as 1919 Popper began to draw the philosophical consequences of this revolution. He saw that the "inductive method," hitherto supposed to be the distinguishing mark of science, was a myth. Empirical evidence was used in science, not to establish cautious hypotheses, which is impossible, but to refute bold ones. The mark of a scientific theory was its refutability, and the scientific pretensions of those other contemporary revolutions in thought, the theories of *Marx, *Freud, and Adler, were suspect on this count. Popper's revolutionary philosophy of science was eventually published in *Die Logik der Forschung* (1934; *The Logic of Scientific Discovery*, 1959). He had close contact in these early years with the logical positivist movement. He criticized the postivists' inductivism, and their attempt to dismiss all metaphysics as meaningless. This, he argued, ignored the suggestive value of many metaphysical ideas for science. Popper wrote *The Open Society and Its Enemies* (2 vols., 1945, 1965), which criticized the authoritarian political philosophies then in vogue. He attacked their belief in the inexorable laws of history, and the idea that the task of the social sciences was to discern these laws and to prophesy the future development of society. His elaboration of these criticisms, and his positive views on the method of the social sciences, later appeared in his book *The Poverty of Historicism* (1957). From the time Popper began working in England a stream of articles issued forth, witnessing to his new, more metaphysical interests in such things as indeterminism and emergent evolutionism. A collection of these, entitled *Conjectures and Refutations: The Growth of Scientific Knowledge*, appeared in 1963. Popper also wrote an interesting autobiography, *Unended Quest* (1976). Popper's influence, through his fertile and original contributions to a wide variety of problems, has been great: his concept of *critical fallibilism* is an important trend in contemporary philosophy. His view that to be scientific a theory must be falsifiable, and his insistence that the so-called "scientific socialism" of Marxism is not scientific, have had profound effects upon postwar Western thought. Popper is often grouped with such influential writers in Britain as George Orwell and Frederick von Hayek whose key works, which also appeared in the mid-late 1940s, undermined the intellectual attractiveness of Marxism in the West and, eventually, everywhere.

BIBLIOGRAPHY: M.A. Bunge (ed.), *Critical Approach to Science and Philosophy* (1964), incl. his bibl.; K. Popper, in: C.A. Mace (ed.), *British Philosophy in the Mid-Century* (1957), 155–91 (philosophical autobiography); P. Edwards (ed.), *Encyclopedia of Philosophy* (1967), index. **ADD. BIBLIOGRAPHY:** M.H. Hacohen, *Karl Popper: The Formative Years, 1902–1945* (2000).

[Alan E. Musgrave]

POPPER, SIEGFRIED (1848–1933), Austro-Hungarian rear admiral and naval engineer. From 1871 to 1904 he served as an engineer on battleships and was then appointed head of naval construction with the rank of rear admiral. Popper developed new methods of naval warfare and almost all the Austrian battleships of his time, as well as torpedo boats and fast destroyers, were constructed under his direction. After his retirement he served in the Technische Hochschule in Vienna but was dismissed through Nazi pressure in 1933.

POPPER, WILLIAM (1874–1963), U.S. Orientalist and biblical scholar. Born in St. Louis, Missouri, Popper served from 1902 to 1905 as an associate editor of the *Jewish Encyclopedia* and acting head of the Oriental Department of the New York Public Library. During this period and again in 1919/20, he also lectured on Semitic languages at Columbia University. From 1905 onward he taught at the University of California, Berkeley, becoming a full professor and head of the Semitic department in 1922. He retired in 1945.

Popper's biblical research centered on the literary and stylistic aspects of Isaiah (*Parallelism in Isaiah*, 1923), whose text he tried to reconstruct, publishing with an English translation of his own (*The Prophetic Poetry of Isaiah*, 1931). In the field of Arabic studies his critical editions and translations of Arabic historical texts of the 15th century have made this period accessible to non-Arabist historians. Among his works are: parts of the critical edition of Yūsuf ibn Taghrī-Birdī's *Al-Nujūm Al-Zâhira fī Mulûk Miṣr waal-Kâhira* (History of Egypt; 1909) and part of his *Hawādith al-Duhūr* (4 vols., 1930–42). *History of Egypt* (8 vols., 1954–63) is the English translation to Taghrī-Birdī's Arabic Annals. *The Cairo Nilometer* (1951) presents studies in Ibn Taghrī-Birdī's "Chronicles of Egypt." *Egypt and Syria under the Circassian Sultans 1382–1468* (2 vols., 1955–57) offers systematic notes to Ibn Taghrī-Birdī's chronicles. In the field of Jewish scholarship he wrote *The Censorship of Hebrew Books* (1899, reprinted with introduction by M. Carmilly-Weinberger, 1969). On the occasion of his 75th birthday, Popper was presented with a Jubilee Volume (*Semitic and Oriental Studies*, ed. by W.J. Fischel, 1951).

BIBLIOGRAPHY: W.J. Fischel, in: JAOS, 84 (1964), 213–220.

[Walter Joseph Fischel]

POPPER BOZIAN, WOLF (d. 1625), merchant and banker in Cracow. His father, Israel Gershon ha-Kohen, was from *Checiny; and his wife, Cyrl, was the daughter of Judah Lewek *Landau, one of the heads of the Jewish community in Kazimierz. Popper Bozian engaged in import, especially of cloth from *Cologne, and in financial transactions in a number of fairs which took place in several towns in Poland and Schleswig, from which businesses he became very rich. His will revealed that his financial transactions, which amounted to many thousands of zlotys, were often carried out with use of special promissory notes (*mamram). His success in business was used as an excuse for blaming the Jews for a period of commercial strife in Cracow in the second decade of the 17th century. In a pamphlet entitled *Zwierciadło korony polskiej* ("The Mirror of the Polish Kingdom," Cracow, 1618), the antisemite Sebastian *Miczyński describes Popper Bozian as a businessman who owned seven stores in Cracow and whose transactions extended to many towns and amounted to more than 300,000 zlotys. In order to incite mob hatred, Miczynski also implicated him in a blood libel. In 1620 Popper Bozian financed the construction of a synagogue (Popper Shul, destroyed by the Nazis) and a *bet midrash*.

BIBLIOGRAPHY: M. Balaban, *Historja żydów w Krakowie i na Kazimierzu*, 1 (1931), 75, 199, 238, 270–6.

[Arthur Cygielman]

POPPERS (Popers), JACOB BEN BENJAMIN HAKOHEN (d. 1740), German rabbi. Born in Prague, Poppers studied under his father and in various yeshivot. He was subsequently appointed rabbi of Coblenz and of Trier, in the Rhineland. He declined an invitation to Halberstadt in 1718 but accepted the rabbinate of Frankfurt where he headed a large yeshivah. His disciples included Jacob Berlin, Joseph *Steinhardt, and Joseph Wassertrilling. Poppers corresponded with the great scholars of his time on halakhic and contemporary problems. He was among those who imposed a ban on Moses Hayyim *Luzzatto in 1725 for teaching Kabbalah and on suspicion that he adhered to the Shabbatean doctrine. Compelled to leave Italy, Luzzatto arrived in Frankfurt, where he was summoned before the *bet din* of Poppers and, after much discussion, was obliged again to promise not to teach Kabbalah nor to engage in its study until he was 40 years old. Poppers was the author of *Shav Ya'akov* (Frankfurt, 1741–42), responsa in two parts. Some of his novellae are included in *Minḥat Kohen* (Fuerth, 1741) by Shabbetai b. Moses. Poppers died in Frankfurt.

BIBLIOGRAPHY: M. Horovitz, *Frankfurter Rabbinen* (1969^2), 117–24.

[Jacob Rothschild]

POPPERS, MEIR BEN JUDAH LOEB HA-KOHEN (d. 1662), kabbalist of Ashkenazi descent who was active in Jerusalem after 1640. A pupil of Jacob Ẓemaḥ, he became the last editor of the Lurianic writings. He divided the mass of Vital's different versions of Luria's teachings into three parts, *Derekh Eẓ Ḥayyim*, *Peri Eẓ Ḥayyim*, and *Nof Eẓ Ḥayyim*. Poppers' version became the one in most widespread use in Poland and Germany. After 1640 he composed a large number of his own kabbalistical writings in the vein of Lurianic Kabbalah. They are said to have comprised 39 books, each of which contained the word *or* ("light") in its title, the entire corpus being called *Kokhevei Or*.

Several parts have been preserved (Ms. Jerusalem no. 101, Ms. R. Alter of Gur no. 170). They included commentaries on *Sefer Bahir*, on Naḥmanides' Torah commentary, on the Zohar, and on Luria's writings according to his own edition (Ms. Jerusalem no. 102). In the latter manuscript Poppers reports that he had studied Luria's writings for 17 years. Only two of these books have been published: *Or Ẓaddikim* (Hamburg, 1690), written in Jerusalem in 1643, and later incorporated in Moses *Katz's compilation, *Or ha-Yashar* (Amsterdam, 1709); and *Me'orei Or*, a dictionary of kabbalistic symbolism, published with copious notes by Jacob Vilna and Nathan Neta Mannheim under the title *Me'orot Natan* (Frankfurt, 1709). In addition, *Mesillot Ḥokhmah*, a booklet summarizing Lurianic metaphysics in 32 paragraphs, later published under Poppers' name (Shklov, 1785), was first printed anonymously (Wandsbeck, c. 1700). Poppers is credited with the authorship of a graphic description and summary of the Lurianic system, in the form of a scroll, published under the title *Ilan ha-Gadol* (1864). This tree, however, shows the distinct influence of Israel *Sarug's version of Lurianism, which is not to be found in Poppers' other writings. Part of his homilies on the Torah were published as *Tal Orot* (1911).

He mentions as his teachers one R. Israel Ashkenazi and his father-in-law, Azariah Ze'evi (probably from Hebron). During the 1650s Poppers spent about two years in Constantinople. He died in Jerusalem.

BIBLIOGRAPHY: Azulai, 1 (1852), 120 no. 27; Frumkin-Rivlin, 2 (1928), 38–39; G. Scholem, *Kitvei Yad be-Kabbalah* (1930), 146–9.

[Gershom Scholem]

POPULATION.

Methodological Uncertainties

Because of the great difficulties in ascertaining human population data in general, and Jewish data in particular, especially in ancient and medieval times, a word of caution is even more necessary here than in most other areas of historical and sociological research. Even the size of the world Jewish population is questionable because the two largest countries of Jewish settlement, the United States and the Soviet Union, were supplying only inadequate estimates, rather than scientifically verifiable facts (see below). The same holds true for many other countries embracing substantial numbers of Jews.

In their report to the International Congress of Historical Sciences in 1950 Carlo Cippola and his associates reported on behalf of their Committee that "in the eyes of demographers bent on scientific precision and certainty all demographic research undertaken for any period before the 18th century runs the risk of appearing as a mere fantasy." Nevertheless, the Committee felt impelled to present some results of their investigations, as have many other scholars dealing with population statistics of past ages. They have felt that the rise or fall of populations, and the concomitant facts relating to natality and mortality rates, sex and age distribution, marriages and divorces, and so forth, are too vital for the understanding of all other socioeconomic, political, and even intellectual developments for scholarship to be satisfied with a resigned *ignoramus et ignorabimus*. Many demographers and historians are, indeed, convinced, to cite the Spanish sociologist Javier Ruiz Almanza's pithy epigram, that "history without demography is an enigma, just as is demography without history."

Population *censuses were not completely absent in the ancient and medieval worlds. As a matter of fact, an Egyptian record of about 3000 B.C.E., preserved on the so-called Palermo Stone, gives us a fair idea of how the population was counted at that early age. Egyptian censuses were rather frequently conducted during the Middle Kingdom; they went into such details as naming all members of the respective families. In ancient Israel, too, the censuses attributed to Moses and David have a high degree of probability as to fact, if not with respect to the actual results. However, these counts were much too sporadic to serve as reliable guides. Even modern censuses become truly dependable only when they are periodically repeated and employ the same basic methods. If their final results are not absolutely accurate, they at least reveal some fundamental trends in growth or decline and other variations during the intervening periods. Ancient and medieval censuses, even when recorded, were taken too far apart, and used unknown or, at least, variable statistical methods. Hence they furnish almost no guidance for the prevailing trends. The resultant figures, moreover, are frequently available to us only in texts reproduced by successive copyists over many generations, or even centuries. It is a well-known fact that copyists are more likely to err with respect to numbers than in regard to almost any other words, because such changes, as a rule, do not make the meaning of the entire phrase or sentence incomprehensible. It is enough, for example, for a Hebrew copyist to omit a *lamed* in *shalosh* to produce the word *shesh* which immediately doubles the figure. In its abbreviated form a change from a *dalet* (representing four) to a *resh* (two hundred), or vice versa, can play havoc with any number intended by the author. Nor does any proofreader or ordinary reader, unless well-informed about the particular situation, notice such changes which, by constant repetition, sometimes assume the appearance of dependability.

Even informed students, moreover, often approach the recorded figures with set presuppositions. Until the 18th century Jewish, as well as general, European opinion believed that ancient times were in all aspects more glorious than the Middle Ages or the modern period. They assumed that ancient populations were far larger than those familiar to them from observation or readings of more recent events. Even so critical a thinker as Montesquieu was convinced that the world population of his day did not total more than one-tenth of what it had been in antiquity. The first scholar to question these assumptions was David Hume. Subsequently, the pendulum swung to the other extreme. As in other areas of life, most scholars were convinced of mankind's gradual progress, despite occasional relapses, and believed that the size of human populations, too, as a rule showed an upward curve. In time, however, more careful studies revealed that there were constant ups and downs, with periods of growth followed by those of decline, and the other way around. Another drawback of the recorded censuses and other population records consisted in their underlying purposes. Ancient and medieval governments rarely, if ever, undertook counting population out of general scientific curiosity. They did it principally in order to secure lists of prospective taxpayers, soldiers, or both. Understandably, since they often served as instruments of greater fiscal oppression and more effective military levies, censuses were heartily disliked by the masses of the population. Thus readily grew the widespread superstition that censuses caused divine wrath and retribution. Even King David's census provoked the biblical writer to observe: "And again the anger of the Lord was kindled against Israel, and He moved David against them, saying: 'Go, number Israel and Judah'" (II Sam. 24:1). In fact, it is related, the king later repented his irreligious act. As a result of this popular resentment many persons undoubtedly succeeded in evading the count, thus greatly reducing its value. A remarkable talmudic anecdote states that when Persian tax collectors arrived in a city to number the Jews subject to the capitation tax, the latter were forewarned by their leaders to go into hiding until the collectors departed. The community at large had a self-interest in reducing the figures thus obtained because it afterwards had to negotiate with the government for some lump-sum payment to cover the total tax due.

Bearing all these deficiencies in mind, scholarship must nevertheless make concerted efforts to come to grips with the demographic facts of life in both the past and the present. Wherever possible a number of convergent hypotheses, even if by themselves none too reliable, may offer at least some more or less acceptable approximations. Yet in the summary here presented its often extremely tentative nature must never be lost sight of.

Ancient Israel

There are only a few direct pieces of information about the population of ancient Israel. Some of it is quite dubious. The well-known figure of 600,000 adult male Israelites (601,730 men aged 20 or over in addition to 23,000 male levites, including minors, according to Num. 26:51 and 62), who are said to have been counted by Moses after the Exodus from Egypt, has long been discounted by critical scholars. Including the women and minors, this number would have represented a population of about 2,500,000, much too large for the small province of Goshen in northeastern Egypt where the majority of Israelites had lived before their departure. The addition of some non-Israelites of the "mixed multitude" (Ex. 12:37–38) who joined the Exodus was undoubtedly more or less balanced by those Israelites who refused to leave the "fleshpots" of Egypt and remained behind. It is to them and their descendants that some Egyptian papyri of the 12th century B.C.E. refer when they speak of some "Hebrew" (*apiru*) still living in Egypt at the time. Moreover, a mass of 2,500,000 persons crossing the "Red Sea" and migrating through the desert for 40 years staggers the imagination. Even if we accept the extreme emendation by some scholars which reduces the figure to 6,000 adult males, it would still leave a considerable number of 25,000 or more persons finally entering Canaan, where they may have joined some descendants of the ancient Ḫabiru ("Hebrews") who had never left Palestine for Egypt but had slowly been occupying Canaanite territory from the days of the El-Amarna Letters in the 15th and 14th centuries B.C.E.

Much more informative are the figures yielded by the census conducted by Joab at the behest of King David. Here there is a major difficulty in having two apparently contradictory records. The figures given in II Samuel 24:9, namely that "there were in Israel eight hundred thousand valiant men that drew the sword; and the men of Judah were five hundred thousand men," seem to be controverted by the report in I Chronicles (21:5) that "all they of Israel were a thousand thousand and a hundred thousand men that drew sword; and Judah was four hundred three-score and ten thousand men that drew sword." Whichever figure is taken – and with some difficulty they can be harmonized – it indicates a population of well over 5,000,000, which is possible, if at all, only if Joab counted the population, including the subject peoples, of the entire Davidic empire from parts of Syria to the border of Egypt. In that case, the Israelite population doubtless formed but a minority of those counted. If, in the following generations, Israel rapidly assimilated some of the subject tribes in its midst, the area under its control had shrunk considerably under Solomon and his successors. Another figure of great interest is given in the Assyrian king Sennacherib's boast that at the time of his siege of Jerusalem in 701 B.C.E. he had deported 200,150 men, women, and children from the Judean kingdom, all of which except the capital had been occupied by the Assyrian troops. This number too, has been subjected to much carping by modern critics. One of them, Karl Ungnad, suggested that it be reduced to 2,150 persons – a number which would have rendered the royal boast entirely meaningless. While Sennacherib's grandiloquent inscription may indeed have exaggerated considerably the number of prisoners taken back to Assyria, it must to some extent have approximated reality.

Some of the figures here quoted are partially supported by the existence in the country of a large number of "cities." As early as the 15th century B.C.E. the famous Egyptian inscription by Thutmoses III named more than 100 Palestinian cities conquered in an area covering only about one-fourth of what was later to become the land of Israel and Judah, which bears out the development of some 400 "municipalities" under the Israelitic regime indicated by both the ancient *Onomastica* and modern geographic research. These cities were for the most part very small. Even in Israel's heyday their vast majority embraced only 1,000 inhabitants or less, but from Canaanite times on they had served the purpose of protecting the farming population against raids from hostile outsiders. Most farmers seem indeed to have lived within walled cities while cultivating their soil by "going out" to their fields or vineyards in the morning and returning in the evening. (This is, therefore, the sequence of the well-known biblical phrase.) Incidentally, this situation explains why ancient Palestine did not have any such major cleavage between the urban and rural populations as has characterized the medieval and modern West.

Finally, there is also some interesting data concerning the kingdom of Judah during the Babylonian conquests and its aftermath in the years 597–582 B.C.E. One source reports that 3,023 Judeans had been deported in the seventh year of Nebuchadnezzar, 832 Jerusalemites in the 18th year, 745 Judeans in the 23rd year, together "all the persons were four thousand and six hundred" (Jer. 52:28–30). In contrast, II Kings (24:14–16) states that the Babylonians "carried away all Jerusalem, and all the princes, and all the mighty men of valor, even ten thousand captives, and all the craftsmen and the smiths." Somewhat differently, the figure of 7,000 is mentioned in the same context. These contradictory data have been subjected to a variety of interpretations, but with some effort and ingenuity they can be harmonized. In any case, both sets of figures evidently refer only to a small elite of landowners, priests, and craftsmen whose absence would deprive the subject population of leadership and the supply of arms, but the Babylonians must have simultaneously deported a great mass of captives from the lower classes. Archaeological discoveries have confirmed the fact that after 586 B.C.E. the Judean countryside was quite deserted, although the conquerors may have brought in some replacements in addition to maintaining their own garrisons on the spot. This exchange of populations had long been practiced by the Assyrians in order to stem irredentist movements and, a century and a quarter before the fall of Jerusalem, they had deported a great many Northern Israelites before and after the fall of Samaria in 733–719 B.C.E.

In short, on the basis of these and numerous other scattered data, supported by a number of demographic considerations, the present writer ventured to propose the highly tentative Table 1, Ancient Population for the approximate population of ancient Israel and Judah between 1000 and 586 B.C.E.: The decline in the population, here assumed, may well be explained by the general deterioration in the political and economic strength of the two kingdoms in the intervening four centuries. It did not seriously affect, however, the number of "cities" (about 300–400 in the whole country and about 60–70 in Judah alone), the population of which may have been greatly reduced, but which continued to function as more or less autonomous municipalities. These avowedly extremely tentative "guesstimates," made more than 40 years ago, still seen to offer the most acceptable approximations. The enormous amount of additional archaeological and other source material and interpretation which have since been brought forth by biblical scholars has, if anything, helped to support them.

Table 1. Ancient Israel: Approximate Population of Ancient Israel and Judah between 1000 and 586 B.C.E.

	1000	733/701	586
Judah	450,000	300,000–350,000	150,000
Israel	1,350,000	800,000–1,000,000	–
Total Israelite and Judean population	1,800,000	1,100,000–1,350,000	150,000
Per square mile	40	28–32	24

Second Commonwealth

During the restoration period the recovery of Palestine's Jewish population was very slow. At first the Second Commonwealth embraced only an area of some 1,200 square miles in and around Jerusalem. According to Ezra (2:64–65), "the whole congregation [of returning exiles] together was forty and two thousand three hundred and threescore, besides their manservants and their maidservants, of whom there were seven thousand three hundred thirty and seven; and they had two hundred singing men and singing women." Even adding to these figures a number of survivors from the pre-Exilic period, the population of the Commonwealth could not have amounted to much more than 60,000–70,000. In time, this population must have increased considerably so that, writing in the third century B.C.E., Pseudo-Hecataeus could estimate the number of Jerusalem's inhabitants alone at 120,000 (Jos., Apion, 1:197). There also were growing Jewish settlements outside the boundaries of the autonomous Jewish province, particularly in Galilee (still called the Gelil Ha-Goyim; "the district of gentiles"), along the coast, and in Transjordan. Yet at the outbreak of the Hasmonean Revolt in 165 B.C.E. the total Jewish population in the country still was very small. It grew by leaps and bounds, however, after the establishment of the sovereign Judean state by Simeon Maccabee in 140 B.C.E. and particularly after the annexation of large territories conquered by his successors, John *Hyrcanus and Alexander *Yannai. It now included a considerable number of Idumeans and others forcibly converted to Judaism by these conquerors, whose amalgamation with the older Jewish inhabitants proceeded apace with great speed. In the days of Jesus and the *tannaim* Galilee was as Jewish as the environs of Jerusalem. This growth was not stemmed by the occupation of the country by the Romans under Pompey in 63 B.C.E. and the conversion of Judea into a sub-province of the Roman Empire. Only some cities, organized along the lines of a Hellenistic polis along the coast and in Transjordan, were now under the control of their "Greek" city councils, with the Jews often constituting but a tolerated minority.

During the two centuries of Hasmonean and Herodian rule over Palestine the Jewish people expanded numerically to an unprecedented degree not only in Palestine but also in other lands, in part by active proselytization. Curiously, the Phoenician-Carthaginian Diaspora, long a major factor throughout the Mediterranean world, suddenly vanished at the beginning of the Common Era. It has been suggested that, with their ancient kinship to the Canaanite-Hebrew civilization, these offshoots of enterprising Tyre and Sidon were now submerged within the Jewish Dispersion. Be this as it may, unquestionably, many new communities now sprang up as far west as Italy and Tunisia and possibly even Spain and Morocco. Few reliable figures, however, are available for either the total Jewish population of any Roman province or that of individual communities. Not even Palestine has left behind records from which one could derive dependable statistics. Babylonian Jewry fell almost totally silent from the days of Ezra and Nehemiah to the second century C.E., although the presence there of great masses of Jews is not subject to doubt. Josephus' attempt to justify his behavior during the great Roman-Jewish War of 66–70 by first writing his history of that war in Aramaic is definite proof of the importance of those communities outside the Roman Empire. But numerically there are only such vague assertions as Josephus' statement that "myriads upon myriads" of Jews lived in the Euphrates Valley, while admitting that their "number could not be ascertained" (Ant., 11:133). Egypt, next to Palestine harboring the most culturally creative Jewish community of the time, embraced about a million Jews in the first century C.E., according to a casual remark by the well-informed Philo Judaeus. Other sources show that Jews probably predominated in two of the five quarters of Alexandria, that great emporium of trade and cultural activity, the population of which is variously estimated at 500,000 to 1,000,000. They may, indeed, have formed almost 40% of the population, in which case the Alexandrine community may well have exceeded in size that of Jerusalem in its heyday. There are also glimpses of such lesser Egyptian communities as the *Elephantine Jewish colony under the Achaemenids and Apollinopolis Magna or Edfu under the Ptolemies and Romans.

To be sure, certain data reported by the rabbis seem vastly exaggerated. For instance, the figures given for the attendance at the Passover sacrifices at the Temple of Jerusalem shortly before its destruction (Tosef., Pes. 4:3; Pes. 64b) cannot be taken at their face value. The Temple could not possibly have accommodated at any time a bare fraction of that number even if the Jews offered their sacrifices in frequent relays. A little more informative are the reports of the casualties in deaths and prisoners sustained by Jerusalem during the Roman siege. The figures transmitted by such distinguished historians as Josephus and Tacitus ranging between 600,000 fatalities and 1,197,000 dead and captured (Jos., Wars, 6:420; Tacitus, *Historiae*, 5:13) are not quite so out of line as they appear at first glance. Jerusalem's population before the siege had been swelled by countless numbers of pilgrims from all over the Dispersion and refugees from the provinces previously occupied by the Roman legions.

A new factor was injected into the discussion by the report of Gregory bar Hebraeus, a 12th-century Syrian chronicler of Jewish descent, about a census of the Jewish population taken by Emperor Claudius in 48 C.E. (*Historia compendiosa dynastiarum*, ed. by E. Pococke, 75, 116; ed. by A. Salhani,

115). According to this report, first brought to the attention of students of ancient Jewish history by Jean Juster, Claudius found no less than 6,944,000 Jews within the confines of the empire. To be sure, some scholars denied the authenticity of this report, or attributed the census to one of Roman citizens, rather than of Jews. However, the weight of evidence still favors the acceptance of that figure as the most likely approximation of the number of Jews living within the empire. To them must be added the numerous Jews of Babylonia, the Iranian Plateau, the Yemen, and Ethiopia. It stands to reason, therefore, that shortly before the fall of Jerusalem the world Jewish population exceeded 8,000,000, of whom probably not more than 2,350,000–2,500,000 lived in Palestine. Other major countries of Jewish settlement included Egypt, Syria, Asia Minor, and Babylonia, each probably embracing more than 1,000,000 Jews. Even Rome, the capital of the empire, seems to have included a Jewish community of about 40,000 in a total population of some 800,000, if we accept the figure of 8,000 Roman Jews accompanying a Palestinian delegation in the year 4 B.C.E., and 4,000 Jewish youths reputedly deported by Tiberius to the salt mines of Sardinia, as reported by Josephus (Ant., 17:300; 18:84) and Tacitus (*Annales*, 2, 85). This numerical strength of the Jewish population was important not only for the subsequent destinies of the Jewish people but also for the rise and expansion of Christianity. No less an authority than Adolf Harnack developed the theory that only where Jewish communities existed in the first century were there substantial Christian congregations before Constantine the Great in the early fourth century.

Unfortunately, after the fall of Jerusalem the demographic sources relating to Jews almost completely dried up. Unquestionably, the total number of Jews rapidly declined. As a result of the war ravages in 66–70, during the uprisings against Trajan in 115–117 and the *Bar Kokhba War in 132–35 the population of Palestine, Egypt, Cyprus, and other areas diminished sharply. Jerusalem for a while ceased to be a Jewish city altogether. After Trajan, Egyptian Jewry, though not completely suppressed, became almost totally silent for nearly a century; it never recovered from that mortal blow until centuries after the Muslim conquest. The conversion of some Jews to the new Christian religion was further aggravated by the more or less continuous Roman oppression culminating in the anti-Jewish legislation of the Christian Roman emperors from the fourth to the sixth centuries. Nor could the Jews entirely escape the impact of the biological decline of the empire as a whole from the third century on. Ultimately, in 632 Emperor Heraclius outlawed Judaism altogether. At the same time, through both immigration and natural growth, the Jewish population in Babylonia and elsewhere throughout the resurgent Persian Empire under the Sassanid dynasty (after 226) grew rapidly and, by the fourth century, may have equaled in size that of Rome and Byzantium. But no estimates of any kind, nor even informed guesses, can be made for the actual numbers of Jews inhabiting either empire.

Characteristically, however, the Jewish dispersion continued to expand in all directions. During those centuries some Jews seem to have penetrated India, as well as parts of Africa outside of Rome's control, while, if tradition is to be believed, some individuals even reached China. In the West there is some documentary and epigraphic evidence about Jewish settlements in Gaul, Germany, Hungary (Pannonia), Romania (Dacia), and perhaps even Britain. But these outlying Jewries were, for the most part, very small, and influenced the size of the world Jewish population to but a minor extent.

Medieval Islam and Byzantium

Curiously, for the long medieval period (from 313 or 476 C.E. to 1492) there is no global figure for the Jewish population of any year even comparable to the reconstruction, however uncertain, of the Claudian census in the mid-first century. There are only stray records pertaining to individual communities in different areas and periods which rarely lend themselves to any overall "guesstimates." The following medieval data are, therefore, even more tentative than those for the Ancient period. Palestine Jewry, though greatly decimated by the wars and Roman persecutions, seems nevertheless to have recovered sufficiently to be able to stage several revolts against their oppressive masters. According to one Christian chronicler even 4,000 Jews living in neighboring Tyre were able to start a revolt in 610, with the aid of 20,000 Jewish soldiers assembled from Palestine, Damascus, and Cyprus (Eutychius ibn Baṭrīq, *Annales*, in J.P. Migne's *Patrologia graeca*, 111:1084f.; and in Arabic text, ed. by L. Cheikho et al., 1:216). Another large-scale uprising, supported by an invading Persian army, was so successful that for three years the Jews seem to have exercised control over large parts of the country including Jerusalem and Tiberias (614–617). The repression in 629–632, however, was sharp and swift. Yet the total outlawry of Judaism in 632 hardly began to be implemented when five years later the Arab armies overran the country.

Jerusalem, which since the days of Bar Kokhba's defeat had only a sporadic and largely surreptitious Jewish settlement, was gradually reopened to Jewish residents under the Muslim domination. At first, Caliph Omar I admitted only 70 Jewish families. But this number increased considerably in the following generations owing to both Rabbanite and Karaite immigration. Similarly Caesarea, which in the Byzantine period had served as the administrative capital of the province, continued to harbor a substantial Jewish population, although the figures given by Balādhurī (200,000 Jews, 30,000 Samaritans, 700,000 Byzantine soldiers) and Yāqūt (100,000 Jews, 80,000 Samaritans, 100,000 soldiers) are fantastically exaggerated. This evolution was cut short by the bloodbath perpetrated by the conquering Crusaders in 1099 from which the Jewish community but slowly recovered. Some 70 years later the traveler Benjamin of Tudela found in Jerusalem a small community of perhaps 1,000 persons (the extant manuscripts differ between 4 and 200 families), while in 1218 Judah Al-Ḥarizi noted the presence there of three Jewish congregations.

A similar divergence may be observed between Benjamin's estimate of 3,000 Jews in Damascus and the 10,000 Jews quoted, a decade later, by another visitor, Pethahiah of Regensburg.

The other great center of Jewish life, Babylonia, seems more successfully to have conserved its biological strength. Despite the numerous sufferings inflicted upon the Jews by the Mazdakite movement during the chaotic fifth century, the figure of 90,000 Jews welcoming the arrival of the Arab general Ali (*Iggeret Sherira Ga'on*, ed. by B.M. Lewin (1921), 101) is not out of the range of historical probability. Under the Muslim administration the Jews of Babylonia and the neighboring Iranian Plateau continued to expand. The city of Sura, for example, the seat of a famous rabbinic academy, was found by a tenth-century Muslim investigating committee to have a large Jewish majority (Ibn abī Uṣaybiʿa, *Ṭabaqāt al-aṭibbāʾ*, ed. by A. Mueller, 1:221). The original Aramaic name of Mosul, Ḥesna Ebraya ("Hebrew Castle": the Jews themselves called it Ashshur) was undoubtedly deserved before the city grew into a major administrative and economic center. These old communities were speedily overshadowed by Baghdad after 762 when it became the capital of the vast Caliphate. In spite of the empire's dissolution and the chaotic conditions which prevailed there in the tenth century, Benjamin still found in the Baghdad of the 1160s a flourishing Jewish community of perhaps 40,000 persons. According to the Arab writer, Ibn al-Naqqāsh, the Mongolian invaders of Baghdad in 1258 counted there no less than 36,000 Jewish taxpayers – doubtless an exaggeration. In any case Jews constituted but a small segment of a population which at times may have ranged from 1,000,000 to 2,000,000 in size.

Egyptian Jewry, too, seems to have gradually recovered from its sharp decline of the second century. Although the glorious community of Alexandria had never recovered its former size and intellectual eminence and, in 414, had suffered from a serious, if unauthorized, expulsion, the conquering Arabs exaggeratingly claimed to have found there in 640 no less than "400,000 poll-tax paying Jews" (Eutychius, *Annales*, in: PG 111: 1107; in the Arabic text, ed. by Cheikho, 2:26). Here, too, the recovery proceeded apace under the Muslim rule, particularly the friendly Fatimid and Seljuk regimes of the 11th and 12th centuries. In the newly developed capital of Fostat (Old Cairo) Benjamin found 7,000, and in Alexandria, 3,000 Jewish families. He also saw or heard of numerous other Jewish communities throughout the land. Taking these figures as representing persons, rather than families, some careful historians calculated that all of Egypt had a Jewish population of no more than 20,000–40,000, which is probably too conservative a ratio in the country's general population of perhaps 7,000,000–8,000,000. While Benjamin's estimates do not quite tally with the evidence of local sources, particularly those preserved in the Cairo **Genizah*, they all give the impression of populous and often flourishing Jewish settlements.

To the west of Egypt there were growing Jewish communities in Kairouan (Tunisia), Morocco, and particularly Muslim Spain. However, no precise data are available on the demographic situation in most of these communities. Only here and there are there some figures, as a rule none too reliable, in the writings of Arab chroniclers and geographers or in rabbinic sources. The famous Moroccan community of Fez, for example, is said to have sustained 6,000 Jewish fatalities during the massacre of 1032–33. In Spain, al-Idrīsī calls the frontier town of Tarragona a "city of Jews" (*Description de l'Afrique*, ed. and trans. by R. Dozy and M.J. de Goeje, 191 (Ar.) and 231 (Fr.)). In addressing the Jewish leaders of Lucena the ninth-century Babylonian *Gaon*, Natronai b. Hilai, casually mentions that "there are no gentiles living among you at all" (Responsum, reproduced in B.M. Lewin's *Oẓar ha-Ge'onim*, vol. 3, 1, 24f. no. 64). Even the celebrated city of Granada is, doubtless for good reason, called by al-Ḥimyarī *Ighranāṭat-al-Yahūd* ("Jewish Granada"; in *La Peninsule Ibérique*, ed. by E. Lévi-Provençal, 23, 42f. (Ar.), 29ff., 53ff. (Fr.)). Córdoba, the metropolis of Muslim Spain, also included a very sizable Jewish community. Although these stray data do not allow for any comprehensive estimate of the Jewish population of the whole country, it appears that here, too, Ely Ashtor's estimate of but 50,000–55,000 Jews in the whole Iberian Peninsula around 1050 (in a general population of some 7,000,000–9,000,000) is the result of excessive caution. Even under the intolerant Almohad domination of the 12th century many, perhaps most, Jews continued secretly to profess Judaism. They "rolled with the waves" until the 13th-century reconquest by the Christian Spaniards, when they could once again overtly profess Judaism and resume their demographic as well as socioeconomic and cultural expansion.

Similar uncertainties beset the demographic historian trying to ascertain the size of the Jewish population in the Byzantine Empire. It is a remarkable testimony to the enormous vitality of the Jewish people that, despite four successive total outlawries of Judaism in 632, 722–3, 873–4, and 930, it survived and resumed its historic evolution, without noticeable breaks in its continuity. At any rate, when around 1160 Benjamin of Tudela visited Constantinople, he found there no less than 2,000 Rabbanite and 500 Karaite families. For that time this was an impressive estimate of 12,000–15,000 Jews, although they evidently constituted but a small minority of the capital's population which, ranging between 50,000 and 100,000 persons, by far exceeded that of any Christian city of the period. Some ten to fifteen years later, Pethahiah of Regensburg, on arriving in Byzantium, was so overawed by the number and size of its Jewish communities, which sharply contrasted with the underpopulated cities and Jewish settlements of his German homeland, that he exclaimed: "There are there [in the Byzantine Empire] so many congregations that the land of Israel could not contain them, were they to be settled therein." Nonetheless, there is no way of closely estimating the total Jewish population of the empire, both before or after the Arab expansion of the 630s.

Here, too, much of the demographic information depends on data supplied by Benjamin of Tudela. Regrettably, different manuscript of his travelogue quote figures with considerable variants. The question whether he had in mind persons, taxpayers, or families still is largely unresolved. It is quite possible that some of his figures represented different entities and that he merely reported numbers as they were given to him by local informants in the towns he happened to visit. Though displaying unusual interest in Jewish demography and probably quite accurately transmitting the information he received, he was, needless to say, unable to check it. With all these weaknesses, Benjamin is relatively the most reliable guide. It has been shown that the sum total of his figures was 512,532. Since he did not visit all communities and did not record figures even in many of those he had seen, these numbers must at least be doubled. In short, at the end of the 12th century the world Jewish population may well have embraced 1,000,000, perhaps even close to 2,000,000 persons, the large majority of whom still resided in countries under the domination of Islam. This situation began changing rapidly in the 13th century, when the center of gravity of the Jewish people shifted to the Western lands. With the rest of the population, the Eastern Jewries declined sharply, to be revitalized only under the Ottoman Empire of the late 15th and the 16th centuries.

Medieval West

Despite the availability of much more ample and better-investigated source materials, population studies of medieval Western Jewry are likewise affected by great uncertainties. Apart from the general decline of population during the Barbarian invasions, many Jewish settlements were totally destroyed during the wave of intolerance which, in the seventh century, swept through Visigothic Spain, Merovingian France, and Langobard Italy. Thereafter the total number of Jews in Western Europe, including Germany, must have been very small indeed. The only continuous major settlements carried over from Antiquity were in the Papal States, southern Italy, parts of Spain, and southern France. However, here, too, the general population decline is well illustrated by the city of Rome which, from a metropolis embracing some 1,000,000 inhabitants at the end of the second century, was reduced to but 35,000 eight centuries later. Nonetheless, in the 1160s Benjamin could find substantial Jewish communities in Rome, Naples, Messina, and particularly in Palermo, whose 1,500 Jewish families undoubtedly formed the largest Jewish community under Roman Catholic Christianity. Rome itself may also have embraced at that time about 1,000 Jews.

Relatively, the best information deals with the conditions in medieval England. Owing to the comparatively small number of Jews, the availability of large and well-preserved source material, and untiring research by scholars, Christian and Jewish, over several decades, the evolution of the medieval Anglo-Jewish community has been fairly well elucidated. Its demographic aspects, however, have left many questions open. It appears that, beginning with the Norman Conquest of 1066, the number of Jewish settlers gradually reached about 2,500 persons before the massacres of 1190–91 and the ensuing flight of numerous Jews to the Continent. Within a few years English Jewry recovered its strength, however, and resumed its growth in the first half of the 13th century. Yet the endless fiscal exactions of Henry III and the general hostility of the population, which found expression in a number of cities securing privileges *de non tolerandis Judaeis*, before long began taking their toll. Even at the expulsion of 1290 there were probably no more than about 10,000 Jews in a total population of about 3,500,000 in the country. This is avowedly a compromise figure between the decided underestimate by George Caro of no more than 3,000 Jewish residents and the records of contemporary chroniclers, whose reports about the Jews effected by the decree of expulsion of 1290 ranged from 15,000 to 17,500. Even that relatively small number was scattered over 91 cities, of which 21 (at their heyday, 27) were sufficiently important to contain royal *archae* where records of all Jewish loans were officially kept. In addition, there were more than 100 other localities in which individual Jews were mentioned in the sources. A few individuals seem also to have penetrated Wales, Scotland, and Ireland, though no organized community existed in any of these areas in the Middle Ages.

On the Continent Jewish demography depends for the most part on sporadically preserved tax records. In the case of capitation taxes it is relatively easy to multiply the number of taxpayers by whatever quotient is derived from our knowledge, otherwise obtained, of their ratio to minors, indigents, and other non-paying groups. Of course, here, too, it was in the best interest of the Jewish communities to underestimate the number of taxpayers whereas the government authorities sought to exaggerate them. In addition, there were sporadic censuses of population, including Jews, such as was instituted in Aix-en-Provence in 1341 on orders of King Robert of Anjou. It revealed that, at that time, 1,205 Jews occupied 203 houses and constituted some 10% of the city's population. A Jewish taxpaying "hearth" averaged 5.9 members, while individual households included a membership of up to 30 persons. In contrast, a similar census in Carpentras in 1471 revealed a Jewish average of only 4.3 per "hearth," as against 5.2 persons per Christian "hearth." The latter discrepancy is explainable only by the intervening trials and tribulations of Carpentras Jewry which was always treated more harshly by both the populace and the city council than that of its larger neighbor, Avignon. Here no less than 210 Jewish heads of households were called upon in 1358 to take an oath of allegiance to the pope, which indicates the presence of a Jewish community of well over 1,000 persons. In general, the Jewish population of Provence and the papal possessions in France exceeded the general ratio of Jews in the rest of France and for that matter anywhere in Europe north of the Alps and Pyrenees. Already in the days of Benjamin the community of Arles, with its 200 families, seems to have formed some 20% of the city's population. The smaller town of Tarascon embraced 125 Jewish families in 1442, 183 families in 1487. On the other hand, Narbonne, once the leading southern French community and, in Carolingian times, the seat of a "Jewish king," steadily declined and, shortly before the 1306 expulsion, numbered no more than 1,000 Jews among the city's 15,000 inhabitants. Similarly, Toulouse in 1391 had only 15 Jewish families in a population of 25,000–30,000. All of Gascony under English domination apparently never exceeded that total of 1,000 Jews before their banishment in 1288. More remarkably, the "great city" of Paris (Benjamin), where, before the expulsion of 1182, some chroniclers spoke exaggeratingly of Jews forming half the city's population and owning half its real estate, in fact embraced at no time before the final expulsion of 1394 many more than the 124 taxpayers (in 86 households) among the 15,200 taxpayers recorded in 1292 in a total population of 80,000 or more counted in 1328.

No house-to-house canvasses are recorded in the Holy Roman Empire. There we depend principally on tax records which, however, are almost invariably incomplete. Even the very significant list of taxpaying Jewish communities in 1241 omits such large Jewish settlements as that of Nuremberg. On the other hand, Germany has preserved a number of examples of the *memorbuch* which, by recording victims of persecutions by name, are the most dependable, if partial, sources of demographic information. In Nuremberg, for example, 628 such fatalities are recorded as a result of the *Rindfleisch massacres of 1298; despite the community's subsequent recovery, 570 more Jews lost their lives in the massacre of 1349. Wuerzburg sustained in 1298 no less than 900 casualties, of whom 100 are specifically mentioned as nonresidents. Even smaller communities like Weissensee or Ueberlingen could lose 125 and over 300 Jews respectively, in massacres resulting from local *blood libels in 1303 and 1332. However, such incidental records give us but a remote approximation of the total Jewish population in the respective periods. The only conclusion one may draw from these stray references is that, especially after 1350, most German Jewish communities were very small.

In Jewish, as in general West and Central European life, the 14th century was a period of great crisis, both economically and biologically. The recurrent famines (1315–17, etc.) and pestilences – the greatest of the epidemics, the *Black Death of 1348–49, was but one of a series of destructive diseases – resulted in a long-lasting decline in population. During many decades an annual birthrate of 39 per 1,000 population was exceeded by a mortality rate of 41 per 1,000. Hence life expectancy of newly born children in many areas sank as low as 17–20 years. Jews not only fell victim to these widely spreading contaminations, but were often massacred in advance of the plague by their panic-stricken Christian neighbors, as alleged "poisoners of the wells" responsible for the contagion. Not surprisingly, their numbers declined frightfully even in a city like Vienna, which was restrained by its rulers from attacking Jews, despite its daily losses of 500 (occasionally up to 1,200) dead to the plague. Its Jewry, considered by some informed contemporaries the largest Jewish community in the empire, 70 years later had only 92 male and 122 female martyrs during the persecution (the so-called *Gezerah*) of 1421. The celebrated Jewish community of Augsburg listed only 17 and 21 Jewish taxpayers in 1401 and 1437, and in the following year banished the whole community of 300 persons. Erfurt, which a short time before possessed four or five synagogues and four slaughterhouses for the supply of ritually permissible meat, dwindled to a total of only 50–86 taxpayers in 1357–89. Similarly Frankfurt, which was destined to play so great a role in German Jewish history in the following centuries, embraced only a few Jewish families in the 1360s, and as late as 1462, when its new ghetto was formally established, it counted no more than about 200 inhabitants. If during that period many German Jews found shelter in the neighboring lands of Poland, Lithuania, and Hungary (each destined to occupy an imposing place in the modern history of the Jewish people), before 1500 C.E. their total numbers, even when augmented by the earlier settlers in part stemming from territories further east, still were quite small before the end of the Middle Ages.

The largest agglomerations of Jews under medieval Christendom were to be found on the Iberian and Apennine peninsulas together with the adjacent Balearic Islands and Sicily. Spain, the largest and most influential focus of medieval Judaism, has preserved a great many demographically relevant records, some of which are yet to be explored. However, their evaluation by modern scholars has diverged very greatly. While the first careful investigator of the subject, Isidore Loeb, estimated the Jewish population of Castile at 160,000 around 1300 C.E., Yitzḥak Baer, the outstanding student of Spanish Jewish history, attributes to that kingdom only some 3,600 Jewish families at that time. Together with Navarre and Aragon, he believes, the combined Jewish population did not exceed 40,000. Once again the truth seems to be somewhere in between, and a total of 150,000 would seem to offer a much closer approximation. Remarkably, neither the Jewish nor the general population suffered permanently irretrievable losses as a result of the Black Death of 1348–49, or the subsequent major plagues of 1394–96 and 1490. Despite various setbacks, especially after 1391, the Iberian Jewish population continued to grow, particularly in Castile, and there is somewhat more agreement about the number of Jews affected by the expulsion of 1492. The best approximation was given by Meir Melammed, son-in-law of "Chief Rabbi" Abraham Senior, and another Jew (both of whom preferred conversion to exile) who estimated the number of Jewish families affected by the decree of expulsion at 35,000 in Castile and 6,000 in Aragon (Andrés Bernaldez, *Historia de los Reyes Catolicos*, cx ff.). Not very much higher is the figure of 300,000 Jewish inhabitants of Spain, cited by Isaac Abrabanel, the leader of the departing exiles (*Ma'yenei ha-yeshu'ah*, introd.). If it be true that some 120,000 of these expatriates proceeded to neighboring Portugal (Abraham Zacuto, *Sefer Yuḥasin*, 277a), the total Jewish population of the smaller country may have reached 200,000 to be affected by the forced conversion of 1496–97. These large figures lent themselves to easy exaggeration and even such a well-informed and careful 16th-century historian and political theorist as Juan Mariana glibly speaks of 800,000 Spanish Jews affected by the expulsion (*Historia general de España*, ed.

by J.M. Gutiérrez, vol. 5, 440). In the Iberian case, moreover, there is a major problem of estimating the number of Conversos (including numerous secret Judaizers) who lived under the reign of Ferdinand and Isabella and whose number was greatly increased by those Jews who in 1492 preferred baptism to exile. These Conversos were to furnish a considerable number of members to the growing Marrano dispersion in the West, while others found ways of speedily returning to Judaism by settling in Muslim lands.

Somewhat less controversial is the size of the large Jewish population of Sicily and the kingdom of Naples. Sicily alone doubtless had a Jewish population of more than 50,000 in the 15th century, many of whom departed in 1492 for Naples, Rome, and other localities. Combined with refugees from Spain, the Sicilian exiles may well have temporarily doubled the Jewish population of the kingdom of Naples before the expulsion of Jews in 1511 and 1541. At the same time, the resettlement of Jewish communities in Italy north of the Papal States was proceeding rather slowly and the glorious Renaissance republics of Florence, Ferrara, Venice, and others became really important areas of Jewish settlement only in the early modern period.

In short, after considering these and many other complicated factors and in full realization of the perilous nature of any computation, S. Baron has submitted Table 2, Jewish Population in European Countries before 1500 C.E. covering the Jewish population in Western and Central Europe during the last centuries of the Middle Ages.

1500–1800

The three centuries of the early modern period were at first marked by a simultaneous expansion and contraction of Jewish settlement, which of course had an important bearing on Jewish demography as well. On the one hand, the wave of expulsions from England, France, the Iberian Peninsula, and many Italian and German territories of the period from 1290 to 1500 now continued unabated. Jews were ousted permanently from the kingdom of Naples in 1511 and 1541; from the duchy of Milan in 1597; and from the Papal States (except Rome and Ancona) on a more temporary basis, in 1569 and 1593. The banishment of the Jews from Regensburg in 1519 and Rothenburg in 1520 was followed during the early Reformation period by expulsion from Saxony in 1536, Brandenburg (after their readmission in 1540) in 1571, and many other German principalities, bishoprics, and free cities. The result was a greater diffusion of Jews into smaller localities, even villages, in both Italy and Germany – a trend which was reversed only during the Thirty Years' War. At the same time there was not only a great expansion of the Jewish people into Poland-Lithuania, the Ottoman Empire, and other Muslim countries, but through the Marrano dispersion there was the incipient resettlement of Jews, first secret and later overt, in Western Europe. There was also the beginning of Jewish participation in the colonization of the New World, as well as of the Far East and some African territories by the great colonial powers.

If, on balance, the Jewish settlement in the middle of the 17th century extended over a much larger area than that of 1500 C.E., the growth of Jewish population did not keep pace with that geographic expansion. Certainly those New Christians, who by 1660 had formally returned to Judaism, were but a small fraction of the descendants of the original Conversos on the Iberian Peninsula. The small size of the Jewish or Marrano settlements did not prevent, however, unfriendly observers from magnifying the Jewish presence beyond measure. Even a great scholar like Erasmus of Rotterdam, who had had hardly any contacts with living Jews, could exclaim with abandon: "Jews are very numerous in Italy; in Spain there are hardly any Christians. I am afraid that when the occasion arises that pest, formerly suppressed, will raise its head again" (*Opus epistolarum*, 3:253; 4:114). More recklessly, temperamental Martin Luther once contended that Italy was so full of Jews that, for instance, Cremona had no more than 28 Christians among its inhabitants (*Tischreden*, 3:369f.; 4:619f.). These comments were made at a time when Italy's most populous areas of Naples and Sicily no longer had any professing Jews. After 1569, moreover, the Papal States, too, but grudgingly admitted Jews outside Rome and Ancona but never in sufficient numbers to justify the maintenance of some 115 synagogues such as had existed before the 1569 expulsion. Similarly, the Jews readmitted to Brandenburg in 1540 formed but tiny commu-

Table 2. The Jewish Population in European Countries before 1500 C.E.

Country	1300 C.E.		1490 C.E.	
	Jews	General population	Jews	General population
France (including Avignon)	100,000	14,000,000	20,000	20,000,000
Holy Roman Empire (including Switzerland and the Low Countries)	100,000	12,000,000	80,000	12,000,000
Italy	50,000	11,000,000	120,000	12,000,000
Spain (Castile, Aragon, and Navarre)	150,000	5,500,000	250,000	7,000,000
Portugal	40,000	600,000	80,000	1,000,000
Poland–Lithuania	5,000	500,000	30,000	1,000,000
Hungary	5,000	400,000	20,000	800,000
Total	450,000	44,000,000	600,000	53,800,000

nities of eight to ten families in Berlin, Stendal, and Frankfurt on the Oder when they were once again banished 31 years later. It was only in the 17th and particularly the 18th century that the German-speaking Jewry of the Holy Roman Empire, aided by immigration from Eastern Europe and later by the inclusion in Prussia and Austria of formerly Polish territories through the partitions of Poland in 1772–95, started rising significantly throughout the country.

At the same time, the "Golden Age" of both Polish Jewry and Poland as a whole in the 16th and early 17th centuries was largely terminated in the era of the Chmielnicki uprising (1648–49) and the Swedish-Muscovite wars of 1648–56. Not only did Polish Jewry sustain very severe losses in human lives but, combined with the general economic decline of the country, these disturbances set in motion a Jewish mass emigration which kept the growth of the population at a relatively low rate. Nevertheless the Jewish numerical strength continued gaining and the area of what was Poland-Lithuania in 1648 may well have embraced a Jewish population twice as large in 1800. The majority was now included in the Russian Empire which, after many centuries of refusing to admit Jews – as late as 1740 the whole Jewish population of 292 men and 281 women, scattered through 130 manorial estates in the Ukraine and Belorussia, was expelled – thus suddenly became the largest country of Jewish settlement.

Unfortunately, dependable demographic data on Jews are available only in very few areas. Italy, to be sure, often conducted population censuses, and information concerning Jews in various Italian communities of the early modern period is quite illuminating. The emergent Jewish communities in France, England, and particularly Holland can also be estimated with close approximation to the truth. On the other hand, the Holy Roman Empire, until its dissolution in 1806, offers only sporadic insights into the number of its Jewish inhabitants. In Poland-Lithuania the Jewish population in certain cities can be estimated with a fair degree of accuracy, while vast areas in the country are subject to more or less questionable estimates based on the yield of the capitation tax which in 1560 amounted to only 6,186 florins (on an assessment of 1.50 florins per family), but rose to 80,000 florins in 1634 and to 220,000 florins in 1714 (both representing collections of 3 florins per person). There were also a number of regional censuses (so-called *lustracje*), but only those of 1764–65 shortly before the partitions of Poland have left behind more comprehensive and reliable records; they have also been subjected to closer scrutiny by modern scholars.

In contrast, the enormously important Jewish settlement of the Ottoman Empire, with its western Asiatic and North African provinces, offers an almost hopeless problem to the demographic historian. It stands to reason that, since the empire had seen its glory progressively dimmed from 1600 on and its Jewish subjects suffered serious setbacks several decades later in the era of the Shabbatean movement, the forward motion of both the Jewish and the general populations also greatly slowed down. Yet it appears that, as in Poland, such retardation did not completely halt the numerical expansion of the Jewish masses. However, this assumption cannot be supported by precise statistical data despite the fact that the Ottoman archives have preserved many records of detailed censuses, some of which go back to the 15th century. These records are in many ways far superior to what is preserved in most Western countries of that period. Yet even with the aid of so-called *defters*, or brief summaries kept in the archival registries, these sources have thus far been scrutinized only to a very slight extent. The few Jewish studies heretofore published relate almost exclusively to Palestine's population under the early Ottoman regime. They have opened up new vistas and whetted the appetite for more information but they have supplied only disjointed fragments which do not add up to a total picture. Equally unsatisfactory is knowledge of Jewish demography in the North-African countries. Only here and there do the sources, often derived from casual observation by foreign visitors, mention figures pertaining to the size of Jewish communities. Yet with some effort and ingenuity Maurice Eisenbeth succeeded in compiling, on the basis of such reports, approximate statistics of Jewish inhabitants in the city of Algiers. His estimates for the 16th century range from 1,000 to 5,000 Jews. About 1600 their number rises to 8,000 or 9,000 persons, while about 1700 it reaches a peak of 10,000–12,000. In the course of the 18th century the Jewish population declines to some 7,000 and is further reduced to but 5,000 by 1818 (M. Eisenbeth, *Les Juifs en Algerie et en Tunisie à l'epoque turque (1576–1830)*, 147ff.).

In the following we can refer, therefore, only to a number of illustrations of Jewish communities which have undergone extraordinary expansion, while others have lagged behind. In Italy the papal capital under the Renaissance popes allowed its Jewry to grow, so that it may have reached the number of 2,500–3,000 Jews before the expulsion from the rest of the Papal States in 1569. Although locked in a formal ghetto since 1555, the Rome community continued to grow because after 1569 it had to absorb a great many refugees from the provinces. It is estimated that in 1592 it embraced 3,500 persons in a total population of 97,000. A century later the Jewish population is said to have reached a peak of 10,000–12,000 persons which was never exceeded thereafter even in the 20th century. In the 18th century the Jewish population dropped back to a median of 3,076 persons, according to the official records of 1775–1800. Venice, after the expulsion of Jews in the Middle Ages, did not tolerate them at all until 1509 and in 1516 shut them off in a ghetto, the first to bear that name. But subsequently it allowed the Jewish community to grow rather speedily so that by the middle of the 17th century it may have reached a total of 5,000 persons. Even more remarkably, Leghorn, which had few Jews before 1593, embraced 114 in 1601, 711 in 1622, and 1,175 in 1642. It continued to grow in the following decades; the official censuses refer to a Jewish population of 3,476 in 1738, 4,327 in 1784, and 4,697 in 1806. Leghorn thus competed with Rome and Venice for the designation of the largest Jewish community in Italy. Even a medium-sized community, such as that of

Verona, grew to 400 persons in 1600 and over 1,000 in 1751. In contrast, many cities, including Genoa, never admitted more than a handful of Jews. The constant ups and downs in the size of respective communities are well illustrated by the following estimates for the three neighboring Jewish centers in the duchy of Urbino. In 1628 Pesaro had 610 Jewish inhabitants, Urbino 370, Senigallia 200. By 1700 the respective figures were about 600, 200, 600, Senigallia assuming the cultural, as well as numerical, leadership. Historically, the relatively small Jewish communities of Piedmont (its capital Turin first reached a Jewish population of 500 in 1563) were to play an important role in the 19th century when their country marched in the vanguard of Italian unification. All of Italy embraced some 25,000 Jews in 1638, according to the well-informed apologist Simone Luzzatto (*Discorso circa il stato degl' hebrei*, 91). At this level Italian Jewry remained more or less stabilized during the following two centuries while the general Italian population grew from about 11,000,000 in the 17th century to 18,125,000 in 1800, and 23,000,000 in 1850.

In Germany, too, some startling increases contrasted with declines or, at best, demographic stagnation. In Frankfurt, which had only 110 Jews at the time when the community moved into its assigned quarter in 1462, the number grew to 250 in 1520, 900 in 1569, 2,200 in 1600. By 1613 the assailants of Jews led by Vincent Fettmilch complained that the 454 Jewish families in the city engaged in too sharp a competition with the Christian artisans and traders. The concentration of about 3,000 Jews within the original quarter throughout the 17th and 18th centuries caused that tremendous overcrowding which made the Frankfurt ghetto a byword in Jewish literature. Hamburg admitted a few New Christians in the 16th century but did not legally recognize the presence of a Jewish community until 1612. Its Jewry, both Sephardi and Ashkenazi, grew rapidly (together with the sister communities of Altona and Wandsbeck which jointly formed the single tri-community of Altona-Hamburg-Wandsbeck, abbreviated into AHU according to its Hebrew initials) during the following two centuries, reaching in 1810 the number of 6,299 Jews, according to the official census. It thus was second only to the community of Prague among the Jewish settlements in the empire. The Bohemian capital, a much older community, which had maintained its historic continuity despite several decrees of expulsion in the 16th century and again in 1744 (often not seriously implemented), was throughout the early modern period a major center of Central European Jewish life and learning. By 1729 it embraced, according to an official census, 10,507 persons.

At the same time a great many German Jews of the 16th and early 17th centuries lived scattered through countless hamlets and villages. An investigation conducted in 1541 in the Memmingen district revealed the presence of but 40 Jewish families living in 11 localities. Throughout Germany there were such small Jewish settlements with but one to ten families trying to eke out a meager livelihood and yet instilling in their children a pride in, and knowledge of their Jewish heritage. This great dispersal was largely the result of the preceding wave of expulsions of Jews from the major cities, including their famous medieval settlements of Mainz, Speyer, Cologne, and Regensburg, and their finding shelter, however precariously, under the domination of the petty lords. This trend was reversed, however, during the Thirty Years' War (1618–48) when Jews fleeing before the marching armies and pillaging marauders often had to be admitted to the larger cities, which in turn found that they often benefited greatly from Jewish trade and taxation. Thus was ushered in the era of progressive urbanization of German Jewry, which was to make tremendous strides in the 19th and early 20th centuries. An example of such growing concentration in German metropolitan areas is offered by Prussia of the days of Frederick the Great. While no reliable data for Jews in that rapidly expanding state are available, a well-informed student, Friedrich Wilhelm August Bratring, estimated that in 1750 Berlin had 2,188 Jews (in a population of 133,520), while the rest of the Kurmark accommodated only 1,685 of their coreligionists. Twenty years later the Berlin Jewish community embraced 3,842 persons (an increase of nearly 80%), whereas the provincial communities together totaled only 1,996 persons (an increase of but 20%). In the subsequent three decades, to be sure, Berlin's Jewish inhabitants numerically declined in contrast to both the city's general population and the provincial Jewries, but this was a mere temporary interruption in the process of rapid growth which brought the size of Berlin Jewry up to 172,672 in 1925.

The Netherlands, emerging from the War of Liberation as a forward-looking and relatively liberal state, embraced but a few New Christians in the late 16th century. But, beginning in 1593, the country witnessed a tremendous expansion in the number and size of Jewish settlements which, two centuries later, embraced a population of well over 50,000. Amsterdam alone accommodated in 1795 no less than 21,000 Ashkenazi and 2,400 Sephardi Jews. Its community, often styled the "New Jerusalem," exceeded in size any contemporary or earlier European Jewish community, except perhaps those of ancient Rome and early modern Constantinople.

France's total Jewish population at the outbreak of the Revolution in 1789 amounted to less than 40,000. Their majority was concentrated in Alsace – which at the time of its annexation by France after 1648 included a number of older Jewish communities. Lorraine's Metz speedily developed into a major center of some 3,000 Jews, whereas Strasbourg, the metropolis of the area, saw its privilege *de non tolerandis Judaeis* breached only in the 1780s. A governmental census of 1784, probably incomplete, enumerated 182 Alsatian localities embracing a Jewish population of 3,913 families and 19,707 persons (9,945 males and 9,762 females). The actual figures were a bit higher; Z. Szajkowski estimates the total at between 22,570 and 23,800 persons. It may also be noted that, in contrast to the German areas, Alsace under French domination witnessed a continued dispersal of Jewish settlements from 95 in 1689, to 129 in 1716, and 182 in 1784. Simultaneously, southern France, particularly Bordeaux and Saint Esprit, a suburb of Bayonne, in the 18th century accommodated a total of some 4,500 Jews. Characteristically, Paris, the very heart of French life and culture, barely tolerated 500–800 Jews at the outbreak of the French Revolution.

England's Jewish population, too, still was very small, as was that of the New World. It is estimated that English Jewry embraced some 6,000 persons in 1730, and 12,000 in 1791. Other contemporary estimates raise this figure to 20,000 and more at the end of the 18th century. The large majority was concentrated in London (R.D. Barnett, in: V.D. Lipman (ed.), *Three Centuries of Anglo-Jewish History* (1961), 60f.). In contrast, the six known communities in the United States during the American Revolution counted among them only little more than 2,000 Jews. Possibly the same number was scattered through the Caribbean Islands and Surinam; the largest community among them, that of Kingston, Jamaica, numbered some 500 Jews, and thus rivaled New York in continental North America. On the other hand, the community of French Martinique, which was allegedly reinforced by 400 Jewish refugees from Brazil in 1654, was wiped out by the French decree of expulsion of 1683. In Latin America, under its intolerant Spanish and Portuguese regimes, only New Christians were sometimes grudgingly allowed to settle. In some areas they were quite numerous. Out of them subsequently emerged groups of professing Jews who helped populate the Western Hemisphere. The largest of these groups lived in Recife, Brazil; more than 1,000 of them publicly professed Judaism during the short-lived Dutch domination (1630–54). Upon the return of the Portuguese, the majority found refuge in Surinam, the Caribbean Islands, New Amsterdam (later New York, where 23 of them in 1654 laid the foundations for the largest Jewish community in history), as well as Holland.

1800–1939

A new phase of Jewish demography began with the 19th century. More and more countries now conducted regular censuses; many included a column relating to religious faith. The vast majority of Jews unhesitatingly indicated their Jewish allegiance to the census takers. In the early 1800s, to be sure, when censuses were still taken primarily for fiscal and military purposes, numerous Jews hesitated to appear before the enumerators. Their fears of discriminatory treatment were enhanced by the old folkloristic apprehensions, nurtured by the biblical references to the effects of David's census. According to Gustav Adolf Schimmer, one of the early pioneers in Jewish population studies (1873), there were many localities in Eastern Europe, where upon the advent of the census takers the entire Jewish youth vanished from the scene, to reappear only after the enumerators' departure. In time, however, as the censuses became more purely administrative and scholarly undertakings and were periodically repeated, their accuracy usually improved by the use of more refined techniques. Apart from supplying definite figures of the Jewish population and such other relevant information as that of the Jewish birth and mortality rates, sex and age distribution, marriages and divorces, they offered periodic data revealing the prevailing trends.

Regrettably, this practice was not universal. Czarist Russia, where before 1914 almost half of the world Jewry resided, had no such dependable investigations until 1897 when the government and the Alliance Israélite Universelle from its Paris headquarters collaborated in the attempt to obtain more detailed statistical information about the Russian Jews who, because of recurrent pogroms and discriminatory legislation, had attracted world-wide attention. This endeavor was not repeated, however, except for a valiant but incomplete effort by the ORT in 1921, until 1926 when the Soviet Union took a comprehensive census of its own. Here the Jews were listed as a national, rather than religious group; however, removing some elements of comparison with the earlier accounts. Even worse was the situation in the Ottoman Empire and the other Muslim lands, where before World War I all population statistics were in a deplorable state.

Not much better was the situation in the United States, the burgeoning world center of the Jewish people, which after World War I became the largest country of Jewish settlement. Because of the constitutional separation of state and church, the governmental censuses conducted every ten years since 1790 did not include a question on the person's religious allegiance. For a time the government collected data on the number of congregations affiliated with each denomination, their membership, and other pertinent factors. After 1890, however, the combination of these inquiries with the official decennial censuses was abandoned and a special "census of religious bodies" was instituted in the middle of each decade following the general census of 1900. The first such specific survey was made in 1906; it was followed by others in 1916, 1926, and 1936. However, the preparation of replies was left to the respective denominations themselves, many of which used different criteria for counting their members. In the case of Jews the religious censuses of 1906 and 1916 by definition counted only Jews who were members of congregations. In 1926 and 1936 a new definition was employed. The instructions given to the agent in charge read: "The Jews… now consider as members all persons of the Jewish faith living in communities in which local congregations are situated" (U.S. Census Bureau, *Religious Bodies Summary*, 1 (1926), 16). This definition greatly increased the totals from 357,135 in 1906 to 4,081,242 in 1916 and thereby removed the most important element for comparing the new results with the earlier accounts. The census itself admitted it by deleting any reference to Jews in the column recording the membership growth over the preceding two decades. Since the Jewish communities were unable to undertake a house-to-house enumeration, they had to rely upon information supplied by more or less informed local leaders whose estimates, frequently mere "guesstimates," often widely differed. The result was that the compilers of the census had to reach median numbers of such diverse estimates. The general result was that many figures, including the total membership of 4,641,184 in 1936, tended toward exaggeration. When almost simultaneously with the census of 1936 a more detailed canvass of ten important communities was conducted by local leaders under the sponsorship of the Conference on Jewish Relations, it turned out that the resulting more accurate figures ran between 8% and 20% below those suggested in the census. Of course, no one could be sure that the experience of these ten cities was typical of the whole country, particularly of the New York metropolitan area which apparently embraced some 40% of American Jewry.

Even in those Western European countries, such as France, Belgium, the Netherlands, Switzerland, or Italy, where the governmental censuses included a query concerning the inhabitants' religious preference, the returns are not completely reassuring. In the first place, all census bureaus (including that of the United States which uses highly refined statistical techniques) count with a margin of error of at least 1–1.5%. In the case of Jewish respondents the difficulty is aggravated by the uncertainty of "who is a Jew." Many persons who considered themselves Jews refused to give the enumerator straight answers about their religious preference, either because they felt that religion should be treated as a "private" concern which no government had any right to probe, or because, for a variety of reasons, they personally tried to hide their Jewishness. There is also the problem of children of mixed marriages who, according to rabbinic law, are automatically considered Jews if their mother is Jewish – a distinction which in practice is often disregarded, positively as well as negatively. Baron has suggested, therefore, that for practical reasons everyone be regarded as a Jew "who (1) is born of Jewish parents and has never been converted to another faith; (2) is born of mixed parentage but declares himself a Jew and is so considered by the majority of his neighbors; and (3) one who by conscious will has adopted Judaism." In view of these largely subjective criteria it has been found doubly imperative to supplement the official census data, wherever such exist, by more searching sample studies.

Another complication has arisen in various countries as a result of the new Jewish national movement. Some Jews, professing no religion, nevertheless counted themselves as belonging to the Jewish "nationality," while others, even if staunchly Orthodox, regarded themselves as members of a different "nationality." Still other Jews who neither professed Judaism nor regarded themselves as nationally Jewish nonetheless thought of themselves as Jews and were thus regarded by their neighbors, Jewish and non-Jewish. The confusion arising from these varying definitions was well illustrated in 1921 in the first Czechoslovakian census. "The official figures showed that there were 336,520 Czechoslovak nationals [in addition to 17,822 foreigners] professing the 'Israelite' religion. Their majority, 180,616, declared themselves to be members of the Jewish nationality (this majority was larger in Slovakia and Carpathian Ruthenia but it turned into a minority in the main provinces of Moravia, Bohemia, and Silesia). Of the rest, 73,371 signed up as members of the Czech nationality, 49,123 as Germans, 29,473 as Magyars, 3,751 as Russians, 74 as Poles, and 112 as belonging to other nationalities. In addition, there were 100 persons who professed no religion but were members of the Jewish nationality. More astonishingly, there also were some members of the Jewish nationality who professed the Roman Catholic faith (74), Greek Catholicism (23), Greek Orthodoxy (12), Protestantism (19), and one woman, who was an adherent of the new Czechoslovak national faith. Thus the 180,616 members of the Jewish nationality who also professed the Jewish faith were joined by 229 co-nationals who professed other religions or none. There probably were many more thousands of Jews who never signed up as Jews by either nationality or religion and thus did not appear as such in the census" (S.W. Baron, "Who Is a Jew?" in *History and Jewish Historians*, 16f.).

The matter was far more serious in the Soviet Union. With its anti-religious bias the government eliminated all references to religious preference from the census, leaving only the Jewish nationality as a criterion. While most Jews declared themselves Jews by nationality, in each case the decision depended on the nationality entered in the passports of the respective heads of households. For one example, Leon Trotsky always signed up as a Russian by nationality, whereas Maxim Litvinov, even while serving as Soviet ambassador to the United States or as a Soviet foreign minister, always carried with him a passport marking his membership in the Jewish nationality. There is no way of telling how many Jews thus escaped being counted in the censuses of 1926, 1939, and again, in 1959. If the first Soviet census, even with respect to the territories which had formerly been part of Czarist Russia, was not quite comparable to the 1897 enumeration, the one of 1939 came on the eve of World War II and the German invasion of Russia. It has been subjected, therefore, to little detailed scrutiny and its Jewish aspects in particular have been inadequately explored.

Nonetheless, the situation was not hopeless. Many countries such as Austria-Hungary and its successor states, Germany, interwar Poland, the Baltic states, Romania, the emergent settlement in Palestine under the Mandate, and others had regular censuses which yielded relatively reliable information also on all aspects of Jewish demography. From these data one may deduce much also concerning the conditions in countries lacking satisfactory official census records. At any rate, quite apart from the accuracy of specific figures, certain major trends in the rise or decline of the Jewish population clearly manifested themselves throughout the Jewish world in the course of the 19th and the first third of the 20th centuries. This period was characterized by a "population explosion" of the Western world. In the relatively peaceful period of 1815–1914 Europe's population more than doubled (from some 190,000,000 to over 400,000,000), while European émigrés helped populate the Western Hemisphere and other continents. The United States alone increased its population from 7,240,000 in 1810 to 91,972,000 in 1910. Growth of this rapidity was owing less to increase in natality than to a sharp decrease in the death rate – a result of the great progress of medical science and the spread of more hygienic ways of life among the European and American masses.

In the Jewish case these factors operated with redoubled intensity. Like their neighbors in Eastern Europe, Jews still married quite early, definitely earlier than the average couples in Central and Western Europe. Marriages of boys aged between 15 and 18 with 14–16-year-old girls were quite common. An 18th-century Polish census mentions a Jewish wife aged eight. (Even in the West the burgomaster of Amsterdam had to prohibit in 1712 a marriage of a Jewish couple under the age of 12.) These conditions prevailed through most of the 19th century. As late as 1891, Arnold White, an English visitor to the Jewish agricultural colonies in the Ukrainian province of Kherson, was told by some Russian landowners who employed Jews that "they have no vice, unless early, improvident, and fruitful marriages can be deemed a vice" (*New Review*, 5, 98). Moreover, more than their neighbors, East European Jews (and many West Europeans as well) took the rabbinic interpretation of the blessing in Genesis (1:28) "Be fruitful, and multiply, and replenish the earth" as the first commandment in the Bible, rather than a blessing. A great many did not even consider the "moral restraint," propagated by Thomas Robert Malthus, as truly moral and hence shunned any form of birth control. More importantly, while their natality may more or less have equaled that of their equally fruitful East European neighbors, mortality, particularly the most decisive one of infants under one year of age and of children between two and five, was decidedly lower. In Czarist Russia's European provinces, for example, where general mortality per 1,000 inhabitants had declined from 37.1 to 31.2 between 1861–70 and 1895–1904, respectively, of 1,000 newly born children no less than 268 died before reaching their first birthday – a figure practically unchanged for several decades. Suffice it to mention that by 1967 the United States reduced its infant mortality to 22.1 per 1,000 and the U.S.S.R. to 26.3. Nor can these two superpowers boast of leading the world in this respect; they lag far behind Sweden, the Netherlands, New Zealand, Australia, and Japan. The Jewish population of Israel had in 1966 an infant mortality of only 21.6 per 1,000. Among the reasons for the long-term Jewish record of keeping newly born children alive was the extreme rarity of illegitimate births among Jews. As late as 1929 and 1930 among 100 Jewish children born in Vilna only 0.5 and 0.9 were illegitimate, whereas the ratio among the Catholics was 14%. More generally, even in the crowded East European ghettos medical help was much more readily available, while better hygienic conditions prevailed owing to the numerous requirements for religious ablutions and ritual food controls. There also was relatively greater family cohesiveness and devotion of Jewish parents to their children. Moreover, because of the strong sense of responsibility for each member by the community at large and the presence of numerous charitable societies specifically devoted to help the indigent sick, even the destitute groups were rarely deprived of basic nourishment and medical care. The result was that even in New York City, where the gap between Jews and non-Jews was constantly narrowing, Jewish infant mortality in 1915 was only 78 for each 1,000 births, whereas that for the rest of the population amounted to 105.

Similarly favorable, at least between 1800 and 1914, was the Jewish ratio in deaths occasioned by violence, particularly wars. It so happened that even most of the great Napoleonic battles took place outside territories densely inhabited by Jews. The same held true for the rest of the century until World War I. Jewish fatalities among combatants were relatively small because the two large centers of Jewish population, Czarist Russia and the Ottoman Empire, did not begin drafting Jews into the army until 1827 (in Congress Poland, 1845) and 1908, respectively. While in previous centuries Jews had suffered numerous casualties as a result of uprisings and massacres, the period of 1800 to 1914 was relatively quiescent in this respect. The Russian pogroms of 1881, 1891, 1903, and 1905, though highly significant in their psychological impact upon Jews and non-Jews, did not cause enough fatalities significantly to retard the growth of the Russian Jewish population. The situation changed abruptly during World War I when Poland, Galicia, Lithuania, Romania, as well as Salonika, Palestine, and other areas with large Jewish concentrations, were turned into theaters of war. Jewish combatants in the various armies also were quite numerous, probably exceeding 500,000 in the Russian, Austrian, German, and the Western Allied armies. Their high ratio of fatalities was exemplified by the death in battle of about 12,000 German Jewish soldiers. The aftermath of the war, particularly during the Communist Revolution and the civil war in Russia, and the following massacres of Ukrainian Jews, likewise caused much destruction of Jewish lives. However, the biological vitality of the people was still so great that losses thus sustained were quickly made up by the continuous natural increase in the world's Jewish population.

Incipient signs of retardation became noticeable in the Western countries toward the end of the 19th century, however. As is well known, the French population during the first decades of the 20th century had become practically stationary. Germany, England, and the United States also had declining birthrates which progressively narrowed down the surplus of births over deaths. Because of their increased concentration in urban, even metropolitan areas, which revealed these tendencies most pronouncedly, Jews were ahead of their neighbors in reducing their birthrate. At the same time their death rate, which had long declined, began to be stabilized owing to the relatively larger segment of old persons in the Jewish population, the result of the previous decline in Jewish mortality. Even in Polish Lodz, in 1919–29, where Jewish infant mortality of 134–54 contrasted favorably with the corresponding non-Jewish mortality of 171–203 per 1,000 births, the ratios were reversed in the case of persons over 70. At the beginning of the 20th century these trends had become so manifest that in 1908 Felix A. Theilhaber (in *Der Untergang der deutschen Juden*) warned his German coreligionists that, if these demographic weaknesses were to continue unabated, German Jewry, without the aid of immigration from the outside, would decline rapidly and ultimately die out.

These tendencies became more pronounced during and after World War I. In the years 1911–24 the general Prussian population still had an excess of births over deaths of 3,019,100 persons, but the Jewish population, on the contrary, had an excess mortality of 18,252. In 1925–28 Prussia's general population gained 1,182,056 persons, while the Prussian Jews lost 5,090 through natural causes (H. Silbergleit, *Bevoelkerungs*..., p. 39). These losses were made up only by the continued influx of Jews from Eastern Europe, as well as from the province of Posen (Poznan), which was allotted by the peace treaties to Poland. These adverse factors gradually unfolded also among the Jews of Western Europe and the United States. For example, a Jewish census taken in Buffalo in 1938 testified to a marked decline of the Jewish birthrate, much larger than that of non-Jews. While in the total population the age group under 15 amounted to 26.4% (1930), in the Jewish population it amounted to only 23.2%. The ratios of children under five were more unfavorable: 8.3 versus 6.3% (U.Z. Engelman, in: S. Robinson's *Jewish Population Studies*, 40). Most remarkably, these trends began affecting also the main reservoir of Jewish manpower in East-Central Europe. In 1926 the Soviet Jews had a birthrate of only 24.6 per 1,000 (as against 35.9 30 years before, and 43.3 of the 1926 Soviet population as a whole), the lowest of all major nationalities in the Union. Such large cities as Vienna and Budapest actually had an excess of Jewish mortality over natality (2,709 deaths vs. 1,343 births in Vienna in 1929 and a still larger surplus of 1,588 deaths in Budapest in 1932). Even in Warsaw in 1925–29 the Jewish ratio of 15.5 births vs. 11.1 deaths per 1,000 contrasted with that of 22.4:15.4 among the city's Christians. On a world scale these retarding tendencies still were partially made up by an increasing growth of the Jewish population in North Africa and some other Oriental communities. There the introduction of improved sanitary conditions and health services by the colonial powers before and after World War I created conditions similar to those of the European nations in the preceding century. With the speedily declining death rate, particularly among infants and children, and continued high birthrate, the surplus of births over deaths constantly increased. Nonetheless, the disquieting demographic trends in the much larger Ashkenazi communities were so great that in the 1930s sociologists began to warn the Jewish people that, before very long, their world population would become stationary and begin declining at an accelerated pace thereafter.

Other socioreligious factors, especially conversions and mixed marriages, further aggravated the decline in the rate of increase in Jewish population. In the history of the Jewish dispersion both in the East and the West there always existed converts out of Judaism to Christianity and Islam. For the most part this was a one-way street, since conversions from the dominant faiths to Judaism were outlawed, often under the sanction of capital punishment. Such prohibitions continued throughout the 19th century in Czarist Russia and the Ottoman Empire. Elsewhere, too, social and economic pressures led many more Jews to adopt Christianity than vice versa. Even in Russia, with its staunchly Orthodox Jewish majority, strong conversionist impulses were generated by the Re*krutchina* (forcible draft for long-term military service, often involving young children) over the three decades of 1827–56 (see *Cantonists). Under these and other pressures the number of baptized Jews increased substantially during the 19th century. According to the Berlin missionary, Johannes de la Roi, a biased but informed student of the missionary movements, no less than 84,500 Russian Jews found their way to the baptismal front in the 1800s ("*Judentaufen im neunzehnten Jahrhundert, ein statistischer Versuch*," in *Nathanael*, vol. 15, 65–118). The ratio was understandably higher in such a Western country as Prussia, where the number of Jewish converts to Christianity seems to have reached a peak of 3,771 in the years 1812–14, according to A. Menes' computation.

Elsewhere the statistics are not very good but the number of Jews who left their community often increased threateningly. In Austria-Hungary, before World War I the second-largest center of the Jewish population, most of those who took that step were not necessarily converts. Many of them simply declared themselves persons without religion (*konfessionslos*). In Vienna alone the number of such losses to the community often amounted to 1,000 annually in the period after World War I. In Prussia, on the other hand, as a result of the Jewish Community Law of 1876 many Jews severed their ties with the existing communities because of real or alleged "religious scruples." While some of these Jews merely wished to separate themselves from the middle-of-the-road communities and to join special Orthodox groupings (the so-called *Trennungsorthodoxie*), most others did it for financial or other secularist reasons. In other countries, too, conversions to Judaism were relatively rare; they were far outweighed by conversions of Jews to other faiths, or their simple disappearance within the majority without formal action. Many of the *konfessionslos* persons, particularly in Austria, adopted this status in order to marry out of the faith, since until the interwar period the marriage of a Catholic to a Jew was legally invalid. In Germany, France, and Italy, too, mixed marriages were quite frequent. In one year (1927) 52% of marriages entered into by the Jews of Trieste had a non-Jewish partner. Demographically, intermarriage interfered with the growth of Jewish population in two ways. Unlike in the United States in recent years, European couples, when denominationally divided, as a rule raised their children as Christians rather than as Jews. Secondly, perhaps to avoid further complications, many intermarried couples refrained from having children altogether or were satisfied with but a single child. The end result was a further diminution of the Jewish numbers.

Under these circumstances only tentative estimates can be given for many figures in Table 3, Jewish Population 1820–1939. They relate to the three periods of 1820–25 (rather than 1800, because after the rapid changes during the Napoleonic Wars the frontiers of the countries of Jewish settlement essentially stable until (World War I), 1900 (before World War I), and 1939 (on the eve of World II).

Table 3. Jewish population 1820–1939

	1820–25		1900		1939	
	Jewish population	Total population	Jewish population	Total population	Jewish population	Total population
			(in thousands)			
Europe						
Russia (including Congress Poland)	1,600.0	46,000	5,190.0 (1897)	126,368		
U.S.S.R. (including Asiatic parts)	–	–	–	–	2,825.0	132,519
Poland (including Galicia, Posen, etc.)	–	–	–	–	3,250.0	32,183
Lithuania (1923)	–	–	–	–	155.0	2,029
Latvia (1935)	–	–	–	–	95.0	1,951
Estonia (1934)	–	–	–	–	4.56	1,126
Romania (enlarged after 1918)	80.0	3,335	267.0	5,956	850.0	18,053
Austria–Hungary (before 1918)	568.0	26,000	2,069.0	44,400	–	–
Austria (1934)	–	–	–	–	191.0	6,760
Czechoslovakia (1930)	–	–	–	–	357.0	14,730
Hungary (1930)	–	–	–	–	445.0	8,688
Yugoslavia (1931)	–	–	5.1	2,494	68.0	13,934
Greece	–	–	5.8	2,434 (1896)	73.0 (1928)	6,205
Turkey (European, 1935)	–	–	–	–	50.0	1,266
Germany	223.0	26,624	520.0	56,367	504.0 (1933)	65,988
Switzerland (1837)	2.0	2,190	12.5	3,315	18.0 (1930)	4,066
Italy	25.0	19,000	35.0	32,449	48.0 (1936)	42,528
Great Britain and Northern Ireland	20.0	21,130	200.0	41,457	300.0 (1931)	46,190
France (including Alsace–Lorraine)	50.0	30,000	115.0 (A.L.) 35.0	38,961	260.0 (1936)	41,906
Netherlands	45.0	2,460	104.0	5,179	112.0 (1930)	7,936
Belgium	2.0	3,500	20.0	6,693	60.0 (1930)	8,092
Europe (as a whole)	2,730.0	190,000	8,690.0	423,000	9,480.0	512,849
The Americas						
United States	8.0	5,308	1,000.0	75,995	4,975.0 (1940)	131,669
Canada	–	–	16.0	4,833	155.7.0 (1931)	10,377
Mexico	–	–	1.0	13,600	9.0 (1930)	16,523
Argentina	–	–	30.0	4,900	275.0 (1935)	12,958
Brazil	–	–	2.0	17,300	35.0 (1930)	40,273
Uruguay	–	–	0.9	840	12.0 (1931)	1,903
The Americas (as a whole)	10.0	–	1,175.0	144,000	5,537.0	261,985
Asia						
Palestine	45.0	–	78.0	650	475.0	1,467
Asiatic Turkey	–	–	300.0	16,134	30.0	14,935
Iraq	–	–	–	–	91.0	3,560
Syria and Lebanon	–	–	–	–	26.0 (1935)	3,630
Yemen and Arabia	–	–	30.0	7,000	50.0 (1935)	1,000
Iran	–	–	35.0	9,000	50.0 (1935)	15,000
India	–	–	18.2	232,000	24.0 (1931)	352,838
China	–	–	2.0	402,680	10.0 (1936)	457,835
Japan	–	–	–	43,760	2.0	72,876
Asia (as a whole)	300.0	–	420.0	857,000	1,047.0	1,094,524

Table 3. Jewish population 1820–1939 (cont,)

	1820–25		1900		1939	
	Jewish population	Total population	Jewish population	Total population (in thousands)	Jewish population	Total population
Africa						
Egypt	–	–	30.7	9,734	70.0 (1937)	15,905
Morocco	–	–	103.7 (1904)	5,000	162.0 (1936)	7,096
Algeria	20,000.0 (1851)	–	51.0	4,729	110.0 (1931)	7,235
Tunisia	–	–	62.5	1,500	59.5 (1936)	2,608
Ethiopia	–	–	50.0	5,000	51.0 (1935)	10,000
Union of South Africa	–	–	40.0	1,100	90.7 (1936)	9,590
Africa (as a whole)	240.0	–	300.0	120,000	627.5	157,650
Oceania						
Australia	–	–	15.0	3,036	23.6 (1933)	6,630
New Zealand	–	–	1.6	773	2.7 (1936)	1,574
Oceania (as a whole)	1.0	–	17.0	4,730	33.0	–
World total	3,281.0	1,171,000	10,602.5	1,608,000	16,724.0	2,296,000

From the table's figures, however unreliable in detail, one may obtain an approximation of both the growth and the shifts of the Jewish population over the 120 years from 1820 to 1939. They are largely cited here from the works of Jacob Lestschinsky, notwithstanding serious reservations as to the accuracy of all such computations. The most startling evolution was, of course, that of the Jewish population in the Western Hemisphere which was owing more to Jewish migrations than to natural increase. The United States, in particular, in the half-century preceding World War I became the great magnet for immigrants from Eastern Europe, as well as from almost all other European and Middle Eastern countries. Suffice it to say that in the course of merely 24 years, from 1890 to 1914, some 30% of all East European Jews changed their residence to some overseas country, particularly the United States. In addition, there were major migratory movements of Jews within their countries of settlement. Many Russian Jews moved into the newly annexed neo-Russian territories in the south, including a number of agricultural colonies established for them on the initiative of the Czarist regime. They also spoke in the 1830s of the Jewish "discovery of Volhynia" which brought many new Jewish settlers from the western provinces into that area which had made noteworthy contributions to Jewish culture already in pre-partition Poland. On the other hand, a great many Russian Jews, often simply called Litvaks, settled in Congress Poland in the years before World War I. After the removal of the *Pale of Settlement as a result of that war and the Communist Revolution, there was a great exodus of Jews from the original Pale into the interior of Russia, particularly the two metropolises of Moscow and Leningrad, as well as such newly founded industrial centers as Magnitogorsk in the Urals. There also was a small Jewish movement to Far Eastern *Birobidzhan, more significant ideologically than numerically. Similarly, there was a constant transplantation of Jews from Galicia to other parts of Austria-Hungary, particularly to neighboring Bukovina and Slovakia and the two capitals of Vienna and Budapest. The same holds true for the formerly Polish possessions incorporated into Prussia in the years 1772–95 but subsequently lost to resurrected Poland in 1919. The majority of Jewish residents of that area had been leaving it for other parts of Germany, England, and the United States throughout the 19th century, but their departure was accelerated after 1918.

These migratory movements gave additional stimuli to the process of Jewish urbanization which had long been under way. The settlement of Jews in many major cities and metropolitan areas far exceeded their ratio in the respective populations. The climactic urban and metropolitan concentration of Jews continued in the course of the 20th century.

1940–1971

These three decades belong to the most portentous periods of human history, general and demographic. They also were of decisive historic importance in the destinies of the Jewish people. Begun with the great Holocaust, which destroyed thousands of European Jewish communities and ended eight centuries of European Jewish hegemony, the decade of the 1940s ended with the rise of the State of Israel. This ushered in an entirely new period of Jewish history which has already had demographic effects of enormous importance.

Despite the ever-growing literature on the Holocaust, certain aspects have not yet been sufficiently explored. Among the questions still incompletely resolved is the precise number of victims of the Nazi extermination squads. The accepted figure of 6,000,000 Jews, along with many more millions of non-Jews slain by the Nazis, has often been challenged, especially by some German writers. One of the major difficulties in obtaining definitive and precise figures consists in the fact that, in pursuing their "final solution" of the Jewish question, the Nazi authorities were quite careful in simultaneously destroying human lives and the records pertaining to them. In his oft-quoted Posen speech of Oct. 4, 1943, Heinrich Himmler alluded to the "very grave matter" of exterminating Jews and declared: "Among ourselves it should be mentioned quite frankly, and yet we shall never speak about it publicly… I mean… the extirpation of the Jewish race. This is a page of glory in our history which has never been written and is never to be written."

Yet not only does the partial evidence from various localities confirm the 6,000,000 estimate, but it also emerges as the most likely figure from the demographic changes in European and world Jewish population during the war and postwar periods (see *Holocaust). If on the eve of World War II the Jewish people numbered some 16,750,000, by 1945 this number was reduced to about 11,000,000. True, in addition to their victimization at the hands of Nazi extermination squads, Jews suffered considerable losses in manpower as combatants in the Soviet, U.S., and other armies, as well as from the numerous other adverse by-products of the great war. But these losses should easily have been made up by the natural growth of the Jewish population during the six war years, especially in the Western Hemisphere and other continents where the war touched only the periphery of Jewish life. Moreover, even the defeated nations of Germany, Italy, and Japan quickly recovered their biological strength and in the two decades of 1940–60 increased their populations by 25–33%. But the Jewish people which, if allowed to continue its population growth of the preceding two decades, by 1960 should have reached a total of 19,000,000–20,000,000 persons, counted instead no more than 12,800,000 persons. Even today, another decade later, it still is very far from returning to its populousness of 1939. As a result of the Holocaust and World War II there was a complete shift of the center of gravity of the Jewish people from the Old to the New World. With Russian Jewry not only weakened, but subject to a severe antisemitic onslaught especially during the declining years of Stalin's regime in 1948–52, its isolation from the rest of Jewry became even tighter than before. Its influence on the historic progress of the entire people, particularly in the cultural sphere, declined rapidly. The demographic picture, too, of the entire European Continent was affected adversely, although Western Europe, particularly France, has staged a steady recovery in the postwar era: in the French case because of the growing immigration of North African Jews. During the prolonged Algerian uprising the Jewish communities of that country reaching back to antiquity and glorying in a great historic tradition were nearly emptied; their majority found shelter in either France or Israel. So did many refugees from other Arab countries.

In reaction to the rise of the State of Israel in 1948 anti-Jewish pressures on the declining Jewries in all Arab countries became unbearable. With the exception of Morocco and Tunisia where substantial remnants of the Jewish inhabitants have carried on against tremendous odds, the other Arab countries almost totally lost their long-established Jewish populations. On the other hand, the very rise of Israel opened untold new possibilities for the concentration of Jews in that country. By absorbing the majority of Jewish émigrés from the Arab lands, as well as most of the surviving remnants of victims of Nazi persecution in continental Europe located in the displaced persons camps, together with migrants from many other countries, Israel's unparalleled population growth more than redressed the balance as far as the continent of Asia was concerned. But Africa continued to be in the losing column also in many of the newly arisen black republics, where the small Jewish communities were further reduced in size by emigration.

Regrettably, during the 1940–70 period the demographic facts relating to Jews became less rather than more thoroughly investigated. To begin with, such leading European countries as Poland, Czechoslovakia, Austria, Germany, and Holland, which before World War II offered, through their governmental censuses, excellent source material for Jewish demography, became so depopulated of Jews that between them they accommodated but little more than 1% of world Jewry. Their place was taken only by Israel, whose excellent censuses and annual statistical estimates have in many ways become a mainstay of Jewish demographic research. Israel scholarship has even helped to stimulate such investigation in other lands. In the largest country of Jewish settlement, the United States, the situation likewise improved somewhat. Although the governmental censuses still fail to supply adequate information, the awareness of U.S. Jewry of the need to be acquainted with the demographic facts of life had been sufficiently aroused to call forth a number of local surveys in the 1950s and the 1960s. While these were consistently enough pursued so as to furnish successive data from decade to decade, nor conducted with the same methods so as to make them fully comparable with one another, they managed to assemble a substantial body of material from which statistical conclusions of a sort could be derived with somewhat greater assurance. All this was merely a beginning, but it appeared, at least, to be a step in the right direction. Similar hesitant steps were made in Western Europe, Argentina, and most successfully, in Canada, where the governmental censuses help supply many vital statistics relating to Jews.

At the same time figures for the second-largest Jewish community, that of the Soviet Union, were still almost exclusively dependent on foreign Jews analyzing the results of the official censuses. That of 1959 was published by the government in 16 volumes, together with some additional data periodically supplied by the official census bureau in regular bulletins. One of the most puzzling problems concerning that census was the question of the extent to which the figures given for Jewish "nationality" really covered Soviet Jewry. Though every Soviet citizen had to carry a "passport" indicating his "nationality" many Jews could escape registering as members of that nationality in the presence of enumerators, since the census takers were instructed to register only the indications made orally by the inhabitants without checking their documents. A good case was made, therefore, for raising the results of the 1959 census which gave the total number of Jews as 2,267,814 and to postulate that their total really came close to 3,000,000.

On April 17, 1971, the Soviet press published the first summaries of the population census taken on Jan. 15, 1970. According to the figures quoted, the Jewish population fell from 11th to 12th in size among 100 nationalities in the Soviet Union, and the overall number of Jews declined from 2,267,814 (January 1959) to 2,151,000.

Despite all the obscurities and uncertainties, one may perhaps venture to propose the Table: World Population, Jewish, largely based (with all due reservations) upon the estimates annually published in the *American Jewish Year Book* and the United Nations' *Statistical Yearbook*.

Regrettably, some of the above data refer to censuses or estimates of populations in the cities proper, while others cover metropolitan districts of a wider area. In the same 1969 edition of *The World Almanac* (pp. 578f., 604ff., and 651), for example, the number of inhabitants in New York City, according to the census of 1960, was given as 7,781,984, and in Greater New York (embracing an additional 8 New Jersey and 5 New York counties) as 14,114,927. In Los Angeles the respective 1960 figures were 2,479,015 and 6,488,791; in Chicago: 3,550,404 and 6,488,791; in Buenos Aires: 2,966,816 and 6,762,629; in Paris: 2,811,171 and 7,369,387 (1962 census) or 9,811,171 (1968 estimate), and so forth. (Incidentally, the same issue of the *Almanac*, p. 602, offers somewhat different estimates of the Jewish population by counties and cities, as prepared by Dr. S.H. Linfield.) Jews had fully participated in that postwar movement, some call it flight, from the core cities to the suburbs, making estimates between official censuses or several years after the completion of communal surveys quite hazardous. It is quite evident that in 1970 about one-half of world Jewry lived in the Western Hemisphere, the United States embracing far more Jews than any other country. In 1970, the second- and third-largest concentrations were found in the U.S.S.R. and Israel. Together, the United States, the U.S.S.R., and Israel between them embraced more than 80% of world Jewry.

The progress of Jewish settlement in major cities during the period of 1900–69 proceeded apace at a tempo even more rapid than that of the general population. Already before 1939 about one quarter of the entire Jewish people lived in metropolitan areas of over 1,000,000 each. Another quarter lived in cities with populations of between 100,000 and 1,000,000 inhabitants. Thirty years later the latter ratio still was approximately correct. But the percentage of "metropolitan" Jews had risen to about 40% of the whole people, leaving barely a third for localities, urban and rural, with less than 100,000 inhabitants. In many countries, moreover, the metropolitan ratios were considerably exceeded; for instance, in England, France, and Argentina, the majority of Jews have long lived in the capitals, while in the United States such a majority may be found in a radius of 100 miles from Times Square in New York. This evolution would not have been surprising even under more normal circumstances, since this is indeed a world-wide trend. Even the Soviet Union, which in the 1920s started as an overwhelmingly rural country, had an urban majority. The Holocaust, however, greatly accelerated that trend, inasmuch as it put an end to most of the agricultural colonies and other rural Jewish settlements in Russia, Carpathian Ruthenia (where originally more than one quarter of the Jewish population engaged in agriculture), and elsewhere. It also eliminated most of the hamlets which still accommodated a large segment of the East European Jewish population. Even in the United States postwar developments were not favorable to Jewish agricultural colonization. The same held true for Israel, where the mass immigration of the first 20 years of statehood strengthened the trend toward urban concentration.

The increase in Jewish population from 1948 to 1968 lagged far behind that of the world population as well as that of most environmental peoples. Mankind as a whole increased by around 36% between 1948 and 1968, but world Jewry added less than 20% to its numbers. This is clearly not the result of increased mortality, but rather of a relatively lower birthrate. The phenomenon of the declining Jewish birthrate so manifest in the Western countries in the interwar period gave way to a growing natality in the 1940s and the 1950s. However, this trend seems not to have lasted to the same extent into the 1960s. While conversions to other religions greatly diminished, the relative demographic ravages caused by intermarriage increased, particularly in the U.S.S.R. and Western Europe, where the offspring of mixed marriages were more likely permanently to sever its ties with the Jewish community. Under these circumstances, it was clear that it would take many more years before the Jewish people recovered its population strength of 1939.

For developments in the last third of the 20th century, see *Demography; *Vital Statistics.

BIBLIOGRAPHY: J. Jacobs, *Studies in Jewish Statistics* (1890); A. Nossig, *Juedische Statistik* (1903), incl. extensive bibl.; U.O. Schmelz (comp.), *Jewish Demography and Statistics: Bibliography for 1920–1960* (1961), Heb. and Eng., with R. Shebath, addenda and index of names (1961); *Zeitschrift fuer Demographie und Statistik der Juden* (1905–1919); AJYB, index; JSOS, index; JJS; Baron, Social and Social²; idem, in: L. Feldman (ed.), *Ancient and Medieval Essays*; E. Ashtor, in: JJS, vols. 18–19 (1967–68); idem, in: *Zion*, 28 (1963); I.S. Revah, in: REJ, 122 (1963); R. Bachi, in: RMI, 12 (1938); idem, in: JJS, 4 (1962); G. Kleczyński and Z. Kluczycki, *Licba głów żydowskich w koronie, z taryf roku 1765* (1898); R. Mahler, in: *Lodzer Visenshaftlekhe Shriftn*, 1 (1938); B. Wasiutyński, *Ludność żydowska w Polsce w wiekach XIX i XX* (1930); J. Unna, *Statistik der Frankfurter Juden bis zum Jahre 1866* (1931); A. Ruppin, *Soziologie der Juden*, 2 vols. (1931–32); idem, *Jewish Fate and Future* (1940); L. Livi, *Ebrei alla luce della statistica* (1920); J. Lestschinsky, in: *Historishe Shriftn*, 1 (1928); idem, in: UJE, 10 (1943), s.v. *Statistics*; idem, *Tefuẓot Yisrael Aḥarei ha-Milḥamah* (1948); I. Cohen, *Contemporary Jewry* (1950); A. Tartakower, in: HUCA, 23 (1950–51); idem, *Ha-Ḥevrah ha-Yehudit* (1957); *Annual of the Institute of Jewish Affairs* (1956), 315–44; S. Shaul (ed.), *Am Yisrael be-Dorenu* (1964); idem, *La vie juive dans l'Europe contemporaine* (1967, also in Heb.); U.Z. Engelman, in: JSOS, 9 (1947); H.S. Linfield, *Jews in the*

United States 1927 (1929); S.M. Robinson, *Jewish Population Studies* (1943), with J. Starr; I. Rosenberg, *Canada's Jews* (1939); I. Rosenwaite, in: JSOS, 22 (1960); M. Friedman (ed.), *A Minority in Britain* (1955); F. Bosse, *Die Verbreitung der Juden im Deutschen Reich... 1880* (1885); H. Silbergleit, *Bevoelkerungs – und Berufsverhaeltnisse der Juden im Deutschen Reich*, 1 (1930); G.A. Schimmer, *Statistik des Judenthums der im Reichsrate vertretenen Koenigreiche und Laender* (1873); L. Goldhammer, *Die Juden Wiens* (1927); B. Blau, in: *Yidishe Ekonomik*, 3 (1939); I. Schiper, *Żydzi w Polsce odrodzonej*, 2 vols. (n.d.), with a demographic study by A. Tartakower; I. Canter, *Di Yidishe Bafolkerung in Ukraine* (Kharkov, 1929); L. Zinger, *Dos Banayte Folk* (Moscow, 1941); M. Altschuler, in: *Gesher*, nos. 47–48 (1966); J. Rothenberg, in: JSOS, 29 (1967), 234–40; 31 (1969), 37–39; Palestine, Department of Statistics, *Vital Statistics, Tables 1929–1945* (1947); Israel, Central Bureau of Statistics, *Statistical Abstract of Israel*; United Nations, Statistical Office, *Statistical Yearbook*; U.O. Schmelz and P. Glikson (ed.), *Jewish Population Studies 1961–1968* (1970). For the 1970–2005 period, see Bibliography in *Demography.

[Salo W. Baron]

PORAT, ORNA (1924–), Israeli actress. Born in Germany of non-Jewish parents, Orna Porat was an established actress when she decided to settle in Israel. After learning Hebrew, she joined the *Cameri Theater and became a leading player. Among her important parts were Shaw's Saint Joan, Schiller's Mary Stuart, and the leading role in *The Good Soul of Sechuan* by Brecht. She also participated in the management of the Cameri, and was head of the company's children's theater. She was awarded the Israel Prize in the arts (theater) in 1979.

PORATH, ISRAEL (1886–1974), rabbi. Israel Porath (son of Aryeh Lieb and Sara Sharashevsky) was born in Jerusalem, the second of seven children. His grandfather Yosef and his grandmother Malka came to Palestine from Lithuania in 1837. Malka came from 15 generations of rabbis. His grandfather and father were among the best-known painters and decorators in Jerusalem, who, according to family tradition, had decorated both the Cave of Machpelah in Hebron and Jerusalem's Hurvah Synagogue. Moses Montefiore had presented a citation to them for being self-employed, rather than living off of the *ḥalukkah*, the funds of the community. As a young boy he studied at the Eẓ Ḥayyim Yeshivah and at Yeshivat Ohel Moshe. When Rabbi Abraham Isaac *Kook arrived in Jaffa in 1904, he traveled to meet him and became one of his preferred students. Rabbi Kook said of him that from all of his students he received the most pleasure from Rabbi Porath and Rabbi Jacob Ḥarlap. In 1905 he married Peshe Miriam Tiktin, the sister of Rabbi David Tiktin, who was the *mashgi'aḥ* (spiritual advisor) at Eẓ Ḥayyim Yeshivah. He received ordination from Rabbi Kook as well as from Rabbi Chaim Berlin and Rabbi Jacob David Willowsky (the Slutzker Rav).

In 1906 he founded a spiritual center for young Torah scholars called Beit Va'ad le-Ḥakhamim and served as the principal and director of Doresh Ẓiyyon, a school system for Sephardi students. He became increasingly involved in religious and political issues of the *yishuv* and in 1911 was the Ashkenazi candidate for the position of *ḥakham bashi* (chief rabbi); however, time-honored tradition won out and only Sephardi chief rabbis were selected (Rabbi Ouziel was chosen). At the behest of the leadership of the *yishuv* he was encouraged to learn foreign languages and was sent to Constantinople to secure draft deferments for yeshivah students from the Turkish army.

During World War I he was responsible for emergency welfare, food, and clothing in Jerusalem, in conjunction with the American Jewish Joint Distribution Committee. He participated in founding many new neighborhoods on the western side of Jerusalem, including Bayit ve-Gan.

In light of post-war economic difficulties as well as internal political strife between the pro- and anti-Zionist factions in the *yishuv*, he left Palestine in 1922, first for Liverpool, England and then for the United States, to head an office for the Eẓ Ḥayyim Yeshivah, where he was joined by his family (in September 1923). He served as a rabbi at Congregation B'nai Israel in Plainfield, New Jersey, and in 1925 moved to Cleveland to become the rabbi of Congregation Oheb Zedek, where he served for 14 years. He then moved to Congregation Neve Zedek, and in 1945 went to New York to head the Rabbi Israel Salanter Yeshivah. He returned to Cleveland within the year where he was rabbi at the Cleveland Heights Jewish Center until his death in 1974.

He was regarded as one of the outstanding leaders of Orthodox Jewish life in Cleveland. In addition to his serving as one of the founders and chairman of the Orthodox Rabbinical Council of Cleveland (Merkaz Harabanim) he was active in the general Jewish community, including the Board of the Jewish Welfare Federation, the Board of Jewish Education, and B'nai B'rith. He was instrumental in the establishment of the Telz Yeshiva in Cleveland. He was an ardent Zionist and a member of the Mizrachi (Religious Zionists of America); he was honored by numerous Zionist organizations for his work on behalf of the State of Israel, including Bar-Ilan University and the Jewish National Fund. He served as the dean of the Cleveland rabbinate for more than 50 years.

He wrote numerous scholarly articles on rabbinic literature. His major contribution was the *Mavo ha-Talmud* (seven volumes), which he composed at the inspiration of his great teacher and mentor, Rabbi Kook, who had encouraged him many years previously (already in 1913) to dedicate himself to writing a new introduction to the Talmud, based on careful research and presentation of the classical sources.

Rabbi Israel Porath died in Cleveland and was buried in Jerusalem. His beloved wife of 68 years, Peshe Miriam, had passed away four months previously. They had six sons and a daughter (Samuel, Josef, Tzvi Haim, Benjamin, Benzion, David, and Shoshana Haas). Many of his descendants returned to Israel including three of his children, nine of his grandchildren, and dozens of great grandchildren. A street is named for him in Jerusalem's Ramot neighborhood (Rehov Harav Yisrael Porath). Three of his sons became rabbis: Samuel Porath, who became a rabbi in Niagara Falls; Benjamin Porath;

and Tzvi Porath, who was rabbi for nearly half a century in Chevy Chase, Maryland. Two of his grandsons also became rabbis, Gerald Porath and Jonathan Porath, who directs the JDC programs in West Russia.

[Jonathan D. Porath (2nd ed.)]

°PORCHETUS SALVAGUS (Victor Porchetto de Salvatici; d. c. 1315), Italian Carthusian of Genoa. Porchetus wrote an anti-Jewish work entitled *Victoria adversus impios Hebraeos, in qua tum ex sacris litteris tum ex dictis Talmud ac cabbilistarum et aliorum omnium authorum quos hebraei recipiunt monstratur veritas catholicae fidei.*

The first part (24 chapters) enumerates proofs to demonstrate the truth of Christianity from the Holy Scriptures, and the second part (16 chapters) similarly instances proofs from the Kabbalah and rabbinic sources. Porchetus' material was not original, being copied mostly from the *Pugio fidei* of Raymond *Martini. His book in turn was copied by later writers such as Pietro *Galatinus Columna and others. The book by Porchetus appeared in Paris in 1520. Its introduction (*prologus*) was reprinted by J.C. Wolf in his *Bibliotheca Hebraea* (vol. 2, 1124–27).

BIBLIOGRAPHY: P. Browe, *Die Judenmission im Mittelalter und die Juden* (1942), 104, 108; A. Posnanski, *Schilo* (1904), 370–8; H. Merhavia, *Ha-Talmud bi-Re'i ha-Naẓrut* (1970), index.

[Judah M. Rosenthal]

PORGES, HEINRICH (1837–1900), writer and conductor. Born in Prague, Porges became coeditor with K.F. Brendel of the *Neue Zeitschrift fuer Musik*, Leipzig (1863) and in 1867 he was responsible, with the editor Julius Froebel, for the arts pages of the *Sueddeutsche Presse*. From 1863, he was drawn into Richard Wagner's circle and became a staunch champion of the composer, and at Wagner's request, he documented in detail in *Die Bühnenproben zu den Bayreuther Festspielen des Jahres 1876* (Leipzig, 1881–96). After living for a while in Vienna he was called to Munich by Wagner's patron, Ludwig II of Bavaria, for whom he had written a study of Wagner's *Tristan und Isolde* (publ. 1906). In 1886 he founded the Porges Choral Society, which promoted the works of Berlioz and Bruckner.

BIBLIOGRAPHY: Grove Music Online.

[Israela Stein (2nd ed.)]

PORGES, MOSES BEN ISRAEL NAPHTALI (17th century), rabbi and emissary of the Ashkenazi community of Jerusalem. Born in Prague, he was a relative of Isaiah ha-Levi *Horowitz, whom he followed to Ereẓ Israel, settling in Jerusalem, where he became a scribe. When, after the *Chmielnicki massacres of 1648–49, the contributions from Poland to Jerusalem ceased, and the Ashkenazi community in Jerusalem was overwhelmed with debt, Porges was sent as their emissary to Germany. During this mission he published, in Prague or in Frankfurt, his small work *Darkhei Ẓiyyon* designed to arouse sympathy and obtain support for the Jewish community in Ereẓ Israel.

This work, one of the best examples of this type of literature, is divided into four sections: the virtue of living in Ereẓ Israel, prayer, study, memorial prayers. The first section is a kind of guidebook for new immigrants to Israel, in which Moses draws upon his personal experiences and advises them on what to take for the journey, the easiest routes, how to conduct themselves on the way and the like. In this section he also gives practical details on prices and currency, describes the foods available in Ereẓ Israel, recounts in detail how much is needed for living, rent, and taxes, and lists customs of dress and conduct in everyday life. In the second section he describes in detail the liturgical customs of Jerusalem, in the third section, the methods of study there, including various details about the holy places, and in the fourth, customs then practiced in Jerusalem, among them those of reciting memorial prayers for the departed and of obtaining contributions from generous individuals outside of Ereẓ Israel, in whose honor lights were kindled in the synagogues on Sabbaths and festivals and for whom blessings were invoked. The book was directed to the masses, and therefore was written in the language they knew best – Yiddish. It succeeded admirably in its aim of presenting an attractive picture of Israel. *Darkhei Ẓiyyon* has only been published once and is very rare.

BIBLIOGRAPHY: A. Yaari, *Masot Ereẓ Yisrael* (1946), 267–304, 770f.; Yaari, Sheluḥei, 275–6.

[Avraham Yaari]

PORGES, NATHAN (1848–1924), rabbi, scholar, and bibliographer. Born in Prossnitz, Moravia, Porges received his rabbinical diploma at the Breslau seminary, in 1874. He served as rabbi in Nakel, Mannheim, Pilsen, and Karlsbad (Karlovy Vary), and from 1888 to 1917 in Leipzig, where he was awarded the title of professor in 1913. His important library contained many incunabula and rare books, which were dispersed and sold through book dealers (cf. Shunami, Bibl, index s.v.).

He wrote articles on Hebrew bibliography which appeared in the *Revue des Etudes Juives*, the *Zeitschrift fuer hebraeische Bibliographie*, and other periodicals. Porges was an expert in medieval Hebrew philology and literature, publishing essays on *Dunash ibn Labrat, Judah *Hayyuj, and Joseph *Bekhor Shor, as well as *Bibelkunde und Babelfunde* (1903) and some sermons.

BIBLIOGRAPHY: M. Brann, in: *Breslau Festschrift zum 50-jaehrigen Jubilaeum der Anstalt* (1904), 188 (includes bibliography).

PORIYYAH (Heb. פּוֹרִיָּה), two urban quarters and a village in northern Israel, on the Poriyyah Ridge, just S. of *Tiberias. Poriyyah was founded in 1912 as a fruit farm, mainly based on almond plantations, by a group of American Zionists. A few of these Zionists went to settle on the site which was worked by Jewish laborers. The place was abandoned in World War I. In 1940 kibbutz *Alummot temporarily settled on the site. In 1949 a work village (*kefar avodah*) was established there by immigrants from Yemen. In 1952 it became an affiliate of Tenu'at ha-Moshavim but later left the association and remained unaffiliated. A government regional hospital was built further north in 1949, as well as housing projects of Upper Tiberias. A youth hostel, named after the veteran Tiberias inhabitant, Y. Taiber, was opened at Poriyyah. In 1968 the village had 180 inhabitants, the Poriyyah Illit quarter had 790, and the Neveh Oved quarter, 750. In 2002 the village population was 288, the Poriyyah Illit population 529, and Neveh Oved had 888 inhabitants.

[Efraim Orni]

°**PORPHYRY** (233–305 C.E.), Greek philosopher, disciple of Plotinus, and one of the most versatile thinkers of his day. Porphyry displayed considerable interest in Judaism, both as one of the ancient religions of the Orient and as the source of Christianity, to which he was hostile. His attitude to Judaism is sympathetic. In his *De Abstinentia* he cites Josephus (the only pagan writer to do so), drawing upon his description of the Essenes, and he describes with commiseration the misfortunes suffered by the Jews during the reign of *Antiochus Epiphanes and under Roman rule. In his life of Pythagoras, he features him as a disciple of the Hebrews. In his lost polemic against Christianity, Porphyry did not confine himself to criticism of the books of the Bible and of the New Testament, but conducted an empirical investigation which revealed a knowledge of biblical sources even greater than that of *Celsus, his predecessor in this field. Porphyry devoted an entire book to discussion of the Book of Daniel (referred to in Jerome's commentary), concluding that it was written by a Jewish contemporary of Antiochus Epiphanes, and that it can, therefore, only be regarded as "prophecy after the event."

BIBLIOGRAPHY: J. Bidez, *Vie de Porphyre* (1913); A.B. Hulen, *Porhyry's Work against the Christians* (1933); Schroeder, in: *Welt als Geschichte*, 17 (1957), 196–202; Reinach, Textes, 203–6.

[Menahem Stern]

PORTAL. The design of a single or double doorway, with flanking columns, appeared early in Jewish funerary art, synagogue mosaics, and paintings, and on glass, lamps, and later in textiles and manuscripts. At first it signified a physical symbol of the concept of the heavenly abode and, later, came to represent the Torah Shrine and the destroyed Temple of Jerusalem. Together with the **menorah*, snuff shovel, **etrog*, **lulav*, and **shofar*, the portal is one of the most common Jewish symbols found from the first centuries of the Common Era. The meaning of the design goes back to the ancient Oriental symbol for the residence of the gods on high. The doorway represented and signified the entrance to the heavenly precincts. Gods were portrayed standing or sitting in the doorway while the sun god Shamash from second-millennium-B.C.E. Akkadian art was frequently shown rising in the eastern mountains from between open double doors. These were the "portals of the sky" from which Shamash called out to the world. In Egypt, too, gods made their appearance standing between pillars that symbolized the heavenly sky. Later, in pagan art the portal was formed into a cult niche (*aedicula* or *naos*) holding the god and indicating his divinity. The early Jews conceived of a portal of heaven opening onto the house of God (Gen. 28:17). The Temple of Solomon is spoken of as the earthly residence of the Divine; the "glory of the Lord" enters, as did the image of Shamash in the Mesopotamian world, through its East Gate (Ezek. 43:4–7). The twin pillars that flanked the Temple, called *Jachin and Boaz, are also found in pagan temples of the Palestinian period. Probably the visual device of the portal was adopted into Jewish art from the neighboring Canaanites and Phoenicians, among whom the portal enclosed and sanctified the cult image. The Jews, having no cult idol, substituted Jewish symbols between the columns of the doorway. This is seen in the Jewish catacombs in Rome on the Via Torlonia where the portal was made in the form of a miniature Roman temple. It is shown with open doors, exposing the ends of scrolls, thus indicating the holy nature of the Torah. Painted directly above the Torah niche on the wall of the third-century-C.E. synagogue at *Dura Europos is a classicized portal probably symbolizing Solomon's Temple. Two columns supporting an arched lintel on a lead coffin from the first- and second-century necropolis at *Bet She'arim in Israel enclosed the *menorah*, thereby signifying the sacred aspect of the candelabrum. Other sepulchers are ornamented with elaborate portals and stone doors that probably retain some of the symbolic value of the heavenly portal. The sixth-century-C.E. synagogues at Bet Alfa and Tiberias have mosaic representations of the pedimented portals surrounded by other Jewish symbols. When the portal was used in Jewish funerary art it probably represented not only the holiness of the tomb, but also the gates of heaven through which the deceased had passed.

BIBLIOGRAPHY: B. Goldman, *The Sacred Portal* (1966), includes bibliography.

[Bernard Goldman]

PORTALEONE, family in N. Italy which originated in the Portaleone quarter of Rome; the *Sommo (or Sommi) family also belonged to it. From the last half of the 14th century the family produced rabbis, physicians, authors, and poets. Among the first important members was ELHANAN BEN MENAHEM (14th and 15th centuries), rabbi of Fano. He is mentioned in 1399 in connection with a bill of divorce (Responsa of Isaac b. Sheshet, no. 127, New Responsa no. 27; Responsa of Simeon b. Zemaḥ Duran, no. 1). In 1416 he represented the town of Ferrara at a synod held in *Bologna, and he is last mentioned in Fano in 1428. His son BENJAMIN PORTALEONE and his grandson JUDAH PORTALEONE were both physicians. Elhanan's brother, MORDECAI (Angelo), is mentioned in Ferrara in 1420. The latter's son, BENJAMIN (Guglielmo Mizolo; d. before 1432), lived in Ferrara, and his grandson, MORDECAI (Angelo) was mentioned there in 1432. BENJAMIN (Guglielmo Mizolo; c. 1420 – c. 1500), Mordecai's son, was born in Mantua and was a renowned physician, well thought of by his Christian colleagues. He completed his studies in Sienna and served as physician to a number of princes; in Naples he served Ferdinand I who knighted him (thereafter he was often referred to as the Jewish knight), and in Milan, Galleazzo Maria Sforza. By 1446 Benjamin returned to his native town, where he served as the physician of the dukes of Mantua: Ludovico Gonzaga, Federico, and Francesco.

Benjamin's son, ABRAHAM, was the physician of the duke of Urbino, Guida Baedo, later returning to Mantua, where he served as the physician of the noble Federico and other nobles. He was regarded as one of the best physicians of his generation and also won the esteem of Pope Clement VII. His other son, ELEAZAR, also engaged in medicine in Mantua. In 1499 he received a permit to practice from Pope Alexander VI, and he, too, became physician to a number of noblemen, among them Prince Carlo Giovanni Sassatelli, commander of the army of the Venetian Republic. In 1530, when David *Reuveni visited Italy, he met Eleazar in Sabbioneta and some time later was entertained by Abraham in Mantua. Eleazar had two sons, DAVID and ABRAHAM. In 1518 both were authorized to practice medicine by Pope Leo X, the former in Mantua and the latter in Sermide. The sons of Abraham were JUDAH, MEIR, and SOLOMON. The first two practiced as physicians in Sermide and served the princes of the house of Gonzaga. Despite an injunction forbidding Jewish physicians to attend Christians, they received special permits from the pope and the rulers to do so. (Meir received such permits in 1593 and 1598.) David's son was the well-known physician, Abraham *Portaleone, author of *Shiltei ha-Gibborim*. Abraham had three sons, ELIEZER, JUDAH, and DAVID; the last was also a physician authorized by popes Clement VIII and Gregory XV to attend Christians. In 1596 David was in Padua but later he returned to Mantua. David's son, BENJAMIN (D.C. 1683), studied medicine at the University of Sienna, receiving his diploma in 1639, with the special authorization of Pope Urban VIII. His brother's son-in-law, SOLOMON, was a well-known surgeon (though without a degree in medicine) serving until 1727. The author of the first Hebrew play, Judah Leone *Sommo, also belonged to this family.

BIBLIOGRAPHY: M. Steinschneider, in: HB, 6 (1863), 48–49; M. Mortara, in: REJ, 12 (1886), 113–6; L. Luzzatto, in: *Vessilic Israelitico*, 43 (1895), 154–5; D. Kaufmann, in: JQR, 10 (1898), 445–56; idem, *Gesammelte Schriften*, 3 (1915), 303–14; I. Abrahams, JQR, 5 (1893) 505–515; W. Colorni, in: *Annuario di Studi Ebraici*, 1 (1934), 176–82; idem, in: *Scritti in Memoria di Sally Mayer* (1956), 38ff.; H. Friedenwald, *The Jews and Medicine*, 2 (1944), 597–9; S. Simonsohn, *Toledot ha-Yehudim be-Dukkasut Mantovah*, 2 vols. (1962–64), index; Roth, Italy, index.

[Abraham David]

PORTALEONE, ABRAHAM BEN DAVID II (1542–1612), Italian physician and author. After graduating in philosophy and medicine at the University of Pavia in 1563, he was admitted to the College of Physicians in Mantua in 1566, and was authorized to practice in his father's place; in 1573 he was appointed body physician to the ducal house. Three years later he escaped from an assassination attempt. In 1591, he received papal authorization to attend Christian patients notwithstanding the current restrictions. He built up a considerable practice both among Jews and non-Jews and enjoyed a great reputation. At the duke's request he composed a Latin work containing medical guidance (*consilia medica*) as well as *Dialoghi tres de duro* (Venice, 1584) on the application of gold in medicine. He also mentions his volume of selected remedies. When in 1605 he had a stroke and was half-paralyzed, he composed for the use of his children his great work *Shiltei ha-Gibborim* ("Shields of the Mighty"; Mantua, 1612), the first Hebrew book using European punctuation. In this, he attempted to elucidate the details of the Temple, its service, and everything pertaining to it, in order to make the prescribed daily recitals of the relevant passages more intelligible. His treatment is so discursive as to make the work a compendium of all branches of science known in his day, in which all of the 10 languages which he knew were amply used.

He begins by describing the architecture of the Temple, this serving as the basis for discussing the architectural measurements and scales and the relationships of parts of a building and their proportions. In discussing the songs of the Levites in the Temple service and the musical instruments they used, he deals with music in general and instrumental music in particular, as well as poetic meter. The division into priests, Levites, and Israelites offers him the opportunity to discuss the social order and general structure of an ordered society or "political unit." Returning to a discussion of Temple sacrifices, he touches upon the cubic measurements of solids and liquids, their weights and the relationship between the two, and attempts to clarify it through his own experiments. For example, he determines the specific gravities of liquids such as wine, oil, and honey, and solids such as wheat, sifted wheat flour, and barley flour (e.g., the *Omer*). The salting of the sacrificial meat gives him an opportunity to give a lengthy description of salts in general, which, together with precious stones and medicinal herbs, were his favorite topics. Salts interested him also as ingredients of explosives, and he therefore describes in detail how saltpeter was produced, and also how to prepare gold salts and silver salts and their use in medicine, and the use of other salts in medicine. The chapter on salts thus becomes a kind of pharmacopeia.

Having completed his scientific excurses, Portaleone returns to his main topic… urging his children to be sure to recite the account of the sacrificial service and the incense burning included in the daily prayers, and he gives in three of the "shields" the order of sacrifices for each day, the passages for evening study of the Torah for each day in the year, arranged according to the days of the week and according to the weekly Scriptural portions, as well as a complete list of the chapters from Pentateuch, Prophets, Hagiographa, Mishnah, Talmud, Midrash, and Zohar. Finally, as a kind of introduction to the list of errata, Portaleone discusses reading, writing, and all aspects of the art of printing, and alphabets, Hebrew as well as others. His method of linking different subjects resulted in confusing the important with the trivial in the light of the goal he set himself, but this very confusion increases the importance of his book as a cultural-historical document, both

Jewish and general, in addition to its value as a biographical document. He combines the faith of his forefathers and the traditional Jewish intellectual preoccupations with the theories and accomplishments of the technology and science of the Renaissance and the Italian humanism of his time.

BIBLIOGRAPHY: C. Roth, *Jews in the Renaissance* (1959), 315–9; D. Kaufmann, in: JQR, 4 (1892), 333–41; 10 (1898), 455; *Oẓar Neḥmad*, 3 (1860), 140–1; N. Shapiro, in: *Ha-Rofe ha-Ivri*, 33 (1960), 137ff.

[Meir Hillel Ben-Shammai]

PORT ELIZABETH, port city in Eastern Cape Province, Republic of South Africa. Jewish families were among the founding British settlers of 1820. A congregation was formed in 1861 (or 1862) and the first synagogue building (a converted Lutheran church) was acquired in 1862. Port Elizabeth became an important center of the wool trade, in the development of which Jewish merchants, notably the *Mosenthal brothers, played a leading part. Hyman Henry Salomon was mayor in 1873–75 and Max Gumpert in 1900. Ministers of Port Elizabeth were: Samuel Rapoport 1873–94, Jacob Philips 1897–1912, and Abraham Levy 1912–54 (with a short break). In 1923 Adolph Schauder, merchant and industrialist, was elected to the city council and remained a member for more than 40 years. He served as mayor in 1940–42; a township for colored people was named after him in recognition of his work for nonwhites. He was also president of the Orthodox Hebrew Congregation for some years. Solly Rubin served as mayor in 1972–3. The United Hebrew Institutions include a *ḥevra kaddisha* and a benevolent society. There are two Orthodox synagogues, the Port Elizabeth Hebrew Congregation and the Summerstrand Hebrew Congregation was founded in 1947, and one Progressive Congregation (Temple Israel), founded in 1949. There is a Jewish day school (Theodor Herzl), although today over 80% of its pupils are non-Jewish. The headquarters of both the Eastern Cape Committee of the Jewish Board of Deputies and the Eastern Province Zionist Council are in Port Elizabeth. In 1969 the Jewish population of Port Elizabeth numbered 2,811 (1.1% of the general population). This had declined to approximately 450 by 2004.

[Lewis Sowden]

PORTELLA, DE, a family of courtiers in the kingdom of Aragon, Spain, who flourished at the close of the 13th century, at the time the Jews were removed from the royal administration. Its most distinguished members were the brothers Muça and Ishmael. MUÇA (d. 1286) was the royal *baiulus* ("baliff") and *merino* in *Tarazona. He first held these functions during the last years of James I (1213–76), who granted him and his family the privilege of not having to pay more than a fifth of the tax which was imposed on the Jewish community of Tarazona (1267). Even though he was considered the private official of the king, he was recognized as the chief administrator of the state's incomes during the reign of Pedro III (1276–85), who also entrusted him with the repair and maintenance of the fortifications of the border regions. In November 1286 he was assassinated in unknown circumstances. His property was at first confiscated by Alfonso III (1285–91) but after negotiations his family succeeded in redeeming both property and status and settled in Albatar, near Borja.

His brother ISHMAEL (d. c. 1312) also participated in the administration of the state incomes, especially after the death of MUÇA. Until 1289 he acted as dispensator (administrator of the household) of the infante Pedro. In appreciation of his numerous services James II (1291–1327), who entrusted him with various diplomatic missions, granted him many privileges and favors, such as exemption from the payment of taxes. He appointed him rabbi of all the Jewish communities of Aragon. After Ishmael's death, his family settled in Navarre. Its decline marked the end of the presence of Jews in the royal administration of Aragon during the period of the Christian reconquest.

BIBLIOGRAPHY: Baer, Spain, index; Baer, Urkunden, index; Neuman, Spain, index; D. Romano, *Los funcionarios Judíos de Pedro el grande de Aragón* (1970), 19–20.

PORTER, SIR LESLIE (1920–), British businessman. Porter joined his family's textile business (J. Porter and Company), of which he became managing director in 1955. In 1959 he joined as director the supermarket chain, Tesco, which had been founded by Sir John Edward *Cohen, and after being appointed assistant managing director in 1964 and deputy chairman in 1970, served as chairman from 1973 to 1985. He was president of the Institution of Grocery Distribution from 1977 to 1980. A noted philanthropist, Porter also served as the Chancellor of Tel Aviv University. In 1949 he married (DAME) SHIRLEY (1930–), daughter of Sir John Edward *Cohen. In addition to company directorships, including that of Capital Radio, an independent broadcasting company in London, Lady Porter was active in Conservative local politics, serving as a Westminster city councilor from 1974 and as leader of the council from 1983 to 1991. She was especially concerned about the promotion of the campaign for a cleaner London. She was awarded a knighthood in 1991. From the late 1990s she received much publicity resulting from her conviction in a so-called "homes for votes" scandal, arising out of the sale of council houses in Westminster during her time as leader of the local council, which resulted in the controversial fine of £37 million being levied on her.

[Vivian David Lipman / William D. Rubinstein (2nd ed.)]

PORTLAND, Oregon's largest city with a population of approximately 1.5 million, situated at the confluence of the Willamette and Columbia rivers on the west coast of the United States; Jewish population (2005) approximately 25,000. The earliest Jewish settlers arrived from Central Europe in the early 1850s. The first Jewish woman, Mrs. Weinshank, opened a boarding house in 1854. Early occupations included peddling and storekeeping. Pioneer Jews, mostly concerned with making a living, recognized that the community would grow only if religious needs could be met. On May 2, 1858, eight men gathered in Portland's National Hotel to establish Beth Israel. The congregation officially organized with 21 male members. Reverend Samuel M. Laski conducted services above a livery stable and blacksmith shop. Congregation Emanu-El in San Francisco loaned the *torah* and *shofar,* which were eventually purchased. In a town that sported five churches, one school and 55 saloons, Portland's first synagogue emerged. Portland quickly became Oregon's major Jewish community. Prussian and Polish Jews founded Ahavai Shalom in 1869. In 1883 a group of Russian Jews, formerly of North Dakota, established what is now the Conservative congregation Talmud Torah. Neveh Zedek, Portland's Orthodox congregation, was established in 1900, merging with Talmud Torah two years later. Ahavai Shalom and Neveh Zedek Talmud Torah merged in 1962 to form Congregation Neveh Shalom, Portland's major Conservative synagogue. Russian Jews established the Orthodox Congregation Shaarie Torah in 1905. In 1911 a group of Sephardi Jews from the island of Rhodes founded Congregation Ahavat Achim, and in 1912 Eastern European immigrants founded Kesser Israel, the only Portland synagogue still in its original location. Reconstructionist Havurah Shalom was founded in 1979. P'nai Or, founded in 1992, is an egalitarian, Jewish Renewal congregation.

Eastern European immigrants had begun arriving around 1900 and became the core of the Portland Jewish community. Settling at the southern end of the center of Portland's downtown, they formed a nearly self- sufficient community lasting more than 50 years. Everything – a kosher shopping district, five synagogues and a community center – contributed to a lively Jewish culture that intermixed with other immigrant groups who also lived in South Portland. The neighborhood changed radically in the late 1950s with an urban renewal project designed to replace residences with a business and commercial district. By this time, many of the second and third generation had moved to the suburbs. Most remaining residents were forced to move. Shops closed or relocated, buildings were razed and a unique part of Portland's history ended.

By the time the immigration from Eastern Europe halted in 1924, Portland Jews worked mostly as merchants and storekeepers or in family networks. Although Portland Jews faced discriminatory practices in country clubs and certain residential areas, for the most part acceptance came easily. Following World War II, as shifts in economic mobility provided more occupational choices, Jews gained access to the middle class and positions in the non-Jewish world in professions such as doctors, lawyers, and upper level managers.

In the early 21st century Portland's vibrant Jewish community supported numerous communal institutions including a Jewish community center, established in 1914 by the local B'nai B'rith Lodge (founded 1879), the Jewish Federation of Greater Portland, two elementary day schools, Cedar Sinai Park (a Jewish facility for the elderly), the Oregon Jewish Community Foundation, Jewish Family and Child Service, Northwest Campus of Jewish Life/Chabad Lubavitch of Oregon, the Institute for Judaic Studies and the Oregon Jewish Museum. Reed College and Portland State University both have Jewish Studies faculty positions. Portland has had many distinguished rabbis, including Stephen S. *Wise and Jonah B. *Wise (Beth Israel) and in recent years, Emanuel Rose (Beth Israel), Joshua Stampfer (Neveh Shalom), and Yonah Geller (Shaarei Torah) each of whom served their communities for more than 40 years. In 2005, Portland sustained 17 congregations. Prominent Jewish civic, business, and cultural leaders have made Portland their home (see *Oregon). The city has seen five Jewish mayors – the first was Bernard Goldsmith (1869–1871) and the most recent was Vera Katz (1992–2004).

[Judith Margles (2nd ed.)]

PORTNOY, JEKUTHIEL (**Noah**; **Yuzef**; 1872–1941), one of the pioneers of the *Bund. Portnoy joined a revolutionary circle at the Jewish teachers seminary in Vilna (1888–92). As a teacher in Kovno (Kaunas), he was active among the Jewish workers and in contact with Polish and Lithuanian socialists. Sent to Siberia for revolutionary activities, he managed to escape in 1899 and shortly thereafter joined the central committee of the Bund. He edited its paper, *Arbeter Shtime,* and directed its organizational matters, settling internal differences of the Bund and lending direction to its program. After 1908 he lived permanently in Warsaw. During World War I he worked for cooperation of the Bund with the Polish socialist parties, but was imprisoned by the Germans. After World War I, in independent Poland, he headed the central committee of the Bund, and in 1925 and 1930 was sent as an emissary to the United States. When the Nazis occupied Poland, he succeeded in escaping to the United States and served as head of the U.S. delegation of the Bund of Poland.

BIBLIOGRAPHY: J.S. Hertz (ed.), *Doyres Bundistn,* 1 (1956), 68–122. **ADD. BIBLIOGRAPHY:** G. Pickhan, *"Gegen den Strom," Der allgemeine Juedische Arbeiterbund – Bund in Polen 1918–1939* (2001) (index.)

[Moshe Mishkinsky]

PORTO, Italian family prominent during the 16th and 17th centuries. Its members were scattered in various Italian towns, notably Mantua, Venice, Verona, and Rome. The family originated in Germany, from the Rafa (Rabe, "raven") family, which settled in the town of Porto in the province of Verona, and from which the noted *Rapoport family was descended. Its members include Abraham Menahem ben Jacob ha-Kohen *Porto, one of the heads of the family. ABRAHAM (d. 1593) was a rabbi of Mantua, and author of *Ammudei ha-Golah* (in manuscript). His sons were JEHIEL (1532–1577), a pupil of Meir *Katzenellenbogen of Padua, and GERSHON (1538–after 1593), also a scholar of Mantua. Gershon's son, SIMḤAH, was a pupil of Samuel Judah Katzenellenbogen in Venice, where he worked as a proofreader until 1589. In 1602 he left for the Moravian town of Prossnitz (Prostejov), where he published *Kol Simḥah* (1603), a rhymed work on the Sabbath laws. From there he went on to Vienna.

Other members of the family include MENAHEM ZION (EMANUEL) PORTO (d. c. 1600), rabbi and mathematician.

Born in Trieste, he held rabbinical office in Padua, and wrote a number of works on mathematics and astronomy in Italian, and one in Hebrew entitled *Over la-Soḥer* on various mathematical subjects (Venice, 1627). ZECHARIAH BEN EPHRAIM MAHALALEL (d. 1672) lived in Urbino, Rome, and Florence. He was a wealthy philanthropist and many Italian communities benefited from his generosity. He wrote *Asaf ha-Mazkir*, a reference book of sayings and legends of the Talmud (Venice, 1675). ISAAC BEN DAVID (d. c. 1577) was rabbi in Mantua. Toward the end of his life he was imprisoned, having been slandered by his opponent R. Abraham Jagel Gallico. ẒEMAḤ BEN ISAAC (d. c. 1666) was appointed rabbi in Mantua in 1637. (See also *Rapoport family.)

BIBLIOGRAPHY: E. Carmoly, *Ha-Orevim u-Venei Yonah* (1861), 1–13; A. Berliner, *Hebraeische Grabschriften in Italien* (1881), 10, 26; Mortara, Indice, 51; I.T. Eisenstadt and S. Wiener, *Da'at Kedoshim* (1897–98), 144ff.; S. Simonsohn, *Toledot ha-Yehudim be-Dukkasut Mantovah*, 2 vols. (1962–64), index; A. Yaari, in: KS, 20 (1933–34), 48/50; idem, in: *Meḥkerei Sefer* (1958), 303–6.

[Abraham David]

PORTO (Rafa-Rapaport), ABRAHAM MENAHEM BEN JACOB HA-KOHEN (1520–after 1594), one of the important rabbis of Verona. In his youth he studied in Venice where he became acquainted with Elijah *Levita and where he was a proofreader for the printing press of *Bragadini. Porto witnessed the burning of the Talmud in Venice on the 13th and 14th of Marḥeshvan 1553, and appointed these days annually as days of mourning and fasting. In 1555 he published his *Ẓafenat Pane'aḥ*, containing a cypher-code of his own invention. He left Venice not later than 1574 and may have gone to Cremona where he is known to have been in 1574 and where he stayed until at least 1582. From 1584 to 1592 he was rabbi of Verona. The period of his rabbinate in Verona was that of its crowning glory, and the yeshivah which he conducted there became famous. In 1593 he was in Cologne (Germany).

He was the author of *Minḥah Belulah* (Verona, 1594), a commentary on the Pentateuch based upon the Midrashim. It was reprinted together with the text of the Pentateuch (Hamburg, 1795). He compiled similar commentaries on several other books of the Bible and on *Avot* which have never been published, although they have been preserved in manuscript with some of his writings (the ms. is in Hekhal Shelomo, Jerusalem). Some of his responsa and rulings are scattered in the works of contemporary scholars; additional responsa are extant in manuscript (H. Hirschfeld, *Descriptive Catalogue of the Hebrew Mss. of the Montefiore Library* (1904) nos. 480–481).

Abraham Menahem Porto was among those who forbade the reading of Azariah de *Rossi's work, *Me'or Einayim*, which had been published in Mantua in 1573 (his letter to Menahem Azariah *Fano). However, after the rabbis of Mantua, David b. Abraham *Provencal and Judah b. Joseph *Moscato, allowed it to be read, he retracted and joined them in permitting this (his letter to Azariah de Rossi). His signature appears on *takkanot* forbidding gambling (1573) and the infringement of moneylending franchises held by fellow Jews.

BIBLIOGRAPHY: E. Carmoly, *Ha-Orevim u-Venei Yonah* (1861), 1, 5–8; J. Reifmann, in: *Ha-Shaḥar*, 3 (1872), 353–76; S.Z.H. Halberstam, in: *Tehillah le-Moshe* dedicated to M. Steinschneider (1896), 1–3 (Heb. part); A. Kahane, *Sifrut ha-Historyah ha-Yisre'elit*, 2 (1923), 252–5; D. Kaufmann, *Gesammelte Schriften* 3 (1915), 86ff; I.T. Eisenstadt and S. Wiener, *Da'at Kedoshim* (1897–98), 144; I. Sonne, in: *Kobez al Jad*, 3 (1940), 147, 169–78; S. Simonsohn, in: KS, 35 (1960), 265.

[Tovia Preschel / Abraham David]

PORTO ALEGRE, capital of the State of Rio Grande do Sul, Brazil; population: 1,416.363 (2004); estimated Jewish population: 9,000 (2004). After São Paulo and Rio de Janeiro, Porto Alegre has the third most important Jewish community in Brazil, with a solid institutional network and an active social and cultural life.

The Jewish community was established in Porto Alegre in the 1910s, when immigrants from Eastern Europe founded the local association União Israelita. In 1915, the first Jewish newspaper to appear in Brazil, *Di Mentshhayt*, written in Yiddish, was published in Porto Alegre. The Centro Israelita Porto-Alegrense (Jewish Center of Porto Alegre) was founded in 1917, while the Centro Hebraico Rio-Grandense (Jewish Center of Rio Grande do Sul, 1922) and Sociedade Beneficente das Damas Israelitas Sefaradis (Beneficent Society of Jewish Sephardic Women, 1931) were founded by Sephardi immigrants.

The pattern of Porto Alegre's Jewish community follows the general pattern established in the most important urban centers in Brazil: a well-organized institutional life; successful economic, social, and cultural integration; and a Jewish-Brazilian identity. The local community has created a school and several cultural, sport, and social welfare entities. Among them are Associação Israelita Damas de Caridade (1922), Cooperativa de Crédito Popular (1922, providing its 2,000 members with credit and banking services), Colégio Israelita Brasileiro (1922), Grêmio Esportivo Israelita (1929), Círculo Social Israelita (1930), Sociedade Beneficente de Socorros Mútuos Linath Hatzedek (1932), Sociedade Israelita Brasileira de Cultura e Beneficência – Sibra (1936), founded by German Jews who arrived during the 1930s, and the youth movements Yavne, Ha-Bonim Dror, Betar, Ha-Shomer ha-Ẓa'ir and Chazit Ha-Noar.

Located in a region with considerable economic development and large ethnic minorities (Germans, Italians, Poles), the Jewish community of Porto Alegre flourished and developed its institutions. In 1941, the Jews had a radio program. A second one came into existence in 1968. After World War II, new institutions were created: Organização Sionista (1945), WIZO (1947), Naamat Pioneiras (1948), Clube Campestre (1958), Federação Israelita do Rio Grande do Sul (1961), and a Jewish sport club (inaugurated in 1966). After 1956, scores of refugees from Egypt and Hungary, as well as immigrants from Israel, joined the community.

In 1992, there were around 3,300 Jewish families living in Porto Alegre and 310 in other small towns located in the State of Rio Grande do Sul. In the 1920s most of the colonists from ICA colonies moved to Porto Alegre and also created small communities in the hinterland of Rio Grande do Sul: Santa Maria (1915), Pelotas (União Israelita Pelotense, 1920), Rio Grande (Sociedade Israelita Brasileira, 1920, many from Philipson), Passo Fundo (União Israelita Passo-Fundense, 1922), Erechim (Sociedade Cultural e Beneficente Israelita, 1934, with many colonists from Quatro Irmãos), and also Erebango, Cruz Alta, and Uruguaiana.

Moacyr *Scliar (1937–) the most important Jewish-Brazilian writer, was born and lived Porto Alegre. He was the main literary voice of the Brazilian Jewish experience in the 20th century. Physician and member of the Academia Brasileira de Letras (Brazilian Academy of Literature), some of his books take place in the Jewish neighborhood of Bom Fim, where the author creates an atmosphere of fantastic realism. Some of his most famous books are *A Guerra no Bom Fim* ("The War in Bom Fim," 1972), *Balada do Falso Messias* ("Ballad of the False Messiah," 1976) and *A Estranha Nação de Rafael Mendes* ("The Strange Nation of Rafael Mendes," 1983).

Cintia Moscovich (1958–), from Porto Alegre, is an important Jewish-Brazilian writer from the new generation and has published titles like *O reino das cebolas* ("The Kingdom of the Onions," 1996) and *Duas Iguais – Manual de amores e equívocos assemelhados* ("The Identical Two – Manual of Loves and Similar Mistakes," 1998). Carlos Scliar (1920–2001) was a distinguished artist, being one of the most important Brazilian engravers. The local community had also a soccer player idol in the 1950s: David Russowsky, the "Russinho" (1917–1958), who played for "Internacional" and was also a lawyer.

Instituto Cultural Judaico Marc Chagall (1985) is a very active Jewish-Brazilian cultural institution, promoting different kinds of activities. Marc Chagall has a Memoirs Department with a well-organized historical archive about Jewish immigrants in Rio Grande do Sul.

Antisemitism

Antisemitism was a significant question in Porto Alegre during the 1990s due to the activity of local Editora Revisão, a publishing house that translated and edited some antisemitic titles such as *The Protocols of the Elders of Zion*; antisemitic works by Gustavo Barroso (a fascist leader in the 1930s), such as *Brasil, colônia de banqueiros* ("Brazil, a Colony of Bankers," first published in the 1930s), and Holocaust-denial books such as *Holocausto judeu ou alemão? Nos bastidores da mentira do século* ("Jewish or German Holocaust? The Framers of the Century's Lie," written by S.E. Castan, pseudonym of the editor Siegfried Ellwanger); and *Quem escreveu o diário de Anne Frank?* ("Who Wrote the Diary of Anne Frank?"). In 1989, when the books achieved commercial distribution and political repercussions, a group of Jews and other activists, including Afro-Brazilians, launched Movimento Popular Anti-Racismo – Mopar to respond to the diffusion of antisemitism. Editora Revisão participated in several book events in Brazil, and this provoked discussions between those who were in favor of "absolute" freedom of expression and those who denounced the racism and the antisemitism. After a legal battle of many years, the publisher S.E. Castan, owner of Revisão, was condemned for the crime of racism and antisemitism in 2004. It was the first Brazilian court conviction for antisemitism, establishing an important precedent in the matter.

In 2005, three young Jews were attacked in a bar in Porto Alegre by a skinhead group, in a rare episode of violent and open antisemitism in the country.

BIBLIOGRAPHY: A. Brumer, *Identidade em mudança. Pesquisa sociológica sobre os judeus do Rio Grande do Sul* (1994); E. Nicolaiewsky, *Israelitas no Rio Grande do Sul* (1984); I. Gutfreind. *A imigração judaica no Rio Grande do Sul. Da memória para a história* (2004); J.A. Wainberg (ed.), *100 Anos de Amor. A imigração judaica no Rio Grande do Sul* (2004); J.H. Lesser, *Pawns of the Powerful. Jewish Immigration to Brazil 1904–1945* (1989); J.H. Lesser, *Jewish Colonization in Rio Grande do Sul, 1904–1925* (1991); J.S. Halpern, *Contribuição para a história da imprensa judaica no Rio Grande do Sul* (1999); L. Milman (ed.), *Ensaios Sobre o Anti-Semitismo Contemporâneo. Dos mitos e da crítica aos tribunais* (2004).

[Roney Cytrynowicz (2nd ed.)]

PORTO-RAFA (Rapaport), MOSES BEN JEHIEL HAKOHEN (d. 1624), Italian scholar. Moses was a member of the German family Rafa that settled in the town of Porto in the vicinity of Verona and became the progenitors of the renowned *Rapaport family. In 1602 Moses served as rabbi of Badia Polesine in Piedmont. Subsequently he became rabbi of Rovigo. While he was there a great controversy broke out about the validity of its **mikveh*. He was among those, headed by his relative Avtalyon b. Solomon of *Consiglio, who prohibited its use. Moses collected, edited, and published all the rulings of those who took a stringent view in the dispute in a work entitled *Palgei Mayim* (Venice, 1608), appending to it a criticism of the *Mashbit Milḥamot*, which gave all the rulings of those who permitted the use of the *mikveh*. Moses was on friendly terms with Leone *Modena. He died in Venice.

His brother, ABRAHAM MENAHEM PORTO (b. 1569), studied in his youth under members of his family in Cremona and Mantua. He appears to have been one of the rabbis of Verona.

He was the author of *Ḥavvot Ya'ir* (Venice, 1628), giving epigrams and other witty deductions of rabbinic sayings in alphabetic order. He corrected and published the *Minḥah Belulah* (Verona, 1594), a commentary on the Pentateuch by his relative Abraham Menahem b. Jacob Ha-Kohen *Porto (Rafa-Rapaport). The following works by him have remained in manuscript: *Gat Rimmon*, a collection of poems; *Shimmush Avraham*, a commentary on the Pentateuch; and *Ḥasdei David*, a commentary on the Psalms. A few of his responsa have been published in the works of his contemporaries.

BIBLIOGRAPHY: Ghirondi-Neppi, 35; E. Carmoly, *Ha-Orevim u-Venei Yonah* (1861), 9–11; I.T. Eisenstadt and S. Wiener, *Da'at Kedoshim* (1897–98), 145; L. Blau (ed.), *Leo Modenas Briefe und Schriftstuecke* (1905), Heb. part, 87f.; A. Yaari, *Meḥkerei Sefer* (1958), 420–9.

[Abraham David]

PORTO-RICHE, GEORGES DE (1849–1930), French playwright. Born in Bordeaux into an assimilated family of Italian origin, Porto-Riche began his literary career with some collections of poetry: *Prima Verba* (1872), *Pommes d'Eve* (1874), and *Tout n'est pas rose* (1877). After writing two plays in verse – *Le Vertige* (1873) and *Un Drame sous Philippe II* (1875) – he turned his dramatic talent to plays dealing with the psychology of love. The most successful of these witty and well-constructed dramas were *La chance de Françoise* (1888), *Amoureuse* (1891), *Le passé* (1898), *Le vieil homme* (1911), and *Le marchand d'estampes* (1918). Collected as *Théátre d'amour* (1928), his plays fill four volumes.

Porto-Riche's view of love was the 17th-century classical concept of a tyrannical and destructive passion. His success was due largely to what was, at the time, a daring novelty: the presentation on the stage of the most intimate problems of people in love. This won him great popularity with many critics as well as with the public, but it also earned biting criticism from some of the more conservative. This, in the case of the extreme reactionaries of the "Action française," often took an antisemitic turn.

In 1906 Porto-Riche was appointed director of the Bibliothèque Mazarine. He was elected to the Académie francaise.

BIBLIOGRAPHY: E. Sée, *Porto-Riche* (Fr., 1932), includes bibliography; W. Mueller; *Georges de Porto-Riche, 1849–1930* (Fr., 1934)

[Moshe Catane]

PORTRAITS OF JEWS. Portraits were known among the Jews in the classical period: Josephus (Ant., 17:6) records that *Alexandra sent portraits of her sons to Mark Antony in order to rouse his sympathy. The Jewish "zoographos" Eudoxios who lived in Rome was presumably a portrait painter. No such portraits have survived, though an extant statue of the classical period has been said to represent *Josephus. In the Middle Ages there are numerous representations of Jews in biblical (especially New Testament) scenes, but none that can be identified with any specific living person. What has been described as the earliest Jewish portrait is the Scharfzandt window of the Church of Our Lady in Munich but it is no more than a vivid representation of a Jewish type. The earliest actual representations of identifiable Jews are presumably the medieval Anglo-Jewish caricatures of Isaac of Norwich (1233) and of Aaron 'fiz Diaboli' of Colchester (1277). In a late 14th-century Spanish prayer book in the Vatican library (Ms. Vat. ebr. 324) there are a number of crude sketches of various members of the community, similarly caricatures rather than portraits.

The earliest identifiable portraits of Jews in the full sense are those of Daniel da Norsa and his family at the foot of the painting of the Madonna made for the Basilica di Sant' Andrea in Mantua in 1495, built on land confiscated from him. Somewhat later is the portrait of *Joseph of Rosheim in a contemporary German document. It is somewhat curious that the earliest known specially commissioned portraits of Jews are three medals of the Renaissance period, for the religious prohibition was considered to apply more strictly to plastic art than to a plane surface. Leone *Modena stated that in his day Jews had portraits in their homes, but his own portrait, prefixed to his *Riti Ebraici*, was made as an exercise by a gentile acquaintance.

From about this time portraits of prominent Jews, including rabbis, became commonplace in the northern European Sephardi communities, where presumably the former traditions to which they had become accustomed as *Marranos had become deeply engrained. On occasion the Jews went to the most eminent artists of their time for the purpose: while *Rembrandt's portraits of *Manasseh Ben Israel may have been executed as an act of friendship, there is every reason to believe that his *Dr. Ephraim Bueno* was commissioned. In 18th-century England, artists of the caliber of Reynolds and Gainsborough carried out portrait commissions for wealthy Anglo-Jewish families. Sculptured portraits begin to emerge in the Jewish communities only in the late 18th century. To this day some of the extreme Orthodox object to having their portraits taken even by photography, because of their stern interpretation of the biblical prohibition. On the other hand, portraits of the dead persons in high relief are to be found in the Jewish cemetery of Curaçao, and in some parts of the U.S. photographs are incorporated into tombstones. In recent times, eminent Jewish portraitists include P. de *Laszlo and S.J. *Solomon, and the sculptor Jacob *Epstein.

BIBLIOGRAPHY: A. Rubens, *A Jewish Iconography* (1954); *Anglo-Jewish Portraits* (1935); Frankel, in: HJ, 5 (1943), 155–64; Friedman, in: HUCA, 23 pt 2 (1950–51), 433–48; Mayer, Art, index, s.v. *Medals, Portraits*.

[Cecil Roth]

PORT SAID, city N.E. of *Cairo on the Mediterranean, at the entrance to the Suez Canal. With the construction of the Port Said harbor in 1856 Jews began to settle there. The Anglo-Jewish traveler S. Samuel found about 20 families (70 souls) in the town in 1879, earning their livelihood as tailors, retail traders, and money lenders. The community in Port Said prospered after the building of the Suez Canal. In 1882 there was a blood libel against the Jews of Port Said, but the local governor protected them. In April 1892 there again was a blood libel which resulted in the death of a Jewish merchant and an attack on the synagogue. Some Jews then left the city. Nevertheless, the census of 1897 showed that the Jewish population had increased to 400 (out of a total of 42,972 inhabitants). In 1901, 1903, and 1930, there were further blood libels. The community was organized at the end of the 19th century and obtained the patronage of the Austro-Hungarian Empire. In 1890 the members of the local Jewish court of law were R. Joseph Buskila, Rabbi Bechor Abraham Bitran and the *shoḥet* Jacob Aaron Luria. At the beginning of the 20th century an Ashkenazi woman had a pub in the city. In 1901 the rabbis of Cairo traveled to Port Said and published there their new regulation on *kiddushin*. In the same year seven children from Port Said studied at the Alliance Israélite Universelle school in Jerusalem. The community was subordinate to the Jewish court of law in *Alexandria. The census of 1907 found 378 Jews in Port Said; the majority were of *Aden and Yemenite origin and a minority of Egyptian origin, Ashkenazi and Sephardi Jews. In 1917 594 Jews lived in the city. During World War I, the Jewish population temporarily increased. At that time, there were also some Zionist activities in the town. During the 1920s, the community had two synagogues and a school built by the Binyan family of Aden. It closed down in the 1930s. In 1927 there were 1,009 Jews in Port Said; in 1937 they numbered 767 and in 1947, 864. The rabbi of the community in 1918–35 was Nissim Benjamin Ohana, who was born in Algeria (died in Haifa in 1966). He published a responsa collection called *Na'eh Eshiv* (published in Jerusalem; 1958) and a halakhic book about *sheḥitah*, *Ze Torat Ha-Zevaḥ* (published in Jerusalem in 1959). In 1956 the number of Jews in the town was estimated at 300, most of whom were compelled to leave as a result of the Suez campaign in 1956. In 1960 only six Jews lived in Port Said. In 2005 there were no Jews in Port Said.

ADD. BIBLIOGRAPHY: J.M. Landau, *Jews in Nineteenth-Century Egypt* (1969), index.; S. DellaPergola, in: J.M. Landau (ed.), *Toledot ha-Yehudim be-Miẓraim ba-Tekufah ha-Otmanit* (1988), 41; L. Bornstein-Makovetsky, in: *ibid.*, 143, 152, 166; J. Hassoun, in: *ibid.*, 567; Z. Zohar, in: *ibid.*, 592, 600–801; A. Rodrigue, *Ḥinukh, Ḥevrah ve-Historiyah* (1991), 156; Z. Zohar, in: *Pe'amim*, 86–87 (2001), 109.

[Haim J. Cohen / Leah Bornstein-Makovetsky (2nd ed.)]

PORTSMOUTH, seaport and naval base in Hampshire, S. England. The Jewish community, perhaps the oldest in continuous existence in England outside London, was founded in 1746 and a cemetery was acquired in 1749. Among early settlers were a family of engravers, a jeweler, navy agents, and small tradesmen. In a boat disaster in 1758 11 Jews were drowned, the only survivor being Samuel Emanuel, ancestor of a family later prominent in civic life. A communal split occurred in 1766 over the recognition of the rabbi of the Great Synagogue or the rabbi of the Hambro' Synagogue as spiritual leader. A reconciliation in 1771 led to reunion of the two groups in 1789. In 1780, the original synagogue was reconstructed and was still in use until 1936, when it was replaced by a new building in Southsea, the residential suburb. Portsmouth's prosperity as a naval and garrison town during the Napoleonic Wars attracted large numbers of Jews, but with the decline of the town after 1815 the community also decreased. A Jewish day school, Aria College, existed in Portsmouth for many years. In 1969 the Jewish population was estimated at 600 (out of a total of 215,000). The only communal institutions apart from the synagogue were the benevolent institution and a Board of Guardians for the poor. In the mid-1990s the Jewish population was estimated at approximately 385. The 2001 British census found 235 declared Jews in Portsmouth.

BIBLIOGRAPHY: C. Roth in: JHSET, 13 (1936), 157–87; idem, *Rise of Provincial Jewry* (1950), 94–95; Newman, in: JHSET, 17 (1953), 251–68; JYB.

[Vivian David Lipman]

PORTUGAL, southwesternmost country of continental Europe, in the Iberian Peninsula. Jewish settlement in the area began prior to Portugal's emergence as a nation. The existence of a significant Jewish settlement on the peninsula by 300 C.E. is apparent from the edicts of *Elvira which proscribe "taking food with the Jews" and single out the Jewish group in a number of dicta. A tradition among the Sephardi Jews ascribes their arrival in Iberia to Roman times, in the wake of the destruction of the Temple in 70 C.E. and subsequent dispersion toward Europe. James *Finn endeavored to make a case for dating the initial Jewish involvement in the area as early as 900 B.C.E., based on reports of two ancient Hebrew inscriptions, one mentioning *Amaziah, king of Judah, and a second marking the grave of King Solomon's treasurer, *Adoniram.

When Portugal emerged as a distinct national entity under Affonso (Henriques) I (1139–85), a number of wholly Jewish districts existed, including communities in *Lisbon, *Oporto, *Santarém, and *Beja. Affonso employed as his treasurer Yaḥya ibn Ya'ish, thereby initiating the pattern of Portuguese rulers enlisting Jewish talent in the management of affairs of state. Under King Affonso III (1248–79) Portugal attained total independence and fixed its historic geographic boundaries, and during his reign the classic Portuguese model of Jewish communal life emerged. The crown recognized the Jewish community as a distinct legal entity, headed by the royally appointed *arraby mor. The *arraby mor*, in turn, named seven **dayyanim*, one for each of seven regional centers; Santarém, Oporto, *Moncorvo, *Viseu, *Faro, *Evora, and *Covilhã, each with his own administrative staff to adjudicate both civil and criminal cases. Their decisions were subject to appeal before the *arraby mor*, who visited the district courts annually for this purpose, accompanied by an **av bet din* ("chief justice") and an executive staff. The vast power of the *arraby mor* was balanced by the right of the people to select the local rabbis – who, however, were paid by the crown and required its confirmation – and to elect the *tovei ha-ir* (see *Community, *Elders) who directed the daily functions of the community. In the larger towns Jews generally lived together in a *juderia* (see *Jewish Quarter) such as Oporto's Jews' Hill or Loulé's Jews' Vale.

Portuguese Jewry prospered under these separatist conditions, continuing the attentiveness to learning that marked the peninsula's formative years. The community's autonomy amid officialness was the crucible in which the proud, enduring Portuguese Sephardi heritage was shaped. By the 15th century the Jews were playing a major role in the country's monarchical capitalism, as that economic system has been characterized. The concentration of Jews in Lisbon and other

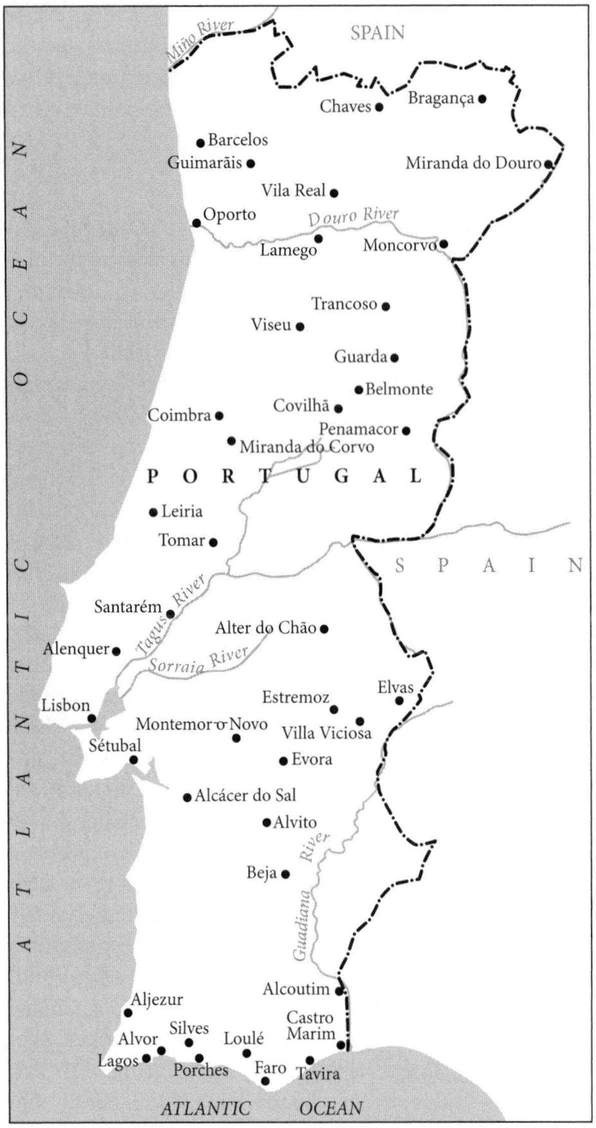

Places of Jewish settlement in Portugal, 1200–1497.

population centers rendered obvious the group's business success and – as a result of their access to royalty – their disproportionate prominence in society. At the same time, Portuguese Jews were fastidious in loyalty to their faith and reciprocated the distant posture assumed by their devout Catholic neighbors, making way for the suspicions that feed on envy. Furthermore, the independence enjoyed by the Jewish community, in the otherwise Christian state, aroused the ire of the clergy. Their efforts to erode Jewish civil rights were resisted by the cultured King Diniz (1279–1325), who retained the *arraby mor* Don Judah as his treasurer and reasserted that the Jews need not pay tithes to the church. In any event the Jews were heavily taxed as the price of remaining unmolested, including a special Jews' tax intended to redeem the "accursed state of the race," and a tax based on the number of cattle and fowl slaughtered by the *shoḥatim*. The unsympathetic Affonso IV (1325–57) increased the direct tax load to bring him an annual state income of about 50,000 livres. He also reinstituted the dormant requirement that Jews wear an identifying yellow *badge, and restricted their freedom to emigrate. The emboldened clergy accused the Jews of spreading the *Black Death in 1350, inciting the populace to action. During the short rule of Pedro I (1357–67) – who employed as his physician the famed Moses *Navarro – the deterioration of the Jewish position was halted. The situation then fluctuated from ruler to ruler until the reign of Affonso V (1438–81), who gave the Jews his conscientious protection, affording them a last peaceful span of existence in Portugal. The general populace was seething with envy and religious hate. In 1449 there occurred a riot against the Jews of Lisbon; many homes were sacked and a number of persons were murdered. Local assemblies in 1451, 1455, 1473, and 1481 demanded that steps be taken to reduce the national prominence of the Jew.

Somehow the Jews of Portugal never considered their predicament as hopeless, and when *Spain expelled its Jews in 1492, some 150,000 fled to nearby Portugal, where both the general and Jewish culture approximated their own (see *Spanish and Portuguese Literature). King John II (1481–95), eager to augment his treasury, approved their admission. Wealthy families were charged 100 cruzados for the right of permanent residence; craftsmen were admitted with an eye to their potential in military production. R. Isaac *Aboab was permitted to settle with a group of 30 important families at Oporto. The vast majority, however, paid eight cruzados per head for the right to remain in Portugal for up to eight months. When this unhappy group found that a dearth of sailings made their scheduled exit impossible, John II proclaimed them automatically his slaves. Children were torn from their parents, 700 youths being shipped to the African island of São Tomé (Saint Thomas) in an unsuccessful scheme to populate this wild territory.

With the accession of Emanuel I the Fortunate (1495–1521), the harsh distinctions between the displaced Spanish and the native Portuguese Jews began to be erased, and hopes for a tranquil period were raised. Instead, Emanuel's reign signaled the end of normative Jewish life in Portugal, for within a year of his accession he contracted a marriage with the Spanish princess Isabella – hoping thereby to bring the entire peninsula under a single monarch – and Spanish royalty made its consent dependent on his ridding Portugal of all Jews. Consenting reluctantly, on Dec. 4, 1496, Emanuel ordered that by November of the following year no Jew or Moor should remain in the country. Forthright action was not taken against the Moors, if only because Christians in Moorish lands would then be subject to reprisals. As the departures proceeded Emanuel reconsidered the loss of the Jewish citizenry and the attendant economic losses. He resolved to keep them in the country by turning the Jews into legal Christians. He tried persuasion and torture, but with little success, and the chief rabbi, Simon *Maimi, died resisting conversion. Accordingly on March 19, 1497, all Jewish minors were forcibly baptized and detained, a move that tended to prevent their parents from attempting to flee. The order then went out for all who were still intent on embarkation to assemble at Lisbon. Some 20,000 gathered there, but instead of being evacuated they were ceremonially baptized and declared equal citizens of the realm. Bewildered, these *Conversos cautiously began to emigrate, prompting Emanuel to respond on April 21, 1499, by withholding the right of emigration from the *New Christians, as this new class was officially designated, but technicalities aside, the Portuguese majority continued to regard them as Jews. In the spring of 1506, over 2,000 New Christians were massacred during a Lisbon riot. If the Conversos had had any thoughts of finding solace in the religion thrust upon them, such riots dissuaded them. Consequently even those who were otherwise weak of spirit tended to cling to their God, with the resultant emergence of *Crypto-Judaism, or Marranoism. While attending church and conducting themselves outwardly as Catholics, in secret they maintained Jewish observances, to whatever extent was possible.

As early as 1516 King Emanuel, suspecting that such a situation existed, proposed to Pope *Leo x that an *Inquisition – on the Spanish model – be authorized to ferret out backsliding New Christians. John III (1521–57) enlisted Enrique *Nuñez, an apostate from the Canary Islands, to mingle with the Marranos and report on their practices. In 1527 Nuñez presented King John with an exposé of Marrano life, appending a list of Crypto-Jews. Popular support for a Portuguese Inquisition surfaced in 1531, when the populace attributed the earthquake of that year to divine retribution for New Christian duplicity. Unable to resist these pressures, Pope Clement VII authorized the Inquisition, with King John's confessor Diogo da Silva as the first inquisitor general. Attempting to counter this, the Marranos dispatched Duarte de *Paz to Rome. Armed with unlimited funds, Paz was to attempt, at the very least, to deny the Inquisition the right to confiscate the property of those condemned, recognizing that this would be an incitement to prosecution. The ensuing diplomatic fray lasted half a century. On April 5, 1533 the Marranos won a suspension of the Inquisition, but on May 23, 1536 it was reauthorized, to be effective three years hence. A first *auto-da-fé took place in Lisbon on Sept. 20, 1540, but in 1544 the Inquisition was again suspended. Finally Emperor *Charles v brought his influence to bear and King John offered the bribe of Viseu's total tax revenue; irrevocable papal consent was given on July 16, 1547. Permanent tribunals were established at Lisbon, Evora, *Coimbra, and in Portugal's Far East outpost *Goa. Ultimately, in 1579, the right to confiscate the culprit's property also accrued to the inquisitors, so that every wealthy Portuguese not certified as pure-blooded (*limpieza de sangre) lived in terror. The Portuguese Inquisition became inspired more by greed than by piety, as Padre Antonio *Vieira charged. Soon the tribunal authorities were able to construct lavish palaces, to proffer large sums to receive condemnatory testimony, and to produce spectacular autos-da-fé, which competed with the bullfights in drawing crowds of tens of thousands. Accused Marranos could escape death by repentantly admitting to Judaizing, but in such an event they would be forced into implicating family and friends, thus providing a spiraling supply of victims. Occasionally even a genuine Christian was martyred for Judaizing, young Don Lope de *Vera y Alarcon (1620–1644) being the most notable example. Crypto-Jews sought precarious safety among the ruling classes and clergy; in time this tendency resulted in a significant percentage of Marrano blood being found within Portugal's ruling circles – as bitterly documented by Mario Saa.

The surest method of evading the Inquisition was to abandon the peninsula, and a constant flow of Conversos escaped – some with daring (see Samuel *Nunez), some with luck – to the communities of the *Marrano Diaspora, where many of them quickly reverted to normative Judaism. Some ex-Marranos, however, such as Spinoza's teacher Juan de *Prado, were not found acceptable by congregational leaders, giving rise to a responsa literature debating the status of the New Christians and ex-Marranos in Jewish law. The leading city of the Portuguese Diaspora was *Amsterdam, with *Salonika ranking first in the Ottoman East, but the former Marranos became ubiquitous in all the Old and New World centers of trade, to the extent that "Portuguese" became synonymous with "Jewish" – much to the consternation of gentile Portuguese travelers. The stream of refugees continued until the end of the inquisitional period. As late as 1795, immigrants to London cited flight from the Inquisition on their aliens' certificates. In 1791 Isaac Lopes Simões fled Lisbon to enter the covenant of Abraham at Bordeaux, France.

The Inquisition was brought to an end during the reign of Joseph Emanuel I (1750–77) through the initiative of Sebastião José de Carvalho ê Mello, Marques de Pombal (1699–1782), who was the power behind the titular monarch. In a series of acts from 1751 to 1774 Pombal deprived the Holy Office of real power, placing it under secular control, and restored the civil rights of the New Christian class, even bullying certified Old Christian families into contracting marriages with New Christians. A last auto-da-fé took place in 1791; on March 31, 1821, the Inquisition was abolished in Portugal. During the nightmare centuries of Portugal's Inquisition, over 40,000 persons were implicated, of whom 30,000 were sentenced at autos-da-fé. A total of 750 of these were staged, at which 29,000 persons were reconciled to the Church, 600 persons burned in effigy, and 1,200 persons burned at the stake. The majority of the victims were accused of Judaizing. The terror that weighed on the Marranos who managed to avoid detection cannot be measured.

Historians writing at the beginning of the 20th century supposed that the last Marranos had by then disappeared. In 1917, however, a mining engineer named Samuel *Schwarz discovered a community of Marranos in the remote northern region near *Belmonte. Apparently they had succeeded in maintaining their identity in the remote mountain areas, marrying among themselves, harboring memories of Jewish observances, being called Jews by their neighbors, and holding to the belief in a single, personal Deity who would redeem His people at the end of days. While Schwarz was publicizing his discovery, a Portuguese hero of Marrano descent, Captain Arturo Carlos de *Barros Basto, openly espoused Judaism and undertook to revitalize the spiritual life of the Marranos. World Jewry took a warm interest in the Barros Basto enterprise, with British Jews taking the lead in a plan to forge a link between the Marranos and the Jewish community that had sprung up in Portugal since the end of the Inquisition.

[Aaron Lichtenstein]

Resettlement

Jewish settlement in Portugal was renewed around 1800: a corner of the British cemetery in Lisbon contains Hebrew tombstones dating from 1804. The first settlers, who held British nationality, had been buried in a separate plot allotted to them in the English cemetery. Later, in March of 1833, a Portuguese nobleman by the name of António de Castro let to Abraham de José Pariente, at an annual rent of 4,000 reis, a plot of land to serve "as a cemetery for the tenant, Abraham de José Pariente, his descendants, and relatives." It was used as a general Jewish cemetery. By a decree published in 1868, the Jews of Lisbon were permitted to "construct a cemetery for the burial of their coreligionists." Official recognition was not accorded to the Jewish community until 1892, when a decree was published entitling it "to hold religious services, maintain a cemetery for the burial of Jews resident in or in transit through Portugal, to establish funds for the assistance of the poor, and to keep registers of births, deaths, and marriages." After the establishment of the republic by the revolution of Oct. 5, 1910, the government of Portugal approved the community's statute presented to it in 1912. In accordance with the approved statute, the community was authorized to maintain places of worship, a cemetery, and a *ḥevra kaddisha*, to slaughter in accordance with the Jewish law, to keep registers of births, deaths, and marriages, and to establish charity funds. Beginning in the 1920s, cases of conversion to Catholicism were not infrequent and several families were split into Jewish and Catholic branches. However, after 1950, this tendency declined to a great extent.

[Reuven Nall]

Holocaust Period

At the outbreak of World War II, Portugal had an organized Jewish community of about 380 Portuguese nationals, in addition to another 650 Jews, many of whom were refugees from Central Europe, who were granted "resident" status. The Jewish community was headed by Moses *Amzalak, a personal friend and associate of President Salazar. After the fall of France, Portugal adopted a most liberal visa policy under which thousands of refugees, including a large proportion of Jews, were allowed to enter the country as immigrants. This policy, however, excluded those of Russian origin or birth. Starting late in 1940, and particularly from the Spring of 1941, Portuguese immigration policy became increasingly stringent as a result of the limited sailings from Portuguese ports. During the second half of the war, Portugal agreed to grant entry visas as part of various rescue operations, on the condition that its territory be used only for transit purposes. For reasons outside Portugal's control, these plans were never realized. During this period, however, Portugal saved all of its 245 Jewish citizens and those Jews in occupied countries to whom it granted consular protection, forcing the Germans to return part of their confiscated property. Portugal joined the other neutral countries in saving Hungarian Jews (see *Hungary, Holocaust) in late 1944, by granting them her protection. Throughout the war Lisbon served as a base for the operations of Jewish organizations in and beyond the Iberian Peninsula.

[Haim Avni]

Contemporary Period

In 1971 the Jewish community of Portugal consisted of 650 persons, about half of them Sephardim and the others Ashkenazim. Of these, 630 lived in Lisbon, 15 in Oporto, and five in Algarve. Most of the Ashkenazim (mainly of German and Polish origin) took up residence in Portugal after World War II, with such notable exceptions as Kurt Jacobsohn, the vice rector and the interim rector of Lisbon University, who settled in Portugal in the late 1920s. The majority of the Jews were in the liberal professions, or engaged in business, real estate, construction, and private employment. Several occupied high positions in the academic and medical fields. There were four synagogues in Portugal, one in Lisbon opened in 1902, one in Oporto, built with the assistance of the Portuguese communities in London and Holland and the generous donation of the Kadoorie family, and two private synagogues in Faro, one belonging to Semtob Sequerra and the other to the Amram family. Apart from the Lisbon synagogue, these were seldom frequented. The former community center in Lisbon was used as a prayerhouse by the Ashkenazim.

At the outset of the 21st century about half of Portugal's 600 Jews lived in Lisbon, maintaining two synagogues, a cultural center, and a home for the aged. Most Portuguese Jews came from North Africa. There was also a small number of Ashkenazi Jews, some of whom arrived in the country during World War II. Their most serious problems were common to other communities, especially the small ones: assimilation and mixed marriages. In certain mountainous regions far to the north, the remaining *Crypto-Jews maintain old customs, ways of praying, and special festivities. They were able to survive thanks to the preservation of their tradition and a high rate of endogamic marriages. In 1917, the community of *Belmonte in the Estrella Mountains was discovered. In 1983, a film was produced about those "judeos" of Belmonte, portraying their fidelity to Jewish customs. Around 100 were living there at the beginning of the 21st century, some of them returning to Orthodox Judaism.

[Reuven Nall]

Relations with Israel through the 1960s

Diplomatic relations were not established between Portugal and Israel. In 1958, after diplomatic contacts had been made in other European capitals, Israel established a consulate general in Lisbon on the understanding that this step would be followed by the establishment of full diplomatic relations. The expectation did not materialize, however, probably due to Portugal's fear of Arab reactions. In 1959 an agreement was signed between the Bank of Israel and the Bank of Portugal, and trade relations developed in the 1960s. In 1969 Israel's exports to Portugal amounted to $1,542,000, mainly in cotton and diamonds, and imported commodities reached $297,000, mainly copra and wood. In the United Nations, Portugal usually abstained on issues related to Israel or supported the Arab viewpoint. Israel voted against Portugal several times on questions of colonialism.

[Shimeon Amir]

After the 1974 Revolution

The troubled period between the outburst of the revolutionary disturbances of April 1974 (the "Carnation Revolution"), and the establishment of a regular constitutional government in 1976 was characterized by a flare-up of extremist and anarchist movements directed against parliamentarian democracy, freedom of speech and free enterprise. As a result, about half of the 600 Jews of Portugal left, migrating to Israel, Brazil, Canada, and the United States, in that order; the 300 who remain reside mostly in Lisbon, with a handful in Oporto.

During the political struggle for power in 1974–76, accusations of "collusion" with Israel with its (then) governing Labor Party were hurled at the leadership of the Portuguese Socialist Party (PS) led by Dr. Mario Soares by its Communist and leftist opponents. The MRPP, a Maoist militant party, gave its agitation a "Jewish" slant; its organization in the Beira Baixa province, where several thousand Marranos lived, waged its political campaign under the slogan "Hitler killed your brethren, do not back Fascism and reaction." But they gained no support whatsoever in the region.

With the end of Portuguese rule in Angola and Mozambique, the few Jews resident there emigrated to Brazil and South Africa. All the institutions of the Lisbon community still function, including two synagogues, a Jewish cultural center, a kosher butcher, a special slaughter-house, and a home for the aged.

The Soares government established diplomatic relations on ambassadorial level with Israel at the beginning of 1977, after a successful exploratory mission to Jerusalem headed by Jaime Gama, future minister of the interior of Portugal. The chairman of the Portuguese parliament, Salgado Zenha, who visited Israel as an official guest of the Israeli Labor Party, was also warmly received by the representatives of all the political parties in Israel. As a result, an Israeli embassy was established in Lisbon, the first ambassador being Ephraim Eldar. But anti-Israeli tendencies, embodied mainly in circles having commercial relations with Arab countries, and in the Supreme Revolutionary Council, where the former Foreign Minister, Major Melo Antunes, exercised a dominant influence, prevented the opening of a Portuguese embassy in Israel.

The cultural and economic links between Portugal and Israel were noticeably strengthened. Israeli specialists in agriculture and fisheries (mainly experts in the raising of fresh-water carp in artificial ponds) worked in Portuguese villages; the Gulbenkian Foundation, the main scientific and cultural institution of Portugal, granted scholarships to Israeli scientists.

In 1978 Israel's exports to Portugal amounted to $21.6 million (mainly machinery, chemicals, medicaments, textiles), a nearly twenty-fold increase over the 1969 figures. The value of imports from Portugal reached $9.4 million (raw materials, especially wood), a 31-fold increase over 1969. In 1980 the sums were $61 million and $16.1 million, respectively, and in 2004, $76.1 million and $70.1 million.

[Michael Harsgor]

During the early 1980s there was a considerable increase in cultural exchange between Portugal and Israel. The Institutos de Relacioes Culturais Portugal-Israel (Institutes for Portuguese-Israel Cultural Relations) was active in Porto and Guarda. In 1983, the Mayor of Lisbon, Nuno Kruz Abecassi, visited Israel to participate in the Fourth Jerusalem Conference of Mayors. Dr. Jorge Sampaio, who visited Israel twice as mayor of Lisbon, has served as president of Portugal since 1996. His maternal grandmother was from a Moroccan Jewish family. His cousin is president of the Lisbon Jewish community.

[Jose Luis Nachenson and Noemi Hervits de Najenson]

BIBLIOGRAPHY: A. Herculano de Carvalho e Araujo, *History of the Origin and Establishment of the Inquisition in Portugal*, tr. by J.C. Branner (1926); I.M. Ford (ed.), *Letters of John III, King of Portugal, 1521–1557* (1931), introd. in Eng., letters in Portuguese; H.V. Livermore, *A History of Portugal* (1947), index s.v. *Jews*; M.A. Cohen, *Samuel Usque's Consolation for the Tribulations of Israel* (1965), introd.; C.R. Boxer, *Four Centuries of Portuguese Expansion, 1415–1825* (1969), 47f. 52; Baron, Social, 13 (1969), 44–158; Graetz, Hist, index; E.N. Adler, in: JQR, 15 (1902/03), 413–39; *The American Sephardi*, 4, no. 1–2 (Autumn 1970); J. Mendes dos Remedios, *Os Judeus em Portugal*, 2 vols. (1895); A. Novinsky and A. Paulo, in: *Commentary* (May 1967), 76–81; M. Kayserling, *Geschichte der Juden in Portugal* (1867); A. Baião, *Episodios dramáticos da inquisação portuguesa*, 2 vols. (1919–24); J. Lucio d'Azevedo, *Historia dos Christaos Novos Portugueses* (1921); S. Schwarz, *Inscrições hebraicas em Portugal* (1923); idem, *Os Cristãos-novos em Portugal no seculo XX* (1925); A.C. de Barros Basto, *Os Judeus no velho Porto* (1929); N. Slouschz, *Ha-Anusim be-Portugal* (1932); E.H. Lindo, *History of the Jews of Spain and Portugal* (1970). **ADD. BIBLIOGRAPHY:** M.J.P. Ferro Tavares, *Os judeus em Portugal no século XIV*, (1970); idem, *Os judeus em Portugal no século XV*, 2 vols. (19882–4); idem, *Judaismo e Inquisição; estudos*, (1987); I.S. Révah, in: *Annuaire (École pratique des hautes étudeas, IVe section: Sciences historiques)* (1970–71), 469--84; (1971–72), 423–31; A. Novinsky, *Cristãos novos na Bahia*, (1972), 3–22, 23–55; idem, *Inquisição I: inventários de bens confiscados a cristãos novos* (1976); idem, in: *Sefárdica*, 2 (1984), 51–68; I. Steinhardt, in: *Língua cultura*, 2 (1972), 131–41; H.P. Salomon, *Novos pontos de vista sobre a Inquisição em Portugal* (1976); idem, in: *Arquivos do Centro Cultural Portugués*, 17 (1982), 41–64; F.E. Talmage, in: *Association for Jewish Studies Newsletter*, 13 (Feb. 1975), 13–15; F.E. Talmage and E. Vieira (eds. & trans.), *The Mirror of the New Christians (Espelho de cristãos novos)* by F. Machado (1977);

G. Nahon, in: *Annuaire (École pratique deshautes études, Ve section: Sciences religieuses)*, 88 (1979–80), 258–70; 90 (1981–82), 260–1; C.A. Hanson, *Economy and Society in Baroque Portugal, 1668–1703*, (1981), 70–107; P. Gomes, *A filosofia hebraico-portuguesa* (1981); E. Lipiner, *Santa Inquisição, terror e linguagem*, (1977); idem, *O tempo dos judeus, Segundo as Ordenções do reino*, (1982); idem, in: Y. Kaplan (ed.), *Jews and Conversos; Studies in Society and the Inquisition* (1985), 124–38 (in Portuguese); E.C. de A. Mea, in: *ibid.*, 149–78; H.B. Moreno, in: *ibid.*, 62–73; idem, in: *Ler história*, 3 (1984), 3–11; idem, in: *Revista altitude*, 2. sér., ano IV, 9–10 (1983–84), 49–53; L.R. Torgal, *Revista Altitude*, 2. sér., ano II, 4 (dez. 1981), 5–15; A. Paulo, *Os judeus secretos em Portugal* (1985); A.Y.M. Levin (ed.), in: *Oraita*, 15 (1986), 27–43 (Heb.); E.C. de A. Mea, in: *Revista de Facudade de Letras: História*, 2. sér., 4 (1987), 151–77; E. Samuel, in: R.D. Barnett and W.M. Schwab (eds.), *The Sephardi Heritage*, vol. 2, *The Western Sephardim* (1989), 100–4; J.M. Abecassis, *Genealogia hebraica: Portugal e Gibraltar, sécs. XVII a XX* (1990–1), 5 vols.

PORTUGALOV, BENJAMIN OSIPOVICH (1835–1896), Russian physician and publicist. He was imprisoned for his activities in the *Narodnaya Volya* movement in 1860 in the fortress of St. Peter and Paul. After his release he qualified as a physician but was arrested again in 1874 and exiled to the Urals. Later he settled in Samara (Kuibyshev). Portugalov devoted a great deal of his time to philanthropic work and to combating drunkenness. He was the first physician in Russia to advocate social medicine. A fanatic assimilationist, Portugalov was opposed to the rituals of *sheḥitah and *circumcision and even asked the authorities to forbid them. He took an active part in the Jewish-Christian movement initiated by Jews in southern Russia in the 1880s. He considered the pogroms in the 1880s as a social movement against the injustice perpetrated by leading classes. Portugalov was also opposed to Zionism, seeing the solution of the Jewish problem in social religious reform, based on a general humanistic religion free of ritual ceremonies.

BIBLIOGRAPHY: E. Tcherikower, in: *Historishe Shriftn*, 3 (1939), 81–82; S. Ginsburg, *Meshumodim in Tsarishn Rusland* (1946), 256.

PORUMBACU (Schwefelberg), VERONICA (1921–1977), Romanian poet and novelist. Born in Bucharest, Veronica Porumbacu grew up in an intellectual circle, and studied psychology and sociology. A member of the anti-Fascist underground during World War II, she began her literary career under the postwar Communist regime, first publishing children's books in 1946.

Like many of her subsequent publications, her first collection of verse *Visele Babei Dochia* ("The Dreams of Baba Dochia," 1947) dealt with contemporary political questions. She also wrote lyrical works, notably *Intoarcerea din Cythera* ("Return from Cythera," 1966). Her volumes of poetry include *Generația mea* ("My Generation," 1955), *Lirice* ("Lyrics," 1957), *Diminețele simple* ("Simple Mornings," 1961), *Memoria cuvintelor* ("Recollections of Worlds," 1963), and *Histriana* (1968). Many of her poems have been translated into other languages. In 1968 she published a much-praised autobiographical novel, *Porțile* ("Gates"). Set in the period of the pre-Nazi Antonescu regime, the book tells of her reaction to antisemitism and of the exclusion of Jewish children from the Romanian educational system. Despite her assimilated upbringing, Veronica Porumbacu became aware of her Jewish heritage and was impressed by the traditional loyalties of her ancestors, whom she describes sympathetically. She also published translations from Hebrew poetry (N. Alterman, A. Shlonsky, and Y. Amichai) and from English the 19th-century U.S. author E. Dickinson.

BIBLIOGRAPHY: G. Călinescu, in: *Națiunea* (1945) no. 1; O. Crohmălniceanu, in: *Contemporanul* (1961), no. 12; P. Georgescu, in: *Viața Romînească* (1964), no. 10; Perpessicius, in: *Gazeta Literară* (Dec. 1, 1966).

[Dora Litani-Littman]

PORUSH, ISRAEL (1907–1991), Australian rabbi. Porush was born in Jerusalem and, after receiving a traditional religious education in the talmud torah and yeshivah Eẓ Ḥayyim of the old *yishuv*, he proceeded to Berlin to study at the Hildesheimer Rabbinical Seminary, where he received his rabbinical diploma in 1932, and at the universities of Berlin and Marburg, where he received his doctorate in mathematics. On Hitler's rise to power in 1933, Porush moved to London and was appointed rabbi of the Finchley Synagogue (1934–1940). In the latter year, he was appointed to the Great Synagogue of Sydney, the mother congregation of Australian Jewry, and became *Av bet din*, retaining that position after his retirement at the end of 1972. Porush was regarded as the Orthodox spiritual head of Australian Jewry and rabbinic representative of the community in state and civic affairs. In 1952, he founded the Association of Jewish Ministers of Australia and New Zealand, of which he was president. He was also president of the Jewish Historical Society of Australia from 1948. He retired in 1975 when he also resigned as president of the association and was appointed honorary life president. Porush wrote *Today's Challenge to Judaism* (1972) and *The House of Israel, A History of the Sydney Great Synagogue* (1977), published on the occasion of its centenary (1878–1978). His manuscript autobiography, *Memoirs of an Australian Rabbi*, was published posthumously by the Australian Jewish Historical Society in 1993.

BIBLIOGRAPHY: W.D. Rubinstein, Australia II, index.

PORUSH, MENACHEM (1916–), *ḥaredi* politician and public figure, member of the Fourth to Thirteenth Knessets. Porush was born in Jerusalem. He studied at the Eẓ ha-Ḥayyim yeshivah in Jerusalem. In the years 1932–38 he was a reporter for *ḥaredi* papers. In 1949–63 he was appointed editor of *Kol Yisrael*, and in the years 1950–51 was editor of *Ha-Mevasser*. In 1951 Porush founded a network of nurseries for *ḥaredi* children. In 1953 he was one of the founders of the independent education system of Agudat Israel, and served as one of its directors. In 1954 he became a member of the Agudat Israel Center in Israel, and a member of the Executive of the World Agudat Israel. In 1955 he was appointed chairman of

LEFT: **Mallow.** © *Dr. David Darom.* *RIGHT:* **Almond tree.** © *Dr. David Darom.*

THE BIBLE MENTIONS ABOUT 100 NAMES OF PLANTS, THE BULK OF THEM FROM EREẒ ISRAEL, THE OTHERS BEING TREES OF LEBANON AND TROPICAL PLANTS THAT YIELD AN AROMATIC SUBSTANCE OR ARE USED IN INCENSE. ISRAEL IS AT THE CONVERGENCE OF THREE FLORAL REGIONS, WHICH RESULTS IN A WIDE VARIETY OF PLANT LIFE.

PLANTS OF THE BIBLE

Almonds. © *Dr. David Darom.*

Apple blossom. © *Dr. David Darom.*

Anise. © *Dr. David Darom.*

Broad bean blossom. © *Dr. David Darom.*

Cattail. © *Dr. David Darom.*

Balm. © *Dr. David Darom.*

Barley. © *Dr. David Darom.*

Briar. © *Dr. David Darom.*

Cedar. © *Dr. David Darom.*

Citron. © *Dr. David Darom.*

Coriander. © *Dr. David Darom.*

Cumin. © *Dr. David Darom.*

Flax. © *Dr. David Darom.*

Garlic. © *Dr. David Darom.*

Gourds. © *Dr. David Darom.*

Hemlock (gall). © *Dr. David Darom.*

Lily. © *Dr. David Darom.*

Mandrakes. © *Dr. David Darom.*

Common millet. © *Dr. David Darom.*

Leeks. © *Dr. David Darom.*

Lentils. © *Dr. David Darom.*

Millet (sorghum). © *Dr. David Darom.*

Mint. © *Dr. David Darom.*

Mulberry. © *Dr. David Darom.*

Mustard. © *Dr. David Darom.*

Myrrh. © *Dr. David Darom.*

Nettle. © *Dr. David Darom.*

Onions. © *Dr. David Darom.*

Palm dates. © *Dr. David Darom.*

Acorn. © *Dr. David Darom.*

Oak tree. © *Dr. David Darom.*

Olive tree. © *Dr. David Darom.*

Pine tree. © *Dr. David Darom.*

Pistachio. © *Dr. David Darom.*

Pistachio nuts. © *Dr. David Darom.*

Plane tree. © *Dr. David Darom.*

Pods (Carob). © *Dr. David Darom.*

White poplar. © *Dr. David Darom.*

Reeds. © *Dr. David Darom.*

Rue. © *Dr. David Darom.*

Saffron. © *Dr. David Darom.*

Tamarisk. © *Dr. David Darom.*

Thistles. © *Dr. David Darom.*

Thorns. © *Dr. David Darom.*

Weeds. © *Dr. David Darom.*

Willow. © *Dr. David Darom.*

the Agudat Israel Center in Israel. Porush was first elected to the Fourth Knesset in 1959 on the Agudat Israel list. He was a member of the Knesset Education and Culture Committee from the Fourth to Ninth Knessets, and of the Constitution, Law, and Justice Committee from the Fifth to Eighth Knessets. In the Ninth and Tenth Knessets he served as chairman of the Labor and Welfare Committee, and in the Twelfth Knesset as a member of the Foreign Affairs and Security Committee and the Interior and Environment Committee. In the years 1984–85 he served as deputy minister of labor and welfare, and again in 1990–92, after the Labor Party left the National Unity Government.

Simultaneously with his membership in the Knesset Porush was elected to the Jerusalem municipality in 1969, and served as deputy mayor of Jerusalem under mayor Teddy *Kollek until 1974. In 1973 he established Kiryat ha-Yeled – a center for *ḥaredi* children.

The son of Menachem Porush, MEIR, was a member of the Jerusalem City Council in the years 1983–96, and deputy mayor under both Teddy Kollek and Ehud *Olmert in the years 1989–96. He has been a member of the Knesset on behalf of Agudat Israel within Yahadut ha-Torah since the Fourteenth Knesset, and served as deputy minister of construction and housing in the years 1996–2003.

[Susan Hattis Rolef (2nd ed.)]

PORZECANSKI, TERESA (1945–), Uruguayan anthropologist, poet, and writer of Ashkenazi and Syrian descent. Her professional works includes nine books on anthropology and social sciences, among them *Historias de vida de inmigrantes judíos al Uruguay* ("Life Stories of Jewish Immigrants to Uruguay," 1986), based on oral history. Porzecanski is lecturer and researcher in social sciences at the Universidad de la República, Montevideo. Her novels and short stories frequently deal with small, unimportant people in their desperate struggle for happiness and sense in life, which is frequently related to mythic motifs and impulses deeply rooted in the human soul. Her Jewish characters (Ashkenazi and Sephardi, following her own roots) show the transformations of traditions and beliefs in a modern and often alien environment, and the forging of a new, Latin American Jewish identity. Her main books are *Construcciones* ("Constructions," 1979); *La invención de los soles* (1982; *Sun Inventions and Perfumes of Carthage, Two Novellas*, 2000); *La respiración es una fragua* ("Breath Is a Forge," 1989); *Mesías en Montevideo* ("Messiah in Montevideo," 1989); *Perfumes de Cartago* (1994); *Una novela erótica* ("An Erotic Novel," 1986); *La piel del alma* ("The Soul's Skin," 1996); *Nupcias en familia y otros cuentos* ("Marriage in the Family and Other Stories," 1998); and *Felicidades Fugaces* ("Shooting Happiness," 2002). She has received many national and international awards, including the Fulbright and Guggenheim scholarships. Her works have been translated into English, Portuguese, German, and Dutch, and included in anthologies of Uruguayan, Jewish, and women's writing.

BIBLIOGRAPHY: M. Agosin, *Taking Root. Narratives of Jewish Women in Latin America* (2002); L. Baer Barr, *Isaac Unbound: Patriarchal Traditions in the Latin American Jewish Novel* (1995); D.B. Lockhart, *Jewish Writers of Latin America – A Dictionary* (1997); J. Payne, *Conquest of the New Word: Experimental Fiction and Translation in the Americas* (1993); E. Valverde, *Perfumes letales y banquetes eróticos: los mundos de Teresa Porzecanski* (2005).

[Florinda F. Goldberg (2nd ed.)]

POSEKIM, a Hebrew term for scholars whose intellectual efforts were concentrated on determining the *halakhah* in practice (for whom the word "decisors" is sometimes used) in contrast to those commentators who applied themselves to study for its own sake, and in order to facilitate the understanding of the subject under discussion and who are called *mefarshim* (expositors or commentators). This distinction was already recognized by early authorities who stressed, for instance, that *halakhah* should not be derived from *Rashi's commentary on the Talmud – since Rashi did not introduce into his commentary various ancillary considerations without which no practical decision can be arrived at, except perhaps for those few instances where Rashi explicitly states that the *halakhah* is in accordance with his exposition.

In the early period, especially in Germany, the term *posekim* was identical with the teachers and leaders of the generation in every locality. It included the heads of the yeshivot, *avot battei din*, rabbis and talmudic scholars generally, on condition that their statements were made "by way of *pesak*," on actual cases which arose. The ruling of the *posek* was binding only upon those subject to his authority, since he laid down the *halakhah* in accordance with local tradition and for the people who accepted his authority. A ruling was never successfully imposed upon communities outside the area of the jurisdiction of the *posek*. The authority of the *posek* during this period depended on his being a competent talmudic scholar, possessing a comprehensive knowledge in every field on his subject, and on the fact that he continued the tradition of his locality and of his teachers transmitted to him while he studied under them. In the course of time this situation gradually changed, as a result of the dissemination of the codes, which afforded easy access to sources necessary for deciding the *halakhah*. From the second half of the 16th century with the beginning of the spread of the Shulhan Arukh, the character of the works by the *posekim* changed fundamentally. Henceforth the outstanding *posekim* hardly engaged at all in theoretical exposition, and to the extent that they did do so their commentaries were generally forgotten and ignored. The *posek* during this period won general recognition by virtue of the extensive practical experience he accumulated and by gaining the approbation of contemporary scholars, by devoting the whole of his intellectual and physical energy to this goal, and by virtue of "divine aid," the charisma with which he was endowed. For a survey of the *posekim* and their development see *Codification of Law.

BIBLIOGRAPHY: C. Tchernowitz, *Toledot ha-Posekim* (1947); Waxman, Literature, 2 (1960^2), ch. 4; H.Z. Benedikt, in: KS, 25 (1950),

164, 76; I.Z. Kahana, in: *Sinai*, 34 (1954), 311–24; idem in: *Bar-Ilan Sefer ha-Shanah*, 1 (1963), 270–81; A. Goldrat, in: *Tagim*, 1 (1969), 22–31; Friedberg, Eked, 4 (1956^2), nos. 1212–14, 1222–26; Shunami, Bibl. 181–3.

POSENER, GEORGES HENRI (1906–1988), French Egyptologist. Born and educated in Paris, Posener was a member of the Institut Française d'Archéologie Orientale in Cairo from 1931 to 1935. In 1945 he was named directeur d'études of the Ecole Pratique des Hautes Etudes (4th section). From 1961, he held the chair of Egyptian philology and archaeology of the Collège de France. He was elected president of the Société Française d'Egyptologie in 1963.

Posener's work concentrated on ancient texts. He published for the French Institute in Cairo the *Catalogue des ostraca hiératiques littéraires de Deir el Medineh* (2 vols., 1934–52). His *La première domination Perse en Egypte* (1936) collected the hieroglyphic inscriptions relating to the Persians in Egypt. In *Princes et pays d'Asie et de Nubie* (1940) he studied the hieratic texts written on figurines, believed to have magic properties. *Littérature et politique dans l'Egypte de la XIIe dynastie* (1956) continued his interest in the use of literature in historical studies. He also wrote *De la divinité du pharaon* (1960), but is probably best known for the *Dictionnaire de la civilisation egyptienne* (1959; A Dictionary of Egyptian Civilization, 1962).

[Irwin L. Merker]

POSENER (Pozner), SOLOMON (1876–1946), social historian and writer. Born in Minsk, Posener began to write for the Russian-Jewish press under the name of Stellin.

He contributed to the report prepared by *ICA on the economic position of Russian Jewry (1904). He also wrote a study on Jews in government schools in Russia for *Novy Voskhod* (printed separately in 1913). In Paris from 1903, he contributed to the French press on conditions in Russia and on Russian Jewry, as well as editing *La Correspondence Russe* and *La Tribune Juive*. He published articles in French on the history of Jews in France in various journals. His most important work is a biography of Adolphe *Cremieux (French, 1933–34, 1939; English, 1940).

[Yehuda Slutsky]

°**POSIDONIUS** (c. 135–c. 51/50 B.C.E.), Greek philosopher, ethnologist, scientist, and historian from Apamea in Syria, one of *Cicero's teachers. He lived on the island of Rhodes. No book of his survives, though his influence was great. His voluminous writings included a history and ethnology of the Jews, who were treated also in his book on Pompey. The antisemitic accusations he retailed in his writing (on Jewish asocial behavior, misanthropy, impiety, inhumane religion and rites) reflected common Hellenistic opinions and attitudes, and later found wide echoes, e.g., in Apion (according to Jos., *Apion*, 2:79). His antisemitic remarks can be reconstructed from the more or less close paraphrase of Posidonius by Diodorus Siculus (as quoted in Photius, *Bibliotheca*, 244; 379), including the story that Antiochus Epiphanes found a statue of a bearded man seated on an ass in the Holy of Holies. However, if, as is likely, the respectful appraisal of Moses and his beliefs found in Strabo 16:2, 35ff. also derives from Posidonius, it is probable that the latter did not concur fully in the slanders he related.

BIBLIOGRAPHY: Reinach, Textes, 56–59; F. Jacoby, *Fragmente der griechischen Historiker* 2A (text, 1926), 222–317, no. 87; 2A (1926), 154–220 no. 87.

[Daniel E. Gershenson]

POSNANSKI (Poznański), family of scholars. ADOLF POSNANSKI (1854–1920) was a rabbi and a scholar. Born in Lubraniec, Poland, Posnanski served as rabbi at Reichenberg (Liperec) and Pilsen, Bohemia, and from before World War I as teacher of religion in high schools in Vienna.

Posnanski's scholarly work was mainly concerned with the messianic idea in Judaism and Christianity; his major contribution in this field was *Schilo, ein Beitrag zur Geschichte der Messiaslehre* (1904). He also published an edition of Profiat *Duran's anti-Christian work, *Kelimat ha-Goyim* (in HHY, vols. 3–4, 1914–15), and prepared *Abraham b. Ḥiyya's *Megillat ha-Megalleh*, for publication (1924). Posnanski's study of the *Tortosa Disputation also appeared posthumously (in REJ, vols. 74–76, 1922–23); other editions of polemical literature which Posnanski was working on at the time of his death remained unpublished.

SAMUEL ABRAHAM POZNANSKI (1864–1921), rabbi, scholar, and bibliographer, the younger brother of Adolf Posnanski. Born in Lubraniec, Poland, he studied at Berlin University and at the *Lehranstalt (Hochschule) fuer die Wissenschaft des Judentums, where he came under the influence of M. *Steinschneider. In Poland he served as spiritual leader of the Tlomacka "choir" synagogue in Warsaw. There he took great interest in Hebrew education and culture, founding a government-supported training college for Jewish teachers. He was an early and ardent Zionist, and was a delegate to the First Zionist Congress.

Poznański's scholarly interests and achievements were catholic and were greatly helped by his linguistic propensities. His interests covered the history of Hebrew grammar and philology in the Middle Ages, the cognate field of Bible exegesis in the geonic, Spanish, and French periods, the Palestinian and Babylonian *geonim*, the North African communities, Jewish-Arabic literature, and others.

As a Karaitologist

Poznański's interest in early geonic literature led him as a young man to the study of Karaite history and literature, first of the geonic period, and subsequently as a whole, from the earliest times to the modern period. The result of this lifelong attention was a vast amount of published material, mostly in the form of papers contributed to learned journals (for the most part the *Jewish Quarterly Review*, the *Revue des Études Juives*, and the *Zeitschrift fuer Hebraeische Bibliographie*), jubilee and memorial volumes, and similar publications. Some of these were also issued separately, as reprints. As a Karaitologist Poznański ranks with Abraham *Harkavy, and indeed surpasses him in the overall range of his interest. His erudition in rabbinic literature, his command of Arabic philology, his extensive use of original manuscript sources, and his accuracy and industry have endowed his works in this field with a value which has not succumbed to the passage of time. They include, among others, studies of *Anan and his immediate successors, of the various writers of the golden age of Karaite learning (10–12th cent.), and of *Saadiah's Karaite opponents (from Saadiah's time to the 19th cent.); a pioneering survey of Karaite printing and book production; a genealogy of the eminent Karaite family *Firūz; an annotated list of copyists and owners of Karaite manuscripts; and an edition of the *Zekher Ẓaddikim* by the 19th-century Karaite historian Mordecai *Sultansky. As a frequent reviewer of Karaitological publications by other scholars, Poznański often enriched his reviews with extensive and valuable corrections and annotations. His long article on Karaism in Hasting's *Encyclopedia of Religion and Ethics* (1915) is still the best available general sketch of Karaite history and literature. For many years Poznański assembled material for his major work in this field, a comprehensive bio-bibliographical dictionary of Karaite writers, of which a file of some 8,000 cards had been prepared by the time of his death.

[Leon Nemoy]

The extensive bibliography of his works, prepared by his son Edward Poznański (see below) and A. Marx (see bibl.), runs into many hundreds of items. His countless book reviews are an indispensable commentary on modern Jewish scholarship. In 1908 Poznański, together with D.J. Simonsen and A. Freimann, reorganized the *mekiẓei Nirdamim society and continuously stimulated its activities. His excellent relations with scholars and directors of libraries the world over made his vast knowledge and generous advice and assistance in all scholarly matters invaluable assets for all concerned. A memorial volume in his honor was published in 1927 (repr. 1970). EDWARD (ISAAC JACOB) POZNAẐSKI (1901–1974), the son of Samuel Abraham Poznański, was a bibliographer and lecturer in philosophy at the Hebrew University, of which he was academic secretary from 1946 to 1964.

BIBLIOGRAPHY: A. Posnanski: J. Rosenthal, in: S. Mirsky (ed.), *Ishim u-Demuyyot be-Ḥokhmat Yisrael* (1959), 275ff. S.A. Poznaẑski: A. Marx, in: Festschrift… S. Poznanski (1927), 7ff. (= REJ, 74 (1922), 169ff.); idem and E. Poznański, *ibid.*, xxixff. (= REJ, *ibid.*, 184ff.); M. Balaban, *ibid.*, ixff. (separately publ. in Polish as *S. Poznański*, 1922).

POSNER, AKIVA BARUKH (Arthur; 1890–1962), rabbi, scholar, librarian, and bibliographer. Born in Samter (Szamotuly), Poznan, Posner taught at Mainz, Halle, and Vienna, and he served as rabbi at Kiel, Schleswig-Holstein, from 1924 to 1934. He was an outspoken and courageous critic of Nazism. After being forced to leave Germany, he settled in Jerusalem where he worked as a librarian, first at the E.L. Prinz Library of the Mizrachi Teachers' Seminary (until 1954), and then at the central rabbinical library at Heikhal Shelomo in Jerusalem.

While still in Germany, Posner published *Das Buch das Propheten Micha* (1924); *Die Psalmen, des Religionsbuch der Menschheit* (1925); *Prophetisches und Rabbinisches Judentum* (1925); and *Die Freitag-Abendgebete* ("Friday Night Prayers," 1929), with translation and commentary. He later prepared similar editions in Hebrew of the Sanctification of the Moon and Sanctification of the New Moon liturgies (1945, 1948), as well as a *siddur* of domestic prayers (*Le-Veit Yisrael*, 1957). Posner wrote communal histories on Czarnkow (Heb. and Eng., 1957), Gniezno (Heb. and Eng., 1958), and Rawicz (with Eng. abstract, 1962) – all towns in his native Poznan. His literary legacy included 35 such histories in manuscript. Among his bibliographical studies were a biography of the book collector E.L. Prinz (*E.L. Prinz, Ḥayyav ve-Avodato ha-Sifrutit*, 1939); a bibliography of E.M. *Lipschuetz (*E.M. Lipschitz, Reshimah Bibliografit*, 1941); a monograph on the Hebrew printer Monasch of Krotoszyn (in *Aresheth*, 1 (1958), 260–78); and a supplement to the index of the first 75 volumes of the MGWJ, which is extant in manuscript. A memorial brochure, *Zikkaron ba-Sefer la-Rav A.B. Posner*, published by Heikhal Shelomo and edited by A. Piczenik (1964), contains a biography of Posner by A.Z. Givon and a bibliography by Rachel Posner.

POSNER, DAVID BEN NAPHTALI (mid–17th cent.), talmudist. David lived in Posen and then in Krotoschin. He was the author of *Yalkut David* (Dyhernfurth, 1691), a collection of Midrashim serving as a kind of supplement to the *Yalkut Shimoni*. The material, edited by his father, Naphtali Hirsch Shpitz, is arranged in the order of the weekly Torah portions. Fuenn holds that David Posner is to be identified with David Tevele Posner, author of the *Sha'arei Ẓiyyon* (Hamburg, 1615).

BIBLIOGRAPHY: Steinschneider, Cat Bod, 863; Fuenn, Keneset, 248; Braun, in: MGWJ, 40 (1896), 524f.

POSNER, RICHARD ALLEN (1939–), U.S. jurist, law professor, and author. Posner graduated from Yale College *summa cum laude* in 1959 and Harvard Law School (where he was president of the *Harvard Law Review*) *magna cum laude* in 1962. He was a law clerk to Supreme Court Justice William J. Brennan, Jr. (1962–63) and to Federal Trade Commissioner Philip Elman (1963–65), and an assistant to Solicitor General Thurgood Marshall (1965–67). In 1967 he became general counsel to the President's Task Force on Communications Policy. He began teaching law at Stanford Law School in 1968 and moved to the University of Chicago Law School in 1969, where he continued full-time teaching until his appointment by President Reagan to the Court of Appeals for the Seventh Circuit in December 1981. He was chief judge of that court from 1993 to 2000, while he continued teaching part-time at the University of Chicago.

Posner is a prolific writer on the law, economics, and social sciences. By 2005, he had written over 2,200 judicial opinions, 38 books, and more than 300 articles and book reviews. His original ideas regarding the interplay of economics and law were presented in volumes titled *Antitrust Law: An Economic Perspective* (1976), *Economic Analysis of Law* (1977), and *The Economics of Justice* (1981). These books, as well as his articles in the *Journal of Legal Studies,* which he founded, encourage economic analysis of law and had a major influence on American judicial thought in the final decades of the 20th century. Between 1977 and 1981 he was the president of Lexecon, Inc., a firm of lawyers and economists that he created to provide economic and legal litigation research. In 1991, a national legal periodical reviewing potential candidates for the Supreme Court called Posner "the most influential legal scholar and the most brilliant judge in the country."

The most notorious of his unconventional proposals was to eliminate the black market in adoptions by abolishing adoption agencies, buying and selling babies on the open market, and paying pregnant unwed mothers not to have abortions. Following the 9/11 terrorist attacks on the United States, he turned his attention to national security and intelligence reform, publishing books on those subjects in 2004 and 2005.

A case that demonstrated Posner's innovative approach to Jewish religious rights concerned a public high school basketball association's prohibition against the wearing of headgear by basketball players. An Orthodox Jewish team that wore yarmulkes fastened with bobby pins challenged the rule as a violation of freedom of religion. While upholding the general applicability of the rule when yarmulkes are "insecurely" fastened with bobby pins during a game, Posner directed that the team be permitted alternative means of securing the yarmulkes during play with chin straps or by sewing them onto headbands.

[Nathan Lewin (2nd ed.)]

POSNER, SOLOMON ZALMAN BEN JOSEPH (c. 1778–1863), rabbi and author. Posner studied under his father, the rabbi of Poznan (Posen), and under Akiva *Eger, Solomon Zalman of Warsaw, and his own uncle, Zeeb Wolf Kalafri. He occupied himself mainly with commerce in the city of Lubraniec and amassed great wealth, but nevertheless found time for extensive study. He wrote many works, some of which have remained in manuscript.

Among his unpublished workers are *Zemir Ariẓim*, against those who regarded the study of Talmud as unnecessary; *Gal-Ed*, 33 (the numerical equivalent of "*Gal*") letters on educational topics addressed to his children when they left home to study in yeshivot; *Tal Yaldut*, a letter to his young children; *Nir Rash*, on the Torah, containing in particular explanations of obscure allusions in Rashi's commentary; and *Dodo Yigalenu*, on the Book of Esther. His *To'ar Penei Shelomo* (1870) is a valuable and unique book describing his own life and the lives of his forebears as far back as the 17th century, and contains many interesting details of the civilization of the period. This book also includes educational directives to his children. His testament is appended to it. It has been claimed that this book is not his own, but that of his son, Moses, who was also rabbi of Poznan and that Solomon gave his name to it. Of his other sons, Aryeh Leib became rabbi of Pniewy, and Elijah, rabbi of Wodzislaw.

BIBLIOGRAPHY: *Ha-Meliẓ* (1887), 906.

[Itzhak Alfassi]

POSQUIÈRES, ancient name of the present town of Vauvert, S. France. The earliest record of the presence of Jews in Posquières is from 1121: the dowry that Ermensinde, daughter of the viscount of Béziers and Nîmes, brought to her husband, the lord of Posquières, included a Jew of Béziers, Benjamin. According to *Benjamin of Tudela, there were 40 Jews (or 40 heads of families) in the town in about 1165. It appears that the lords of the town employed the Jews in public office: After an admonition of Pope *Innocent III in 1209, the lord of Posquières solemnly swore not to entrust such offices to Jews. The Jews lived in a quarter known as *Carrière des Juifs.* Wealthy Jews who possessed more than 100 sols paid an annual tenure of one gold florin to the lord. After the expulsion of 1306 the Jews of Posquières migrated to *Provence, *Comtat Venaissin, and *Perpignan. Of the scholars of the town named by Benjamin of Tudela, the only one known from other sources was the renowned *Abraham b. David, head of the yeshivah of Posquières.

BIBLIOGRAPHY: Gross, Gal Jud, 446–50; P. Palgairolle, *Histoire de la ville de Vauvert* (1918); S. Kahn, in: *Mémoires de l'Académie de Nîmes*, 35 (1912), 1–23; G. Scholem, *Ursprung und Anfaenge der Kabbala* (1962), index; I. Twersky, *Rabad of Posquières* (1962).

[Bernhard Blumenkranz]

POSTAN, MICHAEL MOISSEY (1899–1981), British economic historian. Postan, who was born in Tighina, Bessarabia, began his teaching career in 1927 at University College, London. He was a lecturer on economic history at the London School of Economics from 1931 to 1935, when he became a lecturer at Cambridge University. From 1938 to 1965 he held the professorship of economic history at Cambridge and from 1934 to 1960 served as editor of the *Economic History Review* at a time when this discipline grew strongly in size. Postan's lucid style, searching inquiries and comprehensive analyses of economic problems of the past made him one of the world's leading historians in his field. His major contribution, in addition to many publications, was the coeditorship of the *Cambridge Economic History of Europe* from 1952 onward. Postan received a knighthood in 1980.

ADD. BIBLIOGRAPHY: ODNB Online.

[Joachim O. Ronall]

°**POSTEL, GUILLAUME** (1510–1581), French Orientalist and philosopher, and an outstanding exponent of the Christian *Kabbalah. A self-taught prodigy, Postel was appointed in 1538 professor of mathematics and philology at the College of the Three Languages in Paris and thereafter produced an enormous output of books, tracts, and pamphlets. Four years later he abandoned his post following the first of several mystical visions. His first major work, *De orbis terrae concordia* (1544), made room for Islam in its universal scheme and Postel thereafter exploited rabbinic and kabbalistic literature in support of his pretensions, notably his "immutation" as Elijah and Balaam and as the "Angel-Pope." Postel traveled constantly in search of rare manuscripts and prophetic writings. In Venice he met Elijah *Levita and Daniel *Bomberg, the Christian pioneer of Hebrew printing, whose Jewish publications he was engaged to censor during his second visit to Venice in 1546–49. Here he began his first translation of the *Zohar and published an extraordinary mystical treatise on the significance of the **menorah* ("candelabrum"), first in a Hebrew broadsheet entitled *Or Nerot ha-Menorah* (undated; 1547?) and then in a modified Latin version, *Candelabri typici in Mosis Tabernaculo... interpretatio* (1548). A Latin-Hebrew copy made by Conrad *Pellicanus has been preserved in Zurich, and unpublished versions in French and Italian are also extant. During the next few years, Postel's millenarianism reached frenzied heights. He visited Ereẓ Israel (1549–50), accepted the emperor's invitation to teach in Vienna (1554–55), and multiplied his publications in anticipation of the messianic year 1556. In his Hebrew *Candelabrum*, Postel had styled himself *Ish Kefar Sekhanya u-Shemo Eliyyahu Kol-Maskalyah she-Nitgayyer le-Ḥibbato shel Yisrael...* ("A man of Kefar Sekania, named Elijah Kol-Maskalyah, who converted [to Judaism] out of love for Israel..."), which suggests that he had then become some kind of Judeo-Christian (cf. Av. Zar. 27b; and see *Jacob of Kefar Sakhnayya). During his imprisonment by the Inquisition at Ripetta (1555–59), he was said by a Jewish fellow-captive to have prayed in Hebrew. Postel returned to Paris in 1562 and spent the rest of his life in protective custody. However, he continued his voluminous writing and correspondence, and also influenced such younger scholars as G. *Génébrard, A. *Maes, and the French poet Guy *Le Fèvre de la Boderie, through whose agency Postel's approach even penetrated the "Catholic" Antwerp Polyglot Bible printed by Christophe *Plantin (*Biblia Regia*, 1568–72). His published works include many of Jewish interest – grammatical and philological compendia, a guide to the Holy Land (1562), and a Latin version of the Sefer *Yeẓirah (1552), with his own mystical comments. Postel's unpublished Latin translations of the Zohar on Genesis and of other Jewish classics have in recent years been discovered and discussed by François Secret. Long derided as a heretic or madman, Postel has emerged as one of the impressive and influential personalities of the Renaissance.

BIBLIOGRAPHY: W.J. Bouwsma, *Concordia Mundi: The Career and Thought of Guillaume Postel* (1957); S.K. Stahlmann, *Guillaume Postel* (Ger., 1956); C. Clair, *Christopher Plantin* (1960), 34–35, 247; I. Zaneh, *Mi-Paulo ha-Revi'i ad Pius ha-Ḥamishi* (1954), 71ff.; F. Secret, *Guillaume Postel (1510–1581) et son Interprétation du Candélabre de Moyse* (1966); idem, in: *Archivio di Filosofia*, 3 (1963), 91–118; idem, *Kabbalistes Chrétiens de la Renaissance* (1964), 171ff.; idem, in: REJ, 124 (1965) 174–6; Baron, Social[2], 13 (1969), 177–8, 394, 398, 403–4; G.E. Silverman, in: JC (Jan. 8, 1960); idem, in: JC (Oct. 23, 1964).

[Godfrey Edmond Silverman]

POSTOLSKY, SHALOM (1893–1949), composer. Born in Siedlce, Poland, he went to Ereẓ Israel in 1920 and was among the founders of kibbutz En-Harod in 1921. Some years later he began composing songs for the needs of the kibbutz and also arranged the *omer and *seder ceremonies of En-Harod. Later he settled in Bet Yiẓhak. His songs include *Kumah Eḥa, Elef Laylah ve-Od Laylah, Ba-Ḥashai Sefinah Gosheshet (Olim), Bikkurim Peri Hillulim* (all to texts by Y. *Shenhar), *Ha-Shibbolim Penimah, Im Garin Zarata* (*Levi Ben-Amitai), and *Ein Zeh Pele* (N. *Alterman), generally corrupted to *Eizeh Pele*.

POTIPHAR (Heb. פּוֹטִיפַר), Egyptian royal official who purchased *Joseph (Gen. 37:36; 39:1). His wife attempted unsuccessfully to seduce Joseph and then brought false charges against him, as a result of which Potiphar had him incarcerated. The name reflects an underlying Egyptian prototype *Pa-diu-pa-Re*, "The one whom the sun god Re has given." The Egyptian name occurs on a stele from the Late period (c. 1087–664 B.C.E.), during which time the near variant *pa-di* followed by the name of a god is most commonly found. Potiphar's titles, "servant of Pharaoh" and "chief [or "master"] of the cooks," while not Egyptian in themselves, may well be Hebrew translations of two Egyptian titles. The former could have been a general term for almost any servant, official, or courtier, and the latter appears to be a translation of the Egyptian *wpdw nsw* or *wb 3 nsw* ("butler/cook of the king"). In any event, the title did not imply that its bearer was a lowly servant, but rather a very high official. It first comes to prominence very late in the Twentieth Dynasty, and its bearers are attested as leading military expeditions, heading royal commissions, and exercising high administrative functions. Both Potiphar's name and his title strongly suggest that the writing down of the Joseph story should be dated no earlier than the later Twentieth Dynasty (and possibly even to the Twenty-First to Twenty-Second dynasties), a suggestion substantially supported by other Egyptian elements occurring in it, particularly the Egyptian names. Further support for this dating is given by the parallel between the attempted seduction of Joseph by Potiphar's wife and the opening portion of an Egyptian literary text, "The Tale of the Two Brothers," which is dated, on paleographic grounds, to about 1225 B.C.E.

[Alan Richard Schulman]

In the *Aggadah*

Potiphar is regarded as identical with *Poti-Phera (Gen. 41:45), indicating different aspects of his idolatrous behavior. "Potiphar" refers to his practice of rearing bullocks, *mefattem parim*, for idolatrous sacrifices; and "Poti-Phera" to his habit of indecently exposing himself (*pore'a*) in honor of his gods. He purchased Joseph in order to perform sodomy with him, but was castrated by God (or by the angel Gabriel; Sot. 13b.), in order to prevent him fulfilling his desire and for this reason is called the "eunuch of Pharaoh" (Gen. 37:36). From the fact that the light-skinned Joseph was offered for sale by the negroid Midianites, he realized that Joseph had been kidnapped. The conflicting scriptural account of the purchase indicates that Potiphar insisted that the Midianites prove prior purchase, in order that he should not be party to a theft (Gen. R. 86:3). Two of Potiphar's actions are favorably commented on. He saw that "the Lord was with [Joseph]" (Gen. 39:3), although he personally was a sun worshiper. Secondly, he was extremely skeptical of his wife's account of Joseph's attempted seduction; had he believed it he would have put Joseph to death instead of imprisoning him. He apologized to Joseph for his action, explaining that his purpose was to prevent a stigma upon his children (Gen. R. 87:9).

In Islam

Qiṭfīr (also Quṭayfar) of Muslim legend is the biblical Potiphar, who bought Joseph from the Midianites or the Ishmaelites (Gen. 37:36; 39:1). Although his name is not mentioned in the tale of Joseph in the *Koran, there is no doubt as to his identity, in spite of the error in the first letter of the source, which is due to the Arabic script. Ṭabarī calls him Aṭfīr. Thaʿlabī counts Qiṭfīr among the three valiant ("afras"): al-ʿAzīz, i.e., Qiṭfīr, for his defense of Joseph; the woman who brought Moses to her father; and the caliph Abū-Bakr, when he appointed ʿOmar.

[Haïm Z'ew Hirschberg]

BIBLIOGRAPHY: Janssen, in: *Jaarbericht van het Vooraziatisch-Egyptisch Gezelschap "Ex Oriente Lux,"* 14 (1955–56), 67–68; J. Vergote, *Joseph en Egypte* (1959). IN THE AGGADAH: Ginzberg, Legends, 2 (1946), 13, 38, 56–58; 5 (1947), 338–39, 341, 369; I. Ḥasida, *Ishei ha-Tanakh* (1964), 360. IN ISLAM: *Ta'rikh*, 1 (1357 A.H.), 236–7; Thaʿlabī, *Qiṣaṣ* (1356 A.H.), 98–99 and passim in the story of Yūsuf; Kisāʾī, *Qiṣaṣ* (1356 A.H.), 161–2 (Quṭayfar).

POTI-PHERA (Heb. פּוֹטִי פֶרַע), father-in-law of *Joseph. According to Genesis 41:45, 50, and 46:20, Joseph was married to *Asenath the daughter of Poti-Phera, "the priest of On." Since On, the city of *Heliopolis, was the center of the Egyptian solar cult, the "priest of On" could hardly have been any other than the high priest of the sun god Re. The name Poti-Phera contains the same underlying elements as that of Joseph's former master, *Potiphar, but in a transcription more fully and more accurately reflecting the original Egyptian form.

[Alan Richard Schulman]

POTOCKI, VALENTINE (**Abraham ben Abraham**; d. 1749), Polish count martyred as a proselyte. According to legend, Potocki, a gifted scion of the celebrated Potocki family, while studying in Paris became friendly with Zaremba, another young Polish aristocrat. Once, while in a tavern, they noticed the owner, an old Jew, immersed in the study of the Talmud, and expressed a desire to be instructed in the principles of Judaism. The two vowed that they would become Jews if convinced of the error of Christianity. Zaremba married and forgot both his vow and his friend. Potocki, however, after spending some time at the papal academy in Rome, went to Amsterdam and became a Jew. When Zaremba heard the report, which had spread throughout Lithuania, of Potocki's disappearance from Rome, he recalled his vow, and, taking his family with him to Amsterdam, also became a Jew there, and subsequently settled in Ereẓ Israel. Potocki went to Lithuania and settled as a Jew in *Ilya, near Vilna.

Once Potocki scolded a boy for disturbing the prayers in synagogue. The boy's father, a coarse tailor, took umbrage and reported the existence of the proselyte to the authorities, thus leading to his arrest. Potocki was put on trial, and despite the pleas of fellow aristocrats refused to recant. On the second day of Shavuot, 5509 (1749), he was burned at the stake at the foot of the fortress of Vilna, on his lips the prayer, "Blessed art Thou, O Lord,… who sanctifiest Thy name before multitudes." A local Jew, Eliezer Ziskes, pretending to be a Christian, succeeded through bribery in collecting some of the ashes and a finger from the corpse, and these were eventually buried in the Jewish cemetery. From the soil over the grave of Potocki, who was called by them the *Ger Ẓedek* ("the righteous proselyte"), there grew a big tree which drew vast pilgrimages of Jews. The grave was demolished by Polish vandals. The first to publish the story of the *Ger Ẓedek* was the Polish writer J. Kraszewski in 1841. He claimed to have found it in a Hebrew manuscript. Later it was published by I.M. *Dick in Hebrew (1862) and in Yiddish (n.d.) under the title *Gerei ha-Ẓedek* (see YIVO *Bleter*, 1 (1931), 331–3). So far no historical evidence for the story has been discovered, although it is generally believed to have been true. The story served as a theme for a drama in Yiddish, called *Dukus* ("Prince"), by Alter *Kacyzne and for some novels. The Jews of Vilna celebrated the anniversary of Potocki's death by reciting the *Kaddish* and by making pilgrimages to his purported grave on the Ninth of Av and on the High Holy Days.

BIBLIOGRAPHY: I. Cohen, *Vilna* (1943), 73–74, 416, 484–6; M. Balaban in: *Nayer Haynt* (1925), nos. 68, 80, 81, 94, 99, 113, 119, 134; *Yevreyskaya Biblioteka*, 3 (1873), 229–37; A. Litvin, *Yidishe Neshomes*, 1 (1916), 1–8; *Gerei ha-Ẓedek* (Vilna, 1862); *Gerei Ẓedek* (Berlin, 1921).

[Arthur Cygielman]

POTOFSKY, JACOB SAMUEL (1894–1979), U.S. labor leader. Potofsky, who was born in the Ukraine, went to Chicago in 1908. His trade union career began almost immediately. From 1916 to 1946 he held a succession of important posts in the Amalgamated Clothing Workers Union and during these years worked closely with union leader Sidney *Hillman. Upon Hillman's death in 1946, Potofsky was elected as the president of the union and continued the major programs developed under Hillman's leadership. Thus, the Amalgamated Clothing Workers continued the policy of avoiding strikes and substituting arbitration wherever possible, a policy over which it clashed with such militant labor unions as John L. Lewis' United Mine Workers. It expanded its insurance programs, increased the number of its group health centers, maintained two banks, and led in sponsoring cooperative housing. Potofsky headed the United Housing Foundation, a combine of his and other trade unions and organizations, which erected large cooperative housing developments.

Under Potofsky's leadership, the Amalgamated continued to play an active political role in national, state, and municipal elections, normally in support of the candidates of the Democratic Party. As a member of the CIO Political Action Committee after 1947 and a vice president of the AFL-CIO after 1955, as well as a leading figure in New York State's Liberal Party, he was one of the prominent, most influential U.S. labor leaders. Potofsky was a supporter of the State of Israel, and the Amalgamated has established a close relationship with the Histadrut. He was also a delegate to many international labor conferences. A vigorous opponent of all forms of prejudice, Potofsky was closely associated with the efforts of the American Jewish Committee and the Anti-Defamation League of B'nai B'rith. He served on a number of public bodies, including the New York Temporary State Commission on Economic Expansion (1959–1960) and the New York City Temporary Commission on City Finances (1965). In both cases, he dissented freely from recommendations that seemed to compromise the interests of wage earners.

BIBLIOGRAPHY: Finkelstein (ed.), *American Spiritual Autobiographies, Fifteen Self-portraits* (1948), 226–242.

[Irwin Yellowitz]

POTOK, CHAIM, (1929–2002) novelist and editor. Born and raised in New York City, Chaim Potok graduated from Yeshiva University in 1950 with a B.A. *Summa Cum Laude* in English literature. In 1954 he was ordained as a Conservative rabbi at the Jewish Theological Seminary.

Potok was a member of the faculty of the University of Judaism in Los Angeles; in 1964 he became managing editor of *Conservative Judaism*. He received his doctorate from the University of Pennsylvania in 1965, and in 1966 he became editor for the Jewish Publication Society of America. Among his works are *The Chosen* (1967), *The Promise* (1969), *My Name is Asher Lev* (1972), *In the Beginning* (1975), *Wanderings* (1978), *The Book of Lights* (1981), *Davita's Harp* (1985), *The Gift of Asher Lev* (1990), and *I Am the Clay* (1992).

The recurrent theme in Chaim Potok's work is the moment of radical change in traditional Jewish existence – a change personified by a son and not usually entailing an actual break with the basic Judaism of the father. Such rebellions have been depicted before in various degrees of severity. Potok's scene differs in that it takes place within an elitist society of learning, the yeshivah, in which all members, fathers and sons, have a deep-rooted respect for each other, and hierarchies of study and knowledge take precedence over familial hierarchies. This mutual respect between fathers and sons, as scholars, many of them *musarniks* in a sphere where, in Potok's words, "the fusion of the sacred and the secular seems almost effortless," therefore creates an impasse when a son chooses a totally different vocation: painting in *Asher Lev*, psychiatry in *The Chosen*, scientific examination of the Oral Law in *The Promise*. In the final reckoning the father is usually reconciled to the son's role in the world, thereby affirming the fluidity of Judaism and its basic tenet of "*ele ve'ele divre Elokim ḥayyim*" (both these and those are the words of the one Living God).

It has been argued that Potok's rebel sons do not venture very far; they shave off beards and sidelocks and work in a secular world, but their basic Orthodoxy does not suffer from any serious modern doubt. Yet Potok's yeshivah may well be seen as a parable for any community with a consequent way of living, the total destruction of which would be equivalent to the destruction of sanity. Chaim Potok proposes a sociological change without a change of values. In Freudian terms, Chaim Potok's sons rebel against the father without actually killing him, thereby assuring cultural continuity.

Potok works within the framework of Jewish value concepts, including the *ḥakham*, the *ẓaddik*, and the overall supremacy of study. His fictional style is uncluttered, his dialogue credible, and he loves his protagonists. Absorbed in father-son, teacher-student relationships, Potok is far less vivid in depicting women who seem in his work to have fewer spiritual doubts, and their existence is delineated mainly by their men.

ADD. BIBLIOGRAPHY: E. Abramson, *Chaim Potok* (1986); S. Sternlicht, *Chaim Potok – A Critical Companion* (2000).

[Shulamith Hareven]

POTTERY. Pottery appears for the first time in the Neolithic period, around the middle of the sixth millennium B.C.E. For two reasons, it serves as a major tool for the archaeological study of the material culture of ancient man: first because of its extensive use in everyday life and second because of its durability; for although the vessels break easily, the material survives as potsherds. Pottery is of great value for acquiring the knowledge of the technological progress of various periods, the trends in the development of early plastic art, and international cultural and commercial relations which form the basis of the comparative chronology of different cultures in the ancient Near East. On the basis of stratigraphic finds at archaeological excavations, pottery is seen to have undergone changes in different periods as well as in different phases of the same period – changes in form, decoration, techniques of working the clay, and firing. As a result, pottery serves as a major index of the relative chronological framework of a given culture. For protohistoric cultures and periods containing no written remains or coins, which are the primary sources of absolute chronology, the relative chronology constructed on pottery sequence serves as a substitute. Once the absolute date of a potsherd is established, the stratum in which it was found can be dated, and thus it also becomes an aid in fixing the absolute chronology (see *Archaeology).

POTTERY MANUFACTURE

The clay from which pottery is produced is an aluminum silicate mixed with various additions such as iron oxides, alkalies, quartz, and lime. Two kinds of clay have been differentiated: clean clay, of pure aluminum silicate, which is not found in Ereẓ Israel, and a rich clay, consisting of aluminum silicate mixed with iron ozides, carbon compounds, etc. The material was prepared for use by sifting and removing foreign matter, mixing it with water and levigating it. If the clay was too rich and not sufficiently plastic, it was tempered by the addition of substances such as sand and quartz grit. The wet sifted clay was then wedged by hand or treaded; after it was well mixed it was ready for shaping. The earliest pottery was handmade. In the Neolithic period, pottery was made by joining together coils of clay, smoothing the junction line by hand. The pottery was shaped on a base or stand of wood, stone, or matting. A technical innovation was shaping pottery from a ball of clay. In the Chalcolithic and Early Bronze periods primitive potter's wheels consisting of a turning board (tournette) were used. Examples of the next stage in the development of the potter's wheel have been found in excavations in Palestine. It consists of two horizontal stone disks placed one on top of the other, the lower one with a conical depression and the upper with a conical projection which could be turned by hand. Several types of pottery were thrown on the wheel in the Early Bronze Age but it was used extensively only in the Middle Bronze Age. After the pot was shaped it was removed from its stand and set aside to dry until its water content was not more than 15%. The pot was then of a leather hard consistency and handles, base, spout, projecting decorations, etc. were applied and various types of ornamentation were added: slips and burnishing, paint, incisions, relief and impressed markings. When the pot was completely fashioned it was dried a second time until it retained only about 3% of its water content. Afterwards it was fired in an open or closed kiln at a temperature of 450°–950° C. The best wares were produced at the highest temperatures. The earliest pottery was fired in open pits, in which combustible material was laid over the pottery, leaving blistering or patches on the sides of vessels. At a later stage the pottery was separated from the fuel by a perforated clay partition built above the fuel compartment. With the invention of the closed kiln it was possible to use an oxidizing fire, which produced pottery of a red color, or a reducing fire, without oxygen, which turned the pottery black.

NEOLITHIC PERIOD

The invention of pottery is believed to have taken place first in the northern Levant, together with the plaster-based White Ware ("vaisselles blanches"), and slowly it began appearing in Palestine as well. Crude attempts at making pottery (sun-dried or low-fired) were found at Pre-Pottery Neolithic C levels at Ain Ghazal and Basta (c. 5800–5500 B.C.E.). At Yiftahel (Stratum III) the White Ware and the early pottery was visually indistinguishable, and some distinctions could only be made by petrographic analysis.

The pottery of the Late Neolithic period (5500 to 4000 B.C.E.) is handmade, coarse, and badly fired. The pottery types include jars, cooking pots, bowls and storage jars decorated with a red-burnished slip or painted triangular and zigzag lines, and with incised and painted geometric designs (such as chevron and herring-bone patterns). The main finds of this period come from the Jordan Valley, Sha'ar ha-Golan, Jericho, etc. The Wadi Rabbah pottery is a more accomplished type of pottery, known particularly in the coastal region.

CHALCOLITHIC PERIOD

In the Chalcolithic period (4000–3300 B.C.E.). several new forms are added to the pottery repertoire of the previous period. The pottery is handmade, sometimes made on a tournette (particularly bowls), and decorated with a rope ornament and occasionally painted with bands of red paint. Tiny lug handles are characteristic of the period, and the shapes include cornets, V-shaped bowls, goblets, jugs, and kraters. Mat impressions are found on the bases of the storage jars. A bird-shaped pot with a lug handle at each end has been named "churn" since it apparently served for making butter, though it may have been a water container. The largest assortment of Chalcolithic pottery was found in the Ghassulian and Beer-Sheba cultures. Additional pottery types are known from the Golan. There also appears to be an earlier phase of Chalcolithic ("Middle Chalcolithic") pottery from the Jordan Valley and from the central highland regions.

EARLY BRONZE AGE

The Early Bronze Age 3300 B.C.E. to 1200 B.C.E. may be subdivided into three or four secondary phases:

(1) Early Bronze I – the typical pottery of the period is gray burnished ware, band-slip (grain-wash) ware, and burnished red-slip ware. Gray burnished ware has a more northerly distribution. Imports of Egyptian vessels are also known, with local imitations, particularly at southern sites (e.g., En Besor).

(2) Early Bronze II – the most distinctive pottery type is the so-called "Abydos (Egyptian) ware," a group of pitchers and storage jars with burnished red-slips on the lower half and triangles and dots painted brown-black on the upper half. This pottery is named after the site where it was first found – the royal tombs of the First Dynasty at Abydos in Upper Egypt. It is of great value for correlating the chronology of Egypt and Palestine. Another important pottery group consists of storage jars with two loop handles and surfaces decorated with pattern combing.

(3) Early Bronze III – the characteristic pottery of this phase is called Khirbat Karak ware (named after Bet Yeraḥ (Khirbat Karak) where it was first found). The pottery types include kraters, bowls, pitchers, and stands. The ware is made of a poor-quality clay and is covered throughout with a highly burnished slip. Occasionally it has a red slip all over but often the rim and interior are red and the exterior is black. The decoration consists of incised lines or groups of lines in relief.

Intermediate Bronze Age

The Intermediate Bronze Age (also known as the Early Bronze IV, 2300–2000 B.C.E.) constitutes a transitional stage between the Early Bronze Age and the Middle Bronze II period. Its material remains are known from villages, campsites, and tombs. The pottery of the period is globular or cylindrical in shape, with wide flat bases, and lacks shoulders and handles. The handles which do occur – enveloped ledge handles and lug handles between the neck and the body – are apparently a continuation of the Early Bronze ceramic tradition. The body of this type of vessel is handmade while the neck, which flares outward, is formed on the wheel; the line where the two are joined together is decorated with combing or with single incised grooves. A group by itself is an assortment from the Megiddo tombs, which consists of "teapots" and goblets made on the wheel of black clay decorated with yellow bands and also jugs with red slips. There are no distinctive cooking pots; hole-mouth jars were apparently used for cooking. The typical lamp of the period is a small bowl with four pinched corners.

MIDDLE BRONZE AGE

With the renewed urbanism of the Middle Bronze Age (2000–1550 B.C.E.) the pottery assemblage flourished with common wares matched by luxury vessels, and greater regionalism in ware types now becomes apparent. All the pottery is now produced on the wheel, which allowed for great artistic development. The period is subdivided generally into the Middle Bronze IIA and Middle Bronze IIB.

Middle Bronze II A

In the Middle Bronze IIA period a glossy red slip decoration – produced by burnishing with a shell or pebble – appears on many vessels, such as small and closed carinated bowls with disk bases (perhaps imitations of metal prototypes); open bowls with flat or disk bases; jugs and juglets with double or triple handles, often set on the shoulder, and dipper juglets. The storage jars are elliptical with a flattened base and often have two loop handles in the center of the body. The cooking pot has straight sides with a thumb-indented projecting band surrounding the body and some are perforated above the band. An interesting group are the storage jars, jugs, and juglets decorated on the upper part of the body with black and red bands, triangles, or circles on a white slip. This ware was thought to be similar in ornamentation to that found in the Khabur region and at Byblos.

Middle Bronze IIB

The red burnished slip ceases to be dominant in the Middle Bronze IIB period and many vessels are undecorated. The technique of manufacture is highly developed and many vessels are produced with thin walls and complicated shapes, such as open carinated bowls with disk or trumpet bags, made of a well-fired, levigated clay. The storage jars have elongated elliptical bodies with two to four loop handles. A special group consists of pear-shaped (pyriform) juglets with a button base and red, brown, or black burnished slips. In the final phase of the period, the characteristic juglet is cylindrical with a flat base. The lamps are small pinched bowls with one wick hole. The cooking pots are shallow with rounded bases and rounded flaring rims. An unusual group of pyriform juglets are known as Tell al-Yahūdiyya ware – named after the site where they were first found in the Nile Delta (many types are now known from Tell ed-Daba'). These juglets have black, gray, or red burnished slips and a white puncture-filled decoration on the surface made with a pointed tool.

LATE BRONZE AGE

The Late Bronze Age (1550–1200 B.C.E.) extends from the conquest of Palestine by the first pharaohs of the 18th Dynasty to the appearance of the Israelites. Palestine in this period was under Egyptian rule, and its culture was influenced both by Egypt as well as by extensive trade connections with the Aegean and East Mediterranean civilizations. It is possible to subdivide the period into three phases (according to Egyptian chronology): Late Bronze I (c. 1550–1400 B.C.E.), the beginning of the 18th Dynasty; Late Bronze IIA (c. 1400–1300 B.C.E.), mainly the Tell el-Amarna period; Late Bronze IIB (c. 1300–1200 B.C.E.), 19th Dynasty.

Late Bronze I

The pottery types and technique of manufacture of the Middle Bronze IIB period persist partly in the Late Bronze I period. The pottery repertoire includes carinated bowls with ring bases or high ring bases; kraters with two loop handles and a ring base, often with a rope decoration as in the previous period; storage jars with elongated bodies, rounded bases, and flaring rims. The ceramic tradition of the Middle Bronze IIB period is also seen in the jugs, juglets, cooking pots, and lamps. Two new groups of ware appear in this period: pilgrim flasks and the so-called "biconical" vessels. The latter have one loop handle. The upper part is decorated with metopes painted red, black, or brown. A new class of vessels first appearing in the transition period between the Middle and Late Bronze Age and continuing into the Late Bronze I is the Bichrome Ware. Made of finely levigated and well-fired clay it is slipped and burnished. The group includes jugs, kraters, and bowls decorated with metopes formed by bands painted red and black. The metopes contain animal decoration – birds, fishes, oxen – and geometric patterns. The character of the ware, which contains a number of unique forms, the decoration, and the uniform method of production indicate that this pottery may have been created by a group of artists in a single center, possibly Tell al-ʿAjūl, south of Gaza.

Late Bronze II

In the Late Bronze II period the previous pottery tradition continues on the whole but shows a certain degeneration in form and quality. The workmanship of the carinated bowls is cruder. The bowls are mainly simple flat vessels with flat or disk bases. The storage jar now shows a sharp shoulder and thickened button base (this type of storage jar was exported from Ereẓ Israel and has been found, together with imitations, in countries in the Aegean Sea and Egypt). The typical jug has a prominent neck with the handle from the rim to the shoulder, and the most common juglet is a dipper juglet generally with trefoil mouth. A new style of painted pottery develops in this period. The ornamented ware – biconical vessels, jugs, kraters – are painted in a single color, red, black, or brown, and a typical decoration has two gazelles facing each other with a palm tree between them. This style degenerates in the second half of the period, Late Bronze IIB, and becomes more schematic and cruder. The pilgrim flasks are flattened and generally decorated with painted concentric circles. In the Late Bronze IIA the neck is attached to the handles of the flask like a flower among leaves while in the second half of the period the flasks are lentoid shaped and the attachment of the neck to the handles is effaced. The lamps have an elongated sharply pinched rim; the cooking pots are shallow with a rounded base and have an ax rim and no handles

There is an abundance of imported pottery in this period, mostly of Mycenean and Cypriot origin. All the Cypriot pottery occurs in Palestine parallel with its appearance in Cyprus. The most distinctive feature of this pottery is the technique of manufacture – it is all handmade and the handles are inserted inside the body of the vessels. This pottery falls into two main groups – White Slip Ware, which includes the "milk bowls," half-globular bowls with wishbone handles and a white-slip and ladder decoration painted brown or black. The second type is called Base Ring Ware and is characterized by a high ring base. This ware is made of well-fired clay and has a metallic ring when struck; it is covered with a reddish brown slip. Its most common types are bowls with wishbone handles and jugs with high tilted necks called *bilbil*. Groups of Monochrome Ware are also found in Palestine as well as the knife-pared type – usually dipper juglets – and other groups. The bulk of the Mycenean pottery appears in Late Bronze II. It is wheel-made of a light-colored, finely levigated clay, and well fired. The vessels are covered with a light slip and painted with bands of geometric patterns and floral and animal motifs. Aside from a number of shards and a cup decorated with an ivy-leaf design which are attributed to the Late Bronze I (Mycenaean II), the entire assortment belongs to the Mycenaean IIIA–B period. The vessels include cups, pear-shaped amphoriskoi, stirrup-jars, pilgrim flasks, juglets, bowls, pyxides, etc. A small amount of pottery imported from Syria and Egypt is also found in this period.

IRON AGE

The Iron Age is divided into two main parts: the Early Iron Age (or Iron Age I, 1200–1000 B.C.E.) and the Late Iron Age (Iron Age II A–C, 1000–586 B.C.E.). The history of this period encompasses the appearance of the Philistines, Israelites, and other peoples in the region, and subsequently, the period of the United Monarchy, the Kingdoms of Israel and Judah, and the destruction of Jerusalem in 587/586 B.C.E. The collective term for pottery in the Bible is *kelei ḥeres* (כְּלֵי חֶרֶשׂ, Lev. 6:21; Num. 5:17; Jer. 32:14), while pottery sherds are called *ḥeres* (חֶרֶשׂ, Job. 2:8). Pottery vessels were used for cooking (Lev. 6:21), as containers for liquids (Num. 5:17), and containers for scrolls (Jer. 32:14). There are references in the Bible to some of the methods that the potter used in his work – "the potter treads clay" (Isa. 41:25) and "I went down to the potter's house, and there he was working at his wheel. And the vessel he was making of clay was spoiled in the potter's hand, and he reworked it into another vessel, as it seemed good to the potter to do" (Jer. 18:3–4). Only two types of vessels in the Bible are designated as pottery. They are: "earthen pots" (*nivlei ḥeres*; Lam. 4:2) and "earthen flasks" (*bakbuk yoẓer ḥeres*; Jer. 19:1). Other vessels that presumably were made of clay are, e.g., *aggan, agganot*, "bowl, cup" (Song 7:3 (2); Isa. 22:24); *asukh*, "jar" (II Kings 4:2); *gavʿia*, "pitcher" (Jer. 35:5); *kad*, "jar" for water (Gen. 24:14) or flour (I Kings 17:14); *kos*, "cup" (Jer. 35:5); *sir*, "pot" (Ex. 16:3); *sefel*, "bowl" (Judg. 6:38); *pakh*, "vial" (of oil; Jer. 25:28; I Sam. 10:1); *ẓappaḥat*, "cruse" (I Kings 17:14); *kubbaʿat*, "cup" (Isa. 51:17, 22); *keʿarah*, "bowl" (Num. 7:85).

Early Iron

In the areas not settled by the Israelites, the Late Bronze pottery tradition seems to continue in the first phase of the period. At the same time new types of pottery appear in the highlands and inland regions of the country. This pottery is associated in the central highlands with the appearance of the Israelites, but in Galilee there are pottery types that indicate Phoenician influence as well. The pottery types which continue the Late Bronze tradition include kraters with two loop handles and painted metope decoration, cooking pots which continue the ax-shaped rim and are without handles, lentoid flasks which are decorated with painted concentric circles, and lamps. The pottery attributed to the area of the appearance of the Israelites, mostly coarse in shape and carelessly made, includes simple, crude bowls, storage jars mostly with a collar rim, many-handled kraters (up to eight) with a rope or incised decoration. The cooking pot shows numerous variations of the ax-shaped rim. During this period there also appear carinated bowls, especially in the south of the country, often with a pair of degenerated horizontal handles. Toward the end of the period new pottery features develop-two loop handles are added to the cooking pot which also has a ridge beneath the rim on the outside; tiny juglets appear with a black or red burnished slip; red-slipped vessels are also common with irregular hand burnishing which is the hallmark of the period. A very distinctive pottery assortment occurs in the 12th–11th centuries B.C.E., called Philistine Ware; it is found mainly in the area inhabited by the Philistines. The shapes and decorative motifs of the pottery are derived from the Aegean pottery tradition, mainly Mycenean IIIC 1. The typical Philistine shapes include kraters with two horizontal loop handles; stirrup jars; jugs with long narrow necks, loop handles, and strainer spouts, which are known as "beer jugs"; long-necked jugs influenced by Egyptian pottery; elongated pyxides; and horn-shaped vessels. Some vessels are covered with a whitewash on which metopes are painted in red and black and ornamented with geometric designs, or even with animals and birds. With the consolidation of the Philistines into the material culture of Palestine in the late 11th century B.C.E., the typical animal motifs disappear and their pottery is no longer differentiated from other pottery types of the period.

Late Iron

Although many differences are found in the pottery of the north and south of the country in various periods, a sharper differentiation occurs with the division of the Monarchy and recent research has been able to highlight various aspects of regionalism. The excavation of Lachish was instrumental in establishing the character and date of pottery assemblages from Level III (destroyed in 701 B.C.E.) and Level II (destroyed in 587/586 B.C.E.). In Judah red-slip and wheel-burnished vessels are more common; the bowls are carinated with enveloped rims toward the end of the period; the kraters have from two to four handles, are covered with a red slip, and are wheel-burnished on the inside, and on the rim of the outside; the rims of the cooking pots are ridged on the outside, and toward the end of the period a special type of cooking pot with a high ridged rim appears; the typical storage jar (in Lachish III) has four ridged loop handles, often stamped with *la-melekh* ("of the king") seal impressions, an elliptical body, and a rounded base; the hole-mouth jars have a round bottom and a wide enveloped or ridged rim; the jugs have bulging bodies and thick necks; at the end of the period the lamps have high bases. In Israel not only the red-slip burnished ware is dominant but red- and black-slip pottery is also very common. The typical storage jar has an elongated globular body, prominent shoulder, and pointed base; bowls and kraters are often decorated with bar handles under the rim. A distinctive northern group is known as Samaria Ware, appearing in two groups – thick-walled and thin-walled ware. This pottery is characterized by a very high standard of workmanship. The walls of the thin ware are of eggshell thinness; it is slipped and burnished throughout in red or in alternating concentric circles of red and yellow. The thick ware, made of a creamy clay, has thick walls and either ring, high ring, or stepped bases, The bowls are covered with a red, yellow, or black burnished slip. The pottery common to both Israel and Judah includes water decanters, spouted jugs, carinated bowls, dipper juglets, etc. Several types of imported pottery also occur in this period – the most prominent is known as Cypro-Phoenician Ware which first appears in Palestine toward the end of the Iron I period and continues until the eighth century B.C.E. This pottery includes bowls with two degenerated horizontal handles and juglets with a flat base and one or two handles. The vessels are decorated with black stripes and concentric circles on a lustrous red slip ("Black on Red"). Some imports from Assyria are also found.

PERSIAN PERIOD

This period (586–330 B.C.E.) is identical with the post-Exilic period, and covers the half century of Babylonian rule after the destruction of the Temple, as well as the subsequent two centuries of Persian rule. Some scholars have suggested that the material culture of the Iron Age II did not cease with the destruction of Jerusalem in 586 B.C.E., but that it continued during the time of Babylonian rule, at least until 530/520 B.C.E., with others suggesting lowering the terminal date well into the fifth century B.C.E.

The pottery of the Persian phase includes coarse bowls with a high ring base and ribbed sides; storage jars with an elongated stump base and two loop handles rising above the shoulders; carrot-shaped juglets; storage jars with two deformed loop handles, elongated pointed base, straight shoulders, and slightly projecting rim. Towards the end of this period kraters and holemouth jars appear with a decoration of bands of reed incisions on their shoulders. The lamps have flat bases with one elongated wick hole and a wide rim around the bowl. A number of pottery types imported from Greece are found in Palestine.

HELLENISTIC PERIOD

Palestine in the Hellenistic period (330–63 B.C.E.) was for most of the time part of an empire and under its cultural influence. The local pottery made for ordinary domestic use was on the whole coarse and clumsy, with regional production centers, but two groups of imported ware are found: fine luxury ware and amphorae for storing imported goods, especially wine. The most characteristic of the local ware are bowls with inverted or outward flaring rims and ring or flat bases; spindle-shaped juglets; cooking pots with two handles and a low erect neck which are reminiscent of the Iron Age pots. There is also a group of open pinched lamps with one wick hole. Both classes of imported ware are widely distributed in this period, the most widespread being the Rhodian wine amphora with stamped handles. The luxury ware included Megarian bowls which were cast in molds; various types of black-glazed bowls ("fish plates") with impressed or roulette decoration. At the end of the period appears the terra sigillata ware – fine red-glazed pottery with impressed and roulette decoration.

ROMAN PERIOD

The pottery of the Roman period (63 B.C.E.–325 C.E.), is divided into the Early Roman period (63 B.C.E.–135 C.E.), with some types disappearing with the fall of Jerusalem in 70 C.E., and the Middle Roman and/or Late Roman (135–325 C.E.). The typical local pottery of the Herodian period (first century C.E.) includes pilgrim flasks with twisted handles; bottles with high necks and thick bodies; juglets with flaring rims; closed lamps cast in molds with pared horned nozzles. The cooking pots follow the tradition of the previous period. Changes occur in the storage jars which divide into elongated bag-shaped jars and bell-shaped jars. Of the imported ware the most common type is the terra sigillata ware, mainly platters and flat bowls with ring bases; they are covered with a red glaze and have a roulette and impressed decoration. Both eastern and western sigillata appear in Palestine. The western, Arretine style (30 B.C.E–30 C.E.) is outstanding in workmanship and finish. Nabatean Ware also appears in this period – eggshell-thin bowls decorated with red floral patterns on an orange background. A local painted variety of bowl – resembling slightly Nabatean examples – appears in Jerusalem. In the Late Roman period these shapes continue to develop – the discus lamps are round and closed, cast in a mould, with a handle or a knob. Numerous Mediterranean types of amphorae appear in the region.

THE BYZANTINE PERIOD

Pottery types of the previous period continue into the Byzantine period (325–640 C.E.). From the beginning of the period, red gloss bowls ("Late Roman Wares") make their appearance. Hayes (1972) produced a dated series of these LRW types (but changes in this dating system is now being assumed by scholars). Local examples, such as bowls with rouletted decorations on their rims, also make their appearance. Various kinds of storage jars are typical of the period, particularly the so-called "Gaza" jar which was made at kilns sites along the lower coast region, from Ashkelon towards north Sinai. Numerous imported jars are also known for this period. Closed cooking pots with two ear-like handles give way to shallow cooking pots with two horizontal handles and a lid. There are also clay pans with only one horizontal handle. The lamps are closed, cast in molds, and elongated in form. Most of them are decorated. The pottery of the Byzantine period did not change with the invasion of the Hejaz Arabs in the early seventh century C.E., but continued with very small changes until the Abbasid period, i.e., in the mid-eighth century. It is at this point that major changes in the pottery assemblages of the Islamic period first become apparent.

BIBLIOGRAPHY: R. Amiran, *The Ancient Pottery of Palestine* (1970). **ADD. BIBLIOGRAPHY:** GENERAL (see also bibliography under *Archaeology); D. Homes-Fredericq and H.J. Franken, *Pottery and Potters – Past and Present* (1986); M. Peleg, *A Bibliography of Roman, Byzantine and Early Arab Pottery from Israel and Neighbouring Countries* (1990); L.G. Herr, *Published Pottery of Palestine.* (1996); S. Gitin (ed.), *The Ancient Pottery of Israel and its Neighbors: from the Neolithic through the Hellenistic Period.* (2006). TECHNOLOGY AND RESEARCH METHODS: D.E. Arnold, *Ceramic Theory and Cultural Process* (1985); C. Orton, P. Tyers, and A. Vince, *Pottery in Archaeology* (1993); I. Freestone and D. Gaimster (eds.), *Pottery in the Making* (1997); CHALCOLITHIC TO PERSIAN: Y. Garfinkel, *Neolithic and Chalcolithic Pottery of the Southern Levant* (1999); J.A. Callaway, *Pottery from the Tombs at ʿAi (Et-Tell)* (1964); M.F. Kaplan, G. Harbottle, and E.V. Sayre, "Multi-disciplinary Analysis of Tell el-Yahudiyeh Ware," in: *Archaeometry,* 24 (1982), 127–42; R. Bonfil, "MB II Pithoi in Palestrine," in: *Eretz-Israel,* 23 (1992), 26–37 (Heb.); M. Artzy and E. Marcus, "Stratified Cypriot Pottery in MBIIa Context at Tel Nami," in: G.C. Ionnides (ed.), *Studies in Honour of Vassos Karageorghis* (1992), 103–10; D. Ilan, "Middle Bronze Age Painted Pottery From Tel Dan," in: *Levant,* 28 (1996), 157–72; P. Magrill and A. Middleton, "A Canaanite Potter's Workshop in Palestine," in: I. Freestone and D. Gaimster (eds.), *Pottery in the Making* (1997), 68–73; J.S. Holladay, "Of Sherds and Strata: Contributions Toward an Understanding of the Archaeology of the Divided Monarchy," in: F.M. Cross (ed.), *Magnalia Dei: The Mighty Acts of God* (1976), 253–93; S. Bunomovitz and A. Yasur-Landau, "Philistine and Israelite Pottery: A Comparative Approach to the Question of Pots and People," in: *Tel Aviv,* 23 (1996); A. Mazar and N. Panitz-Cohen, *Timnah (Tel Batash) II: The Finds from the First Millennium BCE* (2001); D. Ussishkin (ed.), *The Renewed Archaeological Excavations at Lachish (1973–1994),* 5 vols. (2004). HELLENISTIC TO BYZANTINE: A. Berlin and K.W. Slane, *Tel Anafa II, i: The Hellenistic and Roman Pottery* (1997); T. Levine, "Pottery and Small Finds From the Subterranean Complexes 21 and 70," in: A. Kloner, *Maresha Excavations Final Report I* (2003); D. Regev, "Typology of the Persian and Hellenistic Pottery Forms at Maresha – Subterranean Complexes 70, 21, 58," in: A. Kloner, *Maresha Excavations Final Report I* (2003); G. Finkielsztejn, *Chronologie détaillée et révisée des eponyms amphoriques rhodiens de 270 à 108 av. J.C. environ. Premier bilan* (2001); P.W. Lapp, *Palestinian Ceramic Chronology 200 B.C.–A.D. 70* (1961): D.P.S. Peacock and D.F. Williams, *Amphorae and the Roman Economy* (1991); J. Eiring and J. Lund (eds.), *Transport Amphorae and Trade in the Eastern Mediterranean* (2004); J.W. Hayes, *Handbook of Mediterranean Roman Pottery* (1997); D. Adan-Bayewitz, *Common Pottery in Roman Galilee* (1993); D. Barag and M. Hershkovitz, "Lamps," in: *Masada IV: The Yigael Yadin Excavations 1963–1965: Final Reports* (1994); S. Loffreda, *Cafarnao: II. La Ceramica* (1974); S. Loffreda, *La Ceramica: di Macheronte e del' Herodion (90 A.C.–135 D.C.).* (1996); R. Bar-Nathan, *Hasmonean and Herodian Palaces at Jericho: Vol. III: The Pottery.* (2002); J. Magness, *The Archaeology of Qumran and the Dead Sea Scrolls* (2002); M. Hershkovitz, "Jerusalem Painted Pottery from the Late Second Temple Period," in: R. Rosenthal-Higenbottom (ed.), *The Nabateans in the Negev.* (2003): 45–50; M. Killick, "Nabatean Pottery," in: *Artists Newsletter* (Nov. 1986), 16–17; J.W. Hayes, *Late Roman Pottery* (1972); F. Vitto, "Pottery and Pottery Manufacture in Roman Palestine," in: *Bulletin of the Institute of Archaeology,* 23 (1986), 47–64; U. Zevulun and Y. Olenik, *Function and Design in the Talmudic Period* (1979); J. Magness, *Jerusalem Ceramic Chronology circa 200–800 CE* (1993); LATER PERIODS: G.M. Crowfoot, "Pots, Ancient and Modern," in: PEFQST (1932), 179–87; A.D. Grey, "The Pottery of the Later Periods from Tel Jezreel," in: *Levant,* 26 (1994), 51–62; D. Whitcomb, "Khirbet al-Mafjar Reconsidered: The Ceramic Evidence," in: BASOR, 271 (1988), 51–67; D. Pringle, "The Medieval Pottery of Palestine and Transjordan (AD 636–1500): An Introduction, Gazetteer and Bibliography," in: *Medieval Ceramics,* 5 (1981), 45–60. LAMPS: R. Rosenthal and R. Sivan, *Ancient Lamps in the Schlossinger Collection.* (1978); Y. Israeli and U. Avida, *Oil Lamps from Eretz Israel* (1988); J. Goodnick Westenholz, *Let There Be Light: Oil Lamps from the Holy Land,* Bible Lands Museum (2004).

[Isaak Dov Ber Markon / Shimon Gibson (2nd ed.)]

°POUND, EZRA LOOMIS (1885–1972), U.S. poet and critic. Born in Idaho, Pound left the United States in 1907 and lived in London and in Paris before settling in Rapallo, Italy, in 1925. By then he had already won international acclaim as a modern poet. A prolific writer, he published over 40 volumes of poetry, verse translations, and literary criticism whose influence on 20th-century poetic style has been enormous. In Italy, Pound became an admirer of Mussolini and came to adopt an increasingly pro-Fascist, anti-British, and antisemitic tone. He developed an ardent, if amateur, interest in economics and became an advocate of the Canadian C.H. Douglas' social credit doctrine, which vocalized agrarian discontent and blamed human misery on the financial manipulations of a small capitalistic class, largely Jewish in composition and inspiration. Pound's *Money Pamphlets* (6 vols., 1950–52), published in Italy in the 1930s, spoke repeatedly of the "Jewish poison," and in 1939 he wrote an article for the Italian press entitled "The Jew, Disease Incarnate." Many of his poems are also violently anti-Jewish. During World War II Pound broadcast pro-Axis propaganda over the Italian radio.

He was arrested by the American army in 1945 and returned to the United States to face an indictment of treason, but was judged mentally unfit to stand trial and was committed to a mental hospital in Washington, D.C., in 1946. In 1958, following the intervention of many noted poets, he was released, and returned to Italy.

BIBLIOGRAPHY: M. Reck, *Ezra Pound* (1967); C. Norman, *Case of Ezra Pound* (1969), includes bibliography; N. Stock, *Poet in Exile* (1964), includes bibliography; N. Stock, *Life of Ezra Pound* (1970); J. Cornell (ed.), *Trial of Ezra Pound* (1966).

[Charles Reznikoff]

POUPKO, BERNARD (1918–), U.S. Orthodox rabbi. Poupko, who was born in Russia, was ordained by the Rabbi Isaac Elchanan Theological Seminary in 1941 and was appointed rabbi of Pittsburgh's Sha'are Torah Congregation in 1942. He served there for more than 60 years until 2004. He completed his Ph.D. at the University of Pittsburgh on alternatives in adult Jewish education. He was a founder of the Hillel Academy in Pittsburgh. Poupko visited the U.S.S.R. several times after 1964. He was one of the first rabbis to visit the Soviet Union and wrote extensively on Soviet Jewry. He edited or co-edited a 38-volume series for the Rabbinical Council of America including volumes in memory and in honor of Bernard Revel and Norman Lamm, Chief Rabbi Herzog of Israel and The Rav, Rabbi Joseph B. Soloveitchik. A collection of his articles based on his Russian visits was published as *In the Shadow of the Kremlin* (1969). In 1970 he became president of Mizrachi in the U.S. He was a national vice president of the Rabbinical Council of America and for 50 years was president of the Rabbinical Council of Pittsburgh, where he was a most influential Orthodox leader.

[Louis Bernstein / Michael Berenbaum (2nd ed.)]

POVERTY. Distinctions between rich and poor predate recorded history. In Israel, however, these differences do not seem to have become pronounced until the eighth century B.C.E., following the social revolution produced by the monarchy and the dissolution of the earlier tribal solidarity. The expansion of trade and foreign conquest brought an influx of wealth into the land, while urbanization and the rise of favored classes resulted in the amassing of fortunes (Isa. 2:7; Hos. 12:9; Amos 3:15) and the cruel impoverishment of many families (Amos 8:5; Micah 2:2).

The gross social injustice drew stinging rebukes from the prophets (e.g., Isa. 1:23; 3:14; Amos 4:1; 5:11), who called for obedience to the divine command for righteous living (Isa. 1:16–17; Amos 5:14–15) and loyalty to His covenant (Hos. 12:7ff.). Unlike the authors of the wisdom literature, the prophets did not condemn the poor for having brought poverty on themselves through sloth (Prov. 6:6–7; 10:4) and irresponsibility (13:18; 23:21). At the same time, they did not idealize the poor, recognizing that they, too, were often guilty of ignoring God's commands (Isa. 9:12–16; Jer. 5:3–5; 6:13).

Those who were in a better economic position were expected to treat the poor with compassion in order to avoid the further aggravation of their wretchedness (Ex. 22:24–26). Indeed, God Himself was their protector and His blessing to Israel was contingent upon the generous treatment they received (Deut. 15:7–11). Accordingly, Israel's laws – for example, those concerning the prompt payment of wages (Deut. 24:14–15), the prohibition of usury (Ex. 22:24; Lev. 25:36; Deut. 23:20), allotments from vintage and harvests (Lev. 19:9–10), the right to enjoy the Sabbatical fruits (Ex. 23:11) and third-year tithes (Deut. 14:28–29; 26:12–13), and the privilege of eating one's fill from a neighboring vineyard or field (Deut. 23:25–26) – provided for the amelioration of their conditions. It was the duty of the judge to protect the rights of the lowly (Ex. 23:6ff.; Lev. 19:15), as it was that of the more fortunate citizen to enable them to participate in the festivals (Deut. 16:11, 14). The king could assure the stability of his rule by concerning himself with the just treatment of the humble (Prov. 29:14).

The Torah recognized that poverty as such could not be eliminated (Deut. 15:11). At the same time, it sought to avoid the evils of pauperism by providing for periodic remission of debts during the Sabbatical Year (Deut. 15:1ff.), and the return of ancestral landed properties in the Jubilee Year as well as the manumission of Israelite slaves (Lev. 25:8ff.). In this way, it was hoped, the ancient covenant fellowship of Israel could retain its original force, as the tribal solidarity was reaffirmed and restored to the social conditions of pre-monarchical times.

Social oppression, however, did persist, and a "spiritual transposition of vocabulary" is apparent in the later literature, with *ʿani* (עני) and *ʿanaw* (ענו) becoming functionally equivalent to "God-fearing" and "pious" (Zeph. 2:3; 3:12–13), the opposite of *rashaʿ*. By this time, though, the term had lost its sociological significance. In any event, neither before nor after the Exile did the poor constitute a religious party or social class.

[David L. Lieber]

In the Talmud

The Talmud reveals a distinctly ambivalent attitude toward poverty. It would appear that poverty was so widespread and was regarded as so irremediable that it was raised to the level of a virtue which had its positive value. Poverty appears to have been particularly endemic in Babylonia. "Of ten measures of poverty which descended to the world, Babylonia took nine" (Kid. 49b) and it was stated that the poverty of the Jews there was the reason that the festivals were celebrated with special joy (Shab. 145b). Both the negative and positive aspects are equally stressed. The former finds its expression in such statements as that "grinding poverty deprives a man of his mental balance" (Er. 41b) and it is the worst of all sufferings in the world (Ex. R. 31:12). "Poverty in a man's house is worse than 50 plagues" (BB 116a). The statement in the Talmud (Ned. 64b) that the "poor man" is one of the four who are regarded as dead has to be amended, as the context shows, to "he who has lost his property," i.e., the man who was once wealthy and is reduced to poverty. Rav's daily prayer, which included "a life of wealth and honor" (Ber. 16b), is only one of a host of statements which extol the contrary desirable ideal of wealth, or at least the absence of poverty.

On the other hand poverty is extolled as having a positive value, from the point of view of its salutary effect both upon the character of the poor and upon the sense of generosity which it engenders in those who relieve it. All the various statements in the Talmud which emphasize both aspects are collated in one statement in a late Midrash, "the Holy One Blessed be He considered all the boons which He could confer upon Israel, and selected poverty, since as a result of poverty they fear the Lord. Righteousness derives only from poverty; *gemilut ḥasadim* derives only from poverty; a man becomes godfearing only through poverty; a man studies Torah only through poverty" (EHZ 24). For the last, compare "take special care of the children of the poor; from them comes Torah" (Ned. 81a). Indeed "Poverty is as becoming to Israel as red trappings on a white horse" (Ḥag. 9b). The parallel passage (Lev. R. 35:6) which has "the daughters of Israel" is ascribed to R. Akiva and it is he who answers the other aspect of the positive value of charity. "If your God loves the poor why does he not support them?" asked *Tinneius Rufus, and Akiva answered, "so that through them [i.e., by relieving their wants] we may be delivered from Gehinnom" (BB 10a). A particular aspect of the virtue of poverty is found in the statement "the men of the Great Synagogue fasted 24 fasts that scribes of Torah scrolls, **tefillin*, and **mezuzah* should not become prosperous" (Pes. 50b). The Midrash enumerates eight names for the poor man in the Bible. The comprehensive one is *ani*; the *evyon*, as the root of the word conveys, is the needy man in the literal sense ("he who is in need of something"); while the *misken* is "the most despised of all" (Lev. R. 34:6). The poor man who was entitled to receive food from the public soup kitchen (*tamḥui*) was one who did not have sufficient for two meals a day (Shab. 118a).

Poverty was almost predetermined and was regarded as independent of man's efforts. "R. Meir said: One should always pray to Him to whom all wealth and property belong, for there is not a craft in which are not [the potentialities] of poverty and of wealth, for neither poverty nor wealth is due to the craft, but all depends upon one's [spiritual] merit" (Kid. 4:14).

The relief of the poor had to be effected with the utmost delicacy and consideration. "God stands together with the poor man at the door, and one should therefore consider whom one is confronting" (Lev. R. 34:9). One of the earliest talmudic authorities, Yose b. Johanan of Jerusalem, made as his maxim: "Let the poor be members of thy household" (Avot 1:5); "he who is openhanded to the poor will be vouchsafed male children" (BB 10b). The previous circumstances of the poor man were taken into consideration, and the story is told of Hillel who, when a poor man who had once been in prosperous circumstances came to him for help, provided him with a horse and a "servant to run before him" since that was the minimum to which he was accustomed, and when he could not find (or afford) a servant he acted himself in that capacity (Ket. 67b). Applicants for food were examined as to the genuineness of their needs, but not applicants for clothes, but the contrary view also has its advocates (BB 9a). In the dispensation of charity the local poor took precedence over those from other towns (BM 71a). A peripatetic mendicant was provided with a minimum of a loaf of bread of a certain value, and lodging for the night (BB 9a). It was stated that most poor are descendants of the tribe of Simeon; this being the effect of Jacob's curse "I will scatter them in Israel" (Gen. 4, 9:7; Gen. R. 98:5).

[Louis Isaac Rabinowitz]

BIBLIOGRAPHY: A. Kuschke, in: ZAW, 57 (1939), 31–57; de Vaux, Anc Isr, 72–74; H.J. Muller, *Freedom in the Ancient World* (1961), 34; S.N. Kramer, *The Sumerians* (1963), 77; Baron, Social^2, index, 234; M. Lazarus, *The Ethics of Judaism* (1900).

POVICH, SHIRLEY LEWIS (1905–1998), sports reporter, editor, and columnist for the *Washington Post* for 76 years. Born in Bar Harbor, Maine, the eighth of ten children to Lithuanian immigrants Rosa (Orlovich) and Nathan, Povich was named after his grandmother Sarah, or "Sorella" in Yiddish, thus "Shirley," which accounted for his listing in *Who's Who of American Women* in 1962. Povich's father, who arrived in the U.S. in 1878 at age 20 with his grandfather, owned a furniture store frequented by the wealthy families who maintained summer homes in the area, including Edward McLean, owner of the *Washington Post*, for whom Povich caddied at the Kebo Valley Country Club. After graduating from Morse High School in Bath, Maine, in 1922, 17-year-old Povich was persuaded by McLean to move to D.C. to serve as his caddy and to work at the *Washington Post*. Povich's first day in Washington found him caddying for President Warren Harding, and on his second day he started working in the *Post*'s city room – first as a copyboy and then a police reporter and a rewrite man, before moving to the sports department in 1924. Povich attended Georgetown University – paid for by McLean – from 1922 to 1924, when he left without a degree. His first byline appeared on August 5, 1924, above a report on the Washington Senators.

In 1926, at age 20, Povich was named *Post* sports editor, the youngest sports editor of a metropolitan daily in the nation. His column, "This Morning With Shirley Povich," ran from August 1926 until 1974, interrupted only by a stint as a war correspondent in the South Pacific during World War II. In 1933, Povich gave up his position as sports editor to concentrate on his column, logging more than 15,000 columns during his career, including some 50 a year after his "retirement" in 1973. Povich, who covered 60 World Series and 20 Super Bowls, was an eyewitness to most of the significant sporting events of the 20th century: the 1927 Dempsey-Tunney "Long

Count" fight; Ruth's "called shot" in the 1932 World Series; and Cal Ripken breaking Lou Gehrig's consecutive-game streak. Povich wrote with clarity, style, grace, and wit, and some of his writings are considered sports journalism classics. At Lou Gehrig's retirement speech at Yankee Stadium in 1939 he wrote: "I saw strong men weep this afternoon, expressionless umpires swallow hard, and emotion pump the hearts and glaze the eyes of 61,000 baseball fans in Yankee Stadium. Yes, and hard-boiled news photographers clicked their shutters with fingers that trembled a bit."

Povich was an early voice for the integration of sports, writing a column advocating the integration of Major League Baseball in 1939, eight years before Jackie Robinson broke the color barrier. When he finally signed, Povich wrote: "Four hundred and fifty-five years after Columbus eagerly discovered America, major league baseball reluctantly discovered the American Negro..." He regularly criticized then-Washington Redskins owner George Preston Marshall for refusing to hire any black players. On one occasion, Povich wrote: "Jim Brown, born ineligible to play for the Redskins, integrated their end zone three times yesterday."

Povich wrote until, literally, the day before he died, and his last column appeared the following day. He was the recipient of the Baseball Writers Association of America's J.G. Taylor Spink Award, the Baseball Hall of Fame honor for sportswriters, in 1975, and he is the only sportswriter to receive the National Press Club's prestigious Fourth Estate Award (1997). The University of Maryland created the Shirley Povich Chair in Sports Journalism in his memory. He was elected to the National Sportswriters Hall of Fame in 1984.

Povich, the father of American television personality Maury Povich, is the author of *The Washington Senators* (1954) and *All These Mornings* (1969). A collection of his columns, *All Those Mornings ... At the Post*, was published in 2005.

[Elli Wohlgelernter (2nd ed.)]

POWDERMAKER, HORTENSE (1896–1970), pioneering scholar in American anthropology. Powdermaker was born in Philadelphia, one of four children of Minnie (Jacoby) and Louis Powdermaker, a German-Jewish middle class family. She attended Goucher College, where she became interested in the labor movement; after graduation she worked for the Amalgamated Clothing Workers of America and organized workers in Cleveland and Rochester. In 1925 Powdermaker enrolled in a graduate course in social anthropology with Bronislaw Malinowski at the London School of Economics. Strongly influenced by Malinowski, she went on to receive a Ph.D. in 1928, writing a thesis on leadership in "primitive society." Powdermaker's first book, *Life in Lesu* (1933), was based on fieldwork in Melanesia; her second study, *After Freedom* (1939), reflecting her research in Indianola, Mississippi, was among the first anthropological studies of a modern American community. Her psychological analysis of black-white relations in the context of the larger communal dynamics in a racially divided city made this book a landmark achievement.

In 1938 Powdermaker founded the Department of Anthropology and Sociology at Queens College in New York City and during World War II she also taught at Yale in an army training program focusing on the Pacific. During this time, her writing was focused on racial problems and included *Probing Our Prejudices* (1944), for high school students. In 1946–47, Powdermaker served as a part-time visiting professor at the University of California at Los Angeles, while conducting research on the Hollywood movie industry. The resulting book, *Hollywood, The Dream Factory* (1950) remains the only serious anthropological study of American filmmaking. In the 1950s, Powdermaker did research in a mining town in Northern Rhodesia and published her analyses in *Coppertown* (1962). Her 1966 volume, *Stranger and Friend*, compared and evaluated her four very different fieldwork experiences. Following her retirement from Queens College, Powdermaker moved to Berkeley, California. Among other honors, Powdermaker served as president of the American Ethnological Society and received an honorary doctorate from Goucher College. She also was awarded the Distinguished Teacher Award from the Alumni Association of Queens College.

BIBLIOGRAPHY: B. Johnson. "Hortense Powdermaker," in: P.E. Hyman and D. Dash Moore (eds.), *Jewish Women in America*, vol. 2 (1997), 1099–1100; S. Silverman. "Hortense Powdermaker," in: U. Gacs, A.Khan, J. McIntyre, and R. Weinberg (eds.), *Women Anthropologists: A Biographical Dictionary* (1988), 291–96.

[Judith R. Baskin (2nd ed.)]

POZNAN (Ger. **Posen**), city in historical *Great Poland; in Prussia 1793–1807 and 1815–1919; now in Poznan province, W. Poland. One of the most ancient and leading Jewish communities of Poland-Lithuania, it was probably one of those for whom the charter of rights granted by Prince Boleslav the Pious (1264) was intended. Jews are known to have lived in Poznan in 1379; a *blood libel is mentioned in 1399. The development of the community was interrupted in 1447 when a fire ravaged the town, impoverishing the Jews. The first signs of economic recovery appeared during the second decade of the 16th century, inaugurating a period of progress and spiritual efflorescence which lasted until approximately the close of the century. Then one of the largest communities in Poland-Lithuania, with 3,000 persons (about 10% of the city's population) and 137 wooden and stone houses, Poznan became the Jewish center of Great Poland. Its rabbis, among the most prominent authorities of the generation, were recognized throughout the country and the "sages of Poznan" were renowned. Nevertheless this period of prosperity was marked by a severe struggle with the local townspeople and the monks. The townsmen repeatedly (1521, 1523, 1554, 1556) endeavored to hinder the retail trade of the Jews, to restrict the number of houses in the Jewish quarter and beyond it (1532, 1537, 1545), and to expel new Jewish settlers (1549). Students of the Jesuit seminary organized bloody attacks (*Schuelergelaeuf*, 1575) on the Jewish quarter. During riots in 1577, 20 Jews lost their lives and after a fire in 1590 the Jewish quarter was abandoned for two years.

Through further misfortunes the community began to decline. Jesuit persecutions were renewed in 1607, and in the wake of another fire (1613) the Jews temporarily settled on the outskirts of the town, from where they were expelled in 1620. The plague known as St. Anthony's Fire claimed a number of victims and those who fled at this time did not return. Signs of decline became apparent in the middle of the 17th century with a one-third decrease in the population, although the proportion of Jews within the general population rose to 15%. The burden of taxation became severe and attempts to raise funds by new lease methods did not alleviate the financial plight. There was constant recourse to loans but these were insufficient for the growing needs and settlement of former debts (not finally settled until the middle of the 19th century). As German merchants from Silesia penetrated the region, trade rivalry grew. Jewish traders at the fairs (*Brandenburg, *Gniezno, Frankfurt on the *Oder) met with difficulties that reduced their sources of livelihood. In riots in 1639 some lost their lives and property was destroyed. Famine and plagues following the Swedish War (1655–60) and renewed riots (1687) brought economic ruin and accelerated the depletion of the community. A call for assistance to the communities of Germany and Bohemia (1674) failed to raise sufficient funds for charity or for redemption of the *Sifrei Torah*, mortgaged in payment of debts (which amounted to 60,000 zlotys to the nobility alone). Economic distress was accompanied by social and cultural decline: Tension prevailed and quarrels became endemic; even education was neglected.

Deterioration continued during the 18th century. In 1709 there was a renewed outbreak of St. Anthony's Fire, and an attack by the army of the so-called Tarnogrod Confederation (1716–17) further depleted the community. A severe fire (1717), the flooding of the Warta River, and a blood libel (1736) had disastrous consequences, and rehabilitation of the community became beyond its means. Growing numbers of Jews left the city, some for Swarzęc, a subsidiary community of Poznan. Those who remained could not halt the process of disintegration in all aspects of Jewish communal, social, and economic life. In 1759 the conquering Prussian army imposed an enormous fine of 2,676 guilders. Another fire in 1764 destroyed 76 houses and claimed many victims. The debts of the community increased to unprecedented figures (686,081 guilders, with 27,800 guilders annual interest). A royal commission failed to solve the problem of the debts. The majority of the members of the community, which numbered 3,000 persons (about 40% of the population) at the end of the 18th century, were poor recent arrivals, unable to bear the burden of taxation and payment of debts.

When Poznan was under Prussian rule (1793–1807), *Prussia's legislation relating to the Jews and its general legislation affected Jewish life in Poznan in many new spheres, e.g., it restricted communal jurisdiction in favor of the local Prussian tribunal. General elementary and secondary schools were opened to Jews. Haskalah and Germanization received considerable impetus. The municipality attempted to induce the new rulers to restrict the numbers and activities of Jews in the city, and seized the opportunity after the fire of 1803, in which the Jewish quarter was severely damaged, to submit proposals for the confinement of the Jews to their original quarter. For hygienic reasons, however, the Prussian government decided not to rebuild the Jewish quarter and to allow the Jews to settle in any part of the town, with the sole reservation that they should have no more houses than they had previously owned. The purchase of houses from Christians was permitted. This decision could not take effect because of the outbreak of the Napoleonic War, and so the Jews of Poznan returned to their quarter and rebuilt a number of houses. A minority, presumably *maskilim*, settled outside the Jewish quarter.

The situation of Poznan's Jews was certainly not improved during the period of the Grand Duchy of Warsaw (1807–13); the *maskilim* were disillusioned by the abrogation of emancipation (1808), while the general Jewish population was burdened by new taxes (the recruits' tax and the kosher meat tax). The community viewed with suspicion the activities of David *Caro. A member of the Berlin Haskalah and contributor to *Ha-Me'assef*, he called for reforms in education and Divine Worship and disseminated Haskalah literature. When Prussian rule was reestablished (1815), a conflict broke out within the community over the election of the rabbi. The *maskilim* were opposed to the candidacy of Jacob Moses Eger, whose scholarly authority and social influence worked against their plans for the closure of the *ḥadarim* in favor of public schools and the opening of a teachers' seminary. Toward the end of his life (1833), these questions were again raised by the Prussian government in the form of "temporary directives," aimed at achieving a Germanic assimilation to counter the Polish element in the city. The resistance of the community prevented their implementation and the *ḥadarim* were not replaced until 40 years later. Another article of the "temporary directives" granted equality to that tiny section of the community whose education (knowledge of the German language), length of residence (from 1815), or act of Prussian patriotism entitled them to state citizenship. The overwhelming majority of the Jewish population (85%) was merely "tolerated," a status which was not changed until 20 years later. Germanization of the Jewish community was partially achieved during the 1850s, under the pressure of the Prussian authorities, who forced the German settlers to consent, and in the face of growing hostility of the Poles. When delegates of the Jews were elected to municipal institutions in 1853, Poles for the first time were in the minority. Relations between Germans and Jews improved and, as a result, Germanization was intensified. The ties between the community of Poznan and those of Prussia and central Germany were strengthened while those with communities to the east weakened. The Jewish population increased (about 6,000 in the 1860s) and its economic situation improved. Communal authority confined itself to religious and philanthropic spheres: A magnificent synagogue was built and rabbinical conventions were held there in 1876, 1877, 1897, and 1914.

The defeat of Germany in World War I and the annexation of Poznan by Poland came as a severe blow to the Jews, who had supported Germany in the struggle (1918–19). The renewal of Polish rule was marked by riots and clashes and the community rapidly declined. By the late 1930s, about 2,000 Jews remained in the city.

The Organization of the Community (16th–18th Centuries)

The records of the Poznan community (the memorial volumes and the lists of *kesherim* ("eligibles")) provide a detailed picture of its organization and of the activities of its institutions (1611–1833). Communal officials were chosen by means of eligible arbitrators or by the community council (there were about 100 delegates every year). The eligible arbitrators were elected by the outgoing community council from among the members of the community and they in turn elected the higher officials by secret ballot and majority vote: the *parnasim*, the elders, the council, the *dayyanim*, and the treasurers (about 35 people). The new community council selected the lower officials: the city representatives, the initiators of regulations, various functionaries, the superintendents of the guilds, assessors, the council of the *bardan* (a specific tax levied partly on food consumption and partly on trade turnover), accountants, and those responsible for relief work (about 65 people). Election procedures followed very elaborate rules designed to fulfill certain halakhic requirements while embodying various methods designed to ensure a moderate oligarchical regime in the community. The salaried community officials – rabbis, preachers, *shtadlanim*, *ḥazzanim*, and beadles – were selected by 32 men (13 from the council and 19 from the three classes: the wealthy, the middle class, and the poor) and their term of office was from one to three years, fixed by letter of appointment. As the rabbi of Poznan also acted as rabbi of the province of Great Poland, the arbiters of the province assisted at his election; an inhabitant of Poznan was disqualified from holding this office. Later, after obstruction by the province, the election of the rabbi was entrusted to 32 men. The *kesherim* also had legislative power, formally in pursuance of their electoral power. Their ordinances were intended as guidance for the higher and lower officials. The overt legislation (the regulations) and the hidden legislation ("secret letters") were decreed by the *kesherim* themselves at their meetings (these constituted about 85% of the whole legislation), sometimes on the initiative of the "initiators of the regulations." The *kesherim* advised and passed regulations in the spheres of economy, jurisdiction, relief, and education. Sumptuary regulations were also included. The *kesherim* also undertook the supervision of the community's institutions. It was considered their task to ensure that the regulations were executed to the full, in letter and spirit. Thus the *kesherim* became one of the most distinctive and firmest institutions of the Poznan community, but because they were selected annually and about 50% were newcomers every year, they did not become a closed ruling group. Through them the members of the community felt that their leadership was under permanent control and that their selection was a responsible public act.

The community determined the number of permanent and temporary residents, as well as the number of dwelling houses in the community. In general they acted according to principles accepted in Jewish society (see **Ḥerem ha-Yishuv*) but there were special considerations prevailing in the Poznan community. Acceptance of new settlers was dependent on the agreement of the 32-member committee or a commission acting in its name. Their decision was based on two considerations: the quota of Jewish inhabitants permitted by the municipal council and the number of poor members, which could not be increased. Community membership was granted to a new settler after three years' residence and after payment of special fees. Those living "outside the community" as a result of wars, floods, plagues, and fires became once more full-fledged members when they had equipped themselves with a letter of residence granting its bearer the right to trade in Poznan in exchange for his sharing the burden of taxation. The optimum number of houses in the Jewish quarter was fixed. In 1641 there were 80 wooden houses (40 housing one family, 39 two families, and one three families) and another 57 stone houses (48 housing two families and nine three families). In 1710 the number of houses decreased to 98, but in 1714 it increased to 109. The ownership of many dwellings by the wealthy during the community's period of prosperity and their refusal to rebuild after various calamities resulted in a shortage of houses, a rise in rents, and the demand that rents be paid in advance. Because of the opposition of the municipal authorities it was difficult to find temporary lodging – especially after wars, plagues, and fires – beyond the Jewish quarter. Specialized community institutions dealt with fiscal problems, with the collection and assessment of taxes. The collection of "gifts for the authorities" (to the *wojewoda*, the ministers, the municipal council, and the monks) was borne by the communal institutions. To achieve greater efficiency in the collection of charity donations and payments for *mitzvot*, a list of the needy was drawn up and collection methods and procedures for the distribution of allocations were established.

The community intervened in the regulation of trade competition. The *kesherim* supported the merchants against the craftsmen (butchers, tailors, hatters, furriers, buttonhole makers), the brokers, and the moneylenders. The attitude of the *kesherim* toward the middleman, i.e., the itinerant broker in the town or at the fair, was based on the extent of his usefulness or the damage caused by his economic activities to commerce and moneylending. The merchant class waged a fierce struggle against the permanent brokers to non-Jews, against the middleman between one non-Jew and another, and against the brokers who acted as messengers or attracted customers from one trader to another. Loans for consumption were not encouraged, but a loan for trading purposes was viewed favorably. A loan which surpassed the means of the borrower was condemned and invalidated. Guarantees for loans were defined (*pledge, agreement by handing over an object (*kinyan sudar*), mortgage, and **mamram*) and a rate of interest was fixed (in towns 22%; at fairs 33%; for squires 15%; for monks 8%). In the legal and judicial field, special and detailed attention was given to procedures, such as summons to court, the actual trial, and the execution of the sentence. The community tried to impose sumptuary laws based on the principles of: "everyone according to his wealth and prevailing conditions"; "a man is only authorized to spend according to his status"; and "the Torah took pity on the money of Israel." These restrictions were applied to clothes and religious celebrations in accordance with financial means (middle class, lower class, and religious officials). The poor were supported by various funds, most important being the charity fund for the poor, and assistance funds for poor brides, the needy aged, guests, youth, the sick, and paupers. The youth of Poznan attended two educational institutions: the *bet midrash* (or the synagogue) and the yeshivah. In the *bet midrash* they studied in three classes and the teachers were supervised by the community. In the yeshivah the number of students was predetermined and limited. Adults also studied in these institutions under the guidance of the *av bet din*, the preacher, the *dayyan*, and learned laymen. Public religious life was centered around the numerous synagogues. The larger synagogues enjoyed more extensive rights with regard to the status of their treasurers, the selection of *ḥazzanim*, the distribution of *etrogim*, and the determination of the seat of the *Gaon* or preacher.

[Dov Avron]

Holocaust Period

At the outbreak of World War II there were about 1,500 Jews in Poznan. Many of them escaped before the entry of the Germans or in the first weeks of the occupation. Poznan became the capital of the Reichsgau Wartheland under the Nazi occupation. The Jewish community in occupied Poznan existed for only three months. In that time the synagogue was transformed into a stable, Jewish property was systematically plundered, and the Jews were driven out of the better residences. On Nov. 12, 1939, the S.S. and police chief of Warthegau, Wilhelm Cappy, ordered that Poznan be made "*judenrein*" within three months. On Dec. 11–12, 1939, the Jews were deported to Ostrow Lubelski and other towns of the General Government. Some of the refugees reached Wloszczowa; others went to Grodzisk Mazowiecki, Zyrardow, Wiskitki, and Blĩnie. On April 15, 1940, the Nazi paper *Ostdeutscher Beobachter* reported the solemn, symbolic, ceremonial removal of the Star of David from the last synagogue in Poznan. From November 1939 until August 1943 Jewish forced labor camps existed in the town and vicinity. The inmates, who came from various towns in Warthegau, worked on road building, land estates, and other work sites.

[Danuta Dombrowska]

Postwar Period

A report issued in 1947 by the Central Committee of the Jews of Poland (set up immediately after the liberation of the country) showed that 224 Jews were living in Poznan in January 1946 (148 men, and 76 women), and 343 in June of the same year (208 men, and 135 women).

No significant Jewish community developed in subsequent years.

BIBLIOGRAPHY: M.M. Zarchin, *Jews in the Province of Posen* (1939), incl. bibl.; B.D. Weinryb, *Texts and Studies in the Communal History of Polish Jewry* (1950); J. Lukaszewicz, *Historisch-statistisches Bild der Stadt Posen* (1878); A. Heppner and J. Herzberg, *Aus Vergangenheit und Gegenwart der Juden und der juedischen Gemeinden in den Posener Landen* (1909); T. Ereciński, *Prawo przemysłowe miasta Poznania w XVIII wieku* (1934); D. Avron, *Pinkas ha-Kesherim shel Kehillat Pozna* (1966); J. Perles, in: MGWJ, 13–14 (1864–65); Berliner, *ibid.*, 17 (1868), 174–8; D. Kaufmann, *ibid.*, 38 (1894), 184–92; 39 (1895), 38–46, 91–96; P. Bloch, *ibid.*, 47 (1903), 153–69, 263–79, 346–56; J. Jacobsohn, *ibid.*, 64–65 (1920–21); T. Nożyński, in: *Kronika miasta Poznania*, vol. 10; W. Feilchenfeld, in: *Zeitschrift der historischen Gesellschaft fuer die Provinz Posen*, 10–11 (1895–96); J. Landesberger, in: *Festschrift ... Dr. Wolf Feilchenfeld* (1907), 40–46; idem, in: JJLG, 10 (1912), 361–71; J. Jacobsohn, in: *Menorah – juedisches Familienblatt*, 7 (1929); F. Kupfer, in: BŻIH, no. 2–3 (1953), 56–121. Ḥ.D. Friedberg, *Ha-Defus ha-Ivri be-Polanyah* (1950^2), 61; L. Lewin, in: *Soncino-Blaetter*, 1 (1925/26), 171ff. HOLOCAUST: *Megillat Polin*, 5 pt. 1 (1961), 158, 160; I. Trunk, in: *Bleter far Geshikhte*, 2 no. 1–4 (1949), 78; D. Dabrowska, in: BŻIH, no. 13–14 (1955), 122–84, passim.

POZNAŃSKI, EDWARD (1901–1974), philosopher. Poznański, the son of Samuel Abraham Poznański (*Posnanski), was born in Warsaw, and studied philosophy and mathematics at the local university. While in Poland he was the secretary and moving spirit of the Friends of the Hebrew University in Poland. His principal concern was the building of the Jewish National and University *Library, and many thousands of books arrived at the library through his good offices, bound and catalogued – since among his fields of expertise and hobbies were bibliography and librarianship.

He immigrated to Palestine in 1939, and was appointed academic secretary of the Hebrew University in 1946, holding the position until his retirement in 1964. One of his major concerns was the advancement of junior staff through administering funds for fellowships and scholarships. He was instrumental in defining the university's policy for enabling younger scholars to visit great universities abroad and return with enhanced experience and deepened scholarship to join the ranks of the Hebrew University faculties.

During his tenure of office as academic secretary, Poznański taught logic, philosophy of science, and philosophy of mathematics at the Department of Philosophy. After his retirement he devoted all his time to this department as teacher, administrator, student counselor, and as principal editor of the Hebrew philosophical quarterly *Iyyun.* He wrote extensively in the field of his specialization.

Poznański established a wide-spread network of contacts with philosophers all over the world. During and after the Yom Kippur War of 1973 he disseminated information and analyses of the situation in many of his letters, some of which also reached the Soviet Union.

Poznański was rooted in Jewish culture, was widely read in the literatures of several languages, and was interested in poetry, music, children's books, and photography. His friendship with the renowned Jewish educator Janusz *Korczak was an important part of his life and a source of inspiration to him as a man and educator.

[Nathan Rotenstreich (2nd ed.)]

POZNANSKI, GUSTAVUS (1804–1879), Jewish religious leader and reformer. Born in Storchnest, Poland, and educated in Hamburg, he immigrated to the United States in 1831 and served for a time as the *shoḥet* of Shearith Israel in New York, blowing the *shofar* and serving as assistant *ḥazzan* as well. In 1837 he went to Congregation Beth Elohim of Charleston, SC, then the wealthiest and most cultured Jewish community in America as *ḥazzan*. He came to a divided community between Reformers and an Orthodox group well recommended by Isaac Leeser, then the leading Orthodox figure in the United States. He came as an Orthodox Rabbi on probation but soon earned the admiration of his congregation and was given life tenure. Leeser was soon to regret his recommendation when Poznanski's views changed radically. In 1838, his synagogue burned and when the new building was constructed an organ was introduced, the first organ ever used in a U.S. synagogue. It divided the synagogue and the case was taken to court by 40 members who had left the congregation because of their objection to the organ. When he recommended the abolition of the second day of Jewish Festivals more members withdrew. Poznanski offered to step aside to bring peace but returned to the pulpit for four additional years until 1847. His successor could not be chosen until 1850 because the community remained divided. Among those who applied for the position was Isaac Mayer Wise. After retirement, Poznanski remained in the community for some 15 years and later divided his time between New York and Charleston. In New York, he was a member of Shearith Israel, which was an Orthodox Congregation still retaining his Reform membership in Charleston.

BIBLIOGRAPHY: Minute Books of the Congregation Beth Elohim, 1838–43, 1846–1852; B.A. Elzas, *The Jews of S.C.* (1905); D. Philipson, *The Reform Movement in Judaism* (rev. ed., 1931); Jewish Marriage Notices ... Charleston, SC (1917); *Occident and Am. Jewish Advocate*, vols. 1–4, 8, 9; *Sinai* (Balt., Md., 1856); *Jewish Messenger* (Jan. 17, 1879; Reproduced in Biography Resource Center. Farmington Hills, Mich.: Thomson Gale (2006), *http://galenet.galegroup.com/servlet/BioRC*; K.M. Olitzsky, L.J. Sussman, and M.H. Stern, *Reform Judaism in America: A Biographical Dictionary and Sourcebook* (1993).

[Barnett A. Elzas (2nd ed.)]

POZNANSKY, MENAḤEM (1887–1956), Hebrew writer. Born in Kamenets-Podolski (Russia), Poznansky emigrated to Palestine as a result of his close friendship with J.H. *Brenner, who was one of the main influences in his life. Besides teaching, Poznansky wrote stories, which were posthumously collected together with his sketches in *Demuyyot Melavvot* (1958). After Brenner was killed, Poznansky devoted himself to Brenner's literary estate, and published the first complete edition of his works (8 vols. in 9 books, 1924–30). This was followed by an abridged edition (3 vols., 1946–51), and a revised complete edition (1961), of which Poznansky succeeded in preparing only the first volume. All these editions included introductions and notes by Poznansky. He also published an annotated collection of Brenner's letters (vols. 1–2, 1941). Poznansky translated into Hebrew works by Turgenev, Goncharov, and Gogol. One of his stories appears in English translation (Goell, Bibliography, 74, no. 2349).

BIBLIOGRAPHY: G. Kressel, Leksikon, 2 (1967), 575–6.

[Getzel Kressel]

PPS (**Polska Partia Socjalistyczna**), Polish Socialist Party. Founded in Paris in 1892, the PPS began activities in Poland despite Russian political restrictions. While in Galicia, then under Austrian control, the movement formed a legally recognized popular party, the PPSD (Polish Socialist Democrat Party). In Congress Poland, as a result of czarist oppression, the PPS became an underground movement. The PPS also was in conflict with the general Social Democratic movement in Poland and Lithuania, which on cosmopolitan principles opposed the nationalist tendency among the leaders of the PPS. During World War I the right wing of the PPS organized its own military units (the "legions") to act for the liberation of Poland. With the attainment of Polish independence, the PPS organized a national convention in April 1919 which brought about the establishment of the party throughout the country.

From the outset many Jews were active in the PPS. However, in the wake of ideological conflicts during and after the war a considerable number of Jewish activists left the party to join the extreme left. Three Jews became prominent in the party in the interwar years: (1) Feliks Perl (1871–1927), a native of Warsaw, who influenced the program of the united movement by his adherence to the party's socialist views as opposed to its rightist nationalist tendencies; (2) Herman *Diamand (1860–1931) of Lvov, lawyer and economist, who was a PPS member in the Austrian parliament between 1907 and 1914, and the party's economic expert in the Polish *Sejm (parliament); and (3) Herman *Lieberman (1870–1941), lawyer, journalist and outstanding speaker, member of the Austrian parliament and the Polish Sejm, and later (1940) minister of justice in the Polish government-in-exile in London. All three considered that the solution to the Jewish problem lay in Polish patriotism and eventual assimilation; they were opposed to the principles of Zionism and the efforts of Jewish leaders to preserve Jewish cultural identity.

The PPS made efforts to approach the mass of Jewish workers through Yiddish publications. It tended to regard the Jewish socialist parties, such as the *Bund and the leftist Po'alei *Zion, as potential competitors for voters, accusing them of separatism and nationalism. In its attitude to actual discrimination against Jews, the PPS showed a willingness to assist them in principle. However it was cautious in the extent of its support so as not to be suspected of "serving Jewish interests." In the trade unions the PPS showed a tendency to make difficulties in the admission of Jewish workers to industrial enterprises, even where the owners themselves were Jews.

It was only in the late 1930s that the PPS showed more courage in the struggle against antisemitism, then being overtly exploited by the reactionary successors of *Pilsudski, as a means of hitting at the opposition.

BIBLIOGRAPHY: I. Schiper et al. (eds.), *Żydzi w Polsce odrodzonej*, 1 (1932), 531–41; **ADD. BIBLIOGRAPHY:** J.M. Majchrowski et al., *Kto byl kim wdrugiej Rzeczypospolitej* (1994), (F. Perl) No. 1045, (H. Diamand) No. 251, (H. Lieberman) No. 769; C. Kozlowski, *Zarys Dziejow Polskiego Ruchu Robotniczego do 1948 roku* (1980), index; J. Holzer, *Mozaika poliyczna drugiej Rzeczypospolitej* (1974), 207–22, 481–510; J. Zarnowski, "PPS w latach 1935–1939," in: *Najnowsze Dzieje Polski III*, 93–160; idem, *Polska Partia Socjalistyczna 1935–1939* (1965).

[Moshe Landau]

PRAAG, SIEGFRIED EMANUEL VAN (1899–2002), Dutch novelist and writer. He studied French language and literature at the Municipal University of Amsterdam, became a schoolteacher, married Hilda Sanders, and started a career as a writer. After 1933 they initiated a German department in the Allert de Lange publishing house in Amsterdam. They moved to Brussels in 1936. In 1940 they succeeded in reaching England, where Van Praag worked for the Belgian radio. After the war they returned to Brussels and Van Praag again taught school but mainly spent his time in writing. When he passed away in Brussels he could look back on a long life in letters – having written more than 60 books.

Van Praag wrote on literature: *De West-Joden en hun letterkunde sinds 1860* (1926), *In eigen en vreemden spiegel. Uit de letterkunde van en over Joden* (1928).

He excelled in writing (historical) novels on women, *Maria Nunes* (1928), *La Judith. Een groot actrice* (1930; Ger., *Judith, der Roman einer Schauspielerin*, 1931), *Julie de Lespinasse. Een groote minnares* (1934), *Madame de Pompadour. Roman van eerzucht en liefde* (1936), *Een vrouw van tact* (1947), *De Hebreeuwse lichtekooi* (1954), and his last novel *De lieve glorie van Truitje Bonnettemaker* (1988). Moreover he was fascinated by people and by the animals of the Amsterdam Zoo ("Artis"), so he wrote articles on "Artis in de kunst" (1926) and on the topic of the animal in literature, *Wij en de dieren* (1932).

Along with the published recollections of Jaap Meijer, Meyer J. Perath, Mozes H. Gans, Meyer Sluyser, and Eddy van Amerongen, Van Praag's descriptions of pre-war Jewish Amsterdam have been decisive for younger generations. On this topic he wrote among others *Jeruzalem van het Westen* (1961; seventh pr., 1985), *De oude darsjan. Over Jodenbuurten en joodse buurten* (1971), and *Een lange jeugd in Joods Amsterdam* (1985), a companion volume (with about 100 photographs) to a film by Willy Lindwer made the previous year. The book covers his years 1899–1935 in Amsterdam. Van Praag wrote more extensively on his life in *De arend en de mol. Autobiografische schetsen* (1973). The memoirs of his wife, Hilda van Praag-Sanders, followed: *Meedoen. Persoonlijk en nietpersoonlijke ervaringen van een journaliste* (1975).

In 1995 he entrusted his library, manuscripts, correspondence and photographs to the Bibliotheca Rosenthaliana, Amsterdam University Library.

BIBLIOGRAPHY: *Siegfried E. van Praag. Een schrijver en zijn werk*. Comp. by Bea Polak-Biet (1969), Preface by R. Bulthuis. Includes a short autobiography, an anthology, and a bibliography. ON THE ACQUISITION OF HIS LIBRARY AND ARCHIVE: *Studia Rosenthaliana*, 29 (1995), 205f.

[F.J. Hoogewoud (2nd ed.)]

PRACTICE AND PROCEDURE.

CIVIL

Court Sessions

The courts of three (judges) exercising jurisdiction in civil matters (see bet *din) held their sessions during the day, but – following Jethro's advice to Moses that judges should be available "at all times" (Ex. 18:22) – they would continue sitting at night to complete any proceedings commenced during the day (Sanh. 4:1). The session started early in the morning, with the judges robing themselves – they had special robes "wrapped around them," so that they would not look around too much (*Sma*, ḤM 5 n. 16) – and usually continued for six hours until mealtime (Shab. 10a). While originally the session was not interrupted even for prayers, the law was later revised so that in this case it may be interrupted (ḤM 5:4). No court was held on the Sabbath or holidays, lest any writing was done. On the eves of the Sabbath or holidays the courts would sit only in exceptionally urgent cases (*Rema*, ḤM 5:2), but a party summoned was not punished for failing to appear on such a day (ḤM 5:2). The court may sit on the intermediate days of a festival (*Ḥol ha-Mo'ed*, MK 14b).

Parties

Any person, male or female (Sif. Deut. 190), may sue and be sued, except minors, deaf-mutes, and lunatics (see Legal capacity). Actions brought by or against guardians on behalf of such incapacitated persons may be heard by the court, but any judgment rendered is binding only if in their favor (Git. 52a). Non-Jews who sue or are sued in a Jewish court may demand that their own non-Jewish law be applied to them (Yad, Melakhim 10:12); a Jew litigating with a non-Jew was originally entitled to claim any benefit of non-Jewish law, but this discrimination was later abolished (cf. *Beit ha-Beḥirah* thereto).

The rule is that parties must litigate in person and may not be represented; and even when and where representation is allowed, the parties are required to attend in person so as to enable the court to form a direct opinion of them (*Sma*, ḤM 13 n. 12, 17 n. 14). An exception was made in favor of women defendants: if such women were accustomed to stay at home and not to be seen in public they were allowed to make their statements to a scribe of the court in their own homes (Tos. to Shevu. 30a). When suing for his own usufruct in his wife's property, a husband may also sue for the principal without special authorization, but not otherwise (Git. 48b; ḤM 122:8).

Joint claimants may sue jointly or separately (Ket. 94a; ḤM 77:9, 122:9), but in an action by one of them, the others will normally be included by order of the court. In cases of joint liabilities each defendant can be sued only for his share of the debt, unless he expressly or by implication guaranteed the whole debt (ḤM 77:1); such a guarantee is implied in the debts of partners, joint contractors, and joint tort-feasors (*ibid.*).

Venue

The plaintiff "follows the defendant," i.e., the claim has to be lodged in the court of the place where the defendant resides (*Rema*, ḤM 14:1); but if the plaintiff finds the defendant at a place where there is a court in session, he may sue him there and then (Resp. Maharik no. 14). The ancient rule that a party had the right to insist on trial by the Great Court at Jerusalem (Yad, Sanh. 6:7), though obsolete (*ibid.* 9), has been interpreted in many countries as enabling the plaintiff to compel the defendant to stand trial outside his place of residence in a court of higher repute or authority (Sanh. 31b; Tur ḤM 14; ḤM 14:1 and *Rema* thereto). The debtor's property may be attached by order of the court sitting at the place where the property is situated (*Rema*, ḤM 73:10).

Summonses

On the plaintiff's application a summons is issued to the defendant to appear in court on a day named in the summons (MK 16a; ḤM 11:1). A plaintiff need not disclose particulars of his claim before the defendant stands in court to answer the summons (BB 31a), and, if he does, he is not bound by any such summons unless he repeats them in court (ḤM 80:1). This rule was devised in order that the defendant should not have time, before coming into court, to fabricate a defense (*Rashbam*, BB 31a); but later jurists held this purpose to be outweighed by the more desirable opportunity of an out-of-court settlement if the claim was disclosed in advance (*Siftei Kohen*, ḤM 11, n.1).

The issue of a summons requires an order of the full court (Sanh. 8a), but one judge may make the order if the others are present in court. The summons is delivered by the officer of the court, either orally or by a written notice endorsed by the court (ḤM 11:6). It must specify not only the exact time the defendant is required to appear in court, but also the name of the plaintiff suing him (Nov. Ritba thereto). It may specify alternative dates of hearing (MK 16a), so that if the defendant fails to appear at one date, he must appear at the next specified date (*Rashi* thereto). Originally, such alternative summonses were issued for the next following Monday, Thursday, and Monday (Yad. Sanh. 25:8), these being the fixed court days in talmudic times (Ket. 3a). If not drawn up as alternative summonses, they could be issued subsequently one after the other in case of nonappearance (*Rashi*, BK 113a).

The court has discretion on whether or not to issue a summons; it may refuse to summon scholars of great eminence (Kid. 70a), practicing rabbis, and women who live in seclusion (ḤM 124). Each summons contained a warning that, failing his appearance in court on the date (or one of the dates) specified, the defendant was liable to be declared under a ban (see *Rashba*, BK 113a). A defendant who had to go on a journey or was otherwise prevented from attending court had to send an apology and request an adjournment (ḤM 11:1 and *Rema* thereto). Failing both appearance and apology, the court would issue a bill of attainder (*petiḥah*) to be served on the defaulter, and a ban would be imposed on him, unless he appeared in court within one week, paid the expenses of the *petiḥah*, and produced it to be torn up (BK 112b–113a). A less rigorous mode of enforcing court summonses was the attachment of the defaulter's property (Resp. Rosh 73:1, 97:4).

Default Procedure

It is forbidden to adjudicate the plaintiff's case in the absence of the defendant (though duly summoned) except where the plaintiff's claim is prima facie valid, e.g., where it is based on a bill signed by the defendant and confirmed by witnesses (BK 112b; Tur ḤM 106 and *Beit Yosef* thereto), or where the defendant is abroad more than 30 days' journey away (Yad, Malveh 13:1; ḤM 106). The reason for this deviation from the general rule that there shall be no adjudication unless both parties stand before the court (cf. Deut. 19:17), is said by Maimonides to be "that not everybody should take the money of other people and then go and settle abroad, with the result that borrowers will find all doors closed to them" (Yad, Malveh 13:1). Judgments in civil cases may always be given in the absence of the parties (ḤM 18:6).

Cause List

Hearing out "high and low alike," and fearing no man (Deut. 1:17) was interpreted as prohibiting any preference of major over minor cases (Sash. 8a; Yad, Sanh. 20:10): the case that came in first must be heard first, whatever its relative importance (Rashi, Sanh. 8a; ḤM 15:1). There are several exceptions to this rule: the case of a scholar is given preference, so that he should not be kept too long from his studies (Ned. 62a); orphans and widows are given preference even over scholars, for it is by judging them that justice is done (Isa. 1:17); and cases in which one of the parties is a woman are advanced so as not to keep her waiting in court (Yev. 100a).

Subject Matter

The court will not entertain a claim for anything of less than minimal value (BM 55a; Yad, Sanh. 20:11). Opinions were divided on whether the court, once seized of a claim for *shaveh perutah*, could proceed to deal with other (ideal and non-valuable) matters between the same parties; the leading view is that it could (BM 55b; Yad, loc. cit.; ḤM 6:1).

Settlement

When the parties stand before the court, they must first be advised to settle their dispute by a friendly *compromise (Sanh. 6b), which is the "judgment of peace" alluded to by the prophet (Zech. 8:16). Failing such compromise, the court will ask them whether they insist on adjudication according to law, or whether they would not rather empower the court to adjudicate between them by way of fair compromise (Yad, Sanh. 22:4; ḤM 12:2); and courts were admonished to do everything in their power to dissuade parties from insisting on adjudication according to law (ḤM 12:20). However, so long as a compromise had not actually been implemented by *kinyan or by performance, the parties might go back on their agreement and resort to law (ḤM 12:7, 19).

Court Decorum

The parties are required to stand up before the court (cf. Deut. 19:17), and so are the witnesses (Shev. 30a), and they may not sit down except with the court's permission (Yad, Sanhedrin 21:3; ḤM 17:1). Maimonides comments sadly upon the fact that the post-talmudic courts always allow parties and witnesses to be seated – there being no longer sufficient strength in us to conduct ourselves according to the law (loc. cit. 21:5; ḤM 17:3). Permission to be seated may not be given to one party unless it is also given to the other (Tosef., Sanh. 6:2; TJ, Sanh. 3:10, 21c). Even where a scholar is permitted to be seated out of respect for him, his opponent must be given the same permission, and it is up to him whether he avails himself of it or not (Shev. 30b; Yad, Sanh. 21:4; ḤM 17:2).

There is no rule requiring parties (or attorneys) to be dressed in any particular manner; but where one party is more richly dressed than the other, he will be ordered to dress in the same manner as the other before being allowed to address the court (Shev. 31a). This rule has been said to be now obsolete, because differences in dress are no longer so ostentatious (*Siftei Kohen*, ḤM 17 n. 2); others have held that instead of ordering the party to change his dress, the court should rather assure the other party that his adversary's showy appearance makes no impression on it (Maharshal, quoted in *Baḥ.*, ḤM 17:1 and in *Be'er ha-Golah*, ḤM 17, n. 4).

Equality of Parties

The injunction: "Judge your neighbor fairly" (Lev. 19:15) was interpreted as prescribing equal treatment by the court for all parties before it (Shev. 30a; Yad, Sanh. 21:1; ḤM 17:1). In particular, the parties must all be given the same opportunity and the same time of audience (*ibid.*); no party may be heard in the absence of the other (Shevu. 31a; Sanh. 7b; Yad, loc. cit. 21:7; ḤM 17:5). Where one party desires to be represented or to be accompanied by friends, relatives, or partners, the other party may be so represented or accompanied too, and will be heard to oppose such representation or escort through lack of equal facilities (ḤM 17:4 and *Pitḥei Teshuvah*, ḤM 17 n. 7). Where there are several plaintiffs and one defendant (or vice versa), they will be asked to choose one of them to argue for all, so as to keep the proportions even (*Sma*, ḤM 17 n. 8).

The injunction not to favor the poor or to show deference to the rich (Lev. 19:15; cf. Ex. 23:3) was elaborated as follows:

No judge should have compassion for the poor and say, this man is destitute and his adversary is rich – why should he not support him? I will give judgment for the poor man and thus cause him to be honorably provided for; nor should a judge favor the rich: when there are before him a wealthy notable and a poor ignorant man, he should not greet the notable and show him any respect, lest the other may be embarrassed; nor should he say to himself, how can I decide against him and cause him disgrace? I will rather send him away now and tell him in private later that he ought to satisfy the other party – but he must give true judgment forthwith. And when there are before him two men, one good and one evil, he may not say, the one is a criminal and probably lies, and the other is virtuous and will stick to the truth – but he must regard both as if they were potential evildoers who might lie in order to strengthen their own case, and he must judge them according to his best conscience; and, having so judged them, he should then regard them both as perfectly in order (ḤM 17:10).

Pleadings

The rule is that the parties must plead for themselves (see *Attorney), orally, but if both so agree, they may be allowed to put their arguments into writing, either by dictating them to the scribe of the court or by filing written briefs (*Rema*, ḤM 13:3); in the latter case, they cannot be allowed to go back on anything they have written (*ibid.*), and it appears that the courts have resorted to written pleading so as to prevent parties from changing their positions every now and then (cf. *Rema*, ḤM 80, n. 2). The costs of all such written records are borne equally by both parties (BB 10:4; 168a).

The court may not put any argument in a party's mouth or teach him how to argue his case (Avot 1:8; Yad, Sanh. 21:10; ḤM 17:8), nor may the court express an opinion presupposing a hypothetical argument ("if A would plead this way, judgment might be given for him"; *Rema*, ḤM 17:5). On the other hand, the court is admonished to open the mouth of the dumb for him (Prov. 31:8), i.e., to help a litigant who is intellectually or emotionally unable to express himself to formulate his argument (Yad, Sanh. 21:11; ḤM 17:9). This rule applies especially to orphans and imbeciles (cf. *Baḥ*, ḤM 17, n. 12).

The plaintiff pleads his case first (BK 46b; ḤM 24), but he may be allowed by the court to postpone his pleading in whole or in part if he so desires (*Rema*, ḤM 24). There is a curious exception to the rule: if by hearing the plaintiff first, the property of the defendant may depreciate (e.g., by rumors in the market that the title is disputed), the defendant is heard first (ḤM 24 and *Siftei Kohen* thereto, n. 1). When the plaintiff has stated his case, the defendant is bound to reply forthwith, but the court may, in a suitable case, give him time to think and prepare his defense (*Rema*, ḤM 16:2). For the various pleadings open to litigants and their respective effects, see *Pleas.

Evidence

Where a case cannot be disposed of on the pleadings and has to be proved by *evidence, the parties must be ready with their witnesses and documents on the day of the pleading, but the court may allow them up to 30 days' grace to produce their witnesses or documents (Sanh. 3:8; BK 112b; ḤM 16:1). Opinions were divided on what should happen if they failed to do so within this time limit (Sanh. 3:8), and the law was eventually settled to the effect that while the court would not extend the time limit (except where the witnesses are known to reside at a distance of more than 30 days' journey; ḤM 16:1), any judgment given on the pleadings was subject to review, and could be annulled, if and when warranted by any further evidence being adduced (ḤM 20:1). Where a party had declared in court that there were no witnesses or documents available to prove his case, he would not afterward be allowed to adduce such evidence, the suspicion being that it would be fabricated (Yad, Sanh. 7:7–8; ḤM 20:1); but where a party declared that there were witnesses or documents in existence but he could not trace them, the court would make a public announcement threatening a *ḥerem* on any person who withheld evidence (ḤM 16:3); such an announcement would even be initiated by the court where evidence was lacking to prove claims or defenses by representatives of estates (ḤM 71:8). Before testifying, witnesses were warned by the court of the consequences of perjury and the moral turpitude this involved (Yad, Edut 17:2; ḤM 28:7).

For the burden of adducing evidence, and presumptions in lieu of evidence, see *Evidence.

Deliberations

Having heard the parties and their witnesses, the judges confer with each other. According to ancient Jerusalem custom, the conference is conducted in private (Yad, Sanhedrin 22:9; ḤM 18:1); but while the parties always had to be excluded, primarily because they ought not to know how each judge voted (Maim. *Comm. to Mishnah*, Sanh. 3:7), it appears that some courts allowed the general public to be present while they conferred (*Baḥ.*, ḤM 18:1); and there is a talmudic tradition that the judges' students were allowed not only to be present but also to participate in the discussions (Sanh. 33b, and *Rashi* thereto). Witnesses who testified in the case could express their opinion on the merits of the case while giving testimony, but could not be heard during the judges' conference, because "no witness is made a judge" (Yad, Edut 5:8).

The conference starts with the oldest (or presiding) judge stating his opinion (Sanh. 4:2, Yad, Sanhedrin 11:6); but the view was expressed that, as in criminal cases, it should rather be the youngest member of the court who states his opinion first, the same reasons applying in civil cases as well (*Rema*, ḤM 18:1; see also below). Any judge may, in the course of deliberations, change any opinion he previously expressed (Sanh. 4:1). If a judge cannot make up his mind, he must say so, and need not apologize or give reasons for saying so (Yad, Sanhedrin 8:3). Two more judges will then be added to the court (Sanh. 3:6), as the judge unable to form an opinion is regarded as being absent and the remaining two judges, even if of one mind, are not regarded as a court (*Rashi*, Sanh. 29a). The augmented court (of five) will start deliberations anew, but need not hear the case once more (ḤM 18:1).

Judgment

At the close of the deliberations, the parties are called back into court and asked to stand up (Shevu. 30b; Yad, Sanh. 21:3; ḤM 17:1); the presiding judge announces the decision, without disclosing whether or not the judgment is unanimous, or how each judge voted. If the judgment is unanimous, so much the better; if not, the majority prevails (Sanh. 3:6, Sanh. 3b; et al.). If (owing to the judges being unable to form an opinion) the court has been increased time and again up to the maximum of 71 members and is still almost equally divided, judgment will be given for the defendant as the plaintiff has not established his case to the satisfaction of a clear majority (Yad, loc. cit. 8:2; ḤM 18:2).

Any party may ask the court for a record of the judgment in writing (Sanh. 30a; Yad, loc. cit. 22:8, ḤM 19:2) and for a written statement of the reasons behind it (BM 69b and Tos. thereto; Sanh. 31b; Tur ḤM 14 and *Beit Yosef* thereto), if only for the purposes of appeal to the Great Court (Yad, Sanhedrin 6:6). The written judgment (and the reasons for it) must be signed by all the judges, including the dissenter (R. Johanan in TJ, Sanh. 3:1, 21 ḤM d). While judgment is given on the day the case was heard (Sanh. 4:1; Maim. *Comm. to Mishnah*, Avot. 5:8; ḤM 17:11), and any delay of justice is regarded as a violation of "Ye shall do no unrighteousness in judgment" (Lev. 19:15), the written record of the judgment and the reasons for it may be given whenever a party applies for it, without any time limit (*Rema*, ḤM 14:4). Where the judgment has not been put into writing, the fitness of the judges to say what judgment they gave ceases when the parties no longer stand before them (Kid. 74a; ḤM 23:1), i.e., when they are no longer associated with the case (Tosef., BM 1:12). This rule apparently caused great hardship and was later restricted, first to discretionary judgments given without pleadings and without evidence, and then to judgments given by a single judge (ḤM 23:1; Resp. *Rosh* 6:15, 56:4; *Mordekhai* Kid. 541), and was thus virtually abolished.

The judgment may not exceed the amount of the claim (*Rema* ḤM 17:12); but where the court is satisfied that the plaintiff was genuinely ignorant of the real extent of his rights, it may impose fines and other sanctions on the defendant to compel him to satisfy the plaintiff even beyond his claim (*Sma*, ḤM 17:26; *Baḥ* ḤM 17).

For the effect of judgments *inter partes* and *inter alios*, see *Ma'aseh.

Revision

A judgment is always subject to revision, normally by the court that made it in the first place, if new evidence has come to light disproving the facts which the judgment was based on, provided the party seeking to adduce such new evidence is not debarred from so doing (see above; Sanh. 3:8; Yad, Sanhedrin 7:6; ḤM 20, 1). Every judgment is also subject to revision for errors of law. Originally the rule appears to have been general and to have applied in all civil cases, whatever the quality of the error (Sanh. 4:1); later it was confined to erroneous judgments of nonprofessional and non-expert judges (Bek. 4:4); finally, the rule was confined to errors of mishnaic (i.e., clear and undisputed) law, as distinguished from "errors of discretion" (Sanh. 6a, 33a; Ket. 84b, 100a). While "discretion" was originally understood in its wide literal sense (cf. Sanh. 29b; TJ, Sanh. 1:1, 18a), it was eventually confined to matters on which there were different views in the Talmud and the *halakhah* had not been decided; whatever view the judge followed, his judgment would not (for that reason alone) be subject to revision. It might otherwise be where the court followed one opinion in ignorance or disregard of the fact that another opinion had been accepted and put into practice "throughout the world" (Yad, Sanh. 6:2; ḤM 25:2). The revisable error could (in certain well-defined circumstances) be of great moment to the judge personally, as he might find himself saddled with the obligation to pay out of his own pocket any irrecoverable damage caused by his error (Yad, loc. cit. 6:3; ḤM 25:3).

Apart from revisable error, unwarranted assumption of judicial authority (whether it resulted in error or not) is a cause for having the judgment set aside, but it stands until set aside (Yad, loc. cit. 6:4; ḤM 25:4). The finding of unwarranted assumption of judicial authority is tantamount to a finding of a trespass, and counts in damages (*ibid.*). In many countries, the revision of judgments of errors of law was reserved to courts of appeal, i.e., mostly courts presided over by the leading scholars of the community.

Modern Law

While the procedure in Israel civil courts is mainly based on English law, the procedure in the rabbinical courts is governed by the *Takkanot ha-Diyyun* which were enacted by the chief rabbinate of Israel in 1960 (revising earlier *takkanot* of 1943). They purport to reflect talmudic and post-talmudic law, but actually deviate from it and follow modern procedural concepts in many important particulars; for example, the requirement of written statements of claim, representation by attorneys, cross-examination of parties (in addition to witnesses), reduction of judgments into writing before delivery, and discretion in the matter of costs.

PENAL

For the composition of courts competent to adjudicate in criminal cases, see Bet *din. The composition of the court and certain matters of procedure differ in capital and non-capital cases. While the following account deals with capital cases (unless otherwise indicated), practice and procedure were modeled on them as far as possible (cf. Maim., Yad, Sanh. 16:1–4).

Court Sessions

In criminal cases, the court sits only during the day and adjourns at sunset (Sanh. 4:1; Yad, Sanh. 11:1). If the proceedings have been concluded during the day, a judgment of acquittal will be announced forthwith, but a judgment of conviction and sentence may not be announced until the following day (Sanh., loc. cit.; Yad, loc. cit.), since there is a chance that the judges may change their minds during the night (*Rashi*, Sanh. 32a). No criminal sessions may therefore be held on the eves of the Sabbath and holidays (Sanh. 4:1; Yad, Sanhedrin 11:2); and either because a trial is regarded as potentially a first step in an execution, which may not take place on a Sabbath (TJ, Sanh. 4:7, 22b), or because the trial involves writing prohibited on the Sabbath (Tos. to Beẓeh 36b and Sanh. 35a), no criminal trials may be held on the Sabbath or holidays.

In the Temple precincts (see Bet *din), criminal sessions started after the morning sacrifices and ended with the late afternoon sacrifice (Sanh. 88b); otherwise the time of court sessions is the same in criminal as in civil cases. The following is a mishnaic account of the manner in which courts of 23 held criminal trials:

The court sat in the form of a half-circle, so that the judges could all see one another. The two court scribes stood before them, one at the right and one at the left, and recorded the words of the judges – one the words of those in favor of conviction, and the other the words of those in favor of acquittal. Three rows of learned disciples sat before them, each knowing his place; when the seat of a judge became vacant, his place would be filled with the first sitting in the first row (Sanh. 4:3–4 – According to Maim., Yad, Sanhedrin 1:9; but Rashi (to Mishnah, Sanh. 36b) states that the two scribes write the words both of those in favor and those against, so that if one scribe errs the other can correct him).

The public and the disciples would be already in court when the judges entered – the presiding judge last – and everyone present would rise and remain standing until the presiding judge gave them leave to sit down (Tosef., Sanh. 7:8).

Duplicity of Trials

Only one capital case may be tried on any one day in any one court (Sanh. 6:4; Tosef., Sanh. 7:2). An exception was made where there were several participants in one crime, provided they were all liable to the same penalty (Sanh. 46a). However, where participants in one crime were liable to execution by different methods, as, e.g., in *adultery where the male adulterer was liable to strangulation and the female adulteress, if a priest's daughter, to burning, they had to be tried separately on different days (Yad, Sanh. 14:10).

Arrest

The arrest and detention of persons awaiting trial is reported in the Bible (Lev. 24:12; Num. 15:34), and the appointment of judges presupposed the concomitant appointment of police officers (*shoterim*: Deut. 16:18). Maimonides describes *shoterim* as officers equipped with sticks and whips who would patrol streets and marketplaces, and bring any criminals they caught before the court; these officers would also be dispatched by the court to arrest any person against whom a complaint had been brought ("they act upon the judges' orders in every matter": Yad, Sanhedrin 1:1). In capital cases the accused would be detained pending trial (Sif. Num. 114; Yad, Sanhedrin 11:2), if he was caught *in flagranti delicto* or there was at least some *prima facie* evidence against him (TJ, Sanh. 7:8). However, the fact that the available evidence was as yet insufficient to put a man on trial was no reason not to detain him until sufficient evidence was available (Sanh. 81b). Or, where death had not yet ensued but the victim was dangerously wounded, the assailant would be detained until the degree of his offense could be determined (Sanh. 78b; Ket. 33b). The accused would always be held in custody (Yad, Sanh. 12:3). Opinions were divided on whether an arrest could be made on the Sabbath.

Bail

The release of an accused person on bail pending trial is already mentioned in early sources (Mekh. Nezikin 6). The rule evolved that in capital cases no bail should be allowed (*ibid.*; and Resp. Ribash no. 236, quoted in *Beit Yosef*, ḤM 388, n. 5), from which it may be inferred that in non-capital cases bail would be granted as a matter of course.

Default Proceedings

No criminal proceeding may be conducted in the absence of the accused (Sanh. 79b; Yad, Roẓe'ah 4:7, Sanh. 14:7).

Prosecution

There is good authority for the proposition that in cases of *homicide the *blood-avenger acted as prosecutor (Nov. Ran; Sanh. 45a). Where no blood-avenger was forthcoming, the court would appoint one for this purpose (Sanh. 45b). By analogy, it may be assumed that in cases other than homicide the victim of the offense acted as complainant and prosecutor. In offenses of a public nature, the court initiated the proceedings and dispensed with prosecutors. Such proceedings were normally prompted by witnesses who came forward and notified the court that an offense had been committed; if they could identify and name the accused and satisfy the court that a *prima facie* case could be made out against him, the court would take action (Yad, Sanh. 12:1).

Defense

In criminal matters, any person who wished to plead in favor of the accused was allowed and even encouraged to do so (Sanh. 4:1). If a disciple of the judges wished to plead for the accused, he was raised to the bench and allowed to stay there until the end of the day (Sanh. 5:4), clearly a potent encouragement. There are records in post-talmudic times of defense attorneys having been appointed by the court (e.g., Ribash Resp. no. 235).

Evidence

Unlike civil trials, criminal trials started with the interrogation of the witnesses. Before this, each witness had to be warned separately by the court in the following terms:

If you are going to tell us anything which you only believe or opine, or anything you may have heard from any other person, however trustworthy he may seem to you, or anything you know from rumors – or if you are not aware that this court is going to examine you by a probing cross-examination – you had better know that a criminal trial is not like a civil trial; in a civil case, a false witness pays money to the man he has wronged and will then be discharged; but in a criminal case, his blood and the blood of his children will be on him until the end of the world. Man was created single in this world, to show you that whoever causes one single soul to perish from this world is regarded as if he had caused the whole world to perish; and he who keeps one single soul alive in this world is regarded as having kept the whole world alive. Are not all men created in the form of Adam, the first man, and still the form of each man is different from that of anybody else? Therefore can each and everybody say, it is for me that the world was created. And do not say, why should we bring this calamity upon ourselves? for it is written, whoever is able to testify from what he has seen or known, and does not do so, will be punished [Lev. 5:1]; nor may you say, it is more convenient for us to incur punishment for our silence, than to bring upon ourselves the blood of that criminal; for it is written, there is rejoicing when the wicked perish (Sanh. 4:5; Yad, Sanh. 12:3).

The evidence of at least two witnesses (Deut. 17:6) is required to prove not only that the accused was seen to have committed the act constituting the offense (Ket. 26b; Sanh. 30a; Git. 33b), but also that, immediately before committing it, he had been warned of its unlawfulness and of the exact penalty he would incur (Sanh. 12:2). No circumstantial evidence is ever sufficient to support a conviction (Sanh. 37b; Tosef., Sanh. 8:3; see *Evidence; Penal *law). The accused must be present during the examination of the witnesses, but opinions are divided on whether he must stand up or may be seated. The judges, are of course, seated when hearing evidence (ḤM 28:6), while the witnesses stand (Shevu. 30a; ḤM 28:5).

For the methods of examination of witness, see *Witness.

Deliberations

It is only if and when the evidence of all the witnesses heard is first found consistent, i.e., if it is established to the satisfaction of the court that the witnesses do not contradict themselves or each other in any material particular, that the deliberations (in the technical sense) start (Sanh. 5:4; Yad, Sanh. 12:3). If the evidence is found to be inconsistent, the accused is acquitted and discharged there and then. The rule is that the youngest member of the court has the first say in the deliberations (Sanh. 4:2; Yad, Sanh. 11:6), in case the junior members be unduly impressed and influenced by what their elders have to say (Yad, Sanh. 10:6; Rashi to Ex. 23:2 and to Sanh. 36a); but this rule yields to another that the deliberations must always start with a view propounded in favor of the accused (Sanh. 4:1, 5:4; Yad, Sanh. 11:1, 12:3). Talmudic scholars wondered how anything could be said in favor of the accused once the evidence against him had been found to be consistent, and they solved the problem by suggesting that "opening in favor of the accused" really meant asking the accused whether he could adduce any evidence in rebuttal (Sanh. 32b; TJ, Sanh. 4:1), or reassuring the accused that if he was innocent he had nothing to fear from the evidence adduced against him (*ibid.*;

Yad, Sanh. 10:7). Deliberations were thus held in the presence of the accused, and it would appear that at this stage he was given the opportunity of saying anything he wished in his defense: "If he says, I wish to plead in favor of myself, he is heard, provided there is some substance in his words" (Sanh. 5:4). According to Maimonides, he is even raised to the bench for this purpose (Yad, Sanh. 10:8). However, he is not allowed to say anything to his detriment, and as soon as he opens his mouth to admit his guilt or otherwise prejudice himself, he is silenced and reprimanded by the court (Tosef., Sanh. 9:4). Where the accused is not capable of speaking for himself, the court or a judge will do so for him (Sanh. 29a).

It appears that the credibility and weight of the evidence, even though it was found consistent (and hence admissible), was an open issue for the deliberation of the judges, as was the legal question whether the act committed by the accused constituted a punishable offense (Yad, Sanh. 10:9). Having once expressed his view in favor of an acquittal, a judge is not allowed to change his view during the deliberations (Sanh. 4:1, 5:5, 34a; Yad, Sanh. 10:2); but having expressed his opinion condemning the accused, a judge may change his mind even during the deliberations (*ibid.*; Yad, Sanh. 11:1). Judges ought not to follow the opinion of other, greater judges, especially in criminal cases, but must decide solely according to their own knowledge and personal conviction (Tosef., Sanh. 3:8; Yad, Sanh. 10:1).

If, at the end of the day, a majority for an acquittal has been reached, the accused is acquitted forthwith; if no such majority has emerged, the case is adjourned to the next day (see above), the judges conferring, in groups of two, throughout the night, abstaining from too much food and from all alcohol. The next morning, back in court, the scribes checked the judges' views with those they had expressed the day before, so that the number of those arguing in favor of an acquittal could meanwhile only have increased (Sanh. 5:5, Yad, Sanh. 12:3). If a clear majority for conviction has eventually been reached, judgment will be pronounced accordingly; but a "clear majority" presupposes some minority and accordingly, where the whole court is unanimous that the accused be convicted, proceedings are adjourned and deliberations continued until at least one judge changes his view and votes for an acquittal (Sanh. 17a; Yad, Sanh. 9:1). It is believed that this rule applied only to the Great Sanhedrin of 71 (Maim., Yad, *ibid.*, speaks of the "Sanhedrin" as distinguished from the "Small Sanhedrin" in the immediately following paragraph), while in courts of 23 and of three unanimity was as good as, or even better than, a majority.

Judgment

The sentence pronounces the accused guilty and specifies the punishment to be inflicted on him; it is not reasoned. Unlike in civil cases (see above), the accused knows which of the judges were in the majority and which in the minority, and what were the reasons which prompted each judge in his voting, since he had been present at their deliberations.

Once a capital sentence is pronounced, the accused is in law deemed to be dead (Sanh. 71b), and a person killing him would not be guilty of homicide (Yad, Mamrim 7, 9), nor would a person wounding him be guilty of any offense or liable for damages (Tosef., BK 9:15). The theory was propounded that it is this legal fiction which enables the court and the executioners to execute capital sentences without incurring liability as murderers.

On the other hand, as long as the sentence has not been carried out, the judgment is subject to revision: on the way from the court to the place of execution, a herald announces that *A* son of *B* is going to be executed for having committed the offense *C*, and witness *D* and *E* have testified against him; whoever has anything to say in his defense should come forward to say it (Sanh. 6:1). The case is returned to court for a retrial not only if any such person is forthcoming but even if the accused himself wishes to plead again in his own defense – provided there is some substance in what he says (*ibid.*). In order to find out whether or not there is some substance in what the accused wishes to say, two men learned in the law are seconded to accompany him on his way to the place of execution (Yad, Sanh. 13:1), and if they are satisfied that there is some such substance, they will have him brought back into court even two and three times (*ibid.*). If, on retrial or redeliberation, the accused is acquitted, the sentence is deemed to be annulled *ex tunc*, as if it had never been passed.

Where the accused escapes after sentence and before execution and then is caught and brought before the court which had sentenced him, his trial is not reopened, but the sentence stands (Mak. 1:10). It might be different if he were brought before a court in Ereẓ Israel, and the court which had sentenced him had sat outside Ereẓ Israel (Yad, Sanh. 13:8). For the purpose of establishing that sentence had duly been pronounced against him, two witnesses must testify that in their presence sentence had been passed on this particular accused and they had also heard the evidence given against him by two named witnesses (Mak. 1:10; Yad, Sanh. 13:7). Before the sentence is finally executed, the accused is asked to confess in order that he may have a share in the world to come (Sanh. 6:2). If he does not know how to make confession, he is asked to repeat the words, "may my death expiate all my sins" (*ibid.*).

For the various modes of execution, see Capital *Punishment.

[Haim Hermann Cohn]

RULES OF PROCEDURE OF THE RABBINICAL COURTS OF THE STATE OF ISRAEL

The promulgation of the Rules of Procedure for the Rabbinical Courts in Ereẓ Yisrael marked the first attempt in the history of halakhic literature to provide a modern compilation of the rules of procedure. The Council of the Chief Rabbinate published the Rules of Procedure, based largely on the Shulḥan Arukh and responsa literature, in 1943. The Rules have been revised several times over the years. As of 2006 the last revision was made in 1993, and all references in this article are to those Rules.

The Court's Intervention in Litigation

In this article, we present the primary findings of a comprehensive study of the rabbinical court's intervention in litigation in general, and in pleadings and the examination of witnesses in particular (Y. Sinai, *Me'uravut Bet ha-Din be-Halikh ha-Diyyuni be-Mishpat ha-Ivri* (Ramat-Gan, 2003)).

Sources of Jewish Law dealing with the intervention of judges in pleadings paint a complex picture, drawing upon several procedural systems that developed at different times and in different places. In this context, we find tension between the adversarial principle, "Do not play the part of an advocate" (M. Avot 1.8), and the inquisitorial principle – "Open thy mouth for the mute" (TJ Sanh. 3:6).

In general, one may distinguish between two primary procedural approaches, which developed against different legal and historical backgrounds. While these approaches were clearly enunciated by medieval scholars in Spain and Ashkenaz, they were already hinted at in talmudic literature. One approach, emphasized primarily in the classical Spanish tradition, took an adversarial view, and tended to shy away from the court providing any assistance to a litigant's pleadings, whether factual or legal, in the course of the proceedings (see, e.g., Yad, Sanh. 21:10–11). This approach sees in the live, spontaneous conflict between the parties a means for uncovering the factual truth. The proceedings are conducted primarily by the parties themselves, who present their arguments before the court. Any uncontrolled intervention in that spontaneous dispute by third parties (whether the court or lawyers) may seriously impede the process of uncovering the truth. Nevertheless, this approach does permit the court to intervene in the proceedings in exceptional circumstances. We thus find the rule that the court may raise arguments for the benefit of an heir or a buyer (Git. 58b).

The second approach, emphasized in the Ashkenazi tradition, prefers an inquisitorial view. This approach recognizes numerous situations in which the court is required to assist in raising factual and legal arguments (see, e.g., *Teshuvot u-Fesakim me'et Ḥakhmei Ashkenaz*, sec. 99). However, even the supporters of this system did not adopt an extreme inquisitorial approach, and limited court intervention to some degree. Similar to the supporters of the first approach, their aim was that the truth be uncovered with the assistance of the court. The Ashkenazi scholars developed and perfected a comprehensive theory to distinguish between common and uncommon arguments, so that the court was allowed to take the initiative to raise only the more common arguments that might reasonably reflect the truth.

Talmudic and post-talmudic sources reveal a clear, fundamental distinction between factual and legal arguments. In general, the Sages were in favor of judges raising legal argumentation and safeguarding the rights of defendants in criminal cases, and of litigants in civil monetary cases (in the framework of arbitration). Raising arguments is part of a judge's role, in accordance with the duty to apply the law in the case before him. In light of Maimonides' statement at the beginning of Chapter 6 of *Hilkhot To'en ve-Nit'an*, we must distinguish between two stages of the proceedings. During the first stage, the parties raise their factual claims. The legal arguments are only addressed at the second stage, that of rendering judgment, and the court decides in accordance with the legal principles. The court's role is to draw the legal conclusions that flow from the litigants' factual pleadings. At the stage of rendering judgment, the court is required to raise legal arguments deriving from *halakhah*, even if a litigant was mistaken in this regard or failed to raise the arguments.

Under the rules of procedure of Jewish Law, witnesses are examined by the court and, in principle, litigants and their attorneys may not question the witnesses. On the subject of examining witnesses, see *Witness.

ADHERENCE TO THE RULES OF PROCEDURE. Many scholars have noted that, although the courts operate in accordance with established rules of procedure, the approach of the Sages and of judges is fundamentally informal. While the rules of procedure are intended to establish appropriate order in the normal course of the court's work, they are not sacrosanct, and breach of a rule will not result in any unnecessary loss of rights or any harm to a litigant that does not serve the interests of justice (N. Kirsch, "*Le-Mahut ha-Proẓess ha-Ivri*," in: *Yavneh*: 3 (1949), 128–36; A.H. Shaki, "*Kavvei Yiḥud be-Sidrei ha-Din ha-Rabbanyyim u-ve-Gishat ha-Dayyanim le-Tti'un Formalisti: le-Or Pesikat Batei ha-Din ha-Rabbaniyyim be-Yisrael*," in: *Sefer Sanhedrai* (Tel Aviv, 1972), 248; S. Darnes, "*Ḥoser Formalizim be-Sidrei ha-Din be-Vatei ha-Din ha-Rabbaniyyim be-Yisrael*," in: *Dinei Yisrael*, 10–11 (1981–83), 27).

In this regard, the Israeli Supreme Court stated (CA 561/77 *Ḥevrat Ram Ltd. v. Bank Leumi Ltd.*, 32 (2) PD 639, 643, *per* Justice Elon):

> The importance of the rules of procedure requires no emphasis, as they are the guarantor of legal stability and of the search for truth. Nevertheless, the commandment to do true justice may require that the court show leniency when one of the litigants errs in a matter of procedure, when it will not harm the opposing litigant…We may learn from the words of the Rabad of Posquières … one of the great halakhists of the 12th century, who stated in a certain matter in which a litigant erred in one of his pleadings: "We must not decide in accordance with his pleading but pronounce true judgment…and therefore it is up to the court, if it sees that he pleaded mistakenly or foolishly…not to follow it to its conclusion but to correct it" (*Tamim De'im*, 56).

In the following we will examine other subjects in the order that they appear in first part of this entry.

COURT SESSIONS. The Talmud states: "The day is for the beginning of the trial, the night is for the conclusion of the trial" (Sanh. 34b), and that is the rule established in the Shulḥan Arukh (ḤM 5.2). This is taken to mean that the parties are not to be summoned to court at night. However, if the proceedings – i.e., the pleadings and taking of testimony – are concluded while it is still day, the trial may be concluded – i.e., the judgment may be read – at night. Various opinions have been expressed as to whether the judges must conclude their deliberations during the day, or whether they may continue them at night (*Pitḥei Teshuvah* on Sh. Ar., ḤM 5.7). Opinions differ as to the validity of the decision of a court that breaches this rule (*Hagahot ha-Rema, ad loc.*). Nevertheless, the litigants may give their consent to conducting proceedings at night (*Responsa of Rabbi Meir b. Baruch of Rottenburg* (Cremona, 1557) 29).

Ending the court's session at noon is dictated by the prohibition of sitting in judgment without eating, because the judges cannot devote their undivided attention to the proceedings if they are hungry (*Arukh ha-Shulḥan*, ḤM 5.11). If the judges choose to reconvene after the noon meal, the litigants must comply (*Be'er Eliyahu al Bi'ur ha-Gra*, Sh. Ar., ḤM 5.7). When a judge is a public appointee, his work hours are set by agreement or by the customary rules (Resp. R. Joseph ibn Migash, 127).

In the State of Israel, the rabbinical courts are in recess for one month of the year (from the ninth of Av until the tenth of Elul), during which period only emergency cases are heard.

PARTIES. There is a fundamental tendency in Jewish Law opposing representation by lawyers. The court must hear the pleadings from the litigants themselves in order to obtain an impression from their appearance and their behavior as an aid in determining who is telling the truth. Despite the fundamental tendency to reject representation by counsel, the institution nevertheless found its way into Jewish Law by virtue of practical realities that overcame the theoretical objections (see in detail, Rackover, *ha-Sheliḥut ve-ha-Harsha'ah ba-Mishpat ha-Ivri*, Chap. 8). Granting a defendant the possibility of appointing an attorney to argue on his behalf derives from a custom that was roundly criticized by several *poskim*, but that garnered the support of others (*Sema* on Sh. Ar., ḤM 17.14). In the modern period, the said custom ultimately crystallized into a rule included in the Rules of Procedure of the Rabbinical Courts of Israel permitting litigants to appoint representatives to appear before the court on their behalf. Nevertheless, the regulations do not entirely ignore the negative view of the majority of *posekim* in regard to representation. Thus, under rule 57, the appointment of a legal representative does not exempt the appointing party from personally appearing in court. Rule 60 (1) further establishes that, in general, the litigant shall initially plead on his own behalf, and only thereafter are his representatives permitted "to explain and reason their pleadings."

The court's authority to order a joinder of parties can be based upon the basic procedural principle of judicial economy: "it would not be proper to trouble the Court of Law so much for nothing" (BK 89b), namely, that the court should not be troubled without reason, and should be saved from unnecessary annoyance. It would therefore appear that, where there is a question before the court that is common to several parties, the joinder of those parties in a single action is within the competence of the court, and is even desirable under the procedural rules of Jewish Law, even if the parties do not all share an interest in every element of the case (Shochetman, *Seder ha-Din*, 58).

VENUE. The basic rule is that the appropriate venue for litigation between parties residing in the same city is the court of that city (Sanh. 31b). Even if both parties are present in another city, one cannot compel the other to submit to the court of that city, but must file suit before the court of their permanent place of residence (Naḥmanides' *Torah Commentary* to Deut. 16:18). The ancient rule that a lender could demand that his case be heard before the Great Court in Jerusalem (Yad., Sanh. 6:6) was interpreted by the Shulḥan Arukh to mean that, in the case of a debt for which the plaintiff is the defendant's creditor, the rule that the case be heard in their own city applies only if it is acceptable to the plaintiff, who is at liberty to choose that the matter be brought before a higher court in another place (ḤM 14:1). However, the plaintiff can demand that the defendant go to the Great Court only if he first brings evidence or testimony before the local court showing that there is substance to his suit. This is the law, and Rema adds in his gloss to the Shulḥan Arukh that the prevailing custom is that no litigant may demand that his case be heard by a court in another city, even if it be a greater court. This custom is based on the fear of abuse by dishonest plaintiffs who might file baseless suits against wealthy victims, in the expectation that the defendants would prefer to offer a settlement rather than travel to a distant city in order to present a defense (Resp. Maharik, no.21). Another reason given for the custom is to prevent disputes as to which court is greater (Resp. Maharshdam, ḤM 7). If the litigants do not reside in the same city, the applicable rule is that "the plaintiff follows the defendant" (Rema, ḤM 14:1).

Rule 7 of the Rules of Procedure of the Rabbinical Courts of Israel establishes that "the place of the defendant shall be deemed to refer to his permanent place of residence, permanent place of work, or primary place of business." Where there is no court in the defendant's city, the plaintiff must file suit in the court closest to the defendant's place of residence (*Piskei Mordekhai le-Sanhedrin*, Chap. 3, end of §709).

Although the general rule is that the plaintiff follows the defendant, if the defendant comes to the plaintiff's place of residence, the plaintiff may require the defendant to submit to the jurisdiction of the local court, as this will not cause the defendant to incur added expense. If both litigants are present in another city, the plaintiff can require the defendant to submit to the jurisdiction of the local court in order to frustrate a suspicion of evasion by the defendant (Rema, ibid; *Pitḥei Teshuvah*, ibid., §2). Other exceptions to the rule are that a son sued by his father must appear in the court of his father's place of residence (*Rema* on Sh. Ar., YD 240:8), and that a student must appear in the court of his teacher's residence (*Knesset ha-Gedolah le-Ḥoshen Mishpat* 14; *Hagahot ha-Tur*, §8).

DEFAULT PROCEDURE. Some scholars are of the opinion that the demand that a litigant be present at the proceedings is the preferred rule, but that a case may be tried in absentia (*Kezot ha-Ḥoshen*, ḤM 13:1). On this basis, Rule 101 of the Rules of Procedure of the Rabbinical Courts of Israel establishes that if a litigant does not appear in court, "the court may decide to hear the suit, including hearing testimony and evidence, in the defendant's absence, and render judgment or adjourn the proceedings to a later date." Examples of various rules that granted courts in the Diaspora the authority to hear cases in the defendant's absence may be found in Assaf, *Batei ha-Din ve-Sidreihem le-Aḥar Ḥatimat ha-Talmud*, 36–37.

The halakhic sources do not refer to situations in which the two parties failed to appear at the trial, or in which the plaintiff did not appear, but these situations are contemplated in the Rules of Procedure of the Rabbinical Courts of Israel. Where both parties fail to appear, Rule 100 grants the court the power to adjourn to a later date, or to dismiss the case without prejudice. The court is not empowered to dismiss the case with prejudice and prevent reinstituting the suit, inasmuch as such a dismissal is possible only after hearing the pleadings and the witnesses (Resp. Maharam Schick, ḤM no. 1). If the plaintiff fails to appear, Rule 102 states: "If the defendant appears and the plaintiff does not appear after having been duly summoned, the court will dismiss the case at the defendant's request, unless the court finds that, under the circumstances, the case should not be dismissed, in which case it shall adjourn the proceedings." Here, too, the court is not authorized to dismiss with prejudice and rule in favor of the defendant.

CAUSE LIST. Some scholars are of the opinion that the laws presented in this regard were intended to address a reality that required the personal appearance of the various parties before the court in order to submit complaints. Thus, the rules established that certain persons be granted priority. However, in modern practice the court sets the dates for hearings only after the submission of written complaints, so that it would appear that there would be no affront to the dignity of scholars or women if their cases were not granted precedence (Shochetman, *Seder ha-Din*, 38).

SETTLEMENT. The preference for compromise over judicial decision is rooted in the fact that the parties agree to a compromise, whereas in the latter the winning side welcomes the judicial decision and the loser is always left dissatisfied. In addition, there is a fear that if the judge is left to decide in accordance with Torah law, he may err as to the true intent of the Torah. As Rabbi Jacob ben Asher wrote: "The judges must do all in their power to distance themselves from having to decide in accordance with Torah law, as the minds have greatly diminished" (Tur ḤM 12:6). Handing down judgment in accordance with a compromise removes this fear, as the judge is not required to seek the truth under the law of the Torah. Nevertheless, a judge is not at liberty to suggest an arbitrary compromise. Even the suggested compromise must reflect the law, and a mechanical compromise of fifty-fifty division is invalid (BB 132b and Rashi there). The *halakhah* informs us that, as long as the proceedings have not ended, the court may – and even must – suggest that the parties agree to a compromise (*Sema* on Sh. Ar., ḤM, ad loc., §§6, 9).

The court's authority to settle the issue before it in accordance with a compromise was given statutory expression in Israeli law in 1992, in Sec. 79A of the Courts Law [Consolidated Version], 5744 – 1984. The court's obligation to suggest a compromise was emphasized by Judge Kister in a decision of the Tel Aviv District Court (MA (TA) 288/57 *Blin v. Officers of Execution Office*, 20 PM 60, 63, 79).

PLEADING. The reasons underlying the *halakhah*'s opposition to written pleadings, and its preference for oral arguments, are that requiring written pleadings presents a burden for the parties, and that hearing oral arguments from the parties themselves may aid the court in ascertaining who is telling the truth, while written pleadings are usually prepared by lawyers who are professionally proficient (Resp. Ribash no. 98).

The need for a written complaint as a general requirement is an innovation of the Rules of Procedure of the Rabbinical Courts of Israel (chapter 3). Like the accepted rules of procedure in civil courts, the Rules establish a general requirement of a written complaint, even if the defendant does not request it.

We find a broad, original approach to the principle "open thy mouth for the mute," even where a party is represented by counsel, in an Israeli Supreme Court decision (CA 634/76 *Estate of Gerltz v. Aharon*, 33 (1) PD 253, 255–256, *per* Justice H. Cohn):

> There are judges who are unwilling to make themselves "play the part of an advocate" but, consistent with my own approach that we not punish clients for the sins of their attorneys, and in order to do justice with the party standing before it, the court will uphold the maxim "open thy mouth for the mute," even in regard to a lawyer who does not know how to plead.

There is no express source in *halakhah* for the right of litigants to question one another, inasmuch as the examination of witnesses is carried out primarily by the court. Nevertheless, the Rules of Procedure of the Rabbinical Courts of Israel (rule 63 (1)) provide that, after the parties present their arguments, each side may examine the other in regard to its claims. These examinations must be aimed at aiding the court in uncovering the truth.

EVIDENCE. On developments in contemporary Israeli law in regard to warning witnesses and the abolition of oaths, see *Witness.

Testimony cannot be taken in the absence of the concerned party (Sh. Ar., ḤM 28:15) because, when a witness speaks in the presence of the person about whom he is testifying, he is careful not to testify about things of which he is not certain (*Sema* on Sh. Ar, ḤM, ibid., §48).

The court may call witnesses upon its own motion, even if they have not been summoned by the parties (Rule 93 of the Rules of the Rabbinical Courts of Israel).

On the examination of witnesses in civil law, see *Witness.

FRAUDULENT CLAIMS. Halakhic literature presents a variety of approaches, not necessarily contradictory, with regard to the manner in which a court should proceed when it believes that it is faced with a fraudulent claim. The early Palestinian view assumed that a judge must refrain from attempting to contend in the usual manner with a case that he feels will lead to an untrue result, and that he must either refuse to adjudicate or adopt the alternative means of compromise (TJ Sanh. 94.1; Y. Sinai, "*Me'uravut Bet ha-Din be-Halikh ha-Diyyuni be-Mishpat ha-Ivri*," pp. 286–93). This approach is consonant with the desire to distance the judge from fraudulent claims, as expressed in the *baraita* in Shevu'ot 30b. Some see this approach as consistent with the dominance of the concept of *yir'at ha-hora'ah* (reluctance to render decisions for fear of making a mistake in *halakhah*) in Palestine during the period of the Sages (Sinai, *ibid.*, 293–98).

A later period saw the development of the activist Babylonian approach, expressed by R. Papa, which held that, if a judge senses that he is confronted with a fraudulent claim, then he should – and, it would seem, must – continue with the legal proceedings as usual, and contend with the fraud by means of a careful examination of the witnesses that will help him uncover the truth and correctly decide the law (TB Sanh. 32b). Here, too, one scholar has demonstrated that the conceptual roots of R. Papa's approach to fraudulent claims are grounded in the activist conduct of his predecessors (Sinai, *ibid.*, 304–7).

These approaches became more sharply distinguished in the post-Talmudic period (Yuval Sinai, "Judicial Treatment of Fraudulent Claims (*Din Merummeh*): An Examination of Legal Traditions," in: *Jewish Law Annual* (see bibliography)). On the theoretical level, there is not necessarily any clear, fundamental dispute among medieval scholars. Most would appear to agree, that in cases of fraudulent claims, there are instances in which the judge carefully examines the witnesses, and there are other instances in which he refuses to adjudicate. However, in practice, the scholars differ as to the emphasis they give to each of the said approaches as well as to the tendency toward judicial activism or restraint.

The *geonim* and the Spanish *rishonim* developed the Babylonian activist approach, supporting an aggressive judicial approach toward fraud (Responsa Rambam, ed. Blau, 58; Responsa Rashba, vol. 2 no. 148). This may reflect the aggressive authoritarianism characteristic of these authorities, who enjoyed a broad measure of judicial autonomy enabling them to contend even with problematic cases of fraud without fear (Sinai, ibid.). As opposed to this, the traditional approach in medieval Ashkenaz and France tended toward judicial restraint, and saw refusal to adjudicate a fraudulent case as a practical, legitimate course of action (see Resp. Maharam mi-Rothenburg (ed. Prague), no. 319; *Resp. Mahari Bruna* no. 213). This approach may be related to *yir'at ha-hora'ah* as a dominant factor in these countries, as is also expressed in the desire of the scholars of Ashkenaz and France to avoid adjudicating monetary claims. The matter is also linked to the limited judicial autonomy in Ashkenaz, and to the fact that the appointing of arbitration tribunals was common, and took the place of a permanent court. It is only natural that an arbitrator who is not a professional judge, and who has been selected to decide a particular case, will refrain from addressing fraudulent claims (Sinai, *ibid.*). Rabbenu Asher disagreed with the idea of leaving the case in dispute, and of not deciding in cases of fraud. He deviated from the traditional Ashkenazi approach, and adopted an activist position much closer to, although not identical with, the Spanish approach (Resp. Rosh, rule 107.6).

The judge's duty to decide *din emet le-amito* ("the true law truthfully"; Shab. 10a) was interpreted by the Tosafot as follows: "'true' – this excludes a deceitful judgment… 'truthfully' – one may not distort the law" (Tosafot, BB 8b, s.v. *din emet le-amito*). On the basis of this interpretation, Justice Elon wrote in one of his decisions that "'True' (*emet*) – is the factual truth; 'truthfully (*le-amito*) – is the legal truth. The judge must adjudicate in accordance with both truths, and put them into effect one upon the other" (Cr. A. 115/82 *Moadi v. State of Israel*, 38 (i) PD 197, 259). On fraudulent claims, also see *Witness.

JUDGMENT. The prevailing custom in the rabbinical courts in Israel is to publish judgments in the name of the judge who wrote the opinion (Shochetman, *Seder ha-Din*, 373). In an Israeli Supreme Court decision (HC 228/64 *Plonit v. Beit ha-Din ha-Rabbani ha-Eizori*, 18 (4) PD 141, 156), Justice Haim Cohn brought support for the importance of publishing the minority opinion from R. Judah's statement that the minority view is preserved along with that of the majority so that it may be relied upon should the need arise (Tosefta Eduyyot 1.4).

Although *halakhah* does not strictly require that a decision be delivered in writing, special *takkanot* requiring written decisions were instituted in various places (*Takkanot Medinat Mehrin* (Jerusalem, 1952) §379, p. 125; *Takkanot Nikolsberg* (Jerusalem, 1962) §126, p. 135). The Rules of Procedure of the Rabbinical Courts of Israel also establish that both the decision and the judgment must be rendered in writing (Rule 112).

The overwhelming majority of judgments issued by rabbinical courts over the generations did not state the reasoning (E. Shochetman, "The Obligation to State Reasons for Legal Decisions in Jewish Law," in: *Shenaton ha-Mishpat ha-Ivri*, 6–7 (1979–80), 335–38). The establishment of courts of appeal by the Chief Rabbinate of Israel institutionalized the right of appeal, and thus made it necessary that courts reason their decisions. The Rules of Procedure of the Rabbinical Courts of Israel establish a general rule requiring them to record the reasoning for their decisions (rule 114), as is the accepted practice in civil courts.

REVISION. Many legal systems recognize the doctrine of *res judicata*, according to which a matter will not be reopened once all avenues have been exhausted and a final decision has been rendered. Jewish law adopts an entirely different approach and does not recognize such a doctrine. An expression of the preference of this approach to that of English law may be found in an opinion by Justice Berenson (CA 395/60 *Amrani v. Attorney General*, 15 PD 594, 602), in which he states that "it would be preferable to make recourse to this rule [Sh. Ar., ḤM 20] that is better suited to the conditions of Israel than to be loyal to the severe, rigid English rule."

In order to challenge a decision, the petitioner must show that the new evidence was not in his possession and that he was unaware of it (Resp. Rosh, 13.20). Relying upon sources in Jewish law, Justice Kister held that new evidence cannot be introduced after the rendering of a decision if it could have been brought earlier (CA 211/65 *Attorney General v. Mazan*, 19 PD 32, 42–44).

There is a difference of opinion as to whether a party may challenge a decision on the basis of new arguments that were not raised at trial. One view is that a decision can only be challenged on the basis of new evidence (*Sho'el ve-Nish'al le-Rabbi Khalfon Moshe ha-Kohen*, Pt. 5, ḤM § 8, s.v. *ve-khen yesh le-hokhi'aḥ*). However, the prevailing view would appear to be that a decision can be challenged on the basis of new arguments (*Sefer Me'irat Einayim* on Sh. Ar., ḤM 20:1; *Arukh ha-Shulḥan*, ḤM 20:3).

Where there is a suspicion that the court may have erred in rendering judgment, the challenge need not originate with one of the parties. The court itself may – and even must – take the initiative to reverse the judgment (Sh. Ar., ḤM 17:8).

APPEAL. Halakhic sources make no mention of appellate courts as a permanent institution, nor is there any recognition of a doctrine of *stare decisis* (= binding precedent). Nevertheless, appeals courts were established at various times and places, through communal edict (*takkanah*; see Assaf, *Batei ha-Din ve-Sidreihem le-aḥar Ḥatimat ha-Talmud* (Jerusalem, 1924) 74ff.). This is also the basis for the establishment of a permanent court of appeals in the rabbinical court system, and is one of the important innovations of the Rules of Procedure of the Rabbinical Courts of Israel. Although some rabbinical court judges reject the authority of the Supreme Rabbinical Court of Appeals to order them to act contrary to their own opinions, the position of the Supreme Rabbinical Court of Appeals is that it is empowered to reverse the decisions of the district rabbinical courts, and that the district rabbinical courts are subject to the orders of the Supreme Rabbinical Court of Appeals (Shochetman, *Seder ha-Din*, 447–450). See also *Appeal.

Criminal Procedure

DEVIATION FROM PROCEDURE. Just as, in an emergency, it is possible to inflict punishment upon those whom the *halakhah* exempts from punishment, it is similarly possible to deviate from established procedure in an emergency. Strict adherence to the established rules of procedure may impede bringing criminals to justice and punishing them. It is therefore permissible to deviate from the rules and to impose punishment that is not grounded in the Torah. Thus, we are told that Simeon ben Shetaḥ hanged 80 women in one day (Mish. Sanh. 6:4), contrary to the rule that one may judge only one person a day. Rashi explains that this was carried out in an emergency situation, so that "the relatives not conspire to save them" (Rashi, at Sanh. 45b).

ARREST. Imprisonment is not always carried out by force of a court order. This was the case, for example, in regard to a tax debtor who is "imprisoned in jail and is not brought before the court, but the city dignitaries judge him according to their custom" (Resp. Rosh 7:11). Nevertheless, the rules of Valladolid of 1432, governing the congregations of the Kingdom of Castile, included the following rule with regard to arrests: "We establish that a judge may not order the arrest of a Jew or Jewess except by an arrest order issued in writing, signed by the judge and two witnesses. In every order – other that an arrest order for informing or for capital crimes – the judge must state the specific reasons for issuing the order" (see M. Elon, *Ha-Mishpat Ha-Ivri*, 1:647).

Israel Supreme Court Deputy President M. Elon relied upon the principles of Jewish Law in rendering important decisions on the subject of the arrest of suspects (see, e.g., MA 335/89 *State of Israel v. Lavan*, 43 (2i) PD 410; MA 71/78 *State of Israel v. Abukasis*, 32 (2) PD 240). In greater detail, see *Detention.

DEFAULT PROCEEDINGS. Nevertheless, one of the great decisors ruled with regard to an informer that, although a person cannot be tried in absentia, if "the court is of the belief that this involves a danger, then, in an emergency, the court may deviate from the law for the purpose of creating a fence around the Torah" and hear the case in the absence of the defendant (Resp. Rivash, no. 237).

PROSECUTION. The role of prosecutor was generally fulfilled by the witnesses who observed the criminal conduct (Num. 15:32–33). Where the death penalty was imposed, the witnesses executed the judgment, inasmuch as they had actually seen the commission of the offense with their own eyes (Rambam's *Mishnah Commentary*, at Sanh. 7:3).

DEFENSE. From certain verses in the Torah (Num. 35:22–25), the Sages concluded that a court serves two functions – judging and defending the accused (M. Sanh. 1.6; Yad, Sanh. 5:3). The Sages were of the opinion that defending the accused was one of the court's primary roles. Thus, a significant part of criminal procedure is devoted to the defense of the accused against conviction for an offense, and the court serves as the defendant's guardian and advocate.

The principle that we "begin in favor" of the defendant was put into effect by the Israeli Supreme Court in an interesting way (HC 3412/91, *Sufian v. IDF Commander*, 47 (2) PD 843, 851) by Deputy President Menachem Elon, who wrote "that today the principle 'begin in favor' in criminal law includes, first and foremost, both the right of an arrested suspect to know that he has a right to meet with counsel, and the duty of the authorities to inform him of that right."

The principle that a person who has been acquitted cannot be convicted upon appeal was expressed by the Israeli Supreme Court (Cr. A. 348/78 *State of Israel v. Mishali*, 32 (3) PD 245, 250) when Justice Menachem Elon wrote: "This far-reaching principle [of Jewish Law] does not exist in our criminal law, by which we must rule, but the concept it embodies was given some expression in the accepted principle that an appellate court must not act to the full extent of the law in the framework of an appeal by the state against the leniency of punishment."

EVIDENCE. Testimony is not to be heard through a translator (Mish. Makkot 1:9), for fear that the judges and the translators may not adequately understand the witness's intent. For details on the examination of witnesses in criminal law, see Witness.

JUDGMENT. Supreme Court Justice Tirkel grounded the principles of open court in the verse "and be guiltless before the Lord, and before Israel" (Num. 32:22). From this verse, the Sages learned "that a person must fulfill his obligations to his fellow beings in the manner that he fulfills his obligations before the Divine" (Yoma 38a). This rule applies, in particular, to those fulfilling judicial and public functions, in order to keep them above suspicion. Infringement of the open court principle might lead to suspicion that the judge is not objective. Nevertheless, Justice Turkel added that "even the sources of Jewish Law recognized the principle of open court to be a relative principle that may, at times, retreat before defined rights and interests," among these security interests (HC 4841/04 *Ra'id Salaḥ v. State of Israel*, Takdin Elyon 2004 (2), 3304, para. 6).

Nevertheless, it would appear as if the parties were not present at the critical juncture of the judges' deliberations (in this regard, see N. Rakover's article on criminal procedure [*Ha-Praklit* 18, p. 322], in which he cites sources indicating that the involved parties and others were not present during the judges' deliberations, and as if the parties were not aware of who voted for conviction and who voted for acquittal (325)).

The possibility of appealing a sentence was established in Lithuania in the 17th century. The defendant was granted 24 hours to give notice of his intention to file an appeal. If notice was given, execution of the sentence was stayed for eight weeks, which would appear to have been the time estimated for completing the appeal (Assaf, *Batei ha-Din*, 83–84).

[Yuval Sinai (2nd ed.)]

BIBLIOGRAPHY: CIVIL: H.B. Fassel, *Das mosaisch-rabbinische Gerichts-Verfahren in civilrechtlichen Sachen* (1859); M. Bloch, *Die Civilprocess-Ordnung nach mosaisch-rabbinischem Rechte* (1882); J. Kohler, in: *Zeitschrift fuer vergleichende Rechtswissenschaft*, 20 (1907), 247–64; Juster, Juifs, 2 (1914), 93–126; T.S. Zuri, *Mishpat ha-Talmud*, 7 (1921); Gulak, Yesodei, 4 (1922); S. Assaf, *Battei ha-Din ve-Sidreihem Aḥarei Ḥatimat ha-Talmud* (1924); idem, in: *Ha-Mishpat ha-Ivri*, 1 (1925/26), 105–20; M. Frank, *Kehillot Ashkenaz u-Vattei Dineihem* (1937); N. Kirsch, in: *Yavneh*, 3 (1948/49), 128–36; B.M. Rakover, in: *Sinai*, 38 (1955/56), 312–20; A. Weiss, *Seder ha-Diyyun* (1957); Elon, Mafte'aḥ, 190–9; idem, in: ILR, 3 (1968), 426–8, 437f.; 4 (1969), 103f. Penal: H.B. Fassel, *Das mosaisch-rabbinische Strafgesetz und strafrechtliche Gerichts-Verfahren* (1870); J. Fuerst, *Das peinliche Rechtsverfahren im juedischen Alterthume* (1870); M. Bloch, *Das mosaisch-talmudische Strafgerichtverfahren* (1901), Juster, Juifs, 2 (1914), 127–214; T.S. Zuri, *Mishpat ha-Talmud*, 7 (1921); H.E. Goldin, *Hebrew Criminal Law and Procedure* (1952); A. Weiss, *Seder ha-Diyyun* (1957); J. Ostrow, in: JQR, 48 (1957/58), 352–70; N. Rakover, in: *Ha-Peraklit*, 18 (1961/62), 264–72, 306–30; Elon, Mafte'aḥ, 190–9; Mendelsohn, *The Criminal Jurisprudence of the Ancient Hebrews* (1968[2]); H.E. Baker, *Legal System of Israel* (1968), 197–231. **ADD. BIBLIOGRAPHY:** CIVIL: M. Elon, *Ha-Mishpat ha-Ivri* (1988), 1:180, 247, 321f., 434f., 497–504, 533f., 568f., 603, 617f., 622, 633, 639f., 645–647, 663, 667–76, 669, 715, 757, 810f., 816f.; 2:856, 862, 885, 1138, 1264; 3:1420, 1442, 1473, 1486; idem, *Jewish Law: History, Sources, Principles* (1994), 1:202, 287, 384f; 2:529, 605f., 609, 649f., 698f., 747, 763f., 769, 783, 791f., 800f., 820, 824, 827, 834, 876–77, 883, 933, 992f., 1000f; 3:1047, 1053, 1079, 1366, 1533; 4:1692, 1703–4, 1715, 1753, 1767–70, 1812–14; M. Elon and B. Lifshitz, *Mafte'aḥ ha-She'elot ve-ha-Teshuvot shel Ḥakhmei Sefarad u-Ẓefon Afrikah* (legal digest) (1986), (2), 312–315; B. Lifshitz and E. Shochetman, *Mafte'aḥ ha-She'elot ve-ha-Teshuvot shel Ḥakhmei Ashkenaz, Ẓarefat ve-Italyah* (legal digest), (1997), 214–218; S. Albeck, *Law Courts in Talmudic Times* (Heb., 1980); S. Darnes, "*Ḥoser Formalizim be-Sidrei ha-Din be-Vatei ha-Din ha-Rabbaniyym be-Yisrael*," in: *Dinei Yisrael*, 10–11 (1981–83), 27–124; Y. Haba, "*Etikah shel Nihul Hitdayyenut ba-Mishpat ha-Ivri*," in: *Mishpatim*, 25 (1995), 333–72; N. Rackover, *Ha-Sheliḥut ve-ha-Harsha'ah ba-Mishpat ha-Ivri* (1972), chp. 8; A.H. Shaki, "*Kavvei Yiḥud be-Sidrei ha-Din ha-Rabbaniyyim u-ve-Gishat ha-Dayyanim le-Ti'un Formalisti le-Or Pesikat Batei ha-Din ha-Rabbaniyyim be-Yisrael*," in: *Sefer Sanhedrai* (1972), 275f.; M. Silberg, *In Inner Harmony* (Heb., 1982), 207–24; E. Shochetman, *Seder ha-Din be-Mishpat ha-Ivri* (1988); E. Shochetman, "*Ḥovat ha-Hanmakah be-Mishpat ha-Ivri*," in: *Shenaton ha-Mishpat ha-Ivri*, 6–7 (1979--80), 319–97; Y. Sinai, "*Me'uravut Bet ha-Din be-Halikh ha-Diyyuni be-Mishpat ha-Ivri* (2003); idem, "Judicial Treatment of Fraudulent Claims (*Din Merummeh*): An Examination of Legal Traditions," in: *Jewish Law Annual* (2006); idem, "*Koḥo shel Dayyan de-Din Merummeh u-ve-Kim Leih be-Gavei be-Mishnat ha-Geonim ve-ha-Rambam*," in: *Ma'aliyot*, 25 (Kovez le-Ẓiyyun Shemoneh Me'ot Shanah li-Fetirat ha-Rambam; 2005), 269–92; Z. Warhaftig, *Studies in Jewish Law* (Heb., 1985), 13–77. CRIMINAL: M. Elon, *Ha-Mishpat ha-Ivri* (1988), 568–69, 647–49; A. Kirschenbaum, *The Criminal Confession in Jewish Law* (Heb., 2005); idem, "Aspects of Criminal Defense in Jewish Law," in: *Dinei Israel*, 22 (2003), 9–48 (Heb.).

PRADO, JUAN (Daniel) DE (c. 1615–c. 1670), *Marrano physician. Born in Spain, probably at Alcalá de Henares, Prado studied at the university there and then at the University of Toledo, where he received a medical diploma in 1638. Outspoken by nature, Prado felt impelled to leave inquisitorial Spain and made his way to Picardy, in northern France. By 1655 he had moved to Holland, where he proclaimed himself a Jew and took the name of Daniel. A dozen contemporaneous documents reveal how upon settling in Amsterdam, Prado formed a circle of young intellectuals and led them in the development of unorthodox philosophical ideas. One of the group was Baruch *Spinoza, then 22. As early as 1656, Prado was charged with being publicly critical of the Bible, derogating the distinctiveness of Jewish people, denying the authority of rabbinic tradition, and preaching the supremacy of Natural Law. To avoid being condemned, Prado read the required statement of regret for heresy. Nevertheless, he was excommunicated in 1657. Unlike Spinoza, however, he strove to have the ban (*ḥerem*) lifted. A full review of Prado's expulsion in 1657 resulted in a reaffirmation of the ban. Inquisition arrest warrants for the "tall, black-bearded" Prado and for Spinoza were circulated twice during 1659. The Inquisition had been an indirect factor in their excommunications, for the congregation had feared that their liberal pronouncements would offend the Church and would serve as pretexts to force the Dutch authorities into restricting the freedom of Amsterdam Jewry. After 1659 there was no apparent contact between Prado and Spinoza. Spinoza, content in the *ḥerem*, went on to develop his pantheistic philosophy, in which Prado had no share; Prado continued to grapple with the problems of universalism versus Jewish identity, still seeking reentry into the Jewish fold.

Three letters attacking Prado were written around 1665 by Isaac *Orobio de Castro. Legalistically thorough and longest is the *Epistola Invectiva Contra Prado, un Philosopho Medico, que Dubitava, o no Creya la Verdad de la Divina Escritura, y Pretendió Encubrir su Malicia con la Affecta Confaesion de Dios y Ley de Natureza* ("Epistle against Prado, philosopher/physician who doubted or disbelieved the truth of Divine Writ, maliciously hiding behind affectations of faith in God and natural law"). Another Spanish Marrano, the poet Daniel Levi de *Barrios, took Prado as his subject, condemning him in three poems composed during 1665–72. The most ironic was occasioned by Prado's death, with Barrios bidding good riddance "to that master of false dogmas."

BIBLIOGRAPHY: C. Gebhardt, in: *Chronicon Spinozanum*, 3 (1923), 269–91; I.S. Revah, *Spinoza et le Dr. Juan de Prado* (1959); Roth, Marranos, 300; JE, s.v. *Castro, Balthasar (Isaac) Orobio de.*

PRAEFECTUS JUDAEORUM (Hebraeorum supremus, Obrister der Judischkait, prince des juifs, etc.), office of the leader of Jews in Hungary during the Middle Ages. It may be assumed that the position of *Praefectus Judaeorum* was established by the Hungarian king, Matthias Corvinus, at the suggestion of János Ernuszt, a treasurer of Jewish origin, at the time of the financial reforms (1467–76). The principal function of the *Praefectus* was the collection of taxes for the royal treasury. In exchange for this he enjoyed royal privileges and could effectively defend the rights of the Jews against any attack. On festive occasions, he was authorized to accompany the king with much splendor at the head of a battalion. The *Praefectus* governed the Jews of the country and was exempted from wearing distinctive signs. Until its abolition in 1539, this position was held by members of the *Mendel family.

BIBLIOGRAPHY: S. Kohn, *A zsidók története Magyarországon*, 1 (1884), 212–22; S. Buechler, *A zsidók története Budapesten a legrégibb időktől 1867-ig* (1901), 48–51; S. Balog, *A magyarországi zsidók kamaraszolgasága és igazsászolgáltatása a középkorban* (1907), 68–72; J. Hajnik, in: *Akadémiai Értesitő*, 5 (1866), 203–49; S. Scheiber, in: *Mult és Jővő*, 33 (1943), 107–8; L. Zolnay, *Buda középkori zsidósága* (1968), 23–26; *Magyar Zsidó Lexikon* (1929), s.v. *Zsidó prefektura*; P. Gruenwald, in: *Sefer ha-Yovel ... N.M. Gelber* (1963), xiii–xx (Ger.).

[Andreas Kubinyi]

PRAGER, DENNIS (1948–), U.S. author, radio commentator. Prager was born in Brooklyn, N.Y., and received his B.A. from Brooklyn College in 1970. He did his graduate work as a Fellow at the Russian and Middle East Institutes of the Columbia University School of International Affairs and was awarded an honorary doctorate of laws from Pepperdine University in 1996. He taught Russian and Jewish history at Brooklyn College (1972–73); and following a trip to the Soviet Union to meet with Soviet Jews, during which he brought out names of those wishing to emigrate, and brought in Jewish religious and cultural materials, he was sent out to speak on the plight of Soviet Jewry by the Student Struggle for Soviet Jewry, who named him their national spokesman. In 1976, Dr. Shlomo *Bardin appointed Prager to succeed him as director of what became known as the Brandeis-Bardin Institute in Simi Valley, California. During his tenure (1976–83), BBI programs enjoyed unprecedented success, attracting up to 1,000 people on the Sabbath and some 90 college students to attend the Brandeis Collegiate Institute. He also launched a singles group, leading to several marriages, and a group for interfaith couples to bring them closer to Judaism.

In 1982 Prager became a radio talk show host on KABC Radio in Los Angeles. For 10 years, he conducted a weekly interfaith dialogue on radio with representatives of virtually every religion in the world. Beginning in 1985, he began writing a quarterly journal, *Ultimate Issues*, which in 1995 became the bi-weekly *The Prager Perspective*. As his popularity increased, his radio show was nationally syndicated by the Salem Radio Network in 1999. The following year he discounted the newsletter and began writing a weekly column, syndicated nationally by Creators Syndicate and appearing in newspapers throughout North America. His radio show, now broadcasting from KRLA in Los Angeles, is heard on approximately 100 radio stations in the United States as well as over the Internet.

Prager's reputation in the Jewish community was built largely on the success of his first book, *Eight Questions People Ask about Judaism* (1975), which he authored with Rabbi Joseph *Telushkin. Their self-published effort was so well received that prominent publisher Simon & Schuster picked up its revised version, with one added question. *Nine Questions*

People Ask about Judaism remains in print, has been translated into nearly a dozen languages, and is one of the most widely used introductions to Judaism in the world. Their second collaboration, *Why the Jews? The Reason for Antisemitism* (1983) was revised in 2003 to reflect more recent global developments.

Prager's first solo book, *Think a Second Time* (1996), is a collection of 44 essays on as many topics. He then wrote *Happiness Is a Serious Problem: A Human Nature Repair Manual* (1998), which became a number one bestseller on the *Los Angeles Times* bestseller list. His *The Case for Judeo-Christian Values* appeared in 2006.

Prager's writings have appeared in major national and international publications and won significant awards, including the Amy Foundation First Prize and the American Jewish Press Association's Excellence in Commentary Award for his columns in *Moment* magazine (2005). An eloquent speaker, Prager lectures to Jewish communities in North America and abroad about 50 times a year. He also often speaks to Christian groups – especially those identified with fundamentalism and evangelism – with whom he shares a common worldview.

From 1992, Prager taught the Bible verse-by-verse at the *University of Judaism. He also led a weekly Sabbath service for a small congregation he defined as "Hassidic Reform." In 1986, he was appointed by President Ronald Reagan to the U.S. Delegation to the Vienna Review Conference on the Helsinki Accords.

In 2002, Prager produced a documentary, *Israel in a Time of Terror,* telling the story of the Intifada from the standpoint of Israelis under the daily threat of terrorist attacks. He also wrote and produced three comedy videos on values: *For Goodness Sake* (directed by Hollywood director David Zucker); *For Goodness Sake II*, and *Character: What It Is and How to Get It.*

Although Prager describes himself as a "passionate centrist" and a "JFK liberal," he is a critic of contemporary liberalism (and of the Democratic Party) and has become identified with the conservative wing of the Republican Party. His outspoken support of many of the Bush administration's policies – he considered running for the U.S. Senate as a Republican with White House backing in 2004 – as well as his ties to conservative Christian ideologues have caused him to become a more controversial figure in the Jewish community. He was the first to break with the Christian right in regard to Mel Gibson's *The Passion of the Christ,* indicating that he wished the film was never made. His break may have given some cover for those Jews on the right who oppose the film. Moreover, unlike most of the Jewish mainstream, he defends references to God, the Ten Commandments, and the Christian cross in public facilities such as schools, parks, and courthouses and has criticized the stance of the *Anti-Defamation League on the issue of church (religion) and state.

[Bezalel Gordon (2nd ed.)]

PRAGER, RICHARD (1883–1945), German astronomer. Prager was born in Hanover. In 1908 he joined the Berlin Academy of Sciences; and in 1909 was appointed head of a department in the National Observatory in Santiago, Chile. From 1913 onward he worked as scientific collaborator, and from 1924 as observer at the Berlin University Observatory at Babelsberg. He made an important contribution to photoelectric stellar photometry, and also extended, by several volumes, the large enterprise of a complete history and bibliography of the light variations of variable stars. He was imprisoned in Potsdam by the Nazis in 1938, an experience from which he never recovered. His friends in Britain and the United States were able to free him and brought him to England and America, where he applied his talents to pure astronomy and war work for the U.S. Navy.

BIBLIOGRAPHY: A. Beer, in: *The Observatory*, 66 (1945), 186–7; J.C. Poggendorff, *Biographisch-literarisches Handwoerterbuch*, 7A (1961), s.v.

[Arthur Beer]

PRAGUE (Czech **Praha**), capital of the *Czech Republic; it has the oldest Jewish community in *Bohemia and one of the oldest communities in Europe, for some time the largest and most revered. Jews may have arrived in Prague in late Roman times, but the first document mentioning them is a report by *Ibrahim ibn Yaʿqūb from about 970. This may be interpreted as showing that Jews had either settled in Prague or carried on business there without necessarily settling permanently. The first definite evidence of the existence of a Jewish community in Prague dates to 1091. From an analysis of medieval commerce in Prague, it is reasonable to assume that its beginnings date from about the middle of the tenth century. Jews arrived in Prague from both the East and West around the same time. It is probably for this reason that two Jewish districts came into being there right at the beginning, one in the suburb of the Prague castle (*Suburbium Pragense*) and the other close to the second castle, Wissegrad (*Vicus Wissegradensis*).

The relatively favorable conditions in which the Jews at first lived in Prague were disrupted at the time of the First Crusade in 1096. The Crusaders murdered many of the Jews of Prague, looted Jewish property, and forced many to accept baptism. During the siege of the Prague castle in 1142, the oldest synagogue in Prague and the Jewish quarter below the castle were burned down and the Jews moved to the right bank of the river Moldau (Vltava), which was to become the future Jewish quarter, and founded the Altschul ("Old Synagogue") there.

The importance of Jewish culture in Prague is evidenced by the works of the halakhists there in the 11th to 13th centuries. The most celebrated was *Isaac b. Moses of Vienna (d. c. 1250), author of *Or Zaruʿa*, a native of Bohemia who spent part of his life in Prague. Since the Czech language was spoken by the Jews of Prague in the early Middle Ages, the halakhic writings of that period also contain annotations in Czech. From the 13th to 16th centuries, the Jews of Prague increasingly spoke Ger-

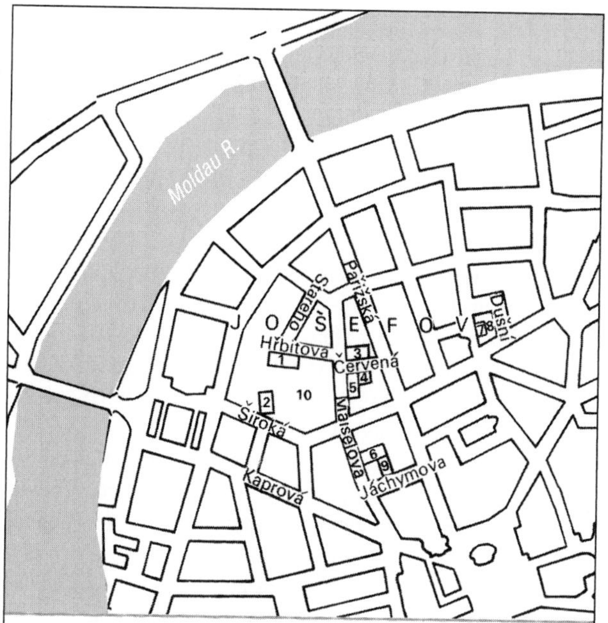

1. Klaus Synagogue, built 1680.
2. Pinkas Synagogue, built 1535.
3. Altneuschul Synagogue, built 1270, still in use today.
4. High (Town Hall) Synagogue, built second half of 16th century.
5. Jewish Town Hall, residence of the Prague Jewish community today, last reconstruction 1765.
6. Maisel Synagogue, reconstructed 1885–1913.
7. Dušní Synagogue, formerly Altschul Synagogue; built 1605 and reconstructed 1866.
8. State Jewish Museum, formerly the Sephardi Synagogue.
9. State Jewish Museum, formerly Bet Sefer ha-Torah.
10. Jewish Cemetery.

The Jewish quarter in Prague.

man. At the time of persecutions, which began at the end of the 11th century, the Jews of Prague, together with all the other Jews in Europe, lost their status as free people. From the 13th century on, the Jews of Bohemia were considered servants of the Royal Chamber (**servi camerae regis*). Their life in Prague was subject to the most humiliating conditions (the wearing of special dress, segregation in the ghetto, etc.). The only occupation that Jews were allowed to adopt was moneylending, since this was forbidden to Christians and considered dishonest. Socially the Jews were in an inferior position, but economically many of them were relatively well off. Against payment of high taxes they were protected by the king by means of special privileges (e.g., the privilege issued by *Přemysl Ottokar II in 1254).

Protection by the kings made it possible for larger numbers of Jews to settle there, particularly from Germany. In the 13th century a new Jewish settlement was founded in Prague, in the vicinity of the Altneuschul (the "Old-New Synagogue"), construction of which was completed in 1270. The synagogue, which still exists, is the oldest remaining in Europe. By the 13th century the Jewish community of Prague owned a cemetery, which was then situated outside the city walls (on the present Vladislav street), and also served other Jewish communities in Bohemia. It was sold, under pressure, to the citizens of Prague as a building plot in the 15th century.

The community suffered from persecutions accompanied by bloodshed in the 13th and 14th centuries, particularly in 1298 and 1338. Charles IV (1346–78) protected the Jews, but after his death the worst attack occurred in 1389, when nearly all the Jews of Prague fell victims. The rabbi of Prague and noted kabbalist Avigdor *Kara, who witnessed and survived the outbreak, described it in a *seliḥah: Et Kol ha-Tela'ah*. It was also described in a Christian work *Passio Judaeorum Pragensium secundum Joannem rusticum quadratum*. Under *Wenceslaus IV the Jews of Prague suffered heavy material losses following an order by the king in 1411 canceling all debts owed to Jews.

At the beginning of the 15th century the Jews of Prague found themselves at the center of the Hussite wars (1419–36; see *Hussites). An analysis of Hussite biblical interpretation shows possible Jewish influence. The attitude of German Jews toward the Hussites reveals a certain sympathy on the part of the Jewish communities for this movement (as expressed, e.g., by Jacob b. Moses *Moellin, the "Maharil" of Cologne). The attitude of the Hussites to the Jews was not entirely friendly. Some Hussite ideologists (e.g., Jacobellus of Stříbro (Mies) in the treatise *De usura*) demanded that Jewish moneylending be prohibited. However, no such prohibition was ever issued in Prague during the time of the Hussites. The Jews of Prague also suffered from mob violence (1422) in this period. The unstable conditions in Prague compelled many Jews to emigrate. Nevertheless, the Jewish community continued to exist there throughout the Hussite period, and this in itself may be considered proof of the relatively tolerant attitude of the Hussites toward the Jews.

The position of the Jews in Prague in the second half of the 15th century remained insecure. There were also attacks in that period (as in 1448 and 1483). Following the legalization, at the end of the 15th century, of moneylending by non-Jews in Prague, the Jews of Prague lost the economic significance which they had held in the medieval city and had to look for other occupations in commerce and crafts. Thus the Jews began to compete economically with the citizens, at a time when the traditional crafts were in a state of crisis.

The tension between the Jews and the citizens brought about a considerable change in the position of the Jews in Prague. From the beginning of the 16th century the citizens repeatedly attempted to obtain the expulsion of the Jews from the city. Their demands to this effect, in 1501, 1507, 1517, etc., were unsuccessful, however. Despite the growing tension between the Jews and the citizens of Prague, the position of the Jews began to improve at the beginning of the 16th century, mainly owing to the assistance of the king and the nobility. The Jews found greater opportunities in trading commodities and monetary transactions with the nobility. As a consequence, their economic position improved. The number of Jews in Prague increased from the beginning of the 16th century. In 1522 there were about 600 Jews in Prague, but by

1541 they numbered about 1,200. At the same time the Jewish quarters were extended. At the end of the 15th century the Jews of Prague founded new communities in the New Town and on the *Kleinseite*. At the beginning of the 16th century they left these districts and concentrated on extending the Jewish quarter in the Old Town. At the turn of the 15th and early in the 16th centuries they rebuilt the devastated Altschul and built the Pinkas Synagogue (the construction of which was completed in 1535).

Under pressure of the citizens, King *Ferdinand I was compelled in 1541 to approve the expulsion of the Jews. The elegy *Anna Elohei Avraham*, composed by *Abraham b. Avigdor, is related to that expulsion. The Jews had to leave Prague by 1543 but were allowed to return in 1545. Following the defeat of the first anti-Hapsburg rebellion in Bohemia in 1547, in which the towns played an important part, the latter lost a great deal of their political importance in the country and were no longer able to threaten the Jews of Prague seriously. However, in 1557 Ferdinand I once again, this time upon his own initiative, ordered the expulsion of the Jews from Prague. They had to leave the city by 1559. Only after the retirement of Ferdinand I from the government of Bohemia were they allowed to return in 1562.

The progress of the Jewish community of Prague had been noticeable also in the cultural sphere even before their expulsion when the Gersonides (successors of Gershom Kohen) founded a Hebrew printing establishment before 1512 (see Hebrew printing in Prague, below). During the reign of Rudolf II (1576–1611), who transferred his court to Prague, and of his successor Matthias (1611–19), the position of the Jews was particularly favorable. L. *Zunz called that period the golden age of Prague Jewry. Some Jews attained fabulous wealth and became the patrons of the Jewish community, notable among them Marcus Mordecai *Meisel (1528–1601), the Gersonide Mordecai Ẓemaḥ Kohen (d. 1592), and Jacob *Bassevi von Treuenberg (d. 1634).

The favorable position of the Jewish community of Prague during the reign of Rudolf II is reflected also in the flourishing Jewish culture. Among illustrious rabbis who taught in Prague at that time were *Judah Loew b. Bezalel (the "Maharal"); *Ephraim Solomon b. Aaron of Luntschitz; Isaiah b. Abraham ha-Levi *Horowitz, who taught in Prague from 1614 to 1621; and Yom Tov Lipmann *Heller, who became chief rabbi in 1627 but was forced to leave in 1631. The chronicler and astronomer David *Gans also lived there in this period. At the beginning of the 17th century about 6,000 Jews were living in Prague. To extend the Jewish quarter, the community acquired in 1627 the so-called Lichtenstein houses, thus almost doubling the area.

In 1648 the Jews of Prague distinguished themselves in the defense of the city against the invading Swedes. In recognition of their acts of heroism the emperor presented them with a special flag, which is still preserved in the Altneuschul. Its design, with a Swedish cap in the center of the Star of David, became the official emblem of the Prague Jewish community.

After the Thirty Years' War, government policy was influenced by the Church Counter-Reformation, and measures were taken to separate the Jews from the Christian population, to reduce the number of Jews and segregate them in ghettos, to limit their means of earning a livelihood, and to extort larger contributions and higher taxes from them. The ultimate aim of this "antisemitism of the authorities" was to reduce the importance of the Jews in Prague. A number of resolutions and decrees were promulgated; among them, the resolution of the provincial diet of Bohemia passed in 1650, and the *Familiants Law of 1727 were particularly oppressive. According to the latter, only the eldest son of every family was allowed to marry and raise a family, the others having to remain single or leave Bohemia.

In 1680, more than 3,000 Jews in Prague died of the plague. Shortly afterward, in 1689, the Jewish quarter burned down, and more than 300 Jewish houses and 11 synagogues were destroyed. The authorities initiated and partially implemented a project to transfer all the surviving Jews to the village of Lieben (Libén) north of Prague, later a suburb of the capital. The clergy fanned anti-Jewish feelings. Great excitement was aroused in 1694 by the murder trial of the father of Simon Abeles, a 12-year-old boy who, it was alleged, had desired to be baptized and had been killed by his father. Simon was buried in the Tyn (Thein) church, the greatest and most celebrated cathedral of the Old Town of Prague. Concurrent with the religious incitement against the Jews, an economic struggle was waged against them.

The anti-Jewish official policy reached its climax after the accession to the throne of *Maria Theresa (1740–80), who in 1744 issued an order expelling the Jews from Bohemia and Moravia. This was actually carried out against the Jews of Prague, who were banished (1745–48) but were subsequently allowed to return as a result of influential intervention on their behalf and after they promised to pay high taxes. In 1754 a great part of the Jewish quarter burned down. Despite all these persecutions, Jewish culture continued to flourish in Prague. In the Baroque period, noted rabbis were Simon Spira; Elias Spira; David *Oppenheim; and Ezekiel *Landau, chief rabbi and *rosh yeshivah* (1755–93).

The position of the Jews greatly improved under *Joseph II (1780–90), who issued the **Toleranzpatent* of 1782 and other decrees connected with it. The new policy in regard to the Jews aimed at gradual abolition of the limitations imposed upon them so that they could become more useful to the state in a modernized economic system. At the same time, the new regulations were part of the systematic policy of Germanization pursued by Joseph II. Jews were compelled to adopt family names and to establish schools for secular studies; they became subject to military service and were required to cease using Hebrew and Yiddish in business transactions. Wealthy and enterprising Jews made good use of the advantages of Joseph's reforms. Jews who established manufacturing enterprises were allowed to settle outside the Jewish quarter. Among the first Jewish industrialists of Prague, who were engaged particularly in the textile industry, were the Porges (later Porges of Portheim), Dormitze, and Epstein families.

Subsequently the limitations imposed upon Jews were gradually removed. In 1841 the prohibition on Jews owning land was rescinded. In 1846 the Jewish tax was abolished. In 1848 Jews were granted equal rights, and by 1867 the process of legal *emancipation had been completed. In 1852 the ghetto of Prague was abolished and united with four other "cities" as the fifth district of Prague, called Josefov (Ger., Josefstadt). Because of the unhygienic conditions in the former Jewish quarter, the Prague municipality decided in 1896 to pull down the old quarter, with the exception of important historical sites. Thus the Altneuschul, the Pinkas and Klaus, Meisel and Hoch synagogues, the famous Radnice, or Rathaus (Jewish town hall), erected by Mordecai Meisel, the larger part of the old cemetery, and some other places of historical and artistic interest remained intact. Many Jews moved out of the old quarter and dispersed throughout the city. Whereas in 1870 more than half of Prague Jewry lived in the old quarter, in 1900 less than one-quarter remained.

In 1848 the community of Prague, numbering over 10,000, was still one of the largest Jewish communities in Europe (Vienna then numbered only 4,000 Jews). In the following period of the emancipation and the post-emancipation era, the Prague community increased considerably in numbers but did not keep pace with the rapidly expanding new Jewish metropolitan centers in Western, Central, and Eastern Europe. While an increasing proportion of Bohemian Jewry concentrated in Prague, the importance and size of Bohemian Jewry within world Jewry began to dwindle. In the period 1880 to 1900, Jewish natural increase reached its peak in the world, whereas the number of Jews in Bohemia reached its maximum in 1880 and subsequently decreased. The table "Number of Jews in the Jewish Community in Prague" shows the numerical development of the Jewish population of Prague (including the suburbs incorporated in the city, some only after World War I).

During the revolutionary period of 1848 there were violent anti-Jewish outbreaks in Prague. In consequence, the emigration of Bohemian Jews to America and Western Europe that had begun in the 1840s increased and gained momentum.

After emancipation had been achieved in 1867, emigration from Prague abroad ceased as a mass phenomenon; movement to Vienna, Germany, and Western Europe continued, but in Prague the loss had been offset by the influx of Jews from the smaller provincial communities. Jews contributed to the economic progress of the city. They were now represented in industry, especially the textile, clothing, leather, shoe, and food industries, in wholesale and retail trade, and in increasing numbers in the professions and as white-collar employees. Some Jewish bankers, industrialists, and merchants achieved considerable wealth. The majority of Jews in Prague belonged to the middle class, but there also remained a substantial number of poor Jews.

Emancipation brought in its wake a quiet process of secularization and assimilation. In the first decades of the 19th century Prague Jewry, which then still led its traditionalist Orthodox way of life, had been disturbed by the activities of the followers of Jacob *Frank. The situation changed in the second half of the century. The chief rabbinate was still occupied by outstanding scholars, such as Solomon Judah *Rapaport (Shir; officiated from 1840 to his death in 1867), the leader of the Haskalah movement; Markus *Hirsch (officiated 1880–89); Nathan *Ehrenfeld (1890–1912); and Heinrich (Ḥayyim) *Brody (1912–30), but the mainstream of Jewish life was no longer dominated by the rabbinate. Many synagogues introduced modernized services, a shortened liturgy, the organ, and a mixed choir, but did not necessarily embrace the principles of the *Reform movement.

Jews availed themselves eagerly of the opportunities to give their children a secular higher education. The table "Number of Jews of Prague among the University Students" shows the participation of Jewish university students at Prague (the famous Charles University, founded in 1348, was split in 1882 into a German and a Czech university).

Emancipation was accompanied by a strong tendency to adopt the German language, and by assimilation to German

Number of Jews in the Jewish Community in Prague

Year	No. of Jews	% of Jewish population of Bohemia	% of total population of Prague
1880	20,508	21.7	6.52
1890	23,473	24.8	5.91
1900	27,289	29.4	5.31
1910	29,107	33.9	4.72
1921	31,751	39.8	4.69
1930	35,463	46.4	4.17

Percent of Jews of Prague who Declared their Nationality

	% of the Jews of Prague who declared themselves to be:		
Year	Czech	German	Jewish
1900	55.3	44.4	
1921	53.5	25.3	20.1
1930	54.8	18.1	27.0

Percent of Jews of Prague among the University Students

Year	% of Jews among university students	
1852	7.2	
1862	11.2	
	German University	Czech University
1860	44.6	0.67
1900	46.5	1.60
1925	29.8	9.70

culture and national consciousness. Jews formed a considerable part of the German minority in Prague, and the majority adhered to liberal movements. David *Kuh founded the German Liberal Party of Bohemia and represented it in the Bohemian Diet (1862–73). Despite strong Germanizing factors, many Jews adhered to the Czech language, and in the last two decades of the 19th century a Czech assimilationist movement (see Čechů-židů, Svaz) developed which gained support from the continuing influx of Jews from the rural areas. Through the influence of German nationalists from the Sudeten districts antisemitism developed within the German population and opposed Jewish assimilation. At the end of the 19th century Zionism struck roots among the Jews of Bohemia, especially in Prague. The table "Number of Jews of Prague who Declared their Nationality other than Jewish," showing the national affiliation of the Jews of Prague, indicates the extent of assimilation there (Jews were entitled to declare their nationality as Jewish from 1920).

Growing secularization and assimilation led to an increase of *mixed marriages and abandonment of Judaism. Whereas under Austrian rule cases of baptism were not very frequent, at the time of the Czechoslovak Republic, established in 1918, many more people registered their dissociation of affiliation to the Jewish faith without adopting another. The proportion of mixed marriages in Bohemia was one of the highest in Europe, amounting to 24.3% in 1927 and 30.73% in 1933 of the marriages of all Jewish males and 22.1% and 25.25% respectively of Jewish females. The proportion in some small communities may have been higher than in Prague, but the difference could not change the overall picture substantially, since almost half of Bohemian Jewry resided in Prague. The consequences of this development are clearly demonstrated in the census of 1939, conducted under the German occupation. Of those classified as Jews in Prague according to the Nazi racial laws, 12.1% did not profess the Jewish faith.

After the establishment of the Czechoslovak Republic, when the suburbs were incorporated in the municipality of Prague, the Jewish communities did not similarly affiliate. The paradoxical situation therefore developed that there were seven Jewish communities in Prague, one covering the inner city (districts I–VII) with approximately one-half of the Jewish population of Prague, and the other six in the various suburbs. These seven communities were federated in the Union of Jewish Religious Communities of Greater Prague, cooperated on many issues, and also established joint institutions; among these the most important was the Institute for Social Welfare, established in 1935. There were many Jewish associations, organizations, and institutions in Prague. Among associations of a religious character the most important was the *ḥevra kaddisha* existing from the early 16th century. The *Afike Jehuda Society for the Advancement of Jewish Studies was founded in 1869. There were also the Jewish Museum and the Jewish Historical Society of Czechoslovakia. A five-grade elementary school was established with Czech as language of instruction. The many philanthropic institutions and associations included the Jewish Care for the Sick, the Center for Social Welfare, the Aid Committee for Refugees, the Aid Committee for Jews from Carpatho-Russia, orphanages, hostels for apprentices, old-age homes, a home for abandoned children, free-meal associations, associations for children's vacation centers, and funds to aid students. Zionist organizations were well represented. There were three *B'nai B'rith lodges, several other fraternities, women's organizations, youth movements, student clubs, sports organizations, and a community center. Four Jewish weeklies were published in Prague (three Zionist; one Czecho-assimilationist), and several monthlies and quarterlies. Most Jewish organizations in Czechoslovakia had their national headquarters in Prague.

Jews first became politically active, and some of them prominent, within the German orbit. David Kuh and the president of the Jewish community, Arnold Rosenbacher, were among the leaders of the German Liberal Party in the 19th century. Bruno *Kafka and Ludwig *Spiegel represented its successor in the Czechoslovak Republic – the German Democratic Party – in the chamber of deputies and the senate respectively. Many Jews also joined the German Social Democratic Party and some rose to leadership; Emil Strauss represented that party in the 1930s on the Prague municipal council and in the Bohemian Diet. From the end of the 19th century an increasing number of Jews joined Czech parties, especially T.G. *Masaryk's Realists and the Social Democratic Party. In the latter party Alfred Meissner, Lev Winter, and Robert Klein rose to prominence, the first two as ministers of justice and social welfare respectively. Klein, leader of the white-collar employees, participated in the founding of the World Jewish Congress; he was tortured to death in a concentration camp. Meissner (d. 1952) was a member of the last Council of Elders in *Theresienstadt, and survived the Holocaust.

The Zionists, though a minority, soon became the most active element among the Jews of Prague. Before World War I the students' organization *Bar Kochba, under the leadership of Samuel Hugo *Bergman, became one of the centers of cultural Zionism. At the same time Zionism also spurred Jewish political activity. The Prague Zionist Arthur *Mahler was elected to the Austrian Parliament in 1907, though as representative of an electoral district in Galicia. Under the leadership of Ludvik *Singer the Jewish National Council was formed in 1918. Singer was elected in 1929 to the Czechoslovak Parliament, and was succeeded after his death in 1931 by Angelo *Goldstein. Singer, Goldstein, František Friedmann, and Jacob Reiss represented the Zionists on the Prague municipal council also. Some important Zionist conferences took place in Prague, among them the founding conference of *Hitaḥadut in 1920, and the 18th Zionist Congress in 1933.

Jews were prominent in the cultural life of Prague. Their contribution to German literature was most significant. Of the older generation Salomon *Kohn dealt mainly with Bohemian Jewish topics; Friedrich *Adler, Auguste Hauschner, and Hugo *Salus were among the most prominent authors; Heinrich Teweles was important as an author, editor, and director of the theater. The group of Prague German-Jewish authors which emerged in the 1880s, known as the "Prague circle" (*Der Prager Kreis*), achieved international recognition and included Franz *Kafka, Max *Brod, Franz *Werfel, Oskar *Baum, Ludwig Winder, Leo *Perutz, Egon Erwin *Kisch, Otto Klepetar, and Willy *Haas. Among Jews who contributed to Czech literature a pioneer was the poet Siegfried *Kapper; he was later considered the herald of Czech-Jewish assimilation. To this group also belonged at a later time Eduard Lederer *(Leda), Vojtēch *Rakous, celebrated for his novels about Jewish life in the Czech countryside, and Jindřich *Kohn, the philosopher and ideologist of assimilation. Other important authors were Otakar *Fischer, Richard *Weiner, František *Langer, his brother Mordecai Jiří *Langer, Jiří *Weil, František *Gottlieb, and Egon *Hostovský. Important scientists teaching at Prague universities included Arnold Piek, Max Saenger, and Edmund Weil (medicine), Samuel *Steinherz (history), Ludwig *Spiegel (constitutional law), Moritz *Winternitz (Sanskrit), Otakar Fischer (German literature), Oskar Engländer (economics), and Guido *Adler (musicology). Albert *Einstein taught in Prague in 1911–12, and Hans *Kelsen, a native of Prague, taught there in 1936–38. The composer Jaromir *Weinberger was born in Prague and lived there until his emigration in 1937; Gustav *Mahler, a native of Bohemia, spent several years in Prague as a conductor. Among many other noted Jewish conductors and musicians from Prague were Walter Suesskind, Frank *Pelleg, George Singer, and Karel Ančerl. The German theater in Prague knew its most glorious period under the directorships of Angelo Neumann, Heinrich Teweles, and Leopold Kramer. Ernst *Deutsch and Franz Lederer were among the most celebrated actors on the German stage, and Hugo Haas and Jiří Voskovec on the Czech stage. Emil *Orlik and Hugo Steiner-Prag were outstanding artists.

Jewish topics, and particularly the history and legends of Prague Jewry, were a frequent theme in the work of non-Jewish authors and artists, more so in the Czech cultural sphere than in the German. Retrospectively, the Jewish ghetto has been considered part and parcel of Prague's history. The statue of Judah Loew b. Bezalel at the entrance to the new City Hall, and a statue of Moses near the Altneuschul, both works of Czech sculptors commissioned by the Prague municipality, are monuments to this attitude. The Jews of Prague responded with gratitude and pride in their history; but latterly only a minority was still capable of living a meaningful Jewish life, much less of forging a creative Jewish future.

[Jan Herman / Chaim Yahil]

Holocaust Period

From 1935, two years after Hitler's seizure of power in Germany, a constant influx of refugees arrived in Prague from Germany, followed in 1938 by refugees from Austria and the German-speaking occupied parts of Czechoslovakia. As a result the number of Jews in Prague on March 15, 1939, the day of the Nazi occupation, amounted to about 56,000. On July 22, 1939, *Reichsprotektor* Constantin von Neurath ordered the establishment of a Zentralstelle fuer juedische Auswanderung in Boehmen und Maehren ("Central Office for Jewish Emigration in Bohemia and Moravia"). Its director in fact was Adolf *Eichmann. Initially the office dealt only with Prague's Jews but as of Feb. 16, 1940, it affected all the Jews in the protectorate.

At the outbreak of the war (Sept. 1, 1939), prominent Prague Jews were arrested and deported as hostages to *Buchenwald concentration camp. Various anti-Jewish measures, e.g., deprivation of property rights, prohibition against religious, cultural, or any other form of public activity, expulsion from the professions and from schools, a ban on the use of public transportation and the telephone, affected Prague Jews much more than those still living in the provinces. Jewish organizations provided social welfare and clandestinely continued the education of the youth and the training in languages and new vocations – in preparation for emigration. The *Palestine Office in Prague, directed by Jacob *Edelstein, enabled about 19,000 Jews to emigrate legally or otherwise until the end of 1939. In March 1940, the Prague Zentralstelle extended the area of its jurisdiction to include all of Bohemia and Moravia. In an attempt to avert the deportation of the Jews to "the east," Jewish leaders, headed by Jacob Edelstein, proposed to the Zentralstelle the establishment of a self-administered concentrated Jewish communal body; the Nazis eventually exploited this proposal in the establishment of the ghetto at *Theresienstadt (Terezin). The Prague Jewish community was forced to provide the Nazis with lists of candidates for deportation and to ensure that they showed up at the assembly point and boarded deportation trains. In the period from Oct. 6, 1941, to March 16, 1945, 46,067 Jews were deported from Prague to the east or to Theresienstadt. Two leading officials of the Jewish community, H. Bonn and Emil Kafka (a former president of the community), were dispatched to *Mauthausen concentration camp and put to death after trying to slow down the pace of the deportations. The Nazis set up a Treuhandstelle ("Trustee Office") over evacuated Jewish apartments, furnishings, and possessions. This office sold these goods and forwarded the proceeds to the German *Winterhilfe* ("Winter Aid"). The Treuhandstelle ran as many as 54 warehouses, including 11 synagogues (as a result, none of the synagogues was destroyed). The Zentralstelle brought Jewish religious articles from 153 Jewish communities to Prague on a proposal by Jewish scholars. This collection, including 5,400 religious objects, 24,500 prayer books, and 6,070 items of historical value, the Nazis intended to utilize for a "Central Museum of the Defunct Jewish Race." Jewish historians engaged in the creation of the museum were deported to extermination camps just before the end of the war. Thus the Jewish Museum had acquired at the end of the war one of the richest collections of Judaica in the world. The Pinkas Synagogue, which is included in the museum complex, contains inscriptions of the names of 77,297 Jewish victims of the Nazi extermination campaign in Bohemia and Moravia.

In April 1945 the Prague representative of the International Red Cross (IRC), Paul Dunant, negotiated with *Reichsprotektor* Karl Hermann Frank for the transfer of the Theresienstadt ghetto to IRC auspices. When the Czechoslovak government-in-exile in London returned to Prague, a Jewish member of the State Council, Arnošt Frischer, also came back; under his leadership, the Prague Jewish community was reconstituted and a council of Jewish communities in Czechoslovakia established. According to the monthly *Věstník*, the official Jewish community publication, Prague had a Jewish population of 10,338 in 1946, of whom 1,396 Jews had not been deported (mostly of mixed Jewish-Christian parentage); 227 Jews had gone underground; 4,980 returned from prisons, concentration camps, or Theresienstadt; 883 returned from Czechoslovak army units abroad; 613 were Czechoslovak Jewish émigrés who returned; and 2,233 were Jews from Ruthenia (Carpatho-Ukraine), which had been ceded to the U.S.S.R., who decided to move to Czechoslovakia.

Contemporary Period

In the three years following the end of the war, the Jewish population of Prague rose to 11,000, after the return of Prague Jews and the settlement of other survivors of the Holocaust. Thus a basis for Jewish life again existed in the city, and Chief Rabbi Gustav Sicher, who had returned from Palestine, sought to establish firm foundations for the further development of Jewish activities. The Communist takeover of 1948, however, put an end to these endeavors and marked the beginning of a period of stagnation. By 1950 about half of the Jewish population had gone to Israel or immigrated to other countries. The Slańský Trials and the officially promoted antisemitism had a destructive effect upon Jewish life. Nazi racism of the previous era was replaced by political and social discrimination. Most of the Jews of Prague were branded as "class enemies of the working people" and suffered from various forms of persecution, including imprisonment, exile, forced labor, and, in some cases, execution. During this period (1951–64) there was also no possibility of Jewish emigration from the country. The assets belonging to the Jewish community – estimated at 100 million Czech crowns – had to be relinquished to the state, the charitable organizations were disbanded, and the budget of the community, provided by the state, was drastically reduced. The general anti-religious policy of the regime resulted in the cessation, for all practical purposes, of such Jewish religious activities as bar mitzvah religious instruction, and wedding ceremonies. Two Prague rabbis – E. Davidovi and E. Farkas – left the country, and in 1964 the office of the chief rabbi also became vacant; only two cantors and two ritual slaughterers were left. Services were held in only two of Prague's nine synagogues, while the other seven were used as exhibition halls and warehouses for the State Jewish Museum. The Hebrew inscription on the wall of the Talmud Torah Synagogue was removed by the museum director. The museum's collection of Jewish art and religious articles were used by the Czechoslovak Travel Bureau as a tourist attraction. Officials of the Jewish communal organizations achieved their positions by manipulated elections.

The social, cultural and, above all, political activity of Jewish communal officials was strictly supervised, and the officials themselves were agents of the authorities – in charge of supervising the members of the congregation, the people who attended prayers and festivities, and clients of the kosher restaurant. The officials participated in propaganda projects such as the World Peace Movement. They abstained, however, as much as they could from attacking the State of Israel and Zionism. The Rada zidovskych nabozenskych obci (Council of Jewish Religious Congregations) cooperated with the central federation of Jewish religious congregations in Slovakia, but the cooperation did not always go smoothly. While Bratislava complained that Prague was monopolizing the representation of Czechoslovak Jewry, Prague charged that Bratislava was getting a disproportionate amount of assistance from abroad. The bulletin *Věstník* ("The Informer") represented both Czech and Slovak Jewry, both sides supplied material for the publication, and both covered the expenses.

The liberalization of the regime during 1965–68 held out new hope for a renewal of Jewish life in Prague. At the end of March 1967 the president of the *World Jewish Congress, Nahum *Goldmann, was able to visit Prague and give a lecture in the Jewish Town Hall. Among the Jewish youth, many tended to identify with Judaism. In August 1968, however, the Soviet invasion of Czechoslovakia put an end to this trend. The festivities that were to mark the millennium of Jewish life in Prague were canceled four times. A new wave of emigration began, and the Jewish population of Prague was further reduced to about 2,000.

The period of "normalization" after the invasion of the Warsaw Pact forces in August 1968 heralded renewed discrimination and oppression of the Jewish minority. The liberals who led the Prague Spring of 1967 granted the Jewish community freedom. Jewish institutions were free to act as they pleased. These liberals approved the Israeli and Jewish polices of President Novotny and his people. After the occupation on August 21, 1968, Jewish policies and Jewish institutions once again became targets of suspicion and attack. President Husak and the conservatives who surrounded him earmarked the Jews for special treatment. Prague's Jewry and foreign Jewish institutions were under surveillance. After the wave of hasty emigration in 1968–70, the authorities would not permit Jews to leave, particularly to the State of Israel. The close governmental ties with Arab countries had a strong impact on Czechoslovak foreign and domestic policies.

Czech dissent was by and large inclined to understand local Jewry and objected to governmental policies. The anti-Zionist campaign, which increased after 1970 and sometimes turned into overt antisemitism, affected the life of Prague's Jewish community. The conditions improved somewhat when Mikhail Gorbachev assumed the reins of power in Moscow. When the student demonstrations occurred in Prague in the fall of 1989 and the police displayed unusual brutality, numerous Prague organizations protested and the Council published a special communiqué. During the Samet Revolution, Prague Jewry identified with the protesters. After the change of the regime, the council was reorganized, personnel changes took place, and a young rabbi took over the vacant seat of the chief rabbi. Rabbi Karol Sidon, who had studied in Heidelberg and in Jerusalem and was trained there for the rabbinate, was installed in the position. He had cooperated with the dissent in the past and proved to be a prolific and respected writer.

The authorities handed back to the Prague congregation its jurisdiction over the Altneuschul synagogue and the adjacent ancient cemetery, as well as other synagogues and properties. These became a source of considerable income from visitors and tourists. The congregation renewed the regular services in the Altneuschul. There was a certain unrest in the early years when Jews, and youth in particular, wanted to return to Judaism. The veteran Orthodox synagogue goers – some immigrants from Carpatho-Rus – would not recognize the newcomers as Jews. Those not recognized as Jewish according to *halakhah* had to fight for their rights. In Prague, the younger generation identified with Judaism and the State of Israel and was forced to face the apprehension of the Conservatives.

The social function of the congregation and the desire to enjoy reparation, and indemnity monies from Germany and elsewhere led the elderly in particular to join the congregation. Also, cultural activities sponsored by the congregation and by the Jewish Museum gave the impetus for more extensive Jewish life; and many who had hitherto hidden their Jewish ancestry began to avail themselves of the services provided by the congregation. These included the activities of the Center for Educational and Cultural Activities, organized by the Jewish Museum. Consequently, Jewish life saw a revival. The center organized conferences, hosted exhibitions, and published books and other material. The bulletin *Rosh Chodesh* serves the Jewish communities in the Czech lands and in Slovakia, as does the annual magazine *Zidovsk rocenka*. The Czech Jewish communal institutions do not enjoy inner consolidation. Frequent quarrels, resignations, election campaigns, and confrontations disturb the congregation's peace and the communal life. Rabbi Sidon has been unable to remedy the situation. In 2005 around 1,300 Jews were affiliated with the community.

[Erich Kulka / Yeshayahu Jelinek (2nd ed.)]

Hebrew Printing in Prague

Prague was the first city north of the Alps where Hebrew books were printed. The earliest, printed in 1512, was a book of miscellaneous prayers. Of the early printers Gershom *Kohen emerged as the leading figure; from 1526 he and his sons carried on the printing business which for several generations remained one of the outstanding Hebrew presses in Europe. Gershom Kohen, with his brother Gronim (Jerome), produced independently in 1526 the famous illustrated Passover *Haggadah* (facsimile edition, 1926). In the following year (under the name of Herman) he obtained from King Ferdinand of Bohemia a printing privilege, which at his death in 1545 was reissued to his son Moses and in 1598 to his great-grandson Gershom b. Bezalel. He and his brother Moses after him were active until the middle of the 17th century. The Gersonides printed mainly liturgical items in this period, but also such important works as Jacob b. Asher's *Turim* (1540) and Moses Isserles' *Torat ha-Olah* (1569). Another printing press was founded by Jacob Bak who was printing in Prague by 1605. Jacob died in 1618, and after him eight generations of Baks printed Hebrew books in Prague up to the threshold of the 19th century. Their productions were mostly liturgical and for local use, and they, like other Hebrew printers, suffered much under the Jesuit censorship (from 1528) and occasional book burnings (1715, 1731). Jonathan *Eybeschuetz obtained permission to print the Talmud at Bak's (1728–41).

Besides Kohen and Bak, other Hebrew printers of note in Prague included Abraham Heide-Lemberger and his sons (1610–41). From 1828 Moses Landau printed independently, in particular a Talmud edition (8°, 1830–35).

BIBLIOGRAPHY: The standard guide is O. Muneles, *Bibliographical Survey of Jewish Prague* (Ger. and Czech, 1952); M. Kreutzberger (ed.), *Bibliothek und Archiv*, 1 (1970), and the bibliographies appended to the *Yearbook of the Leo Baeck Institute* (1956–) offer additional information. New material on Prague appears mainly in the communal journal *Věstník*, the scholarly *Judaica Bohemiae* (since 1965), and in works commissioned by the Jewish State Museum of Prague. GENERAL WORKS: S. Steinherz, *Die Juden in Prag* (1927); G. Klemperer, in: HJ, 12 (1950), 33–66; 13 (1951), 55–82; G. Kisch, *Die Prager Universitaet und die Juden* (1969); L. Schnitzler, *Prager Judendeutsch* (1966); *Gesher*, no. 2–3, 15 (1969); *The Jews of Czechoslovakia* (1968); *Jewish Studies. Essays in Honor of Dr. Gustav Sicher* (1955). MIDDLE AGES: Germ Jud, 1 (1963); 2 (1968); S. Steinherz, in: *B'nai B'rith Monatsblaetter*, 6 (1927), 433–8; idem, in: JGGJ, 1 (1929), 1–37; J. Proke, *ibid.*, 41–224; R. Kestenberg, *ibid.*, 8 (1936), 1–25; V. Rynes, in: *Judaica Bohemiae*, 1 (1965), 9–25; P. Trost, *ibid.*, 4 (1968), 138f. RENAISSANCE: M. Wischnitzer, in: JSOS, 16 (1955), 335–50; idem, *Jewish Crafts and Guilds* (1965), index; O. Muneles (ed.), *Prague Ghetto in the Renaissance Period* (1965); F. Thieberger, *The Great Rabbi Loew of Prague* (1954). PRAGUE EXPULSION: B. Brilling, in: *Zeitschrift fuer die Geschichte der Juden*, 1 (1964), 37–42; A. Newman, in: JHSET, 22 (1968), 30–42; B. Mevorah, in: *Meḥkarim be-Toledot Am-Yisrael ve-Ereẓ Yisrael* (1970), 187–232; idem, in: *Zion*, 28 (1963), 125–64. MODERN ERA: F. Weltsch (ed.), *Prag vi-Yrushalayim* (1954); H. Tramer, in: YLBI, 9 (1964), 305–39; F. Meissner, *German Jews of Prague* (1961; = AJHSP, 50 (1960/61), 98–120); R. Kestenberg-Gladstein, *Neuere Geschichte der Juden in den boehmischen Laendern* (1969); idem, in: YLBI, 9 (1964), 295–304; M. Brod, *Der Prager Kreis* (1966); W. Benda, in: *Zeitschrift fuer die Geschichte der Juden*, 2–3 (1966), 85–94; J. Urzidil, in: BLBI, 10 (1967), 276–97; G. Kisch, in: *Judaica Bohemiae*, 3 (1967), 87–100; J. Vyskočil, *ibid.*, 36–55; K. Baum, in: MGWJ, 73 (1929), 349–65. HEBREW PRINTING: Zunz, Gesch, 261–303; S.H. Lieben, in: *Die Juden in Prag…* (1927); A. Freimann, in: *Soncino-Blaetter*, 3 (1929–30), 113–43 (189–219); Ḥ.D. Friedberg, *Toledot ha-Defus ha-Ivri ba-Arim she-be-Eiropah ha-Tikhonah* (1935), 1–29 [see also KS, index to vols. 1–40 (1967), nos. 126, 176, 213]. HOLOCAUST PERIOD: M. Moskowitz, in: JSOS, 4 (1942), 17–44; M.Y. Ben-Gavriel, *Bayit bi-Prag* (1945); O. Kraus and E. Kulka, *The Death Factory* (1966), index; *Juedisches Nachrichtenblatt* (Prague, 1939–44); Juedische Kultusgemeinde Prag, *Wochen, Monats-und Vierteljahresberichte*, 10 vols. (1933–42); H.G.

Adler, *Theresienstadt 1941–45* (Ger., 1960), passim. CONTEMPORARY JEWRY: A. Charim, *Die toten Gemeinden* (1966), 1321; R. Iltis (ed.), *Die aussaeen unter Traenen mit Jubel werden sie ernten* (1959). MUSEUM, GHETTO, AND CEMETERY: *Historica Hebraica* (1965); H. Volavkov, *Story of the Jewish Museum in Prague* (1968); idem, *The Pinkas Synagogue* (1955); J. Lion and J. Lukas, *The Prague Ghetto* (1960); idem, *The Old Prague Jewish Cemetery* (1960); I. Herrmann, J. Tege and Z. Winter, *Das Prager Ghetto* (1903); S. Muenzer, in: JGGJČ, 4 (1932), 63–105; A. Deutsch, *Die Zigeuner-Grossenhof-und Neusynagoge in Prag* (1907); S. Hock and D. Kaufmann, *Die Familien Prags* (1892); B. Wachstein, in: *Jewish Studies... G.A. Kohut* (1935), 25–40. **ADD. BIBLIOGRAPHY:** J. Fiedler, *Jewish Sights of Bohemia and Moravia* (1991).

PRATO, DAVID (1882–1951), rabbi and Zionist leader. Born in Leghorn, Prato was chief cantor in Florence, rabbi of Alexandria (Egypt) from 1927 to 1936, and chief rabbi of Rome from 1936 to 1938. Conditions became impossible for him when the Fascist regime began its antisemitic policy, and Prato moved to Ereẓ Israel. He resumed his post in Rome in 1945. An ardent Zionist, Prato played a prominent part in the administration of the *Jewish National Fund and *Keren Hayesod in Italy. In 1929 he founded in Alexandria the French-Hebrew review *L'Illustration Juive*, which was followed by *Cahiers Juifs* in 1933. He published two collections of sermons, *Cinque anni di Rabbinato* (1933), and *Dal pergamo della Comunità di Roma* (1950), covering his activities in Rome.

BIBLIOGRAPHY: *Ha-Rav David Prato* (1940).

[Giorgio Romano]

PRATT, RICHARD (1934–), Australian businessman. One of the most successful contemporary Australian businessmen, Pratt was born in Danzig, migrating to Australia in 1939 from London, where his father, a retailer, had moved. In 1948 Pratt's father, Leon, opened a cardboard factory in Melbourne, which was developed by Richard Pratt after his father's death in 1969. Known as Visy Board (now Visy Industries), it grew into one of the largest producers of packaging and waste recyclers in the world. By the 1990s it employed 8,000 staff in a hundred plants around the world. Pratt, a powerful, athletic man, was also a notable Victorian Rules football player in his youth and was then an actor, starring in the noted Australian play *The Summer of the Seventeenth Doll.* By 2004 Pratt was regarded as the second wealthiest man in Australia (jointly with Frank *Lowy), worth an estimated A$4.2 billion (US$3.5 billion). With his wife, Jeanne, he was the founder of the Pratt Foundation, one of the major Australian philanthropies. Pratt received numerous awards. He became a Companion of the Order of Australia (AO) and, in 2004, was named Australian Humanitarian of the Year.

BIBLIOGRAPHY: R. Ostrow, *The New Boy Network* (1987), 200–4; "The Rich 200," in: *Business Review Weekly* (Melbourne, May 20–26, 2004), 115; W.D. Rubinstein, Australia II, index.

[William D. Rubinstein (2nd ed.)]

PRAWER, JOSHUA (1917–1990), Israel historian. Born in Bedzin, Poland, Prawer settled in Palestine in 1936. He began teaching at the Hebrew University of Jerusalem in 1947 and was promoted to the chair of medieval history in 1958. From 1962 to 1966 he was dean of the faculty of humanities. Prawer also served the Israel Ministry of Education as chairman of the pedagogical council for the planning of national education (1957–59) and headed the committee that recommended reforms in secondary education, which constituted the basis of the reform law adopted by the Knesset in 1968. He was also a co-founder and first dean of the Haifa University College, whose academic chairman he was from 1966 to 1968. Prawer's scholarly interests centered mainly on the Crusades. He wrote *Mamlekhet Yerushalayim ha-Ẓalbanit* ("The Crusader Kingdom of Jerusalem," 1946–47), *Toledot Mamlekhet ha-Ẓalbanim be-Ereẓ-Israel* ("A History of the Latin Kingdom of Jerusalem," 2 vols., 1963), and *The History of the Jews in the Latin Kingdom of Jerusalem* (1988). He was a member of the Israel Academy of Sciences and Humanities and from 1967 chief editor of the *Encyclopaedia Hebraica*. In 1969 he was awarded the Israel Prize for humanities.

[George Schwab]

PRAWER, SIEGBERT (1925–), British professor of literature. Born in Cologne, Prawer came to Britain in the late 1930s and attended King Henry VIII School in Coventry and Oxford and Cambridge Universities. A distinguished scholar of German and other literatures, he was professor of German at London University and then at Oxford Universities. He wrote noted works on Heine, Marx, Thackeray, and others and received many awards, including the Goethe Medal (1973), the Isaac Deutscher Prize (1977), and the Gold Medal of the Goethe Gesellschaft (1977). He was a fellow of the British Academy.

BIBLIOGRAPHY: R. Robertson, "An Appreciation of the Work of Siegbert Prawer, J.P. Stern, and George Steiner," in: S.P. Dowden and M.G. Werner (eds.), *German Literature, Jewish Critics* (2002).

[William D. Rubinstein (2nd ed.)]

PRAYER, the offering of petition, confession, adoration or thanksgiving to God.

In the Bible

The concept of prayer is based on the conviction that God exists, hears, and answers (Ps. 65:3; cf. 115:3–7) – that He is a personal deity. In a sense it is a corollary of the biblical concept that man was created "in the image of God" (Gen. 1:26–27), which implies, inter alia, fellowship with God (see *Man, Nature of). Although prayer has an intellectual base, it is essentially emotional in character. It is an expression of man's quest for the Divine and his longing to unburden his soul before God (Ps. 42:2–3 [1–2]; 62:9[8]). Hence prayer takes many forms: petition, expostulation, confession, meditation, recollection (anamnesis), thanksgiving, praise, adoration, and intercession. For the purpose of classification, "praise" is distinguished from "prayer" in the narrower, supplicatory sense, and "ejaculatory" from formal, "liturgical" prayer. But the source is the same; in its irresistible outpouring, the human heart merges all categories in an indivisible "I-Thou" relationship. Thus prayer and praise may intermingle (I Sam. 2:1–10) and supplication and thanksgiving follow in close succession (Ps. 13:1–5, 6). Indeed many scriptural passages might be called "para-prayers" – they seem to hover between discourse and entreaty (Ex. 3:1–12), meditation and petition (Jer. 20:7ff.), or expostulation and entreaty (Job, passim). It has been estimated (Koehler-Baumgartner) that there are 85 prayers in the Bible, apart from 60 complete psalms and 14 parts of psalms that can be so termed; five psalms are specifically called prayers (Ps. 17, 86, 90, 102, 142). But such liturgical statistics depend on the definition given to prayer.

TERMINOLOGY. The variegated character of biblical prayer has given rise to a rich nomenclature for praying. The rabbis already noted that "prayer is called by ten different expressions" (Sif. Deut. 26), but on closer examination even more can be found. The most common word for prayer is *tefillah* (Isa. 1:15); the corresponding verb is *hitpallel* (I Kings 8:42). The stem, *pll*, has been explained to mean "to cut oneself" and to refer to the primitive pagan custom of slashing oneself in a frenzy during worship. This etymology is not only hypothetical, but is wholly irrelevant to the biblical situation. It was the idol-worshipers who cut themselves (I Kings 18:28) and the verb used is *wa-yitgodedu*; the Torah forbids such practices (Deut. 14:1). In Scripture the stem *pll* signifies "to interpose, judge, hope." These meanings are eminently suited to the biblical conception of prayer as intercession and self-scrutiny leading to hope. Other terms are: *qara*ʾ ("to call" on the name of the Deity, i.e., worship – Gen. 4:26); *zaʿaq* ("to cry out" for redress of wrongs – Judg. 3:9); *shiwwʿa* ("to cry aloud" for help – Ps. 72:12); *rinnah* ("ringing cry" of joy or sorrow – Ps. 17:1); *darash* ("to seek" God – Amos 5:4); *biqqesh penei* ("to seek the face of" God – Hos. 5:15); *shaʾal* ("to inquire" – Ps. 105:40); *nasa*ʾ ("to lift up" – Jer. 7:16); *pagʿa* ("to encounter," i.e., to appease, gain favor – Jer. 7:16); *hitḥannen* ("to seek favor," i.e., beseech – Deut. 3:23); *shafakh lev* ("to pour out heart" – Ps. 62:9[8]); and *siaḥ* ("complaint" – Ps. 142:3[2]).

THE CHARACTER OF PRAYER. Despite its multifaceted character, biblical prayer is essentially a simple human reaction. The rabbis called it "the service in the heart" (Taʾan. 2a); the expression has its roots in biblical thought (Hos. 7:14; Ps. 108:2; 111:1). But the needs of man are so numerous and complex that prayer inevitably came to reflect the vast range of human moods, fears, hopes, feelings, desires, and aspirations. In early times – in the patriarchal age – a simple invocation, a calling upon the name of the Lord (Gen. 12:8; 21:33), would suffice. The approach to God at this stage was marked by spontaneity, directness, and familiarity – God was near. Yet the future was veiled by mystery; man was often undecided how to act. Hence the request for a sign or oracle addressed directly to God (Gen. 24:12–14), or indirectly through a priest (I Sam. 14:36–37) or prophet (II Kings 19:2ff.). From this stratum grew the magnificent prayers for understanding and guidance (Num. 6:24–26; I Kings 3:6ff.; Ps. 119:33ff.).

But in emergency man does not merely want to know the future; he seeks to determine it by entreating God's help. Thus Jacob (in a votive supplication) prayed for essential material needs (Gen. 28:20ff.); Eliezer for the success of his mission (Gen. 24:12–14); Abraham for the salvation of Sodom (Gen. 18:23–33); Moses for erring Israel (Ex. 32:31–32); Joshua for divine help in the hour of defeat (Josh. 7:6–9); Hezekiah for deliverance from Sennacherib (II Kings 19:15–19); the prophets on behalf of their people (Jer. 14:1ff.; 15:1ff.; Amos 7:2ff.); Daniel for Israel's restoration (Dan. 9:3–19); Ezra for the sins of his people (Ezra 9:6–15); and Nehemiah for the distress of his people (Neh. 1:4–11). Solomon's noble dedication prayer at the consecration of the Temple (I Kings 8:12–53) includes almost every type of prayer – adoration, thanksgiving, petition, and confession. It also strikes a universal note (8:41ff.) so often echoed by the prophets. The spectrum of biblical prayer thus ranges from the simplest material needs to the highest spiritual yearnings (Ps. 51:1ff.; 119:1ff.), transcending, like prophecy, the horizon of history and reaching to the realm of eschatology (Isa. 66:22–23).

There was an early relationship between *sacrifice and prayer (Gen. 13:4; 26:25), which persisted until the destruction of the Second Temple. The sacrifice suggested man's submission to the will of God; the prayer often provided a commentary on the offering. But the two are not necessarily linked. It is noteworthy that the sacrificial regulations make no liturgical provisions (except for the Day of Atonement, Lev. 16:21); but actually the offerings were themselves a dramatic form of prayer. Contrariwise, prayer could replace sacrifice (Ps. 141:2). In the synagogue, prayer, accompanied by Scripture reading and exposition, entirely took the place of altar offerings.

Examples of prayers of intercession have already been cited. The intercessor, whether prophet, priest, king, or national leader, does not point to the need for an intermediary in worship: "The Lord is near to all who call upon Him in truth" (Ps. 145:18). The intercessor is one who, by his innate spiritual attributes, lends weight to the entreaty. The ultimate criterion still remains not the worthiness of the pleader but of those for whom he is pleading (Ezek. 14:14, 20).

THE ACCESSORIES OF PRAYER. Prayer, unlike sacrifice, could be offered up anywhere (Gen. 24:26; Dan. 6:11 in the upper chamber; Ezra 9:5ff.), but there was a natural tendency to prefer a sacred site (e.g., Shiloh or Gibeon). Eventually the Temple at Jerusalem became the major place of prayer (Isa. 56:7); those who could not be there physically at least turned toward it when worshiping (Dan. 6:11; cf. Ps. 5:8 [7]). In time to come the Temple would be a house of prayer for all nations (Isa. 56:7). The synagogue had its origin during the Babylonian exile; originally a place of assembly, it became in due course a house of prayer and study. The emphasis on congregational prayer began to grow but private prayer was never abolished. The heart and not the hour dictated the occasion for prayer. Day and night the Heavenly Father could be entreated (e.g., I Sam. 15:11; Ps. 86:3; 88:2[1]). But the need for regularity brought about a synchronization of the times of prayer and of sacrifice: morning worship corresponded to the morning oblation (Ps. 5:4[3]), afternoon orisons to the late afternoon sacrifice (I Kings 18:36; Ezra 9:5). Nightfall provided yet another occasion for worship, so that prayers came to be offered thrice daily (Ps. 55:18; Dan. 6:11; though twice in I Chron. 23:30). The seven times mentioned in Psalms 119:164 mean "often" or "constantly."

In the Bible no particular gestures are prescribed in connection with prayer. But certain postures developed naturally to lend emphasis to the content of the prayer: standing, which is normal (I Sam. 1:26; I Kings 8:22); kneeling (Dan. 6:11; Ezra 9:5); prostration (Josh. 7:6); head bowed (Gen. 24:26; Neh. 8:6); hands stretched out or uplifted (I Kings 8:22; Ps. 28:2); face between knees (I Kings 18:42); and even sitting (II Sam. 7:18). More important accompaniments of prayer were fasting, mourning, and weeping (Isa. 58:2–5; Joel 2:12); but the ultimate criterion remained earnestness of heart (Joel 2:13).

Originally prayer was undoubtedly spontaneous and personal; but the need to organize religion gave rise to liturgical patterns and musical renderings (Ezra 2:65; I Chron. 16). Prayer formulas are found already in the Pentateuch (Deut. 21:7ff.; 26:5–15). The Psalms provide examples of fuller liturgical development, including choral and instrumental features (see *Psalms). The response "Amen" occurs in Numbers 5:22, Psalms 41:14, etc.; a prayer before the reading of the Torah in Nehemiah 8:6; a doxology in Nehemiah 9:5, 32; a typical review of God's dealings with Israel leading to a confession and a pledge in Nehemiah 9:6–10:1 (9:38).

ANSWER TO PRAYER. That prayer is answered is an accepted biblical verity (e.g., Gen. 19:17–23; Num. 12:9ff.); but Scripture is no less emphatic that not all prayers are answered (Gen. 18:17ff.; Isa. 29:13ff.). Ritual is not enough, while hypocritical worship is an abomination (Isa. 1:15; Amos 4:4ff.); and there are occasions when intercession is forbidden (Jer. 7:16; 11:14). It is at this point that the biblical concept of prayer is seen in its true inwardness. Paganism regarded worship as a form of magic, whereby the deity could be compelled to fulfill the worshiper's wishes; the moral element was wholly absent. In biblical faith the divine response is essentially linked to ethical and spiritual values. Man, as it were, answers his own prayer (Gen. 4:7), and fundamentally the answer is a significant change of spirit and outlook. Abraham learned the lesson of faith (Gen. 15:1–6); Moses became his people's deliverer (Ex. 3:2–4:18); Isaiah was transformed into a prophet (Isa. 6:5–8). Prayer and prophecy were probably closely correlated, the former providing spiritual soil in which the revelatory seed took root (Jer. 1:6ff.; Hab. 1:13–2:3). In many instances prayer assumes a tempestuous character (Jer. 12; Ps. 22; Job, passim [cf. 16:17]), but the storm always ends in newfound faith and peace. At times, moreover, God answers before He is appealed to (Isa. 65:24; cf. Dan. 9:20ff.), for man not only beseeches God, but God also seeks man (Isa. 50:2; 65:12). The "I-Thou" relationship is reciprocal.

In sum, the Bible conceives prayer as a spiritual bridge between man and God. It is a great instrument of human regeneration and salvation, worthy even of martyrdom (Dan. 6:11). Rooted in faith (Ps. 121) and moral integrity (Ps. 15), it banishes fear (Ps. 23) and asks, in its noblest formulations, only the blessing of divine favor (Num. 6:24–26). Clothed in language of simple but matchless beauty, it is imbued with religious love and a sense of sweet fellowship with God. Both the Christian and Muslim liturgies have been profoundly influenced by the spirit, thought, and forms of biblical prayer.

[Israel Abrahams]

In the Apocryphal Literature

There are a number of references to prayer in the apocryphal books, including the idea of the living offering up prayers on behalf of the dead (II Mac. 12:44–45). The apocryphal work, The Prayer of Manasseh, is a penitential prayer. The biblical concept that God is near to those who suffer is also developed (Ecclus. 35:13–17). Prayer is associated with the giving of alms (Ecclus. 7:10), and there is a national prayer for deliverance from an enemy (Ecclus. 36:1–17).

In Rabbinic Thought

On the biblical verse "And serve Him with all your heart" (Deut. 11:13), the rabbis commented "What is service of the heart? This is prayer" (Ta'an. 2a). "Service" (*avodah*) in this context is connected with the Temple and its worship, for which prayer is seen as a substitute. On the other hand, the saying of R. Eleazar that prayer is dearer to God than good works and sacrifices (Ber. 32b), though hyperbolic, may nonetheless be intended to express the real superiority of prayer. Possibly, the tension in this matter is to be perceived in the two reasons given for the statutory prayers of the day. According to one opinion, these were ordained by the patriarchs, while another view has it that they correspond to the perpetual offerings in Temple times (Ber. 26b).

The obligation of offering up prayer, though supported by a scriptural verse, is considered to be rabbinic, not biblical (Ber. 21a). Prayers are to be recited three times a day: morning, afternoon, and night (Ber. 4:1). In addition to the statutory prayers and private prayers of various kinds, public prayers were offered in times of distress; prayers for rain, for instance, in times of drought (Ta'an. 2:1–5).

THE VALUE OF PRAYER AND CONCENTRATION IN PRAYER. Prayer stands high in the world of values (Ber. 6b). God Himself prays, His prayer being that His mercy might overcome His judgment (Ber. 7a). Nevertheless, the study of the Torah occupies a higher rung than prayer, and some scholars, whose main occupation was study, only prayed periodically (Shab. 11a; RH 35a). A rabbi who spent too much time on his prayers was rebuked by his colleague for neglecting eternal life to engage in temporal existence (Shab. 10a). Communal prayer is of greater significance than private prayer (Ber. 8a; Deut. R. 2:12). Too much reflection on one's prayers in the expectation that these will be answered was discouraged (Ber. 32b). Prayer should be offered with proper concentration (*kavvanah*) on the words uttered in God's presence (Ber. 31a). R. Eliezer said: "He that makes his prayer a fixed task, his prayer is not supplication" (Ber. 4:4). R. Simeon b. Nethanel said: "...and when thou prayest make not thy prayer a fixed form, but [a plea for] mercies and supplications before God" (Avot 2:13). One way of avoiding the deadening familiarity of a "fixed form" was to recite a new prayer each day (TJ, Ber. 4:3, 8a). When R. Eliezer was asked by his disciples to teach them the ways of life that they might learn them and by following attain the life of the world to come, part of his reply was: "When you pray, know before Whom you stand" (Ber. 28b). A person who has just returned from a journey and is consequently unable to concentrate properly, should not pray until three days have elapsed (Er. 65a).

PROPER FORMS OF PRAYER. Not every prayer is valid. A prayer for God to change the past, for instance, is a "vain prayer" (Ber. 9:3). The impossibility of God answering every prayer addressed to Him is acknowledged in the account of the prayer of the high priest on the Day of Atonement who used to pray before the rainy season that the prayers of the travelers who required fair weather should not be allowed to enter God's presence (Yoma 53b). A man should not only pray for himself but should also think of others, using the plural form "grant us" rather than the singular "grant me" (Ber. 29b–30a). If a man needs something for himself but prays to God to grant that very thing to his neighbor who needs it, such an unselfish prayer causes God to grant him his wish first (BK 92a). Man should never despair of offering supplication to God "even if a sharp sword rests upon his neck" (Ber. 10a). In praising God, man should be circumspect, using only the standard forms of praise found in Scripture and established for use in prayer (Ber. 33b). Prayers of thanksgiving, particularly in the form of the benediction (*berakhah*), are repeatedly enjoined by the rabbis (Ber. 6:1–3), as well as praise of God for His wondrous works and the marvelous beings He has created (Ber. 9:1–2; Ber. 58b).

THE ADDRESSING OF PRAYERS DIRECTLY TO GOD. R. Judah said that if a human being is in trouble and wishes to invoke the aid of his patron he must first stand at the door and call out to a servant or a member of the patron's family and he may or may not be allowed to enter. But it is otherwise with God. God says, "When a man is in trouble, do not cry out to the angel Michael or to the angel Gabriel but to Me and I will answer immediately" (TJ, Ber. 9:1, 13a). On the other hand, R. Johanan said: "When one petitions for his needs in Aramaic, the ministering angels do not heed him, for they do not understand Aramaic" (Shab. 12b). Possibly a distinction is to be made between the angels bringing man's prayers to God and direct intercession, with the angels as intermediaries between man and God (cf. Tob., 12:12, 15). Some men were renowned for their capacity to pray and to have their prayers answered, so that great scholars, less gifted in this direction, would ask these saints to pray on their behalf (Ber. 34b). A number of miracle tales are told to illustrate the immediacy of God's response to the prayers of such men (Ta'an. 3:8; Ta'an. 23a–b).

In Medieval Thought

Although medieval Jewish thinkers profoundly considered major theological problems, there is surprisingly little discussion in their writings of the intellectual difficulties involved in prayer. One of the few discussions as to why prayer should be necessary, since God knows man's needs, is that of Joseph *Albo (Ikkarim 4:18). Albo replies that the act of turning to God in prayer is itself one of the conditions upon which God's help depends, just as it depends on other forms of human effort.

MAIMONIDES. True to his doctrine of theological negation, *Maimonides in the standard liturgy only permits the use of those divine attributes in prayer which have been ordained by the "prophets," and he is opposed to the indiscriminate writing of hymns (Guide, 1:59; cf. Ibn Ezra to Eccles. 5:1). In spite of the talmudic statement that the obligation to pray is of rabbinic origin (*mi-de-rabbanan*), Maimonides observes that this only applies to the number, form, and times of prayer, and that it is a biblical duty for the Jew to pray daily (Yad, Tefillah, 1:1). The need for adequate concentration in prayer (*kavvanah*) is particularly stressed in the Middle Ages and formed part of the general tendency prevalent among medieval Jewish thinkers who stressed greater inwardness in religious life. *Baḥya ibn Paquda (*Ḥovot ha-Levavot*, 8:3, 9) remarks that prayer without concentration is like a body without a soul or a husk without a kernel. Maimonides' definition of *kavvanah* reads: "*Kavvanah* means that a man should empty his mind of all other thoughts and regard himself as if he were standing before the Divine Presence" (Yad, Tefillah, 4:16; cf. H.G. Enelow, in: *Studies in Jewish Literature Issued in Honor of Prof. Kaufmann Kohler* (1913), 82–107).

THE KABBALISTS. The kabbalists stress the difficulty of petitionary prayer to a God who is unchanging. They advance the view that prayer cannot, in fact, be offered to God as He is in Himself (*Ein Sof*), but only to God as He is manifested in the ten divine potencies (the *Sefirot*). God Himself is, therefore, not entreated directly to show mercy, for example, but prayer is directed to God as He is manifested in the *Sefirah* of loving-kindness. As a result of the power of man's prayer, this potency might function on earth. The magical nature of kabbalistic prayer and the dangers of setting up the *Sefirot* as divine intermediaries were the topic of much subsequent debate (Ribash, Resp. no. 157). The kabbalists, in fact, substituted for the older doctrine of *kavvanah* the concept of special intentions (*kavvanot*) i.e., meditations on the realm of *Sefirot*. Instead of concentrating on the plain meaning of the prayers, the kabbalist dwells on the realm of divine potencies and directs his mind, when reciting the words, to the supernal mysteries which govern and are controlled by them (see I. Tishby, *Mishnat ha-Zohar*, 2 (1961), 247–306).

The Ḥasidim

In Ḥasidism, the kabbalistic type of *kavvanot* yields to a far more emotional involvement and attachment (*devekut*) to God. "The metamorphosis which took place in the meaning of *kavvanot* at the advent of Ḥasidism, and more explicitly after the Great Maggid [*Dov Baer of Mezhirech], consists in this – that an originally intellectual effort of meditation and contemplation had become an intensely emotional and highly enthusiastic act" (Weiss, in: JJS, 9 (1958), 163–92). In Ḥasidism, prayer is a mystical encounter with the Divine, the heart leaping in ecstasy to its Source. Violent movements in prayer were not unusual; some of the ḥasidic groups even encouraged their followers to turn somersaults during their prayers (Dubnow, *Ḥasidut*, 112–5).

Prayer is frequently seen in Ḥasidism as man's most important religious activity. R. Shneur Zalman of Lyady, the founder of the intellectual *Ḥabad sect in Ḥasidism, writes: "For although the forms of the prayers and the duty of praying three times a day are rabbinic, the idea of prayer is the foundation of the whole Torah. This means that man knows God, recognizing His greatness and His splendor with a serene and whole mind, and an understanding heart. Man should reflect on these ideas until his rational soul is awakened to love God, to cleave to Him and to His Torah, and to desire His commandments" (M. Teitelbaum, *Ha-Rav mi-Ladi u-Mifleget Ḥabad*, 2 (1914), 219).

In Ḥabad Ḥasidism, the true meaning of prayer is contemplation on the kabbalistic scheme whereby God's infinite light proceeds through the whole chain of being, from the highest to the lowest. Man should reflect on this until his heart is moved in rapture, but he should not engage in prayer for the sake of the pleasure such rapture will bring him; he must take care not to confuse authentic ecstasy with artificial spiritual titivation (Dov Baer of Lubavitch, *Kunteres ha-Hitpa'alut*). Many ḥasidic groups, otherwise strictly conformist, disregarded the laws governing prayer at fixed times on the grounds that these interfere with the need for adequate preparation and with the spontaneity which is part of the prayer's essence.

THE PRACTICE OF SWAYING IN PRAYER. During the Middle Ages, the practice of swaying during prayer is mentioned. The Zohar (3:218b–219a) refers to the difference between Israel and the nations. It states that the soul of the Jew is attached to the Torah as a candle is attached to a great flame, and hence Jews sway to and fro while studying the Torah. *Judah Halevi (*Kuzari* 2:79–80) also refers to the custom as practiced during the study of the Torah, but makes no mention of prayer. Isserles, however, quoting earlier authorities, also mentions the custom for prayer, while other authorities disagree (see Sh. Ar., OḤ, 48:1 and *Magen Avraham*, ad loc.). The explanation given by Simeon Brainin (quoted by Judah David Eisenstein in JE 11 (1907), 607), that swaying during study and prayer was intended to afford the body with exercise, is incredibly banal. Bodily movements during prayer are, of course, not unusual among the adherents of most religions.

In Modern Thought

The early reformers were much concerned about such questions as prayers for the restoration of sacrifices or the return to Zion, and whether prayer might be recited in the vernacular. Very few challenges, however, were presented to the idea of prayer as such in its traditional understanding. In the 20th century, Jewish thinkers began to consider the basic philosophical problems surrounding prayer. Petitionary prayer was felt to be especially difficult in the light of scientific views regarding cause and effect. A definite move away from the idea of prayer as a means of influencing God and toward its function as a way to affect man's attitudes can be observed. "Self-expression before God in prayer has thus a double effect; it strengthens faith in God's love and kindness, as well as in His all-wise and all-bountiful prescience. But it also chastens the desires and feelings of man, teaching him to banish from his heart all thoughts of self-seeking and sin, and to raise himself toward the purity and the freedom of the divine will and demand" (K. Kohler, *Jewish Theology* (1918), 275).

The tendency in some circles to reinterpret the God-idea itself in impersonal terms has cast prayer into a different light. It is seen as an attempt by man to attune himself to those powers in the universe which make for human self-fulfillment and as a reaching out to the highest within his own soul. Defenders of the traditional view of God and of prayer to Him have, however, not been lacking. (See *Proceedings of the Rabbinical Assembly of America*, 17 (1953), 151–238, for these two opinions).

[Louis Jacobs]

Women and Prayer

Biblical examples of female prayer include the songs of Miriam (Ex. 15:20–21) and Deborah (Judg. 5:1–31). Hannah's entreaty at Shiloh (I Sam. 2) became the rabbinic exemplar of supplicatory prayer for women and men (Ber. 31a–b).

Although Berakhot 20a–b is clear that women are obligated to pray (since prayer is a supplication "for mercy," necessary for all), rabbinic Judaism exempted women from communal prayers which were to be recited at specific times. Women's prayer was to follow the spontaneous model of Hannah's worship from the heart and could be uttered at any time and in any language (Sot. 32a–33a). However, rabbinic literature has little to say about the content of women's personal worship. Some authorities have claimed that women were not obligated in rabbinic time-bound commandments, including prayer, because regular synagogue attendance would interfere with their primary domestic roles. However, women not responsible for home and family were also exempt from communal prayer. Others have suggested that women were not obligated in time-bound public rituals because, like slaves and minors, they are of subordinate status: In the system of rabbinic Judaism, male heads of households perform religious acts on behalf of women, children, and other dependents under their aegis.

An exception to Judaism's normative exemption of women from participation in communal prayer occurred in medieval Ashkenaz, between the 11th and 13th centuries, when Jewish women's central roles in economic and social life, coupled with a concurrent religious revival in Christian Europe, empowered women to demand more significant participation in Jewish worship (Grossman, *Pious and Rebellious …*). This included fulfilling time-bound positive commandments such as shaking the *lulav* and sitting in a *sukkah* as well as regular participation in synagogue worship on the Sabbath and holidays. Medieval rabbis, among them R. Jacob *Tam, permitted these innovations. A century later, some Ashkenazi sages agreed to include women in the quorum of three or ten needed for the invitation to recite grace after meals. *Dulcea of Worms (d. 1196), wife of R. *Eleazar of Worms (the Roke'aḥ), was one of a number of Ashkenazi women, including Richenza and Urania, described by contemporaries as serving as "prayer leaders of the women." These women stood in the women's section of the synagogue near a small window which was connected to the main sanctuary and repeated the cantor's prayers aloud so that the women could follow the service.

In East European synagogues of the early modern era, women called *firzogerin* (Yiddish for "foresayers") led prayers among women in the synagogue. Some may have composed **tkhines*, vernacular petitionary prayers written for and sometimes by women.

In the modern era, particularly in North America, gender issues in prayer have defined the differences among Jewish denominations. Nineteenth-century American Reform Judaism introduced a number of changes, including family pews, mixed choirs, and the confirmation ceremony (initially intended to replace the bar mitzvah), directed at reducing women's inequality in prayer. Penina *Moise of Charleston, South Carolina, was the author of America's first Jewish hymnal, published in 1842; many of her contributions were used in Reform worship well into the 20th century.

Women's roles in prayer in Conservative Judaism were circumscribed until the 1950s, when the Committee on Jewish Law and Standards first raised the possibility of women being called to the Torah. By the 1980s and 1990s, after Jewish feminists agitated for change, women were counted in the *minyan* and called to the Torah in a majority of Conservative synagogues. Havurot (prayer and study groups without professional clergy, which arose in the 1960s) promoted egalitarian worship and opportunities for women's religious leadership. The Reconstructionist movement established gender equality as a founding principle. By the late 20th century, Orthodox women also expanded traditional roles by forming women's prayer groups where women led services, read the Torah, and celebrated life cycle passages. However, such groups did not say those prayers for which a *minyan* is required. By the first decade of the 21st century, new prayer communities in Israel and North America included women as much as possible in traditional worship. In these prayer groups, a *meḥizah* separates men and women but divides the room evenly between them. With a traditional *minyan* of ten men (or, in some cases, ten men and ten women), women lead certain parts of the service (the introductory morning blessings and the prayers welcoming the Sabbath) and fully participate in the Torah service, including reading from the Torah.

In the last quarter of the 20th century, feminism had a significant impact on Reform, Conservative, and Reconstructionist liturgies. Changes included eliminating references to the community of worshipers as male and adding the names of the matriarchs to those contexts in which the patriarchs were traditionally invoked. Other innovations focused on gender neutral ways to address God, using both English translations and new Hebrew epithets such as *Mekor ha-Ḥayyim* ("Source of Life").

In the last decades of the 20th century, women also constructed new prayers and rituals for events in their lives not previously sanctified in Judaism, such as onset of menstruation, pregnancy, childbirth, weaning children, and menopause. Others created liturgical roles for women and girls in traditional lifecycle passages, such as egalitarian wedding ceremonies, lesbian commitment ceremonies, and rituals acknowledging separation and divorce. Healing ceremonies addressed women's pain and losses from violence and abuse, illness, miscarriage, infertility, abortion. Other life cycle innovations, such as bat mitzvah and *simḥat bat* (baby naming/covenant ceremonies), were female complements to existing rituals centered on males.

[Susan Sapiro (2nd ed.)]

BIBLIOGRAPHY: K. Kohler, *The Psalms and Their Place in the Liturgy* (1897); A. Greiff, *Das Gebet im Alten Testament* (1915); F. Heiler, *Das Gebet* (1923); A. Wendel, *Das freie Laiengebet im vorexilischen Israel* (1932); Idelsohn, Liturgy; P.A.H. de Boer, in: OTS, 3 (1943); S.H. Blank, in: HUCA, 21 (1948), 331–54; 32 (1961), 75–90; idem, *Jeremiah, Man and Prophet* (1961), 92–93, 105ff., 234ff.; F. Hesse, *Die Fuerbitte im Alten Testament* (1951); M.D. Goldmann, in: *Australian Biblical Review*, 3 (1953), 1ff.; D.R. Ap-Thomas, in: *Scottish Journal of Theology*, 9 (1956), 422–9; idem, in: VT, 3 (1956), 225–41; J. Scharbert, in: *Theologie und Glaube*, 50 (1960), 321–38; J. Has-Paecker, in: *Bibel und Leben*, 2 (1961), 81–92, 157–70; E.A. Speiser, in: JBL, 82 (1963), 300–6; H. Ḥamiel (ed.), *Ma'yanot* (1964); H.A. Broncers, in: ZAW, 77 (1965), 1–20; L. Krinetzki, *Israels Gebet im Alten Testament* (1905); A. Gonzáles, *La oración en la Biblia* (1968); M. Kadushin, *Worship and Ethics: A Study in Rabbinic Judaism* (1964); R. Schatz-Uffenheimer, in: *Studies in… Gershom G. Scholem* (1967), 317–36. **ADD. BIBLIOGRAPHY:** R. Biale, *Women and Jewish Law* (1984); J. Baskin, *Midrashic Women* (2002); M. Bar-Ilan. *Some Jewish Women in Antiquity* (1998); T. Cohen, "Women's Spiritual Alternatives," in: J. Harlow et. al., *Pray Tell: A Hadassah Guide to Jewish Prayer* (2003); S.B. Fishman, *A Breath of Life* (1995); A. Grossman, *Pious and Rebellious: Jewish Women in Medieval Europe* (2004); J. Hauptman, *Rereading the Rabbis* (1998); D. Orenstein (ed.), *Lifecycles* (1998); S. Grossman and R. Haut (eds.), *Daughters of the King* (1992). **WEBSITE:** www.dnoam.org (Darkhei Noam); http://www.geocities.com/shira_hadasha/.

PRAYER BOOKS. Books containing the texts of the customary daily prayers did not exist in ancient times. Sources of tannaitic and amoraic times take it as understood that prayer is by heart (e.g., Ber. 5:3–5; RH 4:5–6; Ta'an. 2:2). In public prayer the reader prayed aloud before the congregation, which responded "*amen*" to the blessings. The writing down of the text of blessings and prayers was considered forbidden ("writers of blessings are [like] those who burn the Torah," Tosef. to Shab. 13:4; Shab. 115b; TJ, Shab. 16:1, 15c). After the completion of the Talmud, however, this prohibition was disregarded, and in the geonic era written prayer books undoubtedly existed already (L. Ginzberg, *Geonica*, 1 (1909), 119ff.). In Babylon it was permitted, at first, to use them only on the Day of Atonement, and on other fast days, but later they were permitted generally. This development was complete at the beginning of the eighth century. The Cairo *Genizah* has preserved fragments of prayer books both from Ereẓ Israel and the countries bordering it from this period (see *Liturgy).

Siddur and Maḥzor

The book that included the regular prayers for the whole year was called *seder (siddur) tefillah* – a name fixed by the *geonim* themselves – or, according to the cycle of the year, *maḥzor* (i.e., the cycle of prayers). At first there was no difference between the two names, and in the early period (in certain communities, until the present time) they were used indiscriminately. In the course of time the additions for special days (i.e., the *piyyutim*) were also included. However, the present Ashkenazi custom (and, through their influence, that of certain Sephardi communities as well) to differentiate between the *siddur* (pl. *siddurim*) – containing only the regular prayers – and the *maḥzor* (pl. *maḥzorim*) – containing also the *piyyutim*, in most cases only those of the festivals – came into being at a very late period, and is without foundation. The (Arabic-speaking) Jews of Yemen call the comprehensive *siddur, Tikhlal*. All the *siddurim* that have been preserved are designed for a particular rite. In the manuscripts there are a greater number of rites than those of the countries or the cities which finally came to be established or which later reached publication.

Early Siddurim

The beginnings of the order of prayer are found in the second part of tractate *Soferim*, which is a compilation from the period of the first *geonim*.

SEDER RAV AMRAM GAON. The first true prayer book, however, is the *Seder Rav Amram Gaon* from the ninth century. This prayer book (compiled at the request of the Jews of Spain) contains the regular prayers, according to the order of the whole year – weekdays, Sabbath, New Moon, fast days, Ḥanukkah, Purim, and all the festivals – together with the relevant *halakhot* preceding each section. At the end are the *benedictions and special prayers for occasions such as marriage, circumcision, redemption of the firstborn, and the burial service. Unfortunately this text of the prayers cannot serve as an authentic source for the custom of the *geonim* since all the extant manuscripts of this *seder* differ greatly from one another, in accordance with the rite of the copyist (ed. by N.N. Coronel, 1865, A.L. Frumkin in 1912, partially by D. Hedegård, 1951).

SIDDUR SAADIAH GAON. The *Siddur Saadiah Gaon*, which was written 100 years later, and which also contains the relevant *halakhot* along with the text of the prayers – the former written in Arabic for the benefit of the Jews of Egypt – is apparently, in the sole extant manuscript (ed. by I. Davidson, S. Assaf, and B.I. Joel, 1941), the rite of the Babylonian *geonim* (with some influence of the rite of Egypt). In contrast the *Genizah* fragments of the *siddur* contain the text of the prayers in a different and adapted version. The logical, methodical order of this prayer book, however, which differs from the ordinary calendar order, was not generally accepted (except by Maimonides); its order possibly explains as well the limited circulation of this *siddur*. Another prayer book compiled in the 11th century by *Hai b. Sherira Gaon, has been lost except for some quotations from it in halakhic literature.

The work entitled *Siddur Rashi*, which emerged in the 11th/12th centuries from the school of *Rashi (ed. by S. Buber, 1911), does not contain the text of the prayers at all, but only the halakhic material, with full talmudic treatment. Also the *Seder ha-Tefillot* that *Maimonides (12th century) attached to his *Mishneh Torah* is not a true prayer book but a collection of versions of prayers from which it is possible to compile a *siddur*; his rite is apparently that current in Egypt in his time, very different from that of the Spanish Jews; it was also adopted in Yemen.

MAḤZOR VITRY. In contrast to these works, the *Maḥzor Vitry, compiled in the 11th century by *Simḥah b. Samuel of Vitry, a pupil of Rashi, is a prayer book in the full sense of the word. It contains the text of all the regular prayers, in accordance with the rite of northern France, which is close to that of Germany. The laws of prayer precede each section in great detail. In the halakhic part, which is mainly consistent with the *Siddur Rashi*, large sections have been copied from the *Seder Rav Amram Gaon*, but later *geonim* are also cited. The edition of S. Hurwitz, published in 1889–93, is based on a London manuscript, amplified by additions of the 13th and 14th centuries. Besides the regular prayers, the *Maḥzor Vitry* includes only a limited number of *piyyutim*, namely *ma'arivim* and *hoshanot*; added to it are the Passover *Haggadah* and the prayers for Simḥat Torah; it lacks all the *kerovot* (which were, however, already in use at that time), and thus cannot be regarded as a complete *maḥzor*. It seems, however, that this format came about through a certain logic; beginning with the Middle Ages, prayer books were copied mostly in a small format for individual use, and it was usual among Germans and French to include in them *ma'arivim* and *hoshanot*, while the *maḥzorim* including the *kerovot*, mainly in large format (folio), were designed for the cantors. The prayer books themselves, apart from a few differences in text, do not differ from one another in their scope. The sole difference is in the laws of the prayers, which are sometimes brought at length and sometimes briefly. In place of the full talmudic explanation of the themes and the discussion of the various opinions found in the *Seder Rav Amram Gaon* and the *Maḥzor Vitry*, the final ruling alone came to be given.

MANUSCRIPTS FROM OTHER RITES. From this period prayer books of other rites have also been preserved (see *Liturgy) in manuscript: those of the Jews of Italy (*Roman Maḥzor*) mainly in small folio format, and also of the Jews of the Balkans, and of the Jews of Spain, mostly in quarto. Among the Jews of Yemen (where there was no printing press at all) the writing of prayer books continued (mostly *Tikhlalim* in small folio) until the beginning of the 20th century. This wealth of manuscripts, most of which are in the large libraries, has not yet been fully exploited for scientific editions and for research into the history of the text. There is still no critical text of any of the well-known rites constructed out of the actual texts in the manuscripts.

Commentaries on the text of the prayers began simultaneously with the composition of the ancient prayer books. In the prayer books of the *geonim* there is as yet no explanation of the texts of the prayers but the *Maḥzor Vitry* contains explanations of a number of prayers, such as *Kaddish*, **Nishmat Kol Ḥai*, *hoshanot*, and the Passover *Haggadah*. The greatest rabbinic authorities, such as Rashi, Joseph *Caro, *Eliezer b. Nathan of Mainz (Raban), *Ephraim b. Jacob of Bonn, Baruch the father of *Meir of Rothenburg, Judah he-Ḥasid of Regensburg, *Eleazar b. Judah of Worms, author of *Ha-Rokeʾaḥ* (see Abraham b. Azriel, *Arugat ha-Bosem*, ed. by E.E. Urbach, 4 (1963), introd., passim), participated in the exposition of the prayer books. Their comments were transmitted anonymously from place to place and passed into the customary manuscript expositions, and then into print in the margins of the *siddurim* and *maḥzorim*.

Printed Prayer Books

With the advent of printing, prayer books for different customs, both *maḥzorim* for the whole year as well as *siddurim* in small format for use of the individual, were printed. Among the *incunabula there are already many prayer books (see A. Freimann, *Thesaurus Typographiae Hebraicae Saecue*; XV, Suppl. to pt. 1, 1967–69; list of incunabula). Prayer books of the Roman rite were published first (*Maḥzor Roma*, Soncino-Casalimaggiore 1485/86; *Siddur Katan* called "Sidorello," 1486), then those of the Spanish rite (*Seder Tefillot*, 1490). Printed Spanish and Portuguese books have come down only in fragments. In the 16th century, German and Polish prayer books were published (*maḥzorim*, beginning with 1521, 1522, and *siddurim*, about 1508), and those of the Romaniot custom (*maḥzorim*, from 1510, *siddurim*, later still). Prayer books for the communities of southern France were not printed until the 18th century (*Maḥzor* Avignon 1765–66, Carpentras 1739–62), while the *Tikhlal* of the Yemenite Jews was published only at the end of the 19th century (Jerusalem, 1894–98). Certain categories of prayers such as *seliḥot* and *kinot* for the Ninth of *Av were printed long ago in special editions (e.g., *seliḥot* according to the German custom, Soncino 1496; *kinot* for the Ninth of Av according to the Polish custom, Cracow 1584), although in the main they were also incorporated in the *maḥzorim*.

Types of Prayer Books

In the course of time the following types of prayer book became established among Ashkenazi Jews:

(1) *Ha-Maḥzor ha-Gadol* in folio (also called *Kol Bo*), containing, according to the ancient custom, all the prayers of the year – weekday, Sabbath, festivals, and special days;

(2) the so-called *Maḥzor*, which included only the festival prayers, usually a separate volume for each festival;

(3) the small *siddur*, containing only the regular prayers;

(4) *Ha-Siddur ha-Shalem*, completed by the addition of the *yoẓerot* for the special Sabbaths, the *hoshanot*, *seliḥot* for fast days, *maʿarivim* for the nights of the festivals, and supplemented at times by the Book of Psalms and *maʿamarot*.

The Sephardi Jews, on the other hand, arrived at the following subdivision:

(1) *Tefillat ha-Ḥodesh*, comprising the prayers for weekdays, Sabbath, the New Moon, Ḥanukkah, and Purim;

(2) *Moʿadim*, consisting of the prayers for the three pilgrim festivals;

(3) *Rosh Ha-Shanah*, for the New Year;

(4) *Kippur* for the Day of Atonement;

(5) *Taʿaniyyot*, which also included the Ninth of Av and its *kinot*.

Only the Jews of Italy and Yemen maintained the original form of the *Maḥzor ha-Shanah*, which contained all the prayers in cyclical order; small *siddurim* were, however, also published by them.

Textual Editions

As to the text of the regular prayers, the *siddur* of the Sephardi Jews was edited in the 16th century in accordance with the "intentions" (**kavvanah*) of Isaac *Luria; as a result hardly any pre-Lurianic prayer books are extant. In many editions they made the divine names conform with the Lurianic "intentions" by a different pointing or by interlacing the ineffable name with various forms of the word *Adonai*. The text of the Ashkenazi *siddur* occupied several scholars, particularly in the 17th to 19th centuries, who published the prayer book in new editions or wrote books in which they justified substantiation or amendment of the text: Naḥman Lieballer (Dyhrenfurth, 1690); Azriel and his son, Elijah of Vilna (*Derekh Siʾaḥ ha-Sadeḥ*, Frankfurt on the Main, 1704); Solomon Zalman Katz Hanau (*Kunteres Shaʿarei Tefillah* and the ed. *Beit Tefillah*, Jesnitz, 1725); Jacob Emden (Yaveẓ; *Luʾaḥ Eresh*, an appendix to his prayer book, Altona, 1769); Mordecai Duesseldorf (*Kunteres Hassagot al Siddur Shaʿarei Tefillah*, published after his death, at Prague in 1784); Isaac Satanow (*Va-Yeʿetar Yiẓḥak*, Berlin 1785, who polemicizes with all his predecessors); Judah Leib Ben Zeʾev (*Tikkunei ha-Tefillah*, published after his death with the edition *Tefillah Zakkah*, Vienna, 1816); Wolf Heidenheim (*Siddur Safah Berurah* with notes at several points, Roedelheim, 1806). In the course of time Heidenheim's text was accepted as a sort of standard text. All disputes about the text, however, turn on such grammatical niceties as the insertion of a *dagesh* or *meteg* and matters of pointing, and only very rarely on establishing the text. In the case of Heidenheim, particularly, and those following him, it should be pointed out that they preferred, to too great an extent, the language of the Bible to Mishnaic Hebrew.

Critical Editions

Critical treatment of the prayer book begins with the activity of E.L. Landshuth who contributed to the *Siddur Hegyon Lev* (published by Z.H. Edelmann, 1845) the commentary *Mekor Berakhah*, in which he consistently gathered the sources of the prayers and tried to establish the date of their compilation and composition. This method was continued by W. Jawitz (*Mekor ha-Berakhot*, 1910), A. Berliner (*Randbemerkungen zum taeglichen Gebetbuch*, 2 vols., 1909–12), and S. Elbogen (*Der juedische Gottesdienst*, 1913, 1931^3).

Commentaries

Commentaries to the prayer book appeared in fairly large numbers, and it is impossible to mention here even an appropriate part of them. The old commentaries, based upon manuscript commentaries, were printed in the folio editions of *maḥzorim* (e.g., *Hadrat Kodesh*, Venice, 1554, et al.; *Ma'gelei Ẓedek*, Venice 1588, et al.; to the *maḥzor* of Rome, *Kimḥa de-Avshuna*, Bologna 1540). There are commentaries with a kabbalistic approach (like that of Lipmann *Muehlhausen, in *Siddur Dikduk Tefillah*, Thiengen 1560; the *Sha'ar ha-Shamayim* of Isaiah *Horowitz, Amsterdam 1717; *Beit Tefillah*, with the commentary of Isaac Luria and Moses *Zacuto to the Sephardi *siddur*, Amsterdam 1712, et al.; and the *siddur Ha-Gra* of *Elijah b. Solomon, the Gaon of Vilna, Jerusalem 1895). Other commentaries deal more with explanations of the words and themes, such as *Beit-El Sha'ar ha-Shamayim* (Altona, 1745/47) of Jacob Emden, though here too comments of an esoteric nature are intermingled; *Iyyun Tefillah* (1857) of Jacob Ẓevi Meklenburg: *Avodat Yisrael* (1868) of Isaac Seligman *Baer, containing sources of the prayers, many notes on grammatical topics, and comparisons of the texts of different rites, as well as a short exposition of the *seliḥot* and *yoẓerot; Ishei Yisrael* (c. 1900) following the rite of Elijah b. Solomon, with two commentaries – *Avnei Eliyahu* of Elijah Landau, and *Si'aḥ Yiẓḥak* of Isaac Malzan; *Oẓar ha-Tefillot* (1915, et al.) with the commentaries of A.L. Gordon and Enoch Zondel b. Joseph, to the sections of *piyyut*, too, and with a special section, "*Tikkun Tefillah*," on the textual variations – apparently the most complete prayer book; *Siddur Tefillah* (1912) with the commentaries "*Magen ha-Elef*" and "*Mekor ha-Berakhot*" of A.L. Frumkin (in his edition of the *Seder Rav Amram Gaon*); *Avodat ha-Levavot* (1922) with the commentary of Wolf Jawitz, dealing mainly with the dependence of the language of the prayer book upon that of the Bible; *Olat Re'iyyah* (1939–49), with the commentary of Abraham Isaac Kook; *Ẓelota de-Avraham* (1957–62), in accordance with the usage of Abraham Landau, rabbi of Czechanow (d. 1875), with the commentary of his grandson M.M.H. Landau, and with additional exposition by Jacob Werdiger, the latter's grandson, containing important studies of the sources of the prayers and of the various rites. To these should be added the commentary "*Ez Ḥayyim*" of Yaḥya b. Joseph Ẓelaḥ to the Yemenite *Tikhlal* (1894–98). The ancient connection between the text of the prayers and their laws was renewed in the 19th century when the *Derekh ha-Ḥayyim* (1828) of Jacob *Lorberbaum of Lissa and the *Nehora ha-Shalem* (1827) of Jehiel Michael of Michailishki (Vilna region), author of the *Korban Aharon* on the *maḥzor*, were accepted into the prayer books; both have been published innumerable times. The Sephardi Jews created similar editions for the use of their congregations, when they added to their prayer books the *Kesher Godel* (Leghorn, 1802) of Ḥ.J.D. Azulai, dealing with the laws of the prayers, and the *Shelemut ha-Lev* of an anonymous author.

Ḥasidic Siddurim

In the 18th century the Sephardi tradition with certain modifications was adopted by the ḥasidic communities of Poland and Russia. From that time on ḥasidic prayer books were published, i.e., Ashkenazi prayer books with the regular prayers adapted to the needs of the Ḥasidim. A careful editing of this version was executed by the founder of the Chabad ḥasidic sect, *Shneur Zalman of Lyady – he called this version specifically the Lurianic version (*Nosaḥ ha-Ari*). It was published and disseminated in many editions, in part enlarged by commentaries in the form of lectures to the Ḥasidim (Kapust, 1816, reprinted New York, 1965, with full printing history).

[Ernst Daniel Goldschmidt]

Modern Prayer Books (English Editions)

Mention should be made of some of the better known translations of the prayer books in English. The *Authorized Daily Prayer Book* (1890) by S. *Singer has been a standard for the English speaking world for many years. It went through many editions and by 1970 had sold nearly 500,000 copies (a revised edition was published in 1962). A companion to this prayer book was published by (1914) and an annotated edition by J.H. Hertz (1941) with the addition of occasional prayers. In the U.S. another version with notes was edited by P. *Birnbaum (*Daily Prayer Book* (1949, and many editions)), and the *High Holyday Prayerbook* (1951, and many editions). A prayer book that grew considerably in popularity in the 1990s was the ArtScroll Siddur. The best-known modern Sephardi prayer book and *maḥzor* were the ones edited by David de Sola *Pool.

Reform Prayer Books

Liturgical reform began in the practical sphere, with most of the attention being given to the external aspects of worship. During the initial stages the aesthetics of the synagogue service occupied the minds of the early Reformers more than the doctrinal content of the prayer book. The major emphasis as exemplified by the efforts of Israel *Jacobson, I.S. *Fraenkel, and M.I. *Bresselau, was placed on the form of worship rather than on serious grappling with theological issues. In 1810 Jacobson, a financier and philanthropist, provided a simplified, decorous service for boarding-school children in Seesen, and in 1815, opened a synagogue in Berlin in which he installed an organ and instituted the confirmation ceremony (see *Bar Mitzvah), while the editorial labors of Fraenkel and Bresselau created the Hamburg *Gebetbuch (Sefer ha-Avodah, Ordnung der oeffentilichen Andacht*, first ed. 1819). However, the more scholarly contributions of Wolf *Heidenheim's *"Mendelssohn des Gebetbuches"* (Elbogen) were not ignored by the early Reformers. The closing pages of the Hamburg volume contain learned notes citing dissenting views in older sources that might lend support to Reform. Yet the emphases of the first Reformers were practical, and it was not until later that the burgeoning *Wissenschaft des Judentums*, as well as recent developments in Jewish theology, left their influence on the reformulated *siddur*. While the German Reform Rabbinical Conferences (1844–46) were in session, lending shape and direction to the amorphous variety of liturgical changes then in the making, the founders of the Berlin Reform community broke company and began to devise its own radical, predominantly German rite which limited the Hebrew to a few selected biblical verses. When the congregation secured Samuel *Holdheim as its spiritual leader, he was authorized to revamp its liturgical manuals. While keeping much of their dissentient character, Holdheim brought classical and traditional forms and recent liturgical research into greater play, thus moderating the excesses of the Reform community's ritual. D.W. Marks, a remarkably well-versed layman, edited *Seder ha-Tefillot – Forms of Prayer*, published in 1841–43. A spiritual offspring of the Hamburg *Gebetbuch*, the prayer book was used in the West London Synagogue of British Jews of which Marks was the spiritual leader. Although in the introduction the editor admits his debt to the scholarship of *Zunz, *Rapoport, and others, in actuality, he relied very little upon the content of their works. Rather Marks derived from these learned men the encouragement and inspiration for his own original endeavors. Unlike its continental counterparts, *Forms of Prayer* evinces an almost Karaitic scriptural fundamentalism. Marks imitates his Hamburg predecessors, however, in some choices of Hebrew prayers to be read in the vernacular, in shunning repetitions, in the offhand treatment of the *haftarah*, in slight abbreviations of the standard text, and in the partiality toward Sephardi *piyyutim*. Apart from occasional pseudo-Karaizing, *Forms of Prayers* may be said to stand in the Orthodox tradition. Only infrequently did Marks contribute original Hebrew compositions. These works were often written in a felicitous classical style, as in his unique *Birkat ha-Mo'adim* which replaces the festival additional service. The prayer books of the aforementioned Reform community were probably the first to pay particular attention to the theological principles underlying the prayer text and to make emendations accordingly. In line with his evolutionary view of Judaism, Abraham *Geiger was the first consistently to introduce Reform principles into the body of the traditional Hebrew text. Historical consciousness and theological integrity are the hallmarks of Geiger's liturgical works (the first edition of his prayer book was published in 1854) that became the major characteristics of the moderate Reform (Liberal) liturgy in Germany for nearly a century.

During the middle of the 19th century, German Jewish immigrants to the U.S. brought with them the liturgical reforms that were then emerging in Central Europe. The single formative influence to dominate all others was the Hamburg *Gebetbuch*. The principal U.S. prayer books of the day, Leo *Merzbacher's *Seder Tefillah – The Order of Prayer for Divine Service* (1855), David *Einhorn's *Olat Tamid – Book of Prayers for Israelitish Congregations* (1856), and Isaac M. *Wise's *Minhag Amerikah – The Daily Prayers for American Israelites* (1857), which varied in degree of reform, revealed the tastes and talents of their authors, and reflected the demands of their respective congregations, nevertheless, bore the stamp of the Hamburg *Gebetbuch*, the parent Reform prayer book. *Seder Tefillah, Olat Tamid*, and *Minhag Amerikah* contain similar treatments of *Ausheben* (*Hoẓa'at ha-Torah*) and have either the expanded Hamburg Mourner's Kaddish and/or an elaborate *Todtenfeier* (*Hazkarat Neshamot*) for the Day of Atonement, rendered almost entirely in the vernacular. (For sentiment's sake, Wise kept his German version even in his English translation). All of the prayer books have recourse to hymns from the Hamburg *Gesangbuch*. Each carries the Sephardi *hashkavah*, usually replacing *El Male Raḥamim* of Ashkenazi tradition, and all delete *Kol Nidrei* in favor of Leopold Stein's *O Tag des Herrn* ("O Day of God") or some other appropriate substitute. *Piyyutim* of Spanish-Portuguese origin take precedence over the more recondite and allusive Ashkenazi *piyyutim*. Influenced by a process already begun in the Hamburg rite, Einhorn progressed further than his German-American counterparts by making his ritual bilingual, although German predominated, especially in the new, protracted pieces recited by the rabbi in oratorical style. Merzbacher pared his Hebrew service to mishnaic simplicity and occasionally recast phrases or whole sections in unexceptionable Hebrew, saving the vernacular for extra-liturgical, non-statutory prayers and hymns. Both Merzbacher and Einhorn dropped the **Musaf*, the former, however, reserving it for the day-long worship on the *Day of Atonement. Wise, however, kept the order intact, concentrating chiefly on revising the text in accordance with Reform doctrine. (On rare occasions he permits himself such liberties as replacing the **Pesukei de-Zimra* on the festivals with the *Hallel* psalms and creating an unusual private service for *yahrzeit*.) All of these rites were incorporated in the most important Reform work of the following century, *The Union Prayer Book for Jewish Worship – Seder Tefilot Yisrael* (first ed. 1894–95). Of particular importance in the compilation of *The Union Prayer Book* were the transitional works of Adolph *Huebsch (e.g., his prayer book for Congregation Ahawath Chesed (1889) in New York, translated by A. Kohut) and Isaac S. *Moses. Huebsch combined Holdheim's work with Wise's *Minhag Amerikah*; while Moses combined *Seder Tefillah, Olat Tamid*, and later, Huebsch's synthesis as well. The end of the 19th century witnessed the writing of many new vernacular compositions. Some from predominantly English formularies, beginning with Joseph *Krauskopf's *The Service Ritual* (1888) and *The Service Manual* (1892), Gustav *Gottheil's *Morning Prayer* (1889), and Kaufmann *Kohler's *Sabbath Eve Service* (1891), found their way into the *Union Prayer Book*. After much weighing and harmonizing of texts, the result was an abbreviated and simplified liturgy with both languages kept in balance, interspersed with prayers and responses in the language of the country. The *Union Prayer Book* represents the cumulative efforts of the American Reform movement to achieve a uniform rite that would meet the needs of diverse congregations throughout the nation. The remarkable durability of the prayer book in its various editions testifies to the success of those efforts. Each edition mirrors changes in theological views and reflects the vicissitudes of the Jewish community both in the U.S. and abroad. The second edition (1922), for example, shows an increased interest in ceremonial life which hitherto had been substantially eliminated. Neither Merzbacher's volume nor Einhorn's contains the ritual *berakhot* for the blowing of the *shofar* or the kindling of the Ḥanukkah candles, whereas the second edition of the *Union Prayer Book* readmits them. The greater quality of the Hebrew in the revised 1940 edition attests to a heightened ethnic consciousness. Jewish group solidarity is expressed by the inclusion of Hebrew prayers from all eras and places, which enhance the diminished rabbinic *stammgebete* (regular prayers). The 1975 edition, *Shaarei Tefillah: The Gate of Prayer – The New Union Prayer Book* affirms Jewish tradition, culture, and nationhood in its choice of prayers and supplements. In the 1990s a gender-sensitive edition appeared as well.

OUTSIDE U.S. IN 20TH CENTURY. Reform in the U.S. was generally dependent upon Central European prototypes for doctrinal reformulations until the early 20th century, when American Reformers took the lead in liturgical renewal. Two cases in point, Caesar *Seligmann's *Israelitisches Gebetbuch* (1910) and the French Union Libérale Israélite's *Tefillot Kol ha-Shanah – Rituel des Prières Journalières* (1925), which take considerable liberties with the historical text and the directions for the performance of the ritual, were inspired by American models. While there is no slavish imitation – distinctively European requirements having been given attention – the desire to forestall monotony during the service by introducing variety and meaningful alternation of languages was substantially derived from the U.S. *The Liberal Jewish Prayer Book* (1923–26) by Israel I. *Mattuck, former U.S. Reform rabbi and a founder of English Liberal Judaism, displays unique and wide-ranging literariness. (The same disposition toward variety is maintained in *Avodat ha-Lev – Service of the Heart* (1967).) Largely influenced by the *Union Prayer Book*, the emended West London Synagogue's *Seder ha-Tefillot – Forms of Prayer* (1931) exhibits renewed appreciation for both traditional rabbinic arrangement and religious liberalism in being shorn of its eccentric and ostensibly fundamentalist character. This is seen in the selection of benedictions for the weekday *Amidah*, in the choice of the *Aleinu* text, and in the reinstitution of *berakhot* for rabbinic ordinances. The *Einheitsgebetbuch* (edited by C. Seligmann, I. Elbogen, and H. Vogelstein, 1929) deserves special mention not only because it appropriated a variety of texts from the *Union Prayer Book*, but, more significantly, because it succeeded in achieving unity among the Liberal congregations of Germany before World War II. This major accomplishment serves as a becoming *Memorbuch* to a decimated German Jewry.

Conservative and Reconstructionist Prayer Books

The Conservative and Reconstructionist manuals adhere to the classical outlines, although also constituting a departure from traditional Judaism, representing what J.J. *Petuchowski calls "Reform from within." *Maḥzor le-Shalosh Regalim – The Festival Prayer Book* (United Synagogue of America, 1927), a Conservative publication, is closer to the enlightened Orthodoxy of Hermann *Adler and Joseph H. *Hertz, former chief rabbis of Great Britain, than to any publication of the moderate Reform or proto-Conservative movement such as Benjamin *Szold's and Marcus *Jastrow's *Avodat Yisrael – Israelitish Prayer Book* (first ed. 1865), or Aaron Wise's *Shalhevet Yah – The Temple Service* (1891). A reason for this may lie in the Conservative movement's loyalty to Solomon *Schechter's motto "catholic Israel." Dependence upon the official British books can be seen in the use of the festival *piyyutim* and of the introductory memorial prayer at *Hazkarat Neshamot*. This anglophile penchant gave way approximately 20 years later to a more independent *Seder Tefillot Yisrael le-Shabbat u-le-Shalosh Regalim – Sabbath and Festival Prayer Book* (Rabbinical Assembly of America and United Synagogue of America, 1946), wherein a minimum of textual reforms are permitted as in some of the preliminary benedictions of the morning service and in the middle benediction of the additional service where *sham na'aseh ve-nakriv* is altered to *sham asu ve-hikrivu*. With unity of Conservative congregations their overriding aim, the editors were determined not to add unnecessarily to the plethora of variations on controverted texts. Among the more innovative features of the *Sabbath and Festival Prayer Book* are the supplementary readings and explanatory notes at the end of the volume. The most far-reaching of the Conservative liturgical publications in hard-cover is the *Siddur li-Ymot ha-Ḥol – Weekday Prayer Book* (1961). The editors introduce significant changes in wording to bring the prayers into closer harmony with the consensus of Conservative belief. Apart from obvious Zionist sentiment, the rewritten *Musaf* for the festivals and for Rosh Ḥodesh reads materially as a 19th-century German Liberal reconstruction. The 1985 Siddur *Sim Shalom* preserves much of the traditional liturgy while again addressing itself to contemporary concerns. It too came out with a gender-sensitive edition in the 1990s. The Reconstructionist *siddurim* (*Seder Tefillot le-Shabbat – Sabbath Prayer Book*, 1945; *Maḥzor le-Yamim Nora'im – High Holy Day Prayer Book*, 1948; *Festival Prayer Book*, 1958; and *Seder Tefillot li-Ymot ha-Ḥol – Daily Prayer Book*, 1963) also make extensive use of supplementary readings. Reconstructionist tenets, such as the denial of the idea of the Chosen People, and the diminution or deletion of supernatural and anthropomorphic references, set them apart from the Conservative prayer books.

Prayers for Contemporary Events

It has taken time for the events of World War II, the Holocaust, and the rebirth of the State of Israel to be fully comprehended and treated in adequate liturgical form, but none of the official prayer books of American Jewry alludes to any of these momentous happenings except the Reconstructionist *Daily Prayer Book*, and the Conservative *Siddur li-Ymot ha-Ḥol – Weekday Prayer Book* (1961), which includes a newly composed *Al ha-Nissim* for Israel Independence Day. That these events have not been forgotten is proven by the fact that individual congregations and communities mark these occasions by circulating mimeographed prayers, privately or locally printed. Because Europe was the battleground, the remnant of Progressive Jewish communities in Europe have already responded to this chain of circumstances. Virtually all of the latest European Liberal and Reform prayer books include at least an entreaty on behalf of the State of Israel. Within the last two decades, as the shock of the Holocaust has been absorbed and its implications assimilated, a number of new prayer books have been compiled both in Europe and in Israel that give proper weight to the twin experiences touching world Jewry. The majority of these prayer books show an awareness of the scope of tradition and clearly enunciate principles of 20th-century Reform (e.g., Zionism is obviously no longer the taboo it once was). A modern and uniform liturgy is beginning to emerge in which the mishnaic nucleus of the *Stammgebete* is preserved and the *Musaf* dismissed. Differences consist mainly in wording, in selections from the opening sections of the prayer book, i.e., *Birkhot ha-Shaḥar* and *Pesukei de-Zimra*, and in the length of individual prayers. Variety is emphasized even within this simplified and relatively fixed framework. Novel and unexpected developments have been taking place in the U.S., including experimentation with jazz, rock, and multi-media in the performance of the liturgy.

[Eric Lewis Friedland]

There have been many innovations by the Rabbinate in Israel with regard to certain events. The most extensive of these new prayers concerns Israel Independence Day (see Prayers for *Independence Day). In addition the Israel rabbinate has composed special prayers for Holocaust Remembrance day (Nisan 27) and for the day of general *yahrzeit* for victims of the Holocaust (Tevet 10). They have also produced special *El Male Raḥamim* prayers for victims of the Holocaust and for those who fell in the defense of the State of Israel, and special prayers on behalf of Soviet and Arab Jewry. The Israel Army Rabbinate composed a special *Tefillat ha-Derekh* for paratroopers (written by the Chief Chaplain Rabbi Shelomo *Goren). After the Six-Day War the religious kibbutz movement Ha-Kibbutz ha-Dati issued a new version of the *naḥem* prayer (which mourns the destruction of Jerusalem) recited on the Ninth of Av, emphasizing the opportunity to rebuild Jerusalem.

BIBLIOGRAPHY: GENERAL: Zunz, Ritus; Elbogen, Gottesdienst; Benjacob, Oẓar and Friedberg, Eked, s.v. titles of prayer books; JE, 10 (1907), 174 (list of principal prayer books); J.J. Cohen, in: S.D. Luzzatto, *Mavo le-Maḥzor Benei Roma*, ed. by E.D. Goldschmidt (1966), 105–36; Goldschmidt, in: *Sefunot*, 8 (1964), 207–36 (Romaniot rite). REFORM: Abrahams, Companion; S.S. Cohon, in: CCARY, 38 (1928), 246–70; M. Davis, *Emergence of Conservative Judaism* (1963); Elbogen, Gottesdienst; S.B. Freehof, in: *Reform Judaism: Essays…* (1949); E.L. Friedland, *Historical and Theological Development of Non-Orthodox Jewish Prayerbooks in the United States* (1967); E.D. Goldschmidt, in: YLBI, 2 (1957), 119–35; J. Heinemann, *Ha-Tefillah bi-Tekufat ha-Tanna'im ve-ha-Amora'im* (1966^2); Idelsohn, Liturgy; B. Italiener, in: HUCA, 26 (1955), 413–24; J.J. Petuchowski, *Prayerbook Reform in Europe* (1968); D. Philipson, *Reform Movement in Judaism*; G.W. Plaut, *Growth of Reform Judaism* (1931); idem, *Rise of Reform Judaism* (1963); M. Silverman, in: *Proceedings of the Rabbinical Assembly of America*, 4 (1933), 322–43. **ADD. BIBLIOGRAPHY:** N. Wieder, *The Formation of Jewish Liturgy in the East and the West*, 2 vols. (Heb.; 1998).

PREACHING.

In the Talmudic Period

NATURE AND PURPOSE OF THE SERMON. The sermon, delivered in the synagogue or in the house of study, mainly on Sabbaths and festivals, is a very ancient institution. Nothing is known of its beginnings. It may have originated in the *Targum, i.e., the translation of the lections from Scripture into the Aramaic vernacular for the benefit of those who could not follow the Hebrew reading. The Targum in days of old was paraphrastic and the biblical texts were embellished with much aggadic material. Eventually, the Targum was curtailed and additions to the text were no longer allowed (Tosef., Meg. 4:41). Its former function of instruction and edification was then taken over by the sermon. By the end of the Second Temple period, sermons were a well-established custom both in Palestine and in the Diaspora.

The importance of the sermon can hardly be overestimated. Not only did it serve as the chief means of instructing all the people – peasants, women, and children – and imparting to all and sundry at least an elementary knowledge of the Torah and its teachings, but it also provided the sages with a means of guiding the people, strengthening their faith, and refuting heretical views.

By using at times daring methods of interpretation, the preachers succeeded in making the Bible an unceasing source of ever-new meaning and inspiration in which answers to the problems of every generation could be found. Thus when the unquestionable biblical faith in the rewards of the righteous in this life could no longer satisfy the people in times of disasters and persecutions, the rabbis would unhesitatingly substitute for it the belief of reward in the world to come: "He has given food unto them that fear Him, He will ever be mindful of His covenant" (Ps. 111:5) became – by means of a play on the words *teref*, "food," and *teruf*, "confusion" – "He has given confusion to those who fear Him in this world; but in the future to come He will ever be mindful of His covenant" (Gen. R. 40:2). To the outcry of those who witnessed the destruction of the Temple, and who, on reading such a verse as "Who is like unto Thee, O Lord, among the mighty?" (Ex. 15:11) would ask: "Where then is His might, if he looks on while His Temple is destroyed and keeps silent?" The rabbis answered: "Who is like unto Thee among the mute ones" (a play on the words אֵילִים, *elim*, "the mighty ones," and אִלְּם, *illem*, "mute"). The explanation was: "His very restraint and silence is the proof of His strength and power: for who is mighty? He who conquers his passions!" (TJ, Ber. 7:4, 11c; Mekh., Shira, 8; Yoma 69b; Avot 4:1).

THE SERMON AND AUDIENCE. Through their reinterpretations of the Bible, their bold use of the biblical material to give expression to the burning issues of their own times, and the application of ancient traditions to new circumstances, the rabbis succeeded in keeping the Bible alive and meaningful for their own generations.

Entertaining Devices Used in Sermons. In addition to the use of exegesis, the preachers would amplify and recreate stories, would enliven their preaching by ample use of folktales and parables, and employ dramatization and various rhetorical means to make their sermons attractive and challenging. They would modulate their voices in presenting dialogues and imitate the different characters represented. The "entertainment value" of the sermon was often no less important than its educational and edifying aspects. Some critics indeed compared the Jewish preachers to actors whose "performances" were too "theatrical" for their liking. Small wonder then that the people would come in masses to hear sermons, especially of well-known preachers (TJ, Hor. 3:7, 48b). They would come even from outlying villages, and would make special arrangements beforehand to permit them to exceed the "Sabbath-limit" of 2,000 cubits (Er. 3:5).

The rabbis contrasted the synagogues and the houses of study and their sermons with the attractions of the circus and of the theater of the Roman-Hellenistic world. Remarkably enough, they succeeded in making the bulk of the people prefer the former: "They that sit in the gate talk of me" (Ps. 69:13) was given two different interpretations: "those are the gentiles who sit in their theaters and circuses … scoffing me"; and "those are Israel who sit in the synagogues and houses of study … reading dirges and lamentations and *Eikhah*" (Lam. R., Proem 17). However, the well-to-do would, at times, stay away from such "vulgar" gatherings (Git. 38b). The audience expressed their approval and enjoyment; at times, they reacted with laughter, or, when the preacher did not succeed in arousing them, with indifference. The preachers would adapt their interpretations and examples to the level of the audience, and when addressing simple people they would not refrain from using very telling, even ribald, phrases or illustrations (Lev. R. 18:1; S. Lieberman, *Greek in Jewish Palestine* (1942), 161–2). The popularity of the aggadic sermon emerges clearly from the following statement: "In times of old when the *perutah* [a small coin] was easy to come by, a man would desire to hear words of Mishnah and of Talmud; but now when the *perutah* is no longer easily found, and moreover we are suffering from the kingdom [i.e., Roman rule], a man desires to hear words of Scripture and words of *aggadah*" (PdRK 101b).

Time of Delivery of Sermon. Sermons were delivered, whenever possible, on every Sabbath and on other special occasions, including fast days, especially on the Ninth of *Av. They would be based mostly on the Torah sections read on the days when they were delivered, i.e., the *sidra* of the so-called *triennial cycle on ordinary Sabbaths and the special lections on festivals. On special Sabbaths (e.g., before and after the Ninth of Av), the prophetic readings might provide the texts for the homilies. The exact time of the sermon varied. It is known that there were sermons delivered on Friday nights (TJ, Sot. 1:4, 16d), on Sabbath mornings after the readings from Scripture (Luke 4:16ff.), or on Sabbath afternoons (Yal. Prov. 964). It appears that many sermons were given before the scriptural readings, serving as introductions to, and preparations for, the latter (see below). Probably, such sermons were rather brief.

The Preacher. If one of the great sages delivered the sermon, he would make his appearance only after the whole audience had assembled; in the meantime, younger rabbis, acting as auxiliary preachers, would keep the people occupied (TJ, Suk. 5:1, 55a; Gen. R. 98:11; but also Deut. R. 7:8). The preacher made use of a *turgeman* ("translator"), or of several, whose task it was to broadcast the words of the preacher in a loud voice which could be heard by all sections of the audience. This served not so much a practical purpose, for some of the preachers at least must have had voices powerful enough to make themselves heard, but was a token of respect (I.M. Kosowsky, in *Sinai*, 45 (1959), 233 – 43). The preacher would take care to prepare his sermon properly; but in some places, at least, it was customary for members of the audience to address questions to him which he was expected to answer on the spot. Some inexperienced preachers found this custom disconcerting and were unable to reply (Gen. R. 81:2).

The Openings of Sermons. The sections opening with a halakhic question, preceded by the formula *yelammedenu rabbenu* ("may our master teach us") or the like, which appear at the beginning of homilies, especially in the **Tanḥuma* Midrashim, reflect the custom of introducing a sermon by a question posed by a member of the audience. The challenge to the preacher was not so much in finding the answer – for mostly the questions referred to well-known *halakhot* – but to improvise a way of linking up both the question and the answer with the real subject matter of his sermon, concerned usually with an aggadic interpretation of the Bible reading for the day. It is, however, quite possible that often the question posed to the preacher had been prompted and was known to him beforehand.

FORMS OF THE SERMON. Though the "classical" Midrashim undoubtedly drew the bulk of their material from the tens of thousands of sermons which had actually been preached in the synagogues of Palestine during the first four or five centuries C.E., they have hardly ever preserved these sermons in their original form. In many cases, they present mere outlines of actual sermons or of parts of them, while, on the other hand, they take sections from many separate sermons and weld them into new and larger units.

The Proem Type. One of the rhetorical forms, found frequently in practically all of the old Midrashim, the proem (*petiḥta*), undoubtedly had its origin in the live sermon. It opened with a quotation from Scripture, not taken from the text read on that day, but mostly from the Hagiographa. Through a series of aggadic interpretations and stories, the quotation was gradually linked up with the first verse of the pericope (or the prophetic lesson) of the day. Often, the preacher intentionally chose a verse which seemed completely unconnected with the weekly portion so as to arouse the curiosity of the audience and increase its interest. Sometimes the connection would be established by means of a play on words or similar rhetorical device. Nearly always, the opening verse chosen expressed a general idea which was subsequently illustrated by the specific example provided by the contents of the pericope. Such proems served originally either as opening sections of complete sermons (according to Maybaum, Bacher) or, more likely, were sermons complete in themselves (according to Bloch, Baeck) and were preached, presumably, immediately before the readings from Scripture, serving as introductions to the latter (Heinemann).

Other Types. But the proem type was by no means the only kind of sermon in vogue. Apart from the *yelammedenu* form, already mentioned, there were sermons opening with a form of benediction, praising God for giving Torah to Israel, and proceeding from this to the specific theme to be developed (J. Heinemann, *Ha-Tefillah bi-Tekufat ha-Tanna'im ve-ha-Amora'im* (1964), 160 – 2). Undoubtedly, other sermons took for their point of departure the first verse of the weekly portion itself; the section in *Mekhilta*, beginning with "And Moses took the bones of Joseph with him" (Ex. 13:19), may serve as an example of this type. Another type of opening of the sermon has been preserved in passages in which the first verse of the pericope is immediately followed by a reference to a verse elsewhere, in the light of which the former is interpreted, e.g., "'Then came Amalek'... This verse is to be ... explained in connection with the passage in Job where it is said 'Can the rush shoot up without mire ...'"(Mekh., Amalek, 1 beginning).

Conclusions of Sermons. The concluding sections of homilies in the Midrashim mostly sound the messianic theme, contrasting the suffering and the troubles of "this world" with the joys of "the world to come." It stands to reason that these sections also represent perorations of actual sermons. Other sermons appear to have ended in prayers which expressed either thanks to God for the giving of the Torah or a request for the speedy coming of redemption or both (Heinemann, loc. cit.). One example of such a concluding prayer is the **Kaddish*.

Example of a Complete Sermon. One of the few sermons whose entire structure appears to have been preserved (though probably only in outline) is the one by R. Tanḥum of Nevay (Shab. 30a–b): It starts with the halakhic question of whether one may extinguish a light on the Sabbath for the sake of a person dangerously ill. It then proceeds to discuss the relation of life and death on the basis of scriptural quotations, illustrating its argument with poignant stories from the lives of David and Solomon and making the point, among others, that even one day in the lives of the righteous is of supreme value in the eyes of God. It concludes by answering the question posed at the beginning that man's soul "is the lamp of the Lord" (Prov. 20:27) and it is better that a lamp made by man be extinguished on the Sabbath rather than the soul (life), the lamp made by God. In form this sermon is unique, for in spite of its affinities with the *yelammedenu* type, it differs from it by placing the answer to the halakhic question at the conclusion of the entire sermon.

HOMILIES IN THE MIDRASHIM. It follows that in different times and places sermons exhibited a variety of structures and patterns. Against this, in the so-called homiletic Midrashim all homilies are constructed more or less in a uniform pattern: after a series of proems there follows the "body" of the sermon (whose structure is not clearly defined), and finally the messianic peroration (Lev. R.; PdRK). In Midrashim of the *Tanḥuma-yelammedenu* type, the parts mentioned are preceded by the section opening with a halakhic question. Such homilies do not represent single, actual sermons as preached in public. Even if the proems are considered to be mere opening sections, no preacher would have used a whole series of such introductions, independent of one another, consecutively, in order to arrive again and again at the same point which he had already reached with the first one, i.e., the first verse of the pericope. Hence these homilies must be taken as creations of the editors of the Midrashim who made use of a number of sections, especially proems, taken from different sermons, and combined them into a new form, the "literary homily," which must not be confused with the actual live sermon as preached in the synagogue (in a variety of forms).

J. Mann developed a highly ingenious theory that both the halakhic question (in the *yelammedenu* type of homily) and the Bible verses with which the proems open were chosen for the sake of verbal tallies to the prophetic reading (*haftarah*) for the day. Thus a system of associations with the *haftarah* provides the hidden links between the various sections of the sermon (even though the *haftarah* itself is not quoted, as a rule). Pertinent objections to this theory have been raised by S. Lieberman (*Kovez̦ Madda'i le-Zekher M. Schorr* (1944), 186) and by Ḥ. Albeck (Zunz-Albeck, Derashot, 473–4, n. 180). Among the weaknesses of Mann's hypothesis is the fact that associations consisting of a mere verbal link – provided often by very common words – could presumably be discovered in practically all cases, even if they had not been intended. What is more, where the required tally with the known *haftarah* cannot be found, Mann unhesitatingly stipulates a different one. Even the actual *yelammedenu* sermons, to the analysis of which Mann's book (see bibliography) is devoted, are frequently not the ones found in fact in the Midrashim, but sermons reconstructed by Mann himself by combining parts taken from different sources. Moreover, Mann assumes that such homilies were invariably composed of a good many parts: the halakhic openings, series of proems, the bodies of the sermons, and the perorations. Although he occasionally states that some of these parts (e.g., the proems) may be more ancient than others, he remains ambiguous as regards the all-important question of whether such complex structures represent live sermons actually preached, or are mere literary creations of the editors of the Midrashim.

[Joseph Heinemann]

Medieval Period

Through the *derashah*, or homily, the medieval synagogue pulpit could respond to and influence communal life on the pressing issues of the day and reinforce the traditions and ethics of the Torah. It served, too, as a vehicle for social criticism and reform, arousing concern and giving encouragement in times of trial and gloom. The sermon also provided scholars with the opportunity to show their worth, erudition, and acuteness. The *derashah*, while always based on biblical verses and rabbinic sayings, and utilizing the approach of the traditional commentary, aims, nevertheless, to interpret its subject matter according to contemporary needs and concepts. For the most part, the preacher also attempts to attune his homilies to the level and tastes of his listeners.

THE PREACHER. Over the generations, especially at times of crisis, scholars arose who regarded the sermon as their chief interest and duty. Many of them served as peripatetic preachers among the various communities and lands. Preachers appointed by particular communities received fixed salaries, while itinerant preachers usually had to rely on irregular contributions and, on occasion, congregational allotments for their support. The majority of homilies have survived in the forms in which they were composed and written down by the preachers themselves, which are undoubtedly different from the forms in which they were originally delivered. The *darshan* ("preacher") organized the written text and made it more scholarly than the original oral version. The language, also, was different, since the homily was preached in the tongue spoken by the Jews of the locale, while it was written down in Hebrew.

CONTENTS. Because the sermon was directed at the congregation as a whole, the *darshan* was frequently faced with the problem of reconciling the different levels of education within his audience, being caught between the use of a simple, clear approach on the one hand, and his desire for an original, innovative, and profound manner of preaching on the other. At times the focus on nuances of interpretation would far outweigh the ethically instructive and socially beneficial aspects of the homily, which while pleasing the learned members of the community worked to the detriment of the simple folk, as well as impairing the effectiveness of the sermon itself. Midrashim from the early Middle Ages indicate that ethical teachings and commentaries touching on matters of communal interest were also at this time closely related to Torah reading in the synagogue. During that period anthologies of such material were prepared specifically for preachers. Their purpose was "to broaden the scope of Scripture and interpret it in terms of the world scene, thereby showing that God has from the very beginning of time foretold the end of days, and that we may learn many things about the commandments from the conversations of the Patriarchs" (*Midrash Lekaḥ Tov, Va-Yeẓe*). The chronicle of *Ahimaaz relates that a certain learned preacher from Ereẓ Israel had a number of prepared sermons written in rhymed Hebrew. The exegetical method as well as the socioreligious function of the *darshan* was already well established and defined for the Mediterranean Jewish communities from the time of Isaac *Alfasi and *Maimonides (11th and 12th centuries). The latter even ruled that "each Jewish congregation must arrange to have a respected and wise elder who has been known for his piety from his youth and is beloved by the people, who will publicly admonish the community and cause them to repent" (Yad, Teshuvah 4:2; cf. also Tefillah 11:3; Maim. Responsa, ed. by J. Blau, 1 (1957), no. 67). Judah *Hadassi in his *Eshkol ha-Kofer* records that by the 12th century the *Karaites had recognized the importance of the homily and accepted it as a standard practice: "The learned preacher would expound and comment upon the current Scriptural reading and Psalm before the people, who piously sought his presence and interpretation on Sabbaths, festivals, fast days, in the house of mourning, at weddings, and at circumcisions … and turns many away from transgression" (para. 18).

The homily likewise had become an accepted part of Jewish life in Germany by the first half of the 12th century. Accounts of Jews martyred in 1096 include an actual *derashah* publicly delivered to "the first to be slain" and urging them to accept martyrdom. A substantial number of the stories and ethical teachings in *Sefer Ḥasidim* appear to have been passages from sermons, parables, and the like. R. *Eleazar b. Judah b. Kalonymus of Worms ruled that "one must preach in words more precious than gold on the Sabbath … one must assemble the people at that time and preach to them" (Comment. to Prayers, Mss. Bodleian, Opp. 110; see also A.M. Habermann, *Gezerot Ashkenaz ve-Ẓarefat* (1945), 166). After the carnage during the *Black Death, the homily in Germany in the late 14th and early 15th centuries became mainly a means to exhort the people to remain observant, as well as to teach laws and commandments as they should be practiced. In the second half of the 13th century, *Moses b. Jacob of Coucy, France, personally described a journey which he made throughout Spain giving sermons of admonition. His purpose was to strengthen the ritual practices of *tefillin*, *mezuzot*, and *ẓiẓit*; to persuade the men to give up their non-Jewish wives and to prevent them from profaning the name of God through abusing the gentile (*Sefer Mitzvot ha-Gadol*, 1, 2, 112; 11, introd.). He also records a complete sermon in a style very similar to the manner in which it was delivered, obviously directed to a group particularly in need of spiritual awakening. For this he used the system of explaining biblical verses, raising the threat of divine punishment as well as the promise of a heavenly reward. This wandering halakhist and *darshan* is the first known preacher in the Middle Ages to appear as a moral and ethical preceptor of the masses. Most of the ethical works of *Jonah Gerondi appear to be the literary residue of fiery preaching. The homilies of *Naḥmanides which have been preserved (as, e.g., for Rosh Ha-Shanah and in the debate with the king of Aragon in the synagogue on the Sabbath) are in reality profound, comprehensive essays on ethical theory, an indication of the high level of his Spanish audience. The rationalist followers of Maimonides in 14th-century Provence also publicly delivered philosophical-allegorical homilies (compare Jacob *Anatoli in his *Malmad ha-Talmidim*).

In Spain, by the 14th century, the *derashah* had attained a well-developed methodology and compact structure. To the halakhic and philosophical content of the *derashah* were now added mystic elements (e.g., cf. the *Kad ha-Kemaḥ* of R. *Baḥya b. Asher). One of the most renowned preachers of this period was *Nissim b. Reuben Gerondi. The 15th-century sermon reflects the struggle with Christianity and points up the social crises that arose at a time of persecution. The homilies of the most illustrious *darshan* of the generation of the Expulsion, R. Isaac *Arama, show that periods of vigorous anti-Jewish Christian preaching have called forth an equally strong reaction from contemporary Jewish preaching (introd. to *Akedat Yiẓḥak*). Arama's sermons in *Akedat Yiẓḥak* combine a more difficult speculative analysis with popular appeal in order to strengthen the faith, be alert against Christian slanders, and safeguard the character of his hearers during the calamities threatening them.

STRUCTURE AND STYLE. Joel *Ibn Shuaib, a *darshan* who taught the transposition of laws from theory to practice, summed up the architectural and aesthetic tradition of the *derashah* in Spain around the time of the Expulsion. The preacher, he counseled, should concern himself with two essentials in his sermons: (1) the integrity of the subject matter, and (2) the perfecting of his manner of expression.... Regarding the first, he must be careful ... that, whatever he will say, his listeners will derive benefit. Though his sermons be very profound, he must make them clear enough for the masses of the people to gain something from them on their level. Yet no less must he have regard for the special interests of the more intellectually inclined who may be present when his subject is mostly directed to the simple folk. On the second principal concern, the form of the sermon, three considerations are paramount:

(1) the length – it should not be the least bit longer than is absolutely necessary to convey the intended *derashah*;

(2) the structure – the sermon should be well organized, not lacking in proper order, now in the streets, now in the broad places (Prov. 7:12);

(3) his phrases and words should possess grace and dignity, and they ought to be delivered in a pleasing and proper way according to the following conditions: Along with an attractive style and an inherent order within the sermon, the preacher must also make proper use of his voice in addressing the people so that they should understand even from his external manner of speaking that his words have value for them (Introd. to *Olat Shabbat*, Venice, 1577).

An interesting illustration of the actual style of the *derashah* as it was preached has been preserved in the homily delivered by Isaac *Aboab, the last principal of the yeshivah of Lisbon, in 1492–93, to the exiles from Spain:

> How can I endure so much suffering? A man can exist in this world for one of two reasons: either because he is in his own land, or because the Lord is watching over him. About the first reason, Cain said: "Behold, Thou hast driven me out this day from the face of the land" (Gen. 4:14). Regarding the second, he added, "whosoever findeth me will slay me" (*ibid.*), meaning, whatever may befall me, whether through the air or from some other part of the world, may be a reason for Him to kill me. The Holy One will have mercy on us.... There is a parable of a father and son walking together. Tired and feeling weak, the son asks the father if they are far from the city... and the father explains to him how he may know: once you see a cemetery, then you will be near the city.... When we see many misfortunes at hand, it signals the coming of the Messiah (*Nahar Pishon*, Constantinople, 1538, 11a).

This homily is an immediate, live reaction to the expulsion from Spain.

The *derashah* developed further in the 16th and 17th centuries among the exiles, and Jews in Italy influenced by them, who were all nourished to some extent by Renaissance culture. The sermons of the most prominent 16th-century preacher in Italy, Judah *Moscato, intersperse references to music and astronomy and Italian phrases with rabbinic aphorisms. Within this milieu, Leone *Modena compared the preacher to "a stone engraver carving out a fine statue" (*Midbar Yehudah*, Venice, 1602, 5a). To the Venetian Jewish community the homily was a work of art valued for the perfection of its form.

Homiletics underwent a more turbulent development in Poland and Lithuania, reflecting communal dissension and social problems. A number of Polish-Jewish preachers openly declared that they had the right to interpret Scripture freely in order to admonish and instruct their congregants. Yet some scholars complained about the preachers who would take liberties with biblical verses not in order to reprove their communities but to prove their own dialectical subtlety and to satisfy the eagerness of their listeners for novel and clever interpretations. This tendency led to confusion and awkwardness in the *derashah*. From the same period there are many *midreshei-peli'ah* ("wonder tales") invented by preachers who attributed them to early Midrashim. *David b. Manasseh, an itinerant often-persecuted preacher, wrote *Ketav Hitnaẓẓelut la-Darshanim* ("Writ of Apology for Preachers") in 1574, in which he argues for homiletic license to interpret and use various rhetorical devices to influence listeners. The *darshan* *Berechiah (Berakh) b. Isaac Eisik of Cracow testifies (in his *Zera Berakh*) that the homily provided the learned with a means of persuading the leaders of the community to their point of view.

SOCIAL IMPACT. Some preachers battled openly and vigorously in communal affairs. Outstanding among these was Ephraim Solomon of *Luntshits, whose sermonic works (*Ir Gibborim, Olelot Efrayim, Ammudei Shesh*, and *Oraḥ le-Ḥayyim*) influenced his own as well as later periods. R. Ephraim forcefully attacked egotism, the avaricious pursuit of wealth, the haughtiness of the rich, and their self-righteous hyprocrisy. Formerly a wandering *darshan*, frequently derided and little known, by his dynamic preaching Luntschitz achieved such recognition that he was invited to deliver a homily before the *Council of Four Lands in session at Lublin. He later served as rabbi of Prague, succeeding *Judah Loew b. Bezalel, who was himself an eminent preacher.

The pervasive influence of the *derashah* is apparent, too, from regulations and communal actions in Poland-Lithuania. In 1638 and 1648 the salary of the preacher appointed by the Poznan community was set as second only to that of the *av bet din*, and the difference between the two was negligible. In 1717, the Jews of Cracow defined the ideal preacher as one who "in his pleasant utterances gives joy to both God and man, and quenches the spiritual thirst of every class of people according to the depth and breadth of their understanding. Sometimes he teaches the Law in depth, explaining the words of our rabbis, distilling the strong waters of *Gemara*, codes, and *tosafot*. Yet he can still clarify, instill into his hearers a sense of reverence, sweeten the bitterness of life through his pleasant manner of speaking with straightforwardness…, in sermons open and understood by all, including those whose minds cannot fathom the depth of his words" (D. Weinryb, *Te'udot le-Toledot ha-Kehillot ha-Yehudiyyot be-Polin* (1950), 185).

The regulations issued by the Council of Lithuania indicate that the communal leadership was apprehensive of the potential force of the *derashah*, which they could not control. In 1628, they instituted supervision over all sermons in reaction to the freedom which the itinerant preachers had assumed. In 1667, during the agitation which followed the appearance of *Shabbetai Ẓevi, they again protested that "a number of men go around in this region, preaching publicly in synagogues and other places, pompously delivering open reproofs. However, their preaching appears in some part for their own self-glorification." The Council placed supervision of the sermons under "the local rabbi and seven city elders. If a man attempts to preach without their express permission, they may say to him: 'Step down from the pulpit,' aside from imposing additional penalties" (S. Dubnow (ed.), *Pinkas ha-Medinah* (1925), no. 596). In Moravia, too, the governing body issued regulations regarding "the acceptability of preachers who station themselves at houses of learning," and in 1701 they felt it necessary to warn the local leaders not to allow such *maggidim* ("wandering preachers") to deliver sermons without the approval of the local *av bet din* (I. Halpern, *Takkanot Medinat Mehrin* (1951), 100, 168).

18th to Early 19th Century

The changes which occurred in Jewish life as a result of the partitions of Poland, the rise of *Ḥasidism, the development of *Haskalah, and *Emancipation brought a modification of the character and status of the homily. Significantly, even in the 18th century, preaching in the medieval style still retained its importance. Just as the Jewish leaders in Poland had epitomized their concept of the ideal preacher of the past in 1717, *Elijah b. Solomon ha-Kohen of Izmir in his homiletic work *Shevet Musar* (Constantinople, 1712) summed up the method of admonition which invokes the fear of Gehinnom and sufferings in the afterlife. His work was widely read, and translated into Yiddish. Jonathan *Eybeschuetz achieved fame in his lifetime as well as posthumously for his homilies (*Ya'arot Devash*). In the 18th century, Jacob *Kranz, the Dubno *Maggid*, exerted a profound effect upon his listeners through the effective use of parables. Some scholars believe that in 18th-century Poland these itinerant *maggidim* made up an intelligensia opposed to the existing intellectual establishment, who indirectly aided the rise of Ḥasidism. Yet the ḥasidic movement gradually substituted "the saying of Torah" by the ḥasidic rabbis for the standard *derashah*, thereby eventually replacing the wandering preachers.

Within the cultural sphere of the *Mitnaggedim the homily continued to play a role. Itinerant *darshanim* like *Moses b. Isaac ha-Darshan of Kelmy, and Ḥayyim Zadok, the *Maggid* of Rumschischki, were influential in Jewish society. Their chief concern focused on the struggle against Ḥasidism and Haskalah, as well as the founding of charitable institutions in the small towns of Lithuania and White Russia. They often intoned their sermons using a special plaintive melodic mode, and the parable was one of their most essential homiletic tools. For the *derashah* given by the boy who had become bar mitzvah, see *Bar Mitzvah. Also there was a custom that the bridegroom or the scholar give a *derashah* under the wedding canopy or at the festivities following.

[*Encyclopaedia Hebraica*]

In Modern Times (From the Beginning of the 19th Century)

THE MODERN SERMON. Part of the aim of Zunz's most famous work, *Gottesdienstliche Vortraege der Juden* (1832), was to demonstrate, when this was challenged by the Prussian government (under the influence of Orthodox groups who saw the sermon in the vernacular as the beginnings of Reform), that preaching is not an innovation but an ancient Jewish institution. While this is true, the traditional *derashah* was, in fact, replaced in the 19th century by a new type of Jewish sermon, the *Predigt*, as it was called in Germany. There were a number of important changes in language, style, and content which, first in Germany and then in other European countries, gave a completely new cast to the sermon. This new type of sermon was delivered in the vernacular and unlike the occasional *derashah*, it was a regular feature of the service. It sought to express Jewish values in a contemporary idiom and in the thought patterns of the day. Woven around one central theme, the modern sermon developed in orderly fashion, without academic digressions on the texts quoted, emphasizing edification rather than pure instruction. Although the early 19th-century preachers in Germany were not rabbis, preaching, instead of being delegated to a special functionary, eventually became the preserve of the rabbi and one of his most important duties in Western countries. Among the well-known preachers in 19th-century Germany were: Eduard *Kley, Gotthold *Salomon, Abraham *Geiger, Samuel *Holdheim, Jehiel Michael *Sachs, Samson Raphael *Hirsch, and David *Einhorn; and in the 20th century: Siegmund *Maybaum, Nehemia Anton *Nobel, and Leo *Baeck.

A. Altmann (see bibl.) has demonstrated the influence of the Protestant pulpit on the development of the modern Jewish sermon. The early German preachers consciously modeled their sermons on the patterns of Christian homiletics and used Christian guides to the art of preaching. Even Isaac Noah *Mannheimer, the most outstanding 19th-century preacher, who pleaded for a closer link with the Jewish homiletical tradition, admitted "that we as pupils and disciples, as novices in the art of preaching which we have been practicing only a little while, can learn a great deal from the masters of the art, and we have gratefully to accept every guidance and instruction offered to us in their schools." Zunz, in his brief career as a preacher at the New Synagogue in Berlin (1820–22), was influenced by *Schleiermacher. It is even on record that the most popular Christian preachers of the time, such as Ritschl and Schleiermacher, used to hear the young preachers at Israel *Jacobson's temple in Berlin and give them, after the sevice, "manifold hints and directives."

A reaction soon set in. There was a persistent demand for a truly Jewish homiletic, arguing, in Mannheimer's words, that "it is always better to feed on one's own resources than to live from alms." But, generally speaking, the reaction in the 19th century only amounted to a greater use of rabbinic, especially midrashic, material, as exemplified in the sermons of the illustrious preacher Adolf *Jellinek in Vienna. Jellinek's preaching attracted many of the intellectuals of his day who, in their quest for Jewish identity, needed his reassurance that Judaism was supremely worthwhile and still capable of making important contributions. Jellinek was fond of preaching that too many were saying: "Now Israel's eyes were dim with age; he could not see" (Gen. 48:10), whereas the truth was that Moses still spoke and God still answered him in thunder (Ex. 19:19). Jellinek's methods and strong Jewish emphasis influenced Jewish preaching everywhere. A later occupant of Jellinek's pulpit, Hirsch (Ẓevi) Perez *Chajes, for example, preached to a bar mitzvah the story of the woman whose vessels were miraculously replenished by the oil (II Kings 4:1 – 7). The never-ending power of Judaism is always available if only Jews will provide the vessels with which to contain it. No matter how great the Jew's spiritual demands, Judaism is capable of satisfying them (*Ne'umim ve-Harẓa'ot* (1953), 400).

Tobias *Goodman is credited with being the first Jew to preach in the English language. Two of his printed sermons are: *A Sermon on the Universally Regretted Death of the Most Illustrious Princess Charlotte*, preached on Wednesday, Nov. 19, 1817, at the synagogue, Denmark Court, London (the first sermon to be both delivered and printed in English), and *A Sermon Occasioned by the Demise of Our Late Venerable Sovereign, King George the Third*, preached on Wednesday, Feb. 16, 1820, at the same synagogue (A. Barnett, *The Western Synagogue Through Two Centuries* (1961), 48 – 51). In December 1828 a Committee of Elders was appointed at the Bevis Marks Sephardi Synagogue in London to inquire into the best means of elevating the tone of public services. Among their recommendations was that an English sermon based on a text taken from Scripture should be delivered every Saturday afternoon. Before delivery every sermon should be examined by a committee of three elders for statements contrary to Jewish doctrines or hostile to the institutions of the country (J. Picciotto, *Sketches of Anglo-Jewish History* (1956^2), 318–20). In the U.S., preaching in the English language was introduced much later. Some preachers, like the Reform Rabbi David Einhorn, preferred to give sermons in their native German. Einhorn declared that "Where the German sermon is banned, there the reform of Judaism is nothing more than a brilliant gloss, a decorated doll, without heart, without soul, which the proudest temples and the most splendid theories cannot succeed in infusing with life." The Jewish sermon in English was developed to a fine art by such preachers as Simeon *Singer, Morris *Joseph, Joseph Herman *Hertz, Israel *Mattuck, A.A. Green, Abraham *Cohen, and Ephraim Levine in England; Stephen S. *Wise, Israel Herbert *Levinthal, Abba Hillel *Silver, Solomon *Goldman, and Solomon Bennett *Freehof in the U.S. Two annual collections of sermons in English are those published by the Rabbinical Council of America (Orthodox) since 1943; and since 1954, the collection by rabbis from all three groups in *Best Jewish Sermons*, edited by Saul I. Teplitz.

In Eastern Europe the older type of *derashah* delivered in Yiddish by the *maggid* still predominated, but certain new features manifested themselves even here. The winds of change in the Jewish world moved the *maggidim* to find a rather more sophisticated approach. Preaching in Yiddish became directed to the needs of the individual as well as the community. The Haskalah movement was frequently fought by the *maggidim* with the weapons of pulpit oratory. With the rise of Zionism, many of its opponents used the same weapons to combat it, while others sympathetic to Zionism preached the love of the Holy Land and the legitimacy of Jewish nationalistic aspirations with new fervor. In fact, a new type of nationalistic preacher emerged and was given the name *mattif* ("speaker";

Micah 2:11), to distinguish him from the old-type *maggid*. Under the influence of the Lithuanian Musar movement, with its strong moralistic concern, the *derashah* began to place greater emphasis on ethical matters. The hellfire preaching of Moses *Isaac, the Kelmer *Maggid* (1828–1900), the most popular of the folk preachers, was directed largely against dishonesty in business and general unethical conduct (D. Katz, *Tenu'at ha-Musar*, 2 (c. 1958), 395–407). Many of the *maggidim* went to the U.S., England, and South Africa where their preaching was directed against the widespread desecration of the Sabbath and neglect of the dietary laws, abuses unknown in their native countries. *Maggidim* still flourish in the State of Israel, but there has been little development of the sermon in Hebrew and the rabbi-preacher is virtually unknown there as a regular and respected synagogue functionary. Among the Yiddish preachers of renown were: Ḥayyim Zundel, H.Z. *Maccoby (the Kamenitzer *Maggid*), J.L. Lazarov, Ẓ.H. *Masliansky, Isaac *Nissenbaum, M.A. *Amiel, Zalman *Sorotzkin, and Ze'ev *Gold.

PREACHING TECHNIQUES. Simeon Singer in "Where the Clergy Fail," an address delivered to young preachers on Jan. 17, 1904 (*Lectures and Addresses* (1908), 203 – 25), describes the aim of the Jewish preacher thus: "to teach the word of God to their brethren, young and old; to help them to the perception of the highest truths of religion; to uplift their souls out of the rut of the common, the sordid, the selfish, in life; to speak a message of comfort to the sorrowing, of hope to the despondent, of counsel to the perplexed, of courage to the struggling and aspiring." In the belief that the art of preaching can be taught, the major rabbinical seminaries have departments of homiletics. Sigmund Maybaum taught homiletics at the Hochschule in Berlin, Israel *Bettan at Hebrew Union College, Mordecai Menahem *Kaplan at the Jewish Theological Seminary, and Abraham Cohen at Jews' College.

The modern Jewish sermon is usually based on a text chosen from the portion (the *sidra* or *haftarah*) read in the synagogue on the day the sermon is delivered. Books of the Bible which are not read in public, like Job, rarely furnish texts for sermons, though they may be quoted in support of a position the preacher adopts. Normally the sermon is delivered toward the end of the service. While the note of exhortation is never entirely absent from the sermon, many preachers nowadays prefer to use the sermon chiefly as a means of instruction, imparting information about Jewish faith, history, and teachings. The length of the sermon varies from preacher to preacher but on the average is about 20 minutes. Preaching from a prepared manuscript is the rule for some preachers while others prefer to speak extemporaneously. Adequate preparation is counseled by the best preachers. In the preface to his *Faith of a Jewish Preacher* (1935), Ephraim Levine compares the preacher who waits for Providence to put words into his mouth to Balaam who said the very opposite of what he intended to say. Oratory has now generally yielded to an easier conversational tone. Few preachers would today follow the example of Leo Baeck of whom it was said that he never used the personal pronoun "I" in the pulpit.

Sermon illustrations are taken from the personal experience of the preacher, Jewish history, the Midrash, natural science and psychology, and, latterly, ḥasidic lore. L.I. Newman's *Hasidic Anthology* (1934) and M. Buber's *Tales of the Hasidim* (1947–48) have come to serve as sources for sermon illustrations. Quotations from secular literature are used to develop themes. In a typical sermon outline on *Kol Nidrei* by Milton *Steinberg (*Sermons*, B. Mandelbaum, ed. (1954), 58–63) there are references to the *geonim*, Walter Pater, Tennyson, Leibnitz, Omar Khayyam, and W.L. Phelps. Louis I. *Rabinowitz (*Out of the Depths* (1951), 332–5) builds a *Kol Nidrei* sermon around a poem by the modern Hebrew writer Zalman *Shneur. In a Day of Atonement sermon by Israel H. Levinthal (*Steering or Drifting – Which?* (1928), 128–35), there are quotations from *Judah Halevi, the Talmud, the prayer book, a Christian legend, folk language, the Bible, and the Midrash. Preachers in the U.S. frequently take for their sermon theme a book, movie, or play that has received much attention for its treatment of some moral or religious question. Some sermons conclude with a prayer. This and other pulpit pretensions, however, were severely criticized by Franz *Rosenzweig in his scathing attack on preaching in *Sermonic Judaism* (N.N. Glatzer, *Franz Rosenzweig* (1953), 247–50). The chosen text and the way it is treated depend on the individual bent of the preacher but, judging by published sermons, certain themes are constant. Each of the festivals, for example, has its particular message so far as the preacher is concerned. The theme of Passover is freedom; of Shavuot Jewish education (in Orthodox pulpits the immutability of the Torah); of Sukkot trust in God and thankfulness for His bounty; of Ḥanukkah spiritual light; of Purim Jewish peoplehood; of Rosh Ha-Shanah the need for renewal; and on the Day of Atonement sin and atonement. In addition to the weekly Sabbath sermon the rabbi preaches on the special occasions in the life of his congregation: anniversaries, weddings, funerals, installation of officers, bar mitzvahs, and his own induction. A number of rabbinic manuals contain sermonic material in capsule form for the rabbi's use on special occasions (e.g., H.E. Goldin, *Ha-Madrikh*, 1939).

ISSUES OF THE DAY IN PREACHING. The modern Jewish sermon frequently addresses itself to particular problems which agitate the Jewish community as well as to wider issues of universal import. There is much discussion on the extent to which politics should be introduced, but few Jewish preachers accept a total ban on political questions. There are numerous instances of preachers seeking to influence their congregants either when a topic is a source of controversy in the community or when they feel that widely held views are contrary to Jewish teaching. Themes treated in the contemporary pulpit are the controversy between religion and science, the role of the State of Israel, the permissive society, intermarriage, Jewish education, war and peace, social injustice, racial discrimination, the use and abuse of wealth, and Judaism and its relation to other faiths. The 1968 edition of *Best Jewish Sermons* contains sermons against the taking of drugs; on the "death of God" movement, fair housing, the estrangement of the Jewish intellectual from Judaism, recreation, and the need to care for the hungry of the world. Rabbis have fought to free the pulpit from control by the lay leaders of the congregation. When Stephen Wise was being considered for the influential post of rabbi of Temple Emanu-El in New York, Louis *Marshall, the president, held that in controversial matters the pulpit must remain under the control of the trustees. Wise refused to consider the post under such conditions and eventually founded the Free Synagogue to uphold the principle of pulpit liberty.

In 19th-century America the slavery issue was echoed from the Jewish pulpit. Morris J. *Raphall preached that slavery was a divinely ordained institution since it is sanctioned in the Bible. David Einhorn, however, attacked slavery from the pulpit as "the greatest crime against God." As a result, his life was placed in jeopardy and on April 22, 1861, Einhorn and his family were secretly escorted out of Baltimore.

With the rise of the *Reform movement the issue of Reform was hotly debated from the pulpit. A favorite text for the Reform sermon, used by Geiger and others, was: "One generation passeth away, and another generation cometh; but the earth abideth for ever" (Eccles. 1:4). The "earth" represents the essential, unchanging spirit of Judaism, which must be interpreted by each generation in the light of its own needs and insights. Often the same set of texts would be used by both Orthodox and Reform preachers in support of their positions. The "wicked son" of the Passover *Haggadah* was, for the Orthodox preacher, the Reform Jew who asks "What is this service to you?" For the Reform Jew the son who represented their point of view was the "wise son" who was ready to ask the intelligent questions demanded by the new age. Chief Rabbi N.M. *Adler preached in London, on the second day of Passover in 1868, a sermon against the abolition of the second day of festivals in the Diaspora, a matter which at that time had begun to be an issue in the struggle between Orthodoxy and Reform. His son and successor, Hermann *Adler, at the beginning of the 20th century, refused to permit a synagogue under his jurisdiction to appoint Morris *Joseph as preacher because the latter had published views "at variance with traditional Judaism." Solomon *Schechter, living at that time in Cambridge, pointed out that if doctrines were to become the test of a minister, then the greatest names in Jewish learning – Zunz, Graetz, Herzfeld, Joel, Gotthold Salomon, Rapoport and others – would never have been permitted to preach in a United Synagogue (R. Apple, *The Hampstead Synagogue* (1967), 23–27). Chief Rabbi J.H. *Hertz preached a series of sermons, *Affirmations of Judaism* (1927), attacking the new Liberal movement founded by Claude Goldsmid *Montefiore and others.

[Louis Jacobs]

BIBLIOGRAPHY: GENERAL: Zunz-Albeck, Derashot; N.R. Rabinowitz, *Deyokena'ot shel Darshanim* (1967). TALMUDIC PERIOD: Aptowitzer, in: MGWJ, 76 (1932), 558–75; Ḥ Albeck, *Mavo u-Mafteḥot le-Midrash Bereshit Rabba*, 1 (1965^2), 11–19 (in *Midrash Bereshit Rabba* ed., by J. Theodor and Ḥ. Albeck, 3 (1965^2)); L. Baeck, *Aus drei Jahrtausenden* (19582), 158; W. Bacher, *Die Prooemien der alten juedischen Homilie* (1913); Bloch, in: MGWJ, 34 (1885), 166–84, 210–24, 257–69, 385–404; 35 (1886), 165–87, 389–405; J. Heinemann, *Derashot be-Ẓibbur bi-Tekufat ha-Talmud* (1970); idem, in: *Divrei ha-Kongress ha-Olami ha-Revi'i le-Madda'ei ha-Yahadut*, 2 (1960), 3–47; idem, in: JJS, 19 (1968), 41–48; J. Mann, *The Bible as Read and Preached in the Old Synagogue*, 1 (1940); J. Mann and I. Sonne, *The Bible as Read and Preached in the Old Synagogue*, 2 (1966); S. Maybaum, *Die aeltesten Phasen in der Entwicklung der juedischen Predigt*, 1 (1901); M. Kadushin, *The Rabbinic Mind* (1965^2), 59ff.; Stein, in: *Sefer ha-Yovel… Schorr* (1935), 85–112; H.L. Strack, *Introduction to the Talmud and Midrash* (1945), 210ff.; Theodor, in: MGWJ, 28 (1879), 97–112, 164–75, 271–8, 337–50, 408–18, 455–62; 29 (1880), 19–23; 30 (1881), 500–10. Medieval Period: I. Bettan, *Studies in Jewish Preaching* (1939); S.Y. Glicksberg, *Ha-Derashah be-Yisrael* (1940); S.B. Freehof, *Modern Jewish Preaching* (1941); Baron, Community, index, s.v. *Preaching*; A. Steinman, *Kitvei ha-Maggid mi-Dubno* (recast in modern style), 2 vols. (1952); H.H. Ben-Sasson, *Hagut ve-Hanhagah* (1959), 34–54; J. Katz, *Tradition and Crisis* (1961), 173–5. Modern Times: A. Altmann, in: YLBI, 6 (1961), 3 – 59; idem (ed.), *Studies in Nineteenth-Century Jewish Intellectual History* (1964), 65–116; A. Cohen, *Jewish Homiletics* (1937); New York Board of Jewish Ministers, *Problems of the Jewish Ministry* (1927), 1–43; The Rabbinical Assembly of America, *Proceedings*, 10 (1946), 85–102; L. Treifel, in: *Festschrift zum 75 Jaehrigen Bestehen des Juedisch-Theologischen Seminars Breslau*, 2 (1929), 373–6.

PRECIOUS STONES AND JEWELRY.

In the Bible

Precious stones are mentioned in various contexts in the Bible, the most comprehensive list appearing in the description of the breastpiece worn by the high priest. The breastpiece was set with 12 precious stones arranged in four rows with three stones in each row to represent the 12 tribes: "set in it mounted stones, in four rows of stones. The first row shall be a row of *'odem, piṭdah*, and *bareqet*; the second, of *nofekh, sappir*, and *yahalom*; the third of *leshem, shevo*, and *'aḥlamah*; and the fourth, of *tarshish, shoham*, and *yashfeh*…" (Ex. 28:17–20). Most of these stones are mentioned again as present in the Garden of Eden where the king of Tyre originally abode (Ezek. 28:13).

(See Table: Gems in High Priest Breastplate.)

From the talmudic period onward, biblical translators and commentators have attempted to determine the mineralogical nature of these stones and to identify them in terms of the names of modern minerals. However, the identity of the stones of the breastpiece cannot be established by a mineralogical study, since there is no statement even about their colors except in the late Midrash (in *Midrash Rabbah*). Philological research is of assistance only in a few cases. Archaeological excavations can help somewhat by establishing which minerals were utilized as precious or semiprecious stones in pre-Exilic times. The chart presented here summarizes a few of the different identifications of the stones of the breastpiece found in ancient and modern Bible translations, and advanced by the modern scholars N. Shalem and R. Sverdlov. There is also disagreement between the Palestine Targum (followed

Precious Stones in the High Priest's Breastplate in the Hebrew Bible and its Versions

Hebrew Bible	Targum Onkelos	Targum Jonathan	Palestine Targum	Ex. Rabbah 38, 10	LXX	J.P.S.A.	New English Bible
אֹדֶם	סַמְקָן	סִימוּקְתָא	סַמְקָתָא	שרדנגין (שדרננין)	σάρδιόν	carnelian	sardin
פִּטְדָה	יַרְקָן	יַרְקְתָא	יַרְקָתָא	טומפזין (שומפזין)	τόπάζιον	chrysolite (topaz)	chrysolite
בָּרֶקֶת	בַּרְקָן	בַּרְקְתָא	בַּרְקָתָא	דיקינתון	σμάραγδος	emerald (smaragd)	green felspar
נֹפֶךְ	אִזְמַרְגְּדִין	אִיזְמֹרַד	כַּדְכְּדָנָא	ברדינין	ἄνθραξ	turquoise (carbuncle)	purple garnet
סַפִּיר	שַׁבְזִיז	סַפִּירִינוֹן	סִמְפּוֹרְיָנָא	סאפירינון	σάρΦείρος	sapphire	lapis lazuli
יַהֲלֹם	סִבְהֲלוֹם	כַּדְכּוֹדִי	עֵין עִיגְלָא	אזמרגדין	ἴαστις	amethyst (emerald)	jade
לֶשֶׁם	קַנְכֵּרִי	קַנְכִּרִינוֹן	זוֹזִין	כוכלין (בוחלין)	λιγύριον	jacinth	turquoise
שְׁבוֹ	טַרְקְיָא	טַרְקִין (ערקין)	בִּירְזְלִין	אכאטיס	ἀχάτης	agate	agate
אַחְלָמָה	עֵין עֶגְלָא	עֵין עֵיגֶל	זְמַרְגַּדִין	(המטוסיון) הימוסיון	ἀμέθυστος	crystal (amethyst)	jasper
תַּרְשִׁישׁ	כרום יַמָּא	כְּרוּם יַמָּא רַבָּא	כְּרוּם יַמָּא	קרומטסין	χρυσόλιθός	beryl	topaz
שֹׁהַם	בוּרְלָא	בֵּירְלֵיוַת חַלָּא	בְּדוֹלְחָא	פראלוקין	βήρύλλιον	lapis lazuli (onyx)	cornelian
יָשְׁפֵה	פַּנְטֵירֵי	אַפַּנְטוֹרִין מַרְגְּנִיַּית	מַרְגָּלִיתָא	מרגליטים	ὀνύχιον	jasper	green jasper

by Maimonides and Baḥya) and the Targum Jonathan (followed by Rashi) as to the order of the names of the tribes on the stones. According to the Palestine Targum, the six sons of Leah appear first, then the sons of the maidservants, and lastly the sons of Rachel. Targum Jonathan, on the other hand, claims that they followed the order of their birth, i.e., the sons of the maidservants preceded Issachar and Zebulun. The only source specifying a mineralogical property is the description found in *Midrash Rabbah* (Num. R. 2:7):

"There were distinguishing signs for each prince; each had a flag and a different color for every flag, corresponding to the precious stones on the breast of Aaron … Reuben's stone was *ʾodem* and the color of his flag was red; and embroidered thereon were mandrakes. Simeon's was *piṭdah* and his flag was of a yellow (or green) color … Levi's was *bareqet* and the color of his flag was a third white, a third black, and a third red … Judah's was *nofekh* and the color of his flag was like that of the sky … Issachar's was *sappir* and the color of his flag was black like stibium … Zebulun's was *yahalom* and the color of his flag was white … Dan's was *leshem* and the color of his flag was similar to *sappir* … Gad's *ʾaḥlamah* and the color of his flag was neither white nor black but a blend of black and white … Asher's was *tarshish* and the color of his flag was like the precious stone with which women adorn themselves … Joseph's was *shoham* and the color of his flag was jet black … Benjamin's was *yashfeh* and the color of his flag was a combination of all the 12 colors …"

If this ancient Midrash is accepted, it appears that the color of the stones was the most accurate mark of identification that popular Jewish tradition could preserve. Ibn Ezra (Ex. 28:9), on the other hand, sharply criticizes the translations of Saadiah Gaon: "and we have no way of clearly knowing the 'stones for setting' because the Gaon rendered them as he wished, and he has no tradition which he can rely on…"

Through a comparison of the various translations and commentaries, reasonable identification may be advanced for some of the stones; with others, an identification is impossible. Some of the stones may be identified mineralogically, but because they are different in color they were called by different names.

ʾODEM. (אֹדֶם; Ex. 28:17; 39:10; Ezek. 28:13), a red stone. *ʾOdem* is rendered as *samqan* (סַמְקָן), i.e., "red," in Aramaic translations; as *sardion* in the Greek versions; and *aḥmar* in Arabic. This stone is probably carnelian sard, one of the red cryptocrystalline varieties of quartz (SiO_2). It is found in excavations. Some regard it as the opaque red jasper found in Egypt and in the vicinity of Eilat.

PIṬDAH. (פִּטְדָה; Ex. 28:17; 39:10; Ezek. 28:13), according to the commentators, a green stone, and generally identified in the versions as the green-yellow topaz. According to Pliny, however, what was known as the topaz in antiquity was not identical with the modern stone called topaz $Al_2F_2SiO_4$, but with the modern chrysolite or peridot belonging to the olivine group. This mineral is usually green in color and is used as a gem. The identification of topaz or chrysolite with *piṭdah* is rejected by N. Shalem who proposed plasma, a green variety of cryptocrystalline quartz. *Piṭdah* is also mentioned in Job 28:19 as *piṭdah* of Ethiopia, which is used as a symbol of the value of wisdom. This is apparently a reference to *piṭdah* imported from Ethiopia.

BAREQET. (בָּרֶקֶת; Ex. 28:17; 39:10; Ezek. 28:13), a similar term in Akkadian, *barraqtu*, also means a precious stone. Both words may share a common etymology in the Semitic root *brq* or may be borrowed from the Sanskrit *marakata* which means smaragd. Most Greek versions explain *bareqet* as smaragd, which is a variety of beryl $Al_2Be_3Si_6O_{18}$ with small additions of other elements, i.e., the emerald. Emerald-smaragd mines were located in ancient times in Kosseir in Egypt. Smaragd was considered the most valuable green stone, and it has been found in the form of gems in the tombs of the pharaohs. U. Cassuto and others identify *bareqet* with malachite, which is similar in color to smaragd and was easier to work in ancient times. According to these explanations, *bareqet* is green and thus does not fit the description in the Midrash which states that *bareqet* is found in three colors. N. Shalem therefore proposed to identify *bareqet* with jasper (SiO_2).

NOFEKH. (נֹפֶךְ; Ex. 28:18; 39:11; Ezek. 27:16; 28:13). *Nofekh* is mentioned as one of the stones on the breastpiece, in the description of the precious stones belonging to the king of Tyre in the Garden of Eden, and also among the valuable goods brought to Tyre by the Arameans. *Nofekh* has been identified by some scholars as the red mineral pyrope $Mg_3Al_2(SiO_4)_3$ of the garnet group. According to the Midrash, it was sky blue in color and N. Shalem, therefore, proposed to identify it with turquoise ($Cu_3Al_2O_3 \cdot 2P_2O_5 \cdot 9H_2O$) which was well known in Sinai as early as the time of the first pharaohs.

SAPPIR. (סַפִּיר). This stone appears in the Bible as the second stone in the second row of the breastpiece (Ex. 28:18; 39:11) and also in other passages as a very costly gem. It is included among the precious stones brought to Tyre by the Arameans (Ezek. 28:13); the firmament is said to have the appearance of the *sappir* stone (Ezek. 1:26); it is used as a symbol of beauty (Song 5:14; Lam. 4:7) and of value – "It cannot be valued in the gold of Ophir, in precious onyx, or *sappir*" (Job 28:16). The Midrash describes the *sappir* as "black, like stibium." Most translations identify the *sappir* with the present-day blue sapphire (Al_2O_3); this stone, however, was apparently unknown in antiquity. In contrast to the Midrash, which regards the *sappir* as blue, Saadiah Gaon calls it white, on the basis of the verse "the likeness of *livnat ha-sappir*" (Ex. 24:10), where he interprets *livnat* as "whiteness." Ibn Ezra disagreed with Saadiah, explaining that the *sappir* is red on the basis of the verse "their bodies were more ruddy than coral, the beauty of their form was like *sappir*" (Lam. 4:7). Despite these sources, most scholars identify *sappir* with lapis lazuli, a translucent blue mineral of the lazulite group, which was used as a decorative stone in antiquity. Lapis lazuli was known in Cyprus as a natural stone and in ancient Egypt also as an artificial gem.

YAHALOM. (יַהֲלֹם), the third stone in the second row of the breastpiece (Ex. 28:18; 39:11), also mentioned in Ezekiel 28:13 as one of the precious stones found in the Garden of Eden. The *yahalom* was a white stone according to the Midrash, and Ibn Ezra rendered it as diamond "which breaks all stones and precious *bedolaḥ*" (on Ex. 28:9). Although in modern Hebrew *yahalom* means diamond, the hardest mineral found in nature, it is not likely that the Bible refers to this stone, which was apparently unknown in biblical times. N. Shalem has proposed chalcedony, a variety of quartz (SiO_2), which is a relatively hard white mineral which fits the midrashic description.

LESHEM. (לֶשֶׁם), the first stone in the third row of the breastpiece (Ex. 28:19; 39:12). Scholars disagree as to the identity of this stone: Sverdlov attributed it to the zircon family, whereas Shalem identifies it with aventurine; others regard it as amber. The name Leshem and the tribe of Dan are connected by means of the *leshem* stone on the breastpiece as well as by means of the city Leshem, also called Laish, which was settled by the tribe of Dan in the north of Israel (Josh. 19:47).

SHEVO. (שְׁבוֹ), the second stone in the third row of the breastpiece (Ex. 28:19; 39:12). According to the Midrash, it is neither white nor black but of a mixed color. *Midrash Rabbah* renders it as *achatis*, as does the Septuagint. This corresponds to the agate, a variety of chalcedony (SiO_2) which has variegated colors as a result of impurities – sometimes in the form of stripes and sometimes in other forms. Agate, a very common mineral, was known in Near Eastern countries in biblical times.

ʾAḤLAMAH. (אַחְלָמָה), the third stone in the third row of the breastpiece (Ex. 28:19; 39:12). Most translators and commentators identify it with amethyst, a transparent purple stone of the SiO_2 group. The Septuagint, Vulgate, and most other versions render it as amethyst. It was believed in antiquity that wine drunk from an amethyst cup would not intoxicate, since the word amethyst in Greek apparently means "not drunken." Ibn Ezra connects the word *ʾaḥlamah* with *ḥalom*, "dream": "whoever wears this stone on his finger never fears dreams," and goes on to say that the *ʾaḥlamah* possesses a magic power which influences dreams, just as there is "a stone which attracts iron" (magnet) and "a stone which flees from vinegar" (the influence of acid on certain minerals). The identification of *ʾaḥlamah* with amethyst, which was well known in antiquity, is generally accepted by most scholars.

TARSHISH. (תַּרְשִׁישׁ), the first stone in the fourth row of the breastpiece (Ex. 28:20; 39:13). The *tarshish* apparently had an unusual luster and brilliance and is thus mentioned several times in the Bible: "the appearance of the wheels… was like the gleaming of a *tarshish*" (Ezek. 1:16; 10:9); "his arms are rounded gold set with *tarshish*" (Song 5:14); "his body was like *tarshish*, his face like the appearance of lightning" (Dan. 10:6). The Targums Onkelos and Jonathan translate *tarshish* as "color of the sea." In all probability, the reference is to the mineral known today as aquamarine, a transparent, bluish green variety of beryl which was considered a very beautiful and costly stone. The aquamarine stone was apparently known in southern Egypt and Spain. This explanation also seems to agree with the Midrash which states that its color resembles a precious stone, since aquamarine was known from earliest times as a precious stone. N. Shalem, in 1931, identified *tarshish* with opal, but later suggested it was mother-of-pearl, perhaps because of the connection between the "color of the sea" and the "sea stone" of Targum Onkelos, which can refer only to pearls. No connection should apparently be sought between the *tarshish* stone and the country or island of the same name to which boats were sent to bring back metals (1 Kings 10:22) and to which Jonah fled. It seems that aquamarine is the most correct suggestion.

SHOHAM. (שֹׁהַם), the second stone in the fourth row of the breastpiece (Ex. 28:20; 39:13). *Shoham* is mentioned as one of the stones of the land of Havilah in the Garden of Eden (Gen. 2:12). The translations are not agreed on any one definition: the Septuagint renders it as beryl, as apparently does Onkelos ("burla"); the Palestine Targum translates it as *bedolaḥ* and Josephus, in *The Jewish Wars*, as onyx. According to the Midrash, it was very black in color, whereas Ibn Ezra calls it white (on Ex. 28:9). Onyx is also a variety of silica and usually has different shades and colors. There is no evidence to substantiate the ancient translation of beryl. There is no doubt that *shoham* was considered one of the precious stones of the Garden of Eden (Ezek. 28:13), and it also appears in Job as a symbol of wealth and importance: "wisdom… cannot be valued… in precious *shoham*" (Job 28:16). It was apparently a very costly, hard, and rare stone, but as yet no well-founded identification has been proposed.

YASHFEH. (יָשְׁפֵה), the third stone in the fourth row of the breastpiece (Ex. 28:20; 39:13) and one of the precious stones of the Garden of Eden (Ezek. 28:13). This stone appears with the same name in many ancient documents, including the Tell el-Amarna letters, and is apparently identical with the mineral jasper. This is the only case where one of the stones of the breastpiece is identified with a modern mineral through a similarity of names (that is, if we accept the above theory that the biblical *sappir* is not the modern sapphire). *Yashfeh* was translated as jaspir or jasper from very early times, although the Targums Onkelos and Jonathan do not mention them. Jasper is also a variety of silica.

ʾELGAVISH. (אֶלְגָּבִישׁ) appears in the Bible in connection with heavy rains: "there will be a deluge of rain, great *ʾelgavish* stones will fall" (Ezek. 13:11; 38:22). The Septuagint translates *ʾelgavish* stones both as hail and as slingstones. It is very likely that hail was seen as the slingstones of God, and for this reason the term was used in both senses. Some scholars read it as *ʾel gavish, gavish*, as in Job 28:18, probably meaning crystal as in modern Hebrew. The common crystal is quartz, also known as rock crystal. Hail was called *ʾelgavish* since it was similar in form to real crystal, but as it was only water it could not be called *gavish* but only *ʾelgavish*.

ʾEQDAḤ. (אֶקְדָּח), mentioned only once in the Bible: "I will make your pinnacles of *kadkod*, your gates of *ʾeqdaḥ*" (Isa. 54:12). It has not been identified. Some commentators associate the word *ʾeqdaḥ* with a sparkling, lustrous stone, on the basis of the verse: "you are all kindlers of fire (*qodḥe ʾesh*), who set brands alight" (Isa. 50:11). According to Rashi, *ʾeqdaḥ* is not a mineral but a gate constructed from a large stone in which an opening was made by drilling (*qidduʿaḥ*).

KADKOD. (כַּדְכֹּד), a term that appears twice in the Bible: "I will make your pinnacles of *kadkod*" (Isa. 54:12) and in the list of precious goods brought to Tyre by the Arameans (Ezek. 27:16). *Kadkod* apparently denotes a shiny, sparkling stone, and it is possible that it does not refer to one specific mineral but is a name based on the expression *kiddode ʾesh*, "sparks of fire" (Job 41:11). The Septuagint substituted the letter *resh* for *dalet* which makes the word closer to *karkond*, the Arabic name for spinel, a red precious stone. Some identify *kadkod* with the hyacinth, a transparent orange, red, or brown precious stone which is a variety of zircon.

BAHAṬ, SHESH, DAR, SOḤARET. (בַּהַט, שֵׁשׁ, דַּר, סֹחָרֶת), four terms appearing in the description of the floor of Ahasuerus' palace (Esth. 1:6). This floor was apparently a mosaic pavement containing these four stones. *Bahaṭ* is possibly a type of marble. Alabaster, which was very common in all Near Eastern countries, is sometimes called *bahaṭ* in modern Hebrew. *Shesh* is marble. *Dar*, which means "pearl" in Arabic, may designate stones with a pearl-like luster. The identity of the last term, *soḥaret*, is unknown. These four terms denote decorative building stones which could be polished, but apparently not precious stones.

RAʾMOT. (רָאמוֹת), mentioned in the Bible in various contexts. It is listed among the precious goods brought by the Arameans to Tyre (Ezek. 27:16); as a precious stone which is compared to wisdom in the eyes of a fool: "Wisdom is for a fool as *raʾmot*" (Prov. 24:7); and again as a very costly stone whose value is nevertheless surpassed by wisdom (Job 28:18). *Raʾmot* is clearly a precious stone; its identity, however, is unknown.

[Uri Shraga Wurzburger]

In Rabbinical Literature

Talmud, Midrash, Aramaic and other versions as well as the medieval commentators give translations or interpretations of the two *shoham* (onyx?) stones on the high priest's Ephod and of the 12 precious stones that make up the "Breastplate of Judgment" (Ex. 28:6–12; 15–30). Rav Assi (Meg. 12a) endeavored to explain "stones of a crown, glittering over His land" (Zech. 9:16) and the *bahaṭ* of Esther 1:6 by אבנים שמחוטטות על בעליהן ("stones that flash back at their owner," but see Rashi and He-Arukh, s.v. חט). Another explanation given (*ibid.*) reads המחיטטות לעיניים במקומן ("which dazzle the eyes in the place where they are found" (see Jastrow, Dict, s.v. חטט). The precious stones mentioned in Job 28:18 are translated in the Targum by סנדלכון (corrupted from Greek σαρδόνυχ) and בירולין or בירוצין (beryl), the former also being used in the Talmud as a generic term for precious stones (Sanh. 59b; ARN1[1], 5 and 38, 114). The onyx stone (אנך) is mentioned (Av. Zar. 8b, 11b and Tosef. Kel. BM 1:3).

Under the influence of beliefs prevalent among other peoples and cultures, Talmud and Midrash attach magical, in particular medical but also psychological, influences to precious stones, ideas which continued to prevail among medieval Jewish Bible commentators like Abraham Ibn Ezra, David Kimḥi, Baḥya b. Asher and also in the Zohar (see *Astrology). Simeon b. Ẓemaḥ Duran (14th–15th centuries) in his *Magen*

Avot 2, 1 refers to the more than 400 precious stones and their qualities mentioned by Aristotle, and Abraham b. David Portaleone (16th century) devoted a special chapter to this subject in his *Shiltei ha-Gibborim* (1612). Abraham wore a precious stone, hanging from his neck, which healed all those who looked at it (BB 16b); cf. the pearl-bag worn by animals (Sanh. 68a and Rashi ad loc.). Josephus mentions that the Essenes used precious stones for healing purposes (Wars, 2:136). Many legends have been woven round the *Shamir* stone (or worm?) which was said to have been used to cut stones for Solomon's Temple and to engrave the Ephod and breastpiece stones (Avot 5:6; Sot. 48a–b; Git. 68a). Similar qualities were ascribed to the sapphire (PdRK 135b) which was believed to be indestructible and out of which the Two Tablets of the Law (the Ten Commandments) were said to have been made (Tanḥ. Ki Tissa 26; Song. R. 5:14, 3). Precious stones almost invariably occur together with gold and silver as signs of wealth throughout rabbinic literature, and are the subjects of numerous legends (see Ginzberg, Legends, index, s.v. Stone (Stones), Precious). Precious stones were also used for *seals and signet rings.

The expression תכשיט (esp. תכשיטי נשים) = finery, covers not only jewelry but also *cosmetics. Women's finery as a means of seduction was said to have been the invention of the daughters of Cain (see Krauss, TA I. 198), yet women were entitled to possess and wear it (Ket. 65a). Jewelry formed part of the marriage settlement (Song R. 4:12; TJ, Ket. 6:3, 30d), and was sometimes given in lieu of betrothal money (Kid. 48a); cf. certain restrictions on Sabbath wear and some purity regulations (Shab. 6:1; Tanh. Gen. 34, 1; Kel. 11:8, 9; cf. Shab. 62b; Tosef., Kid. 1:11). A bride in particular, was to adorn herself lavishly (Song R. 4:10, 1; Tanḥ. Ex. 31, 18). Jewelry was of gold, silver, precious stones, pearls, and sometimes coral. There are full details of the treatment of pearls, their size, color, and shape and the manner in which they were pierced. They were strung together into necklaces sometimes consisting of several rows. Pearls were also set in diadems, together with precious stones; they were also inset in them or vice versa. In general pearls rated above jewels as the most precious objects, and served as presents between royalty (Artaban of Persia to Judah ha-Nasi, TJ, Pe'ah 1:1, 15d). Not only men wore these but even animals were sometimes adorned with precious stones as amulets as can be seen from the story of the ass bought by Simeon b. Shetaḥ (TJ, BM 2:5, 8c).

The main types of jewelry mentioned are signets (see *seals) usually worn as finger rings; women generally wore no signet rings, only ordinary rings (Shab. 6:1, 3; 62a; Kel. 11:8). Metal rings with a seal made of sandalwood or vice versa are mentioned. Rings, probably as other jewelry, were acceptable as loan-pledges (TJ, Shev. 10:9, 39d). They could also contain poison (Deut. R. 2:24). Women, brides in particular, wore as diadems a "City of Gold" (representing Jerusalem, Shab. 6:1; Kel. 11:8; Sot. 49b) such as Akiva once gave to his wife (Shab. *ibid.*; TJ, Shab. 6:1, 7d; ARN[2] 12:30). Above all, women wore necklaces (*catella*), some of the "choker" type which were made of precious metal or stones, pearls, glass beads, or sandalwood. Ear- and nose rings were very common among women and also children of both sexes. An amulet-text was inserted in a capsule worn round the neck; children wore also small tablets or scrolls containing a Bible verse. Officials and tradesmen wore the insignia of their office or trade as adornments. Other ornaments included anklets, bracelets, and also strings of coins, worn, by children in particular, on the forehead, as a necklace, or on the upper part of the dress. Women also wore bells around the neck or attached to their dress.

BIBLIOGRAPHY: Eisenstein, Yisrael, 1 (1907), 71–74 (with bibliography); I. Loew, *Fauna und Mineralien der Juden* (1969); N. Shalem, in: *Leshonenu*, 3 (1931), 291–9; idem, in: *Kovez ha-Ḥevrah ha-Ivrit la-Ḥakirat Erez Yisrael va-Attikoteha*, 2 (1935), 197–214; U. Cassuto, *A Commentary on the Book of Exodus* (1967); S. Tolansky, *The History and Use of Diamond* (1962); E.S. Dana, *A Textbook of Mineralogy*, ed. by W.E. Ford (1966[4]); S. Shefer (ed.), Abraham b. David Portaleone, *Bigdei Kehunnah* (1964); R.Z. Sverdlov, *Yesodot ha-Minerologyah…* (1948), 177–87; A. Rosenzweig, *Kleidung und Schmuck in Bibel und talmudischen Schriften* (1905).

PREGER, JACOB (1887–1942), Yiddish playwright, poet, and short story writer. Preger was born in Kobrin, Belorussia, and raised in Drogichin and Warsaw. His reputation is based largely on two highly successful plays, *Der Nisoyen* ("The Temptation," 1925) and *Simkhe Plakhte* ("Simkhe the Rag," 1935), a comedy produced by Maurice Schwartz in the U.S. under the title *Der Vasertreger* ("The Watercarrier"). His published verse includes *Oyf di Vegn* ("On the Roads," 1914), *Oyfn Veg* ("On the Road," 1919), and *Shloyme Hameylekh* ("King Solomon," 1932), a "dramatic poem in three acts." Preger's art is rooted in folklore and the popular imagination. He is reported to have been killed by the Germans in Otwock.

BIBLIOGRAPHY: LNYL, 7 (1968), 227–8; Z. Zylbercweig, *Leksikon fun Yidishn Teater*, 3 (1959), 1888–94. **ADD. BIBLIOGRAPHY:** M. Ravitch, *Mayn Leksikon*, 1 (1945).

[Leonard Prager]

PREIL, ELAZAR MEIR (1881–1933), rabbi. Born in Birz, Lithuania, he studied with his bother Rabbi Joshua Joseph before going to Slabodka. After ordination he joined the faculty of the yeshivah in Sadove and then moved with Rabbi Bloch to Telshe. In 1907 he became the rabbi of Beit Midrash Hagadol in Manchester, England, and then immigrated to the United States in 1911 where he became a rabbi in Trenton. A fellow graduate of Telshe, Rabbi Bernard Revel invited Preil to teach at the Rabbi Isaac Elchanan Theological Seminary where he taught from 1912 onward, first while serving in Trenton and then as rabbi in Elizabeth, New Jersey. During World War I he worked with the Central Relief Committee and became secretary of Agudath ha-Rabbonim and chairman of its *Vaad Kashrut*. He was widely published in Torah journals and published a book on family purity law in Yiddish. He was succeeded by his son-in-law Rabbi Pinchas Teitz, who strengthened the Elizabeth Jewish community.

BIBLIOGRAPHY: M.D. Sherman, *Orthodox Judaism in America: A Biographical Dictionary and Sourcebook* (1996).

PREIL, GABRIEL JOSHUA (1911–1993), U.S. Hebrew poet. Born in Dorpat, Estonia, Preil was taken to the United States in 1922. Though he published essays from time to time, wrote in Yiddish and English, and translated from Hebrew into English and from English into Hebrew, he was mainly a modernist Hebrew poet who introduced new themes and cadences into Hebrew literature in America. His lyrical pieces, which form the bulk of his collected poems, usually move in subtle, unrhymed rhythms on the boundary of prose and poetry. He is a poet of things and facts: a map, a mailbox, Lincoln Center in New York City, a Chinese sketch, a picture of Vincent van Gogh serve as foci for poetical aperçus and reflective moods. Though influenced by Whitman, Frost, and Sandburg, whose "Prairie" he translated into Hebrew, he was mainly an introspective lyricist. The New Hampshire and Vermont landscapes fascinated him: The cool sobriety of the north corresponded to his temperament which never ventured into flights of pathos.

Preil's poetry appeared in the following volumes: *Nof Shemesh u-Kefor* (1944); *Ner Mul Kokhavim* (1954); *Mappat Erev* (1961); and *Ha-Esh ve-ha-Demamah* (1968). A volume of his Yiddish poems, *Lider*, including his translations of his Hebrew poems, appeared in 1966. Other books of his poems are *Mi-tokh Zeman ve-Nof* (1973), *Shirim mi-Shenei ha-Keẓavot* (1976) and *Yalkut Shirim* (1978), *Adiv le-Aẓmi* (1981), *Ḥamishim Shir ba-Midbar* (1987). Dan Miron collected the later poems and wrote an essay on Preil's poetry in *Asfan Setavim* (1993). Preil also published a monograph in English on *Israeli Poetry in Peace and War*, in 1959.

BIBLIOGRAPHY: A. Epstein, *Soferim Ivrim ba-Amerikah*, 1 (1952), 229–36; A. Shabtay, *Gavri'el Preil* (Heb., 1965); A. Marthon, in: *Bitzaron*, 43 (1961), 49–53; 54 (1966), 163–7. **ADD. BIBLIOGRAPHY:** Y. Rabinovitz, *"Darko shel G. Preil ba-Shirah,"* in: *Hadoar*, 48 (1969), 354–355, 358; D. Rudavsky, "G. Preil: A Hebrew Poet in America," in: *Judaism*, 25 (1976), 188–200; A. Komem, in: *Yedioth Aharonoth* (January 21, 1977); Y. Akaviahu, *"Ha-Shir be-Aspaklariyyat ha-Shir,"* in: *Moznayim*, 47:2 (1978), 129–31; M. Peri, *"Ha-Onah ha-Me'uzenet: Al Mivneh ha-Omek shel Shirei Preil,"* in: *Siman Keriah*, 9 (1979), 369–88; 453–462; E. Sharoni, "Weary Single of Exile: G. Preil's 'Courteous to Myself'," in: *Modern Hebrew Literature*, 7:1–2 (1981/82), 50–55; Y. Feldman, *Modernism and Cultural Transfer: Gabriel Preil and the Tradition of Jewish Literary Bilingualism* (1985); D. Pinto, *Ha-Hekerut im Shirim Kodmim ke-Misgeret Yeda Relevantit: Le-Miẓui Mashma'ut ha-Shir ha-Boded be-Shirat Gabriel Preil* (1997); A. Holtzman, *"Ha-Meẓayyer be-Millim: G. Preil ve-ha-Omanut ha-Plastit,"* in: *Migvan* (1989), 127–140; E. Spicehandler, "Gabriel Preil," in: *CCAR Journal*, 50:3 (2003), 76–84.

[Eisig Silberschlag]

PREMINGER, OTTO LUDWIG (1905–1986), U.S. film and stage director and producer. Born in Vienna, Preminger worked at Max *Reinhardt's Josefstadt Theater in Vienna in 1923, and in 1928 was engaged by Reinhardt as director. He went to the U.S. in 1935 and gained prominence in the theater with productions that included the anti-Nazi play *Margin for Error* (1943). Taking up film work, he became one of the most controversial and important directors.

His successes include *Laura* (1944); *Daisy Kenyon* (1947); *Angel Face* (1952); *The Moon Is Blue* (1953), which led to a Supreme Court decision that prohibited local censors from stopping distribution; *Carmen Jones* (1954), an African American version of Bizet's opera *Carmen*, starring Harry Belafonte and Dorothy Dandridge, whose performance earned her an Oscar nomination for Best Actress – the first for an African American actress in a leading role; *The Man with the Golden Arm* (1956); *Saint Joan* (1957); *Bonjour tristesse* (1958); *Anatomy of a Murder* (1959); *Exodus* (1960), based on Leon *Uris' novel that dealt with the pre-1948 migration of European refugees to Israel; *Advise and Consent* (1962); *In Harm's Way* (1965); *Bunny Lake Is Missing* (1965); *Hurry Sundown* (1967); *Skidoo* (1968); *Tell Me That You Love Me, Junie Moon* (1970); *Such Good Friends* (1971); *Rosebud* (1975); and *The Human Factor* (1979), all of which he produced and directed. Preminger also directed such films as *Forever Amber* (1947); *River of No Return* (1954); and *Porgy and Bess* (1959).

Despite condemnation of several of his films by the Roman Catholic Legion of Decency, Preminger was later decorated by the Vatican for his film *The Cardinal* (1963). Both *Laura* and *The Cardinal* earned him Academy Award nominations for Best Director, and *Anatomy of a Murder* was nominated for a Best Picture Oscar.

Preminger's autobiography, *Preminger*, appeared in 1977.

BIBLIOGRAPHY: A. Sarris (ed.), *Interviews with Film Directors* (1967), 339–49; *Current Biography Yearbook 1959* (1960), 369–71. **ADD. BIBLIOGRAPHY:** N. Grob, *Otto Preminger* (1999); W. Frischauer, *Behind the Scenes of Otto Preminger* (1974); G. Pratley, *The Cinema of Otto Preminger* (1971).

[Harvey A. Cooper / Rohan Saxena and Ruth Beloff (2nd ed.)]

°**PŘEMYSL OTTOKAR II** (c. 1230–1278), margrave of Moravia in 1247, duke of Austria in 1251, and king of Bohemia in 1253. Following his general policy of developing the cities, Přemysl protected the Jews in his dominions. The city privilege of *Jihlava (Iglau), which he signed in 1249, contained clauses concerning Jews. In 1254 he issued a charter, based on the 1244 declaration of *Frederick II of Babenberg and even more liberal than the earlier proclamation. It was valid for all his dominions. Among other provisions, it added sacred vestments to the articles forbidden as pledges, but it left the adjustment of the rate of interest to the contracting parties. Though omitting the provisions about capital punishment for desecration of cemeteries, it laid down that the Jews were not to be disturbed on their holidays with the return of pledges. Another provision was that an oath taken by a Jew was itself sufficient to absolve him of responsibility in the case of a pawn that was accidentally destroyed. Moreover, Přemysl included the bulls of *Innocent IV against the blood libel. He employed two Jewish *comes camerae*, and Jewish tax collectors and mintmasters. His favorable treatment of the Jews was opposed by the clergy. In 1268, apparently as a reaction to the Vienna Church Council of 1267, he renewed the Jewish rights "of his youth"; since the

Jews belonged to his chamber, he indicated, they came under his protection. Between 1273 and 1278 he exempted the *Brno (Bruenn) community from all taxes for one year.

BIBLIOGRAPHY: J.E. Scherer, *Die Rechtsverhaeltnisse der Juden in den deutsch-oesterreichischen Laendern*, 1 (1901), 336–8; B. Bretholz, *Quellen zur Geschichte der Juden in Maehren* (1935), 2–10; idem, *Geschichte der Juden in Maehren im Mittelalter*, 1 (1934), index s.v. *Přemysl Otakar II*; Bondy-Dworský, 1 (1906), 17–32; M. Grunwald, *Vienna* (1936), index, s.v. *Ottakar II*; H. Tietxe, *Die Juden Wiens* (1935), index, s.v. *Przemysl Ottokar von Boehmen*.

[Meir Lamed]

PRESBYTER JUDAEORUM (arch-presbyter, or *le prestre* in Norman French), secular head of the exchequer of the Jews in 13th century England who supervised the collection of taxes and fees for the crown. He has been variously identified by historians as chief rabbi, high priest, bishop, or judge. As one of the most prominent Jews in England, he was often called upon by the king to advise on a variety of matters affecting his people, and was sworn "to look after the administration of justice on behalf of the king and to explain the king's laws," largely, presumably, on administrative matters. Six such arch-presbyters are known, all of them wealthy. Jacob of London, appointed in 1199, was followed in 1207 by Josce fil' Isaac, who was succeeded by *Aaron of York in 1236. *Elias le Eveske assumed the position in 1243. After protesting against the onerous taxes and fines, he was deposed in 1257 and eventually became an apostate. The king then offering the Jews the right to select a successor, they chose Hagin (Ḥayyim), son of Master Moses of Lincoln, in 1258. The last arch-presbyter, who held office from 1281 until the expulsion of the Jews from England a decade later, was Cok Hagin, son of Deulecresse of London.

BIBLIOGRAPHY: H.P. Stokes, *Studies in Anglo-Jewish History* (1913), 23–43; Roth, England, 112n., 30–31, 79–80; A.M. Hyamson, *History of the Jews in England* (1928²).

[Isaac Levitats]

PRESENCE, DIVINE. The notion of the Divine Presence is expressed in the Bible in two different senses: (1) in the corporeal sense, i.e., the actual dwelling (*shakhan*, שָׁכַן) of God in His abode; (2) in the abstract sense, i.e., symbolic representation by means of calling or establishing His name (*shikken shem*, שִׁכֵּן שֵׁם) upon the Sanctuary or the people.

The Corporeal Notion

God's presence, according to the ancient view, is confined to the Tabernacle/Sanctuary and to other visible phenomena serving as the vehicles of God, such as the Ark and the *cherubim or the cloud enveloping the Godhead in its movements. That the Tabernacle was considered an indicator for God's presence in ancient Israel may be learned from the words of Nathan the prophet to David: "… I have been moving about [*mithalekh*] in a Tabernacle and tent [*be-ohel u-ve-mishkan*] … All the time I was moving about among the Israelites…" (II Sam. 7:6–7). The same concept is given expression in the Priestly source of the Pentateuch: "I will establish My abode [*mishkani*] in your midst… and I will be moving about[i.e, be present]in your midst: I will be your God and you shall be my people" (Lev. 26:11–12). Similar statements are found in other parts of the Priestly literature, where *shakhan*, "dwelling," is used instead of *hithalekh*, "moving about," as in Exodus 25:8: "Let them make me a Sanctuary that I may dwell [*we-shakhanti*] among them," and at the end of the inauguration of the Tabernacle in Exodus 29:45–46: "And I will dwell among the Israelites and I will be their God." The rabbinic term *Shekhinah is actually an abstraction of this concept of "dwelling," which in the sources just quoted is understood literally. Indeed the Tabernacle, as depicted in the Priestly tradition, represents a royal house with all its necessary facilities.

Within the inner recesses of the Tabernacle, removed and veiled from the human eye sits the Deity ensconced between the two cherubim and the entire conception of the service is anthropomorphic (see below). It is performed "before the Lord" (לפני ה') that is, in His presence.

The presence of the Deity in the Sanctuary demands a rigorous observance of all rules concerning holiness and purity; any laxity might incur the wrath of the Deity and thus invite disaster. The divine seclusion must be respected. Thus in an adjoining chamber, the high priest, the most intimate of God's ministrants, attends to His essential needs. Only the priest who ministers to the Lord may approach the divine sanctum; the "stranger" who draws near must die (Num. 17:28 etc.). Drawing near to the Deity here signifies entrance into the actual sphere of the Divine Presence and for this reason is fraught with great physical danger (cf. Lev. 10:1–2; Num. 16:35).

This anthropomorphic theology derives from early sacral conceptions. The Ark was conceived as the footstool of the Deity and God as sitting enthroned upon the cherubim (I Sam. 4:4; Ps. 80:2; 99:5, etc.) The shewbread (לחם הפנים) laid out before the Lord by the high priest, the lamp kindled before Him to furnish light, the sweet incense burned mornings and evenings for His pleasure, the offerings consumed by the Divine fire, and the danger that accrues from approaching the Divinity are all alluded to in the early historiographic narratives.

In the ancient Israelite traditions God's presence is manifested mainly by the Ark and the pillar of cloud (see below). The Ark guided the people in the desert (Num. 10:33–34) and preceded the Israelites in the crossing of the Jordan before entering the Holy Land (Josh. 3:3ff.). The Ark also accompanied the people in their battles with their enemies (Num. 10:35–36), a fact which is well exemplified in the story of the critical encounter between the Israelites and the Philistines in Aphek (I Sam. 4). When the Ark was brought into the camp, the Israelites shouted with a great shout so that the whole earth stirred (4:5), and the Philistines, hearing the shout, became terrified, saying that "God has come into the camp" (4:7). The most common expression for the manifestation of God's presence is *Kevod* YHWH.

THE KAVOD OF THE LORD. The Godhead and its appearance are associated with the term *kavod*, a term underlying the imagery of the Divine Presence in the Bible and paralleling the term *Shekhinah* in rabbinic literature. The Tabernacle is said to be sanctified by the "*Kavod* of the Lord" (Ex. 29:43) and indeed when God enters the Tabernacle after its inauguration the Tabernacle is said to be filled with the *kavod* (Ex. 40:34–35). The dedication of the Jerusalem Temple is described in similar terms in I Kings 8:11. In both cases the *kavod* enters the holy abode, accompanied by the cloud, up to the Holy of Holies during which time Moses, on the one hand, and the Jerusalem priests, on the other, could not come in to minister. Only after the cloud departed and the *kavod* arrived at its place between the cherubim could Moses or the Jerusalem priests reenter the holy House.

The cloud serves as an envelope which screens the Deity from mortal view. Only Moses, who converses with God face to face, may enter into the cloud (Ex. 24:18). To the Israelites, however, God manifests Himself only when covered by a cloud. Unlike Moses they see only flames flashing forth from the cloud (Ex. 24:17). Only once does God manifest Himself to Israel without His screen of cloud – on the day of the inauguration of the Tabernacle (Lev. 9:23), an event whose importance parallels the Sinaitic revelation. The cloud departs from the Deity only when He assumes another mode of concealment, namely the Tent of Meeting or the Sanctuary. When the *kavod* enters the Tabernacle, the cloud remains outside and covers the tent. When the Tabernacle is dismantled, the *kavod* leaves the tent which is enveloped once again by the cloud which awaits Him and rises upward (Num. 9:15ff.).

THE NATURE OF THE KAVOD. Knowledge of the underlying imagery of the concept of *kavod*, which is embedded in Priestly tradition, is provided by Ezekiel whose ideology and divine imagery is grounded on Priestly doctrine. In Ezekiel 1, the *kavod* is described as an envelope of fire and brightness conveyed on a chariot. From afar, the apparition is like a blazing fire upon a great cloud swept by a storm wind (1:4). It is this radiance and brightness of the *kavod* which made Moses' face radiant after he spoke with God (Ex. 34:29–35).

This characteristic feature of God, i.e., His being surrounded by an aureole or nimbus, is salient in the description of gods in Mesopotamia. The terms denoting the halo of the gods in Mesopotamia, *pulḫu-melammu*, actually correspond to the Hebrew *kavod-yir'ah* and indeed refer to the flame and fire enveloping the Godhead. Like the Tabernacle and Temple in Israel, the Mesopotamian shrines and chapels were clad with the *melammu*, i.e., the divine splendor. The *kavod* is said to cover (cf. Hab. 3:3, *ksh*) and fill (Num. 14:21; Isa. 6:3, *ml'*) heaven and earth. The same idea occurs in connection with the *pulḫu-melammu* in Akkadian expressed by the verbs *katāmu* and *malû* which are identical with the Hebrew *ksh* and *ml'*. The Akkadian *pulḫu-melammu* is often employed in connection with overwhelming the enemy and terrifying him. This is in fact expressed in Isaiah 2 where on the "day of the Lord" God appears in "terror" and "majestic glory" (*paḥad* YHWH *ve-hadar ge'ono*) a pair of concepts which can now be better understood on the basis of the Mesopotamian parallels.

The correspondence of *pulḫu-melammu* to *kavod-yir'ah* may be discerned in some other biblical descriptions. The Mesopotamian god imparts his *melammu* to the king who is the god's representative and thus endows him with divine power. When the god rejects the king and deprives him of the *melammu*, the king no longer continues to reign by divine grace. Reflections of these beliefs may also be discerned in biblical literature. Though the Priestly document describes only Moses as being endowed with the divine radiance, biblical wisdom and psalmodic literature describe man in general, in contexts in which he is likened to a king, as being endowed with the divine *kavod* and splendor: "Thou hast made him little less than God, and dost crown him with *kavod* and splendor" (Ps. 8:6). If man becomes unworthy then God deprives him of the divine *kavod*: "He has stripped me of my *kavod* and taken the crown from my head" (Job 19:9).

Ezekiel in his divine chariot vision describes the divine animals as endowed with terror (*yir'ah*; 1:18). The passage appears to employ the term in the sense of a dazzling and awe-inspiring covering or dress of heavenly and divine beings as does its Akkadian counterpart in Babylonian and Assyrian literature (see Oppenheim, in bibl.). The obscure expression in the Song of the Sea *nora' tehillot* (Ex. 15:11a) is also best rendered in this sense. The word *tehillot* in this verse does not mean "praises" but "radiance" (cf. Job 29:3; 31:26, 41:10) as it does in Habakkuk 3:3: "His splendor covered the heavens and the earth was full of his *tehillah*." The *tehillah* of God fills the universe as does His *kavod* (cf. Num. 14:21; Isa. 6:3). The terms *yir'ah* and *kavod*, then, are used synonymously in biblical literature as are their Akkadian counterparts *pulḫu* and *melammu* in Babylonian literature.

The Abstract Notion

In contradiction to this corporeal representation of the *kavod*, Deuteronomy promulgates the doctrine of the "Name." The Deity cannot be likened to any form whatever, and He cannot therefore be conceived as dwelling in a Temple. God has caused the Temple to be called by His name or has caused His name to dwell therein, but He Himself does not dwell in it. The Deuteronomic school used the word *shem*, "name," to indicate the incorporeal aspect of God in a very consistent manner and never made the slightest digression from it. There is not one example in the Deuteronomic literature of God's dwelling in the Temple or the building of a house for God. The Temple is always the dwelling of His "name." This consistency is seen most clearly when a Deuteronomic text is interwoven with an earlier text which does not know the "name theology." Thus the account of the building of the Temple and the ancient story of its dedication speak plainly about building a house for God (I Kings 6:1, 2; 8:13), while the Deuteronomist whenever he mentions the building, describes it as being for the "name" of God (I Kings 3:2; 5:17, 19; 8:17, 18, 19, 20, 44, 48).

The most definitive expression of this theology is to be found in the prayer of Solomon in I Kings 8. The Temple is not God's place of habitation but serves only as a house of worship in which Israelites and foreigners alike may deliver their prayers to the Lord Who dwells in heaven. The idea that God's habitation is in heaven is here articulated most emphatically to eradicate the belief that the Deity sat enthroned between the cherubim in the Temple. Whenever the expression "Thy dwelling place" (*mekhon shivtekha*) is employed it is invariably accompanied by the word "in heaven" (8:39, 43, 49). The Deuteronomic editor is here disputing the older view implied by the ancient song that opens the prayer (8:12–13) and that designates the Temple as God's "exalted house and dwelling place [or pedestal] forever." The word *ba-shamayim*, "in heaven," is consistently appended to the expression *mekhon shivtekha* to show that it is heaven which is meant and not the Temple as the ancient song implies.

In actual fact, however, the term "thy dwelling place" in the early sources as well as in Solomon's song (8:12–13) denotes the Sanctuary; it is the editor who is here attempting to alter this meaning and thereby wrest the song from its natural sense. This may be apprehended from the Song of the Sea (Ex. 15) in which the poet declares: "Thou wilt bring them in, and plant them on Thy own mountain, the foundation, O Lord, which Thou hast made for Thy abode [*makhon le-shivtekha*] the Sanctuary, O Lord, which Thy hands have established" (15:17). The Israelites can only be planted in YHWH's own mountain. The latter denotes not the Temple mount alone but the entire Holy Land (cf. Isa. 11:9; 14:25; 25:6, 7, 10; see *Isaiah), but "the place for You to dwell in" and "the Sanctuary" means naturally the Temple, and one suspects an adaptation of Solomon's dedication with "you made" substituted for an original "I made" and "Your hands" for an original "my [i.e., Solomon's] hands" (cf. *Eretz-Israel*, 9 (1969), 45 n. 4). Indeed, Isaiah who visualizes God as seated upon a throne in the Temple (chapter 6), designates the Temple as the "foundation [*mekhon*] of Mount Zion" (4:5) and elsewhere explicitly describes the Lord as dwelling on Mount Zion (*ha-shokhen be-har Ẓiyyon*; 8:18; cf. 31:9). The expression "a place to dwell in," or rather the concept of a permanent abode for the Deity, goes back to the period of the United Monarchy when the House of the Lord was first erected, and constitutes an innovation in the Israelite conception of the Divinity. The psalms which extol Zion and Jerusalem, most of which are rooted in the court theology of the United Monarchy, consistently stress the idea that Jerusalem and its house of worship are the place of God's domicile (Ps. 46:5; 48:9; 50:2; 76:3, etc.). Thus, Psalms 132, which describes the transfer of the Ark to Jerusalem, expressly declares that "the Lord has chosen Zion, for He has desired it for His habitation [*moshav*]" (132:13). It is in the Temple of Jerusalem that God found, in a sense, His true place of rest, hence the Psalmist declares in the name of the Lord: "This is My resting place for ever, here will I dwell, for I have desired it" (132:14).

This conception appears to have been first contested during the period of the Hezekian-Josianic reforms, in all probability by the circle which was then engaged in the final crystallization of Deuteronomy. It is interesting that the very book which elevates the chosen place to the highest rank of importance in the Israelite cult should at the same time divest it of all sacral content and import. With remarkable consistency it resorts again and again to the phrase "the place where He shall choose to cause His name to dwell" (*le-shakken/la-sum shemo*) so as to emphasize that it is God's name and not God Himself who dwells within the Sanctuary, as against the Priestly tradition which speaks of God's dwelling in the midst of the children of Israel (Ex. 25:8; 29:45; Num. 16:3).

It appears then that it was the Deuteronomic school that first initiated the polemic against the anthropomorphic and corporeal conceptions of the Deity and that it was afterward taken up by the prophets Jeremiah and Deutero-Isaiah. It is by no means coincidental that the only passages which reflect a quasi-abstract conception of the Deity and negation of His corporeality are to be found in Deuteronomy and Deutero-Isaiah: Deuteronomy 4:12: "You heard the sound of words, but saw no form [*temunah*]" (cf. 4:15) and Isaiah 40:18: "To whom will you liken God or what likeness compare Him," and similarly in Isaiah 40:19 and 46:5.

These later conceptions, then, are diametrically opposed to the earlier views articulated in the JE and P documents and in the prophetic books antedating Deuteronomy. Thus Exodus 24:9–11 refers to the leaders, elders, and so on seeing God; in Exodus 33:23 Moses is said to have beheld God's back, and Numbers 12:8 speaks even more strikingly of Moses as gazing upon "the form [*temunah*] of the Lord." Amos similarly sees the Lord "standing beside the altar" (9:1), and Isaiah beholds God sitting upon a throne with His train filling the Temple (6:1; cf. I Kings 22:19–20).

REVELATION AND THE ARK IN DEUTERONOMIC LITERATURE. In contrast to the account in Exodus 19 of God's descent upon Mt. Sinai (19:11, 20), Deuteronomy 4:36 says: "Out of heaven He let you hear His voice, that He might discipline you; and on earth He let you see His great fire and you heard His words out of the midst of the fire." In other words, the commandments were heard from out of the midst of the fire that was upon the mount, but they were uttered by the Deity from heaven. Deuteronomy has, furthermore, taken care to shift the center of gravity of the theophany from the visual to the aural plane. In Exodus 19, the principal danger confronting the people was the likelihood that they might "break through to the Lord to gaze" (19:21); it was to prevent this that there was need to "set bounds for the people round about" (19:12) and to caution them not to ascend the mountain. Indeed, the pre-Deuteronomic texts always invariably speak of the danger of seeing the Deity: "For man shall not see Me and live" (Ex. 33:20), and similarly in Genesis 32:30: "For I have seen God face to face, and yet my life is preserved" (cf. Judg. 13:22; Isa. 6:5). Deuteronomy, on the other hand, cannot conceive of the possibility of seeing the Divinity. The Israelites saw only "His great fire" which symbolizes His essence and qualities (Deut. 4:24: "For the Lord your God is a devouring fire, a jealous God"; cf. 9:3), whereas God Himself remains in His heavenly abode. In Deuteronomy the danger threatening the people and the greatness of the miracle is that of hearing the voice of the Deity: "Did any people ever hear the voice of a god speaking out of the midst of the fire as you have heard, and survived" (4:33; cf. 5:23).

This attempt to eliminate the inherent corporeality of the traditional imagery also finds expression in Deuteronomy's conception of the Ark. The specific and exclusive function of the Ark, according to Deuteronomy, is to house the tables of the covenant (10:1–5); no mention is made of the Ark cover, *kapporet*, and the cherubim which endows the Ark with the semblance of a divine chariot or throne (cf. Ex. 25:10–22 [P]). The holiest vessel of the Israelite cult performs, in the Deuteronomic view, nothing more than an educational function: it houses the tablets upon which the words of God are engraved, and at its side the Book of the Torah is laid from which one reads to the people so that they may learn to fear the Lord (Deut. 31:26; cf. 31:12, 13). The Ark does not serve as God's seat upon which He journeys forth to disperse His enemies (Num. 10:33–36), but only as the vessel in which the tables of the covenant are deposited. This becomes quite clear when Deuteronomy 1:42–43 is compared with Numbers 14:42–44, a tradition on which the Deuteronomic account is based. Numbers 14:44 states that after the incident of the spies "the Ark of the Covenant of the Lord departed not out of the camp" and that this was the reason for the Israelites' defeat in their subsequent battle with the Amalekites and Canaanites. The Deuteronomic account, on the other hand, completely omits the detail of the Ark and ascribes the Israelite defeat to the fact that God was not in their midst, without referring to the whereabouts of the Ark.

The author of Deuteronomy similarly relates that it was God who went before the people to seek out new resting places (1:33), whereas the earlier source, upon which Deuteronomy was dependent, relates that it was the Ark which journeyed forth before the people to seek out new resting places for them (Num. 10:33). The absence of the Ark is especially striking in the Deuteronomic law of warfare (23:15). One would expect a passage which speaks of the presence of the Divinity within the military encampment to make some mention of the Ark which accompanied the warriors on their expeditions, as in I Samuel 4:6–7 (see above). The Deuteronomic law, however, speaks of the Lord as moving about the camp but does not make any allusion to the Ark or the holy vessels.

A similar conception is encountered in Jeremiah, for example, in 3:16–17: "They shall say no more, 'The Ark of the Covenant of the Lord.' It shall not come to mind… At that time Jerusalem shall be called the throne of the Lord." In other words, the Ark of the Covenant shall no longer serve as God's seat, as the people were previously accustomed to believe, but all of Jerusalem shall be "the seat of YHWH," that is in a symbolic sense. In another passage the prophet declares: "Do I not fill heaven and earth, says the Lord" (23:24), recalling the words of Deutero-(or Trito-) Isaiah when he expressly repudiates the notion of the Sanctuary as the place of God's habitation: "Heaven is My throne and the earth is My footstool, what is the house which you build for Me, and what is the place of My rest" (66:1). This view is also encountered in the Deuteronomic prayer of Solomon: "Behold, heaven and the highest heaven cannot contain Thee; how much less this house which I have built" (I Kings 8:27). The Sanctuary is here conceived as a house of prayer and not as a cultic center.

Although the abstract notion of the Divine Presence associated with the so-called "Name" theology found its full expression in Deuteronomy and in the Deuteronomic school, it should be pointed out that traces of it are already found in some of the earlier sources, especially in E (see *Pentateuch). The latter source does not contain theophanies in which God appears visibly in human form but revelations through various media, such as the dream or the angel. In one particular case, the angel, representing God, is said to contain God's "name" in himself (Ex. 23:21), which is at least an anticipation of the Deuteronomic "Name" theology.

BIBLIOGRAPHY: A.L. Oppenheim, in: JAOS, 63 (1943), 31–34; G.E. Wright et al., in: BA, 7 (1944), 158–84; 10 (1947), 45–68; G. von Rad, *Studies in Deuteronomy* (1953), 37–44; M. Haran, in: IEJ, 9 (1959), 30–38, 89–98; idem, in: *Scripta Hierosolymitana*, 8 (1961), 272–302; R.E. Clements, *God and Temple* (1965); M. Weinfeld, in: *Tarbiz*, 37 (1968), 116–20, 131–2; idem, *Deuteronomy and the Deuteronomic School* (1971); J. Milgrom, *Studies in Levitical Terminology*, 1 (1970).

[Moshe Weinfeld]

PRESIDENT OF ISRAEL, the official head of the State of Israel, resembling a constitutional monarch in function and powers, bears the ancient Hebrew title of "*nasi." According to the Basic Law: President of the State, passed by the Knesset on June 16, 1964, any citizen of Israel resident in the country is eligible for the office and may hold it for no more than two consecutive terms. The seat of the president is Jerusalem. With the exception of these two provisions, the Basic Law does not differ substantially from the Presidency of the State Law, 1951, which provides that the president must be elected by a majority of all members of the Knesset (i.e., by at least 61 votes) for a five-year term beginning on the day when he makes and signs the declaration of allegiance before the Knesset. He cannot be called to account before any court but he may be deposed by the Knesset for unbecoming behavior or in the case of ill-health, which makes it impossible for him to carry out his duties.

The president signs all laws (other than those concerned with his own powers) and treaties ratified by the Knesset. He appoints (upon the recommendation of the foreign minister) the diplomatic representatives of the state, and accepts the credentials of diplomatic representatives of foreign states accredited to Israel. Upon the recommendation of the appropriate governmental authorities, he appoints the state comptroller, the governor of the Bank of Israel, the members of the civil judiciary, and the judges of the religious courts. The president receives the resignation of the government and sets in motion the process of forming a new government by consulting representatives of all the political parties in the Knesset and then entrusting a member of the Knesset with the task of setting up a government. He is also given reports of government meetings. The president is empowered to pardon offenders and to mitigate sentences.

The first president of the state, Chaim *Weizmann, was elected on Feb. 16, 1949, at the opening session of the First Knesset – held with symbolic significance in Jerusalem, though the seat of the Knesset and government was still in Tel Aviv. He brought to the presidency his extraordinary experience in Zionist leadership and diplomatic negotiation, but illness restricted his activities to the formal duties of the office. Weizmann died on Nov. 9, 1952, and was succeeded by Izhak *Ben-Zvi. Under President Ben-Zvi, the official residence and office of the president were established in Jerusalem. There for two full terms and part of a third, until his death on April 23, 1963, Ben-Zvi filled the office with rich human, spiritual, and scholarly content. He and his wife Raḥel made the residence a meeting place for the diverse "tribes of Israel," aiding notably in the process of national amalgamation during those years of mass immigration from Europe and the Islamic countries. The monthly "New Moon" meetings of groups from particular countries and the "Open House" held annually during Sukkot week were typical of the direct contact established with the masses of Israel's citizens, including the Muslim, Druze, Christian, Bahai, and Samaritan communities. President Ben-Zvi paid state visits to Belgium and Holland, to Burma, and to Congo Brazzaville, the Central African Republic, and Liberia.

When Zalman *Shazar was elected president on May 21, 1963, he brought with him the qualities of a historian, Israel and Zionist leader, and orator, who had devoted himself to the world Jewish community, its educational problems, and its literature in Hebrew, Yiddish, and other languages. All these interests were expressed in the activities of the president's residence. The Bible Study Circle, originally led by the Prime Minister, David *Ben-Gurion, met there regularly, as did the Circle for the Study of the Diaspora under the aegis of the Hebrew University's Institute of Contemporary Jewry. The president instituted a special fund for the encouragement of literature and scholarship and invited outstanding writers, artists, and thinkers from abroad to visit Israel as his guests. He and his wife Raḥel, a writer and women's leader, paid state visits to Nepal, Uruguay, Chile, and Brazil in 1966, and Canada in 1967.

[Shulamit Nardi]

Shazar was succeeded by Ephraim *Katzir in 1973, Yitzhak *Navon (1978), Chaim *Herzog (1983), Ezer *Weizman (1993), and Moshe *Katzav (2000). Katzir, a renowned scientist, promoted science and higher education as president as well as encouraging the spirit of volunteerism. Navon, a member of the Knesset from 1965 to 1978, was the first Israeli president to take a public stand on a controversial political issue, calling for a commission of inquiry to investigate the events surrounding the Sabra and Shatilla massacre in the Lebanon War. He also made state visits to Egypt under Sadat and the U.S. at President Reagan's invitation. Herzog too spoke out on the issues and played a key role in the formation of the 1984 and 1988 coalition governments. He visited over 30 countries, including first-time presidential visits to Germany and China. Weizman brought a brash, down-to-earth style to the presidency, more than once putting his foot in his mouth. He frequently visited the wounded in hospitals and bereaved families in their homes. He resigned the office midway through his second term because of failing health and public criticism concerning his personal finances. His successor, Moshe Katzav, took a more low-key conciliatory approach.

PRESOV (Slovak. **Prešov**; Hung. **Eperjes**; Germ. **Preschau**; Ukr. **Prjasev**), town in E. Slovakia. From the late Middle Ages, foreigners attended the fairs of Presov, but the Jews had to leave in the evenings. The official rationale was that Jews were a different creed, but documents indicate that the burgers and guilds feared business competition. In the decree of Hungarian King Mathias II Corvinus, the guilds prohibited members from doing business with Jews. Austrian Empress Maria Theresa (1740–48) permitted Jews to stay in the city for the fair, but local law specified that a burger who provided a Jew accommodation would be fined. The Jew would be beaten, deprived of his wares, and expelled. So Jews settled in nearby villages. Things improved during the reign of Emperor Joseph II (1780–90) but declined again after his death.

In 1780 a Jewish businessman from Tarnopol, Poland, settled in Presov. Prosperous and well connected with the imperial court in Vienna, Markus Holaender (1760–1849) could not be expelled by the burgers, who were determined to oust him. In 1789 he received permission to live in Presov. Soon other Moravian Jews arrived. In 1830 a prayer room was established in Holaender's house, and in 1847 the first synagogue was erected. In 1855 the *ḥevra kaddisha* was established; in 1857 a primary school was opened; and in 1870 the *mikveh* opened. In 1887 the old cemetery, dating back to 1827, was replaced.

During the Magyar Revolution of 1848–49, many Presov Jews enlisted in the army. In 1868 Holaender's son, Leo, presided over the Hungarian Jewish Congress in Budapest, and led the Neolog (Reform) faction there. The Presov congregation joined the congress (Neolog organization of Hungarian Jewry). In 1871 the Orthodox split and established a new congregation. The influx of Orthodox Jews from Galicia and neighboring villages soon overshadowed the Neologs. In 1892 the Orthodox erected their own synagogue. The Neologs constructed a new synagogue in 1888 after theirs had been burnt in a townwide fire.

In 1836 there were 89 Jews in Presov; in 1844 there were 120; in 1851 there were 170. The community increased fast and in 1880 there were 1,221; in 1900 there were 1,211; in 1910 the number reached 2,673. In 1930 there were 4,858. In 1940, on the eve of the deportations, the official number of Jews was 4,308.

In 1860 the Neologs elected Dr. Mayer Austerlitz to serve as rabbi. Officiating until his death in 1913, he had a lasting impact on his congregation and the Jewish community. In 1912 a *nusaḥ "sefarad"* Ḥasidic group left the Orthodox congregation and organized one of their own. They hired a rabbi, created their own yeshivah, and built a synagogue, a *talmud torah*, and other Jewish installations. Each congregation had its own school system. In 1931 the Orthodox established a Beth Jacob girls' elementary school. Presov also had a vocational school for metal work.

During World War I many young men enlisted in the army. After the war, a wave of antisemitism swept upper Hungary. In Presov, all Jewish stores on the main street were looted and demolished. As a result, Zionist political parties and youth movements were formed. The Czechoslovak Communist Party was also engaged in political activity among the Jewish public and Jewish youth.

On the eve of the deportations, there were 6,000 Jews in Presov. In addition to the local population, the city hosted Jewish refugees from Germany, Austria, and Poland.

In October 1938, Hlinka's Slovak People's Party, a clerical nationalistic and Fascist party, proclaimed Slovakia's independence under Nazi supervision. One of their first orders of business was to persecute the Jews. In November 1938 Slovakia lost a part of its mainland, which was annexed to Hungary. The party blamed the Jews for the loss. On March 14, 1939, Slovakia proclaimed independence under the name the Slovak State. Again, the Jews were persecuted as violent demonstrations accompanied the proclamation. Jews were assaulted in the streets and their property vandalized. Soon all Jewish institutions and organizations were shut down. Jews were expelled from schools, and the Presov community was charged with the responsibility of teaching the children. The next year, appropriation of Jewish property under the pretext of "Aryanization" began. Jews were losing their property and sources of income. In the spring of 1941, the Hlinka Party ordered Jews to wear a yellow armband. Six months later, all Slovakian Jews had to wear a yellow Star of David. In January 1941 a mob burned down the Orthodox synagogue. During the winter of 1941–42 Jews who lived on main streets were forced to leave their apartments. Consequently, Jews expelled from Bratislava sought accommodation in Presov.

In March 1942, deportation to the camps in Poland began. In Presov, the deportations started on May 12. Some 6,000 of Presov's Jews perished in the Holocaust. While still crowded around Lublin, the home communities did their best to provide the deportees with money, medicine, and food. The remaining community organized a network of smugglers to transfer goods, money, and letters to the exiles. Jews who manage to escape from the camps and reach Slovak borders were transferred to safety in Hungary. In the spring of 1944, with the approaching front, the Jews of eastern Slovakia were ordered to resettle in central and western Slovakia.

At the end of August 1944, an anti-Fascist uprising took place in Slovakia; 26 Presov Jews participated. Among the six Presov Jews killed in the attempt was Egon Roth, leader of the Ha-Shomer ha-Ẓa'ir movement and head of the effort to help the Jews who had escaped from Poland.

In 1947 there were 548 Jews in Presov. There was only one congregation. The Orthodox synagogue was restored, as was the *mikveh*. A memorial was erected for the Holocaust victims. A kosher kitchen and restaurant supplied meals for those who returned but had no place to stay, as well as those on their way home. In the spring and summer of 1945, mobs attacked and vandalized Jewish installations, shouting antisemitic slogans. This prompted the remaining Jews to immigrate abroad.

In 1957 the synagogue underwent restoration and the cemetery was cleaned. During the Velvet Revolution, there were 60 Jews in Presov, who faced an unexpected problem: an American Jewish company wanted to purchase the Orthodox synagogue and transfer it to the United States. The Jews deterred their government from selling out. The Jewish Museum was reconstructed and opened in November 1993. The Orthodox synagogue is occasionally used for services. All other synagogues are used mainly as warehouses.

BIBLIOGRAPHY: M. Atlas, in: *Zeitschrift fuer die Geschichte der Juden*, 4 (1967), 17–32, incl. bibl. **ADD. BIBLIOGRAPHY:** G. Amir, *Presov the Story of a Jewish Community: One among Many* (2002); E. Bárkány-L. Dojc, *Zidovské nábozenské obce na Slovensku* (1991), 335–41; *Yizkor, Pietné odhalenie pamätnika martyrov v Presove*, 18 augusta 1991 (1992), 3–5; A.J. Licht, *Galed* (Tashmad).

[Yeshayahu Jelinek (2nd ed.)]

PRESS.

This article is arranged according to the following outline:

Introduction
In Australia and New Zealand
In Belgium
In Canada
In Czechoslovakia
In England
YIDDISH PRESS
In France
In Germany and Austria
BETWEEN THE TWO WORLD WARS
AFTER WORLD WAR II
IN VIENNA
In Holland
In Hungary
In India
In Italy
Ladino Press
ZIONISM
IN THE U.S.
ISRAEL
In Latin America

Introduction

The first Jewish newspaper is generally considered to be the *Gazeta de Amsterdam*, which appeared in 1675. Holland had by then become an important Jewish center, having attracted many Spanish-Portuguese and Polish Jews seeking a refuge from persecution, and some years earlier *Manasseh Ben Israel had set up the first Hebrew *printing press there. The appearance of the *Gazeta* was no accident. It was issued by a Sephardi printer, was written in Judeo-Spanish or Ladino, the language of the exiles, and carried dispatches from other countries. The next notable publication, *Dinstagishe un Fraytagishe Kurant* in Yiddish, appeared twice a week and then once a week as the *Dinstagishe Kurant* in 1686 and 1687. The first Jewish periodical was *Peri Eẓ Ḥayyim*, also of Amsterdam, a monthly bulletin containing rabbinical decisions of the Sephardi community. It appeared from 1728 to 1761.

As Emancipation and Haskalah gained ground among European Jewry in the middle of the 18th century, Jewish journals appeared in Germany and other countries. Their numbers increased with the revival of Hebrew, the growth of Yiddish literature, and the continued flight of Jews from Eastern Europe. The rise of modern Zionism and the emergence of political parties among the Jews stimulated printing and publishing, and by 1882 Isidore Singer of Vienna, in the brochure *Presse und Judenthum*, was able to list 103 extant Jewish newspapers and journals. Thirty of them were in German, 19 in Hebrew (three of them appearing in Jerusalem), 15 in English, 14 in Yiddish, six in Ladino, five in French, and the rest in eight other languages.

The first successful Jewish newspaper in the modern sense was the **Allgemeine Zeitung des Judentums*, launched in Leipzig in 1837 and surviving until 1922. The *Jewish Chronicle*, founded in London in 1841, was to prove even more successful and in 2006 has flourished as the oldest Jewish newspaper in the world. On Jan. 17, 1896, it published the first Zionist article by Theodor *Herzl. Herzl himself launched **Die Welt* in 1897. These two weeklies published the latest Jewish and Zionist news and served as sources for other newspapers before the Zionist Organization established its own press bureau to supply the Jewish press with the latest news from Ereẓ Israel and the Diaspora. The first Jewish news agency was the Neue Juedische Korrespondenz, which was founded in Berlin in 1907 and served the Jewish press until shortly after the outbreak of World War I. In order to keep in touch under war conditions with communities in other parts of the world, some Jewish organizations established offices in neutral countries. The World Zionist Organization, with headquarters in Berlin, opened offices in Copenhagen where an information bulletin appeared under its auspices in English, French, and German, and reached (sometimes in reprint) the countries of both the Allied and Central powers. Another well-organized agency was the Juedische Presse Zentrale in Zurich. The main function of these agencies was to scan the world press for information of Jewish interest and pass it on to the newspapers. They were mostly short-lived; but the *Jewish Telegraphic Agency, established in The Hague in 1914 by Jacob *Landau and reestablished in London in 1919 by Landau and Meir *Grossman, proved more permanent. In 1922 its headquarters were transferred to New York. It had correspondents and bureaus in many countries, and it issued a *Jewish Daily Bulletin* in English and other languages; in 1962 it began a weekly bulletin, *Community News*.

Until World War II, Europe had the largest number of Jewish periodicals. There were Yiddish dailies in Warsaw, Lvov, Cracow, Lodz, Bialystok, Vilna, Riga, Kovno, and other large East European towns, including Soviet Yiddish newspapers in Moscow, Kharkov, and Minsk. There were also Jewish Polish dailies, more than two dozen weeklies in Yiddish, Hebrew, and Polish, and nearly 100 monthlies. There were more than 100 Jewish German-language weeklies, fortnightlies, and monthlies in Germany and Austria. A Jewish German-language daily appeared in Vienna, 1919–27. The rise of Nazi power brought most of these papers to an end. When the Nazi forces overran any country, one of their first acts was to close down the Jewish publications. "Underground" newspapers also appeared in the ghettos, among the partisans in the forests, and even, if rarely, in the concentration camps.

In 1967 there were 580 Jewish newspapers and periodicals in the world, outside Israel: 178 in Europe, 245 in the U.S., 82 in Central and South America, 29 in Africa, 21 in Canada, 19 in Australia and New Zealand, several in Asia, and two in the Soviet Union. English was the language of the largest number (300), with Yiddish coming second (112). The position of the Yiddish language presented a paradox. Though Yiddish was regarded as generally losing ground, all the Jewish daily papers outside Israel, ten in number, were in Yiddish. Efforts to establish a Spanish Jewish daily in Argentina were without success, and an English Jewish daily in London proved unsuccessful. In 2006 there were around 50 weekly newspapers and a large number of bi-weekly and monthly publications in the U.S. There were 15 weekly Jewish newspapers in Europe, seven in Canada, three in Latin America, and two elsewhere in the world. In addition, there were many which appeared bi-weekly or monthly in different centers of Jewish population. The former Soviet Union saw a rebirth of the Jewish press with over 40 publications among the republics associated with the Federation of Jewish Communities.

[Lewis Sowden and Josef Fraenkel / Yoel Cohen (2nd ed.)]

In Australia and New Zealand

The Voice of Jacob, founded in Sydney in 1842, was the first Jewish newspaper in Australia, and before the end of the century several others, all in English, had run their brief careers and ceased publication. A few, however, became firmly established, notably the *Australian Jewish Herald* (1879), the *Australian Jewish Times* (1893), and *Hebrew Standard* (1894). There was no significant growth in the Jewish press until the middle decades of the 20th century, when the Jewish population rose from about 27,000 in 1938 to 67,000 in 1960. The *Australian Jewish News*, founded in Melbourne in 1933 as a bilingual English and Yiddish weekly, published a Sydney edition under the name of *The Sydney Jewish News*. In 1967 the two editions had a combined circulation of 20,000.

The Jewish press attained a high standard under the guidance of Newman Rosenthal, O. Rubinstein, and Reuben Havin, its leading editors during the 1930s and 1940s. They made it an important factor in molding opinion both in the Jewish community and among prominent non-Jews. Leading political figures gained their knowledge of Zionism, the Holocaust, and Israel from pages of the *Australian Jewish Herald* and the *Australian Jewish News*. This bore fruit in the pro-Jewish stand taken by Dr. C. Evatt of Australia, as chairman of the UN Advisory Committee on Palestine in 1947. Within the community, the press exercised a strong influence on the development of representative bodies, particularly the state Boards of Deputies and the Executive Council of Australian Jewry. It also influenced the decision in favor of establishing the Melbourne day school, Mount Scopus College, and later the Jewish day-school movement generally.

The strong support which the Jewish press gave to Zionism influenced the outlook of the Jewish community, eventually winning over old-established families who had opposed political Zionism in the pre-State era. The pro-Israel opinion thus formed eventually led to the downfall of the *Australian Jewish Herald* and its Yiddish subsidiary, the *Australian Jewish Post*. In 1968 the *Australian Jewish Herald*, the oldest existing Jewish paper in Australia, published an article with an anti-Israel bias. During the controversy that followed, David Lederman, publisher of the *Herald* and the *Post*, also attacked the Victoria Jewish Board of Deputies. Pressure by the board and the immediate loss of popularity compelled both papers, with a total circulation of 12,500 weekly, to cease publication. Among the other publications which appeared in Australia were *The Bridge*, a literary quarterly, and Yiddish periodicals, *Der Landsmann* and *Unzer Gedank*.

In New Zealand, the *Jewish Times*, a monthly, appeared in Wellington in 1931, and was succeeded by the *New Zealand Jewish Chronicle*, a bimonthly, in 1944. A monthly, *Hashofar*, was founded in 1959.

[Lewis Sowden]

In Belgium

The small size of the Jewish community of Belgium for long limited the publication of Jewish periodicals. The first, *Revue Orientale*, edited from 1841 to 1846 by Eliakim *Carmoly, did not have enough local interest to last. No others were published until shortly before World War I, when several publications were sponsored by Jews of East European origin.

By 1959, however, no fewer than 225 Jewish periodicals had appeared in Belgium, reflecting the vitality of the community in the 20th century. Of these, 46 were in a mimeographed or lithographed form; 97 were in Yiddish, four in Hebrew, 80 in French, two in German, one in Russian, one in English, and 27 in more than one language. Four were published between 1900 and 1918, 137 from 1919 until the German occupation of Belgium in 1940, seven illegally during the German occupation of 1940–44, and 70 after the liberation of Belgium. Most of these were intended for the membership of an organization, rather than for the public at large.

In 1970 there were five Jewish journals in Belgium: the weekly *Belgisch Israelietisch Weekblad*, founded in 1954; the bimonthly *Tribune Sioniste*, founded in 1951 and having a circulation of 5,500; three monthlies, *Centrale* (circulation 8,000), *Regards* (*Cahiers du Centre Communautaire Laic Juif*), and *Kehilatenou*; and a quarterly, *Central* in Flemish and Yiddish.

In Canada

The earliest Jewish newspaper to appear in Canada was the *Jewish Times*, a weekly first, published in 1897. In 1909 its name was changed to *Canadian Jewish Times*, and in 1915 it merged with the weekly *Canadian Jewish Chronicle* of Montreal, which had been founded in 1914. The *Chronicle* amalgamated with the *Canadian Jewish Review* and appeared as the *Canadian Jewish Chronicle Review* from 1966 in both Toronto and Montreal, becoming a monthly in 1970. There was no Yiddish press until 1907, when *Der Kanader Adler* (The Canadian [Jewish] Eagle) began daily publication in Montreal. Other Yiddish newspapers, such as the Toronto-based daily *Yiddisher Zhurnal* (Hebrew Journal) established in 1911, emerged in the wake of increased immigration from Eastern Europe. After several false starts, a weekly Yiddish paper *Dos Yiddishe Vort* (The Jewish Word) started up in Winnipeg,

Driven by a strong political agenda, Canadian Jewish communists began publishing a Yiddish newspaper starting from the 1920s that went through several name changes emerging as the Vokhenblat after World War II. A monthly *Congress Bulletin*, by the Canadian Jewish Congress from 1943 and the *Canadian Zionist*, in English and Hebrew, was published by the Zionist Organization beginning in 1931; the English/Yiddish *The View-Dos Vort* by the Canadian Labour Zionist movement beginning in 1940 and *Orah* of the Canadian Hadassah Organization. In addition a French monthly, *Bulletin du Cercle Juif*, was published by the Canadian Jewish Congress from 1954, and a quarterly in English and Spanish, *Newsletter*, founded by the International Council of Jewish Women, were both widely distributed.

[Lewis Sowden]

The Yiddish language press no longer existed in Canada in the 21st century, but the Anglo-Jewish press was alive and well. The *Canadian Jewish News* was by far the largest weekly Jewish newspaper in Canada with separate Toronto editions and Montreal editions. The Montreal edition offered readers some French articles. With a combined weekly subscriber count of about 41,000 households, the paper is read from coast to coast across Canada. It is privately-owned but effectively functions as the national community-based newspaper featuring diverse points of view on topics of Jewish interest, national and foreign. The weekly *Jewish Independent*, published between 1930 and 2005 as the *Jewish Western Bulletin*, serves the Jewish communities of British Columbia, especially Vancouver, and is largely circulated by mail. Serving Winnipeg and surrounding communities since 1925 is the weekly *Jewish Post and News*. Similarly *The Jewish Free Press* is an independent newspaper published in Calgary which addresses the interests of Jew in southern Alberta. *The Jewish Tribune* is published twice a month by B'nai B'rith Canada, and deals with local, national and international concerns. A left-leaning monthly magazine, *Canadian Jewish Outlook*, is currently published out of Vancouver, with the assistance of "collectives" in other communities. Increasingly, all these publications have online editions. Across Canada, many Jewish organizations, synagogue, Jewish campus groups and smaller communities also have their own newspapers or regular bulletins and there are several Jewish-community–focused radio and television programs broadcast in centers of heavier Canadian Jewish population.

[Richard Menkis and Harold Troper (2nd ed.)]

In Czechoslovakia

Jewish journalists worked in papers of all political parties in Czechoslovakia. There were Conservatives like Josef Penížek, Liberals like Josef Kodícek, Karel Poláček, and Richard Weiner; Social Democrats like Gustav Winter; and Communists like Rudolf Slánský. There were also baptized Jewish editors on the Catholic press, among them Alfred Fuchs and Pavel Tigrid. Adolf Stránský founded the daily *Lidové Noviny*. The *Prager Tagblatt* had many Jews on its staff (Max *Brod among them) and a large Jewish readership.

The Jewish press itself was characterized by vehement public discussion between the Zionists and the organized assimilationist movement, which created its first paper, *česko-židovské Listy*, in 1894. In 1907 it amalgamated with a similar periodical published by Viktor Vohryzek and appeared then as a weekly under the name *Rozvoj* until 1939. The first Zionist organ was the German weekly for youth, *Jung Juda*, which was established in 1899 by Filip Lebenhart and survived until late in the 1930s. Another weekly, *Selbstwehr*, edited from 1918 by Felix *Weltsch, assisted later by Hans Lichtwitz (Uri Naor; d. 1988), became one of the outstanding Zionist periodicals in Europe, and from the 1920s issued a woman's supplement edited by Hanna Steiner. Another Zionist weekly, *Juedische Volksstimme*, edited by its founder Max Hickl and later by Hugo *Gold, appeared in Brno. The paper was established in 1901 and appeared until 1939.

The first Zionist organ in Czech, *Židovské Listy pro čechy, Moravu a Slezsko*, appeared in 1913, but was suspended during World War I and replaced in 1918 by the weekly *Židovské zpravy*, edited by Emil Waldstein, František Friedman, Gustav Fleischmann, Zdeněk Landes, and Viktor Fischl (Avigdor *Dagan). In Slovakia and Carpathorussia the Jewish press included Orthodox organs and papers in Hungarian and Yiddish. In Slovakia were the Zionist weekly *Juedische Volkszeitung* (with a Slovak supplement), edited by Oskar Neumann, and the Mizrachi organ *Juedisches Familienblatt*; in Carpathorussia the Zionist weekly *Juedische Stimme*, the Revisionist *Zsidó Néplap*, and the journal of the rabbi of Munkacz, *Yidishe Tsaytung*, had the largest circulation. Of the many other Jewish periodicals the following were notable: the historical review *Zeitschrift fuer die Geschichte der Juden in Boehmen und Maehren* (editor Hugo Gold); *B'nai B'rith Blaetter* (editor Friedrich Thieberger); the Revisionist *Medina Iwrit-Judenstaat*, edited by Oskar K. *Rabinowicz (1934–39); the *Po'alei Zion paper *Der Neue Weg* (editor Karl Baum); and the sports monthly *Hagibor-Hamakabi*. The Jewish youth and student movements also published periodicals of varying duration in the different languages of the country. The *Juedische Revue* was issued by emigrants from Germany in the late 1930s. Between 1945 and the Communist take-over in 1948, attempts were made to revive some Jewish periodicals, but eventually all that remained of the extensive Jewish press in Czechoslovakia was the organ of the Prague congregation; *Věstník židovské náboženské obce v Praze*, edited by R. Iltis (d. 1977), who also edited the almanac *Zidovská ročenka*.

[Avigdor Dagan]

In England

The Anglo-Jewish press had its beginnings in the first half of the 19th century. During the next 100 years and more, numerous publications appeared both in London and the provinces. Many of them were short-lived, but some had long and influential careers, and in 1968 the Jewish press in Britain comprised about 60 publications.

The first periodical was *The Hebrew Intelligencer*, printed and published by J. Wertheimer in London. Intended as a monthly, it first saw light in January 1823, but published only three issues. More successful was *The Hebrew Review and Magazine of Rabbinical Literature*, also a monthly, which lasted from 1834 to 1837, under the editorship of Morris Jacob *Raphall. Persecution of Jews abroad demonstrated the need for a channel of expression in England and brought about the first effective enterprise in Anglo-Jewish journalism. *The Voice of Jacob*, edited by Jacob *Franklin, was initiated in September 1841 as a fortnightly, and was followed two months later by the *Jewish Chronicle*. The two papers were in competition until 1848, when the *Jewish Chronicle* gained the field for itself and was destined to become the most long-lived of Jewish newspapers. Among other papers that appeared in the ensuing years were *Sabbath Leaves* (1845) sponsored by Haim *Guedalla; *The Cup of Salvation* (Liverpool, 1846–47); *The Hebrew Observer* (1853), which merged with the *Jewish Chronicle* in the following year; *The Jewish Sabbath Journal* (1855); and the *Hebrew National* (1867).

The first Jewish penny paper, *The Jewish Record*, was a weekly that ran for four years (from 1868). *The Jewish World*, established in 1873, was edited by the novelist S.L. *Bensusan in 1897, when its circulation rose to 2,000. In 1931 it was acquired by the *Jewish Chronicle* and was amalgamated with it in 1934. Other papers were *The Jewish Times*, a penny weekly of 1876; *The Jewish Standard*, also a penny (1888–91); and *Jewish Society* (1888–91), under the nominal editorship of Frank Danby (the novelist Julia *Frankau). Provincial Jewry had periodicals such as *Jewish Topics* (Cardiff, 1886), *The Jewish Record* (Manchester, 1887), and *The South Wales Review* (1904). A Hebrew weekly *Ha-Yehudi* appeared in London 1897–1913 issued by Isaac *Suwalski.

The period after World War I produced *The Jewish Woman* (1925–26); *The Jewish Family* (1927); *The Jewish Graphic* (1926–28); *The Jewish Echo* (Glasgow, 1928–); *The Jewish Gazette* (Manchester, 1928–); *The Jewish Weekly* (1932–36); *World Jewry* (1934–36); and *The Jewish Guardian* (1920–36), which was founded under the editorship of Laurie *Magnus by a group of anti-Zionists. In 1968 the Jewish press of Great Britain included a branch of the Jewish Telegraphic Agency; the *Press Survey* of the World Jewish Congress, founded in 1945; the Jewish World News Agency (Yiddish), founded in 1940; and the *Jewish Chronicle* Feature and News Service, founded in 1948. There were weeklies in Glasgow, Manchester, Leeds, and Newcastle. In London, another weekly, *The Jewish Observer and Middle East Review*, was founded in 1952, as a successor to the *Zionist Review*. The fortnightlies included the Mizrachi *Jewish Review*, the Po'alei Zion's *Jewish Vanguard*, and *The Jewish Tribune* in English and Yiddish. The others varied widely from monthly trade journals to learned quarterlies and annuals.

YIDDISH PRESS. Attempts to establish Yiddish newspapers in England preceded the mass immigration from Eastern Europe in the 1880s. The *Londoner Yiddish-Deitche Zeitung* was started in 1867 and the socialist *Londoner Israelit* in 1878, but both were short-lived. Later enterprises were more successful. The weekly *Peilisher Yidel* (later *Die Zukunft*) was founded in 1884 and lasted for two years. As the immigrant communities increased in numbers in London, Leeds, and Manchester, they were served by dailies and weeklies, mostly socialist in outlooks – *Der Arbeter, Arbeter Fraynd* (1886–91), *Germinal* (anarchist fortnightly), *Der Veker* (anti-anarchist), *Di Naye Velt* (1900–01), and humorous periodicals such as *Pipifax, Der Bluffer*, and *Der Ligner*. It was not until the 20th century that Yiddish newspapers like the *Advertiser* and the *Yidisher Telefon* began to flourish. The *Advertiser* was absorbed by the *Yidisher Zhurnal*, founded in 1907, which was itself absorbed in 1914 by the *Yiddisher Ekspres*. The *Ekspres* began publication in Leeds in 1895 and became a London daily in 1899. The *Yidisher Tageblat* appeared from 1901 to 1910, and **Di Zeit*, a daily founded in 1913, survived until 1950. A Yiddish fortnightly, *Yidishe Shtime*, founded in 1951, was edited in 1970 by I.A. Lisky. There was also a Yiddish literary journal *Loshn un Lebn*.

[Lewis Sowden]

In France

There was no Jewish press in France before the French Revolution. The first Jewish publication was the *Caitung*, a weekly in Alsatian Yiddish issued by a Metz printer for five months from November 1789. Several later journals were also short-lived, and it was not until the early 1840s that a monthly, *Les Archives Israélites de France*, showed any capacity for survival. It was founded by S. Cahen and advocated reform. This stimulated J. *Bloch to launch a rival conservative monthly, *L'Univers Israélite*, in 1844. For nearly 100 years both periodicals exercised considerable influence on Jewish life, *Les Archives* surviving until 1935 and *L'Univers* continuing as a weekly until 1940. This 100-year period, however, saw the birth and demise of more than 300 other publications. A total of 374 appeared from 1789 to 1940. Only 38 of these saw the light before 1881; the largest number, 203, came into being after 1923. Of the total, 134 were in French, 180 in Yiddish, and nine in Hebrew; 56 of them (21 in Yiddish) were Zionist, and 28 (all in Yiddish) were communist. Many of them were stable and influential. Two of them were Yiddish dailies. During World War II a few underground papers were published in Yiddish and French. After the war, the Jewish press recovered its prewar character. In 1957 the illustrated *L'Arche*, edited by Joseph Samuel and published by the Fonds Social Juif Unifié, the leading Jewish welfare and fund-raising organization in France, began to appear. *L'Arhe* was intended to express the revival of French Jewry after World War II by reflecting its religious, intellectual, and artistic life. In 1967 there were three Yiddish dailies, among them *Unzer Vort* (Po'alei Zion) and *Unzer Shtime* (*Bund), and a large number of weeklies and monthlies in French and Yiddish.

In Germany and Austria

Jewish periodicals appeared in Germany from the middle of the 18th century, when they became an expression of the era and its movements – Enlightenment, Reform, and Emancipation. One of them, the *Dyhernfurther Privilegierte Zeitung*, published in 1771–72 in the Lower Silesian town famous for its Hebrew printing presses, was a German-language journal written in Hebrew script. A few years later **Ha-Me'assef* (Berlin, 1784–1811), was founded by Moses *Mendelssohn and used Hebrew as its medium. The first periodical intended for Jews published in the German language and script was *Sulamith*, which appeared in Dessau from 1806 to 1833. Apart from this, the only periodical before 1850 that lasted for any significant length of time was the *Wissenschaftliche Zeitschrift fuer Juedische Theologie*, which Abraham *Geiger edited in Frankfurt from 1835 to 1847. The longest-lived journal in German Jewish press history – 85 years – was the religiously liberal weekly *Allgemeine Zeitung des Judentums*, founded in 1837 by R. Ludwig Philippson of Magdeburg, and edited by him for 50 years.

Of the 75 Jewish newspapers and periodicals that came into existence during the 60 years before World War I, only 16 of those appearing at least once a month held out for more than 12 years. They were the following:

(1) the **Monatsschrift fuer Geschichte und Wissenschaft des Judentums* (1851–1939);

(2) **Jeschurun* (Frankfurt, 1854–70), founded by Samson Raphael *Hirsch;

(3) the Hebrew **Ha-Maggid* (Lyck, 1857–92);

(4) the Orthodox **Israelit* (Mainz and Frankfurt, 1860–1938);

(5) the *Juedische Zeitschrift fuer Wissenschaft und Leben* (Breslau, 1862–75);

(6) the **Juedische Presse* (Berlin, 1869–1923), edited by Hirsch *Hildesheimer;

(7) the Conservative *Israelitische Wochenschrift fuer die religioesen und sozialen Interessen des Judenthums* (Breslau and Magdeburg, 1870–94);

(8) the *Monatsblaetter zur Belehrung ueber das Judentum* (Frankfurt, 1881–1908);

(9) the liberal *Allgemeine Israelitische Wochenschrift* (Berlin, 1891–1906);

(10) *Im deutschen Reich* (Berlin, 1895–1921), the organ of the Central Union of German Citizens of Jewish Faith;

(11) the independent *Juedisches Volksblatt* (Breslau, 1896–1923);

(12) the Zionist **Juedische Rundschau* (Berlin, 1896–1938, see below);

(13) the Mizrachi *Israelitisches Familienblatt* (Frankfurt, from 1900) called after 1920 *Neue Juedische Presse*;

(14) the arts periodical *Ost und West* (Berlin, 1901–22);

(15) the *Zeitschrift fuer Demographie und Statistik der Juden* (Berlin, 1904–22);

(16) the *Israelitisches Familienblatt* (Hamburg, 1898–1938).

BETWEEN THE TWO WORLD WARS. The Jewish political press was at its most flourishing after World War I, when German Jewry enjoyed a cultural revival. This political press consisted mainly of weeklies, such as (1) the Zionist *Juedische Rundschau*; (2) the **C.V. Zeitung* (Berlin, 1922–38) edited by Ludwig Hollaender, Alfred Weiner, Alfred Hirschberg, and others, founded in Berlin in 1922 as an outgrowth of the Central Union's monthly *Im Deutschen Reich*; (3) the *Israelitisches Familienblatt*, established in Hamburg in 1898 by Max and Leo Lessmann; (4) the **Israelit*; and (5) *Der Schild*, founded in 1921 by the Jewish ex-servicemen's association.

Of more than three dozen community papers that appeared at various periods, most of them neutral in their handling of Jewish politics, the most prominent ones were those appearing in Berlin from 1911, Frankfurt from 1922, and Munich (serving the Bavarian region) from 1924. A considerable number of papers served the special interests of youth, women, teachers, cantors, social workers, and other groups. In addition to these, a large number of periodicals – published, practically without exception, in German – dealt with religious, scientific, and politico-cultural affairs. Among these was *Der Morgen* (Darmstadt, later Berlin, 1925–38), which had a "German-Jewish" or assimilationist policy. **Der Jude* was the name given to a periodical published by Gabriel *Riesser during his campaign for Jewish Emancipation (Altona, 1832–35). The same name was used some 75 years later for another periodical, directed by Martin *Buber in Berlin from 1916 to 1924 and supporting Jewish nationalism. The title *Zion* was given first to a religious fortnightly (Berlin, 1833–35), then to a Reformist monthly (Frankfurt, 1840–43), later still to a Zionist monthly (Berlin, 1895–99), and finally to a Mizrachi periodical (Berlin, 1929). In this connection J. *Ettlinger's monthly *Der Zionswaechter* (Altona, 1845–55) should be mentioned.

Until *Kristallnacht* (Nov. 10, 1938), as a direct result of which the entire Jewish daily and periodical press of the Reich was wiped out, there were about 12 regular publications in Berlin and nearly three dozen more outside the capital. The *Juedisches Nachrichtenblatt*, established on the orders of the Nazi authorities shortly after the general ban on Jewish publications, first appeared on Nov. 23, 1938. It was restricted to announcements of official decrees, bulletins of the Nazi-enforced organization of the Jews in Germany (Reichsvereinigung der Juden in Deutschland), and of the larger Jewish communities, and the issue of important notices about emigration and welfare matters. This paper, which had none of the characteristics of a Jewish publication, appeared until 1943.

AFTER WORLD WAR II. The Jewish press revived in West Germany after World War II was little more than a shadow of what had existed in pre-Nazi days. The first journal to appear, in 1946, was the Duesseldorf *Mitteilungsblatt fuer die juedischen Gemeinden der Nordrheinprovinz*. In the following year the *Juedisches Gemeindeblatt fuer die britische Zone* was published in the same city. The German journalist Karl Marx founded the popular *Allgemeine Unabhaengige Juedische Wochenzeitung* in 1946. In 1951 two pro-Israel weeklies were founded: the *Muenchner Juedische Nachrichten* and the Yiddish *Naye Yidishe Tsaytung*. By 1970 these three were the only three Jewish newspapers in the whole of the German Federal Republic, including West Berlin. Apart from occasional publications, a monthly bulletin published by the *Juedischer Pressedienst* of Duesseldorf (the JPD) has appeared from 1965. In the German Democratic Republic one newspaper, the *Nachrichtenblatt*, has been issued since 1961 by an editorial board divided between East Berlin, Dresden, Erfurt, and Schwerin, its full title being *Nachrichtenblatt der juedischen Gemeinde von Gross-Berlin und des Verbandes der juedischen Gemeinden in der Deutschen Demokratischen Republik*.

IN VIENNA. The German language was also predominant in the Jewish papers of Austria, all of which were published in Vienna. The first weekly came into existence in the second half of the 19th century. It was the politically liberal *Neuzeit* (1861–1904), a paper well disposed to religious reform, founded by Leopold *Kompert and Simon Szánto and vigorously promoted by Adolf *Jellinek. The *Oesterreichische Wochenschrift*, founded in 1884 by R. Joseph Samuel *Bloch, several times a member of the Austrian parliament, lasted for 37 years. This was for a time the organ of the Vienna Jewish community, and as such it actively opposed both the antisemitic Christian Social movement and early Zionism. *Die Wahrheit*, the weekly organ of the Union of Austrian Jews, which first appeared in 1885, was emphatically assimilationist and anti-Zionist; its last editor was Oscar Hirschfeld. *Die Welt* (1897–1914), founded by Theodor Herzl, which appeared in Cologne and Berlin as well as in Vienna, was the weekly organ of the Austrian Zionist movement; in 1918–19 Robert *Weltsch edited the Zionist *Juedische Zeitung* (1907–21). He was also associated with the only Jewish daily ever to appear in Vienna, the *Wiener Morgenzeitung* (1919–27). The weekly *Die Neue Welt* (1928–38) was directed by Robert *Stricker, the founder of the Jewish People's Party. The weekly *Juedische Presse* (1915–34) represented the interests of the Agudat Israel; and the *Juedische Welt*, founded in 1929, was close to the Austrian Mizrachi movement. *Die juedische Front* (1931–38) was the organ of the Jewish ex-servicemen.

On Nov. 10, 1938, all Jewish newspapers and periodicals in Austria were forced to close down. A Vienna edition of the official Nazi *Juedisches Nachrichtenblatt* appeared from the end of 1938. After World War II the Austrian Jewish press was confined to monthlies. By the end of the 1960s there were a half dozen in existence, the two leading ones being *Neue Welt*, founded in 1948 and directed by Georg Kuenstlinger (1892–1969), and *Die Gemeinde*, founded by the Vienna Jewish community in 1958 and edited by Wilhelm Krell.

[Ernst Gottfried Lowenthal]

In Holland

The *Gazeta de Amsterdam*, which was issued in 1675, is generally regarded as the first Jewish newspaper. It was printed by David de Castro Tartas, a Sephardi Jew, and though its contents were not specifically Jewish, its language, Judeo-Spanish, shows that it was intended for the Spanish-Portuguese or Marrano community. The first Yiddish paper was the *Dinstagishe un Fraytagishe Kurant*, which appeared first as a semiweekly from Dec. 5, 1680, and then as a weekly, *Dinstagishe Kurant*, in 1686–87. It was issued by the Amsterdam Jewish printer Uri Phoebus Halevi. In 1797–98 the secession of a number of Amsterdam Jews from the *alte kehile* ("the old congregation") and their formation of the new congregation called Adath Yeshurun led to the publication of a polemical Yiddish weekly *Diskursen fun di Naye Kehile*, which appeared for 24 issues (November 1797–March 1798). Its rival, *Diskursen fun di Alte Kehile*, appeared for 13 issues.

During the next 50 years, several yearbooks or almanacs appeared for short periods, but there was no regular Jewish press until about 1850, when a number of Jewish weeklies made their appearance under various titles. The first was the *Nederlands Israëlitisch Nieuws-en Advertentieblad* (1849–50), started by A.M. Chumaceiro (1813–1883), who became chief rabbi of Curaçao in the Dutch West Indies in 1855. It then continued as *Israëlitisch Weekblad*, under a new editorial committee. The original editors established the *Weekblad voor Israëlieten* (1855–84), which was continued as *Nieuwsblad voor Israëlieten* (1884–94). As the *Weekblad voor Israëlieten* it defended Reform Judaism, while a rival Orthodox weekly, the *Nieuw Israëlitisch Weekblad* (NIW) was started in 1865 "to advocate the real love of truth." Its founder and first editor was the bibliographer M.M. *Roest. During the last quarter of the 19th century, it was one of several Jewish weeklies in Holland and had a circulation of 3,000. By 1914 its circulation had risen to 13,000 and in 1935 to 15,000 among a Jewish population of about 120,000. Publication was interrupted by the Nazi occupation of Holland but was resumed in 1945, when its policy, formerly anti-Zionist, became pro-Israel, while its approach remained Orthodox. By 1970 it was the only Jewish weekly in Holland and had a circulation of about 4,500 among a Jewish population of about 20,000.

Contemporary with the NIW until 1940 were the *Weekblad voor Israëlietische Huisgezinnen* (1870–1940), edited by the firm of Haagens in Rotterdam, and the *Centraal Blad voor Israëlieten in Nederland* (1885–1940), published by Van Creveld in Amsterdam. These three publications carried detailed reports of local Jewish events, and readers' letters, with foreign Jewish news usually in a subordinate place. Different was the approach of the weekly, later a bimonthly, *De Joodse Wachter*, established in 1905, which became the official publication of the Netherlands Zionist Federation. Its editors, always unpaid honorary officers of the federation, included Fritz (later Peretz) *Bernstein in the 1920s. From 1967 until 1969 it existed only as a one-page supplement to the NIW, appearing once every two or three weeks, but has since become independent again as a monthly. Other Zionist periodicals were *Tikvath Israel* (1917–40), the official monthly of the Zionist Youth Federation; the Zionist youth leaders' *Baderech* (1925–38) which continued as *Ḥerutenu* (1938–40); the woman's monthly *Ha Ischa* (1929–40), and *Het beloofde Land* (1922–40), later called *Palestine*, and issued by the Keren Hayesod. An important cultural journal, opening horizons far beyond the confines of Holland, was *De Vrijdagavond* (1924–32), established by Izak M. Prins, J.S. da Silva Rosa, librarian of Eẓ Ḥayyim, and Justus Tal, then chief rabbi of Utrecht.

By order of the Germans, most Jewish journals had to cease publication in October 1940. Only one Jewish weekly was allowed, *Het Joodse Weekblad*, which first appeared in August 1940 and which, from April 1941 until September 1943, was issued under the auspices of the Joodse Raad ("Jewish Council"). It published official announcements.

After the liberation of the southern part of the Netherlands in the autumn of 1944, Jews started publishing *Le-Ezrath ha-Am*. This periodical merged with NIW in 1946. Postwar publications of a more than ephemeral nature include *Habinjan* (1947–1999), the monthly of the Portugees-Israëlitische Gemeente Amsterdam (the Sephardi Congregation of Amsterdam); *Hakehilla* (1955–1998), the monthly of the Joodse Gemeente Amsterdam (the Ashkenazi Jewish Community of Amsterdam); and *Levend Joods Geloof* (1955–), the monthly of the Verbond van Liberaal-Religieuze Joden in Nederland (Union of Liberal Synagogues in the Netherlands). In 1998 *Hakehilla* merged with *Hakehillot*, the new monthly of the Nederlands-Israëlitisch Kerkgenootschap (Organization of Jewish Communities in the Netherlands). In 1999 *Habinjan*, too, merged with *Hakehillot*.

Studia Rosenthaliana (1966–) is a scholarly journal, devoted to Dutch Jewish history and related subjects, published by the Bibliotheca Rosenthaliana of the Amsterdam University Library. Until 2002 it was published biannually, from 2002 onward annually.

Around 2000 several new publications came into being: the glossy quarterly *Joods Journal* (1997–); *Grine medine* (2000–), a literary quarterly about and partly in Yiddish; *Orange Juice* (2004), a bimonthly for young Jews. In 2000 the website Joods.nl started, which mainly publishes Jewish news from Dutch and foreign newspapers.

[Henriette Boas / Hilde Pach (2nd ed.)]

In Hungary

The beginning of a Jewish press in Hungary dates back to the 1840s. A few issues of a Hungarian-language quarterly, *Magyar Zsinagóga*, appeared in Papa in 1846–47, and a German-language weekly, *Der Ungarische Israelit*, appeared in 1848. The first journal of any importance was Ben *Chananja, a German-language quarterly which had originated in Leipzig but from 1858 was published in Szeged, Hungary, by R. Leopold Loew, who used it in the struggle for Jewish Emancipation; in 1861 it became a weekly in reduced format. There had hitherto been little demand for Jewish newspapers in Hungary, where capable Jewish journalists usually found employment in the general press. But now the position underwent a change. Several short-lived papers appeared in the 1860s, and in 1869 a Yiddish paper, *Pester Juedische Zeitung*, was founded in Budapest. It appeared five times weekly and continued publication until 1887, when it was converted into a German-language weekly, *Allgemeine Juedische Zeitung* (in Hebrew characters), which lasted until 1919. More significant was the Hungarian-language weekly **Egyenlőség* (1881–1938), which, during the *Tiszaeszlár blood libel case of 1882–83, appeared daily with reports of the proceedings. An important contemporary was the monthly **Magyar Zsidó Szemle* ("Hungarian Jewish Review"), which was founded in 1884 and appeared until 1948. It was produced by members of the Budapest rabbinical seminary and also joined in the struggle for Jewish Emancipation and religious equality. The same personnel simultaneously published a review in Hebrew, which was at first entitled *Ha-Ẓofeh le-Ḥokhmat Yisrael* ("Judaic Studies Observer"), later *Ha-Ẓofeh me-Ereẓ Hagar* ("Hungarian Observer"), and finally *Ha-Soker* ("The Observer"). This review provided a forum for Hebrew writers at a time when almost all Jewish publications in Central Europe were in German.

Between 1846 and World War I, many periodicals appeared for short periods, most of them weeklies and most of them in German or Hungarian. During the early years of Zionism, the authorities refused permission for the publication of a Zionist paper. This was largely the result of the attitude of Jewish organizations which were opposed to the development of Hungarian Zionism. The first Zionist weekly was the German-language *Ungarlaendische Juedische Zeitung* which appeared from 1908 to 1914. A Zionist periodical in Hungarian, *Zsidó Néplap*, appeared from 1903 to 1905 and reappeared in 1908 as *Zsidó Élet* ("Jewish Life"). In 1909 the Hungarian Zionist Federation founded its own organ, *Zsidó Szemle* ("Jewish Review"), which was banned in 1938. The poet J. *Patai published a literary monthly **Mult és Jövő* from 1912 to 1939 and opened its columns to Zionist discussion.

Between the two world wars, there were only about 12 effective weeklies and monthlies in Hungary. The Jewish press practically came to an end in 1938, after which time the Hungarian totalitarian regime (whether Nazi or Communist) authorized only one Jewish periodical. The periodical *Új Élet* ("New Life") was founded in November 1945 by the Central Board of Hungarian Jews, and from 1948 reflected the policies of the Communist rulers, giving no space to the subject of Israel. Its circulation in 1967 was 10,000.

[Baruch Yaron]

In India

The first Jewish periodicals of India were in Judeo-Arabic. *Doresh Tov le-Ammo*, edited by David ben-Ḥayyim had a short life around 1870 and was followed by the Calcutta weeklies, *Mevasser; the Jewish Gazette* (1873–77), edited by Ezekiel Solomon; and *Maggid Meisharim* (1889–1900) edited by Solomon Abed Twena. Bene Israel publications in Marathi begun appearing in the late 1870s. There was an almost continuous succession of periodicals, sometimes more than one at a time, in Marathi and English. These contributed substantially to the education of the community. *The Bene Israelite* appeared in English and Marathi (the mother tongue of the *Bene Israel) from 1896, and reported the rejection by the Bene Israel leaders in Bombay of Theodor Herzl's invitation to send two delegates to the First Zionist Congress in 1897. It gave as the main reason the community's support for the "**Protestrabbiner*" of Germany and the extremely Orthodox section of Anglo-Jewry.

The first national periodical to appear in India was *The Jewish Advocate*, an independent monthly published by the Bombay Zionist Association from 1923 to 1951. Another Zionist paper, *The Jewish Tribune*, appeared in Bombay from 1933 to 1939. *India and Israel* was owned and edited from 1949 to 1953 by F.W. Pollack, who in 1952 became Israel trade commissioner and consul in Bombay. In 1968 there were three regular Jewish periodicals. The fortnightly *News from Israel*, founded in 1954 and published in Bombay by the Israel consulate, had a circulation of 2,000. The *Maccabi* monthly, founded in 1947, was published in both English and Marathi. Other organizations published house journals from time to time.

[Percy S. Gourgey]

In Italy

The Italian Jewish press dates from the middle of the 19th century. The first newspaper, *La Rivista israelitica*, edited by Cesare Rovighi, appeared in Parma in 1845 and continued until 1848. Jewish journalism in the 19th century gave rise to such short-lived publications as Leghorn's *L'Israelita* in 1866, and Pitigliano's *Il romanziere israelitico* in 1895. It also produced two important reviews, *L'educatore israelita* and *Il Corriere israelitico*. The first, founded in Vercelli in 1853 by the rabbis Giuseppe Levi (1814–1874) and Esdra Pontremoli (1818–1888), published articles on religious affairs and news from the Jewish communities abroad. Among its contributors were Elijah *Benamozegh, S.D. *Luzzatto, and Lelio della *Torre. In 1874 *L'educatore israelita* became *Il Vessillo israelitico*, which appeared at Casale Monferrato under the editorship of Flaminio *Servi and lasted until 1922. *U Corriere israelitico*, founded in Trieste by A.V. *Morpurgo in 1862 and later edited by A. Curiel and then by Dante *Lattes, was a publication sensitive to the pressing problems of Jewish life. This newspaper staunchly supported the Zionist movement when it came into being.

In 1901 the rabbinical college at Leghorn launched the short-lived review, *L'Antologia ebraica*. *L'Idea sionista* appeared in Modena from 1901 to 1910. In 1904 the journal *Lux*, edited by Arrigo Lattes and Alfredo *Toaff, appeared in Leghorn, but ceased publication after ten numbers. *La Rivista israelitica*, published in Florence from 1904 to 1915, was edited by the chief rabbi S.H. *Margulies and became a source of great interest for Italian studies. Umberto *Cassuto, P.H. *Chajes, Ismar *Elbogen, S. *Colombo, and E.S. *Artom were among the contributors. In 1910 Rabbi Margulies also founded *La Settimana israelitica*, a weekly in the style of the Florentine cultural weeklies, which appeared until 1915, edited by Alfonso *Pacifici, Carlo A. *Viterbo, Q. Sinigaglia, and G. *Ottolenghi. In 1916 the *Corriere israelitico* and *La Settimana israelitica* were amalgamated in Florence under the title *Israel* and was edited by Carlo A. Viterbo. Offshoots of *Israel* were *Israel dei ragazzi* (1919–39) and **La Rassegna mensile di Israel* (from 1925).

Other publications with considerable circulation in 1970 were *Bollettino della Comunità israelitica di Milano*, founded in 1945 and edited by Raoul Elia; *Shalom*, a monthly of Roman Jewry since 1952; *Ha-Tikvah*, the monthly organ of the Federation of Jewish Youth (1953); *Karnenu*, the semimonthly publication of the Jewish National Fund (1948); and *Hed ha-Ḥinnukh*, an educational monthly.

[Yoseph Colombo]

Ladino Press

One of the reasons for the growth of a Ladino press was the reluctance or inability of the exiles from Spain to learn the languages of the countries in which they found themselves. Before World War II – during which the Sephardi communities of the Balkan countries were either entirely or partly destroyed – a considerable number of Sephardi Jews, mainly of the older generation and especially women, spoke Ladino. They had only an elementary knowledge of the local language – enough for local business and social intercourse with the surrounding population. There was, therefore, a growing need for some kind of Ladino reading material.

As mentioned above, the first Jewish newspaper appeared in 1675 in Amsterdam and it was *Gazeta de Amsterdam*, printed in Ladino. It lasted less than a year and had no Ladino successors until the beginning of the 19th century. The main reason for this delayed development of the Ladino press, in spite of its early start, is to be found in the social environment of the Ladino-speaking Jews, the bulk of whom lived in the countries of the Balkans and the Middle East. During the 18th century these countries were socially and culturally retarded, and their newspapers were neither many nor widespread. Like the population around them, the Jews, even the educated exiles from Spain among them, felt little need for the stimulus or enlightenment that newspapers could give. All this changed gradually in the 19th century and when in 1882 Isidore Singer of Vienna listed 103 extant Jewish newspapers, six of them were in Ladino.

Newspapers in Judeo-Spanish, transcribed in *Rashi type, had appeared in Jerusalem, Smyrna, Constantinople, Salonika, Belgrade, Paris, Cairo, and Vienna. One of them was the Smyrna journal, *La Puerta del Oriente* ("Gateway of the Orient"), which first appeared in 1846 under the Hebrew name *Sha'arei Mizraḥ*. Edited by Rafael Uziel, it contained material of general interest, commercial notices, and literary articles. It lasted just one year. *El Luzero de la Paciencia* ("The Light of Patience"), the first Judeo-Spanish newspaper to appear in Latin characters, was started in 1885 by Elia M. Crespin, in the Romanian city of Turnu Severin. It was a bimonthly and continued publication until 1889. The reason for publishing in Latin characters, according to the editor, was that the writing of Spanish had become greatly corrupted because Rashi often spelled words of different meaning in the same way. The corruption of Ladino by the violation of the rules of Spanish, from which it derived, was a subject often discussed in the Ladino press. Thus *El Tiempo* ("The Times") of June 28, 1907, ridiculed the Ladino used by a Bulgarian Ladino paper. *El Tiempo*, a literary, political, and financial paper, was first published in Constantinople in 1871 under the editorship of Isaac Carmona, and continued to appear until 1930. Its last editor was David *Fresco, one of the best-known Ladino writers of his time. Fresco was also the editor of *El Sol* ("The Sun") of Constantinople (1879), a scientific and literary bimonthly. It seems to have lasted for about two years. He also edited *El Amigo de la Familia* ("The Friend of the Family"), an illustrated periodical, which was published in Constantinople in 1889.

There were journals which were published partly in Ladino and partly in other languages. *Salonik* ("Salonika"), which appeared from 1869 to 1870, was published in Ladino, Turkish, Greek, and Bulgarian, the Bulgarian part being edited in Sofia. It seems to have been the official newspaper of the Turkish authorities in Salonika under the editorship of Rabbi Jacob Uziel. *Djeridie y Lesan* ("The Journal of the Language") appeared in Constantinople in 1899 in Ladino and Turkish. Its purpose was to make Turkish a living language among the Jews.

Ladino found considerable support among the Jewish socialists of the Balkans, who claimed that it was the language of the Sephardi masses and should be preserved and encouraged. They insisted, therefore, that it should be the medium of instruction in Jewish schools. A number of Ladino newspapers were exponents of the socialist idea. Among them the best known was *Avante* ("Forward"), which began publication in 1911 in Salonika under the name *La Solidaridad Ouvradera* ("Workers' Solidarity"). It may be said that the history of this journal, which began as a biweekly and during the Balkan Wars (1912–13) became a daily, is the history of socialism among the Jewish workers of Salonika. Its first editor was Abraham ben Aroya, who was succeeded by Alberto Arditi. In 1923 the paper became the mouthpiece of the Jewish Communists with its editor Jack Ventura, for some time one of the Communist representatives in the Greek Parliament. *Avante* ceased publication in 1935. *El Azno* ("The Donkey"), a satirical journal which appeared as a weekly for three months in 1923, was apparently designed to counter *Avante* when the latter became communistic. Another important Ladino journal published in Salonika was *La Epoca*, edited by Bezalel Sadi Halevi. It appeared from November 1875, first as a weekly, then twice a week, and finally as a daily, until 1912.

In Bulgaria, where a number of Ladino newspapers and periodicals appeared under the auspices of the community and the rabbinate (*El Eco Judaico, La Luz*) the best-known Zionist journal was *El Judio* ("The Jew"), whose editor was David Elnecave, one of the most prominent Zionist leaders in the Balkans. It first appeared in 1909 in Galata, and was later published in Varna and Sofia. It ceased publication in 1931, when Elnecave immigrated to Buenos Aires where he launched *La Luz*. On his death, the editorship was taken over by his son, Nissim.

ZIONISM. With the rise of Zionism, Hebrew was revived as a spoken language among the Jews of the Balkans, and newspapers made their appearance in both Hebrew and Ladino. *Yosef ha-Da'at* or *El Progresso*, a bimonthly, was published in Adrianople in 1888 in Hebrew and Ladino under the editorship of Abraham *Danon. Devoted mainly to historical research among the Jews of Turkey, it was published for about a year. Another Adrianople periodical was *Karmi Shelli* ("My Vineyard"), a literary and national monthly (1881), published under the editorship of David Mitrani. Among the better-known Zionist Ladino journals was *El Avenir* ("The Future"), started in 1897. It existed for 20 years under the editorship of David Florentin. The organ of the Zionist Federation of Greece, the weekly *La Esperansa* ("The Hope"), appeared in Salonika from 1916 to 1920. A Zionist weekly which was predominantly French but also contained articles in Ladino was *Lema'an Yisrael – Pro Israel*, founded in Salonika in 1917 and edited from 1923 to 1929 by Abraham Recanati, who eventually settled in Israel.

A number of satirical Ladino journals also appeared. At the beginning of the 20th century, *El Kirbatj* – the Turkish word for "whip" that found its way into Ladino – appeared in Salonika as a "liberal, humorous, independent weekly journal" under the editorship of Moise Levy. It was followed in 1918 by *El Nuevo Kirbatj* ("The New Whip") under the editorship of Josef Karaso, which ceased publication in 1923.

Altogether, about 43 satirical and humorous journals were published among the Balkan communities at various times. Among them were *El Burlon* ("The Joker"), of Constantinople, edited by Nisim Behar; and *La Gata* ("The Cat"), a satirical journal established in Salonika in 1923 with M. Matarasco as editor.

At no time were the incentives for the creation or maintenance of Ladino newspapers in any sense great or compelling. The Sephardi Jews found themselves mostly in countries of little cultural development and they long retained the desire for knowledge inherited from Jewish life in Spain. This enabled them to resist for some time the primitive influences of their surroundings, to which in time, however, they succumbed. The intellectual classes of Sephardi Jews, educated in the cities of Central Europe, spoke the vernacular and other languages such as French and German. They, therefore, did not feel the need for Ladino newspapers. Finally, to most of the Sephardim in the Balkans the study of the Holy Scriptures, the Talmud and the Codes, and above all the daily recitals of prayers, were not merely religious duties: they also provided almost all their educational and cultural needs. The Bible, the prayer books, and certain rabbinical works were available in Spanish or Ladino. Textbooks were also available for the learning of Hebrew. Aspirations for a wider world outlook did not exist among the Sephardim, largely because the countries in which they lived were on the whole cut off from the mainstream of European intellectual life. There was, therefore, little scope for newspaper activity. According to Moshe David Gaon in his *Ha-Ittonut be-Ladino* (1965) there were 296 publications in Ladino between 1845 and World War II, most of them in the Balkans and the Middle East, with Salonika as the greatest center. In 1968 there was hardly any regular Ladino press, except for two weeklies in Israel and one, partly in Ladino, in Turkey.

IN THE U.S. Although Sephardim were the first Jews to settle in the New World and founded the first Jewish congregation there in 1654, Ladino newspapers did not appear in the United States until the beginning of the 20th century, when the second wave of Sephardi immigrants began to arrive, mainly from the Balkan countries. The daily *La Aguila* ("The Eagle") and the weekly *La America* appeared under the editorship of Moshe Gadol between 1911 and 1925. Moshe Gadol, a native of Bulgaria, and his partners Jacob Farhi, Asher Benveniste, Eliyahu Hananya, and Josef Abulafia, acquired their own printing press in New York. In 1926 *El Luzero* ("The Dawn"), an illustrated monthly, was launched by the Sephardic Publishing Company, its editors being Albert Levy and Moise Sulam. Only 12 issues appeared. The weekly *La Vara* ("The Stock") existed from 1928 until 1948, advertised as "the only Spanish Jewish newspaper in America"; the editors were the same as those of *El Luzero.* A weekly journal edited by Nisim and Alfred Mizraḥi appeared from 1915 under the name *El Progresso* and later took the name *La Boz del Pueblo* ("The Voice of the People"). In 1919 it became *La Epoca de New York* but survived for only one more year.

For all practical purposes the Ladino press in the United States had come to an end by 1948. A new English-speaking generation was taking the place of the older people, and even when the young Sephardim knew Ladino, their use of it approximated to modern Spanish.

ISRAEL. Before World War II there was a constant *aliyah* of Sephardim from the Balkan countries and the Middle East. Many of these immigrants had acquired a good knowledge of Hebrew in their native countries and when they settled in the Holy Land it required no special effort for them to use Hebrew in their daily life, while preserving Ladino in their family circles and among friends. For this reason there was a real need for Ladino papers, which were usually concerned with the preservation of Sephardi culture, customs, and literature. *Ḥavaẓẓelet-Mevasseret Yerushalayim* was published in 1870, its editor being Ezra Benveniste. During the year of its existence 25 issues appeared.

After the establishment of the State of Israel, a number of Ladino journals appeared, mostly sponsored by political parties. In 1968 there were two weeklies, *El Tiempo* (affiliated to Mapai) and *La Verdad.*

[Salomon Gaon]

In Latin America

The Jewish press plays an important part in the life of Latin American Jewry. Though it started almost exclusively in Yiddish, it had been going over to Spanish, although as late as 1970 Yiddish still held a predominant position. The first Jewish papers appeared in Argentina in 1898; one of them, *Folks Shtime*, lasted for 16 years. There were many other short-lived publications, but in 1914 the first daily, *Di Yidishe Tsaytung*, came into being, and was followed in 1918 by *Di Prese.* They continued to appear into the 1970s. Until the 1920s *Di Prese* was inclined toward the left, but both papers supported Zionism, and after the establishment of the State of Israel the ideological differences between them diminished. Although exercising political and social importance, neither paper ever achieved a circulation of more than 10,000. The only Jewish daily in Spanish, *Amanecer*, appeared in 1957. It was supported by most Jewish writers in the Spanish language, but lasted only until the following year.

Besides the Yiddish dailies, Argentine Jewry produced also a variety of weeklies and other publications. Their contents ranged from popular medicine to humor, literary criticism, and philosophical essays in quarterly reviews. Some of them, like *Ilustrirte Literaishe Bleter*, a monthly which started in 1953, and *Davke*, a philosophical quarterly founded in 1949, were in publication in 1970. Jewish weeklies and monthlies in Spanish, *Juventud* and *Vida Nuestra*, made their first appearance before or during World War I. The monthly *Israel* was established in 1917, serving especially Jews of Sephardi or Near Eastern origin, among whom it found lasting support. Other enduring weeklies were *Mundo Israelita* ("Israel World"), founded in 1923; *La Luz*, which started as a fortnightly in 1930; *Davar*, issued from 1945 by Sociedad Hebraica; and the literary quarterly *Comentario*, founded in 1953. Although closely identifying itself with Zionism and Israel, Argentine Jewry has produced few periodicals in Hebrew. *Ha-Bimah ha-Ivrit* ("Hebrew Forum"; 1921–30), *Atidenu* ("Our Future"; 1926), and *Darom* ("South"), founded 1938 and amalgamated with *Ẓohar* ("Window") in 1964, were the most important. Only the last mentioned survives. By 1970 the circulation of the popular press had declined considerably, but two dailies, about seven weeklies, 20 monthlies, and a dozen other periodicals, most of them representing political parties, were still flourishing in *Argentina.

In Brazil, Jewish newspapers date from the period of World War I. Subsequently there were Yiddish and Portuguese weeklies and biweeklies of varying duration. Attempts at establishing a Yiddish daily were only partly successful, but the others were more enduring. In 1970 *Der Nayer Moment* (Yiddish) appeared three times a week, the *Yidishe Prese* appeared as a weekly, and a paper in Portuguese appeared biweekly. São Paulo and Rio de Janeiro were the main centers of publication (see also *Brazil). There was practically no Jewish press in Mexico until the *Meksikaner Yidish Lebn* appeared in 1927. In 1970 *Der Veg* appeared weekly and *Di Shtime* (1939–) biweekly, both in Yiddish. There was also a Zionist Spanish-language weekly, *Prensa Israelita* (1948), and several fortnightlies (see also *Mexico). A daily, *Yidishe Tsaytung*, appeared in Uruguay shortly after World War I, but was short-lived. The weekly *Unzer Lebn* was initiated in 1926, but a Jewish press was not firmly established in Uruguay until the daily *Unzer Fraynd* was launched in 1935. *Haynt*, a daily with Zionist affiliations, began publication in 1957. Several weeklies were also flourishing in 1970 (see also *Uruguay). Since the 1970s, however, Yiddish has almost disappeared from the print media in favor of Spanish.

In the years of Argentine dictatorship the weekly *Nueva Presencia* (1977) was founded, which started as a Spanish offshoot of the Yiddish daily *Di Prese.* Under the editorship of Herman Schiller, it adopted an opposition stance against the repression in Argentina. This journal became one of the referents of the Argentinean Human Rights Movement, and Schiller, who participated in the organization of the Jewish Movement for Human Rights, was recognized as one of its leaders. Other new Jewish publications in Argentina were *Comunidades* (1980s), and *La Voz Judía* (1990s). In recent years there were also daily news publications on the Internet such as Iton Gadol and ShalomOnLine. In Brazil the Jewish written press lost much of its circulation and turned inward to the community. Most of the main organizations had their own newsletters. In Mexico, too, communities had their own bulletins, though here were some independent organs such as the *Foro* magazine available by subscription and *Kesher* with free distribution in all the communities.

In the Middle East and North Africa

Oriental Jewish newspapers emerged only during the first half of the 19th century, but they soon acquired importance among the communities they served. Some of them were published in two or more languages; Hebrew, which was rarely used, was sometimes employed not because there were many Hebrew readers, but with the aim of reviving the language. The Hebrew press in the Middle East was in fact preceded by Jewish papers in Ladino, from 1841, and papers in the colloquial Arabic of the Baghdadi Jewish dialect, such as *Doresh Tov le-Ammo*, from 1855. The first Hebrew paper to appear in Baghdad was *Ha-Dover* (1863), which was published by Moses Baruch Mizraḥi. At a rough estimate, the circulation of Jewish papers in the Middle East, even though these served communities beyond the city or land in which they appeared, never exceeded 5,000. Many papers were shortlived, surviving for no more than a year or two, with only a few appearing regularly for more than five years. Jewish papers appeared in Turkey, Tunisia, Algeria, Ereẓ Israel, Egypt, Syria, Lebanon, Iraq, and Persia. The languages used were literary Arabic, colloquial Arabic, Jewish dialects (i.e., local languages written in Hebrew characters), Hebrew, French, English, Ladino, Spanish, Turkish, and Persian.

In Turkey, only a few papers appeared in languages other than Ladino, such as Hebrew or French, and these had a Zionist orientation, first making their appearance after 1910. In North Africa, Egypt, and Lebanon many Jewish papers appeared in French, some examples being *La Renaissance Juive* (Cairo, 1912), the fortnightly *L'Israélite algérien* (Oran, 1900), and the religious *Gazette de Jérusalem* (Jerusalem, 1882). Another Jewish newspaper which had a long career was the Zionist weekly *L'Aurore*, founded by Lucien Sciuto in 1908. It appeared in Istanbul until 1919, but from 1924 to 1931 was published in Cairo. It then came under the control of Jacob Elmaleh, who, with the support of the B'nai B'rith, transformed it after the rise of Hitler into the organ of the League for War on antisemitism, based in Egypt.

Among the longer-lived Oriental Jewish newspapers was the weekly *Israel*, which first appeared in French, Hebrew, and Arabic (Cairo, 1920). Although the Hebrew section was soon dropped, the Arabic section survived with some interruption for 14 years. In 1939 the paper was amalgamated with *La Tribune Juive*, which had been established at Alexandria in 1936. In Tunisia most Jewish papers appeared in French (e.g., *La Justice*, 1917–), and in Turkey a B'nai B'rith monthly, *Ha-Menorah*, appeared in Turkish and French. The English-language press was mainly confined to India (see above), but in Baghdad there was also the *Iraq Times*.

After the papers appearing in Hebrew, the largest number of Jewish newspapers appearing in Arab countries were published in Arabic. The origins of this press may be traced to Yaʿqūb *Ṣanūʿ, who issued an Egyptian Jewish paper in Arabic in the 1870s. These papers were both religious and secular and were irregular and short-lived. Most of them were ardent supporters of the Zionist cause and defended Zionism and the idea of a Jewish national home against the attacks of the general Arabic press. Papers that survived for some years included the monthly (later weekly) *al-ʿĀʾila* ("The Family"), founded by Esther *Moyal in 1898; the weekly, *al-Miṣbāḥ* (Baghdad, 1924–29); the literary and cultural weekly *al-Ḥāṣid* (Baghdad, 1924–39); the Lebanese *ʾĀlam al-Isrāʾīlī (L'Univers Israélite*, Beirut, 1921–46); the Egyptian Karaite paper *al-Ittiḥād al-Isrāʾīlī* (Cairo, 1924–30); and *al-Shams* ("The Sun," Cairo, 1934–48), published in literary Arabic.

Christiane Souriau's research on the Tunisian and Algerian press brought to light a large number of Jewish papers that had appeared in colloquial Arabic and in Arabic characters from the year 1878, when the dual-language (Judeo-Arabic and French) *al-ʿAmāla al-Tūnisiyya* first appeared. From then until 1900, as many as 22 papers were established, most of them lasting no more than a year or two. The Zionist *al-Bustān* ("The Garden," 1888–97) was exceptional. During the years 1901–19, a further 37 Jewish newspapers and periodicals in colloquial Arabic were published in Tunisia, only two of which lasted for more than four years: *al-Ṣabāḥ* ("The Morning," 1904–29) and *al-Sion* ("The Voice of Zion," 1913–20). The number of papers declined from 1920, although the life-span of those that remained became longer, e.g., *al-Najma* ("The Star," 1920?–38). Souriau mentions 37 Jewish papers in colloquial Arabic appearing in Tunisia. After the establishment of the State of Israel, the Arabic Jewish press in the Arab lands ceased to exist. Instead, the number of papers appearing in Arabic in Israel increased as a result of the immigration of Jews from the Arab countries.

[Shmuel Moreh]

In Poland

For the period up to World War I, see below: In Russia. The great development of the Jewish press in Poland that took place in the years immediately after the war reflected the vigorous life of the Jewish population. More than 200 newspapers and periodicals appeared in the 1920s, and many of them were still flourishing when the Nazi armies overran Poland in September 1939. The papers represented all shades of opinion; most of them were in Yiddish, but a few were in Hebrew and some in Polish. During this period, about 20 daily papers appeared, three in Vilna – *Letste Nayes* (1915), which became *Der Tog* (in 1920), *Avend-Kurier* (from 1924, and *Tsayt* (1924); two in Bialystok – *Dos Naye Lebn* (1919), and *Bialystoker Telegraf*; three in Lodz – *Lodzer Tageblat* (1908, under J. Unger, having a circulation of 20,000); *Dos Morgenblat* from 1912, and *Naye Folksblat* (1923); in Lublin the *Lubliner Tageblat* (1918); and in Grodno, the *Grodne Moment* (1924). Lvov had two, one in Polish, *Chwila* (1919), and one in Yiddish, *Der Morgen* (1926);

and Cracow had two, one in Polish, *Nowy Dziennik* (1918), first under Wilhelm Berkelhammer and from 1921 to 1924 under Isaac *Schwarzbart.

The others were published in Warsaw, where *Haynt* and *Der Moment* had the largest circulations and were in close competition. Other Warsaw dailies were *Der Yid* (later, *Dos Yidishe Vort*, from 1917), *Varshever Ekspres* (1926), *Naye Folkstzaytung* (1926), and *Unzer Ekspres* (1927). The daily *Nowy Czas* (1929) was in Polish, as was the Zionist daily *Nasz Pzeglad* (1923). Besides these publications there were literary weeklies like *Literarishe Bleter* (Warsaw, from 1924), *Kino-Teater-Radio* (1926), *Veltshpigl* ("World Mirror," 1927), and the Yiddish PEN *Klub Nayes of Vilna* (1928). The scientific *Land un Lebn* (1927) appeared monthly; a popular science fortnightly, *Der Doktor*, appeared in Warsaw from 1929; and another, *Folksgesunt*, in Vilna from 1923. A humorous weekly, *Der Blufer*, was prominent in Warsaw journalism from 1926. This body of newspapers and periodicals, employing thousands of people, was closed by the Germans in 1939, and its editors, contributors, and printers fled or perished as the Nazi terror fastened on the country.

[Artur Fiszer]

AFTER WORLD WAR II. The first Jewish newspaper in postwar Poland, *Dos Naye Lebn*, appeared in Lodz on April 10, 1945. At first it was published weekly, then semiweekly and on March 1, 1947, at the conference of the Jewish regional committees, it was decided to make *Dos Naye Lebn* a daily paper and the official organ of the Central Committee of Polish Jews, which comprised all existing Jewish parties. Between 1945 and 1949 there were also weekly and semiweekly publications of various Jewish parties, e.g., the *Arbeter Tsaytung* of the Po'alei Zion, the *Iḥud* of the Liberal Zionists, *Di Folkshtime* connected with the Communist Polish Labor Party (PPR), the *"Głas Młodzieży,"* of the Ha-Shomer ha-Ẓa'ir, and *Yidishe Shriftn*, a publication of the Jewish Writers' Association. After the liquidation of the Jewish political parties in November 1949, most of the Jewish press was gradually closed down by the authorities (see *Poland). The literary monthly *Di Yidishe Shriftn* continued to be published by the Jewish Cultural Society as an organ of the Jewish writers, who elected its editorial board. *Di Folkshtime* alone remained as a newspaper appearing four times a week and serving officially as the Yiddish organ of the ruling party, controlled to a large degree by the Jewish Cultural Society. By 1968 *Di Folkshtime* became a weekly, publishing a Polish section once in two weeks, and *Di Yidishe Shriftn* ceased its publication after its 25th issue.

[David Sfard]

In Romania

The Jewish press in Romania developed with the social and intellectual life of the Romanian Jews. Two short-lived publications made their appearance in the middle of the 19th century and were followed in 1857 by the weekly *Israelitul Român* ("Romanian Israelite") of Bucharest and in 1874 by the review *Revista Israelită* of Jassy. In 1890 Moses *Schwarzfeld, publicist and historian, founded the weekly *Egalitatea* ("Equality"), which lasted until the rise of the Fascist regime. Other publications of that period were the weekly *Ha-Yo'eẓ* ("The Adviser"), which leaned toward the Ḥovevei Zion, appearing from 1876 to 1920, and the review *Likht* ("Light," 1914), both in Yiddish. In 1906, Horia *Carp founded the weekly *Curierul Israelit* ("Israelite Messenger"), which became the official organ of the group Uniunea Evreilor Pământeni (Union of Native Jews; after 1918, Uniunea Evreilor Romani – Union of Romanian Jews) and continued until 1941.

After World War I most of the Jewish newspapers in Romania had Zionist leanings. Major influences in forming a Zionist outlook among the Jewish population were two weeklies: *Mañtuirea* ("The Deliverance"), founded by A.L. *Zissu in 1922 and republished, after a long break, from 1945 to 1949; and *Renaşterea Noastră* ("Our Revival"), founded by S. Stern, publicist and Zionist, in 1928. The weekly *Viata Evrească* ("Jewish Life," 1944–49) had a Zionist Socialist tendency. In addition to these weekly publications, there were literary and political reviews. The monthly *Hasmonaea*, founded in 1915, was the official organ of the association of Zionist students. The review *Adam* (1929–39) founded by I.O. Ludo, attracted to its pages Jewish writers in the Romanian language.

Except for a brief period in 1877, there was never a daily Jewish press in Romania because there was no autonomous national Jewish life. The information published by the Jewish weekly and monthly papers in Yiddish, German, and Romanian, was limited to Jewish international and local life. Political outlook was centered on events of specific Jewish interest, and the Jewish press had a rather polemic character. The weekly Zionist paper *Renaşterea Noastră* resumed publication in 1944. Five more papers that appeared in 1945 were similarly oriented. In the years that followed, various attempts were made to maintain other Jewish papers, several in Yiddish and one in Hebrew, but by the end of 1953 all had ceased publication. From 1956 the Jewish population in Romania was served by a review published by the Jewish community in Bucharest, **Revista Cultului Mozaic* ("The Mosaic Cult's Review"), edited by Moses *Rosen, the chief rabbi.

[Isac Bercovici]

In Russia

The history of the Jewish press in Russia before the Bolshevik Revolution falls into two periods: the mid-19th century to the 1905 Revolution – years during which severe restrictions and censorship were in force; and 1906 to 1917 – a period during which restrictions were partially relaxed. Jewish newspapers in czarist Russia appeared in four languages: Hebrew, Yiddish, Russian, and (in Warsaw) Polish. During the first period, the publication of Jewish periodicals was beset with obstacles. A license to publish was obtained only with great difficulty, and when granted, the official censor controlled the paper's contents. This situation accounted for the strange practice of publishing journals intended primarily for Russian Jews in places outside the country, mainly in Prussia and Austria. Even these newspapers had to pass the Warsaw censor, who deleted any item he did not approve. In spite of its distance from the centers of Jewish population, many newspapers were published in St. Petersburg because the censor there held more liberal attitudes.

Efforts at establishing a Jewish press in the early decades of the 19th century resulted in such short-lived publications as *Beobachter an der Weichsel*, a Yiddish weekly issued in Warsaw in 1823, and *Pirḥei Ẓafon*, an annual that published two volumes in Vilna in the 1840s. The first enduring Hebrew periodical intended for Russian Jewry was *Ha-Maggid*, published from 1856 to 1891 in Lyck (later Elk), a Prussian border town. It contained news and essays, whose prominent tone was a moderate approach to the Haskalah. In 1860, Alexander *Zederbaum, who became a leading figure in the Jewish press, founded a Hebrew weekly, *Ha-Meliẓ*, which was published until 1871 in Odessa and then for another three years in St. Petersburg. Its stated purpose was to be "the mediator (*ha-meliẓ*) between the Jews and government and between faith and Haskalah." Zederbaum also published the first weekly in Yiddish, *Kol Mevasser* (1862–71), which grew to become very popular. In Vilna S.J. *Fuenn issued *Ha-Karmel*, intended mainly for local consumption, which ran as a weekly from 1860 to 1870 and as a monthly until 1880. In Warsaw, **Ha-Ẓefirah*, edited by Ḥ.S. *Slonimski, began as a weekly in 1862 but was published for only six months. In Odessa, Russian-speaking members of the Jewish intelligentsia published Russian-language weeklies, such as *Razsvet*, renamed *Sion* (1860–61), and later *Den* (1869–71). These papers had the dual purpose of serving as a forum for the discussion of Jewish themes and for presenting Jewish problems to the general Russian public in order to combat antisemitism. In 1871 Zederbaum launched a Russian-language weekly in St. Petersburg, *Vestnik russkikh yevreyev* ("Russian Jewish Herald") which, however, was boycotted by the Jewish intelligentsia and ceased publication in 1873. The first Jewish weekly in Polish, *Jutrzeńka*, was published in Warsaw in 1861–63; it had a pronounced assimilationist tendency and was eventually replaced by *Izraelita*, which appeared from 1866 to 1906. A Hebrew monthly, *Ha-Boker Or*, was published by Abraham *Gottlober in Lemberg and later in Warsaw (1876–86). Eight volumes of a Russian annual, containing a variety of literary works and named *Yevreyskaya Biblioteka*, edited by Adolph *Landau, appeared in the period 1871–80.

Ha-Ẓefirah resumed publication in 1874, first in Berlin and from 1875 in Warsaw. In addition, *Ha-Meliẓ* was revived in 1878. The Balkan Wars of 1877–78, the pogroms of the early 1880s, and the anti-Jewish restrictions that followed aroused greater interest in newspapers among the Jewish public. In 1879 two Russian-language weeklies made their appearance in St. Petersburg: **Razsvet* (1883), which pioneered in awaking the national consciousness of Russian Jewish youth, and *Russkiy yevrey* (1884). Another weekly, **Voskhod* (1881–1906), edited by Adolph Landau until 1899, served as the major forum for Russian Jewish intellectuals. Because of the oppressive restrictions placed on them, Yiddish publications were constantly in difficulties, and only the indefatigable Zederbaum succeeded in issuing a Yiddish weekly in St. Petersburg, *Yidishes Folksblat* (1881–90). A revolutionary development in Hebrew journalism took place in 1886, when the first Hebrew daily, *Ha-Yom*, edited by Judah Leib *Kantor, made its appearance in St. Petersburg. Although its career was short (two years), *Ha-Yom* exerted a profound influence on the style employed by the Hebrew press, hastening the transition from florid phraseology to practical prose. The two competing weeklies, *Ha-Meliẓ* and *Ha-Ẓefirah*, were forced to become dailies. The spread of the *Ḥibbat Zion movement in the 1880s resulted in the publication of a considerable number of annuals which served as a forum for the movement's ideology. Among the annuals were *Ha-Asif*, edited by Nahum *Sokolow (1884–88, 1893); *Keneset Yisrael*, edited by Saul Phinehas *Rabbinowitz (Warsaw, 1886–88); and *Ha-Pardes* in Odessa (1892–96, three vols.). They were followed by *Ha-Shilo'aḥ* (1896–1905 in Berlin and Cracow, 1902–19 in Odessa, and until 1926 in Jerusalem). Under the editorship of *Aḥad Ha-Am, and later J. Klausner, *Ha-Shilo'aḥ* became the leading Hebrew monthly, printing articles of a literary and general nature. Attempts which were made by D. Frischmann to publish the intellectual literary weekly *Ha-Dor* (1901, 1904) were unsuccessful as the readership required for this kind of publication was as yet too small.

The need for Yiddish reading matter was met by such annuals as *Hoysfraynd*, edited by Mordecai *Spector (Warsaw, 1888–96); *Yidishe Folks-Bibliothek*, edited by *Shalom Aleichem (Kiev, 1888–89); and *Yidishe Bibliotek*, edited by I.L. *Peretz (3 vols., Warsaw, 1891–95). A. Zionist weekly, *Der Yid*, directed at the educated reader, was published in Cracow from 1899 to 1902, and a popular weekly (vocalized for easy reading), *Yidishe Folkstsaytung*, also in Cracow (1902–03), had a women's supplement, *Di Yidishe Froyen Velt*. These weeklies paved the way for the first Yiddish daily to appear in Russia – *Der Fraynd* (1903–08 in St. Petersburg, 1909–13 in Warsaw), which gained immediate acceptance by the Jewish masses and had a circulation of tens of thousands.

In the beginning of the 20th century, the older Hebrew dailies ceased publication (*Ha-Meliẓ* in 1904 and *Ha-Ẓefirah* in 1906) and were replaced by more modern newspapers, *Ha-Ẓofeh* (Warsaw, 1903–05) and *Ha-Zeman*, the latter founded by Benzion *Katz (St. Petersburg, 1903–04; Vilna, 1905–15), which tried to keep pace with the general Russian press in reporting the latest news and commenting upon it. At the end of the 19th century, the Bund undertook the publication of underground newspapers such as *Arbeter Shtime, Der Yidishe Arbeter*, and *Posledniye Izvestia*, which were printed in the West and smuggled into Russia.

At the end of 1905 censorship was abolished and the press enjoyed a short period of freedom. It soon turned out, however, that the authorities still retained means of controlling the press by administrative measures, ranging from economic reprisals (such as prohibiting advertising, stopping the sale of single copies, closing down the printing press) to temporary or permanent suspension of publication. The immediate result of the short interval of freedom was the appearance of party newspapers. The Bund published *Der Veker*, and, when this was closed down, *Folks Tsaytung* and other newspapers. The Zionist Socialists issued *Der Yidisher Proletarier*, *Der Nayer Veg*, and *Dos Vort*. Another workers' party, the *Sejmists, sponsored the *Folks Shtime*. *Po'alei Zion had a Yiddish weekly, *Der Proletarisher Gedank*, and a Russian periodical, *Yevreyskaya Rabochaya Khronika*. All these party publications disappeared in 1907, when the revolutionary movement was suppressed. The Zionist press, nevertheless, continued to flourish. There were Zionist newspapers in Yiddish (*Dos Yidishe Folk*, Vilna, 1906–08); in Hebrew (*Ha-Olam*, Cologne, 1907; Vilna, 1908; Odessa, 1912–14), and in Russian. The first Zionist Russian-language monthly was *Yevreyskaya Zhizn* (1904–06), followed by *Razsvet*, which became the most popular Russian Jewish weekly with a circulation of tens of thousands. Attempts were made to revive the Hebrew press in Warsaw with the dailies *Ha-Yom* (1906–07) and *Ha-Boker* (1909). In 1910, *Ha-Ẓefirah* also reappeared as a daily, and, with the support of the Zionist Organization, attained a circulation of 15,000.

The most significant development of this period, however, was the growth of a popular Yiddish press centered in Warsaw. At the end of 1905, a Yiddish daily, *Der Veg*, edited by Ẓevi *Prylucki, was founded in the Polish capital and became the forerunner of the popular Yiddish press in Poland. It was succeeded by *Haynt* (1908–39) and *Der Moment* (1910–39), two Yiddish dailies which catered to popular taste and reduced the price of the papers. Along with the news and literary articles they printed sensational items and fostered the cheap novel. The papers enjoyed a circulation of many thousands and acquired great influence. Politically they supported Jewish nationalism and Zionism. Yiddish periodicals also appeared in the large provincial cities (Odessa, Lodz, Vilna, Kiev) but were of local character. An extreme Orthodox weekly, *Ha-Modi'a*, made its appearance in Poltava from 1909.

The non-Zionist Russian Jewish intelligentsia issued its own weeklies, such as *Yevreyskiy Mir* (1910–12) and *Novy Voshkod* (1910–17), both published in St. Petersburg. There were also magazines devoted to special subjects, such as the educational magazines *Yevreyskaya Shkola* (1904–05) and *Vestnik*, the latter founded in 1910 by the Society for the Spread of Enlightenment; *Yevreyskiy Meditsinskiy Golos*, a medical quarterly founded in Odessa in 1908; *Perezhitoye*, a history annual; *Yevreyskaya Starina*, a scientific quarterly (1909–30); and *Vestnik Yevreyskoy Obshchini* (1913–14), which dealt with community administration. There were children's magazines in Hebrew, Russian, and Yiddish (see *Children's Literature). In 1913 a literary magazine *Di Yidishe Velt*, edited by S. *Niger and maintaining high standards, was founded in Vilna.

The outbreak of World War I caused a crisis in the Jewish press: the price of paper and printing rose sharply, and military censorship restricted freedom of expression. The advance of the Central Powers into Poland and Lithuania also separated the masses of readers from the sources of their newspapers. In July 1915 a government decree ordered all Hebrew and Yiddish journals to cease publication. Jewish papers in the Russian language, especially the Zionist-oriented *Razsvet*, did their best to fill the void. The ban was lifted with the outbreak of the February 1917 Revolution.

IN THE U.S.S.R. (1917–1970). The February 1917 Revolution ushered in a short period of freedom of the press which lasted until the Bolshevik Revolution in October. Newspapers independent of the Communist Party continued to appear until September–October 1918 and in some regions (such as Ukraine and Belorussia) until Soviet rule was established there in 1920. This brief period proved to be the golden era of the Jewish press in the U.S.S.R. The leading newspapers were the Zionist Hebrew daily *Ha-Am* in Moscow (July 1917–June 1918), which had a circulation of 15,000 at its height, and the Zionist Yiddish daily *Tagblat* in Petrograd (May 1917–August 1918). Kiev had no less than four papers: the Bundist *Folks Tsaytung* (August 1917–May 1919), the United Socialists' *Naye Tsayt* (September 1917–May 1919), the Po'alei Zion's *Dos Naye Lebn* (December 1917–March 1919), and the Zionist *Der Telegraf* (November 1917–January 1918). Minsk had *Der Yid* (December 1917–July 1918) and *Far'n Folk* (September 1919–January 1920), which were both Zionist in outlook, and the Bundist *Der Veker* (first published in May 1917, and becoming a Communist paper in April 1921).

Hebrew periodicals were also revived after a two-year lapse. In Odessa, *Ha-Shilo'aḥ* resumed publication in June 1917 and continued until banned by the Soviet authorities in April 1919. In the same city, *Barkai*, the last of the Hebrew weeklies, appeared until the beginning of 1920. There were educational magazines such as *Ha-Ginnah* in Odessa, *Ha-Moreh* in Kiev, and *Ha-Makkabbi*, dealing with physical education. A children's magazine in Hebrew, *Shetilim*, was published in Petrograd. A number of annuals served as the forum literary and scientific work, such as *Keneset*, *Massu'ot*, and *Ereẓ* in Odessa and *Olamenu* in Petrograd. Outstanding for size and quality was the quarterly *Ha-Tekufah*, the first three issues of which appeared in Moscow in 1918. Collections were devoted to history and ethnography: *He-Avar* (2 vols., Petrograd), *Reshumot* (1 vol., Odessa), and *Sefatenu* (Odessa). Publication of Hebrew periodicals ended with the ban on the use of Hebrew in the Soviet Union.

Before long, the Jewish press in the Russian language also ceased to exist. *Raszvet* was closed down in September 1918 and *Khronika Yevreyskoy Zhizni* in July 1919. In the period 1924–26, when *He-Ḥalutz was a legal organization, it published the central organ of the movement, *He-Ḥalutz*, in Moscow. The left Po'alei Zion was permitted to publish its central organ, *Yevreyskaya Proletarskaya Mysl*, until 1926 (with a Yiddish edition appearing until 1927). A group of writers and scholars, members of the long-established *Society for the Promotion of Culture and the Historical Ethnographical Society, published several collections of literary and historical pieces in the 1920s, including *Yevreyskaya Starina* (vols. 9–13, occurs (mostly as a free variant of [*t*]). When it is soft, it is realized as [*s*] by the Ashkenazi communities, as interdental voiceless [*ṯ*] by the Yemenite community, the Arabic-speaking Iraqi community, and the Aramaic-speaking community of Zakho in northern Iraq; as [*d*] by the communities of Italy (but for the Sephardi communities of this country); and as voiced interdental or postdental [*ḏ*] by the Cochin community of India. All other communities have [*t*] as the realization of both hard and soft ת, but for some communities of Morocco which have the affricate [*ts*] for both hard and soft ת.

Only relatively few communities differentiate the realization of soft ד from that of hard ד. Soft ד is realized as an interdental [*ḏ*], whereas hard ד is [*d*], by the Yemenite community, by the Aramaic-speaking Zakho community of northern Iraq (where [*z*] appears as a free variant), and by a number of communities in the Balkan countries. The Arabic-speaking community of Iraq has [*ḏ*] as the realization of soft ד only in a few words: in the divine name [*ʾaḏonay*] and in the word [*ʾeḥaḏ*], "one," but only when occurring in the first verse of *Qeriat Shema*. In all other words [*d*] is the realization of both hard and soft ד in the Iraqi community.

כ is realized as a voiceless velar stop, [*k*], when hard, and as a voiceless velar fricative [*ḵ*], when soft, by all communities but for the Samaritan, who has [*k*] for both hard and soft כ.

ג, when soft, is realized as a voiced velar fricative, [*ḡ*], by most Arabic-speaking communities, as well as by some communities of the Balkans. The Dutch-Portuguese community has a voiceless velar fricative, [*ḵ*], as the realization of soft ג. All communities not mentioned here have only one realization, [*g*], for both hard and soft ג. This is also the realization of hard ג in the above communities who do maintain this differentiation, except for certain Yemenite communities. The communities of central Yemen have a voiced prepalatal affricate, [*ǧ*], as the realization of hard ג; those of extreme eastern Yemen, and some of those of northern Yemen – a voiced prepalatal plosive, [*g'*].

THE GUTTURALS. *The Laryngeals.* The letter א is realized as a glottal stop, [ʾ], in most pronunciations. It should be noted, however, that in the Ashkenazi pronunciation, and occasionally, but much less frequently, also in some Sephardi (including the Italian) and Yemenite pronunciations, it may be realized as zero, that is, it is not represented by any sound. In some Ashkenazi pronunciations the contact between two vowels caused by the elision of א in medial intervocalic position gives birth to a glide. In the Georgian-speaking community as well as in some North African communities, and in the community of Cochin (India), [*h*] appears as free variant of א.

The letter ה is realized as a glottal fricative [voiced or voiceless] by most communities. In the Italian-speaking communities its realization is, however, zero, as that of א. In some Ashkenazi communities, as well as in some communities of the Balkan countries, and in a great number of communities located in the area stretching from Libya to southeast Morocco, it varies freely with the realizations of א, that is also with zero.

Final consonantal הּ (ה with a *mappiq*) is realized as [*h*] in the Yemenite pronunciation and in those of some other Arabic-speaking communities. In the Ashkenazi communities and in most Sephardi communities of Europe it is generally realized as zero. In the Dutch-Portuguese community it is realized as [*aha*].

The Pharyngeals. The realizations of the letters ח and ע as voiceless and voiced pharyngeal fricatives, [*ḥ*] and [ʿ], respectively, are found in all Arabic-speaking communities and in most Aramaic-speaking communities. Most of the Persian-speaking communities, however, have [*h*] as the realization of ח, and zero as that of ח. ע is realized as a voiceless velar fricative, [*ḵ*], by all European communities, both Ashkenazi and Sephardi, and by the Georgian-speaking community. ע is realized as [ʾ] or zero by all of the European communities, with the exception of those of Italy and the Dutch-Portuguese of Amsterdam. The latter communities have a voiced velar nasal, [ŋ] – the sound of *ng* in the English word "king" – as the realization of ע. The Georgian-speaking community has for this letter a voiceless glottalized uvular plosive, [*q'*], in initial and final position; intervocally it is realized as a voiced laryngealized uvular fricative.

THE EMPHATICS. ט is realized identically to its non-emphatic counterpart, ת in the pronunciations of the Ashkenazi, Italian, Dutch-Portuguese, and Sephardi communities of Europe, as well as in the pronunciation of the communities of Persia and eastern Kurdistan (in the pronunciation of the Kurdish communities, however, a historical ט is reflected in the quality of the phones of the word, which became emphatic). In the Arabic-speaking communities, the Aramaic-speaking community of Iraqi Kurdistan and in the Georgian-speaking community the realization of ט differs from that of ת: it is a velarized dental (or alveolar) voiceless (or fortis) plosive, [*ṭ*], in most Arabic-speaking communities and in the aforementioned Aramaic-speaking community; either [*ṭ*] or [*ḍ*], the voiced (or lenis) counterpart of voiceless (or fortis) [*ṭ*], in the Yemenite community, and [*t'*], a voiceless glottalized dental plosive in the Georgian-speaking community.

צ is realized as a voiceless dental affricate [*ts*] by the Ashkenazi, Italian, and Dutch-Portuguese communities; as [*ṣ*], a velarized hissing sound, in the Arabic-speaking communities and the Aramaic-speaking community of Iraqi Kurdistan; as a non-emphatic [*s*] – its realization being identical to that of ס – in the Persian-speaking communities, in the Aramaic-speaking communities of eastern Kurdistan and Azarbaijan, in the Georgian-speaking community, in the community of Cochin (India), and in some communities of the Balkan and North African countries.

ק is realized identically to its non-emphatic counterpart, כ, in the Ashkenazi, the Italian, the Dutch-Portuguese, and the other Sephardi communities of Europe, in some Algerian and east Moroccan communities, and a number of Persian-speaking communities. In the following communities ק is realized in a way different from כ: in the communities of central, north-

Table 3: The Realizations of Hebrew Graphemes (letters, vowel-signs, gemination signs) in the Traditional Pronunciations

Hebrew grapheme	Samaritan pronunciation	Yemenite pronunciation					Sephardi pronunciation							Ashkenazi pronunciation		
							European communities			Asian (Yemenite excepted) and African communities						
		Central	Northern	South-western	Aden	Eastern	Ladino speaking	Italian speaking	Dutch-Portuguese	Arabic speaking	Aramaic speaking	Persian speaking	Georgian speaking	North-eastern	South-eastern	Central
א	ʾ, "zero"	ʾ, "zero"	ʾ	ʾ	ʾ	ʾ	"zero"	"zero"	"zero"	ʾ, "zero"	ʾ, "zero"	ʾ, "zero"	ʾ, h	"zero"	"zero,"(h)	"zero"
בּ	b, (β)	b	b	b	b	b	b	b	b	b, β	b, β	b	b	b	b	b
בֿ	b, (β)	v	v, b	v, b	v, b	v, b	v	v	b	b, β	b, β, v	β, v, w	v	v	v	v
גּ	g	ğ	g'	g	g	g'	g	g	g	g	g	g	g	g	g	g
גֿ	g	ḡ, q^x	ḡ	ḡ	ḡ	ḡ, q^x	g	g	x	ḡ	ḡ	ḡ	g	g	g	g
דּ	d	d	d	d	d	d	d	d	d	d	d	d	d	d	d	d
דֿ	d	ḏ	ḏ	ḏ	ḏ	ḏ	d	d	d	d	ḏ[1]	d	d	d	d	d
הּ	ʾ, "zero"	h	h	h	h	h	h, "zero"	h, "zero"	h	h	h	h	"zero"	h	"zero," h	"zero," h
ה	"zero"	h	h	h	h	h	h, "zero"	h, "zero"	ha	h, "zero"	h, "zero"	h, "zero"	"zero"	"zero"	"zero"	"zero"
ו	b,(w)	w	w	w	w	w	v	v, w	v	w, v[1]	w, β	β, v, w	v	v	v	v
ז	z	z	z	z	z	z	z	z, s, dz, ts	z	z[2]	z	z	z	z	z	z
ח	ʾ, "zero"	ḥ	ḥ	ḥ	ḥ	h	x	x	x	ḥ	ḥ	ḥ, h	x	x	x	x
ט	ṭ, t	ṭ, ḍ	ṭ, d	ṭ, ḍ	ṭ, ḍ	ṭ, ḍ	t	t	t	ṭ	ṭ, t	t	tʾ	t	t	t
י	y	y	y	y	y	y	y	y, (ğ)	y	y	y	y	y	y	y	y
כּ	k	k	k	k	k	k	k	k	k	k	k	k	k	k	k	k
כֿ	k	ḵ	ḵ	ḵ	ḵ	ḵ	ḵ	ḵ	ḵ	ḵ	ḵ	ḵ	ḵ	ḵ	ḵ	ḵ
ל	l, (ḷ)	l	l	l	l	l	l	l	l	l	l	l	l	l	l	l
מ	m	m	m	m	m	m	m	m	m	m	m	m	m	m	m	m
נ	n	n	n	n	n	n	n	n	n	n	n	n	n	n	n	n
ס	s, (ṣ)	s	s	s	s	s	s	s	s	s[3]	s	s	s	š[4]	s	s
ע	ʾ, "zero," ʿ	ʿ	ʿ	ʿ	ʿ	ʿ	"zero"	ŋ	ŋ	ʿ	ʿ	ʿ, ʾ, "zero"	qʾ	"zero"	"zero"	"zero"
פּ	b, f	p	p	p	p, f	f	p	p	p	p, f	p, f	p	p	p	p	p
פֿ	b, f	f	f	f	f	f	f	f	f	f	f	f	p	f	f	f

צ	ṣ, s	ṣ	ṣ	ṣ	ṣ	ṣ	ts	ts	ts	ṣ	ṣ, s	s	s	ts	ts	ts
ק	q, ʾ	g, g̱	g, g̱	q	q, ʁ	g, g̱	k	k	k	q, ʾ	q	g, ʁ, (k)	kʾ	k	k	k
ר	r	r	r	r	r	r	r	r	r	r	r	r	r	r, ḡ	r, ḡ	r, ḡ
שׁ	š	š	š	š	š	š	š	š, s	š	š[5]	š	š	š	see ס	š	š
שׂ	š	s	s	s	s	s	s	s	s	s[5]	s	s	s	see ס	s	s
תּ	t	t	t	t	t	t	t	t	t	t, (t^s)	t	t	t	t	t	t
ת	t	ṯ	ṯ	ṯ	ṯ	ṯ	t	d	t	t, (t^s), ṯ[6]	t, ṯ[1]	t	t	s	s	s
dageš forte	CC	CC	CC	CC	CC	C	C	CC	C	CC	CC, C	C	C	C	C	C

šureq-qibbuṣ	u, o[7]	u, (ü), (ʉ)	u	u	u	u	u	u	u	u	u, (ü)	u, (ü), (ʉ)	u	u	i, (ü), (ʉ)	i, (ü), (ʉ)
ḥolem	u, o[7]	ö	ö	e	e	ö	o	o	o	o[8]	o	o	o	ey	y	oy[9]
qameṣ	a, å	å	å	å	å	ɒ	qameṣ (except when coming in closed unstressed syllable: "qameṣ qaṭan") is identical to pathaḥ, both being realized as a; "qameṣ qaṭan" is realized as o.							o	u	u
pathaḥ	a, å	a, ä	a, ä	a, ä	a, ä	a, ä	Exception: some Persian speaking communities realize the qameṣ as å.							a	a	a
ṣere	ε[10]	e	e	e	e	e	In all varieties ṣere and segol are realized alike, as e ~ ε							ey	ay	ay
segol	ε[10]	realization is identical to that of pathaḥ												ε	ey, e	ey, e
ḥireq	i	i	i	i	i̯	ə	i	i	i	i	i	i	i	i	i, ə	i, ə
mobile šewa		basic realization = ă; when preceding y = i̯; when preceding ʾ, h, ḥ or ʿ = ultrashort vowel, identical in quality to the vowel of the following consonant					e ~ ε	e ~ ε	e ~ ε[11]	e ~ ε	e ~ ε[12]	a, (ʌ)	e	e, ə	e, ə	e, ə
ḥatef-pathaḥ		ă	ă	ă	ă	ă	a	a	a	a	a	a	a	a	a	a
ḥatef-segol		ă	ă	ă	ă	ă	e ~ ε	e ~ ε	e ~ ε	e ~ ε	e ~ ε	e ~ ε	e	ε	ey, e	ey, e
ḥatef qameṣ	å̆	å̆	å̆	å̆	å̆	å̆	o	o	o	o	o	o	o	o	u	u

1. In some communities.
2. In some North African communities a sound intermediate between z and ž.
3. In some North African communities a sound intermediate between š and s (for these communities see also footnote 4).
4. No distinction between ס (and שׂ) and שׁ; both realized as š or as a sound intermediate between š and s.
5. For North African communities see ס.
6. In Iraq.
7. Merger of šureq-qibbuṣ and ḥolem into one phoneme, whose allophones are o, u.
8. In North African communities merger of ḥolem and šureq-qibbuṣ into one phoneme, whose allophones are o, u.
9. In German-speaking communities: aw.
10. Merge of these phonemes into one phoneme: ε; allophones: e, a.
11. Šewa ga'ya = a: šewa preceding y=i.
12. In some communities as in the Yemenite pronunciation, but less consistently.

Notes to Table 3.

1. Two or more phonetic signs are given as the realizations of any letter (or of a vowel sign) in a specific community, when the letter has two or more realizations, the relationship between them being that of "free" or "positional" allophones (that is, sounds whose articulation depends on their position in the word, the preceding and the following sounds, the structure of the syllable, etc.).

One of the phonetic signs that represent the realizations of a letter comes in brackets when it is less common than the other realizations, or when it is used only by a part of the community in question.

2. C stands for "consonant." CC = a geminated, double, consonant.

3. The sign ˘ above a letter representing a vowel, denotes that the vowel is ultrashort, e.g. [ă] = ultrashort [a].

4. A long vowel is denoted by a line above it, e.g. [ā] = long [a].

---

ern, and eastern Yemen it is realized as a voiced velar or uvular plosive [*g*] or [*g̣*]. In the communities of southwest Yemen and Aden it is realized as a voiceless uvular plosive, [*q*], which has, particularly in the community of Aden, a voiced uvular fricative, [ʁ], as its variant in certain positions. In some Persian-speaking communities ק is realized as a voiced uvular stop, [*g̣*], which has as its variant a voiced uvular fricative [ʁ]; other Persian-speaking communities realize ק as [*k*]. Many Arabic-speaking communities and those speaking Aramaic have a voiceless uvular plosive, [*q*], as the realization of ק. In the community of Aleppo, as well as in some communities of Algeria and Morocco, ק is realized as a glottal stop, [ʾ]; in these communities, however, this realization of [ʾ] exists alongside with [*q*]. In the communities of southern Algeria and Cochin, ק has a velar, or uvular, voiceless fricative, [*k*], as its realization (along with the realization [*q*]). In the Georgian-speaking community ק is realized as a velar-uvular affricate, [*k*ʁ].

THE SIBILANTS. No community maintains the distinction that existed in biblical Hebrew between the phonemes represented by the letters שׁ, ס, and שׂ. In the Samaritan community the realization of שׂ is identical to that of שׁ; in all other communities the realization of שׂ is equal to that of ס. Most communities realize שׁ as an unvoiced hushing sound, [*š*], and ס (as well as שׂ) as an unvoiced hissing sound, [*s*]. Exceptions are the following:

(1) In the northeastern ("Lithuanian") Ashkenazi and some North African communities, no distinction was made between the realization of שׁ on the one hand and that of ס (and שׂ) on the other, the exact articulation of the sound representing both שׁ and ס (and שׂ) – whether [*š*] or a sound intermediary between [*š*] and [*s*] – varying locally. This pronunciation, which corresponds to dialectal features of northeastern Yiddish, tended to disappear after about 1930. A similar phenomenon occurs in some Moroccan communities in which both שׁ and ס (and שׂ) are realized as a sound intermediary between [*š*] and [*s*], or as [*s*].

(2) In some communities of Greece the realization of שׁ as [*š*] has a variant [*s*].

(3) In the communities of northwest Italy, and to a lesser extent in the communities of northeast Italy, שׁ is realized as [*s*].

ז is realized by most communities as a voiced hissing sound, [*z*]. In some Italian-speaking communities it is realized as a voiceless hissing sound, [*s*]; in other communities as an affricate, voiced, [*dz*], or voiceless, [*ts*]. In both categories of these communities, the exact realization of ז depends on the position of the letter in the word. In some communities of Morocco it is realized as a sound intermediary between [*z*] and [*ž*].

RESH. The letter ר is realized as an apical flap or trill, [*r*], by most of the Arabic-speaking, Aramaic-speaking, and Persian-speaking communities as well as by the Sephardi communities of Europe. Most of the Ashkenazi communities, on the other hand, realize it as a voiced velar fricative [*ğ*], or a velar frictionless continuant; some Ashkenazi communities, however, realize ר as an apical flap or trill, [*r*].

THE SEMIVOWELS. The letter ו is realized by most Arabic-speaking communities as the semivowel [*w*]; in some communities of Syria and Egypt, as well as in northwest Morocco, it is realized as a labiodental voiced fricative, [*v*]; in the communities of northeast Morocco the realization [*w*] has the variant [*v*]; in some communities of Algeria [*w*] is realized as a bilabial voiced stop, [*b*]. In the Aramaic-speaking communities ו is realized as [*w*]; this realization, however, has a bilabial voiced fricative, [β], as its variant. In the Persian-speaking communities the realization of ו is identical to that of soft ב: it is either a bilabial voiced fricative, [β], or a labiodental voiced fricative, [*v*]; in the environment of a back vowel it has as its variant the semivowel [*w*]. Some Italian-speaking communities realize as [*v*] when it comes in initial and medial position, but as [*w*] in final position.

All Ashkenazi communities have [*v*] as the realization of ו.

The letter י is realized by the great majority of the communities as the palatal semivowel [*y*]. Some communities have for this realization the variants [*i*] or [ʾ*i*], the particular positions in which these variants occur differing for the various communities. In some communities in northeast Italy, י, when occurring at the beginning of a syllable, is realized as the voiced prepalatal affricate, [*ğ*]. According to the medieval grammarians Profiat Duran and Abraham de Balmes, such was the realization of geminated י in Provence and Italy.

GEMINATION. The *dageš forte* is realized by doubling the consonant in the Arabic-speaking communities and the Aramaic-speaking communities of eastern Kurdistan. However, a single consonant occurs in some of these communities as the realization of a letter which has a *dageš forte*, particularly in an unstressed syllable. Most of the Italian-speaking communities also have a doubling of the consonant as realization of the *dageš forte*; the communities of northeast and northwest Italy, however, tend to realize a letter with a *dageš forte* in a way identical to that of a letter not possessing a *dageš forte*.

All the Ashkenazi communities, as well as the Persian-speaking communities, disregard the *dageš forte* in their traditional pronunciations.

The Vowels

The basic features of the vowel systems of the three major groups of the traditional pronunciations, in their relation to the Tiberian system of vocalization, were described above. We shall now present the realizations of the vowels in the various pronunciations.

ŠUREQ-QIBBUṢ וּ, ֻ. The Ashkenazi communities of the regions in which southeastern and central Yiddish was spoken – that is the Ukraine, Poland, Western Hungary, Western Slovakia, etc. – realize the *šureq* and the *qibbuṣ* as [*i*], or, some of them, as [*ü*] (rounded [*i*]). A realization of the *šureq* and the *qibbuṣ* as [*ü*], or as a centralized variant of this vowel, [ʉ], also exists in a number of other communities – in some communities of Yemen, in Shiraz (Persia), Azarbaijan, in western Kurdistan, in some communities of northwestern Morocco, in northwestern Italy – but in most of these communities the realizations in question, rounded [*i*] and [ʉ], are in fact variants of [*u*]. Since *qibbuṣ* appears in the vocalization of the Bible mostly in closed unstressed syllable, some scholars stated that in these communities a realization of the *qibbuṣ* is found – rounded [*i*] or [ʉ] – which differs from that of the *šureq*, which is [*u*]. But the situation is not so. Today a consistent and regular differentiation between the realization of the *šureq* and that of the *qibbuṣ* does not exist in any community.

For communities in which the difference between the realizations of the *šureq* (and the *qibbuṣ*) and that of the *ḥolem* was neutralized, see below.

ḤOLEM וֹ, ֹ. In two groups of communities, which were geographically located quite apart, the realization of the *ḥolem* was identical with that of the *ṣere*: in the communities of the regions in which northeastern ("Lithuanian") Yiddish was spoken, and in the communities of southwest Yemen (as well as in the community of Aden): in the former group both the *ḥolem* and the *ṣere* were realized as [*ey*], in the latter as [*e*]. From a historical point of view, however, there is no relation between the realization of *ḥolem* as *ṣere* in these two groups of communities. In the "Lithuanian" communities this realization apparently resulted from an interference of Yiddish in the traditional pronunciation of Hebrew. In the pronunciation of the aforementioned Yemenite communities, the realization of *ḥolem* as *ṣere* constitutes a feature of the pronunciation that prevailed in some Babylonian communities of the geonic period (see above).

The communities of the regions in which central and southeastern Yiddish was spoken realized the *ḥolem* as [*oy*], some German-speaking communities as [*au*], English-speaking communities as [*ou*]. In the communities of central, northern, and eastern Yemen – that is, in all Yemenite communities but for these in which *ḥolem* is realized as *ṣere* (see above) – the *ḥolem* is realized as a lower-mid rounded central vowel, [*ö*] (quite similar to the realization of *eu* in French *peur*). A similar realization of the *ḥolem* is attested in the Aramaic-speaking communities of Persian *Azerbaijan.

QAMEṢ AND PATHAḤ ָ, ַ. All the Sephardi communities of Europe, the Italian communities, the Dutch-Portuguese communities of Amsterdam, and all the Asian and African communities – but for the Yemenite and the Persian (to some extent – see below) – do not differentiate between the realization of *qameṣ gadol* (that is, a *qameṣ* not occurring in a closed unstressed syllable) and that of a *pathaḥ*: they are both realized as a low front (or, in some communities, low central) vowel, [*a*]. This is a feature typical of the Sephardi pronunciation. In the Aramaic-speaking communities of eastern Kurdistan and Persian Azerbaijan a historical *qameṣ gadol* (which is realized as [*a*]) is reflected by the emphaticization of the phones of the word in which it occurs. All the above-mentioned communities realize *qameṣ qaṭan*, i.e., *qameṣ* which comes in a closed unstressed syllable (and which historically reflects the phoneme [*u*]) *as* [*o*], that is as a *ḥolem*. It should be noted, however, that the communities in question make two exceptions to the realization as [*o*] of *qameṣ* which historically reflects the phoneme [*u*], namely:

(1) A *qameṣ* preceding a *ḥatef-qameṣ*, e.g., in נָעֳמִי, is consistently regarded by these communities as a *qameṣ gadol*, and is realized as [*a*]. This realization of the *qameṣ* originated in the fact that these communities regard the *metheg* that follows a *qameṣ* preceding a *ḥatef-qameṣ* as indicating that the **qameṣ* is a *qameṣ gadol* (whereas in fact it indicates that the syllable is open and that it has secondary stress).

(2) In the word כָּל, but only in two instances in the Bible (Ps. 35:10; Prov. 19:7) the *qameṣ* is realized as [*a*], that is, this word is pronounced [*kal*]. The reason for this lies in the fact that in these two instances the word כָּל has an accent, and this has been taken by the communities whose pronunciation is Sephardi to indicate that the *qameṣ* is a *qameṣ gadol*, which is realized as a *pathaḥ*, namely [*a*] (see Z. Ben-Ḥayyim, *Studies in the Traditions of the Hebrew Language* (1954), 71–72).

The Ashkenazi, the Yemenite, and some Persian communities differentiate between the realizations of *qameṣ* (*qameṣ gadol* as well as *qameṣ qatan*: no distinction is made in these communities between these entities) and that of *pathaḥ*. In the Ashkenazi communities the *qameṣ* is realized as [*o*] or [*u*] (the latter realization prevailing in communities of the region in which central and southeastern Yiddish is spoken). Most of the Yemenite communities realize the *qameṣ* as a rounded lower-mid back vowel, [*å*]; the communities of Ḥabbān and Ḥāḍina in Ḥaḍramaut realize the *qameṣ* as an unrounded low back vowel, [ɒ]. Some Persian-speaking communities realize the *qameṣ* as a rounded lower-mid back vowel, [*å*].

ṢERE AND SEGOL ֵ, ֶ. All the communities which follow the Sephardi pronunciation have one realization for both *ṣere* and *segol* (see above). This realization is a front higher-mid or lower-mid vowel, [*e*] or [ɛ]. In some North African communities no distinction is made between the realizations of *sere* (and *segol*) and that of *hireq*. This applies also, to some extent, to the Iraqi community. In the Yemenite pronunciation the realization of the *segol* is identical with that of the *pathaḥ*. The Ashkenazi pronunciations are divided into two major groups as to the realizations of *ṣere* and *segol*:

(1) The communities of the area of northeastern Yiddish (the "Lithuanian" communities), as well as some other Ashkenazi communities, realized the *segol* (in a stressed syllable) as a front unrounded higher-mid vowel, [*e*]; the *ṣere* is realized as the diphthong [*ey*].

(2) Many communities of the areas of central and southeastern Yiddish realize the *segol* in a stressed syllable as [*ey*] and the *ṣere* as [*ay*]. No community makes any distinction between the realization of a defective *ṣere* and that of full ("plene") *ṣere*, as well as between the realization of a defective *segol* and that of a full ("plene") *segol*.

ḤIREQ ִ. All communities realize the *ḥireq* as a high front vowel, [*i*], with some positional variants. In eastern Yemen the *hireq* is realized as a central vowel, [ə].

THE ŠEWA ְ. In presenting the realizations of the *šewa* two points should be considered: the principles that guide the various communities in differentiating a *mobile šewa* from a *quiescent šewa*; the realizations of the *mobile šewa* in the various communities.

Mobile Šewa and Quiescent Šewa in the Various Communities. The Yemenite community and the communities that adhere to the Sephardi pronunciation, including the Italian community, regard the *šewa* sign as denoting *mobile šewa* when it belongs to one of the following categories:

(1) when it appears in the beginning of a word;

(2) when it follows another *šewa*;

(3) when it comes with a letter that has a *dageš forte*;

(4) when it comes with the second of two identical letters, as in the word הִנְנִי (to this rule, however, there are exceptions);

(5) when it follows, in medial position, *qameṣ, ṣere, ḥolem, šureq*, or *ḥireq* which do not come in a syllable that has a primary stress, but may have a secondary stress (the reading traditions of many communities regard the *metheg* as a sign denoting secondary stress), and after which a *dageš forte* does not come (this applies mostly to the *ḥireq*). It should be noted that there is no general consistency as to the realizations of the *šewa* of this category as a *mobile šewa*. In Hebrew grammar this *mobile šewa* is known as "a *šewa* following a 'long vowel'"; in the traditional pronunciation of these communities, however, there is no consistent differentiation between "long" and "short" vowels in accordance with the opposition between these two categories of vowels in Hebrew medieval grammatical theory (primarily, in the grammatical theory of the school of the Kimḥis). Therefore, for the actual pronunciation of the communities in question this kind of *mobile šewa* cannot be defined in terms of "a *šewa* following a 'long vowel.'"

In some Yemenite pronunciations the second of two final *šewas* is regarded as *mobile*.

In the reading of the post-biblical literature the communities who adhere to the Sephardi tradition disclose some deviations from the ways they follow in differentiating the *mobile šewa* from the *quiescent šewa* in the reading of the Bible. The most prominent among these deviations is the realization as a *quiescent šewa* of the *šewa* in forms of the *qatĕla, qatĕlu, qotĕlim*, and *qotĕlot* patterns.

In the pronunciations of the Ashkenazi communities a *šewa* which historically should be regarded *mobile* is in fact *quiescent* in many cases. This is always the case with a *šewa* coming with a letter that has a *dageš forte* (see above, category (3)); these communities do not geminate the consonants) and with a *šewa* that follows a so-called "long vowel" (above, category (5)). As to an initial *šewa* (above, category (1)), its realization either as a vowel (that is, as a *mobile šewa*) or as zero (that is, as a *quiescent šewa*) depends on the phonological rules according to which initial clusters may or may not exist in the vernaculars of the various communities.

The Realizations of the Mobile Šewa. In the Yemenite community there exist three categories in the realizations of the *mobile šewa*:

(1) when it comes with a letter which is not followed by י or by a guttural (that is, a laryngeal – ה, א, or a pharyngeal – ע, ח), the *šewa* is realized like an ultrashort *pathaḥ*, namely, [ă];

(2) when it comes with a letter which is followed by י, the *šewa* is realized as an ultrashort *ḥireq*, namely [ĭ];

(3) when it comes with a letter which is followed by a guttural (but is not itself a guttural), the *šewa* is realized as an ultrashort vowel, whose quality is identical to that of the vowel of the following guttural. Thus, when the vowel of the following guttural is a *qameṣ*, the *šewa* is realized as an ultrashort *qameṣ* namely, [ŏ]; when it is a *šureq*, the *šewa* is realized as an ultrashort *šureq*, namely [ŭ]; when it is a *ḥolem* the *šewa* is realized as an ultrashort *ḥolem*, namely [ŏ̆].

A *šewa* followed by a *gaʿya* ("*šewa-gaʿya*") is realized by the Yemenite community as a short (not an ultrashort) vowel, its quality being determined by the nature of the following consonant as stated above, in categories (1), (2), (3). The realizations of the *mobile šewa* in the traditional pronunciation of the Yemenite community disclose complete agreement with the realizations of the *mobile šewa* in the pronunciation that prevailed in the Tiberian school. To these latter realizations a number of medieval grammatical treatises bear evidence. Very few communities except the Yemenite have preserved the above realizations that the *mobile šewa* had in the Tiberian school: they exist – but much less consistently than in the Yemenite community – in the Aramaic-speaking communities of western Kurdistan. Some Persian-speaking communities, as well as the Aramaic-speaking communities of Persian Azerbaijan (see above) have the realization [*a*], or [^], a lower-mid unrounded back bowel, for the *mobile sewa*. This realization is identical, in quality, to category (1) of the realizations of the *sewa* in the Yemenite community; but whereas in the Yemenite community this realization occurs when the *šewa* comes in certain positions only (see above), in the above-mentioned communities it is the regular realization of the *mobile šewa*. The Dutch-Portuguese community realizes the *šewa -gaʿya* as [*a*] and a *šewa* preceding **י** as [*i*], an ordinary *mobile šewa* as [*e*]. All the communities that follow the Sephardi tradition – except the Dutch-Portuguese community and the above-mentioned Aramaic- and Persian-speaking communities, which can be regarded as following the Sephardi tradition in as much as they realize the *qameṣ* as *pathaḥ* and the *ṣere* as *segol* – realize the *šewa* as a phone which is qualitatively identical to the realization of the *ṣere* and the *segol*. Quantitatively, the *ṣere* and the *segol*, when they come in stressed syllables, may be realized as long vowels, whereas the *šewa*, which does not come in a stressed syllable, is always realized as a short vowel.

In the Ashkenazi communities, the *šewa*, in those instances in which it is realized as a vowel (see above) is realized as [*e*] or [*ə*]. The Samaritan community has usually a vowel as the counterpart of a *mobile šewa* of the Tiberian vocalization.

THE ḤATEFS. The Yemenite community is the only one to have preserved the quantitative difference between the realization of a *ḥatef* and that of a vowel which is its counterpart, that is between *ḥatef-pathaḥ* and *pathaḥ*, between *ḥatef-segol* and *segol*, between *ḥatef-qameṣ* and *qameṣ*; the *ḥatefs* are realized as ultrashort vowels which are qualitatively identical with the vowels which are their counterparts – *ḥatef-pathaḥ and ḥatef-segol* as [ă], *ḥatef-qameṣ* as [å̆]. The reason for the identity of the realizations of the *ḥatef-pathaḥ* and the *ḥatef-segol* is that in the Yemenite pronunciation the realizations of the *pathaḥ* and *segol* are identical.

In the Sephardi and Ashkenazi pronunciations the *ḥatefs* are realized as the vowels which are their counterparts: *ḥatef-pathaḥ* is realized as [*a*], *ḥatef-segol* as [*e*] (or as a variant of this phone, in accordance with the variants of the realizations of the segol in the various communities), *ḥatef-qameṣ* as [*o*].

VOWEL QUANTITY. No community maintains, in the realizations of the vowels, the distinction between a "long" and a "short" vowel ("*tenuʿah gedolah*" and "*tenuʿah qeṭanah*"), a distinction prevalent in later medieval grammatical theory. In most communities long realizations of the vowels occur in stressed syllables. The Yemenite community maintains the distinction between ultrashort and ordinary vowels, the *mobile šewa* and the *ḥatefs* being realized as ultrashort vowels.

Stress

The communities which follow the Sephardi tradition follow, in reading the Bible, the Tiberian rules of stress distribution, as regards both primary and secondary stress. In reading the post-biblical literature there are, in these communities, quite a few cases of deviations from these rules (detailed studies as to the stress distribution in the reading traditions of post-biblical literature in the Sephardi communities are, as yet, missing).

The Yemenite community generally maintains in reading the Bible the Tiberian rules of stress distribution in words which have disjunctive accents; words which have conjunctive accents, on the other hand, quite frequently have stress patterns differing from those of the Tiberian tradition. This latter phenomenon is manifest in the fact that words, which in the Tiberian tradition have an ultimate stress ("*milleraʿ*"), have in the Yemenite pronunciation the stress on the penultimate syllable ("*milleʿl*"), and occasionally on the antepenultimate, when they come with a disjunctive accent. In the reading of post-biblical literature the number of the words having a penultimate or an antepenultimate stress, and which according to the Tiberian rules of stress distribution should have an ultimate stress, is greater than in the reading of the Bible.

The Ashkenazi communities do not adhere to the Tiberian rules of stress distribution. Quite frequent is the occurrence of penultimate (or, in some communities, antepenultimate) stress where the Tiberian tradition has ultimate stress.

Samaritan Hebrew has, as a rule, penultimate primary stress (with concomitant secondary stress on the second syllable preceding the one which has the primary stress; secondary stress may fall on the syllable directly preceding the syllable which has the primary stress – this is the case when the former syllable has a long vowel). It may be, however, proven that the actual stress patterns of Samaritan Hebrew are rather late, and that the stress patterns that Samaritan Hebrew formerly possessed were identical with those of Tiberian Hebrew (Z. Ben-Ḥayyim, *Sefer Ḥanokh Yalon* (1963), 149–160).

SPECIMEN TEXTS

The text of Genesis 47:28–31 is given here in the traditional pronunciations of several communities

1. ′= primary stress; , = secondary stress. Both signs appear before the stressed syllable. When a word has no stressed syllable, no space is left in the transcription between this word and either the preceding or the following word. Since in the Samaritan pronunciation, stress usually falls on the penultimate syllable, it is not marked in specimen text no. 1, unless it occurs in the last syllable.

2. A colon that follows a letter representing a vowel denotes that the vowel is ultralong, e.g. [ā:] = ultralong[a].

1. The Samaritan Community

(transcription kindly provided by Professor Z. Ben-Ḥayyim)

Gen. 47:28: wyī yå:qob bårəṣ miṣrəm šåba ʿåšåra šēna wyåyyu yåmi yå:qob šēni ʿayyo šåba šēnəm war′bīm wmåt šēna.

29: wyiqrābu yåmi yišråʾəl almot wyiqra albēno alyūsəf wyåʾūmər lū am nā måṣåtti ån bīnək šim nā yēdåk tēt yirki waššītå nā immådi ēsəd wåmət al nā tiqbårinni båmiṣrəm.

30. wšåkåbti am åbūti wnåšåttåni mimmiṣrəm wqåbårtåni afqēbirråtimma wyå̊ʾūmər å̊nåki ēšši kådēbårək.

31. wå̊yʾūmər iššāba li wyiššāba lū wyištabbi yišrå̊ʾəl ʿal rēʾoš ammēṭå.

2. The Yemenite Community (Ṣanʿa)

28. wayh′ḥi ,yaʿa′göv bă′ʾāraṣ miṣ′rāyim šă′vaʿ ʿas′re šå′nå way′ḥi yă′me ,yaʿă′göv šă,ne ḥay′yow ′šāvaʿ šå′nim wă′ʾarbåʾim ʾum′ʾat ,šå′nå.

29. Wayyigră′vu yă′me yisrå′ʾel lå′mūṯ wayyig′rå liv′nö lĭyö′sef way′yömar ′lö ʾim′nå må′ṣåṯi ′ḥen beʿe′nāḵå ′simnå ,yåḏă′ḵå ′tāḥaṯ yăre′ḵi wåʿå′sīṯå ′immåḏi ′ḥāsaḏ waʾă′maṯ ′ʾalnå ṯigbă′rēni bamiṣ′rå̊yim.

30: wašåḵav′ti ʿim ʾavö′ṯay ʾunså′ṯāni mimmiṣ′rāyim ʾugvar′tāni big,vūrå′ṯåm way′yömar ,ʾånö′ḵi ′ʾaʿăsa ḵiḏ′vå rāḵå.

31: way′ yömar hiš,šåvå̆′ʿå li way,yiššå′vaʿ ′lö wayyiš′taḥu yisrå′ʾēl ′ʿalröš ,hammī′ṭṭå̊.

3. The Iraqi Community (Baghdad)

28: way′ḥi ′yāʿa′qob be′ʾēreṣ məṣ′rāyəm šəbaʿ ʿəs′re ša′na way′hi ye′me ,yāʿa′qob še′ne ḥay′yaw ′sēbaʿ ša′nim weʾarba′ʿim ʾum′ʾaṯ šā′nā.

29: wayyiqre′bu ye′me yisra′ʿēl la′mūṯ wayyəq′rā ləb′no leyo′sef way′yomer ′lo ′ʾimna ma′ṣāṯi ′ḥen beʿe′nēḵa sim′na yade′ḵa ′taḥaṯ yere′ḵi weʿa′siṯa ′ʿəmmadi ′ḥesed weʾe′mēṯ ʿal′na ṯəgbe′rēni beməṣ′rāyəm.

30: we,šāḵab′ti ʿimʾabo′ṯay wunsa′ṯāni məmməs′rāyəm wuqbar′tani biq,bura′ṯam wayyoʾmar ′ʾano′ḵi ʾeʿ′se ,kədba′reḵa.

31:way′yōmer həš,šābe′ʿa ′lī way,yišša′bāʿ ′lō wayyiš taḥu yisrå′ʾēl ′ʿalrös ,hammī′ṭṭā.

4. The Aleppo (Syria) Community

28: way′ḥi[1] ′yāʿa′qob be′ʾēreṣ məṣ′rāyim ši,vaʿes′re ša′na way′hi ye,me yaʿa′qov še′ne ḥa′yav ′ševaʿ ša′nim weʾarba′ʿim um′at ša′nā. note: Var.: vayhi [v] and [w] both appear in the pronunciation of the Aleppo community as the realizations of Heb. ו.

29: wayiqrə′vu ye,me yisra′ʾēl la′mut wayəq′rā lĭb′no leyo′sēf wa′yomer ′lo ʾəm′na ma′ṣati ′ḥen ,beʿe′nēḵa ,sim′na ,yade′ḵa ′taḥat yere′ḵi veʿa′sita ʿəmma′di ′ḥesed ,veʾe′met ʾal′na təqbe′rēni beməṣ′rāyim.

30: we,šaḵav′ti ʿəmʾavo′tay wunsa′tāni məməṣ′rāyim wuqbar′tani bəq,būra′tam wayo′mar ,ʾano′ḵi ʾeʿ′se ,kədba′rēḵa.

31: wa′yomer hiš,šaveʿal′li wayiš,ša′vāʿlo wayiš′taḥu yisra′ʾel ʿal′roš hamməṭ′ṭā.

5. The Community of Lithuania

28: vay′ḵi ′yankev beʸeḡets mits′ḡaim ′švaesrey ′šono va′yi yemey′yankev šney ′ḵayov ′ševa ′šonim veaḡ′boim u′meas ′šono.

29: va′yikḡvu yemey yis′ḡoel lo′mus va′yikḡo liv′ney le′yeyeʸ seyf va′yeymaḡley im′no mo′tsosi ′ḵeyn bey′nēḵo ′simno ′yodḵo ′taḵas ye′ḡeyḵi veʸ o′siso i′modi ′ḵesed ve′ʸemes ′alno tigbe′ḡeyni bemitsḡaim.

30: vešo′kavti ima′veysay unso′sani mimits′ḡaim ukvaḡ ′tani bikvu′ḡosom va′yeymaḡ o′neyḵi ee′se kidvo ′ḡēḵo.

31: va′yeymeḡ i′šovoli vayi′sovaley vayiš′taḵu yis′ḡoel al′ḡeyš a′mito.

BIBLIOGRAPHY: I. GENERAL (includes works dealing with the pronunciations of more than one community): J. Cantineanu, *Essai d'une phonologie de l'hébreu biblique*, in: BSL, 46 (1950), 82–133; I. Garbell, *Quelques observations sur les phonèmes de l'hébreu biblique et traditionnel, ibid.*, 50 (1954), 231–43; idem, *Mesorot ha-Mivta ha-Ivri shel Yehudei Asya ve-Afrika la-Ḥativoteihen*, in: *Fourth World Congress of Jewish Studies, Papers*, 2 (1968), 453–4 (Eng. summ., 212); G. Garbini, *Il Consonantismo dell' Ebraico attraverso il Tempo*, in: *Annali dell' Istituto Universitario Orientale di Napoli*, 14 (1964), 165–90; S. Morag, *Ha-Ivrit Shebbefi Yehudei Teiman* (1963); idem, "Oral Tradition as a Source of Linguistic Information," in: *Substance and Structure of Language*, ed. by J. Puhvel (1969), 127–46; G.M. Schramm, *The Graphemes of Tiberian Hebrew* (1964); S. Morag, Review of Schramm, *The Graphemes*, in: KS, 42 (1967/68), 78–86; M. Ẓ. Segal, *Yesodei ha-Fonetika ha-Ivrit* (1918); M. Sister, *Probleme der Aussprache des Hebraeischen* (1937). II. SPECIFIC COMMUNITIES: (1). The Samaritan: Z. Ben-Ḥayyim, *Ivrit va-Aramit Nosaḥ Shomron*, 1–5 (1957–77); for pronunciation see particularly 3, pt. 1 (1961), 13–27; idem, "Some Problems of a Grammar of Samaritan Hebrew," in: *Biblica*, 52 (1971), 229–52; R. Macuch, *Grammatik des samaritanischen Hebraeisch* (1969). (2). The Yemenite: S. Morag, *Haivrit* (see 1; Bibliography pp. 295–305); I. Garbell, Review of Morag, *Ha-Ivrit*, in: KS, 40 (1964/65), 323–30; E.Y. Kutscher, *Yemenite Hebrew and Ancient Pronunciations*, in: JSS, 11 (1966), 217–25. (3). Sephardi, Italian, and Oriental Communities (except the Yemenite): I. Garbell, *Mesorot ha-Mivta* (see 1); M.J. Premsela (Perat), in: *Ha-Olam* (Sept. 11, 1941), on the pronunciation of the Dutch-Portuguese community; A.S. Corré, *The Anglo-Sephardic Pronunciation of Hebrew*, in: JJS, 7 (1956), 85–90; E.S. Artom, *Mivta ha-Ivrit eẓel Yehudei Italia*, in: *Lešonenu*, 15 (1946/47), 52–61; idem, *La pronuncia dell'ebraico presso gli Ebrei della Tripolitania*, in: *Vessillo Israelitico*, 70 (1922), 5; H. Zafrani, *La lecture traditionelle de l'hébreu chez les Juifs arabophones de Tiznit (Maroc)*, in: GLECS, 10 (1964), 29–31; I. Garbell, *Mivta ha-Izzurim ha-Ivriyyim befi Yehudei Iran*, in: *Lešonenu*, 15 (1946/47), 62–74. (4). The Ashkenazi: M. Altbauer, "*Meḥkar ha-Masoret ha-Ivrit haAshkenazit ve-Zikato la-Dialektologyah shel ha-Yidish*," in: *Fourth World Congress of Jewish Studies, Papers*, 2 (1968), 455; D. Leibel, "On Ashkenazic Stress," in: *The Field of Yiddish*, ed. by U. Weinreich, 2 (The Hague, 1965), 63–72; M. Weinreich, "Prehistory and Early History of Yiddish," *ibid.*, 1 (New York, 1954), 73–101; idem, "*Reshit ha-Havara ha-Ashkenazit be-Zikatah li-Veayot Kerovot shel ha-Yidish ve-shel ha-Ivrit ha-Ashkenazit*", in: *Lešonenu*, 27–28 (1966/67), 131–47, 230–51, 318–39. III. HISTORICAL PROBLEMS (in addition to the bibliography given in 1): I. Garbell, "The Pronunciation of Hebrew in Medieval Spain," in: *Homenaje a Millás-Vallicrosa*, 1 (1954), 647–96; Y.G. Gumperz, *Mivtaʾei Sefatenu* (1952/53); S. Morag, "*Sheva Kefulot* BGD KPRT," in: *Sefer Tur-Sinai* (1959/60), 207–42; H. Yalon, "*Shevilei Mivtaʾim*," in: *Kuntresim le-Inyenei ha-Lashon ha-Ivrit*, 1 (1937), 62–78; 2 (1938), 70–76; idem, "*Hagiya Sefaradit be-Ẓarefat ha-Ẓefonit*," in: *Inyenei Lashon* (1941/42), 16–31; "*Al Hagiyat ha-Kameẓ ve-ha-Kameẓ he-Ḥatuf be-Ashkenaz*," *ibid.*, 31–36; idem, "*Le-Toledot Hagiyat ha-Ivrit be-Ashkenaz*," in: *Inyenei Lashon* (1942/43), 52–58. See also the series *Eda ve-Lashon* and *Massorot*.

[Shelomo Morag]

PROOPS, family of Hebrew printers, publishers, and booksellers in Amsterdam. SOLOMON BEN JOSEPH (d. 1734), whose father may have been a Hebrew printer as well, was established as a bookseller in Amsterdam and associated with other printers from 1697 to 1703. In 1704 he set up his own Hebrew press, which produced mainly liturgical books but also a wider range of works in *halakhah, aggadah*, Kabbalah, ethics, and history. In 1714 Proops began to print a Talmud edition in competition with that planned by Samuel b. Solomon Marches and Raphael b. Joshua de Palasios, but was forced by them to discontinue in view of their prior rabbinic monopoly. From 1715 productions by Proops carried advertisements of books he had published, and in 1730 he issued a sales catalog (*Appiryon Shelomo*), the first such Hebrew publication.

At his death, appointed guardians continued to operate the press, and even when his sons JOSEPH (d. 1786), JACOB (d. 1779), and ABRAHAM (d. 1792) took over, they traded under the old name until 1751. Between 1752 and 1765 the sons – now under their own name – printed a Talmud edition with interruptions, which were due in part to attempts to print a Talmud in *Sulzbach, against which they successfully asserted their own rabbinical monopoly. In 1761 they bought the typographical material of the *Athias press, but business declined. In 1785 Joseph Proops sold most of his work to Kurzbeck of Vienna, and when he died a year later his widow and sons – for some time in partnership with Abraham Prins – continued printing on a small scale until 1812. From 1774 to his death Jacob Proops worked on his own; his widow and sons continued along until 1793 and until 1797 in partnership with SOLOMON (d. 1833), son of Abraham Proops; Solomon worked alone until 1827. Abraham Proops had been active on his own in 1776–79; afterward he removed his business to *Offenbach, but his son, who worked with him, returned to Amsterdam at his father's death. DAVID, a son of Jacob Proops, printed from 1810 to 1849 in partnership with H. van Emde and his widow, when the press was sold to Levisson who continued it until 1869; the Levisson brothers remained active until 1917.

BIBLIOGRAPHY: Steinschneider, Cat Bod, 3021–22; Ḥ.D. Friedberg, *Toledot ha-Defus ha-Ivri be-Eiropah* (1937), 36–40; R.N.N. Rabinovicz, *Ma'amar al Hadpasat ha-Talmud* (1887), 94, 103–5.

PROOPS, MARJORIE (1911–1996), British advice columnist and journalist. Born Rebecca Marjorie Israel in Tottenham, London, the daughter of salesman, she went to art school and became a freelance fashion artist, known as Marjorie Proops after her marriage. Around 1945 she became fashion editor of the London *Daily Mirror* newspaper and soon after began the advice column which made her nationally known, "Ask Marje." Emulating such American advice columnists as Abigail Van Buren, Proops became probably the best-known "Agony Aunt" (as such columnists are known) in Britain. She was especially noted for her extreme frankness on sexual matters and is seen as having a role in initiating the more liberal attitudes of the 1960s. A 1992 biography by Angela Patmore, *Marje: The Guilt and the Gingerbread*, revealed her own failing marriage and many affairs. Proops was named Woman Journalist of the Year in 1969 and was the author of an autobiography, *Dear Marje* (1976).

BIBLIOGRAPHY: ODNB online.

[William D. Rubinstein (2nd ed.)]

PROPERTY.

Classification

Property may be divided into different classes in accordance with the various legal principles applicable thereto. One common division is between immovable property and movables, distinguished from each other in the following respects among others: in their different modes of *acquisition, since there cannot be a "lifting" (*hagbahah*) or "pulling" (*meshikhah*) etc., of land; the law of overreaching (see **Ona'ah*) applies to the sale of movables but not land, apparently because land is always distinctive by virtue of its quality and situation and frequently it is of varying value for different people (see *Sefer ha-Ḥinnukh*, no. 340); in the case of land a rival claim to ownership may be resisted upon proof of three-year possession (see **Ḥazakah*), whereas movables which are in a person's possession for any period of time are presumed to belong to him; litigants are only required to swear an *oath if the dispute concerns movables and not land; unlike movables, land can never be stolen (see *Theft and Robbery) since it cannot be removed or carried away – and it is for this reason that originally only the debtor's land and not his movables became subjected to the creditor's *lien (although later, as a result of changed economic circumstances, the lien was extended by the Babylonian *geonim* to both categories, probably because the majority of Jews had ceased to be landowners at that time). The laws relating to slaves resemble those applicable to land in some respects – for instance as regards overreaching – and in other respects resemble the laws applicable to movables – for instance as regards incidental acquisition (*kinyan aggav*, Tos. to BK 12a).

For the purposes of debt recovery, land is divided into best, median, and poorest quality (*iddit*, *beinonit*, and *zibburit*, respectively). A claim arising from tort is recovered from land of the best quality, the creditor's claim from the median, and the wife's *ketubbah* from the poorest (Git. 5; see also *Execution). In biblical times land was further classified according to location, thus, "a dwelling house in a walled city," "land of one's holding," "land that is purchased" (Lev. 25:25ff.; 27:16ff.).

Movables may be classified by a number of criteria:

(1) *perot* ("fruits" or "produce") and *kelim* ("vessels" or "utensils"), the one for consumption and the other for use respectively; the latter serve for the purpose of acquiring by barter by way of *kinyan sudar*, the former not (see *Acquisition, Modes of);

(2) animals and other movables, the former requiring three-year possession for establishment of title whereas *ḥazakah* of the latter is immediately acquired (Sh. Ar., ḤM 133–5);

(3) coins which are legal tender constitute a special category of movables which cannot be acquired or alienated by barter and can only be given as a loan for consumption but not for use and return (i.e., the borrower need not return the very coins of the loan);

(4) deeds are another separate category of movables since these are not in themselves property but only serve as evidence

of their contents, and they differ from other movables in their modes of acquisition (see *Shetar*; *Assignment).

A criterion unrelated to physical differences is one between property that is owned and ownerless property (*hefker*), for which there are different modes of acquisition. Owned property is further subdivisible into public property (see Meg. 26; BB 23a and *Tosafot*) and private property (including joint ownership (see *Partnership)); and into consecrated property (*hekdesh*) as distinct from property of the common man (*nikhsei hedyot*). It is forbidden for the common man to derive a benefit from consecrated property as long as it retains its sanctity of which there are different categories (see *Hekdesh*).

Consecrated property is further distinguished from property of the common man as regards the modes of acquisition and the applicable laws of overreaching, tort, etc. Land which is owned may be classified into free, unencumbered property (*nekhasim benei ḥorin*) and encumbered and mortgaged property (*nekhasim meshu'badim*), the latter being land sold by the debtor to others but remaining charged in favor of his creditors for the repayment of debts which cannot be recovered out of his free property (see *Lien).

Another separate category is property from which no enjoyment may be derived, such as *ḥameẓ* ("leaven") on Passover, the ox that is condemned to death by stoning, fruit of the *orlah* (i.e., the first three years), etc. Such property is not considered to be in the possession of its owner, nor apparently does the latter have a full proprietary right thereto since it not only cannot be enjoyed but may not even be purchased or sold (see *Lien).

Property is further divisible into capital, fruits or profits, and improvements (*keren, perot*, and *shevaḥ*, respectively). The capital is the property as it is at any given time; the fruits are the profits derived therefrom; and the improvement is the increase in market value of the property – whether deriving from actual improvement, natural or effected, or from increase in market price without such.

Proprietary Rights

OWNERSHIP. This is the most common proprietary right and is closely connected with possession. A person is the owner of property if he has possession thereof for an unlimited period, or if it is out of his possession for a limited period only and thereafter is due to be restored to him for an unlimited period – for instance when it had been let, lent, or even when it has been lost or stolen or robbed from the owner in circumstances where it may be surmised that he will regain possession of the property; if not, his ownership of the property will likewise terminate. Since the same property may be in the possession of different people – for instance, one in possession of a dwelling and another of its upper floor – it follows that ownership may be shared by different people with each owning a defined part of the property. The owner does not have unrestricted freedom to deal as he pleases with his property. In biblical times for instance it was not possible to sell a field in perpetuity, but only until the Jubilee Year. Other restrictions have applied at all times, including the following: a person may not use his land in such a manner as to disturb his neighbors in the normal use of their land (see *Nuisance); in certain special circumstances a person is obligated to allow others the use of his land (BK 81a).

RIGHTS IN THE PROPERTY OF OTHERS. Short of ownership, a person may have proprietary rights in the property of others (*jura in re aliena*). Such rights are not exhausted by the recognized legal categories thereof, but may be freely created by the parties thereto in a form and on conditions suited to their needs, without restriction. Broadly, however, these rights may be classified as falling into one of the following three categories: a right to the use of another's property along with its possession as in the case of hire (see *Lease and Hire), loan, and bailment; a right to the enjoyment of another's property without its possession – such as the right to project a bracket into the space of the neighboring courtyard; a right in the form of a charge on another's property, such as a mortgage, and the abutter's rights (see *Maẓranut*; *Execution). All the above proprietary rights have in common the fact that they avail against the whole world, including the owner of the property concerned, continue to attach to the property even if it be sold to a third party, and cannot be cancelled without the right-holder's consent. Hence these rights are like a form of limited or partial ownership for a specific purpose – their acquisition being a "transfer of the body for its fruits," such as transfer of a tree for its fruit, a dovecote for the fledglings, or land for a road or thoroughfare (see *Servitude). Similarly, hire is like a sale for a limited period and loan like a gift for a limited period (Yad, She'elah 1:5; Sekhirut 7:1). However, this does not really amount to full, nor even limited, ownership (*Nimmukei Yosef*, BM 56b, in the name of Ran), but only to a real right in the property, available against the whole world.

The most common of the first of the above-mentioned categories of *jura in re aliena*, i.e., with possession, is hire or *lease. The lessor, like the lender or bailor, may not withdraw during the subsistence of the contract and the lessee's rights are protected against all comers, including the lessor. A contract of lease may take various forms and, in the case of land, may be for monetary remuneration or the right to work the land for a proportional part of the produce (Yad, Sekhirut 8:1) – the latter right either for a fixed period or passing on inheritance; the lease may even take the form of a sale of the land for return after a number of years. The "sale for the fruit" is so close to the transfer of ownership that the *amoraim* disputed whether acquisition for the fruits was an acquisition of the land itself (*kinyan ha-guf*; Git. 47b), i.e., whether the sale of a field for its fruits involved transfer of the field's ownership or not. When the law of Jubilee Year was observed, any sale of a field was in fact no more than a sale for its fruits.

The proprietary rights attaching to the above relationships carry also corresponding personal rights or obligations. Thus in the case of movables it is the duty of the hirer to take care of the hired property and he assumes liability for damage arising from his negligence, or from the loss or theft of the property, and – in the case of loan – even from inevitable accident. These obligations are separate from the proprietary right in question and the two may even come into effect at different times (see Tos. to BM 99a). Thus an unpaid bailee who has mere custody or detention, but not possession, of the deposit – since it may be removed by the owner at any time – apparently has not proprietary right in the deposit but only the obligation to take proper care thereof and to compensate for his neglect to do so. Other similar obligations may be circumscribed by agreement in the same way as are the terms of the real rights, since both may be created by the parties in a manner they think fit.

The second of the above-mentioned categories of proprietary rights are those which allow a person the enjoyment of another's property without its possession. These include a man's right to cause a nuisance to his neighbor or to project an abutment into the airspace of his neighbor's court (see *Servitude). Similarly, a man buying a tree has the right of having it stand in the land of the seller (BB 81b), or the owner of a vine or shrub to have it cling to the tree of his neighbor (BM 116b). These too are proprietary rights which are transferable to others and available against purchasers of or heirs to the servient property, the owner whereof may not withdraw from or cancel the said rights.

Acquisition and Transfer of Proprietary Rights

The usual transfer of proprietary rights is by the parties' will. There are two categories of voluntary acquisition of ownership, the first involving the acquisition of ownerless property, and the second acquisition of property from its former owner. For acquisition of the former, i.e., original acquisition, it is necessarily required that the person becoming entitled thereto have possession of the property together with the intention of acquiring its ownership. Hence in this case the formality of acquisition is satisfied by way of a "lifting" or "pulling" of the property, or by its presence within his "premises which are guarded for him" or his "four cubits" (*arba ammot*), or, in the case of land, by acts revealing his control thereover (i.e., *ḥazakah*).

For the acquisition of property from its former owner, it is not necessary that the acquirer have possession of the property, which may be at any place whatever. In this case acquisition takes place by consent of the parties and their making up their minds to the transaction so as to exclude withdrawal therefrom. Here too it is not sufficient that the parties make up their minds, but this fact must also be revealed in a manner that is recognized by all. In general it is customary for the parties to make up their minds and complete the formal acquisition by the same modes as those applicable to the acquisition of ownerless property; additional modes of acquisition in this case are those which naturally reveal that the parties have made up their minds – including by way of money, deed, delivery (*mesirah*), barter, or by way of an act or formality which for historical reasons had become recognized as an act of acquisition, such as *kinyan sudar* (acquisition by means of the "kerchief") and *kinyan aggav* (incidental acquisition). These acts are not symbolic of anything else, but are acts bringing about the making up of the parties' minds and its revelation. Hence if in a particular locality some other act is equal legal validity (as, e.g., in the case of *kinyan* customary in the closing of a transaction, it will be of *sitomta*, i.e., affixing of a mark).

For details, see *Acquisition, Modes of.

Extinction of Ownership

A person's ownership of property is extinguished when he is reconciled (makes up his mind) to the fact that he no longer has permanent possession of the property or that it will no more return to his permanent possession. Here too his state of mind must be revealed and recognizable to all, save that no formal act is required and it may be indicated by speech or conduct alone. Thus ownership terminates upon (1) **ye'ush* ("despair"), i.e., when the owner abandons hope of recovering possession of property of which he has been deprived, for example through loss or theft; (2) abandonment or reunification, whereby the owner reveals his intention to terminate his ownership, whether or not the property be in his possession (see **Hefker*); (3) transfer or alienation of property to another, whereby the owner reveals his intention to terminate ownership thereof but only through its acquisition by a specific person and only from the moment of such acquisition. Transfer of ownership other than by the will of the parties concerned, takes place on a person's death (see *Succession), or upon forfeiture by order of the court, or by the operation of law (see *Confiscation, Expropriation, Forfeiture). Ownership is also extinguished upon the destruction of property or its transmutation (*shunnui, specificatio*).

In the State of Israel

Property law in the State of Israel is governed mainly by Knesset laws, such as the Water Law, 5719 – 1959; the Pledges Law, 5727 – 1967; the Bailee's Law, 5727 – 1967; the Sale Law, 5728 – 1968; the Gift Law, 5728 – 1968; the Land Law, 5729 – 1969; etc. Some of the provisions of the above laws are in accordance with Jewish law on the particular subject.

BIBLIOGRAPHY: T.S. Zuri, *Mishpat ha-Talmud*, 4 (1921); Gulak, Yesodei, 2 (1922), 172–6; idem, *Le-Ḥeker Toledot ha-Mishpat ha-Ivri bi-Tekufat ha-Talmud*, 1 (*Dinei Karka'ot*, 1929); G. Webber, in: *Journal of Comparative Legislation*, 10 (1928), 82–93; Herzog, Instit, 1 (1936); Elon, in: ILR, 4 (1969), 84f., 90–98, 104f. **ADD. BIBLIOGRAPHY:** M. Elon, *Ha-Mishpat ha-Ivri* (1988), 1:69, 101f., 476f., 482f., 822f.; 3:1364f.

[Shalom Albeck]

PROPHETS, LIVES OF THE, name given to one of the few examples of ancient Jewish hagiographic writings (another example being the "Martyrdom of Isaiah"). Although in its present form the book contains some Christian elements, there is a general consensus among scholars as to the antiquity and the basic Jewish character of the work. Many of the traditions, such as that of Isaiah's death at the hands of Manasseh, find echoes in Jewish apocryphal and rabbinic literature (see also Martyrdom of *Isaiah).

The primary text is preserved in Greek. The Greek version falls into four recensions, two attributed to Epiphanius of Cyprus (hence the title "Pseudo-Epiphanius" sometimes given to this work), one to Dorotheus, and one anonymous. The anonymous recension is to be found in Codex Morchalianus (Codex Q of the Septuagint). It is generally considered to be the oldest extant form of the work. Certain of the other recensions, especially that attributed to Dorotheus, are much expanded, containing the lives of various New Testament figures, apostles, and so forth. The "Lives of the Prophets" is also known in a number of the Oriental Churches in translation. There are various Syriac forms of the book which all appear to be developments of a single original translation from Greek. Although it is attributed to Epiphanius, Nestle and Schermann were of the opinion that the form of the Syriac "Lives" contained in the Syrohexaplar Code represents a different translation, but this is denied by Torrey. The "Lives" are also extant in Armenian, in a number of forms, but little is known of this version. Most scholars consider the Greek to be original, although Torrey posited a Hebrew original for the book.

The recension of Q contains the lives of Isaiah, Jeremiah, Ezekiel, and Daniel, followed by the lives of the Twelve Minor Prophets. These are followed by the lives of Nathan, Ahijah, Joed (identified with the anonymous prophet who is mentioned in I Kings 13), Azariah (son of Oded – II Chron. 15:1ff.), Zechariah b. Jehoiada (II Chron. 24:20–22; cf. Matt. 23:35; Luke 11:51), Elijah, and Elisha. Some of these "Lives" are quite extensive, containing many traditions of extra-biblical character touching on the circumstances of birth, acts, or death of the prophet concerned. Others seem to be limited to the very barest of details of place of birth and death. The traditions contained in these brief narratives are of considerable interest. Some of them are found in other sources, others are extant only in the "Lives." It is plausible that the "Lives" preserve references to lost apocryphal documents or at least traditions in common with them. The popular character of many of the traditions also adds to their interest. The "Lives" abound with geographical names, not all of which can be identified.

BIBLIOGRAPHY: E. Nestle, *Marginalien und Materialien* (1893), 1–64, 2nd pagination; T. Schermann, *Propheten-und Apostellegenden* (1907); idem, *Prophetarum Vitae Fabulosae…* (1907); C.C. Torrey, *The Lives of the Prophets* (Gr. and Eng. 1946).

[Michael E. Stone]

PROPHETS AND PROPHECY. This article is arranged according to the following outline:

IN THE BIBLE

Classifications

The second division of the Hebrew Canonical Scriptures is today subdivided into "The Former Prophets," i.e., the books of Joshua, Judges, Samuel, and Kings (the term is taken from Zech. 1:4, where it has a different sense), and "The Latter Prophets," i.e., the books of Isaiah, Jeremiah, Ezekiel, and the Twelve Minor Prophets.

This division is basically a chronological one. A preferable nomenclature would be the pre-classical, or popular, prophets and the classical, or literary, prophets. The latter terminology is reserved for those prophets whose oracles were preserved in writings either by themselves, their disciples, or their scribes (e.g., Jer. 36:4, 18). The primary literary remains of the pre-classical, prophets, in contrast, are the stories and accounts of their lives transmitted at first, no doubt, orally by followers and admirers. Though several third-person biographical accounts of the classical prophets have also been preserved in their respective books (e.g., Isa. 36–39; Jer. 26ff.; Amos 7:10–17), these stories are secondary to their prophetic pronouncements. The terminological division serves as a formal external criterion for distinguishing between the two.

Nature of Prophecy

The institution of prophecy is founded on the basic premise that God does not abandon humans to their own devices, but provides them with divine guidance. A prophet is a charismatic individual endowed with the divine gift of both receiving and imparting divine messages. In biblical theory, the prophet does not choose his profession but is chosen, often against his own will, to convey the work of God to his people regardless of whether or not they wish to hear it (Ezek. 3:11). A prophet does not elect to prophesy, nor does he become a prophet by dint of a native or an acquired faculty on his part. Prophecy is not a science to be learned or mastered. There is no striving to be one with God, no *unio mystica*, no indwelling of God within the spirit of the prophet through rapture, trances, or even spiritual contemplation. The prophet is selected by God and is irresistibly compelled to deliver His message and impart His will, even if he personally disagrees with it. He is to some extent set apart from his fellowmen and is destined to bear the responsibility and burden of being chosen. The prophet stands in the presence of God (Jer. 15:1, 19) and is privy to the divine council (Isa. 6; Jer. 23:18; Amos 3:7). He speaks when commanded, but once commanded, must speak (Amos 3:8). Appointed messenger, he must translate his revelatory experience into the idiom of his people. For though the prophet is overwhelmed by the divine word and becomes "word possessed," he does not lose his identity nor does he suffer from any effacement of personality. The "word of YHWH" and not His "spirit" is the primary source of prophecy. The "spirit" may prepare the prophet to receive divine revelation, may evoke the revelatory state of mind, but the "word" is the revelation itself. What makes him a prophet is not the spirit which envelops or moves him – for this spirit also motivated elders, judges, Nazirites, and kings – but the word that he has heard and which he transmits to others. In fact, the "spirit" or the "hand" of God (see below) is mentioned only occasionally in the writings of the classical prophets (a major exception being Ezekiel), and then it constitutes the stimulus, not the content, of revelation. The prophet, although conscious of being overwhelmed by the divine word and of being involved in an encounter with God, is still capable of reacting and responding and may even engage God in a dialogue. The divine constraint does not exclude the prophet's personal freedom; his individuality is maintained, and the divine message is accented by his own tones.

The prophetic experience is one of confrontation. The prophet is both a recipient and a participant. Armed solely with the divine word and as conveyor of the divine will, he views the world *sub specie dei*. He is concerned not with the being of God but with the designs of God. He has knowledge not about God but from God concerning His actions in history. The prophet is neither a philosopher nor a systematic theologian, but a mediator, often a covenantal mediator, who delivers the word of God to his people in order to shape their future by reforming their present. He is not the ultimate source of the message nor its final addressee; he is the middleman who has the overpowering experience of hearing the divine word, and who must perform the onerous task of bearing it to a usually indifferent if not hostile audience.

The individuality of the prophet is never curtailed. No two prophets prophesied in the same style. Their unique literary styles, whether expressed in prayers, hymns, parables, indictments, sermons, dirges, letters, mocking and drinking songs, or legal pronouncements, bear the mark of independent creativity. The divine message is refracted through the human prism. This is dramatically brought out by the striking image of the prophets' receiving, literally eating, God's word, and then bringing it forth (Jer. 15:16ff.; Ezek. 3:1ff.). God speaks to the prophet and the prophet speaks out. The divine revelation is delivered by a human agent.

ORIGIN AND FUNCTION. The Hebrew term for a prophet, *navi'*, cognate of the Akkadian verb *nabû*, "to call," i.e., "one who has been called," is first applied to Abraham. He merits this title because of his role as intercessor (see below): "But you [Abimelech] must restore the man's wife [Sarah] – since he is a prophet, he will intercede for you – to save your life" (Gen. 20:7). The origin of the office of prophecy, according to Deuteronomy, is rooted in the event at Horeb. Since the people were afraid of receiving God's word directly in a public theophany (divine manifestation), they requested Moses to "go closer and hear all that our Lord our God tells you… and we will willingly do it" (Deut. 5:24). The account serves as an etiological explanation of why ordinary Israelites do not have direct access to the divine word. This etiology is elaborated in the words of Moses: "I stood between the Lord and you at that time to convey the Lord's word to you, for you were afraid of the fire and did not go up the mountain" (Deut. 5:5; cf. Ex. 19:19). Thus Moses in Deuteronomy serves as the inaugurator of prophecy in Israel (se further Deut. 18:15–19).

The term *navi'*, translated in the Septuagint by the Greek word *prophētēs* ("prophet"), which means "one who speaks on behalf of" or "to speak for" "speak before," is a "forthteller" and spokesman as well as a "foreteller" and prognosticator. He is God's mouthpiece (Jer. 15:19); the one to whom God speaks, and who, in turn, speaks forth for God to the people. This, indeed, is the very definition of the prophet's role found in several places in the Bible. In Exodus 4:15–16 the roles that Moses and Aaron are to assume before Pharaoh are delineated: "You [Moses] shall speak to him [Aaron] and put the words in his mouth… and he shall speak for you to the people. Thus he shall be your spokesman and you shall be an oracle [*'elohim*]." In Exodus 7:1, "The Lord replied to Moses, 'See I make you an oracle [*'elohim*] to Pharaoh, and your brother Aaron shall be your spokesman' [*navi'*]." So, too, in Deuteronomy 18:18, "I will raise up a prophet for them among their own people, like yourself. I will put My words in his mouth, and he will speak to them all that I command him."

DREAMS. Moses, though he is called a *navi'* for the first time only in Deuteronomy (18:15; 34:10), is cast as the prophet par excellence. He is distinguished by God's revealing Himself directly to him, "mouth to mouth, plainly and not in riddles," while to other prophets, God revealed Himself only in visions or dreams (Num. 12:6–8). This distinction between *dreams and prophecy is made because of the universal belief that gods communicate their will to humans through the medium of dreams. Several instances of divine revelation through dreams are attested in the Bible, e.g., the dreams of Abimelech (Gen. 20:3; cf. Gen. 31:10–13); Solomon (I Kings 3:5–14); Joel (3:1); and Job (33:14–18).

In Deuteronomy 13:2ff. dreams are directly linked to prophecy. It is no wonder, then, that they are considered a possible means for determining the will of God, e.g., I Samuel 28:6 (cf. 28:15). Nevertheless, this means for revealing the will of God is frowned upon by some prophets (see Jer. 23:28; 27:9; Zech. 10:2; cf. Jer. 29:8). Dream interpretation existed in ancient Israel as shown by I Samuel 28:6, 15 and by the stories of Joseph and Daniel. Even though classical Judaism viewed prophecy as a thing of the past, dream interpretation persisted in rabbinic literature (Bar 101–7).

DIVINATION. In the aforementioned quotations from the books of Jeremiah and Zechariah, the medium of dream communication is coupled with that of divination, a science that was well known and widely spread throughout the entire Ancient Near East. It was a highly specialized skill, which enabled the expert practitioner to peer into the world of the future by fathoming the inexplicable will of the gods. The art of divination was extremely elaborate and encompassed many different fields, including hepatoscopy, extispicy, lecanomancy, libanomancy, necromancy, belomancy, reading entrails, bird omens, astrology, and so on. Against these common practices of Israel's neighbors the Bible inveighs, "You shall not practice divination or soothsaying" (Lev. 19:26); "Do not turn to ghosts and do not inquire of familiar spirits" (Lev. 19:31; cf., also, 20:6, 27). The most comprehensive prohibition is found in Deuteronomy 18:10–11: "Let no one be found among you who consigns his son or daughter to the fire, or who is an augur, a soothsayer, a diviner, a sorcerer, or one who casts spells, or who consults ghosts or familiar spirits, or who inquires of the dead." The prohibition is a clear indication that these practices obtained in Israel (see I Sam. 28:7; II Kings 23:24; Isa. 2:6; 8:19; 29:4). In keeping with their attribution of practices of which the biblical writers disapprove (e.g., forms of sexual activity) to the Canaanites, the biblical legislator of Deuteronomy 18:10–11 expresses disapproval of some divinatory practices by identifying them with the Canaanites. The Bible is well aware of divination in other nations as well, e.g., Philistines (I Sam. 6:2; Isa. 2:6); Babylonians (Isa. 47:9, 12–13; Jer. 10:2; 50:35; Ezek. 21:26–28), and Egyptians (Isa. 19:3). It is of interest that the Bible never says that these practices are ineffective. When a prophet vilifies other prophets, he may link them rhetorically with sorcerers (Jer. 27:9).

Biblical opposition to divination is selective. There are several biblical analogues to various forms of divination, e.g., hydromancy or oleomancy (Gen. 44:5, 15), and tree oracles (II Sam. 5:24). Other biblically sanctioned, legitimate means through which God discloses His will are dreams (I Sam. 28:6; see above), the *Urim and Thummim placed in the priest's breastplate (Ex. 28:30; Lev. 8:8; Num. 27:21; I Sam. 14:41; Ezra 2:63), and the *ephod (I Sam. 23:9ff.). In fact, it seems that prophets may have, at times, fulfilled the same function as the last two. This is suggested by the manner of framing questions in the simple form of alternatives in I Samuel 14:37, 42 (cf. Greek version); 23:11, and I Kings 22:6. Lots (Num. 26:55–56) and the ordeal (Num. 5) were also occasionally resorted to.

Pre-Classical Prophets

TERMINOLOGY. The pre-classical prophets are referred to by four different names: *ḥozeh, ro'eh*, both meaning "seer"; *'ish ha-'Elohim*, "man of God" (I Kings 13:1; Elijah, I Kings 17:18, 24; II Kings 1:10; Elisha, II Kings 4:7, 9, 21; 8:4, 8, 11; 13:19; cf. Moses, Deut. 33:1; Josh. 14:6; Ps. 90:1; Ezra 3:2; I Chron. 23:14; II Chron. 30:16); and *navi'*, "prophet." (The last is also the standard term for the classical prophets.) The seer was one who possessed the ability to reveal that which was concealed from ordinary mortals; he was also able to foretell the future. The term *ro'eh* is first applied to Samuel in I Samuel 9, when Saul, in search of his father's asses, seeks the aid of the seer Samuel and is prepared to pay a fee of one-quarter of a shekel. Samuel, who in this narrative (9:6) is also called *'ish ha-'Elohim*, and who had been previously informed by the Lord of Saul's arrival, provides the necessary information and, in addition, anoints Saul king of Israel (I Sam. 10). He then informs Saul of the events which are about to befall him on his way home. It is within this account that the editor of the narrative adds an important historical-chronological footnote (9:9): "He who now is called *navi'* was formerly called *ro'eh*." The title *ro'eh* is later applied to Samuel in I Chronicles 9:22; 26:28; and 29:29. The only other one clearly designated by this title is Hanani (II Chron. 16:7, 10; some also attribute it to the priest Zadok (II Sam. 15:27), but this is highly dubious). In I Chronicles 29:29 the three diversely titled prophets of the period of David, Samuel the *ro'eh*, Nathan the *navi'*, and Gad the *ḥozeh*, are named together.

The title *ḥozeh* is first applied to Gad in II Samuel 24:11, where he is called the *ḥozeh* of David (so, also in I Chron. 21:9), where he once again is distinguished by protocol from Nathan the *navi'*. (On the interchangeability of these two terms, however, one may note that Gad is also called *navi'* in I Sam. 22:5, and in II Sam. 24:11 he is accorded the dual title *navi'* and *ḥozeh*.) According to Chronicles, several other kings kept in their courts men who bore the title *ḥozeh*: I Chronicles 25:5, Heman is mentioned as a *ḥozeh* for David; II Chronicles 9:29, Jedo (Iddo) for Jeroboam (in II Chron. 12:15, he is distinguished from Shemaiah the *navi'*); II Chronicles 19:2, Jehu son of Hanani, for Jehoshaphat; II Chronicles 33:18, anonymous men for Manasseh; and II Chronicles 35:15, Jeduthun, Heman, and Asaph for Josiah. Since only the term *ḥozeh* (and not *ro'eh* or *navi'*) is found when reference is made to a king (*ḥozeh ha-melekh*), it most probably indicates that the seers who bore this title were officially attached to the court, the so-called court prophets.

The term *ḥozeh* was at times also connected with *navi'*: positively, in II Samuel 24:11 and II Kings 17:13, and negatively, in Isaiah 29:10 (cf. 28:7); Amos 7:12; and Micah 3:7. That this technical term was not confined to Israel, but was a common West Semitic title for such seers is attested by the inscription of King Zakkur of Hamath (early eighth century B.C.E.), who declares: "I lifted up my hands to Baʿalsha[may]n and Baʿalshamayn answered me [and spoke] to me through seers [חזין] and diviners" (lines 11–12; Pritchard, Texts3, 655; COS II, 155).

GROUP PROPHECY. The first story in the Bible that makes reference to a seer also mentions bands of prophets. When Saul consults the seer Samuel as to the whereabouts of his father's lost asses, he is told that he is to become "prince over his people Israel" (I Sam. 10:1). To substantiate the authenticity of this prediction, he is informed that upon arriving at Gibeah he will meet "a band of prophets coming down from the high place with harp, tambourine, and lyre before them." And when he did subsequently meet them, a "spirit of God came mightily upon him and he spoke in ecstasy among them." This encounter became the source for the proverbial question "Is Saul also among the prophets?" (I Sam. 10:12). I Samuel 19:18–24 relates this proverb to another instance of the contagious nature of group prophecy: Saul sends men to capture David, who was then in the company of Samuel. However, when the men "saw the company of prophets with Samuel standing as head over them, the spirit of God came upon the messengers of Saul and they also prophesied." This incident is repeated two more times as subsequent messengers are overcome by their contact with the band of prophets. Finally, Saul himself goes to capture David, but the spirit of God comes upon him and he, too, prophesies before Samuel, strips off his clothes, and lies naked all that day and night. Hence, it is said, "Is Saul also among the prophets?"

ECSTASY. The ecstatic nature of these groups of prophets is illuminated by Numbers 11:16ff., a narrative whose purpose may have been the legitimation of the phenomenon of ecstatic prophecy. Moses gathered 70 of the people's elders and stationed them around the Tent of Meeting. "Then the Lord came down in a cloud and spoke to him. He drew upon the spirit that was on him and put it upon the 70 elders. And when the spirit rested upon them they spoke in ecstasy" (11:25; cf. 11:16–27).

Another instance of group ecstasy is found in I Kings 22, where some 400 prophets rage in ecstasy before kings Jehoshaphat and Ahaz on the eve of their attack against Ramoth-Gilead. This feature of collective dionysiac frenzy is not confined to early Israelite prophets. In I Kings 18 it is recorded that 450 Canaanite prophets (referred to as *navi*) of Baal (and 400 prophets of Asherah, verse 19) "cried aloud and cut themselves after their manner with swords and lances till the blood gushed out upon them. And it was so, when midday was past, that they prophesied in ecstasy until the time of the evening offering…" (18:28–29). Ecstatic seizures, moreover, were not limited to groups; individuals, too, could have them. Thus, the seizure of Elijah: "The hand of the Lord was upon Elijah… and he ran before Ahab['s chariots]" (I Kings 18:46; see also *Ecstasy).

An extra-biblical reference to an ecstatic prophet is attested in the 11th-century tale of the Egyptian Wen-Amon, which takes place in Byblos. It relates that "while he [Zakar-Baal, king of Byblos] was making offering to his gods, the god seized one of his youths and made him possessed. And he said to him, 'Bring up [the] god! Bring the messenger who is carrying him! Amon is the one who sent him out! He is the one who made him come!' And while the possessed [youth] was having his frenzy on this night…" (Pritchard, Texts, 26; COS I, 90). Additional examples of this phenomenon are found among the Hittite *šiunianza* and the pre-Islamic *kāhins*.

In such a state one turns, as Saul did, into "another man" (I Sam. 10:6) and may behave madly, as witnessed by Saul's attempt to take the life of David in I Samuel 18:10ff. The irrational and ecstatic behavior of such possessed individuals makes them appear to be madmen. Thus, when Elisha goes to Ramoth-Gilead to anoint Jehu king of Israel, Jehu was asked, "Is all well? Why did this madman come to you?" (II Kings 9:11). A juxtaposition of "madman" and "ecstatic prophet" is found in Jeremiah 29:26; and in Hosea 9:7 the parallel to "prophet" is "madman." (The Hebrew term for madman, *meshuggaʿ* in these verses may very well be a *terminus technicus*, related to the Akkadian *muḫḫûm*, "crazy/frenzy," found in *Mari).

According to the Bible, an ecstatic seizure might be induced by external means, e.g., music. In II Kings 3:15 Elisha requests a musician, "and when the musician played, the power of the Lord came upon him." Specific mention of various musical instruments of the band of prophets is found in I Samuel 10:5 and II Chronicles 35:15. (Dancing in order to induce a prophetic frenzy is mentioned in connection with the Canaanite prophets of Baal, I Kings 18:26.) Of course, prophetic seizure is conceived of as dependent on God, otherwise it would simply be madness. It is ascribed directly to Him and is caused either by "the hand [*yad*] of YHWH," "the spirit [*ruaḥ*] of YHWH" or "the spirit [*ruaḥ*] of God." The term "the hand of YHWH" to indicate divine inspiration is employed when Elisha resorts to music to help induce this state (II Kings 3:15). It is also found in I Kings 18:46 in the description of Elijah in an ecstatic fit running before Ahab's chariot (cf. Jer. 15:17). The term "the spirit of God" appears in both I Samuel 10:6, 10 and 19:20, 23, where the spirit "came mightily" upon Saul and his messengers (cf. I Sam. 18:10). In I Kings 22:21–24 the "spirit" is responsible for inducing false prophecy. Azariah son of Oded in II Chronicles 15:1 and Jahaziel son of Zechariah in II Chronicles 20:14 are both inspired by "the spirit of God/YHWH," which comes upon them (cf. Neh. 9:30).

GROUP LIFE OF PROPHETS. The pre-classical prophets as a group were distinguished by several prominent personalities, e.g., Samuel, Nathan, Elijah, and Elisha, and by their number, at times in the hundreds. They were often banded together in groups of "disciples of the prophets" (Heb. *benei ha-nevi'im*) who may or may not have been located at a shrine. Such groups first appear when Saul encounters a "band of prophets" (I Sam. 10:5, 10) and reappear in the Elijah and Elisha cycles. Though in II Kings 4:38 it is stated that they have their meals in common, some of their members are married and have families. Elisha performed a miracle for the widow of one of the members of this order (II Kings 4:1–7). Some of them owned their own houses (I Kings 13:15ff.). One group was found at Beth-El, and another at Jericho, the latter consisting of 50 members (II Kings 2:3, 5, 7, 15). Elisha performed miracles on behalf of his coterie at Gilgal (II Kings 4:38–44, where 100 are mentioned), and sent one of them to anoint Jehu (II Kings 9:1ff.). He is also called their master (lit., "father," II Kings 6:21). Obadiah, the chief steward of Ahab, saved 100 of them, during the siege of Jezebel (I Kings 18:3–4, 13), and kings Ahab and Jehoshaphat consulted some 400 prophets prior to their attack against Ramoth-Gilead (I Kings 22:6). There is also one possible, but far from certain, indication that heredity may have played some role in such circles, for Jehu, the *ḥozeh*, was a son of Hanani, presumably the same Hanani who was himself a *ro'eh* (II Chron. 16:7; 19:2; I Kings 16:1, 7).

Some of these prophets had attendants in their service. Elisha ministered to Elijah (I Kings 19:21), and Elisha had an attendant (*mesharet*) himself (II Kings 4:43; 6:15). A synonymous term, *na'ar* is also employed for the servants of Elijah (I Kings 18:43; 19:3), of Elisha (II Kings 4:38; 9:4), who was also attended by Gehazi (II Kings 4:12, 25; 5:20; 8:4), and of the attendant of the "man of God" in II Kings 6:15.

ROLE IN SOCIETY. These early prophets played a prominent role in communal affairs and were often sought out and consulted for advice, and asked to deliver oracles in the name of God. In I Kings 14:5, the wife of Jeroboam turns to Ahijah; in I Kings 22:8, Jehoshaphat and Ahab to Micaiah (cf. verses 5ff.); in II Kings 3:4ff., Jehoshaphat and Jeroboam to Elisha; in II Kings 8:8, Ben-Hadad (king of Aram!) to Elisha; and in II Kings 22:13, Josiah to Huldah. Prophets, like ordinary people needed to make a living. There are several references to remunerations for prophetic services, sometimes amounting to as little as one quarter of a shekel (I Sam. 9:8) or ten loaves of bread, some cakes, and a jar of honey (I Kings 14:3); or as much as 40 camels bearing the treasures of Aram (II Kings 8:9). Prophets in Israel, as was true earlier in Mari, delivered their oracles whether asked to or not. In II Kings 1:3ff. Elijah stops Ahaziah's messengers on their way to inquire of Baal-Zebub; Ahijah the Shilonite tears his new garment when he confronts Jeroboam and announces the division of the United Kingdom (I Kings 11:29ff.); and Shemaiah announces to that same king that he should not go to war against his kinsmen of Israel (I Kings 12:22ff.). In Israel (as in Mari and Assyria) prophets could be female as well as male (Ex. 15:20; Judg. 4:4; II Kings. 22:14; Isa. 8:3; Neh. 6:12).

Politics. The prophets greatly influenced the political destiny of Israel. Samuel chose both Saul (I Sam. 9) and David (I Sam. 16) to be kings over Israel. Nathan castigated David for his conduct with Bath-Sheba and Uriah, her husband (II Sam. 12:7ff.), and later instigated the scheme to have David recognize her son, Solomon, as the next king (I Kings 1:8ff.). Ahijah announced both the selection and the rejection of Jeroboam as king of Israel (I Kings 11:29–39; 14:1–18; 15:29). Another "man of God" declared to Jeroboam the future birth of Josiah, who would destroy the idolatrous priests of the high places (I Kings 13:1–2). Shemaiah, mentioned above, forbade that king to attempt to regain the ten tribes of the North (I Kings 12:22–24; II Chron. 11:2–4). Azariah son of Oded influenced King Asa to institute a reform in Judah and to rely on God (II Chron. 15:1ff.), but the seer Hanani reprimanded Asa for requesting Ben-Hadad's aid against the blockade set up by Baasha, king of Israel (II Chron. 16:1ff.). Jehu denounced Jehoshaphat, king of Judah, for allying himself with Ahab (II Chron. 19:2–3). (He also chronicled that king's career, II Chron. 20:34.) In I Kings 22 both Ahab and Jehoshaphat turn to the prophets for an oracle to instruct them whether or not to go to war, and they receive an answer from Micaiah. ("Shall I go to battle against Ramoth-Gilead, or shall I forbear"; the alternative form of this question is reminiscent of the type formerly addressed to the Urim and Thummim.) Elisha foretells the defeat of Moab at the hands of Jehoshaphat and Jehoram (II Kings 3:16ff.). Elisha has one of his colleagues anoint Jehu king of Israel, inspires the latter's rebellion against Jehoram (II Kings 9), and later (II Kings 13:14ff.) by means of a symbolic act (see below) helps insure the victory of Joash over the Arameans.

Prophets were so important to the crown that several kings had their own court prophets. Both Nathan (II Sam. 7; I Kings 1:8ff.) and Gad (I Sam. 22:5; II Sam. 24:11; I Chron. 21:9; 29:29; II Chron. 29:25) served with David. Also in David's court were the sons of Asaph, Heman, and Jeduthun "who could prophesy with lyres, harps, and cymbals" (I Chron.

25:1ff.; II Chron. 29:30; 35:15 – the interesting connection between the prophets and musical guilds may be noted). According to the Chronicler, both Nathan and Ahijah wrote accounts of Solomon's career (II Chron. 9:29); Jedo (Iddo) wrote of either Solomon or Jeroboam (II Chron. 9:29); Iddo and Shemaiah recorded Rehoboam's acts (II Chron. 12:15); and Iddo did the same for Abijah, Rehoboam's successor (II Chron. 13:22).

CLAIRVOYANCE AND PREDICTION. The prophets were both clairvoyant and capable of predicting future events. For example, Ahijah predicted the overthrow of Jeroboam's house and the death of his son (I Kings 14:6ff.); Elijah predicted a drought (I Kings 17:1), and the death of Ahaziah (II Kings 1:4); and Elisha predicted a famine for seven years (II Kings 8:1), and many other events. The prophetic groups in Beth-El and Jericho knew that the Lord would take Elijah away that very day to die (II Kings 2:3ff.). Elisha was aware that Gehazi had accepted a remuneration, for "did I not go with you in spirit when the man turned from his chariots to meet you? Is it a time to receive money…?" (II Kings 5:26). He also knew where the Arameans were encamping (II Kings 6:9) and hears their very words (6:12). Only in exceptional cases does he not foresee events, e.g., when the Shunamite's son died and he declared, "the Lord has hid it from me, and not told me" (II Kings 4:27). Elisha even falls into a trance and foretells the future harm that Hazael, king of Aram, is going to cause Israel (II Kings 8:11ff.). Even if some of these events are *vaticinium ex eventu*, "prophecy after the events," the narratives make it abundantly clear that the people believed in the prophet's ability to foresee the future. Some prophets are also visionaries, e.g., in I Kings 22:19ff., Micaiah sees God enthroned on high; in II Kings 6:17, Elisha sees a mountain full of horses and chariots.

SYMBOLIC ACTS. The prophets did not merely predict the future, however. They often performed symbolic acts, which dramatized and concretized the spoken word. Though the dynamism of the spoken word is considered to have a creative effect in and of itself, it is given further confirmation by this act, which is efficacious and actually plays a role in bringing about the event. Ahijah rends his garment into 12 pieces and bids Jeroboam take ten of them for "thus says the Lord of Israel: 'Behold I will rend this kingdom out of the hand of Solomon and will give you ten tribes, but he shall take one tribe for my servant David's sake…'" (I Kings 11:29ff.). Elisha, in turn, orders Joash to take bow and arrows, open the window eastward, and shoot: "The Lord's arrow of victory, the arrow of victory over Aram! For you shall fight the Arameans in Aphek until you have made an end of them" (II Kings 13:14ff.).

WONDERS. These prophets were also wonder workers. The two most famous are Elijah and Elisha. Elijah causes the jar of meal and the cruse of oil not to fail the widow of Zarephath, "according to the word of the Lord which he spoke" (I Kings 17:8ff.); later, he brought her son back to life (17:17–24). He succeeded in bringing fire down from heaven in his famous contest with the Canaanite prophets (I Kings 18); split the Jordan River by striking it with his mantle (II Kings 2:8); and was swept up on high into heaven by a whirlwind (II Kings 2:11). His successor, Elisha, was no less successful in performing miracles. He, too, split the waters of the Jordan into two with Elijah's mantle (II Kings 2:13–14), made a small jug of oil fill many large vessels (4:1–7), and brought back to life a child who had died (4:8ff.). When the inhabitants of Jericho complained that "the water is bad and the land is unfruitful," he requested a new bowl and salt, which he then threw into the water and said, "Thus says the Lord: 'I have healed these waters; henceforth neither death nor miscarriage shall come from it.' And so the waters were healed" (II Kings 2:19–22). Once in Gilgal during a famine, the prophetic guild complained that the pottage they were eating had the taste of death. By pouring some flour into the pottage, he effected a miracle and made the food edible (II Kings 4:38–41). Another miracle made a small allotment of food suffice for 100 men, "For thus says the Lord, 'They shall eat and leave some'" (4:42–44). His potency for producing miracles continued even after his death. A dead man was reported to have come back to life when his corpse was thrown into Elisha's grave and touched his bones (II Kings 13:20–21). The stories of Elijah and Elisha influenced the New Testament portrayals of Jesus.

These prophets did not always enjoy the security and immunity that their prophetic position should have assured them. Ahab persecuted or permitted Jezebel to persecute Elijah (I Kings 17ff.); Micaiah was put into prison because he foretold the defeat of Israel and the death of Ahab (I Kings 22:27); and Asa, king of Judah, put Hanani, the seer, in the stocks, because the prophet reprimanded him for not relying on God but accepting the help of the king of Aram (II Chron. 16:7–10).

EXTRA-BIBLICAL PROPHECY: MARI. In the pre-biblical period, apostolic prophets, i.e. prophets who declare that a god has sent them, appear in Syria at *Mari in the early second millennium, while late second millennium *Emar texts have the tantalizing *nābû* and *munabbiātu* among their cultic personnel who call upon god. Seers are attested by name outside of Israel (cf. above, the Zakkur inscription). In the neo-Assyrian period favorable oracles are delivered personally to Kings Esarhaddon and Assurbanipal by individuals, mostly women, who address Esarhadddon in the name of Ishtar, and Assurbanipal in the name of Mullissu (Ninlil).

Comparison of Pre-Classical and Classical Prophets

Earlier scholars attempted to draw strong distinctions between the pre-classical prophets such as Samuel, Elijah, and Elisha and such classical prophets as Isaiah and Jeremiah. Among the alleged distinctions are the following:

(1) The classical prophets rejected the cult and ritual and called for ethical monotheism.

(2) They rejected the nationalistic outlook of the popular prophets and replaced it with their concept of universalism.

(3) Whereas the popular prophets functioned as part of guilds, the classical prophets always appear alone (e.g., Amos 7:14).

(4) The popular prophets were ecstatics, given to intoxication of the senses (I Sam. 19:20–24), and they employed musical accompaniment to induce or heighten their frenzy (II Kings 3:15). The classical prophets, however, for the most part pronounced their oracles soberly in clear control of their senses.

It was thought that there was an unbridgeable gap between the two, and with *Amos, the first of the literary prophets, the watershed was reached. Yet, there are many points of contact and continuation in the lives and writings of the classical prophets. Classical prophecy, like every other institution in ancient Israel, did not exist in a vacuum but came into being with an ancestry. The classical prophets were indebted in many ways to the heritage of their predecessors. The technical title *navi'* is applied to both. Both speak solely in the name of the God of Israel, who reveals His will directly to them. They are both sent by God, hear the divine word, and are admitted into His council; their messages are sometimes rooted in the Covenant. These and the following considerations lead to the conclusion that there was one continuous religious tradition. More likely the difference between the pre-classical and classical prophets is the literary form in which the prophetic traditions have reached us.

RITUAL VERSUS MORALITY. The prophet Nathan rebukes King David for his breach of the moral law in his conduct with Bath-Sheba, and Elijah takes Ahab to task for the Naboth incident, in which Ahab was an accessory to murder. True, both indictments concern a primary breach of the moral law, adultery and murder, and are leveled against kings; but they are still an integral part of the ethical-moral dimension. Here, too, may be added Samuel's rebuke of Saul "Has the Lord as great delight in burnt offerings and sacrifices, as in obeying the voice of the Lord? Behold to obey is better than sacrifice, and to hearken than the fat of rams" (I Sam. 15:22). The classical prophets for the most part, do not reject the cult per se any more than they absolutely reject prayer or any other type of worship. To them the cultic obligations are secondary to, and dependent upon, the fulfillment of the moral code of behavior. There is a decided change in the degree of emphasis in the preexilic literary prophets, but not in the principle. Moreover, the words of castigation leveled against the cult are found in the writings of the pre-Exilic prophets; in contrast, in the books of the Exilic and post-Exilic prophets the ritual is often highly emphasized and favorably viewed (see below).

NATIONALISM VERSUS UNIVERSALISM. Nationalistic as well as universalistic tendencies are present in greater or lesser degree in the writing of both. This can be seen in Elijah's command that Elisha anoint Hazael king of Aram (I Kings 19:15), for YHWH is considered equally responsible for events in Aram and in Israel. Other universalistic themes in the early prophets are exemplified in I Kings 20:28, in which a man of God says to the king of Israel, "Thus says the Lord, 'Because the Arameans have said, "the Lord is a god of the hills but he is not a god of the valleys," therefore I will deliver all of this great multitude into your hand, and you shall know that I am the Lord,'" and in I Kings 5:15 in which Naaman, the commander of the Aramean army, after being cured by immersing himself in the Jordan River as prescribed by Elisha, confesses, "Behold, I know that there is no God in all the world but in Israel." The universalistic prophecies of the classical prophets on the other hand, do not preclude, of course, their predominant number of nationalistic oracles.

MANTICS VERSUS REPROVERS. Mantic behavior was not restricted to the pre-classical prophets. For example, Isaiah foretells the future for Hezekiah (Isa. 37:1ff.; 38:1ff.), and Jeremiah, for Zedekiah (Jer. 32:4–5, and see below). The latter also predicts the death of his prophetic rival, Hananiah (Jer. 28:16–17). At the same time, the early prophets Nathan, Elijah, and Elisha do not restrict their activity to merely predicting the future and the answering of queries, but are themselves messengers, apostles, and chasteners who deliver the word of God.

GROUP VERSUS INDIVIDUALS. Although Samuel, Elijah, and Elisha are followed by bands of prophets, when they fulfill their missions, they do it alone as individuals just as the later prophets did. The latter, too, may have had their followers (e.g., the difficult verse, Isa. 8:16), for it is most likely that it was the disciples of these prophets who recorded their masters' words (e.g., Jer. 36:4).

ECSTATICS VERSUS NON-ECSTATICS. Ecstasy, too, is not limited to the pre-classical prophets. The classical prophets had visions and unnatural experiences during their prophetic "seizures." Ezekiel, in particular, was prone to various ecstatic fits; Hosea is called a "madman" (Hos. 9:7) and so too, by direct implication, is Jeremiah (Jer. 29:26).

ROLE IN SOCIETY. The classical prophets played an extremely important role in the Israelite society, as is well known. Like the earlier prophets, they were consulted by those who wanted information from God. Jeremiah is requested by King Zedekiah's messengers to "inquire of the Lord for us, for Nebuchadnezzar, king of Babylon, is making war against us…" (Jer. 21:1–2; cf. similar requests in Jer. 37:7ff.; 42:1ff, and the advice given in Jer. 23:33ff.; Ezek. 8:1ff.; 14:1ff.; 33:30ff.; and contrarily, Isa. 30:1–2).

SYMBOLIC ACTS. The classical prophets, too, performed significant symbolic acts which not only presaged future events but were efficacious in initiating their process of realization. In this category may be included the symbolic names which Isaiah gave his children: "a remnant shall turn back" (Isa. 7:3), and "pillage hastens, looting speeds" (Isa. 8:3), and most probably his own name (Isa. 8:18; cf. the child's name, "God is with us," Isa. 7:14). Isaiah walked about naked and barefoot for three years as a sign that the king of Assyria would lead the Egyptians and Cushites naked into exile (Isa. 20:2ff.). Jeremiah (16:1ff.) refrained from marrying and having children as a portent that both the parents and children of Israel would perish by the sword and famine. He buys a linen waistcloth, wears it, and then buries it in a cleft of the rock, and later upon recovering it, he finds that it has become spoiled, "good for nothing": "Thus will the Lord spoil the pride of Judah and Jerusalem who were made to cling to God but would not obey" (Jer. 13:1ff.). He buys a potter's earthen flask and promptly smashes it to signify that the Lord "will break this people and this city, as one breaks a potter's vessel so that it can never be mended" (Jer. 19:1ff.). He is commanded by the Lord to make thongs and yoke bars and put them on his neck as a portent that any nation or kingdom that does not put its neck under the yoke of Nebuchadnezzar, king of Babylon, will be punished, and only those who submit will be left alone to till their own land (Jer. 27:2ff.; cf. the same act performed by Zedekiah, I Kings 22:11).

The "false" prophet Hananiah, as a symbolic act of his own, breaks these very bars and says, "Thus says the Lord: 'Even so will I make the yoke of Nebuchadnezzar king of Babylon break from the neck of all the nations within two years.'" Jeremiah subsequently replaces his wooden yoke with one of iron and repeats the same message (Jer. 28). During the very last months of the siege of Jerusalem, he purchases a field from his uncle as a sign that "houses and fields and vineyards shall again be bought in this land" (Jer. 32:6ff.). In Jeremiah 43:8ff. the prophet is commanded to take large stones and hide them in the mortar in the pavement which is at the entrance to Pharaoh's palace in Tahpanhes as a sign that the Lord will set the throne of Nebuchadnezzar over these stones. In Jeremiah 51:61–64, when Seraiah comes to Babylon, Jeremiah commands him to read the book he has written concerning all the evil that would befall Babylon. He is then to bind a stone to it and cast it into the Euphrates and say, "Thus shall Babylon sink, to rise no more, because of the evil I am bringing upon her." Both the recitation of curses and the sinking of the scroll portend the final downfall of Babylon. Ezekiel (4:1ff.) takes a brick, portrays upon it the city of Jerusalem, puts siege works against it, builds a siege wall, casts a mound, sets camps against it, and plants battering rams round about. He then takes an iron plate and places it as an iron wall between himself and the city and presses the siege against the city, "a sign for the house of Israel." He also lies alternately on his left and right sides for an extended period of time, presaging the oncoming days of punishment of Israel and Judah. He eats and drinks during those days only a very small amount of food including barley cake baked on human dung to indicate that the people of Israel and Jerusalem "shall eat their bread unclean among the nations" and "shall eat bread by weight… and water by measure" (Ezek. 4:9ff.). In chapter 5 he takes a sharp knife, uses it as a barber's razor to cut the hair of his head and beard, takes balances and weights, and divides the hair for impending judgment. And in chapter 12 he conspicuously prepares for exile in full sight of his people.

SIGNS AND WONDERS. The literary prophets, following their predecessors, also resorted to the use of signs and wonders to authenticate their prediction of impending events. Isaiah tells King Ahaz that since the latter did not put his complete confidence in the Lord in order to withstand the Syro-Ephramite coalition, "The Lord Himself will give you a sign: Behold a young woman is with child and shall bear a son and shall call his name, Immanuel." Before this lad reaches maturity, the kingdoms of Aram and Ephraim would be destroyed (Isa. 7:10–25). The same prophet gives a sign to King Hezekiah in order to prove to him that the Lord has heard his prayer; 15 years would be added to his life, and he would be delivered from the hand of the king of Assyria: "This is the sign to you from the Lord, that the Lord will do this thing that he has promised: Behold I will make the shadow cast by the declining sun on the dial of Ahaz turn back ten steps" (Isa. 38:5–8). He also cures the king by rubbing a cake of figs over his inflammation (38:21–22; II Kings 20:7). In the previous chapter he gives the following sign to that same king: "And this shall be the sign for you: This year eat what grows of itself, and in the second year what springs of the same; then in the third year sow and reap, and plant vineyards" (Isa. 37:30). This is a sign that the surviving remnant of Judah would take root and bear fruit.

Jeremiah, in an embarrassing confrontation with the "false" prophet Hananiah, who later smashed the wooden yoke bars of Jeremiah and subsequently replaced them with bars of iron, says, "Thus says the Lord… 'This very year you shall die, because you have uttered rebellion against the Lord'." The next verse tells that in that very year Hananiah died (Jer. 28:15–17). In one instance Ezekiel himself becomes a sign to the people, when God predicts and then executes the death of the prophet's wife and forbids him to mourn for her as an omen of what the people are about to experience (Ezek. 24:15ff.).

VISIONS. Both the pre-classical and classical prophets share the common oracular terminology "Thus says YHWH." Though the latter are more "hearers" than "seers," they, too, often report visions, e.g., those of Amos (7:8); Isaiah (6); Jeremiah (1:11ff.; 24:1ff.), and the extraordinary visions of Ezekiel (particularly in chapters 1–3, 8–10); and Zechariah (5–6). Indeed, visions play an important role in the classical prophetic writings, as the following quotations further attest:

> I spoke to the Prophets;
> It was I who multiplied visions (Hos. 12:11).
> And it shall come to pass in the future
> that I will pour out my spirit in all flesh;
> your sons and daughters shall prophesy,
> your old men shall dream dreams, and your young
> men shall see visions (Joel 3:1).
> For they are a rebellious people, lying sons,
> sons who will not hear the instruction of the Lord;
> who say to the seers, 'See not!' and to the prophets,
> 'Prophesy not to us what is right' (Isa. 30:9–10; cf. Isa. 29:10; Amos 7:12 in negative contexts).

Like their pre-classical forerunners, the literary prophets occasionally employ the terms "the hand of YHWH" (Isa. 48:16; 59:21; 61:1; Joel 3:1; Micah 3:8; Zech. 7:12; cf. Isa. 11:2; Hos. 9:7) and "the spirit of YHWH" to describe the power that activates and evokes their revelatory state of mind. The ecstatic character of literary prophecy is documented in the various trances of Ezekiel. Finally, classical prophets also, at times, bore the consequence of their dire predictions. Just as Ahab persecuted Elijah (I Kings 17ff.) and had Micaiah imprisoned, because he foretold the destruction of Israel and the death of the king (I Kings 22:27), so too Jeremiah was put into the stocks (Jer. 20:2) as well as in prison (Jer. 32ff.), and Uriah was put to death (Jer. 26:20–23).

Classical Prophecy

The classical prophets, thus, cannot be fully understood without knowledge of their antecedents. Some prophets are connected with the literature of the Torah, e.g., Jeremiah with Deuteronomy and Ezekiel with the Priestly Code. Hosea was indebted to traditions about Jacob; and he, Micah, and Jeremiah knew traditions of Exodus and wilderness wanderings. Isaiah was indebted to traditions of David and Zion. Nevertheless, they cannot be entirely explained by their predecessors or by earlier traditions. For in the middle of the eighth century B.C.E., a new dimension was added to Israelite religion, which definitively shaped the character of the nation. Commencing with Amos, a herdsman from Tekoa, there arose a series of great religious teachers and thinkers, inspired spokesmen who became the passionate bearers of the word of God.

HISTORICAL SCOPE. Their appearance was engendered by specific historical and political events. The temporal limits of the classical apostolic prophets can be placed in a historical framework extending over some 300 years and highlighted by two cataclysmic events. The first prophets appeared a few decades before the fall of Northern Israel (722 B.C.E.), after the conclusion of the 100-year war with the Arameans – a war which produced a vast societal cleavage between the impoverished masses and the wealthy minority, and they disappeared approximately a century following the destruction of Jerusalem (587/6 B.C.E.). Within this period three major empires successively dominated the world scene: Assyria, Babylonia, and Persia.

The prophets, however, always addressed their message to the contemporary situation. Amos, living in the time of Jeroboam II before the rise of Tiglath-Pileser (745 B.C.E.) and the neo-Assyrian empire, foretold exile and destruction for Israel, but he never indicated that it would be executed by Assyria. Second *Hosea (chs. 4–14), a somewhat later contemporary, also foresaw destruction, but although he was aware of both pro-Egyptian and pro-Assyrian factions, he did not designate Assyria as the enemy par excellence. Isaiah's call, in contrast, came at the time of the peak of Assyrian ascendancy. He called that nation the rod of God's wrath and considered it the last of the world powers. Simultaneous with the fall of Assyria would come the demise of arrogance, the root of all idolatrous behavior. Micah and *Zephaniah, too, knew of the Assyrian menace, but except for one late interpolation in the former (Micah 4:10), they, like Isaiah, did not include Babylonia within their historical purview. *Nahum, coming a bit later, rejoiced over the fall of Assyria, but was silent about Babylonia. The Book of *Habakkuk reflects the transition period between Assyrian and Babylonian hegemony. Jeremiah, who received his call to prophecy in 627 B.C.E., identified the enemy described as the "nation from the north" with Babylonia only after the battle of Carchemish in 605 B.C.E. When he portrays the eventual defeat of Babylonia, however, he once again resorts to his initial image of a "nation from the north." Persia is never mentioned as the successor to Babylonia in Jeremiah. Ezekiel, living in the time of Nebuchadnezzar, prophesied the fall of Babylonia but never specified Persia as the conqueror. (Persia is mentioned only once in this connection and then incidentally, 38:5.)

Only with the advent of the anonymous prophet of the Exile who is called Deutero-Isaiah (Isa. 40ff.), was Cyrus, king of Persia, specifically mentioned and then favorably so (Isa. 44:28; 45:1). The three last prophets of Israel, *Haggai, *Zechariah, and *Malachi, were active during the post-Exilic period under the Persian rule and were not aware of the future ascendancy of the Greek Empire. (For the dating of all these prophets as well as *Jonah, *Joel, and *Obadiah, see the individual articles under their names.) Though there are supplements and interpolations, the oracles of the prophets are oriented to their own contemporary situation.

Thus, classical prophecy arose and reached its zenith during the rise and fall of world empires. In the period of the pre-classical prophets, the political-historical horizon was of limited local significance. The enemies of those days – Ammonites, Moabites, Edomites, Philistines, and Arameans – did not strive for world dominion. The age that witnessed the emergence of great empires bore witness to the unique religious phenomenon of classical prophecy, which interpreted these world-significant events in the light of its own theological viewpoint. The Lord of Israel was seen as the director of the drama of world history. His ever-changing cast included the leading historical figures of those days – Sargon, Sennacherib, Nebuchadnezzar, Cyrus – but his attention was continually focused on Israel; her destiny within the divinely controlled arena of world politics was his main concern. The prophets provided an answer to the "why" of destruction and the "how" of future restoration. One implication of classical prophetic teaching was that Israel's defeats did not indicate Yahweh's weakness, but his strength. He could move all the peoples of the earth to punish his people or reward them, depending on their behavior.

DEDICATION AND COMMISSIONING OF THE PROPHET. The dedication and commissioning of a prophet has its own literary motif; the account of his being called. Such commissioning or re-commissioning accounts are found in Isaiah 6 (which does not describe the prophet's original call to prophecy, but rather his re-commissioning, so Kaufmann); Jeremiah 1:4ff. and 15:19–21 (the latter, too, being a re-dedication; see below); Ezekiel 1–3; and perhaps Deutero-Isaiah 40:6–8.

The lengthy prophetic dedication of Moses (Ex. 3–4) contains motifs that recur from time to time in the descriptions of the dedication of other prophets: (1) the humble occupation of the prophet (so, too, Amos, who was taken from his flocks to become a prophet, Amos 7:14); (2) the human response; (3) a protest of inadequacy for the mission; and (4) the divine reassurance. Moses made several attempts to dissuade God from selecting him, since he felt that he did not possess sufficient credentials for his mission. He pleaded inadequacy: "Who am I that I should go to Pharaoh and free the Israelites from Egypt" (Ex. 3:11) and "Please, O Lord, I have never been a man of words… I am slow of speech and slow of tongue" (Ex. 4:10).

Isaiah, in chapter 6, which describes his re-dedication to the prophetic office, after complaining of "unclean lips," first has his mouth sanctified, and then upon hearing God's question, "Whom shall I send?" volunteers his services, "I am ready, send me." (In an augural vision, the prophet would most likely not be asked to volunteer but would be compelled to go willy-nilly.) Jeremiah, who was prenatally designated and consecrated for his calling, recounts how God touched his mouth, too, and put His words into his mouth (Jer. 1:9). Ezekiel describes his consecration as the devouring of a scroll written by God (Ezek. 3:1ff.). The organ of speech is specifically mentioned in all of these prophetic accounts, because the prophet becomes, upon dedication, God's "mouthpiece." Not only the lips, however, but the prophet's whole being becomes dedicated to the service of God.

His Reluctance and God's Reassurance. The prophets, however, were often reluctant to accept their calling. The most dramatic example by far is the unsuccessful flight of Jonah. The unwillingness of Moses, Isaiah, and Jeremiah to accept the divine call is also concentrated on their organ of speech: "I have never been a man of words" (Ex. 4:10); "Woe is me, for I am lost; for I am a man of unclean lips" (Isa. 6:5); "Alas, Lord God, I do not know how to speak, for I am inexperienced" (Jer. 1:6). God, in turn, responds with encouraging assurances, for Moses (Ex. 4:11), for Isaiah (Isa. 6:7), and, in particular, for Jeremiah, "Gird up your loins… Do not be dismayed… They will fight against you; but they shall not prevail against you, for I am with you, says the Lord, to deliver you" (Jer. 1:17–19; cf. 15:19–21).

LIFE OF THE PROPHET. Why such initial opposition? Why, too, such an outpouring of divine encouragement? The prophet's distinction of being chosen by God was matched only by his frustration and rejection on the part of his fellowman. The prophetic office was not easy to bear. The description of the prophet's emotional experience upon receiving a "stern vision" is at times graphic and overwhelmingly frightening: his loins are filled with anguish; his pain is comparable to birth pangs; he is tortured, anguished, terror-stricken; he reels, and he is filled with the wrath of God (Isa. 21:3–4; Jer. 4:19; 6:11; 15:17; Hab. 3:16).

Of far greater significance, however, is the fact that such a selected messenger sometimes becomes a solitary individual, whose life is marked by loneliness and bitterness: "I sat not in the company of merrymakers, nor did I rejoice; I sat alone because Your Hand was upon me" (Jer. 15:17); "Oh that I had a lodge in the wilderness that I might leave my people and go away from them, for they are all adulterers, a troop of treacherous men" (Jer. 9:1). Jeremiah, whose personal tribulations and confessions are better known than those of any other prophet, became the paradigm of one who suffers for his mission. It is no wonder that he was not euphoric about being selected for such a task. Rejected and spurned, he bemoans his fate, "Woe unto me, my mother, that you bore me, a man of strife and contention to the whole land. I have neither a lender nor borrower been, yet everyone belittles me" (15:10). Even his own kinsmen and family are counted among his chief antagonists (12:6; cf. 20:10). Enemies were continually plotting against his life (11:19). Eventually, he even cursed his fate, "Cursed be the day on which I was born. Let the day my mother bore me not be blessed… Why did I come forth from the womb to experience trouble and grief and to waste my days in chagrin" (20:14–18).

Some prophets were fated to become harbingers of their nation's downfall. Messengers of doom, they were doomed to suffer from their very message: "Lord, how long!" (Isa. 6:11); "Let me weep bitterly. Seek not to comfort me for the destruction of the daughter of my people" (Isa. 22:4); "For this I will lament and wail. I will go stripped and naked… For incurable are her blows, for it has come to Judah, has reached the gate of my people, to Jerusalem" (Micah 1:8–9); "O that my head were water and my eyes a fountain of tears, that I might weep day and night for the slain of the daughter of my people" (Jer. 8:23). The prophet bemoans their imminent tragedy and weeps over their tragic rejection of his words: "But if you will not listen, I will weep in secret for your pride; my eyes will weep bitterly and run down with tears because the Lord's flock has been taken captive" (Jer. 13:17; cf. 10:19ff.; 14:17–18).

The life story of a prophet is liable to be one of anguish, fear, rejection, ridicule, and even imprisonment (Isa. 28:9–10; Jer. 11:18–23; 12:1ff.; 15:10, 15; 17:14–18; 18:18–23; 20:7–18; 37:12–21; Ezek. 21: 11–12; Hos. 9:8; Amos 7:12–13; Micah 2:6). Some did not escape their assassins (Jer. 26:20–23; Uriah). Though the prophet weeps with his destined victims and takes up the cry of his compatriots, he is not understood by them. Great yet unbearable is the fate of one who claims that he was seduced, even forced into his role: "O Lord you have seduced me, and I was seduced; you have raped me, and have prevailed" (Jer. 20:7). Nevertheless he cannot cease from being a prophet: "If I say, 'I will not mention Him or speak any more His name,' there is in my heart as it were a burning fire shut up in my bones, and I am not able to hold it in" (Jer. 20:9). Yet paradoxically when he does prophesy, he may be silenced by God (Jer. 7:16; 11:14; 14:11) or mocked and spurned by man. Jeremiah is eventually led to curse his people and demand vengeance against his adversaries (11:20b; 12:3b; 15:15a; 18:21–23).

Reproaching God. He is even driven in extremis to reproach God: "Why are you like a man dumbfounded, like a mighty man who cannot save?" (Jer. 14:9); "You are to me like a deceitful stream, like waters that fail!" (15:18). With this last outburst the prophetic protest reached its ultimate, as is indicated by the response of God, "If you return, I will restore you, and you shall stand before me" (15:19). Paradoxically, he who dedicated his life to persuading the people to return must now "return" himself. And why? So that he can once again perform the role of God's emissary, "You shall be my spokesman" (15:19). Thus, it seems that for a short period of time Jeremiah had actually lost prophetic office. This "demotion" is further substantiated by the remainder of God's response, where He repeats in almost exactly the same words the original encouragement at the time of the prophet's initial call, "I will make you before this people an impregnable wall of bronze; They will attack you, but they will not prevail over you, for I am with you to save you and deliver you, says the Lord" (15:20). Jeremiah, after his defiant outcry of reproach, was re-commissioned to deliver the word of God.

False Prophets. The problem of how to distinguish a prophet who was truly commissioned by God from a "false" prophet is perplexing. A prophet may speak falsely but there is no term for a false prophet in the Bible. The distinction, which is found in rabbinic literature, was introduced by the Greek translation of the Bible into some verses in the books of Jeremiah (6:13:26 (= Greek 33); 7, 8, 11, 16; 27 (= Greek 34):9; 28 (= Greek 35):1) and Zechariah (13:2), as *pseudoprophētēs*. In the Hebrew Bible, however, both "false" and "true" prophets are called *navi'*, and both claim inspiration and a mission.

In Deuteronomy there are several, not too useful, attempts to provide infallible criteria for distinguishing between them. Deuteronomy 18:20–22 reads "Any prophet who presumes to speak in My name a prophetic word that I did not command him to utter, or who speaks in the name of other gods – that prophet shall die. And should you ask yourselves, 'How can we know that the prophetic word was not spoken by the Lord?' – if the prophet speaks in the name of the Lord and the word does not come true, that word was not spoken by the Lord; the prophet has uttered it presumptuously: do not stand in dread of him." Deuteronomy 13:2 ff. goes one step further: even if the prophet utters prophecies after providing signs and wonders, should his message be to worship other gods, that prophet, too, is not to be heeded, since his appearance is only a test to determine whether the people really love and revere the Lord alone.

However, examples of an Israelite prophet delivering his message in the name of another god (Jer. 2:8; 23:13) are rare and not one demands that an alien god be worshiped. Most of them spoke, apparently with sincerity and conviction, in the name of God. As for the chronological criterion of the fulfillment of the oracle, this was of no value whatever at the moment the prophecy was uttered. How could the people suspend judgment if Hananiah told them not to submit to the king of Babylon and foretold the release from Babylonian captivity within two years, while Jeremiah declared that it was God's plan that Israel surrender and remain in exile for 70 years (Jer. 27–28)? Jeremiah, himself, was completely perplexed and left the scene of confrontation without further contradicting Hananiah (28:11). Furthermore, several occasions are specifically recorded in which an oracle delivered by an acknowledged true prophet did not materialize in the manner in which he predicted – even within his own lifetime! Only a few examples of unfulfilled prophecies need be cited: Jeremiah predicted an ignominious end for King Jehoiakim (Jer. 22:19); yet II Kings 24:6 clearly belies this oracle. Ezekiel predicted the destruction of Tyre by Nebuchadnezzar (26:7–14), but later he acknowledged that the king's siege of the city was unsuccessful (29:17–20). Both Haggai's (2:21–23) and Zechariah's (4:6–7) glorious anticipations and designs for Zerubbabel never materialized.

Jeremiah sought another objective criterion for distinguishing between a true and false prophet when he was dramatically confronted and confuted by Hananiah son of Azzur (Jer. 28). Hananiah declared in the name of YHWH that the Lord was going to break the yoke of Babylon, and that within two years the exiled community in Babylon and their king Jehoiachin would return to Israel. Jeremiah sincerely wished that Hananiah's words were true. He did not question his sincerity nor did he call him a false prophet, but he merely pointed out that "the prophets who were of old, before my time and yours, prophesied against many countries and great kingdoms of war, disaster, and plague." Only the future would vindicate the prediction of a prophet who foresaw peace; "As for the prophet who prophesies of well-being, when that prophet's word comes to pass, then it can be acknowledged that he is the prophet whom YHWH really sent." But then again how could one suspend judgment until history decided?

Jeremiah, more than any other prophet, was in constant combat with these prophets. He attacks three different types of "false" prophets (Jer. 23): (1) those who have dreams and report them as though they were the word of God and thus mislead the people, "The prophet who has a dream, let him tell his dream"; (2) those who are plagiarists "who keep stealing My words from one another" and pretend that they have had direct revelation; and (3) those "who using their own speech" concoct their own oracles and pass them off as prophecy. Nevertheless, when prophet clashed with prophet not only were the people confounded, but Jeremiah himself, in the case of Hananiah, was left speechless, and was unable to point to any irrefutable objective standard by which to verify or disqualify his opponent (Jer. 28).

To confound matters even more, a true prophet might be misled by a "false" prophet (I Kings 13), and false prophecy might even be inspired by God in order to deceive and entice Israel (I Kings 22:21 ff.). According to Ezekiel 14:9–11, moreover, God might actually seduce a bonafide prophet to deliver a false message!

If the individual prophet had a questionable moral character – if he was a drunkard (Isa. 28:7), an adulterer, or a liar (Jer. 23:14); if he used his office to make a living by telling the people what they wanted to hear and not what they ought to hear (Micah 3:11); or if he was a "professional" prophet attached to the staff of temple personnel (the joint denunciation of priest and prophet may be noted in Isa. 28:7; Jer. 23:11, 34; Micah 3:11; Zech. 7:2–3), his veracity obviously would be highly dubious. But what of the others? If there was no difference in the technical form of the prophecy, what of the contents? Apparently the only, and by no means infallible, criterion would be the nature of the message, whether it was one of weal or woe. Proclamations of national-religious salvation were suspect for over 250 years (cf. I Kings 22:11ff.; Jer. 6:14; 8:11; 14:13; 23:17; 28:2ff.; Ezek. 13:16; Micah 3:5ff.). It is also possible that such prophecies were related to the national interests of the crown and the cult – Hananiah predicted the early return of the cult vessels (Jer. 28:3).

But this, too, was not an absolute definition, for both pre-Exilic, e.g., Nahum 2:1, Jeremiah 30–33 (if these chapters stem from the early part of his career), and Exilic, e.g., Deutero-Isaiah, as well as post-Exilic prophets, Haggai, Zechariah, and Malachi, brought messages of comfort, and some also took a positive view of the cult (see below). Hence, the falsity or veracity of prophecies could not be determined on the external basis of form or content. They could only be judged by the person who had true insight into the intentions of God at that historical moment. A prophet "who has My word, let him faithfully speak My word. What has straw to do with wheat?... Is not My word like fire... like the hammer that shatters the rock" (Jer. 23:28–29).

The Prophet as Intercessor. The irresistible character that such a religious experience has on a "God-intoxicated" individual (Jer. 23:9), "who has stood in YHWH's council and seen and heard His word..." (Jer. 23:18), not only constrains him to deliver the divine message but compels him, at times, to intercede on behalf of his people. Herein lies one possible means of distinguishing between the two kinds of prophets: the function of the prophet as an intercessor. In this role, as distinct from his role as a messenger, the prophet attempts through prayer to offset the impending doom. The first individual in the Bible to be designated a prophet, Abraham, does not merit this title because he delivered oracles in the name of God, but because he was ready to intercede: "Since he is a prophet, he will intercede for you to save your life" (Gen. 20:7). Abraham also valiantly attempted to save the twin cities of Sodom and Gomorrah, and with unbridled daring challenged God: "Shall not the judge of all the earth deal justly" (18:25).

The paragon of prophets, Moses, paradigmatically and eloquently exemplifies this aspect of his prophetic mission several times:

(1) After the incident of the golden calf, "Let not Your anger, O Lord, blaze forth against Your people, whom You delivered from the land of Egypt with great power and with a mighty hand... Turn from Your blazing anger, and renounce the plan to punish Your people. Remember Your servants, Abraham, Isaac, and Jacob, how You swore to them by Your Self and said to them: 'I will make your offspring as numerous as the stars of heaven, and I will give to your offspring this whole land of which I spoke, to possess for ever'" (Ex. 32:11–13). Moses' plea was successful. "And the Lord renounced the punishment He had planned to bring upon His people" (Ex. 32:14).

(2) At Taberah, "The people cried out to Moses. Moses prayed to the Lord and the fire died down" (Num. 11:2).

(3) After the incident of the spies, Moses prayed, "Therefore, I pray, let my Lord's forbearance be great... Pardon, I pray, the iniquity of this people according to Your great kindness, as You have forgiven this people ever since Egypt" (Num. 14:13ff.). Once again he met with success, "And the Lord said, 'I pardon, as you have asked'" (Num. 14:20). (For Moses' personal intervention on behalf of Miriam and Aaron, see Num. 12:13 and Deut. 9:20, respectively.)

Next in line in the Bible's narrative tradition of prophetic intercession stands Samuel, who prayed on behalf of his people after their defeat at the hands of the Philistines (I Sam. 7:5–9), on their behalf after their request for a king, which so embittered God (I Sam. 12: 19, 23), and on behalf of Saul after God rejected his election as king of Israel (I Sam. 15:11).

In the Book of Jeremiah, both Moses and Samuel are singled out as the exemplars of great intercessors on behalf of their people (Jer. 15:1; cf. Ps. 99:6). Jeremiah proved a worthy, though unsuccessful, successor to these two. That he prayed to God on behalf of his nation is explicitly stated several times, e.g., in a time of drought, when he was driven by the enormity of his task to defy God, "Why are You like a man confused, like a mighty man who cannot save" (Jer. 14:1ff.; cf. his words in 4:10; 15:11; and his confession in 18:20, "Remember how I stood in Your presence speaking good on their behalf so as to avert Your anger from them"). Even more impressive are God's express commands to Jeremiah not to intercede! "Do not pray for this people, or lift up cry or prayer for them, and do not intercede with Me, for I do not hear you" (Jer. 7:16; cf. 11:14). When God attempts to silence Jeremiah in 14:11–12, the prophet, nevertheless, blurts out a plea on their behalf (verse 13). The die, however, was cast; the nation was doomed. Even Moses and Samuel (Jer. 15:1) would be helpless in such a situation. Intercession would no longer avail, or more properly stated, God would not permit any further intercession, because it just might have been successful in diverting Him from His self-prescribed course.

The passages cited above and the pleas of Amos (Amos 7:1–3, 4–6) make it patently clear that a prime function of the prophet was to defend his people and to act as mediator on behalf of his nation. Kings Hezekiah and Zedekiah also requested Isaiah (Isa. 37:2ff. = II Kings 19) and Jeremiah (Jer.

37:3; cf. 42:2, 20) respectively, to intercede on behalf of Israel in the face of an enemy onslaught.

Intercession, thus, is an integral component of the true prophet's mission. To be a prophet means to speak for the people to God, represent their case, and take up their cause. Should one shirk from such a duty by refusing to engage God in polemics and confine himself to merely speaking to the people for God, he would be belying his prophetic call. He would then be a "false" prophet. This interpretation finds confirmation in Ezekiel, who himself carries on the tradition of intercession (cf. 9:8; 11:13). In Ezekiel 13:4–5, God declares, "Your prophets have been like foxes among ruins, O Israel. You have not gone up into the breaches to prepare the broken wall around the Israelites, that it may stand firm in battle on the day of the Lord." The prophet's mission was to stand in the breach of the nation's wall, a breach caused by the sin of his people. He was to prevent God from entering; for entrance spelled doom and destruction. This is explicitly stated in Ezekiel 22:30–31, "I looked for a man among them who could build up a barricade, who could stand in the breach before Me to defend the land from ruin; but I found none. Thus I poured out my indignation upon them and utterly destroyed them in the fire of My wrath…" It is of interest to note that the very same imagery is employed in Psalms 106:23 (Y. Muffs).

In sum, though some of the "false" prophets did have revelations and visions, performed symbolic actions (Jer. 28:10ff.), imparted oracles (23:31), and prophesied in YHWH's name (14:14; 29:9), since they promised good fortune and prosperity and thereby lulled the people into false security (6:14; 8:11; 14:13; 23:17; 28:2ff.), they were accused by Jeremiah of not having been sent by God (14: 14–15; 23:21, 32; 28:15; 29:9), of not having been admitted to the divine council (23:18), and of not interceding with God on behalf of the people (27:18). However, after all, the final verdict could only be given by a true prophet, and even he was not always completely certain.

HISTORY

Universalism and Election

To the prophets, events of history disclosed the finger of God. God revealed Himself in the language of history. It is true that other nations in the Ancient Near East also regarded their gods as being active in history on significant occasions, but none of them conceived of a panoramic world outlook in which all of history was seen to be governed by the will of one God, nor did they interpret the history of their nation as a unified sequence governed by one, all-encompassing divine plan. Though the God of Israel addressed Himself to all humanity (see, e.g., Isa. 13:23; Jer. 27:2ff.; 28:8; 46–51; Ezek. 25–32; Amos 1:3–2:3; 9:7; Obad.; Nah. 3), the concept of election was unique to Israel: "Only you have I chosen from amongst the nations; therefore I shall punish you for all your sins" (Amos 3:2). Election was not a bona fide guarantee of special protection. Some prophets actually fought against this popular conception of inviolability (e.g., Isa. 28:15; Jer. 5:12; Amos 5:14). The consequence of being chosen was not immunity but heightened responsibility.

Whereas the nations of the world were held culpable solely for gross violations of the established order, Israel alone was taken to task for any and every infringement of the moral and ethical code of behavior. Indeed, one of the distinctive characteristics of the writings of the classical prophets is their insistent and adamant denunciation of corruption in the moral, ethical, and social fields. No one was impervious to their attack: not kings, priests, prophets, judges, women, creditors, wealthy landowners, or even the poorer classes. They leveled severe criticisms against murder, juridical corruption, violence, cruelty, dishonesty, greed, oppression, exploitation, bribery, harlotry, degeneracy, debauchery, arrogance, luxury, callousness, apathy, lust for power, and militarism. Each and every one of these vices exemplifies a "forgetting of God," which leads to the disintegration and the eventual condemnation of the nation (e.g., Isa. 3:14–15, 16–24; 5:8, 11–12, 18–19, 20–23; 9:8–9, 16; 31:1; Jer. 5:26; 7:9; Ezek. 22; Hos. 1:7;4:2,6, 11–13; 6:8–10; 7:1–7; 8:14; 10:13; 12:8–9; 13:6; Amos 2:6–8; 3:10–11; 4:1; 5:7; 6:1–7, 13; Micah 3:1–3, 11; Zeph. 1:12). Idolatry, too, was subjected to its usual severe criticism (e.g., Isa. 65:3–4; Jer. 7:18, 30–31; 19:4–5; Ezek. 8; Hos. 2:15; Amos 8:14; Zeph. 1:4–6).

Supremacy of Morality

Special attention should be given to the prophets' new concept of the cult and their novel idea of the supremacy of morality. The problem of the relationship of the prophets to cultic worship has gone through several stages of interpretation. One of the basic axioms of biblical scholarship was the notion that the priest and prophet were fundamentally opposed to one another. The major contribution of the prophets was considered to be the de-ritualization of religion. The basic message of the prophets was "ethical monotheism," with the stress on morality rather than ritual. Thus, it was thought that the independent spirit of the prophet conflicted head-on with the priest, the professional officiant of organized religion. The former was interested in right; the latter in rites. The prophet was "word-possessed" – he brought the word of God to man. The priest was "cult-possessed" – he raised man's sacrifice to God.

The development of form-critical studies brought a partial scholarly reversal, and the attempt was made to demonstrate the positive attitude of the prophets toward the cult. Their utterance of divinely inspired oracles was supposed to be an integral component of Israelite worship. The time, and later even the content, of these oracles were understood to be liturgically fixed. The prophets were identified as members of the cultic personnel.

Both views, especially the latter, are extreme and are constantly being debated. What can be said with certainty is that the prophetic attacks on the cult did introduce a new principle into the religion of Israel: The essence of God's demand is not to be found in the cult but in the moral and ethical spheres of life. In the Torah and pre-classical prophetic literature there is no sharp distinction between cultic and moral prescriptions. Both are equally important, and both are essential to the continued existence of the nation. With the words of the classical prophets, however, a new aspect was introduced. While Samuel argued for the primacy of obedience over sacrifice (I Sam. 15:22), Amos and his fellow prophets stressed the primacy of morality (Isa. 1:11–17; 66:1ff.; Jer. 6:20; 7:21–23; 14:12; Hos. 6:6; Amos 5:21–25; Micah 6:6–8). The prophets were no more unequivocally opposed to the cult than they were to song and psalm (Amos 5:23) or prayer, festival, and Sabbath (Isa. 1:13–15), all of which they mentioned in their attacks. On the contrary, Isaiah's call came apparently while he was in the Temple (Isa. 6). The Exilic (Isa. 44:28; 52:11; 66:20–24; Jer. 33:11, 18; Ezek. 20:40–44; 22:8, 26; 40–48), as well as the post-Exilic prophets Haggai and Zechariah, had a very positive attitude toward the Temple and its cult. They advocated the rebuilding of the sanctuary, with the restoration of sacrificial worship, and stressed ceremonial law. The prophets did not denounce the practice of sacrifice per se, but they did adamantly oppose the absolutization of the cult.

Attitude Toward Ritual

In Israel, ritual is conceived of as God's gift, an act of grace intended for the good of humanity. It affords man means by which to draw closer to God. Worship and ritual are means, justice and righteousness are ends. "God requires devotion, not devotions" (S. Spiegel, *Amos versus Amaziah* (1957), 43), right not rite. When cult becomes a substitute for moral behavior, it is to be condemned. Religion is not to be equated with formal worship, nor is it to be restricted to certain specified times during the calendar year; it is to encompass all of life. Hence, any cultic act performed by a worshiper whose moral or ethical character is not beyond reproach is considered an abomination to God. It is no wonder that, after disparaging independent importance of the cult, the prophets clashed with the acknowledged heads of established religion, the priests. Clashes such as of Amos with Amaziah (Amos 7:10ff.), Jeremiah with Pashhur (Jer. 20), or with Zephaniah son of Maaseiah (Jer. 29:25ff.), are unheard of in stories set in pre-classical times. In the dramatic, near tragic confrontation of Jeremiah with his antagonists (Jer. 26) the priests are among the forefront in demanding the death sentence for the prophet, who was accused of "blasphemy" for repudiating the inviolability of the Temple (Jer. 7).

Moreover, it should be recalled that in other religions of the Ancient Near East the correct observance of the cult was of paramount importance, since it was thought that the welfare of the gods was dependent on both the maintenance of their temples and the daily upkeep of their sacrifices. The prophets, however, devaluated the intrinsic significance of ritual, and stressed God's ultimate concern with correct behavior. Justice, righteousness, kindness, integrity, and faithfulness were among God's chief demands (e.g., Jer. 9:22–23; 22:15–16; Hos. 6:6; Amos 5:15, 24; Micah 6:8).

Morality and Destiny

The prophets took yet another step. Not only was morality of ultimate importance but it became the decisive factor in determining the national destiny of Israel. The classical prophets differ in emphasis from the view expressed in the Torah literature and in the Former Prophets, according to which the sin of idolatry was the primary transgression. Not only were the worship of other gods than Yahweh and the cardinal sins of murder and incest denounced as before, but the everyday immoral acts of society were condemned as well. With the emergence of the classical prophets a new criterion became operative – moral rectitude. The destiny of the nation was bound up with it, and unrighteousness would spell the end of Israel.

Repentance

The prophets consistently pleaded with Israel to seek God that they might live (Amos 5:4, 14). They demanded piety and faithfulness to the covenant between God and Israel, and threatened punishment and fulfillment of the covenant's curses for those who were disloyal to it. Yet all of their denunciations and frightful maledictions were not meant as ends in themselves. They were, rather, a vain attempt to arouse the people from their lethargic status quo; they were didactic means to achieve the desired end – repentance. The objective of the prophetic threat of dire punishment was that it should not take place. Paradoxically, the prophets wished to make their own calling self-defeating by persuading man to return to God. They censured, warned, and admonished their audiences to forsake their immoral ways in order to avoid imminent destruction.

The prophets were not always ready to accept the finality of divine judgment (for Amos and Jeremiah, see above). They prayed that repentance would have the desired effect: "Who knows, God may yet have a change of heart and turn from His fierce anger so that we shall not perish" (Jonah 3:9, the words of the king of Nineveh expressing the prophetic sentiment; cf. the "perhaps" of the sailors in 1:6). There are other examples: "Who knows whether He will not turn and change His decision and leave a blessing behind Him" (Joel 2:14). "It may be that the Lord, the God of hosts, will be gracious to the remnant of Joseph" (Amos 5:15). "Perhaps you may find shelter on the day of the Lord's anger" (Zeph. 2:3). The future is contingent on human response to the prophetic word. Divine plans are not unchangeable; human actions tip the scales of justice and mercy: "If at any time I declare concerning a nation or a kingdom, that I will pluck up and pull it down and destroy it, and if that nation, concerning which I have spoken, turns from its evil, I will repent of the evil that I intended to do it. And if at any time I declare concerning a nation or a kingdom that I will build and plant it, and if it does evil in My sight, not listening to My voice, then I will repent of the good which I intended to do to it" (Jer. 18:7–10; cf. Ezek. 3:17–21; 33:7–20). Even the possibility of a "divine turning" not predicated upon the prior repentance of the people was contemplated, "How can I give you up, Ephraim! [How can I] hand you over, Israel! How can I treat you like Admah or make you like Zeboim! My heart is changed within Me; My compassion grows warm and tender, I will not execute My fierce anger, I will not again destroy Ephraim…" (Hos. 11:8–9). Compassion may overcome wrath (cf. Jer. 33:8; Micah 7:18–19).

SUSPENSION OF FREEDOM AND GOD'S INACCESSIBILITY. Yet the prophets were not often so optimistic. They knew very well the futility of chastisement (e.g., Amos 4:6–11; Isa. 1:5ff.; 9:12; Jer. 2:30; 5:3). This incurable stubborness and hardheartedness of the people (Jer. 5:21; Isa. 42:18–20; 43:8; 46:12; 6:10, 17; 9:25; Ezek. 2:4; 12:2) led one prophet to take the most radical step of all: the suspension of freedom. Isaiah was commissioned to "make the heart of this people fat, their ears heavy, and their eyes dim, lest they see with their eyes, and hear with their ears, and understand with their hearts, and turn and be healed" (Isa. 6:10). The prophet became God's messenger to harden their hearts and thereby to prevent the people from repenting! Since Israel had so often spurned the words of God and since they had not returned to Him, the privilege of repentance was to be denied them (until only one-tenth of the population remained). The only "cure" for obdurate hardness was to intensify it.

At other times God would make Himself inaccessible to the people as a punishment (e.g., Hos. 5:6; Amos 8:11–12), or to the prophet himself. Jeremiah had no immediate answer for Hananiah (Jer. 28:11) and had to wait once for ten days for the word of God (Jer. 42:7).

New Covenant

The frustration of waiting for human response and the realization that human effort alone could not effect a total return to God led to the development of an entirely new idea. If humans would not initiate the process, God would. He would not only initiate it but finalize it as well. This is the thought implicit in the concept of a "new covenant." Since the old covenant was broken, God despairing of further futile warnings and punishments, would implant His will directly into the human heart, thereby changing human nature by a divine "grafting." The human heart of stone would be turned into a heart of flesh. People would have their whole being filled with the "knowledge of God," and thus he could not but obey God; they would no longer be capable of rejecting God's teachings. This new covenant would be unbreakable and would presage final redemption (Isa. 55:3; Jer. 24:7; 31:30–33; 32:38–41; Ezek. 16:60; 34:25ff.; 36:26ff.; 37:26ff.; cf. Deut. 30:6; Isa. 11:9; 54:13).

Future of Israel

With the covenant renewed, the future community of Israel, constituted by the *remnant (e.g., Isa. 4:3–4; 8:16–17; 10:20–21; Jer. 31:31ff.; Amos 9:8ff.; Micah 7:8; Zeph. 2:3, 9), which will have survived the "*Day of the Lord" (see also *Eschatology), would live in peace, no longer troubled by oppression, injustice, or war (e.g., Isa. 2:1–5; 10:27; 11:1–9; 60:5–16; 61:4–9; Hos. 2:21ff.; Micah 4:3–4). It would be an age in which God's glory would be manifested to all mankind (Isa. 40:5), and so all the nations would come to reject idolatry and recognize and revere the God of Israel alone (Isa. 19:18–25; 45:22ff.; Jer. 3:17; 12:16; Ezek. 17:24; Micah 7:16ff.; Hab. 2:14; Zeph. 2:11; Zech. 2:15; 8:20–23; 14:16–21). Jerusalem would become the spiritual center of the world (Isa. 2:2), from which would flow God's instruction to all mankind (Isa. 2:3; 51:4ff.). Israel, would, according to Deutero-Isaiah, become a prophet nation (49:2–3; 51:16; 59:21), spreading the teaching of God to all humanity (42:1–4) and recounting His glory (43:21). It would become "a light to the nations" (42:6; 49:6) and bring God's blessing and beneficence to the ends of the earth (45:22–24).

[Shalom M. Paul / S. David Sperling (2nd ed.)]

In the Talmud

Despite the many aggadic elements in the references to prophecy or the prophets in rabbinical literature, there emerges a clear picture of the rabbinic view of the prophets. Substantially it is based upon two main principles. The first is that Moses was the "master of the prophets" and no prophet after him succeeded as did Moses in penetrating into the nature of the Divine, communing with Him, and receiving His message while in full possession of his normal cognitive faculties. This is of course clearly expressed in the Bible (Num. 12:6–8) but it is extended to apply to all future prophecy. This concept is expressed in various ways, the most striking being that whereas Moses beheld the Divine as through a clear mirror, the other prophets did so through a distorted mirror ("a mirror which does not shine," Yev. 49b; cf. "through a glass darkly," I Cor. 13:12).

However, there is noticeable a definite tendency to give Isaiah precedence over all other prophets. Although it is stated that of the four near-contemporary prophets, Isaiah, Amos, Micah, and Hosea, the last was first both in time and in importance (Pes. 87a), it is stated that of all the prophets only Moses and Isaiah "knew what they were prophesying" (Mid. Ps. 90:1, no. 4). Both are referred to together as "the greatest of the prophets" (Deut. R. 2:4). Isaiah is responsible for more prophecies than any other prophet and he prophesied not only to Israel but to mankind as a whole (PR 34:158a); he received revelation direct from God and his prophecies were "doubled" (Pd–RK 125b). If Ezekiel was vouchsafed a revelation of the Divine Essence equal to that of Isaiah, he saw Him as "a villager sees the person of the king," while Isaiah saw Him as an "inhabitant of a metropolis [*kerakh*] who sees the person of the king" (Ḥag. 13b).

The second principle is a corollary of the first. It is to the effect that the prophets were not responsible for any religious innovations or novel doctrines, their function being confined to expounding and clarifying the teachings of the Pentateuch. The Talmud interprets the verse (Lev. 27:34) "these are the commandments which the Lord commanded Moses for the children of Israel in Mount Sinai," to mean that "henceforth a prophet may make no innovations" (Shab. 104a). "The prophets neither took away from, nor added to, aught that is written in the Torah, save only the commandment to read the *megillah*" and even for that they sought biblical sanction (Meg. 14a). In conformity with this view, in the chain of tradition with which tractate *Avot* opens, the prophets appear merely as the tradents of the Torah of Moses, the successors to the elders after Joshua, and the predecessors of the men of the Great Synagogue. It is highly probable that this view was influenced by the contrary Christian view of progressive revelation through the ages, culminating in Jesus, though one need not go so far as does Weiss (Dor, 2 (1904[4]), 8) in seeing in it a polemic against the antinomianism of Paul. Consequently statements of the prophets which have no pentateuchal confirmation or support cannot normally be made the basis of the *halakhah*.

According to the rabbis the number of prophets was innumerable ("double the number of the children of Israel who went forth from Egypt") and every tribe produced them (Suk. 27b). However only the prophecies of those which contained a lesson (lit. "were required for") future generations were recorded. They amount to 48 prophets and seven prophetesses: to Miriam (cf. Ex. 15:20 and Num. 12:2), Deborah, and Huldah, the rabbis add Sarah, Hannah, Abigail, and Esther (Meg. 14a). There were also seven gentile prophets: Balaam, his father Beor (Sanh. 105a), Job and his three companions, and Elisha the son of Barachel (BB 15b), but of them Balaam was incomparably the greatest. He was even regarded as the equal of Moses (see *Balaam in Aggadah) and the gentile nations cannot therefore claim that they were not vouchsafed prophecy (Yalk 966; Num. R. 14:34). Nevertheless prophecy came to them only by night and in "half words" and from "behind the curtain" (Gen. R. 52:5). All the prophets prophesied only concerning the messianic age (i.e., the present world in its ideal state) but were not vouchsafed to see the celestial world to come (Ber. 34b). The statement "the same message [*signon*, lit. "sign"] is given to a number of prophets but no two prophets prophesy in the same *signon*" (Sanh. 89a) is probably to be taken to refer to the fact that although they all reveal the word of God, each one has his own particular message or doctrine. The daring use of anthropomorphisms by the prophets is regarded as a sign of their "greatness" (Num. R. 19:4). With the exception of Jeremiah, all the prophets conclude their prophecies on a note of hope and comfort (TJ, Ber. 5:1, 8d). Where the patronymic of the prophet is given, it is to show that his father was also a prophet; when his place of origin is not given he was a Jerusalemite (Meg. 15a).

The prophets are divided into the Early and Later Prophets, but the former encompass all those of the period of the First Temple, only the post-Exilic – Haggai, Zechariah, and Malachi – constituting the latter (Sot. 48b). All the prophets were wealthy. An interesting proof is given with regard to Amos. Since he was both a herdsman of Tekoa (Amos 1:1) and a dresser of sycamore trees (7:14), and sycamores grow only in the Shephelah but not in the hilly country of Tekoa, he must have been a wealthy landowner with flocks in Judea and plantations in the Shephelah (Ned. 38a). When prophecy came to an end, the **Shekhinah* departed from Israel and the **Bat Kol* became a partial substitute (Yoma 9b).

For the order of the prophets according to the Talmud (BB 14b) see *Bible Canon.

[Louis Isaac Rabinowitz]

IN JEWISH PHILOSOPHY

Philo

The teaching of *Philo concerning prophecy has to be reconstructed from discussions scattered throughout his writings. Philo conceives of the prophet as priest, seer, and lawgiver all in one. Prophetic understanding is the highest form, transcending reason, which is based on sense perception. When the divine prophetic spirit rests on a man, he is "possessed" by it in a kind of frenzy or "sober intoxication." All prophecy is by grace of God, but prophecy through the divine spirit, in contrast to communication through angels or the divine voice, demands preparation in the recipient, be he Jew or non-Jew: he must be refined, wise, and just, and emancipated from bodily concerns.

[Ralph Lerner]

Medieval Jewish Philosophy

Prophecy is a critical subject in medieval Jewish philosophy. This is hardly surprising. Where a religious community defines itself by a divinely revealed law and regards the teachings of the biblical prophets as the Word of God, the nature and significance of revelation, the manner of its transmission, and the qualities of the human recipient of the divine message are issues of primary importance. The early medieval Jewish philosophers developed their approaches to prophecy in the broader context of Greek philosophical thought as it was received and shaped in the Islamic world. A fundamental question they wrestled with as a result of this influence is how can the incorporeal, transcendent Deity appear to human beings and communicate with them. As we shall see, their approaches vary greatly in addressing this problem. While all the philosophers agreed that God has no body and hence cannot be seen, nor does He possess any organs of speech, some continued to view Him as directly involved in every bestowal of prophecy, while others developed naturalistic explanations for understanding the phenomenon.

SAADIAH GAON. The early 10th-century Babylonian *gaon* *Saadiah in his *Book of Beliefs and Opinions* (Books 2 and 3) deals with a number of issues related to prophecy, particularly the problem raised by the corporeal descriptions of God in biblical literature, and the problem of the purpose of prophecy and the manner of its verification. Since God, in Saadiah's view, is incorporeal and is not to be characterized by any of the categories that pertain to matter (e.g., time, place, quantity, affections), most of the prophets' corporeal descriptions of Him are not to be interpreted literally but allegorically. In regard to the instances when the prophet reports actually seeing God, Saadiah, however, presents a different explanation. These visions are to be interpreted literally – the prophet in fact sees with his eyes what he is describing – but they are not of God. Rather their object is a special created entity made from the purest luminous matter and called the Created Glory or the *Shekhinah*. God sends this special entity to the prophet in order to confirm that the message heard indeed comes from Him. The message itself consists of words created by God, Created Speech, and conveyed through the air to the hearing of the prophet. Prophecy hence is an experience that the recipient attains and verifies by means of the external senses, which, in Saadiah's view, are a source of reliable knowledge. Prophecy is verified by others by their beholding this special entity in one of its manifold forms, or by miracles that accompany the relaying of the divine message and which only God is capable of performing. This explanation serves to preserve the integrity of Scriptures by limiting the necessity for introducing allegorical interpretations which undermine its literal meaning. Allegorical interpretations are to be accepted only when there is a blatant contradiction between the literal meaning and the other sources of reliable knowledge.

The Created Glory receives a more extensive treatment in Saadiah's earlier *Commentary to the Book of Creation*, where he identifies it with the Holy Spirit (**Ru'aḥ ha-Kodesh*) which is the first of God's creations. In addition to being the instrument for transmitting prophecy, it also fills the entire world and plays a crucial role as an intermediary for divine governance. One can detect in this work overtones to the Philonic idea of the *Logos*. Saadiah in his *Book of Beliefs and Opinions* greatly reduces the stature of the Glory, stressing instead God's direct governance of the world.

As for the purpose of prophecy, Saadiah underlines its role in revealing to all of humanity the fundamental truths of reason, such as the existence of God and the creation of the world, so everyone will possess these beliefs with full confidence even prior to being able to prove them. He also sees a necessity for prophecy with respect to the commandments dictated by the intellect, in addition to those known only by way of revelation (see Reasons for *Commandments). While the former commandments are known by reason and obligatory upon all human beings, reason dictates only general moral principles. Revelation lays down specific commandments which translate these principles into a body of law.

JUDAH HALEVI. While Saadiah views prophecy primarily in terms of a mission, the early 12th-century philosopher Judah *Halevi in his *Kuzari* identifies this phenomenon as the ultimate perfection of the individual. Halevi at the beginning of his treatise indicates that the Islamic Aristotelian philosophers posit the following criteria for attaining human perfection: possessing the proper potential inherited from one's parents, living in a moderate geographical clime conducive to actualizing this potential by attaining the moral virtues and mastering all of the sciences. They define ultimate perfection in terms of conjunction with the Active Intellect resulting in the eternal felicity of the intellect, as well as attainment of knowledge of hidden matters by way of prophetic visions. As opposed to this view, while at the same time drawing heavily from it, Halevi maintains that prophecy is unique to the Jewish people due to a special inherited quality they possess and which is actualized by living in the Land of Israel and observing the divinely revealed commandments with the proper intent. God alone knows the actions that will perfect the soul and they are those given in the Torah. Halevi describes prophecy in terms of conjunction with the *Amr Ilahi* (Divine Matter), though he never offers a clear definition of this term (some scholars maintain that it refers to the *Logos* while others see it as an epithet for God in those instances where there exists an unmediated connection between the Deity and His creatures). The prophet attains the rank of the angels. By means of prophetic intuition, labeled by Halevi "the inner eye," the prophet sees the divine world and experiences an immediate relation with God leading to an overpowering love of the deity, described also in terms of the sense of "taste" (4:3, 15–17) – a state reminiscent of Islamic mystical descriptions of ecstatic rapture.

Halevi, however, does not present a single model for understanding the prophetic phenomenon. In passages where it is important for him to show that prophecy is an empirically verifiable phenomenon proving that God is cognizant of individuals and acts in history, Halevi adopts Saadiah's view of the Created Speech and Created Glory. In this manner he explains the Revelation at Sinai (1:87). In other cases of prophecy he wavers between this approach and the one that treats prophecy as an internal experience. Halevi goes so far as to leave open the possibility that the visions themselves are the product of the prophet's imagination acting under the control of the intellect, a view that follows the Aristotelian philosophers (4:3).

In treating prophecy more in terms of ultimate perfection than a divinely bestowed mission, Halevi himself may have sought to attain this state. Certainly his intention to move to Israel and revive the Jewish community there was part of his plan to bring about the conditions leading to the reappearance of prophecy. His aspiration for achieving this state also finds expression in his liturgical poetry.

MAIMONIDES. Prophecy is a central topic in all of *Maimonides' major writings. It is integrally related in his thought to a host of issues – the nature of God, divine knowledge, providence, divine law, politics, human perfection and biblical exegesis. Already in his early legal writings Maimonides presents a naturalistic approach to prophecy drawn from the Islamic Aristotelians. In his *Commentary to the Mishnah: Introduction to Perek Ḥelek* (Sixth Principle of Faith), Maimonides describes prophecy as follows: "There are human beings possessing a superior nature and great perfection. They prepare their souls till they receive the form of the intellect. The human intellect then conjoins with the Active Intellect. From it [the Active Intellect], a noble emanation emanates upon them. These are the prophets; this is prophecy and this is its essence." The "form of the intellect" is a reference to the "acquired intellect," which according to Alfarabi (see *Farabi, Abu Nasr Muhammad, Al-) is attained only after mastery of all the sciences and apprehension of the essence of the intellect itself. This intellect is an immortal entity, not dependent upon the body for its existence, and it conjoins with the Active Intellect. A similar description of prophecy is presented by Maimonides in his *Mishneh Torah: Laws of the Principles of the Torah* (7:1). In both of these legal works he goes on to deal with the imagination's role in prophecy, which accounts for the prophetic visions.

The naturalistic approach to prophecy characterizes also *The Guide of the Perplexed.* Maimonides dismisses the view of the masses that God bestows prophecy upon whom He chooses even if the individual is not perfect. He insists that only a perfect individual – one who possesses a perfect physical temperament and imagination, the moral virtues, and a perfect intellect – can attain prophecy. He introduces the proviso, however, that God can miraculously withhold prophecy from the worthy individual (2:32). In this manner he leaves room for the workings of divine will, though he ascribes to it a negative role. Maimonides defines prophecy as an emanation from God to the Active Intellect and from there to the individual's rational faculty and imaginative faculty (2:36). This emanation results in the apprehension of metaphysical truths, principles of governance and the ability to divine the future. Philosophers and non-prophetic rulers and diviners possess perfection in only one of these two faculties, while one alone attains the Active Intellect's emanation (2:37) – the rational faculty in the case of the philosophers enabling them to master the sciences and the imaginative faculty in the case of the others enabling them to govern and divine the future (though imperfectly). The prophet for Maimonides thus reaches the pinnacle of human perfection and achieves the rank of the perfect philosopher, statesman and diviner. His account suggests that the emanation to the prophets does not consist of specific information, the Active Intellect has no cognizance of the recipient or his circumstances; rather it strengthens the prophet's own faculties to apprehend those matters about which he is thinking and to represent them in a figurative manner. Even the prophetic mission is explained by Maimonides in a naturalistic manner. While for many, if not most, prophets this attainment is a private one, for some the emanation is so strong that the recipient feels inwardly compelled to extend his perfection to others by assuming a leadership role despite the dangers involved (2:37). Maimonides stresses that one attaining intellectual perfection and prophecy in truth prefers the solitary existence in which he can continuously enjoy the state of contemplation. The private longings of the individual who attains perfection to detach himself from society together with the overpowering feeling that he must assume a public role is reflected in Jeremiah's initial prophetic vision in which he tries to refuse the divine mission but is commanded to undertake it nevertheless. The vision itself reflects the conflict in Jeremiah's own soul. Maimonides attempts to reconcile the dilemma facing the public prophet by positing a state in which the prophet continues to live in his own private space, contemplating God and the order of the world, even while engaged in interacting with others and leading them.

In Maimonides' approach to prophecy one can detect his wavering between viewing prophecy primarily in terms of an intellectual attainment and viewing it primarily in terms of the perfection of the imagination. In his most lengthy treatment of this phenomenon in the *Guide of the Perplexed* (2:36–48) he stresses the latter dimension. His distinction between prophetic dreams, which occur while the recipient is asleep, and the higher level prophetic visions, which occur while awake, is based on the functioning of the imagination. A similar consideration marks his division of prophetic levels based on whether the prophet saw only parables in his dream, heard a voice without seeing anything, beheld a human being speaking, beheld an angel speaking, or beheld God speaking (2:45). His discussions of prophecy in the introduction to his treatise and towards its conclusion (3:51), on the other hand, describe prophecy as the ultimate intellectual attainment, surpassing the metaphysical knowledge possessed by the philosophers. The stress on the imaginative dimension of prophecy is not only important in explaining the biblical visions but also in order to draw a categorical distinction between Moses and all other prophets.

From his discussion of prophecy Maimonides excludes Mosaic prophecy and the Revelation at Sinai. He insists that as opposed to all other prophets, Moses' imaginative faculty was not involved in his prophetic experience, only his intellect. The uniqueness of Moses' prophecy has as its most important corollary the fact that his prophecy alone involves divine legislation. No other prophecy, past or future, results or will result in the laying down of a divine law (2:39). Maimonides appears to maintain that Moses received the Torah directly from God, word for word, and not from the Active Intellect. Furthermore, at Sinai an audible voice was heard by all of Israel, though only Moses heard the actual words (2:33). Maimonides clearly builds on Saadiah's view of Created Speech. Whether this stance reflects his true opinion on the subject or is designed solely for public consumption has been a source of controversy among Maimonidean scholars. His views on the nature of Mosaic prophecy and the Revelation at Sinai are clearly intended to uphold the supernatural origin of the Torah, its uniqueness and inviolability in a manner that would appeal to the masses of Jews. Despite this apparent fundamental departure from the naturalism of the Aristotelian philosophers, Maimonides continues to follow in their footsteps in his conception of the goal of the Torah. He maintains that it is designed to lead society to human perfection in the best possible manner by preventing wrongdoing, instilling the moral virtues and inculcating true beliefs, particularly the monotheistic idea and all this idea entails, which directs one to the path of intellectual perfection (2:49; 3:27). Even all the ceremonial commandments play a crucial role in this regard. All other legislations fall short in attaining this goal.

GERSONIDES. Maimonides' approach to prophecy, as well as *Averroes' account of divination in his *Epitome to Parva Naturalia* had a decisive impact on subsequent treatments of this topic among the Jewish philosophers in Provence and in Spain. The most analytical discussion of this phenomenon is to be found in the early 14th-century treatise by Gersonides (*Levi ben Gershom), *Wars of the Lord.* Gersonides deals with prophecy in Book Two of his treatise in the context of his discussion of veridical dreams. He was more interested than his predecessors in understanding the details of this phenomenon – what exactly is the nature of the emanation from the Active Intellect and how does it come about that the prophet receives it as a particular message relating to his own historical circumstances. While Gersonides views prophets as perfect philosophers, he treats prophecy itself as primarily concerned with knowledge of the future. The prophet has no advantage over the philosopher *qua* prophet when it comes to theoretical knowledge.

The fact that prophecy primarily involves future contingent events raises in its wake certain fundamental philosophic problems for Gersonides: Can the future be known while humans at the same time enjoy free will? Can God's knowledge which is unchanging nevertheless encompass all particulars throughout history? Since Gersonides does not feel that the future can be known absolutely without sacrificing the idea of human freedom, even God in his view does not know what occurs as a result of free choice. The implications of this point are profound. Since God's knowledge is unchanging, not only does He not know the future but also does not know the past. In short, God does not know any individual *qua* individual nor any of his particular circumstances. The same is true also of the knowledge of the Active Intellect. This position is certainly exceptionally radical (and problematic) from a theological perspective. It also does not explain the empirical fact that diviners and prophets often see the future, including events that are contingent upon human choice.

Gersonides resolves this dilemma by ascribing to God and to the Active Intellect knowledge of the entire order of the world, including all the specific influences of the stars and planets upon human events. God does not know individuals as such, but has knowledge of all the influences that the heavenly bodies exert upon any person born at any given time and place. One may say that according to Gersonides, God and the Active Intellect possess knowledge of all possible horoscopes without knowing which horoscope applies to any particular person. Since most people act in accordance with the influences of the heavenly bodies, and do not exercise their freedom to act in a manner contrary to them, their future can be predicted with a fair amount of confidence. Hence all predictions are not absolute but conditional; they are contingent upon the fact that those involved will act in accordance with the celestial influences.

This view still does not explain how the Active Intellect transmits specific knowledge to a particular individual regarding other particular individuals or groups, without at all being cognizant of the individual and his circumstances. According to Gersonides, all information pertaining to the world order emanates continuously from the Active Intellect. The rational and imaginative faculties of the prophet, while "withdrawn" from the other faculties of the soul in the state of sleep, attain the information that applies to an individual or group who the prophet has in mind. One may think of the Active Intellect as a giant transmitter which transmits on all frequencies at once all information regarding celestial influences on all places on earth through all time. The prophet receives only the information on the frequency to which his mind is attuned, that is to say, which people and groups he is thinking about. In this manner he learns their probable future without the Active Intellect being aware who receives this information, who and what is the subject of the information, and what actually occurs in the domain of human events.

Gersonides deals with Moses' perfection within the context of his discussion of prophecy, but he does not discuss in his philosophic treatise the most important facet of Moses' attainment – the divine law. He turns to this subject in his commentary on the Torah, where he sees the Torah as resulting from a miraculous and unique act of divine providence. Both the topics of providence and miracles are treated in the *Wars of the Lord*. They are seen as resulting from the impersonal activity of the Active Intellect vis-à-vis the person who has attained the level of perfection that triggers off this activity on his behalf.

ḤASDAI CRESCAS. The late 14th-century Spanish philosopher, Ḥasdai *Crescas sought to restore to Jewish philosophy the notion of God's personal involvement in the bestowal of prophecy as well as the primacy of the prophetic mission. In short, he sought to counter the naturalistic approaches to prophecy that characterize Maimonides' and Gersonides' approaches by treating prophecy primarily as a supernatural phenomenon. In his philosophic treatise, *Light of the Lord*, he defines prophecy as follows [Book 2, Section 4]: "Prophecy is a spiritual emanation of knowledge. It emanates from God to the intellect of the person, with or without an intermediary. It informs him, even without [his possessing] the necessary premises, of a certain matter or matters of which he is ignorant. It extends to all subjects. Its purpose is to guide him or others properly." For Crescas, prophecy categorically differs from divination which is received by the imagination. It does not entail the recipient possessing any previous knowledge of the subject of the message. Prophecy is a gift of God, who knows all particulars through all time including all contingent events, to the perfect individual with the purpose of correct guidance. In the case of Moses, the prophecy came directly from God, who is the Author of each word of the Torah. Crescas accepts Saadiah's notion that the voice heard by Moses and by Israel at Sinai was a created audible one. Even in those cases where prophecy came through the mediation of the Active Intellect and was received by the internal faculties of the individual, God determined the message to be received.

Crescas does not abandon the naturalistic approach to prophecy entirely. The attainment of prophecy in his view is contingent upon the attainment of perfection. Yet this perfection for Crescas, as for Halevi before him, does not lie primarily in one's level of theoretical knowledge but in the level achieved of love of God, which is dependent also upon observance of the commandments. As a result of the prophetic experience, the individual not only attains a specific message but achieves an even more passionate love of God and ultimate felicity. This experience in turn leads to the overpowering desire to call upon others to serve and love God. For Crescas, even more than for Maimonides, the prophetic mission is integral to the prophetic experience itself.

BARUCH SPINOZA. In the *Tractatus Theologico-Politicus* by the 17th-century philosopher Baruch *Spinoza we find a reaction to the medieval Jewish philosophic tradition regarding prophecy at the same time that he incorporates into his treatise many of its ideas. For Spinoza there can be no "supernatural" activity or supernaturally attained knowledge, for the eternal laws of nature are inviolable Spinoza depicts the prophets as simple-minded individuals, sharing with their contemporaries the same false beliefs about the world, but possessing a superior imagination that translates these beliefs into images. Hence their prophecies as presented in the Bible contain no theoretical truths, and Scripture should not be read as presenting such truths in figurative form. Moses, too, possessed a completely false conception of reality. The law that he laid down led to a well-ordered society of former slaves but certainly not to true virtue and felicity. In this manner Spinoza seeks to undermine completely the authority of the Bible (at least the Old Testament) as a source of knowledge beyond philosophy, and with it the authority of its religious interpreters. Only philosophers left unrestrained in their activity can attain true knowledge of the world. Only they are capable of achieving true virtue and the intellectual love of God. In a crucial sense they are for Spinoza the true prophets.

[Howard Kreisel (2nd ed.)]

Modern Jewish Thought

Depending on their attitude toward *revelation, modern Jewish philosophers treat prophecy either as a subjective experience or as a supernatural phenomenon. Those philosophers who regard prophecy as a subjective experience account for the phenomenon in a variety of ways. Some dismiss it as a form of psychological delusion; others view it as a mystical experience or an "inspired" insight, deriving from excellence of moral, intellectual, or imaginative faculties. Those who treat prophecy as a supernatural phenomenon differ over the nature of the prophetic experience. Of those philosophers who accept the notion that revelation constitutes a supernatural communication of content, some regard prophecy as the authentic disclosure of a message received word by word from God, a view referred to as "the doctrine of verbal inspiration," and others regard it as the record of a human response to a divine revelation of content. According to the latter view, human and divine elements are intermingled in prophecy. Other philosophers, while accepting supernatural revelation, deprive it of any ideational or instructive content and restrict it to the manifestation of the Divine Presence; they look upon the words of the prophet as a personal response to a revelatory experience.

As a dogmatic rationalist, Moses *Mendelssohn maintained that reason could supply man with all the theoretical insights needed for salvation. Therefore, he restricted the function of prophecy to the practical sphere, to the divine communication of instruction for human action (*Jerusalem* (1852), pt. 2, ch. 3).

The idealistic philosophers, emphasizing the cognitive aspects of prophecy, viewed it as a special aptitude for moral and religious insight. Hermann *Cohen regarded the prophets as pioneering thinkers who removed the mythical elements from religion and developed Judaism from a tribal religion into a universal ethical monotheism. The essence of the universal ethical monotheism is belief in God and adherence to the moral law (*Juedische Schriften*, 1 (1924), 310–6). Kaufmann *Kohler, like many other exponents of the doctrine of "progressive revelation," viewed the "inspired" moral and religious insights of the prophets as important milestones in the evolution of the human spirit toward higher ethical and metaphysical truths.

Sharply reacting to idealistic theories that reduce prophecy to a function of the human spirit, Solomon Ludwig *Steinheim insisted that revelation cannot be explained solely in terms of rational or spiritual insight. The central religious affirmations of Judaism could not have originated within our own cognitive faculties because of their inherent limitations. The primary function of prophecy is to disclose religious truths that can be known only through supernatural revelation (*Die Offenbarung nach dem Lehrbegriffe der Synagoge*, 5ff.). However, Steinheim assigned reason an important function in determining which parts of Scripture represent the revelation of eternal truth.

Samson Raphael *Hirsch and other Orthodox thinkers subscribed to the doctrine of verbal inspiration of the Scriptures. Bitterly objecting to any form of biblical criticism, Hirsch insisted that one must look upon the Scripture as a basic datum in the same manner scientists look upon natural phenomena as given (*Nineteen Letters* (1960), note to letter 18). As a staunch exponent of the traditional view, he rejected the evolutionary theory, according to which the contributions of later prophets are an advance over earlier formulations (*Horeb* (1962), 7).

Naturalist thinkers, such as *Aḥad Ha-Am and Mordecai *Kaplan, ruled out all supernatural elements in prophecy. However, because of their positive attitude toward Jewish nationalism, they could not follow Hermann Cohen in treating the prophet merely as an exponent of ethical universalism. According to Aḥad Ha-Am, who regarded the nation as the bearer of true ethical universalism, the prophet personifies the finest manifestation of the Jewish national spirit.

Jewish existentialist thinkers characterize prophecy as a dialogic relationship between man and God, rather than as the disclosure of a message. Martin *Buber in his book *The Prophetic Faith* (1949) maintained that the prophet is involved in a divine-human encounter. The prophet's message reflects the prophet's personal subjective response to his encounter with God. In the view of Franz *Rosenzweig, although revelation is a supernatural event occurring at specific times to particular individuals, the words of the prophet are nonetheless a purely human "interpretation" of a revelatory experience in which God reveals His love to man. Abraham J. *Heschel contends that the prophet experiences not merely the presence or the love of God, but a revelation of the "divine pathos." However, although prophecy is a revelatory experience in which God's concerns and designs for man are apprehended (*The Prophets* (1962), 307–23), the expression of this experience is affected by the cultural background as well as the personal style of the prophet (*God in Search of Man* (1965), 258–62).

Of the most recent Orthodox thinkers, Joseph B. *Soloveitchik, maintains in his article "The Lonely Man of Faith" (*Tradition*, summer 1965) that the prophetic encounter, a dialogue initiated by God, makes possible the establishment of a "covenantal community" between God and man. Unlike the mystical experience, however, prophecy cannot be limited to religious feelings or intuitions, but entails a normative content. Abraham Isaac *Kook's treatment of prophecy, in his work *Orot ha-Kodesh* (pt. 1 (1963), 267–72), reflects his mystical orientation. Genuine metaphysical insights, according to Kook, cannot be obtained by reason alone. When properly cultivated by a life of piety and holiness, man's imaginative faculties enable him to attach himself to the Divine Source and apprehend reality in the light of the **Shekhinah*, or "Divine Presence." Illumination derived from union with the Divine reaches its highest level in prophecy. Thus, Kook regarded prophecy as the ultimate religious goal.

[Walter S. Wurzburger]

BIBLIOGRAPHY: G. Hoelscher, *Die Profeten* (1914); T.H. Robinson, *Prophecy and the Prophets in Ancient Israel* (1932); R.B.Y. Scott, *The Relevance of the Prophets* (1944); S. Mowinckel, *Prophecy and Tradition* (1946); M. Buber, *The Prophetic Faith* (1949); Y.A. Seligmann, in: *Eretz Israel*, 3 (1954), 125–32 (Heb.); A. Malamat, *ibid.*, 4 (1956), 74–84 (Heb.); 5 (1958), 67–73 (Heb.); 8 (1967), 231–40 (Heb.); idem, in: VT *Supplement*, 15 (1965), 207–27; Kaufmann Y., Religion, 87–101, 343–446; A.J. Heschel, *The Prophets* (1962); J. Lindblom, *Prophecy in Ancient Israel* (1962); O. Eissfeldt, *The Old Testament, An Introduction* (1965), 76–81, 146–52, 301–443 (incl. bibl.); G. von Rad, *Old Testament Theology*, 2 (1965), 3–300; H.M. Orlinsky, in: *Oriens Antiquus*, 4 (1965), 153–74. **ADD. BIBLIOGRAPHY:** R. Wislon, *Prophecy and Society in Ancient Israel* (1980); (S.) D. Sperling, in: A. Green (ed.), *Jewish Spirituality from the Bible to the Middle Ages* (1986), 5–31; M. Fishbane, in: *ibid.*, 62–81; A. Rofé, *Introduction to the Prophetic Literature* (1992); H. Huffmon, in: ABD, 5, 477–82; J. Schmitt, in: *ibid.*, 482–89; J. Barton, in: *ibid.*, 489–95; D. Fleming, in: JAOS, 113 (1993), 175–83; idem, in: BA, 58 (1995), 139–47; S. Parpola, *Assyrian Prophecies* (SAA IX; 1997); J. Tigay, in: M.V. Fox et al. (eds.), *Texts, Temples and Traditions... Tribute to M. Haran* (1996), 137–43; M. Nissinen, *References to Prophecy in Neo-Assyrian Sources* (SAAS VII; 1998); S. Geller, *Sacred Enigmas* (1998); idem, in: A. Berlin and M. Brettler (eds.), *The Jewish Study Bible* (2004), 2021–40; S. Bar, *A Letter That Has Not Been Read. Dreams in the Hebrew Bible* (2001). IN MEDIEVAL JEWISH PHILOSOPHY: S. Pines, introduction to M. Maimonides, *Guide of the Perplexed* (1963), lvii–cxxxiv; L. Strauss, *Philosophie und Gesetz* (1935), 87–122; idem, in: REJ, 100 (1936), 1–37; Husik, Philosophy, 224–6 and index s.v. *Prophecy*; Guttmann, Philosophies, 216–8 and index s.v. *Prophecy* and *Prophets*; H.A. Wolfson, *Philo*, 2 (1947), 11–72; B. Netanyahu, *Don Isaac Abravanel* (1968²), 121–3; Reines, in: HUCA, 31 (1960), 107–35; 33 (1962), 221–53; 38 (1967), 159–211; idem, *Maimonides and Abrabanel on Prophecy* (1970). **ADD. BIBLIOGRAPHY:** C. Sirat, *Les théories des visions surnaturelles dans la pensée juive du moyen-âge* (1969); A. Reines, *Maimonides and Abrabanel on Prophecy* (1970); H. Wolfson, *Studies in the History of Philosophy and Religion*, 2 (1977), 60–119; S. Feldman, *Levi ben Gershom: The Wars of the Lord*, 2 (1987), 5–73; L. Strauss, *Philosophy and Law* (1995); H. Kreisel, *Prophecy: The History of an Idea in Medieval Jewish Philosophy* (2001). MODERN JEWISH PHILOSOPHY: Guttman, Philosophies, index s.v. *Prophecy* and *Prophets*; S. Noveck (ed.), *Great Thinkers of the Twentieth Century* (1963), index; N. Rotenstreich, *Jewish Philosophers in Modern Times: From Mendelssohn to Rosenzweig* (1968), index.

PROPPER, DAN (1941–), Israeli Industrialist, CEO of Israeli food giant Osem International Ltd., founded by his father in 1942. Propper and his brother GAD (1944–) hold 13% of Osem stock, with Nestlé the majority shareholder. The group produces more than 1,000 different food products in ten plants located throughout Israel. Exports went primarily to Europe. Net sales in 2004 reached nearly NIS 2.5 billion ($550 million).

Propper studied food engineering and worked for a few years in the industry in England. He joined the firm in the age of 26, starting off in product development and becoming director-general at the age of 37. During the 1990s he served as president of the Israel Manufacturers Association, establishing himself as a highly visible spokesman for Israeli industry. In 2006 he announced that he was stepping down as Osem CEO while remaining chairman of the board.

[Shaked Gilboa (2nd ed.)]

PROSBUL (Heb. פרוזבול or פרוסבול), a legal formula whereby a creditor could still claim his debts after the *Sabbatical Year despite the biblical injunction against doing so (Deut. 15:2). The text of the prosbul reads, "I declare before you, so-and-so, the judges in such-and-such a place, that regarding any debt due to me, I may be able to recover any money owing to me from so-and-so at any time I shall desire." The prosbul was signed by witnesses or by the judges of the court before whom the declaration was made (Shev. 10:4, Git. 36a). The principle underlying the prosbul was based on the passage "and this is the manner of the release: every creditor shall release that which he hath lent unto his neighbor; he shall not exact it of his neighbor and his brother... Of a foreigner thou mayest exact it; but whatsoever of thine is with thy brother thy hand shall release" (Deut. 15:2, 3). From this the law was deduced that the operation of the year of release did not affect debts of which the bonds had been delivered to the court (*bet din*) before the intervention of the Sabbatical Year (Shev. 10:2), since the Court was regarded as a corporate body to which the words "thy brother," suggesting an individual, did not apply. The court would therefore collect its debts after the Sabbatical Year (Yad, Shemittah ve-Yovel 9:15). Through a slight extension of this precedent, the prosbul was instituted, which in effect amounted to entrusting the court with the collection of the debt. Without actually handing over the bond to the court as previously required, the creditor could secure his debt against forfeiture by making the prescribed declaration.

The prosbul was instituted by Hillel. The Mishnah states that when he saw that the people refrained from giving loans one to another before the Sabbatical Year, thereby transgressing "Beware that there be not a base thought in thy heart," etc. (Deut. 15:9), he instituted the prosbul (Shev. 9:3). The Talmud therefore explained prosbul as *pruz buli u-buti*, meaning an advantage for both the rich and poor. It benefited the rich since it secured their loans, and the poor since it enabled them to borrow (Git. 37a). The word seems, however, to be an abbreviation of the Greek expression πρὸς βουλῇ βουλευτῶν meaning "before the assembly of counselors" (cf. *Boule). The rabbis later explained that Hillel only abrogated the Mosaic institution of the release of all debts every seventh year since the law of release itself was only of rabbinic authority during the Second Temple period when the Jubilee was not operative because the land was not fully occupied by Israel (Git. 36a–b). It was only permitted to write a prosbul when the debtor possessed some real property from which the debt could be collected. The rabbis were very lenient with this rule, however, and permitted the writing of a prosbul even when the debtor possessed a minute amount of land such as a flowerpot or the trunk of a tree. The creditor was also permitted temporarily to transfer to the debtor a small parcel of land so that the prosbul could be written (Shev. 10:6, 7; Git. 37a). An antedated prosbul was considered valid, but a postdated one was void (Shev. 10:5).

During the Hadrianic persecutions, all religious practices were forbidden on the penalty of death and it was hazardous to preserve a prosbul. The rabbis therefore ruled that a creditor could collect his debt even if he did not produce a prosbul since it was assumed that he previously wrote one, but had destroyed it out of fear (Ket. 9:9). This temporary provision later became the established law, and the creditor was believed when he alleged that he had lost his prosbul (Git. 37b; Sh. Ar., ḤM 67:33). Orphans were not required to execute one since they were considered wards of the court. Money owed to them was therefore automatically considered as being owed to the court (Git. 37a). The *amoraim* debated the virtue of Hillel's institution. Samuel declared that if he had the power he would abolish it, while R. Naḥman held that even if no prosbul was actually written it should have been regarded as written. Samuel also maintained that only the leading courts of each generation could supervise the writing of a prosbul. Subsequent practice, however, entrusted all courts with this responsibility (Git. 36b; Isserles to Sh. Ar., ḤM 67:18). During the Middle Ages, the writing of prosbuls was widely disregarded since there was an opinion that the laws of the Sabbatical Years were no longer operative (Rema to Sh. Ar., ḤM 67:1 and commentaries). Nevertheless, meticulous individuals continued to write prosbuls even in modern times (e.g., *Pe'er ha-Dor: Ḥayyei Ḥazon Ish*, 2:245; see also *Takkanot; *Usury).

[Aaron Rothkoff]

PROSE, FRANCINE (1947–), U.S. novelist and short story writer. Prose was born in Brooklyn, New York, and educated at Radcliffe and Harvard. Among her works devoted to Jews and Judaism is *Judah the Pious* (1973), which is a story within a story. The work is a fable dealing with the religious quest that leads to moral transformation and a changed way of viewing the empirical world. *Hungry Hearts* (1983), with its homage to *An-Ski, focuses on a Yiddish theater troupe in which a dybbuk possesses an actress. In *Guided Tours of Hell: Novellas* (1997), the title story examines with caustic wit the uses of authenticity as a famed Holocaust survivor helps lead a tour of a concentration camp, spurring the envy of a minor American playwright. *A Changed Man* (2005) depicts with comic irony the ethical metamorphosis of a member of a neo-Nazi group; he becomes a spokesman for a Jewish organization promoting understanding and peace.

BIBLIOGRAPHY: J.P. Steed, "Francine Prose," in: *Contemporary American Women Fiction Writers* (2002), 312–17.

[Lewis Fried (2nd ed.)]

PROSELYTES. There is ample evidence of a widespread conversion to Judaism during the period of the Second Temple, especially the latter part of the period, and the word *ger*, which in biblical times meant a stranger, or an alien, became synonymous with a proselyte (see *Strangers and Gentiles).

Among the notable converts to Judaism may be mentioned the royal family of Adiabene, Aquila and/or Onkelos, Flavius Clemens, the nephew of Vespasian, and Fulvia, wife of Saturninus, a Roman senator. Unique, as the only case of forced conversion in Judaism, was the mass conversion of the Edomites by John Hyrcanus.

In addition to those outstanding figures, however, it is obvious that proselytism was widespread among the ordinary people. The statement of the New Testament that the Pharisees "compass sea and land to make one proselyte" (Matt. 23:15), suggesting a vigorous and active proselytization may possibly be an exaggeration, but on the other hand, the near pride which the rabbis took in the claim that some of their greatest figures were descended from proselytes (see below) point to an openhanded policy toward their acceptance. Such incidents as the different approach of Shammai and Hillel to the request to be taught the principles of Judaism by a potential proselyte (Shabb. 31a) and the incidental mention of "Judah the Ammonite proselyte" (Ber. 28a) point to the fact that the movement was not confined to the upper classes. In fact Josephus states explicitly that in his day the inhabitants of both Greek and barbarian cities evinced a great zeal for Judaism (Contra Ap. 2. 39).

It was during this period that the detailed laws governing the acceptance of proselytes were discussed and codified, and they have remained standard in Orthodox Judaism.

Laws of Conversion

The procedure, established by the *tannaim*, according to which a non-Jew may be accepted into the Jewish faith, was elucidated as follows: "In our days, when a proselyte comes to be converted, we say to him: 'What is your objective? Is it not known to you that today the people of Israel are wretched, driven about, exiled, and in constant suffering?' If he says: 'I know of this and I do not have the merit,' we accept him immediately and we inform him of some of the lighter precepts and of some of the severer ones… we inform him of the chastisements for the transgression of these precepts… and we also inform him of the reward for observing these precepts… we should not overburden him nor be meticulous with him…" (Yev. 47a; cf. Ger. 1, in: M. Higger, *Sheva Massekhtot Ketannot* (1930), 68–69). This text refers to a person who converted through conviction. The *halakhah* also accepts a posteriori, proselytes who had converted in order to marry, to advance themselves, or out of fear (Yev. 24b, in the name of Rav, see TJ, Kid. 4:1, 65b–d; Maim. Yad, Issurei Bi'ah 13:17; Sh. Ar., YD 268:12). The acceptance of a proselyte "under the wings of the Divine Presence" is equivalent to Israel's entry into the covenant, i.e., with circumcision, immersion, and offering a sacrifice (Ger. 2:4, in: M. Higger; loc. cit. 72).

A proselyte had to sacrifice a burnt offering either of cattle or two young pigeons. R. Johanan b. Zakkai instituted that in those times when sacrifice was no longer possible, a proselyte was not obliged to set aside money for the sacrifice (Ker. 9a). Therefore, only circumcision and immersion remained. R. Eliezer and R. Joshua disagreed as to whether someone who immersed himself but was not circumcised or vice versa could be considered a proselyte. According to R. Eliezer, he is a proselyte, even if he performed only one of these commandments. R. Joshua, however, maintained that immersion was indispensable. The halakhic conclusion is that "he is not a proselyte unless he has both been circumcised and has immersed himself" (Yev. 46). The act of conversion must take place before a *bet din*, consisting of three members; a conversion carried out by the proselyte when alone is invalid (Yev. 46b–47a). There is a suggestion that the three members of the *bet din* must be witnesses only to his acceptance of the precepts but not to the immersion. Maimonides, however, decided (Yad, Issurei Bi'ah 13:7), that a proselyte who immersed himself in the presence of two members only is not a proselyte. The schools of Shammai and Hillel differed on the issue of a proselyte who had already been circumcised at the time of his conversion: "Bet Shammai states: 'One must draw from him the blood of circumcision'; Bet Hillel states: 'One need not draw the blood of circumcision from him'" (Tosef., Shah. 15:9; TB, Shab. 135a). Most of the rabbinic authorities decide in favor of Bet Shammai (Tos. to Shab. 135a; Maim. Yad, Issurei Bi'ah 14:5; Sh. Ar., YD 268:1), and "who hast sanctified us with Thy commandments and hast commanded us to circumcise proselytes and to draw from them the blood of the covenant" (Shab. 137b) is said in the circumcision benediction of proselytes.

A proselyte must observe all the precepts that bind Jews. The statement: "There shall be one law for the citizen and for the stranger that dwelleth amongst you" (Ex. 12:49), which refers to the paschal lamb, the sages interpreted to mean that the stranger (proselyte) was the equal of the citizen concerning all the precepts of the Torah (Mekh. Pisha, 15). They tried to equalize the status of the proselyte and that of the Jew; certain differences stemming from the origin of the convert, however, remained. According to an anonymous Mishnah, a proselyte may not confess himself after taking out the tithes since the statement occurs in the confession "the land which Thou hast given to us"; nor does he read the section on the first fruits, where the statement is: "which the Lord hath sworn unto our fathers to give unto us." The proselyte, praying by himself must say: "the God of the Fathers of Israel"; in the synagogue he says: "the God of your Fathers" (Ma'as. Sh. 5:14; Bik. 1:4). According to one tradition, R. Judah permitted a proselyte to read the section on the first fruits, claiming that Abraham was the father of the whole world (TJ, Bik. 1:4, 64a; but in Tosef., Bik. 1:2 this permission is only extended to the Kenites). The Palestinian *amoraim*, R. Joshua b. Levi and R. Avihu, agreed with R. Judah. The authorities (particularly R. Samson in his commentary to *Bikkurim* (*ibid.*), and Maimonides in his letter to Obadiah the Proselyte, below) in permitting a proselyte to say "the God of our Fathers" in the prayers based themselves on the same rationale.

A proselyte terminates all former family ties upon conversion and "is considered a newly born child." His Jewish name is not associated with that of his father and he is referred to as "the son of Abraham (our father)." Later, it became the custom to name the proselyte himself after the first Jew who knew his Creator "Abraham the son of Abraham." According to the letter of the law, a proselyte may marry his relatives. The sages, however, decreed against this "So that they should not say: 'We have come from a greater sanctity to a lesser sanctity'" (Yev. 22a, Yad, Issurei Bi'ah 14:12). The disqualifications pertaining to testimony of relatives in judicial cases of family members do not apply to the proselyte; his relatives also may not inherit from him. If no heirs were born to him after his conversion, his property and his possessions are considered not to belong to anyone, and whoever takes hold of them becomes their owner (BB 3:3, 4:9; Git. 39a; Yad, Zekhi'ah u-Mattanah 1:6).

A proselyte may marry a Jewish woman, even the daughter of a priest (Kid. 73a; Yad, Issurei Bi'ah 19:11; Sh. Ar., EH 7:22). A female proselyte, however, cannot marry a kohen, unless she was converted during childhood, not later than the age of three years and one day (Yev. 60b; Kid. 78a). R. Yose permits the marriage of the daughter of a male or female proselyte to a kohen; R. Eliezer b. Jacob, however, disputes the matter. The statement "From the day of the destruction of the Temple, the kohanim have preserved their dignity and followed the opinion of R. Eliezer b. Jacob" shows that tradition tended toward the latter's opinion. The *amoraim*, however, decided that he be followed only in those cases where the marriage has not yet taken place. If a female proselyte is already married to a kohen, she is not bound to leave him (Kid. 4:7; TB, Kid. 78b; Yad, Issurei Bi'ah 19:12). A proselyte may also marry a *mamzer* ("bastard"). According to some opinions, the permission may extend over ten generations, while others claim it should be only until his heathen origin is forgotten (Kid. 72b, 75a).

A proselyte cannot be appointed to any public office. The rabbis based their decision on the verse: "Thou shalt appoint over thee a king from among thy brothers – appointments shall be only from among thy brothers." This injunction does not apply to a proselyte whose mother or father are of Jewish origin (Yev. 45b; Kid. 76b; Tos. Sot. 41b, Yad, Melakhim 1:4). A proselyte may not hold the office of judge in a criminal court; he may act as such in a civil court (Sanh. 36b) and also judge a fellow proselyte, even in a criminal law case (Rashi to Yev. 102a). Unless one of his parents was born Jewish, most authorities bar a proselyte from acting as judge even in a civil court (Alfasi on Sanh. 4:2, Yad, Sanh. 2:9, 11:11). Others are of the opinion that even in a civil court he can only judge a fellow proselyte (Tos. Yev. 45b; Ra-Sh-BA on Yev. 102a).

Appreciation of the Proselyte

In the Talmud and the Midrashim, as well as in other contemporary literature, the accepted attitude toward proselytes is usually positive. There is, however, strong evidence in rabbinic sources that some authorities were opposed to the concept of conversion and proselytes. Those scholars who ignore or obliterate such evidence cannot be justified. The differences in outlook found in rabbinic sources can partly be explained by disparities in character and temperament. However, the deciding factors were usually contemporary conditions and the personal experiences of the rabbis. R. Eliezer b. Hyrcanus, who was under ban, objected to the acceptance of proselytes (Eccles. R. 1:8). When Aquila the Proselyte wondered and asked: "Is this all the love which the Lord hath given unto the proselyte, as it is written 'and He loveth the stranger to give him bread and clothing?'" R. Eliezer was angry with him, but R. Joshua comforted him, saying: "Bread means Torah… clothing means the *tallit*: the man who is worthy to have the Torah, will also acquire its precepts; his daughters may marry into the priesthood and their grandsons will sacrifice burnt offerings on the altar." (Gen. R. 70:5). It is possible that R. Eliezer's negative attitude may have been influenced by his contacts with the first Christians. He may have seen that many of the new heretics were proselytes who had relapsed and it is only concerning these that he said, "They revert to their evil ways" (BM 59b). The same R. Eliezer also states: "When a person comes to you in sincerity to be converted, do not reject him, but on the contrary encourage him" (Mekh. Amalek 3). From his time, proselytes out of conviction were mentioned in the benediction for the righteous and the pious in the *Amidah* (Meg. 17b). The bitter experience of Jews with proselytes in times of war and revolt influenced the negative attitude to conversion. Proselytes and their offspring became renegades, often slandering their new religion and denouncing the Jewish community and its leaders to the foreign rulers. In Josephus there is a description of Hellenist proselytes who apostatized and returned to their evil ways (Jos., Apion 2:123). Reference to the situation which existed after the destruction of the Temple and the abortive revolt which followed it is made in the *baraita* statement: "Insincere proselytes who wear *tefillin* on the heads and on their arms, *zizit* in their clothes, and who fix *mezuzot* on their doors – when the war of Gog and Magog will come… each one of them will remove the precepts from himself and go on his way…" (Av. Zar. 3b). At the time of the revolt of Bar Kokhba the expression "they impede the arrival of the Messiah" (Nid. 13b), referred to such proselytes. At the same epoch, R. Nehemiah taught: a proselyte who converted in order to marry or converted to enjoy the royal table or to become a servant of Solomon, proselytes who converted from fear of the lions (see: II Kings 17:24–28), proselytes who converted because of a dream, or the proselytes of Mordecai and Esther, are not acceptable as proselytes, unless they convert themselves (as) at the present time (Yev. 24b), i.e., by conviction in times of political decline, oppressions, persecutions, and lack of any material benefit. R. Simeon b. Yohai, upon seeing Judah b. Gerim ("a son of proselytes"), who was responsible for the rabbi's criticism of the Romans reaching the ears of the rulers, said: "Is this one still in the world!" and set his eyes upon him, turning him into a heap of bones (Shab. 33b–34a). This experience throws light on the commentary of R. Simeon: "Those who feared the Lord were a hindrance to Israel… the best of the gentiles, you should put to death…" (Mekh. Va-Yehi 2). His real opinions, however, found expression in the commentary (Mekh. Nezikim (Mishpatim) 18): "It is said – 'And those that are beloved by Him are compared to the sun when it rises in all its strength'; Now who is greater – he who loves the king or he whom the king loves? One must say – he whom the king loves, as the verse says: 'and He loves the stranger [proselyte]'"; the statement of R. Hiyya: "Do not have any faith in a proselyte until 24 generations have passed because the inherent evil is still within him" (Mid. Ruth Zuta on 1:12); and other statements of *amoraim* who despised proselytes: "Proselytes are as hard for Israel [to endure] as a sore" (Yev. 47b) were prompted by the bad experiences Jews had with proselytes who had turned national or religious recreants. To these the rabbis referred: "The proselytes who left Egypt with Moses, made it [the Golden Calf] and said to Israel: These are your gods" (Ex. R. 42:6). The rabbis distinguished between three categories of proselytes: "Proselytes are of three types: There are some like Abraham our Father, some like Hamor, and some that are like heathens in all respects" (SER 27). In the teachings of the *amoraim* the basic tone is that of the tannaitic statement: "Proselytes are beloved; in every place He considers them as part of Israel" (Mekh. *ibid.*). They too made efforts "not to close the door before the proselytes who may come" (*ibid*). In the third century, R. Johanan and R. Eleazar separately deduced from different verses that "the Holy One, Blessed be He, exiled Israel among the nations only in order to increase their numbers with the addition of proselytes" (Pes. 87b). R. Eleazar also said: "Whoever befriends a proselyte is considered as if he created him" (Gen. R. 84:4). There are numerous other statements which praise proselytes (e.g., Tanh. Lekh Lekha 6; Num. R. 8:9; Mid. Ps. 146:8). A tendency to increase the honor of the proselytes and to glorify conversion can perhaps be found in the tradition which traces the origins of such great personalities as R. Meir, R. Akiva, Shemaiah, and Avtalyon to proselytes. They were descendants of such wicked men as Sisera, Sennacherib, Haman, and Nero (Git. 56a, 57b; Sanh. 96b). The name of R. Akiva's father does not appear explicitly in the Talmud, but *Dikdukei Soferim, ibid.*, 9 (1878), 283 and also Maimonides' introduction to *Mishneh Torah* relate that Joseph, the father of R. Akiva, was a proselyte by conviction. The last of the Babylonian *amoraim*, R. Ashi, said that the destiny of the proselytes had also been determined at Mount Sinai (Shab. 146a). Most of the rabbis of the Talmud observed the tradition: "When a proselyte comes to be converted, one receives him with an open hand so as to bring him under the wings of the Divine Presence" (SER 7; Lev. R. 2:9).

Two of the three paradigmatic biblical proselytes in midrashic tradition, Ruth and Rahab (Joshua 2), are female. *Pesikta Rabbati* 40:3 links these two women with Jethro, Moses's father-in-law, as examples of "upright" gentiles who chose to join the Jewish people. Ruth, the ancestor of King David, is praised for her loving-kindness and for her complete devotion to Jewish law and practice (Ruth R. 2:22, 2:23). Rahab, the beneficent Jericho harlot who preserved Joshua's spies from capture, became the pre-eminent rabbinic model of the righteous proselyte who went beyond all others in her proclamation (Josh. 2:11) of divine ubiquity and omnipotence (*Mekhilta* Amalek 3; Deut. R. 2:26–27). She is said to have married Joshua and their descendants became prophets and righteous men in Israel (Sifrei Numbers 78; Meg. 14b; Num. R. 8:9; Ruth R. 2:1). It may be that Rahab, a woman with a lurid past, assumed this special importance in a rabbinic setting looking for engaging female figures of repentance and conversion (Zev. 116a–b).

Post-Talmudic

During the following era the proponents of the two ruling monotheistic religions – in contrast to polytheism – regarded abandonment of their faith and transfer to another religion as a capital offense. The canons of the Church forbade proselytism and Christian rulers fiercely opposed any tendency to adopt Jewish religious customs. The number of proselytes diminished in Christian countries, and those who endangered their lives by adherence to Israel were generally compelled to flee to lands beyond the bounds of the rule of the Church.

At the commencement of this period, however, during the period of transition from polytheism to belief in One God, Judaism also succeeded in winning the hearts of the upper classes of two peoples, as formerly occurred with the kingdom of Adiabene. In the fifth century the kings of Himyar in southern Arabia adopted Judaism, and in the first half of the eighth century the upper classes of the Khazars. There is no information about Muslim proselytes, but the adoption of Judaism by Christians in Muslim countries was not forbidden, and even common. The sources chiefly mention Christian male and female slaves in the houses of Jews whose owners were enjoined by Jewish law to circumcise them and have them undergo ritual immersion. The *geonim* Sar Shalom and Zemah Zedek b. Isaac were asked about a "gentile woman slave who was conversant with the idolatry of the Christians and was compelled to undergo ritual immersion by her owner," and about "a slave woman who says I am a Jewess, but acts in all respects like a gentile" (*Ozar ha-Ge'onim*, Yev. 114). They also mention that there are some slaves "who become proselytes immediately and some eventually. Some of these do not want to convert at all; most are such and do not convert but there are some who say: 'Wait until we see your laws and learn them, and we shall convert…'" (*ibid.*, 199). It may be assumed that many of these slaves became assimilated into the Jewish community. Sometimes Jews became sexually involved with women slaves and had them undergo ritual immersion for the purpose of proselytism; their children were regarded as full-fledged proselytes. The best known of these cases concerns the Exilarch Bustanai b. Haninai (*ibid.*, 39–43, 173).

Besides such converts, there were also proselytes from conviction in Christian countries who voluntarily adopted Judaism out of love for Jewish law and about whom only fragmentary information has been preserved. Such proselytes were mainly members of the Christian clergy, whom theological study, and especially comparison of the New Testament with its roots in the Old, brought to Judaism. After becoming proselytes some even attempted to win over souls for their new religion. Bodo-Eleazar, court deacon of Louis the Pious in the ninth century, escaped to Muslim Spain and wrote sharp polemics attacking Christianity (B. Blumenkranz, in: RHPR, 34 (1954), 401–13). In 1012 the priest Vicilinus in Mainz became a proselyte, and he, too, wrote works to prove from the Bible the correctness of his course and the truth of the religion of Israel. Some scholars consider that his action was the cause of the expulsion of the Jews from Mainz by Emperor Henry II (Aronius, Regesten, nos. 144, 147). From about the same period record has been preserved about a wealthy Christian woman of distinguished family who became a proselyte, settled in Narbonne, and married R. David, a member of the family of the *nasi* Todros.

One remarkable case of proselytism in the Middle Ages concerns the Norman proselyte Obadiah (c. 1100), a member of a noble family of Oppido in Lucano, southern Italy. The events that befell him are known from a number of fragments preserved in the Cairo *Genizah*. This proselyte left notes in which he introduces himself by his gentile name Johannes and relates first concerning "the archbishop Andreas, chief priest of the province of Bari… in [whose] heart God placed love of the Torah of Moses. He left his land and priesthood, and all his glory, went to the province of Castantinia and circumcised himself. Troubles and evils befell him. He arose and fled for his life because the uncircumcised sought to kill him, and God delivered him from their hands… strangers arose after him, saw his deeds, and acted as he had done, and they too entered the covenant of the Living God. This man then went to Egypt and dwelt there until his death. The name of the king of Egypt at that time was Al-Mustanzir…" News of the action of Andreas, bishop of Bari from 1062 to 1078, spread throughout Greece and Italy and reached the ears of Johannes while he was a youth. In the first year of his entering the priesthood he had a dream which influenced him to follow in the path of Andreas. In 1102 he was circumcised and began to observe the Sabbath and the festivals, and even wrote pamphlets calling upon all religious people to return to the religion of Israel. The authorities, however, imprisoned him and threatened to kill him unless he repented of his deeds. He succeeded in escaping, arrived in Baghdad, and dwelt in "the home of Isaac b. Moses, head of the Academy." He also visited Jewish communities in Syria, Erez Israel, and Egypt, and wrote the events of his life.

There were also proselytes who remained in Christian countries and apparently succeeded in concealing themselves from the vigilance of the Church by roaming from one country to another. There is also mention of a proselyte family at the time of Jacob Tam which originated in Hungary and was living in northern France or Germany. The father, Abraham the proselyte, interpreted the rabbinic dictum "Proselytes are as hard for Israel [to endure] as a sore" (Yev. 47b) in favor of proselytes: because they are meticulous in observing the precepts they are hard for the Jews since they recall their iniquities. He and his two sons Isaac and Joseph, engaged in biblical interpretation, taking issue with Christian exegesis, and also criticizing the Gospels and the Christian prayers. A pupil of Jacob Tam, Moses b. Abraham of Pontoise, tells of a proselyte who used to study "Bible and Mishnah day and night." Six *piyyutim* composed by the *paytan* Josephiah the proselyte who lived in France in the 12th century are known (Zunz, Lit Poesie, 469). Toward the end of the 12th century a proselyte living in Wuerzburg who knew "the language of the priests" (i.e., Latin) but not Hebrew made a copy of the Pentateuch for his own use from "a rejected book belonging to priests." R. Joel permitted this proselyte to act as reader for the congregation.

A talmudist who was a proselyte by conviction sent halakhic queries to Maimonides, who addressed him in respectful terms: "Master and teacher, the intelligent and enlightened Obadiah, the righteous proselyte," and wrote to him, "You are a great scholar and possess an understanding mind, for you have understood the issues and known the right way." In his letters to this proselyte, Maimonides expresses high appreciation of proselytism and the proselyte: he permits him to pray: … as every native Israelite prays and recites blessings… anyone who becomes a proselyte throughout the generations and anyone who unifies the Name of the Holy One as it is written in the Torah is a pupil of our father Abraham and all of them are members of his household… hence you may say, Our God, and the God of our fathers; for Abraham, peace be upon him, is your father… for since you have entered beneath the wings of the Divine Presence and attached yourself to Him, there is no difference between us and you.… You certainly recite the blessings: Who has chosen us; Who has given us; Who has caused us to inherit; and Who has separated us. For the Creator has already chosen you and has separated you from the nations and has given you the Torah, as the Torah was given to us and to proselytes.… Further, do not belittle your lineage: if we trace our descent to Abraham, Isaac, and Jacob, your connection is with Him by Whose word the universe came into being.

(Resp. Rambam (ed. Freimann), no. 42). Concerning the vexations and humiliating words violently addressed to this proselyte by certain Jews, Maimonides writes to him:

Toward father and mother we are commanded honor and reverence, toward the prophets to obey them, but toward proselytes we are commanded to have great love in our inmost hearts.… God, in His glory, loves proselytes.… A man who left his father and birthplace and the realm of his people at a time when they are powerful, who understood with his insight, and who attached himself to this nation which today is a despised people, the slave of rulers, and recognized and knew that their religion is true and righteous… and pursued God… and entered beneath the wings of the Divine Presence… the Lord does not call you fool [Heb. *kesil*], but intelligent [*maskil*] and understanding, wise and walking correctly, a pupil of Abraham our father… (*ibid.*, no. 369). There were proselytes who suffered martyrdom (*Kiddush ha-Shem*) and even those who became proselytes with this intention. Among those who suffered martyrdom during the massacres of the First Crusade in 1096 was a man whose "mother was not Jewish"; before his martyrdom he said: "hitherto you have scorned me." In 1264 the burning took place at Augsburg of "Abraham, son of Abraham our Father, of Ishpurk, who rejected the gods of the nations, broke the heads of the idols… and was tormented with severe tortures." This proselyte had conducted a campaign for Judaism among the Christians and attacked the symbols of Christianity. Elegies on his death were written by the great scholars of the generation; Mordecai b. Hillel ha-Kohen described how the man became a proselyte: "And Abraham journeyed, reaching the Hebrew religion, attached himself to the house of Jacob and cut his foreskin," and related that the words spoken by the proselyte in public against his former religion were the cause of his being burned at the stake: "when he proclaimed his ideas… in the town, he was taken to the stake." Another elegist spoke of his courage during his life and at his death: "He walked in purity and broke images… he revealed the glory of the Creator to the nations, denying belief in the crucified one; to martyrdom he walked like a bridegroom to the bride." In 1270 Abraham b. Abraham of France was burned in Wiesenburg. He was a respected monk and fled from his country after he became a proselyte: "he rejected images and came to take refuge in the shadow of the wings of the Living God." In 1275 it was noted that a monk, Robert of Reading, became a proselyte in England.

It is difficult to ascertain with certainty the extent of proselytism in the Middle Ages. The historical sources mention isolated cases only. However, the fact that such cases recurred in every generation, as well as the preachings and admonitions by the heads of Church against Judaizing and the many regulations and decrees they issued to prevent this danger, testifies to the persistence of the phenomenon, at least to a limited extent. Some scholars regard proselytism as being of quantitative significance also during the Middle Ages and explain the marked anthropological differences between the various Jewish communities, and the resemblance of every community to the ethnic type of its environment, as being due in great measure to the inflow of external ethnic elements which continued at least throughout the first half of the Middle Ages.

With the decline in the number of proselytes by conviction, the fundamental attitude of the medieval Jewish scholars toward proselytism as a phenomenon of profound religious significance did not change, and some of them continued to consider that the purpose of Israel's dispersion among the nations was to gain proselytes. Moses b. Jacob of Coucy (mid-13th century) explains to his contemporaries that they must act uprightly toward gentiles since "so long as they [i.e., Jews] act deceitfully toward them, who will attach themselves to them?" (*Semag*, Asayin 74). Isaiah b. Mali di Trani the Younger permits the teaching of the books of the Prophets and the Hagiographa to gentiles, because he regards them as consolation spoken to Israel, "and as a result he [the gentile] may mend his ways" (*Shiltei Gibborim*, Av. Zar., ch. 1).

In Modern Times

The Jewish attitude to proselytism at the beginning of the modern period was inclined to be negative; aspirations to win over people of other faiths to Judaism dwindled. However, the *bet din* has no authority to repudiate proselytes wishing to convert despite the admonitions concerning the gravity of such a step; the Shulhan Arukh and the other *posekim* of the period left the laws concerning proselytism in force, but examination of the texts reveals, and at times it is even expressly stated, that it was only a formal duty to accept proselytes, and, indeed, attempts at active conversion were infrequent. However, isolated cases of conversion continued to occur. Proselytes were associated with the Hebrew press in Amsterdam, in various cities in Germany, in Constantinople and Salonika (see A. Yaari, in: KS, 13 (1936/37), 243–8). A Christian who visited Jerusalem in 1494–96 relates that he found there two monks "who had three years before gone over from the Christian faith to the Jewish religion" (*Die Pilgerfahrt des Ritters Arnold von Harft* (ed. by E.V. Groote (1860), 187). On the other hand, there is no real evidence to indicate attempts at actual conversion or proselytizing activity in the "Jewish heresy" (see *Judaizers) that was reported in the Orthodox Church in the principality of Moscow at the end of the 15th and beginning of the 16th century.

Solomon Luria warned against receiving proselytes, and the Jewish councils of Lithuania and Moravia even threatened to impose severe penalties on anyone who began to proselytize or gave protection to converts. The reason for this in part stemmed from the fear of the consequences and dangers this activity entailed, since it was severely prohibited by the authorities. The Jewish communities in Poland and Lithuania were more than once obliged to clear themselves of the charge of proselytizing, and it is not always clear whether this was the result of a false accusation by agitators or of the prevalent public opinion in regard to actual occurrences.

When Lutheranism began to spread in Poland in the 16th century, many who inclined to "reforms" were accused by the Catholics of "Judaizing." In 1539 an old woman of 80, Catherine Weigel, the wife of a citizen of Cracow, was burned at the stake for having embraced Judaism; the clarification of her case took ten years. Before she perished she said: "God had neither wife nor son… we are His children and all who walk in His ways are His children." Jews were falsely accused of smuggling proselytes into Turkey, and an official investigation of this matter took place in Lithuania causing great harm to the Jews of that country. Nevertheless, it appears that most Jews not only refrained outwardly from engaging in proselytizing activities as the result of external pressures and penalties, but the attitude of Judaism itself in that period formed an important factor. The Jews increasingly withdrew from the outside world; the difference between Judaism and the other faiths was regarded as an inherent, radical distinction between two unbridgeable worlds with scarcely any points of contact. The general tendency of that entire period is expressed in the words of Solomon Luria: "Would that the seed of Israel continue to stand fast and hold its own among the nations throughout the days of our exile and no stranger be added to us who is not of our nation."

With the relative toleration that began to prevail in the ruling circles and among intellectuals in the 17th century, especially in Western Europe, the negative attitude to Christianity among Jews diminished. There was a growing tendency not to regard Christianity as an idolatrous religion but to look upon its adherents as Noachides who are absolved from the belief in absolute monotheism. Such a view left no room for conversion efforts to bring Christians under the wings of the *Shekhinah*. This abandonment of conversionary activity on the part of Jews was thus given a theoretical, intellectual basis. However, individual proselytes continued to find their way to Judaism by their own inner conviction. At the end of the 16th century a pious Christian who embraced Judaism on his own initiative is known (Moes Germanus). In 1716 two Christian women were put to death in Dubno because they became Jews; in 1738 the naval officer Alexander Voznitsyn was publicly burned to death in Russia for having become a Jew, together with the Jew, Baruch b. Leib, who persuaded him to take this step. The memory of the "*Ger Ẓedek* of Vilna," Count Valentine Potocki, who was allegedly burned in Vilna in 1746, is preserved in popular folklore. Another notable 18th-century proselyte was the English politician Lord George Gordon.

The Enlightenment strengthened this inclination to religious contraction. The slogan of religious toleration discouraged propaganda activities among the different faiths. The *maskilim* pointed with pride to the resemblance between the principles of Enlightenment and the aims of Judaism – which, in their opinion, were tolerance. Emphasis on Jewish tolerance and abandonment of all active proselytizing became a fixed principle in modern Jewish apologetics. This apologetical attitude even influenced study of the past, and historical accounts tended to ignore that active Jewish proselytizing had occurred, as if Judaism had never desired to make converts. There was no change from the psychological point of view in the self-defensive attitude of Judaism even after it had been granted a status of juridical equality with the other religions of the state. Even though no legal obstacles now prevent proselytizing little attempt has been made to propagate conversion.

A certain number of proselytes came from the sects of the Sabbath Observers in Russia (see *Judaizers; *Somrei Sabat), who adopted a number of Jewish customs and finally went over to Judaism completely. Others embraced Judaism because of an experience or religious conviction, but chiefly it was the result of unhampered social contacts that ended with intermarriage (see also *San Nicandro).

[*Encyclopaedia Hebraica*]

Recent Trends

Whereas in some countries of the Diaspora, particularly England and South Africa, there was a distinct tendency to adopt more stringent regulations for the acceptance of proselytes in the Orthodox community, it was generally appreciated that a greater leniency could be permitted in the State of Israel, since the prospective proselytes, most of whom were either partners in, or the children of, mixed marriages, would become much more integrated in the Jewish people than would be likely in the Diaspora. Despite this the rabbinical authorities were slow to alleviate the difficulties in the way of applicants for proselytization. They normally insisted on a year's postponement of consideration after making application, and on the ability and undertaking of the candidate to adhere to the requirements of Orthodox Judaism. From 1948 to 1968, 2,288 proselytes were accepted by the rabbinical courts of Israel, out of a total of 4,010 who applied. A tendency toward leniency became more pronounced at the beginning of the 1970s as a result of two factors. One was the expectation of an increased immigration from Soviet Russia where, owing to prevailing circumstances, intermarriage had taken place on an unprecedented scale; and the other was the situation created by the amendment to the Law of Return adopted by the Knesset in 1970. Two provisions made the need for an acceleration of proselytization urgent. The first was that the law was extended to include the partners, children, and grandchildren of mixed marriages who were not Jews according to *halakhah*, and the second that, whereas in Israel only those converted in accordance with *halakhah* were registered as Jews, in the case of immigrants, conversion by Reform and Conservative rabbis was accepted by the civil authorities for these immigrants to be registered as Jews. The resulting anomaly, that these non-Orthodox proselytes were regarded as Jews by the civil authorities while their conversion was not accepted by the Orthodox rabbinate, which was the only legal body determining personal status, had to be reduced as much as possible. In 1971 the Ministry for Religious Affairs, for the first time, established schools for prospective proselytes in Israel, at the Orthodox kibbutzim of Sa'ad and Lavi, where candidates may undergo an intensive course in Judaism.

There have also been a number of instances of the conversion of Muslims to Judaism (see A. Rotem, in: *Mahanayim*, no. 92 (1964), 159).

In 1955 a World Union for the Propagation of Judaism was established in the belief that the time had come for Jews to undertake conversionist activity, and it published a brochure, *Jedion*. There was, however, little response to this suggestion from the public, and some of the steps taken in that direction, particularly among the Chuetas, proved abortive.

[Louis Isaac Rabinowitz]

In the U.S.

In 17th-century colonial America Jewish slaveholders, following ancient custom, converted their slaves to Judaism. A number of Black Jewish congregations in the United States are made up, in part, of the descendants of these early proselytes. During the first quarter of the 18th century a community of German Baptists, in what is now Schaefferstown, Pennsylvania, voluntarily "Judaized." They observed dietary laws and the Sabbath, built a "schul" and a home for their *hazzan* from rough logs, and in 1732 laid out a cemetery. The community lasted from about 1720 to 1745. The cemetery – now destroyed – was still intact in 1885; the home of the *hazzan* still stood in 1926 but was destroyed later. Whether or not these "Judaizers" actually became Jewish proselytes is uncertain.

The earliest well-known U.S. proselyte was a Quaker, Warder Cresson, who became U.S. consul in Jerusalem in 1844. There, in 1848, he converted and assumed the name of Michael Cresson Boaz Israel. His American wife divorced him and he then married a Palestinian Jewess. He was a prominent member of the Jerusalem Sephardi community and is buried on the Mount of Olives.

The first incorporated Jewish missionary society in modern times, the United Israel World Union (UIWU), was established in New York City in 1944 by the journalist David Horowitz. Groups of UIWU proselytes have their own congregations in Wilbur, West Virginia, and West Olive, Michigan. Another such missionary society, the Jewish Information Society of America, was founded in Chicago in 1962. U.S. Reform Judaism has maintained that Jews have an obligation to teach their religion to all mankind and to attract like-minded non-Jews into the Jewish community. This theoretical determination was followed by the establishment in 1951 of a Committee on the Unaffiliated, by the Central Conference of American Rabbis, to develop "practical means for extending the influence and acceptance of the Jewish religion." The Conservative rabbinate declined to undertake such efforts, although it accepted prospective converts. The Orthodox remained extremely reluctant to accept converts, making stringent demands of all prospective candidates.

Reports from 785 U.S. congregational rabbis in 1954 regarding conversions to Judaism in the United States showed that approximately 3,000 persons were then being converted annually to Judaism. The number increased yearly. In 95 percent of the conversions, an impending or existing marriage to a Jew was involved; female proselytes outnumbered males five to one.

[David Max Eichhorn]

Non-Orthodox Views

Reform rabbis have insisted upon instruction in Judaism and study of selected books as prerequisites for conversion. However, in conflict with the traditional Jewish attitude they have stressed the importance of the declaration of faith by the convert, disregarding the ritual aspects of conversion to Judaism (*tevilah*, and in the case of male converts, circumcision). In 1892 the Central Conference of American Rabbis (CCAR) decided that any Reform rabbi in conjunction with two colleagues could accept as a convert any person without any initiatory rite, and also published manuals for guiding their rabbis in regard to conversion. Nor did Reform follow the *halakhah* with regard to children – children of converted parents born prior to their conversion are considered Jews if the parents declare they will raise them as Jews. With regard to children of school age their confirmation at the end of their schooling is considered the ceremony of their official entry into Judaism. Children past confirmation age are considered adults, and have to undergo instruction prior to conversion. However, attitudes were changing at the beginning of the 21st century. In 2001, the Central Conference of American Rabbis approved new guidelines recommending that all Reform rabbis require *bet din*, *tevilah* for all converts, and a symbolic circumcision for male converts.

The Conservative movement has always officially upheld the *halakhah* as regards the ceremonies of conversion. They demand that three rabbis be present, but they emphasize the preparation of the proselyte in Jewish sources and texts on Jewish history and customs. In 1970 the Rabbinical Assembly committee on Jewish Law and standards reaffirmed that its members "may not conduct a conversion *ab initio* without *tevilah*."

BIBLIOGRAPHY: J. Bamberger, *Proselytism in the Talmudic Period* (1968²); W.G. Braude, *Jewish Proselytizing in the First Five Centuries* (1940); D.M. Eichhorn (ed.), *Conversion to Judaism: A History and Analysis* (1965); JSOS, 16 (1954), 299–318. H. Graetz, *Die juedischen Proselyten im Roemerreiche…* (1884); A. Bertholet, *Die Stellung der Israeliten und der Juden zu den Fremden* (1896); I. Lévy, in: REJ, 50 (1905), 1–9; 51 (1906), 1–31; Juster, Juifs, 1 (1914), 253–90; A.S. Herschberg, in: *Ha-Tekufah*, 12 (1920/21), 129–48; 13 (1921/22), 189–210; I. Lévy, in: *Ha-Goren*, 9 (1922), 5–30; G. Rosen, *Juden und Phoenizier…* (1926); M. Guttmann, *Das Judentum und seine Umwelt*, 1 (1927), 43–97; S. Bialoblocki, *Die Beziehungen des Judentums zu Proselyten und Proselytentum* (1930); Z. Kasdai, *Ha-Mityahadim* (1930²); A.Z. Markus, *Le-Toledot Dat Nazerat* (1937, 1950²), pt. 1: *Gerin*; G. Alon, in: KS, 23 (1946/47), 37–42; A.M. Habermann, *Sefer Gezerot Ashkenaz ve-Zarefat* (1945), 186–90; S. Assaf, *Mekorot u-Mehkarim be-Toledot Yisrael* (1946), 143–54; I.A. Seligmann, in: EM, 2 (1954), 546–9; ET, 6 (1954), 21–32, 253–304, 426–49; A. Scheiber, in: KS, 30 (1954/55), 93–98; E.E. Urbach, *Ba'alei ha-Tosafot* (1955), 112, 180, 193f., 265, 388; J. Katz, *Exclusiveness and Tolerance* (1961, repr. 1969). **ADD. BIBLIOGRAPHY:** S.J.G. Cohen, *The Beginnings of Jewishness* (2001); G.G. Porton, *The Stranger Within Your Gates* (1994).

PROSKAUER, JOSEPH MEYER (1877–1971), U.S. lawyer and community leader. Proskauer, who was born in Mobile, Alabama, was a partner in the law firm Elkus, Gleason, and Proskauer from 1903 to 1923, then served as judge in the Appellate Division of the First Department of the Supreme Court of New York (1923–30). A close associate of Alfred E. Smith, whom he first met through his political activities for the Citizens Union in New York, Proskauer served with Belle *Moskowitz and Robert *Moses on the non-Tammany faction of the "War Board" which helped Smith plan his gubernatorial campaigns, and later worked closely with Smith in his 1928 presidential campaign. In 1935 Proskauer served on the New York City Charter Revision Commission.

Early in the Nazi regime, he joined the *American Jewish Committee. He became its president in 1943 on the platform "Statement of Views with Respect to the Present Situation in Jewish Life," prepared by him, Irving *Lehman, Samuel I. *Rosenman, and George Z. *Medalie, which proposed free Jewish immigration into Palestine and an international trusteeship status but opposed a Jewish state. From October 1947, however, the committee publicly supported creation of a Jewish state in the form proposed by the UN Special Commission on Palestine. Proskauer led it in the thrust for a Jewish state. Elected essentially as an anti-Zionist, his 1948 presidential address, "Our Duty as Americans – Our Responsibility as Jews," marked his complete commitment to political Zionism. The desire to find a common Jewish front on settlement of the Palestine question and the need for continued support from the U.S. Jewish community for the committee's primary interest in Jewish defense probably contributed to Proskauer's change of direction. In his *Segment of My Times* (1950), he describes his pre-1943 anti-Zionist stand as based on instinctive opposition to a state identified with a religion; once he began to study the problem as committee president, he found that the U.S. form of national allegiance he was committed to could not apply in Eastern Europe, where Jews were accorded only partial rights. He thus came to believe that a state in which they could be free was essential. Proskauer remained committee president until 1949. He had served as consultant to the U.S. delegation to the 1945 UN Conference in San Francisco. Proskauer returned to private law practice as senior member of Proskauer, Rose, Goetz, and Mendelsohn. He was chairman of the New York State Crime Commission in 1951–53 and also served as director of the National Refugee Service.

BIBLIOGRAPHY: S. Halperin, *Political World of American Zionism* (1961), index.

PROSKUROV (from 1954 **Khmelnitzki**), capital of the Khmelnitski district, Ukraine. Jews are mentioned in 1629;

they suffered at the hands of the Cossacks of Khmelnitski in 1648. In 1765 there were 750 Jews in the city who paid poll tax; by 1847 the number had risen to 3,107. After the town was linked by the railway, wholesale trade flourished, mainly in grain, timber, and textiles. Jews owned factories for sugar, bricks, roof tiles, ceramics, and tobacco. Toward the end of the 19th century, the Jewish population increased, reaching 11,411 (50% of the total population) in 1897. There were in town 18 *ḥadarim*, a *talmud torah*, a library, and a theater. After the February revolution some 24 Jews (out of 50 members) served on the local council. In Februrary 1919, as Semosenko's Ukrainian troops retreated before the Red Army, they committed in Proskurov one of the most vicious pogroms of the civil war period. On February 15 Semosenko's forces marched into the city, methodically killing every Jew they could find. A local priest who begged the soldiers to stop was killed at the door of his own church. Three and a half hours after the soldiers had entered the city, a telegraphed order came from headquarters, calling a halt to the slaughter, but by then 1,600 people had been murdered and thousands wounded. Despite the demands made by representatives of the Jewish community to the *Petlyura government, Semosenko was never punished. There were 13,408 Jews (42% of the population) in Proskurov in 1926. Yiddish was used in documents issued by the municipality and by the court of law. A Jewish school existed at this time. In 1939 the Jews numbered 14,518 (39% of the total population). The Germans occupied Proskurov on July 7, 1941, and by the end of August they had killed 800 Jews. Jews from the environs were brought into a labor camp in the town. In August 1942 8,000 were murdered, and on November 30, 1942, another 7,000 were killed. About 18,000 Jews were murdered in Proskurov. The 1959 census recorded 6,200 Jews (10% of the total population). In 1970 there was no synagogue but kosher poultry was available. In the 1990s most Jews left for Israel and the West.

BIBLIOGRAPHY: *The Pogroms in the Ukraine* (1927), 58–61, 176–95; E. Tcherikower, *Di Ukrainer Pogromen in Yor 1919* (1965), 118–60; B. West, *Be-Ḥevlei Kelayah* (1963), 124.

[Yehuda Slutsky]

PROSODY, HEBREW. This article is a survey of the history of Hebrew poetic forms from the Bible to the present time. The entry is arranged according to the following outline:

INTRODUCTION

Hebrew poetry throughout the ages has used many forms of verse, rhyme, sound patterns, and strophic structure which changed from period to period, often from country to country, and from genre to genre. Since the close of the Bible, an enormous number of Hebrew poems have been written in Palestine and throughout the Diaspora, most of them following strict forms which were often quite complex and elaborate. To date no history of these forms has been published and while for the major periods some central concepts are known, they are usually framed in normative terms. The following survey should therefore be considered merely as a tentative outline.

The term "form," used here in a limited sense, refers to all poetic patterns which employ sound elements for the organization of the language material of a poem, such as rhyme, acrostic, meter, stanza, and other principles of composition. The term "poem" here refers to any text composed in such forms and does not necessarily imply aesthetic values in a modern sense. In the Middle Ages thousands of Hebrew texts, written as liturgy, chronicles, rhymed letters, dedications, etc., used the same formal norms employed in works which could be classified from a modern or aesthetic point of view as "poetic."

Of the few ancient literatures that have continued uninterruptedly throughout the ages, Hebrew poetry is the most variegated and versatile in its forms, due to its permanent creativity and to its interaction with different systems of language and poetry: Arabic, Italian, German, Russian, Yiddish, English, and others. The pronunciation of Hebrew as well as the norms of writing have undergone considerable changes during the wanderings of the centers of this literature. On the other hand, there were strong tendencies of continuity and conservatism in Hebrew forms and poetic genres, as well as in the language itself.

Unlike other languages, Hebrew, as a semi-"dead" tongue, has never changed the core of its vocabulary, or the written form of its words, its basic morphology, certain patterns of syntax and of idiomatic formulations, or the fundamental framework of its historical, semantic, and mythological allusions. Hebrew poems separated by a time span of a thousand years are from the point of view of their language comparable, and may be intelligible to the same reader. The major changes in the language (insofar as this survey) occurred in the field of pronunciation, but even these did not alter the basic form of the written word. However, due to its interaction with a variety of foreign prosodic and aesthetic norms, most known systems of verse have been created in Hebrew over the past 2,000 years.

The Variety of Formal Systems

The following prosodic systems are found in Hebrew poetry: (1) a purely *accentual* poetry with a free variation of the verse units (primarily in the Bible); (2) a meter based on a regular *number of accents* (in post-biblical poetry); (3) a meter based on the *number of words* (in the major tradition of liturgy); (4) a *quantitative* meter based on the opposition of short and long syllables (especially in medieval Spain and Italy); (5) a *syllabic* meter (in Italy since the Renaissance and in Central and Eastern Europe in the 19th century); (6) an *accentual-syllabic* system (in modern poetry in Eastern Europe, Israel, and the U.S.); (7) an *accentual meter with restricted syllabic freedom*, influenced by the verse of Russian modernism (in Israeli poetry since World War I); (8) a variety of *free verse* forms, based largely on a rhythm of phrase groups (which evolved in Europe in the 1920s during the vogue of Expressionism and in Israel since the 1950s under the impact of English imagism).

The earliest known systematic use of rhyme in poetry was invented in Hebrew sometime between the fourth and the sixth centuries C.E. It grew out of a cluster of principles of repetition, based on semantic, morphological, and sound elements. During its long history, Hebrew verse passed through a gamut of rhyme norms: terminal or accentual, continuous or discontinuous, grammatical or sound-autonomous, based on suffixes or on the lexical morpheme, using word repetition or excluding it. The same kind of variety runs through the rhyme patterns, strophic forms, and through the principles of composition of a poem.

The Specific Nature of Hebrew Literary History

A study of the changes in the forms of Hebrew verse should take into account the peculiar nature of its history. A Hebrew poet, regardless of his time, was at the crossroads of three lines of development. (1) There was the historical factor common to all literatures: the tension between synchrony and diachrony, i.e., trends of the poet's generation as juxtaposed to norms of the immediate past as well as classical works. The other two factors are specific to the geographic and sociological situation of the Hebrew writer: (2) the influence of Hebrew poetry written in other countries; (3) the impact of non-Hebrew poetry of his own time and place.

The tension between the three systems, of which the Hebrew poet was aware, was of primary importance to the history of Hebrew poetic forms. Quite often cardinal differences existed between the three. Thus, the 13th-century Hebrew poets in Rome wrote in the strophic forms of Byzantine Ereẓ Israel (canonized long before any Italian language existed) in which words rather than syllables were counted and in which each rhyme had multiple members but did not alternate with other rhymes. But they were confronted with two other poetic systems as well: Contemporary Italian poets used stanzas with alternating rhymes and syllabic meters; the Hebrew poets in Spain used a purely quantitative versification mostly without any strophic forms. It took time until Hebrew poets in Italy changed their poetic system and, typically enough, they adapted quantitative meters (developed in Spain in genres of Hebrew secular poetry) to write Hebrew strophic poetry in the Italian sonnet form. Similar dilemmas faced Jewish poets in other generations and countries.

A Jewish poet was closer to each of the three traditions than poets usually are when experiencing influences of a foreign literature. Thus, the impact of Hebrew poetry written in other countries was enhanced by the closeness of the language and the mobility of men of letters and of written and printed texts. The influence of aesthetic norms dominant in other languages was particularly strong, in spite of traditional Hebrew conservatism, because most Hebrew poets did not speak primarily Hebrew, but were intimately acquainted with other languages which they read and used in everyday life. In many cases they knew at least one more Jewish language and one or two foreign languages, e.g., Arabic and Spanish (in Christian Spain), or Yiddish and Italian (in 16th-century Venice), or Yiddish and Russian (in 19th-century Eastern Europe), or Yiddish, Russian, and English (in America since the late 19th century). Shifts in the forms of Hebrew poetry, whether gradual or drastic, were wrought by such factors as the influence of literary authorities, changes in the relationship to another culture, or changes in the system of genres of Hebrew writing itself. Such changes were usually accompanied by a sudden leap from one way of writing to another, brought about by a realization of a potential influence from one of the three above-mentioned directions.

The influences, however, were implemented neither automatically nor immediately. There was a strong awareness of the peculiar Hebrew tradition, and there usually was neither eclecticism nor chaos of forms. Forms created under the influence of one culture were transposed by Hebrew poetry into the domain of quite a different foreign culture; e.g., (1) quantitative meters, developed in Spain under Arabic influence, were used for centuries in Christian Europe where no such meters had been employed; (2) syllabic versification, developed in Italy, dominated 19th-century Hebrew poetry in Germany and Russia where such meters were no longer used. Even adaptations of poetic elements and themes from other literatures were not automatically introduced in their original forms.

Moreover, there was not necessarily an acceptance of a whole system of forms from the influencing source, but quite often a reconciliation, or a readjustment, of several traditions. Thus, (1) *Immanuel (b. Solomon) of Rome combined the form of the Italian sonnet with the Hebrew-Spanish quantitative meter which was of Arabic origin; (2) Italian strophic forms were used for several centuries with their original rhyme patterns but without the requirement of stress accord, which is compulsory in Italian rhyme.

Foreign influences on Hebrew poetry were not necessarily contemporaneous, e.g., while accentual-syllabic versification was introduced into Hebrew under Russian influence, it occurred only toward the end of the 19th century when this metrical system began to fall into disuse in Russian poetry. These influences should also not be considered as organic transplantations or imitations of a literary trend or poetic school. Belated as such an impact may have been, it was not necessarily accepted in all its aspects. Thus, Judah Leib *Gordon, though influenced by his Russian contemporary Nekrasov as to theme, genre, and even tone of language, did not accept the Russian verse system; the poetry of Abraham *Shlonsky of the 1920s and 1930s was strongly influenced by the imagery of Russian futurism, but in meter it was as classical as the verse of Pushkin. On the other hand, many Hebrew poets were very much aware of the relativity of prosodic systems. They knew how to use diverse, and sometimes even opposing, systems for different genres (such as religious and secular poetry) or for different languages (especially in the case of bilingual poets, such as Elijah Baḥur *Levita and J.L. *Gordon). Despite these complex circumstances and the great body of rhymed and versified Hebrew texts, the varying norms of Hebrew poetry can be described exactly, since in most ages these norms were conventional rather than individual and constituted a firm part of the language of Hebrew verse. The history of these forms epitomizes the worldwide scope of Hebrew poetry; the tensions between tradition and openness which were basic to its evolution; and the symbiotic, but autonomous, nature of Hebrew culture throughout the ages.

The Major Periods of Hebrew Prosody

The peculiar nature of Jewish history does not permit the development of Hebrew poetic forms to be divided into pure historical "periods," but rather into "areas," determined by a combination of historical, geographic, and generic factors. Since the close of the Bible, the following major areas of Hebrew poetic traditions may be distinguished:

(1) POST-BIBLICAL POETRY. This is a rather amorphous area consisting of several distinct trends: *Wisdom poetry (*Ben Sira), the poetry of religious sects, the formulation of the basic prayers, and the beginnings of liturgy. A variety of rhythmic formulae, occasional rhyme, patterns of sound, and parallelism were widely used, but no established formal system of any kind can be discerned.

(2) THE RHYMED PIYYUT. Created in Byzantine Ereẓ Israel sometime between the fourth and the sixth centuries C.E., the rhymed *piyyut* comprehends some clearly defined poetic genres which have specific functions in Jewish liturgy. Fundamental to it are large poetic cycles of a complex structure in which the poems use strophic patterns and obligatory rhyme. This kind of *piyyut* spread to the East (Babylonia and Egypt) and to Italy and Ashkenaz (the German Rhine area).

A vigorous strain in this tradition, which used the difficult "Kallirian" rhyme, flourished in the 10th century and determined the formation of the Italian and Ashkenazi *maḥzor. The rhythm crystallized in this evolution was based on a strict number of words.

(3) THE SPANISH TRADITION. It is based on quantitative meters (under Arabic influence), which were used mainly in secular poetry but also in religious genres. Developed in Islamic Spain since the 10th century, it flourished in Christian Spain and Provence until the 15th century and dominated Hebrew poetry in Italy and throughout the Islamic East almost until the present time. Besides the long metrical poems which use one single rhyme, a peculiar strophic tradition evolved in Spain ("girdle" poems), as well as a major genre of rhymed prose (*maqāmat*).

(4) ITALY. Created from the 9th to the 20th century, Hebrew poetry in Italy passed through all possible stages of Hebrew poetic forms: several periods of forms stemming from the Palestinian *piyyut*; Italian strophic patterns; Spanish quantitative meters, which in time were transformed into Italian-like syllabic verse; and even onsets of accentual-syllabic iambs.

(5) THE AREA OF ASHKENAZI JEWRY. Hebrew poetry was written throughout the Middle Ages by Ashkenazi Jews, at first in Germany and France, then in the Slavic countries. The Palestinian-Italian tradition formed its early stages (10th to 12th centuries). A "weaker" line descending from the Palestinian *piyyut*, followed and continued until modern times, especially in several shorter genres (notably the *selihah and the *kinah). The forms of this tradition influenced other genres too, such as the Hebrew verse chronicle and some Yiddish poems.

(6) THE EAST. Babylonia, North Africa, and other countries under Islamic rule passed easily from the old *piyyut* forms to the Spanish tradition (similar to Arabic forms). In the 16th century, however, the influence of Turkish song forms may be discerned in the writings of Hebrew poets in the Ottoman Empire (including Ereẓ Israel itself).

(7) HASKALAH. Toward the end of the 18th century in Central and Eastern Europe purely syllabic versification was introduced. It continued to be the medium of Hebrew verse until the end of the 19th century.

(8) THE PERIOD OF "REVIVAL." Since the early 1890s Hebrew poetry in Russia, using the Ashkenazi pronunciation, accepted accentual-syllabic meters and became receptive to all forms of modern European poetry. The system spread immediately from its Russian center to all countries of Hebrew creativity: Germany, Ereẓ Israel, the U.S., etc.

(9) "CLASSICAL" VERSE IN ISRAEL. Accentual-syllabic meters, transferred to the Israeli (basically "Sephardi") pronunciation, appeared at the beginning of the 20th century, but started to dominate Hebrew poetry only since the late 1920s. The system spread from its center in Israel to other countries where Hebrew literature was being written (Poland, U.S.S.R., U.S.).

(10) FREE VERSE. There are two varieties: (1) the Russian influenced strophic and rhymed free verse which is close to regular meters (the so-called Russian Dolnik); (2) free irregular verse beginning with some poems by H.N. Bialik (written in period 8), developed in Europe in the 1920s and in Israel and the U.S. especially since the 1950s.

These forms followed both foreign examples (English, German) and Hebrew antecedents (notably some of the so-called biblical verse of the Period of "Revival").

Approaching the present day, the periods become shorter; different forms, traditions, and influences become more intermingled, frequently coexisting in time, in place, often in one literary journal, and even in the writings of one poet.

SOME PRINCIPLES OF BIBLICAL VERSE

The forms of biblical poetry constitute a world of their own, at the same time however, a discussion of post-biblical verse must consider the Bible which had an overpowering influence on Hebrew poetry of all periods. The language of the Bible has dominated the language of Hebrew poetry, more often than it did prose, in a variety of poetic conceptions, at least since *Saadiah Gaon (10th century) and almost to the present. Despite this fact, however, post-biblical Hebrew poetry has not relied on biblical rhythm and verse forms. With few exceptions, post-biblical Hebrew prosody at every stage of its development was based on highly formal conventions, and it could not have been satisfied with the fluid, though rich orchestration of biblical verse. Nevertheless the patterns of biblical poetry, its syntactic-rhythmical tendencies, its typical word groups, its alliterations, loomed large behind the language of the Hebrew poets in subsequent generations. These patterns did not prevail or mold the new forms, but embellished and imbued Hebrew poems with the power of internal rhythm. The strength of the biblical example was not merely in its sanctified status, but in the very "weakness" of "impurity" which its rhythm had from any normative or classicistic point of view: the intimate, almost inseparable relationship between the semantic, syntactic, and accentual aspects of its rhymic patterns of language.

Though including writings which range nearly over a millennium, the Bible has been viewed by later ages as primarily a unified work with basically a common language. Whatever may have been the developments in phonetics and prosody during the time of its creation, the Bible for post-biblical readers was the canonized text with its system of stresses, intonation marks, and vocalization. In this survey of post-biblical poetry the major principles of biblical verse, as seen from the point of view of a reader of later times, shall merely be mentioned and illustrated.

Parallelism

The foremost principle dominating biblical poetry is parallelism. Usually two versets (sometimes three or even four) are parallel to each other in one or several aspects. The parallelism may be either complete or partial; either of the verset as a whole or of each word in it; of words in the same order or reversed. It may be a parallelism of semantic, syntactic, prosodic, morphological, or sound elements, or of a combination of such elements. In most cases there is an overlapping of several such heterogeneous parallelisms with a mutual reinforcement so that no single element – meaning, syntax, or stress – may be considered as completely dominant or as purely concomitant. The parts of the parallelism may be equal or unequal in their size or form; they may be related to each other in a variety of ways: synonymous, antithetic, hierarchic, belonging to a category of some kind, etc. The principles of the parallelism used may change from verse to verse. The basis of this type of rhythm may be described as semantic-syntactic-accentual. It is basically a free rhythm, i.e., a rhythm based on a cluster of changing principles. Its freedom, however, is clearly confined within the limits of its poetics. The following is an example of a rather ordered type:

הַאֲזִינוּ הַשָּׁמַיִם וַאֲדַבֵּרָה   וְתִשְׁמַע הָאָרֶץ אִמְרֵי־פִי.
יַעֲרֹף כַּמָּטָר לִקְחִי   תִּזַּל כַּטַּל אִמְרָתִי,
כִּשְׂעִירִם עֲלֵי־דֶשֶׁא   וְכִרְבִיבִים עֲלֵי־עֵשֶׂב.

Give ear, o, ye heavens, and I will speak;
And hear, O earth, the words of my mouth.
My doctrine shall drop as the rain,
My speech shall distil as the dew,
As the small rain upon the tender herb,
And as the showers upon the grass
(Deut. 32: 1–4).

There are 3:3 stresses in the first two pairs of versets, and 2:2 stresses in the last pair. But syntactically the last two pairs are linked. The words הַאֲזִינוּ ("give ear"), and וְתִשְׁמַע ("hear") are synonymous in meaning though not in morphology; "I will speak" and "the words of my mouth" are not synonyms, but their meanings are parallel. "Heavens" and "earth" are parallel by opposition. "Rain" and "dew" both express fruition by water, but one is strong and the other is subtle, these are two poles of one scale. There is also a concatenation of the three parts: versets 3 and 4 unfold the theme of the first pair ("the words of my mouth"); versets 5 and 6 develop the images of 3 and 4. But the versets of the last pair are parallel only to one member of the previous pair ("the rain" or "the dew").

The parallelism of meaning in the last four versets is chiastic: the water is strong (3) – weak (4) – weak (5) – strong (6). In the last pair דֶשֶׁא and עֵשֶׂב are on one level, but שְׂעִירִים and רְבִיבִים, though morphologically alike, are quite different in degree. Some additional devices of rhythm and sound reinforce the effect of this passage.

Rhythm

If the equivalent meaning or syntactic pattern of parallel versets draws the reader's attention to the parallelism and its reinforcing quality, it is the rhythmical structure proper which embodies it. The major rhythmic element is stress. The rhythm is accentual, but the number of stresses in each verset is not necessarily fixed or permanent. There may be an exact repetition: 3:3 stresses, or a freer relationship: 3:4, as well as changing numbers throughout the poem. The specific numerical relationship is however important. The numbers are quite often equal or similar. Moreover, whenever there is freedom it is confined within fixed boundaries. Each verset is usually a phrase, a basic syntactic and logical unit, consisting of 2, 3, or 4 stressed words. The smallness and compactness of the verset lends each stress conspicuous force. The condensed, laconic nature of biblical Hebrew also contributes to the prominence of each word within the line, the more so when it is reinforced by the parallel verset. The versets are static, independent units, well balanced against each other. This is supported by the nature of biblical syntax which favors parataxis to the subordination of clauses and phrases.

Is stress the only sound element determining biblical rhythm? For many generations scholars have argued over the "secrets" of biblical prosody; there have been attempts to correct or rewrite the text so that it might conform with pseudo-classic ideas of rhythm which require strict numbers of some kind: regularized "feet," equalized hemistichs, or stanzas of recurring numbers of lines. Such attempts seem pointless today since no exact regularity of any kind has been found and since rhythm need not be based on strict numerical regularity. Considering the rhythm to be based on free variation, it is clear, however, that stress is not enough to describe the effects of biblical rhythm. The number of unstressed syllables between two stressed ones, though not fixed in the sense of modern accentual-syllabic versification, is certainly limited: By rule no two stresses are permitted to follow each other, on the other hand long words have secondary stresses. Thus, each stress dominates a group of 2, 3, or 4 syllables; there are 2, 3, or 4 such groups in a verset, and 2, 3, or 4 parallel versets in a sentence. It is a three-stage hierarchy of simple, indivisible, though flexible groups. Within this free framework there are clearly functional specific patterns, such as the so-called rhythm of elegy based on an opposition of 3:2 stresses. The rhythm of major stresses is so strong that sometimes it may be the only supporter of the parallelism of two versets, without any actual repetition of meaning or syntax.

Sound

Within this framework of rhythmical parallelism there is a whole gamut of sound repetition and sound patterns, freely distributed, but clearly embellishing the text. Whatever the origins of Hebrew rhyme and puns or sound patterns in later poetry, the later poets were able to draw on a variety of such devices in the Bible. There is (1) simple alliteration: (2) ;הוֹד וְהָדָר, חֵן וָחֶסֶד a chain of one repeated sound: צַדִּיק מִצָּרָה נֶחֱלָץ; (Prov. 11:8); (3) a repetition of the same root which is syntactically justified: אָחוּדָה־נָּא לָכֶם חִידָה ("I will riddle you a riddle," Jud. 14:12), חוּדָה חִידָתְךָ וְנִשְׁמָעֶנָּה ("riddle your riddle and we will hear," *ibid.* 14:13); (4) puns on similar sounding roots: אַל תַּחֲרוֹשׁ עַל רֵעֲךָ רָעָה (Prov. 3:29); (5) אִשָּׁה – אֵשׁ – אִישׁ; פַּחַד – פַּחַת פָּח; root rhyming בָּבֶל – בָּלַל

(cf. Gen. 11:9), צְדָקָה־צְעָקָה (cf. Isa. 5:7); (6) occasional rhymes in modern sense שְׁלְחָנָהּ – יֵינָהּ (cf. Prov. 9:4), צֶמַח־קֶמַח (cf. Hos. 8:9), etc.

Rhyme is sometimes obviously linked to the parallel structure, e.g.,

פֶּן־תִּתֵּן לַאֲחֵרִים הוֹדֶךָ/ וּשְׁנוֹתֶךָ לְאַכְזָרִי
פֶּן־יִשְׂבְּעוּ זָרִים כֹּחֶךָ/ וַעֲצָבֶיךָ בְּבֵית־נָכְרִי

Lest thou give thy vigor unto others,
And thy years unto the cruel;
Lest strangers be filled with thy strength,
And thy labors be in the house of an alien.
(Prov. 5:9–10).

The two sentences are similar in rhythm (3:2 stresses) and are linked by an anaphora, as well as by parallel syntax, meaning, morphology, and rhyme. Though the symmetry is pervasive and multiple, it is however neither regular nor permanent: the first versets of each line are parallel in meaning as a whole but not in each word; אחרים ("others") and זרים ("strangers") are parallel in morphology and rhyme but not in their syntactical function; וּשְׁנוֹתֶךָ ("thy years") and וַעֲצָבֶיךָ ("thy labors") are not parallel in the same sense as אחרים ("others") and זרים ("strangers"); אכזרי ("the cruel") and בית־נכרי ("the house of an alien") are not synonymous in the language but become so when enforced by this context. In the same way all parallel words rhyme with each other, except for the second word.

This is an extreme example of order; usually the patterns are less symmetrical and the sentence that follows may not have any of the above devices. Rhyme, as it is known at present, i.e., as a regular organizing principle of a poem which is not an internal ornament of a line but links lines together, was created as concomitant to an unequivocal strophic structure and a formalization of poetic patterns. This occurred centuries later in the Palestinian *piyyut* of *Yannai and Eleazar *Kallir.

THE CLASSICAL PIYYUT

Piyyut (from *paytan* (poet) from the Greek Ποιητής) is the common term applied to a variety of genres of Hebrew liturgical poetry which originated in Ereẓ Israel under Byzantine rule. Some scholars distinguish between *piyyut* and *seliḥah* (a penitential prayer), including under the former all kinds of hymns and under the latter several types of elegies, supplicating or exhortative religious poems. For the purposes of this survey it is convenient to include the entire range of Hebrew religious poetry of the Middle Ages under the general term *piyyut*. The chronological division of the earlier periods of the *piyyut* from a formal point of view is as follows: (1) the so-called beginnings of the *piyyut*, primarily in Ereẓ Israel and in Babylonia from the close of the Bible until the creation of the formal rhymed *piyyut*; (2) the formal period, employing formalized, strophic, and rhymed poems patterned in highly complex *piyyut* cycles, apparently originating in their complete form in Byzantine Ereẓ Israel somewhere between the fourth and sixth centuries C.E. Only the latter will be discussed here.

The Formal Period

Various forms of rhythm, sound patterns, sporadic rhyme, acrostic, and strophic patterns have been developed in biblical literature and during the first centuries of the *piyyut*. But only by an act of formalization were the new complex structures created. Even if it were possible to trace every single device of the formal *piyyut* to earlier examples, there is no precedent to any of the complex structures as a whole. Rhyme, refrain, stanza, etc., whatever had been sporadic, was now formalized and organized in complex cycles of poems, governed by strict rules which set the formal conventions of all poems belonging to a given genre.

In the same way as the period is characterized by the introduction of unequivocal rules of formal structure, differences in genres are marked by differences in form. Moreover, some diversities between poets, or successive generations, or local traditions are marked by minor or major changes both in the complex structures, as well as in the use of particular devices or genres of the *piyyut*.

The large variety of genres, formal differences, and historical changes in these structures does not permit a complete, even schematic, description here. Since the complex structures are determined by the genre, it is preferable to describe the formal structure together with the thematic aspect of each genre, its liturgical function and the particular way of its inclusion in the basic text of the prayer book. The difficulty of such a detailed description is underlined by the present limited knowledge of the history of the *piyyut*. While there are many scattered studies and insights, there is no detailed up-to-date historical description of the whole field. The objective circumstances were a contributing factor to this state of scholarship: tens of thousands of poems and fragments, found in the Cairo *Genizah*, are in the process of being deciphered. These poems, written over many centuries, are by and large undated, often fragmentized or written in a cryptic language, and are either anonymous or only have the first name of the poet who in most cases is unknown from other historical sources. On the other hand a considerable number of *piyyutim* were known for centuries because they were included in the prayer book. More and more of them have been published in recent years. Below only the principles of some basic patterns employed in the complex structures will be outlined and only schematic examples of major formal principles will be given.

The Structure of One Cycle

The widespread forms of the older formal *piyyut*, especially the **kerovah* with its varieties and the **yoẓer*, are cycles of a complex nature, e.g., a *kerovah* by Yannai is a superstructure of nine parts with a permanent set of rules for each. Yannai wrote hundreds of *kerovot* – a different cycle for each week of the triennial cycle of the Torah reading. The structure of each of these poems is governed to the smallest detail by one set of rules. Other poets wrote cycles of poems for the Sabbath, the festivals, and often several different sets of poems for the same purpose, apparently written for the services of different years or different synagogues.

Yannai's *kerovot* are mostly of the *kedushta* type. The *kedushta* is a poetic cycle incorporated in the prayer in which the *Kedushah* is recited. The *kedushta* has a fixed theme for every week based on the weekly biblical portion. The theme and its language are integrated into the poems of the cycle. It consists of the following parts:

(1) A poem to the first benediction of the *Amidah* composed of 3 stanzas of 4 versets each. Every stanza has a separate fourfold end rhyme, linking all its versets. Every verset begins with a separate letter following the order of the Hebrew alphabet; the poem is thus linked by an unfinished acrostic from the letters א to ל. The concluding verset alludes to the first sentence of the weekly portion which follows and introduces a series of biblical sentences in their original form, having neither rhyme nor meter. The biblical passage gives, as it were, authoritative support to the content of the poem. This chain of biblical sentences is linked to a closing stanza of 3 or 4 versets, with the last word of the chain of sentences repeated at the beginning of the closing stanza. The last verset of this stanza is again linked to what follows, alluding to the *Magen Avot* benediction (the second) recited after this poem.

(2) A poem to the second benediction which is similar in its strophic structure to the first poem. It continues the interrupted acrostic (from the letter מ to ת) and uses the last two letters twice in order to fit the 22-letter Hebrew alphabet into a framework of a series of four-verset stanzas (altogether 24 versets). This poem too is linked to the weekly portion with the final verset alluding to its second sentence. A chain of explanatory sentences also lead toward a closing stanza in which the final verset anticipates the following benediction, *Meḥayyeh ha-Metim*.

(3) A short poem of 4 stanzas, each starts with a letter which is part of an acrostic of the poet's name ינאי. Every stanza consists of 4 short cola of 2 or 3 words each, rhymed either with a fourfold rhyme or with a twofold rhyme. The poem ends with an allusion to the first word of the *haftarah* which follows, together with an explanatory passage.

(4) A poem of a rather free structure, having no fixed rules for its rhyming though usually consisting of 3 fourfold stanzas. Concluding the first part of the *piyyut*, the poem is marked by the obligatory use of the final word – *Kadosh*.

(5) A poem traditionally called *asiriyyah* because it is composed of 10 stanzas which are linked by an acrostic of the first 10 letters of the Hebrew alphabet. The stanzas are rhymed couplets having quite often a large variety of internal rhymes.

(6) A poem consisting of 11 stanzas, each using a separate fourfold rhyme. Every couple of versets is linked to a complete alphabetical acrostic. The poem introduces a group of poems and is preceded by the biblical statement which it discusses. Frequently, the biblical statement or parts of it are interwoven into the poem either as beginnings of the first lines of the poem or of its stanzas.

(7) This part consists of 1 to 3 pattern poems (*rehitim*), each of which has an individual structure, usually of a complex form, which permeates the text in every detail. Variegated and individual in their composition, they follow a fixed set of rules (described below). Only in this category is the poet allowed to use strictly organized poems without rhyme.

(8) The *silluk*, a kind of free verse poem that introduces the *kedushah*. It has a free structure which varies from *kerovah* to *kerovah* and is richly rhymed in an unrestricted manner. In the poetry of Yannai's follower (or disciple), Eleazar Kallir, the *silluk* developed into a very long, exuberant, richly orchestrated, yet unrestricted poem. Yannai's *silluk*, however, is rather short.

(9) The *Kedushah*; it has neither rhyme, nor strophic structure. In the period of Yannai there was no fixed version as yet, and the poet was free to formulate his *Kedushah* in every cycle anew. It was based on an exegesis and elaboration of the formula *Kadosh, Kadosh, Kadosh* (*Holy, Holy, Holy*).

The above is a simplified account of a poetic cycle, as described by M. *Zulay. It is impossible to delineate here in detail the forms of other cycles, their liturgical functions, and their development throughout the ages. Each cycle is determined by a combination of certain thematic, verbal, and formal elements. Though the intricate rules for each cycle changed from genre to genre, there was no free combination in each new creation: The basic forms used in these compositions were quite restricted. Some of these basic forms are discussed below:

Forms of Composition

Within a given cycle the form and length of each poem was restricted, depending on its place in the cycle, its use of acrostic, and its strophic form. The following strophic forms existed in the *piyyut*:

(1) AN UNDIVIDED POEM. One single end-rhyme runs throughout the poem (*ḥaruz mavri'aḥ*). At the beginnings of the lines there is a compulsory acrostic which covers the whole Hebrew alphabet, each letter is repeated one or several times; the number of versets being either 22, 44, or 88.

(2) REGULAR STROPHIC STRUCTURE. Each poem is composed of a number of stanzas of a permanent form and length. Every stanza has its own independent rhyme both differing from and not interfering with members of other rhymes: *aaaa bbbb cccc*, etc. The length of stanzas may vary from 2 to 10 versets. A stanza of 4 versets became the major form of the *seliḥah*, especially in the variety created throughout the ages in Ashkenazi Europe. The multiple (fourfold or eightfold) repetition of each rhyme and the lack of rhyme alternation in the rhyming *piyyut* create an effect quite distinct from standard European strophic poetry which uses its rhymes in alternation.

Stanzas may have an additional internal structure and may be molded by means additional to rhyme, primarily meter, acrostic, and the refrain. Thus, in Kallir's *kerovah* to the *Musaf* prayer of the Day of Atonement (in the Ashkenazi prayer book), one of the poem *Essa De'i le-Meraḥok* is based on a stanza of 9 versets. The following is one stanza of the poem:

יְשַׁלְּגוּ אָדְמֵי שָׁנִים/ שֶׁל כָּל־יְמוֹת הַשָּׁנִים/ חֲדָשִׁים וְגַם יְשָׁנִים
יַלְבִּינוּ כִּתְמֵי שׁוֹשַׁנִּים/ וְיוֹשִׁבוּ לְתַעֲרָם שְׁנוּנִים/ בִּפְלוּל אֲשֶׁר מְשַׁנְּנִים
רַחֲצוּ וְהִזַּכּוּ מֵעִשּׁוּנִים/ לְאִוֶּלֶת מִהְיוֹת שׁוֹנִים/ וְעַל מִבְטָחֵימוֹ שְׁעוּנִים

Each verset has 3 words, 3 versets form a line, each line begins with a letter from the acrostic (in this case it is the end of the poet's name קליר, the י repeated twice), 3 lines form a stanza by means of the particular rhyme which is repeated 9 times.

This particular poem belongs to the *kiklar* (from the Greek κύςκλο, cycle) genre, in which there is a refrain-like shorter stanza of 3 versets after each regular stanza. There are 3 different refrains in the above poem, alternating between the 7 regular stanzas. In the following general scheme of the poem each verset of the regular stanzas shall be represented by letters from *a* to *g*, according to the rhyme patterns; the refrains by letters *p* to *r*; capital letters represent versets linked by an acrostic:

Aaa	Ddd	Ggg
Aaa	Ddd	Ggg
Aaa	Ddd	Ggg
ppp	ppp	ppp
Bbb	Eee	
Bbb	Eee	
Bbb	Eee	
qqq	qqq	
Ccc	Fff	
Ccc	Fff	
Ccc	Fff	
rrr	rrr	

The poem is organized, as it were, both vertically and horizontally. The triadic principle is dominant throughout: 3 words make a verset, 3 versets a line, 3 lines a stanza, 3 stanzas complete a refrain cycle. The third refrain cycle is, however, not completed since there are 7 stanzas.

(3) PATTERN POEMS. An unusual kind of formal poem – the pattern poem – was developed in the *piyyut*, especially by Yannai. A pattern of a line elaborated in all its details – syntactic, semantic, morphological, and sound devices – was established in the poem and was then repeated throughout its 22 lines (the number being determined by the acrostic). A great variety of such patterns appear in Yannai's poetry, all in the seventh part of the *kerovah* cycle. The following is an example of a very simple kind:

If you loved who would hate? אִם אָהַבְתָּה מִי יַשְׂנִיא
If you blessed who would curse? אִם בֵּירַכְתָּה מִי יָאֳרֹר
If you fenced who would break out? אִם גִּדַּרְתָּה מִי יִפְרוֹץ
If you joined who would separate? אִם דִּבַּקְתָּה מִי יַפְרִיד

Every line is a rhetorical pattern with two fixed and two free words. The initial letter of the first free word depends on the place of the word in the alphabetically arranged poem; this word is a verb in the second person past, and its meaning has a positive connotation. The second free word is opposite in meaning, it has a strongly negative connotation, and is a verb in the third person future.

There are more complex patterns, such as this:

תּוֹלְדוֹת אָהוּב וְשָׂנאוּי אָהוּב (ל...) חס וְשָׂנאוּי לְמַאֵס
תּוֹלְדוֹת בָּחוּר וּבָזוּי בַּחוּר לְסֶגֶל וּבָזוּי לְסֶגֶר
תּוֹלְדוֹת גְּדִי וְנָמֵר גְּדִי לְרִצּוּי וְנָמֵר לְנִיצּוּי

The story of a loved one and a hated one/
loved for respect and hated for neglect
The story of a chosen one and despised one/
chosen for virtue and despised for rejection
The story of a lamb and a tiger/
a lamb for pleasing and a tiger for strife

Every line consists of two parts, of 3 and 4 words, respectively. The first part refers to a story of two personae: one positive, the other negative. The second part elaborates on the first, repeating the two personae and modifying the description of each. The first word is permanent, creating an anaphoric chain ("the story of…"); the second word is positive in meaning and is strung on an acrostic; the third word is either a direct or indirect opposite of the second. The other hemistich repeats words (2) and (3) and qualifies them, explaining the reason for the opposition: In what perspective are the personae to be cast. The modifiers do not provide a full explanation, but allude to a biblical text. Both modifiers – words (5) and (7) – are introduced by a preposition of purpose (-ל) and are linked to each other by some kind of rhyme, though the rhyming principle changes throughout the poem. It may be:

a terminal sound rhyme רִצּוּי – נִיצּוּי
or an initial rhyme עזוז – לעזאזל, סגל – סגר
or a semantic rhyme זכות – חובה, חיים מות

Since the morphology of most words of the pattern is fixed, in all cases where suffixes are used the rhyme is inevitable, e.g.,

וירא אהובים ויאמל ואבה לאררם
וירא באים ויבעת וביקש לבלעם
וירא גרים ויגר וגמר לגרשם

The meaning of the pattern is "He saw ("positive personae") and he was frightened (or shocked, or worried, etc.) and he wished (or planned, or hurried, etc.) to curse them (or swallow them, or uproot them, etc.)." All four changing words are linked to the acrostic, the second and the fifth, using plural suffixes, create each a chain of rhymes. In the rhyming chain of the second words there are, however, two exceptions: המון, רבבה – words which designate plurality but do not have the grammatical plural form. Indeed, rhyme is concomitant to grammatical parallelism but is not an absolute necessity. It is possibly the only structured poem in a Yannai cycle which may have no rhyme, if rhyme does not appear with the grammatical form. In most cases there is rhyme, but of a peculiar variety; a morphological rhyme based on a suffix.

The form of the pattern poem is derived from biblical parallelism, but two new principles were applied: (a) the symmetry of two versets was turned into a chain of synonymous sentences; (b) there was a rigorous formalization of the pattern, and all deviations are excluded.

(4) FREE STROPHIC FORMS. These are of two kinds: (a) the unrhymed *piyyut*, an exceptional form, fulfilling strict liturgical functions and employing phrases of a formulaic nature; (b) the rhymed free poem, especially the *silluk*, developed by Kallir into a long chain of rhymed versets, with changing rhymes and shifting rhyme principles and without any strophic structure or measure of length. Each rhyme usually has many members (e.g., 25 LAKH+20 MU+18 ŠEV+13 MEM, etc. – in Kallir's *silluk* to *Parashat Zakhor*). Besides sound rhyme there may be in the rhyming position semantic rhymes (names of rivers or of time periods), word repetition, words of one root, etc.

Rhyme

THE ORIGINS OF RHYME IN EUROPEAN POETRY. Rhyme, the great innovation of the *piyyut*, had impact on the history of world poetry. Since not many *piyyutim* were known before the recent studies of the *Genizah* (where over 50,000 liturgical poems were discovered), and also since the external circumstances of the *piyyut* were obscure and its language almost puzzling, it was not until recently that scholars have become aware of this original contribution of Hebrew poetry. All its aspects, however, have not yet been fully explored.

It is clear by now that rhyme grew out of the internal development of Hebrew poetry and became in Hebrew a permanent, even obligatory, feature of poetry earlier than in any other language. It is assumed that the principle of rhyme was then transferred to the poetry of the Syriac Church, written in Aramaic (a language closely related to Hebrew, spoken *inter alia* by Jews and written in the same area; i.e., in the Middle East) and through this mediation introduced into Latin poetry and then into all other languages of Europe.

THE MAJOR NORM: THE DISCONTINUOUS RHYME. Not one, but several kinds of rhyme existed in the *piyyut*, each associated with different strophic forms. The most important was the rhyme of the strophic poems. The basic norm of this rhyme is unknown in the poetry of other languages. Each rhyme of a strophic *piyyut* had to meet two requirements: (1) parallelism of all the sounds of the last syllable, beginning with the consonant preceding the last vowel; (2) parallelism of two consonants belonging to the root of each rhyming word, e.g., in Eleazar Kallir's stanza quoted above (from the *piyyut Essa De'i le-Meraḥok*), the rhyming words are: ŠaNIM – ha-ŠaNIM – ye-ŠaNIM – Šo-ŠaNIM – ŠenuNIM – mešaneNIM – meiŠuNIM – So-ŠaNIM – ŠenuNIM – mešaneNIM – meiŠuNIM – Šo-NIM – ŠeuNIM. For the sake of identification capital letters represent the rhyme (all the sounds repeated in all members of one rhyme).

The rhymeme in this system is both terminal and discontinuous. The principle of terminality implies that the rhymeme covers the final syllable of each rhyming member whereas in European or in modem Hebrew poetry its basis is the stressed syllable rather than the final one. In most cases in Hebrew, though, the two overlap, but in instances of discrepancy, stress in the rhyme of the *piyyut* is disregarded. The principle of discontinuity of the rhymeme is unique in rhyming systems and is based on the nature of the Hebrew lexical morpheme, which is discontinuous, consisting merely of consonants. Thus, the changes of vowels in such Hebrew words as Ša-Var – Še-Ve-R – Šo-Ve-R cause morphological differences only (Š+V+R is a root meaning "break," the vowels in the example creating: past, noun, present), whereas in English the differences between, e.g., "lever – liver – lover" are lexical.

Though rhyme may have had, as one of its sources the puns on words of one root, rhyme became an autonomous pattern, independent of grammar or word repetition. The discontinuous rhyme is merely similar in structure to the Hebrew root, but is not necessarily based on words of one root. In the above case the rhyme is S+NIM. Between the discontinuous sounds of the rhymeme there appeared changing vowels and even consonants, though usually consonants of the kinds found in the rhymeme (as in our case).

Thus, rhyme was based on sound parallelism of the roots of words as well as of their endings. Since a Hebrew root can have no more than three sounding consonants, only one (at most) is given to variation. In stanzas with many rhyme members, it is extremely difficult to find enough words which may meet such requirements, especially when the rhyming words are at short distances from each other. Such rhyming was possible in the *piyyut* due to the difficult "Kallirian" style which allowed, on the one hand, for an almost unlimited number of neologisms and, on the other hand, was abundant in allusions and ellipses which permitted the bringing together of words from quite distant semantic areas.

There are in this system five major forms of rhyme, dependent upon the morphological structure of the rhyming words:

(1) if the final syllable is open (e.g., LA), an additional preceding consonant was necessary, e.g., in Kallir's rhyme: GoLA – Geula – beGiLA – niGLA – GiLA – veeGLA – aGuLA – meGiLA – veGoLA (the rhymeme is G + La); (2) if the final syllable is closed (e.g., NIM) and one consonant belongs to a suffix, a root consonant has to be preceded as in the above case with plural endings: ŠaNIM – haŠaNIM – ŠenuNIM, etc. The rhymeme is Š+NIM; (3 and 4) if the final syllable has no root consonants, two discontinuous root consonants are added, e.g., צוּרֵינוּ – נַעֲצָרְנוּ – יוֹצְרֵינוּ – מְצָרָתֵינוּ – ẒuReNU – naaẒReNU – yoẒReNU – ẒaRateNU (the rhymeme is Ẓ+R+NU). The same holds for a suffix in a closed syllable (e.g., M+R+HEM); (5) if the final syllable is closed and includes no suffix, then it meets in itself both requirements. There is no discontinuity, but the difficulty in finding or inventing rhyme words remains, e.g.,

the famous stanza which served as a symbol of Kallir's unintelligible (or even cacophonous) style:

אץ קוצץ בן־קוצץ / קצוצי לקצץ / בדבור מפוצץ /
רצוצי לרצץ / לץ בבוא ללוצץ /
פלץ ונתלוצץ / כעץ מחצצים לחצץ / כנץ על צפור לנצץ.

Due to the neologisms, allusions, and the elliptic syntax, this passage is almost unintelligible without a commentary. On the other hand, the richness of rhyme and sound effects is obvious.

Using the symbols N – the norm; R – a root consonant; C – a morphological consonant; V – a vowel; + – a possible discontinuity in the sound string, the above five forms of the Kallirian rhyme may be summarized as follows:

$N_1 = R+RV$
$N_2 = R+RVC$
$N_3 = R+R+CV$
$N_4 = R+R+CVC$
$N_5 = RVR$

A typical case of discontinuous rhyme can be found in the *Hoshanot* read on the first and second days of Sukkot where the poet rhymes 22 times שׁ + עִי (in the poem אֶעֱרוֹךְ שַׁוְעִי) or 22 times שׁ + עוֹת (in the poem אֵל לְמוֹשָׁעוֹת מוֹשָׁעוֹת – שְׁבוּעוֹת – בְּשַׁוְעוֹת שׁוּעוֹת – שַׁעְשְׁעוֹת, etc.

In Yannai's poetry, repetitions of four equivalent or similar words are often found in rhyme (such as פָּנִים – פָּנִים לְפָנִים – לִיפְנִים). A repeated word obviously meets both requirements of the rhyme norm. But Yannai's pupil Kallir excluded word repetition as a substitute for a strophic rhyme, thus enforcing his difficult norm. Word repetitions remained a device of rhyming, but in a distinct kind of rhyme chain.

LANGUAGE AND RHYME. The rhyme norm described above was primarily based on sound. Sound was not identical with letter or with the later canonized vocalization. For the sake of rhyme the *qameš* (ָ) and the *pattaḥ* (ַ) were equivalent (*a*); also the *ṣere* (ֵ) and *segol* (ֶ) (*e*). The letters א, ה, ח, ע lost their consonantal qualities and in the rhyme of the *piyyut* they are interchangeable and may be either disregarded or counted as consonants. Kallir rhymes אֱלוֹהַּ – לִשְׁלוֹחַ, טְמֵאָה – קְמְעָה, etc., ב and ו seem to be equivalent מַחֲשָׁבָה – שָׁוָה, אֵבָה – גַּאֲוָה, etc. On the other hand, however, consonants with or without a *dageš* rhyme freely with each other, thus פּ פ, e.g., נֶפֶשׁ – טְפֵשׁ and בּ ב, e.g., מַרְבֵּץ – רוֹבֵץ – מַשְׁבֵּץ – קוֹבֵץ. The equivalence of בּ ב, according to the graphic principle, and that of ב ו, according to the sound principle, established a new equivalence for the sake of rhyme: בּ וְ, e.g., Kallir rhymes דְּבָרִים – שְׁוָרִים – גִּבּוֹרִים or רְבִיד – מַעֲבִיד – לְהַאֲבִיד – הִרְבִּיד – דָּוִד.

This tradition of equivalents for the sake of rhyme was carried with the *piyyut* into Italy and Franco-Germany. Thus, *Meshullam b. Kalonymus of the 10th century (born in Italy, lived in Mainz) rhymes freely הִרְבָּה – רָוָה – מְרִיבָה; בִּבְּן, etc.; Rabbi *Meir b. Baruch of Rothenberg in the 13th century rhymes: טְבוּעִים – מַצְבִּיעִים – מְשׁוּעִים , etc.

THE HISTORY OF KALLIRIAN RHYME. The forms of "Kallirian" *piyyut* spread throughout the Diaspora to the East and to the West. In the East they were superseded in the 10th and 11th centuries by the forms of Arabic versification, especially as adapted by the Hebrew poetry of Spain. In Italy and Franco-Germany they dominated the basic form of the *maḥzor* and do so to the present day. With time, the difficult rhyme norm was simplified: poets dropped the requirement to include two root consonants; rhyme was based on a repetition of the final syllables and became *terminal*, i.e., the standard Hebrew rhyme of the Middle Ages. The process of simplification apparently originated in Ereẓ Israel. (Thus, in the ninth century the Palestinian-influenced *piyyut* of southern Italy was based on final syllables only.) But the "strong" norm prevailed again in the 10th century in Babylonia, Italy, and Franco-Germany to be dropped finally toward the end of the 11th century.

OTHER KINDS OF RHYME. In Yannai's poetry the discontinuous rhyme of the strophic poem is not the only rhyme form. All aspects of the Hebrew word were employed in one form or another for the sake of rhyme: the root, the suffix, the meaning, the sound. In pattern poems it is obvious: not only the final sounds of the parallel words are repeated, but also their meaning and morphological structure. In this genre, however, rhymes, as other kinds of repetition, are tied: they serve the composition of the poem not independently but as a whole cluster. For the later development the untied free rhyme is of primary interest.

The following kinds of rhyme may be discerned: (1) *Sound Rhyme*, a rhyme based on parallelism of sounds especially in the discontinuous terminal form described above. (2) *Morphological Rhyme*. This rhyme is based on a suffix. It appears sporadically in the Bible and was used several times at considerable length in the Dead Sea Scrolls and in Ben Sira. It became a legitimate variety of rhyme in non-strophic *piyyutim*, especially in the pattern poems. (3) *Semantic Rhyme*. The relations of the rhyming members are in parallelism of meaning rather than in sound: זמר – רנן אכילה – שתיה, etc. Even in a strophic poem, in a chain of sound rhymes, Yannai writes suddenly: סוס – סוס – חמור – חמור rhyming horse with donkey! (4) *Root Rhyme*. Found in the rhyming of words of one root, they do not necessarily have similar sound endings, e.g., גָּאָה – גָּאֶה – גַּאֲוָה – גֵּאִים or תּוּצְדַּק – יִצְדַּק – צַדִּיק – צֶדֶק. Semantic rhyme and root rhyme are used only occasionally, especially in free strophic forms, such as the *silluk*, or as an additional device within the line. They are of particular interest for the understanding of the origins of sound rhyme which grew in an environment of repetition of any possible aspect of the language. (5) *Word Rhyme*. This rhyme is based on the repetition of one word, usually a key word (life, death, night, war, etc.), throughout a poem. It is older than systematic rhyme and is often employed in *piyyutim* – either in poems of 22 lines or in free strophic patterns.

A distinct kind of *piyyut* uses a word rhyme together with sound rhymes in one single rhyme chain of a long poem, such as Kallir's rhyme of the word טל ("dew") (in his "prayer for dew" "תפלת טל"), repeated endlessly and interwoven with words ending with same sounds: טלטל, נטל, etc.

Rhythm

Biblical rhythm was accentual but with free variation of the numbers of stresses in parallel versets. It seems that later developments led in two directions:

(1) The rhythm as found in the poetry of Ben Sira where there are usually 2 versets to a line, with 4 metrical stresses being the optimal limit of a verset. A 4-stress pattern is achieved if long words are seen as having two metrical stresses (in a way quite similar to our reading of iambs in modern Hebrew poetry), e.g.,

אחרי תאותיך אל תלך   ומחמדותיך המנע
אם תעשה רצון נפשך   תשיגך שמחת שונא

This was apparently a tradition of a poetry which sensed an inherent semi-regular meter, approaching syllabic regularity. (The syllabic principle is said to be underlying Syriac poetry of the early Christian centuries.)

(2) The tradition of early liturgical poetry which was based on the number of major stresses. Here, too, 4 stresses were a common optimal frame, but these were major stresses, each dominating a word or a group of words. Thus, *Yose b. Yose, in his famous *Avodah le-Yom Kippur* has regular stanzas of 4 lines each (determined by a fourfold repetition of each letter in the alphabetical acrostic). Each line consists of two versets (or hemistichs), each verset having 4 major stresses:

אתה כוננת עולם ברוב-חסד / ובו יתנהג עד קץ הימים,
אשר לא ימוט מעון יצורים / ולא ימעד מכבד פשעים וחטאים

In Ben Sira there are often two stresses on one long word; in Yose b. Yose two smaller words are linked by one stress. The number of stresses is similar, but the interpretation of the rhythm in the language is quite different.

Yannai usually has no regular rhythm, except for pattern poems in which the number of words is fixed by the pattern. Neither is there any syllabic regularity, similar to the one which is supposed to govern Syriac meters, discernible. But in Kallir's poetry there are already *piyyutim* (beyond the pattern poems) which have a fixed meter, based on the number of words, such as the meter of the *kiklar* analyzed above. In Italy, this meter became obligatory from the ninth century. While this meter may have grown out of earlier stress regularity, it was now strictly based on the graphic division of words, requiring a permanent number of words in each verset. It became the dominant form of the Ashkenazi *piyyut* in the Middle Ages. Some genres had norms peculiar to them, e.g., the *seliḥah* was usually written in Italy and in Franco-Germany in 5-word lines and 4-line rhymed stanzas.

MEDIEVAL HEBREW POETRY IN SPAIN

Hebrew poetry entered a new era with its emergence in Islamic Spain, in the 10th century. The Arabic rules of versification were adopted by the Hebrew verse; quantitative meter became the dominant system in Hebrew poetry in Spain from its beginnings, through the "Golden Age," until the destruction of Jewish life in Spain at the end of the 15th century. Due to the authority and the achievements of Hebrew culture and poetry in Spain, its poetic language and metrical system spread to other countries. It dominated Hebrew poetry throughout the Islamic world – Egypt, Babylonia, Yemen, North Africa, the Ottoman Empire – until recent times. It ruled Hebrew poetry in Provence, spread throughout Europe, and reigned in Italy until the 19th century.

Hebrew literature in the East in the first centuries of Arabic rule, though flourishing in the very heart of Islamic culture and strongly influenced by Arabic science and literature, shows no trace of having come under the sway of the forms of Arabic poetry. *Saadiah Gaon of Babylonia (10th century), a distinguished philosopher and linguist in Arabic, followed the norms of the pre-Islamic *piyyut* in his Hebrew poetry. He used the strophic structure of the *piyyut* in fourfold or manifold rhymes which change from stanza to stanza and there was no trace of any syllable-counting meter. However, Saadiah Gaon's pupil, *Dunash b. Labrat, a native of Fez, who was educated in Baghdad and went to Cordoba, Spain, introduced there in the middle of the 10th century the Arabic quantitative metrical system into Hebrew poetry. Ben Labrat's innovation, which became the subject of a fierce polemic, was seen as violating the nature and grammar of the Hebrew language. But even Ben Labrat's opponents used quantitative meters in their caustic polemical poems against this very same system. Arguments against quantitative metrics, raised time and again, especially emphasized the biblical tradition and the accentual nature of the Hebrew language. The opponents themselves, however, notably *Judah Halevi, seldom strayed from this metrical system in their secular poetry.

Kinds of Verse

Hebrew literature in Spain was written in a variety of genres, secular as well as liturgical. Generic properties included theme, forms of composition, attitude of the speaker, use of language. But hardly any thematic genre had its own peculiar meter or rhyme scheme. On the other hand, there was a strong distinction between several kinds of literature, based on principles of meter, rhyme, and strophic structure. The following major types may be discerned: (1) Non-strophic poems using one single rhyme throughout, linking all the lines of the poem. In this type quantitative meter in one of the classical regular forms was obligatory (used in most of Spanish Hebrew poetry, especially secular poetry). (2) Strophic poetry of the type of the "girdle" poem, employing a quantitative metrical pattern which may be irregular in itself but permanent throughout the poem. (3) Poems with a plain syllabic meter, primarily in strophic forms. (4) Strophic poetry in "free" verse, i.e., without syllable counting, used primarily in liturgical genres. (5) Rhymed prose, used primarily in genres of Oriental storytelling.

The Hebrew Quantitative Meter

A quantitative meter is based on a regular pattern of short and long (rather than stressed and unstressed) syllables. Hebrew quantitative meters though derived from Arabic versification were quite different from their prototypes as well as from Greek quantitative patterns. This was basically due to the different properties of the Hebrew language.

Traditional descriptions of Hebrew verse in Spain did not distinguish between problems of diachrony and synchrony. The derivation of a particular meter from this or that Arabic prototype seemed to be more relevant than the assessment of its place in the synchronic system of Hebrew verse. The existing classification of medieval Hebrew meters, basically unchanged for the past 800 years, relies on medieval Arabic cataloguing. One finds usually long taxonomic lists of patterns rather than structural rules to explain the nature of the Hebrew quantitative meters.

Twelve of the 16 basic meters codified in the theories of classical Arabic versification were adopted by Hebrew poets (the other being impossible to imitate in Hebrew). With their many derivations, the number of particular regular meters runs into several dozens (Yellin's list has 67), whereas the irregular patterns of the "girdle" poems may account for several hundred forms. No explanation is usually given as to why no other meters existed.

The traditionally identified meters will not be enumerated here but rather an attempt will be made to explain the basic rules and tendencies. One reason for the large number of metrical types is that each is used as a label for a pattern of a whole line which has not been analyzed into its distinctive features. Three such features should be considered: (a) the basic metrical units, or recurring groups of syllables ("feet"); (b) the number and order of such groups (i.e., the length of the line); (c) the form of the final group – whether complete, short, or changed (cf., in accentual-syllabic poetry an analytical term such as "iambic pentameter" – one word signifies the basic foot, the other the length of the line, whereas the nature of the end of the line is described in terms of rhyme gender: "feminine" or "masculine"). Thus, the difference between the two traditionally distinct meters *ha-merubbeh* (/ ◡ – – – / ◡ – – – / ◡ – – /) and *ha-marnin* (◡ – – – / ◡ – – –) (◡ stands for a short syllable, – for a long, the direction of the symbols here is from left to right) is one of length of line only; whereas for a parallel difference between (– ◡ – – / – ◡ – – / – ◡ – –) and (– ◡ – – / – ◡ – –) only one term (*ha-kalu'a* a' and b') has been used. While a difference in the length of a line may be an important rhythmic factor, it should not justify the use of unanalyzed terms.

THE BASIS OF HEBREW QUANTITATIVE METERS. The Hebrew poets in Spain did not resort to the distinction between short and long vowels of the biblical vocalization. Only the mobile *šewa*, the *ḥataf*, and the conjunction ו (when pronounced *u*) were considered short vowels. All full vowels were considered long, e.g., in Ibn *Gabirol's poem (from right to left; short syllables are unmarked):

מְלִיצָתִי בְדאָגָתִי הֲדוּפָה, / וְשִׂמְחָתִי בְאַנְחָתִי דְחוּפָה

In comparison with Arabic or Greek quantitative meters, the number of short syllables in Hebrew is conspicuously small. Moreover, whereas in Greek verse a long (i.e., a strong) syllable constitutes the distinguishing element of a foot, in Hebrew it is a short (i.e., a weaker) element. It is hard to conceive how such a weaker element could provide a rhythmic basis for a foot. Indeed, there was a different way of describing this kind of meter, through use of another kind of contrast, namely that of cord (C = –) (*tenu'ah*, i.e., vowel) and peg (P = / ◡ – /) (*yated*). A short followed by a long was called a peg. (In traditional Hebrew grammar a peg is considered one syllable.) All other syllables are cords. The above quoted line from Ibn *Gabirol can be rewritten (from left to right): PCC PCC PC/PCC PCC PC, the basic foot consisting of one peg and two cords (rather than one short and 3 longs). Besides the rhythmic factor considered above, this system of description is justified because in Hebrew there is practically no short "syllable" which is not followed by a long one, i.e., a short is not an independent unit (even though modern pronunciation may create such an illusion). Except for experimental poems, there are no meters of pegs only. Thus, a quantitative meter may be described as based on a regulated opposition of pegs and cords.

The basic group of syllables recurring several times in a line is called a foot. A foot may consist of either 2 or 3 syllables. The basic feet are:

Number of Syllables	Place of the Peg
Binary:	PC (initial)
	CP (final)
	CC (neutral)
Ternary:	PCC (initial)
	CPC (medial)
	CCP (final)

No foot has more than one peg. (In some meters there may be a substitute of 2 pegs: PP, but not as a regular recurring unit.) In Hebrew, as opposed to Arabic, there was a meter without pegs, the so-called *mishkal ha-tenu'ot* (meter of cords) of 8 long syllables, but it retained the quantitative opposition, since the text avoids all pegs in the language (i.e., all the mobile *šewa'im* and the like). No ternary foot without pegs may constitute a regular metrical scheme (though CCC may occur as a substitute within a meter with pegs).

The verse form of classical poetry is a distich (*bayit*) consisting of 2 lines identical or differing slightly at the end: the first line is called *délet*, the second *soger*. At the end of the *soger* there is a rhyme member linking it to the whole poem, which has one rhyme with a long chain of members, connecting the ends of the distichs as a string. A poem often consists of several dozens of distichs repeating again and again the same rhyme, with the typical effect of emphasis and monotony. In the first distich usually both lines are rhymed.

Any meter in this system is based on the principle of rhythmic impulses of recurring groups of pegs and cords, combined with a tendency to repeat each group at least twice, but an exact repetition of the same group more than twice in each line is avoided in most meters. The variations are codified within the metrical pattern of a line. This pattern, however, is in all its details permanent throughout the poem.

In each line the basic foot is repeated several times, but the last foot may be incomplete. The feet of a line may be of one kind only (as in the accentual-syllabic system of modern poetry), or of two kinds, unknown in modern poetry. If the first two feet are identical, the meter is *regular*; if they are different, the meter is *variegated*.

The length of a line is not as varied as in Hebrew or European poetry of modern times. There is a strong interrelation between the nature of the feet and their number. The rules governing the length of a line are the following: (a) if one of the first two feet is binary, there are 4 feet in a line; (b) if both first feet are ternary, there are 2 or 3 feet in a line, and the third may be either complete, shortened, or changed.

The last foot of a line can be described separately; if it is the third foot, it is either complete, shortened, changed, or avoided. But for this element, the length of a line can be seen as automatic. Indeed, there are 5 basic regular meters. These can be illustrated by using the list of all meters and variants which appear in J. Schirmann's famous anthology of Hebrew poetry in Spain and Provence (see following table).

REGULAR METERS

PC binary initial	PC·PC·PC·PC	המתקרב	*ha-mitkarev*
CC binary neutral	CC·CC·CC·CC	משקל התנועות	*mishkal ha-tenu'ot*
PCC ternary initial	PCC·PCC·PC	המרובה	*ha-merubbeh*
	PCC·PCC	המרנין	*ha-marnin*
CPC ternary medial	CPC·CPC·CP	הקלוע א'	*haa-kalu'a (a)*
	CPC·CPC	הקלוע ב'	*ha-kalu'a (b)*
CCP ternary final	CCP·CCP·CCP	השלם א'	*ha-shalem (a)*
	CCP·CCP·CC·P/C	השלם ב'	*ha-shalem (b)*
	CCP·CCP·CCC	השלם ג'	*ha-shalem (c)*
	CCP·CCP·CPC	השלם ז'	*ha-shalem (g)*
	CCP·CCP·CPCC	השלם ח'	*ha-shalem (h)*
	CCP·CCP·CP	המהיר א'	*ha-mahir (a)*
	CCP·CCP·CC	המהיר ב'	*ha-mahir (b)*
	CCP·CCP·C	השלם ד'	*ha-shalem*
	CCP·CCP -/C	השלם ה'	*ha-shalem*
	CCP·CCP·C	השלם ו'	*ha-shalem*

(The symbol P/C shows two differing endings of the two lines in a distich.) In spite of the different labels, all the variations are in the third foot and can be described separately. Binary meters have practically no variations (due to rule a) and there is practically no binary final meter. Only the rule of length (a) can explain why the meter of cords (binary neutral) uses 8 syllables. There is no regular ternary meter of cords. Moreover, the ternary medial meter is rare in Hebrew. No other regular meters are possible. In the ternary meters the third foot may be complete only if the peg is at the very end. But this weak position of the last peg calls for a great variety of substitutes.

VARIEGATED METERS. From the rules of length follows also the structure of the variegated meters of which there are two kinds:

(1) Alternating meters: if one of the first two feet is binary and one is ternary there are 4 feet in a line (according to rule a); the whole pattern is repeated twice (e.g., PC PCC PC PCC in the meter *ha-arokh*).

(2) Changing meters: if both first feet are ternary (and different) there cannot be 4 feet (according to rule b), i.e., there can be no repetition of the whole group within each line. In this case, if there is a third foot it either repeats the first or is changed (as the last foot of a line).

Alternating Meters. In alternating meters the following rules hold for the basic patterns: (1) there are 4 feet in a line; (2) the meter is based on a regular alternation between ternary and binary feet; (3) both kinds of feet are either initial or final; (4) in each hemistich, if there are 2 pegs they are removed from each other by only one cord. From rules (3) and (4) follows that there may be only 2 basic meters:

alternating initial PC PCC PC PCC הארוך *ha-arokh*
alternating final CCP CP CCP CP המתפשט *ha-mitpashet*

There can be no medial feet since there must be a common rhythmical denominator; if it is not the foot, it is its direction. Since each line has two symmetrical hemistichs, variations of the scheme may be accepted at the end of the line as well as in the second foot, e.g., the alternating falling meter has a variant PC CCC PC CCC (the meter of Dunash b. Labrat). The variants will not be listed here.

Changing Meters. If the first two feet are different but ternary, the whole group cannot be repeated twice. Only two ternary feet combine: the medial and the final. Hence the two basic metrical schemes are as follows:

medial and changing CPC CCP CPC הקל א' *ha-kal (a)*
final and changing CCP CPC הקטוע *ha-katu'a*

Variations occur in the third foot (the end of the line) and in the second (the end of the basic group). These meters are however rare and will not be enumerated here.

THE METERS USED IN HEBREW POETRY. All the basic meters practically used in Hebrew poetry may be summed up as in the following table.

Feet \ Meter	Regular		Variegated	
	binary	ternary	alternating	changing
Initial	PC	PCC	PC·PCC	–
Medial		CPC	–	CPC·CCP
Final	–	CCP	CCP·CP	CCP·CPC
Neutral	CC	–		

The structural symmetry is obvious. There are practically no meters beginning with a binary final foot; no medial foot in the alternating patterns, and no initial foot in the changing meters (rare exceptions may be found).

In actual poetry the situation is even simpler. Indeed, some poets liked experimenting. As Yellin has shown, *Samuel ha-Nagid used 57 different metrical schemes. The bulk of Hebrew poetry in Spain, however, employed only a small number of basic meters, with some variations, of which the most widespread are (in this order): initial and final ternary meters and the meter of cords. More precisely:

(1)	ternary initial, esp.	PCC PCC PC	הַמְּרֻבֶּה	*ha-merubbeh*
	but also	PCC PCC	הַמַּרְנִין	*ha-marnin*
(2)	ternary final, esp.	CCP CCP CC P/C	השלם ב'	*ha-shalem* (b)
	also	CCP CCP CC	המהיר ב'	*ha-mahir* (b)
(3)	cords (binary neutral)	CC CC CC CC	התנועות	*ha-tenu'ot*

These three groups, with a few variations, account for 94% of Moses *Ibn Ezra's meters in his secular poetry. The major meter, *ha-merubbeh*, found in about half of the Hebrew poems in Spain, later gave way to *ha-shalem* (b).

Following these three groups, though far behind, are the alternating meters, initial (PC PCC PC PCC – *ha-arokh*), and final (CCP CP CCP CP – *ha-mitpashet*). The preference of initial over final meters is due to the structure of the Hebrew word; the majority of vocal *šewa'im* are at the beginnings of words and a *šewa* may easily be added before a word with a preposition or conjunction (ב, כ, ל, ו). Medial or changing meters are quite rare.

The bulk of the poetry uses ternary meters, with 3 (incomplete) feet in a line. Since the length of the line is regulated, it varies only within narrow limits. There are only lines of 6 to 10 syllables. If the short syllables are also counted (as they were later, in Hebrew poetry in Italy), the limits are 8–14. Since in contemporary Israeli poetry about half of the *šewa'im* are considered syllables, those limits are comparable with 7 to 12 syllables today. If the special effect of the *ha-marnin*, which has the typical rhythm of a short line, is excluded, all other meters compare well with the variations given in modern poetry between 4 iambics and 4 anapests. Thus, the length of a line in Spanish Hebrew poetry as well as its rhythmic-syntactical form are similar to the length of typical lines in modern poetry. The optimal line has 8 to 9 long syllables (or 11, counting the short ones), which is similar to a line of 4 or 5 iambs.

VERSE ENDINGS. There are many variations of verse endings in the last foot of the basic metrical schemes. Any such variant creates a permanent pattern, repeated in all the lines of a poem. As opposed to modern poetry or to Greek and Arabic quantitative meters, Hebrew poets allowed very rarely for changes from line to line (feet-substitutes) or deviations from a given metrical scheme (i.e., changes occurring only in some lines, e.g., in Hebrew in the changing meter CPC CCP CPC the second foot may be substituted by PP). The variations in Hebrew in the third foot are felt not against the pattern of the poem but against the rhythmic impulse of the first 2 feet of the same line.

Variations of feet in verse endings are of several kinds: (1) the last foot is short (catalectic), PCC→PC, CPC→CP; CCP→CC; this change occurs almost only in ternary meters where it is the usual case (unless it is the last peg which is shortened, as in the final *ha-shalem*);

(2) hypercatalectic: CCP→C which is very rare; (3) a peg substituted by a cord: CCP→CCC; CP→CC, which occurs quite often since short syllables are scarce in Hebrew; (4) two cords are substituted by a peg, CCP→PP; PPC→PP; a rare variation, occurring in changing meters, especially in the second foot; (5) a peg is advanced, CCP→CPC (or: CP), e.g., in *ha-shalem* (g) CCP CCP CPC. The most widespread changes are a catalectic foot (1) or a substitute by a cord (3) (cf., instances in the list of regular ternary meters).

RHYTHM. The quantitative opposition provides the Hebrew poet with a metrical framework rather than with a pervasive rhythmic movement. The role of short syllables in the Hebrew language is much less than in Arabic. Thus, the two major meters in Arabic, *tawil* and *basīt* (equivalent to our alternating final and initial meters) are far from being major meters in Hebrew. Moreover, every possible substitution of longs for shorts is resorted to in Hebrew. Thus, the scheme of the Arabic *basīt* is (from left to right):

/ ◡ – ◡ – / ◡ ◡ – / ◡̄ – ◡ – / ◡̄ ◡ – /

its Hebrew derivation: / – - ◡ – / – ◡ – / -- ◡ – / – ◡ – /

CCP CP CCP CP

Instead of 8 shorts to 6 longs, the proportion became 4:9. A common variation of this meter has even less shorts:

/ C̄C̄ P̆ – / C̄C̄ / C̄C̄ P̆ – / C̄C̄ /

No two consecutive short syllables are possible in Hebrew, therefore some Arabic meters could not be reproduced. There is also the favorite Hebrew innovation: the meter of cords in which all short syllables are avoided.

On the other hand, in many Hebrew poems can be distinguished a strong tendency of regulating stress order and word boundaries. Although no permanent laws hold in this area, the tendencies are clearly felt, e.g., in the poem by Solomon ibn *Gabirol (short syllables are unmarked):

נחר / בקר אי גרוני / דבק לח / כי לשוני
היה לב בי סחרחר מרב כא בי ואוני

The formal division of the quantitative meter in this poem (*katua'*), though consistent, seems artificial. The language of the poem follows quite clearly a different pattern:

נֵחַר ׀ בִּקְרָאִי ׀ גְּרוֹנִי ׀ דְּבַק ׀ לְחִכִּי לְשׁוֹנִי

The accents are clearly regulated, and so are the word boundaries. Though it is not an absolute rule in this poem, in 85% of the cases there are word boundaries in marked places (whereas only 36% observe the formal foot boundaries of the meter). This kind of regularity in stress order and word boundaries is partly due to the correlation between the following factors: (1) short syllables cannot be stressed in Hebrew; (2) short syllables are most common at the beginning of a word, therefore, a boundary usually precedes them. It seems, however, that the major force behind this tendency is the subconscious rhythmical sense for stress order felt especially in the works of the great poets, Ibn Gabirol and Judah Halevi.

Relative regularity in stress order may be felt as a rhythmic substitute in meters without the peg/cord alternation. Thus, in the meter of cords there are lines which are clearly "iambic" in the modern sense:

כֻּתְנוֹת פַּסִּים לָבַשׁ הַגַּן ׀ וְכֻסּוֹת רִקְמָה מְדֵי דְשָׁאוֹ

Girdle Poems

Though the bulk of Hebrew poetry in Spain used regular meters and one rhyme running throughout the poem (with as many as 60 or 80 rhyming members – distichs), several kinds of strophic forms also flourished.

The *muwaššaḥ*, or "girdle" poem (שִׁיר אֵזוֹר, *shir ezor*), an original development of Arabic Andalusian poetry, was represented in Hebrew poetry almost from its beginnings (11th century) and was the form of some of the best Hebrew lyrical poems in the 12th century. Though originally used in love poetry, it was employed widely for religious poems. The girdle poem combines in its composition both the strophic principle of changing rhymes and the principle of the "running" rhyme, which runs through all parts of the poem in a refrain-like manner. There are two kinds of stanzas: (1) the changing stanzas with changing rhymes. Every stanza has one or several distinct rhymes, different from the rhymes of other stanzas;

(2) the girdle stanza, a strophic pattern recurring after every changing stanza, with the same rhyme or rhymes repeated in all girdle stanzas throughout the poem. A girdle stanza often appears at the beginning of the poem; it is the "guiding" stanza. In many poems the final girdle, the so-called *ḥarǧa*, is written not in Hebrew but in popular Arabic or in the old Romance language of Spain. Usually it is a quotation of a love conversation. The *ḥarǧa* thus determines the meter and rhyme of the girdle, as well as the melody (most girdle poems were apparently created as songs).

The meter of the changing stanzas and of the girdle may be identical, but often is not. Each line may consist of 1, 2, or 3 parts, rhymed or unrhymed. The metrical pattern may either be regular or highly irregular: Within the line there is a free combination of all kinds of feet, which seems often to be a kind of "free verse." But the same irregular pattern is repeated throughout the poem, in the stanzas of each kind

separately. The two metrical schemes are often related to each other, in a variety of ways, e.g., one may include a partial repetition of the other. A simple example, in Judah Halevi's song "בִּי הַצְּבִי בִּי אֲדֹנִי" (*"Bi ha-Ẓevi, Bi Adoni"*)

the meter of the changing stanza is   CCP CPC
and that of the girdle: CC CPC/CCP CPC

The stanza has a simple but irregular scheme. The metrical pattern of the girdle repeats the meter of the stanza in its second part, but the first part of the girdle is different (in this case a slight variation).

An example of a complex rhyme scheme can be found in a poem by Joseph ibn Jacob ibn *Ẓaddik (1075–1149), which begins with a guiding girdle,

נוּמִי, אֲהָהּ, נִגְזַל ׀ – בָּרַח, אֲהָהּ, גּוֹזָל ׀ מֵאָהֳלִי!
דִּמְעִי, אֲהָהּ, יִזַּל ׀ – עָפְרִי אֲהָהּ, אָזַל ׀ – מִי גוֹאֲלִי?

נוֹגֵן, שְׁלַח אֶצְבַּע ׀ לַעֲוֹת חֲלִילֶךְ ׀ טוֹב מַעֲנֶה!
אִלֵּם – אֲבָל יַבַּע ׀ צְחוֹת, כְּקוֹלֶךְ, ׀ כֵּן יַעֲנֶה.
שָׁלֹשׁ וְגַם אַרְבַּע ׀ עַל פִּי נְבָלֶיךָ ׀ בִּשְׂמֹאל מִנֶּה.

שִׁירִים נִצֹּר עַל דָּל ׀ – שָׂפָה, וְאַל יֶחְדַּל ׀ מִפִּי כְלִי־
שִׁיר – קוֹל, אֲשֶׁר יִגְדַּל עִתִּים, וְעֵת יִדַּל – לֹא מַחֲלִי!

The rhyme pattern is seen in the following table (capital letters represent the girdle rhymes):

PPR	abc	def	ghi	jkl	mno
PPR	abc	def	ghi	jkl	mno
	abc	def	ghi	jkl	mno
	PPR	PPR	PPR	PPR	PPR
	PPR	PPR	PPR	PPR	PPR

The principles of the girdle poem were widely used in Hebrew religious poetry, especially by the great poets *Judah Halevi and Abraham *Ibn Ezra.

Other Metrical Principles Used in Strophic Poems

In the genres of religious poetry the metrical principles varied: (1) the quantitative principle, using regular or irregular patterns of pegs and cords; (2) patterns using free numbers of cords where no pegs appeared; (3) syllabic meter where the opposition P/C was disregarded (i.e., the short syllables *šewa* and *ḥataf* appeared irregularly, but were not counted); (4) a free verse in the vein of older Hebrew liturgy, though usually tending toward a syllabic semi-regularity.

Rhymed Prose

The *maqāma* is a genre of rhymed prose, usually written as a chain of stories in the Oriental manner, and interwoven with anecdotes, fables, and metrical poems. Many books in this genre were written during the Middle Ages or translated and adapted from Arabic (notably by Judah b. Solomon *Al-Ḥarizi and *Immanuel of Rome). Usually the prose text of the *maqāma* rhymes throughout, though it has no meter. The number of members of each rhyme is not fixed; the distance between the rhyming members constantly changes and the sound patterns of such rhymes also vary, from a mere minimum to near-homonyms. On the other hand, the poems, which are frequently introduced into this rhymed prose, are clearly marked by their strict adherence to classical meters and rhyming.

A typical case of a different kind of rhymed prose is the religious philosophical poem "*Keter Malkhut*" by Ibn *Gabirol. Though rhyme and rhythm play an important role in this work, their use is neither permanent nor regular; it may be considered a kind of richly adorned free verse, changing its rhythmical tone from a densely rhymed sound-orchestration to mere prose employing parallelism.

Rhyme in Medieval Poetry

TERMINAL RHYME. Rhyme in Hebrew poetry in Spain, and throughout the Diaspora in the Middle Ages, was terminal. It disregarded stress or morphology. The rhymeme included all sounds from the consonant preceding the last vowel to the end of the line:

DO	נוּדוֹ	לְהַגִּידוֹ –	הוֹדוֹ –
DOT	חֲרָדוֹת	חִידוֹת –	חֲמוּדוֹת –
DOD	וּנְדוֹד	כִּידוֹד –	מְדוֹד –

The norm is N=CV (C). The number of sounds (2 or 3) depends on the language: whether the final syllable is open or closed. The principle was obviously derived from the rhyme of the Palestinian *piyyut*, after it dropped the requirement of including two root consonants in the rhymeme.

In order to make rhyming easier, the poets made wide use of rhymemes with open syllables or with suffixes (as in the first two of the above examples), thus having to change only one root consonant. This tendency was motivated by other principles of medieval poetics. Since there was no requirement for individuality in imagery or theme, the poets could widely use the Hebrew plural suffixes throughout their long poems. The same holds for possessive particles, such as ־ַיךְ (yours, when addressed to God) אַיִךְ (to Zion), etc.

The obligatory requirement that a consonant precede the final vowel, similar to the French *consonne d'appui*, was peculiar to medieval Hebrew poetry and was not required in other languages. It was, as it were, a compensation for the missing stress principle required in modern Hebrew poetry. A typical example is found in the following table:

Medieval Hebrew				Modern Hebrew	
	סוֹרֵג		מְדַלֵּג	סוֹרֵג – מְדַלֵּג	ÉG
REG		LEG			
	דֶּרֶג		שֶׁלֶג	שֶׁלֶג – פֶּלֶג	ÉLEG

In modern Hebrew ÉG is a perfectly sufficient rhymeme, in medieval poetry an additional preceding consonant had to be included in the rhyme. On the other hand, in penultimately stressed (feminine) rhymes in modern poetry the inclusion of one syllable is not enough. The principles changed, but the overall proportion between the vocabulary of the language and the rhyming patterns remained similar.

This relationship between modern and medieval Hebrew rhyme may be compared to the difference between English and French rhyme. Whereas in French *rime riche* (using *consonne d'appui*) was highly welcome, in English it was often excluded from rhyme. The situation is similar: French rhymemes are based practically on the last syllable, the words are longer, and an addition to the minimal rhymeme is welcome in order to avoid trite rhyming. Only in Hebrew, however, was the use of the *consonne d'appui* obligatory; hence it may be called the Hebrew terminal rhyme. Its peculiar impact was felt especially against the background of Italian, German, Yiddish, or Russian rhyme, where such enrichments were discouraged.

THE RULE OF MAXIMUM. If the final syllable was based on a suffix, the poets often strove to enrich the rhymeme, adding to it at least some part of the root. Though this was not a necessary rule (there appeared rhymemes of pure suffixes too), it was a strong tendency.

But rich rhyming was limited by unwritten rules:

(1) if the normally required final syllable (N) had two root consonants, no sound could be added to N; rhymemes such as מִיד, דוֹד, בָּל are both minimal and maximal;

(2) if the final syllable (N) included one root consonant, a preceding vowel could be added; thus, there are rhymemes, such as: לִי, כִּי, לִים, רִים; but also ־ָלִי, ־ָרִים, etc.;

(3) if the final syllable (N) included no root consonant, one root consonant could also be added; thus, besides rhymemes such as הֵם, נוּ, ־ַיךְ there are: ־ֵיהֶם, ־ֵינוּ and ,נֵינוּ לֵיהֶם, רַיִךְ.

"FEMININE" RHYME. Though stress was disregarded, in meter as well as in rhyme, a secondary tradition developed a "feminine" rhyme, which is based on penultimately stressed endings (which are a small minority in the language, but are represented in several suffixes and in word endings with ח ,ע (־ֵעַ, וֹעַ, ־ֵחַ, וּחַ).

Feminine rhyme became obligatory on one kind of meter composed of unequal hemistichs in which the final foot had a cord instead of a peg appearing in the first hemistich, e.g., the *ha-shalem* (b): CCP CCP CCP / CCP CCP CCC. The end presents a change in the regularity of the meter – where a P was expected a C appeared instead. As a compensation for this frustrated expectation, the poet used in this case feminine rhyme.

Feminine rhyme appeared occasionally in other meters too. But with the meter *ha-shalem* (b) it became prominent in Romance-speaking countries, especially in Italy, where feminine rhymes were the dominant rhyming form.

Elsewhere, i.e., in the majority of Hebrew medieval poems, stress was disregarded, words ultimately and penultimately stressed rhymed freely with each other.

The Dispersion of the Hebrew Terminal Rhyme

The Hebrew terminal rhyme originated in the Palestinian liturgy as an alleviated form of its "difficult" rhyme. It may be found both in Ereẓ Isael after Kallir and in ninth-century Byzantine in Southern Italy. It developed again, as a simplification of the "Kallirian" rhyme in 10th-century Babylonia (Saadiah Gaon) and in 11th-century Germany. It was strengthened by the comparison with the Arabic rhyming norm (basically requiring a consonant and the vowel following it) and later with European terminal rhyme which knew no discontinuous rhymeme.

This norm persisted in Hebrew throughout the world until the end of the 18th century, except for Italy, where stress was accepted in rhyme since the 17th century (but in Italy, too, no violation of the Hebrew norm could be found). The norm also remained obligatory throughout the Ashkenazi domain (Germany, Poland), though Hebrew had become a penultimately stressed language there. The penultimate stress caused a neutralization of all final vowels. Nevertheless rhyme remained exclusively in the final syllable. Thus, Meir b. Samuel of Sczebrzeszyn in his historical chronicle rhymes in 8-line stanzas words such as: פָּקִיד – נִפְקָד – עוֹקֵד, apparently pronounced: *pokəd-nifkəd-oykəd*. Though the original *i, o, ey* (or *i, a, e*) were blurred in an unstressed position, rhyme remained terminal: a repetition of final sounds. This Hebrew conservatism is even more astounding in bilingual poems, such as the *Megillat Vinẓ* (1616), with regularly alternating Hebrew and Yiddish stanzas. In the Yiddish stanzas all rhymes are stress-bound (feminine and masculine), according to the standard European norm; even Hebrew words follow this rule. But in the Hebrew stanzas the same Hebrew words disregard stress: terminal rhyme is preserved.

Only in some cases under the influence of foreign poetry did Hebrew rhyme relinquish the requirement of the *consonne d'appui* (in closed syllables only), rhyming N=VC. Such was the case in some of the girdle poems (patterned on rhymes in a foreign language), e.g., Judah Halevi rhymes: צַח – פַּח – נֶאֱנָח, (AḤ). The same holds for the bilingual Hebrew-Arabic strophic poems of the Yemenite classical poet Shalem *Shabazi and for the strophic songs the 16th-century kabbalist poet of Safed, Israel b. Moses *Najara, who was apparently influenced by Turkish songs.

HEBREW POETRY IN ITALY

The Jewish community in Italy was probably the oldest in Europe; though small in number, it was an important center throughout the Middle Ages. Located in a central position, between Israel, Yemen, and Babylonia in the East and Spain in the West, between North Africa in the South and Germany and France in the North, Italy was on the crossroads of the major cultural trends in Jewish history. Hebrew poetry in Italy, the first examples of which are from the ninth century, continued to flourish uninterrupted until the 20th century. The changes of poetic systems in Italy may be representative of the shifts in Hebrew prosody throughout the centuries. The major formal periods in Italy will be briefly listed below:

(1) The poetry of Byzantine Southern Italy in the ninth century consisted of strophic *piyyutim*, from 2 to 10 lines in a stanza, each stanza having one separate rhyme. The rhymes were simple (terminal norm). Usually an acrostic was required and sometimes a permanent refrain was used to close all stanzas of a poem. Contrary to the "Kallirian" *piyyut*, the early Italian *piyyut* required a compulsory meter, based on a constant number of words in a line.

Though strophic poems were known in Latin and in Greek-Byzantine poetry of the period, in these languages rhyme was not yet a required, regular, or permanent device. Only in Hebrew did rhyme serve as a criterion for strophic structure and was obligatory.

(2) In the 10th and beginning of the 11th centuries Italy accepted again the "difficult" "Kallirian" rhyme. It was, as it were, a "reversed evolution." But strict meters were required too. *Solomon b. Judah ha-Bavli and other poets of this period composed in this vein. Their followers who moved to the Rhine area introduced this norm into the Hebrew *piyyut* of Franco-Germany. These circles edited the *maḥzor* and apparently included in it only such rhymed strophic poems which were written by Kallir or followed his rhyming norm. A number of *yoẓerot* and a large number of *seliḥot* were created in this style.

(3) In the 11th and 12th centuries the norms of the ninth century were again revived: The *piyyut* used strophic poems with changing but separate rhymes, written in exact meters, based on the number of words. The simplification of rhyme was apparently due to a variety of factors, the foremost being (a) The influence of the Hebrew rhyme of Spain and Provence (though neither the pattern of one running rhyme nor the quantitative meter was accepted). The Spanish scholar and poet Abraham *Ibn Ezra propagated the simpler rhyme in Rome in the 11th century. (b) The decline of the difficult enigmatic style of Ha-Bavli, which occurred in Franco-Germany too. Without this style "Kallirian" rhyming was almost impossible.

In the 13th century Italian poetry in the vernacular emerged and flourished. Hebrew poets living in Rome could not have been unaware of the differences in the respective prosodic systems: (a) Hebrew strophic poems used changing but separate rhymes (*aaaa bbbb cccc*, etc.), whereas Italian rhymes were usually alternating (*abba; aba bcb*, etc.); (b) Hebrew meter was based on the number of words, Italian – on the number of syllables; (c) Hebrew rhyme was terminal but required a *consonne d'appui*: N=CV(C), whereas Italian rhyme was stressed, usually feminine: N=V́CV. Thus, Hebrew rhyme was based on one syllable, Italian on two. Hebrew leaned primarily on consonants, Italian on vowels. In these three respects Hebrew poetry in Italy adopted the Italian norms, but it was done over a period of centuries, primarily through the transformation of forms existent in some Hebrew tradition.

(4) Alternating rhyme was introduced into Roman Hebrew poetry in the 13th century. The major poet who initiated this change was Benjamin b. Abraham *Anav. But Benjamin Anav did not directly imitate Italian forms; he switched to alternating rhymes, meeting thus an Italian aesthetic norm by

adopting the patterns of the girdle poem which had been developed in Hebrew poetry in Spain and Provence. However the poets of this generation did not transfer the system of quantitative meters from Spain; only a semi-regular syllabic meter, as in many a strophic *piyyut* of Judah Halevi or Isaac *Ibn Ghayyat, was employed. Many such poems, both of Italian and Spanish origin, were by that time absorbed into the Italian *maḥzor.*

(5) *Immanuel of Rome (end of 13th–beginning of the 14th century) was the major Hebrew poet who shifted to the use of both quantitative syllabic meters as well as of Italian strophic forms, primarily the sonnet. In both techniques he had predecessors, but the major achievement was his. With him Hebrew poetry in Italy switched from liturgy to secular poetry. It seems that in order to find an equivalent for Italian poetic forms, Immanuel had to seek a language for secular poetry in Hebrew; this he found in the Spanish tradition, which he accepted with its rhymed prose (*maqāma*), quantitative meters, Oriental storytelling, and imagery. Suddenly Hebrew poetry discovered exact syllabic meters, required by the Italian aesthetic taste, in its own language and tradition. Though the distinction between long and short syllables, a vestige of Arabic influence, was apparently disregarded in the Italian Hebrew pronunciation, its patterns persisted until the 20th century: Isaac Ḥayyim (Vittorio) *Castiglioni wrote his poem on the death of Theodor Herzl in 1904 in a quantitative meter.

Moreover, Hebrew poets in Italy found in the Spanish tradition meters which fitted the lengths of line favored in Italian poetry. The major meter, especially in the sonnets, was the endecasyllabic line for which a Hebrew poet was able to use either *ha-merubbeh* or *ha-shalem* (b), counting both "long" and "short" as whole syllables. *Ha-shalem* (b): / – – ∪ – / – – ∪ – / – – – / became the major meter of Hebrew poetry in Italy, due to its compulsory feminine rhyme which fitted both Hebrew-Spanish and Italian taste. Immanuel accepted it for his sonnets, breaking each distich into two lines, with a rhyme for each; lines with an even number of syllables had a masculine rhyme, and those with uneven numbers – a feminine rhyme.

But Immanuel introduced stressed rhyme and alternating rhyming only for his Italian strophic forms. In other parts of his book he completely accepted the Spanish Hebrew tradition, employed widely the running rhyme, rhymed prose, disregarded stress, etc. His was a combination of two systems with a common denominator: the quantitative metrical system.

(6) After Immanuel of Rome, Hebrew poetry adopted a variety of other Italian strophic forms (besides the sonnet which became the most popular), the ottava rima, Dante's *terza rima*, the *sestina*, the *canzonetta*, and some others. Nevertheless, strophic forms of the *piyyut* on the one hand and the Spanish running rhyme on the other lived on for centuries:

(7) Despite the domination of the quantitative meter, a new syllabic meter evolved. Its first major poet was Moses b. Isaac *Rieti (beginning of the 15th century) called "Il Dante Ebreo" for his book *Mikdash Me'at* written in the form of Dante's *terza rima*. Rieti understood that Hebrew had to rhyme primarily in the ultimately stressed form (masculine rhymes) and accordingly reduced his line to 10 syllables.

Whereas previous Italian attempts at syllabic meters (13th century) disregarded short syllables altogether, according to their Spanish prototypes, Rieti counted short syllables as completely equivalent to long ones. Hence he abolished the limitation of short syllables to particular spots in the metrical scheme. But Rieti's innovation, i.e., syllabic meters without quantitative distinctions, did not become prominent in Italian Hebrew verse until the 18th century.

(8) For several centuries Hebrew poets proceeded to retain in their rhyme forms the distinction between Italian strophic patterns and the Spanish or the liturgical tradition. On the whole, rhyme was terminal, stressed rhyme being reserved for the sonnet and other Italian patterns. Thus, *Joseph ha-Zarefati (12th century) writes his octaves in masculine rhymes but still follows the Hebrew rule of a required *consonne d'appui* (thus, פֵּר and בֵּר are for him two different rhymemes). Only in the 17th century was the change completed; stressed rhyme according to the European norm became compulsory. Despite the nature of the Hebrew language, which favored masculine rhymes, under Italian impact feminine rhyme became dominant. Since the 18th century feminine rhyme was almost exclusive. It was employed primarily in the *ha-shalem* meter, or in derivations of it: either dropping one or both short syllables, or shortening the line, e,g., in Moses Ḥayyim *Luzzatto's *La-Yesharim Tehillah* there are two kinds of verse line: (a) the 11-syllabic: – – ∪ – / – – – – / – – – –, and (b) the 7-syllabic: – – ∪ – / – – – – each retaining merely one short syllable. Some of his followers in Italy and in Amsterdam dropped this last vestige of quantitative metrics, thus paving the way for the forms of the new era, the Haskalah.

(9) Another Italian development of great interest should be noted: the earliest invention of accentual iambs in Europe was accomplished in Yiddish rhymed romances by the Venetian poet Elijah Baḥur Levita, about 1508/09. Northern Italy was at that time a center of Yiddish literature. Elijah Levita, a grammarian, a versatile scholar, and a poet was fluent in several languages. He wrote Hebrew verse both in the Sephardi pronunciation, using quantitative meters, and in the Ashkenazi vein, using free accentual verse. When adapting long Italian strophic romances, such as *Buovo d'Antona* (the *Bove Bukh*) and *Paris un Viene*, and creating stanzas in pure ottava rima in a quite modern Yiddish, he merged the Italian syllabic principle with the Germanic accentual principle (which ruled Yiddish poetry until his time) and developed his iambic tetrameter. The process of this invention is of major interest to comparative prosody, but with the decay of the Italian center, it did not last in Yiddish poetry. Accentual-syllabic meters reappeared in Yiddish and in Hebrew under Russian influence only as late as around 1890 (with the one exception discussed below).

(10) In the later centuries of Italian Hebrew poetry iambic pentameters began to appear.

The combination of principles from three metric systems in one verse line – the Hebrew quantitative, the Italian syllabic, and the biblical accentual – did not hamper but encouraged the creation of a fourth system in the same verse: the accentual-syllabic meter, in its iambic form. How did it come about? The major quantitative meter used in Italy was: – – ◡ – / – – ◡ – / – – –. Since short syllables cannot be stressed in Hebrew, the third and seventh syllables were unstressed. Italian poetry opposed a stress on the fifth syllable. On the other hand, the 10th syllable was stressed by the rule of rhyme. Since the biblical rule precluded two adjacent syllables from being stressed (if it happens, the first stress would move backward) and the ninth and 11th were also excluded from stress, the following pattern – with the third, fifth, seventh, ninth, and 11th positions unstressed – emerged: – – ◡ – – – ◡ – – – – – . Thus, only even syllables were allowed to receive a stress and a perfect iambic pentameter evolved. (The first foot only was free for variation, but this is the case in English or German iambics too.) Only when the Italian requirement for not stressing the fifth syllable was disregarded did these iambs not materialize.

Hebrew stress was apparently strong and this tendency was felt and spread to other meters too (primarily meters without fixed short syllables). Despite this obvious iambic tendency, it was never formulated as such, being rather an automatic, unintentional result of rules of quite a different nature. The 19th-century Haskalah poets were strongly influenced by late Italian Hebrew poetry, but having a different pronunciation (Ashkenazi as opposed to the Italian "Sephardi"), they could not feel this underlying iambic meter. Though they dropped entirely all distinctions of a quantitative nature, they interpreted this verse as purely syllabic. Only poets in Ereẓ Israel of the 1930–40s, such as J. *Fichmann writing again in a "Sephardi" dialect, rediscovered the iambs of their Italian predecessors.

HASKALAH

The modern age of Hebrew literature began with the revival of Hebrew poetry in Germany in the second half of the 18th century. It is regarded as a "secular" period (though many of the poets were religious and some of their themes were of a religious nature) since there was a conscious creation of poetry and prose written in the genres of contemporary European literature which were conspicuously different from the genres of liturgy. Haskalah poetry was a direct descendant of Hebrew poetry in Italy and Holland. However, since this poetry emerged with a new social and cultural trend, the Enlightenment movement, and flourished closer to the center of the Jewish population in Eastern Europe, it expressed a reorientation of Hebrew literature and may rightly be considered a new period.

Haskalah literature was written and published by small groups of writers and their followers in Germany, Austria, Hungary, and Russia (including Poland) throughout the 19th century. Though their ideas were, to some extent, typical of the European Enlightenment of the 18th century, Haskalah poetry cannot be considered of a monolithic nature, but rather as an eclectic body of verse. This new poetry was indeed, from its beginnings, influenced primarily by 18th-century German literature, especially in the typical genres of epic and fable. It embraced, however, also genres developed previously in Hebrew, in Italy, such as allegorical drama, and absorbed themes and motifs from 19th-century European lyrical and social poetry.

It seems that Hebrew literature lagged considerably behind the evolution of European poetry, going into the stages of the development of neighboring literatures only after those had been established as "classical." Thus, one of the major Hebrew writers of the Haskalah in Russia, Judah Leib *Gordon, who knew Russian well and lived for many years in the capital of Russia, wrote poetry in the vein of the Haskalah in the 1860s and 1870s, i.e., in the time of Tolstoy and Dostoevski and after Pushkin, Lermontov, and Tyutchev. But though Haskalah verse seemed to be a fossilized remnant of the 18th century, untouched by the poetics of Russian classical poetry, Gordon also absorbed some influences from the social and "civic" poetry of his Russian contemporary Nekrasov. On the other hand, he continued to use forms which antedated the Haskalah.

The meter of Hebrew poetry throughout the Haskalah was syllabic. Thus, the poets continued the basic form of Hebrew versification in Italy in spite of the fact that their prototypes in German and Russian were written in accentual-syllabic meters. Even translations from German poetry were transposed in Hebrew into syllabic meters, regardless of the German prototype, e.g., Schiller's *Glocke* (written in accentual-syllabic meters) was translated into Hebrew in syllabic meters, without stress regularity, and into Yiddish in accentual meters, without syllable counting. Stress, strangely enough, played no role in the Hebrew meters of this period, despite the fact that it was prominent in the speech of these writers and even dominant in the meter of folk song in their spoken language, Yiddish, as well as in the small amount of Yiddish poetry which they wrote, and despite the fact that it ruled the versification of German and Russian poetry which they strove to imitate. There was no traditional Hebrew poetic authority to back up this choice of syllabic versification – the venerated poetry of the Bible was accentual and relatively free in its verse forms. The only explanation could be the sense of continuity and the typical conservatism of Hebrew verse.

A few attempts were made in the second half of the 19th century to introduce accentual-syllabic meters (notably by A.B. *Gottlober). But only S. *Frug, well-known as a Russian poet, transferred the Russian system of versification into Yiddish when he started writing in this language. Ḥ.N. *Bialik in the 1890s, strongly influenced by Frug, was among the first to use predominantly accentual-syllabic versification in his Hebrew poetry.

The new meter, influenced by the Russian prototype, swept Hebrew and Yiddish poetry in the 1890s, paradoxically enough at the same time when the symbolist movement, which tried to break away from meter altogether, emerged in Russia.

The Syllabic System of Versification in Hebrew

Haskalah poetry used the pure syllabic system, which had developed in Hebrew literature in Italy, after the last vestiges of quantitative versification have been dropped. Every poem had its own meter, i.e., a permanent number of syllables in each line, with a stress on the penultimate syllable. Otherwise, stress was not regulated. A permanent caesura was rarely implemented.

Apart from marginal uses of quantitative meters, inherited from medieval Spanish Hebrew poetry, the poetry of the Haskalah did not apply the distinction between short and long syllables. The traditionally short syllables, *šewa* and *ḥataf*, confused the poets and were considered sometimes as syllables and sometimes as non-syllables. Naphtali Hirz *Wessely, who introduced this system, used the *ḥataf* at the beginning of words as a syllable and in the middle of words as a non-syllable; the mobile *šewa* as a syllable in the middle of a word and as a non-syllable at the beginning. It seems that Wessely tried to avoid the mobile *šewa* at the beginning of words in order to eschew the problem. With time, however, it became impossible to refrain from using a whole group of words (beginning with the mobile *šewa*) in Hebrew poetry.

Shirei Tiferet, Wessely's epic, was the classical prototype of all the poetry of the Haskalah. The prologues to each of the 18 parts of his epic were written in 11-syllabic rhymed stanzas, but the epic itself was composed in 13-syllabic unrhymed verse. Wessely used feminine endings exclusively both in his rhymed and unrhymed poetry. Unrhymed feminine endings in his poem conformed with the Hebrew tradition inherited from Italy (where the penultimate syllable was stressed) and with Wessely's German prototype, Friedrich Gottlieb Klopstock's *Der Messias*. Wessely, however, in accordance with his Italian prototypes, resorted only to words which were penultimately stressed in the Sephardi pronunciation; these constitute a small and very specific part of the Hebrew vocabulary.

The firm grip of tradition led to the exclusive use of penultimately stressed (*mille'eil*) endings in the Sephardi pronunciation in much of Haskalah poetry; it was an absolute rule in the higher genres of poetry, especially poetic drama and epic verse, and in the "higher" circles of the Haskalah, such as the centers of Germany and Vilna, though not in Galicia or Hungary. The paradox of this use of *mille'eil* in the Sephardi pronunciation is underscored by the fact that in other respects Hebrew was obviously pronounced according to the Ashkenazi dialect, even in specific Ashkenazi subdialects. Thus in the poetry of Lithuania (a major center of Haskalah literature in the second half of the 19th century), the rhymes often betray the poet's pronunciation: חֹפֶשׁ – נֶפֶשׁ (both *ḥolam* and *segol* being pronounced as *ei*), רַעַשׁ – כַּעַס (שׂ and ס being equal to *s*). Though Lithuanian Ashkenazi pronunciation is evident in their poetry and the penultimate stress was the general rule of the Hebrew words in all varieties of the Ashkenazi dialect, the Haskalah poets did not dare use Hebrew in their own pronunciation as a natural resource for the compulsory use of feminine rhymes. Consequently most of the vocabulary of their language was excluded from final verse positions.

When the young poet Mikhal (Micah Joseph *Lebensohn) was negligent in this respect and rhymed words which were perfectly equivalent in his own dialect, but appeared as a mixture of *millera* and *mille'eil* (masculine and feminine) to a distant Sephardi ear, he was scolded by the Italian scholar S.D. *Luzzatto. Both Mikhal and J.L. *Gordon, in his later period, broke the rule and on and off used words which are feminine only according to the Ashkenazi pronunciation. But even then the majority of rhymes were still based on words which are considered *mille'eil* in the Sephardi pronunciation: What used to be a compulsory rule became a habit, or a matter of merit in poetic style.

This phenomenon had a strong effect on the style of Haskalah poetry. Words of the *mille'eil* form exist only in several specific groups: (1) a small group of nouns penultimately stressed (אֶרֶץ – פֶּרֶץ – קֶרֶץ) which recurred endlessly in the rhymes of the Haskalah and became trite symptoms of this poetry; (2) a variety of archaic forms (אֱלוֹמָה, בָּמוֹ, לָמוֹ, מֶנְהוּ); (3) several forms of the verb (הפריעה, אמרתי), notably in the biblical end-stop pronunciation (יִנְהָרוּ, יִבְעָרוּ); (4) a group of feminine endings (אוֹמֶרֶת, תָּבִינִי). Since other sources were limited, the penultimately stressed forms of the verb became prominent in the rhymes of Haskalah poetry. As a further result, the rules of rhyme caused sentence inversion, since the verb was closing a verse line, and enjambement was excluded; all complements of the verb, similes, etc., preceded the verb rather than followed it (as the usual word-order would require). The following is a typical stanza of this kind:

וּבֵין כֹּה וָכֹה הַדְּמָמָה הִפְרִיעוּ
תּוֹפְשֵׂי הַמָּשׁוֹט בַּמַּיִם יַחְתּוֹרוּ;
גַּם קוֹל עַל הַמַּיִם עַם רָב הִשְׁמִיעוּ,
גַּם דָּוִד גַּם רֵעוֹ מִשְּׁנָת נֵעוֹרוּ.

Meantime the silence they interrupted,
The crew who in the water rowed;
A voice on the water a multitude emitted,
And David and his friend from their sleep awoke

Thus, in spite of the accepted Ashkenazi pronunciation in the later poetry of J.L. Gordon, most of the words in his poetry were excluded from rhyme position: a group of words constituting 8% of the normal language continuum was used in 90% of his rhymes. With the abolition of the restriction to the Sephardi stress, no revolutionary change occurred in the rhymes of the Haskalah since the typical rhymes became part of poetic style as such. Only a fundamental change in poetic style and in the very conception of poetic language, introduced by Ḥ.N. Bialik and his generation, was to alter radically the resources of Hebrew rhyme, making available for rhyme practically the whole range of the Hebrew language. During the Haskalah, this freedom was enjoyed only sometimes in minor genres and by poets on the geographical "periphery" (poets from Galicia or Hungary).

Though the tradition of epic poetry in the Haskalah began with Wessely's blank verse, in time rhyme became dominant in this domain too, especially in the Lithuanian center. The poets of the Haskalah used a variety of strophic forms very often of more than 4 lines, notably the stanza developed by Wessely consisting of 6 lines and rhyming *aabccb*, the ottava rima inherited from Italy, and other strophic patterns, especially of 6 or 8 lines. The 4-line stanza was also widespread, primarily in the form of *abab*, but it was not as predominant as in the poetry of later generations.

The strophic forms in all their variety usually used alternating rhymes, the members of one rhyme alternating with the members of another rhyme. Rarely did a Haskalah poet systematically use one rhyme more than twice without alternating. In this respect Hebrew poetry conformed to the prevalent European sense of rhyme variation. On the other hand, there was no alternation whatsoever or rhymes insofar as their rhythmical properties. Though Russian poetry alternated, as a rule, not only the rhymes, but also their rhythmic patterns, i.e., combining throughout a poem feminine and masculine, or masculine and dactylic rhymes, Hebrew poetry of this period did not accept this norm. Feminine rhymes were the absolute rule, except for sporadic, non-systematic uses of masculine-rhyming words.

In Italy such a restriction of the language could be understood as influenced by a taste formed through the reading of Italian poetry in which predominantly feminine rhymes are used; this is a concomitant of the structure of the Italian language. In Russia, however, the restriction made no sense and can only be explained through the compulsion exerted by the internal Hebrew tradition. Paradoxically enough, this requirement continued to obtain even at a time when feminine rhymes were drawn merely from the words regarded as feminine according to the Sephardi pronunciation, i.e., when the bulk of the language could have been used for the purpose of masculine rhymes. It was only the generation of Bialik that, again paradoxically enough, attempted to alternate between feminine and masculine rhymes, in spite of the scarcity of the latter in the Ashkenazi dialect, which became in this generation the accepted language of Hebrew verse.

Nevertheless, though stress was disregarded by the syllabic system, it may subconsciously have played a role in forming the rhythmic nature of Hebrew verse in the Haskalah period. The most widespread meters were 13 and 11 syllables. Such a length of lines conformed very well with the structure of 4 major accents, or 4 words, grouped mostly in 2 pairs. This condition may have played a role in the acceptance of Haskalah poetry, for there was, to the ear, as it were, an underlying quasi-biblical meter, felt even more because of the biblical language used in this poetry. A line of 11 or 13 syllables, using 4 major stresses, in a language in which the average number of syllables to each stress is about 3, can easily be brought to approximate an amphibrachic tetrameter, e.g., the first stanza of A.D. *Lebensohn's poem לַבֹּקֶר רִנָּה in the Ashkenazi pronunciation can be read (unstressed syllables are unmarked):

קוֹל תִּשְׁמַע נַפְשִׁי // הֲמוֹן צִבְאוֹת חַיִל
רִנַּת כּוֹכָבִים // וּבְרֹאשָׁם יָרֵחַ;
עַל מִשְׁמֶרֶת אֶרֶץ // עָמְדוּ בַּלָּיִל;
עַתָּה כִּי בָא שַׁחַר // לִבָּם שָׂמֵחַ;
גַּם נָגַע זֶה // עַל עֵינַי וַיְּעוֹרוּ,
וּמְלֹא כָל הָאָרֶץ // אֶרְאֶה כִּי אוֹרוּ

This is a typical Haskalah stanza (*aba bcc*), rhyming Sephardi *mille'eil*. But an Ashkenazi reading reveals the underlying dactylic-amphibrachic meter, sidestepped only in the first hemistichs of lines 3, 4, and in the second hemistich of line 5.

Toward the end of this period the unregulated stresses within the line became more and more often "ordered," many lines approximating 4 amphibrachs (such were, for example, the poems of S.L. Gordon in the early 1890s).

Thus, for the second time in its history, Hebrew syllabic verse developed again toward an accentual-syllabic meter, dominated however by the amphibrach rather than the iamb, prevalent in Italy, and it followed the Ashkenazi rather than the Sephardi pronunciation.

Such is the story of the transformations of a major Hebrew metrical form: The quantitative meter of Spanish Hebrew poetry, originating in Arabic versification, was reinterpreted in Italy as syllabic, under the influence of Italian versification. Hebrew syllabic poetry stretched over a period of centuries (from the 12th to the 19th), adopting Italian strophic forms without relinquishing the quantitative patterns of the Arabic heritage, but shifting time and again into accentual-syllabic iambs. The Haskalah took up the same syllabic verse forms, continued to use them in spite of a literary environment which accepted exclusively accentual-syllabic meters and imbued them with an underlying semi-biblical (that is accentual) rhythm. It finally brought Hebrew poetry again to the verge of accentual-syllabic meters.

The development of Hebrew poetry should be considered as a chain in transformation rather than a series of totally opposed and separate periods. In regard to sentence structure and syntactical rhythm, there was no fundamental change: Similar groups of words could constitute a verse line, since a line of 11 syllables was the most frequent length in all these periods.

THE MODERN PERIOD

The Historical Setting

Though echoes of European literature and of European poetics of the modern age had reverberated in Hebrew poetry since the days of Dante in Italy, and throughout the literature of the Haskalah, Hebrew poetry had not accepted fully, until the very end of the 19th century, the consequences of the lyrical revolution accomplished by *Goethe, Pushkin, or the English romantics.

From the limited point of view of this survey, one can observe the striking fact that Hebrew meter was based, until the end of the 19th century, on syllable-counting rather than on the subtle and complex instrument developed in other languages with "free" stress in the form of accentualsyllabic (or tonic-syllabic) versification. English poetry since the 16th century, German poetry since Opitz (17th century), Russian poetry since the middle of the 18th century – the whole modern period of these poetries – cannot be imagined without the metrical system. It is an instrument whose exact structures made possible the clear-cut distinction of a large variety of forms and also provided the background for clearly pronounced effects of particular rhythmical variations. These two assets were of primary importance for a poetry characterized by the individuality of the writer, the individuality of the poem, the reliance on a living language, and the immediate appeal in concrete sensuous images to the imagination of the reader. Even free verse was rich and effective when playing on this background. Such a poetics was accepted and absorbed by the Hebrew poets who, through an externist's secondary education, came to know the classical Russian heritage of Pushkin, Lermontov, and their followers. The first poet to write consistently in accentual-syllabic meters was Ḥ.N. Bialik whose first poem "*El ha-Ẓippor*" ("To the Bird") was published in 1894, in the very year when Russian symbolism emerged, i.e., a movement which strove to break away from the regularities of this very same metrical system.

In Odessa before World War I where Hebrew poets wrote some of the best of Hebrew poetry in the poetic mode of Russian literature of the 1830s, young Jewish poets, writing in Russian, launched modernistic journals such as *The Flying Omnibus*. The beginning and end of the major cycle of modern Russian poetry seemed to meet at one time and in one place. Obviously, Hebrew poetry could not for long be excluded from the general developments, the more so because Yiddish poetry was sometimes written by the same poets in a language more alive and actual and therefore absorbed the waves of modernism more rapidly. Thus, in one generation Hebrew poetry not only caught up with the European classical heritage as conceived by the early 19th century, but at the same time landed, in one grand leap, into the European 20th century. The struggle and interaction between a variety of poetic trends – evolution turned into contemporaneity – make it one of the most panoramic and interesting periods of Hebrew poetry. But, as regards this survey, it is a handicap: It is difficult to keep apart the "generations" of poetry in which unequivocal norms persist. Free verse was developed almost contemporaneously with exact meters or Greek verse forms. Modernistic rhymes were intermingled with exact "classical" rhyming and with blank verse. Hence it is advisable to discuss forms and formal systems – "regular" or "modernistic" – rather than periods of poetry.

A second objective difficulty in discussing the rhythms of Hebrew poetry in the 20th century is due to the revolution in the pronunciation of the Hebrew language which undermined its whole prosodic foundation. The rhythm and sound orchestration, so essential to the concept of poetry of the classics of the last generation – Ḥ.N. Bialik, S. *Tchernichowsky, J. *Fichmann, J. *Steinberg, Z. *Shneour – is lost to the ears of Israeli readers. The poetry of the Hebrew revival in Russia at the end of the 19th century, which is concrete and sensuous and employed the Russian sensibility for subtleties of rhythm and sound, unfolded the sound values of the language in the Ashkenazi dialects. But almost at the same time there was in Israel a revival of Hebrew as a spoken language, which used the "Sephardi" or "Israeli" pronunciation. The clash between the two dialects was sometimes fierce. The changing laws of language will be discussed below. Here one example may suffice. The two words עֹז־רֵתֶת were a perfect rhyme in the Lithuanian Ashkenazi Hebrew of U.N. *Gnessin E YS-rs-E YS (both *ḥolam* and *ẓere* being pronounced *ey*; ת sounding like *s*; and *z* = *s* in rhyme, according to the Russian convention of neutralizing voiced consonants in an end position); but the same rhyming pair lost all sound identities to the ears of an Israeli who reads it: *oz-retét*. The Sephardi pronunciation was also employed in Hebrew meters in this period, as early as 1900 (not to count some experiments during the Haskalah period as well as the unintentional iambs of Hebrew poetry in Italy). The Ashkenazi pronunciation was still dominant in the 1920s and was alive with some poets until the 1960s. This coexistence again complicates our discussion.

The shift of dialects was a revolution in the sound system of a language, which did not occur elsewhere in such an abrupt manner. In this process most of the poetry of the period of Revival was lost from the point of view of its musicality and rhythm. But the poets who moved from one Hebrew tongue to quite a different one, despite the pangs of readjustment, remained the same, and so did the poetic ideals and norms. These had no time to change. It was simply a matter of readjusting to the new sound system, of regaining a *modus vivendi* with the spoken language. Therefore it is possible, despite the crucial shift, to discuss the prosodic norms, using at first illustrations from Hebrew poems in the contemporary Israeli pronunciation.

The Two Dialects of Modern Hebrew

When Hebrew became a spoken language in Ereẓ Israel, it adopted the principles of the "Sephardi" pronunciation in which the location of stress is based on the accentuation marks of the Bible. The majority of words in this Israeli pronunciation have a stress on their final syllable. Only a small group of words are penultimately stressed; these are of two varieties; the so-called *segoliyyim* having two *e* vowels, patterned like *dégel*, and words with the furtive *pattaḥ* ending in an originally guttural consonant, like תַּפּוּחַ (*tappú'aḥ*), רֵיחַ (*rei'aḥ*) לָנוּעַ (*lanu'a*). A larger group of penultimately stressed words is provided by several suffixes, such as the feminine forms אוֹמֶרֶת (*omeret* – versus the masculine *Omer*), verbs in some perfect forms: אָמַרְנוּ, אָמַרְתָּ, אָמַרְתִּי (*amarti, amarta, amarnu*), or nouns in the plural with some possessive pronouns

(דְּבָרֶיךָ, דְּבָרַיִךְ – *devarekha, devarayikh*). A new group of penultimately stressed words consists of foreign borrowings: *akadémya, gemnázya*, etc. On the other hand, several distinctions in the quality of sounds marked in the biblical vocalization system, are blurred in the Sephardi dialect. Thus, both *pattaḥ* and *qameṣ* are pronounced *a; ṣere* and *segol* are pronounced *e*; ת and תּ are both *t*.

The Ashkenazi pronunciation of Hebrew, developed in Europe since the 14th century, is based primarily on the penultimate stress. With a few exceptions, a penultimate stress is absent only when it is impossible to implement it: (a) in monosyllabic words (a small group in Hebrew); (b) in bisyllabic words, if the first syllable is a short one (*ḥataf* or *šewa*), e.g., אֲנִי, בְּנִי; (c) in longer words where the penultimate syllable is a short one, the stress moves to the third-to-last syllable, e.g., הַמְּחוֹנְנִים (*ha-meḥónenim*), נַעֲרָה (*náarah*). In (b) and (c) there are exceptions, based on the fact that historically short syllables became normal and may be stressed, like in Hebrew words in Yiddish (e.g., חֲלוֹם should be *khalóym*, but it is often pronounced as in Yiddish: *khólem*). On the other hand, there is in Ashkenazi a wider range of vowel qualities: *qameṣ* is distinguished from *pattaḥ*; *ḥolam* and *ṣere* are diphthongs. The weak ת is pronounced *s* (rather than the Israeli *t*). Within the Ashkenazi domain there were several dialects, on the whole resembling the dialects of Yiddish. In poetry these sub-dialects are felt not in the meter but in the rhyme.

Ashkenazi Hebrew with its diphthongs and penultimate stress was felt by the poets to be "softer" and more "musical" than the "harsh" Israeli Hebrew which is ultimately stressed and in which *a* makes up 50 percent of its vowels. Until the late 1930s some tried to keep poetry in the traditional Ashkenazi dialect, but finally they had to give in to the spoken language of Israel. Several poets attempted "translating" their poetry into the new dialect. On the whole they succeeded in making a mechanical meter, but in most cases the poem was severely harmed in the process. A variety of interesting transitional forms developed. Thus, U.Z. *Greenberg, though still writing in Ashkenazi Hebrew, let the Israeli workers in his poems speak in their authentic Israeli pronunciation.

Accentual Syllabic Meter in Hebrew

The dominant system of Hebrew prosody since the 1890s was accentual-syllabic, though throughout the period other forms also existed. Accentual-syllabic versification came to Hebrew poetry under the influence and in the forms of the Russian tradition of the 19th century. However, some rhythmical characteristics of these meters are due to the structural properties of the Hebrew language. Accentual-syllabic meters are based on the ordering both of the number of syllables and of the location of stresses in a verse line. But it is rare, especially in Hebrew poetry, that the actual stresses in the language of a line constitute a neatly ordered pattern, copying exactly the metrical scheme. There is a discrepancy between the units of the language and the units of meter: stress and word boundaries on the one hand and metrical accents and feet on the other. A meter exists in a poem if its actual stresses and word boundaries meet certain rules of correlation with the underlying metrical scheme.

TYPES OF METERS. A meter is a permanent order of accented and unaccented syllables, underlying all lines of a poem (or part of it). The sign (–) represents a metrically accented syllable, the sign (◡) an unaccented one. The elementary recurrent group of syllables is called a "foot." Thus, in a line of the type: ◡◡ – ◡◡◡ – ◡ – there are three feet / ◡◡ – /. A foot is not a rhythmical unit; its boundaries do not mark any stop in reading; it is a mere abstraction of the basic principle underlying the pattern of a line. Each foot has one accented and one or two unaccented syllables.

There are two binary feet:	iamb / ◡ – /
	trochee / – ◡ /
and three ternary feet:	anapest / ◡◡ – /
	amphibrach / ◡ – ◡ /
	dactyl / – ◡◡ /

A meter of a line is determined by the kind of feet and their number, e.g., an iambic pentameter is a line of five iambs. The number of feet is determined by the number of accents; the last foot may be incomplete and may vary throughout a poem. Thus, in an iambic pentameter there may be either 10 or 11 syllables: ◡ – ◡ – ◡ – ◡ – ◡ – (◡) (depending on the gender of rhyme or on the line ending). Usually in Hebrew poetry there is only one kind of foot in a poem, i.e., one form of alternating accented and unaccented syllables (binary or ternary).

DEFINITION OF METER. A poem has a certain meter, when it can be read according to a metrical pattern without contradicting its language. The general rule of correlation is: If a word receives metrical accents, at least one of them must fall on the stressed syllable. This rule implies that a word (1) may be unaccented; or (2) may have an accent on its stressed syllable; or (3) may have several accents, one of them falling on the stressed syllable, e.g., *Nŏshĕv, ērĕv ăfŏr vĕ-ŏr(e)vim ăl t(e)rănăv*. This is a line of four anapests (by *Alterman) in which the stress (marked) of the first word is disregarded by the meter, the stresses of other words are employed by the meter as regular accents. The following is an example of a Hebrew stanza meter of 4 iambs (by Alterman):

Ăz ḥivvărŏn gădŏl hē'ir
Ĕt ha-r(e)hŏvŏt vĕ-hā-sh(e)vakim
Ămăd nătŭi ăl p(e)nĕi
Năḥshŏl shămăyĭm yērŭkim

The first word of the first line is unaccented by the meter, the second word has 2 accents (one of them on the stressed syllable). The second line provides only two stresses in its language.

RHYTHMIC VARIATION. Obviously, an expressive reading of a poem will consider language stress and word boundaries rather than the mechanical pattern of the metrical accents.

Thus, rhythmical variation is created primarily by the fact that not all accents of the meter are realized in the language, the division of actual stresses and word boundaries may vary from line to line, e.g., a trochaic stanza (Alterman):

Dumiyyáh la-merḥavím shoreket
Bóhak ha-sakkín be-éin ha-ḥatulím
Láylah, kámmah láylah! Ba-shamáyim shéket
Kokhavím be-ḥittulím

It has 5–6–6–4 trochees, but the number of stresses is 3–4–5–2, irregularly dispersed. When read according to its language, every line seems to be rhythmically different (every box represents a word, X denotes a syllable, Y an accented syllable).

X X·Y	X·X·X·Y	X·Y·X		
Y·X	X·X·Y	Y·Y	X·X·X·Y	
Y·X	Y·X	Y·X	X·X·Y·X	Y·X
X·X·Y	X·X·X·Y			

In modern Hebrew there is, on the average, one stress to each three syllables. In binary meters, which constitute the bulk of modern Hebrew metrical verse, rhythmical variation is based primarily on avoiding stresses in accented positions. This tendency usually follows the Russian symmetrical pattern of variation. Thus in a meter of four iambs or trochees, the fourth and the second accents are almost always stressed, the third and the first are quite often unstressed. (This is obviously different from English binary meters where variation is largely based on the opposite possibility: stressing unaccented syllables.) In short, Hebrew iambs and trochees are not based on a regular number of stresses to each line, but on changing deviations from a regular abstract scheme.

Limited Free Verse: The "Ternary Net"

Whereas in binary meters variation is built into the system (a 3:2 relationship between accent and stress), in ternary meters almost all accents coincide with stresses. In the Israeli pronunciation where in most words stress coincides also with word boundary, the effect becomes tedious, especially in the anapestic meters where almost every foot is a word and every accent a stress. Poets did their best to create variation here too, but the solution came in the form of a kind of free verse adapted from Russian modernist poetry (Blok, Akhmatova, Yessenin). In this system, the number of accents in a line remains regular, but the number of syllables is free to a certain extent. Usually an impulse of a ternary meter is created, to be disturbed on and off; instead of two unaccented there are occasionally one or none (and in some poets also three). The abstract pattern looks like a "net": a ternary scheme with "holes" in it which appear without any regularity, but rarely enough, so as not to destroy the underlying ternary pattern. Beginnings of lines are usually free too, thus abolishing any distinction between anapest, amphibrach, or dactyl, e.g., two stanzas by the poetess Raḥel:

Hen damáh be-dami zorém	∪ ∪ – ∪ ∪ – o ∪ –
Hen koláh bi rán	∪ ∪ – o ∪ –
Rahél, ha-ro'áh ẓón laván	o ∪ – ∪ ∪ – ∪ ∪ –
Rahél – em ha-ém	o ∪ – ∪ ∪ –
Ve-al kén ha-bayit li ẓar	∪ ∪ – o ∪ – ∪ ∪ –
Ve-ha-ir zarah	∪ ∪ – o ∪ –
Ki hayah mitnoféf, sudaráh	∪ ∪ – ∪ ∪ – ∪ ∪ –
Le-ruḥot ha-mid-bár	∪ ∪ – ∪ ∪ –

The conversational tone is achieved here by breaking the anapestic flow. But the same principle may be used for a variety of rhythmic tendencies and poetic themes and tones. It became a major form of Hebrew poetry since the 1920s, developed by *Raḥel, Alterman, Zusman, Lea *Goldberg, *Bat-Miriam, and other poets of the Russian tradition.

Free Verse

Since the beginnings of Hebrew accentual-syllabic meters, varieties of freedom from their strictures were sought. Thus, Tchernichowsky used widely the dactylic hexameter, varying often two or one unaccented syllables. The effect was similar to the ternary net, but the "excuse" was an interpretation of the Greek meter followed by German poets, which varied the dactyls by using trochees (instead of the Greek spondee). Bialik developed his so-called biblical rhythms; but, unlike in the Bible, the number of accents was fixed and the number of unaccented syllables varied in a limited way: 1 or 2 (and occasionally 3) syllables in each interstress interval. About 10 years after the initiation of the accentual-syllabic meters, a Hebrew poet appeared who wrote purely free verse: Avraham *Ben Yiẓḥak. This trend, based on the balancing of small word groups and phrases, was enhanced by the influence of German expressionism (exerted on such poets as David *Vogel). It was renewed in some of the young poets of the Palmaḥ generation (1948) and in the 1950s, under the influence of English modernism. The forms of free verse are too varied to be discussed here. Basically they lean on syntactic patterns, strengthened by parallelism and sound orchestration. At present the whole scale from strict meters to prose-like free verse is productive in Hebrew poetry.

Rhyme in Modern Poetry

Though rhyme in Hebrew was older than in any of the surrounding languages, and though its forms changed throughout the centuries, it was not before the 1890s that Hebrew rhyme accepted fully the European rhyme system. (As has been seen, the principle of stressed rhyme was adopted already in Hebrew poetry in Italy in the 17th century, but it actually applied to feminine rhymes only and did not involve the whole language until the end of the 19th century.)

In modern Hebrew poetry it is convenient to distinguish "exact" from "inexact" rhymes. In "exact" rhymes the rhymeme always extends to the very end of the rhyming members (*x=ḥ* or *kh; c=ẓ*): *sma MA-ey-MA, novÉYAX- KerÉYAX*; in "inexact" rhymes some of the final sounds are not identical, i.e., the rhymeme does not always reach the end of the verse line:

meso-RÉGEt- baRÉGEv; la ḥaDSÍ- kiDuŠIn; ba-xÓFEn- haOFEk, etc. The inexact rhyme, a symptom of modernism, should be discussed after the basic "exact" norm from which it deviated.

THE BASIC NORM OF THE EXACT RHYME. The rhymeme is the basic norm in modern Hebrew poetry, as it is in most European languages; it includes all sounds from the last stressed vowel to the end of the line: N=V́ ( ). (The parentheses represent all sounds, which may come after the stressed vowel.) As opposed to the terminal Hebrew rhyme of the Middle Ages, this is an accentual-terminal rhyme norm, e.g., *šovÁX- heÁX; šenavÓXA- kamÓXA; dÁY LA- LÁYLA; lirKOŠET- xarOSET*. The rhyme in these cases includes 2, 3, or 4 sounds (V́C, VCV, V́CCV, VCVC). All of these are minimal rhymemes: they may be enlarged, but deducting one sound destroys the rhyme. Thus, the basic norm is not determined by the number of sounds but by their position. The number of sounds following the stressed vowel depends on the structure of the words; it is a matter of language rather than of rhyming norm. In this system, a *rime riche* is based not on the number of sounds in the rhymeme, but on the employment of sounds additional to the required norm. Thus, *tic-Nax – aNAX* (תִּצְנַח – אֲנָךְ) is a rich rhyme, though its rhymeme *Nax* has only three sounds, since *AX* would be good enough; whereas *ESET* in *IESET – nogÉSET* (לֶסֶת – נוֹגֶסֶת) is not rich, though it has four sounds, since it is the minimal sound group in such feminine rhymes.

SECONDARY NORMS. In addition to the basic norm, several secondary norms are at work, some are more general, others less obligatory or more restricted to certain poets or trends.

The Numeric Norm. Hebrew poetry in the Israeli pronunciation requires a minimum of two sounds in the rhymeme. In English, German, or Yiddish poetry, one stressed vowel is enough, if it comes at the end of the word: *free – tranquility – sea, be – we, go – snow* are perfect rhymes in English. But in Israeli Hebrew, as in Russian, in such cases, a consonant has to precede the final vowel: *bitfi-LÁ-leo-LÁ* is a minimal rhyme (N2 = CV). Two sounds are enough, even when there is no consonant: *ligvÓA- elÓA*.

Hebrew poetry in the Ashkenazi pronunciation did not require this numeric norm. Bialik rhymed *lÍ – bnÍ* (לִי – בְּנִי), *hazE – hapE* (הַזֶּה – הַפֶּה), etc. The reason is obvious: there are in the Ashkenazi pronunciation very few ultimately stressed words (primarily monosyllables, a rather small group in Hebrew) and even fewer such words with open syllables. With the additional rule it would be almost impossible to rhyme these words. On the other hand, in the Israeli pronunciation most of the words are ultimately stressed, the number of vowels has been reduced to 5, and there are an enormous number of words which terminate in (resulting both from the historical *pattaḥ* and *qameṣ*). The use of such an á as a rhyme would be too easy and trite to be effective.

The Historical Factor. There was a historical factor to this development, too. Bialik and many of his contemporary "Ashkenazi" poets at the end of the 19th and the beginning of the 20th century (Z. Shneour, I. *Katzenelson, Jacob Steinberg, J. Fichmann) wrote Yiddish as well as Hebrew poetry. Yiddish, as other Germanic languages, does not require the numeric norm. But the Israeli poets of the next generation (Raḥel, A. *Shlonsky, Lea Goldberg) were overwhelmingly influenced by Russian poetry where this norm is required.

The historical factor is felt again in the "young" Israeli poetry of the 1950s. Hebrew poetry now moved from the Russian to the English sphere of influence and away from rich "colorful" rhyming to a rather "prose-like" poetics. Here again rhymes appeared, based on a single stressed vowel: *kÍ-civonÍ; lezokhrÓ be-motÓ*, etc.

The Morphological Norm. In the Israeli pronunciation *sIR – kabIR, niM – alIM* (נִים – אֲלִים) are perfect rhymes, but *mex-usIM – alIM* (מְכוּסִים – עָלִים) is not, since *IM* in this case is a morphological ending: the non-feminine plural suffix of nouns, verbs, and adjectives. This secondary norm requires the participation of at least one stem consonant in a rhyme: *mesuSIM – ma'aSIM* or *aLIM – keLIM* are minimal rhymes in this case.

Three Criteria of the Rhyming Norm. The basic norm with the secondary norms may now be combined: "exact" rhyme in modern Hebrew poetry in the Israeli pronunciation requires in its rhymeme all the sounds from the last stressed syllable to the end of the verse line, provided that there are at least two sounds and at least one is part of the root of the rhyming word. This complex rule makes three kinds of demands: (a) a norm for the *place* of the rhymeme; (b) a norm for its minimal *size*; (c) a norm concerning its *morphological* structure.

THE RELATIVITY OF THE MORPHOLOGICAL NORM. The three heterogeneous norms have different degrees of validity in different poets or generations. The morphological subnorm seems to be the most flexible. Some suffixes are less susceptible to this norm. Thus, Raḥel, a poetess of the 1920s who preceded the "young" generation in the use of "prosaic" language in her lyrical poetry (influenced not by English Imagism but by the Russian Acmeists, especially the poetry of Akhmatova), strictly applies the morphological norm to the non-feminine plural suffix *Im* (e.g., *raVIM – asaVIM*), but disregards this requirement for the feminine plural *OT* (*kallOT – netivOT*) and other suffixes. Some "young" poets of the 1950s use even obvious grammatical rhymes, with the plural suffix *IM* as a rhymeme.

On the whole, the more widespread the use of a suffix in a language, the stronger is the tendency not to rely upon that suffix alone. The opposition to grammatical rhyme, inherited from Russian poetry, was strongest in the plural *IM*. On the other hand, the requirement to add a root consonant is entirely weak in two-syllabic suffixes, which are penultimately stressed, such as the dual: *áyim*.

The "mistrust" of grammatical rhyme is often expressed in poetry far beyond the required norm. Thus, Shlonsky uses rich rhymes especially when a suffix occurs, as if to compensate for the very use of a suffix in rhyme: *DIRIM – aDIRIM, MeDuROT – MiDoROT* (where *RIM* or *ROT* would be sufficient), etc.

MINIMUM AND MAXIMUM. The norm described above concerns the minimal group of sounds required in a rhymeme. In Hebrew poetry in the Israeli pronunciation there is a wide discrepancy between the minimum sounds required and the maximum actually used. Some poets, such as Shlonsky or Alterman, influenced by the poetics of Russian modernism, employ rhymes as rich as possible: *tiKTEFÉNU – Ktefenu, AKuMÓT – hAKOMÓT*, etc. The words in modern Hebrew, having no secondary stress, are usually long (3 syllables and more). Most of the sounds in the rhyming words of the poets under discussion are employed in the rhymeme. This tendency is doubly connected with the poetics of Hebrew "imagistic" poetry: (a) It is part of the general "colorful" aesthetics which abounds in striking imagery, rich sound patterns, "strong" themes, etc. There is a strongly expressed "set toward the message," a high "density" of the poetic language. (b) Since many sounds are involved in each rhyme, it is quite difficult to find words rhyming with each other; only a poetic language with a high degree of flexibility in imagery and elliptic combination could enable such freedom in connecting rhyming words drawn from distant spheres of meaning.

The maximal limit for a rhymeme consists in leaving a minimal difference between the rhyming members. In such rhymes as Yehudah *Karni's *K'ILU MAT – KIL'UMAT* (כְּאִלּוּ־מַת – כִּלְעוּמַת) or *YIF'AM – YIF AM* (יִפְעָם – יִיף עָם), the difference may only be a junction between words. In Alterman's rhyme בְּגוּמַת לְחָיַיִךְ – אֶת יֵינָן הַלּוֹהֵט לְחַיַּיִךְ (*LEXAYAYIX*), the difference lies merely in the different morphological structure: in the first case ("your cheeks") the *l* is part of the root לחי, in the second case ("for your life") the *l* is a separate morpheme ("for") connected only graphically with the word חיים.

A COMPARATIVE PERSPECTIVE. Rich rhyme in Israeli Hebrew can be explained not merely by the influence of one kind of modernist poetics. The properties of the language also encourage this trend. Most of the words in this pronunciation are stressed ultimately and most of the words are multisyllabic. Rhyming merely one syllable time and again would be tedious. Moreover, since most of the words are stressed ultimately, there is a multitude of words available for each rhyme ending. It may be compared to other languages. In Russian, where many words are also multisyllabic, stresses may occur on any syllable of a word, there-fore the number of words rhyming ultimately is relatively smaller, and multisyllabic rhyme is usual. In Yiddish, too, the number of feminine and dactylic rhymes is incomparably higher.

In English the number of monosyllables is so high that masculine rhymes are usual, as in Hebrew. But the "neutral" sounds of each number are not felt strongly, since they are few. In a usual Hebrew word one or three syllables do not participate in a minimal rhymeme: cf., the English pARTS – mARTS (though the rhymeme is monosyllabic most sounds of each member are covered by it) with the Hebrew *mešuxrÁR – veaxzÁR* where the nonparticipating, "neutral," sounds of each member are conspicuous. Moreover, English has some 13 different rhyming vowels (as compared to the mere five of Israeli Hebrew) and many consonant clusters, preceding and following the vowel, which make the number of possible rhyme endings incomparably higher and the number of words available for each relatively much smaller. Since there are very few possible rhyme endings in Israeli Hebrew, it is much easier to meet the minimal rhyme requirements and also easier, and more necessary, to add sounds and "enrich" the rhymeme. French with its ultimate stress, though it is more abundant in rhyme endings than Hebrew, also tends to prefer *rime riche*.

RHYME IN THE ASHKENAZI PRONUNCIATION. The basic norm of the accentual-terminal rhyme is identical in the poetry of the "Sephardi" pronunciation (in Italy since the Renaissance) or in the Israeli, as well as in the Ashkenazi, pronunciation, which was accepted in European Hebrew from the 14th century, but entered rhyme only in the 19th century. But the realization of the norm differed strongly due to the difference in the rhythmic structure of the Hebrew word.

Since the Ashkenazi stress falls on the second or third syllable from the end, most rhymes were automatically polysyllabic and most sounds of a word were included in the rhymeme. Thus, *mÍDBOR – nÍDBOR* is a very common rhyme in Bialik's poetry, but the same pair makes a very rich rhyme in the Israeli pronunciation: *mIDBÁR – nIDBÁR* (since *AR* would be enough). Therefore, rich rhymes are few in Ashkenazi but may abound in Israeli Hebrew (at least in the practice of some poets). Moreover, the necessity to include in most cases at least two syllables in the rhymeme leads the poets to search for alleviating devices. Thus, Bialik in his early poetry tends to use grammatic rhymes which have already one syllable given in the morphological suffix, and the poet has to find words which differ in one syllable only. This necessity also leads to the use of archaic endings, feminine forms, etc. In short: any *manqué* form of a word, e.g., the Israeli rhyme צוֹהֵל – נוֹזֵל is not a rhyme in Ashkenazi (*cohel – nozel*), but the feminine form, with an added syllable, is צוֹהֶלֶת – נוֹזֶלֶת (*coheles – nozeles*). Therefore Bialik uses not אוֹר נוֹזֵל ("running light") but a more archaic form, which is feminine אוֹרָה נוֹזֶלֶת. Feminine verbs or adjectives in rhyme position obviously bring about feminine nouns in the middle of the line. The same holds for plurals and archaic forms.

"Modernistic" Rhyme

THE "INEXACT" RHYME. Modernistic Hebrew poetry uses a large number of inexact rhymes, such as Alterman's *ŠKuFÁ hI-miŠKaFAyIM: KoS Ha-MÁyIM – KSuMÁ hI*, etc. In such rhymes at least one member ends with a "neutral" sound not participating in the rhymeme. But the effect is strong, since such rhymes usually have many sounds. There is a great variety of concrete forms, but in all cases the stressed vowel is constant, i.e., it is an accentual rhyme. In most cases the rhymeme is discontinued and the system may be called: *accentual-discontinuous*. The rhymeme, in addition to the fixed-stressed vowel, is based primarily on consonants. This phenomenon of the discontinuous rhymeme, particular to Hebrew poetry, is based on the nature of the Hebrew lexical morpheme, which is discontinuous and purely consonantal.

This system, representing a strong break from the standard European norm where rhyme is *accentual-terminal* and is usually continuous, had its forerunner in the earliest system of rhyme, in old Hebrew liturgy (the *piyyut*). But the concrete immediate influence which created this norm in Hebrew modernism came from the poetry of Mayakovski and *Pasternak, where rhymemes were also inexact in their endings and moved deeper into the middle of the line. While discontinuity in Russian rhyme was an occasional form of deviation rather than the rule, for Alterman and his contemporaries it became the norm, based on the characteristics of the Hebrew language. Alterman uses both exact and inexact rhymes in the same poems. The minimal requirement for a rhymeme now is: two sounds, at least one of which is the last stressed vowel. But only rarely was the minimal rhymeme employed (e.g., an exact rhyme: *zahÁV – yadÁV*; an inexact rhyme: *koXÓ harXÓv*). Most of the rhymes are very rich. The sound contrast between the rhyming members was strongly emphasized through the introduction of neutral sounds in between the sounds of the (discontinuous!) rhymeme, e.g., *SiPuNÉXA – kaSE PaNÉXA, LEORÉR – LEOR nER*; or by changing the order of the parallel sounds, e.g., *miTPARECET – TRAPECIo-T* (*TPAR* Trap).

In short, modernist rhyme cannot be described merely in negative terms, as a deviation from a "classical norm." The norm of the *accentual-discontinuous* rhyme creates a system as consistent and as effective as the *accentual-terminal* one, though the range of variation given to particular poets may be considerably wider now.

SUMMARY

A Pan-Historic Synopsis of Hebrew Prosodic Systems

The preceding historical survey, though simplified as much as possible, presents a long chain of changes. When pan-historical comparisons are made, one finds logical relationships; similarities and contrasts between systems which are distant in time and place, but created in the forms of one language and culture. The table below, The Major Systems of Hebrew verse, may present the basis of such a comparison. The major systems of Hebrew verse are arranged in this diagram clockwise, in the order of their emergence in the history of Hebrew poetry. Except for a meter based on pitch, all known verse systems were productive in Hebrew. As can be seen from the diagram, there is a logical pattern, a kind of cyclic movement in this history. The major basis of the meter moved from *phrase* to *word* to *syllable* and vice versa.

The earliest and the latest verse systems were based on a free rhythm of phrase groups, though in the Bible there was a strong symmetricity of parallelism, whereas in modernist free verse there is a typical flow of continuity and lengths of lines may be highly varied. On the other hand, in modernist free verse poets often employ changing segments of accentual-syllabic meters as well as effects of irregular rhyme. It is not the freedom of "primitive" poetry, preceding any system, but the freedom of a "late" post-classical period, which is also free to employ any device developed in the "classical" rules of previous periods.

From biblical rhythm, based on semantic-syntactic-accentual free parallelism of phrases, the development of Hebrew verse moved toward basing its meters on more and more exact measures, i.e., ordering smaller elements of the language from phrases to the number of stresses, through the exact number of words, to the number of syllables, to a distinction of syllables according to their prosodic features.

Meters based on syllable counting ruled Hebrew poetry from about 950 almost to 1950. These were the most exact and variegated systems of Hebrew versification. Within this tradition, the change in the internal organization of the verse line from a quantitative principle to an accentual principle represented the general development of European poetry, but marked also the shift from the artificial "high" style of reading poetry to the intrusion of the cadences of the spoken language. (In religious poetry of Franco-Germany throughout the Middle Ages, a system based on the number of words persisted, i.e., a rhythm which, though numerically rigorous, was closer to representing some phrase patterns and clearly resembled the rhythm of medieval Yiddish and German poetry.)

In modernist poetry the movement of the early centuries of the Christian era was reversed: from strict syllable counting through a semi-regular meter, relying almost exactly on the number of major word stresses (though with a still limited freedom of syllable numbers 7), to a free verse system, based primarily on a rhythm of phrase groups, relying on the tension between the verse line and syntactic units. But in this period, even within the domain of free verse (8), the previous regular norms (6 accentual-syllabic and 7, accentual net) were still widely employed. On the other hand, the essential difference between the major systems of Hebrew verse should not lead to the overlooking of some basic consistent trends which cut across several systems. Within each system not all possibilities were equally employed. In any system, a rather small number of all possible forms were prevalent in poetry. Observing the syntactic possibilities of Hebrew verse in different periods, one finds a predilection for a certain optimal length of line, persistent throughout the ages: three or four major stresses in the Bible, four or five graphic words, 11 or 13 syllables (including short ones), three or four amphibrachs, and five iambs which are very similar in length of line and conveniently accommodate similar groups of words and phrases.

The Major Systems of Hebrew Verse (in their logical and chronological order)

Length of a line	**Free**	**Fixed**		
Major Basis of the Meter	**Phrase**	**Word**		**Syllable**
Antiquity and Middle Ages (From phrase to syllable)	I. *Bible: free accentual* (Phrase – parallelism group of stresses)	II. *Early Piyyut: accentual* Number of major stresses	III. *Rhymed Piyyut:* word meter Number of words	IV. *Spain: quantitative* Number of syllables order of long/short syllable
				V. *(Italy) Haskalah: syllabic* Number of syllables
Modern Age (From syllable to phrase)	VIII. *Modernist: Free Verse* Changing balance of phrase groups	VII. *Modernist ("Russian") accentual net* Number of major stresses (+ limited freedom of syllables)		VI. *Modern: accentual=syllabic* Number of syllables order of stressed/ unstressed

Regular Rhyme

No Regular Rhyme	**Form of Rhymeme** / **Decisive Vowel**	**Discontinuous**	**Discontinuous**
I. *Bible* Free sound orchestration	final	II. *Kallirian Piyyut:* *terminal-discontinuous* RVR רִיק R+RV מ + רִי R+RVC מ + רִיס R+R+CV(C) מ + ר + הם (תִּי)	III. *Medieval: terminal* CVC רִיק CV רִי CVC רִים CV(C) הֵם (תִּי)
VI. *Modernist* ("Free") Scattered Rhymes	stressed	V. *Modernist ("Russian"):* *accentual-discontinuous* מַבְרִיק CV́+ רִי + מוֹרִי דְּבָרִים V́C (V)+ וֹר + (אֹרַת עוֹרֶק) CV́C(V) דֶר + (דֶּרֶךְ-קוֹדֵר-אַץ) C+C+CV́+(V)+ ק + ס + מָ + ? (Ko-S ha Malm-KSu-MAhl)	IV. *(Italy, Haskalah) Modern:* *accentual-terminal* V́C יק CV́ רִי RV́C רִים V́CVC וֹרֶק

The Major Systems of Hebrew Rhyme

A similar pattern can be discerned in the history of Hebrew rhyme norms. Here, again, Hebrew poetry completed a whole cycle in its development. But rhyme was not as obligatory as meter. The earliest and the latest periods have no regular rhyme, i.e., no rhyme in the strict sense of a sound device used regularly for the strophic composition of a whole poem. The Regular Rhyme section of the table Major Systems of Hebrew verse represents typical rhymemes, using the following symbols: V – vowel, C – consonant, R – root consonant (only where relevant), V´ – stressed vowel, ł – discontinuity in the rhymeme. When read clockwise, the diagram represents the history of Hebrew rhyme.

Disregarding some secondary developments, there were four major rhyme systems. The similarities and the differences between these systems are related to the form and location of the rhymeme. The upper part of the diagram is opposed to the lower part from the point of view of the decisive vowel: in the Middle Ages the rhymeme relied on the final vowel, in the modern age on the stressed vowel. On the left hand (the extremes of this history) the rhymeme could be discontinuous, whereas on the right hand (in the "classical" periods) the rhymeme had to be a continuous and a terminal chain of sounds.

There is also a correlation (though not overlapping) between the corresponding major systems of meter and rhyme, as may be seen from a comparison of both diagrams. At the extreme ends of this cycle, when rhythm was based primarily on phrases, i.e., was dominated by a balancing of syntactic and semantic patterns, no regular rhyme was necessary. In the "classical" periods, when meter was based on the number of syllables, rhyme, too, was syllabic: the medieval rhymeme was based on one (terminal) syllable; modern rhyme based its major distinction of rhyme gender (masculine-feminine) on the number of syllables. Typically enough, in verse systems in which the prominence of the word was basic, discontinuous rhyme developed, i.e., rhyme based on the nature of the Hebrew word. However, this parallelism, essential as it was, was by no means automatic, e.g., word meter continued a long time after the suppression of the early discontinuous rhyme.

BIBLIOGRAPHY: GENERAL: (There is no general history or survey of Hebrew versification). On rhyme: B. Hrushovski, "*Ha-Shitot ha-Rashiyyot shel he-Ḥaruz ha-Ivri min ha-Piyyut ad Yameinu*," in: *Hasifrut*, 4 (1971), 721–49. **ADD. BIBLIOGRAPHY:** E. Cogan, "*Migilgulei Mishkal ha-Hat'amot be-Shiratenu*," *Heker ve-'Iyyun be-Madda'ei ha-Yahdut – Sifrut, Mikra, Lashon* (1976), 107–117; T. Carmi (ed.), *The Penguin Book of Hebrew Verse* (1981). BIBLE: W.H. Cabb, *A Criticism of Hebrew Metre* (1905); J. Begrich, *Zur hebraeischen Metrik*, in: *Theologische Rundschau*, 4 (1932), 67–89; I. Gabor, *Der hebraeische Urrythmus* (1929); B. Levin, *Zivvug ha-Millin ba-Tanakh* (1926). **ADD. BIBLIOGRAPHY:** F.M.Cross, "Toward a history of Hebrew prosody," *Fortunate the Eyes That See* (1995), 298–309 (=*From Epic to Canon* (1998)). PIYYUT: J. Schirmann, *Hebrew Liturgical Poetry and Christian Hymnology*, in: JQR, 44 (1953/54), Zunz, Lit Poesie; A. Mirsky, "*Maḥzavtan shel Ẓurot ha-Piyyut*," in: YMḤSI, 7 (1958), 1–129; M. Zulay, *ibid.*, 2 (1936), 213; idem, *Piyyutei Yannai* (1938); E. Fleischer, "*Le-Ḥeker Tavniyyot ha-Keva be-Fiyyutei ha-Kedushta*," in: *Sinai*, 65 (1969), 21–47; idem, "*Iyyunim bi-Ve'ayot Tafkidam ha-Liturgi shel Sugei ha-Piyyut ha-Kadum*," in: *Tarbiz*, 40 (1971), 41–63; idem, "*Mivnim Strofiyyim Me'ein-Ezoriyyim ba-Piyyut ha-Kadum*,", in: *Hasifrut*, 2 (1970), 194–240; B. Hrushovski, "*Ẓurot ha-Piyyut ha-Kadum ve-Reshit ha-Ḥarizah ha-Ivrit*," in: *Hasifrut*, 3 (1971). **ADD. BIBLIOGRAPHY:** E. Fleischer, *The Yoẓer – Its Emergence and Development* (Heb., 1984); J. Yahalom, *Poetic Language in the Early Piyyut* (Heb., 1985); S. Elizur, *Poet at a Turning Point – Rabbi Yehoshua Bar Khalfa and His Poetry* (Heb., 1984); A. Mirsky, *Ha-Piyyut – The Development of Post Biblical Poetry in Ereẓ Israel and the Diaspora* (Heb., 1990); M. Zulay, in: E. Hazan (ed.), *Ereẓ Israel and its Poetry – Studies in Piyyutim from the Cairo Genizah* (Heb., 1995); N. Katusmata, *The Liturgical Poetry of Nehemiah ben Shelomoh ben Heiman ha-Nasi* (Heb., 2002); idem, *Hebrew Style in the Liturgical Poetry of Shemuel ha-Shelishi* (Heb., 2003). SPAIN: Schirmann, Sefarad; idem, "La métrique quantitative dans la poesie hebraique du Moyen-Age," in: *Sefarad*, 8 (1948), 323–32; B. Halper, "The Scansion of Mediaeval Hebrew Poetry," in: JQR, 4 (1913/14), 153–224; D. Yellin, *Torat ha-Shirah ha-Sefaradit* (1940); idem, "*Ha-Mishkalim be-Shirat Shemu'el ha-Nagid*," in: YMḤSI, 5 (1939); I. Davidson, in: JQR, 30 (1939/40), 299–398; N. Aloni, *Torat ha-Mishkalim* (1951); S. Almoli, *Shekel ha-Kodesh* (1965); K. Heger, *Die… Ḥarǧas…* (1950); A. Mirsky, "*Mashmaut he-Ḥaruz be-Shirat Sefarad*," in: *Leshonenu*, 33 (1969). **ADD. BIBLIOGRAPHY:** E. Hazan, *The Poetics of the Sephardi Piyut, according to the Litrugical Poetry of Yehuda Halevi* (1986); J. Schirmann, in: E. Fleischer (ed.), *The History of Hebrew Poetry in Muslim Spain* (Heb., 1996); idem, in. E. Fleischer (ed.), *The History of Hebrew Poetry in Christian Spain and Southern France* (Heb., 1997); Y. Yahalom (ed.), *Judaeo-Arabic Poetics – Fragments of a Lost Treatise by Eleazar ben Jacob of Baghdad* (Heb., 2001). ITALY: A Mirsky, *Mishkal ha-Tenu'ot ha-Italki*, in: *Sefer Ḥanokh Yalon* (1963), 221–7; B. Hrushovski, "The Creation of Accented Iambs in European Poetry and their First Employment in a Yiddish Romance in Italy (1508–09)," in: *For Max Weinreich, on his Seventieth Birthday* (1964), 108–46. YIDDISH POETRY. U. Weinreich, *On the Cultural History of Yiddish Rime*, in: *Essays on Jewish Life and Thought* (1959), 423–42; B. Hrushovski, "On Free Rhythms in Modern Yiddish Poetry," in: U. Weinreich (ed.), *The Field of Yiddish* (1954), 219–66. THE MODERN AGE: B. Benshalom, *Mishkalav shel H.N. Bialik* (1945), idem, "*Keri'at Deror la-Ḥaruz ha-Monosilabi*," in: *Hasifrut* (1968–69), 161–75; S. Span, *Massot u-Meḥkarim* (1964); B. Hrushovski, "'*Ritmus ha-Raḥvut' Halakhah u-Ma'aseh be-Shirato ha-Ekspresyonistit shel U.Z. Greenberg*," in: *ibid.*, 176–205. **ADD. BIBLIOGRAPHY:** U. Shavit, "*Bein Ḥaruz le-Mashma'ut – le-Ofyah ve-li-Mkomah shel ha-Siyomet ha-Daktilit be-Shirat Bialik*," in: Z. Malachi (ed.), *Al Shira ve-Sipporet – Meḥkarim be-Sifrut ha-Ivrit* (1974), 229–262; R. Zur, "*Ḥaruz Anti-Dikduki u-Khshirut Leshonit*," in: *Ha-Sifrut* 22 (1976), 59–62; M. Barukh, "*Iyyun Nosaf al ha-Kesher bein Ḥaruz u-Mashma'ut [besifrut yeladim ivrit]*," in: *Sifrut Yeladim va-No'ar*, 7 (1980), 10–14; D. Bregman, *The Golden Way – The Hebrew Sonnet during the Renaissance and the Baroque* (Heb. 1995); idem, *A Bundle of Gold – Hebrew Sonnets from the Renaissance and the Baroque* (Heb., 1997).

[Benjamin Hrushovski-Harshav]

PROSSNITZ, JUDAH LEIB BEN JACOB HOLLESCHAU (c. 1670–1730), Shabbatean prophet. Born in Uhersky Brod, he settled in Prossnitz (Prostejov) after his marriage. An uneducated man, he made his living as a peddler. About 1696 he underwent a spiritual awakening and began to study the Mishnah, and later the Zohar and kabbalistic writings. Believing that he was visited by the souls of deceased, he claimed that he studied Kabbalah with Isaac *Luria and *Shabbetai Ẓevi. Whether his Shabbatean awakening was connected with the movement in Moravia around *Judah Ḥasid, Heshel *Ẓoref, and Ḥayyim *Malakh is still a matter of conjecture. Possibly he was won over by Ẓevi Hirsch b. Jerahmeel *Chotsh, who spent some time in Prossnitz in 1696. Judah Leib first turned to teaching children but later his followers in Prossnitz provided for him and his family. Taking up residence in the *bet midrash* of Prossnitz, he led a strictly ascetic life; he became generally known as Leibele Prossnitz. Before long he started to divulge kabbalistic and Shabbatean mysteries and to preach in public in the manner of a revivalist preacher (*mokhi'aḥ*). He found many adherents, his most important supporter for some years being Meir *Eisenstadt, a famous rabbinic authority who served as rabbi of Prossnitz from 1702. At the same time his Shabbatean propaganda, especially since it came from an uneducated lay mystic, aroused strong hostility in many critics. Between 1703 and 1705 he traveled through Moravia and Silesia, causing considerable agitation in the communities. Along with other Shabbatean leaders of this period, he prophesied the return of Shabbetai Ẓevi in 1706. His open Shabbatean propaganda led to clashes in Glogau and Breslau, where the rabbis threatened him with excommunication unless he returned to Prossnitz and stayed there. As 1706 approached his agitation reached a pitch. He assembled a group of 10 followers who studied with him and practiced extravagant mortifications.

Judah Leib was widely credited with magical practices connected with his attempts to bring to an end the dominion of *Samael and is reported to have sacrificed a chicken as a kind of bribe to the unclean powers. The facts concerning this and his promise to reveal the *Shekhinah* to some of his followers, including Eisenstadt, are shrouded in legend, but they contain some kernel of historical truth. Since by then he was widely considered by his foes to be a sorcerer, Eisenstadt left him and Prossnitz was put under a ban by the rabbinical court and sentenced to exile for three years; however, he was allowed to return after several months. He persisted at the head of a secret Shabbatean group in Prossnitz, again working as a children's teacher. Maintaining connections with other Shabbateans, in

1724 he tried to obtain the appointment of one of his closest followers, R. Sender, to the rabbinate of Mannheim (L. Loewenstein, *Geschichte der Juden in der Kurpfalz* (1895), 198–9). Jonathan *Eybeschuetz, a pupil of Meir Eisenstadt in Prossnitz for several years, is said to have studied secretly with Judah Leib, who was then propagating teachings close to the radical wing of Shabbateanism. Along with others in this group, he supported heretical teachings regarding divine providence. When Leib b. Ozer wrote his memoir on the state of Shabbateanism in 1717, Judah Leib was refraining from public manifestations of Shabbatean faith and was said to be working on a kabbalistic commentary on the Book of *Ruth. With the resurgence of Shabbatean activities in 1724, in the wake of the emissaries from Salonika, Judah Leib again appeared publicly on the scene, claiming to be the Messiah ben Joseph, the precursor of the Messiah ben David. Once more, he found many followers in Moravia and even in Vienna and Prague. Some of his letters to Eybeschuetz and Isaiah Mokhi'aḥ in Mannheim were found among the papers confiscated from Shabbatean emissaries. In the summer of 1725 Judah Leib was again excommunicated by the rabbis of Moravia in Nikolsburg (Mikulov) and after that led a vagrant life. When he came to Frankfurt on the Main in early 1726 he was not allowed to enter the Jewish quarter, but he was given material assistance by one of his secret supporters. His last years were reportedly spent in Hungary. Whereas the friendly contact between Judah Leib and Eybeschuetz is well established, there is no conclusive proof of Jacob *Emden's claim that Judah Leib saw Eybeschuetz as the future leader of the Shabbateans (J. Emden, *Beit Yonatan ha-Sofer* (Altona, 1762 (?), 1b), or that he would even be the Messiah after Shabbetai Ẓevi's apotheosis (*Shevirat Luḥot ha-Aven* (Zolkiew, 1755), 18b). After Judah Leib's death a strong group of Shabbateans survived in Prossnitz during the 18th century.

BIBLIOGRAPHY: J. Emden, *Torat ha-Kena'ot* (Amsterdam, 1752), 34bf., 41a–42a; A. Neubauer, in: MGWJ, 36 (1887), 207–12; D. Kahana, *Toledot ha-Mekubbalim ve-ha-Shabbeta'im*, 2 (1914), 168–75, 184; M.A. Perlmutter (Anat), *R. Yehonatan Eybeschuetz, Yaḥaso el ha-Shabbeta'ut* (1947), 43–47; Chr. P. Loewe, *Speculum Religionis Judaicae* (1732), 80–82.

[Gershom Scholem]

PROSSTITZ (Prossnitz), DANIEL (Steinschneider; 1759–1846), Hungarian rabbi. Born in Tobitschau near Prossnitz (Prostejov), Daniel studied first in Moravia and later in Pressburg under the rabbi of the town Meir b. Saul *Barby and was later appointed by Meshullam *Igra to his *bet din* there. Eventually he succeeded Rabbi M. Toska, the head of the *bet din*. In addition he was appointed rabbi to a society for the study of the Talmud (*Ḥevrah Shas*) established in Pressburg. He served the Pressburg community in these capacities for 50 years. Prosstitz recommended Moses *Sofer for the vacant position of rabbi of Pressburg and it was largely due to his conduct of the negotiations that Sofer was appointed. Prosstitz also occupied himself with Kabbalah and used to fast frequently, especially after a dream.

He published the *Sefer ha-Yashar* of Jacob Tam, and left responsa and novellae to the Talmud in manuscript. Responsa addressed to him are found in the Resp. Ḥatam Sofer, in Ezekiel *Landau's *Noda bi-Yhudah*, and in the responsa of his other great contemporaries.

BIBLIOGRAPHY: D. Prosstitz Steinschneider, *Dan mi-Daniel*, 1 (1881), introd.; I. Weiss, *Avnei Beit ha-Yoẓer* (1900), nos. 1:11, 2:11; S. Sofer, *Iggerot Soferim*, pt. 2 (1928), 5; H. Gold, *Die Juden und die Judengemeinde Bratislava in Vergangenheit und Gegenwart* (1932).

[Samuel Weingarten-Hakohen]

PROSTEJOV (Czech **Prostějov**, Ger. **Prossnitz**, Heb. פרוסטיץ), city in central Moravia, Czech Republic. From the Middle Ages Prostejov was a center for the textile and ready-made clothing industries, in which Jews played an important part. A Jew is mentioned in a document of 1445. The Jewish community, founded by people expelled from nearby *Olomouc (Olmuetz) in 1454, was, from the 17th to the 19th century, second only to *Mikulov (Nikolsburg) among the communities of Moravia. The Jews dealt in luxury goods and locally made textiles. In 1584 the Jews' right of residence was confirmed but the branches of trade open to them were restricted. The community then numbered 31 families. A minute book (*pinkas*) opened in 1587 began with the *takkanot* of *Judah Loew b. Bezalel regulating synagogal arrangements. A compendium of Sabbath hymns, *Kol Simḥah*, was printed in 1602 by a short-lived local printing house.

The Jewish community and its importance in local industry increased after the Protestant inhabitants had left when the town became Roman Catholic under duress. In 1639 there were 143 Jewish men in Prostejov and 64 houses in the town were owned by Jews. Prostejov absorbed many refugees after the *Chmielnicki massacres in 1648 and the Vienna expulsion in 1670. The community numbered 64 families in 1669. The synagogue was dedicated in 1676. The first known rabbi was Isaac Ḥayyut b. Abraham (d. 1639); among his successors were Meir b. Isaac Ashkenazi and Wolf Boskowitz. The Prostejov rabbinate was a steppingstone to the office of *Landrabbiner* for Menahem *Krochmal and Nahum *Trebitsch. The names of almost 30 rabbis have been recorded since the late 16th century. In 1785–94 the local yeshivah was led by Rabbi Moses *Sofer (Schreiber), called Ḥatam Sofer (1762–1839). A compromise reached in 1677 (and supplemented in 1688) concerning the extent of trade between Jews and gentiles testifies to the importance of Jewish participation in the textile and clothing trades. The community numbered 318 families in 1713, 1,393 persons in 1787, and 1,495 in 1798. In 1804 the number was 1,704, representing about a quarter of the total population. The population continued to grow to about 2,000 in 1875 but then dropped to 1,553 and 1,442 in 1930. The number of families allotted under the *Familiants Law was 328. The Prostejov community was strongly influenced by the Shabbatean movement, and one of its leaders, Judah Leib *Prossnitz, lived in the town. The community was also affected by *Frankism and was one of the first to absorb the ideas of the *Haskalah. The first sermon in German in the Hapsburg dominions was preached there by Loew *Schwab (1835). In 1843 a Jew founded a private elementary school for Jewish and Christian children. In 1831 Feith *Ehrenstamm founded a factory, the beginning of Jewish enterprise in modern textile industry. By 1842 there were 135 Jewish textile merchants in Prostejov. The first factory for ready-made clothes on the European continent was founded by Mayer and Isaac Mandel in 1859. The 200 Jews in the National Guard units were lauded for their conduct in fighting during the anti-Jewish riots in 1848. Prostejov became a political community (*politische Gemeinde) in 1849. In 1880 there were 1,804 Jews in Prostejov. The community absorbed many World War I refugees from Eastern Europe. Between the two world wars the community was one of the most active in Czechoslovakia and the first to arrange modern Hebrew courses. The clothing industry, represented mainly by the Sborowitz firm, which had 108 sales establishments throughout Czechoslovakia and a vast export business, brought affluence to the community which attracted many new members from *Sub-Carpathian Ruthenia (Carpatho-Russia). In 1930 the community numbered 1,442 (4.3% of the total). Among the natives of the town were Menahem Katz, rabbi of the *Deutschkreutz community and leader of Hungarian *Orthodoxy; Gideon Brecher, physician and author of a booklet on circumcision; his son Adolph, author and physician; and the bibliographer Moritz *Steinschneider. Jonathan *Eybeschuetz and Adolf and Hermann *Jellinek were among the pupils of the Prostejov yeshivah. The well-known philosopher and founder of phenomenology Edmund *Husserl (1859–1938) was born there.

Many refugees from the Sudeten area arrived in Prostejov in autumn 1938. After the German invasion (March 1939) Jews suffered from Gestapo raids, mainly in July when the synagogue also was closed. Many Jews left Prostejov during 1940. Those who remained were deported to the Nazi extermination camps in 1942. Over 1,200 local Jews perished in the Holocaust. The synagogue appurtenances were transferred to the Jewish Central Museum in Prague. In 1945 a small congregation administered by the Olomouc community was reestablished, mostly by Jews from Sub-Carpathian Ruthenia. A memorial to the victims of the Holocaust was consecrated in 1950. The congregation was still active in 1980. Few Jews remained in the early 21st century.

Three synagogues were active in Prostejov: the first, from about 1676, was demolished before 1905; the second synagogue served as a *bet midrash* before being converted into a synagogue; it was in service until World War II; in 1953–64 it was used by the Orthodox church and in 1970 it was converted into an exhibition hall; the third synagogue was built in 1904; services were held there until World War II and from 1949 it was used by the Hussite church.

The prayer house established in 1945–46 has been used by the Plymouth Brethren's Church since 1982. Prostejov had three cemeteries: the first known from the 17th century and closed down after 1800; the second from about 1801 and destroyed by the Nazis in 1943; and the last founded in 1908.

BIBLIOGRAPHY: J. Freimann, in: JJLG, 15 (1923), 26–58; B. Wachstein, *ibid.*, 16 (1924), 163–76; L. Goldschmied, in: H. Gold (ed.), *Juden und Judengemeinden Maehrens* (1929), 491–504; B. Heilig, in: JGGJČ, 3 (1931), 307–448, incl. bibl.; idem, in: BLBI, 3 (1960), 101–22; R. Iltis (ed.), *Die aussaeen unter Traenen…* (1959), 71–76; *The Jews of Czechoslovakia*, 1 (1968), 417–8; R. Kestenberg-Gladstein, *Neuere Geschichte der Juden in den boehmischen Laendern*, 1 (1969), index; Y. Toury, *Mehumah u-Mevukhah be-Mahpekhat 1848* (1968), index.

[Meir Lamed / Yeshayahu Jelinek (2nd ed.)]

PROSTITUTION (Heb. זְנוּת, *zenut*), the practice of indiscriminate sexual intercourse for payment or for religious purposes. Prostitution was practiced by male and female prostitutes. The word *zenut*, applied to both common and sacred prostitution, is also often used metaphorically.

Biblical

The prostitute was an accepted though deprecated member of the Israelite society, both in urban and rural life (Gen. 38:14; Josh. 2:1ff.; I Kings 3:16–27). The Bible refers to Tamar's temporary harlotry and to the professional harlotry of Rahab without passing any moral judgment. The visits of Samson to the harlot of Gaza (Judg. 16:1) are not condemned, but conform with his picaresque life. Harlots had access to the king's tribunal, as other people (I Kings 3:16ff.). Nevertheless, harlotry was a shameful profession, and to treat an Israelite girl like a prostitute was considered a grave offense (Gen. 34:31). The Israelites were warned against prostituting their daughters (Lev. 19:29), and priests were not allowed to marry prostitutes (21:7). The punishment of a priest's daughter who became a prostitute, thus degrading her father, was death through fire (Lev. 21:9). According to the talmudic sages, however, this law applies only to the priest's daughter who is married or at least betrothed (Sanh. 50b–51a). Prostitutes might be encountered in the streets and squares, and on street corners, calling out to passersby (Prov. 7:10–23); they sang and played the harp (Isa. 23:16), and bathed in public pools (I Kings 22:38). Their glances and smooth talk were dangers against which the immature were warned (Jer. 3:3, Prov. 2:16; 5:3, 6:24–25, 7:5, et al.).

In the Ancient Near East, temple women, of whom one class was called *qadištu*, probably served as sacred prostitutes. Sometimes dedicated by their fathers to the deity, they had special statutes, and provisions were made for them by law (Code of Hammurapi, 178–82). Customs connected with them are likely to underlie Herodotus' lurid and misleading statement that in Babylon every woman was to serve once as a sacred prostitute before getting married, thus sacrificing her virginity to the goddess Mylitta (Ishtar; 1:199). In Israel the sacred prostitutes were condemned for their connection with idolatry. Deuteronomy 23:18–19 forbids Israelites, men and women alike, to become sacred prostitutes, and states that their wages must not be used for paying vows.

It has been supposed that "the women who performed tasks at the entrance to the Tent of Meeting," mentioned in I Samuel 2:22, were sacred prostitutes – though this hardly suits their other occurrence in Exodus 38:8. There were male and female prostitutes in Israel and Judah during the monarchy, and in Judah they were, from time to time, the object of royal decrees of expulsion (cf. I Kings 14:24; 15:12; 22:47; II Kings 23:7; Hos. 4:14). Sacred prostitution, because of its association with idolatry, was the object of numerous attacks in the Bible, especially in the historical and prophetic books (cf., e.g., II Kings 23:4–14; Jer. 2:20; Ezek. 23:37ff.). Terms connected with harlotry are used figuratively to characterize unfaithfulness toward the Lord (Num. 25:1–2; Judg. 2:17; 8:27, 33; Jer. 3:6; Ezek. 6:9; Hos. 4:12; et al.).

[Laurentino Jose Afonso]

Post-Biblical

The many warnings of Ben Sira against prostitution is evidence that it was widespread in the Hellenistic period. According to II Maccabees 6:4, Antiochus Epiphanes introduced sacred prostitutes into the Temple. Throughout the whole of the apocryphal and pseudepigraphical literature, in the Damascus Document, in the documents of the Dead Sea sects (Serekh ha-Yahad 1:6), in Josephus (Ant. 4:206), and by Philo (Jos. 43, Spec. 3:51), prostitution is vigorously denounced.

In Talmud and Halakhah

Different opinions are expressed in the Talmud with regard to the prostitute of the Bible, both concerning her hire and her marriage to a priest. Some were of the opinion that these references apply only to a professional prostitute, but there were also other opinions. With regard to her hire (Deut. 23:19) the *halakhah* was decided in accordance with the opinion of R. Judah ha-Nasi that it was not forbidden except to those for whom "cohabitation is a transgression" (Tosef., Tem. 4:8; see Prohibited Marriage). With regard to the unmarried woman who engages in prostitution, however, "her wage is permitted" (i.e., for use in the Temple; Maim. Yad, Issurei ha-Mizbe'ah 4:8). Some were of the opinion that her wage is forbidden only with regard to such reward "the like of which can be offered on the altar," but not to money (Tem. 6:4; but Philo refers explicitly to a prohibition on money). The term *be'ilat zenut* ("intercourse of prostitution") was, however, applied not only to those relations forbidden in the strict legal sense (see also Yev. 8:5) but also to any intercourse not expressly for the purpose of marriage (TJ, Git. 7:448d; Git. 81b), and even to a marriage not celebrated in accordance with the *halakhah*.

The *halakhah* imposed a general prohibition on the professional prostitute, and the term came to include any woman who abandoned herself to any man even if not for pay, and states that "Whoever hands his unmarried daughter [to a man] not for the purposes of matrimony," as well as the woman who delivers herself not for the purposes of matrimony, could lead to the whole world being filled with *mamzerim* since "from his consorting with many women and not knowing with whom, or if she has had intercourse with many men and does not know with whom – he could marry his own daughter, or marry her to his son" (see *Mamzer*; Sifra, Kedoshim 7, 1–5). The ruling is based on the verse "Profane not thy daughter, to make her a harlot" (Lev. 19:29), as well as the verse "There shall be no harlot of the daughters of Israel" (Deut. 23:18; *kedeshah* being taken as referring to every prostitute (Sanh. 82a)). The penalty for both parties is flogging (Maim. Yad, Ishut 1:4; Na'arah Betulah 2:17). Abraham b. David of Posquières in his gloss (*ibid.*) stressed that this law applies only to the woman "who is ready to prostitute herself to every man," and he makes an express exception in the case of a woman "who gives herself solely to one man without benefit of marriage." The rabbis were eloquent in their condemnation of the prostitute and her like, but in most cases their strictures apply to every kind of licentiousness. They warned particularly against approaching a harlot's door (Ber. 32a; Av. Zar. 17a) and passing through a "harlots' market" (ARN[1] 2, 14; ARN[2] 3, 13), such as were to be found in large cities (Pes. 113b; Ket. 64b), especially in Ereẓ Israel, where the Romans "built marketplaces in which to set harlots" (Shab. 33b). Sometimes inns served as brothels. The Targum gives *pundekita* ("woman innkeeper") as the translation of the "harlot" of the Bible (also Yev. 122a). After the destruction of the Temple and during the Hadrianic persecutions, the Romans placed Jewish women in brothels (ARN[1] 8, 37; Av. Zar. 17–18), and even men were taken captive for shameful purposes (Lam. R. 1:16, no. 45; cf. Or. Sibyll. 3:184–6, and 5:387–9). Some succeeded in maintaining their virtue and were ransomed; others committed suicide to avoid being forced into prostitution (Git. 57b). But there were also Jewish women who willingly engaged in prostitution (TJ, Ta'an. 4, 8, 69a) and Jews who were pimps (*ibid.* 1:4). There are even stories in the *aggadah* about sons of scholars who were very dissolute (BM 85a). The *halakhot* of ritual purity and impurity mention several garments which were peculiar to prostitutes: a "net" for the hair and a harlot's shift made like net work (Kel. 24:16, 28:9). The sages, who realized that the urge to prostitution is greater than that to idolatry (Song R. 7:8), considered it one of the important causes of the destruction of the Temple, and its spread as a sign of the advent of the Messiah (Sot. 9:13, 15). But there are also stories about prostitutes who repented completely (Av. Zar. 17a; SEZ 22), as well as about a gentile prostitute who converted to Judaism out of conviction (Sif. Num. 115; Men. 44a). Extensive aggadic material about the biblical Rahab portrays both her dissolute behavior as a harlot and her complete spiritual and social transformation when she accepted the truth of Jewish beliefs (Zev. 116a–b; Sif. Num. 78).

[Moshe David Herr]

Post-Talmudic

Jews in the pre-modern world lived, with few exceptions, in Jewish communities and under the yoke of Jewish tradition and *halakhah*. This affected every aspect of their lives, including sexual relations. As stated above, every sexual act between a man and woman outside marital relations was considered as coming within the definition of prostitution (*be'ilat zenut*), and the rabbis strongly condemned manifestations of sexual license in the Jewish community. Many regulations were issued by the various communities to fight prostitution in all its forms. Relations between Jews and gentiles were regarded as especially dangerous, because in most places they were against the laws of the land and the Church, and were therefore apt to evoke an undesirable reaction by non-Jews and involve the whole community.

Jewish communities were never reconciled to the existence of prostitution among them, especially organized prostitution on a commercial basis. They reacted energetically to every attempt to maintain a brothel in the Jewish quarter. There is mention of brothels actually being closed down by order of the communities in various German and French cities in the 17th and 18th centuries. Heavy fines were imposed on landlords who rented their houses for the purpose of prostitution. Anybody who knew of such a case was obliged to report it to the community. The Jews did not always manage to prevent brothels being opened within their neighborhoods, although protests against their establishment sometimes brought about their removal. In many places the laws of the country forbade their being maintained in the cities, so that they were relegated to the outskirts. Sometimes they were located in the vicinity of the Jewish quarter merely by chance, but in some cases they were established there deliberately, out of contempt for the Jews. At times the rabbis closed their eyes to the visits of unmarried men of the community to the brothels, in order to prevent other forms of lewdness.

There is evidence in the responsa literature that Jewish women engaged in prostitution, and no doubt there were also Jews who lived on pimping, but there is no data to the extent. The *halakhah* literature in the Middle Ages mentions several regulations against Jewish prostitutes and against Jews who frequented gentile prostitutes, but the prostitute was entitled to claim her fee (Rema). At the end of the Middle Ages it was laid down that a married man who frequented prostitutes was obliged to give his wife a divorce.

[Max Wurmbrand]

Modern Period

Prostitution is known to increase in times of chaos and upheaval and this was certainly true for East European Jews at the end of the 19th century. Violence and other forms of antisemitism, economic deprivation, and massive emigration led to various forms of significant Jewish involvement in the white slave trade, a euphemism for the trafficking of women across international borders for the purpose of prostitution.

Drastic impoverishment had always led some Jewish women, especially widows or abandoned wives, to occasional or part-time prostitution. The sexual mores of the Jewish community also meant that young women who had been seduced or had chosen to have premarital sexual relations, as well as unmarried older women, often had difficulty finding marriage partners. As it was nearly impossible for an uneducated single woman to support herself by other means, prostitution was often the only viable option. With the increasingly difficult situation in Eastern Europe in the late 19th century, and the large and mostly unregulated movement of population, it was particularly easy for profiteers to induce or entrap Jewish women to travel abroad and serve as prostitutes.

Traffickers used local agents to point them to young widows, abandoned wives, spinsters, or "ruined women," who were offered an escape from their poverty and shame and the promise of riches in distant lands. The procurers would then rely on a string of colleagues to obtain papers and tickets, arrange passage through borders, and accompany the women to their destinations. Upon arrival the women were usually placed in brothels where they had to work, initially without pay in order to pay back all of the fees incurred through their travels. Some professional procurers courted and married attractive women from poor families with promises of a prosperous new life abroad. The "groom" would then consummate the marriage and bring his "bride" to a large city before disclosing her fate. Procurers would often comb entire regions, collecting brides and depositing them with an agent in a larger city before transport abroad. The young women, even when not physically forced to serve as prostitutes, were often too ashamed to return to their homes and had no other alternative. Other procurers specialized in wooing and seducing young domestic servants working far from their families. Some Jewish women became prostitutes of their own volition to escape the drudgery of factory or domestic work or the grinding poverty of family life.

Jews neither controlled nor dominated the white slave trade but they did oversee the large and lucrative traffic in Jewish women. By the turn of the 20th century Jewish criminal gangs managed a complex system of routes, personnel, brothels, and corrupt officials. Obtaining accurate statistics on Jewish prostitution is nearly impossible. Although prostitution was legal in most European states in the late 19th century, it carried a social stigma and legal consequences, such as the need to submit to regular medical examinations. Additionally, many women engaged in prostitution only on an occasional basis. Nonetheless it is estimated that the proportion of Jews among prostitutes was never, even at its height, greater than the proportion of Jews in the population.

Jewish women from Europe were sent as far as southern Africa and the Far East, with England and Constantinople serving as major transit points, but one of the main destinations was South America. South American countries were eager to attract European immigrants and imported thousands of young men to serve in their growing economies. Open borders and underdeveloped law enforcement capacities led to rampant prostitution. In 1900, shortly after having been excluded by the local burial society, the Polish Jewish pimps of Buenos Aires chartered a mutual aid society and obtained their own cemetery. The groups that came to be known as the Zwi Migdal Society later had a synagogue as well. This was only the most infamous of a series of Jewish communal institutions established by and for criminal elements around the world.

America was another destination of the white slave trade, as well as a recruiting ground. Crowded and poor immigrant neighborhoods in cities across the United States provided ideal conditions. Polly *Adler, a prominent brothel-keeper in the first half of the 20th century, described in her memoirs (*A House Is Not a Home*, 1950) how her rape by a co-worker, the extreme privations of working-class existence, and her attraction to the trappings of success led her gradually toward a career as a madam.

The uneasy alliance between official toleration of prostitution and public discomfort with its visible aspects began to deteriorate as prostitution, and especially large-scale trafficking, grew across Europe and the United States. Yiddish literature of the early 20th century contains a number of powerful portrayals of the social and personal costs of widespread prostitution including Sholem *Asch's *God of Vengeance* and Perets *Hirschbein's *Miriam*. A 1908 performance of the latter in Buenos Aires led to a bloody public riot.

Already in the 1880s outraged individuals involved in social purity movements in Britain and the United States had begun to sound the alarm about the problems of the white slave trade. By the beginning of the 20th century, the public began to listen. Sensational press stories about kidnappings of young girls contributed to raising public ire. Much of the press coverage focused on Jewish involvement. While major news outlets published unfounded reports of salacious deeds and hinted that Jews masterminded these events, the antisemitic press went even further in exploiting the association between Jews and the white slave trade. These antisemitic polemics gave the impression that Jewish men were raping and stealing Christian girls in a modern version of the ancient *blood libel. In fact, although Jewish involvement in the white slave trade is not in question, Jewish traffickers dealt almost exclusively in Jewish women. The trade in non-Jewish women was generally overseen by their own countrymen and correligionists.

Public opinion, however, was not limited to placing blame, and Jewish and non-Jewish organizations began to form to combat the white slave trade. In 1899, Britain's fiery evangelical campaigner William Coote toured Europe trying to raise awareness about the need to regulate cross-border traffic and protect women. His trip was financed in part by the Rothschild family. Only several years previously the formation of the Jewish Association for the Protection of Girls and Women had created a central agency for British Jewish action. The group was ably and energetically run by Arthur Moro for the next several decades.

In Germany, Bertha *Pappenheim tirelessly fought for the rights of women. Combating the trade in women was one of the central platforms of her *Juedischer Frauenbund, established in 1904. Hers and other voluntary association across Europe established travelers aid stations at major terminals and worked to have laws changed to prevent the free movement of human traffic. Equally important, they established international communication lines. The National Council of Jewish Women in the United States undertook similar initiatives in the American immigrant community. Although these networks were never as sophisticated as those of the traffickers, they were still able to cause disruptions by sending advance warning to law enforcement and other voluntary societies around the world. The Jewish community in South America was particularly grateful for the monetary and informational support of their correligionists in Europe. At times Jewish and non-Jewish groups worked together on such projects but often their relations were soured by antisemitism.

In the early 20th century, the success of social work and legal activism in Western Europe, and the awareness that the root of the problem lay further east, led to calls to treat the blight of prostitution at its source. In 1913 a group of Jewish social workers and nurses were preparing to travel to Galicia and Romania to establish institutions to help Jewish women avoid the snares of poverty and the white slave trade. This work, however, ended as Europe descended into war.

The onset of World War I meant a severe deterioration in Jewish life in Europe, as well as the closure of escape routes. Both increased presence of soldiers and failing economic conditions led to an increase in non-professional prostitution among Jews and non-Jews on the continent. At the same time the international white slave trade routes were interrupted, and would never fully recover. World War I essentially put an end to the period of major Jewish involvement in prostitution. Jewish prostitution, and even small scale procuring and trafficking continued, but the conditions were no longer ripe for large-scale activities as emigration slowed down and Jews in western countries increasingly moved up the economic ladder.

Prostitution once again came to the fore in Jewish communal concerns following the collapse of the Soviet Union and the large-scale immigration of former Soviet citizens to Israel in the 1990s. Among the many immigrants was a small minority of individuals involved in a variety of criminal activities, including trafficking and prostitution. The relatively open immigration policies contained in the *Law of Return made Israel a useful hub for international criminal enterprise. Vulnerable women from all ethnic groups in the former Soviet Union were brought into Israel either voluntarily, or in some cases by deception, to serve as prostitutes in Israel or to be shipped elsewhere. Following time-tested methods, many of the women were forced to serve their procurers for lengthy periods to repay the cost of their travel. Others had their personal papers confiscated and were imprisoned in brothels or intimidated through the use of violence.

As the scope and size of the problem became clear, the Israeli government worked with internal non-governmental organizations and women's groups as well as international bodies to craft appropriate policies on judicial and criminal matters as well on as issues of rehabilitation and repatriation. Although these efforts did not end the international traffic in women, by 2004 they had proven effective in increasing both the prosecution of leaders of criminal rings and the rehabilitation of their victims.

[Eliyana R. Adler (2nd ed.)]

BIBLIOGRAPHY: M.G. May, in: AJSLL, 48 (1931–32), 73–98; B.A. Brooks, in: JBL, 60 (1941), 227–53; R. Patai, *Sex and Family in the Bible and the Middle East* (1959), 145–52; L.M. Epstein, *Sex Laws and*

Customs in Judaism (1948), 152–78. **ADD. BIBLIOGRAPHY:** J. Baskin, *Midrashic Women* (2002), 113–14, 154–60; Y. Assis, "Sexual Behavior in Medieval Hispano-Jewish Society," in: A. Rapaport-Albert and S. Zipperstein (eds.), *Jewish History* (1998), 25–59; A. Grossman, *Pious and Rebellious: Jewish Women in Medieval Europe* (2004), 133–47; E. Bristow, *Prostitution and Prejudice: The Jewish Fight against White Slavery 1870–1939* (1983); R. Gershuni, "Trafficking in Persons for the Purpose of Prostitution: The Israeli Experience," in: *Mediterranean Quarterly* (Fall 2004), 133–46; N. Glickman, *The Jewish White Slave Trade and the Untold Story of Raquel Liberman* (2000); R. Rosen, *The Lost Sisterhood: Prostitution in America, 1900–1918* (1982).

PROSTITZ, ISAAC BEN AARON (d. 1612), Hebrew printer. Isaac was born in Prossnitz, Moravia, and learned the printing trade in Italy, working with G. Cavalli and G. Grypho in *Venice. There he met the proofreader Samuel Boehm (d. 1588), who later joined Isaac in *Cracow, where he printed from 1569. From Italy they had brought with them typographical material, decorations etc., and in the privilege issued in 1567 to Isaac by King Sigmund August II of Poland for 50 years he is called an "Italian" Jew. In spite of initial intrigues by the Jesuits, Isaac and later his sons – Aaron and Issachar – and grandsons were able to print for nearly 60 years some 200 works of which 73 were in Yiddish, using fish and a ram (symbol for the offering of Isaac) as printer's mark. The productions covered a wide field: rabbinics, Bible, Kabbalah, philosophy, history, and even mathematics. The Babylonian Talmud was printed twice (1602–08; 1616–20); these were poor editions after an earlier and more auspicious beginning in 1579. The Jerusalem Talmud of 1609 has become standard in the form it was reissued in Krotoschin in 1886. Isaac was printer to the great scholars of the time: Moses *Isserles of Cracow, Solomon *Luria of Lublin, and Mordecai *Jaffe of Prague and Poznan. In 1602 he returned to his native Prossnitz, where he printed some works until 1605, while his son Aaron remained active in Cracow to 1628 printing apart from the Talmuds, the *Zohar (1603), and the *Shulḥan Arukh (1607, 1618–20), Turim with Joseph *Caro's commentary (1614–15), and **Ein Ya'akov* (1614, 1619). Isaac's descendants were working as printer's assistants until nearly the end of the 17th century.

BIBLIOGRAPHY: Steinschneider, Cat Bod, 2901–02; idem, *Juedische Typographie* (1938), 34–35; H.D. Friedberg, *Toledot ha-Defus ha-Ivri be-Polanyah* (1950^2), 5–25; M. Balaban, in: *Soncino Blaetter*, 3 (1929/30), 9–11, 47–48; R.N.N. Rabbinovicz, *Ma'amar al Hadpasat ha-Talmud* (1877), 70–75.

PROTESTANTS.

Up to World War II

Seen in perspective, the attitude of the Protestant movement toward Jews and Judaism was ambivalent and unstable. For the earlier periods see *Luther, *Calvin, and *Reformation. By the beginning of the 18th century the Protestant churches had amassed a vast amount of material on the Jews and on Judaism. The traditional hostility of more than a millennium was fully recorded in books such as *Entdecktes Judentum* (1700), an immense storehouse of learning and abuse collected by Johannes Andreas *Eisenmenger. The Jewish response in polemic and apologetic was equally comprehensively dealt with in *Tela Ignea Satanae* (1681) by Johann Christoph *Wagenseil. Of more interest was the appearance of material of a different kind – material which for the first time described Jews, Jewish customs, and Judaism sympathetically and objectively, and without either a controversial or theological bias.

In the historical field the most important work was *L'Histoire et la Religion des Juifs depuis Jésus Christ jusqu'à Présent*, by the Huguenot diplomat and scholar Jacques *Basnage. It appeared at the beginning of the century, and was immediately plagiarized by the Jesuits, who altered or omitted all his references to Christian responsibility for Jewish sufferings. The increase of travel led to an interest in Jewish customs, social, domestic, and religious; and books describing these customs in Europe, Africa, and the Middle East became part of the stock of any well-equipped library. But the most attractive field for Protestant study was rabbinic, and almost every university claimed a chair in Hebrew. Leiden and Franeker in Holland, Cambridge in England, and Jena in Germany were among the most distinguished. While the Christian Hebraists wrote much that was of little value, their studies of the Talmud removed the atmosphere of mystery and even blasphemy which medieval scholars had imparted to it. John *Selden in *De Synedriis et Praefecturis Juridicis veterum Hebraeorum* (1650–55) laid the foundation for the serious study of Jewish legal procedures. At the beginning of the 18th century, Wilhelm *Surenhuys of Amsterdam, in his introduction to a Latin edition of the Mishnah and in other writings, was the first to speak of rabbinic Judaism as the natural and proper development of the Judaism of the Bible.

Side by side with this interest in rabbinic Judaism was the concern of some of the Protestant sects with biblical Judaism as an ideal expression of natural law. John *Toland in *Nazarenus* (1718) made the first study of Judaic Christianity as something distinct from its gentile brother, and more valuable in that it retained the laws of Moses. But as the century progressed, this attitude of the free-thinking sects changed to violent hostility which saw "Jehovah" as the model of all tyranny. Hermann Samuel Reimarus (1694–1768) subjected the Scriptures to so detailed a critical examination that he can be regarded as the father of much of 19th-century biblical scholarship.

Missionary Activities

While these various developments helped to maintain a general interest in the Jews, it was not until the very end of the century that any organized approach to them evolved. Protestantism had been slow to develop missions in any field, and still slower to create organized missions to Jews. But individual authors, some of them converts from Judaism, exhorted the Jews to recognize the truth of Christianity. Traditionally such writings were filled with mockery and hatred; but in the 18th century, although there was a good deal of writing in the old style, a new approach of friendliness and respect appeared.

This contradiction was also manifested in the 18th-century view as to the general status of the Jews in a Christian society. In 1753 a bill was passed through the British Parliament to facilitate the naturalization of Jews. It provoked an immense flow of pamphleteering; of those pamphlets written from a Christian standpoint some were hostile and others favorable. When full political emancipation became an issue a hundred years later, the archbishop of Canterbury opposed it, while the archbishop of Dublin supported it. Even with individual Jewish converts to Protestantism the same contradiction was apparent, and in many cases they were received with scarcely veiled hostility and suspicion.

The leading figure in the emergence of organized Protestant missionary activity was Lewis *Way. He had unexpectedly inherited an enormous fortune upon the sole condition that he used it for the glory of God; and events led him to fulfill this condition in work for the conversion of the Jews. In 1809 the London Society for Promoting Christianity among the Jews had been founded, largely through the enthusiasm of a German Jewish convert, J.S.C.F. Frey. Way wished to increase his understanding of the whole question, and traveled extensively. He was horrified by the treatment that Jews received in Christian countries, and came to the conclusion that full emancipation was the fundamental preliminary to a missionary approach. He visited St. Petersburg and so impressed Czar Alexander I that he was invited to the Congress of Aix-la-Chapelle by the emperor, and succeeded in getting a resolution passed commending the idea of emancipation to the governments of Europe. Emancipation came slowly, but Way's influence brought into existence throughout the Protestant world societies which devoted themselves to sending missions to the Jews. Jewish life at that period was at a low ebb; and while actual conversions were few, many communities in eastern Europe, as well as in Palestine and North Africa, profited from the schools and hospitals established by the missions.

In 1910 an International Missionary Council was formed, and it included a special committee on missions to the Jews. (In 1961 the Council was incorporated in the World Council of Churches; and under its new name of "Committee on the Church and the Jewish People" it to some extent disavowed its proselytizing activity.)

Converts' Participation in Academic Life

Alfred Edersheim (1825–1889), the son of Viennese Jewish parents, first served the Scottish mission in Jassy, and then had a distinguished academic career at Edinburgh and Oxford. His *Life and Times of Jesus the Messiah* was the first scholarly picture of the Jewish environment of the Gospels. Even more distinguished was the son of a Jewish peddler of Goettingen by the name of Emmanuel Mendel, who on his baptism took the name of Neander (new man). As August Johann Wilhelm *Neander, he became a prolific historian of the Christian Church and professor of theology at Berlin University. More interesting than individual scholars was the group of distinguished converts who published a short book absolutely denying the authenticity of the ritual murder accusation at the time of the Damascus Affair in 1840. The accusation had first originated with a converted Jew of Cambridge in the 12th century, but this was the first time that a group of Jewish converts turned to defend their old religion. The most valuable contribution to the scholarly work of the missions was made by social institutes for Judaic studies (1650 in Strasbourg and 1702 in Halle) and chiefly by Franz *Delitzsch, who wrote extensively on post-biblical Judaism; in 1880 the Institutum Delitzschianum was founded in his honor, and it continued to produce scholarly works until the time of the Nazis.

While the leadership in missionary work was largely British, in the field of scholarship it was unquestionably German. Freedom of criticism was inevitably more possible in the Protestant than in the Catholic universities, and from the end of the 18th century onward Protestant German scholars made great contributions to the understanding of the literature, history, and religion of the people of Israel. The list begins with Johann Gottfried *Eichhorn, professor at Jena, and continues down to the present day. Among many famous names those of Karl Heinrich *Graf and Julius *Wellhausen are conspicuous; and their theory of how different sources were combined in the Pentateuch held the field until the emergence of the contemporary "formcritical school" pioneered by Herman *Gunkel. While German scholarship often tends to extremes which others find unnecessary and unacceptable, it has immensely enriched knowledge by its research, even for those who reject its conclusions.

At the very end of the 19th century, the work of *Selden and Surenhuys in recognizing and defining the spiritual validity of Judaism was taken up by two scholars – George Foot *Moore in America, who published his two volumes on *Judaism in the First Centuries of the Christian Era* in 1927, and R. Travers *Herford, an English Unitarian, whose first work *Pharisaism* appeared in 1912, and was, during the next 30 years, followed by a whole series on talmudic Judaism.

Jewish Return to the Land of Israel

The 19th century witnessed a new understanding between Jews and Protestants in another field. As far back as the millenarians of the 17th century there had been a fluctuating interest in a Jewish return. John Toland predicted that this would lead to the creation of a society of unparalleled power and prosperity. Many other 18th- and 19th-century writers did so too. In 1839, under the influence of the deeply religious Earl of Shaftesbury, Lord Palmerston set up a British consulate in Jerusalem with a special mandate to protect Jews who had no other source of defense. From then onward until the Balfour Declaration in 1917, there were always some members and even whole sects of the Protestant churches who, motivated partly by eschatological beliefs, gave their support to Zionism.

To all this varied work there was a reverse side. The Protestant Church in Germany produced powerful support for the new *antisemitism in the Christian Socialist Workingmen's Union, founded and led by a court chaplain, Adolf *Stoecker;

and its failure to speak and act against Nazi antisemitism was a lasting disgrace.

[James W. Parkes]

From 1945

(For the 1939–45 period, see Holocaust and the Christian *Churches.) A new era in the development of relations between Protestantism and the Jewish people opened in 1945, and had four major causes:

(1) the influence of the Holocaust, which led many Christians to question the responsibility of the Church's "teaching of contempt" (Jules *Isaac's phrase) which had nurtured antisemitism;

(2) the establishment of the State of Israel;

(3) the general reconciliation between different churches and religions and the rise of ecumenism; and

(4) the consolidation of pluralism in Western culture.

Declarations Against Antisemitism

The foundations of the new attitude toward Jews were laid at the International Emergency Conference of Jews and Christians which was held in 1947 in Seelisberg in Switzerland and was attended by 64 theologians, educators, and thinkers, Jewish, Catholic, and Protestant. They deliberated on methods of fighting antisemitism through educational, political, religious, and social channels. At the conclusion of the conference, the "Ten Points of Seelisberg" were drafted and adopted. These were principles to assist the Churches "to show their members how to prevent any animosity toward the Jews which might arise from false, inadequate or mistaken presentations or conceptions of the teaching and preaching of the Christian doctrine, and how on the other hand to promote brotherly love toward the sorely-tried people of the old covenant." The conference thus established the lines for the new process of reconciliation between Jews and Christians, which was to be developed in two spheres: the struggle against antisemitism and a new form of dialogue.

At its foundation conference in Amsterdam in 1948, the World Council of Churches (WCC; the roof organization of the majority of larger Protestant, Anglican, and Orthodox churches) moved a resolution strongly condemning antisemitism. The organization again passed this resolution at its third world conference in New Delhi (1961), with the additional recommendation that Christians should repudiate the idea of the collective guilt of the Jews for the crucifixion of Jesus. However, the texts of both these resolutions are ambiguous, because there is an evangelist-missionary undertone in their attitude toward the Jews.

In 1964, further declarations condemning antisemitism were issued by several important Protestant organizations: the roof organization of the Protestant churches in the United States (National Council of the Churches of Christ in the United States) passed a "Resolution on Jewish-Christian Relations," calling among other things for the fostering of a dialogue between Jews and Christians. The Lutheran World Federation also made a declaration, following an international consultation in Denmark on the subject of "The Church and the Jews"; and the House of Bishops of the Protestant Episcopal Church in the United States drafted a statement of condemnation of antisemitism in extremely strong terms. The Lutheran and Episcopalian declarations also contained expressions of regret for past persecutions of the Jews fomented by the churches.

Liquidation of Theological Antisemitism

As seen above, the Churches recognized that some of the roots of antisemitism were implanted in their religious literature and that it was their duty to uproot them. In a number of countries, a fundamental examination of religious literature, teaching manuals of the Church, prayers, and so on was carried out in order to assist the Church in purifying this material from all versions or commentaries which were liable to create hatred of Judaism or prejudices about it. The Protestants' most comprehensive research was carried out at Yale University under the direction of the sociologist B.E. Olson, who published his findings in *Faith and Prejudice* (1963). This work brings to light the various aspects of the "teaching of contempt" in the curriculum of the Fundamentalist, the Conservative, the Neo-Orthodox, and the Liberal Protestants in the United States. Further research into the religious roots of antisemitism, especially within Protestantism, was carried out by the sociologists Ch. Y. Glock and R. Stark of the University of California at Berkeley and published in their work *Christian Beliefs and Anti-semitism* (1966).

Church Committees for the Fostering of Relations with the Jews

The interest shown by Protestantism in a dialogue with the Jews led to the establishment of new Church bodies for this specific purpose. A special committee to the Jews known as the Committee on the Christian Approach already existed in 1932 as part of the International Missionary Council (IMC; the world roof organization of Protestant missions). In 1961, the IMC amalgamated with the WCC, and the committee for Jews became an integral part of the WCC, its name being changed to CCJP (Committee on the Church and the Jewish People). This committee, which considers that its aim is "to further the Church witness to the Jewish people by study and other appropriate means," has in fact principally taken upon itself the duty "to study the Jewish world in its various aspects in order to develop an effective program to combat antisemitism and arouse Christian responsibility toward the Jews." The CCJP has convened a number of international conferences (usually held at the Ecumenical Institute of the WCC at the Château de Bossey, near Geneva) which have been attended by theologians of many countries, in order to lay down a new theological standpoint toward Judaism and the State of Israel. However, to the regret of the promoters, the recommendations agreed upon at the end of these deliberations have never become official decisions of the WCC and are therefore not binding upon the member Churches. It should also be noted that Protestant institutions have always shown reticence in adopting a clear theological stance toward the existence of the State of Israel. The declaration made in 1956 by the WCC is characteristic. It states: "We cannot say a plain yes, nor can we say a plain no, because the Church does not stand for a vague cosmopolitanism."

Special committees for the fostering of relations with the Jews have also been formed within the Protestant churches of a number of Western European countries, independently of the framework of the world organization. An outstanding example is that of the Reformed Churches of the Netherlands, which have concentrated their efforts for the strengthening of contacts with the Jews by means of a joint coordination committee ("Interchurch Contact for Israel"), which publishes its own bulletin. The Reformed Church of the Netherlands was also the first to mold a more positive theological approach to Judaism, in one of its publications, *Israel and the Church* (1960), and to advocate the adoption of a dialogue in place of missionary activities.

The Evangelical Church of Germany has also worked intensively toward a Jewish-Protestant reconciliation. During the national conferences of the Church (Evangelische Kirchentage) in 1961 (Berlin), 1963 (Dortmund), and 1965 (Cologne), study days were dedicated to the "Jewish-Christian problem" under the direction of joint working groups of Protestant delegates and specially invited Jews. The lectures and discussions were published by the German Church in two volumes which contain extensive documentation and an exhaustive bibliography on the Protestants' attitude toward the Jews since 1945 (*Der ungekuendigte Bund*, 1962; *Das gespaltene Gottesvolk*, 1966).

In comparison with the situation in Europe, organized Protestantism in the United States and Canada has shown less interest and initiative in furthering relations with the Jews; and activity in this field is led by a small group of "concerned Christians." Although their numbers include theologians and members of the clergy, they are not generally representative of the churches (see below).

The Protestant Mission

Most of the Protestant Churches view the "Christian witness to the Jewish people" as a fundamental religious obligation. However, as a result of a recommendation of the WCC that it was preferable for the mission to the Jews to engage in its activity "as a normal part of parish work, rather than by special agencies, and with avoidance of all 'unworthy pressures'" the majority of the member Churches, especially those of the United States, decided to abolish all organizations devoted especially to the evangelization of the Jews. The Lutheran, Reformed, and Anglican Churches of Europe continue to maintain separate missionary agencies in many countries, including Israel, for activities among the Jews. Even within these Churches, however, there is growing opposition to the antiquated methods of conversion, although Evangelicals and Fundamentalist Protestants still continue to attach the utmost importance to the evangelization of the Jews. These denominations, as well as many organizations of converted Jews (Hebrew Christians), carry on intensive and sometimes even aggressive missionary activities.

In recent years a new conception has been evolved repudiating the theological value of the missions; but it has been expressed by only a limited number of Protestant thinkers, the most notable among them being Reinhold *Niebuhr, Roy *Eckhardt, and James *Parkes. These theologians believe in the Jewish religion's right to independent existence as a road to Redemption, and they deny validity to all forms of evangelization of the Jews.

Development of the Interfaith Movement

The dialogue between Jews and Christians is also conducted independently of the organizational framework of the churches. In the British Isles, most European countries, in the United States, Canada, and Australia, as well as in Israel, councils composed of Jews and Christians have been formed for the advancement of understanding and for holding a dialogue between the two religions. These bodies function in many countries under various names and employ different methods. Some of them publish bulletins dedicated to the aims of their activities. In 1961, a roof organization of all these councils, the International Consultative Committee of Organizations for Christian-Jewish Cooperation, was established. A number of Jewish organizations, such as the World Jewish Congress, the Anti-Defamation League of B'nai B'rith, and the American Jewish Committee, have created special departments for the advancement of interfaith activities. Reform and Conservative Jews, especially in the United States, attach especial importance to the achievement of a deeper understanding between Jews and Christians and have set up their own organizational frameworks to this end.

Since 1950, there has been a growing tendency among the promoters of interfaith contacts to change the character of their interreligious relationships and to translate such expressions as "good will" and "brotherhood" into an honest and fruitful dialogue adjusted to the requirements of a pluralistic society. Upon the initiative of interested Jews and Christians, interfaith dialogues have been held in academic and theological institutions, with important religious and intellectual personalities of both faiths taking part. As a result of these numerous encounters, there has emerged a ramified literature on the question of dialogues in general and Jewish-Protestant relations in particular. Within Orthodox Judaism there are many reservations toward the movement, considered on principle unacceptable. Some other Jewish circles have also expressed their suspicions that these dialogues may become a means of disguised missionary activity on the part of some churches. Moreover, despite the extensive activity carried on by the promoters of the dialogues, the interfaith movement has only succeeded in winning over to its cause a limited elite among Protestant believers. This was no doubt one of the reasons for the crisis in Jewish-Protestant relations, which broke out in 1967 after the Six-Day War. The silence of the Churches that had preceded the war and the unfriendly, even hostile, declarations of the Protestant leadership concerning Israel and her postwar policies proved that the dialogue, as conducted previously, was a disappointment. It also became evident that Christians who had participated in these dialogues, due to their ignorance of the true essence of Judaism as a synthesis of a people and a religion bound to the Land of Israel and the Holy City of Jerusalem, had no understanding of the way in which Diaspora Jews identified themselves with the Jews of Israel. Those Jews and Christians who despite all these setbacks insisted on continuing the dialogue arrived at the conclusion, expounded by Rabbi Marc Tanenbaum (d. 1992), one of the leaders of interfaith in the United States, that "no future dialogue will take place without Jews insisting upon the confrontation on the part of Christians on the profound historical, religious, and liturgical meaning of the Land of Israel and of Jerusalem to the Jewish people."

[Yona Malachy]

In the U.S.

Throughout its history the vast but decreasing majority of the inhabitants of the United States was classed as Protestant (about 98% in 1776 and 66% in 1965), in contrast to the very small Jewish minority. Despite a strong evangelical and missionary outlook in American Protestantism, the two groups have maintained a relatively harmonious relationship. The reasons for this are embedded in the social and religious history of the U.S. Since U.S. independence (1776) was achieved in an age of religious laxity and suspicion of ecclesiastical authority, Jews were from the very first accorded a measure of hospitality. Constitutional guarantees of religious freedom and the separation of church and state assured U.S. Jews a legal security unprecedented in Western history. Concentrated in urban areas, Jews also possessed a regional influence disproportionate to their actual numbers. Creedal and denominational diversity within U.S. Protestantism also meant that this majority group could rarely approach U.S. Jewry, and Catholics, with a single voice.

Cognizant of their organizational weaknesses, spokespersons for U.S. Protestantism periodically made great efforts to strengthen and unify their position. Prior to the 20th century many Protestants believed that the U.S. was "chosen" to be a Christian light to the world; and because of the lack of official public support they were determined to lean upon their own resources to Christianize the U.S.

As long as Protestant efforts were aimed to "convert" the West, U.S. Jews, sparse in that region, were not seriously touched by their efforts. After 1870, however, when Protestant revivalism turned toward the more Eastern cities, its impact was felt more sharply. Protestant Christianizing programs included street corner preaching, distribution of Bibles and Christian tracts, efforts to inject Christian teaching into public education, the erection of Young Men's and Young Women's Christian Associations, institutional churches, and Christian-oriented settlement houses. In part to counteract the possible influence of these efforts, U.S. Jews created their own settlement houses, YMHAs, Hebrew schools, and Jewish centers. Increasingly, U.S. Protestants began to associate social reform with the conversion of the U.S.

The years 1880–1914 witnessed the most intense involvement of the Church in social and economic problems. During these years Protestantism also adopted a new theological outlook, which emphasized the goodness of man rather than his depravity, a new view of God as an Immanent Deity directly involved in human history, and stressed the moral and ethical aspects of theology. A rising interest in comparative religious studies and Higher Criticism motivated Protestants to examine more critically ancient Jewish life. This period, referred to as the Social Gospel, elicited considerable interest, especially among Reform Jews, who believed that the Jewish tradition shared many similar social and theological beliefs. An ecumenical outlook, which first manifested itself in the World Parliament of Religions, held in Chicago in 1893, facilitated a dialogue between Protestants and Jews. During the early years of the 20th century some liberal spokesmen of both camps exchanged pulpits and joined in worship. Nevertheless, despite such outbursts of friendship, an undercurrent of suspicion persisted within both religious groups; and even the most liberal Protestants, be they Unitarians, Transcendentalists, Social Gospelers, or mid-Twentieth Century ecumenicists, continued to view Judaism as merely a bridge from paganism to Christianity.

Recent decades have witnessed the creation of new Protestant-Jewish bonds which, however, were periodically severed. Both have joined in opposing Communism, the outspoken enemy of all organized religions. Involvement in the 1960s in the Civil Rights movement and in the Vietnam debate forged ties between rabbis and ministers of all denominations. Among the leading voices of Protestantism, Paul Tillich and Reinhold Niebuhr evinced an abiding respect for Judaism. Yet Protestant silence in the face of Nazi destruction of Europe's Jews was disturbing. Antisemitism persists among U.S. Protestants and continues to be disseminated in religious literature. As mentioned above, the response of Protestants to the Six-Day War was disappointing and disillusioning to U.S. Jews and seriously threatened the dialogue between the two faiths. On the theological level, Jews and Protestants have also parted roads. The "God-is-dead" theological movement among liberal Protestants, a group which in the past significantly influenced Jewish thought-to secularize theology, was completely rejected by virtually all Jewish religious thinkers.

[Egal Feldman]

Protestants and Israel

The World Council of Churches, a fellowship of mainstream Protestant churches, was established in 1948, a few weeks after the founding of the State of Israel. In 2005 the coalition numbered 347 denominations in 120 countries. However, the member bodies of the WCC have experienced a significant decline in numbers the last half of the 20th century. As of the early 21st century, the constituencies of Evangelical and Pentecostal churches throughout the world comprise the majority of Protestant churchgoers.

Despite its gradually diminishing size, the WCC, headquartered in Geneva, continues to exert a strong influence in political and social justice issues throughout the world. In particular, since early 2005, the WCC has recommended divestment from Israel and opposition to the building of the security wall. A small group of Protestants, most notably the Presbyterians Concerned for Jewish and Christian Relations and the National Christian Leadership Conference for Israel, have opposed this stance, together with evangelical denominations who, on the whole, do not see these steps as an appropriate church response to the quest for stability in Israel-Palestinian relations. The WCC in addition has called for a return to pre-1967 borders and for an unlimited right of return for "Palestinian refugees."

Despite Israel's efforts, both in resuming serious negotiations with the Palestinian Authority and the withdrawal from Gaza, there has been no significant change in the WCC's position.

[Claire Pfann (2nd ed.)]

BIBLIOGRAPHY: J.F.A. de Le Roi, *Geschichte der evangelischen Judenmission*, 2 vols. (1899); H.J. Schonfield, *History of Jewish Christianity* (1936); D. Mc-Dougall, *In Search of Israel* (1941); J. Parkes, *Judaism and Christianity* (1948); idem, *Anti-semitism* (1963); P.W. Massing, *Rehearsal for Destruction* (1949, 1967); G. Hedenquist (ed.), *Church and the Jewish People* (1954); S.S. Schwarzschild, in: *Judaism*, 13 (1964), 259–73; *Conservative Judaism*, 19 (1964/65), no. 3, 1–56; G.A.F. Knight (ed.), *Jews and Christians* (1965); JBR, 33 (1965), 101–65; H.J. Schoeps, *The Jewish-Christian Argument* (1965); P. Schneider, *Sweeter than Honey* (1966); U. Tal, *Yahadut ve-Naẓerut ba-Reich ha-Sheni* (1970); C.Y. Glock and R. Stark, *Christian Beliefs and Anti-semitism* (1966); A.R. Eckardt, *Elder and Younger Brothers* (1967); A. Gilbert, in: *Journal of Ecumenical Studies*, 4 (1967), 280–9; M.H. Vogel, *ibid.*, 684–99; Y. Malachy, in: WLB, 23 (1969); *Lutheran Quarterly*, 20 (1968), 219–89; F. Heer, *God's First Love* (1970). IN THE U.S.: A.P. Stokes, *Church and State in the United States*, 3 (1950); B.H. Levy, *Reform Judaism in America* (1933); C.H. Hopkins, *The Rise of the Social Gospel in American Protestantism, 1865–1915* (1940); E. Feldman, in: *Journal of Church and State*, 9 (1967), 180–9; M. Davis, in: L. Finkelstein (ed.), *The Jews*, 1 (1949), 488–587, incl. bibl.; W. Herberg, *Protestant, Catholic, Jew* (1955); W.S. Hudson, *American Protestantism* (1961); J. Hershcopf Banki, *Christian Reactions to the Middle East Crisis* (1968); B.E. Olson, *Faith and Prejudice* (1962). **ADD. BIBLIOGRAPHY:** P.C. Merkley, *Christian Attitudes toward the State of Israel* (2001).

PROTESTRABBINER ("Protest Rabbis"), phrase coined by Theodor *Herzl (in an article in *Die *Welt*, 1, no. 7 (July 16, 1897)), as a designation for the five German rabbis who had signed a trenchant protest letter against Zionism and the Zionist Congress in the name of the German Rabbinical Association. This association comprised two opposing wings – Orthodox and Reform (liberal) – united in their opposition to Zionism. Their attitude as formulated in the protest letter contained three postulates: the intention to establish a Jewish state in Palestine contradicts the messianic destiny of Judaism; Judaism obligates all her believers to be faithful to their native land, serving it as best they can; philanthropic support for agricultural settlers in Palestine is permissible, since it is not connected with the establishment of a Jewish national state. The letter closes with the assertion that love for one's country obligates all those who care for Judaism to shun Zionism and in particular the Zionist Congress.

It was mainly because of this letter that the first Zionist Congress was held in Basle rather than in Munich, as was originally planned. The letter also aroused an unusual amount of agitation because of its hints about the Zionists' unfaithfulness to Germany. Herzl severely criticized the signatories (two Orthodox rabbis – M. Horowitz of Frankfurt and A. Auerbach of Halberstadt – and three liberals – S. Maybaum of Berlin, J. Gutmann of Breslau, and K. Werner of Munich) – and a great number of Zionist rabbis, Orthodox, and liberal, wrote letters and articles condemning the "protest rabbis." The protest letter was endorsed, however, by the general assembly of the Rabbinical Association, convened in Berlin a year later (July 1–2, 1898), with only one rabbi – Selig Gronemann (Samuel *Gronemann's father) – voting against it. Seventy years after the publication of the protest letter, a survey discovered that almost all the children, grandchildren, and great-grandchildren of the "protest rabbis" had settled in Israel.

BIBLIOGRAPHY: *Zionistisches A-B-C Buch* (1908), 227–30; *Ma'ariv* (July 16, 1968).

[Getzel Kressel]

°PROUDHON, PIERRE JOSEPH (1809–1865), French Socialist and anti-Jewish theorist. For Proudhon, the Jew was the "source of evil," as "incarnated in the race of Shem" (*Césarisme et christianisme*, 1 (1883^2), 139). He accused the Jews of "having rendered the bourgeoisie, high or low, similar to them, all over Europe" (*De la justice dans la Révolution et dans l'Eglise* (1858), 458). In his "diary," published posthumously, he called them an "unsociable race, obstinate, infernal… the enemy of mankind. We should send this race back to Asia, or exterminate it" (*Carnets*, 2 (1961), 23, 337). Proudhon's unremitting hatred of the Jews was probably influenced by *Bonald and by *Fourier, but above all by his own xenophobic passion for France, which he saw as "invaded by the English, Germans, Belgians, Jews," and other foreigners (*France et Rhin* (1867^2), 258). In the France of the first half of the 19th century, Proudhon was the mainstay of a grass-roots socialism, which has been seen as an early version of National-Socialism.

BIBLIOGRAPHY: L. Poliakov, *Histoire de l'antisémitisme*, 3 (1968), index; R.F. Byrnes, *Anti-semitism in Modern France*, 1 (1950), index; E. Silberner, *Sozialisten zur Judenfrage* (1962), index.

PROUST, MARCEL (1871–1922), French novelist. Proust was born in Paris to Adrien Proust, a successful non-Jewish physician, and Jeanne (née Weil), a member of an old Alsatian-Jewish family. Through his mother, Proust was related to the eminent statesman Adolphe *Crémieux and to the wife of Henri *Bergson, whose theories of time and memory were a possible influence on him. By 1893 it became obvious that Proust's delicate health would not allow him to follow any profession, and he thereafter devoted himself to writing and to the pursuit of social advancement. His wealth and personal qualities gave him an entrée into the high society that was to form the background to his literary works. He became a contributor to literary reviews, helped to found the short-lived *Le Banquet* (1892) and in 1896 published two books – *Portraits de peintres*, a volume of poems, and *Les Plaisirs et les jours*, a collection of poems, stories, and sketches. Proust's outstanding work, *A la Recherche du temps perdu* (15 vols., 1913–27), one of the masterpieces of 20th century literature in its representation of the nature and texture of memory and its evocation of *fin de siècle* French society, consists of seven parts: *Du côté de chez Swann* (1913); *A l'Ombre des jeunes filles en fleurs* (1918); *Le Côté de Guermantes* (1920); *Sodome et Gomorrhe* (1921); *La Prisonnière* (1923); *Albertine disparue* (1925); and *Le Temps retrouvé* (1927). Though not strictly autobiographical, the novel cycle contains much material based on personal recollections and encounters. During the last 17 years of his life he was an invalid, and spent most of his time locked up in his Paris apartment, feverishly working on his manuscripts and revising his published work. Raised as a Catholic, Proust alludes to his Jewish ancestry in his writings, describing his mother and maternal grandparents, and mentioning his grandfather's practice of placing a pebble on his parents' grave. In *Du côté de chez Swann*, his grandfather admits a preference for his Jewish friends and Proust himself remained on the closest terms with Jews such as Léon *Brunschvicg, and the convert Daniel *Halévy. He always retained some Jewish sympathies, and it was he who persuaded Anatole France to intervene in the *Dreyfus Affair. *A la recherche du temps perdu* contains three major Jewish characters: the actress *Rachel; the aggressive unsympathetic intellectual Albert Bloch; and the assimilated Charles Swann, a member of the exclusive Jockey Club, who has been seen as Proust's own alter ego. The snobbishness of Proust's Jewish characters masks their basic insecurity and, like his creator, Swann finally discovers his identity when he sides with Dreyfus and detaches himself from high society. The contrasting titles of *Du Côté de chez Swann* ("the Side of Swann") and *Le Côté de Guermantes* ("the Side of Guermantes") reflect the conflicting Jewish and non-Jewish sides of Proust's own heritage. Other works published after his death include the fragmentary novel, *Jean Santeuil* (3 vols., 1952), and the critical study *Contre Sainte-Beuve* (1954).

C.K. Scott Moncrief produced the first English translation of *A la recherch du temps perdu* in the 1920s under the title *Remembrance of Things Past*, reworked by Terence Kilmartin and subsequently revised by D.J Enright as *In Search of Lost Time*. Pléiade published its second, definitive French edition in 1987–89. *Correspondance de Marcel Proust* appeared in 1970–93 in 21 volumes (ed. Philip Kolb).

BIBLIOGRAPHY: A. Spire, *Quelques juifs et demi-juifs* (1928), 45–61; Quenell, in: H. Bolitho (ed.), *Twelve Jews* (1934), 177–99; L. Pierre-Quint, *Marcel Proust, sa vie, son oeuvre* (1936); Moss, *The Magic Lantern of Marcel Proust*, (1980); Van Praag, in: *Revue juive de Genève*, 5 (May-July, 1937); A. Maurois, *The Quest for Proust* (1950); Mesnil, in: E.J. Finbert (ed.), *Aspects du Génie d'Israël* (1950), 297–300; G. Cattavi, *Marcel Proust* (Fr., 1958); C. Lehrmann, *L'Elément juif dans la littérature française*, 2 (1961), 134–41; G.D. Painter, *Marcel Proust, a Biography*, 2 vols. (1965); C. Mauriac, *Proust par lui-même* (1953); de Silva Ramos, in: *Les cahiers Marcel Proust*, 6 (1932), 13–86 (incl. bibl.). **ADD. BIBLIOGRAPHY:** H. Bloom (ed.), *Remembrance of Things Past* (critical essays; 1992); J.-Y. Tadie, *Marcel Proust: A Life* (2000); W.C. Carter, *Marcel Proust: A Life* (2000).

[Georges Cattaui]

PROVENÇAL, ABRAHAM BEN DAVID (16th century), scholar of Mantua. He was the son of David b. Abraham *Provençal. Abraham was the teacher of Azariah dei Rossi and Abraham Portaleone, who refer to him in terms of the highest praise and make mention of his extensive knowledge of Torah and Talmud, Latin, philosophy, and medicine. The titles of doctor of philosophy and doctor of medicine were conferred upon him, and from 1563 he started to become widely known as an outstanding physician. At the same time he served as rabbi in various Italian towns, including Ferrara and Mantua. With his father, he planned, in 1564, the founding of a university for the study of Judaism and the general sciences. Both David and Abraham Provençal belonged to a group of Italian scholars who aspired toward a beneficial merger between the curricula of Jewish religious studies and of general knowledge in order to strengthen religious education among Jews and to minimize the influences of general education.

BIBLIOGRAPHY: M. Guedemann, in: *Festschrift… A. Berliner* (1903), 164–75; J.R. Marcus, *Jews in the Medieval World* (1938), 381–8; H. Friedenwald, *Jews and Medicine* (1944), 221f.; C. Roth, *Jews in the Renaissance* (1959), 42f., 247f., 254, 331; S. Simonsohn, in: KS, 37 (1962), 106, 115, 118f.; M.A. Shulvass, *Ḥayyei ha-Yehudim be-Italyah bi-Tekufat ha-Renaissance* (1955), 239f.

[Yehoshua Horowitz]

PROVENÇAL, DAVID BEN ABRAHAM (b. 1506), rabbi of Mantua, preacher, and linguist. He was the brother of Moses *Provençal. Provençal had the idea of establishing a Jewish university in Mantua because he feared a decline in the study of Torah in Italy after the burning of the Talmud. In 1564 he addressed an appeal on this subject to the Italian communities (later published in *Ha-Levanon*, 5 (1868), 418f., 434f., 450f.). According to his plan the curriculum was to include the written and oral law, philosophy, Hebrew grammar, Hebrew poetry, Latin and Italian, grammar, medicine, and astronomy. There are differences of opinion as to the extent to which the proposed program was carried out. The traditional view is that many of the fundamental points were implemented, even though the atmosphere of intolerance on the part of the Catholic Church toward the Jews of Italy undoubtedly served to hinder the fulfillment of the university program.

Provençal was the author of *Ir David*, a commentary on the Pentateuch, and a commentary on the Song of Songs; *Dor Haflagah*, on the Hebrew words adopted in foreign languages;

and *Migdal David*, on Hebrew grammar. All three books have been lost, though they were seen by Azariah dei Rossi. Provençal's defense of Philo against Azariah dei Rossi's criticisms is not extant either. His commentary to *Avot* has been preserved in manuscript (N. Weisz, *Kataloge… D. Kaufmann* (1906), no. 131). He also proofread the Venice 1565 edition of the *Paḥad Yiẓḥak*.

BIBLIOGRAPHY: M. Guedemann, in: *Festschrift… A. Berliner* (1903), 164–75; S. Assaf, *Mekorot le-Toledot ha-Ḥinnukh be-Yisrael*, 2 (1930), 115–20; J.R. Marcus, *Jews in the Medieval World* (1938), 381–8; M.A. Shulvass, *Ḥayyei ha-Yehudim be-Italyah bi-Tekufat ha-Renaissance* (1955), index; C. Roth, *Jews in the Renaissance* (1959), 42f., 247f., 331; S. Simonsohn, *Toledot ha-Yehudim be-Dukkasut Mantovah*, 2 (1964), 422f., 450, 458, 533f.

[David Tamar]

PROVENÇAL, JACOB BEN DAVID (15th century), scholar of France and Italy. It is probable that Jacob was the ancestor of the Provençal (Provenzale) family that settled in Mantua in the 16th century. He resided first in Marseilles, where he engaged in maritime trade, but subsequently went to Naples, where he is mentioned in c. 1480 as one of its rabbis.

It was from Naples that he wrote a letter to Messer David b. Judah *Leon of Mantua, in which he expressed his opinion on the value of secular studies, particularly medicine (see *Divrei Ḥakhamim* (1849) edited by Eliezer Ashkenazi). He gave an approbation for the *Agur* of Jacob Baruch b. Judah *Landau which appears in the Rimini edition of 1526. He also seems to have written a commentary on the *Song of Songs which was published together with the commentaries of *Saadiah Gaon and Joseph ibn *Kaspi in about 1577.

BIBLIOGRAPHY: Ghirondi-Neppi, 215; Gross, Gal Jud, 383f.; M.A. Shulvass, *Ḥayyei ha-Yehudim be-Italyah bi-Tekufat ha-Renaissance* (1955), 75, 142, 238; C. Roth, *Jews in the Renaissance* (1959), 43n.

[Yehoshua Horowitz]

PROVENÇAL, MOSES BEN ABRAHAM (1503–1575), rabbi. He is sometimes referred to as Moses da Rosa from the town near Vicenza in which he was apparently born. Brother of David *Provençal, Moses was considered one of the greatest talmudists and one of the most illustrious scholars of Italian Jewry in the Renaissance period. For many decades he was rabbi of the Italian community of Mantua, which therefore became a center of talmudic study. Rabbis turned to him from all over Italy and beyond with halakhic problems. With the Catholic Counter-Reformation a sociocultural ferment was set off in Italy, which spread even to the ghettos, with the result that zealous rabbis began to persecute such liberally minded scholars as Moses. Matters reached a head when Moses introduced a new formula for the **Havdalah* when a festival immediately followed the Sabbath. The innovation so aroused the wrath of Meir *Katzenellenbogen of Padua and Moses Basilea that they secured his expulsion from office, although for some unknown reason they later repealed the ban. Another ruling, in which he invalidated Samuel Venturozzo's divorce of his wife, the daughter of Joseph Tamari, on the grounds of its having been given under duress – brought down upon him the censure of many Italian rabbis. He appealed with the help of the Court impresario Judah Leone *Sommo to Duke Guglielmo, who granted him a hearing before an impartial rabbinical tribunal. In 1566 he was banned by the rabbis of Venice from holding office for three years. Rabbis in Turkey and Greece also associated themselves with the ban, and even the scholars of Safed entered into the controversy. Moses *Trani supported the excommunication, but many of the outstanding rabbis of Safed, including almost certainly Joseph *Caro, supported Provençal. This was apparently the reason that his second dismissal also was not implemented, since he continued to act as rabbi of Mantua until his death. In 1560 he was asked to decide on the permissibility of playing tennis on the Sabbath. In his reply, which sheds much valuable information on the development of the game, he permitted tennis on the Sabbath provided that there was no betting, that rackets were not used, and it was not played at the time of the sermon. The approbation he gave to the Mantua (1558–60) edition of the Zohar shows him to have been in favor of the publication of kabbalistic works, which was the subject of a dispute in Italy at the time.

Moses' works include: *Be'ur Inyan Shenei Kavvim*, a dissertation on the Theorem of Apollonius, on two straight lines which never meet, which is discussed by Maimonides and published in the Sabionetta (1553) edition of Maimonides' *Guide of the Perplexed*. His commentary on this dissertation was translated into Italian by Joseph Shalit (Mantua, 1550) and from Italian into Latin with a commentary by F. Barocius (Venice, 1586); *Elleh ha-Devarim*, and a commentary, *Be'ur Zeh Yaẓa Rishonah* (Mantua, 1566), on the Tamari-Venturozzo divorce; *Hassagot* ("notes") to *Me'or Einayim* (Mantua, 1573) of Azariah dei Rossi, published at the end of the book; *Be-Shem Kadmon* (Venice, 1596), abridged rules of Hebrew grammar in poetic form; responsa published in various works. Moses' major literary legacy, responsa, and commentaries on various tractates of the Talmud, and a commentary to Maimonides' *Guide of the Perplexed* are almost entirely unpublished.

BIBLIOGRAPHY: Rivkind, in: *Tarbiz*, 4 (1933), 366–76; C. Roth, *Jews in the Renaissance* (1959), 28–29, 236, 266; R.W. Henderson in: JQR, 26 (1935/36), 1–6; Benayahu, in: *Rabbi Yosef Caro*, ed. by Y. Raphael (1969), 304–5; S. Simonsohn, in: *Tarbiz*, 28 (1958), 381–92; idem, *Toledot ha-Yehudim be-Dukkasut Mantovah*, 2 vols. (1962–64), index; I. Tishby, in: *Perakim*, 1 (1967–68), 140: E. Kupfer, in: *Sinai*, 63 (1968), 137–60; idem, in: *Tarbiz*, 38 (1969), 54–60.

[Abraham David]

PROVENCE (Heb. פרובינצא), region and former province of S.E. France corresponding to the present departments of Bouches-du-Rhône, Var, Basses-Alpes, and parts of Vaucluse and Drôme. In rabbinical literature the name of Provence is frequently applied simultaneously to a part of Languedoc, a practice also adopted by some modern scholars which has given rise to numerous confusions. *Comtat Venaissin and

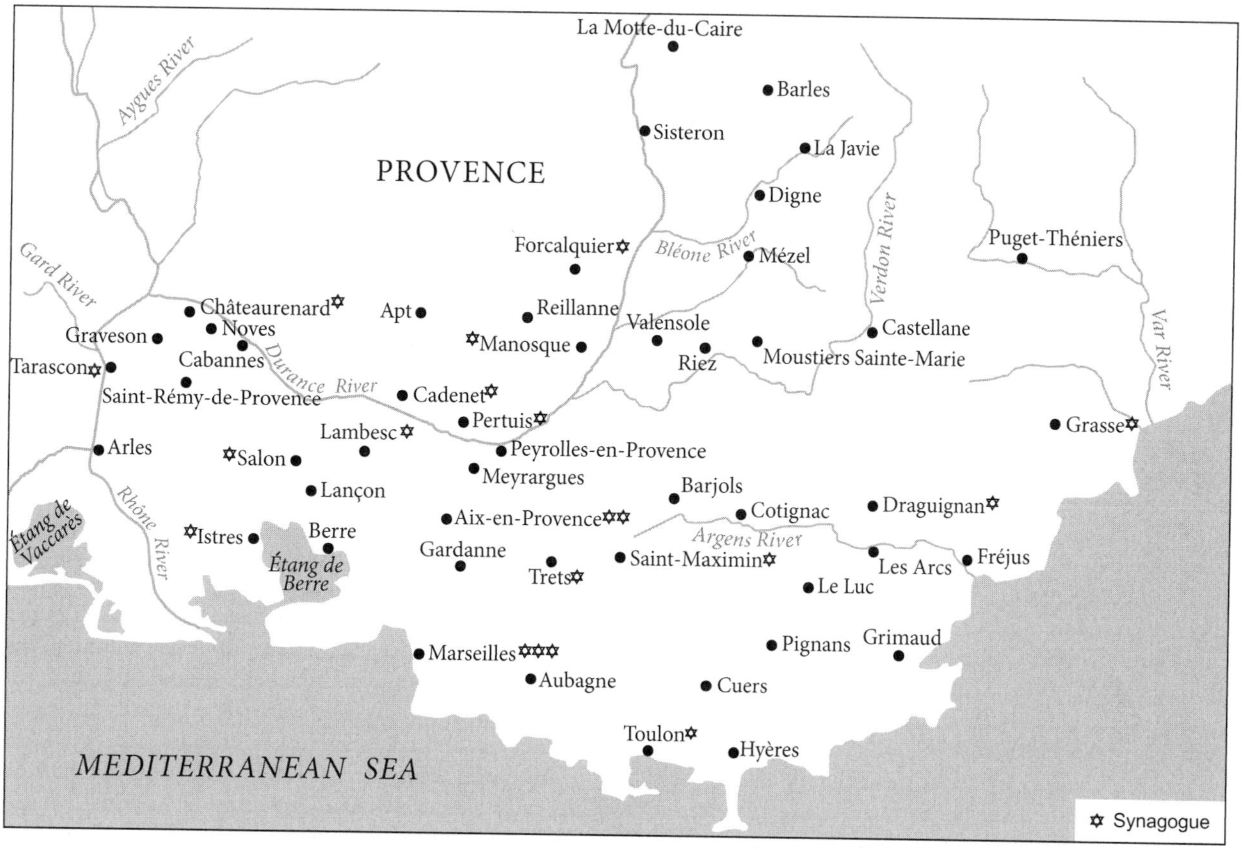

Principal Jewish settlements in medieval Provence.

the county of *Nice were detached from Provence from the administrative point of view at an early date and are therefore mainly excluded from this survey. Recent archaeological discoveries prove that the settlement of Jews in Provence is of ancient date and goes back to at least the end of the first century C.E. The earliest documentary evidence for the presence of Jews dates from the middle of the fifth century in *Arles. They were to be found in large numbers in *Marseilles at the close of the sixth century. It was not until the 13th and especially the 14th century that Jews were to be found in numerous localities of Provence, between 80 and 100, more particularly in *Aix-en-Provence, *Apt, Aubagne, Berre, Cadenet, Castellane, Chateaurenard, Cotignac, *Digne, *Draguignan, Forcalquiers, Fréjus, Grasse, *Hyères, Istres, Lambesc, *Manosque, Moustiers-Sainte-Marie, Pertuis, Peyrolles-en-Provence, Saint Maximin, *Saint-Rémy, Salon, *Tarascon, *Toulon, and Trets. The Jewish population reached a peak on the eve of 1348, when it probably numbered about 15,000.

Regulations governing the activity and administration of the communities in Provence are known from 1215 on, as evidenced from the community of Arles. Later the first sumptuary regulations appear in Provence, as well as charitable confraternities and the introduction of compulsory education. From at least the end of the 13th century an inter-community organization existed, though imposed by the government to facilitate the collection of the tax rendered by Jews to the sovereign of Provence. From the beginning of the 15th century, a special official, the "Conservateur des Juifs," was responsible for their protection and adjudication; the office was coveted by the leading families of Provence, because of the considerable revenue it brought in.

The principal occupation of the Jews in Provence was *moneylending; the rate of interest charged was very low for that period, from 10 to 25%. However they only lent small sums destined for expenses and did not possess the capital required for commercial loans on a large scale; the latter was furnished by Christians of Provence and Languedoc, Italians, and Catalans. Hence, not a single Jew is found among the creditors of King René of Provence (1434–80) although members of the Forbin family of Provence and of the Doria family of Genoa are frequently recorded. Jewish participation in commerce was also dependent on this factor. Jews did not have the capital required to engage in large business upon their own initiative but often acted as brokers. They were therefore involved in most transactions of wheat and wine. They also traded in spices and textiles and the sale or lease of houses. The number of Jewish physicians in Provence was particularly great and in some towns they formed 5% of the Jewish working population; this would have amounted to one physician for every 100 persons if their services had been restricted to the Jewish community, but they also treated Christians, often holding the official function of municipal physician, and were particularly in demand when epidemics broke out. Their fees were nevertheless far lower than those of their Christian colleagues. In agriculture, Jews in Provence often cultivated vineyards. They also owned and worked fields, as well as market gardens, especially in the vicinity of Digne.

From having been subject to the direct authority of local lords, particularly the bishops, the Jews were placed under the jurisdiction of the count from the time of Charles of Anjou's suzerainty (1246–85). In 1276 he limited the jurisdiction over the Jews which had been assumed by the Inquisition. In contrast, his successor Charles II (1285–1309) issued a regulation in 1294 which reintroduced several anti-Jewish measures of ecclesiastical origin: the employment of Christians by Jews was forbidden; the Jews were barred from public functions; they were compelled to wear the distinctive *badge. At the time of the expulsion of the Jews from France in 1306, those of Provence were exposed to vexations of a fiscal nature. In 1310 King Robert (1309–45) ordered his officers to assist the Jews to collect the debts which were due them. He refused to consider a request of several ecclesiastics to expel the Jews, but stringently applied the separationist measures which had been issued against them. Jewish quarters had developed in various towns spontaneously, but from 1341 at the latest, Jewish residence was confined to a separate quarter in the towns of Provence. The first anti-Jewish disturbances on a large scale broke out in Provence in 1331. In 1340 other disturbances occurred in Moustiers and Forcalquiers. The severest anti-Jewish riots of the 14th century took place in 1348, at the time of the *Black Death; in Toulon, the community was almost completely annihilated; there were also attacks in Apt and throughout Provence. The loss of life and property suffered by the Jews was so considerable that Queen Jeanne (1343–82) reduced the tax of the Jews of Provence to one-half of its usual rate for ten years. Before the end of this reprieve, new persecutions broke out in several towns in 1355.

The 15th century on the whole was an extremely favorable period for the Jews of Provence. In an edict of 1423, Queen Yolande extended protection to the Jews from arbitrary arrest if there were no reliable witnesses; every accuser of a Jew was required to identify himself by name and provide a surety; a Jew was not to be imprisoned if he could provide bail, unless for crime liable to corporal punishment. King René was known as "the good king," a sobriquet which applied to his treatment of the Jews as well. In 1443 he renewed the edicts of Queen Yolande which had been so favorable to the Jews. In 1454 he authorized the admission of Jews to every category of commerce, trade, and craft, as well as to certain public functions of a fiscal nature. He reduced the size of the Jewish badge and exempted the Jews from wearing it while traveling. He expressed his opposition to instances of forced baptism and even penalized those who had perpetrated such acts.

Within France

In 1481, after the death of René, Provence became united with the Kingdom of France, from which the Jews had been "definitively" expelled in 1394. The privileges of the Jews of Provence were nevertheless renewed in 1482. However, from 1484, anti-Jewish disturbances broke out in Arles, Aix, and Marseilles. This looting and violence was perpetrated by bands of laborers hired for the harvest season from Dauphiné, Auvergne, and the mountain regions of Provence. In Tarascon, where they threatened the Jews, the latter were effectively protected by the officials of the town. Charles VIII, who, although aged only 14, already nominally governed France, took the Jews under his protection. However, a voluntary exodus began and was accelerated when similar disorders were repeated in 1485. On this occasion, the bands of seasonal workers were reinforced by the inhabitants of the town who took part in looting the Jewish quarter. The Jews once more took refuge in the castle. From 1484, one town after another called for their expulsion. In Marseilles, which had also demanded their expulsion, a veritable gang had been organized to rob the Jews, although protests were voiced against their departure. New anti-Jewish disorders broke out in Tarascon in 1489, in Arles before July 1493, and in Manosque in 1495, led by the Carmelites and Franciscans. Louis XII finally issued a general expulsion order against the Jews of Provence in 1498. Not enforced at the time, the order was renewed in 1500 and again at the end of July 1501. On this occasion, it was definitively implemented.

The only alternative to exile offered to the Jews of Provence was conversion to Christianity and a number chose such a solution. However, after a short while – if only to compensate partially for the loss of revenues caused by the departure of the Jews – the king imposed a special tax on them, referred to as "the tax of the neophytes." A roster dating from 1512 enumerates 122 to 164 persons (probably heads of families) subjected to this tax living in 16 important localities of Provence. These converts and their descendants soon became the objects of social discrimination, a situation against which the parliament of Provence reacted in 1542. The campaign of discrimination was nevertheless maintained. A pamphlet published in 1611 attributed the miserable condition of the parliament of Provence to the neophytes. Around the beginning of the 18th century a lampoon entitled "Critique du nobiliare de Provence," which accused a large number of aristocratic families of being of Jewish origin, gained notoriety. To this campaign must also be attributed the adaptation to Provençal of a forgery of Spanish origin: this was a mere literary farce in the form of an exchange of letters between the Jews of Arles and those of Constantinople. The correspondence was supposedly conducted at the close of the 15th century, when the Jews of Provence asked how they were to act in order to avoid expulsion. The Jews of Constantinople, according to this, counseled them to accept baptism while inwardly remaining Jews, stating that once they had attained the powerful positions to which the Christian religion admitted them, they would be able to avenge all the former miseries which they had endured.

During the second half of the 17th century a number of Jews attempted to reestablish themselves in Provence, following the edict issued by the minister Colbert in March 1669 which granted Marseilles the status of a "tax-free port." However, on complaints of the chamber of commerce of that town the parliament of Provence renewed the prohibitions against the residence of Jews there. Although the parliament authorized their temporary residence during the 18th century to enable them to trade at the fairs, a further attempt by a number of Jews to settle permanently, on this occasion in Aix, was prevented. Before the French Revolution abolished the administrative entity of Provence, the first community outside the southwest, Alsace-Lorraine and Comtat Venaissin, was formed in Marseilles.

For later history see *France.

[Bernhard Blumenkranz]

Cultural Life

The fortuitous geographical circumstance in which Provence was situated between three great intellectual centers – Spain, Italy, and Franco-Germany – had a decisive effect on the development of Provence as a major center for Jewish learning and literature. The incorporation of Provence into the Christian Carolingian Empire severed it from contact with Jews in Muslim lands until the 12th century. As a result the early cultural life of Provence was closely allied with that of the Franco-German center. Unlike their contemporaries in Spain, Provençal scholars focused entirely on the Talmud in the development of their cultural life. Their achievements were of some importance. While scholars in Arles at one time turned to those in Lucca, Italy, for guidance, Torah centers in France, Germany, and Italy often looked to Provence for the solution of halakhic difficulties and exchanged responsa with Provençal scholars. Provençal halakhic traditions were expressed largely in oral rather than in written form. Provence had an important influence on the development of Midrash, both in their creation of new Midrashim and the editing of older ones; of equal importance were its *minhagim*, some merging Babylonian and Palestinian influences.

At the beginning of the 12th century a large part of Provence was incorporated into Catalonia, bringing Provençal scholars into contact with those of *Barcelona. The result was a greater spirit of enlightenment in Provence and the broadening of its intellectual horizon to include interest in the sciences and language. That development was speeded up considerably with the invasion of Spain by the *Almohads in the middle of the 12th century and the consequent flight of many Spanish thinkers to Provence when Jewish centers in Spain were destroyed. The cultural life of Provence was considerably enriched as a result. Major changes took place in biblical exegesis; scholars increasingly engaged in the natural sciences; there was a flowering of interest in poetry, lexicography, grammar, and philosophy. Major effort was expended on the translation of literature from Arabic to Hebrew. Nevertheless, the halakhic knowledge of Provençal scholars was not lost, Ashkenazi influences remained, and the contact with Ashkenazi scholarship was deepened. Through the work of Spanish scholars the influences of Isaac *Alfasi and the Babylonian *geonim* were deeply felt in Provence; Ashkenazi and Spanish approaches to the *halakhah* found a new synthesis in the work of Provençal halakhists. Unlike Spain it was in Provence that the philosophers and grammarians also wrote works on *halakhah*. Great interest was kindled in mysticism, also, and philosophical knowledge was profound enough to make Provence a major focus of the *Maimonidean controversy. Into the 14th century Provence remained the meeting point of different intellectual systems and an area of considerable intellectual ferment.

Prominent among the scholars of Provence were R. Moses of Arles, a correspondent of Kalonymus of Rome; R. Judah b. Moses of Arles, his son, mentioned by Rashi in *Sefer ha-Pardes*; *Gershon b. Solomon of Arles, author of the metaphysical work, *Sha'ar ha-Shamayim*; *Kalonymus b. Kalonymus (1281–after 1328), translator and author of *Even-Bohan*; Kalonymus b. David b. Todros, 14th-century Bible commentator; *Isaac b. Abba Mari of Marseilles (12th century), author of a commentary to the Code of Alfasi as well as *Sefer ha-Ittur*; Joseph of Marseilles, Bible commentator mentioned by Judah Messer Leon; Aaron b. Abraham b. Isaac and Shem Tov Falcon, the correspondents of Solomon b. Abraham *Adret; Samuel b. Judah, 14th-century scientist and translator of the commentary of Averroes on Aristotle's *Ethics*; Moses de Salon, philosopher and teacher of Kalonymus b. Kalonymus; Bonjudas Nathan Crescas, physician, noted through the medical work, *Sod ha-Sodot*; and *Nissim b. Moses of Marseilles, 14th-century author of a commentary on the Pentateuch entitled *Ma'aseh Nissim*.

[Alexander Shapiro]

BIBLIOGRAPHY: Gross, Gal Jud, 489ff.; R. Busquet, in: *Mélanges Institut Historique de Provence*, 4 (1927), 68–86; A. Kober, in: JSOS, 6 (1944), 351–74; Z. Szajkowski, *ibid.*, 31–54; idem, *Franco-Judaica* (1962), index; Schirmann, Sefarad, passim; E. Camau, in: *La Provence à travers les âges* (1928), 249–367; A.Z. Aeskoly, in: *Zion*, 10 (1945), 102–39; B. Blumenkranz, in: *Evidences*, 12 (March–April 1961), 29–33; idem, in: *Bulletin Philologique et historique* (1965), 611–22; B. Benedict, in: *Tarbiz*, 22 (1951), 85–109.

PROVERB (Heb. מָשָׁל, *mashal*; pl. מְשָׁלִים, *meshalim*). The term "proverb" as a translation of the biblical Hebrew word *mashal* denotes certain specific literary forms, particularly of wisdom literature. Several of these forms are also referred to by the words *pitgam* and *mikhtam* in post-biblical Hebrew (although in the Bible these two terms have other connotations). The literary forms referred to in the Bible by the term *mashal* are of different types, and scholars are divided on the question of the connection between these forms, as well as on the basic meaning of the biblical term *mashal*. In post-biblical Hebrew, *mashal* signifies several poetic forms, i.e., figures of speech or types of ornate style. The nature of these poetic forms, which are found particularly in classical literature, has been elucidated in Western thought. Parallels to these poetic forms are found in the Bible, although its authors were not conscious of them. Discussions of the term *mashal*, therefore, may fall into two sections: the first, devoted to *mashal* in its broader post-biblical sense, i.e., as referring to poetic forms in general, and the second, to *mashal* in its more limited sense, i.e., in its specific use in the Bible as a concept associated principally with wisdom literature.

Poetic Forms

Many examples of basic figures of speech, such as similes and metaphors, occur in the Bible. These are common in every language, and occur even in daily conversation. The complex literary forms known as *meshalim* in post-biblical Hebrew are structured on these basic figures of speech.

ALLEGORY. An allegory is a metaphor expanded to the dimensions of a narrative in which all the details reflect the actual subject of the metaphor. Examples of allegory in the Bible are to be found, in particular, in Ezekiel's account of the great eagle and the top of the cedar (17:3–12), of the lioness and her whelps (19:2–9), of the vine that was uprooted and withered (19:10–14), of the pot set on fire (24:3–5), of the cedar in Lebanon that was cut down (31:3–17), and of the shepherds who neglected the sheep (34:2–31), as well as others. The description of old age at the end of Ecclesiastes (12:2–6) is not allegorical, but consists rather of a series of metaphors which do not combine to form a narrative. On the other hand, there are expressions which, while they are not allegories, contain the elements of allegory, being extended metaphors which do not reach the proportions of an actual narrative, for example, Balaam's comparison of Israel to a lion (Num. 24:8–9).

PARABLE. A parable is an independent narrative in which a particular detail contains a moral that is applicable beyond the content of the narrative itself. Examples of parables in the Bible are Nathan's tale of the poor man's ewe lamb (II Sam. 12:1–4), and, to some extent, Jehoash's story of the thistle and the cedar in Lebanon (II Kings 14:9). Isaiah's song of the vineyard (5:1–6) may be either an allegory or a parable.

FABLE. A fable is a story whose figures are taken from the animal or vegetable realm and are endowed with human characteristics; it has a moral which is applicable beyond the content of the narrative itself. Examples of fables in the Bible are Jotham's tale of the trees that sought a king for themselves (Judg. 9:8–15), and, to a certain extent, Jehoash's account of the thistle and the cedar in Lebanon (II Kings 14:9). The sayings drawn from the animal realm in Proverbs (6:6–8; 30:24–31) and the descriptions of animals in God's reply to Job (38:39–39:30; 40:15–41:26) cannot be considered fables because they do not contain personification; they are rather didactic statements based on observation of natural phenomena.

Mashal in the Bible

The term *mashal* in the Bible can be elucidated either by means of etymological investigation or by examining its actual usage and combining the features common to all the literary forms to which it refers. These two methods have been accompanied by conjecture and differences of opinion among scholars, and neither has as yet produced any definitive results.

ETYMOLOGY. The root *mšl*, from which the word *mashal* is derived, has two etymologies, both of which have been used to explain the nature of the biblical *mashal*. Some scholars base their interpretation of *mashal* on one meaning of the root *mšl*, which is "resemblance" or "the equating of one thing to another," found in the Arabic *mithl*, and the Aramaic *mtl*. While some scholars maintain that this meaning indicates the primary tendency of the *mashal* which is to compare and allegorize (Koenig, Eissfeldt, Johnson, et al.), others find it an allusion to the element of sympathetic magic prevalent in the ancient proverb (Godbey). This meaning of the root *mšl* does not occur in Canaanite, but a trace of it is to be found in the Bible: "Upon earth there is not his like" (Job 41:25[33]), although the absolute state of the noun here is *moshel* (מֹשֶׁל), not *mashal* (מָשָׁל). The Bible contains examples of *meshalim* that are not allegorical in character but simply songs (see below). Another meaning of the root *mšl* implies government and rule; equivalents are found in Canaanite inscriptions, and in the Bible *mšl* commonly has this meaning. On the basis of this meaning of the root, some scholars seek to explain the primary significance of the *mashal* as the statement of an influential man who is endowed with authority (Pedersen, Bostroem, Bentzen). However, this explanation, too, is forced and cannot be completely reconciled with the examples of *meshalim* in the Bible.

LITERARY FORMS. The following are the literary forms called *mashal* in the Bible:

The Folk Saying. The characteristic features of the folk saying are its widespread use and its pithy, concentrated formulation, which gives pointed expression to popular experience and wisdom. In the Bible, such sayings are prefaced by expressions attesting to their popular character. At times the identical saying occurs in two different passages, further evidence of its widespread use. The saying, "Is Saul also among the prophets?" is quoted in two narratives and is introduced by the statements: "Therefore it became a *mashal*" and "wherefore they say" (I Sam. 10:12; 19:24). A folk saying of the period of the Babylonian Exile, "The fathers have eaten sour grapes, and the children's teeth are set on edge," is mentioned in two prophetic books (Jer. 31:29; Ezek. 18:2–3). Another contemporary saying current in Palestine is quoted by Ezekiel (12:22–23), while David repeats to Saul the *mashal* of the Kedemites, "Out of the wicked comes forth wickedness" (I Sam. 24:13). There are introductory expressions hinting at other folk sayings quoted in the Bible which, by analogy, may presumably also be regarded as *meshalim*, although they are not called such in the Bible, for example: "Like Nimrod a mighty hunter before the Lord" (Gen. 10:9). There are other statements which have the characteristics of folk sayings even though they are not prefaced by introductory expressions, for example, "For as the man is, so is his strength" (Judg. 8:21) and "Let not him that girds on his armor boast himself as he that puts it off" (I Kings 20:11).

The Literary Saying. The literary saying does not differ in form from the folk saying, except that it is not in common use, being coined by a wisdom writer who uses a fixed formula in which to cast conventional thoughts of his school. Compilations of literary sayings are extant in the second and fifth collections of the Book of Proverbs (10:1–22:16; chs. 25–29) and segments of them are embodied in other collections of that book (see *Proverbs). These sayings inculcate the particular outlook of wisdom literature. Groups of literary sayings have also been incorporated in Ecclesiastes as quotations from its author's wisdom compositions, their conventional contents frequently contradicting Ecclesiastes' essentially pessimistic reflections. One passage attests that Koheleth "also taught the people knowledge, weighing, and studying, and arranging proverbs [*meshalim*] with great care" (12:9), that is, he redacted and composed many *meshalim* that are not included in this book. At times it is impossible to know whether a saying is literary or popular, such as the following statement by Ezekiel concerning Jerusalem: "Everyone who uses proverbs will use this proverb about you saying, 'Like mother, like daughter'" (Ezek. 16:44), and Jeremiah's remark, "What has straw in common with wheat?" (Jer. 23:28). It cannot be determined whether in these passages the prophets are quoting current sayings or coining new ones. Sometimes a literary saying may be adopted and widely used by the people, as is the case with many biblical verses which in the course of time became popular sayings.

The Poetic Utterance. The poetic utterance is also called *mashal* in the Bible. Sometimes such an utterance contains obvious metaphorical and allegorical features, as in Ezekiel's statements about the great eagle and the top of the cedar (17:2–10), the forest of the South (21:1–5), and the pot set on the fire (24:3–11), all of which he calls *meshalim*. Sometimes, although the poetic utterance lacks these features it is still termed a *mashal*. It may have been popular – a sort of folk saying, like the song which the ballad singers uttered on the overthrow of Heshbon by Sihon king of the Amorites (Num. 21:27–30). In some cases the poetic utterance may not even have been popular and yet been called a *mashal*. The first collection in Proverbs (1–9) contains about a dozen poetical-rhetorical units, all of them literary compositions bearing the imprint of the wisdom school; most of these have no allegorical features; their contents are evident and explicit, yet all are called *meshalim* (Prov. 1:1). Two psalms that are referred to as *meshalim* have neither a folk character nor employ allegory – the one speaks of the fate of the wicked (Ps. 49), the other reviews the history of Israel from the Exodus until the building of the Temple in Jerusalem (Ps. 78). Job's last two monologues are similarly called *meshalim*, and from their superscriptions: "And Job took up his *mashal*, and said" (Job 27:1; 29:1), it seems that his earlier utterances during the discussion are also regarded as *meshalim*. At the same time, several poetic utterances that are called *meshalim* do not even seem to belong to wisdom literature, e.g., Balaam's songs (Num. 23:7–10, 18–24; 24:3–9, 15–24); the derisive elegy on the fall of the king of Babylon (Isa. 14:4–22); and the song of the ballad singers on the overthrow of Heshbon, referred to above.

CONCLUSION. To understand more fully the meaning of *mashal* in the Bible, the features common to all the above-mentioned literary forms may be combined and in this way the essential characteristics of the concept determined. The first, and indispensable, characteristic of the *mashal* is its poetic form. All the *meshalim* quoted or alluded to in the Bible take the form of a song, while the *mashal* and the song (*shir*) are mentioned as analogous concepts in I Kings 5:12. Folk sayings of a few words (see above) must thus be understood as versets of poetry. Prose statements are never termed *meshalim* in the Bible. Thus the story of Jotham in Judges 9:8–15 and that of Nathan in II Samuel 12:1–4 are not called *meshalim*. The difference between a *mashal* and a song (*shir*) apparently lies in the fact that the song was set to a tune and its recitation accompanied by musical instruments, whereas the *mashal* may have been associated with some melody, but was generally simply declaimed. The wisdom psalm is an exception, however, insofar as it has the form of a *mashal* and yet is at the same time a psalm (Ps. 49:5). Another characteristic of the *mashal* is its rhetorical aspect. It is intended for oral recitation only. Every *mashal* quoted in the Bible is accompanied by a statement indicating that it was, or was supposed to be, uttered aloud. Frequently it is prefaced by the phrase "to take up a *mashal*" (Num. 23:7, 18; 24:3; Isa. 14:4; Micah 2:4; Hab. 2:6; Job 27:1; 29:1). In Ezekiel, the usual phrase employed is "to use [or speak] a *mashal*" (Ezek. 12:23; 16:44; 17:2; 18:2–3, et al.). The Bible says that Solomon "spoke three thousand *mashal*" (I Kings 5:12). Of the literary compositions assembled in Proverbs and called *meshalim* – the poetic units in the first collection (Prov. 1–9) and the literary sayings in the second and the fifth (10:1–22:16; chs. 25–29) – some bear a clear rhetorical stamp, and all were apparently intended to be declaimed and memorized in the wisdom schools (see *Proverbs). Also characteristic of the *mashal* is its essentially secular nature. It is not the word of God but specifically the product of human "wisdom." A prophetic statement in the name of God, even if in the form of a poem, is never called a *mashal*, unless the prophet is commanded to compose *meshalim*, as in Isaiah 14:4 and in Ezekiel. In such instances, the prophet employs, as it were, his own wisdom and creative talents to proclaim the word of God specifically in the form of a *mashal*. Balaam's *meshalim* are similarly to be understood as the product of his occult science, as the expression of his skill in cursing and blessing (cf. Num. 22:6; Josh. 13:22; see *Balaam). These characteristics lend probability to the view that the *mashal* originated either in wisdom circles, or in those close to it, or in ancient folk wisdom (as distinct from aristocratic wisdom whose compositions have been assembled in the Book of Proverbs), the occurrence of the *mashal* in the prophetic books being explained as the use by the prophets of ready-made formulas. The figures of Balaam and of the ballad singers who on important occasions expressed themselves in *mashal* (Num. 21:27) point to pre-Solomonic times. The figure of Balaam also suggests that the ancient *mashal* was connected with sorcery and magic, those who practiced them being likewise included in the category of wise men (cf. Gen. 41:8; Ex. 7:11; Isa. 44:25; Ps. 58:6; cf. Isa. 3:3: "the skillful enchanter"). In the course of time the *mashal* apparently developed in several directions. Mention has been made above of the pithy saying and the poetic utterance. Other changes of nuance in the character of the *mashal* are expressed in the Bible by combining *mashal* with another word thus producing hendiadys or parallelism. The words *mashal* and *ḥidah* ("riddle") in parallelism allude to a *mashal* whose contents are somewhat obscure and for whose comprehension some knowledge and ability are necessary (Ezek. 17:2; Hab. 2:6; Ps. 49:5; 78:2; Prov. 1:6). Accordingly, it may be inferred that the *ḥidah*, too, in particular one which is in the form of a poem and whose solution takes a poetic form (cf. Judg. 14:14, 18), is in essence close to the *mashal*. The combination of *mashal* and *sheninah* ("byword"; Deut. 28:37; I Kings 9:7; Jer. 24:9; II Chron. 7:20; and in elliptic form in Ps. 69:12) refers to a *mashal* marked by derision and irony. This characteristic is also alluded to in the combination of *ʾot*, "sign," and *meshalim* (Ezek. 14:8) and of *mashal* and *menod rosh* ("shaking of the head"; Ps. 44:15). An example of the derisive *mashal* occurs in Isaiah 14:4–23. Another term used in the Bible to express irony is *meliẓah*, "taunt," and hence the combination of *mashal* and *meliẓah* (Hab. 2:6; Prov. 1:6). Some maintain that the *moshelim*, mentioned by the prophet in Isaiah 28:14, refer to composers of *meshalim*. According to this interpretation, they composed taunting *meshalim*, as is also evident from the verses that follow. The parallelism of *mashal* and *nehi*, "lamentation" (Micah 2:4), alludes to a *mashal* which has the characteristics of an elegy. An example of this type of *mashal* occurs in Isaiah 14:4–23, and to some extent in Numbers 21:27–30. Another possible tendency in the development of the *mashal* is the emphasis on metaphorical and allegorical features, which are the determining characteristics of Ezekiel's *meshalim* and are found, to a certain extent, in other *meshalim* as well. The verse which says of Solomon that "he spoke of trees, from the cedar that is in Lebanon to the hyssop that grows out of the wall; he spoke also of beasts, and of birds, and of reptiles, and of fish" (I Kings 5:13 [4:33]) may refer to *meshalim* of an allegorical and fabulous nature. On the other hand, it may simply refer to didactic sayings and poems. It is difficult to assume that originally the allegorical aspect determined the essential character of *meshalim*.

BIBLIOGRAPHY: E. Koenig, *Stylistik, Rhetorik, Poetik in Bezug auf die biblische Literatur* (1900), 77–110; A. Wuensche, *Die Schoenheit der Bibel* (1906); O. Eissfeldt, *Der Maschal im Alten Testament* (= BZAW, 24 (1913)); idem, in: *Einleitung in das Alten Testament* (1964), 89, 109–13, 123–6, 166–70; J. Pedersen, *Der Eid bei den Semiten* (1914), 12; A.H. Godbey, in: AJSLL, 39 (1922–23), 89–108; G. Bostroem, *Paronomasi i den aeldre Hebreiska Maschalliteraturen* (1928); M. Hermaniuk, *La parabolé évangélique* (1947), 62–189; J. Pirot, in: *Recherches de science réligieuse*, 37 (1950), 565–80; A. Bentzen, *Introduction to the Old Testament* (1952), 167–77.

[Menahem Haran]

PROVERBS, BOOK OF (Heb. סֵפֶר מִשְׁלֵי, *Sefer Mishlei*), one of the three "wisdom books" of the Hagiographa, representing the affirmative and didactic element in wisdom (*ḥokhmah*), in contrast to the radical questioning of Job and Ecclesiastes. In its present form the book appears to have served as a manual for the moral and religious instruction of the young. Comprising materials of various kinds gleaned from the long tradition of wisdom, the book was used in schools by professional sages (cf. Eccles. 12:9–12; Ecclus. 6:23–28). The teacher's objectives and methods are outlined in Proverbs 1:2–6, namely, cultivation of the mind and training in ethical principles by the use of *proverbs (*mashal*), epigrams (*meliẓah*), sayings of the sages, and riddles (*ḥidah*) or puzzling questions. The teacher's basic theme is summed up in the motto with which he begins and ends the introduction to the older materials – "The fear of the Lord is the beginning [or first requirement, chief part] of knowledge [wisdom]" (1:7; 9:10).

Title

In the Masoretic Text the title *Mishle Shelomo ben David Melekh Yisrael* is usually abbreviated *Mishle* (so LXX, Vulg.). Solomon is here named as the traditionally supreme sage and patron of wisdom; this neither proves nor necessarily implies a claim of authorship. According to I Kings 5:12–13, Solomon authored 3,000 proverbs, which are said to have addressed the nature of trees and animals, presumably as fables illuminating the behavior of humankind. There are, however, very few examples of this genre preserved in the Book of Proverbs itself (e.g., 6:6–8; 30:24–31). Statements such as Proverbs 20:2, 8, 26 are not such as would come from a king's own lips. Two divisions of the book are each headed *Mishle Shelomo*, which would be redundant if the title in 1:1 were intended to be comprehensive. Other authors are named in 22:17, 24:23; 30:1; and 31:1. It is therefore probable that the title of the book was taken over and adapted from 10:1 when chapters 1–9 were prefixed to the previously existing materials. The word *mashal*, literally "likeness, comparison" (cf. Akkadian *mašālu*, "to be similar to"), would most obviously refer to proverbial expressions employing similes (e.g., Ezek. 16:44, "like mother, like daughter"). In practice however, *mashal* is applied to a wide variety of compositions characterized by elevated language or rhetorical style, such as prophetic speeches, parables, and even extended series of oaths (e.g. Num. 23:7; Ezek. 17:2; Job 27:1). Indeed, in the Hebrew Bible itself, *mashal* appears alongside and is linked to such disparate designations as *kelalah*, "curse"; lit., "deprecation" (Jer 24:9), *neginah*, "(taunt) song" (Ps. 69:13), *nehi*, "lament" (Mic. 2:4), and *ot*, "sign," "symbol" (Ezek. 14:8). In Proverbs 10–22:16 and chapters 25–29 the heading *Mishle Shelomo* may have designated the literary form characteristic of these sections, namely, a single-line proverb in poetic parallelism, as distinguished from the half-line or prosaic form of colloquial sayings (cf. I Sam. 10:12; 24:14).

The Wisdom Tradition

The cultivation of *ḥokhmah* as an understanding of the good and satisfactory life had a long history in ancient Israel. In and of itself, the term has no ethical content, but means simply a special skill or superior ability. The moral and religious element, broadly speaking, is an expansion of its meaning. In Job 38:36 and 39:17 it denotes simply intelligence. The "wisdom" of Bezalel was his expertness as a craftsman (Ex. 35:30–35). The word is used even of the disgraceful cunning of Jonadab (II Sam. 13:3). In I Kings it refers successively to Solomon's cleverness (2:6), his moral discernment (3:12), his encyclopedic knowledge (5:9), and his special ability as a king (5:21). The wise women of Tekoa and Abel in II Samuel 14:2ff., and 20:16ff. are characterized chiefly in terms of their rhetorical skills and mastery of the art of persuasion. The "wise" with whom Isaiah and Jeremiah disputed were powerful courtiers (Isa. 29:13–16; Jer. 9:22). However, wisdom as embracing ethical qualities in personal and social life found expression in the divinely given moral obligations of the covenant people (Deut. 4:5–6), and in the prophetic picture of the ideal king (Isa. 11:1–2). It finally took literary form in the piety of wisdom psalms, e.g., Psalms 1 and 34, of the author of Proverbs 1–9 and of Ben Sira, and in the dogmatism against which the writers of Job and Ecclesiastes revolted (see also *Wisdom).

International Wisdom

Hebrew wisdom was distinctive but not unique, as is recognized in the Bible itself. Solomon's wisdom is compared to his advantage with that of Egypt and of the people of the East (I Kings 5:10–11). Edom was famous for its sages (Jer. 49:7; Obad. 8), as was Tyre (Ezek. 28:2ff., 12ff.). Surviving wisdom literature from Egypt and Mesopotamia exhibits the same kind of divergence as between Proverbs and Ben Sira on the one hand, and Job and Ecclesiastes on the other – the first conservative, affirmative, didactic, and practical, the second skeptical of traditional values and radically speculative. The lengthy "instruction" (Eg. *sb'yt*) addressed by a pharaoh or high official to his son and expected successor was a well attested genre in Egypt from the Old Kingdom on. The oft-repeated warnings in Proverbs 1–9 against the danger posed by the "strange woman" find their parallel in the Instructions of Ani (New Kingdom). The influence of this form has been traced in the admonitory discourses in Proverbs 1–8, and more certainly in 22:17–24:22. The latter has a demonstrable literary connection with the Egyptian *Instruction of Amen-em-ope* (New Kingdom). A late example of the instruction, ascribed to *Onchsheshonqy*, contains many sayings and proverbs of which some recall those of Proverbs, including examples of antithetical parallelism. In Sumerian literature the instruction genre (NA.RI.GA) is attested as early as 2400 B.C.E. in the *Instructions of Suruppak*. This composition, which exists in a number of versions, as well as in an Akkadian translation, includes both positive instructions and prohibitions on a wide variety of subjects. These are introduced, and regularly reintroduced, with the formula "Suruppak gave instructions to his son." Various kinds of advice offered here, some quite distinctive in content, are likewise found in Proverbs: warnings against going surety for another (Prov. 6:1–5), involvement in quarrels (Prov. 25:8), drinking beer when administering justice (Prov. 31:4–5), or partaking of "stolen food" (metaphorical; Prov. 9:17). Study of the recensional history of this long-lived Mesopotamian wisdom collection may well have specific application for understanding how the biblical book of Proverbs was composed. Similar to the Sumerian *Instructions of Suruppak* is the later Akkadian composition referred to as *The Counsels of Wisdom*, which in some cases offers the identical advice, but more consistently favors longer, more extensive topical units. The discovery of an Akkadian tablet at Ras Shamra in Syria containing the *Instructions of Shube-awilim*, itself related to the more ancient *Instructions of Suruppak*, attests to the availability of traditional Mesopotamian wisdom literature in the Canaanite cultural sphere as early as the 15th pre-Christian century. A millennium later a fifth-century Aramaic papyrus from the Jewish military colony at *Elephantine in Egypt contains the maxims of the famed Assyrian court sage Ahiqar. This collection presents numerous parallels in both content and form to the practical advice offered in the biblical Book of Proverbs. Particularly remarkable is the cluster in one column of the papyrus of close to 10 individual proverbs counseling caution in dealing with kings, whose unlimited power and volatile wrath are fraught with danger for the ordinary courtier. This topical cluster is most reminiscent of analogous groupings on the identical theme in Proverbs 16:10, 12–15; 25: 2–7 (cf. 20:2, 8, 26, 28).

Precepts and Proverbs

Inherent in the biblical idea of wisdom was that it could be taught to those capable of learning (Ex. 35:34). The *peti* in Proverbs 1:4 is "simple," "untutored"; he is not a "fool" (*'evil*) unless he despises learning (1:7). There were two methods of education – the authoritative *musar* ("training, precept") of the parent and of the teacher in a parent's role, and *'eẓah*, the "counsel" of the sage and of the teacher as sage. *Musar* is found in Proverbs in peremptory "dos and don'ts" (e.g., 3:25–32; 22:22ff.), and in longer discourses in chapters 1–9 and 30:1–9. *'Eẓah* is expressed in the sentence-long sayings about how life is lived well or badly, which form the substance of the "Solomonic" proverbs in 10:1–22:16 and chapters 25–19. The precept speaks in the imperative mood, the proverb in the indicative, with the occasional variant of a rhetorical question. The one seeks to impose the teacher's will and knowledge on the student; the other to elicit from him a free and positive response. They have the same objectives of forming the mind, building the moral character, and training the judgment of the pupils (1:2–4). The form of extended instruction differs from that of the shorter precept by including a motive clause indicating the welcome or unwelcome results that would follow from obedience or disobedience respectively. In this it resembles many proverbs describing the character and behavior of men, and thus serving as indirect precepts encouraging virtue and holding up vice to contempt. "A little sleep, a little slumber, a little folding of the hands to rest – and poverty will come upon you like a robber" (24:33–34) has the same effect as "Love not sleep lest you come to poverty" (20:13). The precept in 25:16 is the equivalent of the saying in 25:27a. Precepts reflect the imperatives of social order and religious values. Proverbs were rules of another kind, pointing to a right order in life which exists or should exist, expressed in the stylistic pattern: "this is like that," "this is better than that," "this results in that." Happy or unhappy consequences of actions occur in accordance with an unseen order of justice. The observations and counsels of the proverbs in 10–22:16 and chapters 25–29 are on two levels of moral and religious understanding. On one level they are exhortations to personal piety and probity, and affirmations that the Lord is master in human affairs and guarantor of the moral order (e.g., 10:3; 11:1; 12:2; 16:1). With these are associated the encomiums on wisdom and wise men, and the identification of the latter with "the righteous" and of fools with "the wicked" (e.g., 10:6–8; 12:1, 15; 13:20; 16:22). On the second level are the more secular sayings, caustic comments on antisocial behavior, and pathetic reflections on "the way things are" (e.g., 13:7; 14:13; 20:14; 26:6–16). Some short colloquial sayings seem to have been recast in verse form, as when an identical saying in 10:15a and 18:11a has been differently supplemented in the second half of the line. In 15:33 and 18:12, what looks like a simple parental admonition has been given different parallel lines. Other sayings possibly of popular origin are 11:2a; 12:4a; 17:14a; 22:8a; 27:7b, 10c. A special type of proverb compares phenomena in a culminating numerical series. "Three things are never satisfied, four never say, 'Enough!': Sheol, the barren womb, the earth ever thirsty for water, and the fire which never say 'Enough'!" (30:15b–16; cf. 30:18–19, 21–31). Since a whole number cannot have an exact synonym, it is paired with the number next lower when used in synonymous parallelism (see *Poetry). The form originated in the effort of early wisdom thinkers to classify phenomena by common characteristics. It is a kind of riddle: "What do such similarities mean for man's understanding of the world about him?"

Structural Outline of the Book

PART 1. Chapters 1–9. Didactic discourses and "wisdom poems."

Title, preface and motto: 1:1–7.

Ten instructional discourses: 1:8–19; 2:1–22; 3:1–12; 3:21–26 + 31–35; 4:1–9; 4:10–19; 4:20–27 + 5:21–23; 5:1–14; 6:20–21 + 23–35; 7:1–27.

Five poems:

(a) the rewards of wisdom: 3:13–20;

(b) personified Wisdom addresses men in rebuke, appeal and self-affirmation: 1:20–33; 8:1–36; 9:1–6 (+ Folly, 13–18).

Precepts, direct or implied: 3:27–30; 5:15–20; 6:1–19, 22;9:7–12.

PART 2. Chapters 10–22: 16. First Collection of "Solomonic Proverbs."

PART 3. (A): Chapters 22:17–24:22. The "Thirty Precepts" of the Sages; an "Instruction" modeled on the Egyptian *Instruction of Amen-em-ope.*

(B): Chapter 24:23–34. Other Sayings of the Sages; an appendix to (A).

PART 4: Chapters 25–29. Second Collection of "Solomonic proverbs," transmitted by Hezekiah's scribes. Appendixes to the book:

(1) Chapter 30:1–9. The skepticism of Agur, and a believer's reply.

(2) Chapter 30:10–13. Warnings and numerical proverbs.

(3) Chapter 31:1–9. A queen mother's diatribe.

(4) Chapter 31:10–31. Acrostic poem on the Excellent Wife.

Subject Matter

Since none of the main divisions of the book is entirely homogeneous in spite of the clear distinctions from one another, some further comments are called for.

In Part 1 the points where each of the 10 discourses begins are clearly marked, but their extent and possible expansions are less certain. Each opens with an exhortation to learn wisdom because of its value for living. All except no. 2 have as their pivotal point a specific precept, with corresponding promises or threats. In no. 2 the casuist form ("if you… then") replaces the imperative. In nos. 3, 5, and 7 the counsel is positive and general: "learn wisdom, and keep to the right path." In nos. 1, 4, and 6 the pupil is sternly warned against casting his lot with evildoers, and in 2, 8, 9, and 10 against the seductions of adultery. The latter evidently has here both a literal meaning and a metaphorical reference to religious unfaithfulness. A notable feature in nos. 1, 6, 8–10 is the vividness of the descriptions of temptation and the fateful consequences of yielding to it. The poems in 1:20–33, 8:1–36, and 9:1–6 not only conceptualize Wisdom but personify her in striking fashion. Chapter 8, arranged in three strophes and an epilogue, is one of the most remarkable passages in the wisdom literature, picturing Wisdom as YHWH's associate in the creation of the world. This poem appears to be based on the shorter one in 3:13–20, which, however, speaks of Wisdom in the third person. The short poem on Folly in 9:13–18 is a companion piece to that on Wisdom in 9:1–6. Following the eighth discourse, four short warnings against particular vices are inserted, together with a numerical list of hateful sins (4:15–20; 6:1–19). Again in 9:7–9 three proverbs intrude into the context.

Part 2 brings together about 375 single-line metrical proverbs or "wisdom sayings," haphazardly arranged except for one or two small groups on related topics (16:1–15). Some formal differences can be noted between chapters 10–15 and 16–22:16, though the point of division is indefinite and the teaching of both halves of the collection is essentially the same. In 10–15 there is a much higher incidence of antithetical parallels than later; "righteous" and "wicked" are contrasted most frequently in chapters 10–12, and "wise man" and "fool" most often in 12–15. After chapter 15 synonymous and extended parallelism predominates, together with scornful descriptions of the fool. References to YHWH's overruling providence and to divine sanctions on man's conduct are most frequent in 15 and 16. These may have been inserted by the teacher who prefaced 1–9 to the earlier collection of proverbs.

The literary relationship of Part 3 (A) to Amen-em-ope is clear, but difficult to spell out in detail. The structure of the two is the same: a summons to hear "thirty" (*sheloshim*, for MT vocalization *shalishim*) admonitions, a series of extended negative precepts. The first six and the ninth of these have topical and some verbal echoes of their Egyptian counterparts, but in a different order. The most striking verbal correspondence is the counsel against avarice in Proverbs 28:4–5: for wealth "grows wings, like an eagle it flies away into the sky." Amen-em-ope gives the same counsel but uses the simile "geese" rather than an "eagle." Because the order of corresponding sections is different, and 21 of the Egyptian precepts have no counterparts in the Hebrew work, it seems that the Hebrew scribe was depending on what he remembered from an earlier acquaintance with the Egyptian work. Part 3 (B) is a brief miscellaneous section attributed like 3 (A) to "the wise men," that is, to tradition. The first seven verses have enough points of contact with (A) to raise the possibility that they were left over from an earlier or alternative form of (A).

Part 4, the second collection of "Solomonic proverbs," resembles the first in some particulars and differs in others. It also falls into two parts unmarked in the text, 25–27 and 28–29. Chapter 25 opens with a series of precepts of double length, and chapter 26 has groups of sayings that pillory the fool and the sluggard. Throughout 25–27 precepts and similes predominate, rather than the declarative sentences common in the first collection. The tone also is more secular and less moralizing; the name YHWH occurs only once, and then in a supplementary line. The topical unit 27:23–27 is devoted to the seemingly unusual subject of animal husbandry, but similar subject matter appears in the Sumerian *Instructions of Suruppak* and in an Akkadian composition styled *The Counsels of a Pessimist*. This venerable tradition of combining advice on one's behavior together with helpful hints on the care of farm and flock survives in Hesiod's *Works and Days*, Virgil's *Georgics*, and beyond. In 28–29 the resemblance to 10–22:16 is greater both in form and content. Parts 2 and 4 have six proverbs in common, seven others are nearly identical, and four more have identical half-lines. The virtues extolled and the vices held up to scorn are much the same. The four appendices differ markedly from each other and from the rest of the book. In 30:1–9 the challenge of Agur the agnostic is answered (either in dialogue or as a later addendum) by a believer who affirms his faith and adds a humble prayer. In 30:10–33 there are five numerical sayings or riddles, a numbered list of sinners in the same style as 6:16–19, and some miscellaneous proverbs. In 31:1–9 the mother of an otherwise unknown King Lemuel cautions her son against dissolute behavior and neglect of his duties to his people. The fourth appendix is an acrostic poem on the excellent wife; it is remarkable for the light it throws on domestic activities in well-to-do homes and on the managerial responsibilities undertaken by the woman.

Text and Dating

The questions of the text and its dating are interrelated. The Hebrew text is relatively well preserved. The Septuagint seems to have been derived from essentially the same text, in spite of the idiosyncracies of that version. The only significant difference is in the order of some sections, indicating that the text was still not finally fixed in the first century B.C.E. One problem of dating is that an atomistic work, of which so much of Proverbs consists, was peculiarly susceptible to minor expansions. Hence the rare occurrence of Aramaic words may be meaningless for dating. There are no Persian or Greek words, and it is no longer necessary to posit the Greek period on philosophical or theological grounds. The customary post-Exilic dating of the book may have been influenced more than is realized by its association with Ben Sira. The book is composed throughout in classical Hebrew, with the exception of some Phoenicianisms, chiefly in chapter 8, which may have resulted from the use of older sources. Material as early as the time of Solomon may be included in the numerical proverbs of 30:15–31 and many of the more secular sayings. If reliable, 25:1 indicates that older materials were assembled in Hezekiah's reign. The activity of Wisdom teachers in the eighth century B.C.E. is evident in Isaiah (cf. Prov. 19:11–12; 21:2), in the prophet's adoption of a wisdom form for his oracle in Isaiah 28:23–29, and in apparent references to schools (Isa. 28:9–10; cf. 6:9–10). The literary influence of the Egyptian instructions and the optimistic serenity of tone point to a time when concern for individual conduct and education were not crowded out by alarm over national security. However, both older and later materials undoubtedly are included. Although the evidence is inconclusive, the late monarchical period seems as likely as any for the completion of the work in substantially its present form.

Ethical and Religious Teachings

The contents of Proverbs range from purely intellectual observations about natural phenomena, to "secular" comments on how men behave and life's occurrences, as well as a final positive association of right conduct with true wisdom and piety. The teacher's introduction in chapters 1–9 emphasizes the spirit in which the older wisdom materials are to be approached. Virtues and vices which had been discerned in the long experience of the community and by its older sages were still valid. The principal new emphasis is on resisting the temptation to fall into the ways of hardened evildoers and adulterous women. The "wise" and the "fools" have become the "righteous" and the "wicked" in newly composed moralistic couplets, inserted in the Solomonic collections. Whereas in the older wisdom it was asserted on grounds of experience that good conduct generally led to prosperity and its opposite to ruin, the reason for each now is seen to be that "the eyes of the Lord are in every place, keeping watch on the evil and the good" (15:3). In the older parts of the book, wisdom means simply the state of being wise. Its conceptualization begins with the idea in the Solomonic sayings that wisdom is an inner fountain of life (13:14). The teacher in 1–9 further develops both ideas: The state of being wise is attained by training, but it is also a gift of divine grace (2:1–6), and will act as a personal guide through life. This personification of Wisdom is dramatically enhanced in 1:20–33 and 8:1–31, yet still within the limits of poetic imagery (cf. Ps. 85:11–12). Wisdom here addresses men in her own name and in the guise of a goddess; she is a living power in the order of the world and has been YHWH's associate in its creation. Scholars differ as to whether in 8:22ff. Wisdom has become a full-blown hypostasis of YHWH, or whether it is an imaginative image of what is said in 3:19: "YHWH by [His] wisdom founded the world." The structure of the whole passage 8:12–31, when compared to 3:13–20, favors the latter alternative, though the picture may be colored to some degree by mythic language. However, the oft-posited identification of *ḥokhmah*, "Lady Wisdom," and the Egyptian goddess Maat has yet to be demonstrated beyond a superficial similarity. At the same time, the personification of Wisdom and her characterization as one who is herself not divine but nevertheless "dear to the gods" are found in the Aramaic proverbs of Ahiqar cited above.

BIBLIOGRAPHY: R. Gordis, in: HUCA, 18 (1843–44), 77–118; C.I.K. Story, in: JBL, 64 (1945), 319–37; Kaufmann, Y., Toledot, 2 (1960), 631–46; C.T. Fritsch, and R.W. Schloerb, in: *Interpreter's Bible*, 4 (1955), 767–957; Pritchard, Texts, (1955²), 405–52; W.G. Plaut, *Book of Proverbs* (1961); B. Gemser, *Sprueche Salomos* (1963); M. Haran, in: *Tarbiz*, 39 (1969–70), 116–18, 130–32; W. McKane, *Proverbs* (1970), incl. bibl. **ADD. BIBLIOGRAPHY:** W.G. Lambert, *Babylonian Wisdom Literature* (1960); *Ugaritica*, 5 (1968; Text 163 = R.S. 22.439); B. Alster, *The Instructions of Suruppak* (*Mesopotamia* 2; 1974); idem, *Studies in Sumerian Proverbs* (Mesopotamia 3; 1975); J.M. Lindenberger, *The Aramaic Proverbs of Ahiqar* (1983); B. Porten and A. Yardeni, in: TADAE, 3 (1993), 24–53; R.J. Clifford, *Proverbs*, incl. bibl.; 1999; M. Fox, *Proverbs 1–9* (AB; 2000), incl. bibl.

[Robert B.Y. Scott / Murray Lichtenstein (2nd ed.)]

PROVERBS, TALMUDIC. The Talmud abounds in proverbs of all kinds. Important sources are the tractates *Avot, Avot de-Rabbi Nathan, Derekh Ereẓ Rabbah*, and *Derekh Ereẓ Zuta*, and numbers of proverbs occur together in several smaller collections (BK 92a–b; Bek. 17a; et al.), although they are scattered through all rabbinical literature.

Scholarly and Popular Proverbs

The proverbs of scholars are usually introduced with the words, "it was customary for A to say" or "he used to say," and their popular ones by "as the rabbis say." In most cases these proverbs have an ethical and didactic character. The Talmud also contains many popular proverbs which are quoted with the opening words "the proverb says" (in Hebrew and in Aramaic), "they say," "as people say," "the proverb says," "the common proverb says," and in "the language of the people." These popular proverbs are mainly expressed in Aramaic. In many cases there is no clear distinction between scholarly and popular proverbs, and it is then difficult to determine their source. For example, the saying of Rabban Simeon b. Gamaliel, "One who gives bread to a child must inform its mother" (Shab. 10b), is also cited in the Midrash (Num. R. 19:33) as "a popular proverb." The words "he used to say" merely indicate that a particular scholar quoted it frequently. Thus the saying of Samuel the Younger, "Rejoice not when thine enemy falleth, and let not thine heart be glad when he stumbleth" (Avot 4:19), is a verse from Proverbs (24:17). The dictum of Shammai, "Receive all men with a cheerful countenance" (Avot 1:15), is quoted with a slight variation by Ishmael (3:13). The dictum of Hillel on the Feast of Water Drawing, "Whither I desire to go thither my feet lead me" (Tosef., Suk. 4:2), was originally a popular saying which Hillel applied to God (S. Lieberman, *Tosefta ki-Feshutah*, ad loc.). This is probably why Rashi quotes "walls have ears" as a popular proverb (Ber. 8b), although it is given in the Midrash in the name of R. Levi (Lev R. 32:2; Eccles. R. 10:21). Sometimes contradictory proverbs appear to be directed at one another. An example is found in the ethical dictum, "Be rather a tail to lions than a head to foxes" (Avot 4:15), which contradicts the popular saying, "The proverb says: Be a head to foxes rather than a tail to lions" (TJ, Sanh. 4:10, 22b), and indeed parallels to this popular version are found in Hellenistic literature.

The rabbis spared no effort to introduce beautiful popular proverbs into the world of scholarship. They sought authority for them in early sources, in the Bible and in the tannaitic literature (BK 92a–b), and also derived proverbs from the interpretation of biblical verses, although in these cases it is also possible that the proverb anticipated the interpretation (cf. "From here we see that the ignorant person pushes himself to the front" (Meg. 12b); "When wine enters, counsel departs" (Er. 65a; Sanh. 38a); "Woe is me because of my Creator [*yoẓer*], woe is me because of my [evil] inclination" (*yeẓer*; Ber. 61a)).

Proverbs and *Halakhah*

The sages did not hesitate to utilize the worldly wisdom in the proverbs for halakhic ruling. "Once a man borrowed a cat to deal with mice, but the mice killed the cat. The case came before Ashi for judgment. Thereupon a certain Mordecai, who was present, intervened, quoting Rava: A man killed by women gets neither judgment nor judge," i.e., the cat was itself responsible and the owner can have no claim (BM 97a). They applied the proverb "It is not the mouse that is the thief, but the hole" (Git. 45a) in halakhic discussions. From the ancient, pointed proverb, "An olive's bulk of the paschal offering, yet the rejoicing splits the roof," expressing the popular attitude toward an inflated ceremony, Ḥiyya inferred a *halakhah* in connection with ritual uncleanness (TJ, Pes. 7:10, 35b). The reverse also occurred, namely that the proverb was created through the halakhic ruling, as in the case of a ruling of Akiva expressed in a proverbial form: "You have dived into the depths and brought up only a potsherd" (BK 91a). The rabbis utilized the dictum: "That which made you unclean, did not make me unclean, yet you have made me unclean" as a mnemotechnic chain connecting a collection of *mishnayot* on the laws of ritual defilement (Par. 8:2–7).

Rabbinic Study of Proverbs

The sages engaged in the study of proverbs. Mention has been made of a series of dialogues in which *amoraim* searched for the classical source of popular sayings, and it is worth noting that for one of them (BK 92b) they discovered five possible sources. They also compared the dicta of Ereẓ Israel and Babylon: "Here [in Babylon] they say, 'Tobias sinned and Ziggas was flogged.' There [in Ereẓ Israel] they say, 'Shechem married and Mabgai was circumcised'" (Mak. 11a; i.e., because Shechem – Gen. 34 – wished to marry Jacob's daughter the whole population had to undergo circumcision).

Ereẓ Israel and Babylon

Undoubtedly much use was made of proverbs in Ereẓ Israel; but for some reason the number of them in the Jerusalem Talmud is relatively meager in comparison with those in the Babylonian, and most of those quoted in the Jerusalem Talmud are also found in the Babylonian Talmud.

Translations from Aramaic to Hebrew

In the late Midrashim there occur translations into Hebrew of the Aramaic proverbs in the Babylonian Talmud. At times the translation is inferior to the original. Thus the dictum (BK 92b), "Into the well from which you have drunk water do not throw clods," becomes in the Midrash (Num. R. 22:4), "Into the well… do not throw stones." The Aramaic word for "clod" is more suitable, since it suggests the defiling of the water.

Comparison with Biblical Proverbs

Talmudic proverbs surpass the biblical ones in pungency and appositeness but are inferior in sophistication and poetry. Thus the biblical (Eccles. 10:8), "He that diggeth a pit shall fall into it," parallels, "If a man spits into the air, it will fall on his face" (Eccl. R. 7:9, no. 1), and the verse (Prov. 17:10), "A rebuke entereth deeper into a man of understanding than a hundred stripes into a fool," parallels, "A hint is sufficient for a wise man but a fool needs the fist" (Mid. Prov. 22:15).

Animal Proverbs

The sages made extensive use of the animal world for their proverbs. The miser is compared to "a mouse lying upon the coins" (Sanh. 29b). Of a coward who treats harshly those subservient to him, it says: "One who cannot hit the donkey [lest it kick], hits the saddle" (Tanḥ. Pekudei 4). A warning against women occurs in the saying: "If the dog barks – enter; if a bitch – leave" (Er. 86a; from which Rav exemplified a *halakhah* in the laws of *Eruvin* based upon the difference in a man's relationship to his son-in-law and to his daughter-in-law). Of a weak character it says, "He never controlled two flies" (Deut. R. 1:5).

Stylistic Characteristics

Alliteration occurs in several dicta, such as "A man's character can be recognized in his cup, his purse, and his anger" (Heb. *koso, kiso, ka'aso* – Er. 65b). In some instances the alliteration is somewhat rhymed such as, "He who eats the fat tail [*allita*] must hide in the loft [*alita*], but he who eats cress [*kakule*] may lie by the dunghill [*kikle*] of the town" (Pes. 114a); and "When a Jew must eat carobs [*ḥaruva*], he repents [*tetuva*]" (Lev. R. 13:4). Ingenious homiletical interpretations of words occur: "Why are some coins called *zuzim*? Because they are removed [*zazim*] from one and given to another. Why are other coins called *ma'ot*, because they signify *mah la-et* [what of the future time?]" (Num. R. 22:8).

Eulogistic Dicta

The Talmud cites dicta uttered by professional mourners. Thus, "if the flame has fallen upon the cedars [the great] what avails the hyssop on the wall!" (the lowly; MK 25b); "Many have drunk the cup of death; many shall drink" (Ket. 8b). Tawiow noted that the Bible and the Talmud contain no derogatory proverbs about deformed persons such as occur in abundance in the sayings of other peoples.

Rabbinic Proverbs in Popular Parlance

Hundreds of rabbinic dicta have found their way into popular usage. In many of them changes have occurred which are worth noting. Very many others originally quoted in a halakhic or theoretical framework have become popular sayings with a meaning different from the original. Thus, "A man may see any leprous signs except his own" (Neg. 2:5), taught originally as a law that a leprous priest must be examined by some other priest, received the popular psychological meaning that no man is objective with reference to himself. The expression *dikdukei aniyyut* ("the minutiae of poverty"; Er. 41b), first used of the sufferings of poverty, is used already by Ibn Ezra (Eccles. 12:5) with reference to a forced explanation, i.e., the writer is lacking imagination. "*Damim tarte mashma*," in the original means "the word *damim* [blood] applies to two kinds of blood" and is popularly used to express both "blood" and "money." Hundreds of rabbinic sayings found their way into the spoken language in the form in which they occur in more popular works, such as Rashi's commentary, *piyyutim*, etc. The expression, "The Omnipresent has many agents of death" (Ta'an. 18b), is current among people in the form it occurs in Rashi (to Ex. 16:32): "The Omnipresent has many agents." The dictum, "Four count as if dead: a poor man, a blind man…" (Ned. 64b), is better known in the abridged form of Rashi (to Ex. 4:19): "A poor man is regarded as dead." Akiva's dictum, "No pity may be shown in a lawsuit" (Ket. 9:2), is popularly known by the form in which it occurs in a *silluk* (type of *piyyut*) for the first day of the New Year: "[The Supreme King preserves the world through justice, for] there is no pity in judgment." The changes popularly introduced did not result from ignorance but from didactic grounds whether consciously or unconsciously. These changes gave greater clarity and accuracy to the dicta, furnished a general and abstract form to dicta that needed it, and also added interpretation where necessary. The talmudic dictum, "In the place where penitents stand, the wholly righteous do not stand" (Ber. 34a) was popularly revised into the clearer dictum, "In the place where penitents stand, the wholly righteous are unable to stand," stressing the superiority of the penitent more clearly than in the original. The statement of Rava (Meg. 16a) that the help given Mordecai was given "not because of the love for Mordecai but because of the hatred for Haman" received a general abstracted meaning in the mouth of the people: "not from love of Mordecai but from hatred of Haman" (a version already found in the *Massekhet Purim* attributed to *Kalonymus b. Kalonymus, ed. by J. Willheimer (1871), 43). The expression "R. Yose always has his reason" (Git. 67a) became through the influence of Rashi, "his justification and reason are with him," i.e., he always has good reason. During recent years many works have appeared comparing talmudic sayings with those of other peoples (see bibliography) which prove that among cultures and languages far from Ereẓ Israel and Babylonia, such as the Far East, independent proverbs similar to those in the Talmud were common.

BIBLIOGRAPHY: I.H. Tawiow, *Oẓar ha-Meshalim ve-ha-Pitgamim* (1922), 10–25; L. Taubes, *Talmudishe Elementn inem Yidishn Shprikhvort* (1928), 9–16; M. Waxman, *Mishlei Yisrael* (1933), 23–31; I. Davidson, *Oẓar ha-Meshalim ve-ha-Pitgamim* (1957); M. Glueck, in: *Hadoar*, 36 (1957), 484–6 (= *Leshonenu la-Am*, 8 (1957), 260–6); 9 (1958), 20–27); S. Ashkenazi, in: *Leshonenu la-Am*, 11 (1960), 261–65; 12 (1961), 99–105; E. Blankenstein, *Mishlei Yisrael ve-Ummot ha-Olam* (1964); I. Davidson, in: *Jivobleter*, 13 (1938), 354–72 (bibl.); Y.L. Zlotnik, in: *Barkai*, 66 (1940), 14f. (additions to bibl.).

[Arie Strikovsky]

PROVIDENCE, in religion and philosophy, God's guidance or care of His creatures, emanating from His constant concern for them and for the achievement of His purposes. Providence includes both supervision of the acts of men and the guidance of the actors in specific directions. Its object is also to deal out fitting retribution – in order to establish justice in the world, retribution itself often serving as a means of guidance (see below). Hence there is a connection between providence and the principle of *reward and punishment. The origin of the term providence is Greek (πρόνοια, lit. "perceiving beforehand") and first appears in Jewish literature in the Wisdom of Solomon, 14:3; 17:2.

In the Bible

The basis of the belief in a constant and eternal divine providence is the biblical conception of God. In polytheism there is generally a belief in a fixed "order" of nature, which is above the gods. This "order" serves to some extent as a guarantee that right prevails in the world (this is the Greek θέμιζ or μοῖρα; the Egyptian *ma'at*; and the Iranian-Persian *artha*, "truth"). However, in this type of belief the right is, as it were, a product of action (this is also the Buddhist belief in "karma") and is not dependent on a divine providence with a universal moral purpose. On the contrary, through the use of certain magical acts, man can even overcome the will of the god. In any case, there is a basic belief in fate and necessity. By contrast, the belief in providence is in the first instance a belief in a God who has cognition and will, and who has unlimited control over nature and a personal relationship with all men – a relationship which is determined solely by their moral or immoral behavior. Biblical belief does not deny the existence of a fixed natural order – "the ordinances" of heaven and earth, of day and night (Jer. 31:35–36; 33:25) – but since God is the creator of nature and is not subject to its laws (e.g. Jer. 18:6ff.), He can guide man and reward him according to his merit, even through the supernatural means of miracles. Such guidance may be direct (through divine *revelation) or indirect – through a prophet or other animate or inanimate intermediaries ("Who maketh His angels spirits; His ministers a flaming fire," Ps. 104:4; cf. Joel 2:1ff.; Amos 3:7; Ps. 103:20–22). God's providence is both individual – extending to each and every person (Adam, Abel, Cain, etc.), and general-over peoples and groups, especially Israel, His chosen people. The guarding and guidance of the Patriarchs (Abraham, Isaac, and Jacob) and their families (Sarah in the house of Pharaoh, Hagar in the desert, Joseph in Egypt, etc.) aimed at the ultimate purpose of creating an exemplary people exalted above all other nations (Deut. 26:18). The whole history of the Israelites, beginning with the Exodus from Egypt, is, according to the biblical conception, a continuous unfolding of divine providence's guidance of the people as a whole as well as of its individual members in the way marked out for them. Even the sufferings undergone by the people belong to the mysteries of divine providence (cf. e.g., the doctrinal introductions in Judg. 2:11–23; 3:1–8; 6:7–10, 13–17; 10:6–15; II Kings 14:26–27; 17:7ff.).

It can be said that the entire Bible is a record of divine providence, whether general or individual. While the Pentateuch and the Prophets emphasize general, national providence, Psalms and Proverbs are based on the belief that God is concerned with the individual, hears the cry of the wretched, desires the well-being of the righteous, and directs man, even against his will, to the destiny which He has determined for him ("The lot is cast into the lap, but the whole disposing thereof is of the Lord," Prov. 16:33; "The king's heart is in the hand of the Lord, as the rivers of water; He turneth it whithersoever He will," Prov. 21:1; etc.). Prophets (Jeremiah, Ezekiel, Habakkuk) and psalmists (Ps. 9; 71; 77; 88) sometimes question the ways of providence and divine justice, but they ultimately affirm the traditional belief in providence. In the last analysis, this position is also maintained by the author of Ecclesiastes, who otherwise expresses the gravest doubts regarding providence ("But know that for all these things God will bring thee to judgment," Eccles. 11:9). This is true also of Job, but his doubts and misgivings are confined to the question of a divine providence which rules the universe, and particularly mankind.

The unlimited belief in providence would seem to conflict with the doctrine that man can freely choose good and evil (for which God rewards or punishes him), which is also integral to the biblical world view. This issue was grappled with only in later times, with the development of religious philosophy in the Middle Ages.

In the Apocrypha

In the Apocrypha, too, the belief is widespread that God watches over the deeds of mortals in order to requite the wicked and the righteous according to their deserts. The suffering of the righteous is but a temporary trial in order that they be well rewarded in the end. Tobit, for instance, for dealing kindly with the living and with the dead is persecuted by the authorities. It appears as if the hand of God, too, was turned against him but his righteousness is rewarded. In the end he is vindicated and is vouchsafed the victory of righteousness. The same applies to the community of Israel – the enemy invariably receives his punishment and the righteous nation is saved, almost unexpectedly. According to I Maccabees (9:46), Judah Maccabee urged the people to pray because he knew that God pays attention to prayer ("Now therefore cry unto Heaven that you may be delivered out of the hand of your enemies"). Similarly, the inhabitants of Jerusalem were convinced that their prayer saved them in time of trouble (II Macc. 1:8). As in ancient times, so too in the time of the Hasmoneans, God continued to save His people by means of angels sent by Him (Heliodorus, who went to desecrate the Temple, fell into a faint at the hand of angels: II Macc. 3; angels in heaven hastened to the assistance of Judah Maccabee: *ibid.* 10:29–30). Lysias also realized that the Hebrews were invincible because God helped them (*ibid.* 11:13).

In the concept of providence in the apocalyptic works, particularly in the writings of the *Dead Sea sect, one can detect a tendency toward an important innovation. In these works the idea is expressed that God, who has preknowledge of everything, also decrees everything in advance; both the wicked and the righteous are formed at their creation ("all the sons of light each one to his fortune according to the counsel of the Lord…; all the sons of darkness each one to his guilt according to the vengeance of the Lord," – Manual of Discipline 1:9–10; "From the Lord of Knowledge, all is and was… and before they came into being he prepared all their thought… and it is unchangeable," – *ibid.* 3:15–16; "and unto Israel and the angel of his truth [Michael?] [they] are a help to all the sons of light," while "the angel of darkness" rules over "all the dominion of the sons of wickedness," – *ibid.* 20–24; and see Jub. 1:20 and 2:2). According to Jubilees everything is also written beforehand in the "tablets of the heavens" (3:10). Josephus, too (Ant., 13:171–3, 18:11f.; Wars, 2:119f.), distinguishes between the different sects that arose in the time of the Second Temple, primarily on the basis of the difference between them in the concept of providence. According to him, "the Pharisees say that some things but not all depend on fate, but some depend upon us as to whether they occur or not" (Ant., 13:172). "The Essenes hold that fate rules everything and nothing happens to man without it; while the Sadducees abolish fate, holding that it does not exist at all, that human actions do not occur through its power, and that everything is dependent upon man himself who alone is the cause of the good, and evil results from man's folly" (*ibid.*; see also *Essenes; *Sadducees; *Boethusians; *Pharisees). If the definitions of Josephus are accurate, one may say that the Sadducees deviated from the biblical concept and believed in providence in general but not in detail; something of the same can be said of the Essenes in what pertains to their belief in predestination, but judging from the writings found in Qumran, this belief was not without qualifications and exceptions.

In the Talmud

The outlook of the scholars of the Mishnah and Talmud on the nature and purport of divine providence is summarized in the dictum of Akiva (Avot 3:15): "All is foreseen, but freedom of choice is given; and the world is judged with goodness, and all is in accordance with the works." It is apparent that the first part of this dictum expresses an attempt to reconcile the principle of providence on the one hand with freedom of choice on the other; but it is possible that the idea here expressed is identical with that contained in the dictum: "Everything is in the hand of heaven except for the fear of heaven" (Ber. 33b), which is intended to build a bridge between freedom of choice and the idea of predestination. From various dicta in the Talmud it is possible to infer that the idea of providence during this era embraced not only all men but even all creatures. For the gazelle that is wont to cast its seed at parturition from the top of the mountain, the Holy One prepares "an eagle that catches it in its wings and places it before her, and were it to come a moment earlier or a moment later [the offspring] would die at once" (BB 16a–b); in similar vein is: "The Holy One sits and nourishes both the horns of the wild ox and the ova of lice" (Shab. 107b). Of man it was said: "No man bruises his finger on earth unless it is decreed in heaven" (Ḥul. 7b); and all is revealed and known before God: "even the small talk of a man's conversation with his wife" (Lev. R. 26:7). Similarly: "The Holy One sits and pairs couples – the daughter of so-and-so to so-and-so" (Lev. R. 8:1; Gen. R. 68:4; and cf. MK 18b), or: "He is occupied in making ladders, casting down the one and elevating the other" (Gen. R. 68:4).

The continuation of Akiva's dictum ("and the world is judged with goodness") accords apparently with the traditional outlook of the Talmud. Thus, for example, it was said that even if man has 999 angels declaring him guilty and only one speaking in his favor, God assesses him mercifully (TJ, Kid. 1:10, 61d; Shab. 32a); that God is distressed at the distress of the righteous and does not rejoice at the downfall of the wicked (Sanh. 39b; Tanh., be-Shallaḥ 10) and does not deal tyrannically with His creatures (Av. Zar. 3a); and he sits and waits for man and does not punish him until his measure is full (Sot. 9a).

[Yehoshua M. Grintz]

In Medieval Jewish Philosophy

The treatment of providence (*hashgaḥah*) in medieval Jewish philosophy reflects the discussion of this subject in late Greek philosophy, particularly in the writings of the second-century C.E. Aristotelian commentator Alexander of Aphrodisias, and in the theological schools of Islam. The Hebrew term *hashgaḥah* itself was apparently first coined by Samuel ibn Tibbon as a translation of the Arabic word *ʿanāʾyah.* In his *Guide of the Perplexed* (trans. by S. Pines, 1963), Maimonides uses the latter synonymously with *tadbīr,* the Hebrew equivalent of which is *hanhagah* (i.e., governance of the world). In most Hebrew philosophical works, however, *hanhagah* designates the universal providence which determines the natural order of the world as a whole, while *hashgaḥah* is generally used to designate individual providence. For the latter, Judah *Al-Ḥarizi also used the Hebrew term *shemirah* ("safekeeping"), and it should be noted that originally Ibn Tibbon, too, preferred this, as is shown in a manuscript copy of a letter to Maimonides (see below).

*Saadiah Gaon deals with the problem of providence in treatise 5 of his *Emunot ve-De'ot* (*Book of Beliefs and Opinions*, trans. by S. Rosenblatt, 1948), whose subject is "Merits and Demerits." In chapter 1, he identifies providence with the reward and punishment meted out by God to the individual in this world, which is "the world of action"; though, ultimately, reward and punishment are reserved for the world to come. Echoes of the philosophical debate on the problem of providence may be found in other parts of Saadiah's book. Thus, he asks how it is possible that God's knowledge can encompass both the past and the future and "that he knows both equally" in a single, eternal, and immutable act of knowing (*ibid.*, 2:13). His reply is that it is impossible to compare man's knowledge, which is acquired through the medium of the senses, with God's, which "is not acquired by any intermediate cause" and is not derived from temporal facts, but rather flows from His essence. This linking of the problem of providence with that of the nature of God's knowledge originated with Alexander of Aphrodisias, as did the question of the reconciliation of God's foreknowledge with man's freedom of the will. Saadiah's solution to the latter problem is to point out that the Creator's knowledge of events is not the cause of their occurrence. If that were the case, all events would be eternal, inasmuch as God's knowledge of them is eternal (*ibid.*, 4:4). Abraham *Ibn Daud devotes an entire chapter of his book *Emunah Ramah* (6:2; ed. by S. Weil (1852), 93ff.) to the problems involved in the concept of providence. Ibn Daud, too, was considerably influenced by Alexander of Aphrodisias, who upheld "the nature of the possible," thereby allowing for human choice, in opposition to the absolute determinism of the *Stoics. Like Alexander, he limits God's knowledge to that which stems from the necessary laws of nature through natural causes, to the exclusion of the effects of accident or free will which are only possible. He argues that God's ignorance of things that come to be as a result of accident or free will does not imply an imperfection in His nature, for whatever is "possible" is also only possible for God, and hence He knows possible things only as possible, not as necessary.

Maimonides deals with the question of providence in light of the philosophic teachings on "governance" (*hanhagah, tadbīr*), which identify it with the action of the forces of nature (*Guide*, 2:10). He fully discusses *hashgaḥah* (*ʿanāʾyah; ibid.*, 3:16–24), listing five main views on the matter: those of *Epicurus, *Aristotle, the Ash'arites, the Mu'tazilites (see *Kalām), and, lastly, of the Torah, which affirms both freedom of the human will and divine justice. The good and evil that befall man are the result of this justice, "for all His ways are judgment," and there exists a perfect correspondence between the achievements of the individual and his fate. This is determined by the level of man's intellect, however, rather than by his deeds, so that it follows that only he whose perfected intellect adheres to God is protected from all evil (*Guide*, 3:51). Such a man realizes that governance, providence, and purpose cannot be attributed to God in a human sense, and he will, therefore, "bear every misfortune lightly, nor will misfortunes multiply doubts concerning God… but will rather increase his love of God." Maimonides argues against Alexander of Aphrodisias and Ibn Daud that God's knowledge instantaneously encompasses the numerous things subject to change without any change in His essence; that God foresees all things that will come to be without any addition to His knowledge; and that He therefore knows both the possible ("privation," i.e., that which does not yet exist but is about to be) and the infinite (i.e., individuals and particulars which are unlimited in number). The philosophers, he states, arbitrarily asserted that it is impossible to know the possible or the infinite, but they overlooked the difference between God's knowledge and human knowledge. Just as man's intellect is inadequate to apprehend God's essence, so it cannot apprehend His knowledge (*ibid.*, 2:20).

In his letter to Maimonides (published by Z. Diesendruck in: HUCA, 11 (1936), 341–66), Samuel ibn Tibbon calls attention to a contradiction between Maimonides' treatment of providence in *Guide*, 3:17ff., and his discussion at the end of the *Guide* in chapter 51, where, departing from the philosophical approach that providence is relevant only to the welfare of the soul, Maimonides expresses the conviction that the devout man will never be allowed to suffer any harm. Shem Tov ibn *Falaquera (*Moreh ha-Moreh*, 145–8), Moses ibn *Tibbon, in a note to his father's letter (ed. Diesendruck, *op. cit.*), *Moses of Narbonne, in his commentary on the *Guide* (3:51), and Efodi (Profiat *Duran), in his commentary on the same chapter, all dwell on this point. Shem Tov b. Joseph *Ibn Shem Tov, in his book *Emunot* (Ferrara, 1556, 8b–10a) and Isaac *Arama, in his *Akedat Yiẓḥak*, take Maimonides to task for having made the degree of providence exercised over man dependent on perfection of the intellect rather than on performance of the commandments. The Karaite *Aaron b. Elijah devotes several chapters of his book *Eẓ Ḥayyim* (ed. by F. Delitzsch (1841), 82–90) to the subject of providence, and he, too, criticizes Maimonides. Once the position has been taken that God's knowledge cannot be restricted, the activity of providence likewise cannot be made to depend only upon the degree of development of man's intellect. Just as God knows everything, so He watches over all things (ch. 88).

Isaac *Albalag, in his *Tikkun De'ot*, discusses providence in the course of his critique of the opinions of *Avicenna and al-*Ghazālī. It is impossible, he contends, to comprehend God's mode of cognition, but it is possible to attribute to Him a knowledge of things which are outside the realm of natural causation, i.e., free will and chance. God's knowledge and providence also provide the subject of a penetrating analysis in the *Milḥamot Adonai* of *Levi b. Gershom (treatises 2 and 3), who returns to the Aristotelian position as understood in the light of Alexander of Aphrodisias' commentary. It is inadmissible, he states, that God should know the possible and the numerically infinite, that is, the particulars qua particulars, but He does know all things through the order embracing them all.

In contrast to this view, Ḥasdai *Crescas argues in his *Or Adonai* (2:1–2) that the belief in individual providence is a fundamental principle of the Mosaic Law, according to which God's knowledge "encompasses the infinite" (i.e., the particular) and "the non-existent" (i.e., the possible) "without any change in the nature of the possible" (i.e., without His knowledge nullifying the reality of free will). Crescas maintains that the biblical and talmudic faith in providence is based on a belief in individual providence. His disciple, Joseph *Albo, also deals extensively with God's knowledge and providence in his *Sefer ha-Ikkarim* (4:1–15), during the course of his discussion concerning reward and punishment.

[Alexander Altmann]

In the Kabbalah

The question of divine providence almost never appears in the Kabbalah as a separate problem, and therefore few detailed and specific discussions were devoted to it. The idea of providence is identified in the Kabbalah with the assumption that there exists an orderly and continuous system of government of the cosmos, carried out by the Divine Potencies – the *Sefirot* – which are revealed in this government. The Kabbalah does no more than explain the way in which this system operates, while its actual existence is never questioned. The world is not governed by chance, but by unceasing divine providence, which is the secret meaning of the hidden order of all the planes of creation, and especially in the world of man. He who understands the mode of action of the *Sefirot* also understands the principles of divine providence which are manifested through this action. The idea of divine providence is interwoven in a mysterious way with the limitation of the area of action of causality in the world. For although most events which happen to living creatures, and especially to men, appear as if they occur in a natural way which is that of cause and effect, in reality these events contain individual manifestations of divine providence, which is responsible for everything that happens to man, down to the last detail. In this sense, the rule of divine providence is, in the opinion of *Naḥmanides, one of the "hidden wonders" of creation. The workings of nature ("I will give you your rains in their season," Lev. 26:4 and the like) are coordinated in hidden ways with the moral causality determined by the good and evil in men's actions.

In their discussions of divine providence, the early kabbalists stressed the activity of the tenth *Sefirah*, since the rule of the lower world is principally in its hands. This *Sefirah* is the *Shekhinah*, the presence of the divine potency in the world at all times. This presence is responsible for God's providence for His creatures; but according to some opinions the origin of divine providence is actually in the upper *Sefirot*. Symbolic expression is given to this idea, particularly in the *Zohar, in the description of the eyes in the image of **Adam Kadmon* ("Primordial Man"), in his two manifestations, as the *Arikh Anpin* (lit. "The Long Face" but meaning "The Long Suffering") or *Attikah Kaddishah* ("the Holy Ancient One"), and as the *Ze'eir Anpin* ("The Short Face," indicating the "Impatient"). In the description of the organs in the head of *Attikah Kaddishah*, the eye which is always open is taken as a supernal symbol for the existence of divine providence, whose origin is in the first *Sefirah*. This upper providence consists solely of mercy, with no intermixture of harsh judgment. Only in the second manifestation, which is that of God in the image of the *Ze'eir Anpin*, is the working of judgment also found in the divine providence. For "…the eyes of the Lord… range through the whole earth" (Zech. 4:10), and they convey his providence to every place, both for judgment and for mercy. The pictorial image, "the eye of providence," is here understood as a symbolic expression which suggests a certain element in the divine order itself. The author of the Zohar is refuting those who deny divine providence and substitute chance as an important cause in the events of the cosmos. He considers them to be fools who are not fit to contemplate the depths of the wisdom of divine providence and who lower themselves to the level of animals (Zohar 3:157b). The author of the Zohar does not distinguish between general providence (of all creatures) and individual providence (of individual human beings). The latter is, of course, more important to him. Through the activity of divine providence, an abundance of blessing descends on the creatures, but this awakening of the power of providence is dependent on the deeds of created beings, on "awakening from below." A detailed consideration of the question of providence is set forth by Moses *Cordovero in *Shi'ur Komah* ("Measurement of the Body"). He, too, agrees with the philosophers that individual providence exists only in relation to man, while in relation to the rest of the created world, providence is only directed toward the generic essences. But he enlarges the category of individual providence and establishes that "divine providence applies to the lower creatures, even animals, for their well-being and their death, and this is not for the sake of the animals themselves, but for the sake of men," that is to say, to the extent to which the lives of animals are bound up with the lives of men, individual providence applies to them as well. "Individual providence does not apply to any ox or any lamb, but to the entire species together… but if divine providence applies to a man, it will encompass even his pitcher, should it break, and his dish, should it crack, and all his possessions – if he should be chastized or not" (p. 113). Cordovero distinguishes ten types of providence, from which it is possible to understand the various modes of action of individual providence among the gentiles and Israel. These modes of action are bound up with the various roles of the *Sefirot* and their channels which convey the abundance (of blessing) to all the worlds, in accordance with the special awakening of the lower creatures. He includes among them two types of providence which indicate the possibility of the limitation of divine providence in certain instances, or even its complete negation. Also, in his opinion, things may happen to a man without the guidance of providence, and it may even happen that a man's sins cause him to be left "to nature and to chance," which is the aspect of God's hiding his face from man. In fact, it is uncertain from moment to moment whether a particular event in an individual's life is of this latter type, or whether it is a result of divine providence: "And he cannot be sure – for who will tell him if he is among those of whom it is said: 'The righteous man is as sure as a lion' – perhaps God has hidden His face from him, because of some transgression, and he is left to chance" (p. 120).

Only in the Shabbatean Kabbalah is divine providence seen once again as a serious problem. Among *Shabbetai Ẓevi's disciples was handed down his oral teaching that the Cause of Causes, or the *Ein-Sof* ("the Infinite") "does not influence and does not oversee the lower world, and he caused the *Sefirah Keter* to come into being to be God and *Tiferet* to be King" (see Scholem, Shabbetai Ẓevi, p. 784). This denial of the providence of *Ein-Sof* was considered a deep secret among the believers, and the Shabbatean Abraham *Cardozo, who was opposed to this doctrine, wrote that the emphasis on the secret nature of this teaching arose from the Shabbateans' knowledge that this was the opinion of Epicurus the Greek. The "taking" (*netilah*) of providence from *Ein-Sof* (which is designated in these circles by other terms as well) is found in several Shabbatean schools of thought, such as the Kabbalah of Baruchiah of Salonika, in *Va-Avo ha-Yom el ha-Ayin*, which was severely attacked for the prominence it gave to this opinion, and in *Shem Olam* (Vienna, 1891) by Jonathan *Eybeschuetz. The latter work devoted several pages of casuistry to this question in order to prove that providence does not actually originate in the First Cause, but in the God of Israel, who is emanated from it, and who is called, by Eybeschuetz, the "image of the ten *Sefirot*." This "heretical" assumption, that the First Cause (or the highest element of the Godhead) does not guide the lower world at all, was among the principle innovations of Shabbatean doctrine which angered the sages of that period. The Orthodox kabbalists saw in this assumption proof that the Shabbateans had left the faith in the absolute unity of the Godhead, which does not permit, in matters pertaining to divine providence, differentiation between the emanating *Ein-Sof* and the emanated *Sefirot*. Even though the *Ein-Sof* carries out the activity of divine providence through the *Sefirot*, the *Ein-Sof* itself is the author of true providence. In the teachings of the Shabbateans, however, this quality of the First Cause or the *Ein-Sof* is blurred or put in doubt.

[Gershom Scholem]

BIBLIOGRAPHY: IN THE BIBLE: E. Koenig, *Theologie des Alten Testaments* (1923), 208ff.; K. Kohler, *Jewish Theology* (1928²), 167ff.; W. Eichrodt, *Theologie des Alten Testaments*, 2 (1935), 177ff.; M. Pohlenz, *Die Stoa* (1948), passim; O. Procksch, *Theologie des Alten Testaments* (1950), 503ff.; E.E. Urbach, in: *Sefer ha-Yovel le Y. Kaufmann* (1960), 122–48; idem, *Ḥazal-Pirkei Emunot ve-De'ot* (1969). IN KABBALAH: I. Tishby, *Mishnat ha-Zohar*, 1 (1957²), 265–8; M. Cordovero, *Shi'ur Komah* (1883), 113–20; Scholem, Shabbetai Ẓevi, 779, 784; M.A. Perlmutter, *R. Yehonatan Eybeschuetz ve-Yaḥaso el ha-Shabbeta'ut* (1947), 133–41, 190–1. IN MEDIEVAL JEWISH PHILOSOPHY: Strauss, in: MGWJ, 45 (1937), 93–105; Pines, in: PAAJR, 24 (1955), 123–31; Moses Maimonides, *The Guide of the Perplexed* (1963), introd. by Pines, lxv–lxxviii, lxxvi–lxxvii; idem, *Le guide des égarés*, ed. and trans. by S. Munk, 3 (1866), 111, 116ff.; J. Guttmann, *Dat u-Madda* (1955), 149–68; S. Heller-Wilensky, *R. Yiẓḥak Arama u-Mishnato* (1956), 132–6; G. Vajda, *Isaac Albalag, Averroïste juif, traducteur et annotateur d'Al-Ghazali* (1960), 15–17, 64–71, 144–7, 121–3; Guttmann, Philosophies, index; Husik, Philosophy, index.

PROVINS, town in the department of Seine-et-Marne, France. The earliest evidence of the presence of Jews in Provins dates from 1201. Concentrated in two streets, Rue de la Vieille-Juiverie and the Rue des Juifs, the Jews rapidly increased in number. They owned at least two synagogues and a cemetery. The importance of the market of the Provins Jewish community is described in the polemic work of Joseph "the Zealot" (*le Zélateur*). The extent of Jewish financial activity in Provins is apparent from the use of a special seal for ratifying documents in business transactions which involved Jews. The town itself, as well as the Jewish community – which disappeared entirely after the expulsion of 1306 – began to decline with the reign of *Philip the Fair and the transfer of the town (which had formerly belonged to *Champagne) to royal authority.

In the early 13th century, the yeshivah of Provins was under the direction of Jacob b. Meir author of a biblical commentary (not preserved) sometimes erroneously attributed to a certain Jacob of Provence. Some medieval remains have been found in a modern house on the Rue des Juifs; these include a hall with ogive vaults, which local tradition claims is the remains of a medieval synagogue.

BIBLIOGRAPHY: Gross, Gal Jud, 493ff.; F. Bourquelot, *Histoire de Provins* (1840); M. Veissière, *Une communauté à Provins* (1961), 116f.

[Bernhard Blumenkranz]

PRUEWER, JULIUS (1874–1943), conductor. Born in Vienna, Pruewer became a close friend of Brahms during his studies there. He worked as a conductor at Bielitz, in Cologne, and at the Breslau Municipal Theater (1896–1923), where he became director in 1920. At Breslau he gained a high reputation and produced many modern works. He later became professor at the Berlin Hochschule fuer Musik and conducted the popular concerts of the Berlin Philharmonic. In 1933 he left Germany and in 1939 settled in New York where he taught at the New York College of Music.

PRUSINER, STANLEY S. (1942–), U.S. medical investigator and Nobel laureate. Prusiner was born in Des Moines, Iowa, and graduated A.B. (1964) and M.D. (1968) from the University of Pennsylvania. He was trained in scientific methodology in Earl Stadtman's laboratory at the National Institutes of Health in Bethesda (MD) (1968–72) and in neurology at the

University of California, San Francisco (1972–74). From 1974 he was on the staff of UCSF, becoming professor of neurology and biochemistry and the founder and director of the Institute for Neurodegenerative Diseases. His lifelong interest in degenerative neurological diseases was initiated by clinical experience. He showed that certain neurodegenerative diseases of sheep and other species, formerly attributed to a "slow virus" infection, are caused by proteinacious infectious particles lacking nucleic acids, which he called "prions." Because of Prusiner's persistence the prion concept, once heretical, is now accepted. Prions cause disease by inducing structural changes in proteins of similar sequence to those found in normal brains. In man, prions cause disease in three ways: through genetic variation in the normal protein, sporadically from unproven causes (Creutzfeld-Jacob disease), and probably through ingesting prions of other species (new variant Creutzfeld-Jacob disease). The discovery of a human disease occurring on a genetic or an infectious basis was unprecedented. His discoveries have fundamental implications for other human neurodegenerative diseases, including Alzheimer's disease. He was awarded the Nobel Prize in medicine in 1997. His many honors include the Gairdner award (1993), the Lasker award (1994), the Wolf Prize from the State of Israel (1996), and membership in the U.S. National Academy of Sciences as well as foreign membership in the Royal Society of London.

[Michael Denman (2nd ed.)]

PRUSSIA (Ger. **Preussen**), former dukedom and kingdom, the nucleus and dominant part of modern united *Germany (1870). The name came to signify a conglomerate of territories whose core was the electorate of *Brandenburg, ruled by the Hohenzollern dynast from the capital, *Berlin.

1300–1740

The order of Teutonic Knights, who ruled East Prussia from the 13th century, in 1309 expressly prohibited Jews from entering their territory. From the 15th century East Prussia was dominated by Poland and became economically dependent on it. As Jews constituted an important section of the merchant class in Poland, East Prussia acquiesced to the presence of Jewish merchants (exporters of furs, leathers, wax, and honey) although prohibiting them from settling and repeatedly threatening them with expulsions, which were rarely enforced. It was only with the complete secularization of the Teutonic order under Duke Albert I of Prussia (1522–77) that two Jewish physicians were allowed to settle temporarily in *Koenigsberg (1538–41). From the 17th century Jews came in ever increasing numbers to the then staunchly Protestant region, where they were welcomed by the ruling circles. In 1664 Moses Jacobson de Jonge of Amsterdam received very favorable commercial privileges (subsequently renewed) in *Memel, where he became the most important merchant, paying more customs dues than any of his Christian counterparts. He became a *Court Jew in 1685 and his sons inherited the function. In Koenigsberg, capital of East Prussia, Jews were permitted to graduate in medicine from the university in 1658, and Jewish merchants were encouraged to settle soon after. A synagogue was built there in 1680 and a cemetery opened in 1703. The community grew during the 18th and 19th centuries, remaining the economic, social, and religious center of the region. In the latter half of the 18th century Jewish communities were founded in *Elblag, Marienwerder, *Lyck, and elsewhere.

Jews were expelled from Brandenburg in 1573 by Elector Joachim II. The great elector, Frederick William (1640–88), who became absolute master of East Prussia, inherited principalities in Western Germany where Jews had already settled (see *Cleves, Behrend *Levi); subsequently he acquired *Halberstadt and *Minden (1648), and at a later date *Magdeburg and *Halle (1680) where Jews were granted rights of residence soon after the annexation. Frederick William, anxious to repair the havoc wrought by the Thirty Years' War and influenced by mercantilistic and tolerant ideas, encouraged foreigners to settle on his lands. In 1650 he permitted Polish Jews to trade in Brandenburg for seven years but not to settle there; this privilege was renewed in 1660. Israel Aron, a military contractor and purveyor to the mint (see *Mintmasters) received permission to settle in Berlin in 1663 and became Frederick William's Court Jew.

The basis for a Jewish settlement, however, was created by the expulsion from Vienna (1670). Through his resident agent in Vienna, Andreas Neumann, the elector, declared that he was not opposed to receiving 40–50 "rich and wealthy persons, prepared to bring and invest their means here"; on May 21, 1671, he permitted 50 families to settle, buy houses and shops, and engage in trade almost unrestrictedly. They could not, however, open a synagogue. The leaders of the small and interrelated group, Benedict Veit and Abraham Ries, and the richer Jews were encouraged to remain in Berlin. Other families settled in the cities of *Brandenburg, *Frankfurt on the Oder, and Landsberg (*Gorzow Wielkopolski) where the first **Landrabbiner*, Solomon Kajjem Kaddish, and his successor had their seat. The elector disregarded his subjects' objections to Jewish settlement, being concerned with the economic benefits he derived from direct taxation of the **Schutzjuden* and indirect taxation through customs, tolls, and excise, which the Jews paid at a higher rate. During his reign the Berlin Jewish community grew to 40 families, that of Halberstadt to 86, that of Frankfurt to 43, while 15 families had settled in Pomerania.

His son Frederick I (1688–1713; crowned king of Prussia in 1701) confirmed existing Jewish privileges on his succession; new communities were founded and existing ones grew. A noted collector of gems, Frederick patronized jewel purveyors such as Jost and Esther *Liebmann and Marcus *Magnus. Under his son Frederick William I (1713–40), a generally harsh regime was introduced. On his accession he ordered a thorough inquiry into Jewish affairs, the outcome of which was the law of 1714 restricting to one the number of sons who could inherit their father's right of residence (*Schutzbrief*); to be granted this right the second son had to possess 1,000 ta-

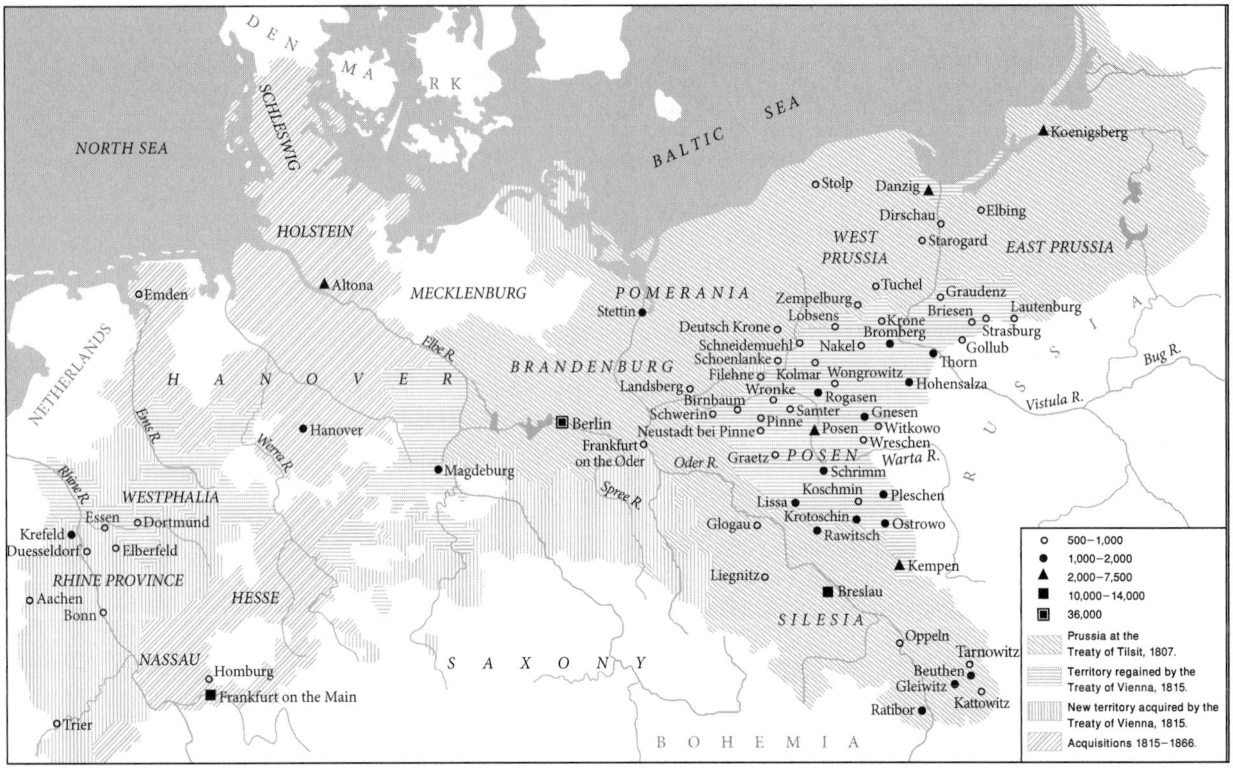

Major Jewish communities in Prussia in 1871, with historic place names. Based on S. Neumann, Zur Statistik der Juden in Preussen von 1816 bis 1880, *Berlin, 1884.*

ler and pay 50, and the third son twice these amounts. Thus a dominant theme in Prussian-Jewish relations, the attempt to restrict and even to reduce the number of Jews, was formally introduced. In 1717 the king appointed Moses Levin *Gomperz as *Oberaeltester* ("chief elder," *parnas*) of Berlin and Prussian Jewry, an appointment probably connected with the supervision of the just distribution of the tax load, conducted by representatives of communities and *Landjudenschaften. In 1728 the sum was fixed at 15,000 taler annually, to be reapportioned every five years. In 1730 a new Jewry law was promulgated: the eldest son was now obliged to own 1,000 and pay 50 taler and the second twice these amounts; all were subject to the condition that the number of protected Jews (*Schutzjuden*) in any given locality should not increase. Foreign Jews in possession of at least 10,000 taler were allowed to settle in Prussia. The law also prohibited Jews from engaging in all crafts (except seal engraving) competing with Christian guilds; it prohibited them from dealing in a large number of goods (mainly local produce). *Peddling, in particular, was suppressed. Commerce in luxury wares (expensive textiles, spices, etc.) was permitted, as was moneylending and dealing in old clothes. The law applied not only to Brandenburg but to all Prussian territories, creating uniform conditions for the Jews and defining (in article 24) their juridical relationship to the state. The regular tax load was raised, in addition to extraordinary exactions. Jewish merchants were encouraged to become entrepreneurs and invest in manufacture, particularly of textiles (silk, ribbons, satin, lace, etc.). These businessmen were granted highly favorable conditions. Thus the king passed on to his son a basically contradictory policy, at the same time mercantilist and anti-Jewish; needing and encouraging Jews for their economic contribution he attempted to restrict their rights and numbers.

From Frederick II to Emancipation

*Frederick II, the Great, enforced his father's policies even more rigorously. By his conquest of Silesia (1742) his rule extended over a sizable Jewish population; appreciating their economic importance he exempted them from his otherwise obnoxious Jewish legislation. In 1750 Frederick promulgated his *Revidiertes Generalprivilegium und Reglement*, prompted by the results of an inquiry which showed the number of privileged Jewish families in Prussia (excluding Silesia) in 1749 at 2,093, almost double the 1728 figure. The preamble stated that the law was intended to help both Christians and Jews, whose livelihood was being threatened by the increasing number of Jews. It created two types of *Schutzjuden*: an unrestricted number of "extraordinary" ones whose rights could not be inherited, and a restricted number of "ordinary" *Schutzjuden* who could pass on their rights to one son only. As in 1730, Jews were excluded from almost all professions and expressly prohibited from brewing, innkeeping, and farming. Trade in livestock, wool, leather, and most local produce was prohibited; the permitted occupations were moneylending and dealing in luxury wares and old clothes. The strictures against peddling were made more severe, as were those against beggars. During the Seven Years' War (1756–63) Frederick relied on monetary manipulations effected by Daniel *Itzig, V.H. *Ephraim, and other purveyors to the mint. His armies were provisioned by Jewish military *contractors (supplying horses, grain, fodder, wine, etc). After the war he encouraged a newly created, sparse layer of very wealthy Jews to invest their capital in industry and manufacture. Frederick levied onerous and distasteful taxes. In 1766 he introduced the *Silberlieferung*: 12,000 silver marks to be delivered annually at below face value to the royal mint; the 15,000 marks annual tax (from 1728) was increased to 25,000 in 1768. In 1769 he ordered every Jew to purchase and export a certain quantity of local porcelain (expensive, inferior wares produced by the royal factory) whenever he needed a royal concession or privilege (e.g., for marriage).

During Frederick's reign the Berlin community gradually became preponderant in Prussian Jewry. The *Landrabbinat* was occupied by such leading authorities as David Fraenkel (1742–62), Aaron Mosessohn (1762–71), and Hirschel *Levin. The dual office of *Oberlandes-Aeltester* was successively occupied by elders of the Berlin community, V.H. Ephraim (1750–75), Daniel Itzig (1775–99), and Jacob Moses (1775–92). In Berlin, Breslau, and Koenigsberg the upper strata of the Jews, who were rich and influential, took the first steps toward assimilation, acquiring the *General-Privilegium*, which granted them the rights of Christian merchants (such as freedom of movement and settlement). Through the First Partition of Poland (1772) Prussia's Jewish population had almost doubled, and Frederick feared above all an influx of Jews from the newly annexed province of West Prussia.

Frederick's nephew, Frederick William II (1786–97), inaugurated a period of liberalization and reform in Prussia. As crown prince he had borrowed large sums from Berlin's Jewish financiers. An admirer of *Mendelssohn and *Mirabeau, in the first years of his reign he abolished the porcelain law and repealed the **Leibzoll* for foreign Jews. On May 2, 1791, Daniel Itzig and his family received the first *Naturalisations-patent*, which granted them full citizenship. A year later the *solidarische Haftung* (collective responsibility and liability of the Jewish community for non-payment of taxes and crimes of theft) was abolished. The king nominated a commission to draft a new and liberal Jewry law but due to the procrastination of his counselors, his own hesitations, and his increasing preoccupation with foreign affairs this was never carried out. New problems were created by the Second (1793) and Third (1795) Partitions of Poland, which respectively added about 53,000 and 75,000 Jews to the Prussian realm. New legislation became urgent. Shortly before his death Frederick William II passed a Jewry law for the new territories, which was in some respects more progressive than previous laws. His early death and the conservative nature of his son, *Frederick William III, disrupted all reformatory activity until Napoleon's defeat of Prussia at Jena (1806), when far-reaching reforms were carried out under the leadership of Karl August von *Hardenberg and Wilhelm von *Humboldt. In 1808 municipal citizenship and offices were opened to all, irrespective of religion.

The decisive step was taken with the promulgation in March 11, 1812, of an edict concerning the civil status of the Jews. The first article declared all legally resident Jews to be full citizens. All occupations were declared open to Jews, as were academic positions. Article 9, however, postponed the question of Jewish eligibility to state offices; the *oath *more Judaico* also remained in force. Marriage to a Prussian Jewess did not bestow citizenship and foreign Jews were prohibited from becoming communal employees. The edict was received with thanksgiving by the elders of the main Jewish communities, Berlin, Breslau, and Koenigsberg. A year later, during the War of Liberation, Prussian Jews expressed their patriotism by volunteering in large numbers (see *Military service). The high expectations of Prussian Jewry were not put to the test until after the Congress of *Vienna, at which Prussia was given back the province of Posen (*Poznan) and received the Rhineland and part of *Westphalia (where Jews had been fully emancipated).

As King Frederick William III had no intention of carrying out the 1812 edict, he repudiated his express promise that volunteers, irrespective of their religion, would be eligible for state offices. On Sept. 18, 1818, Jews were excluded from all academic positions (causing Heinrich *Heine, Eduard *Gans, and others to apostatize); the following January Jewish officials in Westphalia and the Rhineland were dismissed (including Heinrich Marx, father of Karl *Marx). The benefits of the 1812 edict had not been applied to Posen (where the laws of 1750 and 1797 remained in force), while its restrictions were applied to the western territories. Thus the Napoleonic "infamous decree," which by then had lapsed in France, was renewed by Prussia in 1818 to cover the Rhineland for an indefinite period. Prussian Jewry's legal position was encumbered by the coexistence of 22 different legislative systems with the various provinces. The king actively encouraged conversion to Christianity and prohibited conversion to Judaism; between 1812 and 1846, 3,171 Jews in Prussia converted. In addition he closed down Israel *Jacobson's private Reform prayer room in Berlin; on Sept. 12, 1823, he made the minister of the interior responsible for ensuring that "no sects among the Jewries (*Judenschaften*) of my lands be tolerated." The king's policy toward the Jews of Posen province – the historical *Great Poland (where they were 6.4% of the population and 42% of all Prussian Jews in 1816) – was even more restrictive. Severe steps were taken to keep them within the boundaries of the province. In 1833 a new Jewry law was promulgated for Posen; its main feature was the division of the province's Jews into naturalized citizens, whose rights were conditional on their economic, moral, and educational achievements (command and use of German), and the remainder, who remained deprived of basic rights. By 1846, 80% of Posen Jews were still not citizens and one-third of Prussian Jews had not attained that status.

The accession of *Frederick William IV (1840) was accompanied by rising hopes, which were soon dashed when he took steps to implement his medieval conception of a corporationist "Christian state." In this crisis Prussian Jewry, led by Moritz *Veit and Ludwig *Philippson, was supported by the liberal majorities in the provincial estates. Nevertheless, with the aid of the upper house and Friedrich Julius *Stahl, the king succeeded in passing the 1847 Jewry constitution which recognized the corporate status of individual Jewish communities. It permitted Jews to occupy "offices not carrying executive, juridical, or law enforcement powers"; at universities all chairs in the humanities were closed to them, as were the senate and rectorate; Jews owning landed estates could not enjoy the rights accorded the gentry. The law, introduced for the benefit of the Jews the king declared, was not applicable to Posen. It had barely been introduced when the 1848 revolution proclaimed the principles of religious freedom and equality for all, reconfirmed in 1869 for the whole North-German Confederation. In practice, however, discrimination in the army, bureaucracy, and university remained the rule.

During the 19th century the geographic, demographic, social, and economic makeup of Prussian Jewry underwent great changes. Their number increased from 123,823 in 1816 to 194,558 in 1840. In 1840 about two-fifths of Prussian Jewry were concentrated in Posen province (where they formed about 6% of the population), and another two-fifths in Silesia, the Rhineland, and West Prussia (where they constituted about 1% of the population). Posen had the largest Jewish community (6,748), with Berlin (6,458) and Breslau (5,714) following. The majority of Prussian Jewry lived in rural and semi-rural conditions; peddling, shop- and innkeeping, commerce, and the livestock trade were the main occupations. In 1816 Prussia contained 48.2% of German Jewry; in 1871, 325,000 Jews were natives of Prussia (69.2% of German Jewry), including the Jews of the recently (1866) annexed territories of *Hanover, *Schleswig-Holstein, *Hesse-Nassau, and *Frankfurt on the Main. Due to internal migration the percentage of Posen Jews had declined proportionately, to 22.8% in 1871, and also absolutely, so that by 1910 only 26,512 remained (about 7.7% of Prussian Jewry). A similar process of depletion occurred in West Prussia. As a result of industrialization and urbanization, Brandenburg (Berlin) attracted a greater proportion of Prussian Jewry, increasing from 6.5% in 1816, to 17.5% in 1871, and 43.9% (151,356) in 1910. In the other provinces, Westphalia, Rhineland, and Silesia, the number of Jews remained proportionately stable while increasing at a regular rate. Demographically, Prussian Jewry reached its peak around 1870–80. The process of urbanization continued, causing small-town communities to remain stable or decline while village communities gradually vanished. By 1925, 60% of Prussian Jewry (342,765) was to be found in the four largest communities and another 15% in communities with more than 1,000 persons.

Prussia within the German Empire

In spite of the noteworthy cultural, economic, and social achievements of Prussian Jews within the new German Empire, Prussia retained a specific conservative, anti-Jewish, social and political attitude, which found expression in the influence of the Prussian mentality within the empire and in its political parties (see *Bismarck, E. *Lasker, I.D. *Bamberger, and *Central-Verein). Until World War I the majority of Prussian communities were organized within the *Deutsch-Israelitischer Gemeindebund (DIGB). The organization's main difficulties were caused by differences between the numerous small, rural, and needy communities and the large wealthy ones, primarily Berlin. Thus, when a common communal organization did not immediately emerge after the war the Berlin community entrusted Ismar *Freund with organizing the Preussischer Landesverband juedischer Gemeinden. Its opening session (1921) was attended by 110 communities, who soon numbered 656 (96% of Prussian Jewry), making it the largest regional communal organization in Germany. Its charter and activities were modeled on the defunct DIGB; although a Prussian official was present at its founding and it received state subsidies, it was not officially recognized by the government of Prussia.

Throughout the late 19th and 20th centuries the Prussian reactionary mentality found a persuasive anti-Jewish argument in the "*Masseneinwanderung*," the alleged mass immigration of unwanted East European Jews (*Ostjuden*) into Prussia, particularly into Berlin and the major cities. Their number was greatly magnified by antisemitic propaganda which eventually caused the expulsion of 30,000 Russian Jews, mainly refugees from the 1883 pogroms. In fact, the number of Prussian Jews was decreasing, due to a low birth rate and emigration. After World War I the problem of the unwanted East European Jews again became a political issue; in fact, the majority of these were Jews from Posen, then once more in Poland, who had preferred to be repatriated to Prussia (one-third of c. 45,000 Jews). When the Nazis seized power, H. *Goering was appointed prime minister of Prussia, where he enforced the Nazi anti-Jewish measures (see *Germany).

BIBLIOGRAPHY: Wiener Library, *German Jewry* (1958), 62–66 (bibl.); BJCE (bibl.); LBI, *Bibliothek und Archiv*, 1 (1970), index (bibl); *Gesamtregister zur MGWJ* (1966), index; I. Freund, *Die Emanzipation der Juden in Preussen*, 2 vols. (1912); S. Stern, *Der preussische Staat und die Juden*, 4 vols. (1925–1975); H.D. Schmidt, in: YLBI, 1 (1956), 28–47; H. Strauss, *ibid.*, 11 (1966), 107–36; H. Fischer, *Judentum, Staat und Heer im fruehen 19. Jahrhundert* (1968); H. Schnee, *Die Hoffinanz und der moderne Staat*, 1 (1953); 5 (1965), 15–53; M. Aschkewitz, *Zur Geschichte der Juden in Westpreussen* (1967); H. Neubach, *Die Ausweisungen von Polen und Juden aus Preussen 1885/86* (1967); S. Wenzel, *Juedische Buerger und kommunale Selbstverwaltung in preussischen Staedten 1808–1848* (1967); A. Sandler, in: YLBI, 2 (1957), index; H. Strauss, *ibid.*, 11 (1966), 107–38; M. Lamberti, in: LBIYB, 17 (1972), 5–17; M. Birnbaum, *Staat und Synagoge*, 1918–1939 (1981); A. Bruer, *Geschichte der Juden in Preussen (1750–1820)* (1991); S. Volkov, *Jahadut Prussia – Mythos u-Męziut* (Hebr.; 1994); Clark, in: *Past and Present*, 147 (1995), 159–79; C. Clark, in: *Protestants, Catholics and Jews in Germany* (2001), 67–93.

[Henry Wasserman]

PRUZHANY (Pol. **Pružana**), city in Brest district, Belarus. Situated on the road which leads from Brest-Litovsk to Moscow, it was under Polish rule until 1795; in the third partition of Poland it was incorporated into Russia, and in 1919 regained by Poland until 1939. Jews lived in Pruzhany during the middle of the 15th century and around 1450 there was a *ḥevra kaddisha* which noted its activities in a register. In 1463 the first synagogue (destroyed by fire in 1863) was erected near the center of the Jewish quarter. In 1495 the Jews of Pruzhany were included in the general expulsion of Jews from Lithuania, but they returned after a few years. In 1563 there were 11 Jewish families and 276 Christian families. Both Christians and Jews earned their livelihood primarily from agriculture and livestock, although there were some engaged in commerce and crafts. In 1588 the town was granted autonomous rights according to the *Magdeburg Law. The rights of the Jews were formally drawn up and ratified by Ladislaus IV in 1644 and subsequently, on several occasions, by his successors. According to these rights Jews were authorized to reside in Pruzhany, to practice their religion and freely engage in their occupations. At the close of the 17th century there were 571 Jews (42% of the population); in 1868, during the period of Russian rule, there were 2,575 Jews (61% of the total), and in 1897 there were 5,080 (of a total population of 7,633). By the close of the 19th century the Jewish community enjoyed a vigorous social and cultural life in which all trends and parties were active. During German occupation (1915–1917) Jews were taken for forced labor, and suffered from a typhoid epidemic. In 1921 the Jewish population was 4,152 (about 57% of the total). With the establishment of independent Poland, Jews also participated in the municipal government. In 1927, 16 of the 24 delegates elected to the administration were Jews. In the elections of the Jewish community in 1928, M. Goldfein, a delegate of the merchants, was elected president. There were in town a Jewish orphanage, an old-age home, a Hebrew and Yiddish schools, and a yeshivah; two weeklies were published.

Distinguished rabbis served in the town. At the close of the 16th century, R. Joel *Sirkes, the renowned author of the *Baḥ* (*Bayit Ḥadash*), officiated as rabbi and *rosh yeshivah* for some time. R. *David b. Samuel ha-Levi, author of the *Turei Zahav* (*Taz*) also held the rabbinical office for a brief period. Among the last rabbis of the town, one of the most prominent was R. Elijah Feinstein (1842–1929) who was appointed in 1884. Active in the affairs of Polish Jewry, he wrote *Sefer Halikhot Eliyahu* ("Book of the Demeanors of Elijah," 1932), and a novella on Maimonides which was published in 1929. He was succeeded by his son-in-law R. David Feigenbaum, who perished in the Holocaust.

[Shimshon Leib Kirshenboim]

Holocaust Period and After

Under Soviet rule (1934–41) the Jewish communal bodies were disbanded. Private enterprise was gradually liquidated as merchandise was sold and no new stock made available. Cooperatives were set up for the skilled craftsmen. Educational institutions were reorganized, and a Yiddish-language school set up. The Jewish orphanage was combined with its Christian-run counterpart and placed under the municipality.

On June 27, 1941, after war broke out between Germany and the U.S.S.R., the Germans entered Pruzhany. They immediately exacted a fine from the Jewish community of 500,000 rubles, 2 kg. of gold, and 10 kg. of silver, to be paid within 24 hours. A Judenrat was set up, first chaired by Welwel Schreibman and later by Yiẓḥak Janowicz, which tried to cope with the emergency. The Germans set up a ghetto on Sept. 22, 1941. Workshops were created in the hope that the economic utility of the Jews to the Germans would forestall deportations. The Judenrat combated the decrees against the Jewish inhabitants, gaining the confidence of members of the community. The ghetto swelled when 4,000 Jews were brought in, 2,000 from Bialystok and 2,000 from towns in the vicinity. In the latter half of 1942 an underground resistance organization was formed in the ghetto. Cells were established, arms acquired, and contacts sought with the partisans on the outside. On Jan. 27, 1943, two Jewish partisans approached the Judenrat to strengthen contact with the underground. Germans caught them there by surprise, but with the help of some of the Judenrat members the partisans escaped. The Judenrat was then charged with collaborating with the partisans. The following day the Germans began the deportation of the 10,000 inmates of the ghetto, 2,500 being dispatched daily to *Auschwitz. Within four days the community was destroyed. Some groups of Jews fled to the forests and joined the Jewish partisans who operated in the vicinity. In the late 1960s there was a Jewish population of about 60 (12 families). The former Great Synagogue was turned into an electric power plant. A mass grave of Jewish victims massacred by the Nazis was repeatedly desecrated and a road was built through its site.

[Aharon Weiss]

BIBLIOGRAPHY: *Pinkes fun Funf Fartilikte Kehiles: Pruzhana, Bereza…* (1958), 3–323, 599–690.

PRYLUCKI, NOAH (1882–1941), Yiddish philologist and journalist, and Polish political leader. Born in Berdichev, Ukraine, he grew up in Kremenets and in Warsaw, and practiced as a lawyer after 1909. Having published a collection of erotic lyrics, *Farn Mizbeakh* (1908), he gave up poetry and devoted himself to journalism and Yiddish philology. He was a pioneer of research into the Yiddish language and helped to classify the various dialects of Eastern, Central, and Western Yiddish. His closest collaborators were the linguist M. *Weinreich, the literary historian Z. *Rejzen, and the folklorist Shmuel Lehman. At the Czernowitz Language Conference of 1908, he fought unsuccessfully for an extreme resolution declaring Yiddish as the national Jewish language. In 1905, together with his father, Ẓevi *Prylucki, he founded the Warsaw Yiddish daily *Der *Moment*, which existed until the German occupation of Warsaw in 1939. Active in politics from 1916, he was the defender of the impoverished Jews and of the middle-class artisans. He founded the Folkspartei, which fought for Jewish autonomous rights in Poland. In 1918 he was elected as the party's representative in the Polish Sejm. Besides publishing philological studies, he influenced the modernization of Yiddish orthography, helped to found the *YIVO Institute for Jewish Research, edited YIVO's organ *Yidish far Ale* (1838–1939), and published articles and reviews in *YIVO Bleter.* When World War II began, he fled to Vilna, where he lectured on Yiddish philology until 1941. When the Germans marched into Vilna he was arrested, compelled to classify YIVO's treasures for the Gestapo, and tortured to death.

BIBLIOGRAPHY: Rejzen, Leksikon, 2 (1927), 954–66; M. Ravitch, *Mayn Leksikon* (1945), 174–6. **ADD. BIBLIOGRAPHY:** J. Gothelf, *Ittonut Yehudit she-Hayeta* (1973), index.

[Melech Ravitch]

PRYLUCKI, ẒEVI HIRSCH (1862–1942), Hebrew and Yiddish journalist, one of the first members of Ḥovevei Zion. Born in Kremenets, Ukraine, Prylucki began his journalistic career with a series of critical essays in Hebrew criticizing *Aḥad Ha-Am's "Truth from Ereẓ Israel." From then on he wrote for Hebrew, Yiddish, and Russian-Jewish journals. In 1905 he moved to Warsaw, establishing the first Yiddish daily there, as well as a Hebrew daily, *Ha-Yom*. Both newspapers were of a Zionist and literary character. After several failures, at the end of 1910 Prylucki began to publish the daily *Der Moment*, whose circulation amounted to more than 60,000 copies on the eve of World War I. Prylucki, the editor, wrote the weekly political review. The newspaper was Jewish nationalist in a general sense, giving expression to non-Zionist opinions as well (Folkism, Yiddishim). Prylucki died in the Warsaw ghetto during the German occupation.

BIBLIOGRAPHY: J. Heftman, in: A.S. Stein et al. (eds.), *Pinkas Kremenets* (1954), 189–90; S.L. Zitron, *Leksikon Ẓiyyoni* (1924), 544–8. **ADD. BIBLIOGRAPHY:** J. Gothelf, *Ittonut Yehudit she-Hayeta* (1973), index.

[Yehuda Slutsky]

°**PRYNNE, WILLIAM** (1600–1669), Puritan barrister and pamphleteer. Prynne first came to notice through his vehement opposition to the theater. A fierce tirade against the stage coincided, unfortunately for him, with Queen Henrietta Maria's appearance in a court play. After he had been imprisoned in the tower for one year, his ears were struck off.

While in the tower Prynne wrote an essay, published in 1654, entitled *A Briefe Polemical Dissertation*, concerning the "true time of the Inchoation and determination of the Lordsday – Sabbath… that the Lordsday begins and ends in evenings and ought to be solemnized from evening to evening: against the novel errors of such who groundlessly assert that it begins and ends at midnight or daybreaking…" At that time the question of the observance of Sunday was a highly controversial issue between Catholics and Protestants. The Church of England inclined toward the Catholic view, maintaining that Sunday, being essentially the commemoration of the resurrection of Jesus, had no connection with the Jewish Sabbath. This infuriated the Puritans, who insisted that Sunday had taken over the characteristics of the Jewish Sabbath. Prynne contended that all days in Scripture begin and end at evening, the Sabbath being no exception. Furthermore, the beginning and termination of days is perpetual and was not altered by the resurrection of Jesus in the morning. These points were proved by a wealth of citations from the Bible, the Church Fathers, and subsequent medieval writers, among whom was the Franciscan *Nicholas of Lyra, whom Prynne declared to be a convert from Judaism, possibly because of his knowledge of Hebrew and his use of Rashi. But, as Prynne amply demonstrates, Puritans could admire Judaism while still hating Jews. At the time the sabbatical pamphlet was published, the question of the official readmission of the Jews into England was being discussed, and during the following year Prynne produced yet another pamphlet entitled *A Short Demurrer to the Jewes Long Discontinued Remitter into England, Comprising an Exact Chronological Relation of Their First Admission into, Their Ill Deportment, Misdemeanours, Condition, Sufferings, Oppressions, Slaughters, Plunders… With a Brief Collection of Such English Laws, Scriptures, as seem strongly to plead and conclude against their Readmission into England, especially at this Season*. The *Demurrer* is an important source for the study of medieval Anglo-Jewish history.

BIBLIOGRAPHY: A. Saltman, in: *Jewish Academy*, 4 (1947), 35–39; Roth, Mag Bibl, index; D. Bush, *English Literature in the Earlier Seventeenth Century 1600–1660* (1962²), index. **ADD. BIBLIOGRAPHY:** ODNB online; W. Lamont, *Marginal Prynne* (1963).

°**PRYSTOR, JANINA**, deputy in the Polish Sejm; wife of Alexander Prystor (1874–1941), premier of Poland from 1931 to 1933. With the growing influence of the reactionary anti-Jewish elements in leading circles after the death of Marshal Piłsudski (1935), Janina Prystor proposed in 1936 that *sheḥitah* should be prohibited, claiming that it contradicted Christian moral and religious principles. The proposal had an obvious economic aim for it would have broken the Jewish monopoly on trade in cattle destined for slaughtering. After a struggle in which the Jews boycotted buying meat and strong objections were voiced by all Jewish circles, the proposal, which would have prevented Jews from eating *kasher* meat, was rejected. After prolonged discussions the government adopted a compromise, allowing limited *sheḥitah* in areas of dense Jewish population and prohibiting it in districts where the Jewish population was less than 3% of the total. Although intended to reduce political tension, the compromise succeeded in breaking the Jewish livestock monopoly.

BIBLIOGRAPHY: H.M. Rabinowicz, *The Legacy of Polish Jewry* (1965), 179–82; Y. Gruenbaum (ed.), EG, 1 (1953), 116. **ADD. BIBLIOGRAPHY:** J. Majchrowski et al., *Kto byl kim w drugiej Rzeczypospolitej* (1994), 404.

PRYWES, MOSHE (1914–1998), Israeli physician and medical educator, born in Warsaw, Poland, to a distinguished Jewish family. He studied medicine at the University of Tours, France, from 1931 to 1933 and at the University of Warsaw from 1933 to 1939. In 1939 he was mobilized into the Polish army as a medical officer and from 1940 to 1945 was a prisoner in the U.S.S.R. As a prisoner, he became the medical director of a 350-bed hospital. From 1945 to 1946, he was head of surgery in the Kherson hospital in Ukraine and later became a chief assistant in the department of surgery, University Hospital, Gdansk, Poland. In Paris, from 1947 to 1951, he headed the medical services of the Union OSE, international Jewish medical organization, and organized preventive and curative services for Jewish communities in Europe, Morocco, Tunisia, and Libya. He immigrated to Israel in 1951, joined the Hebrew University-Hadassah Medical School as assistant dean and later became associate dean (1955), and associate professor and head of the department of medical education in 1965. In 1968, he was appointed vice president, resigning in 1973 to take up his appointment as president of the University of the Negev (now the Ben-Gurion University of the Negev), to devote himself to acting as dean of the Faculty of Health Sciences of the university, as well as director of Health Services for the Negev region on behalf of both Kuppat Ḥolim and the Ministry of Health. Prywes was a delegate to the World Conference on Medical Education and a member of the World Health Organization's Advisory Board on Medical Research. He was chairman of the scientific subcommittee of the France-Israel Cultural Agreement, and was made a Chevalier of the Legion of Honor by the French government for his work in this capacity. He served as editor-in-chief of the *Israel Journal of Medical Sciences*, and edited a number of works, including *Medical and Biological Research in Israel* (1960), *Health Problems in Developing States* (1968; with A.M. Davies), and *Topics in Basic Immunology* (1969; with M. Sela). He was elected senior member of the Institute of Medicine, National Academy of Sciences, U.S., 1983, and in 1990, Prywes received the Israel Prize in life sciences for his pioneering work in medical education. In 1995 he was awarded the Ben-Gurion Foundation's Ben Gurion prize.

[Bracha Rager (2nd ed.)]

PRZEDBORZ (Pol. **Przedbórz**), town in Kielce province, S. central Poland. Jews lived in Przedborz from the time of the town's earliest development. At the beginning of the 15th century, urban population increased when King Ladislaw II Jagello granted the merchants of the town privileges according to the *Magdeburg Law. In the years 1550 and 1570 King Sigismund II Augustus further aided the town's Jews by exempting them from customs duties and certain other payments. In 1595 King Sigismund III restricted their rights to own houses. The restriction was lifted, however, in 1638 when a fire destroyed the town and it had to be rebuilt. A second fire destroyed Przedborz in 1834. The Jewish population increased during the 19th century when Jews established trade relations with markets of the Russian empire. In 1865 about 75% of the town's population were Jews; in 1921 Jews numbered 3,749 (63.6% of the total population).

[Shimshon Leib Kirshenboim]

Holocaust Period

Before the outbreak of World War II, there were about 4,500 Jews in Przedborz. The Jewish community was liquidated on Oct. 9–12, 1942, when all Jews were deported to *Treblinka death camp. After the war, the Jewish community of Przedborz was not reconstituted.

PRZEDBORZ, ḥasidic dynasty founded by ISAIAH OF PRZEDBORZ (d. 1830). He was one of the closest disciples of *Jacob Isaac, Ha-Ḥozeh ("the Seer") of Lublin, and a companion of Jacob Isaac, the *Yehudi ha-Kadosh* ("Holy Jew") of *Przysucha (Pshiska), with whom he studied at the renowned yeshivah of *David Tevele b. Nathan of Lissa (*Leszno). Rabbi in Przedborz from 1788, in 1815 Isaiah became a ḥasidic *ẓaddik*. His son, IMMANUEL WELTFREID (1802–1865), officiated as rabbi in Przedborz from 1850, and was famed as a miracle worker. He married the granddaughter of Jacob Isaac Ha-Ḥozeh of Lublin and was a disciple of Dov Baer of Radoshits. His son, ABRAHAM MOSES OF ROZPRZE (d. 1918), became leader of the ḥasidic community after his father's death. He had three sons, EMMANUEL OF LODZ, ISAIAH OF KALISH (Kalisz; both d. 1939), and SOLOMON OF TOMASZOW who perished in the Holocaust.

BIBLIOGRAPHY: M. Friedensohn, in: *Elleh Ezkerah*, ed. by I. Levin, 5 (1963), 229–33; Z.M. Rabinowitz, *Ya'akov Yiẓḥak mi-Pshiskhah* (1960), 10, 29, 57, 125–6; M. Buber, *Gog u-Magog* (1967^2), 28, 80–83; L.H. Grossmann, *Shem u-She'erit* (1943), 81.

[Esther (Zweig) Liebes]

PRZEMYSL (Pol. **Przemyśl**), city in Rzeszow province, S.E. Poland; after the partition of Poland, it passed to Austria (1772–1919), subsequently reverting to independent Poland. In 1939–40 the German-Soviet borderline ran through Przemysl. A Jewish community existed in the city by 1367. In 1542 some 18 Jewish families were living there. The community numbered 1,558 by 1775. A Jew of Przemysl, Moses (Moshko) Shmuhler, was sentenced to death in 1630 following a *Host desecration libel. In 1638 the communities in the vicinity were ordered to pay their taxes through the Przemysl community, and from 1670 Przemysl became a leading community for the region of "Red Russia" within the framework of the *Councils of the Lands. Przemysl Jewry was granted detailed charters of rights by King Sigismund II Augustus (March 29, 1559) and King Stephen Báthory (June 27, 1576) enabling the Jews to trade despite opposition from the municipality. The economic position of Przemysl Jewry declined in the 18th century and the community fell heavily into debt. When in 1772 the community passed to Austrian rule its autonomy was curtailed, and the Jews in Przemysl, like the rest of the Jews in the territories incorporated into Austria, came under the Austrian system of supervision limiting their numbers and marriages (see *Familiants Laws). On the other hand they also benefited from the more favorable Austrian attitudes toward the Jews and legislation concerning them. The Austrian authorities gave support to the *Haskalah movement, directed Jews to attend government schools, and were inimical to *Ḥasidism. Half of the members of the Przemysl city council were Jews. Among the heads of the Jewish community the most influential was Moshe Sheinbah, an active member of both the municipal and community councils before World War I. The Jewish population numbered c. 5,692 in 1870; 16,062 in 1910 (29.6% of the total population); 18,360 (38.3%) in 1921; and 17,300 (34.0%) in 1931. Wealthy Jews of Przemysl engaged in the wholesale commerce of wheat and timber; some were purveyors to the Austrian army garrison in the town. Jews also engaged in banking, small- and large-scale industry, and agriculture. A large section of the Jewish population was impoverished.

Among rabbis of Przemysl in the 19th century Samuel Heller and Isaac Judah *Schmelkes were prominent. In 1875 the Yishuv Ereẓ Israel organization was founded, and from 1897 many Jews in Przemysl joined Zionist organizations, prominent among them Aguddat Herzl. The *Bund, *Agudat Israel, and the *Folkspartei were also active in Przemysl. H. *Lieberman was active in organizing the Polish Socialist Party (PPS). In World War I Przemysl was occupied for a short time in 1915 by the Russians. Many Jews then left the city and some were expelled by the Russians.

After the war Przemysl was incorporated in independent Poland. In the municipal elections of 1928 the Jewish National bloc in coalition with the Polish Sanacja party won 18 seats out of 40; a Jew was elected deputy mayor. In the communal elections of 1928 Agudat Israel gained the majority. In the 1936 elections it was defeated by the Zionists whose representative, Jacob Rebhan, was elected president of the community organization.

[Shimshon Leib Kirshenboim]

Holocaust Period

There were approximately 20,000 Jews living in Przemysl in 1939. When war broke out that year, many Jews from areas further west took refuge in the city. On Sept. 14, 1939, Przemysl fell to the Germans and within a few days some 500 Jews, about half of them refugees, were murdered on a trumped-up charge that 12 Germans had been shot by Jews. On September 18 Przemysl was handed over to the Soviet Union; two days prior to this, the Jews of Zasanie, which remained under German occupation, were expelled to the eastern sector of the city. Under Soviet rule all Jewish communal activities ceased. Jewish artisans were organized in cooperatives; Jews in the professions (except physicians) faced difficulties in finding employment. In April and May 1940, 7,000 Jews were deported to Russia. Most of them were refugees from the western parts of Poland.

Following the German attack on the Soviet Union in June 1941, Przemysl fell to the Germans on June 28, 1941. Subsequently a Judenrat was set up, headed by Ignacy Duldig. In June 1942 the Germans shot 45 of the Jews from Zasanie. This was followed by the expulsion of 1,000 Jews to the camp of Janowska in *Lvov and the transfer, by Aug. 3, 1942, of 12,500 Jews to *Belzec extermination camp. On Nov. 18, 1942, a further 4,000 Jews were sent to the same camp. Some 10 months later, on Sept. 2–3, 1943, 3,500 Jews were sent to *Auschwitz. In subsequent months the remaining Jews in Przemysl – some 2,000 persons – about half of whom had been in hiding, were murdered by the Nazis.

The Jews made an attempt at armed resistance. In April 1943 a group of young Jews went to the nearby forests with the intention of joining the partisans. They were all captured and murdered.

The Soviet army reentered the city on July 27, 1944, and a few days later some 250 Jewish survivors gathered in Przemysl. A Jewish council was established under the leadership of Mordechai Schatner and later of Ẓevi Rubinfeld to assist the survivors; in 1947 its activities were limited to religious needs only. Przemysl Landsmannschaften had been established in Israel and in New York. A memorial book on the Jewish community of Przemysl has been published (*Sefer Przemysl*, Heb. and Yid., 1964).

[Aharon Weiss]

BIBLIOGRAPHY: M. Schorr, *Żydzi w Przemyślu do końca XVIII wieku: opracowanie ... materyału archiwalnego* (1903).

PRZEWORSK, town in Rzeszow province, S.E. Poland. The town was overrun by the Turks in 1498, it endured the invasion of the Swedes in 1656 during the reign of John Casimir, and recovered after 1677 when the Polish *Sejm decided to lend its assistance in its development. From then on it enjoyed economic prosperity. In 1865 its total population was 4,000 and in 1921 it was 3,371 of which 1,457 were Jews. Moses *Sofer (d. 1805), a rabbi of the community, achieved fame in his lifetime and was regarded as a saint after his death. After World War I its library played a prominent role in the cultural life of the Jewish population. After the great fire of 1930 many of the town's Jews were left homeless and dependent on support from charitable institutions. With the increase of antisemitism during the 1930s the community organized a protest campaign and a self-defense group. Elections to the community were held in 1934. No information is available on later years.

[Shimshon Leib Kirshenboim]

PRZYSUCHA, city in Kielce province, S.E. central Poland. The Jewish population of the city increased during the 19th century. In 1865 there were 2,907 inhabitants; this number grew and in 1921, 3,238 inhabitants, including 2,153 Jews (66%) lived in Przysucha. The ancient synagogue, which stood in the town until the Holocaust, testified to the antiquity of the Jewish community. The Jewish settlement became renowned through its *ẓaddikim*. One such prominent ḥasidic leader, R. Jacob Isaac b. Asher *Przysucha (*ha-Yehudi ha-Kadosh*; see next entry), acquired a world reputation among Jews. Another renowned ḥasidic leader of Przysucha was R. *Simḥah Bunem, the disciple of the *Yehudi ha-Kadosh*. After World War I there was a considerable amount of communal activity. Upon the eve of World War II the Jewish community was headed by Joseph Meisels. Its rabbi was R. Elhanan Fuks.

[Shimshon Leib Kirshenboim]

Holocaust Period

On the outbreak of World War II there were about 2,500 Jews in Przysucha. The Jewish community was liquidated on Oct. 27–31, 1942, when 4,000 Jews from Przysucha and its vicinity were deported to *Treblinka death camp. After the war the Jewish community of Przysucha was not reconstituted.

PRZYSUCHA (Pshishkha), JACOB ISAAC BEN ASHER (ha-Yehudi ha-Kadosh, "the holy Jew"; 1766(?)–1814), ḥasidic rebbe, the founder of Pshiskha Ḥasidism, in Poland. R. Jacob Isaac was born in *Przedborz, Poland, to a rabbinic family. In his youth he was a student of R. David Tevele b. Nathan of Lissa and R. Aryeh Leib Halperin, whom he followed to Apta. His first wife was his confidant until her early death. His second marriage, to her sister Sheindel, the mother of his children, was bitter. He started teaching in the local yeshivah, after which he wandered in poverty, teaching children. It was in Apta that he joined Ḥasidism after becoming acquainted with R. *Moses Leib of Sasov and R. David of *Lelov. The latter became a life-long friend and their children married. It was David of Lelov who influenced him to travel to see to R. *Jacob Isaac Horowitz – "Ha-Ḥozeh" (the Seer) of Lublin – in what would be a decisive event in both of their lives. The Ḥozeh recognized him as his great disciple, and Ha-Yehudi ha-Kadosh accepted the Ḥozeh as his rebbe. It was probably then that he began to be called Ha-Yehudi ha-Kadosh, so that he would not be called by his rebbe's name. The mutual admiration continued throughout their lives, nevertheless their relationship was tangled and complex.

Ha-Yehudi ha-Kadosh arrived in Lublin at a relatively young age but as a fully developed personality. The Ḥozeh asked him to become a mentor to the young elite students that arrived in Lublin. Soon brilliant youngsters along with older Ḥasidim were looking to him to guide them in their religious life. The very presence of a new charismatic teacher in the Ḥozeh's inner circle attracted hostility from some of the older disciples who were overshadowed by him, and from the Ḥozeh's family. A major cause of the opposition was his original religious teaching and leadership, which was in conflict with the Ḥozeh's.

Under the influence of his surroundings the Ḥozeh's dealings with him vacillated between intimacy and bitter hostility and even persecution. The schism was inevitable. Ha-Yehudi ha-Kadosh moved to Przysucha to become a rebbe and to found his own school. Some of the most distinguished Ḥasidim of Lublin joined him, among them R. *Simḥah Bunem of Przysucha and R. Menahem Mendel of *Kotsk. Ha-Yehudi ha-Kadosh died in Przysucha as he was in the midst of his ecstatic daily prayers. After his death, R. Simḥah Bunem of Przysucha was recognized by most of his disciples as his successor.

Teachings

The first expressions of Ha-Yehudi ha-Kadosh's religious orientation can be traced back to his childhood and youth, when he concealed his acts of charity and engaged in diligent Torah learning and fervent praying which led him to give up praying in a *minyan* as a child. Hiding his deeds should be understood as part of his emphasis on purifying one's motives and eliminating socially influenced behavior from one's actions so that they will express the inner-self. An individual should reexamine his intentions to cleanse them, so that they will be truthful. "God's seal is 'truth,' it can not be forged, since if it is forged it is true no more" (*Tiferet ha-Yehudi*, 50). This inner process is the route that leads to repair (*tikkun*). It was in this respect that the religious dispute with the Ḥozeh manifested itself strongly. The Ḥozeh recognized the Napoleonic wars as the "War of Gog and Magog" and understood his religious duty to use kabbalistic means to bring about the redemption. Although the Ḥozeh put all of his weight on Ha-Yehudi ha-Kadosh to join this spiritual endeavor, the latter refused, believing that the road to redemption passes, rather, through personal struggle for perfection.

Humility is the characteristic virtue of a person who truly knows himself, recognizing his own imperfection. At the same time one should not be influenced by social conventions and public opinion: "Each person should have two figs (Yid. *feigen*), after showing one to himself he will not be troubled by others and will be able to show the other to the rest of the world" (*Tiferet ha-Yehudi*, 76). The search for a true path to God's worship involves critical judgment of religious routine. In this spirit Ha-Yehudi ha-Kadosh understood that there are many routes in the search for God and taught that "all the rules that a person makes for himself to worship God are not rules, and this rule is not a rule either" (*Tiferet ha-Yehudi*, 93). Behaving in this unconventional way, he broke the halakhic rules, delaying the time of his ecstatic prayer, finding that he needed time to prepare for it. This conduct provoked great antagonism and fueled his opponents. His religiosity was both ecstatic and ascetic. He had outstanding physical strength but his intensive, ascetic life exhausted him. He removed himself from earthly desires, in particular eating, sex, and money, aiming at what he viewed as the end of all the *mitzvot – devekut*.

The Ḥozeh and other Polish rebbes of his time emphasized their duty to provide the masses with materialistic and spiritual comfort, by conventional means and through miracles. Though Ha-Yehudi ha-Kadosh did not oppose this altogether, he changed the emphasis dramatically, criticizing the ḥasidic leadership of his time. He understood their way as leading Ḥasidism to degeneration and mediocrity – subverting it under its very own principles. He taught that the main role of the rebbe was to guide his disciples in their struggle for spiritual depth, while responsibility lies primarily with the disciple. This teaching suited his followers, an elite group with outstanding mental and spiritual qualities who were willing to sacrifice their material well-being as well as their inner peace for a demanding religious quest.

R. Uri of Sterlisk described Ha-Yehudi ha-Kadosh's innovation as "worshiping God by unifying Torah learning and praying" (*Imrei Kadosh*, 68). Learning Talmud became central to the worship of God, as Ha-Yehudi ha-Kadosh taught that "learning Talmud and Tosafot purifies the mind and makes one ready for praying" (*Tiferet ha-Yehudi*, 29), stating that "through the learning of Torah one can attain all spiritual levels" (*Nifla'ot ha-Yehudi*, 1992, p. 60).

While his innocent mystical religiosity did not spawn successors in Pshishkha Ḥasidism, other aspects of his legacy marked the routes of the diverse branches of Pshishkha Ḥasidism, creating a new ethos in Polish Ḥasidism. This ethos is characterized by: (a) the critical search for truth; (b) a critical attitude to conventions; (c) understanding the rebbe's main role as challenging his elite followers rather than comforting the masses with miracles; (d) the centrality of studying Talmud for religious growth.

Some of his teachings were collected and published, the earliest almost a hundred years after his death, in *Nifla'ot ha-Yehudi* (1909), *Tiferet ha-Yehudi* (1912), *Kitvei Kodesh* (1906), and *Torat ha-Yehudi* (1911). His figure stands in the center of Martin Buber's novel *Gog u-Magog* (1941).

BIBLIOGRAPHY: A. Marcus, *Ha-Ḥasidut* (1980), index; W.Z. Rabinowitsch, *R. Ya'akov Yiẓḥak mi-Pshishkhah* (1932); A.Z. Eshcoly, *Ha-Ḥasidut be-Polin* (2000), 50–72; M. Buber, *Or ha-Ganuz* (1965), 52–53, 395–403.

[Yehuda Ben-Dor (2nd ed.)]

PRZYTYK, town near Radom, E. central Poland. In 1936, 90% of its 3,000 inhabitants were Jews. Przytyk became notorious because of the pogrom which occurred there in 1936 and aroused sharp reaction from Jewish public opinion throughout the world. After the death of Marshal *Pilsudski in May 1935, the strength of his followers in the government weakened, and they were unable to check the virulent antisemitism which erupted as a result of reactionary and nationalist pressure from the *Endecja party. A series of bloody riots broke out against Jewish students in metropolitan universities and against small Jewish shopkeepers, who were regarded as competitors by impoverished peasants who had been driven to seek a livelihood in the cities. Anti-Jewish *boycott propaganda was followed by several attacks on Jews, which the authorities took no measures to prevent.

Against this background of tension, a pogrom broke out in Przytyk. In March 9, 1936, when the peasants came to the seasonal fair, they were incited to attack Jewish stallkeepers and even break into Jewish homes; three Jews were killed and 60 wounded. The Jews organized a self-defense group, and in the ensuing clashes one Pole was shot and killed. In the subsequent trial no attempt was made to distinguish between attackers and defenders. The Jew accused of the shooting was found guilty and given a harsh sentence. As a mark of Jewish protest, the Bund announced a general strike starting on March 18, 1936; the majority of Jews in Poland, as well as many Polish workers, joined in the strike.

[Moshe Landau]

Holocaust Period

On the outbreak of World War II there were about 2,500 Jews living in Przytyk (about 70% of the total population). The German army entered the town on Sept. 4, 1939, and initiated persecution of the Jews. A decree of March 5, 1941, ordered the immediate evacuation of the Jewish population from Przytyk and about 160 surrounding villages. Their passive resistance prolonged the deportation action for over a month. The Jewish refugees settled in about 30 different places in the Kielce province, but within a short time were again ordered to concentrate in two towns only – Przysucha and Szydlowiec. All of them were afterward deported to Treblinka death camp and exterminated, in part together with the Jewish population of Przysucha (Oct. 31, 1942), and that of Szydlowiec (Jan. 13, 1943). The community was not reestablished after the war.

[Stefan Krakowski]

BIBLIOGRAPHY: H.M. Rabinowicz, *The Legacy of Polish Jewry* (1965), 57–58; Y. Gruenbaum (ed.), EG, 1 (1953), 116. **ADD. BIBLIOGRAPHY:** E. Melzer, *No Way Out: The Politics of Polish Jewry 1935–1939* (1997), index; J. Zyndul, *Zajscia antyzydowskie w Polsce w latach 1935–1937* (1994), 21–27.

PSALMS, APOCRYPHAL. Syrian manuscripts have preserved a group of five apocryphal Psalms, one of which is also contained in the Septuagint version of the canonical Book of Psalms. This Psalm, which occurs as a "supernumerary" in the Septuagint, found its way into the *Vetus Latina* and the *Syrohexapla* (see *Bible, Versions) as well. It was not known whether the five apocryphal Psalms were a translation from an original Hebrew version or whether they were originally composed in some other language in imitation of the Hebrew Psalms.

An answer to this problem came in 1962 with the publication of the Psalms Scroll found among the *Dead Sea Scrolls in Qumran Cave 11 (11QPsa), which included, among the canonical Psalms, three of the five apocryphal Syrian Psalms. This unexpectedly confirmed the supposition, of M. Noth, of the Hebrew origin of (at least some of) the Syrian Psalms. Moreover, the fact that the apocryphal Psalms were included in 11QPsa among the canonical Psalms raised the possibility that the members of the Qumran sect regarded them as part of the Canon. This assumption, if correct, would imply that shortly before the beginning of the Common Era – when 11QPsa was written – a great flexibility existed in the books of Psalms in circulation in Ereẓ Israel both as regards the Psalms they included and as regards the internal arrangement of the biblical Psalms themselves. This is a further indication that the final crystallization of the Book of Psalms, in its present form, is comparatively late. Thus the boundary line between canonical and apocryphal materials – at least as far as the Book of Psalms is concerned – becomes rather blurred. Some scholars however maintain that 11QPsa does not represent the Book of Psalms, as generally understood, but rather a liturgical compilation used in religious services. This "liturgical theory" removes two major difficulties for those scholars rejecting such a late date for the final canonization of the Biblical Psalter:

(1) a compilation of this nature would naturally contain various non-biblical excerpts without any intention of ascribing to them a canonical status;

(2) the biblical chapters quoted in such a liturgical compilation would not necessarily follow the order in which they occur in the Bible. Hence the Qumran Psalms Scroll cannot, at this stage, confirm the canonicity of the apocryphal Psalms even among certain Jewish circles at the turn of the Common Era. It can however prove the existence of an original Hebrew text from which (some of) the Syrian Psalms were translated.

Date and Place of Origin

The content of these Psalms do not provide a clear solution for the problem of their date and place of origin, since they too exhibit those nontemporal features characteristic of the canonical Psalms. The attemps to find in them traces of "an Orphic influence" or indications of "an Essene origin" cannot be conclusively proved. Linguistic criteria, although insufficient for fixing any definite dating, at least furnish grounds for stating that in their present form the apocryphal Psalms (including the Septuagint Psalm 151, apparently the earliest of them) were possibly composed in Hellenistic times and certainly not before the Persian period. This is borne out by the use not only of characteristically postclassical Hebrew idioms and phraseology but also of terms and epithets typical of rabbinic and post-biblical literature: "sons of the covenant"; "a faithful judge" (*dayyan emet*); "the Lord of all" (but this reading is disputed). The apocryphal Psalms also display significant parallels to the Wisdom of Ben Sira and to Qumran post-biblical writings, as do other "Psalms" contained in other scrolls.

If it should be proved that the apocryphal Psalms are Hellenistic, and if it is true that none of those in the canonical Psalter originated after the Persian period, it may well be contended that (one of) the reason(s) for the exclusion of the apocryphal Psalms from the canonical Psalter is due to the fact that the rabbis did recognize the late origin of these compositions. This is however a question that can be clearly and unequivocally decided only on the basis of new facts and the discovery of further apocryphal writings.

BIBLIOGRAPHY: J.A. Sanders, *Psalms Scroll of Qumrân Cave 11* (1965); idem, *Dead Sea Psalm Scroll* (1967), incl. detailed bibl. (pp. 151–3); Yalon, in: *Molad*, 22 (1964), 463–5; B. Uffenheimer, *ibid.*, 69–81, 328–42; Talmon, in: *Tarbiz*, 35 (1965/66), 214–34; idem, in: *Textus*, 5 (Eng., 1965), 11–21; Goschen-Gottstein, *ibid.*, 22–23; A. Hurvitz, in: *Eretz Israel*, 8 (1967), 82–87.

[Avi Hurvitz]

PSALMS, BOOK OF

This article is arranged according to the following outline:

TITLE

The English name Psalms is derived from the Latin Vulgate *Liber Psalmorum or Psalmi* for short. The Latin, in turn, was borrowed from the Greek ψαλμοι which is the title found in most Greek manuscripts and by which the book is cited in the New Testament (Luke 20:42; 24:44; Acts 1:20). It meant "a song sung to a stringed instrument" and seems to be a translation of the Hebrew term *mizmor* which occurs 57 times in the individual Hebrew captions of the book. A variant title, derived from the same Greek root, is ψαλτήριον, found in the fifth-century Codex Alexandrinus (GA), which is the source of the Latin *Psalterium* and the English Psalter. No Hebrew name which might have served as the origin of the Greek is known, but there is evidence of a Palestinian practice to refer to all psalms as *mizmorot*, even when the technical term *mizmor* is absent (cf. TJ, Ber. 4:3, 7d–8a; Shab. 16:1, 15c; Ta'an. 2:2, 65c). Closest to this is the Syriac title of the book, *Kēthaba de-mazmūrē*.

The Hebrew Bible does not preserve any original title for the compilation as a whole. The editorial note, Psalm 72:20, would indicate that at some period "The Prayers of David son of Jesse" designated a smaller collection of psalms, although the Hebrew term *tefillah* in its usual supplicatory meaning would be inappropriate to much of the contents of the present Books I and II. Perhaps it was used in a more generalized sense of the articulated communication of man with God (cf. I Sam. 2:1; Hab. 3:1).

The universally accepted Hebrew name for the book in rabbinic and subsequent literature is *Sefer Tehillim* (cf. BB 14b), often contracted to *Tillim* (Av. Zar. 19a; TJ, Suk. 3:12, 53d; Ket. 12:3, 35a) or *Tille* and reflected in the transliterations of the Palestinian Church Fathers as Σφαρ θελλέιμε (Origen, in Eusebius, *Historia Ecclesiastica*, 6:25) and *Sephar Tallim* (Jerome, *Psalterium juxta Hebraeos*).

This Hebrew title poses several difficulties. In the first place, there is the use of the normally masculine plural ending *-im* for a feminine noun as against the regular feminine plural *-ot* (i.e., *tehillot*), which the word *tehillah* takes in the Bible (cf. Ps. 22:4; 78:4; cf. Ex. 15:11; Isa. 60:6; 63:7). Then, only a single psalm (145) is actually entitled *tehillah* and this, curiously, is replaced by *tefillah* in the Qumran scroll (11QPs[a] 16:1, 7). Lastly, a title based on *tehillah*, a song of praise, would seem to be applicable only to a selection of the compositions that make up the collection.

The oft-repeated assumption that *Tehillim* was artificially coined to differentiate the title of the canonical book (i.e., Psalms) from the ordinary plurality of *tehillah* (i.e., psalms) must now be discarded in view of the presence of *tehillim* in the aforementioned Qumran scroll (11QPs[a] 27:1, 4) in the simple sense of liturgical compositions. It must be supposed that the masculine plural form represents an internal, post-biblical Hebrew development parallel to the development of *tefillim/n* as the plural of *tefillah* in the sense of "phylactery." In any case, medieval Hebrew writers such as Mishael b. Uzziel (*Kitāb al-Khilaf*) and Abraham Ibn Ezra (*Iggeret ha-Shabbat*, 3) refer to the book as *Sefer Tehillot*, though whether they do so by some tradition or out of a desire to preserve the biblical Hebrew form, it is difficult to tell.

The Hebrew title itself was selected or emerged doubtless because the root *hll* in biblical usage is overwhelmingly characteristic of the language of psalms and, in fact, seems to have acquired in the post-Exilic books the specialized connotation of "Temple worship" (cf. Ezra 3:10–11; Neh. 5:13; 12:24; I Chron. 16:4, 36; 23:5, et al.). The popular liturgical refrain *Hallelujah, which is exclusive to the Book of Psalms, was probably an additional influence, as was the fact that the hymn plays a leading role among the categories of psalms (see discussion of technical terms, below).

PLACE IN THE CANON

According to an anonymous tannaitic source, the proper place of Psalms in the corpus of *Ketuvim* is second, following Ruth and succeeded by Job and Proverbs (BB 14b; see *Bible). The source does not give any explanation for the sequence, but the precedence of Ruth is undoubtedly due to the closing genealogy of David (Ruth 4:18–22), the reputed author of Psalms. For an exploration of the other features of the arrangement, see *Job, beginning. The importance of the book in the canon may be gauged by the fact that despite the great variety in the order of the books of the *Ketuvim* exhibited by the manuscripts, Psalms invariably either heads the list or is preceded only by Ruth and/or Chronicles. In the early printed editions the book always comes first and this has become the universal practice in Hebrew printed Bibles (see *Bible, table 2, cols. 829–30).

It is quite likely that this represents the oldest order of the *Ketuvim* for II Maccabees 2:13 refers to "books about the kings and prophets and the writings of David…," and Philo similarly speaks of "Laws and oracles delivered by prophets and hymns and other writings" (Cont. 25). The New Testament likewise invokes "the law of Moses and the prophets and the psalms" (Luke 24:44). It is reasonable to infer from this early testimony that the Psalter was looked upon as being the most important among the books of the *Ketuvim*.

NUMBER OF PSALMS

Current editions of the Psalter universally contain 150 psalms. The ancient Greek version of the Jews of Alexandria has the same number even though it exhibits some different internal divisions, combining into single psalms the Hebrew 9–10 and 114–115, while dividing the Hebrew 116 and 147 each into two psalms. The Hebrew-Greek correspondences are as follows:

MT	LXX
1–8	1–8
9–10	9
11–113	10–112
114–115	113
116:1–9	114
116:10–19	115
117–146	116–145
147:1–11	146
147:12–20	147
148–150	148–150

The coincidence of 150 psalms in the two versions, despite the differences, would seem to be significant, particularly since the Greek contains an additional composition which it designates as "supernumerary," thereby exhibiting a conscious desire to limit the canonical psalms to 150.

At the same time, there is a wealth of evidence for the existence of widely varying traditions. A Psalter of 147 chapters is mentioned as early as amoraic times (TJ, Shab. 16:1, 15c; cf. Sof. 16:11; Mid. Ps. to 22:4) and is to be found in manuscripts (C.D. Ginsburg, in bibl., 18, 777) and in the first edition of the *Yalkut Shimoni* (Salonica, 1521–26; cf. also Jacob b. Asher, *Ba'al ha-Turim*, Gen. 47:28). The Leningrad Codex B and the Brescia (1494) and Naples (1491–94) Bibles all feature a division into 149 psalms, an arrangement also known to Mishael b. Uzziel (*Kitāb al-Khilaf*) and to Samuel ha-Nagid (J.H. Schirmann, in bibl.) and present in some Hebrew manuscripts (I. Joel, in bibl.). Others comprise divisions of 148 (*ibid.*), 151, 159, and even 170 psalms (C.D. Ginsburg, in bibl., 583, 536, 725).

These variations have nothing to do with the content of the Psalter which remains the same in all the editions. They merely register differences in the divisions and combinations of psalm units. That our Psalms 1 and 2 were very early conjoined is explicitly attested in rabbinic sources (Ber. 9b–10a; TJ, Ber. 4:3, 8a; Ta'an. 2:2, 65c) and in New Testament manuscripts (Acts 13:33) and may possibly also be reflected in a Qumran scroll (4Q 174 col. 1). The truncated alphabetic acrostic that spans Psalms 9–10 shows that the two originally constituted a single psalm in the Hebrew just as they do in the Greek. It is very likely that such a combination is behind a Palestinian *amora's* citation of Psalm 20:2 as belonging to the 18th psalm (TJ, Ber. 4:3, 8a; Ta'an. 2:2, 65c), thus showing that a pair of our short units apart from 1 and 2 must have counted as a single entity in his Psalter.

Other documented examples of the conjoining in earlier times of what appear in our texts as individual psalms are 42–43 (cf. 42:6, 12; 43:5; Yal., Ps. 745; C.D. Ginsburg, in bibl., 725); 53–54 (*ibid.*); 70–71 (*ibid.*, 18, 777); 93–94 (I. Joel, in bibl.); 94–95, 104–105, 114–115, 116–117, 117–118:4 (C.D. Ginsburg, in bibl., 18, 536, 777, 853, 873). In the case of 117, the idea of a two-versed psalm seemed preposterous (cf. Tos. to Pes. 117a) and led to its merging with either the preceding or following psalm. Yet, just as the Greek displays the breakdown of 116 and 147 each into two separate compositions, so there are manuscripts in which 118 and 119 are subdivided (C.D. Ginsburg, in bibl., 536–7, 583, 725–6).

All in all, it is quite clear that no fixed and uniform system of chapter divisions existed in ancient times. Except where a superscription intervenes, the manuscripts frequently do not in any way mark the transition from one psalm to another, thus easily permitting varieties of verse groupings. What is not clear is the significance to be attached to the variant numbers of the psalms. The most plausible explanation is that which relates them to the custom of reading the Torah each Sabbath in the Palestinian synagogues in a triennial cycle (cf. Meg. 29b). It is presumed that there also existed a similar cycle of weekly Psalter readings in association with the Torah and prophetical readings. Since the latter were not stable, but varied from community to community, this would account for the diversity in the numeration of the psalms.

VERSE DIVISION

In the Qumran scroll (11QPs[a]), all the psalms are written in prose form with nothing to indicate verse division, except for Psalm 119 where the alphabetic arrangement provides a natural indication. However, the verse division must be quite early. Other Qumran Psalms manuscripts, especially from cave 4, do reflect a practice of transmitting the text in a form in keeping with the verse structure.

According to a tannaitic report, the number of verses in the Psalter is 5,896 (Kid. 30a). This is over twice the sum of 2,527 specified in the western masorah's note at the end of the book. The eastern masorah details only three fewer due to the combination of each of the following two verses into one: 22:5–6; 52:1–2; 53:1–2; and 129:5–6, and the division of verse 1 in Psalm 90 into two (C.D. Ginsburg, in bibl., 101; Lewin, in bibl., 84). The great discrepancy between the masoretic and tannaitic traditions is to be explained by varying concepts of "verse." The former enumerates the larger poetic unit which may contain two or three stichs and which is marked off by a major stop or caesura; the latter is most likely based on a peculiar mode of writing biblical poetry in which the spacing of words and their alignment, column by column, was important (cf. Meg. 16b; TJ, Meg. 3:8, 74b; Sof. 12:9). The *tannaim* evidently counted as a "verse" each compact cluster of words and even a caption of one or two words (S.D. Luzzatto, in bibl., 281–2). In this connection, incidentally, it should be noted that our printed editions, following the pattern fixed in the Torah (cf. Gen. 26:6), may accept three words, but not less, as a separate verse, so that a superscription of three words or more receives a separate enumeration. This is never the case in the English versions and accounts for the frequent difference of one between the Hebrew and English verse numberings.

One other distinction between the talmudic and masoretic traditions lies in the location of the middle verse of the book which is stated by the note at the end of the Psalter to be Psalm 78:36, but two verses ahead in the rabbinic computation (Kid. 30a).

DIVISION INTO BOOKS

The Psalter is divided into five books, each of the first four being marked off by a doxology, or formulaic expression of praise to God, as follows:

Book I, Ps. 1–41
41:14 Blessed is the Lord, God of Israel,
From eternity to eternity.
Amen and Amen.

Book II, Ps. 42–72
72:18–20 Blessed is the Lord God, God of Israel,
Who alone does wondrous things;
Blessed be His glorious name for ever,
And let His glory fill the whole world.
Amen and Amen. End of the prayers of David son of Jesse

Book III, Ps. 73–89
89:53 Blessed be the Lord to eternity.
Amen and Amen.

Book IV, Ps. 90–106
106:48 Blessed is the Lord, God of Israel,
From eternity to eternity.
And let all the people say
Amen, Hallelujah.

Book V, Ps. 107–150

This last book bears no closing formula. It is likely that Psalm 150 was regarded as a doxology for the entire Psalter.

These liturgical formulas which distinguish the various books that now make up the Book of Psalms are present in the Greek and are therefore at least as old as the second half of the second century B.C.E., by which time that translation was certainly completed. They are also definitely post-Exilic in origin as can be determined by some stylistic and terminological peculiarities. Indeed, three of the four doxologies are not integrated with the psalms to which they are attached, but form an appendage to them. It is thus reasonable to assume that they signify the close of what were once independent collections. Further support for this inference may be derived from the colophon to Book II. It is hardly conceivable that an editor who was aware of the 18 psalms attributed to David in the subsequent books would have written that "the prayers of David son of Jesse" had come to an end (Ps. 72:20; cf. Jer.

51:64; Job 31:40). It is also unlikely that a single compiler would have duplicated individual psalms. If Psalm 14 appears again in Book II (Ps. 53) which also repeats Psalm 40:14–18 (Book I) in the form of Psalm 70, and if parts of two psalms of Book II (57:8–12; 60:7–14) become Psalm 108 in Book V then it should be conceded that the various books existed at some time or other as independent entities. In other words, the division of the Psalter into books may represent successive stages in the growth of the work as a whole.

There are good reasons for believing, however, that the doxology to Book IV (Ps. 106:48) constitutes the exception to the rule and that the division between Books IV and V is artificial. These books share certain characteristics which put them in contrast with the preceding ones. Eighteen of their 61 psalms bear no superscriptions as opposed to only six psalms without superscriptions in all the foregoing 89 psalms. On the one hand, not a single musical reference is to be found in the headings, while such otherwise characteristically technical terms as *La-Menaẓẓe'aḥ* and *Selah* are almost totally absent, the former occurring only three times and the latter four. On the other hand, Hallelujah appears exclusively in these two collections. In addition, the subject matter of the two is very much alike; they contain predominantly praise and thanksgiving psalms suitable for the public service in the Temple. Most telling is the fact that the doxology of Book IV seems really to be an integral part of the last psalm and need not originally have applied to the entire collection. The first and last two verses of Psalm 106 are cited in I Chronicles 16:34–36 together with the peculiar invocational rubric. Since the latter fits naturally into the situation there described it is likely that the presence of the rubric, slightly varied, at the end of Psalm 106 has been due to the influence of the Chronicles passage.

The cumulative effect of the evidence here presented is to cast grave doubt upon the originality of the book division after Psalm 106. In this connection it is of interest that the Qumran scroll (11QPs[a]) intersperses in Book V selections from Book IV, although in an order differing slightly from ours. While it is not at all certain that the scroll is not a sectarian liturgy or hymn book, rather than a canonical Psalter, the phenomenon may reflect a period of time before the division of Psalms 90–150 into two. At any rate, the extension of a fourfold into a pentateuchal arrangement was probably suggested by the analogy of the Torah, and may have been the result of the reading of the Psalms, week by week, in association with the triennial cycle of Torah readings. An echo of this is to be found in the rabbinic observation that "Moses gave the five books of the Torah to Israel, and David gave the five books of the Psalms to Israel" (Mid. Ps. to 1).

At all events, the liturgical character of the doxologies would seem to prove that the book divisions were originally fixed for purposes of public worship, and it can hardly be accidental that the Book of Psalms opens with a reference to the study of the Torah.

COMPOSITION OF THE PSALTER

From the foregoing data it becomes evident that the present pentateuchal division is only the crystallization of a long and complex history involving the emergence of several small collections and their combination into larger units. The process of development can only be partially discerned and any reconstruction must of necessity remain conjectural to a certain extent.

The earliest collection is undoubtedly Book I, or rather Psalms 3–41 within it. Except for Psalms 10 and 33 which are anonymous, every unit is "Davidic." As has been pointed out above (on the number of psalms) the alphabetic arrangement, supported by contextual and stylistic considerations, confirms the tradition of the rabbis, the Greek translation, and several Hebrew manuscripts, that Psalms 9 and 10 originally were one. Psalm 33 has a "Davidic" superscription in the Greek which may have gotten lost in the Hebrew, although it is more likely that the psalm was inserted into Book I at a later date. (Perhaps it was influenced by the similarities between 32:11 and 33:1; *kōnes* (33:7) is a vocable characteristic of post-Exilic Hebrew and a late composition for Psalm 33 is also suggested by the fact that the summons to sing a new song to the Lord is put off to verse 3 instead of coming at the beginning as in Psalms 96, 98, etc.) The "Davidic" psalms would thus constitute the very first stage in the compilation of the Psalter.

The second collection is the group comprising Psalms 42–83 which is distinguished by the rarity of the use of YHWH and the frequency of the appearance of *Elohim* (in its absolute or suffixed forms) in its place, in striking contrast to the situation in the rest of the Psalter. Within this group of 42 psalms, the Tetragrammaton occurs some 45 times and *Elohim* 210 times. However, in the remaining 118 psalms (1–41, 84–150) *Elohim* appears only 94 times altogether, while YHWH occurs 584 times. This overwhelming preference for *Elohim* is so consistent that it even influences two psalms of Book I as they reappear in a second recension in this group. YHWH in Psalm 14:2, 4, 7 becomes *Elohim* in Psalm 53:3, 5, 7 and the same switch occurs between Psalm 40:14a, 17 and Psalm 70:2a, 5 (cf. also Ps. 50:7 with Ex. 20:2; Ps. 68:2, 8–9 with Num. 10:35 and Judg. 5:4–5). Furthermore, such otherwise unknown combinations as *Elohim Elohai* (Ps. 43:4) and *Elohim Elohekha* (Ps. 45:8; 50:7) make their appearance.

Since this phenomenon is restricted to Books II and III (up to Ps. 83), it is evident that the "elohistic" Psalms 42–83 once constituted an independent collection. Their superscriptions show, however, that this development resulted, in turn, from the combination of smaller "elohistic" groupings. Psalms 51–65 and 68–70 make up a second "Davidic" collection which quite probably once followed the first and to which the subscription of Psalm 72:20 was attached. Insofar as no additional psalms are ascribed to David in the "elohistic" Psalter, the colophon is accurate. The other constituents are the "Korahite" Psalms 42–49 (42–43 were originally a unit) and the "Asaphic" Psalms 50, 73–83, both collections internally arranged according to the technical terms of the superscriptions. Four other psalms (66, 67, 71, 72) belong to the "elohistic" Psalter, three of which are anonymous in the received Hebrew text; Psalm 67 is ascribed to David in some Greek manuscripts; Psalm 71 is conjoined with Psalm 70 to form one psalm in many Hebrew manuscripts, but is "Davidic" in the Greek; Psalm 72 is "Solomonic." The presence of the colophon at the end of Psalm 72 naturally influenced the bisection of the "elohistic" Psalter so that it marked off Book II and received a doxology. To the rest of the "elohistic" group was added an appendix (Ps. 84–89) consisting of four more "Korahite" psalms, one "Davidic" psalm, and one attributed to "Ethan" to complete Book III.

The distinguishing characteristics of Psalms 90–150 and their artificial bisection into Books IV and V have been discussed earlier. Here it may be added that this group of psalms must postdate the "elohistic" Psalter because Psalm 108 is constituted from it (Ps. 57:8–12; 60:7–14) and still retains its "elohistic" character despite its presence in a collection otherwise differentiated by the preferred use of YHWH as the divine name. Within the group of Psalms 90–150 some originally smaller collections are still discernible. The most obvious example is that comprising 15 psalms (120–134) entitled *Shir ha(la)-Ma'alot*. There also seems to have existed still another "Davidic" collection from which were extracted Psalms 101, 103, 108–110, and 138–145. In contrast, Psalms 90–100 are practically all anonymous and although some of them have features in common, they can hardly be said to derive from a recognizable source. Whether the "Hallelujah" psalms (104–106, 111–117, 135, 146–150) were once a separate hymnbook is a question impossible to decide with any degree of confidence.

It is extremely improbable that Psalm 1 or Psalm 2 originally formed part of Book I, if only for the reason that they are anonymous. It is far more likely that when Psalm 2 came to be messianically interpreted and associated with David it was affixed to the "Davidic" collection, just as Ruth was placed immediately before Psalms in many orders of the *Ketuvim* because of its concluding Davidic genealogy (see discussion on place in Canon, above).

After the Psalter had been completed, Psalm 1 was added as a sort of introduction to the entire work, for a combination of various factors made it an ideal choice for the purpose. In the first place, the psalm affirms the governance of the world by a divinely ordained moral order so that the operation of providence is both inevitable and effective. It thus gives expression to the fundamental and indispensable presupposition for all meaningful communication with God, in the biblical view. At the same time it formulates the basic Pharisaic notion of the preoccupation with Torah as the response of Israel to the Divine demand, with the consequent interdependence of study and piety. In addition, the canonical form of the Hebrew Bible indicates the supremacy of Torah over the other divisions by beginning the first prophetic book, Joshua, with an injunction to Joshua to keep the Torah of Moses and read it day and night (Jos 1:7–8) and concludes the last prophetic book, Malachi, with the injunction to be mindful of the Torah of Moses with its laws and statutes (Mal. 3:22). As such Psalm 1 is the appropriate beginning for the third division of the Hebrew Bible.

The selection of what became Psalm 1 also proved to be felicitous from an external literary viewpoint, for it exhibits striking verbal associations with both Psalm 2 (Table 1) and Psalm 41 (Table 2). It could simultaneously be unified with the former, if need be (see discussion on the number of psalms above), and serve with Psalm 41 as a literary framework to Book II.

Table 1

Ps. 1	verse	1	אַשְׁרֵי
		2	תּוֹרָה
		2	יֶהְגֶּה
		6	דֶּרֶךְ... תֹּאבֵד
Ps. 2	verse	12	אַשְׁרֵי
		7	חֹק
		1	יֶהְגּוּ
		12	תֹאבְדוּ דֶרֶךְ

Table 2

Ps. 1	verse	1	אַשְׁרֵי
		2	חֶפְצוֹ
		5	לֹא־יָקֻמוּ
		6	תֹּאבֵד
Ps. 41	verse	2	אַשְׁרֵי
		12	חָפַצְתָּ
		9	לֹא־יוֹסִיף לָקוּם
		6	אָבַד

DATE OF THE PSALTER

Critical scholarship in the 19th century generally regarded the Psalms as the product of the Maccabean-Hasmonean era. This view was grounded in the conviction of the late development of pure monotheism in Israel with its concomitant that the Psalms postdated the prophets. The numerous traces of Psalms' language in the prophetic literature were explained by the influence of the latter on the former, while the extremely individualistic consciousness that is mirrored in the psalms was taken as sure evidence for a highly developed, and hence late, stage in the history of the religion of Israel. Granted these assertions, it was not difficult to interpret allusions to historic events in the Psalter as reflections of internal and external affairs in Judea in the course of the second century B.C.E.

The 20th century witnessed the weakening of this position on the part of biblical scholars for whom the convergence of several lines of independent evidence led to a far more conservative reevaluation of the problem of the age of the Psalter.

In the first place, renewed attention has been paid to the testimony provided by the Greek version. The unchallenged prestige and prominence of the Psalter among the books of the Hagiographa (cf. II Macc. 2:13; Philo, Cont., 25; Luke 24:44) would of itself have been a factor in its early translation into Greek. In addition, the known fact that this version was made in response to the needs of the synagogue worship makes it virtually certain that the Psalms were turned into the vernacular in Alexandria even before much of the Prophets. Ben Sira itself amply attests a knowledge of the Psalms and it may be taken for granted that his grandson, writing around 132 B.C.E., had in mind a Greek Psalter when he referred to the translation into that language of "the law, the prophecies, and the rest of the books." Since the Greek Book of Psalms is identical in order and number with the received Hebrew, the canonization of the corpus must have taken place well before the beginning of the second century B.C.E., by which date the Greek translation is now generally agreed to have existed. It is apparent, moreover, that the translators often encountered difficulty with the original language and were quite ignorant of the meaning of the Hebrew technical terminology which had become completely obsolete. This loss of the living tradition presupposes a considerable passage of time between the composition of the psalms and their rendition into Greek. It is significant that whereas Daniel 3:5ff. contains a list of characteristic musical instruments of the Hellenistic period, not one of these appears among the more than ten instruments referred to in the psalms.

All this, of course, precludes the possibility of any significant number of Maccabean psalms, influences, or historical references. Some Psalms use language that belongs to Late Biblical Hebrew (LBH). Among these are Ps. 119; 133; 144. Nonetheless, the Hebrew Psalter is completely free of Greek linguistic influences and its theology is wholly devoid of Hellenistic concepts.

This conclusion fits in precisely with the evidence to be derived from various types of literature recovered from the Judean Desert. A second-century B.C.E. Psalter (4QPs[a]), although fragmentary, clearly demonstrates that at least Books I and II of the Hebrew Psalms collection had been fixed by Hasmonean times. In fact, the Psalter had gained such wide currency that it had generated an imitative literature in the form of psalms (or hymns) of thanksgiving (4QH) which are replete with the phraseology of the canonical Psalter. Nevertheless, linguistic, stylistic, structural, thematic, and theological differences between the two bodies of literature are so large as to leave no doubt of the far greater antiquity of the biblical Psalms. Moreover, the recovery of parts of the original Hebrew version of the Ben Sira from Qumran and Masada has clearly shown that the style of the Psalms belongs to a much earlier stratum of the language than that of an educated Jew of approximately 200 B.C.E.

As to historic allusions, explicit references to national events are to be found in but a handful of psalms, e.g., Ps. 137 which refers to the Babylonian exile. Of the Judahite or Israelite kings, David alone is favored with a mention in the body of a psalm (Ps. 18:51; 89:4, 36, 50; 132:1, 11, 17). Otherwise, there are allusions to foreign invasions of Israel (cf. Ps. 2, 48, 74, 79, 83, 89), but no way of pinpointing the specific event. The references to "God-Fearers" as a group distinct from Israel and the (post-Exilic) "house of Aaron" (Ps. 115:11, 13; 118:4; 135:20) reflect the post-Exilic conditions of semi-conversion to Judaism. The emphasis on Torah (Ps. 19:8–12) and its study (Ps. 1, 119) is likewise post-Exilic. In contrast, the picture of internal corruption and social injustice reflected in many of the psalms could as well mirror the same conditions inveighed against by the literary prophets as the state of affairs in Second Temple times. It is probably fair to say that the Book of Psalms has an ancient foundation, with additions made in the period of the Second Temple.

Above all, it is in the realm of the religious ideas of the Psalter, or rather in the inexplicable omission of certain concepts, that a late date for the collection becomes highly dubious. There is no clear notion of eschatological judgment upon the wicked and no trace of the characteristic eschatological terminology such as "the end of days," "the day of the Lord," "in that day." The motif of national sinfulness is lacking, and the theme of the absolute supremacy of morality over the cult, which has no intrinsic worth without morality, does not find unambiguous expression. There are no prayers for the restoration of the Davidic line or for the ingathering of the exiles. Were the prophetic activities and teachings indeed the source of inspiration for the psalmist, and if he composed during the life of the Second Temple, then the absence of all these would be very strange, especially since they all appear as characteristically dominant features of the known literature of the period. There is an exception which proves the rule. The lateness of the Books IV and V of Psalms was stressed above; and near the very end of Book V it is found that Psalm 147, which, among other signs of lateness, borrows extensively from older psalms, is also replete with echoes of Deutero-*Isaiah, including, at the beginning, praise of the Lord for rebuilding Jerusalem (cf. Isa. 44:28) and for healing the brokenhearted (cf. Isa. 57:15, 18; 61:1). But even when the other echoes from Deutero-Isaiah are added they fall far short of the extent to which Deutero-Isaiah and other prophets make use of various psalms, which are thereby proved to antedate them (see, e.g., Ginsberg, in bibl.).

The argument concerning the supposedly late date of the highly individualistic and personal spirit that animates the religion of Psalms has increasingly lost its validity in the wake of the progressive discovery of a huge psalms' literature of the Ancient Near East. Most of it antedates by far the appearance of Israel on the scene of history, yet it exhibits exactly the same individualized and personal qualities as does the Hebrew Psalter.

Finally, there are several psalms and parts of psalms that combine genuinely archaic language with religious concepts that undermine the Jewish monotheism of the post-Exilic period. Psalm 29 has the *bene elim*, "the sons of the gods," blessing Yahweh in phraseology at home in the cult of the ancient Syrian storm god (Ginsberg, 1969), while Ps. 19:2–7 uses sun-god imagery (Sarna).

ASCRIPTION TO DAVID

The Book of Psalms contains neither superscription nor colophon and nowhere in the Hebrew Bible is there any indication of its Davidic authorship. Seventy-three of 150 psalms are designated *le-David*, but the precise connotation of this term is uncertain. It could well have reflected a tradition of authorship ("by David"); it might equally have related to some tradition connecting the content with an event in the life of David ("concerning David"; cf. *la-Nevi'im* in Jer. 23:9 and the headings of Jer. 46:2; 48:1; 49:1, 7, 23, 28). The existence of such exegesis is apparent in the superscriptions to Psalms 3, 7, 18, 34, 51, 52, 54, 56, 57, 59, 60, 63, and 142. That it was once more widespread is evident from the headings in the Greek version of Psalms 27, 71, 97, 143, and 144. However, such an interpretation of *le-David* might be of secondary origin and in any case does not of itself preclude an original understanding of the phrase as implying Davidic authorship of the individual psalms involved. Other possibilities include a dedication to David, a tune or style supposedly Davidic in origin, or a composition taken from the repertoire of a Davidic guild of singers.

If *le-David* indeed originally indicated authorship, then it is of interest that the form is unique to the psalms' literature (cf. Hab. 3:1) for the ascription of no other biblical book to a historic personality ever involves the use of the *lamed* formula (cf. Song, Proverbs). Yet the Psalter is internally consistent in its employment of the same construction with other names such as the Korahites (Ps. 42, et al.), Asaph (Ps. 50, et al.), Solomon (Ps. 72), Heman (Ps. 88), Ethan (Ps. 89), and Moses (Ps. 90).

Whatever its original meaning, there cannot be any doubt that *le-David* was very early interpreted in the sense of authorship. This can be demonstrated by the heading of Psalm 18 which explicitly declares that David "addressed the words of this song to the Lord" (cf. the parallel in II Sam. 22:1 which lacks *le-David*). Another proof is provided by the editorial colophon to the second book of Psalms (72:20): "End of the prayers of David son of Jesse." Since 56 of the 73 occurrences of the formula appear in the first two books, it must be assumed that this remark is a sure indication of how that term was understood very early in the history of the development of the canon of Psalms.

In the course of time, the claim for Davidic composition was extended to the entire Psalter. II Maccabees 2:13 mentions "the writings of David," apparently in reference to the Book of Psalms. The Greek version extends the Davidic heading to psalms not so marked in the received Hebrew text (viz., 33, 43, 71, 91, 93–99, 104, 137). How the idea of Davidic authorship could be applied to the entire collection can now be illustrated by the epilogue of the large Qumran scroll (11QPs[a], 27:4–5, 9–10) which ascribes to David a library of 3,600 "psalms" (*tehillim*) and 450 "songs" (*shirim*), although its use of the Davidic superscription does not differ greatly from that of the standard Hebrew text. The first explicit claim to the Davidic origin of the entire Psalter is to be found in rabbinic literature which draws a comparison between the five books of Davidic psalms and the Pentateuch of Moses and was not perturbed by the incidence of other names in the headings (Mid. Ps. to 1:2; BB 14b, 15a; cf. Pes. 117a).

There can be no doubt that the association of David with psalmody rests upon very ancient traditions. The king had a reputation as a skillful player on the lyre in his early youth (I Sam. 16:16–23), an inventor of musical instruments (Amos 6:5; Neh. 12:36; I Chron. 23:5; II Chron. 29:26–27), as a composer of dirges (II Sam. 1:17; 3:33), and as a "sweet singer of Israel" (II Sam. 23:1; cf. 6:5). His role in the establishment of Jerusalem as the supreme, national, religious center (6:2–17; I Chron. 13:3–14; 15:1–16:2) is beyond dispute, and although the sources making David responsible for the organization of the guilds of Temple singers and musicians and for the institution of the liturgy are post-Exilic (Neh. 12:24; I Chron. 6:16ff.; 16:4–7, 41–42; 25:1, 5; II Chron. 7:6; 8:14; 23:18; 29:26–27, 30), there is every reason to believe that they rest upon a solid kernel of historical fact. Indeed, other ancient Near Eastern kings were credited with the composition of hymns including Ammiditana (1683–1647) of Babylon and Assurbanipal of Assyria (669–627; COS I, 445).

TYPES OF PSALMS

The Psalter presents a picture of unusual variety and complexity in its literary typology. Any attempt, however, to effect a systematic generic classification based upon considerations of a commonality of theme, mood, occasion, and style is bound to be more an exercise in convenience than precision. The choice of categories will be influenced by subjective or exegetical factors; sometimes the lines between one class and another cannot be clearly drawn; sometimes a single psalm can be simultaneously subsumed under more than one heading; many psalms are a fusion of two or more types; many are susceptible of diverse interpretations; the tense system, for example, is still imperfectly understood and it is difficult at times to decide whether one is dealing with a prayerful description of present troubles or grateful enumeration of afflictions now happily over; lastly, external criteria might favor one arrangement, whereas a determination of the original life-setting (*Sitz im Leben*) of a psalm might disclose an unsuspected generic affinity with other compositions.

The leading genre is the hymn. Broadest in scope, it invades other groups as well and its preeminence helped provide the most popular title of the book (see discussion on title, above). In essence, it is a poem of praise celebrating the majesty, greatness and providence of God. Examples of such include Psalms 8, 19a, 29, 33, 65, 66, 92, 100, 104, 113, 114, 117, 135, and 145–150. Several psalms specifically extol God's royal role in the universe and so may be regarded as forming a special category within the hymn (Ps. 47, 93, 96–99). They are often referred to as "enthronement psalms." Another group (Ps. 46, 48, 76, 84, 87, 122) glorifies God's city, His holy mount in which He has placed His abode, and is thus designated "Zion Songs." Two psalms (19b, 119; cf. 1) acclaim God's Torah and laud its attributes and its beneficial effects on those who study and observe it.

About one third of the Psalter is given over to laments in which the speaker may be either the individual or the community. The latter type bewails situations of national oppression or misfortune (e.g., Ps. 44, 60, 74, 79, 80, 83, 89c, 94); the former comprises about 40 psalms in all and is distinguished by personal complaints of bodily or mental suffering which may frequently be accompanied by protestations of innocence and integrity and are usually coupled with a strong plea for divine help (Ps. 3, 5, 6, 7, 9–10, 13, 17, 22, 25–28, 31, 35, 36, 38, 39, 41, 42–43, 51, 52, 54–57, 59, 61, 63, 64, 69, 71, 77, 86, 88, 102, 120, 123, 130, 140–143). A distinctive feature of many of the laments is the expression by the worshiper of the absolute certainty that His prayers will be heard. These "psalms of confidence" may be both collective (e.g., Ps. 46, 125, 129) or individual in nature, the latter being more frequent (e.g., Ps. 4, 11, 16, 23, 27, 62, 91, 121).

Closely related to the hymn and the lament is the genre of thanksgiving psalms. Here, again, community songs are relatively rare (e.g., Ps. 66, 67, 118, 136). This may be due to the fact that many of the hymns may have had their origin in a national song of thanksgiving. Psalms in which the speaker is an individual are 9–10, 18, 30, 34, 40, 111, and 138. In Psalm 107 it is difficult to know whether the speaker is a single worshiper or the congregation as a whole. Similarly, in Psalm 144 the speaker employs both the singular and plural forms of address. Many psalms of thanksgiving also contain descriptions of the original misfortune which has now given way to new circumstances. They thus combine two or more types of psalmody into a cohesive union (e.g., 6, 13, 22, 28, 30, 31, 36, 41, 54, 55, 56, 61, 63, 64, 69, 71, 86, 94, 102, 130).

A class in itself is the "royal psalms" in which the center of attention is the anointed one of God, the earthly king of Israel. His relationship to God, his ideal qualities, the misfortunes that befall him, and the woes that afflict him may all be the themes of the song (Ps. 2, 18, 20, 21, 45, 72, 89, 110, 132, 144; cf. 28, 61, 63, 84). Psalms 44 and 101, which, in contrast to royal psalms in the greater ancient Near East contain no direct reference to the reigning monarch (see Starbuck) but which appear to have been liturgies recited by him, probably belong within this same category. The numerous royal hymns in the Psalter are in marked contrast to the scarce references to the king in the Torah (Deut. 28:14–20; 28:36).

One other major category is provided by those compositions which betray the influence of wisdom literature or which have a distinctly pedagogic function or character. They may be reflective or sententious (Ps. 1, 34, 36, 37, 49, 73, 78, 112, 127, 128, 133) or descriptive of the kind of conduct pleasing to God (Ps. 15, 24, 32, 40, 50). They may also be historical retrospectives which either directly or inferentially project the lessons to be derived from the past and which are deemed to be relevant to the occasion of the psalm (Ps. 78, 81, 105, 106, 114).

PSALMS AND THE CULT

The detailed and elaborate prescriptions of the Pentateuch's Priestly Code contain almost no reference to any recitations by the priest or the worshiper in the course of the performance of the daily and festival rituals. Conversely, none of the psalms provides any explicit information on the type of cultic priestly ceremony to which it might have been attached. It is not clear whether this reflects differences in the cult as conceived respectively by the writers of the Torah and the psalmists, or whether the explanation for the difference is literary.

It is of interest that the Chronicler carefully and consistently differentiates the origin of the sacrificial system which he ascribes to Moses, from the institution of its musical-recitative accompaniment which is attributed to Davidic innovation (II Chron. 23:18; see section on ascription to David, above). The Psalter, significantly, never associates any psalm with the Aaronide priests. Given the post-Exilic origin of the priesthood of *Aaron, this is a further argument for the early date of much of the book of Psalms.

There is ample evidence to show that the verbal element did constitute an aspect of the worship of both the pre-Exilic period and the post-Exilic periods. The pre-Exilic priestly benediction (Num. 6:22–26) is one example, the cultic liturgy of the first fruits offering (Deut. 26:1–11) is another. Hannah's personal prayer in the Sanctuary at Shiloh (I Sam. 1:10–13) could not have been exceptional. Solomon's post-Exilic Temple dedication address repeatedly refers to "prayer and supplication" (I Kings 8:28ff.), and both early and late evidence from Isaiah shows the Temple to have been, indeed, a place of a multitude of prayers (Isa. 1:15; cf. 56:7). Amos (5:23) makes it quite clear that song set to musical accompaniment was part of the cult at the temple at Beth-El. It is not regarded as illegitimate as such, and there is no reason to believe that it was unique to this place. Jeremiah describes the chanting of a well-known refrain during the bringing of the *todah* offering to the Jerusalem Temple (Jer. 33:11; cf. Ps. 100:1, 4–5; 107:1; 118:1, 29; 136:1ff.). The prophet of the late Babylonian Exile describes the Temple as "a house of prayer" (Isa. 56:7).

All this suggests a close and ancient connection between cult and liturgy. In fact, without some association between the two it would be extremely difficult to account for the preservation and transmission of the individual compositions over long periods of time until they became gathered into collections and ultimately canonized as a corpus.

Two basic forces operated simultaneously in anchoring the psalms to the cult. First, most of them clearly answer to specific situations in the life of the individual or the community. The ability to categorize them according to a relatively few major and minor types (see above) and to recognize a recurrent use of a limited number of fixed patterns and conventional modes of expression strongly suggest standardized liturgies available for recitation, when the need arose, either at the central Temple or at the provincial shrines that existed throughout most of the period of the Monarchy. The great national festivals which were fundamental to the religious life of Israel would have been the natural occasions for the public recitation of many of the psalms.

Once a liturgical tradition is assumed within the Israelite cult, and it must be so assumed, then the analogy of Near Eastern temples can be drawn upon. In Egypt, Mesopotamia, Ugarit, and Canaan, guilds of singers and musicians connected with the temples enjoyed official status and were highly organized. There is good reason to believe that similar guilds existed in Israel, and there is ever-increasing evidence to support the view that the Davidic date for their establishment as claimed by the Chronicler may not be very wide of the mark (I Chron. 6, 15, 16, 25, 29; II Chron. 35:15), if anachronistic in detail.

Proof for the well-rooted and extensive tradition of music and psalmody in Israel in the period of the First Temple comes from several sources. King Hezekiah of Judah included male and female musicians among the tribute he paid to Sennacherib of Assyria (c. 701 B.C.E.; Annals of Sennacherib, 3:46–48; Pritchard, Texts, 288; COS II, 303) and no fewer than 200 lay singers of both sexes were among those who returned from the Babylonian Exile with Zerubbabel (Ezra 2:65, 70), apart from the 148 Asaphites (Ezra 2:41; Neh. 7:44). The latter are connected with several psalms (Ps. 50, 73–83) and are said to have been appointed by David to be in charge of the service of the song in the Temple at Jerusalem (I Chron. 6:16, 24). At any rate, their presence in the list of returnees can prove that they had functioned as professional singers in the First Temple. Another guild of Temple servitors from the same period is called "the Korahites" (I Chron. 6:7, et al.) and their name, too, appears in the superscriptions of several psalms (Ps. 42, 44–49, 84–85, 87–88). Their existence as Temple functionaries, in the times of the late Monarchy at least, is now attested by the appearance of their name among the inscribed Hebrew ostraca discovered in the temple of Arad.

There can be no doubt of the involvement of musical guilds in the public worship of Israel in the days of the kings. Inevitably, each guild would develop its own liturgical repertoire and thus constitute another important factor in the presentation and transmission of Hebrew psalmody, rooted in the cult as it naturally was anyway.

THE TEXT

It is unlikely that the standard Hebrew text is free of the corruptions that inevitably beset all ancient literature in the course of scribal transmission. Hundreds of years elapsed between the editio princeps of a given psalm and its earliest witnesses, and while the special circumstances of its connection with the cult must certainly have reduced its susceptibility to gross error, it cannot be gainsaid that many of the textual cruxes owe their origin to the carelessness of intermediaries. At the same time, so long as no autograph is available there can be no way of knowing the extent, if any, of editorial activity behind the smoothest text. That such occurred is the inescapable conclusion from a comparison of Psalms doublets (Ps. 14 = Ps. 53; Ps. 18 = II Sam. 22; Ps. 31:2–4 = Ps. 71:1–3; Ps. 40:14–18 = Ps. 70; Ps. 57:8–12 = Ps. 108:2–6; Ps. 60:7–14 = Ps. 108:7–14).

At the same time, there can also be no doubt that the consonantal text of Psalms has proved to be far more reliable than an earlier age of textual criticism had judged. Northwest Semitic inscriptions and comparative Near Eastern literature have opened up new vistas in the understanding of the biblical poetic idiom and in ancient Hebrew orthography, lexicography, grammar, and syntax. The result has been a considerable diminution in the number of instances previously deemed to be corruptions of the text.

This conclusion intermeshes with the observation that, unlike the case with some other biblical books, a comparison of the received Hebrew of Psalms with the Greek, Latin, Aramaic, and Syriac versions shows that all known witnesses to the text basically constitute a single recension. This conclusion is, in turn, in perfect agreement with the evidence from the scrolls of the Judean Desert. About 30 exemplars in various stages of preservation have been uncovered in the library of Qumran, more copies than of any other part of the Scriptures. While numerous variations from the standard Hebrew text may be registered, the overwhelming number are merely orthographic in character and very rarely present significant differences in meaning or interpretation. In no instance can a recension different from that of the earliest Ben Asher manuscripts be detected. The text of the Massadah Scrolls is, in fact, virtually identical in content and orthography with the received Hebrew text.

It is clear that this latter enjoys a traceable history of over 2,000 years. Its great prestige and constancy must derive from its use in the liturgy of the Second Temple times, a powerfully conservative factor in the preservation of a text.

SUPERSCRIPTION AND TECHNICAL TERMINOLOGY

Only 24 psalms have no headings of any sort. Psalms 1, 2, 10, 33, 43, 71, 93–97, 99, 104, 105, 107, 114–119, 136, and 137 may thus be termed "orphan psalms" (Av. Zar. 24b). In each instance, the LXX repairs the Hebrew deficiency, though in Psalms 105, 107, 114–119, and 135 the addition consists solely of an initial "Hallelujah." In all but Psalms 115 and 118 this term belongs in the Hebrew to the preceding composition.

The titles of the psalms are for the most part obscure. For the sake of convenience they may be classified as follows:

Those Containing Personal Names (with Affixed *Lamed*)

Usually the preposition *le* must indicate either authorship or a collection identified with a guild. However, in Psalm 72 it must mean "about" or "dedicated to," and Psalm 102 *le-ʿani* can only mean, "for [recitation by] the afflicted man."

DAVID. Seventy-three psalms are connected with the name David, distributed as follows:

Book I, 37 (3–9, 11–32, 34–41).
Book II, 18 (51–65, 68–70).
Book III, one (86).
Book IV, two (101, 103).
Book V, 15 (108–110, 122, 124, 131, 133, 138–145).

The LXX omits the Davidic reference in Psalms 122, 124, 131, and 133, but adds it to Psalms 33, 42 (GA), 43, 67, 71, 91, 93–99, 104, and 137. It is of interest that 96, 105, 106, and 107 are connected with Davidic activity in I Chronicles 16, yet they do not have Davidic superscriptions in the Hebrew text.

A unique feature of the Davidic ascription is the tendency, found 13 times, to connect a psalm with some event in the life of that king: Psalms 3 (II Sam. 15–19), 7 (? II Sam. 18:21), 18 (II Sam. 22), 34 (I Sam. 21:14), 51 (II Sam. 11–12), 52 (I Sam. 22:9), 54 (I Sam. 23:19; 26:1), 56 (?I Sam. 21:11; 27:2), 57 (I Sam. 22:1; 24:3), 59 (I Sam. 19:11), 60 (II Sam. 8:13; I Chron. 18:1–12), 63 (I Sam. 23:14; 24:1; 26:2), 142 (I Sam. 22:1; 24:3). Here, again, the LXX extends this practice by connecting Psalms 27, 71, 97, 143, and 144 with David's biography, but apart from 144 (cf. I Sam. 17) the references are indeterminate.

It should be noted that in some instances the connection between the Hebrew superscription and the body of the psalm is very tenuous. It is possible that the reference may often be to some tradition rooted in a biography of David not included in the biblical narratives and now lost.

ASAPH. Twelve psalms are associated with Asaph (50, 73–83). If the reference is to Asaph rather than to the Asaphites (Ezra 2:41; 3:10, et al.) it is probably because he was a contemporary of David, appointed by him to a prominent position in the leadership of the Temple (Neh. 12:46; I Chron. 6:24; 15:19, et al.).

THE KORAHITES. There are 11 Korahite psalms (42, 44–49, 84–85, 87–88). The Korahites (cf. Num. 26:11) are first recorded as participating in the public worship of the Temple in the time of Jehoshaphat (II Chron. 20:19). They are not listed among the returnees from Babylon (Ezra 2; Neh. 7), so that they operated only during the First Temple period. The appearance of the Korahites among the ostraca of Arad confirms the existence of the guild in the Monarchy period.

HEMAN, ETHAN. Only one psalm each is assigned to Heman and Ethan (Ps. 88, 89). Both are entitled "Ezrahite" (LXX, "Israelite"). They are both leaders of the Temple musicians under David (I Chron. 2:6; 6:18, et al.). Both names are otherwise mentioned as personages famous for their wisdom (I Kings 5:11). Psalm 88 is also ascribed to the Korahites, indicating a double tradition.

SOLOMON. It appears that in the case of Psalm 72 the reference to Solomon is to the content rather than the authorship and was so understood by the Greek translators. In Psalm 127 the presence of "Solomon" in the title (omitted in LXX) was conditioned by the mention of "the building of the house."

MOSES. The attribution to Moses in Psalm 90 is probably based on the affinities between verse 1 and Deuteronomy 33:27, verse 10 and Exodus 7:7, and verse 13 and Exodus 32:12.

JEDUTHUN. At first sight Psalms 39, 62, and 77 appear to be ascribed to Jeduthun who, according to the Chronicler, was a levitical singer in David's time (I Chron. 16:38, 41, 42; 25:1, 3, 6; II Chron. 5:12). However, not only are the first two also attributed to David and the third to Asaph, implying a combination of variant traditions, but the preposition *ʿal* (62–77) is difficult to reconcile with a personal name. It is possible, therefore, that a musical instrument is intended.

Another interpretation connects the term with the verb *ydh*, "to confess," and presumes some confession liturgy or ritual.

Eight names are listed, at most, to which the Septuagint adds "Zechariah" in Psalm 137 and "Haggai and Zechariah" in Psalms 146, 147:1, 147:12, and 148.

Titles with Liturgical Application

The heading of Psalm 30 mentions "the dedication of the Temple" which must be an allusion to the occasion of its public recitation. The identification of the reference, however, is not clear (cf. Sof. 18:2). Psalm 100 implies a liturgy for the *todah* offering (cf. Jer. 33:11). Psalm 92 indicates a Sabbath reading. The Greek Psalter further reflects liturgical traditions by affixing additional superscriptions indicating that Psalms 24, 48, 94, and 93 were read, respectively, on the first, second, fourth, and sixth days of the week (cf. Tam. 7:4; RH 31a). It also, strangely, designates Psalm 38 "for the Sabbath" and appends to Psalm 29 the notice, "on the going forth of the Tabernacle," perhaps a reference to a custom of reading this hymn on the last day of the Feast of Tabernacles. However, the rubric may also allude to a tradition connecting Psalm 29 with David's bringing of the ark to Jerusalem, since the verses supposedly sung on that occasion (I Chron. 16:28–29) betray a close affinity with verses 1–2. Another possibility in explanation of the Greek annotation may be that the original Hebrew rubric containing the term *ʿaẓeret* was mistakenly identified with the eighth day of Tabernacles (cf. Lev. 23:36), whereas it is the rabbinic term for Pentecost. Indeed, the reading of Psalm 29 on this festival is attested (Sof. 18:3).

The Greek rubric to Psalm 96, "when the house was built after the captivity," would imply some tradition not otherwise known. Totally obscure is the Septuagint annotation to Psalm 97, "when the land was established."

Technical Terms in the Headings

The superscriptions are remarkably rich in the number and variety of technical terms, most of which are shrouded in obscurity. Their meanings were already lost in early times for the Greek translators were generally ignorant of them, even in the days of the Second Temple, and rabbinic literature and medieval commentators present an assortment of interpretations. The explanation for this severance of tradition may lie, at least partially, in the fact that the terminology was rooted in the technical jargon of the different guilds of singers and musicians who jealously guarded their professional secrets until they, themselves, went out of existence (cf. Yoma 3:11).

Mizmor. The term *mizmor* appears exclusively in the Book of Psalms, always as a title and never in the body of a psalm. It is never attached to those psalms found elsewhere in biblical literature. With a single exception (Ps. 98:1, but LXX adds "of David") it is always used in conjunction with a proper name preceded by *lamed*. Why it is restricted to 57 psalms cannot be known. It was translated *psalmos* by the Septuagint and by Theodotion and so came down in English as "psalm" lending its name to the entire book (see discussion on title, above). The verbal form appears outside Psalms only in Judges 5:3, II Samuel 22:50 (= Ps. 18:50), Isaiah 12:5, and I Chronicles 16:9 (= Ps. 105:2) and always in a liturgical context (cf. Isa. 51:3). It appears 44 times alone, 13 times together with *shir*, and also frequently in parallelism with that term (cf. Ps. 21:14; 27:6; 57:8; 68:5, 33; 104:33; 108:2; Judg. 5:3; Amos 5:23). It is also used in connection with the lyre (Ps. 71:22; 98:5; 147:7; 149:3), the harp (33:2; 144:9; cf. Amos 5:23), and the timbrel (81:3; 149:3). There can be no doubt that *mizmor* refers to liturgical music.

La-Menaẓẓe'aḥ. The title *la-menaẓẓe'aḥ* occurs in 55 psalms invariably in the initial position. Outside the book it appears only in Habakkuk 3:19, also a liturgy. Its absence from II Samuel 22 and its presence in Psalm 18 shows that it has to do with the liturgical performance. Medieval Jewish commentators generally point to the verbal usage in the sense of overseeing labor (Ezra 3:8, 9; I Chron. 23:4; II Chron. 2:1, 17; 34:13) and so understand the term to mean "director, overseer, choirmaster" or the like. Its connection with music is established by I Chronicles 15:21 and II Chronicles 34:12. However, the Septuagint took it to mean "eternity" (cf. Heb. *la-neẓaḥ*), the other Greek versions and Jerome connecting it with victory (cf. Heb. *niẓẓaḥon*). The Targum understood it to mean "to praise."

Shir. Thirty psalms are entitled *shir*. The feminine *shirah* appears but once (Ps. 18:1; cf. Ex. 15:1; Num. 21:17; Deut. 31:19, et al.). *Shir* is not restricted to psalms and may be used for secular as well as religious songs (cf. Isa. 23:16). However, the invocation "sing ye!" (*shiru*) is exclusively liturgical. The term *shir*, unlike *mizmor*, may also appear in the body of the psalm itself (Ps. 18:1; 28:7; 33:3, et al.). Only in Psalm 46 is it found alone. In five instances it is followed by *mizmor* (Ps. 48, 66, 83, 88, 108) and in seven (or eight) others the order is reversed (30?, 65, 67, 68, 75, 76, 87, 92). The significance of the sequence is unknown. The emphasis in its use would be on the words set to a rhythm since the Hebrew uses the phrase "to speak a song" (Judg. 5:12; cf. 11QPs[a] 27:9, 11), but whether it indicates a special mode of presentation is a matter of conjecture.

Shir ha-Ma'alot. Shir ha-ma'alot appears at the head of a cluster of 15 psalms (Ps. 120–134; Ps. 121 *la-ma'alot*). LXX and Jerome translate it "degrees" (cf. II Kings 20:911), but what was understood by that is not clear. Some assume a reference to some peculiar gradational style of musical execution. The rendering "ascents" assumes a connection with the return from Babylon (cf. Ezra 7:9), but only Psalm 126 would be suitable to such a context for in Psalms 122 and 134 the Temple is still standing. Similarly, only Psalm 122 would be appropriate to a "pilgrim psalm" interpretation which would better fit other psalms (e.g., 15, 24, 43, 84) not so designated. The Mishnah appears to understand *ma'alot* as "steps" (cf. Ex. 20:26 [23]; I Kings 10:19, 20) and to find a connection with the 15 steps joining the court of the Israelites to the court of women in the Second Temple on which the levitical musicians used to stand during the ceremony of the "drawing of water" on Sukkot (Suk. 5:4; Mid. 2:5). These psalms may also have derived their designation from their use in some festal procession.

Maskil. Featured in the headings to 13 psalms, *maskil* never appears without a proper name with a prepositional *lamed* (Ps. 32, 42, 44, 45, 52–55, 74, 78, 88, 89, 142). The LXX understood it to mean "instruction" (cf. Ps. 32:8). It must be assumed to refer to some special skill required in the manner of musical performance (cf. Ps. 47:8). From the context of Amos 5:13 and the contrast between the *maskil* and the mourning rites (5:16–17), the term might well indicate some type of song.

Neginot. The term *neginot* appears six times (Ps. 4, 6, 54, 55, 67, 76) preceded by *la-menaẓẓe'aḥ* and with the preposition *be-* (cf. Hab. 3:19), and once in the singular preceded by *'al* (Ps. 61). From I Samuel 16:16, 23 it would clearly seem to indicate stringed instruments (cf. Ps. 68:33; Isa. 23:16; Ezek. 33:32).

Mikhtam. All six appearances of the term *mikhtam* are attached to *le-David* (Ps. 16, 56–60). LXX and Theodotion rendered it *stēlographia* which most likely represents its original meaning as "an inscription upon a slab." It is probably interchangeable with the title *mikhtav* in Hezekiah's thanksgiving psalm (Isa. 38:9). Some connect the word with the Akkadian verb *katāmu*, meaning "to cover," "to conceal," and assume a connection with some ritual.

Tefillah. Despite the epilogue to the second book of Psalms (72:20) which speaks of "the prayers [*tefillot*] of David" and the more than a score of appearances in the body of the psalms, the term *tefillah* is found only in the superscriptions to five psalms (17, 86, 90, 102, 142) and to Habakkuk 3.

Al Shoshannim. Al Shushan Edut, El Shoshannim Edut. Al shoshannim may be translated "On the lilies" (Ps. 45, 69), *al shushan edut* "On the lily of testimony" (Ps. 60), and *el shoshannim edut* "To the lilies of testimony" (Ps. 80). They may be cue-words, i.e., the incipits or titles of some well-known songs to the tune of which the psalm was sung. The reference may also be to a six-stringed or six-bell instrument shaped like the lily.

Al Tashḥet. Found in the headings of Psalms 57–59, *al-tashḥet* means "do not destroy" and may be an incipit, perhaps of some old vintage song (cf. Isa. 65:8). Since it is accompanied by *mikhtam* (see above) in three of its four occurrences, it has been suggested that it may be an adjuration against altering or destroying inscriptions.

Al ha-Gittit. The ancient versions generally connect the term *al ha-gittit* in Psalms 8, 81, 84 with the winepress (*gat*). It may indicate a tune sung by the grape treaders (cf. Isa. 16:10; Jer. 25:30), or it may be a musical instrument derived from the Philistine city of Gath (so Targum).

Al ha-Sheminit. Meaning literally, "on the eighth," *al ha-sheminit* may refer to an eight-stringed instrument in Psalm 6, 12 (cf. Ar. 13b; Tosef., Ar. 2:7). It cannot mean an octave as the division into eight modes was unknown. The reference in I Chronicles 15:21, "with lyres on the *sheminit*" in parallel with verse 20, "with harps on *ʿalamot*" (see below) has suggested a quality of the voice, perhaps a low bass.

Lehazkir. The appearance of the term *lehazkir* in I Chronicles 16:4 in a context of public worship strongly suggests a liturgical or cultic meaning in the headings of Psalms 38, 70. However, the precise circumstances cannot be determined for the verb is elsewhere used of invoking the divine name (cf. Ex. 20:21; Isa. 26:13; 48:1; 62:6; Amos 6:10; Ps. 20:8), of recalling sinfulness (cf. Gen. 41:9; Num. 5:15; I Kings 17:18; Ezek. 21:28, 29; 29:16), and in connection with the meal offering or incense burning (cf. Lev. 2:2; 24:7; Num. 5:15, 26; Isa. 66:3).

Al Maḥalat. If *al maḥalat* is not a cue-word identifying the tune to which Psalms 53, 88 were to be sung, it may indicate a wind instrument (cf. I Kings 1:40, et al.) or some choreographic direction (cf. Judg. 21:23, et al.). It might also be translated, "for sickness" (cf. I Kings 8:37) and imply some accompanying ritual.

Al Alamot. The term *al alamot* is found as a heading only once (Ps. 46). However, another occurrence of *al alamot* may be the obscure *al-mut* in our received Hebrew text of Psalm 48:15, which might belong to the next psalm, as well as in the title of Psalm 9 (see below *al mut la-ben*). Its connection with public worship is attested by I Chronicles 15:20. It could refer to a musical instrument such as a small flute or pipe or express a quality of the voice, i. e., "youthful" (cf. *almah*, "a maiden"), perhaps high pitched or soprano.

Al Mut la-Ben. Al mut la-ben could either mean "male soprano" or be a cue-word in its single appearance (Ps. 9).

El ha-Neḥilot. Either a wind instrument (cf. *al-maḥalat* above) or a cue-word could be intended by *el ha-neḥilot* in Psalm 5. The variant *ʾel* for the frequent *al* cannot be explained.

Al Ayyelet ha-Shahar. Al ayyelet ha-shaḥar is almost certainly a cue-word, the psalm (22) being set to the tune of a well-known song entitled, "On the hind of the morning."

Al Yonat Elem Reḥokim. Al yonat elem reḥokim too (Ps. 56) must be a cue-word that may be translated, "On the speechless dove far-off," or, "On the dove of the far-off terebinths [*elim*]." The Septuagint seems to have understood "dove" as an epithet for the people of Israel and have read *elim*, and construed it as "gods" or "holy beings."

Shir Yedidot. The title *shir yedidot*, "a love song," is appropriate to the occasion of Psalm 45 which celebrates the marriage of an Israelite king to a Tyrian princess.

Lelammed. Lelammed means literally "to teach." Its use in Psalm 60 is reminiscent of the similar introductions to songs in Deuteronomy 31:19 and II Samuel 1:18.

Leʿannot. The meaning "to afflict" indeed connects with the theme of Psalm 88. *Leʿannot* might refer to some ritual of penance (cf. Lev. 23:27, 29). It could also be an intensive form of the verb *anah* ("to chant"; cf. Ex. 15:21; 32:18), and might indicate some antiphonal arrangement in the performance of the psalm.

Shiggayon. Shiggayon (Ps. 7) also appears in the plural form in the heading to Habakkuk 3. On the basis of the Akkadian *šigû*, "lamentation," "type of prayer" (CAD, Š / II, 413–14) it has been understood as meaning a psalm of lamentation, and is an Akkadian loanword.

Tehillah. The term *tehillah*, which gave the book its most popular Hebrew title, occurs only in Psalm 145 (see discussion on title, above).

Hallelujah. Ten psalms begin with the term Hallelujah (106, 111–113, 135, 146–150) which is not strictly a title but an invocation (see *Hallelujah).

Technical Terms Within the Psalms

Two terms appear within the body of the psalms themselves.

Selah. The term *selah* occurs 71 times in 39 psalms mainly in the "elohistic" psalms, and three times in Habakkuk 3 (verses 3, 9, 13). In 31 of these psalms *la-menaẓẓeʾaḥ* also appears, as it does in Habbakkuk 3. It is never to be found at the beginning of a verse, but occasionally comes in the middle (Ps. 55:20; 57:4; cf. Hab. 3:3, 9). Otherwise, its position is at the end of the verse and four times even at the end of the entire psalm (Ps. 3, 9, 24, 46). It may appear more than once in the same psalm (Ps. 3, 32, 46, 66, 68, 77, 89, 140). The LXX adds *selah* also at Psalms 34:11; 39:8; 50:15; 80:8; 94:15.

There is no agreement among the ancient versions and medieval Jewish commentators as to its meaning and function. There is no certainty that its current position in a psalm is always original and not sometimes the work of a later scribe or editor. The etymology is obscure and even the masoretic vocalization seems to be secondary.

The Septuagint, Theodotion (usually), and Symmachus all translated *selah* as διάψάλμά. However, the meaning of the Greek is as enigmatic as the Hebrew, and the usual rendering "interlude" is not at all sure. The Targum, Aquila, and Jerome all understood it as part of the text of the preceding verse in which it appears and rendered it as "always," or "for eternity." The present vocalization of the Hebrew word seems to reflect this tradition for it is the same as that of the usual word for eternity (*neẓaḥ*), and the accentuation connects the term with the preceding. The same interpretation is to be found in the Talmud (Er. 54a), and in the employment of *selah* in the Hebrew prayer book. It also finds support in the comments of Saadiah, Jonah ibn Janaḥ, and Rashi.

A different explanation is given by Kimḥi (*Sefer Shorashim*) who connects it with the use of the Hebrew root *sll* in the sense of raising up (cf. Isa. 57:14; Ps.68:5). The term would then be an instruction for the singers or musicians. Abraham

Ibn Ezra (to Ps. 3:3) believes it to be a liturgical response on the part of the worshipers, affirming the truth of the sentiments previously stated in the psalm.

Some scholars have suggested a derivation from *sal* ("basket"), concluding that at certain points in the service a basket-shaped drum was beaten. Others believe the term to be an acrostic. No solution to the enigma of *selah* is possible in the present state of our knowledge.

Higgayon. The term *higgayon* appears together with *selah* in Psalm 9:17 and with a musical instrument in Psalm 92:4. It is found as part of the text in Psalm 19:15 where it implies "utterance," or "musings." The basic root meaning seems to be "to make a sound" (cf. Isa. 16:7; 31:4; 39:14). *Higgayon* may therefore be an instruction to the musicians to produce a murmuring glissando or a flourish.

The Psalms, with their messianic references real and imagined, played a significant role in Jewish-Christian polemic as early as the New Testament (Matt. 22:21–46). The responses of the medieval Jewish biblical commentators to Christian Psalms interpretation, extremely valuable resources for the history of Jewish-Christian relations, were censored out of earlier editions of rabbinic Bibles but are now available in the excellent edition of M. Cohen (ed.), *Mikra'ot Gedolot "ha-Keter" Tehillim* (2 vols., 2003).

[Nahum M. Sarna]

IN THE TALMUD AND MIDRASH

The rabbis reduced the traditional number of psalms to 147 (Mid. Ps. 22:19; 104:2) merely for homiletical purposes as is evident from the passage in *Berakhot* 9b–10a. The Talmud explains that Psalm 19:15 was instituted to be recited after the 18 benedictions of the **Amidah* since it comes at the end of the 18th Psalm. Whereupon the Talmud asks, "But this is the 19th Psalm, not the 18th," and answers that Psalms 1 and 2 constitute one psalm. It brings evidence for this in the statement that David first uses the word Hallelujah at the end of the 103rd Psalm, where in fact it is in Psalm 104:35. It is therefore evident that at that time Psalms 1 and 2 normally constituted two psalms, and Psalms 19 and 104 were numbered as they are today. That homiletical purpose seems clear. It is reflected in the statement "Moses gave the five books of the Torah to Israel, and corresponding to them, David gave the five books of the Psalms to Israel" (Mid. Ps. 1:2). In order to emphasize this relationship, the number of psalms was reduced to 147, probably in order to make it correspond to the number of *sedarim* in the Bible according to the triennial cycle current in Ereẓ Israel. The other two cases of two psalms which were combined in one were probably 114 and 115 (see Kimḥi in loc.) and 117 and 118 (see Buber in Mid. Ps. 22 note 88).

The Book of Psalms includes the compositions of ten earlier authorities, Adam, Melchizedek, Abraham, Moses, Heman, Jeduthun, Asaph, and the three sons of Korah (BB 14b, 15a, variants are given in Eccles. R. 7:19.4). Nevertheless the Book of Psalms was called after David because "his voice was pleasant" (Songs R. 4:4 no. 1 referring to II Sam. 23:1). All the psalms were inspired (Pes. 117a) and music helped to bring the inspiration: "A harp was suspended above the bed of David. When midnight came the north wind blew on it and it produced music of its own accord. Immediately David arose and occupied himself with Torah." That "Torah" consisted of songs and praises, however, since "until midnight he occupied himself with Torah; and from then with songs and praises" (Ber. 3b). The psalms are both individual and general; those in the singular are personal, those in the plural are of general application (Pes. 117a).

Various psalms and groups of psalms are singled out for special mention in the Talmud. They are the **Hallel*, Psalms 113–118, the only psalms which formed part of the liturgy in talmudic times (see below; Psalms in Liturgy) and also known as the "Egyptian *Hallel*" (Ber. 56a), to distinguish it from Psalms 145–150 and Psalm 136 which are also variously referred to as *Hallel* (Shab. 118b), or, the latter, *Hallel ha-Gadol* (Pes. 118a); the seven psalms which were "the psalms which the levites used to recite in the Temple" (Tam. 7:4) and which have been included in the liturgy; and the Fifteen Songs of Degrees 120–134 (*shir ha-ma'alot*). Such importance was attached to the alphabetical Psalm 145, that it was stated that "he who recites it three times a day is certain to be vouchsafed the world to come" (Ber. 4b). Psalm 16 compresses into 11 principles the whole of the Torah (Mak. 24a). The *Tamnei Appei* (lit. "eight faces"), i.e., Psalm 119, the eightfold alphabetical acrostic psalm which in later ages is given a special importance (see below), is only mentioned en passant (*ibid.*).

The almost complete neglect of the psalms in the liturgy during talmudic times may give a wrong impression of the enormous importance with which the psalms were invested by the rabbis. A suggestion has been made that in some places there was a triennial cycle of the reading of psalms, corresponding to the triennial cycle of the reading of the Pentateuch, which would explain, inter alia, the comparison made between the Five Books of Moses and the Five Books of Psalms, and the equalization of the number of psalms with the pericopes of the Pentateuch. It was, however, in their homilies and preaching that the psalms were most heavily relied upon. The Midrash states that Ben Azzai "strung together [as a row of pearls] the words of the Pentateuch with those of the prophets, and of the prophets with the Hagiographa, and words of Torah rejoiced as on the day they were given at Sinai" (Lev. R. 16:4). Although it refers to the Hagiographa in general, there is no doubt but that Psalms was the favorite book of that section of the Bible employed. This method of "stringing together" the verses of Psalms with those of the Pentateuch is reflected in the proems to the classical *Midrashim, the overwhelming majority of which are expositions of verses of the psalms which are linked with the pentateuchal verse under discussion. As a result, even disregarding **Midrash Tehillim* (*Midrash Psalms*), which is a running commentary on the whole Book of Psalms, and which in any case is largely a compilation based on earlier material, there is not a single chapter of Psalms and hardly a single verse which is not expounded in the Talmud and Midrash (cf. A. Lavat, *Beit Aharon ve-Hosafot*, 1881).

IN THE LITURGY

The penetration of the psalms into the liturgy represents a gradual process extending over the centuries, the effect of which can be seen in the fact that whereas in the talmudic period the statutory prayers included no psalms whatsoever on Sabbaths and weekdays, and the only psalms recited were the *Hallel* on the three Pilgrim Festivals and Ḥanukkah, and later, despite a specific rubric to the contrary (Arukh 10a), on the *New Moon, the authorized Daily Prayer Book of the United Hebrew Congregation of England (Singer) gives an index of 73 psalms and part of another included in the various services. In part, at least, this inclusion of the psalms into the liturgy came as a result of popular demand. Of the Daily Psalm, for instance, there is the statement that "the people have adopted the custom of including it" (Sof. 18:1) and with regard to the choice of Psalm 136 as the psalm for the Passover "the people have adopted the custom of reciting this psalm, though it is not the best choice" (*ibid.* 18:2).

Statutory Prayers

The process whereby the recitation of psalms became an integral part of the statutory prayers consisted of regarding every reference to the recitation of psalms in the Talmud, either as acts of special piety performed by individuals, or as part of the Temple service, as a justification for making them part of the statutory service. To this class belong the **Pesukei de-Zimra* and the Daily Psalm. The *Pesukei de-Zimra* consisted originally only of the six last psalms, the Hallelujah Psalms 145–50. The process of inclusion is clearly seen in the fact that whereas their recitation is mentioned in the Talmud by R. Yose as an act of especial piety (Shab. 118b; and it is the later authorities who decide that the *Hallel* to which he refers are those psalms), in the post-talmudic tractate **Soferim*, they are called simply "the six daily psalms" which are already part of the statutory service (Sof. 17:11). Both these passages, however, confine the *Pesukei de-Zimra* to those six psalms. On the principle, however, that there was more leisure on Sabbaths and festivals, both the Ashkenazi and Sephardi rites add a considerable number on those days: the former adds nine (19, 34, 90, 91, 135, 136, 33, 92, and 93) and the Sephardi 14 (103, 19, 33, 90, 91, 98, 121–124, 135, 136, 92, 93; some rites include the first two in the weekday service).

The same process is seen with regard to the Daily Psalm. They are mentioned in the Midrash as "the psalms which the levites used to sing in the Temple" (Tam. 7:4). By the time of *Soferim* they are already part of the daily prayers, "the people having adopted the custom" (18:1). However, here again, once the transfer was made to the synagogue, it was extended to special psalms for every festival (for the text see *Soferim* 18 and 19 and for a variant, Baer, *Avodat Yisrael*, last unnumbered page). In the course of time a large number of individual psalms were added: Psalm 30 before the *Pesukei de-Zimra*, Psalm 100 on weekdays in the *Pesukei de-Zimra*, Psalm 6 in the supplicatory prayers, Psalm 24 on weekdays when the *Sefer Torah* is returned to the ark, and 29 on Sabbaths and festivals. Psalm 20 was included in the last portion of the daily service. Some rites have psalms added to the evening service parallel to the Daily Psalm in the morning (see Singer, 133–40). Psalm 27 was instituted for the penitential period from the second day of Elul to *Hoshana Rabba, 144 and 67 for the Service of the Termination of the Sabbath, etc.

Two groups of psalms have to be mentioned: Psalms 104 and the Fifteen Songs of Degrees, included in the Sabbath afternoon service during the winter months, instituted in the 12th century, and the latest addition of all, which spread with remarkable rapidity, Psalms 95–99 and 20, for the Inauguration of the Sabbath. Instituted by the kabbalists of Safed in the 16th century – although the author of the liturgical work *Matteh Moshe* published in 1615 makes no mention of it, and 15 years later the author of *Yosef Omeẓ*, while praising it as "a good and beautiful custom," refers to it as "a new one, lately come up" – it has become standard in all Ashkenazi services (most Sephardi rites confine themselves to 29). This list, however, though incomplete, does not exhaust the inclusion of Psalms in the statutory service. Some of the prayers consist merely of a mosaic of single verses from Psalms of which the most notable are two passages which precede the Psalms of the *Pesukei de-Zimra*, called by their opening words *Romemu* and *Yehi Khevod*. Both consist entirely of verses from Psalms (except for one verse from Prov. 19:21 and one composite verse (*Adonai Melekh*) consisting of three parts, two of which are from Psalms) and of verses selected from the five books into which Psalms is divided. Only the second book has no verse in the *Yehi Khevod*, but the Yemenite rite adds Psalm 46:12 from this book, and this is probably the original version, already mentioned in *Soferim* (17:11). It would appear that this selection is deliberate. In all, no less than 250 individual verses from Psalms are thus added to the liturgy (A. Berliner, *Randbemerkungen*, p. 9).

Non-Statutory Prayers

It can safely be said that there is no special or non-statutory service which does not include one or more psalms. They include the introduction to the Grace after Meals, prayers for drought (Baer, appendix, p. 87), before going on a journey, the night prayer before retiring to rest, prayers for and by the sick, the burial service, the prayer in the house of mourning, the memorial service for the dead, and the service at the consecration of a tombstone which, apart from the memorial prayer, consists of a selection of psalms. The custom has been followed in all forms of service added in recent years, of which Singer includes the services on the occasion of making collections for hospitals, of thanksgiving of a woman after childbirth, and on the consecration of a house. They are naturally included in the prayers for Independence Day. Custom has developed, under the influence of the Kabbalah, especially in Israel, with regard to Psalm 119, the eightfold alphabetical psalm. At memorial services the verses are recited which make up the name of the deceased and his father, with the addition of the verses the letters of which form the word *neshamah* ("soul").

Various

The regular reading of Psalms was not confined to services. The recital of the whole Book of Psalms is widespread, whether as an act of piety by saintly individuals, or by groups of unlearned people. For this purpose "societies of reciters of psalms" (*ḥevrot tehillim*) were formed, and in recent times a special society has been formed in Jerusalem whereby two separate groups recite the whole Book of Psalms daily at the Western Wall. The Psalms are included in their entirety in all large prayer books. A prayer has been composed to be recited prior to and at the conclusion of each of the five books as well as for its reading on Hoshana Rabba which specifically equates them with the Five Books of Moses (Baer, Introduction to Psalms in *Avodat Yisrael*, pp. 5–8). Baer concludes with a list of psalms which it is customary to recite on Sabbath to correspond with the weekly portion "in the manner of the *haftarah*," thus "stringing together" Pentateuch, Prophets, and Psalms (last page, unnumbered).

[Louis Isaac Rabinowitz]

IN THE ARTS

In Literature

From the early Middle Ages the Book of Psalms has had an incalculable influence on literature, art, and music. Its impact has, perhaps, been greatest on writers. J.G. *Herder stated that "it is worth studying the Hebrew language for ten years in order to read Psalm 104 in the original" and Israel *Zangwill even claimed that the psalms "are more popular in every country than the poems of the nation's own poets. Besides this one book with its infinite editions… all other literatures seem 'trifles light as air'…" (1895). Literary treatment of Psalms has taken several forms: translation and paraphrase in verse and prose, imitation, and the composition of hymns and epics inspired by the themes and style of the original. Many of the first European translations of Psalms possess considerable literary merit and importance and some helped to mold the languages in which the sense of the Hebrew was conveyed. Among the earliest known are the versions in Anglo-Saxon (eighth century), Old Church Slavonic (ninth century), and Old High German (tenth century). During the 13th–15th centuries many more versions of the Psalter appeared in lands throughout Europe; and translations of Psalms were among the first books printed in some countries, notable examples being Jacques Lefèvre d'Etaples' French Psalter (1509), Jan Kochanowski's *Psałterz Dawidów* (1578) and Maciej Rybiński's *Psalmy monarchy i proroka świątego Dawida* (1598) in Poland, and the Psalter of the Brasov friar Coresi (1578–80) in Romania. Together with other portions of the Old Testament, the Psalms were translated from the Hebrew by 15th-century Judaizing sects in Russia, and a version in Yiddish was published in Venice by the pioneer Hebrew grammarian and author Elijah *Levita (1545).

From the early 16th century the Psalms inspired the highest degree of literary creativity in England and France. Thomas Sternhold headed a team of scholars who published *The Whole Booke of Psalmes; collected into Englysh metre… conferred with the Ebrue…* (London, 1551^2, 1562), which ran to literally hundreds of editions during the 16th–18th centuries; and this version was first used for the Church of Scotland's metrical *Psalms of David* (Edinburgh, 1650), which has remained one of the standard collections for Protestants throughout the English-speaking world. Another verse translation of the 16th century was that by Sir Philip Sidney and his sister, Mary Herbert, Countess of Pembroke, whose *Psalmes of David* was, however, only published in 1823. The pioneering French translation was that prepared by the poet Clément Marot (later in collaboration with the Geneva Reformer Théodore de Bèze): *Trente Pseaulmes de David mis en francoys* (1541) and *Cinquante Pseaulmes de David* (1543), which ran to dozens of editions from 1560 onward. Marot's version, with its "sober, solemn music," became an integral part of the French Protestant liturgy and enjoyed an extraordinary vogue, not only at the Protestant court of Navarre but even at the Catholic French court, where it was officially banned by the Sorbonne. French writers who paraphrased or reinterpreted the Book of Psalms include Agrippa d'Aubigné, Jean Antoine de Baïf, Jean Bertaut, Honorat de Bueil, Jean de la Ceppède, Jean Baptiste Chassignet, Philippe Desportes, Guy *Le Fèvre de la Boderie (whose works include many verse paraphrases from the Hebrew), and François de Malherbe.

During the 17th century, too, the Psalms retained their fascination for many writers. They inspired German hymns by Paul Gebhardt; the so-called *Teitsch-Hallel*, a Yiddish composition based, at least in part, on contemporary Protestant hymnology; and the first important work printed in New England, the *Bay Psalm Book* (Cambridge, 1640), a metrical (and highly literal) translation from the Hebrew for those who wished to "sing in Sion the Lord's songs of prayse according to his own wille." In the 18th century a Spanish verse paraphrase (*Espejo fiel de Vidas que contiene los Palmos de David in Verso*, London, 1720) was published by the ex-Marrano Daniel Israel Lopez *Laguna; and a German Jewish translation was prepared by the philosopher Moses *Mendelssohn (1783). Directly and indirectly many writers of the 19th and 20th centuries have been influenced by the Book of Psalms. Thomas Carlyle maintained that the Psalms of David "struck tones that were an echo of the sphere-harmonies." Even greater praise was expressed by the British statesman William Ewart Gladstone, who unfavorably contrasted "all the wonders of Greek civilization" with "the single Book of Psalms," claiming that the "flowers of Paradise… blossomed in Palestine alone" (*The Place of Ancient Greece*, 1865). The same source has provided perennial inspiration for Jewish writers, including Penina *Moise, whose metrical renderings of the Psalms were adopted by U.S. Reform congregations; Heinrich *Graetz; and Samson Raphael *Hirsch, whose German neo-Orthodox edition of the Book of Psalms appeared in 1882. Jewish writers of the 20th

century who dealt with the same theme included Nachman Heller, who published an edition of the Psalms together with a rhymed Hebrew paraphrase, English and Yiddish translations, and English notes (1923); Izak *Goller, whose original verse translation of Ps. 113–118, *Hallel – Praise*, was published in 1925; and the U.S. rabbi Gershon Hadas who published a new translation for "the modern reader" (1964).

[Godfrey Edmond Silverman]

In Art

Among Christians of the Middle Ages the Book of Psalms was the most popular section of the Hebrew Bible and it was frequently illustrated in illuminated manuscripts such as Psalters, Bibles, breviaries, and Books of Hours. A particularly popular subject was King David the Psalmist playing on his harp or, occasionally, on other instruments. In the English 13th-century Rutland Psalter he is shown playing the organ. Carolingian Psalters and Bibles and manuscripts of the following two centuries often depict David surrounded by Asaph, Heman, Ethan, and Jeduthun, his four musicians, symbolizing Jesus with the four evangelists. A charming representation of David the Psalmist is the introductory miniature to a 15th-century north Italian Book of Psalms, part of a Hebrew miscellany volume in the Israel Museum, Jerusalem. The king is shown seated in a garden near a wood from which deer emerge, charmed by his playing. The subject was revived in northern Europe in the 17th century. There are paintings by Rubens (Staedelmuseum, Frankfurt), Pieter Lastman (Gallery Brunswick), and *Rembrandt (Kaplan Collection, New York). Modern works include those by Dante Gabriel Rosetti (Llandaff Cathedral) and by Jozef *Israels (Stedelijk Museum, Amsterdam).

The Middle Ages have also left manuscript illuminations of other subjects taken from the Psalms; and these are often extremely literal in interpretation. Some illustrations to Psalm 27:1 ("The Lord is my light") show David turning toward Jesus or the hand of God, and pointing to his own eyes. Psalm 53:2 ("The fool hath said in his heart: 'There is no God'...") is illustrated by a half-naked medieval jester with a bauble in his hand or wearing a jester's long-eared cap. Sometimes he swallows a stone or bites a dog by the tail. In the 16th-century *Henry VIII Psalter* (British Museum) David is shown as Henry and the fool as his court jester. In some cases, however, the fool is David himself feigning madness before Abimelech. Psalm 69:2–3 ("Save me, O God; For the waters are come in even unto the soul...") takes the form of a naked crowned monarch submerged up to the waist or shoulders, his hands raised in supplication. Psalm 81:2 ("Sing aloud unto God, our strength") is illustrated by David striking on bells with a hammer, playing his harp, or dancing before the ark. Psalm 137 ("By the rivers of Babylon") likewise formed the subject of manuscript illustrations, but also of paintings by the 19th-century French Romantic artist Eugène Delacroix (in the dome of theology of the Palais Bourbon, Paris) and the German academician Eduard Bendemann (Wallraf-Richartz Museum, Cologne). Psalm 150:1 ("Praise God in His sanctuary") inspired the bas-reliefs of choristers by Luca della Robbia (15th century; Florence Cathedral).

In Music

The singing of psalms was the chief medium of personal and communal devotion during the formative period of Christianity and has retained an important position in its liturgy ever since. In both the old Eastern and Western denominations, as in Jewish traditions, the melodies of the psalms are built on the principle of psalmody and show many similarities (see Musical Rendition, below). In the Christian traditions they are correlated with a rigid system of melodic theory, that of the Eight Modes or Tones, i.e., eight basic melodic-scalar patterns. The roots of this system also lie in the Near East; the psalmodic patterns have been the least affected by changes in style or creative initiative, since they were to all effect "canonized" no less than the liturgical texts. Their earliest notation in the West is found in the anonymous treatise, *Commemoratio brevis de tonis et psalmis modulandis*, dating from about the second half of the ninth century, and their final forms, preserved thereafter by notation and usage, are those established shortly after the turn of the first millennium. As in Jewish tradition, the performance of the Psalms in the Christian liturgies shows many forms of responsorial and antiphonal divisions (soloist-group, group-group) and various relationships and means of musical linkage with the hymns and prayers of the service. An important feature is the florid rendition of the *Alleluia*, interpolated between the half clauses or the verses (cf. *Hallelujah), often spun out into a long, wordless melisma on the final *a*, the so-called *Jubilus*, and the extension of the psalmodic principle to form the very melismatic chants of the *Tractus* ("drawn-out") category. Special psalmodic formulas are also used for the rendition of certain hymns from the Bible and the New Testament, such as the Songs of Moses – *Audite coeli (Ha'azinu*, Deut. 32:1–43) – and the Song of Mary – the *Magnificat* (Luke 1:46–55).

The Protestant Reformation and its related movements, basing its liturgy on the vernacular, created rhymed paraphrases of the Psalms, which were furnished with new melodies, i.e., newly composed, taken over from secular songs, or reshaped to the meter from a traditional ("Gregorian") melody. The major composers who took part in the creation of this new tradition were Loys Bourgeois (c. 1510–c. 1561), Claude Le Jeune (1528–1600), and Claude Goudimel (c. 1515–1572), in France and Switzerland, for the psalm paraphrases by Marot and Calvin; Jacobus Clemens Non Papa (c. 1510–c. 1556) in Holland, with his three-part arrangements of folk tunes to the Dutch rhymed Psalter (the *Souterliedekens* – "little Psalter songs"); and Martin *Luther and the members of his circle for the psalm paraphrases among the German chorales. The continental tunes were largely taken over into the English and Scottish repertoire (Sternhold Psalter, 1563), and then with local additions, migrated with the Puritans to North America, where the earliest book of music instruction published was *A very plain and easy introduction to the whole Art of Singing Psalms* by John Tufts (1712, 1744[11]). Almost from the outset, the Protestant and related movements linked their psalm and hymn collections with art music (and no doubt also popular harmonizing practices) by publishing them in three- or four-voice part settings, a practice which still continues.

Art music compositions for the Psalms appear much later than for the other parts of the service, in the early 15th century, since most of the Psalm texts appear in those parts of the service which are less frequently the occasion for artistic elaboration, such as Vespers. The polyphonic settings of the Psalms "do not constitute a musical category, but are the sum of all those musical categories and forms which stand in any relationship to the biblical Psalms, to their text (original, translated, paraphrased, rhymed, reinterpreted, or taken as the base for an instrumental interpretation), or, in a more narrow sense, to their liturgical melodies" (L. Finscher). It is therefore hardly possible to trace the history of these compositions separately from the mainstream of European art music, from the strictly liturgical-functional harmonizations of the Psalm tones, through the golden ages of the continental motet and the English verse anthem (16th–17th centuries), to the free settings of modern composers. The Psalms have always appealed to composers not only as the "essence of sacred music" but also through their balance of the individual and communal expression of joys and sorrows, which challenges each composer anew. Psalm settings are found in the works of almost all major composers from the 16th century onward. The tradition has been continued by such works as Igor Stravinsky's *Symphony of Psalms* (1930, to the Latin text), and Leonard *Bernstein's *Chichester Psalms* (1965, specified by the composer to be sung only in Hebrew).

[Bathja Bayer]

MUSICAL RENDITION IN JEWISH TRADITION

Historical Sources

It is most probable that some of the components of the so-called psalm titles, i.e., the verses or half verses prefaced to many of the psalms, indicate certain musical aspects: *shir, mizmor,* and their combinations (see above; see also *Music). The simple recurring response *ki le-olam ḥasdo* ("For His mercy endures forever") in Psalms 136, 118:1–4, 106:1, etc., may have been sung to an equally simple melodic formula (by the levitic choir or by the public) after the more elaborate rendition of the first part of the verse by a soloist or by the choir. The refrain or response verses did not have to be written out explicitly if the performers and the public knew them by tradition, and the same was true for the practice of interjecting the praise Hallelujah, once, or several times, after each verse or group of verses. Present-day traditional usages show many instances of the use of one verse as response or refrain, the intercalation of extraneous sentences as refrains, and the addition of Hallelujah in both Jewish and Christian traditions.

The version of Psalm 145 found in Cave 11 at Qumran (11QPs[a]) may be an early documentation of the practices. A refrain-like clause ("Blessed be God and blessed be His Name forever and ever"), not found in the masoretic text or in the versions, is added after each verse. This refrain is obviously related to verse 1 and could have been intoned as a response. The talmudic sources offer a number of fairly detailed references to psalm singing. Especially important are those references that refer to the various possible divisions of performance between soloist and choir (or public) in the *Hallel* (Sot. 5:4, elaborated in Tosef., Sot. 6:2; TJ, Sot. 5:6, 20c; Sot. 30b; Mekhilta Shirata 1). The discussion centers upon the rendition of the Song of the Sea which is said to have been performed "as the *Hallel* is sung." The information may therefore be applied to the contemporary performance of the *Hallel*.

The historical notated sources begin rather late, as compared to the notations of masoretic cantillation (see *Masoretic Accents). A specimen of psalm-cantillation motives according to the masoretic accents was notated sometime during the first half of the 17th century by Jacob Finzi, cantor in Casale Monferrato. Four psalm melodies – three Italian-Sephardi and one Italian-German – were among the 11 synagogal melodies notated by Benedetto Marcello in Venice and published in his *Estro poetico armonico* (1724–27 and subsequent editions). More than half of the compositions in Salamone de' *Rossi's *Ha-Shirim asher li-Shelomo* (Venice, 1622–23) are settings of psalms (for three or more voices) with Psalms 92 and 111 set for a double choir of four-plus-four voices. Many freely composed settings of *Hodu* (Ps. 136) appear in the early cantor's manuals, beginning with the manuscript of Juda Elias of Hanover (1740). Similar to Rossi's works, these also belong to the province of art music; but the cantoral specimens frequently feature the beginning of the traditional intonation as a point of departure for their late-baroque flights of fancy.

Since the practice of psalm singing was taken over by Christianity from the synagogues of the surrounding Jewish communities in the Near East (and not from the art music of the Second Temple), many fruitful – and often problematic – attempts have been made to discover the "common heritage" by comparative methods. A survey of the oral traditions shows that the melodic content of psalm singing is extremely varied. On the other hand, all the truly traditional styles and practices of psalm singing do fall into a very limited number of categories as regards the melodic structure, relationship between melody and text, response and refrain, usages, and the influence of external musical and non-musical factors.

Melody

About 90% of the existing melodies follow the pattern which musicologists call psalmody (Gr. Πσάλμὸδίά, "singing of psalms"), i.e., a simple two-wave melodic curve corresponding to the parallel-clause structure of the majority of the psalm verses (two hemistichs). According to the still accepted definition established by medieval European church-music theory, psalmody consists of the following: *initium*, the opening rise; *tenor* (or *tonus currens*, or *tuba*) the holding tone for the recitation of the main parts of the verse; *mediant* (or *flexa*), the midpoint "dip" between the two hemistichs, with a kind of secondary *initium* leading to the reappearance of the *tenor* for the second hemistich; and *finalis* (or *punctum*), the closing formula (see ex. 1). The tenor may be repeated for as long as necessary to cover a varying number of words, and the system is applied with enough flexibility to cover even those psalm verses which are actually not bipartite but tripartite. The realization of the psalmodic principle in the Jewish traditions is frequently more complex than in the Christian ones in several respects:

(1) many melodies have not one but two tenors, and there are also some "double" melodic formulas (see ex. 2);

(2) the tenor, or tenors, are often covert, appearing as one or several long notes, or as the axis of a series of melismatic movements, or otherwise hidden beneath a florid elaboration;

(3) in the second half of the verse, the structure is often disturbed by subtraction, addition, or other departures from the pattern; the ending, however, will always come to obey the convention of the *finalis* (see ex. 3). On the other hand, there are also many very simple and presumably archaic melodies which follow the psalmodic pattern faithfully: examples are known from Tunisia, Morocco, Persia, Yemen, and even Europe.

The character and complexity of the melody are linked with the liturgical function. A certain psalm may thus be sung to various melodies. The exceptions are the two psalms of national mourning ("Asaph, O God the heathen are come into Thine inheritance"), and Psalm 137 ("By the rivers of Babylon") and Psalm 79 ("A psalm of often Psalm 91 ("Psalm of the afflicted individual"). The traditional intonations these have acquired in each community are so strongly associated with their contents that they cannot be transferred to the more joyful and festive texts of other psalms. The daily reading in the synagogue, or in private devotions, is the simplest and most closely follows the principle of psalmody. For the group of psalms sung in the morning prayer (*Pesukei de-Zimra*), different melodies are chosen for weekdays, Sabbath, and feasts. With the increasing festiveness of the occasion, the melodies tend to become more elaborate, especially when the rendition is given to the *ḥazzan*. Examples are the *Hallel* in the synagogue and psalms sung at weddings (especially Ps. 45). On extraordinarily festive occasions, the ritual will consist mostly of appropriately chosen psalms, and here virtuoso composition and performance are given the freest rein – as in a festive prayer for the sovereign (which will feature Ps. 21 and similar texts) and in the ceremony for the dedication of a new synagogue (where Ps. 118 is prominent).

In home rituals, such as in the *Hallel* sung at the *seder*, or

Hau - du la-dau-noj, kir - u wisch-mau, hau-di - u wo-am - mim a - li - lau-ssow.

Example 1. Simple psalmody, Ps. 105, Frankfurt tradition. From F. Ogutsch and J.B. Levy, Der Frankfurter Kantor, *1930, p. 4.*

Example 2. Psalmody with two tenors (i.e., holding-notes), Ps. 114, Djerba tradition. The melodic pattern analyzed here has also been preserved in the Western Christian tradition, where it is called tonus peregrinus. *Recorded in Jerusalem, 1955, by A. Herzog. Transcription by A. Herzog, from* Yuval 1, *1968, music examples booklet, no. 14.*

Example 3. Psalmody with free expansion of the second half-clause. Ps. 95, East Ashkenazi tradition for the Friday evening service. Verses 1–9 and the first half-clause of verse 10 are sung to the strict psalmodic pattern. The melody then takes over elements of the Adoshem malakh **shtayger, but returns to the psalmodic closing-formula. From Idelsohn,* Melodien, *vol. 8, no. 27.*

for those parts of the above-mentioned ceremonies in which the congregation is expected to participate the simplest psalmodic melodies will retain their place by the force of tradition and for obvious practical reasons (cf. Volunio Gallichi's manuscript score for the inauguration of the Siena synagogue in 1786 (ed. I. Adler, 1965)) which, in addition to an elaborate composition of *Open to me the Gates of Righteousness* (Ps. 118) and of various poems, has also preserved the traditional intonation for the "obligatory" prayers of the ceremony, including those for Psalms 32 and 95 (*Lekhu nerannenah*).

The psalmodic pattern may be overlaid by non-psalmodic elements as an effect of liturgical function. In the Ashkenazi *Lekhu nerannenah*, for example, the original psalmody seems to have been stretched by successive generations of *ḥazzanim* toward the *nusaḥ* of the "Reception of the Sabbath" (cf. Idelsohn, Melodien 8, no. 27, and A. Baer, *Ba'al T'fillah*, no. 320). "If…a psalm was used as an introduction to or interlude between prayers in a certain mode, that mode was, as a rule, transferred also to the Psalms – a procedure called by the precentors *me-inyana* [מעניינא – "of the relevant subject," a talmudic technical term]" (Idelsohn, Music, p. 60). The all-important end clause in the Ashkenazi **nusaḥ* intonation is truly psalmodic and it has been maintained that the *nusaḥ* system itself developed out of psalmody. Another instance of *me-inyana* is the singing of Psalms 92 and 93 in Yemen at the onset of the Sabbath, in the intonation of the study of the Mishnah, since the mishnaic passage *Ba-Meh Madlikin* is read there, as in many other communities, immediately preceding, as a kind of bridge between the afternoon and evening prayer.

Psalmodic melodies are also used for texts which are not psalms, as in the **Seliḥot* (of all communities) and in various prayers for Rosh Ha-Shanah and the Day of Atonement (among the Ashkenazim). Some of these may be better classified as a litany, which is an even simpler form than psalmody but closely related to it. In any case this again supports the contention of the relationship between prayer and psalmody.

Although the psalms are furnished with accents in the masoretic texts, the question, whether they were ever, or still are, sung according to the accents is still moot. Even the 17th-century Italian notation of accent motives for Psalms and the claims of present-day informants that they sing according to the accents are not conclusive. Most scholars think that the system of the accents is too sophisticated to be followed precisely or that there was a "lost art" of psalm cantillation. It may even be that some present-day practices of following the accents approximately are a back-formation phenomenon: since the accents were there, it was felt that they had to be obeyed somehow, and after many generations some characteristic motives became attached to the accent-signs in coexistence with the overall psalmodic line. Some modifications, such as those which occur in *Mizmor Shir le-Yom ha-Shabbat* (Ps. 92) in many communities, can only be explained by the influence of the accents.

Performance

In traditional group singing the psalm is sung in unison (or, as in Yemen, in the *organum*-like folk polyphony of that community). In most non-Ashkenazi communities the text is "metricized" in a precisely proportioned succession of the short and long syllables, as done with almost all prose or prose-like liturgical texts when sung by the congregation. As the oldest sources attest and contemporary practices still show, the psalms are also frequently sung in various forms of alternation: solo and group (responsorial psalmody), alternating or succeeding soloists, group against group (antiphonal psalmody), with response and refrain verses and intercalations of Hallelujah between the verses or even after each half clause (see *Music, ex. 4). The point of alternation is not always at the end of the verse or after each half clause: often the performers alternate only at the half-clause point, apparently disregarding the primary verse divisions. In some cases a singer will end his part with the word bearing a masoretic accent of major divisive status inside the verse (not the *etnaḥta* at the half clause). For the waving of the *lulav* (palm branch) on *Sukkot, verses of Psalm 118 are sung to an extended melody to allow for the waving in six directions (cf. Suk. 37b; A. Baer, *Ba'al T'fillah*, no. 814ff., for the Western and Eastern Ashkenazi melodies; and ex. 4 a melody from Djerba).

Example 4. End of Ps. 117 and beginning of Ps. 118, as sung during the waving of the palm branches on Hoshana Rabba, Djerba tradition. Recorded at moshav Berekhyah, 1955, by A. Herzog. Parallel strict and simple transcription. From A. Herzog, Renanot, *10, 1963, p. 8.*

Some communities are particularly rich in psalm melodies: Yemen, Morocco, Tunisia, Cochin, Syria, Turkey, Italy, and the "Portuguese communities" of Western Europe. In Yemen groups of psalms are sung most artistically in the prayer meetings called *ashmorot* (at dawn on the Sabbath), very similar to the singing of hymns by the Near Eastern communities in the **bakkashot*. The Egyptian repertoire is less varied, but many of the melodies are extremely florid and linked to the **maqāma* system; it is a moot point whether the practice is rooted in the same old tradition from which Christianity derived its extended "Jubilus" (the wordless prolongation of Hallelujah) or acquired more recently from Arabic art song. Among the Ashkenazi communities hardly any true psalmodies have survived, and the home rituals for the singing of the psalms have absorbed many folk tunes from the surrounding cultures. In the realm of the ḥasidic *niggun*, psalm verses furnish some of the texts, with no particular distinction as to the choice of melody (cf. the well-known "neo-ḥasidic" *Yismeḥu ha-Shamayim*).

In the "ordered *ḥazzanut*" of the 19th century in Western Europe, the psalms were set to music in a manner not different from the style of the prayers and often as showpieces for the choir, somewhat in the manner of the Anglican anthem. In Reform Judaism where the text was paraphrased as a rhymed poem in Western meters, the result followed the precedents of the Protestant chorale and even utilized its tunes. At this stage the survey of the traditions of the musical rendition of the Psalms passes into the history of musical composition, discussed under Psalms in the arts (see above).

[Avigdor Herzog]

BIBLIOGRAPHY: GENERAL: Kaufmann Y., Toledot, 2 (1947), 200–6, 646–727; A.R. Johnson, in: H.H. Rowley (ed.), *The Old Testament and Modern Study* (1951), 162–209; S. Mowinckel, in: VT, 5 (1955), 13–33; M.H. (Z.) Segal, *Mevo ha-Mikra*, 4 (1955), 517–85; A.S. Kapelrud, in: *Annual of the Swedish Theological Institute*, 4 (1965), 74–90; H.H. Rowley, *Worship in Ancient Israel* (1967); N.M. Sarna, in: M. Buttenwieser, *The Psalms* (1969), xiii–xxxviii. TITLE: B. Jacob, in: ZAW, 16 (1896), 162–3. PLACE IN CANON: C.D. Ginsburg, *Introduction to the Massoretico-Critical Edition of the Hebrew Bible* (1966), 1–8. NUMBER OF PSALMS: Schirmann, Sefarad, 1 (1954), 92, 101; I. Joel, in: KS, 38 (1962), 125; J. Heinemann, in: *Tarbiz*, 33 (1963/64), 362–8; C.D. Ginsburg, *Introduction…* (1966), 18, 777. VERSE DIVISION: S.D. Luzzatto, *Peninei Shadal* (1888), 281–2; Lewin, Oẓar, 9 (1939), 84; P.W. Skehar, in: VTS, 5 (1957), 153–5. DIVISION INTO BOOKS: I. Abrahams, in: JQR, 16 (1903–04), 579; H. St. J. Thackeray, *The Septuagint and Jewish Worship* (1921); A. Hurwitz, *The Identification of Post-Exilic Psalms by Means of Linguistic Criteria* (1966); J.A. Sanders, *The Psalms Scroll of Qumran Cave 11 (11QPsa)* (1965); idem, *The Dead Sea Psalms Scroll* (1967). COMPOSITION OF THE PSALTER: R.G. Boling, in: JSS, 5 (1960), 221–55; W.F. Albright, *Yahweh and the Gods of Canaan* (1968), 31–33. DATE OF THE PSALTER: C.L. Feinberg, in: *Bibliotheca Sacra*, 104 (1947), 426–40; M. Tsevat, *A Study of the Language of the Biblical Psalms* (1955); S. Holm-Nielson, *Studia Theologia*, 14 (1960), 1–53. ASCRIPTION TO DAVID: Albright, Arch Rel, 121–5. TYPES OF PSALMS: H. Gunkel and J. Begrich, *Einleitung in die Psalmen* (1933); S. Mowinckel, *The Psalms in Israel's Worship*, 1–2 (1962); C. Westerman, *The Praise of God in the Psalms* (1965). PSALMS AND THE CULT: H.L. Ginsberg, in: BASOR, 72 (1938), 13–15; idem, in: *L. Ginzberg Jubilee Volume* (1945), 159–71; W.F. Albright, in: *A. Marx Jubilee Volume* (1950), 66; Albright, Arch Rel, 121–5; A. Weiser, *The Psalms* (1959), 23–35; H.J. Kraus, *Worship in Israel* (1966); Y. Aharoni, in: BA, 31 (1968), 11; idem, in: IEJ, 17 (1967), 272; J. Liver, *Perakim be-Toledot ha-Kehunnah…* (1968). SUPERSCRIPTION AND TECHNICAL TERMINOLOGY: B. Jacobs, in: ZAW, 16 (1896), 129–82; R.B.Y. Scott, in: *Bulletin of the Canadian Society of Biblical Literature*, 5 (1939), 17–24; R. Gyllenberg, in: ZAW, 58 (1940–41), 153–6; H.G. May, in: AJSL, 58 (1941), 70–83; H.L. Ginsberg, in: *L. Ginzberg Jubilee Volume* (1945), 169–71; N.H. Snaith, in: VT, 2 (1952), 43–56; A. Guilding, in: JTS, 3 (1952), 41–55; H.D. Preuss, in: ZAW, 71 (1959), 44–54; W. Bloemendaal, *The Headings of the Psalms in the East Syrian Church* (1960); S. Mowinckel, *The Psalms in Israel's Worship*, 2 (1962), 207–17; J.J. Glueck, in: *Studies on the Psalms* (1963), 30–39; L. Deleket, in: ZAW, 76 (1964), 280–97; S.E. Loewenstamm, in: VT, 19 (1969), 464–70; J. Blau and J.C. Greenfield, in: BASOR, 200 (1970), 11–12. IN THE TALMUD AND MIDRASH: L. Rabinowitz, in: JQR, 26 (1935/36), 350–68; idem, in: HJ, 6 (1944), 109–22; K. Kohler, *Studies, Addresses and Personal Papers* (1931). MUSICAL RENDITION IN JEWISH TRADITION: Sendrey, Music, nos. 982–1058, 1079–1297, 6760–6912; Idelsohn, Music, 58–64; E. Gerson-Kiwi, in: *Festschrift Bruno Stablein* (1967), 64–73; Adler, Prat Mus, 36, 48, 49, 256; A. Herzog, in: M. Smoira (ed.), *Yesodot Mizraḥiyyim u-Ma'araviyyim ba-Musikah be-Yisrael* (1968), 27–34; E. Werner, in: MGWJ, 45 (1937), 319–416; idem, in: HUCA, 15 (1940), 335–66; idem, in: *Review of Religion*, 7 (1943), 339–52; H. Avenary, in: *Tatzlil*, 5 (1965), 73–78; idem, in: *Musica Disciplina*, 7 (1953), 1–13; A. Herzog and A. Hajdu, in: *Yuval*, 1 (1968), 194–203; L. Levi, in: *Scritti sul' Ebraismo in memoria di Guido Bedarida* (1966), 105–36; *Dukhan*, 5 (1954), papers of conference devoted to Psalms. **ADD. BIBLIOG-**

RAPHY: H.L. Ginsberg, in: ErIsr, 9 (1969), 45–50; P. Craigie, *Psalms 1–50* (Word; 1983); L. Allen, *Psalms 101–150* (Word; 1983); J. Kugel, in: A. Green (ed.), *Jewish Spirituality from the Bible through the Middle Ages* (1986), 113–42; M. Tate, *Psalms 51–100* (Word; 1990); J. Limburg, in: ABD, 5:522–36; P. Miller, Jr., *They Cried to the Lord: The Form and Theology of Biblical Prayer* (1994); N. Sarna, *On the Book of Psalms* (1995); D. Howard, Jr., in: D. Baker and B. Arnold, *The Face of the Old Testament: A Survey of Contemporary Approaches* (1999), 329–68; R. Starbuck, *Court Oracles in the Psalms: The So-Called Royal Psalms in the Ancient Near East Context* (1999); idem, in: B. Batto and K. Roberts (ed.), *David and Zion ... Studies J.J.M. Roberts* (2004), 247–65; A. Greenstein, in: *EncRel*, 11 (2005), 7460–66 (incl. bibl.).

PSANTIR, JACOB (1820–1902), historian of Romanian Jewry. Born in Botosani, Romania, Psantir was orphaned in childhood and received no formal education apart from a few years in a Jassy *talmud torah*. He earned a meager living in a variety of occupations, including that of singer in a gypsy band. In this way he traveled throughout Romania and several other Balkan countries, and his great desire for knowledge coupled with an acute sense of observation enabled him to fill the gaps in his education. In his wanderings Psantir learned about the life of Jewish communities at first hand, investigating their history, their organization, their means of livelihood, and their relations with their non-Jewish neighbors. He supplemented his findings from communal and municipal archives and by deciphering inscriptions on gravestones. The results of his research are contained in two books written in Hebrew, *Divrei ha-Yamim le-Arẓot Rumanyah* ("Chronicles of the Lands of Romania," 1871) and *Korot ha-Yehudim be-Rumenyen* ("History of the Jews in Romania," 1873), and the Yiddish *Sefer Zikhroynes* ("Memoirs," 1875).

Although Psantir's work lacks any scientific discipline, being the product of a self-taught writer whose imagination exceeds his critical faculty, it has important historical value because the sources completely disappeared after the Nazi Holocaust.

BIBLIOGRAPHY: M.A. Halevi, in: YIVOA, 7 (1952), 204–11.

[Isac Beercovici]

°**PSEUDO-LONGINUS**, name ascribed to the author of the Greek treatise "On the Sublime." The oldest manuscript of the treatise ascribes it to Dionysius Longinus. The only Longinus known, however, was named Cassius not Dionysius, and the opening of this manuscript notes the author as "Dionysius or Longinus." The work must therefore be regarded as of uncertain date and authorship. The book tries to answer the question: "What are the characteristics of great writing?" In 9.9, the author cites Genesis as an example of greatness of thought: "Similarly, the lawgiver of the Jews, no ordinary man – for he understood and expressed God's power in accordance with its worth [cf. Jos., Ant. 1:15 for similarity of language] – writes at the beginning of his Laws: 'God said' – what? – 'Let there be light,' and there was light; 'let there be land,' and there was land." The fact that Longinus gives only the substance of the biblical passage suggests an intermediate source, and since Longinus' treatise was written explicitly in answer to a work of *Caecilius of Calacte, who was apparently a Jew, the latter may well be the source. Another possible source is *Philo, whose language and sentiments resemble those of "Longinus" in chapter 44.

PSEUDO-PHOCYLIDES, a Hellenistic Jewish didactic poet, author of 230 hexameters falsely ascribed to the sixth-century B.C.E. Greek lyric poet Phocylides. The few fragments of Phocylides that have survived suggest a reputation for moral wisdom which Pseudo-Phocylides seems to have drawn upon to lend authority to his own moral apothegms. The poem of Pseudo-Phocylides was apparently considered an authentic work of the Greek poet from the time of its earliest citation in Stobaeus (fifth century C.E.). In the later Byzantine Empire this poem became quite popular and it was widely distributed as a school textbook in the period of the Reformation. There are many Byzantine manuscripts; the first printed edition is of 1495; there are many 16th-century translations and reprints. In 1856 Jacob *Bernays wrote a definitive study on the subject demonstrating that the author was Jewish and dependent on the Bible. Since then others have argued for Christian elements in the poem (A. Harnack), pagan elements (A. Ludwich, W. Kroll), and that the work is by a convert to Judaism (M. Roissbroich).

The contents are primarily ethical maxims of such general content that they might easily be taken to be the work of a non-Jew. Their Jewishness can be recognized occasionally as, for example, in the injunction to let the mother bird escape and keep only the young when a nest is taken (84ff.; cf. Deut. 22:6ff.) or the prohibition against eating the flesh of an animal killed by a beast of prey (147ff., cf. Ex. 22:30 and 139, cf. Deut. 14:21). Most of the poem, however, preaches a universal moral code rather than a particular theology or ceremonial law. Even though many parallels can be made between passages in Pseudo-Phocylides and the Pentateuch, the spirit of the poem as well as some of its phraseology is more akin to the wisdom literature in the Bible and the Apocrypha, especially the Apocryphal books of *Ben Sira* and *Wisdom of Solomon*.

Absent from the poem is any specific attack on idolatry, which Bernays ascribes to the cowardice or indifference of the author. There is also little or nothing which can be considered as anti-Christian, thus placing it in the period before the anti-Christian polemics, i.e., before 70 C.E., if it is assumed that the author was a Jew. Some verses (103ff.) speak of physical resurrection and say that "those who rise up again afterward become gods." This is taken to be a Christian reference (Harnack), or a pagan reference (Kroll). Little else can be distinctly identified with any specific religious view. There are similarities between the moral admonitions of Pseudo-Phocylides and a moral manual of the early Church known as the *Didaché*. Rendel Harris, in his edition of the *Didaché* (1887, p. 46), suggests the possibility that both Pseudo-Phocylides and the *Didaché* go back to an earlier Jewish manual of morality. Part of Pseudo-Phocylides (5–79) was excerpted, with few variants and omissions, and incorporated into the *Sibylline Oracles

(2:56–148). Since the text is sometimes dependent on the Septuagint, the dating of the work would be in the second or first century B.C.E. (or, if Christian, in the first century C.E.). The metrics and the poetry are not very inspiring and the corruption of the text presents many problems. An exaggerated importance has been attached to the work.

BIBLIOGRAPHY: T. Bergk (ed.) *Poetae Lyrici Graeci*, 2 (1882[4]), 74–109 (critical edition of the Greek text); J. Bernays, *Ueber das Phokylideische Gedicht* (1856); M. Roissbroich, *De Pseudophocylideis* (1910); Schuerer, Gesch, 3 (1909[4]), 617–22; W. Kroll, in: Pauly-Wissowa, 39 (1941), 506–10; *Anglican Theological Review*, 14 (1932), 222–8 (translation by B.S. Easton).

[Marshall S. Hurwitz]

°**PSEUDO-SCYLAX** (fl. c. 350 B.C.E.), pseudonym of the Greek author of a seafarers' manual (*Periplus*), which includes a description of the Mediterranean and Black Sea coastlines. The work, entitled "Periplus of the sea of inhabited Europe, of Asia, and of Libya," refers to Scylax of Caryanda, a contemporary of Darius I (521–485 B.C.E.). However, the work was composed about the middle of the fourth century B.C.E. It has survived in almost complete form. The author charts, inter alia, the coastal cities of Palestine and Syria, such as Joppa (Jaffa), Doris (Dora), and Ascalon (Ashkelon). The latter two are described, respectively, as a city of the Sidonians and as a royal city of the Tyrians. He also mentions a mountain and temple of Zeus, which seems to refer to Mt. Carmel. He describes the boundaries of "Coele-Syria" as extending from Ascalon to the river Thapsacus, and states the distance between them.

BIBLIOGRAPHY: C. Mueller, *Geographi Graeci Minores*, 1 (1855): A. Baschmakoff, *La Synthèse des Périples Pontiques* (1948), text and French translation.

[Solomon Rappaport]

PSYCHIATRY.

The Biblical Period

References to states of mental disturbance are frequently found in the Bible. Deuteronomy 28:28, 34 views madness as punishment for disobeying the commandments. The tragedy of Saul's last years is ascribed to an evil spirit that troubled Saul when the Lord departed from him. Saul's paranoidal fears and jealousy of David could not be assuaged by David's attempts to help and reassure him by playing the harp (I Sam. 16:14–23; 18:10ff.; 19:9–10). Later, David himself, in order to escape from Achish, simulated insanity, "scribbling on the doors of the gate and letting his spittle fall upon his beard" (21:11–16). The Bible does not speak of treatment of mental illness or recognize insanity as illness. On the contrary, it was enjoined that the person who was seen to be possessed by spirits should be stoned to death (Lev. 20:27); yet the Bible abounds in counsel for mental health, usually with an ethical intention. In Proverbs it is held that understanding is "a wellspring of life" (16:22) and that "a merry heart doeth good like medicine" (17:22).

In the Talmud

In the Talmud mention of mental illness is generally of a legal nature. The episodic nature of mental illness is taken into account on several occasions and there are references to periods when the person is of lucid or of unsound mind. There are also suggestions of a possible classification of mental illness such as a mental defect, confusion, acute and cyclical psychoses, and those which result from physical illness. The Talmud recognizes mental illness and is chary of accepting popular definitions such as: "he who goes out alone at night, who sleeps in the cemetery and tears his clothes" (Tosef., Ter. 1:3, and cf. Ḥag 3b). The word *shoteh* which contains the idea of walking to and fro without purpose is used to describe the mentally ill. The legal and social implications of insanity are frequently referred to in the Talmud. The mentally ill are not responsible for the damage they cause and those who injure them must bear the responsibility; the insane are not responsible for the shame they cause. They may not marry but, contrary to Greek concepts, in periods of lucidity the individual is considered healthy and capable from every other point of view. The Talmud sets very little store by magical medicines and cures for mental illness which were then current among the nations and were frequently found among Jews in the Middle Ages. It prefers to admit frankly the lack of effective treatment.

The Medieval Period

In the Middle Ages Jewish physicians no less than others were dependent on the humoral theories of Greek and Roman medicine (Hippocrates and Galen). Some Jewish physicians made original discoveries and contributions. *Asaph, the earliest Jewish physician known by name who lived apparently in the sixth or seventh century, felt that the heart is the seat of the soul and vital spirit. In his work, *The Book of Medicines*, he refers to the disturbed behavior of epileptics and to psychosis–phreneticus. Shabbetai *Donnolo, who lived in the tenth century, wrote in one of his medical books an analysis of the psychiatric conditions of melancholia and of nightmare. His description of mania contains a complex of conditions and undoubtedly included schizophrenia. Donnolo's psychiatric views while avoiding the magical element are derivative from the humoral theory of the Greeks. Nevertheless, though some of his explanations could be termed psychological his treatment was almost purely medicinal.

*Maimonides in the 12th century added to the genius of exegetical and philosophic work the brilliant practice of medicine and the exposition of it. His work *Pirkei Moshe* ("The Aphorisms of Moses") distinguishes clearly between motor and sensory nerves and voluntary and automatic activity. This book also deals with the anatomy of the brain and organic conditions such as epilepsy, weakness, contractions, and tremor. Maimonides' view of the influence of emotion on bodily function, in producing illness and retarding cure, was unique in his time. He was thus the father of psychosomatic medicine. In *Hanhagat ha-Beri'ut* ("The Regimen of Health") he sets out these views and instructions for attention to and the mitigation of the emotional state of the patient. He does, however, recognize the limitations of psychiatric care. *Sefer ha-Nimẓa*, which deals with mental illness, is questionably attributed to him. The "*Sefer Madda*" in Maimonides' Code sets out clearly his views on the promotion of individual mental health. His orientation to it is, of course, profoundly ethical, yet he relates mental health no less to the pragmatic functioning of the body and its appetites and effects. In essence this view recommends the middle road between indulgence and asceticism. He abjures all magical procedures.

The medieval flowering of Jewish medicine was followed by a prolonged period of folk medicine practiced by peripatetic healers. They acquired a reputation for healing as wonder-workers through incantations, *amulets, etc. They treated mental patients as if they were afflicted by spirits, devils, and impure influences. The founder of the ḥasidic movement *Israel ben Eliezer, in the 18th century, acquired his medical reputation by a rapid cure of a mental case. After him there ensued a further period of decadence in which the healers encouraged and exploited superstition.

The Modern Period

The reconstruction of psychiatry as a moral practice and a rational system after medieval times was accomplished in Europe only after a prolonged struggle against the demonological beliefs of the Church and the people. Phillipe Pinel's work in France after the Revolution was a turning point. The 19th century saw the progressive definition and classification of mental illness, of the psychoses and the neuroses, and the humanization of treatment in hospital. The first Jewish medical psychologist to join this European movement was Cesare *Lombroso who in 1864 published his *Genius and Insanity*. He described the delinquent personality carefully and related it to anatomical phenomena and genetic causes rather than moral factors. He thus became a pioneer in human and rational corrective measures for criminal behavior. His work also contributed much to the promotion of scientific thought and methods in psychiatry. Hippolyte *Bernheim's name is linked with the investigation of the neuroses which took precedence in the last two decades of the century. Although a careful observer, his interest was not in theory but in the cure of the patient. He was the first psychologist to advocate the principle of the "irresistible impulse" in legal medicine.

In 1889 Sigmund *Freud was a spectator of Bernheim's astonishing experiments in the treatment by hypnosis of mental hospital patients. Freud decided to use hypnosis in the treatment of neurotic patients and was associated in this task with Josef *Breuer, a practitioner in Vienna. In 1895 their epoch-making book, *Studien ueber Hysterie*, appeared. This work embodied the discovery of the unconscious. Freud soon found that he could dispense with hypnosis by letting the patient talk at random and obtained better therapeutic results. This new method Freud called free association. With the publication in 1900 of his *Interpretation of Dreams*, Freud invaded the field of normal psychology, and the borderland between abnormal and normal psychology began to disappear. Freud's theory and technique of psychoanalysis, after much resistance, not only revolutionized psychiatric therapy but was the final and decisive medium in which education, child care, and the treatment of criminals was humanized and made rational.

Alfred *Adler challenged the validity of Freud's concepts of basic sexual drives and repression as prerequisites for neurotic symptom formation. In 1912 he coined the term "individual psychology." He reduced the significance of childhood sexual factors to a minimum. For the school which developed around Adler, neurosis stems from childhood experience of over-protection or neglect or a mixture of both. This leads to a neurotic striving for superiority. His intuitive thinking may have been confirmed by thinkers subsequently who have defined the interaction between the goals of the individual and his social group and environment. Sandor *Ferenczi made a singular contribution to psychoanalysis which has been considered second only to that of Freud with whom he was associated. He attempted to correlate biological and psychological phenomena in his scientific method – bioanalysis. Karl *Abraham, one of the founders of psychoanalysis, contributed greatly through his researches to the clinical understanding of the neuroses and the psychoses especially of manic-depressive insanity. A.A. *Brill was responsible for the introduction of psychoanalysis into the United States and into the practice of psychiatry there. Max *Eitingon founded the first psychoanalytic training institute and polyclinic in Berlin in 1920. This became the model for all psychoanalytic training. He settled in Palestine in 1933 where he founded the psychoanalytic society and institute. Freud's inner circle or "Committee" by 1919 comprised Ferenczi, Abraham, Eitingon, Otto *Rank, Hans *Sachs, and the only non-Jew among them, Ernest Jones. Jones has commented on the effect of Freud's Jewishness on the evolution of his ideas and work; he attributed the firmness with which Freud maintained his convictions, undeterred by the prevailing opposition to them, to the "inherited" capacity of Jews to stand their ground in the face of opposition and hostility. That also held true for his mostly Jewish followers. Freud believed that the opposition to the inevitably startling discoveries of psychoanalysis was considerably aggravated by antisemitism. Early signs of antisemitism appeared in the Swiss analytic group. Freud felt that it was easier for Abraham to follow his thought than for Jung, because Jung as a Christian and the son of a pastor could only find his way to Freud through great inner resistance. Hans Sachs joined Freud in 1909. He abandoned law for the practice of psychoanalysis. Sachs was an editor and trained analyst whose main work was in the application of psychoanalysis to understanding the creative personality.

There were several other Jewish psychiatrists and lay psychoanalysts associated with the earlier phases of the development of psychoanalysis. Among them was Paul *Federn who met Freud in 1902 and was the fourth physician to become an analyst. Theodor *Reik was associated with Freud from 1910. Probably his major theoretical contribution was in the field of masochism. Helene *Deutsch as a psychiatrist and analyst made the pioneer exploration of the emotional life of women and constructed a comprehensive psychology of their life cycle. Melanie *Klein and Anna *Freud, both lay analysts, were originators of the psychoanalytical treatment of children, which they carried from the Continent to England.

In the United States, Erik Homberger *Erikson developed concepts of the development of the identity of the individual and his effort to maintain its continuity while seeking solidarity with group ideals and group identity. Margaret *Mahler added to the understanding of normal development in earliest infancy, describing the separation process from the mother. Perhaps the greatest contribution to child psychiatry was made in the United States by Leo *Kanner who, in 1943, first described and named the infantile psychosis, "early infantile autism." Lauretta *Bender believed that genetic factors determine the infants' vulnerability to a schizophrenic type of disorder and further related the onset of the psychosis to a biological crisis. Her visual Motor Gestalt Test was widely used to reveal organically based problems. Moritz *Tramer, the Swiss child psychiatrist, maintained that childhood schizophrenia exists as a hereditary entity in childhood and runs its course into the adult form. The psychoanalyst Paul *Schilder's dynamic concept of the "body image" contributed much to psychological thinking in the study of schizophrenia, especially in children. Beata Rank, while stressing the hereditary and constitutional factors in atypical emotional development, in therapy treated the early parent-child relationship. Rene *Spitz, a psychoanalyst, made important contributions in his studies of emotionally deprived infants and those separated from their mothers.

Many Jewish psychoanalysts, psychiatrists, and psychologists have been involved in the further development of child psychiatry and therapy especially in the United States. These include Phyllis *Greenacre, Herman *Nunberg, Ruth Eissler, Edith Buxbaum (c. 1895–1982), Bertha Bornstein (c. 1890–), Marianne R. Kris, William Goldfarb (1915–1995), David Levy (1892–1977), Stella Chess (1914–), Augusta Alpert, S.R. *Slavson, Peter B. Neubauer (1913–), Reginald Lourie, Fritz *Redl, and Martin Deutsch (1923–).

The effect of analytic theory and practice on psychiatry in the United States received an historic impulse after the Nazi accession and the transplantation of the psychoanalytic centers and practitioners from Europe. Franz *Alexander from Berlin had already added much to ego psychology and that of the criminal before developing, in his Chicago School, concepts of psychosomatic medicine and modifications of psychoanalytic treatment methods. Sander *Rado, who had studied drug addiction and developed "ego analysis" in New York, developed his modifications of it in "adaptational psychodynamics." Heinz *Hartman laid the foundations for the theoretical understanding of the interaction of the ego with personal, biological, and social reality. With Ernst *Kris and Rudolph *Loewenstein he explored the ways in which cultural differences produced variations of behavior. Géza *Roheim applied psychoanalytic principles to anthropological research. Otto *Fenichel is remembered as a teacher of psychoanalysis. Ernst Simmel was noted for his contribution on war neuroses and on antisemitism. Wilhelm *Reich made a basic contribution in his analysis of character before his defection from psychoanalysis. Sander Lorand is noted for his teaching in technique. Kurt *Lewin made a notable contribution to the understanding of personality within its psychological environment; Erich *Fromm to the appreciation of the passions and behavior of men as determined by the creativity and frustrations of society; Kurt *Goldstein's studies have applied principles of perception and reaction of Gestalt psychology.

Among the U.S. psychiatrists and others who have contributed much to psychiatry the following should be mentioned here: F.J. Kallmann, for his genetic studies; Jules *Masserman, for his "biodynamic" methods; David *Rapaport, in his psychological researches; Melitta Schmideberg, for her treatment of major criminals; Manfred *Sakel who discovered insulin therapy; Roy *Grinker, for his integrative approach; and Nathan *Ackerman, for his family therapy. Other notable practitioners, teachers, and researchers were Eduardo Weiss, Milton Greenblatt (1914–), Paul Lemkau (1909–), Felix *Deutsch, Greta L. Bibring (1899–1977), Melvin Sabshin (1925–), Lewis *Wolberg, Theresa *Benedek, Lawrence S. Kubie (1896–1973), Leon Salzman (1915–), David A. Hamburger (1925–), David Shakow (1901–1981), Abraham *Kardiner, Frieda *Fromm-Reichman, Theodore Lidz (1910–2001), Thomas *Szasz, Samuel Beck (1896–), Bruno *Bettelheim, David Wechsler (1896–1981), J.S. Kasanin (1897–1946), Samuel Ritvo, Ralph Greenson (1911–1979), Rudolf Ekstein (1912–2005), Milton Rosenbaum (1910–2003), Eugen Brody (1921–), Eric D. Wittkower (1899–1983), Iago Galdston (1895–), M. Ralph Kaufman (1900–1977), Howard P. Rome (1910–1992), J.R. Linton (1899–), Frederick Redlich (1910–2004), and J.L. *Moreno who developed psychodrama.

Social scientists who contributed to mental health were Marvin and Morris *Opler, Melford Spiro (1920–), Leo Srole (1908–1993), Morris and Charleen Schwartz, Bert Kaplan (1919–), and Daniel Lerner (1917–1980).

In England the psychoanalytic approach was represented by Michael *Balint, Kate *Friedlander, Willie *Hoffer, Susan *Isaacs, August Bonnard, Joseph J. Sandler (1927–), W.G. Joffe, and Liselotte Frankl. Erwin Stengel (1902–1973) made remarkable contributions on suicide and M.D. *Eder, an early member of the movement, was also a devoted Zionist. Jews in psychiatry are ably represented by Sir Aubrey *Lewis, W. Mayer-Gross, Emanuel *Miller (1894–1970), and H.J. Eysenck (1916–1997), who represents the school of "behavior therapy" and psychology. In South Africa, Wulf Sachs (1893–1949) pioneered psychoanalysis and analyzed the first African subject. In France, Eugene *Minkowski was a pioneer in psychiatry and existentialist psychotherapy. In the Soviet Union L.M. Rozenshteyn developed preventive methods in neuropsychiatry. M.O. Gurevich (1906–) shared the writing of a well-known textbook of psychiatry. The noted Soviet psychiatrist T.I. Yudin wrote an outline of the history of Russian psychiatry. O.B. Feltsman tried to popularize psychoanalysis through a psychotherapy journal and Moshe Woolf attempted this through his activities. The psychologist L. Vygotski and his coworker Luria contributed fundamentally to the understanding of disturbed thought processes. Psychoanalysis was brought to Palestine by Eitingon Moshe Woolf and Ilya Shalitd. Its influence was extended into the practice of psychiatry by Henri Winnik, Ruth Jaffe, Eric Gumbel (1908–), and Shmuel Nagler (1914–). The establishment of the State of Israel led to a rapid expansion of psychiatric facilities, initially in the army and later in communities. Notable contributions were made in this respect and in others by Yeshayahu Baumatz (1897–1964), Erich *Neumann, Shmuel Golan (1901–1966), Janus Schossberger (1914–), Shlomo Kulcar (1901–), Abraham Weinberg (1891–1972), Julius Zellermayer (1910–), F.S. *Rothschild, Franz Bruell (1904–), Ludwig Tramer (1923–), Miriam Gay (1917–), Phyllis Palgi (1917–), and Nehama Barzilai (1918–).

The impact of Jews in modern Western psychiatry probably relates to their personal analytic gifts fostered by their own historic culture. Two events of the 19th century contributed to their entry into psychiatry in the 20th century: the political emancipation of Jews in Europe which permitted their entry into the universities and into the valued profession of medicine in which they had been involved in medieval times; and the freeing of psychiatry from its cloak of irrationality and prejudice, speeded by the discoveries of Freud. Ernest Jones has remarked that historically psychoanalysis was not a particularly Jewish movement in England. Neither psychoanalysis nor psychiatry in England are so even today. Psychoanalysis was not essentially attractive to Jews in the United States until the displacement to the U.S. of the largely Jewish Viennese and German schools and their attraction of Jews there to the profession. In psychiatry in Western countries, Jews were on the whole under-represented but they are especially today well represented in the U.S.

BIBLIOGRAPHY: J.M. Leibowitz, in: *Harofe Haivri*, 1 (1961), 167–75; D. Margalit, *Ḥakhmei Yisrael ke-Rofe'im* (1962); G. Zilboorg, *History of Medical Psychology* (1941), 484–570.

[Louis Miller]

PSYCHOLOGY, the science of the mind or of mental phenomena and activities.

Psychological Concepts in the Bible

"Psychology has a long past, but only a short history" (H. Ebbinghaus, *Abriss der Psychologie*, 1908). Nowhere is this aphorism better exemplified than in the many centuries during which Jewish physicians and thinkers dealt with the problems of behavior and behavior disorders. Many current notions on classification and therapy were foreshadowed in biblical and talmudic literature, and Jewish philosophers wrestled with the same psychological concepts that still occupy attention today.

The Jewish art of healing always emphasized mental as well as physical health. Behavior disorders were well known to the early Hebrews, who were noteworthy for their observance of the laws of preventive medicine and hygiene. From the beginning Jewish monotheism excluded all kinds of magic practices. The Bible opposed occult healing as "Amorite customs" and prescribed as therapy for all mental and physical ills prayer to "God your healer" (Ex. 15:26) and the use of medicine (Ex. 21:19; I Kings 17:21; II Kings 4:32–35; Ezek. 30:21).

Cases of mental disorder described in the Bible include King Saul's paranoia, depression, and epileptic seizures, treated by music therapy, and Nebuchadnezzar's lycanthropy. Various types of insanity are cited in the Pentateuch, such as phobia and panic (Lev. 26:17).

Post-Biblical and Talmudic Period

The talmudic description of *shoteh* ("the mentally insane") approaches the symptomatology of several psychoses (Ḥag. 2b; Sanh. 65b; Nid. 17a). The rabbis saw in the act of transgression a *ru'aḥ shetut* ("a mental deviation," Sot. 3a). Other psychological conditions mentioned are: epilepsy (Yev. 64b); hysteria (Hag. 3a); phobias (Git. 70a); hereditary traits (Bek. 8a; Yev. 64b) versus environment (Suk. 56b), melancholia (Shab. 2:5; see Maim.), defense mechanisms such as repression, sublimation, and projection (Meg. 25b; Kid. 70a), and the concept of catharsis cited in both the Bible (Prov. 12:25) and the Talmud (Sanh. 100b). Talmudic and midrashic literature also discussed ideas related to individual and social behavior, attitudes and values, systems of learning, discipline, and punishment. The need for "group belongingness" in the spirit of Hillel (Avot 2:4) was always stressed, and social acceptance was considered an indicator of divine approval (Avot 3:10). In the realm of education, the Talmud approached the training of children in the light of an awareness of differing learning abilities and the relation of learning to stages of development (Ber. 28a; Kid. 30a; Yoma 27a; Avot 5:12). The Talmud understood and stressed such principles as the need for psychological understanding of the mentally sick, individual differences in personality assessment (Sanh. 38a; ARN[1] 4, 17), and the role of habit formation (Yoma 27a).

*Dreams were regarded as being of divine provenance. In antiquity Jews were famous as "dream interpreters," from Joseph to Daniel, and later the Essenes. The Talmud considers the dream "a sixtieth part of prophecy," that also contained irrelevant material, which "if not interpreted is like a letter which was not opened" (Ber. 55a). Halakhic literature deals with dreams related to oaths and promises, and with anxiety over a "bad dream," for which one is permitted to fast a *ta'anit ḥalom* even on the Sabbath (Shab. 11a). Hebrew "dream books" similar to those of the old Egyptians and Greeks were written by R. Hai.

The nature and function of the *soul, reason, and intellect were treated by Jewish philosophers (under Greek influence) and in the Kabbalah. Judaism believes that the soul and the body comprise the total personality in the divine image and do not represent an essential duality. Although the biblical terms *ru'aḥ*, *nefesh*, and *neshamah* are used synonymously, the rabbis identified the *neshamah* as the human psyche – the higher spiritual substance. In recognizing the conflict between the *yeẓer ha-ra* (the orgiastic drive to sin) and the *yeẓer ha-tov* (the positive inclination to control it), Judaism believes in the *liber arbitrum* (the principle of free choice), whereby man can master the id forces of the destructive *yeẓer ha-ra* (Suk. 52a) for the sake of the emergence of a healthy ego. *Maimonides attributed to the divine soul five different faculties: the nutritive, the sensitive, the imaginative, the emotional, and the rational (*Shemonah Perakim*, 1), the last being the distinctive, discriminating trait of man enabling him to apprehend and create ideas (*Guide* 1:70).

Medieval Period

Medieval Jewish philosophers who wrote on psychology included the eclectic Isaac b. Solomon Israeli who wrote *Sefer ha-Yesodot* ("The Book of Elements"), and discussed the interaction of mind and body and identified epilepsy and melancholia with insanity; Baḥya b. Joseph ibn Paquda; Solomon ibn Gabirol; Joseph ibn Ẓaddik; Judah Halevi; Abraham ibn Daud; and the rationalist Maimonides.

The Jewish share in the spread and development of medieval culture and the sciences is well known. Jewish works in medicine and science became the ultimate source of European medicine in the schools of Salerno and Montpellier. *Asaph's earliest medical work in Hebrew contains the first medical notice of the hereditary character of mental diseases and of psychosomatics. A description of mania was given by the earliest Italian physician Shabbetai Donnolo who was born in 913 C.E. Although ideas about psychological illness were historically attributed to Ḥibat Allah ibn Jumay (c. 1180), who was the Jewish physician to Saladin, Jewish genius in this field really begins with that remarkable physician of mind and body, Moses Maimonides, the most modern in approach of all medieval physicians.

Maimonides advocated research through experiment. He emphasized the high regard a physician should have for the human mind, and stressed the psychosomatic approach in therapy (*Regimen Sanitatis*, 3:13). He also differentiated between constitutional and environmental sources of behavior, urging the mentally sick to avail themselves of a "physician of the mind" (Code, 1:2). He warned against excessive use of tranquilizers or any radical changes in behavior (*Shemonah Perakim*, 1). Quite modern from the psychotherapeutical point of view, Maimonides insisted on complete psychological harmony between couples during sexual union for the benefit of the offspring, and viewed "physical health as a prerequisite to mental health and excellence" (Code, 1:4). In his treatise on the manic-depressive state Maimonides proposed "a strict hygiene of the soul" based on self-discipline and mental calm (*Shemonah Perakim*, 3).

The 13th-century rabbi Gershon b. Solomon of Arles identified the brain as the center of motility and not the heart. He is said to have experimented by removing the heart of a monkey and to have made similar tests on birds. In the same century Shem Tov b. Joseph *Falaquera wrote *Battei Hanhagat Guf ha-Bari ve-ha-Nefesh* and *Sefer ha-Nefesh* dealing with the psychic forces. Philosophical and physiological psychology is treated by *Hillel b. Samuel of Verona in *Tagmulei ha-Nefesh* ("Rewards of the Soul"). Moses Narbonni (11th century) and Nathan b. Joel Falaquera wrote on mental hygiene. Sleep was analyzed by the tenth-century Karaite Jacob al-*Kirkisani, and later by Jedaiah (ha-Penini) Bedersi as "a state when the sense of comprehension comes to a standstill" (*Ketav ha-Da'at*, "Treatise of the Intellect"). The medical works of *Amatus Lusitanus (16th century) and of Jacob *Ẓahalon (17th century) contain ample references to psychological issues.

Responsa Literature

The responsa literature also deals with mental diseases, in connection with matrimonial suits. Among the topics discussed were: melancholia, hysteria, "lunacy," manic-depressive states, megalomania, and character disorders. Isaac Lampronti of Ferrara permitted the desecration of the Sabbath "to prevent a state of emotional anxiety" (Resp. *Naḥalat Shivah*, 83). Music therapy, already used by King Saul and later treated separately by both Saadiah Gaon and Maimonides, is discussed by Ḥ.J.D. *Azulai in the Responsum *Ḥayyim Sha'al* (53), while hypnotism was noted by R. Jacob Ettlinger (d. 1871) in *Binyan Ẓiyyon* (67). Prison psychology was first introduced by the 18th-century Marrano Ribeira Sanchez. Jewish religious law requires strict consideration and good care for the mentally deficient (Sh. Ar., YD 240:10; Sh. Ar., EH 119:6). Even before Pinel's pioneering work in France, Jewish law required communal care for the insane, who "are not held responsible for their actions, yet, injuring them is legally prohibited" (Sh. Ar., ḤM 924:8). Suggestive therapy "to pacify a patient's mind" is permitted by Maimonides and Caro on psychological grounds (Sh. Ar., YD 179:6).

Ḥasidism

The ḥasidic movement of the 18th century again introduced suggestive therapy. Mental disorders were often treated by early *ẓaddikim*. The Ḥasid's identification with his ego-ideal, the *ẓaddik*, a humane, divinely inspired messenger, and the strong belief in this spiritual leader, had phenomenal therapeutic effects. Much psychological insight is to be found in the writings of R. Israel Ba'al Shem Tov, R. Dov Baer, the Maggid of Mezhirech, R. Naḥman of Bratslav, R. Shneur Zalman of Lyady, and their disciples. Ḥasidic teaching with its kabbalistic overtones and its strong emotional appeal and emphasis on the humane and mystical factors is the most psychologically oriented of all the expressions of Judaism.

[Menachem M. Brayer]

Modern Period

Psychology as a science and a profession emerged in the second half of the 19th century. Before the birth of psychology as an independent discipline, there had been a long period during which the subject matter of psychology – mental activity, human nature, and the relationship of mind and body – had been the province of philosophy. Jewish thinkers, ranging from Philo, who attempted to reconcile Greek and Hebrew thought, to the Jewish philosophers in the Arab countries during the Middle Ages, and from *Spinoza and his laws of the mind to *Husserl and his phenomenology, played an important role in this history. But modern, scientific psychology could only come into being when the progress of physiology had provided the biological basis and physics, the methods to make psychology an experimental science.

PSYCHOLOGICAL PIONEERS. The last two decades of the 19th century saw the founding of academic departments of psychology in most major universities in Europe and the United States. As it was difficult for Jews to obtain university appointments because of official and unofficial discrimination, there were relatively few Jewish pioneer psychologists involved in the founding of laboratories. G.F. *Heymans participated in the establishment of a laboratory at Louvain in Belgium in 1891 and went on to found the first Dutch laboratory at Groningen in 1892. Hugo *Muensterberg founded the laboratory at Freiburg in Breisgau, Germany, and was called to Harvard in 1892 to reactivate and take charge of the laboratory there. Joseph *Jastrow received the first doctorate in psychology granted in the United States, at Johns Hopkins University in 1886. Doubly handicapped by the absence of academic departments and the fact that he was Jewish, he circularized the major university departments with his proposals for a psychology curriculum. He was successful in gaining an appointment at the University of Wisconsin, thus founding the second psychological laboratory in the U.S. in 1888. In England, where resistance to the new experimental psychology was especially strong, C.S. *Myers was the first psychologist to be in charge of the laboratory at Cambridge.

THE SCHOOLS. After its initial phase, psychology passed through a period in which various schools advanced their claims to be its true representative. Although most psychologists remained eclectic, it was the schools which provided the chief directions for the development of psychological theory. Joseph Jastrow of Wisconsin was typical of this trend. Otto *Selz was a prominent member of the so-called "Wuerzburg" school which investigated the psychology of thinking processes. The next generation of psychologists rejected many of the theoretical concepts and experimental techniques of the older schools. The European movement, in opposition to the older schools, successfully challenged the earlier elementaristic concepts, substituting an emphasis on relationships and phenomenological methodology. It was influenced by the work of David *Katz and Edgar *Rubin on perception. The founders of the new school, known as Gestalt psychology, were Max *Wertheimer and his associates, including Kurt *Koffka. Other important early members of this school were Kurt *Goldstein and Kurt *Lewin. Gestalt psychology was particularly affected by the fact that most of its founders were Jewish. It was originally primarily a European school, but the forced emigration of most of its important contributors to the U.S. (including Koehler, who was not Jewish, but in sympathy with his Jewish colleagues) with the advent of the Nazis, introduced it into U.S. psychology. There it gained further support through the work of Hans Wallach in perception, Abraham Luchins in problem solving, and Solomon Asch in social psychology. In the 1920s and 1930s the acceptance of psychoanalytic and allied concepts in psychology grew rapidly and the ideas of Sigmund *Freud began to penetrate all facets of psychology, as well as literature, history, and the arts. The development of clinical psychology as a field of study and treatment of personality disorders can be traced primarily to the influence of psychoanalytic thinking.

Contemporary Period

Contemporary psychology has discarded the approach of the schools, with their attempt to bring all of psychology into one harmonious framework. It has substituted, in its systematic part, an emphasis on specific theories and models, and in its work, an emphasis on the investigation of specific problems and their applications. Many of the ideas of the schools have been incorporated into these modern approaches. Jewish psychologists have significantly contributed to the development of these theories. German and Austrian psychology was practically destroyed by the measures adopted by the Nazi regime, many of the displaced psychologists emigrating to the U.S. and making their contribution through teaching and research. Besides the Gestalt psychologists already mentioned, these included such important figures as Charlotte *Buhler, William *Stern, Heinz *Werner, Werner *Wolff, Erich *Fromm, Adhémar Gelb, and Else Frenkel-Brunswik (see Albert Wellek, "The impact of the German immigration on the development of American psychology," in *Journal of the History of the Behavioral Sciences*, 4 (1969), 207–29). A selective sample of prominent Jewish contributors to the development of present-day theoretical positions shows that practically all the psychological specialties are represented. Abram Amsel, Howard Kendler, Joseph Notterman, Leo Postman, William Schoenfeld, and Richard Solomon engaged in the study of learning with human and animal subjects. In the field of perception and sensory functions, leading names include Julian Hochberg, Hershel Leibowitz, Carl Pfaffman, and Irvin Rock. Comparative and physiological psychology are represented by Daniel Lehrman and David Krech, and by Murray Jarvik in the allied field of psychopharmacology. Jerry Hirsch made important contributions to psychogenetics, and Joshua *Fishman and Kurt Salzinger to the study of language. Melvin Marx worked in the field of learning, but is better known for his contribution to systematics. Abraham *Maslow figured prominently in the development of a humanistic psychology. The social field includes Leonard Berkowitz, Morton Deutsch, Leon Festinger, Otto Klineberg, and Daniel *Katz, with George Katona working in the allied area of the relation of economics and psychology.

Saul Rosenzweig, after work in personality and projective testing, became primarily interested in the history of psychology, as did Benjamin Wolman. In the development of projective testing Samuel Beck and Bruno Klopfer became known as experts on the Rorschach test. Personality theory has gained through the work of Milton Rokeach. David Wechsler originated the standard tests of intelligence named after him, while Boris Levinson used intelligence tests to discover the characteristic patterns of the mental development of Jewish children. Joseph Zubin attempted to devise objective tests of abnormal behavior. Jewish psychologists constitute a large segment of the U.S. clinical field. Their various contributions to theory and practice can be exemplified by the work of Perry London, Emanuel Schwartz, and Hans Strupp in clinical psychology, and Morton Seidenfeld in counseling.

The Jewish contribution to all branches of psychology has been very important from the start, and Jews make up a disproportionate number of the profession. The diversity of viewpoints and the distribution of psychologists in the past indicate that psychology has attracted Jewish professionals because it presented an opportunity for intellectual advancement that was denied in some of the better-established fields. Without the Jewish contribution it may safely be said that psychology would not have reached its present state of development and would be seriously handicapped in its future course.

[Helmut E. Adler]

Women in Psychology

Jewish women are well represented in the field of psychology; they have been particularly prominent in clinical psychology and the social psychology of intergroup relationships, especially as it involves socially marginalized groups. Female Jewish psychologists hoping to work in the academic world, particularly prior to the 1960s, often faced both antisemitism and discrimination based on their gender that made it difficult to find tenured professorships. A number of Jewish women psychologists in the second half of the 20th century came from working-class households imbued with socialist political convictions; many of these women were advocates of social justice and equity in their scholarly work and in their lives. A disproportionate number of Jewish women have been active scholars and practitioners in the field of the psychology of women. Seven of the 12 recipients of the Association for Women in Psychology's distinguished career awards through 2005 have been Jewish women. These include sociologist Jessie Bernard in 1977; Ethel Tobach in 1979; Jean Baker Miller in 1980; Florence *Denmark in 1986; Rhoda Unger in 1994; Bernice Lott in 1998; and Lenore Tiefer in 2004. A number of these women also received distinguished publication awards from that organization. In addition, 10 of the 23 recipients of the Carolyn Wood Sherif Award, the most important award offered by the Division of the Psychology of Women of the American Psychological Association, are Jewish women whose work is mentioned in this article. Rhoda Unger received the first such award in 1984 followed by Barbara Wallston in 1986 (posthumously), Martha Mednick in 1988, Florence Denmark in 1991, Phyllis Katz in 1994, Bernice Lott in 1996, Sandra Schwartz Tangri in 1999, Michelle Fine in 2000, Judith Worell in 2001, and Laura Brown in 2004. A Jewish male, Arnold Kahn, received this award in 2002.

EARLY PIONEERS. The first major Jewish women psychologists were trained in Europe in the first few decades of the 20th century; many fled to the United States to escape the Nazis in the mid- or late 1930s. Like their male counterparts, many of these women, including Frieda *Fromm-Reichmann (1889–1957) and Else Frenkel-Brunswick (1908–1958), made their most important contributions in psychoanalytic and psychodynamic theory; others had an impact on the developing field of clinical psychology. These female refugees from Nazism helped to change the focus of American social psychology by giving it a more "outsider" perspective. These women, who were also early activists for various social causes, included the following:

Tamara Dembo (1902–1993) ultimately became a full member of the faculty at Clark University. Her major contributions were in the field of rehabilitation psychology, in which she advocated adapting environments to people rather than the other way around.

Erika Fromm (1910–2003) emigrated to the U.S. with her husband in 1938. Although confronted with gender discrimination that hampered her academic career, Fromm had an important impact on psychoanalysis through her work on dream interpretation and on hypnosis as a key to the unconscious.

Eugenia Hanfmann (1905–1983) studied conceptual thinking in schizophrenics and the role of projective tests in the assessment of personality. After a number of impermanent faculty positions, Hanfmann was invited to begin a counseling service for students at the newly formed Brandeis University in 1952.

Marie Jahoda (1907–2001) spent the war years in England but had an illustrious career in the U.S. beginning in 1945.

Margaret Mahler (1897–1985), a native of Hungary, worked in object relations theory.

Four U.S.-born Jewish women also made significant contributions to the field of psychology in the period directly after World War II:

Thelma Alper (1908–) was the 11th woman (and the first Jewish woman) to receive a psychology Ph.D. from Harvard University. After several years as a non-tenure track lecturer at Harvard, Alper accepted a tenured position at Wellesley in 1952. Her research combined elements of clinical and social psychology. She did a great deal of applied work with children and adolescents.

Mary Henle (1913–), who was born in Cleveland, was committed to experimental and theoretical issues involving Gestalt psychology. A member of the Graduate Faculty of the New School for Social Research in New York City, her research shifted to experimentation on perception and cognition in later years.

Bernice Levin Neugarten (1916–2001) received her Ph.D. from the interdisciplinary program on child development at the University of Chicago; this was the first degree in human development conferred by any institution.

Jane Loevinger (1918–) completed her graduate work at the University of California at Berkeley. Unable to obtain an academic position in St. Louis, where her husband was on the faculty of Washington University, Loevinger conducted a variety of research studies in the areas of measurement and psychoanalysis supported by outside grants. In 1971, she finally became a tenured professor at Washington University. Well known as a pioneer in the study of the structure of personality, she published work on the construction of projective tests as well as on the meaning and measurement of ego development.

SOCIAL ACTIVISTS. This group of women (born in the 1920s or early 1930s) began their careers after World War II when discrimination against Jews and women had become less overt. Social activism, as well as research on the personal and social costs of societal inequities, was the central focus of their professional lives. As the feminist movement in the late 1960s and early 1970s made positions of leadership for women more acceptable, a number of Jewish women became presidents of the Society for the Psychological Study of Social Issues (SPSSI).

Cynthia Deutsch (1928–), who succeeded June Tapp as president of the SPSSI, received her Ph.D. from the University of Chicago in 1953. Deutsch was primarily concerned with the psychological consequences of early intervention in the lives of children at risk.

Marcia Guttentag (1932–1977), was born in New York City and received her Ph.D. from the clinical psychology doctoral program at Adelphi University in 1960. Her scholarship focused on mental health evaluation and gender and racial inequity in education. In 1972 Guttentag became the Richard Clarke Cabot Visiting Professor of Social Ethics in the Department of Psychology and Social Relations at Harvard University as well as Director of the Social Development Research Center and the Center for Evaluation Research at its School of Education.

Lois Wladis Hoffman (1929–), who was born in Elmira, New York, and received her Ph.D. from the University of Michigan in 1958, spent most of her professional career at the University of Michigan where she became a professor of psychology in 1975. Her earliest work was on child development, but she also investigated the effect of maternal employment on children. Her books include *The Employed Mother in America* (1963/1976) and *Working Mothers: Evaluative Review of the Consequences for Wife, Husband, Child* (1974). She later collaborated with Martha Mednick and Sandra Tangri on a book called *Women and Achievement: Social and Motivational Analyses* (1975).

Phyllis Katz (1938–), born in New York City, received her Ph.D. in developmental and clinical psychology from Yale in 1961. She founded and edited the feminist journal *Sex Roles* and edited the *Journal of Social Issues*. She was a professor at the Graduate School of City University of New York and went on to maintain her own research institute in Boulder, Colorado. Her major work in psychology was on the socialization of gender roles in children and she also edited two books on eliminating racism (1976; 1988).

Clara Weiss Mayo (1931–1981) received her Ph.D. in psychology from Clark University in 1959. After she joined the faculty at Boston University, Mayo was involved in one of the first studies to examine the effect of busing on school integration. She was also interested in the way nonverbal communication patterns helped or hindered relationships between individuals from different social groups.

Martha Mednick (1929–) was an influential pioneer in the study of women and gender.

June Tapp (1929–1992) was born in New York City but grew up in Los Angeles. After graduating from the University of Southern California, she completed her Ph.D. in social and political psychology at Syracuse University in 1963. A major researcher in psychology, law, and public policy, Tapp held a number of short-term positions before becoming a professor at the Institute of Child Development at the University of Minnesota in 1972. Her co-authored books include *Ambivalent America* (1971) and *Law, Justice, and the Individual in Society* (1977); she was also an effective social activist.

Ethel Tobach (1921–) is unique among this group, because of her field of comparative psychology as well as her European birth.

PROMINENT LATER PRACTITIONERS. Judith Alpert (1944–), who received her Ph.D. in school psychology from Teacher's College of Columbia University in 1973, did her research in school psychology and women and psychoanalysis. She was associated with the School Psychology Program in the School of Education at New York University for virtually all of her career.

Sandra Lipshitz Bem (1944–), a Pittsburgh native, moved with her husband Darryl Bem to University of Michigan, where she received her Ph.D. in developmental psychology in 1968. Bem did early collaborative work with her husband on the internalization of gender stereotypes as a source of gender inequality; she also originated the concept of "androgyny" – a measure of personality which views "masculine" and "feminine" traits as independent of each other. Her 1993 *The Lenses of Gender* examined the way gender is constructed by societal constraints.

Annette Brodsky (1938–) followed Florence Denmark and Martha Mednick as the fifth president of the APA's division on women (1977–1978). Born in Chicago, Brodsky received her Ph.D. in clinical psychology from the University of Florida in 1970. She initiated the first women's studies course at the University of Alabama and co-edited the first book on psychotherapy and women and also conducted important research on sexual contact between therapists and clients. She later lived in Los Angeles where she was director of clinical training for a large hospital and an expert witness on sexual abuse in psychotherapy.

Laura Brown (1952–), a Cleveland native, received her Ph.D. from Southern Illinois University in 1977. A clinical professor of psychology at the University of Washington and a private practitioner, Brown served as president of the APA

Division on the Psychology of Women following her term as president of the APA's Division on Gay and Lesbian Psychology. Brown is the author of *Subversive Dialogues* (1994) and other books on diversity issues in feminist therapy and feminist perspectives on personality and psychopathology.

Nancy Datan (1941–1987) emigrated to Israel in 1963, two years after receiving her master's degree from the human development program at the University of Chicago where she worked with Bernice Neugarten. She completed her Ph.D. from the same program while in Israel and returned to the U.S. in 1973. She taught at the University of Wisconsin at Green Bay with her second husband for the few years before her death. Datan and several colleagues conducted a pioneering study of aging among women from five subcultures in Israel, which ranged from traditional to modern in their conceptions of women's roles (Datan et al., 1981). She later reconsidered the research questions they had asked and their implications for gender roles within a religious and cultural framework (Datan, 1986). Datan also edited an important series of books on adult development and aging.

Florence Denmark (1932–) was the first Jewish woman to be elected president of the American Psychological Association (1980).

Michelle Fine (1953–), who grew up in suburban New Jersey, received her Ph.D. in 1980 from Teacher's College of Columbia University. A professor of psychology at the Graduate Center of the City University of New York, Fine's scholarship has focused on women and disability; black and Latina high school dropouts; and problematizing whiteness.

Frances Degen Horowitz (1932–), New York City-born, received her Ph.D. from the University of Iowa in 1959. Much of her professional career was spent at the University of Kansas where she rose from professor of psychology to dean of the Graduate School. She became president of the Graduate School of the City University of New York in 1991. Horowitz's research focused on early childhood development and children in poverty. President of the APA Division of Developmental Psychology in 1977–78, and president of the Society for Research on Child Development in 1996–97, she received the Weizmann Institute's Women in Science award in 1994.

Hannah Lerman (1936–), the twelfth president of the APA Division of the Psychology of Women (1984–85), was born in New York City and received her Ph.D. in clinical psychology from Michigan State University in 1963. A therapist in private practice in the Los Angeles area, she co-founded the Feminist Therapy Institute. Lerman wrote a well-received book critiquing Freudian theory (1986) as well as a critique of the psychodiagnosis of women in the late 20th century (1997). She also co-edited an important book on feminist ethics in psychotherapy (1990).

Bernice Lott (1930–), a president of the APA Division on the Psychology of Women (1990–91), taught at the University of Rhode Island. Her career shows discontinuities similar to those of other women who are/were married to prominent men in the field. Following her second marriage to Albert Lott, she began to publish research regularly both in collaboration with him and by herself. Her work focused on prejudice and discrimination against women and on the social learning of gender.

Judith Seitz Rodin (1944–) was born in New York City and received her Ph.D. in social psychology from Columbia University in 1970. She did important work on obesity, aging, and social control while a professor of psychology at Yale where she became dean of the Graduate School before becoming president of the University of Pennsylvania. She made important contributions to research and policy issues involving women's health.

Marilyn Safir (1938–) moved to Israel shortly after receiving her Ph.D. in clinical psychology from Syracuse University. Born and raised in New York City, Safir was an activist on racial issues. Disenchanted with the treatment of women in the civil rights movement, she went to Israel because she believed that there would be more sexual equality there than in the U.S. In Israel, Safir was an early advocate of feminism and fostered dialogue between U.S. and Israeli scholars. Her research challenged myths of sexual equality in Israel.

Sylvia Scribner (1923–1991) worked as a union organizer and an anti-establishment activist for many years. After receiving her Ph.D. in 1970 under the direction of Mary Henle, Scribner became professor of developmental psychology at the Graduate Center of the City University of New York at the age of 59. Her extensive scholarly contributions were primarily in the area of cross-cultural psychology, cognitive science, and the history of science.

Sandra Schwartz Tangri (1937–2003) received her Ph.D. from the University of Michigan's interdisciplinary social psychology program in 1967. Tangri held faculty appointments at Douglass College of Rutgers University and Richmond College of the City University of New York. Between academic jobs, she was director of the Office of Research for the U.S. Commission on Civil Rights for four years and senior research associate at the Urban Institute for three more years. She later became professor of psychology at Howard University. Tangri conducted longitudinal research on women's careers and also investigated sexual harassment in the federal work force and ethical issues in population programs.

Rhoda Kesler Unger (1939–), who received her Ph.D. in experimental psychology from Harvard University in 1966, was the eighth president of the APA Division of the Psychology of Women (1980–81). Co-author of an early text on the psychology of women with Florence Denmark (1975), she became professor of psychology and director of the All-College Honors Program at Montclair State University in New Jersey in 1972. Her primary work was on the relationship between ideological values, theory, and methodology within psychology.

Lenore Walker (1942–), the 17th president of the APA Division of the Psychology of Women (1989–90), received her Ed.D. from Rutgers University and is best known for her groundbreaking work on battered women. She received a

Distinguished Award for Contributions to the Public Interest from the American Psychological Association for her lobbying efforts in this area.

Barbara Strudler Wallston (1943–1987) received her Ph.D. in social psychology from the University of Wisconsin in 1972. She spent her entire career as an academic researcher at George Peabody College of Vanderbilt University, where she served as chair of the Department of Psychology and Human Development and as coordinator of its graduate program in psychology. She was a leader in the Association for Women in Psychology and chair of APA's Committee on Women in Psychology in 1980; in 1987 she received the Carolyn Wood Sherif Lectureship Award for her achievements in and commitment to feminist scholarship, teaching, and mentoring and to professional leadership in feminist psychology (O'Leary, 1988). Wallston developed a health locus of control scale with her then husband, Kenneth Wallston, which is used internationally to measure people's beliefs about what controls their health status and she also worked in the area of dual-career couples, stereotyping (Wallston and O'Leary, 1981), and feminist methodology in psychology.

Naomi Weisstein (1940–), born in New York City, received her Ph.D. in cognitive psychology from Harvard University. Academic gender discrimination initially limited her employment to an adjunct lectureship at the University of Chicago. She finally joined the faculty at the State University of New York at Buffalo in 1973 where her research life was cut short by chronic fatigue and immune dysfunction syndrome. Weisstein contributed to the understanding of the neuropsychology of visual perception as well as to feminist scholarship.

Judith Worell (1928–) was born in New York City and received her Ph.D. in clinical psychology from Ohio State in 1954. She served as chair of the Department of Counseling Psychology at the University of Kentucky and edited *Psychology of Women Quarterly*. Worell's research interests focus on the development of a feminist model for counseling psychology; she also conducted extensive research on women's roles throughout their lifespan and on their satisfaction with their choices.

[Rhoda K. Unger (2nd ed.)]

BIBLIOGRAPHY: J. Preuss, *Biblisch-talmudische Medizin* (1911); M. Perlmann, *Midrash ha-Refu'ah*, 3 vols. (1926–34); H.J. Zimmels, *Magicians, Theologians, and Doctors* (1952); M.M. Brayer, in: *Harofe Haivri*, 1 (1964), 285–98; 2 (1965), 248–54; E.G. Boring, *History of Experimental Psychology* (1950²); H. Misiak and V.S. Sexton, *History of Psychology: An Overview* (1966); A.A. Roback, *History of American Psychology* (1952); R.I. Watson, *Great Psychologists* (1968²); M. Wertheimer, *Brief History of Psychology* (1970); B. Wolman (ed.), *Historical Roots of Contemporary Psychology* (1968); R.S. Woodworth and M.R. Sheehan, *Contemporary Schools of Psychology* (1964³). **ADD. BIBLIOGRAPHY:** *Association for Women in Psychology Newsletter* (Winter, 1997); E.T. Beck, "Judaism, Feminism, and Psychology: Making the Links Visible," in: K. Weiner and A. Moon (eds.), *Jewish Women Speak Out* (1995), 11–26; C.P. Deutsch, "Gender Discrimination as an Intergroup Issue: Comment on Capshew and Lazlo," in: *Journal of Social Issues*, 42 (1986), 185–89; M. Fine, *Disruptive Voices: The Possibilities of Feminist Research* (1992); A.N. O'Connell and N.F. Russo, *Models of Achievement: Reflections of Eminent Women in Psychology* (1983); idem, *Women in Psychology* (1990); E. Scarborough and L. Furumoto, *Untold Lives: The First Generation of American Women Psychologists* (1987); G. Stevens and S. Gardner, *The Women of Psychology* (1982); S.S. Tangri, "Living with Anomalies: Sojourns of a White American Jew," in: K.F. Wyche and F.J. Crosby (eds.), *Women's Ethnicities: Journeys through Psychology* (1996), 129–43; L. Tiefer, *A Brief History of the Association for Women in Psychology (AWP), 1969–1991* (1991); R.K. Unger, "Psychology," in: P.E. Hyman and D.D. Moore (eds.), *Jewish Women in America: An Historical Encyclopedia* (1997), vol. 2, 1104–13; idem, "Looking toward the Future by Looking at the Past: Social Activism and Social History," in: *Journal of Social Issues*, 42 (1986), 215–27.

PTASHNE, MARK STEPHEN (1940–), U.S. biochemist. Born in Chicago, Ptashne graduated with a B.S. from Reed College in Portland, Oregon, and received his Ph.D. from Harvard University under the direction of Matthew Meselson. He joined the faculty of biochemistry and molecular biology at Harvard (1965) where he became professor (1971), chairman (1980–83), and Herschel Smith Professor from 1993. He was later a faculty member of the Molecular Biology Program at Memorial Sloan-Kettering Cancer Center, New York. His early research concerned the relationship between a virus called phage lambda and the bacteria it infects. There are two possible outcomes to infection. The virus may multiply and destroy the infected bacteria, a process termed lysis. Alternatively, the viral genetic information may persist without destroying the bacteria, a process called "lysogeny." However the quiescent phage DNA may subsequently be reactivated and lead to bacterial lysis. Ptashne identified and characterized the protein which determines the outcome of infection and he elucidated the mechanisms by which it operates. These discoveries were the basis for the new field of "transcriptional regulation" which explores the control of genetically determined programs in cells. It has crucially important implications for understanding the molecular basis of normal development and the abnormal events underlying cancer. He continued to work on gene regulation in normal and cancer cells. He reviewed his research in *A Genetic Switch: Phage Lambda Revisited* (2004³). His work has been recognized by many honors, including election to the U.S. National Academy of Sciences, the Gairdner Award (1985) and the Lasker Award for Basic Medical Science (1997). Ptashne is an accomplished violinist.

[Michael Denman (2nd ed.)]

PTOLEMY, the common name of monarchs of the Macedonian (or Thirty-First) Dynasty who ruled in Egypt from 323 to 30 B.C.E. It is unclear precisely how many such sovereigns there actually were; some scholars give a total of 14 and some 16. Most important for Jewish history were: PTOLEMY I (called Soter), reputed son of Lagus, founder of the dynasty. Ruler of Egypt as satrap from 323 B.C.E., he assumed the title of king in 305 and remained in power until his death in 283. Josephus states (Apion, 1:209 ff., and cf. Ant. 12:2 ff.) on the authority of Agatharchides of Cnidus that Ptolemy, after gaining admittance to Jerusalem on the pretext of wishing to make a sacrifice, captured the city on the Sabbath day when the Jews did not fight (320 B.C.E.). Agatharchides comments derisively that the Jews "persevering in their folly" of not defending their city on this day, were given over to a "harsh master." The second part of his statement is of especial interest, for scholars differ over whether Ptolemy was indeed a "harsh" master or whether his attitude toward the Jews was essentially benevolent. Whether the Jews in Egypt during his reign were indeed granted equal rights with Macedonian *clerouchoi* ("settlers") must remain an open question.

PTOLEMY II (called Philadelphus) reigned from 283 to 245 B.C.E. According to the Letter of *Aristeas he was responsible for two important actions, the one of immediate and the other of lasting consequence: he freed numerous Jewish slaves (themselves evidence of his father's military actions in Palestine) and initiated the Greek translation of the Bible – the *Septuagint. Both the foregoing statements may well have a historical basis. Philadelphus' literary interests are attested from other sources, and the Bible project may conceivably have been begun during his reign. The construction of several cities in Ereẓ Israel must also be attributed to his reign, including Philoteria (near Lake Kinneret) and Ptolemais, near present-day Acre (Arist. 115) as well as Philadelphia in Transjordan. He gained important victories in the first Syrian war against the Seleucid sovereign, *Antiochus I, and gave his daughter Berenice's hand in marriage to Antiochus II upon completion of the second Syrian campaign (c. 253 B.C.E.).

PTOLEMY III (called Euergetes) reigned from 246 to 221 B.C.E. Some scholars identify this Ptolemy with the king of that name mentioned by Josephus with regard to Joseph the Tobiad (Ant. 12: 154ff.), while others are of the opinion that it was Ptolemy V (Epiphanes). If the king was Euergetes, then he must be credited with a favorable attitude toward his Jewish subjects. Josephus goes so far as to claim that after Euergetes' great victory over the Seleucids during the third Syrian war (246–241 B.C.E.) he offered incense at the Temple in Jerusalem. A possible reference to some of the king's actions during and after his campaigns in the Seleucid realm may be found in Daniel 11:7–9 where it is related that the Egyptian king removed idols from the conquered territories and restored them in his own country.

PTOLEMY IV (called Philopator) reigned from 221–203 B.C.E. A "wretched debauchee" according to E. Bevan, this monarch has fared less well than his predecessors in Jewish annals. Philopator is often associated with the following events described in III Maccabees: On the conclusion of the (fourth Syrian) war and his victory over Antiochus at Raphia (present-day Rafa) in 217 B.C.E., Philopator paid a visit to Jerusalem with the intention of entering the Temple. God intervened and he was felled to the ground. As revenge, when he returned to Egypt he ordered the Jews to be massacred in the Alexandrian arena by a horde of elephants, but the beasts turned on the royal troops instead. The day of deliverance was commemorated by the Jews as an annual feast day, which seems to be the only historically verifiable aspect of the story, though Josephus places it in a later context.

PTOLEMY V (called Epiphanes) reigned from 203 to 181 B.C.E. This monarch irretrievably lost the whole of Palestine to Antiochus III at the battle of Paneas (present-day Banias) c. 200 B.C.E.

PTOLEMY VI (or VII; called Philometor) reigned from 181 to 145 B.C.E. (from then on until the death of the last of the Ptolemies in 30 B.C.E., dates of birth and regnal years become increasingly uncertain). Philometor appears to have been generally well disposed toward the Jews, though he invaded Palestine to intervene in the disputes over the succession to the Syrian throne. His relations with *Jonathan the Hasmonean were cordial. II Maccabees 1–10 states that Philometor's mentor was a Jewish philosopher and biblical exegete, Aristobulus by name. Under this same ruler the high priest *Onias IV, having fled from Jerusalem, built a temple at Leontopolis (c. 161 B.C.E.), while Philometor's military garrisons were commanded by two Jews, Onias and Dositheus.

PTOLEMY VII (or IX; called Euergetes II) reigned from 145 to 116 B.C.E. According to Josephus the Jews were persecuted during his rule, yet a synagogue was dedicated to him by the Egyptian Jewish community. It was in the 38th year of Euergetes' reign that the grandson of *Ben Sira went to Egypt where he translated his grandfather's work into Greek.

PTOLEMY VIII (or X; called Lathyrus and Soter II) reigned intermittently from 116 to 80 B.C.E. He launched an attack on the Hasmonean Alexander *Yannai shortly after the latter had come to the throne, only to be driven back by his mother, *Cleopatra III, who, with his brother Ptolemy IX (or XI; called Alexander I), later planned their own assault on Yannai.

BIBLIOGRAPHY: A. Bouché-Leclercq, *Histoire des Lagides*, 4 vols. (1903–07), passim; Schuerer, Gesch, 3 (1909^4), 24–52; E.R. Bevan, *A History of Egypt…* (1927), passim; Schalit, in: *Scripta Hierosolymitana*, 1 (1954), 64–77; J. Gutman, *Ha-Sifrut ha-Yehudit-ha-Hellenistit*, 1 (1958), 115ff.; V. Tcherikover, *Hellenistic Civilization and the Jews* (1959), index; M. Stern, *Ha-Te'udot le-Mered ha-Ḥashmona'im* (1965), 11–27; W.W. Tarn and G.T. Griffith, *Hellenistic Civilization* (1966^3), passim.

[David Solomon]

PTOLEMY (c. 135 B.C.E.), son of Ḥabub (Abubus) and son-in-law of *Simeon b. Mattathias (the Hasmonean). Ptolemy was *strategos* (i.e., military and local commander) at Jericho. Plotting to overthrow the Hasmonean House in 135 B.C.E., he invited Simeon and his entourage to a banquet while they were on a visit to the Jericho area, and treacherously murdered him and later two of his sons. He then sent messengers to Gazara (Gezer) to kill Simeon's other son John *Hyrcanus. At the same time, he set out to capture Jerusalem, dispatching a message to the Syrian king, Antiochus Sidetes, to inform him of the developments and to enlist his aid. Hyrcanus succeeded, however, in killing his assailants and hastened to Jerusalem where he won the trust of the people, who remained loyal to the Hasmonean dynasty. Having ensured his succession, Hyrcanus pursued Ptolemy and besieged him in a fortress in the vicinity of Jericho to which he had retreated. Ptolemy was able to defy Hyrcanus by holding his mother as a hostage. Eventually Hyrcanus had to lift the siege as a result of the onset of the Sabbatical year which led to a food shortage. Ptolemy fled to Philadelphia (Rabbath Ammon), after putting Hyrcanus' mother to death, and he is not heard of again.

BIBLIOGRAPHY: I Macc. 16; Jos., Ant., 13:228–35; Jos., Wars, 1:54–60; Schuerer, Hist, 66–68.

[Lea Roth]

°PTOLEMY (Son of Mennaeus), king of Chalcis, in the region of the Lebanon (c. 85–40 B.C.E.). *Josephus relates that the inhabitants of Damascus despised Ptolemy, and preferred as king of Coele-Syria the Nabatean king, Aretas. Ptolemy's position in the area, however, was firmly established, and the Judean queen *Alexandra's armed attempt to weaken that influence brought no results. During Pompey's campaign in Syria, the territory under Ptolemy was devastated, but Ptolemy held fast to his principality though he was compelled to pay a ransom of 1,000 talents to the Roman conqueror. Following the Roman conquest of Judea, Ptolemy assumed guardianship over *Antigonus, the son of the Hasmonean prince, Aristobulus, and his sisters. They were brought to Ptolemy at Ashkelon by his son, Philippion, who eventually married one of the princesses, Alexandra. Philippion, however, was subsequently slain by his father on account of Alexandra, after which Ptolemy married the princess himself. Meanwhile, with the gradual subjugation of Judea under Herod, Antigonus gathered an army and with Ptolemy's assistance returned to his country, only to be defeated by Herod and again driven out of Judea. Ptolemy was succeeded as king of Chalcis by his son, Lysanias, who continued to support Antigonus.

BIBLIOGRAPHY: Klausner, Bayit Sheni, 3 (1950²), 169 f., 257 f.; Schuerer, Hist, 112; A. Schalit, *Koenig Herodes* (1969), 819 f. (index), s.v. *Ptolemaios, Sohn des Mennaios.*

[Isaiah Gafni]

°PTOLEMY THE BIOGRAPHER, brother of *Nicholas of Damascus. Like his brother, Ptolemy was a highly esteemed member of the literary circle which surrounded Herod I. After Herod's death, he sided with Antipas (Jos., Ant. 17:225; Wars 2:21). A fragment of a work about Herod stating that the Idumaeans were Phoenician and Syrian in origin and were forcibly converted to Judaism (cf. Jos., Ant. 18:257–8) has been ascribed to him by Reinach (Textes, 88–89) but it may possibly belong to another Ptolemy.

°PTOLEMY THE GEOGRAPHER (second century C.E.), Alexandrian astronomer and geograher. Among his many works was a "Geography" in eight books in which he fixed the longitude and latitude of thousands of places, including many in Palestine: Ptolemais (Acre), Sycaminon (Haifa), Mount Carmel, Caesarea Stratonis (Caesarea), Iope (Jaffa), Ascalon (Askelon), Tiberias, Neapolis (Nablus), Gaza, Lydda, Hierosolyma (Jerusalem). However, Ptolemy's locations are often in error.

°PTOLEMY MACRON, a general under *Antiochus IV (Epiphanes). The author of II Maccabees (10:12) explicitly states that Ptolemy "had taken the lead in preserving justice" for the Jews. As a result, he was accused before *Antiochus V (Eupator) and eventually took his life by poison. Some commentators accept the fact that the Ptolemy in question is synonymous with the Ptolemy son of Dorymenes, mentioned by Josephus (Ant. 12:298), in I Maccabees 3:38 and II Maccabees 4:45. The difficulty lies in equating this benevolent reputation with that in the foregoing passages (and cf. II Macc. 8:8–11). In these he is depicted as taking the field against *Judah Maccabee and being instrumental in the execution of a three-man Jewish deputation which had leveled charges against the Hellenizer *Menelaus. Polybius (27, 13) and Suidas (s.v. Πτόλέμάΐός) refer to Ptolemy as former governor of Cyprus under Ptolemaic rule. He was later awarded the governorship of Coele-Syria and Phoenicia by the *Seleucids.

BIBLIOGRAPHY: Meyer, Ursp, 2 (1921), 161 f.; H. Bévenot, *Die beiden Makkabaeerbuecher* (1931), 30, 75, 218 f.; Pauly-Wissowa, 46 (1959), 1763–65, nos. 48 and 49.

[David Solomon]

°PTOLEMY OF CHENNOS (early second century B.C.E.), of Alexandria, author of a lost "new" compilation of interesting facts, summarized in Photius. He derived Moses' supposed nickname, "Alpha," from the Greek word for leprosy, *alphoi* (cf. Nicarchus).

°PTOLEMY OF MENDE (date unknown), an Egyptian priest who wrote in Greek a lost work on Egyptian chronology, quoted by Tatian in *Oratio ad Graecos*, 38, on the date of the Exodus. Apion made use of this work.

PUBERTY. It was estimated that puberty, defined by the appearance of two pubic hairs, began in women early in the 13th year, and in men about the start of the 14th year, and for that reason maturity was regarded as beginning legally from the age of 12 years and one day in the case of females and 13 and one day in the case of males (Nid. 5:6; Nid. 52a). The rabbis reckoned religious responsibility to begin with the onset of puberty. From this period onward one was recognized as an adult, responsible for the observance of the precepts and the discharge of communal obligations. In the case of females, the rabbis delineated several distinct stages: *ketannah* ("minor"), from the age of three to the age of 12; the *na'arah* ("young woman"), for six months following the initial period; and the *bogeret* ("adult"), which begins at the expiration of these six months (Nid. 5:7). No such distinctions were made for the males who were simply *ketannim* ("minors") before 13 and *gedolim* ("adults") after their 13th birthday.

The attainment of the age of maturity did not automatically render one an adult, since the physical characteristics of puberty were also necessary in order to establish adulthood. However, when an examination for the signs of puberty was not made, it was presumed that a minor who reached the age of maturity had also developed the necessary signs (Nid. 46a). A young man past his *bar mitzvah is therefore counted for a *minyan even without an examination (Isserles to Sh. Ar., OḤ 55:5). A woman's maturity was deemed sufficiently established if she bore a child (Yev. 12b). In the event that signs of puberty did not appear by the age of maturity, the person retained the status of a minor until the age of 20. After that age, if signs of impotence developed, thus accounting for the absence of secondary sex characteristics, the person was considered an adult (Nid. 5:9). If such signs did not develop, the person retained the status of a minor until the age of 35, which was considered the major portion of a person's life-span (Nid. 47b).

After attaining the age of maturity, young adults were held responsible in ritual, civil, and criminal matters, and were held punishable by the courts for their transgressions or breaches of contract. It was believed, however, that heavenly punishment was not forthcoming for sins committed before the age of 20 (Shab. 89b, cf. BB 121b) and only those above the age of 20 were liable for military service (Num. 1:3) or obligated to pay the half-shekel when the people were counted (Ex. 30:14).

See *Child Marriage for marriages entered into by minors or arranged for them.

BIBLIOGRAPHY: Krauss, Tal Arch, 3 (1911), 23f., 449f.; J. Preuss, *Biblisch-talmudische Medizin* (1923³), 146–8; M. Perlmann, *Midrash ha-Refu'ah*, 1 (1926), 36–38; ET, 5 (1953), 137–52, 168–79.

[Aaron Rothkoff]

PUBLIC AUTHORITY, in the context of this article, a term referring to an authoritative body composed of representatives of the public – whether appointed or elected by the latter – and entrusted with the duty and power to arrange various matters of common concern to this public. (For particulars concerning a personal authority, see *King and Kingdom; **Nasi*; *Exilarch.) It has been stated that "the foundations of the community, as they remained in existence until the modern Enlightenment, were laid mainly in the first generations of the Second Temple period" (Y. Baer, in: *Zion*, 15 (1950), 1). Attributable to this early period are a number of tannaitic sources incorporating *halakhot* concerning the "townspeople" (*benei ha-ir* or *anshei ha-ir*, Shek. 2:1; BB 1:5), as well as certain *beraitot* concerning the authority of the townspeople to compel each other toward the satisfaction of public needs in various fields (Tosef., BM 11:23ff.; BB 8a). At the head of such public authority stood the "seven good [elder] citizens" (*tovei ha-ir*, Jos., Ant., 4:214; TJ, Meg. 3:2, 74a; Meg. 26a). However, it was only with the rise of the Jewish community in various parts of the Diaspora from the tenth century onward that Jewish law came to experience its main development in the field of the laws concerning a public authority. This article deals with aspects of a public authority such as its legal standing, composition and powers, the legal relationship between itself and individual members of the community, and so on. For further particulars concerning the legislative institutions of the community and the related administration of the law, see **Takkanot ha-Kahal*; as regards the legal aspects of communal administration in fiscal and financial matters, see *Taxation; **Hekdesh*.

Qualifications, Duties, and Standing of Communal Leaders

The qualifications and duties of public representatives are discussed in the Bible and in the Talmud, mainly from the social, moral, and ideological aspects. The ways of the Patriarchs and other leading Jewish figures – such as Moses, Aaron, Samuel, and David – in dealings with the people serve as a basic source of guidance for the relationship between the people and their leaders, between the citizen and the public authority. It has been stated that appointment of "a good public leader [*parnas tov*] is one of the three things proclaimed by the Almighty Himself" (Ber. 55a; Kal. R. 8); that the Almighty had already shown to Adam "every generation with its leaders" (*dor dor u-farnasav*, Av. Zar. 5a), and to Moses, "all the leaders destined to serve Israel from the day of its leaving behind the wilderness until the time of the resurrection of the dead" (Sif. Num. 139); that in time to come, "when the Almighty shall renew His world, He shall stand Himself and arrange the leaders of the generation" (Yal., Isa. 454).

The requirements demanded of the leader representing a public authority are many and stringent: "In the past you acted only on your own behalf, from now on [i.e., upon appointment] you are bound in the service of the public" (Yal., Deut. 802); "a leader who domineers over the public" is one of those "whom the mind does not tolerate" (Pes. 113b) and over whom "the Almighty weeps every day" (Ḥag. 5b). It is not only forbidden for a leader to impose undue awe on the community if not intended "for the sake of Heaven" (*le-shem shamayim*; RH 17a), but he must himself stand in awe of the public (Sot. 40a). The scholars described in various ways the mutual interdependence between the citizen and the public authority: "A leader shall not be imposed on the public unless the latter is first consulted" (Ber. 55a), but once appointed, "even the most ordinary… is like the mightiest of the mighty" (RH 25b), to whom the public owes obedience and honor. This interdependence is illustrated in the difference of opinion between Judah Nesi'ah (grandson of Judah ha-Nasi) and other scholars as to whether the stature of a leader follows that of his generation – *parnas le-fi doro* – or whether the generation is influenced by its leaders – *dor le-fi parnas*.

These, and other similar concepts scattered in halakhic and aggadic literature, guided the halakhic scholars in their determination of the principles of Jewish administrative law. A person engaged in public affairs is as one studying the Torah (TJ, Ber. 5:1). Moreover, "If he be engaged in studying the Torah and the time comes for recital of the *Shema* ["morning prayers"], he shall leave off studying and recite the *Shema*… if he be engaged in the affairs of the public, he shall not leave off but complete this work, and recite the *Shema* if there remain time to do so" (Yad., Keri'at Shema 2:5; Sh. Ar., OḤ 70:4; based on Tosef., Ber. 1:4, 2:6; see also Lieberman, *Tosefta ki-Feshutah*, Berakhot, p. 3). Hence it followed that it was not merely a privilege to represent the public but also a duty. Thus in a case where a member of the community was elected to public office, contrary to his own declared wishes in the matter (namely, appointment as a tax assessor; see *Taxation), it was decided that "no person is free to exempt himself… since every individual is bound in the service of the public in his town… and therefore anyone who has sought to exclude himself from the consensus has done nothing and is bound to fulfill the duties of his office because the community has not agreed that he be excluded" (Resp. Rashba, vol. 3, no. 417; cf. also vol. 1, no. 769; vol. 7, no. 490; *Tashbeẓ*, 2:98).

In post-talmudic times the legal standing of a public authority was given precise definition based on the central legal doctrine accepted by the scholars of this period as the source of the community's standing and authority to make enactments; namely, that the standing of the communal leadership is assimilated to that of a court (*bet din*; see **Takkanot ha-Kahal*). In a certain case a person sought appointment to a public office; he had previously sworn a false oath with regard to his tax declaration, was fined for so doing, and came to an arrangement with the community concerning this tax payment. It was held by Israel *Isserlein (15th-century scholar of Vienna) that since such a person was unfit for appointment as a *dayyan*, he was also unfit to be numbered among the leaders of the community: "the leaders of the community fulfill the role of a court when they sit in supervision over the affairs of the public and private individuals" (*Pesakim u-Khetavim*, no. 214). This principle set a guide standard for the qualifications required of communal leaders (see, e.g., *Terumat ha-Deshen*, Resp. no. 344): "communal leaders appointed to attend to the needs of the public or private individuals are like *dayyanim*, and it is forbidden to include among them anyone who is disqualified from adjudicating on account of his own bad conduct" (*Rema*, ḤM 37: 2). A further reason given by the scholars for assimilating the standing of communal leaders to that of *dayyanim* is that the duties of the former are largely concerned with providing for the social needs of the community, determination of the measure of support and relief for each being a task of a judicial nature (BB 8b and Rashi thereto; Sh. Ar., YD 256:3; *Mishpetei Uziel*, ḤM no. 4).

The assimilation of the communal leader's standing to that of *dayyan* is naturally limited to such powers as he enjoys in his official capacity only. Hence communal leaders who have been empowered to elect a body to supervise public affairs must do so themselves, since they have no power to delegate this authority to others (see below), even though an ordinary court has authority to appoint an agent and entrust him with the execution of certain tasks (Resp. Ribash no. 228).

The Public Authority and Laws of Property and Obligation

The aforementioned assimilation facilitated the solution of a number of problems arising in Jewish law with regard to legal relations between the public authority and the individual. Thus, for instance, the general requirement in Jewish law of a formal act of *kinyan* (see *Acquisition; *Contract) in order to lend a transaction legal effect would normally have constituted a serious obstacle to the efficient administration of a public authority's multiple affairs. However, beginning in the 13th century, the new legal principle of the validity of any legal transaction effected by a public authority, even without a *kinyan*, came to be recognized. Apparently this was first laid down by *Meir b. Baruch of Rothenburg in a case concerning the hire of a teacher by the community (quoted in *Mordekhai*, BM 457. 8). Normally the parties would have been entitled to retract, since no formal *kinyan* had been effected and the teacher had not yet commenced his work (see *Labor Law), but Meir of Rothenburg decided that there could be no retraction from the contract of hire "because a matter done by the public requires no *kinyan* – although this would be required in the case of an individual." He based this innovation on a wide construction of a number of talmudic rulings from which it may be inferred that the public has to be regarded differently from the individual, even though these contain no suggestion whatever that a *kinyan* might be dispensed with in a transaction effected by a public body (Meg: 26a; Git. 36a); in addition he compared the case of a transaction effected by a public body to that of a small *gift, although in this case withdrawal from the transaction is prohibited as amounting to a breach of faith and not because the transaction has full legal validity (i.e., when effected without a formal *kinyan*; BM 49a; Yad, Mekhirah 7:9; Sh. Ar., ḤM 2; see also *Contract). He further decided that a *suretyship for the fulfillment of the contract of employment between the community and the teacher was valid, even though it had been undertaken without a *kinyan* and in a manner in which the suretyship would otherwise be of no legal effect (*ibid.*). This decision is also given as the source of the rule that a gift by a public body is fully valid even if it is made without a formal *kinyan* (Sh. Ar., ḤM 204:9, and see also *Ha-Gra* thereto, n. 11). The law was similarly decided in regard to other legal matters affecting the public (see, e.g., Resp. Ribash no. 476; *Rema*, ḤM 81:1). This principle took root in the Diaspora: "The custom is widespread that whatever the communal leaders decide to do is valid and effective… and neither *kinyan* nor deed is required" (Resp. Rosh 6:19 and 21); similarly, in Constantinople in the 15th century it was held: "The widely accepted *halakhah* is that all matters of the public and anything that is done by or before the public is valid, even without *kinyan*, nor do the laws of alienation and acquisition [*hakna'ah*] apply in respect of such transactions" (*Mayim Amukkim*, no. 63); it was likewise decided by Isserles that "All matters of the public require no *kinyan*" (*Rema*, ḤM 163:6).

Other fundamental requirements of the law of *kinyan* were also relaxed with reference to a public authority. It was thus laid down, e.g., that the public may validly acquire something not yet in existence and alienate to someone not yet in existence (*Mayim Amukkim*, no. 63; see also *Acquisition, Modes of; *Contract); and also that in a public matter **as-*

makhta constitutes no defect (Resp. Mabit, vol. 2, pt. 2, no. 228). One of the explanations given for this fundamental innovation was that it had to be assumed that in any transaction with which the public was connected the parties would make up their minds absolutely (*gemirut ha-da'at*), even without a *kinyan* and notwithstanding the fact of *asmakhta* and so on (see, e.g., Resp. Ribash no. 476; *Rema*, ḤM 81:1; *Sma*, ḤM 204, n. 14); However, the main explanation given for this innovation is the fact that the legal standing of a public authority has to be assimilated to that of a court, that is "because it is influenced by the rule of **hefker bet din*… and a public authority, in its dealings with the public, is as a court for the whole world" (Resp. Rashbash no. 566, also no. 112; cf. the statement of Meir of Rothenburg quoted in *Mordekhai*, BM 457–8; idem, Resp., ed. Prague, no. 38). For the same reason it was held that a public body might not plead that it had not seriously intended a particular transaction, nor that it had erred and not properly understood the nature thereof (Rashbash, loc. cit.).

Relaxation of the requirements of the law of *kinyan*, of the rule of *asmakhta*, and so on, in the case of public matters naturally extended not only to the public body but also to the individual transacting with that body, so that he too was not free to withdraw from the transaction, even if it was effected without a *kinyan*, etc. (Resp. Rashbash no. 112; *She'ot de-Rabbanan*, no. 14; *Ba'ei Ḥayyei* ḤM, pt. 2, no. 81; PDR 6: 172f., 180f.).

The Public Authority and the Exercise of its Own Discretion

A basic question of administrative law concerning the power of a public authority to delegate authority in a matter requiring the exercise of its own discretion was extensively dealt with in a responsum of *Isaac b. Sheshet Perfet (Resp. Ribash no. 228). A certain Catalonian community was granted a royal privilege in terms of which three communal trustees, together with the court, were authorized to nominate 30 persons to supervise the affairs of the community, particularly tax matters. The trustees and the court were unable to reach agreement on the execution of their task and instead agreed to elect two persons and delegate to them authority to appoint the 30 communal leaders. When this was done, a section of the community objected on the ground that authority could not be delegated by a body required to exercise its own discretion. In upholding this objection Isaac b. Sheshet held that even if in general an agent could delegate his authority to another – in circumstances where it could be assumed that the principal was not particular about the matter (see *Agency, Law of) – this was not so in the case of a public authority, even though the latter is in a sense an agent of the public. The explanation offered is that no express power to delegate authority was given in the royal privilege, and the matter was of great importance since all the affairs of the community depended on selection of its 30 leaders, and those responsible for their selection had to choose leaders possessing suitable qualities; wise, just, and peace-loving persons, knowledgeable in the affairs of the community: "it is not the intention of the community that those who have to select them [the 30] shall be able to appoint others to act in their own place, even if these others equal them in wisdom and standing"; if, however, the responsible parties had been given express authority to delegate their powers, "then it would be as if the community itself had chosen these two."

In the same matter Isaac b. Sheshet went on to give an important ruling concerning resort to the law of the land in the interpretation of the royal privilege. In his opinion, even if it were to be said that the privilege had been given with the intention that it be construed "only according to the law of the land," and even if according to this "anyone entrusted with a matter may in turn entrust this matter to anyone he chooses," yet in the case under consideration the delegation of authority remained invalid, because the rules of administrative law, so far as the Jewish community was concerned, derived their authority from Jewish law also, which did not allow for the delegation of authority in the case at hand. This ruling also involved no conflict with the law of the land in accordance with which the privilege had been given, since the general authorities were not concerned if the Jewish public failed to avail itself of the powers given under the law of the land, but were only concerned when the Jewish collective interpreted the privilege in such a manner as to lend itself wider authority than was available under this law: "the king is only particular about an extension of authority, not about a narrowing of it" (*ibid.*).

The Public Authority as an Employer

The great development of Jewish public law that followed on the rise of the Jewish community also made itself felt in the field of master and servant, in relation to employment by a public body. Special requirements relating to a public-service contract had already been emphasized in talmudic law. Thus, it was laid down that if a public-bath attendant, barber, or baker was the only one available and a festival was approaching, he could be restrained from leaving his employment until he provided a replacement (Tosef., BM 11, 27; see also *Contract). In addition, in order to avoid harm to the public, it was laid down that an individual fulfilling his duties to the public in a negligent manner might be dismissed immediately, as in the case of a public gardener, butcher, or bloodletter, a scribe, a teacher of young children, "as well as other like artisans who may cause irretrievable harm, may be dismissed without warning, since they are appointed by the public for as long as they carry out their duties in a proper manner" (Yad, Sekhirut 10:7, based on BM 109a and BB 21b). The majority of the *rishonim* interpret the rule of the *Gemara* as also extending to a private servant, considering that he too may be dismissed during the duration of his service contract if he has caused irretrievable damage (*Hassagot Rabad*, Sekhirut 10:7; *Beit ha-Beḥirah*, BM 109a; Tur and Sh. Ar., ḤM 306:8; *Rema* thereto; *Sma* thereto, n. 19). It was, however, laid down that a servant might not be dismissed without proper warning unless he was continually guilty of slackness in his work, and it must also be proved in the presence of the worker that he was indeed failing in his duties (*Rema* loc. cit.; *Maggid Mishneh*, Sekhirut 10:7; *Nimmukei Yosef*, BM 109a; see also below).

In post-talmudic times the halakhic scholars had to contend with the converse question: namely, whether it was permissible for a public authority to dismiss its servant without justifiable reason, on expiry of the agreed period of service, in the same way as could a private employer, who is free to refrain from renewing his servant's employment. (In modern times Jewish law has come to recognize the master's duty to pay severance pay to his servant on his dismissal: see **Ha'anakah*.) The talmudic rule that the high priest may not be dismissed from his office (TJ, Sanh. 2:1) did not serve as an analogy for public servants in general (see Assaf, *Mi-Sifrut ha-Ge'onim*, 73f.; *Sha'arei Teshuvah*, nos. 50, 51). From the 12th century, Jewish law consistently tended toward recognition of the principle that a public servant may not be dismissed from his employment except for justifiable reason. Maimonides laid down the general rule: "a person is not removed from a public position in Israel unless he has offended" (Yad, Kelei ha-Mikdash 4:21); also that "it is not proper to dismiss any officeholder from office on account of mere rumors concerning him; this cannot be done even if he has no enemies, all the less so if there are people in the town who are his enemies and have ulterior motives" (his Resp. (ed. Blau) no. 111; this was also the view of Meir ha-Levi and R. *Yom Tov b. Abraham Ishbili (Ritba), see Nov. Ritba to Mak. 13a). This principle was explained on the ground of "avoiding suspicion," that is, termination of the servant's employment with the public may arouse suspicion that the servant is being dismissed on account of his improper conduct (Resp. Rashba, vol. 5, no. 283; quoted also in *Beit Yosef*, OḤ 53, conclusion).

At the same time, it is held to be permissible to dismiss a public servant whenever it is customary to appoint people in charge of public matters for a fixed period, "so that at the end of it these men depart and are replaced by others, whether they be appointed in charge of food supplies, the charity fund, tax, or any other public service, and whether or not they receive any remuneration for their service; even if no fixed period of service be stipulated for them, the terms of their appointment shall be similarly in accordance with the custom… because of their practice to replace [officials], the suspicion mentioned above is eliminated" (Rashba loc. cit.). In his responsum Solomon ibn Adret confirmed that such was in fact the custom in his time: "that the competent in each generation carry out tasks on behalf of the public, and thereafter depart to be replaced by others." The statement of this twofold principle – that a public servant may not be dismissed without justifiable cause except when it is the custom to hold office for a fixed period only – was accepted as *halakhah* in the Shulḥan Arukh (OḤ 53:25–26) and was applied in the different centers of Jewish life in respect of all persons employed by a public authority (*keneset ha-gedolah*, OḤ 53, *Beit Yosef; Arukh Ha-Shulḥan*, OḤ 53:26; *Mishnah Berurah*, OḤ 53, no. 73ff.; *Even ha-Ezer*, Sekhirut 10:7). In modern times attempts have been made to distinguish between different categories of public servants, although there is no apparent justification for this in the halakhic sources (see PDR 3:94ff.).

The discussions concerning dismissal of a public servant also embraced the related and more far-reaching proposition that a public office be transmitted from father to son by way of inheritance. In this respect too there was already the tannaitic rule, on the analogy of a king succeeded by his son (Deut. 17:20), that "all the leaders [*parnasim*] of Israel have their places taken by their sons" (Sif. Deut. 162; cf. Sifra Ẓav 5). Also Maimonides laid down that "Not only the kingship, but all offices and appointments in Israel are an inheritance from father to son for all time" (Yad, Melakhim, 1:7; Kelei ha-Mikdash, 4:20). In later times a trend toward restriction of this widely stated rule asserted itself. Thus, some scholars held that the rabbinate too was an office that could be passed by inheritance (Resp. Ribash no. 271; *Rema*, YD 245:22). Others disagreed, taking the view that "the crown of Torah is not an inheritance" (Reap. Maharashdam, YD, no. 85; Shneur Zalman of Lyady, Sh. Ar., OḤ 53:33, et al.). This was also Moses Sofer's original opinion, which he later reversed (Resp. Ḥatam Sofer, OḤ 12 and 13). It was laid down that local custom concerning inheritance of an office was to be followed (*Rema* loc. cit.). A son can in no event inherit a public office unless he is qualified for it and worthy of doing so (Sifra, loc. cit.; Maim. Yad, Melakhim, 1:7; *Rema*, Sh. Ar. YD 245:22; Ḥatam Sofer loc. cit.; for further details see OPD 46, 112; PDR 4:211; see also *Labor Law).

Election of Public Officeholders

Questions such as the nomination of candidates, their number, their manner of election, etc., are extensively dealt with in post-talmudic halakhic literature (see **Takkanot ha-Kahal*; *Taxation). In modern times, with the renewal of Jewish autonomy in Ereẓ Israel and the establishment of the State of Israel, halakhic discussion has been resumed in relation to various problems arising in connection with the election of officeholders to representative state and municipal bodies. The primary sources relied upon in this discussion are found in the post-talmudic halakhic literature dealing with the leadership and administration of the community and its institutions; sometimes, when these sources do not deal specifically with the subject discussed by modern scholars, a conclusion is reached by way of analogy.

MAJORITY AND MINORITY. The principle of electing a public representative by majority vote was based by the scholars on the doctrine of *Aḥarei rabbim le-hattot* ("to follow a multitude": Ex. 23:2; see *Majority Rule), which was interpreted to mean "that in all matters to which the community consents the majority is followed" (Resp. Rosh 6:5; in talmudic *halakhah* the doctrine was interpreted as pertaining to a majority of the court in giving its decision, or to the concept of majority as a legal presumption; see **Takkanot ha-Kahal; *Ḥazakah*). At various times extensive discussions and sharp disputes centered around the question of the weight to be attached to the vote of individual members of the community. Many scholars objected to a scale graded in accordance with social and economic standing: "and it makes no difference whether this majority was composed of rich or poor, of scholars or the common people" (Resp. Re'em no. 53). An illiterate person was held to be eligible even for certain public appointments (Resp. Rashba, vol. 3, no. 399).

An informative description of some such disputes is to be found in a responsum of Menahem Mendel *Krochmal (mid-17th-century leader of Moravian Jewry; *Ẓemaḥ Ẓedek* no. 2). It had been the custom in a certain community for all taxpayers, regardless of their financial standing or education, to participate in the election of communal leaders and the appointment of public officials. Some of the "respected citizens" sought to depart from this custom and to have it laid down that only a person paying tax in excess of a certain rate, or a *talmid ḥakham* ("at least qualified as a *ḥaver"), could participate in the elections. Krochmal mentions that the "respected citizens" supported their demand with the argument that "most of the needs and affairs of the public involve the expenditure of money; how is it likely that the opinion of a poor man shall be as weighty as that of a rich man, or the opinion of an *am ha-areẓ* who is not wealthy be considered in the same way as that of a *ḥaver*." They further contended that what they were seeking was anyhow customary in "large and important communities." The rest of the community objected to such a change in the system: "the poor, the masses of the people cry out against the derogation of their rights, since they also pay tax and contribute their share, and even if the rich pay more, the poor at any rate find the little they pay to be a greater burden than do the rich in paying much more."

In his decision Krochmal strongly condemned the discriminatory nature of the proposed change in the election system and held that – at the very least – "the little of the poor is balanced against the much of the rich." He nevertheless upheld the custom prevailing in most of the communities of striking a balance between a majority based on the number of souls and a majority based on financial contribution. He also rejected the proposition that those lacking in knowledge of the Torah be deprived of their vote, "lest they separate themselves from the public… which will lead to increased strife in Israel." A change involving discrimination against any section of the public was forbidden except with the unanimous consent of all members of the community, and, added Krochmal, in communities where there was such discrimination it had to be assumed that this had been instituted with the unanimous approval of the entire community. In recent times halakhic scholars have accepted as binding the view that every vote is to carry equal weight (see, e.g., *Mishpetei Uziel*, ḤM no. 3).

ELIGIBLE AGE. The question of the age at which the right to elect and be elected to public office is acquired has in recent times come to be discussed by analogy with the criterion of age in other fields of the law. The general view is that the usual age of legal capacity – namely 13 years and one day for a man and 12 years and a day for a woman – is not to be relied upon as decisive with regard to the right to participate in elections, since in Jewish law the age of legal capacity is dependent on the specific nature of the legal act involved (see Elon, ILR, 1969, p. 121ff.) and exercise of the voting right carries with it legal consequences affecting the public as a whole – a factor calling for greater maturity on the part of the voter. According to one view, the active right to elect is acquired at 18 years: at this age a person has legal capacity to adjudicate in matters of civil law (*dinei mamonot*; Sh. Ar., ḤM 7:3) and to perform public religious duties, for instance as a ritual slaughterer (*Rema*, YD 1:5). Another view is that the right to vote is acquired from the age of 20, paralleling the biblical military age (Ex. 30: 14; Num. 1:3) and the age of full majority, for instance for the purpose of the sale of paternal land which has been inherited (Yad, Mekhirah, 29: 13; Sh. Ar., ḤM 235:9).

In the case of the passive right to be elected, the general view is that the minimal age is 20 years and over. At this age a person has the right to adjudicate in matters of criminal law (*dinei nefashot*; TJ, Sanh. 4:7) and even – for the purpose of permanent appointment as a *dayyan* – in matters of civil law (*Pitḥei Teshuvah*, ḤM 7, n. 4). Other scholars arrive at this age (20) following the minimal age for permanent appointment as a cantor (Sh. Ar., OḤ 53:8) or as an *apotropos (cf. Resp. Ribash no. 20). There is also an opinion that distinguishes between a person elected to a state body, such as the Knesset (by virtue of whose far-reaching substantive powers the function of its representatives is held to be analogous to that of a *dayyan* adjudicating in matters of the criminal law), and a person elected to a municipal body (whose function is held to be analogous to that of the *dayyan* adjudicating in matters of the civil law, and who is therefore eligible from the age of 18 years).

WOMEN. A woman's right to elect and be elected to public office has been the subject of much halakhic discussion in recent times. In particular a great deal of opposition has been expressed to granting women the passive right to be elected, such opposition being based on tannaitic and amoraic law (Sif. Deut., 157 and Ber. 49a, respectively): "A woman is not appointed to the kingship, as it is said, 'set a king over thee' (Deut. 17:15) and not a queen; similarly for all offices in Israel none but men are appointed" (Yad, Melakhim 1:5). Some scholars took a different view, basing themselves on the fact that Deborah "judged Israel" (Judg. 4:4), i.e., that she functioned not only as a judge but was also the leader of the people. The *rishonim* had already commented on the contradiction between the fact of Deborah's leadership and the rule excluding women from public office, a contradiction they sought to reconcile by the qualification that the objection to a woman's leadership is eliminated when she is accepted by the will of the people (Nov. Rashba and Ran, Shevu. 30a; cf. also Tos. to BK 15a and Nid. 50a). On this basis some latter-day scholars have decided that a woman is entitled to elect and be elected (see, e.g., *Mishpetei Uziel*, ḤM no. 6), their conclusion being influenced by the consideration that under existing social conditions "men and women meet daily in business transactions" (*ibid.*). Although at the time he gave this decision (in the 1940s) R. Uziel wrote that it was of a purely theoretical nature and was not to be applied in practice (*ibid.* and see p. 292), it has nevertheless been accepted in practice in the state of Israel by the decisive majority of religious Jewry so far as concerns Knesset and municipal elections.

PERIOD OF RESIDENCE. The period of residence qualifying a person to elect and be elected has generally followed the period laid down for tax liability (see *Taxation; see also Resp. Maharit, vol. 1, no. 569; *Mishpetei Uziel*, ḤM no. 3).

PROPORTIONAL REPRESENTATION. In detailed decisions, scholars such as Rabbi *Kook, Jacob *Meir, and Ḥayyim *Brody expressed the opinion that the system of elections on a proportional basis answers the requirements of Jewish law, one of their main reasons being that in this way representation in the government of the state and its institutions is offered to all sections of the people (see *Sinai*, 14 (1943/44), 100–14).

In the State of Israel

IN THE SUPREME COURT. A number of Jewish law principles, concerning the legal standing of a public body and the relationship between the latter and its employees, have been considered and relied upon in decisions of the Supreme Court of Israel. In one case a municipal employee who had been dismissed on a charge of improper conduct applied to the Supreme Court – sitting as a high court of justice – to have his dismissal set aside on the ground that he had been given no opportunity to make himself heard and to answer the charge against himself prior to his dismissal. The court rejected the municipality's plea that in terms of the municipalities' ordinance it had been under no obligation to hear the employee prior to his dismissal and upheld the employee's application, relying mainly on the following principles of Jewish law:

(1) a person appointed to a public office, or holding a position with a public institution, may not be dismissed without a reasonable cause;

(2) municipal councilors are as judges and therefore may not act arbitrarily but must consider a case on its merits;

(3) since the councilors are like judges they have to follow a procedure that accords with natural justice, and a basic principle of Jewish law is that a person subjected to an inquiry must be enabled to appear and state his case (see PD 20, pt. 1 (1966), 29; cf. Resp. Rema no. 108).

In another case the court applied the Jewish law principle that – for the good of the public – there is an obligation to dismiss a public servant who is proved to have neglected his duties after he has been given due warning (see PD 20, pt. 1 (1966), 41). In another instance the court, relying on the principle that a member of a public body is as a judge, concluded that no fault was to be found with a publicly elected official for not always following the opinions of those by whom he had been elected, since he has to act as a judge seeking the truth of a matter (PD 21, pt. 1 (1967), 59), provided only that he does so upon mature consideration and does not irresponsibly and often change his views (PD 20, pt. 1 (1966), 651). Another principle of Jewish law which the court has applied precludes a judge from adjudging a matter from which he stands to derive personal benefit, and in terms of this the court set aside the decision of a local council which had been taken with the participation of a councilor who had a personal interest in the matter (*ibid.*, 102; see also PD 19, pt. 3 (1965), 393).

IN THE RABBINICAL COURTS. There is among others a decision of the rabbinical court on a basic problem that has arisen in recent years, touching on the above-mentioned rules of Jewish administrative law (the court in this instance sitting as an arbitral body since its jurisdictional authority is confined to matters of personal status; see **Mishpat Ivri*). Three political parties entered the municipal elections under a joint list, having agreed that if only two of their candidates were elected then the second one on the list resign in favor of the next candidate on the list; only two candidates were elected and the second one refused to resign as agreed. It was contended before the court that the agreement was invalid because it had not been effected by means of a *kinyan*, because it related to something not yet in existence (the agreement having been concluded prior to the elections), and because it was defective on account of *asmakhta* (i.e., since the parties had been confident that more than two of their candidates would be elected, there had been no *gemirut ha-da'at*). The court rejected all these contentions and upheld the validity of the agreement, relying on the principles discussed above governing a public authority. The court emphasized that these principles applied not only to a public authority administering municipal affairs, but also to the public constituting a political party: "If it is the rule that in public matters there is no need for a *kinyan*, and the power of the public in its doings is so great that it is not restricted by the limitations imposed on the legal act of an individual – for instance as regards something that is not yet in existence, *asmakhta*, etc. – then there is no matter that is more eminently of a public nature than the matter under consideration, namely the composition of the public leadership" (PDR 6:176). It was accordingly held that the second one of the elected representatives was obliged to resign, as undertaken in the agreement. The decision was confirmed on appeal (*ibid.* 178ff.) and in addition the following guiding principle in the field of Jewish administrative law was laid down: "We have to add and say to the litigants that public leaders should not, in the course of their public duties, avail themselves of the plea that they are not bound by their own undertakings because of their questionable legal validity. Statements and undertakings, particularly in public affairs, are sacred matters which have to be observed and fulfilled wholeheartedly, in letter and spirit… for the public is always bound by its statements and may not retract" (*ibid.*).

[Menachem Elon]

Court Rulings on Issues Relating to Public Authority

The courts in the State of Israel, particularly the Supreme Court, have on more than one occasion had recourse to Jewish law when discussing various issues relating to public authorities. In this respect, one may draw a distinction between two different periods in time. Until the mid-1970s, the policy in this area was characterized by judicial restraint and moderation. The court limited its grounds for reviewing public authorities almost exclusively to those cases where the latter exceeded its authority, and avoided intervening in the decisions themselves or an examination of their reasonability.

During this period, Jewish law served as a reference for a number of legal procedures in the area of administrative law. Thus, for example, Justice Silberg laid down the obligation of the public sector to consult with the public prior to making appointments to public office (*Aboudi* case, see below). In a number of other cases, the court discussed issues of dismissal of public employees (see below).

In the late 1970s, a major change came about in Israeli public law. The public authorities, with all its institutions and employees, became one of the most conspicuous focuses of Supreme Court rulings in Israel. This effect also became apparent in other judicial instances. The broadening of the "right of standing" in the High Court of Justice and the development of additional grounds for judicial review of the actions of the public sector (such as reasonability, arbitrariness, discrimination, unlawful considerations and so forth) led to massive intervention on the part of the judicial authorities in the actions of the public sector, and to the development of many new laws in this field.

In view of the little legislation governing public law in Israel, it has developed mainly by means of court rulings. More than once, those sitting in judgment have taken into account sources of Jewish law when studying various related issues. In 1980 the Foundations of the Law Act was enacted (see *Mishpat Ivri: The Law in the State of Israel), requiring the court to refer to the principles of "justice, freedom, integrity and peace of Israel's heritage" in all those cases where no answer could be found in the standard legal sources (e.g., legislation, case law, analogy). In 1992, two Basic Laws were passed – Basic Law: Human Dignity and Freedom; and Basic Law: Freedom of Occupation – that also required that the sources of Jewish law be examined for the interpretation of various basic rights included therein in accordance with "the values of a Jewish state." These acts of legislation made a very significant contribution to increasing the degree of recourse to the sources in Jewish law dealing in constitutional and administrative law.

In this context, a most important contribution was made by court rulings, especially those of the Supreme Court justices, who anchored many of the procedures they established in sources of Jewish law. The basis for this was the considerable quantity of material in the field of administrative law in Jewish law which, according to Justice Menachem Elon, saw "great development and rich creativity with the rise in power and status of the Jewish community from the 10th century onward. The Jewish community in various parts of the Diaspora enjoyed broad internal and judicial autonomy and, as a result of the diverse activities of community leadership in various public and administrative spheres, numerous principles of Jewish administrative law were developed and formulated. In some cases this internal autonomy was given, not only to an individual community within its own borders, but to associations of communities in many parts of the Diaspora, or a large number of communities within the bounds of the same association" (HC 702/79, *Goldberg v. Ramat Hasharon Municipal Council Head*, 34 (4) PD 89; HC 376/81, *Lugasi v. Minister of Communication et al.*, 36 (2) PD 467; cf. M. Elon, *Ha-Mishpat Ha-Ivri*, 547ff; 558ff; HC 333/78, *Bank Leumi Le-Israel Trust Company v. Estate Duty Administration*, 32 (3) PD I. 212; HC 323/81 *Wilozni v. Jerusalem Rabbinical Court of Appeals*, 36 (2) PD 741ff.). On the basis of this valuable material, the Israel Supreme Court had recourse to various aspects of Jewish law when establishing the procedures of Israeli public law. We shall present below a general review of the subjects discussed in these rulings, in the different judicial instances.

PUBLIC FIGURES AS "TRUSTEES." One of the governing principles of administrative law in Israel is the conception of public figures as "trustees" of the community's assets and rights. The status of "trustee," is known in many legal systems, with its origin in the laws of trusteeship in private law, and it imposes special obligations on public employees and elected public officers.

With the large-scale creation and development of Jewish administrative law from the 10th century onwards, alongside the increase in strength and status of the community within the framework of internal Jewish autonomy, the concept of trusteeship as the essence of the role of the public official was also expressed in the terminology of Jewish public administration. Justice Elon (HC 4566/90, *David Dekel v. Minister of Finance et al.*, 45 (1) PD 34) pointed out that a foreshadowing of the application of the laws of trusteeship with regard to public figures is already found in Jewish law, in which community leaders and people filling public positions in different areas of community life were known as "trustees" or "trustees of the congregation" (*parnasim* or *parnasei ha-ẓibbur*; see, for example, the responsum of Rabbi Joseph Bonfils (Tov Elem) in Resp. Maharam of Rothenberg, 23; cf. Resp. Rashba, vols. 3:398; 4:112; 5:259, 7:353; Resp. Ribash, 33, 61, 198, 228, 399; Tashbeẓ, 1.23; Resp. Rashbash, 287; and cf. *Digest of Responsa of the Sages of Spain and North Africa*, ed M. Elon, *Legal Digest*, vol. 2, s.v. Congregation, 414–15).

This quality of "trustee" was already identified by the Sages as attributable to Moses, the leader of Israel (see Prov. 28:20; *Exodus Rabbah* 51.1). As "trustee of the community," according to the Midrash, he took care to ensure that two other people would calculate and supervise the money he expended from the people's donations for the Tabernacle (see Ramban, Sforno, and *Ha-Emek Davar* to Gen 47:14). This title for public leaders and rulers in the Jewish community expresses the essential nature of their authority as being entrusted with power for the welfare of the community, and everything evolved from the obligations of this trusteeship, in accordance with the principles of justice and integrity of the Jewish heritage.

THE OBLIGATION OF CONSULTING THE COMMUNITY PRIOR TO MAKING AN APPOINTMENT. In one case that came before it, the Supreme Court was asked to intervene in the actions of the Elections Committee for the Chief Rabbinate (FH 12/60 *Aboudi v. Minister of Religious Affairs et al.*, PD 14, 2084). In this context, Justice Silberg insisted upon the obligation of the public authority to consult with the community prior to appointing people to public positions (see below). This principle is derived from the work of the Tabernacle, prior to which God asked Moses to turn to the people of Israel for their opinion as to whether he was worthy of the exalted position of building the Tabernacle (Ber. 55b). The court quoted the response of R. Moses Sofer, who was fiercely critical of the appointment of a rabbi against the wishes of the community (Resp. Ḥatam Sofer ḤM, 19). This principle was also discussed by the Supreme Court in a case relating to the appointment of a rabbi to the local council. The presiding judge, Justice Türkel, ruled that, given that the obligation of consulting the community is a fundamental principle in Jewish law for the appointment of public officials (see Ber. 55b; Sh. Ar., ḤM. 3; Resp. Ribash, 271), and this obligation had not been fulfilled, the appointed rabbi should be disqualified from serving in the position.

Rights and Obligations of Elected Officials and Employees of the Public Authorities

With regard to the employees of the public sector, Jewish law applies the fundamental principle by which authority "was entirely created merely to serve the common good, and it has nothing of its own." Consequently, the fundamental instruction given to those appointed to communal positions is: "In the past you were your own master; from now on you are enslaved to the community" (*Sifre*, at Deut 1:16); and therefore those receiving an appointment to serve in a public position are told: "Perhaps you think I am giving you a position of power? I give you slavery!" (TB Horayot 10a–b) and, according to Rashi's interpretation (ad loc.): "Authority is bondage for a man, imposing on him the yolk of the public." Consequently Justice Elon, speaking for the Supreme Court (in the above-cited Dekel judgment), drew attention to the Sages' severe criticism of "those who accept authority in order to derive benefit from it" (*Pesikta Rabbati* 22.2, Ish-Shalom edition, p. 111). According to this, the Sages' denunciation of the community leader and member of the public sector who "raises himself up above the community" is also understandable (Ḥag. 5b; cf. Maharal of Prague, *Netivot Olam*, pt. 2, *Netiv ha-Onah*, ch. 5 (Jerusalem, 5731), 12b). From all these, Justice Elon concluded there that: "Until a person becomes a public figure, he is his own master; from the time he becomes a public figure, he belongs to the community. He belongs to the community, but the community does not belong to him. The authority he undertakes is in order that the community may benefit from it, not for his own benefit. The appointed community leader must support the community, rather than himself, the community leader, being supported by the community and raising himself above the community."

On the basis of these sources, the Supreme Court concluded that political appointments made by virtue of connections rather than talent are invalid, as:

> A public authority that appoints an employee in public service acts as a trustee of the public. And it is an important rule that this trusteeship must act with integrity, without extrinsic considerations, and for the benefit of the community, by whose power and on whose behalf the mandate to make the appointment is given to the appointing authority… When a public figure appoints an employee to the public service on the basis of extraneous considerations of political interests, such an appointment is invalid and is a form of breach of trust with regard to the community that has empowered the appointing authorities (ibid.).

In one of its judgments (Cr. A 884/80 *State of Israel v. Grossman*, 35 (1) PD 412) the Court discussed the State's appeal against the acquittal of a senior employee of the Bank of Israel charged with fraud and breach of trust after acquiring debentures, intended for banking institutions and further education funding, for members of his own family. Justice Tirkel, in a minority opinion, allowed the respondent's acquittal to stand, but spoke at length of the obligation of members of public authorities to avoid any act that might cast suspicion on themselves or their actions. In this context, he cited the rules concerning the watchmen of the Temple Guard, who were enjoined from any action – even the most legitimate – which might cast the slightest suspicion of their defrauding the community's trust, in order to fulfill the obligation "that you shall be clear before the Lord and before Israel" (Num. 32:22). From this verse, the sages inferred that "a man must perform his obligations to the community in the same way as he must perform his obligations to God" (TJ Shek. 3.2; BT Yoma 28a).

In another case, the special obligation of the public figure to be incorruptible and honest is discussed (HC 400/87 *Kahana v. Speaker of the Knesset*, 41 (2) PD 729). Based upon the words of Rabbi Israel Isserlein (*Terumat ha-Deshen, Pesakim u-Ketavim*, 214; Rema, Sh. Ar., ḤM, 37: 22), Justice Elon derived this obligation from the analogy made by the Sages between the public figure and the judge sitting in judgment.

A PUBLIC FIGURE AS A WITNESS. The special status of the public figure dictates the upholding of his dignity. This matter was discussed in a Supreme Court case concerning a litigant's request to call a judge as witness and to examine him on the stand in the course of a civil suit (LCA 3202/03 *State of Israel v. Hagai Yosef et al.*, 58 (3) PD 544–545). In rejecting the request, Justice Tirkel based his decision, inter alia, on Jewish law, which discusses the importance of maintaining the dignity of public figures. He quoted Maimonides' ruling that "The community must act with respect towards judges, and be in awe of them, nor should he degrade himself or act frivolously in their presence, for when a person is appointed as a leader over the community, he may not engage in [manual] labor in the presence of three people so as not to be degraded before them; all the more so may he not eat and drink in the presence of the public" (ḤM 8:4; and see also Yad, Sanh. 25.1, 4).

THE PUBLIC AUTHORITIES' DUTY OF GOOD FAITH. One of the fundamental rules in law is the duty to act in good faith. This duty applies not only to the individual but also, and in particular, to the public authorities, who are required to act in good faith in their dealings with those who turn to them. In one of the appeals to the Supreme Court (HC 376/81 *Lugasi et al. v. Minister of Communications*, 36 (2) PD 465), Justice Elon based this obligation on the principles of Jewish law: "The principle of acting in good faith, both towards the individual and towards the community, is based on the ancient precept of 'and you shall do that which is right and good' (Deut. 6:18). By virtue of this precept, the principle of good faith crystallized in the legal system of the State of Israel in the aforementioned provisions of the Contract Law (General Section). The term 'good faith,' both in its Jewish sources and in ordinary contemporary usage, is synonymous with integrity, and represents an overall guiding principle, a kind of 'royal decree,' in the entire world of procedure." Justice Elon further wrote that: "Assistance in understanding this concept may be found in the sharp and incisive words of Naḥmanides (one of the Spanish Sages at the end of the 12th century), defining the essence of behavior which is the opposite of that which is righteous and good: Namely, that anyone acting according to the technical and formal meaning of the laws of the Torah alone, that is, who takes care to adhere only to that which is explicitly stated and not to that which is not explicitly mentioned but is implied by the general spirit of the Torah is, in the words of the Ramban, a 'scoundrel with the permission of the Torah' (Naḥmanides, Torah Commentary, on Lev 19:2). Thus, a lack of good faith on the part of the public authorities in discharging an obligation is the behavior of 'a scoundrel in the service of the public.'"

THE PUBLIC AUTHORITIES' OBLIGATION TO KEEP THEIR PROMISES. The duty of good faith also obliges public authorities not to renege on promises they have made. Accordingly, the Supreme Court has ruled that even a "political agreement" binds its signatories, even if it is not treated in the same way as a private legal contract. Since no solution was found to this matter in the Contracts Law, the Supreme Court turned to sources of Jewish law and established this basic principle as derived from Jewish Law (HC 1635/90 *Jerczewski v. the Prime Minister et al.*, 45 (1) PD 780–781). Thus, for example, Ribash wrote that the community is not entitled to renege on a promise that has been given, "public authorities do not make statements in jest [i.e., act as a joker and recant]" (Resp. Ribash, no. 476), and this was the basis of the Rema's ruling in the Shulḥan Arukh (ḤM 81:1). Justice Elon refers to a golden rule in this matter that appears in the response of the Rashbash (Rabbi Solomon ben Simeon Duran), who ruled: "If you examine the conduct of all the communities in such a matter, you will see that they never revoke or rescind [an agreement] …as it is unseemly for the community to say 'we were mistaken'" (Resp. Rashbash, no. 566; and cf. the response of the Ra'anah, Resp. Mayim Amukim, Teshuvot, no. 63). Justice Elon found an instructive explanation of the binding legal validity of a public agreement in the words of Rabbi Joseph Colon, one of the greatest respondents of 15th century Italy: "that the agreement of many is pleasant and its paths are the paths of peace, and therefore it was said that their words would be fulfilled when all were in agreement and together, and none of them would be able to recant and destroy the state of truth and peace" (Resp. Maharik no. 179 in Lemberg 1797 ed.; in Warsaw, 1870 ed., no. 181).

THE DUTY TO GIVE REASONS FOR A DECISION. Like other legal systems, Israeli law also states that, apart from exceptional cases, all public authorities must give reasons for their decisions. One of the appeals before the High Court of Justice discussed a case in which one of the institutions of the Bar Association failed to give the reasons for a certain decision. Justice Kister, who discussed this matter (HC 142/70 *Shapira v. the District Committee of the Bar Association*, 25 (1) PD 333), based the public authority's obligation to give reasons on the basis of Jewish law, and the duty of the law court to give reasons for its decisions. The source for this appears in the Talmud (Sanh. 31b), which says that if one of the litigants says "write and tell me for what reason I have been judged – you write and tell him." The obligation and conditions of reasoned explanation are also set out in the literature of the rabbinical authorities (Yad, Sanh. 6.6; Tur & Sh. Ar., ḤM 14.4, in Rema).

A number of reasons are given for this in Jewish law: (a) to ensure the possibility of review by the *Bet Din ha-Gadol* (High Court) or by another body (*Bet ha-Va'ad*) that may be able to determine whether there has been an error in the decision or not; (see *Appeal); (b) the overall principle, guiding all persons, and especially those holding public office, "then you shall be clean before the Lord and before Israel" (Num. 32:22).

In view of these considerations, the rabbinical authorities ordered that, in those cases where both parties had agreed to be involved in litigation before any body, there was usually no reason to give an explanation, unless there was cause for suspicion that an error had been made. In addition, the rabbinical authorities distinguished between the duty to give a broader verbal explanation for the sake of the litigants, and the requirement to provide a written explanation.

With regard to written reasons, which for the most part are not necessarily intended to explain to the litigants the reasoning behind the judgment but rather to enable review, it is stated in the *Nimmukei Yosef Baba Meẓi'a* (ibid): "One does not write 'for this reason and for this evidence' [i.e., in the sense of an argument or proof from halakhic literature], but one writes 'so-and-so claimed this and so-and-so responded that, and as a result so-and-so was acquitted, and in the Court they knew the reasons.'" The same ruling was given by the Rema (R. Moses Isserles – in the Sh. Ar., ḤM 14: 4. One of the commentaries on the Shulkhan Arukh, the *Sema* (ibid., 26), explains: "When they (i.e., the judges) hear the arguments, they know how to rule on them, because there is one law for all of us."

On the other hand, Rabbi Jair Ḥayyim Bacharach, author of Resp. Ḥavvot Yair (whose comments are partially cited in *Pitḥei Teshuvah* in Sh. Ar., ḤM 14:10), questioned the Rema's ruling and ruled that a description of the argument or, as it might been described in modern legal terms – a description of the facts as presented in court, was not sufficient and that it was necessary to add the actual legal reasons for the decision. In Justice Kister's opinion, the considerations mentioned in the above sources hold true today. Today, as in the past, authorities discussing the rights of the citizen – and not necessarily in the courts – should act according to the rule "then you shall be guiltless before the Lord and before Israel" or, as it is commonly said, "that justice must not only be done, it must be seen to be done." In any event, today too it is difficult to provide appropriate review of any decision if the reasons for the decision are not known.

When translating the *posekim*'s dispute regarding the scope of the reasoned explanation into modern terms Justice Kister stated that in order to enable review of a particular decision, it is sufficient for the deciding authorities to provide the applicant the set of facts upon which the decision is based; the authority reviewing the case will then be able to determine whether the authority that decided was in error or not. This is the minimum requirement with regard to reasoned explanation; it may be expected that the authorities will also state its legal reasoning, at least in brief.

The regulations of the rabbinical courts in Israel state that "every judgment, in addition to the decision regarding the case, must also include: (a) a brief summary of the arguments of the parties; (b) determination of the important facts; (c) reasons for the decision."

THE CLAIM OF ESTOPPEL IN ADMINISTRATIVE LAW. One of the governing principles of administrative law is that a person who was a partner to a particular act may not raise arguments against the legality of the act in which he himself participated. This doctrine is known as "estoppel," and has implications for different areas of law, including public law. In one of the cases heard before the High Court of Justice, the court was required to hear an appeal of a company that had participated in the tender issued by a public authority, and complained that its bid was not accepted (HC 632/81 *Migda Ltd. v. Minister of Health et al.* 35 (2) PD 688). Contrary to the positions of Justices Barak and Netanyahu, who sat in judgment, Justice Elon was of the minority opinion that the appeal should be rejected, on the basis of the theory of *estoppel* set down in Jewish law: "In cases such as this, the Talmud of the Sages says 'embellish yourself and then embellish others' (BM 107b), and in the words of the ancient maxim, when one says to another: 'take the toothpick out of your teeth, the other responds: first take the beam out of your eye' (BB 15b; and see Rashi, BB ibid.).

ONUS ON THE PUBLIC AUTHORITIES EVEN IN THE ABSENCE OF A KINYAN. One of the characteristics setting the public sector apart from others is its obligation to keep promises it has made even in the absence of an act of acquisition (*kinyan*) (unlike private law, in which Jewish law demands an act of acquisition to create a legal obligation – see entry *Acquisition).

In a ruling dealing with the authority's obligation to honor its undertaking to provide telephones to the country's residents (HC 376/81 *Lugasi et al. v. Minister of Communications et al.* 36 (2) PD 449), Justice Elon based this obligation on the sources of Jewish law: "Beginning from the thirteenth century the principle was established that any legal transaction made by the community is binding, even if no such act of acquisition (*kinyan*): 'for whatever is done by the public does not require a *kinyan*, even if it is something which for a *kinyan* is necessary in the case of an individual'" (Resp. Maharam of Rothenburg, cited in Mordechai, BM 457–458). This new principle was applied to various types of legal transactions, such as employee-employer relations, the laws of guarantee and gifts, and other legal matters in which the public is a party (see, for example, Resp. Maharam b. Baruch, Prague, no. 38; Resp. Ribash, no. 176; Rema, Sh. Ar., ḤM 163:6, in Rema; 204:9; Resp. Mayim Amukkim, section with Responsa of Resp. Ra'anah – R. Eliyahu b. Ḥayyim, no. 63). The rule that was laid down and accepted was: "It is a simple custom, that whatever the community leaders agree to do is completely valid even without a *kinyan*" (Resp. Ha-Rosh, 6:19, 21). In addition, a number of other fundamental requirements of the laws of acquisition in Jewish law, were drastically relaxed for public authorities. Thus it was settled that a public authority can purchase or transfer a thing that has not yet come into existence and, contrary to the rule in Jewish Law that an agreement affected by an *asmakhta* (i.e., absence of a deliberate and unqualified intent to be bound) is not valid, (see *Asmakhta) it was established that there is no defect in *asmakhta* where the public is involved (Resp. Mayim Amukkim, ibid.; R. Moses Di Trani, Resp. Mabit, vol.3. no. 228; and see *Contract, the Laws of Contract).

Based on this fundamental assumption, Justice Elon further states (HC 376/81 *Lugasi*, ibid, p. 470) that "a greater degree of seriousness, integrity, and propriety is demanded of the public authorities in fulfilling its undertakings than is demanded of an individual in the field of private law. For this reason, when a representative of a public authority agrees that an individual citizen is exempt from a certain payment, this admission is binding and has full legal force. If, however, an individual makes a similar admission, it is not binding unless he has made it before two witnesses to whom he says 'you are my witnesses,' because we presume that admissions given only in the presence of the two litigants themselves lacks the necessary resolve to constitute valid, admissions, as the party making the admission may claim 'I made the admission in jest' (Sanh. 29a). This is not, however, the case with regard to an admission made by a public authority. Why is this so? Because 'although an individual making an admission may claim this, it may not be said… of the community making an admission, because the community does not make statements in jest" (Isaac b. Sheshet Perfet, Resp. Ribash, no. 476 (14th century, a leading halakhic authority in Spain and Algiers; and see also Rema to Sh. Ar., ḤM 81:1). To support this, Justice Elon cited two incidents recorded in the responsa literature. In the first, a question was brought before Rabbi Solomon b. Simeon Duran (Rashbash; the spiritual leader of the Jewish community of Algiers, 15th century), with regard to "a community whose custom was to a particular kind of concession for one year, as was the practiced in all the communities; and the custom of that community was to sell it for one year, but on that occasion the treasurers of the community sold if for four years, and they wished to revoke the sale. May they recant or not?" (Resp. Rashbash no. 566). From the responsum, it appears that the leaders of the community wanted to revoke the sale because, in their opinion, the concession had been sold at a price lower than should have been obtained for such a period of time. Selling for either more or less than the accepted price is called in the Talmud "over-reaching" and when the deviation from the accepted price is more than one-sixth below the fair price, the seller, who is the injured party is entitled to rescind the transaction (BM 49b; and see *Ona'ah). It was further claimed that the concession was sold without an act of acquisition, and therefore is invalid, because it relates to something that has not yet come into existence. The Rashbash rejected the arguments of the community, and denied them the right to rescind their agreement:

> A sale by the public, even without an act of acquisition, and even regarding something that is not yet in existence, and even to someone not yet in existence, is valid…. And even if it was their custom to sell it [the concession] for one year and they sold it for four [years], they cannot rescind the sale… And there is no ground for rescinding the sale for this reason, unless the treasurers sold it privately, not in the presence of the community, for then the community may rescind the sale, as they sold it contrary to their custom. But if the sale was made in the presence of the members of the community, or the majority of them, then it may not be rescinded and it is valid; and there is no element of over-reaching. If you examine the conduct of all the communities in this matter you will see that they never revoke or rescind [an agreement], neither because it concerns an object not yet in existence, nor because of over-reaching… because it is unseemly for the community to say: we were mistaken.

From these words of Rashbash, the High Court of Justice concluded, *per* Justice Elon, that the transaction would have been invalid had the treasurers not been authorized to engage in a transaction of this kind at their own discretion and without the explicit authority of the community. However, if the representatives of the public body did not deviate from their authority and are authorized, by the accepted practice of that body, to engage in transactions on behalf of the public body at their own discretion, then the transaction is valid and the public body may not rescind it, even though a transaction of this kind, carried out by an individual, in the field of private law, may be rescinded for reasons of mistaken price under the laws of over-reaching. Why? Because a greater degree of integrity and propriety is demanded of a public authority and its representatives; they do not recant the undertakings they have made and for which they request the validity of a legal transaction, because it is unseemly for them to say that they were mistaken in their undertaking.

Justice Elon also finds support for this fundamental principle concerning the public authorities in another responsum by Rabbi Elijah b. Ḥayyim, the Ranaḥ (Resp. Mayyim Amukkim, ibid.). In this case, the community leaders agreed with one of the town's residents as to the amount of the tax to be paid on his father's estate. After a while, the community requested to rescind the agreement made by its representatives, claiming that there had been a mistake in the evaluation of the estate made by the community representatives. The respondent objected to a reappraisal and argued that the agreement he had reached with the community leaders was binding with regard to the entire community. Ranaḥ first examined the duty imposed upon the court to be most meticulous in ensuring that public funds are not misused. Nevertheless, he rejected the arguments of the public authorities, by virtue of the fundamental principle that "every act undertaken by the leaders of the community to whom the affairs of the community are entrusted is valid, and the community may not retract, even if it is evident that the community leaders erred in the matter." On the basis of this response, Justice Elon established a basic principle in public law: "The undertaking made by a public authority or its representatives within the framework of their powers, with the intention that it have legal force, is binding on the public authority, and it cannot retract it, even if such an undertaking, were it to be made by an individual in the area of private law, could have been rescinded and revoked. A public authority which has assumed an undertaking must fulfill it with a greater degree of integrity and propriety, over and above what the law requires of an individual as to such an undertaking in private law." This guiding principle, based upon Jewish law, has served as the foundation for many other rulings in later years and determined the obligation of the administrative authorities to fulfill promises it has made, even if these are not accompanied by a formal undertaking as is customary in private law.

THE OBLIGATION OF PUBLIC AUTHORITIES TO ACT OVER AND ABOVE THE LETTER OF THE LAW. Alongside the obligation of the public authorities to uphold their undertakings even if given in the absence of any formal act of acquisition, there are other cases in which the public authority is relieved of fulfilling duties that exist in private law. In the *Lugasi* ruling mentioned above (HC 376/81 *Lugasi et al. v. Minister of Communications et al.* 36 (2) PD 449), Justice Elon further states that, notwithstanding the fact that in the world of Jewish law there is a duty, in special circumstances, to act over and above the letter of the law, even when the litigant is exempt from this by the law (see, for example, BM 83a; BK 55b–56a), this duty does not always exist in the case of a public authority. The reason is that the individual is required, in certain circumstances, to uphold the general rule "Favor him with your own property and give it to him" (Ḥul. 154a); but this is not the case for a public authority which, when exempted by the law, may not make payment to an individual from public funds on the basis of an extra-legal obligation. In this case, the public authority would be favoring an individual at the expense of the general public – since the public authority acts as a trustee for the funds and rights of the general public – and it is not entitled to do so. The rule is "Favor him with your own property and give it to him but not from public funds" (see also the discussion in the Rabbinical Court on this subject, in File 517/5714 (Jer) p. 171.)

CAPACITY AND DISMISSAL OF PUBLIC EMPLOYEES. The subject of the capacity of public employees to serve in a public position, and their dismissal, has come up before the Supreme Court on a number of occasions, and more than once the court has had recourse to the sources of Jewish law to support its rulings. Thus, for example, a particular case (HC 290/65 *Altgar v. Head of the Municipality*, 20 (1) PD 29) concerned a municipality employee dismissed from his position due to inappropriate behavior. Among other arguments, the employee claimed that he had been dismissed without being given an appropriate "right to plead" and to respond to the charges against him. In his discussion of this matter, Justice Kister set out the reasons for dismissal of a public employee in Jewish law. The talmudic rule is that "one never removes [a person] from leadership within Israel," but this rule does not apply to an employee who has "sinned" – i.e., who was involved in a serious transgression or behaved in a way that is not fitting to his position – nor does it apply to one who was initially appointed for a fixed period of time.

On the basis of Maimonides' rulings (*Klei Mikdash* 4:21), Justice Kister wrote that a public employee may not be dismissed merely because of a bad rumor that has been spread about him (Resp. Rambam no. 111), and that the public authorities should act with propriety and in good faith in the dismissal process (with regard to the public authorities obligation to act in good faith, see above). Since members of the public sector are like judges, they must be scrupulous in upholding legal procedure and in providing an appropriate opportunity for the employee to make his arguments heard before deciding in his case (see below).

In another case, the Supreme Court ruled, *per* Justice Kister, that in the interests of the public's benefit there was a duty to dismiss a public employee who was negligent in his job and did not carry it out properly despite being cautioned, and to employ in his stead someone who was fair and honest. This rule is based upon the words of the Ḥazon Ish, Rabbi Abraham Isaiah Karelitz (second half of the 20th century) (HC 218/65 *Gabbai v. Jerusalem Municipality*, 20 (1) PD 48).

In discussing these issues, the Supreme Court included the obligation to consider, inter alia, the damage that may ensue to the family of an employee threatened with dismissal, who is dependent upon him for its livelihood. This consideration has an important place in the sources of Jewish law, and expresses the balance between the interests of the community and the interests of the individual (See HC 192/68 *Bashkin v. Mayor of Tel Aviv*, 22 (2) PD 748; Rabbi Avraham Halevi Horovitz, *Ẓur Ya'akov*, end of §195).

Another case (ALA 1/68 *Anon. v. Attorney General*, 22 (1) PD 676), discusses the terms set in Jewish law for restoring a public employee to his position after serving a sentence. In this matter, the authority must be convinced that the employee has completely repented of his ill deeds (ḤM 34.33, in the words of Rema). In extreme cases, such as the case of a man who has committed murder, he is never returned to his position (Yad, Sanh. 17:8).

Justice Kister emphasized that, notwithstanding that Jewish law regards the rehabilitation of those who repent as an overarching principle (see *Punishment) and believes in the possibility of complete rehabilitation, it is cautious with regard to one who has transgressed and repented serving in a public position of trust. Rambam already ruled that people in various public positions who have failed in carrying out their position, even in error, "are dismissed without notice, for there is permanent notice upon them, as they act as public agents" (Yad, Sekhirut 10.7, according to BM 109a; and see also Sh. Ar., ḤM 306). With regard to restoration to their former position, Justice Kister says that, according to Jewish law, when the case in question involves dismissal due to a crime, a particularly stringent examination is carried out, to assure that they may be regarded as trustworthy in the future, as to whether repentance is indeed complete, or whether the court is being deceived or not (Sh. Ar., ḤM 34.33, end of the Rema's comments; and cf. *Bet Yosef* ad loc. See also the article by Justice Kister, "*Gishat ha-Yehadut la-Avaryan u-le-Shikkumo* ("The Jewish Approach to the Criminal and his Rehabilitation" (Hebrew), *Ha-Praklit*, 25, 485–86).

This issue was discussed at length in another Supreme Court ruling dealing with the capacity of a criminal who has served his sentence to return and serve in public office (HC 1935/93 *Mahfoud v. Minister of Religious Affairs et al.*, 48 (1) PD 768–769). Based on Jewish law, Justice Elon writes about the duty to balance between the desire to prevent a stain on the reputation of the public service and a loss of public trust in it, and the basic principle of rehabilitation in Jewish law, which has even been anchored in legislation by the Knesset in the Crime Register and Rehabilitation of Offenders Law, 5741 – 1981 (on this issue, see also: ALA 18/84 *Carmi v. State Prosecutor*, 44 (1) PD 373–381).

RULES OF NATURAL JUSTICE AND THE RIGHT TO PLEAD. One of the basic rules in the theory of administrative law requires the public authorities to uphold "the rules of natural justice" – among which, the right to hear a person's arguments before making a decision liable to affect his rights. Justice Silberg, who discussed this issue (HC 3/58 *Berman v. Minister of Interior,* 12 PD 1493), noted that English law of the 18th century (*The King against the Chancellor, Master and Scholars of the University of Cambridge (1723)*, 93 ER 698, 704) already regarded the Torah as the source of this obligation, in the words God spoke to Adam before his expulsion from the Garden of Eden (Genesis 3: 9–11). Justice Silberg expanded and extended this obligation to "hear the other party" when talking about a judicial or quasi-judicial authorities, based upon many sources in Jewish law, including the words of Rabbi Moses Isserles (leading rabbinic authority in Poland, 16th century), who discussed it at length in his responsa (Resp. Rema, no. 108). The Rema saw this principle as already well-established in the Torah precept of "hearing your brothers." In addition to the aforementioned proof from Adam, the Rema adds that it is also possible to learn this principle from other cases: e.g., God calling upon Cain to hear his arguments before imposing the punishment. Similarly, in the case of Sodom the Sages derived from God's words "I will go down and see" (Gen. 18:21), that the judge may not make his ruling until he has heard and understood the arguments of the accused (HC 10/59 *Vicky Levy v. The Rabbinical Court,* 13 PD 1187; and see the High Court judgment in *Altgar* cited above. Judge Leron of the Beersheba District Court also based his decision upon the source in App.31/81 *Ben-Simon v. State of Israel,* PSM 5742 (1) 438).

The basic principle of the "duty to hear" was among the reasons invoked by Justice Elon in stating the husband's right to be a party to his wife's application to terminate a pregnancy, as one liable to be affected by a decision on this matter (CA 413/80 *Plonit v. Ploni,* 35 (3) PD 88). (See *Abortion). Justice Elon based this decision, among other things, on a statement by the Sages to the effect that "there are three partners in the creation of man: God, his father and his mother" (Kid. 30b), which requires that the husband's position be heard prior to taking a decision with regard to aborting the fetus.

PROHIBITION AGAINST CONFLICT OF INTEREST. One of the basic rules in the theory of public authority and administrative law, arising from the "rules of natural justice," is the prohibition against a public employee being in a position of "conflict of interest" when coming to decide on a certain matter. This conflict of interests may arise from a personal interest that he has in a particular matter under discussion, or from an institutional interest on the part of the entity he is representing. In a number of Supreme Court rulings (HC 291/72 *Rubinstein v. Elections Committee for the Chief Rabbinate Council,* 26 (2) PD 279; HC 91/74 *Gabara et al. v. The District Court,* 28 (2) PD 526; HC 21/66 *Katabi v. Chairman of Kiryat Ekron Local Council,* 20 (2) PD 108), the Supreme Court (per Justices Haim Cohn and Kister) referred to the sources of Jewish law in order to highlight this prohibition, and in particular to a ruling concerning judges, by which a judge cannot sit in judgment on any issue in which he has any kind of benefit (Sh. Ar., ḤM 8.12). The Talmudic sages went to the extent of disqualifying a judge whose interest in the case was no more than that of any other inhabitants of a town whose Torah scroll had been stolen:

> If a scroll of the Law belonging to the inhabitants of a town has been stolen, the judges of that town must not try him [the alleged culprit]. If a man says: Distribute a *maneh* to the inhabitants of my town [and it is stolen], the judges of that town must not try him [the alleged culprit] (BB 43a). And Rosh ruled that if a person avoided paying tax, the town's judges, to whom the tax was paid, were not entitled to judge him: "it is obvious that he should not be judged by them, because how can they judge themselves as they have a part in the claim" (Resp. Ha-Rosh, 58.7). The analogy between elected public figures and judges implies that the obligation to avoid conflict of interest applies both to employees in public services and to elected public figures.

In another case (SSA 2/73, *Ploni v. State of Israel,* 28 (1) PD 370), Justice Kister stated, again on the basis of sources in Jewish law, that every public employee must avoid making use of his subordinates for his own personal purposes. According to Rabbi Jonah Gerondi (a contemporary of Naḥmanides) in his book *Sha'arei Teshuvah,* (Sect. 3. 60), one who is in charge of others is entitled, and even required, to demand of these employees that they carry out their work in the service, and no more than that.

PROHIBITION AGAINST "LEAKS." In one case (HC 264/70 *Mizrachi v. the Committee for Appointing Dayyanim,* 24 (2) PD 229), the High Court of Justice, per Justice Kister, established the obligation on the part of the public authorities to maintain confidentiality with regard to information, which if disclosed might harm another. Justice Kister based this obligation on the verse "He that goes about as a talebearer reveals secrets" (Prov. 11:13), and on the words of Rabbi Israel Meir Ha-Cohen of Radin, in his famous book *Hafeẓ Hayyim* (*Hilkhot Lashon ha-Ra,* 2.11).

NON-JUSTICIABILITY. Alongside judicial review of the actions of the implementing authorities by the court, there are certain areas that "are not justiciable" and which the court avoids dealing with, such as military considerations, foreign policy and so forth. In one case, the High Court of Justice discussed the question of the judicial review of orders issued by the security authorities (HC 302/72 *Abu Hilu v. Government of Israel,* 27 (2) PD 184–185). In rejecting the petition, the Supreme Court, in a decision by Justice Kister, ruled that the Court would not pass issues of this kind under its judicial review. Among other things, he based this position on the distinction that exists in Jewish law in this respect: alongside the provision that the king may embark on a voluntary war only with the consent of the Sanhedrin, in the case of a just war, such as "saving Israel from a foreign power," he does not require the permission of the Sanhedrin, and his decision is not subject to judicial review (Yad, Melakhim 5:1–2; S. Arieli, *Mishpat ha-Milḥamah,* pp. 96, 179; E.Y. Waldenberg, *Hilkhot Medinah,* vol. 2, chs. 4–5).

DEVIATING FROM AUTHORITY. One of the most important grounds for judicial review is *ultra vires.* The basic rule in public law, known as the "principle of legality," states that, unlike a private individual, a public authority may not carry out any action whatsoever unless it has obtained explicit authority to perform this action by law or by virtue of the law. In an appeal hearing in the Supreme Court, the issue of the ability of a local authority to impose imposts on a resident without explicit authorization to do so by law was discussed (Cr. A 656/76 *Ha-Giva ha-Aduma Co. v. Rishon le-Zion Municipality*, 30 (3) PD 823). Justice Haim Cohn stated that not only was this impost improper, as a deviation from authority, but that it even involved an element of robbery. He supported this position with Maimonides' words with regard to the King's Law: "'that the king may cut down trees and destroy houses, and even more so collect taxes so as to build roads or bridges. In what case? That of a king whose coin is valid… But if his coin is not valid, then he is like a robber with a strong arm or a gang of armed bandits whose laws are not law, and this king and all who work for him are robbers in every respect' (Yad, Gezeilah ve-Aveidah 5.18). The king's 'coin is valid' when he carries out actions and decrees with the authorization of the people of that land; consequently, one can say that the municipality's 'coin' is valid when it imposes taxes and collects money, either with the authorization of the legislator or with the consent of the taxpayer. Without explicit and unequivocal authorization and without the agreement of the taxpayer, a requirement to pay for the sake of providing a deposit is a form of 'royal robbery' which does not justify taking money from its owner."

DELEGATION OF AUTHORITY. Administrative law has developed various rules relating to the right of a public figure to delegate authorities to another person. The basic principle is that, so long as the authority in question is mainly technical (such as the erection of signposts) there is nothing to prevent one person from delegating authority to another. By contrast, an authority involving an element of discretion may not be delegated, as it has been granted to a particular person and not to another. The Supreme Court had recourse a number of times to the sources of Jewish law in this matter. In one case (HC 380/74 *Salman v. National Labor Court in Jerusalem*, 30 (1) PD 501) the issue of the dismissal of an employee was discussed. Justice Berenson held that where a local authority has a number of panels authorized to make decisions, not every matter needs to come before the highest instance. He anchored this decision in a verse from the Torah, regarding the advice given to Moses by Jethro (Exod. 18:22): "and it shall be, that every great matter they shall bring unto thee, but every small matter they shall judge themselves."

In another ruling (HC 702/79 *Goldberg v. Sherman*, 34 (4) PD 85), discussing the ability of the head of a local authority to delegate authority to his deputies, Justice Elon developed the doctrine of "delegation of authority" in administrative law, utilizing the response of Rabbi Isaac ben Sheshet Perfet (Ribash, halakhic authority, Spain–North Africa, end of 14th century–beginning of 15th century) to a question asked by the leaders of the Barcelona community (Resp. Ribash 228). The question concerned a public regulation (see *Takkanot ha-Kahal) enacted in a particular community in the Catalonia district, in which three of the community's leaders, called "trustees," were authorized, along with the community's court, to select a group of 30 people to supervise various community matters, in particular matters relating to the division of the tax burden and the manner of its collection. The trustees, who did not succeed in reaching an agreed position, attempted to delegate their authorities to two other people, but certain members of the community objected to this. Ribash accepted the arguments of those who objected to the delegation, stating that the authority conveyed upon a person elected by the community, whose performance involved a degree of "reasoning and consideration," must be carried out by that individual, unless there is an explicit provision enabling the position holder to delegate his position to another (see also HC 2303/90 *Philipovitz v. Ministry of Justice*, 46 (1) PD 425–426).

ADMINISTRATIVE DISCRETION. One of the most important issues in administrative law concerns the obligation of a public authority to exercise its discretion before taking a decision on any matter. The components of this discretion and the scope of judicial review over the manner in which it is exercised are frequently discussed in court rulings. In one case, the basic principle of independent exercise of discretion was established, based upon sources of Jewish law. The court held that the obligation of trust imposed upon an official elected to a given institution, required it to act in accordance with relevant considerations and in accordance with his convictions, even if this contradicted the partisan interests of the body that elected him and sent him to that elected institution (HC 24/66, *Malkah v. Seri Levy*, 20 (2) PD 657); cf. Elon, *Authority and Power in the Jewish Community* (Hebrew) p. 29).

INCORRUPTIBILITY AND SINCERITY. One of the laws concerning public administration states that the court will not review an action involving an appellant wishing to appeal the decision of a public authority if he appears before the court with "unclean hands" – that is, if he is himself a criminal or is concealing facts from the court. Justice Tirkel based this ruling on a passage from Psalms (24:3–4): "Who shall ascend into the mountain of the Lord, and who shall stand in his holy place? He that hath clean hands and a pure heart; who hath not taken my name in vain and hath not sworn deceitfully" (LCA 5072/00 *Izzy Yogev Industries Ltd. v. Abu Bros. Locksmiths*, 55 (2) PD 309).

Takkanot Kahal (community enactments) and the Responsa Index

A major contribution to the rules and laws concerning public authorities in Jewish law was made by a number of digests appearing in recent years. Among these, we should particularly note the *Legal Digest of Responsa Literature from Spain and North Africa* (edited by M. Elon), and its counterpart from Ashkenaz, France, and Italy (edited by B. Lifschitz and

A. Shochetman), containing many entries (such as community, community regulation) dealing with various aspects of public administration law. An important source concerning the legal status of the public authorities and its employees are the community records (see *Takkanot ha-Kahal) which have been published in recent years, containing rich material on the history of public authority, its rules and procedures, rights and obligations.

[Aviad Hacohen (2nd ed.)]

BIBLIOGRAPHY: T.S. Zuri, *Mishpat ha-Talmud*, 8 (1922), 52–60; idem, *Toledot ha-Mishpat ha-Ẓibburi ha-Ivri*, 1 (1931), 301ff.; E.J. Waldenberg, *Ẓiẓ Eli'ezer*, 2 (1947), no. 24; Z. Warhaftig, in: *Sinai*, 23 (1948), 24–49; M. Findling, in: *Yavneh*, 3 (1949), 50–56, 63; A. Karlin, in: *Ha-Torah ve-ha-Medinah*, 1 (1949), 58–66; J. Pilz, *ibid.*, 2 (1950), 55–58; J.H. Asafi, *ibid.*, 4 (1951), 241–3; N.Z. Friedmann, *ibid.*, 7–8 (1954/57), 63–71; T.A. Agus, in: JQR, 43 (1952/53), 153–76; M. Feinstein, in: *Ha-Ma'or*, 12 (1960), issue 2 (English numbering: 10 (1960), issue 10), 4–7; M. Amsel, *ibid.*, 7–10; M. Vogelmann, in: *Sinai*, 48 (1960/61), 196–203; M. Elon, in: *Meḥkerei Mishpat le-Zekher Avraham Rosenthal* (1964), 1–54; idem, in: *Fifth World Congress of Jewish Studies*, 3 (1969), 90f. (Eng. Abstract). **ADD. BIBLIOGRAPHY:** M. Elon, *Ha-Mishpat ha-Ivri* (1988), 1:49f., 399, 548f., 558f., 571f; 2:1255, 1280, 1283, 1288; 3:1319; idem, *Jewish Law* (1994), 1:55f; 2:487, 667f., 679f., 703f.; 3:1501, 1527, 1531, 1537; 4:1576; M. Elon and B. Lifshitz, *Mafte'aḥ ha-She'elot ve-ha-Teshuvot shel Ḥakhmei Sefarad u-Ẓefon Afrikah* (legal digest), 2 (1986), 397–424; B. Lifshitz and E. Shochetman, *Mafte'aḥ ha-She'elot ve-ha-Teshuvot shel Ḥakhmei Ashkenaz, Ẓarefat ve-Italyah* (legal digest) (1997), 266–85; M. Elon: "Authority and Power in the Jewish Community: A Chapter in Jewish Public Law," in: *Shenaton ha-Mishpat ha-Ivri*, 3–4 (1976–77), 34–37 (Heb.) [also printed in D. Eleazar (ed.), *Kinship and Consent*, Jerusalem, 1991]; idem; "*Darkei ha-Yeẓirah ha-Hilkhatit be-Pitronan shel Be'ayot Ḥevrah u-Mishpakhah ba-Kehillah*," in *Sefer ha-Zikkaron le-Y. Baer* [also printed in *Zion*, 44 (1979)]; idem, "*Demokratyah, Zekhuyyot Yessod u-Minhal Takin bi-Pesikatam shel Ḥakhmei ha-Mizraḥ be-Moẓe'ei Gerush Sefarad*," in: *Shenaton ha-Mishpat ha-Ivri*, 18–19 (1992–94), 9–63; A. Grossman, "*Rov u-Mi'ut be-Mishpatam shel Ḥakhmei Askenaz ba-Me'ah ha-Yud-Alef*," in: *Proceedings of the 6th World Congress of Jewish Studies*, vol. 2 (1973), 135–40; "The Attitude of Early Scholars of Ashkenaz towards the Authority of the 'Kahal,'" in: *Shenaton ha-Mishpat ha-Ivri*, 2 (1975), 175–99 (Heb.); A. Hacohen, "*Ve-Khi ha-Rabbim Gazlanim Hem? Al Hafka'at Mekarkein u-Pegiyah bi-Zekhut ha-Kinyan be-Mishpat ha-Ivri*," in: *Sha'arei Mishpat*, 1 (1997), 39–54; idem, *Mishpat Ḥukkati u-Minhali be-Mishpat ha-Ivri – Koveẓ Mekorot* (source book; 1997); idem, "*Ḥovotehem u-Zekhuyyotehem shel Meshartei Ẓibbur*," in: *Koveẓ ha-Ẓiyyonut ha-Datit* (2000), 462–69; idem, "*Ad Me'ah ve-Esrim!? Ḥovat ha-Perishah le-Gimla'ot be-Misphat ha-Ivri*," in: *Daf Parashat ha-Shavu'a*, Ministry of Justice, no.44 (Elul, 2001); D. Hacohen, "*Ha-Kehillah be-Livorno u-Mosedoteha (ba-Me'ah ha-Yud Zayin)*," in: R. Bonfil (ed.), *Sefer ha-Zikkaron le S.A. Nakhon* (1978), 107–28; R.S. Klainman, "Conflict of Interest of Public Officials in Jewish Law: Prohibition, Scope and Limitations," in: *Jewish Law Association Studies*, 10 (1998), 93–116; idem, "*Yekholet ha-Kefiyyah al ha-Ẓibbur li-Nhog li-Fenim mi-Shurat ha-Din*," in: *Megal*, 12 (1998), 349–58; idem "*Kefiyyat Normot shel 'li-fenim mi-shurat ha-din' al Gufim Ẓibburiyyim*," in: *Sefer Shamgar*, 1 (200), 469–500; Y. Kaplan, "*Hilkhot Kahal be-Ashkenaz bi-Ymei ha-Beinayim ad Shilhei ha-Me'ah ha-Tet-Zayin*" (diss., Jerusalem 2004); idem, "*To'elet ha-Ẓibbur*," in: *Dinei Yisrael*, 17, 27–91; idem, "*Li-Kefifuto shel ha-Ẓibbur le-Migbalot ha-Mishpat ha-Perati be-Mishpat ha-Ivri*," in: *Mishpatim*, 25 (1995) 377–434; idem, "*Kabbalat Hakhra'ot bi-Kehillah ha-Yehudit le-Da'at Rabbenu Tam le-Halakhah u-le-Ma'aseh*," in: *Zion*, 60 (1995); idem "*Samkhut u-Ma'amad Manhigei Ẓibbur bi-Kehillah ha-Yehudit bi-Ymei ha-Beinayim*," in: *Dinei Yisrael*, 18 (1996), 295–319; idem, "*Rov u-Mi'ut be-Hakhra'at ha-Kehillah ha-Yehudit bi-Ymei ha-Beinayim*," in: *Shenaton ha-Mishpat ha-Ivri*, 20 (1997); N. Rakover, *Shilton ha-Ḥok be-Yisrael*, (1989); E. Shochetman, "*Diyyun be-Herkev Ḥaser u-Pesikah Lekuyah bi-She'elat Tovat ha-Yeled – Ilah le-Hitarvut Bagaẓ?*" in: *Mishpatim*, 15 (1985), 287; idem "The Obligation to State Reasons for Legal Decisions in Jewish Law," in: *Shenaton ha-Mishpat ha-Ivri*, 6–7 (1979–1980), 319; idem, "*Rov Mitokh Kullo – Tokfam shel Ḥukkim ha-Mitkabbelim be-Meli'at ha-Knesset she-Einah Mele'ah*," in: *Teḥumin*, 9 (1988), 82–102.

PUBLIC RELATIONS. Public relations as a profession developed in the 20th century, mainly in the U.S. Until the beginning of the 20th century public relations was a refined form of propaganda employed almost exclusively to defend a movement, cause, or individual or institution, regardless of merit or social significance. Among the first Jews in the field were Moses Lindo of South Carolina, who made skillful use of publicity to promote the export of American indigo in the years before the Revolution, and Henry Castro, a French Jew who publicized Texas among European Jews in 1844 as an agent of the Republic of Texas. Henry Zeltner was a U.S. government press agent in New York City during and after the 1863 draft riots. Twenty years later his son, Louis, served as publicity man for Theodore Roosevelt when he was police commissioner of New York City. The country's first financial publicity agency was founded by Albert Frank in 1872 to obtain free newspaper space for stockbrokers. Rudolph Guenther set up a similar agency in 1892, and later the Albert Frank-Guenther law firm became the leading financial publicity organization. Gus J. Karger (1866–1924), a vice president of the firm, was the press chief of William Howard Taft's 1908 presidential campaign and director of the Republican Party's press bureau in the 1912 presidential election.

Modern public relations took shape during World War I with the formation of the U.S. Committee on Public Information. This first organized use of all the tools and techniques of publicity as an offensive measure for mobilizing the power of mass opinion demonstrated to business, industry, government, and private institutions the value of public relations. This committee was the training ground for two young men, Carl Byoir (1888–1957) and Edward L. *Bernays, who became major forces in raising public relations to a profession. Byoir helped distribute 40,000,000 of the famous red, white, and blue texts on war aims abroad, publicized the draft, interpreted American war objectives throughout the world, and was on Woodrow Wilson's press staff at the Versailles Peace Conference. He also served as public relations adviser to Thomas G. *Masaryk, first president of Czechoslovakia. He was the originator of the Franklin D. Roosevelt birthday balls that raised millions for polio victims and led to the establishment of the National Foundation for Infantile Paralysis.

It was Bernays who coined the term "public relations counselor" and gave the profession its first code and set of principles. He also wrote the first book on the subject, *Crystallizing Public Opinion*, in 1923, and taught the first college course in public relations at New York University in 1930. Before his retirement in the late 1950s, Bernays represented some of the nation's largest corporations and newspapers as well as government agencies and social and health organizations.

The Europe of World War I was also the training ground for Benjamin Sonnenberg (1901–), who began his flamboyant career as a writer of publicity stories for the *American Jewish Joint Distribution Committee. He launched his own firm in 1924 and became a highly successful adviser to corporations, entertainment and literary personalities, and big businessmen. George Weissman (1919–1978), who rose from public relations director to president of the Philip Morris Co., learned the art in the Sonnenberg office. Out of the Byoir firm came Kalman Druck, later head of his own firm, and Edward Gottlieb. Druck was one of the key figures in uniting the Public Relations Society of America and the American Public Relations Association (APRSA) into a single professional organization. He headed the committee that developed the system for accrediting practitioners. Gottlieb, famed for coining the permanent-wave slogan "Which twin has the Toni?" was responsible for popularizing French champagne in the U.S.

Public Relations in Entertainment and Sport

In the 1920s and 1930s, most Jews in public relations were not in industry but in the world of entertainment, in the film industry. One of the earliest motion picture press agents was Mike Newman, promotion director for Columbia Pictures, who made Mary Pickford an international celebrity. Howard Dietz was the publicity agent who in 1917 devised Leo the Lion as the Metro-Goldwyn-Mayer trademark. He spread the malapropisms of Samuel *Goldwyn for many years before becoming press chief for *Loew's. Another film public relations pioneer was Charles Einfeld (1901–1974) of Warner Bros. Studios, who trained scores of people in motion picture promotion. He introduced the movie trailer and the premiere junket. Harry Reichenbach was an outstanding press agent from 1915 to 1930, as was Irving Strouse in the 1930s. Bernard Sobol was the man who made Flo *Ziegfeld's Follies a national institution before World War II. Sydney Eiges and Sid Garfield were publicity chiefs for the National Broadcasting Company and Columbia Broadcasting System respectively. Many of the leading stage and movie personalities were represented by Henry C. Rogers of Hollywood. The public relations resourcefulness of Henry Meyer converted Miami Beach from a winter playground for the rich to a year-round resort for people of modest means. The bathing beauty contests that became internationally famous were Meyer's brain children. Hal Cohen, Meyer's successor, built up the Florida resort even more.

Many of the best-known professional sports enterprises had Jewish public relations directors. Haskell Cohen was the public relations chief of the National Basketball Association. Robert Fishel and Harold Weisman were the public relations directors of the New York Yankees and the New York Mets respectively. Joe Goldstein, who promoted Roosevelt Raceway, began as a publicity man at the old Madison Square Garden. Irving Rudd, who handled public relations at Yonkers Raceway, grew up in small-time boxing club publicity. Harry Markson was for years the public relations man for Mike Jacobs, the leading fight promoter of Madison Square Garden. Joe Reichler handled public relations for the Baseball Commissioner of America.

Public Relations in Politics and Public Affairs

Events flowing from the depression of the 1930s and the New Deal, and later from World War II, were responsible for the immense expansion of public and private public relations in which Jews came to play an increasingly significant role. Charles Michelson (1869–1947), brother of the scientist Albert A. *Michelson, who became press director of the Democratic National Committee in 1929, was the ablest political publicist of his time. Mike Straus, who went to Washington with the New Deal, was the highly effective public relations director of the Department of the Interior under Harold C. Ickes.

One of the founders of the American College Public Relations Association in 1917 was Bernard Sobel, information director of Purdue University. An early president of this oldest organized group of publicists was Louis Boochever, public relations director of Cornell University in the 1920s, and later national public relations director of the American Red Cross. George Hecht, publisher of *Parents Magazine*, was the founder in 1919 of *Better Times*, the first publication to publicize social work. Six years later he established the Social Legislation Information Service as a public relations lobby. Louis Resnick (1892–1941), for 15 years public relations director of the National Society for the Prevention of Blindness, set many of the standards used in social welfare publicity during his years as information director of the National Safety Council. In 1935 he became the first information director of the newly established U.S. Social Security Administration. Harold Levy, for many years on the staff of the Russell Sage Foundation, was one of the pioneers of social work publicity. Irving Rimer was the third executive director of the National Public Relations Council on Health and Welfare, and his successor was Harold Weiner. Rimer later became public relations director of the American Cancer Society. Sol Lifson was for a long time director of public information for the National Tuberculosis and Respiratory Diseases Association. Another pioneer in social work publicity was Viola Paradis, who headed public relations for the *National Council of Jewish Women. Bernard Roloff introduced the "crusade for mercy" theme as public relations director of the United Fund for Chicago, one of the largest community chests. Victor Weingarten made the Child Welfare League widely known. From 1923 to 1936 Herbert Seligman was public relations director of the National Association of Colored People, and Frances Adlerstein directed public relations for the Travelers Aid Association.

Anna *Rosenberg, who served as assistant secretary of defense under President Truman, later became a highly successful public relations expert for big business. When he retired from newspaper work, Herbert Bayard *Swope, the renowned managing editor of the *New York World*, was public relations adviser to Bernard M. *Baruch and to many government agencies and business firms. In the 1950s, Sydney S. Baron was the publicity director of Tammany Hall. The CIO Political Action Committee's public relations director was Allan Reitman, and David B. Charney had the same post with the International Teamsters' Union. Frank Mankiewicz was the press director for Senator Robert F. Kennedy, and held the same post in the unsuccessful effort of Senator George McGovern to win the 1968 Democratic presidential nomination.

Public Relations in the Jewish Community

The rise of the public relations man in Jewish communal life was a post-World War I phenomenon directly attributable to major events and developments in Jewish history. The relief campaigns on behalf of war-stricken European Jewry, the struggles against the antisemitism of Henry Ford and the Ku Klux Klan in the 1920s, the growth of national membership organizations and Jewish federations, the building-fund campaigns for synagogues, Jewish community centers, old folks homes and institutions of Jewish higher learning, the fight against Nazism, and the dramatic efforts to establish the State of Israel, all called between 1917 and 1948 for the unprecedented mobilization of Jewish public opinion as well as the winning of support from the general population.

The first public relations bureau serving the Jewish community was formed in 1919 by Louis Popkin (1894–1943) and his wife Zelda (née Feinberg). A reporter on the *American Hebrew*, Popkin had been drafted in 1914 to handle publicity for the newly-organized American Joint Distribution Committee. In 1917 he took on the same job for the wartime National Jewish Welfare Board. After the war the Popkin established Planned Publicity Service, which did public relations for a number of Jewish organizations. Their first assignment was the drafting of the cable to Woodrow Wilson at the Versailles Peace Conference asking for the protection of Jewish rights. For the New York Federation of Jewish Philanthropies they set up the first organized permanent public relations department in any Jewish agency. In 1922 Abraham H. Fromenson (1874–1935), editor of the English page of the Yiddish-language daily, the *Tageblatt*, who had been publicity head of the Zionist Organization of America when Louis D. *Brandeis controlled it, joined the Popkin firm, which trained many of the people who later became the first public relations directors of major Jewish organizations. David A. Brown, the Detroit business executive who turned into the leading Jewish fund-raiser of the 1920s and 1930s, pioneered many of the public relations techniques on which later public relations experts built.

As public relations chief of the Federation of Jewish Philanthropies from 1934 to 1945, Elliott Cohen, founder of **Commentary*, introduced to the field of public relations people of professional competence and familiarity with Jewish life and traditions, who were able to interpret health and welfare with intelligence, style, and clarity. He established the high standards of production and art that set the pattern of fund-raising literature for the whole Jewish community. One of Cohen's predecessors was Isidore Sobeloff (1899–), who went on to become a Federation executive in Detroit and Los Angeles.

Henry *Montor (1905–1982) became publicity director of the United Palestine Appeal in 1931, and was a genius in persuading American Jewish communities to provide unprecedented sums for Palestine by the use for the first time of all the tools and techniques of modern public relations. In 1939, when the JDC and UPA joined forces in the United Jewish Appeal, Montor was elevated to national campaign director. He and his successor, Meyer Steinglass, broke new ground by running full-page advertisements in the daily press and using radio for campaign publicity. When Montor left UJA to assume direction of the Bonds for Israel campaign, Steinglass went with him as public relations director. Raphael Levy and Ben Hanft (d. 1985), Steinglass' successors at UJA extended their methods to television and films.

The public relations techniques first tested by UJA and Bonds for Israel were adapted with some modifications but equal success by the American offices of Israel organizations as well by virtually every other national Jewish agency. The American Jewish Committee, the Anti-Defamation League, and the American Jewish Congress varied in approach and emphasis, but they all saw public relations as a significant element of their overall educational role in bringing to public attention the nature of prejudice, the evils of antisemitism and bigotry, and the importance of understanding among men of all races and ethnic groups.

A unique public relations instrument created by the Jews of America was the Jewish Welfare Board Public Relations Committee, formed during World War II by the American Jewish Committee, the Anti-Defamation League, the American Jewish Congress, the Jewish War Veterans, and the Jewish Labor Committee. This combined operation developed within the Jewish community an understanding of the war issues, and built up support for a program of religious and morale services to Jewish military personnel.

Through public relations of the most dignified character, the Jewish Theological Seminary of America helped establish Judaism as one of the major religious traditions in America. The Seminary's radio and TV program, "The Eternal Light," was a highly effective public relations instrument. Skilled public relations played significant roles in the expansion of Yeshiva University, Albert Einstein College of Medicine, Brandeis University, the growth of mass Jewish membership organizations such as Hadassah and B'nai B'rith, and the raising of hundreds of millions of dollars for new synagogues, community centers, hospitals, and other communal institutions.

By 1940 there were enough people professionally employed as public relations specialists by Jewish organizations to warrant the organization of the Jewish Publicity Directors Council. In 1956 this was reorganized as the American Jewish Public Relations Society. In 1968 it was estimated that more than 500 people were engaged in some phase of public relations for local and national American Jewish organizations and by international Jewish agencies with offices in the U.S. In the 1960s a number of commercial public relations firms headed by Jews were called in as short-or long-term consultants by several Jewish organizations. Ruder and Finn served the Jewish Theological Seminary in this capacity, while Kalman Druck's firm took over full public relations responsibility at UJA in 1968. Of the more than 15,000 public relations firms operating in the U.S. in 1968, some twenty percent were reported to be Jewish in ownership or management.

[Bernard Postal]

In the latter years of the 20th century, Howard J. Rubenstein became one of the most influential public relations practitioners in the country. As an individual and with his firm he represented important political figures, winning recognition as an adviser to Mayor Abraham *Beame of New York City. At the same time, he became close to the governors and successor mayors of New York State and City and he advised politicians of both major parties. Among his clients were such controversial figures as George Steinbrenner, principal owner of the New York Yankees, who was constantly in the news during that time. Other public relations practitioners of note were Richard Manoff, who had many clients in the theater, and Morton Yarmon, who became one of the highest officials in the American Jewish Committee.

[Stewart Kampel (2nd ed.)]

In Israel

The Public Relations Association of Israel was established in 1958 in Tel Aviv as the Public Relations and Tourism Coordinators. Each of the three major cities set up their own organization designed to serve the special interests in that area. Jerusalem members called their organization "The Spokesmen's Circle" and limited membership to government public relations and information officers.

In 1961 it was decided to create a national organization with all three branches maintaining a special autonomous status covered by a new constitution and the national body run by an Executive Committee drawn from all three branches. There are national conventions every year, professional activities on both a local and national scale, and courses either sponsored or controlled by the organization. In 1970 the Israel Association was host to the Fifth Public Relations World Congress. There were over 200 members in the Public Relations Association of Israel.

[Zvi Harry Zinder]

With the introduction of television in Israel in the late 1960s, and the understanding of the power of its images, the role of the media adviser became central in all campaigns geared to a viewing audience, particularly in politics. By the 1990s, leading candidates could be divided into those who understood the medium and those who did not, understanding often coming courtesy of advisers imported from the United States. And as in the United States, though the viewer recognized the artificiality of the presentation, he was often taken in by it in spite of himself. The handling of public relations was also thought to be a central element in the way Israel was perceived around the world in its clashes with the Palestinians. Generally, Israel was given poor marks, for using ineffective spokesmen, failing to have a comprehensive PR plan, and failing to accommodate foreign media representatives. However, some would argue that the management of news and the manipulation of images might not necessarily make Israel a more popular country, for clearly the eagerness with which many attacked Israel might lead one to believe that their views were not necessarily a response to good or bad public relations, not to mention simple facts.

PUBLISHING

PUBLISHING. This article is arranged according to the following outline:

MODAN
RAV KOOK INSTITUTE
SCHOCKEN
YEDIOTH AHARONOTH

GENERAL PUBLISHING

Jews joined the European publishing industry little more than three decades after its pioneering efforts, notably in Italy, Spain, and Portugal. The first recorded Jewish printer of non-Hebrew books (possibly *Abraham b. Garton of Reggio di Calabria) published the outstanding fourth edition of Dante's *Divina commedia* (Naples, 1477), as a result of which he was bitterly attacked by a Christian rival who appended *Erubescat Judeus infelix* ("Let the unhappy Jew blush for shame") to his own edition of the *Purgatorio* (c. 1478). By this time Jews were evidently active in the Naples book trade, as they had been for some years as Hebrew printers in Italy as a whole. In its early stages, the printing industry was combined with book publishing, printers accepting, printing, and selling their works in one commercial venture. Prior to the expulsion from Spain (1492), Jews probably played an equally important part in printing there. During the 1470s, Juan de Lucena issued a prayer book (*cituri*, i.e., *siddur*) in Spanish, for which he was years later (as a New Christian) persecuted by the Inquisition. A more significant publishing achievement was that of Solomon b. Maimon Zalmati of Jativa, who in 1483 entered into partnership with two Christian printers with the aim of producing Christian theological works for the general market. They subsequently published Jaime Perez's commentary on Psalms (Valencia, 1484) and other works by the same writer, including his antisemitic *Tractatus contra judaeos* (1485). In neighboring Portugal, Jewish printer-publishers also attained eminence as pioneers before the general expulsion of 1497. Samuel de Ortas issued *Tabulae tabularum coelestium motuum: sive almanach perpetuum* (Leiria, 1496), a classic by the great astronomer Abraham *Zacuto.

Jewish activity in the sphere of general publishing was centered in Italy from the beginning of the 16th century. The *Soncino family, famous in early Hebrew printing, also produced a host of works in other languages. Gershom Soncino the elder, who studied the art of printing in Mainz, published a series of books in Latin and Italian from 1502 and for 25 years thereafter issued about 100 titles – about as many as he published in Hebrew over a longer period. As Hieronymus Soncinus, he produced only non-Hebrew works in Ancona and Cesena. Gershom's new edition of Petrarch (Fano, 1503) was dedicated to Cesare Borgia, and his literary editor, the humanist Lorenzo Abstemio (Bevilaqua), urged other Italian scholars to patronize the Soncino press. Gershom Soncino later published the statutes of the cities of Fano (1508), Jesi (1516), and Rimini (1525), as well as many other works for Christians, including the "Rules of the Franciscan Order" (Pesaro, 1507). Gershom Soceino produced his non-Hebrew books for non-Jewish readers. He was, however, compelled to abandon this activity in about 1527.

From the early 1550s onward, Yom Tov b. Levi *Athias (Jeronimo Vargas) published Spanish versions of Jewish liturgical works at Ferrara and, in collaboration with Abraham *Usque, issued the famous Ferrara Bible (1553) which appeared in separate editions for Jews and Christians. Abraham Usque later published other liturgical books for Jewish immigrants as well as works by Bernardim *Ribeiro, Alfonso de la *Torre, and his kinsman Samuel *Usque. The self-imposed Jewish censorship of Hebrew books after the burning of the Talmud in Rome (1553), the temporary persecution of newly arrived Marranos, and Church interference in Jewish affairs all led to the eventual abandonment of vernacular publishing by Italian Jews. However, the physician Jacob Marcaria, who operated a Hebrew press in Riva di Trento (1558–62), was the unofficial publisher of speeches and works by many of the churchmen assembled at the Council of Trent (1545–63). The scene of Jewish activity in general publishing thereafter shifted to Amsterdam, where a host of works in Spanish and Portuguese was written and published from the beginning of the 17th century.

The "Dutch Jerusalem"

The earliest Jewish vernacular publications in the Netherlands were written in Spanish for Marrano immigrants unfamiliar with Hebrew and often took the form of translations of biblical and liturgical texts. The first work of this type was a reissue of Yom Tov Athias' Ferrara prayer book (1552), published at Dordrecht ("Mainz") in 1584 and evidently intended for the crypto-Jewish community of Antwerp. The first work in Spanish to appear in Amsterdam dates from 1612 and during the next two centuries hundreds of books in Spanish and Portuguese were issued by the city's Jewish publishers. These included *Manasseh Ben Israel, whose press, founded in 1626, produced books in Spanish and Portuguese as well as Hebrew; Joseph *Athias; and Isaac Cohen de *Lara, a leading bookseller. The messianic frenzy roused by the claims of *Shabbetai Ẓevi led to a spate of publications in Spanish in 1666. Spanish substituted for Hebrew as the language of study and prayer among Marranos, while Portuguese was reserved for poetry and other secular literature.

In time, however, Dutch Jews began writing and publishing works in the vernacular. Two of the oldest Jewish publishing houses of Amsterdam, both noted for their Hebrew printing, also engaged in producing books in Dutch for the Jewish reader: the firms of the brothers *Proops, which flourished during the 18th–19th centuries, and J.L. Joachimsthal, which was still active in the 1970s and issued the Dutch Jewish weekly *Nieuw Israëlietisch Weekblad*. The bookseller L. Simons (1862–1932) founded the *Wereldbibliotheek*, while Isaac *Keesing established the firm of N.V. Keesing, noted for its production of reference books and archive material. Another Amsterdam Jewish publisher was the minor writer Emmanuel Querido (18711943), a victim of the Nazis, whose brother was the novelist Israël *Querido.

[Godfrey Edmond Silverman]

In Germany and Austria

During the Middle Ages, Jews played an active part in the European book trade, which assumed increasing importance in the German-speaking lands after the introduction of printing. From the 16th century onward, Jews naturally promoted Hebrew publishing, of which Frankfurt became the principal center, and from the early 19th century they were active in the general sphere of German book production (Berlin, Breslau, Frankfurt, Koenigsberg, Leipzig, Prague, and Vienna). Probably the earliest such enterprise was the Prague firm of Taussig (founded in 1783), which ceased its activities under the Nazis. Other pioneering firms were those of Julius Eduard *Hitzig (Berlin, 1808–14); Friedrich Cohen (Bonn, 1829); Joseph and Felix Lehmann (1832); and Moritz *Veit, president of the Berlin Jewish community, whose scientific publishing house, Veit & Co., flourished between 1834 and 1858. Also prominent in Berlin was the Schlesinger'sche Buch- und Musikalienhandlung (1810), headed by Adolf Martin Schlesinger (1768–1848), which issued some of the compositions of Beethoven.

In general publishing, however, Jews only achieved real importance from about 1835 during the heyday of the *Jung Deutschland* literary group. The leading literary publisher of this era was Karl (Zacharias) Loewenthal, who changed his name to Loening after abandoning Judaism. A close friend and admirer of Karl Gutzkow, the leader of *Jung Deutschland*, Loewenthal founded his publishing house in Mannheim in 1835 and published Gutzkow's periodical *Deutsche Revue* and his novel *Wally, die Zweiflerin* (1835). When the works of the *Jung Deutschland* group, including those of Heinrich *Heine, were proscribed and their authors and publisher brought to trial, Loewenthal did not abandon his friends, despite antisemitic slanders. In 1844 he moved to Frankfurt and, together with the apostate author Joseph Jacob Ruetten (Rindskopf, 1805–78), reestablished his firm under the name of Rueten und Loening, producing philosophical and sociological books as well as fiction. The firm still operated in Munich in the 1970s. Other 19th-century enterprises included those of R. Levi (Stuttgart, 1840), J. Guttentag (Berlin, 1842), Moritz Perles (Prague, 1844; later moved to Berlin and Vienna), M. Glogau (Hamburg, 1850), J. Taubeles (Prague, 1861), Albert Goldschmidt (Hamburg, 1863), S. Cronbach (Berlin, 1867), R.L. Prager (Berlin, 1872), and the Enoch Brothers (Hamburg, 1875). In Vienna, a literary firm was established by Leopold Rosner (1838–1903).

During the 1880s, the champion of the school of realism was Otto *Brahm, who in 1889 founded the Freie Buehne, which later became the literary periodical *Die Neue Rundschau*. Closely connected with this new literature was the Berlin publishing house of Samuel *Fischer. The S. Fischer Verlag (1886) rapidly became a center of avant-garde literary life. Under the Nazis, this publishing house moved overseas but after World War II reopened in Frankfurt. In 1895 George Bondi (1865–1935) established a firm in Berlin specializing in works by members of the Stefan George circle, such as Friedrich *Gundolf, Ernst Bertram, and Ernst Kantorowitsch (*Blaetter fuer die Kunst*). When George decided to make his own poetry available to the general public, Bondi became his publisher. Paul *Cassirer founded a publishing house in 1908 as a branch of his art gallery. He issued books mainly about modern artists (Herman *Struck, Ernst Barlach, Max Pechstein, Oskar Kokoschka), but also published literary works by Else *Lasker-Schueler, Ernst Barlach, Walter *Hasenclever, René Schickelé, and Kasimir Edschmid. Another field in which Cassirer became interested was cultural socialism, represented by the works of Ferdinand *Lassalle, Kurt *Eisner, and Gustav *Landauer. His cousin Bruno Cassirer (1872–1942) also founded a publishing house in 1898. Bruno Cassirer's book production, which was of the highest intellectual standard, ranged through art, philosophy, and literature. His art books were written by leading historians and critics of the fine arts; his journal, *Kunst und Kuenstler*, edited by Karl Scheffler, became the leading German art journal during the early 20th century. Bruno Cassirer also published all the writings of another cousin, the eminent philosopher Ernst *Cassirer. He issued the complete edition of Kant's works, edited by Ernst Cassirer, and those of Hermann *Cohen, the founder of neo-Kantianism. During the years before the rise of Hitler, he turned to modern fiction, where he was assisted by Max *Tau, who introduced several modern Scandinavian authors to the German reader. Bruno Cassirer finally immigrated to England. His publishing house, refounded in Oxford, now specializes in illustrated books about foreign countries.

Erich Reiss founded his Berlin publishing house in 1908 and was a keen enthusiast of the beautiful, well-printed book. He published German editions of Jonathan Swift's works, the writings of Georges *Brandes, and the political essays of Maximilian *Harden. For a time Reiss also issued Siegfried *Jacobsohn's periodical *Die Schaubuehne* (later *Die Weltbuehne*) and *Blaetter des deutschen Theaters*. After 1933 he tried to publish books of Jewish interest only, but soon abandoned the project and immigrated to New York.

All attempts to make Vienna a center of the publishing trade on a par with Leipzig and Berlin failed until Paul von Zsolnay established the Paul Zsolnay Verlag in 1924. In a very short time, this firm assembled the works of some of the most distinguished European novelists, including Sholem *Asch, Henri Barbusse, Max *Brod, John Galsworthy, Heinrich Mann, and Franz *Werfel. After the *Anschluss* of 1938, Zsolnay immigrated to England; his firm was refounded in Vienna after World War II. The Austrian capital was also the home of the Internationaler Psychoanalystischer Verlag, established by the *Freud family and later transferred to London, and of E.P. Tal (1919), a firm specializing in modern German and foreign literature.

Bela Horovitz (1898–1955), who was devoted to the study of Greek, Roman, and Jewish antiquity, established his Phaidon Verlag in Vienna (1923) with the aim of popularizing works on the ancient world. His publications included Plato, Petrarch, Shakespeare, Klabund, Friedell, and Unamuno. In later years, the Phaidon Verlag republished illustrated editions of the great German historians, such as Mommsen, Grimm, and Ranke. Assisted by Ludwig Goldseheider, Horovitz also issued many low-price art books which appeared in several languages and made Phaidon known in many countries. After 1938 he established the Phaidon Press in London, following the same line as in Vienna. The Nazi onslaught on the Jews led him to establish a new publishing house in London, the East and West Library, entirely devoted to Jewish literature. From 1955 onward, his family continued to run both publishing houses until these were sold to other companies in the late 1960s.

Other firms active between the world wars were Ernst Salter's literary Verlag die Schmiede in Berlin, which introduced Marcel *Proust to the German public; Erich Lichtenstein's Weimar house, devoted especially to new editions of classic writers (e.g., Annette von Droste-Huelshoff); and Victor Fleischer's Frankfurter Verlags-Anstalt, which published books on literary criticism and history.

Salman *Schocken, who headed a chain of department stores, founded the Berlin Schocken Verlag in 1931. This firm's publications dealt largely with Jewish philosophy, theology, Hebraica, and poetry, but also included the works of Franz *Kafka and Alfred *Mombert. Wide popularity was achieved by the "little Schocken books" and the works of Martin *Buber, particularly his German Bible. In 1933, Schocken, a leading German Zionist, emigrated to Jerusalem and his publishing house now operates in New York and in Tel Aviv, where it published, among others, the works of the Nobel Prize winner S.Y. *Agnon. In scientific publishing, firms like Carl Heymann (1815), Julius Springer (1842), S. Karger (1890), and the Akademische Verlagsbuchhandlung (1906) were in Jewish hands.

The Jewish publishers of the great liberal newspapers such as the *Frankfurter Zeitung* and the *Berliner Tageblatt* also entered book publication. Rudolf *Mosse established his firm in 1867 and, apart from his newspaper empire (*Berliner Tageblatt, Berliner Volkszeitung, 8-Uhr Abendblatt*), produced books of a popular character. The entire business was confiscated by the Nazis. Leopold *Ullstein founded the Ullstein Verlag in 1877. Besides a vast number of newspapers and magazines, the firm published popular fiction. Ullstein's Propylaeen Verlag (1919), under the direction of Emil Herz, who later emigrated to the United States, grew into a versatile publishing house of the highest standard, publishing an edition of Goethe's works in 45 volumes. It also issued the serialized *Klassiker des Altertums, Propylaeen-Weltgeschichte, Werke der Weltliteratur,* and *Klassiker des Altertums*, as well as the works of Brecht, Remarque, and *Zuckmayer. After World War II the corporation returned to family ownership, but it was eventually sold to Axle Springer in 1960. The Frankfurter Societaetsdruckerei, publishers of the liberal *Frankfurter Zeitung*, which was founded in 1856 by the democratic Jewish politician Leopold *Sonnemann, also published works by modern German writers.

[Rudolf Kayser]

In Scandinavia

The only major house in Scandinavia was the Albert Bonniers Förlag of Stockholm (established in 1837). Its founder, Albert Bonnier (1820–1900), was the son of a Dresden Jew who settled in Copenhagen. Albert and his brother Adolf moved to Sweden, where they set up a publishing and printing enterprise that became the largest in the country. It was subsequently run by Albert's son, Karl Otto Bonnier (1856–1941), and, with associated firms, remained under family control. In Denmark, the Gad publishing house of Copenhagen specialized in Judaica, while Norway's leading publishers included the German refugee Max Tau, who began his career with Bruno Cassirer in Berlin.

The Swedish-Jewish publishing house Hillel started offering books on the subject of Judaica in 1963. For the first couple of decades, Hillel worked closely with the Chinuch educational organization. In those early days, the publishing house's foremost purpose was to produce Swedish-language educational materials for use in Stockholm's Hillelskolan Jewish school. As of 2001, Hillel is housed on the premises of the Stockholm Jewish Community. With its sights set firmly on a wider reading public, Hillel produces Jewish literature of a religious, historical, and socio-political nature.

The Megilla publishing house started up in 1990 and has published several Swedish-language books since then, all with a specifically Jewish connection – novels, poetry anthologies, and fact books.

Megilla has also published a number of books on the subject of Yiddish as well as books in Yiddish, in the form of textbooks, songbooks, books of proverbs, etc. Megilla is run on a purely voluntary basis.

In Italy

As mentioned above Italian Jews were among the pioneers of general publishing activity in the country, but Jewish participation in the trade declined sharply from the mid-16th century. It was not until the 1840s that Jews again became prominent in the general sphere, with the establishment of the Florence publishing house of Felice Paggi (1823–1895) and his brother Alessandro (1818–1893). This issued many works of popular education and other books by leading authors, including Carlo (Lorenzini) Collodi's children's classic, *Pinocchio* (1880). The firm was joined by Alessandro Paggi's son-in-law, Roberto Bemporad (d. 1891), whose son, Enrico *Bemporad, eventually assumed control, changing its name to R. Bemporad & Figlio. Under his direction it soon became one of the most important publishing houses in Italy. A firm associated with Bemporad was that founded by Simone Lattes in Turin.

Italy's greatest publishing house, however, was that established in Milan by Emilio *Treves and his brother Giuseppe (1838–1904). Fratelli Treves (1864) published newspapers and works by leading Italian and foreign authors. In 1886, Leo S. Olschki (1861–1944), a Prussian immigrant, established himself in Florence, where he later became the leading antiquarian bookseller and publisher of scholarly works in Italy. After his death the business remained under family control. Jews continued this close association with Italian publishing during the 20th century. Among them was Angelo Fortunato *Formiggini, a staunch anti-Fascist, whose firm was first established in Bologna (1908) and who published Italy's first "Who's Who." Luciano Morpurgo (b. 1886) founded his Casa Editrice Dalmatia in 1928, and this publishing house was still operating under the name in the second half of the 20th century.

In France

Jews only began to achieve prominence in the field of general publishing toward the middle of the 19th century. The two pioneering firms were those established by the *Alcan and *Lévy (Calmann-Lévy) families. Moyse Alcan's publishing house was active in Metz from about 1840 and was later headed by his son Félix, who specialized in works on philosophy. The brothers Michel, Alexandre-Nathan, and Calmann Lévy founded their enterprise in Paris in 1842 and, as Michel Lévy Frères, succeeded in building up one of the leading French publishing firms, issuing the works of writers such as Balzac, Dumas, Heine (in translation), and *Renan. From 1875 the business changed its name to Calmann-Lévy. Paul Ollendorf, the Paris-born son of a Polish immigrant, published *Gil Blas*, a political and literary newspaper that flourished between 1880 and World War I. In 1881 Fernand Nathan established a firm (still under family management) specializing in classics, reference works, and educational and children's books. Four other modern firms were Rieder (Crémieux), Bernheim-Jeune, Camille Bloch, and Fernand Hazan (1945).

[Godfrey Edmond Silverman]

In Czechoslovakia

Although, compared with Germany and Austria, Jewish publishing firms in what was Czechoslovakia were few and limited in scope, they included some pioneering enterprises, such as Taussig und Taussig (see Germany and Austria, above). The first Jewish bookseller and antiquarian in Prague was Wolf (Ze'ev) *Pascheles, who founded S. Pascheles & Son in 1836. A branch of this famous house was established in Breslau (1899) by his son-in-law, Jacob B. Brandeis (relative of Louis D. *Brandeis). Both firms specialized in Judaica, but also published biographies and fiction in German (Sacher-Masoch, M.G. Saphir, M. Rosenfeld, etc.) under the imprint of the Juedische Universal-Bibliothek. Also active in Prague was the firm of Josef Flesch, which produced scholarly works between the world wars, while Julius Fuerth managed the Melantrich publishing house and the liberal paper *Lidové noviny* at about the same period, later transferring his interests to London. Outside of Bohemia, the influence of German diminished, and most Jewish publishing enterprises were founded only from the late 19th century onward.

In Yugoslavia

The first translations and editions of world classics issued in Croatia were by the pioneer Jewish publisher and bookseller Lavoslav Hartmann (1813–1881). The Yugoslav book trade was later revolutionized by Geca Kon (1873–1941) of Belgrade, who headed the country's greatest publishing house between the world wars.

In Romania

From about 1880 until 1940 Jews made an outstanding contribution to the development of the Romanian publishing industry. In Jassy, Elias Şaraga established an important firm, in partnership with his brother Samuel, in 1878. Three other Jewish publishing houses in the same town were those of A. Berman, Cuperman, and H. Goldner. The family business of Samitca in Craiova (c. 1895) specialized in low-cost editions and books of Jewish interest. In Bucharest, low-price books were also produced by Leon Alcalay (1900–34). Other firms included Simon Benvenisti, I. Ciornei, H. Steinberg, Carol Segal, and Emmanuel Ocneanu. Literary works were also published by the house of Virgil Montaureanu, which later transferred its activities to Israel.

In Hungary

Jews played an important part in the Hungarian publishing industry from its very inception. A pioneer in the field was Sámuel Révai (Rosenberg; 1833–1908), who began trading as a bookbinder and later as a bookseller in Eperjes (now Prešov, Slovakia). In 1869, he and his brother Leó established the Budapest publishing house of Révai Testvérek, which was later run by Sámuel's sons. In time, this became one of the leading firms in Hungary, its publications including the works of such eminent writers as Mór Jókai and Kálmán Mikszáth and an important reference work, *Révai Nagy Lexikona* ("Révai's Great Encyclopedia"). Earlier still, the Wodianer family, late 18th-century immigrants from Wodian, in Moravia, had achieved prominence when Fülöp Wodianer, a printer turned publisher, became the official publisher of the revolutionary government of Kossuth in 1848. He acquired the R. Lámpel firm in 1874 and was ennobled for his services to the state. Wodianer's business remained under family control after his death, the Lámpel house issuing books on a wide variety of subjects and publishing various newspapers. A firm specializing in the publication of musical works and scores was that founded by Gyula Rózsavölgyi (1822–1860), whose father was the eminent composer Márk Rózsavölgyi. Other leading Jewish publishers were József Wolfner, Lipót Hirsch de Örményes, and Andor Miklós, who took over the Athenaeum publishing house, which issued books by modern Hungarian writers. One of Athenaeum's directors was Viktor Ranschburg (1862–1930), who later moved to the firm of Pantheon. His brother, Gusztáv Ranschburg, was the editor of the Müveltség Könyvtára ("Library of Culture") and of the Athenaeum Könyvtár ("Athenaeum Library"). Izidor Kner (1860–1935) of Gyoma specialized in belles lettres and was awarded the gold medal at the Leipzig Exhibition of 1914 for his publications, mostly works by contemporary writers. His son, Imre Kner (1890–1944), a victim of the Nazi Holocaust, published the historical series *Monumenta Litterarum*, as well as other Hungarian and European classics, and gained first prize at the

Paris Exhibition of 1937. As in Romania, Jewish publishers in Hungary were subjected to increasing restrictions from the late 1930s onward.

[Baruch Yaron]

In Poland

One of the earliest Jewish influences in Polish literary life from the first quarter of the 19th century was the activity of Jewish, or converted Jewish, publishers. Side by side with the Jews who pioneered the printing and publishing of Hebrew and Yiddish works, there were a few who achieved distinction in the general field, notably Nathan Gluecksberg (1780–1831) and sons, Samuel Orgelbrand (1810–1868) and son, and S. Lewental. Orgelbrand is mainly remembered for the first modern Polish encyclopedia, which he issued in 28 volumes (1859–68). In the 20th century, particularly between the world wars, Jews made an increasingly important contribution to the Polish publishing industry with firms such as those headed by H. Altenberg, M. Arct, J. Mortkowicz, J. Przeworski, K. Wild, and W. Zukerkandel. Others, notably the well-known firm of Rój, had important Jewish managing interests, although they did not bear recognizably Jewish names. Even after the Communist takeover following World War II, there were Jews among the founders and directors of state publishing houses, of whom J. Borejsza of Czytelnik was one of the most prominent.

[Moshe Altbauer]

In Russia

During the last decades Jews published on specifically Jewish topics in Russian, as well as Hebrew and Yiddish. After the Bolshevik Revolution, these activities tended to be transferred overseas. In the general sphere of pre-Revolutionary Russian publishing, the outstanding names were the brothers I.N. and A.N. Granat, who issued an important encyclopedia, and Ilya Abramovich *Efron, who began his activity in 1880. Efron's enterprise, which became one of the largest in Russia, mainly produced scholarly works and is best remembered for its massive 86-volume *Novy entsiklopedicheskiy slovar* (1907) and for the 16-volume Russian-Jewish *Yevreyskaya Entsiklopediya* (1907–13), in which the publisher himself took an active interest. (For Russian-language publishing in Israel from the 1990s see "In Israel" below.)

[Godfrey Edmond Silverman]

In Spain and Latin America

Despite the numerical insignificance of Spain's Jewish population in the 20th century, Jewish activity in the book trade was seen in the establishment of the Madrid firm of Aguilar (1923), which also operated in Latin America. It was only after World War I that Jews began to figure in the Latin American publishing industry (mainly in Argentina, Brazil, and Mexico). In Argentina, the Buenos Aires firm of Candelabro, established by Abrahám Mibashán and specializing in Judaica, was taken over by José Mirelman and Máximo G. Yagupsky, who also controlled the firm of Israel. Jews have played a more important role in the general publishing life of Brazil. Here the major names were Aizen, Bloch, Iussim, Koogan, and Weissman, with Adolfo Aizen publishing comic books and strip cartoons (*Brasil, América*), Nathan Waissman heading the Rio de Janeiro publishing house of Guanabara, and Henrique Iussim (who was also a writer) controlling the Biblos firm. Abrahão Koogan published literary, medical, and scientific books and, through the firm of Delta, world classics and encyclopedias. Almost all of the Jewish enterprises were based in Rio de Janeiro, one exception being Perspectiva of São Paulo. The largest Brazilian publishing firm under Jewish control was run by the Bloch family (Adolfo, Arnaldo, and Boris Bloch) and incorporated Fatos & Fotos and Manchete. It was later managed by Oscar Bloch Sigelman, Pedro Jack Kapeller, and H.W. Berliner.

In Great Britain

Three 19th-century pioneers were Samuel Lewis (d. 1865), who published topographical dictionaries and atlases; John Wertheimer (1799–1883); and William Swan Sonnenschein (1855–1931). The latter, son of a refugee Hungarian revolutionary, founded Swan Sonnenschein & Co. (1878), which specialized in reference books, and also traded under his non-Jewish mother's name of Stallybrass, becoming senior managing director of the Routledge publishing firm. The Franklin family subsequently obtained a controlling interest in Routledge's (George Routledge and Kegan Paul, 1934).

Two prominent figures, both with marked Socialist leanings, were Leonard *Woolf and Sir Victor *Gollancz. Woolf co-founded the Hogarth Press (1917), which issued works by modern writers (including his wife, Virginia Woolf); while Gollancz, who established the firm bearing his name in 1928, also co-founded the Left Book Club (1936) and helped to stimulate the production of low-cost quality literature. Gollancz specialized in modern fiction and religious books and threw his prestige behind several unpopular causes. Oliver Simon (1895–1956), the typographer, was a director of the Soncino Press and managed another house, Curwen Press, from the 1930s until his death. He was succeeded by his brother Herbert Simon. Another printer and publisher was Ellis Paul Howe. Among those who established publishing firms between the world wars were John *Rodker (Ovid Press, Imago Press), who issued works by Freud. T.S. Eliot, and Ezra Pound; Frederick Muller (1933); Michael Joseph (1935), a specialist in general fiction and mysteries; and *Frederick J. Warburg of Secker & Warburg, founded in 1936.

Soon after World War II Jewish activity in the British publishing world increased with the establishment of many new publishing houses catering for a wide variety of interests. *André Deutsch (1917–2000), who had immigrated from Hungary as a youth, entered the trade in 1942 and, after operating as Allan Wingate (1945–50), founded his own company in 1951, specializing in history, biography, and paperback editions. Deutsch founded African publishing firms in Nigeria (1962) and Kenya (1964). Sir George *Weidenfeld, Baron Weidenfeld, an Austrian refugee, founded *Contact* (1945), a journal of contemporary affairs and arts, and three years later established the firm of Weidenfeld and Nicolson in association with Nigel Nicolson. Weidenfeld, a keen Zionist, published many books by Israel writers and founded a subsidiary company in Jerusalem (1969). His firm specialized in books on literature, art, and archaeology (many in illustrated editions). Another postwar publisher of importance was Anthony Blond (1930–), who established his publishing house in 1958, specializing in new writers, paperbacks, and works for young people. Blond is the author of an autobiography, *Jew Made in England* (2004). Other names in postwar British publishing were Sidney Bernstein, Baron Bernstein (1899–1993), the television pioneer, whose enterprises included the Granada Publishing company; Robert *Maxwell, who headed Pergamon Press (1948) and built a publishing empire; and Paul Hamlyn, Baron Hamlyn (1926–2001), who controlled Ginn & Co., Newnes, Odhams, and Spring Books, Temple Press, the Paul Hamlyn "coffee table books," and (in association with EMI) Music For Pleasure Records. Other British publishing firms under Jewish management or with important Jewish interests include H. Pordes (1947), Thomas Yoseloff, W.H. Allen, Frank Cass, Peter Owen, Paul Elek, and a large group containing Cresset Press, Berrie and Rockliff, and Hammond, Hammond.

[Godfrey Edmond Silverman]

In the United States

Before the 20th century, Jews played an insignificant part in the general book publishing industry of the United States. In 1897 the bookselling firm founded by August *Brentano in 1858 started a publishing division. Brentano was the original U.S. publisher for the plays of George Bernard Shaw, but the firm discontinued publishing in 1933. Another pioneer, Ben[jamin] W. Huebsch (1873–1964), son of Adolph *Huebsch, began publishing under his own imprint from 1900 and introduced the writings of Hauptmann, Strindberg, Chekhov, and Gorki to the American public. He also published works by James Joyce and Sherwood Anderson. In 1925 his firm merged with the Viking Press. Alfred A. *Knopf began publishing in 1915 and quickly established a reputation for excellence in design and materials. His list featured many prominent authors, both foreign and American. The firm merged with Random House in 1960. Boni and Liveright was established by Albert Boni (1892–1981) and Horace Briabin Liveright (1896–1933). Their most successful project was the Modern Library, a reprint series now issued by Random House. Boni soon left the firm, but the original name was retained until 1928. In 1923 Boni became a partner in Albert and Charles Boni, a pioneer of paperback books. Albert Boni, who founded the Washington Square Players (now the Theatre Guild), invented Microprint and the Readex reading projector and from 1940 was president of the firm that produced these devices. Horace Liveright was a lavish promoter of authors such as Theodore Dreiser and Eugene O'Neill, but later worked mainly as a stage producer.

Men who had worked for Boni and Liveright established several important publishing firms. Thomas Seltzer formed his own firm in 1920 and Richard L. Simon organized Simon and Schuster with M. Lincoln *Schuster in 1924. In 1925 Liveright sold the Modern Library to Bennett A. *Cerf and Donald S. Klopfer (d. 1986). Two years later they and Elmer *Adler formed Random House. In 1965 when Cerf became chairman of the board, the presidency was assumed by Robert L. Bernstein. The poet and literary critic Joel Elias *Spingarn was a founder of Harcourt, Brace & Co. and the firm's literary adviser from 1919 to 1932.

Other book publishing firms established by Jews in the 1920s and 1930s included that of Greenberg Publisher (1924) by Jacob Walter Greenberg (1894–1976); Viking Press (1925); and the short-lived Covici-Friede, which specialized in limited editions. When this last firm was dissolved, Donald Friede joined the World Publishing Company as a senior editor, and Pascal Covici became an editor for Viking Press. William Bernard Ziff (1898–1953), a founder of the Ziff-Davis Publishing Company (1933), was also president of the Zionist Revisionist Organization of America. From Greenberg, Nat Wartels and Robert Simon bought the Outlet Book Company, which disposed of publisher's overstocks, and they began publishing under the imprint of Crown Publishers. Max Salom of the Harlem Book Company, who pioneered the sale of publishers' overstocks through drugstores, acquired the Dial Press in 1934. George W. Joel was editor-in-chief of Dial Press (1939–51) and president and publisher from 1951 until his death in 1959. Stanley Burnshaw (1906–2005) was founder, president, and editor-in–chief of Dryden Press (1936).

Several other publishing houses were established by Jews or had Jews in leading managerial positions. Roger W. Straus, Jr. was founder and president of Farrar, Straus, and Giroux (1945); Abelard-Schuman was headed by Lew Schwartz; Arthur J. Rosenthal was president editor-in-chief of Basic Books, Inc. (1952); Oscar Dystal was president of Bantam Books, a subsidiary of Grosset and Dunlap whose president from 1944 was Manuel Siwak; Joseph Gaer (1897–1969) served as editor-in-chief of the Federal Writers Project. With Charles Boni, Gaer formed Boni and Gaer (1946), which soon changed its name to Gaer Associates. Jeremiah Kaplan, an executive of the Free Press of Glencoe from 1947, became president of the Macmillan Company in 1965. Harry N. Abrams, Inc., specialized in art books. Robert Salomon headed Citadel Press; Paul Steiner, Chanticleer Press; Arthur B. Frommer headed Arthur Frommer, Inc.; Harold H. Hart, Hart Publishing Co.; A.L. Furman, Lantern Press; Philip F. Cohen, Oceana Publications; Jacob Steinberg, Twayne Publishers; Milton Gladstone, Arco Publishing Co.; Richard L. Grossman, Grossman Publishers; and Sol Stein, Stein and Day.

The decades in which American Jews became active in book publishing saw tremendous changes in the book world in the United States. Alfred A. Knopf and Simon and Schuster did much to invigorate book promotion and advertising. Huebsch, Knopf, Seltzer, and their successors introduced many new European authors, but at the same time sought fresh American and British talents. The new publishers had high production standards, Knopf and Viking in particular insisting on attractive, well-made books.

BOOK CLUBS, REPRINTS, AND CHILDREN'S LITERATURE. Three publishing developments during the first half of the 20th century greatly expanded the market for books and in these Jews were prominent. The basic idea of membership in a club for the publication and distribution of books was not new. The *Jewish Publication Society of America (1888) was the successor to at least two earlier membership schemes, and several other groups had been established to publish special editions for members. Harold K. *Guinzburg, founder of the Viking Press (1925), was impressed by the popularity of recently-formed book clubs in Germany. He developed a plan for an American book club, The Literary Guild, which began active operations in 1927; it was sold to Doubleday in 1934. Harry Scherman (1887–1969) who was born in Montreal, Canada, had successfully promoted the Little Leather Library (1916), a mail-order firm, and felt that people living far from bookshops would subscribe to books as to magazines. With Robert K. Haas (1890–1964) and Maxwell B. Sackheim, he organized the Book-of-the-Month Club (1926), which by 1970 had distributed 250 million books. In 1929 George Macy started the Limited Editions Club, limited to 1500 members; and he also founded several others (Heritage Club, Junior Heritage Club, Readers Club). Thomas Yoseloff (1913–) has operated many book clubs, including the Jewish Book Guild, Military Science Book Club, Natural History Book Club, Book Collectors' Society, Art Book Guild, and the Science Book Club. He also established or bought several publishing houses (Beechurst Press, A.S. Barnes and Co., Sagamore Press, Thomas Yoseloff, Inc.) and was the U.S. publisher of the Ben-Yehuda Hebrew dictionary.

Another important development was in the area of low-price reprints, many publishers issuing inexpensive editions of popular works with several firms specializing in this field. The Modern Library was a notable addition to the hard-cover reprint world, and the World Publishing Co. of Cleveland, founded by Alfred Cahen as the Commercial Book Bindery (1905), became prominent, particularly after Benjamin David Zevin (1901–1984) joined the firm. However, the revolution in the industry really began with paperback books. As editor and publisher of Little Blue Books, Emanuel Halderman-Julius (1889–1951) had issued and distributed millions of small paperbound books through the mail for as little as five cents a copy. Occasionally, too, Simon and Schuster had issued a book in paper binding, while the paperbacks published by Albert and Charles Boni and by the *New Republic*, though praised for their content and format, made little impact on sales. In 1939, Pocket Books Inc. was organized by Robert F. de Graff, an expert in the cloth reprint field, with H. Lincoln Schuster, Leon Shimkin, and Richard L. Simon (1899–1962). The first printing of each of the ten titles in the initial list was about 10,000 copies. Twenty years later, 1,000,000 paperbacks a day were sold in the United States. By 1957 only Leon Shimkin remained active in Pocket Books. Others who entered the field were Joseph Meyers, who founded Avon Publications in 1940, and Ned L. Pines, who published under the Popular Library imprint. Doubleday opened a new era in paperback publishing in 1953 with its Anchor Books. The first editor of this serious fiction and non-fiction series was Jason Epstein, later an editor with Random House. Other higher-priced, serious paperback series were the Viking Press's Compass Books and those issued by Schocken Books.

During the 20th century, children's books became one of the most important divisions of American publishing. Knopf, Viking, and Random House were all leaders in the field, but the establishment by Simon and Schuster of Little Golden Books in 1942 brought low-cost books to young people for the first time. More than 400,000,000 Golden Books were sold in the first 13 years. Golden Press Inc., headed by Albert R. Leventhal, formerly a Simon and Schuster executive, became a division of Western Printing Co.

[Israel Soifer]

AFTER THE 1970S. The huge changes that continue to engulf the general book publishing field in the United States, and indeed throughout the world, also had a sharp impact on the specialized area of Jewish publishing. In 1950 it was thought that there were some 600,000 Jewish youngsters attending some kind of Jewish school in the U.S. and Canada, offering a market for textbooks and supplementary reading books that attracted substantial numbers of Jewish publishers. In 1970, it was estimated that the number of such students was closer to 300,000, of whom one-third were enrolled in largely Orthodox yeshivot. The results were almost predictable: the innovative Orthodox house, Artscroll, serviced the Orthodox market; Behrman House continued to be the leader of modern texts for the Conservative area; and the publishing arm of the Reform movement, the Union of American Hebrew Congregations, provided books for the Reform congregations' school needs.

The one area in Jewish school enrollment that saw a steady rise remained the pre-school nurseries, where children aged three and four are introduced to Judaic concepts through a wide variety of educational material, including video cassettes. It was this slice of the Jewish market that seemed to attract both general and Jewish publishers, as the number of full-color illustrated books for very young children continued to mount.

Although an estimated 700 new Jewish books appear every year in the United States, many of these are highly specialized titles meant for limited academic or professional library use. While the number of general Jewish books remains relatively high, and the number of Jewish-theme novels, biographies, general non-fiction, books on Israel, the Holocaust, etc. remains impressive, many publishers are not at all certain how much longer this phenomenon will last, especially as the total number of Jews in the United States is declining for various reasons.

This is not to say that publishers – both general houses and Jewish houses – have given up on Judaica publishing. Jews still buy books in disproportionately large numbers, and every publisher is trying to turn out titles that will capture the community's imagination and become perennial bestsellers. Jewish Book Month, which is sponsored by the Jewish Book Council, an affiliate of the National Jewish Welfare Board, takes place annually in November, with many hundreds of book fairs being held throughout the country.

In New York, a major fair attracted some 15,000 visitors. Some of the authors featured had written general books but since they were themselves well-known Jews, they helped bring in people. A number of authors spoke about such esoteric topics as "The Jewish Detective," "The Jewish Voter" (the fair was held just before the national elections in the U.S.), "How to Care for Your Parents," and "The Jewish Holiday Kitchen." The new books featured at 1988 fairs ranged from a new coffee table volume on Israel published on the state's 40th anniversary, with text by A.B. Yehoshua, to a new volume by Israel's Lova Eliav, titled *New Heart, New Spirit: Biblical Humanism for Modern Israel*, plus a series of new first-person memoirs of the Holocaust, a new series of brief biographies of Rashi, Buber, Bialik and Heine, the autobiography of a former Soviet dissident, fiction by Leon Uris, Amos Keinan, and David Grossman, and scholarly works with such titles as *Jewish Values in Psychotherapy: Essays on Vital Issues of Man's Search for Meaning* by Rabbi Levi Meier.

Although the trend in the last quarter of the 20th century was toward smaller numbers of vast publishing empires (Doubleday, once a major general publisher of large numbers of Jewish titles, is now part of the German-owned Bertelsman-Bantam-Doubleday group, while Random House has absorbed Crown, and Macmillan was taken over by Britain's vast Maxwell empire), the number of tiny one or two-man publishing houses has exploded, and now numbers in the thousands. Modern computer technology and desktop publishing have attracted literally thousands of people to set up shop in their homes, basements, and garages, where they issue local, regional or national titles at the rate of two or three a year. This radical new concept has also caught on in the Jewish community.

In addition to the well-known Jewish houses like the Jewish Publication Society, Behrman, Hebrew Publishing, Bloch Publishing, Feldheim, Ktav, Artscroll, and the publishing arms of various religious/educational/rabbinical organizations, one can now find a growing number of small, new Jewish houses: Micah Publications, Alpha Publishing, Bet Shamai Publications, Biblio Press, Bezalel Art, Jewish Historical Society of Oregon, Kar-Ben Copies, Hunter Publishing, Markus Weiner Publishing, Quartet Books, Madison Books, Edwin Mellen Press, Wandering You Press, Mensch Makers Press, Judaica Press, Peartree, Jason Aronson.

The number of Jewish titles appearing on the regular lists of large and small university presses, as well as in the offerings of Christian religious houses, remains high. Abingdon Press, a noted Christian house, issued *A Grammar for Biblical Hebrew* by C.L. Seow in 1988, while Wayne State University Press published a study by Amnon Linder titled *Jews in Roman Imperial Legislation*.

The Jewish Publication Society of America celebrated its 100th anniversary in 1988, noting that it had issued more than 700 titles in that period aggregating more than nine million volumes that it had distributed to its members and the public at large.

A glance at the catalogs of general houses and Jewish houses will quickly demonstrate that certain broad subjects remain on top of the community's reading agenda: Israel, the Holocaust, antisemitism, assimilation, Jewish ethics, culture, and philosophy. From the last quarter of the 20th century, a number of publishers began to issue titles dealing with a subject that is often peripheral in Jewish life – Kabbalah, or Jewish mysticism. Whether this was a reflection of the times or a deep spiritual hunger is hard to say.

A major problem in Jewish publishing in America – distribution – was not fully resolved in the traditional manner. Books of Jewish interest reviewed in daily or Jewish media, recommended by friends or referred to by a rabbi during a Sabbath sermon, were often very hard to come by in general book stores. Although there were some 250 strictly Jewish book shops in all parts of the U.S., and many hundreds of (primarily Conservative and Reform) congregations sold limited numbers of Judaica titles from their volunteer-manned "gift shops," no one was been able to work out an effective method of getting Jewish books into the hands of book buyers on a nationwide scale.

With the coming of the Internet in the 1990s Jewish books became available online at innumerable sites, obviating the longstanding problem of distribution among publishers of Jewish books.

[David C. Gross]

PUBLISHING OF HEBRAICA AND JUDAICA

Central and Western Europe

The first publishers – in the modern sense – of Judaica were in Germany, which for a long time remained the center of Jewish (mainly non-Hebrew) publishing. The pioneer was W. *Heidenheim, who was succeeded by M. Lehrberger, in Roedelheim, the producer of famous editions of the Jewish liturgy. In the first half of the 19th century Jewish bookshops were opened in the larger towns and many of their owners later became publishers. M.W. Kaufmann established himself in Leipzig in 1828, later specializing in publishing synagogue music. J. *Kaufmann established himself in Frankfurt on the Main in 1832 and his firm was the leading Jewish publisher (and bookseller) in Germany for three generations, taking over Lehrberger in 1899. In Prague W. Pascheles was active from 1836. Several firms were established in Berlin in the course of the 19th century, some of which, like *Asher and Co., later gave up Jewish publishing; others did not stay the course (A. Cohn, J. Sittenfeld, Springer and Co., Veit and Co., and others). M. Poppelauer (est. 1860) and C. Boas (est. 1863) remained of importance for some decades. The firm of B.L. Monasch was active in Krotoschin from 1835 to 1910 and that of Zirndorfer published works in Fuerth.

In the 20th century the most important publishing house became the *Juedischer Verlag, which not only produced Zionist literature but also a great variety of Hebrew and Yiddish works in the original and in translation. After World War I the concentration of Jewish writers and scholars from Eastern Europe in Germany, in Berlin in particular, produced a Jewish intellectual revival, and many publishing houses sprang up, producing both Hebraica and Judaica. Louis Lamm was already established in 1903; the Weltverlag followed it in 1919. The *Philo Verlag (1919–38), the publishing arm of the *Centralverein deutscher Staatsbuerger juedischen Glaubens, fought against the rising antisemitism, but its activities covered a wide range of Jewish literature, including the publication of periodicals like *Der Morgen and Zeitschrift fuer die Geschichte der Juden in Deutschland*. The Akademie Verlag was a branch of the Akademie fuer die Wissenschaft des Judentums. The Eschkol Verlag published the *Encyclopaedia Judaica* in German (10 vols., to 1934 unfinished) and in Hebrew (2 vols., 1929–32, also unfinished) and other important works such as J. Klatzkin's *Thesaurus Philosophicus Linguae Hebraicae* (4 vols., 1928–33). Other firms included Reuben Mass in Berlin, who later continued publishing in Jerusalem; Schocken Verlag, also in Berlin (see above); Saenger und *Friedberg (the bibliographer) in Frankfurt; the Hermon Verlag, which was connected with the Orthodox weekly *Israelit*; the Juedischer Verlag (1901); and the *Soncino Gesellschaft (1924). After 1938 Schocken Verlag published in Israel and the U.S. Some Hebrew publishers, like *Devir, *Moriah, and *Stybel, transferred to Germany, later moving to Ereẓ Israel or the U.S. Similarly, the Omanut Hebrew publishing house, established in Moscow in 1917 by H. *Zlatopolski and his daughter Shoshannah *Persitz, moved to Odessa in 1918, Homburg (near Frankfurt) in 1920, and Tel Aviv in 1928. Other firms include Chorev, which published small-size reproductions of the great rabbinic texts, Yavneh, Ayyanot, and Yuval, the latter specializing in Jewish music. Klal and Vostock published Yiddish literature. The economic conditions in post-World War I Germany led to the closing of several smaller firms.

In Vienna Benjamin Harz republished, among other works, L. Goldschmidt's Talmud edition and German translation. The firm of R. Loewitt, active there from 1833, later issued mainly Jewish belletristic works. Joseph Schlesinger founded his firm in 1858 – with a branch in Budapest at a later date – and became a leading publisher of prayer books and other items, supplying several European countries as well as North Africa.

In Leghorn, Italy, the house of *Belforte was active from 1838 to 1939 as publishers of liturgical literature for the Italian, North African, and Levantine market. In France (Paris), E. Durlacher and M. Lipschuetz published Hebraica and Judaica; the former was still active in 1970.

NON-JEWISH PUBLISHERS OF JUDAICA. In pre-Hitler Germany a number of non-Jewish publishers were responsible for some works of Hebraica and Judaica: the Insel Verlag (Brody-Wiener's *Anthologia Hebraica*, 1924), Langenscheidt (Eliezar Ben-Yehuda's *Thesaurus*), O. Harrassowitz in Leipzig, Toepelmann, Giessen, and others. In Holland the house of Brill in Leiden has been active for nearly 100 years. In France some general publishing houses published books dealing with Jews and Judaism, e.g., F. Rieder, Fernand Nathan, Albin Michel, Payot, Au-bier Montaine, Flammarion, and Presses Universitaires de France.

In Great Britain

The pioneers of Jewish publishing in Great Britain were members of the London Sephardi community who issued works on philosophy, literature, and Jewish liturgy in Spanish and Portuguese from the early 18th century onward. Daniel Israel Lopez *Laguna's *Espejo Fiel de Vidas* ("Faithful Mirror of Life"), a Spanish metrical version of Psalms planned in the cells of the Inquisition and completed in Jamaica, was published in London in 1720. Long after Marrano immigration had virtually come to an end, Spanish and Portuguese remained the official languages of the Sephardim, with the result that Isaac *Pinto's English translation of the prayer book had to appear in New York (1761–66) because of the disapproval of the London *mahamad*. One of the first Anglo-Jewish publishers whose name has survived was Alexander b. Judah Loeb Alexander (d. 1807), who issued a *Haggadah* (1770) and a Sephardi prayer book with English translation (1788), as well as other works of a liturgical nature. This activity was maintained by his son, Levy Alexander (1754–1853), who also proved to be an indifferent translator with his pioneering, but defective, Hebrew-English Bible (1824). Levy, however, did not confine himself to religious publications, producing an account of Anglo-Jewish social scandals in 1808.

By about the middle of the 19th century Jews were becoming more prominent in the general field of publishing, founding several important family business concerns. Isaac Vallentine (1793–1868), the Belgian-born son of a rabbi, was a leading communal figure as well as a printer, publisher, and bookseller of note. In 1841 he founded the predecessor of the weekly *Jewish Chronicle* and also established *The Hebrew Almanack and Calendar* (1848), a forerunner of the *Jewish Year Book*. The firm of Vallentine & Co. later underwent a merger, becoming the bookselling and publishing firm of Shapiro, Vallentine, which remained in business until 1971.

[Godfrey Edmond Silverman]

Other Jewish publishers of Hebraica and Judaica, who became active from the late 19th century included the booksellers M. Cailingold, R. Mazin (later Jack Mazin), and Edward Goldston. In the 1920s Jacob Davidson founded the Soncino Press, which was responsible for the publication of classic Jewish texts in English. They issued (35- and 11-volume editions) the Talmud edited by I. *Epstein, Midrash Rabbah (10 vols.), Zohar (5 vols.), the Bible (text, translation, and commentary,

13 vols.), a one-volume edition of J.H. Hertz's Pentateuch and Haftarot, the minor tractates of the Talmud (2 vols.), a collection of S.R. Hirsch's essays (2 vols., edited by I. *Grunfeld), and Hirsch's *Horeb* (2 vols.; also edited by I. Grunfeld). From the 1930s onward the East and West Library (see above) brought out a series of Jewish classics. In the 1940s and 1950s a number of books in Hebrew and Yiddish, as well as the journal *Metsudah*, were produced by the Ararat Publishing Company. Since World War II the firm of Valentine Mitchell (associated with the *Jewish Chronicle*) has published a large variety of books of Jewish interest. Literature pertaining to Anglo-Jewish history was published by the *Jewish Historical Society of England.

General publishing firms as well, some of them owned by Jews, have published Hebraica and Judaica. George Routledge and Sons published the Davis-Adler *Maḥzor* (6 vols., 1904), which has gone through many editions and reprints, and other books of Jewish interest. Eyre and Spottiswoode have issued the popular Singer's *Prayer Book* since 1890; it has sold over half a million copies.

In Eastern Europe

In Eastern Europe publishing gradually emerged as distinct from Hebrew printing. Great printing houses signed contracts with authors, e.g., Romm in Vilna with I.M. *Dick and K. *Schulman. Important booksellers also began to publish works, e.g., A. Zuckermann and A.J. Shapiro in Warsaw; I. Ginzburg in Bobrisk; and Rawnitzki in Odessa. Newspaper owners, learned societies, and patrons published works, hitherto in manuscript or unsatisfactory editions. The first noncommercial publishing house was Aḥiasaf, founded in Warsaw in 1892–93 on the initiative of the *Bnei Moshe and under the direction of E.E. Kaplan and the guidance of *Aḥad Ha-Am. Aḥi'asaf, which was active until 1923, published works of modern Jewish scholarship and youth literature as well as the annual *Lu'aḥ Aḥi'asaf* and the periodicals *Ha-Shilo'ah* and *Ha-Dor.* One of the founders of Aḥi'asaf, A. Ben-Avigdor, set up the Tushiyyah company in 1895, which extended its activities to Hebrew belles lettres, both original and translated, works in the natural and social sciences, and modern school books.

In 1899, in Warsaw, J. Lidzki founded the "Progres" publishing firm for Yiddish literature. B. Schimin, also in Warsaw, brought out books both in Hebrew and Yiddish as did S. Scherberk in Vilna (established 1901–02), who published the popular Bible commentary *Mikra Meforash*. In order to further original Hebrew literature P. Lachower set up the Sifrut company in Warsaw in 1908. In 1910 in Vilna B. Klatzkin began to publish scientific books, as well as original and translated literature in Yiddish. A year later Tushiyyah, Progres, Schimin, and Scherberk merged under the name of Merkaz ("Zentral"). In 1901 Ḥ.N. Bialik, S. Ben-Zion, and Yehoshua Ḥana Rawnitzki founded the *Moriah publishing house in Odessa for classical Hebrew literature and textbooks for schools, while Turgeman concentrated on translations from other languages.

World War I brought with it a severe crisis in the Jewish book market in Russia, which was aggravated by an edict in 1915 prohibiting all printing in Hebrew types. After the March 1917 revolution two Hebrew publishing houses were set up in Moscow: *Stybel, under the direction of D. *Frischmann, for classical world literature in Hebrew, and Omanut (see above). Moriah also renewed its activities. After the October Revolution and the subsequent anti-Jewish measures of the Soviet government, all these ceased. Stybel moved to Warsaw and later to Berlin, New York, and finally Tel Aviv. In the early years of the Soviet regime some private Yiddish publishing continued, e.g., by the Kultur-Lige (founded in 1917 in Kiev), but these businesses were soon absorbed by the state corporation Der Emes in Moscow; the Ukrainian state publishers and the Belorussian state publishers year after year issued many hundreds of Yiddish books, most of them propagating communist ideology. With the outbreak of World War II this output was severely reduced, ceasing altogether with the liquidation of Jewish writers in the years 1942–48. From 1958 onward only very few books in Yiddish were published in Soviet Russia.

In Poland the centers of Jewish publishing between the two world wars were Warsaw and Vilna. In Warsaw "Zentral" continued its activities; S.L. *Gordon published his Bible commentary, and Stybel *Ha-Tekufah*, and hundreds of books. A Kultur-Lige, founded in 1921, issued the best of Yiddish literature, school books, and Dubnow's "World History of the Jewish People." B. Klatzkin moved from Vilna to Warsaw and expanded its activities. Other publishers include A. Gitlin, H. Bzoza, S. Goldfarb, Katzanellenbogen, and Armkraut and Freund (Przemysl). The brothers Lewin-Epstein, who had published religious literature from 1880, began to issue belles lettres in Hebrew as well as in Yiddish. In Vilna "Tomor" produced I. Zinberg's history of Jewish literature. The various political parties also published books, as did newspapers (*Literarishe Bleter*) and scholarly societies such as *YIVO. With the invasion of Poland by Nazi Germany this activity came to an end. After the war a state corporation under the control of Jewish communists, Dos Yidishe Bukh, produced some important studies on the Holocaust.

[Yehuda Slutsky]

In the United States

Until the early 19th century, Jews in the United States imported books of specifically Jewish interest (chiefly Bibles, prayer books, and instructional material for the young) from Europe. However, a Hebrew Bible, a reprint of Joseph *Athias' unpointed text, was printed in Philadelphia in 1814. In 1845 Isaac *Leeser established the American Jewish Publication Society for the dissemination of Jewish literature. Fourteen books were published under the general title "Jewish Miscellany," but the society collapsed in 1851 when a fire destroyed the building in which the books and plates were stored. The firm now known as the Bloch Publishing Co. was founded in Cincinnati in 1854 by Isaac M. *Wise and Edward Bloch (1816–1881) to print and publish books on Jewish subjects. The *Bloch family has retained control of the firm, which has been in New York since 1901. Edward H. Bloch (1899–), grandson of the founder, was president from 1940, and Solomon Kerstein (1901–1969), a founder of the Jewish Book Council, was vice president from 1947 onward. By 1970 over 1,000 titles had appeared on the firm's catalogs. The Hebrew Publishing Company came into being in New York in 1883, when Joseph L. Werbelowsky and some associates began to publish prayer books and school texts. In 1901 the firm was known as Rosenbaum and Werbelowsky, Inc. Menahem Menschel, an agent for the Stybel (Hebrew) Publishing House and a partner in the Jewish bookselling firm of Reznick, Menschel and Co., was manager from 1938. The firm published new Hebrew-English editions of the *siddur* and the *maḥzor* by Philip *Birnbaum. The third of these pioneering Jewish publishing houses, the Jewish Publication Society, was established in Philadelphia in 1888, and its many titles include authoritative translations of the Bible (1917; 1963–). Unlike the others, this is a membership organization with many features of the modern book clubs. The *Jewish Encyclopedia* (1901–06) was issued by the non-Jewish publishing house of Funk and Wagnall (see *Encyclopedias: Jewish).

National Jewish organizations in the United States have sponsored various publication programs. The *Union of American Hebrew Congregations (Reform) developed an extensive program under its own imprint. Emanuel *Gamoran, educational director of the UAHC and its Commission on Jewish Education (1923–1958), developed text and reference books catering for all age groups. The Conservative movement (*United Synagogue of America) also established its own publishing divisions. Burning Bush Press and the United Synagogue Book Service serve the needs of the affiliated synagogues and schools. The *Union of Orthodox Jewish Congregations of America has also published text materials, while many works for both adults and children have appeared under the imprint of the Ḥabad ḥasidic Merkos l'Inyonei Chinuch of New York. The viewpoint of *Reconstructionism is presented in the bound books and paperbacks of the Reconstructionist Press. The Herzl Press has issued Zionist classics, handbooks, and yearbooks. In 1967 the *B'nai B'rith Commission on Adult Education contracted with the W.W. Norton Co. for a 50-book series of "Jewish Heritage Classics."

The Anti-Defamation League of B'nai B'rith usually employs a general publisher for its major works, pamphlets and shorter publications normally appearing under the organization's own imprint. The B'nai B'rith Hillel Foundation has also published books and pamphlets, while *Commentary*, the monthly sponsored by the American Jewish Committee, operates its own book club. Other publishers active in the field include Pardes, the Jewish Agency, various Zionist bodies (ZOA, Farband, Mizrachi) and university presses (Dropsie College, HUC, JTS, Yeshiva University, Brandeis) and the National Jewish Welfare Board. The *Histadrut Ivrit publishes Hebrew literature and *YIVO, the Yiddish Scientific Institute, has issued several important Yiddish works. Several regional educational bodies have also entered publishing. The JEC Press of the Jewish Education Committee of New York has issued a library of Hebrew story books for American children, while the bureaus of Jewish education of Chicago and Cleveland also have their own publishing divisions.

Establishing these institutional publishing firms or the sponsoring of individual books under the imprint of a general publisher has tended to discourage privately owned publishing houses from specializing in the Jewish field. Indeed, practically all the privately owned Jewish publishing firms also run bookshops where Jewish books under various imprints are sold. They include Behrman House (1920), founded by Louis Behrman and later directed by his son, Jacob; the Ktav Publishing House, which issued text and story materials from 1924 (with Asher Scharfstein as president), and which has latterly published and reprinted serious scholarly works; the Furrow Press (1933), which issued festival plays and literature for Jewish schools; and the U.S. branch of Schocken Books (1945), known particularly for its serious paperback program. Other privately owned firms specializing in Judaica are Shengold Publishers (Moshe Sheinbaum); the Jonathan David Publishing Co. (Alfred J. Kolatch); Philipp Feldheim, which published English translations of the works of Samson Raphael *Hirsch; and Hermon press. The established firm of Shulsinger Brothers also prints Jewish publications. Morris *Silverman, a Conservative rabbi in Hartford, edited and published a series of Conservative prayer books with English translations under the Prayer Book Press imprint. Most publishers active in the Jewish field belong to the Association of Jewish Book Publishers. The chief publication of Yiddish works include *YIVO, *Congress for Jewish Culture, and Der Kval, a private firm.

Several general publishers have displayed continuous interest in Jewish books and their authors. Rinehart (now Holt, Rinehart, and Winston) issued a series of Jewish anthologies edited by Leo W. Schwarz, and Abelard-Shuman operates a separate division, Ram's Head Books, for Jewish books. Maurice *Samuel's books have been published by Knopf, and those of Isaac *Bashevis Singer and Bernard *Malamud by Farrar, Straus, and Giroux. Meridian Books (established by Arthur A. Cohen) first distributed the paperbacks of the Jewish Publication Society, a function later performed by Harper and Row. Another area of cooperation is the joint issue of a title by a Jewish and a general publisher. Many JPSA titles appear under the joint imprint of the Society and a general publisher. Thus Columbia University Press collaborated in Salo W. *Baron's multivolume *Social and Religious History of the Jews*, while Herzl Press and Doubleday have also cooperated on several publications.

In 1925, Fanny *Goldstein, a librarian, organized a Jewish Book Week in Boston. The movement grew gradually, and the Jewish Book Council, sponsored by the *National Jewish Welfare Board, was established in 1942. Jewish Book Week was later expanded to Jewish Book Month. The *Jewish Book Annual* has been issued since 1942 and a series of annual prizes for authors in the Jewish field was established.

[Solomon Kerstein]

IN ISRAEL

Printing and publishing developed slowly in Ereẓ Israel. Eliezer ben Yitzhak *Ashkenazi, a printer of Hebrew books from Prague, together with his brother Abraham, established the first printing plant in the Upper Galilee city of Safed in 1577. Their first publication was *Lekaḥ Tov* ("A Worthy Inspiration"), a commentary on the biblical Book of Esther by R. Yom Tov Ẓahalon. The Ashkenazi press remained in Safed for some 10 years during which time only five books were printed, and in 1605, the type was sold to a printer in Damascus. It took another two and a half centuries before a printing house was again established, that of Israel *Bak, in 1831, also in Safed. The publishing and printing business was subsequently transferred to Jerusalem where it continued to function until 1878. With the growing Jewish immigration to Palestine in the latter half of the 19th century, Jerusalem began to develop into a center for the printing of religious and liturgical works in Hebrew. By the turn of the century, more than a dozen Jerusalem printers – most of whom also acted as booksellers – were producing Hebrew books and periodicals, most of them in the field of Judaica, rabbinic studies, and prayer books.

Professional publishing in the modern sense really began only during the period of the British Mandate in the 1920s and 1930s, with the move to Palestine of some of the major Jewish imprints of Europe. Moriah, which had been established in Odessa early in the century by Ḥayyim Naḥman *Bialik and Yehoshua *Rawnitzky merged in 1923 with *Dvir, which had been founded in Berlin by Bialik, Rawnitzky, and Shmaryahu *Levin a year earlier. The workers' periodical *Ha-Poel ha-Ẓa'ir* introduced the writings of contemporary luminaries of Hebrew literature such as Asher *Barash, A.D.*Gordon, and Moshe *Smilansky among others and issued a series of books under the title "The People's University Library." Shlomo Sreberk, a publisher in Vilna and Warsaw, moved to Palestine in 1933 reestablishing his imprint and founding a new one named Izreel. Omanut, specializing in the arts and books for children, was founded in Moscow in 1916 by Shoshanah *Persitz (who subsequently became a member of the Israel Knesset) and was transferred to Tel Aviv in 1925. Rubin Mass, founded in Berlin in 1927, moved to Palestine in 1933. The Schocken publishing house, founded in Berlin in 1927, moved to Palestine in 1938, where it also established Israel's leading daily newspaper, *Haaretz*. Most of the publishing houses mentioned above still exist in one form or another (for details see below).

At the same time that many of the old-established European houses were being reborn in Palestine, new indigenous publishing houses were also being set up. Three veterans of the *Jewish Brigade of the British Army in World War I, Joshua Chachik, Mordechai Newman, and Joseph Sreberk, inaugurated Mitzpeh in 1925; in 1944 the partnership dissolved and each of them set up their own imprint. In 1930, one of the pioneers of early Tel Aviv, Naḥum Twersky, established his own publishing house as did Z. Zack in Jerusalem in the same year. Schachna Achiasaf founded his eponymous publishing house in Jerusalem in 1933. Joshua Orenstein's Yavneh Publishing House has been active in Tel Aviv since 1932. One of the most important publishers in pre-state Palestine and during the first four decades of the state was Massadah, founded in 1931 by Bracha Peli, who had left Russia with her family and immigrated to Palestine 10 years before. The company, which began as a lending library in 1922, then becoming a chain of bookstores, eventually developed into one of the dominant publishing houses in the Israeli book trade and it also owned one of the biggest printing plants in the Middle East. The company was split up and its assets disposed of following the death of Bracha Peli in 1986. Under the direction of Alexander Peli, the son of Bracha, Massadah was publisher of the 38-volume *Encyclopedia Hebraica*, unquestionably the single most important and complex publishing project in the history of the state.

Israel has had a tradition of publishing by institutions with a strong ideological motivation. From 1939, the two major kibbutz movements Ha-Kibbutz ha-Arẓi and Ha-Kibbutz ha-Me'uḥad operated their own publishing houses (respectively Sifriat Poalim and Ha-Kibbutz ha-Me'uḥad) combining general publishing with books having a clear ideological affinity with their respective kibbutz movements. Another institutional publisher is Am Oved, founded and owned by the Histadrut (the General Federation of Labor in Israel). For details of these publishing houses, see below.

While the Hebrew language is by far the dominant force in Israeli publishing, there is a certain amount of quality Arabic publishing in the country, some of it sponsored by institutions and there are also several independent publishers, including Dar el-Huda of Kafr Kara, Al-Mushreq of Shefaram, and al-Aswar of Acre. In addition there is a limited amount of original publishing of books and journals in English and other languages (much of it of a scholarly and academic nature).

With the influx of nearly one million new immigrants from the former Soviet Union between 1989 and 2000, the cultural face of Israel has been transformed in many ways, and the Russian influence is very apparent in music, theater, dance, and, of course, literature. There has been a flowering of newspapers and magazines, and some 250 outlets throughout the country sell books in Russian. It has been asserted that Israel has one of the world's largest publics for Russian language books and magazines – second only to Russia itself. Among the leading Russian language publishers are Gishrei-Tarbut ("Cultural Bridges") based in both Jerusalem and Moscow, which publishes an extensive list of original and translated books in Russian including the works of many contemporary Hebrew writers. Its main publication is the multi-volume *Bibliotheca Judaica* published in cooperation with the Center of Jewish Studies in Russian of the Hebrew University, Jerusalem. Other leading Russian-language publishers include Mahanayim, for religious publications including the Bible, Talmud, and prayer books. Merkur, Beseder, and Moskva/Kfar Saba are three general publishers. Sifriat Aliya has published the *Shorter Jewish Encyclopedia* in Russian, based on the *Encyclopaedia Judaica*.

Although official government statistics with reference to the book trade have not been compiled for several years, it is estimated that some 4,500 new books were being published annually in Israel in the early 21st century – the overwhelming majority of which in Hebrew. While there are hundreds of individuals, companies and institutions who publish the occasional book or two, there are approximately 100 publishing houses which can be considered as "professional" (those publishing from 15 to 100 or even more new titles a year). A brief account of some of the leading publishers is given below.

Some 90 publishers belong to the Book Publishers' Association of Israel founded in 1939. In addition to acting as a lobby for the promotion of Israeli books, the Association also organizes and administers Hebrew Book Week (see below). It also operates a joint paper-purchasing company which negotiates reduced prices for its members. Another smaller group of about 25 publishers is organized in the Israel Publishers' Union. The Book and Printing Center of the Israel Export Institute promotes Israeli publishing and printing abroad and is responsible for organizing Israel's national stand at the Frankfurt Book Fair and other international book trade events.

The major event in the Israeli publishing world is the annual Hebrew Book Week. This event, first held in 1952, takes place in the early summer in all of the country's major cities. It takes the form of open-air markets and is a very popular occasion attended by hundreds of thousands of people who take advantage of the many special offers and bargains that the publishers display on their own stands. The event in effect lasts a whole month with all the local bookstores participating and offering books at the same reduced prices as on the publishers' stands.

The Jerusalem International Book Fair is a biennial event that began in 1963. Over the years it has become one of the most popular events on the international publishing circuit and is attended by publishers from all over the world who seek new projects and authors in Israel or who wish to sell Hebrew rights or make distribution arrangements. A key event of the Fair is the Editorial Fellowship Program, which is internationally regarded as the most important forum in the world today for young editors. Since its establishment in 1985, more than 250 editors from some 25 countries (as of 2005) have participated in the program. Today many of its alumni hold key positions in publishing houses the world over. The Fair is also the occasion of the awarding of the Jerusalem Prize for the Freedom of Mankind in Society – Israel's premier international literary award. Prominent past recipients of the Jerusalem Prize include Bertrand Russell, Isaiah *Berlin, Jorgé Luis Borges, Simone de Beauvoir, Milan Kundera, Mario Vargas Llosa, Don DeLillo, and Susan *Sontag.

While some of Israel's leading writers are represented by literary agents abroad, two agents in Israel represent the bulk of Israeli authors. The Institute for the Translation of Hebrew Literature is a public company founded in 1962 for the purpose of promoting Hebrew literature including poetry and children's books into other languages. It represents a wide range of Israeli writers of quality fiction. The Institute also publishes the highly regarded magazine, *Modern Hebrew Literature*, edited by Gershon *Shaked, which features short stories, extracts, and chapters from important recently published or forthcoming books. It also publishes catalogues of Israeli books, biographies of leading writers, and a series of bibliographies of Israeli publications both in the original and in translation.

The Harris/Elon Agency, founded in Jerusalem by Deborah Harris in 1991, also represents an important cross-section of Israeli authors of both fiction and non-fiction, as well as those writing in languages other than Hebrew. Three agencies specialize in the marketing of foreign rights to Israeli publishers for translation into Hebrew: the Harris/Elon Agency referred to above; the Pikarsky Agency in Tel Aviv, founded in 1975 by the American/Israeli writer, Barbara Rogan; and a literary agency belonging to the Israel Book Publishers' Association, which caters to its members.

Israel's printing industry measures up to the most rigorous and advanced modern standards and several publishers specialize in packaging co-productions for publishers overseas. The availability of advanced digital printing processes has led to the short-run reissuing of many rare books, especially in the fields of Judaica and rabbinic studies.

Israel's retail book trade is dominated by the Steimatzky chain. Founded by Ezekiel Steimatzky in Jerusalem and Beirut in 1925, this is the oldest and most diversified bookselling enterprise in Israel. It imports books and magazines, videos and CDs and its business extends to over 160 shops throughout the country. It also acts as a wholesaler to another 1,000 retail outlets. Steimatzky also acts as a publisher and issues co-editions of books having a particular reference to Israel, such as illustrated albums, books by prominent local personalities, etc. While Steimatzky still enjoys a near monopoly over imported general books and magazines, the Tzomet Sefarim chain, founded in 1996 and owned by the Kinneret/Zmora/Dvir publishing conglomerate, is a major force for Hebrew books with some 30 shops mostly but not exclusively situated in the country's shopping malls.

A relatively small, third chain, Tamir, has seven shops in the Jerusalem area. The main sources for scientific, medical, and academic books are Academon, belonging to the Hebrew University of Jerusalem, and Dyonon, belonging to Tel Aviv University and with branches in the Ben-Gurion University of the Negev in Beersheba and the Multi-Disciplinary Center of Herzliyyah. Despite the competition from the chains, there are still many smaller traditional bookstores throughout the country, although their numbers are declining. There are electronic companies selling books through the internet, including dbook and Mitos. Gefen, a primarily English- language publisher, has a subsidiary company called Israbook, with a branch in New York, which supplies libraries, institutions and individuals throughout the world with Israeli publications.

The Publishers

The following brief list gives some of the leading, most prolific, or best-known Israeli publishers (the list is by no means exhaustive nor does it imply any value judgment).

AM OVED. One of Israel's leading publishers of quality literature and non-fiction. Founded by the Histadrut (the General Federation of Labor) in 1942, it publishes in an exhaustive range of subjects. As a major publisher of paperback books, it promotes new and classical Israeli and world literature in Hebrew through its series *Sifriyyah le-Am* ("The Peoples' Library").

BIALIK INSTITUTE. This distinguished non-profit making institution, was established by the World Zionist Organization in 1935 and was named in honor of the national poet Ḥayyim Naḥman Bialik. Its aim is to promote Hebrew literature, particularly in the field of Jewish studies, biblical research, philosophy, and sociology. Its publications cover scholarly and popular editions of classical Jewish works, archaeology, Judaica, art and art history, and Hebrew literature.

CARTA. Founded in 1958, the company specializes in the publication of maps, atlases, encyclopedias, and other reference books in Hebrew, English, German, Russian, and other languages, many of them in co-production with overseas publishers, concentrating on the geography, history, and archaeology of the Bible, the Holy Land, and the Land of Israel today.

HA-KIBBUTZ HA-ME'UḤAD/SIFRIAT POALIM. A merger of two publishing houses owned respectively by the National Federation of Collective Settlements (kibbutzim) and the Kibbutz Artẓi movement. Sifriat Poalim was founded in 1939 and Ha-Kibbutz ha-Me'uḥad in 1945. Both are public cultural institutions with a broad general publishing vision and a prolific and eclectic list with a strong emphasis on children's books, as well as books of an ideological nature representing the social and political beliefs of the two pioneering movements. The series *Ha-Sifriyyah ha-Ḥadashah* ("New Library") is one of the country's most distinguished lists of original and translated fiction. The two houses merged their publishing activities in 2000.

THE INSTITUTE FOR THE TRANSLATION OF HEBREW LITERATURE. The Institute for the Translation of Hebrew Literature (ITHL) was founded in 1962 to create a bridge between modern Hebrew literature and the non-Hebrew–speaking world. Over the years its range of activities has expanded far beyond translation (into 66 languages). ITHL's current activities include publication of author/book directories and catalogues; a unique bibliographic center listing all published translations of Hebrew literature; a website including an index of Hebrew authors in English (about 450 to 2006); yearly publication of *Modern Hebrew Literature*, a journal in English; literary agency services to more than 200 leading authors of adult, young adult, and children's literature; participation in major book fairs, financial support to foreign publishers; initiating anthologies of Hebrew literature in a variety of languages (about 200 to 2006); organizing international translation and literary events in Israel and abroad.

JERUSALEM PUBLISHING HOUSE. Founded in 1966, the company initiates and packages co-publishing projects with leading publishers overseas under whose imprints the books are published. Its profusely illustrated publications, concentrating on biblical research, archaeology, and general history, have made it a world leader in the production of Jewish English-language encyclopedias and dictionaries. Among its major publications are the *Dictionary and Concordance of the Bible*; *Guide to Biblical Holy Places*; *Archeological Dictionary of the Holy Land*; *Continuum Political Encyclopedia of the Middle East*; *Encyclopedia of the Holocaust*; *New Encyclopedia of Judaism*; *Encyclopedia of Jewish Life Before and After the Holocaust*; and *Encyclopedia of the Righteous Among the Nations*. It is co-publisher of the second edition of the *Encyclopaedia Judaica* (2006), responsible for all editorial content.

KETER. The company began as the Israel Program for Scientific Translations, established in 1958 by the U.S. National Science Foundation in Washington and the Israel Prime Minister's Office to translate scientific literature from Russian and other languages into English. In the 1960s it began to diversify its publishing activities under the imprints Israel Universities Press and Keter Books. Keter was purchased from the government in 1966 and has been a public company since 1987. It is Israel's largest integrated publishing, manufacturing (with its own printing plant), and book marketing concern and one of the country's major publishers in a wide range of genres. Its Israeli authors include Amos *Oz, Aharon *Appelfeld, Savyon *Liebrecht, and Uri *Orlev, and foreign authors include Paul *Auster, Paolo Coelho, Boris Pasternak, Salman Rushdie, Susan Sontag, and Mario Vargas-Llosa. Keter's major achievement was the magisterial English-language *Encyclopedia Judaica* first published in 16 volumes in 1971. The revised and updated second edition was co-published by Thomson Gale (Macmillan) in 2006.

KINNERET/ZMORA/DVIR. This house is a merger dating from 2002 of three well-known publishers and is today Israel's most prolific publisher in terms of annual number of titles. The group is also part owner of the Tsomet Sefarim bookselling chain (see above). Kinneret was founded as a general publisher in 1979 and Zmora (previously Zmora/Bitan/Modan), founded in 1973, was a leading publisher of original and translated fiction, as well as a broad general list. One of the most distinguished names in Israeli publishing, Dvir was established in Berlin in the early 20th century by some of the leading Hebrew literary figures of the time and moved to Palestine in 1924. It has published many of the classics of Modern Hebrew literature, several of which are now being re-issued.

MAGNES PRESS. Founded in 1929, the publishing house of the Hebrew University of Jerusalem is the oldest and largest scholarly publishing house in the country. It publishes books and journals, in English and Hebrew, on Jewish studies, Bible, history, contemporary Jewry, archeology, law, mathematics, among other subjects. Many of its publications are published in cooperation with academic and university publishing houses overseas.

MODAN. The successor to the Lewin-Epstein publishing house founded in 1930, Modan, established in 1974, is a large general publisher specializing in cookbooks, general fiction, and "how-to" books.

RAV KOOK INSTITUTE. This scholarly publishing house was founded in 1936 to perpetuate the memory of the chief rabbi of Palestine, Abraham Isaac Kook. It is a non-profit institution whose aim is to publish scholarly works in traditional religious Jewish studies, especially Bible commentary, the Talmud, Jewish history, philosophy, and Jewish law. Among its major publications are several editions of the Bible, a Bible commentary in 30 volumes, and the collected works of Maimonides.

SCHOCKEN. Schocken Verlag was founded in Berlin in 1931 by Salman *Schocken, owner of a chain of prosperous department stores. He immigrated to Palestine in 1934 and established two publishing houses: Schocken Tel Aviv for books in Hebrew and Schocken New York for books in English. The Israeli company is one of the most distinguished publishing houses in the country and numbers among its writers some of its leading literary figures such as Yehuda *Amichai, Yeshayahu *Leibowitz, Meir *Shalev, A.B.*Yehoshua, and Shmuel Yosef *Agnon, Israel's only winner of the Nobel Prize for literature (in 1966). Among its foreign authors are Franz *Kafka, Herman Hesse, Ted Hughes, D.H. Lawrence, Dylan Thomas, Gabriel Garcia Marques, Philip *Roth, and Alexander Solzhenitsyn. Schocken has acquired the rights to reissue a new an updated edition of the monumental *Encyclopedia Hebraica*, originally published by Massadah.

YEDIOTH AHARONOTH. Wholly owned by the mass-circulation daily newspaper of the same name, the publishing house, established in 1952, began with the publication of basic Jewish texts including the Bible, but since then has branched out into a wide range of subjects with a strong emphasis on books on the history of the State of Israel, political and military affairs, biographies of prominent individuals, encyclopedias, and children's books. The house has an imprint called Proza for quality original and translated fiction, philosophy, psychology, etc.

[Asher Weil (2nd ed.)]

BIBLIOGRAPHY: F. Kapp and J. Goldfriedrich, *Geschichte des deutschen Buchhandels*, 4 vols. (1886–1913); R. Hamburger, *Rudolf Mosse* (1928); A.M. Hyamson, in: *Anglo-Jewish Notabilities* (1949), 4–73; H. Lehmann-Haupt, *The Book in America* (1951²); Y. Pograbinsky, in: *Ha-Sefer ha-Ivri*, 9 (1951), 37–56; 10 (1952), 37–53; K. Schottenloher, *Buecher bewegten die Welt*, 2 vols. (1952); A. Levinson, *Toledot Yehudei Varshah* (1953), 306–10; S.Z. Sreberk, *Zikhronot* (1954); A. Litai, in: *He-Avar*, 3 (1956), 51–54; C. Roth, *Jews in the Renaissance* (1959), 165–85; Roth, Marranos, ch. 13, 269, 322ff.; idem, in: JJS, 4 (1953), 116–30; J. Toury, in: BLBI, 3 (1960), 58–69; Ch. Shmeruk, *Pirsumim Yehudiyyim bi-Verit ha-Mo'azot* (1960); S.H. Steinberg, *Five Hundred Years of Printing* (1961²); S. Kaznelson, *Juden im deutschen Kulturbereich* (1962³), 131–46; H.G. Adler, *Juden in Deutschland* (1962); G. Berman-Fischer, *Der Fischer Verlag* (1967); M. Faeber, in: *Jews of Czechoslovakia*, 1 (1968), 532–8; A.M. Habermann, *Ha-Sefer ha-Ivri be-Hitpatteḥuto* (1968), incl. bibl.

PUERTO RICO, island in the Caribbean 1,000 miles southeast of Miami. In 2005 there were 1,500–2,000 Jews in Puerto Rico among its population of 4,000,000. The Jewish experience in America begins with the actual "Discovery" in 1492. The first Jews to come to Puerto Rico were mainly Spanish and Portuguese. The existing Jewish community consists mainly of immigrants who had arrived in the United States during the post-World War II years and Cuban families who settled there in the 1960s and 1970s.

In the 19th century several records were located in the form of anecdotes in personal letters mentioning Jews of the 19th century. Sources dating back to 1898 confirm that there were a number of American Jews residing in Southern Puerto Rico at the time. A census conducted for that year includes the names of Jacob Benjamin and Samuel Levi as the Ponce residents.

Jews then arrived in Puerto Rico most often in conjunction with war. Among the soldiers who took part in the Spanish American War, there were several Jews.

Between 1899 and 1905, Rabbi Adolph Spiegel tried to organize the first Jewish congregation in the island. There was a slight increase in Jewish immigration when, as a result of the Spanish American War, Puerto Rico became a territory of the United States. During this period and before World War I, several Jewish men were involved in the drafting of the Island's first legal and fiscal codes. They aided in the creation of the court system and recruitment for it. Their contributions were crucial in the forming of the island's infrastructure.

World War I added to the presence of Jewish soldiers in the military bases. But at the end of the war the Jewish population once again decreased. Still, several government workers remained along with a pioneering group of businessmen who saw the island as a fertile ground for building their home and future.

Among the most prominent of the Island's Jews was Louis Sulzabacher, president of the Supreme Court of Puerto Rico and a strong supporter of United States citizenship for the Puerto Rican people.

The end of the 1920s and early 1930s brought a new surge of Jews from Central and Eastern Europe suddenly excluded from the United States by quotas. Other Jews continued to arrive on the Island; many represented American companies such as the Consolidated Tobacco Company. The 1930 generation consisted of men and women with a desire to make Puerto Rico their permanent home. They organized the first Jewish Community Center and the first synagogue in San Juan.

By 1940, there were only 150 Jews living in Puerto Rico. World War II brought a large number of soldiers to Puerto Rico and they included some Jews. About 400 Jewish soldiers were living in military bases in Puerto Rico at the time. The Jewish Welfare Board coordinated the rental of various meeting halls around San Juan in order to provide the soldiers with the opportunity to celebrate Sabbath services. They held the first Passover Seder in 1942.

The beginning of the 1950s was marked by the creation of Operation Bootstrap, an initiative by the local government based on the concept of "industrialization by invitation." The program indirectly encouraged the arrival of more Jews to the island. They were attracted by a series of incentives offered to American manufacturing companies. Jews were among the architects of the economic development of the Island and also prominent in the legal and medical professions. Cecil Snider was named by President Roosevelt associate justice of the Supreme Court of Puerto Rico. Eleven years later he was named by Governor Luis Muñoz Marín chief justice of the Supreme Court.

The emergence of the Cuban communist regime in 1958, headed by Fidel Castro, produced the third migration of Jews to Puerto Rico. Thousands of families abandoned the island of Cuba. Many of them wanted to move to the United States eventually, while others sought a social and cultural environment similar to that of Cuba.

Upon their arrival in Puerto Rico, most of these Jewish families joined the Jewish Community Center. At the time, the center embraced 200 families and the Hebrew school had 125 registered students. The inclusion of Cuban families gave the Jewish Community Center a new Hispanic outlook. These Orthodox families exerted a significant influence in the development of the Shaare Zedek Synagogue and the Hebrew school. They came to stay in Puerto Rico.

In the 1970s and the 1980s a new Jewish migration arrived in Puerto Rico. Close to 200 Israeli farmers came to the Island as part of an agricultural program developed by companies such as April-Agro, Isprac, HDC, and Fruits International. This project utilized 2,500 acres in the Santa Isabel region. A new revolutionary irrigation system was introduced by a group of agronomists from Israel. In the 1960s a new group of Argentinean Jews began to arrive in Puerto Rico.

Synagogues in San Juan

The first attempt to establish a Jewish congregation in Puerto Rico proved unsuccessful. The second effort in 1935 gathered some 26 families. They would meet in private homes and commercial spaces, such as the offices above La Esquina Famosa store in Santurce, the San Juan Casino, and El San Juan Hotel.

In 2005 there were three synagogues in San Juan, representing the three ideologies within Judaism: Orthodox, Conservative, and Reform Judaism.

In 1953 the Jewish Community acquired a private residence and transformed it into a synagogue and site of the first congregation. Nowadays, the Shaare Zedek Temple is the largest synagogue in the Island. The first religious school was started in 1952.

The Shaare Zedek Temple, founded in 1953, became the first Conservative synagogue. Its name means "Gates of Justice," and was taken from a synagogue that was destroyed in Leipzig, Germany. It is headed by Rabbi Gabriel Isaías Frydman, originally from Argentina. The Jewish Community Center also operates as a Hebrew and Judaic studies school as well as a pre-school center and meeting facility. It houses the Morris Rothenberg Library, the most complete Judaic library in the Caribbean. The center currently has 255 members.

The second Jewish organization established in Puerto Rico is Temple Beth Shalom, the Reform Jewish Congregation of Puerto Rico, which was established in 1967. The synagogue has among its Torahs one that had been rescued from the Holocaust. For most of its congregational life, Temple Beth Shalom has relied on retired rabbis from the mainland who have served for all or part of the period from Rosh Hashanah to Shavuot. Currently a series of distinguished rabbis serve for six weeks at a time. The congregation owns a beautiful building on the corner of Loiza and San Jorge Streets in the Condado section of San Juan. Many of its members are "snowbirds," who spend their winters in Puerto Rico. There are, however, enough all year around attendees to hold services every Friday evening and Saturday morning, maintain a flourishing Religious School and provide a very active Adult Education Program. Tourists and other visitors are always made to feel very welcome.

The third synagogue, Sharei Torah, was founded in 1999; it is one of the Chabad Lubavitch synagogues and educational centers around the world. During its early period, the group would rent meeting rooms in the Marriott Resort to conduct prayers and activities. The synagogue was officially inaugurated on February 2, 2000. A few years later a larger property was purchased in Isla Verde, making it more accessible for Jewish tourists and communities from nearby Caribbean islands.

The Chabad Lubavitch Center and its synagogue Sharei Torah operate under the direction of Rabbi Mendel Zarchi and his wife Rachel Zarchi. Chabad Lubavitch of Puerto Rico features a school to educate children and adults. It also offers religious services and coordinates community activities such as visits to hospitals, activities related to Jewish festivities, assistance in the immersion rituals of *mikveh*, lectures and provision of kosher food products. The Center is to expand to accommodate the first and only *mikveh* in Puerto Rico.

[Museum of San Juan Staff (2nd ed.)]

PUGLIESE, EMANUELE (1874–1967), Italian soldier. His military career began when he took part in the Italo-Turkish war (1911–12). With the entry of Italy into World War I, Pugliese rose rapidly. In 1917, he took part in the battle of Vittorio Veneto. At the end of the war, he became a divisional commander and as such he fought in the war in Albania in 1920. In 1931, he was appointed military commander of Sardinia and in 1934 reached the rank of lieutenant general and corps commander. Pugliese received the highest military decoration of his own country and many foreign honors.

ADD. BIBLIOGRAPHY: A. Rovighi, *I Militari di Origine Ebraica nel Primo Secolo di Vita dello Stato Italiano* (1999), 87.

[Mordechai Kamrat]

PUGLIESE, UMBERTO (1880–1961), Italian-Jewish patriot and scientist, a genius in the field of naval architecture. Pugliese was born in Alessandria, Piedmont, and joined the Italian navy in 1898, later being transferred to the naval corps of engineering. After various positions both in the royal arsenal and aboard ship he served for ten years on the committee for naval projects, and was appointed general inspector of the Naval Corps of Engineers. Pugliese planned and was responsible for the construction of most of the great Italian battleships ("Garibaldi," "Vittorio Veneto," "Roma," "Impero," "Littorio," and others). His most remarkable invention was a device known as the Pugliese Water-Line capable of enabling bombed battleships to float and, in many instances, to resume service.

On December 31, 1938, while his battleships were still in the dockyards, Pugliese was dismissed from the navy because of his Jewish origin, in compliance with the new racial laws. He nevertheless remained in Italy and, when the British bombed the Italian Navy out of service in November 1940, the chief of staff, Admiral Cavagnari, did not hesitate to appeal to Pugliese for his assistance in refloating the battleships. Pugliese fulfilled the mission and, when asked what reward he demanded for his services in saving the Italian Navy, he requested the honor to don his naval uniform again. His request was partially granted in 1942.

In 1943, he was arrested and questioned by the Germans, who had hoped to use his valuable knowledge in Germany, but Pugliese was adamant in his refusal, declaring that he was, and would stay faithful to, the oath he had given to the monarchy. When the Germans occupied Rome in 1943, they sent the Jewish Admiral Augusto *Capon to Auschwitz, where he was gassed despite the fact that he had a personal letter from Mussolini, but Pugliese was spared. When he died in Sorrento in 1961, Pugliese was buried with full military honors.

[E.L. Touriel]

PUKHACHEWSKY, MICHAEL ZALMAN (1863–1947), pioneer of Jewish agriculture in Ereẓ Israel. He was born in Brest-Litovsk in 1885. Pukhachewsky was one of six young men chosen by Ḥovevei Zion in Russia (at Baron Edmond de *Rothschild's suggestion) to specialize in agriculture in the Baron's settlements and become agricultural instructors for settlers. He established a farm in Rishon le-Zion and worked for many years as an agricultural instructor, specializing in viticulture in the Jordan Valley, the Jezreel Valley, and other areas. He published articles in Palestinian agricultural journals and wrote his memoirs on the early days of Jewish settlement (*Bustanai*, 1 (1929/30), nos. 6–44). His wife, NEḤAMAH (1869–1934), was a writer active in the public life of Palestine. She joined Ḥovevei Zion at the age of 17 and went to Ereẓ Israel together with her husband. She wrote essays under the pen name Nefesh.

BIBLIOGRAPHY: Tidhar, 3 (1958), 1281–82.

[Yehuda Slutsky]

PUKHOVITSER, JUDAH LEIB (c. 1630–after 1700), rabbi, scholar, and preacher in Lithuania, Poland, and Germany. His father had settled in Pinsk by the end of the 1620s. Judah Leib studied under Naphtali b. Isaac Katz, the rabbi of Pinsk (1639–44). His surname appears to have been derived from the townlet of Pukhovichi, near Minsk. In 1659, when he was rabbi of *Bykhov, he was an eyewitness to the conquest of the town by Muscovite soldiers, who massacred the Jews and killed one of his daughters. After 1667 Pukhovitser returned to his native Pinsk where he acted as rabbi and preacher. From time to time he left Pinsk, preaching in the communities of Pinsk province and the large communities of Lithuania and Poland. In 1681–82 he stayed in Frankfurt on the Oder, where he published his homiletic works in two parts, *Keneh Ḥokhmah* and *Derekh Ḥokhmah*. His work *Divrei Ḥakhamim* (in two parts) on Shulḥan Arukh was published in Hamburg (1692–93), and *Kevod Ḥakhamim* in Venice (1699–1700). Leaving Venice, he went to Jerusalem, where he died after 1700.

Pukhovitser lived during a period which saw tremendous changes in the lives of the Jews of Poland and Lithuania as a result of the massacres of 1648–49 and 1666–67. One of the fundamentals of his homiletic teaching is that the study of the Torah for its own sake must lead to good deeds and repentance. In his sermons, he urged that *battei midrash* in which Torah would be permanently studied should be maintained and every Jew obliged to fix regular times for Torah study; he thus gave a great impetus to the formation of study groups in Lithuania. Criticizing the prevailing methods of study in the *ḥadarim* and yeshivot, he called for a gradual progression from easier subjects to more difficult ones. He also attacked the situation which prevented the poor from studying in the yeshivot and demanded that several well-established members of the community provide for the upkeep of a Torah student. At the same time he condemned the method of study based on *pilpul*. Pukhovitser's works are imbued with kabbalistic motifs, containing many Lurianic elements. In a letter to the scholars of Jerusalem (Hamburg, 1692), he developed the idea that the future redemption of Israel would be effected by the community of Jerusalem when it had reached the degree of *kenishta ḥada* ("a unified community").

BIBLIOGRAPHY: E. Pines, *Tanna de-Vei Eliyahu* (1753); Ḥ.N. Dembitzer, *Kelilat Yofi*, 1 (1888), 49–50; 2 (1893), 122; Frumkin-Rivlin, 2 (1928), 88ff.; A. Ya'ari, *Meḥkerei Sefer* (1958), 102–3; idem, *Ta'alumat Sefer* (1954), 17–21; G. Scholem, in: *Beḥinot*, 8 (1955), 79–95; A. Shochat, in: *Ha-Ḥinnukh*, 28 (1956), 410–2; M. Benayahu, in: *Sefunot*, 3–4 (1960), 134; I. Tishby, *Netivei Emuna u-Minut* (1964), 110ff.

[Mordekhai Nadav]

PULAWY (Pol. **Pulawy**; Yid. **Pilev**; Rus. **Novaya Aleksandriya**), a town in Lublin province, Poland. The first Jews to settle in Pulawy came from the neighboring townlets (mostly Wlostowice) at the beginning of the 19th century when the area developed rapidly upon the initiative of its owner, Prince A.K. *Czartoryski. There was an organized Jewish community in Pulawy from 1820. In 1897 it numbered 3,883 (about 73% of the population). The principal Jewish occupations were shoemaking, gardening, furniture-making and shopkeeping. From the middle of the 19th century, the influence of Ḥasidism became widespread among the Jews of Pulawy; they were attached to the ḥasidic courts of *Lublin and *Kotsk and later to those of Gut (*Gora Kolwariya) and *Sokolow. From 1875 to 1884 the rabbinical seat of Pulawy was held by Elijah Lerman, the author of *Devar Eliyahu* (1884). In 1888, Ḥayyim Israel Morgenstern, the grandson of Menahem Mendel of *Kotsk, founded a ḥasidic court in Pulawy. At the close of the 19th century, enterprises established by Jewish initiative included iron industries, machinery and shoe manufacture. Jewish workers found employment in them and organized themselves into trade unions. From 1875 Jewish students studied at the Higher Institute of Agriculture of Pulawy; many of the students participated in revolutionary social democratic activities. From 1907 a Jewish cooperative bank functioned in Pulawy with much success. In 1910 there were 6,111 Jews (61% of the population). During World War I, the Jewish population of the town decreased because of persecutions and a fire. From 1917 branches of all parties then active on the Jewish scene were organized in Pulawy. At first, the *Bund and *Agudat Israel wielded the greatest influence, but *Po'alei Zion circles, other Zionist parties, and communists soon grew strong. Jewish craftsmen and merchants established unions in 1920. In 1921 there were 3,221 Jews (45% of the population) living in the town. Between the two world wars there was a private Hebrew secondary school, as well as *Tarbut, Yavneh and Beth Jacob schools, and a Jewish library.

[Arthur Cygielman]

Holocaust Period

At the outbreak of World War II there were 3,600 Jews in the town. At the end of October 1939, an open ghetto was established. On Dec. 29, 1939, the entire Jewish population was expelled to the nearby town of Opole Lubelskie, where all were in turn deported to the *Sobibor death camp in May 1942 and exterminated. No Jewish community was reconstituted in Pulawy.

[Stefan Krakowski]

BIBLIOGRAPHY: B. Wasiutyński, *Ludnaść żydowska w Polsce…* (1930), 34, 63, 72, 77, 78; *Słownik geograficzny Królestwa Polskiego*, 9 (1888), 287–9; 13 (1895), 720; N. Gasiorowska (ed.), *Zródła do dziejów klasy robotniczej na ziemiach polskich* (1962), nos. 354, 376, 377; J. Bernstein, *Yisker Bukh Pulav* (1964); R. Bender, in: BŻIH, 34 (1960), 45–46.

PULCELINA OF BLOIS, 12th-century female moneylender to the court of Blois. Pulcelina (also Pucellina) was implicated in the first ritual murder accusation in France and was burnt at the stake along with her two daughters and 30 other co-religionists in 1171. These events are documented in a variety of Hebrew sources, including five surviving letters, a chronicle, two memorial lists, and eight poems; this literary productivity indicates the degree to which this tragedy shocked the Jews of Ashkenaz. In his account in *Sefer Zekhirah* ("Book of Remembrance"), the chronicler and liturgical poet Ephraim ben Jacob of Bonn (1132–c. 1200) used the verb *ohav* ("love") to describe the affection of Count Thibaut of Blois (1152–1191) for Pulcelina; most historians have assumed that the two were involved in a romantic relationship. (See the translation in J. Marcus, ed., *The Jew in the Medieval World* (rep. 1990), pp. 127–30.) This theory has been challenged by S. Einbinder (1998), who suggests that *ohav* in this instance implies that the count "favored" Pulcelina as a lender and perhaps as a trusted financial advisor. Einbinder believes that Thibaut's wife, Countess Alix, who is described as hating Pulcelina and swaying the count against her, was motivated not by sexual jealousy but because she herself, and others close to her, owed significant sums to Pulcelina and resented her influence over the Count. The surviving documents make it clear that Pulcelina behaved arrogantly and was widely disliked by members of Thibaut's court. That a ritual murder accusation could be brought against Pulcelina, and Blois Jewry, when there was no corpse and no missing child, also indicates the level of animosity her position of power had generated. Ephraim wrote that once she was arrested she was prevented from speaking with the count for fear that she might convince him to change his mind and release the Jews. Although Jews from other communities attempted to ransom the prisoners, they were unable to offer sufficient funds to prevent their martyrdom. While in many ways this catastrophe represents a cautionary instance of the fall of a court Jew, with tragic consequences for the larger community, Pulcelina's gender and the possibility that she had an intimate relationship with Count Thibaut give the story added dimensions as an extreme example of the independence and entrepreneurship of Jewish women in Askenaz in the 11th and 12th centuries. The tragedy was the subject of a Hebrew drama by S.D. *Goitein, *Pulzelinah* (1927).

BIBLIOGRAPHY: R. Chazan, "The Blois Incident of 1171…," in: *Proceedings of the American Academy of Jewish Research* (1968), 13–31; idem, "Ephraim ben Jacob's Compilations of Twelfth Century Persecutions," in: JQR, 84:4 (1994), 397–416; S. Einbinder, *Beautiful Death* (2002), 45–69; idem, "Pucellina of Blois: Romantic Myths and Narrative Conventions," in: *Jewish History*, 12:1 (1998), 29–46.

[Judith R. Baskin (2nd ed.)]

PULITZER, JOSEPH (1847–1911), American editor and publisher who bought declining newspapers and restored them to national influence. Born in Mako, Hungary, son of a Jewish father and a Roman Catholic mother, Pulitzer emigrated to the U.S. at the age of 17 to serve in the Union Army during the Civil War. Discharged from the cavalry in 1865, he went to St. Louis and in 1868 became a reporter for the German-language daily *Westliche Post*. Three years later he bought an interest in the paper, became managing editor, and sold back his shares at a vast profit. In 1878 Pulitzer took his first big step toward creating a newspaper empire when he bought the St. Louis *Dispatch* at an auction for $2,500 and merged it with the St. Louis *Post* into the *Post-Dispatch*. By 1881 it was yielding profits of $85,000 a year. He left for New York in 1883 and bought *The World* from Jay Gould, the financier, for $346,000.

Three years later, revived by Pulitzer's innovations in mass appeal journalism, *The World* was earning more than $500,000 a year. He established a sister paper in New York, the *Evening World*, in 1887. All three newspapers succeeded on a formula of vigorous promotion, sensationalism, sympathy with labor and the underdog, and innovations in illustration and typography. In 1869 Pulitzer served in the lower house of the Missouri legislature, and in 1885 was elected to the U.S. House of Representatives from New York, but served only briefly. A man of intellect and energy, he worked himself into a condition which compelled him to live his last years as a totally blind invalid. However, he still directed his newspapers. He endowed the Pulitzer School of Journalism at Columbia University and the famous Pulitzer Prizes for journalism. His son, JOSEPH JR. (1885–1955), continued the policies of his father with success as the publisher of the St. Louis *Post-Dispatch*, but under his other two sons, Ralph (1879–1959) and Herbert (1897–1957) the two New York papers declined and were sold in 1931 to Scripps-Howard.

BIBLIOGRAPHY: W.A. Swanberg; *Pulitzer* (1967); K. Stewart, *Makers of Modern Journalism* (1952), 86–102.

[Irving Rosenthal]

PULKAU, small town in Lower Austria; it became notorious in the 14th century as the scene of a *Host desecration libel, which was followed by a wave of massacres of the Jews. A bleeding Host was allegedly found concealed in front of a Jew's house on Easter Sunday, April 12, 1338, the day following the last day of Passover. Rumors spread that the Host had performed miracles; crowds came to venerate it, and on April 23 they burned the Jews at the stake and plundered their property. The disorders spread, and Jews were massacred in 27 localities as far away as *Jindrichuv Hradec (Neuhaus) in Bohemia, *Trebic (Trebitsch) in Moravia, and St. Poelten. Duke *Albert II expressed his doubts about the accusation and asked Pope Benedict XII for an investigation. The pope ordered the bishop of Passau to conduct an inquiry, but its results are unknown. A church called Zum Heiligen Blut ("The Holy Blood") was built on the site; decorated with representations of the alleged occurrence, it attracted many worshipers throughout the years. The pictures were later painted over. The site where the Jews were burned is well marked. At the time of the massacres, Jewish books were confiscated; possibly some of the parchment manuscripts confiscated in 1338 were utilized for binding city records in 1622 and 1623.

BIBLIOGRAPHY: J.E. Scherer, *Rechtsverhaeltnisse der Juden*, 2 (1968), 363–9; *Germania Judaica*, 2 (1968), 665–7.

[Meir Lamed]

PULTUSK (Pol. **Pułtusk**), town in Warzawa province, Poland. Although there were some Jews in Pultusk in 1486 a settlement as such did not develop because of the privilege *de non tolerandis Judaeis* granted to the Masovia region during the 16th century by the Polish king, Sigismund II Augustus. Even temporary residence for Jews was authorized only by special permit. The prohibition was temporarily abrogated after the Grand Duchy of Warsaw was created in 1807 but renewed with the establishment of the Polish kingdom in 1815, according to the decision of the Congress of Vienna. The decree was finally abolished in 1866. During the 19th century the Jewish population increased; there were 118 Jews in 1810 (5.1% of the total population), 4,769 in 1856, and 6,950 (45.7%) in 1909. During World War I many Jews fled to Warsaw, so that by 1921 the number had decreased to 5,919 (about 46% of the total population). In independent Poland the Jewish population rose again and by 1931 there were 8,300 Jews (49.2% of the total) in the town.

Despite its proximity to Warsaw, Pultusk did not develop as a center of commerce and crafts mainly because it was removed from railway junctions. Nevertheless, a considerable number of Jews were craftsmen, particularly tailors. Because of the surrounding forests, there were a number of sawmills so that carpentry as well as trade in wood and furniture developed. However, economic difficulties led many Jews to emigrate. In 1894 many wealthy Jews left when a cholera epidemic broke out. During the 19th century the community supported various activities, the most important of which was social relief to the needy. Between the two world wars a Jewish educational program was developed. It attracted most of the community's elementary and secondary school students. Jews were represented in the municipal administration; about one-half of the delegates elected in 1922 and 1927 were Jews. The leadership of the Jewish community itself was elected democratically for the first time in 1927. The oldest synagogue was erected between 1805 and 1815. It burnt down and was rebuilt in 1854. Of the rabbis of Pultusk, the most renowned were R. Joshua *Trunk (from 1853 to 1861), R. Ḥanokh Zundel b. Jacob Grodzinski, who belonged to the **Mitnaggedim* (appointed in 1878), and R. Ḥayyim Meshullam ha-Kohen (1909–1929), known for his Zionist tendencies. The last rabbi of Pultusk was R. Israel Ber Lowenthal, who immigrated to Palestine at the outbreak of World War II and died there in 1942.

[Shimshon Leib Kirshenboim]

Holocaust Period

The city was captured by the Germans on Sept. 7, 1939, and by September 11, 14 Jews had been shot. During the holiday of Sukkot 1939, the Germans deported all the Jews to the other side of the Narev River, in the Soviet zone of occupation. All Jewish property was looted, and on the way to the border Jews were maltreated and many were killed. Many of the deportees found temporary shelter in Bialystok and surrounding cities under the Soviet administration, where they were subjected to administrative restrictions and met with difficulties in finding housing and work. In the summer of 1940 many were deported to the Soviet interior.

[Aharon Weiss]

PULVERMACHER, OSCAR (1883–1958), British editor. Pulvermacher's father came to England from East Prussia. Oscar Pulvermacher was born in London and started work with the

London *Daily Mail* at the age of 17, rising to be editor in 1929. Pulvermacher apparently remained editor for only one year, although he continued to be employed by the *Daily Mail* in a period when the paper achieved what was then the highest circulation in the world. In 1933 he disagreed with the sympathetic policy toward Hitler of the paper's owner Lord Rothermere and resigned. A month later he was engaged by the *Daily Telegraph* to reorganize its news services and during World War II was its northern editor in Manchester.

[William D. Rubinstein (2nd ed.)]

PULZER, PETER G.J. (1929–), British political historian. Born in Vienna, Pulzer was a lecturer in politics at Oxford University from 1952 and, in 1985–91 was Gladstone Professor of Government and Administration at Oxford and a fellow of All Souls College. Pulzer's best-known work, *The Rise of Political Antisemitism in Germany and Austria* (1964), was a pioneering study of the emergence of modern political hostility towards the Jews in German-speaking Central Europe. He wrote widely on German and German-Jewish history, in such works as *Jews and the German State* (1992) and *Emancipation and Its Discontents: The German-Jewish Dilemma* (1997). A *Festschrift* in his honor, edited by Henning Tewest and Jonathan Wright, *Liberalism, Anti-Semitism, and Democracy* (2001), includes a biography.

[William D. Rubinstein (2nd ed.)]

PUMBEDITA, town in Babylonia. Pumbedita was situated on the bank of the River Euphrates on the site of the Shunya-Shumvata (Git. 60b), the most northerly of the canals joining the Euphrates and the Tigris. A canal called Nehar Papa also passed through Pumbedita itself (Yoma 77b), and situated near it was the town of Peruz-Shavur. The area had an exceptionally abundant water supply and a pleasant climate, and commerce flourished there, the caravan route to Syria passing nearby. Crops included cereals and fruits, dates being especially plentiful (Pes. 88a), and the flax grown there (Git. 27a; BM 18b) was the basis of the local textile industry. The Jewish settlement in Pumbedita apparently already existed during the period of the Second Temple and was included by Sherira Gaon among those settlements which were centers of the study of Torah during that period (*Iggeret Rav Sherira Ga'on*, ed. by B.M. Levin (1921), 40). However, its importance as a communal and religious center dates only from the middle of the third century C.E. In 259, after Nehardea was destroyed by Papa b. Naser (see *Odenathus and Zenobia), commander in chief of Palmyra, Judah b. Ezekiel founded an academy there. This academy and its *bet din* were the central religious authority for Babylonian Jewry until the middle of the fourth century C.E. During that period some of the best known **amoraim* of Babylonian Jewry headed the academy – Rabbah b. Nahamani, Joseph, Abbaye, and Rava. During the time of Rava the academy was transferred to Maḥoza, where Rava resided. During this period, when the academy began to flourish, exceptionally strong ties were established between it and its sister academy at Tiberias through the medium of the **neḥutei*. The aforementioned heads of the academy, with the exception of Joseph, were distinguished for their teaching methods which were marked by acumen and even casuistry (Hor. 14a; BM 38b). As a result of this intellectual acumen, which in their opinion was an efficient method to discuss *halakhah* and arrive at correct decisions, they came to be called "uprooters of mountains," and it was said of them that "they could draw an elephant through the eye of a needle" (BM 38b).

From the death of Rava in 352 until the first half of the geonic period, the Pumbedita academy did not occupy a central place in the scholastic and halakhic world. It was subordinate to *Sura, which was granted more privileges than Pumbedita. Life in a large, bustling, commercial city full of connections with foreign merchants had a deleterious influence on the character of the Jews of Pumbedita. The Babylonian Talmud has preserved many adverse evaluations of their moral character. Mention is made of the cheating by workers (BB 46a; Ḥul. 127a), and Rava refers to the thieves who would come to the city, as well as the resident thieves (Av. Zar. 70a). In fact, the dishonest practices of the people of Pumbedita became a byword among the Jews of Babylon (Ket. 82a), and it is therefore not surprising that scholars were not popular among them, since the scholars rebuked them for their deeds (Shab. 153a). One scholar advised his son not to dwell in affluent Pumbedita (Hor. 12a).

[Moshe Beer]

During the Post-Talmudic Period

Sherira Gaon related that as the result of religious persecution under Persian rule, the Pumbedita academy was transferred to Peruz-Shavur, in the vicinity of Nehardea. It remained there during the period of the **savoraim*; when the Arabs conquered Babylonia (c. 634 C.E.), it returned to Pumbedita. R. Isaac, the *Gaon* of Pumbedita, who lived in Peruz-Shavur, went out to welcome the conquering caliph ʿAli ibn Abi Ṭāleb. During the Arab period Pumbedita was known as Anbar, and the academy was called *yeshivah shel ha-golah* ("academy of the Diaspora"). Until the beginning of the ninth century Pumbedita was overshadowed by *Sura. During the 830s the *ḥakhamim* of the Pumbedita academy backed the candidacy of David b. Judah as exilarch against Daniel, who had the support of the *ḥakhamim* of Sura. The former's election as exilarch also resulted in the consolidation of the Pumbedita academy. From his time the Jews gathered in Pumbedita on the occasion of the *Shabbeta de-Rigla* (*Iggeret R. Sherira*, p. 93). In an extant letter of his son, the exilarch Judah, he seeks contributions for the academy, which is described "as having many **allufim*, *ḥakhamim*, elders, Mishnah scholars, Talmud scholars, and *tannaim*: there are seven *allufim* …" (Abramson, Merkazim, 18).

An important head of the academy in this period was *Paltoi b. Abbaye (842–52), the first to be styled *Gaon* of Pumbedita, who maintained contacts with the communities of Spain and North Africa. From Spain, they turned to him "to write the Talmud and its interpretation down for them, and upon his order it was written for them" (Sherira Gaon, *Iggeret...*, ed. by M.N. Adler (1907), xxiii (2nd Roman pagination)). During his son *Ẓemaḥ's (872) lifetime these ties were strengthened and the status of the academy surpassed that of Sura. In the *Kaddish* the name of Ẓemaḥ b. Paltoi was mentioned before that of the *gaon* of Sura, *Ẓemaḥ b. Ḥayyim.

During the days of the *Gaon* Hai b. *David (890–98), who had previously been a *dayyan*, the academy was transferred to Baghdad. In the first half of the tenth century contributions to the academy decreased – the centers of the Diaspora established their own Torah institutions and their attachment to the Babylonian center was thus weakened. The contest for the gaonate between R. Aaron Sargado and R. *Nehemiah b. Kohen Ẓedek from the 940s to 960s and the dispute between the latter and R. Sherira were also responsible for the decline in the status of the academy. The situation changed under Sherira *Gaon, a powerful personality, who renewed the contacts with the communities of North Africa and called upon them to support his academy. The period of office of Sherira Gaon (968–98) and that of his son *Hai Gaon (998–1038) was the period of Pumbedita's efflorescence. The greatest number of extant responsa to the Diaspora, especially to the communities of North Africa (e.g., Kairouan, Fez, etc.), was written by these two *geonim*. Students came from abroad to study with R. Hai and later went on to hold important positions. These included *Shemariah b. Elhanan of Egypt, who was "the first in the 'great' [first] row of the three rows of the academy"; Maẓliaḥ b. Albaẓak of Sicily; the *gaon* Solomon b. Judah's son from Palestine; and students from Byzantium and Italy. After R. Hai's death the exilarch *Hezekiah b. David headed the Pumbedita academy for 20 years (until 1058).

According to sources found in the Cairo *Genizah*, the *divan* of Eleazar b. Jacob ha-Bavli, and Arab sources, it appears that the Baghdad academy continued in existence until the 13th century. The names of nine *geonim* who lived during the 12th and 13th centuries and considered themselves the heirs of the Pumbedita academy are known. The last *Gaon* was Samuel b. Daniel ha-Kohen (1288). According to Benjamin of Tudela, who visited Babylonia in the 1170s, there were about 3,000 Jews in Pumbedita. Even though this number seems to be exaggerated, it appears that an important community still existed there.

[Moshe Beer and Eliezer Bashan (Sternberg)]

BIBLIOGRAPHY: TALMUD: Neubauer, Géogr, 349; A. Berliner, *Beitraege zur Geographie und Ethnographie Babyloniens im Talmud und Midrasch*, 57f., in: *Jahres-Bericht des Rabbiner-Seminars zu Berlin pro 5643* (1882/83); J. Obermeyer, *Die Landschaft Babylonien* (1929), 226–42; M.D. Yudilewitz, *Yeshivat Pumbedita bi-Ymei ha-Amora'im* (1932); idem, *Ha-Ir Pumbedita bi-Ymei ha-Amora'im* (1939). POST-TALMUDIC: S. Schechter, *Saadyana* (1903), 117–21; L. Ginzberg, *Geonica*, 1 (1909), 14–22, 62–66; G. Margoliouth, in: JQR, 14 (1901/02), 307–11; A. Cowley, *ibid.*, 18 (1905/06), 399–403; 19 (1906/07), 104–6; J. Mann, *ibid.*, 8 (1917/18), 341–62; 9 (1918/19), 139–47; 11 (1920/21), 419–21; idem, in: *Tarbiz*, 5 (1933/34), 148–79; Mann, Texts, 1 (1931), 75–145, 179–201; B.M. Lewin (ed.), *Iggeret R. Sherira Ga'on* (1921), 99–100, 109–14, 119–22; Dinur, Golah, 1 pt. 2 (1961²), 106–9; Abramson, Merkazim, index; S. Assaf, in: *Ha-Shilo'ah*, 39 (1921), 218–20; Assaf, Ge'onim, 42–70, 261–78; B.M. Lewin (ed.), *Ginzei Kedem*, 2 (1923), 46–48; H.Z. Taubes, in: *Sefer Zikkaron li-Shelomo S. Mayer; Kovez le-Toledot Yehudei Italyah* (1956), 126–41; Benjamin of Tudela, *Masa'ot...*, ed. by M.N. Adler (1907), 34, 46 (Heb. pagination); Neusner, Babylonia, passim.

PUNISHMENT. While there is no modern theory of punishment that cannot, in some form or other, be traced back to biblical concepts, the original and foremost purpose of punishment in biblical law was the appeasement of God. God abhors the criminal ways of other nations (Lev. 20:23) whose practices the Israelites must not follow (*ibid.*) and from whose abominations they must not learn (Deut. 20:18); by violating His laws, His name is profaned (Lev. 22:31–32); and not only are criminals abhorrent to God (Deut. 18:12; 22:5; 25:16; 27:15), as well as crimes (Lev. 18:27–29), but God's own holiness obliges man to be holy like Him (Lev. 19:2). By taking "impassioned action" (Num. 25:13) to punish violators of His laws, expiation is made to God and God's "fierce anger" (Deut. 13:18) turned away from Israel (Num. 25:4). Closely related to the appeasement of God is another expiatory purpose of punishment: a crime, and more particularly the shedding of blood, pollutes the land – "and no expiation can be made for the land for the blood that is shed therein but by the blood of him that shed it" (Num. 35: 33). Excrement must be covered because the land being holy demands that "thy camp be holy,... "(Deut. 23:15), so that God would "see no unseemly thing" occurring there (*ibid.*).

Still another aspect is reflected in the talionic punishment of death for *homicide, as originally formulated: "Whoso sheddeth man's blood, by man shall his blood be shed; for in the image of God made He man" (Gen. 9:6). Man being created in the image of God, it is an affront to God to kill him and killing the killer is the only acceptable expiation to God. Similarly, purging Israel of the blood of the innocent (Deut. 19:13) by killing the killer appears to be necessary in order to avoid blood guilt attaching to the land and to the people forever (cf. Deut. 21:9; 19:10); and it is for this reason that a murderer must be taken even from God's very altar to be put to death (Ex. 21:14).

All talionic punishment as such reflects its underlying purpose, namely the apparent restitution of the *status quo ante* by inflicting on the offender the injury inflicted by him (Lev. 24:20) and by doing to him what he had done to another (Lev. 24:19). This sort of sanction (see *Talion), where the character and measure of punishment is precisely commensurate with those of the crime, is intended to represent exact justice. It was, indeed, by proving that this kind of "exact justice" necessarily involved unavoidable injustice, that some talmudical jurists justified the abolition of talionic punishment except for murder (BK 84a). And while they did not abolish it for murder, whether by reason of the many express biblical injunctions that murderers must be killed (especially Num. 35:31), or in order to retain the deterrent effect of the death penalty, many of them held that judges must do everything in their power to avoid passing death sentences (cf. Mak. 1:10), e.g., by rigorously cross-examining the witnesses long enough to have them contradict themselves or each other in some particular (Mak. 7a) and thus render their evidence unreliable (see *Evidence, *Witness). The warning was already sounded then that any reticence in imposing capital punishment would result in an increase of crime and bloodshed (Mak. 1:10). Maimonides comments on the talmudical discussion, that while it was true that the courts must always satisfy themselves that the incriminating evidence was credible and admissible, once they were so satisfied, they ought to order the execution even of a thousand men, day after day, if that is what the law (the Torah) prescribes (his commentary to the Mishnah, Mak. 1:10).

The most common purpose of punishment, as found in the Bible, is "to put away the evil from the midst of thee" (Deut. 17:7, 12; 19:19; 21:21; 22:24; 24:7). While such "putting away" is applied in the Bible to capital punishment only (which indeed constitutes the only effective total elimination), the principle underlying the elimination of evil, as distinguished from that of the evildoer (cf. Ps. 104:35 and Ber. 10a), provides a theory of punishment of universal validity and applicable to all criminal sanctions. It means that the act of punishment is not so much directed against the individual offender – who is, however, unavoidably its victim – as it is a demonstration of resentment and disapproval of that particular mode of conduct. By branding that conduct as worthy of, and necessitating, judicial punishment, it is outlawed and ostracized. Similarly, punishment is inflicted on the offender not so much for his own sake as for the deterrence of others: that all people should hear and be afraid (Deut. 17:13 – rebellious elder; 19:20 – perjury; 21:21 – rebellious son). From the point of view of criminal law enforcement policies, the deterrent aspect of punishment in Jewish law is already the most important of all: people who hear and see a man heavily punished for his offense are supposed to be deterred from committing the offense and incurring the risk of such punishment (they "will do no more presumptuously" – Deut. 19:20). Hence the particular injunction to have the offender impaled on a stake after having been put to death (Deut. 21:22), so as to publicize the execution as widely and impressively as possible; but note that the corpse must be taken off the gibbet before nightfall, "for he that is hanged is a reproach to God" and defiles the land (Deut. 21:23) – and no concession made to policies of law enforcement can derogate from the affront to God involved in killing and impaling a human being.

It is not only the principle known in modern criminology as "general prevention," the deterrence of the general public, but also that of "special prevention," the prevention of the individual offender from committing further crimes, that is reflected in Jewish law. It has been said that the imposition of capital punishment on such offenders as the rebellious son (Deut. 21:18–21), the rebellious elder (Deut. 17:12), the abductor (Ex. 21:16), and the burglar (Ex. 22:1) is justified on the ground that these are all potential murderers (cf. Maim., Guide 3:41); and rather than let them take innocent human lives, they should themselves be eliminated. That the deterrent effect of punishment on the offender himself was a consideration which weighed heavily with the talmudical jurists is illustrated also by the rule that where punishment had proved to have had no beneficial deterrent effect on the offender and he has committed the same or some similar offenses over and over again, he would be liable to be imprisoned and "fed on barley until his belly bursts" (Sanh. 9:5).

The talmudical law reformers also achieved the substitution for the ever-threatening divine punishment by the judicial punishment of *flogging, making it clear that whoever underwent judicial punishment would not be visited with any further *divine punishment (Mak. 3:15). They went so far as to lay down that even though God had Himself expressly proclaimed that a criminal would not be "guiltless" and escape divine wrath (Ex. 20:7; Deut. 5:11), the judicial authorities in imposing the flogging were authorized by the Torah itself to clear him: if God would never clear him, a court of justice could (Shevu. 21a). The measure of punishment must always conform to the gravity of the offense on the one hand, and the blameworthiness of the individual offender on the other: "according to the measure of his wickedness" (Deut. 25:2). Even here the talmudical law reformers found cause for some mitigatory improvement: they interpreted "wickedness" as the yardstick for the measure of punishment, as including also the physical capacity of the offender to undergo and suffer punishment (cf. Maim., Comm. Mak. 3:10 and Yad, Sanhedrin 17:1). In several instances, the particular turpitude of the offense is expressly stressed as reason for heavy penalties (e.g., "because she hath wrought a wanton deed in Israel" – Deut. 22:21; "it is wickedness" – Lev. 20:14); and in post-talmudic times, the imposition of severe punishments (such as *capital punishment) was always justified by stressing the severity of the particular offense and the public danger of mischief thereby caused.

Maimonides laid down that the gravity and measure of punishment are to be determined, first, by the gravity of the offense: the greater the mischief caused, the heavier must be the penalty; second, by the frequency of the offense: the more widespread and epidemic the offense, the heavier must the penalty be; third, the temptation prompting the offense: the more easily a man is tempted to commit it, and the more difficult it is for him to resist the temptation, the heavier must the penalty be; and fourth, the secrecy of the offense: the more difficult it is to detect the offense and catch the offender, the more necessary is it to deter potential offenders by heavy penalties (Maim., Guide 3:41).

[Haim Hermann Cohn]

In the Framework of Jewish Autonomy

Within the framework of the Jewish *autonomy structure, a great variety of penalties could be imposed on wrongdoers, including *fines, *imprisonment, **ḥerem*, and – extremely rarely – capital punishment, according to judgment passed by a *bet din* under the ordinances of the community or a **ḥevrah*. New and previously unknown penalties were resorted to in the Middle Ages, sometimes for crimes not provided for in talmudic law. This development was especially evident in Muslim and Christian Spain. Capital punishment was openly imposed in Spain with the sanction of the state authorities, and somewhat clandestinely in other countries on rare occasions; the death penalty was reserved mainly for *informers, and it was imposed with the aid and often the urging of the very authorities to whom the denunciation had been made. The manner of execution usually followed that obtaining in the host country, such as bloodletting from an arm, drowning, strangulation, or stoning. Some of the talmudic rules of evidence were waived. In 1380 the Jews of Castile were denied the right of capital punishment. Other bodily penalties – again mainly in Spain – were amputation and mutilation of limbs (mainly for sexual offenses), cutting off the nose and ears, cutting out the tongue (in the case of informers), gouging out the eyes, shaving of head and beard, and stripes. Flogging was most common, particularly in lands like Germany where capital punishment was not resorted to. There were two kinds of lashes: the biblical statutory 39 stripes and the discretionary rabbinic penalty, which could be severe or very light, aimed at inflicting not pain but rather public shame. In Babylonia the person punished in this way had his hands and feet tied as he lay on a bench in the courtroom. More customary was the symbolic penance at the threshold of the synagogue between the afternoon and evening daily services. Shaving the head or beard, which was dreaded more than bodily mutilation, was reserved mainly for assault and battery, adultery, or fornication with a gentile maiden.

The most severe social penalty was the *ḥerem*, with its associated "donkey's burial," interment by the fence of the cemetery, far from respectable graves. Another punishment was expulsion – most customary in Spain and Poland-Lithuania – from the town or even from the country for a stated period or permanently. Sometimes a man's entire family was banished with him. This penalty was imposed on suspected murderers who had only one witness to testify against them, for assault and battery resulting in death, for wife-beating, fornication, stealing, and forgery. The *Mahamad community council of the Sephardi Jews of Hamburg expelled moral or business offenders for several years to Amsterdam or elsewhere. For card-playing and similar offenses German Jewry was accustomed to banish the recalcitrant from the local synagogue. A bankrupt was sometimes ordered to sit for three years behind the *almemar*. For libeling a friend, a woman was ordered to change her seat periodically in the women's gallery of the synagogue. Various penalties involving loss of title or prestige were imposed. For insulting a fellow Jew the culprit would be denied the title of *morenu* or *ḥaver* in Ashkenazi Jewry. The right to be called to the reading of the Torah was withdrawn in certain cases. Often an announcement would be made in all synagogues that for a stated offense a person could not be trusted as a witness or to take an oath.

Institutionally imposed punishment ran parallel to punishment self-inflicted by people who wanted to do penance for their sins. The *Ḥasidei Ashkenaz, in particular Eleazar b. Judah of Worms, developed a detailed and exacting system of penance, the *teshuvat ha-mishkal*. Throughout the Middle Ages and early modern times such offenders as mothers who smothered their infants in sleep, people who killed unwittingly, or persons who committed undetected sexual transgressions would ask the rabbi to impose on them strict penances, which included public confession and self-vilification. Denial of participation in and benefit from communal and religious services was considered a severe penalty. The sinner could also be deprived of certain citizenship rights, such as membership in the plenary assembly and the right to vote. Most damaging socially and economically – especially in Eastern Europe – was expulsion from a *ḥevrah* by the *kahal*, since expulsion from a guild could also mean the loss of livelihood. The *kahal* was especially strict with its own employees or other communal functionaries. A **badḥan* ("jester") would be forbidden to perform at weddings and musicians to solicit their customary holiday gifts. The *kahal* possessed much more serious weapons against persons who refused to cooperate: exorbitant taxes, frequent billeting of troops, and, in Russia during the *Cantonist troubles, drafting the son into military service. Fines and confiscation of property were very common.

With the weakening of Jewish autonomy in modern times these penalties became, in various stages in different countries, obsolete and inoperative.

See also *Banishment; *Reward and Punishment.

[Isaac Levitats]

Forms of Punishment: Biblical Law; Extra-Legal Punishment; "The King's Law"

Jewish criminal law as crystallized in talmudic literature, includes, inter alia, the following characteristics:

1. Before commission of an offense, the prospective offender *must have been admonished by two witnesses*, who explain to the prospective offender the specific offense he is about to commit, and the offender must answer them, stating that he is aware of the offense and that he is nevertheless deliberately committing the offense (Yad, Sanhedrin 1–2);

2. Strict evidentiary law, which prevents the admission of many forms of testimony and evidence (see *Witness; *Evidence). These two requirements made it very difficult to maintain a system of criminal judgment that could realistically deter criminal behavior. In order to cope with these difficulties, in both the societal and legal arenas, Jewish law recognizes two additional tracks of judgment and punishment. The first is that of "punishment not in accordance with Torah law" (*anishah shelo min ha-din*), which authorizes the court, in accordance with the exigencies of the times, to impose punishment, as well as to legislate enactments with regard to punishment, on a far broader scale than that prescribed by biblical law (for an extensive discussion regarding the implementation of this power by rabbinic courts throughout various periods of

history, see: *Capital Punishment). The second track is "the King's Law" (*mishpat ha-melekh*), which was defined in great detail by Rabbi Nissim of Gerona (*Derashot ha-Ran*, no. 11). The "King's Law" is a legal system that operates concurrently with biblical law, and that complements the law of the Torah by adjudicating and punishing those offenses or cases regarding which punishment cannot be imposed and enforced under strict biblical law. If such a parallel system did not exist, says Rabbenu Nissim, "the social order would collapse entirely, and murderers would proliferate without fear of punishment; therefore God, may He be blessed, commanded that Kings be appointed, so that public order might be maintained ... a king may judge a case without [prior] admonition, as he sees fit, for the benefit of the public" (*ibid.*).

These two tracks – punishment not prescribed by the Torah, and the King's Law – are characterized by the fact that they grant considerable discretionary authority to the courts both in prescribing punishment in specific instances, and in legislating general enactments in criminal law. One important distinction between these two systems and the Torah's penal system is that, when the law of the Torah prescribes a specific punishment for a particular transgression, the rabbinic court may not deviate from the prescribed punishment (Yad, Sanhedrin 14.1). In the extra-legal system of punishment and in the King's Law, on the other hand, the judges are not limited by any such restriction. It follows, therefore, that these two legal systems enable the courts to adjudicate and punish even in those situations not punishable under biblical law, as well as to impose more lenient sentences than those prescribed by the Torah, in accordance with the specific circumstances.

Instructions to Judges in Imposing Sentence

Once this broad authority has been bestowed on the courts, the judges are instructed, with regard to each and every case presented to them, to carefully consider the appropriate punishment, and the degree to which it should be imposed. Maimonides affirms that rabbinical judges are indeed vested with the authority to impose punishment which deviates from the strict law of the Torah, and proceeds to summarize a judge's obligations in exercising that authority:

> All these matters are carried out in accordance with what the judge deems necessary in accordance with the exigencies of that time, and his acts should always be for the sake of heaven and he should not take a frivolous attitude to human dignity... This applies with even greater force to the dignity of the children of Abraham, Isaac, and Jacob, who adhere to the true Law. The judge must be careful not to do aught calculated to destroy their dignity, but his sole concern should be to enhance the glory of God... (Yad, Sanhedrin 24:10).

Similarly, Rashba warned judges that the law should be adjusted and imposed in a manner appropriate to the situation of the public. A judge needs to take into account the public's ability to accept the punishments imposed on offenders, rather than be carried away by the passion for revenge: "moderation, consideration, and consent are required, and then the public will be led in the name of Heaven; the greater the act, and the more powerful its execution, the greater the need for consideration, observation and controlled anger; the judge must be on guard lest he be consumed by the heat of his zeal for the Holy God that may have caused him to abandon the appropriate path" (Resp. Rashba, 5: 238).

The Israeli Supreme Court was guided by Rashba's comments when considering the appropriate punishment for criminals (CA 212/79 *Anon. v State of Israel*, 34 (2) 421, 426–428; Cr. A. 156/80 *Binyamin v. State of Israel*, 35 (4) PD 744, Justice Menachem Elon.)

Avoiding Discrimination in Imposing Punishment

The discretionary authority enjoyed by the judges in imposing punishment does not release them from their responsibility to refrain from discrimination between offenders in doing so. This obligation appears repeatedly in the Torah and in rabbinic literature, in various contexts. Judges are warned not to discriminate for socioeconomic reasons – neither on behalf of the rich, in deference to their dignity, nor in favor of the poor, out of inappropriate compassion (Exod. 23:6; Lev. 19: 15; Deut. 24:17). The Torah certainly grants special consideration to the poor man, even when he has broken the law in order to deal with his predicament, as in the words of King Solomon, "Do not despise a thief if he steals to satisfy his appetite when he is hungry" (Prov. 6:30). This is, however, not a legal instruction, but a moral one: "It is written: 'justify the poor and the downtrodden' (Ps. 82:3). What is meant by 'justify'? If this were meant to justify him legally, is it not written, 'you shall not show preference to a poor person in his suit'?! Rather, exact justice [by giving him] from your own property and give it to him." That is, the judge must bestow his own property to the poor person, after the legal process has been completed, as an act of charity.

The Torah emphasizes that there must be no discrimination between man and woman with regard to punishment. The Torah states, "when a man or woman may do any in transgression" (Num. 5:6), which the Rabbis understood to mean that "Scripture considers women equal to men with regard to all of the punishments in the Torah" (Bava Kamma 15a; Yad, *Genevah*, 1:7; Tur, Sh. Ar., ḤM, 349:1). Similarly, discrimination between Jews and proselytes as it states: "you shall not pervert the judgment of a proselyte" (Deut. 24:17).

Talmudic *halakhah* determines that public figures are not immune from the law or from punishment. A high priest is not punished differently than a layman in any respect (Sanh. 18a), and a president (*nasi*) who sins may be flogged (JT Horayot 3:1). The same applies to a rabbinic scholar (*talmid ḥakham*). The one exception to this rule is the king who, according to the Mishnah, may not be judged (Sanh. 2.2). According to the Babylonian Talmud, this exception was introduced as a rabbinic enactment in wake of an episode in which King Yannai was summoned to court but the members of the Sanhedrin would not judge him because they were afraid of him (Sanh. 19a–b; Yad, Sanh. 2:5). This exceptional enactment applies only to "kings of Israel," i.e., to Hasmonean Kings, to their contempt for the Sanhedrin's authority, and not to the kings of the Davidic dynasty, who are judged as any other individual would be. According to the Jerusalem Talmud (Sanh. 2.3), the exemption from judgment applies to any king, whether or not from the House of David, because the king is not subject to any authority whatsoever, other than that of God Himself. It would seem that in our era the president or prime minister of the State of Israel would not be included in this classification, and that they would be judged as any other individual, according to Jewish law. This is because, first, they are not "kings," but rather, at best enjoy a status similar to that of the "*Nasi*"; second, because they are indeed governed by other institutions, unlike the king who is subject to God alone (see bibliography, Fogelman, and editors notes, ibid.).

Sentencing in Accordance with the Offender's Circumstances

The obligation to avoid discrimination does not mean that the personal circumstances of an offender may not be taken into account when imposing punishment. While the same punishment might be meted out to different offenders, it may not have the same implications. Thus, when imposing flogging, for example, the rule is that the degree of the punishment should correspond to the physical capacity of the offender (see *Flogging). This rule was cited by the Israeli Supreme Court in when establishing a fundamental principle in sentencing policy (CA 419/81, *Kalman Feibish v. State of Israel*, PD 35(4)701; per Justice Shilo). In discussing the tension between the need to impose punishment appropriate to the offender, and the desire that punishment be perceived as being consistent and uniform – i.e., that all offenders receive the same punishment for the same offense – Justice Shilo pointed out that "the origin of the concept of setting the degree of punishment in accordance with the offender's circumstances" is indeed to be found in the principle discussed above, i.e., that an offender may not be flogged to a greater degree than he is able to tolerate (p. 708 and 709 of the judgment).

Collective Punishment

The rule in Jewish law is that the offender, and he alone, is liable for his actions, and that he alone may be punished for his behavior. Since the era of the Tannaim, this rule has been clear and unequivocal. In the Bible, however, we find seemingly contradictory statements in this respect. On the one hand, the Bible warns that "The fathers shall not be put to death for the children, neither shall the children be put to death for the fathers: every man shall be put to death for his own sin." (Deut 24:16). During the era preceding the Destruction of the First Temple, the prophets confronted the complaint that the people were being punished by God for the sins of their fathers; the prophets rejected those accusations, and attempted to convince the people that, according to Divine law, only the sinner himself, and not his offspring, could be punished (Jer. 31:28–29; Ezek. 18:2–3). On the other hand, Scripture describes God as "visiting the iniquity of the fathers upon the children, and upon the children's children, unto the third and to the fourth generation." (Exod. 34:7), implying that He indeed punishes descendants for the sins of their fathers. The Rabbis, however, interpreted this as applying to descendents who "continue to perform the actions of their fathers" (Sanh. 27b).

An additional case in which the Torah ostensibly mandates collective punishment is the law of the "condemned city" (*ir ha-nidaḥat*; Deut. 13:13–19), a city in which, according to the Biblical description, all of the city's inhabitants are punished because certain individuals incited the other inhabitants to worship idols. But according to the rabbinic interpretation of these passages, this is not a case of collective punishment at all; the halakhic Midrash interprets the verses as requiring a standard legal process, in which each and every individual among the city's inhabitants receives his punishment by a court of law, and even then only after testimony and admonition by witnesses (*Midrash Tannaim*, ed. Hoffmann, 13.15; *Sifre Devarim*, 93) – that is to say, punishment identical to that of any other case of capital punishment (see *Capital Punishment). The dissenting opinion in this regard is that of Maimonides (Yad, Ovedei Kokhavim 4:6), who rules that it is sufficient that the majority of the city be idolatrous for all of its inhabitants be sentenced to death. Maimonides' ruling was the subject of heated debate among the leading scholars of the generation that followed him. It is also important to note that a view was expressed in the Talmud, that a condemned city ever actually existed, and that its laws were never intended for concrete application, but rather as a hypothetical concept for the sake of theoretical study and drawing moral lessons alone (Sanh. 71a).

The Appropriate Attitude Toward the Offender During and After His Punishment

The obligation to respect the dignity of every individual applies even when the individual in question is an offender who is serving a sentence, and this obligation applies even during the process of the sentence itself. The rabbis ordered that even the execution of a person sentenced to death must be carried out in such fashion that minimizes suffering and does not include humiliation. The well-known great principle of the Torah, "you shall love your fellow as yourself" (Lev. 19:18; *Sifra*, *Kedoshim* 2) was interpreted by the rabbis of the Talmud as obligatory even with regard to an offender awaiting punishment, even capital punishment. The rabbis ruled: "choose (i.e., rule in favor of) a pleasant death for him" (Ket. 37b). Even an individual sentenced to death is considered "your fellow." The rabbis also taught that the dignity of an individual who is sentenced to imprisonment must be preserved. In a responsum by Rabbi Hayyim Palaggi (19th century – Resp. Ḥikekei Lev, vol. 2 ḤM 5), we find a ruling that prisoners may not be incarcerated in "dirty and desolate cells," because "even though they have sinned, they are still Jews," and they must therefore be kept in a "dignified prison." This requirement of Jewish law formed the basis for the Israeli Supreme Court's judgment in the *Tamir* case, which dealt with conditions of imprisonment of prisoners in the State of Israel (CAA 4/82, *State of Israel v. Tamir*, PD 37(3)201; Justice

Elon; for further information and additional legislation regarding this matter, see *Imprisonment; *Human dignity).

Jewish law seeks to prevent any offender being permanently stigmatized. Rather, after being punished the offender once again becomes a regular citizen for all intents and purposes. This reflects his position in relation to his Creator: the truly repentant offender is accepted by God as pure and unblemished: "Yesterday, this one [i.e., the offender] was hated by the Holy One blessed be He – and was considered a detestable outcast, rejected, and abhorred... but today, he is beloved, near to him, and a friend... Yesterday he was separated from the God of Israel.... he cries [prays] and is not answered...; today he is cleaved to the *Shekhinah*... he cries out and is answered immediately..." (Maimonides, Hilkhot Teshuvah 7:6–7), and this is similarly the case in human criminal law. Regarding punishment by flogging, the Torah states that an offender may not be flogged more than is necessary, so as not to create a situation in which "your brother shall be debased before your eyes" (Deut. 25:3). The rabbis expounded this verse as meaning that "once he has been flogged – he is to be considered as your brother" (M. Makkot 3.15). In another source, we read: "all day the Torah calls him as "a wicked person," as it is stated "If the wicked one is to be flogged" (Deut. 25:2). However once he has been flogged, the Torah refers to him as 'your brother' as it is stated 'Lest your brother be degraded'" (*Sifre Devarim*, 286).

This fundamental rule served as the basis for a set of laws and *halakhot* intended to rehabilitate offenders who have borne their punishment, a concept known as "the Enactment for the Encouragement of Penitents" (*Takkanat ha-Shavim*: Mishnah Gittin 5:5). The Mishnah cites the testimony of Rabbi Johanan ben Gudgada (end of 2nd century, C.E.) concerning a law stipulating that one who stole a wooden beam and built it into his house is not required to dismantle his house in order to return the actual beam to its rightful owner, but rather may restore its monetary value, "so as to enable the encouragement of penitents." The reasoning behind this enactment is that if the thief is required to destroy his house in order to return the specific beam to its owner, he might refrain from repentance altogether (Rashi, on Gittin 55a). This enactment was accepted as legally binding, in accordance with the opinion of the School of Hillel, and in opposition to the dissenting view of the School of Shammai, who maintained that the thief must in fact take down his home in order to return the original beam to its owner.

There are exceptions to this rule: where the offense is particularly grave, or involves a position demanding an especially high level of moral integrity and reposition of trust in the position holder, the offender may not continue to serve in that position even if he has served his sentence and repented. Maimonides (Yad, 17:7–9) rules that:

> Whoever sins and has been flogged returns to his state of propriety, as it is stated: "Lest your brother be degraded before your eyes" (Deut. 25:3) – once he has been flogged, he is to be considered [again] as your brother... If the High Priest sins, he is flogged and is reinstated to his high position... But if the head of the academy [i.e., the President (*nasi*) of the Sanhedrin] sins, he is flogged, and he does not return to his position, and cannot even resume a position as an ordinary member of the Sanhedrin....

The same holds true for crime of involuntary manslaughter. An individual who killed another involuntarily must flee to a city of refuge. The Mishnah (Makkot 2:8) records a dispute between the Sages regarding the status of the prisoner exiled to the city of refuge: May an exile who has served his punishment and returned from the city of refuge, return to a position of authority he formerly held? The halakhic ruling cited by Maimonides (Yad, Roẓe'aḥ u-Shemirat ha-Nefesh 7:13–14) is that the individual may not return to his former position for the rest of his life "since it was through him that this great misfortune came about" (cf. Nov. Ritba to Makk. 13a; and see *City of Refuge).

In addition, it is forbidden to remind an individual who has served his sentence and/or repented of his former offenses; this is considered "oppression by means of words" (*ona'at devarim*; Mishnah, BM 4:10; Yad, Teshuvah 7:8; Mekhirah 14:13). Rabbenu Gershom Meor ha-Golah actually imposed a ban on any person who reminded a former offender of his bygone deeds. The reason invoked by Rabbenu Gershom for this prohibition is the desire to make it easier for offenders to reform their ways and to reintegrate into society as honest citizens (*Teshuvot Rabbenu Gershom Meor ha-Golah*, 4; see also under *Apostate).

The "Rehabilitation of Penitents" in the State of Israel

Jewish law's basic approach – that the past life of an offender who has been punished is to be forgotten – is the basis of the legislation of the Rehabilitation of Offenders and Crime Register Law, 5741 – 1981. This law imposes restrictions on divulging information from the Crime Register regarding crimes committed by an individual after the period of limitations has passed as well as ordering the deletion of such information from the Register after an additional period of time has passed. Nonetheless, the law regarding the aforementioned statute of limitations differentiates between various offenses, depending on their severity, and it also differentiates between various bodies to whom such information may be divulged. During the parliamentary debate that preceded the enactment of the law, the justice minister emphasized that "the proposed law is consistent with the principles of Jewish law as mentioned above, i.e., on the one hand, it forbids the use of information regarding an individual's past history when it is possible to conclude – without harming the public interest – that for certain purposes and under certain circumstances, the past history of an individual who has transgressed, but did not return to his former ways, is immaterial; on the other hand, it allows use of information concerning the individual's past history in those cases where preserving the public interest is of greater importance than rehabilitation of the offender. For this reason it allows for preserving the information, without erasure, even after the passage of time (*Divrei ha-Knesset* 75 (5736) 301).

In the *Carmi* case (ABA 18/84, *Carmi v. Attorney General of the State of Israel*, 44(1) PD 53); Justice Menahem Elon), the issue of the interpretation of the Crime Register and Rehabilitation of Offenders Law was raised before the Israeli Supreme Court in the wake of an appeal submitted by a lawyer who, long after he had been found guilty of criminal activity, was suspended by the disciplinary court of the Israel Bar Association. The court conducted an extensive study of the sources of the law, which are rooted in Jewish law and part of which have been cited above, with particular attention to the matter in general, as well as to cases in which exceptions were determined.

[Menachem Elon (2nd ed.)]

BIBLIOGRAPHY: E. Goitein, *Das Vergeltungsprincip im biblischen und talmudischen Strafrecht* (1893); S. Gronemann, in: *Zeitschrift fuer vergleichende Rechtswissenschaft*, 13 (1899), 415–50; J. Wohlgemuth, *Das juedische Strafrecht und die positive Strafrechtsschule* (1903); J. Herrmann, *Die Idee der Suehne im Alten Testament* (1905); I.S. Zuri, *Mishpat ha-Talmud*, 6 (1921), 1–27; A. Pomeranz, in: *Ha-Mishpat*, 3 (1928), 23–27; A. Buechler, *Studies in Sin and Atonement in the Rabbinic Literature* (1928); J. Lipkin, in: *Haolam*, 16 (1928), 281–3; T. Ostersetzer, in: *Sefer ha-Shanah li-Yhudei Polanyah*, 1 (1938), 35–60: H.H. Cohn, in: ILR, 5 (1970), 53–74. IN THE FRAMEWORK OF JEWISH AUTONOMY: S. Assaf, *Ha-Onshin Aḥarei Ḥatimat ha-Talmud* (1922); Dubnow, Hist Russ, index, s.v. *Kahal Courts*; I. Levitats, *Jewish Community in Russia* (1943), 198–217; Baron, Community, index; Baer, Spain, index s.v. *Criminal Jurisdiction of Jewish Community*. **ADD. BIBLIOGRAPHY:** M. Elon, *Ha-Mishpat ha-Ivri* (1988), 1:10, 65, 97, 119, 156, 180, 307, 423ff, 437, 438, 499, 558, 568, 649, 692, 693, 720, 11, 841, 111, 1464; idem, *Jewish Law* (1994), 1:9, 73, 109, 134, 173, 202, 367; 2:516ff, 534, 535, 608, 679, 698, 803, 854, 855, 888; 3:1029, 4:1739; idem, *Jewish Law (Cases and Materials)* (1999), 567–83; idem, "*Ha-Ma'asar ba-Mishpat ha-Ivri*," in: *Sefer Ha-Yovel Le-Pinḥas Rozen* (1962); M. Elon and B. Lifshitz, *Mafte'aḥ ha-She'elot ve-ha-Teshuvot shel Ḥakhmei Sefarad u-Ẓefon Afrikah* (legal digest) (1986), (2), 329–45; B. Lifshitz and E. Shochetman, *Mafte'aḥ ha-She'elot ve-ha-Teshuvot shel Ḥakhmei Ashkenaz, Ẓarefat ve-Italyah* (legal digest) (1997), 228–36; M. Frishtick, *Anishah ve-Shikkum be-Yehadut* (1986); A. Kirshenbaum, "*Mekomah shel ha-Anishah ba-Mishpat ha-Ivri ha-Pelili*," in: *Iyyunei Mishpat*, 12 (1987), 253–73; A. Desberg, "*Ha-Hatra'ah, Mekor ha-Din ve-Ta'amo*," in: *Teḥumin*, 12 (1991) 307–26; A. Enker, "*Yesodot ba-Mishpat ha-Pelili ha-Ivri*,": in: *Mishpatim*, 24 (1995), 177–206; S. Albeck, *Yesodot ha-Averah be-Dinei ha-Talmud* (1997), 100–40; M. Halbertal, *Mahapekhot Parshaniyyot be-Hithavutan* (1997), 128–44; M. Fogelman, "*Ha-Nasi Lo Dan ve-lo Danim Oto*," in: *Be-Ẓomet ha-Torah ve-ha- Medinah*, vol. 1 (1991).

PUNON (Heb. פּוּנֹן), encampment of the Israelites in Edom, between Zalmonah and Oboth (Num. 33:42–43). It is identified with Khirbat Faynān, the Greek Phainon, in the Arabah. Remains of ancient copper mines abound in the area, the richest being at Umm al-ʿAmad. The copper ore of Punon was exploited from Chalcolithic times onward. There is evidence of extensive settlement at the end of the Early Bronze Age and in Iron Age I. The name of the Edomite prince Pinon (Gen. 36:41; I Chron. 1:52) may be connected with the locality. The mines were reopened in Nabatean times and continued to be exploited throughout the Roman and Byzantine periods. They were worked by condemned criminals, as well as Christian martyrs and bishops. Remains at the site include the foundations of a basilica and an inscription mentioning a bishop Theodorus. According to the Madaba map, the place where the Israelites were saved by the *copper serpent was located near Punon. The place was included in the fortifications of the Roman *limes*, Ala Prima miliaria Sebastena being stationed there (*Notitia dignitatum*, 73:32).

BIBLIOGRAPHY: Frank, in: ZDPV, 57 (1934), 218–19, 221–24; Alt, in: ZDPV, 58 (1935), 6ff.; Glueck, in: AASOR, 15 (1935), 32–35.

[Michael Avi-Yonah]

PURIM (Heb. פּוּרִים), the feast instituted, according to the Book of *Esther (9:20–28), by *Mordecai to celebrate the deliverance of the Jews from *Haman's plot to kill them. Purim (Akk. *pūrū*, "lots") is so called (Esth. 9:26) after the lots cast by Haman in order to determine the month in which the slaughter was to take place (Esth. 3:7). Purim is celebrated on the 14th of Adar, and in Hasmonean times it was known as the "Day of Mordecai" (II Macc. 15:36). The Jews of Shushan celebrated their deliverance on the 15th of Adar (Esth. 9:18), and this day became known as Shushan Purim. Out of respect for Jerusalem, it is said, the day is still kept by Jews living in cities which had a wall around them "from the days of Joshua" (Meg. l:1). Thus in present-day Israel Purim is celebrated in Jerusalem on the 15th, but in Tel Aviv on the 14th. In leap years Purim is celebrated in the second month of *Adar.

The chronological difficulties such as the identity of King *Ahasuerus and the absence of any reference in the Persian sources to a king having a Jewish consort; the striking resemblance between the names Mordecai and Esther to the Babylonian gods Marduk and Ishtar; the lack of any reference to Purim in Jewish literature before the first century B.C.E.; the language of the Book of Esther, which suggests a later date – all these have moved the critics to look elsewhere than the account in Esther for the true origin of the festival. Various conjectures have been made (see *Scroll of Esther) but the problem still awaits its solution. In any event the festival had long been established by the second century C.E. when a whole tractate of the Mishnah (*Megillah) was devoted to the details of its observance, especially to the rules governing the reading of the Scroll of Esther, called in the rabbinic literature the *megillah* ("scroll"). Purim is a minor festival in that work on it is permitted, but it has been joyously celebrated in Jewish communities as a reminder of God's protection of His people. However, the widespread acceptance of the festival as only minor is reflected in the popular Yiddish saying that as a high temperature does not denote serious illness neither is Purim a festival.

The main feature of Purim is the reading of the Book of Esther, the *megillah*, with a special cantillation. *Megillot* are frequently decorated, sometimes with scenes from the narrative. Since according to the midrashic interpretation the word *ha-melekh* ("the king"), when it is not qualified by Ahasuerus, refers to the King of the universe, some *megillot* are so written that each column begins with this word. It would seem that originally the *megillah* was read during the day, but eventually the rule was adopted to read it both at night and during the day (Meg. 4a). It is customary to fold the *megillah* over and spread it out before the reading since it is called a "letter" (Esth. 9:26, 29). The four verses of "redemption" (2:5; 8:15–16; and 10:3) are read in louder voice than the other verses. The custom of children to make a loud noise with rattles and the like whenever the name of Haman is read, in order to blot out the "memory of Amalek" (see Deut. 25:19; and Esth. 3:1 and I Sam. 15:8–9 for Haman was a descendant of Amalek) is ancient and still persists, though frowned upon as undecorous by some authorities. It is the practice for the reader to recite the names of the 10 sons of Haman (Esth. 9:7–9) in one breath (Meg. 16b) to show that they were executed simultaneously. The custom has also been seen, however, as a refusal by Jews to gloat over the downfall of their enemies (C.G. Montefiore and H. Loewe (ed.), *A Rabbinic Anthology* (1938), 53). The Torah reading for Purim morning is Exodus 17:8–16.

The Book of Esther (9:22) speaks of "sending portions" (*mishlo'aḥ manot* – abbreviated to *shelakhmones*) to friends on Purim and of giving gifts to the poor. The rule is to send at least two "portions" of eatables, confectionery, and so forth, to a friend and to give a present of money to at least two poor men. A special festive meal is eaten on Purim afternoon toward eventide. Among the special Purim foods are boiled beans and peas, said to be a reminder of the cereals Daniel ate in the king's palace in order to avoid any infringement of the dietary laws, and three-cornered pastries known as *hamantashen* ("Haman's ears"). There has been much discussion around the saying of the Babylonian teacher Rava (Meg. 7b) that a man is obliged to drink so much wine on Purim that he becomes incapable of knowing whether he is cursing Haman or blessing Mordecai. The more puritanical teachers tried to explain this away, but the imbibing of alcohol was generally encouraged on Purim and not a few otherwise sober teachers still take Rava's saying literally (see, e.g., H. Weiner: *9½ Mystics* (1969), 207). The laws of Purim and the reading of the *megillah* are codified in Shulḥan Arukh, OḤ 686–97. Various parodies of sacred literature were produced for Purim, the best known of which, *Massekhet Purim*, is a skillful parody of the Talmud with its main theme the obligation to drink wine merrily and to abstain strictly from water. The institution of the Purim rabbi, a kind of lord of misrule, who recites Purim Torah, the frivolous manipulation of sacred texts, was the norm in many communities. Some have seen in all this an annual attempt to find psychological relief from what otherwise might have become an intolerable burden of loyalty to the Torah (Druyanow, *Reshumot*, 1 and 2). Under the influence of the Italian carnival it became customary for people to dress up on Purim in fancy dress, men even being permitted to dress as women and women as men. The *Adloyada carnival in Tel Aviv has been a prominent feature of Purim observance in modern Israel.

In the kabbalistic and ḥasidic literature much is made of Purim as a day of friendship and joy and as the celebration of God at work, as it were, behind the scenes, unlike Passover which celebrates God's more direct intervention. (God is not mentioned in the Book of Esther.) The "lots" of Purim are compared with the "lots" cast on the Day of Atonement (Lev. 16:8), what human beings call "fate" or "luck" being, in reality, only another manifestation of God's providential care. So highly did the kabbalists esteem Purim that they reported in the name of Isaac Luria that the Day of Atonement is "like Purim" (*Yore ke-Furim*).

While some Reform congregations abolished Purim, others continued to celebrate it as a day of encouragement and hope, some even arguing that it helped Jews to express their aggressive emotions and to sublimate their feelings of wrath and hatred (W.G. Plaut, *The Growth of Reform Judaism* (1965), 224).

BIBLIOGRAPHY: N.S. Doniach, *Purim* (Eng., 1933); S. Zevin, *Ha-Mo'adim ba-Halakhah* (1963[10]), 188–214; J.D. Epstein, *Oẓar ha-Iggeret* (1968); P. Goodman, *Purim Anthology* (1960), incl. bibl.; J.L. Fishman, *Ḥagim u-Mo'adim* (1944), 119–68: J.H. Greenstone, *Jewish Feasts and Fasts* (1945), 135–78; H. Schauss, *Jewish Festivals* (1938), 237–71.

[Louis Jacobs]

PURIM KATAN (Heb. פּוּרִים קָטָן; "minor Purim"), the name given to the 14th and 15th days of the first month of *Adar in a leap year, when *Purim is celebrated during the second month of Adar. (The Karaites were the only sect to celebrate Purim during the first Adar in a leap year.) According to talmudic tradition, Purim should be celebrated in the second Adar because that was the date of the original Purim (which occurred in a leap year). The rabbis also wanted to bring the period of the redemption of Esther closer to that of the redemption of the Israelites from Egypt celebrated in the following month of Nisan (Meg. 6b). Purim Katan has none of the ritual or liturgical features of Purim: The *megillah* is not read, and no gifts are sent to the poor (Meg. 1:4). The *Al ha-Nissim prayer is not said, but fasting and funeral eulogies are prohibited (Meg. 6b). Also, *Taḥanun is not recited on these days, which are considered a minor occasion of rejoicing (Sh. Ar., OḤ 697:1).

BIBLIOGRAPHY: Eisenstein, Dinim, 337; G. Ki-Tov, *Sefer ha-Toda'ah*, 1 pt. 1 (1958), 297.

PURIM MESHULLASH ("Triple Purim"). As stated in the article on *Purim, Purim is celebrated on the 15th of Adar ("Shushan Purim") in Jerusalem, which "has been a walled city from the days of Joshua ben Nun," whereas elsewhere it is celebrated on the 14th of the month. When, however, the 14th of Adar falls on Friday, the celebration in Jerusalem and other cities said to be "walled cities from the time of Joshua" extends over three days, and is thus called Purim Meshullash. The *megillah*, the Scroll of Esther, is read on the 14th but the additional prayers for Purim are included in the Sabbath service on the 15th and the *haftarah* of the previous Sabbath, *Shabbat Zakhor* (I Sam. 15. 2–34), is repeated. The special festive meal however is held on the Sunday, so as to distinguish it from the normal Sabbath festive meal, and it is on this day gifts are exchanged ("*mishlo'aḥ manot*," popularly called "*shelakhmones*") and donations to the poor are made.

PURIMS, SPECIAL. Following the talmudic injunction that one must recite a special thanksgiving benediction on returning to the place where one was once miraculously saved from danger (Ber. 54a), the custom evolved for Jewish communities or families to celebrate the anniversary of their escape from destruction by reciting special prayers and with a ritual similar to that of Purim. (See: A. Gumbiner's note to Sh. Ar., OḤ 686.) These special communal Purims are called *Purim Katan ("minor Purim"), or Mo'ed Katan ("minor holiday") or Purim… (followed by the name of the community or the special event). In many cases special Purims were preceded by a fast comparable to the Fast of *Esther. In addition, on the Purim Katan itself the story of the personal or communal salvation was often read from a scroll (**megillah*) in the course of a synagogue service in which special prayers of thanksgiving, in the style of *piyyutim*, were offered. Sometimes the *Al ha-Nissim prayer and the *Hallel were inserted into the ritual. The traditional Purim observances of enjoying a festive meal and giving charity to the poor were also applied to special Purims. (See Table: List of Special Purims.)

The Karaites observe a special Purim on 1st Shevat, in memory of the release from prison of one of their leaders, Yerushalmi. The exact date of the event is unknown. The followers of Shabbetai Ẓevi observed a special Purim on 15th Kislev, because on this day in 1648 Shabbetai Ẓevi proclaimed himself Messiah.

BIBLIOGRAPHY: C. Roth, in: HUCA, 10 (1935), 451–82; 12–13 (1937–1938), 697–99; Y.T. Lewinski (ed.), *Sefer ha-Mo'adim*, 6 (1956), 297–321; M. Steinschneider, in: MGWJ, 47 (1901–21) ff.; A. Danon, in: REJ, 54 (1907).

List of Special Purims

Purim of…	Observed on	Established in	Reason for Observance
Algiers (called Purim Edom)	4th Ḥeshvan	1540	Saved from destruction in Spanish-Algerian wars of 1516–1517 and 1542.
Algiers (called Purim Tammuz)	11th Tammuz	1774	Saved from danger.
Alessandria Della Paglia (Italy)	25th Av	1779	Saved from massacre.
Ditto	2nd Ḥeshvan	1797	Saved from riots during revolutionary war.
Ancona	21st Tevet	1690	Saved from earthquake.
Ancona	15th Tishri	1741	Synagogue escaped destruction by fire.
Ancona	24th Adar	1775	Jewish quarter saved from conflagration.
Ancona	12th Shevat	1797	Saved from riots in revolutionary war.
Angora/Ankara/(called: Purim Angora or Purim Sari-Kiz)	21st Elul	?	Saved from blood libel accusation.
Angora, called Purim Abazza	11th Iyyar	?	?
Angora, called Purim de la Turquito	14th Tammuz	1775	Saved from blood libel accusation.
Avignon	24th Tammuz	?	?
Avignon	28th Shevat	1757	Escaped dangers of a riot.
Baghdad	11th Av	1733	Relieved from Persian oppression.
Belgrade	19th Sivan	1822	Saved from destruction during Turko-Serbian war.
Breche (Champagne, France)	14th Adar	1191	Chief Jew-baiter executed.
Cairo	18th Shevat	?	?
Cairo, called Purim Miẓrayim	28th Adar	1524	Saved from extermination.
Candia (Crete)	18th Tammuz	1583	Saved from collective punishment for treason, during Turco-Venetian conflict.
Carpentras	16th Kislev	1512	Saved from riot.
Ditto	9th Nisan	1692	Saved from annihilation.
Ditto, called Yom va-Yosha	21st Nisan	1651	Saved from threat of massacre.
Casablanca, called Purim Hitler	2nd Kislev	1943	Escape from riot and Nazi occupation.
Castille (Spain) called Purim Martinez	1st Adar	1339	Saved from annihilation following accusations by Jew-baiter Gonzales Martinez, king's adviser.
Cavaillon (Provence)	25th Iyyar	1631	Plague ended.
Ditto	29th Sivan	1677	Saved from blood libel accusation.
Cento (Italy)	12th Av	1820	Escaped from fire.
Chieri (Italy)	1st Av	1797	Saved from danger of war.
Chios (Greece), called Purim de la Senora ("Purim of the Good Lady")	8th Iyyar	1595 (or 1820)?	Saved from death during Franco-Turkish war.
Cuneo (Italy)	5th Kislev	1799	Synagogue saved from destruction by shell.
Ettingen (Germany)	18th Iyyar	1690	Saved from destruction by enemies.
Ditto	29th Sivan	1713	?
Ferrara	24th Kislev	?	Saved from destruction by fire.
Ditto	18th Iyyar	1799	Escaped war riots.

List of Special Purims (cont.)

Purim of...	Observed on	Established in	Reason for Observance
Fez	22nd Kislev	1840	Saved from destruction.
Florence	27th Sivan	1791	Escaped sacking and riots.
Fossano (Italy)	18th Nisan	1796	Saved from bomb explosion during war.
Frankfurt on the Main, also called: Purim Winz or Purim Fettmilch	20th Adar	1616	Expelled Jews readmitted to town and chief Jew-baiter, Fettmilch, executed.
Fulda	15th Elul	?	?
Gumeldjina (Thrace) called: Purim de los ladrones ("Purim of the thiefs")	22nd Elul	1786	Saved from collective punishment for instigating robbers to sack town.
Hebron	1st Av	?	Saved from collective punishment and execution by Ibrahim Pasha.
Ditto, called Purim Takka ("Window Purim")	14th Tevet	1741	Saved from annihilation by miraculous ransom money on the windowsill of synagogue.
Ivrea (Italy)	1st Shevat	1797	Escaped plundering during revolutionary war.
Komotini (Gumurjina, Gumuldjina) (Greece)	22nd Elul	1768	Saved from destruction during Turkish suppression of Greek revolt.
Kovno	7th Adar (II)	1783	Privileges of civic freedom granted by King Stanislaus II
Leghorn	12th Shevat	1742	Saved from destruction in earthquake.
Ditto	25th Tevet	1810	Plague ends.
Ditto	16th Adar	1813	?
Lepanto (Greece)	11th Tevet	1699	Saved from destruction during Turkish war.
Medzibezh (Poland)	11th Tevet	1648 or 1649	Saved from annihilation by Chmielnicki's bands.
Morocco	13th Nisan	1771	Saved from annihilation.
Mstislavl (Russia)	4th Shevat	1744	Saved from slaughter by Cossacks.
Ditto	3rd Kislev	1844	Saved from collective punishment for alleged rebellion against authorities.
Narbonne	20th Adar	1236	Saved from riots.
Oran	6th Av	1830	Saved from massacre before arrival of French troops.
Ostraha	23rd Nisan	1734 or 1768	Saved from pogrom.
Ditto	7th Tammuz	1792	Saved from destruction during Russo-Polish war.
Padua called Purim di fuoco ("Fire Purim")	11th Sivan	1795	Saved from fire.
Ditto, called Purim di Buda	10th Elul	1684	Saved from massacre during Austro-Turkish (in Budapest).
Ditto, called Purim dei Sassi (?)	Shabbat "Bo"	1748	?
Pesaro/see also: Urbino and Senigallia	?	1799	Escaped damages of war.
Pitigliano (Italy)	15th Tammuz	1757	Collapse of school roof, no casualties.
Ditto	15th Sivan	1799	Saved from damages during revolutionary war.
Posen	1st Ḥeshvan	1704	Saved from death during Polish-Swedish war.
Prague	14th Ḥeshvan	1620	Saved from sacking and riots by protection of Emperor Ferdinand.
Ditto, called Vorhang Purim ("Curtain Purim")	22nd Tevet	1622	Beadle of synagogue saved from hanging for keeping stolen curtains.
Purim Byzanc (observed by Jews of Thrace)	14th Adar	1574	Saved from extermination.
Ragusa	?	1631	Saved from accusation of blood libel.
Rhodes	14th Adar	1840	Saved from annihilation.
Ritova (Lithuania) called Purim Jeroboam b. Nebat.	14th Adar	1863	Jew-baiter Count Aginsky died.
Rome	1st Shevat	1793	Ghetto saved from assault and fire.
Sa'na	18th Adar	?	Saved from extermination.
Sarajevo	4th Ḥeshvan	1819	10 leaders of Jewish community freed from prison and saved from execution.
Senigallia (Italy)/see also: Urbino and Pesaro	15th Sivan	1799	Saved from annihilation during war by escaping to Ancona.
Sermide (Italy)	25th Tammuz	1809	Saved from earthquake.
Shiraz, called Purim Mo'ed Katan	2nd Ḥeshvan	1200 or 1400	Permitted to practice Judaism after having being forced to convert to Islam.

List of Special Purims (cont.)

Purim of…	Observed on	Established in	Reason for Observance
Sienna	15th Sivan	1799	Saved from destruction during revolution.
Spoleto	21st Sivan	1797	Saved from annihilation during revolutionary war
Ditto	7th Adar	?	?
Syracuse (Sicily), called Purim Saragossa	17th Shevat	1425	Saved from destruction for alleged treason by honoring King Alfonso with empty cases of Torah Scrolls.
Tetuan and Tangiers, called Purim de las bombas, or Purim de los Christianos	2nd Elul	1578	Saved from destruction during Moroccan Portuguese war.
Tiberias	7th Elul	1743	Saved from danger of war.
Ditto	4th Kislev	?	?
Trieste	14th Adar	1833	Leading Jew-baiter died.
Tripoli and Tunisia	25th Shevat	?	?
Ditto, called Purim Sheriff or Purim Kadebani ("False Purim")	24th Tevet	1705	Saved from destruction by hostile ruler, Khalil Pasha.
Ditto, called Purim Borgḥel	29th Tevet	1793	Saved from destruction during occupation by Bourgel Phasa of Turkey.
Tunisia, called: Purim Sheleg ("Purim of Snow")	24th Tevet	1891	Jewish quarter saved from natural disaster
Tunisia	15th Shevat	?	?
Turino	1st Av	1797	Saved from war and sacking.
Urbino	11th Sivan	1799	Saved from war and riots.
Verona	20th Tammuz	1607	Permission granted to lock ghetto gates from inside instead of from outside.
Vidin, Bulgaria, called Purim de los borrachones ("Purim of the Drunken")	4th and 5th Ḥeshvan or 9th–10th	1806	Saved from annihilation following accusation that the ruler had been poisoned by his Jewish physician.
Ditto	2nd Adar	1878	Saved from destruction during Russo-Turkish (Balkan) war.
Vilna	15th Av	1794	Saved from destruction during Russo-Polish war.
Zborow (Galicia)	12th Tevet	?	Saved from annihilation because of blood libel accusation.
Family Purims			
Altschul family of Prague	22nd Tevet	1623	Head of family, Hanokh Moses, saved from death.
Brandeis family of Jungbunzlau (Bohemia), called Povidl Purim "Plum Jam Purim"	10th Adar	1731	David Brandeis and family saved from accusation of having killed gentiles by poisoning plum jam.
Danzig family of Vilna, called Pulverpurim ("Powder Purim")	15th Kislev	1804	Family of Abraham Danzig author of "Ḥayyei Adam" saved from explosion of magnesium.
Elyashar family of Jerusalem	2nd Nisan	?	Saved from death.
Heller family of Prague	1st Adar	1629	Head of family, Yom Tov Lipman, rabbi of Prague saved from death sentence.
Jonathan ben Jacob of Fulda (Germany)	17th Tammuz	?	?
Maimon family of Lithuania	?	1750	Grandfather of Solomon Mimon saved from death sentence for blood libel.
Meyuḥas family of Jerusalem	16th Adar	1724	Head of family, Raphael Meyuḥas, escaped death by highwaymen.
Samuel Ha-Nagid of Spain	1st Elul	1039	Saved from death plot of conspirators.
Segal family of Cracow	1st Iyyar	1657	Family saved from drowning in river while escaping from pogrom.
Treves family (?)	Shabbat "Va-Yeẓe"	1758	Escaped from fire.

PURIM-SHPIL (Yid. lit. "Purim play"), monologue or group performances given at the traditional festive family meal held on the festival of *Purim. There is definite evidence that use of the term *Purim-shpil* was widespread among all Ashkenazi communities as early as the mid-16th century. The earliest written record in which the term appears is at the beginning of a lengthy poem relating the events of the Book of Esther with the aid of appropriate midrashic material, composed about 1555 in Venice by a Polish Jew (*Lieder des Venezianischen Lehrers Gumprecht von Szczebrszyn*, ed. by Moritz Stern (1922), 18). From the context it appears that the poem was intended as a *Purim-shpil*. However, there are extant manuscripts of Yiddish poems on the Purim story dating from at least the 15th century, and from the start of the 16th century printed versions began to circulate. Well into the 19th century this type of poem continued to be defined as a *Purim-shpil* (e.g., *Purim-Shpil*, Warsaw, 1869 and 1874). At first the term *Purim-shpil* was used to define a monologue during which the performer sometimes appeared in costume. The monologues were mostly rhymed paraphrases of the Book of Esther, as well as parodies on liturgical and other holy texts, such as a "kiddush" or a "sermon" for Purim, composed to entertain the audience. Together with the more complex forms, the monologue form of *Purim-shpil* continued to appear in Eastern Europe until World War II.

Manuscript fragments and other evidence from the second half of the 16th century attest to the gradual enlarging of the *Purim-shpil* to include presentations by several performers. One such fragment includes a contest between cantors from Poland, Italy, and Germany; it may be assumed that this is a combination of three earlier satirical monologues. Other fragments show evidence of growing complexity in dramatic expression blended with the traditional parody. Judging from the extant material it is probable that during the 16th century and until at least the mid-17th century, the subject matter of the *Purim-shpil* was drawn from contemporary Jewish life and was based on well-known humorous tales. This type of *Purim-shpil* also survived in Eastern Europe until World War II (16 *Purim-shpil* texts of this non-biblical type were published in the collection, *Yidisher Folklor* (1938), 219–74). In its initial and developing stages, the *Purim-shpil* often parallels the German *Fastnachtspiel*, as evidenced from texts of the 15th and 16th centuries. The *Purim-shpil* in all its varieties was usually presented in private homes during the festive family meal; the performers, who wore masks or primitive costumes, were generally recruited from among yeshivah students. In the course of time the *Purim-shpil* became the object of competition between groups of performers recruited not only from among students but also from among apprentices, craftsmen and mendicants; even professional entertainers saw in the *Purim-shpil* a field for their activity. By the 16th century, the prologues to the *Purim-shpil* had developed a conventional form, which included blessings for the audience, an outline of the contents of the performance, and an introduction of the actors; conventional epilogues had also developed, including parting blessings and appeals for an ample reward. (One of the shorter prologues reads in part: "Good Purim, good Purim, my worthy audience! And do you then know of Purim's significance?…" And an excerpt from an epilogue reads: "Today Purim has come in, tomorrow it goes out. Give me then my single groschen and kindly throw me out!…") Like the *Fastnachtspiel*, the Purim performance was introduced, conducted, and concluded by a narrator (leader of the performance), traditionally called *loyfer*, *shrayber*, or *payats*, and, as in the *Fastnachtspiel*, profanity and obscenity of an erotic nature are outstanding elements of the humorous effects.

Well-developed texts on biblical themes presented as *Purim-shpils* began to appear in the late 17th century. Naturally, the subject of the oldest surviving text of this type, a manuscript of 1697, is the story of the Book of Esther, popularly known as the *Akhashverosh-shpil*. In the 18th century the repertoire expanded to include *The Selling of Joseph* and *David and Goliath*, and in the 19th and 20th centuries East European performers presented *The Sacrifice of Isaac, Hannah and Penninah, The Wisdom of Solomon*, etc. (A collection of this genre of *Purim-shpil* was edited by Noah Prylucki in *Zamlikher far Yidishn Folklor* (1912), 125–88; (1917), 143–5.) Most of these biblical works retain the conventional form of *shpil* with prologues, epilogues, parodies, vulgar language, the traditional narrator, and, often, stories unconnected with any biblical theme. These older forms are very apparent in the above-mentioned text of 1697 and in a similar version of an *Akhashverosh-shpil* printed at Frankfurt in 1708 (which appears in J.J. Schudt's *Juedische Merckwuerdigkeiten*, 3 (Frankfurt and Leipzig (1714), 202–25). The printed version of the *Akhashveroshshpil* was burned by the city fathers of Frankfurt presumably because of the play's indecent elements. This was probably the reason for a public notice of 1728 in which the leaders of the Hamburg community banned the performance of all *Purim-shpils*. To assure compliance with the ban, fines were threatened and special investigating officers were posted.

As early as the beginning of the 18th century, the biblical *Purim-shpil* reflected many trends of the contemporary European theater in its literary style, choice of subject, and scenic design. Previously marked by extreme brevity, not exceeding a few hundred rhymed lines, and by the limited number of performers, the *Purim-shpil* became a complex drama with a large cast, comprising several thousand rhymed lines performed to musical accompaniment in public places for a fixed admission price. Nonetheless, the plays maintained a connection with Purim and were performed during the appropriate season. From the early 18th century there are extant texts of such plays and evidence of performances in Frankfurt, Hamburg, Metz, and Prague, and, later in the century, in Amsterdam and Berlin. Although there is an historical tie between the traditional *Purim-shpil* and the more developed biblical dramas of a later era, the term *Purim-shpil*, if strictly applied, refers only to those early, short performances at family gatherings.

ADD. BIBLIOGRAPHY: Sh. Epstein, in: JQ, 28:1 (1980), 34–36; idem, in: *Judaism Viewed from Within and from Without* (1987), 1952–17; idem, in: *New World Hasidim* (1995), 237–55; L. Carrracedo, in: WCJS, 8,4 (1982), 7–12; Ch. Daxelmueller, in: *Paradeigmata*, 1 (1989), 431–63; J. Baumgarten, in: *Pardès*, 15 (1992), 37–62; idem, in: *Perspectives*, 10 (2003), 127–42; E. Rozik, in: *Diálogo*, 24 (1994), 56–61; idem, in: *European Legacy*, 1:3 (1996), 1231–235; A. Belkin, in: *Assaph* – C2 (1985), 40–55; idem, in: *Assaph* – C12 (1996), 45–59; idem, in: *Cahiers du Judaïsme*, 6 (1999–2000), 105–12; idem, in: *Yiddish Theatre* (2003), 29–43.

[Chone Shmeruk]

PURITY AND IMPURITY, RITUAL (Heb. טֻמְאָה וְטָהֳרָה, *tumah ve-toharah*), a symbolic system according to which a pure person or object is qualified for contact with the Temple and related sancta (holy objects and spaces) while an impure person or object is disqualified from such contact. Ritual impurity arises from physical substances and states associated with procreation and death, not in themselves sinful. Ritual impurities are in general permitted (if not unavoidable or obligatory) and in this they can be distinguished from moral impurities, which arise from prohibited acts. Both types of impurity are denoted by Hebrew terms of defilement (forms of *tame*) but context and associated terms indicate that different kinds of impurity are intended.

Ritual, or permitted, impurity is distinguished by the following features: (1) it is contagious, transferred from one person or object to another in a variety of ways, such as physical contact or sharing space within a covered area; (2) impurity contracted from a source of ritual impurity is impermanent and can be reduced and removed by some combination of ablutions, time, and/or the performance of specified rituals; (3) ritual impurity can defile sancta and must be kept separate from it. More severe forms of ritual impurity can also defile common (non-sacred) objects as well, and thus may require isolation or exclusion.

By contrast, moral impurity arises from the commission of certain heinous sins, specifically idolatry, bloodshed, and sexual transgressions. These sins are said to generate a moral impurity that symbolically defiles a range of sancta including the land of Israel itself and the sanctuary. In addition to originating in sin, moral impurity differs from ritual impurity in that it is not contagious (one does not contract impurity by touching a murderer), and it is not generally removed by rituals of bathing, laundering, and the like. Moral impurity is sometimes removed through a process of atonement. In some cases, a repentant sinner may bring a sacrificial offering to purge the sanctuary of the defilement caused by his sins. In severe cases, however, moral impurity is absolved only with punishment and/or death. The Yom Kippur rite is designed to purge the sanctuary of the defilement caused by unrepentant sins of the community at large.

The concept of ritual – as distinct from moral – purity and impurity is by no means exclusive to the Jewish religion; indeed it was a central and integral feature of most, if not all, ancient religions (see below). It is generally believed that impurity is a concurrent of the belief in evil spirits and a part of the taboo concept. Whatever its origins, the system of ritual purity and impurity as crafted in the priestly writings of the Hebrew Bible represents an attempt to "monotheize" the community's purity practices. In these writings, impurity is generally divorced from any association with evil spirits and functions as a symbol of that which is anathema to the holy.

In the Bible

The main source for the biblical laws of ritual purity and impurity is Leviticus 11–17 and Numbers 19. Other specific purity laws are also found in Leviticus 5:2–3; Numbers 31:19–20, Deuteronomy 14:3–21; 23:10–15; 24:8; 26:14. The ritual purity system limned in the priestly writings of the Hebrew Bible does not reflect a concern with health or hygiene. Only one set of diseases generates ritual impurity and many substances widely considered unhygienic, such as human and animal excrement, are not deemed to be ritually impure. While there is no theoretical definition of purity and impurity in the Bible, its function and symbolism can be readily deduced from the antithetical relationship between impurity and holiness (Lev. 11:43–47). Only God is inherently holy. Things that are nonholy, or common, may acquire holiness by being brought into God's realm (being sanctified or consecrated). The realm of the common is subject to two possible states connoting compatibility and incompatibility with holiness: purity and impurity. Under normal circumstances, common objects are pure and compatible with the holy. However, contact with certain sources of ritual impurity will defile common objects and render them incompatible with the holy. That which is holy is by definition pure and must never come in contact with the impure. If defiled, a sanctum loses both its holiness (becomes common) and its purity (becomes ritually impure). To be fully restored, it must first be purified (making it pure but common) and then resanctified (making it holy once again).

What are the sources of ritual impurity that are incompatible with the holiness of God? The three main sources of impurity are (1) corpses and certain animal carcasses, (2) *ẓara'at* – skin diseases in humans (a decomposition of the flesh associated with death; see Num. 12:12, Job 18:13) and fungal growths in fabrics and houses, and (3) genital discharges. Many scholars have noted that the physical substances and states labeled impure, and thus deemed to be anathema to God, are associated with death and procreation. The God of the Hebrew Bible does not die and does not have sexual relations. These are characteristic of humans. To be eligible to approach the sanctuary, God's residence among the Israelites, humans must separate from that which makes them least Godlike: death and procreation. The ritual purity laws requiring separation from sources of impurity are thus essential to the frequent priestly exhortation to be like God (*imitatio dei*) and to strive for holiness.

According to Leviticus 10:10, the priests must teach Israel the distinction between pure and impure on the one hand, and holy and common (or profane) on the other, in order to prevent impermissible contacts between the holy and the impure. Maintaining a ritually pure and holy area in the community (the sanctuary compound) is essential if God is to dwell in Israel's midst. During the wilderness period, the entire camp of the Israelites was a kind of holy war camp with the ark in the center; thus, it was subject to stricter purity regulations than the ordinary settled habitation. This accounts for the exclusion of severe impurity bearers from the camp (Num. 5:2–3 and 31:13–44), even though such persons are not excluded from their communities in the laws for ordinary settled habitation (see below).

CORPSES AND CARCASSES. The most severe source of ritual impurity is the human corpse, which communicates to persons and objects that contact it or enter an enclosed space with it (Num. 19:14ff.) an impurity that lasts seven days and can in turn defile others with a milder one-day impurity. Human bones and graves also convey ritual impurity. Corpse impurity is so severe that some sources exclude the corpse-defiled from the holy camp for the period of impurity (Num. 5:2–3, Num. 31:13–24). Numbers 19, which reflects the situation in settled communities generally, rather than the holy camp, does not. The corpse-defiled are purified by a ritual process that includes sprinkling with a mixture of water and ashes from a ritually burned red heifer on the third and seventh days, bathing, laundering and waiting till sundown. Corpse-defiled objects are purified by fire or immersion in water as appropriate, though defiled earthenware cannot be purified and is simply destroyed.

The carcasses of all large land animals and eight types of smaller land animals (e.g., mice, lizards) convey a one-day ritual impurity. One who touches or carries them becomes impure until nightfall (Lev. 11:24ff.). The purity laws pertaining to animals are complicated by the fact that many defile by ingestion (see *Dietary Laws). The only living beings to contract corpse impurity are humans, both Israelite and non-Israelite (Num. 19:11). Food may also become impure if it has first been in contact with water (which makes it "receptive" to impurity; Lev. 11:34).

SCALE-DISEASE OR "LEPROSY". "Leprosy" is a conventional but erroneous rendering of Hebrew *ẓara'at*. The term covers a set of skin lesions in humans that feature scaling of the skin as well as fungal growths in clothes and residential buildings; these are detailed in Lev. 13–14. Skin lesions of human beings generate a most severe impurity (defiling to both sancta and common objects) and can be subdivided: one type is immediately declared as impure, another as pure (including a case where the symptoms appear over the whole body). A third type requires isolation for a week or a fortnight, and if there is no deterioration the bearer is considered pure. Because the scale-diseased person can defile even common objects and persons, he is either restricted within or excluded from the community (Lev. 13:46; Num. 12:14–15). Scale-disease of clothes and buildings always requires isolation of the afflicted entity for a week or a fortnight and only following this period is it decided whether it is pure or not. The purification ritual for persons is carried out by the priest only after healing is complete (hence, the ritual is not curative). It is more intricate and complicated than for other impure persons, and bears certain similarities to the Azazel (scapegoat) ceremony on the Day of Atonement (Lev. 16:5–11). Impurity is removed by sprinkling a mix of bird blood and water, and then carried away by a live bird. The person bathes, launders, and shaves, waits a week, and then bathes, launders, and shaves again before offering a special sacrifice at the sanctuary. Houses from which *ẓara'at* has been removed are purified by sprinkling and dispatch of a live bird; fabrics are purified by washing.

In many narrative texts of the Hebrew Bible, *ẓara'at*, like death, can be deployed as a divine punishment for sin (Ex. 4:6; Num. 12:10–15; Deut. 28:27, 35; II Sam. 3:29; II Kings 5). Nevertheless, the priestly discussion of scale-disease impurity makes no mention of a state of sinfulness, only of ritual impurity preventing contact with sancta. There is slight evidence for a biblical association of scale-disease with death (Num. 12:12, Job 18:13), supporting the claim that biblical impurities arise from substances and conditions associated with procreation and death.

ISSUE FROM THE SEXUAL ORGANS. Emissions of semen, pus, or blood from the genitals of either sex convey ritual impurity. Emissions may be divided into two main classes: normal emissions (discharges of semen from the male and menstrual blood from the female) and abnormal emissions (diseased discharges of non-menstrual blood or pus).

Normal emissions are less severe, conveying impurity only for the period of the discharge itself: one-day for an emitter of semen and (an idealized) seven-days for a menstruant. Semen (the least defiling genital flux) defiles clothing, but since emitters of semen do not convey a secondary impurity, the semen-defiled are restricted only from the sphere of the holy (the sanctuary area and holy items outside the sanctuary such as sacrificial meats). Purification for a semen emitter is achieved by bathing, laundering, and waiting until evening. Sexual intercourse conveys a one-day semen impurity to the female partner as well as the male. This is removed by bathing and waiting until evening. The ritual impurity of a menstruant (*niddah*) is slightly more severe, defiling both persons and objects for one day. The bed and chair of the menstruant are defiled (probably due to the possibility of actual contact with the flux) and can convey a one-day impurity to persons or things by contact. Objects or furniture on which a menstruant sits or lies can convey impurity by contact. Sexual intercourse with a menstruant conveys an equivalent seven-day impurity to the male partner (Lev. 15:24; but Lev. 18:19 prohibits sex with a menstruant). Purification from menstrual impurity does not require a sacrifice; we may deduce that the menstruant bathes and launders on the seventh day and waits until evening although this is not explicitly stated. Lev. 15, which contains the impurity regulations for genital emissions, normalizes and regularizes menstruation on analogy to the emission of semen. These regulations do not banish the menstruant from her home and they contain none of the rhetoric of disgust for menstruation evidenced in other biblical texts (such as Isaiah 30:22 which suggests a practice of physical expulsion for menstruants; or Ezekiel 7:19–20; 36:17) and in ancient literature generally (see Pliny, *The Natural History*, Book VII, chapter 13).

Abnormal emissions convey a more severe form of ritual impurity that resembles in its effect the other severe impurities of *ẓara'at* and corpse contamination. First, the impurity continues for a period of seven days beyond the time of the discharge itself (similar to the week between healing and purification of scale-disease). Second, the purification ritual, like that prescribed for *ẓara'at* and corpse contamination, requires sacrificial offerings. Third, the *zav* and *zavah* (male and female with an abnormal emission) are excluded from the sanctuary camp (Num. 5:2–3). The regulations in Leviticus 15, presumably intended for settled habitation, do not include expulsion from the community. The *zav/ah* conveys to a bed, chair, or saddle on which he sits or lies a one-day impurity that can defile other persons or things. Touching a *zav/ah* or being touched by a *zav/ah* with unwashed hands leads to a one-day impurity. The spittle of a *zav* also conveys a one-day impurity. Purification from abnormal genital emission, beginning seven days after the condition has healed, involves bathing in "living water" (*mayyim ḥayyim*; (Lev. 15:13)), laundering, waiting until evening, and bringing a burnt offering and a purification offering (*ḥattat*) on the eighth day.

Lochial discharge (genital emissions attending and following the birthing process) also convey ritual impurity. For seven days after the birth of a male and fourteen days after the birth of a female, a woman defiles like a menstruant. For an additional 33 or 66 days (for a male or female child respectively), the mother bears a lesser impurity and is restricted only from contact with sancta, not ordinary objects or persons (presumably sexual intercourse is permitted). The new-born child is not considered impure. Purification from post-partum impurity is not detailed and must be deduced from comparable impurities, but likely included bathing and laundering after both the first and second stages. When the purification period is over, the woman brings a burnt-offering sacrifice and a purification (*ḥatta't*) sacrifice to the sanctuary (Lev. 12:6–8).

Other permitted ritual defilements occur in the context of the cult when those engaged in certain purification rituals absorb or otherwise incur a one-day impurity.

PURIFICATION FROM PERMITTED (RITUAL) IMPURITIES REGARDING PERSONS AND OBJECTS. Common to all purifications for ritual impurity is the time factor. One must wait until the evening for the lesser degrees of impurity (e.g., Lev. 11:24, 25, 27) and seven days for the greater degrees (e.g., Lev. 12:2). Rituals increase with the severity of the impurity. Thus, ablutions, bathing for persons and washing for objects, are a basic purification rite for all permitted ritual impurities even where not expressly specified. Slightly more severe forms of contact with a source of impurity (carrying rather than mere touching) and impurities lasting longer than one-day also require laundering (Lev. 11:25, 28). Sprinkling, another form of cleansing, is prescribed for the severe impurities (sprinkling with water and blood for the scale-diseased, with water and the ashes of a red heifer for corpse-defilement). The more severe ritual impurities of abnormal genital emissions and scale-disease require a *ḥattat* (purification offering) to purify the sanctuary, not the offerer, of impurity generated by his or her condition. (The offerer's personal impurity has been removed by the passage of time and by ablutions following the healing of his or her condition.) On occasion, additional sacrifices are prescribed as appeasements that enable the full reintegration of the offerer (e.g., a burnt offering for the *zav/ah*, Lev. 15:14–15, 29–30). The *asham* offering required of the scale-diseased person is normally brought for cases of sacrilege and may reflect an ancient idea that scale-disease is a punishment for sacrilege.

Objects defiled by contact with a corpse are passed through fire if they can endure it; if not they are immersed in water (Num. 31:19–24). Earthenware vessels cannot be purified but must be broken, as must even stoves and ovens. Various modes of destruction or disposal are prescribed for other impurities that cannot be removed. For example, corpses must be buried outside the settlement, fabrics infected by *ẓara'at* are burned and *ẓara'at* infected building materials are deposited in an impure place outside the camp.

Defiled sancta are fully restored with a two-step process of purification followed by reconsecration. Purification rituals also elevate persons to positions of increased access to the sacred. Priests undergo ablutions (washing hands and feet) before serving in the sanctuary and special ablutions attend the high priest's performance of the Yom Kippur ritual. Levites are purified by shaving, laundering, and sprinkling with "waters of purification" (*me ḥattat*; Num. 8:6–7, 15, 21) before assisting the priests and performing sanctuary labors.

PROHIBITED (MORAL) IMPURITIES AND THEIR PURIFICATION. Leviticus 18, 20, and related texts (most belonging to a set of writings known as the Holiness Code) employ impurity terminology in a moral context. (In addition to the term *tame*, the terms *to'evah* and *ḥanaf* are used in reference to moral, and not ritual, impurity.) According to these texts, moral impurity arises from the commission of sin and defiles the sinner himself (with a non-removable degradation) and the sanctuary. Unlike ritual impurity, moral impurity is not conveyed to others; it is not subject to rites of purification (such as ablutions). Moral purity of persons can be achieved only by punishment for heinous sins (such as *karet*, the divine penalty of "cutting-off"), atonement for lesser sins, or abstention from defiling immoral acts in the first instance. Where ritual impurity defiles persons, some objects, and the outer altar of the sanctuary, severe moral impurity defiles the innermost areas of the sanctuary as well as the land. Land that is repeatedly defiled by sexual transgressions will eventually "vomit out" those who dwell upon it, a reference to exile (see Lev. 18:25, 28).

Three classes of heinous moral transgression are singled out as sources of a moral impurity that defiles the land. These transgressions, which incur severe punishment, include various sexual sins, homicide, and idolatry. According to Leviticus 18 and 20, sexual sins such as incest (18:6–18), adultery (18:20), homosexuality (18:22), bestiality (18:23), and intercourse with a menstruant (18:19, 20:18), result in *karet* for the offender and defilement of the land (exposing the community to the danger of expulsion). In other texts, victims of sexual violations incur a personal moral defilement (a non-contagious condition of degradation), as in the case of rape (Gen. 34:5, 13, 27) and incest (Ezek. 22:11). So, too, do those who remarry after an intervening union (Deut. 24:1–4).

Illicit (i.e., non-judicial, non-military) homicide, whether intentional or unintentional, also defiles the land (Num. 35:33–34). The manslayer bears "bloodguilt," a kind of moral impurity, and his life is forfeit. In cases of murder, the personal defilement of the murderer and the defilement of the land are removed only by the death of the murderer. In instances of accidental homicide, the death of the perpetrator at the hands of the victim's blood avenger also removes bloodguilt and impurity from the land. However, the accidental manslayer may take refuge in one of five cities designated for this purpose until the death of the high priest, which serves to remove the impurity of the homicide.

Two idolatrous actions are described as defiling in Leviticus (offering a child to Molech in Leviticus 20:2–5 and consulting the dead in Lev. 19:31). However, numerous biblical texts speak of idolatry, idols, and idolatrous utensils more broadly as defiling the worshipper (e.g., Josh. 22:17, Jer. 2:23, Ezek. 20:7, 18, 26, 31), the sanctuary (Jer. 7:30, Ezek. 5:11), and the land (Jer. 2:7–9; Ezek. 36:17–18). Offenders are subject to stoning and the divine penalty of *karet* (cutting off). In many passages, idols and their cultic appurtenances must be destroyed or disposed of (for burning see Ex. 32:20, Deut. 7:5, 25, II Kings 10:26; for burying see Gen. 35:4).

In addition to the three classes of heinous sin, lesser transgressions generate a moral impurity that defiles the sanctuary. The defiling effect of these transgressions is calibrated to the sinner's intentionality (deliberate or inadvertent sin) and the presence or absence of repentance. The sanctuary defilement of inadvertent sins is purged by bringing a *ḥattat* sacrifice. Repentance reduces deliberate sins to a status equal to that of unintentional sin, allowing the removal of sanctuary defilement by *ḥattat* also. Brazen, unrepented sins and unintentional sins of which the perpetrator is unaware remain unremedied. Thus, Leviticus 16 describes an annual ritual process designed to purify the sanctuary from the accumulated defilements accruing to it as a result of these trespasses. On the Day of Atonement (or Yom Kippur) a *ḥattat* sacrifice is brought on behalf of the community. The high priest confesses all of the sins of the Israelites over the head of a goat which is then dispatched into the wilderness.

Although ritual impurities are not sinful, failure to purify oneself from a permitted ritual impurity (e.g., corpse-defilement) is sinful and defiles the sanctuary with a moral impurity. If inadvertent, the situation can be rectified by bringing a *ḥattat* (purification offering) in addition to the normal purification procedures for the ritual impurity. If deliberate and unrepented, the punishment is *karet*.

The purity requirements for Nazirites and priests are higher than those for ordinary Israelites because of the greater holiness of the former. Thus, while Israelites may become impure from any corpse, priests may not defile themselves by any corpse but that of close kin. The high priest and Nazirite must avoid corpse-defilement altogether. Nazirite contact with a corpse is a sin that defiles the sanctuary. If done inadvertently, a *ḥattat* must be offered to purify the sanctuary, but if done deliberately the Nazirite is punished with *karet*.

Both ritual and moral impurity appear in biblical sources as real and potent forces. While their sources and modes of transfer differ, they are deemed to have real (albeit different) effects in the world. There are, however, secondary non-literal applications of terms of impurity that should be understood as mere metaphor. For example, "a pure heart" (Jer. 4:14, Ps. 24:4, 51:12, 73:1) and "pure hands" (Gen. 20:5, II Sam. 22:21, Ps. 18:21, 25) are clearly metaphors for righteousness while "impure lips" (Isa. 6:5) is a metaphor for impious speech.

GENERAL. Several scholars have stressed the similarity between the laws of purity and impurity in the Bible and those of the ancient Near East, including Egypt, Mesopotamia, and the ancient Hittites. According to Herodotus (1,198), it was customary in Babylon to bathe in water after cohabitation and it was forbidden to touch any utensil prior to this. According to an ancient Babylonian text, a man touching a menstruating woman was unclean for six days. The pig was considered unclean, although it was not considered forbidden food. In Egypt it was forbidden for a man to enter the temple after cohabitation unless he first bathed, and the priests bathed twice daily and twice nightly. The king of Egypt purified himself every morning (cf. Ex. 7:15). Among the Hittites a corpse was considered impure and there is evidence of a detailed ritual for the purification of a mother after giving birth. Despite these significant similarities and the ancient, pre-monotheistic roots for many Israelite purity practices, any effort to understand the purpose and meaning of these practices as systematized by the monotheizing priestly writings in Lev. 12–16 must attend to the larger symbolism of impurity and holiness in those writings. Thus, although Babylonian purity rites are accompanied by healing incantations, it cannot be assumed that biblical purification rites as crafted by the priestly writers are designed to heal, since they occur only *after* the diseased condition (abnormal genital emission, *ẓara'at*) has already ceased.

In some cultures purity regulations serve as tools of subordination. There is little evidence to suggest that Israelite purity regulations served this function. Ritual impurity is not a permanent or long-lasting stigma applied to certain groups selectively. The biblical system of ritual impurity is impermanent and applies to all Israelites – priests and lay Israelites, men and women.

In the Halakhah

A general concern for ritual purity is attested in the Second Temple Period. Ritual purity was important when handling consecrated food or objects and impurity had restrictive consequences, such as disqualification from eating sacrificial food, or participating in the Passover celebration. Purity observance, however, was important for reasons that extended beyond cultic practice and access. For example, groups like the Essenes and Pharisees voluntarily adopted the purity regulations of priests, striving to eat their food in a state of purity, as part of their quest for holiness. Moreover, strong biblical sanctions attended the failure to purify from severe impurities (e.g., Num. 19:13 threatens those who do not purify from corpse impurity with *karet* or "cutting off"). Finally, the larger Hellenistic milieu was one in which corpse impurity was feared and avoided. In Greek tradition, priests could not attend funerals and were defiled by even looking at a corpse. Houses of the dead contracted impurity and were to be cleansed with sea water. Tombs, bones, and uncovered graves were to be avoided. According to Roman law, corpse impurity traveled along blood lines so that relatives of the dead were defiled even if physically distant. For Jews to observe their own ritual purity laws in such an environment would be rather unremarkable, as evidenced by passages in Philo and Josephus. All of these non-cultic inducements to the observance of purity regulations while the Temple still stood, help explain rabbinic interest in the laws of purity in a post-Temple world.

The *tannaim* continue the biblical distinction between ritual impurity and moral impurity, recognizing that ritual impurity arises from natural, unavoidable and even obligatory circumstances and not from sin. While the biblical laws of ritual impurity and purity are systematized and extended in rabbinic *halakhah* (at least ⅓ of the Mishnah deals with the laws of ritual purity in some fashion), moral impurity and the consequences of sin are matters of moral instruction rather than legal formulation; they are treated in aggadic rather than halakhic texts. (The rabbis expand on the list of morally defiling transgressions, as in *Mekhilta, ba-Ḥodesh* 9: "anyone who is arrogant causes the land to become impure").

The following discussion of rabbinic and later halakhic impurity regulations focuses exclusively on the treatment of ritual impurity.

RABBINIC SYSTEMATIZATION OF BIBLICAL IMPURITY REGULATIONS. Twelve complete tractates in the Mishnah and the Tosefta, scores of *mishnayot* in other tractates, and many *beraitot* in the halakhic Midrashim and in the two Talmuds, as well as the studies of *amoraim* connected with them, are devoted to these *halakhot*. The rabbinic authors assume that the biblical regulations are not random, but form a system whose principles can be discerned and extrapolated. Through exacting exegesis, comparison of parallel passages and logical inference, they fill the gaps in the biblical material and produce a fully elaborated scheme of ritual purity and impurity. For example, as regards purification, rabbinic authors realize that: (1) the requirement of bathing can be assumed even where not specified (supported by such parallels as Lev. 11:39–40, Lev. 17:15, and Lev. 22:5–6); (2) ablutions or immersion of some kind are a minimal purity requirement for any defiled person or object even when not specified; (3) more intense contact with impurity (carrying and eating rather than merely touching a carcass; lying down or eating rather than merely stepping in a *ẓara'at* afflicted house) necessitates laundering as well as bathing (compare Lev. 11:39–40 with 17:15; Lev. 14:36,46 with 14:47); (4) since more intense contact with impurity necessitates laundering as well as bathing, the requirement to launder assumes the need to bathe even where not specified (supported by such parallels as Num. 19:19 and Num. 31:24); (5) logic demands that females with genital discharges of any description must bathe even where not specified since (a) bathing is required of those they defile and (b) the bathing requirement indicated in the first case of genital discharge discussed in Leviticus 15 (the *zav*) extends to all cases, male and female, subsumed thereunder (see Lev. 15:33); (6) for more severe impurity bearers ablutions remove layers of impurity (supported by Lev. 14:8, Lev. 15:11), a biblical idea that generates the rabbinic category of *tevul yom* – one who has undergone immersion and is awaiting sunset for complete purification. The *tevul yom* is no longer defiling in the common sphere (hence he may reenter the camp; cf. Lev. 14:8) and is a threat only to sancta and food that must be eaten in purity,

The Categories of Impurity. Rabbinic systematization may also be seen in the categorization of the biblical impurities. The ritual impurities mentioned in the Torah (corpses, carcasses, genital emissions, and scale-disease) are regarded in rabbinic texts as "fathers of impurity" (*avot ha-tumah*). Impurity affects persons, vessels, clothing, food, liquid, and, in some cases, beds and chairs. Entities that contract ritual impurity from a father of impurity are called "children" (*yeladot*) or "offspring of impurity" (*toledot ha-tumah*) and are impure in the first degree. These offspring of impurity render only foods and liquids impure in the second degree (BK 2b; Yad, Tumat Met 5:7). In the common sphere the chain of impurity ceases in the second degree, but hands, food and liquid which are impure in the second degree still transmit impurity to dedicated or sacred produce. *Terumah* contracts a third degree impurity but does not transmit impurity further. Sacred produce (*kodoshim*, dedicated to Temple use) can contract a third degree impurity and transmit an impurity to foods and liquids to the fourth degree (Sot. 5:2; Toh. 2:3–5; Yad, Avot ha-Tumah 11:1–4). The exception to this descending series is that which contracts impurity from a corpse, which (based on an ambiguity in Num. 19:22) is deemed by the rabbis to be a father of impurity which is itself able to defile both persons and objects. In order to differentiate the corpse from the corpse-defiled, the corpse itself is called a "father of fathers" (*avi avot*) of impurity by Rashi (Pes. 14b, 17a, et al.) and other commentators (R. Samson to Kel. 1:1; Oho. 1:2).

Methods of Contracting Impurity. Corpses and related matter (bones, graves). Rabbinic texts are careful to define and prescribe minimum specifications for corpse matter, graveyards, and bones that convey impurity according to Num. 19:16. They also define the "tent" that conveys the impurity of a corpse reposing within it according to Num. 19:11. The rabbis recognize that the power of a tent in which a corpse reposes to convey impurity lies in its overhang and declare other overhangs capable of conveying impurity (a tree or awning for example). Impurity by overshadowing (Kel. 1:4) is caused whether the corpse or corpse related item (such as a bone) overshadows the person or utensil, these overshadow the corpse, or something a handbreadth wide overshadows both the corpse and the object (Oho. 3:1; Naz. 53b; Maimonides, Yad, Tumat Met 1:10). However, significant limitations of the corpse impurity law are effected by the rabbinic determinations that (1) corpses defile in a vertical direction only and (2) the only items in a corpse-defiled house susceptible to defilement are unsealed vessels, foods, and liquids (interpreting Num. 19:11 in light of Lev 11:32 and Num. 31:20). The latter leniency stands in stark contrast to Qumranic law in which every single item in a corpse-defiled house contracts impurity.

Ẓara'at Impurity. The rabbinic material pertaining to the scale-diseased person (*meẓora*) reveals a desire to reduce the incidence of *ẓara'at* as far as possible. The rabbinic definition of the disease is narrowed to exclude certain persons (e.g., resident aliens) and places (e.g., Jerusalem in Tosef., Neg. 6:1 and later all of Babylonia in Ket. 77b). Certification of a *meẓora* is subject to stringent criteria concerning minimal size, time of examination, location of affliction, and so on. *Ẓara'at* for garments is limited by excluding all naturally colored or dyed fabrics, and houses are susceptible to *ẓara'at* only if the original stone or wood is affected (Sifra, Neg. 5:3). An extra week is added to the quarantine period for *ẓara'at*, and doubtful cases must be decided leniently (in opposition to the general rule that doubts in matters of Torah law are decided stringently; cf. Neg 7:14). That the purpose of these rules is to reduce the incidence of *ẓara'at* impurities is attested by the pronouncement in Tosefta, *Nega'im* 6:1 that "there never was and never will be a case of a *ẓara'at* infected house."

At the same time, the actual impurity of a *meẓora* is elaborated in a relatively stringent manner in rabbinic *halakhah*. The biblical text offers very little on the conveyance of impurity by a *meẓora*, and the rabbis fill in this gap by comparative exegesis. Thus the *meẓora* is said to defile others present in the same house on analogy with the *ẓara'at* affected house, which defiles its contents. The *meẓora*'s defilement by overhang is analogized to that of a corpse. Since the spittle and shifting (see below) of the less severely defiled *zav* conveys impurity, the rabbis rule that the spittle and shifting of the more severely defiled scale-diseased person must also convey impurity. Thus a *meẓora* defiles others by touching, shifting, carrying without contact, spitting, and according to *Zav* 5:6, breathing. According to *Niddah* 34, all fluids of a *meẓora* are impure. Rabbinic sources also define legal minima for the conveyance of impurity. For example, a scale-diseased person must put his head and the greater part of his body into a house in order to defile by overhang; a person must put his head and the greater part of his body into a house afflicted with *ẓara'at* in order to contract impurity from it; a *ẓara'at* diseased garment must be the size of an olive or more to defile a house in which it is put (Neg. 13:8); building materials from a house afflicted by *ẓara'at* must be the size of an olive or more to convey impurity to humans and vessels by contact, carrying, and overhang (Neg. 13:6; Tosef., Neg. 6:11; Yad, Tumat Ẓara'at 16:1).

The *meẓora* is subject to some restrictions. He is not allowed within walled cities, and the Mishnah states that a partition 10 handbreadths high and four cubits wide was made in the synagogue to segregate the *meẓora* from other congregants, and he was required to enter first and exit last (Neg. 13:12). The Mishnah shows greater stringency in its treatment of the *meẓora* than the *Sifra* or the Babylonian Talmud (the latter declaring that there is no *ẓara'at* in Babylonia at all). Some aggadic traditions express the older view that *ẓara'at* is a divine punishment for transgression (Lev R. 15:5, 16:1, 17:3).

Genital Emissions. The rabbinic systematization of impure genital emissions is complex and there are differences among the sources. In general, the semen emitter is distinguished from other dischargers in that the former conveys impurity to persons only through sexual intercourse and not by contact. This is because the semen, and not the semen emitter, is an *av tumah* (the semen emitter being impure in the first degree). The other dischargers are analogized by virtue of their having a flux. While rabbinic texts recognize a hierarchy among the *zav*, *zavah*, *niddah*, and first-stage *yoledet*, they nevertheless equate their potential to defile to a large degree. A unique feature of discharge impurity is the ability of its bearers to defile by pressure (*midras*), based on the attention in Lev. 15 to the impurity of items upon which these persons have sat or lain. Because Lev. 15 specifically mentions seats and beds, the rabbis limit *midras* impurity to items used for sitting or lying (Nid. 49b). However, Lev. 15:10 attributes impurity to "all that is under" (the *zav*), and not merely beds and seats. The rabbis choose to read this verse as attributing impurity to "all that [the *zav*] is under" (a grammatically possible reading), generating the concept of "*maddaf*" (impurity of items located above the *zav*. Although it is not clear what these items are in tannaitic texts, the Babylonian Talmud limits *maddaf* to the bed covering of the *niddah*. *Maddaf* uncleanness is understood to be of rabbinic origin and is considered a light impurity. Persons with a genital discharge also defile by shifting or being shifted (*hesset*). *Hesset* is when an object is supported or carried by one with a flow without direct contact.

While rabbinic *halakhah* extends the defiling power of bodily discharges by systematic analogizing, there is evidence of a simultaneous desire to limit impurity. Susceptibility to *midras* impurity by flux-bearers is limited to beds and seats. Earthenware and items that cannot be purified are not considered susceptible to defilement by flux-bearers. In addition, comparison with Qumranic exegesis of the same biblical laws reveals a lenient tendency on the part of the rabbis. At Qumran, all women, not merely menstruants, are excluded from Jerusalem; excrement is also viewed as a defiling discharge, and semen-emitters contract a three-day impurity. Although the reference to "places of impurity" in Mishnah *Niddah* 7:4 may point to a custom in tannaitic times of isolating menstruants in special places, the practice is not robustly attested in rabbinic *halakhah*. In general, while sectarian exegetes fill scriptural gaps in a stringent manner, creating a purity system that ultimately requires separation and isolation in a desert community, the rabbis fill scriptural gaps in a less stringent manner, enabling observance to continue in the course of everyday existence.

Things susceptible to impurity are Israelites, utensils, food, and drink. Although biblically, a *ger* (gentile resident alien) can contract corpse uncleanness (see Num. 19:10b–14), the rabbis understand the term *ger* to refer to a proselyte, and conclude that only a convert and not a gentile contracts corpse impurity (Naz. 61b; Yad, Tumat Met 1:13). All human corpses convey impurity, but whether a gentile corpse defiles by contact and carrying only (Yev. 61a; Maim. *ibid.*, 1:12) or also by overshadowing (Oho. 18:7) is disputed. All utensils, except those made of stone, unfired clay, or dung, are susceptible to impurity no matter what their shape. Some, however, such as flat wooden or bone utensils, contract impurity by rabbinic law only (Men. 69b; Kel. 11:1; 15:1; Yad, Kelim 1:6, 10). Glass vessels are the subject of a special decree (Shab. 14b, 15a, 16b; Yad, Kelim 1:15). Metal vessels that contact a corpse take on its degree of impurity (based on exegesis of Num. 19:16). Utensils can contract impurity only when they are completed and the sages defined what stage of manufacture marks completion for the different types of vessels. Broken vessels likewise are not susceptible to impurity but some, on being repaired or reassembled, revert by a special rabbinic decree to their original impurity (Shab. 16b).

Purifications. As in the Bible, impurity is removed by sacrifices, immersions or ablutions, waiting for sunset, and in some cases special cultic acts. An individual with a genital discharge counts seven pure days and then has to bathe in living waters, i.e., a spring (Mik. 1:8). A *meẓora* whose signs of impurity have disappeared brings two birds that have lived in freedom, and the priest (or in another view, any person) slaughters one over a new earthenware bowl, then takes cedar wood, hyssop, and scarlet wool and binds them together. He then brings the tips of the wings and the tail of the second bird near to them, dips them in the blood and sprinkles it seven times on the back of the hand (and some say also on the forehead) of the *meẓora*. After sending away the living bird the priest shaves the *meẓora*. After seven days, during which the *meẓora* may enter within the wall of Jerusalem but is still regarded as a "father of impurity," the priest shaves him a second time and the *meẓora* must then wash his garments and bathe (Neg. 14:1–2; Yad, Tumat Zara'at 11:1–2). He who contracts impurity from a corpse is sprinkled on the third and seventh days of his impurity with purification-offering water, and after the sprinkling on the seventh day is obliged to bathe. Bathing alone is sufficient for all others who are impure and can be purified. Wherever bathing is mentioned in connection with those who are impure, except in the case of one with a flux, the bathing takes place in a **mikveh*. The purification of the impure is completed at the going down of the sun (Lev. 22:6–7). On the day the impure individual bathes, he is called a *tevul yom* (immersed that day) and is disqualified from *terumah* and hallowed things. The bathing of the hands for (the eating of) hallowed things also requires a *mikveh*. Otherwise those needing to wash their hands must pour a quarter *log* of water (about a quarter liter) over the hands (see *Ablution).

The priest who was to burn the red heifer and the high priest who was to serve on the Day of Atonement were separated from their households seven days beforehand and sprinkled with the purification-offering water (Par. 3:1). The duty of every Israelite to purify himself for the festival (Sifra, Shemini 4; RH 16b) is also because of the pilgrimage to the Temple (Yad, Tumat Okhelim 16:10). Immersions are sometimes required even of the ritually pure to mark the transition to a sacred context: "None may enter the Temple court for the service, even though he is pure, until he has immersed himself" (Yoma 3:3; TJ, Yoma 40b). Certain sects habitually immersed themselves even though they were not impure. According to Josephus (Wars, 2, 129), the Essenes used to immerse their bodies in cold water before their communal meals at noon and in the evening. The immersion of the "morning bathers," too, was unconnected with seminal impurity, but was a regular daily immersion. The Pharisees opposed this custom, and responded to the complaint of the morning bathers that "they mention the Divine Name in the morning without immersion," to the effect that, "I complain against you morning bathers who mention the Divine Name out of a body in which impurity resides."

Food. All foods set apart for human consumption can contract impurity, once they are detached from the ground and have been made susceptible through being moistened, to the satisfaction of their owners, by one of the following seven liquids: water, dew, oil, wine, milk, blood, honey (Uk. 3:1; Makhsh. 1:1; 6:4). These liquids themselves also contract impurity (Yad, Tumat Okhelim 1:4 and commentaries), in an even stricter degree than foodstuffs (Par. 8:7; Toh. 2:6, Yad, Avot ha-Tumah 10:10). Liquids are the most potent conveyers of impurity. If defiled by an item, even in the third degree, they contract and convey a first degree impurity.

Fathers of Impurity on the Authority of the Scribes. In addition to the Pentateuchal sources of ritual impurity, the rabbinic sages ascribed irregular forms of ritual impurity to the *bet ha-peras* ("burial area," see below), to gentile countries, to idols and related items, and to gentiles. These impurities bear the signs of rabbinic innovation, including controversy over the details, sporadic enforcement, resolution of doubtful cases on the side of leniency, conceptual irregularity, and the use of analogical formulations ("x conveys impurity *like* a menstruant or *like* a corpse").

Burial Area. A burial area (*bet ha-peras*) is defined as land in which a ploughed-over bone, a lost grave, or burial niches (*kukhim*) may be present. By rabbinic decree, such areas are deemed to be impure by reason of the doubt that attaches to them. These fields have special laws for building, sowing, planting, and impurity removal (Oho. 17:1, 18:1–5; Tosef., Oho. 17:1–2).

Gentile Countries. Gentile lands are decreed by the rabbis to be ritually impure (the decree is attributed in later sources to Yose b. Yoezer and Yose b. Yohanan; see b. Shab. 14b; Tosef., Par. 3:5). In the Mishnah and Tosefta, the juxtaposition of the impurity of gentile lands with the impurity of the *bet ha-peras* indicates that gentile lands were likewise deemed impure because of doubt about the possible presence of bones, corpses, and graves (Tosef., Ahilot 17:6–7, 18:1–5, 14–17, Tosef., Kel. 7:1). In the Hebrew Bible, land is defiled *morally*, by sinful deeds such as idolatry, but not ritually. The few biblical verses that refer to gentile lands as impure (Amos 7:17 and Josh. 22:18) should be understood as references to moral impurity (stemming from the idolatry that occurs there). Thus, the rabbinic decree of *ritual* impurity is a true innovation. The degree to which and the precise manner in which gentile lands convey ritual impurity is not explicit in the halakhic sources (see Maimonides, Yad, Tumat Met 2:16; Rashi, Shah. 14b s.v. *Al ha-Ereẓ*). The conjecture that the purpose of this decree was to discourage emigration from Ereẓ Israel following the persecutions and exterminations in the time of Antiochus has no basis in the sources. The decree did not prevent emigration: not only do we find scholars in Alexandria (Joshua b. Perahya and Judah b. Tabai), but the Mishnah also assumes that people could be in foreign countries legitimately. Frequent contact with various countries and the existence of Jewish settlements outside the land of Israel made the observance of this decree a burden and in consequence it was lightened in various ways (Tosef., Oho. 18:2; Yad, Tumat Met 11:6). The paths taken by the pilgrims from Babylon on their festival pilgrimages, even in gentile lands, were declared pure (Tosef., Oho. 18:3; Yad, Tumat Met 11:12; see Maim. comm. to Oho. 18:7). Gentile towns within the land of Israel (Tosef., *ibid.*, 18:4; Yad. *ibid.*) were also declared free from impurity. Similarly, gentile dwellings are declared to be impure, pending inspection, because of doubt about the possible presence of a buried fetus (Ohal. 18:7–8; see the Temple Scroll, 11 QT 48:11–12, for the sectarian belief that gentiles bury their dead indiscriminately and even in the middle of their houses).

Idols/idolatry. In the Bible, idols and idolatry are strictly prohibited. While idols are strongly associated with moral impurity capable of defiling persons, land, and sanctuary, they are not among the biblical sources of ritual impurity. However, by the rabbinic period, idols and associated items are deemed to be ritually impure and to convey ritual impurity to sacred and profane places, objects, and persons. Rabbinic sources explicitly assert that the ritual impurity of idols and related items is rabbinic rather than from the Torah, as seen by the lack of consensus on the nature and degree of the impurity, the leniency governing the construction of these laws (Shab. 9:1, 11d and b. Shab. 83b), and the use of analogies to express this impurity. Drawing on biblical metaphors, R. Akiva asserts that, like a menstruant, the idol defiles by carriage. The sages, on the other hand, assert that an idol defiles only by physical contact, like a dead creeping thing (Shab 9:1). Elsewhere, the idol is said to defile by overhang like a *meẓora* (Tosef., Zav 5:5). The law that one passing under an *asherah* (idolatrous tree) becomes impure (Av. Zar. 3:8) is explained in conformity with this view, i.e., the likely presence of an idolatrous offering beneath it (Av. Zar. 48b).

Gentiles. According to the biblical purity system, all humans are subject to moral impurity arising from certain heinous sins, but only those under the covenant (Israelites and gentiles who join the covenant community) are subject to ritual impurity from the physical states and substances detailed in Lev. 12–15. Rabbinic texts are consistent and unanimous in asserting that biblical law excludes gentiles from the ritual purity system of Lev. 12–15 (Sifra, Zavim 1:1; Sifra, Tazria 1:1). Gentiles neither contract nor communicate ritual impurity through genital emissions (Mik. 8:3–4, Zav. 2:1, 2:3, Nid. 4:3, Ed. 5:1, cf. Tosef., Nid. 5:5, Nid. 7:3); nor are they, their houses or their garments susceptible to scale-disease impurity (Neg. 1:1, 3:1, 7:1, 11:1, 12:1). The consensus of rabbinic texts is that gentiles are also not susceptible to corpse impurity. Nor do gentiles bear an intrinsic ritual impurity, as some scholars have argued, as evidenced by the fact that they may separate *terumah* (Ter. 3:9) and make sacrificial offerings and donations to the sanctuary (Sifra, Emor 7:2, Shek. 7:6, Zev. 4:5, Men. 5:3, 5:6, 6:1 and 9:8). Many rabbinic passages assume commensality of Jews and gentiles without concern for ritual impurity (Ber. 7:1, Av. Zar. 5:5) and others assume other interactions (Shab. 1:9) and even collaboration in the production of wine (a liquid that is very susceptible to defilement; Av. Zar. 4:9–12). The exclusion of gentiles from the Temple rampart is not due to an alleged intrinsic ritual impurity but to a hierarchical gradation of holiness in the sanctuary precincts that determines different degrees of access even for the pure (ranging from pure gentiles who have the least access to pure Israelite women, followed by pure Israelite men, Levites, priests, and finally the high priest who has the most intimate access).

Nevertheless, some rabbinic sources hold that gentiles bear a ritual impurity by rabbinic decree. "Israelites defile by *zav* and not gentiles, but the rabbis decreed concerning them that they defile like *zavim*" (Sifra, Zav 1:1). Later sources suggest that this decree dates to the early first century C.E. All sources agree that the ritual impurity of gentiles is not biblical but rabbinic. Doubtful cases are decided leniently, observance appears to have been sporadic, and the impurity itself is irregular. Specifically, the gentile does not defile like a *zav* in every respect. Scattered traditions assume the gentile can convey impurity by carriage, *hesset*, or *madras*, but in most instances this statutory impurity is understood to mean that the spittle and urine of a gentile convey impurity (Zav. 5:7, Mak. 6:6, Shek. 8:1, Toh. 5:8, Tosef., Toh. 5:4, Mak. 2:3, Toh. 5:2, and Tosef., Mik. 6:7). Some scholars believe that the rabbinic decree of statutory impurity for gentiles was a political decree intended to segregate the Jews from Romans and neighboring peoples during the time of the war. However, the mild impurity contracted from the spittle or urine of a gentile would not have been a major inconvenience and would not have prevented interaction between Jews and Romans (as evidenced by many laws regulating everyday transactions with gentiles). The rabbinic position seems lenient when compared with the sectarian rule of bathing after any contact with an alien.

Impurity of Hands. The idea that hands should be washed before contacting sacred items is probably quite ancient. Rabbinic tradition attributes a decree concerning the impurity of hands to Shammai and Hillel (early first century C.E.) (TJ Shab. 1:7, 3d; Shab. 14b). Despite the Babylonian Talmud's assertion that Hillel and Shammai were merely extending to *terumah* an older Solomonic regulation requiring hand washing before contact with holy things (in view of the fact that "hands are fidgety" and may be presumed to contact impure things; Shab. 15a), the nature and extent of this decree is not clear. Tannaitic sources do refer to hand washing before eating *terumah* (Sifrei Num. 116; Bik. 2:1). However, in Second Temple times, some Jews strove not only to maintain the purity of priestly food, but also to eat their own ordinary food in a state of purity. Josephus (Wars 2:129) relates that the Essenes were wont to bathe before their meal. In non-sectarian circles hand washing was more common. New Testament sources attest to the Pharisaic practice of washing hands before consuming ordinary food (Mark 7; Luke 11:38; washing the hands before a meal is referred to in Matthew 15:2 as a "tradition of the elders."). In some tannaitic traditions, the impurity of hands is assumed even for ordinary meals (Ḥag. 2:5, cf. TJ Ḥag. 78b, Ḥag. 18b). That Bet Shammai and Bet Hillel are said to have debated the timing of the hand washing rite at ordinary meals, suggests the ritual was accepted practice in the first century C.E. (Ber. 8:2; but cf. Tosef., *ibid.* 6 (5):3, and S. Lieberman, *Tosefta ki-Feshutah, ad loc.*). However, other tannaitic sources indicate that only the pious considered hands to be impure, even for ordinary food. Thus, one who eats ordinary food in purity is called a *ḥaber*, and one who does not is called an *am ha-areẓ* (Tosef., Av. Zar. 3 (6):10; Tosef., Dem. 2:2–3; Tosef., Dem. 2:20–22). By eating ordinary food in the same state of purity required for priests who were eating sacred food, Pharisees and *ḥaverim* aspired to a higher level of holiness. Pouring water over the hands before a meal may reflect the influence of a similar ancient Greek custom (Yad 1:2 and Tosef., Yad 1:12).

In a number of cases, the sages decreed a statutory ritual impurity upon the hands as a protective measure. For example, it was decreed that all sacred writings and *tefillin* with straps render hands impure (Yad, Avot ha-Tumah., 3:3–5: and see Kel. 15:6). The desire to discourage (mis)handling and storage near food are cited as reasons. Of the sacred writings, "their importance is the cause of their impurity, that they not be made into covers for animals" (Tosef., Yad 2:19 and cf. Shab. 14a). To prevent the loss of sacred meats, it was said that hands do not render impure in the Temple (Pes. 19a–b, Rashi; Yad, Avot ha-Tumah 8:6).

THE CONSEQUENCES OF IMPURITY. The most immediate and direct consequences of ritual impurity attach to the realm of the sacred. According to rabbinic sources, priests in Second Temple times were especially strict about the purity of the Temple. If a dead reptile was found in the Temple "a priest may remove it with his girdle even on the Sabbath" (Er. 10:15). "If a priest served [at the altar] in a state of impurity, his fellow priests did not bring him to the *bet din*, but the young priests took him outside the Temple court and split open his brain with clubs" (Sanh. 9:6; cf. Tosef., Kel. 1:6). In Jerusalem itself, precautions were taken to guard the hallowed things and the priests from impurity. No burials were permitted there, and corpses were not allowed to be kept in the city overnight. In conformity with this view, the biblical requirement to send severe impurity bearers out of the camp was understood as meaning the area of Jerusalem and the Temple Mount (Kel. 1:8–9; Sifre Num.1). The *mezora* was sent out of walled cities only (Kel. 1:7) but "they may go throughout the land" (Sifrei Zuta to 5:2). Impure persons were expected to take care not to impart impurity to the people of Jerusalem and lenient rulings made it possible for pilgrims to maintain purity during pilgrimage festivals (e.g., Shek. 8:1: "any spittle found in Jerusalem may be deemed free from impurity excepting what is found in the upper market" frequented by gentiles). The verse (Lev. 11:8): "of their flesh you shall not eat, and their carcasses you shall not touch; they are impure for you," directed to all Israel, is explained as referring only to the time of the festivals (Sifra, Shemini 4, 9; RH 16b), "since they must be ready to enter the Temple and eat of the hallowed things" (Yad, Tumat Okhelim 16:10).

Nevertheless, there is considerable evidence that impurity was deemed to have consequences outside the Temple context, though to what extent is unclear. Certainly, the *ḥaver* was obliged to undertake "to eat [even] common food in purity" (Tosef., Dem. 2:2). This *halakhah* might be regarded as merely the custom of individuals who were strict with themselves, something like the report of Johanan b. Gudgada that "he always ate [even common food] in accordance with the purity of hallowed things" (Ḥag. 2:7; cf. Tosef., Ḥag. 3:2–3). On the other hand, some sources teach the *halakhot* of common food purity with no differentiation between *ḥaverim* and others (Ḥul. 2:5; Tosef., Ber. 6:2–4; et al.). The prohibition against causing impurity to common food in the land of Israel is also taught as incumbent upon all people (Tosef., Maksh. 3:7). In addition to their impact on the eating of common food, certain impurities had an effect in regard to prayer (Ber. 3:4–6; Ter. 1:6). The prohibition against praying where there is corpse impurity is inferred from the *baraita*, "If he were busy with a dead body in a grave and the time of reading the *Shema* arrives, he removes himself to a pure place, puts on *tefillin*, reads the *Shema* and says his prayers" (TJ, Bet. 2:3, 4c). The practice of bathing after sexual intercourse and before Torah study mentioned in some rabbinic sources has been mistakenly interpreted as a ritual purity requirement. However, there is no blanket prohibition against studying Torah in a state of ritual impurity. Tosef., Ber. 2:13 states explicitly that severe impurity bearers are not prohibited from Torah study: "males and females who have an abnormal genital discharge, menstruants, and women after childbirth are permitted to read the Torah, and to study Mishnah and Midrash, *halakhot* and *aggadot*, but men who have had an emission of semen may not" (Tosef., Ber. 2:13). The prohibition of the semen emitter and the Palestinian practice of immersion after sex and before Torah study is linked to a perceived incompatibility between sexuality and holy activity (TJ, Ber. 3:4, 6c; Ber. 22a states that the requirement of immersion is to ensure that scholars do not frequent their wives like roosters). Some sages in the land of Israel were so meticulously careful to comply with bathing before their learning, that Ḥanina, who came from Babylon, ridiculed them with the title "morning bathers" (TJ, *ibid.*). In the Babylonian Talmud the practice of immersion after sex and before Torah study was abolished. During the geonic era it was considered a point of difference between Ereẓ Israel and Babylon (M. Margalioth, *Ha-Ḥillukim she-Bein Anshei Mizraḥ u-Venei Ereẓ Yisrael*, pp. 78 and 108ff.). The view attributed to R. Judah ben Bathyra, that "the words of Torah are not susceptible to impurity," (b. Ber 21b) was eventually normative in this respect. As regards menstruants, however, more restrictive views prevailed and in a later period some local customs included prohibitions against menstruants praying or entering the synagogue or being present as blessings are recited (see the late source *Baraita de-Messekhta Niddah*, ed. Horowitz pp. 3 and 17; and see **Baraita de-Niddah*; **Niddah*). Such extensions of the laws of impurity and purity liken prayers to Temple sacrifices, and extend the sanctity of the priesthood to all Israel.

Despite such extensions, some maintain that the laws of impurity and purity have no relevant consequences of any substance except for priests and the affairs of the Temple and its hallowed things. This view has been summarized in the words of Maimonides (Yad, Tumat Okhelim 16:8–9): "Whatever is written in the Torah and in traditional teaching about the laws relating to things impure and pure is relevant only to the Temple and its hallowed things and to heave-offering and second tithe, for it warns those impure against entering the Temple or eating anything hallowed, or heave-offering, or tithe. However, no such prohibition applies to common food, and it is permitted to eat common food that is impure and to drink impure liquids.... Similarly, it is permissible to touch things that are impure and to incur impurity from them, for Scripture warns none but the sons of Aaron and the Nazirite against incurring impurity from a corpse, thereby implying that for all others it is permissible, and that even for priests and Nazirites it is permissible to incur impurity from other impure things, but not from a corpse."

REASONS FOR PURITY AND IMPURITY. There is not a great deal of discussion of the reasons for purity and impurity in rabbinic literature. It is certain that the rabbis did not regard the impurities as infectious diseases or the laws of purification as quasi-hygienic principles. In a late narrative Johanan b. Zakkai is described as denying any efficacy to impurity and rites of purification: "By your lives! The corpse does not cause impurity, nor do the waters purify, but it is a decree of the Supreme King of Kings" (*Pesikta de-Rav Kahana* 40a–b). Ritual purity is a religious ideal. It is said of the patriarch Abraham that he ate common food in purity (BM 87a). In describing the ideal era of the time of King Hezekiah, Isaac Nappaḥa says, "Search was made ... from Gabbat to Antipris and no boy or girl, man or woman, was found who was not well versed in the laws of impurity and purity" (Sanh. 94b). In Avodah Zarah 20b, purity is listed as one of the grades on the path to holiness.

Impurity and Purity at the Present Time.

The cessation of most of the laws of impurity and purity in the contemporary era is the consequence of a prolonged process, which is only in part connected with the destruction of the Temple. Already in rabbinic times, the laws of *ẓara'at* in houses was weakening and even in the laws concerning the *meẓora* a clear trend to limit and lighten their impact is noticeable (Neg. 3:1–2; 5:1; "Any condition of doubt in leprous signs is deemed pure," in opposition to the rule: "Doubts in Torah law are decided stringently"; cf. 7:4). The law that when a *meẓora* enters the synagogue "they must make for him a partition ten handbreadths high and four cubits wide; he must enter first and come out last" (Neg. 13:12 and cf. Tosef., Neg. 8:2) is not directed especially to the era of the Temple. The laws of scale-disease were not in force in Babylon in the geonic era, as can be inferred from the summary of an unknown *gaon*: "Nowadays if a disciple or scholar is *meẓora*, he is not thrust forth from the synagogue or *bet midrash*, for there is not now the law that thy camp shall be holy" (*Sha'arei Teshuvah*, no. 176 and S. Assaf (ed.), *Teshuvot ha-Ge'onim* (1942), 123). Although immersion after sex and before learning was abolished in the Babylonian Talmud, the *geonim* in Babylon, under the influence of Muslims who were accustomed to bathe before every prayer, were also strict "because of cleanliness and in order to sanctify the Name before gentiles" (*Sha'arei Teshuvah*, no. 298). It became "the common custom in Shinar and Spain that none from whom semen issues prays before washing his whole body in water" (Yad, Tefillah 4:6). The custom was not followed in Christian Europe "and all Jews among the uncircumcised are not accustomed to wash" (*Teshuvot ha-Ramban* (Leipzig, 1859), no. 140; see Tur, OḤ 88 and 613). Some were strict, however, even in those countries, and required bathing at least for the reader and the priest reciting the priestly blessing (Resp., Maharam of Rothenberg (Berlin, 1841), 137). The ḥasidim reintroduced the duty of bathing for one from whom semen issues (see *Ablution). For various reasons, including the biblical prohibition against intercourse with a menstruant, halakhic prohibitions and practices designed to preserve men from contracting ritual impurity from their menstruating and post-partum wives, have continued in traditional Judaism (see **Niddah*). This is the only element of the biblical ritual purity system that retains serious contemporary relevance.

Purification from corpse impurity was possible as long as purification-offering water prepared from the ashes of a red heifer was available. Mishnah Parah 3:5 claims that some red heifers were burnt in Second Temple times. Some of the ashes of the red heifer were distributed to each of the priestly courses (*mishmarot* – Par. 3:11) and Israelites were sprinkled with it (Tosef., *ibid.*, 3:14). In Galilee there may have been purification-offering water even in the time of the *amoraim* (Nid. 6b; see also TJ Ber. 6, 10a). With the cessation of purification-offering water, all Israel are assumed to have incurred corpse impurity. Priests are forbidden to contract corpse impurity even today (Sh. Ar., YD 369), but even so they are not pure, since they cannot guard against impurity from a metal utensil overshadowed by a corpse (see comm. Samson of Sens to Ḥul. 4:8). These facts have consequences also in the laws of *terumah* and *ḥallah* (*ibid.*; Sh. Ar., YD 322:4), and are the reason for the prohibition against entering the Temple area even nowadays (*Yere'im ha-Shalem*, no. 297; *Magen Avraham* to Sh. Ar., OḤ 561:2).

BIBLIOGRAPHY: H. Harrington, *The Impurity System of Qumran and the Rabbis* (1993); C. Hayes, *Gentile Impurities and Jewish Identities* (2002); J. Klawans, "Notions of Gentile Impurity in Ancient Judaism," in: *AJS Review,* 20:2 (1995), 285–312; idem, *Impurity and Sin in Ancient Judaism* (2000); J. Milgrom, *Leviticus 1–16*, Anchor Bible Series (1991); idem, *Leviticus 17–22*, Anchor Bible Series (2000). D. Wright, *The Disposal of Impurity* (1987).

[Christine Hayes (2nd ed.)]

PUT (Heb. פּוּט), one of the sons of Ham, son of Noah. In the Table of Nations, Put is mentioned, along with Cush, Egypt, and Canaan (Gen. 10:6; I Chron. 1:8). However, whereas the genealogies of the other three are recorded, nothing further is said of Put. However, the people is mentioned several times in the prophetic literature. Referring to the impending conquest of Egypt by Nebuchadnezzar, Jeremiah mentions the "men of Cush and Put, who handle the shield, men of Lud, skilled in handling the bow" (Jer. 46:9). Ezekiel mentions Put along with Persia and Lud as serving in the army of Tyre (Ezek. 27:10). In his prophecy against Egypt, he cites Put, together with Ethiopia (Cush), Lud, Arabia, and Cub (Gr. Libya), as doomed to fall by the sword (Ezek. 30:5), and in his oracle against Gog, he again places Put alongside Persia and Cush (Ezek. 38:5). From the passages cited the exact identity of Put cannot be decided, but an African location is strongly suggested. In all the prophetic passages cited above, except Ezekiel 30:5, the Septuagint translates Put by "Libyans." It would seem then that Put was identified with Libya or possibly some neighboring area such as Cyrene.

BIBLIOGRAPHY: A. Reuveni, *Shem, Ḥam ve-Yafet* (1932), 85–87; U. Cassuto, *A Commentary on the Book of Genesis* (1964), 200ff.

[Shlomo Balter]

PUTIEL (Heb. פּוּטִיאֵל). The name Putiel occurs only once in the Bible (Ex. 6:25), where it is stated that Eleazar the son of Aaron married one of Putiel's daughters, and that their son was Phinehas.

The rabbis identify Putiel with Jethro and give two homiletical interpretations of the name, one praiseworthy and the other derogatory. The first one, connected with the view that he became converted to Judaism, is that he "emancipated" (*patar*) himself from idolatry (Mekh., Amalek 1) and the other that he fattened (*pittem*) calves for the purpose of idolatrous worship. The same passage, however, also makes it refer to Joseph, who overcame (*pitpet*) his passion, and concludes that Phinehas was descended from both (Sot. 43a). It has been suggested that Putiel is in fact a Hebraized version of Poti-Phera, the "priest of On" whose daughter Joseph married (Gen. 41:45), "ph" being the definite article in Egyptian, and Ra the Egyptian god.

BIBLIOGRAPHY: Kohut, Arukh, 6 (1926^2), 310f.

PUTNAM, HILARY (1926–), U.S. scholar. Born in Chicago, Putnam is the son of Samuel Putnam, a writer and translator. Hilary Putnam received his bachelor's degree from the University of Pennsylvania in 1948 and his Ph.D. from the University of California at Los Angeles in 1951. He was a Rockefeller Foundation research fellow in 1951 and 1952.

From 1952 to 1953 Putnam taught at Northwestern University as an instructor in philosophy, then joined the faculty of Princeton University as an assistant professor, becoming an associate professor in 1960. From 1961 to 1965 he was a professor of philosophy at the Massachusetts Institute of Technology.

In 1965 Putnam became a professor of philosophy at Harvard. He was named the Walter Beverly Pearson Professor of Modern Mathematics and Mathematical Logic in 1976. In 1995 he was appointed the Cogan University Professor in the department of philosophy; he became professor emeritus in 2000.

Putnam wrote extensively on the philosophy of mathematics, the philosophy of natural science, the philosophy of language, and the philosophy of mind. His many notable works include *Philosophy of Logic* (1971); *Meaning and the Moral Sciences* (1978); *The Many Faces of Realism* (1987); and

Realism with a Human Face (1990). In the philosophy of mathematics, Putnam advanced the view that mathematics does not use only strictly logical proofs but "quasi-empirical" methods, and he contributed to the resolution of Hilbert's tenth problem. In the philosophy of language, Putnam addressed external, as opposed to inherent, meaning. His work on the philosophy of mind has evolved through an early embrace of functionalism, which he later recanted.

Putnam was actively involved in the antiwar movement of the Vietnam era and for a time was a member of the Progressive Labor Party (PLP), a left-wing political organization. He received numerous awards and honors. He was a fellow of the National Science Foundation (1957 and 1968–69), a Guggenheim Foundation fellow (1960), and a fellow of the National Endowment for the Humanities (1975–76). He was a fellow of the American Academy of Arts and Sciences and a president of the American Philosophical Association.

[Dorothy Bauhoff (2nd ed.)]

PUTTERMAN, DAVID (1903–1979), U.S. cantor. Born in New York, Putterman was one of the first American-trained cantors to establish a reputation for himself. In his youth he sang and studied with the leading cantors of the time, including Zeidel Rovner (Jacob Samuel *Morogowsky) and Josef *Rosenblatt. From 1921 to 1933 he was cantor of Temple Israel, Washington Heights, New York, and then moved to the Park Avenue Synagogue. He had a pleasing tenor voice and was a popular soloist in concert and radio programs. Putterman strove to interest Jewish and non-Jewish composers alike in composing for the synagogue, and commissioned a series of "Services of Contemporary Liturgical Music." An anthology of 38 of these works, *Synagogue Music by Contemporary Composers*, was published in 1951 and includes compositions by Leonard *Bernstein, Darius *Milhaud, Morton Gould, Kurt *Weill, Mario *Castelnuovo-Tedesco, Alexander Gretchaninoff, Roy Harris, and the African-American composer William Grant Still. Putterman was also instrumental in the establishment of the Cantors Assembly of the United Synagogue of America and the Cantors Institute of the Jewish Theological Seminary.

[David M.L. Olivestone]

In 1979 the Cantor's Assembly of New York issued *Mizmor le-David*, containing compositions by Putterman which he sang during his 43 years (1933–76) as cantor to the Park Avenue synagogue.

[Akiva Zimmerman]

BIBLIOGRAPHY: Jewish Ministers Cantors' Association of America, *Di Geshikhte fun Khazzones* (1924), 165; *Cantors' Voice* (Dec. 1952), 7; I. Rabinovitch, *Of Jewish Music* (1952), 306–7.

PUY (-EN-VELAY), LE, town in the department of Haute-Loire, S. France. The Jewish quarter of Le Puy, on the site of the Rue de la Juiverie, is first mentioned in 1212. There is no other information available on the early medieval community there. Following the return of the Jews to the kingdom in 1315 after the expulsion of 1306, a Jew of Le Puy was accused in 1320 of having killed a chorister of the church of Notre-Dame, the murder having been revealed by a miracle. The accused was murdered by the populace, and the other Jews were banished from Le Puy. In 1325 Charles IV granted the choristers of Le Puy the jurisdiction over any Jew found within the town.

BIBLIOGRAPHY: Theodore, *Histoire angél... du Puy* (1693), 316ff.; M. Schwab, in: REJ, 33 (1896), 277–82; A. Jacotin, *Nomenclature historique... des rues du Puy* (1928).

[Bernhard Blumenkranz]

PYE (Mendez), JAEL HENRIETTA (c. 1737–1782), English writer. Apparently the daughter of a wealthy London merchant named Mendez and the niece of Moses *Mendez (c. 1690–1788), the playwright and poet, in 1762 she married John Neil Campbell, a barrister, and, in 1766, Robert Hampden Pye, the son of a member of Parliament and the brother of the Poet Laureate Henry Pye. Her anonymous book of verse, *Poems. By a Lady* (1767), and her novel, *Theodosius and Arabella* (1768), are the earliest recorded contributions of a Jewess to English literature. She lived much of her life in France, where she died.

BIBLIOGRAPHY: ODNB online; Katz, England, 255.

[William D. Rubinstein (2nd ed.)]

PYRRHUS, DIDACUS (originally **Diogo Pires**; also known as **Pyrrhus Lusitanus** and, from his birthplace, Évora, as **Flavius Eborensis**; 1517–1607), Portuguese Marrano poet. He is not to be confused with the more famous Diogo Pires (Solomon *Molcho) who was martyred in 1532. In order to escape the Portuguese Inquisition, Pyrrhus left Évora for Salamanca in Spain, where he began to study medicine in 1535 and eventually qualified as a physician. His movements during the following two decades are relatively confused, but he is known to have fled to Antwerp in about 1540. From there he made his way to Venice and Ferrara, and then lived for a time in Ancona; but the persecution of the local Marrano colony in 1555 obliged him to take refuge in the Dalmatian town of Ragusa (Dubrovnik), where he formally reverted to Judaism under the name of Isaiah Kohen. Pyrrhus, who had first achieved literary distinction with his volume of *Carmina* (Ferrara, 1545), spent about 50 years of his life in Ragusa, then a center of Neo-Latin poetic culture, and was mainly active as a teacher and writer. According to some authorities, Pyrrhus made a pilgrimage to Jerusalem in his last years before returning to Ragusa, where he died.

He published two humanistic works in praise of his new home: *De illustribus familiis quae hodie Rhacusae exstant* (Venice, 1582; 1709^2) and *Excerpta ex Flavii Jacob Eborensis Carminibus ad Historiam Sacram Rachusinam aliquo modo facientibus* (1596); *Cato Minor* (Venice, 1592), moralizing verse for children; and *Jacobi Flavii Eborensis seu Didaci Pirrhi Lusitani Elegiarum Libri Tres...* (Venice, 1596). Pyrrhus ranks among the outstanding Neo-Latin poets of the Renaissance. One of his rare works of Jewish interest was a Latin elegy composed for the tombstone of *Amatus Lusitanus in Salonika, but unfortunately no trace of it survives.

BIBLIOGRAPHY: A. Ribeiro, *Portugueses das sete partidas* (1950), 223–85; M. Gruenwald and A. Casnacich, *Didacco Pyrrho… ein Lebensbild* (1883); JE, s.v. *Flavius Eborensis*; Roth, England, 137–8; Roth, Marranos, 298; idem, *Jewish Contribution to Civilization* (1940), 113; (1956^{3}), 82n.; idem, *Jews in the Renaissance* (1959), 109–10.

°**PYTHAGORAS** (late sixth century B.C.E. (?)), Greek philosopher. Pythagoras founded a religious community incorporating strict rules of ritual and ethical purity. This perhaps led ancient Jewish, Christian, and pagan authors to claim that he owed his theories to the Jews and other Eastern peoples with whose teachers he had studied during his travels. The idea seems to have originated with *Hermippus of Smyrna (late third century B.C.E.), who only referred to the Jews. The idea that Greek philosophers were indebted to the East for their views was popular in Hellenistic times. Conversely, it has been suggested by Levy that the legends surrounding the life of Pythagoras influenced the account of Moses' life found in *Philo and *Josephus. Influence of the Pythagorean brotherhood on the Essenes and on the Dead Sea Sect have likewise been postulated. The five-pointed star found on some Pythagorean coins and in some Jewish inscriptions probably derives from a common Babylonian source.

BIBLIOGRAPHY: I. Levy, *Recherches sur les sources de la légende de Pythagore de Grèce en Palestine* (1927); C.J. de Vogel, *Pythagoras and Early Pythagoreanism* (1966), 28–51.

[Daniel E. Gershenson]

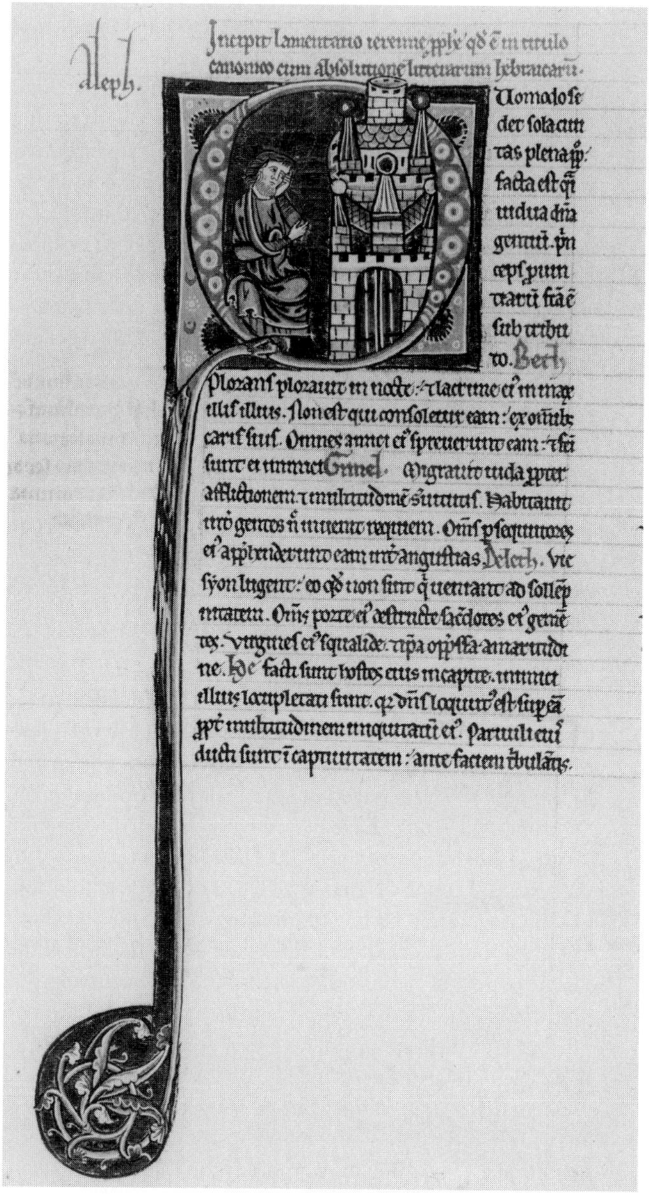

Initial letter "Q" for Quomodo *at the beginning of Lamentations, from a Latin Bible, N. France, c. 1200. Within the letter is Jeremiah mourning Jerusalem. Amiens, Bibliothèque Nationale, Ms. 21, fol. 132v. Photo Caron, Amiens.*

QA-QU

QAL'AT ḤAMMĀD, city formerly situated S.W. of *Constantine, *Algeria. It was founded in 1007 by a branch of the *Zirids (Banu Zīrī) who reigned in *Kairouan. Its population included Christians, Jews, and members of the Jerāwa tribe, *Berbers formerly converted to Judaism. Qal'at Ḥammād received the majority of the inhabitants of Kairouan when that city was sacked by Arab nomads in 1057, and it inherited the importance of the former metropolis. As capital of a vast kingdom in the 11th century, it possessed a Jewish elite among whom was Solomon ha-Dayyan b. Formash. Abraham *Ibn Daud knew of Solomon and also reported the tradition which stated that Isaac *Alfasi was born in Qal'at Ḥammād. The city was completely destroyed by the *Almohads in 1152.

BIBLIOGRAPHY: Neubauer, Chronicles, 1 (1887), 73, 75; L.M.E. de Beylie, *La Kalaa des Beni-Hammad* (1909); Poznański, in: REJ, 58 (1909), 297–8; Hirschberg, Afrikah, 1 (1965), 167, 259.

[David Corcos]

QAṢR IBN HUBAYRAH (Kasr ibn Hubayrah), town that was situated south of the ruins of ancient Babylon, west of the Euphrates (i.e., then its eastern arm, which was known as the Sura River). Qaṣr ibn Hubayrah was founded by Omar ibn Hubayrah, the last governor of Babylonia appointed by the

*Ummayyad caliphs; the town bears his name. A report by the Arab geographer al-Muqaddasī, dating from the end of the tenth century, states that Qaṣr ibn Hubayrah had a large Jewish community. According to *Nathan ha-Bavli, it was the original home of *David b. Zakkai, the *exilarch who had a bitter controversy with R. *Saadiah Gaon. At the beginning of the 12th century, when the town of *Ḥilla was founded and became a transit point for the district's caravans and its trade center, Qaṣr ibn Hubayrah lost its importance and eventually fell into a state of ruin.

BIBLIOGRAPHY: G. Le Strange, *The Lands of the Eastern Caliphate* (1930), 70f., 83.

[Eliyahu Ashtor]

QAYNUQĀʿ, BANŪ, a large, strong Jewish tribe in *Medina (pre-Islamic Yathrib) that became famous in Islamic historiography through its conflict with *Muhammad in the battle of Buʿāth several years before Muhammad's arrival at Medina. The Qaynuqāʿ fought against the other two large Jewish tribes of Medina, *Naḍīr and *Qurayẓa. Before *Islam the market of the Qaynuqāʿ was the central market of Medina. But when Muhammad attempted to gain a foothold there, it was the Naḍīr leader *Kaʿb ibn al-Ashraf who prevented him from doing so. The Qaynuqāʿ were goldsmiths; their *bayt al-midrās* was located in their town, al-Quff. They owned at least two fortresses as well as an unknown number of date orchards (*amwāl*, sing. *māl*) that were seized by Muhammad. Unlike the Naḍīr and Qurayẓaʿ, the Qaynuqāʿ did not own large agricultural lands.

The Qaynuqāʿ lived in the *Sāfil*a of Medina or Lower Medina, close to Muhammad's first territorial basis. Consequently, when the conflict between Muhammad and the Jews began, they found themselves in a precarious situation, the more so since they were allied with the strong Arab tribe of Khazraj that was far more loyal to Muhammad than the other large Arab tribe, the Aws. The sources provide a variety of reasons for Muhammad's attack on the Qaynuqāʿ where one good reason would have sufficed. But one has to bear in mind that Muhammad's biography is not only a history book and that for its compilers justification of Muhammad's actions was at least as important as historical fact. The fall of the Qaynuqāʿ is connected to internal Arab tribal politics. Qaynuqāʿ's allies from among the Khazraj were the ʿAwf ibn al-Khazraj, who were divided into two subsections led respectively by ʿAbdallāh ibn Ubayy and ʿUbāda ibn al-Ṣāmit. ʿAbdallāh, arguably the strongest Arab leader in Medina before Muhammad's arrival, was steadfast in his support of his Jewish allies, reportedly reasoning that he feared that the Jews might gain the upper hand over Muhammad. ʿUbāda, who was younger, repudiated his alliance with them. This left them exposed to Muhammad's attack, because internecine fighting within the ʿAwf over the alliance with the Qaynuqāʿ would have been inconceivable. However, Ibn Ubayy managed to prevent the execution of the Qaynuqāʿ men, literally compelling Muhammad to let them go into exile. The many weapons found in their fortress included some fine items that are often listed among Muhammad's own weapons. One of them was a coat of mail called al-Sughdiyya or "the Soghdian" that had belonged to ʿUkayr al-Qaynuqāʿī; allegedly it had been carried by David when he killed Goliath. With regard to the expulsion of the Qaynuqāʿ, Muhammad's biography is probably not nuanced enough, since there are indications that a significant number of them lived in Medina after the supposed expulsion of the whole tribe. One assumes that part of the Qaynuqāʿ, perhaps even a whole subsection, was not expelled. Jews from the Qaynuqāʿ participated in Muhammad's expedition against Khaybar in 7/628, receiving a modest share of the spoils. In due course they converted to Islam, although some of them were branded hypocrites who had embraced Islam outwardly only.

BIBLIOGRAPHY: The chapter on the siege of the Qaynuqāʿ in Muhammad's Arabic biographies; A.J. Wensinck, "Ḳainuḳā," in: EIS, 4, 645b–646a; idem and R. Paret, "Ḳainuḳā," in: EIS², 4, 824a–b; M. Lecker, *The "Constitution of Medina": Muhammad's First Legal Document* (2004), index; idem, *Jews and Arabs in Pre- and Early Islamic Arabia* (1998), index.

[Michael Lecker (2nd ed.)]

QAZZĀZ, MANASSEH BEN ABRAHAM IBN (AL-) (tenth century, also known as **Menashe b. al-Farrar**), Jewish silk trader and governor in *Damascus from 990 to 996. In the year 980 he engaged in administering Yaʿqūb ibn Killis' property. He must have played a leading part in the military administration of Syria. Al-Qazzāz was appointed by the *Fatimid caliph al-ʿAzīz (975–96) as deputy to the Coptic Christian vizier ʿĪsā b. Nestorius (995–96), whose seat was in Cairo. These two high officials made use of their positions for the benefit of their coreligionists. The discontented Muslims complained to the caliph, and he imprisoned the two officials and their subordinates. After some time the Christian vizier was reinstated. The fate of al-Qazzāz is unknown. A poem discovered in the *genizah* praises his son, ʿAdiya (d. after 1037). It describes the exalted position of Manasseh and his activities, including his support of the Palestinian *geonim* and the exilarchs. Another source mentions that he was one of the opponents of the Jerusalem *gaon* R. *Salomon b. Judah. Al-Qazzāz' son ʿAdiya, who also held an important position in Damascus and protected his coreligionists, was employed as government secretary (*kātib*). ʿAdiya's sons Samuel and Ishmael held the position of **nagid*.

BIBLIOGRAPHY: Mann, Egypt, 1 (1920), 19–23; 2 (1922), 11–13; idem, in: HUCA, 3 (1926), 257–8; Fischel, Islam, 62–64; S. Assaf and L.A. Mayer (eds.), *Sefer ha-Yishuv*, 2 (1944), 51, 73–75; Ashtor, Toledot, 1 (1944), 29. **ADD. BIBLIOGRAPHY:** S.D. Goitein, *A Mediterranean Society*, II (1971), 354.

[Abraham David]

QITTNER, ZSIGMOND (1857–1918), Hungarian architect. After studying in Munich and traveling in three continents he settled down in Budapest. In collaboration with L. and J. *Vago he designed the Gresham Palace for an English insurance company (1907), a landmark in Budapest and an example of early Secessionism. Among other public appointments he was also president of the Association of Hungarian Architects.

[Eva Kondor]

°**QUADRATUS, UMMIDIUS CAIUS**, Roman governor of *Syria (50–60 C.E.). During the administration of Quadratus a series of disturbances erupted between the Jews and Samaritans of Palestine. *Cumanus, the Roman procurator of Judea at the time, was unable to cope with the situation, and the leaders of both camps presented their arguments before the Syrian governor at Tyre. Whereas the Samaritans accused Jewish bands of sacking their villages and thus taking the law into their own hands, the Jewish delegation, including the high priest J *Jonathan b. Anan, alleged that Cumanus had been bribed by the Samaritans to ignore the murder of Jewish pilgrims on their way to Jerusalem through Samaritan territory. According to Josephus, Quadratus at first deferred judgment. He subsequently proceeded to Caesarea where he crucified the prisoners taken by Cumanus from both sides. From there he went to Lydda and granted a second hearing to the Samaritan case. As a result of this, several Jews, including Doetus, were executed for their part in the rising. Numerous Samaritan and Jewish dignitaries, among them the high priest *Ananias, were ordered to appear before the emperor Claudius and account for their actions. Quadratus then left for Jerusalem, found the people peaceably celebrating Passover and returned to Antioch (52 C.E.).

BIBLIOGRAPHY: A. Schalit, *Namenwoerterbuch zu Flavius Josephus* (1968), 39, s.v. 4 Δοσίθεος.

[Isaiah Gafni]

QUAIL (Heb. שְׂלָו), the bird *Coturnix coturnix*, the smallest of the pheasant family. The quail is approximately seven inches (about 18 cm.) long and weighs some 3½ ounces (100 gr.). The color of its plumage is like that of the house sparrow, a fact indicated in the Talmud, which also states that the quail is one of four species of pheasant (the other being the *pheasant and two species of *partridge), that its flesh is very fatty and its taste inferior to that of the other species (Yoma 75b). Large flocks of quail provided food for the Israelites in the wilderness having been blown across the sea by a wind which "let them fall by the camp, about a day's journey on this side, and a day's journey on the other side, round about the camp, and about two cubits above the face of the earth." Some were eaten fresh, the rest being spread out on the ground to dry in the sun (Num. 11:31–33; cf. Ex. 16:3–4; Ps. 78:26–27; 105:40). According to Josephus, flocks of quails from the Arabian gulf "came flying over this stretch of sea, and, alike wearied by their flight and withal accustomed more than other birds to skim the ground, settled in the Hebrews' camp" (Ant. 3:25). This description is factual. The phenomenon repeats itself in spring and in fall when large flocks of quail pass over the Mediterranean Sea on their migration from northern countries to Africa in fall and on their return in spring. Weary from their lengthy flight, the flocks settle on the southern coast of the country (between Gaza and El-Arish), to be caught in nets spread out before they settle, into which they fall exhausted. The local population eats them, selling most of them in city markets. Until the 1930s and 1940s millions of quails were caught in this way at these seasons but their number has since decreased. In addition to the migratory flocks of quails, some of them breed in cereal and fodder fields in various regions of Israel, building their nests on the ground. Their grayish-brown color conceals them from human sight and only when approached do they rise in noisy flight, coming to rest in a nearby field, since their comparatively short wings make it difficult for them to fly high.

BIBLIOGRAPHY: Lewysohn, Zool, 210f., no. 260; F.S. Bodenheimer, *Animal and Man in Bible Lands* (1960), 59; J. Feiks, *Animal World of the Bible* (1962), 56.

[Jehuda Feliks]

°**QUARESMIUS, FRANCISCUS**, a 17th-century Franciscan friar. Quaresmius was born at Lodi, Italy, and from 1619 to 1626 was custodian and apostolic commissary for the Holy Land. He later served as the general procurator of the Franciscan Order and from 1637 as custodian of St. Angelo, Milano.

He was the author of two folio volumes *Elucidatio Terrae Sanctae historica, theologica et moralis* (1639) which contain the most complete survey of the remains and legends of the Holy Land as accepted in Catholic circles. Quaresmius painstakingly copied inscriptions and used the archives of the Mt. Zion monastery for his description of the traditions and monastic institutions of 17th-century Palestine.

[Michael Avi-Yonah]

QUASTEL, JUDAH HIRSCH (1899–1987), British biochemist. Quastel, born in Sheffield, was a fellow of Trinity College, Cambridge (1924). Quastel was a descendant of Solomon Judah Leib *Rapoport (Shir). He was director of research at the Cardiff City Mental Hospital from 1929 to 1941, and director of the soil metabolism unit of the Agricultural Research Council from 1941 to 1947. In 1947 he went to Canada to become professor of biochemistry at McGill University and director of the McGill-Montreal General Hospital Research Institute. In 1966 he became professor of neurochemistry and biochemistry at the University of British Columbia, Vancouver. Quastel is recognized as a founder of modern neurochemistry. His fields of research were the chemistry of enzymes, microorganisms and soils, phytobiochemistry, and the biochemistry of mental disorders. In 1970 he was made a Companion of the Order of Canada (COC), Canada's highest decoration. In 1974 he was the recipient of the Gairdner International Award for Medical Research, and from 1976 to 1977 was visiting professor at the National Hospital for Nervous Diseases, London, and in 1979 was appointed honorary president of the International Congress of Biochemistry, Canada.

He was editor and coauthor of *Neurochemistry* (1955, 1962^2), *Methods in Medical Research*, vols. 8–9 (1960–61), *Metabolic Inhibitors*, vols. 1–2 (1963–64), vol. 3 (1972) and vol. 4 (1973), and coauthor of *The Chemistry of Brain Metabolism in*

Health and Disease (1961). Quastel was a fellow of the British Royal Society and of the Royal Society of Canada, and president of the Canadian Biochemical Society. He was on the Board of Governors of The Hebrew University of Jerusalem from 1950 and honorary secretary of the Canadian Friends of The Hebrew University for 19 years.

[Samuel Aaron Miller]

QUE, the Assyrian (*Quwe*) and biblical Hebrew (קְוֵא, קְוֵה), name of Cilicia, the classical name of the Mediterranean littoral south of the Taurus Mountains in Turkey, from Paphlagonia in the west to the Amanos Mountains in the east. At its eastern end, this littoral broadens into a fertile valley watered by the rivers Pyramus (Ceyhan), Sarus (Seyhan), and Cydnus (Tarsus); this portion was known in classical times as *Cilicia Pedias* or *Campestris*, or simply *Cilicia* proper, to the Egyptians as *Kode* or *Qedi*, to the Hittites as *Kizzuwatna* (*Kizwatna*), and to the neo-Babylonians as *Ḫume*. According to some Egyptologists, the western portion of Cilicia (*Cilicia Aspera* or *Tracheia*) was called *Keftiu* (the biblical Caphtor), though this name is more generally held to designate Crete and perhaps the Aegean coasts as well. The name Cilicia is probably derived from that of the Ḫilakkû people who were the dominant ethnic group in the neo-Assyrian period (as identified by Herodotus). Like much of the surrounding littoral, Que was an important link in the trade routes of the ancient Near East and subject to influences, by land and sea, from all its neighboring cultures (see below).

Political History

The political history of Que begins in about 1650 B.C.E. Kizzuwatna, eastern Que, was clearly under Hittite control, for Ḫattušili I and Muršili I, the outstanding Old Hittite kings, seem to have moved freely down the Pyramus River (Hittite *Purna*) on their campaigns into Syria. However, with the death of Muršili about 1590 B.C.E., the Hurrians asserted themselves in Que, as elsewhere, and Que enjoyed two precarious centuries of independence. The first attested king of Que, Išputaḫšu, son of Paria-watri, is known both from his own inscription and from a Hittite record. His bilingual bull from Tarsus proclaims him a "great king." In the time of Arnuwanda I (c. 1440–1420 B.C.E.), Kizzuwatna even expanded beyond the borders of Que as far east as Uršu and Wašukanni (see *Hittites). However, the increasing power of the new Hittite Empire and the rise of rival Hurrian states, particularly Mitanni, soon put an end to these pretensions.

An interesting light is thrown on western Que at this time. Texts from *Ugarit in the 14th and 13th centuries mention a number of merchants from Ura, the capital of the later Pirindu (see below). One in particular regulated their status at Ugarit, where they apparently enjoyed "extra-territorial" rights under Hittite protection.

Que After Hittite Times

With the collapse of the Hittite Empire under the onslaught of the Sea Peoples (c. 1200 B.C.E.), Que too was plunged into obscurity. It is conceivable that as the remnants of Hittite culture and population sought refuge in northern Syria, those of Kizzuwatna migrated into Anatolia, and that the later name Katpat-uka (Cappadocia) preserves the ancient tribal name of Kizwatna. Que-Cilicia (or better, a part of it) reemerged into history at first through biblical sources. I Kings 10:28 and II Chronicles 1:16 state that royal merchants imported, and perhaps even transported and resold, horses from Que and *Miẓrayim* (= Muṣri, a neighbor of Que) for the king's personal use and for the other northern kings of Aram and of the Hittites (the petty successors of the Hittite Empire; cf. II Kings 7:6). The word *mi-qweh* ("from Que") in these passages was generally misunderstood. From the ninth century on, Que and the other parts of Cilicia are taking part in northern coalitions against Assyria. At this period, Que appears to have been settled by new ethnic elements, known to the Assyrians collectively as Ḫilakkû, though many individuals, including particularly the petty princes who ruled various parts of the area, still bore Luwian names comparable to those of the second millennium. The name of Kizzuwatna survived in the name of the city Kisuatni, but the principal site of Que in this period is Karatepe at Ceyhan (classical Pyramus in the Amanus mountains). According to the monumental bilingual inscriptions of Azittawdda, the contemporary king, in Phoenician and Hittite hieroglyphics, this site was the capital of Awar(a)ku king of the Danunites (Homer's Dannaeans?) of Que (identical with the Urikki king of Que in Tiglath-Pileser III's annals). The growing involvement of Que with Assyria began in Shalmaneser III's time, when the northern coalition was crushed by him. On the other hand, Que did not participate in the southern coalition (see *Karkar where the corrected lines of the inscription are cited). Que's connections with Assyria continued through *Esarhaddon's time down to that of Neriglissar.

BIBLIOGRAPHY: E.D. Forrer, in: *Klio*, 30 (1937), 135–86; H. Goldman, in: R.W. Ehrich (ed.), *Relative Chronologies in Old World Archeology* (1954), 69–82; C.H. Gordon, in: JNES, 17 (1958), 28–31; A. Goetze, in: JCS, 16 (1962), 48; M.J. Mellink, in: *Bibliotheca Orientalis*, 19 (1962), 219–26; H. Tadmor, in: JEJ, 11 (1961), 143–50.

QUEBEC, Canadian province. Quebec is Canada's second largest province and the only one of Canada's provinces with a French-speaking majority. It is also home to Canada's longest-established Jewish community. In 2005 it has a Jewish population of approximately 94,000, making it the province with the second largest Jewish community in the country.

Quebec's first Jewish settlers accompanied the British military during the Seven Years' War when it captured the vast territory from the French in 1760. While Jews concentrated in Montreal, they were also present in other parts of what was then known as Lower Canada. Mainly involved in the fur trade and other commercial activities, as many as one out of 10 merchants in the city were of the Jewish faith. Canadian Jewish communal and organizational life traces its origins to Montreal, where in 1768 the first congregation was established – Shearith Israel – more commonly known as the Spanish and Portuguese Synagogue. By 1830 there were about 100 Jews in Lower Canada.

Because they enjoyed British legal status, Jews benefited from the privileges of the early colonial regime. But their status became the object of debate. The first major test emerged in 1807 with the election of the first Jew, Ezekiel Hart, to the Legislature by the voters of Trois-Rivières. Hart's right to sit was challenged by French Catholics who argued that a Jew could not legitimately take an oath of office which included the words "on the faith of a Christian." As a consequence he was prohibited from assuming office. It took some 25 years but on January 31, 1831, the Bill of Equal Rights was adopted by the Assembly of Lower Canada granting Jews the right to hold public office. Championed by the prominent French Canadian political reformer Louis Joseph Papineau, the Bill was received favorably by England's Parliament and became law within a year. The granting of freedoms to Jews proved to be a catalyst for the freedoms of others within the colony, directly resulting in the abolition of certain religious restrictions for Catholics.

The Jewish population continued to grow slowly and in middle of the 19th century, institutions were established to facilitate the absorption of Jewish settlers. In 1847, the Hebrew Philanthropic Society of Canada was founded and replaced in 1863 by the Young Men's Hebrew Benevolent Society (YMHBS). In the 1870s Jews from Eastern Europe began arriving in Montreal. By 1886 there were some 3,000 Jews in the province and by 1890 the imminent influx of immigrants prompted the established Jewish community to enhance relief efforts. With significant financial aid from Maurice Baron de *Hirsch, the YMHBS was renamed the Baron de Hirsch Institute with a mission to provide services to the new immigrants.

In the early 20th century, Montreal's Jewish leadership was confronted by the challenge of assisting a large influx of East European Jewish immigrants. Between the mid-1890s and the onset of World War I in 1914 the Jewish community of Quebec, largely centered in Montreal, increased nearly fourfold from 7,600 to 30,000. The fast-growing numbers contributed to rising demands for service from Montreal's existing Jewish community. In 1916 the established Jewish leadership consolidated the major Jewish community institutions with the creation of the Montreal Federation of Jewish Philanthropies.

By far the largest percentage of the early 20th century immigration was Yiddish speaking and such individuals often looked to their own **landsmannshaften*, labor and political organizations and congregations, for support rather than to the Federation. The massive immigration of the Yiddish-speaking group not only altered the composition of the Montreal Jewish community but the city on the whole. By the 1920s, Yiddish had become the third most widely used language in Montreal after French and English. Based in Montreal, the country's only daily Yiddish newspaper, the *Keneder Odler* ("Canadian Eagle") was established in 1907 with a growing readership. Conflicts emerged between the predominantly immigrant working-class Yiddish speakers (commonly referred to as "downtowners") and the mainly English-speaking community establishment (referred to as "uptowners").

Given the demographic and political importance of the "downtowners" their views could not be ignored. Within the province's biconfessional structure of Catholics and Protestants, Jews were considered Protestant for educational purposes. This situation resulted in certain limits on the rights of Jewish students in publicly funded schools. In the late 1920s, the downtowners pressed for the creation of a publicly funded Jewish school board alongside the existing Catholic and Protestant school systems, a proposal to which the established Jewish leadership was less favorable. Although the Quebec government submitted a bill in support of the initiative, the negative reaction from the province's Catholic hierarchy prompted the administration to reverse course.

By 1931 the Quebec Jewish population grew to nearly 60,000. The economic depression of the 1930s was characterized by a significant rise in antisemitism in the province. Elements within the Quebec Catholic hierarchy disseminated antisemitism through various publications. Influenced by European fascism Catholic intellectuals such as Lionel Groulx propagated anti-Jewish sentiment. A concrete expression of the antisemitism of the decade was the "*achat chez nous*" ("buy from your own kind") movement which under the guise of promoting French Canadian economic progress urged a boycott of Jewish-owned businesses. Antisemitism was not confined to the French Canadian population, as certain programs at McGill University imposed quotas on the admission of Jewish students.

Despite the challenges of the 1930s, Jewish community leaders aimed to address the problem of badly needed services. The construction of the Jewish General Hospital with a substantial financial contribution from Sir Mortimer B. *Davis ensured quality health care for subsequent generations of Jews. Today the Jewish General is Quebec's most multiethnic hospital.

During the 1930s, conflict within the Jewish community appeared to wane as the growing threat of antisemitism both locally and abroad drew the community together. In 1934 the reactivation of the Canadian Jewish Congress (which first convened in 1919) under the leadership of Montreal's Samuel *Bronfman aimed to reinforce the political influence of the Canadian Jewish community to help address the plight of European Jewry. Locally, the already strained relations between Jews and French Canadians suffered a further setback around the issue of military involvement in World War II. While the Jewish community was committed to greater involvement in the war effort, French Canadians were overwhelmingly opposed to military conscription.

In 1943 the persistent ideological divisions within the Quebec Jewish community surfaced around the election of the Communist candidate, Fred *Rose (Rosenberg), in the federal riding of Cartier. Rose contended that a vote for the Communist Party would support Russia and the war effort and was thus a vote in support of the Canadian war effort. After the war, political divisions within the Jewish community diminished further as the leadership turned its attention to providing relief to East European Jews. Between 1947 and 1952, more than 4,500 Holocaust survivors settled in Montreal and benefited from the assistance of Jewish immigration aid services.

As in the rest of Canada in the aftermath of World War II, there was some reexamination on the part of the Quebec Catholic hierarchy of its attitude towards the Jewish population. Dialogue between Jews and French Catholics were organized through the Council of Christians and Jews. But the dialogue encountered ongoing difficulties and thus initiatives aimed at fostering interfaith and intergroup understanding were spearheaded by Quebec intellectuals, writers, and elected officials. The postwar period and the challenges to which it gave rise proved a source of great cultural inspiration for Quebec Jews. Based in Montreal, such writers as Leonard *Cohen and Mordechai *Richler achieved international status with their literary works. In his popular book *The Apprenticeship of Duddy Kravitz*, Richler offered some insight into the often difficult relationship between Jews and both English and French Canadian communities in Montreal.

During the 1950s through the 1970s, the Quebec Jewish community welcomed yet another wave of immigrants. Jews from Middle Eastern and North African countries, mainly French-speaking, further modified the composition of the community. Aside from their largely Sephardi religious traditions, these Sephardi Jews often brought with them the customs of their particular countries of origin. As well as the adaptation effort put forward by the institutions of the predominantly English-speaking Ashkenazi Jewish population, the process of integration of the Sephardi population also involved the creation of a series of parallel organizations directed at specific needs of the new immigrants.

During the 1960s the Jewish community witnessed a significant expansion of its Jewish day schools, a network that existed since the early 20th century. The provincial authorities did not offer these Jewish schools public status equal to the Catholic and Protestant sectors, but in 1968 the Quebec government did declare that the funding of private Jewish schools was in the public interest and thus assumed the majority of Jewish school costs. Although funding diminished somewhat in the decades that followed, approximately half of the Quebec Jewish student population are today enrolled in Jewish schools. The Jewish schools are characterized by significant internal diversity and differences in affiliation and include Sephardi establishments and a number of educational institutions for the growing ḥasidic segment of the community.

By 1971 the Quebec Jewish population reached more than 120,000 persons, but declined quite sharply thereafter. During the 1970s the Quebec provincial government was more and more challenged by French-Canadian nationalists to protect and expand French language primacy in Quebec. The government responded by passing legislation aimed at making the French language the province's common language. But this was not enough for the growing body of support for Quebec independence amongst the French-speaking majority. Strongly supportive of Quebec's remaining part of Canada, many in the province's Jewish community were uneasy with the rise in nationalism and the threat of separatism. In the growing atmosphere of political uncertainty, the overwhelming number of Jews in Quebec endorsed the federalist Quebec Liberal party. Certainly the Jewish community in Quebec was unprepared for the 1976 provincial electoral victory of the separatist Parti Québécois. Quebec Jewish community leadership had few contacts with the new government and thus tensions occasionally emerged. During the 1980 referendum on sovereignty, the Canadian Jewish Congress (CJC) chose to remain officially neutral though community members voted massively in favor of Canadian unity. During the 1995 referendum on Quebec sovereignty, the CJC chose to officially endorse the federalist position. In both cases the federalist side won, but only by the slimmest of majorities in 1995. Despite the often difficult political climate in Quebec, relations between Jews and increasingly urban, secular, and educated French Quebecers have much improved and although antisemitic expression has not altogether disappeared, it is but a pale shadow of what it was less than a generation ago.

However, political uncertainty has cost the Quebec Jewish community dearly. During the 1970s through the turn of the century, as many as 35,000 Jews left the province, notably the younger, better educated, and more mobile segment of the community. By 2001 the number of Quebec Jews dropped below 95,000. This out-migration had significant consequences for the demographic condition of the community and the establishment of priorities. Amongst other issues, the departure of so many younger Jews has contributed to the aging profile of the population and the need to direct greater attention to service provision for the elderly. More than one out of five Quebec Jews are over the age of 65. Other priorities included trying to stem the departure of young Jewish professionals through enhanced youth employment services.

In 2001, immigrants constituted some one-third of the Quebec Jewish population. More recently efforts have been directed at attracting Russian and Argentinian immigration. The community profile continues to possess characteristics that set it apart from Jewish communities elsewhere in Canada and for that matter in North America. While most Quebec Jews are English speaking, Quebec has both the largest French-speaking Jewish population on the continent and the largest share of Holocaust survivors of any Jewish community in Canada. Moreover it is one of the few Jewish communities in the world where Yiddish is still spoken almost as much as Hebrew. As a result of the pressure on the population to acquire the French language, Quebec Jews are the most trilingual group in North America.

On a national scale, the exodus of many Quebec Jews, a large number to Toronto, resulted in the decline of the Jewish population of Quebec. It dropped from around 40% of the total Canadian Jewish population in 1971 to just above one-quarter in 2001. As a result, the center of national Jewish decision-making has increasingly shifted away from Montreal as witnessed by the move of the national headquarters of the CJC from Montreal to Ottawa. Still, the Jewish historic contribution of Jews to Quebec life qualifies Jews as one of the province's founding peoples.

[Jack Jedwab (2nd ed.)]

QUEEN OF SHEBA. The biblical account of the queen of Sheba (I Kings 10:1–10, 13; II Chron. 9:1–9, 12) describes how when the queen of Sheba heard of the fame of Solomon, she went to Jerusalem with a great train of camels, bearing spices, gold, and precious stones, "to prove him with hard questions," all of which Solomon answered to her satisfaction. They exchanged gifts, after which she returned to her land. For details, see *Solomon.

In the Aggadah

Talmudic references to the queen of Sheba are sparse. A most elaborate account, however, is given in *Targum Sheni* to Esther, which can be supplemented by details found in the Alphabet of Ben Sira and Josephus (Ant. 8:165–73). A hoopoe informed Solomon that the kingdom of Sheba was the only kingdom on earth not subject to him and that its queen was a sun worshiper. He thereupon sent it to Kitor in the land of Sheba with a letter attached to its wing commanding its queen to come to him as a subject. She thereupon sent him all the ships of the sea loaded with precious gifts and 6,000 youths of equal size, all born at the same hour and clothed in purple garments. They carried a letter declaring that she could arrive in Jerusalem within three years although the journey normally took seven years. When the queen arrived and came to Solomon's palace, thinking that the shining floor was a pool of water, she lifted the hem of her dress, uncovering her legs. Solomon informed her of her mistake. When she arrived she asked him three (Targ. Sheni to Esther 1:3) or, according to another source, 19 riddles to test his wisdom.

In Islam

Sheba (Ar. Sabāʾ) was the most important kingdom in ancient southern *Arabia with its capital Mārib (in inscriptions: Mayrab, east of Sanʿa), the largest city in that area. This kingdom existed from the beginning of South Arabian civilization, and the oldest stone inscription dates back to the eighth century B.C.E., already referring to the kingdom as quite an established one. Its history is divided into two periods: (a) from its beginning until the first centuries B.C.E., dominated by caravan economy linked with Mesopotamia and the Land of Israel; (b) from the first century B.C.E. until the sixth century C.E., when it was controlled in general by the highland kingdom of Ḥimyar. Owing to the frankincense and many other spices exported to ancient lands, Sheba was quite known in the classical world, and its country was called Arabia Felix. Its disappearance resulted from the destruction of the Great Dam built seven kilometers north of Mārib, by which it had been possible to irrigate up to 10,000 hectares.

The biblical story, unattested by any other source, including hundreds of inscriptions from the Kingdom of Sheba, was adopted by the Ethiopic Church claiming that Ethiopian kings were descendants of the kingly couple King Solomon and Queen of Sheba. The Muslim sources, especially the *Koran, just copy the Bible and other Jewish sources, although they call this queen Bilqīs and add the tradition that the first Jews arrived in Yemen at the time of King Solomon, following the politico-economic alliance between him and Queen of Sheba. However, this tradition is suspected to be an apologetic fabrication of Jews in Yemen later transferred to Islam, just like many other traditions. The ancient Sabaic Awwām Temple, known in folklore as *Maḥram* (the Sanctuary of) *Bilqīs*, was recently excavated by archaeologists, but no trace of Queen of Sheba has been discovered so far in the many inscriptions found there.

[Yosef Tobi (2nd ed.)]

BIBLIOGRAPHY: IN THE AGGADAH: Ginzberg, Legends, 3 (1911), 411; 4 (1913), 143–9; (1928), 288–91. IN ISLAM: Thaʿlabī, *Qiṣaṣ* (1356 A.H.), 262–4; Kisāʾī, *Qiṣaṣ* (1356 A.H.), 285–92; G. Weil, *The Bible, the Koran, and the Talmud…* (1846); M. Gruenbaum, *Neue Beitraege zur semitischen Sagenkunde* (1893), 211–21; H. Speyer, *Die biblischen Erzaehlungen im Qoran* (1931, repr. 1961), 390–9; EIS, s.v. *Bilḳis*. **ADD. BIBLIOGRAPHY:** C. Robin, "Saba and the Sabaens," in: A.C. Gunther (ed.), *Caravan Kingdoms: Yemen and the Ancient Incense Trade* (2005), 9–19; M. Phillips Hodgson, "The Awam Temple: Excavations in the Mahram Bilqis Near Marib," in: *ibid.*, 60–66; W. Daum (ed.), *Die Königin von Saba: Kunst, Legende und Archäeologie zwischen Morgenland und Abendland* (1988).

QUELER, EVE (1936–), U.S. conductor. Born in New York City, Queler studied horn and piano at Mannes College and conducting with Joseph *Rosenstock, Carl Bamberg, Walter *Susskind, Leonard *Slatkin, Igor Markevich, and Herbert Blomstedt in Europe. Her career was temporarily interrupted following her marriage in 1956 but she later returned to study conducting and she became a rehearsal pianist for the New York City Opera. Her conducting debut in opera came in 1966, at Fairlawn, N.J. Because of the few opportunities offered to women conductors, she founded the Opera Orchestra of New York in 1968 with the aim of giving opera in concert performances and it met with increasing success and popularity. A leading exponent of forgotten opera, she worked to make them known with the participation of many major singers, including June Anderson, Carlo Bergonzi, Montserrat Caballé, Placido Domingo, Jane Eaglen, René Fleming, and Renata Scotto. A combination of determination in the face of great odds and a natural flair for opera gained Queler a position in the front rank of women conductors. She also appeared as a guest conductor at the New York City Opera, the Kirov Mariinsky Opera, the Hamburg Staatsoper, and the Frankfurt Opera as well as with the Philadelphia Orchestra, Montreal SO, and Honolulu SO. Queler also wrote a number of journal articles and supervised critical editions of three Donizetti operas. She made recordings of *Jenůfa*, Strauss's *Guntram* and Boito's *Nerone*.

BIBLIOGRAPHY: Grove Music Online.

[Max Loppert / Israela Stein (2nd ed.)]

QUERIDO, ISRAËL (1872–1932), Dutch novelist and author. He belonged to an Amsterdam Sephardi family and displayed a generally ambivalent attitude toward his Jewish background. In an early novel, *Levensgang* ("Life," 1901), he vividly portrays the diamond workers and merchants of Amsterdam and contrasts virtuous Christians with venal Jews. His autobiographical novel *Zegepraal* ("Triumph," 1904) was less successful. *Aron Laguna* (1916) is a lively recreation of Sephardi life which preserves the everyday speech of Sephardi Jewry of his generation.

His most important work was the cycle of novels published as *De Jordaan* (4 vols., 1912–25), a study of life in an Amsterdam working-class neighborhood. He wrote a number of novels and plays on biblical themes, including the lyrical drama *Saul en David* (1914) and a trilogy entitled *De oude waereld* ("The Old World"), which comprises three novels: *Koningen* ("Kings," 1918), *Zonsopgang* ("Sunrise," 1920), and *Morgenland* ("The Orient," 1921). Another biblical work was the novel *Simson* ("Samson," 2 vols., 1927–29). Toward the end of his life Querido published another novel cycle dealing with the Sephardim. It consisted of two books, *Van armen en rijken* ("Of the Rich and the Poor," 1931) and *Menschenharten* ("Human Hearts," 1932). They reappeared together as *Het volk Gods* ("God's People," 2 vols., 1932). Other works by Querido include *Misleide Majesteit* ("Misled Majesty," 1926), an animal story based on an Indian epic, and volumes of criticism.

His brother, the publisher EMANUEL QUERIDO (1871–1943), wrote a semi-autobiographical novel dealing with the development of Amsterdam during the years 1880–1910. This work, *Het geslacht der Santeljano's* ("The Santeljano Family," 10 vols., 1918–29), contains much important biographical material on his brother. After the Nazi occupation, Emanuel Querido was deported and died in the Sobibor death camp.

BIBLIOGRAPHY: J.L. Boender, *Israël Querido en het begrip literatuur* (1927); A.M. de Jong, *Israël Querido, De mens en de kunstenaar* (1933).

[Gerda Alster-Thau]

QUERIDO, JACOB (c. 1650–1690), Shabbatean leader in *Salonika. The son of R. Joseph Filosof, he was later generally known as Jacob Querido (Sp. "the beloved"). His sister became *Shabbetai Ẓevi's last wife. When she returned to Salonika after Shabbetai's death in 1676, she allegedly claimed that her brother was the recipient of her late husband's soul. Querido's father and R. Solomon Florentin supported his assertions which led, in 1683, to the mass apostasy of a large group of Salonika families. Together with the earlier converts to Islam among Shabbetai's followers, this group formed the nucleus of the *Doenmeh sect. Taking the Turkish name Abdullah Yacoub, Querido became the most prominent leader of the sectarians. An apocryphal letter attributed to Shabbetai confirmed his claims. His extravagant leadership led to dissension within the group as earlier converts had become dissatisfied with his innovations and therefore opposed his leadership. Insisting on outward demonstration of strict Muslim piety, he undertook a pilgrimage to Mecca in 1688, accompanied by one of his leading followers, Mustafa Effendi. Returning from Mecca, he died in Egypt, in either Alexandria or Bulak. When his companion returned, the schism among Querido's followers became final; according to tradition 43 families formed a subsect called Jacobites. As Querido had no male children, his adherents were led by chiefs who maintained a very strong control over the affairs of their group. They treasured several relics of Shabbetai Ẓevi and Querido and administered the personal fortune left by Shabbetai. The members of their subsect were mostly merchants and lower officials. No writings by Querido and his followers have survived, but one of the pamphlets written against him by another apostate between 1690 and 1695 is extant. Querido's followers took no part in the further divisions within the *Doenmeh sect that led to yet another schism. Their organization existed down to the 20th century.

BIBLIOGRAPHY: Tobias Rofe, *Ma'aseh Toviyyah* (Venice, 1707); A. Struck, in: *Globus*, 81 (1902), 221–2 (Ger.); J. Nehama, in: *Revue des écoles de l'Alliance Israélite* (1902), 308–9; A. Galanté, *Nouveaux documents sur Sabbetaï Sevi* (1935), 58–62; G. Scholem, in: *Zion*, 7 (1942), 14–20 (on the apostasy in 1683); idem, in: *Sefunot*, 9 (1965), 195–207.

[Gershom Scholem]

QUETSCH, SOLOMON (1798–1856), Moravian Orthodox rabbi. A native of *Mikulov (Nikolsburg) and pupil of Mordecai *Banet, he officiated as rabbi at Piesling and *Lipnik (1832–54). He was the last representative of the old Orthodoxy and the chief opponent of Samson Raphael *Hirsch as Moravian *Landesrabbiner. In May 1855 he became rabbi of Mikulov, but the position was not combined with that of *Landesrabbiner.* His death in January 1856 caused the closing of the Mikulov yeshivah.

A few of his novellae were published as *Ḥokhmat Shelomo* together with the Prague edition of Mordecai Banet's *Har ha-Mor* (1862). S.J. Rapoport wrote a commemorative poem on him in *Kokhevei Yiẓḥak*, (22, (1856), 3).

BIBLIOGRAPHY: A. Schnitzer, *Juedische Kulturbilder* (1904), 38–56.

[Meir Lamed]

°QUIETUS, LUSIUS (second century C.E.), Roman general. Quietus, who was of Moorish origin, was commander of the Moorish cavalry in the Roman army as early as the time of Domitian. He especially distinguished himself in the wars during Trajan's reign and was one of his principal commanders in the Parthian campaign. Among his activities in Mesopotamia was the subduing of the Jews there, who were hostile to Rome. Trajan ordered Lusius Quietus to crush them. He conducted the attack craftily, killing many. As a reward for this success he was appointed ruler of Judea in 117 C.E. (Eusebius, *Historia Ecclesiastica*, 4:2). Apparently Quietus also subdued the Jews in Judea who revolted against Rome. Details are lacking of this action, but a reference to them has been preserved in the talmudical accounts of "the war of Quietus." When Hadrian became emperor he removed Quietus from his command of the Moors and from the army, and shortly after he was executed for participating in a conspiracy against the emperor.

BIBLIOGRAPHY: Schuerer, Hist., 277f., 292f.; Pauly-Wissowa, 26 (1927), 1874–90, no. 9; Allon, Toledot, 1 (1958[3]), 255ff.; E.M. Smallwood, in: *Historia*, 11 (1962), 500–10; S. Appelbaum, *Yehudim vi-Yvanim be-Kirini ha-Kedumah* (1969), 255–61, 273–4.

[Uriel Rappaport]

QUINCE, name of both a tree, *Cydonia oblonga*, and its fruit. It is not mentioned in the Bible, but in rabbinic literature it is referred to under three names: *ḥavush, parish*, and *aspargal. Ḥavush* (Aram. *ḥavusha*) is mentioned as being given to the sick (Tosef., Ter. 7:13). It is an aromatic fruit and is enumerated together with the *etrog* among the fruits over whose fragrance a blessing should be recited (Ber. 43b). The name *parish* is found in a discussion as to the permissibility, in time of emergency, of substituting some other large and beautiful fruit for the *etrog* in order to fulfill the precept of the Four Species, and it was decided in the negative (Tosef. Suk. 2:9, 31a–b). According to the Jerusalem Talmud (Kil. 1:3, 27a), it was so called because it is the only fruit reserved (*parush*) for the pot, i.e., it is inedible in its raw state and must be cooked. The same passage notes that its Aramaic name is *aspargal* which is the Arabic name for the quince. The Mishnah lays down that the quince belongs to the same species as the hawthorn (*uzrar*). Apparently the ancients took the latter to be a degenerate quince.

BIBLIOGRAPHY: Loew, Flora, 3 (1924), 240ff.; J. Feliks, *Kilei Zera'im ve-Harkavah* (1967), 93–96. **ADD. BIBLIOGRAPHY:** J. Feliks, Ha-Ẓome'aḥ, 128.

[Jehuda Feliks]

°**QUINTILIAN** (**Marcus Fabius Quintilianus**; first century C.E.), Roman rhetorician. In language reminiscent of Tacitus he berates the founder (Moses?, though some have thought, probably wrongly, that Jesus is meant) for having concentrated his people in cities as a curse to others (*Institutio Oratoria* 3:7, 21).

[Jacob Petroff]

°**QUINTILIUS VARUS** (d. 9 C.E.), Roman consul in 13 B.C.E. and governor of Syria from 6 to 4 B.C.E. Varus first appeared in Judea during the last years of *Herod the Great, and on that occasion he participated in the king's trial of his son Antipater, accused of attempted patricide. After hearing lengthy denunciations of the prince and verification that the poison allegedly prepared for the plot was in fact potent, Varus went into private consultation with Herod, drafted a report to Augustus, and departed for Antioch. Antipater was put into chains, and it was assumed by the populace that Herod in so doing was acting upon the advice of the Syrian governor, although Antipater was eventually executed. With the death of Herod in 4 B.C.E., his primary heir Archelaus was unable to control the serious disturbances that broke out throughout the country. Following a bloody attempt on Passover at quieting the unrest, Archelaus departed for Rome and disturbances reached a new peak with the appearance of Sabinus, finance officer (procurator) of Syria, for the purpose of taking charge of Herod's estate. During the festival of Pentecost the Jews in Jerusalem rose up in open rebellion, which eventually spread to all of Palestine, Sabinus, realizing his inability to cope with the situation, was forced to appeal to Varus for help. The Syrian governor appeared at Acre with the three legions at his disposal, together with auxiliary troops supplied by the citizens of Berytus, and from there proceeded to subdue the whole country. Cities such as Sepphoris and Emmaus were reduced to ruins, and thousands of rebels were crucified. The invasion under Varus was so devastating that Josephus lists it together with the wars of Antiochus Epiphanes, Pompey, and Vespasian (Apion 1:34). The rabbinic chronology *Seder Olam Rabbah* also cites a *pulmus shel Asveiros* taking place 80 years before the war of Vespasian, and since Graetz historians have interpreted this as "the war of Varus." Varus was eventually killed by the Germans at the battle of the forest of Teutoburg.

BIBLIOGRAPHY: Jos., Wars, 1:617ff., 2:16ff.; Jos., Ant., 17:89ff., 221ff.; Schuerer, Gesch, 1 (1901[4]), 322, 420f., 3 (1909[4]), 296.

[Isaiah Gafni]

°**QUIRINIUS, P. SULPICIUS**, Roman commander and administrator at the beginning of the first century C.E. Quirinius did not belong to an aristocratic family; his rise to power was due to his own abilities and the support of Augustus and his stepson Tiberius with whom he enjoyed a relationship of unwavering friendship. He achieved his reputation as a result of his military exploits in Africa and Asia Minor. He reached the peak of his public career in the year 6 C.E. when he was appointed governor of Syria. He was responsible for laying the foundations of the organization of the new province of Judea, after *Archelaus, son of Herod, had been dismissed from the post of ethnarch of Judea. Quirinius himself, accompanied by Coponius, newly appointed governor of Judea, arrived in order to conduct a general census of property in the new province, and to deal with the possessions of Archelaus (Jos., Ant., 18:1ff.). The census aroused widespread opposition among the Jews, but thanks to the influence of the high priest, *Joezer b. Boethus, it was carried out without serious disturbances. However, extremist circles, headed by *Judah the Galilean and *Zadok the Pharisee, who incited the people to rebellion maintained that the institution of the census symbolized servitude to the Romans. Quirinius also introduced changes into the high priesthood. He dismissed Joezer b. Boethus and replaced him by *Anan b. Seth (Jos. Ant., 18:26), the first high priest of the house of Anan. Scholars dispute the passage in Luke 2:1–2 where the census of Quirinius is mentioned in connection with the birth of Jesus. An inscription discovered in Tibur Tivoli, Italy, has been regarded as referring to Quirinius and as a result an attempt has been made to maintain that Quirinius served twice as governor of Syria, the first time being during Herod's lifetime. But even if the inscription refers to Quirinius, it fails to prove that he served twice as governor of Syria.

BIBLIOGRAPHY: T. Mommsen, *Res gestae Divi Augusti* (1865), 115ff.; Schuerer, Hist, 197; R. Syme, *The Roman Revolution* (1939), 399; Roos, in: *Mnemosyne*, 9 (1941), 306–18; H. Dessau, *Inscriptiones Latinae Selectae* 1 (1892), no. 918; D. Magie, *Roman Rule in Asia Minor*, 2 (1950), 1322–23; E. Gabba, *Iscrizioni greche e latine per lo studio della Bibbia*, no. xviii, 52–61.

[Menahem Stern]

°QUISLING, VIDKUN ABRAHAM LAURITZ JONSSØN (1887–1945), Norwegian who openly met the conquering Nazis as their collaborator; since he was the first to do so, the British press used his name as the symbol of all collaborators and traitors during World War II. Born in Fyresdal (southern province of Telemark), where his father was a priest, he graduated with distinction from the military academy of Norway and served as an officer in the General Staff (1911–18). His special interest in Russia – and his fluent Russian – brought about his appointment as military attaché to the Soviet Union and a diplomatic post in Petrograd (St. Petersburg, 1918–19) and Helsinki (1920–21). He became an assistant to Fridtjof Nansen fighting starvation in Ukraine in 1922 and after fulfilling humanitarian tasks on behalf of the League of Nations returned to Norway after Nansen's death in 1930. In his politics he veered from the Soviet-oriented left to the fascist right. He was minister of defense in 1931–33 in the government of the Farmers' Party. In 1933 Quisling founded his own party, Nasjonal Samling (National Union), which never gained popular support. The Nazi leaders took an interest in him while the invasion into Norway was planned, when he was received by Hitler on whom he made a favorable impression. On the day of the invasion he declared himself prime minister but was removed six days later by the German authorities, who installed Josef Terboven as a military police governor. In February 1942 Quisling succeeded in being named prime minister, but although his influence was nil, he committed enough crimes, including the preparations for the deportation of the Jews, to be condemned to death by a Norwegian tribunal in 1945, and was executed on October 24. The Norwegian government earmarked the mansion in which Quisling lived during World War II and until his arrest for a Center for Holocaust and Minorities Studies, comprising a research center and a museum. The Center is financed by Norwegian Holocaust restitution funds and was opened in 2006.

[Leni Yahil]

QUMRAN, region on the northwest shore of the Dead Sea, which has become famous since 1947 as the site of the discovery of the *Dead Sea Scrolls. The name belongs more particularly to Wadi Qumran, a precipitous watercourse which runs down to the sea from the west, and to Khirbet Qumran, a ruin standing less than a mile west of the sea on the marl terrace north of the wadi. Visitors to the region in earlier days, impressed by the fortuitous similarity of names, thought that Khirbet Qumran might be all that was left of Gomorrah. In 1873 C.S. *Clermont-Ganneau inspected the ruin, but was more interested in a cemetery lying between it and the sea. He came to no positive conclusions as a result of his inspection.

Occupation of Khirbet Qumran

In 1949, the possibility was raised of a connection between the discoveries in the first manuscript cave and Khirbet Qumran. A trial excavation was made on the site, but nothing was found which suggested any connection. In November and December 1951, three rooms were excavated. In the floor of one of them was found a jar of the same type as those in which the scrolls in Cave 1 had been placed, and along with it was a coin bearing a date equivalent to 10 C.E. Systematic campaigns of exploration were mounted in 1953, 1954, 1955, and 1956, in which the Jordan Department of Antiquities, the Palestine Archaeological Museum, and the French Dominican Ecole Biblique collaborated.

It soon became evident that the building complex had formed the headquarters of a fairly large and well-organized community. R. de Vaux, soon after the excavations began, expressed the belief that these were the headquarters of the *Essenes referred to by *Pliny the Elder in his *Natural History* (5:73), partly on the ground that nothing else in that region could correspond to Pliny's description. Pliny says that "below" the Essene headquarters lies *En-Gedi; since he is describing the Jordan Valley and Dead Sea region from north to south he may mean that En-Gedi lies south of the Essene headquarters; En-Gedi in fact lies some 22 miles (34 km.) south of Khirbet Qumran. But the identification of the community or *Yaḥad that occupied Khirbet Qumran cannot be determined on archaeological grounds alone.

The cemetery to the east of Khirbet Qumran proved to contain about 1,200 graves, laid out in parallel rows lying north and south, with the head to the south. The burials were as simple as possible; the bodies were neither placed in coffins nor accompanied by funeral offerings. In an eastern extension of the cemetery, skeletons of four women and one child were found. Skeletons of women and children were also identified in two other subsidiary cemeteries lying north and south respectively of Wadi Qumran. Pottery in the earth-filling of the graves indicated that the burials belonged to the same general period as the community occupation of Khirbet Qumran.

The site of Khirbet Qumran had been occupied at various times in antiquity. At a low level were found the remains of walls and pottery of Iron Age II (8th–7th centuries B.C.E.). A potsherd inscribed with Phoenician characters and a royal seal stamped on a jar handle belonged to this period, as did also a deep circular cistern which, centuries later, was incorpo-

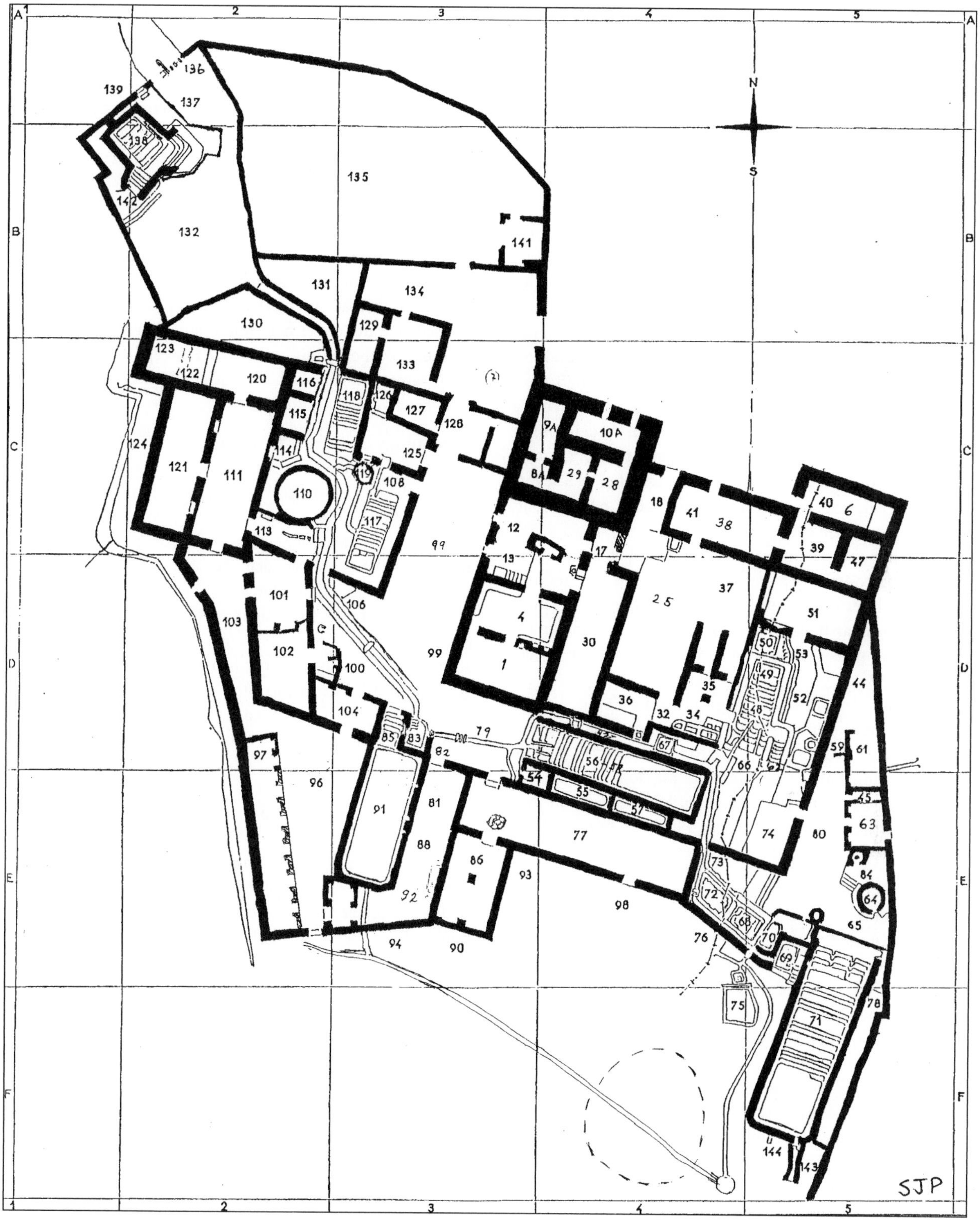

Khirbet Qumran: Schematic Plan and Position of the Loci in Period Ib.

rated in an elaborate system of aqueducts and reservoirs. This phase of occupation may be correlated with the statement that Uzziah king of Judah (c. 790–740 B.C.E.) "built towers in the wilderness and hewed out many cisterns" (II Chron. 26:10). M. Noth has suggested that at this period the site was known as Ir ha-Melaḥ ("city of salt," Josh. 15:61).

Chief interest attaches to the abundant evidence for the occupation of the site in the Greco-Roman period. In this period Roland de Vaux, the excavator, distinguished the following phases of occupation:

IA. May have been constructed by John Hyrcanus I (134–104 B.C.E.) or more likely by one of his predecessors, i.e., Jonathan (152–142 B.C.E.) or Simon (142–134 B.C.E.), due to the presence of a relatively significant number of coins of John Hyrcanus I and Antiochus VII (138–129 B.C.E.). It was occupied at that time by a people who cleared the circular cistern, built two rectangular stepped pools beside it, constructed a few rooms around these, and installed two pottery kilns in the Iron Age enclosure.

IB. Occupation of a much enlarged area, with two- and three-storey buildings, and an elaborate system of ritual immersion pools and cisterns (incorporating the earlier ones) connected by channels and supplied by an aqueduct from a dam built to store the water which runs down Wadi Qumran in the rainy season. This phase began quite possibly during the reign of John Hyrcanus I and was terminated by a severe earthquake (almost certainly the famous one of 31 B.C.E.) followed by an extensive fire.

II. After about a quarter of a century of abandonment, the building complex was reoccupied and was restored following the lines of phase IB but was reinforced at various points against earthquake damage. Based upon numismatic evidence this phase came to an end during the First Revolt, in the year 68 C.E.

III. Non-Jewish coins ranging from 67/68 C.E. until 72/73 C.E. seem to indicate that a Roman garrison was stationed among the ruins of the site from 68 until 73 C.E., and withdrew immediately after the fall of Masada.

The site was again abandoned until the Bar Kokhba War (132–135 C.E.), as evidenced by coins, when the site served revolutionaries as a hiding place or center of resistance.

Description of Khirbet Qumran

The main building of the complex in phases Ib and II was roughly 37 meters square, of large undressed stones, with a strong tower at the northwest corner. There were several large rooms suitable for assembly rooms or refectories. Adjoining the largest of these rooms (on the south side of the building) was a smaller room containing over 1,000 earthenware vessels – all the varieties necessary for kitchen and refectory use. They may have been manufactured on the spot, since the excavations brought to light the best preserved pottery factory thus far found in ancient Palestine, complete with kilns and levigating pit. A first-storey room in the southwest part of the building (upper loc. 30) was evidently furnished with inkwells and plastered writing tables as a writing room (*scriptorium*). Flour mills, storage bins, ovens, a laundry, a stable, furnaces, and workshops with metal implements were also uncovered. The occupants apparently aimed at being as self-sufficient as possible. The building complex does not seem to have included sufficient sleeping quarters; tents or the neighboring caves may have served the occupants for rest and shelter.

The elaborate series of pools, designed to ensure a plentiful water supply, has excited special interest; there has been a tendency to relate these to the prescriptions regarding cleansing in water laid down in the Manual of *Discipline found in the Qumran caves. It is especially in one of these pools that the damage from the earthquake is still most clearly visible. The 14 stone steps of the largest pool (loc. 85/86), to the east of the site, show a central crack running down from top to bottom, so that their eastern half has sunk nearly half a meter below the level of the western half. When the site was reoccupied some 30 years after the earthquake, this pool could not be used as it no longer held water; a new one was excavated southeast of the building. Other major repairs were effected at the same time: the walls were strengthened and the northwestern tower was reinforced.

Chronology of Khirbet Qumran

The record of the phases of the occupation of Khirbet Qumran is indicated most clearly by the coins found in the course of excavations on the site. About 650 coins of the Greco-Roman period have come to light. The coin record starts with Antiochus VII of the Seleucid dynasty (139–129 B.C.E.) and his contemporary John Hyrcanus (135–104 B.C.E.) and goes on without a break to Antigonus, the last Hasmonean king (40–37 B.C.E.). Coins of Alexander Yannai (103–76 B.C.E.) are especially frequent. Only five coins from Herod's reign (37–4 B.C.E.) have come to light. The record is resumed with coins of Archelaus (4 B.C.E.–6 C.E.) and continues with those of the procurators and a particularly large number of Herod Agrippa's coins (37–44 C.E.). There are 73 coins from the second year of the war against Rome (67–68 C.E.) and several from the following year, contemporary with these are coins minted in the coastal cities of Caesarea, Dora, and Ashkelon; later are a coin of Agrippa II (86 C.E.), one of Vespasian (69–79 C.E.), three of Trajan (98–117 C.E.), one of the type struck by the liberation leaders during the second revolt. It is doubtful whether a hoard of 563 silver coins hidden in three pots in a floor to the west of the building can be related to the occupation of Khirbet Qumran. The hoard was comprised primarily of tetradrachmas and didrachmas of Antiochus VII (earliest dated 139/138 B.C.E.) and Demetrius II (later reign) along with shekels and half shekels of Tyre, the latest of which was dated 10/9 B.C.E. These coins may have been hidden there toward the end of the period of abandonment between Phases Ib and II or at the very beginning of Period II.

A sample of charcoal from the room where the large number of earthenware vessels (Loc. 89) was found was subjected to the radiocarbon test, which yielded a date of 16 C.E. (with a margin of deviation of 80 years either way) for the age of the wood, and a date of 66 C.E. (with a similar margin of deviation) for the burning. Phase II of the occupation of Khirbet Qumran was brought to an end not by earthquake but by fire and sword. The destruction was much more thorough than that caused by the earthquake 100 years earlier. The walls were demolished, a layer of black ash covered the site, and a quantity of arrowheads added their silent testimony to the picture. De Vaux concluded that that the building was attacked and stormed by the Romans in the summer of 68 C.E. because of the paucity of First Revolt bronzes which date to that year. (However it should not be discounted that perhaps the site was destroyed by revolutionaries, who were known for their "scorched earth" policy, on the eve of the Vespasian's scourge of Judea.)

A few rooms were built over the ruins and occupied by a Roman garrison which appears to have been stationed there for a few years. The brief occupation of the site by an insurgent garrison during the second revolt was followed by the complete destruction of its surviving fortifications.

The chronology of the occupation of Khirbet Qumran, archaeologically established, agrees remarkably well with that of the nearby manuscript caves and their contents, paleographically established.(The paleographical evidence is supplemented by the application of pottery dating to the jars in which the manuscripts of Cave 1 were placed and by the application of the radiocarbon test to some of the linen in which these manuscripts were wrapped before being placed in the jars, although the radiocarbon test involves too large a margin of deviation to be helpful when precise dating within decades is required.) A close connection between the occupants of the building and the manuscripts in the caves is cogently indicated; the community described in the "community documents" and the community which manifestly occupied Khirbet Qumran must have been one and the same community; at least, it would require specially conclusive arguments to make it probable that they were two separate communities.

Additional Phases

After 50 years, the time has come to reassess De Vaux's proposed phases, based on data from recent excavations of Qumran's immediate periphery (sequentially: Y. Magen and Y. Peleg; M. Broshi and H. Eshel; O. Guttfeld and R. Price), in which refuse dumps and agricultural terraces were examined in the immediate vicinity. Along with these investigations, a fresh review of De Vaux's excavation and its associated material culture by Donçeel, Humbert, and Chambon, along with new light from recent scientific analyses (Humbert and Gunneweg (eds.), *Khirbet Qumrân et 'Ain Feshkha*, vol II., 2003) provide evidence for three additional phases at the site, and at least four separate sources in the caves.

INTERIM PERIOD. De Vaux's "Period of Abandonment" (ca. 31–10 B.C.E.), during which the site was *not* entirely abandoned. A large pit containing hundreds of carbonized dates which cuts through the southern drainage system suggests that date farmers (perhaps lay Essenes), occupied the site during this period.

PERIOD IIB. During the last years of Period II (ca. 66–68 C.E.), during a period of social upheaval, political strife, and war, Qumran was taken over by another group, likely revolutionaries. Hoards of Revolt coins, stoneware, new pottery forms (differing in form and proportions from the communal pantries of loci 89 and 114), and light weapons (including knives and arrow heads) were recovered from this period, which preceded the Roman occupation of the site.

PERIOD IIIB. Another "Period of Abandonment" according to De Vaux (ca. 73–132 C.E.). Numerous items, including late first and early second century coins (Vespasian and Trajan), numerous shards of glass, a spindle whorl, a stone vase and white strainer jugs indicate that a non-military occupation at the site extended well beyond that of the Roman garrison (which ended ca. 73 C.E. according to De Vaux), an occupation that seems to have extended into the early second century.

The Caves of Qumran

After the first two "scroll caves" were discovered in 1947 (Cave 1Q) and 1952 (Cave 2Q), a survey of the cliffs in the vicinity of Qumran was conducted during March 1952. Upon completion of the survey, the caves and sites which contained archaeological remains were numbered, from north to south, "Survey Cave GQ1" through "Survey Cave GQ40." Certain scroll caves that were found in the cliffs (specifically, 1Q, 2Q, 3Q, and 6Q) were also assigned Survey cave numbers (GQ14, GQ19, GQ8 and GQ26, respectively). Subsequent caves in which manuscripts were discovered were numbered in the sequence of their discovery, yielding Scroll caves 1Q through 11Q, the last being discovered in January 1956. These two separate numbering systems were conceived at that time and continue to be used for all Qumran caves of archaeological import identified between 1947 and 1956. However, the two categories of caves and their numbers have often become confused in the literature. In April 1956 two adjacent caves without manuscripts were discovered and excavated to the northeast of cave 3Q (= GQ8) and were called "Cave A" and "Cave B." In 1963, an additional cave with abundant remains, but no manuscripts, was discovered by John Allegro and his team as part of the "Copper Scroll Expedition" and was dubbed "The Christmas Cave," since King Hussein of Jordan visited the cave on that day. A third system of enumeration has arisen with the cave surveys and excavations of Y. Patrich between 1984 and 1991, for which we will use the numbers "PQ1–PQ24."

The Caves of Qumran can be divided into five distinct clusters:

Cave Cluster of the Marl Terrace Adjacent to the Qumran Site. Southwest Caves 4 Spur. Qa, 4Qb, 5Q and 10Q. The complex is located 80 meters southwest of the buildings of Qumran on a spur of the marl formation separated from the site by a narrow ravine. The Bedouin discovered caves 4Qa and 4Qb simultaneously, with the result that the fragments from the two caves arrived at the museum mixed and indistinguishable. Thus these adjacent but separate caves were delineated "4Q" by de Vaux with regard to the manuscripts and other items collected by

Phases of Occupation at Qumran and their Character

Dates	De Vaux's Phases	Modified de Vaux	Nature of Occupation	Datable Loci	Coins	Lamps	Pantry	Characteristic Material Culture	Cave/Manuscript Collection (Time of Deposition)
8th–6th cent. B.C.E.	Iron II	Iron II	Settlement, perhaps farmstead; cf. II Chron. 26:10	Below 73, 80, 68, 86, 88; outside 6, 40; north of 38	Not applicable	Late Iron Age	(unknown)	LMLK jar handles; hole mouth jars	11Q; GQ6, 13, 27, 39; GQA, B; Christmas Cave
c 150–130	Ia	Ia	Pre Essene, farmstead	Under 30; under 66	Demetrius I (early reign)	Hellenistic: Tr A, delfiniform; west trench (Broshi/Eshel)	(unknown): includes fish plates (cf. loc. Under 30)	Villa rustica with agricultural terraces	(unknown)
c 130–31	Ib	Ib	Essene (mainly Yahad)	89, 48/49, 52, 53, 16	Antiochus VII, John Hyrcanus I	Qumran type: loc 130, 1Q.1; Hellenistic Radial	Communal: loc. 86/89; 1 cup : 3 dishes : 10 bowls	Ritual communal meals; numerous mikvaot; lots	1Q Phase A (part of 4Q, 5Q)
31–4	Abandoned	Interim	Lay Essenes? Date farmers	South 75 (pit with dates)	Shekel hoards A, B & C	Herodian Radial	(unknown)	Pit full of dates	(unknown)
4 B.C.E.– 66 C.E.	II	IIa	Essene (first Yahad then Lay)	114	Procurators, Agrippa I	Herodian A and B	Communal: loc. 114; 1 cup : 3 dishes : 10 bowls	Ritual communal meals; numerous mikvaot; lots	1Q Phase B; 6Q (part of 4Q, 5Q)
66–68	II	IIb	Revolutionaries	2, 4, 30, 45a–c, 59, 61	1st Revolt coin hoards	Herodian C	Personal: loc. 2, 4, 45a–c, 59, 61, upper 77; 10 cups : 10 dishes : 10 bowls	Stoneware; numerous spherical juglets; carinated bowls	2Q; ostracon 1 (Year 2)
67–83	III	IIIa	Roman Outpost	(none)	Roman provincial coins 67-73 CE	(none)	(unknown)	Hob nails (on paths)	Northern Cluster; includes 3Q, 11Q (c 70 C.E., likely Zealot); not associated with Qumran site.
c 73–132	Abandoned	IIIb	Post-Essene occupation	14, 15, 16, 20, 21, 24, upper 34	Vespasian, Agrippa II (86 CE), Trajan	Discus lamp 4Q, molded lamps	(unknown)	Glass, stoneware, pseudo-Nabatean painted; white strainer jugs, spindle whorl	None
c 132–135	Bar Kokhba	IIIc	Revolutionaries	29	Second Revolt coins	(unknown)	(unknown)	(unknown)	Christmas Cave

the Bedouin. However, when describing the findings from his own excavations, De Vaux was able to distinguish them as "4Qa" and "4Qb".

Southern Spur: Caves 7Q, 8Q and 9Q. The complex is located at the southern end of the same marl terrace, 90 meters directly south of the building complex of Qumran and connected to it by the southern enclosure. The three caves, whose roofs had collapsed, are accessible only from within the confines of the enclosure wall.

Cave Cluster of the Northern Cliffs. Caves 3Q and 11Q; Survey Caves GQ1–11; Caves A and B; PQ13, PQ. The northern cliffs lie between the wadi that divides the cliffs two kilometers to the north of Qumran and the Rijm al-Asbah "the rock of the thumb," about one kilometer further north.

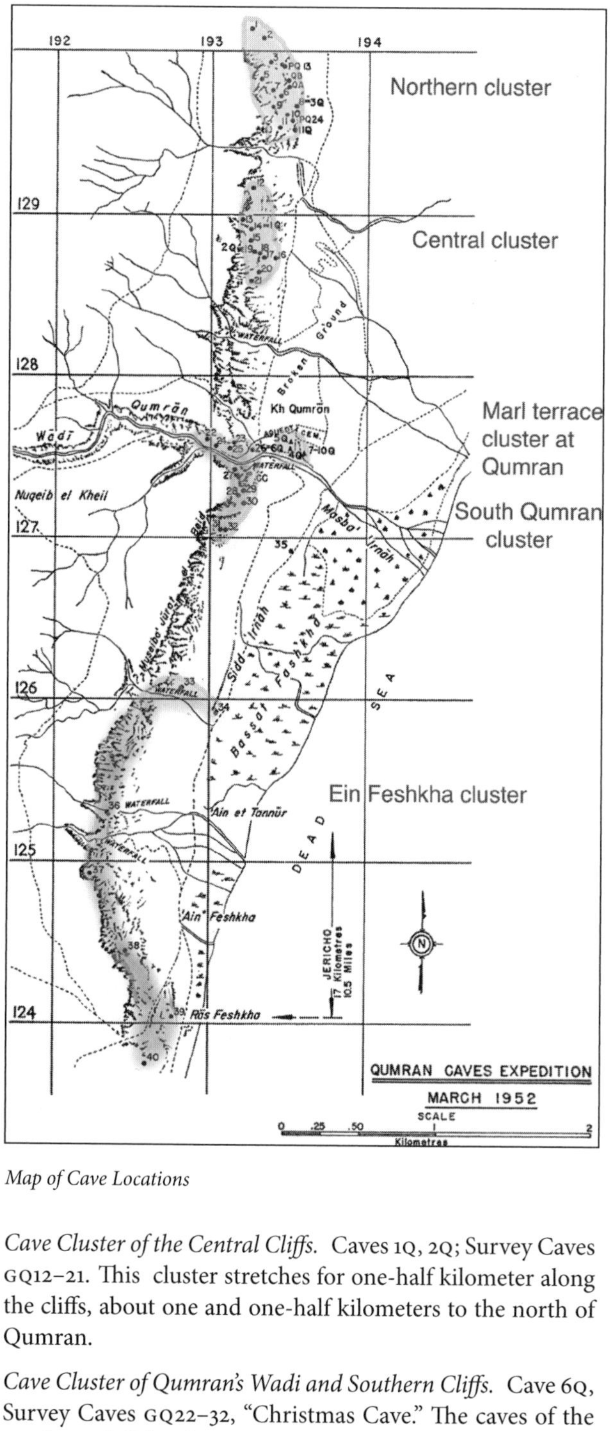

Map of Cave Locations

Cave Cluster of the Central Cliffs. Caves 1Q, 2Q; Survey Caves GQ12–21. This cluster stretches for one-half kilometer along the cliffs, about one and one-half kilometers to the north of Qumran.

Cave Cluster of Qumran's Wadi and Southern Cliffs. Cave 6Q, Survey Caves GQ22–32, "Christmas Cave." The caves of the southern cliffs lie along a one-half kilometer stretch south of the Wadi Qumran.

Cave Cluster of the Ein Feshkha Cliffs. Survey Caves GQ. This stretch of cliffs begins 33–40. 2.75 kilometers south of Qumran and extends southward for 2.5 kilometers, ending at Ras Feshkha, with the spring of Ein Feshkha at the center.

Pottery and Dating of the Caves

The caves in the cliffs contained material from the Pre-Pottery Neolithic B (flint blades), Chalcolithic (pottery sherds), Iron II (lamps and bowls), Hellenistic, Roman, Byzantine, and Islamic periods. The most substantial and widespread remains were from the first century C.E., including the typical cylindrical jars and, less commonly, lamps, cooking pots, tableware and, of course, the scrolls themselves. Many of the caves were visited on more than one occasion in antiquity, providing remains from more than one period in the same cave. Most periods represented by the remains from the caves have counterparts in the stratified remains of Khirbet Qumran.

In certain cases, the date of the remains in the cliffs reflects a time of hiding and transition in the occupation of the site. This is also true of the various hidden scroll deposits, the approximate date of the deposition being concurrent with the latest paleographically dated manuscript in the collection. On the other hand, the remains from the caves in Khirbet Qumran's marl terrace have a different history of use than those in the cliffs. The deposition of manuscripts there took place continuously over a long period of time and can be dated within a limited frame: no earlier than the late second century B.C.E. and no later than the end of the first century C.E. (roughly concurrent with periods IB and II).

On occasions when domestic pottery has been found in a cave – including collections of lamps, cooking pots, tableware, and food remains – this would indicate that individuals hid in or used the caves as temporary lodging (although these occupants should not necessarily be identified as those who hid the scrolls). Domestic pottery, especially lamps, provides an important means toward pinpointing periods of occupation, as in Iron II lamps (caves 11Q and GQ39), Hellenistic lamps (1Q), and lamps from the second half of the first century C.E. or First Revolt (caves 1Q, 3Q, 4Q, 8Q, 10Q, 11Q, GQ29, GQ39, PQ13, PQ24).

Cylindrical Jars

From the initial moment that the first scrolls were said to have been found in a certain, cylindrically shaped jar in Cave 1, it was assumed that those hitherto unknown jars were manufactured specifically to store scrolls. Even though the original excavator consistently called the jars "cylindrical jars," scholars preferred to utilize the term "scroll jars" whenever a new jar of this type was found. The facts, however, show that the jars were not all intended for carrying scrolls. This is clear from the fact that most of these jars were not found with scrolls in them and very few scrolls that were discovered were actually found in jars. Also, most caves which contained cylindrical jars or their lids had no trace of even a single manuscript inside the cave (e.g., GQ1–3, 7, 10, 12, 15, 17–18, 21, 22, 28–32, 39, 40; PQ13, PQ24).

It also has been assumed that these jars were manufactured at Qumran. However, after recent chemical analyses of the cylindrical jars by Gunneweg and Bala, it was concluded that at least 75% of the cylindrical jars from the caves, and more than 50% of those from the site of Qumran, were derived from the Jerusalem area, having been made from clay from the Jerusalem/Motsa flow. The remainder were proven to derive primarily from the regions of Qumran and Jericho and were further distinguished by detectable variations in form, color and manufacture. Those in the caves which derived from Jerusalem were often accompanied by lamps or domestic wares dating to the second half of the first century C.E., indicating that they were most likely hidden there during the period of the First Revolt.

The fact that most of the jars were found empty, and yet had been purposely hidden, seems to indicate that they were valued aside from their contents. Furthermore, it appears that most of the jars, especially the tall cylindrical jars, were not originally intended to contain scrolls. Rather, they were intended for the collection of levitical tithes. They are designated by the term *kelei dema'*, "tithe jars," and are frequently listed among the hidden treasures in the Copper Scroll (3Q15) without any reference to their actual contents (if they had any). One of the jars from cave 3Q was marked twice with the letter *tet* which characterizes certain jars of this type as similarly found at Masada. (Cf. M. *Ma'aser* 4:11, "If a vessel was found on which was written a *kof*, it is *korban*; if a *mem*, it is *ma'aser*; if a *dalet*, it is *demai*; if a *tet*, it is *tevel*.") It is more likely that only the shorter jars with handles were used for archival purposes. The handles were actually used as anchors for tying down the lid; parallels of such practices have been found in Egypt. However, the scrolls of an active community library were not placed in archive jars for extended periods of time but were normally stored on shelves inset into the walls of a room (compare, e.g., the Celsus library at Ephesus, the library at Nizanna, and, apparently, Qumran loc. 2). The only reason the contents of a library might be found in a cave, whether in jars or not, would be to set aside worn or damaged scrolls in a *genizah* or to temporarily hide the scrolls from imminent danger. If the latter case is true for the cliffs of Qumran, those who hid them did not survive to retrieve them according to plan.

Diverse Caves and Libraries of Qumran

It has been generally assumed that the numerous manuscripts from the Qumran caves (and those from Masada!) were once part of a single library, produced and kept by a singular movement of people, known within the scrolls as the "Yaḥad" or the "Sons of Light" (and by their contemporaries as the "Essenes"). The various manuscript deposits, however, when examined by content and context, by what unites them and what divides them, tell a different story. Their unique and dissimilar features reveal that their owners actually came from diverse groups, who hid the scrolls at different times.

A survey of the contents of each manuscript collection confirms that, in all cases, the Books of Moses were central to each collection, reflecting the common Jewish background of the peoples who deposited the manuscripts. However, the Torah manuscripts were supplemented in each collection by other Jewish writings, which reveal the views of its owners and help to define each group. This feature along with certain variations in material remains from each scroll cave provides evidence as to the identity of individual groups who harbored each manuscript collection.

The general character of a group, whether priestly or lay, is indicated by a number of predictable elements. If, for example, a library predominantly contains works such as rulebooks, liturgies, and multiple copies of the Book of Psalms – a collection which helps to define and support the role of priesthood – then priests must have comprised the core group (e.g., the collections of caves 1Q and 11Q). If the supplemental material contains rule books, copies of the "five *megillot*" (pocket scrolls read by the laity during the feasts), and legendary texts which define and support the role of the laity, then the collection likely belonged to a lay group (e.g., the collections from caves 2Q, 3Q, 6Q and perhaps 5Q). If the collection contains a mixture of these features, then it might represent a *genizah* for both priestly and lay communities (e.g., the contents of cave 4Q and perhaps 5Q), or the library of a community which composed of both priestly and lay elements (e.g., Masada).

The specific sectarian leanings of the owners can be discerned by the contents of their rulebooks and the supplemental literature they preserve within the collection, or even possibly by which texts are excluded. These leanings appear to go in two directions: (1) Caves 1Q, 4Q, 5Q and 6Q, which as a group preserve libraries of the two divisions of the "Sons of Light," the priestly *Yaḥad* "Community" and the laity Israelites (both divisions of which are, by nature, ideologically and typically "Essene" as described by Josephus; the term "Qumran Community" is inappropriate since the movement, as described in the scrolls, was not confined to this site), and (2) Caves and sites which preserve libraries which ideologically support and belong to various groups involved in the First Revolt (potentially including especially the Sicarii, the followers of Simon bar Giora, the Zealots and others described by Josephus in his *Jewish Wars*).

CAVES 1Q, 4Q, 5Q, AND 6Q. Cave 1Q: This *Yaḥad* collection, in addition to being of a priestly character, is all written on parchment, and contains one copy each of all of the major works identified with the Yahad and its founder the Moreh Ẓedek, especially the *Rule of the Community*, two copies of the *Thanksgiving Hymns* and most of the community's commentaries (lacking, however, the *Temple Scroll* and *Ben Sira*, which support divergent views). The group also avoids authoring pseudepigraphic works. 1Q contained at least 75 manuscripts from about 125 B.C.E. to 25 C.E., with two peaks in accession (14% from c. 100–75 B.C.E. and 43% from 31–1 B.C.E.). Since accessions ended by 25 C.E., this must be the approximate date that this library was removed from Qumran and hidden in the cave. This may provide a *terminus ad quem* for the presence of the priestly *Yaḥad* at Qumran. The textiles from 1Q were of unbleached, "off-white" linen, often with blue dyed indigo or *tekhelet* pin-stripes woven into the fabric.

Cave 6Q: This Essene collection of lay character (including a *megillah* of the Song of Songs) is written primarily on papyrus and contains one copy of the lay rule book, the *Damascus Document*.

Cave 4Q: The special case of cave 4Q is that, as a *genizah*, it contains more than 700 worn copies of parchment and papyrus scrolls, sometimes from diverse sources, copied over long periods of time (in this case, dating from the late third cent. B.C.E. to the late first cent. C.E., with at least 70% deriving from the period between 75 B.C.E. and 25 C.E.). The cave contains books of Essene institutional interest, both from a priestly and a lay perspective. There is a broad and mixed offering of scrolls topically (Bible, Apocrypha, parabiblical, liturgical, legal, calendrical, and legendary texts), yet an avoidance of works which would be considered errant, such as *Ben Sira*, the *Books of Maccabees*, and all works of the Pharisees and the Sadducees.

Cave 5Q may also belong to the adjacent cave 4Qa/4Qb *genizah* complex, as it contains parchment scrolls (including both the *Community Rule* and the *Damascus Document*), though of a more limited age span. (If it is not a *genizah*, then a lay character might be assigned to this collection, since it contains two *megillot* of the book of Lamentations)

CAVES 11Q AND 3Q. Cave 11Q: A non-Essene collection of a priestly character, located in the northern cave cluster, Cave 11Q contains three copies of the pseudepigraphic rulebook the *Temple Scroll*, a chapter of *Ben Sira* (in 11Q Psalms[a]), and promotes Ezekiel among the prophets (perhaps due to its emphasis on the future temple and its promotion of the Zadokites). The library contains no certain works that promote the history or views of the Moreh Ẓedek and his followers. The textiles derived from this cave were almost exclusively bleached white (as opposed to the usual natural off-white, as in Cave 1Q and elsewhere) and often with blue indigo pin-stripes woven in.

Cave 3Q, located in the same cave cluster as 11Q, is of non-Essene, lay character (including a Lamentations *megillah*). It is likely connected with the Zealots, the self-appointed protectors of the Temple and its treasures, since it contained the *Copper Scroll*, which enumerates the locations where priestly paraphernalia, Temple treasures, and tithe jars were hidden.

Sixty-five percent of the at least 46 manuscripts from caves 11Q and 3Q come from the last 25 years before the fall of Jerusalem and 90% of the manuscripts come from the 1st century C.E. It would seem that these, and the other caves of the northern cluster, were inhabited briefly at the end of the First Revolt. The best candidate for ownership of these manuscript collections would seem to be the group of rebels led by the Zealot general Judah ben Jair who came down from Jerusalem to the jungle of the Jordan to take their last stand, along with another group of refugees from Machaerus (Jos., Wars, 7:210–15).

CAVE 2Q. Cave 2Q, although it is in the same cluster as cave 1Q, is not likely connected with the Essenes since it contains no community documents and includes *Ben Sira*. It is of lay character (containing two *megillot* of the Book of Ruth) and is likely connected with the revolutionaries (perhaps with Simeon bar Giora's group).

THE CASE OF MASADA. Early during the revolt Masada became the sole stronghold and residence of the Sicarii. The founder Judah the Galilean and his successors were called "teachers" by Josephus (Wars, 2:118). There is no reason to believe that this group would not keep an institutional library. The cache of scrolls found at Masada that once were thought to connect with the Qumran scrolls are no longer considered to be either Yaḥad or Essene in character. The corpus of manuscripts from Masada should be viewed as the remnants of a Sicarii library, written mainly on parchment, with certain lay and priestly components. (The various extraneous papyrus documents derived from the Roman occupation of the site must be treated separately.)

CAVES 7Q, 8Q, 9Q, AND 10Q: The remains from cave 7Q, which contained only Greek manuscripts, and cave 8Q, which contained Psalms, a liturgical work, a phylactery and a *mezuzah*, although having a definable character, are too sparse to be able to connect them with the other caves. The manuscripts from Caves 9Q and 10Q are not definable. However, in light of the food remains and lamps from all four of these caves, they all appear to have been used at the end of period IIb as residences for the rebels. This is also true with respect to most of the caves throughout the cliffs. In the Ein Feshkha cluster most of the caves contain remains from the post-70 C.E. period.

BIBLIOGRAPHY: R. de Vaux, *L'Archéologie et les manuscrits de la mer morte* (1961); J. van der Ploeg, *The Excavations at Qumran* (1958); J.T. Milik, *Ten Years of Discovery in the Wilderness of Judaea* (1959); Zeuner, in: PEFQS, 92 (1960), 27ff. **ADD. BIBLIOGRAPHY:** ARCHAEOLOGY OF QUMRAN AND EIN FESHKHA: R. de Vaux, *Archaeology and the Dead Sea Scrolls* (1972); R. de Vaux, with J.-B. Humbert and A. Chambon, *Fouilles de Khirbet Qumran et de Aïn Feshkha I* (1994). S. Pfann, *The Excavations of Qumran and Ein Feshkha* (2003; annotated English edition of R. de Vaux's excavation notes); J.B. Humbert and J. Gunneweg (eds.), *Khirbet Qumrân et 'Ain Feshkha II: Etudes d'anthropologie, de physique et de chimie* (2003) – Y. Magen and Y. Peleg; M. Broshi and H. Eshel; O. Guttfeld and R. Price; ARCHAEOLOGY OF THE QUMRAN CAVES: 1Q: Harding, de Vaux, Crowfoot, *Discoveries in the Judaean Desert I* (1955). 2Q–3Q, 5Q–11Q; Survey Caves 1–40; Caves A and B: R. de Vaux and J.T. Milik, *DJD III* (1962); 4Qa and 4Qb: de Vaux, Carswell and Barnes, *DJD VI* (1977). SURVEY CAVES: S. Pfann, *The Excavations of Qumran and Ein Feshkha* (2003); "Sites in the Judean Desert Where Texts Have Been Found," *The Dead Sea Scrolls on Microfiche: A Comprehensive Facsimile Edition of the Texts from the Judean Desert* (in collaboration with Emanuel Tov, 1993); "*Kelei dema*," Tithe Jars, Scroll Jars, and Cookie Jars," in: G. Brooke and P. Davies (eds.), *Proceedings of the Manchester Copper Scroll Conference* (2002); J. Patrich, "Khirbet Qumran in Light of New Archaeological Explorations in the Qumran Caves," in: *Methods of Investigation of the Dead Sea Scrolls and the Khirbet Qumran Site: Present Realities and Prospects* (1994). THE CHRISTMAS CAVE: J. Allegro, *Search the Desert* (1964). M. Bélis, "Des textiles: catalogues et commentaries: Les Textiles de *Christmas Cave*," in: J.B. Humbert and J. Gunneweg (eds.), *Khirbet Qumrân et 'Ain Feshkha II*, 211–221 (includes a list of other remains from the cave in *Tablau 2*).

[Frederick Fyvie Bruce / Stephen Pfann (2nd ed.)]

QUNAYṬIRA, AL- (**Kuneitra**), central town in *Ramat ha-Golan, at the crossroads where the highway connecting the Benot Ya'akov bridge with Damascus intersects roads to Mt. Hermon and Lebanon, to Sheikh Miskīn and the southern Bashan, and to *Ḥammat Gader on the Iarmuk River. The town lies in a shallow valley, approximately 2,950–3,100 ft. (900–950 m.) above sea level. Remains from the Byzantine period were found there, e.g., a granite column and three tombstones with legends in Greek. An archaeological survey in 1968 revealed additional Greek inscriptions, some of which testify to a Jewish population there in the Byzantine period, e.g., the legend "Archelaus ben Hananiah" on a tombstone. Until the mid-19th century al-Qunaytira was only a wayfarers' inn (*khān*). With the settlement of Circassians in Golan the town became a regional center, and by the end of the 19th century had 1,800 inhabitants, almost all Circassian Muslims. Water from a spring was collected in a reservoir dating from the Byzantine period and conducted to ponds at several places in the town, and the houses were built along broad, paved roads. The Circassians regarded al-Qunayṭira as their national center. The economy was based on administrative services, commerce, small workshops, and auxiliary farming. In the 1950s, when the town belonged to Syria, it began to lose its Circassian character as Arab merchants settled there. In the 1960s al-Qunayṭira was made the district town of Golan, when the population approached 15,000 and the economy was increasingly geared to the Syrian military installations. A large headquarters for the "Palestinian Front" was erected at the town's western entrance. The Circassians by then constituted no more than 15–20% of the total population. When al-Qunayṭira was captured by Israel forces on the last day of the *Six-Day War (June 11, 1967), it was found abandoned by almost all its inhabitants. According to the Israel census (1967), there were still 206 people, but they subsequently left. Kibbutz Merom Golan was established at the town's western entrance. Al-Qunayṭira has a place in Theodor *Herzl's prophetic novel *Altneuland*. The town, which he envisioned as accessible by an electric train rising from the shores of Lake Kinneret, became a junction of Transjordanian railways.

[Mordkhai Neishtat]

QURAYẒA, BANŪ, One of the three major Jewish tribes in *Medina (pre-Islamic Yathrib) that became famous in Islamic historiography through their conflict with *Muhammad. Their defeat in 627 came after that of the *Qaynuqāʿ and the *Naḍīr. Following Qurayẓa's siege and unconditional surrender, hundreds of their men were beheaded and their women and children were sold into slavery. The tribe of Qurayẓa was divided into two subdivisions, the ʿAmr and the Kaʿb, each having its own assembly (*majlis*). They had tower-houses used for residence that were owned by leaders such as al-Zabīr ibn Bāṭā, "the last of the Qurayẓa" in Saul *Tchernichowsky's famous poem, and Kaʿb ibn Asad, their chief at the time of Muhammad. In addition, they had a central fortification, al-Muʿriḍ, which was large enough to shelter the whole tribe in wartime. As was always the case in a settled tribal society, Qurayẓa's defense was also based on alliances. When these alliances collapsed, their fall was only a matter of time.

The dramatic events surrounding Qurayẓa's demise dominate the reports about them in Islamic literature. They were preceded by the Battle of the Ditch (Khandaq) in which Medina was besieged by a coalition of Muhammad's enemies that included his own tribe, Quraysh, and several nomadic tribes. The Qurayẓa who had a non-belligerency agreement with Muhammad – not to be confused with the so-called "Constitution of Medina" in which they did not participate – probably remained neutral: they lent the Muslims tools for digging the defensive ditch, but also sold provisions to the besiegers. After their surrender their fate was reportedly decided not by Muhammad, but by the fatally wounded Saʿd ibn Muʿādh of the Aws. His decision was met with opposition among the Aws with whom the Qurayẓa had an old alliance. One of the Quraẓī women taken captive was Rayḥāna, who became Muhammad's wife or concubine. The Quraẓī boys who were spared because they had not yet reached puberty were literate, and hence an asset for the emerging Islamic culture. When we read Qurayẓa stories "from within" that favorably describe certain Quraẓī leaders, otherwise known as Muhammad's enemies, they should be attributed to the role of these survivors as Muslim informants. The son of one such survivor achieved great fame a century after Muhammad: it was Muhammad ibn Kaʿb al-Quraẓī who was a leading authority on *Koran exegesis.

BIBLIOGRAPHY: W.M. Watt, "Ḳurayẓa," in: EIS², 5, 436a–b.; M.J. Kister, "The Massacre of the Banū Qurayẓa: A Re-Examination of a Tradition," in: *Jerusalem Studies in Arabic and Islam*, 8 (1986), 61–96. Reprinted in: idem, *Society and Religion from Jāhiliyya to Islam*, (1990), no. 8; M. Lecker, "On Arabs of the Banū Kilāb Executed together with the Jewish Banū Qurayẓa," in: *Jerusalem Studies in Arabic and Islam*, 19 (1995), 66–72. Reprinted in: *Jews and Arabs in Pre- and Early Islamic Arabia* (1998), no. 10.

[Michael Lecker (2nd ed.)]

Abbreviations

•

ABBREVIATIONS

GENERAL ABBREVIATIONS

This list contains abbreviations used in the Encyclopaedia (apart from the standard ones, such as geographical abbreviations, points of compass, etc.). For names of organizations, institutions, etc., in abbreviation, see Index. For bibliographical abbreviations of books and authors in Rabbinical literature, see following lists.

*	Cross reference; i.e., an article is to be found under the word(s) immediately following the asterisk (*).
°	Before the title of an entry, indicates a non-Jew (post-biblical times).
‡	Indicates reconstructed forms.
>	The word following this sign is derived from the preceding one.
<	The word preceding this sign is derived from the following one.

ad loc.	*ad locum*, "at the place"; used in quotations of commentaries.
A.H.	*Anno Hegirae*, "in the year of Hegira," i.e., according to the Muslim calendar.
Akk.	Addadian.
A.M.	*anno mundi*, "in the year (from the creation) of the world."
anon.	anonymous.
Ar.	Arabic.
Aram.	Aramaic.
Ass.	Assyrian.
b.	born; *ben, bar.*
Bab.	Babylonian.
B.C.E.	Before Common Era (= B.C.).
bibl.	bibliography.
Bul.	Bulgarian.
c., ca.	Circa.
C.E.	Common Era (= A.D.).
cf.	*confer*, "compare."
ch., chs.	chapter, chapters.
comp.	compiler, compiled by.
Cz.	Czech.
D	according to the documentary theory, the Deuteronomy document.
d.	died.
Dan.	Danish.
diss., dissert,	dissertation, thesis.
Du.	Dutch.
E.	according to the documentary theory, the Elohist document (i.e., using Elohim as the name of God) of the first five (or six) books of the Bible.
ed.	editor, edited, edition.
eds.	editors.
e.g.	*exempli gratia*, "for example."
Eng.	English.
et al.	*et alibi*, "and elsewhere"; or *et alii*, "and others"; "others."
f., ff.	and following page(s).
fig.	figure.
fl.	flourished.
fol., fols	folio(s).
Fr.	French.
Ger.	German.
Gr.	Greek.
Heb.	Hebrew.
Hg., Hung	Hungarian.
ibid	*Ibidem*, "in the same place."
incl. bibl.	includes bibliography.
introd.	introduction.
It.	Italian.
J	according to the documentary theory, the Jahwist document (i.e., using YHWH as the name of God) of the first five (or six) books of the Bible.
Lat.	Latin.
lit.	literally.
Lith.	Lithuanian.
loc. cit.	*loco citato*, "in the [already] cited place."
Ms., Mss.	Manuscript(s).
n.	note.
n.d.	no date (of publication).
no., nos	number(s).
Nov.	Novellae (Heb. *Ḥiddushim*).
n.p.	place of publication unknown.
op. cit.	*opere citato*, "in the previously mentioned work."
P.	according to the documentary theory, the Priestly document of the first five (or six) books of the Bible.
p., pp.	page(s).
Pers.	Persian.
pl., pls.	plate(s).
Pol.	Polish.
Port.	Potuguese.
pt., pts.	part(s).
publ.	published.
R.	Rabbi or Rav (before names); in Midrash (after an abbreviation) – *Rabbah*.
r.	recto, the first side of a manuscript page.
Resp.	Responsa (Latin "answers," Hebrew *She'elot u-Teshuvot* or *Teshuvot),* collections of rabbinic decisions.
rev.	revised.

Rom.	Romanian.
Rus(s).	Russian.
Slov.	Slovak.
Sp.	Spanish.
s.v.	*sub verbo, sub voce*, "under the (key) word."
Sum	Sumerian.
summ.	Summary.
suppl.	supplement.
Swed.	Swedish.
tr., trans(l).	translator, translated, translation.
Turk.	Turkish.
Ukr.	Ukrainian.
v., vv.	*verso*. The second side of a manuscript page; also verse(s).
Yid.	Yiddish.

ABBREVIATIONS USED IN RABBINICAL LITERATURE

Adderet Eliyahu, Karaite treatise by Elijah b. Moses *Bashyazi.

Admat Kodesh, Resp. by Nissim Ḥayyim Moses b. Joseph |Mizraḥi.

Aguddah, Sefer ha-, Nov. by *Alexander Suslin ha-Kohen.

Ahavat Ḥesed, compilation by *Israel Meir ha-Kohen.

Aliyyot de-Rabbenu Yonah, Nov. by *Jonah b. Avraham Gerondi.

Arukh ha-Shulḥan, codification by Jehiel Michel *Epstein.

Asayin (= positive precepts), subdivision of: (1) *Maimonides, *Sefer ha-Mitzvot;* (2) *Moses b. Jacob of Coucy, *Semag.*

Asefat Dinim, subdivision of *Sedei Ḥemed* by Ḥayyim Hezekiah *Medini, an encyclopaedia of precepts and responsa.

Asheri = *Asher b. Jehiel.

Aeret Ḥakhamim, by Baruch *Frankel-Teomim; pt, 1: Resp. to Sh. Ar.; pt2: Nov. to Talmud.

Ateret Zahav, subdivision of the *Levush*, a codification by Mordecai b. Abraham (Levush) *Jaffe; *Ateret Zahav* parallels Tur. YD.

Ateret Ẓevi, Comm. To Sh. Ar. by Ẓevi Hirsch b. Azriel.

Avir Ya'akov, Resp. by Jacob Avigdor.

Avkat Rokhel, Resp. by Joseph b. Ephraim *Caro.

Avnei Millu'im, Comm. to Sh. Ar., EH, by *Aryeh Loeb b. Joseph ha-Kohen.

Avnei Nezer, Resp. on Sh. Ar. by Abraham b. Ze'ev Nahum Bornstein of *Sochaczew.

Avodat Massa, Compilation of Tax Law by Yoasha Abraham Judah.

Azei ha-Levanon, Resp. by Judah Leib *Zirelson.

Ba'al ha-Tanya – *Shneur Zalman of Lyady.

Ba'ei Ḥayyei, Resp. by Ḥayyim b. Israel *Benveniste.

Ba'er Heitev, Comm. To Sh. Ar. The parts on OḤ and EH are by Judah b. Simeon *Ashkenazi, the parts on YD AND ḤM by *Zechariah Mendel b. Aryeh Leib. Printed in most editions of Sh. Ar.

Baḥ = Joel *Sirkes.

Baḥ, usual abbreviation for *Bayit Ḥadash*, a commentary on Tur by Joel *Sirkes; printed in most editions of Tur.

Bayit Ḥadash, see *Baḥ*.

Berab = Jacob Berab, also called Ri Berav.

Bedek ha-Bayit, by Joseph b. Ephraim *Caro, additions to his *Beit Yosef* (a comm. to Tur). Printed sometimes inside *Beit Yosef*, in smaller type. Appears in most editions of Tur.

Be'er ha-Golah, Commentary to Sh. Ar. By Moses b. Naphtali Hirsch *Rivkes; printed in most editions of Sh. Ar.

Be'er Mayim, Resp. by Raphael b. Abraham Manasseh Jacob.

Be'er Mayim Ḥayyim, Resp. by Samuel b. Ḥayyim *Vital.

Be'er Yiẓḥak, Resp. by Isaac Elhanan *Spector.

Beit ha-Beḥirah, Comm. to Talmud by Menahem b. Solomon *Meiri.

Beit Me'ir, Nov. on Sh. Ar. by Meir b. Judah Leib Posner.

Beit Shelomo, Resp. by Solomon b. Aaron Ḥason (the younger).

Beit Shemu'el, Comm. to Sh. Ar., EH, by *Samuel b. Uri Shraga Phoebus.

Beit Ya'akov, by Jacob b. Jacob Moses *Lorberbaum; pt.1: Nov. to Ket.; pt.2: Comm. to EH.

Beit Yisrael, collective name for the commentaries *Derishah, Perishah*, and *Be'urim* by Joshua b. Alexander ha-Kohen *Falk. See under the names of the commentaries.

Beit Yiẓḥak, Resp. by Isaac *Schmelkes.

Beit Yosef: (1) Comm. on Tur by Joseph b. Ephraim *Caro; printed in most editions of Tur; (2) Resp. by the same.

Ben Yehudah, Resp. by Abraham b. Judah Litsch (ליטש) Rosenbaum.

Bertinoro, Standard commentary to Mishnah by Obadiah *Bertinoro. Printed in most editions of the Mishnah.

[Be'urei] Ha-Gra, Comm. to Bible, Talmud, and Sh. Ar. By *Elijah b. Solomon Zalmon (Gaon of Vilna); printed in major editions of the mentioned works.

Be'urim, Glosses to Isserles *Darkhei Moshe* (a comm. on Tur) by Joshua b. Alexander ha-Kohen *Falk; printed in many editions of Tur.

Binyamin Ze'ev, Resp. by *Benjamin Ze'ev b. Mattathias of Arta.

Birkei Yosef, Nov. by Ḥayyim Joseph David *Azulai.

Ha-Buẓ ve-ha-Argaman, subdivision of the *Levush* (a codification by Mordecai b. Abraham (Levush) *Jaffe); *Ha-Buẓ ve-ha-Argaman* parallels Tur, EH.

Comm. = Commentary

Da'at Kohen, Resp. by Abraham Isaac ha-Kohen. *Kook.

Darkhei Moshe, Comm. on Tur Moses b. Israel *Isserles; printed in most editions of Tur.

Darkhei No'am, Resp. by *Mordecai b. Judah ha-Levi.

Darkhei Teshuvah, Nov. by Ẓevi *Shapiro; printed in the major editions of Sh. Ar.

De'ah ve-Haskel, Resp. by Obadiah Hadaya (see *Yaskil Avdi).*

Derashot Ran, Sermons by *Nissim b. Reuben Gerondi.
Derekh Ḥayyim, Comm. to *Avot* by *Judah Loew (Lob., Liwa) b. Bezalel (Maharal) of Prague.
Derishah, by Joshua b. Alexander ha-Kohen *Falk; additions to his *Perishah* (comm. on Tur); printed in many editions of Tur.
Derushei ha-Ẓelaḥ, Sermons, by Ezekiel b. Judah Halevi *Landau.
Devar Avraham, Resp. by Abraham *Shapira.
Devar Shemu'el, Resp. by Samuel *Aboab.
Devar Yehoshu'a, Resp. by Joshua Menahem b. Isaac Aryeh Ehrenberg.
Dikdukei Soferim, variae lections of the talmudic text by Raphael Nathan*Rabbinowicz.
Divrei Emet, Resp. by Isaac Bekhor David.
Divrei Ge'onim, Digest of responsa by Ḥayyim Aryeh b. Jeḥiel Ẓevi *Kahana.
Divrei Ḥamudot, Comm. on *Piskei ha-Rosh* by Yom Tov Lipmann b. Nathan ha-Levi *Heller; printed in major editions of the Talmud.
Divrei Ḥayyim several works by Ḥayyim *Halberstamm; if quoted alone refers to his Responsa.
Divrei Malkhi'el, Resp. by Malchiel Tenebaum.
Divrei Rivot, Resp. by Isaac b. Samuel *Adarbi.
Divrei Shemu'el, Resp. by Samuel Raphael Arditi.

Edut be-Ya'akov, Resp. by Jacob b. Abraham *Boton.
Edut bi-Yhosef, Resp. by Joseph b. Isaac *Almosnino.
Ein Ya'akov, Digest of talmudic *aggadot* by Jacob (Ibn) *Habib.
Ein Yiẓḥak, Resp. by Isaac Elhanan *Spector.
Ephraim of Lentshitz = Solomon *Luntschitz.
Erekh Leḥem, Nov. and glosses to Sh. Ar. by Jacob b. Abraham *Castro.
Eshkol, Sefer ha-, Digest of *halakhot* by *Abraham b. Isaac of Narbonne.
Et Sofer, Treatise on Law Court documents by Abraham b. Mordecai *Ankawa, in the 2nd vol. of his Resp. *Kerem Ḥamar.*
Etan ha-Ezraḥi, Resp. by Abraham b. Israel Jehiel (Shrenzl) *Rapaport.
Even ha-Ezel, Nov. to Maimonides' *Yad Ḥazakah* by Isser Zalman *Meltzer.
Even ha-Ezer, also called *Raban* of *Ẓafenat Pa'ne'aḥ,* rabbinical work with varied contents by *Eliezer b. Nathan of Mainz; not identical with the subdivision of Tur, Shulḥan Arukh, etc.
Ezrat Yehudah, Resp. by *Isaar Judah b. Nechemiah of Brisk.

Gan Eden, Karaite treatise by *Aaron b. Elijah of Nicomedia.
Gersonides = *Levi b. Gershom, also called Leo Hebraecus, or Ralbag.
Ginnat Veradim, Resp. by *Abraham b. Mordecai ha-Levi.

Haggahot, another name for *Rema.*
Haggahot Asheri, glosses to *Piskei ha-Rosh* by *Israel of Krems; printed in most Talmud editions.
Haggahot Maimuniyyot, Comm,. to Maimonides' Yad Ḥazakah by *Meir ha-Kohen; printed in most eds. of Yad.
Haggahot Mordekhai, glosses to *Mordekhai* by Samuel *Schlettstadt; printed in most editions of the Talmud after *Mordekhai.*
Haggahot ha-Rashash on Tosafot, annotations of Samuel *Strashun on the Tosafot (printed in major editions of the Talmud).
Ha-Gra = *Elijah b. Solomon Zalman (Gaon of Vilna).
Ha-Gra, Commentaries on Bible, Talmud, and Sh. Ar. respectively, by *Elijah b. Solomon Zalman (Gaon of Vilna); printed in major editions of the mentioned works.
Hai Gaon, Comm. = his comm. on Mishnah.
Ḥakham Ẓevi, Resp. by Ẓevi Hirsch b. Jacob *Ashkenazi.
Halakhot = Rif, *Halakhot.* Compilation and abstract of the Talmud by Isaac b. Jacob ha-Kohen *Alfasi; printed in most editions of the Talmud.
Halakhot Gedolot, compilation of *halakhot* from the Geonic period, arranged acc. to the Talmud. Here cited acc. to ed. Warsaw (1874). Author probably *Simeon Kayyara of Basra.
Halakhot Pesukot le-Rav Yehudai Ga'on compilation of *halakhot.*
Halakhot Pesukot min ha-Ge'onim, compilation of *halakhot* from the geonic period by different authors.
Ḥananel, Comm. to Talmud by *Hananel b. Ḥushi'el; printed in some editions of the Talmud.
Harei Besamim, Resp. by Aryeh Leib b. Isaac *Horowitz.
Ḥassidim, Sefer, Ethical maxims by *Judah b. Samuel he-Ḥasid.
Hassagot Rabad on Rif, Glosses on Rif, *Halakhot,* by *Abraham b. David of Posquières.
Hassagot Rabad [on Yad], Glosses on Maimonides, *Yad Ḥazakah,* by *Abraham b. David of Posquières.
Hassagot Ramban, Glosses by Naḥmanides on Maimonides' *Sefer ha-Mitzvot;* usually printed together with *Sefer ha-Mitzvot.*
Ḥatam Sofer = Moses *Sofer.
Ḥavvot Ya'ir, Resp. and varia by Jair Ḥayyim *Bacharach
Ḥayyim Or Zaru'a = *Ḥayyim (Eliezer) b. Isaac.
Ḥazon Ish = Abraham Isaiah *Karelitz.
Ḥazon Ish, Nov. by Abraham Isaiah *Karelitz
Ḥedvat Ya'akov, Resp. by Aryeh Judah Jacob b. David Dov Meisels (article under his father's name).
Heikhal Yiẓḥak, Resp. by Isaac ha-Levi *Herzog.
Ḥelkat Meḥokek, Comm. to Sh. Ar., by Moses b. Isaac Judah *Lima.
Ḥelkat Ya'akov, Resp. by Mordecai Jacob Breisch.
Ḥemdah Genuzah, , Resp. from the geonic period by different authors.
Ḥemdat Shelomo, Resp. by Solomon Zalman *Lipschitz.
Ḥida = Ḥayyim Joseph David *Azulai.
Ḥiddushei Halakhot ve-Aggadot, Nov. by Samuel Eliezer b. Judah ha-Levi *Edels.
Ḥikekei Lev, Resp. by Ḥayyim *Palaggi.
Ḥikrei Lev, Nov. to Sh. Ar. by Joseph Raphael b. Ḥayyim Joseph Ḥazzan (see article *Ḥazzan Family).
Hil. = Hilkhot … (e.g. *Hilkhot Shabbat).*
Ḥinnukh, Sefer ha-, List and explanation of precepts attributed (probably erroneously) to Aaron ha-Levi of Barcelona (see article **Ha-Ḥinnukh*).
Ḥok Ya'akov, Comm. to Hil. Pesaḥ in Sh. Ar., OḤ, by Jacob b. Joseph *Reicher.
Ḥokhmat Sehlomo (1), Glosses to Talmud, *Rashi* and Tosafot by Solomon b. Jehiel "Maharshal") *Luria; printed in many editions of the Talmud.
Ḥokhmat Sehlomo (2), Glosses and Nov. to Sh. Ar. by Solomon b. Judah Aaron *Kluger printed in many editions of Sh. Ar.
Ḥur, subdivision of the *Levush,* a codification by Mordecai b. Abraham (Levush) *Jaffe; *Hur* (or *Levush ha-Hur)* parallels Tur, OḤ, 242–697.
Ḥut ha-Meshullash, fourth part of the *Tashbeẓ* (Resp.), by Simeon b. Zemaḥ *Duran.

Ibn Ezra, Comm. to the Bible by Abraham *Ibn Ezra; printed in the major editions of the Bible *("Mikra'ot Gedolot").*
Imrei Yosher, Resp. by Meir b. Aaron Judah *Arik.
Ir Shushan, Subdivision of the *Levush,* a codification by Mordecai b. Abraham (Levush) *Jaffe; *Ir Shushan* parallels Tur, ḤM.
Israel of Bruna = Israel b. Ḥayyim *Bruna.
Ittur. Treatise on precepts by *Isaac b. Abba Mari of Marseilles.

Jacob Be Rab = *Be Rab.
Jacob b. Jacob Moses of Lissa = Jacob b. Jacob Moses *Lorberbaum.
Judah B. Simeon = Judah b. Simeon *Ashkenazi.
Judah Minz = Judah b. Eliezer ha-Levi *Minz.

Kappei Aharon, Resp. by Aaron Azriel.
Kehillat Ya'akov, Talmudic methodology, definitions etc. by Israel Jacob b. Yom Tov *Algazi.
Kelei Ḥemdah, Nov. and *pilpulim* by Meir Dan *Plotzki of Ostrova, arranged acc. to the Torah.
Keli Yakar, Annotations to the Torah by Solomon *Luntschitz.
Keneh Ḥokhmah, Sermons by Judah Loeb *Pochwitzer.
Keneset ha-Gedolah, Digest of *halakhot* by Ḥayyim b. Israel *Benveniste; subdivided into annotations to *Beit Yosef* and annotations to Tur.
Keneset Yisrael, Resp. by Ezekiel b. Abraham Katzenellenbogen (see article *Katzenellenbogen Family).
Kerem Ḥamar, Resp. and varia by Abraham b. Mordecai *Ankawa.
Kerem Shelmo. Resp. by Solomon b. Joseph *Amarillo.
Keritut, [Sefer], Methodology of the Talmud by *Samson b. Isaac of Chinon.
Kesef ha-Kedoshim, Comm. to Sh. Ar., ḤM, by Abraham *Wahrmann; printed in major editions of Sh. Ar.
Kesef Mishneh, Comm. to Maimonides, *Yad Ḥazakah,* by Joseph b. Ephraim *Caro; printed in most editions of *Yad Ḥazakah.*
Keẓot ha-Ḥoshen, Comm. to Sh. Ar., ḤM, by *Aryeh Loeb b. Joseph ha-Kohen; printed in major editions of Sh. Ar.
Kol Bo [Sefer], Anonymous collection of ritual rules; also called *Sefer ha-Likkutim.*
Kol Mevasser, Resp. by Meshullam *Rath.
Korban Aharon, Comm. to *Sifra* by Aaron b. Abraham *Ibn Ḥayyim; pt. 1 is called: *Middot Aharon.*
Korban Edah, Comm. to Jer. Talmud by David *Fraenkel; with additions: *Shiyyurei Korban;* printed in most editions of Jer. Talmud.
Kunteres ha-Kelalim, subdivision of *Sedei Ḥemed,* an encyclopaedia of precepts and responsa by Ḥayyim Hezekiah *Medini.
Kunteres ha-Semikhah, a treatise by *Levi b. Ḥabib; printed at the end of his responsa.
Kunteres Tikkun Olam, part of *Mispat Shalom* (Nov. by Shalom Mordecai b. Moses *Schwadron).

Lavin (negative precepts), subdivision of: (1) *Maimonides, *Sefer ha-Mitzvot;* (2) *Moses b. Jacob of Coucy, *Semag.*
Leḥem Mishneh, Comm. to Maimonides, *Yad Ḥazakah,* by Abraham [Ḥiyya] b. Moses *Boton; printed in most editions of *Yad Ḥazakah.*
Leḥem Rav, Resp. by Abraham [Ḥiyya] b. Moses *Boton.
Leket Yosher, Resp and varia by Israel b. Pethahiah *Isserlein, collected by *Joseph (Joselein) b. Moses.
Leo Hebraeus = *Levi b. Gershom, also called Ralbag or Gersonides.
Levush = Mordecai b. Abraham *Jaffe.
Levush [Malkhut], Codification by Mordecai b. Abraham (Levush) *Jaffe, with subdivisions: *[Levush ha-] Tekhelet* (parallels Tur OḤ 1–241); *[Levush ha-] Ḥur* (parallels Tur OḤ 242–697); *[Levush] Ateret Zahav* (parallels Tur YD); *[Levush ha-Buẓ ve-ha-Argaman* (parallels Tur EH); *[Levush] Ir Shushan* (parallels Tur ḤM); under the name *Levush* the author wrote also other works.
Li-Leshonot ha-Rambam, fifth part (nos. 1374–1700) of Resp. by *David b. Solomon ibn Abi Zimra (Radbaz).
Likkutim, Sefer ha-, another name for *[Sefer] Kol Bo.*

Ma'adanei Yom Tov, Comm. on *Piskei ha-Rosh* by Yom Tov Lipmann b. Nathan ha-Levi *Heller; printed in many editions of the Talmud.
Mabit = Moses b. Joseph *Trani.
Magen Avot, Comm. to *Avot* by Simeon b. Ẓemaḥ *Duran.
Magen Avraham, Comm. to Sh. Ar., OḤ, by Abraham Abele b. Ḥayyim ha-Levi *Gombiner; printed in many editions of Sh. Ar., OḤ.
Maggid Mishneh, Comm. to Maimonides, *Yad Ḥazakah,* by *Vidal Yom Tov of Tolosa; printed in most editions of the *Yad Ḥazakah.*
Maḥaneh Efrayim, Resp. and Nov., arranged acc. to Maimonides' *Yad Ḥazakah* , by Ephraim b. Aaron *Navon.
Maharai = Israel b. Pethahiah *Isserlein.
Maharal of Prague = *Judah Loew (Lob, Liwa), b. Bezalel.
Maharalbaḥ = *Levi b. Ḥabib.
Maharam Alashkar = Moses b. Isaac *Alashkar.
Maharam Alshekh = Moses b. Ḥayyim *Alashekh.
Maharam Mintz = Moses *Mintz.
Maharam of Lublin = *Meir b. Gedaliah of Lublin.
Maharam of Padua = Meir *Katzenellenbogen.
Maharam of Rothenburg = *Meir b. Baruch of Rothenburg.
Maharam Shik = Moses b. Joseph Schick.
Maharash Engel = Samuel b. Ze'ev Wolf Engel.
Maharashdam = Samuel b. Moses *Medina.
Maharḥash = Ḥayyim (ben) Shabbetai.
Mahari Basan = Jehiel b. Ḥayyim Basan.
Mahari b. Lev = Joseph ibn Lev.
Mahari'az = Jekuthiel Asher Zalman Ensil Zusmir.
Maharibal = *Joseph ibn Lev.
Mahariḥ = Jacob (Israel) *Ḥagiz.
Maharik = Joseph b. Solomon *Colon.
Maharikash = Jacob b. Abraham *Castro.
Maharil = Jacob b. Moses *Moellin.
Maharimat = Joseph b. Moses di Trani (not identical with the Maharit).
Maharit = Joseph b. Moses *Trani.
Maharitaẓ = Yom Tov b. Akiva Ẓahalon. (See article *Ẓahalon Family).
Maharsha = Samuel Eliezer b. Judah ha-Levi *Edels.
Maharshag = Simeon b. Judah Gruenfeld.
Maharshak = Samson b. Isaac of Chinon.
Maharshakh = *Solomon b. Abraham.
Maharshal = Solomon b. Jeḥiel *Luria.
Mahasham = Shalom Mordecai b. Moses *Sschwadron.
Maharyu = Jacob b. Judah *Weil.
Maḥazeh Avraham, Resp. by Abraham Nebagen v. Meir ha-Levi Steinberg.
Maḥazik Berakhah, Nov. by Ḥayyim Joseph David *Azulai.

*Maimonides = Moses b. Maimon, or Rambam.

*Malbim = Meir Loeb b. Jehiel Michael.

Malbim = Malbim's comm. to the Bible; printed in the major editions.

Malbushei Yom Tov, Nov. on *Levush,* OḤ, by Yom Tov Lipmann b. Nathan ha-Levi *Heller.

Mappah, another name for *Rema.*

Mareh ha-Panim, Comm. to Jer. Talmud by Moses b. Simeon *Margolies; printed in most editions of Jer. Talmud.

Margaliyyot ha-Yam, Nov. by Reuben *Margoliot.

Masat Binyamin, Resp. by Benjamin Aaron b. Abraham *Slonik

Mashbir, Ha- = *Joseph Samuel b. Isaac Rodi.

Massa Ḥayyim, Tax *halakhot* by Ḥayyim *Palaggi, with the subdivisions *Missim ve-Arnomiyyot* and *Torat ha-Minhagot.*

Massa Melekh, Compilation of Tax Law by Joseph b. Isaac *Ibn Ezra with concluding part *Ne'ilat She'arim.*

Matteh Asher, Resp. by Asher b. Emanuel Shalem.

Matteh Shimon, Digest of Resp. and Nov. to Tur and *Beit Yosef,* ḤM, by Mordecai Simeon b. Solomon.

Matteh Yosef, Resp. by Joseph b. Moses ha-Levi Nazir (see article under his father's name).

Mayim Amukkim, Resp. by Elijah b. Abraham *Mizraḥi.

Mayim Ḥayyim, Resp. by Ḥayyim b. Dov Beresh Rapaport.

Mayim Rabbim, , Resp. by Raphael *Meldola.

Me-Emek ha-Bakha, , Resp. by Simeon b. Jekuthiel Ephrati.

Me'irat Einayim, usual abbreviation: *Sma* (from: *Sefer Me'irat Einayim*); comm. to Sh. Ar. By Joshua b. Alexander ha-Kohen *Falk; printed in most editions of the Sh. Ar.

Melammed le-Ho'il, Resp. by David Ẓevi *Hoffmann.

Meisharim, [*Sefer*], Rabbinical treatise by *Jeroham b. Meshullam.

Meshiv Davar, Resp. by Naphtali Ẓevi Judah *Berlin.

Mi-Gei ha-Haregah, Resp. by Simeon b. Jekuthiel Ephrati.

Mi-Ma'amakim, Resp. by Ephraim Oshry.

Middot Aharon, first part of *Korban Aharon,* a comm. to *Sifra* by Aaron b. Abraham *Ibn Ḥayyim.

Migdal Oz, Comm. to Maimonides, *Yad Ḥazakah,* by *Ibn Gaon Shem Tov b. Abraham; printed in most editions of the *Yad Ḥazakah.*

Mikhtam le-David, Resp. by David Samuel b. Jacob *Pardo.

Mikkaḥ ve-ha-Mimkar, Sefer ha-, Rabbinical treatise by *Hai Gaon.

Milḥamot ha-Shem, Glosses to Rif, *Halakhot,* by *Naḥmanides.

Minḥat Ḥinnukh, Comm. to *Sefer ha-Ḥinnukh,* by Joseph b. Moses *Babad.

Minḥat Yizḥak, Resp. by Isaac Jacob b. Joseph Judah Weiss.

Misgeret ha-Shulḥan, Comm. to Sh. Ar., ḤM, by Benjamin Ze'ev Wolf b. Shabbetai; printed in most editions of Sh. Ar.

Mishkenot ha-Ro'im, Halakhot in alphabetical order by Uzziel Alshekh.

Mishnah Berurah, Comm. to Sh. Ar., OḤ, by *Israel Meir ha-Kohen.

Mishneh le-Melekh, Comm. to Maimonides, *Yad Ḥazakah,* by Judah *Rosanes; printed in most editions of *Yad Ḥazakah.*

Mishpat ha-Kohanim, Nov. to Sh. Ar., ḤM, by Jacob Moses *Lorberbaum, part of his *Netivot ha-Mishpat;* printed in major editions of Sh. Ar.

Mishpat Kohen, Resp. by Abraham Isaac ha-Kohen *Kook.

Mishpat Shalom, Nov. by Shalom Mordecai b. Moses *Schwadron; contains: *Kunteres Tikkun Olam.*

Mishpat u-Ẓedakah be-Ya'akov, Resp. by Jacob b. Reuben *Ibn Ẓur.

Mishpat ha-Urim, Comm. to Sh. Ar., ḤM by Jacob b. Jacob Moses *Lorberbaum, part of his *Netivot ha-Mishpat;* printed in major editons of Sh. Ar.

Mishpat Ẓedek, Resp. by *Melammed Meir b. Shem Tov.

Mishpatim Yesharim, Resp. by Raphael b. Mordecai *Berdugo.

Mishpetei Shemu'el, Resp. by Samuel b. Moses *Kalai (Kal'i).

Mishpetei ha-Tanna'im, Kunteres, Nov on *Levush,* OḤ by Yom Tov Lipmann b. Nathan ha-Levi *Heller.

Mishpetei Uzzi'el (Uziel), Resp. by Ben-Zion Meir Hai *Ouziel.

Missim ve-Arnoniyyot, Tax *halakhot* by Ḥayyim *Palaggi, a subdivision of his work *Massa Ḥayyim* on the same subject.

Mitzvot, Sefer ha-, Elucidation of precepts by *Maimonides; subdivided into *Lavin* (negative precepts) and *Asayin* (positive precepts).

Mitzvot Gadol, Sefer, Elucidation of precepts by *Moses b. Jacob of Coucy, subdivided into *Lavin* (negative precepts) and *Asayin* (positive precepts); the usual abbreviation is *Semag.*

Mitzvot Katan, Sefer, Elucidation of precepts by *Isaac b. Joseph of Corbeil; the usual, abbreviation is *Semak.*

Mo'adim u-Zemannim, Rabbinical treatises by Moses Sternbuch.

Modigliano, Joseph Samuel = *Joseph Samuel b. Isaac, Rodi (Ha-Mashbir).

Mordekhai (Mordecai), halakhic compilation by *Mordecai b. Hillel; printed in most editions of the Talmud after the texts.

Moses b. Maimon = *Maimonides, also called Rambam.

Moses b. Naḥman = Naḥmanides, also called Ramban.

Muram = Isaiah Menahem b. Isaac (from: Morenu R. Mendel).

Naḥal Yizḥak, Comm. on Sh. Ar., ḤM, by Isaac Elhanan *Spector.

Naḥalah li-Yhoshu'a, Resp. by Joshua Ẓunẓin.

Naḥalat Shivah, collection of legal forms by *Samuel b. David Moses ha-Levi.

*Naḥmanides = Moses b. Naḥman, also called Ramban.

Naẓiv = Naphtali Ẓevi Judah *Berlin.

Ne'eman Shemu'el, Resp. by Samuel Isaac *Modigilano.

Ne'ilat She'arim, concluding part of *Massa Melekh* (a work on Tax Law) by Joseph b. Isaac *Ibn Ezra, containing an exposition of customary law and subdivided into *Minhagei Issur* and *Minhagei Mamon.*

Ner Ma'aravi, Resp. by Jacob b. Malka.

Netivot ha-Mishpat, by Jacob b. Jacob Moses *Lorberbaum; subdivided into *Mishpat ha-Kohanim,* Nov. to Sh. Ar., ḤM, and *Mishpat ha-Urim,* a comm. on the same; printed in major editions of Sh. Ar.

Netivot Olam, Saying of the Sages by *Judah Loew (Lob, Liwa) b. Bezalel.

Nimmukei Menaḥem of Merseburg, Tax *halakhot* by the same, printed at the end of Resp. Maharyu.

Nimmukei Yosef, Comm. to Rif. *Halakhot,* by Joseph *Ḥabib (Ḥabiba); printed in many editions of the Talmud.

Noda bi-Yhudah, Resp. by Ezekiel b. Judah ha-Levi *Landau; there is a first collection *(Mahadura Kamma)* and a second collection *(Mahadura Tinyana).*

Nov. = Novellae, Ḥiddushim.

Ohel Moshe (1), Notes to Talmud, *Midrash Rabbah,* Yad, *Sifrei* and to several Resp., by Eleazar *Horowitz.

Ohel Moshe (2), Resp. by Moses Jonah Zweig.
Oholei Tam. Resp. by *Tam ibn Yaḥya Jacob b. David; printed in the rabbinical collection *Tummat Yesharim.*
Oholei Ya'akov, Resp. by Jacob de *Castro.
Or ha-Me'ir Resp by Judah Meir b. Jacob Samson Shapiro.
Or Same'aḥ, Comm. to Maimonides, *Yad Ḥazakah,* by *Meir Simḥah ha-Kohen of Dvinsk; printed in many editions of the *Yad Ḥazakah.*
Or Zaru'a [the father] = *Isaac b. Moses of Vienna.
Or Zaru'a [the son] = *Ḥayyim (Eliezer) b. Isaac.
Or Zaru'a, Nov. by *Isaac b. Moses of Vienna.
Orah, Sefer ha-, Compilation of ritual precepts by *Rashi.
Oraḥ la-Ẓaddik, Resp. by Abraham Ḥayyim Rodrigues.
Oẓar ha-Posekim, Digest of Responsa.

Paḥad Yiẓḥak, Rabbinical encyclopaedia by Isaac *Lampronti.
Panim Me'irot, Resp. by Meir b. Isaac *Eisenstadt.
Parashat Mordekhai, Resp. by Mordecai b. Abraham Naphtali *Banet.
Pe'at ha-Sadeh la-Dinim and Pe'at ha-Sadeh la-Kelalim, subdivisions of the *Sedei Ḥemed,* an encyclopaedia of precepts and responsa, by Ḥayyim Hezekaih *Medini.
Penei Moshe (1), Resp. by Moses *Benveniste.
Penei Moshe (2), Comm. to Jer. Talmud by Moses b. Simeon *Margolies; printed in most editions of the Jer. Talmud.
Penei Moshe (3), Comm. on the aggadic passages of 18 treatises of the Bab. and Jer. Talmud, by Moses b. Isaiah Katz.
Penei Yehoshu'a, Nov. by Jacob Joshua b. Ẓevi Hirsch *Falk.
Peri Ḥadash, Comm. on Sh. Ar. By Hezekiah da *Silva.
Perishah, Comm. on Tur by Joshua b. Alexander ha-Kohen *Falk; printed in major edition of Tur; forms together with *Derishah* and *Be'urim* (by the same author) the *Beit Yisrael.*
Pesakim u-Khetavim, 2nd part of the *Terumat ha-Deshen* by Israel b. Pethahiah *Isserlein' also called *Piskei Maharai.*
Pilpula Ḥarifta, Comm. to *Piskei ha-Rosh, Seder Nezikin,* by Yom Tov Lipmann b. Nathan ha-Levi *Heller; printed in major editions of the Talmud.
Piskei Maharai, see *Terumat ha-Deshen,* 2nd part; also called *Pesakim u-Khetavim.*
Piskei ha-Rosh, a compilation of *halakhot,* arranged on the Talmud, by *Asher b. Jehiel (Rosh); printed in major Talmud editions.
Pitḥei Teshuvah, Comm. to Sh. Ar. by Abraham Hirsch b. Jacob *Eisenstadt; printed in major editions of the Sh. Ar.

Rabad = *Abraham b. David of Posquières (Rabad III.).
Raban = *Eliezer b. Nathan of Mainz.
Raban, also called *Ẓafenat Pa'ne'aḥ* or *Even ha-Ezer,* see under the last name.
Rabi Abad = *Abraham b. Isaac of Narbonne.
Radad = David Dov. b. Aryeh Judah Jacob *Meisels.
Radam = Dov Berush b. Isaac Meisels.
Radbaz = *David b Solomon ibn Abi Ziumra.
Radbaz, Comm. to Maimonides, *Yad Ḥazakah,* by *David b. Solomon ibn Abi Zimra.
Ralbag = *Levi b. Gershom, also called Gersonides, or Leo Hebraeus.
Ralbag, Bible comm. by *Levi b. Gershon.
Rama [da Fano] = Menaḥem Azariah *Fano.
Ramah = Meir b. Todros [ha-Levi] *Abulafia.
Ramam = *Menaham of Merseburg.
Rambam = *Maimonides; real name: Moses b. Maimon.
Ramban = *Naḥmanides; real name Moses b. Naḥman.
Ramban, Comm. to Torah by *Naḥmanides; printed in major editions. ("Mikra'ot Gedolot").
Ran = *Nissim b. Reuben Gerondi.
Ran of Rif, Comm. on Rif, *Halakhot,* by Nissim b. Reuben Gerondi.
Ranaḥ = *Elijah b. Ḥayyim.
Rash = *Samson b. Abraham of Sens.
Rash, Comm. to Mishnah, by *Samson b. Abraham of Sens; printed in major Talmud editions.
Rashash = Samuel *Strashun.
Rashba = Solomon b. Abraham *Adret.
Rashba, Resp., see also; *Sefer Teshuvot ha-Rashba ha-Meyuḥasot le-ha-Ramban,* by Solomon b. Abraham *Adret.
Rashbad = Samuel b. David.
Rashbam = *Samuel b. Meir.
Rashbam = Comm. on Bible and Talmud by *Samuel b. Meir; printed in major editions of Bible and most editions of Talmud.
Rashbash = Solomon b. Simeon *Duran.
*Rashi = Solomon b. Isaac of Troyes.
Rashi, Comm. on Bible and Talmud by *Rashi; printed in almost all Bible and Talmud editions.
Raviah = Eliezer b. Joel ha-Levi.
Redak = David *Kimḥi.
Redak, Comm. to Bible by David *Kimḥi.
Redakh = *David b. Ḥayyim ha-Kohen of Corfu.
Re'em = Elijah b. Abraham *Mizraḥi.
Rema = Moses b. Israel *Isserles.
Rema, Glosses to Sh. Ar. by Moses b. Israel *Isserles; printed in almost all editions of the Sh. Ar. inside the text in Rashi type; also called *Mappah* or *Haggahot.*
Remek = Moses Kimḥi.
Remakh = Moses ha-Kohen mi-Lunel.
Reshakh = *Solomon b. Abraham; also called Maharshakh.
Resp. = Responsa, *She'elot u-Teshuvot.*
Ri Berav = *Berab.
Ri Escapa = Joseph b. Saul *Escapa.
Ri Migash = Joseph b. Meir ha-Levi *Ibn Migash.
Riba = Isaac b. Asher ha-Levi; Riba II (Riba ha-Baḥur) = his grandson with the same name.
Ribam = Isaac b. Mordecai (or: Isaac b. Meir).
Ribash = *Isaac b. Sheshet Perfet (or: Barfat).
Rid= *Isaiah b. Mali di Trani the Elder.
Ridbaz = Jacob David b. Ze'ev *Willowski.
Rif = Isaac b. Jacob ha-Kohen *Alfasi.
Rif, *Halakhot,* Compilation and abstract of the Talmud by Isaac b. Jacob ha-Kohen *Alfasi.
Ritba = Yom Tov b. Abraham *Ishbili.
Riẓbam = Isaac b. Mordecai.
Rosh = *Asher b. Jehiel, also called Asheri.
Rosh Mashbir, Resp. by *Joseph Samuel b. Isaac, Rodi.

Sedei Ḥemed, Encyclopaedia of precepts and responsa by Ḥayyim Ḥezekiah *Medini; subdivisions: *Asefat Dinim, Kunteres ha-Kelalim, Pe'at ha-Sadeh la-Dinim, Pe'at ha-Sadeh la-Kelalim.*
Semag, Usual abbreviation of *Sefer Mitzvot Gadol,* elucidation of precepts by *Moses b. Jacob of Coucy; subdivided into *Lavin* (negative precepts) *Asayin* (positive precepts).
Semak, Usual abbreviation of *Sefer Mitzvot Katan,* elucidation of precepts by *Isaac b. Joseph of Corbeil.

Sh. Ar. = *Shulḥan Arukh,* code by Joseph b. Ephraim *Caro.
Sha'ar Mishpat, Comm. to Sh. Ar., ḤM. By Israel Isser b. Ze'ev Wolf.
Sha'arei Shevu'ot, Treatise on the law of oaths by *David b. Saadiah; usually printed together with Rif, *Halakhot;* also called: *She'arim of R. Alfasi.*
Sha'arei Teshuvah, Collection of resp. from Geonic period, by different authors.
Sha'arei Uzzi'el, Rabbinical treatise by Ben-Zion Meir Ha *Ouziel.
Sha'arei Ẓedek, Collection of resp. from Geonic period, by different authors.
Shadal [or Shedal] = Samuel David *Luzzatto.
Shai la-Moreh, Resp. by Shabbetai Jonah.
Shakh, Usual abbreviation of *Siftei Kohen,* a comm. to Sh. Ar., YD and ḤM by *Shabbetai b. Meir ha-Kohen; printed in most editions of Sh. Ar.
Sha'ot-de-Rabbanan, Resp. by *Solomon b. Judah ha-Kohen.
She'arim of R. Alfasi see *Sha'arei Shevu'ot.*
Shedal, see Shadal.
She'elot u-Teshuvot ha-Ge'onim, Collection of resp. by different authors.
She'erit Yisrael, Resp. by Israel Ze'ev Mintzberg.
She'erit Yosef, Resp. by *Joseph b. Mordecai Gershon ha-Kohen.
She'ilat Yaveẓ, Resp. by Jacob *Emden (Yaveẓ).
She'iltot, Compilation arranged acc. to the Torah by *Aḥa (Aḥai) of Shabḥa.
Shem Aryeh, Resp. by Aryeh Leib *Lipschutz.
Shemesh Ẓedakah, Resp. by Samson *Morpurgo.
Shenei ha-Me'orot ha-Gedolim, Resp. by Elijah *Covo.
Shetarot, Sefer ha-, Collection of legal forms by *Judah b. Barzillai al-Bargeloni.
Shevut Ya'akov, Resp. by Jacob b. Joseph Reicher.
Shibbolei ha-Leket Compilation on ritual by Zedekiah b. Avraham *Anav.
Shiltei Gibborim, Comm. to Rif, *Halakhot,* by *Joshua Boaz b. Simeon; printed in major editions of the Talmud.
Shittah Mekubbeẓet, Compilation of talmudical commentaries by Bezalel *Ashkenazi.
Shivat Ẓiyyon, Resp. by Samuel b. Ezekiel *Landau.
Shiyyurei Korban, by David *Fraenkel; additions to his comm. to Jer. Talmud *Korban Edah;* both printed in most editions of Jer. Talmud.
Sho'el u-Meshiv, Resp. by Joseph Saul ha-Levi *Nathanson.
Sh[ulḥan] Ar[ukh] [of Ba'al ha-Tanyal], Code by *Shneur Zalman of Lyady; not identical with the code by Joseph Caro.
Siftei Kohen, Comm. to Sh. Ar., YD and ḤM by *Shabbetai b. Meir ha-Kohen; printed in most editions of Sh. Ar.; usual abbreviation: *Shakh.*
Simḥat Yom Tov, Resp. by Tom Tov b. Jacob *Algazi.
Simlah Ḥadashah, Treatise on *Sheḥitah* by Alexander Sender b. Ephraim Zalman *Schor; see also *Tevu'ot Shor.*
Simeon b. Ẓemaḥ = Simeon b. Ẓemaḥ *Duran.
Sma, Comm. to Sh. Ar. by Joshua b. Alexander ha-Kohen *Falk; the full title is: *Sefer Me'irat Einayim;* printed in most editions of Sh. Ar.
Solomon b. Isaac ha-Levi = Solomon b. Isaac *Levy.
Solomon b. Isaac of Troyes = *Rashi.

Tal Orot, Rabbinical work with various contents, by Joseph ibn Gioia.
Tam, Rabbenu = *Tam Jacob b. Meir.
Tashbaẓ = Samson b. Zadok.
Tashbeẓ = Simeon b. Zemaḥ *Duran, sometimes also abbreviation for Samson b. Zadok, usually known as Tashbaẓ.
Tashbeẓ [Sefer ha-], Resp. by Simeon b. Ẓemaḥ *Duran; the fourth part of this work is called: *Ḥut ha-Meshullash.*
Taz, Usual abbreviation of *Turei Zahav,* comm., to Sh. Ar. by *David b. Samnuel ha-Levi; printed in most editions of Sh. Ar.
(Ha)-Tekhelet, subdivision of the *Levush* (a codification by Mordecai b. Abraham (Levush) *Jaffe); *Ha-Tekhelet* parallels Tur, OḤ 1-241.
Terumat ha-Deshen, by Israel b. Pethahiah *Isserlein; subdivided into a part containing responsa, and a second part called *Pesakim u-Khetavim* or *Piskei Maharai.*
Terumot, Sefer ha-, Compilation of *halakhot* by Samuel b. Isaac *Sardi.
Teshuvot Ba'alei ha-Tosafot, Collection of responsa by the Tosafists.
Teshjvot Ge'onei Mizraḥ u-Ma'aav, Collection of responsa.
Teshuvot ha-Geonim, Collection of responsa from Geonic period.
Teshuvot Ḥakhmei Provinẓyah, Collection of responsa by different Provencal authors.
Teshuvot Ḥakhmei Ẓarefat ve-Loter, Collection of responsa by different French authors.
Teshuvot Maimuniyyot, Resp. pertaining to Maimonides' *Yad Ḥazakah;* printed in major editions of this work after the text; authorship uncertain.
Tevu'ot Shor, by Alexander Sender b. Ephraim Zalman *Schor, a comm. to his *Simlah Ḥadashah,* a work on *Sheḥitah.*
Tiferet Ẓevi, Resp. by Ẓevi Hirsch of the "AHW" Communities (Altona, Hamburg, Wandsbeck).
Tiktin, Judah b. Simeon = Judah b. Simeon *Ashkenazi.
Toledot Adam ve-Ḥavvah, Codification by *Jeroham b. Meshullam.
Torat Emet, Resp. by Aaron b. Joseph *Sasson.
Torat Ḥayyim, , Resp. by Ḥayyim (ben) Shabbetai.
Torat ha-Minhagot, subdivision of the *Massa Ḥayyim* (a work on tax law) by Ḥayyim *Palaggi, containing an exposition of customary law.
Tosafot Rid, Explanations to the Talmud and decisions by *Isaiah b. Mali di Trani the Elder.
Tosefot Yom Tov, comm. to Mishnah by Yom Tov Lipmann b. Nathan ha-Levi *Heller; printed in most editions of the Mishnah.
Tummim, subdivision of the comm. to Sh. Ar., ḤM, *Urim ve-Tummim* by Jonathan *Eybeschuetz; printed in the major editions of Sh. Ar.
Tur, usual abbreviation for the *Arba'ah Turim* of *Jacob b. Asher.
Turei Zahav, Comm. to Sh. Ar. by *David b. Samuel ha-Levi; printed in most editions of Sh. Ar.; usual abbreviation: *Taz.*

Urim, subdivision of the following.
Urim ve-Tummim, Comm. to Sh. Ar., ḤM, by Jonathan *Eybeschuetz; printed in the major editions of Sh. Ar.; subdivided in places into *Urim* and *Tummim.*

Vikku'aḥ Mayim Ḥayyim, Polemics against Isserles and Caro by Ḥayyim b. Bezalel.

Yad Malakhi, Methodological treatise by *Malachi b. Jacob ha-Kohen.

Yad Ramah, Nov. by Meir b. Todros [ha-Levi] *Abulafia.
Yakhin u-Vo'az, Resp. by Ẓemaḥ b. Solomon *Duran.
Yam ha-Gadol, Resp. by Jacob Moses *Toledano.
Yam shel Shelomo, Compilation arranged acc. to Talmud by Solomon b. Jehiel (Maharshal) *Luria.
Yashar, Sefer ha-, by *Tam, Jacob b. Meir (Rabbenu Tam); 1st pt.: Resp.; 2nd pt.: Nov.
Yaskil Avdi, Resp. by Obadiah Hadaya (printed together with his Resp. *De'ah ve-Haskel).*
Yaveẓ = Jacob *Emden.
Yehudah Ya'aleh, Resp. by Judah b. Israel *Aszod.
Yekar Tiferet, Comm. to Maimonides' *Yad Ḥazakah,*by David b. Solomon ibn Zimra, printed in most editions of *Yad Ḥazakah.*
Yere'im [ha-Shalem], [Sefer], Treatise on precepts by *Eliezer b. Samuel of Metz.
Yeshu'ot Ya'akov, Resp. by Jacob Meshullam b. Mordecai Ze'ev *Ornstein.
Yiẓhak Rei'aḥ, Resp. by Isaac b. Samuel Abendanan (see article *Abendanam Family).
Ẓafenat Pa'ne'aḥ (1), also called *Raban* or *Even ha-Ezer*, see under the last name.
Ẓafenat Pa'ne'aḥ (2), Resp. by Joseph *Rozin.
Zayit Ra'anan, Resp. by Moses Judah Leib b. Benjamin Auerbach.
Ẓeidah la-Derekh, Codification by *Menahem b. Aaron ibn Zerah.
Ẓedakah u-Mishpat, Resp. by Ẓedakah b. Saadiah Huẓin.
Zekan Aharon, Resp. by Elijah b. Benjamin ha-Levi.
Zekher Ẓaddik, Sermons by Eliezer *Katzenellenbogen.
Ẓemaḥ Ẓedek (1) Resp. by Menaham Mendel Shneersohn (see under *Shneersohn Family).
Zera Avraham, Resp. by Abraham b. David *Yiẓḥaki.
Zera Emet Resp. by *Ishmael b. Abaham Isaac ha-Kohen.
Ẓevi la-Ẓaddik, Resp. by Ẓevi Elimelech b. David Shapira.
Zikhron Yehudah, Resp. by *Judah b. Asher
Zikhron Yosef, Resp. by Joseph b. Menahem *Steinhardt.
Zikhronot, Sefer ha-, Sermons on several precepts by Samuel *Aboab.
Zikkaron la-Rishonim . . ., by Albert (Abraham Elijah) *Harkavy; contains in vol. 1 pt. 4 (1887) a collection of Geonic responsa.
Ẓiẓ Eliezer, Resp. by Eliezer Judah b. Jacob Gedaliah Waldenberg.

BIBLIOGRAPHICAL ABBREVIATIONS

Bibliographies in English and other languages have been extensively updated, with English translations cited where available. In order to help the reader, the language of books or articles is given where not obvious from titles of books or names of periodicals. Titles of books and periodicals in languages with alphabets other than Latin, are given in transliteration, even where there is a title page in English. Titles of articles in periodicals are not given. Names of Hebrew and Yiddish periodicals well known in English-speaking countries or in Israel under their masthead in Latin characters are given in this form, even when contrary to transliteration rules. Names of authors writing in languages with non-Latin alphabets are given in their Latin alphabet form wherever known; otherwise the names are transliterated. Initials are generally not given for authors of articles in periodicals, except to avoid confusion. Non-abbreviated book titles and names of periodicals are printed in *italics*. Abbreviations are given in the list below.

AASOR	*Annual of the American School of Oriental Research* (1919ff.).
AB	*Analecta Biblica* (1952ff.).
Abel, Géog	F.-M. Abel, *Géographie de la Palestine,* 2 vols. (1933-38).
ABR	*Australian Biblical Review* (1951ff.).
Abr.	Philo, *De Abrahamo.*
Abrahams, Companion	I. Abrahams, *Companion to the Authorised Daily Prayer Book* (rev. ed. 1922).
Abramson, Merkazim	S. Abramson, *Ba-Merkazim u-va-Tefuẓot bi-Tekufat ha-Ge'onim* (1965).
Acts	Acts of the Apostles (New Testament).
ACUM	*Who is who in ACUM [Aguddat Kompozitorim u-Meḥabbrim].*
ADAJ	*Annual of the Department of Antiquities, Jordan* (1951ff.).
Adam	Adam and Eve (Pseudepigrapha).
ADB	*Allgemeine Deutsche Biographie,* 56 vols. (1875–1912).
Add. Esth.	The Addition to Esther (Apocrypha).
Adler, Prat Mus	1. Adler, *La pratique musicale savante dans quelques communautés juives en Europe au XVIIe et XVIIIe siècles,* 2 vols. (1966).
Adler-Davis	H.M. Adler and A. Davis (ed. and tr.), *Service of the Synagogue, a New Edition of the Festival Prayers with an English Translation in Prose and Verse,* 6 vols. (1905–06).
Aet.	Philo, *De Aeternitate Mundi.*
AFO	*Archiv fuer Orientforschung* (first two volumes under the name *Archiv fuer Keilschriftforschung)* (1923ff.).
Ag. Ber	*Aggadat Bereshit* (ed. Buber, 1902*).*
Agr.	Philo, *De Agricultura.*
Ag. Sam.	*Aggadat Samuel.*
Ag. Song	*Aggadat Shir ha-Shirim* (Schechter ed., 1896).
Aharoni, Ereẓ	Y. Aharoni, *Ereẓ Yisrael bi-Tekufat ha-Mikra: Geografyah Historit* (1962).
Aharoni, Land	Y. Aharoni, *Land of the Bible* (1966).

Ahikar	Ahikar (Pseudepigrapha).
AI	*Archives Israélites de France* (1840–1936).
AJA	*American Jewish Archives* (1948ff.).
AJHSP	*American Jewish Historical Society – Publications* (after vol. 50 = AJHSQ).
AJHSQ	*American Jewish Historical (*Society) *Quarterly* (before vol. 50 =AJHSP).
AJSLL	*American Journal of Semitic Languages and Literature* (1884–95 under the title *Hebraica,* since 1942 JNES).
AJYB	*American Jewish Year Book* (1899ff.).
AKM	Abhandlungen fuer die Kunde des Morgenlandes (series).
Albright, Arch	W.F. Albright, *Archaeology of Palestine* (rev. ed. 1960).
Albright, Arch Bib	W.F. Albright, *Archaeology of Palestine and the Bible* (1935^{3}*).*
Albright, Arch Rel	W.F. Albright, *Archaeology and the Religion of Israel* (1953^{3}*).*
Albright, Stone	W.F. Albright, *From the Stone Age to Christianity* (1957^{2}*).*
Alon, Meḥkarim	G. Alon, *Meḥkarim be-Toledot Yisrael bi-Ymei Bayit Sheni u-vi-Tekufat ha-Mishnah ve-ha Talmud,* 2 vols. (1957–58).
Alon, Toledot	G. Alon, *Toledot ha-Yehudim be-Ereẓ Yisrael bi-Tekufat ha-Mishnah ve-ha-Talmud,* I (1958^{3}), (1961^{2}).
ALOR	Alter Orient (series).
Alt, Kl Schr	A. Alt, *Kleine Schriften zur Geschichte des Volkes Israel,* 3 vols. (1953–59).
Alt, Landnahme	A. Alt, *Landnahme der Israeliten in Palaestina* (1925); also in Alt, Kl Schr, 1 (1953), 89–125.
Ant.	Josephus, *Jewish Antiquities* (Loeb Classics ed.).
AO	*Acta Orientalia* (1922ff.).
AOR	*Analecta Orientalia* (1931ff.).
AOS	American Oriental Series.
Apion	Josephus, *Against Apion* (Loeb Classics ed.).
Aq.	Aquila's Greek translation of the Bible.
Ar.	*Arakhin* (talmudic tractate).
Artist.	Letter of Aristeas (Pseudepigrapha).
ARN^{1}	*Avot de-Rabbi Nathan,* version (1) ed. Schechter, 1887.
ARN^{2}	*Avot de-Rabbi Nathan,* version (2) ed. Schechter, 1945^{2}.
Aronius, Regesten	I. Aronius, *Regesten zur Geschichte der Juden im fraenkischen und deutschen Reiche bis zum Jahre 1273* (1902).
ARW	*Archiv fuer Religionswissenschaft* (1898–1941/42).
AS	*Assyrological Studies* (1931ff.).
Ashtor, Korot	E. Ashtor (Strauss), *Korot ha-Yehudim bi-Sefarad ha-Muslemit,* 1(1966^{2}), 2(1966).
Ashtor, Toledot	E. Ashtor (Strauss), *Toledot ha-Yehudim be-Miẓrayim ve-Suryah Taḥat Shilton ha-Mamlukim,* 3 vols. (1944–70).
Assaf, Ge'onim	S. Assaf, *Tekufat ha-Ge'onim ve-Sifrutah* (1955).
Assaf, Mekorot	S. Assaf, *Mekorot le-Toledot ha-Ḥinnukh be-Yisrael,* 4 vols. (1925–43).
Ass. Mos.	Assumption of Moses (Pseudepigrapha).
ATA	Alttestamentliche Abhandlungen (series).
ATANT	Abhandlungen zur Theologie des Alten und Neuen Testaments (series).
AUJW	*Allgemeine unabhaengige juedische Wochenzeitung* (till 1966 = AWJD).
AV	Authorized Version of the Bible.
Avad.	*Avadim* (post-talmudic tractate).
Avi-Yonah, Geog	M. Avi-Yonah, *Geografyah Historit shel Ereẓ Yisrael* (1962^{3}).
Avi-Yonah, Land	M. Avi-Yonah, *The Holy Land from the Persian to the Arab conquest (536 B.C. to A.D. 640)* (1960).
Avot	*Avot* (talmudic tractate).
Av. Zar.	*Avodah Zarah* (talmudic tractate).
AWJD	*Allgemeine Wochenzeitung der Juden in Deutschland* (since 1967 = AUJW).
AZDJ	*Allgemeine Zeitung des Judentums.*
Azulai	Ḥ.Y.D. Azulai, *Shem ha-Gedolim,* ed. by I.E. Benjacob, 2 pts. (1852) (and other editions).
BA	*Biblical Archaeologist* (1938ff.).
Bacher, Bab Amor	W. Bacher, *Agada der babylonischen Amoraeer* (1913^{2}).
Bacher, Pal Amor	W. Bacher, *Agada der palaestinensischen Amoraeer* (Heb. ed. *Aggadat Amora'ei Ereẓ Yisrael),* 2 vols. (1892–99).
Bacher, Tann	W. Bacher, *Agada der Tannaiten* (Heb. ed. *Aggadot ha-Tanna'im,* vol. 1, pt. 1 and 2 (1903); vol. 2 (1890).
Bacher, Trad	W. Bacher, *Tradition und Tradenten in den Schulen Palaestinas und Babyloniens* (1914).
Baer, Spain	Yitzhak (Fritz) Baer, *History of the Jews in Christian Spain,* 2 vols. (1961–66).
Baer, Studien	Yitzhak (Fritz) Baer, *Studien zur Geschichte der Juden im Koenigreich Aragonien waehrend des 13. und 14. Jahrhunderts* (1913).
Baer, Toledot	Yitzhak (Fritz) Baer*, Toledot ha-Yehudim bi-Sefarad ha-Noẓerit mi-Teḥillatan shel ha-Kehillot ad ha-Gerush,* 2 vols. (1959^{2}).
Baer, Urkunden	Yitzhak (Fritz) Baer, *Die Juden im christlichen Spanien,* 2 vols. (1929–36).
Baer S., Seder	S.I. Baer, *Seder Avodat Yisrael* (1868 and reprints*).*
BAIU	*Bulletin de l'Alliance Israélite Universelle* (1861–1913*).*
Baker, Biog Dict	*Baker's Biographical Dictionary of Musicians,* revised by N. Slonimsky (1958^{5}; with Supplement 1965).
I Bar.	I Baruch (Apocrypha).
II Bar.	II Baruch (Pseudepigrapha).
III Bar.	III Baruch (Pseudepigrapha).
BAR	*Biblical Archaeology Review.*
Baron, Community	S.W. Baron, *The Jewish Community, its History and Structure to the American Revolution,* 3 vols. (1942).

Baron, Social	S.W. Baron, *Social and Religious History of the Jews,* 3 vols. (1937); enlarged, 1-2(1952^{2}), 3-14 (1957–69).
Barthélemy-Milik	D. Barthélemy and J.T. Milik, *Dead Sea Scrolls: Discoveries in the Judean Desert,* vol. 1 *Qumram Cave* I (1955).
BASOR	*Bulletin of the American School of Oriental Research.*
Bauer-Leander	H. Bauer and P. Leander, *Grammatik des Biblisch-Aramaeischen* (1927; repr. 1962).
BB	(1) *Bava Batra* (talmudic tractate). (2) *Biblische Beitraege* (1943ff.).
BBB	Bonner biblische Beitraege (series).
BBLA	*Beitraege zur biblischen Landes- und Altertumskunde* (until 1949–ZDPV).
BBSAJ	*Bulletin,* British School of Archaeology, Jerusalem (1922–25; after 1927 included in PEFQS).
BDASI	*Alon* (since 1948) or *Hadashot Arkhe'ologiyyot* (since 1961), bulletin of the Department of Antiquities of the State of Israel.
Begrich, Chronologie	J. Begrich, *Chronologie der Koenige von Israel und Juda* (1929).
Bek.	*Bekhorot* (talmudic tractate).
Bel	Bel and the Dragon (Apocrypha).
Benjacob, Oẓar	I.E. Benjacob, *Oẓar ha-Sefarim* (1880; repr. 1956).
Ben Sira	see Ecclus.
Ben-Yehuda, Millon	E. Ben-Yedhuda, *Millon ha-Lashon ha-Ivrit,* 16 vols (1908–59; repr. in 8 vols., 1959).
Benzinger, Archaeologie	I. Benzinger, *Hebraeische Archaeologie* (1927^{3}).
Ben Zvi, Eretz Israel	I. Ben-Zvi, *Eretz Israel under Ottoman Rule* (1960; offprint from L. Finkelstein (ed.), *The Jews, their History, Culture and Religion* (vol. 1).
Ben Zvi, Ereẓ Israel	I. Ben-Zvi, *Ereẓ Israel bi-Ymei ha-Shilton ha-Ottomani (1955).*
Ber.	*Berakhot* (talmudic tractate).
Beẓah	*Beẓah* (talmudic tractate).
BIES	Bulletin of the Israel Exploration Society, see below BJPES.
Bik.	*Bikkurim* (talmudic tractate).
BJCE	Bibliography of Jewish Communities in Europe, catalog at General Archives for the History of the Jewish People, Jerusalem.
BJPES	Bulletin of the Jewish Palestine Exploration Society – English name of the Hebrew periodical known as: 1. *Yedi'ot ha-Ḥevrah ha-Ivrit la-Ḥakirat Ereẓ Yisrael va-Attikoteha* (1933–1954); 2. *Yedi'ot ha-Ḥevrah la-Ḥakirat Ereẓ Yisrael va-Attikoteha* (1954–1962); 3. *Yedi'ot ba-Ḥakirat Ereẓ Yisrael va-Attikoteha* (1962ff.).
BJRL	*Bulletin of the John Rylands Library* (1914ff.).
BK	*Bava Kamma* (talmudic tractate).
BLBI	*Bulletin of the Leo Baeck Institute* (1957ff.).
BM	(1) *Bava Meẓia* (talmudic tractate). (2) *Beit Mikra* (1955/56ff.). (3) British Museum.
BO	*Bibbia e Oriente* (1959ff.).
Bondy-Dworský	G. Bondy and F. Dworský, *Regesten zur Geschichte der Juden in Boehmen, Maehren und Schlesien von 906 bis 1620,* 2 vols. (1906).
BOR	*Bibliotheca Orientalis* (1943ff.).
Borée, Ortsnamen	W. Borée *Die alten Ortsnamen Palaestinas* (1930).
Bousset, Religion	W. Bousset, *Die Religion des Judentums im neutestamentlichen Zeitalter* (1906^{2}).
Bousset-Gressmann	W. Bousset, *Die Religion des Judentums im spaethellenistischen Zeitalter* (1966^{3}).
BR	*Biblical Review* (1916–25).
BRCI	*Bulletin of the Research Council of Israel* (1951/52–1954/55; then divided).
BRE	*Biblical Research* (1956ff.).
BRF	*Bulletin of the Rabinowitz Fund for the Exploration of Ancient Synagogues* (1949ff.).
Briggs, Psalms	Ch. A. and E.G. Briggs, *Critical and Exegetical Commentary on the Book of Psalms,* 2 vols. (ICC, 1906–07).
Bright, Hist	J. Bright, *A History of Israel* (1959).
Brockelmann, Arab Lit	K. Brockelmann, *Geschichte der arabischen Literatur,* 2 vols. 1898–1902), supplement, 3 vols. (1937–42).
Bruell, Jahrbuecher	*Jahrbuecher fuer juedische Geschichte und Litteratur,* ed. by N. Bruell, Frankfurt (1874–90).
Brugmans-Frank	H. Brugmans and A. Frank (eds.), *Geschiedenis der Joden in Nederland* (1940).
BTS	*Bible et Terre Sainte* (1958ff.).
Bull, Index	S. Bull, *Index to Biographies of Contemporary Composers* (1964).
BW	*Biblical World* (1882–1920).
BWANT	*Beitraege zur Wissenschaft vom Alten und Neuen Testament* (1926ff.).
BZ	*Biblische Zeitschrift* (1903ff.).
BZAW	*Beihefte zur Zeitschrift fuer die alttestamentliche Wissenschaft,* supplement to ZAW (1896ff.).
BŻIH	*Biuletyn Zydowskiego Instytutu Historycznego* (1950ff.).
CAB	*Cahiers d'archéologie biblique* (1953ff.).
CAD	*The* [*Chicago*] *Assyrian Dictionary* (1956ff.).
CAH	*Cambridge Ancient History,* 12 vols. (1923–39)
CAH^{2}	*Cambridge Ancient History,* second edition, 14 vols. (1962–2005).
Calwer, Lexikon	*Calwer, Bibellexikon.*
Cant.	Canticles, usually given as Song (= Song of Songs).

Cantera-Millás, Inscripciones	F. Cantera and J.M. Millás, *Las Inscripciones Hebraicas de España* (1956).
CBQ	*Catholic Biblical Quarterly* (1939ff.).
CCARY	Central Conference of American Rabbis, *Yearbook* (1890/91ff.).
CD	*Damascus Document* from the Cairo *Genizah* (published by S. Schechter, *Fragments of a Zadokite Work*, 1910).
Charles, Apocrypha	R.H. Charles, *Apocrypha and Pseudepigrapha . . .*, 2 vols. (1913; repr. 1963–66).
Cher.	Philo, *De Cherubim.*
I (or II) Chron.	Chronicles, book I and II (Bible).
CIG	*Corpus Inscriptionum Graecarum.*
CIJ	*Corpus Inscriptionum Judaicarum,* 2 vols. (1936–52).
CIL	*Corpus Inscriptionum Latinarum.*
CIS	*Corpus Inscriptionum Semiticarum* (1881ff.).
C.J.	Codex Justinianus.
Clermont-Ganneau, Arch	Ch. Clermont-Ganneau, *Archaeological Researches in Palestine,* 2 vols. (1896–99).
CNFI	*Christian News from Israel* (1949ff.).
Cod. Just.	Codex Justinianus.
Cod. Theod.	Codex Theodosinanus.
Col.	Epistle to the Colosssians (New Testament).
Conder, Survey	Palestine Exploration Fund, *Survey of Eastern Palestine,* vol. 1, pt. I (1889) = C.R. Conder, *Memoirs of the . . . Survey.*
Conder-Kitchener	Palestine Exploration Fund, *Survey of Western Palestine,* vol. 1, pts. 1-3 (1881–83) = C.R. Conder and H.H. Kitchener, *Memoirs.*
Conf.	Philo, *De Confusione Linguarum.*
Conforte, Kore	D. Conforte, *Kore ha-Dorot* (1842^{2}).
Cong.	Philo, *De Congressu Quaerendae Eruditionis Gratia.*
Cont.	Philo, *De Vita Contemplativa.*
I (or II) Cor.	Epistles to the Corinthians (New Testament).
Cowley, Aramic	A. Cowley, *Aramaic Papyri of the Fifth Century B.C.* (1923).
Colwey, Cat	A.E. Cowley, *A Concise Catalogue of the Hebrew Printed Books in the Bodleian Library* (1929).
CRB	*Cahiers de la Revue Biblique* (1964ff.).
Crowfoot-Kenyon	J.W. Crowfoot, K.M. Kenyon and E.L. Sukenik, *Buildings of Samaria* (1942).
C.T.	Codex Theodosianus.
DAB	*Dictionary of American Biography* (1928–58).
Daiches, Jews	S. Daiches, *Jews in Babylonia* (1910).
Dalman, Arbeit	G. Dalman, *Arbeit und Sitte in Palaestina,* 7 vols.in 8 (1928–42 repr. 1964).
Dan	Daniel (Bible).
Davidson, Oẓar	I. Davidson, *Oẓar ha-Shirah ve-ha-Piyyut,* 4 vols. (1924–33); Supplement in: HUCA, 12–13 (1937/38), 715–823.

DB	J. Hastings, *Dictionary of the Bible,* 4 vols. (1963^{2}).
DBI	F.G. Vigoureaux et al. (eds.), *Dictionnaire de la Bible,* 5 vols. in 10 (1912); Supplement, 8 vols. (1928–66)
Decal.	Philo, *De Decalogo.*
Dem.	*Demai* (talmudic tractate).
DER	*Derekh Ereẓ Rabbah* (post-talmudic tractate).
Derenbourg, Hist	J. Derenbourg *Essai sur l'histoire et la géographie de la Palestine* (1867).
Det.	Philo, *Quod deterius potiori insidiari solet.*
Deus	Philo, *Quod Deus immutabilis sit.*
Deut.	Deuteronomy (Bible).
Deut. R.	*Deuteronomy Rabbah.*
DEZ	*Derekh Ereẓ Zuta* (post-talmudic tractate).
DHGE	*Dictionnaire d'histoire et de géographie ecclésiastiques,* ed. by A. Baudrillart et al., 17 vols (1912–68).
Dik. Sof	*Dikdukei Soferim,* variae lections of the talmudic text by Raphael Nathan Rabbinovitz (16 vols., 1867–97).
Dinur, Golah	B. Dinur (Dinaburg), *Yisrael ba-Golah,* 2 vols. in 7 (1959–68) = vols. 5 and 6 of his *Toledot Yisrael,* second series.
Dinur, Haganah	B. Dinur (ed.), *Sefer Toledot ha-Haganah* (1954ff.).
Diringer, Iscr	D. Diringer, *Iscrizioni antico-ebraiche palestinesi* (1934).
Discoveries	*Discoveries in the Judean Desert* (1955ff.).
DNB	*Dictionary of National Biography,* 66 vols. (1921–222) with Supplements.
Dubnow, Divrei	S. Dubnow, *Divrei Yemei Am Olam,* 11 vols (1923–38 and further editions).
Dubnow, Ḥasidut	S. Dubnow, *Toledot ha-Ḥasidut* (1960^{2}).
Dubnow, Hist	S. Dubnow, *History of the Jews* (1967).
Dubnow, Hist Russ	S. Dubnow, *History of the Jews in Russia and Poland,* 3 vols. (1916 20).
Dubnow, Outline	S. Dubnow, *An Outline of Jewish History,* 3 vols. (1925–29).
Dubnow, Weltgesch	S. Dubnow, *Weltgeschichte des juedischen Volkes* 10 vols. (1925–29).
Dukes, Poesie	L. Dukes, *Zur Kenntnis der neuhebraeischen religioesen Poesie* (1842).
Dunlop, Khazars	D. H. Dunlop, *History of the Jewish Khazars* (1954).
EA	El Amarna Letters (edited by J.A. Knudtzon), *Die El-Amarna Tafel,* 2 vols. (1907 14).
EB	*Encyclopaedia Britannica.*
EBI	*Estudios biblicos* (1941ff.).
EBIB	T.K. Cheyne and J.S. Black, *Encyclopaedia Biblica,* 4 vols. (1899–1903).
Ebr.	Philo, *De Ebrietate.*
Eccles.	Ecclesiastes (Bible).
Eccles. R.	*Ecclesiastes Rabbah.*
Ecclus.	Ecclesiasticus or Wisdom of Ben Sira (or Sirach; Apocrypha).
Eduy.	*Eduyyot* (mishanic tractate).

EG	*Enziklopedyah shel Galuyyot* (1953ff.).
EH	*Even ha-Ezer.*
EHA	*Enziklopedyah la-Ḥafirot Arkheologiyyot be-Ereẓ Yisrael,* 2 vols. (1970).
EI	*Enzyklopaedie des Islams,* 4 vols. (1905–14). Supplement vol. (1938).
EIS	*Encyclopaedia of Islam,* 4 vols. (1913–36; repr. 1954–68).
EIS[2]	*Encyclopaedia of Islam, second edition (1960–2000).*
Eisenstein, Dinim	J.D. Eisenstein, *Oẓar Dinim u-Minhagim* (1917; several reprints).
Eisenstein, Yisrael	J.D. Eisenstein, *Oẓar Yisrael* (10 vols, 1907–13; repr. with several additions 1951).
EIV	*Enziklopedyah Ivrit* (1949ff.).
EJ	*Encyclopaedia Judaica* (German, A-L only), 10 vols. (1928–34).
EJC	*Enciclopedia Judaica Castellana,* 10 vols. (1948–51).
Elbogen, Century	I Elbogen, *A Century of Jewish Life* (1960^2).
Elbogen, Gottesdienst	I Elbogen, *Der juedische Gottesdienst …* (1931^3, repr. 1962).
Elon, Mafte'aḥ	M. Elon (ed.), *Mafte'aḥ ha-She'elot ve-ha-Teshuvot ha-Rosh* (1965).
EM	*Enziklopedyah Mikra'it* (1950ff.).
I (or II) En.	I and II Enoch (Pseudepigrapha).
EncRel	*Encyclopedia of Religion,* 15 vols. (1987, 2005^2).
Eph.	Epistle to the Ephesians (New Testament).
Ephros, Cant	G. Ephros, *Cantorial Anthology,* 5 vols. (1929–57).
Ep. Jer.	Epistle of Jeremy (Apocrypha).
Epstein, Amora'im	J N. Epstein, *Mevo'ot le-Sifrut ha-Amora'im* (1962).
Epstein, Marriage	L M. Epstein, *Marriage Laws in the Bible and the Talmud* (1942).
Epstein, Mishnah	J. N. Epstein, *Mavo le-Nusaḥ ha-Mishnah,* 2 vols. (1964^2).
Epstein, Tanna'im	J. N. Epstein, *Mavo le-Sifruth ha-Tanna'im.* (1947).
ER	*Ecumenical Review.*
Er.	*Eruvin* (talmudic tractate).
ERE	*Encyclopaedia of Religion and Ethics,* 13 vols. (1908–26); reprinted.
ErIsr	*Eretz-Israel,* Israel Exploration Society.
I Esd.	I Esdras (Apocrypha) (= III Ezra).
II Esd.	II Esdras (Apocrypha) (= IV Ezra).
ESE	*Ephemeris fuer semitische Epigraphik,* ed. by M. Lidzbarski.
ESN	*Encyclopaedia Sefaradica Neerlandica,* 2 pts. (1949).
ESS	*Encyclopaedia of the Social Sciences,* 15 vols. (1930–35); reprinted in 8 vols. (1948–49).
Esth.	Esther (Bible).
Est. R.	*Esther Rabbah.*
ET	*Enziklopedyah Talmudit* (1947ff.).
Eusebius, Onom.	E. Klostermann (ed.), *Das Onomastikon* (1904), Greek with Hieronymus' Latin translation.
Ex.	Exodus (Bible).
Ex. R.	*Exodus Rabbah.*
Exs	Philo, *De Exsecrationibus.*
EẒD	*Enziklopeday shel ha-Ẓiyyonut ha-Datit* (1951ff.).
Ezek.	Ezekiel (Bible).
Ezra	Ezra (Bible).
III Ezra	III Ezra (Pseudepigrapha).
IV Ezra	IV Ezra (Pseudepigrapha).
Feliks, Ha-Ẓome'aḥ	*J. Feliks, Ha-Ẓome'aḥ ve-ha-Ḥai ba-Mishnah* (1983).
Finkelstein, Middle Ages	L. Finkelstein, *Jewish Self-Government in the Middle Ages* (1924).
Fischel, Islam	W.J. Fischel, *Jews in the Economic and Political Life of Mediaeval Islam* (1937; reprint with introduction "The Court Jew in the Islamic World," 1969).
FJW	*Fuehrer durch die juedische Gemeindeverwaltung und Wohlfahrtspflege in Deutschland* (1927/28).
Frankel, Mevo	Z. Frankel, *Mevo ha-Yerushalmi* (1870; reprint 1967).
Frankel, Mishnah	Z. Frankel, *Darkhei ha-Mishnah* (1959^2; reprint 1959^2).
Frazer, Folk-Lore	J.G. Frazer, *Folk-Lore in the Old Testament,* 3 vols. (1918–19).
Frey, Corpus	J.-B. Frey, *Corpus Inscriptionum Iudaicarum,* 2 vols. (1936–52).
Friedmann, Lebensbilder	A. Friedmann, *Lebensbilder beruehmter Kantoren,* 3 vols. (1918–27).
FRLT	*Forschungen zur Religion und Literatur des Alten und Neuen Testaments* (series) (1950ff.).
Frumkin-Rivlin	A.L. Frumkin and E. Rivlin, *Toledot Ḥakhmei Yerushalayim,* 3 vols. (1928–30), Supplement vol. (1930).
Fuenn, Keneset	S.J. Fuenn, *Keneset Yisrael,* 4 vols. (1887–90).
Fuerst, Bibliotheca	J. Fuerst, *Bibliotheca Judaica,* 2 vols. (1863; repr. 1960).
Fuerst, Karaeertum	J. Fuerst, *Geschichte des Karaeertums,* 3 vols. (1862–69).
Fug.	Philo, *De Fuga et Inventione.*
Gal.	Epistle to the Galatians (New Testament).
Galling, Reallexikon	K. Galling, *Biblisches Reallexikon* (1937).
Gardiner, Onomastica	A.H. Gardiner, *Ancient Egyptian Onomastica,* 3 vols. (1947).
Geiger, Mikra	A. Geiger, *Ha-Mikra ve-Targumav,* tr. by J.L. Baruch (1949).
Geiger, Urschrift	A. Geiger, *Urschrift und Uebersetzungen der Bibel* 1928^2).
Gen.	Genesis (Bible).
Gen. R.	*Genesis Rabbah.*
Ger.	*Gerim* (post-talmudic tractate).
Germ Jud	M. Brann, I. Elbogen, A. Freimann, and H. Tykocinski (eds.), *Germania Judaica,* vol. 1 (1917; repr. 1934 and 1963); vol. 2, in 2 pts. (1917–68), ed. by Z. Avneri.

GHAT	*Goettinger Handkommentar zum Alten Testament* (1917–22).
Ghirondi-Neppi	M.S. Ghirondi and G.H. Neppi, *Toledot Gedolei Yisrael u-Ge'onei Italyah ... u-Ve'urim al Sefer Zekher Ẓaddikim li-Verakhah* . . .(1853), index in ZHB, 17 (1914), 171–83.
Gig.	Philo, *De Gigantibus.*
Ginzberg, Legends	L. Ginzberg, *Legends of the Jews,* 7 vols. (1909–38; and many reprints).
Git.	*Gittin* (talmudic tractate).
Glueck, Explorations	N. Glueck, *Explorations in Eastern Palestine,* 2 vols. (1951).
Goell, Bibliography	Y. Goell, *Bibliography of Modern Hebrew Literature in English Translation* (1968).
Goodenough, Symbols	E.R. Goodenough, *Jewish Symbols in the Greco-Roman Period,* 13 vols. (1953–68).
Gordon, Textbook	C.H. Gordon, *Ugaritic Textbook* (1965; repr. 1967).
Graetz, Gesch	H. Graetz, *Geschichte der Juden* (last edition 1874–1908).
Graetz, Hist	H. Graetz, *History of the Jews,* 6 vols. (1891–1902).
Graetz, Psalmen	H. Graetz, *Kritischer Commentar zu den Psalmen,* 2 vols. in 1 (1882–83).
Graetz, Rabbinowitz	H. Graetz, *Divrei Yemei Yisrael,* tr. by S.P. Rabbinowitz. (1928 1929^{2}).
Gray, Names	G.B. Gray, *Studies in Hebrew Proper Names* (1896).
Gressmann, Bilder	H. Gressmann, *Altorientalische Bilder zum Alten Testament* (1927^{2}).
Gressmann, Texte	H. Gressmann, *Altorientalische Texte zum Alten Testament* (1926^{2}).
Gross, Gal Jud	H. Gross, *Gallia Judaica* (1897; repr. with add. 1969).
Grove, Dict	*Grove's Dictionary of Music and Musicians,* ed. by E. Blum 9 vols. (1954^{5}) and suppl. (1961^{5}).
Guedemann, Gesch Erz	M. Guedemann, *Geschichte des Erziehungswesens und der Cultur der abendlaendischen Juden,* 3 vols. (1880–88).
Guedemann, Quellenschr	M. Guedemann, *Quellenschriften zur Geschichte des Unterrichts und der Erziehung bei den deutschen Juden* (1873, 1891).
Guide	Maimonides, *Guide of the Perplexed.*
Gulak, Oẓar	A. Gulak, *Oẓar ha-Shetarot ha-Nehugim be-Yisrael* (1926).
Gulak, Yesodei	A. Gulak, *Yesodei ha-Mishpat ha-Ivri, Seder Dinei Mamonot be-Yisrael, al pi Mekorot ha-Talmud ve-ha-Posekim,* 4 vols. (1922; repr. 1967).
Guttmann, Mafte'aḥ	M. Guttmann, *Mafte'aḥ ha-Talmud,* 3 vols. (1906–30).
Guttmann, Philosophies	J. Guttmann, *Philosophies of Judaism* (1964).
Hab.	*Habakkuk* (Bible).
Ḥag.	*Ḥagigah* (talmudic tractate).
Haggai	*Haggai* (Bible).
Ḥal.	*Ḥallah* (talmudic tractate).
Halevy, Dorot	I. Halevy, *Dorot ha-Rishonim,* 6 vols. (1897–1939).
Halpern, Pinkas	I. Halpern (Halperin), *Pinkas Va'ad Arba Araẓot* (1945).
Hananel-Eškenazi	A. Hananel and Eškenazi (eds.), *Fontes Hebraici ad res oeconomicas socialesque terrarum balcanicarum saeculo XVI pertinentes,* 2 vols, (1958–60; in Bulgarian).
HB	*Hebraeische Bibliographie* (1858–82).
Heb.	Epistle to the Hebrews (New Testament).
Heilprin, Dorot	J. Heilprin (Heilperin), *Seder ha-Dorot,* 3 vols. (1882; repr. 1956).
Her.	Philo, *Quis Rerum Divinarum Heres.*
Hertz, Prayer	J.H. Hertz (ed.), *Authorised Daily Prayer Book* (rev. ed. 1948; repr. 1963).
Herzog, Instit	I. Herzog, *The Main Institutions of Jewish Law,* 2 vols. (1936–39; repr. 1967).
Herzog-Hauck	J.J. Herzog and A. Hauch (eds.), *Real-encyklopaedie fuer protestantische Theologie* (1896–1913^{3}).
HḤY	*Ha-Ẓofeh le-Ḥokhmat Yisrael* (first four volumes under the title *Ha-Ẓofeh me-Ereẓ Hagar)* (1910/11–13).
Hirschberg, Afrikah	H.Z. Hirschberg, *Toledot ha-Yehudim be-Afrikah ha-Zofonit,* 2 vols. (1965).
HJ	*Historia Judaica* (1938–61).
HL	*Das Heilige Land* (1857ff.)
ḤM	*Ḥoshen Mishpat.*
Hommel, Ueberliefer.	F. Hommel, *Die altisraelitische Ueberlieferung in inschriftlicher Beleuchtung* (1897).
Hor.	*Horayot* (talmudic tractate).
Horodezky, Ḥasidut	S.A. Horodezky, *Ha-Ḥasidut ve-ha-Ḥasidim,* 4 vols. (1923).
Horowitz, Ereẓ Yis	I.W. Horowitz, *Ereẓ Yisrael u-Shekhenoteha* (1923).
Hos.	Hosea (Bible).
HTR	*Harvard Theological Review* (1908ff.).
HUCA	*Hebrew Union College Annual* (1904; 1924ff.)
Ḥul.	*Ḥullin* (talmudic tractate).
Husik, Philosophy	I. Husik, *History of Medieval Jewish Philosophy* (1932^{2}).
Hyman, Toledot	A. Hyman, *Toledot Tanna'im ve-Amora'im* (1910; repr. 1964).
Ibn Daud, Tradition	Abraham Ibn Daud, *Sefer ha-Qabbalah – The Book of Tradition,* ed. and tr. By G.D. Cohen (1967).
ICC	International Critical Commentary on the Holy Scriptures of the Old and New Testaments (series, 1908ff.).
IDB	*Interpreter's Dictionary of the Bible,* 4 vols. (1962).
Idelsohn, Litugy	A. Z. Idelsohn, *Jewish Liturgy and its Development* (1932; paperback repr. 1967)
Idelsohn, Melodien	A. Z. Idelsohn, *Hebraeisch-orientalischer Melodienschatz,* 10 vols. (1914 32).
Idelsohn, Music	A. Z. Idelsohn, *Jewish Music in its Historical Development* (1929; paperback repr. 1967).

IEJ	*Israel Exploration Journal* (1950ff.).
IESS	*International Encyclopedia of the Social Sciences* (various eds.).
IG	*Inscriptiones Graecae,* ed. by the Prussian Academy.
IGYB	*Israel Government Year Book* (1949/50ff.).
ILR	*Israel Law Review* (1966ff.).
IMIT	*Izraelita Magyar Irodalmi Társulat Évkönyv* (1895 1948).
IMT	International Military Tribunal.
INB	*Israel Numismatic Bulletin* (1962–63).
INJ	*Israel Numismatic Journal* (1963ff.).
Ios	Philo, *De Iosepho.*
Isa.	Isaiah (Bible).
ITHL	Institute for the Translation of Hebrew Literature.
IZBG	*Internationale Zeitschriftenschau fuer Bibelwissenschaft und Grenzgebiete* (1951ff.).
JA	*Journal asiatique* (1822ff.).
James	Epistle of James (New Testament).
JAOS	*Journal of the American Oriental Society* (c. 1850ff.)
Jastrow, Dict	M. Jastrow, *Dictionary of the Targumim, the Talmud Babli and Yerushalmi, and the Midrashic literature,* 2 vols. (1886 1902 and reprints).
JBA	*Jewish Book Annual* (19242ff.).
JBL	*Journal of Biblical Literature* (1881ff.).
JBR	*Journal of Bible and Religion* (1933ff.).
JC	*Jewish Chronicle* (1841ff.).
JCS	*Journal of Cuneiform Studies* (1947ff.).
JE	*Jewish Encyclopedia,* 12 vols. (1901–05 several reprints).
Jer.	Jeremiah (Bible).
Jeremias, Alte Test	A. Jeremias, *Das Alte Testament im Lichte des alten Orients* 1930^{4}).
JGGJČ	*Jahrbuch der Gesellschaft fuer Geschichte der Juden in der Čechoslovakischen Republik* (1929–38).
JHSEM	Jewish Historical Society of England, *Miscellanies* (1925ff.).
JHSET	Jewish Historical Society of England, *Transactions* (1893ff.).
JJGL	*Jahrbuch fuer juedische Geschichte und Literatur* (Berlin) (1898–1938).
JJLG	*Jahrbuch der juedische-literarischen Gesellschaft* (Frankfurt) (1903–32).
JJS	*Journal of Jewish Studies* (1948ff.).
JJSO	*Jewish Journal of Sociology* (1959ff.).
JJV	*Jahrbuch fuer juedische Volkskunde* (1898–1924).
JL	*Juedisches Lexikon,* 5 vols. (1927–30).
JMES	*Journal of the Middle East Society* (1947ff.).
JNES	*Journal of Near Eastern Studies* (continuation of AJSLL) (1942ff.).
J.N.U.L.	Jewish National and University Library.
Job	Job (Bible).
Joel	Joel (Bible).
John	Gospel according to John (New Testament).
I, II and III John	Epistles of John (New Testament).
Jos., Ant	Josephus, *Jewish Antiquities* (Loeb Classics ed.).
Jos. Apion	Josephus, *Against Apion* (Loeb Classics ed.).
Jos., index	*Josephus Works,* Loeb Classics ed., index of names.
Jos., Life	Josephus, *Life* (ed. Loeb Classics).
Jos, Wars	Josephus, *The Jewish Wars* (Loeb Classics ed.).
Josh.	Joshua (Bible).
JPESB	Jewish Palestine Exploration Society Bulletin, see BJPES.
JPESJ	Jewish Palestine Exploration Society Journal – Eng. Title of the Hebrew periodical *Kovez ha-Ḥevrah ha-Ivrit la-Ḥakirat Erez Yisrael va-Attikoteha.*
JPOS	*Journal of the Palestine Oriental Society* (1920–48).
JPS	Jewish Publication Society of America, *The Torah* (1962, 1967^{2}); *The Holy Scriptures* (1917).
JQR	*Jewish Quarterly Review* (1889ff.).
JR	*Journal of Religion* (1921ff.).
JRAS	*Journal of the Royal Asiatic Society* (1838ff.).
JHR	*Journal of Religious History* (1960/61ff.).
JSOS	*Jewish Social Studies* (1939ff.).
JSS	*Journal of Semitic Studies* (1956ff.).
JTS	*Journal of Theological Studies* (1900ff.).
JTSA	Jewish Theological Seminary of America (also abbreviated as JTS).
Jub.	Jubilees (Pseudepigrapha).
Judg.	Judges (Bible).
Judith	Book of Judith (Apocrypha).
Juster, Juifs	J. Juster, *Les Juifs dans l'Empire Romain,* 2 vols. (1914).
JYB	*Jewish Year Book* (1896ff.).
JZWL	*Juedische Zeitschift fuer Wissenschaft und Leben* (1862–75).
Kal.	*Kallah* (post-talmudic tractate).
Kal. R.	*Kallah Rabbati* (post-talmudic tractate).
Katz, England	*The Jews in the History of England, 1485-1850 (1994).*
Kaufmann, Schriften	D. Kaufmann, *Gesammelte Schriften,* 3 vols. (1908 15).
Kaufmann Y., Religion	Y. Kaufmann, *The Religion of Israel* (1960), abridged tr. of his *Toledot.*
Kaufmann Y., Toledot	Y. Kaufmann, *Toledot ha-Emunah ha-Yisre'elit,* 4 vols. (1937 57).
KAWJ	*Korrespondenzblatt des Vereins zur Gruendung und Erhaltung der Akademie fuer die Wissenschaft des Judentums* (1920 30).
Kayserling, Bibl	M. Kayserling, *Biblioteca Española-Portugueza-Judaica* (1880; repr. 1961).
Kelim	*Kelim* (mishnaic tractate).
Ker.	*Keritot* (talmudic tractate).
Ket.	*Ketubbot* (talmudic tractate).

Kid.	*Kiddushim* (talmudic tractate).
Kil.	*Kilayim* (talmudic tractate).
Kin.	*Kinnim* (mishnaic tractate).
Kisch, Germany	G. Kisch, *Jews in Medieval Germany* (1949).
Kittel, Gesch	R. Kittel, *Geschichte des Volkes Israel,* 3 vols. (1922–28).
Klausner, Bayit Sheni	J. Klausner, *Historyah shel ha-Bayit ha-Sheni,* 5 vols. (1950/512).
Klausner, Sifrut	J. Klausner, *Historyah shel haSifrut ha-Ivrit ha-Ḥadashah,* 6 vols. (1952–582).
Klein, corpus	S. Klein (ed.), *Juedisch-palaestinisches Corpus Inscriptionum* (1920).
Koehler-Baumgartner	L. Koehler and W. Baumgartner, *Lexicon in Veteris Testamenti libros* (1953).
Kohut, Arukh	H.J.A. Kohut (ed.), *Sefer he-Arukh ha-Shalem,* by Nathan b. Jehiel of Rome, 8 vols. (1876–92; Supplement by S. Krauss et al., 1936; repr. 1955).
Krauss, Tal Arch	S. Krauss, *Talmudische Archaeologie,* 3 vols. (1910–12; repr. 1966).
Kressel, Leksikon	G. Kressel, *Leksikon ha-Sifrut ha-Ivrit ba-Dorot ha-Aḥaronim,* 2 vols. (1965–67).
KS	*Kirjath Sepher* (1923/4ff.).
Kut.	*Kuttim* (post-talmudic tractate).
LA	Studium Biblicum Franciscanum, *Liber Annuus* (1951ff.).
L.A.	Philo, *Legum allegoriae.*
Lachower, Sifrut	F. Lachower, *Toledot ha-Sifrut ha-Ivrit ha-Ḥadashah,* 4 vols. (1947–48; several reprints).
Lam.	Lamentations (Bible).
Lam. R.	*Lamentations Rabbah.*
Landshuth, Ammudei	L. Landshuth, *Ammudei ha-Avodah* (1857–62; repr. with index, 1965).
Legat.	Philo, *De Legatione ad Caium.*
Lehmann, Nova Bibl	R.P. Lehmann, *Nova Bibliotheca Anglo-Judaica* (1961).
Lev.	Leviticus (Bible).
Lev. R.	*Leviticus Rabbah.*
Levy, Antologia	I. Levy, *Antologia de liturgia judeo-española* (1965ff.).
Levy J., Chald Targ	J. Levy, *Chaldaeisches Woerterbuch ueber die Targumim,* 2 vols. (1967–68; repr. 1959).
Levy J., Nuehebr Tal	J. Levy, *Neuhebraeisches und chaldaeisches Woerterbuch ueber die Talmudim . . .,* 4 vols. (1875–89; repr. 1963).
Lewin, Oẓar	Lewin, *Oẓar ha-Ge'onim,* 12 vols. (1928–43).
Lewysohn, Zool	L. Lewysohn, *Zoologie des Talmuds* (1858).
Lidzbarski, Handbuch	M. Lidzbarski, *Handbuch der nordsemitischen Epigraphik,* 2 vols (1898).
Life	Josephus, *Life* (Loeb Classis ed.).
LNYL	*Leksikon fun der Nayer Yidisher Literatur* (1956ff.).
Loew, Flora	I. Loew, *Die Flora der Juden,* 4 vols. (1924 34; repr. 1967).
LSI	*Laws of the State of Israel* (1948ff.).
Luckenbill, Records	D.D. Luckenbill, *Ancient Records of Assyria and Babylonia,* 2 vols. (1926).
Luke	Gospel according to Luke (New Testament)
LXX	Septuagint (Greek translation of the Bible).
Ma'as.	*Ma'aserot* (talmudic tractate).
Ma'as. Sh.	*Ma'ase Sheni* (talmudic tractate).
I, II, III, and IVMacc.	Maccabees, I, II, III (Apocrypha), IV (Pseudepigrapha).
Maimonides, Guide	Maimonides, *Guide of the Perplexed.*
Maim., Yad	Maimonides, *Mishneh Torah (Yad Ḥazakah).*
Maisler, Untersuchungen	B. Maisler (Mazar), *Untersuchungen zur alten Geschichte und Ethnographie Syriens und Palaestinas,* 1 (1930).
Mak.	*Makkot* (talmudic tractate).
Makhsh.	*Makhshrin* (mishnaic tractate).
Mal.	Malachi (Bible).
Mann, Egypt	J. Mann, *Jews in Egypt in Palestine under the Fatimid Caliphs,* 2 vols. (1920–22).
Mann, Texts	J. Mann, *Texts and Studies,* 2 vols (1931–35).
Mansi	G.D. Mansi, *Sacrorum Conciliorum nova et amplissima collectio,* 53 vols. in 60 (1901–27; repr. 1960).
Margalioth, Gedolei	M. Margalioth, *Enẓiklopedyah le-Toledot Gedolei Yisrael,* 4 vols. (1946–50).
Margalioth, Ḥakhmei	M. Margalioth, *Enẓiklopedyah le-Ḥakhmei ha-Talmud ve-ha-Ge'onim,* 2 vols. (1945).
Margalioth, Cat	G. Margalioth, *Catalogue of the Hebrew and Samaritan Manuscripts in the British Museum,* 4 vols. (1899–1935).
Mark	Gospel according to Mark (New Testament).
Mart. Isa.	Martyrdom of Isaiah (Pseudepigrapha).
Mas.	Masorah.
Matt.	Gospel according to Matthew (New Testament).
Mayer, Art	L.A. Mayer, *Bibliography of Jewish Art* (1967).
MB	*Wochenzeitung* (formerly *Mitteilungsblatt*) *des Irgun Olej Merkas Europa* (1933ff.).
MEAH	*Miscelánea de estudios drabes y hebraicos* (1952ff.).
Meg.	Megillah (talmudic tractate).
Meg. Ta'an.	*Megillat Ta'anit* (in HUCA, 8 9 (1931–32), 318–51).
Me'il	*Me'ilah* (mishnaic tractate).
MEJ	*Middle East Journal* (1947ff.).
Mehk.	*Mekhilta de-R. Ishmael.*
Mekh. SbY	*Mekhilta de-R. Simeon bar Yoḥai.*
Men.	*Menaḥot* (talmudic tractate).
MER	*Middle East Record* (1960ff.).
Meyer, Gesch	E. Meyer, *Geschichte des Alterums,* 5 vols. in 9 (1925–58).
Meyer, Ursp	E. Meyer, *Urspring und Anfaenge des Christentums* (1921).
Mez.	*Mezuzah* (post-talmudic tractate).
MGADJ	*Mitteilungen des Gesamtarchivs der deutschen Juden* (1909–12).
MGG	*Die Musik in Geschichte und Gegenwart,* 14 vols. (1949–68).

MGG²	*Die Musik in Geschichte und Gegenwart, 2nd edition (1994)*
MGH	*Monumenta Germaniae Historica* (1826ff.).
MGJV	*Mitteilungen der Gesellschaft fuer juedische Volkskunde* (1898–1929); title varies, see also JJV.
MGWJ	*Monatsschrift fuer Geschichte und Wissenschaft des Judentums* (1851–1939).
MHJ	*Monumenta Hungariae Judaica,* 11 vols. (1903–67).
Michael, Or	H.Ḥ. Michael, *Or ha-Ḥayyim: Ḥakhmei Yisrael ve-Sifreihem,* ed. by S.Z. Ḥ. Halberstam and N. Ben-Menahem (1965²).
Mid.	*Middot* (mishnaic tractate).
Mid. Ag.	*Midrash Aggadah.*
Mid. Hag.	*Midrash ha-Gadol.*
Mid. Job.	*Midrash Job.*
Mid. Jonah	*Midrash Jonah.*
Mid. Lek. Tov	*Midrash Lekaḥ Tov.*
Mid. Prov.	*Midrash Proverbs.*
Mid. Ps.	*Midrash Tehillim* (Eng tr. *The Midrash on Psalms* (JPS, 1959).
Mid. Sam.	*Midrash Samuel.*
Mid. Song	*Midrash Shir ha-Shirim.*
Mid. Tan.	*Midrash Tanna'im* on Deuteronomy.
Miége, Maroc	J.L. Miège, *Le Maroc et l'Europe,* 3 vols. (1961 62).
Mig.	Philo, *De Migratione Abrahami.*
Mik.	*Mikva'ot* (mishnaic tractate).
Milano, Bibliotheca	A. Milano, *Bibliotheca Historica Italo-Judaica* (1954); supplement for 1954–63 (1964); supplement for 1964–66 in RMI, 32 (1966).
Milano, Italia	A. Milano, *Storia degli Ebrei in Italia* (1963).
MIO	*Mitteilungen des Instituts fuer Orientforschung* 1953ff.).
Mish.	Mishnah.
MJ	*Le Monde Juif* (1946ff.).
MJC	see Neubauer, Chronicles.
MK	*Mo'ed Katan* (talmudic tractate).
MNDPV	*Mitteilungen und Nachrichten des deutschen Palaestinavereins* (1895–1912).
Mortara, Indice	M. Mortara, *Indice Alfabetico dei Rabbini e Scrittori Israeliti ... in Italia ...* (1886).
Mos	Philo, *De Vita Mosis.*
Moscati, Epig	S, Moscati, *Epigrafia ebraica antica* 1935–1950 (1951).
MT	Masoretic Text of the Bible.
Mueller, Musiker	[E.H. Mueller], *Deutisches Musiker-Lexikon* (1929)
Munk, Mélanges	S. Munk, *Mélanges de philosophie juive et arabe* (1859; repr. 1955).
Mut.	Philo, *De Mutatione Nominum.*
MWJ	*Magazin fuer die Wissenshaft des Judentums* (18745 93).
Nah.	Nahum (Bible).
Naz.	*Nazir* (talmudic tractate).
NDB	*Neue Deutsche Biographie* (1953ff.).
Ned.	*Nedarim* (talmudic tractate).
Neg.	*Nega'im* (mishnaic tractate).
Neh.	Nehemiah (Bible).
NG²	*New Grove Dictionary of Music and Musicians* (2001).
Nuebauer, Cat	A. Neubauer, *Catalogue of the Hebrew Manuscripts in the Bodleian Library ...,* 2 vols. (1886–1906).
Neubauer, Chronicles	A. Neubauer, *Mediaeval Jewish Chronicles,* 2 vols. (Heb., 1887–95; repr. 1965), Eng. title of *Seder ha-Ḥakhamim ve-Korot ha-Yamim.*
Neubauer, Géogr	A. Neubauer, *La géographie du Talmud* (1868).
Neuman, Spain	A.A. Neuman, *The Jews in Spain, their Social, Political, and Cultural Life During the Middle Ages,* 2 vols. (1942).
Neusner, Babylonia	J. Neusner, *History of the Jews in Babylonia,* 5 vols. 1965–70), 2nd revised printing 1969ff.).
Nid.	*Niddah* (talmudic tractate).
Noah	Fragment of Book of Noah (Pseudepigrapha).
Noth, Hist Isr	M. Noth, *History of Israel* (1958).
Noth, Personennamen	M. Noth, *Die israelitischen Personennamen.* ... (1928).
Noth, Ueberlief	M. Noth, *Ueberlieferungsgeschichte des Pentateuchs* (1949).
Noth, Welt	M. Noth, *Die Welt des Alten Testaments* (1957³).
Nowack, Lehrbuch	W. Nowack, *Lehrbuch der hebraeischen Archaeologie,* 2 vols (1894).
NT	New Testament.
Num.	Numbers (Bible).
Num R.	*Numbers Rabbah.*
Obad.	Obadiah (Bible).
ODNB online	*Oxford Dictionary of National Biography.*
OḤ	*Oraḥ Ḥayyim.*
Oho.	*Oholot* (mishnaic tractate).
Olmstead	H.T. Olmstead, *History of Palestine and Syria* (1931; repr. 1965).
OLZ	*Orientalistische Literaturzeitung* (1898ff.)
Onom.	Eusebius, *Onomasticon.*
Op.	Philo, *De Opificio Mundi.*
OPD	*Osef Piskei Din shel ha-Rabbanut ha-Rashit le-Ereẓ Yisrael, Bet ha-Din ha-Gadol le-Irurim* (1950).
Or.	*Orlah* (talmudic tractate).
Or. Sibyll.	Sibylline Oracles (Pseudepigrapha).
OS	*L'Orient Syrien* (1956ff.)
OTS	*Oudtestamentische Studien* (1942ff.).
PAAJR	*Proceedings of the American Academy for Jewish Research* (1930ff.)
Pap 4QSᵉ	A papyrus exemplar of IQS.
Par.	*Parah* (mishnaic tractate).
Pauly-Wissowa	A.F. Pauly, *Realencyklopaedie der klassichen Alertumswissenschaft,* ed. by G. Wissowa et al. (1864ff.)

PD	*Piskei Din shel Bet ha-Mishpat ha-Elyon le-Yisrael* (1948ff.)
PDR	*Piskei Din shel Battei ha-Din ha-Rabbaniyyim be-Yisrael.*
PdRE	*Pirkei de-R. Eliezer* (Eng. tr. 1916. (1965^{2}).
PdRK	*Pesikta de-Rav Kahana.*
Pe'ah	*Pe'ah* (talmudic tractate).
Peake, Commentary	A.J. Peake (ed.), *Commentary on the Bible* (1919; rev. 1962).
Pedersen, Israel	J. Pedersen, *Israel, Its Life and Culture,* 4 vols. in 2 (1926–40).
PEFQS	*Palestine Exploration Fund Quarterly Statement* (1869–1937; since 1938–PEQ).
PEQ	*Palestine Exploration Quarterly* (until 1937 PEFQS; after 1927 includes BBSAJ).
Perles, Beitaege	J. Perles, *Beitraege zur rabbinischen Sprach- und Alterthumskunde* (1893).
Pes.	*Pesaḥim* (talmudic tractate).
Pesh.	Peshitta (Syriac translation of the Bible).
Pesher Hab.	Commentary to Habakkuk from Qumran; see 1Qp Hab.
I and II Pet.	Epistles of Peter (New Testament).
Pfeiffer, Introd	R.H. Pfeiffer, *Introduction to the Old Testament* (1948).
PG	J.P. Migne (ed.), *Patrologia Graeca,* 161 vols. (1866–86).
Phil.	Epistle to the Philippians (New Testament).
Philem.	Epistle to the Philemon (New Testament).
PIASH	*Proceedings of the Israel Academy of Sciences and Humanities* (1963/7ff.).
PJB	*Palaestinajahrbuch des deutschen evangelischen Institutes fuer Altertumswissenschaft,* Jerusalem (1905–1933).
PK	*Pinkas ha-Kehillot,* encyclopedia of Jewish communities, published in over 30 volumes by Yad Vashem from 1970 and arranged by countries, regions and localities. For 3-vol. English edition see Spector, *Jewish Life.*
PL	J.P. Migne (ed.), *Patrologia Latina* 221 vols. (1844–64).
Plant	Philo, *De Plantatione.*
PO	R. Graffin and F. Nau (eds.), *Patrologia Orientalis* (1903ff.)
Pool, Prayer	D. de Sola Pool, *Traditional Prayer Book for Sabbath and Festivals* (1960).
Post	Philo, *De Posteritate Caini.*
PR	*Pesikta Rabbati.*
Praem.	Philo, *De Praemiis et Poenis.*
Prawer, Ẓalbanim	J. Prawer, *Toledot Mamlekhet ha-Ẓalbanim be-Ereẓ Yisrael,* 2 vols. (1963).
Press, Ereẓ	I. Press, *Ereẓ-Yisrael, Enẓiklopedyah Topografit-Historit,* 4 vols. (1951–55).
Pritchard, Pictures	J.B. Pritchard (ed.), *Ancient Near East in Pictures* (1954, 1970).
Pritchard, Texts	J.B. Pritchard (ed.), *Ancient Near East Texts* ... (1970^{3}).

Pr. Man.	Prayer of Manasses (Apocrypha).
Prob.	Philo, *Quod Omnis Probus Liber Sit.*
Prov.	Proverbs (Bible).
PS	*Palestinsky Sbornik* (Russ. (1881 1916, 1954ff).
Ps.	Psalms (Bible).
PSBA	*Proceedings of the Society of Biblical Archaeology* (1878–1918).
Ps. of Sol	Psalms of Solomon (Pseudepigrapha).
IQ Apoc	The *Genesis Apocryphon* from Qumran, cave one, ed. by N. Avigad and Y. Yadin (1956).
6QD	*Damascus Document* or *Sefer Berit Dammesk* from Qumran, cave six, ed. by M. Baillet, in RB, 63 (1956), 513–23 (see also CD).
QDAP	*Quarterly of the Department of Antiquities in Palestine* (1932ff.).
4QDeut. 32	Manuscript of Deuteronomy 32 from Qumran, cave four (ed. by P.W. Skehan, in BASOR, 136 (1954), 12–15).
4QEx^{a}	Exodus manuscript in Jewish script from Qumran, cave four.
4QEx$^{\alpha}$	Exodus manuscript in Paleo-Hebrew script from Qumran, cave four (partially ed. by P.W. Skehan, in JBL, 74 (1955), 182–7).
4QFlor	*Florilegium,* a miscellany from Qumran, cave four (ed. by J.M. Allegro, in JBL, 75 (1956), 176–77 and 77 (1958), 350–54).).
QGJD	*Quellen zur Geschichte der Juden in Deutschland* 1888–98).
IQH	*Thanksgiving Psalms* of *Hodayot* from Qumran, cave one (ed. by E.L. Sukenik and N. Avigad, *Oẓar ha-Megillot ha-Genuzot* (1954).
IQIs^{a}	Scroll of Isaiah from Qumran, cave one (ed. by N. Burrows et al., *Dead Sea Scrolls* ..., 1 (1950).
IQIs^{b}	Scroll of Isaiah from Qumran, cave one (ed. E.L. Sukenik and N. Avigad, *Oẓar ha-Megillot ha-Genuzot* (1954).
IQM	The *War Scroll* or *Serekh ha-Milḥamah* (ed. by E.L. Sukenik and N. Avigad, *Oẓar ha-Megillot ha-Genuzot* (1954).
4QpNah	Commentary on Nahum from Qumran, cave four (partially ed. by J.M. Allegro, in JBL, 75 (1956), 89–95).
IQphyl	Phylacteries *(tefillin)* from Qumran, cave one (ed. by Y. Yadin, in *Eretz Israel,* 9 (1969), 60–85).
4Q Prayer of Nabonidus	A document from Qumran, cave four, belonging to a lost Daniel literature (ed. by J.T. Milik, in RB, 63 (1956), 407–15).
IQS	*Manual of Discipline* or *Serekh ha-Yaḥad* from Qumran, cave one (ed. by M. Burrows et al., *Dead Sea Scrolls* ..., 2, pt. 2 (1951).

IQS^{a}	The *Rule of the Congregation or Serekh ha-Edah* from Qumran, cave one (ed. by Burrows et al., *Dead Sea Scrolls* ..., 1 (1950), under the abbreviation IQ28a).
IQS^{b}	*Blessings* or *Divrei Berakhot* from Qumran, cave one (ed. by Burrows et al., *Dead Sea Scrolls* ..., 1 (1950), under the abbreviation IQ28b).
4QSam^{a}	Manuscript of I and II Samuel from Qumran, cave four (partially ed. by F.M. Cross, in BASOR, 132 (1953), 15–26).
4QSam^{b}	Manuscript of I and II Samuel from Qumran, cave four (partially ed. by F.M. Cross, in JBL, 74 (1955), 147–72).
4QTestimonia	Sheet of Testimony from Qumran, cave four (ed. by J.M. Allegro, in JBL, 75 (1956), 174–87).).
4QT.Levi	*Testament of Levi* from Qumran, cave four (partially ed. by J.T. Milik, in RB, 62 (1955), 398–406).

Rabinovitz, Dik Sof	See Dik Sof.
RB	*Revue biblique* (1892ff.)
RBI	*Recherches bibliques* (1954ff.)
RCB	*Revista de cultura biblica* (São Paulo) (1957ff.)
Régné, Cat	J. Régné, *Catalogue des actes . . . des rois d'Aragon, concernant les Juifs* (1213–1327), in: REJ, vols. 60 70, 73, 75–78 (1910–24).
Reinach, Textes	T. Reinach, *Textes d'auteurs Grecs et Romains relatifs au Judaïsme* (1895; repr. 1963).
REJ	*Revue des études juives* (1880ff.).
Rejzen, Leksikon	Z. Rejzen, *Leksikon fun der Yidisher Literature,* 4 vols. (1927–29).
Renan, Ecrivains	A. Neubauer and E. Renan, *Les écrivains juifs français* ... (1893).
Renan, Rabbins	A. Neubauer and E. Renan, *Les rabbins français* (1877).
RES	*Revue des étude sémitiques et Babyloniaca* (1934–45).
Rev.	Revelation (New Testament).
RGG^{3}	*Die Religion in Geschichte und Gegenwart,* 7 vols. (1957–65^{3}).
RH	*Rosh Ha-Shanah* (talmudic tractate).
RHJE	*Revue de l'histoire juive en Egypte* (1947ff.).
RHMH	*Revue d'histoire de la médecine hébraïque* (1948ff.).
RHPR	*Revue d'histoire et de philosophie religieuses* (1921ff.).
RHR	*Revue d'histoire des religions* (1880ff.).
RI	*Rivista Israelitica* (1904–12).
Riemann-Einstein	*Hugo Riemanns Musiklexikon,* ed. by A. Einstein (1929^{11}).
Riemann-Gurlitt	*Hugo Riemanns Musiklexikon,* ed. by W. Gurlitt (1959–67^{12}), Personenteil.
Rigg-Jenkinson, Exchequer	J.M. Rigg, H. Jenkinson and H.G. Richardson (eds.), *Calendar of the Pleas Rolls of the Exchequer of the Jews,* 4 vols. (1905–1970); cf. in each instance also J.M. Rigg (ed.), *Select Pleas* ... (1902).
RMI	*Rassegna Mensile di Israel* (1925ff.).
Rom.	Epistle to the Romans (New Testament).
Rosanes, Togarmah	S.A. Rosanes, *Divrei Yemei Yisrael be-Togarmah,* 6 vols. (1907–45), and in 3 vols. (1930–38^{2}).
Rosenbloom, Biogr Dict	J.R. Rosenbloom, *Biographical Dictionary of Early American Jews* (1960).
Roth, Art	C. Roth, *Jewish Art* (1961).
Roth, Dark Ages	C. Roth (ed.), *World History of the Jewish People,* second series, vol. 2, *Dark Ages* (1966).
Roth, England	C. Roth, *History of the Jews in England* (1964^{3}).
Roth, Italy	C. Roth, *History of the Jews in Italy* (1946).
Roth, Mag Bibl	C. Roth, *Magna Bibliotheca Anglo-Judaica* (1937).
Roth, Marranos	C. Roth, *History of the Marranos* (2nd rev. ed 1959; reprint 1966).
Rowley, Old Test	H.H. Rowley, *Old Testament and Modern Study* (1951; repr. 1961).
RS	*Revue sémitiques d'épigraphie et d'histoire ancienne* (1893/94ff.).
RSO	*Rivista degli studi orientali* (1907ff.).
RSV	Revised Standard Version of the Bible.
Rubinstein, Australia I	*H.L. Rubinstein, The Jews in Australia, A Thematic History, Vol. I (1991).*
Rubinstein, Australia II	*W.D. Rubinstein, The Jews in Australia, A Thematic History, Vol. II (1991).*
Ruth	Ruth (Bible).
Ruth R.	*Ruth Rabbah.*
RV	Revised Version of the Bible.

Sac.	Philo, *De Sacrificiis Abelis et Caini.*
Salfeld, Martyrol	S. Salfeld, *Martyrologium des Nuernberger Memorbuches* (1898).
I and II Sam.	Samuel, book I and II (Bible).
Sanh.	*Sanhedrin* (talmudic tractate).
SBA	Society of Biblical Archaeology.
SBB	*Studies in Bibliography and Booklore* (1953ff.).
SBE	*Semana Biblica Española.*
SBT	*Studies in Biblical Theology* (1951ff.).
SBU	*Svenkst Bibliskt Uppslogsvesk,* 2 vols. (1962–63^{2}).
Schirmann, Italyah	J.Ḥ. Schirmann, *Ha-Shirah ha-Ivrit be-Italyah* (1934).
Schirmann, Sefarad	J.Ḥ. Schirmann, *Ha-Shirah ha-Ivrit bi-Sefarad u-vi-Provence,* 2 vols. (1954–56).
Scholem, Mysticism	G. Scholem, *Major Trends in Jewish Mysticism* (rev. ed. 1946; paperback ed. with additional bibliography 1961).
Scholem, Shabbetai Ẓevi	G. Scholem, *Shabbetai Ẓevi ve-ha-Tenu'ah ha-Shabbeta'it bi-Ymei Ḥayyav,* 2 vols. (1967).
Schrader, Keilinschr	E. Schrader, *Keilinschriften und das Alte Testament* (1903^{3}).
Schuerer, Gesch	E. Schuerer, *Geschichte des juedischen Volkes im Zeitalter Jesu Christi,* 3 vols. and index-vol. (1901–11^{4}).

Schuerer, Hist	E. Schuerer, *History of the Jewish People in the Time of Jesus*, ed. by N.N. Glatzer, abridged paperback edition (1961).
Set. T.	*Sefer Torah* (post-talmudic tractate).
Sem.	*Semaḥot* (post-talmudic tractate).
Sendrey, Music	A. Sendrey, *Bibliography of Jewish Music* (1951).
SER	*Seder Eliyahu Rabbah.*
SEZ	*Seder Eliyahu Zuta.*
Shab	*Shabbat* (talmudic tractate).
Sh. Ar.	J. Caro Shulḥan Arukh. OḤ – *Oraḥ Ḥayyim* YD – *Yoreh De'ah* EH – *Even ha-Ezer* ḤM – *Ḥoshen Mishpat.*
Shek.	*Shekalim* (talmudic tractate).
Shev.	*Shevi'it* (talmudic tractate).
Shevu.	*Shevu'ot* (talmudic tractate).
Shunami, Bibl	S. Shunami, *Bibliography of Jewish Bibliographies* (1965[2]).
Sif.	*Sifrei Deuteronomy.*
Sif. Num.	*Sifrei Numbers.*
Sifra	*Sifra* on Leviticus.
Sif. Zut.	*Sifrei Zuta.*
SIHM	Sources inédites de l'histoire du Maroc (series).
Silverman, Prayer	M. Silverman (ed.), *Sabbath and Festival Prayer Book* (1946).
Singer, Prayer	S. Singer *Authorised Daily Prayer Book* (1943[17]).
Sob.	Philo, *De Sobrietate.*
Sof.	*Soferim* (post-talmudic tractate).
Som.	Philo, *De Somniis.*
Song	Song of Songs (Bible).
Song. Ch.	Song of the Three Children (Apocrypha).
Song R.	*Song of Songs Rabbah.*
SOR	*Seder Olam Rabbah.*
Sot.	*Sotah* (talmudic tractate).
SOZ	*Seder Olam Zuta.*
Spec.	Philo, *De Specialibus Legibus.*
Spector, Jewish Life	*S. Spector (ed.), Encyclopedia of Jewish Life Before and After the Holocaust (2001).*
Steinschneider, Arab lit	M. Steinschneider, *Die arabische Literatur der Juden* (1902).
Steinschneider, Cat Bod	M. Steinschneider, *Catalogus Librorum Hebraeorum in Bibliotheca Bodleiana*, 3 vols. (1852–60; reprints 1931 and 1964).
Steinschneider, Hanbuch	M. Steinschneider, *Bibliographisches Handbuch ueber die ... Literatur fuer hebraeische Sprachkunde* (1859; repr. with additions 1937).
Steinschneider, Uebersetzungen	M. Steinschneider, *Die hebraeischen Uebersetzungen des Mittelalters* (1893).
Stern, Americans	M.H. Stern, *Americans of Jewish Descent* (1960).
van Straalen, Cat	S. van Straalen, *Catalogue of Hebrew Books in the British Museum Acquired During the Years 1868–1892* (1894).
Suárez Fernández, Docmentos	L. Suárez Fernández, *Documentos acerca de la expulsion de los Judios de España* (1964).

Suk.	*Sukkah* (talmudic tractate).
Sus.	Susanna (Apocrypha).
SY	*Sefer Yeẓirah.*
Sym.	Symmachus' Greek translation of the Bible.
SZNG	*Studien zur neueren Geschichte.*
Ta'an.	*Ta'anit* (talmudic tractate).
Tam.	*Tamid* (mishnaic tractate).
Tanḥ.	*Tanḥuma.*
Tanḥ. B.	*Tanḥuma.* Buber ed (1885).
Targ. Jon	Targum Jonathan (Aramaic version of the Prophets).
Targ. Onk.	Targum Onkelos (Aramaic version of the Pentateuch).
Targ. Yer.	Targum Yerushalmi.
TB	Babylonian Talmud or Talmud Bavli.
Tcherikover, Corpus	V. Tcherikover, A. Fuks, and M. Stern, *Corpus Papyrorum Judaicorum*, 3 vols. (1957–60).
Tef.	*Tefillin* (post-talmudic tractate).
Tem.	*Temurah* (mishnaic tractate).
Ter.	*Terumah* (talmudic tractate).
Test. Patr.	Testament of the Twelve Patriarchs (Pseudepigrapha). Ash. – Asher Ben. – Benjamin Dan – Dan Gad – Gad Iss. – Issachar Joseph – Joseph Judah – Judah Levi – Levi Naph. – Naphtali Reu. – Reuben Sim. – Simeon Zeb. – Zebulun.
I and II	Epistle to the Thessalonians (New Testament).
Thieme-Becker	U. Thieme and F. Becker (eds.), *Allgemeines Lexikon der bildenden Kuenstler von der Antike bis zur Gegenwart*, 37 vols. (1907–50).
Tidhar	D. Tidhar (ed.), *Enẓiklopedyah la-Ḥalutẓei ha-Yishuv u-Vonav* (1947ff.).
I and II Timothy	Epistles to Timothy (New Testament).
Tit.	Epistle to Titus (New Testament).
TJ	Jerusalem Talmud or Talmud Yerushalmi.
Tob.	Tobit (Apocrypha).
Toh.	*Tohorot* (mishnaic tractate).
Torczyner, Bundeslade	H. Torczyner, *Die Bundeslade und die Anfaenge der Religion Israels* (1930[3]).
Tos.	*Tosafot.*
Tosef.	Tosefta.
Tristram, Nat Hist	H.B. Tristram, *Natural History of the Bible* (1877[5]).
Tristram, Survey	Palestine Exploration Fund, *Survey of Western Palestine*, vol. 4 (1884) = *Fauna and Flora* by H.B. Tristram.
TS	*Terra Santa* (1943ff.).

TSBA	*Transactions of the Society of Biblical Archaeology* (1872–93).
TY	*Tevul Yom* (mishnaic tractate).
UBSB	United Bible Society, *Bulletin.*
UJE	*Universal Jewish Encyclopedia*, 10 vols. (1939–43).
Uk.	*Ukẓin* (mishnaic tractate).
Urbach, Tosafot	E.E. Urbach, *Ba'alei ha-Tosafot* (1957²).
de Vaux, Anc Isr	R. de Vaux, *Ancient Israel: its Life and Institutions* (1961; paperback 1965).
de Vaux, Instit	R. de Vaux, *Institutions de l'Ancien Testament*, 2 vols. (1958 60).
Virt.	Philo, *De Virtutibus.*
Vogelstein, Chronology	M. Volgelstein, *Biblical Chronology (1944).*
Vogelstein-Rieger	H. Vogelstein and P. Rieger, *Geschichte der Juden in Rom*, 2 vols. (1895–96).
VT	*Vetus Testamentum* (1951ff.).
VTS	*Vetus Testamentum* Supplements (1953ff.).
Vulg.	Vulgate (Latin translation of the Bible).
Wars	Josephus, *The Jewish Wars.*
Watzinger, Denkmaeler	K. Watzinger, *Denkmaeler Palaestinas*, 2 vols. (1933–35).
Waxman, Literature	M. Waxman, *History of Jewish Literature*, 5 vols. (1960²).
Weiss, Dor	I.H. Weiss, *Dor, Dor ve-Doreshav*, 5 vols. (1904⁴).
Wellhausen, Proleg	J. Wellhausen, *Prolegomena zur Geschichte Israels* (1927⁶).
WI	*Die Welt des Islams* (1913ff.).
Winniger, Biog	S. Wininger, *Grosse juedische National-Biographie ...*, 7 vols. (1925–36).
Wisd.	Wisdom of Solomon (Apocrypha)
WLB	*Wiener Library Bulletin* (1958ff.).
Wolf, Bibliotheca	J.C. Wolf, *Bibliotheca Hebraea*, 4 vols. (1715–33).
Wright, Bible	G.E. Wright, *Westminster Historical Atlas to the Bible* (1945).
Wright, Atlas	G.E. Wright, *The Bible and the Ancient Near East* (1961).
WWWJ	*Who's Who in the World Jewry* (New York, 1955, 1965²).
WZJT	*Wissenschaftliche Zeitschrift fuer juedische Theologie* (1835–37).
WZKM	*Wiener Zeitschrift fuer die Kunde des Morgenlandes* (1887ff.).
Yaari, Sheluḥei	A. Yaari, *Sheluḥei Ereẓ Yisrael* (1951).
Yad	Maimonides, *Mishneh Torah (Yad Ḥazakah).*
Yad	*Yadayim* (mishnaic tractate).
Yal.	*Yalkut Shimoni.*
Yal. Mak.	*Yalkut Makhiri.*
Yal. Reub.	*Yalkut Reubeni.*
YD	*Yoreh De'ah.*
YE	*Yevreyskaya Entsiklopediya*, 14 vols. (c. 1910).
Yev.	*Yevamot* (talmudic tractate).
YIVOA	*YIVO Annual of Jewish Social Studies* (1946ff.).
YLBI	*Year Book of the Leo Baeck Institute* (1956ff.).
YMḤEY	See BJPES.
YMḤSI	*Yedi'ot ha-Makhon le-Ḥeker ha-Shirah ha-Ivrit* (1935/36ff.).
YMMY	*Yedi'ot ha-Makhon le-Madda'ei ha-Yahadut* (1924/25ff.).
Yoma	*Yoma* (talmudic tractate).
ZA	*Zeitschrift fuer Assyriologie* (1886/87ff.).
Zav.	*Zavim* (mishnaic tractate).
ZAW	*Zeitschrift fuer die alttestamentliche Wissenschaft und die Kunde des nachbiblishchen Judentums* (1881ff.).
ZAWB	*Beihefte* (supplements) to ZAW.
ZDMG	*Zeitschrift der Deutschen Morgenlaendischen Gesellschaft* (1846ff.).
ZDPV	*Zeitschrift des Deutschen Palaestina-Vereins* (1878–1949; from 1949 = BBLA).
Zech.	Zechariah (Bible).
Zedner, Cat	J. Zedner, *Catalogue of Hebrew Books in the Library of the British Museum* (1867; repr. 1964).
Zeitlin, Bibliotheca	W. Zeitlin, *Bibliotheca Hebraica Post-Mendelssohniana* (1891–95).
Zeph.	Zephaniah (Bible).
Zev.	*Zevaḥim* (talmudic tractate).
ZGGJT	*Zeitschrift der Gesellschaft fuer die Geschichte der Juden in der Tschechoslowakei* (1930–38).
ZGJD	*Zeitschrift fuer die Geschichte der Juden in Deutschland* (1887–92).
ZHB	*Zeitschrift fuer hebraeische Bibliographie* (1896–1920).
Zinberg, Sifrut	I. Zinberg, *Toledot Sifrut Yisrael*, 6 vols. (1955–60).
Ẓiẓ.	*Ẓiẓit* (post-talmudic tractate).
ZNW	*Zeitschrift fuer die neutestamentliche Wissenschaft* (1901ff.).
ZS	*Zeitschrift fuer Semitistik und verwandte Gebiete* (1922ff.).
Zunz, Gesch	L. Zunz, *Zur Geschichte und Literatur* (1845).
Zunz, Gesch	L. Zunz, *Literaturgeschichte der synagogalen Poesie* (1865; Supplement, 1867; repr. 1966).
Zunz, Poesie	L. Zunz, *Synogogale Posie des Mittelalters*, ed. by Freimann (1920²; repr. 1967).
Zunz, Ritus	L. Zunz, *Ritus des synagogalen Gottesdienstes* (1859; repr. 1967).
Zunz, Schr	L. Zunz, *Gesammelte Schriften*, 3 vols. (1875–76).
Zunz, Vortraege	L. Zunz, *Gottesdienstliche vortraege der Juden ...* 1892²; repr. 1966).
Zunz-Albeck, Derashot	L. Zunz, *Ha-Derashot be-Yisrael*, Heb. Tr. of Zunz Vortraege by H. Albeck (1954²).

TRANSLITERATION RULES

HEBREW AND SEMITIC LANGUAGES:

	General	*Scientific*
א	not transliterated[1]	ʾ
בּ	b	b
ב	v	v, ḇ
גּ	g	g
ג		ḡ
דּ	d	d
ד		ḏ
ה	h	h
ו	v – when not a vowel	w
ז	z	z
ח	ḥ	ḥ
ט	t	ṭ, t
י	y – when vowel and at end of words – i	y
כּ	k	k
כ, ך	kh	kh, ḵ
ל	l	ḻ
מ, ם	m	m
נ, ן	n	n
ס	s	s
ע	not transliterated[1]	ʿ
פּ	p	p
פ, ף	f	p, f, ph
צ, ץ	ẓ	ṣ, ẓ
ק	k	q, k
ר	r	r
שׁ	sh[2]	š
שׂ	s	ś, s
תּ	t	t
ת		ṯ
ג׳	dzh, J	ğ
ז׳	zh, J	ž
צ׳	ch	č
◌ָ		å, o, ȯ (short) â, ā (long)
◌ַ	a	a
◌ֲ		a, ^{a}
◌ֵ		e, ẹ, ē
◌ֶ	e	æ, ä, ę
◌ֱ		œ, ĕ, ^{e}
◌ְ	only *sheva na* is transliterated	ə, ĕ, e; only *sheva na* transliterated
◌ִ ◌ִי	i	i
◌ֹ וֹ	o	o, o, o
◌ֻ וּ	u	u, ŭ û, ū
◌ֵי	ei; biblical e	
‡		reconstructed forms of words

1. The letters א and ע are not transliterated.
An apostrophe (') between vowels indicates that they do not form a diphthong and are to be pronounced separately.
2. *Dagesh ḥazak* (forte) is indicated by doubling of the letter, except for the letter שׁ.
3. Names. Biblical names and biblical place names are rendered according to the Bible translation of the Jewish Publication Society of America. Post-biblical Hebrew names are transliterated; contemporary names are transliterated or rendered as used by the person. Place names are transliterated or rendered by the accepted spelling. Names and some words with an accepted English form are usually not transliterated.

YIDDISH

א	not transliterated
אַ	a
אָ	o
בּ	b
בֿ	v
ג	g
ד	d
ה	h
ו, וּ	u
וו	v
וי	oy
ז	z
זש	zh
ח	kh
ט	t
טש	tsh, ch
י	(consonant) y (vowel) i
יִ	i
יי	ey
ײַ	ay
כּ	k
כ, ך	kh
ל	l
מ, ם	m
נ, ן	n
ס	s
ע	e
פּ	p
פֿ, ף	f
צ, ץ	ts
ק	k
ר	r
שׁ	sh
שׂ	s
תּ	t
ת	s

1. Yiddish transliteration rendered according to U. Weinreich's Modern *English-Yiddish Yiddish-English* Dictionary.
2. Hebrew words in Yiddish are usually transliterated according to standard Yiddish pronunciation, e.g., חזנות = *khazones.*

LADINO

Ladino and Judeo-Spanish words written in Hebrew characters are transliterated phonetically, following the General Rules of Hebrew transliteration (see above) whenever the accepted spelling in Latin characters could not be ascertained.

ARABIC

ا ء	a[1]	ض	ḍ
ب	b	ط	ṭ
ت	t	ظ	ẓ
ث	th	ع	c
ج	j	غ	gh
ح	ḥ	ف	f
خ	kh	ق	q
د	d	ك	k
ذ	dh	ل	l
ر	r	م	m
ز	z	ن	n
س	s	ه	h
ش	sh	و	w
ص	ṣ	ي	y
ـَ	a	ـَا ى	ā
ـِ	i	ـِي	ī
ـُ	u	ـُو	ū
ـَو	aw	ـِيّ	iyy[2]
ـَي	ay	ـُوّ	uww[2]

1. not indicated when initial
2. see note (f)

a) The EJ follows the *Columbia Lippincott Gazetteer* and the *Times Atlas* in transliteration of Arabic place names. Sites that appear in neither are transliterated according to the table above, and subject to the following notes.

b) The EJ follows the *Columbia Encyclopedia* in transliteration of Arabic names. Personal names that do not therein appear are transliterated according to the table above and subject to the following notes (e.g., Ali rather than ʿAlī, Suleiman rather than Sulayman).

c) The EJ follows the *Webster's Third International Dictionary, Unabridged* in transliteration of Arabic terms that have been integrated into the English language.

d) The term "Abu" will thus appear, usually in disregard of inflection.

e) Nunnation (end vowels, *tanwīn*) are dropped in transliteration.

f) Gemination (*tashdīd*) is indicated by the doubling of the geminated letter, unless an end letter, in which case the gemination is dropped.

g) The definitive article *al-* will always be thus transliterated, unless subject to one of the modifying notes (e.g., El-Arish rather than al-ʿArīsh; modification according to note (a)).

h) The Arabic transliteration disregards the Sun Letters (the antero-palatals (*al-Ḥurūf al-Shamsiyya*).

i) The *tā-marbūṭa* (o) is omitted in transliteration, unless in construct-stage (e.g., *Khirba* but *Khirbat Mishmish*).

These modifying notes may lead to various inconsistencies in the Arabic transliteration, but this policy has deliberately been adopted to gain smoother reading of Arabic terms and names.

GREEK

Ancient Greek	*Modern Greek*	*Greek Letters*
a	a	*Α; α; ᾳ*
b	v	*Β; β*
g	gh; g	*Γ; γ*
d	dh	*Δ; δ*
e	e	*Ε; ε*
z	z	*Ζ; ζ*
e; e	i	*Η; η; ῃ*
th	th	*Θ; θ*
i	i	*Ι; ι*
k	k; ky	*Κ; κ*
l	l	*Λ; λ*
m	m	*Μ; μ*
n	n	*Ν; ν*
x	x	*Ξ; ξ*
o	o	*Ο; ο*
p	p	*Π; π*
r; rh	r	*Ρ; ρ; ῥ*
s	s	*Σ; σ; ς*
t	t	*Τ; τ*
u; y	i	*Υ; υ*
ph	f	*Φ; φ*
ch	kh	*Χ; χ*
ps	ps	*Ψ; ψ*
o; ō	o	*Ω; ω; ῳ*
ai	e	*αι*
ei	i	*ει*
oi	i	*οι*
ui	i	*υι*
ou	ou	*ου*
eu	ev	*ευ*
eu; ēu	iv	*ηυ*
–	j	*τζ*
nt	d; nd	*ντ*
mp	b; mb	*μπ*
ngk	g	*γκ*
ng	ng	*γγ*
h	–	ʽ
–	–	ʼ
w	–	*Ϝ*

RUSSIAN

А	A
Б	B
В	V
Г	G
Д	D
Е	E, Ye[1]
Ё	Yo, O[2]
Ж	Zh
З	Z
И	I
Й	Y[3]
К	K
Л	L
М	M
Н	N
О	O
П	P
Р	R
С	S
Т	T
У	U
Ф	F
Х	Kh
Ц	Ts
Ч	Ch
Ш	Sh
Щ	Shch
Ъ	omitted; see note [1]
Ы	Y
Ь	omitted; see note [1]
Э	E
Ю	Yu
Я	Ya

1. Ye at the beginning of a word; after all vowels except ***Ы***; and after ***Ъ*** and ***Ь***.
2. O after ***Ч***, ***Ш*** and ***Щ***.
3. Omitted after ***Ы***, and in names of people after ***И***.

A. Many first names have an accepted English or quasi-English form which has been preferred to transliteration.
B. Place names have been given according to the *Columbia Lippincott Gazeteer*.
C. Pre-revolutionary spelling has been ignored.
D. Other languages using the Cyrillic alphabet (e.g., Bulgarian, Ukrainian), inasmuch as they appear, have been phonetically transliterated in conformity with the principles of this table.